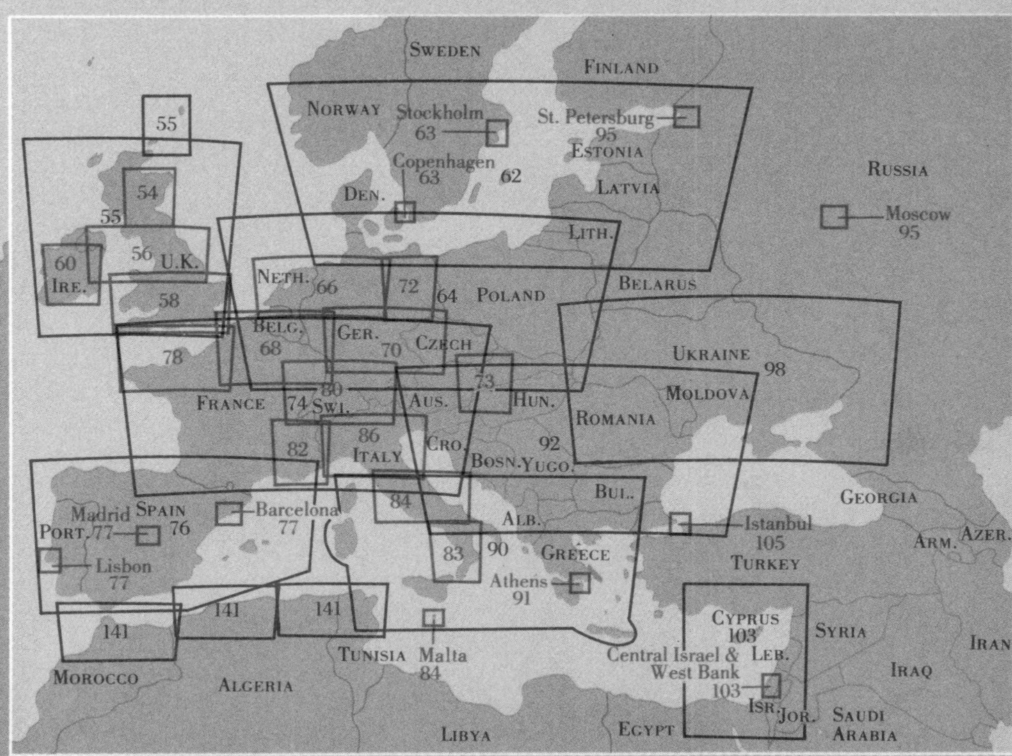




These maps of the World, United States and Europe indicate locations of the regional maps found on pages 52-208. The colored outlines show the scale of each map (per the accompanying legend) and the extent of each map's coverage. Page numbers of the same color are found in the center of each outline. Large scale map insets are noted by outline, name and page number. Small scale maps of continents and large countries are indicated by name and page number only. A map of the world appears on pages 50-51.

OXFORD

HAMMOND

# Atlas of the World

OXFORD
HAMMOND

# Atlas of t

OXFORD UNIVERSITY PRESS

OXFORD • MELBOURNE • TORONTO

# he World

Oxford University Press
Walton Street, Oxford OX2 6DP

Oxford New York Toronto
Delhi Bombay Madras Karachi
Kuala Lumpur Singapore Hong Kong Tokyo
Nairobi Dar es Salaam Cape Town
Melbourne Auckland Madrid

and associated companies in
Berlin Ibadan

Oxford is a trade mark of Oxford University Press

This edition is not available in the USA





British Library
Cataloguing in Publication Data

Data available

Library of Congress
Cataloging-in-Publication Data

Data available

ISBN 0-19-869222-6

# Introduction

In the last one hundred years the world has changed dramatically, but the mechanical process of map-making has changed very little. Creating maps by hand remains a tedious and expensive undertaking; a single map might require forty separate layers of information. And though maps must now be revised constantly to keep pace with world events, updating maps is still a painstaking effort. Equally important, in this age of increasing graphic sophistication, there is a renewed appreciation for maps as art, and a pressing need for a contemporary atlas design which presents geographic information in a more accessible and dynamic fashion.

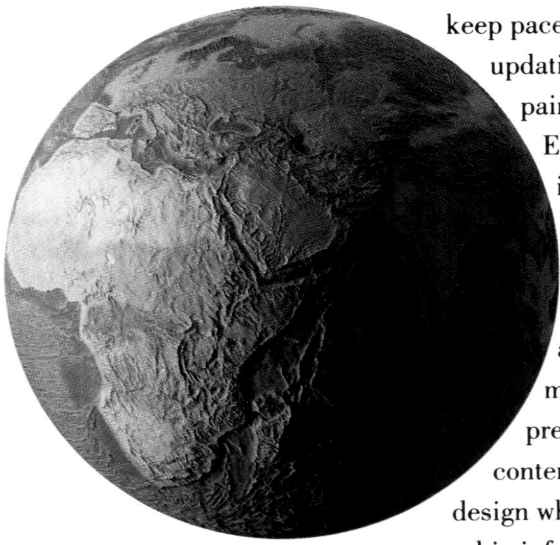

In 1986, Hammond Incorporated saw an opportunity to create such an atlas – and a radically new map-making system. Advances in technology provided a means of producing maps more efficiently and more accurately than ever before. At the heart of the plan was a computerized geographic database – one which would enable maps to be created and changed as desired.

Hammond Incorporated, established in 1900, has long enjoyed a reputation as one of America's finest map makers. Oxford University Press, with its own tradition as an atlas and reference publisher, began discussions with Hammond in 1989, resulting in a unique partnership between an innovative and enterprising family company and one of the world's largest university presses. This new atlas is the first product of that partnership.

The work of creating this atlas has been carried out by a team of talented and pioneering cartographers, researchers, editors, artists, technicians and scholars. In the five years it has taken to develop the new map-making system, the world has undergone huge political changes, to which they have responded, even so far as the most recent events in Czechoslovakia. The publishers wish to acknowledge the fundamental contribution of this team.

We are especially grateful also for the support of our many contributors. In particular, we wish to thank Mitchell Feigenbaum, a brilliant scientist whose talents in physics and mathematics also extend to the art – and science – of cartography. His genius is ever-present in this atlas, from his revolutionary map projection to his pioneering software, which was crucial to the success of our computer mapping system.

For the first time a publisher is able to employ a map-making system that moves as fast as the world is changing. We are committed to maintaining the highest level of quality – in accuracy and timeliness, in design and printing, and in service to our clients and readers. It is our goal to ensure that you can always turn to an Oxford Hammond atlas for the very best in map and atlas design and geographic information.

At the end of the twentieth century we are proud to offer a new presentation of the world as never seen before.

The Publishers
May 1993

# Contents

## Evolution of Cartography

Land-based cartographers used increasingly sophisticated optical instruments and mathematical analysis to survey and measure distances on the ground. Map-making was slow and time consuming, though accuracy was impressive.

Hot air balloons were occasionally used by military observers to map battle areas not accessible by land. More importantly, the application of photography by cartographers early in the 20th century ushered in a new age of map-making.

Airplanes permitted aerial reconnaissance at higher altitudes, greatly reducing surveying time. Meanwhile, advances in photography allowed sharp images of increasingly larger areas.

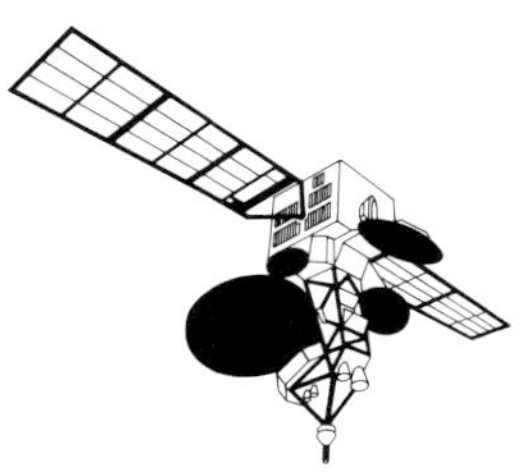

Satellites gave cartographers a global vantage point beyond the earth's atmosphere. Technological advances, many derived from military and aerospace research, permitted images to be systematically sent from space to sophisticated computers, where they were organized and enhanced.

Digital geographic databases are revolutionizing map-making in ways that the ancient Greeks never dreamed of. As this brief history of cartography reveals, maps can now be created and updated with greater accuracy and speed than ever before.

Maps extend our world, and our sense of place and direction within it. From mankind's earliest cave markings, people have drawn lines and sought to define their place within them. Indeed, maps have always been utilitarian tools. As far back as 2300 B.C., Babylonian officials used maps to aid in the collection of taxes.

The foundation of modern-day cartography was laid by the ancient Greeks, who recognized the spherical shape of the earth, developed our system of longitude and latitude, designed the first map projections and calculated the size of the earth — with surprising accuracy. Claudius Ptolemy's *Geographia*, produced in the 2nd century A.D., was the first bound collection of maps designed to serve both scholarship and administration.

During the Middle Ages, mapmakers made little attempt to show the world as it was. The typical medieval map represented a Christian ideal, usually placing Jerusalem in the center of the world. At the same time, however, Arab scholars were improving on Ptolemy's work, making significant advances in map presentation and accuracy.

At the end of the 13th century, the compass came into general use, and with it came a new kind of map, called a portolan chart, created by the Genovese fleet for navigational purposes. Based on compass surveys, these outline maps depicted the Mediterranean and Black seas with great accuracy. An elaborate system of lines indicating compass directions crisscrossed the maps' surfaces. In 1375, the Catalan Atlas used portolans to depict most of the world, following the text of Marco Polo.

Three key events contributed to the renaissance of cartography. First was the rediscovery of Ptolemy's *Geographia* in the West. Carefully preserved by devotees, the text eventually reached the Moorish rulers in Spain.

**This map of Holland was reproduced from an original version of *Theatrum Orbis Terrarum.* (Courtesy of Federico Canobbio-Codelli)**

Second was the invention of printing, which greatly increased the number of available maps, and brought them within reach of the average person. In 1478, Ptolemy's *Geographia* became the first of the classical Greek works to be printed.

**An eminent cartographer of the Age of Exploration, Gerardus Mercator, produced his first world map in 1538. As an aid to seamen, Mercator's map was unsurpassed, because all compass directions appeared as straight lines.**

Third, and perhaps most important, was the age of the great discoveries, which was itself made possible by the development of new three-masted sailing vessels.

### The Age of Exploration

European mariners set sail across the Atlantic beginning in the late 15th century. The great sea-going explorers of this era — Columbus, Cabot, Amerigo Vespucci, Magellan and Sir Francis Drake — all owed much to Ptolemy's ancient text, and to the refinements made at the navigational school founded by Prince Henry the Navigator. Ptolemy and others, however, considerably exaggerated the Eurasian landmass, showing it to occupy nearly half the globe. This error led Columbus to underestimate the distance to Asia; thus he failed to realize that he had reached the new world.

**In 1572 a volume of maps published in Rome added the figure of Atlas holding up the world—hence the name "Atlas".**

Gerardus Mercator, an important cartographer of his age, was the first to produce a true world navigational chart on a flat surface. It became the favored depiction among map publishers.

Many new maps followed as great explorers, and later traders, returned to correct and fill in the blank spaces of the expanding world. The first modern atlas, *Theatrum Orbis Terrarum*, was published in 1570.

The first successful marine chronometer, in use by 1761, offered a reliable means of measuring longitude. By the late 18th century, mapmakers were already producing a reasonable picture of the world as we know it today.

With the invention of photography in the 19th century, cartographers could at last record the landscape with photo-realistic precision and detail.Then, in the early 1900's, airplanes dramatically extended the scope of our view. Advances in photography kept pace, permitting crisp images of ever expanding areas. Aerial reconnaissance became the standard method for gathering cartographic data. Infrared and ultra-violet photography extended the range of perception beyond the visible spectrum, while radar penetrated visual obstacles such as clouds and fog.

A satellite view of the area shown on the map at left. Note the addition of Dutch "polders" or land reclaimed from the sea.

## Images from Space

But a quantum leap forward occurred in the 1970's, when remote sensing satellites launched a new age of cartography, giving us a vantage point beyond the earth's atmosphere. Satellites provided the first exact measurements of the earth's diameter and the distances between continents, and showed the earth to be flattened at the poles by precisely 26.6 miles (42.8 km.).

Today, satellites are mapping the globe. Landsat digital images of the earth are systematically broadcast from space to sophisticated computers, where the images are assembled and enhanced. This marriage of computers and satellites has given birth to radically new geographic information systems.

## Computer-Assisted Maps

Computers were quickly employed in the everyday production of maps. In computer-assisted map-making systems, computers function as electronic versions of traditional drafting tools. Hand-drawn maps are scanned into a computer, where revisions such as name and color changes can be made quickly and easily. However, because these systems must use existing maps as their source material, their ability to output maps at various scales, projections or with different levels of detail is seriously limited.

## Creating a Digital Database

*The Oxford Hammond Atlas of the World* is the first world atlas created directly from a digital database, and its computer-generated maps represent a new phase in map-making technology.

To build the database capable of generating this world atlas, the latitude and longitude of every significant town, river, coastline, natural and political border, transportation network and peak elevation was researched and digitized. Engineering the complex data structure was critical to the success of the system, which relies on powerful computers and enormous data storage capacity. Hundreds of millions of data points describing nearly every important geographic feature on earth are organized into over 1,000 different map feature codes.

Keeping the database current is a never-ending task. Every day, just as map-makers have done for centuries, researchers pore over government publications, maps, international journals and newspapers in search of geographic changes. They record renamed cities, new roads, revamped borders, diverted rivers, and hundreds of other constantly evolving political and topographic details.

## How Computer-Generated Maps Are Made

There are no maps in this unique system. Rather, it consists entirely of coded points, lines and polygons. To create a map, cartographers determine what city, region or continent they want to show and select specific information to include, based on editorial considerations such as scale, town size, population density, and the relative importance of different features. How does a computer plot irregular rivers and mountains — at many different scales? Using fractal geometry to describe natural forms such as coastlines, mathematical physicist Mitchell Feigenbaum developed software capable of re-configuring coastlines, borders and mountain ranges to fit a multitude of map scales and projections.

Even map labeling has finally given way to new technology. Dr. Feigenbaum also created a new computerized type placement program which places thousands of map labels in minutes, a task which previously required days of tedious labor. The program insures that the type carefully follows the curve of the graticule, or map grid, for maximum legibility and aesthetic appeal.

After these steps have been completed, the computer then draws the final map. The benefits of such a system go far beyond producing more timely and accurate maps. For the first time, geographers possess a uniquely creative map-making tool. Map projections can be changed at whim. Revisions that once took months can be completed in hours. Because the maps are digitally created, they can be utilized in a wide variety of electronic media.

Traditional craftsmanship still plays a vital role. To vividly represent a region's topography, hand-sculpted TerraScape™ relief models created by master cartographer Ernst Hofmann are married to the computer-generated world maps.

The database is also the beginning of a unique historical record. Every new town, every redrawn political boundary and reshaped geographic feature will be permanently stored in the digital database, exceeding the predictable life span of printed maps or even archival films.

A traditionally-produced map may require ten to forty film overlays, each containing a portion of the final map. Updating city names and political boundaries in the conventional manner is a tedious manual effort requiring light tables, ink pens and opaquing brushes.

The computer-generated maps in this atlas represent a new phase in cartography. They are derived from a digital world database that contains the precise latitude and longitude coordinates for every significant point on the globe. A single change with the sweep of a mouse can alter the entire look of a map.

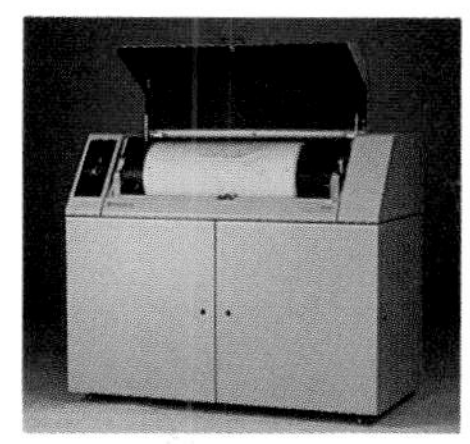

Once the map design is approved, a sophisticated laser plotter prints the final artwork onto film, producing a complete set of film positives for the standard five-color printing process in close to an hour — a savings of many days over conventional methods. Or, the image can be electronically transmitted anywhere in the world.

# Map Projections

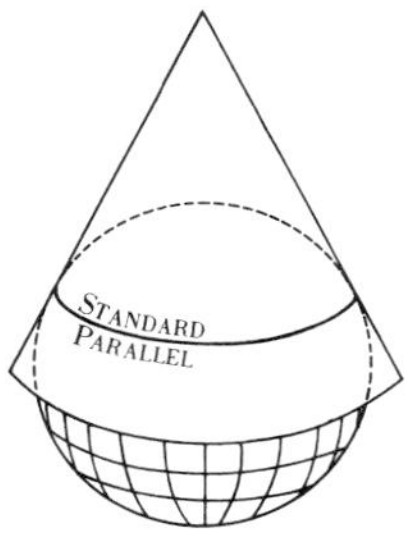


Figure 3
**Conic Projection**
The original idea of a conic projection is to cap the globe with a cone, and then project onto the cone from the planet's center the lines of latitude and longitude (the parallels and meridians). To produce a working map, the cone is simply cut open and laid flat. The conic projection used here is a modification of this idea. A cone can be made tangent to any standard parallel you choose. One popular version of a conic projection, the Lambert Conformal Conic, uses two standard parallels near the top and bottom of the map to further reduce errors of scale.

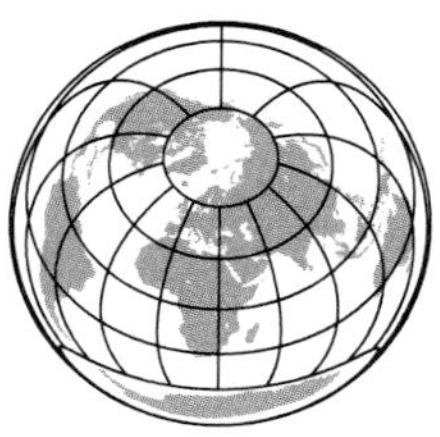

Figure 4
**Lambert Azimuthal Equal Area Projection**
Because this projection shows correct areas with relatively little distortion of shapes, it is commonly used to plot maps of the continents. However, because of improved accuracy, the Optimal Conformal projection was used for all of the continent maps in this atlas.

Simply stated, the map-maker's challenge is to project the earth's curved surface onto a flat plane. To achieve this elusive goal, cartographers have developed map projections — equations which govern this conversion of geographic data.

Since the Age of Exploration, literally hundreds of projections have been created, all attempting to present a view of the world which maintains true geographic relationships across the whole of the Earth. All have failed, for the goal is an impossible one. Yet some projections have achieved a remarkable degree of success.

This section explores some of the most widely used examples. It also introduces a new projection, the Hammond Optimal Conformal.

General Principles and Terms

The earth rotates around its axis once a day. Its end points are the North and South poles; the line circling the earth midway between the poles is the equator. The arc from the equator to either pole is divided into 90 degrees of latitude. The equator represents 0° latitude. Circles of equal latitude, called parallels, are traditionally shown at every fifth or tenth degree.

The equator is divided into 360 degrees. Lines circling the globe from pole to pole through the degree points on the equator are called meridians, or great circles. All meridians are equal in length, but by international agreement the meridian passing through the Greenwich Observatory near London has been chosen as the prime meridian or 0° longitude. The distance in degrees from the prime meridian to any point east or west is its longitude.

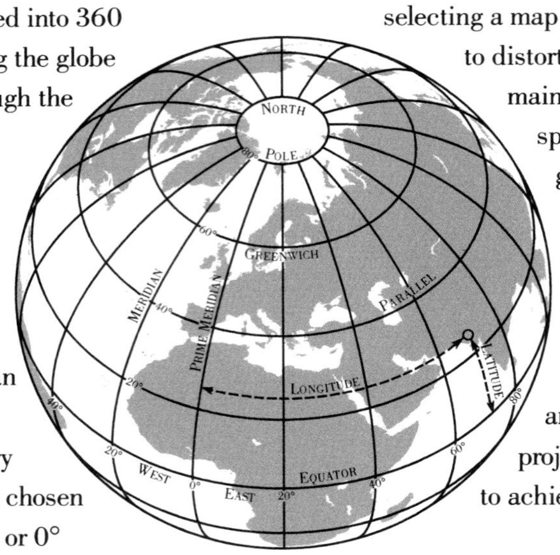


While meridians are all equal in length, parallels become shorter as they approach the poles. Whereas one degree of latitude represents approximately 69 miles (112 km.) anywhere on the globe, a degree of longitude varies from 69 miles (112 km.) at the equator to zero at the poles. Each degree of latitude and longitude is divided into 60 minutes. One minute of latitude equals one nautical mile (1.15 land miles or 1.85 km.).

How to Flatten a Sphere: The Art of Controlling Distortion

There is only one way to represent a sphere with absolute precision: on a globe. All attempts to project our planet's surface onto a plane unevenly stretch or tear the sphere as it flattens, inevitably distorting shapes, distances, area (sizes appear larger or smaller than actual size), angles or direction.

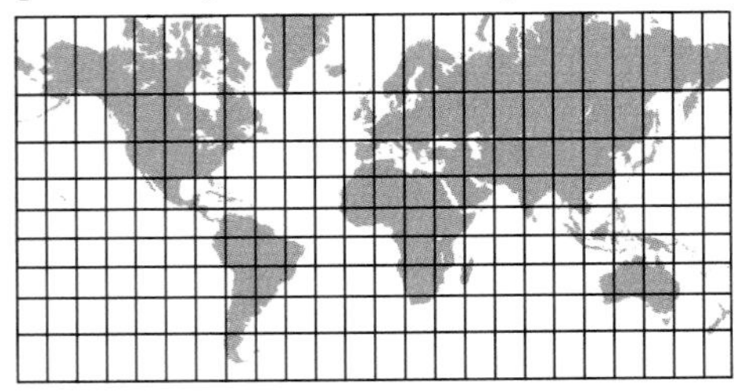

Figure 1 **Mercator Projection**

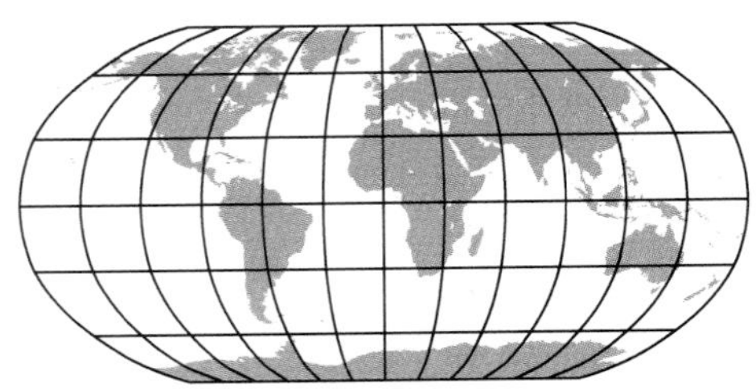

Figure 2 **Robinson Projection**

Since representing a sphere on a flat plane always creates distortion, only the parallels or the meridians (or some other set of lines) can maintain the same length as on a globe of corresponding scale. All other lines must be either too long or too short. Accordingly, the scale on a flat map cannot be true everywhere; there will always be different scales in different parts of a map. On world maps or very large areas, variations in scale may be extreme. The cartographer's concern in creating or selecting a map projection is this: how to distort the map in order to maintain the accuracy of a specific kind of geographic information. Most maps seek to preserve either true area relationships (equal area projections) or true angles and shapes (conformal projections); some attempt to achieve overall balance.

Projections: Selected Examples

Mercator (Fig. 1): This projection is especially useful because all compass directions appear as straight lines, making it a valuable navigational tool. Moreover, every small region conforms to its shape on a globe — hence the name conformal. But because its meridians are evenly-spaced vertical lines which never converge (unlike the globe), the horizontal parallels must be drawn farther and farther apart at higher latitudes to maintain a correct relationship. Only the equator is true to scale, and the size of areas in the higher latitudes is dramatically distorted.

Robinson (Fig. 2): To create the thematic maps in Global Relationships and the two-page world map in the Maps of the World section, the Robinson projection was used. It combines elements of both conformal and equal area projections to show the whole earth with relatively true shapes and reasonably equal areas.

Conic (Fig. 3): This projection has been used frequently for air navigation charts and to create most of the national and regional maps in this atlas. (See side bar).

Hammond Optimal Conformal

As its name implies, this new conformal projection presents the optimal view of an area by reducing shifts in scale over an entire region to the minimum degree possible. While conformal maps generally preserve all small shapes, large shapes can become very distorted because of varying scales, causing considerable inaccuracy in distance measurements. The concept underlying the Optimal Conformal is that for any region on the globe, there is an ideal projection for which scale variation can be made as small as possible. Consequently, unlike other projections, the Optimal Conformal does not use one standard formula to construct a map. Each map is a unique projection — the optimal projection for that particular area.

In practice, the cartographer first defines the map subject, then, working on a computer, draws a band around the region to be mapped. Next, a sophisticated software program evaluates the size and shape of the region to determine the most accurate way to project it. The result is the most distortion-free conformal map possible, and the most accurate projections that have ever been made. All of the continents maps in this atlas (with the exception of Antarctica) have been drawn using this projection.

## Accuracy Compared

| Cities | Spherical (True) Distance | Optimal Distance | Lambert Azimuthal Distance |
|---|---|---|---|
| Caracas to Rio Grande | 4,443 mi. (7,149 km.) | 4,429 mi. (7,126 km.) | 4,316 mi. (6,944 km.) |
| Maracaibo to Recife | 2,834 mi. (4,560 km.) | 2,845 mi. (4,578 km.) | 2,817 mi. (4,533 km.) |
| Fortaleza to Punta Arenas | 3,882 mi. (6,246 km.) | 3,907 mi. (6,266 km.) | 3,843 mi. (6,163 km.) |

**Continent maps drawn using the Lambert Azimuthal Equal Area projection (Fig. 4) contain distortions ranging from 2.3 percent for Europe up to 15 percent for Asia. The Optimal Conformal cuts that distortion in half, improving distance measurements on these continent maps. Less distortion means greater visual fidelity, so the shape of a continent on an Optimal projection more closely represents its True shape. The table above compares measurements on the Optimal projection to those of the Lambert Azimuthal Equal Area projection for selected cities.**

## Projections Compared

Because the true shapes of earth's landforms are unfamiliar to most people, distinguishing between various projections can be difficult. The following diagrams reveal the distortions introduced by several commonly used projections. By using a simple face with familiar shapes as the starting point (The Plan), it is easy to see the benefits — and drawbacks — of each. Think of the facial features as continents. Note that distortion appears not only in the features themselves, but in the changing shapes, angles and areas of the background grid, or graticule.

Figure 6: The Plan

The Plan indicates that the continents are either perfect concentric circles or are true straight lines *on the earth.* They should appear that way on a "perfect" map.

Figure 7: Orthographic Projection

This view shows the continents on the earth as seen from space. The facial features occupy half of the earth, which is all that you can see from this perspective. As you move outward towards the edge, note how the eyes become elliptical, the nose appears larger and less straight, and the mouth is curved into a smile.

Figure 8: Mercator

This cylindrical projection preserves angles exactly, but the mouth is now smiling broadly, and shows extreme distortion at the map's outer edge. This rapid expansion as you move away from the map's center is typified by the extreme enlargement of Greenland found on Mercator world maps (also see Fig. 1).

Figure 9: Peters

The Peters projection is a square equal area projection elongated, or stretched vertically, by a factor of two. While representing areas in their correct proportions, it does not closely resemble the Plan, and angles, local shapes and global relations are significantly distorted.

Figure 10: Gnomonic

Neither conformal nor equal-area, this strange-looking projection is a "perspective" projection made by placing a plane tangent to the sphere at the center of the earth. Though its outer regions are badly distorted, the straight mouth and precise triangle of the nose indicate a key property of this map: all great circles appear as straight lines. This enables the user to find the shortest path between any two points on the map by simply connecting them with a straight line.

Figure 11: Hammond Optimal Conformal

As you can see, this projection minimizes inaccuracies between the angles and shapes of the Plan, yielding a near-perfect map of the given area, up to a complete hemisphere. Like all conformal maps, the Optimal projection preserves every angle exactly, but it is more successful than previous projections at spreading the inevitable curvature across the entire map. Note that the sides of the triangle appear almost straight while correctly containing more than 180°. And though the eyes are slightly too large, it is the only map with eyes which appear concentric. Both mathematically and visually, it offers the best conformal map that can be made of the ideal Plan.

Figure 6
**The Plan**

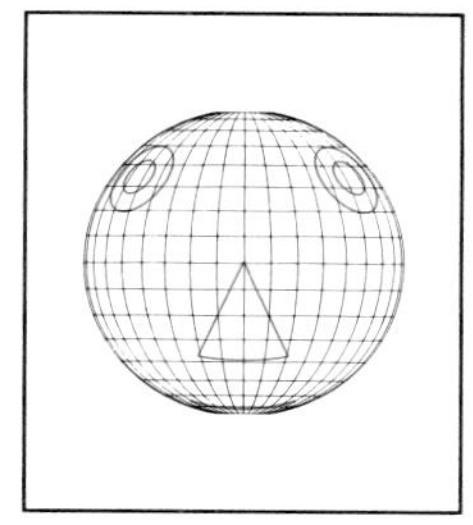

Figure 7
**Orthographic Projection**

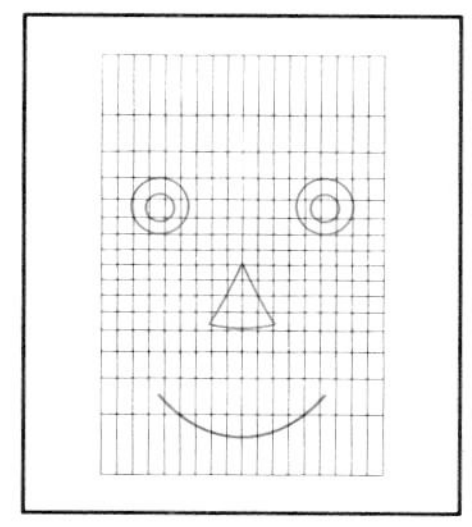

Figure 8
**Mercator Projection**

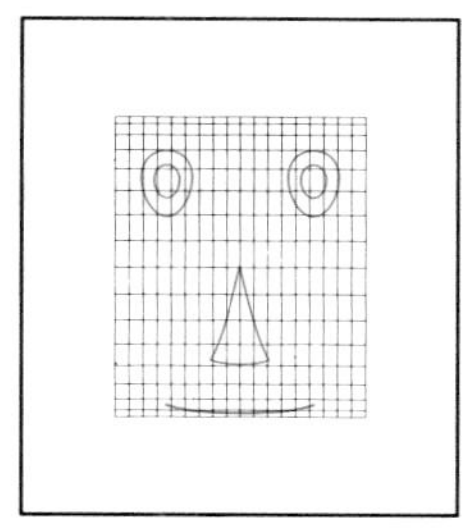

Figure 9
**Peters Projection**

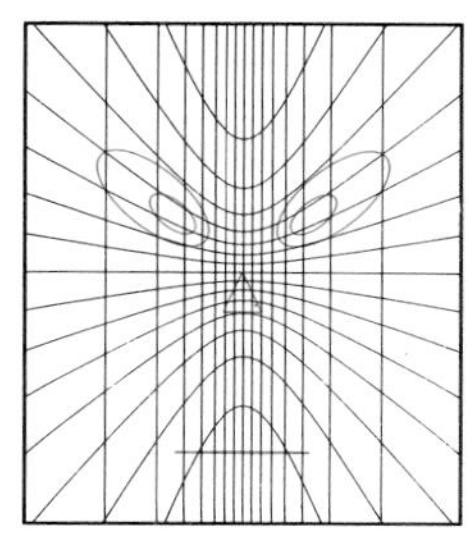

Figure 10
**Gnomonic Projection**

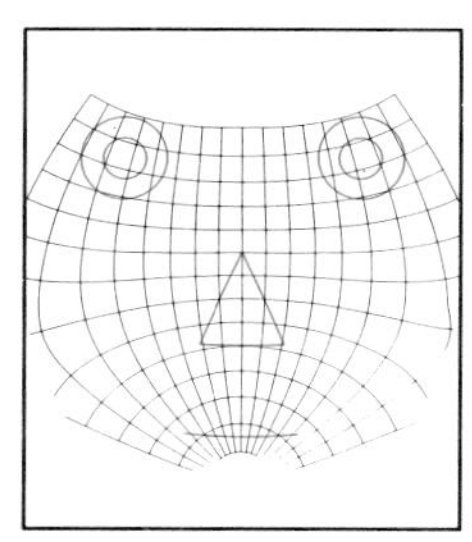

Figure 11
**Optimal Conformal Projection**

# Using This Atlas

**How to Locate Information Quickly**

For familiar locations such as continents, countries and major political divisions, the World Locator Map and Quick Reference Guide help you quickly pinpoint the map you need. For less familiar places, begin with the Master Index.

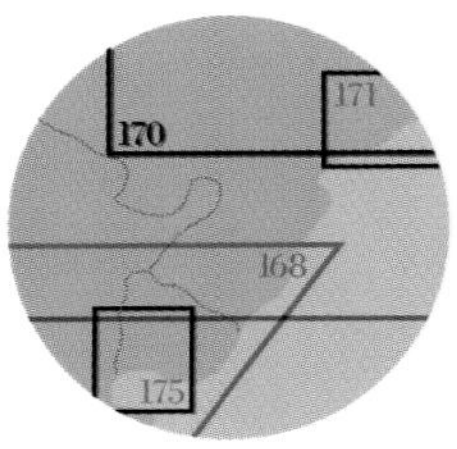


**World Locator Map**

This streamlined world map, conveniently located on the front end sheets, defines the coverage and page numbers of every political map in the atlas. Because it shows the overall arrangement of these maps, it's easy to locate maps of adjacent regions.

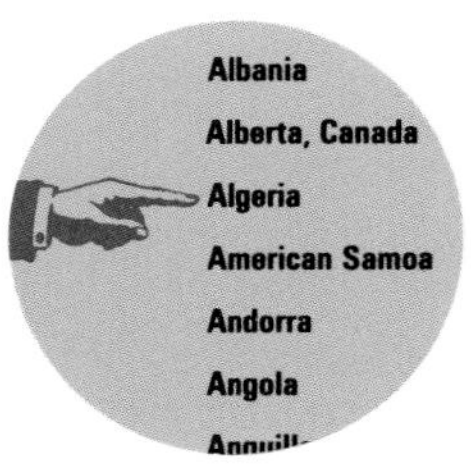


**Quick Reference Guide**

This concise guide lists continents, countries, states, provinces and territories in alphabetical order, complete with the size, population and capital of each. Red page numbers and alpha-numeric reference keys are visible at a glance.

**Master Index of the World**

When you're looking for an unfamiliar place or physical feature, your quickest route is the Master Index. This 115,000-entry alphabetical index lists both the page number and alpha-numeric reference key for every place and feature in Maps of the World.

*The Oxford Hammond Atlas of the World* has been thoughtfully designed to be easy and enjoyable to use, both as a general reference, and for armchair exploration of the globe. A short time spent familiarizing yourself with its organization will help you to benefit fully from its use.

## Global Relationships

This section highlights key social, cultural, economic and geographic factors. Together, these eight succinct chapters — from Population to Standards of Living— provide a fresh perspective on the world today. In the case of complex and rapidly evolving topics such as Environment, data analysis is in a relatively early stage, and projected outcomes are sometimes controversial.

## The Physical World

These relief maps of the continents and major regions of the world depict the topography of the earth's surface, and represent our most current knowledge of the ocean floor. Because the maps are actual photographs of three-dimensional TerraScape™ models, they present the relationships of land and sea forms and the rugged contours of the terrain with startling realism.

## Maps of the World

These detailed regional maps are arranged by continent, and introduced by a political map of that continent. The continent maps, which utilize the new Hammond Optimal Conformal projection, are distinguished by individual colors for each country to highlight political divisions.

On the regional maps, different colors and textures highlight distinctive features such as parks, forests, deserts and urban areas. These maps also provide considerable information concerning geographic features and political divisions. The realistic topography is achieved by combining the computer-generated political maps with the hand-sculpted TerraScape™ relief maps.

## Master Index

This is a complete A-Z listing of every name found on the political maps. It also has its own abbreviation list which, along with other Index keys, appears on page 216.

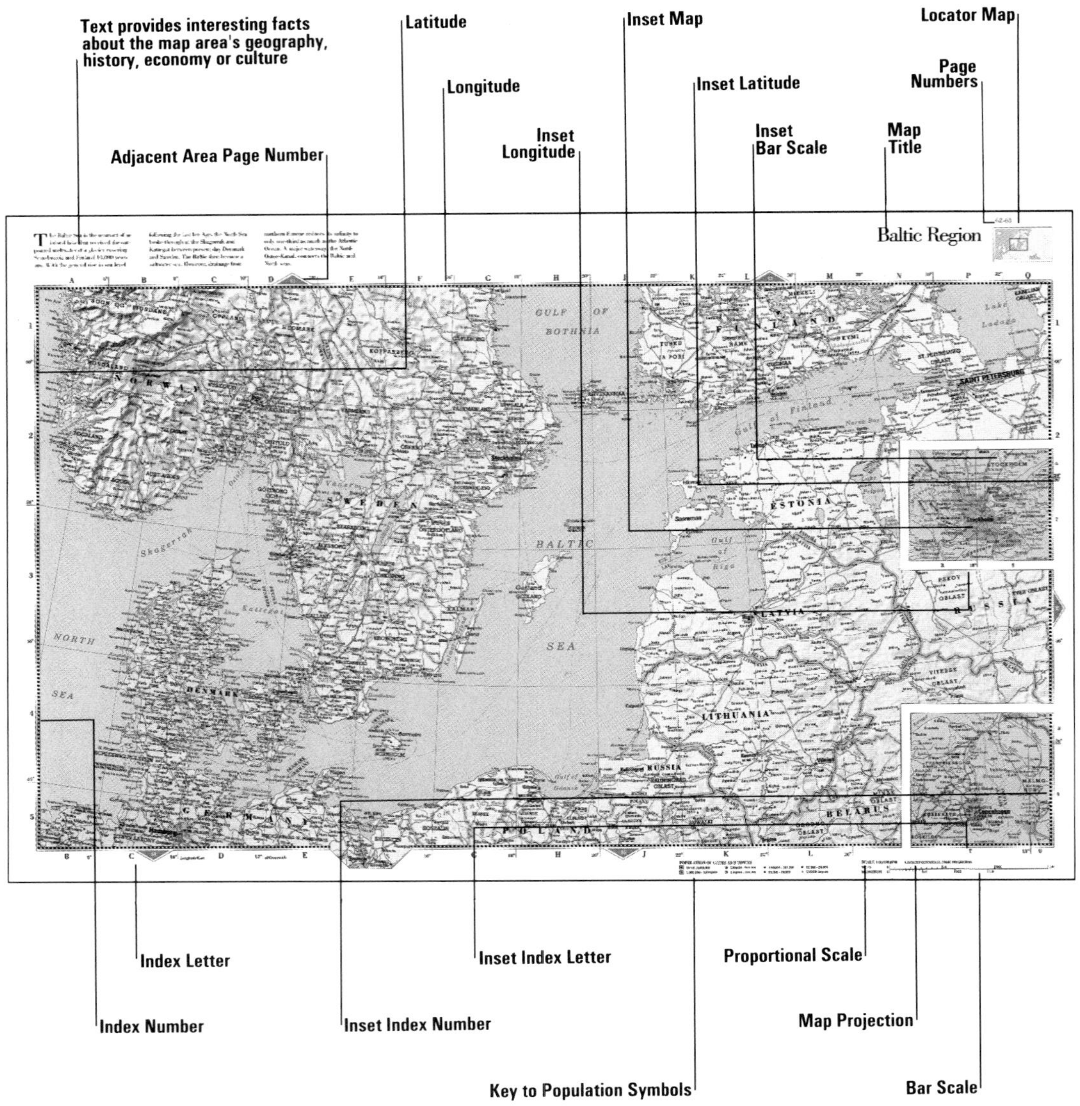


## Symbols Used on Maps of the World

| | | |
|---|---|---|
| First Order (National) Boundary | City and Urban Area Limits | Stockholm — First Order (National) Capital |
| First Order (Water) Boundary | Demilitarized Zone | Lausanne — Second Order (Internal) Capital |
| First Order Disputed Boundary | National Park/Preserve/Scenic Area | Morristown — Third Order (Internal) Capital |
| Second Order (Internal) Boundary | National Forest/Forest Reserve | Neighborhood |
| Second Order Water Boundary | National Wilderness/Grassland | Pass |
| Second Order Disputed Boundary | National Recreation Area/Monument | Ruins |
| Third Order (Internal) Boundary | National Seashore/Lakeshore | Falls |
| Undefined Boundary | National Wildlife/Wilderness Area | Rapids |
| International Date Line | Native Reservation/Reserve | Dam |
| Shoreline, River | Military/Government Reservation | Point Elevation |
| Intermittent River | Lake, Reservoir | Park |
| Canal | Intermittent Lake | Wildlife Area |
| Continental Divide | Dry Lake | Point of Interest |
| Highways/Roads | Salt Pan | Well |
| Railroads | Desert/Sand Area | International Airport |
| Ferries | Swamp | Other Airport |
| Tunnels (Road, Railroad) | Lava Flow | Air Base |
| Ancient Walls | Glacier | Naval Base |

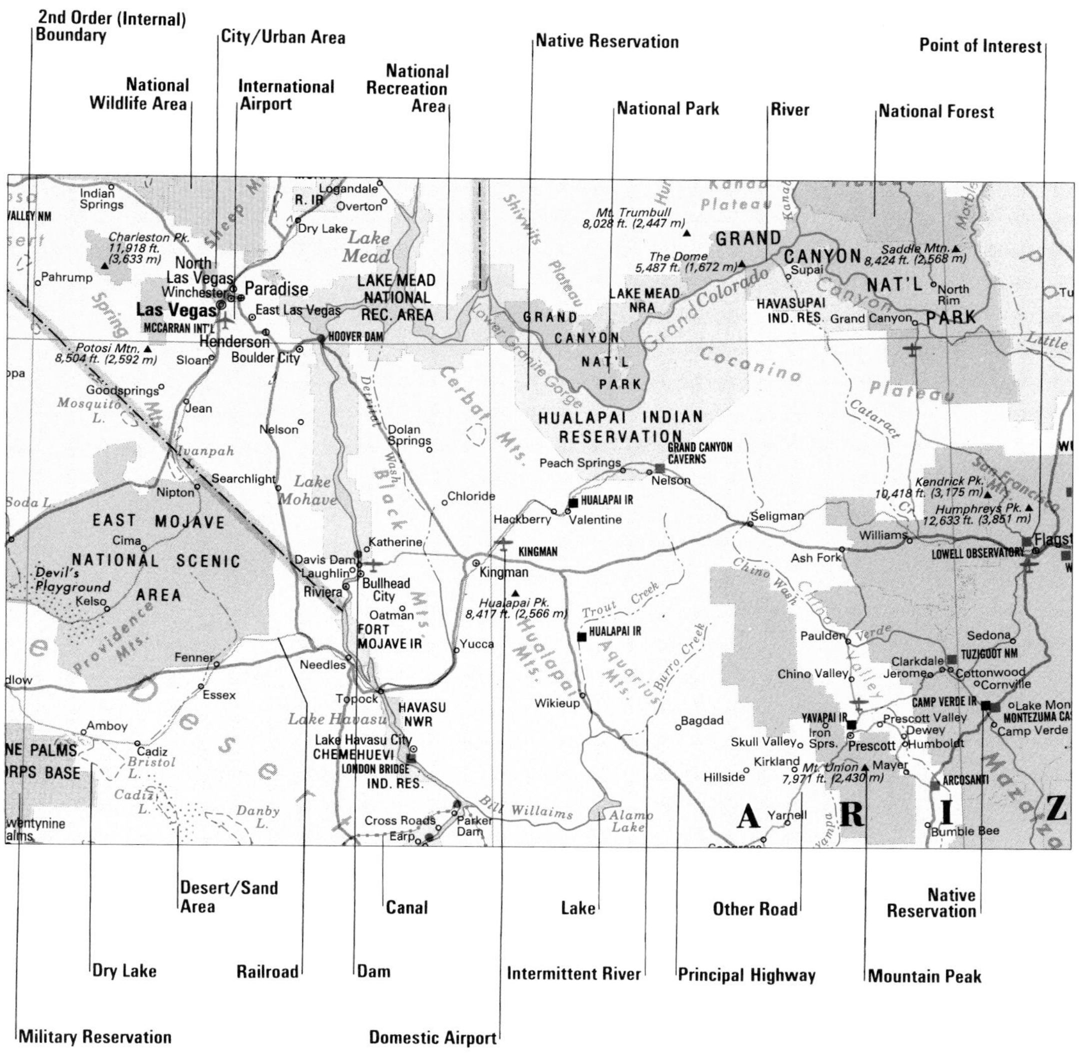


## Principal Map Abbreviations

| | | | | | | | |
|---|---|---|---|---|---|---|---|
| Abor. Rsv. | Aboriginal Reserve | Gd. | Grand | NHPP | National Historical | Passg. | Passage |
| Admin. | Administration | Grsld. | Grassland | | Park and Preserve | Pen. | Peninsula |
| AFB | Air Force Base | Gt. | Great | NHRSV | National Historical | Pk. | Peak |
| Amm. Dep. | Ammunition Depot | Har. | Harbor | | Reserve | Plat. | Plateau |
| Arch. | Archipelago | Hd. | Head | NHS | National Historic | PN | Park National |
| Arpt. | Airport | Hist. | Historic(al) | | Site | Pref. | Prefecture |
| Aut. | Autonomous | Hts. | Heights | NL | National Lakeshore | Prom. | Promontory |
| B. | Bay | I., Is. | Island(s) | NLAB | National | Prov. | Province, |
| Bfld. | Battlefield | Ind. Res. | Indian Reservation | | Laboratory | Prsv. | Preserve |
| Bk. | Brook | Int'l | International | NM | National Monument | Pt. | Point |
| Bor. | Borough | Intst. | Interstate | NMEM | National Memorial | R. | River |
| Br. | Branch | IR | Indian Reservation | NMEMP | National Memorial | RA | Recreation Area |
| C. | Cape | Isth. | Isthmus | | Park | Ra. | Range |
| Can. | Canal | Jct. | Junction | NMILP | National Military | Rec. | Recreation(al) |
| Cap. | Capital | L. | Lake | | Park | Ref. | Refuge |
| C.G. | Coast Guard | Lag. | Lagoon | No. | Northern | Reg. | Region |
| Chan. | Channel | Lakesh. | Lakeshore | NP | National Park | Rep. | Republic |
| Co. | County | Mem. | Memorial | NPP | National Park and | Res. | Reservoir, |
| Consv. Area | Conservation Area | Mil. | Military | | Preserve | | Reservation |
| Cr. | Creek | Miss. | Missile | NPRSV | National Preserve | Rvwy. | Riverway |
| Ctr. | Center | Mon. | Monument | NRA | National | Sa. | Sierra |
| Dep. | Depot | Mt. | Mount | | Recreation Area | Sd. | Sound |
| Depr. | Depression | Mtn. | Mountain | NRIV | National River | Seash. | Seashore |
| Dept. | Department | Mts. | Mountains | NRR | National | So. | Southern |
| Des. | Desert | Nat. | Natural | | Recreational River | SP | State Park |
| Dist. | District | Nat'l | National | NRRA | National River & | Spr., Sprs. | Spring, Springs |
| DMZ | Demilitarized Zone | Nav. | Naval | | Recreational Area | St. | State |
| Dpcy. | Dependency | NB | National | NRSV | National Reserve | Sta. | Station |
| Eng. | Engineering | | Battlefield | NS | National Seashore | Stm. | Stream |
| Est. | Estuary | NBP | National | NSRIV | National Scenic | Str. | Strait |
| Fd. | Fiord, Fjord | | Battlefield Park | | Riverway | Terr. | Territory |
| Fed. | Federal | NBS | National | NSRR | National Scenic & | Tun. | Tunnel |
| Fk. | fork | | Battlefield Site | | Recreational River | Twp. | Township |
| Fld. | Field | NCA | National | NWR | National Wildlife | Val. | Valley |
| For. | Forest | | Conservation Area | | Reserve | Vill. | Village |
| Ft. | Fort | NF | National Forest | Obl. | Oblast | Vol. | Volcano |
| G. | Gulf | NG | National Grassland | Occ. | Occupied | Wild. | Wildlife, |
| Gov. | Governorate | NHP | National Historical | Okr. | Okrug | | Wilderness |
| Govt. | Government | | Park | Par. | Parish | Wtr. | Water |

## Statistics & Other Key Facts

World Statistics lists the dimensions of the earth's principal mountains, islands, rivers and lakes, along with other useful geographic information. Population of Major Cities contains the latest population figures for the world's largest cities, organized by country in alphabetical order. You'll find the size and population of major geographical areas, from states and territories to continents, in the Quick Reference Guide.

## Map Scales

A map's scale is the relationship of any length on the map to an identical length on the earth's surface. A scale of 1:3,000,000 means that one inch on the map represents 3,000,000 inches (47 miles, 76 km.) on the earth's surface. Thus, a 1:1,000,000 scale is larger than 1:3,000,000, just as 1/1 is larger than 1/3.

The most densely populated areas are shown at a scale of 1:1,000,000, while selected metropolitan areas are covered at either 1:500,000 or 1:1,000,000. Other populous areas are presented at 1:3,000,000 and 1:6,000,000, allowing you to accurately compare areas and distances of similar regions. Remaining regions are scaled at 1:9,000,000. The continent maps, as well as the United States, Canada, Russia and the Pacific have smaller scales, in multiples of 3,000,000.

## Boundary Policies

This atlas observes the boundary policies of the U.S. Department of State. Boundary disputes are customarily handled with a special symbol treatment, but de facto boundaries are favored if they seem to have any degree of permanence, in the belief that boundaries should reflect current geographic and political realities. The portrayal of independent nations in the atlas follows their recognition by the United Nations and/or the United States government.

Hammond also uses accepted conventional names for certain major foreign places. Usually, space permits the inclusion of the local form in parentheses. To make the maps more readily understandable to English-speaking readers, many foreign physical features are translated into more recognizable English forms.

**Map Type Styles**

Cartographers use a variety of type styles to differentiate between map features. The following styles are used in this Atlas.

Major Political Areas
**LUXEMBOURG**

Internal Political Divisions
**SAXONY-ANHALT**

Historical Regions
*Polabská Nížina*

Cities and Towns
**Norfolk** Sumter Smyrna

Neighborhoods
BIGGIN HILL

Points of Interest
MISSION SAN BUENAVENTURA

Water Features
*L. Elsinore*

Capes, Points, Peaks, Passes
*Pt. La Jolla* *Pacifico Mtn*

Islands, Peninsulas
*Cape Breton I.*

Mountain Ranges, Plateaus, Hills
*Serra do Norte*

Deserts, Plains, Valleys
*San Fernando Valley*

**A Word About Names**

Our source for all foreign names and physical names in the United States is the decision lists of the U.S. Board of Geographic Names, which contain hundreds of thousands of place names. If a place is not listed, the Atlas follows the name form appearing on official foreign maps or in official gazetteers of the country concerned. For rendering domestic city, town and village names, this atlas follows the forms and spelling of the U.S. Postal Service.

# Quick Reference Guide

This concise alphabetical reference lists continents, countries, states, territories, possessions and other major geographical areas, complete with the size, population and capital or chief town of each. Page numbers and red alpha-numeric reference keys (which refer to the grid squares of latitude and longitude on each map) are visible at a glance. The population figures are the latest and most reliable figures obtainable.

| | Place | Square Miles | Square Kilometers | Population | Capital or Chief Town | Page/ Index |
|---|---|---|---|---|---|---|
| A | **Afghanistan** | 250,775 | 649,507 | 16,450,000 | Kabul | 107/H 2 |
| | **Africa** | 11,707,000 | 30,321,130 | 648,000,000 | ................. | 140 |
| | **Alabama, U.S.** | 51,705 | 133,916 | 4,062,608 | Montgomery | 181/J 5 |
| | **Alaska, U.S.** | 591,004 | 1,530,700 | 551,947 | Juneau | 177 |
| | **Albania** | 11,100 | 28,749 | 3,335,000 | Tiranë | 91/F 2 |
| | **Alberta, Canada** | 255,285 | 661,185 | 2,365,825 | Edmonton | 178/E 3 |
| | **Algeria** | 919,591 | 2,381,740 | 26,022,000 | Algiers | 143/F 3 |
| | **American Samoa** | 77 | 199 | 43,000 | Pago Pago | 139/J 6 |
| | **Andorra** | 188 | 487 | 53,000 | Andorra la Vella | 77/F 1 |
| | **Angola** | 481,351 | 1,246,700 | 8,668,000 | Luanda | 140/D 6 |
| | **Anguilla, U.K.** | 35 | 91 | 7,000 | The Valley | 162/F 3 |
| | **Antarctica** | 5,500,000 | 14,245,000 | ................. | ................. | 137 |
| | **Antigua and Barbuda** | 171 | 443 | 64,000 | St. John's | 162/F 3 |
| | **Argentina** | 1,072,070 | 2,776,661 | 32,664,000 | Buenos Aires | 163/B 7 |
| | **Arizona, U.S.** | 114,000 | 295,260 | 3,677,985 | Phoenix | 187/F 3 |
| | **Arkansas, U.S.** | 53,187 | 137,754 | 2,362,239 | Little Rock | 181/H 4 |
| | **Armenia** | 11,506 | 29,800 | 3,283,000 | Yerevan | 97/H 4 |
| | **Aruba, Netherlands** | 75 | 193 | 64,000 | Oranjestad | 162/D 4 |
| | **Ascension Island, St. Helena** | 34 | 88 | 719 | Georgetown | 140/A 5 |
| | **Ashmore & Cartier Islands, Australia** | 61 | 159 | ................. | (Canberra, Austr.) | 130/A 3 |
| | **Asia** | 17,128,500 | 44,362,815 | 3,176,000,000 | ................. | 102 |
| | **Australia** | 2,966,136 | 7,682,300 | 17,288,000 | Canberra | 128 |
| | **Australian Capital Territory** | 927 | 2,400 | 221,609 | Canberra | 135/D 2 |
| | **Austria** | 32,375 | 83,851 | 7,666,000 | Vienna | 75/L 3 |
| | **Azerbaijan** | 33,436 | 86,600 | 7,029,000 | Baku | 97/H 4 |
| | **Azores, Portugal** | 902 | 2,335 | 275,900 | Ponta Delgada | 77/R 12 |
| B | **Bahamas** | 5,382 | 13,939 | 252,000 | Nassau | 162/B 2 |
| | **Bahrain** | 240 | 622 | 537,000 | Manama | 106/F 3 |
| | **Baker Island, U.S.** | 1 | 2.6 | ................. | ................. | 139/H 4 |
| | **Balearic Islands, Spain** | 1,936 | 5,014 | 655,909 | Palma | 77/F 3 |
| | **Bangladesh** | 55,126 | 142,776 | 116,601,000 | Dhaka | 121/G 4 |
| | **Barbados** | 166 | 430 | 255,000 | Bridgetown | 162/G 4 |
| | **Belarus** | 80,154 | 207,600 | 10,200,000 | Minsk | 52/G 3 |
| | **Belgium** | 11,781 | 30,513 | 9,922,000 | Brussels | 64/C 3 |
| | **Belize** | 8,867 | 22,966 | 228,000 | Belmopan | 160/D 2 |
| | **Benin** | 43,483 | 112,620 | 4,832,000 | Porto-Novo | 145/F 4 |
| | **Bermuda, U.K.** | 21 | 54 | 58,000 | Hamilton | 176/L 6 |
| | **Bhutan** | 18,147 | 47,000 | 1,598,000 | Thimphu | 121/G 2 |
| | **Bolivia** | 424,163 | 1,098,582 | 7,157,000 | La Paz; Sucre | 163/C 4 |
| | **Bonaire, Neth. Antilles** | 112 | 291 | 8,087 | Kralendijk | 162/D 4 |
| | **Bophuthatswana, South Africa** | 15,570 | 40,326 | 1,200,000 | Mmabatho | 156/D 2 |
| | **Bosnia & Hercegovina** | 19,940 | 51,129 | 4,124,256 | Sarajevo | 92/C 3 |
| | **Botswana** | 224,764 | 582,139 | 1,258,000 | Gaborone | 140/E 7 |
| | **Bouvet Island, Norway** | 22 | 57 | ................. | ................. | 51/K 8 |
| | **Brazil** | 3,284,426 | 8,506,663 | 155,356,000 | Brasilia | 163/D 3 |
| | **British Columbia, Canada** | 366,253 | 948,596 | 2,883,367 | Victoria | 178/D 3 |
| | **British Indian Ocean Terr., U.K.** | 29 | 75 | 2,000 | (London, U.K.) | 102/G 10 |
| | **British Virgin Islands** | 59 | 153 | 12,000 | Road Town | 162/E 3 |
| | **Brunei** | 2,226 | 5,765 | 398,000 | Bandar Seri Begawan | 125/A 4 |
| | **Bulgaria** | 42,823 | 110,912 | 8,911,000 | Sofia | 93/G 4 |
| | **Burkina Faso** | 105,869 | 274,200 | 9,360,000 | Ouagadougou | 145/E 3 |
| | **Burma (Myanmar)** | 261,789 | 678,034 | 42,112,000 | Rangoon | 119/G 2 |
| | **Burundi** | 10,747 | 27,835 | 5,831,000 | Bujumbura | 153/G 3 |
| C | **California, U.S.** | 158,706 | 411,049 | 29,839,250 | Sacramento | 180/C 4 |
| | **Cambodia (Kampuchea)** | 69,898 | 181,036 | 7,146,000 | Phnom Penh | 123/D 3 |
| | **Cameroon** | 183,568 | 475,441 | 11,390,000 | Yaoundé | 140/D 4 |
| | **Canada** | 3,851,787 | 9,976,139 | 26,835,331 | Ottawa | 178 |
| | **Canary Islands, Spain** | 2,808 | 7,273 | 1,367,646 | Las Palmas;Santa Cruz | 77/X 16 |
| | **Cape Province, South Africa** | 261,705 | 677,816 | 5,543,506 | Cape Town | 156/C 3 |
| | **Cape Verde** | 1,557 | 4,033 | 387,000 | Praia | 140/A 3 |
| | **Cayman Islands, U.K.** | 100 | 259 | 27,000 | Georgetown | 161/F 2 |
| | **Celebes, Indonesia** | 72,986 | 189,034 | 7,732,383 | Ujung Pandang | 127/E 4 |
| | **Central African Republic** | 242,000 | 626,780 | 2,952,000 | Bangui | 148/C 4 |
| | **Chad** | 495,752 | 1,283,998 | 5,122,000 | N'Djamena | 140/D 3 |
| | **Channel Islands, U.K.** | 75 | 194 | 133,000 | St. Helier;<br>St. Peter Port | 78/C 2 |
| | **Chile** | 292,257 | 756,946 | 13,287,000 | Santiago | 163/B 6 |
| | **China, People's Rep. of** | 3,691,000 | 9,559,690 | 1,151,487,000 | Beijing | 102/J 6 |
| | **China, Republic of (Taiwan)** | 13,971 | 36,185 | 20,659,000 | Taipei | 117/J 3 |
| | **Christmas Island, Australia** | 52 | 135 | 3,184 | Flying Fish Cove | 102/K 11 |
| | **Ciskei, S. Africa** | 2,988 | 7,740 | 635,631 | Bisho | 156/D 4 |
| | **Clipperton Island, France** | 2 | 5.2 | ................. | ................. | 50/D 5 |
| | **Cocos (Keeling) Islands, Australia** | 5.4 | 14 | 555 | West Island | 102/J 11 |
| | **Colombia** | 439,513 | 1,138,339 | 33,778,000 | Bogotá | 164/C 4 |
| | **Colorado, U.S.** | 104,091 | 269,596 | 3,307,912 | Denver | 180/E 4 |
| | **Comoros** | 719 | 1,862 | 477,000 | Moroni | 157/G 5 |
| | **Congo** | 132,046 | 342,000 | 2,309,000 | Brazzaville | 152/C 3 |
| | **Connecticut, U.S.** | 5,018 | 12,997 | 3,295,669 | Hartford | 199/K 4 |
| | **Cook Islands, New Zealand** | 91 | 236 | 18,000 | Avarua | 139/J 6 |
| | **Coral Sea Islands, Australia** | 8.5 | 22 | ................. | ................. | 129/H 3 |
| | **Corsica, France** | 3,352 | 8,682 | 289,842 | Ajaccio; Bastia | 90/A 1 |
| | **Costa Rica** | 19,575 | 50,700 | 3,111,000 | San José | 161/F 4 |
| | **Côte d'Ivoire, see Ivory Coast** | | | | | |
| | **Croatia** | 22,050 | 56,538 | 4,601,469 | Zagreb | 92/B 3 |
| | **Cuba** | 44,206 | 114,494 | 10,732,000 | Havana | 161/F 1 |
| | **Curaçao, Neth. Antilles** | 178 | 462 | 145,430 | Willemstad | 162/D 4 |
| | **Cyprus** | 3,473 | 8,995 | 709,000 | Nicosia | 103/C 2 |
| | **Czech Republic** | 30,449 | 78,863 | 10,291,927 | Prague | 65/H 4 |
| D | **Delaware, U.S.** | 2,044 | 5,294 | 668,696 | Dover | 181/L 4 |
| | **Denmark** | 16,629 | 43,069 | 5,133,000 | Copenhagen | 62/C 4 |
| | **District of Columbia, U.S.** | 69 | 179 | 609,909 | Washington | 206/B 6 |
| | **Djibouti** | 8,880 | 23,000 | 346,000 | Djibouti | 150/B 2 |
| | **Dominica** | 290 | 751 | 86,000 | Roseau | 162/F 4 |
| | **Dominican Republic** | 18,704 | 48,443 | 7,385,000 | Santo Domingo | 162/D 3 |
| E | **Ecuador** | 109,483 | 283,561 | 10,752,000 | Quito | 163/B 3 |
| | **Egypt** | 386,659 | 1,001,447 | 54,452,000 | Cairo | 147/F 3 |
| | **El Salvador** | 8,260 | 21,393 | 5,419,000 | San Salvador | 160/D 3 |
| | **England, U.K.** | 50,516 | 130,836 | 46,220,955 | London | 55/K 10 |
| | **Equatorial Guinea** | 10,831 | 28,052 | 379,000 | Malabo | 152/B 2 |
| | **Estonia** | 17,413 | 45,100 | 1,573,000 | Tallinn | 63/L 2 |
| | **Ethiopia** | 471,776 | 1,221,900 | 53,191,000 | Addis Ababa | 140/F 4 |
| | **Europe** | 4,057,000 | 10,507,630 | 689,000,000 | ................. | 52 |
| F | **Falkland Islands & Dependencies, U.K.** | 6,198 | 16,053 | 1,813 | Stanley | 175/M 8 |
| | **Faroe Islands, Denmark** | 540 | 1,399 | 48,000 | Tórshavn | 52/D 2 |
| | **Fiji** | 7,055 | 18,272 | 744,000 | Suva | 138/G 6 |
| | **Finland** | 130,128 | 337,032 | 4,991,000 | Helsinki | 61/H 2 |
| | **Florida, U.S.** | 58,664 | 151,940 | 13,003,362 | Tallahassee | 203/F 2 |
| | **France** | 210,038 | 543,998 | 56,596,000 | Paris | 74/D 3 |
| | **French Guiana** | 35,135 | 91,000 | 102,000 | Cayenne | 166/C 2 |
| | **French Polynesia** | 1,544 | 4,000 | 195,000 | Papeete | 139/M 6 |
| G | **Gabon** | 103,346 | 267,666 | 1,080,000 | Libreville | 152/B 3 |
| | **Gambia** | 4,127 | 10,689 | 875,000 | Banjul | 144/B 1 |
| | **Gaza Strip** | 139 | 360 | 642,000 | Gaza | 103/C 4 |
| | **Georgia** | 26,911 | 69,700 | 5,449,000 | Tbilisi | 97/G 4 |
| | **Georgia, U.S.** | 58,910 | 152,577 | 6,508,419 | Atlanta | 181/K 5 |
| | **Germany** | 137,753 | 356,780 | 79,548,000 | Berlin | 64/E 3 |
| | **Ghana** | 92,099 | 238,536 | 15,617,000 | Accra | 145/E 4 |
| | **Gibraltar, U.K.** | 2.28 | 5.91 | 30,000 | Gibraltar | 76/C 4 |
| | **Great Britain & Northern Ireland (United Kingdom)** | 94,399 | 244,493 | 57,236,000 | London | 55 |

| | Place | Square Miles | Square Kilometers | Population | Capital or Chief Town | Page/ Index |
|---|---|---|---|---|---|---|
| | **Greece** | 50,944 | 131,945 | 10,043,000 | Athens | 91/G 3 |
| | **Greenland, Denmark** | 840,000 | 2,175,600 | 57,000 | Nuuk (Godthåb) | 176/N 2 |
| | **Grenada** | 133 | 344 | 84,000 | St. George's | 162/F 5 |
| | **Guadeloupe & Dependencies, France** | 687 | 1,779 | 345,400 | Basse-Terre | 162/F 3 |
| | **Guam, U.S.** | 209 | 541 | 145,000 | Agaña | 138/D 3 |
| | **Guatemala** | 42,042 | 108,889 | 9,266,000 | Guatemala | 160/D 3 |
| | **Guinea** | 94,925 | 245,856 | 7,456,000 | Conakry | 144/C 4 |
| | **Guinea-Bissau** | 13,948 | 36,125 | 753,313 | Bissau | 144/B 3 |
| | **Guyana** | 83,000 | 214,970 | 758,619 | Georgetown | 165/G 3 |
| H | **Haiti** | 10,694 | 27,697 | 6,287,000 | Port-au-Prince | 161/H 2 |
| | **Hawaii, U.S.** | 6,471 | 16,760 | 1,115,274 | Honolulu | 180/S 10 |
| | **Heard & McDonald Islands, Australia** | 113 | 293 | ... | ... | 51/P 8 |
| | **Holland, see Netherlands** | | | | | |
| | **Honduras** | 43,277 | 112,087 | 4,949,000 | Tegucigalpa | 160/E 3 |
| | **Hong Kong, U.K.** | 403 | 1,044 | 5,856,000 | Victoria | 117/G 4 |
| | **Howland Island, U.S.** | 1 | 2.6 | ... | ... | 139/H 4 |
| | **Hungary** | 35,919 | 93,030 | 10,558,000 | Budapest | 92/D 2 |
| I | **Iceland** | 39,768 | 103,000 | 260,000 | Reykjavik | 61/N 7 |
| | **Idaho, U.S.** | 83,564 | 216,431 | 1,011,986 | Boise | 180/C 3 |
| | **Illinois, U.S.** | 56,345 | 145,934 | 11,466,682 | Springfield | 181/J 4 |
| | **India** | 1,269,339 | 3,287,588 | 869,515,000 | New Delhi | 118/C 3 |
| | **Indiana, U.S.** | 36,185 | 93,719 | 5,564,228 | Indianapolis | 181/J 4 |
| | **Indonesia** | 788,430 | 2,042,034 | 193,560,000 | Jakarta | 127/E 4 |
| | **Iowa, U.S.** | 56,275 | 145,752 | 2,787,424 | Des Moines | 193/G 2 |
| | **Iran** | 636,293 | 1,648,000 | 59,051,000 | Tehran | 104/H 3 |
| | **Iraq** | 172,476 | 446,713 | 19,525,000 | Baghdad | 104/E 3 |
| | **Ireland** | 27,136 | 70,282 | 3,489,000 | Dublin | 55/G 10 |
| | **Ireland, Northern, U.K.** | 5,452 | 14,121 | 1,543,000 | Belfast | 55/H 9 |
| | **Isle of Man, U.K.** | 227 | 588 | 64,000 | Douglas | 56/D 3 |
| | **Israel** | 7,847 | 20,324 | 4,558,000 | Jerusalem | 103/D 3 |
| | **Italy** | 116,303 | 301,225 | 57,772,000 | Rome | 89/F 2 |
| | **Ivory Coast (Côte d'Ivoire)** | 124,504 | 322,465 | 12,978,000 | Yamoussoukro | 144/D 5 |
| J | **Jamaica** | 4,411 | 11,424 | 2,489,000 | Kingston | 161/G 2 |
| | **Jan Mayen, Norway** | 144 | 373 | ... | ... | 52/D 1 |
| | **Japan** | 145,730 | 377,441 | 124,017,000 | Tokyo | 109/M 4 |
| | **Jarvis Island, U.S.** | 1 | 2.6 | ... | ... | 139/J 5 |
| | **Java, Indonesia** | 48,842 | 126,500 | 73,712,411 | Jakarta | 124/D 4 |
| | **Johnston Atoll, U.S.** | .91 | 2.4 | 327 | ... | 139/J 3 |
| | **Jordan** | 35,000 | 90,650 | 3,413,000 | Amman | 103/D 4 |
| K | **Kampuchea (Cambodia)** | 69,898 | 181,036 | 5,200,000 | Phnom Penh | 123/D 3 |
| | **Kansas, U.S.** | 82,277 | 213,097 | 2,485,600 | Topeka | 181/G 4 |
| | **Kazakhstan** | 1,048,300 | 2,715,100 | 16,538,000 | Alma-Ata | 100/G 5 |
| | **Kentucky, U.S.** | 40,409 | 104,659 | 3,698,969 | Frankfort | 200/E 2 |
| | **Kenya** | 224,960 | 582,646 | 25,242,000 | Nairobi | 140/F 4 |
| | **Kermadec Islands, New Zealand** | 13 | 33 | 5 | ... | 138/G 7 |
| | **Kingman Reef, U.S.** | 0.1 | 0.26 | ... | ... | 139/J 4 |
| | **Kiribati** | 291 | 754 | 71,000 | Bairiki | 138/H 5 |
| | **Korea, North** | 46,540 | 120,539 | 21,815,000 | P'yŏngyang | 113/D 2 |
| | **Korea, South** | 38,175 | 98,873 | 43,134,000 | Seoul | 113/D 4 |
| | **Kuwait** | 6,532 | 16,918 | 2,204,000 | Al Kuwait | 105/F 4 |
| | **Kyrgyzstan** | 76,641 | 198,500 | 4,291,000 | Bishkek | 114/B 3 |
| L | **Laos** | 91,428 | 236,800 | 4,113,000 | Vientiane | 123/C 2 |
| | **Latvia** | 24,595 | 63,700 | 2,681,000 | Riga | 63/L 3 |
| | **Lebanon** | 4,015 | 10,399 | 3,385,000 | Beirut | 103/D 3 |
| | **Lesotho** | 11,720 | 30,355 | 1,801,000 | Maseru | 156/D 3 |
| | **Liberia** | 43,000 | 111,370 | 2,730,000 | Monrovia | 144/C 5 |
| | **Libya** | 679,358 | 1,759,537 | 4,353,000 | Tripoli | 146/C 2 |
| | **Liechtenstein** | 61 | 158 | 28,000 | Vaduz | 81/F 3 |
| | **Lithuania** | 25,174 | 65,200 | 3,690,000 | Vilnius | 63/K 4 |
| | **Louisiana, U.S.** | 47,752 | 123,678 | 4,238,216 | Baton Rouge | 181/H 5 |
| | **Luxembourg** | 999 | 2,587 | 388,000 | Luxembourg | 69/E 4 |
| M | **Macau, Portugal** | 6 | 16 | 446,000 | Macau | 117/G 4 |
| | **Macedonia** | 9,889 | 25,713 | 1,909,136 | Skopje | 91/G 2 |
| | **Madagascar** | 226,657 | 587,041 | 12,185,000 | Antananarivo | 157/H 8 |
| | **Madeira Islands, Portugal** | 307 | 796 | 262,800 | Funchal | 77/V 15 |
| | **Maine, U.S.** | 33,265 | 86,156 | 1,233,223 | Augusta | 196/B 3 |

| | Place | Square Miles | Square Kilometers | Population | Capital or Chief Town | Page/ Index |
|---|---|---|---|---|---|---|
| | **Malawi** | 45,747 | 118,485 | 9,438,000 | Lilongwe | 140/F 6 |
| | **Malaya, Malaysia** | 50,806 | 131,588 | 11,138,227 | Kuala Lumpur | 124/C 1 |
| | **Malaysia** | 128,308 | 332,318 | 17,982,000 | Kuala Lumpur | 126/C 2 |
| | **Maldives** | 115 | 298 | 226,000 | Male | 102/G 9 |
| | **Mali** | 464,873 | 1,204,021 | 8,339,000 | Bamako | 140/B 3 |
| | **Malta** | 122 | 316 | 356,000 | Valletta | 84/H 8 |
| | **Manitoba, Canada** | 250,999 | 650,087 | 1,063,016 | Winnipeg | 178/F 3 |
| | **Marquesas Islands, French Polynesia** | 492 | 1,274 | 5,419 | Atuona | 139/M 5 |
| | **Marshall Islands** | 70 | 181 | 48,000 | Majuro | 138/G 3 |
| | **Martinique, France** | 425 | 1,101 | 345,000 | Fort-de-France | 162/F 4 |
| | **Maryland, U.S.** | 10,460 | 27,091 | 4,798,622 | Annapolis | 181/L 4 |
| | **Massachusetts, U.S.** | 8,284 | 21,456 | 6,029,051 | Boston | 181/M 3 |
| | **Mauritania** | 419,229 | 1,085,803 | 1,996,000 | Nouakchott | 140/A 3 |
| | **Mauritius** | 790 | 2,046 | 1,081,000 | Port Louis | 157/S 15 |
| | **Mayotte, France** | 144 | 373 | 75,000 | Dzaoudzi | 157/H 6 |
| | **Mexico** | 761,601 | 1,972,546 | 90,007,000 | Mexico City | 176/G 7 |
| | **Michigan, U.S.** | 58,527 | 151,585 | 9,328,784 | Lansing | 181/J 2 |
| | **Micronesia, Federated States of** | ... | ... | 108,000 | Kolonia | 138/D 4 |
| | **Midway Islands, U.S.** | 1.9 | 4.9 | 453 | ... | 138/H 2 |
| | **Minnesota, U.S.** | 84,402 | 218,601 | 4,387,029 | St. Paul | 181/G 2 |
| | **Mississippi, U.S.** | 47,689 | 123,515 | 2,586,443 | Jackson | 181/H 5 |
| | **Missouri, U.S.** | 69,697 | 180,515 | 5,137,804 | Jefferson City | 181/H 4 |
| | **Moldova** | 13,012 | 33,700 | 4,341,000 | Kishinev | 98/D 4 |
| | **Monaco** | 368 acres | 149 hectares | 30,000 | ... | 82/D 5 |
| | **Mongolia** | 606,163 | 1,569,962 | 2,247,000 | Ulaanbaatar | 108/D 2 |
| | **Montana, U.S.** | 147,046 | 380,849 | 803,655 | Helena | 180/D 2 |
| | **Montserrat, U.K.** | 40 | 104 | 13,000 | Plymouth | 162/F 3 |
| | **Morocco** | 172,414 | 446,550 | 26,182,000 | Rabat | 142/D 2 |
| | **Mozambique** | 303,769 | 786,762 | 15,113,000 | Maputo | 155/G 3 |
| | **Myanmar, see Burma** | | | | | |
| N | **Namibia** | 317,827 | 823,172 | 1,521,000 | Windhoek | 140/D 7 |
| | **Natal, South Africa** | 33,578 | 86,967 | 5,722,215 | Pietermaritzburg | 157/E 3 |
| | **Nauru** | 7.7 | 20 | 9,000 | Yaren (district) | 138/F 5 |
| | **Navassa Island, U.S.** | 2 | 5 | ... | ... | 161/H 2 |
| | **Nebraska, U.S.** | 77,355 | 200,349 | 1,584,617 | Lincoln | 192/D 3 |
| | **Nepal** | 54,663 | 141,577 | 19,612,000 | Kathmandu | 121/D 1 |
| | **Netherlands** | 15,892 | 41,160 | 15,022,000 | The Hague; Amsterdam | 64/C 3 |
| | **Netherlands Antilles** | 390 | 1,010 | 184,000 | Willemstad | 162/D 5 |
| | **Nevada, U.S.** | 110,561 | 286,353 | 1,206,152 | Carson City | 180/C 4 |
| | **New Brunswick, Canada** | 28,354 | 73,437 | 709,442 | Fredericton | 196/D 2 |
| | **New Caledonia & Dependencies, France** | 7,335 | 18,998 | 172,000 | Nouméa | 138/F 6 |
| | **Newfoundland, Canada** | 156,184 | 404,517 | 568,349 | St. John's | 179/K 3 |
| | **New Hampshire, U.S.** | 9,279 | 24,033 | 1,113,915 | Concord | 199/L 3 |
| | **New Jersey, U.S.** | 7,787 | 20,168 | 7,748,634 | Trenton | 206/D 3 |
| | **New Mexico, U.S.** | 121,593 | 314,926 | 1,521,779 | Santa Fe | 180/E 5 |
| | **New South Wales, Australia** | 309,498 | 801,600 | 5,401,881 | Sydney | 135/C 1 |
| | **New York, U.S.** | 49,108 | 127,190 | 18,044,505 | Albany | 199/J 3 |
| | **New Zealand** | 103,736 | 268,676 | 3,309,000 | Wellington | 136 |
| | **Nicaragua** | 45,698 | 118,358 | 3,752,000 | Managua | 161/E 3 |
| | **Niger** | 489,189 | 1,267,000 | 8,154,000 | Niamey | 140/C 3 |
| | **Nigeria** | 357,000 | 924,630 | 122,471,000 | Abuja | 140/C 4 |
| | **Niue, New Zealand** | 100 | 259 | 3,578 | Alofi | 139/J 7 |
| | **Norfolk Island, Australia** | 13.4 | 34.6 | 2,175 | Kingston | 129/M 5 |
| | **North America** | 9,363,000 | 24,250,170 | 427,000,000 | ... | 176 |
| | **North Carolina, U.S.** | 52,669 | 136,413 | 6,657,630 | Raleigh | 201/G 3 |
| | **North Dakota, U.S.** | 70,702 | 183,118 | 641,364 | Bismarck | 194/D 4 |
| | **Northern Ireland, U.K.** | 5,452 | 14,121 | 1,543,000 | Belfast | 55/H 9 |
| | **Northern Marianas, U.S.** | 184 | 477 | 23,000 | Capitol Hill | 138/D 3 |
| | **Northern Territory, Australia** | 519,768 | 1,346,200 | 154,848 | Darwin | 128/E 3 |
| | **North Korea** | 46,540 | 120,539 | 21,815,000 | P'yŏngyang | 113/D 2 |
| | **Northwest Territories, Canada** | 1,304,896 | 3,379,683 | 52,238 | Yellowknife | 178/E 2 |
| | **Norway** | 125,053 | 323,887 | 4,273,000 | Oslo | 61/C 3 |
| | **Nova Scotia, Canada** | 21,425 | 55,491 | 873,176 | Halifax | 196/E 3 |
| O | **Oceania** | 3,292,000 | 8,526,280 | 23,000,000 | ... | 138 |
| | **Ohio, U.S.** | 41,330 | 107,045 | 10,887,325 | Columbus | 181/K 3 |

| | Place | Square Miles | Square Kilometers | Population | Capital or Chief Town | Page/ Index |
|---|---|---|---|---|---|---|
| | **Oklahoma, U.S.** | 69,956 | 181,186 | 3,157,604 | Oklahoma City | 191/F 3 |
| | **Oman** | 120,000 | 310,800 | 1,534,000 | Muscat | 107/G 4 |
| | **Ontario, Canada** | 412,580 | 1,068,582 | 9,101,694 | Toronto | 178/H 3 |
| | **Orange Free State, South Africa** | 49,866 | 129,153 | 1,833,216 | Bloemfontein | 156/D 3 |
| | **Oregon, U.S.** | 97,073 | 251,419 | 2,853,733 | Salem | 180/B 3 |
| | **Orkney Islands, Scotland** | 376 | 974 | 17,675 | Kirkwall | 55/N 13 |
| P | **Pakistan** | 310,403 | 803,944 | 117,490,000 | Islamabad | 107/H 3 |
| | **Palau** | 188 | 487 | 14,000 | Koror | 138/C 4 |
| | **Palmyra Atoll, U.S.** | 3.85 | 1 | | | 139/J 4 |
| | **Panama** | 29,761 | 77,082 | 2,476,000 | Panamá | 161/F 4 |
| | **Papua New Guinea** | 183,540 | 475,369 | 3,913,000 | Port Moresby | 138/D 5 |
| | **Paracel Islands, China** | ............ | ............ | ............ | ............ | 102/L 8 |
| | **Paraguay** | 157,047 | 406,752 | 4,799,000 | Asunción | 172/D 2 |
| | **Pennsylvania, U.S.** | 45,308 | 117,348 | 11,924,710 | Harrisburg | 199/G 4 |
| | **Peru** | 496,222 | 1,285,215 | 22,362,000 | Lima | 168/C 3 |
| | **Philippines** | 115,707 | 299,681 | 65,759,000 | Manila | 125 |
| | **Pitcairn Islands, U.K.** | 18 | 47 | 54 | Adamstown | 139/N 7 |
| | **Poland** | 120,725 | 312,678 | 37,800,000 | Warsaw | 65/K 2 |
| | **Portugal** | 35,549 | 92,072 | 10,388,000 | Lisbon | 76/A 3 |
| | **Prince Edward Island, Canada** | 2,184 | 5,657 | 126,646 | Charlottetown | 196/F 2 |
| | **Puerto Rico, U.S.** | 3,515 | 9,104 | 3,295,000 | San Juan | 162/E 3 |
| Q | **Qatar** | 4,247 | 11,000 | 518,000 | Doha | 106/F 3 |
| | **Québec, Canada** | 594,857 | 1,540,680 | 6,532,461 | Québec | 179/J 3 |
| | **Queensland, Austraila** | 666,872 | 1,727,200 | 2,587,315 | Brisbane | 134/B 3 |
| R | **Réunion, France** | 969 | 2,510 | 607,000 | St-Denis | 157/R 15 |
| | **Rhode Island, U.S.** | 1,212 | 3,139 | 1,005,984 | Providence | 208/C 2 |
| | **Romania** | 91,699 | 237,500 | 23,397,000 | Bucharest | 93/F 3 |
| | **Russia** | 6,592,812 | 17,075,400 | 147,386,000 | Moscow | 100/H 3 |
| | **Rwanda** | 10,169 | 26,337 | 7,903,000 | Kigali | 153/G 3 |
| S | **Sabah, Malaysia** | 29,300 | 75,887 | 1,002,608 | Kota Kinabalu | 127/E 2 |
| | **Saint Helena & Dependencies, U.K.** | 162 | 420 | 7,000 | Jamestown | 140/B 6 |
| | **Saint Kitts and Nevis** | 104 | 269 | 40,000 | Basseterre | 162/F 3 |
| | **Saint Lucia** | 238 | 616 | 153,000 | Castries | 162/F 4 |
| | **Saint Pierre & Miquelon, France** | 93.5 | 242 | 6,000 | Saint-Pierre | 197/J 2 |
| | **Saint Vincent & the Grenadines** | 150 | 388 | 114,000 | Kingstown | 162/F 4 |
| | **Sakhalin, Russia** | 29,500 | 76,405 | 655,000 | Yuzhno-Sakhalinsk | 101/Q 4 |
| | **San Marino** | 23.4 | 60.6 | 23,000 | San Marino | 87/F 5 |
| | **São Tomé and Príncipe** | 372 | 963 | 128,000 | São Tomé | 152/A 2 |
| | **Sarawak, Malaysia** | 48,202 | 124,843 | 1,294,753 | Kuching | 126/D 3 |
| | **Sardinia, Italy** | 9,301 | 24,090 | 1,450,483 | Cagliari | 90/A 2 |
| | **Saskatchewan, Canada** | 251,699 | 651,900 | 1,009,613 | Regina | 178/F 3 |
| | **Saudi Arabia** | 829,995 | 2,149,687 | 17,870,000 | Riyadh | 106/D 4 |
| | **Scotland, U.K.** | 30,414 | 78,772 | 5,117,146 | Edinburgh | 55/J 8 |
| | **Senegal** | 75,954 | 196,720 | 7,953,000 | Dakar | 144/B 3 |
| | **Seychelles** | 145 | 375 | 69,000 | Victoria | 141/H 5 |
| | **Shetland Islands, Scotland** | 552 | 1,430 | 18,494 | Lerwick | 55/N 2 |
| | **Siam, see Thailand** | | | | | |
| | **Sicily, Italy** | 9,926 | 25,708 | 4,628,918 | Palermo | 90/C 3 |
| | **Sierra Leone** | 27,925 | 72,325 | 4,275,000 | Freetown | 144/B 4 |
| | **Singapore** | 226 | 585 | 2,756,000 | Singapore | 124/C 2 |
| | **Slovakia** | 18,924 | 49,014 | 4,991,168 | Bratislava | 65/K 4 |
| | **Slovenia** | 7,898 | 20,251 | 1,891,864 | Ljubljana | 92/B 3 |
| | **Society Islands, French Polynesia** | 677 | 1,753 | 117,703 | Papeete | 139/K 6 |
| | **Solomon Islands** | 11,500 | 29,785 | 347,000 | Honiara | 138/E 6 |
| | **Somalia** | 246,200 | 637,658 | 6,709,000 | Mogadishu | 141/H 4 |
| | **South Africa** | 455,318 | 1,179,274 | 40,601,000 | Cape Town; Pretoria | 140/E 7 |
| | **South America** | 6,875,000 | 17,806,250 | 297,000,000 | ............ | 163 |
| | **South Australia, Australia** | 379,922 | 984,000 | 1,345,945 | Adelaide | 128/E 5 |
| | **South Carolina, U.S.** | 31,113 | 80,583 | 3,505,707 | Columbia | 201/G 3 |
| | **South Dakota, U.S.** | 77,116 | 199,730 | 699,999 | Pierre | 192/D 1 |
| | **South Korea** | 38,175 | 98,873 | 43,134,000 | Seoul | 113/D 4 |
| | **Spain** | 194,881 | 504,742 | 39,385,000 | Madrid | 76/C 2 |
| | **Spratly Islands** | ............ | ............ | ............ | ............ | 126/D 2 |
| | **Sri Lanka** | 25,332 | 65,610 | 17,424,000 | Colombo | 118/D 6 |
| | **Sudan** | 967,494 | 2,505,809 | 27,220,000 | Khartoum | 140/E 3 |
| | **Sumatra, Indonesia** | 164,000 | 424,760 | 19,360,400 | Medan | 124/D 3 |
| | **Suriname** | 55,144 | 142,823 | 402,000 | Paramaribo | 166/B 1 |
| | **Svalbard, Norway** | 23,957 | 62,049 | 3,431 | Longyearbyen | 100/C 2 |
| | **Swaziland** | 6,705 | 17,366 | 859,000 | Mbabane | 157/E 2 |
| | **Sweden** | 173,665 | 449,792 | 8,564,000 | Stockholm | 61/E 3 |
| | **Switzerland** | 15,943 | 41,292 | 6,784,000 | Bern | 80/D 4 |
| | **Syria** | 71,498 | 185,180 | 12,966,000 | Damascus | 104/D 3 |
| T | **Tahiti, French Polynesia** | 402 | 1,041 | 95,604 | Papeete | 139/X 13 |
| | **Taiwan** | 13,971 | 36,185 | 16,609,961 | Taipei | 117/J 3 |
| | **Tajikistan** | 55,251 | 143,100 | 5,112,000 | Dushanbe | 100/H 6 |
| | **Tanzania** | 363,708 | 942,003 | 26,869,000 | Dar es Salaam | 140/F 5 |
| | **Tasmania, Australia** | 26,178 | 67,800 | 436,353 | Hobart | 135/C 4 |
| | **Tennessee, U.S.** | 42,144 | 109,153 | 4,896,641 | Nashville | 200/D 3 |
| | **Texas, U.S.** | 266,807 | 691,030 | 17,059,805 | Austin | 180/G 5 |
| | **Thailand** | 198,455 | 513,998 | 56,814,000 | Bangkok | 123/C 3 |
| | **Tibet, China** | 463,320 | 1,200,000 | 1,790,000 | Lhasa | 114/D 5 |
| | **Togo** | 21,622 | 56,000 | 3,811,000 | Lomé | 145/F 4 |
| | **Tokelau, New Zealand** | 3.9 | 10 | 1,575 | Fakaofo | 139/J 5 |
| | **Tonga** | 270 | 699 | 102,000 | Nuku'alofa | 139/H 7 |
| | **Transkei, South Africa** | 16,910 | 43,797 | 2,000,000 | Umtata | 156/E 3 |
| | **Transvaal, South Africa** | 109,621 | 283,918 | 10,673,033 | Pretoria | 156/E 2 |
| | **Trinidad and Tobago** | 1,980 | 5,128 | 1,285,000 | Port-of-Spain | 162/F 5 |
| | **Tristan da Cunha, St. Helena** | 38 | 98 | 251 | Edinburgh | 50/J 7 |
| | **Tuamotu Archipelago, French Polynesia** | 341 | 883 | 9,052 | Apataki | 139/L 6 |
| | **Tunisia** | 63,378 | 164,149 | 8,276,000 | Tunis | 143/H 2 |
| | **Turkey** | 300,946 | 779,450 | 58,581,000 | Ankara | 104/C 2 |
| | **Turkmenistan** | 188,455 | 488,100 | 3,534,000 | Ashkhabad | 100/F 6 |
| | **Turks and Caicos Islands, U.K.** | 166 | 430 | 10,000 | Cockburn Town, Grand Turk | 162/D 2 |
| | **Tuvalu** | 9.78 | 25.33 | 9,000 | Fongafale, Funafuti | 138/G 5 |
| U | **Uganda** | 91,076 | 235,887 | 18,690,000 | Kampala | 140/F 4 |
| | **Ukraine** | 233,089 | 603,700 | 51,704,000 | Kiev | 98/F 4 |
| | **United Arab Emirates** | 32,278 | 83,600 | 2,390,000 | Abu Dhabi | 106/F 4 |
| | **United Kingdom** | 94,399 | 244,493 | 57,515,000 | London | 55 |
| | **United States** | 3,623,420 | 9,384,658 | 252,502,000 | Washington | 180 |
| | **Uruguay** | 72,172 | 186,925 | 3,121,000 | Montevideo | 163/D 6 |
| | **Utah, U.S.** | 84,899 | 219,888 | 1,727,784 | Salt Lake City | 180/D 4 |
| | **Uzbekistan** | 173,591 | 449,600 | 19,906,000 | Tashkent | 100/G 5 |
| V | **Vanuatu** | 5,700 | 14,763 | 170,000 | Vila | 138/F 6 |
| | **Vatican City** | 108.7 acres | 44 hectares | 1,000 | ............ | 84/C 4 |
| | **Venda, South Africa** | 2,510 | 6,501 | 450,000 | Thohoyandou | 155/F 4 |
| | **Venezuela** | 352,143 | 912,050 | 20,189,000 | Caracas | 165/E 3 |
| | **Vermont, U.S.** | 9,614 | 24,900 | 564,964 | Montpelier | 199/K 3 |
| | **Victoria, Australia** | 87,876 | 227,600 | 4,019,478 | Melbourne | 135/C 3 |
| | **Vietnam** | 128,405 | 332,569 | 67,568,000 | Hanoi | 123/D 2 |
| | **Virginia, U.S.** | 40,767 | 105,587 | 6,216,568 | Richmond | 201/H 2 |
| | **Virgin Islands, British** | 59 | 153 | 12,000 | Road Town | 162/E 3 |
| | **Virgin Islands, U.S.** | 132 | 342 | 99,000 | Charlotte Amalie | 162/E 3 |
| W | **Wake Island, U.S.** | 2.5 | 6.5 | 302 | Wake Islet | 138/F 3 |
| | **Wales, U.K.** | 8,017 | 20,764 | 2,790,462 | Cardiff | 55/J10 |
| | **Wallis and Futuna, France** | 106 | 275 | 17,000 | Mata Utu | 138/G 6 |
| | **Washington, U.S.** | 68,139 | 176,480 | 4,887,941 | Olympia | 182/D 4 |
| | **West Bank** | 2,100 | 5,439 | 1,105,000 | ............ | 103/D 3 |
| | **Western Australia, Australia** | 975,096 | 2,525,500 | 1,406,929 | Perth | 128/B 4 |
| | **Western Sahara** | 102,703 | 266,000 | 197,000 | ............ | 142/B 4 |
| | **Western Samoa** | 1,133 | 2,934 | 190,000 | Apia | 139/R 9 |
| | **West Virginia, U.S.** | 24,231 | 62,758 | 1,801,625 | Charleston | 181/K 4 |
| | **Wisconsin, U.S.** | 56,153 | 145,436 | 4,906,745 | Madison | 181/H 3 |
| | **World** | (land) 57,970,000 | 150,142,300 | 5,292,000,000 | ............ | 50 |
| | **Wyoming, U.S.** | 97,809 | 253,325 | 455,975 | Cheyenne | 180/E 3 |
| Y | **Yemen** | 188,321 | 487,752 | 10,063,000 | San'a | 106/E 5 |
| | **Yugoslavia** | 38,989 | 102,173 | 11,371,275 | Belgrade | 92/D 3 |
| | **Yukon Territory, Canada** | 207,075 | 536,324 | 23,504 | Whitehorse | 178/C 2 |
| Z | **Zaire (Congo)** | 905,063 | 2,344,113 | 37,832,000 | Kinshasa | 140/E 5 |
| | **Zambia** | 290,586 | 752,618 | 8,446,000 | Lusaka | 140/E 6 |
| | **Zimbabwe** | 150,803 | 390,580 | 10,720,000 | Harare | 155/F 3 |

# Global Relationships

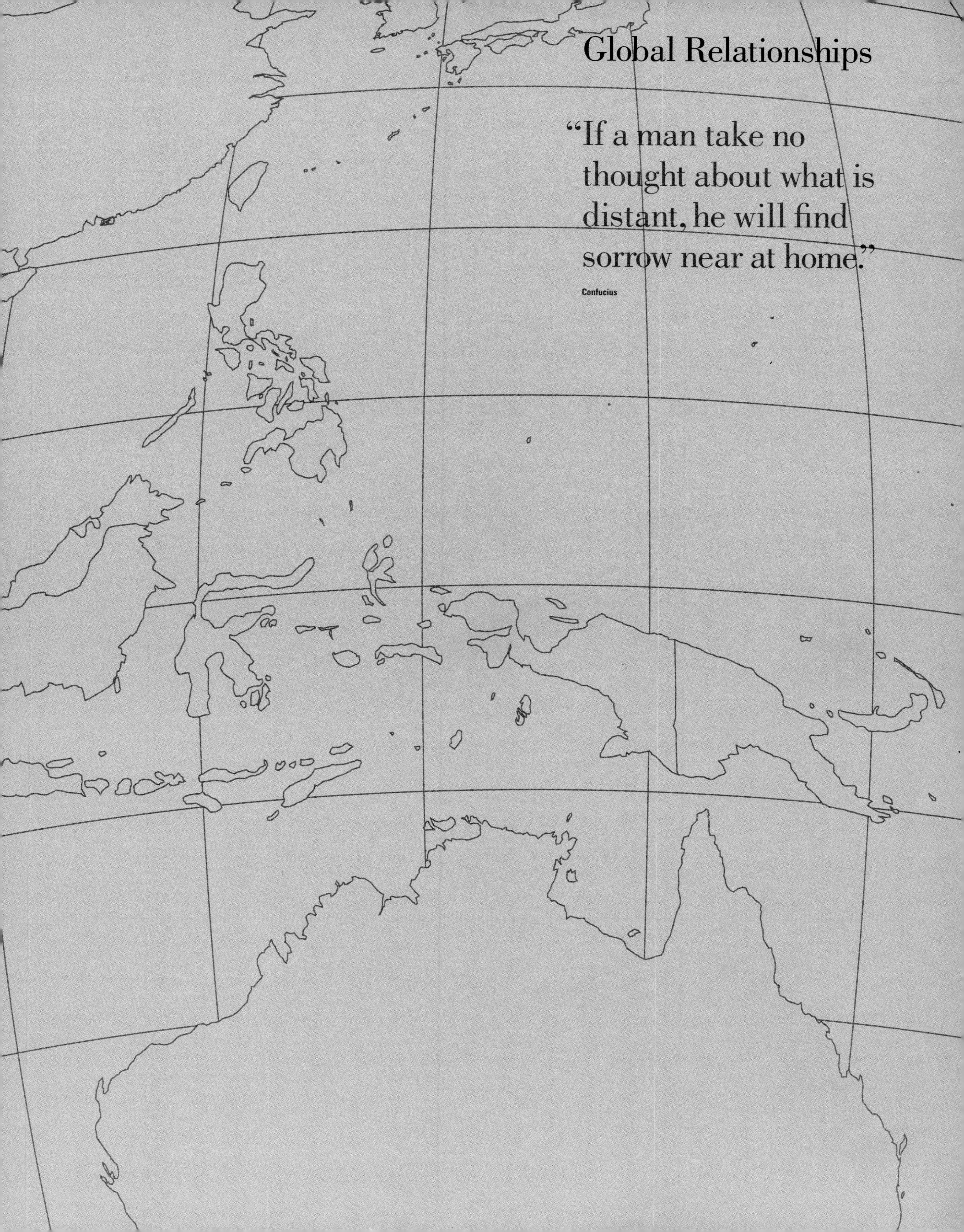

"If a man take no thought about what is distant, he will find sorrow near at home."

**Confucius**

# Environmental

The earth's human population, already 5.5 billion, is growing at the unprecedented rate of 90 to 100 million people a year. This rapid rise is straining the global environment, devouring forests, fresh water and oil reserves while polluting the very resources necessary for survival. Each year, the burning of fossil fuels releases more than 20 billion tons (18 billion metric tons) of carbon dioxide into the air. Man-made chlorofluorocarbons are eating away at the layer of ozone which shields earth from harmful ultraviolet radiation. Highly acidic rains created by fossil fuel emissions are destroying lakes, forests and historic monuments from North America to Africa. "Greenhouse gases" such as carbon dioxide, sulphur and nitrogen oxides trap heat within our atmosphere and warm the planet by absorbing earth's infrared radiation. Tropical rainforests, with their capacity to consume carbon dioxide, generate fresh oxygen and regulate rainfall, might offer an antidote. Yet from South America to Indonesia, they are being levelled for lumber and land at the rate of 100 acres (40 hectares) a minute. Some experts predict that "global warming" could raise the earth's temperature significantly in the next century, leading to unpredictable changes in climate. Soaring temperatures could bring severe recurring droughts, dust storms, forest fires and wildlife extinction. Melting glaciers and rising seas would flood coastal areas, drown wetlands, contaminate estuaries and pollute drinking water. While industrialized nations can afford to invest in environmental preservation, third world countries, home to most of the world's population and rainforests, must focus their limited resources on immediate economic survival. Feeding a nation takes precedence over saving a forest, even if the long-term cost could be incalculable. The solution seems to require nothing less than a unified global effort to transform the way we live, with nature conservation, population control and clean, efficient energy use as our goals.

Breathing in Bombay, India is equal to smoking 10 cigarettes a day.

Is global warming already occurring? During the 1980's, the hottest decade ever recorded, the United States experienced record droughts, floods and forest fires.

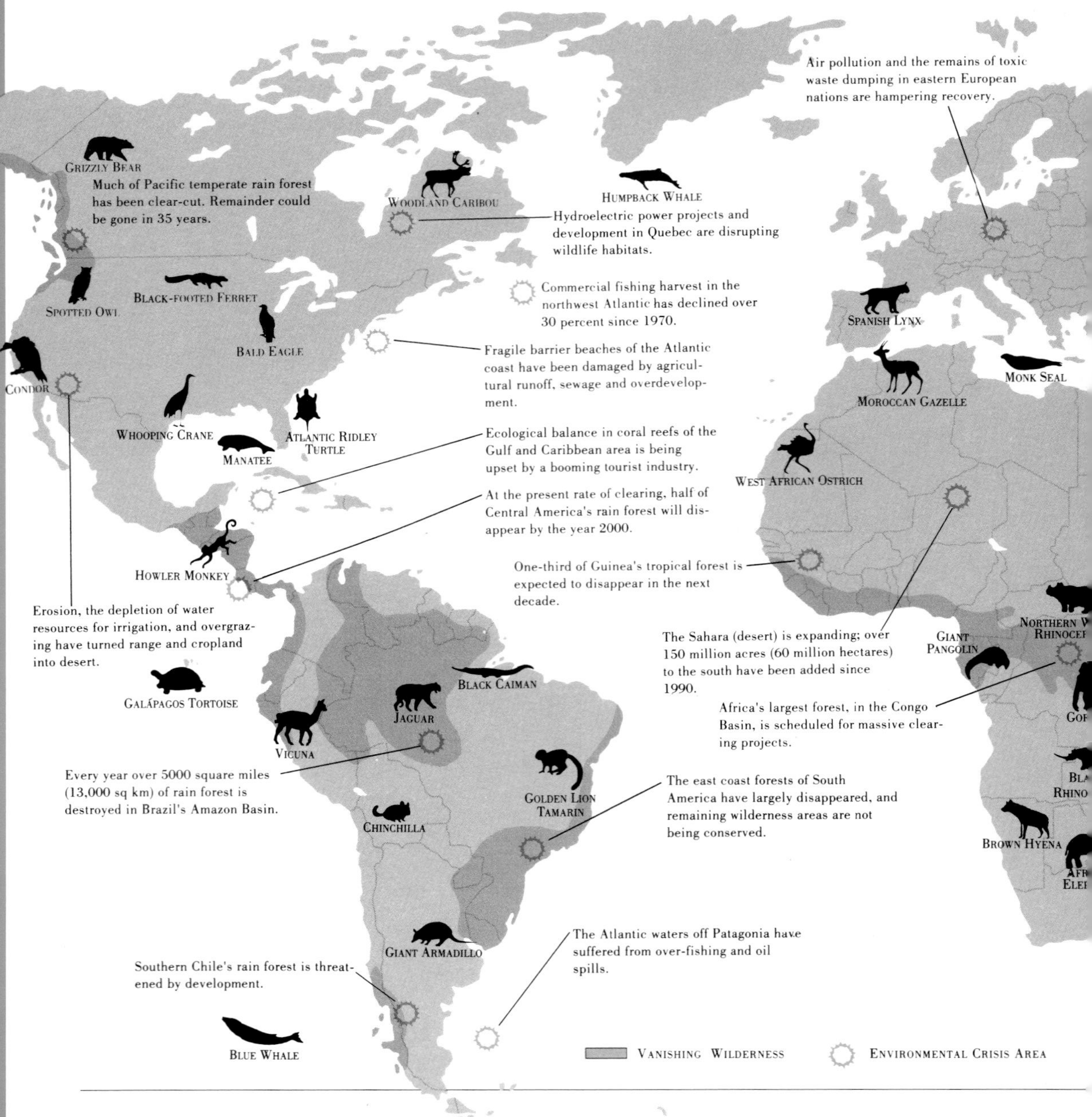

**Air Pollution**

Billions of tons of industrial emissions and toxic pollutants — including carbon dioxide, sulphur, nitrogen oxide, lead, mercury and cadmium — are released into the air each year, depleting our ozone layer, killing our forests and lakes with acid rain and threatening our health: in some parts of the world, lung cancer has become a leading cause of death.

**Water Pollution**

Only 3 percent of the earth's water is fresh. Unfortunately, pollution from cities, farms and factories has made much of it unfit to drink. In the developing world, most sewage flows untreated into lakes and rivers; health officials estimate that 5 million people die each year from diseases caused by unclean water. Regional struggles to secure adequate water are becoming more intense.

**Ozone Depletion**

The layer of ozone in the stratosphere shields earth from harmful ultraviolet radiation. But man-made gases are destroying this vital barrier, increasing the risk of skin cancer and eye disease — with equally harmful effects for all plant and animal species. A hole in the ozone layer over Antarctica is now the size of the continental United States.

# Concerns

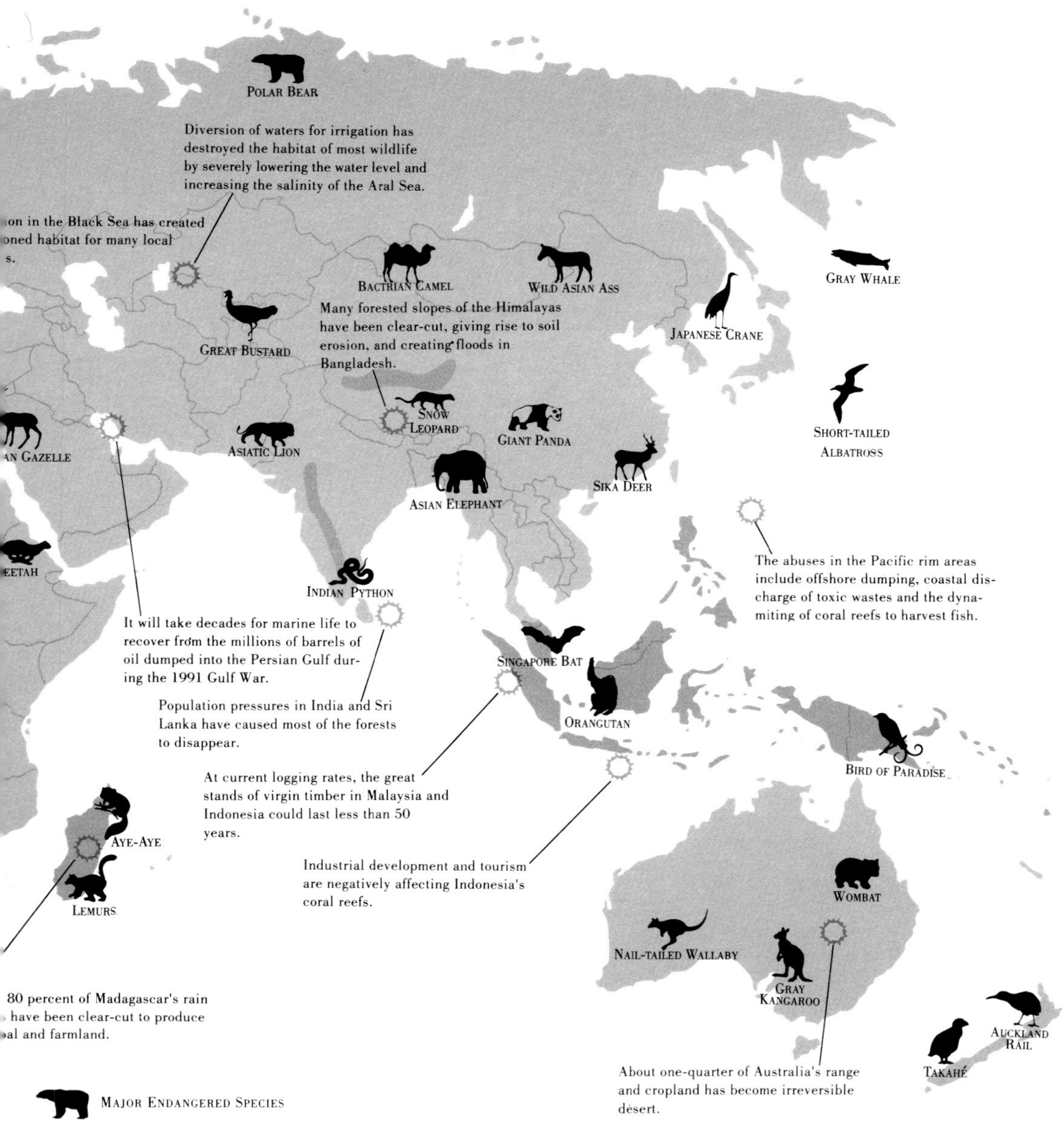


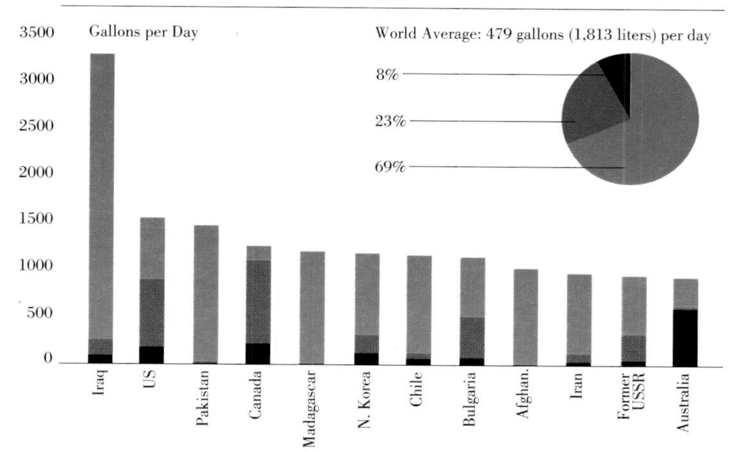


Freshwater Resources—Water Use per Capita

Domestic · Industry · Agriculture

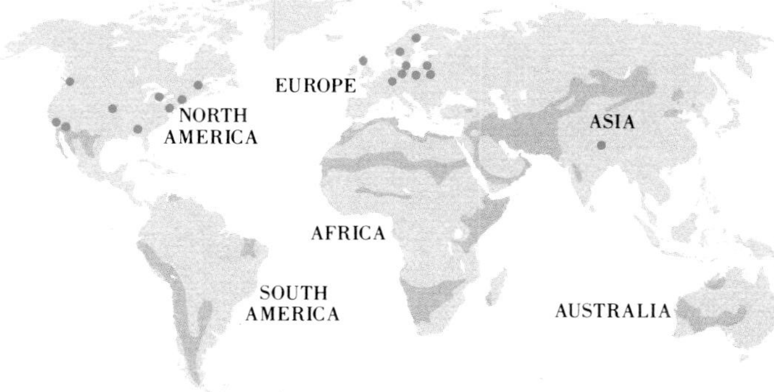


Desertification and Acid Rain Damage

Areas of Productive Drylands Desertified by Early 1980's · Areas of Damage From Acid Rain and Other Airborne Pollutants

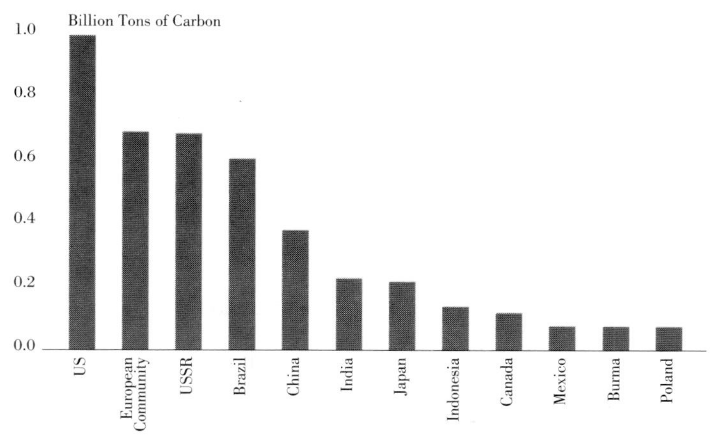


Greenhouse Emissions

Carbon Dioxide Equivalents, 1987 Net Emissions

**Acid Rain**

Acid rain is created when fossil fuel emissions interact with sunlight and water vapor. The resulting clouds of nitric and sulfuric acids are carried thousands of miles. Acid rain has killed all life in thousands of lakes, and over 15 million acres (6 million hectares) of virgin forest in Europe and North America — and even some third world countries — are dead or dying.

**Deforestation**

Each year, 50 million acres (20 million hectares) of tropical rainforests are being felled by loggers — an area larger than Uruguay or Syria. Trees are vital to the prevention of both soil erosion and silting of rivers. They also remove heat-trapping carbon dioxide from the atmosphere.

**Extinction**

Biologists estimate that over 50,000 plant and animal species inhabiting the world's rain forests are disappearing each year due to pollution, unchecked hunting and the destruction of natural habitats. The loss of plant and animal species means fewer potential sources of new foods and medicines.

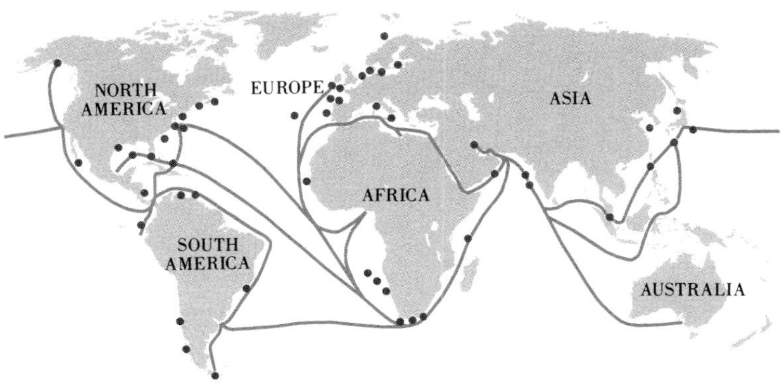


Main Tanker Routes and Major Oil Spills

Routes of Very Large Crude Oil Carriers · Major Oil Spills

# Population

In 6,000 B.C., earth's entire population stood between 5 and 20 million people. It took almost 8,000 years to reach the one billion mark, yet just 100 years more to reach two billion in 1930. Sixty years later, that figure has nearly tripled, to about 5.5 billion people today. This massive expansion has been fueled not by an increasing birth rate, but by a gradual extension of life expectancy and a huge reduction in infant mortality. By 2020, the United Nations projects that our global population could exceed 8.5 billion. Ninety percent of this growth will be concentrated in the poorest countries. The most dramatic increases will take place in sub-Saharan Africa, where fertility rates have remained high. Population shifts are often driven by economic forces. In the late 15th and early 16th centuries, Europe's conquest of the sea spurred trade, exploration and settlements across the globe. The temperate zones of the Americas were especially well-suited to their crops and flocks. Between the 16th and mid-19th centuries, millions of black Africans were brought to the Americas by the Atlantic slave trade, victims of the New World's voracious need for labor. In the industrialized nations of Europe, Japan, Canada and the United States, the trend is towards zero growth. Birth rates have also fallen in India and China, yet 15 percent of the world's people live in India, and 20 percent — 1 of every 5 people — live in China. Aggressive educational programs are helping to change traditional beliefs, which held childbirth as a woman's duty, and viewed large families as proof of wealth, fortification against hardship and security for aging parents. Government-sponsored birth control programs are also showing positive results. Not all of the factors which could limit population growth are so well planned. In the end, the environmental pressures created by rapidly expanding population may deplete the very resources necessary for survival.

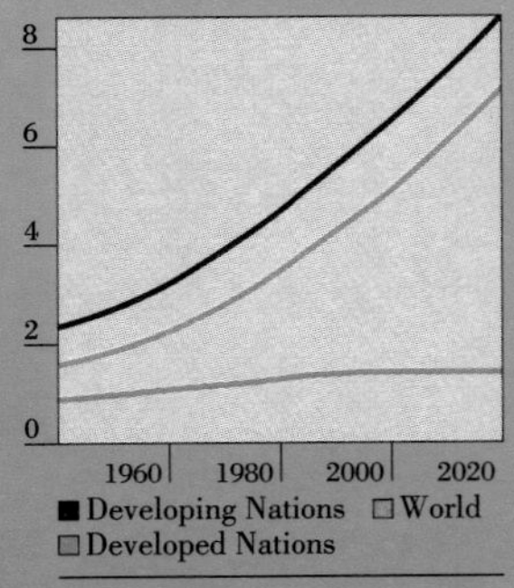


World population in billions

## Crowded Cities

Thousands of Persons per Square Mile (sq. km.)

| City | 1991 | 2000 (estimate) |
|---|---|---|
| Hong Kong, U.K. | 248 (96) | 259 (100) |
| Lagos, Nigeria | 142 (55) | 224 (86) |
| Dhaka, Bangladesh | 138 (53) | 203 (78) |
| Jakarta, Indonesia | 130 (50) | 168 (65) |
| Bombay, India | 127 (49) | 162 (63) |

## Current Population Comparisons

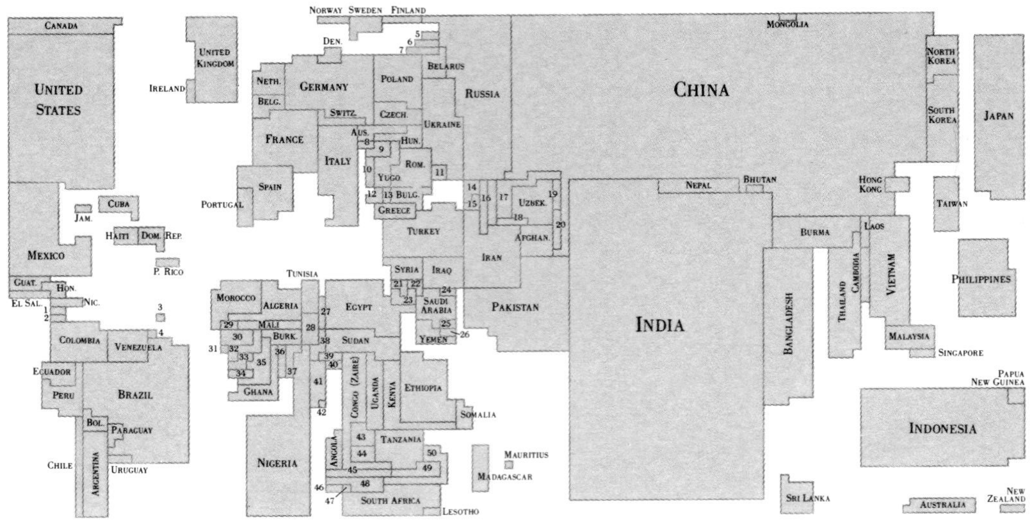


Each Area's Size is Proportionate to Its Population

### Countries Indicated by Number

| No. | Country | No. | Country | No. | Country |
|---|---|---|---|---|---|
| 1 | Costa Rica | 21 | Lebanon | 41 | Cameroon |
| 2 | Panama | 22 | Jordan | 42 | Gabon |
| 3 | Trinidad and Tobago | 23 | Israel | 43 | Rwanda |
| 4 | Guyana | 24 | Kuwait | 44 | Burundi |
| 5 | Estonia | 25 | United Arab Emirates | 45 | Zambia |
| 6 | Latvia | 26 | Oman | 46 | Namibia |
| 7 | Lithuania | 27 | Libya | 47 | Botswana |
| 8 | Slovenia | 28 | Niger | 48 | Zimbabwe |
| 9 | Croatia | 29 | Mauritania | 49 | Mozambique |
| 10 | Bosnia and Hercegovina | 30 | Senegal | 50 | Malawi |
| 11 | Moldova | 31 | Guinea-Bissau | 51 | Cyprus |
| 12 | Albania | 32 | Guinea | 52 | Cape Verde |
| 13 | Macedonia | 33 | Sierra Leone | 53 | Gambia |
| 14 | Georgia | 34 | Liberia | 54 | Equatorial Guinea |
| 15 | Armenia | 35 | Ivory Coast | 55 | Bahrain |
| 16 | Azerbaijan | 36 | Togo | 56 | Qatar |
| 17 | Kazakhstan | 37 | Benin | 57 | Brunei |
| 18 | Turkmenistan | 38 | Chad | 58 | Solomon Islands |
| 19 | Kyrgyzstan | 39 | Central African Republic | | |
| 20 | Tajikistan | 40 | Congo | | |

## Projected Population Comparisons - 2020

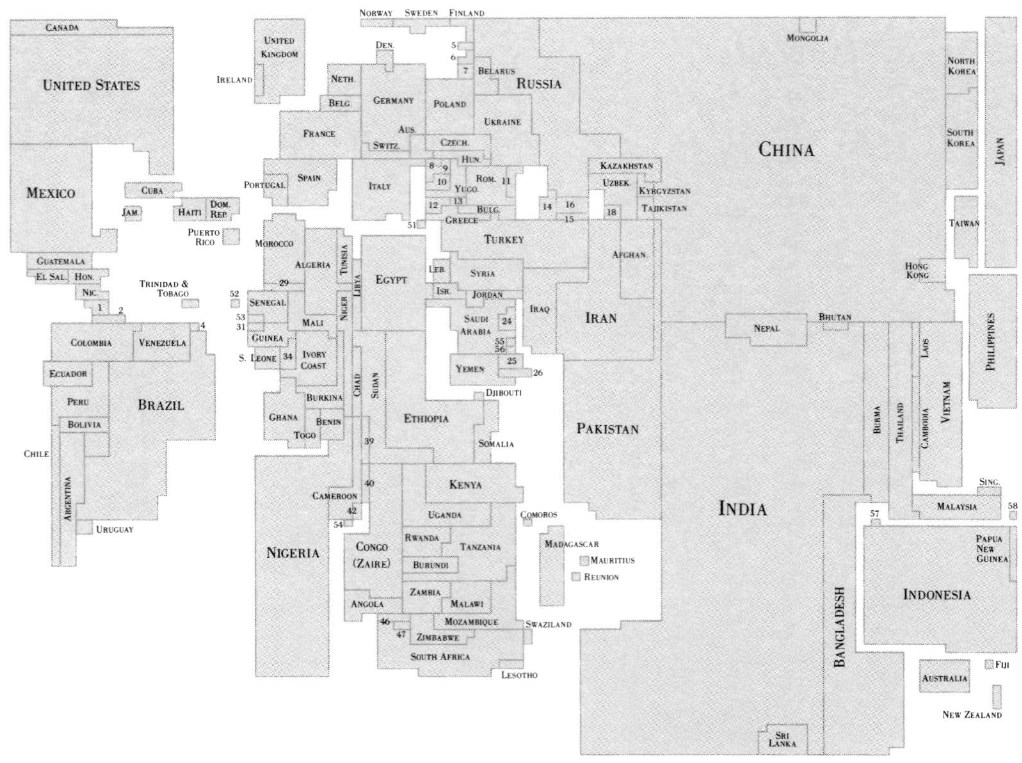


Each Area's Size is Proportionate to Its Population

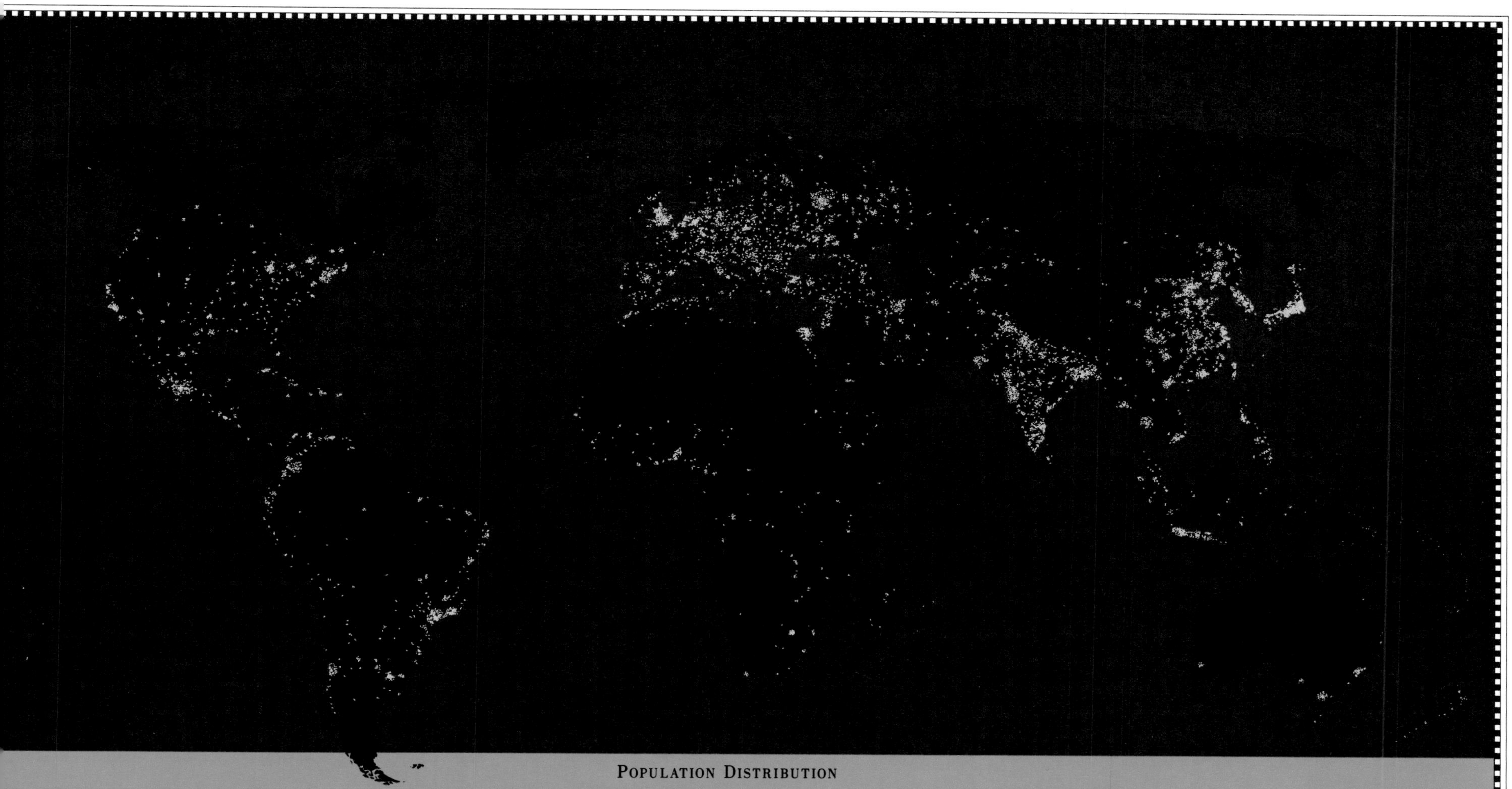

POPULATION DISTRIBUTION

This map provides a dramatic perspective by illuminating populated areas with one point of light per 50,000 residents. Over 2 billion people now live in cities with populations in excess of 500,000. According to the latest census data, there are 10,000 people per square mile (3,860 per sq km) in London. In New York, there are 11,000 (4,250). Tokyo has 25,000 (9,650 per sq km). In Hong Kong, the world's most densely populated city, over 250,000 people pack each square mile of land. During the last decade, the movement to the cities has accelerated dramatically, particularly in developing nations. In Lagos, Nigeria, where there are over 100,000 people per square mile (38,600 per sq km), most live in shantytowns. In Sao Paulo, Brazil, 2,000 buses arrive each day, bringing field hands, farm workers and their families in search of a better life. By the year 2000, the United Nations predicts that 17 of the world's 20 largest cities will be in the third world. Tokyo-Yokohama, Mexico City and São Paulo will top the list.

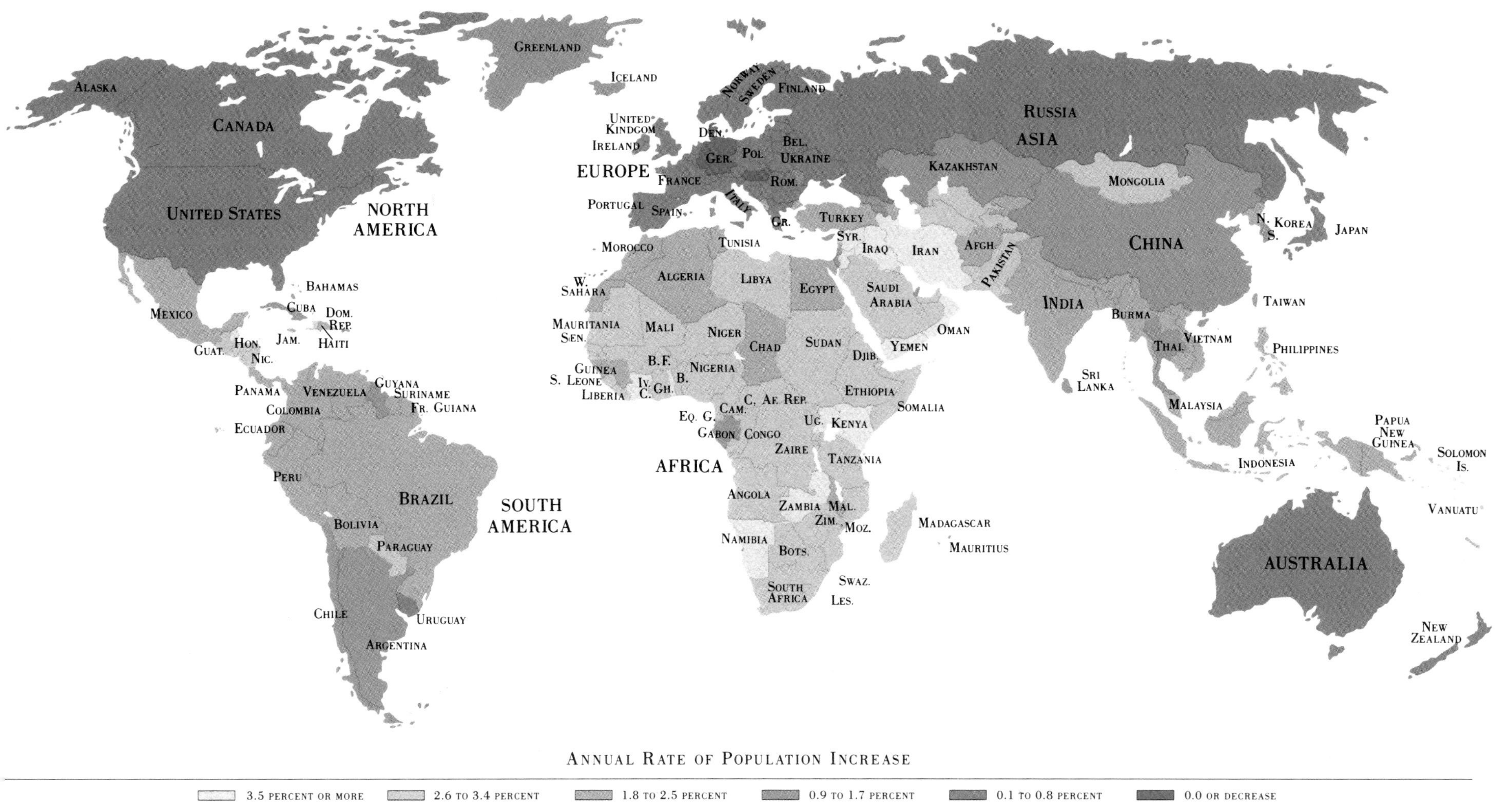


ANNUAL RATE OF POPULATION INCREASE

# Languages & Religions

Over 4,000 languages are spoken in the world today. By searching for the roots of these languages, linguists have reconstructed their origins and charted the migrations of ancient peoples. Indo-European, the ancestral tongue from which modern European languages are descended, may have originated 8,000 years ago in Anatolia, part of modern-day Turkey. By 1000 B.C., Indo-European was spoken over much of Europe, and in parts of southern and southwestern Asia. Today, it is no longer migration, but rather global communications and the media which transport languages across continents. The emerging global business culture, in particular, has created a pressing need for a common tongue. Language and culture are intimately bound and constantly evolving. Many religions are associated with a particular written language: Latin was the primary language of Christianity. For Judaism, it was Hebrew; for Islam, Arabic; and Chinese was the language of Confucianism. Religion has been the chief inspiration for much of the world's greatest music, literature, architecture — and wars. The major religious influence on western civilization was Christianity; Islam and Judaism were also important. These same faiths, and particularly Islam, were also central to the development of Middle Eastern culture. Asian cultures were shaped by Buddhism, Hinduism, Taoism, Confucianism and the Shinto faith. Today, almost one-third of the world's population is Christian; about 17 percent are Muslim; 13.5 percent are Hindus; and 6 percent are Buddhists.

More than 100 languages are spoken by a million or more people. Of these, 19 have over fifty million speakers each.

### Major Languages: Number of Speakers

| Language | Millions of Speakers |
|---|---|
| Chinese | 1,093 |
| English | 450 |
| Hindi | 367 |
| Spanish | 352 |
| Russian | 204 |
| Arabic | 202 |
| Bengali | 187 |
| Portuguese | 175 |
| Malay-Indonesian | 145 |
| Japanese | 126 |
| French | 122 |
| German | 118 |

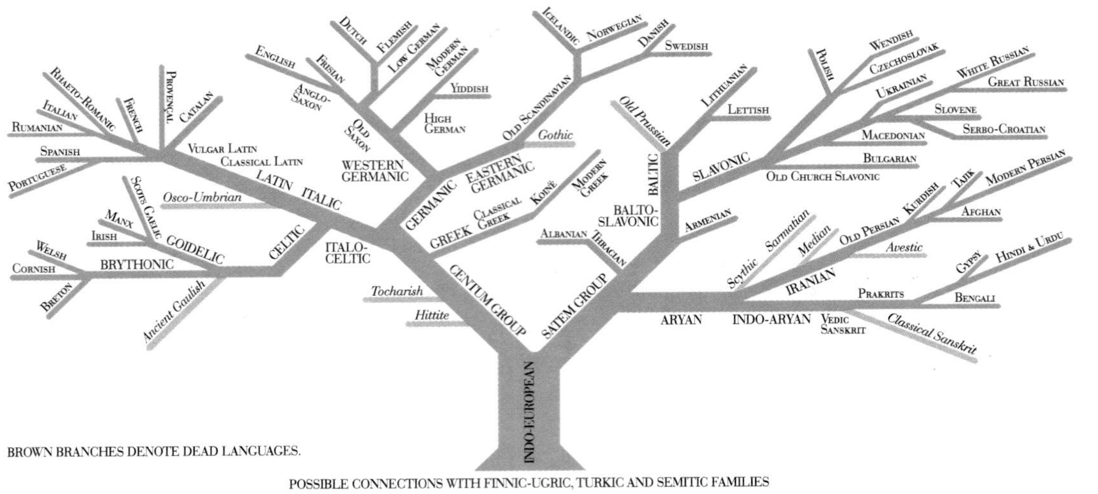


The Indo-European Language Tree

The most well-established family tree is Indo-European. Spoken by more than 2.5 billion people, it contains dozens of languages. Some linguists theorize that all people - and all languages - are descended from a tiny population that lived in Africa some 200,000 years ago.

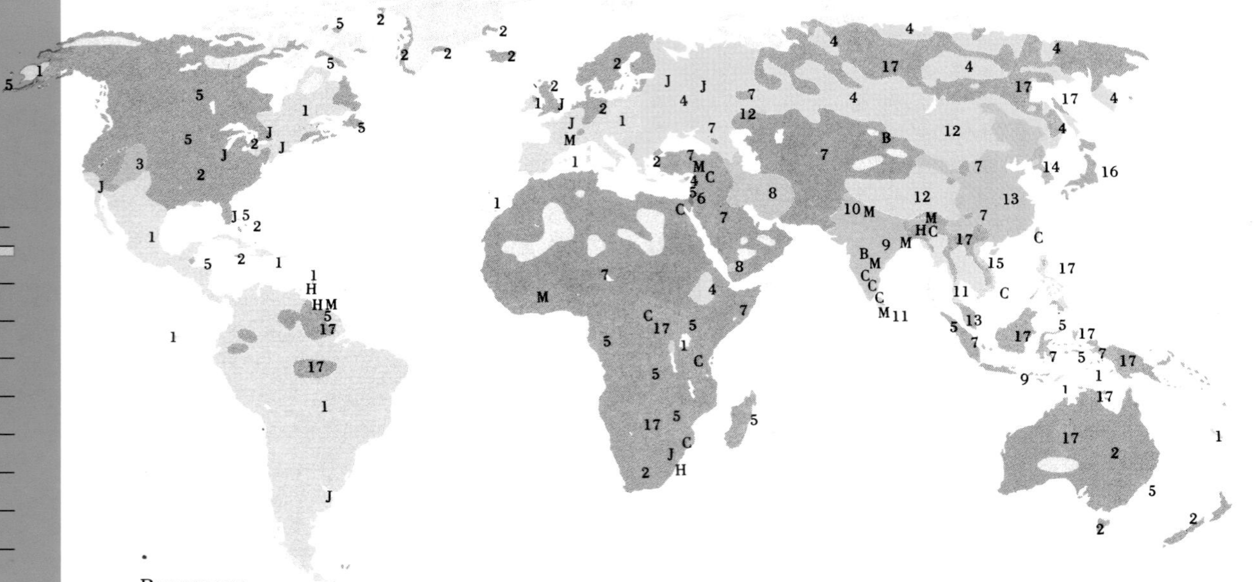

### Religions

C Christianity
- 1-Roman Catholicism
- 2-Protestantism
- 3-Mormonism
- 4-Eastern Churches
- 5-Christianity, sect not distinguished

J 6-Judaism

M Islam
- 7-Sunni
- 8-Shi'a

H 9-Hinduism

10-Sikhism

B Buddhism
- 11-Hinayanian
- 12-Lamaistic

13-Chinese Religious Complex (Confucianism, Taoism, Buddhism)

14-Korean Religious Complex (Buddhism, Confucianism, Christianity, Chondogyo)

15-Vietnamese Religious Complex (Buddhism, Taoism, Confucianism, Cao Dai)

16-Japanese Religious Complex (Shinto and Buddhism)

17-Tribal Religions (Animism or Shamanism)

Unpopulated Areas

Important Local Minorities are Indicated by Letter

LANGUAGE FAMILIES

1-Indo-European
1A-Germanic
1B-Romance
1C-Slavic
1D-Baltic
1E-Celtic
1F-Albanian
1G-Greek
1H-Armenian
1J-Iranian
1K-Indo-Aryan
2-Basque
3-Caucasian Families
4-Burushaski
5-Afro-Asiatic (Hamito-Semitic)
6-Nilo-Saharan
7-Niger-Congo
8-Khoisan
9-Uralic
10-Altaic
11-Paleo-Siberian Families
12-Sino-Tibetan
13-Thai-Kadai
14-Korean
15-Japanese
16-Dravidian
17-Vietnamese
18-Austro-Asiatic
19-Austronesian
20-Papuan
21-Australian
22-Eskimo-Aleut
23-American Indian Families
Unpopulated Areas

LANGUAGES OF EUROPE

Indo-European Family
- Germanic Subfamily
- Romance Subfamily
- Celtic Subfamily
- Slavic Subfamily
- Baltic Subfamily
- Greek
- Albanian

Uralic Family
- Finnic Subfamily
- Ugric subfamily
- Samoyed

Altaic Family
- Turkic Subfamily

Afro-Asiatic Family
- Maltese

Basque

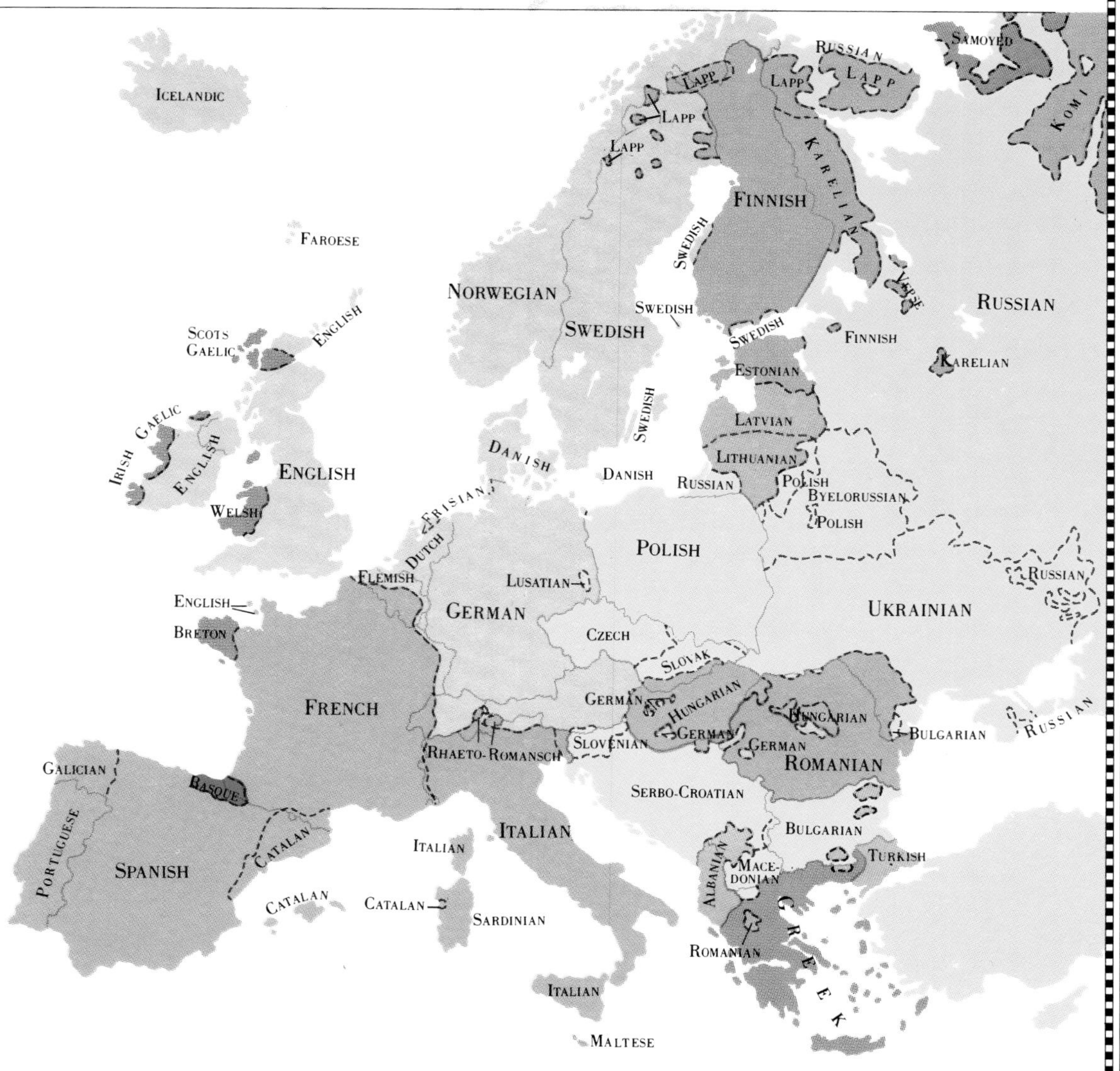

# Standards of

The living standards of less than two dozen highly industrialized nations stand in vivid contrast to conditions in the rest of the world. Though the developed countries represent only about a quarter of the earth's population, they create 80 percent of its wealth. The rest of the world must subsist on one-fifth of the total goods. ❂ Political instability, inadequate education and health care, and the lack or misuse of natural resources all contribute to this disparity. Most people in the developing world still live off the land, leaving them prey to natural disasters and market prices which no longer keep pace with rising costs. Drought, desertification, swelling populations and aggressive development further challenge traditional lifestyles. In third world nations from Mexico to Nigeria, the exodus from rural communities has resulted in intensely overcrowded cities where housing, jobs and clean water are inadequate. ❂ Despite these challenges, advances in education and health care have wrought stunning improvements in average life expectancy. In the developing world, it has risen from 41 years in 1955 to 57 years in 1992. Between 1962 and 1982, life expectancy in China jumped from 39 to 69 years. Antibiotics and immunizations have significantly reduced infant mortality levels in many third world countries. In North America, Western Europe and Japan, the average life expectancy is 73 years for men and 79 years for women. Elsewhere, in Afghanistan and sub-Saharan Africa, average life expectancy still hovers around 40. ❂ Literacy is the cornerstone of a healthy industrial nation. Yet by the year 2000, more than a billion people may be unable to read or write. Most of them will live in the 5 most populous Asian countries: China, India, Indonesia, Pakistan and Bangladesh. Ambitious literacy programs now underway in countries from Iraq to Chile and Mexico have reported significant reductions in their illiteracy rates. With each success comes new hope — for an individual, a family and a nation.

**In Switzerland, the average person earns about $30,000 — the highest per capita Gross National Product in the world. In Mozambique, the same person would earn about $80 in a year.**

**American workers typically get only 2 or 3 weeks of annual paid vacation, while western Europeans enjoy 4 to 6 weeks off. The Japanese are scheduled to work about 200 hours more each year than their American counterparts.**

## Comparison of European, U.S. and Japanese Workers

| Country | Scheduled Weekly Hours | Annual Leave Days/Holidays | Annual Hours Worked |
|---|---|---|---|
| Germany | 39 | 42 | 1708 |
| Netherlands | 40 | 43.5 | 1740 |
| Belgium | 38 | 31 | 1748 |
| Austria | 39.3 | 38 | 1751 |
| France | 39 | 34 | 1771 |
| Italy | 40 | 39 | 1776 |
| United Kingdom | 39 | 33 | 1778 |
| Luxembourg | 40 | 37 | 1792 |
| Finland | 40 | 37 | 1792 |
| Sweden | 40 | 37 | 1792 |
| Spain | 40 | 36 | 1800 |
| Denmark | 40 | 34 | 1816 |
| Norway | 40 | 30 | 1848 |
| Greece | 40 | 28 | 1864 |
| Ireland | 40 | 28 | 1864 |
| United States | 40 | 22 | 1912 |
| Switzerland | 41.5 | 30.5 | 1913 |
| Portugal | 45 | 36 | 2025 |
| Japan | 44 | 23.5 | 2116 |

## Gross National Product Growth Rates

(Per Capita by Percent 1980-1990)

| Best Growth Rates | | Worst Growth Rates | |
|---|---|---|---|
| South Korea | 8.9 | Qatar | -11.4 |
| China | 7.9 | Libya | -9.2 |
| Bhutan | 7.4 | United Arab Emirates | -7.2 |
| Oman | 7.1 | Trinidad & Tobago | -6.0 |
| Maldives | 6.6 | Saudi Arabia | -5.6 |
| Botswana | 6.3 | Suriname | -5.0 |
| Angola | 6.1 | Niger | -4.5 |
| St. Kitts & Nevis | 6.0 | São Tomé & Principe | -4.2 |
| St. Vincent & Grenadines | 5.7 | Bahrain | -4.2 |
| Singapore | 5.7 | Mozambique | -4.1 |
| Thailand | 5.6 | Jordan | -3.9 |
| Hong Kong | 5.5 | Ivory Coast | -3.7 |
| Mauritius | 5.4 | Guyana | -3.2 |
| Grenada | 5.1 | Nigeria | -3.0 |
| Cyprus | 4.9 | Zambia | -2.9 |
| Antigua & Barbuda | 4.7 | Bolivia | -2.6 |
| St. Lucia | 4.2 | Gabon | -2.6 |
| Indonesia | 4.1 | Haiti | -2.3 |
| Luxembourg | 3.9 | Madagascar | -2.3 |
| Malta | 3.6 | Kuwait | -2.2 |
| Japan | 3.5 | Rwanda | -2.2 |

# Living

## Gross National Product per Capita in Dollars

- Over 8000 per Year
- 5000-8000 per Year
- 2000-5000 per Year
- 1000-2000 per Year
- 500-1000 per Year
- Under 500 per Year
- Data not Available

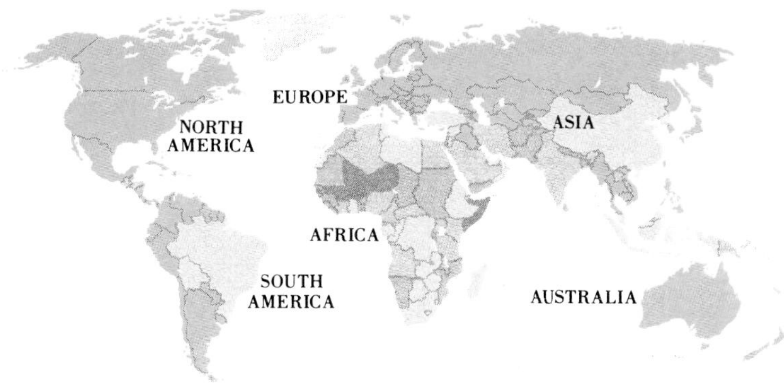


## Literate Percent of Population

- 80 and above
- 60-79
- 40-59
- 20-39
- 0-19

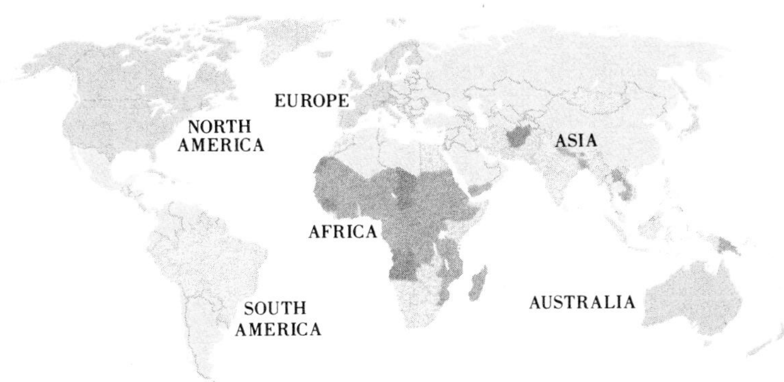


## Years of Life Expectancy (Men and Women)

- 70 and above
- 60-69
- 50-59
- 40-49
- 0-39

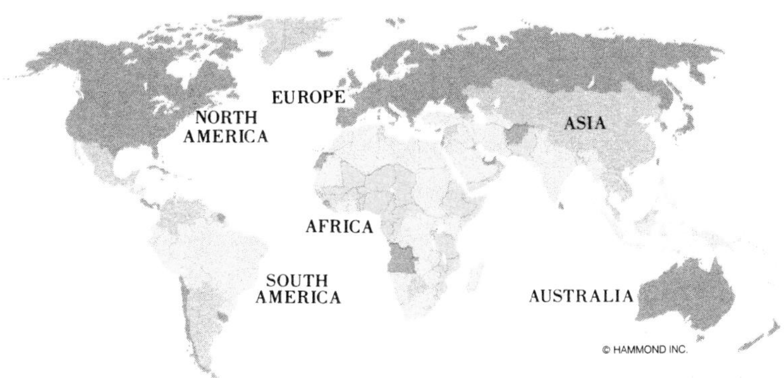




## Infant Deaths per 1,000 Live Births

- 150 and more
- 100-149
- 50-99
- 25-49
- 0-24

## Gross National Product

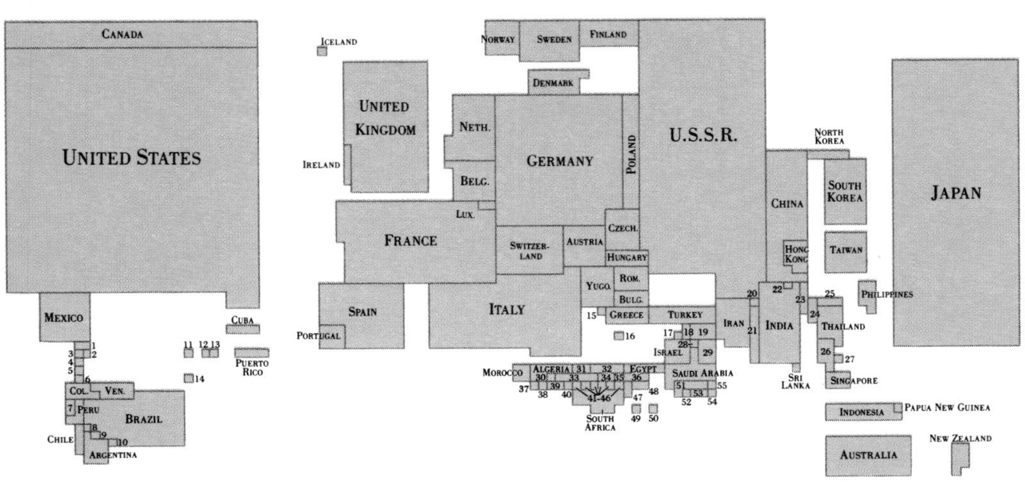


Each Area's Size is Proportionate to its Annual Gross National Product

Countries Indicated by Number

1 Guatemala
2 Honduras
3 El Salvador
4 Nicaragua
5 Costa Rica
6 Panama
7 Ecuador
8 Bolivia
9 Paraguay
10 Uruguay
11 Jamaica
12 Haiti
13 Dominican Republic
14 Trinidad and Tobago
15 Albania
16 Cyprus
17 Lebanon
18 Syria
19 Iraq
20 Afghanistan
21 Pakistan
22 Nepal
23 Bangladesh
24 Burma
25 Vietnam
26 Malaysia
27 Brunei
28 Jordan
29 Kuwait
30 Burkina Faso
31 Tunisia
32 Libya
33 Nigeria
34 Cameroon
35 Niger
36 Sudan
37 Senegal
38 Guinea
39 Ivory Coast
40 Ghana
41 Gabon
42 Angola
43 Tanzania
44 Zaire (Congo)
45 Zambia
46 Zimbabwe
47 Kenya
48 Ethiopia
49 Madagascar
50 Mauritius
51 United Arab Emirates
52 Yemen
53 Oman
54 Qatar
55 Kuwait

For thousands of years, the combustion of natural materials generated heat and light. Coal stoked the iron and steel furnaces of the Industrial Revolution, until eclipsed by oil in the late 19th century. Clean-burning natural gas, found directly above oil reserves, has also grown in popularity, aided by the ability to efficiently transport the gas in liquid form. After World War II, booming cities and industries demanded cheap, abundant energy. In 1956, the first nuclear power station began operation in England, and France soon made nuclear fission its chief source of power. Recently, mounting safety concerns and the problems of disposing spent radioactive materials have slowed new plant construction. Today, a new quest for renewable, environmentally-friendly energy has led to the efficient utilization of natural processes. Clean, inexpensive hydroelectric power currently supplies 7 percent of the world's energy needs — a figure expected to double by the year 2000 — though destruction of surrounding valleys remains an obstacle. In 1981, the world's first solar power station opened in Sicily. Thermal energy from hot springs and geysers is heating buildings and driving power stations from California to Japan. Power stations in Canada and France use tidal waters passing through narrow inlets to generate electricity. A worldwide research effort is now underway to develop a high temperature super conductor capable of transporting energy over vast distances so that these local energy sources can be utilized effectively on a global basis. Technological advances have also expanded the number of elements used in manufacturing. Gold, silver and platinum are vital in the making of electrical components. Steel alloys now include chromium, nickel and cobalt for corrosion resistance; tungsten and vanadium for hardness; and molybdenum for elasticity. Aluminum and titanium are making cars and aircraft lighter and stronger. Nonmetals also play key roles. Diamonds make cutting edges more durable. Potash and phosphates are used to enhance fertilizers. Sulphur is found in gunpowder, insecticides and pharmaceuticals. Perhaps the most important advance in recent years is the development of strong yet lightweight ceramics and carbon fibers. These materials, which can be produced cleanly and efficiently, are now being used to create the next generation of high-tech products.

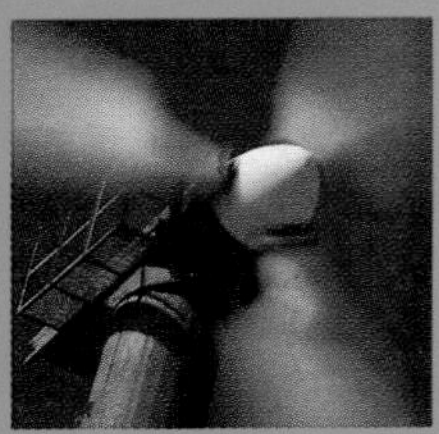

Wind could provide one-fifth of all the United States' energy needs. At Altamont Pass in California, an array of high-tech windmills provides electricity for 5,000 people.

# Energy & Resources

## Top Five World Producers of Selected Mineral Commodities

| Mineral Fuels | 1 | 2 | 3 | 4 | 5 |
|---|---|---|---|---|---|
| Crude Oil | Russia | United States | Saudi Arabia | China | Iraq |
| Refined Oil | United States | Russia | Japan | China | United Kingdom |
| Natural Gas | Russia | United States | Canada | Netherlands | United Kingdom |
| Coal (all grades) | China | United States | Germany | Russia | Poland |
| Mine Uranium | Canada | South Africa | United States | Australia | Namibia |
| **Metals** | | | | | |
| Chromite | South Africa | Kazakhstan | Albania | Finland | India |
| Iron Ore | Brazil | Ukraine | Russia | China | Australia |
| Manganese Ore | Former USSR | South Africa | China | Gabon | Australia |
| Mine Nickel | Canada | Russia | New Caledonia | Australia | Indonesia |
| Mine Silver | Mexico | United States | Peru | Former USSR | Canada |
| Bauxite | Australia | Guinea | Brazil | Jamaica | Former USSR |
| Aluminium | United States | Former USSR | Canada | Australia | Brazil |
| Gold | South Africa | Former USSR | Unites States | Australia | Canada |
| Mine Copper | Chile | United States | Canada | Former USSR | Zaire (Congo) |
| Mine Lead | Australia | Former USSR | United States | Canada | China |
| Mine Tin | Brazil | Indonesia | Malaysia | China | Former USSR |
| Mine Zinc | Canada | Former USSR | Australia | China | Peru |
| **Nonmetals** | | | | | |
| Natural Diamond | Australia | Zaire (Congo) | Botswana | Former USSR | South Africa |
| Potash | Former USSR | Canada | Germany | United States | France |
| Phosphate Rock | United States | Former USSR | Morocco | China | Tunisia |
| Elemental Sulfur | Unites States | Former USSR | Canada | Poland | China |

Names in Green Indicate More Than 10% of Total World Production

## Nuclear Power Production

Percentage of World Total

| Country | % |
|---|---|
| United States | 27.4 |
| France | 15.1 |
| Japan | 11.4 |
| Germany | 8.6 |
| Canada | 4.6 |
| Sweden | 4.1 |
| United Kingdom | 3.3 |
| Belgium | 2.5 |
| Spain | 2.5 |
| South Korea | 2.4 |
| Czechoslovakia | 1.3 |
| Switzerland | 1.3 |
| Finland | 1.2 |
| Bulgaria | 0.7 |
| Hungary | 0.7 |
| Argentina | 0.4 |
| Others | 1.1 |

## Commercial Energy Consumption/Production

Percentage of World Total

0.0 Production ■ 0.0 Consumption

| Country | Production / Consumption |
|---|---|
| Former USSR | 23.2 / 19.3 |
| United States | 19.8 / 24.1 |
| China | 8.8 / 8.3 |
| Canada | 3.3 / 2.7 |
| United Kingdom | 3.3 / 3.0 |
| Saudi Arabia | 3.3 / 0.8 |
| Mexico | 2.5 / 1.5 |
| Germany | 2.5 / 4.9 |
| India | 2.1 / 2.3 |
| Australia | 1.9 / 1.1 |
| Iran | 1.9 / 0.7 |
| Poland | 1.8 / 1.9 |
| Venezuela | 1.7 / 0.6 |
| France | 0.7 / 2.1 |
| Japan | 0.5 / 4.7 |
| Italy | 0.3 / 2.1 |
| Others | 22.4 / 19.9 |

Mineral Fuels

Oil Fields · Natural Gas Fields · ● Major Coal Deposits · ▲ Oil Sands · ✦ Oil Shale · ✶ Major Uranium Deposits · ■ Important Peat Deposits

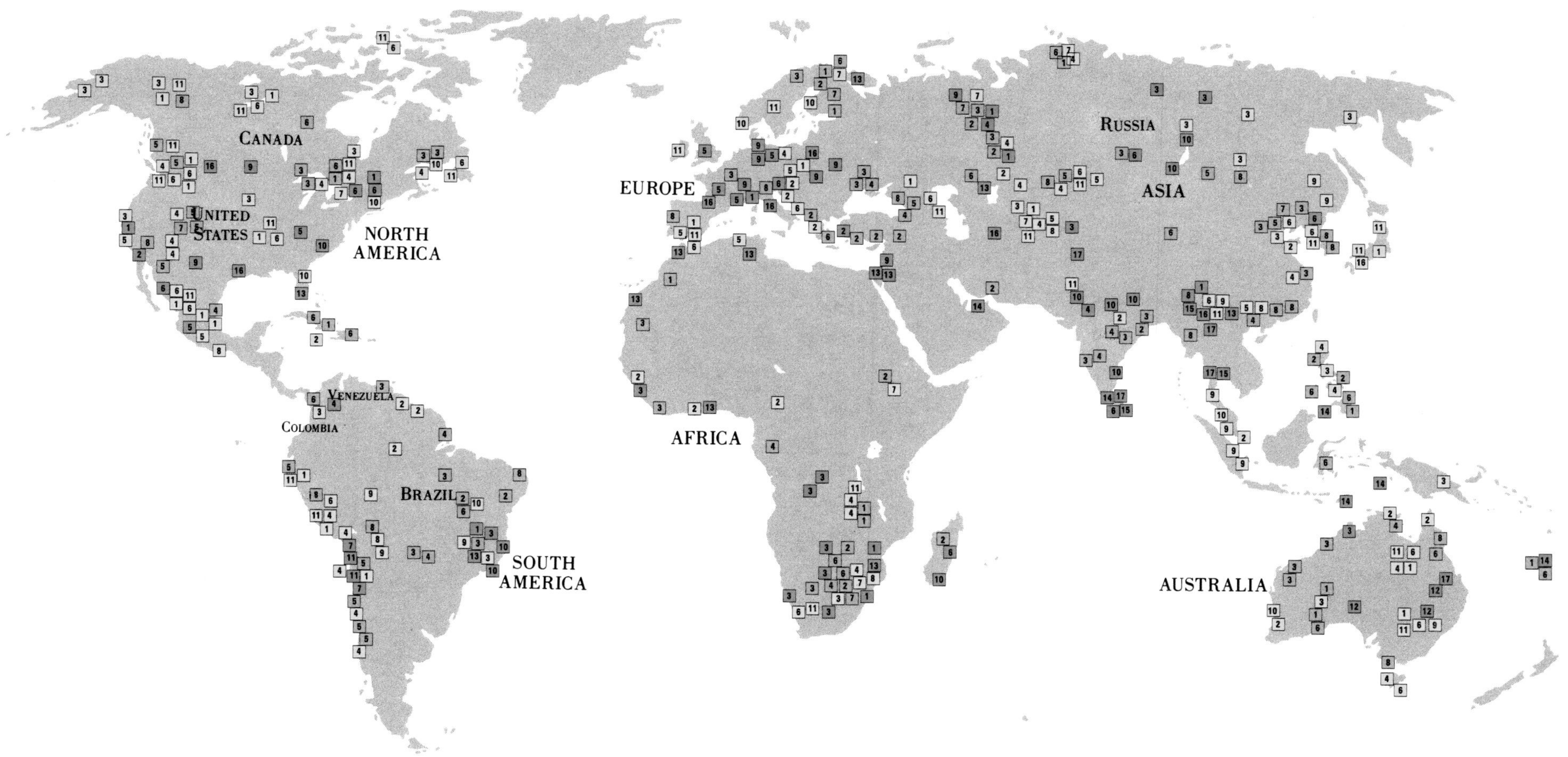


Metals and Nonmetals

**Iron and Ferroalloy Metals**
1 Cobalt
2 Chromium
3 Iron Ore
4 Manganese
5 Molybdenum
6 Nickel
7 Vanadium
8 Tungsten

**Other Metals**
1 Silver
2 Bauxite
3 Gold
4 Copper
5 Mercury
6 Lead
7 Platinum
8 Antimony
9 Tin
10 Titanium
11 Zinc

**Nonmetals**
1 Asbestos
2 Borax
3 Diamonds
4 Emeralds
5 Fluorspar
6 Graphite
7 Iodine
8 Jade
9 Potash
10 Mica
11 Nitrates
12 Opals
13 Phosphates
14 Pearls
15 Rubies
16 Sulfur
17 Sapphires

Today, according to the World Bank, the combined Gross National Products of the United States, United Kingdom, France, Germany and Japan total about 12 trillion dollars. Agriculture and manufacturing are key elements in this total. In 1980, farmers harvested twice as much food as in 1950 — more than enough to feed the earth's population. A key factor has been the development of high-yielding strains of wheat, corn and rice. These three plants account for half of the world's harvest. The sea, too, provides a rich annual harvest — nearly 70 million tons (64 million metric tons) of fish and algae. Deep sea fishing, supported by floating factories to process the catch, is now a major industry. Aquaculture, the breeding of fish and shellfish, contributes an ever-growing portion of the world's seafood. With their adaptable diet and minimal space requirements, hogs are the world's main source of meat. China raises nearly 40 percent of the world's pork. Cattle can be raised in a broad temperate band, but their intensive consumption of grasses, grains and water make them an inefficient food source. Many African economies rely upon a single agricultural commodity for foreign exchange. But deforestation, drought and slash-and-burn farming have kept crop yields at below-subsistence levels. Meanwhile, in the traditional farming nations of China and southeastern Asia, manufacturing activity has increased dramatically, fostered by an educated, low-cost workforce and a global marketplace. Advanced communications and transportation systems now permit companies to disperse production facilities and marketing forces across the globe, accelerating the shift from self-sufficient national economies to a worldwide production system. In the new, international labor market, routine manufacturing jobs, formerly plentiful in the U.S., have developed overseas, where labor is cheaper. Eastern Europe and the former U.S.S.R. are struggling to learn the fundamentals of capitalism while confronting obsolete factories, ineffective distribution systems, inadequate capital, and serious and widespread ethnic conflicts which were suppressed by the previous communist governments. Despite such economic and political instability, the world's richest nations are offering financial support, hoping to avoid the dire prospects of failure and to enjoy the opportunities that success would bring.

Our global food supply is grown on about 11 percent of the earth's total land area. Much of the remaining land lies in areas too dry, cold or mountainous to farm successfully.

# Agriculture & Manufacturing

## Top Five World Producers of Selected Agricultural Commodities

| | 1 | 2 | 3 | 4 | 5 |
|---|---|---|---|---|---|
| Wheat | China | Former USSR | United States | India | France |
| Rice | China | India | Indonesia | Bangladesh | Thailand |
| Oats | Former USSR | United States | Canada | Germany | Poland |
| Corn (Maize) | United States | China | Brazil | Romania | Former USSR |
| Soybeans | United States | Brazil | China | Argentina | Canada |
| Potatoes | Russia | Poland | China | Germany | Ukraine |
| Coffee | Brazil | Colombia | Indonesia | Mexico | Ivory Coast |
| Tea | India | China | Sri Lanka | Kenya | Former USSR |
| Tobacco | China | United States | India | Brazil | Former USSR |
| Cotton | China | United States | Former USSR | Pakistan | India |
| Cattle | Australia | Brazil | United States | China | Russia |
| Sheep | Australia | China | New Zealand | Russia | India |
| Hogs | China | United States | Russia | Germany | Brazil |
| Cow's Milk | United States | Germany | Russia | France | Poland |
| Hen's Eggs | China | United States | Russia | Japan | Brazil |
| Wool | Australia | Former USSR | New Zealand | China | Argentina |
| Roundwood | United States | Russia | China | India | Brazil |
| Natural Rubber | Malaysia | Indonesia | Thailand | China | India |
| Fish Catches | Japan | Former USSR | China | United States | Chile |

Names in Green Indicate More Than 10% of Total World Production

## Percent of Total Employment in Agriculture, Manufacturing and Other Industries

Finance, Insurance, Real Estate Data Included With "Other" for India, China, Indonesia, Pakistan and Nigeria.

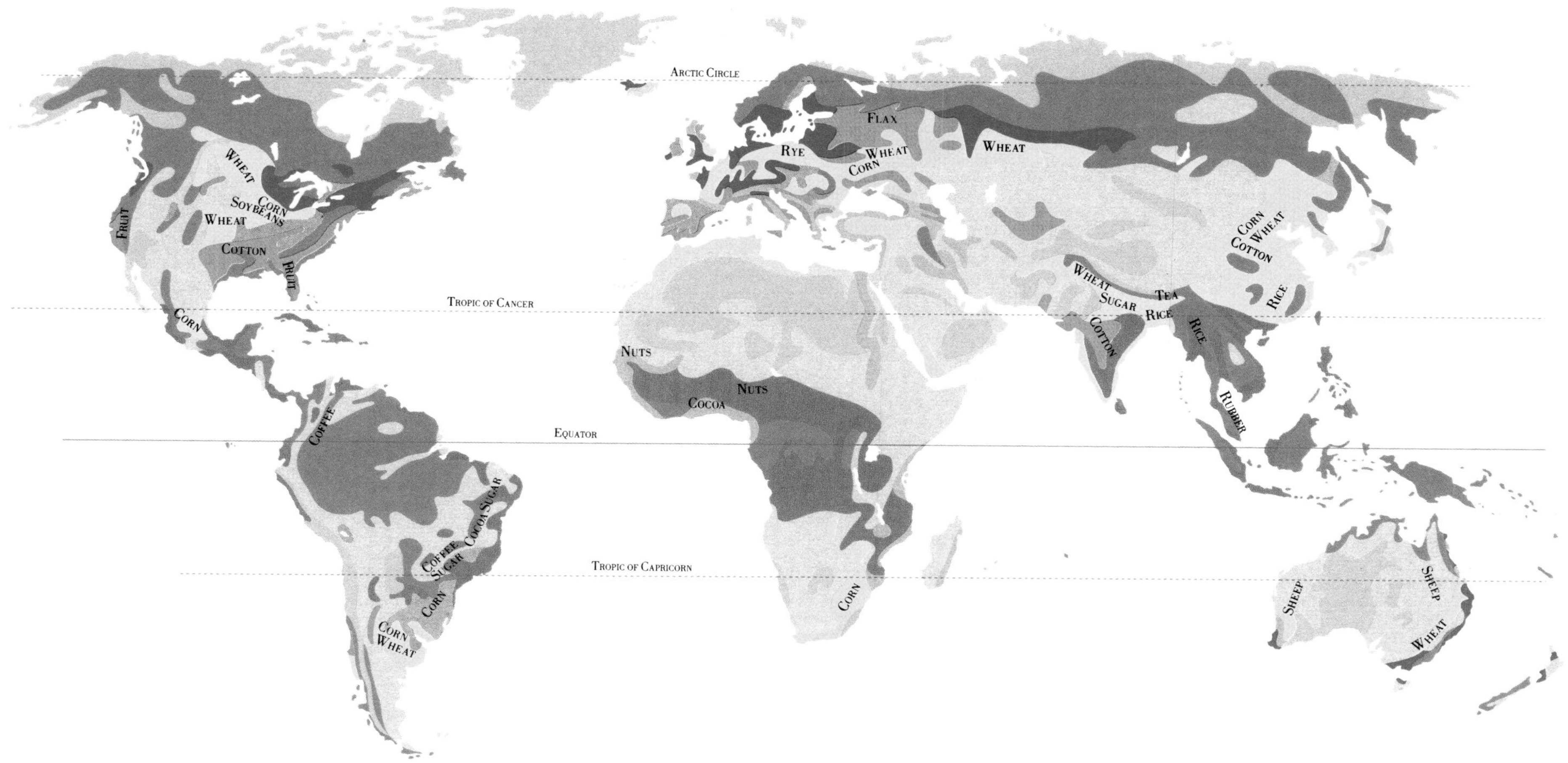


## Land Use

Cereals, Livestock
Cash Crops, Mixed Farming
Dairy, Livestock
General and Mixed Farming
Special Crops
Livestock Ranching and Herding
Diversified Tropical and Subtropical Crops
Forests
Nonproductive Land

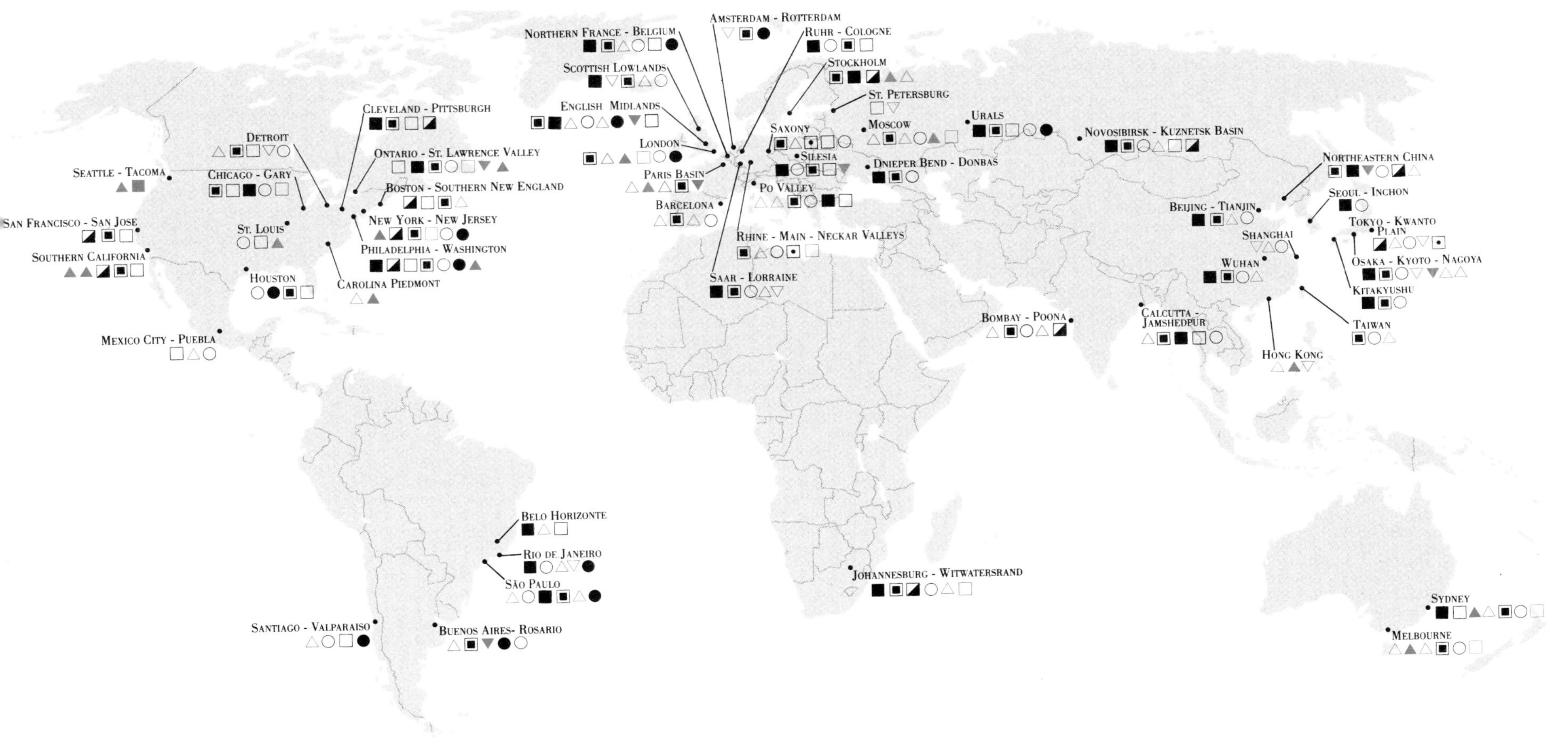


## Manufacturing Regions

Aircraft
Motor Vehicles
Shipbuilding
Transportation Equipment
Iron and Steel
Machinery
Metals and Metal Products
Electrical products
Optical Instruments
Oil Refining
Chemicals
Textiles
Clothing
Rubber Goods
Glass Products
Wood and Wood Products
Printing and Publishing

# Climate

The earth is a living organism. It breathes ceaselessly, as the forces of convection circulate air in an endless stream around the globe. Warm air rises at the equator and flows north or south, while cold air moves down from the poles towards the equator. In this way, global air currents direct the weather. ❂ All weather occurs in the troposphere, the atmospheric level closest to the earth's surface. Chemical exchanges between air and sea help stabilize the oxygen and carbon dioxide content of both. Wind also whips up and carries along invisible droplets of salty water. Water condenses around the salt crystals to produce mists, clouds and rain. ❂ Climate, the average weather in an area as measured over many years, is determined by two key variables: temperature and precipitation. Humidity, sunshine, air pressure and wind play supporting roles. Since temperature depends upon the strength of the sun's rays, the earth's 14 climatic zones (see map) are related to latitude — though winds and elevation can modify these zones. ❂ Climates differ for many reasons, from variations in latitude, elevation and topography to changes in land and water temperatures. Every place on earth has its own climate and ecosystem which, in turn, influences the food, clothing, homes and culture of the local population. ❂ How do climates change? Climatologists point to several causes, from shifts in solar energy to volcanic ash in the atmosphere, which can severely reduce the amount of sunlight reaching the earth's surface — sometimes for years. ❂ Almost 3 billion pounds (1.36 million kg.) of chemicals are released into the air in the United States each year. The sky then transports the pollutants hundreds of miles. During the journey, the atmosphere functions as a complex chemical reactor where fossil fuel emissions interact with sunlight, water vapor and hundreds of man-made compounds. ❂ Our atmosphere, which rises 30 miles (48 km.) above the planet's surface and covers 260 billion cubic miles (1.08 trillion cubic km.), may seem too vast to pollute. But the ability of the atmosphere to warm and cool the earth, to shield us from ultraviolet rays and to enable life to flourish is diminishing. The changes we have wrought are altering our atmosphere, our climate and our lives.

Antarctica, the earth's coldest place, is also one of its driest. Its vast inland plateau is really a desert of ice and snow.

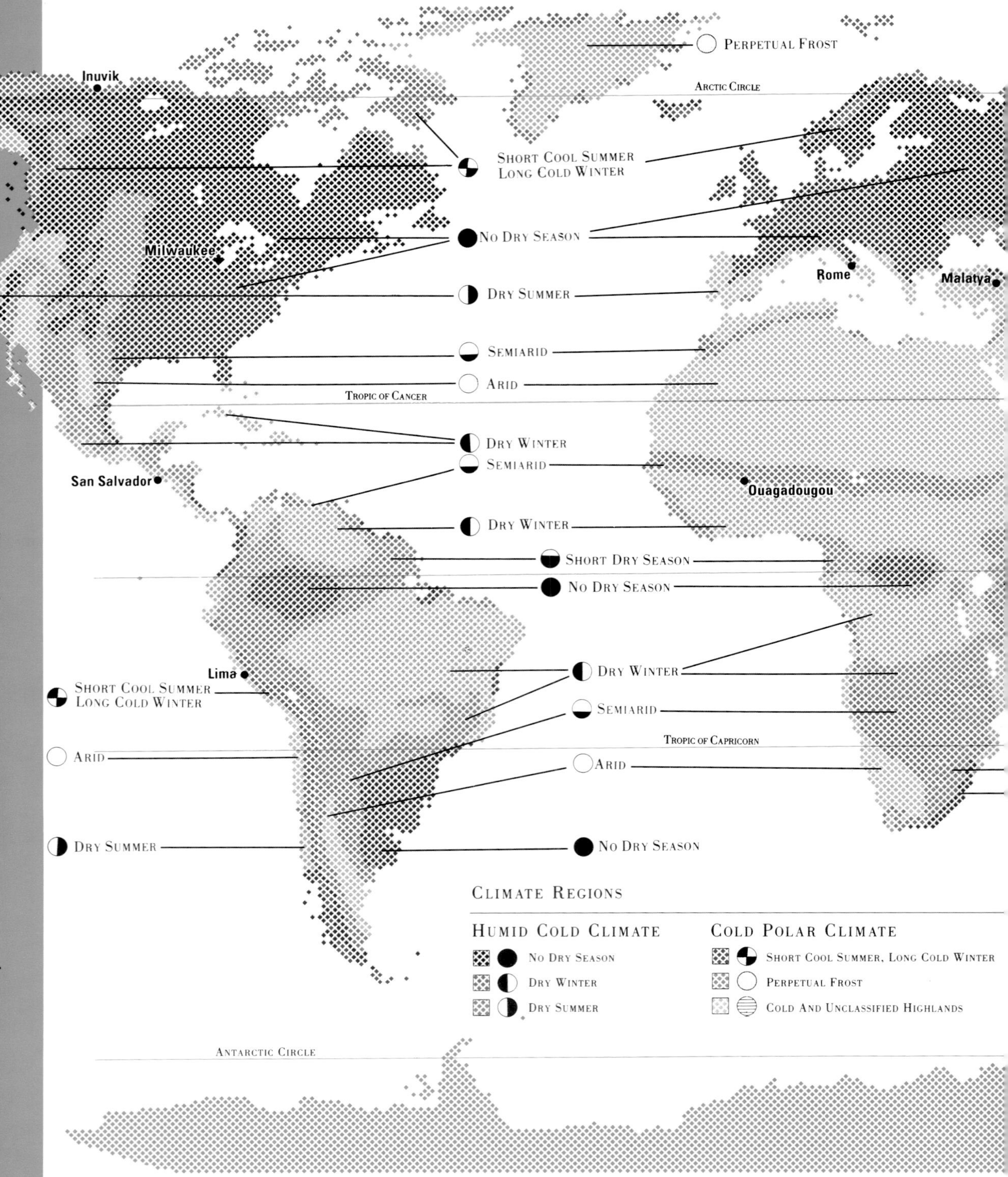


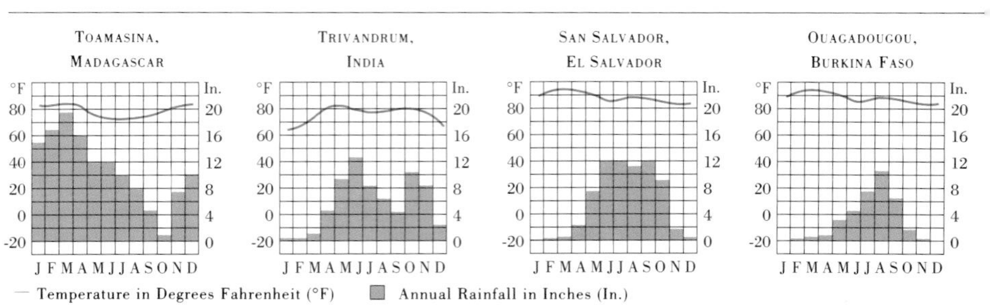

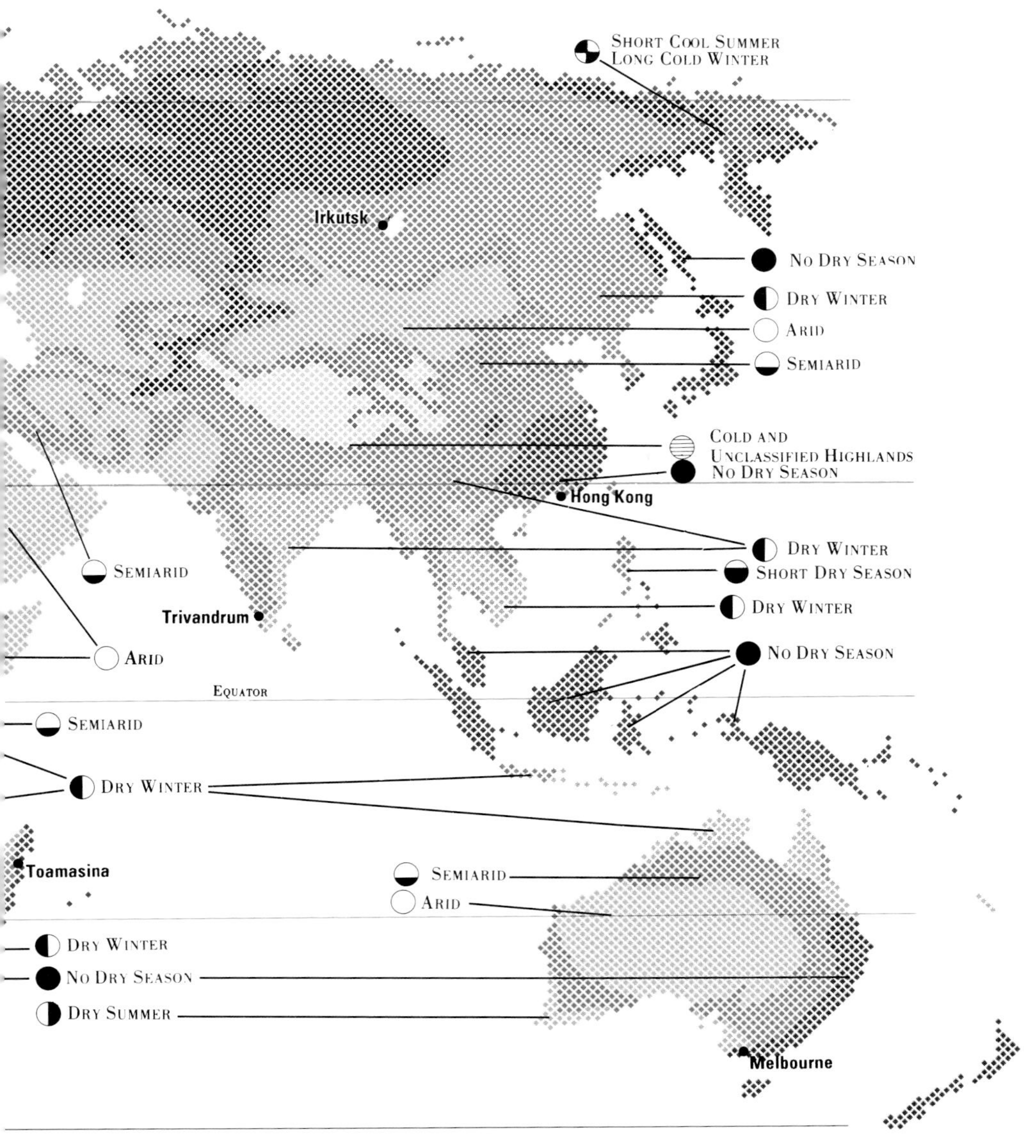


## Humid Tropical Climate

- No Dry Season
- Short Dry Season
- Dry Winter

## Humid Warm Climate

- No Dry Season
- Dry Winter
- Dry Summer

## Dry Climate

- Semiarid
- Arid

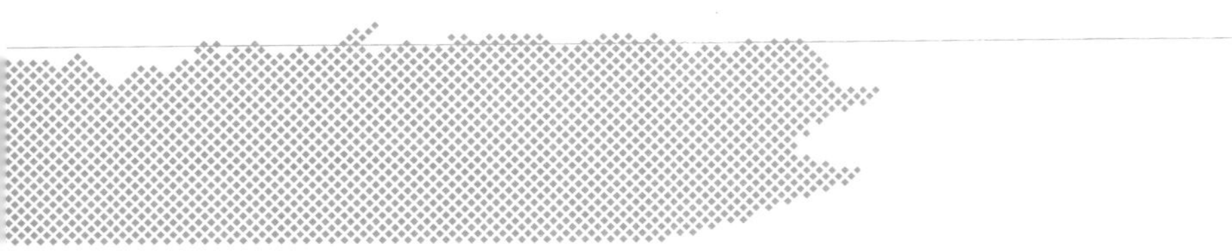

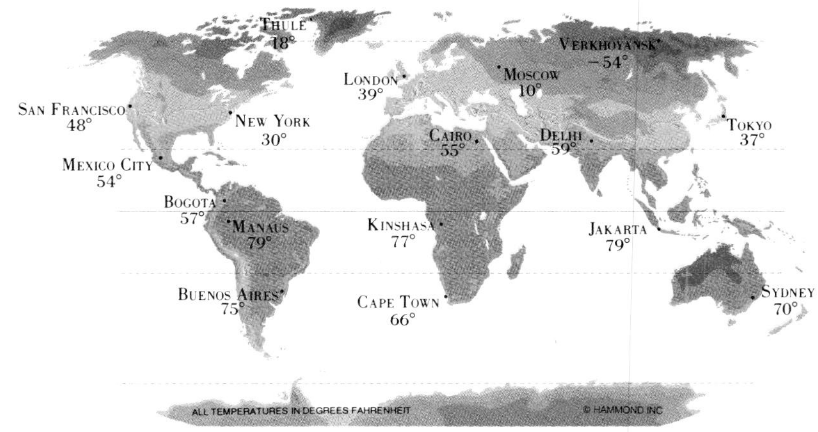


January

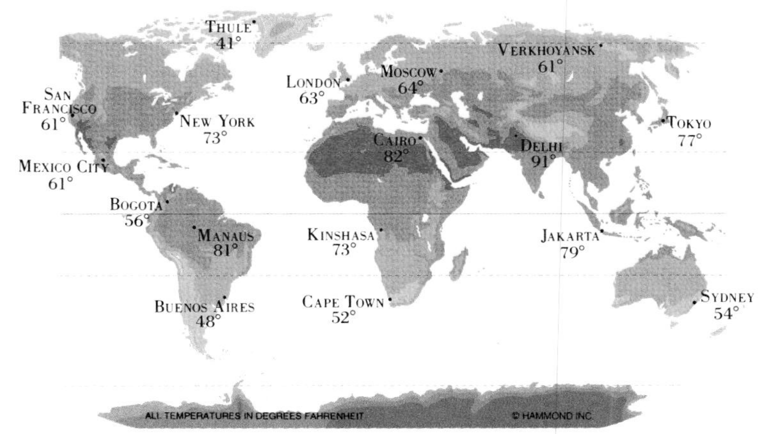


July

## Average Temperatures

| Fahrenheit | Celsius | Fahrenheit | Celsius |
|---|---|---|---|
| Over 86° | Over 30° | -4° to 14° | -20° to -10° |
| 68° to 86° | 20° to 30° | -22° to -4° | -30° to -20° |
| 50° to 68° | 10° to 20° | -40° to -22° | -40° to -30° |
| 32° to 50° | 0° to 10° | Under -40° | Under -40° |
| 14° to 32° | -10° to 0° | | |

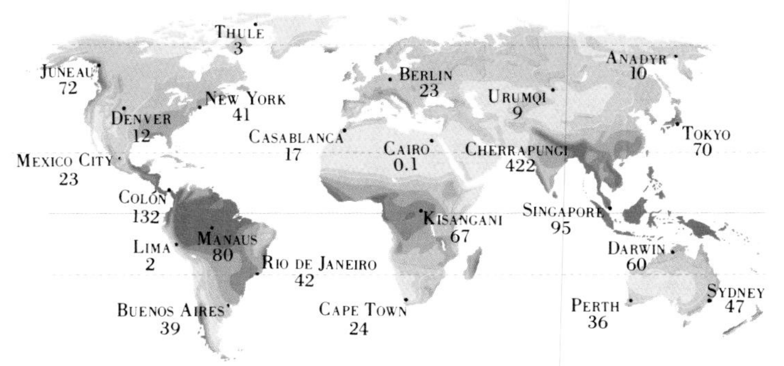


## Average Annual Rainfall

| Inches | Centimeters | Inches | Centimeters |
|---|---|---|---|
| Over 80 | Over 200 | 20 to 40 | 50 to 100 |
| 60 to 80 | 150 to 200 | 10 to 20 | 25 to 50 |
| 40 to 60 | 100 to 150 | Under 10 | Under 25 |

## Selected Climate Stations

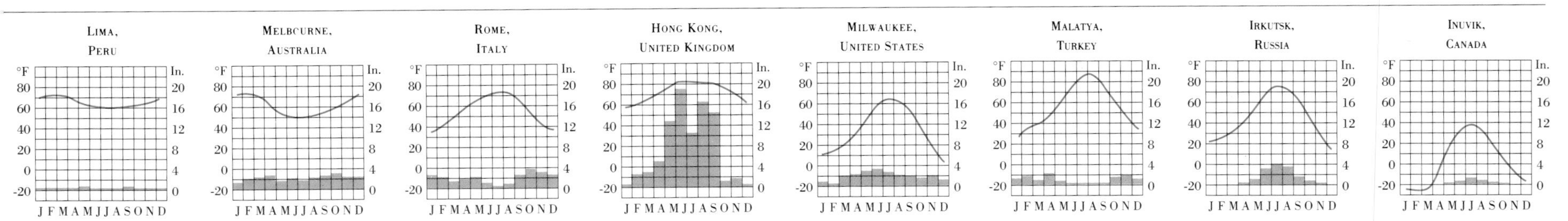

# Vegetation

Fifty years ago, tropical rainforests covered twelve percent of the earth's land; today, half of those forests are gone. Yet rainforests play a crucial environmental role, absorbing the greenhouse gas carbon dioxide while releasing oxygen. The forests also serve as reservoirs for most of the non-glacial fresh water on earth, and are home to more than half of the world's plants, animals and insects. Over 40 prescription drugs can be traced to rainforest plants. The northern hemisphere was once covered by vast stretches of broadleaf, deciduous woodlands. In the eastern and central United States, less than a tenth of the original forested areas remain. However, the older second-growth forests now closely approximate virgin forest conditions. In China, only vestiges of the great forests — and the wildlife that inhabited them — can be seen. Wetlands, too, are quickly being filled in or drained off. These complex environments even out the flow rate of rivers and improve the sub-surface water supply. Attempts to turn wetlands into farmland usually result in very low crop yields. Before the colonization of the Americas, vast prairies stretched across the central plains. Today, most virgin prairie has been plowed for agricultural use, as in the United States, or transformed by domesticated plants, as in the Argentine Pampas. The African savannas are being burned off to make way for farming, though the poor soil is often spent in just a few years. Changes in vegetation usually occur gradually. As one passes from wet to dry regions, dense forests become lighter, trees become small and sparse, and lush undergrowth gives way to small shrubs, then grasslands, and finally desert. About one third of the earth's surface is arid. When the sparse vegetation is destroyed by overuse of the land, the soil is less able to spring back after a drought, and evaporation and rainfall decrease. When rains do occur, they often wash away rather than feed the soil. Each year, about 47,000 square miles (121,700 sq. km.) of agricultural land are lost through creeping desertification, primarily in sub-Saharan Africa, which has been hit hard by two decades of drought.

**The United Nations has designated over 250 Biosphere Reserves, from Australia's Great Barrier Reef to Yellowstone National Park (above), the world's first national park, created in 1872.**

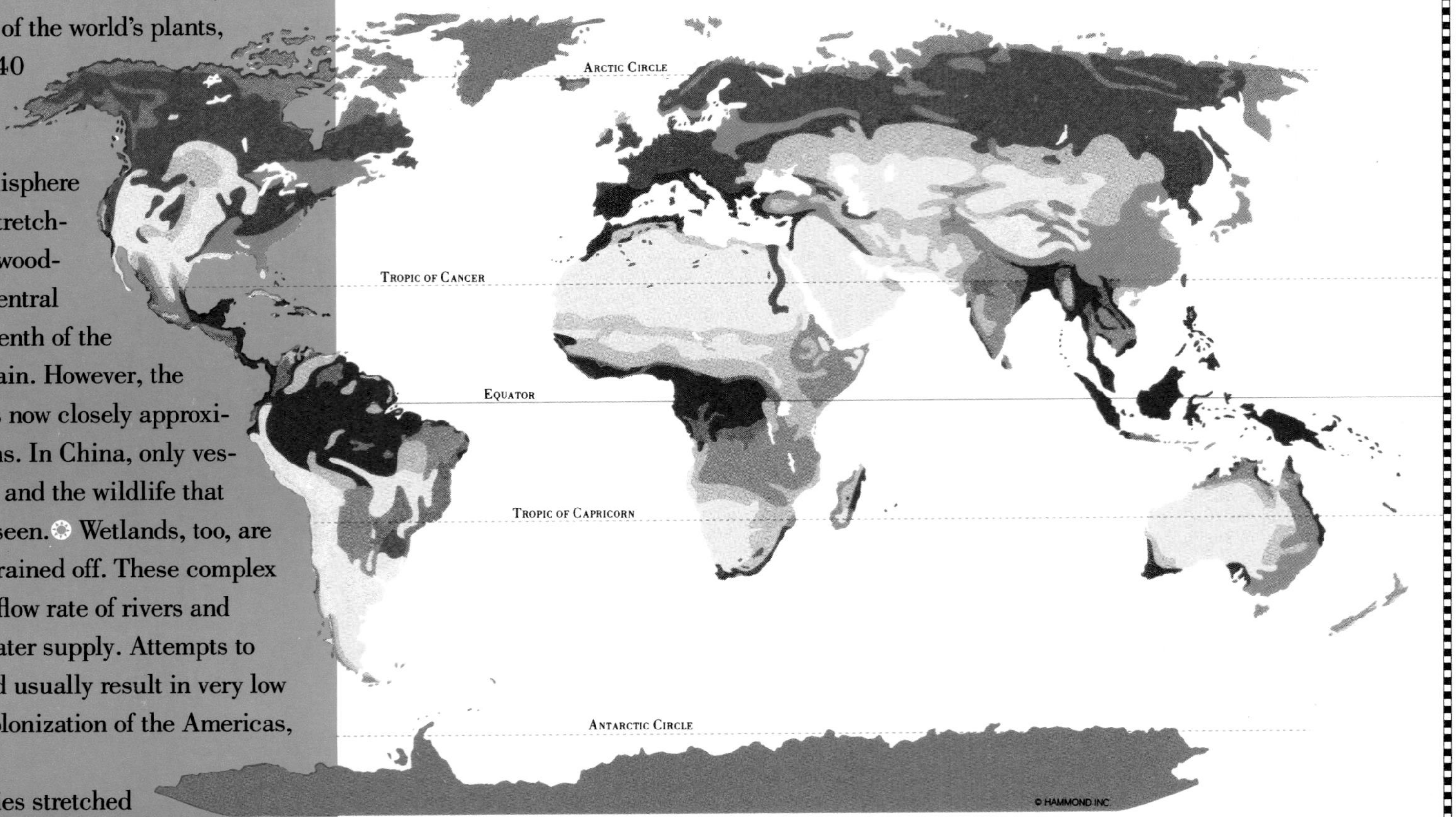


## Natural Vegetation

**Needleleaf Forest**
Found in higher latitudes with shorter growing seasons, and dominated by pure stands of softwood, evergreen conifers (cone-bearing trees) such as pine, fir and spruce. The light undergrowth consists of small shrubs, mosses, lichens and pine needles.

**Broadleaf Forest**
Found in the middle latitudes, this forest of deciduous (seasonal leaf-shedding) trees includes the hardwoods maple, hickory and oak. The forest floor is relatively barren, except for thick leaf cover during colder months.

**Mixed Needleleaf and Broadleaf Forest**
A transitional zone between northern softwoods and temperate hardwoods.

**Woodland and Shrub (Mediterranean)**
A mid-latitude area of broadleaf evergreens, dense growths of woody shrubs and open grassy woodland, characterized by pronounced dry summers and wet winters.

**Short Grass (Steppe)**
A mid-latitude, semi-arid area usually found on the fringe of desert regions, with continuous short-grass cover up to 8" (20cm.) tall, used chiefly to graze livestock.

**Tall Grass (Prairie)**
Mid-latitude, semi-moist areas with continuous tall-grass cover up to 24" (61cm.) in height, used for agricultural purposes. Rainfall is insufficient to support larger plants.

**Tropical Rain Forest (Selva)**
A dense, evergreen forest of tall, varied hardwood trees with a thick broadleaf canopy and a dark, moist interior with minimal undergrowth.

**Light Tropical Forest (Tropical Semideciduous or Monsoon Forest)**
As above, with more widely spaced trees, heavier undergrowth, larger concentrations of single species. Dry season prevents most trees from remaining evergreen. Found in monsoon areas.

**Tropical Woodland and Shrub (Thorn Forest)**
Longer dry season results in low trees with thick bark and smaller leaves. Dense undergrowth of thorny plants, brambles and grasses. Transition belt between denser forests and grasslands.

**Tropical Grassland and Shrub (Savanna)**
Stiff, sharp-edged grasses, from 2' to 12' (0.6m. to 3.7m.) high, with large areas of bare ground. Scattered shrubs and low trees in some areas.

**Wooded Savanna**
A transitional area where savanna joins a tropical or shrub forest, with low trees and shrubs dotting the grasslands.

**Desert and Desert Shrub**
Barren stretches of soft brown, yellow or red sand and rock wastes with isolated patches of short grass and stunted bushes, turning bright green when fed by infrequent precipitation.

**River Valley and Oasis**
River valleys are lush, fertile lands, with varied vegetation. An oasis is a fertile or verdant spot found in a desert near a natural spring or pool.

**Heath and Moor**
A heath is open, uncultivated land covered with low, flowering evergreen shrubs such as heather. Moors are often high and poorly drained lands, with patches of heath and peat bogs.

**Tundra and Alpine**
An area of scarce moisture and short, cool summers where trees cannot survive. A permanently frozen subsoil supports low-growing lichens, mosses and stunted shrubs.

**Unclassified Highlands**
Sequential bands or vertical zones of all vegetation types, which generally follow the warm-to-cold upward patterns found in corresponding areas of vegetation. (Map scale does not permit delineation of these areas.)

**Permanent Ice Cover**
Permanently ice and snow-covered terrain found in polar regions and atop high mountains.

# The Physical World

"In every outthrust headland, in every curving beach, in every grain of sand there is a story of the earth."

**Rachel Carson**

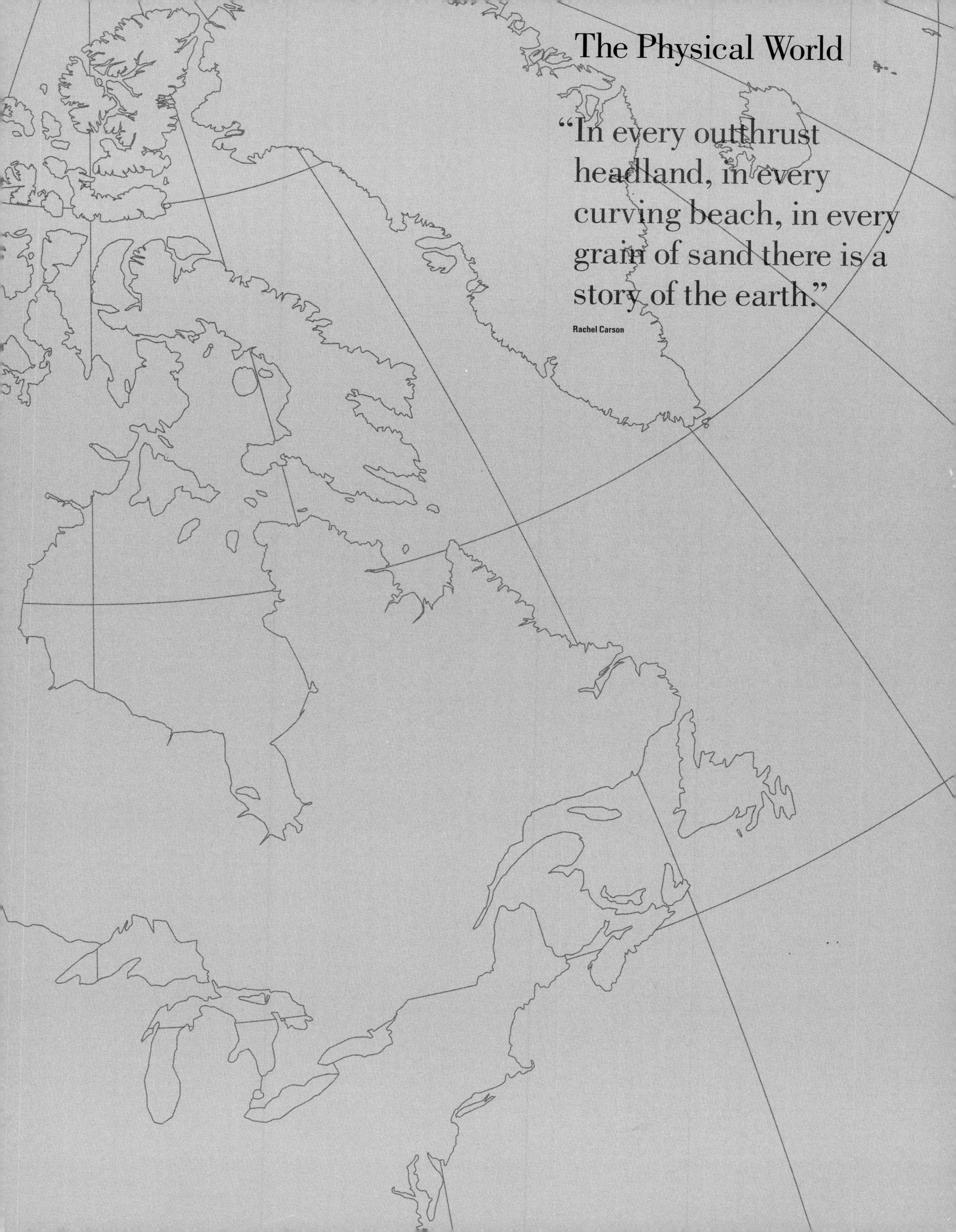

The present continents once formed a single supercontinent which began splitting up about 200 million years ago. Today, the earth's crust consists of eight major plates and a few smaller ones. These slowly drift and collide, and it is at plate boundaries that many of the world's most spectacular landforms occur. These movements within the earth's crust, along with the sculpturing by water, wind and ice, constantly reshape our world. Molten material rises up from below the sea floor, forming mid-ocean ridges and fracture zones that encircle the globe.

# World

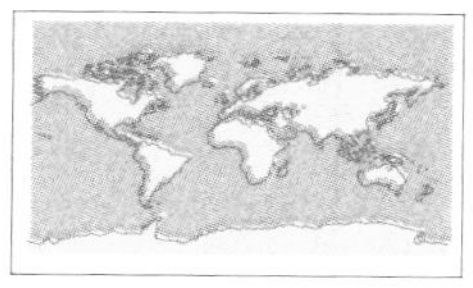

−17,881 ft.
(−5450 m)
ARCTIC
OCEAN
FRANZ JOSEF LAND
SEVERNAYA
ZEMLYA
SVALBARD
NEW SIBERIAN IS.
NOVAYA
ZEMLYA
Laptev
Sea
Nordkapp
Barents
Sea
Kara
Sea
Wrangel I.
Kjølen
Siberia
Lena
Yenisey
Ob'
Ural Mountains
L. Ladoga
Angara
Lena
Aldan
Bering
Sea
ALEUTIAN
BASIN
Kamchatka
Pen.
Baltic Sea
Sea
of
Okhotsk
ALEUTIAN
ISLANDS
ALEUTIAN TRENCH
Volga
Irtysh
Ob'
L. Baykal
EUROPE
ASIA
Dnieper
Amur
Sakhalin
KURIL-KAMCHATKA TRENCH
Danube
Black Sea
Caspian Sea
Aral
Sea
L. Balkhash
Gobi
Sea of
Japan
Honshu
NORTHWEST
PACIFIC
BASIN
JAPAN
TRENCH
Mediterranean Sea
Euphrates
Kunlun
Himalaya
Huang
East
China
Sea
Mt. Everest
Indus
Ganges
Chang
PACIFIC
Nile
Red Sea
Taiwan
Tropic of Cancer
Arabian
Sea
ARABIAN
BASIN
Salween
Mekong
South
China
Sea
PHILIPPINE
BASIN
MARIANA IS.
MARIANA
TRENCH
Luzon
AFRICA
Bay
of
Bengal
Challenger Deep
−36,198 ft.
(−11,033 m)
MARSHALL IS.
CENTRAL
PACIFIC
BASIN
CARLSBERG
RIDGE
C. Comorin
Ceylon
Mindanao
Borneo
CAROLINE IS.
MELANESIAN
BASIN
Equator
CEYLON
PLAIN
L. Victoria
Kilimanjaro
Congo
SOMALI
BASIN
CENTRAL
INDIAN
RIDGE
NINETYEAST RIDGE
Sumatra
Java
New Guinea
Celebes
OCEAN
JAVA TRENCH
24,443 ft.
(−7450 m)
INDIAN
OCEAN
Zambezi
Madagascar
Coral
Sea
Great Barrier Reef
Fiji Is.
Tropic of Capricorn
AUSTRALIA
Orange
BROKEN
PLATEAU
C. Leeuwin
CAPE
Good Hope
BASIN
SOUTHWEST INDIAN RIDGE
SOUTHEAST INDIAN RIDGE
S. AUSTRALIA BASIN
Tasman
Sea
North Cape
North I.
South I.
Tasmania
KERGUELEN
PLATEAU
ENDERBY ABYSSAL PLAIN
AUSTRALIAN-ANTARCTIC BASIN
Antarctic Circle
C. Adare
Amery
Ice Shelf
Ross Sea
ANTARCTICA

ICELAND
Reykjavik
JAN MAYEN RIDGE
NORWEGIAN BASIN
NORWEGIAN SEA
VORING PLATEAU
Arctic Circle
Sørøy
Vesterålen
Lofoten
Vestfjord
Kiruna
Lule
Torne
ICELAND BASIN
ATLANTIC OCEAN
ICELAND-FAROE RISE
FAROE SHELF
Faroe Is. (Den.)
FAROE-SHETLAND CHANNEL
HEBRIDEAN SHELF
ROCKALL PLATEAU
Rockall (U.K.)
ROCKALL BANK
ROCKALL TROUGH
FENI RIDGE
Hebrides
Shetland Is.
Orkney Is.
Moray Firth
Aberdeen
Ben Nevis 4,406 ft. (1343 m)
Glasgow
NORWAY
SWEDEN
Trondheim
Angerman
Sundsvall
Gulf of Bothnia
Glittertind 8,110 ft. (2472 m)
Glama
Ljusnan
Dal
Bergen
Oslo
Klaralven
Hardangerfjorden
NORWEGIAN DEEP
Lindesnes
Åland Is.
Vasterås
Stockholm
Vänern
Vättern
Göteborg
Hiiumaa
Saaremaa
Gotland
Öland
Skagerrak
Kattegat
NORTH SEA
UNITED KINGDOM
U.K.
Belfast
PORCUPINE BANK
IRELAND
Dublin
IRISH SEA
Pennine Chain
Great Britain
Liverpool
Birmingham
C. Clear
St. George's Chan.
CELTIC SHELF
Land's End
Thames
London
Jutland
DENMARK
Copenhagen
Fyn
Sjaelland
BALTIC SEA
Bornholm
Rügen
Gdańsk
Frisian Is.
NETHERLANDS
Amsterdam
The Hague
Ems
Hamburg
Elbe
Berlin
POLAND
Warta
Vistula
Łódź
Oder
PORCUPINE ABYSSAL PLAIN
English Channel
Channel Is. (U.K.)
BELGIUM
Brussels
Cologne
Bonn
GERMANY
Weser
Leipzig
Le Havre
Seine
Paris
Ardennes
Meuse
LUX.
Moselle
Prague
CZECH REP.
Cracow
Nantes
Loire
FRANCE
Vienne
Stuttgart
Rhine
Danube
Brno
SLOVAKIA
Bratislava
Vienna
Munich
BISCAY ABYSSAL PLAIN
IBERIAN ABYSSAL PLAIN
Bay of Biscay
Jura
Bern
SWITZ.
LIECH.
AUSTRIA
Budapest
HUNGARY
Balaton
C. Finisterre
Bordeaux
Dordogne
Garonne
Massif Central
Lyon
Rhône
Mt. Blanc 15,771 ft. (4807 m)
Milan
Po
Turin
Graz
SLOVENIA
Zagreb
CROATIA
Sava
Tisza
Venice
Mino
Cantabrian Mts.
Bilbao
Pyrenees
Ebro
Porto
Douro
ANDORRA
Gulf of Lions
Marseille
MONACO
Genoa
Ligurian Sea
SAN MARINO
BOSNIA & HERCEGOVINA
Belgrade
Sarajevo
YUGOSLAVIA
PORTUGAL
SPAIN
Saragossa
Lisbon
Madrid
Tagus
Barcelona
Corsica
Tiber
ITALY
Apennines
ADRIATIC SEA
Guadiana
Iberian Peninsula
Valencia
Júcar
VATICAN CITY
Rome
C. de São Vicente
Sierra Morena
Guadalquivir
Balearic Is.
Minorca
Majorca
Ibiza
Sardinia
TYRRHENIAN SEA
Naples
Tiranë
ALBANIA
Str. of Gibraltar
Cádiz
Málaga
ALGERIAN PLAIN
11,910 ft. (−3630 m)
G. of Taranto
Tangier
GIBRALTAR (U.K.)
MEDITERRANEAN SEA
C. Teulada
TYRRHENIAN BASIN
IONIAN SEA
Rabat
MOROCCO
Casablanca
Algiers
Oran
ALGERIA
Constantine
Tunis
C. Bon
Palermo
Sicily
Etna 11,053 ft. (3369 m)
Ionian Is.
Pelopon
−16,897 ft. (−5150 m)
C. Passero
IONIAN BASIN
AFRICA
TUNISIA
MALTA
Valletta
RUSSIA
LI
Nie
Gu
Tar
Hammer
Muon
Wars
MACE
GR

# Europe

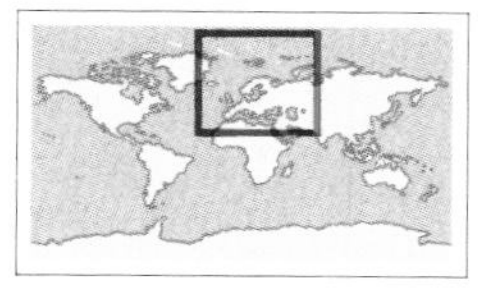

Europe is one large peninsula divided into many smaller peninsulas. The high peaks and glaciated ridges of the Alps form a continental divide across Central Europe from which major rivers flow to the North Sea, the Mediterranean Sea and the Black Sea. Europe's other significant highland area forms the backbone of Scandinavia, Scotland and the north of Ireland.

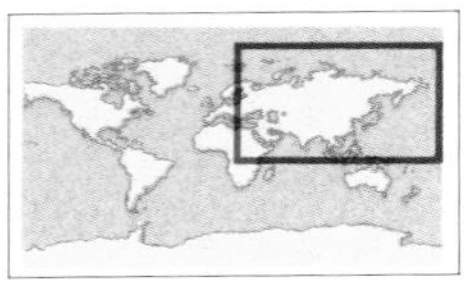

# Asia

Asia and Europe make up the Eurasia plate, which is fringed by jagged peninsulas and island arcs. The Himalayas, crowned by Mt. Everest, form the southern edge of an enormous plateau with numerous ranges. Asia is separated from Europe by the landlocked Caspian Sea and the Urals. Deep ocean trenches mark its boundary with the Pacific Ocean and Australia.

# Near and Middle East

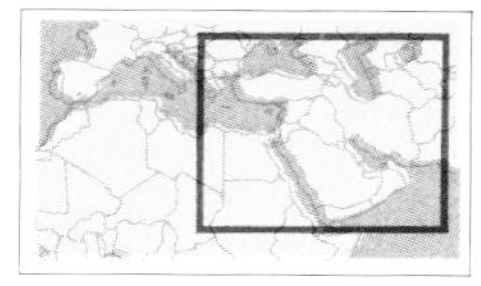

A continuous chain of mountain ranges meanders from Greece to the foothills of the Himalayas. Some 20 million years ago, the Arabian Peninsula pivoted at the Dead Sea and moved away from Africa, creating the Red Sea. Much of the region consists of either rock or sand desert. The Nile, Euphrates, Tigris and Indus river valleys are the most fertile areas.

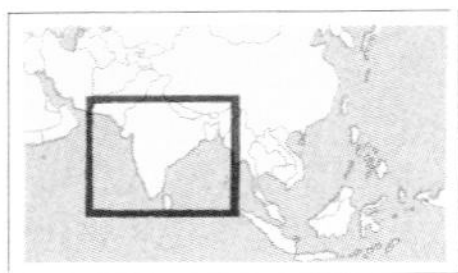

# Southern Asia

The Indian subcontinent is still moving north against Asia, pushing the Himalayas to even greater heights. The sparsely inhabited Plateau of Tibet, flanked by the Taklimakan desert, stretches 800 miles (1280 km.) east to west. The mighty Brahmaputra and Ganges rivers carry waters south from the Himalayas, creating an immense flood plain at the Ganges Delta.

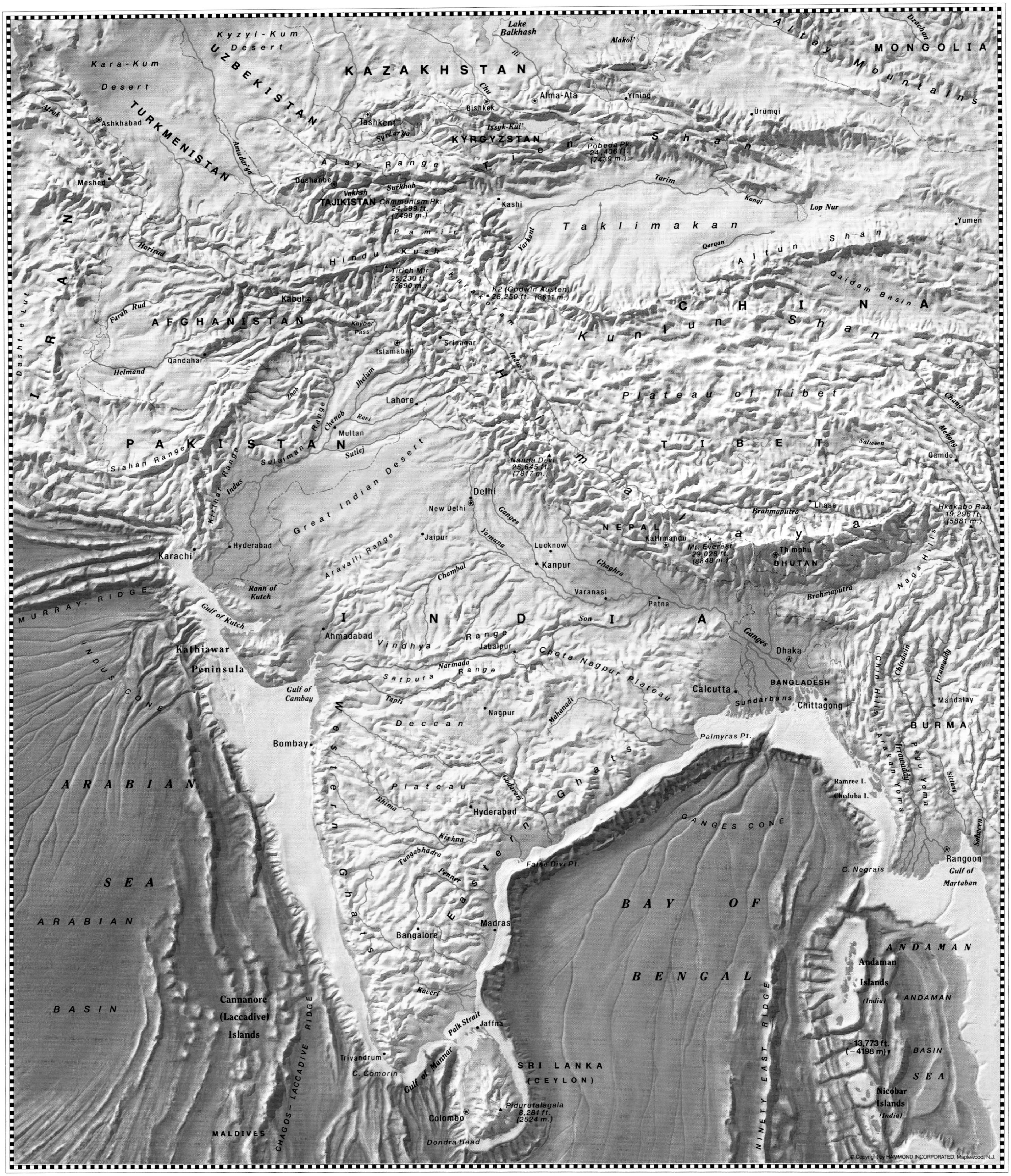

# East Asia

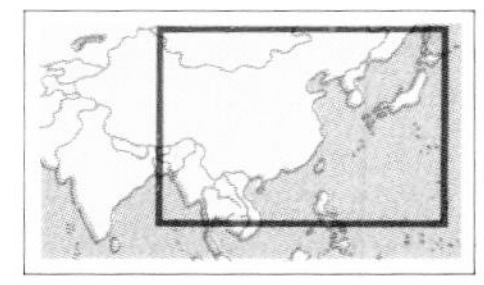

This region extends from the edge of Siberian permafrost to the tropical Philippines. The Plateau of Tibet, a cold rock desert, reaches east with extensive mountain ranges. The outlying islands rise near deep ocean trenches, and are dotted with active volcanoes. The Huang (Yellow) River, with its tributaries in the high plateaus, provides fertile soils to the lower plains.

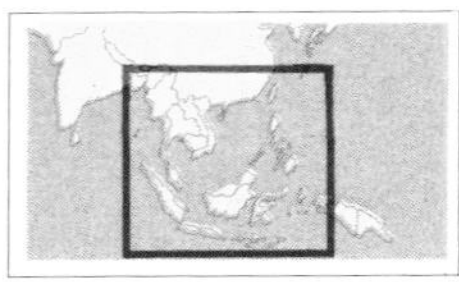

# Southeast Asia

Situated nearly astride the Equator, and on the shallow continental shelf, Southeast Asia is an oceanic realm of peninsulas and thousands of volcanic islands. The island arcs of Indonesia and the adjacent Java Trench are the result of the collision of oceanic crust against the continental plate. The tropical climate and the fertile volcanic soils nurture rain forests and agriculture.

# Australia and Pacific Ocean

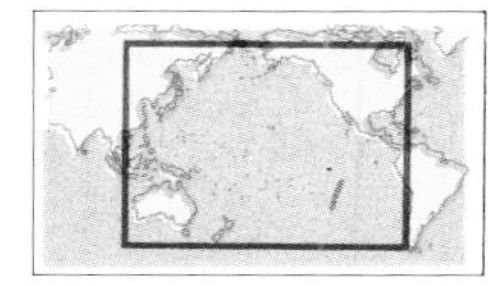

Australia, the smallest continent, borders the Pacific Ocean as part of the Indo-Australian Plate. The Pacific is as large as the Indian, Atlantic and Arctic oceans combined. It contains the ultimate abyss, the 35,000 foot-deep (10,500 m.) Mariana Trench, and numerous islands. It was named by its first European navigator, Magellan, because he experienced calm weather there.

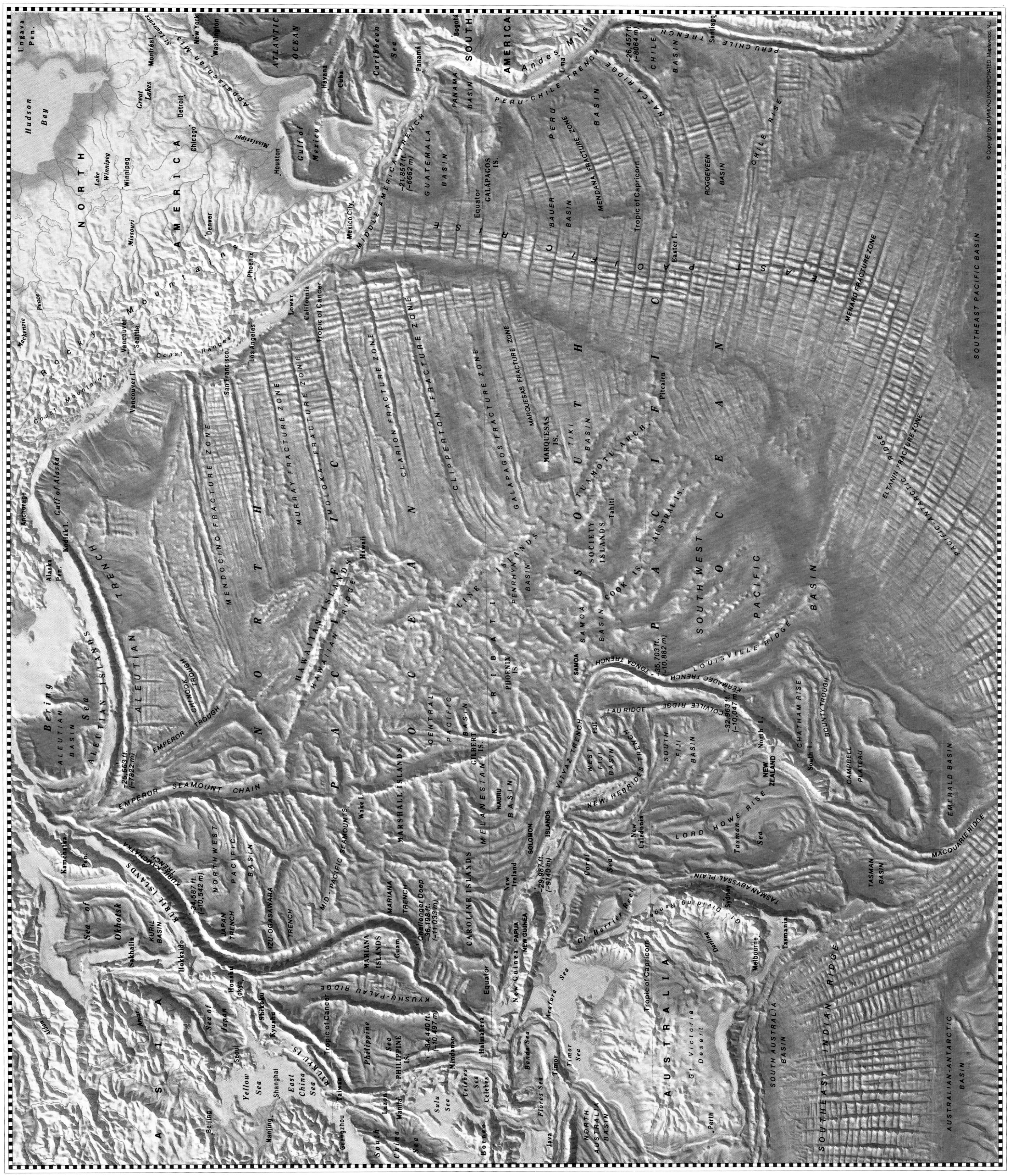

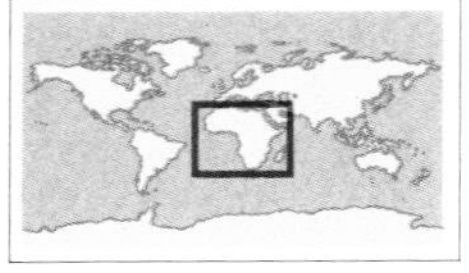

# Africa

Planted squarely on the Equator, Africa is a vast plateau rising steeply from a narrow coast. Fractures in the continent's crust created the Great Rift Valley of East Africa. Africa's vegetation is densest in the Congo Basin, and decreases away from the Equator. The Sahara, an area of 3.5 million square miles (9.1 million sq. km.), is the largest desert in the world.

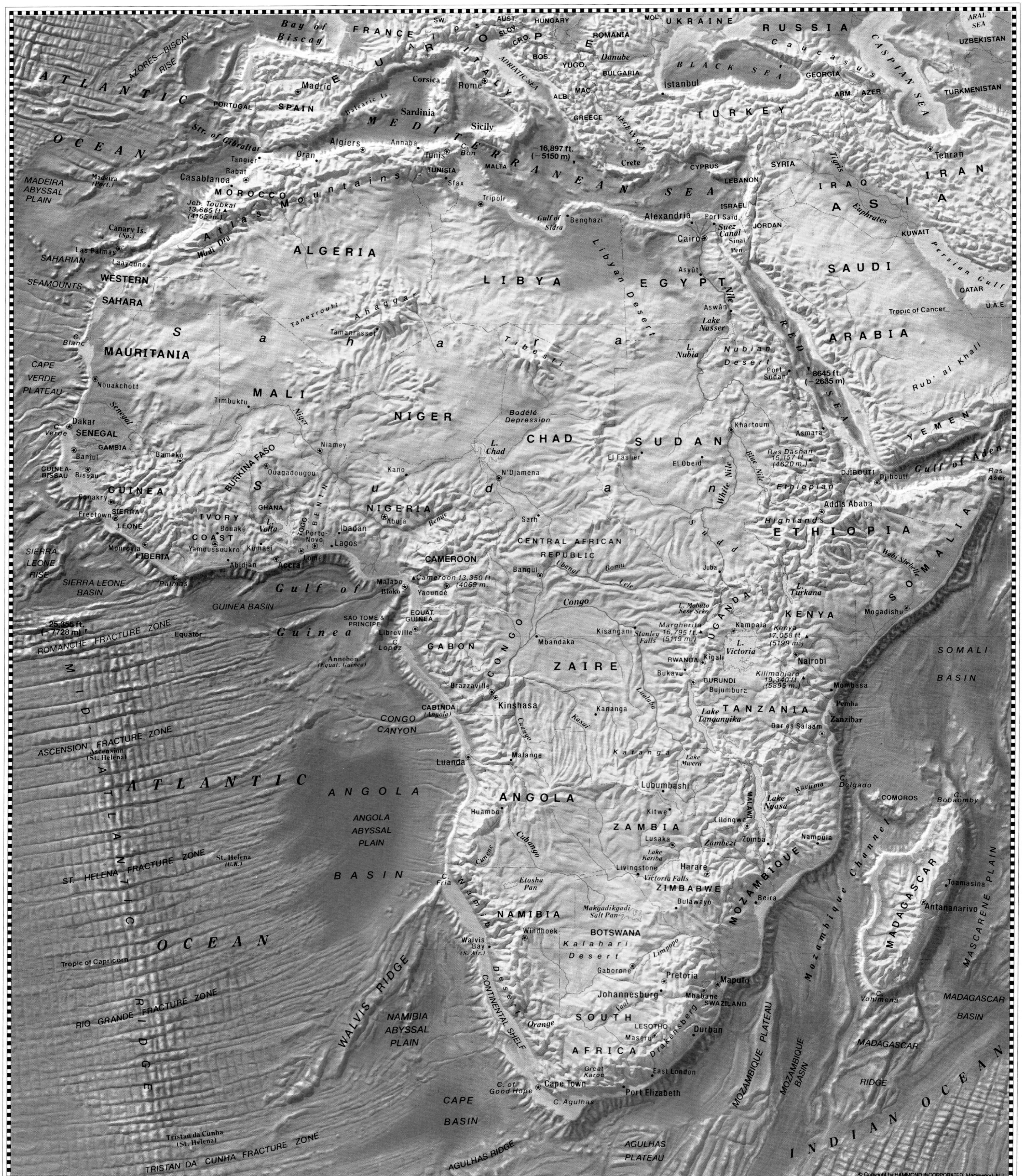

# South America

From a mere trickle in the highlands of Peru, the Amazon swells mightily on its 4,000 mile journey eastward to the Atlantic. The world's largest tropical rainforest lies in its basin, covering about two-fifths of the continent. The towering, snow-capped Andes, second in height only to the Himalayas, form the earth's longest continental range, over 5,500 miles.

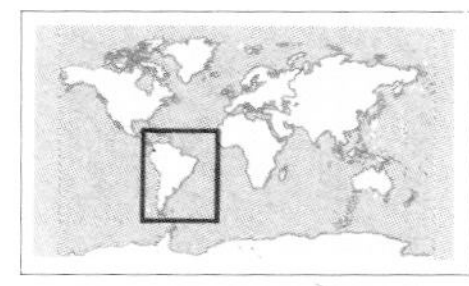

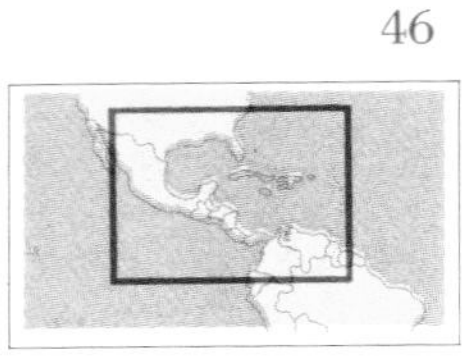

# Middle America

The narrow isthmus between North and South America consists of a mountainous, volcanic spine, flanked by coastal lowlands. At its south end is the Panama Canal, connecting Atlantic and Pacific waters. The Antilles, where Columbus landed, are volcanic islands rising from the depths of the Caribbean Sea. The Puerto Rico Trench has an average depth of 20,000 feet (6000 m.).

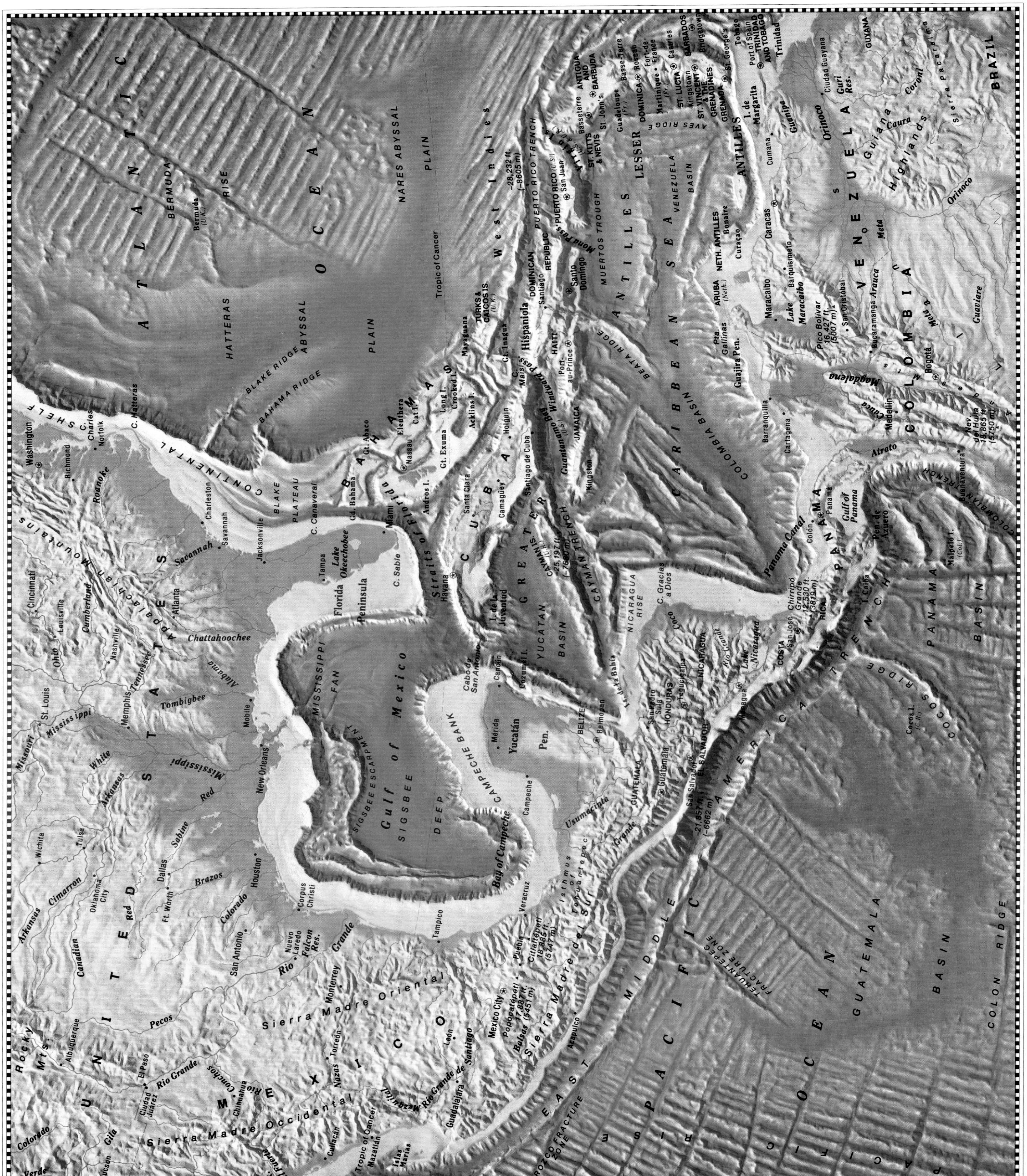

# United States

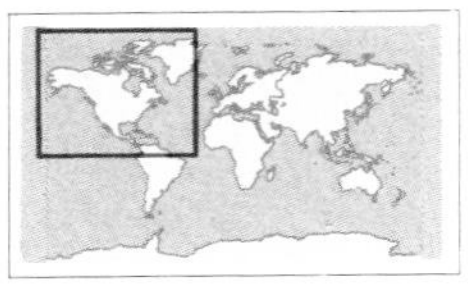

# North America

North America extends over 3,900 miles (6240 km.) from the polar reaches of the Canadian north to the tropics of the Caribbean. Two mountain systems frame a vast interior plain. The younger western ranges, whose summits near 21,000 feet (6300 m.), were formed by the collision of continental plates and ocean crust. Erosion smoothed older eastern mountains into gently rolling hills.

# Maps of the World

"Journey over all the universe in a map without the expense and fatigue of traveling, without suffering the inconveniences of heat, cold, hunger, and thirst."

Cervantes

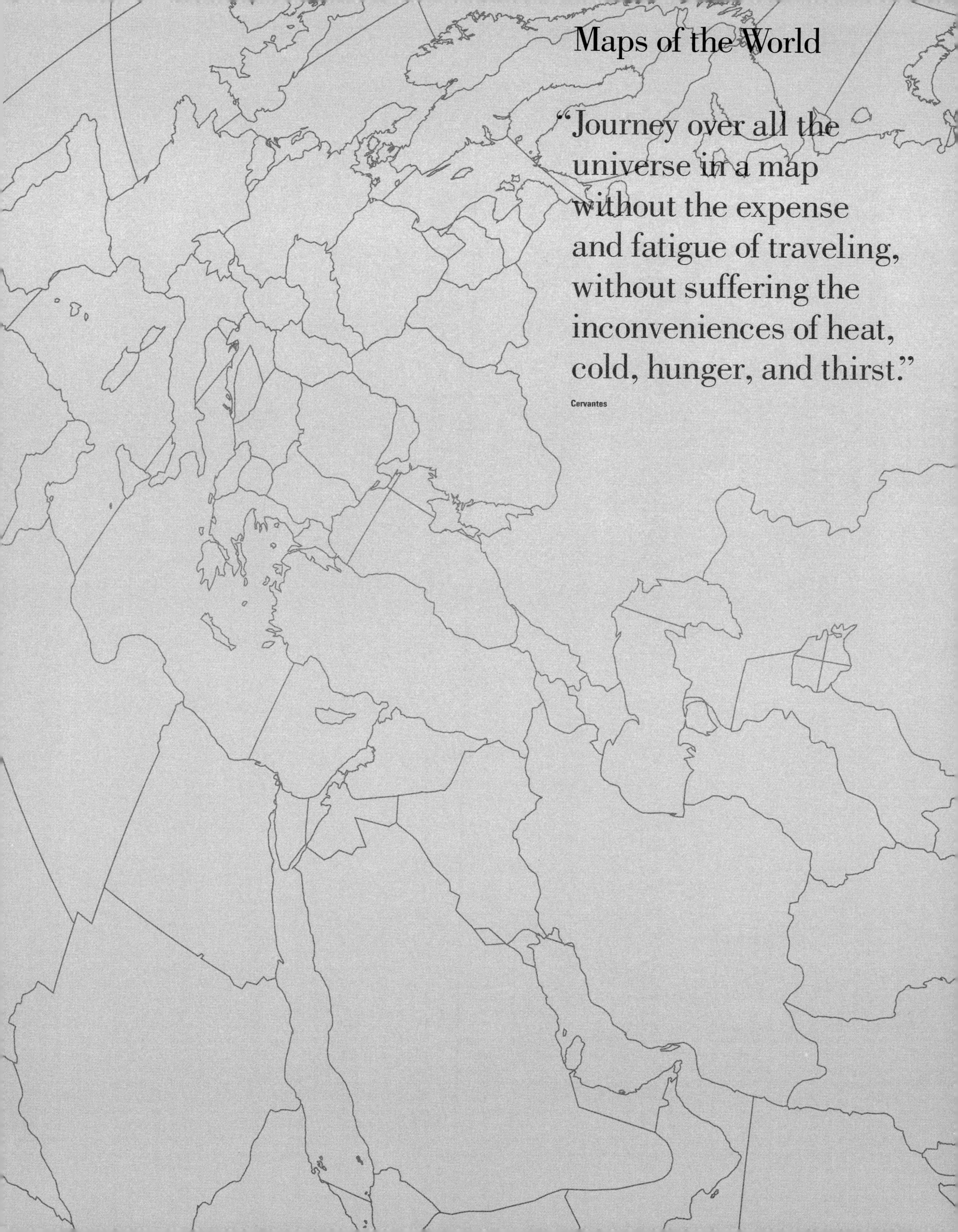

Of the 190 independent countries of the world, more than half have gained their independence since the end of World War II. Country sizes range from the city-states of Monaco and Vatican City to the vastness of Russia. But size often bears little correlation to a nation's population, or to its economic or political power. The world can be divided into three principal power centers: North America, Eastern Asia and Europe. The prospect of a united Europe, and the industrial boom in southeast Asia, may significantly alter geopolitics in the next century.

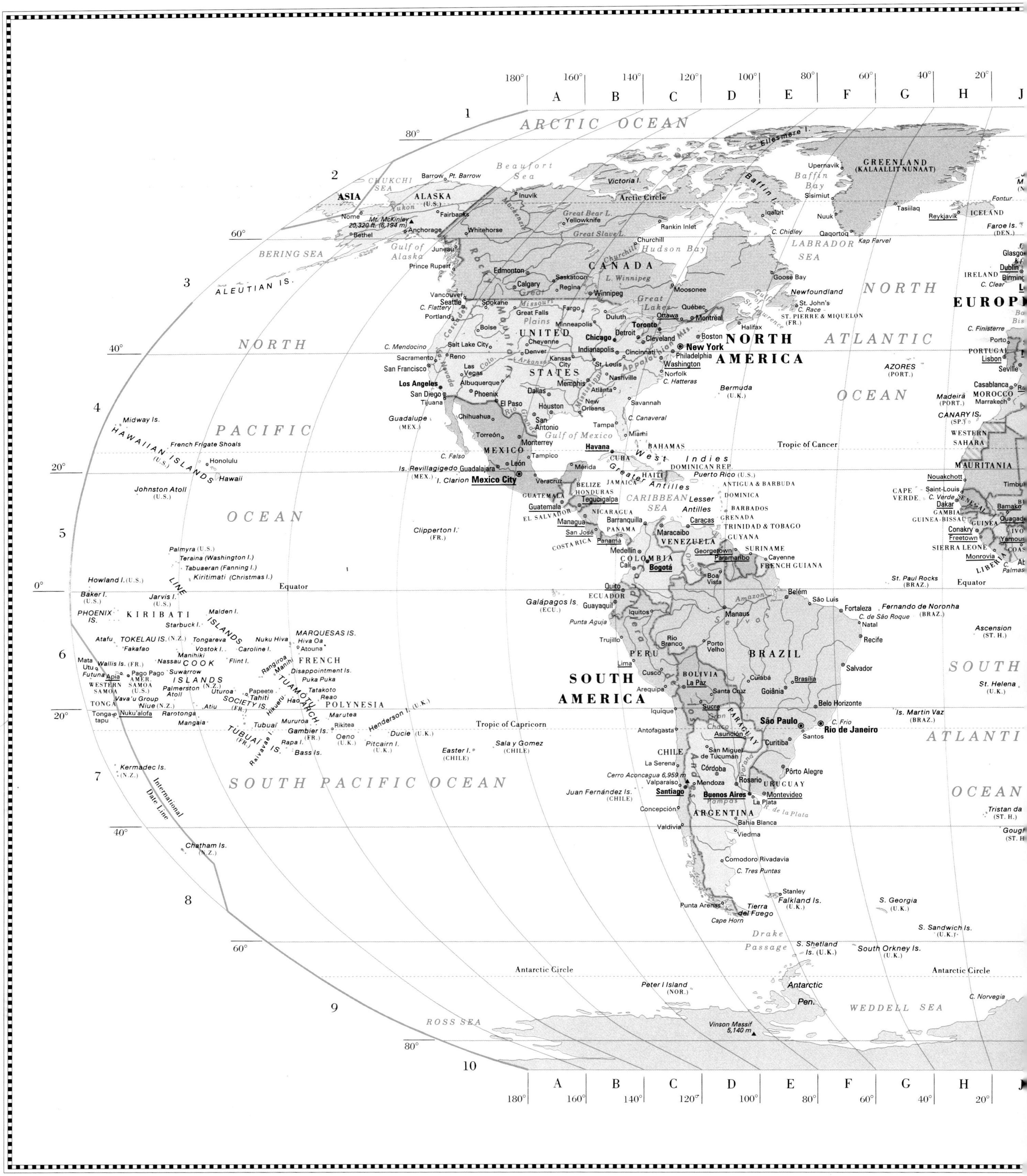

# World

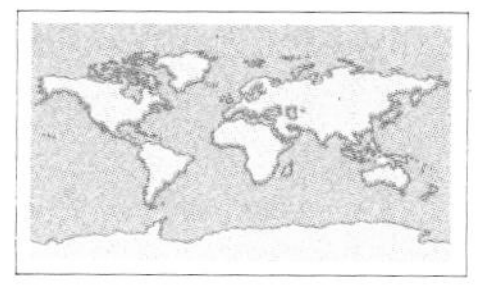

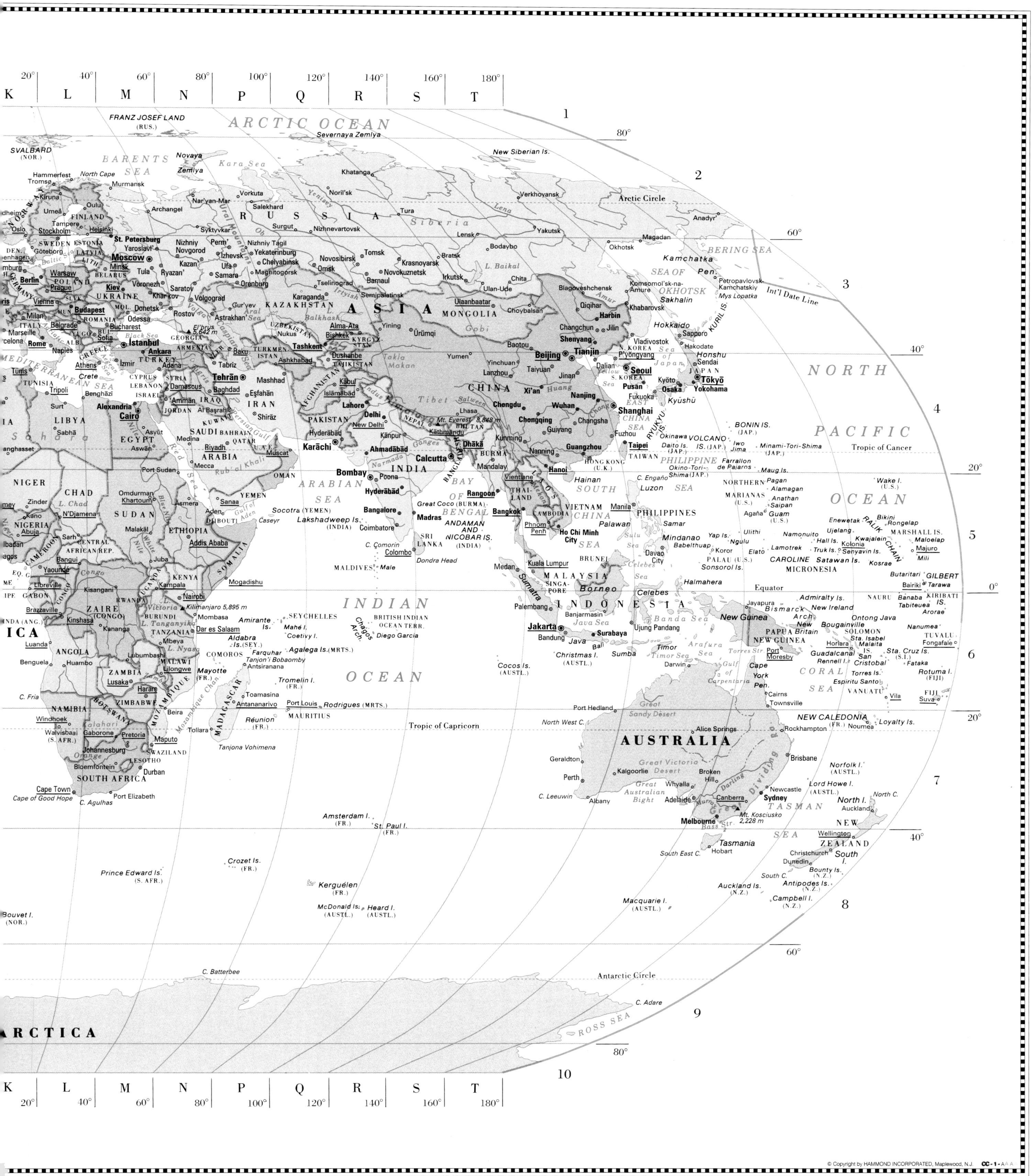




**POPULATION OF CITIES AND TOWNS**

- ◉ OVER 5,000,000
- ⊛ 2,000,000 - 4,999,999
- ⊚ 500,000 - 1,999,999
- ○ UNDER 500,000

SCALE 1:70,000,000 ROBINSON PROJECTION STANDARD PARALLELS 38°N AND 38°S

MILES 0 1000 2000 3000 4000

KILOMETERS 0 1000 2000 3000 4000

The democratic principle was born in Greece, the Renaissance in Italy, and parliamentary government in Great Britain. Europe is the birthplace of many of western civilization's greatest achievements. Europe's multi-faceted character is largely the result of peninsular geography. Mountains, extended lowlands and upland plateaus, joined by a wealth of natural waterways, create varied and distinctive landscapes. Since no mountains run parallel to the Atlantic except in Norway, ocean air currents flow over Europe, fostering a temperate climate throughout most of the continent.

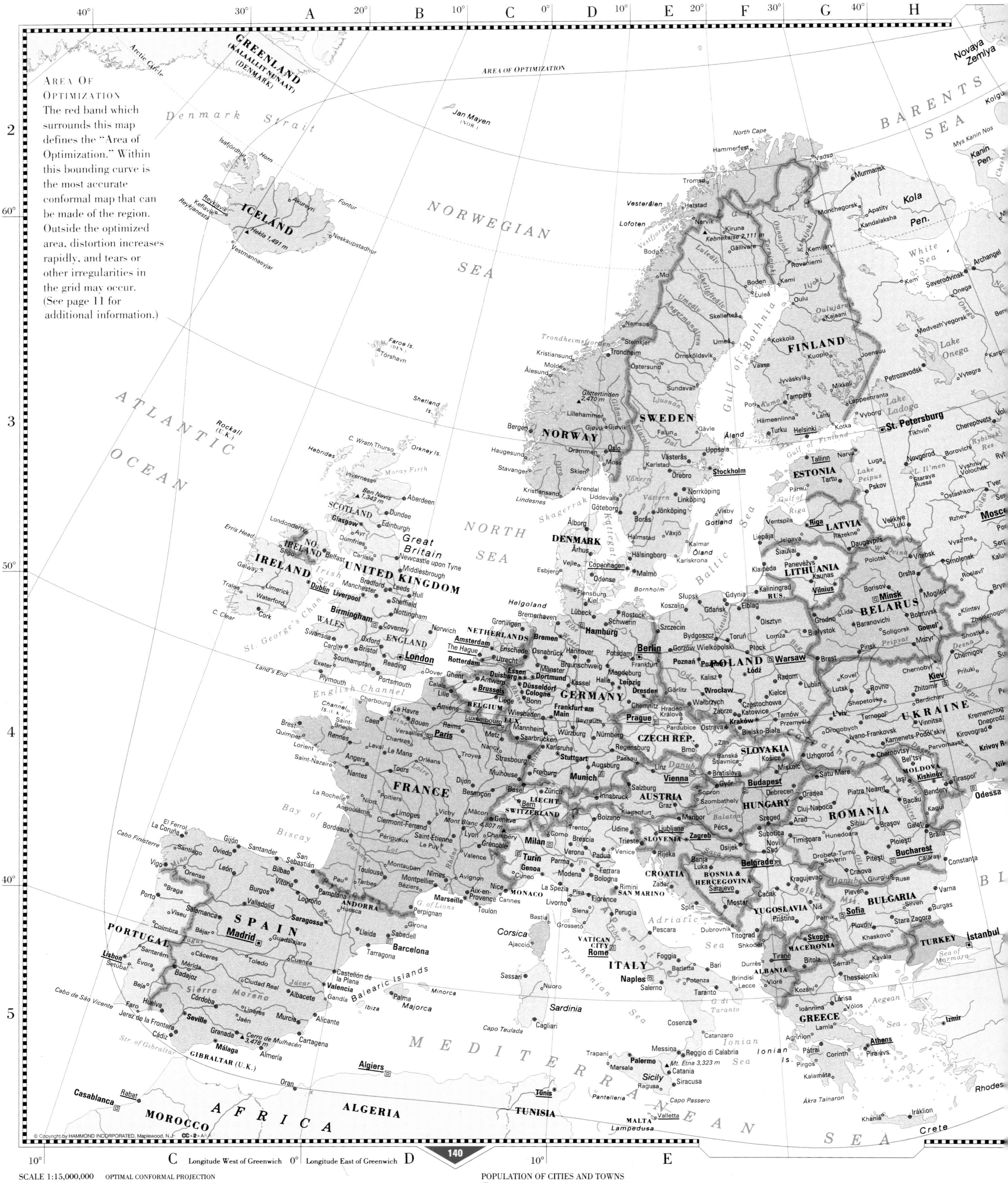




SCALE 1:15,000,000 OPTIMAL CONFORMAL PROJECTION

MILES 0 | 250 | 500 | 750

KILOMETERS 0 | 250 | 500 | 750

POPULATION OF CITIES AND TOWNS

- OVER 3,000,000
- 1,000,000 - 2,999,999
- 500,000 - 999,999
- 100,000 - 499,999
- UNDER 100,000

# Europe

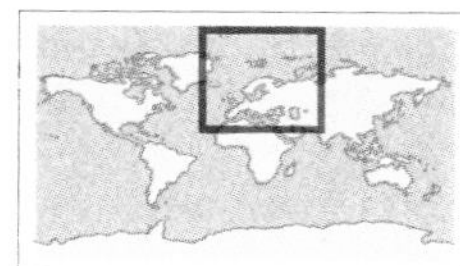

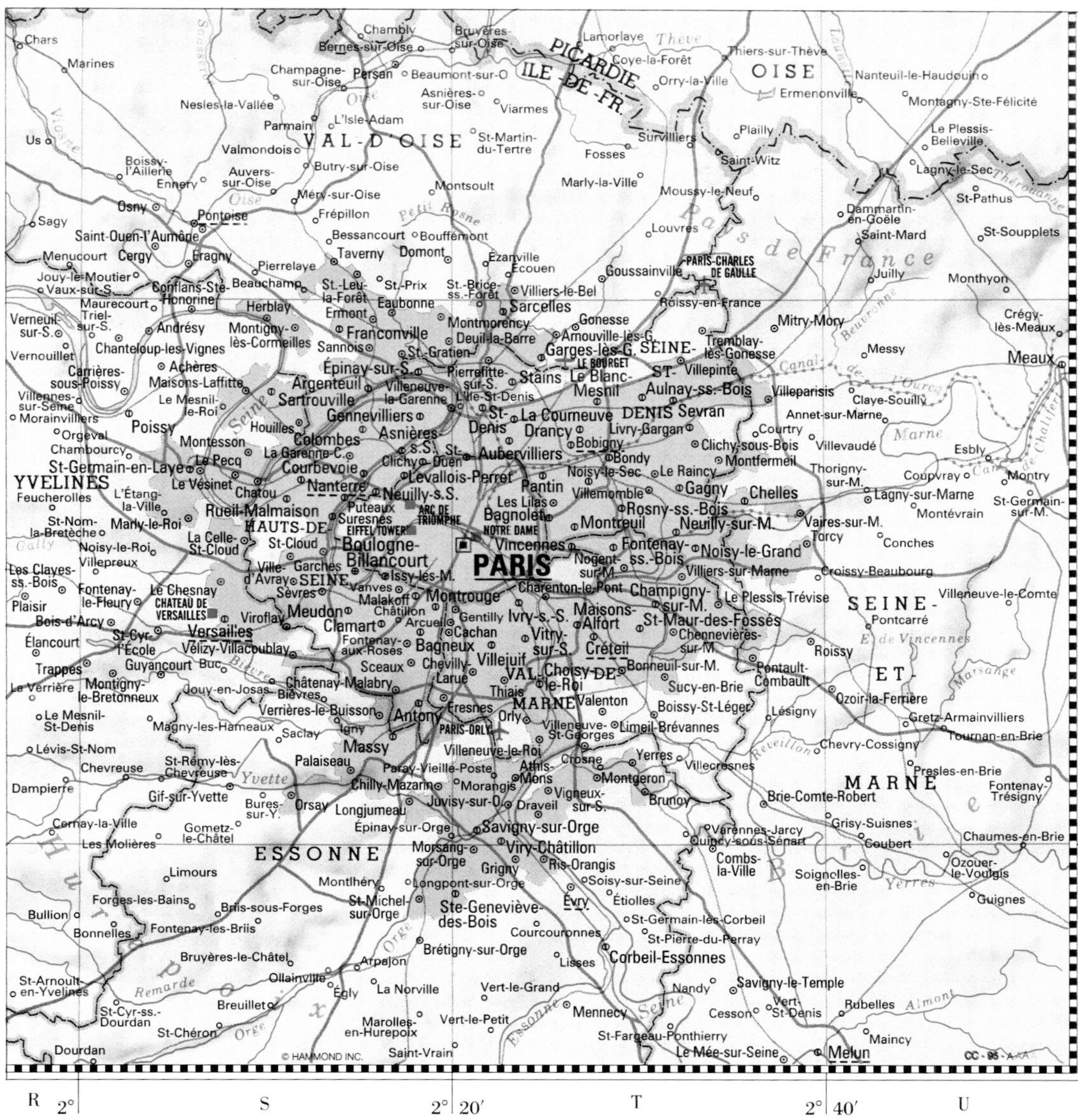


SCALE 1:500,000 LAMBERT CONFORMAL CONIC PROJECTION

MILES 0 10 20

KILOMETERS 0 10 20

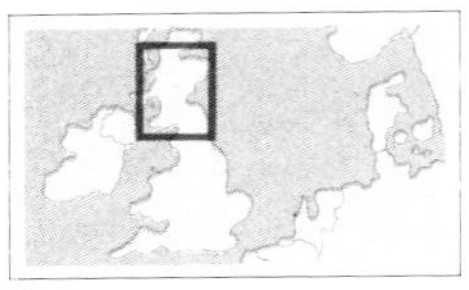

# Central Scotland

The northern Highlands were the rugged home of rival clans until the Highlanders were defeated by the English at the Battle of Culloden in 1746. Coal fields in the narrow waist between the River Clyde and the Firth of Forth brought Scotland into the Industrial Age. More recently, North Sea oil has fueled economic recovery and a resurgent nationalism.

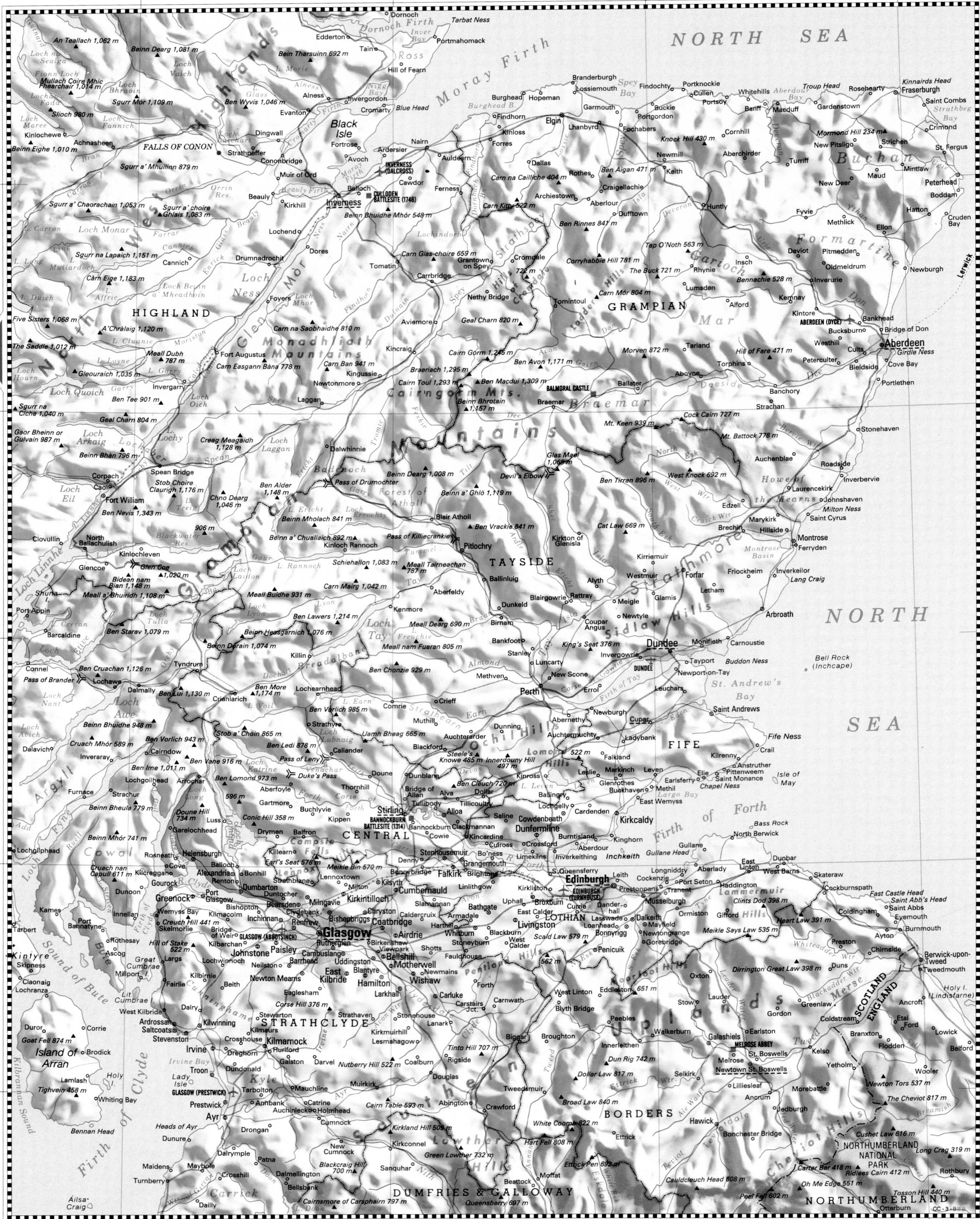


SCALE 1:1,000,000 LAMBERT CONFORMAL CONIC PROJECTION

MILES 0 10 20 30 40 50

KILOMETERS 0 10 20 30 40 50

POPULATION OF CITIES AND TOWNS

- OVER 2,000,000
- 1,000,000 - 1,999,999
- 500,000 - 999,999
- 250,000 - 499,999
- 100,000 - 249,999
- 30,000 - 99,999
- 10,000 - 29,999
- UNDER 10,000

# United Kingdom, Ireland

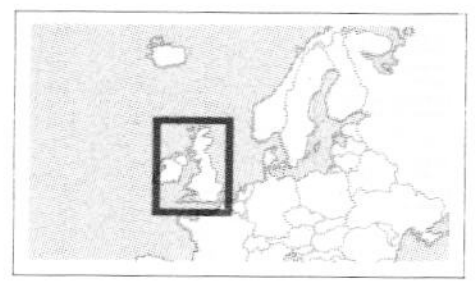

Over the centuries, these islands have been subject to many invasions and migrations. Modern political order began with the union of England and Wales in 1536. In 1707 a parliamentary union with Scotland gave rise to the name Great Britain. Union with Ireland was completed in 1801 under the name United Kingdom. In 1921 Ireland gained independence.

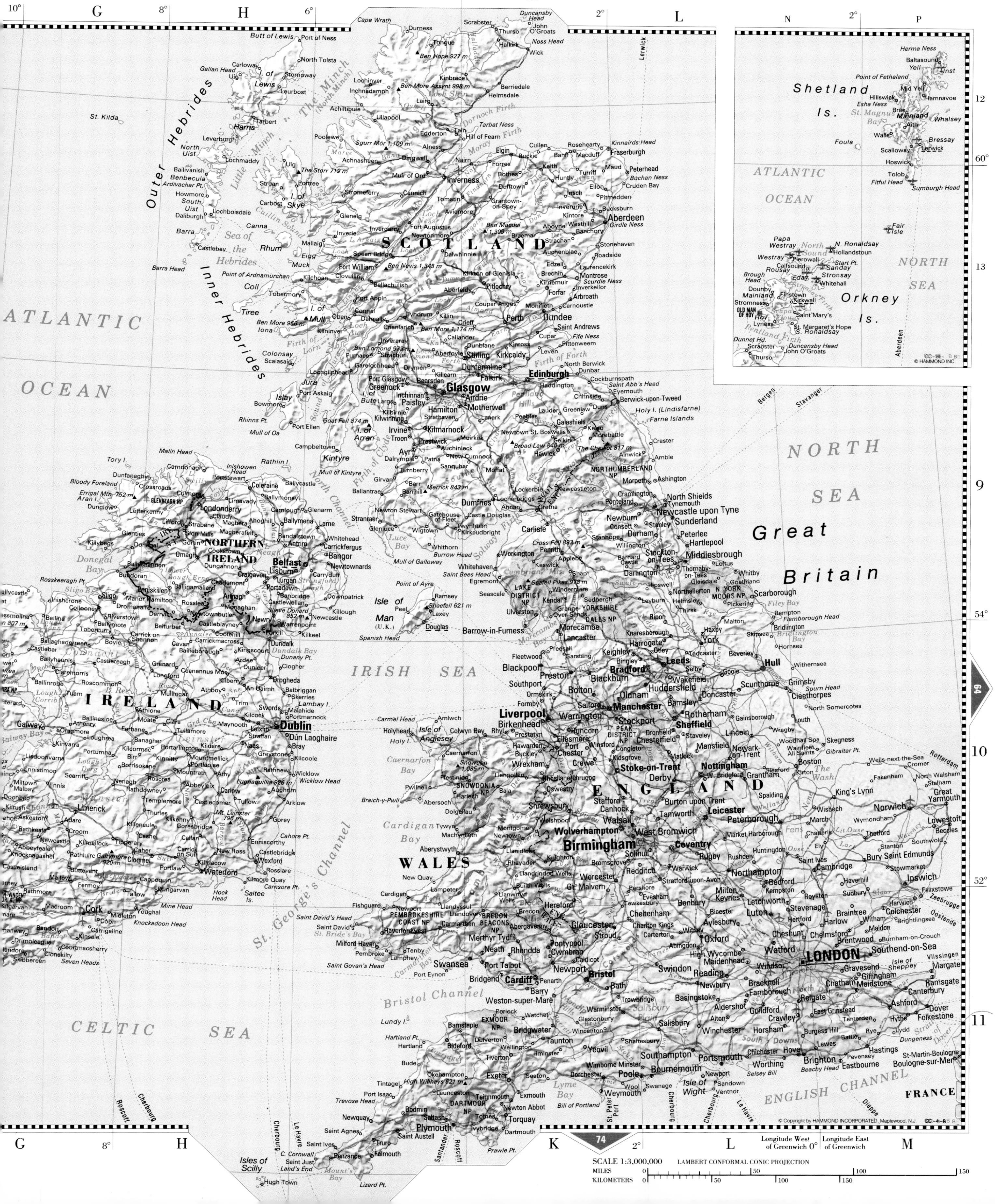

In the late 18th and early 19th centuries, the factory system arose in Lancashire and south Yorkshire, giving birth to the Industrial Age. The cotton and wool processing factories of Manchester and Leeds helped to change dramatically the culture and the economic base of the country. Population growth followed industrial development, and northern England soon became home to half the kingdom's people. Other important centers arose during this time– the shipyards of Belfast, the booming port of Liverpool, the metal shops of Sheffield, and the knitting mills of Nottingham.

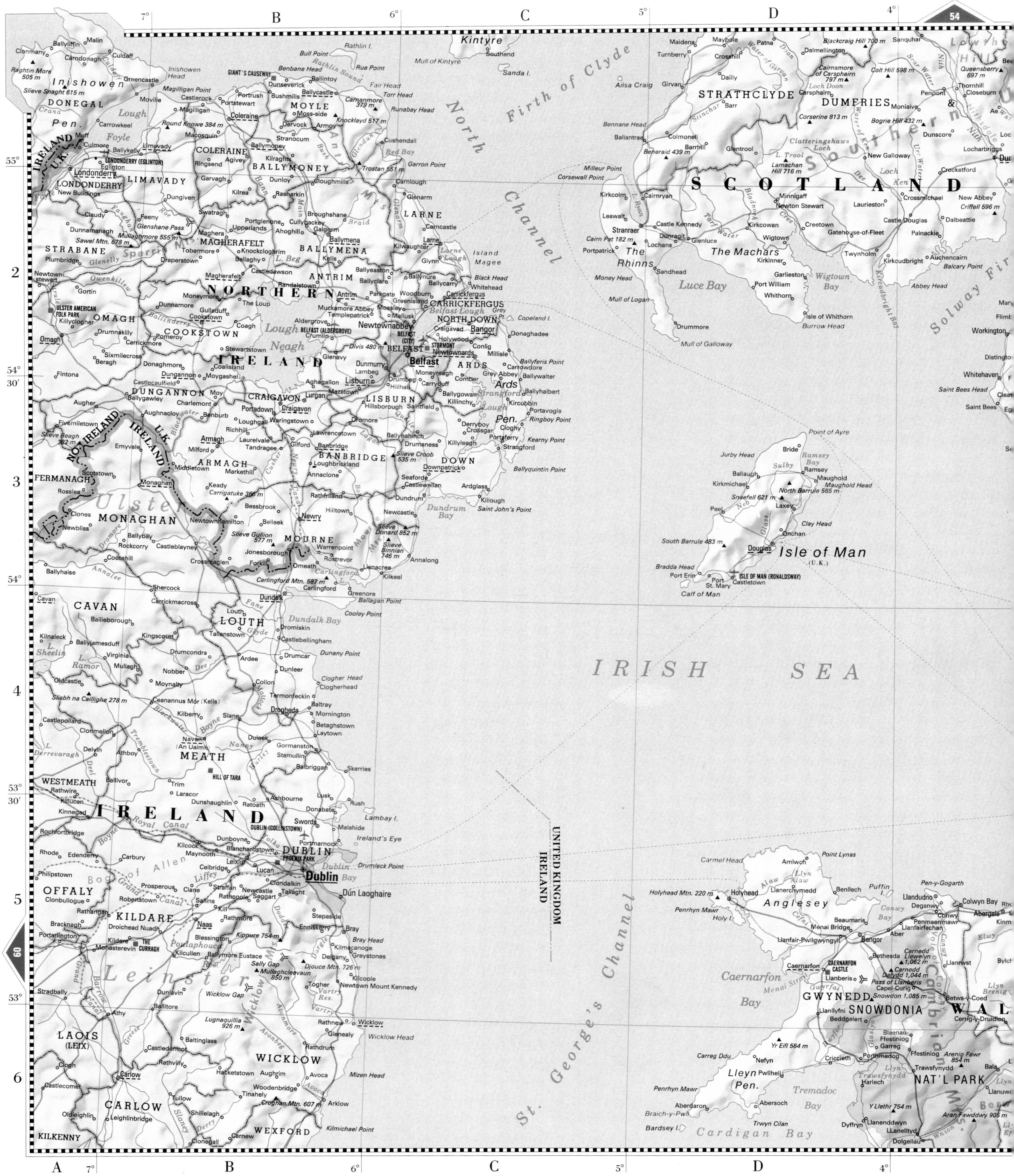

# Northeastern Ireland, Northern England and Wales

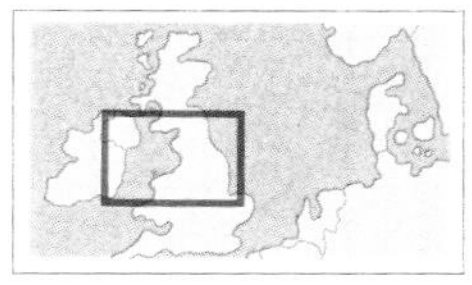

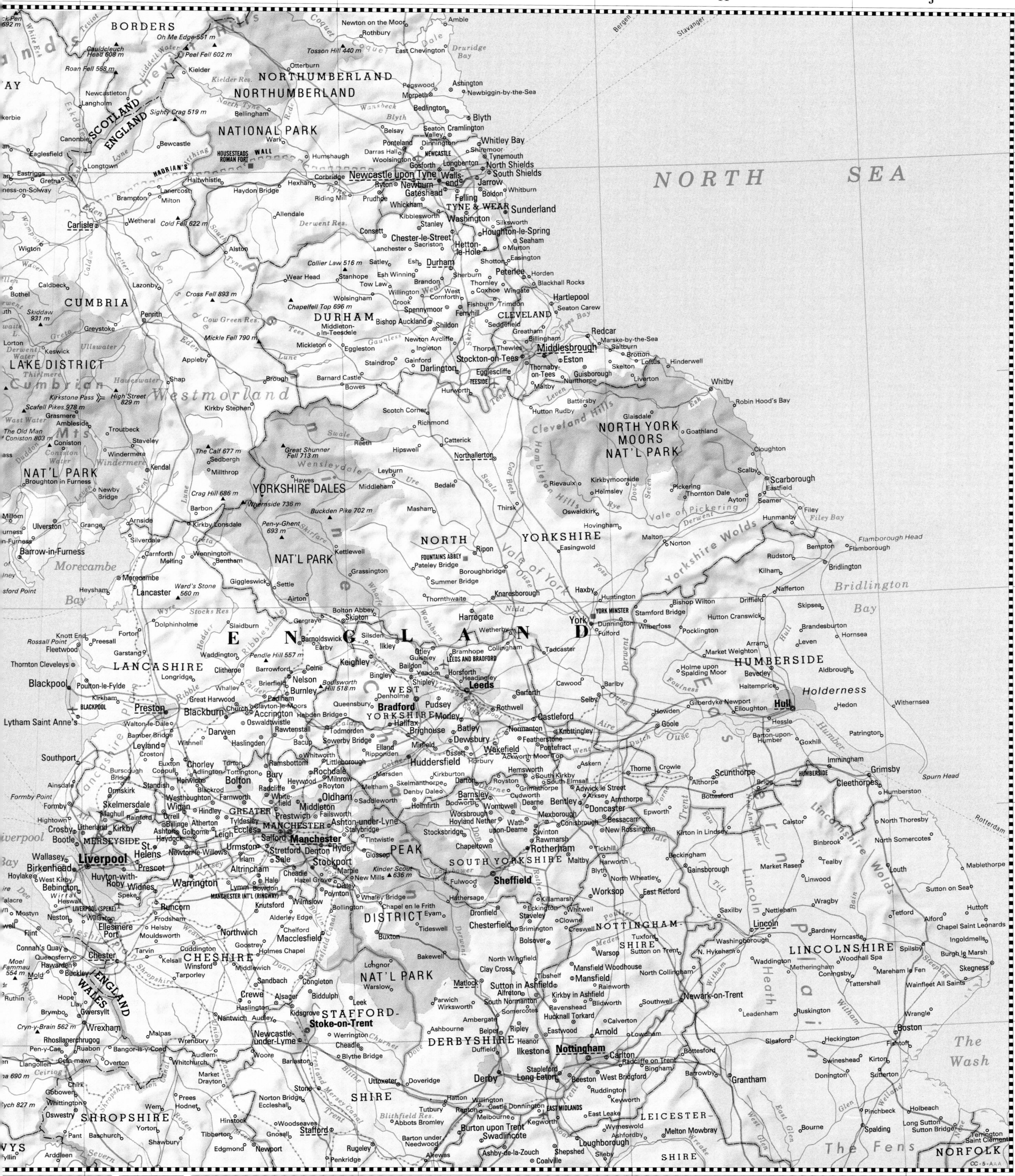




Longitude West of Greenwich

POPULATION OF CITIES AND TOWNS

- OVER 2,000,000
- 1,000,000 - 1,999,999
- 500,000 - 999,999
- 250,000 - 499,999
- 100,000 - 249,999
- 30,000 - 99,999
- 10,000 - 29,999
- UNDER 10,000

SCALE 1:1,000,000 LAMBERT CONFORMAL CONIC PROJECTION

MILES 0 10 20 30 40 50

KILOMETERS 0 10 20 30 40 50

58-59

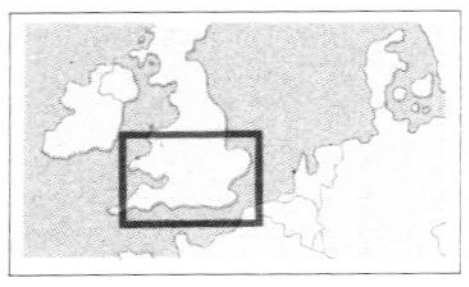

# Southern England and Wales

The major geographical aspect
this region is a dominance of
peninsular forms: Cornwall in the
southwest, Pembroke in the west an
Kent bordering the Strait of Dover.

hese landforms, together with the great stuaries of the Severn and Thames, ace British people, products, ideas nd culture within easy reach of seaports nd the rest of the world. The area is anchored by two great metropolitan complexes: London, the center of government and commerce, and Birmingham, the industrial giant of the English Midlands.

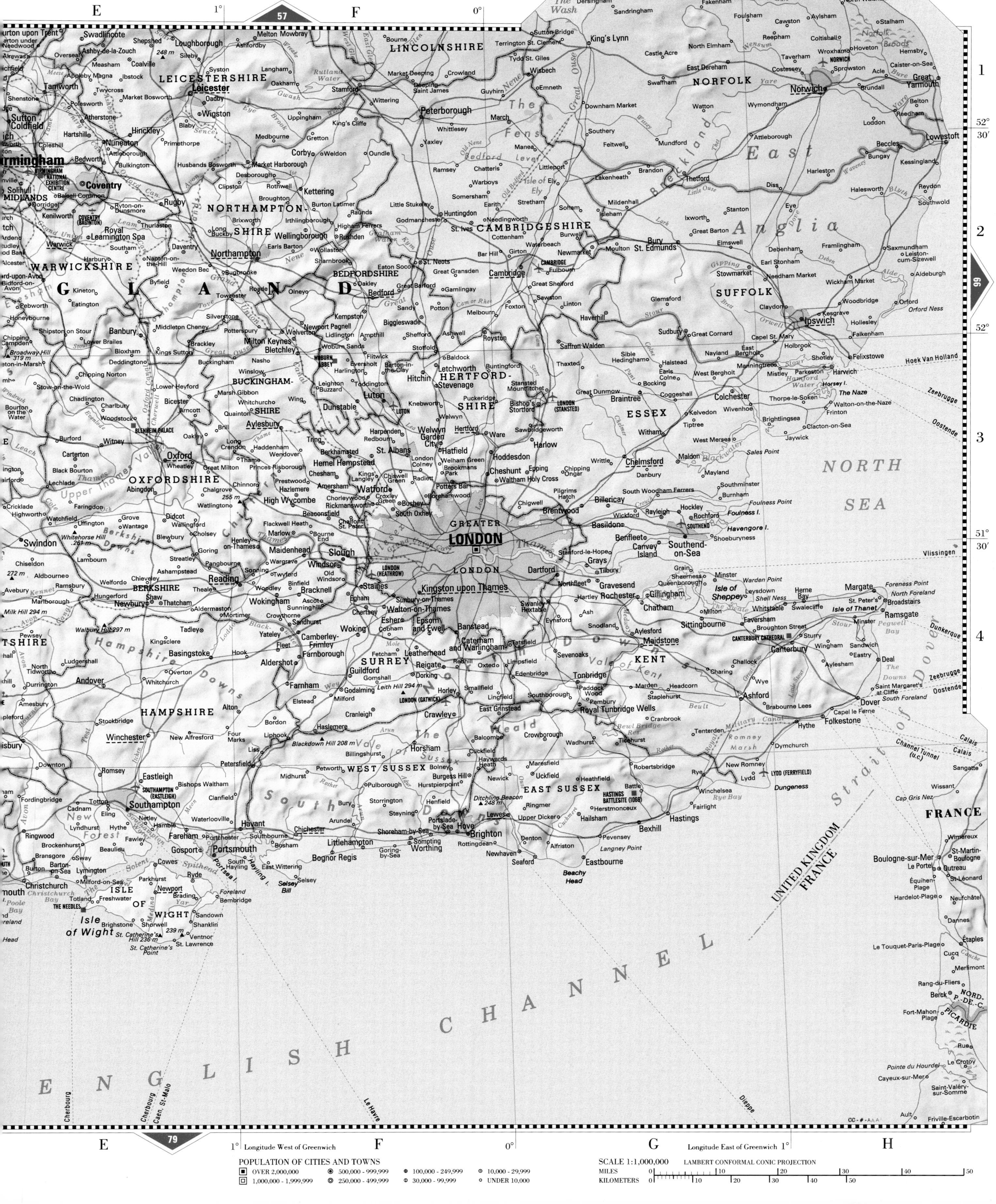

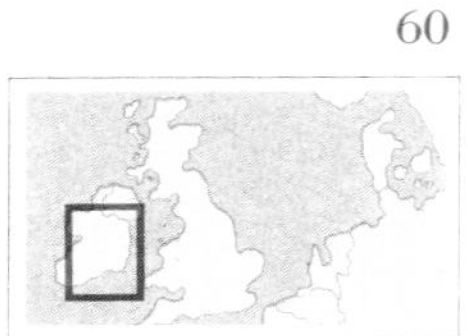

# Central and Southern Ireland

The Celtic culture that once dominated Europe left its most vivid imprint upon Ireland. Though only a small minority claim Irish Gaelic as their mother tongue, the "Emerald Isle" retains its unique Celtic folkways in song, dance, literature and theater. Ireland has joined the European Community and is moving from its agrarian past to a more industrial society.

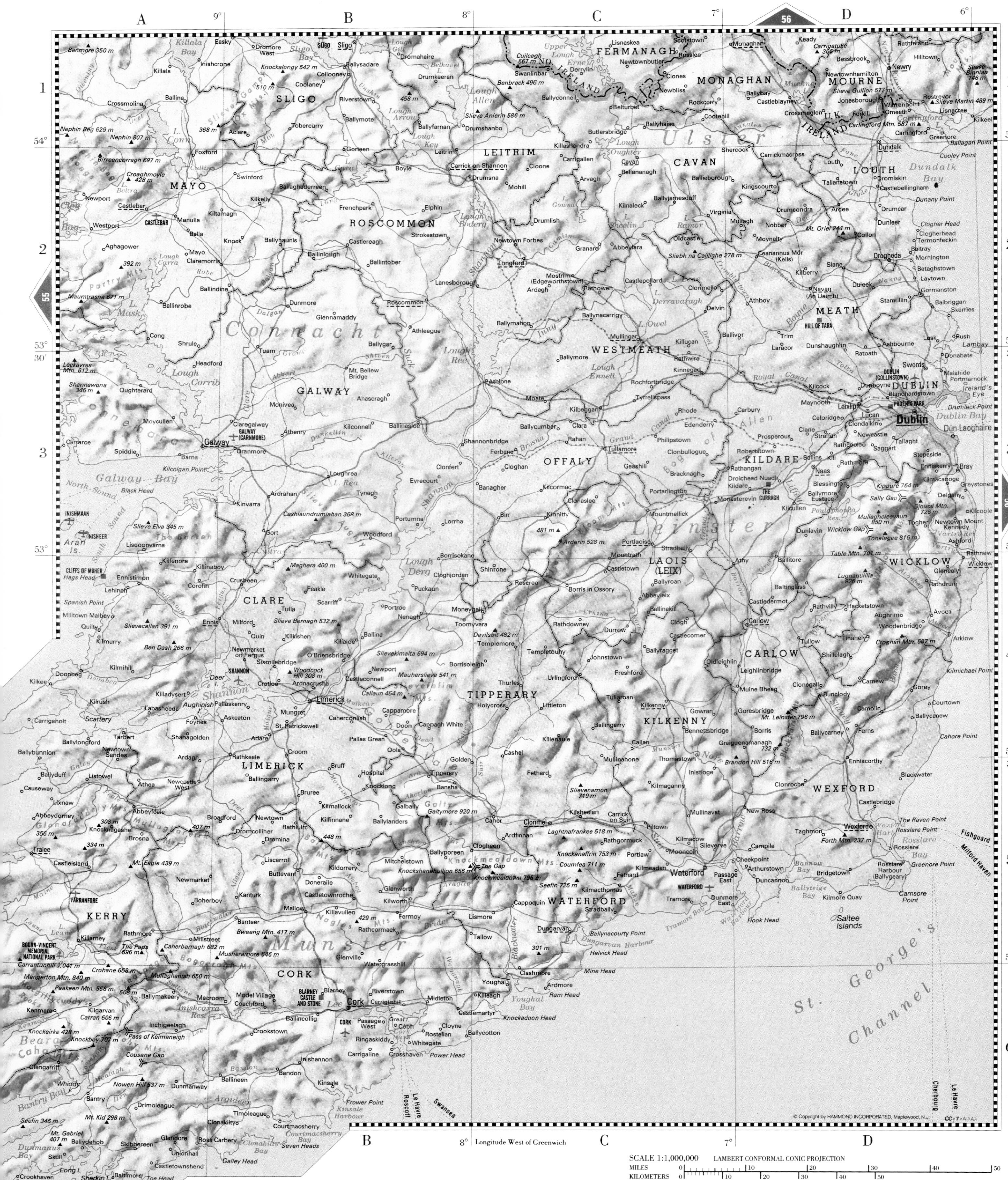


SCALE 1:1,000,000 LAMBERT CONFORMAL CONIC PROJECTION

MILES 0 10 20 30 40 50

KILOMETERS 0 10 20 30 40 50

# Scandinavia and Finland; Iceland

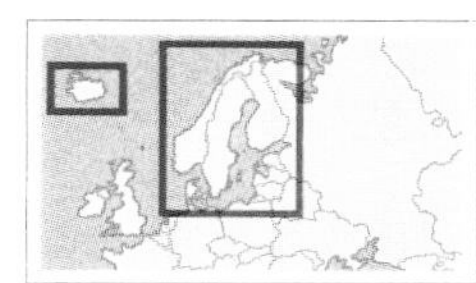

The northern parts of Norway, Sweden and Finland extend beyond the Arctic Circle. The climates of this region, however, are influenced by the North Atlantic Drift, a warm ocean current that brings relatively warm, moist air across most of the peninsula. Iceland straddles the Mid-Atlantic Ridge and is of geologically-recent volcanic origin.

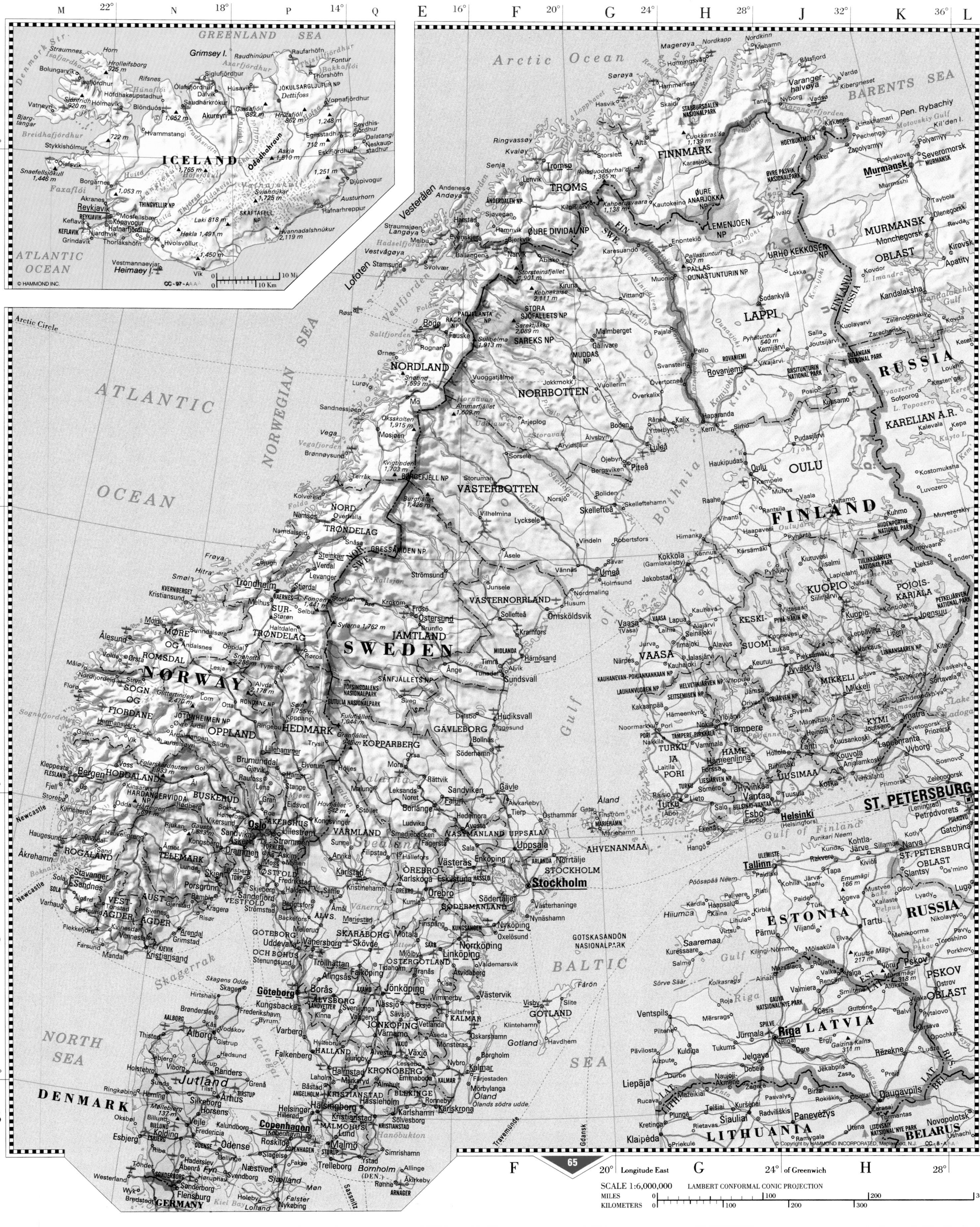

The Baltic Sea is the remnant of an inland lake that received the outpoured meltwater of a glacier covering Scandinavia and Finland 10,000 years ago. With the general rise in sea level following the last Ice Age, the North Sea broke through at the Skagerrak and Kattegat between present day Denmark and Sweden. The Baltic then became a saltwater sea. However, drainage from northern Europe reduces its salinity to only one-third of that in the Atlantic Ocean. A major waterway, the Nord-Ostee-Kanal, connects the Baltic and North seas.

# Baltic Region

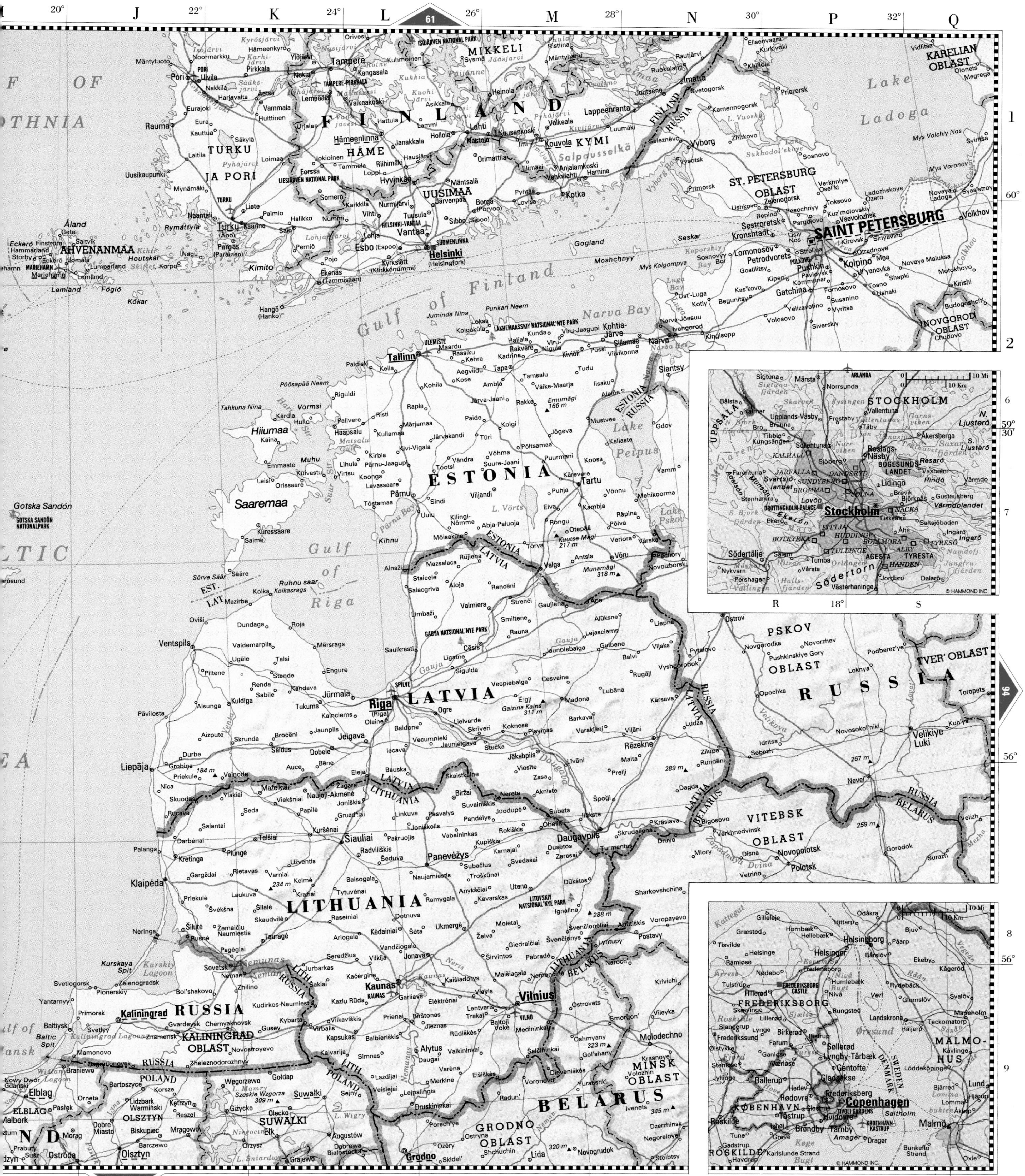

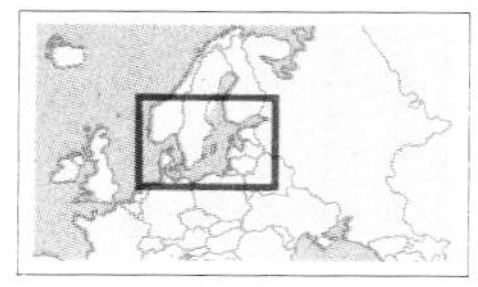


POPULATION OF CITIES AND TOWNS

| | | | |
|---|---|---|---|
| OVER 2,000,000 | 500,000 - 999,999 | 100,000 - 249,999 | 10,000 - 29,999 |
| 1,000,000 - 1,999,999 | 250,000 - 499,999 | 30,000 - 99,999 | UNDER 10,000 |

SCALE 1:3,000,000 LAMBERT CONFORMAL CONIC PROJECTION

MILES 0 50 100 150

KILOMETERS 0 50 100 150

Since the Middle Ages, the great North European Plain has been the scene of numerous conflicts and the pathway for invasions. The lack of mountain barriers along the North Sea and Baltic Coasts has created a stage for marching armies and shifting boundaries well into the 20th century. Modern Germany, created in 1871, experienced major territorial losses in 1919 and, following World War II, was divided into two antagonistic states by the occupying powers. Not until 1990 were East and West Germany reunited as one nation. Berlin is now the capital again.

# North Central Europe

POPULATION OF CITIES AND TOWNS

- ■ OVER 2,000,000
- □ 1,000,000 - 1,999,999
- ◉ 500,000 - 999,999
- ◎ 250,000 - 499,999
- ● 100,000 - 249,999
- ⊙ 30,000 - 99,999
- ⊙ 10,000 - 29,999
- ○ UNDER 10,000

SCALE 1:3,000,000 LAMBERT CONFORMAL CONIC PROJECTION

MILES 0 50 100

KILOMETERS 0 50 100 150

# Netherlands, Northwestern Germany

Since the 1400s the Dutch have drained and reclaimed great stretches of their below-sea level land, using a system of dikes. The vast Zuider Zee (now the "IJsselmeer") has been transformed into a freshwater lake; a massive dam separates it from the North Sea. Parts of the IJsselmeer have been drained to form new land called *polders*.

68
69

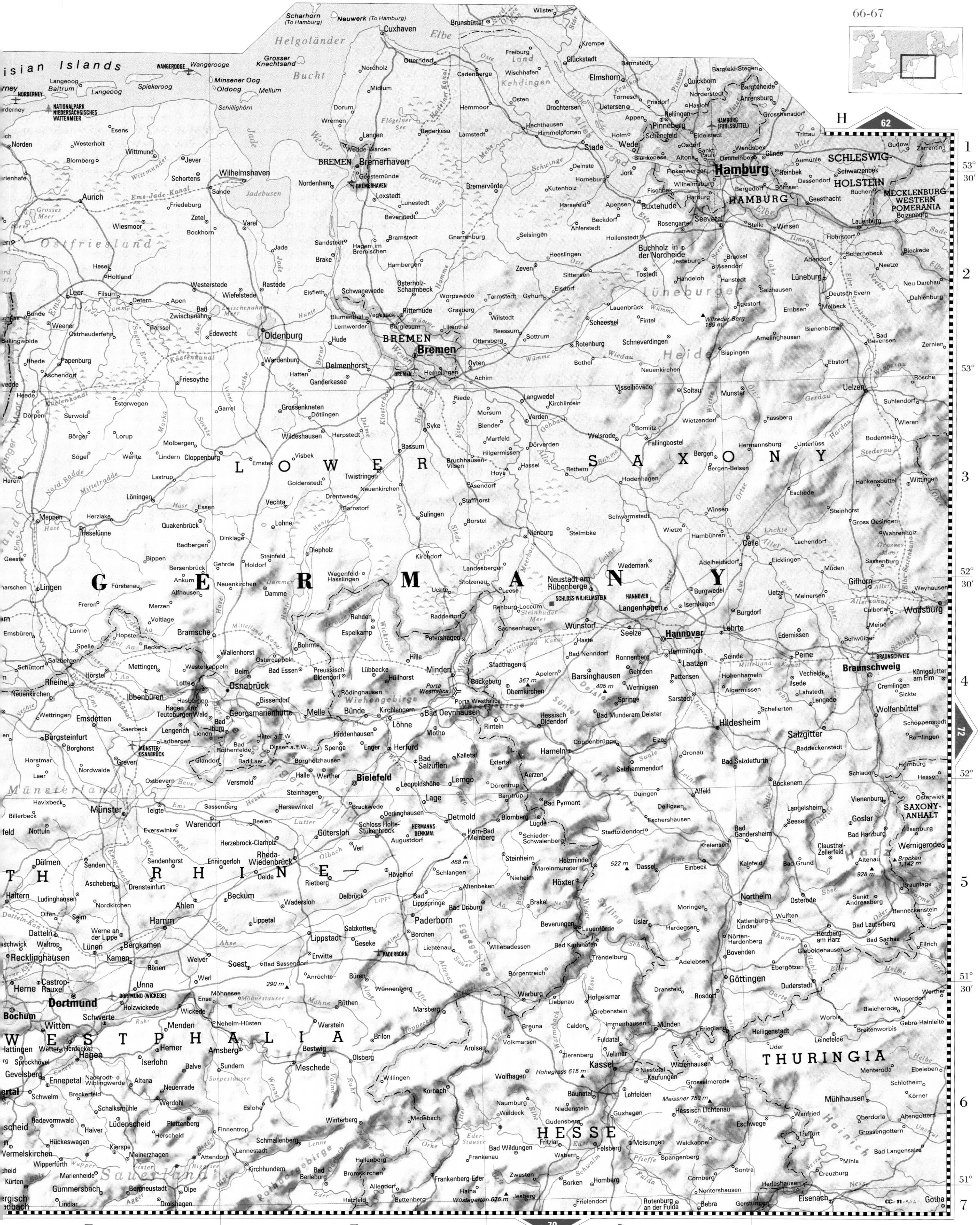


POPULATION OF CITIES AND TOWNS

- OVER 2,000,000
- 1,000,000 - 1,999,999
- 500,000 - 999,999
- 250,000 - 499,999
- 100,000 - 249,999
- 30,000 - 99,999
- 10,000 - 29,999
- UNDER 10,000

SCALE 1:1,000,000 LAMBERT CONFORMAL CONIC PROJECTION

MILES 0 10 20 30 40 50

KILOMETERS 0 10 20 30 40 50

The western German borderlands, Belgium and northern France have been the scene of battles for the last five hundred years as the nation-states that emerged following the Middle Ages clashed and struggled for power. Battle names of the two world wars emphasize the historic nature of the region – Flanders, the Somme, Verdun, the Argonne, Dunkirk (Dunkerque).

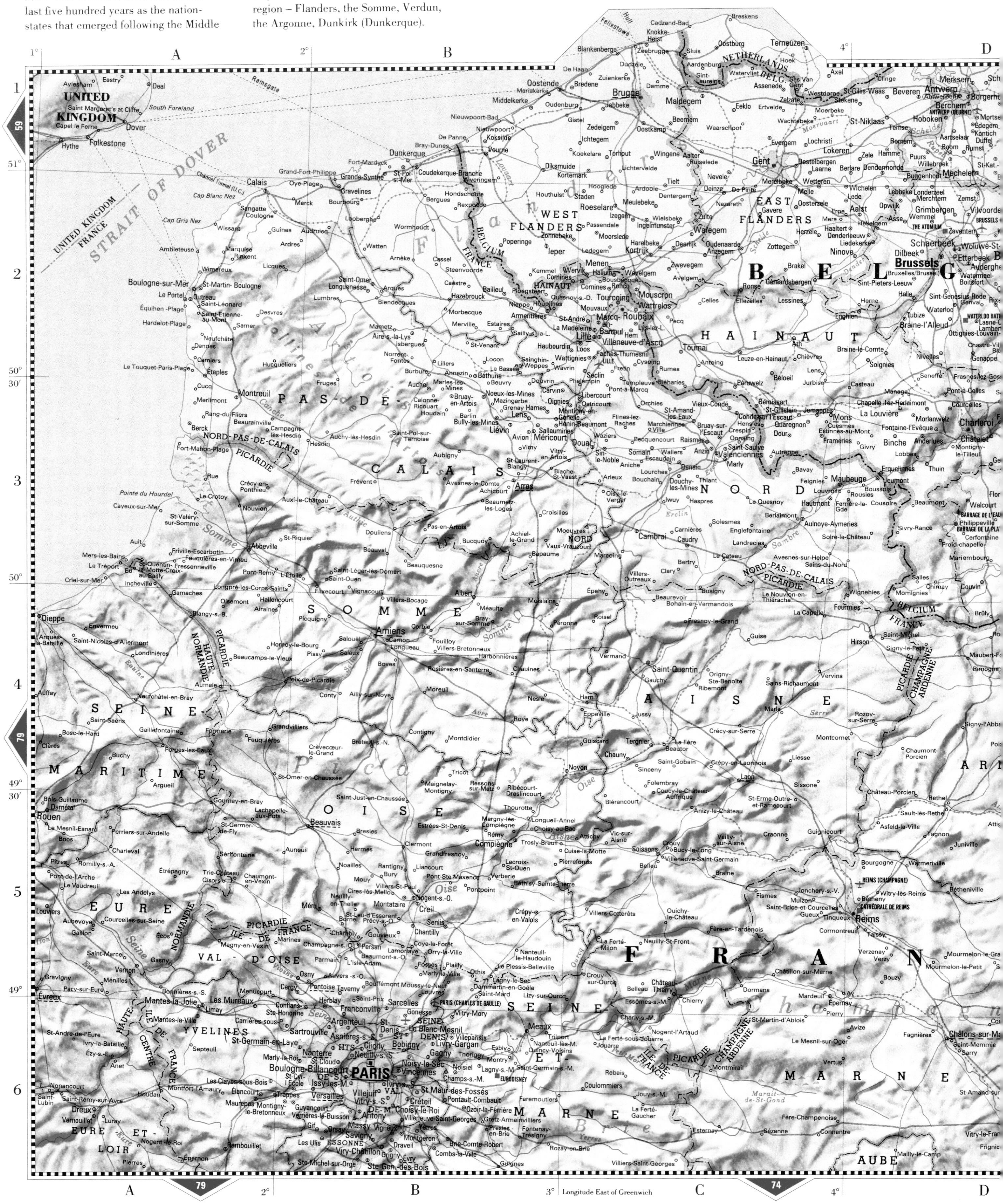

# Belgium, Northern France, Western Germany

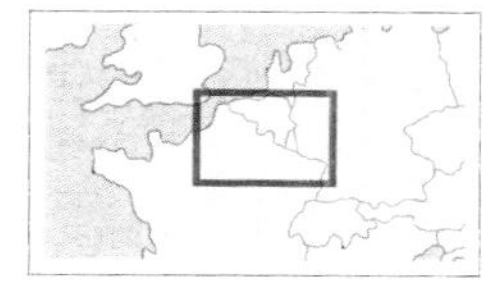

POPULATION OF CITIES AND TOWNS

| | | | |
|---|---|---|---|
| ■ OVER 2,000,000 | ⊛ 500,000 - 999,999 | ⊕ 100,000 - 249,999 | ⊙ 10,000 - 29,999 |
| ▣ 1,000,000 - 1,999,999 | ◎ 250,000 - 499,999 | ⊕ 30,000 - 99,999 | ○ UNDER 10,000 |

SCALE 1:1,000,000 LAMBERT CONFORMAL CONIC PROJECTION

MILES 0 10 20 30 40 50

KILOMETERS 0 10 20 30 40 50

Medieval villages and castles flourished in this mountainous terrain; many survive to this day. On the Neckar River, near the Rhine, stands old Heidelberg. Its famous university dates back to 1386. To the east, a string of towns, from Würzburg to Augsburg, form the "Romantic Way," a picturesque route through a region rich in architecture from the Middle Ages. Munich, which grew from a Benedictine monastery, has numerous historic churches. Czech spas at Karlovy Vary (Karlsbad) and Mariánské Lázně (Marienbad) are world-renowned.

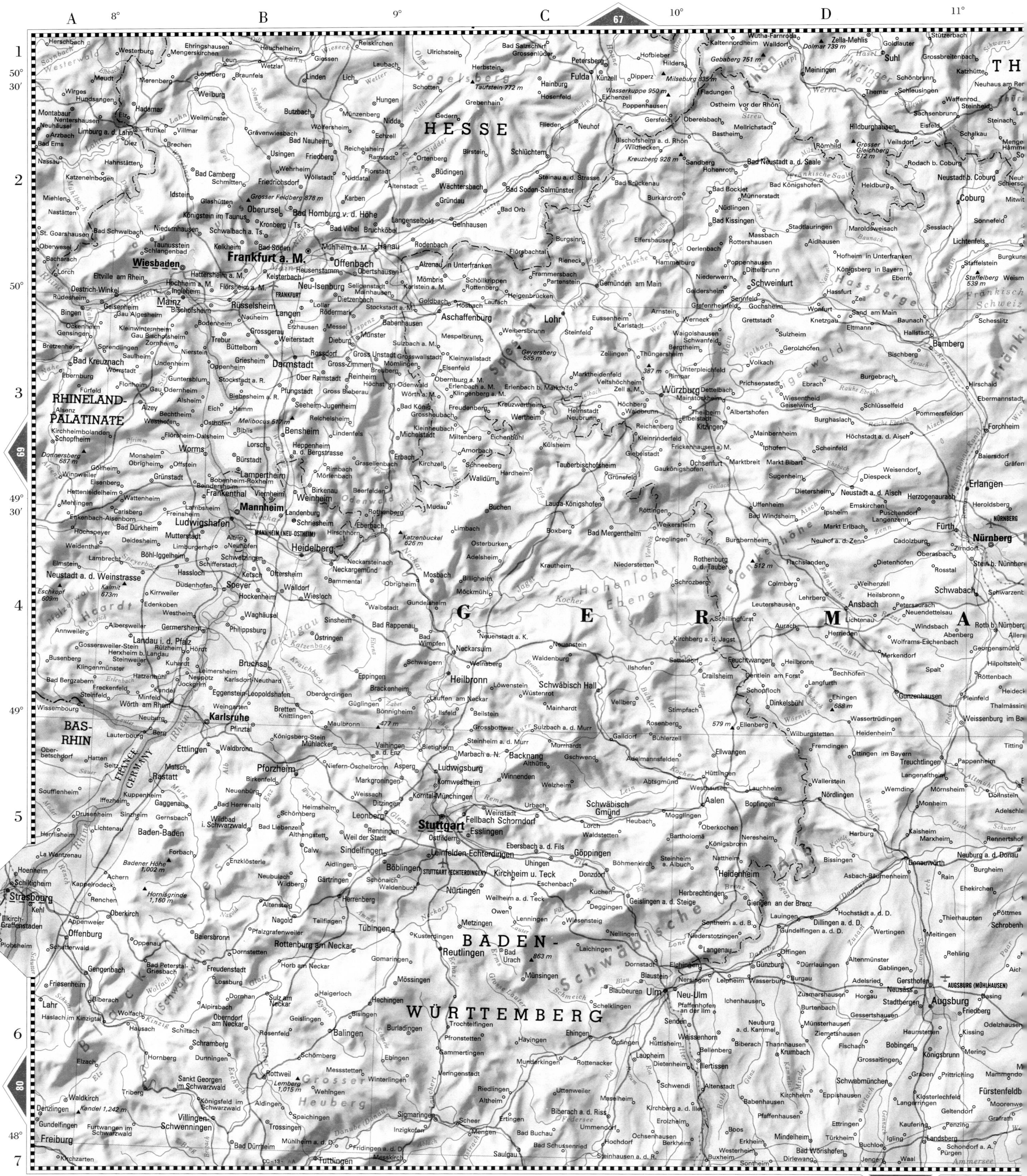


SCALE 1:1,000,000 LAMBERT CONFORMAL CONIC PROJECTION

MILES 0 10 20 30 40 50

KILOMETERS 0 10 20 30 40 50

POPULATION OF CITIES AND TOWNS

OVER 2,000,000 · 1,000,000 - 1,999,999 · 500,000 - 999,999 · 250,000 - 499,999 · 100,000 - 249,999 · 30,000 - 99,999 · 10,000 - 29,999 · UNDER 10,000

# Southern Germany, Czech Republic, Upper Austria

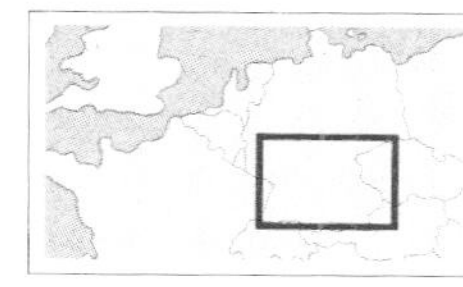

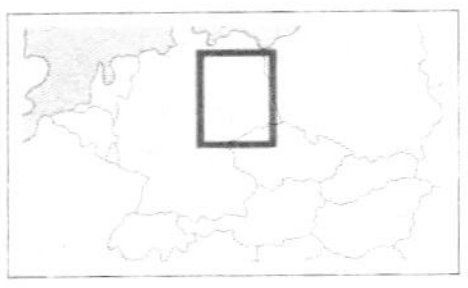

# Eastern Germany

The heart of historic Brandenburg-Prussia, this area is largely comprised of the now-defunct German Democratic Republic. Under that regime the industrial centers of Saxony polluted the air, land and water, becoming one of Europe's most ecologically devastated areas – a challenge now being met by the reunified Germany. Historic Berlin is the region's urban and cultural center.

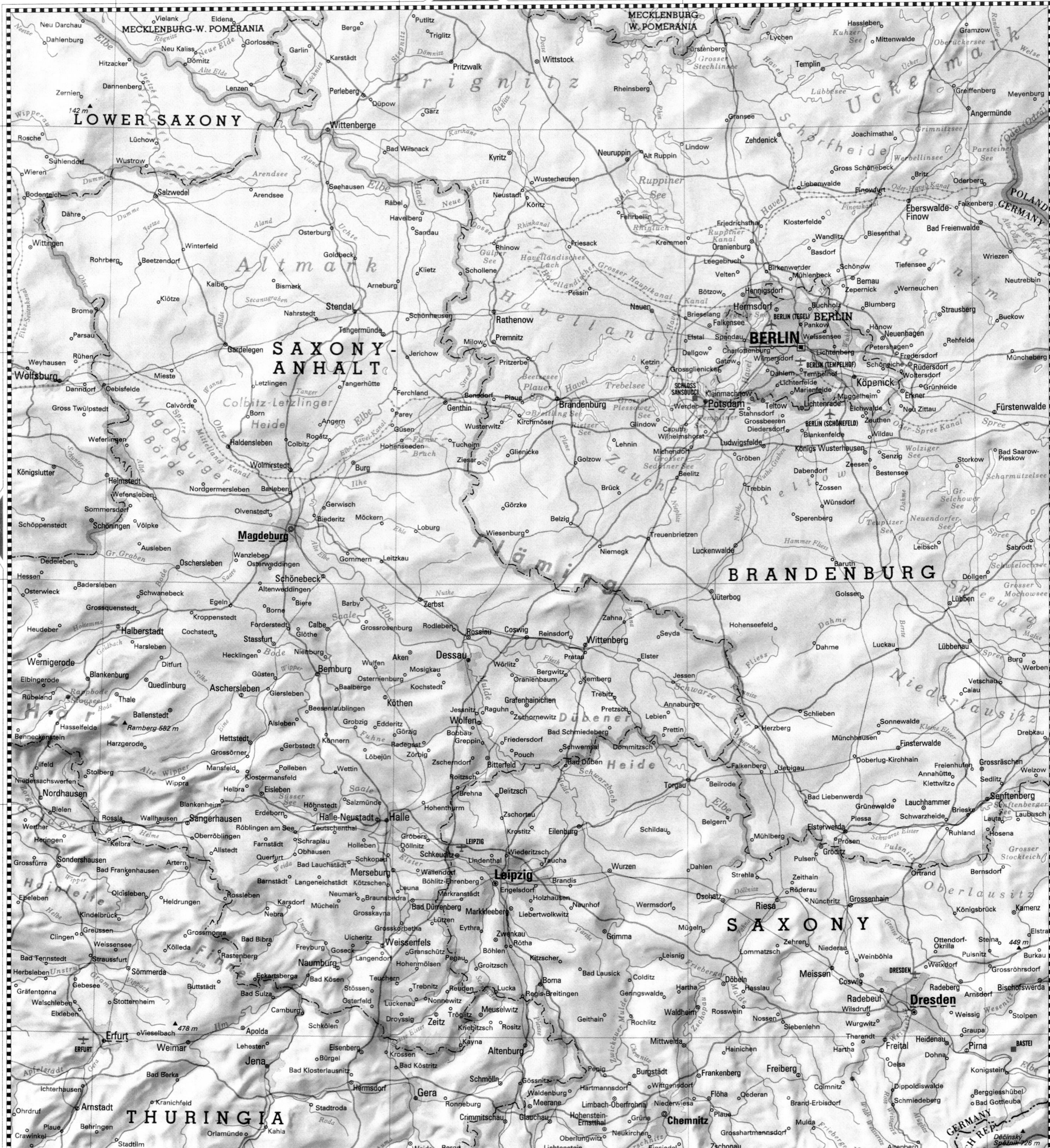


SCALE 1:1,000,000 LAMBERT CONFORMAL CONIC PROJECTION

MILES 0 10 20 30 40 50

KILOMETERS 0 10 20 30 40 50

Longitude East of Greenwich

POPULATION OF CITIES AND TOWNS

- OVER 2,000,000
- 1,000,000 - 1,999,999
- 500,000 - 999,999
- 250,000 - 499,999
- 100,000 - 249,999
- 30,000 - 99,999
- 10,000 - 29,999
- UNDER 10,000

Prior to World War I, Vienna and Budapest were the joint capitals of the Austro-Hungarian empire. Situated on the Danube, these opulent cities were the heart of the Dual Monarchy. After 1918, they presided over the vastly reduced successor states of Austria and Hungary. Today, they are joined by another important city, Bratislava, capital of Slovakia.

# Vienna–Budapest

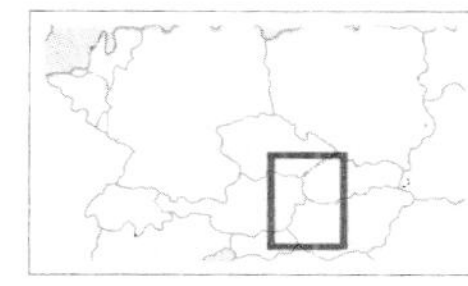

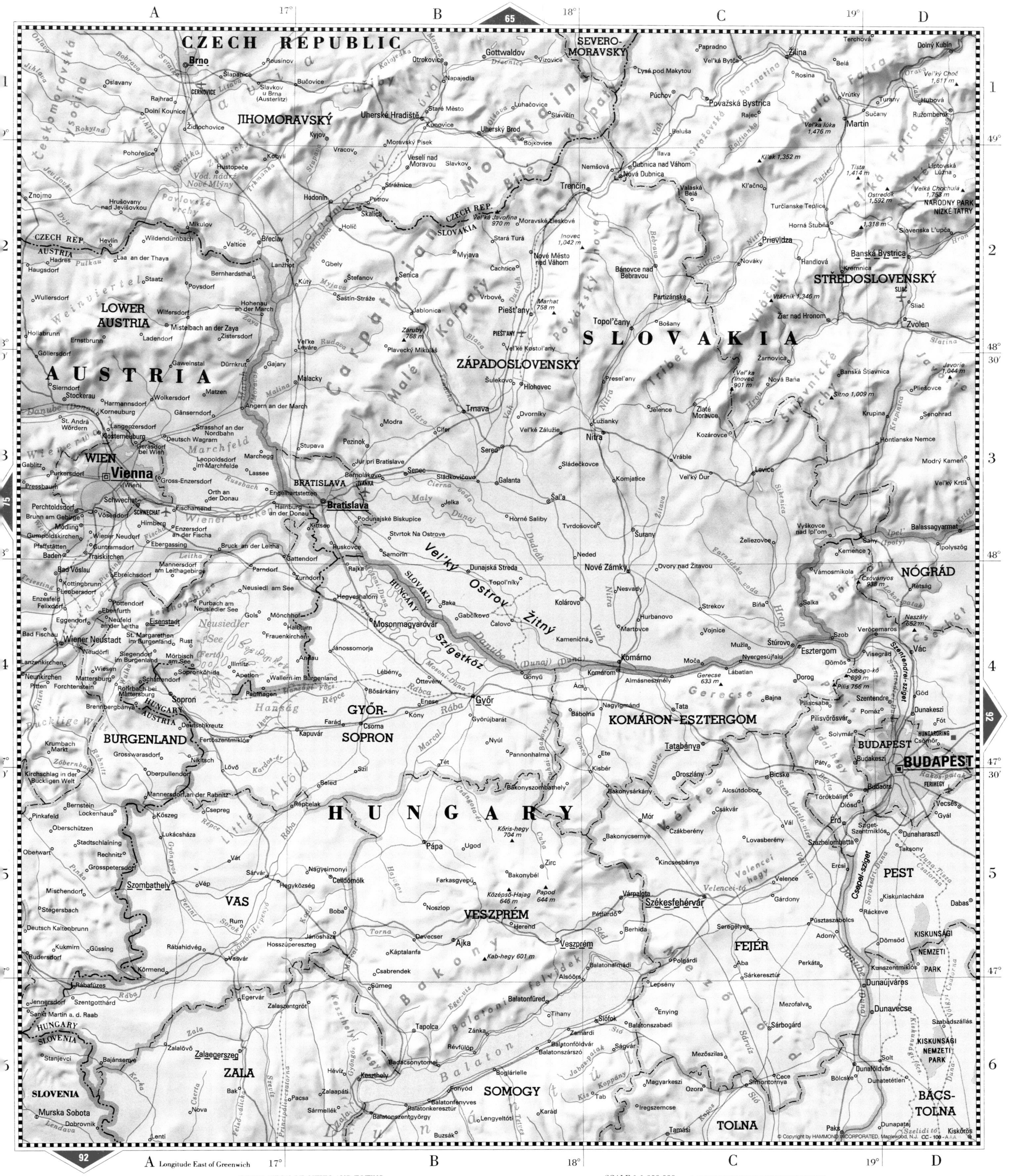


POPULATION OF CITIES AND TOWNS

- OVER 2,000,000
- 1,000,000 - 1,999,999
- 500,000 - 999,999
- 250,000 - 499,999
- 100,000 - 249,999
- 30,000 - 99,999
- 10,000 - 29,999
- UNDER 10,000

SCALE 1:1,000,000 LAMBERT CONFORMAL CONIC PROJECTION

MILES 0 10 20 30 40 50

KILOMETERS 0 10 20 30 40 50

Draw a line northward from central Italy, through the Rhineland and into Belgium. This is the geographical axis along which Western Civilization developed at the end of the Dark Ages. Modern Germany, Italy and France flourished in the millennium following A.D. 1000. Unlike Germany, geography gave France secure boundaries on three sides – the English Channel on the northwest, the Atlantic on the west, and the Pyrenees, Mediterranean and Alps in the south and southeast. As a result, France has enjoyed relatively stable borders in these areas for the last 400 years.

# West Central Europe

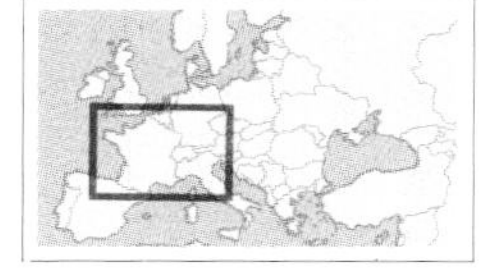

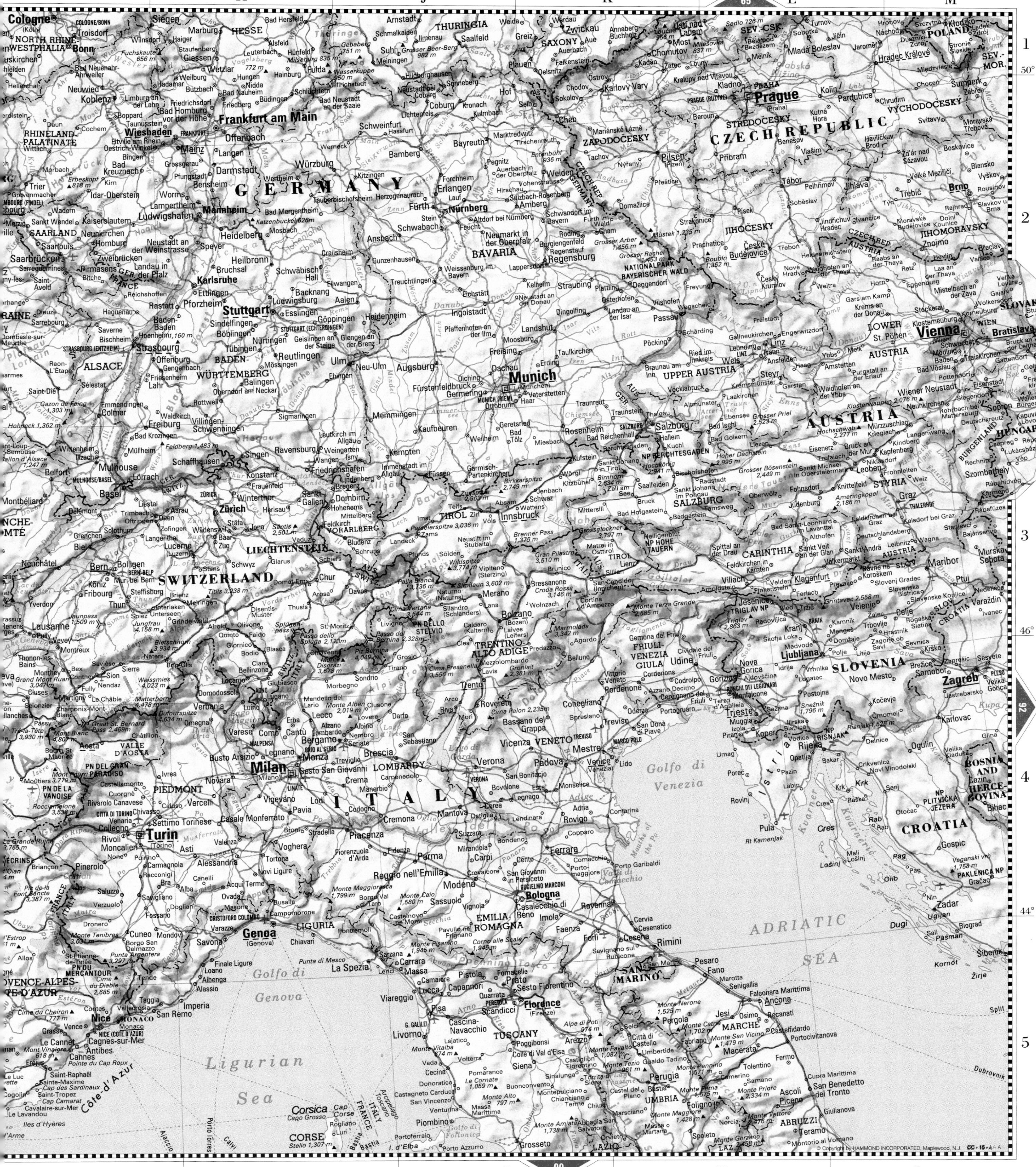


POPULATION OF CITIES AND TOWNS

| | | |
|---|---|---|
| OVER 2,000,000 | 500,000 - 999,999 | 100,000 - 249,999 |
| 1,000,000 - 1,999,999 | 250,000 - 499,999 | 30,000 - 99,999 |
| 10,000 - 29,999 | UNDER 10,000 | |

SCALE 1:3,000,000 — LAMBERT CONFORMAL CONIC PROJECTION

MILES 0 — 50 — 100 — 150

KILOMETERS 0 — 50 — 100 — 150

The Iberian Peninsula (Spain and Portugal) has been described as the meeting place of Europe and Africa. This area was the stage for a 700-year struggle between Christian Europe and Islam. In 711, Islamic Moors swept into Spain from north Africa and eventually conquered the entire peninsula. Moorish power lasted until 1492, and its civilization was one of the finest of Muslim realms. Vestiges of Moorish influence are found throughout the peninsula, the most impressive being the Alhambra, an alcázar (fortress-palace) located in Granada.

# Spain, Portugal

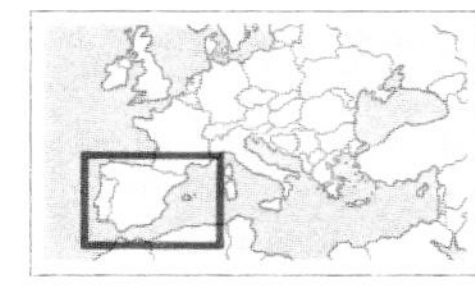

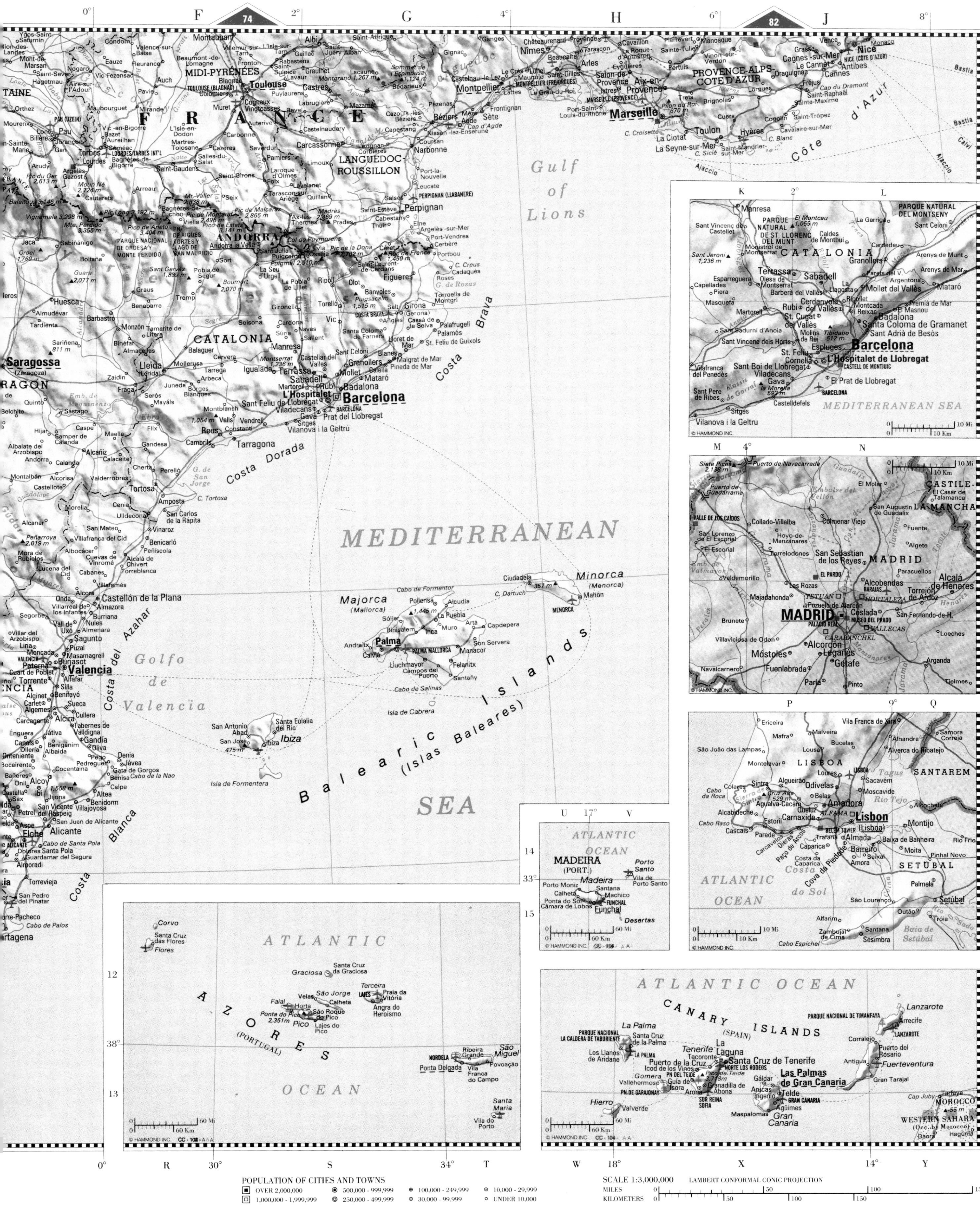


POPULATION OF CITIES AND TOWNS

| | | | | |
|---|---|---|---|---|
| OVER 2,000,000 | 500,000 - 999,999 | 100,000 - 249,999 | 10,000 - 29,999 | |
| 1,000,000 - 1,999,999 | 250,000 - 499,999 | 30,000 - 99,999 | UNDER 10,000 | |

SCALE 1:3,000,000 LAMBERT CONFORMAL CONIC PROJECTION

MILES 0 50 100 150

KILOMETERS 0 50 100 150

78-79

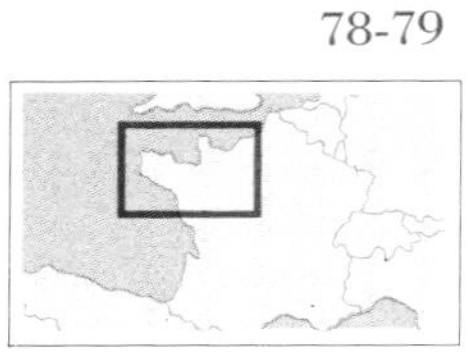

# Northwestern France

Gentle climates make northwestern France a prosperous agricultural region. Fields of grain thr
in the basins of the Seine and Loire. T
valley of the Loire, the longest river in

ance, is famous for its magnificent th and 16th century chateaux. ittany, a prime example of French gionalism, dates from the Dark Ages, en Celtic refugees reached the peninsula from Saxon-overrun England. Normandy began with the Vikings, and traces historic connections to Britain. Normandy is renowned for its apples and *Calvados* (apple brandy).

POPULATION OF CITIES AND TOWNS

| | | | |
|---|---|---|---|
| OVER 2,000,000 | 500,000 - 999,999 | 100,000 - 249,999 | 10,000 - 29,999 |
| 1,000,000 - 1,999,999 | 250,000 - 499,999 | 30,000 - 99,999 | UNDER 10,000 |

SCALE 1:1,000,000 LAMBERT CONFORMAL CONIC PROJECTION

MILES 0 10 20 30 40 50

KILOMETERS 0 10 20 30 40 50

The great mountain system of the Alps, includes the familiar peaks of Mont-Blanc, the Matterhorn , Jungfrau and Dufourspitze (Monte Rosa). It extends in a long semicircle from the Mediterranean seacoast in southeastern France to the outskirts of Vienna. The mountains' central region, which covers more than half of Switzerland, is home to some of the world's most visited glacial regions. These high-elevation "valley glaciers" are all that remain of the vast ice sheet that covered virtually all of the Alps and intervening valleys during the Ice Age of 10,000 years ago.

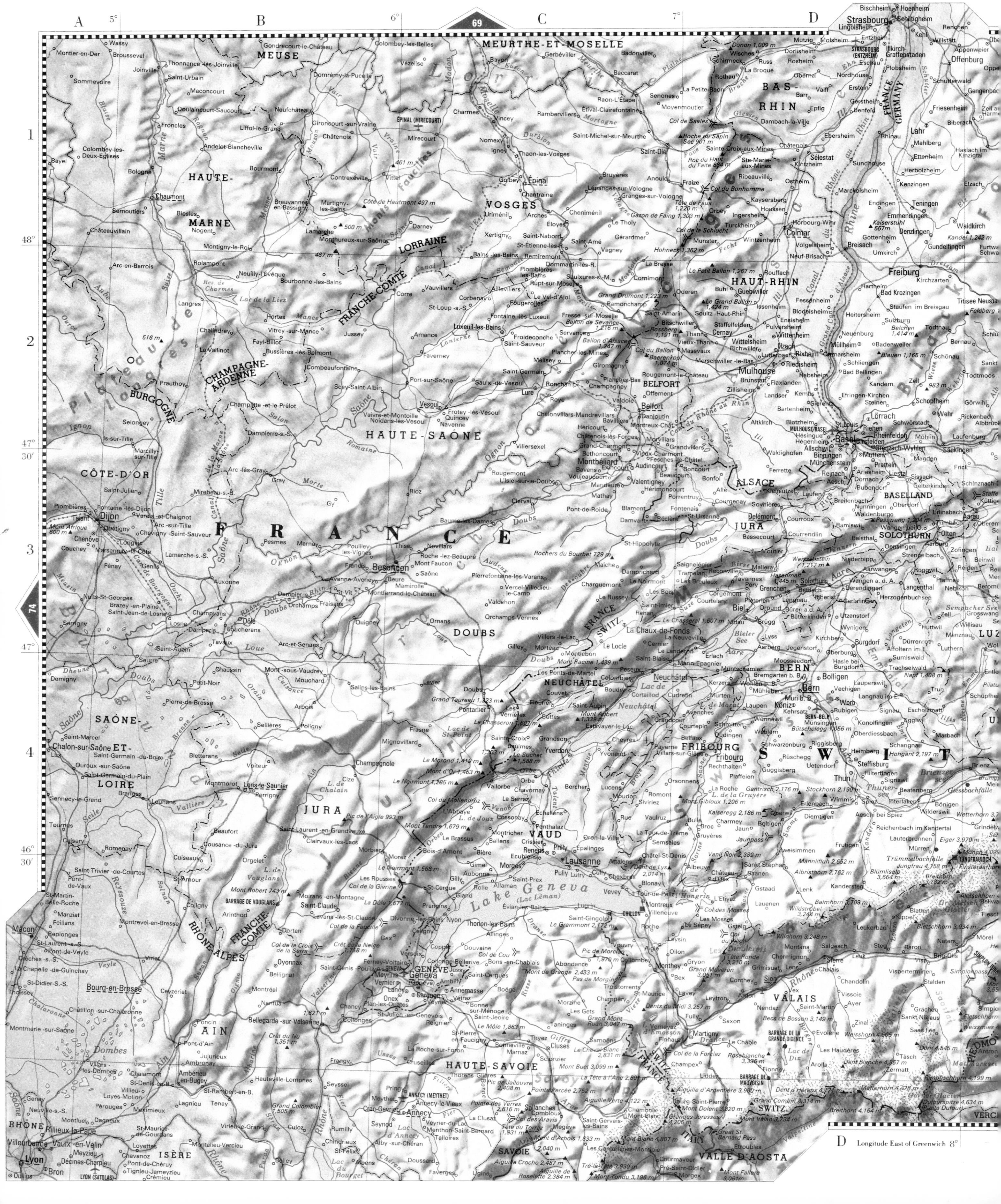

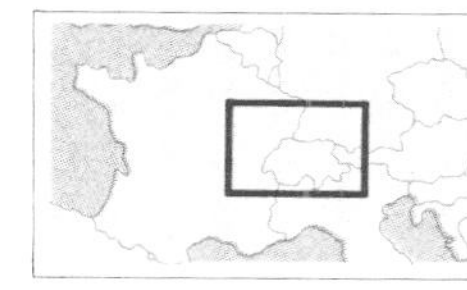

# Central Alps Region

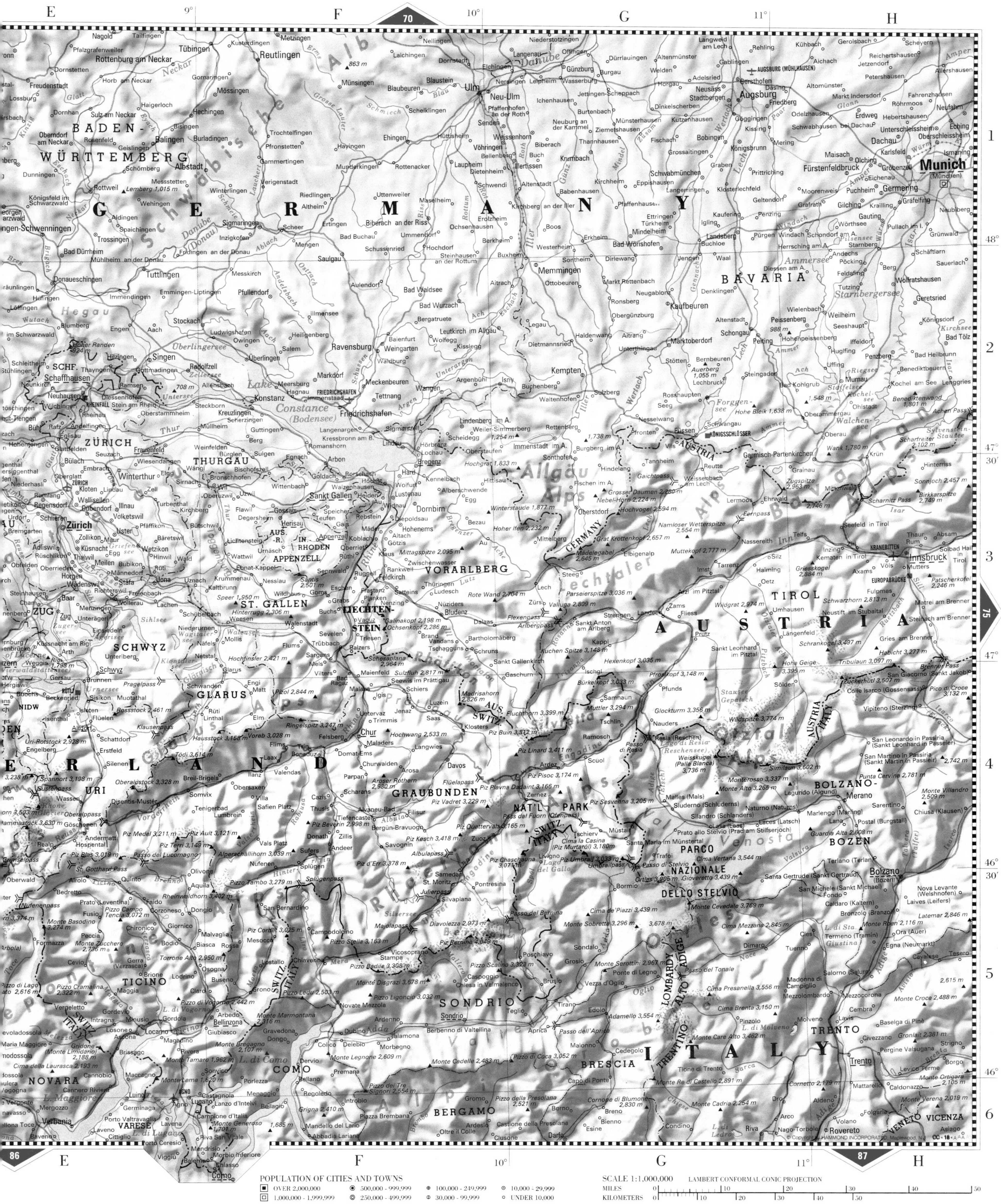


POPULATION OF CITIES AND TOWNS

■ OVER 2,000,000
□ 1,000,000 - 1,999,999
◉ 500,000 - 999,999
◎ 250,000 - 499,999
● 100,000 - 249,999
⊕ 30,000 - 99,999
⊙ 10,000 - 29,999
○ UNDER 10,000

SCALE 1:1,000,000 LAMBERT CONFORMAL CONIC PROJECTION

MILES 0 10 20 30 40 50

KILOMETERS 0 10 20 30 40 50

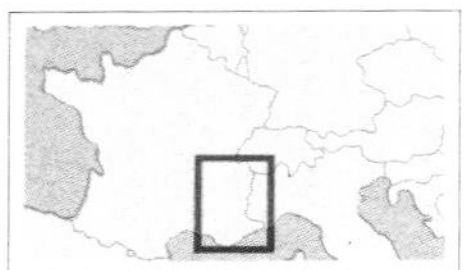

# Southeastern France

During the high Middle Ages, the Provence region was the home of the troubadours, who inspired a courtly culture based on chivalry and lyrical poetry. Today, the coast of Provence is known for the fashionable resorts, hotels and villas of the famed French Riviera (Côte d'Azur), which stretches from St. Tropez, through Cannes and Nice to the Italian border.

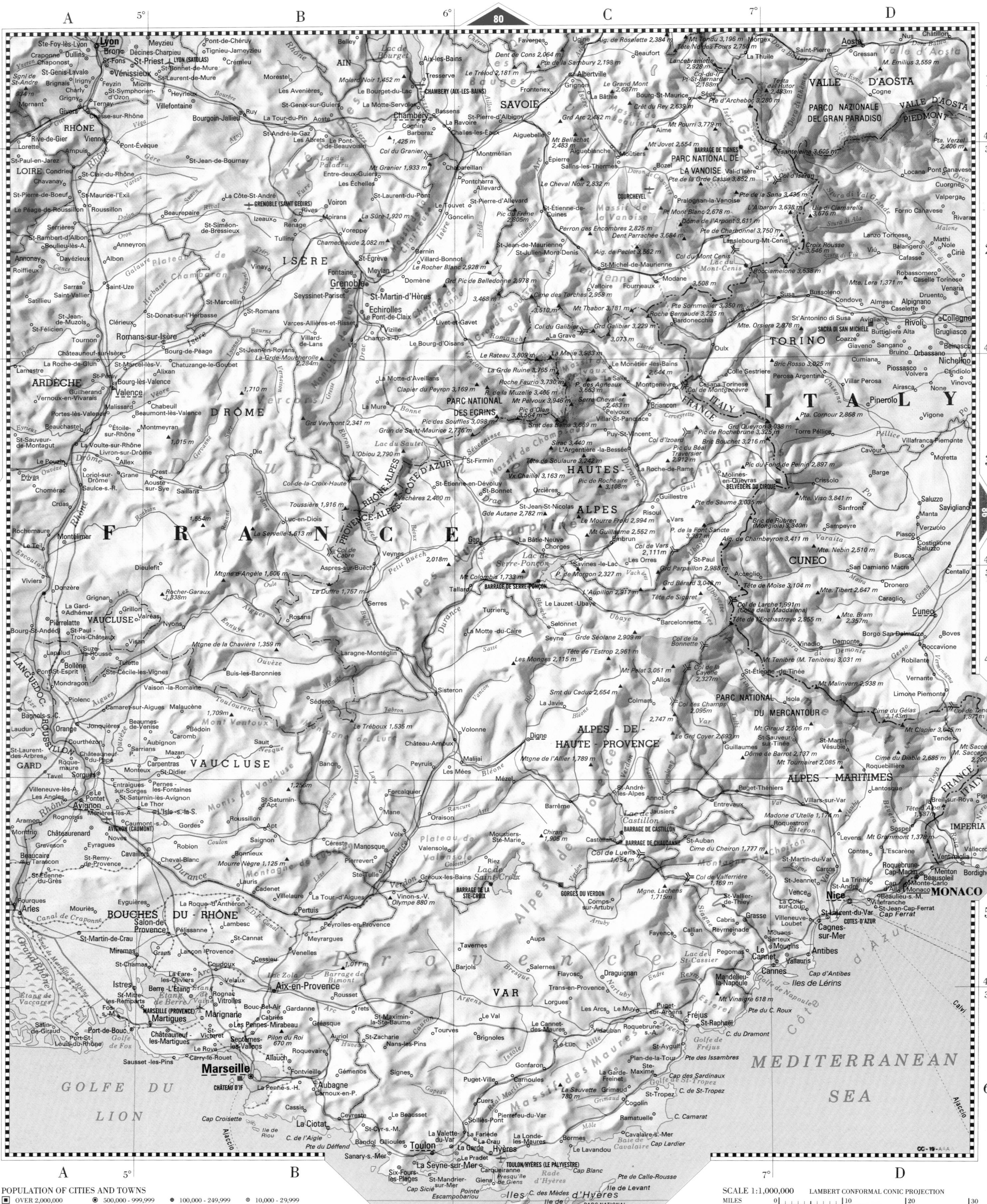


POPULATION OF CITIES AND TOWNS

- ■ OVER 2,000,000
- ◘ 1,000,000 - 1,999,999
- ◉ 500,000 - 999,999
- ◎ 250,000 - 499,999
- ⊕ 100,000 - 249,999
- ● 30,000 - 99,999
- ⊙ 10,000 - 29,999
- ○ UNDER 10,000

SCALE 1:1,000,000 — LAMBERT CONFORMAL CONIC PROJECTION

MILES 0 10 20 30

KILOMETERS 0 10 20 30

# Southern Italy

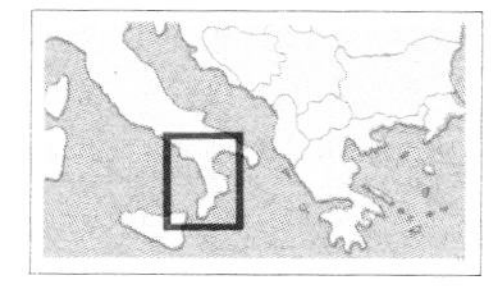

For centuries the Mezzogiorno, which lies south of the Bay of Naples, remained one of Italy's most impoverished regions. Then, after World War II, a redevelopment plan allotted fallow land to peasants, introduced new crops such as cotton, and reclaimed poor and swampy land. Industry was also greatly expanded, especially at Taranto, now a major steel center.

15° 16° 17° Longitude East of Greenwich

**POPULATION OF CITIES AND TOWNS**

- ▣ OVER 2,000,000
- ◫ 1,000,000 - 1,999,999
- ◉ 500,000 - 999,999
- ◎ 250,000 - 499,999
- ⊕ 100,000 - 249,999
- ⊖ 30,000 - 99,999
- ⊙ 10,000 - 29,999
- ○ UNDER 10,000

SCALE 1:1,000,000 LAMBERT CONFORMAL CONIC PROJECTION

MILES 0 10 20 30 40 50

KILOMETERS 0 10 20 30 40 50

This middle portion of the Italian peninsula was once the focus of the Roman Empire. Rome, the Eternal City, reflects a variety of historic influences, depending on the area one visits. Across the landscape of central Italy are found the artifacts of Roman civilization: great aqueducts, straight-as-an-arrow Roman roads, and well-preserved imperial villas. On the Bay of Naples, under the threatening shadow of the volcano Vesuvius, lie the ash-buried ruins of Herculaneum and Pompeii, now excavated to reveal the daily lives of ordinary citizens in A.D. 79.

SCALE 1:1,000,000 LAMBERT CONFORMAL CONIC PROJECTION

MILES 0 10 20 30 40 50

KILOMETERS 0 10 20 30 40 50

POPULATION OF CITIES AND TOWNS

- OVER 2,000,000
- 1,000,000 - 1,999,999
- 500,000 - 999,999
- 250,000 - 499,999
- 100,000 - 249,999
- 30,000 - 99,999
- 10,000 - 29,999
- UNDER 10,000

# Central Italy, Malta



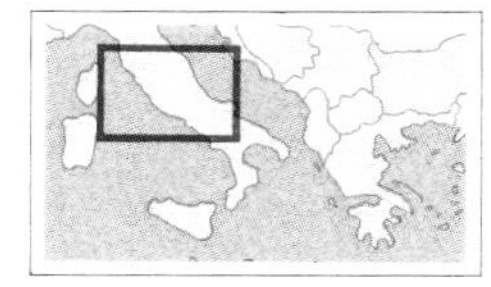

Northern Italy is the nation's industrial, agricultural and recreational heartland. Milan, Italy's primary financial and commercial center, has world-famous textile and machinery industries. Turin is noted for its car industry. The fertile Po Valley is the country's granary, and also leads in dairy farming and sugar beet production. Florence, Siena, Ravenna, Venice and Verona house some of the world's greatest art and architectural treasures. To the north, alpine foothills feature the beautiful glacier-fed lakes Maggiore, Como and Garda.

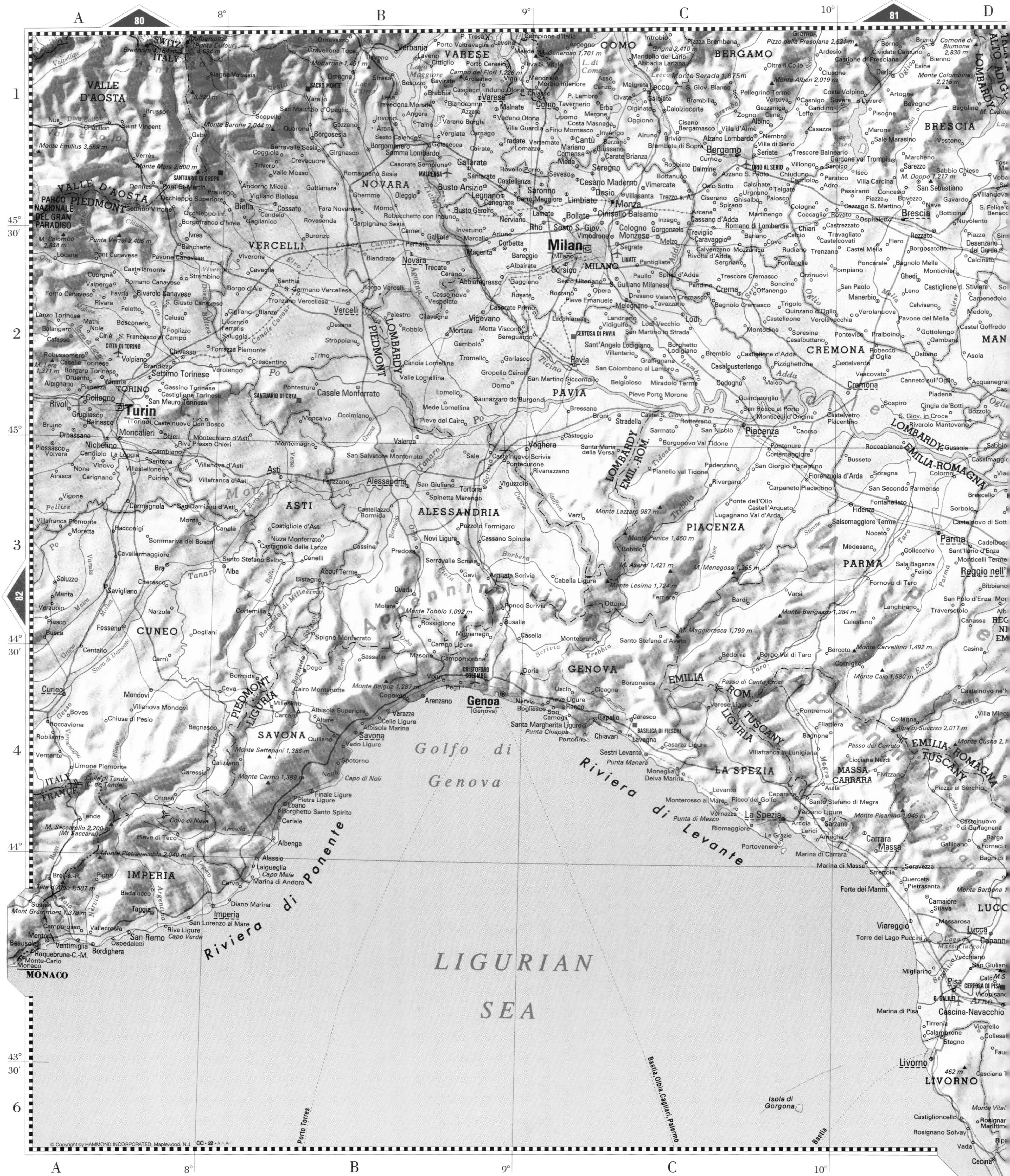

# Northern Italy

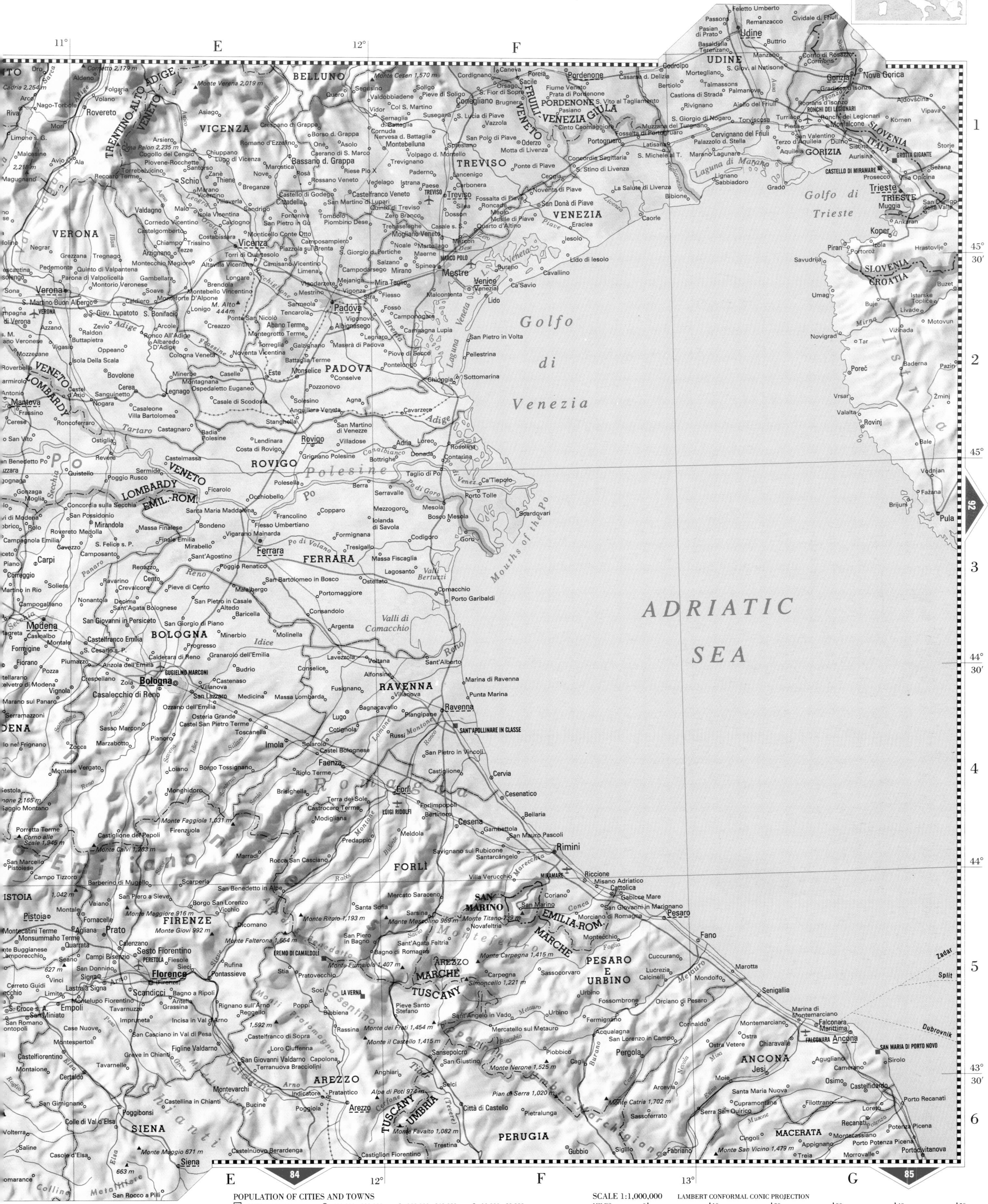


POPULATION OF CITIES AND TOWNS
- OVER 2,000,000
- 1,000,000 - 1,999,999
- 500,000 - 999,999
- 250,000 - 499,999
- 100,000 - 249,999
- 30,000 - 99,999
- 10,000 - 29,999
- UNDER 10,000

SCALE 1:1,000,000 LAMBERT CONFORMAL CONIC PROJECTION

MILES 0 10 20 30 40 50

KILOMETERS 0 10 20 30 40 50

Twenty-one countries border the Mediterranean. Among them are some of the world's richest and poorest nations. Nearly 40 percent of the region's 350 million people live along the 30,000 mile (48,000 km.) coastline. In 30 years, population may double, with most growth occurring in the developing countries of North Africa. Bottled up behind the narrow Strait of Gibraltar, the sea cannot quickly disperse the pollution from human and industrial wastes. The Mediterranean Action Plan has brought disparate nations together to tackle the environmental problems.

# Mediterranean Region

POPULATION OF CITIES AND TOWNS

- OVER 2,000,000
- 1,000,000 - 1,999,999
- 500,000 - 999,999
- 250,000 - 499,999
- 100,000 - 249,999
- 30,000 - 99,999
- 10,000 - 29,999
- UNDER 10,000

SCALE 1:6,000,000 LAMBERT CONFORMAL CONIC PROJECTION

MILES 0 100 200 300

KILOMETERS 0 100 200 300

Classical civilization was born on the northeastern shores of the Mediterranean. Here, in Greece and southern Italy, we find the intellectual and artistic roots of modern Europe. This intricate world of bays, gulfs, channels and lesser seas is crowded with storied places. Homer's Odyssey provides a geography of the area. Ulysses sails from Troy (on the Asian side of the Aegean Sea) and is swept out to sea near the isle of Cythera (Kíthira). Finally, after many landfalls throughout the Mediterranean, he is able to return to his home – the isle of Ithaca (Itháki) on the Ionian Sea coast.

SCALE 1:3,000,000 LAMBERT CONFORMAL CONIC PROJECTION

MILES 0 50 100 150

KILOMETERS 0 50 100 150

POPULATION OF CITIES AND TOWNS

- OVER 2,000,000
- 1,000,000 - 1,999,999
- 500,000 - 999,999
- 250,000 - 499,999
- 100,000 - 249,999
- 30,000 - 99,999
- 10,000 - 29,999
- UNDER 10,000

# Southern Italy, Albania, Greece

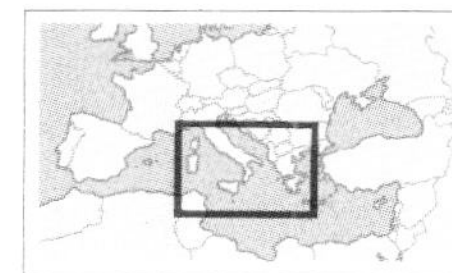

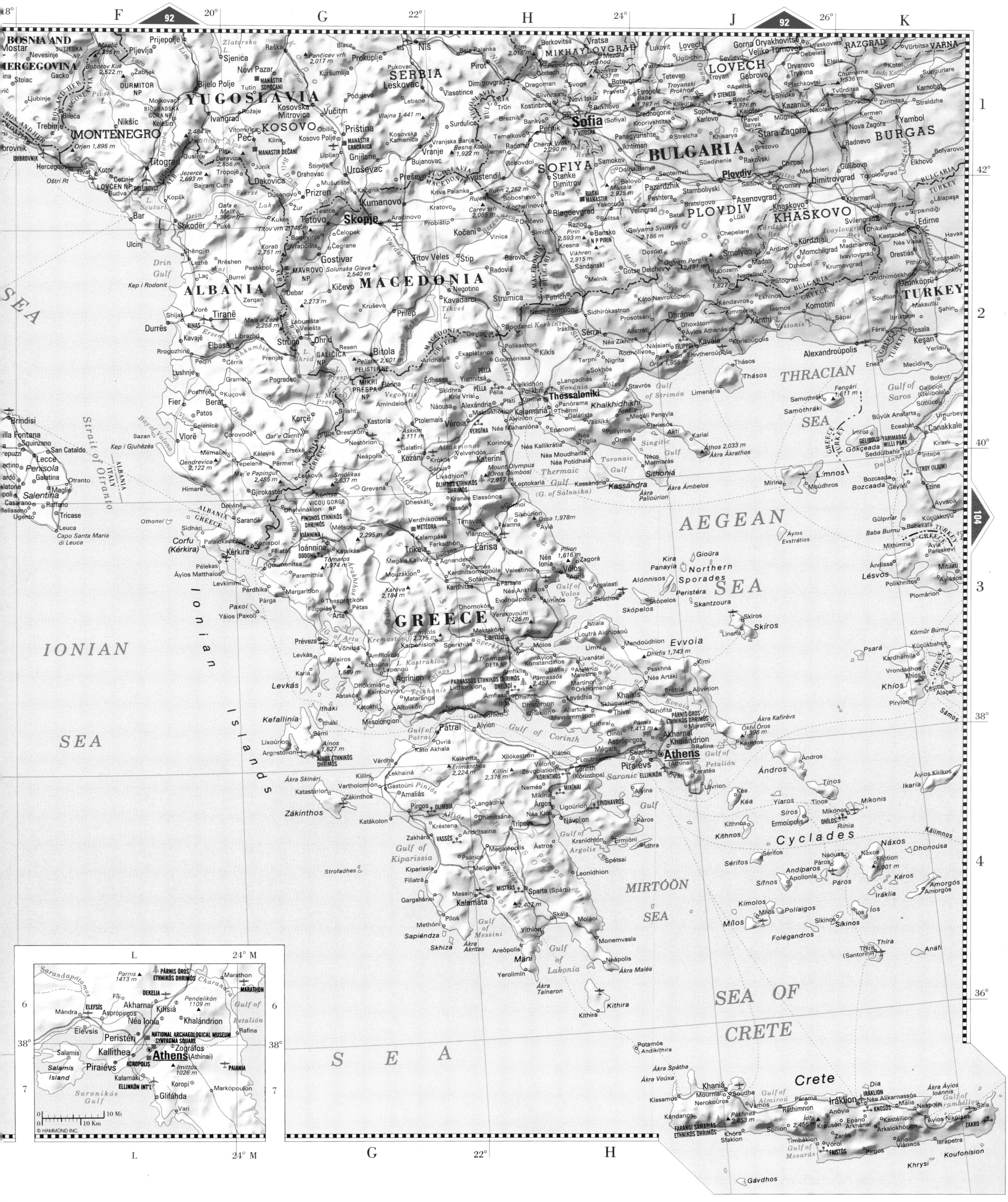

The Balkan Peninsula's rugged mountains and occasional plains are home to a multitude of diverse ethnic groups. Divided by religious, historical and linguistic differences, Slovenes, Croats, Serbs, Bosnians, Montenegrins, Albanians, Macedonians and Turks have, more than once, erupted in conflict. World War I was triggered by the assassination of the Austrian archduke by a Serb at Sarajevo in 1914. The fragmented former republics of Yugoslavia are testament to the competition for territory and the desire for independent ethnic and religious homelands.

SCALE 1:3,000,000 LAMBERT CONFORMAL CONIC PROJECTION

MILES 0 50 100 150

KILOMETERS 0 50 100 150

POPULATION OF CITIES AND TOWNS

- OVER 2,000,000
- 1,000,000 - 1,999,999
- 500,000 - 999,999
- 250,000 - 499,999
- 100,000 - 249,999
- 30,000 - 99,999
- 10,000 - 29,999
- UNDER 10,000

* WHILE THERE IS NO OTHER OFFICIALLY RECOGNIZED NAME FOR
AREA, THE NAME "MACEDONIA" DERIVES FROM ITS FORMER ST
A YUGOSLAV REPUBLIC, AND IS NOT RECOGNIZED BY MANY NAT

# Hungary, Northern Balkan States

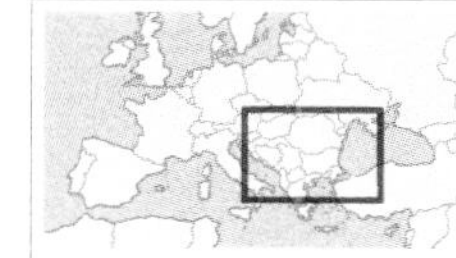

Rivers played a key role in Russian history. Peoples, armies and trade moved throughout Eastern Europe along Russia's famed waterways: the Volga, Don, Dnieper, Dniester, Oka, Kama and the two Dvinas. In the Dark Ages, the Viking Varangians established a trade route from the Baltic to the Black Sea along the Volkhov and Dnieper rivers and founded the first Russian State at Kiev, on the Dnieper. Even Moscow's ascendancy as the center of power can be attributed to its strategic location near the watershed from which the major rivers of European Russia arise.

# Northeastern Europe

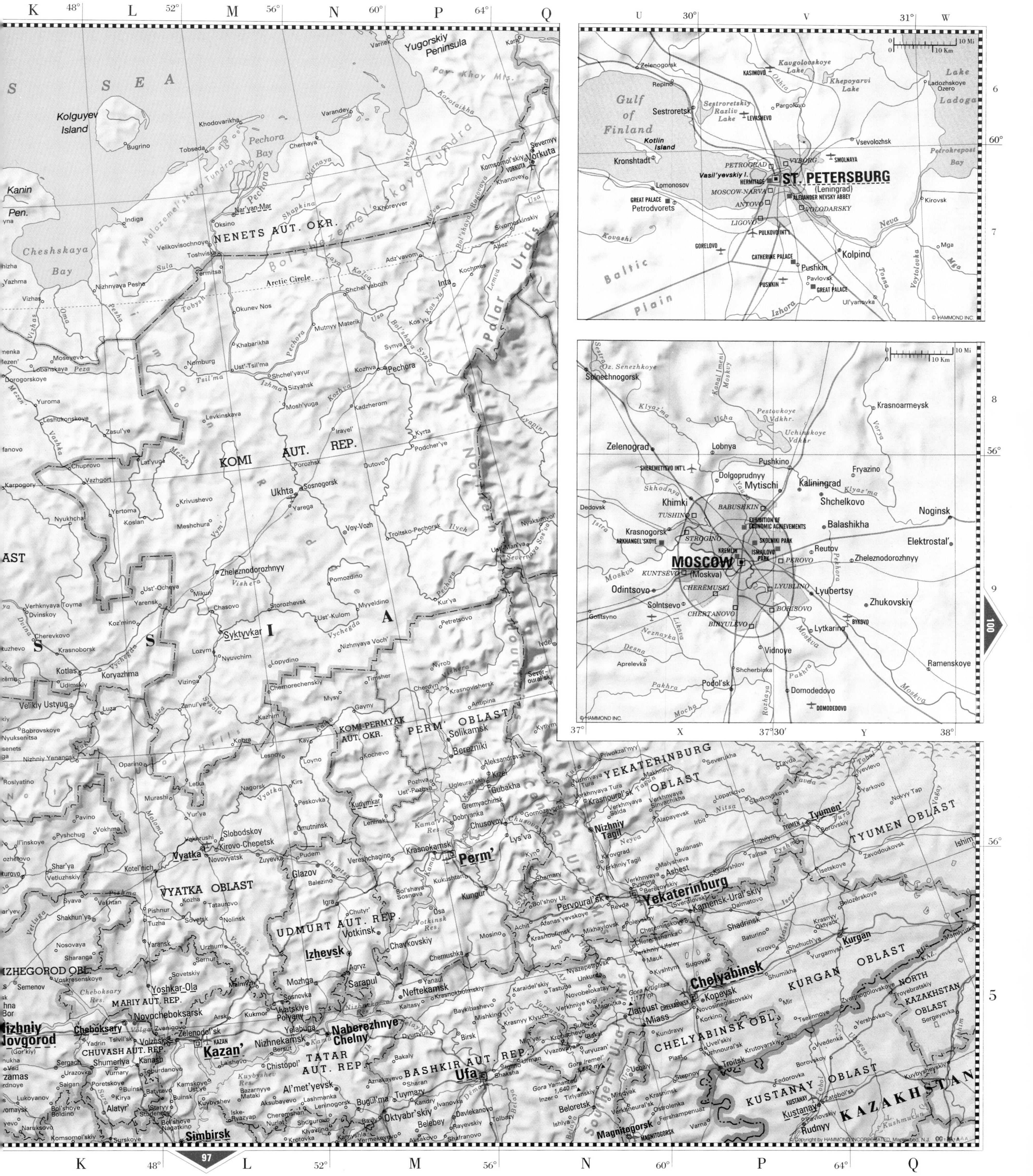


POPULATION OF CITIES AND TOWNS

| | |
|---|---|
| OVER 2,000,000 | 1,000,000 - 1,999,999 |
| 500,000 - 999,999 | 250,000 - 499,999 |
| 100,000 - 249,999 | 30,000 - 99,999 |
| 10,000 - 29,999 | UNDER 10,000 |

SCALE 1:6,000,000 LAMBERT CONFORMAL CONIC PROJECTION

MILES 0 100 200 300

KILOMETERS 0 100 200 300

From the late 1400s Russian expansion moved in two primary directions – east toward the Urals and Siberia, west and south toward the ice-free Baltic and Black Sea. On the west, tsarist Russia clashed with the Polish Kingdom. Farther south, Russian troops battled the Ottoman Empire of the Turks. By the late 1700s Russia had defeated both powers and was firmly established in the Ukraine and Crimea. During the 1800s, the tsars sought to dominate Constantinople (now Istanbul) and the strategic straits leading to the Mediterranean. They never realized their goal.

SCALE 1:6,000,000 LAMBERT CONFORMAL CONIC PROJECTION

MILES 0 100 200 300

KILOMETERS 0 100 200 300

POPULATION OF CITIES AND TOWNS

| | | | |
|---|---|---|---|
| ■ OVER 2,000,000 | ◉ 500,000 - 999,999 | ◉ 100,000 - 249,999 | ○ 10,000 - 29,999 |
| □ 1,000,000 - 1,999,999 | ◎ 250,000 - 499,999 | ⊕ 30,000 - 99,999 | ○ UNDER 10,000 |

# Southeastern Europe

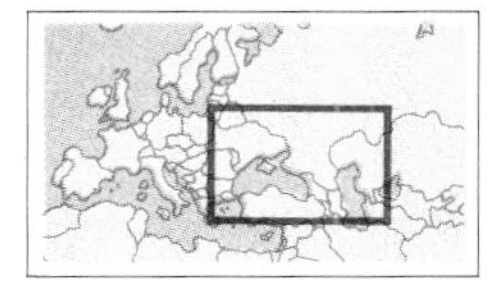

The black soil (chernozem) of Ukraine's vast plains yields one of the world's most bountiful harvests of wheat, barley, sugar beets and sunflower seeds. Important coal deposits in the Donets River basin, and major iron ore resources at Krivoy Rog, proved vital to the economies of the Tsarist Empire and the now-defunct Soviet Union. Europe's sixth most populous nation, Ukraine, could claim to be the birthplace of both the Ukrainian and Russian culture, which was centered at Kiev in the 10th century. Yalta, located on the Crimean peninsula, is a popular Black Sea resort.

# Ukraine

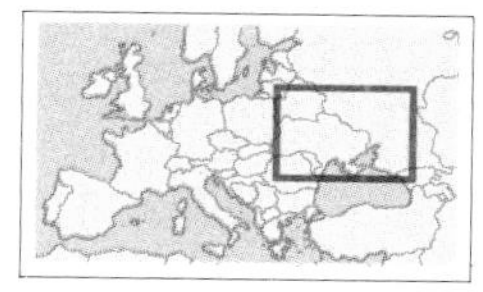

POPULATION OF CITIES AND TOWNS

| | | | |
|---|---|---|---|
| ■ OVER 2,000,000 | ◉ 500,000 - 999,999 | ● 100,000 - 249,999 | ⊙ 10,000 - 29,999 |
| ▣ 1,000,000 - 1,999,999 | ◎ 250,000 - 499,999 | • 30,000 - 99,999 | ○ UNDER 10,000 |

SCALE 1:3,000,000 LAMBERT CONFORMAL CONIC PROJECTION

MILES 0 50 100 150

KILOMETERS 0 50 100 150

The 15 republics of the former Soviet Union stretch from the Polish border to the Bering Strait, spanning 11 time zones and 6000 miles (9600 km.). Their combined landmass – nearly 9 million square miles (23.4 mil. sq. km.) – wraps halfway around the globe. The vast Russian Republic commands 76 percent of the region's land, over 60 percent of its population, most of its petroleum and natural gas, and over half of its iron and coal. With the collapse of the Soviet Union, tensions arose among the diverse ethnic groups in their struggle for greater autonomy.

# Russia and Neighboring Countries

POPULATION OF CITIES AND TOWNS

- OVER 2,000,000
- 1,000,000 - 1,999,999
- 500,000 - 999,999
- 250,000 - 499,999
- 100,000 - 249,999
- 30,000 - 99,999
- 10,000 - 29,999
- UNDER 10,000

SCALE 1:18,000,000 LAMBERT CONFORMAL CONIC PROJECTION

MILES 0 300 600 900

KILOMETERS 0 300 600 900

# Asia

Largest of the continents, Asia is home to more than 40 nations and over half of humanity. The landmass is so large, it is made up of subcontinents: India, Indochina and Arabia. Separated by high mountain ranges, deserts, rivers and seas, its diverse cultures and ethnic groups developed in isolation from one another. Central Asia is one of the harshest and most remote areas in the world.

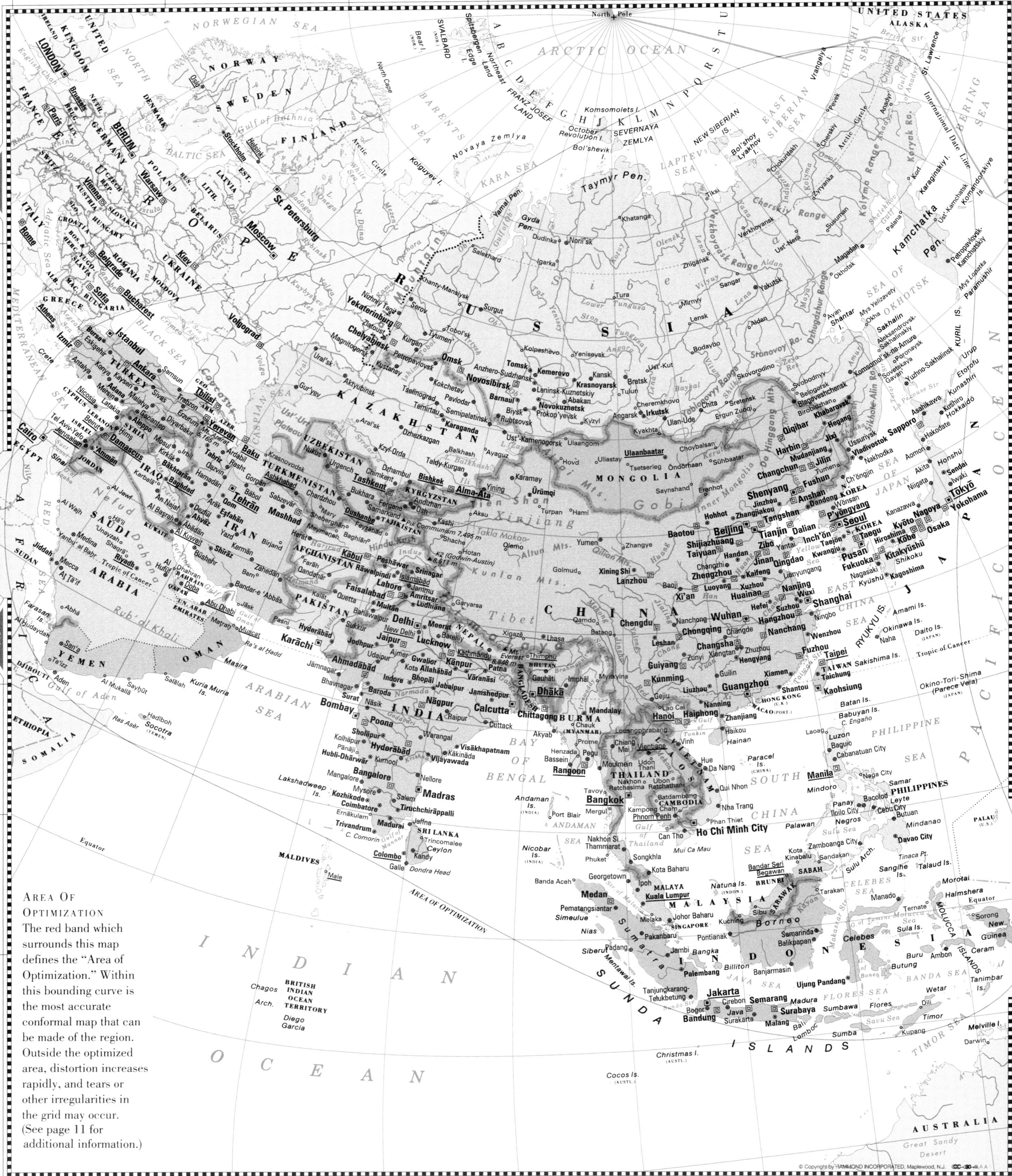


AREA OF OPTIMIZATION

The red band which surrounds this map defines the "Area of Optimization." Within this bounding curve is the most accurate conformal map that can be made of the region. Outside the optimized area, distortion increases rapidly, and tears or other irregularities in the grid may occur. (See page 11 for additional information.)

Longitude East of Greenwich

SCALE 1:42,000,000 OPTIMAL CONFORMAL PROJECTION

MILES 0 700 1400 2100

KILOMETERS 0 700 1400 2100

POPULATION OF CITIES AND TOWNS

- OVER 3,000,000
- 1,000,000 - 2,999,999
- 500,000 - 999,999
- 100,000 - 499,999
- UNDER 100,000

# Eastern Mediterranean Region

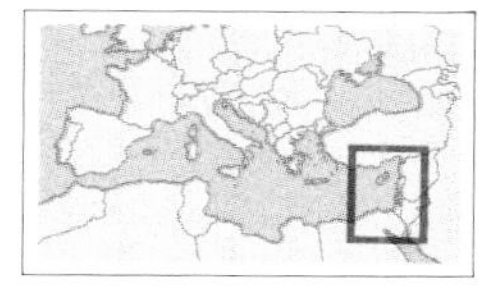

This is the traditional Holy Land of three of the world's great religions, Judaism, Christianity and Islam. Today, the Eastern Mediterranean, or Levant, region suffers from ethnic and religious struggles: Christians vs. Muslims in Lebanon, Greeks vs. Turks on the island of Cyprus, and Israelis vs. Palestinian Arabs in the bitterly contested West Bank area of the Jordan River valley.

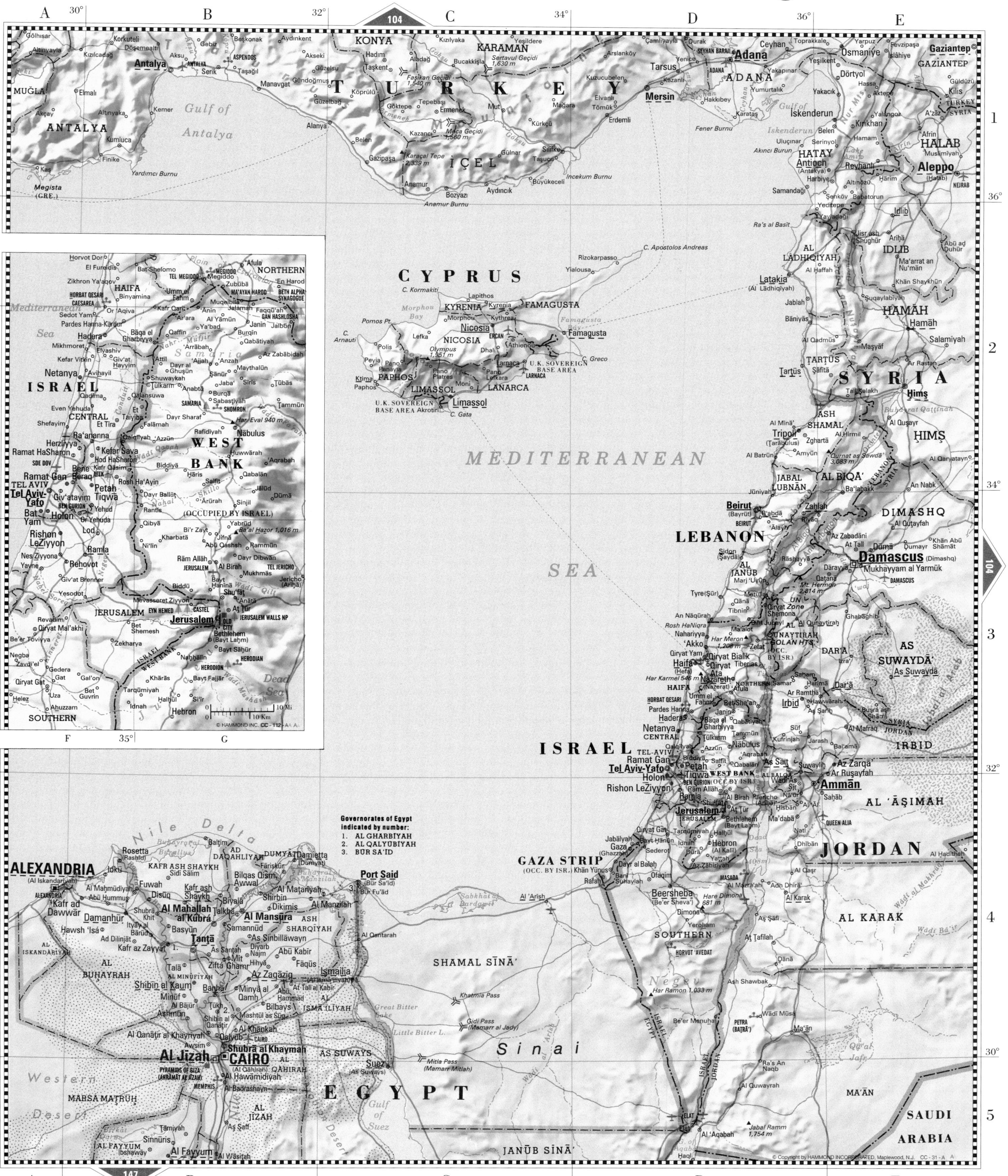


POPULATION OF CITIES AND TOWNS

| | | | |
|---|---|---|---|
| OVER 2,000,000 | 500,000 - 999,999 | 100,000 - 249,999 | 10,000 - 29,999 |
| 1,000,000 - 1,999,999 | 250,000 - 499,999 | 30,000 - 99,999 | UNDER 10,000 |

SCALE 1:3,000,000 POLYCONIC PROJECTION

MILES 0 50 100 150

KILOMETERS 0 50 100 150

Recorded human history began here, on the fringes of the Fertile Crescent. Agriculture evolved along the Mediterranean coast and in the Tigris-Euphrates valleys, nurturing a sequence of great civilizations, from the Sumerian empire to the Babylonians, Egyptians, Hittites, Assyrians, Persians, Saracens and Turks. Today, Muslim fundamentalism is a powerful force throughout the area. Nationalistic aspirations among Armenians, Azerbaijani and Kurds transgress current political boundaries and keep parts of the region in a highly volatile state.

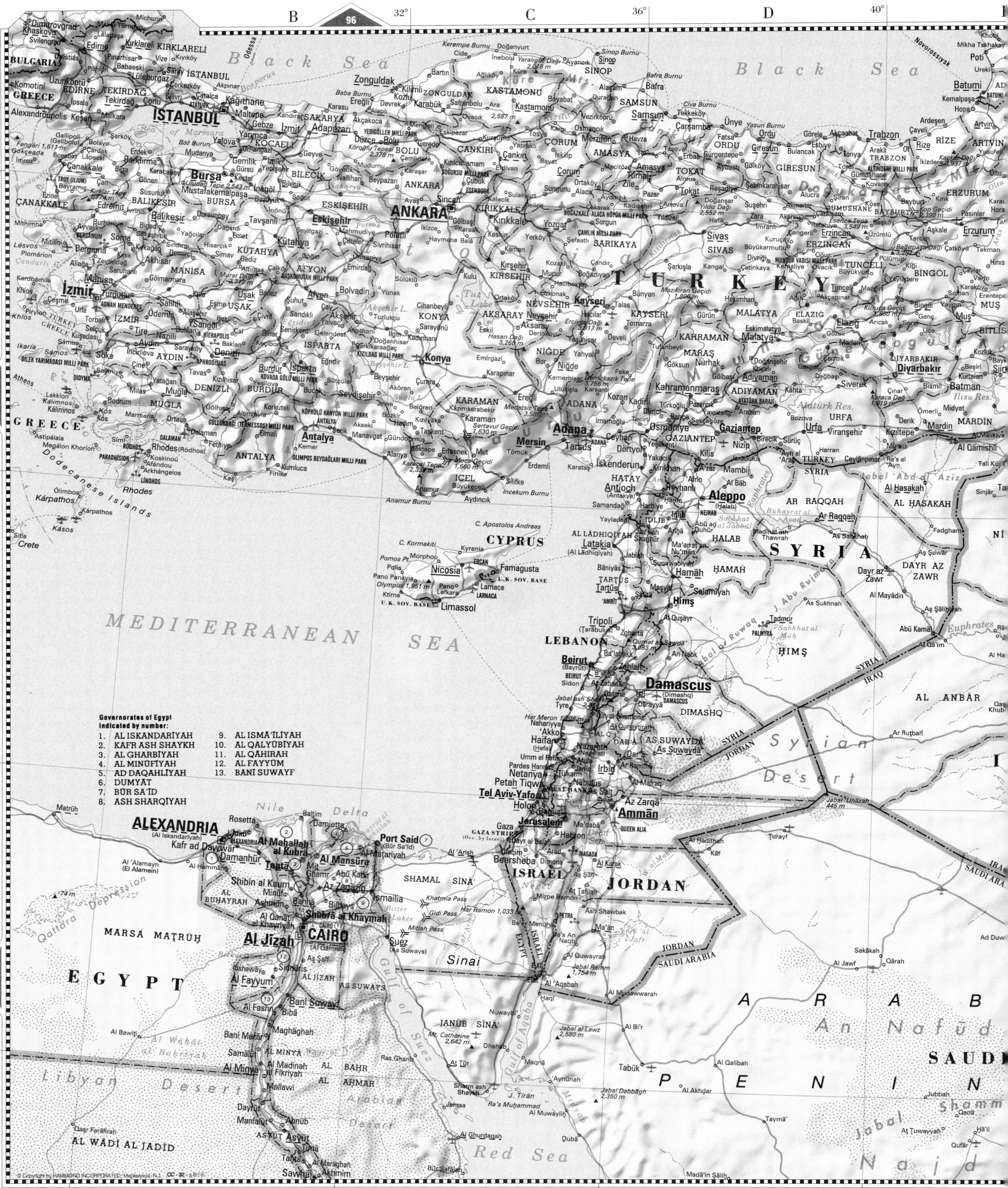


SCALE 1:6,000,000 LAMBERT CONFORMAL CONIC PROJECTION

MILES 0 | 100 | 200 | 300

KILOMETERS 0 | 100 | 200 | 300

POPULATION OF CITIES AND TOWNS

- OVER 2,000,000
- 1,000,000 - 1,999,999
- 500,000 - 999,999
- 250,000 - 499,999
- 100,000 - 249,999
- 30,000 - 99,999
- 10,000 - 29,999
- UNDER 10,000

# Northern Middle East

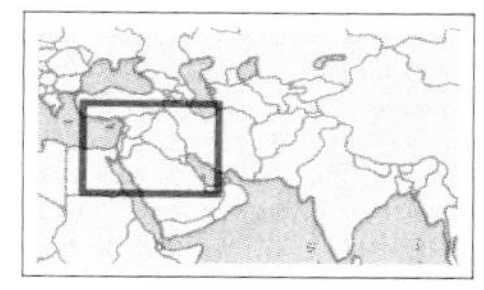

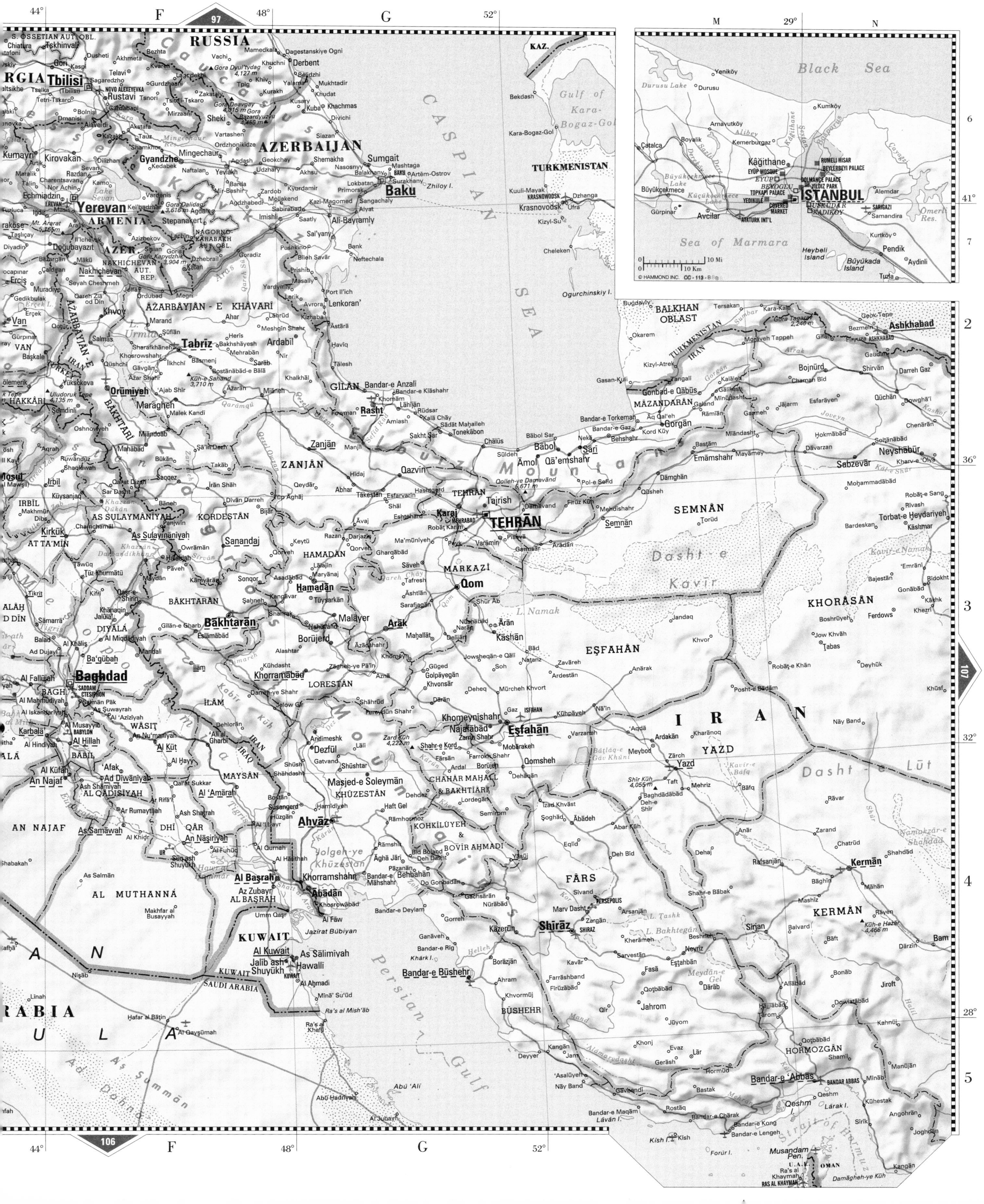

Two great powers rule this parched land: Islam and oil. Barren desert stretches from the Arabian Peninsula to western Pakistan. Three productive river valleys: the Jordan, Tigris-Euphrates, and Indus provide relief. Mohammed, the founder of Islam, lived in Mecca. After his Hegira to Medina, Muslim horsemen swept out of Arabia to conquer the Middle East, North Africa, and beyond. The immense oil wealth of the Persian Gulf region, combined with rising oil demand, has extended the area's influence still further, transforming it into a center of global power.

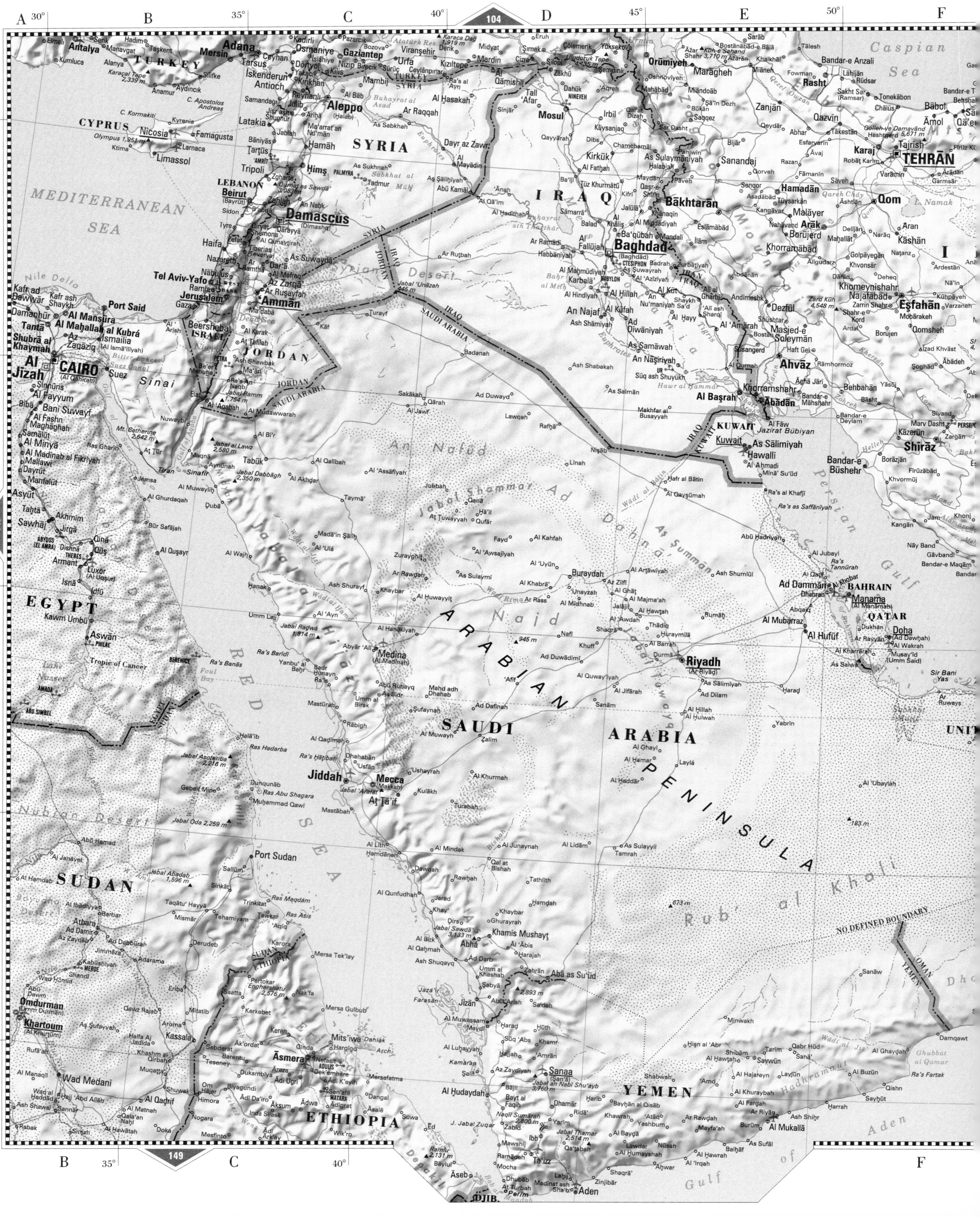

# Southwestern Asia

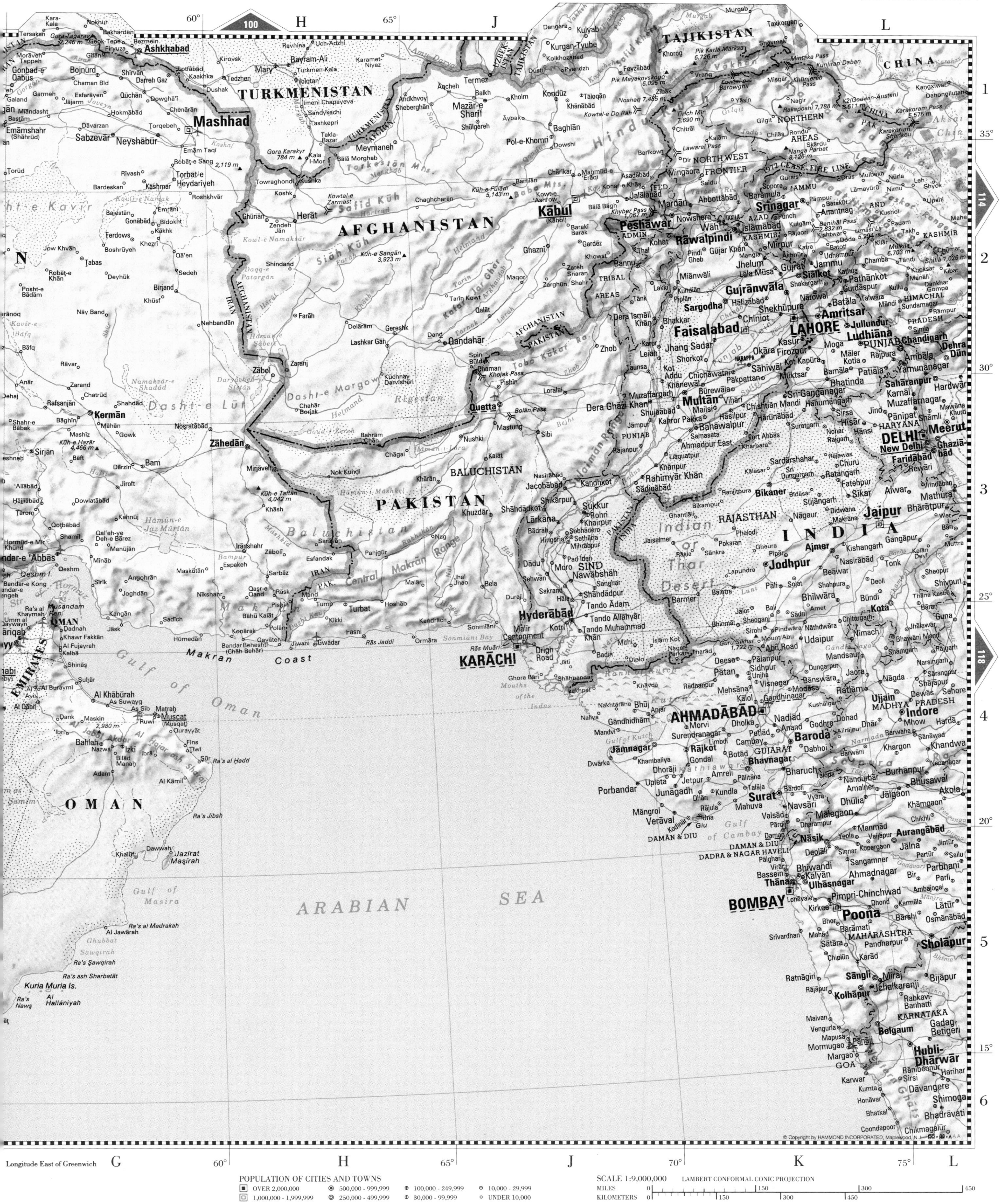


POPULATION OF CITIES AND TOWNS
- ■ OVER 2,000,000
- □ 1,000,000 - 1,999,999
- ◉ 500,000 - 999,999
- ◎ 250,000 - 499,999
- ⊛ 100,000 - 249,999
- ⊕ 30,000 - 99,999
- ⊙ 10,000 - 29,999
- ○ UNDER 10,000

SCALE 1:9,000,000 — LAMBERT CONFORMAL CONIC PROJECTION

MILES 0 150 300 450

KILOMETERS 0 150 300 450

Marco Polo ventured through here on his trek from Venice to the palace of the Great Khan. Chinese, Japanese, Koreans and Russians have vied for strategic advantage and control over the valuable coal and mineral resources of Northern China for over a century. Today the region is one of the world's most productive industrial centers. While Japan successfully exports everything from cars to VCRs, emerging industrial powers such as Taiwan and Korea are joining a high-tech revolution. The Chinese have made Shenyang a center of heavy industry.

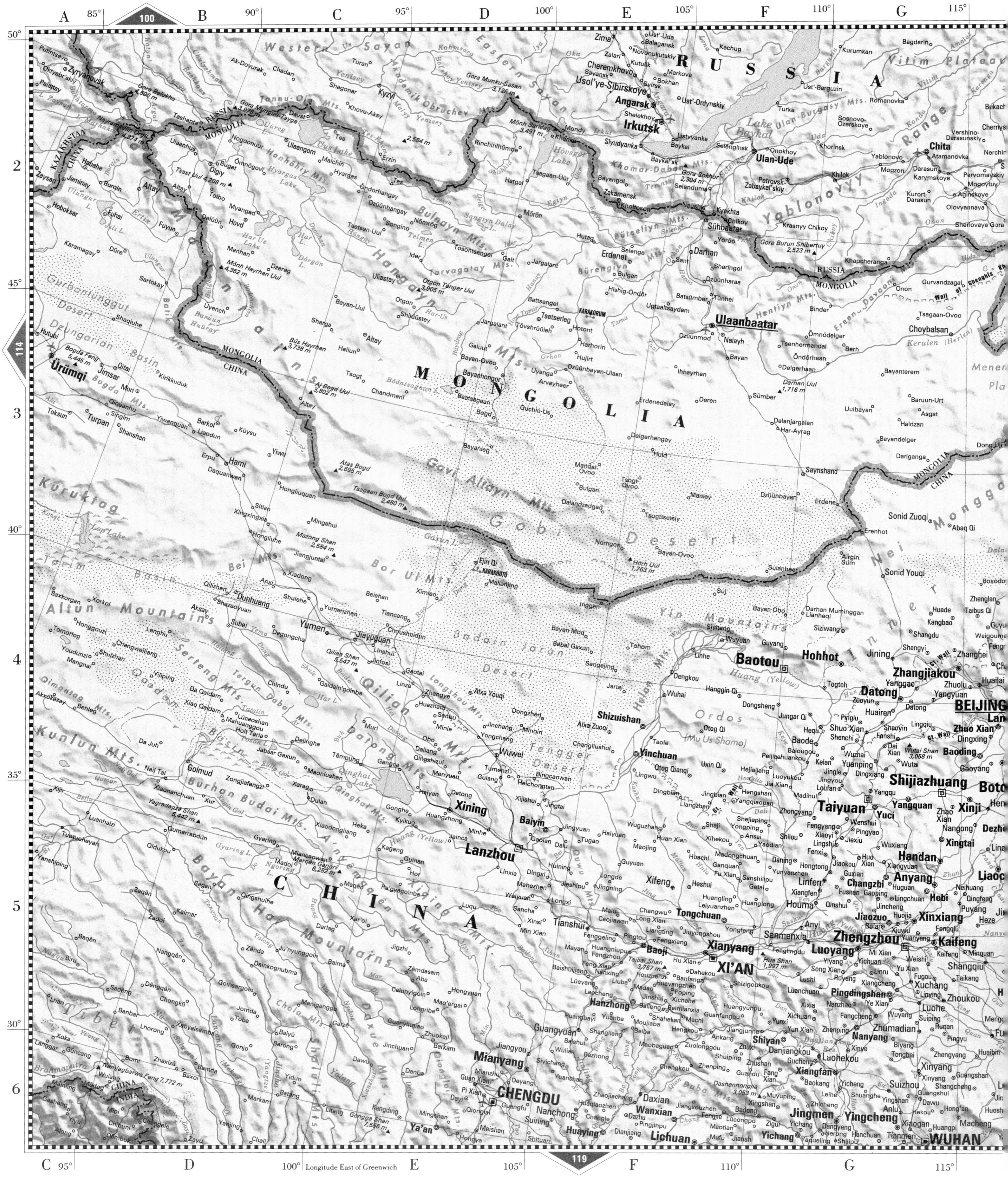

# Eastern Asia

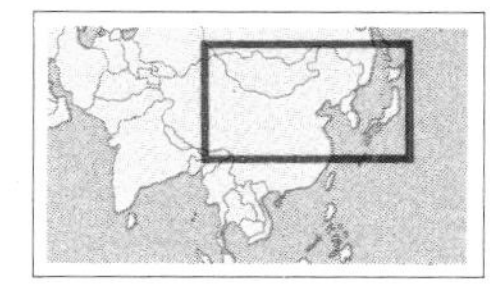

POPULATION OF CITIES AND TOWNS

- OVER 2,000,000
- 1,000,000 - 1,999,999
- 500,000 - 999,999
- 250,000 - 499,999
- 100,000 - 249,999
- 30,000 - 99,999
- 10,000 - 29,999
- UNDER 10,000

SCALE 1:9,000,000 LAMBERT CONFORMAL CONIC PROJECTION

MILES 0 150 300 450

KILOMETERS 0 150 300 450

The heart of Japan's industrial might lies in four highly urbanized clusters in southern Honshu and northern Kyushu. Rebuilt since World War II, Japan has become a major world power despite its lack of iron ore, coal or petroleum, and its limited arable land. It imports raw materials and uses its highly skilled work force to produce the cars, electronics, optical goods, textiles and other well-made products which supply the world market. Tokyo-Yokohama is the leading manufacturing center, followed by the Kobe-Osaka-Kyoto triangle, Nagoya and Kitakyushu.

# Central and Southern Japan

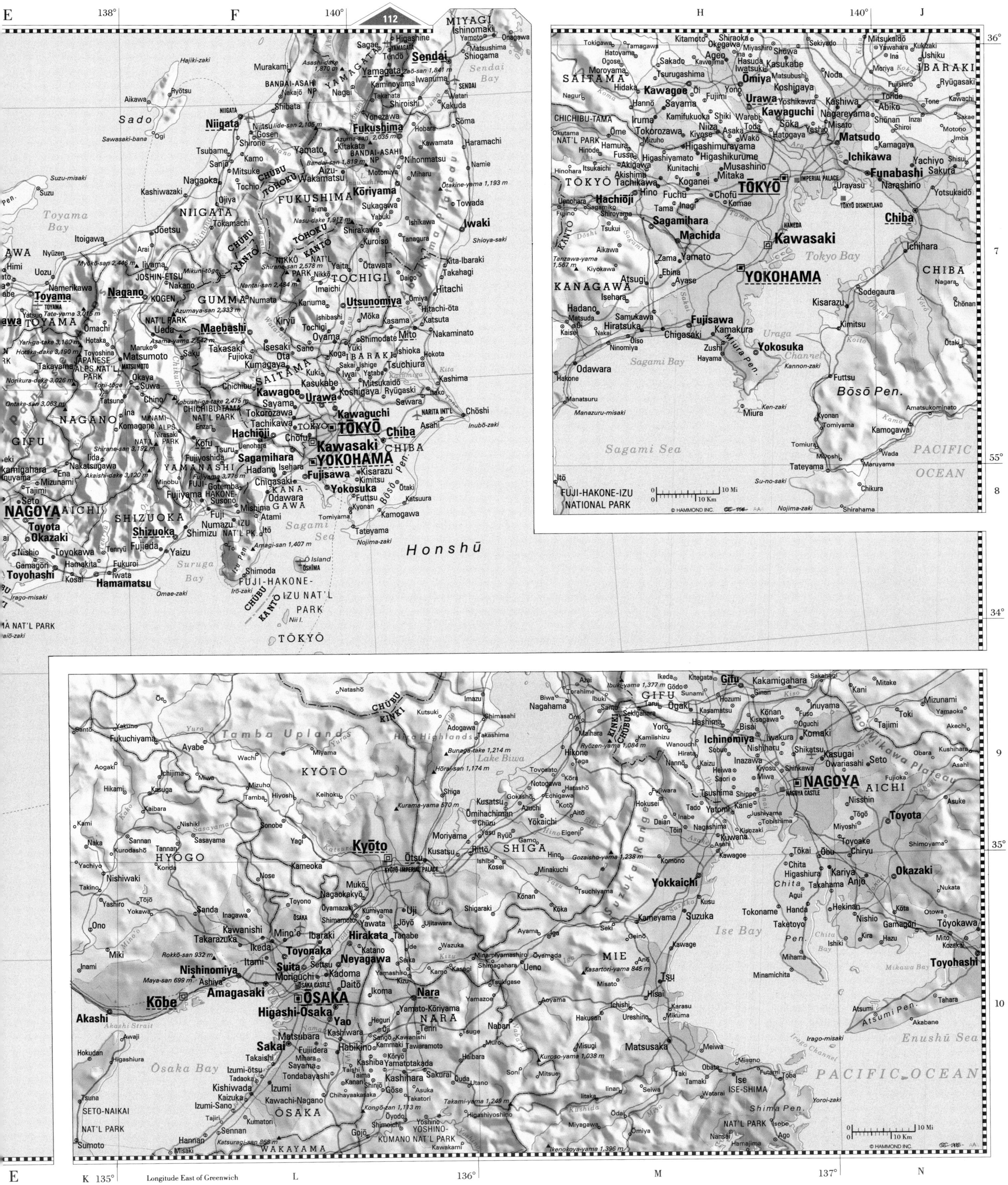


POPULATION OF CITIES AND TOWNS

- ▣ OVER 2,000,000
- ▣ 1,000,000 - 1,999,999
- ◉ 500,000 - 999,999
- ◎ 250,000 - 499,999
- ⊕ 100,000 - 249,999
- ⊙ 30,000 - 99,999
- ⊙ 10,000 - 29,999
- ○ UNDER 10,000

MAIN MAP SCALE 1:3,000,000 LAMBERT CONFORMAL CONIC PROJECTION

MILES 0 50 100 150

KILOMETERS 0 50 100 150

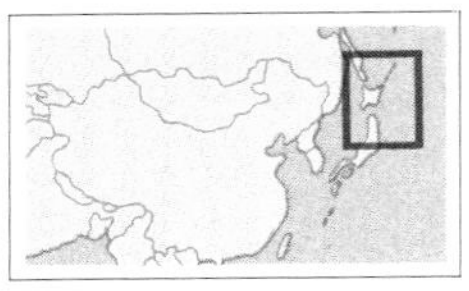

# Northern Japan; Ryukyu Islands

Hokkaido, Japan's northernmost major island, is home to the Ainu, an aboriginal, possibly Caucasian people, unrelated to the Japanese. The Ainu gradually retreated to the island's fertile river valleys to hunt, fish and farm. Fewer than 15,000 Ainu remain. In 1972, Hokkaido hosted the Winter Olympics in the city of Sapporo. The island also contains coal.

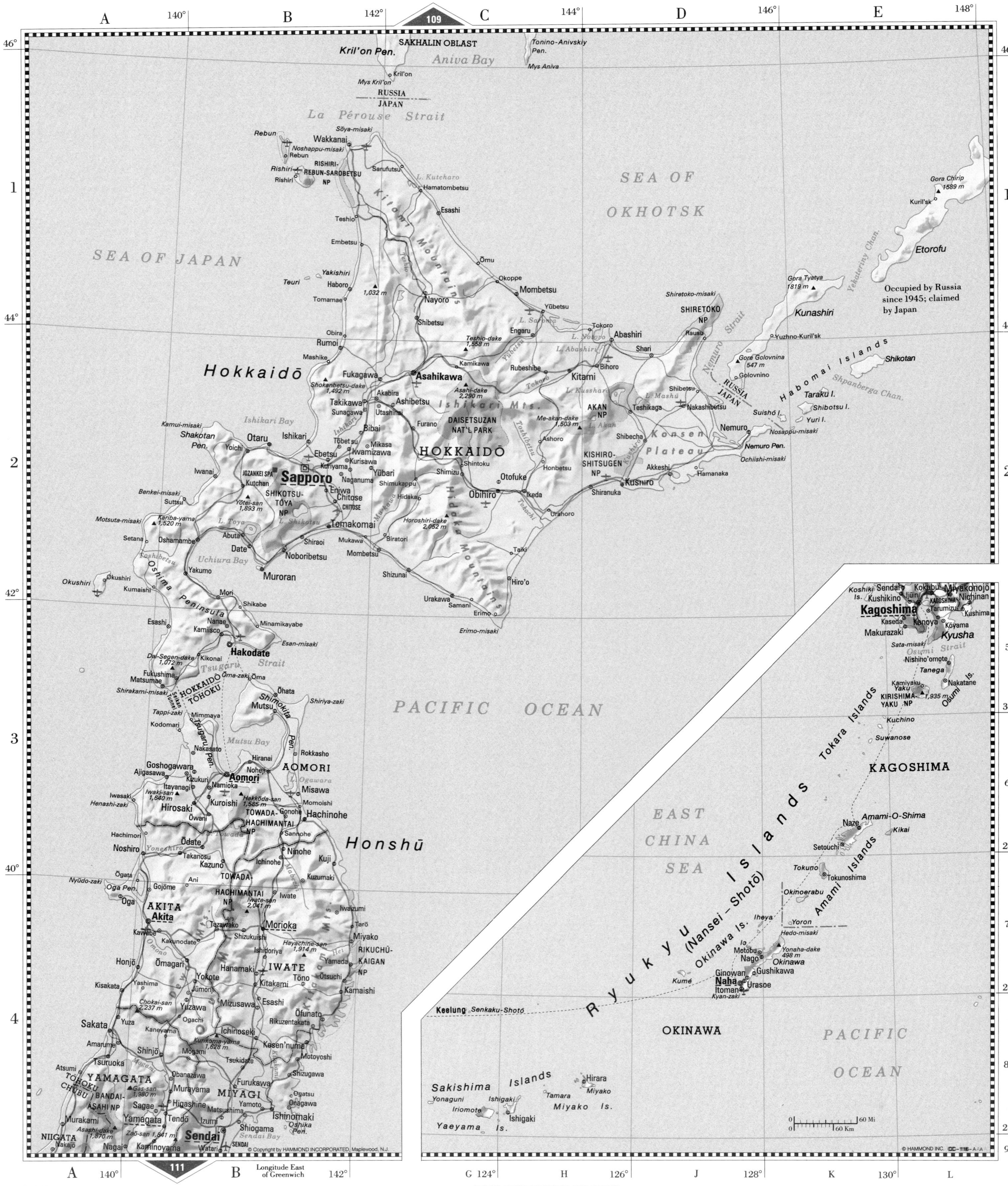


SCALE 1:3,000,000 LAMBERT CONFORMAL CONIC PROJECTION

MILES 0 | 50 | 100 | 150
KILOMETERS 0 | 50 | 100 | 150

POPULATION OF CITIES AND TOWNS

| | | | |
|---|---|---|---|
| ▣ OVER 2,000,000 | ◉ 500,000 - 999,999 | • 100,000 - 249,999 | ◎ 10,000 - 29,999 |
| ▢ 1,000,000 - 1,999,999 | ◎ 250,000 - 499,999 | ◎ 30,000 - 99,999 | ○ UNDER 10,000 |

# Korea

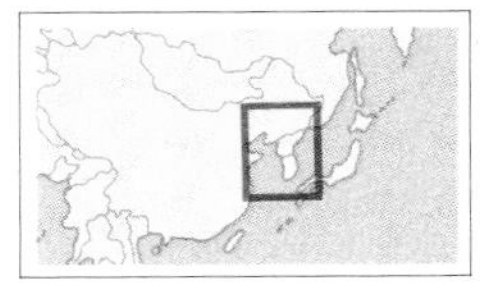

This peninsula has historically served as a bridge between three of the world's major cultures – Chinese, Russian and Japanese. In the early 20th century, Korea was annexed by Japan. After 1945, it was divided into a communist north and a pro-western south. Although devastated by war in 1950, South Korea slowly became a major industrial power after a truce in 1953.

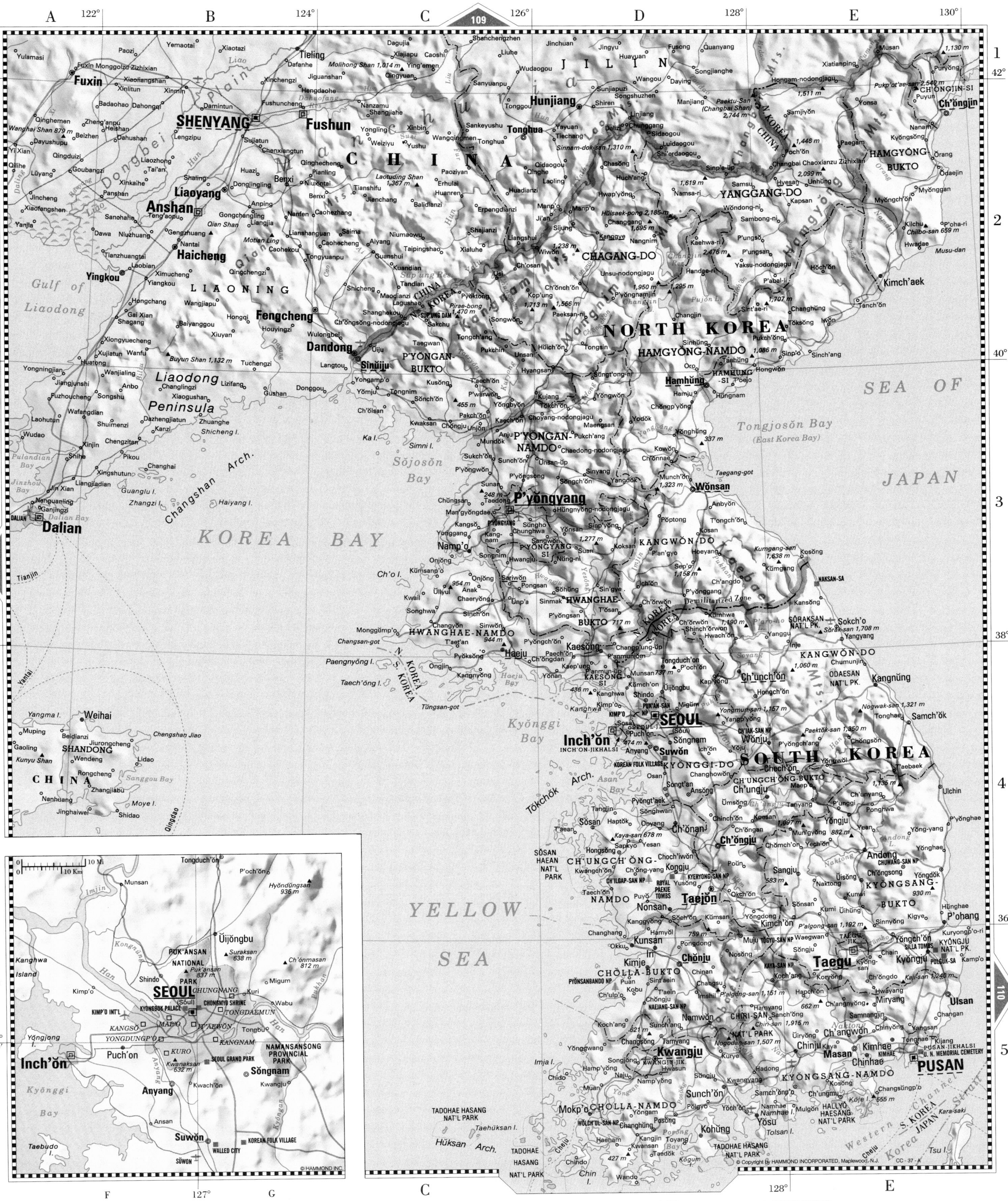


POPULATION OF CITIES AND TOWNS

- OVER 2,000,000
- 1,000,000 - 1,999,999
- 500,000 - 999,999
- 250,000 - 499,999
- 100,000 - 249,999
- 30,000 - 99,999
- 10,000 - 29,999
- UNDER 10,000

SCALE 1:3,000,000 LAMBERT CONFORMAL CONIC PROJECTION

MILES 0 50 100

KILOMETERS 0 50 100 150

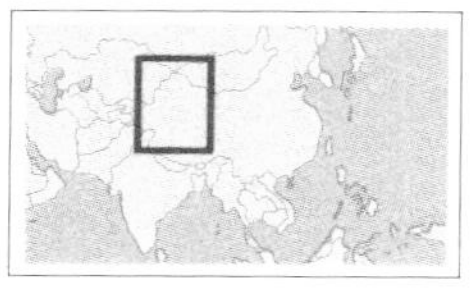

# Central Asia

Known as the "Roof of the World," central Asia is dominated by the vast mountain systems of the Hindu Kush, the Pamir, the Tien Shan and the Himalayas, extending over 1600 miles (2400 km.) from Pakistan to Bhutan. Although isolated, great civilizations – Post-Alexandrian Greece, Imperial China, the Indian empires, the Turks and Mongols – first met in this region.

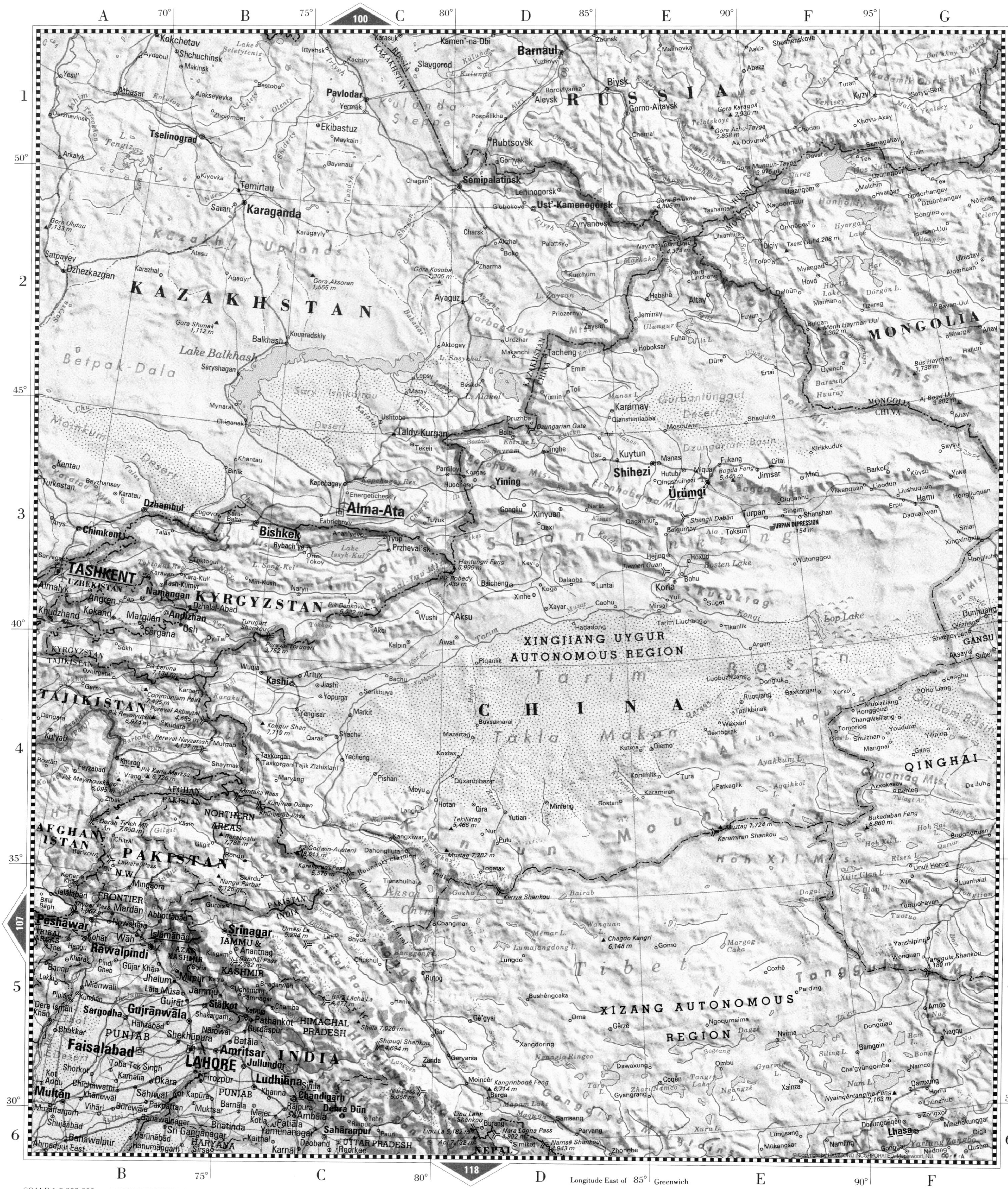


SCALE 1:9,000,000 LAMBERT CONFORMAL CONIC PROJECTION

MILES 0 150 300 450

KILOMETERS 0 150 300 450

POPULATION OF CITIES AND TOWNS

| | | | |
|---|---|---|---|
| OVER 2,000,000 | 500,000 - 999,999 | 100,000 - 249,999 | 10,000 - 29,999 |
| 1,000,000 - 1,999,999 | 250,000 - 499,999 | 30,000 - 99,999 | UNDER 10,000 |

# Northeastern China

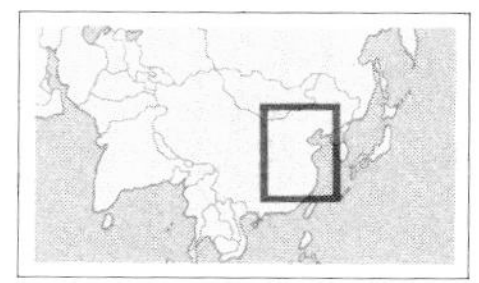

Around 2200 B.C., in the lower Huang (Yellow) River valley, there emerged a high-level Chinese civilization, probably based on the fertile, easily worked soil. Shandong province, a leading center for heavy industry, was once the home of teacher-philosopher Confucius (551-479 B.C.). Shanghai leads in the manufacture of precision and consumer goods.

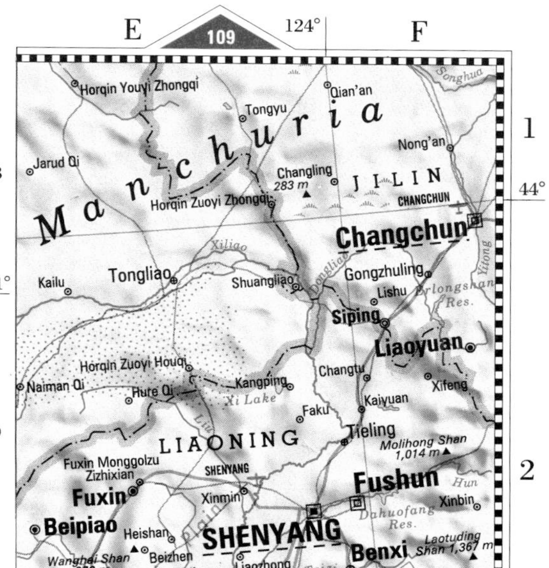

POPULATION OF CITIES AND TOWNS

| | | | |
|---|---|---|---|
| ■ OVER 2,000,000 | ◉ 500,000 - 999,999 | ● 100,000 - 249,999 | ○ 10,000 - 29,999 |
| ◻ 1,000,000 - 1,999,999 | ◎ 250,000 - 499,999 | • 30,000 - 99,999 | ∘ UNDER 10,000 |

SCALE 1:6,000,000 LAMBERT CONFORMAL CONIC PROJECTION

MILES 0 100 200 300

KILOMETERS 0 100 200 300

Southeastern China was once the backward, less developed part of the nation. In the last 20 years, growth has accelerated – particularly in Guangdong Province at Guangzhou (Canton) and nearby in the bustling new city of Shenzhen. Both cities owe their progress to their proximity to the British Crown Colony of Hong Kong, soon to be taken over by the People's Republic. Taiwan, the island refuge of the Nationalist government since 1949, has developed into a major manufacturing power, with a per capita income many times higher than that of the mainland.

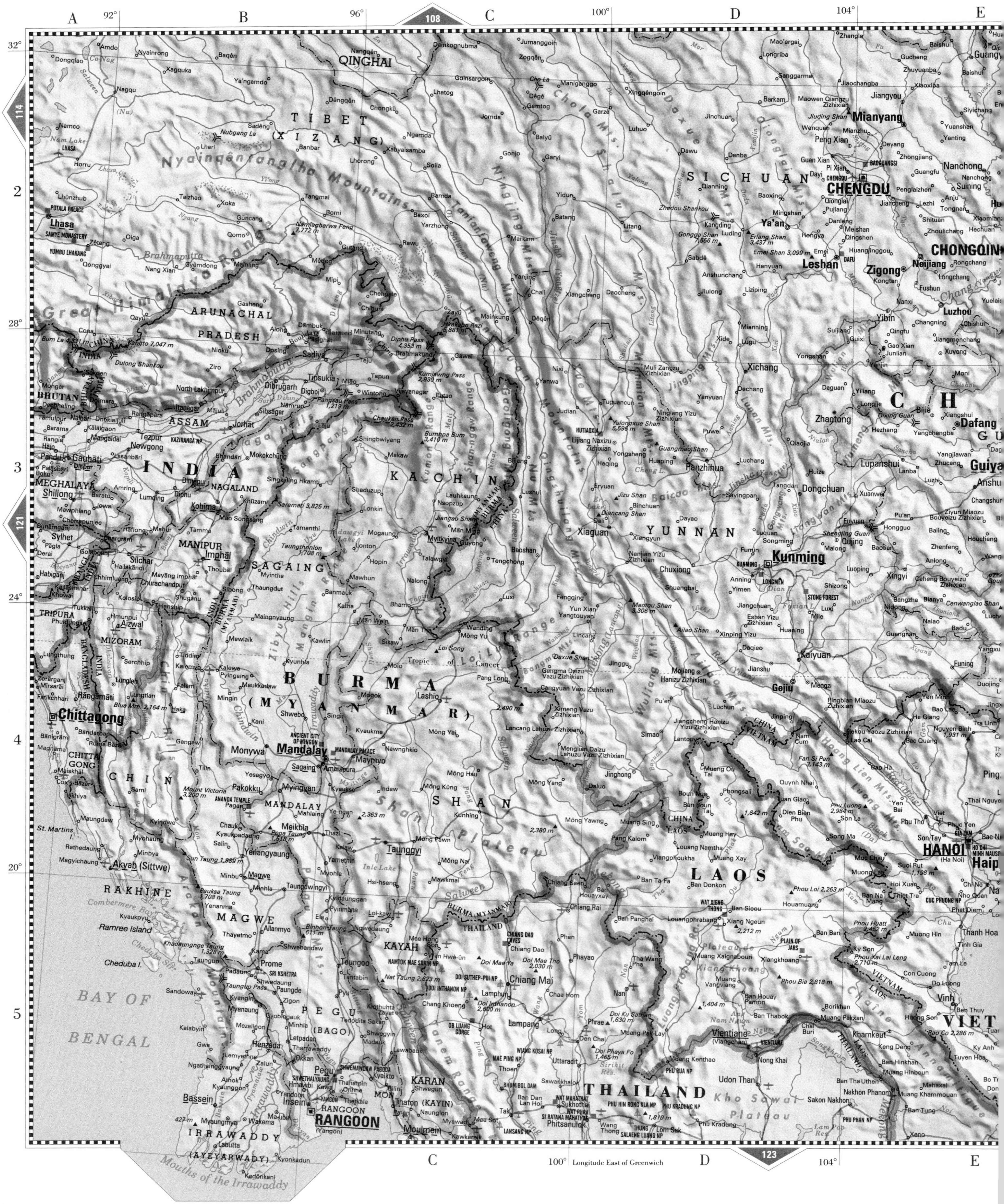

# Southeastern China, Burma

112° Longitude East of Greenwich

**POPULATION OF CITIES AND TOWNS**

| | | | |
|---|---|---|---|
| OVER 2,000,000 | 500,000 - 999,999 | 100,000 - 249,999 | 10,000 - 29,999 |
| 1,000,000 - 1,999,999 | 250,000 - 499,999 | 30,000 - 99,999 | UNDER 10,000 |

SCALE 1:6,000,000 LAMBERT CONFORMAL CONIC PROJECTION

MILES 0 100 200 300

KILOMETERS 0 100 200 300

This is the vast monsoon region of Asia. These yearly rains (monsoon is derived from the Arabic "mausim" or season) bring life-bearing moisture to the rice crops of India, Bangladesh and the Andaman Sea coasts. However, when the monsoon fails, or materializes in the form of great storms, tragedy can come to the populace as famine or flood. About half of the world's population lives in regions affected by monsoons, and the scale of demographic problems exceeds those found anywhere else in the world. Most of the work force is employed in subsistence agriculture.

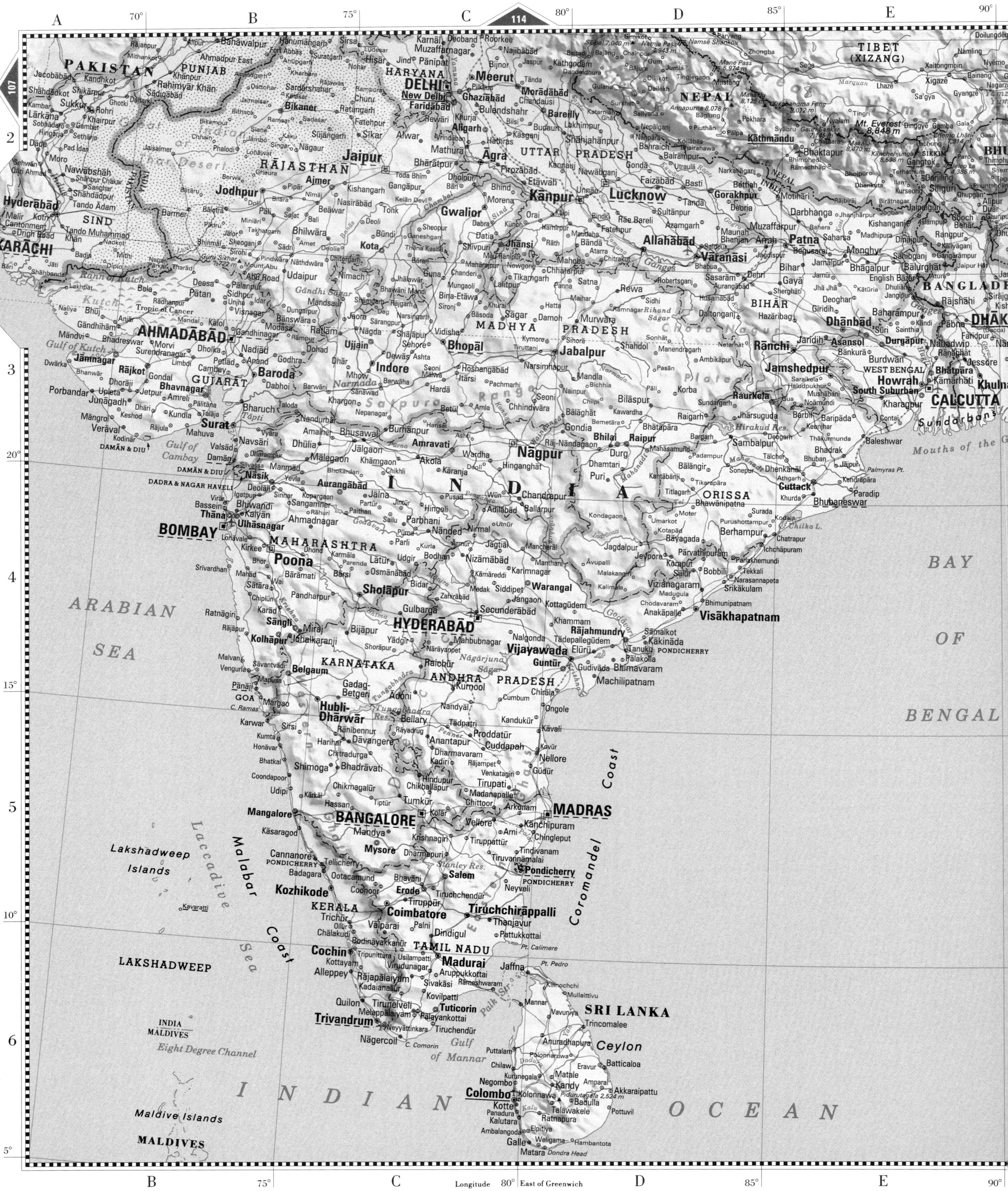

# Southern Asia

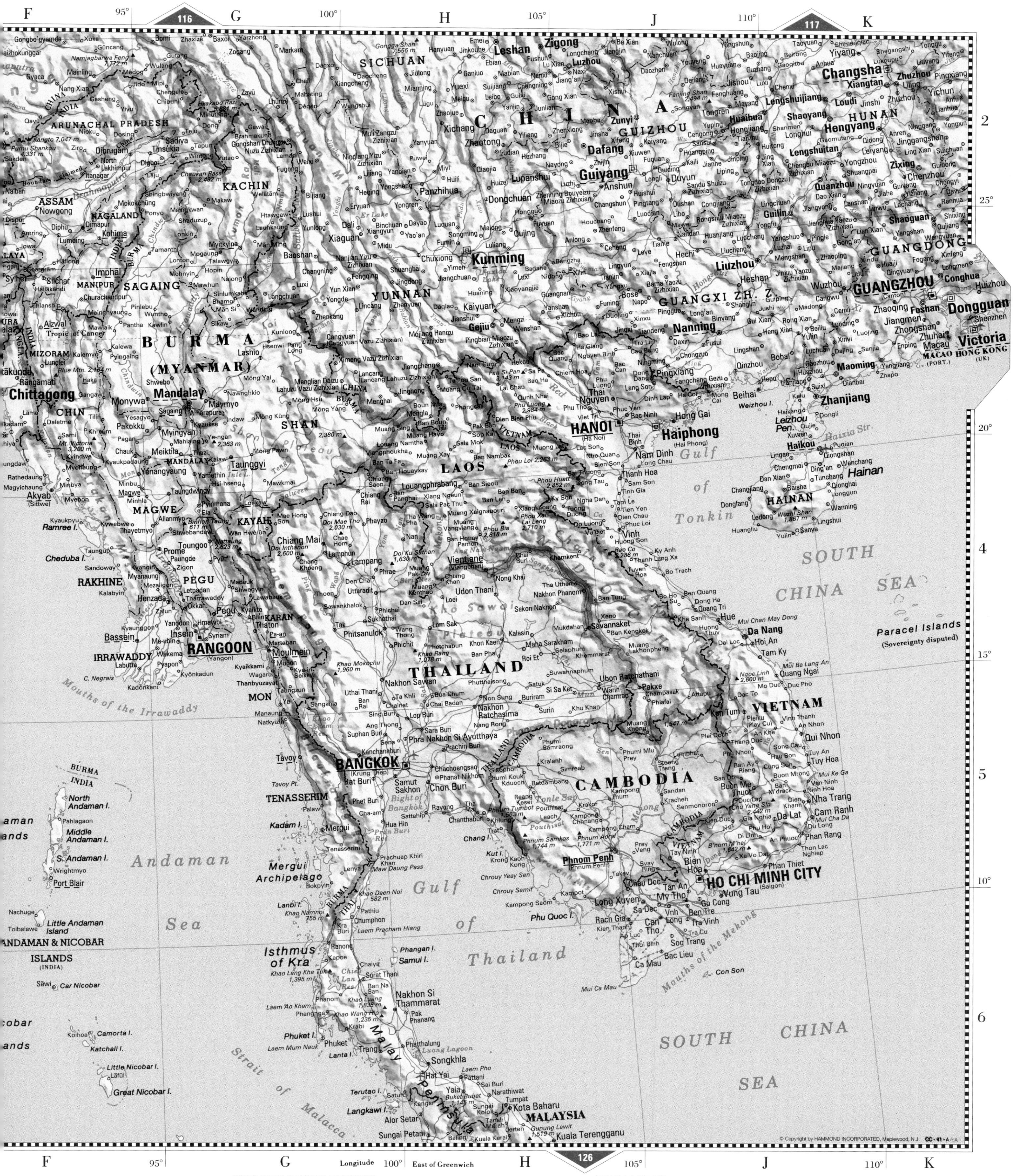


POPULATION OF CITIES AND TOWNS

| | | | |
|---|---|---|---|
| OVER 2,000,000 | 500,000 - 999,999 | 100,000 - 249,999 | 10,000 - 29,999 |
| 1,000,000 - 1,999,999 | 250,000 - 499,999 | 30,000 - 99,999 | UNDER 10,000 |

SCALE 1:9,000,000 LAMBERT CONFORMAL CONIC PROJECTION

MILES 0 150 300

KILOMETERS 0 150 300 450

This densely populated plain along the Ganges River is home to both peasant farmers and city dwellers. Two great Asian religions were born on this fertile soil. The holy city of Hinduism – Varanasi (Benares), sprouted on the banks of the sacred river. Buddha was born 150 miles (240 km.) to the north in Nepal, and attained enlightenment at the Bodh Gaya near Patna. The Ganges swings south, east of Patna, and works its way through the delta to the Bay of Bengal. To the north are the world's highest mountains, the Himalayas, including the great peak of Mt. Everest.

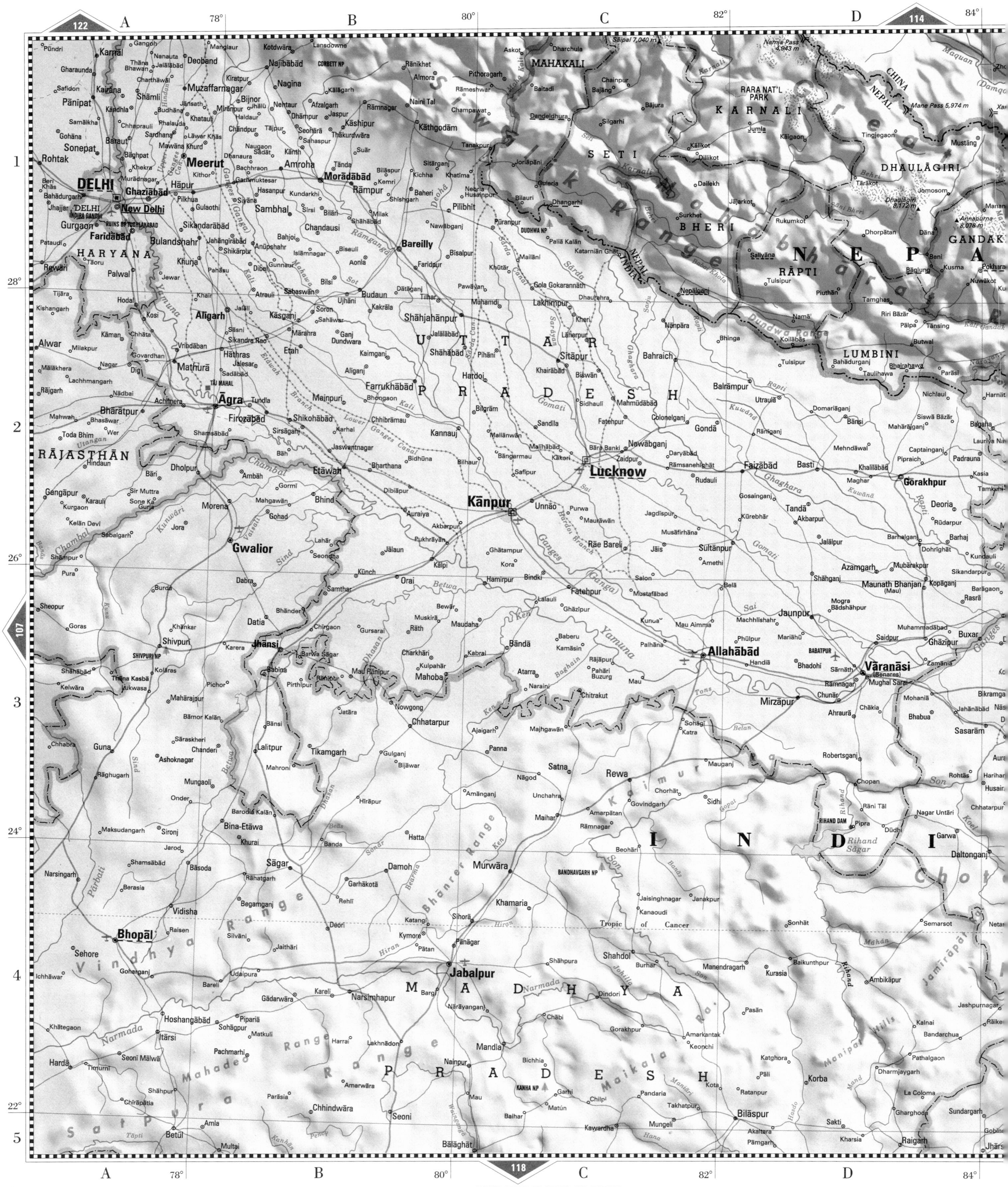


SCALE 1:3,000,000 LAMBERT CONFORMAL CONIC PROJECTION

MILES 0 50 100 150

KILOMETERS 0 50 100 150

POPULATION OF CITIES AND TOWNS

- OVER 2,000,000
- 1,000,000 - 1,999,999
- 500,000 - 999,999
- 250,000 - 499,999
- 100,000 - 249,999
- 30,000 - 99,999
- 10,000 - 29,999
- UNDER 10,000

# Ganges Plain

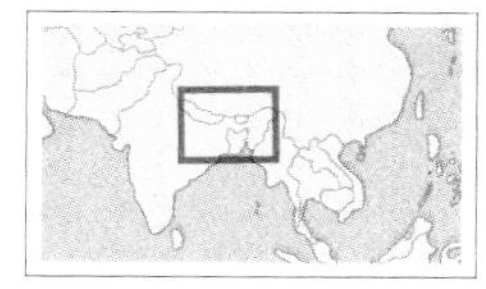

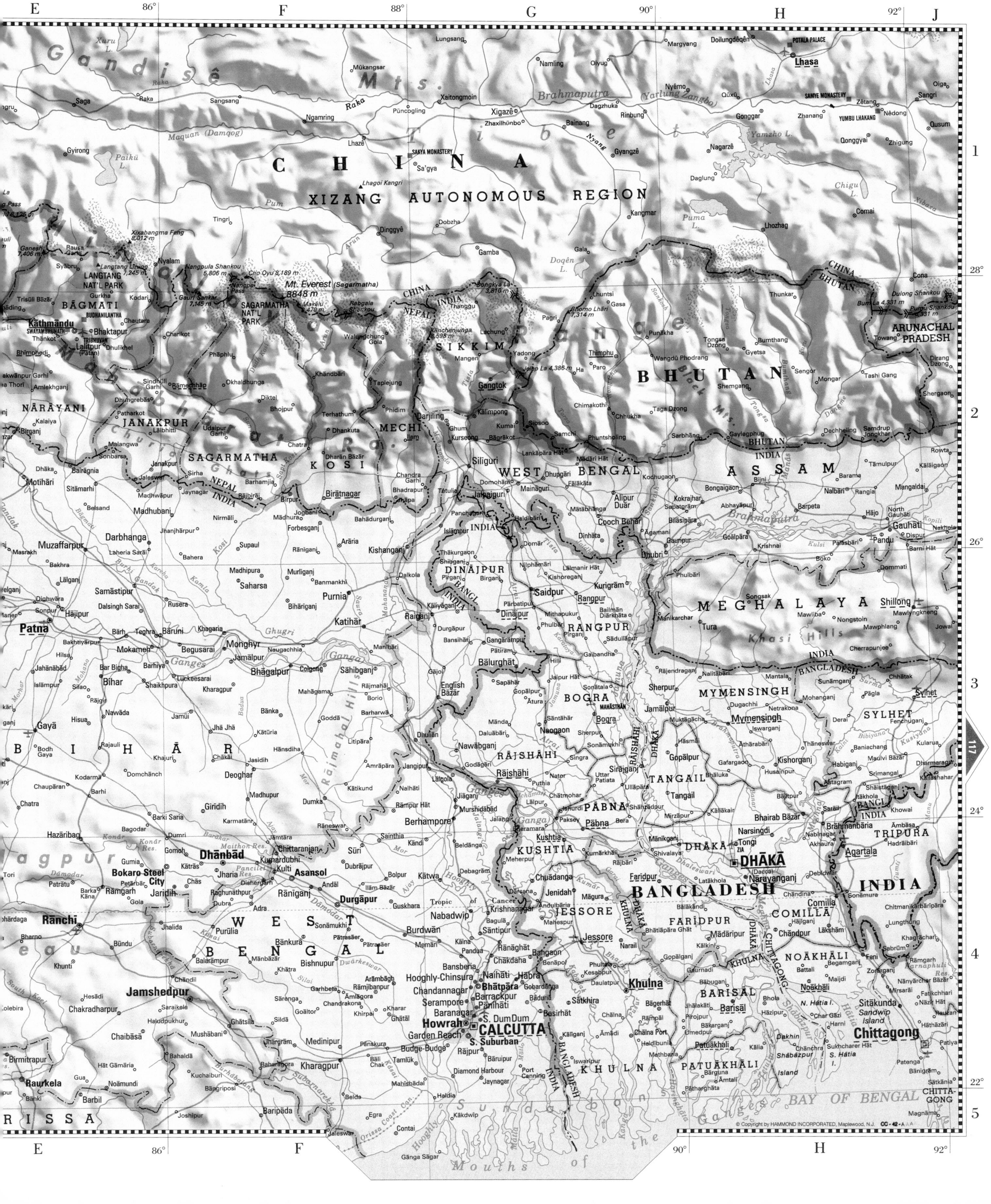

# Punjab Plain; Southern India

The fertile Punjab plain, formed by the Indus River and its tributaries, is the focus of intense religious and political conflict between a Muslim Pakistan and a predominantly Hindu India. India's Sikh separatist movement further compounds the tension. On the southern tip of India, across Palk Strait, Sri Lankan unity is threatened by Tamil separatists' demands.

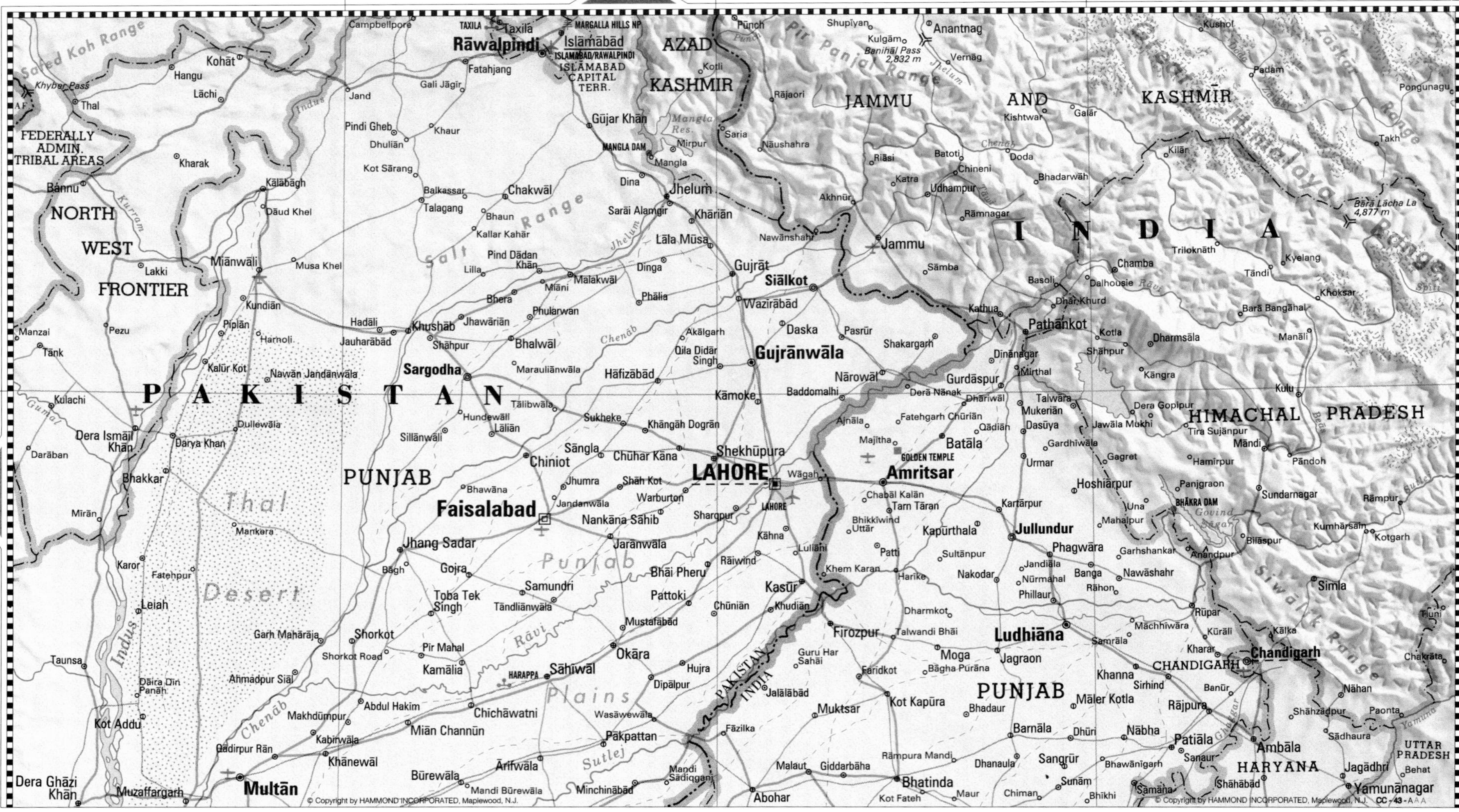


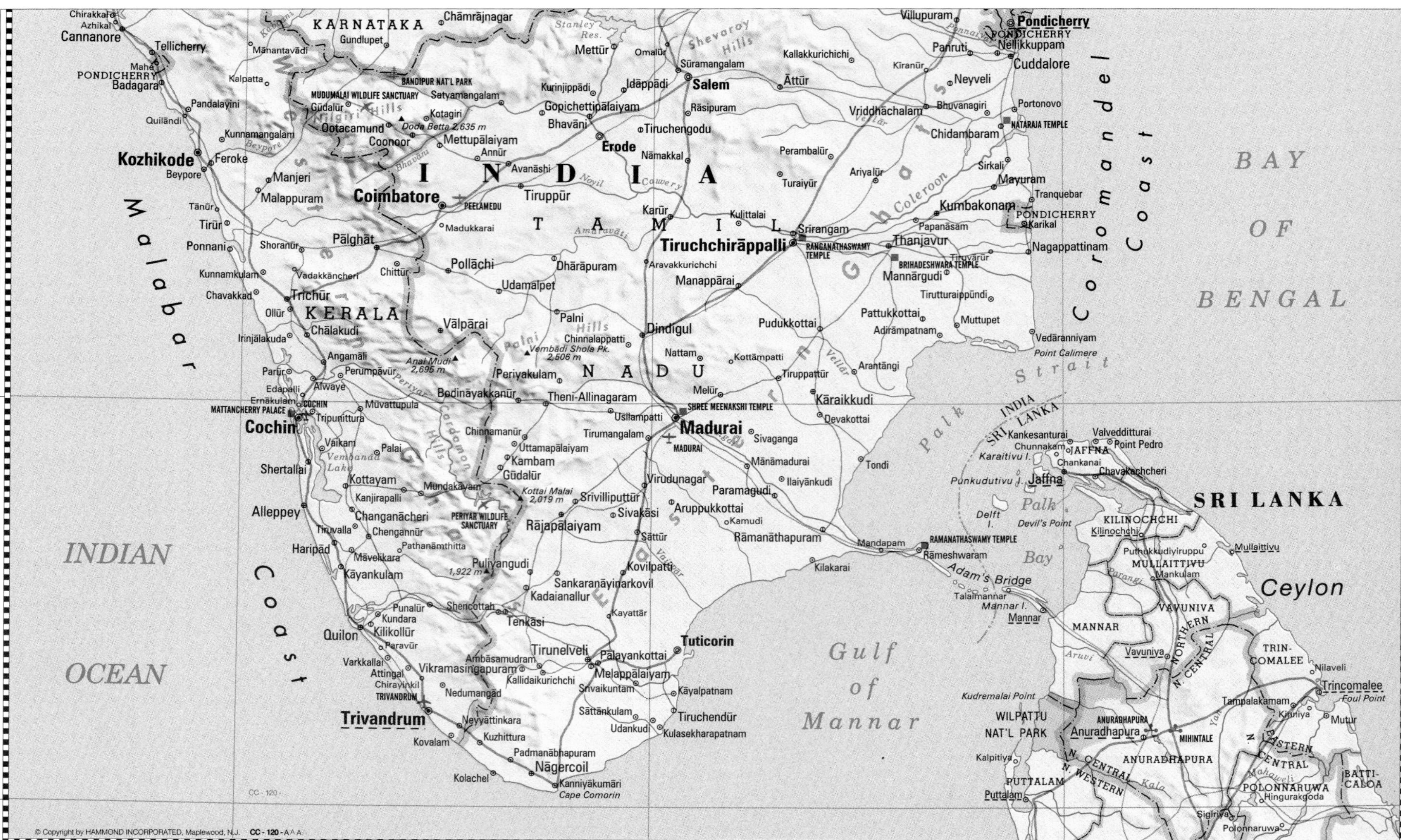


SCALE 1:3,000,000 LAMBERT CONFORMAL CONIC PROJECTION

MILES 0 50 100 150

KILOMETERS 0 50 100 150

POPULATION OF CITIES AND TOWNS

- OVER 2,000,000
- 1,000,000 - 1,999,999
- 500,000 - 999,999
- 250,000 - 499,999
- 100,000 - 249,999
- 30,000 - 99,999
- 10,000 - 29,999
- UNDER 10,000

# Eastern Burma, Thailand, Indochina

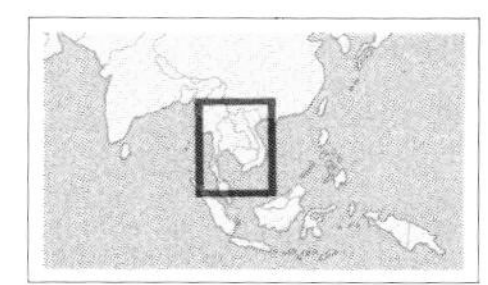

Centuries of conflict have given this rugged yet fertile "shatterbelt" a unique history. Early expansion from India was followed by Thai and Burmese inroads and Vietnamese moves south of the Red River Valley. China also sought control of the region. Britain and France held sway in the 1800s. Intervention in Vietnam is seen in the many speakers of French, English and Chinese.

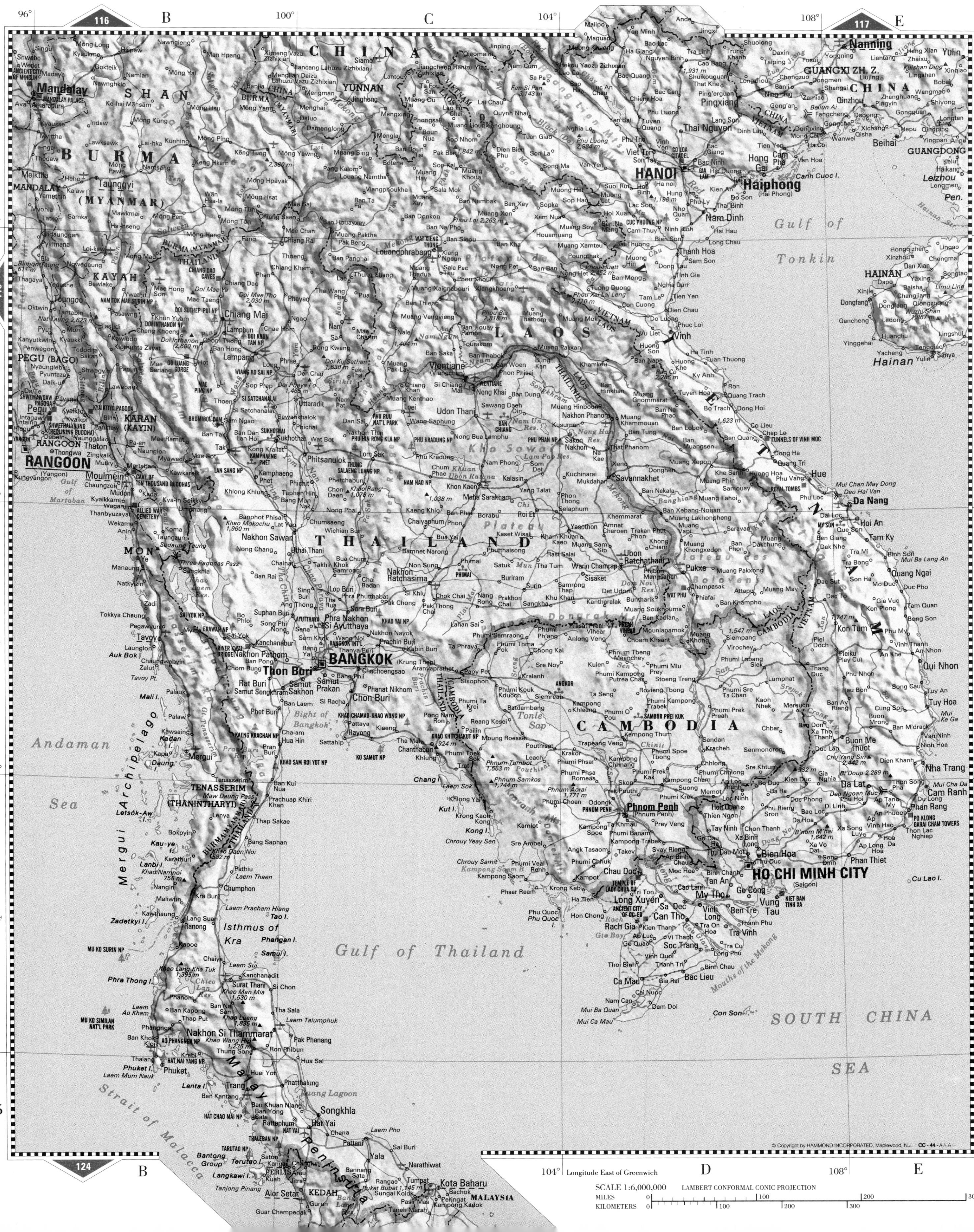


SCALE 1:6,000,000 LAMBERT CONFORMAL CONIC PROJECTION

MILES 0 100 200 300

KILOMETERS 0 100 200 300

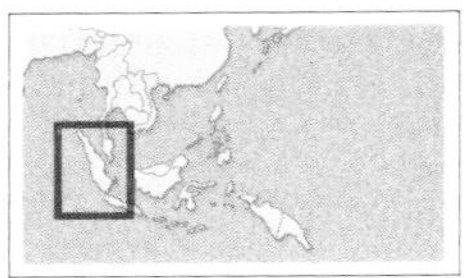

# Malaya, Sumatra, Java

Western Indonesia and mainland Malaysia are the eastern outposts of Islam, which swept the region around A.D. 1100. Today, Indonesia is the most populous Islamic nation on earth; only Bali retains the original Hindu faith of the medieval Indies. Malaysia's maritime location and rich harvests of fish, lumber, tin and rubber have produced one of the region's most successful economies.

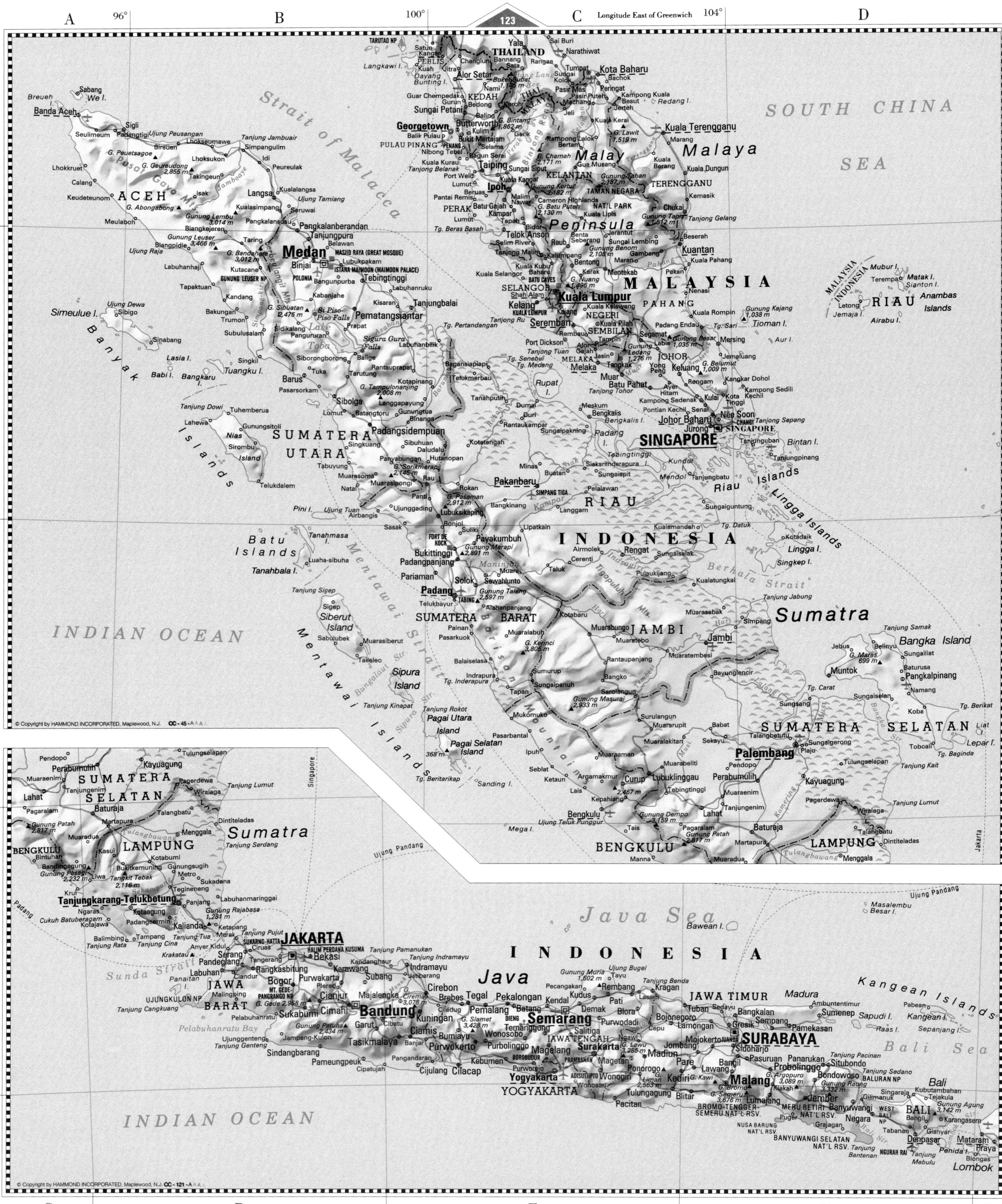


SCALE 1:6,000,000 LAMBERT CONFORMAL CONIC PROJECTION

MILES 0 100 200 300
KILOMETERS 0 100 200 300

POPULATION OF CITIES AND TOWNS

- OVER 2,000,000
- 1,000,000 - 1,999,999
- 500,000 - 999,999
- 250,000 - 499,999
- 100,000 - 249,999
- 30,000 - 99,999
- 10,000 - 29,999
- UNDER 10,000

# Philippines

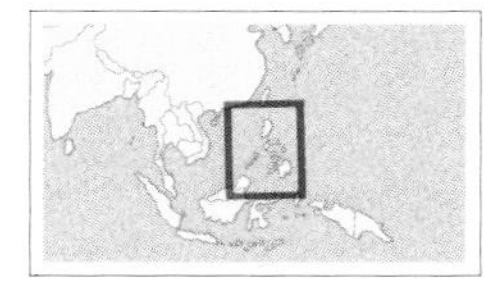

Of the 7,000 islands which make up the Philippines, roughly one in ten are inhabited. The original residents were predominately of Malay stock. From 1565 to 1898, the Philippines were ruled by Spain, which made the Philippines a bastion of Roman Catholicism in East Asia. The following 48 years of United States rule left an equally Western imprint on the national character.

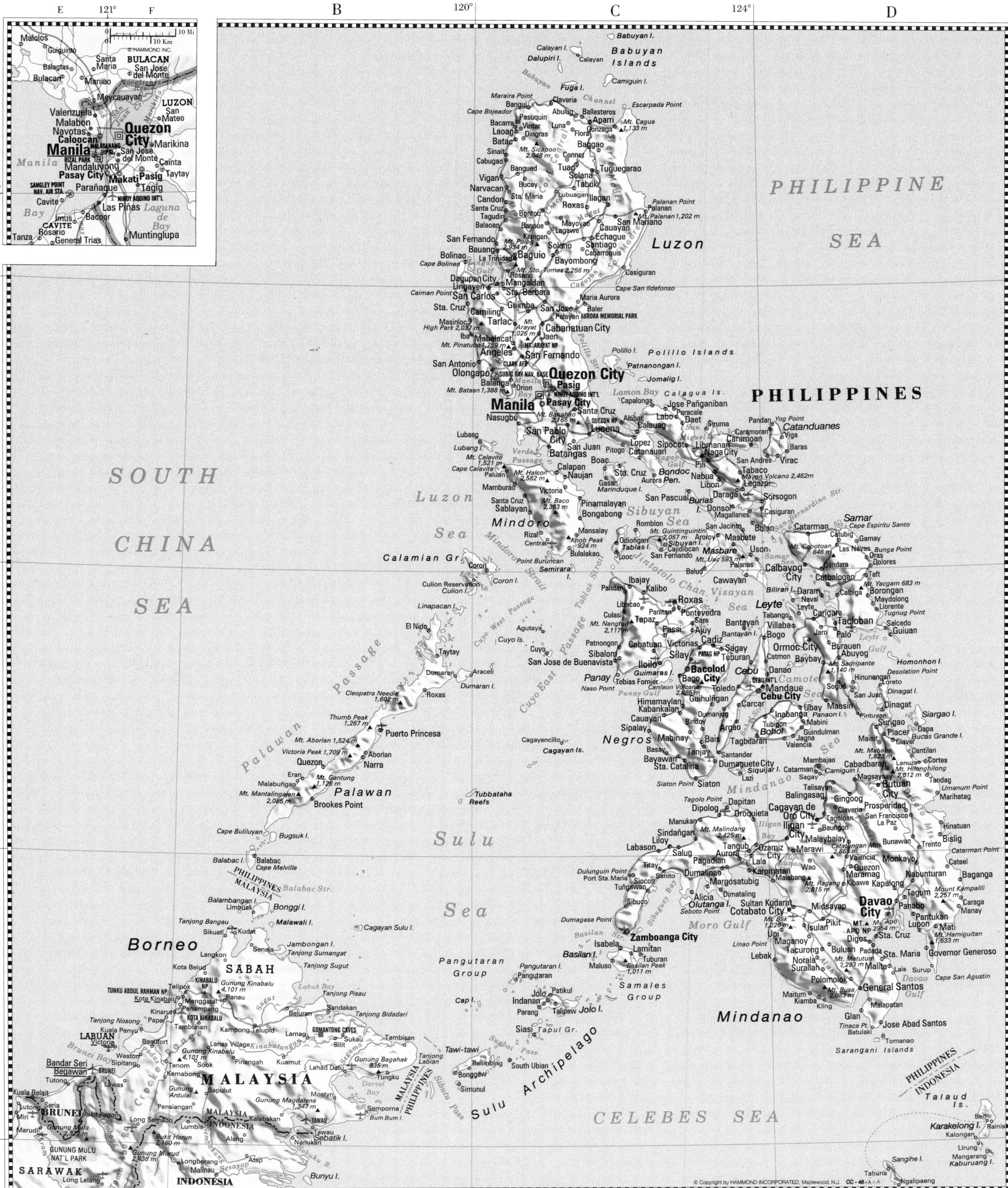


POPULATION OF CITIES AND TOWNS

- OVER 2,000,000
- 1,000,000 - 1,999,999
- 500,000 - 999,999
- 250,000 - 499,999
- 100,000 - 249,999
- 30,000 - 99,999
- 10,000 - 29,999
- UNDER 10,000

SCALE 1:6,000,000 LAMBERT CONFORMAL CONIC PROJECTION

MILES 0 100 200 300

KILOMETERS 0 100 200 300

From "stone age" New Guinea in the east, to mystical Bali, Southeast Asia has been the inspiration for centuries of exotic island fantasies. Here are the Moluccas, the original Spice Islands coveted by European adventurers in the 16th century. Hindu culture that once flourished throughout the archipelago has declined. Java, with its volcano-enriched soils, supports 80 million people. The nearby volcano Krakatoa erupted in 1883, taking thousands of lives. To the north, in Borneo, commercial loggers are stripping away what is left of the rain forest.

SCALE 1:9,000,000 LAMBERT CONFORMAL CONIC PROJECTION

MILES 0 150 300 450

KILOMETERS 0 150 300 450

POPULATION OF CITIES AND TOWNS

- OVER 2,000,000
- 1,000,000 - 1,999,999
- 500,000 - 999,999
- 250,000 - 499,999
- 100,000 - 249,999
- 30,000 - 99,999
- 10,000 - 29,999
- UNDER 10,000

# Southeast Asia

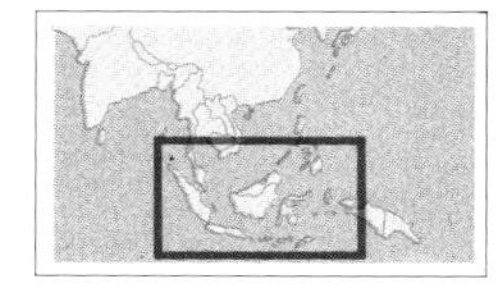

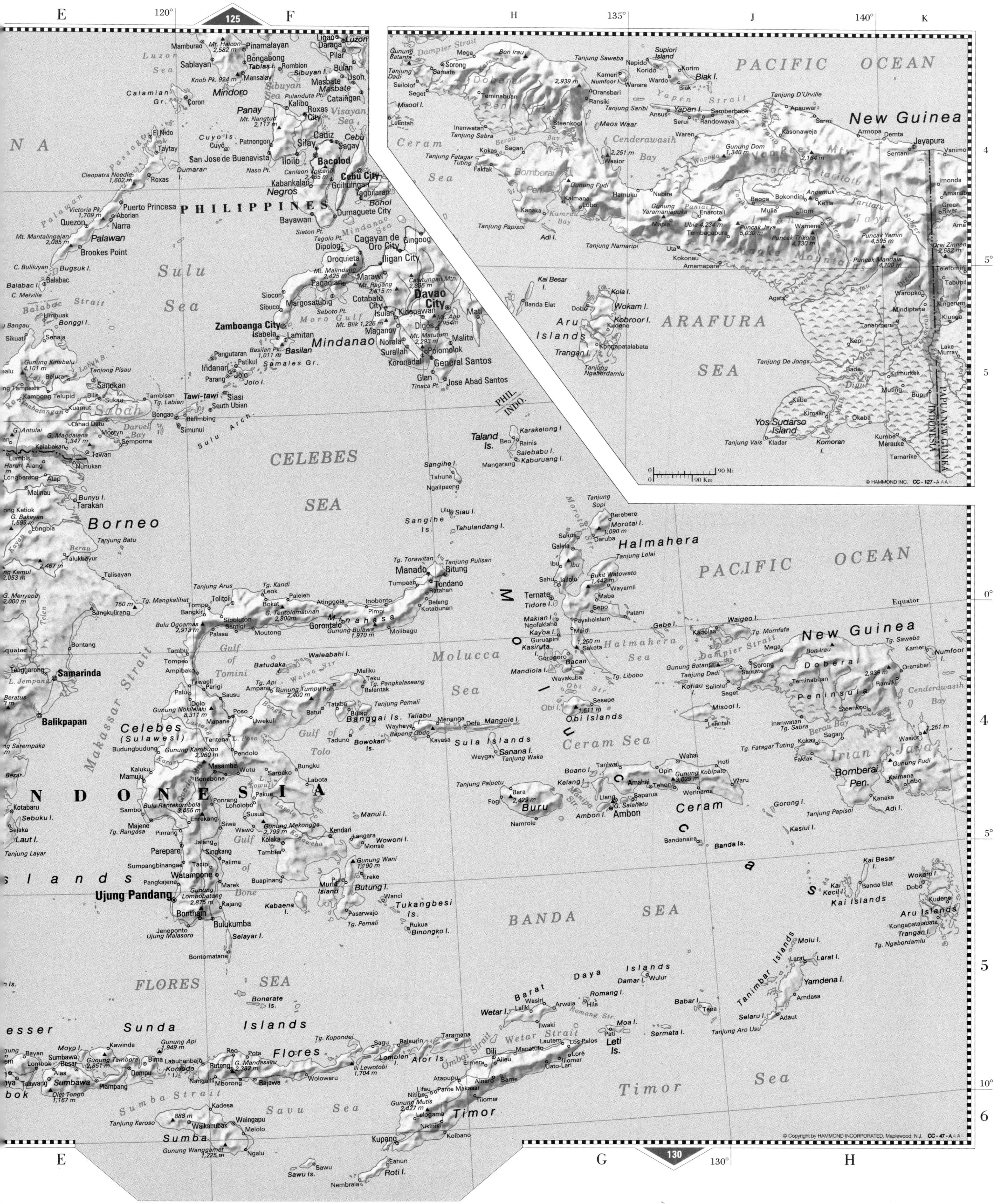

Australia, the world's smallest continent, lies far from its predominantly English cultural roots. Its population is clustered in a few major coastal cities. Long before it was first sighted by European explorers in the 17th century, Australia was inhabited by a number of primitive native groups with various languages and customs. In 1770, Captain James Cook explored the east coast and claimed it for Great Britain. Within 50 years, the whole continent became a British dependency. In 1901 its separate colonies federated into the Commonwealth of Australia.

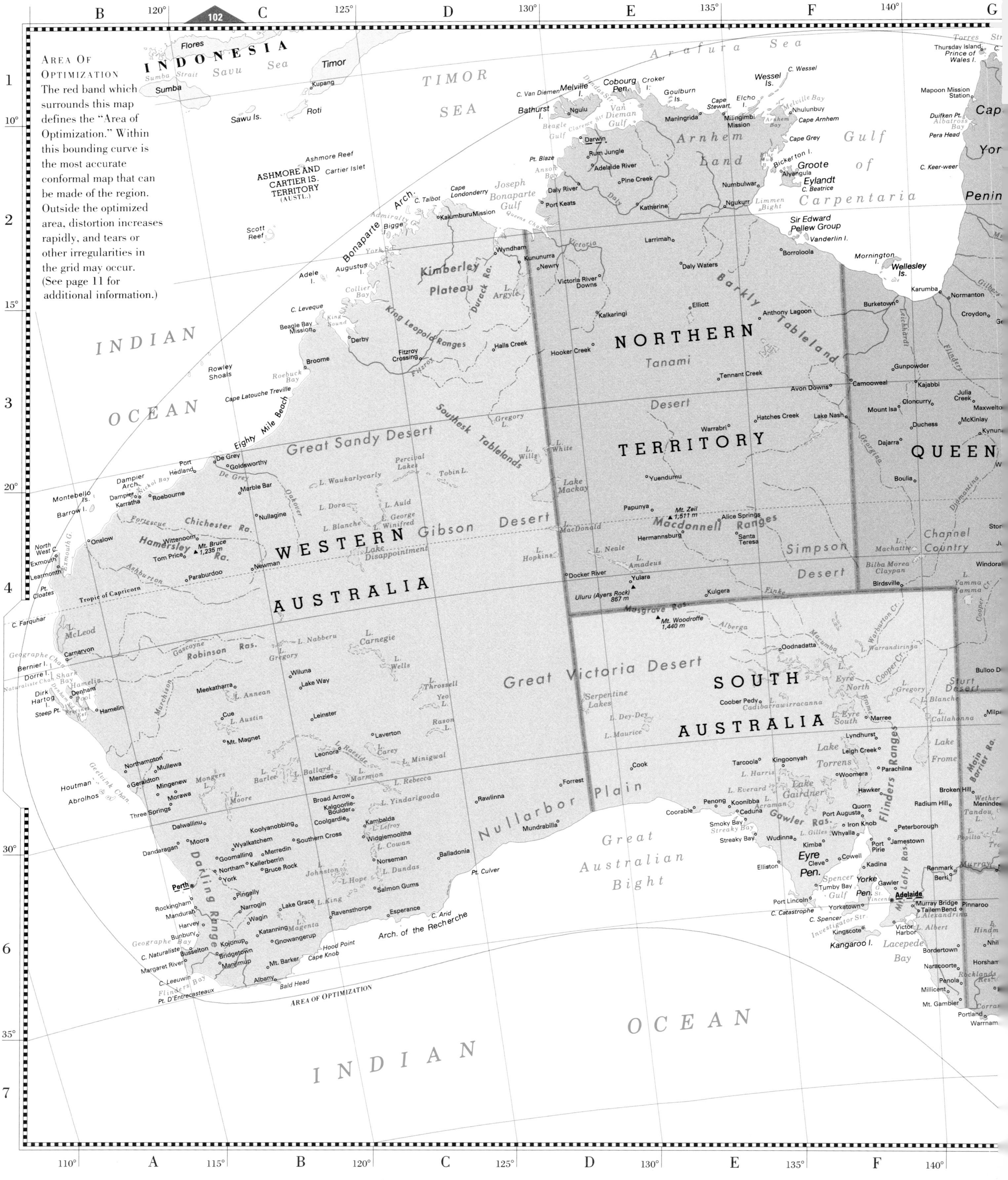

# Australia

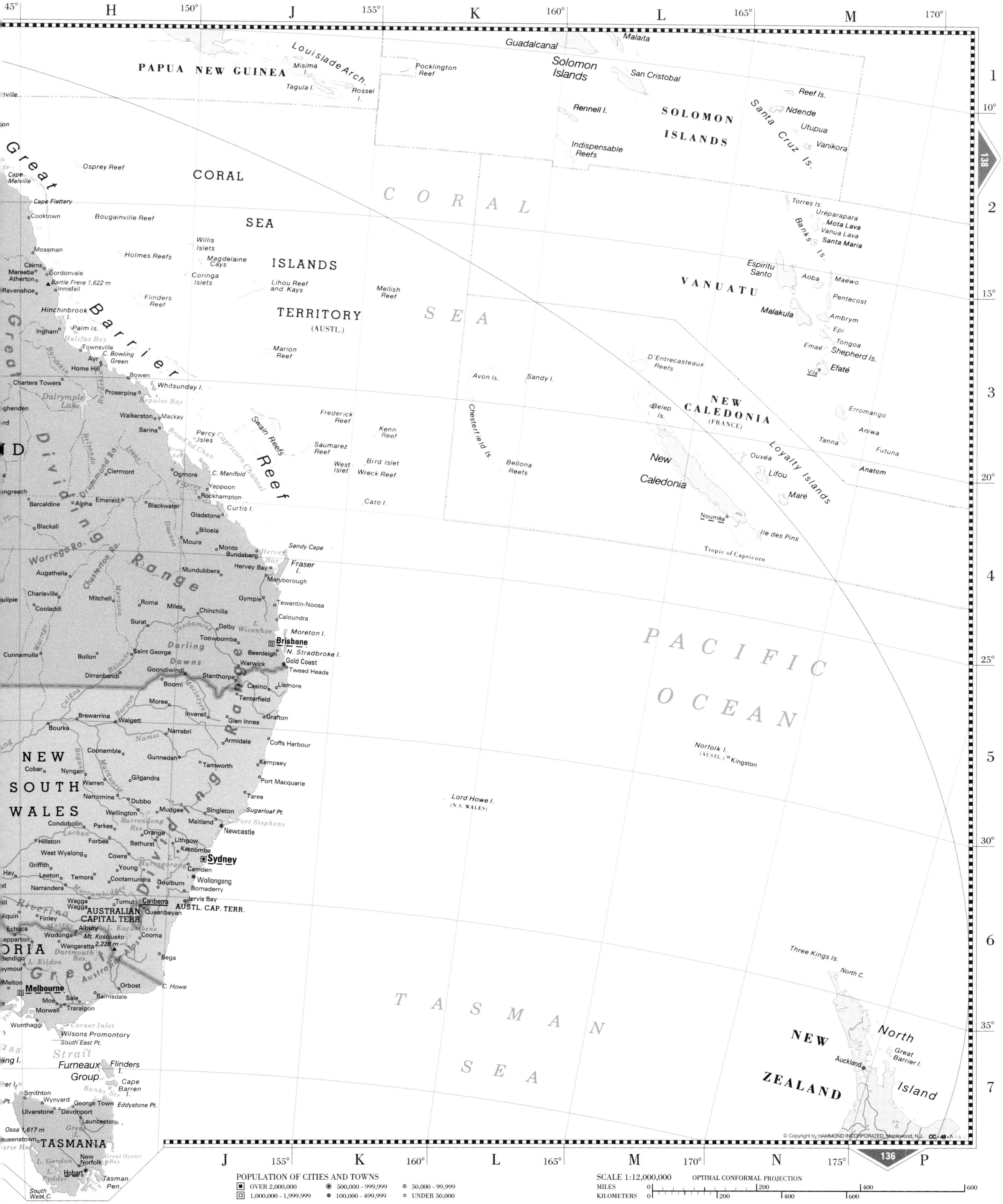

H
J
K
L
M
150°
155°
160°
165°
170°
PAPUA NEW GUINEA
Louisiade Arch.
Misima I.
Tagula I.
Rossel I.
Pocklington Reef
Guadalcanal
Malaita
Solomon Islands
San Cristobal
Rennell I.
SOLOMON ISLANDS
Indispensable Reefs
Reef Is.
Ndende
Utupua
Vanikora
Santa Cruz Is.
138
Osprey Reef
CORAL
SEA
ISLANDS
TERRITORY
(AUSTL.)
Great Barrier Reef
Cape Melville
Cape Flattery
Cooktown
Bougainville Reef
Mossman
Holmes Reefs
Willis Islets
Magdelaine Cays
Coringa Islets
Cairns
Mareeba
Atherton
Gordonvale
Bartle Frere 1,622 m
Innisfail
Ravenshoe
Flinders Reef
Lihou Reef and Kays
Mellish Reef
CORAL SEA
Torres Is.
Ureparapara
Mota Lava
Vanua Lava
Santa Maria
Banks Is.
Espiritu Santo
Aoba
Maewo
VANUATU
Pentecost
Malakula
Ambrym
Epi
Tongoa
Emae
Shepherd Is.
Vila
Efaté
Hinchinbrook I.
Palm Is.
Ingham
Halifax Bay
Townsville
Ayr
C. Bowling Green
Home Hill
Marion Reef
D'Entrecasteaux Reefs
Avon Is.
Sandy I.
Bowen
Whitsunday I.
Charters Towers
Dalrymple Lake
Proserpine
Repulse Bay
Mackay
Walkerston
Sarina
Broad Sd.
Broad Sd. Chan.
Swain Reefs
Frederick Reef
Kenn Reef
Percy Isles
Capricorn Channel
Saumarez Reef
Chesterfield Is.
Belep Is.
NEW CALEDONIA
(FRANCE)
Erromango
Aniwa
Tanna
Futuna
Anatom
Ouvéa
Loyalty Islands
Lifou
Maré
New Caledonia
Nouméa
Ile des Pins
Bellona Reefs
West Islet
Bird Islet
Wreck Reef
Cato I.
Clermont
Drummond Ra.
Belyando
Isaac
Ogmore
C. Manifold
Yeppoon
Fitzroy
Rockhampton
Emerald
Alpha
Barcaldine
Blackwater
Gladstone
Curtis I.
Blackall
Dawson
Biloela
Moura
Monto
Bundaberg
Hervey Bay
Sandy Cape
Fraser I.
Maryborough
Mundubbera
Warrego Ra.
Chesterton Ra.
Augathella
Great Dividing Range
Charleville
Cooladdi
Mitchell
Maranoa
Roma
Miles
Chinchilla
Gympie
Tewantin-Noosa
Caloundra
Surat
Condamine
Dalby
L. Wivenhoe
Toowoomba
Moreton I.
Brisbane
Beenleigh
N. Stradbroke I.
Darling Downs
Warwick
Gold Coast
Tweed Heads
Cunnamulla
Bollon
Saint George
Balonne
Goondiwindi
Dirranbandi
Stanthorpe
Boomi
Macintyre
Casino
Lismore
Tenterfield
Tropic of Capricorn
PACIFIC
OCEAN
Moree
Culgoa
Barwon
Brewarrina
Walgett
Inverell
Glen Innes
Grafton
Bourke
Namoi
Narrabri
Armidale
Coffs Harbour
NEW SOUTH WALES
Coonamble
Bogan
Cobar
Nyngan
Gunnedah
Tamworth
Kempsey
Macquarie
Gilgandra
Warren
Port Macquarie
Norfolk I.
(AUSTL.)
Kingston
Narromine
Dubbo
Taree
Mudgee
Singleton
Sugarloaf Pt.
Wellington
Maitland
Port Stephens
Condobolin
Parkes
Burrendong Res.
Lachlan
Orange
Newcastle
Lord Howe I.
(N.S. WALES)
Hillston
Forbes
Bathurst
Lithgow
Katoomba
West Wyalong
Cowra
Sydney
Griffith
Young
Burragorang
Camden
Hay
Leeton
Temora
Cootamundra
Goulburn
Wollongong
Narrandera
Murrumbidgee
Bomaderry
Riverina
Wagga Wagga
Tumut
Canberra
Jervis Bay
AUSTL. CAP. TERR.
AUSTRALIAN CAPITAL TERR.
Queanbeyan
Deniliquin
Finley
Murray
Echuca
Albury
Wodonga
L. Eucumbene
Mt. Kosciusko 2,228 m
Cooma
Shepparton
Wangaratta
Dartmouth Res.
VICTORIA
Bendigo
L. Eildon
Seymour
Australian Alps
Bega
Three Kings Is.
North C.
Melton
Melbourne
Orbost
C. Howe
Moe
Sale
Bairnsdale
Morwell
Traralgon
TASMAN
SEA
Wonthaggi
Corner Inlet
Wilsons Promontory
South East Pt.
Bass Strait
King I.
Furneaux Group
Flinders I.
Cape Barren I.
Banks Str.
NEW ZEALAND
North Island
Great Barrier I.
Auckland
Smithton
Wynyard
George Town
Eddystone Pt.
Ulverstone
Devonport
Launceston
Ossa 1,617 m
Great L.
Queenstown
TASMANIA
Macquarie Har.
L. Gordon
New Norfolk
Great Oyster Bay
Pedder
Hobart
Tasman Pen.
South West C.
© Copyright by HAMMOND INCORPORATED, Maplewood, N.J.
1
2
3
4
5
6
7
10°
15°
20°
25°
30°
35°
N
P
175°
136
POPULATION OF CITIES AND TOWNS
OVER 2,000,000
1,000,000 - 1,999,999
500,000 - 999,999
100,000 - 499,999
50,000 - 99,999
UNDER 50,000
SCALE 1:12,000,000
OPTIMAL CONFORMAL PROJECTION
MILES 0 200 400 600
KILOMETERS 0 200 400 600

New Guinea was probably first occupied at the same time as Australia, 50,000 to 70,000 years ago. A large population of Papuan highlanders were first encountered by Westerners as late as 1933. A number of intense battles occurred during World War II in New Guinea as the Japanese sought to isolate Australia. Australia's development began with the establishment of colonies in New South Wales in 1788. The native Aborigines were gradually displaced, and their numbers declined. Most now live in the Northern Territory and the Cape York area of Queensland.

# Papua New Guinea, Northern Australia

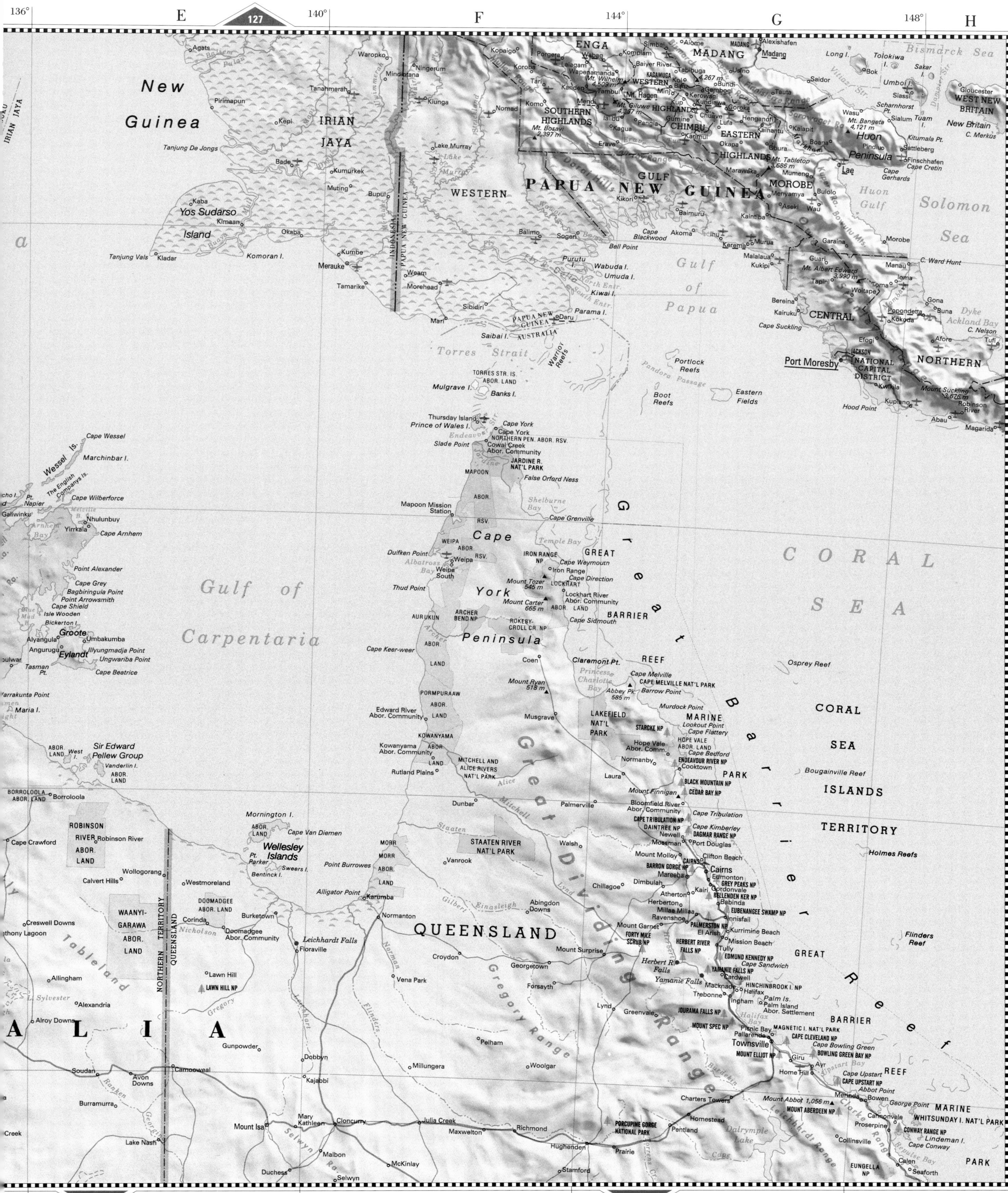


POPULATION OF CITIES AND TOWNS

| | | | |
|---|---|---|---|
| OVER 2,000,000 | 500,000 - 999,999 | 100,000 - 249,999 | 10,000 - 29,999 |
| 1,000,000 - 1,999,999 | 250,000 - 499,999 | 30,000 - 99,999 | UNDER 10,000 |

SCALE 1:6,000,000 LAMBERT CONFORMAL CONIC PROJECTION

MILES 0 100 200 300

KILOMETERS 0 100 200 300

Australia is covered by more desert terrain for its size than any other inhabited continent, most of it in the "outback," home to three distinct deserts and Lake Disappointment. Sheep and cattle graze along the fringes of the arid lands, but moist,parts of coastal lowlands near Perth and Adelaide support cultivation. Major iron ore deposits are found in the Hamersley Range, while gold is mined near the southern town of Kalgoorlie. The isolated scenic monolith, Uluru (Ayers Rock), in the Northern Territory, has strange caves and ancient Aboriginal paintings and carvings.

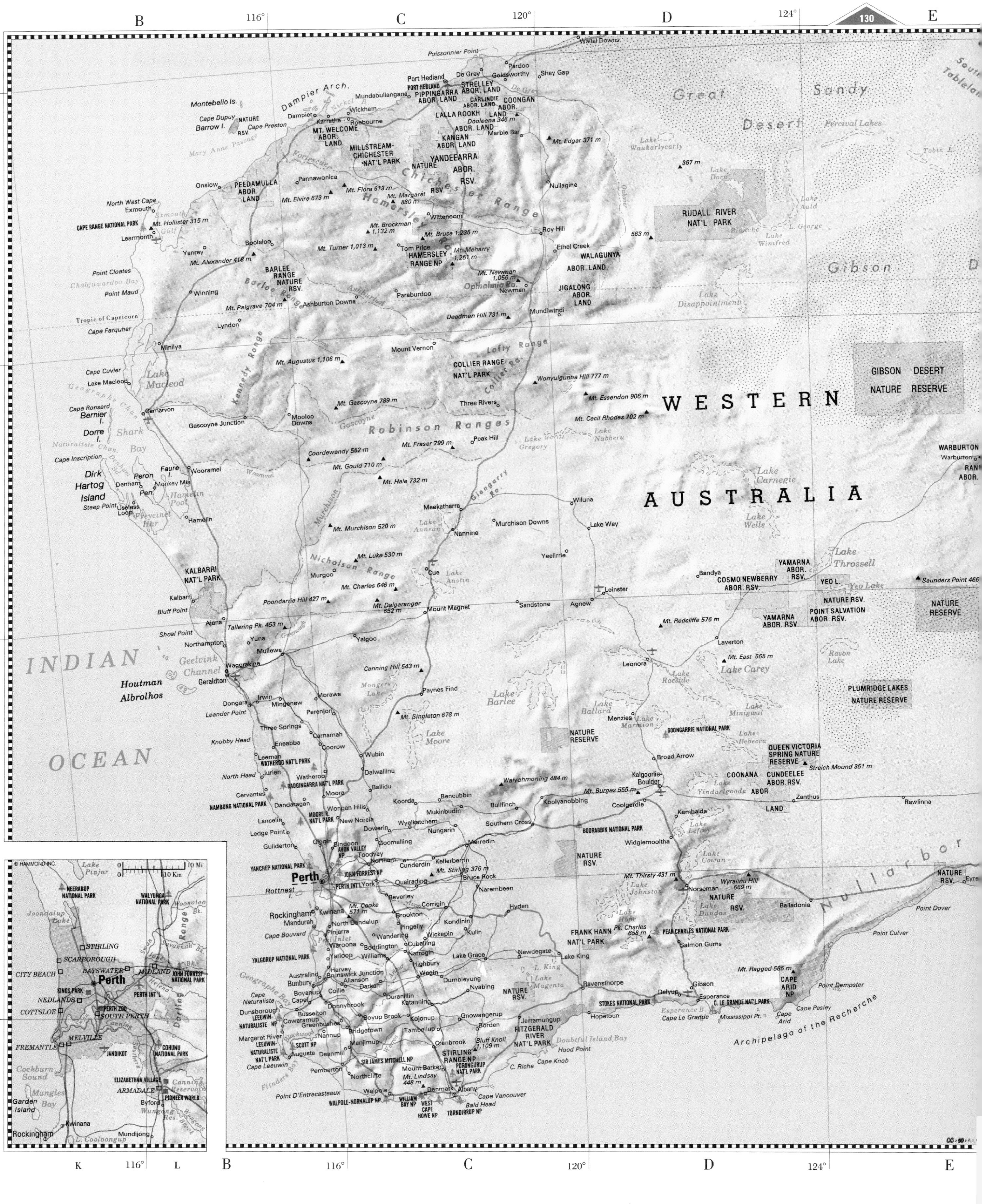

# Western and Central Australia

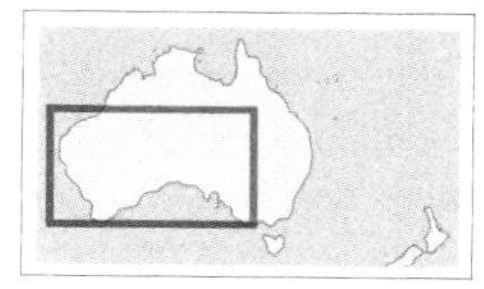

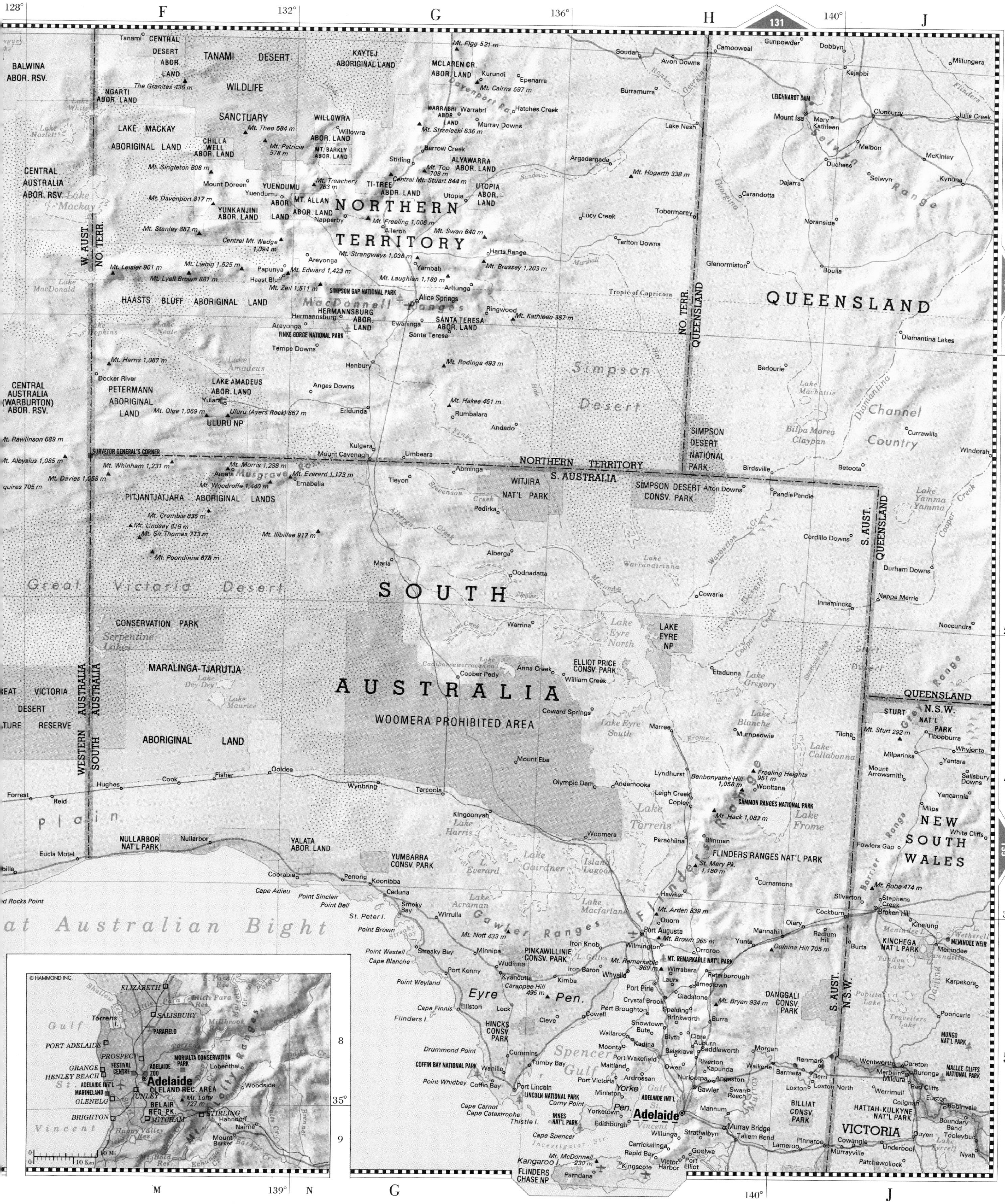


POPULATION OF CITIES AND TOWNS

| | | | |
|---|---|---|---|
| ■ OVER 2,000,000 | ◉ 500,000 - 999,999 | ⊕ 100,000 - 249,999 | ○ 10,000 - 29,999 |
| ▣ 1,000,000 - 1,999,999 | ◎ 250,000 - 499,999 | ⊕ 30,000 - 99,999 | ○ UNDER 10,000 |

SCALE 1:6,000,000 LAMBERT CONFORMAL CONIC PROJECTION

MILES 0 100 200 300

KILOMETERS 0 100 200 300

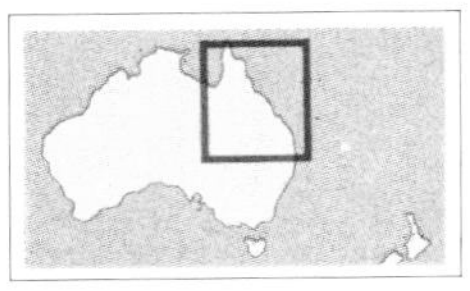

# Northeastern Australia

This is the Australian tropics, complete with rain forests and sugar cane plantations following the coastline as far south as Brisbane. The tropical rain forest thrives along the Queensland coast. Offshore, the Great Barrier Reef – the world's largest complex of coral islands, shoals and atolls, – extends for over 1200 miles (1920 km.), attracting tourists and naturalists.

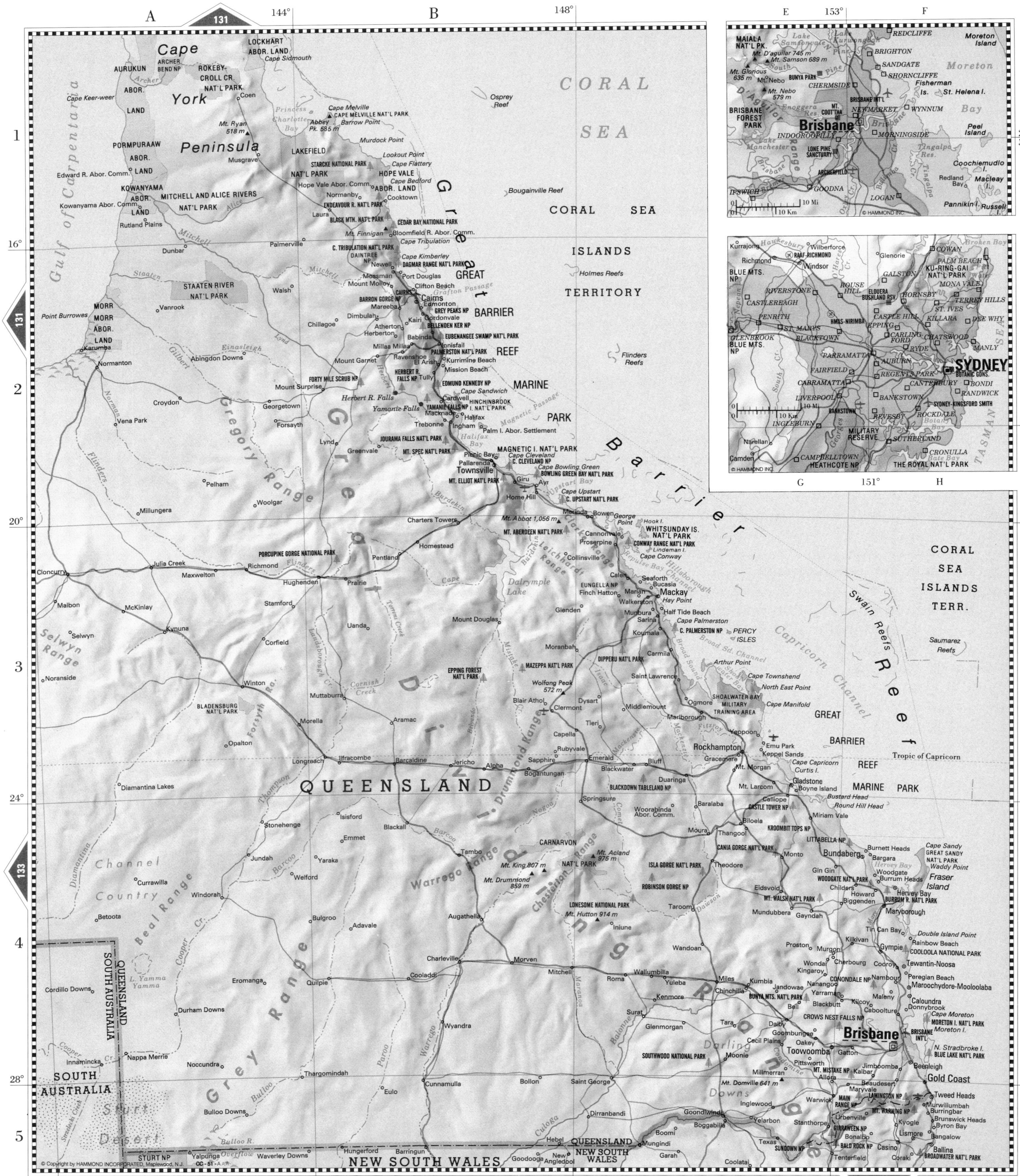


SCALE 1:6,000,000 LAMBERT CONFORMAL CONIC PROJECTION

MILES 0 100 200 300

KILOMETERS 0 100 200 300

POPULATION OF CITIES AND TOWNS

- OVER 2,000,000
- 1,000,000 - 1,999,999
- 500,000 - 999,999
- 250,000 - 499,999
- 100,000 - 249,999
- 30,000 - 99,999
- 10,000 - 29,999
- UNDER 10,000

# Southeastern Australia

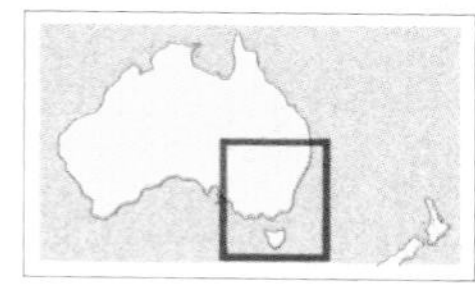

With its relatively comfortable climate and reliable rainfall, this small portion of the continent is home to most Australians. Two hundred years ago, the first European settlement was established near what is now Sydney. Competition between Melbourne and Sydney to become the nation's capital was resolved when the Parliament was transferred in 1927 to Canberra.

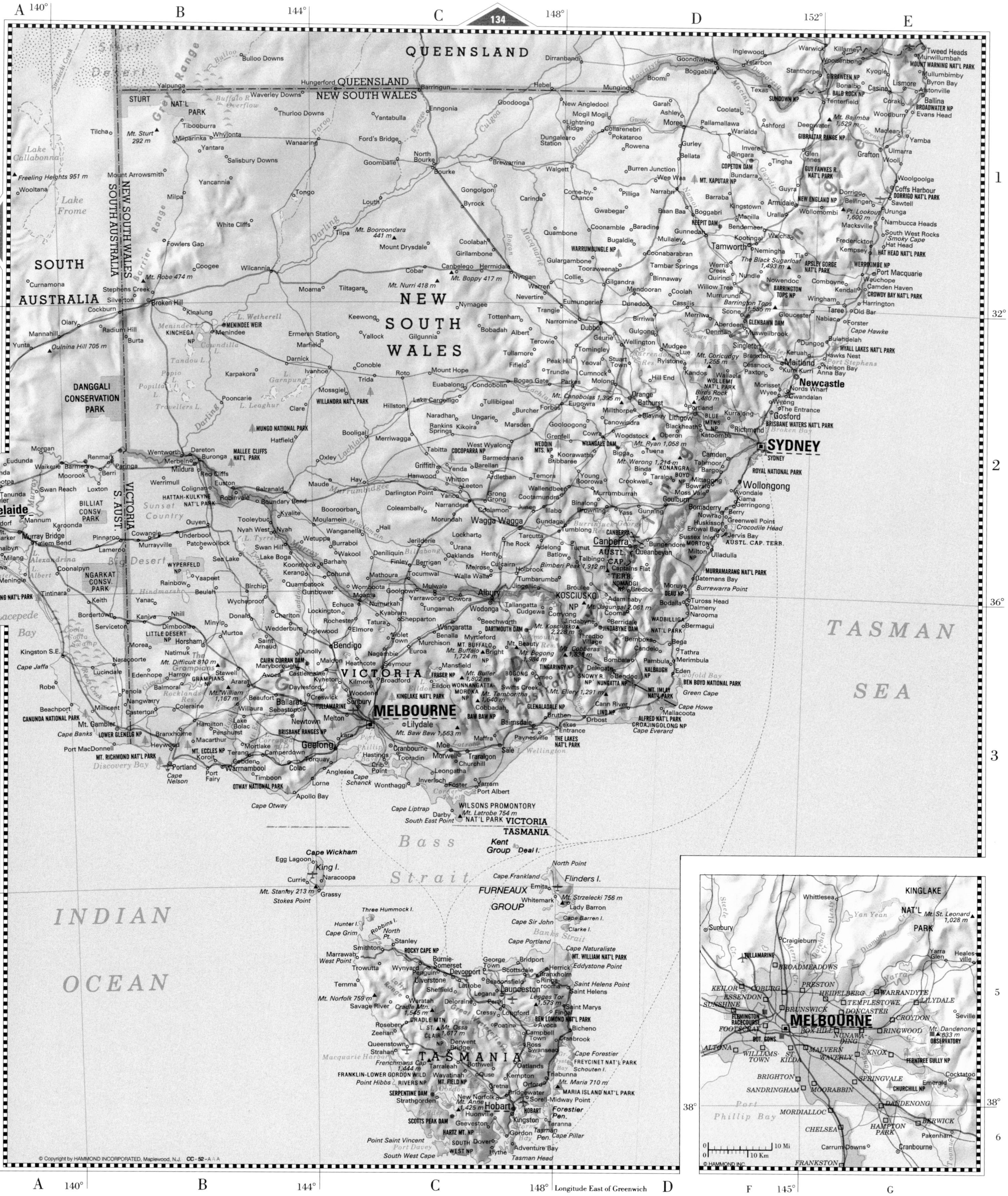


POPULATION OF CITIES AND TOWNS

| | | | |
|---|---|---|---|
| OVER 2,000,000 | 500,000 - 999,999 | 100,000 - 249,999 | 10,000 - 29,999 |
| 1,000,000 - 1,999,999 | 250,000 - 499,999 | 30,000 - 99,999 | UNDER 10,000 |

SCALE 1:6,000,000 LAMBERT CONFORMAL CONIC PROJECTION

MILES 0 100 200 300

KILOMETERS 0 100 200 300

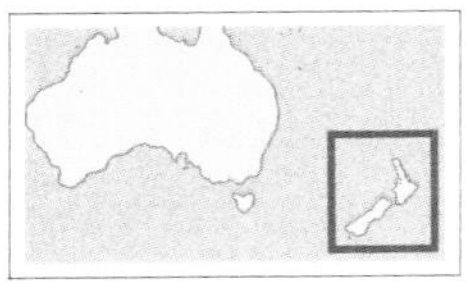

# New Zealand

The sparsely populated South Island boasts magnificent fjords and Alpine scenery. Sheep and cattle are vital to the island's economy. North Island is less agricultural, with its larger cities and hot springs. Geysers have been harnessed to generate electricity. Most New Zealanders are of British descent. Maoris, earlier immigrants from across the Pacific form a small minority.

SCALE 1:6,000,000 LAMBERT CONFORMAL CONIC PROJECTION
MILES 0 100 200 300
KILOMETERS 0 100 200 300

POPULATION OF CITIES AND TOWNS

- OVER 2,000,000
- 1,000,000 - 1,999,999
- 500,000 - 999,999
- 250,000 - 499,999
- 100,000 - 249,999
- 30,000 - 99,999
- 10,000 - 29,999
- UNDER 10,000

# Antarctica

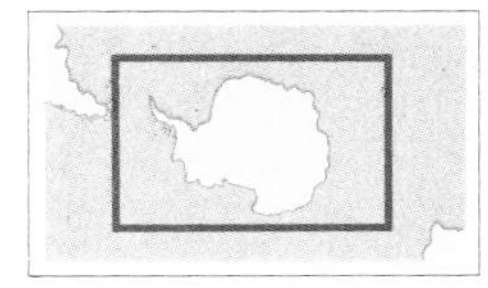

Larger than Europe or Australia, Antarctica covers over 5 million square miles (13 million sq. km.), and contains over 90 percent of the world's permanent ice and snow. Average winter temperatures can plunge below -70°F (-57° C). Summer temperatures along the coasts rise above freezing. Winds are very strong; ice needles and snow are the main forms of precipitation.

X 30° Y 15° Z 0° A 15° B 30° C

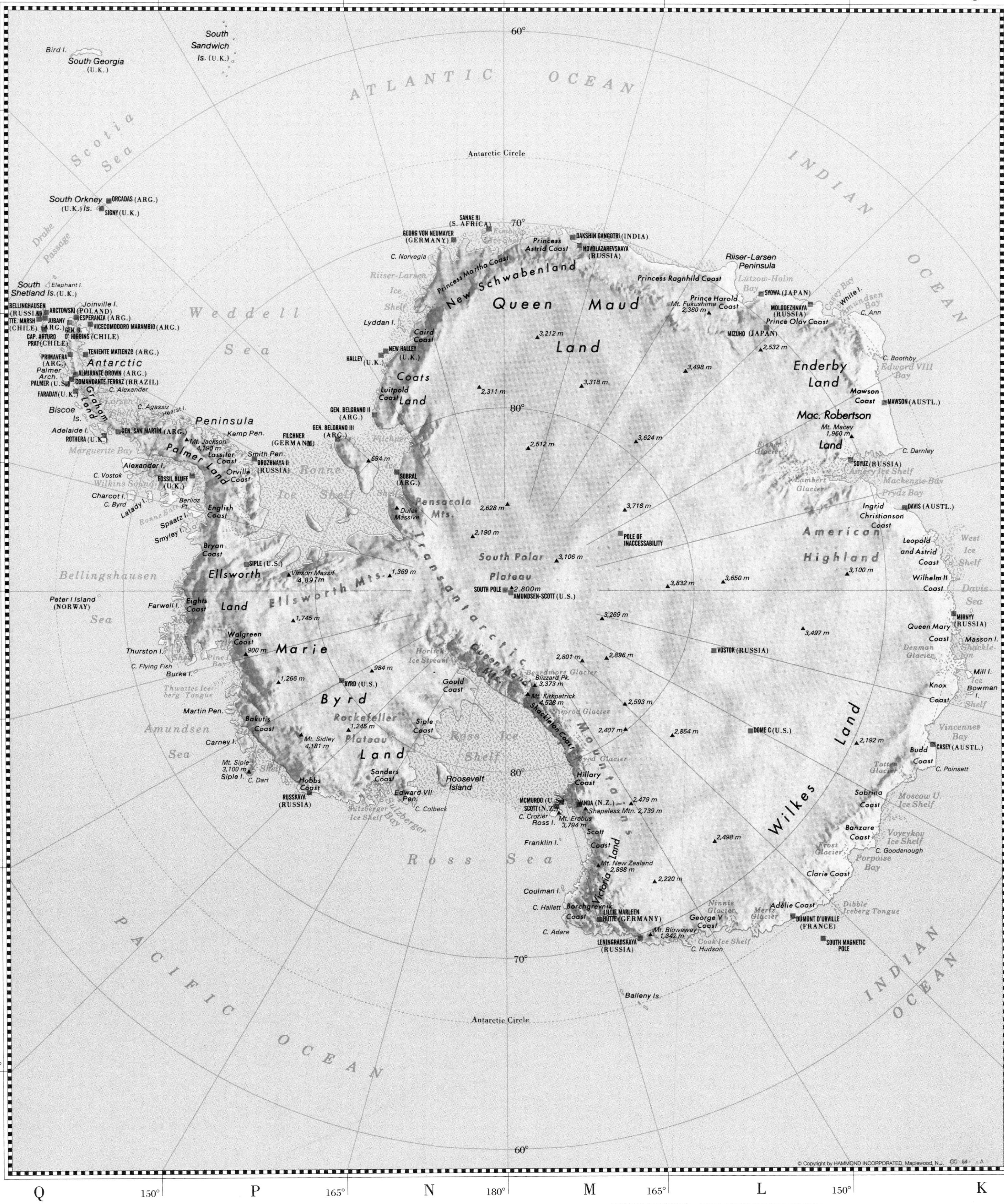


Q 150° P 165° N 180° M 165° L 150° K

SCALE 1:24,000,000 POLAR STEREOGRAPHIC PROJECTION

MILES 0 300 600 900 1200

KILOMETERS 0 300 600 900 1200

The Pacific Ocean is immense: its area covers about 64 million square miles (166 million sq. km.), while the world's land areas cover only 58 million square miles (150 million sq. km.). It is more than twice the size of the next largest ocean, the Atlantic. It occupies about one-third of the world's surface, and holds 46 percent of the world's water. Across this vast area traders moved westward, reaching Fiji by 1300 B.C., and shortly thereafter Tahiti. Between A.D. 400 and A.D. 1000 a distinct Polynesian culture reached virtually every island in the area.

# Central Pacific Ocean

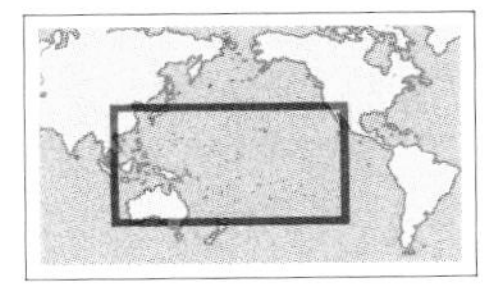

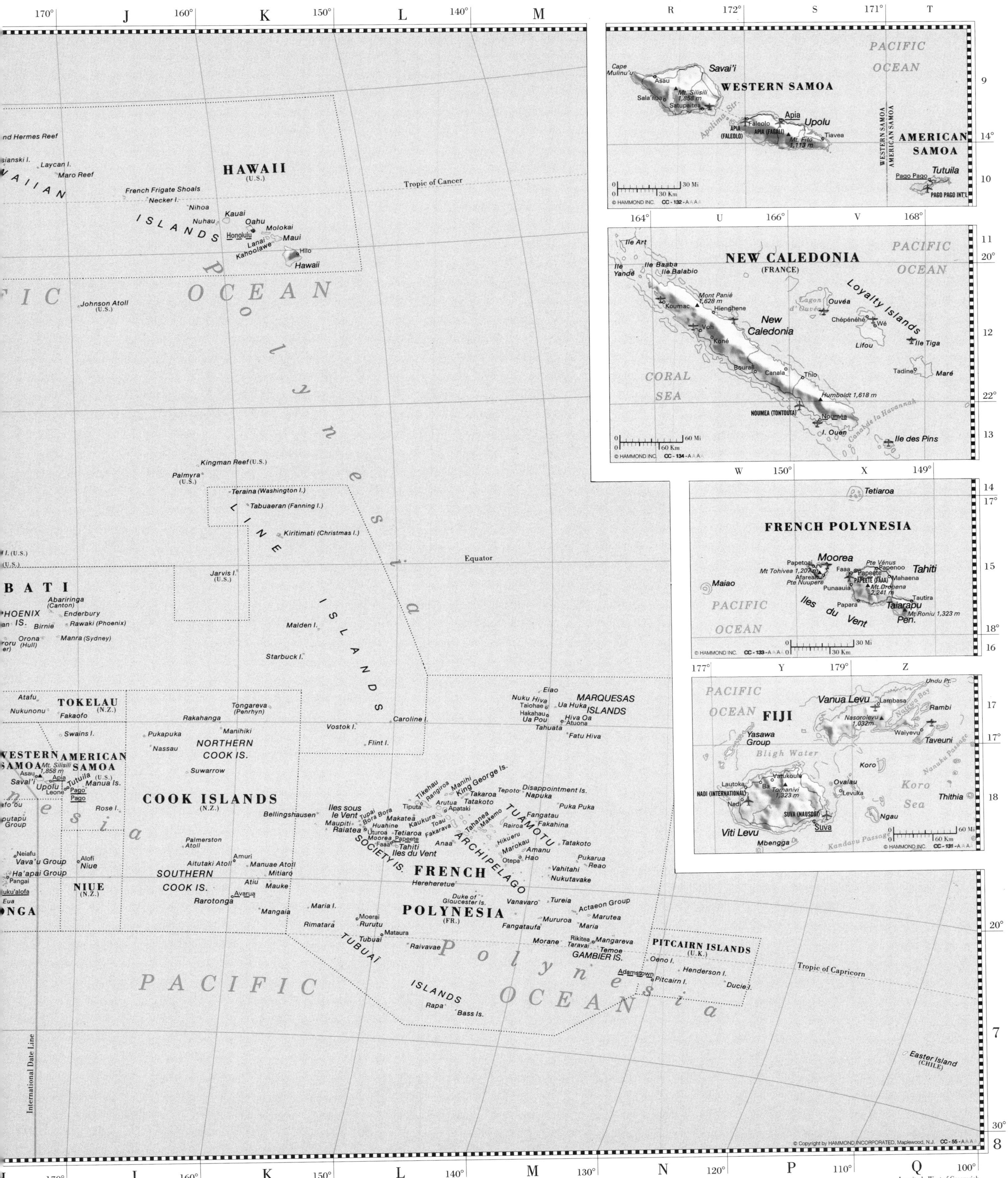


POPULATION OF CITIES AND TOWNS

- OVER 3,000,000
- 1,000,000 - 2,999,999
- 500,000 - 999,999
- 100,000 - 499,999
- UNDER 100,000

SCALE 1:27,000,000 LAMBERT AZIMUTHAL EQUAL-AREA PROJECTION

MILES 0 400 800 1200

KILOMETERS 0 400 800 1200

Longitude West of Greenwich

Africa, the second largest continent, stretches from 37° North Latitude to 35° South Latitude. The regularity of Africa's coast leaves relatively few good harbors and safe anchorages. In 1950 there were four independent African nations, Liberia, Egypt, Ethiopia and the Union of South Africa. Today there are more than fifty, fourteen of which are landlocked. Africa's Arabs live in the north, while south of the Sahara, Black Africans of many different ethnic groups predominate, each group with its own language, beliefs and customs. More than 800 languages are spoken in Africa.

Area Of Optimization
The red band which surrounds this map defines the "Area of Optimization." Within this bounding curve is the most accurate conformal map that can be made of the region. Outside the optimized area, distortion increases rapidly, and tears or other irregularities in the grid may occur. (See page 11 for additional information.)

SCALE 1:27,000,000 OPTIMAL CONFORMAL PROJECTION
MILES 0 400 800 1200
KILOMETERS 0 400 800 1200

POPULATION OF CITIES AND TOWNS
- OVER 3,000,000
- 1,000,000 - 2,999,999
- 500,000 - 999,999
- 100,000 - 499,999
- UNDER 100,000

# Africa

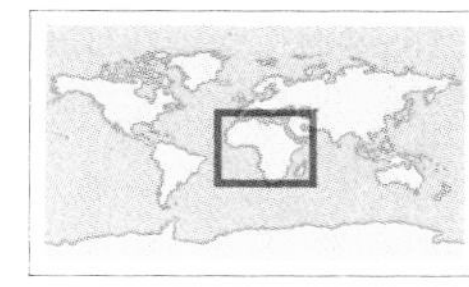

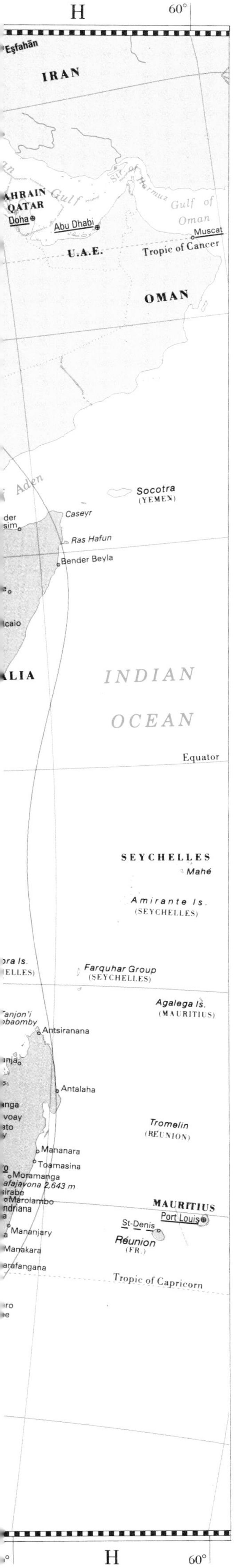

IRAN
QATAR
Doha
Abu Dhabi
U.A.E.
Muscat
Gulf of Oman
Tropic of Cancer
OMAN
Socotra (YEMEN)
Ras Hafun
Bender Beyla
INDIAN OCEAN
Equator
SEYCHELLES
Mahé
Amirante Is. (SEYCHELLES)
Farquhar Group (SEYCHELLES)
Agalega Is. (MAURITIUS)
Antsiranana
Antalaha
Tromelin (RÉUNION)
Toamasina
MAURITIUS
Port Louis
St-Denis
Réunion (FR.)
Mananjary
Tropic of Capricorn


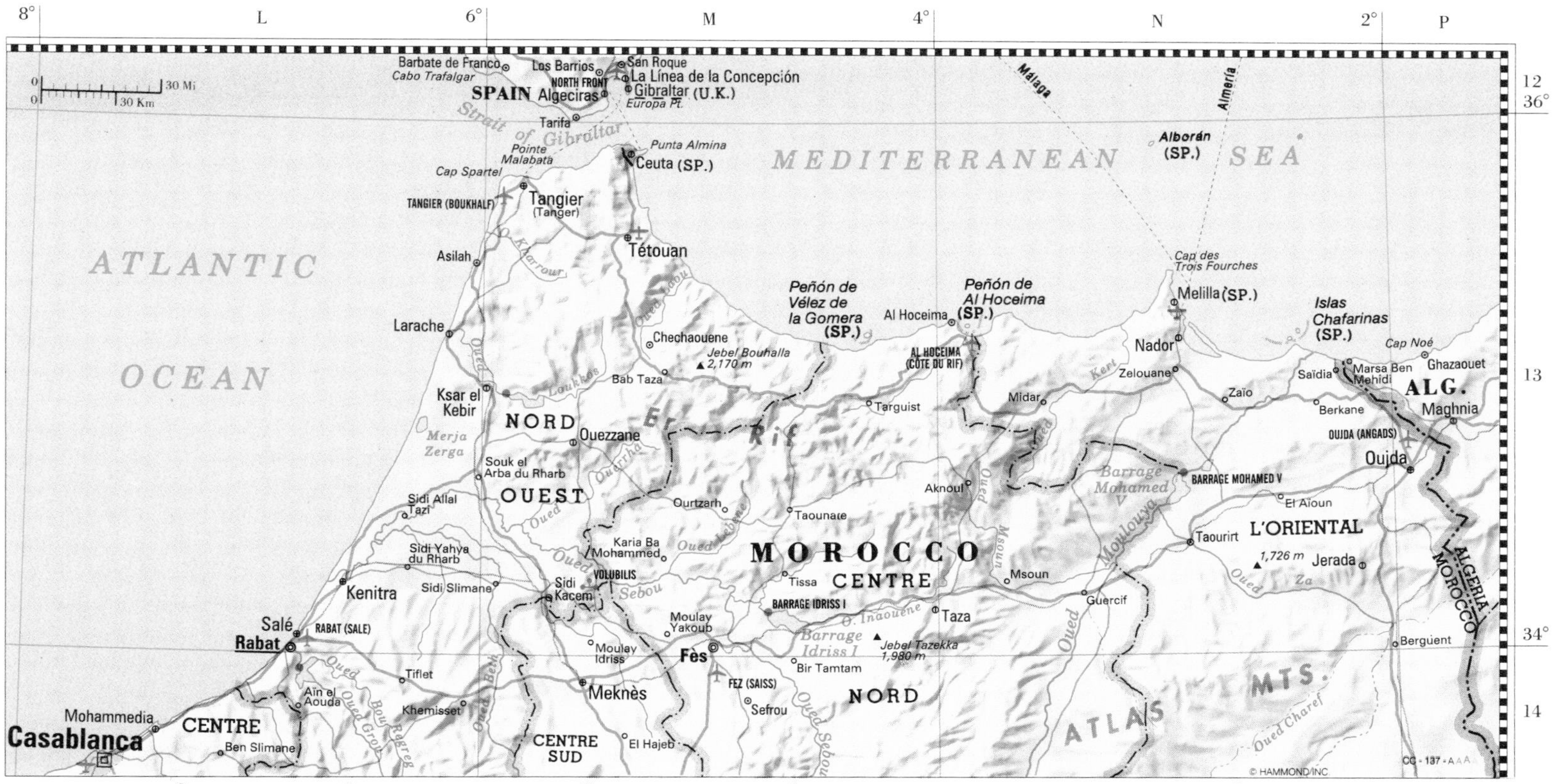

SPAIN
Algeciras
La Línea de la Concepción
Gibraltar (U.K.)
Strait of Gibraltar
Ceuta (SP.)
Tangier
MEDITERRANEAN SEA
Alborán (SP.)
ATLANTIC OCEAN
Tétouan
Larache
Peñón de Vélez de la Gomera (SP.)
Peñón de Al Hoceima (SP.)
Al Hoceima
Melilla (SP.)
Islas Chafarinas (SP.)
Nador
Chechaouene
Ksar el Kebir
NORD OUEST
Ouezzane
Er Rif
Taourirt
L'ORIENTAL
Oujda
ALG.
Maghnia
MOROCCO
CENTRE
Kenitra
Salé
Rabat
Taza
Fès
Meknès
Mohammedia
Casablanca
CENTRE SUD
NORD
ATLAS MTS.
ALGERIA MOROCCO
Jebel Tazekka 1,980 m
Jebel Bouhalla 2,170 m


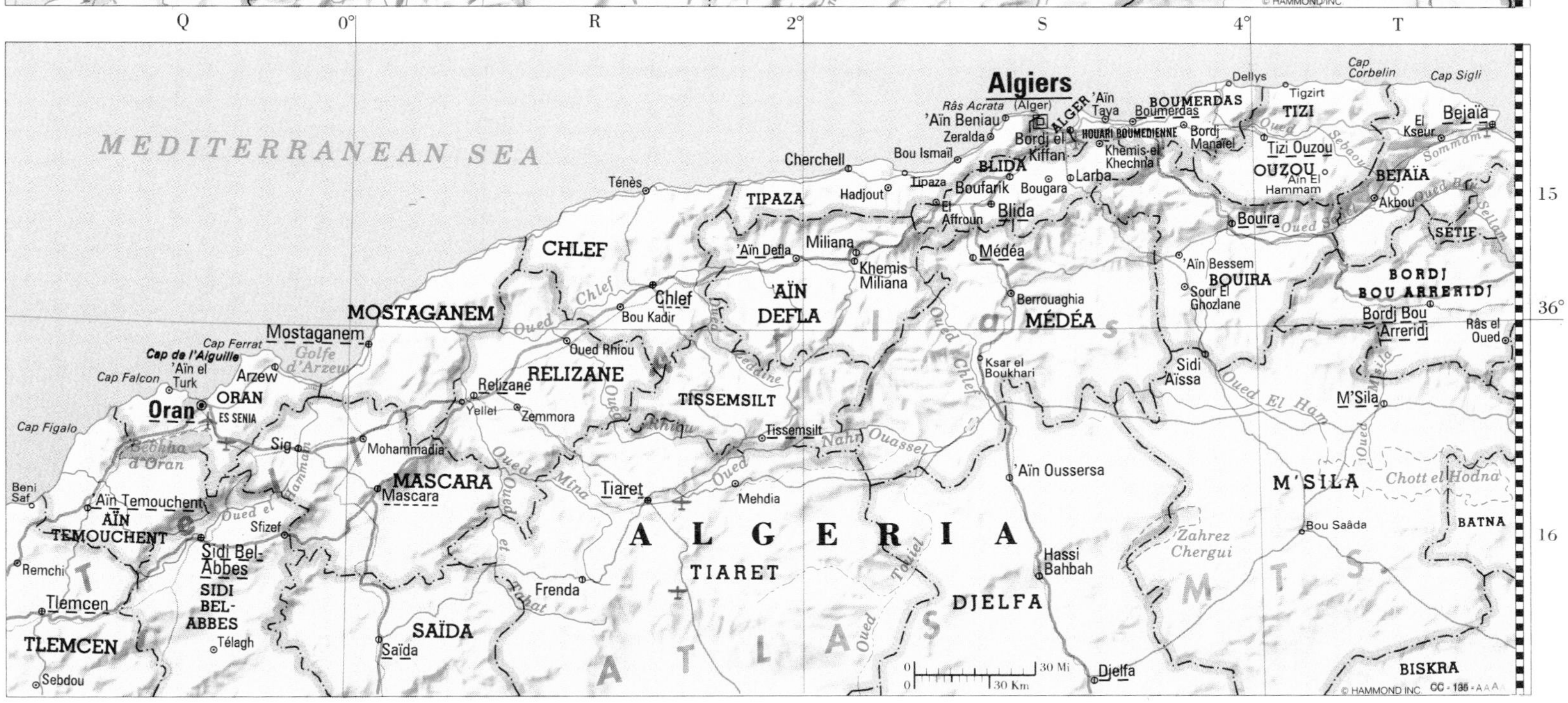

MEDITERRANEAN SEA
Algiers
BOUMERDAS
TIZI OUZOU
Bejaïa
BEJAÏA
BLIDA
Blida
TIPAZA
Cherchell
Ténès
CHLEF
Chlef
AÏN DEFLA
MÉDÉA
Médéa
BOUIRA
BORDJ BOU ARRERIDJ
MOSTAGANEM
Mostaganem
Oran
RELIZANE
Relizane
TISSEMSILT
MASCARA
Mascara
Tiaret
AÏN TEMOUCHENT
Sidi Bel-Abbès
SIDI BEL-ABBES
ALGERIA
TIARET
M'SILA
M'Sila
Chott el Hodna
BATNA
Tlemcen
TLEMCEN
SAÏDA
Saïda
DJELFA
Djelfa
ATLAS
BISKRA


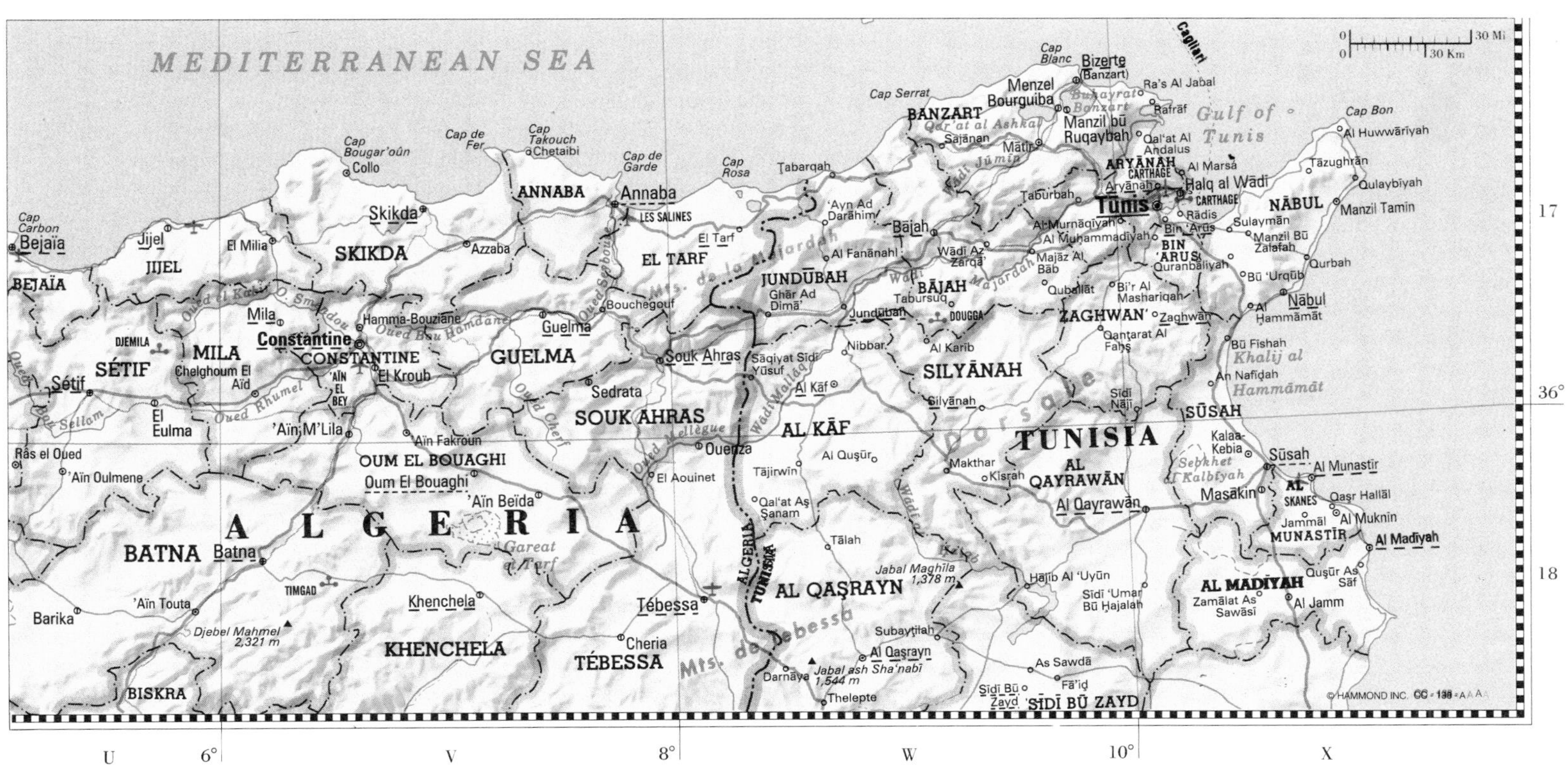

MEDITERRANEAN SEA
Bizerte
BANZART
Gulf of Tunis
Tunis
ARYĀNAH
Cap Bon
NĀBUL
ANNABA
Annaba
Skikda
SKIKDA
JIJEL
Jijel
Bejaïa
BEJAÏA
EL TARF
JUNDŪBAH
BĀJAH
ZAGHWĀN
SÉTIF
Sétif
MILA
Constantine
CONSTANTINE
GUELMA
Guelma
SOUK AHRAS
Souk Ahras
SILYĀNAH
AL KĀF
SŪSAH
Sūsah
TUNISIA
AL QAYRAWĀN
Al Qayrawān
AL MUNASTIR
AL MAHDIYAH
OUM EL BOUAGHI
ALGERIA
BATNA
Batna
KHENCHELA
TÉBESSA
Tébessa
AL QAŞRAYN
SIDI BŪ ZAYD
BISKRA
ALGERIA TUNISIA
Djebel Mahmel 2,321 m
Jabal ash Sha'nabi 1,544 m

The Sahara, the world's greatest desert, covers 3,500,000 square miles (9,100,000 sq. km.) and is 3100 miles (4960 km.) long and 1100 miles (1760 km.) wide. Extreme temperatures, as high as 136° Fahrenheit (58° C), have been recorded here. In addition, this region includes the Atlas Mountains, a structural extension of the Alpine system of Europe. These mountains trap needed moisture for the valleys in Algeria and Tunisia. Mali, Mauritania and Western Sahara are largely desert areas with subsistence-level agricultural economies.

142-143

# Northern West Africa

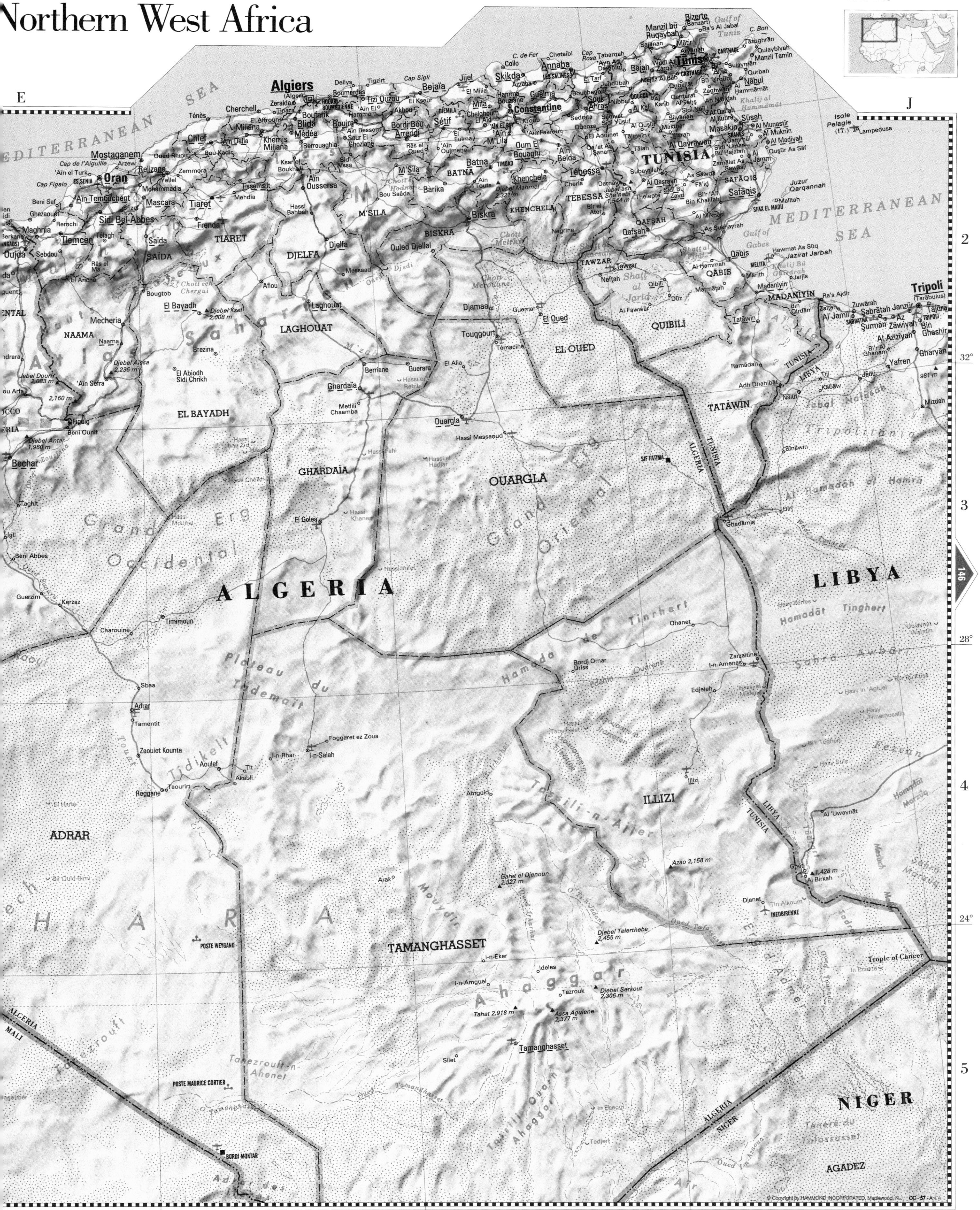


145
146

POPULATION OF CITIES AND TOWNS
- OVER 2,000,000
- 1,000,000 - 1,999,999
- 500,000 - 999,999
- 250,000 - 499,999
- 100,000 - 249,999
- 30,000 - 99,999
- 10,000 - 29,999
- UNDER 10,000

SCALE 1:6,000,000 POLYCONIC PROJECTION
MILES 0 100 200 300
KILOMETERS 0 100 200 300

This region contains a significant diversity in environments, economies and life styles. It includes forests, savannas and deserts. A number of prosperous cities had evolved by the end of the 14th century. European activities in Black Africa began during the 15th century. Trade in slaves, gold, ivory and spices took firm hold in West Africa in part because this area was closest to European colonies in the Americas. African middlemen from coastal areas raided the interior for slaves, which weakened the interior savanna states and strengthened the coastal forest states.

# Southern West Africa

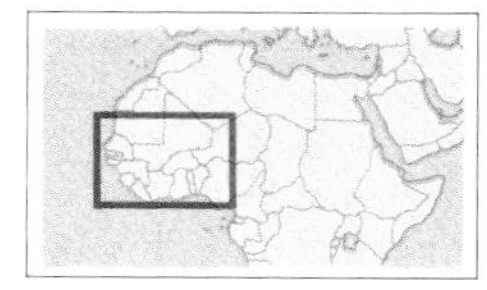

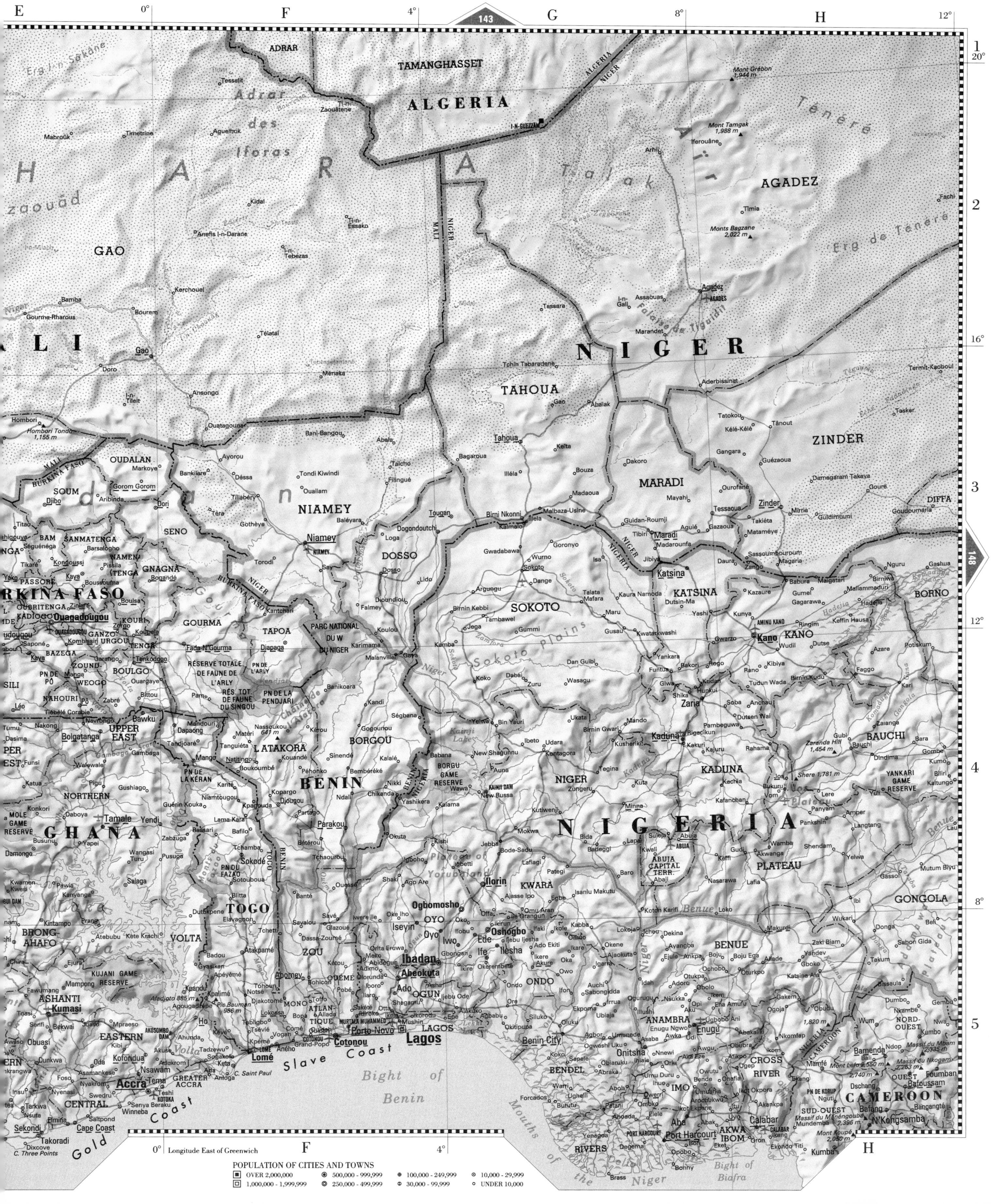


POPULATION OF CITIES AND TOWNS

- OVER 2,000,000
- 1,000,000 - 1,999,999
- 500,000 - 999,999
- 250,000 - 499,999
- 100,000 - 249,999
- 30,000 - 99,999
- 10,000 - 29,999
- UNDER 10,000

Egypt is the second most populous country in Africa. About 95 percent of the population lives within a dozen miles of the Nile River or one of its branches. The world's longest river (4,145 miles or 6632 km.), the Nile, through irrigation, supports almost all of the country's agriculture. Only 5 percent of Egypt's total land area is available for crops, which can provide up to three harvests per year. Oil has profoundly transformed life in this region. Libya, with a small population, has significant oil reserves and has used them to exert political influence.

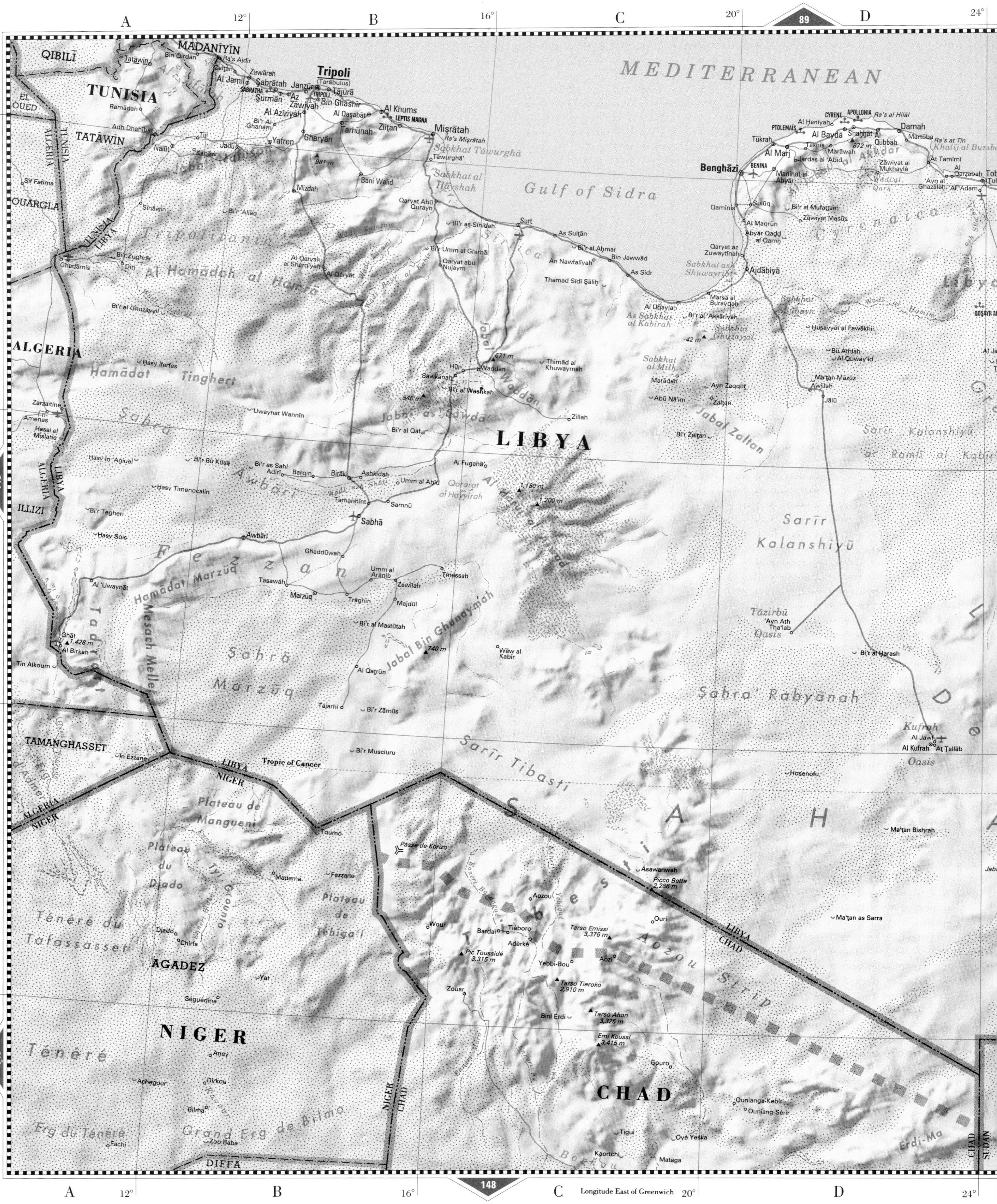

# Northeastern Africa

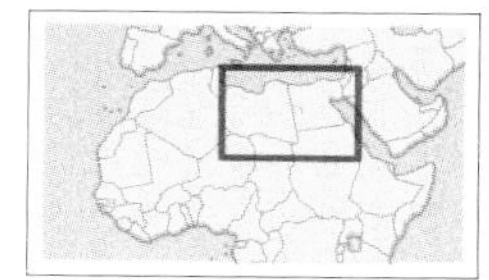

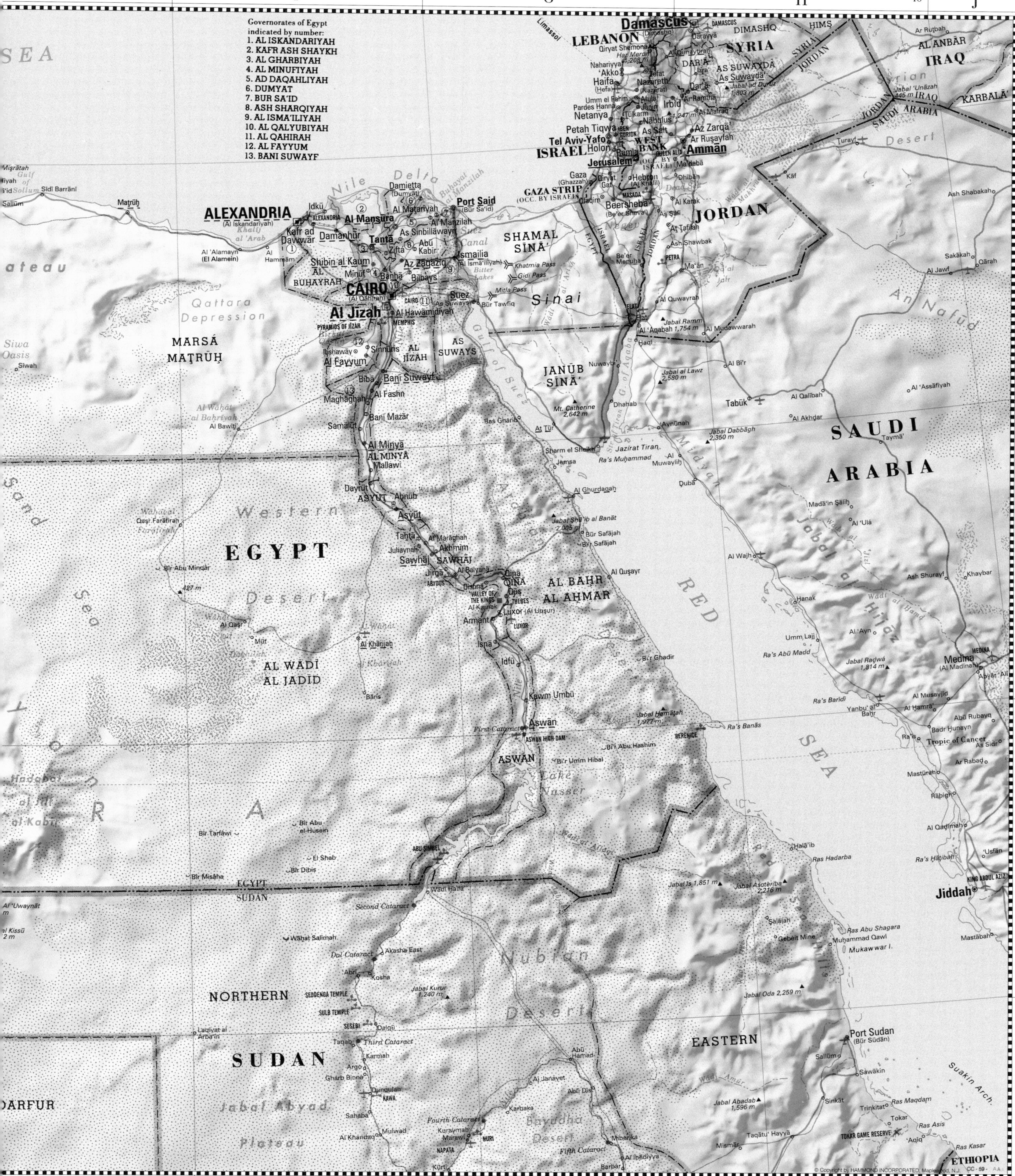


POPULATION OF CITIES AND TOWNS

| | | | |
|---|---|---|---|
| OVER 2,000,000 | 500,000 - 999,999 | 100,000 - 249,999 | 10,000 - 29,999 |
| 1,000,000 - 1,999,999 | 250,000 - 499,999 | 30,000 - 99,999 | UNDER 10,000 |

SCALE 1:6,000,000 POLYCONIC PROJECTION

MILES 0 100 200 300

KILOMETERS 0 100 200 300

The great climatic band of savanna grassland and dry shrub country, stretching east to west north of the Congo Basin, is home to countless herds of cattle. Shifting rainfall patterns, and civil and ethnic wars, have cursed the region with famine, bringing periodic suffering to the peoples of Sudan and Chad. Cameroon and the Central African Republic contain more resources for agriculture, forestry and mining. This region is a transition zone where the cultures of Islam, traditions of Christianity and lifestyles of Black Africa both coexist and struggle with each other.

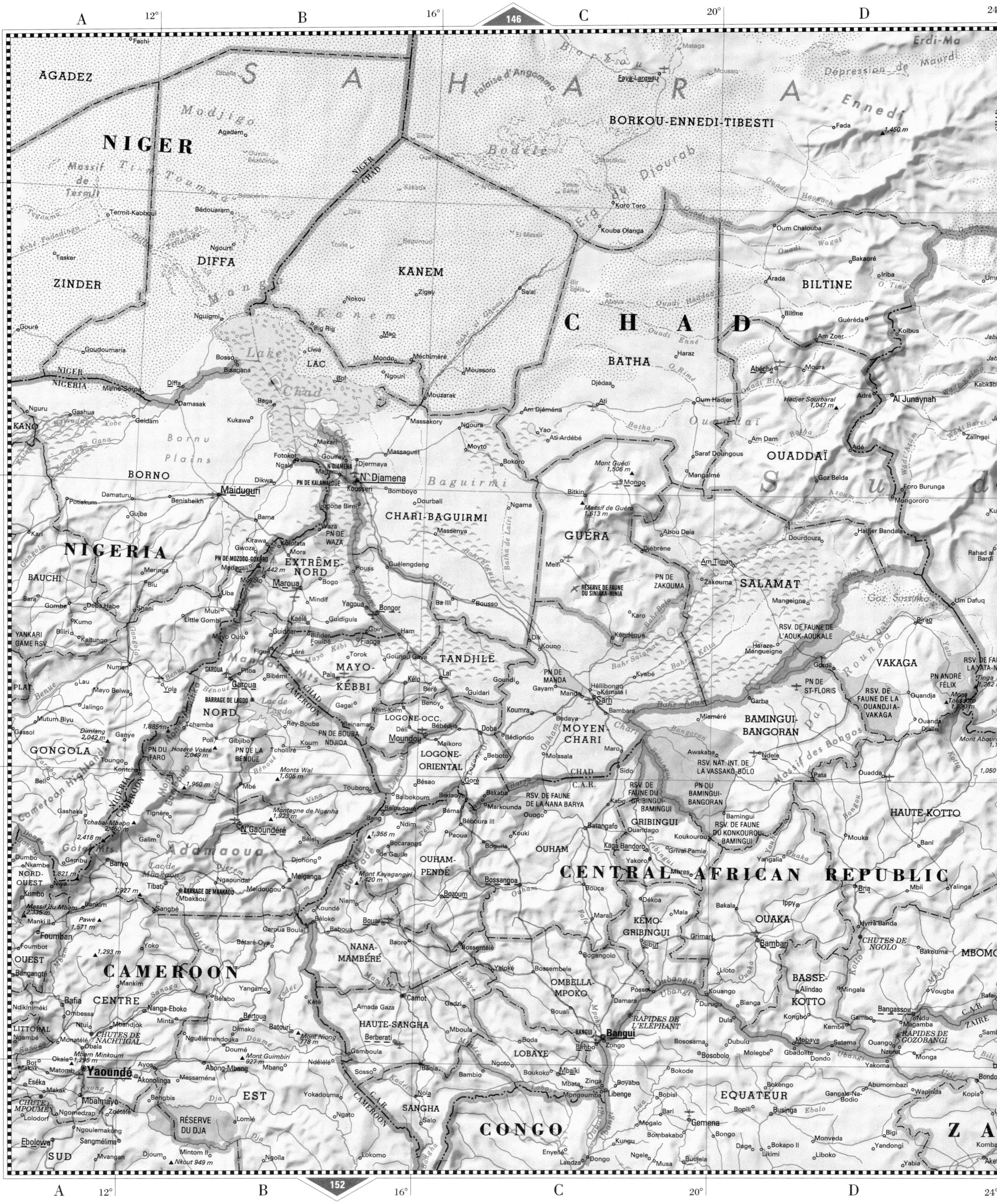

# North Central Africa

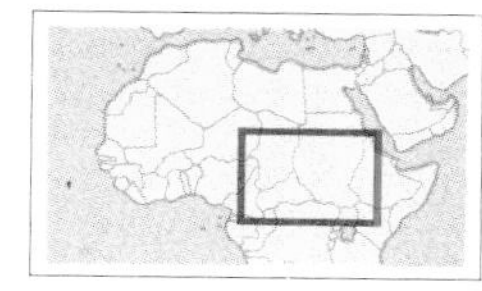

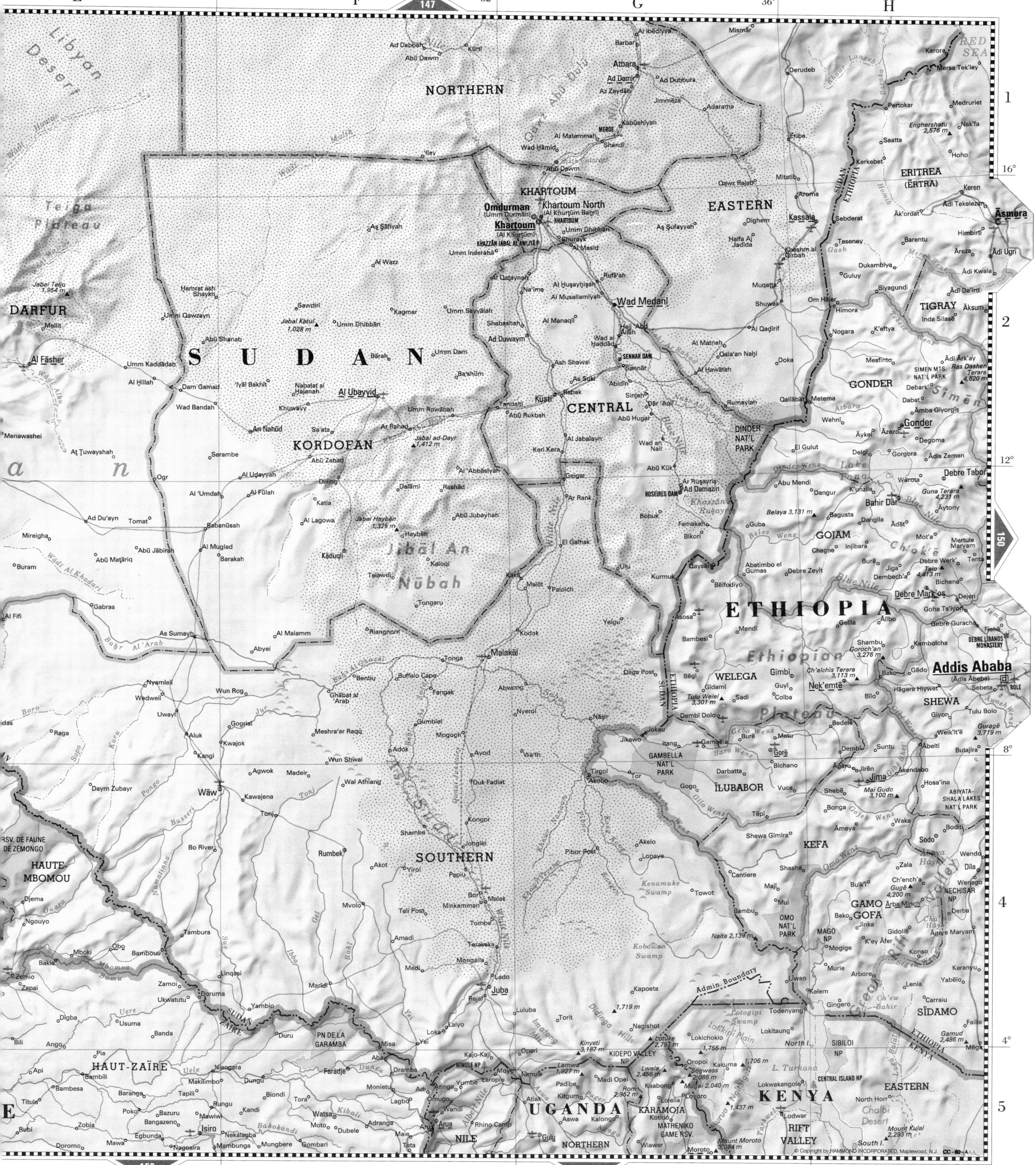


POPULATION OF CITIES AND TOWNS

- ■ OVER 2,000,000
- □ 1,000,000 - 1,999,999
- ◉ 500,000 - 999,999
- ◉ 250,000 - 499,999
- ● 100,000 - 249,999
- ⊕ 30,000 - 99,999
- ◎ 10,000 - 29,999
- ○ UNDER 10,000

SCALE 1:6,000,000 LAMBERT CONFORMAL CONIC PROJECTION

MILES 0 100 200

KILOMETERS 0 100 200 300

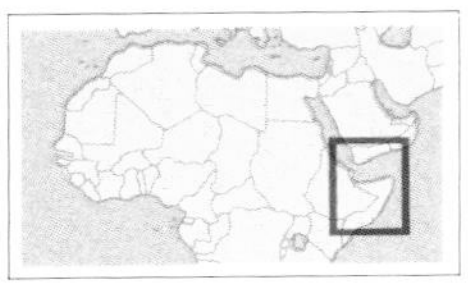

# Ethiopia, Somalia

The historic isolation of Ethiopia by a high mountainous plateau, which protected its unique peoples from outside influences, enabled this country to retain its tradition of Christianity since the 4th century. Ethiopia and Somalia are two of the poorest countries in the world. Agriculture is mostly at subsistence level, and crop failures have resulted in widespread famines.

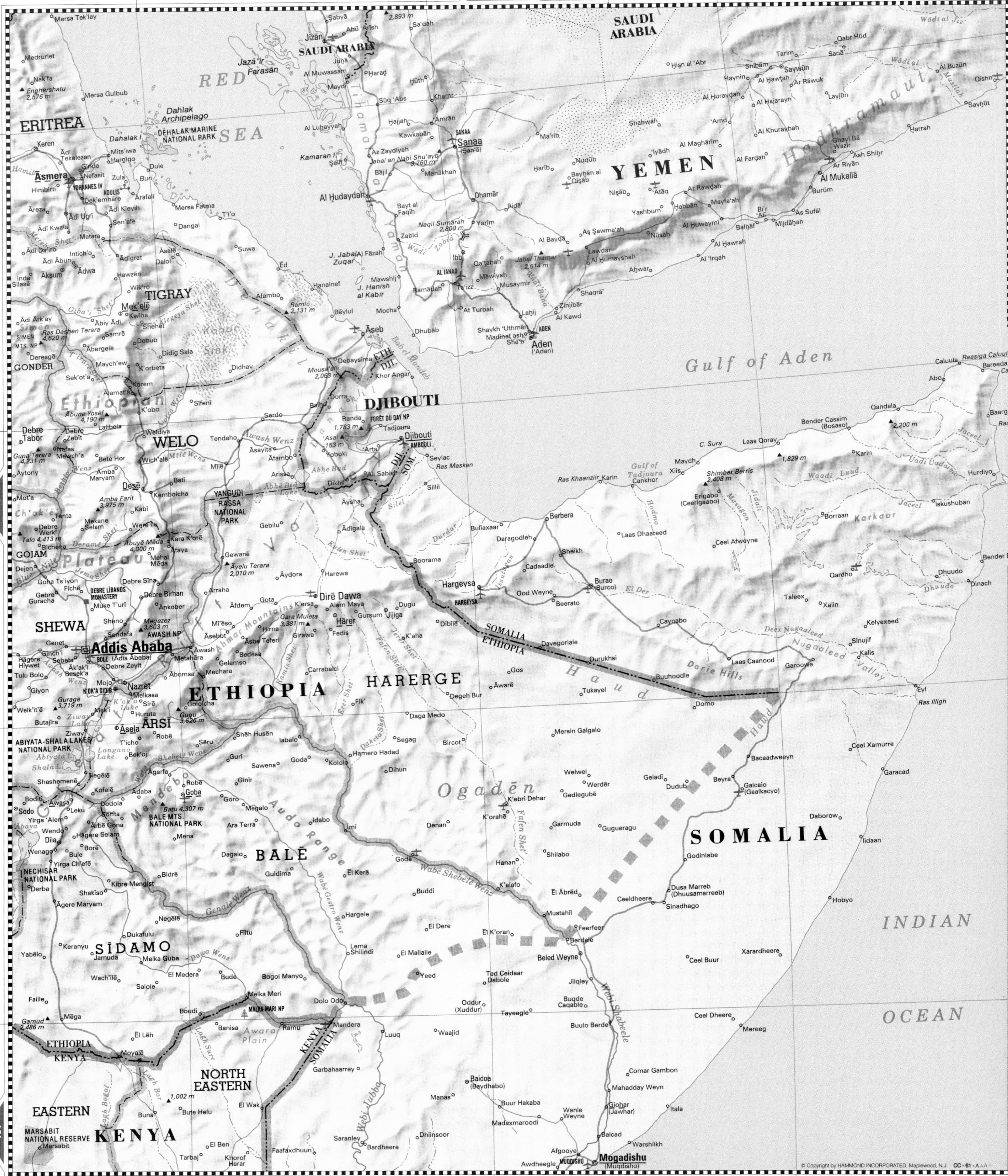


SCALE 1:6,000,000 POLYCONIC PROJECTION

MILES 0 100 200 300

KILOMETERS 0 100 200 300

POPULATION OF CITIES AND TOWNS

- OVER 2,000,000
- 1,000,000 - 1,999,999
- 500,000 - 999,999
- 250,000 - 499,999
- 100,000 - 249,999
- 30,000 - 99,999
- 10,000 - 29,999
- UNDER 10,000

# East Central Africa

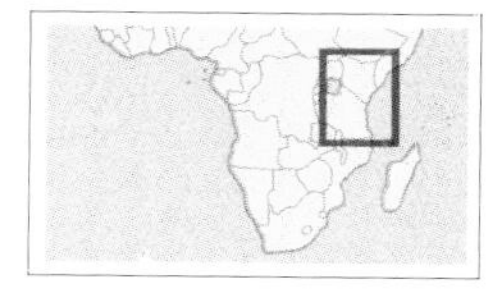

East Africa is the location of the Olduvai Gorge in Tanzania, now considered one of the original homelands of the human race. With limited mineral resources – diamonds in Tanzania and copper in Uganda – most people depend on agriculture and cattle for survival. Kenya has significant numbers of Asians, Europeans and Arabs. By contrast, Tanzania has very few minority groups.

POPULATION OF CITIES AND TOWNS

- OVER 2,000,000
- 1,000,000 - 1,999,999
- 500,000 - 999,999
- 250,000 - 499,999
- 100,000 - 249,999
- 30,000 - 99,999
- 10,000 - 29,999
- UNDER 10,000

SCALE 1:6,000,000 POLYCONIC PROJECTION

MILES 0 100 200 300

KILOMETERS 0 100 200 300

Occupying most of the Congo River Basin, Zaire, with nearly 38 million people in an area of 905,000 square miles (2.4 million sq. km.), has the largest cities, best communications network and the majority of natural resources in this region. Gabon has important mineral deposits, large fore and some oil resources. The Republic the Congo lacks resources and faces

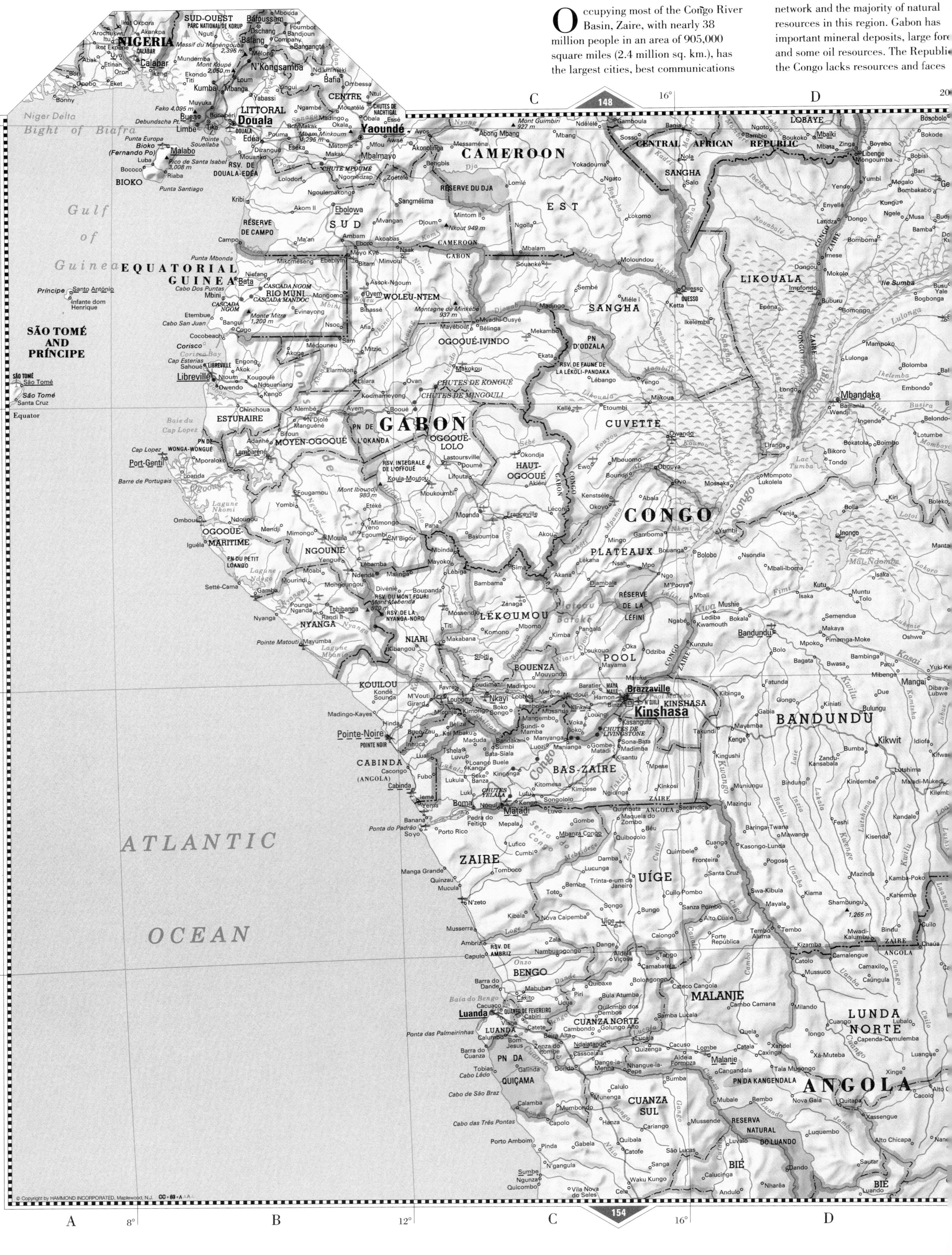

148
154

e expenses to move products to the
st. Angola has significant amounts of
n diamonds and oil and its hydro-
ctric plants generate about three-
rters of the country's total power.



# West Central Africa

POPULATION OF CITIES AND TOWNS

| | | | |
|---|---|---|---|
| OVER 2,000,000 | 500,000 - 999,999 | 100,000 - 249,999 | 10,000 - 29,999 |
| 1,000,000 - 1,999,999 | 250,000 - 499,999 | 30,000 - 99,999 | UNDER 10,000 |

SCALE 1:6,000,000 POLYCONIC PROJECTION

MILES 0 100 200 300

KILOMETERS 0 100 200 300

The southern high country of Africa is a vast plateau, its elevation moderating not only temperatures, but rainfall as well. Semi-arid grassland and desert cover much of the region. The powerful Zambezi River cuts through the highlands of Zambia, Zimbabwe and Mozambique, and forms a wide delta as it empties into the ocean along a tropical coast. Rich deposits of diamonds, copper and nickel brought colonial interests here in the late 1800s. Exploitation of these resources provides an economic foundation for the recently independent nations of today.

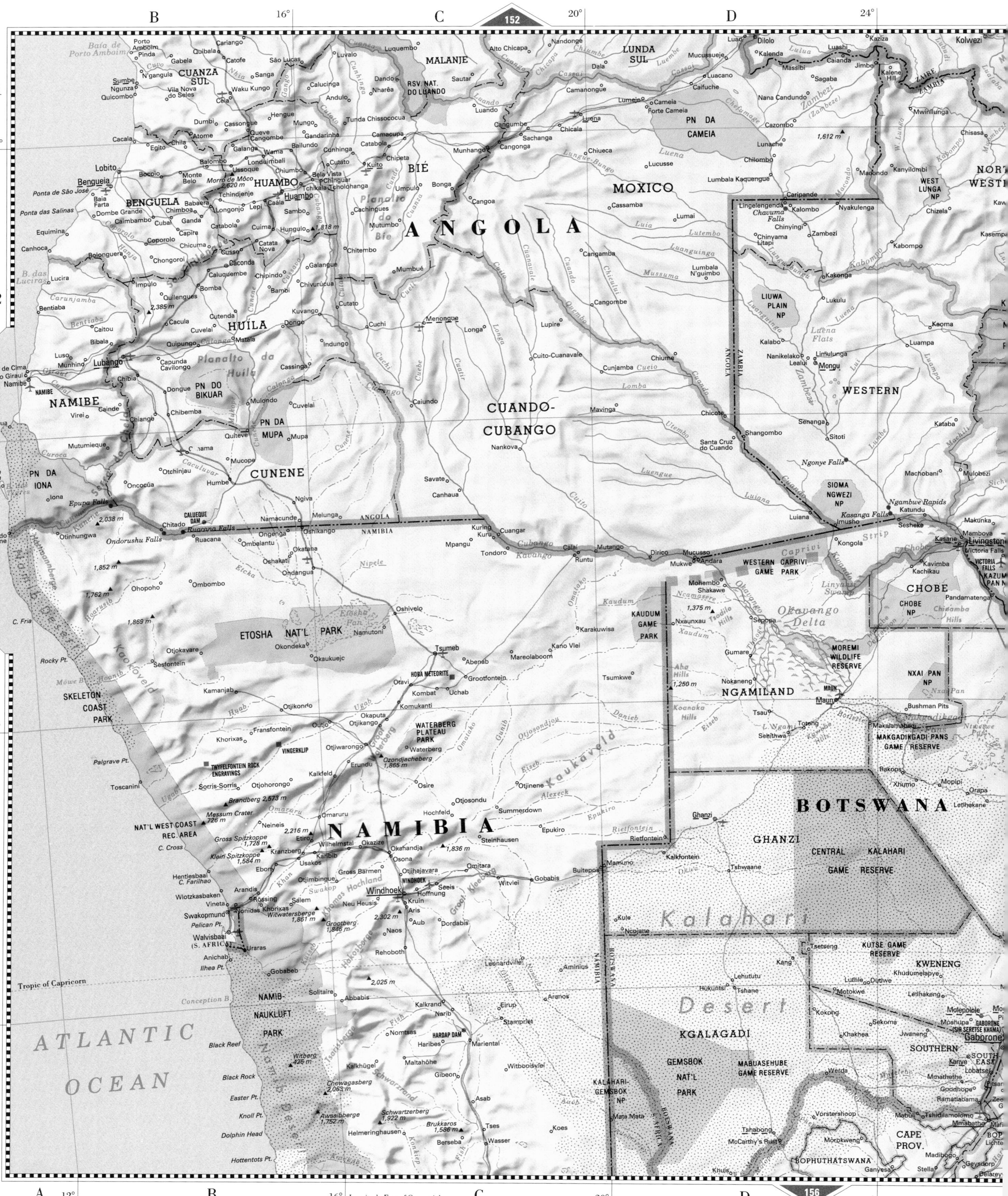


SCALE 1:6,000,000 POLYCONIC PROJECTION

MILES 0 100 200 300

KILOMETERS 0 100 200 300

POPULATION OF CITIES AND TOWNS

- OVER 2,000,000
- 1,000,000 - 1,999,999
- 500,000 - 999,999
- 250,000 - 499,999
- 100,000 - 249,999
- 30,000 - 99,999
- 10,000 - 29,999
- UNDER 10,000

# South Central Africa

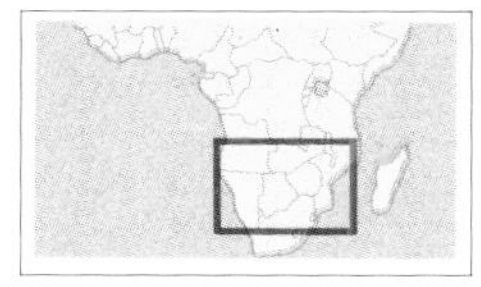

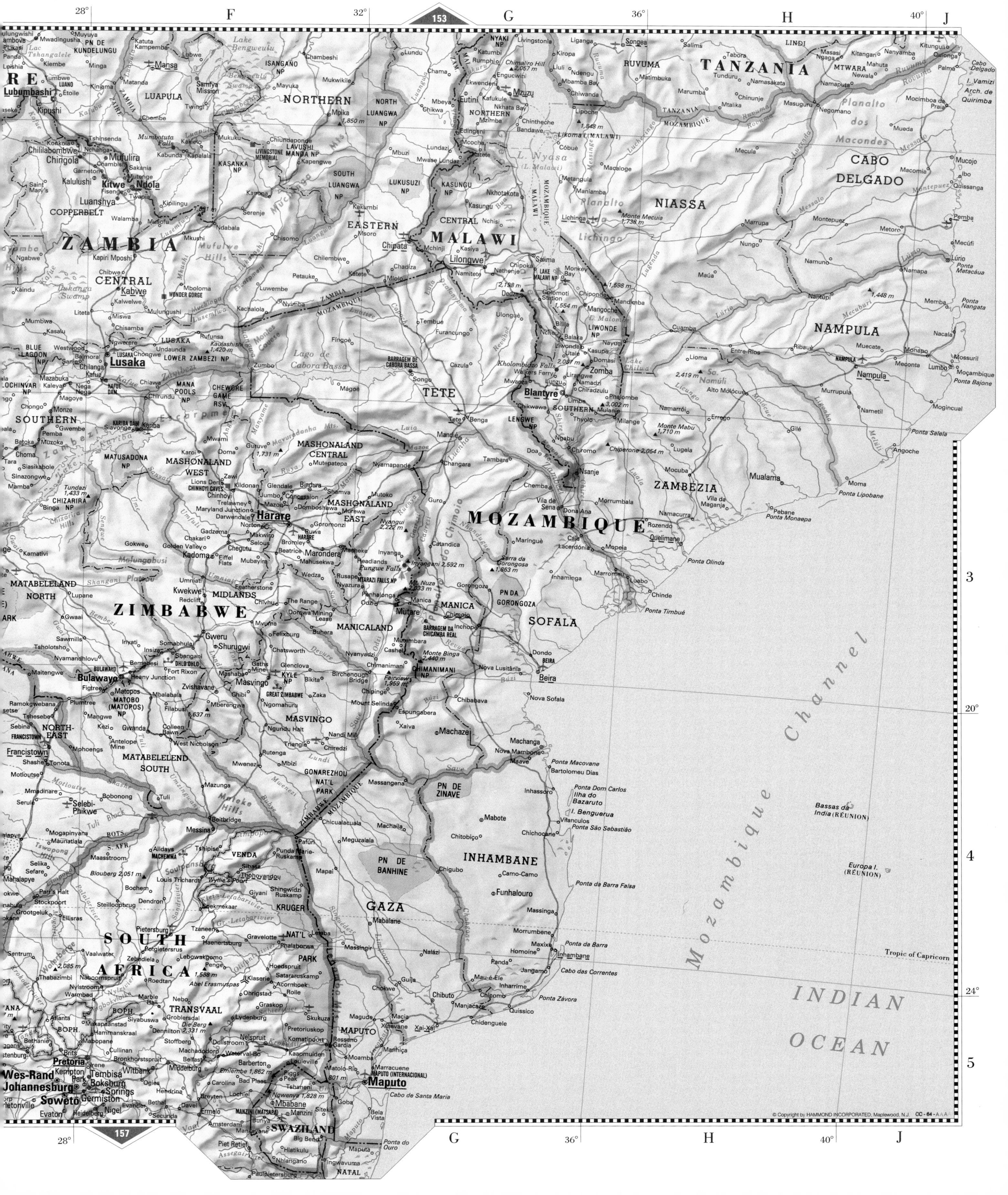

This is Africa's richest region in terms of its natural resources. Gold, chromium, antimony, diamonds, platinum, vanadium and coal are mined in abundance. The favorable climate in South Africa produces a variety of tropical and temperate crops. However, this vast natural wealth is not distributed equally. Botswana, Namibia, Swaziland, Lesotho, and large parts of South Africa itself remain poor. The world's fourth-largest island, Madagascar, was settled by Malayo-Polynesian voyagers from the Sunda Islands of present-day Indonesia. Inhabitants speak the Malagasy language.

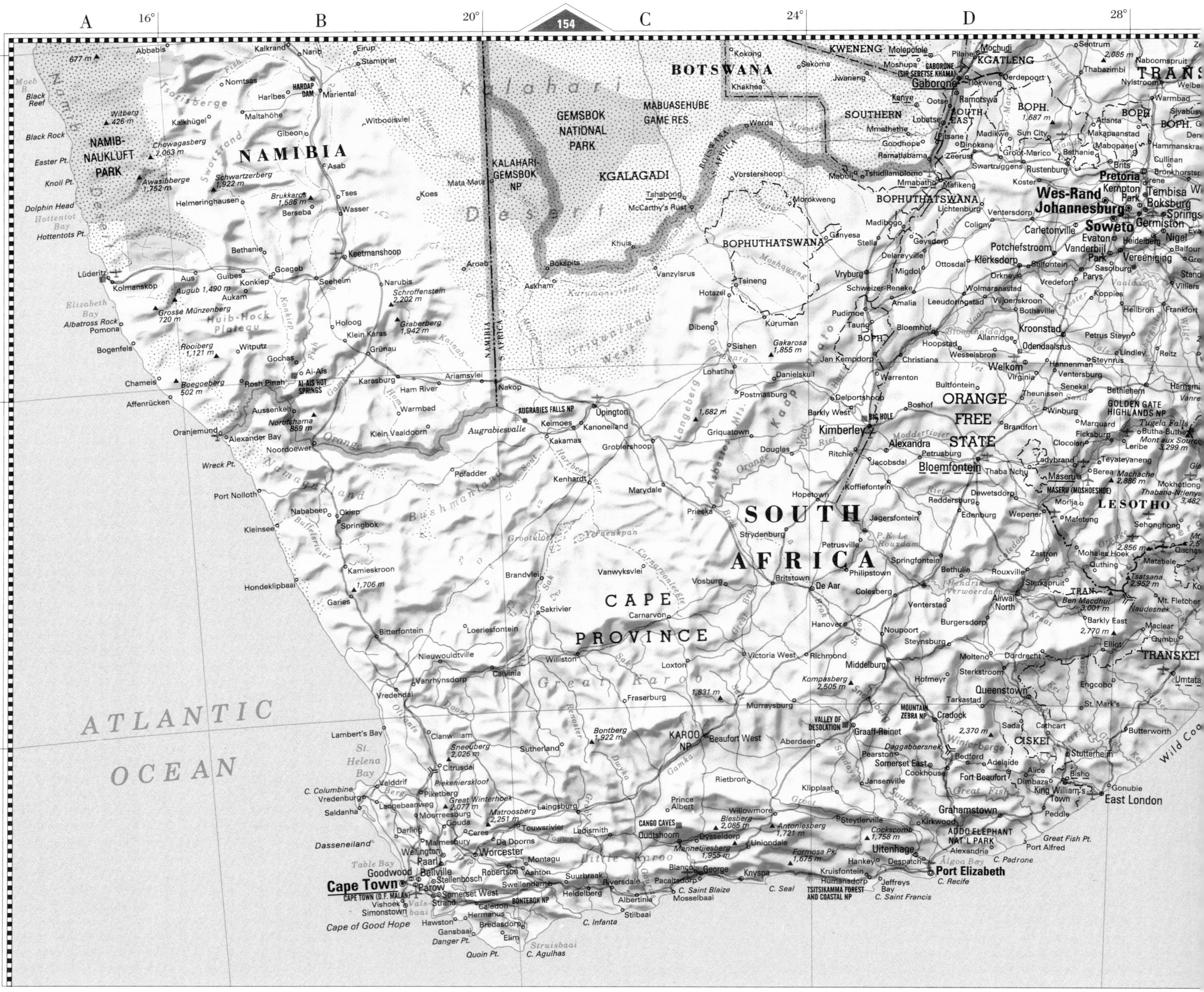


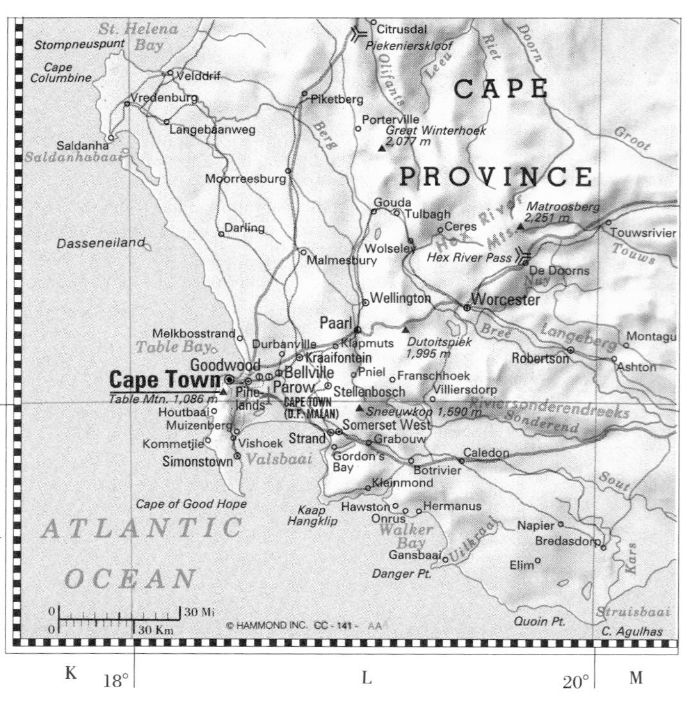


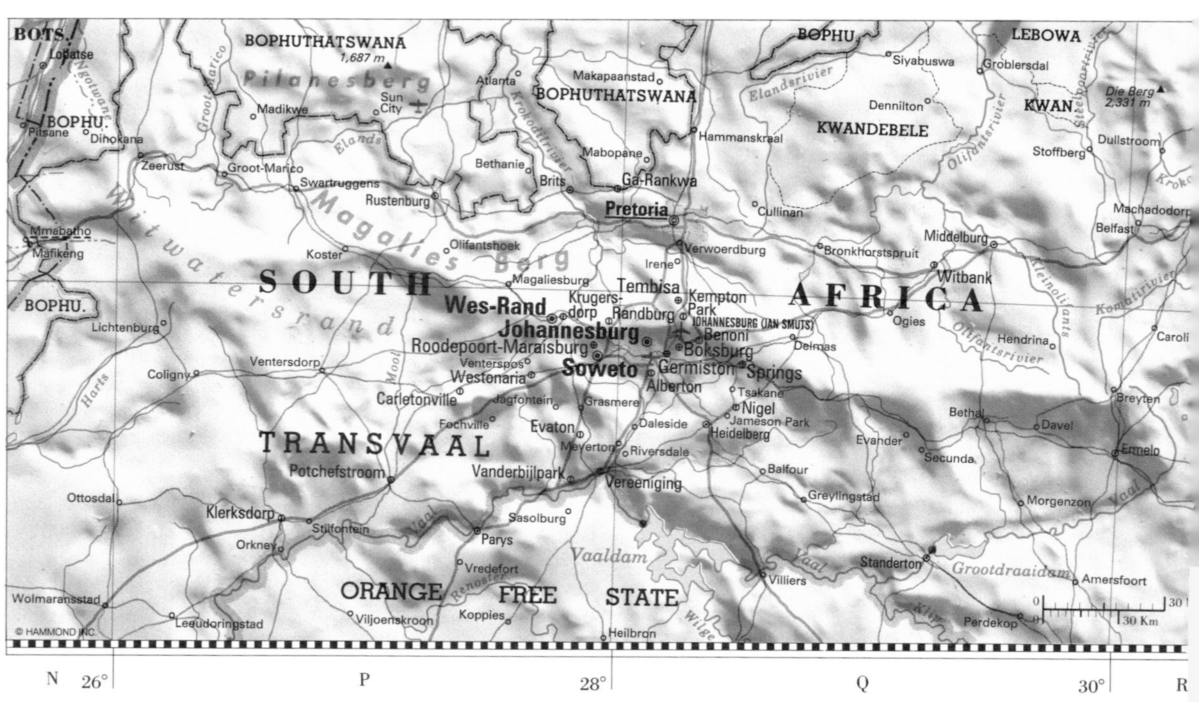

# Southern Africa

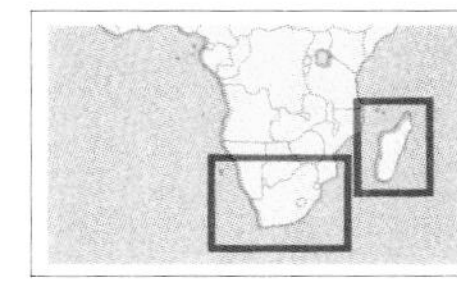

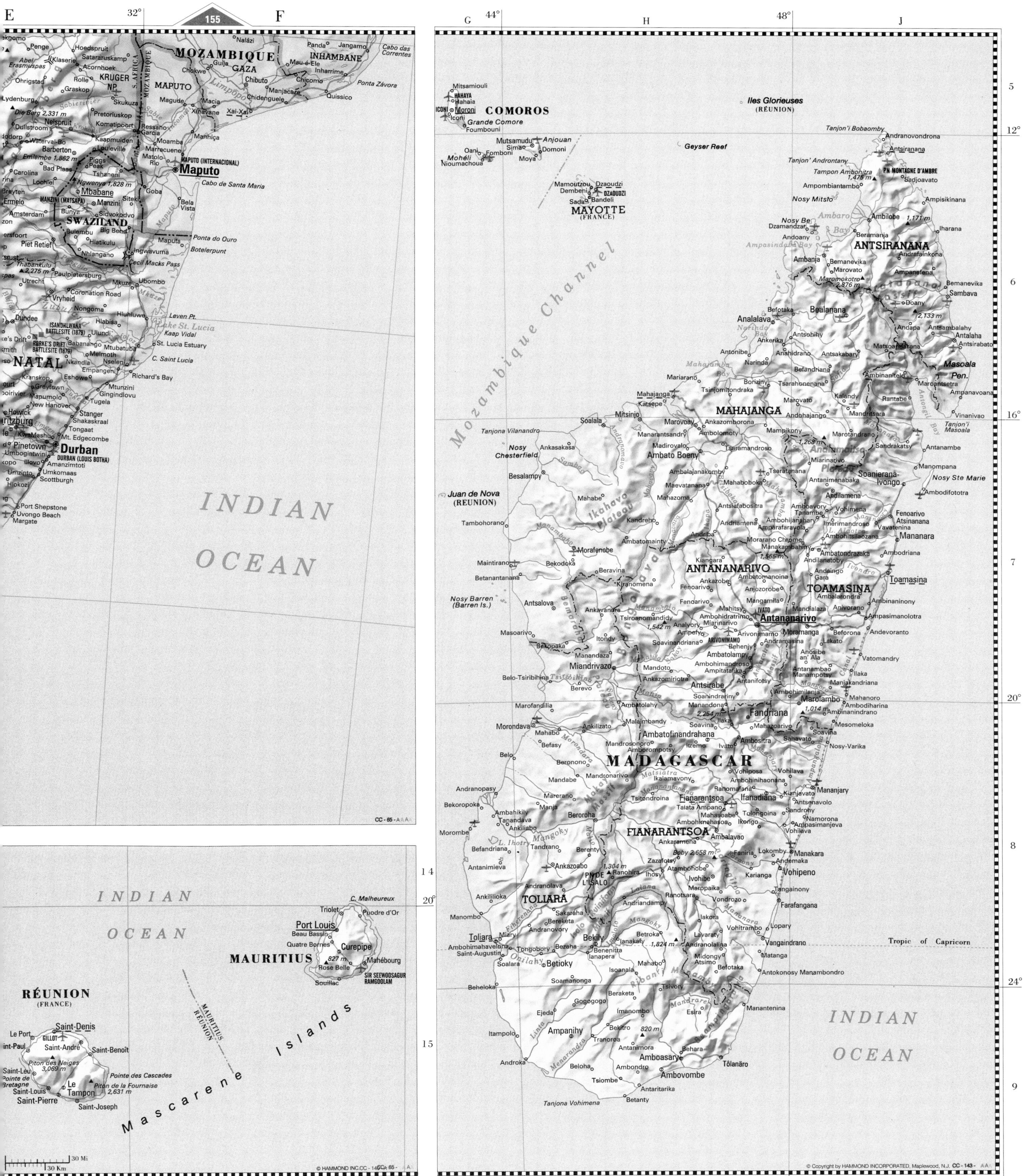


POPULATION OF CITIES AND TOWNS

- OVER 2,000,000
- 1,000,000 - 1,999,999
- 500,000 - 999,999
- 250,000 - 499,999
- 100,000 - 249,999
- 30,000 - 99,999
- 10,000 - 29,999
- UNDER 10,000

SCALE 1:6,000,000 LAMBERT CONFORMAL CONIC PROJECTION

MILES 0 100 200 300

KILOMETERS 0 100 200 300

Mexico has a unique blend of Native American and Spanish cultural heritages. It forms the largest portion of the land bridge which joins North and South America, and played a role in the movements of animals and people. The vast Mexican plateau is bordered on the east and west by high mountain ranges of the Sierra Madres. Despite its size, 50 percent of Mexico's population is concentrated in a zone that centers on Mexico City and stretches from Veracruz to Guadalajara. The population of Mexico City's metropolitan area alone is about 13.8 million people.

# Northern and Central Mexico

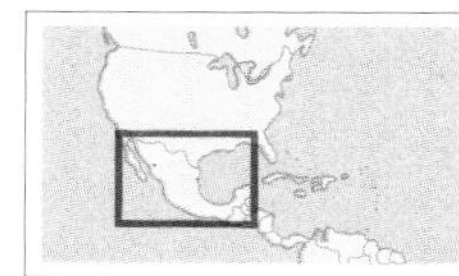

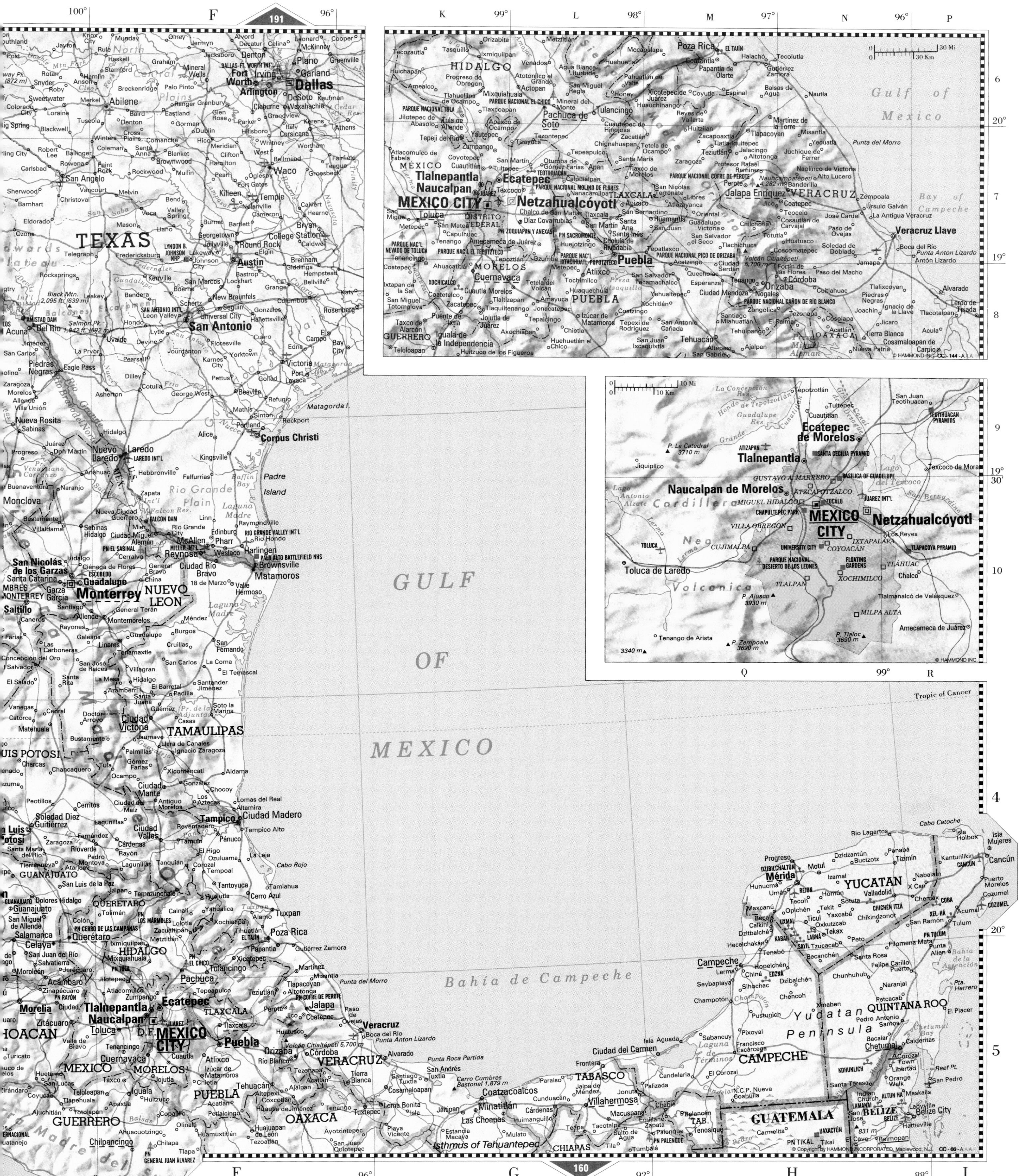


POPULATION OF CITIES AND TOWNS

| | | | |
|---|---|---|---|
| ■ OVER 2,000,000 | ◉ 500,000 - 999,999 | ◉ 100,000 - 249,999 | ◎ 10,000 - 29,999 |
| ▣ 1,000,000 - 1,999,999 | ◉ 250,000 - 499,999 | ◎ 30,000 - 99,999 | ○ UNDER 10,000 |

SCALE 1:6,000,000 LAMBERT CONFORMAL CONIC PROJECTION

MILES 0 100 200 300

KILOMETERS 0 100 200 300

The history of southern Mexico and Central America can be traced back more than 12,000 years, when Paleo-Indian people migrated here. Their descendants created the great pre-Columbian cultures: the Olmec, Teotihuacan, Mayan, Toltec, Zapotec, Mixtec and highly advanced Aztec. Spanish involvement began shortly after Columbus reached the West Indies in 1492. Spanish rule in Mexico lasted until 1821. Guatemala, Costa Rica, Nicaragua, El Salvador and Honduras became independent in 1838. Belize gained its independence in 1981.

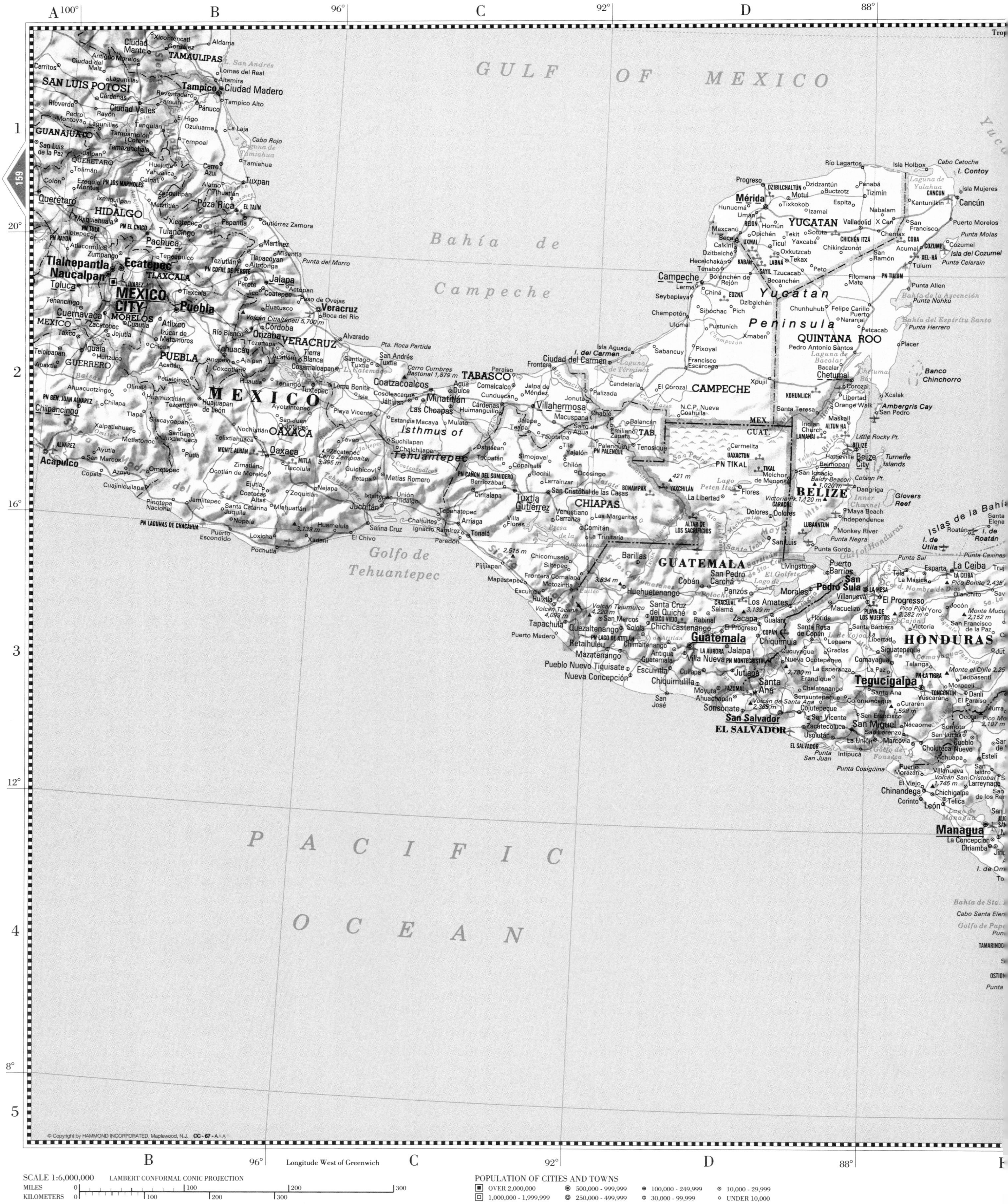


SCALE 1:6,000,000 LAMBERT CONFORMAL CONIC PROJECTION
MILES 0 100 200 300
KILOMETERS 0 100 200 300

POPULATION OF CITIES AND TOWNS
- OVER 2,000,000
- 1,000,000 - 1,999,999
- 500,000 - 999,999
- 250,000 - 499,999
- 100,000 - 249,999
- 30,000 - 99,999
- 10,000 - 29,999
- UNDER 10,000

# Southern Mexico, Central America, Western Caribbean

160-161

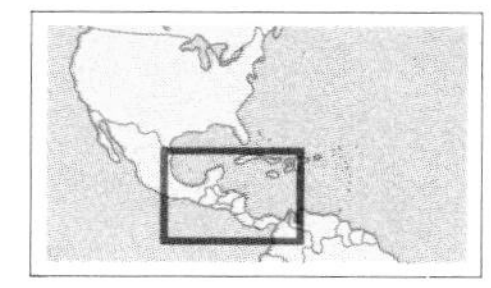

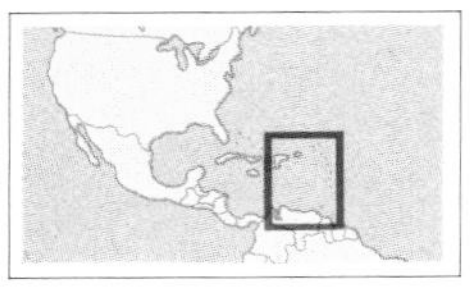

# Eastern Caribbean, Bahamas

The Caribbean islands stretch 1600 miles (2560 km.) from Florida to Venezuela. During the 16th–19th centuries European powers vied for possession of key islands in the Antilles. With its occupation of Puerto Rico in 1898, and the purchase of the western Virgin Islands in 1917, the U.S. also became a regional power. After 1962 many islands became independent nations.

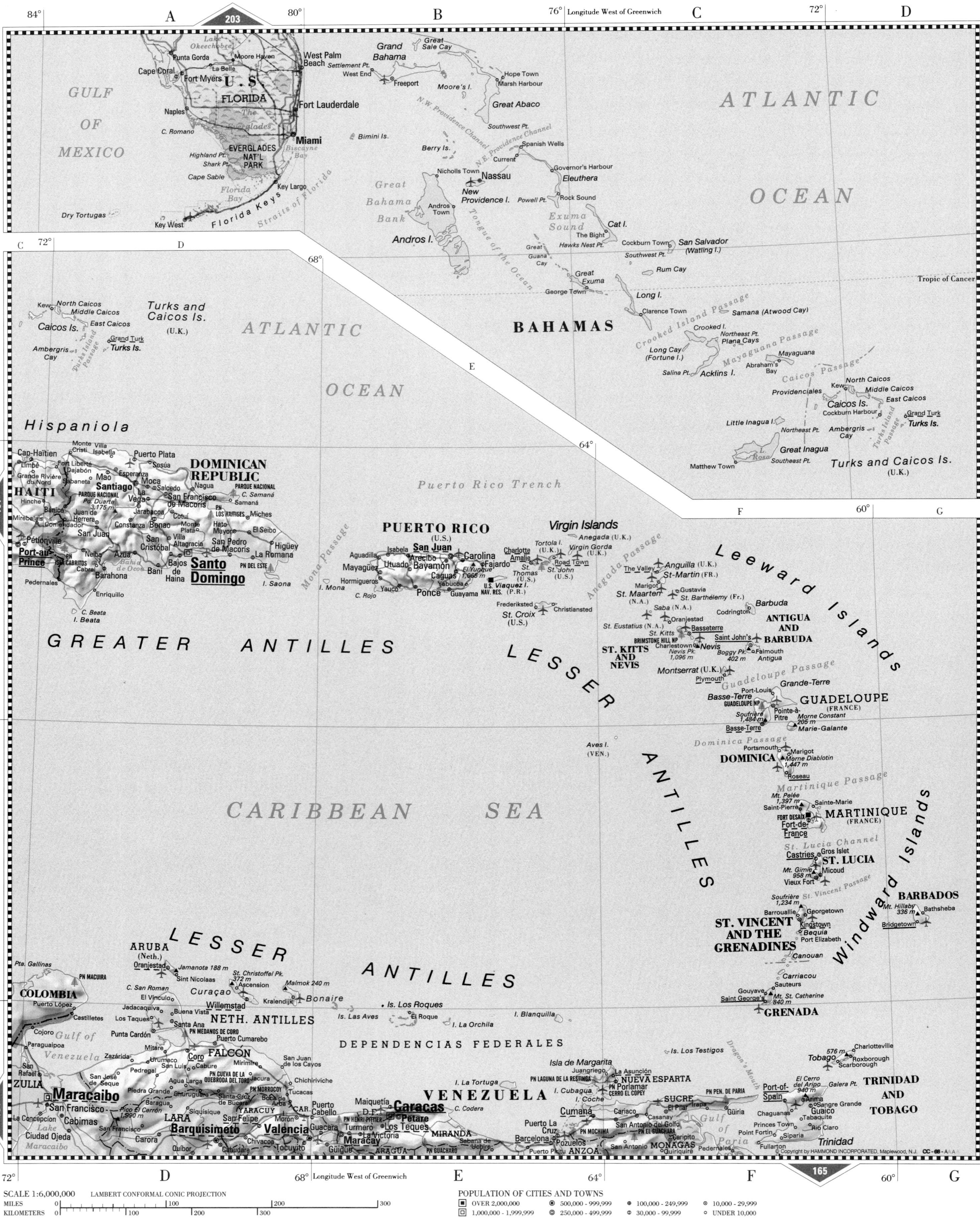


SCALE 1:6,000,000 LAMBERT CONFORMAL CONIC PROJECTION

MILES 0 100 200 300

KILOMETERS 0 100 200 300

POPULATION OF CITIES AND TOWNS

| | | | |
|---|---|---|---|
| ■ OVER 2,000,000 | ● 500,000 - 999,999 | • 100,000 - 249,999 | • 10,000 - 29,999 |
| □ 1,000,000 - 1,999,999 | ● 250,000 - 499,999 | • 30,000 - 99,999 | ○ UNDER 10,000 |

# South America

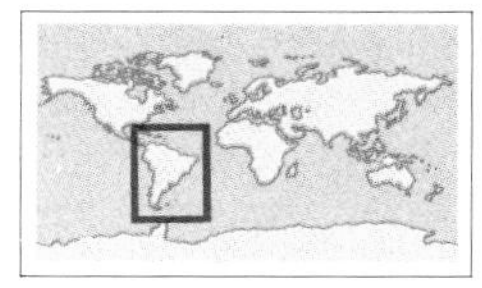

This vast continent extends 4750 miles (7600 km.), from lush rain forests in Venezuela to near-polar conditions at Cape Horn. The major offshore islands include the Galapagos, with their unique wildlife. Before the arrival of the Spanish and Portuguese, Indian civilizations flourished here. The Incan empire spanned Bolivia, Peru, Ecuador, Argentina and Chile.

AREA OF OPTIMIZATION
The red band which surrounds this map defines the "Area of Optimization." Within this bounding curve is the most accurate conformal map that can be made of the region. Outside the optimized area, distortion increases rapidly, and tears or other irregularities in the grid may occur. (See page 11 for additional information.)

POPULATION OF CITIES AND TOWNS

- ■ OVER 3,000,000
- ⊡ 1,000,000 - 2,999,999
- ◉ 500,000 - 999,999
- ● 100,000 - 499,999
- ○ UNDER 100,000

SCALE 1:24,000,000 OPTIMAL CONFORMAL PROJECTION

MILES 0 400 800 1200

KILOMETERS 0 400 800 1200

Coffee and cattle are the chief agricultural commodities of this often mountainous region, although the drug cocaine, made from the coca leaf, has become the most profitable export. Oil is vital to the economies of all three nations: largest reserves are near Lake Maracaibo and the Orinoco tar belt. High inland, the capital cities, Quito, Bogotá and Caracas enjoy cool climates and historic central plazas. The population of mixed Indian and Spanish ancestry is very different from the non-Hispanic Caribbean culture of the "three Guianas," home to a large African and Asian majority.

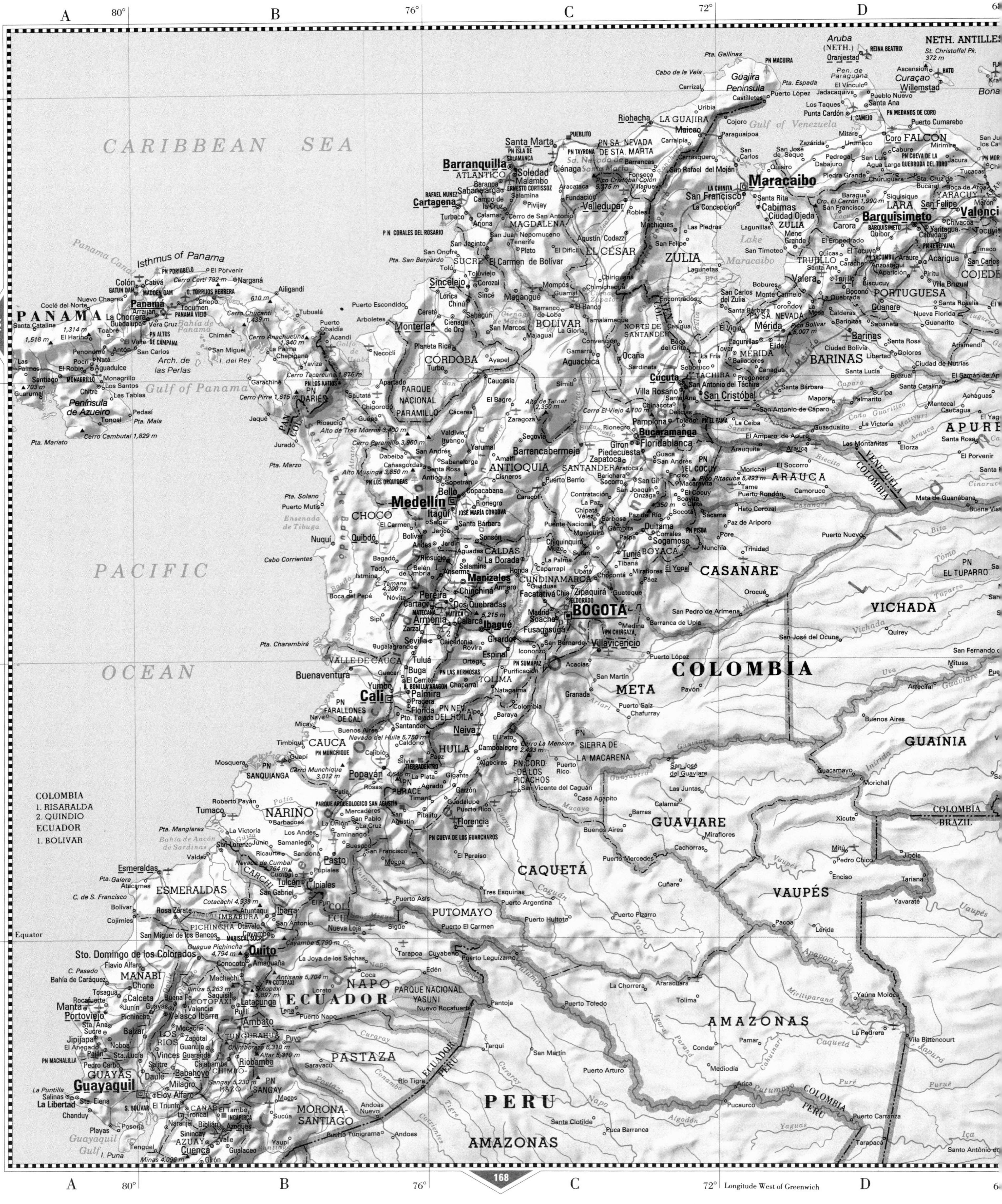

# Colombia, Venezuela, Ecuador

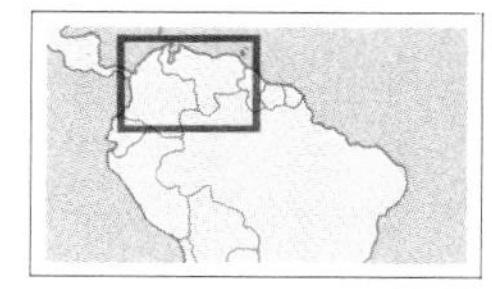

POPULATION OF CITIES AND TOWNS

| | | | |
|---|---|---|---|
| OVER 2,000,000 | 500,000 - 999,999 | 100,000 - 249,999 | 10,000 - 29,999 |
| 1,000,000 - 1,999,999 | 250,000 - 499,999 | 30,000 - 99,999 | UNDER 10,000 |

SCALE 1:6,000,000 LAMBERT CONFORMAL CONIC PROJECTION

MILES 0 100 200 300

KILOMETERS 0 100 200 300

Within the Amazon Basin of Brazil is the world's largest rain forest, home to over a million species of plants and animals. Indian tribes who live here depend on the forest for food and shelter.

The forest is also a nutrient and fresh-water reservoir. Over 40 prescription drugs can be traced to rain forest plants. Two thousand other plants with life-saving properties have been identified.

Every year, over 5000 square miles (13,000 sq. km.) of this vital ecosystem are destroyed. National legislation and international protests are making limited progress in preserving the forest.

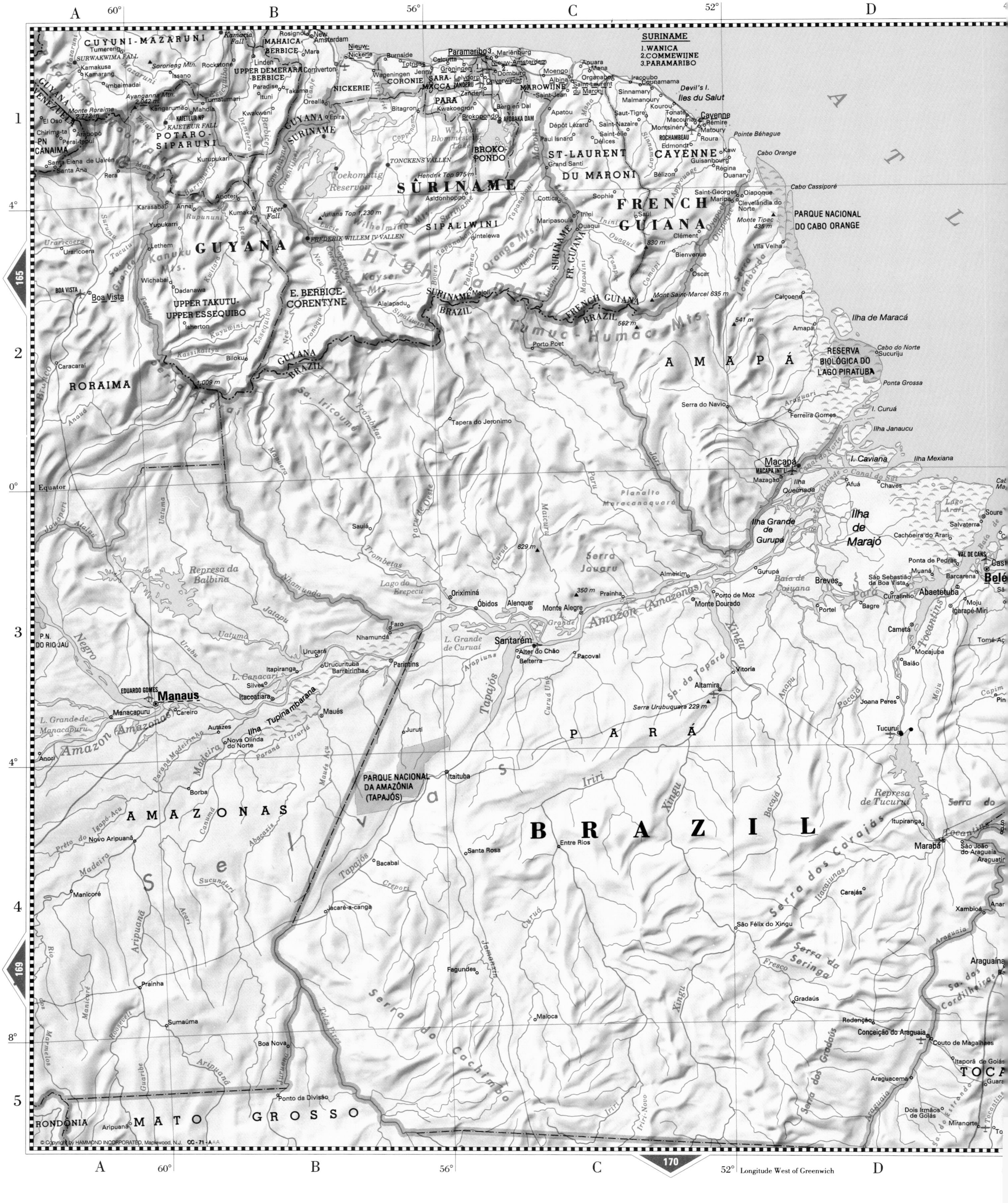

# Guianas, Northern Brazil

POPULATION OF CITIES AND TOWNS

- OVER 2,000,000
- 1,000,000 - 1,999,999
- 500,000 - 999,999
- 250,000 - 499,999
- 100,000 - 249,999
- 30,000 - 99,999
- 10,000 - 29,999
- UNDER 10,000

SCALE 1:6,000,000 LAMBERT CONFORMAL CONIC PROJECTION

MILES 0 100 200 300

KILOMETERS 0 100 200 300

Here are found the ancient ruins of the great native American pre-Columbian civilizations of Andean Peru and Bolivia - the Chavín, the Mochica, the Tiahuanaco, the Chimú and particularly the Inca. The highly developed Inca Empire had a centralized military-political system. It farmed intensively, and utilized domestic animals in economic and transport systems. Unlike major cultures in China and India, the pre-Columbian societies of the Americas fell quickly under the repeated assaults of the conquistadores well before the end of the 16th century.

# Peru, Northern Bolivia, Western Brazil

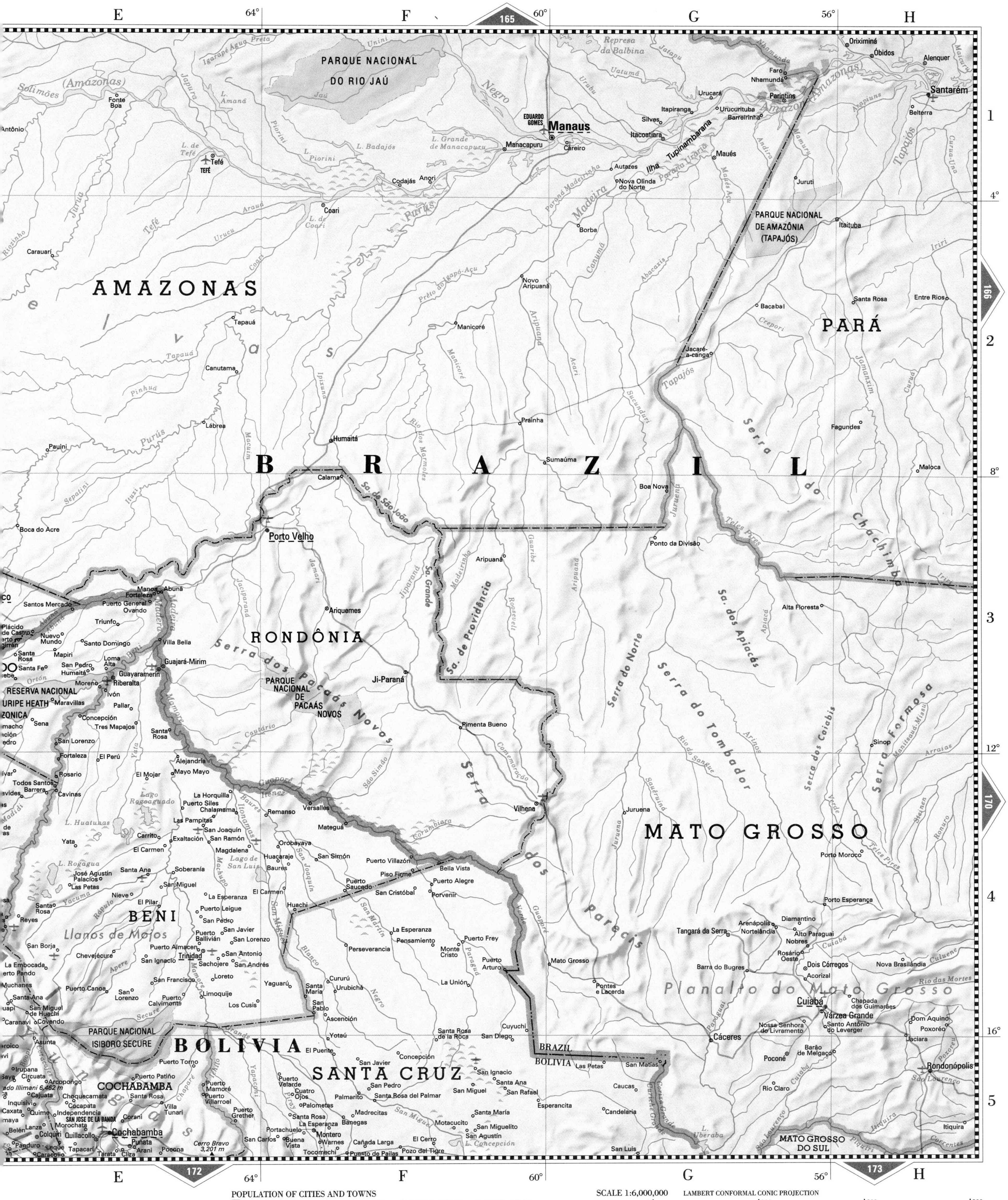


POPULATION OF CITIES AND TOWNS

- OVER 2,000,000
- 1,000,000 - 1,999,999
- 500,000 - 999,999
- 250,000 - 499,999
- 100,000 - 249,999
- 30,000 - 99,999
- 10,000 - 29,999
- UNDER 10,000

SCALE 1:6,000,000 LAMBERT CONFORMAL CONIC PROJECTION

MILES 0 100 200 300

KILOMETERS 0 100 200 300

The largest and most populous South American country, Brazil is the only Portuguese-speaking nation in the Americas. Its tropical to semi-tropical climate and highland areas are ideal for coffee-growing, and Brazil is the world's leading producer. This economic dependence on one key crop – vulnerable to frosts, droughts, and market changes – has been mitigated by the rise of sugar, citrus, cotton, rice and tobacco exports. Brazil's dramatic industrial expansion has been matched by the explosive growth of its major cities – and foreign debt.

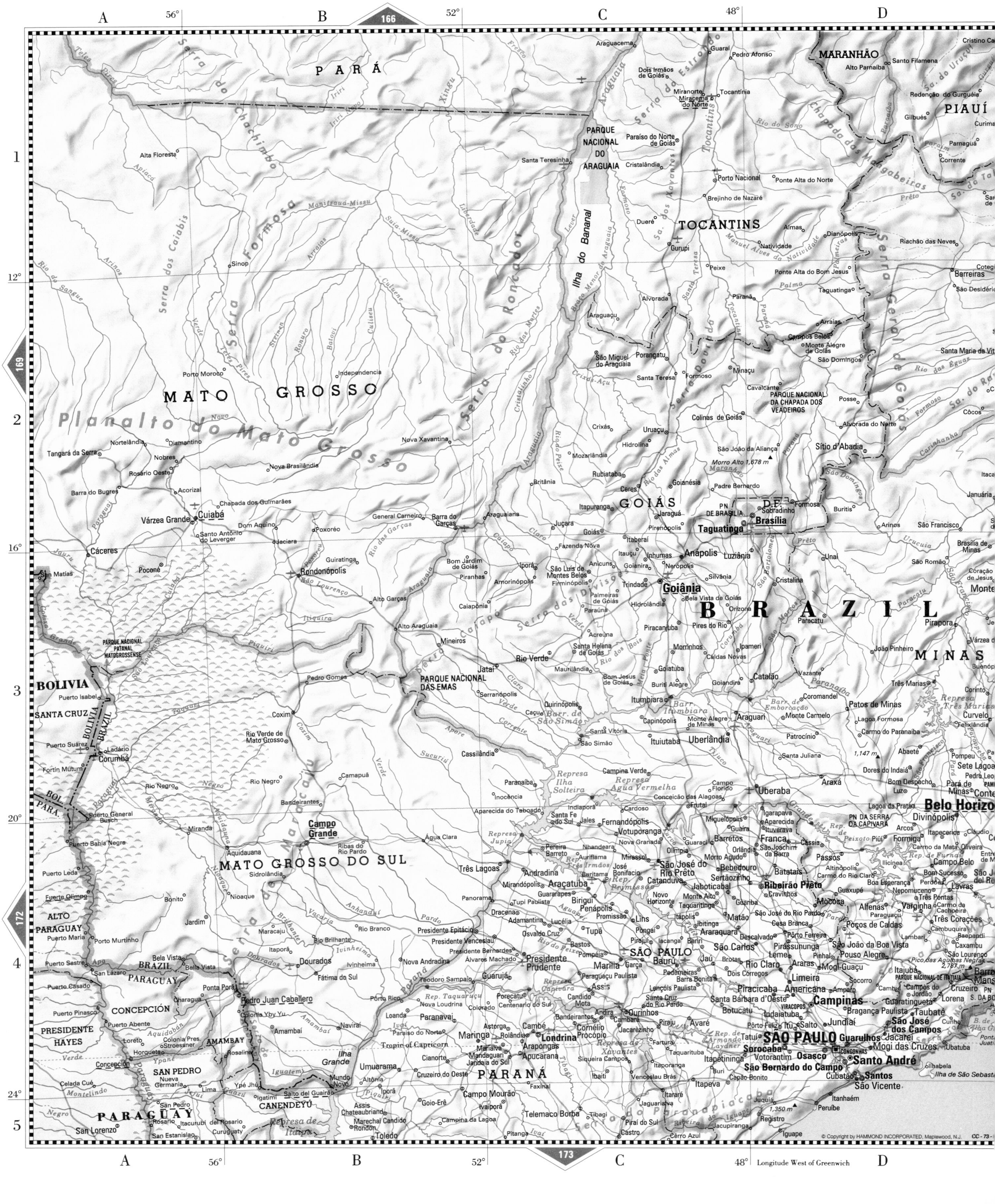

# Eastern Brazil

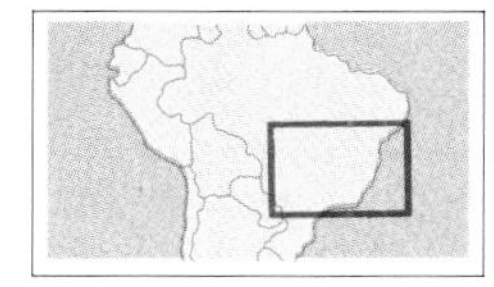

POPULATION OF CITIES AND TOWNS
- OVER 2,000,000
- 1,000,000 - 1,999,999
- 500,000 - 999,999
- 250,000 - 499,999
- 100,000 - 249,999
- 30,000 - 99,999
- 10,000 - 29,999
- UNDER 10,000

SCALE 1:6,000,000 LAMBERT CONFORMAL CONIC PROJECTION

MILES 0 100 200 300

KILOMETERS 0 100 200 300

Great mineral resources are buried within this wide band crossing the continent. Iron ore from the Brazilian state of Minas Gerais and the eastern Amazon basin feeds the growing Brazilian steel industry. Gold has also been discovered here, setting off a modern-day gold rush. Bolivia is one of the world's chief suppliers of tin, and an important supplier of tungsten and antimony. In Chile's northern desert region, copper ore is mined in great quantity. Vast dams on the Paraná and its tributaries supply Brazil and Paraguay with hydroelectric power.

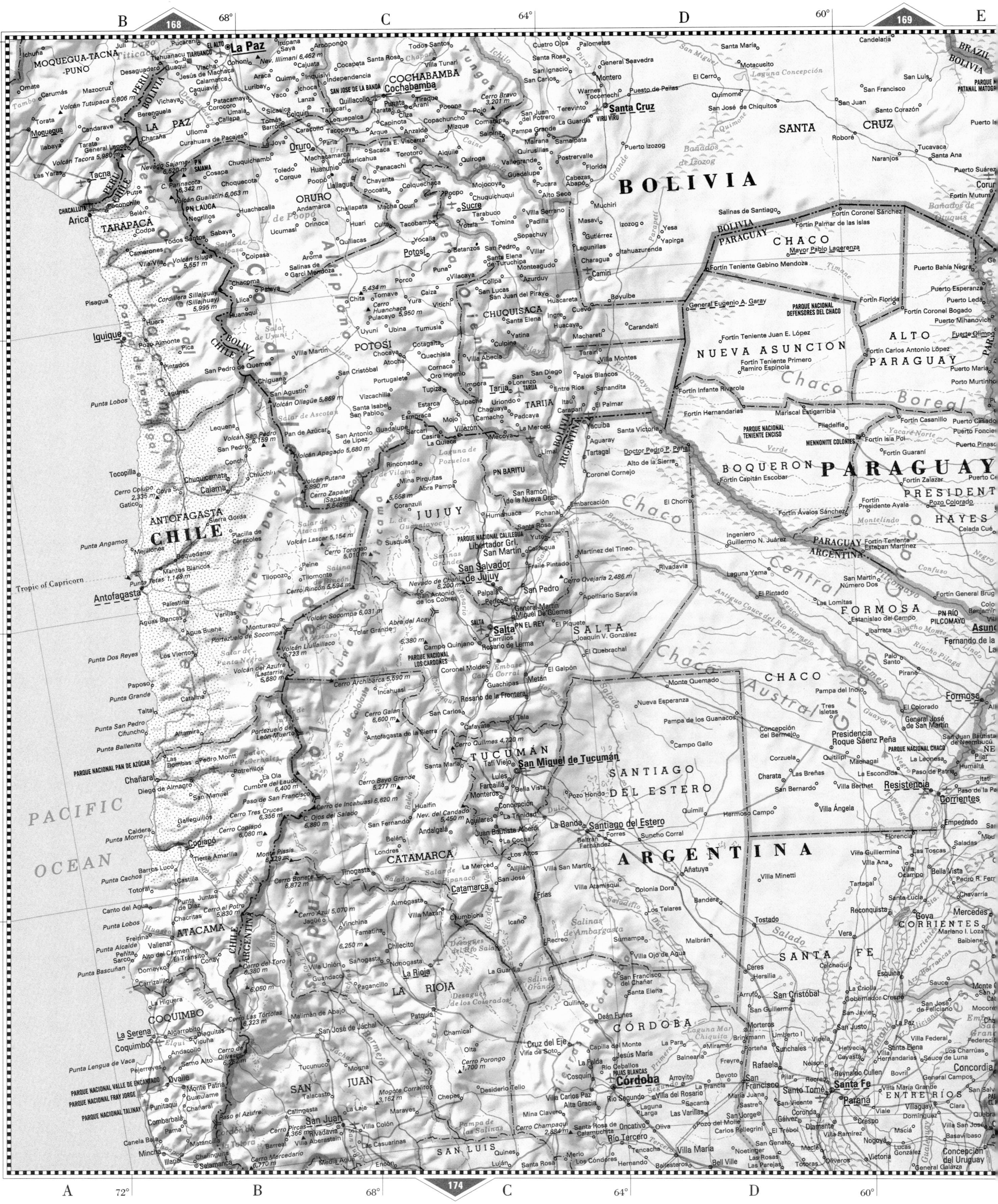

# Central South America

POPULATION OF CITIES AND TOWNS

- OVER 2,000,000
- 1,000,000 - 1,999,999
- 500,000 - 999,999
- 250,000 - 499,999
- 100,000 - 249,999
- 30,000 - 99,999
- 10,000 - 29,999
- UNDER 10,000

SCALE 1:6,000,000 LAMBERT CONFORMAL CONIC PROJECTION

MILES 0 100 200 300

KILOMETERS 0 100 200 300

Agriculture is the hallmark of these two countries. The Argentine Pampas is famed for its cattle, corn, wheat and flax. Sheep graze in the dry scrub country of the southern Patagonian steppe. Despite the country's Indian heritage, most Argentines are of Spanish and Italian descent. Aross the Andes, in Chile, the population is concentrated in a central valley. Chile's mountainous terrain and northern desert preclude farming. But the central region's Mediterranean-type climate yields bountiful fruit crops and fine red wines. The southern coast is heavily forested.

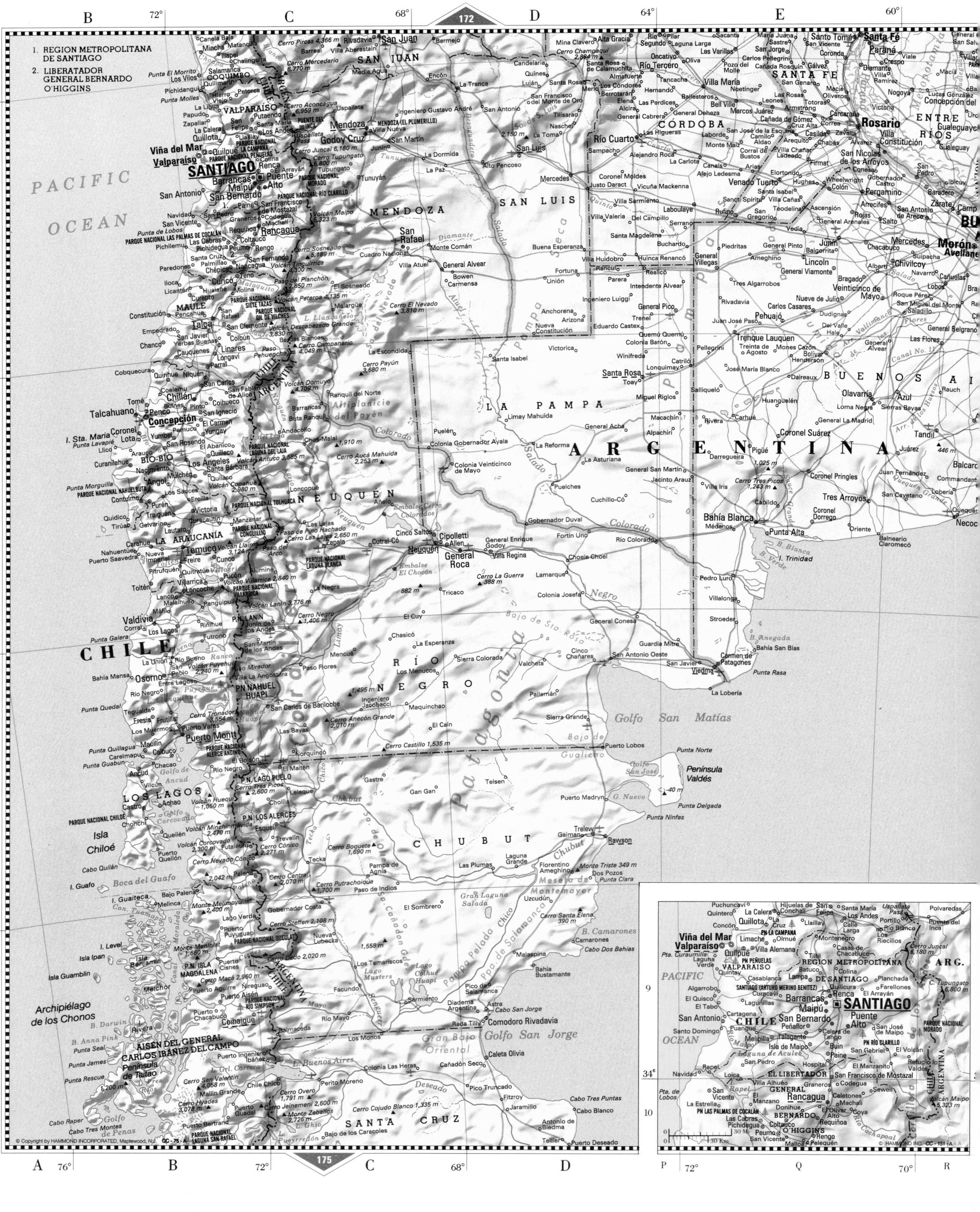

# Southern Chile and Argentina

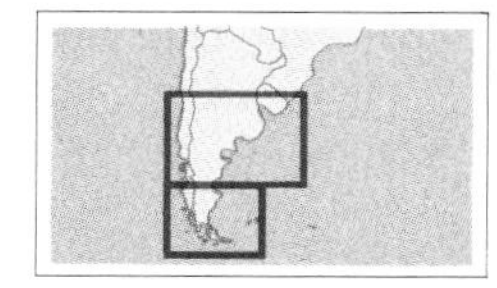

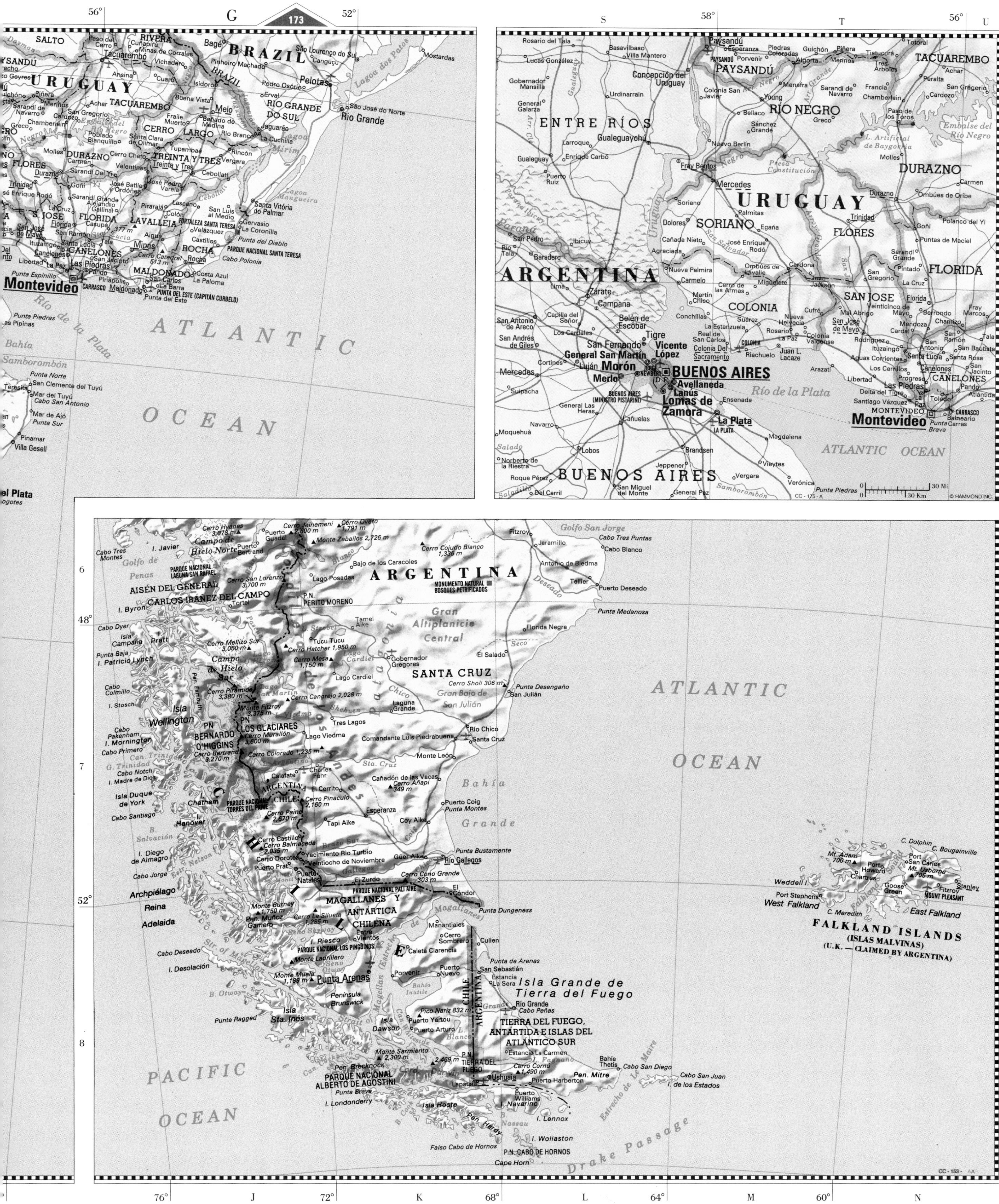


POPULATION OF CITIES AND TOWNS

| | | | |
|---|---|---|---|
| ■ OVER 2,000,000 | ◉ 500,000 - 999,999 | ● 100,000 - 249,999 | ⊙ 10,000 - 29,999 |
| ▣ 1,000,000 - 1,999,999 | ◎ 250,000 - 499,999 | ⊕ 30,000 - 99,999 | ○ UNDER 10,000 |

SCALE 1:6,000,000 — LAMBERT CONFORMAL CONIC PROJECTION

MILES 0 — 100 — 200 — 300

KILOMETERS 0 — 100 — 200 — 300

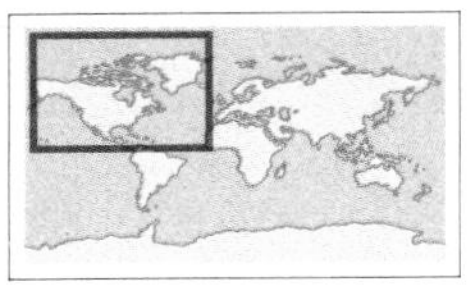

# North America

North America spans a vast range of climates, from the Central American rain forests to the Arctic permafrost. More than 75 percent of Greenland is ice-covered. Culturally, the continent divides along the Rio Grande, with the U.S. and Canada to the north, and Latin America to the south. French-speaking Quebec and the multi-cultural Caribbean islands add ethnic diversity.

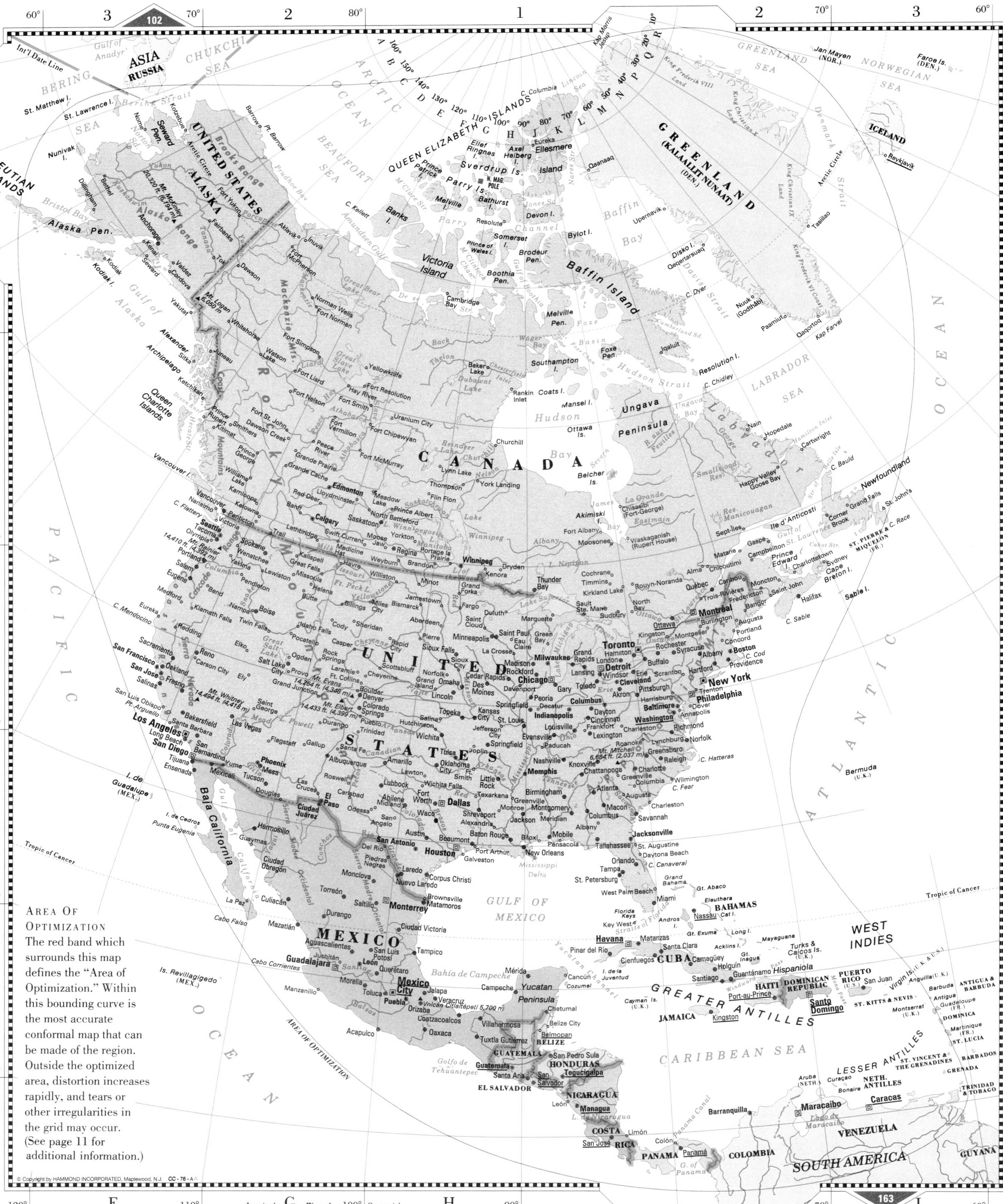


**Area Of Optimization**
The red band which surrounds this map defines the "Area of Optimization." Within this bounding curve is the most accurate conformal map that can be made of the region. Outside the optimized area, distortion increases rapidly, and tears or other irregularities in the grid may occur. (See page 11 for additional information.)

SCALE 1:30,000,000 OPTIMAL CONFORMAL PROJECTION
MILES 0 – 500 – 1000 – 1500
KILOMETERS 0 – 500 – 1000 – 1500

POPULATION OF CITIES AND TOWNS
- OVER 3,000,000
- 1,000,000 - 2,999,999
- 500,000 - 999,999
- 100,000 - 499,999
- UNDER 100,000

# Alaska

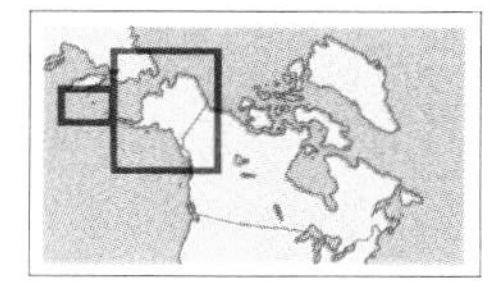

During the last ice age, huge quantities of water were trapped in enormous ice caps. The world's sea and ocean levels sank, and Alaska was joined to Asia at the Bering Sea. Consequently the early ancestors of the native Americans crossed into the continent from here. Alaska's rich mineral resources and natural splendors support and inspire its 550,000 residents.

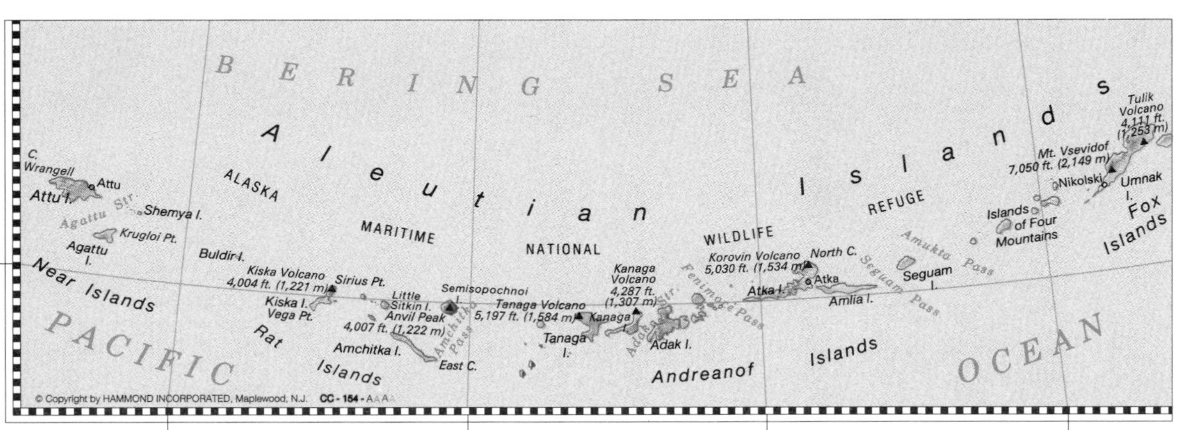


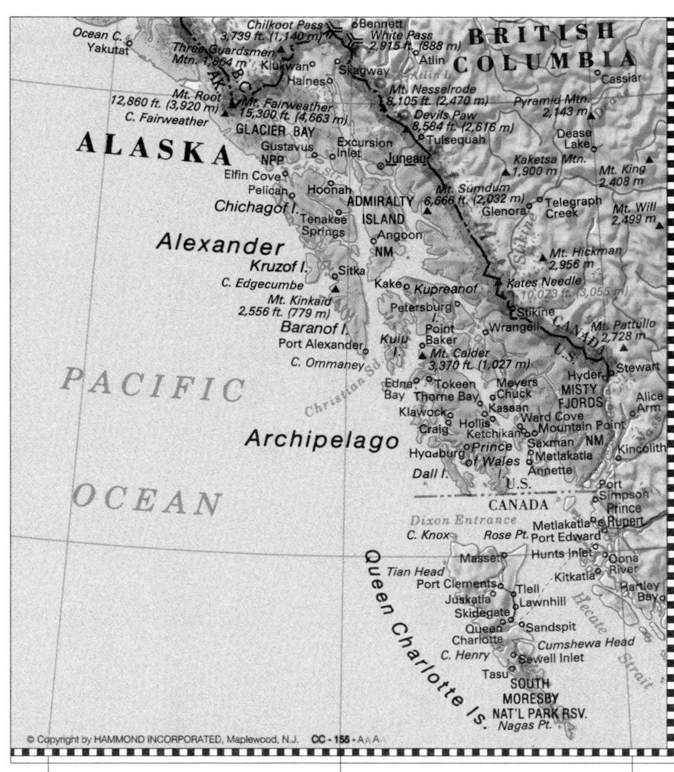


POPULATION OF CITIES AND TOWNS

- OVER 2,000,000
- 1,000,000 - 1,999,999
- 500,000 - 999,999
- 250,000 - 499,999
- 100,000 - 249,999
- 30,000 - 99,999
- 10,000 - 29,999
- UNDER 10,000

SCALE 1:9,000,000 LAMBERT CONFORMAL CONIC PROJECTION

MILES 0 150 300 450

KILOMETERS 0 150 300 450

Canada is larger, but its populati
is only one-tenth that of the U.S
A very short growing season north of 55
North Latitude, the extremely thin soils
north of the St. Lawrence Valley, and th

SCALE 1:12,000,000 LAMBERT CONFORMAL CONIC PROJECTION

MILES 0 200 400 600

KILOMETERS 0 200 400 600

POPULATION OF CITIES AND TOWNS

- OVER 2,000,000
- 1,000,000 - 1,999,999
- 500,000 - 999,999
- 100,000 - 499,999
- 50,000 - 99,999
- UNDER 50,000

recipitation of the northwestern erous forest and tundra region have uraged widespread settlement ghout Canada. In fact, the vast rity of Canadians reside in the south, along a 100-mile-wide (161 km.) zone which stretches from Quebec to Vancouver. English and French are both official languages, while Eskimo-Aleut is spoken in the far north.

# Canada

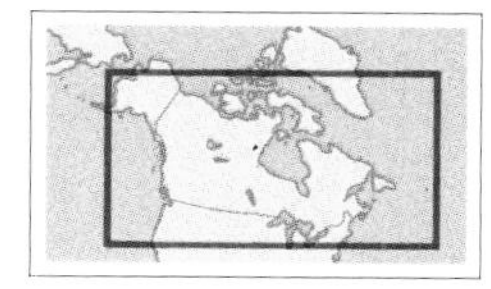

Lying between the 24th and 49th parallels north of the equator (excluding Alaska and Hawaii), the U.S. has a wide range of climates. Although areas in the western states are very dry, the country, has many very productive agricultural regions. A rich natural storehouse of minerals and fuels provided the underpinning for industrial development. Americans continue to move more frequently than the citizens of any other nation. The geographic center of population is now located west of the Mississippi River, as the movement of people is to the west and to the south.

# United States

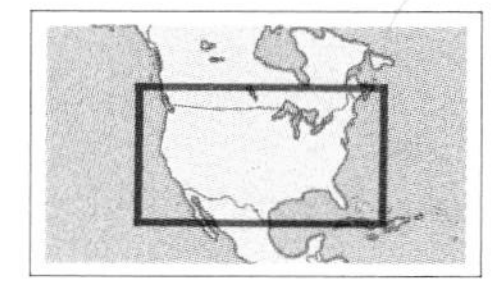

POPULATION OF CITIES AND TOWNS

- OVER 2,000,000
- 1,000,000 - 1,999,999
- 500,000 - 999,999
- 100,000 - 499,999
- 50,000 - 99,999
- UNDER 50,000

SCALE 1:12,000,000 LAMBERT CONFORMAL CONIC PROJECTION

MILES 0 200 400 600

KILOMETERS 0 200 400 600

The Rocky Mountains, Glacier and Olympic national parks and Puget Sound rank among the most beautiful areas of the United States. The Coast Ranges are part of the Pacific "Ring of Fire;" Mt. St. Helens erupted in 1980, and the possibility exists that Mount Rainier might erupt and threaten such metropolitan areas as Seattle and Tacoma. Canada's prairie provinces produce most of the country's grain and livestock. British Colombia has prospered due to its convenient strategic location for both transcontinental and transoceanic trade.

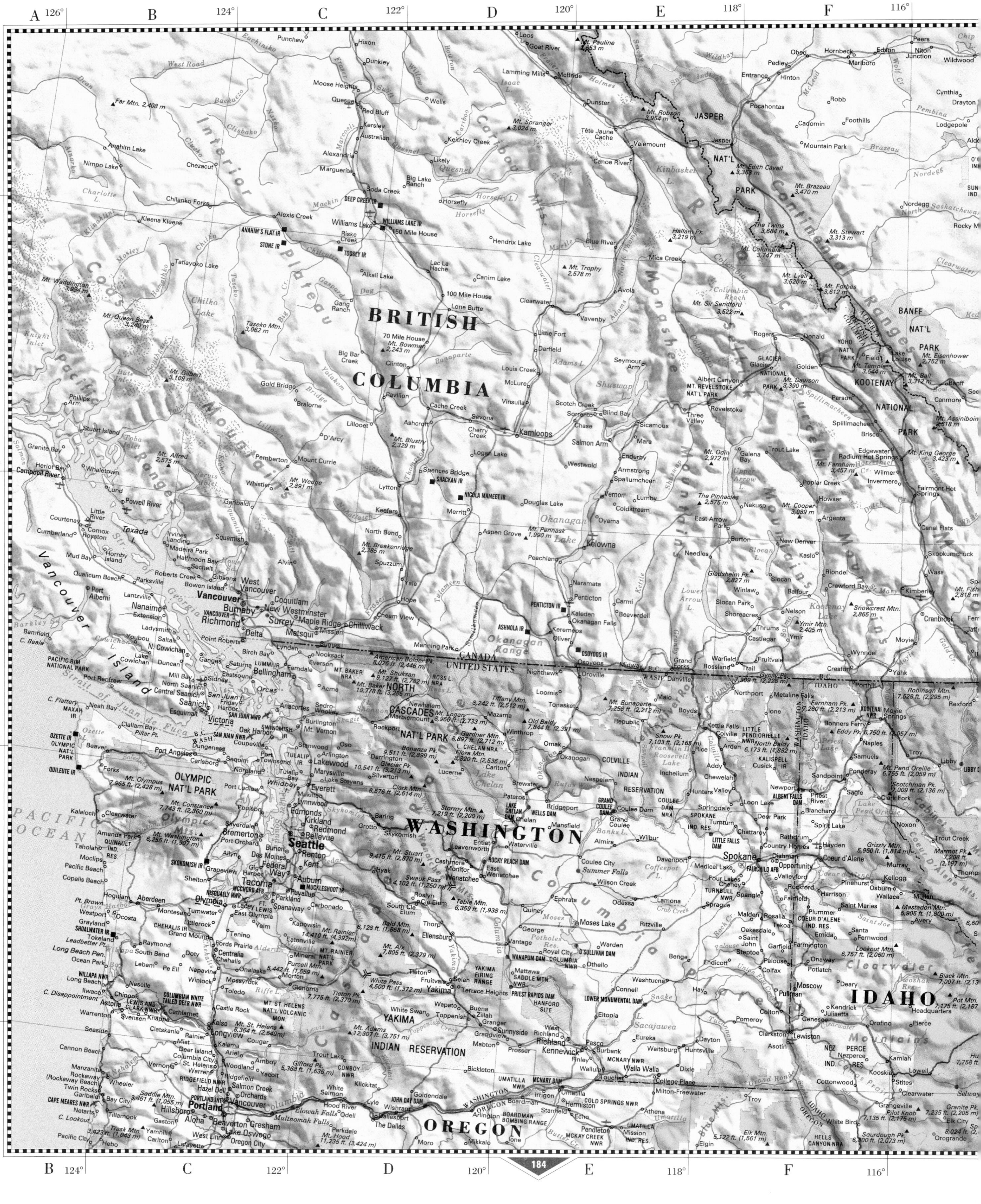

# Southwestern Canada, Northwestern United States

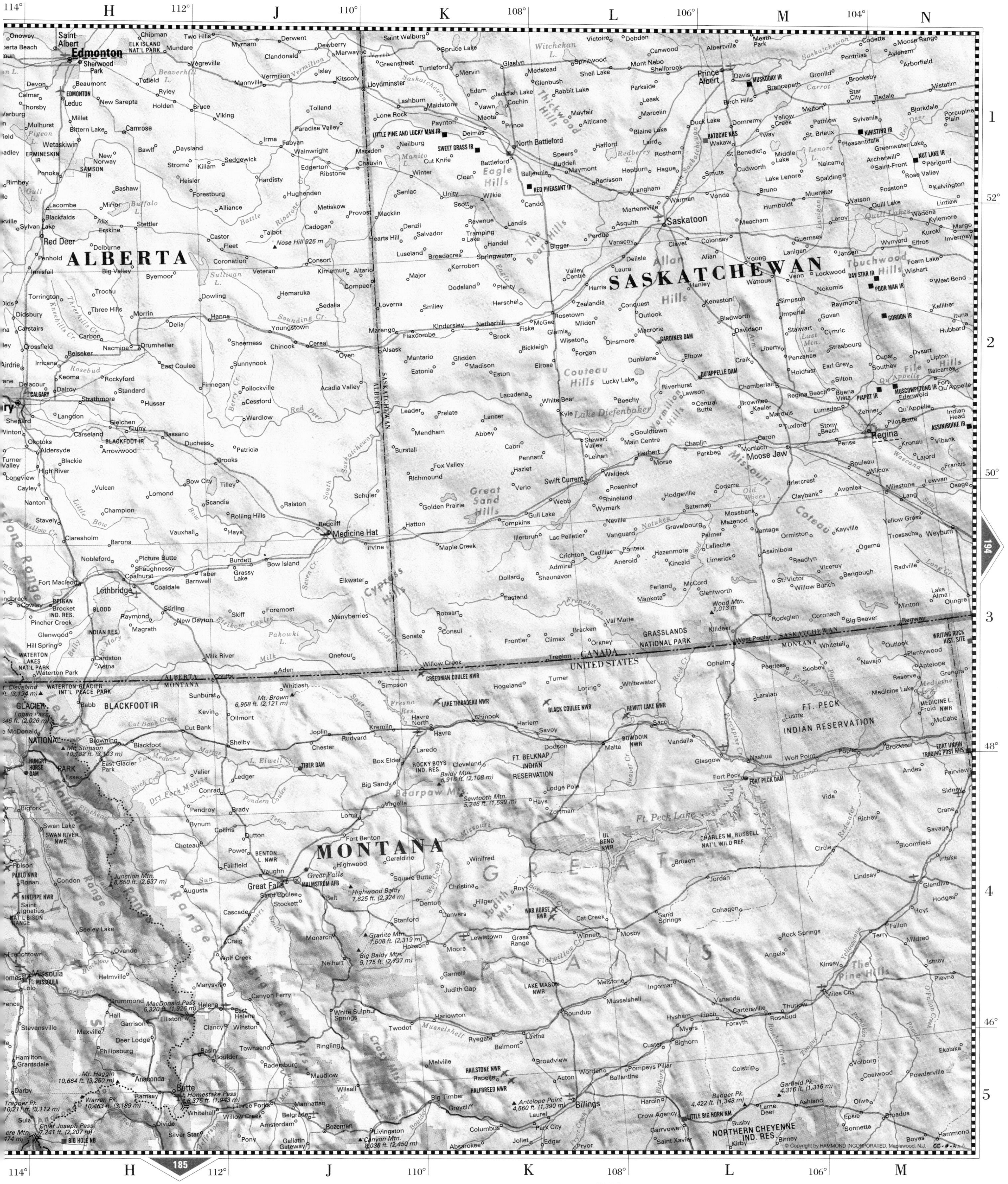


POPULATION OF CITIES AND TOWNS

- OVER 2,000,000
- 1,000,000 - 1,999,999
- 500,000 - 999,999
- 250,000 - 499,999
- 100,000 - 249,999
- 30,000 - 99,999
- 10,000 - 29,999
- UNDER 10,000

SCALE 1:3,000,000 LAMBERT CONFORMAL CONIC PROJECTION

MILES 0 50 100 150

KILOMETERS 0 50 100 150

As in the Southwest, water is the driving human issue in much of this area. Large parts of Nevada and Utah receive, on the average, less than 10 inches (25 cm.) of rainfall a year. Massive irrigation projects over the last hundred years have made Idaho's Snake River Valley fertile. Water from the headwaters of the Colorado River has been diverted by a system of tunnels to agricultural lands east of the Rockies north of Denver. Although production from copper mines in Montana and Utah has dropped drastically, coal and uranium extraction remain important.

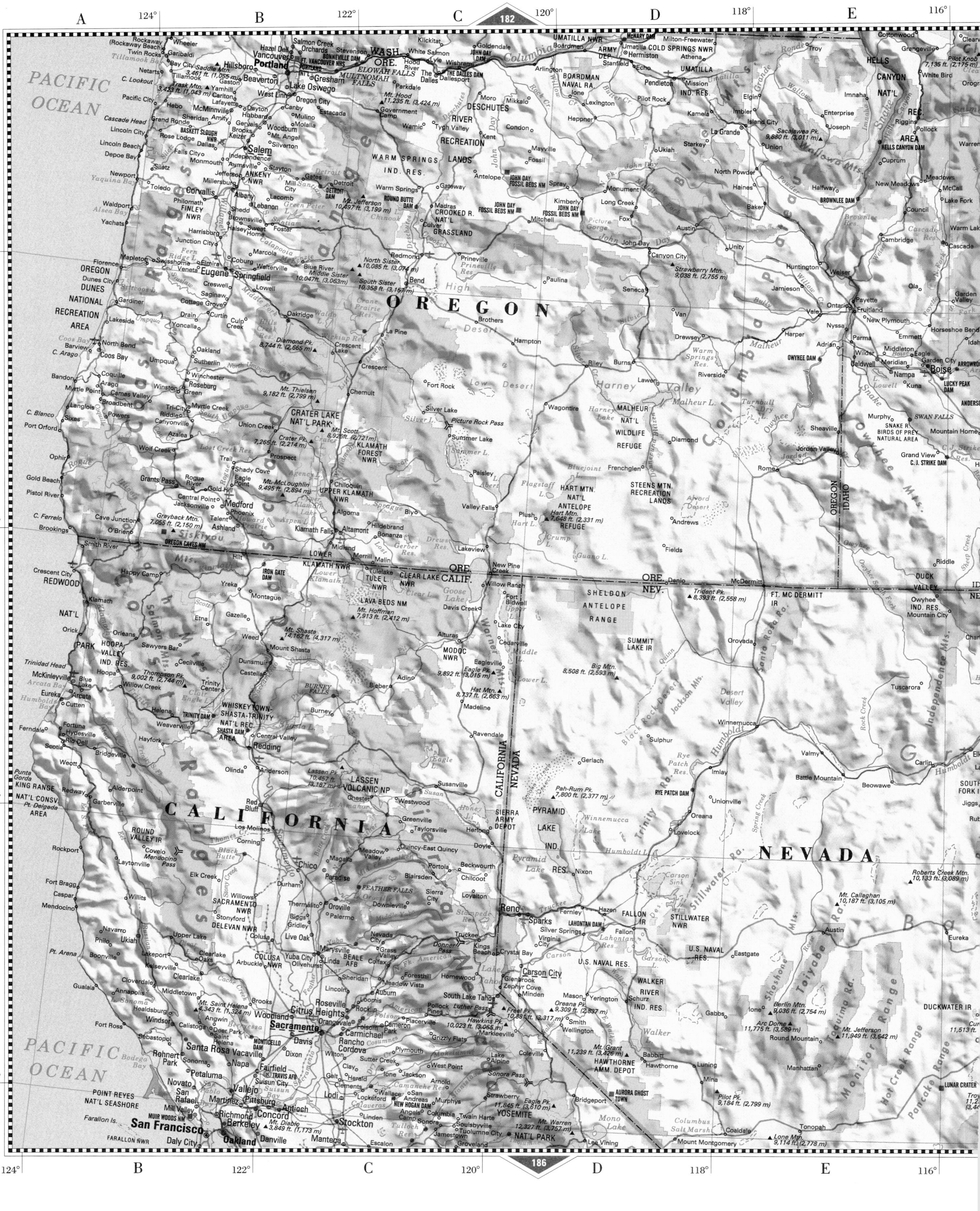

# Central Pacific and Western U.S.

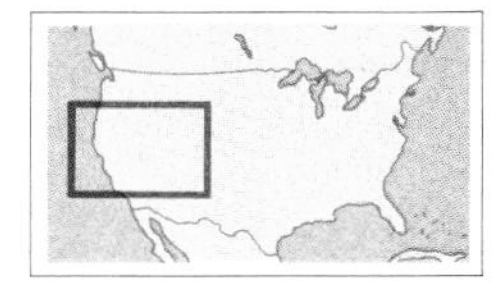

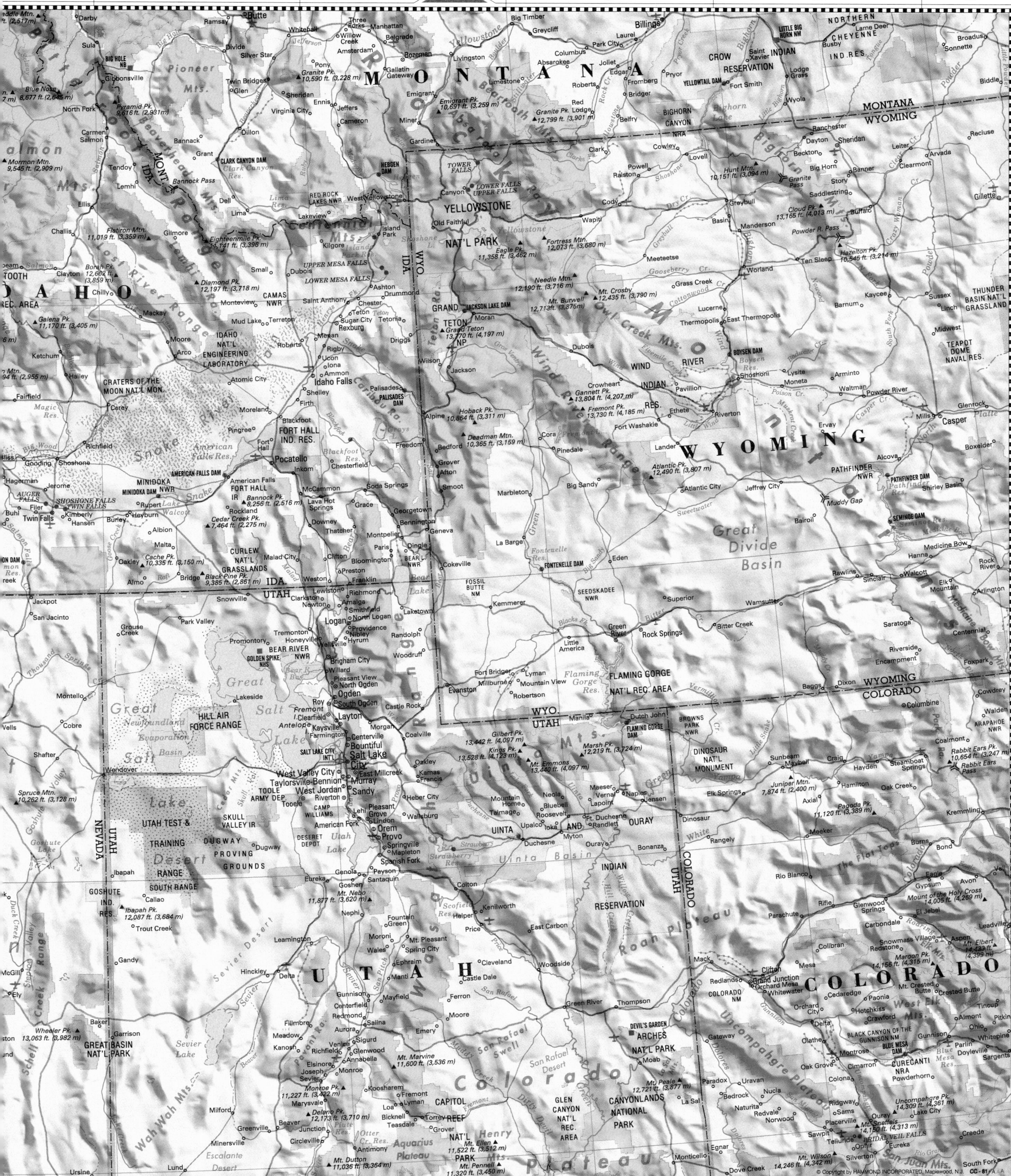


POPULATION OF CITIES AND TOWNS

- OVER 2,000,000
- 1,000,000 - 1,999,999
- 500,000 - 999,999
- 250,000 - 499,999
- 100,000 - 249,999
- 30,000 - 99,999
- 10,000 - 29,999
- UNDER 10,000

SCALE 1:3,000,000 LAMBERT CONFORMAL CONIC PROJECTION

MILES 0 50 100 150

KILOMETERS 0 50 100 150

Some of North America's earlier settlers – the Hopi, Navajo and Pueblo – flourished on the Colorado Plateau. Their ancient ruins echo the grandeur of the spires, arches and canyons nature has carved from the soft, bleached-red rock. The number and scale of national parks, monuments and recreation areas in the Southwest is unparalleled, from California's Sequoia, Death Valley and Yosemite to Arizona's Grand Canyon, Saguaro and Petrified Forest. Today, the overriding concern of this region is water, which is being depleted faster than nature can restore it.

# Southwestern United States

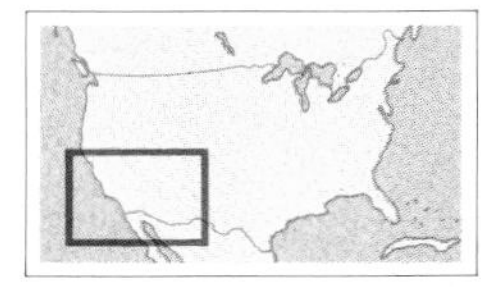

POPULATION OF CITIES AND TOWNS

- OVER 2,000,000
- 1,000,000 - 1,999,999
- 500,000 - 999,999
- 250,000 - 499,999
- 100,000 - 249,999
- 30,000 - 99,999
- 10,000 - 29,999
- UNDER 10,000

SCALE 1:3,000,000 LAMBERT CONFORMAL CONIC PROJECTION

MILES 0 50 100 150

KILOMETERS 0 50 100 150

Like the state of Hawaii, Texas was an independent nation before it became a part of the United States. Thus Texans share a strong sense of state loyalty and pride. Texas entered the 20th century as a cattle and cotton kingdom. Then, following the discovery of the spectacular Spindletop oil field in 1901, the state became the nation's prime source of energy. Today, Texas is also the center of the U.S. chemical industry. With the possible future growth of U.S. - Mexican free trade, Texas occupies a strategic location for inter-American commerce.

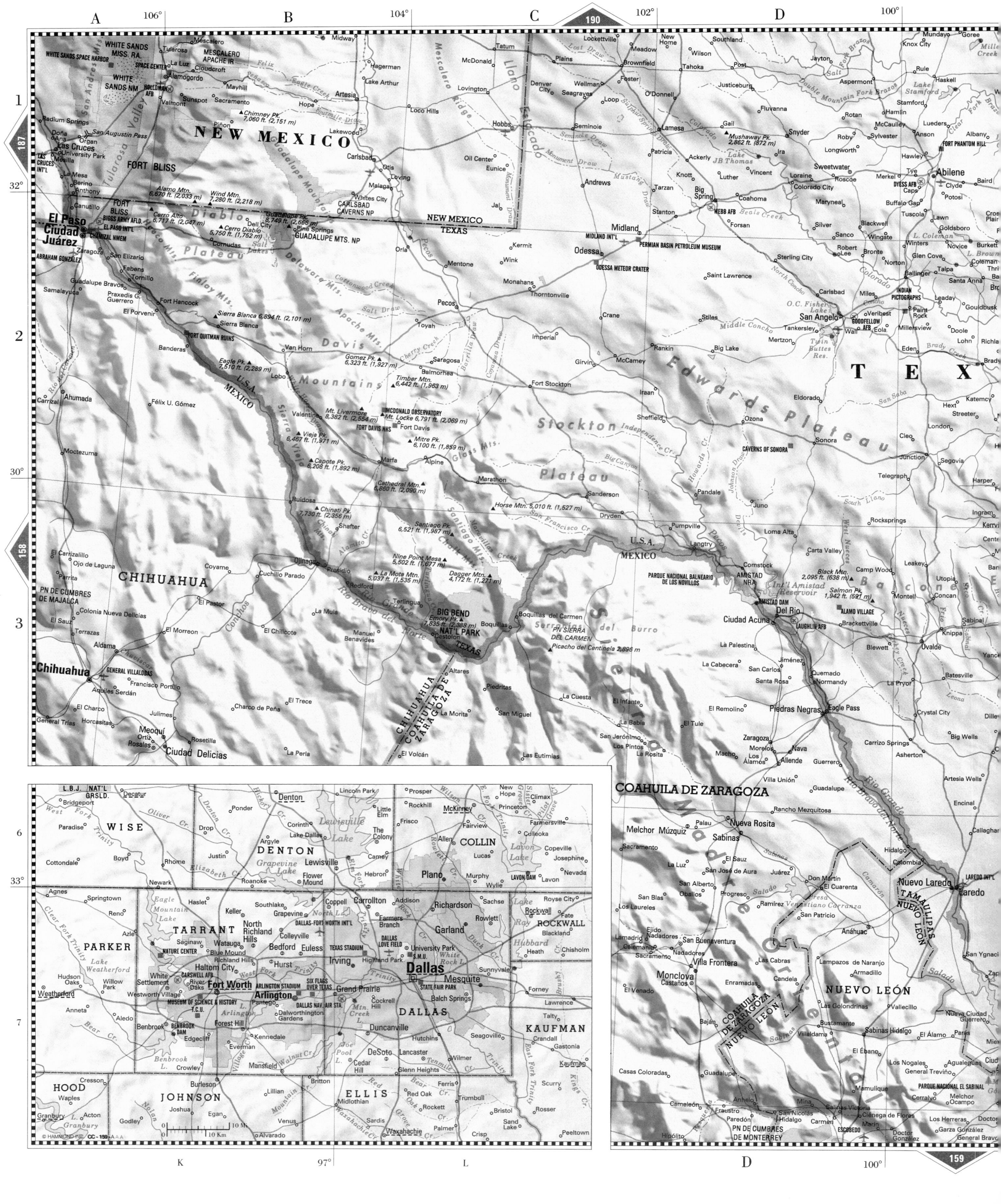

# Southern Texas

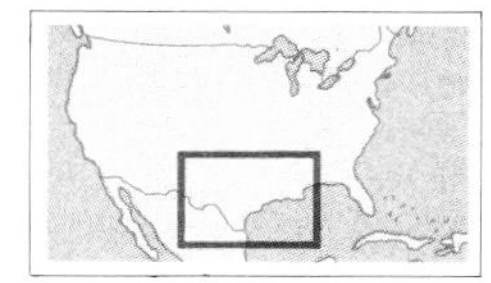

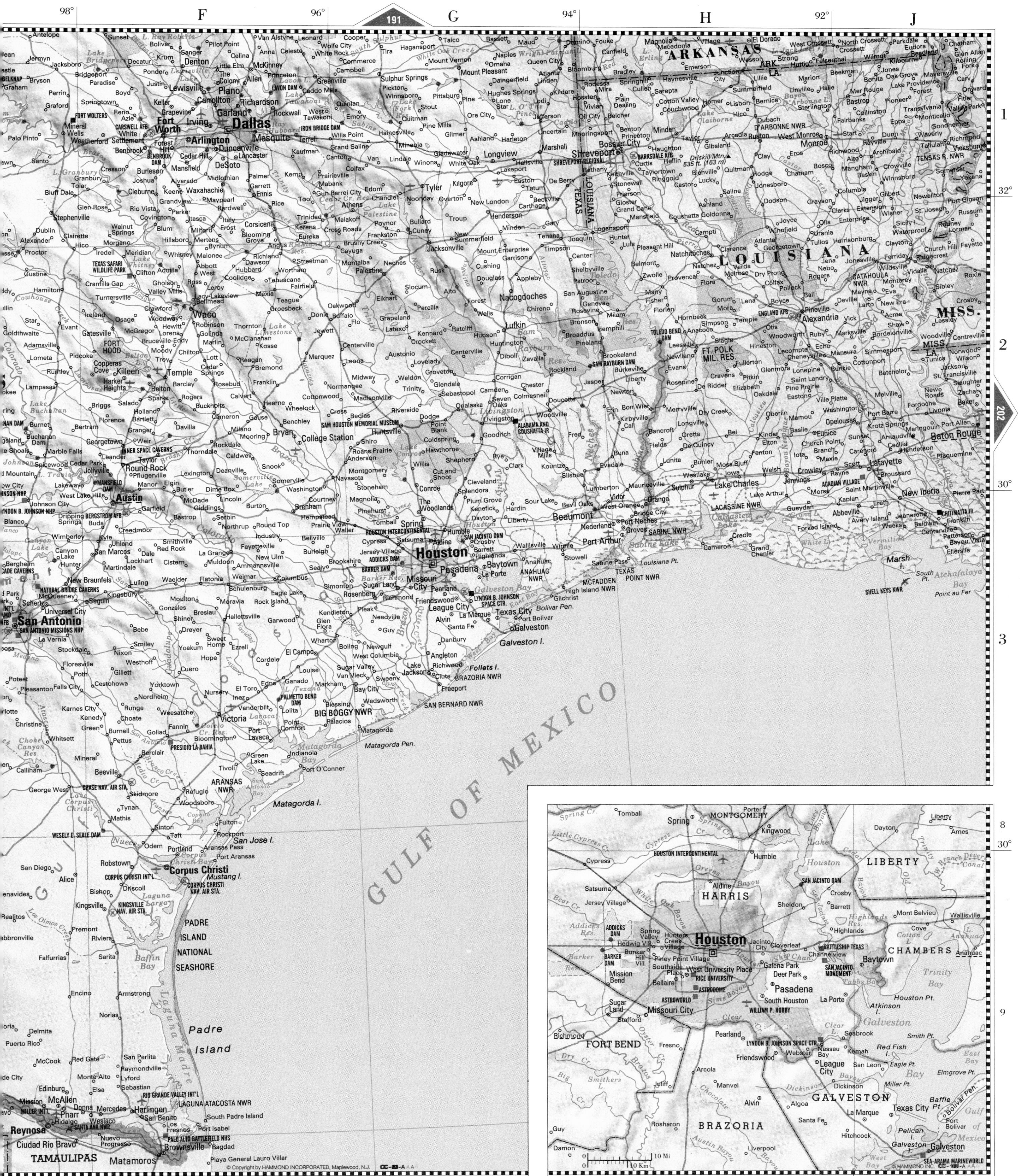


POPULATION OF CITIES AND TOWNS

| | | | |
|---|---|---|---|
| ▣ OVER 2,000,000 | ◉ 500,000 - 999,999 | ⊕ 100,000 - 249,999 | ○ 10,000 - 29,999 |
| ▢ 1,000,000 - 1,999,999 | ◎ 250,000 - 499,999 | ⊙ 30,000 - 99,999 | ○ UNDER 10,000 |

SCALE 1:3,000,000 LAMBERT CONFORMAL CONIC PROJECTION

MILES 0 50 100 150
KILOMETERS 0 50 100 150

Originally, the endless grasslands of the Great Plains were home to the Plains Indians. After horses were introduced to the upper Rio Grande Valley in the 1600s, Native Americans of the region – Comanche, Cheyenne, Kiowa, Pawnee, etc. – adopted a totally new culture based on bison hunting from horseback. The end of the Civil War brought the cattlemen, who dominated the region and created the legendary Cattle Kingdom of the 1870s and 80s. Eventually, homesteaders took over the Plains, producing an abundance of wheat and other grains.

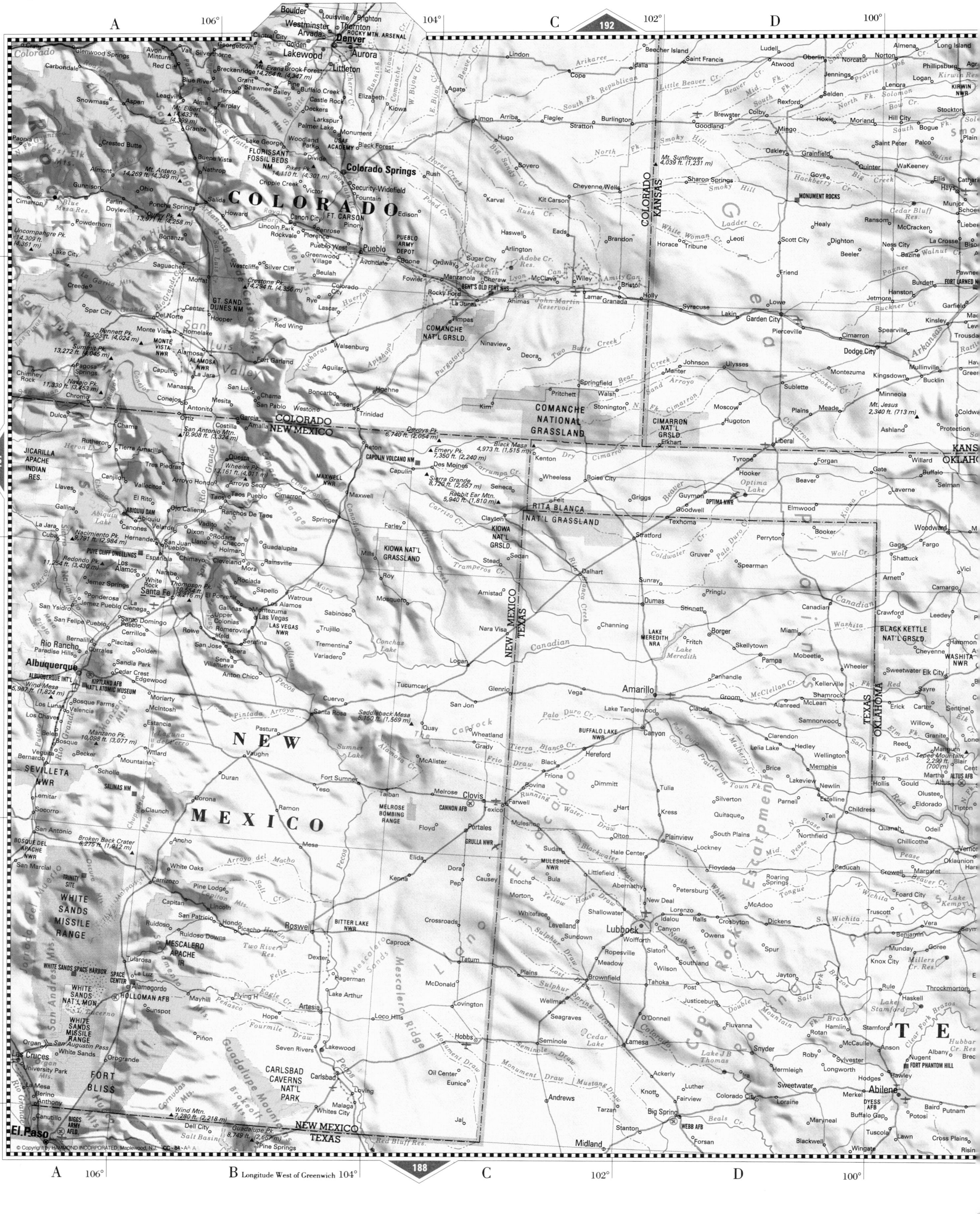

# Southern Great Plains Region

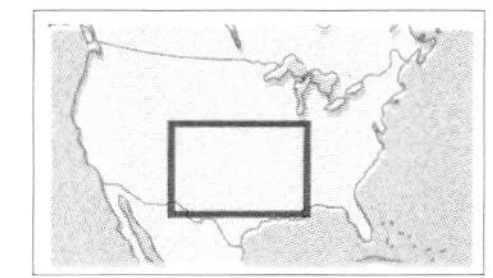

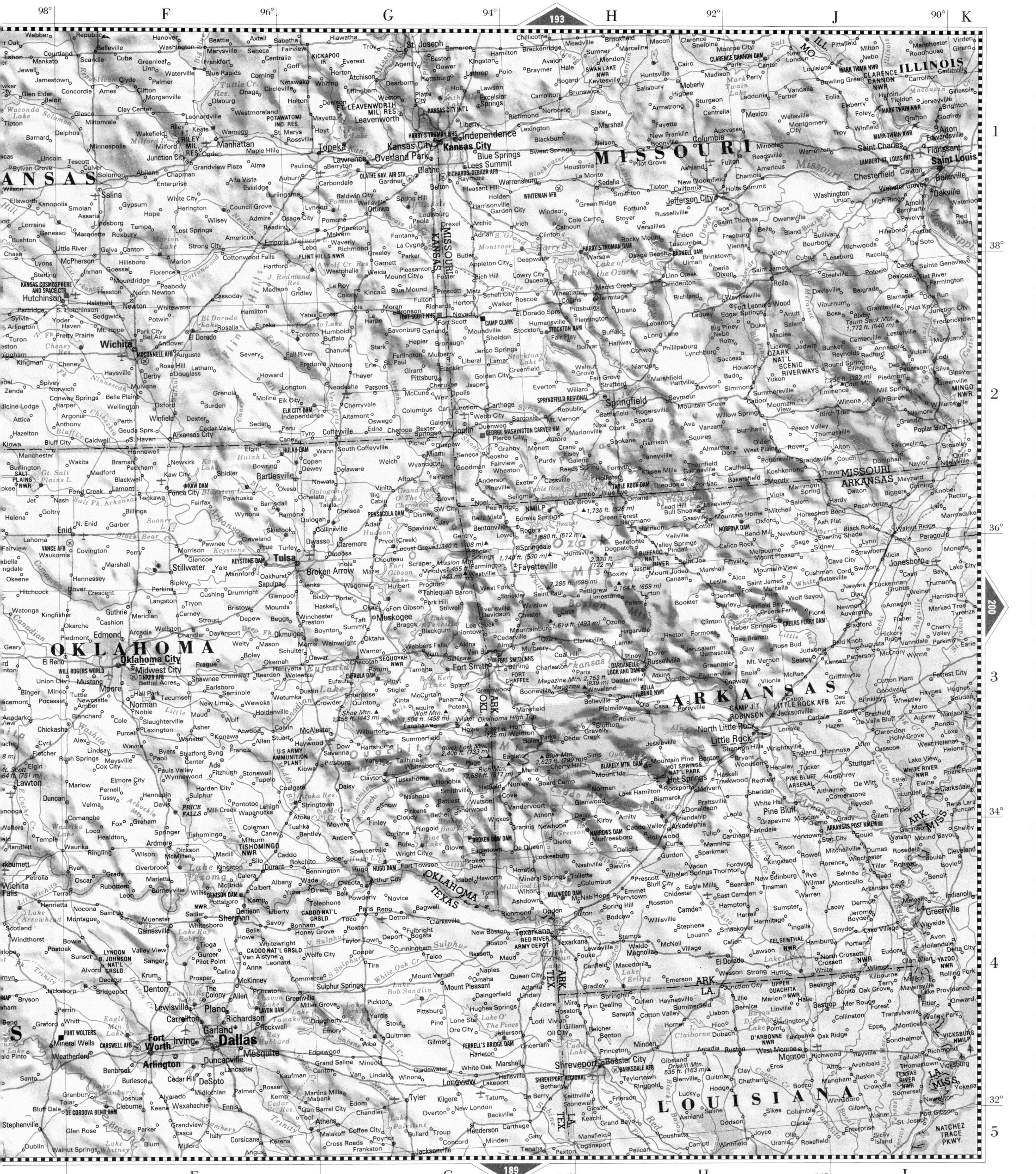


POPULATION OF CITIES AND TOWNS

- OVER 2,000,000
- 1,000,000 - 1,999,999
- 500,000 - 999,999
- 250,000 - 499,999
- 100,000 - 249,999
- 30,000 - 99,999
- 10,000 - 29,999
- UNDER 10,000

SCALE 1:3,000,000 LAMBERT CONFORMAL CONIC PROJECTION

MILES 0 50 100 150

KILOMETERS 0 50 100 150

The American heartland is the nation's breadbasket. The rich, dark soils, combined with advanced farming techniques, yield one of the world's richest harvests of wheat, oats, corn and soybeans. The great prairie cities - Minneapolis, St. Paul, Omaha and Kansas City - grew from feedlots and stockyards to major grain and meat processing centers, and major wholesale and distribution points for goods farmers needed. The mighty Mississippi and Missouri rivers played a major role in the settlement of the region, especially for transportation.

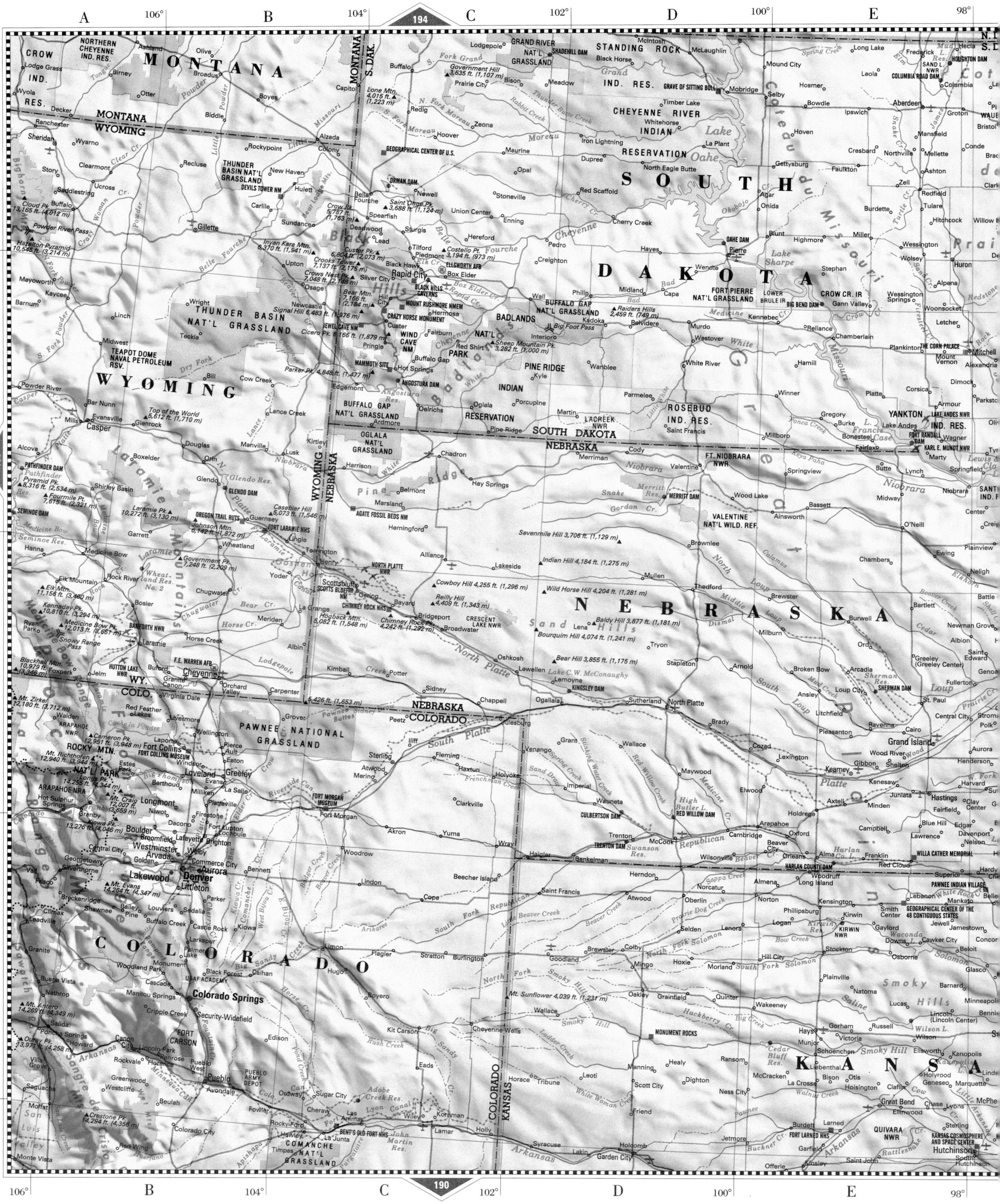

# Central Great Plains Region

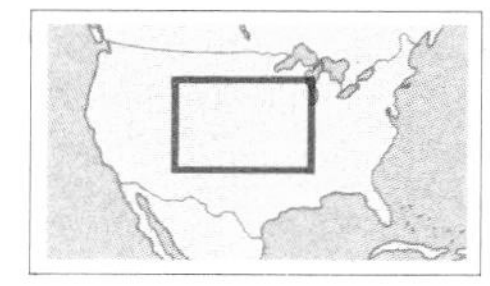

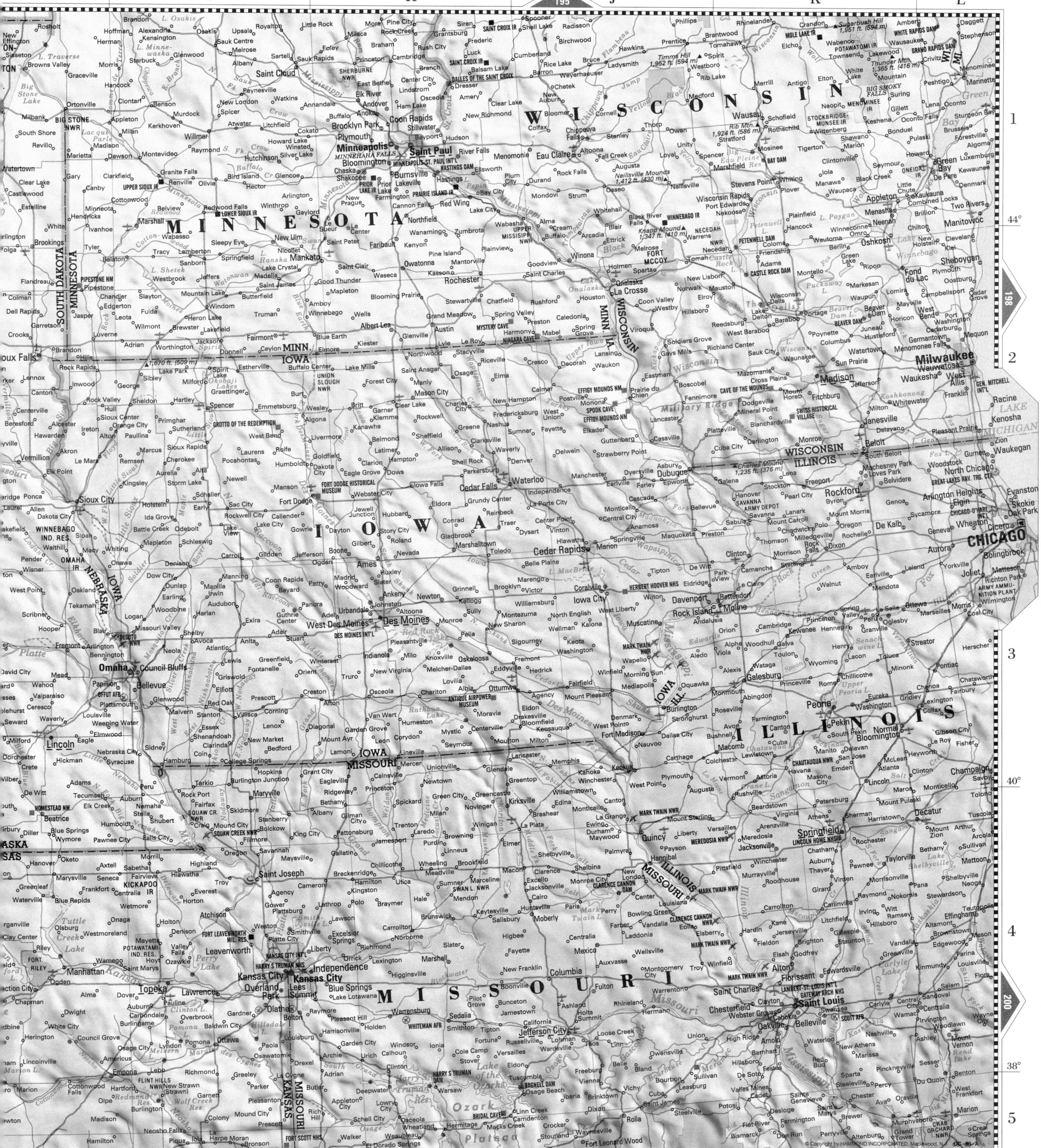


POPULATION OF CITIES AND TOWNS

| | | | |
|---|---|---|---|
| OVER 2,000,000 | 500,000 - 999,999 | 100,000 - 249,999 | 10,000 - 29,999 |
| 1,000,000 - 1,999,999 | 250,000 - 499,999 | 30,000 - 99,999 | UNDER 10,000 |

SCALE 1:3,000,000 LAMBERT CONFORMAL CONIC PROJECTION

MILES 0 50 100 150

KILOMETERS 0 50 100 150

The northern Great Plains, which cover a vast expanse of both the American and Canadian landscape, are clothed in golden fields of spring wheat, barley and flax. In the second half of the 19th century, and in the early 20th century, Minnesota, the Dakotas and the Canadian prairie provinces became home to great numbers of immigrant farmers – Swedes, Norwegians, Volga Germans and Ukrainians. The thin-soiled uplands of northern Minnesota and western Ontario are forest covered and unpopulated except for occasional mining and lumbering communities.

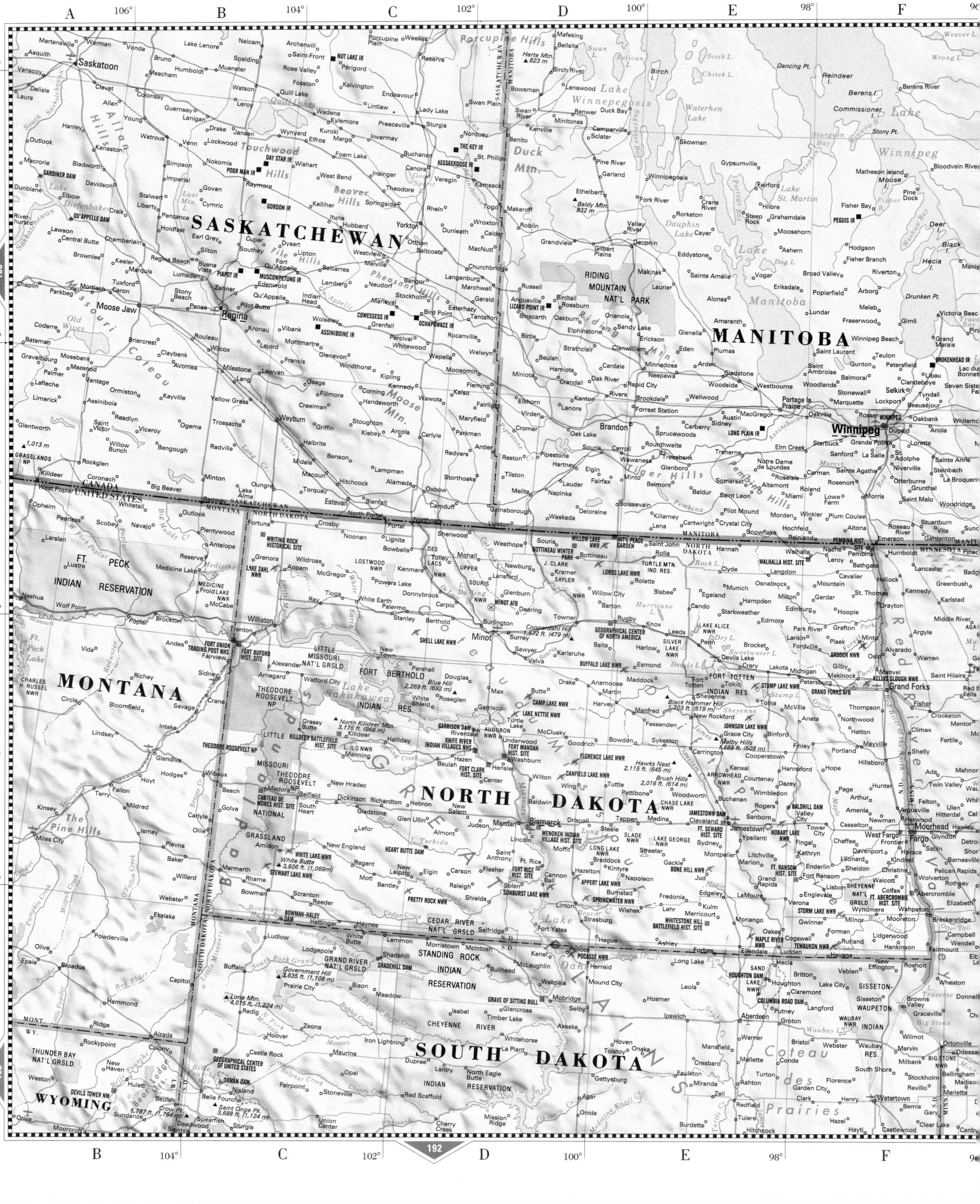

# South Central Canada, North Central U.S.

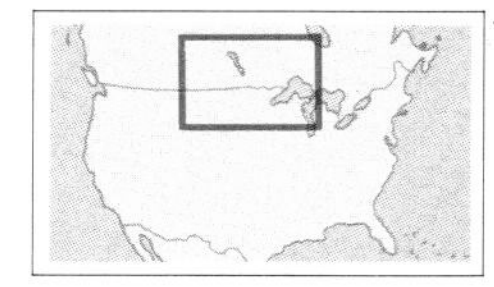

POPULATION OF CITIES AND TOWNS

| | | | |
|---|---|---|---|
| ■ OVER 2,000,000 | ◉ 500,000 - 999,999 | ⊕ 100,000 - 249,999 | ⊙ 10,000 - 29,999 |
| ▣ 1,000,000 - 1,999,999 | ◎ 250,000 - 499,999 | ⊖ 30,000 - 99,999 | ○ UNDER 10,000 |

SCALE 1:3,000,000 LAMBERT CONFORMAL CONIC PROJECTION

MILES 0 50 100 150

KILOMETERS 0 50 100 150

Maritime Canada and New England share a historic, economic and cultural identity that goes back to the first European settlements of the 17th century. The landscape on both sides of the border has remained rural except for the few larger central cities. Fishing, forestry in the uplands and farming in the more fertile valleys continue to be important; recreation and tourism add to the region's economy. French-speaking Quebec has vast amounts of hydro-electric power, minerals, and a growing manufacturing base, in addition to its agriculture and forestry.

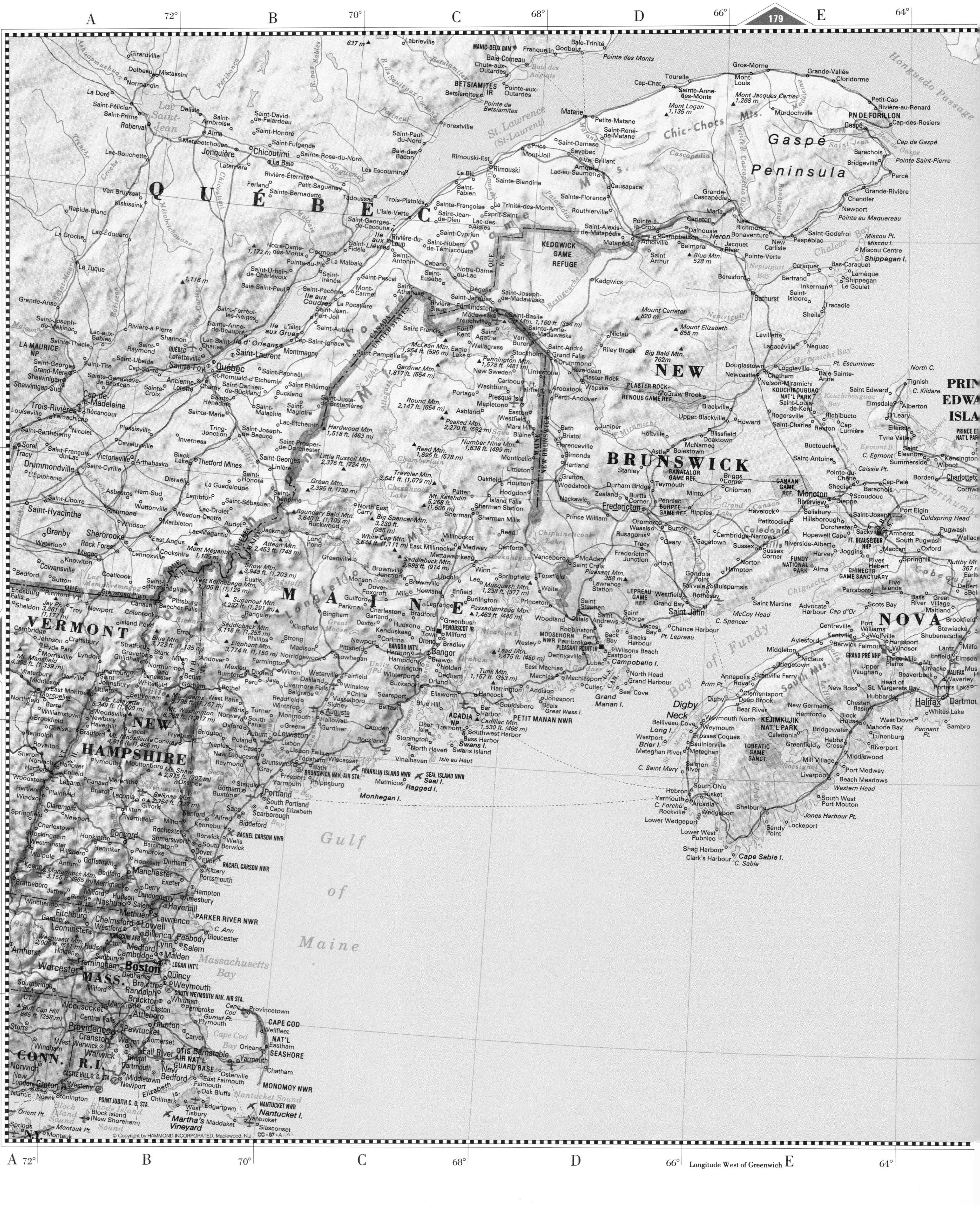

# Southeastern Canada, Northeastern U.S.

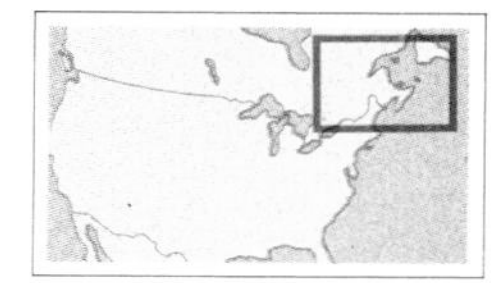

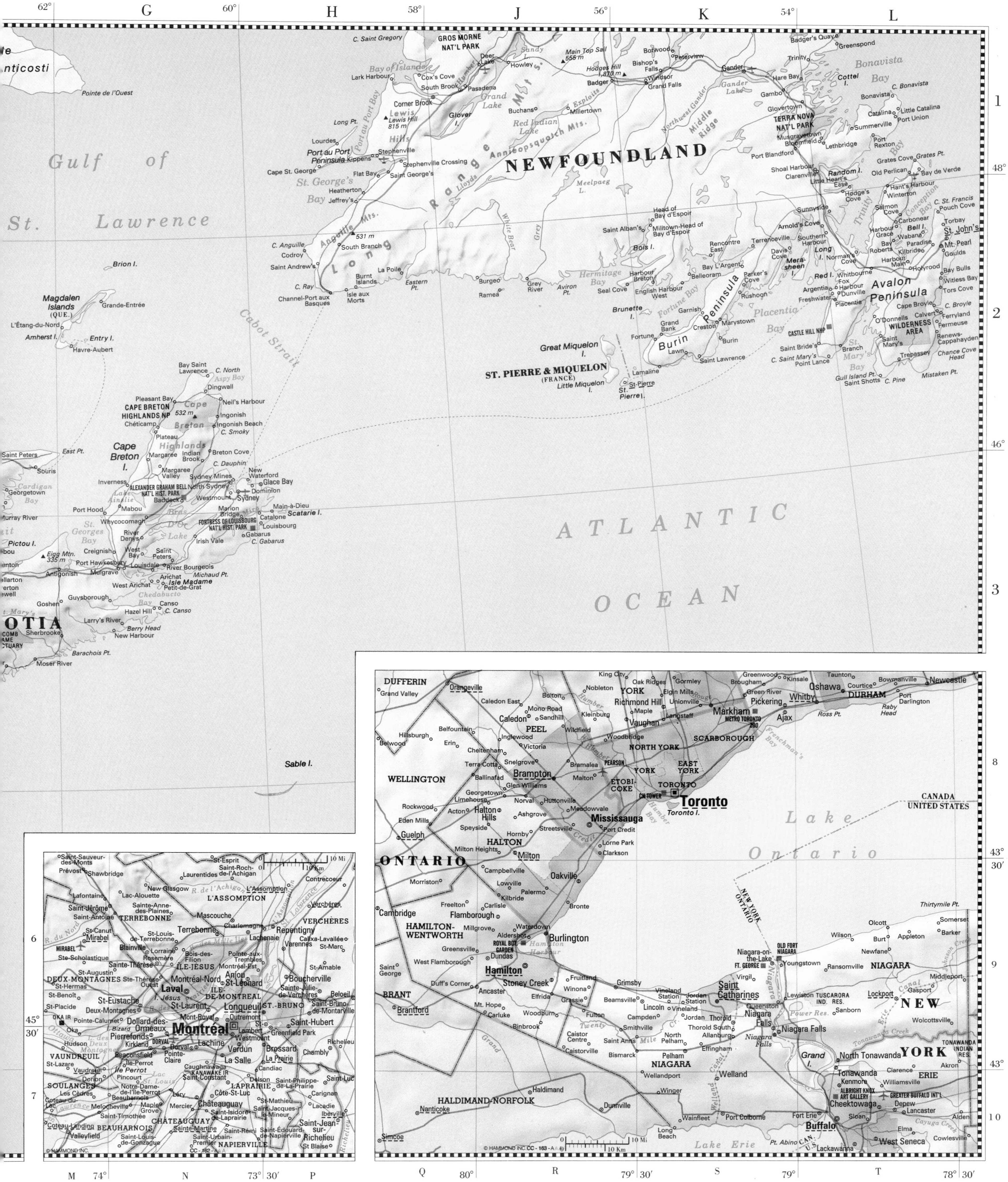


POPULATION OF CITIES AND TOWNS

| | | | |
|---|---|---|---|
| OVER 2,000,000 | 500,000 - 999,999 | 100,000 - 249,999 | 10,000 - 29,999 |
| 1,000,000 - 1,999,999 | 250,000 - 499,999 | 30,000 - 99,999 | UNDER 10,000 |

SCALE 1:3,000,000 LAMBERT CONFORMAL CONIC PROJECTION

MILES 0 50 100 150

KILOMETERS 0 50 100 150

As late as the 1960s, the broad region stretching from New England to the Mississippi was North America's Manufacturing Belt. The East Coast concentrated on textiles, apparel and other non-durables, while the Midwest churned out automobiles and heavy machinery. Appalachian coal fueled the blast furnaces of Pittsburgh, Youngstown, Cleveland, Buffalo and Gary, and ore boats brought iron ore and limestone. Aging plants, and foreign competition led to long term decline. Thirty years later, the "Rust Belt" cities are reviving with alternative industries.

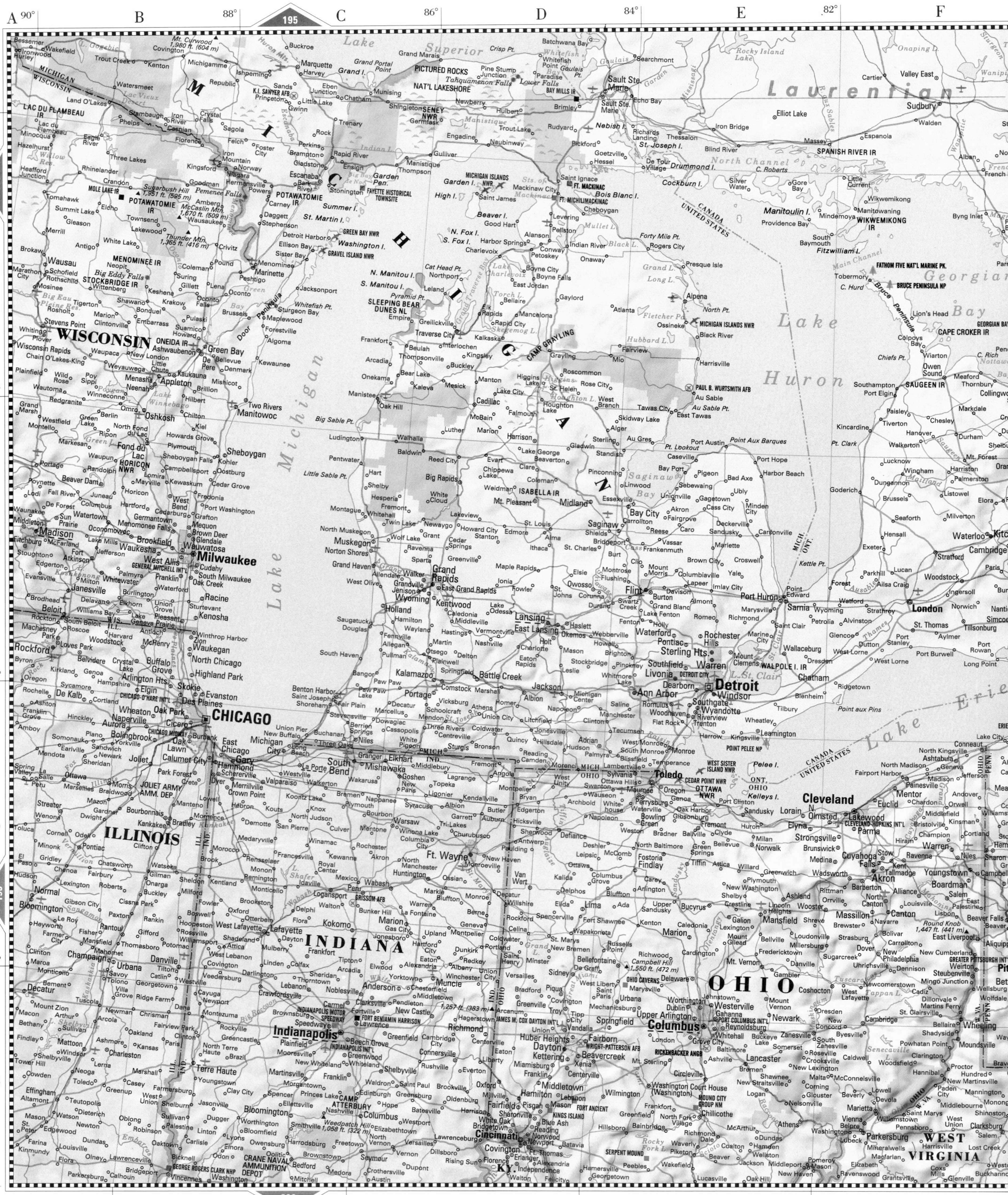

# Great Lakes Region, Middle Atlantic U.S.

POPULATION OF CITIES AND TOWNS

| | | | |
|---|---|---|---|
| ■ OVER 2,000,000 | ◉ 500,000 - 999,999 | ⊕ 100,000 - 249,999 | ○ 10,000 - 29,999 |
| ▣ 1,000,000 - 1,999,999 | ◎ 250,000 - 499,999 | ⊙ 30,000 - 99,999 | ∘ UNDER 10,000 |

SCALE 1:3,000,000 LAMBERT CONFORMAL CONIC PROJECTION

MILES 0 50 100 150

KILOMETERS 0 50 100 150

Settlement by Europeans in this part of the eastern seaboard began at Jamestown in 1607. The first African-Americans arrived in 1619, brought as slaves to work the early tobacco plantations. Later the region became known as the "Cotton Kingdom," and it made up most of the Confederacy of 1861-1865. Long after the ruinous Civil War, this area suffered economic stagnation. The 1970s brought stunning economic growth as part of the Sun Belt phenomenon. People moved here, agriculture shifted to high-value commodities such as beef, and high-tech industry took root.

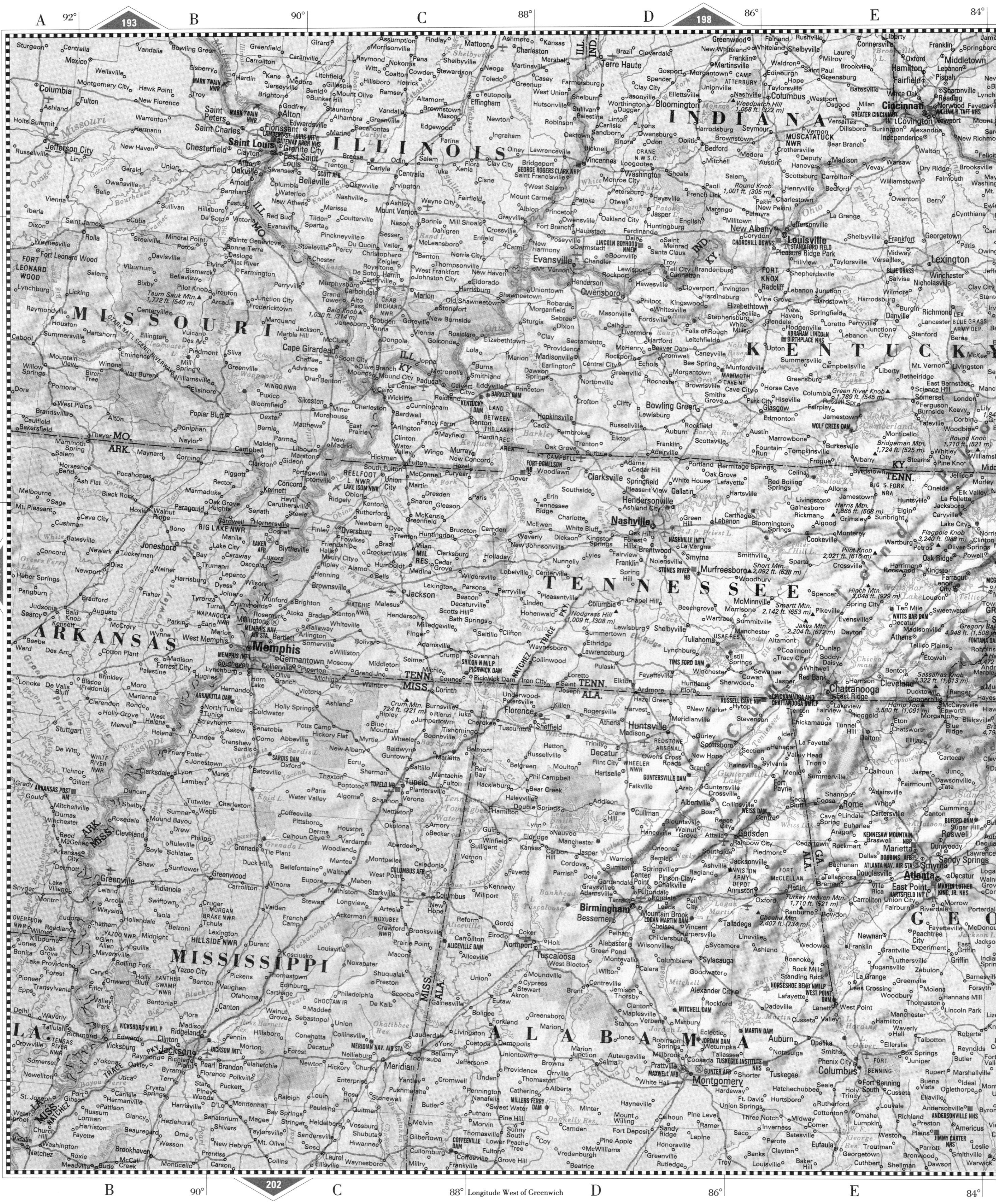

# Mideastern United States

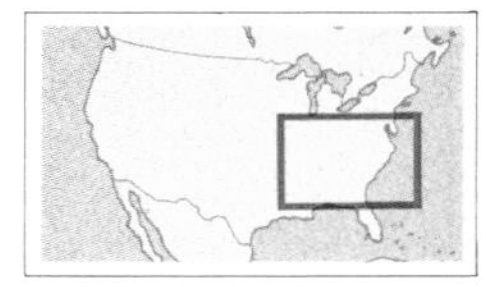

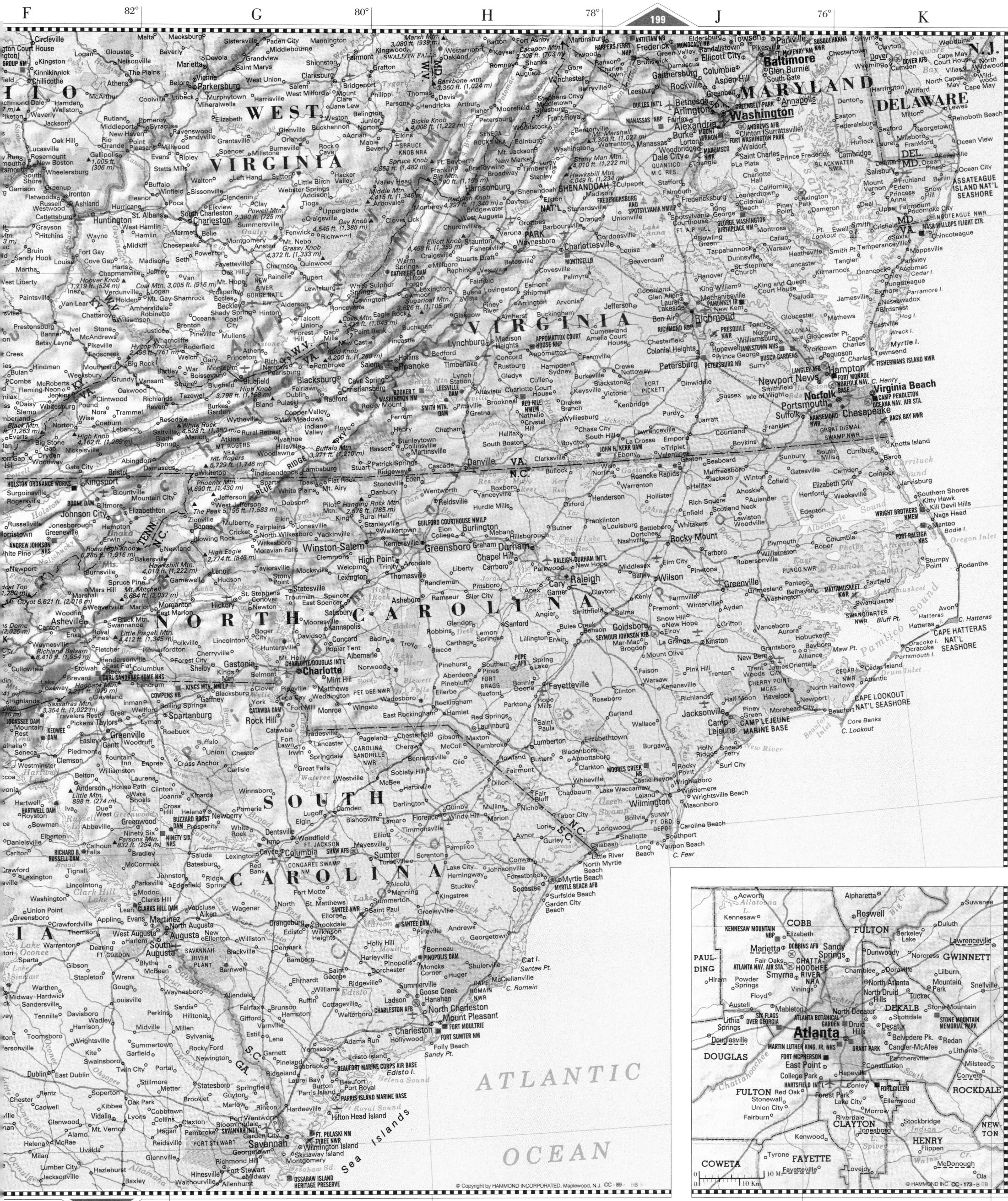


POPULATION OF CITIES AND TOWNS

| | | | |
|---|---|---|---|
| OVER 2,000,000 | 500,000 - 999,999 | 100,000 - 249,999 | 10,000 - 29,999 |
| 1,000,000 - 1,999,999 | 250,000 - 499,999 | 30,000 - 99,999 | UNDER 10,000 |

SCALE 1:3,000,000 LAMBERT CONFORMAL CONIC PROJECTION

MILES 0 50 100 150

KILOMETERS 0 50 100 150

Since the 1950s, this lush and sunny region has boomed. Warm winter climate (with air conditioning to tame the humid summers) has drawn millions to the thriving Miami-Orlando-Tampa Bay triangle. Vacationers and retirees have flocked to the Atlantic and Gulf coasts, as well as the Orlando area, home of the famous Walt Disney World. Miami's Latin American commerce, and Cape Canaveral's space industry, have also spurred impressive growth. Rapid development and sugar farming have created many new challenges for the Everglades.

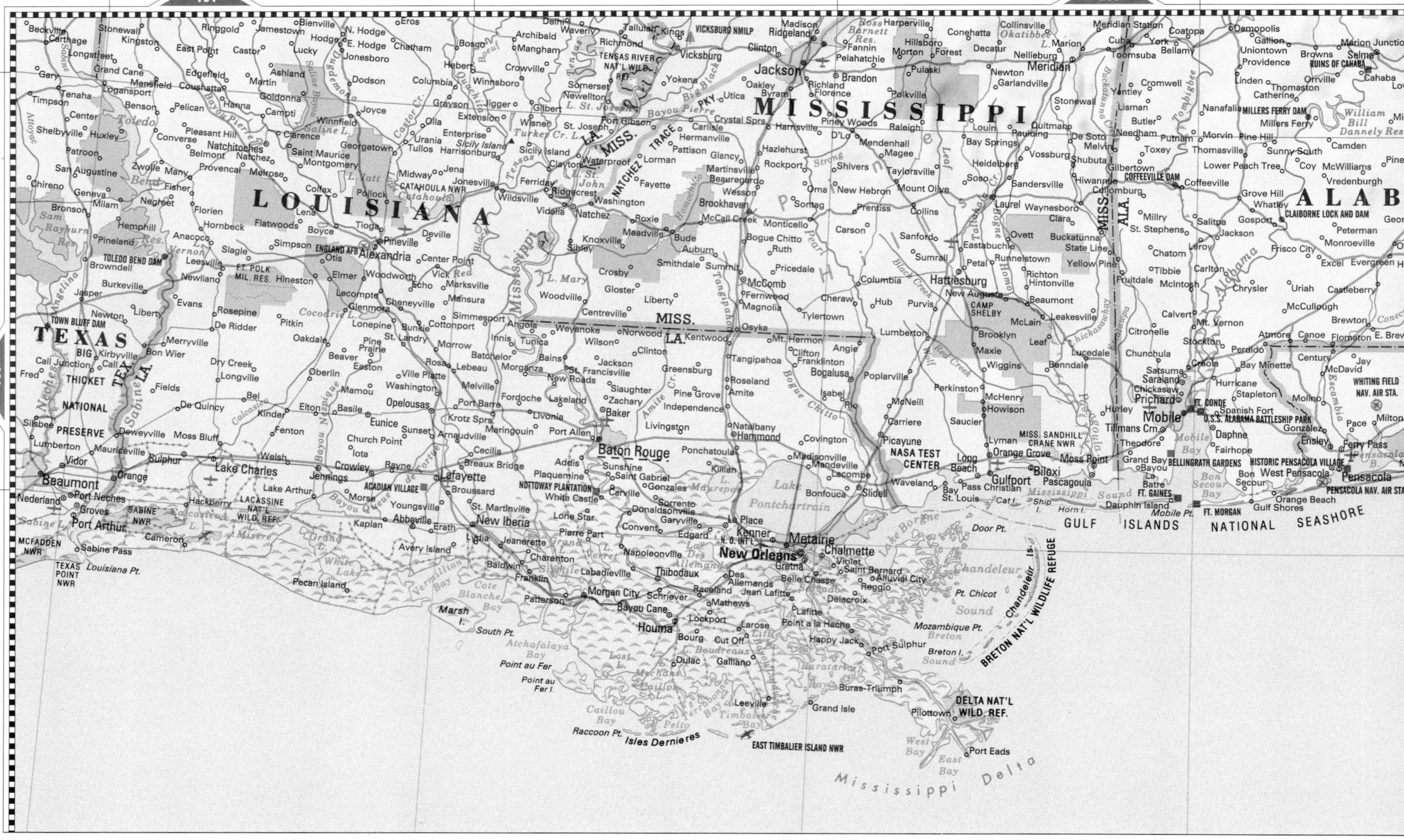


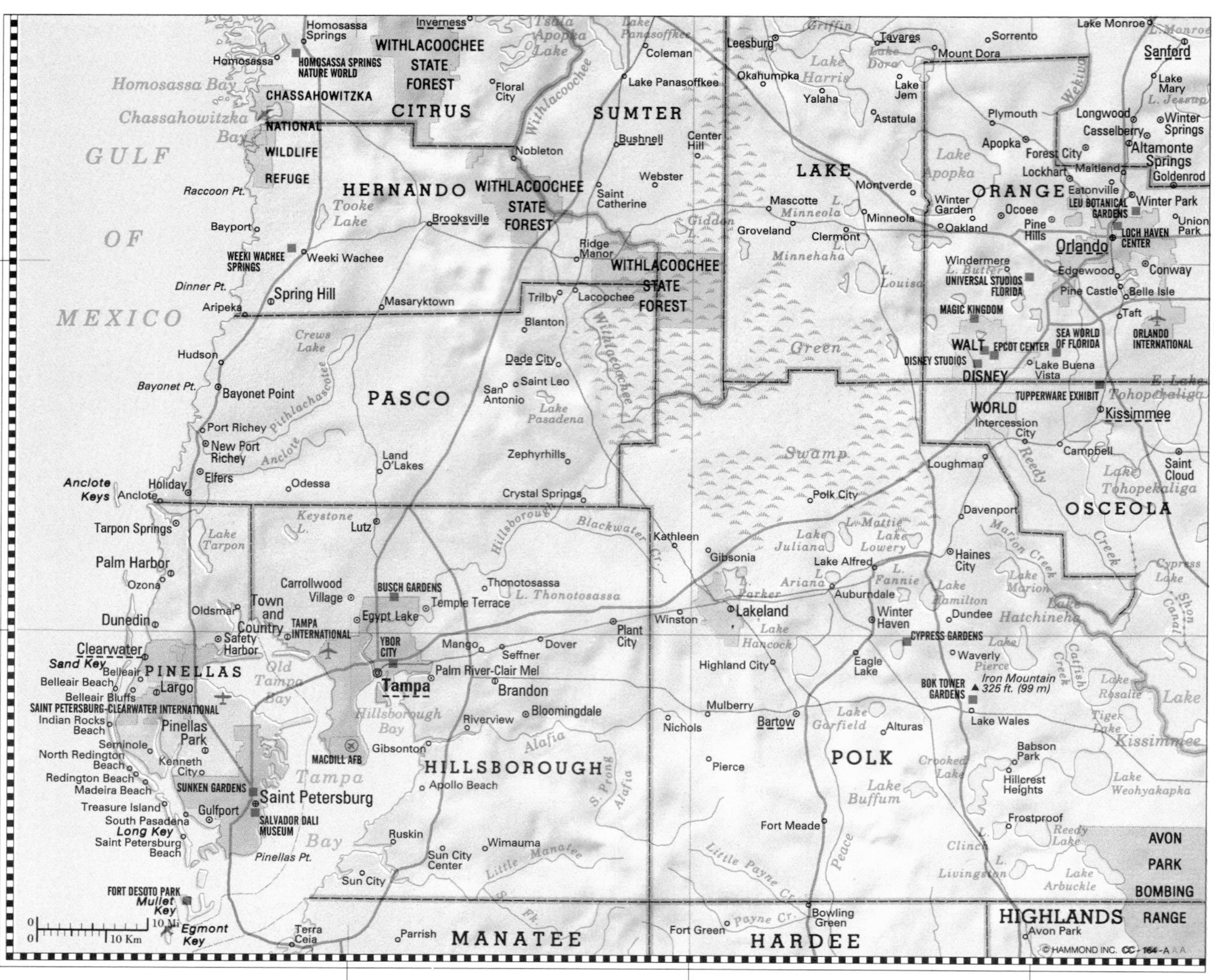


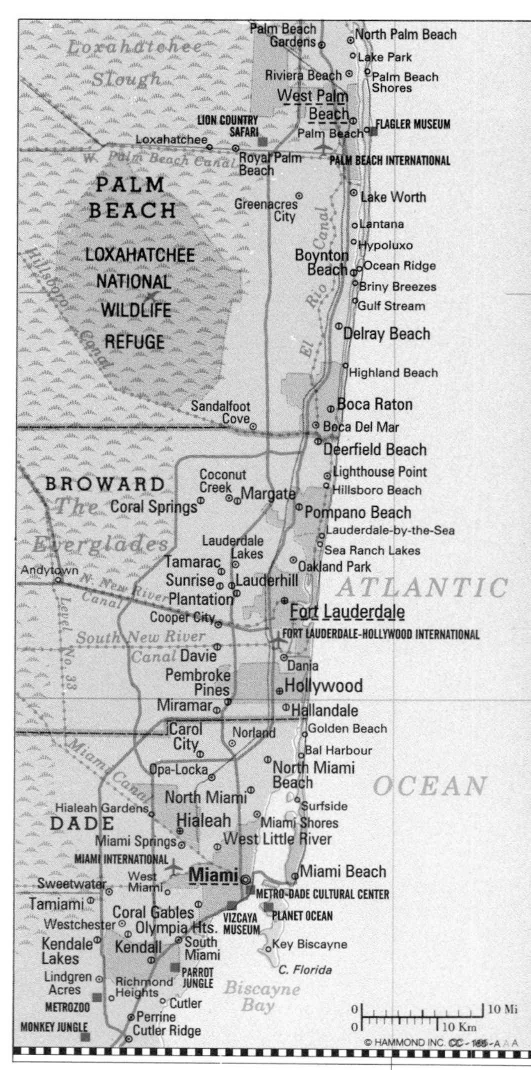


SCALE 1:3,000,000 LAMBERT CONFORMAL CONIC PROJECTION

MILES 0 50 100 150

KILOMETERS 0 50 100 150

POPULATION OF CITIES AND TOWNS

- OVER 2,000,000
- 1,000,000 - 1,999,999
- 500,000 - 999,999
- 250,000 - 499,999
- 100,000 - 249,999
- 30,000 - 99,999
- 10,000 - 29,999
- UNDER 10,000

# Northern Gulf Coast Region

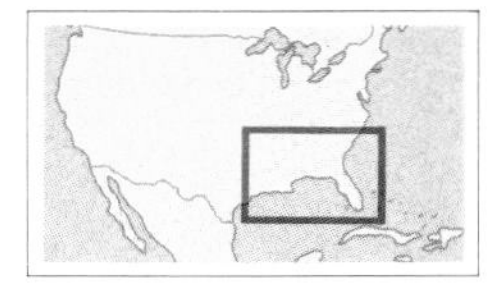

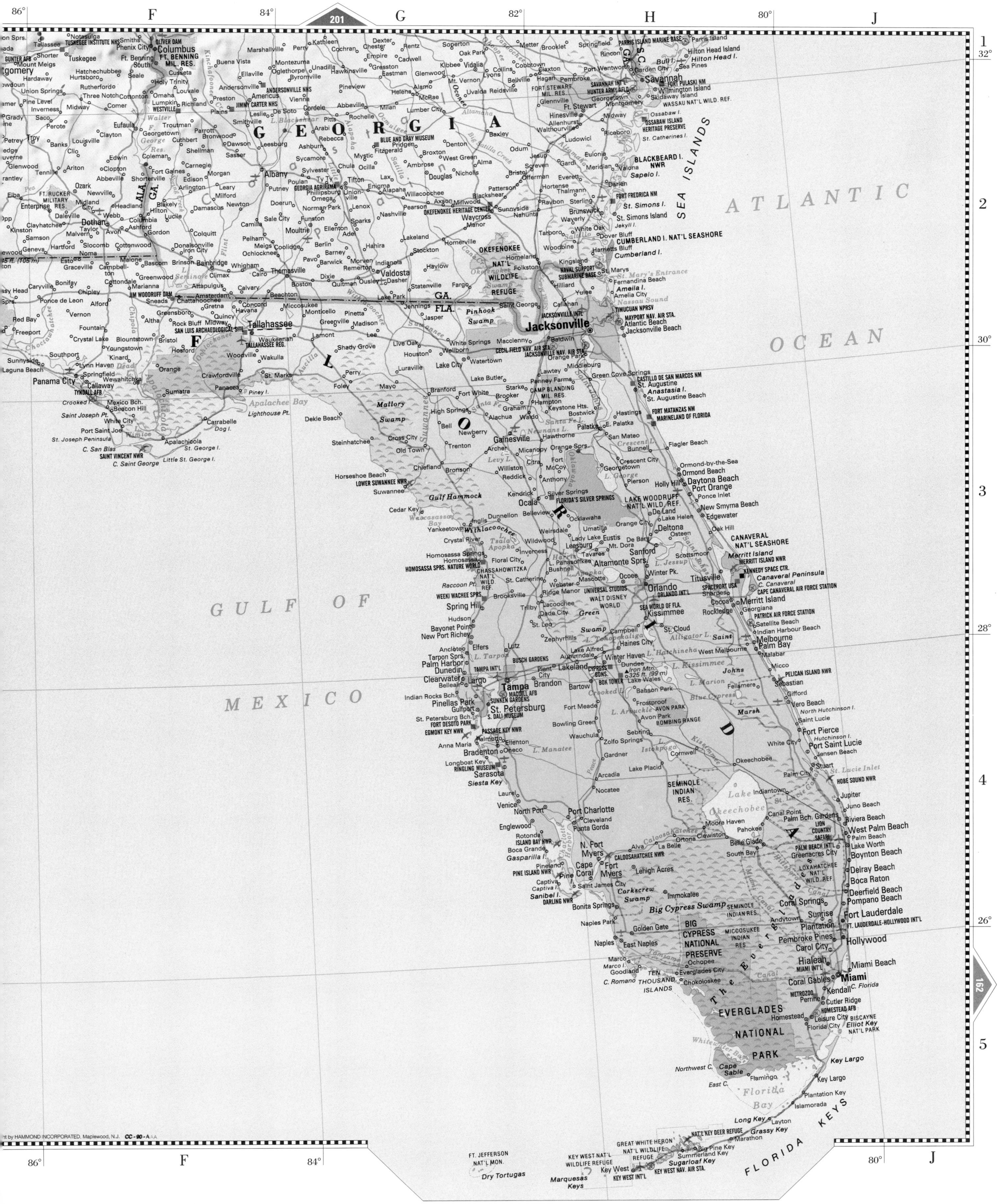

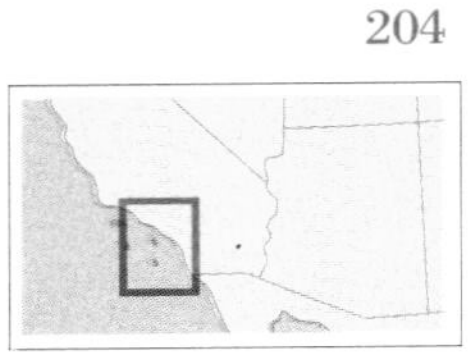

# Los Angeles–San Diego

Metropolitan Los Angeles stretches almost 115 miles (184 km.) from Ventura to San Bernardino. The movie industry, citrus orchards and oil fields fueled the region's early rapid growth. Today, Los Angeles is the aircraft manufacturing capital of the United States, and along with New York and Chicago, leads in manufacturing, international banking and port trade.

POPULATION OF CITIES AND TOWNS
- OVER 2,000,000
- 1,000,000 - 1,999,999
- 500,000 - 999,999
- 250,000 - 499,999
- 100,000 - 249,999
- 30,000 - 99,999
- 10,000 - 29,999
- UNDER 10,000

SCALE 1:1,000,000 LAMBERT CONFORMAL CONIC PROJECTION
MILES 0 10 20 30 40 50
KILOMETERS 0 10 20 30 40 50

# Seattle, San Francisco, Detroit, Chicago

Nestled between Puget Sound and Lake Washington, Seattle is the Northwest's largest city. San Francisco is the West Coast financial center; nearby San Jose is the heart of the "Silicon Valley" computer industry. Detroit is still the nation's automobile capital, while Chicago boasts the world's busiest airport, largest commodities exchange and tallest skyscraper: the Sears Tower.

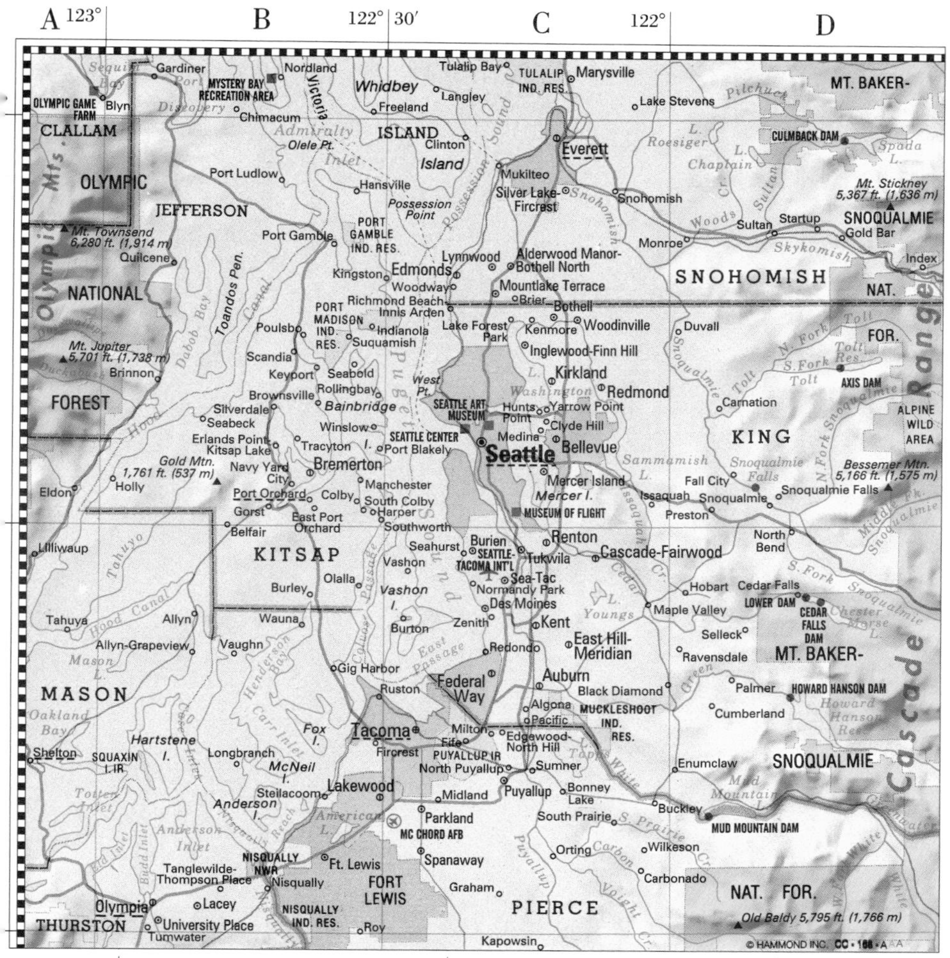


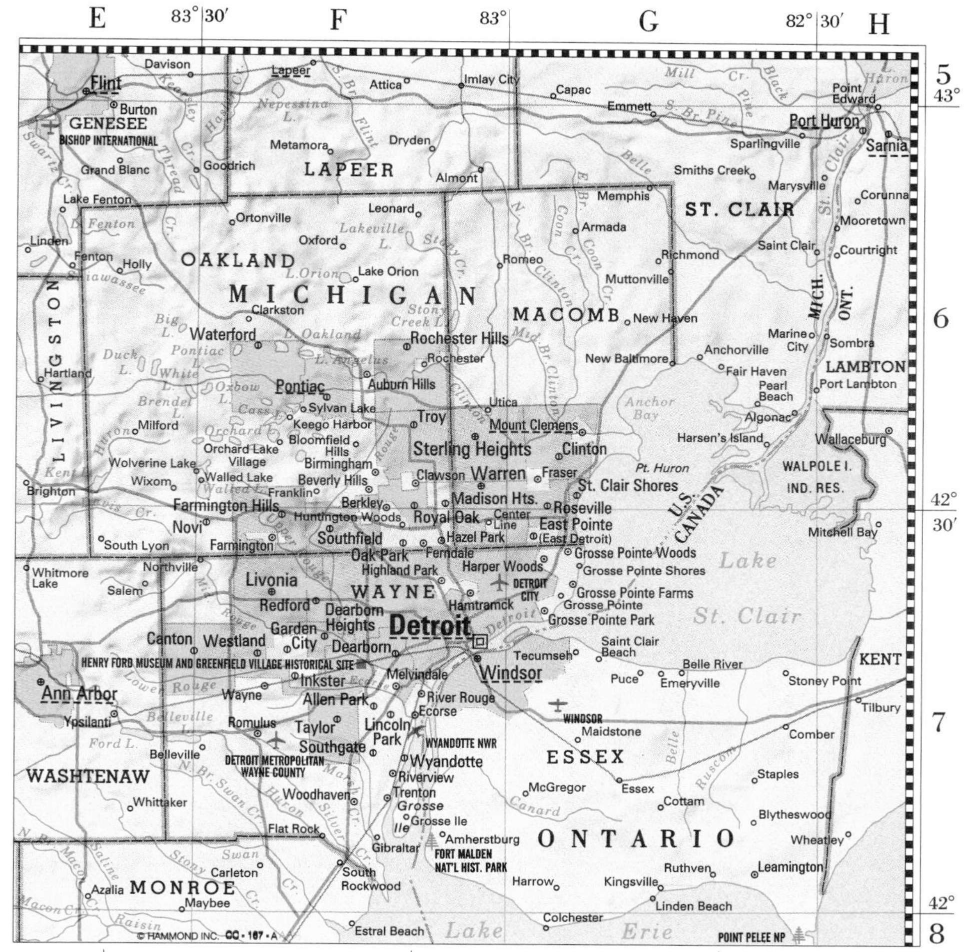


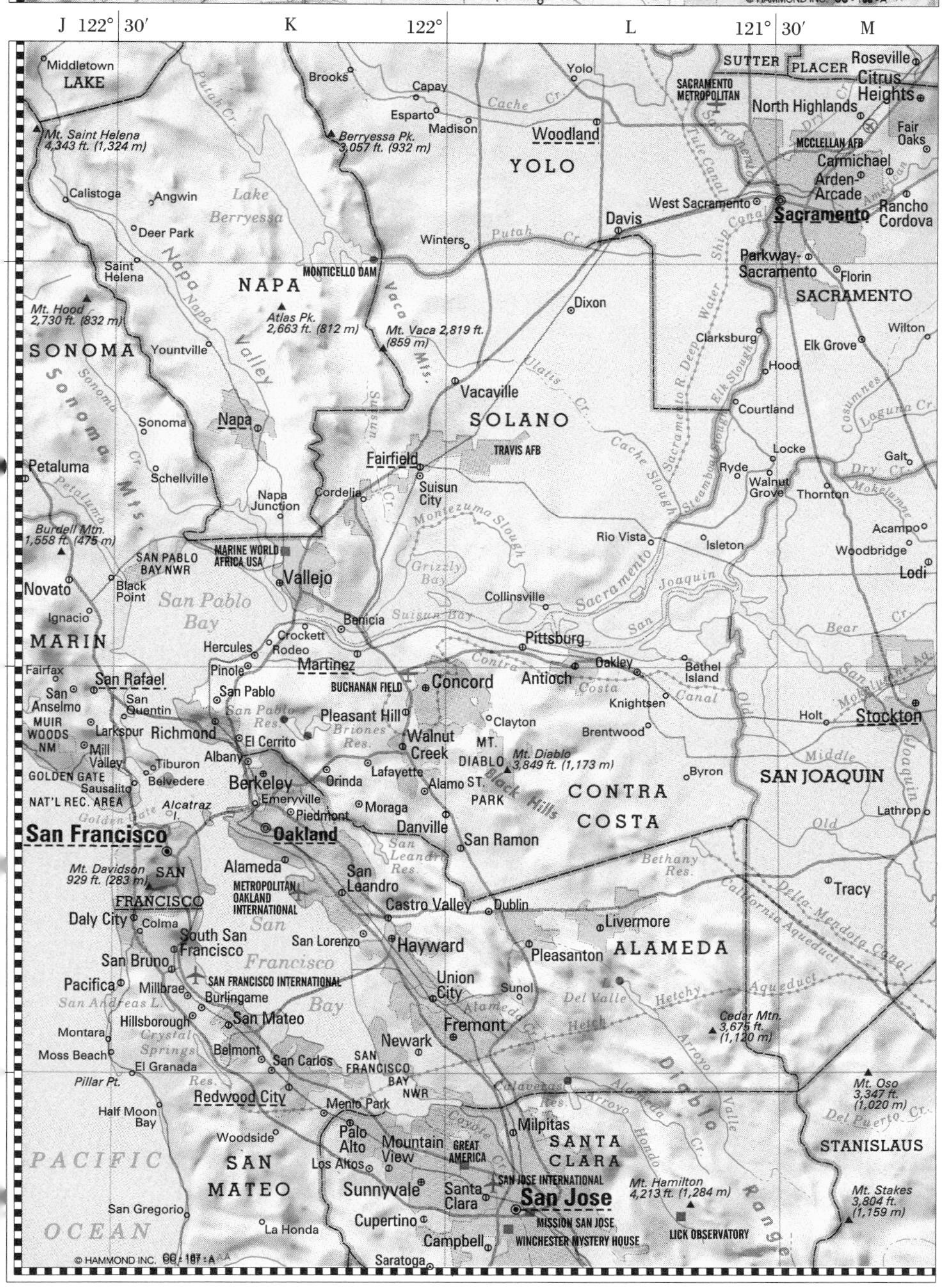


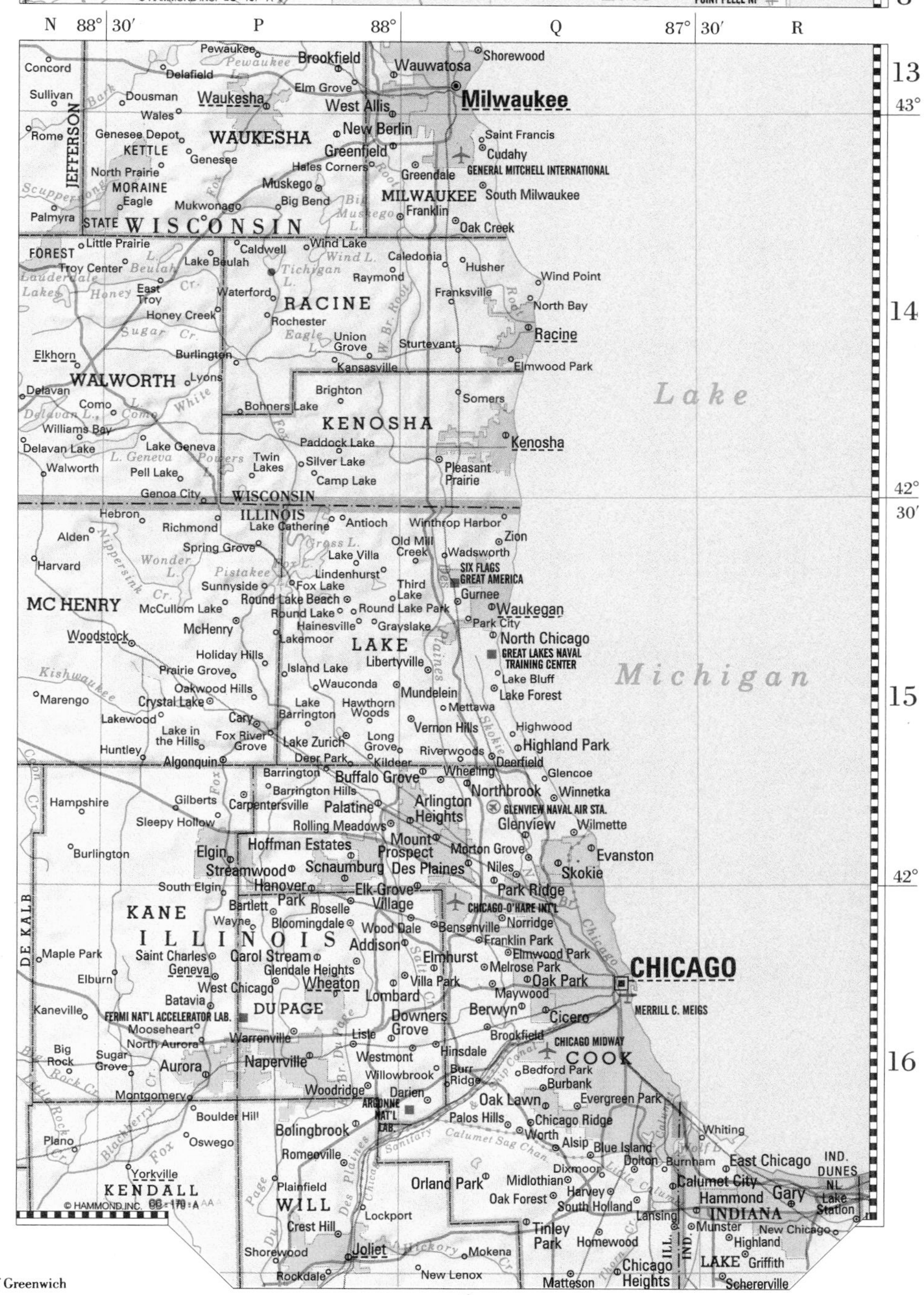


SCALE 1:1,000,000 — LAMBERT CONFORMAL CONIC PROJECTION

MILES 0 10 20 30 40 50

KILOMETERS 0 10 20 30 40 50

Longitude West of Greenwich

The "Northeast Corridor" which links the nation's political capital with its financial and corporate center is the most densely urbanized megalopolis in North America. New York City, the core of a tri-state metropolitan area encompassing 18 million people, is also an international center for theater, the arts and publishing. Historic Philadelphia, a leader in medicine and pharmaceuticals, has one of the highest concentrations of colleges and universities in America. Baltimore's ambitious waterfront development project, including Harborplace, has given that city a new life.

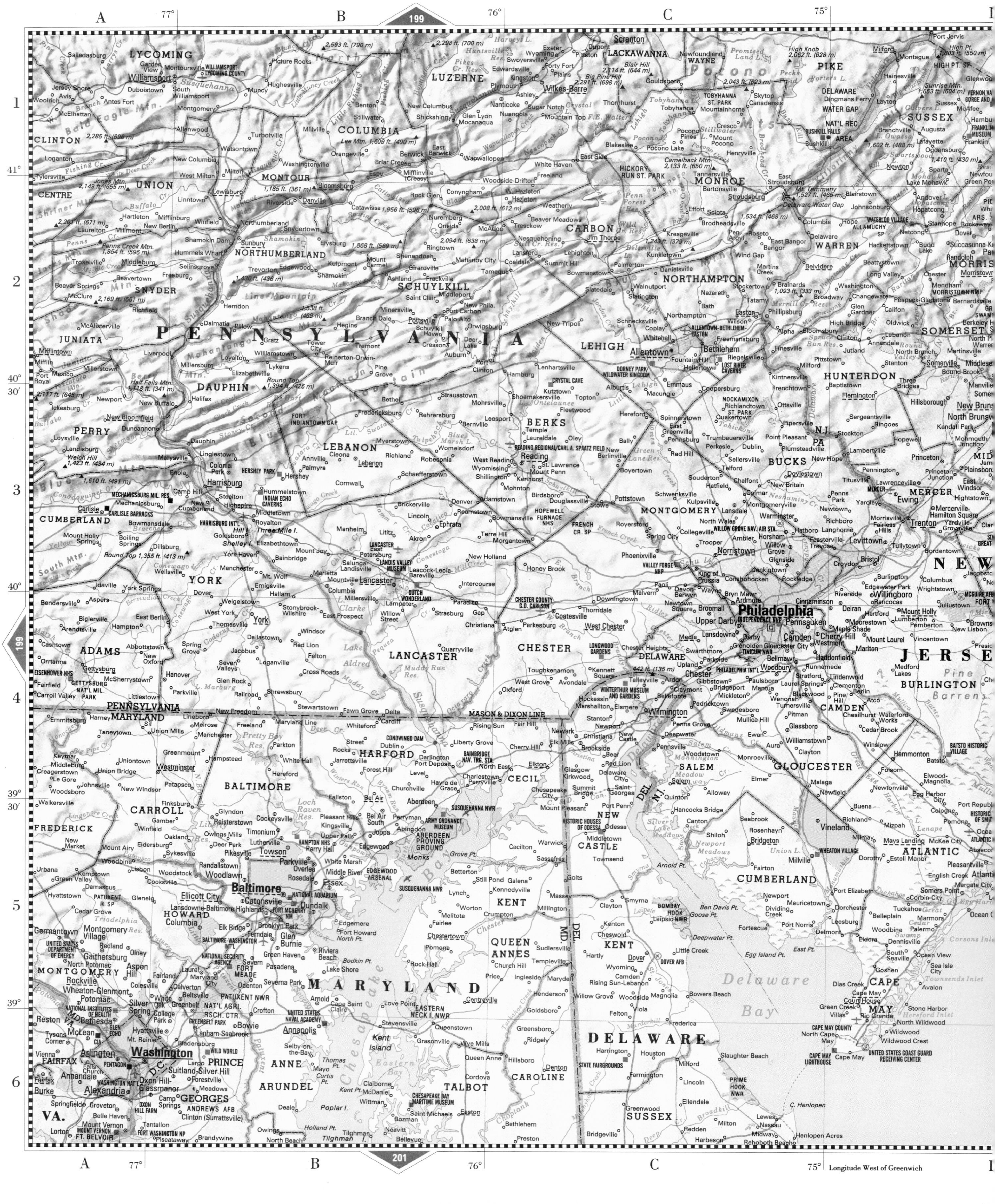

# New York–Philadelphia–Washington

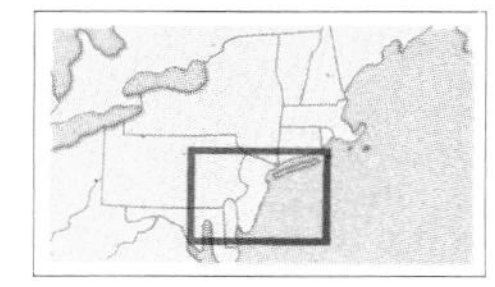

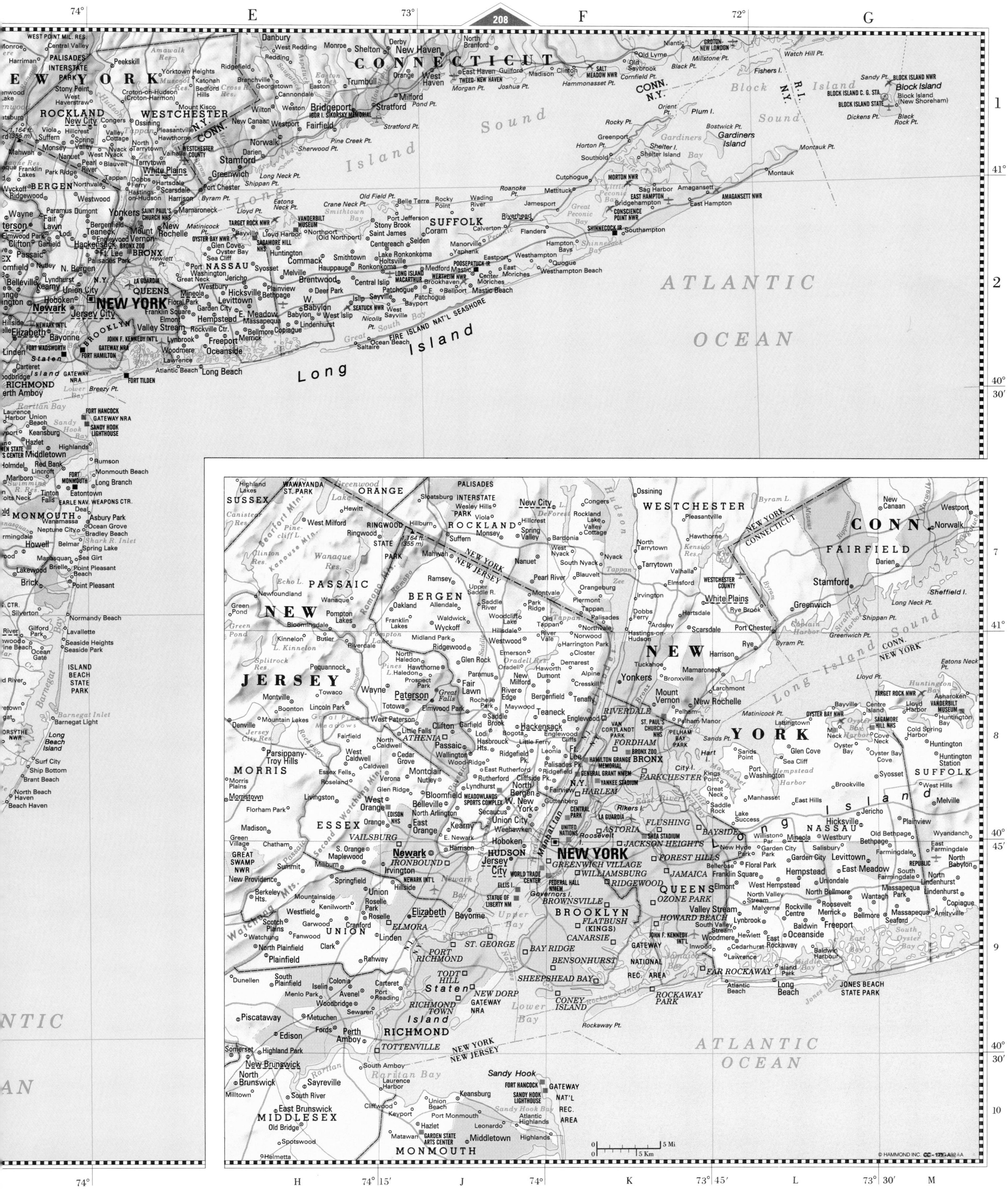


POPULATION OF CITIES AND TOWNS

- OVER 2,000,000
- 1,000,000 - 1,999,999
- 500,000 - 999,999
- 250,000 - 499,999
- 100,000 - 249,999
- 30,000 - 99,999
- 10,000 - 29,999
- UNDER 10,000

SCALE 1:1,000,000 LAMBERT CONFORMAL CONIC PROJECTION

MILES 0 10 20 30 40 50

KILOMETERS 0 10 20 30 40 50

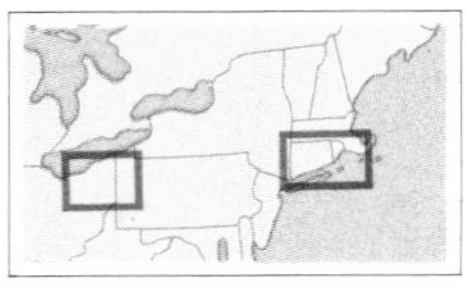

# Hartford-Boston, Cleveland-Pittsburgh

America's industrial revolution was born in the cotton mills, firearm factories and clock works of New England. In the 1970s, the region's academic centers spurred a new wave of high-tech industries. Downtown Cleveland has been revitalized by business investment and urban renewal, and Pittsburgh is now a modern corporate and research center.

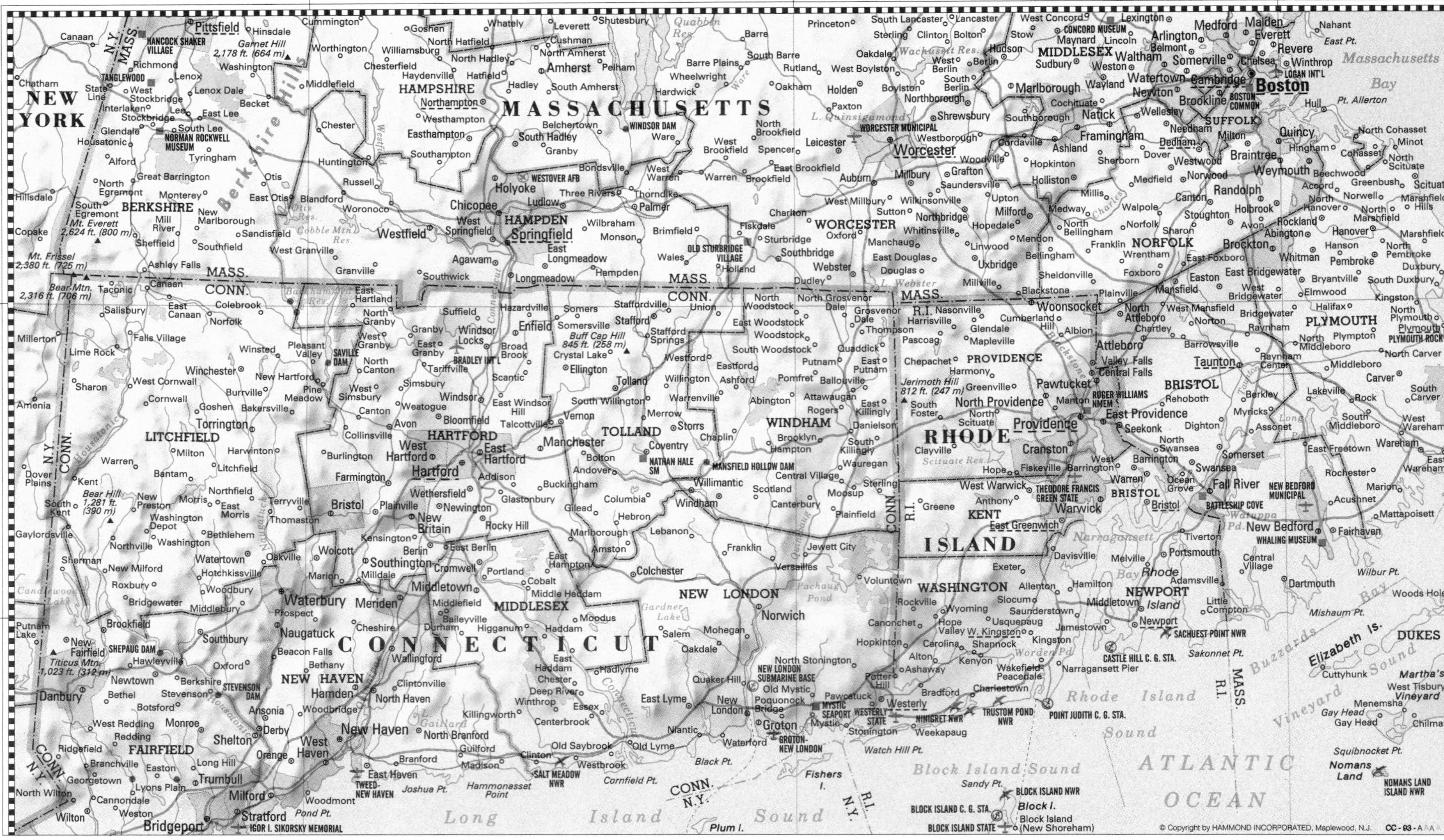


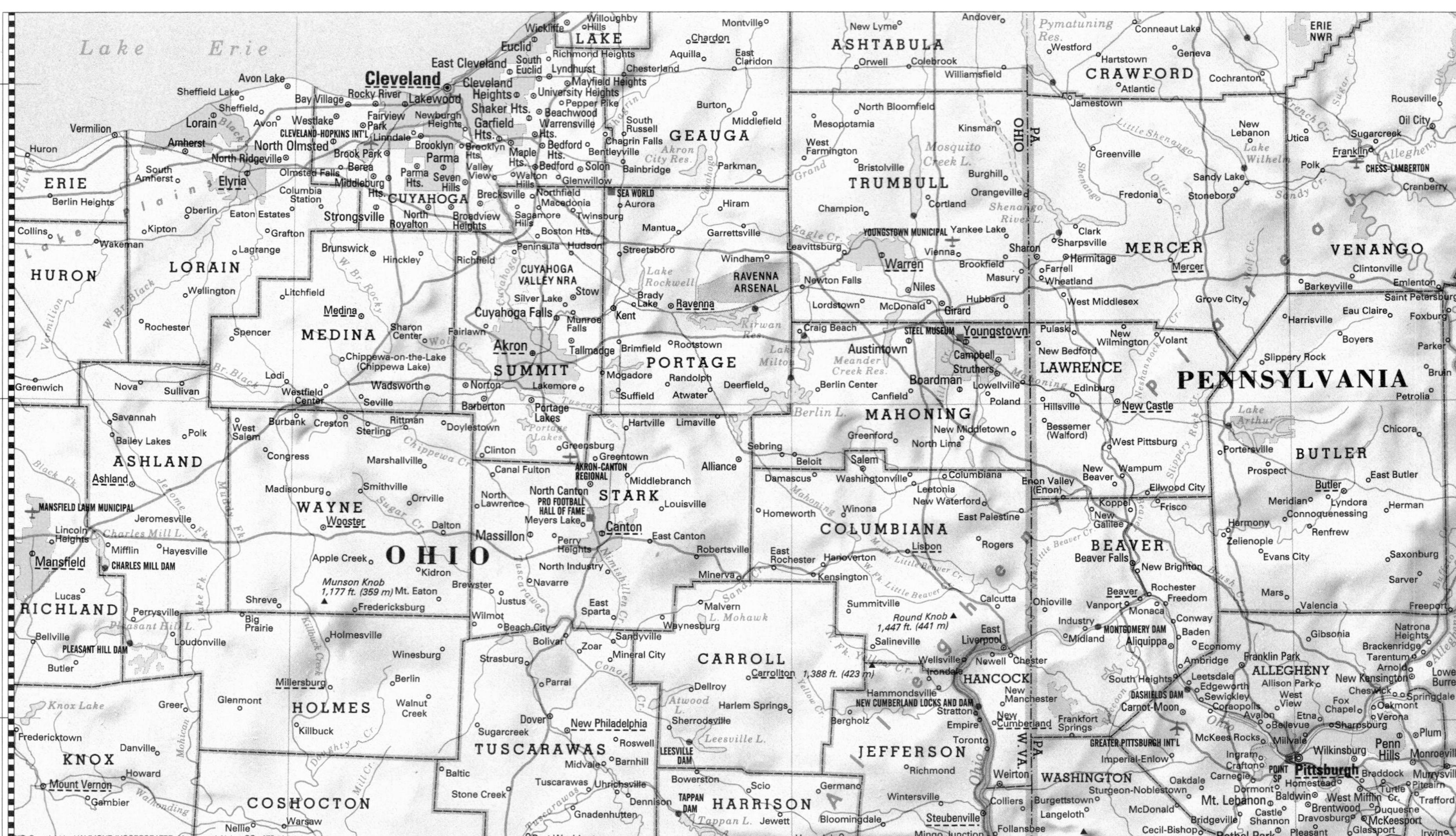


SCALE 1:1,000,000 LAMBERT CONFORMAL CONIC PROJECTION

MILES 0 10 20 30 40 50

KILOMETERS 0 10 20 30 40 50

POPULATION OF CITIES AND TOWNS

- OVER 2,000,000
- 1,000,000 - 1,999,999
- 500,000 - 999,999
- 250,000 - 499,999
- 100,000 - 249,999
- 30,000 - 99,999
- 10,000 - 29,999
- UNDER 10,000

# Statistical Tables and Index

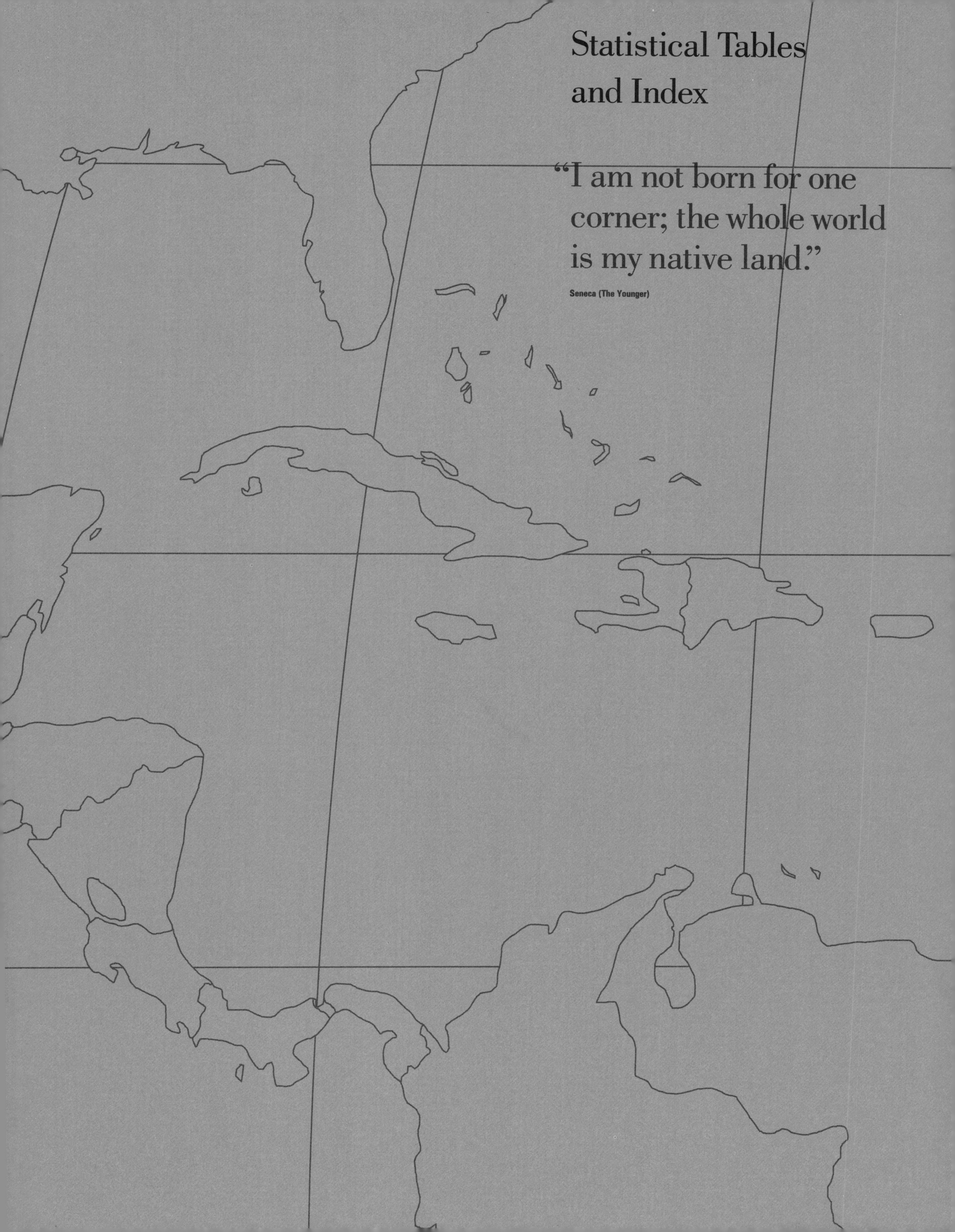

"I am not born for one corner; the whole world is my native land."

**Seneca (The Younger)**

# World Statistics

## Elements of the Solar System

| | Mean Distance from Sun: in Miles | in Kilometers | Period of Revolution around Sun | Period of Rotation on Axis | Equatorial Diameter in Miles | in Kilometers | Surface Gravity (Earth = 1) | Mass (Earth = 1) | Mean Density (Water = 1) | Number of Satellites |
|---|---|---|---|---|---|---|---|---|---|---|
| **Mercury** | 35,990,000 | 57,900,000 | 87.97 days | 59 days | 3,032 | 4,880 | 0.38 | 0.055 | 5.5 | 0 |
| **Venus** | 67,240,000 | 108,200,000 | 224.70 days | 243 days† | 7,523 | 12,106 | 0.90 | 0.815 | 5.25 | 0 |
| **Earth** | 93,000,000 | 149,700,000 | 365.26 days | 23h 56m | 7,926 | 12,755 | 1.00 | 1.00 | 5.5 | 1 |
| **Mars** | 141,730,000 | 228,100,000 | 687.00 days | 24h 37m | 4,220 | 6,790 | 0.38 | 0.107 | 4.0 | 2 |
| **Jupiter** | 483,880,000 | 778,700,000 | 11.86 years | 9h 50m | 88,750 | 142,800 | 2.87 | 317.9 | 1.3 | 16 |
| **Saturn** | 887,130,000 | 1,427,700,000 | 29.46 years | 10h 39m | 74,580 | 120,020 | 1.32 | 95.2 | 0.7 | 23 |
| **Uranus** | 1,783,700,000 | 2,870,500,000 | 84.01 years | 17h 24m† | 31,600 | 50,900 | 0.93 | 14.6 | 1.3 | 15 |
| **Neptune** | 2,795,500,000 | 4,498,800,000 | 164.79 years | 17h 50m | 30,200 | 48,600 | 1.23 | 17.2 | 1.8 | 8 |
| **Pluto** | 3,667,900,000 | 5,902,800,000 | 247.70 years | 6.39 days(?) | 1,500 | 2,400 | 0.03(?) | 0.01(?) | 0.7(?) | 1 |

† Retrograde motion

## Dimensions of the Earth

| | Area in Sq. Miles | Sq. Kilometers |
|---|---|---|
| **Superficial area** | 196,939,000 | 510,073,000 |
| **Land surface** | 57,506,000 | 148,941,000 |
| **Water surface** | 139,433,000 | 361,132,000 |

| | Distance in Miles | Kilometers |
|---|---|---|
| **Equatorial circumference** | 24,902 | 40,075 |
| **Polar circumference** | 24,860 | 40,007 |
| **Equatorial diameter** | 7,926.4 | 12,756.4 |
| **Polar diameter** | 7,899.8 | 12,713.6 |
| **Equatorial radius** | 3,963.2 | 6,378.2 |
| **Polar radius** | 3,949.9 | 6,356.8 |

| | | |
|---|---|---|
| **Volume of the Earth** | $2.6 \times 10^{11}$ cubic miles | $10.84 \times 10^{11}$ cubic kilometers |
| **Mass or weight** | $6.6 \times 10^{21}$ short tons | $6.0 \times 10^{21}$ metric tons |
| **Maximum distance from Sun** | 94,600,000 miles | 152,000,000 kilometers |
| **Minimum distance from Sun** | 91,300,000 miles | 147,000,000 kilometers |

## Oceans and Major Seas

| | Area in: Sq. Miles | Sq. Kms. | Greatest Depth in: Feet | Meters |
|---|---|---|---|---|
| **Pacific Ocean** | 64,186,000 | 166,241,700 | 36,198 | 11,033 |
| **Atlantic Ocean** | 31,862,000 | 82,522,600 | 28,374 | 8,648 |
| **Indian Ocean** | 28,350,000 | 73,426,500 | 25,344 | 7,725 |
| **Arctic Ocean** | 5,427,000 | 14,056,000 | 17,880 | 5,450 |
| **Caribbean Sea** | 970,000 | 2,512,300 | 24,720 | 7,535 |
| **Mediterranean Sea** | 969,000 | 2,509,700 | 16,896 | 5,150 |
| **South China Sea** | 895,000 | 2,318,000 | 15,000 | 4,600 |
| **Bering Sea** | 875,000 | 2,266,250 | 15,800 | 4,800 |
| **Gulf of Mexico** | 600,000 | 1,554,000 | 12,300 | 3,750 |
| **Sea of Okhotsk** | 590,000 | 1,528,100 | 11,070 | 3,370 |
| **East China Sea** | 482,000 | 1,248,400 | 9,500 | 2,900 |
| **Yellow Sea** | 480,000 | 1,243,200 | 350 | 107 |
| **Sea of Japan** | 389,000 | 1,007,500 | 12,280 | 3,740 |
| **Hudson Bay** | 317,500 | 822,300 | 846 | 258 |
| **North Sea** | 222,000 | 575,000 | 2,200 | 670 |
| **Black Sea** | 185,000 | 479,150 | 7,365 | 2,245 |
| **Red Sea** | 169,000 | 437,700 | 7,200 | 2,195 |
| **Baltic Sea** | 163,000 | 422,170 | 1,506 | 459 |

## The Continents

| | Area in: Sq. Miles | Sq. Kms. | Percent of World's Land |
|---|---|---|---|
| **Asia** | 17,128,500 | 44,362,815 | 29.5 |
| **Africa** | 11,707,000 | 30,321,130 | 20.2 |
| **North America** | 9,363,000 | 24,250,170 | 16.2 |
| **South America** | 6,875,000 | 17,806,250 | 11.8 |
| **Antarctica** | 5,500,000 | 14,245,000 | 9.5 |
| **Europe** | 4,057,000 | 10,507,630 | 7.0 |
| **Australia** | 2,966,136 | 7,682,300 | 5.1 |

## Major Ship Canals

| | Length in: Miles | Kms. | Minimum Depth in: Feet | Meters |
|---|---|---|---|---|
| **Volga-Baltic, Russia** | 225 | 362 | – | – |
| **Baltic-White Sea, Russia** | 140 | 225 | 16 | 5 |
| **Suez, Egypt** | 100.76 | 162 | 42 | 13 |
| **Albert, Belgium** | 80 | 129 | 16.5 | 5 |
| **Moscow-Volga, Russia** | 80 | 129 | 18 | 6 |
| **Volga-Don, Russia** | 62 | 100 | – | – |
| **Göta, Sweden** | 54 | 87 | 10 | 3 |
| **Kiel (Nord-Ostsee), Germany** | 53.2 | 86 | 38 | 12 |
| **Panama Canal, Panama** | 50.72 | 82 | 41.6 | 13 |
| **Houston Ship, U.S.A.** | 50 | 81 | 36 | 11 |

## Largest Islands

| | Area in: Sq. Miles | Sq. Kms. |
|---|---|---|
| **Greenland** | 840,000 | 2,175,600 |
| **New Guinea** | 305,000 | 789,950 |
| **Borneo** | 290,000 | 751,100 |
| **Madagascar** | 226,400 | 586,376 |
| **Baffin, Canada** | 195,928 | 507,454 |
| **Sumatra, Indonesia** | 164,000 | 424,760 |
| **Honshu, Japan** | 88,000 | 227,920 |
| **Great Britain** | 84,400 | 218,896 |
| **Victoria, Canada** | 83,896 | 217,290 |
| **Ellesmere, Canada** | 75,767 | 196,236 |
| **Celebes, Indonesia** | 72,986 | 189,034 |
| **South I., New Zealand** | 58,393 | 151,238 |
| **Java, Indonesia** | 48,842 | 126,501 |
| **North I., New Zealand** | 44,187 | 114,444 |
| **Newfoundland, Canada** | 42,031 | 108,860 |
| **Cuba** | 40,533 | 104,981 |
| **Luzon, Philippines** | 40,420 | 104,688 |
| **Iceland** | 39,768 | 103,000 |
| **Mindanao, Philippines** | 36,537 | 94,631 |
| **Ireland** | 31,743 | 82,214 |
| **Sakhalin, Russia** | 29,500 | 76,405 |
| **Hispaniola, Haiti & Dom. Rep.** | 29,399 | 76,143 |

| | Area in: Sq. Miles | Sq. Kms. |
|---|---|---|
| **Hokkaido, Japan** | 28,983 | 75,066 |
| **Banks, Canada** | 27,038 | 70,028 |
| **Ceylon,Sri Lanka** | 25,332 | 65,610 |
| **Tasmania, Australia** | 24,600 | 63,710 |
| **Svalbard, Norway** | 23,957 | 62,049 |
| **Devon, Canada** | 21,331 | 55,247 |
| **Novaya Zemlya (north isl.), Russia** | 18,600 | 48,200 |
| **Marajó, Brazil** | 17,991 | 46,597 |
| **Tierra del Fuego, Chile & Argentina** | 17,900 | 46,360 |
| **Alexander, Antarctica** | 16,700 | 43,250 |
| **Axel Heiberg, Canada** | 16,671 | 43,178 |
| **Melville, Canada** | 16,274 | 42,150 |
| **Southhampton, Canada** | 15,913 | 41,215 |
| **New Britain, Papua New Guinea** | 14,100 | 36,519 |
| **Taiwan, China** | 13,836 | 35,835 |
| **Kyushu, Japan** | 13,770 | 35,664 |
| **Hainan, China** | 13,127 | 33,999 |
| **Prince of Wales, Canada** | 12,872 | 33,338 |
| **Spitsbergen, Norway** | 12,355 | 31,999 |
| **Vancouver, Canada** | 12,079 | 31,285 |
| **Timor, Indonesia** | 11,527 | 29,855 |
| **Sicily, Italy** | 9,926 | 25,708 |

| | Area in: Sq. Miles | Sq. Kms |
|---|---|---|
| **Somerset, Canada** | 9,570 | 24,78 |
| **Sardinia, Italy** | 9,301 | 24,09 |
| **Shikoku, Japan** | 6,860 | 17,76 |
| **New Caledonia, France** | 6,530 | 16,91 |
| **Nordaustlandet, Norway** | 6,409 | 16,59 |
| **Samar, Philippines** | 5,050 | 13,08 |
| **Negros, Philippines** | 4,906 | 12,70 |
| **Palawan, Philippines** | 4,550 | 11,78 |
| **Panay, Philippines** | 4,446 | 11,51 |
| **Jamaica** | 4,232 | 10,96 |
| **Hawaii, United States** | 4,038 | 10,45 |
| **Viti Levu, Fiji** | 4,010 | 10,38 |
| **Cape Breton, Canada** | 3,981 | 10,31 |
| **Mindoro, Philippines** | 3,759 | 9,73 |
| **Kodiak, Alaska, U.S.A.** | 3,670 | 9,50 |
| **Cyprus** | 3,572 | 9,25 |
| **Puerto Rico, U.S.A.** | 3,435 | 8,89 |
| **Corsica, France** | 3,352 | 8,68 |
| **New Ireland, Papua New Guinea** | 3,340 | 8,65 |
| **Crete, Greece** | 3,218 | 8,33 |
| **Anticosti, Canada** | 3,066 | 7,94 |
| **Wrangel, Russia** | 2,819 | 7,30 |

## Principal Mountains

| | Height in : Feet | Meters |
|---|---|---|
| Everest, Nepal-China | 29,028 | 8,848 |
| K2 (Godwin Austen), Pakistan-China | 28,250 | 8,611 |
| Makalu, Nepal-China | 27,789 | 8,470 |
| Dhaulagiri, Nepal | 26,810 | 8,172 |
| Nanga Parbat, Pakistan | 26,660 | 8,126 |
| Annapurna, Nepal | 26,504 | 8,078 |
| Rakaposhi, Pakistan | 25,550 | 7,788 |
| Kongur Shan, China | 25,325 | 7,719 |
| Tirich Mir, Pakistan | 25,230 | 7,690 |
| Gongga Shan, China | 24,790 | 7,556 |
| Communism Peak, Tajikistan | 24,590 | 7,495 |
| Pobedy Peak, Kyrgyzstan | 24,406 | 7,439 |
| Chomo Lhari, Bhutan-China | 23,997 | 7,314 |
| Muztag, China | 23,891 | 7,282 |
| Cerro Aconcagua, Argentina | 22,831 | 6,959 |
| Ojos del Salado, Chile-Argentina | 22,572 | 6,880 |
| Bonete, Chile-Argentina | 22,546 | 6,872 |
| Tupungato, Chile-Argentina | 22,310 | 6,800 |
| Pissis, Argentina | 22,241 | 6,779 |
| Mercedario, Argentina | 22,211 | 6,770 |
| Huascarán, Peru | 22,205 | 6,768 |
| Llullaillaco, Chile-Argentina | 22,057 | 6,723 |
| Nevada Ancohuma, Bolivia | 21,489 | 6,550 |
| Chimborazo, Ecuador | 20,561 | 6,267 |
| McKinley, Alaska | 20,320 | 6,194 |
| Logan, Yukon, Canada | 19,524 | 5,951 |
| Cotopaxi, Ecuador | 19,347 | 5,897 |
| Kilimanjaro, Tanzania | 19,340 | 5,895 |
| El Misti, Peru | 19,101 | 5,822 |
| Pico Cristóbal Colón, Colombia | 18,947 | 5,775 |
| Huila, Colombia | 18,865 | 5,750 |
| Citlaltépetl (Orizaba), Mexico | 18,701 | 5,700 |
| Damavand, Iran | 18,606 | 5,671 |
| El'brus, Russia | 18,510 | 5,642 |
| St. Elias, Alaska, U.S.A.-Yukon, Canada | 18,008 | 5,489 |
| Dykh-tau, Russia | 17,070 | 5,203 |
| Batian (Kenya), Kenya | 17,058 | 5,199 |
| Ararat, Turkey | 16,946 | 5,165 |
| Vinson Massif, Antarctica | 16,864 | 5,140 |
| Margherita (Ruwenzori), Africa | 16,795 | 5,119 |
| Kazbek, Georgia-Russia | 16,558 | 5,047 |
| Puncak Jaya, Indonesia | 16,503 | 5,030 |
| Blanc, France | 15,771 | 4,807 |
| Klyuchevskaya Sopka, Russia | 15,584 | 4,750 |
| Fairweather, Br. Col., Canada | 15,300 | 4,663 |
| Dufourspitze (Mte. Rosa), Italy-Switzerland | 15,203 | 4,634 |
| Ras Dashen, Ethiopia | 15,157 | 4620 |
| Matterhorn, Switzerland | 14,691 | 4,478 |
| Whitney, California, U.S.A. | 14,494 | 4,418 |
| Elbert, Colorado, U.S.A. | 14,433 | 4,399 |
| Rainier, Washington, U.S.A. | 14,410 | 4,392 |
| Shasta, California, U.S.A. | 14,162 | 4,317 |
| Pikes Peak, Colorado, U.S.A. | 14,110 | 4,301 |
| Finsteraarhorn, Switzerland | 14,022 | 4, 274 |
| Mauna Kea, Hawaii, U.S.A. | 13,796 | 4,205 |
| Mauna Loa, Hawaii, U.S.A. | 13,677 | 4,169 |
| Jungfrau, Switzerland | 13,642 | 4,158 |
| Grossglockner, Austria | 12,457 | 3,797 |
| Fujiyama, Japan | 12,389 | 3,776 |
| Cook, New Zealand | 12,349 | 3,764 |
| Etna, Italy | 10,902 | 3,323 |
| Kosciusko, Australia | 7,310 | 2,228 |
| Mitchell, North Carolina, U.S.A. | 6,684 | 2,037 |

## Longest Rivers

| | Length in: Miles | Kms. |
|---|---|---|
| Nile, Africa | 4,145 | 6,671 |
| Amazon, S. America | 3,915 | 6,300 |
| Chang Jiang (Yangtze), China | 3,900 | 6,276 |
| Mississippi-Missouri-Red Rock, U.S.A. | 3,741 | 6,019 |
| Ob'-Irtysh-Black Irtysh, Russia-Kazakhstan | 3,362 | 5,411 |
| Yenisey-Angara, Russia | 3,100 | 4,989 |
| Huang He (Yellow), China | 2,877 | 4,630 |
| Amur-Shilka-Onon, Asia | 2,744 | 4,416 |
| Lena, Russia | 2,734 | 4,400 |
| Congo (Zaire), Africa | 2,718 | 4,374 |
| Mackenzie-Peace-Finlay,Canada | 2,635 | 4,241 |
| Mekong, Asia | 2,610 | 4,200 |
| Missouri-Red Rock, U.S.A. | 2,564 | 4,125 |
| Niger, Africa | 2,548 | 4,101 |
| Paraná-La Plata, S. America | 2,450 | 3,943 |
| Mississippi, U.S.A. | 2,348 | 3,778 |
| Murray-Darling, Australia | 2,310 | 3,718 |
| Volga, Russia | 2,194 | 3,531 |
| Madeira, S. America | 2,013 | 3,240 |
| Purus, S. America | 1,995 | 3,211 |
| Yukon, Alaska-Canada | 1,979 | 3,185 |
| St. Lawrence, Canada-U.S.A. | 1,900 | 3,058 |
| Rio Grande, Mexico-U.S.A. | 1,885 | 3,034 |
| Syrdar'ya-Naryn, Asia | 1,859 | 2,992 |
| São Francisco, Brazil | 1,811 | 2,914 |
| Indus, Asia | 1,800 | 2,897 |
| Danube, Europe | 1,775 | 2,857 |
| Salween, Asia | 1,770 | 2,849 |
| Brahmaputra, Asia | 1,700 | 2,736 |
| Euphrates, Asia | 1,700 | 2,736 |
| Tocantins, Brazil | 1,677 | 2,699 |
| Xi (Si), China | 1,650 | 2,601 |
| Amudar'ya, Asia | 1,616 | 2,601 |
| Nelson-Saskatchewan, Canada | 1,600 | 2,575 |
| Orinoco, S. America | 1,600 | 2,575 |
| Zambezi, Africa | 1,600 | 2,575 |
| Paraguay, S. America | 1,584 | 2,549 |
| Kolyma, Russia | 1,562 | 2,514 |
| Ganges, Asia | 1,550 | 2,494 |
| Ural, Russia-Kazakhstan | 1,509 | 2,428 |
| Japurá, S. America | 1,500 | 2,414 |
| Arkansas, U.S.A. | 1,450 | 2,334 |
| Colorado, U.S.A.-Mexico | 1.450 | 2,334 |
| Negro, S. America | 1,400 | 2,253 |
| Dnieper, Russia-Belarus-Ukraine | 1,368 | 2,202 |
| Orange, Africa | 1,350 | 2,173 |
| Irrawaddy, Burma | 1,325 | 2,132 |
| Brazos, U.S.A. | 1,309 | 2,107 |
| Ohio-Allegheny, U.S.A. | 1,306 | 2,102 |
| Kama, Russia | 1,252 | 2,031 |
| Don, Russia | 1,222 | 1,967 |
| Red, U.S.A. | 1,222 | 1,966 |
| Columbia, U.S.A.-Canada | 1,214 | 1,953 |
| Saskatchewan, Canada | 1,205 | 1,939 |
| Peace-Finlay, Canada | 1,195 | 1,923 |
| Tigris, Asia | 1,181 | 1,901 |
| Darling, Australia | 1,160 | 1,867 |
| Angara, Russia | 1,135 | 1,827 |
| Sungari, Asia | 1,130 | 1,819 |
| Pechora, Russia | 1,124 | 1,809 |
| Snake, U.S.A. | 1,038 | 1,670 |
| Churchill, Canada | 1,000 | 1,609 |
| Pilcomayo, S. America | 1,000 | 1,609 |
| Uruguay, S. America | 994 | 1.600 |
| Platte-N. Platte, U.S.A. | 990 | 1,593 |
| Ohio, U.S.A. | 981 | 1,578 |
| Magdalena, Colombia | 956 | 1,538 |
| Pecos, U.S.A. | 926 | 1,490 |
| Oka, Russia | 918 | 1,477 |
| Canadian, U.S.A. | 906 | 1,458 |
| Colorado, Texas, U.S.A. | 894 | 1,439 |
| Dniester, Ukraine-Moldova | 876 | 1,410 |
| Fraser, Canada | 850 | 1,369 |
| Rhine, Europe | 820 | 1,319 |
| Northern Dvina, Russia | 809 | 1,302 |

## Principal Natural Lakes

| | Area in: Sq. Miles | Sq. Kms. | Max. Depth in: Feet | Meters |
|---|---|---|---|---|
| Caspian Sea, Asia | 143,243 | 370,999 | 3,264 | 995 |
| Lake Superior, U.S.A.-Canada | 31,820 | 82,414 | 1,329 | 405 |
| Lake Victoria, Africa | 26,724 | 69,215 | 270 | 82 |
| Lake Huron, U.S.A.-Canada | 23,010 | 59,596 | 748 | 228 |
| Lake Michigan, U.S.A. | 22,400 | 58,016 | 923 | 281 |
| Aral Sea, Kazakhstan-Uzbekistan | 15,830 | 41,000 | 213 | 65 |
| Lake Tanganyika, Africa | 12,650 | 32,764 | 4,700 | 1,433 |
| Lake Baykal, Russia | 12,162 | 31,500 | 5,316 | 1,620 |
| Great Bear Lake, Canada | 12,096 | 31,328 | 1,356 | 413 |
| Lake Nyasa (Malawi), Africa | 11,555 | 29,928 | 2,320 | 707 |
| Great Slave Lake, Canada | 11,031 | 28,570 | 2,015 | 614 |
| Lake Erie, U.S.A.-Canada | 9,940 | 25,745 | 210 | 64 |
| Lake Winnipeg, Canada | 9,417 | 24,390 | 60 | 18 |
| Lake Ontario, U.S.A.-Canada | 7,540 | 19,529 | 775 | 244 |
| Lake Ladoga, Russia | 7,104 | 18,399 | 738 | 225 |
| Lake Balkhash, Kazakhstan | 7,027 | 18,200 | 87 | 27 |
| Lake Maracaibo, Venezuela | 5,120 | 13,261 | 100 | 31 |
| Lake Chad, Africa | 4,000 – 10,000 | 10,360 – 25,900 | 25 | 8 |
| Lake Onega, Russia | 3,710 | 9,609 | 377 | 115 |
| Lake Eyre, Australia | 3,500-0 | 9,000-0 | – | – |
| Lake Titicaca, Peru-Bolivia | 3,200 | 8,288 | 1, 000 | 305 |
| Lake Nicaragua, Nicaragua | 3,100 | 8,029 | 230 | 70 |
| Lake Athabasca, Canada | 3,064 | 7,936 | 400 | 122 |
| Reindeer Lake, Canada | 2,568 | 6,651 | – | – |
| Lake Turkana (Rudolf), Africa | 2,463 | 6,379 | 240 | 73 |
| Issyk-Kul', Kyrgyzstan | 2,425 | 6,281 | 2,303 | 702 |
| Lake Torrens, Australia | 2,230 | 5,776 | – | – |
| Vänern, Sweden | 2,156 | 5,584 | 328 | 100 |
| Nettilling Lake, Canada | 2,140 | 5,543 | – | – |
| Lake Winnipegosis, Canada | 2,075 | 5,374 | 38 | 12 |
| Lake Mobutu Sese Seko (Albert), Africa | 2,075 | 5,374 | 160 | 49 |
| Kariba Lake, Zambia-Zimbabwe | 2,050 | 5,310 | 295 | 90 |
| Lake Nipigon, Canada | 1,872 | 4,848 | 540 | 165 |
| Lake Mweru, Zaire-Zambia | 1,800 | 4,662 | 60 | 18 |
| Lake Manitoba, Canada | 1,799 | 4,659 | 12 | 4 |
| Lake Taymyr, Russia | 1,737 | 4,499 | 85 | 26 |
| Lake Khanka, China-Russia | 1,700 | 4,403 | 33 | 10 |
| Lake Kioga, Uganda | 1,700 | 4,403 | 25 | 8 |
| Lake of the Woods, U.S.A.-Canada | 1,679 | 4,349 | 70 | 21J2 |

# Population of Major Cities

The following pages include population figures for all cities with more than 100,000 inhabitants, and for all national capitals, regardless of size. Cities are listed alphabetically, and grouped alphabetically by country. Two dependencies, Hong Kong and Puerto Rico, follow the country listing. Capitals are indicated with an asterisk (*). The population figures, given in thousands, represent the most current information available.

| Country<br>City | Population in thousands |
|---|---|
| A | |
| **Afghanistan** | |
| Herāt | 177 |
| Kābul* | 1,424 |
| Mazār-e Sharīf | 131 |
| Qandahar | 226 |
| **Albania** | |
| Tiranë* | 171 |
| **Algeria** | |
| Algiers* | 1,688 |
| Annaba | 228 |
| Batna | 185 |
| Bechar | 107 |
| Bejaïa | 118 |
| Biskra | 130 |
| Blida | 132 |
| Chelif | 130 |
| Constantine | 450 |
| Mostaganem | 115 |
| Oran | 599 |
| Sétif | 186 |
| Sidi Bel-Abbes | 155 |
| Skikda | 129 |
| Tébessa | 108 |
| Tiaret | 106 |
| Tlemcen | 108 |
| **Andorra** | |
| Andorra la Vella* | 12 |
| **Angola** | |
| Luanda* | 475 |
| **Antigua and Barbuda** | |
| Saint John's* | 22 |
| **Argentina** | |
| Avellaneda | 331 |
| Bahía Blanca | 233 |
| Buenos Aires* | 2,908 |
| Concordia | 122 |
| Córdoba | 990 |
| Corrientes | 186 |
| Formosa | 102 |
| General Roca | 210 |
| General San Martin | 384 |
| Godoy Cruz | 142 |
| Lanús | 466 |
| La Plata | 473 |
| Lomas de Zamora | 509 |
| Mar del Plata | 302 |
| Mendoza | 118 |
| Merlo | 293 |
| Morón | 597 |
| Paraná | 224 |
| Posadas | 148 |
| Resistencia | 143 |
| Río Cuarto | 191 |
| Rosario | 935 |
| Salta | 266 |
| San Fernando | 129 |
| San Juan | 118 |
| San Miguel de Tucumán | 393 |
| San Nicolás de los Arroyes | 114 |
| San Rafael | 144 |
| San Salvador de Jujuy | 167 |
| Santa Fé | 375 |
| Santiago del Estero | 163 |
| Tigre | 199 |
| Vicente López | 290 |
| **Armenia** | |
| Kirovakan | 146 |
| Kumayri | 120 |
| Yerevan* | 1,199 |
| **Australia** | |
| Adelaide | 978 |
| Brisbane | 1,149 |
| Canberra* | 247 |
| Geelong | 140 |
| Gold Coast | 135 |
| Hobart | 175 |
| Melbourne | 2,833 |
| Newcastle | 256 |
| Perth | 994 |
| Sydney | 3,365 |
| Wollongong | 207 |
| **Austria** | |
| Graz | 243 |
| Innsbruck | 116 |
| Linz | 198 |
| Salzburg | 138 |
| Vienna* | 1,516 |
| **Azerbaijan** | |
| Baku* | 1,150 |
| Gyandzhe | 278 |
| Sumgait | 231 |
| B | |
| **Bahamas** | |
| Nassau* | 135 |
| **Bahrain** | |
| Manama* | 109 |
| **Bangladesh** | |
| Barisāl | 159 |
| Chittagong | 1,388 |
| Comilla | 126 |
| Dhākā* | 3,459 |
| Jessore | 149 |
| Khulna | 623 |
| Nārāyanganj | 196 |
| Pābna | 101 |
| Rājshāhi | 172 |
| **Barbados** | |
| Bridgetown* | 7 |
| **Belarus** | |
| Baranovichi | 159 |
| Bobruysk | 223 |
| Borisov | 144 |
| Brest | 258 |
| Gomel' | 500 |
| Grodno | 270 |
| Minsk* | 1,589 |
| Mogilëv | 356 |
| Mozyr' | 101 |
| Orsha | 123 |
| Pinsk | 119 |
| Vitebsk | 350 |
| **Belgium** | |
| Antwerp | 186 |
| Brugge | 118 |
| Brussels* | 997 |
| Charleroi | 222 |
| Ghent | 239 |
| Liège | 214 |
| Namur | 102 |
| Schaerbeek | 107 |
| **Belize** | |
| Belmopan* | 3 |
| **Benin** | |
| Cotonou | 383 |
| Porto-Novo* | 144 |
| **Bhutan** | |
| Thimphu* | 12 |
| **Bolivia** | |
| Cochabamba | 205 |
| La Paz* | 635 |
| Oruro | 124 |
| Santa Cruz | 255 |
| Sucre* | 64 |
| **Bosnia & Hercegovina** | |
| Banja Luka | 184 |
| Mostar | 110 |
| Prijedor | 109 |
| Sarajevo* | 449 |
| Tuzla | 122 |
| Zenica | 133 |
| **Botswana** | |
| Gaborone* | 120 |
| **Brazil** | |
| Americana | 122 |
| Anápolis | 161 |
| Aracaju | 293 |
| Araçatuba | 113 |
| Barra Mansa | 123 |
| Baurú | 179 |
| Belém | 934 |
| Belo Horizonte | 1,775 |
| Blumenau | 145 |
| Brasília* | 411 |
| Campina Grande | 222 |
| Campinas | 567 |
| Campo Grande | 291 |
| Campos | 174 |
| Canoas | 214 |
| Carapicuíba | 186 |
| Caruaru | 138 |
| Caxias do Sul | 199 |
| Contegem | 112 |
| Cuiabá | 213 |
| Curitiba | 1,026 |
| Diadema | 229 |
| Divinópolis | 108 |
| Duque du Caxias | 306 |
| Feira de Santana | 225 |
| Florianópolis | 188 |
| Fortaleza | 1,309 |
| Franca | 144 |
| Goiânia | 718 |
| Governador Valadares | 174 |
| Guarulhos | 395 |
| Imperatriz | 112 |
| Ipatinga | 105 |
| Itabuna | 130 |
| Jacareí | 104 |
| João Pessoa | 330 |
| Joinvile | 217 |
| Juazeiro do Norte | 125 |
| Juiz de Fora | 300 |
| Jundiaí | 210 |
| Lages | 109 |
| Limeira | 138 |
| Londrina | 258 |
| Macapá | 138 |
| Maceió | 400 |
| Manaus | 635 |
| Marília | 104 |
| Maringá | 158 |
| Mauá | 206 |
| Mogi das Cruzes | 122 |
| Montes Claros | 152 |
| Mossoró | 118 |
| Natal | 420 |
| Nilópolis | 103 |
| Niterói | 386 |
| Nova Iguaçu | 492 |
| Novo Hamburgo | 132 |
| Olinda | 266 |
| Osasco | 474 |
| Passo Fundo | 103 |
| Pelotas | 197 |
| Petrópolis | 149 |
| Piracicaba | 179 |
| Ponta Grossa | 171 |
| Porto Alegre | 1,126 |
| Porto Velho | 135 |
| Presidente Prudente | 128 |
| Recife | 1,205 |
| Ribeirão Preto | 301 |
| Rio Branco | 117 |
| Rio Claro | 103 |
| Rio de Janeiro | 5,093 |
| Rio Grande | 125 |
| Salvador | 1,501 |
| Santa Maria | 151 |
| Santarém | 102 |
| Santo André | 549 |
| Santos | 411 |
| São Bernardo do Campo | 381 |
| São Caetano do Sul | 163 |
| São Carlos | 109 |
| São Gonçalo | 221 |
| São João de Meriti | 211 |
| São José do Rio Preto | 172 |
| São José dos Campos | 268 |
| São Luís | 450 |
| São Paulo | 8,491 |
| São Vicente | 193 |
| Sorocaba | 255 |
| Taguatinga | 480 |
| Taubaté | 155 |
| Teresina | 378 |
| Uberaba | 180 |
| Uberlândia | 230 |
| Vitória | 208 |
| Vitória da Conquista | 126 |
| Volta Redonda | 178 |
| **Brunei** | |
| Bandar Seri Begawan* | 64 |
| **Bulgaria** | |
| Burgas | 183 |
| Pleven | 130 |
| Plovdiv | 343 |
| Shumen | 100 |
| Sofia* | 1,122 |
| Stara Zagora | 151 |
| Tolbukhin | 109 |
| Varna | 303 |
| **Burkina** | |
| Bobo Dioulasso | 231 |
| Ouagadougou* | 308 |
| **Burma** | |
| Akyab | 108 |
| Bassein | 144 |
| Insein | 144 |
| Mandalay | 533 |
| Monywa | 107 |
| Moulmein | 220 |
| Pegu | 151 |
| Rangoon* | 2,513 |
| Taunggyi | 108 |
| **Burundi** | |
| Bujumbura* | 141 |
| C | |
| **Cambodia** | |
| Phnom Penh* | 300 |
| **Cameroon** | |
| Douala | 784 |
| N'Kongsamba | 102 |
| Yaoundé* | 552 |
| **Canada** | |
| Brampton | 188 |
| Burlington | 117 |
| Burnaby | 145 |
| Calgary | 671 |
| Edmonton | 785 |
| Halifax | 114 |
| Hamilton | 307 |
| Kitchener | 151 |
| Laval | 284 |
| London | 269 |
| Longueuil | 125 |
| Markham | 115 |
| Mississauga | 374 |
| Montréal | 1,015 |
| Oshawa | 124 |
| Ottawa* | 301 |
| Québec | 165 |
| Regina | 175 |
| Richmond | 108 |
| Saint Catharines | 123 |
| Saskatoon | 201 |
| Surrey | 181 |
| Thunder Bay | 112 |
| Toronto | 2,193 |
| Vancouver | 431 |
| Windsor | 193 |
| Winnipeg | 625 |
| **Cape Verde** | |
| Praia* | 57 |
| **Central African Republic** | |
| Bangui* | 474 |
| **Chad** | |
| N'Djamena* | 179 |
| **Chile** | |
| Antofagasta | 203 |
| Arica | 158 |
| Barrancas | 184 |
| Chillán | 127 |
| Concepción | 281 |
| Iquique | 127 |
| Maipú | 118 |
| Osorno | 102 |
| Puente Alto | 126 |
| Puerto Montt | 119 |
| Punta Arenas | 107 |
| Rancagua | 157 |
| San Bernardo | 136 |
| Santiago* | 4,100 |
| Talca | 138 |
| Talcahuano | 218 |
| Temuco | 168 |
| Valdivia | 105 |
| Valparaíso | 273 |
| Viña del Mar | 261 |
| **China** | |
| Anda | 423 |
| Anqing | 449 |
| Anshan | 1,196 |
| Anshun | 201 |
| Anyang | 501 |
| Baicheng | 276 |
| Baiyin | 325 |
| Baoding | 495 |
| Baoji | 341 |
| Baotou | 1,076 |
| Beihai | 174 |
| Beijing* | 5,531 |
| Beipiao | 605 |
| Bengbu | 550 |
| Benxi | 774 |
| Binzhou | 186 |
| Botou | 1,076 |
| Cangzhou | 280 |
| Changchun | 1,747 |
| Changde | 214 |
| Changsha | 1,066 |
| Changshu | 100 |
| Changshun | 1,747 |
| Changzhi | 450 |
| Changzhou | 534 |
| Chaoyang | 207 |
| Chaozhou | 162 |
| Chengde | 327 |
| Chengdu | 2,499 |
| Chenzhou | 166 |
| Chifeng | 293 |
| Chongqing | 2,673 |
| Conghua | 280 |
| Da Xian | 193 |
| Dafang | 962 |
| Dalian | 1,480 |
| Dandong | 545 |
| Daqing | 758 |
| Datong | 962 |
| Da Xian | 193 |
| Dezhou | 259 |
| Ding Xian | 938 |
| Dongguan | 1,230 |
| Dongying | 540 |
| Duyun | 102 |
| Echeng | 119 |
| Fengcheng | 996 |
| Foshan | 274 |
| Fushun | 1,185 |
| Fuxin | 647 |
| Fuyang | 178 |
| Fuzhou | 1,112 |
| Ganzhou | 363 |
| Gejiu | 353 |
| Guangzhou | 3,182 |
| Guilin | 432 |
| Guiyang | 1,350 |
| Haicheng | 992 |
| Haikou | 263 |
| Hailar | 157 |
| Haining | 600 |
| Handan | 930 |
| Hangzhou | 1,171 |
| Hanzhong | 374 |
| Harbin | 2,519 |
| Hebi | 336 |
| Hefei | 795 |
| Hegang | 592 |
| Hengshui | 101 |
| Hengyang | 532 |
| Heshan | 112 |
| Hohhot | 754 |
| Houma | 144 |
| Huaibei | 445 |
| Huaihua | 436 |
| Huainan | 1,029 |
| Huangshi | 376 |
| Huaying | 321 |
| Huizhou | 158 |
| Hunjiang | 694 |
| Huzhou | 953 |
| Jiamusi | 540 |
| Ji'an | 168 |
| Jiangmen | 212 |
| Jiaojiang | 391 |
| Jiaozuo | 484 |
| Jiaxing | 655 |
| Jilin | 1,888 |
| Jinan | 1,359 |
| Jingdezhen | 611 |
| Jingmen | 957 |
| Jinhua | 869 |
| Jining (Nei Mong.) | 159 |
| Jining (Shandong) | 190 |
| Jinzhou | 599 |
| Jiujiang | 351 |
| Jixi | 782 |
| Kaifeng | 602 |
| Kaiyuan | 223 |
| Karamay | 157 |
| Kashi | 257 |
| Korla | 118 |
| Kunming | 1,419 |
| Kuytun | 240 |
| Langfang | 533 |
| Lanxi | 612 |
| Lanzhou | 1,364 |
| Laohekou | 102 |
| Lengshuijiang | 255 |
| Lengshuitan | 371 |
| Leshan | 958 |
| Lhasa | 343 |
| Lianyungang | 397 |
| Liaocheng | 737 |
| Liaoyang | 589 |
| Liaoyuan | 772 |
| Lichuan | 718 |
| Linchuan | 619 |
| Linfen | 208 |
| Liuzhou | 582 |
| Longyan | 347 |
| Loudi | 266 |
| Lu'an | 146 |
| Luohe | 158 |
| Luoyang | 952 |
| Luzhou | 305 |
| Ma'anshan | 352 |
| Manzhouli | 104 |
| Maoming | 413 |
| Meizhou | 111 |
| Mianyang | 769 |
| Mudanjiang | 581 |
| Nanchang | 1,076 |
| Nanchong | 228 |
| Nanjing | 2,091 |
| Nanning | 890 |
| Nanping | 408 |
| Nantong | 403 |
| Nanyang | 288 |
| Neijiang | 271 |
| Ningbo | 479 |
| Pingdingshan | 470 |
| Pingxiang | 1,189 |
| Pingyang | 510 |
| Qingdao | 1,172 |
| Qingjiang | 235 |
| Qinhuangdao | 394 |
| Qiqihar | 1,209 |
| Qitaihe | 283 |
| Quanzhou | 403 |
| Qufu | 545 |
| Quzhou | 981 |
| Renqiu | 591 |
| Rizhao | 988 |
| Sanmenxia | 147 |
| Sanming | 199 |
| Shanghai | 6,293 |
| Shangqiu | 187 |
| Shangrao | 665 |
| Shantou | 718 |
| Shaoguan | 371 |
| Shaoxing | 1,091 |
| Shaoyang | 397 |
| Shashi | 239 |
| Shenyang | 3,944 |
| Shihezi | 564 |
| Shijiazhuang | 1,069 |
| Shishou | 558 |
| Shiyan | 307 |
| Shizuishan | 298 |
| Shuangyashan | 400 |
| Siping | 334 |
| Suizhou | 143 |
| Suzhou | 192 |
| Tai'an | 1,275 |
| Taiyuan | 1,746 |
| Taizhou | 161 |
| Tangshan | 1,408 |
| Tianjin | 5,152 |
| Tianshui | 185 |
| Tieling | 221 |
| Tongchuan | 354 |
| Tonghua | 360 |
| Tongliao | 213 |
| Tongling | 184 |
| Ulanhot | 174 |
| Ürümqi | 961 |
| Wanxian | 267 |
| Weifang | 393 |
| Weihai | 205 |
| Wenzhou | 516 |
| Wuhan | 3,288 |
| Wuhu | 449 |
| Wuxi | 798 |
| Wuzhou | 245 |
| Xiaguan | 117 |
| Xiamen | 507 |
| Xi'an | 2,185 |
| Xiangfan | 323 |
| Xiangtan | 492 |
| Xianning | 406 |
| Xianyang | 502 |
| Xichang | 146 |
| Xifeng | 237 |
| Xingtai | 334 |
| Xining Shi | 567 |
| Xinji | 532 |
| Xinxiang | 525 |
| Xinyang | 240 |
| Xinyu | 622 |
| Xuchang | 219 |
| Xuzhou | 777 |
| Ya'an | 254 |
| Yangquan | 478 |
| Yangzhou | 302 |
| Yanji | 176 |
| Yantai | 385 |
| Yibin | 245 |
| Yichang | 365 |
| Yichun | 756 |
| Yinchuan | 354 |
| Yingcheng | 546 |
| Yingkou | 423 |
| Yingtan | 120 |
| Yining | 257 |
| Yiyang | 165 |
| Yong'an | 272 |
| Yuci | 271 |
| Yueyang | 972 |
| Yumen | 195 |
| Yushu | 150 |
| Yuyao | 778 |
| Zaozhuang | 1,244 |
| Zhangjiakou | 617 |
| Zhangzhou | 283 |
| Zhanjiang | 854 |
| Zhaoqing | 172 |
| Zhaotong | 133 |
| Zhengzhou | 1,404 |
| Zhenjiang | 346 |
| Zhongshan | 135 |
| Zhoukou | 214 |
| Zhuhai | 132 |
| Zhumadian | 150 |
| Zhuo Xian | 478 |
| Zhuzhou | 383 |
| Zibo | 2,198 |
| Zigong | 866 |
| Zixing | 340 |
| Zunyi | 351 |
| **Colombia** | |
| Armenia | 180 |
| Barrancabermeja | 137 |
| Barranquilla | 897 |
| Bello | 206 |
| Bogotá* | 3,975 |
| Bucaramanga | 342 |
| Buenaventura | 160 |
| Cali | 1,324 |
| Cartagena | 491 |
| Cúcuta | 357 |
| Floridablanca | 138 |
| Ibagué | 269 |
| Itagüí | 136 |
| Manizales | 275 |
| Medellín | 1,419 |
| Montería | 157 |
| Neiva | 178 |
| Palmira | 175 |
| Pasto | 197 |
| Pereira | 233 |
| Popayán | 142 |
| Santa Marta | 178 |
| Sincelejo | 121 |
| Soledad | 164 |
| Valledupar | 143 |
| Villavicencio | 161 |
| **Comoros** | |
| Moroni* | 20 |
| **Congo** | |
| Brazzaville* | 299 |
| Pointe-Noire | 142 |
| **Costa Rica** | |
| San José* | 241 |
| **Croatia** | |
| Osijek | 159 |
| Rijeka | 193 |
| Slavonski Brod | 106 |
| Split | 236 |
| Zadar | 116 |
| Zagreb* | 681 |
| **Cuba** | |
| Bayamo | 122 |
| Camagüey | 279 |
| Cienfuegos | 119 |
| Guantánamo | 198 |
| Havana* | 2,078 |
| Holguín | 223 |
| Marianao | 128 |
| Matanzas | 112 |
| Pinar del Río | 117 |
| Santa Clara | 191 |
| Santiago de Cuba | 397 |
| Victoria de las Tunas | 115 |
| **Cyprus** | |
| Limassol | 120 |
| Nicosia* | 167 |
| **Czech Republic** | |
| Brno | 371 |
| Olomouc | 102 |
| Ostrava | 322 |
| Pilsen | 171 |
| Prague* | 1,182 |
| D | |
| **Denmark** | |
| Ålborg | 155 |
| Århus | 182 |
| Copenhagen* | 494 |
| Odense | 137 |

| Country / City | Population in thousands |
|---|---|
| **Djibouti** | |
| Djibouti* | 96 |
| **Dominica** | |
| Roseau* | 8 |
| **Dominican Republic** | |
| Santiago de los Caballero | 279 |
| Santo Domingo* | 1,313 |
| **E** | |
| **Ecuador** | |
| Ambato | 113 |
| Cuenca | 157 |
| Guayaquil | 1,205 |
| Machala | 108 |
| Manta | 104 |
| Portoviejo | 123 |
| Quito* | 890 |
| Santo Domingo de los Colorados | 128 |
| **Egypt** | |
| Alexandria | 2,319 |
| Al Fayyum | 167 |
| Al Jīzah | 1,247 |
| Al Maḩallah al Kubrá | 293 |
| Al Manşūra | 258 |
| Al Minyā | 146 |
| Aswān | 144 |
| Asyūt | 214 |
| Az Zaqāzīq | 203 |
| Banī Suwayf | 118 |
| Cairo* | 5,084 |
| Damanhūr | 189 |
| Ismailia | 146 |
| Kafr ad Dawwār | 161 |
| Port Said | 263 |
| Sawhāj | 102 |
| Shibīn al Kaum | 103 |
| Shubrā al Khaymah | 394 |
| Suez | 194 |
| Tantā | 285 |
| **El Salvador** | |
| San Miguel | 179 |
| San Salvador* | 471 |
| Santa Ana | 228 |
| **Equatorial Guinea** | |
| Malabo* | 37 |
| **Estonia** | |
| Tallinn* | 482 |
| Tartu | 114 |
| **Ethiopia** | |
| Addis Ababa* | 1,413 |
| Āsmera | 275 |
| Dirē Dawa | 105 |
| Gonder | 108 |
| **F** | |
| **Fiji** | |
| Suva* | 70 |
| **Finland** | |
| Esbo (Espoo) | 157 |
| Helsinki* | 486 |
| Tampere | 169 |
| Turku | 161 |
| Vantaa | 144 |
| **France** | |
| Aix-en-Provence | 100 |
| Amiens | 130 |
| Angers | 135 |
| Besançon | 112 |
| Bordeaux | 202 |
| Boulogne-Billancourt | 103 |
| Brest | 154 |
| Caen | 112 |
| Clermont-Ferrand | 146 |
| Dijon | 139 |
| Grenoble | 156 |
| Le Havre | 199 |
| Le Mans | 146 |
| Lille | 168 |
| Limoges | 138 |
| Lyon | 410 |
| Marseille | 868 |
| Metz | 113 |
| Montpellier | 190 |
| Mulhouse | 112 |
| Nantes | 238 |
| Nice | 331 |
| Nîmes | 121 |
| Paris* | 2,166 |
| Perpignan | 108 |
| Reims | 176 |
| Rennes | 191 |
| Roubaix | 101 |
| Rouen | 101 |
| Saint-Étienne | 194 |
| Strasbourg | 247 |
| Toulon | 177 |
| Toulouse | 345 |
| Tours | 131 |
| **G** | |
| **Gabon** | |
| Libreville* | 105 |
| **Gambia** | |
| Banjul* | 49 |
| **Georgia** | |
| Batumi | 136 |
| Kutaisi | 235 |
| Rustavi | 159 |
| Sukhumi | 121 |
| Tbilisi* | 1,260 |
| **Germany** | |
| Aachen | 233 |
| Augsburg | 248 |
| Bergisch Gladbach | 102 |
| Berlin* | 3,305 |
| Bielefeld | 312 |
| Bochum | 389 |
| Bonn | 282 |
| Bottrop | 116 |
| Braunschweig | 254 |
| Bremen | 535 |
| Bremerhaven | 127 |
| Chemnitz | 314 |
| Cologne | 937 |
| Cottbus | 127 |
| Darmstadt | 136 |
| Dessau | 104 |
| Dortmund | 587 |
| Dresden | 520 |
| Duisburg | 527 |
| Düsseldorf | 570 |
| Erfurt | 217 |
| Erlangen | 101 |
| Essen | 621 |
| Frankfurt am Main | 625 |
| Freiburg | 184 |
| Gelsenkirchen | 287 |
| Gera | 113 |
| Göttingen | 118 |
| Hagen | 211 |
| Halle | 236 |
| Hamburg | 1,603 |
| Hamm | 174 |
| Hannover | 498 |
| Heidelberg | 131 |
| Heilbronn | 112 |
| Herne | 175 |
| Hildesheim | 104 |
| Jena | 108 |
| Karlsruhe | 265 |
| Kassel | 189 |
| Kiel | 241 |
| Koblenz | 107 |
| Köpenick | 118 |
| Krefeld | 235 |
| Leipzig | 551 |
| Leverkusen | 157 |
| Lübeck | 211 |
| Ludwigshafen | 158 |
| Magdeburg | 289 |
| Mainz | 175 |
| Mannheim | 300 |
| Moers | 102 |
| Mönchengladbach | 253 |
| Mülheim an der Ruhr | 175 |
| Munich | 1,212 |
| Münster | 249 |
| Neuss | 144 |
| Nürnberg | 249 |
| Oberhausen | 221 |
| Offenbach | 112 |
| Oldenburg | 141 |
| Osnabrück | 155 |
| Paderborn | 114 |
| Pforzheim | 109 |
| Potsdam | 141 |
| Recklinghausen | 122 |
| Regensburg | 119 |
| Remscheid | 121 |
| Reutlingen | 100 |
| Rostock | 249 |
| Saarbrücken | 188 |
| Salzgitter | 112 |
| Schwerin | 128 |
| Siegen | 106 |
| Solingen | 161 |
| Stuttgart | 563 |
| Ulm | 197 |
| Wiesbaden | 254 |
| Witten | 104 |
| Wolfsburg | 126 |
| Wuppertal | 371 |
| Würzburg | 126 |
| Zwickau | 121 |
| **Ghana** | |
| Accra* | 860 |
| Kumasi | 349 |
| Tamale | 137 |
| **Greece** | |
| Athens* | 886 |
| Iráklion | 102 |
| Kallithéa | 117 |
| Lárisa | 102 |
| Pátrai | 142 |
| Peristérion | 141 |
| Piraiévs | 196 |
| Thessaloníki | 406 |
| **Grenada** | |
| Saint George's* | 6 |
| **Guatemala** | |
| Guatemala* | 750 |
| **Guinea** | |
| Conakry* | 526 |
| **Guinea-Bissau** | |
| Bissau* | 109 |
| **Guyana** | |
| Georgetown* | 63 |
| **H** | |
| **Haiti** | |
| Port-au-Prince* | 461 |
| **Honduras** | |
| La Ceiba | 104 |
| San Pedro Sula | 397 |
| Tegucigalpa* | 598 |
| **Hungary** | |
| Budapest* | 2,104 |
| Debrecen | 217 |
| Győr | 131 |
| Kecskemét | 105 |
| Miskolc | 210 |
| Nyíregyháza | 119 |
| Pécs | 182 |
| Szeged | 188 |
| Székesfehérvár | 113 |
| **I** | |
| **Iceland** | |
| Reykjavík* | 96 |
| **India** | |
| Ādoni | 109 |
| Āgra | 747 |
| Agartala | 132 |
| Ahmadābād | 2,548 |
| Ahmadnagar | 181 |
| Ajmer | 376 |
| Akola | 225 |
| Alīgarh | 321 |
| Allahābād | 650 |
| Alleppey | 170 |
| Alwar | 146 |
| Ambāla | 121 |
| Amravati | 261 |
| Amritsar | 595 |
| Amroha | 113 |
| Anantapur | 120 |
| Arrah | 125 |
| Asansol | 366 |
| Aurangābād | 316 |
| Bīkaner | 288 |
| Bally | 148 |
| Bālurghāt | 113 |
| Bangalore | 2,922 |
| Baranagar | 170 |
| Bareilly | 449 |
| Baroda | 745 |
| Barrackpur | 116 |
| Batāla | 102 |
| Belgaum | 300 |
| Bellary | 202 |
| Berhampore | 102 |
| Berhampur | 163 |
| Bhadrāvati | 131 |
| Bhāgalpur | 225 |
| Bharātpur | 105 |
| Bharuch | 121 |
| Bhatinda | 127 |
| Bhātpāra | 265 |
| Bhavnagar | 309 |
| Bhilai | 376 |
| Bhīlwāra | 123 |
| Bhīmavaram | 102 |
| Bhiwandi | 115 |
| Bhiwāni | 101 |
| Bhopāl | 671 |
| Bhubaneswar | 219 |
| Bhusawal | 132 |
| Bihar | 151 |
| Bijāpur | 147 |
| Bilāspur | 187 |
| Bokaro Steel City | 264 |
| Bombay | 8,243 |
| Bulandshahr | 103 |
| Burdwān | 167 |
| Burhānpur | 141 |
| Calcutta | 9,194 |
| Cannanore | 158 |
| Chandannagar | 102 |
| Chandigarh | 423 |
| Chandrapur | 116 |
| Chāpra | 112 |
| Cochin | 686 |
| Coimbatore | 920 |
| Cuddalore | 128 |
| Cuddapah | 103 |
| Cuttack | 327 |
| Darbhanga | 176 |
| Dāvangere | 197 |
| Dehra Dūn | 293 |
| Delhi | 4,884 |
| Dhānbād | 621 |
| Dhārwār | 379 |
| Dhūlia | 211 |
| Dindigul | 164 |
| Dombivli | 103 |
| Durg | 115 |
| Durgāpur | 312 |
| Elūru | 168 |
| Erode | 276 |
| Etāwah | 112 |
| Faizābād | 143 |
| Farīdābād | 331 |
| Farrukhābād | 161 |
| Firozābād | 202 |
| Firozpur | 106 |
| Gadag-Betigeri | 117 |
| Garden Reach | 191 |
| Gauhāti | 152 |
| Gayā | 247 |
| Ghaziābād | 287 |
| Gondia | 100 |
| Gorakhpur | 308 |
| Gulbarga | 221 |
| Guntūr | 368 |
| Gurgaon | 101 |
| Gwalior | 556 |
| Hābra | 130 |
| Hāpur | 103 |
| Hardwār | 146 |
| Hisār | 137 |
| Hooghly-Chinsura | 125 |
| Hospet | 115 |
| Howrah | 744 |
| Hubli-Dhārwār | 527 |
| Hyderābād | 2,546 |
| Ichalkaranji | 134 |
| Imphāl | 157 |
| Indore | 829 |
| Jabalpur | 757 |
| Jaipur | 1,015 |
| Jālgaon | 145 |
| Jālna | 122 |
| Jammu | 223 |
| Jāmnagar | 317 |
| Jamshedpur | 670 |
| Jaridih | 102 |
| Jaunpur | 105 |
| Jhānsi | 284 |
| Jodhpur | 506 |
| Jullundur | 442 |
| Junāgadh | 120 |
| Kākināda | 226 |
| Kalyān | 136 |
| Kāmārhāti | 235 |
| Kānchīpuram | 145 |
| Kānpur | 1,639 |
| Kāraikkudi | 100 |
| Karnāl | 132 |
| Katihār | 122 |
| Khandwa | 115 |
| Kharagpur | 233 |
| Kolār Gold Fields | 144 |
| Kolhāpur | 351 |
| Kota | 358 |
| Kozhikode | 546 |
| Kumbakonam | 142 |
| Kurnool | 206 |
| Lātūr | 112 |
| Lucknow | 1,008 |
| Ludhiāna | 607 |
| Machilipatnam | 139 |
| Madras | 4,289 |
| Madurai | 908 |
| Mālegaon | 246 |
| Mandya | 100 |
| Mangalore | 306 |
| Mathurā | 159 |
| Meerut | 537 |
| Miraj | 105 |
| Mirzāpur | 128 |
| Monghyr | 129 |
| Morādābād | 345 |
| Murwāra | 123 |
| Muzaffarnagar | 172 |
| Muzaffarpur | 190 |
| Mysore | 479 |
| Nabadwīp | 130 |
| Nadiād | 143 |
| Nāgercoil | 172 |
| Nāgpur | 1,302 |
| Naihāti | 115 |
| Nānded | 191 |
| Nāsik | 429 |
| Navsāri | 129 |
| Nellore | 237 |
| New Delhi* | 273 |
| Nizāmābād | 183 |
| Pālghāt | 118 |
| Pānīpat | 138 |
| Pānihāti | 206 |
| Parbhani | 109 |
| Pātan | 105 |
| Pathānkot | 110 |
| Patiāla | 206 |
| Patna | 919 |
| Pimpri-Chinchwad | 221 |
| Pollāchi | 115 |
| Pondicherry | 251 |
| Poona | 1,686 |
| Porbandar | 133 |
| Proddatūr | 107 |
| Purī | 101 |
| Purnia | 110 |
| Quilon | 168 |
| Raichūr | 125 |
| Raipur | 338 |
| Rājahmundry | 268 |
| Rājapālaiyam | 102 |
| Rājkot | 445 |
| Rāmpur | 205 |
| Rānchī | 503 |
| Rānīganj | 119 |
| Ratlām | 156 |
| Raurkela | 321 |
| Rewa | 101 |
| Rohtak | 167 |
| Sāgar | 207 |
| Sahāranpur | 295 |
| Salem | 498 |
| Sambalpur | 162 |
| Sambhal | 108 |
| Sāngli | 269 |
| Secunderābād | 136 |
| Serampore | 127 |
| Shāhjahānpur | 205 |
| Shillong | 175 |
| Shimoga | 152 |
| Sholāpur | 515 |
| Sīkar | 103 |
| Silīguri | 154 |
| Sītāpur | 101 |
| Sonepat | 109 |
| South Dum Dum | 230 |
| South Suburban | 395 |
| Sri Gangānagar | 124 |
| Srīnagar | 606 |
| Surat | 914 |
| Tenāli | 119 |
| Thāna | 390 |
| Thanjavur | 184 |
| Tiruchchirāppalli | 545 |
| Tirunelveli | 178 |
| Tirupati | 115 |
| Tiruppūr | 203 |
| Titāgarh | 105 |
| Trichūr | 170 |
| Trivandrum | 520 |
| Tumkūr | 109 |
| Tuticorin | 251 |
| Udaipur | 233 |
| Ujjain | 282 |
| Ulhāsnagar | 315 |
| Vālpārai | 115 |
| Vārānasi | 797 |
| Vellore | 247 |
| Verāval | 105 |
| Vijayawada | 543 |
| Visākhapatnam | 604 |
| Vizianagaram | 115 |
| Warangal | 335 |
| Yamunānagar | 160 |
| **Indonesia** | |
| Ambon | 209 |
| Balikpapan | 281 |
| Bandung | 1,463 |
| Banjarmasin | 381 |
| Bekasi | 123 |
| Bogor | 247 |
| Ciamis | 105 |
| Cianjur | 132 |
| Cilacap | 119 |
| Cimahi | 157 |
| Cirebon | 224 |
| Jakarta* | 6,503 |
| Jambi | 230 |
| Jember | 115 |
| Kediri | 222 |
| Kuningan | 105 |
| Madiun | 151 |
| Magelang | 123 |
| Malang | 512 |
| Manado | 217 |
| Medan | 1,379 |
| Padang | 481 |
| Padangsidempuan | 135 |
| Pakanbaru | 186 |
| Palembang | 787 |
| Pare | 108 |
| Pekalongan | 133 |
| Pemalang | 110 |
| Pematangsiantar | 150 |
| Pontianak | 305 |
| Probolinggo | 100 |
| Purwokerto | 125 |
| Samarinda | 265 |
| Semarang | 1,027 |
| Sukabumi | 110 |
| Surabaya | 2,028 |
| Surakarta | 470 |
| Tanjungkarang | 284 |
| Tanjungpriok | 148 |
| Tasikmalaya | 136 |
| Tegal | 132 |
| Ujung Pandang | 709 |
| Yogyakarta | 399 |
| **Iran** | |
| Ābādān | 296 |
| Āmol | 118 |
| Ahvāz | 580 |
| Arāk | 265 |
| Ardabīl | 147 |
| Bābol | 115 |
| Bākhtarān | 561 |
| Bandar-e ʿAbbās | 202 |
| Borūjerd | 184 |
| Būshehr | 121 |
| Dezfūl | 151 |
| Eşfahān | 987 |
| Gorgān | 139 |
| Hamadān | 272 |
| Karaj | 275 |
| Kāshān | 139 |
| Kermān | 257 |
| Khomeynīshahr | 105 |
| Khorramābād | 209 |
| Khorramshahr | 147 |
| Khvoy | 115 |
| Malāyer | 104 |
| Marāgheh | 101 |
| Mashhad | 1,464 |
| Masjed-e Soleymān | 105 |
| Najafābād | 129 |
| Neyshābūr | 109 |
| Orūmīyeh | 301 |
| Qā'emshahr | 109 |
| Qazvīn | 249 |
| Qom | 543 |
| Rasht | 291 |
| Sabzevār | 129 |
| Sanandaj | 205 |
| Sārī | 141 |
| Shīrāz | 848 |
| Tabrīz | 971 |
| Tajrīsh | 157 |
| Tehrān* | 6,043 |
| Yazd | 230 |
| Zāhedān | 282 |
| Zanjān | 215 |
| **Iraq** | |
| Al Başrah | 313 |
| An Najaf | 128 |
| Baghdad* | 1,900 |
| Kirkūk | 167 |
| Mosul | 315 |
| **Ireland** | |
| Cork | 133 |
| Dublin* | 503 |
| **Israel** | |
| Bat Yam | 129 |
| Beersheba | 111 |
| Hefa | 226 |
| Holon | 133 |
| Jerusalem* | 429 |
| Netanya | 102 |
| Petah Tiqwa | 124 |
| Ramat Gan | 117 |
| Rishon LeZiyyon | 102 |
| Tel Aviv-Yafo | 327 |
| **Italy** | |
| Bari | 369 |
| Bergamo | 121 |
| Bologna | 455 |
| Bolzano | 103 |
| Brescia | 203 |
| Cagliari | 219 |
| Catania | 380 |
| Cosenza | 101 |
| Ferrara | 118 |
| Florence | 443 |
| Foggia | 150 |
| Genoa | 755 |
| La Spezia | 111 |
| Livorno | 172 |
| Messina | 240 |
| Mestre | 198 |
| Milan | 1,602 |
| Modena | 165 |
| Monza | 123 |
| Naples | 1,210 |
| Padua | 228 |
| Palermo | 698 |
| Parma | 160 |
| Perugia | 104 |
| Pescara | 131 |
| Piacenza | 104 |
| Prato | 157 |
| Reggio di Calabria | 159 |
| Reggio nell'Emilia | 107 |
| Rimini | 112 |
| Rome* | 2,605 |
| Salerno | 150 |
| Sassari | 104 |
| Siracusa | 109 |
| Taranto | 231 |
| Torre del Greco | 104 |
| Trieste | 237 |
| Turin | 1,115 |
| Udine | 102 |
| Verona | 239 |
| Vicenza | 111 |
| **Ivory Coast** | |
| Abidjan | 686 |
| Bouaké | 173 |
| Yamoussoukro* | 36 |
| **J** | |
| **Jamaica** | |
| Kingston* | 494 |
| **Japan** | |
| Abiko | 101 |
| Ageo | 166 |
| Aizu-Wakamatsu | 115 |
| Akashi | 255 |
| Akita | 285 |
| Amagasaki | 524 |
| Anjō | 124 |
| Aomori | 288 |
| Asahikawa | 353 |
| Ashikaga | 166 |
| Atsugi | 145 |
| Beppu | 136 |
| Chiba | 793 |
| Chigasaki | 171 |
| Chōfu | 181 |
| Daitō | 117 |
| Fuchū | 192 |
| Fuji | 206 |
| Fujieda | 103 |
| Fujinomiya | 108 |
| Fujisawa | 300 |
| Fukui | 241 |
| Fukuoka | 1,089 |
| Fukushima | 263 |
| Fukuyama | 346 |
| Funabashi | 479 |
| Gifu | 410 |
| Habikino | 103 |
| Hachiōji | 387 |
| Hachinohe | 238 |
| Hadano | 123 |
| Hakodate | 320 |
| Hamamatsu | 491 |
| Higashikurume | 107 |
| Higashimurayama | 119 |
| Higashi-Ōsaka | 522 |
| Himeji | 446 |
| Hino | 145 |
| Hirakata | 353 |
| Hiratsuka | 214 |
| Hirosaki | 175 |
| Hiroshima | 899 |
| Hitachi | 205 |
| Hōfu | 111 |
| Ibaraki | 234 |
| Ichihara | 216 |
| Ichikawa | 364 |
| Ichinomiya | 253 |
| Ikeda | 101 |
| Imabari | 123 |
| Iruma | 104 |
| Ise | 106 |
| Isesaki | 106 |
| Ishinomaki | 121 |
| Itami | 178 |
| Iwaki | 342 |
| Iwakuni | 113 |
| Izumi | 124 |
| Jōetsu | 128 |
| Kadoma | 139 |
| Kagoshima | 505 |
| Kakamigahara | 115 |
| Kakogawa | 212 |
| Kamakura | 173 |
| Kanazawa | 418 |
| Kariya | 106 |
| Kashihara | 107 |
| Kashiwa | 239 |
| Kasugai | 244 |
| Kasukabe | 156 |
| Kawagoe | 259 |
| Kawaguchi | 379 |
| Kawanishi | 130 |
| Kawasaki | 1,041 |
| Kiryū | 133 |
| Kisarazu | 111 |
| Kishiwada | 180 |
| Kitakyūshū | 1,065 |
| Kitami | 103 |
| Kōbe | 1,367 |
| Kōchi | 301 |
| Kōfu | 199 |
| Kōriyama | 286 |
| Kodaira | 155 |

| Country City | Population in thousands |
|---|---|
| Koganei | 102 |
| Komaki | 103 |
| Komatsu | 104 |
| Koshigaya | 223 |
| Kumagaya | 137 |
| Kumamoto | 526 |
| Kurashiki | 404 |
| Kure | 235 |
| Kurume | 217 |
| Kushiro | 215 |
| Kyōto | 1,473 |
| Machida | 295 |
| Maebashi | 265 |
| Matsubara | 136 |
| Matsudo | 401 |
| Matsue | 136 |
| Matsumoto | 192 |
| Matsusaka | 113 |
| Matsuyama | 402 |
| Mino'o | 104 |
| Mitaka | 165 |
| Mito | 216 |
| Miyakonojō | 129 |
| Miyazaki | 265 |
| Moriguchi | 166 |
| Morioka | 229 |
| Muroran | 150 |
| Musashino | 137 |
| Nagano | 324 |
| Nagaoka | 180 |
| Nagareyama | 107 |
| Nagasaki | 447 |
| Nagoya | 2,088 |
| Naha | 296 |
| Nara | 298 |
| Narashino | 125 |
| Neyagawa | 256 |
| Niigata | 458 |
| Niihama | 132 |
| Niiza | 119 |
| Nishinomiya | 410 |
| Nobeoka | 137 |
| Numazu | 204 |
| Obihiro | 154 |
| Odawara | 177 |
| Ōgaki | 143 |
| Ōita | 360 |
| Okayama | 546 |
| Okazaki | 262 |
| Ōmiya | 354 |
| Ōmuta | 163 |
| Onomichi | 102 |
| Osaka | 2,648 |
| Ota | 123 |
| Otaru | 181 |
| Ōtsu | 215 |
| Oyama | 127 |
| Saga | 164 |
| Sagamihara | 439 |
| Sakai | 810 |
| Sakata | 103 |
| Sakura | 101 |
| Sapporo | 1,402 |
| Sasebo | 251 |
| Sayama | 124 |
| Sendai | 665 |
| Seto | 121 |
| Shimizu | 242 |
| Shimonoseki | 269 |
| Shizuoka | 458 |
| Sōka | 187 |
| Suita | 332 |
| Suzuka | 156 |
| Tachikawa | 143 |
| Takamatsu | 317 |
| Takaoka | 175 |
| Takarazuka | 184 |
| Takasaki | 221 |
| Takatsuki | 341 |
| Tokorozawa | 236 |
| Tokushima | 249 |
| Tokuyama | 111 |
| Tōkyō* | 8,352 |
| Tomakomai | 152 |
| Tottori | 131 |
| Toyama | 305 |
| Toyohashi | 304 |
| Toyokawa | 103 |
| Toyonaka | 403 |
| Toyota | 282 |
| Tsu | 145 |
| Tsuchiura | 113 |
| Ube | 169 |
| Ueda | 112 |
| Uji | 153 |
| Urawa | 358 |
| Utsunomiya | 378 |
| Wakayama | 401 |
| Yachiyo | 134 |
| Yaizu | 104 |
| Yamagata | 237 |
| Yamaguchi | 115 |
| Yamato | 168 |
| Yao | 273 |
| Yatsushiro | 108 |
| Yokkaichi | 255 |
| Yokohama | 2,774 |
| Yokosuka | 421 |
| Yonago | 127 |
| **Jordan** | |
| `Ammān* | 624 |
| Az Zarqā' | 216 |
| Irbid | 113 |
| **K** **Kazakhstan** | |
| Aktyubinsk | 253 |
| Alma-Ata* | 1,128 |
| Chimkent | 393 |
| Dzhambul | 307 |
| Dzhezkazgan | 109 |

| Country City | Population in thousands |
|---|---|
| Ekibastuz | 135 |
| Gur'yev | 149 |
| Karaganda | 614 |
| Kokchetav | 137 |
| Kustanay | 224 |
| Kzyl-Orda | 153 |
| Pavlodar | 331 |
| Petropavlovsk | 241 |
| Rudnyy | 110 |
| Semipalatinsk | 334 |
| Shevchenko | 159 |
| Taldy-Kurgan | 119 |
| Temirtau | 212 |
| Tselinograd | 277 |
| Ural'sk | 200 |
| Ust'-Kamenogorsk | 324 |
| **Kenya** | |
| Mombasa | 247 |
| Nairobi* | 509 |
| **Kiribati** | |
| Bairiki* | 2 |
| **Korea, North** | |
| Ch'ŏngjin | 306 |
| Haeju | 140 |
| Hamhŭng | 484 |
| Kaesŏng | 175 |
| Kimch'aek | 100 |
| Namp'o | 140 |
| P'yŏngyang* | 1,250 |
| Sinŭiju | 300 |
| Wŏnsan | 275 |
| **Korea, South** | |
| Andong | 102 |
| Anyang | 254 |
| Cheju | 168 |
| Chinhae | 112 |
| Chinju | 203 |
| Ch'ŏnan | 121 |
| Ch'ŏngju | 253 |
| Chŏnju | 367 |
| Ch'unch'ŏn | 155 |
| Ch'ungju | 113 |
| Inch'ŏn | 1,085 |
| Iri | 145 |
| Kangnŭng | 117 |
| Kimhae | 203 |
| Kimje | 221 |
| Kohŭng | 217 |
| Kunsan | 165 |
| Kwangju | 728 |
| Kyŏngju | 122 |
| Masan | 387 |
| Mokp'o | 222 |
| Nonsan | 226 |
| P'ohang | 201 |
| Puch'on | 221 |
| Pusan | 3,160 |
| Seoul* | 8,367 |
| Sunch'ŏn | 114 |
| Suwŏn | 311 |
| Taegu | 1,607 |
| Taejŏn | 652 |
| Ulsan | 418 |
| Wŏnju | 137 |
| Yanggu | 278 |
| Yŏsu | 161 |
| **Kuwait** | |
| Al Kuwait* | 182 |
| As Sālimīyah | 153 |
| Ḩawallī | 145 |
| Jalīb ash Shuyūkh | 115 |
| **Kyrgyzstan** | |
| Bishkek* | 616 |
| Osh | 213 |
| **L** **Laos** | |
| Vientiane* | 377 |
| **Latvia** | |
| Daugavpils | 127 |
| Liepāja | 114 |
| Riga* | 915 |
| **Lebanon** | |
| Beirut* | 475 |
| Tripoli | 128 |
| **Lesotho** | |
| Maseru* | 13 |
| **Liberia** | |
| Monrovia* | 167 |
| **Libya** | |
| Benghāzī | 287 |
| Mişrātah | 102 |
| Tripoli* | 550 |
| **Liechtenstein** | |
| Vaduz* | 5 |
| **Lithuania** | |
| Kaunas | 423 |
| Klaipėda | 204 |
| Panevėžys | 126 |
| Šiauliai | 145 |
| Vilnius* | 582 |
| **Luxembourg** | |
| Luxembourg* | 76 |
| **M** **Macedonia** | |
| Bitola | 138 |
| Gostivar | 101 |
| Kumanovo | 126 |
| Skopje* | 507 |
| Tetovo | 162 |
| **Madagascar** | |
| Antananarivo* | 452 |
| Fandriana | 105 |
| **Malawi** | |
| Blantyre | 332 |
| Lilongwe* | 234 |
| **Malaysia** | |
| Georgetown | 248 |
| Ipoh | 294 |

| Country City | Population in thousands |
|---|---|
| Johor Baharu | 246 |
| Kelang | 192 |
| Kota Baharu | 168 |
| Kuala Lumpur* | 920 |
| Kuala Terengganu | 180 |
| Kuantan | 132 |
| Seremban | 133 |
| Taiping | 146 |
| **Maldives** | |
| Male* | 46 |
| **Mali** | |
| Bamako* | 404 |
| **Malta** | |
| Valletta* | 14 |
| **Marshall Islands** | |
| Majuro* | 9 |
| **Mauritania** | |
| Nouakchott* | 135 |
| **Mauritius** | |
| Port Louis* | 134 |
| **Mexico** | |
| Acapulco de Juárez | 302 |
| Aguascalientes | 293 |
| Campeche | 128 |
| Celaya | 142 |
| Chihuahua | 386 |
| Ciudad Juárez | 544 |
| Ciudad Madero | 132 |
| Ciudad Obregón | 166 |
| Ciudad Victoria | 140 |
| Coatzacoalcos | 127 |
| Cuernavaca | 193 |
| Culiacán | 305 |
| Durango de Victoria | 258 |
| Ecatepec de Morelos | 742 |
| Ensenada | 120 |
| Gómez Palacio | 117 |
| Guadalajara | 1,626 |
| Guadalupe | 371 |
| Hermosillo | 297 |
| Irapuato | 170 |
| Jalapa Enríquez | 205 |
| León | 593 |
| Los Mochis | 123 |
| Matamoros | 189 |
| Mazatlán | 200 |
| Mérida | 400 |
| Mexicali | 342 |
| Mexico City* | 8,831 |
| Minatitlán | 107 |
| Monclova | 116 |
| Monterrey | 1,085 |
| Morelia | 298 |
| Naucalpan de Juárez | 724 |
| Netzahualcóyotl | 1,341 |
| Nuevo Laredo | 202 |
| Oaxaca de Juárez | 154 |
| Orizaba | 115 |
| Pachuca de Soto | 110 |
| Poza Rica | 167 |
| Puebla de Zaragoza | 773 |
| Querétaro | 216 |
| Reynosa | 195 |
| Saltillo | 285 |
| San Luis Potosí | 362 |
| San Nicolás de los Garza | 281 |
| Tampico | 268 |
| Tepic | 146 |
| Tijuana | 430 |
| Tlalnepantla de Galeana | 778 |
| Tlaquepaque | 134 |
| Toluca de Lerdo | 200 |
| Torreón | 328 |
| Tuxtla Gutiérrez | 131 |
| Uruapan del Progreso | 123 |
| Veracruz Llave | 285 |
| Villahermosa | 158 |
| Zapopan | 345 |
| **Micronesia**, Federated States of | |
| Kolonia* | 6 |
| **Moldova** | |
| Bel'tsy | 159 |
| Bendery | 130 |
| Kishinëv* | 665 |
| Tiraspol' | 182 |
| **Monaco** | |
| Monaco* | 30 |
| **Mongolia** | |
| Ulaanbaatar* | 515 |
| **Morocco** | |
| Casablanca | 1,506 |
| Fès | 325 |
| Kenitra | 139 |
| Marrakech | 333 |
| Meknès | 248 |
| Oujda | 176 |
| Rabat* | 368 |
| Safi | 129 |
| Salé | 156 |
| Tangier | 188 |
| Tétouan | 139 |
| **Mozambique** | |
| Maputo* | 883 |
| Nampula | 183 |
| **N** **Namibia** | |
| Windhoek* | 96 |
| **Nepal** | |
| Kāthmāndu* | 423 |
| **Netherlands** | |
| Amsterdam* | 695 |
| Apeldoorn | 147 |
| Arnhem | 129 |
| Breda | 121 |
| Dordrecht | 109 |
| Eindhoven | 191 |
| Enschede | 145 |
| Groningen | 168 |

| Country City | Population in thousands |
|---|---|
| Haarlem | 149 |
| Leiden | 109 |
| Maastricht | 116 |
| Nijmegen | 145 |
| Rotterdam | 576 |
| The Hague* | 444 |
| Tilburg | 155 |
| Utrecht | 240 |
| Zaandam | 130 |
| **New Zealand** | |
| Auckland | 149 |
| Christchurch | 168 |
| Manukau | 177 |
| Wellington* | 137 |
| **Nicaragua** | |
| Managua* | 608 |
| **Niger** | |
| Niamey* | 225 |
| **Nigeria** | |
| Aba | 177 |
| Abeokuta | 253 |
| Abuja* | 1 |
| Ado | 213 |
| Benin City | 136 |
| Calabar | 103 |
| Ede | 182 |
| Enugu | 187 |
| Ibadan | 847 |
| Ife | 176 |
| Ilesha | 224 |
| Ilorin | 282 |
| Iseyin | 115 |
| Iwo | 214 |
| Kaduna | 202 |
| Kano | 399 |
| Katsina | 109 |
| Lagos | 1,061 |
| Maiduguri | 189 |
| Ogbomosho | 432 |
| Onitsha | 220 |
| Oshogbo | 282 |
| Oyo | 152 |
| Port Harcourt | 242 |
| Zaria | 224 |
| **Norway** | |
| Bergen | 207 |
| Oslo* | 447 |
| Trondheim | 134 |
| **O** **Oman** | |
| Muscat* | 8 |
| **P** **Pakistan** | |
| Bahāwalpur | 180 |
| Chiniot | 106 |
| Dera Ghāzi Khān | 102 |
| Faisalabad | 1,104 |
| Gujrānwāla | 659 |
| Gujrāt | 155 |
| Hyderābād | 752 |
| Islāmābād* | 204 |
| Jhang Sadar | 196 |
| Jhelum | 106 |
| Karāchi | 5,076 |
| Kasūr | 156 |
| Lahore | 2,953 |
| Lārkāna | 124 |
| Mardān | 148 |
| Mīrpur Khās | 124 |
| Multān | 732 |
| Nawābshāh | 102 |
| Okāra | 127 |
| Peshāwar | 566 |
| Quetta | 286 |
| Rahīmyār Khān | 119 |
| Rāwalpindi | 795 |
| Sāhīwāl | 151 |
| Sargodha | 291 |
| Shekhūpura | 141 |
| Siālkot | 302 |
| Sukkur | 191 |
| Wāh | 127 |
| **Panama** | |
| Panamá* | 432 |
| **Papua New Guinea** | |
| Port Moresby* | 124 |
| **Paraguay** | |
| Asunción* | 388 |
| **Peru** | |
| Arequipa | 108 |
| Callao | 261 |
| Chiclayo | 280 |
| Chimbote | 216 |
| Comas | 287 |
| Huancayo | 165 |
| Ica | 111 |
| Iquitos | 174 |
| Lima* | 376 |
| Piura | 186 |
| Trujillo | 355 |
| **Philippines** | |
| Angeles | 189 |
| Bacolod City | 262 |
| Baguio | 119 |
| Batangas | 144 |
| Butuan | 173 |
| Butuan City | 172 |
| Cabanatuan City | 138 |
| Cadiz | 130 |
| Cagayan de Oro City | 227 |
| Calamba | 121 |
| Calbayog City | 107 |
| Caloocan City | 468 |
| Cebu City | 490 |
| Davao City | 610 |
| General Santos | 149 |
| Iligan | 167 |
| Iligan City | 167 |

| Country City | Population in thousands |
|---|---|
| Iloilo | 245 |
| Lipa City | 121 |
| Lucena | 108 |
| Makati | 373 |
| Malabon | 191 |
| Mandaue | 111 |
| Manila City* | 1,630 |
| Marikina | 212 |
| Olongapo | 156 |
| Ormoc City | 105 |
| Paranaque | 209 |
| Pasay City | 288 |
| Pasig | 269 |
| Quezon City | 1,166 |
| San Carlos | 101 |
| San Fernando | 111 |
| San Pablo City | 132 |
| Silay | 111 |
| Tacloban | 103 |
| Tarlac | 176 |
| Valenzuela | 212 |
| Zamboanga City | 344 |
| **Poland** | |
| Białystok | 268 |
| Bielsko-Biała | 181 |
| Bydgoszcz | 380 |
| Bytom | 230 |
| Chorzów | 132 |
| Częstochowa | 257 |
| Dąbrowa Górnicza | 135 |
| Elbląg | 126 |
| Gdańsk | 462 |
| Gdynia | 251 |
| Gliwice | 212 |
| Gorzów Wielkopolski | 123 |
| Grudziądz | 102 |
| Jastrzębie Zdroj | 102 |
| Kalisz | 106 |
| Katowice | 366 |
| Kielce | 213 |
| Koszalin | 108 |
| Kraków | 746 |
| Legnica | 104 |
| Łódź | 849 |
| Lublin | 349 |
| Olsztyn | 161 |
| Opole | 127 |
| Płock | 121 |
| Poznań | 587 |
| Radom | 226 |
| Ruda Śląska | 169 |
| Rybnik | 142 |
| Rzeszów | 151 |
| Słupsk | 100 |
| Sosnowiec | 259 |
| Szczecin | 411 |
| Tarnów | 121 |
| Toruń | 201 |
| Tychy | 190 |
| Wałbrzych | 142 |
| Warsaw* | 1,651 |
| Włocławek | 121 |
| Wodzisław Śląski | 111 |
| Wrocław | 641 |
| Zabrze | 203 |
| Zielona Góra | 113 |
| **Portugal** | |
| Lisbon* | 818 |
| Porto | 330 |
| **Q** **Qatar** | |
| Doha* | 217 |
| **R** **Romania** | |
| Arad | 188 |
| Bacău | 180 |
| Baia Mare | 140 |
| Botoşani | 109 |
| Brăila | 236 |
| Braşov | 351 |
| Bucharest* | 1,990 |
| Buzău | 136 |
| Cluj-Napoca | 310 |
| Constanţa | 328 |
| Craiova | 281 |
| Galaţi | 295 |
| Iaşi | 313 |
| Oradea | 214 |
| Piatra Neamt | 109 |
| Piteşti | 157 |
| Ploieşti | 235 |
| Reşiţa | 106 |
| Satu Mare | 130 |
| Sibiu | 178 |
| Timisoara | 325 |
| Tîrgu Mures | 159 |
| **Russia** | |
| Abakan | 154 |
| Achinsk | 122 |
| Al'met'yevsk | 129 |
| Angarsk | 266 |
| Anzhero-Sudzhensk | 108 |
| Archangel | 416 |
| Armavir | 161 |
| Arzamas | 109 |
| Astrakhan' | 509 |
| Balakovo | 198 |
| Balashikha | 136 |
| Barnaul | 602 |
| Belgorod | 300 |
| Belovo | 112 |
| Berezniki | 201 |
| Biysk | 233 |
| Blagoveshchensk | 206 |
| Bratsk | 255 |
| Bryansk | 452 |
| Cheboksary | 420 |
| Chelyabinsk | 1,143 |
| Cherepovets | 310 |

| Country City | Population in thousands |
|---|---|
| Cherkessk | |
| Chita | |
| Dimitrovgrad | |
| Dzerzhinsk | |
| Elektrostal' | |
| Engel's | |
| Glazov | |
| Groznyy | |
| Irkutsk | |
| Ivanovo | |
| Izhevsk | |
| Kaliningrad (Kalin.) | |
| Kaliningrad (Moscow) | |
| Kaluga | |
| Kamensk-Ural'skiy | |
| Kamyshin | |
| Kansk | |
| Kazan' | |
| Kemerovo | |
| Khabarovsk | |
| Khimki | |
| Kineshma | |
| Kiselevsk | |
| Kislovodsk | |
| Kolomna | |
| Kolpino | |
| Komsomol'sk-na-Amure | |
| Kopeysk | |
| Kostroma | |
| Kovrov | |
| Krasnodar | |
| Krasnoyarsk | |
| Kurgan | |
| Kursk | |
| Leninsk-Kuznetskiy | |
| Lipetsk | |
| Lyubertsy | |
| Magadan | |
| Magnitogorsk | |
| Makhachkala | |
| Maykop | |
| Mezhdurechensk | |
| Miass | |
| Michurinsk | |
| Moscow* | [illegible] |
| Murmansk | |
| Murom | |
| Mytishchi | |
| Naberezhnye Chelny | |
| Nakhodka | |
| Nal'chik | |
| Neftekamsk | |
| Nevinnomyssk | |
| Nizhnekamsk | |
| Nizhnevartovsk | |
| Nizhniy Novgorod | 1 |
| Nizhniy Tagil | |
| Noginsk | |
| Noril'sk | |
| Novgorod | |
| Novocheboksarsk | |
| Novocherkassk | |
| Novokuybyshevsk | |
| Novokuznetsk | |
| Novomoskovsk | |
| Novorossiysk | |
| Novoshakhtinsk | |
| Novosibirsk | 1 |
| Novotroitsk | |
| Obninsk | |
| Odintsovo | |
| Oktyabr'skiy | |
| Omsk | 1 |
| Orekhovo-Zuyevo | |
| Orël | |
| Orenburg | |
| Orsk | |
| Penza | |
| Perm' | 1, |
| Pervoural'sk | |
| Petropavlovsk-Kamchatskiy | |
| Petrozavodsk | |
| Podol'sk | |
| Prokop'yevsk | |
| Pskov | |
| Pyatigorsk | |
| Rostov | 1, |
| Rubtsovsk | |
| Ryazan' | |
| Rybinsk | |
| Saint Petersburg | 4, |
| Salavat | |
| Samara | 1, |
| Saransk | |
| Sarapul | |
| Saratov | |
| Sergiyev Posad | |
| Serov | |
| Serpukhov | |
| Severodvinsk | |
| Shakhty | |
| Shchelkovo | |
| Simbirsk | |
| Smolensk | |
| Sochi | |
| Solikamsk | |
| Staryy Oskol' | |
| Stavropol' | |
| Sterlitamak | |
| Surgut | |
| Syktyvkar | |
| Syzran' | |
| Taganrog | |
| Tambov | |
| Tol'yatti | |
| Tomsk | |
| Tula | |
| T'ver | |
| Tyumen' | |
| Ufa | 1, |

| Country City | Population in thousands |
|---|---|
| Ukhta | 111 |
| Ulan-Ude | 353 |
| Usol'ye-Sibirskoye | 107 |
| Ussuriysk | 162 |
| Ust'-Ilimsk | 109 |
| Velikiye Luki | 114 |
| Vladikavkaz | 300 |
| Vladimir | 350 |
| Vladivostok | 648 |
| Volgograd | 999 |
| Vologda | 283 |
| Volzhskiy | 269 |
| Vorkuta | 116 |
| Voronezh | 887 |
| Votkinsk | 103 |
| Vyatka | 441 |
| Yakutsk | 187 |
| Yaroslavl' | 633 |
| Yekaterinburg | 1,367 |
| Yelets | 120 |
| Yoshkar-Ola | 242 |
| Yuzhno-Sakhalinsk | 157 |
| Zelenograd | 158 |
| Zhukovskiy | 101 |
| Zlatoust | 208 |
| **Rwanda** | |
| Kigali* | 118 |

| Country City | Population in thousands |
|---|---|
| **Saint Kitts and Nevis** | |
| Basseterre* | 15 |
| **Saint Lucia** | |
| Castries* | 56 |
| **Saint Vincent and the Grenadines** | |
| Kingstown* | 17 |
| **San Marino** | |
| San Marino* | 4 |
| **Sao Tome and Principe** | |
| São Tomé* | 8 |
| **Saudi Arabia** | |
| Ad Dammām | 128 |
| Al Hufūf | 101 |
| Aţ Ţā'if | 205 |
| Jiddah | 561 |
| Mecca | 367 |
| Medina | 198 |
| Riyadh* | 667 |
| **Senegal** | |
| Dakar* | 799 |
| Kaolack | 107 |
| Thiès | 117 |
| **Seychelles** | |
| Victoria* | 16 |
| **Sierra Leone** | |
| Freetown* | 274 |
| **Singapore** | |
| Singapore* | 2,756 |
| **Slovak Republic** | |
| Bratislava* | 380 |
| Košice | 202 |
| **Slovenia** | |
| Ljubljana* | 305 |
| Maribor | 186 |
| **Solomon Islands** | |
| Honiara* | 30 |
| **Somalia** | |
| Mogadishu* | 371 |
| **South Africa** | |
| Bloemfontein | 104 |
| Boksburg | 111 |
| Cape Town* | 777 |
| Durban | 634 |
| East London | 120 |
| Germiston | 117 |
| Johannesburg | 632 |
| Kimberley | 105 |
| Pietermaritzburg | 115 |
| Port Elizabeth | 273 |
| Pretoria* | 443 |
| Roodepoort-Maraisburg | 142 |
| Soweto | 522 |
| Springs | 143 |
| Tembisa | 149 |
| Wes-Rand | 647 |
| **Spain** | |
| Albacete | 116 |
| Alcalá de Henares | 137 |
| Alcorcón | 141 |
| Alicante | 246 |
| Almería | 141 |
| Badajoz | 111 |
| Badalona | 230 |
| Baracaldo | 119 |
| Barcelona | 1,753 |
| Bilbao | 433 |
| Burgos | 153 |
| Cádiz | 157 |
| Cartagena | 168 |
| Castellón de la Plana | 124 |
| Córdoba | 279 |
| Elche | 165 |
| Getafe | 127 |
| Gijón | 256 |
| Granada | 247 |
| Huelva | 128 |
| Jerez de la Frontera | 176 |
| La Coruña | 232 |
| La Laguna | 106 |
| Las Palmas de Gran Canaria | 360 |
| Leganés | 164 |
| León | 127 |
| L'Hospitalet de Llobregat | 295 |
| Lleida | 107 |
| Logroño | 110 |
| Madrid* | 3,159 |
| Málaga | 502 |
| Móstoles | 150 |
| Murcia | 285 |

| Country City | Population in thousands |
|---|---|
| Oviedo | 184 |
| Palma | 290 |
| Pamplona | 178 |
| Sabadell | 186 |
| Salamanca | 154 |
| San Sebastián | 172 |
| Santa Cruz de Tenerife | 186 |
| Santander | 180 |
| Saragossa | 572 |
| Seville | 646 |
| Tarragona | 109 |
| Terrassa | 156 |
| Valencia | 745 |
| Valladolid | 320 |
| Vigo | 261 |
| Vitoria | 190 |
| **Sri Lanka** | |
| Colombo* | 609 |
| Dehiwala-Mount Lavinia | 190 |
| Galle | 109 |
| Jaffna | 127 |
| Kandy | 102 |
| Kotte | 107 |
| Moratuwa | 165 |
| **Sudan** | |
| Khartoum* | 334 |
| Khartoum North | 151 |
| Omdurman | 299 |
| Port Sudan | 133 |
| Wad Medanī | 107 |
| **Suriname** | |
| Paramaribo* | 68 |
| **Swaziland** | |
| Mbabane* | 38 |
| **Sweden** | |
| Borås | 101 |
| Göteborg | 431 |
| Hälsingborg | 107 |
| Jönköping | 110 |
| Linköping | 119 |
| Malmö | 232 |
| Norrköping | 119 |
| Örebro | 120 |
| Stockholm* | 669 |
| Uppsala | 162 |
| Västerås | 118 |
| **Switzerland** | |
| Basel | 182 |
| Bern* | 145 |
| Geneva | 157 |
| Lausanne | 127 |
| Zürich | 370 |
| **Syria** | |
| Aleppo | 977 |
| Damascus* | 1,251 |
| Ḩamāh | 177 |
| Ḩimş | 355 |
| Latakia | 197 |

## T

| Country City | Population in thousands |
|---|---|
| **Taiwan** | |
| Changhua | 186 |
| Chiayi | 252 |
| Kaohsiung | 1,227 |
| Keelung | 348 |
| Pingtung | 189 |
| Taichung | 565 |
| Tainan | 541 |
| Taipei* | 2,108 |
| Taoyuan | 106 |
| **Tajikistan** | |
| Dushanbe* | 595 |
| Khudzhand | 160 |
| **Tanzania** | |
| Dar es Salaam* | 757 |
| Mwanza | 111 |
| Tanga | 103 |
| Zanzibar | 111 |
| **Thailand** | |
| Bangkok* | 4,697 |
| Chiang Mai | 102 |
| Chon Buri | 116 |
| Nakhon Si Thammarat | 102 |
| Songkhla | 173 |
| Thon Buri | 628 |
| **Togo** | |
| Lomé* | 370 |
| **Tonga** | |
| Nuku'alofa* | 18 |
| **Trinidad and Tobago** | |
| Port-of-Spain* | 60 |
| **Tunisia** | |
| Şafāqis | 232 |
| Tūnis* | 597 |
| **Turkey** | |
| Adana | 778 |
| Adapazarı | 152 |
| Ankara* | 2,235 |
| Antalya | 261 |
| Antioch | 108 |
| Balıkesir | 150 |
| Batman | 110 |
| Bursa | 613 |
| Denizli | 169 |
| Diyarbakır | 306 |
| Elazığ | 182 |
| Erzurum | 246 |
| Eskişehir | 367 |
| Gaziantep | 479 |
| İskenderun | 152 |
| İsparta | 101 |
| İstanbul | 5,476 |
| İzmir | 1,490 |
| İzmit | 233 |
| Kağıthane | 164 |
| Kahramanmaraş | 210 |
| Kayseri | 374 |
| Kırıkkale | 208 |
| Konya | 439 |
| Kütahya | 119 |

| Country City | Population in thousands |
|---|---|
| Malatya | 243 |
| Manisa | 127 |
| Mersin | 314 |
| Osmaniye | 104 |
| Samsun | 241 |
| Sivas | 199 |
| Tarsus | 147 |
| Trabzon | 142 |
| Urfa | 195 |
| Van | 111 |
| Zonguldak | 118 |
| **Turkmenistan** | |
| Ashkhabad* | 398 |
| Chardzhou | 161 |
| Tashauz | 112 |
| **Tuvalu** | |
| Fongafale* | 1,500 |

## U

| Country City | Population in thousands |
|---|---|
| **Uganda** | |
| Kampala* | 479 |
| **Ukraine** | |
| Aleksandriya | 103 |
| Belaya Tserkov' | 197 |
| Berdyansk | 132 |
| Cherkassy | 290 |
| Chernigov | 296 |
| Chernovtsy | 257 |
| Dneprodzerzhinsk | 282 |
| Dnepropetrovsk | 1,179 |
| Donetsk | 1,110 |
| Gorlovka | 337 |
| Ivano-Frankovsk | 214 |
| Kamenets-Podol'skiy | 102 |
| Kerch' | 174 |
| Khar'kov | 1,611 |
| Kherson | 355 |
| Khmel'nitskiy | 237 |
| Kirovograd | 269 |
| Kiev* | 2,587 |
| Kommunarsk | 126 |
| Konstantinovka | 108 |
| Kramatorsk | 198 |
| Krasnyy Luch | 113 |
| Kremenchug | 236 |
| Krivoy Rog | 713 |
| Lisichansk | 127 |
| Lugansk | 497 |
| Lutsk | 198 |
| L'viv | 790 |
| Makeyevka | 430 |
| Mariupol' | 517 |
| Melitopol' | 174 |
| Nikolayev | 503 |
| Nikopol' | 158 |
| Odessa | 1,115 |
| Pavlograd | 131 |
| Poltava | 315 |
| Rovno | 228 |
| Sevastopol' | 356 |
| Severodonetsk | 131 |
| Simferopol' | 344 |
| Slavyansk | 135 |
| Stakhanov | 112 |
| Sumy | 291 |
| Ternopol' | 205 |
| Uzhgorod | 117 |
| Vinnitsa | 374 |
| Yenakiyevo | 121 |
| Yevpatoriya | 108 |
| Zaporozh'ye | 884 |
| Zhitomir | 292 |
| **United Arab Emirates** | |
| Abu Dhabi* | 243 |
| Ash Shāriqah | 125 |
| Dubayy | 266 |
| **United Kingdom** | |
| Aberdeen | 190 |
| Belfast | 295 |
| Birkenhead | 156 |
| Birmingham | 1,014 |
| Blackburn | 110 |
| Blackpool | 146 |
| Bolton | 144 |
| Bournemouth | 143 |
| Bradford | 293 |
| Brighton | 135 |
| Bristol | 414 |
| Cardiff | 262 |
| Coventry | 319 |
| Derby | 218 |
| Dudley | 187 |
| Dundee | 174 |
| Edinburgh | 420 |
| Glasgow | 765 |
| Gloucester | 107 |
| Hillingdon | 227 |
| Huddersfield | 148 |
| Hull | 322 |
| Ipswich | 130 |
| Kingston upon Thames | 131 |
| Leeds | 452 |
| Leicester | 324 |
| Liverpool | 539 |
| London* | 7,567 |
| Luton | 163 |
| Manchester | 449 |
| Middlesbrough | 159 |
| Newcastle upon Tyne | 199 |
| Newport | 116 |
| Northampton | 154 |
| Norwich | 170 |
| Nottingham | 273 |
| Oldham | 107 |
| Oxford | 114 |
| Peterborough | 113 |
| Plymouth | 239 |
| Poole | 123 |
| Portsmouth | 174 |
| Preston | 167 |
| Reading | 195 |

| Country City | Population in thousands |
|---|---|
| Rotherham | 122 |
| Saint Helens | 114 |
| Sheffield | 471 |
| Slough | 106 |
| Southampton | 211 |
| Southend-on-Sea | 156 |
| Stockport | 135 |
| Stoke-on-Trent | 272 |
| Sunderland | 195 |
| Sutton Coldfield | 103 |
| Swansea | 172 |
| Swindon | 127 |
| Walsall | 178 |
| Warley | 152 |
| Warrington | 129 |
| Watford | 110 |
| West Bromwich | 154 |
| Wolverhampton | 264 |
| York | 123 |
| **United States** | |
| Abilene | 107 |
| Akron | 223 |
| Albany | 101 |
| Albuquerque | 385 |
| Alexandria | 111 |
| Allentown | 105 |
| Amarillo | 158 |
| Amherst | 112 |
| Anaheim | 266 |
| Anchorage | 226 |
| Ann Arbor | 110 |
| Arlington (Tex.) | 262 |
| Arlington (Va.) | 171 |
| Atlanta | 394 |
| Aurora | 222 |
| Austin | 466 |
| Bakersfield | 175 |
| Baltimore | 736 |
| Baton Rouge | 220 |
| Beaumont | 114 |
| Berkeley | 103 |
| Birmingham | 266 |
| Boise | 126 |
| Boston | 574 |
| Bridgeport | 142 |
| Buffalo | 328 |
| Cedar Rapids | 109 |
| Charlotte | 396 |
| Chattanooga | 152 |
| Chesapeake | 152 |
| Chicago | 2,784 |
| Chula Vista | 135 |
| Cincinnati | 364 |
| Citrus Heights | 107 |
| Cleveland | 506 |
| Colorado Springs | 281 |
| Columbus (Ga.) | 179 |
| Columbus (Ohio) | 633 |
| Concord | 111 |
| Corpus Christi | 257 |
| Dallas | 1,007 |
| Dayton | 182 |
| Denver | 468 |
| Des Moines | 193 |
| Detroit | 1,028 |
| Durham | 137 |
| East Los Angeles | 126 |
| Elizabeth | 110 |
| El Monte | 106 |
| El Paso | 515 |
| Erie | 109 |
| Escondido | 109 |
| Eugene | 113 |
| Evansville | 126 |
| Flint | 141 |
| Fort Lauderdale | 149 |
| Fort Wayne | 173 |
| Fort Worth | 448 |
| Fremont | 173 |
| Fresno | 354 |
| Fullerton | 114 |
| Garden Grove | 143 |
| Garland | 181 |
| Gary | 117 |
| Glendale (Ariz.) | 148 |
| Glendale (Calif.) | 180 |
| Grand Rapids | 189 |
| Greensboro | 184 |
| Hampton | 134 |
| Hartford | 140 |
| Hayward | 111 |
| Hialeah | 188 |
| Hollywood | 122 |
| Honolulu | 365 |
| Houston | 1,631 |
| Huntington Beach | 182 |
| Huntsville | 160 |
| Independence | 112 |
| Indianapolis | 742 |
| Inglewood | 110 |
| Irvine | 110 |
| Irving | 155 |
| Jackson | 197 |
| Jacksonville | 635 |
| Jersey City | 229 |
| Kansas City (Kans.) | 150 |
| Kansas City (Mo.) | 435 |
| Knoxville | 165 |
| Lakewood | 126 |
| Lansing | 127 |
| Laredo | 123 |
| Las Vegas | 258 |
| Lexington | 225 |
| Lincoln | 192 |
| Little Rock | 176 |
| Livonia | 101 |
| Long Beach | 429 |
| Los Angeles | 3,485 |
| Louisville | 269 |
| Lowell | 103 |
| Lubbock | 186 |

| Country City | Population in thousands |
|---|---|
| Macon | 107 |
| Madison | 191 |
| Memphis | 610 |
| Mesa | 288 |
| Mesquite | 101 |
| Metairie | 149 |
| Miami | 359 |
| Milwaukee | 628 |
| Minneapolis | 368 |
| Mobile | 196 |
| Modesto | 165 |
| Montgomery | 187 |
| Moreno Valley | 119 |
| Nashville | 488 |
| Newark | 275 |
| New Haven | 130 |
| New Orleans | 497 |
| Newport News | 170 |
| New York | 7,323 |
| Norfolk | 261 |
| Oakland | 372 |
| Oceanside | 128 |
| Oklahoma City | 445 |
| Omaha | 336 |
| Ontario | 133 |
| Orange | 111 |
| Orlando | 165 |
| Overland Park | 112 |
| Oxnard | 142 |
| Paradise | 125 |
| Pasadena (Calif.) | 132 |
| Pasadena (Tex.) | 119 |
| Paterson | 141 |
| Peoria | 114 |
| Philadelphia | 1,586 |
| Phoenix | 983 |
| Pittsburgh | 370 |
| Plano | 129 |
| Pomona | 132 |
| Portland | 437 |
| Portsmouth | 104 |
| Providence | 161 |
| Raleigh | 208 |
| Rancho Cucamonga | 101 |
| Reno | 134 |
| Richmond | 203 |
| Riverside | 227 |
| Rochester | 232 |
| Rockford | 139 |
| Sacramento | 369 |
| Saint Louis | 397 |
| Saint Paul | 272 |
| Saint Petersburg | 239 |
| Salem | 108 |
| Salinas | 109 |
| Salt Lake City | 160 |
| San Antonio | 936 |
| San Bernardino | 164 |
| San Diego | 1,111 |
| San Francisco | 724 |
| San Jose | 782 |
| Santa Ana | 294 |
| Santa Clarita | 111 |
| Santa Rosa | 113 |
| Savannah | 138 |
| Scottsdale | 130 |
| Seattle | 516 |
| Shreveport | 199 |
| Simi Valley | 100 |
| Sioux Falls | 101 |
| South Bend | 106 |
| Spokane | 177 |
| Springfield (Ill.) | 105 |
| Springfield (Mo.) | 140 |
| Springfield (Mass.) | 157 |
| Stamford | 108 |
| Sterling Heights | 118 |
| Stockton | 211 |
| Sunnyvale | 117 |
| Syracuse | 164 |
| Tacoma | 177 |
| Tallahassee | 125 |
| Tampa | 280 |
| Tempe | 142 |
| Thousand Oaks | 104 |
| Toledo | 333 |
| Topeka | 120 |
| Torrance | 133 |
| Tucson | 405 |
| Tulsa | 367 |
| Vallejo | 109 |
| Virginia Beach | 393 |
| Waco | 104 |
| Warren | 145 |
| Washington* | 607 |
| Waterbury | 109 |
| Wichita | 304 |
| Winston-Salem | 143 |
| Worcester | 170 |
| Yonkers | 188 |
| **Uruguay** | |
| Montevideo* | 1,173 |
| **Uzbekistan** | |
| Almalyk | 114 |
| Andizhan | 293 |
| Angren | 131 |
| Bukhara | 224 |
| Chirchik | 156 |
| Dzhizak | 102 |
| Fergana | 200 |
| Karshi | 156 |
| Kokand | 182 |
| Margilan | 125 |
| Namangan | 308 |
| Navoi | 107 |
| Nukus | 169 |
| Samarkand | 366 |
| Tashkent* | 2,073 |
| Urgench | 128 |

## V

| Country City | Population in thousands |
|---|---|
| **Vanuatu** | |
| Vila* | 5 |
| **Vatican City** | |
| Vatican City* | 1 |
| **Venezuela** | |
| Barinas | 158 |
| Barquisimeto | 661 |
| Cabimas | 162 |
| Caracas* | 1,247 |
| Ciudad Bolívar | 241 |
| Ciudad Guayan | 459 |
| Cumaná | 218 |
| Guarenas | 104 |
| Los Teques | 149 |
| Maracaibo | 1,124 |
| Maracay | 497 |
| Maturín | 205 |
| Mérida | 188 |
| Petare | 396 |
| San Cristóbal | 235 |
| San Francisco | 198 |
| Valencia | 856 |
| Valera | 132 |
| **Vietnam** | |
| Biên Hòa | 187 |
| Cam Ranh | 118 |
| Can Tho | 183 |
| Đà Lat | 105 |
| Đà Nang | 319 |
| Haiphong | 1,279 |
| Hanoi* | 2,571 |
| Ho Chí Minh City | 3,420 |
| Hong Gai | 115 |
| Hue | 166 |
| Long Xuyên | 112 |
| My Tho | 101 |
| Nam yDinh | 160 |
| Nha Trang | 173 |
| Qui Nhon | 127 |
| Thái Nguyên | 110 |
| Vinh | 160 |
| Vũng Tàu | 108 |

## W

| Country City | Population in thousands |
|---|---|
| **Western Samoa** | |
| Apia* | 32 |

## Y

| Country City | Population in thousands |
|---|---|
| **Yemen** | |
| Aden | 240 |
| Sanaa* | 135 |
| **Yugoslavia** | |
| Belgrade* | 1,470 |
| Čačak | 111 |
| Kragujevac | 165 |
| Kraljevo | 122 |
| Kruševac | 133 |
| Leskovac | 159 |
| Niš | 231 |
| Novi Sad | 258 |
| Pančevo | 124 |
| Peć | 111 |
| Priština | 210 |
| Prizren | 135 |
| Šabac | 120 |
| Smederevo | 107 |
| Subotica | 155 |
| Titograd | 132 |
| Uroševac | 114 |
| Zrenjanin | 139 |

## Z

| Country City | Population in thousands |
|---|---|
| **Zaire** | |
| Bukavu | 135 |
| Kananga | 429 |
| Kikwit | 112 |
| Kinshasa* | 1,323 |
| Kisangani | 230 |
| Lubumbashi | 318 |
| Matadi | 110 |
| Mbandaka | 108 |
| Mbuji-Mayi | 256 |
| **Zambia** | |
| Chingola | 146 |
| Kabwe | 144 |
| Kitwe | 315 |
| Luanshya | 132 |
| Lusaka* | 538 |
| Mufulira | 150 |
| Ndola | 282 |
| **Zimbabwe** | |
| Bulawayo | 414 |
| Harare* | 656 |

**Dependency**

| Country City | Population in thousands |
|---|---|
| **Hong Kong (U.K.)** | |
| Kowloon | 2,450 |
| Victoria* | 1,183 |
| **Puerto Rico (U.S.)** | |
| Bayamón | 202 |
| Carolina | 162 |
| Ponce | 159 |
| San Juan* | 426 |
| **Macau (Port.)** | |
| Macau* | 238 |

# Index of the World

This index is a comprehensive listing of the places and geographic features found in the atlas. Names are arranged in strict alphabetical order, without regard to hyphens or spaces. Every name is followed by the country or area to which it belongs. Except for cities, towns, countries and cultural areas, all entries include a reference to feature type, such as province, river, island, peak, and so on. The page number and alpha-numeric code appear in red to the left of each listing. The page number directs you to the largest scale map on which the name can be found. The code refers to the grid squares formed by the horizontal and vertical lines of latitude and longitude on each map. Following the letters from left to right and the numbers from top to bottom helps you to locate quickly the square containing the place or feature. Inset maps have their own alpha-numeric codes. Names that are accompanied by a point symbol are indexed to the symbol's location on the map. Other names are indexed to the initial letter of the name. When a map name contains a subordinate or alternate name, both names are listed in the index. To conserve space and provide room for more entries, many abbreviations are used in this index. The primary abbreviations are listed below.

**Index Abbereviations**

| | | |
|---|---|---|
| A | **Ab,Can** | Alberta |
| | **Acad.** | Academy |
| | **ACT** | Australian Capital Territory |
| | **A.F.B.** | Air Force Base |
| | **Afld.** | Airfield |
| | **Afg.** | Afghanistan |
| | **Afr.** | Africa |
| | **Ak,US** | Alaska |
| | **Al,US** | Alabama |
| | **Alb.** | Albania |
| | **Alg.** | Algeria |
| | **Amm. Dep.** | Ammunition Depot |
| | **And.** | Andorra |
| | **Ang.** | Angola |
| | **Angu.** | Anguilla |
| | **Ant.** | Antarctica |
| | **Anti.** | Antigua and Barbuda |
| | **Ar,US** | Arkansas |
| | **Arch.** | Archipelago |
| | **Arg.** | Argentina |
| | **Arm.** | Armenia |
| | **Arpt.** | Airport |
| | **Aru.** | Aruba |
| | **ASam.** | American Samoa |
| | **Ash.** | Ashmore and Cartier Islands |
| | **Aus.** | Austria |
| | **Austl.** | Australia |
| | **Aut.** | Autonomous |
| | **Az,US** | Arizona |
| | **Azer.** | Azerbaijan |
| | **Azor.** | Azores |
| B | **Bahm.** | Bahamas |
| | **Bahr.** | Bahrain |
| | **Bang.** | Bangladesh |
| | **Bar.** | Barbados |
| | **BC,Can** | British Columbia |
| | **Bela.** | Belarus |
| | **Belg.** | Belgium |
| | **Belz.** | Belize |
| | **Ben.** | Benin |
| | **Berm.** | Bermuda |
| | **Bfld.** | Battlefield |
| | **Bhu.** | Bhutan |
| | **Bol.** | Bolivia |
| | **Bor.** | Borough |
| | **Bosn.** | Bosnia and Hercegovina |
| | **Bots.** | Botswana |
| | **Braz.** | Brazil |
| | **Brln.** | British Indian Ocean Territory |
| | **Bru.** | Brunei |
| | **Bul.** | Bulgaria |
| | **Burk.** | Burkina |
| | **Buru.** | Burundi |
| | **BVI** | British Virgin Islands |
| C | **Ca,US** | California |
| | **CAfr.** | Central African Republic |
| | **Camb.** | Cambodia |
| | **Camr.** | Cameroon |
| | **Can.** | Canada |
| | **Can.** | Canal |
| | **Canl.** | Canary Islands |
| | **Cap.** | Capital |
| | **Cap. Dist.** | Capital District |
| | **Cap. Terr.** | Capital Territory |
| | **Cay.** | Cayman Islands |
| | **C.G.** | Coast Guard |
| | **Chan.** | Channel |
| | **Chl.** | Channel Islands |
| | **Co.** | County |
| | **Co,US** | Colorado |
| | **Col.** | Colombia |
| | **Com.** | Comoros |
| | **Cont.** | Continent |
| | **CpV.** | Cape Verde Islands |
| | **CR** | Costa Rica |
| | **Cr.** | Creek |
| | **Cro.** | Croatia |
| | **CSea.** | Coral Sea Islands Territory |
| | **Ct,US** | Connecticut |
| | **Ctr.** | Center |
| | **Ctry.** | Country |
| | **Cyp.** | Cyprus |
| | **Czh.** | Czech Republic |
| D | **DC,US** | District of Columbia |
| | **De,US** | Delaware |
| | **Den.** | Denmark |
| | **Depr.** | Depression |
| | **Dept.** | Department |
| | **Des.** | Desert |
| | **DF** | Distrito Federal |
| | **Dist.** | District |
| | **Djib.** | Djibouti |
| | **Dom.** | Dominica |
| | **Dpcy.** | Dependency |
| | **DRep.** | Dominican Republic |
| E | **Ecu.** | Ecuador |
| | **Emb.** | Embankment |
| | **Eng.** | Engineering |
| | **Eng,UK** | England |
| | **EqG.** | Equatorial Guinea |
| | **ESal.** | El Salvador |
| | **Est.** | Estonia |
| | **Eth.** | Ethiopia |
| | **Eur.** | Europe |
| F | **Falk.** | Falkland Islands |
| | **Far.** | Faroe Islands |
| | **Fed. Dist.** | Federal District |
| | **Fin.** | Finland |
| | **Fl,US** | Florida |
| | **For.** | Forest |
| | **Fr.** | France |
| | **FrAnt.** | French Southern and Antarctic Lands |
| | **FrG.** | French Guiana |
| | **FrPol.** | French Polynesia |
| G | **Ga,US** | Georgia |
| | **Galp.** | Galapagos Islands |
| | **Gam.** | Gambia |
| | **Gaza** | Gaza Strip |
| | **GBis.** | Guinea-Bissau |
| | **Geo.** | Georgia |
| | **Ger.** | Germany |
| | **Gha.** | Ghana |
| | **Gib.** | Gibraltar |
| | **Glac.** | Glacier |
| | **Gov.** | Governorate |
| | **Govt.** | Government |
| | **Gre.** | Greece |
| | **Grld.** | Greenland |
| | **Gren.** | Grenada |
| | **Grsld.** | Grassland |
| | **Guad.** | Guadeloupe |
| | **Guat.** | Guatemala |
| | **Gui.** | Guinea |
| | **Guy.** | Guyana |
| H | **Har.** | Harbor |
| | **Hi,US** | Hawaii |
| | **Hist.** | Historic(al) |
| | **HK** | Hong Kong |
| | **Hon.** | Honduras |
| | **Hts.** | Heights |
| | **Hun.** | Hungary |
| I | **Ia,US** | Iowa |
| | **Ice.** | Iceland |
| | **Id,US** | Idaho |
| | **Il,US** | Illinois |
| | **IM** | Isle of Man |
| | **In,US** | Indiana |
| | **Ind. Res.** | Indian Reservation |
| | **Indo.** | Indonesia |
| | **Int'l** | International |
| | **Ire.** | Ireland |
| | **Isl., Isls.** | Island, Islands |
| | **Isr.** | Israel |
| | **Isth.** | Isthmus |
| | **It.** | Italy |
| | **IvC.** | Ivory Coast |
| J | **Jam.** | Jamaica |
| | **Jor.** | Jordan |
| K | **Kaz.** | Kazakhstan |
| | **Kiri.** | Kiribati |
| | **Ks,US** | Kansas |
| | **Kuw.** | Kuwait |
| | **Ky,US** | Kentucky |
| | **Kyr.** | Kyrgyzstan |
| L | **La,US** | Louisiana |
| | **Lab.** | Laboratory |
| | **Lag.** | Lagoon |
| | **Lakesh.** | Lakeshore |
| | **Lat.** | Latvia |
| | **Lcht.** | Liechtenstein |
| | **Ldg.** | Landing |
| | **Leb.** | Lebanon |
| | **Les.** | Lesotho |
| | **Libr.** | Liberia |
| | **Lith.** | Lithuania |
| | **Lux.** | Luxembourg |
| M | **Ma,US** | Massachusetts |
| | **Macd.** | Macedonia |
| | **Madg.** | Madagascar |
| | **Madr.** | Madeira |
| | **Malay.** | Malaysia |
| | **Mald.** | Maldives |
| | **Malw.** | Malawi |
| | **Mart.** | Martinique |
| | **May.** | Mayotte |
| | **Mb,Can** | Manitoba |
| | **Md,US** | Maryland |
| | **Me,US** | Maine |
| | **Mem.** | Memorial |
| | **Mex.** | Mexico |
| | **Mi,US** | Michigan |
| | **Micr.** | Micronesia, Federated States of |
| | **Mil.** | Military |
| | **Mn,US** | Minnesota |
| | **Mo,US** | Missouri |
| | **Mol.** | Moldova |
| | **Mon.** | Monument |
| | **Mona.** | Monaco |
| | **Mong.** | Mongolia |
| | **Monts.** | Montserrat |
| | **Mor.** | Morocco |
| | **Moz.** | Mozambique |
| | **Mrsh.** | Marshall Islands |
| | **Mrta.** | Mauritania |
| | **Mrts.** | Mauritius |
| | **Ms,US** | Mississippi |
| | **Mt.** | Mount |
| | **Mt,US** | Montana |
| | **Mtn., Mts.** | Mountain, Mountains |
| | **Mun. Arpt.** | Municipal Airport |
| N | **NAm.** | North America |
| | **Namb.** | Namibia |
| | **NAnt.** | Netherlands Antilles |
| | **Nat'l** | National |
| | **Nav.** | Naval |
| | **NB,Can** | New Brunswick |
| | **Nbrhd.** | Neighborhood |
| | **NC,US** | North Carolina |
| | **NCal.** | New Caledonia |
| | **ND,US** | North Dakota |
| | **Ne,US** | Nebraska |
| | **Neth.** | Netherlands |
| | **Nf,Can** | Newfoundland |
| | **Nga.** | Nigeria |
| | **NH,US** | New Hampshire |
| | **NI,UK** | Northern Ireland |
| | **Nic.** | Nicaragua |
| | **NJ,US** | New Jersey |
| | **NKor.** | North Korea |
| | **NM,US** | New Mexico |
| | **NMar.** | Northern Mariana Islands |
| | **Nor.** | Norway |
| | **NS,Can** | Nova Scotia |
| | **Nv,US** | Nevada |
| | **NW,Can** | Northwest Territories |
| | **NY,US** | New York |
| | **NZ** | New Zealand |
| O | **Obl.** | Oblast |
| | **Oh,US** | Ohio |
| | **Ok,US** | Oklahoma |
| | **On,Can** | Ontario |
| | **Or,US** | Oregon |
| P | **Pa,US** | Pennsylvania |
| | **PacUS** | Pacific Islands, U.S. |
| | **Pak.** | Pakistan |
| | **Pan.** | Panama |
| | **Par.** | Paraguay |
| | **Par.** | Parish |
| | **PE,Can** | Prince Edward Island |
| | **Pen.** | Peninsula |
| | **Phil.** | Philippines |
| | **Phys. Reg.** | Physical Region |
| | **Pitc.** | Pitcairn Islands |
| | **Plat.** | Plateau |
| | **PNG** | Papua New Guinea |
| | **Pol.** | Poland |
| | **Port.** | Portugal |
| | **Poss.** | Possession |
| | **Pkwy.** | Parkway |
| | **PR** | Puerto Rico |
| | **Pref.** | Prefecture |
| | **Prov.** | Province |
| | **Prsv.** | Preserve |
| | **Pt.** | Point |
| Q | **Qu,Can** | Quebec |
| R | **Rec.** | Recreation(al) |
| | **Ref.** | Refuge |
| | **Reg.** | Region |
| | **Rep.** | Republic |
| | **Res.** | Reservoir, Reservation |
| | **Reun.** | Réunion |
| | **RI,US** | Rhode Island |
| | **Riv.** | River |
| | **Rom.** | Romania |
| | **Rsv.** | Reserve |
| | **Rus.** | Russia |
| | **Rvwy.** | Riverway |
| | **Rwa.** | Rwanda |
| S | **SAfr.** | South Africa |
| | **SAm.** | South America |
| | **SaoT.** | São Tomé and Príncipe |
| | **SAr.** | Saudi Arabia |
| | **Sc,UK** | Scotland |
| | **SC,US** | South Carolina |
| | **SD,US** | South Dakota |
| | **Seash.** | Seashore |
| | **Sen.** | Senegal |
| | **Sey.** | Seychelles |
| | **SGeo.** | South Georgia and Sandwich Islands |
| | **Sing.** | Singapore |
| | **Sk,Can** | Saskatchewan |
| | **SKor.** | South Korea |
| | **SLeo.** | Sierra Leone |
| | **Slov.** | Slovenia |
| | **Slvk.** | Slovakia |
| | **SMar.** | San Marino |
| | **Sol.** | Solomon Islands |
| | **Som.** | Somalia |
| | **Sp.** | Spain |
| | **Spr., Sprs.** | Spring, Springs |
| | **SrL.** | Sri Lanka |
| | **Sta.** | Station |
| | **StH.** | Saint Helena |
| | **Str.** | Strait |
| | **StK.** | Saint Kitts and Nevis |
| | **StL.** | Saint Lucia |
| | **StP.** | Saint Pierre and Miquelon |
| | **StV.** | Saint Vincent and the Grenadines |
| | **Sur.** | Suriname |
| | **Sval.** | Svalbard |
| | **Swaz.** | Swaziland |
| | **Swe.** | Sweden |
| | **Swi.** | Switzerland |
| T | **Tah.** | Tahiti |
| | **Tai.** | Taiwan |
| | **Taj.** | Tajikistan |
| | **Tanz.** | Tanzania |
| | **Ter.** | Terrace |
| | **Terr.** | Territory |
| | **Thai.** | Thailand |
| | **Tn,US** | Tennessee |
| | **Tok.** | Tokelau |
| | **Trg.** | Training |
| | **Trin.** | Trinidad and Tobago |
| | **Trkm.** | Turkmenistan |
| | **Trks.** | Turks and Caicos Islands |
| | **Tun.** | Tunisia |
| | **Tun.** | Tunnel |
| | **Turk.** | Turkey |
| | **Tuv.** | Tuvalu |
| | **Twp.** | Township |
| | **Tx,US** | Texas |
| U | **UAE** | United Arab Emirates |
| | **Ugan.** | Uganda |
| | **UK** | United Kingdom |
| | **Ukr.** | Ukraine |
| | **Uru.** | Uruguay |
| | **US** | United States |
| | **USVI** | U.S. Virgin Islands |
| | **Ut,US** | Utah |
| | **Uzb.** | Uzbekistan |
| V | **Va,US** | Virginia |
| | **Val.** | Valley |
| | **Van.** | Vanuatu |
| | **VatC.** | Vatican City |
| | **Ven.** | Venezuela |
| | **Viet.** | Vietnam |
| | **Vill.** | Village |
| | **Vol.** | Volcano |
| | **Vt,US** | Vermont |
| W | **Wa,US** | Washington |
| | **Wal,UK** | Wales |
| | **Wall.** | Wallis and Futuna |
| | **WBnk.** | West Bank |
| | **Wi,US** | Wisconsin |
| | **Wild.** | Wildlife, Wilderness |
| | **WSah.** | Western Sahara |
| | **WSam.** | Western Samoa |
| | **WV,US** | West Virginia |
| | **Wy,US** | Wyoming |
| Y | **Yem.** | Yemen |
| | **Yk,Can** | Yukon Territory |
| | **Yugo.** | Yugoslavia |
| Z | **Zam.** | Zambia |
| | **Zim.** | Zimbabwe |

## A

68/B2 **Aa** (riv.), Fr.
66/D5 **Aa** (riv.), Ger.
67/G5 **Aa** (riv.), Ger.
81/E3 **Aabach** (riv.), Swi.
81/E2 **Aach**, Ger.
81/F2 **Aach** (riv.), Ger.
69/F2 **Aachen**, Ger.
142/B5 **Aaglet Tennuaca** (well), WSah.
142/B4 **Aaglet Yeraifia** (well), WSah.
70/C3 **Aalbach** (riv.), Ger.
62/C3 **Aalborg** (int'l arpt.), Den.
66/C5 **Aalburg**, Neth.
70/D5 **Aalen**, Ger.
66/B4 **Aalsmeer**, Neth.
68/D2 **Aalst**, Belg.
66/D5 **Aalten**, Neth.
68/C1 **Aalter**, Belg.
70/B2 **Aar** (riv.), Ger.
80/E3 **Aarau**, Swi.
80/D3 **Aarberg**, Swi.
80/D3 **Aarburg**, Swi.
66/A6 **Aardenburg**, Neth.
80/D3 **Aare** (riv.), Swi.
80/E3 **Aargau** (canton), Swi.
142/B4 **Aarred, Sebjet** (dry lake), WSah.
69/D2 **Aarschot**, Belg.
68/D1 **Aartselaar**, Belg.
80/D3 **Aarwangen**, Swi.
108/E5 **Aba**, China
73/C5 **Aba**, Hun.
145/G5 **Aba**, Nga.
153/G2 **Aba**, Zaire
106/D5 **Abā as Su'ūd**, SAr.
166/B4 **Abacaxis** (riv.), Braz.
106/C5 **Abadab** (peak), Sudan
147/G5 **Abadab, Jabal** (peak), Sudan
105/G4 **Ābādān**, Iran
105/H4 **Ābādeh**, Iran
143/E3 **Abadla**, Alg.
92/E2 **Abádszalók**, Hun.
170/D3 **Abaeté**, Braz.
166/D3 **Abaetetuba**, Braz.
173/F3 **Abaí**, Par.
138/G4 **Abaiang** (isl.), Kiri.
145/G4 **Abaji**, Nga.
180/D4 **Abajo** (mts.), Ut,US
145/G5 **Abak**, Nga.
145/H5 **Abakaliki**, Nga.
100/K4 **Abakan**, Rus.
152/C3 **Abala**, Congo
145/F3 **Abala**, Niger
145/G3 **Abalak**, Niger
100/K4 **Aban**, Rus.
168/C4 **Abancay**, Peru
152/B2 **Abanga** (riv.), EqG., Gabon
87/E2 **Abano Terme**, It.
172/D1 **Abapó**, Bol.
108/G3 **Abaq Qi**, China
76/E3 **Abarán**, Sp.
139/H5 **Abariringa** (Canton) (isl.), Kiri.
105/H4 **Abar Kūh**, Iran
121/H4 **Ābāsa**, India
112/D1 **Abashiri**, Japan
112/C2 **Abashiri** (lake), Japan
159/E4 **Abasolo**, Mex.
149/G3 **Abatimbo el Gumas**, Eth.
131/H2 **Abau**, PNG
100/H5 **Abay**, Kaz.
150/A4 **Ābaya** (lake), Eth.
149/H4 **Ābaya Hāyk'** (lake), Eth.
114/F1 **Abaza**, Rus.
154/C5 **Abbabis**, Namb.
85/D1 **Abbadia di Fiastra**, It.
86/C1 **Abbadia Lariana**, It.
84/B2 **Abbadia San Salvatore**, It.
78/D5 **Abbaretz**, Fr.
85/D4 **Abbazia di Casamari**, It.
84/D5 **Abbazia di Fossanova**, It.
85/D4 **Abbazia di Montecassino**, It.
84/B1 **Abbazia di Monte Oliveto Maggiore**, It.
60/B3 **Abbert** (riv.), Ire.
68/A3 **Abbeville**, Fr.
203/F2 **Abbeville**, Al,US
201/F5 **Abbeville**, Ga,US
202/B3 **Abbeville**, La,US
200/C3 **Abbeville**, Ms,US
201/F3 **Abbeville**, SC,US
131/G3 **Abbey** (peak), Austl.
183/K2 **Abbey**, Sk,Can
60/A5 **Abbeydorney**, Ire.
60/A5 **Abbeyfeale**, Ire.
56/E2 **Abbey Head** (pt.), Sc,UK
60/C2 **Abbeylara**, Ire.
60/C4 **Abbeyleix**, Ire.
86/B2 **Abbiategrasso**, It.
134/B3 **Abbot** (peak), Austl.
131/H4 **Abbot** (pt.), Austl.
137/T **Abbot Ice Shelf**, Ant.
131/G5 **Abbot, Mount** (peak), Austl.
57/G6 **Abbots Bromley**, Eng,UK
58/D5 **Abbotsbury**, Eng,UK
195/J5 **Abbotsford**, Wi,US
53/M6 **Abbots Langley**, Eng,UK
189/F2 **Abbott**, Tx,US
107/K2 **Abbottābād**, Pak.
201/H3 **Abbottsburg**, NC,US
206/B4 **Abbottstown**, Pa,US
66/B4 **Abcoude**, Neth.
104/D2 **'Abd al 'Azīz, Jabal** (mts.), Syria
105/F3 **Ābdānān**, Iran
122/B2 **Abdul Hakīm**, Pak.
97/K1 **Abdulino**, Rus.
140/E3 **Abéché**, Chad
167/K6 **Abejorral**, Col.
157/E2 **Abel Erasmuspas** (pass), SAfr.
149/H3 **Ābeltī**, Eth.
138/G4 **Abemama** (isl.), Kiri.
154/C3 **Abenab**, Namb.
70/D4 **Abenberg**, Ger.
144/E5 **Abengourou**, IvC.
62/C4 **Åbenrå**, Den.
71/E5 **Abens** (riv.), Ger.
71/E5 **Abensberg**, Ger.
145/F5 **Abeokuta**, Nga.
56/D5 **Aber**, Wal,UK
58/B2 **Aberaeron**, Wal,UK
58/C1 **Aberangell**, Wal,UK
58/B2 **Aberath**, Wal,UK
58/C3 **Abercarn**, Wal,UK
54/D1 **Aberchirder**, Sc,UK
194/F4 **Abercrombie**, ND,US
58/C3 **Aberdare**, Wal,UK
151/B2 **Aberdare Nat'l Park**, Kenya
56/D6 **Aberdaron**, Wal,UK
135/D2 **Aberdeen**, Austl.
178/G2 **Aberdeen** (lake), NW,Can
156/D4 **Aberdeen**, SAfr.
54/D2 **Aberdeen**, Sc,UK
206/B4 **Aberdeen**, Md,US
200/C4 **Aberdeen**, Ms,US
201/H3 **Aberdeen**, NC,US
192/E1 **Aberdeen**, SD,US
182/C4 **Aberdeen**, Wa,US
54/D2 **Aberdeen** (Dyce) (int'l arpt.), Sc,UK
206/B5 **Aberdeen Prov. Gnd.** (mil. res.), Md,US
54/C4 **Aberdour**, Sc,UK
54/D1 **Aberdour** (bay), Sc,UK
58/B1 **Aberdyfi**, Wal,UK
54/C3 **Aberfeldy**, Sc,UK
54/B4 **Aberfoyle**, Sc,UK
58/C3 **Abergavenny**, Wal,UK
150/A2 **Ābergelē**, Eth.
56/E5 **Abergele**, Wal,UK
54/D5 **Aberlady**, Sc,UK
54/C2 **Aberlour**, Sc,UK
190/D4 **Abernathy**, Tx,US
54/C4 **Abernethy**, Sc,UK
58/B2 **Aberporth**, Wal,UK
56/D6 **Abersoch**, Wal,UK
58/C3 **Abersychan**, Wal,UK
184/C2 **Abert** (lake), Or,US
58/C3 **Abertillery**, Wal,UK
78/A3 **Aber Wrac'h** (riv.), Fr.
58/B2 **Aberystwyth**, Wal,UK
95/P2 **Abez'**, Rus.
106/D5 **Abhá**, SAr.
105/G2 **Abhar**, Iran
121/H2 **Abhayāpuri**, India
150/B3 **Abhe Bad** (lake), Djib.
150/B3 **Ābhē Bid** (lake), Eth.
161/G4 **Abide, Serraníade** (range), Col.
149/G2 **'Abidīn**, Sudan
144/D5 **Abidjan**, IvC.
144/E5 **Abidjan** (Port Bouet) (int'l arpt.), IvC.
145/F5 **Abidogun**, Nga.
111/J7 **Abiko**, Japan
191/F1 **Abilene**, Ks,US
188/E1 **Abilene**, Tx,US
59/E3 **Abingdon**, Eng,UK
193/J3 **Abingdon**, Il,US
206/B5 **Abingdon**, Md,US
201/G2 **Abingdon**, Va,US
134/A2 **Abingdon Downs**, Austl.
54/C6 **Abington**, Sc,UK
208/B2 **Abington**, Ct,US
208/D1 **Abington**, Ma,US
197/S10 **Abino** (pt.), On,Can
99/K5 **Abinsk**, Rus.
190/A2 **Abiquiu**, NM,US
190/A2 **Abiquiu** (dam), NM,US
190/A2 **Abiquiu** (lake), NM,US
187/J2 **Abiquiu** (res.), NM,US
61/F1 **Abisko**, Swe.
179/H4 **Abitibi** (lake), On,Can
179/H4 **Abitibi** (riv.), On,Can
150/A2 **Ābiy Ādī**, Eth.
150/A4 **Ābīyata** (lake), Eth.
149/H4 **Abiyata-Shala Lakes Nat'l Park**, Eth.
63/L2 **Abja-Paluoja**, Est.
97/G4 **Abkhaz Aut. Rep.**, Geo.
70/C6 **Ablach** (riv.), Ger.
79/G3 **Ablis**, Fr.
133/G3 **Abminga**, Austl.
147/F3 **Abnūb**, Egypt
150/D3 **Abo**, Som.
145/G5 **Aboh**, Nga.
122/C2 **Abohar**, India
144/E5 **Aboisso**, IvC.
145/F5 **Abomey**, Ben.
150/A3 **Ābomsa**, Eth.
80/C5 **Abondance**, Fr.
124/B1 **Abongabong** (mtn.), Indo.
148/B5 **Abong-Mbang**, Camr.
92/E2 **Abony**, Hun.
125/B3 **Aborlan**, Phil.
125/B3 **Aborlan** (mt.), Phil.
63/K1 **Åbo** (Turku), Fin.
148/C3 **AbouDeia**, Chad
148/E3 **Abourasséin** (peak), CAfr.
97/H4 **Abovyan**, Arm.
54/D2 **Aboyne**, Sc,UK
106/E3 **Abqaiq**, SAr.
125/C1 **Abra** (riv.), Phil.
172/C3 **Abra del Acay** (pass), Arg.
188/A2 **Abraham Gonzalez** (int'l arpt.), Mex.
200/E2 **Abraham Lincoln Birthplace Nat'l Hist. Site**, Ky,US
162/C2 **Abraham's Bay**, Bahm.
145/G5 **Abraka**, Nga.
195/K5 **Abrams**, Wi,US
76/A3 **Abrantes**, Port.
172/C2 **Abra Pampa**, Arg.
158/B3 **Abreojos, Punta** (pt.), Mex.
147/F4 **'Abrī**, Sudan
53/P7 **Abridge**, Eng,UK
82/C4 **Abries** (riv.), Fr.
85/F7 **Abriola**, It.
92/F2 **Abrud**, Rom.
85/D3 **Abruzzese, Appennino** (mts.), It.
85/E4 **Abruzzi** (reg.), It.
85/D4 **Abruzzo Nat'l Park**, It.
81/H3 **Absam**, Aus.
185/H1 **Absaroka** (range), Mt, Wy,US
183/K5 **Absarokee**, Mt,US
206/D5 **Absecon**, NJ,US
70/D5 **Abtsgmünd**, Ger.
103/E2 **Abū aḍ Ḍuhūr**, Syria
106/F4 **Abū al Abyaḍ** (isl.), UAE
105/G5 **Abū 'Alī** (isl.), SAr.
150/B1 **Abū 'Arīsh**, SAr.
149/F1 **Abū Dawm**, Sudan
149/G1 **Abū Dawm**, Sudan
107/F4 **Abu Dhabi** (Abū Ẓaby) (cap.), UAE
147/G5 **Abū Dīs**, Sudan
147/F4 **Abu el-Husein, Bîr** (well), Egypt
148/F2 **Abū Ḥabl** (dry riv.), Sudan
105/G5 **Abū Ḥadrīyah**, SAr.
147/G5 **Abū Ḥamad**, Sudan
103/B4 **Abū Ḥammād**, Egypt
147/G4 **Abu Hashim, Bi'r** (well), Egypt
149/G2 **Abū Hugar**, Sudan
103/B4 **Abū Ḥummuṣ**, Egypt
145/G4 **Abuja** (cap.), Nga.
145/G4 **Abuja** (int'l arpt.), Nga.
149/E3 **Abū Jābirah**, Sudan
145/G4 **Abuja Cap. Terr.** (terr.), Nga.
149/F3 **Abū Jubayhah**, Sudan
103/B4 **Abū Kabīr**, Egypt
104/E3 **Abū Kamāl**, Syria
149/G2 **Abū Kūk**, Sudan
111/G2 **Abukuma** (hills), Japan
111/G2 **Abukuma** (riv.), Japan
125/C1 **Abulug**, Phil.
147/H3 **Abū Madd, Ra's** (pt.), SAr.
149/E3 **Abū Maṭāriq**, Sudan
149/G3 **Abu Mendi**, Eth.
147/E3 **Abu Minqâr, Bîr** (well), Egypt
153/E2 **Abumombazi**, Zaire
169/E3 **Abuná** (riv.), Bol.
169/E3 **Abunã**, Braz.
169/E3 **Abunã** (riv.), Braz.
146/C2 **Abū Nā'im** (well), Libya
150/A2 **Ābune Yosēf** (peak), Eth.
103/G8 **Abū Qashsh**, WBnk.
118/B3 **Abu Road**, India
147/H4 **Abū Rubayq**, SAr.
104/D3 **Abu Rujmayn, Jabal** (mts.), Syria
149/G2 **Abū Rukbah**, Sudan
147/H4 **Abu Shagara, Ras** (cape), Sudan
149/E2 **Abū Shanab**, Sudan
147/F4 **Abu Simbel** (ruins), Egypt
136/B3 **Abut** (pt.), N.Z.
112/B2 **Abuta**, Japan
158/D3 **Abuya**, Mex.
150/A3 **Ābuyē Mēda** (peak), Eth.
125/D3 **Abuyog**, Phil.
149/F2 **Abū Zabad**, Sudan
107/F4 **Abū Ẓaby** (Abu Dhabi) (cap.), UAE
149/G3 **Abwong**, Sudan
62/G2 **Åby**, Swe.
90/A4 **Abyaḍ, Ar Ra's al** (cape), Tun.
147/H3 **Abyār 'Alī**, SAr.
62/C3 **Åbybro**, Den.
147/F3 **Abydos** (ruins), Egypt
149/F3 **Abyei**, Sudan
164/C4 **Acacías**, Col.
196/C3 **Acadia Nat'l Park**, Me,US
202/B2 **Acadian Village**, La,US
183/J2 **Acadia Valley**, Ab,Can
173/E3 **Acahay**, Par.
171/F1 **Acajutiba**, Braz.
159/E4 **Acámbaro**, Mex.
205/M10 **Acampo**, Ca,US
164/B2 **Acandí**, Col.
158/D4 **Acaponeta**, Mex.
158/D4 **Acaponeta** (riv.), Mex.
159/E5 **Acapulco**, Mex.
166/D3 **Acará**, Braz.
166/B2 **Acaraí** (mts., Braz.
165/G4 **Acarai** (mts.), Braz., Guy.
167/F3 **Acaraú**, Braz.
167/F3 **Acaraú** (riv.), Braz.
167/G4 **Acari**, Braz.
166/B4 **Acari** (riv.), Braz.
168/C4 **Acarí**, Peru
164/D2 **Acarigua**, Ven.
158/D3 **Acatita**, Mex.
159/F5 **Acatlán**, Mex.
159/F5 **Acatlán de Pérez Figueroa**, Mex.
159/M8 **Acatzingo de Hidalgo**, Mex.
85/F5 **Accadia**, It.
82/C4 **Acceglio**, It.
83/C2 **Accettura**, It.
168/D4 **Accha**, Peru
83/B2 **Acciaroli**, It.
201/K2 **Accomac**, Va,US
208/D1 **Accord**, Ma,US
145/E5 **Accra** (cap.), Gha.
57/F4 **Accrington**, Eng,UK
175/G1 **Aceguá**, Uru.
124/B1 **Aceh** (prov.), Indo.
85/F6 **Acerenza**, It.
85/F6 **Acerno**, It.
85/E6 **Acerra**, It.
76/B3 **Aceuchal**, Sp.
71/F6 **Ach**, Aus.
71/G6 **Ach** (riv.), Aus.
81/H2 **Ach** (riv.), Ger.
164/D3 **Achaguas**, Ven.
174/B4 **Achao**, Chile
175/F2 **Achar**, Uru.
145/H2 **Achegour** (well), Niger
81/H2 **Achen** (pass), Ger.
109/K2 **Acheng**, China
53/S10 **Achères**, Fr.
70/B5 **Achern**, Ger.
120/A2 **Achhnera**, India
68/B3 **Achicourt**, Fr.
68/B3 **Achiel-le-Grand**, Fr.
197/N6 **Achigan** (riv.), Qu,Can
54/F10 **Achill** (isl.), Ire.
54/F10 **Achill Head** (pt.), Ire.
55/J7 **Achiltibuie**, Sc,UK
67/G2 **Achim**, Ger.
148/C2 **Achim, Ouadi** (dry riv.), Chad
100/K4 **Achinsk**, Rus.
95/N4 **Achit**, Rus.
144/D2 **Achmîm** (well), Mrta.
54/A1 **Achnasheen**, Sc,UK
169/D5 **Achocalla**, Bol.
168/D4 **Achoma**, Peru
54/A2 **A'Chràlaig** (mtn.), Sc,UK
69/G3 **Acht, Hohe** (peak), Ger.
160/E3 **Achuapa**, Nic.
168/B1 **Achupallas**, Ecu.
99/J5 **Achuyevo**, Rus.
78/D4 **Acigné**, Fr.
84/C4 **Acilia**, It.
104/B2 **Acıpayam**, Turk.
90/D4 **Acireale**, It.
188/D1 **Ackerly**, Tx,US
200/C4 **Ackerman**, Ms,US
162/C2 **Acklins** (isl.), Bahm.
57/G4 **Ackworth Moor Top**, Eng,UK
134/C4 **Acland** (peak), Austl.
60/B1 **Aclare**, Ire.
59/H1 **Acle**, Eng,UK
189/J2 **Acme**, La,US
190/B4 **Acme**, NM,US
182/C3 **Acme**, Wa,US
168/C4 **Acobamba**, Peru
168/C3 **Acolla**, Peru
187/J3 **Acoma Ind. Res.**, NM,US
168/B3 **Acomayo**, Peru
168/D4 **Acomayo**, Peru
174/C2 **Aconcagua** (peak), Arg.
158/C2 **Aconchi**, Mex.
167/G4 **Acopiara**, Braz.
168/D4 **Acora**, Peru
170/A2 **Acorizal**, Braz.
157/E2 **Acornhoek**, SAfr.
87/F5 **Acqualagna**, It.
86/D2 **Acquanegra sul Chiese**, It.
84/B2 **Acquapendente**, It.
83/C5 **Acquaro**, It.
85/D2 **Acquasanta Terme**, It.
84/C2 **Acquasparta**, It.
85/D2 **Acquaviva Piceno**, It.
83/A6 **Acquedolci**, It.
79/G2 **Acquigny**, Fr.
86/B3 **Acqui Terme**, It.
133/G5 **Acraman** (lake), Austl.
168/D3 **Acre** (state), Braz.
169/D3 **Acre** (riv.), SAm.
170/C3 **Acreúna**, Braz.
83/C4 **Acri**, It.
91/L7 **Acropolis**, Gre.
73/C4 **Ács**, Hun.
139/M7 **Actaeon Group** (isls.), FrPol.
197/Q8 **Acton**, On,Can
53/N7 **Acton**, Eng,UK
204/B2 **Acton**, Ca,US
196/B4 **Acton**, Ma,US
183/K5 **Acton**, Mt,US
188/K7 **Acton**, Tx,US
159/F5 **Actopan**, Mex.
167/G4 **Açu**, Braz.
159/P8 **Acula**, Mex.
174/Q9 **Aculeo** (lake), Chile
160/E1 **Acumal**, Mex.
188/D3 **Acuña**, Mex.
208/D2 **Acushnet**, Ma,US
201/L6 **Acworth**, Ga,US
145/F5 **Ada**, Gha.
194/F4 **Ada**, Mn,US
198/E4 **Ada**, Oh,US
191/F3 **Ada**, Ok,US
92/E3 **Ada**, Yugo.
150/A4 **Ādaba**, Eth.
179/J1 **Adair** (cape), NW,Can
187/F5 **Adair** (bay), Mex.
193/G3 **Adair**, Ia,US
191/G2 **Adair**, Ok,US
200/E3 **Adairsville**, Ga,US
200/D2 **Adairville**, Ky,US
76/C2 **Adaja** (riv.), Sp.
177/C6 **Adak** (isl.), Ak,US
177/C6 **Adak** (str.), Ak,US
175/M7 **Adam** (peak), Falk.
107/G4 **Adam**, Oman
170/C4 **Adamantina**, Braz.
148/B4 **Adamaoua** (plat.), Camr., Nga.
81/G5 **Adamello** (peak), It.
135/D3 **Adaminaby**, Austl.
97/L2 **Adamovka**, Rus.
182/E2 **Adams** (lake), BC,Can
182/E2 **Adams** (riv.), BC,Can
199/K3 **Adams**, Ma,US
193/F3 **Adams**, Ne,US
199/L2 **Adams** (mt.), NH,US
199/H3 **Adams**, NY,US
206/A4 **Adams** (co.), Pa,US
200/D2 **Adams**, Tn,US
182/D4 **Adams** (mt.), Wa,US
193/K2 **Adams**, Wi,US
122/G4 **Adam's Bridge** (shoals), SrL.
201/G4 **Adams Run**, SC,US
139/M7 **Adamstown**, Pitc.
206/B3 **Adamstown**, Pa,US
200/D4 **Adamsville**, Al,US
208/C2 **Adamsville**, RI,US
200/C3 **Adamsville**, Tn,US
189/E2 **Adamsville**, Tx,US
145/H5 **Adamwa** (plat.), Camr., Nga.
103/D1 **Adana**, Turk.
103/D1 **Adana** (int'l arpt.), Turk.
103/D1 **Adana** (prov.), Turk.
152/B3 **Adanhé**, Gabon
93/K5 **Adapazarı**, Turk.
149/G1 **Adarama**, Sudan
137/M **Adare** (cape), Ant.
60/B4 **Adare**, Ire.
74/C5 **Adarza** (mtn.), Fr.
130/C2 **Adaut**, Indo.
134/B4 **Adavale**, Austl.
54/A4 **Add** (riv.), Sc,UK
86/C2 **Adda** (riv.), It.
148/D3 **Adda** (riv.), Sudan
149/F1 **Ad Dabbah**, Sudan
106/B5 **Ad Dabbūrah**, Sudan
106/D4 **Ad Dafīnah**, SAr.
105/F5 **Ad Dahnā'** (des.), SAr.
149/G3 **Ad Damazin**, Sudan
149/G1 **Ad Damīr**, Sudan
106/F3 **Ad Dammām**, SAr.
103/B4 **Ad Daqahlīyah** (gov.), Egypt
106/D5 **Ad Darb**, SAr.
106/F3 **Ad Dawḥah** (Doha) (cap.), Qatar
105/E3 **Ad Dawr**, Iraq
189/G3 **Addicks** (dam), Tx,US
189/M9 **Addicks** (res.), Tx,US
106/E4 **Ad Dilam**, SAr.
103/B4 **Ad Dilinjāt**, Egypt
202/C2 **Addis**, La,US
150/A3 **Addis Ababa** (Ādis Ābeba) (cap.), Eth.
200/D3 **Addison**, Al,US
208/B2 **Addison**, Ct,US
205/Q16 **Addison**, Il,US
196/D3 **Addison**, Me,US
188/L7 **Addison**, Tx,US
201/G1 **Addison** (Webster Springs), WV,US
105/F4 **Ad Dīwānīyah**, Iraq
53/M7 **Addlestone**, Eng,UK
156/D4 **Addo Elephant Nat'l Park**, SAfr.
149/E3 **Ad Du'ayn**, Sudan
149/G1 **Ad Dubburá**, Sudan
105/F3 **Ad Dujayl**, Iraq
106/D4 **Ad Duwādimī**, SAr.
104/E4 **Ad Duwayd**, SAr.
149/G2 **Ad Duwaym**, Sudan
182/F3 **Addy**, Wa,US
148/D2 **Adé**, Chad
203/G2 **Adel**, Ga,US
193/G3 **Adel**, Ia,US
137/V **Adelaide** (isl.), Ant.
133/H5 **Adelaide**, Austl.
133/M8 **Adelaide** (int'l arpt.), Austl.
130/C3 **Adelaide** (riv.), Austl.
178/G2 **Adelaide** (pen.), NW,Can
156/D4 **Adelaide**, SAfr.
130/C3 **Adelaide River**, Austl.
133/M8 **Adelaide Zoo**, Austl.
204/C1 **Adelanto**, Ca,US
144/D3 **'Adel Bagrou**, Mrta.
128/C3 **Adele** (isl.), Austl.
130/A3 **Adèle** (isl.), Austl.
67/G5 **Adelebsen**, Ger.
67/H3 **Adelheidsdorf**, Ger.
137/K **Adélie** (coast), Ant.
70/D5 **Adelmannsfelden**, Ger.
135/D2 **Adelong**, Austl.
70/E5 **Adelschlag**, Ger.
70/C4 **Adelsheim**, Ger.
63/R7 **Adelsön** (isl.), Swe.
70/D6 **Adelsried**, Ger.
150/C2 **Aden** (gulf), Afr., Asia
102/D8 **Aden** (gulf), Asia
183/J3 **Aden**, Ab,Can
106/D6 **Aden**, Yem.
150/C2 **Aden** (int'l arpt.), Yem.
69/F3 **Adenau**, Ger.
67/H2 **Adendorf**, Ger.
145/G3 **Aderbissinat**, Niger
146/C4 **Adèrké**, Chad
149/H3 **Ādēt**, Eth.
143/H2 **Adh Dhahībāt**, Tun.
103/D4 **Adh Dhirā'**, Jor.
127/H4 **Adi** (isl.), Indo.
153/G2 **Adi**, Zaire
150/A2 **Ādī Ābun**, Eth.
144/E5 **Adiaké**, IvC.
149/H2 **Ādī Ārk'ay**, Eth.
149/H2 **Ādī Da'iro**, Eth.
133/G5 **Adieu** (cape), Austl.
150/B3 **Ādīgala**, Eth.
87/F2 **Adige** (riv.), It.
81/H6 **Adige** (Etsch) (riv.), It.
97/G4 **Adigeni**, Geo.
150/A2 **Ādīgrat**, Eth.
150/A2 **Ādī K'eyih**, Eth.
149/H2 **Ādī Kwala**, Eth.
118/C4 **Adilābād**, India
105/E2 **Adilcevaz**, Turk.
145/F5 **Adimo**, Nga.
184/C3 **Adin**, Ca,US
145/E2 **Adiora** (well), Mali
122/G3 **Adirāmpatnam**, India
146/B3 **Adīrī**, Libya
199/J2 **Adirondack** (mts.), NY,US
149/H3 **Ādīs Ābeba** (Addis Ababa) (cap.), Eth.
124/E4 **Adisutjipto** (int'l arpt.), Indo.
149/H2 **Ādīs Zemen**, Eth.
149/H2 **Ādī Tekelezan**, Eth.
149/H2 **Ādī Ugrī**, Eth.
104/D2 **Adıyaman**, Turk.
104/D2 **Adıyaman** (prov.), Turk.
93/H2 **Adjud**, Rom.
159/F4 **Adjuntas** (res.), Mex.
96/F4 **Adler/Sochi** (int'l arpt.), Rus.
57/F4 **Adlington**, Eng,UK
81/E3 **Adliswil**, Swi.
146/A4 **Admer, 'Erg d'** (des.), Alg.
143/H4 **Admer, 'Erg d'** (des.), Alg., Niger
183/K3 **Admiral**, Sk,Can
179/H1 **Admirality** (inlet), NW,Can
178/C3 **Admirality** (isl.), Ak,US
130/B3 **Admiralty** (gulf), Austl.
138/D5 **Admiralty** (isls.), PNG
205/B2 **Admiralty** (inlet), Wa,US
130/B3 **Admiralty Gulf Abor. Rsv.**, Austl.
177/M4 **Admiralty I. Nat'l Mon.**, Ak,US
191/F1 **Admire**, Ks,US
104/A2 **Adnan Menderes** (int'l arpt.), Turk.
111/L9 **Ado** (riv.), Japan
145/F5 **Ado**, Nga.
192/C4 **Adobe Creek** (res.), Co,US
145/G5 **Ado Ekiti**, Nga.
111/M9 **Adogawa**, Japan
149/F3 **Adok**, Sudan
118/C4 **Ādoni**, India
73/C5 **Adony**, Hun.
71/F2 **Adorf**, Ger.
145/G5 **Adoru**, Nga.
74/C5 **Adour** (riv.), Fr.
121/F4 **Adra**, India
76/D4 **Adra**, Sp.
153/G2 **Adranga**, Zaire
90/D4 **Adrano**, It.
143/E4 **Adrar**, Alg.
143/E4 **Adrar** (wilaya), Alg.
144/B1 **Adrar** (reg.), Mrta.
142/E2 **Adrar bou Nasser** (peak), Mor.
145/F1 **Adrar des Iforas** (mts.), Mali
148/D2 **Adré**, Chad
87/F2 **Adria**, It.
198/D4 **Adrian**, Mi,US
193/G2 **Adrian**, Mn,US
191/G1 **Adrian**, Mo,US
184/E2 **Adrian**, Or,US
201/G1 **Adrian**, WV,US
88/G2 **Adriatic** (sea), Eur.
86/C1 **Adro**, It.
187/G5 **Aduana del Sásabe**, Mex.
145/E5 **Adukrom**, Gha.
150/A2 **Adulis** (ruins), Eth.
59/F5 **Adur** (riv.), Eng,UK
63/M4 **Adutiškis**, Lith.
200/C2 **Advance**, Mo,US
135/C4 **Adventure Bay**, Austl.
196/E3 **Advocate Harbour**, NS,Can
150/A2 **Ādwa**, Eth.
57/G4 **Adwick le Street**, Eng,UK
190/C3 **Ady**, Tx,US
101/P3 **Adycha** (riv.), Rus.
99/L5 **Adyge Aut. Obl.**, Rus.
96/G3 **Adyge Aut. Rep.**, Rus.
97/G4 **Adzhar Aut. Rep.**, Geo.
144/E5 **Adzopé**, IvC.
95/N2 **Adz'va** (riv.), Rus.
95/N2 **Adz'vavom**, Rus.
56/E1 **Ae**, Ire.
91/J3 **Aegean** (sea), Gre., Turk.
63/L2 **Aegviidu**, Est.
62/D4 **Aerø** (isl.), Den.
58/B2 **Aeron** (riv.), Wal,UK
164/D1 **Aeropuerto Hato** (int'l arpt.), NAnt.
80/D3 **Aesch**, Swi.
80/D4 **Aeschi bei Spiez**, Swi.
183/H3 **Aetna**, Ab,Can
63/K1 **Äetsä**, Fin.
56/E1 **Ae, Water of** (riv.), Sc,UK
145/F5 **Afadjoto** (peak), Gha.
105/F3 **'Afak**, Iraq
150/B2 **Afambo**, Eth.
150/B3 **Āfambo**, Eth.
95/N4 **Afanas'yevskoye**, Rus.
89/L3 **Afándou**, Gre.
139/X15 **Afareaitu**, FrPol.
150/B3 **Āfdem**, Eth.
103/F7 **Afek Nat'l Park**, Isr.
78/C5 **Aff** (riv.), Fr.
156/A3 **Affenrücken**, Namb.
80/D3 **Affoltern im Emmental**, Swi.
54/A2 **Affric, Loch** (lake), Sc,UK
200/B1 **Affton**, Mo,US
107/H2 **Afghanistan**
150/C5 **Afgooye**, Som.
152/B2 **Afia**, Gabon
106/D4 **'Afīf**, SAr.
145/G5 **Afikpo**, Nga.
99/K5 **Afipskiy**, Rus.
143/F2 **Aflou**, Alg.
151/C1 **Afmadow**, Som.
166/C1 **Afobaka** (dam), Sur.
167/G4 **Afogados da Ingàzeira**, Braz.
177/H4 **Afognak** (isl.), Ak,US
177/H4 **Afognak** (mtn.), Ak,US
144/C2 **Afollé** (reg.), Mrta.
167/G4 **Afonso Bezerra**, Braz.
131/H2 **Afore**, PNG
85/E6 **Afragola**, It.
167/F5 **Afrânio**, Braz.
140/* **Africa** (cont.)
205/K10 **Africa USA** (Marine World), Ca,US
103/E1 **'Afrīn**, Syria
103/E1 **'Afrīn** (riv.), Syria
103/E1 **Afrin** (riv.), Turk.
80/A3 **Afrique** (mtn.), Fr.
104/D2 **Afşin**, Turk.
66/C2 **Afsluitdijk** (IJsselmeer) (dam), Neth.
67/F5 **Afte** (riv.), Ger.
193/G3 **Afton**, Ia,US
195/Q7 **Afton**, Mn,US
191/G2 **Afton**, Ok,US
185/H2 **Afton**, Wy,US
166/D3 **Afuá**, Braz.
142/B5 **Afuidich, Sebjet** (dry lake), WSah.
103/D3 **'Afula**, Isr.
151/B1 **Afwein, Lac** (dry riv.), Kenya
104/B2 **Afyon**, Turk.
104/B2 **Afyon** (prov.), Turk.
120/B1 **Afzalgarh**, India
148/B1 **Agadem**, Niger
145/H2 **Agades** (int'l arpt.), Niger
145/G2 **Agadez**, Niger
145/H2 **Agadez** (dept.), Niger
142/C3 **Agadir**, Mor.
142/C3 **Agadir** (Inezgane) (int'l arpt.), Mor.
114/B2 **Agadyr'**, Kaz.
153/H2 **Agago** (riv.), Ugan.
141/H6 **Agalega** (isls.), Mrts.
121/G2 **Āgamani**, India
145/F2 **Agamor** (well), Mali
138/D3 **Agana** (cap.), Guam
51/S5 **Agaña** (cap.), Guam
111/F2 **Agano** (riv.), Japan
192/D1 **Agar**, SD,US
150/A4 **Āgarfa**, Eth.
149/H4 **Āgaro**, Eth.
121/H4 **Agartala**, India
137/V **Agassiz** (cape), Ant.
179/T6 **Agassiz** (ice field), NW,Can
194/F3 **Agassiz Nat'l Wild. Ref.**, Mn,US
190/C1 **Agate**, Co,US
192/C2 **Agate Fossil Beds Nat'l Mon.**, Ne,US
131/E1 **Agats**, Indo.
177/A5 **Agattu** (isl.), Ak,US
177/A5 **Agattu** (str.), Ak,US
208/B1 **Agawam**, Ma,US
145/G5 **Agbabu**, Nga.
145/G5 **Agbor**, Nga.
144/D5 **Agboville**, IvC.
97/H5 **Agdam**, Azer.
97/H4 **Agdash**, Azer.
74/E5 **Agde**, Fr.
74/E5 **Agde, Cap d'** (cape), Fr.
142/D3 **Agdz**, Mor.
97/H4 **Agdzhabedi**, Azer.
74/D4 **Agen**, Fr.
193/H3 **Agency**, Ia,US
191/G1 **Agency**, Mo,US
184/B2 **Agency** (lake), Or,US
111/H7 **Ageo**, Japan
71/G7 **Ager** (riv.), Aus.
62/C4 **Agerbæk**, Den.
149/H4 **Āgere Maryam**, Eth.
81/E3 **Agerisee** (lake), Swi.
63/S7 **Agesta** (reg. park), Swe.
96/F1 **Ageyevo**, Rus.
67/E6 **Agger** (riv.), Ger.
92/E1 **Aggteleki Nat'l Park**, Hun.
56/B3 **Aghagallon**, NI,UK
60/A2 **Aghagower**, Ire.
105/G4 **Āghā Jārī**, Iran
158/C3 **Agiabampo** (lag.), Mex.
104/D2 **Ağın**, Turk.
108/G1 **Aginskoye**, Rus.
146/A3 **'Agiuel, Hasy in** (well), Libya
56/B1 **Agivey**, NI,UK
144/C2 **Agjert**, Mrta.
87/E5 **Agliana**, It.
104/C1 **Ağlıköy**, Turk.
74/E5 **Agly** (riv.), Fr.
87/E2 **Agna**, It.
91/G3 **Agnanderón**, Gre.
79/D2 **Agneaux**, Fr.
82/C3 **Agneaux, Pic de** (peak), Fr.
188/K7 **Agnes**, Tx,US
132/D4 **Agnew**, Austl.
144/E5 **Agnibilékrou**, IvC.
93/G3 **Agnita**, Rom.
81/E5 **Agno**, It.
87/E1 **Agno** (riv.), It.
81/E6 **Agno**, Swi.
81/E5 **Agno** (int'l arpt.), Swi.
85/E4 **Agnone**, It.
82/B1 **Agny** (riv.), Fr.
111/M10 **Ago**, Japan
145/F4 **Ago Are**, Nga.
86/B2 **Agogna** (riv.), It.
145/E5 **Agona**, Gha.
78/D2 **Agon-Coutainville**, Fr.
117/J5 **Agoo**, Phil.
75/K3 **Agordo**, It.
145/F5 **Agougadzépe**, Togo
74/D5 **Agout** (riv.), Fr.
120/B2 **Āgra**, India
190/E1 **Agra**, Ks,US
175/S11 **Agraciada**, Uru.
164/C4 **Agrado**, Col.
76/E2 **Ágreda**, Sp.
83/C2 **Agri** (riv.), It.
105/E2 **Ağri** (prov.), Turk.
91/H3 **Agriá**, Gre.
97/H5 **Ağri** (Ararat) (peak), Turk.
90/C4 **Agrigento**, It.
138/D3 **Agrihan** (isl.), NMar.
91/G3 **Agrínion**, Gre.
174/C3 **Agrio** (riv.), Arg.
83/A2 **Agropoli**, It.
95/M4 **Agryz**, Rus.
142/B4 **Agsumal, Sebjet** (dry lake), WSah.
186/E5 **Agua Blanca**, Mex.
159/L6 **Agua Blanca Iturbide**, Mex.
167/F4 **Água Branca**, Braz.
167/G4 **Água Branca**, Braz.
172/B3 **Agua Buena**, Chile
187/F4 **Agua Caliente**, Az,US
186/D4 **Agua Caliente Ind. Res.**, Ca,US
164/C2 **Aguachica**, Col.
170/B4 **Água Clara**, Braz.
164/C3 **Aguadas**, Col.
167/L7 **Agua de Dios**, Col.
162/E3 **Aguadilla**, PR
160/C2 **Agua Dulce**, Mex.
161/F4 **Aguadulce**, Pan.
204/B2 **Agua Dulce**, Ca,US
186/E5 **Agua Flores**, Mex.
187/F4 **Agua Fria** (riv.), Az,US
187/J3 **Agua Fria**, NM,US
204/C4 **Agua Hedionda** (lag.), Ca,US
171/J7 **Aguaí**, Braz.
164/D2 **Agua Larga**, Ven.
188/E4 **Agualeguas**, Mex.
77/P10 **Agualva-Cacém**, Port.
160/E3 **Aguan** (riv.), Hon.
170/C4 **Aguapeí** (riv.), Braz.
173/E3 **Aguapey** (riv.), Arg.
187/H5 **Agua Prieta**, Mex.
172/D2 **Aguaray**, Arg.
164/C5 **Aguarico** (riv.), Ecu.
165/E2 **Aguaro-Guariquito Nat'l Park**, Ven.
171/L6 **Águas** (hills), Braz.
165/F2 **Aguasay**, Ven.
171/F1 **Águas Belas**, Braz.
172/B3 **Aguas Blancas**, Chile
158/E4 **Aguascalientes**, Mex.
158/E4 **Aguascalientes** (state), Mex.
175/T12 **Aguas Corrientes**, Uru.
171/K6 **Águas da Prata**, Braz.
171/K7 **Águas de Lindóia**, Braz.
171/E3 **Águas Formosas**, Braz.
170/C3 **Agua Vermelha** (res.), Braz.
168/C3 **Aguaytía** (riv.), Peru
76/A2 **Águeda**, Port.
76/B2 **Agueda** (riv.), Sp.
145/F2 **Aguelhok**, Mali
142/B5 **Agüenit**, WSah.
142/D5 **Aguêraktem** (well), Mali, Mrta.
87/G5 **Agugliano**, It.
111/M10 **Agui**, Japan
145/G3 **Aguié**, Niger
138/D3 **Aguijan** (isl.), NMar.
187/F4 **Aguila**, Az,US
144/B2 **Aguilâl Faï**, Mrta.
76/C4 **Aguilar**, Sp.
190/B2 **Aguilar**, Co,US
76/C1 **Aguilar de Campóo**, Sp.
172/C3 **Aguilares**, Arg.
76/E4 **Aguilas**, Sp.
158/E5 **Aguililla**, Mex.
77/X17 **Agüimes**, Canl.,Sp.
168/A2 **Aguja** (pt.), Peru
156/C4 **Agulhas** (cape), SAfr.
170/D4 **Agulhas Negras, Pico das** (peak), Braz.
124/F5 **Agung** (vol.), Indo.
125/D3 **Agusan** (riv.), Phil.
164/C2 **Agustín Codazzi**, Col.
125/C3 **Agutaya**, Phil.
153/H2 **Agwata**, Ugan.
149/F4 **Agwok**, Sudan
154/D3 **Aha** (hills), Bots.
140/C2 **Ahaggar** (mts.), Alg.
143/G5 **Ahaggar** (plat.), Alg.
143/G5 **Ahaggar, Tassili Oua-n** (mts.), Alg.
71/F5 **Aham**, Ger.
105/F2 **Ahar**, Iran
60/B3 **Ahascragh**, Ire.
138/G6 **Ahau**, Fiji
136/B3 **Ahaura**, N.Z.
66/E4 **Ahaus**, Ger.
69/F3 **Ahbach** (riv.), Ger.
143/F5 **Ahenet, Tanezrouft-n-** (des.), Alg.
60/B5 **Aherlow** (riv.), Ire.
151/A2 **Ahero**, Kenya
136/C1 **Ahipara**, N.Z.
104/C2 **Ahırlı**, Turk.
104/E2 **Ahlat**, Turk.
67/E5 **Ahlen**, Ger.
67/G2 **Ahlerstedt**, Ger.
118/B3 **Ahmadābād**, India
118/B4 **Ahmadnagar**, India
107/K3 **Ahmadpur East**, Pak.
122/A2 **Ahmadpur Siāl**, Pak.
150/B3 **Ahmar** (mts.), Eth.
146/C2 **Aḥmar, Bi'r al** (well), Libya
142/D4 **Ahmar, 'Erg el** (des.), Mali
142/B5 **Ahmeyine** (well), Mrta.
145/G5 **Ahoada**, Nga.
56/B2 **Ahoghill**, NI,UK
158/C3 **Ahome**, Mex.
146/C4 **Ahon, Tarso** (peak), Chad
201/J2 **Ahoskie**, NC,US
69/F3 **Ahr** (riv.), Ger.
105/G4 **Ahram**, Iran
103/B5 **Ahrāmāt al Jīzah** (The Pyramids of Giza), Egypt
120/D3 **Ahraurā**, India
67/H1 **Ahrensburg**, Ger.
67/F5 **Ahse** (riv.), Ger.
159/K8 **Ahuacatitlán**, Mex.
158/D4 **Ahuacatlán**, Mex.
160/D3 **Ahuachapán**, ESal.
159/F5 **Ahuacuotzingo**, Mex.
159/E4 **Ahualulco**, Mex.
188/A2 **Ahumada**, Mex.
74/E3 **Ahun**, Fr.
145/F5 **Ahunda**, Gha.
62/F4 **Åhus**, Swe.
103/F8 **Aḥuzzam**, Isr.
105/G4 **Ahvāz**, Iran
63/H1 **Ahvenanmaa** (prov.), Fin.
186/C2 **Ahwahnee**, Ca,US
150/C2 **Aḥwar**, Yem.
113/C2 **Ai** (riv.), China
156/B2 **Ai-Ais**, Namb.
156/B2 **Ai-Ais Hot Springs**, Namb.
115/B2 **Aibag Gol** (riv.), China
82/B4 **Aibignan**, Fr.
70/E6 **Aichach**, Ger.
111/E3 **Aichi** (pref.), Japan
70/D2 **Aidhausen**, Ger.
70/B5 **Aidlingen**, Ger.
87/G1 **Aiello del Friuli**, It.
74/C3 **Aiffres**, Fr.
71/G5 **Aigen im Mühlkreis**, Aus.
80/C5 **Aigle**, Swi.
69/D4 **Aiglemont**, Fr.
80/B4 **Aigle, Pic de l'** (peak), Fr.
74/E4 **Aigoual** (mtn.), Fr.
175/G2 **Aiguá**, Uru.
82/C1 **Aiguebelle**, Fr.
82/C1 **Aigueblanche**, Fr.
82/A4 **Aigues** (riv.), Fr.
77/F1 **Aigues Tortes y Lago de San Mauricio Nat'l Park**, Sp.
141/Q16 **Aiguille, Cap de l'** (cape), Alg.
168/B3 **Aija**, Peru
111/F1 **Aikawa**, Japan
201/G4 **Aiken**, SC,US
116/D3 **Ailao** (mtn.), China
116/D4 **Ailao** (mts.), China
133/G2 **Aileron**, Austl.
130/B2 **Aileu**, Indo.
161/G4 **Ailigandí**, Pan.
138/F4 **Ailinglapalap** (atoll), Mrsh.
82/C6 **Aille** (riv.), Fr.
80/C2 **Aillevillers-et-Lyaumont**, Fr.
82/C1 **Aillon** (riv.), Fr.
68/B4 **Ailly-sur-Noye**, Fr.
198/F3 **Ailsa Craig**, On,Can
54/A6 **Ailsa Craig** (isl.), Sc,UK
138/G3 **Ailuk** (atoll), Mrsh.
82/C1 **Aime**, Fr.
117/G2 **Aimen** (pass), China
115/C5 **Aimen Guan** (pass), China
172/C4 **Aimogasta**, Arg.
171/E3 **Aimorés**, Braz.
171/E3 **Aimorés** (mts.), Braz.
82/B1 **Ain** (dept.), Fr.
80/B5 **Ain** (riv.), Fr.
130/B2 **Ainaro**, Indo.
63/L3 **Ainaži**, Lat.
141/V18 **'Aïn Beïda**, Alg.
141/S15 **'Aïn Beniau**, Alg.
142/C4 **Aïn Ben Tili**, Mrta.
141/S15 **'Aïn Bessem**, Alg.
141/R15 **'Aïn Defla**, Alg.
141/R15 **'Aïn Defla** (wilaya), Alg.
141/L14 **Aïn el Aouda**, Mor.
141/V17 **'Aïn El Bey** (int'l arpt.), Alg.
141/T15 **'Aïn El Hammam**, Alg.
141/Q16 **'Aïn el Turk**, Alg.
141/V17 **'Aïn Fakroun**, Alg.
141/V17 **'Aïn M'Lila**, Alg.
91/G3 **Aínos** (peak), Gre.
91/G3 **Ainos Nat'l Park**, Gre.
141/U18 **'Aïn Oulmene**, Alg.
141/S16 **'Aïn Oussersa**, Alg.
57/E4 **Ainsdale**, Eng,UK
143/E2 **'Aïn Sefra**, Alg.
197/G2 **Ainslie** (lake), NS,Can
192/E2 **Ainsworth**, Ne,US
141/S15 **'Aïn Taya**, Alg.
141/Q16 **'Aïn Temouchent**, Alg.
141/Q16 **'Ain Temouchent** (wilaya), Alg.
141/U18 **'Aïn Touta**, Alg.
131/G1 **Aiome**, PNG
164/C4 **Aipe**, Col.
172/C1 **Aiquile**, Bol.
143/G5 **Aïr** (plat.), Niger
145/G2 **Aïr** (plat.), Niger
124/D2 **Airabu** (isl.), Indo.
68/A4 **Airaines**, Fr.
86/A3 **Airasca**, It.
124/B2 **Airbangis**, Indo.
183/G2 **Airdrie**, Ab,Can
54/C5 **Airdrie**, Sc,UK
68/D5 **Aire** (riv.), Fr.
57/G4 **Aire** (riv.), Eng,UK
68/B2 **Aire, Canal de** (can.), Fr.
57/E5 **Aire, Point of** (pt.), Wal,UK
74/C5 **Aire-sur-l'Adour**, Fr.
68/B2 **Aire-sur-la-Lys**, Fr.
179/J2 **Air Force** (isl.), NW,Can
108/G3 **Airgin Sum**, China
124/C3 **Airmolek**, Indo.
85/E5 **Airola**, It.
81/E4 **Airolo**, Swi.
57/F3 **Airton**, Eng,UK
86/C1 **Airuno**, It.
74/C3 **Airvault**, Fr.
70/D3 **Aisch** (riv.), Ger.
68/D3 **Aiseau-Presles**, Belg.
174/B5 **Aisén del General Carlos Ibáñez del Campo** (reg.), Chile
115/E3 **Ai Shan** (mtn.), China
177/L3 **Aishihik**, Yk,Can
69/E3 **Aisne** (riv.), Belg.
68/C4 **Aisne** (dept.), Fr.
68/C5 **Aisne** (riv.), Fr.
140/B1 **Aïssa** (peak), Alg.
143/E2 **Aïssa, Djebel** (mtn.), Alg.
71/H6 **Aist** (riv.), Aus.
138/D5 **Aitape**, PNG
142/D3 **Aït Ben Haddou**, Mor.
71/F5 **Aiterach** (riv.), Ger.
55/P12 **Aith**, Sc,UK
195/H4 **Aitkin**, Mn,US
111/M9 **Aitō**, Japan
91/G3 **Aitolikón**, Gre.
142/D3 **Aït Ourir**, Mor.
81/G2 **Aitrach**, Ger.
81/G2 **Aitrang**, Ger.
139/J6 **Aitutaki** (atoll), Cookls.
167/F4 **Aiuaba**, Braz.
93/F2 **Aiud**, Rom.
171/M6 **Aiuruoca**, Braz.
171/M7 **Aiuruoca** (riv.), Braz.
182/D4 **Aix** (mt.), Wa,US
82/B6 **Aix-en-Provence**, Fr.
82/B1 **Aix-les-Bains**, Fr.
82/B1 **Aix-les-Bains** (Chambery) (arpt.), Fr.
113/C2 **Aiyang**, China
91/H4 **Aíyina**, Gre.
91/H2 **Aiyínion**, Gre.
91/H3 **Aíyion**, Gre.
63/J3 **Aizpute**, Lat.
111/F2 **Aizu-Wakamatsu**, Japan
116/B4 **Aīzwal**, India
105/F2 **'Ajab Shīr**, Iran
90/A2 **Ajaccio**, Fr.
90/A2 **Ajaccio** (gulf), Fr.
120/C3 **Ajaigarh**, India
159/F5 **Ajalpan**, Mex.
132/B3 **Ajana**, Austl.
145/G5 **Ajaokuta**, Nga.
145/G4 **Ajasse Ipo**, Nga.
199/G3 **Ajax**, On,Can
121/F4 **Ajay** (riv.), India
108/D3 **Aj Bogd** (peak), Mong.
114/G3 **Aj Bogd Uul** (peak), Mong.
146/D2 **Ajdābiyā**, Libya
87/G1 **Ajdovščina**, Slov.
112/B3 **Ajigasawa**, Japan
103/G7 **'Ajjah**, WBnk.
147/G5 **Aj Janayet**, Sudan
73/B5 **Ajka**, Hun.
118/B2 **Ajmer**, India
122/C2 **Ajnāla**, India
187/F4 **Ajo**, Az,US
76/D1 **Ajo, Cabo de** (cape), Sp.
158/D3 **Ajoya**, Mex.
159/E5 **Ajuchitlán**, Mex.
159/Q10 **Ajusco** (mt.), Mex.
125/C3 **Ajuy**, Phil.
111/F1 **Aka** (riv.), Japan
111/N10 **Akabane**, Japan
112/C2 **Akabira**, Japan
143/F4 **Akabli**, Alg.
114/F1 **Akademik Obruchev** (mts.), Rus.
145/G5 **Aka Eze**, Nga.
153/G3 **Akagera Nat'l Park**, Rwa.
111/F3 **Akaishi-dake** (mtn.), Japan
149/H3 **Āk'ak'ī Besek'a**, Eth.
122/B1 **Akālgarh**, Pak.
120/D4 **Akaltara**, India
112/D2 **Akan** (lake), Japan
152/C3 **Akana**, Congo
145/H5 **Akankpa**, Nga.
112/D2 **Akan Nat'l Park**, Japan
136/C3 **Akaroa**, N.Z.
62/E4 **Åkarp**, Swe.
104/D2 **Akarsu**, Turk.
147/F4 **Akasha East**, Sudan
110/D3 **Akashi**, Japan
111/K10 **Akashi** (str.), Japan
194/D5 **Akaska**, SD,US
120/B2 **Akbarpur**, India
120/D2 **Akbarpur**, India
114/B4 **Akbaytal** (pass), Taj.
141/T15 **Akbou**, Alg.
104/D1 **Akçaabat**, Turk.
104/D2 **Akçadağ**, Turk.
104/D2 **Akçakale**, Turk.
93/K5 **Akçakoca**, Turk.
93/J5 **Akçaova**, Turk.
104/D2 **Akçapınar**, Turk.
103/A1 **Akçay**, Turk.
144/B2 **Akchâr** (reg.), Mrta.
100/H5 **Akchatau**, Kaz.
104/C2 **Akdağmadeni**, Turk.
106/G4 **Akdar, Al Jabal** (mts.), Oman
89/J4 **Akdar, Al Jabal al** (mts.), Libya
114/F1 **Ak-Dovurak**, Rus.
111/N9 **Akechi**, Japan
195/G4 **Akeley**, Mn,US
149/G4 **Akelo**, Sudan
72/C4 **Aken**, Ger.
62/H2 **Åkersberga**, Swe.
62/D2 **Akershus** (co.), Nor.
153/E2 **Aketi**, Zaire
97/G4 **Akhalkalaki**, Geo.
97/G4 **Akhaltsikhe**, Geo.
91/H3 **Akharnaí**, Gre.
121/H4 **Akhaura**, Bang.
146/D1 **Akhḍar, Al Jabal al** (mts.), Libya
91/G3 **Akhelóos** (riv.), Gre.
177/H4 **Akhiok**, Ak,US
104/A2 **Akhisar**, Turk.
97/H4 **Akhmeta**, Geo.
147/F3 **Akhmīm**, Egypt
122/C1 **Akhnūr**, India
97/J4 **Akhsu**, Azer.
93/H4 **Akhtopol**, Bul.
97/H3 **Akhtuba** (riv.), Rus.
97/H2 **Akhtubinsk**, Rus.
99/H2 **Akhtyrka**, Ukr.
99/K5 **Akhtyrskiy**, Rus.
110/C4 **Aki**, Japan
111/H7 **Aki** (riv.), Japan
177/F3 **Akiachak**, Ak,US
152/C3 **Akiéni**, Gabon
111/H7 **Akigawa**, Japan
176/J4 **Akimiski** (isl.), Can.
179/H3 **Akimiski** (isl.), NW,Can
99/H4 **Akimovka**, Ukr.
103/D1 **Akıncı** (pt.), Turk.
104/D1 **Akıncılar**, Turk.
191/G3 **Akins**, Ok,US
62/F4 **Åkirkeby**, Den.
111/H7 **Akishima**, Japan
112/B4 **Akita**, Japan
112/B4 **Akita** (dept.), Japan
136/D3 **Akitio**, N.Z.
144/B2 **Akjoujt**, Mrta.
142/C3 **Akka**, Mor.
118/D6 **Akkaraipattu**, SrL.
146/C2 **'Akkārīyah, Bi'r al** (well), Libya
62/C2 **Akkerhaugen**, Nor.
112/D2 **Akkeshi**, Japan
103/D3 **'Akko**, Isr.
66/C2 **Akkrum**, Neth.
97/K2 **Akkystau**, Kaz.
177/L2 **Aklavik**, NW,Can
144/D2 **'Aklé 'Aouâna** (dune), Mali, Mrta.
63/L3 **Aknīste**, Lat.
141/N13 **Aknoul**, Mor.
110/D3 **Akō**, Japan
152/C2 **Akoabas**, Camr.
149/G4 **Akobo**, Sudan
149/G4 **Ākobo Wenz** (riv.), Eth.
152/B2 **Akoga**, Gabon

152/B2 Akok, Gabon
118/C3 Akola, India
152/B2 Akom, Gabon
131/G1 Akoma, PNG
152/B2 Akom II, Camr.
148/B5 Akonolinga, Camr.
149/H2 Āk'ordat, Eth.
104/C2 Akören, Turk.
145/F5 Akosombo (dam), Gha.
149/F4 Akot, Sudan
152/C3 Akou, Gabon
144/E5 Akoupé, IvC.
179/K2 Akpatok (isl.), NW,Can
104/D2 Akpazar, Turk.
93/J5 Akpınar, Turk.
114/C3 Akqi, China
97/K2 Akrab, Kaz.
61/M7 Akranes, Ice.
91/J2 Ákrathos, Ákra (cape), Gre.
62/A2 Åkrehamn, Nor.
89/J3 Akrítas (cape), Gre.
91/G4 Akrítas, Ákra (cape), Gre.
200/D4 Akron, Al,US
192/C3 Akron, Co,US
193/F2 Akron, Ia,US
198/C4 Akron, In,US
198/E3 Akron, Mi,US
197/U9 Akron, NY,US
208/F5 Akron, Oh,US
206/B3 Akron, Pa,US
208/F6 Akron-Canton (reg. arpt.), Oh,US
208/F5 Akron City (res.), Oh,US
103/C2 Akrotiri, Cyp.
114/C4 Aksai Chin (reg.), China, India
95/M5 Aksakovo, Rus.
104/C2 Aksaray, Turk.
104/C2 Aksaray (prov.), Turk.
108/C4 Aksay, China
97/K2 Aksay, Kaz.
99/K4 Aksay, Rus.
104/B2 Akşehir, Turk.
104/B2 Akşehir (lake), Turk.
103/B1 Akseki, Turk.
114/C2 Aksoran (peak), Kaz.
105/F1 Akstafa, Azer.
114/D3 Aksu, China
114/C3 Aksu (riv.), China
114/C2 Aksu (riv.), Kaz.
103/B1 Aksu, Turk.
103/B1 Aksu (riv.), Turk.
95/L5 Aksubayevo, Rus.
149/H2 Āksum, Eth.
100/G6 Aktash, Rus.
100/H4 Aktau, Kaz.
103/E1 Aktepe, Turk.
91/J2 Aktí (pen.), Gre.
114/C2 Aktogay, Kaz.
97/L3 Aktumsyk, Kaz.
97/L2 Aktyubinsk, Kaz.
97/L2 Aktyubinsk (int'l arpt.), Rus.
97/L3 Aktyubinsk Obl., Kaz.
145/G5 Aku, Nga.
152/E2 Akula, Zaire
110/B4 Akune, Japan
145/G5 Akure, Nga.
61/N6 Akureyri, Ice.
145/F5 Akuse, Gha.
177/E5 Akutan, Ak,US
177/E5 Akutan (isl.), Ak,US
177/E5 Akutan (passg.), Ak,US
145/G5 Akwa Ibom (state), Nga.
145/H4 Akwanga, Nga.
108/C4 Akxokesay, China
116/B4 Akyab (Sittwe), Burma
97/L2 Ak"yar, Rus.
93/K5 Akyazı, Turk.
114/D2 Akzhal, Kaz.
62/C1 Ål, Nor.
108/B3 Ala (riv.), China
87/E1 Ala, It.
84/A2 Ala (pt.), It.
181/J5 Alabama (state), US
200/D4 Alabama (riv.), Al,US
189/G2 Alabama & Coushatta Ind. Res., Tx,US
200/D4 Alabaster, Al,US
125/C2 Alabat, Phil.
149/F2 Al 'Abbāsīyah, Sudan
106/D5 Āl 'Ābis, SAr.
104/C1 Alaca, Turk.
104/D2 Alacahan, Turk.
93/J5 Alacalı, Turk.
104/C1 Alaçam, Turk.
91/K3 Alaçatı, Turk.
203/G3 Alachua, Fl,US
161/F1 Alacranes, Embalse (res.), Cuba
103/C1 Aladağ, Turk.
146/D2 Al 'Adam, Libya
76/C2 Alaejos, Sp.
202/L8 Alafia (riv.), Fl,US
202/L8 Alafia, South Prong (riv.), Fl,US
97/H4 Alagir, Rus.
86/A1 Alagna Valsesia, It.
74/E4 Alagnon (riv.), Fr.
167/H4 Alagoa Grande, Braz.
171/F1 Alagoas (state), Braz.
171/F2 Alagoinhas, Braz.
77/E2 Alagón, Sp.
76/B2 Alagón (riv.), Sp.
125/D4 Alah (riv.), Phil.
124/C3 Alahanpanjang, Indo.
105/G4 Al Aḩmadī, Kuw.
106/E3 Al Aḩmadī, Kuw.
61/G3 Alajärvi, Fin.
63/M2 Alajõe, Est.
161/E4 Alajuela, CR
177/F3 Alakanuk, Ak,US
104/D4 Al Akhḑar, SAr.
114/D2 Alakol' (lake), Kaz.
145/G5 Alakuko, Nga.
103/D4 Al 'Āl, Jor.
147/F2 Al 'Alamayn, Egypt
166/B2 Alalapadu, Sur.
166/A3 Alalaú (riv.), Braz.
105/E2 Al 'Amādīyah, Iraq
138/D3 Alamagan (isl.), NMar.
105/F4 Al 'Amārah, Iraq
105/H5 'Alāmarvdasht (riv.), Iran
150/A2 Ālamat'ā, Eth.
194/C3 Alameda, Sk,Can
205/K11 Alameda, Ca,US
205/L11 Alameda (co.), Ca,US
205/L11 Alameda (cr.), Ca,US
187/J3 Alameda, NM,US
161/E3 Alamikamba, Nic.
188/B3 Alamito (cr.), Tx,US
159/F4 Alamo, Mex.
187/F3 Alamo (lake), Az,US
205/K11 Alamo, Ca,US
201/F4 Alamo, Ga,US
188/B1 Alamo (mtn.), NM,US
186/E2 Alamo, Nv,US
200/C3 Alamo, Tn,US
187/J3 Alamo Band Ind. Res., NM,US
190/B4 Alamogordo, NM,US
168/A2 Alamor, Ecu.
158/C2 Álamos, Mex.
158/C3 Álamos, Mex.
190/B2 Alamosa, Co,US
190/B3 Alamosa (cr.), NM,US
187/K2 Alamosa East, Co,US
190/B2 Alamosa Nat'l Wild. Ref., Co,US
189/E3 Alamo, The, Tx,US
188/D3 Alamo Village, Tx,US
104/E3 Al Anbār (gov.), Iraq
63/H1 Åland (isl.), Fin.
61/G3 Åland (isls.), Fin.
72/B2 Aland (riv.), Ger.
125/B4 Alang, Indo.
190/D3 Alanreed, Tx,US
198/D2 Alanson, Mi,US
148/B3 Alantika (mts.), Camr., Nga.
103/C1 Alanya, Turk.
157/J7 Alaotra (lake), Madg.
203/G2 Alapaha, Ga,US
203/G2 Alapaha (riv.), Ga,US
95/P4 Alapayevsk, Rus.
93/K5 Alaplı, Turk.
103/D5 Al 'Aqabah, Jor.
149/E3 Al 'Arab, Baḩr (riv.), Sudan
76/D3 Alarcón (res.), Sp.
103/C4 Al 'Arīsh, Egypt
201/F3 Alarka, NC,US
106/E3 Al Arţāwīyah, SAr.
127/E5 Alas, Indo.
104/B2 Alaşehir, Turk.
105/G3 Alashtar, Iran
103/E3 Al 'Āsimah (gov.), Jor.
177/* Alaska (state), US
177/J4 Alaska (gulf), Ak,US
177/F4 Alaska (pen.), Ak,US
177/H3 Alaska (range), Ak,US
177/B5 Alaska Maritime Nat'l Wild. Ref., Ak,US
177/G4 Alaska Pen. Nat'l Wild. Ref., Ak,US
104/D4 Al 'Assāfīyah, SAr.
86/B5 Alassio, It.
85/D4 Alatri, It.
53/H3 Alatyr', Rus.
97/H4 Alaverdi, Arm.
61/G3 Alavus, Fin.
56/D5 Alaw (riv.), Wal,UK
130/D3 Alawa Ngandi Abor. Land, Austl.
106/E3 Al 'Awdah, SAr.
56/D5 Alaw, Llyn (lake), Wal,UK
106/D3 Al 'Awsajīyah, SAr.
103/D3 'Alayh, Leb.
107/G4 Al 'Ayn, SAr.
107/G4 Al 'Ayn, UAE
76/C3 Alayor, Sp.
114/B4 Alayskiy (mts.), Kyr.
101/R3 Alazeya (riv.), Rus.
105/F3 Al 'Azīzīyah, Iraq
146/B1 Al 'Azīzīyah, Libya
70/B5 Alb (riv.), Ger.
86/B3 Alba, It.
93/F2 Alba (co.), Rom.
191/G4 Alba, Tx,US
85/D2 Alba Adriatica, It.
104/D2 Al Bāb, Syria
76/E3 Albacete, Sp.
76/C2 Alba de Tormes, Sp.
103/B5 Al Badrashayn, Egypt
85/D3 Alba Fucens (ruins), It.
147/G3 Al Baḩr al Aḩmar (gov.), Egypt
77/E3 Albaida, Sp.
86/B2 Albairate, It.
93/F2 Alba Iulia, Rom.
103/B4 Al Bājūr, Egypt
62/D3 Ålbæk, Den.
77/E2 Albalate del Arzobispo, Sp.
103/D3 Al Balqā' (gov.), Jor.
147/G3 Al Balyanā, Egypt
198/F1 Alban, On,Can
167/L7 Albán, Col.
74/E5 Alban, Fr.
83/B2 Albanella, It.
167/M6 Albania, Col.
84/C4 Albano (lake), It.
84/C4 Albano Laziale, It.
132/C5 Albany, Austl.
176/J4 Albany (riv.), Can.
205/K11 Albany, Ca,US
203/F2 Albany, Ga,US
198/D4 Albany, In,US
200/E2 Albany, Ky,US
195/G5 Albany, Mn,US
193/G3 Albany, Mo,US
199/K3 Albany, NY,US
191/F4 Albany, Ok,US
184/B1 Albany, Or,US
188/E1 Albany, Tx,US
199/K3 Albany Co. (int'l arpt.), NY,US
87/E2 Albaredo D'Adige, It.
80/B6 Albarine (riv.), Fr.
76/E2 Albarracín, Sp.
106/E4 Al Barrah, SAr.
105/F4 Al Başrah, Iraq
105/F4 Al Başrah (gov.), Iraq
131/F3 Albatross (bay), Austl.
156/A2 Albatross (pt.), Namb.
136/C2 Albatross (pt.), N.Z.
103/D2 Al Batrūn, Leb.
147/F2 Al Bawīţī, Egypt
146/D1 Al Bayḑā, Libya
150/C2 Al Bayḑā, Yem.
80/E2 Albbruck, Ger.
84/B2 Albegna (riv.), It.
168/J6 Albemarle (pt.), Ecu.
201/G3 Albemarle, NC,US
201/J3 Albemarle (sound), NC,US
75/H4 Alben (peak), It.
86/B4 Albenga, It.
86/C1 Alben, Monte (peak), It.
80/B6 Albens, Fr.
76/C2 Alberche (riv.), Sp.
172/E3 Alberdi, Par.
133/G3 Alberga, Austl.
133/G3 Alberga (cr.), Austl.
128/E5 Alberga (riv.), Austl.
204/C3 Alberhill, Ca,US
81/F3 Alberschwende, Aus.
64/E1 Albersdorf, Ger.
70/B4 Albersweiler, Ger.
135/C2 Albert, Austl.
135/A2 Albert (inlet), Austl.
128/F7 Albert (lake), Austl.
69/E2 Albert (can.), Belg.
68/B4 Albert, Fr.
153/G2 Albert (lake), Ugan., Zaire
190/E1 Albert, Ks,US
178/E3 Alberta (prov.), Can.
200/D4 Alberta, Al,US
202/B1 Alberta, La,US
183/G1 Alberta Beach, Ab,Can
182/F2 Albert Canyon, BC,Can
131/G2 Albert Edward, Mount (peak), PNG
174/E2 Alberti, Arg.
156/C4 Albertinia, SAfr.
92/D2 Albertirsa, Hun.
193/H2 Albert Lea, Mn,US
149/F5 Albert Nile (riv.), Sudan, Ugan.
175/J8 Alberto de Agostini Nat'l Park, Chile
196/E2 Alberton, PE,Can
156/Q13 Alberton, SAfr.
183/G4 Alberton, Mt,US
196/E3 Albert-Riverside, NB,Can
70/D3 Albertshofen, Ger.
183/M1 Albertville, Sk,Can
82/C1 Albertville, Fr.
200/D3 Albertville, Al,US
195/N6 Albertville, Mn,US
69/F6 Albestroff, Fr.
80/D4 Albeuve, Swi.
74/E5 Albi, Fr.
193/H3 Albia, Ia,US
83/C3 Albidona, It.
87/E2 Albignasego, It.
192/B3 Albin, Wy,US
154/A2 Albina (pt.), Ang.
166/C1 Albina, Sur.
86/D3 Albinea, It.
84/B2 Albinia, It.
86/C1 Albino, It.
185/G2 Albion, Id,US
200/C1 Albion, Il,US
198/D4 Albion, In,US
198/D3 Albion, Mi,US
192/E3 Albion, Ne,US
199/G3 Albion, NY,US
198/F4 Albion, Pa,US
208/C2 Albion, RI,US
103/E2 Al Biqā' (gov.), Jor.
103/D3 Al Biqā' (Bekaa) (val.), Leb.
104/D4 Al Bi'r, SAr.
103/D4 Al Bīrah, WBnk.
106/D5 Al Birk, SAr.
146/A3 Al Birkah, Libya
86/B4 Albisola Marina, It.
86/B4 Albisola Superiore, It.
66/B5 Alblasserdam, Neth.
77/E2 Albocácer, Sp.
82/A2 Albon, Fr.
88/C4 Alborán (isl.), Sp.
62/C3 Ålborg, Den.
62/D3 Ålborg (bay), Den.
76/D4 Albox, Sp.
197/T10 Albright Knox Art Gallery, NY,US
58/D1 Albrighton, Eng,UK
80/D5 Albristhorn (peak), Swi.
81/F1 Albstadt, Ger.
76/A4 Albufeira, Port.
103/B4 Al Buḩayrah (gov.), Egypt
81/F4 Albula (riv.), Swi.
81/F4 Albulapass (pass), Swi.
76/D4 Albuñol, Sp.
190/A3 Albuquerque, NM,US
187/J3 Albuquerque (int'l arpt.), NM,US
190/A3 Albuquerque (int'l arpt.), NM,US
107/G4 Al Buraymī, Oman
85/F6 Alburno (peak), It.
76/B3 Alburquerque, Sp.
206/C2 Alburtis, Pa,US
135/C3 Albury, Austl.
136/B4 Albury, N.Z.
150/D2 Al Buzūn, Yem.
63/S7 Alby, Swe.
80/C6 Alby-sur-Chéran, Fr.
168/C4 Alca, Peru
77/P10 Alcabideche, Port.
76/A3 Alcácer do Sal, Port.
167/K7 Alcalá, Col.
77/F2 Alcalá de Chivert, Sp.
76/D4 Alcalá de Guadaira, Sp.
76/D2 Alcalá de Henares, Sp.
76/C4 Alcalá de los Gazules, Sp.
76/D4 Alcalá la Real, Sp.
172/B4 Alcalde (pt.), Chile
90/C4 Alcamo, It.
77/E2 Alcanadre (riv.), Sp.
77/E2 Alcanar, Sp.
76/B2 Alcañices, Sp.
77/E2 Alcañiz, Sp.
167/E3 Alcantara, Braz.
83/A7 Alcantara (riv.), It.
76/B3 Alcántara, Sp.
76/B3 Alcántara (res.), Sp.
167/F3 Alcântaras, Braz.
76/E4 Alcantarilla, Sp.
83/A6 Alcara li Fusi, It.
76/D3 Alcaraz, Sp.
88/C3 Alcaraz (mts.), Sp.
76/D3 Alcaraz (range), Sp.
205/K11 Alcatraz (isl.), Ca,US
76/C4 Alcaudete, Sp.
76/C3 Alcázar de San Juan, Sp.
59/E2 Alcester, Eng,UK
193/F2 Alcester, SD,US
174/D2 Alcira, Arg.
77/E3 Alcira, Sp.
93/K5 Alçıtepe, Turk.
191/H3 Alco, Ar,US
200/F3 Alcoa, Tn,US
171/F3 Alcobaça, Braz.
76/A3 Alcobaça, Port.
76/C2 Alcobendas, Sp.
169/E4 Alcoche, Bol.
77/Q10 Alcochete, Port.
201/G4 Alcolu, SC,US
77/E2 Alcora, Sp.
76/D2 Alcorcón, Sp.
77/E2 Alcorisa, Sp.
76/B4 Alcoutim, Port.
185/K2 Alcova, Wy,US
77/E3 Alcoy, Sp.
73/C5 Alcsútdoboz, Hun.
77/G3 Alcudia, Sp.
141/G5 Aldabra (isls.), Sey.
188/B3 Aldama, Mex.
101/N4 Aldan, Rus.
101/N4 Aldan (plat.), Rus.
101/P3 Aldan (riv.), Rus.
114/G2 Aldarhaan, Mong.
59/E4 Aldbourne, Eng,UK
57/H4 Aldbrough, Eng,UK
59/H2 Alde (riv.), Eng,UK
59/H2 Aldeburgh, Eng,UK
152/C5 Aldeia Formoza, Ang.
76/B4 Aldeia Nova de São Bento, Port.
152/C5 Aldeia Viçosa, Ang.
205/N15 Alden, Il,US
197/U10 Alden, NY,US
69/F2 Aldenhoven, Ger.
87/E1 Aldeno, It.
182/C4 Alder (lake), Wa,US
182/G1 Alder Flats, Ab,Can
56/B2 Aldergrove, NI,UK
57/F5 Alderley Edge, Eng,UK
59/E4 Aldermaston, Eng,UK
78/C1 Alderney (isl.), Chl,UK
78/C1 Alderney (The Blaye) (arpt.), Chl,UK
184/B3 Alderpoint, Ca,US
56/B2 Aldersgrove (Belfast) (int'l arpt.), NI,UK
197/R9 Aldershot, On,Can
59/F4 Aldershot, Eng,UK
201/G2 Alderson, WV,US
183/H2 Aldersyde, Ab,Can
205/C2 Alderwood Manor-Bothell North, Wa,US
189/G3 Aldine, Tx,US
70/B6 Aldingen, Ger.
206/B4 Aldred (lake), Pa,US
59/E1 Aldridge, Eng,UK
193/J3 Aledo, Il,US
188/K7 Aledo, Tx,US
144/B2 Aleg, Mrta.
171/E4 Alegre, Braz.
173/F3 Alegrete, Braz.
169/E4 Alejandria, Bol.
175/G2 Alejandro Gallinal, Uru.
174/E2 Alejandro Roca, Arg.
163/A6 Alejandro Selkirk (isl.), Chile
174/E2 Alejo Ledesma, Arg.
177/G4 Aleknagik, Ak,US
99/G3 Aleksandriya, Ukr.
96/G1 Aleksandro-Nevskiy, Rus.
94/H4 Aleksandrov, Rus.
92/E4 Aleksandrovac, Yugo.
97/J2 Aleksandrov Gay, Rus.
99/K4 Aleksandrovka, Rus.
98/G3 Aleksandrovka, Ukr.
95/N4 Aleksandrovsk, Rus.
97/G3 Aleksandrovskoye, Rus.
109/N1 Aleksandrovsk-Sakhalinskiy, Rus.
65/K2 Aleksandrów Kujawski, Pol.
65/K3 Aleksandrów Łódzki, Pol.
114/B1 Alekseyevka, Kaz.
99/K2 Alekseyevka, Rus.
94/H5 Aleksin, Rus.
92/E4 Aleksinac, Yugo.
152/B3 Alembé, Gabon
105/N6 Alemdar, Turk.
150/B3 Alem Maya, Eth.
171/E4 Além Paraíba, Braz.
79/F4 Alençon, Fr.
166/C3 Alenquer, Braz.
83/B2 Alento (riv.), It.
85/E3 Alento (riv.), It.
180/T10 Alenuihaha (chan.), Hi,US
144/E5 Alépé, IvC.
103/E1 Aleppo (Ḩalab), Syria
174/B4 Alerce Andino Nat'l Park, Chile
90/A1 Aléria, Fr.
179/S6 Alert (pt.), NW,Can
92/F2 Aleşd, Rom.
86/B3 Alessandria, It.
86/B3 Alessandria (prov.), It.
62/C3 Ålestrup, Den.
61/C3 Ålesund, Nor.
80/D5 Aletschhorn (peak), Swi.
177/E5 Aleutian (isls.), Ak,US
177/G4 Aleutian (range), Ak,US
54/D6 Ale Water (riv.), Sc,UK
191/F3 Alex, Ok,US
137/V Alexander (cape), Ant.
137/V Alexander (isl.), Ant.
132/B2 Alexander (peak), Austl.
131/E3 Alexander (pt.), Austl.
177/L4 Alexander (arch.), Ak,US
194/C4 Alexander, ND,US
189/E1 Alexander, Tx,US
156/B3 Alexander Bay, SAfr.
200/E4 Alexander City, Al,US
197/G2 Alexander Graham Bell Nat'l Hist. Park, NS,Can
136/B4 Alexandra, N.Z.
156/D3 Alexandra, SAfr.
131/E4 Alexandria, Austl.
167/G4 Alexandria, Braz.
182/C1 Alexandria, BC,Can
140/E1 Alexandria, Egypt
147/F2 Alexandria (int'l arpt.), Egypt
103/A4 Alexandria (int'l arpt.), Egypt
91/H2 Alexándria, Gre.
93/G4 Alexandria, Rom.
155/D4 Alexandria, SAfr.
54/B5 Alexandria, Sc,UK
198/D4 Alexandria, In,US
200/E1 Alexandria, Ky,US
202/B2 Alexandria, La,US
195/G5 Alexandria, Mn,US
193/F3 Alexandria, Ne,US
192/F2 Alexandria, SD,US
206/A6 Alexandria, Va,US
103/A4 Alexandria (Al Iskandarīyah), Egypt
199/J2 Alexandria Bay, NY,US
135/A2 Alexandrina (inlet), Austl.
128/F7 Alexandrina (lake), Austl.
91/J2 Alexandroúpolis, Gre.
154/C4 Alexeck (dry riv.), Namb.
193/J3 Alexis, Il,US
182/C1 Alexis Creek, BC,Can
131/G1 Alexishafen, PNG
114/D1 Aley (riv.), Rus.
114/D1 Aleysk, Rus.
77/E3 Alfafar, Sp.
105/E3 Al Fallūjah, Iraq
77/P10 Alfama, Port.
141/W17 Al Fanānahl, Tun.
150/D2 Al Farḑah, Yem.
77/P11 Alfarim, Port.
76/E1 Alfaro, Sp.
149/E2 Al Fāsher, Sudan
147/F2 Al Fashn, Egypt
93/H4 Alfatar, Bul.
105/E3 Al Fatḩah, Iraq
105/G4 Al Fāw, Iraq
143/H2 Al Fawwār, Tun.
103/B5 Al Fayyūm, Egypt
147/F2 Al Fayyūm (gov.), Egypt
150/B2 Al Fāzah, Yem.
69/F3 Alfbach (riv.), Ger.
67/G5 Alfeld, Ger.
170/D4 Alfenas, Braz.
67/E4 Alfhausen, Ger.
149/E3 Al Fifi, Sudan
91/G4 Alfiós (riv.), Gre.
87/F4 Alfonsine, It.
164/B4 Alfonso Bonilla Aragon (int'l arpt.), Col.
57/J5 Alford, Eng,UK
54/D2 Alford, Sc,UK
203/F2 Alford, Fl,US
208/A1 Alford, Ma,US
182/B2 Alfred (mtn.), BC,Can
196/B4 Alfred, Me,US
199/H3 Alfred, NY,US
135/D3 Alfred Nat'l Park, Austl.
57/G5 Alfreton, Eng,UK
59/G5 Alfriston, Eng,UK
69/G2 Alfter, Ger.
146/C1 Al Fugahā', Libya
105/F4 Al Fuhūd, Iraq
107/G3 Al Fujayrah, UAE
149/F3 Al Fūlah, Sudan
97/L2 Alga, Kaz.
97/K2 Algabas, Kaz.
62/A2 Ålgård, Nor.
172/B4 Algarrobito, Chile
174/Q9 Algarrobo, Chile
164/C4 Algeciras, Col.
76/C4 Algeciras, Sp.
77/E3 Algemesí, Sp.
141/S15 Alger (wilaya), Alg.
198/D2 Alger, Mi,US
141/S15 Alger (Algiers) (cap.), Alg.
143/F3 Algeria
67/G4 Algermissen, Ger.
77/N8 Algete, Sp.
105/F4 Al Ghammās, Iraq
147/F2 Al Gharbīyah (gov.), Egypt
106/E3 Al Ghāţ, SAr.
106/F5 Al Ghayḑah, Yem.
106/E4 Al Ghayl, SAr.
149/F3 Al Ghazāl, Baḩr (riv.), Sudan
90/A2 Alghero, It.
147/G3 Al Ghurdaqah, Egypt
141/S15 Algiers (Alger) (cap.), Alg.
77/E3 Alginet, Sp.
156/D4 Algoa (bay), SAfr.
189/M9 Algoa, Tx,US
164/C5 Algodón (riv.), Peru
76/C4 Algodonales, Sp.
200/C3 Algoma, Ms,US
184/C2 Algoma, Or,US
193/L1 Algoma, Wi,US
193/G2 Algona, Ia,US
205/C3 Algona, Wa,US
205/G6 Algonac, Mi,US
205/P15 Algonquin, Il,US
199/K2 Algonquin (peak), NY,US
200/E2 Algood, Tn,US
175/F2 Algorta, Uru.
77/P10 Algueirão, Port.
81/H4 Algund (Lagundo), It.
104/E3 Al Ḩaddār, SAr.
104/E3 Al Ḩadīthah, Iraq
103/E4 Al Ḩadīthah, SAr.
105/E3 Al Ḩaḑr, Iraq
103/E2 Al Ḩaffah, Syria
107/G4 Al Ḩajar ash Sharqī (mts.), Oman
150/D2 Al Ḩajarayn, Yem.
107/G5 Al Ḩallānīyah (isl.), Oman
76/D4 Alhama de Granada, Sp.
76/E4 Alhama de Murcia, Sp.
106/E4 Al Ḩamar, SAr.
204/B2 Alhambra, Ca,US
200/C1 Alhambra, Il,US
106/B5 Al Ḩamdah, Sudan
143/H2 Al Ḩammah, Tun.
147/F2 Al Ḩammām, Egypt
141/X17 Al Ḩammāmāt, Tun.
147/H4 Al Ḩamrā', SAr.
106/D4 Al Ḩanākīyah, SAr.
167/H4 Alhandra, Braz.
77/Q10 Alhandra, Port.
146/D1 Al Ḩanīyah, Libya
105/F4 Al Ḩārithah, Iraq
104/E2 Al Ḩasakah, Syria
104/E2 Al Ḩasakah (prov.), Syria
76/C4 Alhaurín el Grande, Sp.
103/B5 Al Ḩawāmidīyah, Egypt
149/G2 Al Ḩawātah, Sudan
150/C2 Al Ḩawrah, Yem.
106/E3 Al Ḩawţah, SAr.
150/D2 Al Ḩawţah, Yem.
105/F3 Al Ḩayy, Iraq
104/E4 Al Ḩayyānīyah, SAr.
105/F3 Al Ḩillah, Iraq
106/E4 Al Ḩillah, SAr.
149/E2 Al Ḩillah, Sudan
105/F3 Al Ḩindīyah, Iraq
103/E2 Al Ḩirmil, Leb.
141/N13 Al Hoceima, Mor.
141/N13 Al Hoceima (isl.), Sp.
141/N13 Al Hoceima (Côte du Rif) (int'l arpt.), Mor.
150/B2 Al Ḩudaydah, Yem.
106/E3 Al Ḩufūf, SAr.
106/E4 Al Ḩulwah, SAr.
150/C2 Al Ḩumayshah, Yem.
150/D2 Al Ḩuraydah, Yem.
149/G2 Al Ḩuşayḩişah, Sudan
150/C2 Al Ḩuwaymī, Yem.
106/D3 Al Ḩuwayyiţ, SAr.
141/X17 Al Ḩuwwārīyah, Tun.
90/C4 Alia, It.
76/C3 Alía, Sp.
105/H4 'Alī 'Ābād, Iran
145/H5 Aliade, Nga.
104/A2 Aliağa, Turk.
91/G2 Aliákmon (riv.), Gre.
91/G2 Aliákmonos (lake), Gre.
105/F3 'Alī al Gharbī, Iraq
91/H3 Alíartos, Gre.
105/F3 'Alī ash Sharqī, Iraq
97/J5 Ali-Bayramly, Azer.
149/G1 Al Ibēdiyya, Sudan
105/M6 Alibey (riv.), Turk.
98/F5 Alibey (lake), Ukr.
93/J5 Alibeyköy, Turk.
149/H3 Ālībo, Eth.
77/E3 Alicante, Sp.
77/E3 Alicante (int'l arpt.), Sp.
134/A1 Alice (riv.), Austl.
83/D4 Alice (pt.), It.
156/D4 Alice, SAfr.
189/E4 Alice, Tx,US
134/A1 Alice & Mitchell Rivers Nat'l Park, Austl.
177/N4 Alice Arm, BC,Can
133/G2 Alice Springs, Austl.
200/C4 Aliceville, Al,US
200/C4 Aliceville (dam), Al,US
200/C4 Aliceville (lake), Al, Ms,US
125/C4 Alicia, Phil.
191/J3 Alicia, Ar,US
83/A5 Alicudi (isl.), It.
85/E5 Alife, It.
120/B2 Alīganj, India
120/B2 Alīgarh, India
106/E2 Alīgudarz, Iran
172/C4 Alijilán, Arg.
76/B2 Alijó, Port.
119/F3 Alīkadam, Bang.
152/C3 Alima (riv.), Congo
62/E3 Alingsås, Swe.
118/B2 Alīpur, Pak.
121/G2 Alīpur Duār, India
208/G6 Aliquippa, Pa,US
107/K4 Alīrājpur, India
150/C2 Al 'Irqah, Yem.
150/B3 Ali Sabieh, Djib.
103/A4 Al Iskandarīyah (gov.), Egypt
105/F3 Al Iskandarīyah, Iraq
103/A4 Al Iskandarīyah (Alexandria), Egypt
101/S3 Aliskerovo, Rus.
103/B4 Al Ismā'īlīyah (gov.), Egypt
103/C4 Al Ismā'īlīyah (Ismailia), Egypt
158/C2 Alisos (riv.), Mex.
91/H2 Alistráti, Gre.
83/B6 Ali Terme, It.
91/J3 Alivérion, Gre.
156/D3 Aliwal North, SAfr.
183/H1 Alix, Ab,Can
82/B3 Alixan, Fr.
149/G2 Al Jabalayn, Sudan
146/E2 Al Jaghbūb, Libya
146/B1 Al Jamīl, Libya
141/X18 Al Jamm, Tun.
150/C2 Al Janad (int'l arpt.), Yem.
103/D3 Al Janūb (gov.), Jor.
107/G5 Al Jawārah, Oman
146/D3 Al Jawf, Libya
104/D4 Al Jawf, SAr.
78/A4 Aljezur, Port.
88/F4 Al Jifārah (plain), Alg., Tun.
146/A1 Al Jifārah (plain), Libya, Tun.
106/E4 Al Jifārah, SAr.
103/B4 Al Jīzah, Egypt
103/B5 Al Jīzah (gov.), Egypt
105/G5 Al Jubayl, SAr.
106/D4 Al Junaynah, SAr.
148/D2 Al Junaynah, Sudan
76/A4 Aljustrel, Port.
141/W17 Al Kāf, Tun.
141/W17 Al Kāf (gov.), Tun.
105/E5 Al Kahfah, SAr.
182/C2 Alkali Lake, BC,Can
107/G4 Al Kāmil, Oman
103/E4 Al Karak, Jor.
103/E4 Al Karak (gov.), Jor.
141/W17 Al Karīb, Tun.
147/G3 Al Karnak, Egypt
150/C2 Al Kawd, Yem.
69/E2 Alken, Belg.
106/D3 Al Khabrā', SAr.
107/G4 Al Khābūrah, Oman
103/D4 Al Khalīl (Hebron), WBnk.
105/F3 Al Khāliş, Iraq
147/F5 Al Khandaq, Sudan
103/B4 Al Khānkah, Egypt
97/H4 Alkhan-Kala, Rus.
147/F3 Al Khārijah, Egypt
107/F3 Al Kharrārah, Qatar
105/F4 Al Khiḑr, Iraq
106/F3 Al Khobar, SAr.
146/B1 Al Khums, Libya
150/D2 Al Khuraybah, Yem.
106/D4 Al Khurmah, SAr.
149/G2 Al Khurţūm Baḩrī (Khartoum North), Sudan
149/G2 Al Khurţūm (Khartoum) (cap.), Sudan
66/B3 Alkmaar, Neth.
105/E3 Al Kūfah, Iraq
146/D3 Al Kufrah, Libya
105/F3 Al Kūt, Iraq
149/E2 Alku, Wādī (dry riv.), Sudan
105/F4 Al Kuwayt (Kuwait) (cap.), Kuw.
145/F5 Allada, Ben.
103/D2 Al Lādhiqīyah (dist.), Syria
103/D2 Al Lādhiqīyah (Latakia), Syria
196/C2 Allagash (riv.), Me,US
149/F3 Al Lagowa, Sudan
120/C3 Allahabad, India
120/C3 Allahabad (arpt.), India
78/C5 Allaire, Fr.
177/H2 Allakaket, Ak,US
101/P3 Allakh-Yun', Rus.
80/C5 Allaman, Swi.
186/E4 All-American (can.), Ca,US
206/D2 Allamuchy St. Park, NJ,US
194/A2 Allan, Sk,Can
194/A2 Allan (hills), Sk,Can
197/S9 Allanburg, On,Can
116/B5 Allanmyo, Burma
156/D2 Allanridge, SAfr.
132/C5 Allanson, Austl.
195/J2 Allan Water, On,Can
146/B2 Allāq, Bi'r (well), Libya
147/G4 'Allāqī, Wādī al (dry riv.), Egypt
106/B4 'Allāqī, Wādī al (dry riv.), Egypt
76/B1 Allariz, Sp.
83/C6 Allaro (riv.), It.
200/E3 Allatoona (lake), Ga,US
201/L6 Allatoona (lake), Ga,US
82/B6 Allauch, Fr.
155/F4 Alldays, SAfr.
80/D3 Alle, Swi.
198/D3 Allegan, Mi,US
199/G3 Allegany, NY,US
208/G6 Allegheny (plat.), US
199/G4 Allegheny (riv.), US
208/G6 Allegheny (co.), Pa,US
199/G4 Allegheny Portage Railroad Nat'l Hist. Site, Pa,US
174/D3 Allen, Arg.
136/B4 Allen (peak), N.Z.
58/B5 Allen (riv.), Eng,UK
193/F2 Allen, Ne,US
191/F3 Allen, Ok,US
189/F1 Allen, Tx,US
60/C3 Allen, Bog of (swamp), Ire.
57/F2 Allendale, Eng,UK
198/D3 Allendale, Mi,US
207/J7 Allendale, NJ,US
201/G4 Allendale, SC,US
188/D3 Allende, Mex.
67/F6 Allendorf, Ger.
53/N7 All England Lawn Tennis Club, Eng,UK
201/G5 Allenhurst, Ga,US
60/B1 Allen, Lough (lake), Ire.
205/F7 Allen Park, Mi,US
81/F2 Allensbach, Ger.
208/C2 Allenton, RI,US
206/C2 Allentown, Pa,US
206/C2 Allentown-Bethlehem-Easton (arpt.), Pa,US
65/H4 Allentsteig, Aus.
206/B1 Allenwood, Pa,US
122/F4 Alleppey, India
67/G3 Aller (riv.), Ger.
67/H4 Allerkanal (can.), Ger.
70/E4 Allersberg, Ger.
71/E6 Allershausen, Ger.
208/D1 Allerton (pt.), Ma,US
82/C2 Allevard, Fr.
82/A3 Allex, Fr.
81/G3 Allgäu (mts.), Aus., Ger.
83/C4 Alli (riv.), It.
183/J1 Alliance, Ab,Can
201/J3 Alliance, NC,US
192/C2 Alliance, Ne,US
208/F6 Alliance, Oh,US
106/D4 Al Līdām, SAr.
123/B2 Allied War Cemetery, Burma
74/E3 Allier (riv.), Fr.
131/F4 Alligator (pt.), Austl.
203/H3 Alligator (lake), Fl,US
201/K3 Alligator River (inlet), NC,US
62/D3 Allingåbro, Den.
80/C5 Allinges, Fr.
131/E4 Allingham, Austl.
193/H2 Allison, Ia,US
208/H6 Allison Park, Pa,US
199/G2 Alliston, On,Can
106/D4 Al Līth, SAr.
54/C4 Alloa, Sc,UK
79/F5 Allones, Fr.
79/F6 Allonnes, Fr.
200/E2 Allons, Tn,US
134/C5 Allora, Austl.
82/C4 Allos, Fr.
195/K5 Allouez, Wi,US
60/B5 Allow (riv.), Ire.
206/C4 Alloway, NJ,US
206/C4 Alloway (cr.), NJ,US
80/D2 Allschwil, Swi.
72/B5 Allstedt, Ger.
150/B2 Al Luḩayyah, Yem.
199/H2 Allumettes (isl.), Qu,Can
84/B3 Allumiere, It.
202/D3 Alluvial City, La,US
205/B3 Allyn, Wa,US
205/B3 Allyn-Grapeview, Wa,US
71/G7 Alm (riv.), Aus.
196/E3 Alma, NB,Can
196/B1 Alma, Qu,Can
191/G3 Alma, Ar,US
190/A1 Alma, Co,US
203/G2 Alma, Ga,US
191/F1 Alma, Ks,US
198/D3 Alma, Mi,US
192/E3 Alma, Ne,US
187/H4 Alma, NM,US
199/G3 Alma (hill), NY,US
193/J1 Alma, Wi,US
114/C3 Alma-Ata (cap.), Kaz.
77/F2 Almacelles, Sp.
76/A3 Almada, Port.
76/C3 Almadén, Sp.
104/B5 Al Madīnah al Fikrīyah, Egypt
147/H3 Al Madīnah (Medina), SAr.
143/H2 Al Madīyah, Tun.
90/B5 Al Madīyah (gov.), Tun.
103/E3 Al Mafraq, Jor.
174/D2 Almafuerte, Arg.
150/C2 Al Maghārīm, Yem.
142/E2 Al Maghrib (reg.), Alg., Mor.
76/D3 Almagro, Sp.
103/B4 Al Maḩallah al Kubrá, Egypt
141/X18 Al Mahdiyah, Tun.
141/X18 Al Mahdiyah (gov.), Tun.
141/X18 Al Mahdīyīn, Tun.
103/B4 Al Maḩmūdīyah, Egypt
105/F3 Al Maḩmūdīyah, Iraq
106/E3 Al Majma'ah, SAr.
149/F3 Al Malaṃm, Sudan
104/E2 Al Mālikīyah, Syria
149/F1 Al Malik, Wādī (dry riv.), Sudan
114/A3 Almalyk, Uzb.
106/F3 Al Manāmah (Manama) (cap.), Bahr.
149/G2 Al Manaqīl, Sudan
184/C3 Almanor (lake), Ca,US
77/E3 Almansa, Sp.
103/B4 Al Mansūra, Egypt
76/C1 Almanza, Sp.
103/B4 Al Manzilah, Egypt
76/D4 Almanzora (riv.), Sp.
76/C2 Almanzor, Pico de (peak), Sp.
146/D2 Al Maqrūn, Libya
147/F3 Al Marāghah, Egypt
146/D1 Al Marj, Libya
141/X17 Al Marsá, Tun.
191/H2 Almartha, Mo,US
170/D1 Almas, Braz.
170/C2 Almas (riv.), Braz.
149/G2 Al Masīd, Sudan
73/C4 Almásneszmély, Hun.
171/E2 Almas, Pico das (peak), Braz.
149/G1 Al Matammah, Sudan
103/C4 Al Maţarīyah, Egypt
149/G2 Al Matnah, Sudan
105/E2 Al Mawşil (Mosul), Iraq
104/E3 Al Mayādin, Syria
76/D2 Almazán, Sp.
101/M3 Almaznyy, Rus.
77/E3 Almazora, Sp.
103/D4 Al Mazra'ah, Jor.
67/F5 Alme (riv.), Ger.
76/B2 Almeida, Port.
166/C3 Almeirim, Braz.
76/A3 Almeirim, Port.
66/D4 Almelo, Neth.
190/E1 Almena, Ks,US
171/E3 Almenara, Braz.
77/E3 Almenara, Sp.
76/D3 Almenara (mtn.), Sp.
76/B2 Almendra (res.), Sp.
76/B3 Almendralejo, Sp.
66/C4 Almere, Neth.
76/D4 Almería, Sp.
77/D4 Almeria (gulf), Sp.
82/D2 Almese, It.
53/J3 Al'met'yevsk, Rus.
62/F3 Älmhult, Swe.
106/D3 Al Midhnab, SAr.
143/H2 Al Miknāsī, Tun.
103/D2 Al Mīnā', Leb.
141/M13 Almina (pt.), Mor.
76/C5 Almina (pt.), Sp.
106/D4 Al Mindak, SAr.
103/B4 Al Minūfīyah (gov.), Egypt
147/F2 Al Minyā, Egypt
147/F3 Al Minyā (gov.), Egypt
105/F3 Al Miqdādiyah, Iraq
182/E4 Almira, Wa,US
175/J7 Almirante Montt (gulf), Chile
91/H3 Almirós, Gre.
91/J5 Almiroú (gulf), Gre.
185/G2 Almo, Id,US
76/A4 Almodôvar, Port.
76/C3 Almodóvar del Campo, Sp.
76/C4 Almodóvar del Río, Sp.
76/B3 Almoharín, Sp.
54/C4 Almond (riv.), Sc,UK
53/U11 Almont (riv.), Fr.
190/A1 Almont, Co,US
205/F6 Almont, Mi,US
194/D4 Almont, ND,US
199/H2 Almonte, On,Can
76/B4 Almonte, Sp.
120/B1 Almora, India
77/E3 Almoradi, Sp.
76/C2 Almorox, Sp.
106/E3 Al Mubarraz, SAr.
104/C4 Al Mudawwarah, Jor.
77/E1 Almudévar, Sp.
149/E3 Al Muglad, Sudan
141/X17 Al Muḩammadīyah, Tun.
150/D2 Al Mukallā, Yem.
141/X18 Al Muknīn, Tun.
141/X18 Al Munastīr, Tun.
141/X18 Al Munastīr (gov.), Tun.
76/D4 Almuñécar, Sp.
141/X17 Al Murnāqīyah, Tun.
104/D1 Almus, Turk.
149/G2 Al Musallamīyah, Sudan
147/H3 Al Musayjīd, SAr.
105/F3 Al Musayyib, Iraq
105/F4 Al Muthanná (gov.), Iraq
150/B1 Al Muwassam, SAr.
106/D4 Al Muwayh, SAr.
104/C5 Al Muwayliḩ, SAr.
54/B1 Alness, Sc,UK
54/B1 Alness (riv.), Sc,UK
55/L9 Alnwick, Eng,UK
139/J6 Alofi (cap.), Niue
138/H6 Alofi (isl.), Wall.
182/C5 Aloha, Or,US
153/H2 Aloi, Ugan.
63/L3 Aloja, Lat.
94/C3 Ålond (isl.), Fin.
116/B2 Along, India
109/J1 Alongshan, China
91/H3 Alónnisos (isl.), Gre.
194/E2 Alonsa, Mb,Can
130/B2 Alor (isl.), Indo.
130/B2 Alor (isls.), Indo.
76/C4 Álora, Sp.
124/C2 Alor Gajah, Malay.
124/C1 Alor Setar, Malay.
138/E6 Alotau, PNG
133/F3 Aloysius (peak), Austl.
174/E3 Alpachiri, Arg.
186/C3 Alpaugh, Ca,US
87/E6 Alpe di Poti (peak), It.
86/D4 Alpe di Succiso (peak), It.
66/D5 Alpen, Ger.
198/E2 Alpena, Mi,US
192/E1 Alpena, SD,US
167/E4 Alpercatas (mts.), Braz.
81/F4 Alperschällihorn (peak), Swi.
82/C4 Alpes-de-Haute-Provence (dept.), Fr.
82/D5 Alpes-Maritimes (dept.), Fr.
134/B3 Alpha, Austl.
136/J8 Alpha (mt.), N.Z.
193/J3 Alpha, Il,US
206/C2 Alpha, NJ,US
201/M6 Alpharetta, Ga,US
66/B4 Alphen aan de Rijn, Neth.
76/A3 Alpiarça, Port.
86/A2 Alpignano, It.
187/H4 Alpine, Az,US
207/K8 Alpine, NJ,US
188/C2 Alpine, Tx,US
185/H2 Alpine, Wy,US
205/D2 Alpine Wild. Area, Wa,US
70/B6 Alpirsbach, Ger.
104/D2 Alpköy, Turk.
81/E4 Alpnach, Swi.
76/B4 Alportel, Port.
75/G4 Alps (mts.), Eur.
111/F3 Alps-Minami Nat'l Park, Japan
104/B2 Alpu, Turk.
107/G4 Al Qābil, Oman
147/H4 Al Qaḑīmah, SAr.
149/G2 Al Qaḑīrif, Sudan
105/F4 Al Qādisīyah (gov.), Iraq
103/E2 Al Qadmūs, Syria
103/B4 Al Qāhirah (gov.), Egypt
103/B4 Al Qāhirah (Cairo) (cap.), Egypt
106/D5 Al Qaḩmah, SAr.
104/E3 Al Qā'im, Iraq
143/H2 Al Qal'ah Al Kubrá, Tun.
104/D4 Al Qalībah, SAr.
103/B4 Al Qalyūbīyah (gov.), Egypt
104/E2 Al Qāmishlī, Syria
103/B4 Al Qanāţir al Khayrīyah, Egypt
103/C4 Al Qantarah, Egypt
146/B2 Al Qaryah al Sharqīyah, Libya
146/B2 Al Qaryāt, Libya
103/E2 Al Qaryatayn, Syria
146/D1 Al Qarẕabah, Libya
146/B1 Al Qaşabāt, Libya
105/F3 Al Qāsim, Iraq
147/F3 Al Qaşr, Egypt
103/D4 Al Qaşr, Jor.
141/W18 Al Qaşrayn, Tun.
141/W18 Al Qaşrayn (gov.), Tu
149/G2 Al Qaţaynah, Sudan
106/F3 Al Qaţīf, SAr.
146/B3 Al Qaţrūn, Libya
141/X18 Al Qayrawān, Tun.
141/W18 Al Qayrawān (gov.), Tun.
105/F4 Al Qayşūmah, SAr.
105/E2 Alqōsh, Iraq
146/D1 Al Qubbah, Libya
103/D3 Al Qunayţirah, Syria
103/D3 Al Qunayţirah (dist.), Syria
104/C3 Al Qunaytirah (prov.), Syria
106/D5 Al Qunfudhah, SAr.
105/F4 Al Qurnah, Iraq
147/G3 Al Quşayr, Egypt
103/E2 Al Quşayr, Syria
141/W18 Al Quşūr, Tun.
103/E3 Al Quţayfah, Syria
146/D2 Al Quway'id (well), Libya
106/E4 Al Quway'īyah, SAr.
103/D5 Al Quwayrah, Jor.
59/E1 Alrewas, Eng,UK
131/E4 Alroy Downs, Austl.
62/C4 Als (isl.), Den.
80/D2 Alsace (hist. reg.), Fr
69/G6 Alsace (reg.), Fr.
64/D5 Alsace, Ballon d' (mtn.), Fr.
57/F5 Alsager, Eng,UK
183/K2 Alsask, Sk,Can
76/D1 Alsasua, Sp.
69/F2 Alsdorf, Ger.
184/A1 Alsea (bay), Or,US
70/A3 Alsenz, Ger.
70/A3 Alsenz (riv.), Ger.
64/E3 Alsfeld, Ger.
70/B3 Alsheim, Ger.
205/Q16 Alsip, Il,US
72/B4 Alsleben, Ger.
73/C5 Alsóörs, Hun.
92/E1 Alsózsolca, Hun.
199/K3 Alstead, NH,US
67/H1 Alster (riv.), Ger.
69/F5 Alsting, Fr.
57/F2 Alston, Eng,UK
135/E1 Alstonville, Austl.
63/J3 Alsunga, Lat.
57/F4 Alt (riv.), Eng,UK
61/G1 Alta, Nor.
136/B4 Alta (peak), N.Z.
63/S7 Ålta, Swe.
193/G2 Alta, Ia,US
81/F3 Altach, Aus.
204/B2 Altadena, Ca,US
170/A1 Alta Floresta, Braz.
174/D1 Alta Gracia, Arg.
161/E4 Alta Gracia, Nic.
167/O8 Altagracia de Orituc Ven.
114/D1 Altai (mts.), Asia
73/C4 Által-ér (riv.), Hun.
203/H2 Altamaha (riv.), Ga,U
166/C3 Altamira, Braz.
172/B3 Altamira, Chile
159/F4 Altamira, Mex.
167/E4 Altamira do Maranhão, Braz.
194/E3 Altamont, Mb,Can
193/K4 Altamont, Il,US
191/G2 Altamont, Ks,US
184/C2 Altamont, Or,US
200/E3 Altamont, Tn,US
202/N6 Altamonte Springs, Fl,US
203/H3 Altamonte Springs, Fl,US
90/E2 Altamura, It.
158/C3 Altamura (isl.), Mex.
164/B5 Altar (vol.), Ecu.
158/C2 Altar, Mex.
187/G5 Altar (wash), Az,US
160/D2 Altar de los Sacrificios (ruins), Guat.
86/B4 Altare, It.
183/J2 Altario, Ab,Can
85/E6 Altavilla Irpina, It.
85/F6 Altavilla Silentina, It
87/E1 Altavilla Vicentina,
191/F1 Alta Vista, Ks,US
201/H2 Altavista, Va,US
108/B2 Altay, China
108/B2 Altay, Mong.
108/C3 Altay, Mong.
108/D2 Altay, Mong.
100/J4 Altay Kray, Rus.
81/E4 Altdorf, Swi.
71/E4 Altdorf bei Nürnberg Ger.
77/E3 Altea, Sp.
87/E3 Altedo, It.
72/B3 Alte Elbe (riv.), Ger.
72/B1 Alte Elde (riv.), Ger.
67/E6 Altena, Ger.
69/G2 Altenahr, Ger.
67/H5 Altenau, Ger.
67/F5 Altenau (riv.), Ger.
67/F5 Altenbeken, Ger.
72/D6 Altenberg, Ger.
71/H6 Altenberg bei Linz, Aus.
72/C6 Altenburg, Ger.
193/K5 Altenburg, Mo,US
71/G6 Altenfelden, Aus.
69/G4 Altenglan, Ger.
67/H6 Altengottern, Ger.
69/G2 Altenkirchen, Ger.
70/D6 Altenmünster, Ger.
70/B2 Altenstadt, Ger.
70/D6 Altenstadt, Ger.
70/B5 Altensteig, Ger.
65/G2 Altentreptow, Ger.
72/B4 Altenweddingen, Ge

72/E2 **Alte Oder** (riv.), Ger.
159/F5 **Altepexi**, Mex.
166/C3 **Alter do Chão**, Braz.
76/B3 **Alter do Chão**, Port.
158/E2 **Alteres**, Mex.
66/D5 **Alter Rhein** (riv.), Ger.
67/G1 **Altes Land** (reg.), Ger.
72/B4 **Alte Wipper** (riv.), Ger.
203/F2 **Altha**, Fl,US
71/G6 **Altheim**, Aus.
70/C6 **Altheim**, Ger.
191/J3 **Altheimer**, Ar,US
70/B5 **Althengstett**, Ger.
75/L3 **Althofen**, Aus.
57/H4 **Althorpe**, Eng,UK
70/C5 **Althütte**, Ger.
183/L1 **Alticane**, Sk,Can
104/D1 **Altındere Milli Park**, Turk.
170/D4 **Altinópolis**, Braz.
103/E1 **Altınözü**, Turk.
104/B2 **Altıntaş**, Turk.
103/B1 **Altınyaka**, Turk.
103/A1 **Altınyayla**, Turk.
168/D4 **Altiplano** (plat.), Bol., Peru
80/D2 **Altkirch**, Fr.
72/B2 **Altmark** (reg.), Ger.
71/E5 **Altmühl** (riv.), Ger.
71/G7 **Altmünster**, Aus.
170/D2 **Alto** (peak), Braz.
84/B1 **Alto** (peak), It.
87/E2 **Alto** (riv.), It.
201/F3 **Alto**, Ga,US
189/J1 **Alto**, La,US
189/G2 **Alto**, Tx,US
188/B2 **Alto** (mtn.), Tx,US
170/B3 **Alto Araguaia**, Braz.
152/D5 **Alto Chicapa**, Ang.
152/D4 **Alto Cuale**, Ang.
152/D5 **Alto Cuilo**, Ang.
172/D2 **Alto de la Sierra**, Arg.
172/B4 **Alto del Carmen**, Chile
161/H5 **Alto de Tamar** (peak), Col.
170/B3 **Alto Garças**, Braz.
167/F4 **Alto Longá**, Braz.
159/N7 **Alto Lucero**, Mex.
155/H2 **Alto Molócuè**, Moz.
83/C3 **Altomonte**, It.
87/E2 **Alto, Monte** (peak), It.
70/E6 **Altomünster**, Ger.
59/F4 **Alton**, Eng,UK
193/F2 **Alton**, Ia,US
193/J4 **Alton**, Il,US
191/J2 **Alton**, Mo,US
208/C3 **Alton**, RI,US
187/F2 **Alton**, Ut,US
135/F5 **Altona**, Austl.
194/F3 **Altona**, Mb,Can
67/G1 **Altona**, Ger.
133/H3 **Alton Downs**, Austl.
170/B4 **Altônia**, Braz.
193/H3 **Altoona**, Ia,US
191/G2 **Altoona**, Ks,US
199/G4 **Altoona**, Pa,US
193/J1 **Altoona**, Wi,US
169/G4 **Alto Paraguai**, Braz.
172/E1 **Alto Paraguay** (dept.), Par.
173/F2 **Alto Paraná** (dept.), Par.
167/E5 **Alto Parnaíba**, Braz.
87/D5 **Altopascio**, It.
200/C2 **Alto Pass**, Il,US
174/D2 **Alto Pencoso**, Arg.
168/C3 **Alto Purús** (riv.), Peru
167/F4 **Altos**, Braz.
167/G4 **Alto Santo**, Braz.
161/G4 **Altos de Campana Nat'l Park**, Pan.
172/C1 **Alto Seco**, Bol.
159/F5 **Altotonga**, Mex.
71/F6 **Altötting**, Ger.
168/C3 **Alto Yuruá** (riv.), Peru
57/F5 **Altrincham**, Eng,UK
70/D4 **Altrip**, Ger.
72/C1 **Alt Ruppin**, Ger.
96/E1 **Altukhovo**, Rus.
108/C4 **Altun** (mts.), China
160/D2 **Altun Ha** (ruins), Belz.
184/C3 **Alturas**, Ca,US
202/M8 **Alturas**, Fl,US
190/E3 **Altus**, Ok,US
190/E3 **Altus A.F.B.**, Ok,US
97/K2 **Altykarasu**, Kaz.
97/L4 **Altynkul'**, Uzb.
99/G2 **Altynovka**, Ukr.
106/F4 **Al 'Ubaylah**, SAr.
149/F2 **Al Ubayyiḍ**, Sudan
104/D1 **Alucra**, Turk.
149/F2 **Al Udayyah**, Sudan
149/E3 **Aluk**, Sudan
63/M3 **Alūksne**, Lat.
147/H3 **Al 'Ulá**, SAr.
149/F3 **Al 'Umdah**, Sudan
174/C3 **Aluminé**, Arg.
56/E5 **Alun** (riv.), Wal,UK
62/H1 **Alunda**, Swe.
99/H5 **Alupka**, Ukr.
146/C2 **Al Uqaylah**, Libya
106/F3 **Al 'Uqayr**, SAr.
147/G3 **Al Uqṣur** (Luxor), Egypt
104/E3 **Ālūs**, Iraq
99/H5 **Alushta**, Ukr.
153/F3 **Aluta**, Zaire
146/A3 **Al 'Uwaynāt**, Libya
147/E4 **Al 'Uwaynāt, Jabal** (peak), Sudan
106/D3 **Al 'Uyūn**, SAr.
105/F4 **Al 'Uzayr**, Iraq
54/C4 **Alva**, Sc,UK
203/H4 **Alva**, Fl,US
191/E2 **Alva**, Ok,US
76/A4 **Alvalade**, Port.
81/F4 **Alvaneu-Bad**, Swi.
62/E3 **Alvängen**, Swe.
167/L7 **Alvarado**, Col.
159/G5 **Alvarado**, Mex.
194/F3 **Alvarado**, Mn,US
189/F1 **Alvarado**, Tx,US
170/C4 **Álvares Machado**, Braz.
174/E2 **Álvarez**, Arg.
159/F5 **Alvarez** (int'l arpt.), Mex.
158/C3 **Alvaro Obregón** (res.), Mex.
61/D3 **Alvdal**, Nor.
62/F1 **Älvdalen**, Swe.
173/E4 **Alvear**, Arg.
59/E2 **Alvechurch**, Eng,UK
76/A3 **Alverca**, Port.
77/P10 **Alverca do Ribatejo**, Port.
68/B1 **Alveringem**, Belg.
62/F3 **Alvesta**, Swe.
58/D4 **Alveston**, Eng,UK
84/C2 **Alviano** (lake), It.
85/E5 **Alvignano**, It.
62/B1 **Ålvik**, Nor.
61/F3 **Alvik**, Swe.
182/C3 **Alvin**, BC,Can
189/G3 **Alvin**, Tx,US
195/K5 **Alvin**, Wi,US
198/F3 **Alvinston**, On,Can
76/B3 **Alvito**, Port.
62/G1 **Älvkarleby**, Swe.
170/C2 **Alvorada**, Braz.
170/D2 **Alvorada do Norte**, Braz.
184/D2 **Alvord** (des.), Or,US
191/F4 **Alvord**, Tx,US
62/E3 **Älvsborg** (co.), Swe.
61/G2 **Älvsbyn**, Swe.
147/F3 **Al Wādī al Jadīd** (gov.), Egypt
104/B4 **Al Wāḥāt al Baḥrīyah** (oasis), Egypt
147/H3 **Al Wajh**, SAr.
106/F3 **Al Wakrah**, Qatar
120/A2 **Alwar**, India
103/B5 **Al Wāsiṭah**, Egypt
122/F3 **Alwaye**, India
149/F2 **Al Wazz**, Sudan
108/E4 **Alxa Youqi**, China
108/F4 **Alxa Zuoqi**, China
106/E4 **Al Yamāmah**, SAr.
103/G7 **Al Yāmūn**, WBnk.
131/E3 **Alyangula**, Austl.
97/J5 **Alyat**, Azer.
133/G2 **Alyawarra Abor. Land**, Austl.
54/C3 **Alyth**, Sc,UK
63/L4 **Alytus**, Lith.
92/A1 **Alz** (riv.), Aus.
71/F7 **Alz** (riv.), Ger.
194/B5 **Alzada**, Mt,US
86/C1 **Alzano Lombardo**, It.
70/C2 **Alzenau in Unterfranken**, Ger.
69/F4 **Alzette** (riv.), Lux.
70/B3 **Alzey**, Ger.
71/F6 **Alzkanal** (can.), Ger.
127/K4 **Ama**, PNG
168/D1 **Amacayacú Nat'l Park**, Col.
165/F2 **Amacuro** (riv.), Guy., Ven.
159/K8 **Amacuzac** (riv.), Mex.
106/B4 **Amada** (ruins), Egypt
148/B4 **Amada Gaza**, CAfr.
133/F3 **Amadeus** (lake), Austl.
121/G4 **Āmādi**, Bang.
149/F4 **Amadi**, Sudan
179/J2 **Amadjuak** (lake), NW,Can
187/G5 **Amado**, Az,US
76/A3 **Amadora**, Port.
167/K6 **Amaga**, Col.
207/F2 **Amagansett**, NY,US
207/F2 **Amagansett Nat'l Wild. Ref.**, NY,US
111/L10 **Amagasaki**, Japan
63/T9 **Amager** (isl.), Den.
110/B4 **Amagi**, Japan
111/F3 **Amagi-san** (mtn.), Japan
191/J3 **Amagon**, Ar,US
164/B5 **Amaguaña**, Ecu.
127/G4 **Amahai**, Indo.
159/L6 **Amajac** (riv.), Mex.
110/A4 **Amakusa** (sea), Japan
110/A4 **Amakusa-Unzen Nat'l Park**, Japan
62/E2 **Åmål**, Swe.
151/A2 **Amala** (riv.), Kenya
108/G1 **Amalat** (riv.), Rus.
164/C3 **Amalfi**, Col.
85/E6 **Amalfi**, It.
185/H3 **Amalga**, Ut,US
156/D2 **Amalia**, SAfr.
190/B2 **Amalia**, NM,US
91/G4 **Amaliás**, Gre.
118/C3 **Amalner**, India
168/B2 **Amaluza**, Ecu.
127/J4 **Amamapare**, Indo.
170/B4 **Amambaí**, Braz.
170/B4 **Amambaí** (riv.), Braz.
170/B4 **Amambaí** (mts.), Braz., Par.
173/E1 **Amambay** (dept.), Par.
173/F1 **Amambay** (mts.), Par.
112/K7 **Amami** (isls.), Japan
112/K6 **Amami-O-Shima** (isl.), Japan
153/F3 **Amamula**, Zaire
165/E5 **Amanã** (lake), Braz.
169/E1 **Amanã** (lake), Braz.
127/K4 **Amanab**, PNG
130/C4 **Amanbidji Abor. Land**, Austl.
80/C2 **Amance**, Fr.
182/C4 **Amanda Park**, Wa,US
85/D2 **Amandola**, It.
120/C3 **Amānganj**, India
83/C4 **Amantea**, It.
139/L6 **Amanu** (atoll), FrPol.
157/E3 **Amanzimtoti**, SAfr.
166/D2 **Amapá**, Braz.
166/C2 **Amapá** (state), Braz.
167/F4 **Amarante**, Braz.
76/A2 **Amarante**, Port.
167/E4 **Amarante do Maranhão**, Braz.
194/E2 **Amaranth**, Mb,Can
116/C4 **Amarapura**, Burma
122/F3 **Amarāvati** (riv.), India
76/B3 **Amareleja**, Port.
168/D4 **Amarete**, Bol.
171/F2 **Amargosa**, Braz.
186/D2 **Amargosa** (des.), Ca, Nv,US
186/D2 **Amargosa** (range), Ca, Nv,US
186/D2 **Amargosa** (riv.), Ca, Nv,US
190/D3 **Amarillo**, Tx,US
120/C4 **Amarkantak**, India
83/C5 **Amaro** (peak), It.
85/E3 **Amaro** (riv.), It.
89/G2 **Amaro, Monte** (peak), It.
83/C5 **Amaroni**, It.
120/C3 **Amarpātan**, India
112/A4 **Amarume**, Japan
120/B4 **Amarwāra**, India
84/D5 **Amaseno** (riv.), It.
93/L5 **Amasra**, Turk.
104/C1 **Amasya**, Turk.
104/C1 **Amasya** (prov.), Turk.
133/F3 **Amata**, Austl.
158/D4 **Amatlán de Cañas**, Mex.
83/C5 **Amato** (riv.), It.
85/D2 **Amatrice**, It.
111/J7 **Amatsukominato**, Japan
207/E1 **Amawalk** (res.), NY,US
69/E2 **Amay**, Belg.
159/L8 **Amayuca**, Mex.
109/J1 **Amazar**, Rus.
163/D3 **Amazon** (riv.), SAm.
163/D3 **Amazon** (Amazonas) (riv.), SAm.
169/E2 **Amazonas** (state), Braz.
164/C5 **Amazonas** (comm.), Col.
164/C5 **Amazonas** (dept.), Peru
168/C2 **Amazonas** (dept.), Peru
165/E3 **Amazonas** (terr.), Ven.
163/D3 **Amazonas** (Amazon) (riv.), SAm.
166/B4 **Amazônia** (Tapajós) **Nat'l Park**, Braz.
169/E1 **Amazon** (Solimões) (riv.), Braz.
149/H2 **Āmba Gīyorgīs**, Eth.
120/B2 **Ambāh**, India
157/G8 **Ambahikily**, Madg.
118/C4 **Ambajogai**, India
122/D2 **Ambāla**, India
157/H7 **Ambalajanakomby**, Madg.
118/D6 **Ambalangoda**, SrL.
157/J7 **Ambalarondra**, Madg.
157/H8 **Ambalavao**, Madg.
167/L7 **Ambalema**, Col.
152/B2 **Ambam**, Camr.
150/A3 **Āmba Maryam**, Eth.
141/G6 **Ambanja**, Madg.
172/C3 **Ambargasta** (salt pan), Arg.
94/G2 **Ambarnyy**, Rus.
157/H6 **Ambaro** (bay), Madg.
122/F4 **Ambāsamudram**, India
164/B5 **Ambato**, Ecu.
141/G6 **Ambato Boeny**, Madg.
157/H8 **Ambatofinandrahana**, Madg.
157/H8 **Ambatolahy**, Madg.
157/J7 **Ambatolampy**, Madg.
157/H7 **Ambatomainty**, Madg.
157/H7 **Ambatomanoina**, Madg.
157/J7 **Ambatondrazaka**, Madg.
74/D4 **Ambazac**, Fr.
91/H4 **Ámbelos, Ákra** (cape), Gre.
191/F3 **Amber**, Ok,US
71/E4 **Amberg**, Ger.
193/L1 **Amberg**, Wi,US
57/G5 **Ambergate**, Eng,UK
160/E2 **Ambergris** (cay), Belz.
162/C2 **Ambergris** (cay), Trks.
80/B6 **Ambérieu-en-Bugey**, Fr.
136/C3 **Amberley**, N.Z.
69/E3 **Amberloup**, Belg.
144/C3 **Ambidédi**, Mali
120/D4 **Ambikāpur**, India
80/C5 **Ambilly**, Fr.
157/J6 **Ambilobe**, Madg.
157/J8 **Ambinanindrano**, Madg.
157/J7 **Ambinaninony**, Madg.
157/J6 **Ambinanitelo**, Madg.
63/L2 **Ambla**, Est.
57/F1 **Amble**, Eng,UK
177/B5 **Ambler**, Ak,US
206/C3 **Ambler**, Pa,US
57/F3 **Ambleside**, Eng,UK
68/A2 **Ambleteuse**, Fr.
69/F3 **Amblève**, Belg.
69/F3 **Amblève** (riv.), Belg.
168/B3 **Ambo**, Peru
157/H9 **Amboasary**, Madg.
157/J7 **Amboavory**, Madg.
157/J8 **Ambodifototra**, Madg.
157/J8 **Ambodiharina**, Madg.
157/J7 **Ambodriana**, Madg.
157/H7 **Ambohidratrimo**, Madg.
157/J7 **Ambohijanahary**, Madg.
157/H8 **Ambohimahasoa**, Madg.
157/G8 **Ambohimahavelona**, Madg.
157/H7 **Ambohimandroso**, Madg.
157/H7 **Ambohimilanja**, Madg.
157/H8 **Ambohinihaonana**, Madg.
157/J7 **Ambohitsilaozana**, Madg.
79/F6 **Amboise**, Fr.
157/H7 **Ambolomoty**, Madg.
127/G4 **Ambon**, Indo.
127/G4 **Ambon** (isl.), Indo.
157/H9 **Ambondro**, Madg.
151/B3 **Amboni Caves**, Tanz.
157/H8 **Amborompotsy**, Madg.
151/B2 **Amboseli Nat'l Park**, Kenya
141/G7 **Ambositra**, Madg.
150/B3 **Ambouli** (int'l arpt.), Djib.
141/G7 **Ambovombe**, Madg.
186/E3 **Amboy**, Ca,US
193/K3 **Amboy**, Il,US
193/G2 **Amboy**, Mn,US
182/C5 **Amboy**, Wa,US
208/G6 **Ambridge**, Pa,US
79/E4 **Ambrières-le-Grand**, Fr.
152/C4 **Ambriz**, Ang.
152/C4 **Ambriz Rsv.**, Ang.
97/G4 **Ambrolauri**, Geo.
80/B5 **Ambronay**, Fr.
203/G2 **Ambrose**, Ga,US
138/F6 **Ambrym** (isl.), Van.
121/H4 **Ambsa**, India
124/F4 **Ambuntentimur**, Indo.
177/B6 **Amchitka** (isl.), Ak,US
177/B6 **Amchitka** (passg.), Ak,US
150/C2 **'Amd**, Yem.
148/D2 **Am Dam**, Chad
130/C1 **Amdasa**, Indo.
148/C2 **Am Djéména**, Chad
116/A1 **Amdo**, China
159/K6 **Amealco**, Mex.
158/D4 **Ameca**, Mex.
159/L7 **Amecameca de Juárez**, Mex.
174/E2 **Ameghino**, Arg.
86/C4 **Ameglia**, It.
71/G5 **Ameisberg** (peak), Aus.
69/F3 **Amel**, Belg.
66/C2 **Ameland** (isl.), Neth.
84/C2 **Amelia**, It.
201/G2 **Amelia** (isl.), Fl,US
201/J2 **Amelia C. H.**, Va,US
203/H2 **Amelia City**, Fl,US
199/H2 **Ameliasburg**, Can.
67/H2 **Amelinghausen**, Ger.
83/C3 **Amendolara**, It.
194/F4 **Amenia**, ND,US
208/A2 **Amenia**, NY,US
66/B5 **Amer** (chan.), Neth.
137/F **American** (highland), Ant.
205/M9 **American** (riv.), Ca,US
205/B3 **American** (lake), Wa,US
170/D4 **Americana**, Braz.
182/D3 **American Bolder** (peak), Wa,US
185/G2 **American Falls**, Id,US
185/G2 **American Falls** (dam), Id,US
184/G2 **American Falls** (res.), Id,US
185/H3 **American Fork**, Ut,US
184/C4 **American, North Fork** (riv.), Ca,US
139/T9 **American Samoa**
139/J6 **American Samoa** (terr.), US
186/B1 **American, South Fork** (riv.), Ca,US
200/E4 **Americus**, Ga,US
191/F1 **Americus**, Ks,US
191/J1 **Americus**, Mo,US
75/L3 **Ameringkogel** (peak), Aus.
66/C4 **Amersfoort**, Neth.
156/Q13 **Amersfoort**, SAfr.
59/F3 **Amersham**, Eng,UK
193/H1 **Amery**, Wi,US
137/E **Amery Ice Shelf**, Ant.
193/H2 **Ames**, Ia,US
191/F1 **Ames**, Ks,US
189/N8 **Ames**, Tx,US
59/E4 **Amesbury**, Eng,UK
199/L3 **Amesbury**, Ma,US
118/B2 **Amet**, India
120/C2 **Amethī**, India
149/H4 **Āmeya**, Eth.
91/H3 **Amfíklia**, Gre.
91/G3 **Amfilokhía**, Gre.
91/H3 **Ámfissa**, Gre.
101/N3 **Amga** (riv.), Rus.
101/T3 **Amguema** (riv.), Rus.
143/G4 **Amguid**, Alg.
109/M1 **Amgun'** (riv.), Rus.
119/G4 **Amherst**, Burma
196/E3 **Amherst**, NS,Can
197/F2 **Amherst** (isl.), Qu,Can
208/B1 **Amherst**, Ma,US
199/L3 **Amherst**, NH,US
208/E5 **Amherst**, Oh,US
201/H2 **Amherst**, Va,US
195/K5 **Amherst**, Wi,US
205/F7 **Amherstburg**, On,Can
201/G2 **Amherstdale-Robinette**, WV,US
130/B4 **Amhurst, Mount** (peak), Austl.
84/B2 **Amiata** (peak), It.
194/C4 **Amidon**, ND,US
68/B4 **Amiens**, Fr.
103/E1 **Amik** (lake), Turk.
101/U4 **Amila** (isl.), Ak,US
140/K10 **Amilcar Cabral** (Sal) (int'l arpt.), CpV.
91/G2 **Amindaion**, Gre.
154/C4 **Aminuis**, Namb.
145/H3 **Aminu Kano** (int'l arpt.), Nga.
141/H5 **Amirante** (isls.), Sey.
188/D3 **Amistad** (int'l res.), Mex., Tx,US
190/C3 **Amistad**, NM,US
188/D3 **Amistad** (dam), Tx,US
188/D3 **Amistad Nat'l Rec. Area**, Tx,US
202/C2 **Amite** (cr.), La,US
202/C2 **Amite City**, La,US
191/H3 **Amity**, Ar,US
190/C1 **Amity** (can.), Co,US
184/B1 **Amity**, Or,US
207/M9 **Amityville**, NY,US
120/B5 **Amla**, India
121/F4 **Āmlāgora**, India
105/G2 **Amlash**, Iran
121/E2 **Amlekhganj**, Nepal
62/C2 **Åmli**, Nor.
177/D6 **Amlia** (isl.), Ak,US
56/D5 **Amlwch**, Wal,UK
103/D4 **'Ammān** (cap.), Jor.
58/C3 **Amman** (riv.), Wal,UK
58/C3 **Ammanford**, Wal,UK
189/F3 **Ammannsville**, Tx,US
61/E2 **Ammarfjället** (peak), Swe.
70/B5 **Ammer** (riv.), Ger.
177/K2 **Ammerman** (mtn.), Yk,Can
70/E6 **Ammersee** (lake), Ger.
185/H2 **Ammon**, Id,US
123/D3 **Amnat Charoen**, Thai.
69/F5 **Amnéville**, Fr.
116/D4 **Amo** (riv.), China
105/H2 **Āmol**, Iran
77/P10 **Amora**, Port.
70/C3 **Amorbach**, Ger.
91/J4 **Amorgós**, Gre.
91/J4 **Amorgós** (isl.), Gre.
170/C3 **Amorinópolis**, Braz.
200/C4 **Amory**, Ms,US
179/J4 **Amos**, Qu,Can
62/B2 **Åmot**, Nor.
62/E2 **Amotfors**, Swe.
144/D2 **Amourj**, Mrta.
127/F4 **Ampana**, Indo.
157/J6 **Ampanavoana**, Madg.
157/J6 **Ampanefena**, Madg.
157/J8 **Ampangalana** (can.), Madg.
157/H9 **Ampanihy**, Madg.
157/J7 **Amparafaravola**, Madg.
118/D6 **Amparai**, SrL.
170/D4 **Amparo**, Braz.
157/J8 **Ampasimanjeva**, Madg.
157/J7 **Ampasimanolotra**, Madg.
157/J6 **Ampasindava** (bay), Madg.
168/D4 **Ampato** (peak), Peru
157/H7 **Ampefy**, Madg.
71/E6 **Amper** (riv.), Ger.
145/H4 **Amper**, Nga.
71/E6 **Ampfing**, Ger.
117/G5 **Amphitrite Group** (isls.), China
127/F4 **Ampibako**, Indo.
157/J6 **Ampisikinana**, Madg.
157/H7 **Ampitatafika**, Madg.
83/C4 **Ampollino** (lake), It.
157/J6 **Ampombiantambo**, Madg.
77/F2 **Amposta**, Sp.
59/F2 **Ampthill**, Eng,UK
82/A2 **Ampuis**, Fr.
196/D1 **Amqui**, Qu,Can
150/B2 **'Amrān**, Yem.
121/F3 **Amrāpāra**, India
118/C3 **Amravati**, India
118/B3 **Amreli**, India
116/B3 **Amring**, India
104/C3 **'Amrīt** (ruins), Syria
122/C2 **Amritsar**, India
120/B1 **Amroha**, India
64/E1 **Amrum** (isl.), Ger.
66/B4 **Amstel** (riv.), Neth.
66/B4 **Amstelveen**, Neth.
51/N7 **Amsterdam** (isl.), FrAnt.
66/B4 **Amsterdam** (cap.), Neth.
157/E2 **Amsterdam**, SAfr.
203/F2 **Amsterdam**, Ga,US
191/G1 **Amsterdam**, Mo,US
183/J5 **Amsterdam**, Mt,US
199/J3 **Amsterdam**, NY,US
66/C5 **Amsterdam-Rijnkanaal** (can.), Neth.
66/B4 **Amsterdam** (Schiphol) (int'l arpt.), Neth.
75/L2 **Amstetten**, Aus.
208/B2 **Amston**, Ct,US
121/H4 **Āmtali**, Bang.
148/D3 **AmTiman**, Chad
97/G4 **Amtkel**, Geo.
102/F5 **Amudar'ya** (riv.), Asia
100/G6 **Amu-Dar'ya**, Trkm.
151/A1 **Amudat**, Ugan.
177/D5 **Amukta** (passg.), Ak,US
165/G4 **Amuku** (mts.), Guy.
179/S7 **Amund Ringnes** (isl.), NW,Can
137/D **Amundsen** (bay), Ant.
137/S **Amundsen** (sea), Ant.
176/E2 **Amundsen** (gulf), Can.
137/A **Amundsen-Scott**, Ant.
62/F1 **Amungen** (lake), Swe.
109/M1 **Amur** (riv.), China, Rus.
139/K6 **Amuri**, CookIs.
136/B3 **Amuri** (pass), N.Z.
101/N4 **Amur Obl.**, Rus.
76/D1 **Amurrio**, Sp.
109/M1 **Amursk**, Rus.
147/G5 **'Amur, Wādī** (dry riv.), Sudan
99/K4 **Amvrosiyevka**, Ukr.
103/D2 **Amyūn**, Leb.
148/D2 **Am Zoer**, Chad
139/L6 **Anaa** (atoll), FrPol.
101/L3 **Anabar** (riv.), Rus.
103/G7 **'Anabtā**, WBnk.
204/A2 **Anacapa** (isl.), Ca,US
85/E6 **Anacapri**, It.
161/G4 **Anachucuna** (mtn.), Pan.
165/E2 **Anaco**, Ven.
202/B2 **Anacoco**, La,US
178/E4 **Anaconda**, Mt,US
183/H5 **Anaconda** (range), Mt,US
182/C3 **Anacortes**, Wa,US
191/E3 **Anadarko**, Ok,US
76/A2 **Anadia**, Port.
101/T3 **Anadyr'**, Rus.
101/U3 **Anadyr'** (gulf), Rus.
101/T3 **Anadyr'** (range), Rus.
102/S3 **Anadyr'** (riv.), Rus.
89/K3 **Anafi** (isl.), Gre.
91/J4 **Anáfi** (isl.), Gre.
84/D4 **Anagni**, It.
104/E3 **'Ānah**, Iraq
204/C3 **Anaheim**, Ca,US
204/G8 **Anaheim Stadium**, Ca,US
157/H6 **Anahidrano**, Madg.
182/B1 **Anahim Lake**, BC,Can
182/C1 **Anahim's Flat Ind. Res.**, BC,Can
188/D4 **Anáhuac**, Mex.
189/G3 **Anahuac**, Tx,US
189/N9 **Anahuac** (lake), Tx,US
189/G3 **Anahuac Nat'l Wild. Ref.**, Tx,US
122/F3 **Anai Mudi** (mtn.), India
167/E3 **Anajatuba**, Braz.
113/C3 **Anak**, NKor.
118/D4 **Anakāpalle**, India
177/H2 **Anaktuvuk Pass**, Ak,US
141/G6 **Analalava**, Madg.
157/J7 **Analamaitso** (plat.), Madg.
157/H7 **Analvory**, Madg.
161/G1 **Ana María** (gulf), Cuba
124/D2 **Anambas** (isls.), Indo.
145/G5 **Anambra** (state), Nga.
194/D4 **Anamoose**, ND,US
193/J2 **Anamosa**, Ia,US
103/C1 **Anamur**, Turk.
103/C1 **Anamur** (pt.), Turk.
110/D4 **Anan**, Japan
166/D4 **Ananás**, Braz.
118/B3 **Anand**, India
116/B4 **Ananda Temple**, Burma
118/B2 **Anandgarh**, India
122/D2 **Anandpur**, India
168/D4 **Ananea**, Peru
118/C5 **Anantapur**, India
122/C1 **Anantnag**, India
186/A2 **Ana Nuevo** (pt.), Ca,US
98/E4 **Anan'yev**, Ukr.
114/C3 **Anan'yevo**, Kyr.
99/J5 **Anapa**, Rus.
175/K7 **Añapi** (peak), Arg.
170/C3 **Anápolis**, Braz.
99/J5 **Anapskaya**, Rus.
166/D3 **Anapu** (riv.), Braz.
105/H4 **Anār**, Iran
105/H3 **Anārak**, Iran
203/H3 **Anastasia** (isl.), Fl,US
93/K4 **Anastasiyevka**, Rus.
103/G8 **'Anātā**, WBnk.
138/D3 **Anathan** (isl.), NMar.
104/B2 **Anatolia** (reg.), Turk.
172/D4 **Añatuya**, Arg.
165/F4 **Anauá** (riv.), Braz.
113/B3 **Anbo**, China
117/H4 **Anbu**, China
113/D3 **Anbyŏn**, NKor.
197/R9 **Ancaster**, On,Can
79/D6 **Ancenis**, Fr.
117/H2 **Anchangzhen**, China
145/H4 **Anchau**, Nga.
171/E4 **Anchieta**, Braz.
190/B4 **Ancho**, NM,US
205/G6 **Anchor** (bay), Mi,US
177/J3 **Anchorage**, Ak,US
174/D2 **Anchorena**, Arg.
177/H4 **Anchor Point**, Ak,US
205/G6 **Anchorville**, Mi,US
161/G2 **Anchovy**, Jam.
196/B2 **Ancienne-Lorette**, Qu,Can
186/C2 **Ancient Bristlecone Pine For.**, Ca,US
83/C5 **Ancinale** (riv.), It.
202/K7 **Anclote**, Fl,US
203/G3 **Anclote**, Fl,US
202/K7 **Anclote** (keys), Fl,US
202/K7 **Anclote** (riv.), Fl,US
168/D4 **Ancohuma** (peak), Bol.
168/B3 **Ancón**, Peru
87/G5 **Ancona**, It.
87/G5 **Ancona** (prov.), It.
164/B4 **Ancón de Sardinas** (bay), Col., Ecu.
168/D4 **Ancoraimes**, Bol.
54/E5 **Ancroft**, Eng,UK
54/D6 **Ancrum**, Sc,UK
174/B4 **Ancud**, Chile
174/B4 **Ancud** (gulf), Chile
109/K2 **Anda**, China
174/C3 **Andacollo**, Arg.
172/B4 **Andacollo**, Chile
133/G3 **Andado**, Austl.
168/C4 **Andagua**, Peru
168/C4 **Andahuaylas**, Peru
157/J7 **Andaingo Gara**, Madg.
121/F4 **Andāl**, India
172/C3 **Andalgalá**, Arg.
61/C3 **Åndalsnes**, Nor.
76/C4 **Andalusia** (aut. comm.), Sp.
88/B3 **Andalusia** (reg.), Sp.
203/E2 **Andalusia**, Al,US
193/J3 **Andalusia**, Il,US
119/F5 **Andaman** (sea), Asia
119/F5 **Andaman** (isls.), India
119/F5 **Andaman & Nicobar Is.** (terr.), India
172/C1 **Andamarca**, Bol.
168/C3 **Andamarca**, Peru
133/H4 **Andamooka**, Austl.
157/J6 **Andapa**, Madg.
154/D3 **Andara**, Namb.
171/E2 **Andaraí**, Braz.
73/B4 **Andau**, Aus.
123/D1 **Ande**, China
62/D2 **Andebu**, Nor.
81/H2 **Andechs**, Ger.
81/F4 **Andeer**, Swi.
81/E2 **Andelfingen**, Swi.
68/A4 **Andelle** (riv.), Fr.
80/B1 **Andelot-Blancheville**, Fr.
81/F2 **Andelsbach** (riv.), Ger.
157/H8 **Andemaka**, Madg.
61/F1 **Andenes**, Nor.
69/E3 **Andenne**, Belg.
61/F1 **Ånderdalen Nat'l Park**, Nor.
68/D3 **Anderlues**, Belg.
81/E4 **Andermatt**, Swi.
69/G3 **Andernach**, Ger.
177/N2 **Anderson** (riv.), NW,Can
177/J3 **Anderson**, Ak,US
184/B3 **Anderson**, Ca,US
198/D4 **Anderson**, In,US
191/G2 **Anderson**, Mo,US
201/F3 **Anderson**, SC,US
189/G2 **Anderson**, Tx,US
205/B3 **Anderson** (inlet), Wa,US
205/B3 **Anderson** (isl.), Wa,US
184/F2 **Anderson Ranch** (dam), Id,US
185/F2 **Anderson Ranch** (res.), Id,US
200/E4 **Andersonville**, Ga,US
200/E4 **Andersonville Nat'l Hist. Site**, Ga,US
164/C3 **Andes**, Col.
163/B3 **Andes** (mts.), SAm.
183/M4 **Andes**, Mt,US
157/J7 **Andevoranto**, Madg.
61/F1 **Andfjorden** (fjord), Nor.
118/C4 **Andhra Pradesh** (state), India
66/C3 **Andijk**, Neth.
91/H5 **Andikíthira** (isl.), Gre.
157/J7 **Andilamena**, Madg.
157/J7 **Andilanatoby**, Madg.
105/G3 **Andīmeshk**, Iran
91/J4 **Andíparos** (isl.), Gre.
170/C4 **Andira**, Braz.
169/G1 **Andirá** (riv.), Braz.
91/J3 **Andíssa**, Gre.
114/B3 **Andizhan**, Uzb.
76/D1 **Andoain**, Sp.
157/J6 **Andoany**, Madg.
168/B1 **Andoas**, Peru
164/B5 **Andoas Nuevo**, Ecu.
157/J6 **Andohajango**, Madg.
115/L9 **Andong**, China
113/E4 **Andong**, SKor.
113/D4 **Andong** (lake), SKor.
71/G6 **Andorf**, Aus.
86/B1 **Andorno Micca**, It.
77/F1 **Andorra**
77/E2 **Andorra**, Sp.
77/F1 **Andorra la Vella** (cap.), And.
79/E4 **Andouillé**, Fr.
59/E4 **Andover**, Eng,UK
208/B2 **Andover**, Ct,US
191/F2 **Andover**, Ks,US
196/B3 **Andover**, Me,US
193/H1 **Andover**, Mn,US
195/P6 **Andover**, Mn,US
206/D2 **Andover**, NJ,US
208/G4 **Andover**, Oh,US
61/E1 **Andøya** (isl.), Nor.
171/K7 **Andradas**, Braz.
170/C4 **Andradina**, Braz.
157/J6 **Andrafainkona**, Madg.
77/G3 **Andraitx**, Sp.
157/H7 **Andramasina**, Madg.
157/H8 **Andranolalina**, Madg.
157/H8 **Andranolava**, Madg.
157/H7 **Andranomavo** (riv.), Madg.
157/G8 **Andranopasy**, Madg.
157/J6 **Andranovondrona**, Madg.
157/H8 **Andranovory**, Madg.
177/C6 **Andreanof** (isls.), Ak,US
148/D3 **André Félix Nat'l Park**, CAfr.
170/D4 **Andrelândia**, Braz.
168/C3 **Andres Avelino Caceres** (dept.), Peru
53/S10 **Andrésy**, Fr.
201/F2 **Andrew Johnson Nat'l Hist. Site**, Tn,US
200/F3 **Andrews**, NC,US
184/D2 **Andrews**, Or,US
201/H4 **Andrews**, SC,US
188/C1 **Andrews**, Tx,US
206/B6 **Andrews A.F.B.**, Md,US
97/K1 **Andreyevka**, Rus.
99/J3 **Andreyevka**, Ukr.
99/J4 **Andreyevka**, Ukr.
85/G5 **Andria**, It.
157/H8 **Andriamena**, Madg.
157/H8 **Andriandampy**, Madg.
157/H7 **Andriba**, Madg.
157/H8 **Andringitra** (mts.), Madg.
91/G4 **Andritsaina**, Gre.
157/H9 **Androka**, Madg.
157/J6 **Androntany** (cape), Madg.
162/B1 **Andros** (isl.), Bahm.
91/J4 **Ándros**, Gre.
91/J4 **Ándros** (isl.), Gre.
196/B3 **Androscoggin** (riv.), Me,US
162/B1 **Andros Town**, Bahm.
98/E2 **Andrushëvka**, Ukr.
76/C3 **Andújar**, Sp.
121/G4 **Andulbāria**, Bang.
152/D5 **Andulo**, Ang.
202/P7 **Andytown**, Fl,US
203/H4 **Andytown**, Fl,US
62/F3 **Aneby**, Swe.
174/C4 **Anecón Grande** (peak), Arg.
145/F2 **Anefis I-n-Darane**, Mali
174/E4 **Anegada** (bay), Arg.
162/E3 **Anegada** (isl.), BVI
161/F5 **Anegada** (pt.), Pan.
162/E3 **Anegada Passage** (chan.), West Indies
145/F5 **Anécho**, Togo
138/G7 **Aneityum** (isl.), Van.
174/C3 **Añelo**, Arg.
183/L3 **Aneroid**, Sk,Can
68/A6 **Anet**, Fr.
194/F4 **Aneta**, ND,US
187/H2 **Aneth**, Ut,US
77/F1 **Aneto, Pico de** (peak), Sp.
146/B5 **Aney**, Niger
119/K2 **Anfu**, China
141/P13 **Angads** (Oujda) (int'l arpt.), Mor.
143/E2 **Angads** (Oujda) (int'l arpt.), Mor.
122/F3 **Angamāli**, India
148/C1 **Angamma, Falaise d'** (escarp.), Chad
172/B2 **Angamos** (pt.), Chile
108/E1 **Angara** (riv.), Rus.
108/E1 **Angarsk**, Rus.
133/G3 **Angas Downs**, Austl.
133/H5 **Angaston**, Austl.
173/G2 **Angatuba**, Braz.
61/E3 **Ånge**, Swe.
67/E5 **Angel** (riv.), Ger.
165/F3 **Angel** (falls), Ven.
183/L4 **Angela**, Mt,US
158/B2 **Ángel de la Guarda** (isl.), Mex.
82/B4 **Angèle, Montagnev d'** (mtn.), Fr.
125/C2 **Angeles**, Phil.
204/B2 **Angeles Nat'l For.**, Ca,US
62/E3 **Ängelholm**, Swe.
62/E3 **Ängelholm** (int'l arpt.), Swe.
195/K5 **Angelica**, Wi,US
167/G5 **Angelim**, Braz.
189/G2 **Angelina** (riv.), Tx,US
64/E1 **Angeln** (reg.), Ger.
186/B1 **Angels**, Ca,US
184/C4 **Angels Camp**, Ca,US
205/F6 **Angelus** (lake), Mi,US
204/D2 **Angelus Oaks**, Ca,US
127/J4 **Angemuk** (mtn.), Indo.
86/B1 **Angera**, It.
52/E2 **Angerman** (riv.), Swe.
72/E1 **Angermünde**, Ger.
72/B3 **Angern**, Ger.
73/A3 **Angern an der March**, Aus.
79/E6 **Angers**, Fr.
79/H4 **Angerville**, Fr.
87/F5 **Anghiari**, It.
167/F4 **Angical do Piauí**, Braz.
167/G4 **Angicos**, Braz.
202/D2 **Angie**, La,US
201/H3 **Angier**, NC,US
123/C3 **Angkor Wat** (ruins), Camb.
123/D4 **Angk Tasaom**, Camb.
196/C1 **Anglais** (bay), Qu,Can
79/E4 **Angleine** (riv.), Fr.
195/G3 **Angle Inlet**, Mn,US
136/A4 **Anglem** (peak), N.Z.
77/G2 **Anglès**, Sp.
135/C3 **Anglesea**, Austl.
56/D5 **Anglesey** (isl.), Wal,UK
74/C5 **Anglet**, Fr.
189/G3 **Angleton**, Tx,US
74/D3 **Anglin** (riv.), Fr.
123/C2 **Ang Nam Ngum** (lake), Laos
153/F1 **Ango**, Zaire
155/H3 **Angoche**, Moz.
105/J5 **Angohrān**, Iran
174/B3 **Angol**, Chile
140/D6 **Angola**
198/D4 **Angola**, In,US
202/C2 **Angola**, La,US
199/G3 **Angola**, NY,US
177/M4 **Angoon**, Ak,US
158/C3 **Angostura**, Mex.
160/C2 **Angostura** (res.), Mex.
192/C2 **Angostura** (dam), SD,US
192/C2 **Angostura** (res.), SD,US
74/D4 **Angoulême**, Fr.
77/S12 **Angra do Heroísmo**, Azor.,Port.
170/D4 **Angra dos Reis**, Braz.
114/B3 **Angren**, Uzb.
85/E6 **Angri**, It.
123/C3 **Ang Thong**, Thai.
153/F2 **Angu**, Zaire
162/F3 **Anguilla** (isl.), UK
200/B4 **Anguilla**, Ms,US
84/C3 **Anguillara Sabazia**, It.
87/E2 **Anguillara Veneta**, It.
197/H2 **Anguille** (cape), Can
197/H2 **Anguille** (mts.), Nf,Can
153/F2 **Angumu**, Zaire
131/E3 **Angurugu**, Austl.
189/F1 **Angus**, Tx,US
194/D2 **Angusville**, Mb,Can
177/G4 **Angutikada** (peak), Ak,US
155/F3 **Angwa** (riv.), Zim.
205/K9 **Angwin**, Ca,US
170/B4 **Anhanduí** (riv.), Braz.
173/F1 **Anharduí** (riv.), Braz.
69/D3 **Anhée**, Belg.
188/D4 **Anhelo**, Mex.
62/D3 **Anholt** (isl.), Den.
64/E1 **Anholt By**, Den.
117/F2 **Anhua**, China
115/D4 **Anhui** (prov.), China
111/H7 **Ani**, Japan
177/G3 **Aniak**, Ak,US
177/G4 **Aniakchak** (crater), Ak,US
177/G4 **Aniakchak Nat'l Mon. & Prsv.**, Ak,US
154/B4 **Anichab**, Namb.
68/C3 **Aniche**, Fr.
170/C3 **Anicuns**, Braz.
84/C4 **Aniene** (riv.), It.
97/M2 **Anikhovka**, Rus.
79/F5 **Anille** (riv.), Fr.
187/J2 **Animas** (riv.), Co,US
187/H5 **Animas**, NM,US
187/H5 **Animas** (mts.), NM,US
158/B2 **Ánimas, Punta de las** (pt.), Mex.
123/B3 **Anin**, Burma
103/G7 **'Anīn**, WBnk.
92/E3 **Anina**, Rom.
193/G3 **Anita**, Ia,US
112/C1 **Aniva** (bay), Rus.
109/N2 **Aniva** (cape), Rus.
109/N2 **Aniva** (sea), Rus.
112/C1 **Aniva, Mys** (cape), Rus.
157/J7 **Anivorano**, Madg.
68/C5 **Anizy-le-Château**, Fr.
63/M1 **Anjalankoski**, Fin.
118/B3 **Anjār**, India
111/N10 **Anjō**, Japan
197/N6 **Anjou**, Qu,Can
79/E5 **Anjou** (hist. reg.), Fr.
74/C3 **Anjou** (reg.), Fr.
157/H6 **Anjouan** (isl.), Com.
157/H7 **Anjozorobe**, Madg.
116/E2 **Anju**, China
113/C3 **Anju**, NKor.
66/D2 **Anjum**, Neth.
108/F5 **Ankang**, China
104/C2 **Ankara** (cap.), Turk.
93/K5 **Ankara** (prov.), Turk.
157/H8 **Ankaramena**, Madg.
87/G1 **Ankaran**, Slov.
157/H7 **Ankaratra, massif** (plat.), Madg.
62/G3 **Ankarsrum**, Swe.
157/H7 **Ankasakasa**, Madg.
157/H7 **Ankavandra**, Madg.
157/H8 **Ankazoabo**, Madg.
157/H7 **Ankazobe**, Madg.
157/H7 **Ankazomborona**, Madg.
157/H7 **Ankazomiriotra**, Madg.
193/H3 **Ankeny**, Ia,US
184/B1 **Ankeny Nat'l Wild. Ref.**, Or,US
123/E3 **An Khe**, Viet.
157/H6 **Ankerika**, Madg.
157/G8 **Ankiliabo**, Madg.
157/G8 **Ankililoka**, Madg.
157/H8 **Ankilizato**, Madg.
65/G2 **Anklam**, Ger.
150/A3 **Ānkober**, Eth.
153/F4 **Ankoro**, Zaire
145/G5 **Ankpa**, Nga.
67/E3 **Ankum**, Ger.
117/G4 **Anliu**, China
145/F5 **Anloga**, Gha.
116/E3 **Anlong**, China
119/J2 **Anlong Bouyeizu Miaozu Zizhixian**, China
123/D3 **Anlong Veng**, Camb.
66/D2 **Anloo**, Neth.
115/C5 **Anlu**, China
137/D **Ann** (cape), Ant.
199/L3 **Ann** (cape), Ma,US
99/L2 **Anna**, Rus.
200/C2 **Anna**, Il,US
189/F1 **Anna**, Tx,US
201/J1 **Anna** (lake), Va,US
141/V17 **Annaba**, Alg.
141/V17 **Annaba** (wilaya), Alg.
135/E2 **Anna Bay**, Austl.
185/G4 **Annabella**, Ut,US
71/G1 **Annaberg-Buchholz**, Ger.
103/E2 **An Nabk**, Syria
72/D4 **Annaburg**, Ger.
56/B3 **Annaclone**, NI,UK
133/H4 **Anna Creek**, Austl.
141/X17 **An Nafīḍah**, Tun.
104/D4 **An Nafūd** (des.), SAr.
149/F2 **An Nahūd**, Sudan
72/D4 **Annahütte**, Ger.
165/G4 **Annai**, Guy.
105/F4 **An Najaf**, Iraq
105/E4 **An Najaf** (gov.), Iraq
60/D1 **Annalee** (riv.), Ire.
56/C3 **Annalong**, NI,UK
203/G4 **Anna Maria**, Fl,US
123/D2 **Annamitique** (mts.), Laos, Viet.
119/J4 **Annamitique, Chaine** (chain), Viet., Laos
57/E2 **Annan**, Sc,UK
54/C6 **Annan** (riv.), Sc,UK
195/G5 **Annandale**, Mn,US
206/D2 **Annandale**, NJ,US
206/A6 **Annandale**, Va,US
66/B3 **Anna Pavlowna**, Neth.
174/B5 **Anna Pink** (bay), Chile
130/A4 **Anna Plains**, Austl.
196/E3 **Annapolis** (riv.), NS,Can
184/B4 **Annapolis**, Ca,US
206/B6 **Annapolis** (cap.), Md,US
191/J2 **Annapolis**, Mo,US
196/E3 **Annapolis Royal**, NS,Can
120/D1 **Annapurna** (mtn.), Nepal
106/C3 **An Naqb, Ra's**, Jor.
103/D3 **An Nāqūrah**, Leb.
205/E7 **Ann Arbor**, Mi,US
165/G3 **Anna Regina**, Guy.
105/F4 **An Nāṣirīyah**, Iraq
146/C2 **An Nawfalīyah**, Libya
54/B6 **Annbank Station**, Sc,UK
135/C4 **Anne** (peak), Austl.
132/C3 **Annean** (lake), Austl.
206/B6 **Anne Arundel** (co.), Md,US
80/C6 **Annecy**, Fr.
80/C6 **Annecy** (lake), Fr.
80/C6 **Annecy-le-Vieux**, Fr.
80/C6 **Annecy** (Meythet) (arpt.), Fr.
80/C5 **Annemasse**, Fr.
188/K7 **Anneta**, Tx,US
53/U10 **Annet-sur-Marne**, Fr.
177/M4 **Annette**, Ak,US
82/A2 **Anneyron**, Fr.
68/B2 **Annezin**, Fr.
123/E3 **An Nhon**, Viet.
197/J1 **Annieopsquotch** (mts.), Nf,Can
116/D3 **Anning**, China
116/D3 **Anning** (riv.), China
200/E4 **Anniston Army Dep.**, Al,US
140/C5 **Annobón** (isl.), EqG.
82/A2 **Annonay**, Fr.
82/C5 **Annot**, Fr.
149/F3 **An Nūbah, Jibāl** (mts.), Sudan
105/F3 **An Nu'mānīyah**, Iraq
85/E5 **Annunziata**, It.
122/F3 **Annūr**, India
206/B3 **Annville**, Pa,US
70/A4 **Annweiler**, Ger.
111/M10 **Anō**, Japan
77/K7 **Anoia** (riv.), Sp.
195/H5 **Anoka**, Mn,US
195/P6 **Anoka**, Mn,US
195/P6 **Anoka** (co.), Mn,US
194/F3 **Anola**, Mb,Can
167/L7 **Anolaima**, Col.
166/A3 **Anori**, Braz.
157/J7 **Anosibe**, Madg.
157/J7 **Anosibe an' Ala**, Madg.
80/C1 **Anould**, Fr.
145/G2 **Anou-Zeggarene** (wadi), Niger
91/J5 **Áno Viánnos**, Gre.
91/J5 **Anóyia**, Gre.
123/E4 **An Phuoc**, Viet.
113/B2 **Anping**, China
123/E1 **Anpu**, China
115/D5 **Anqing**, China
115/D3 **Anqiu**, China
119/K2 **Anren**, China
142/D3 **Anrhomer, Jebel** (mtn.), Mor.
67/F5 **Anröchte**, Ger.
69/E2 **Ans**, Belg.
115/B3 **Ansai**, China
113/F7 **Ansan**, SKor.
70/D4 **Ansbach**, Ger.
161/H2 **Anse-à-Galets**, Haiti
161/H2 **Anse-d'Hainault**, Haiti
164/C3 **Anserma**, Col.
161/H2 **Anse Rouge**, Haiti
71/H6 **Ansfelden**, Aus.
113/B2 **Anshan**, China
116/E3 **Anshun**, China
116/D2 **Anshunchang**, China
175/G1 **Ansina**, Uru.
192/E3 **Ansley**, Ne,US
130/C3 **Anson** (bay), Austl.
188/E1 **Anson**, Tx,US
113/D4 **Ansŏng**, SKor.
175/F3 **Ansongo**, Mali
208/A3 **Ansonia**, Ct,US
201/G1 **Ansted**, WV,US
54/D4 **Anstruther**, Sc,UK
127/J4 **Ansus**, Indo.
138/E4 **Ant** (isl.), Micr.
59/H1 **Ant** (riv.), Eng,UK
168/C4 **Anta**, Peru
168/C4 **Antabamba**, Peru
103/E1 **Antakya** (Antioch), Turk.
141/H6 **Antalaha**, Madg.
103/B1 **Antalya**, Turk.
103/B1 **Antalya** (gulf), Turk.
103/B1 **Antalya** (int'l arpt.), Turk.
103/A1 **Antalya** (prov.), Turk.
157/J7 **Antanambao Manampotsy**, Madg.
157/J7 **Antanambe**, Madg.
141/G6 **Antananarivo** (cap.), Madg.
157/H7 **Antananarivo** (prov.), Madg.
157/H7 **Antanifotsy**, Madg.
157/J7 **Antanimenabaka**, Madg.
157/G8 **Antanimieva**, Madg.
157/H9 **Antanimora**, Madg.
137/W **Antarctic** (pen.), Ant.
137/* **Antarctica** (cont.)
137/Z **Antarctic Circle**, Ant.
143/E3 **Antar, Djebel** (mtn.), Alg.
157/H9 **Antaritarika**, Madg.
173/G3 **Antas** (riv.), Braz.
68/D5 **Ante** (riv.), Fr.
54/A1 **An Teallach** (mtn.), Sc,UK
87/E5 **Antella**, It.
183/M3 **Antelope**, Mt,US
183/K5 **Antelope** (peak), Mt,US
184/C1 **Antelope**, Or,US
189/E1 **Antelope**, Tx,US
185/G3 **Antelope** (isl.), Ut,US
204/C1 **Antelope Center**, Ca,US
155/F4 **Antelope Mine**, Zim.
167/G4 **Antenor Navarro**, Braz.
173/E3 **Antequera**, Par.
76/C4 **Antequera**, Sp.
192/A4 **Antero** (mt.), Co,US
206/A1 **Antes Fort**, Pa,US
71/G7 **Anthering**, Aus.
203/G3 **Anthony**, Fl,US
191/E2 **Anthony**, Ks,US
190/A4 **Anthony**, NM,US
208/C2 **Anthony**, RI,US
131/D4 **Anthony Lagoon**, Austl.
142/C3 **Anti-Atlas** (mts.), Mor.
82/D5 **Antibes**, Fr.
82/D5 **Antibes, Cap d'** (cape), Fr.
197/F1 **Anticosti** (isl.), Qu,Can
71/G6 **Antiesen** (riv.), Aus.
199/H5 **Antietam Nat'l Bfld.**, Md,US
79/F1 **Antifer, Cap d'** (cape), Fr.
193/K1 **Antigo**, Wi,US
197/G3 **Antigonish**, NS,Can
162/F3 **Antigua** (isl.), Anti.
142/B3 **Antigua**, Canl.
162/F3 **Antigua & Barbuda**
160/D3 **Antigua Guatemala**, Guat.
159/F4 **Antiguo Morelos**, Mex.
103/D3 **Anti-Lebanon** (mts.), Leb.
185/H4 **Antimony**, Ut,US
115/L8 **Anting**, China
205/L10 **Antioch**, Ca,US
205/P15 **Antioch**, Il,US
103/E1 **Antioch** (Antakya), Turk.
164/C3 **Antioquia**, Col.
164/C3 **Antioquia** (dept.), Col.
95/N3 **Antipina**, Rus.
51/T8 **Antipodes** (isls.), N.Z.
193/H3 **Antique Airpower Museum**, Ia,US

164/B5 Antisana (vol.), Ecu.
194/D3 Antler, Sk,Can
191/G3 Antlers, Ok,US
172/B2 Antofagasta, Chile
172/B1 Antofagasta (reg.), Chile
172/C3 Antofagasta de la Sierra, Arg.
68/C2 Antoing, Belg.
157/H8 Antokonosy Manambondro, Madg.
161/F4 Antón, Pan.
190/B3 Anton Chico, NM,US
157/J6 Antongil (bay), Madg.
157/H6 Antonibe, Madg.
156/C4 Antoniesberg (peak), SAfr.
167/G4 Antonina do Norte, Braz.
159/Q10 Antonio Alzate (lake), Mex.
171/N6 Antônio Carlos, Braz.
175/L6 Antonio de Biedma, Arg.
173/F2 Antônio João, Braz.
190/A2 Antonito, Co,US
159/P7 Antón Lizardo, Mex.
159/G5 Anton Lizardo, Punta (pt.), Mex.
93/H4 Antonovo, Bul.
53/S10 Antony, Fr.
78/D3 Antrain, Fr.
78/D4 Antrain-sur-Couesnon, Fr.
99/K3 Antratsit, Ukr.
56/B2 Antrim, NI,UK
56/B2 Antrim (dist.), NI,UK
56/B1 Antrim (mts.), NI,UK
196/B4 Antrim, NH,US
199/H4 Antrim, Pa,US
84/D3 Antrodoco, It.
80/E5 Antronapiana, It.
157/J6 Antsakabary, Madg.
157/H7 Antsalova, Madg.
157/J6 Antsambalahy, Madg.
157/J8 Antsenavolo, Madg.
157/H7 Antsiafabositra, Madg.
157/J6 Antsirabato, Madg.
141/G6 Antsirabe, Madg.
141/G6 Antsiranana, Madg.
157/J6 Antsiranana (prov.), Madg.
63/M3 Antsla, Est.
157/H6 Antsohihy, Madg.
144/E5 Antubia, Gha.
174/C3 Antuco (vol.), Chile
125/B4 Antulai, Gunung (mtn.), Malay.
69/E1 Antwerp (prov.), Belg.
198/D4 Antwerp, Oh,US
68/D1 Antwerp (Antwerpen), Belg.
68/D1 Antwerp (Deurne) (int'l arpt.), Belg.
68/D1 Antwerpen (Antwerp), Belg.
60/D2 An Uaimh, Ire.
118/B2 Anūpgarh, India
120/B1 Anūpshahr, India
122/H4 Anuradhapura, SrL.
122/H4 Anuradhapura (dist.), SrL.
122/H4 Anuradhapura (ruins), SrL.
191/J2 Anutt, Mo,US
177/F3 Anvik, Ak,US
177/B6 Anvil (vol.), Ak,US
117/H3 Anxi, China
115/G7 Anxin, China
144/D5 Anyama, IvC.
115/C3 Anyang, China
113/D4 Anyang, SKor.
108/D4 A'nyêmaqên (mts.), China
124/D4 Anyer Kidul, Indo.
115/B4 Anyi, China
63/L4 Anykščiai, Lith.
117/G3 Anyuan, China
117/H3 Anyuan, China
109/M2 Anyuy (riv.), Rus.
167/K6 Anzá, Col.
80/E6 Anza (riv.), It.
103/G7 'Anzah, WBnk.
172/C1 Anzaldo, Bol.
85/F5 Anzano di Puglia, It.
115/C3 Anze, China
68/C2 Anzegem, Belg.
100/J4 Anzhero-Sudzhensk, Rus.
115/G7 Anzhou, China
85/F6 Anzi, It.
68/C3 Anzin, Fr.
71/E6 Anzing, Ger.
84/C5 Anzio, It.
167/K7 Anzoátegui, Col.
164/D2 Anzoátegui, Ven.
165/E2 Anzoátegui (state), Ven.
87/E3 Anzola dell'Emilia, It.
111/L9 Aogaki, Japan
76/E1 Aoiz, Sp.
117/J3 Aojiang, China
123/B4 Ao Kham (pt.), Thai.
112/B3 Aomori, Japan
112/B3 Aomori (dept.), Japan
120/B1 Aonla, India
91/G2 Aóos (riv.), Gre.
123/B4 Ao Phangnga Nat'l Park, Thai.
117/G3 Aoquanxu, China
123/D3 Aoral (peak), Camb.
136/J9 Aorangi (mts.), N.Z.
136/B3 Aorangi (reg.), N.Z.
82/D1 Aosta, It.
86/A1 Aosta (prov.), It.
86/A1 Aosta (reg.), It.
86/A1 Aosta (val.), It.
82/D1 Aosta, Valle d' (reg.), It.
82/B1 Aoste, Fr.
166/C1 Aouara, FrG.
144/C2 Aoudaghost (ruins), Mrta.
144/C2 'Aouînat ez Zbil, Mrta.
148/D3 Aouk-Aoukale Fauna Rsv., CAfr.
144/C2 Aoukar (reg.), Mrta.
148/C3 Aouk, Bahr (riv.), CAfr., Chad
143/F4 Aoulef, Alg.
144/C3 Aourou, Mali
82/B3 Aouste-sur-Sye, Fr.
111/M10 Aoyama, Japan
146/C4 Aozi, Chad
146/C4 Aozou, Chad
146/C4 Aozou Strip (reg.), Chad
170/A4 Apa (riv.), Braz., Par.
187/G4 Apache (lake), Az,US
191/E3 Apache, Ok,US
188/B2 Apache (mts.), Tx,US
187/H4 Apache Creek, NM,US
187/G4 Apache Junction, Az,US
172/C2 Apagado (vol.), Chile
203/F3 Apalachee (bay), Fl,US
201/F4 Apalachee (riv.), Ga,US
203/F3 Apalachicola, Fl,US
203/F2 Apalachicola (riv.), Fl,US
159/L7 Apan, Mex.
97/M1 Apanovka, Kaz.
164/D5 Apaporis (riv.), Braz., Col.
173/G4 Aparados da Serra Nat'l Park, Braz.
170/D4 Aparecida, Braz.
170/C4 Aparecida do Taboado, Braz.
164/D2 Aparición, Ven.
125/C1 Aparri, Phil.
164/B3 Apartado, Col.
165/F3 Apaurén, Ven.
139/L6 Apataki, FrPol.
92/E2 Apátfalva, Hun.
92/D3 Apatin, Yugo.
94/G2 Apatity, Rus.
166/C1 Apatou, FrG.
158/E5 Apatzingán, Mex.
127/J4 Apauwar, Indo.
159/K7 Apaxco de Ocampo, Mex.
159/F5 Apaxtla, Mex.
160/B2 Apaxtla de Castrejon, Mex.
123/D4 Ap Binh Chau, Viet.
63/M3 Ape, Lat.
66/C4 Apeldoorn, Neth.
66/D4 Apeldoornsch (can.), Neth.
67/G4 Apelern, Ger.
67/E2 Apen, Ger.
52/E4 Apennines (mts.), It.
67/G2 Apensen, Ger.
169/E4 Apere (riv.), Bol.
73/A4 Apetlon, Aus.
201/H3 Apex, NC,US
145/F5 Apéyémé, Togo
72/A6 Apfelstädt (riv.), Ger.
104/B2 Aphrodisias (ruins), Turk.
126/C3 Api (cape), Indo.
127/F4 Api (cape), Indo.
127/E5 Api (peak), Indo.
114/D5 Api (mtn.), Nepal
153/F2 Api, Zaire
153/F2 Api (riv.), Zaire
167/K6 Apía, Col.
139/H6 Apia (cap.), WSam.
170/A1 Apiacá (riv.), Braz.
169/G3 Apiacás (mts.), Braz.
139/S9 Apia (Fagali) (int'l arpt.), WSam.
139/R9 Apia (Faleolo) (int'l arpt.), WSam.
173/G3 Apiaí, Braz.
192/B5 Apishapa (riv.), Co,US
159/F5 Apizaco, Mex.
168/C5 Aplao, Peru
123/D4 Ap Loc Thanh, Viet.
123/E4 Ap Long Hoa, Viet.
123/D4 Ap Luc, Viet.
125/D4 Apo (mtn.), Phil.
159/E3 Apodaca, Mex.
167/G4 Apodi, Braz.
165/G3 Apoera, Guy.
72/B5 Apolda, Ger.
139/R9 Apolima (str.), WSam.
172/C3 Apolinario Saravia, Arg.
135/B3 Apollo Bay, Austl.
202/L8 Apollo Beach, Fl,US
91/J4 Apollonia, Gre.
146/D1 Apollonia (ruins), Libya
202/M6 Apopka, Fl,US
202/M6 Apopka (lake), Fl,US
203/H3 Apopka (lake), Fl,US
173/F1 Aporé (riv.), Braz.
160/E3 Aposentillo (pt.), Nic.
195/J4 Apostle (isls.), Wi,US
195/J4 Apostle Islands Nat'l Lakesh., Wi,US
173/F3 Apóstoles, Arg.
103/D2 Apostolos Andreas (cape), Cyp.
99/G4 Apostolovo, Ukr.
165/G3 Apoteri, Guy.
181/K4 Appalachian (mts.), US
194/C3 Appam, ND,US
66/D3 Appelscha, Neth.
67/G1 Appen, Ger.
70/A5 Appenweier, Ger.
81/F3 Appenzell, Swi.
194/D4 Appert Lake Nat'l Wild. Ref., ND,US
97/G6 Appignano, It.
66/D2 Appingedam, Neth.
195/Q6 Apple (riv.), Wi,US
57/F2 Appleby, Eng,UK
189/G2 Appleby, Tx,US
59/F1 Appleby Magna, Eng,UK
208/F6 Apple Creek, Oh,US
194/F5 Appleton, Mn,US
197/T9 Appleton, NY,US
193/K1 Appleton, Wi,US
191/G1 Appleton City, Mo,US
204/C1 Apple Valley, Ca,US
195/P7 Apple Valley, Mn,US
201/F4 Appling, Ga,US
201/H2 Appomattox, Va,US
201/H2 Appomattox C. H. Nat'l Hist. Park, Va,US
166/C2 Approuage (riv.), FrG.
81/G5 Aprica, It.
81/G5 Aprica, Passo dell' (pass), It.
85/F4 Apricena, It.
84/C4 Aprilia, It.
93/G4 Apriltsi, Bul.
99/K5 Apsheronsk, Rus.
130/C2 Apsley (str.), Austl.
199/G2 Apsley, On,Can
135/E1 Apsley Gorge Nat'l Park, Austl.
82/B5 Apt, Fr.
123/E4 Ap Tan My, Viet.
186/B2 Aptos, Ca,US
180/U11 Apua (pt.), Hi,US
86/D4 Apuane (mts.), It.
170/C4 Apucarana, Braz.
167/G3 Apuiarés, Braz.
89/H2 Apulia (reg.), It.
167/L7 Apulo, Col.
165/E3 Apure (riv.), Ven.
164/D3 Apure (state), Ven.
163/B4 Apurímac (riv.), Peru
123/E4 Ap Vinh Hao, Viet.
104/C4 Aqaba (gulf), Egypt, SAr.
105/H3 'Aqdā, Iran
147/H5 'Aqīq, Sudan
105/H2 Āq Qal'eh, Iran
114/E4 Aqqikkol (lake), China
103/D3 'Aqrabah, WBnk.
105/E2 'Aqrah, Iraq
158/E3 Aquanaval (riv.), Mex.
173/G1 Aquapei (riv.), Braz.
187/F3 Aquarius (mts.), Az,US
185/H4 Aquarius (plat.), Ut,US
168/B3 Aquia, Peru
170/A4 Aquidabán (riv.), Par.
170/B4 Aquidauana, Braz.
173/F1 Aquidauana (riv.), Braz.
158/E5 Aquila, Mex.
81/E5 Aquila, Swi.
87/G1 Aquileia, It.
188/B3 Aquiles Serdán, Mex.
208/F4 Aquilla, Oh,US
189/F2 Aquilla, Tx,US
85/F6 Aquilonia, It.
161/H2 Aquin, Haiti
85/D5 Aquino, It.
172/G3 Aquiraz, Braz.
74/C4 Aquitaine (reg.), Fr.
108/D4 Ar (riv.), China
60/B5 Ara (riv.), Ire.
111/F2 Ara (riv.), Japan
104/C1 Ara, Turk.
200/D3 Arab, Al,US
147/G2 'Arabah, Wādī (dry riv.), Egypt
104/D2 Araban, Turk.
99/H5 Arabatsk (bay), Ukr.
99/H5 Arabatsk (spit), Ukr.
149/E3 'Arab, Baḥr Al (riv.), Sudan
200/F5 Arabi, Ga,US
106/D3 Arabian (pen.), Asia
107/H5 Arabian (sea), Asia
103/B5 Arabian (des.), Egypt
103/E3 'Arab, Jabal al (mts.), Syria
165/F3 Arabopó, Ven.
147/F2 Arabs (gulf), Egypt
96/E4 Araç (riv.), Turk.
172/C1 Araca, Bol.
165/F4 Araça (riv.), Braz.
171/F1 Aracaju, Braz.
164/C2 Aracataca, Col.
167/G4 Aracati, Braz.
170/C4 Araçatuba, Braz.
125/B3 Araceli, Phil.
76/B4 Aracena, Sp.
92/E4 Aračinovo, Macd.
167/G4 Aracoiba, Braz.
171/E3 Aracruz, Braz.
171/E3 Araçuaí, Braz.
171/E3 Araçuaí (riv.), Braz.
104/C4 'Arad, Isr.
92/E2 Arad, Rom.
92/E2 Arad (co.), Rom.
148/D2 Arada, Chad
106/F4 'Arādah, UAE
105/H3 Ārādān, Iran
105/A2 Arafali, Eth.
106/D4 'Arafāt, Jabal (mtn.), SAr.
130/D2 Arafura (sea), Austl., Indo.
97/H4 Aragats, Gora (peak), Arm.
60/B5 Araglin (riv.), Ire.
184/A2 Arago, Or,US
184/A2 Arago (cape), Or,US
77/E2 Aragon (aut. comm.), Sp.
88/C2 Aragon (reg.), Sp.
76/E1 Aragón (riv.), Sp.
200/E3 Aragon, Ga,US
187/H4 Aragon, NM,US
165/E2 Aragua (state), Ven.
170/C1 Araguacema, Braz.
170/C2 Araguaçu, Braz.
166/D4 Araguaia (riv.), Braz.
170/C2 Araguaiana, Braz.
170/C1 Araguaia Nat'l Park, Braz.
166/D4 Araguaína, Braz.
170/C3 Araguari, Braz.
166/D2 Araguari (riv.), Braz.
170/C3 Araguari (riv.), Braz.
166/D4 Araguatins, Braz.
111/F2 Arai, Japan
167/F3 Araioses, Braz.
143/F4 Arak, Alg.
53/H5 Arak (riv.), Eur., Asia
105/G3 Arāk, Iran
177/D3 Arakamchechan (isl.), Rus.
116/B4 Arakan (mts.), Burma
91/G3 Árakhthos (riv.), Gre.
104/E1 Araklı, Turk.
100/G5 Aral (sea), Uzb., Kaz.
105/F2 Aralık, Turk.
100/G5 Aral'sk, Kaz.
97/H2 Aralsor (lake), Kaz.
134/B3 Aramac, Austl.
189/N9 Arama-Sea Marineworld, Tx,US
121/F4 Arāmbāgh, India
159/F3 Aramberri, Mex.
82/A5 Aramon, Fr.
105/G3 Ārān, Iran
106/F2 Aran, Iran
55/G9 Aran (isl.), Ire.
60/A3 Aran (isls.), Ire.
76/D2 Aranda de Duero, Sp.
158/E4 Arandas, Mex.
92/E3 Arandelovac, Yugo.
154/B4 Arandis, Namb.
172/C1 Arani, Bol.
76/D2 Aranjuez, Sp.
56/E6 Aran Mawddwy (mtn.), Wal,UK
154/C5 Aranos, Namb.
189/F3 Aransas (riv.), Tx,US
189/F3 Aransas Nat'l Wild. Ref., Tx,US
189/F4 Aransas Pass, Tx,US
122/G3 Arantāngi, India
171/M6 Arantina, Braz.
138/G4 Aranuka (isl.), Kiri.
123/C3 Aranyaprathet, Thai.
144/E2 Araouane, Mali
190/E3 Arapaho, Ok,US
192/E3 Arapahoe, Ne,US
192/A3 Arapahoe Nat'l Rec. Area, Co,US
192/A3 Arapahoe Nat'l Wild. Ref., Co,US
136/C3 Arapawa (isl.), N.Z.
172/E4 Arapey, Uru.
168/B1 Arapicos, Ecu.
171/F1 Arapiraca, Braz.
166/C3 Arapiuns (riv.), Braz.
104/D2 Arapkir, Turk.
170/C4 Arapongas, Braz.
103/G7 'Ar'ara, Isr.
164/C5 Araracuara, Col.
173/G4 Araranguá, Braz.
170/C4 Araraquara, Braz.
170/D4 Araras, Braz.
135/B3 Ararat, Austl.
105/F2 Ararat (Ağri) (peak), Turk.
167/E3 Arari, Braz.
166/D3 Arari (lake), Braz.
121/F2 Arāria, India
167/F4 Araripe (uplands), Braz.
167/F4 Araripina, Braz.
167/H4 Araruna, Braz.
104/F2 Aras (riv.), Asia
144/C2 Aratane (well), Mrta.
167/F4 Aratas (res.), Braz.
150/B4 Ara Terra, Eth.
164/C3 Aratoca, Col.
167/G4 Aratuba, Braz.
123/C5 Arau, Malay.
169/E2 Arauá (riv.), Braz.
164/D3 Arauca, Col.
164/D3 Arauca (inten.), Col.
165/E3 Arauca (riv.), Col., Ven.
174/B3 Arauco, Chile
164/D3 Arauquita, Col.
164/D2 Araure, Ven.
122/F3 Aravakkurichchi, India
80/C6 Aravis, Col des (pass), Fr.
138/E5 Arawa, PNG
151/C2 Arawale Nat'l Rsv., Kenya
170/D3 Araxá, Braz.
165/E2 Araya (pen.), Ven.
125/C2 Arayat (mtn.), Phil.
175/T12 Arazati, Uru.
149/H4 Ārba Minch', Eth.
77/F2 Arbeca, Sp.
81/F5 Arbedo, Swi.
150/A4 Ārbē Gona, Eth.
167/L7 Arbeláez, Col.
62/F2 Arboga, Swe.
80/B4 Arbois, Fr.
80/C6 Arbois, Mont d' (mtn.), Fr.
81/E5 Arbola, Punta d' (peak), It.
164/B2 Arboletes, Col.
81/F2 Arbon, Swi.
149/H4 Arbore, Eth.
183/N1 Arborfield, Sk,Can
194/F2 Arborg, Mb,Can
195/K5 Arbor Vitae, Wi,US
201/H1 Arbovale, WV,US
62/G1 Arbrå, Swe.
54/D3 Arbroath, Sc,UK
184/B4 Arbuckle, Ca,US
202/N8 Arbuckle (lake), Fl,US
203/H4 Arbuckle (lake), Fl,US
191/F3 Arbuckle (mts.), Ok,US
82/B5 Arc (riv.), Fr.
82/C2 Arc (riv.), Fr.
184/E4 Arc (mtn.), Nv,US
74/C4 Arcachon, Fr.
74/C4 Arcachon (lag.), Fr.
74/C4 Arcachon, Pointe d' (pt.), Fr.
199/G3 Arcade, NY,US
196/D4 Arcadia, NS,Can
204/B2 Arcadia, Ca,US
203/H4 Arcadia, Fl,US
198/C4 Arcadia, In,US
189/H1 Arcadia, La,US
198/C2 Arcadia, Mi,US
200/B2 Arcadia, Mo,US
192/E3 Arcadia, Ne,US
191/F3 Arcadia, Ok,US
193/J1 Arcadia, Wi,US
198/D5 Arcanum, Oh,US
184/A3 Arcata, Ca,US
184/A3 Arcata (bay), Ca,US
53/S10 Arc de Triomphe, Fr.
85/D4 Arce, It.
171/K6 Arceburgo, Braz.
66/D6 Arcen, Neth.
80/B2 Arc-en-Barrois, Fr.
86/C1 Arcene, It.
87/D3 Arceto, It.
80/B3 Arc-et-Senans, Fr.
87/F6 Arcevia, It.
94/J2 Archangel (Arkhangel'sk), Rus.
94/H3 Archangel Obl., Rus.
198/D4 Archbold, Oh,US
201/H3 Archdale, NC,US
82/C1 Archeboc, Pointe d' (peak), Fr.
76/E3 Archena, Sp.
134/A1 Archer (riv.), Austl.
203/G3 Archer, Fl,US
134/A1 Archer Bend Nat'l Park, Austl.
191/E4 Archer City, Tx,US
151/B1 Archers Post, Kenya
194/C1 Archerwill, Sk,Can
80/C1 Arches, Fr.
185/J4 Arches Nat'l Park, Ut,US
202/C1 Archibald, La,US
172/C3 Archibarca (peak), Arg.
76/C4 Archidona, Sp.
191/G1 Archie, Mo,US
52/C4 Archiestown, Sc,UK
97/L5 Archman, Trkm.
84/B2 Arcidosso, It.
86/B1 Arcisate, It.
80/B3 Arc-lès-Gray, Fr.
87/D1 Arco, It.
185/G2 Arco, Id,US
194/C3 Arcola, Sk,Can
86/C4 Arcola, It.
193/K4 Arcola, Il,US
200/B4 Arcola, Ms,US
189/M9 Arcola, Tx,US
87/E2 Arcole, It.
87/F4 Arçonnay, Fr.
174/C3 Arco, Paso del (pass), Arg.
172/C1 Arcopongo, Bol.
170/D4 Arcos, Braz.
187/F3 Arcosanti, Az,US
76/D2 Arcos de Jalón, Sp.
76/C4 Arcos de la Frontera, Sp.
76/A2 Arcos de Valdevez, Port.
167/G5 Arcoverde, Braz.
80/B3 Arc-sur-Tille, Fr.
50/A1 Arctic (ocean)
177/F2 Arctic (coast. pl.), Ak,US
179/H1 Arctic Bay, NW,Can
177/J2 Arctic Nat'l Wild. Ref., Ak,US
177/M2 Arctic Red (riv.), NW,Can
177/M2 Arctic Red River, NW,Can
177/J2 Arctic Village, Ak,US
93/G5 Arda (riv.), Bul.
86/C3 Arda (riv.), It.
105/G2 Ardabīl, Iran
60/A5 Ardagh, Ire.
60/C2 Ardagh, Ire.
105/E1 Ardahan, Turk.
105/H3 Ardakān, Iran
105/G4 Ardal, Iran
62/B1 Årdalstangen, Nor.
104/E1 Ardanuç, Turk.
94/J5 Ardatov, Rus.
57/E6 Arddleen, Wal,UK
84/C4 Ardea, It.
82/A3 Ardèche (dept.), Fr.
74/F4 Ardèche (riv.), Fr.
60/D2 Ardee, Ire.
133/H5 Arden (peak), Austl.
194/E2 Arden, Can
62/C3 Arden, Den.
206/C4 Arden, De,US
182/F3 Arden, Wa,US
68/D3 Ardennes (for.), Belg.
74/F1 Ardennes (for.), Belg., Fr.
68/D4 Ardennes (dept.), Fr.
69/D4 Ardennes, Canal des (can.), Fr.
81/F5 Ardenno, It.
60/C3 Arderin (mtn.), Ire.
54/B1 Ardersier, Sc,UK
104/E1 Ardeşen, Turk.
86/C1 Ardesio, It.
105/H3 Ardestān, Iran
81/G4 Ardez, Swi.
60/C5 Ardfinnan, Ire.
56/C3 Ardglass, NI,UK
76/B3 Ardila (riv.), Sp.
93/G5 Ardino, Bul.
55/H8 Ardivachar (pt.), Sc,UK
54/C3 Ardle (riv.), Sc,UK
135/C2 Ardlethan, Austl.
60/C6 Ardmore, Ire.
191/F3 Ardmore, Ok,US
206/C3 Ardmore, Pa,US
192/C2 Ardmore, SD,US
200/D3 Ardmore, Tn,US
60/B4 Ardnacrusha, Ire.
55/H8 Ardnamurchan (pt.), Sc,UK
194/F3 Ardoch Nat'l Wild. Ref., ND,US
80/D5 Ardon, Swi.
68/C2 Ardooie, Belg.
83/C6 Ardore, It.
60/B3 Ardrahan, Ire.
68/A2 Ardres, Fr.
133/H5 Ardrossan, Austl.
54/B5 Ardrossan, Sc,UK
56/C2 Ards (dist.), NI,UK
56/C3 Ards (pen.), NI,UK
207/K7 Ardsley, NY,US
61/E3 Åre, Swe.
171/K6 Areado, Braz.
162/E3 Arecibo, PR
167/G4 Areia Branca, Braz.
184/B4 Arena (pt.), Ca,US
158/C3 Arena de la Ventana, Punta (pt.), Mex.
161/E4 Arenal (vol.), CR
169/G4 Arenápolis, Braz.
158/C4 Arena, Punta (pt.), Mex.
76/C2 Arenas de San Pedro, Sp.
175/K8 Arenas, Punta de (pt.), Arg.
62/C2 Arendal, Nor.
66/C6 Arendonk, Belg.
72/B2 Arendsee, Ger.
72/B2 Arendsee (lake), Ger.
206/A4 Arendtsville, Pa,US
56/E6 Arenig Fawr (mtn.), Wal,UK
77/L6 Arenys de Mar, Sp.
77/L6 Arenys de Munt, Sp.
86/B4 Arenzano, It.
193/J4 Arenzville, Il,US
165/F2 Areo, Ven.
91/H4 Areópolis, Gre.
168/D5 Arequipa, Peru
168/C4 Arequipa (dept.), Peru
174/E2 Arequito, Arg.
70/E5 Aresing, Ger.
76/C2 Arévalo, Sp.
133/G2 Areyonga, Austl.
149/H2 Āreza, Eth.
87/E6 Arezzo, It.
87/E5 Arezzo (prov.), It.
105/H3 Arfa' Deh, Iran
74/C5 Arga (riv.), Sp.
133/H2 Argadargada, Austl.
91/H3 Argalasti, Gre.
124/C3 Argamakmur, Indo.
76/D3 Argamasilla de Alba, Sp.
76/C3 Argamasilla de Calatrava, Sp.
114/E3 Argan, China
77/N9 Arganda, Sp.
125/C3 Argao, Phil.
85/D4 Argatone (peak), It.
86/C1 Argegno, It.
74/C5 Argelès-Gazost, Fr.
74/E5 Argelès-sur-Mer, Fr.
167/K6 Argelia, Col.
81/F2 Argen (riv.), Ger.
81/F2 Argenbühl, Ger.
79/E2 Argences, Fr.
82/C6 Argens (riv.), Fr.
182/F2 Argenta, BC,Can
87/E3 Argenta, It.
79/E3 Argentan, Fr.
84/B3 Argentario (mtn.), It.
74/D4 Argentat, Fr.
75/G4 Argentera (peak), It.
53/S10 Argenteuil, Fr.
74/E2 Argenteuil, Paris
197/K2 Argentia, Nf,Can
80/D6 Argentière, Aiguille d' (peak), Swi.
163/B7 Argentina
86/A5 Argentina (riv.), It.
175/J7 Argentino (lake), Arg.
77/L6 Argentona, Sp.
74/D3 Argenton-sur-Creusot, Fr.
79/E4 Argentré, Fr.
93/G3 Argeş (co.), Rom.
93/G3 Argeş (riv.), Rom.
107/J2 Arghandab (riv.), Afg.
60/B6 Argideen (riv.), Ire.
104/B2 Argithani, Turk.
147/F5 Argo, Sudan
91/H4 Argolis (gulf), Gre.
191/F2 Argonia, Ks,US
69/E5 Argonne (for.), Fr.
195/K5 Argonne, Wi,US
205/Q16 Argonne Nat'l Lab., Il,US
124/F4 Argopuro (peak), Indo.
91/H4 Árgos, Gre.
91/G2 Árgos Orestikón, Gre.
91/G3 Argostólion, Gre.
68/A4 Argueil, Fr.
186/B3 Arguello (pt.), Ca,US
78/C4 Arguenon (riv.), Fr.
144/A1 Arguin (bay), Mrta.
142/A5 Arguin, Cap d' (cape), Mrta.
101/M4 Argun' (riv.), China, Rus.
102/L4 Argun (riv.), China, Rus.
145/G3 Argungu, Nga.
194/F4 Argusville, ND,US
114/F2 Argut (riv.), Rus.
104/D2 Arguvan, Turk.
130/C4 Argyle (lake), Austl.
194/F3 Argyle, Mn,US
189/F1 Argyle, Tx,US
54/A4 Argyll (dist.), Sc,UK
145/G2 Arhli, Niger
109/J3 Ar Horqin Qi, China
142/B5 Arhreijît (well), Mrta.
144/C2 Arhrîjît, Mrta.
62/D3 Århus, Den.
62/D3 Århus (co.), Den.
83/A6 Aria (mtn.), It.
156/B3 Ariamsvlei, Namb.
202/M7 Ariana (lake), Fl,US
85/F5 Ariano Irpino, It.
76/C1 Arianza (riv.), Sp.
164/C4 Ariari (riv.), Col.
174/E2 Arias, Arg.
145/E3 Aribinda, Burk.
172/B1 Arica, Chile
164/D5 Arica, Col.
172/B1 Arica (Chacalluta) (int'l arpt.), Chile
104/E2 Arıcak, Turk.
84/C4 Ariccia, It.
197/G3 Arichat, NS,Can
132/D5 Arid (cape), Austl.
110/D3 Arida, Japan
91/H2 Aridhaia, Gre.
204/A1 Arido (mt.), Ca,US
142/B4 Aridal, Sebjet (dry lake), WSah.
74/D5 Ariège (riv.), Fr.
182/C5 Ariel, Wa,US
85/E5 Arienzo, It.
93/K5 Arifiye, Turk.
118/B2 Ārifwāla, Pak.
103/E2 Arīḥā, Syria
103/D4 Arīḥā (Jericho), WBnk.
190/C1 Arikaree (riv.), Co,US
192/C4 Arikaree (cr.), Co, Ne,US
92/E4 Arilje, Yugo.
162/F5 Arima, Trin.
163/D4 Arinas (riv.), Braz.
153/G2 Aringa, Ugan.
170/D2 Arinos, Braz.
170/A1 Arinos (riv.), Braz.
80/B5 Arinthod, Fr.
63/K4 Ariogala, Lith.
165/E3 Aripao, Ven.
202/K7 Aripeka, Fl,US
187/G3 Aripine, Az,US
165/F2 Aripo, El Cerro del (mtn.), Trin.
166/A5 Aripuanã, Braz.
166/A4 Aripuanã (riv.), Braz.
169/F3 Ariquemes, Braz.
154/C4 Aris, Namb.
134/B2 Arish, Austl.
147/G2 'Arīsh, Wādī al (dry riv.), Egypt
164/D2 Arismendi, Ven.
150/B3 Arissa, Eth.
203/F2 Ariton, Al,US
187/G5 Arivaca, Az,US
158/C2 Arivechi, Mex.
157/H7 Arivonimamo, Madg.
157/H7 Arivonimamo (int'l arpt.), Madg.
122/G3 Ariyalūr, India
76/D2 Ariza, Sp.
172/C2 Arizaro (salt pan), Arg.
77/F1 Arize (riv.), Fr.
174/D2 Arizona, Arg.
187/F3 Arizona (state), US
187/G4 Arizona City, Az,US
158/C2 Arizpe, Mex.
62/E2 Årjäng, Swe.
124/F4 Arjasa, Indo.
200/F2 Arjay, Ky,US
61/F2 Arjeplog, Swe.
164/C2 Arjona, Col.
76/C4 Arjona, Sp.
200/B3 Arkabutla (dam), Ms,US
99/M2 Arkadak, Rus.
191/H3 Arkadelphia, Ar,US
54/A3 Arkaig, Loch (lake), Sc,UK
91/J5 Arkalokhórion, Gre.
114/A1 Arkalyk, Kaz.
181/H4 Arkansas (riv.), US
181/H4 Arkansas (state), US
191/J4 Arkansas City, Ar,US
191/F2 Arkansas City, Ks,US
191/J3 Arkansas Post Nat'l Mem., Ar,US
191/F2 Arkansas, Salt Fork (riv.), Ok,US
146/E4 Arkanū (peak), Libya
104/B2 Arkhángelos, Gre.
94/J2 Arkhangel'sk (int'l arpt.), Rus.
94/J2 Arkhangel'sk (Archangel), Rus.
99/L5 Arkhangel'skaya, Rus.
97/G2 Arkhangel'skoye, Rus.
109/L2 Arkhara, Rus.
99/K5 Arkhipo-Osipovka, Rus.
97/G4 Arkhyz, Rus.
60/D4 Arklow, Ire.
65/G1 Arkona, Kap (cape), Ger.
118/C5 Arkonam, India
57/G4 Arksey, Eng,UK
100/H2 Arkticheskiy Institut (isls.), Rus.
62/G2 Ärla, Swe.
62/G2 Arlanda (int'l arpt.), Swe.
76/C1 Arlanza (riv.), Sp.
76/C1 Arlazón (riv.), Sp.
81/G3 Arlbergpass (pass), Aus.
82/A5 Arles, Fr.
80/D3 Arlesheim, Swi.
68/C3 Arleux, Fr.
187/F4 Arlington, Az,US
204/C3 Arlington, Ca,US
190/C1 Arlington, Co,US
203/F2 Arlington, Ga,US
191/E2 Arlington, Ks,US
200/C2 Arlington, Ky,US
208/C1 Arlington, Ma,US
193/G1 Arlington, Mn,US
193/F3 Arlington, Ne,US
199/K4 Arlington, NY,US
198/E4 Arlington, Oh,US
184/C1 Arlington, Or,US
193/F1 Arlington, SD,US
200/C3 Arlington, Tn,US
189/F1 Arlington, Tx,US
188/K7 Arlington (lake), Tx,US
206/A6 Arlington, Va,US
199/K3 Arlington, Vt,US
182/C3 Arlington, Wa,US
185/K3 Arlington, Wy,US
205/Q15 Arlington Heights, Il,US
188/K7 Arlington Stadium, Tx,US
65/L4 Arló, Hun.
69/E4 Arlon, Belg.
133/G2 Arltunga, Austl.
86/B1 Arluno, It.
82/C1 Arly (riv.), Fr.
145/F4 Arly Nat'l Park, Burk.
145/F4 Arly Res., Ben.
183/M2 Arm (riv.), Sk,Can
205/G6 Armada, Mi,US
135/D1 Armadale, Austl.
54/C5 Armadale, Sc,UK
188/D4 Armadillo, Mex.
56/B3 Armagh, NI,UK
56/B3 Armagh (dist.), NI,UK
74/F3 Armançon (riv.), Fr.
170/C4 Armando Laydner (res.), Braz.
147/G3 Armant, Egypt
53/H4 Armavir, Rus.
75/G5 Arme, Cap d' (cape), Fr.
97/H4 Armenia
164/C3 Armenia, Col.
68/B2 Armentières, Fr.
158/E5 Armería, Mex.
164/C3 Armero, Col.
173/E1 Armidabán (riv.), Par.
135/D1 Armidale, Austl.
76/D4 Armilla, Sp.
185/K2 Arminto, Wy,US
186/C2 Armona, Ca,US
127/J4 Armopa, Indo.
192/E2 Armour, SD,US
56/B1 Armoy, NI,UK
174/E2 Armstrong, Arg.
195/K2 Armstrong, Can
182/E2 Armstrong, BC,Can
191/H1 Armstrong, Mo,US
189/F4 Armstrong, Tx,US
195/K5 Armstrong Creek, Wi,US
57/G4 Armthorpe, Eng,UK
118/C4 Armūr, India
93/J5 Armutlu, Turk.
193/K3 Army Ammun. Plant, Il,US
99/G4 Armyansk, Ukr.
206/B5 Army Ordnance Museum, Md,US
79/F5 Arnage, Fr.
62/F4 Arnager (int'l arpt.), Den.
91/H2 Arnaía, Gre.
179/J3 Arnaud (riv.), Qu,Can
202/C2 Arnaudville, La,US
103/C2 Arnauti (cape), Cyp.
105/M6 Arnavutköy, Turk.
59/E3 Arncott, Eng,UK
72/C2 Arneburg, Ger.
76/D1 Arnedo, Sp.
194/C4 Arnegard, ND,US
167/F4 Arneiroz, Braz.
68/B2 Arnèke, Fr.
62/D1 Årnes, Nor.
190/E2 Arnett, Ok,US
195/K4 Arnheim, Mi,US
131/E3 Arnhem (bay), Austl.
131/E3 Arnhem (cape), Austl.
66/C5 Arnhem, Neth.
130/D3 Arnhem Land, Austl.
128/E2 Arnhem Land (reg.), Austl.
118/C5 Arni, India
79/G3 Arnières-sur-Iton, Fr.
86/D5 Arno (riv.), It.
138/G4 Arno (atoll), Mrsh.
130/D3 Arnold (riv.), Austl.
57/G5 Arnold, Eng,UK
186/B1 Arnold, Ca,US
206/B5 Arnold, Md,US
195/L4 Arnold, Mi,US
191/J1 Arnold, Mo,US
192/D3 Arnold, Ne,US
206/C5 Arnold (pt.), NJ,US
208/H6 Arnold, Pa,US
197/K2 Arnold's Cove, Nf,Can
75/K3 Arnoldstein, Aus.
74/E3 Arnon (riv.), Fr.
199/H4 Arnot, Pa,US
53/T10 Arnouville-lès-Gonesse, Fr.
199/H2 Arnprior, On,Can
67/F6 Arnsberg, Ger.
72/D5 Arnsdorf, Ger.
57/F3 Arnside, Eng,UK
72/A6 Arnstadt, Ger.
70/C3 Arnstein, Ger.
71/F5 Arnstorf, Ger.
156/B2 Aroab, Namb.
167/F4 Aroases, Braz.
76/B4 Aroche, Sp.
145/G5 Arochukwu, Nga.
195/L2 Aroland, On,Can
80/D6 Arolla, Swi.
67/G6 Arolsen, Ger.
172/C1 Aroma, Bol.
149/H2 Aroma, Sudan
186/B2 Aromas, Ca,US
79/E4 Aron, Fr.
74/E3 Aron (riv.), Fr.
86/B1 Arona, It.
77/X16 Arona, Canl.,Sp.
68/B4 Aronde (riv.), Fr.
196/D2 Aroostook, NB,Can
138/G5 Arorae (isl.), Kiri.
125/C2 Aroroy, Phil.
81/F4 Arosa, Swi.
81/F4 Aroser Rothorn (peak), Swi.
62/D4 Ærøskøbing, Den.
130/C2 Aro Usu (cape), Indo.
136/C2 Arowhana (peak), N.Z.
201/F5 Arp, Ga,US
105/E1 Arpaçay, Turk.
53/S11 Arpajon, Fr.
74/E4 Arpajon-sur-Cere, Fr.
86/B3 Arquata Scrivia, It.
172/C1 Arque, Bol.
68/B2 Arques, Fr.
68/A4 Arques-la-Bataille, Fr.
147/H4 Ar Rabad, Sudan
103/G7 'Arrābah, WBnk.
121/E3 Arrah, India
150/B3 Arraha, Eth.
149/F2 Ar Rahad, Sudan
105/E3 Ar Raḥḥālīyah, Iraq
170/D2 Arraias, Braz.
170/B1 Arraias (riv.), Braz.
161/G4 Arraiján, Pan.
57/H4 Arram, Eng,UK
105/E3 Ar Ramādī, Iraq
103/E3 Ar Ramthā, Jor.
54/A5 Arran (isl.), Sc,UK
161/E4 Arrancabarba (mtn.), Nic.
149/G3 Ar Rank, Sudan
104/D3 Ar Raqqah, Syria
104/D2 Ar Raqqah (prov.), Syria
68/B3 Arras, Fr.
106/D3 Ar Rass, SAr.
103/E2 Ar Rastan, Syria
77/F1 Arrats (riv.), Fr.
106/D3 Ar Rawḍah, SAr.
150/C2 Ar Rawḍah, Yem.
150/D2 Ar Rāwuk, Yem.
106/F3 Ar Rayyān, Qatar
74/D5 Arreau, Fr.
164/D4 Arrecifal, Col.
142/B3 Arrecife, Canl.
174/E2 Arrecifes, Arg.
78/B4 Arrée (mts.), Fr.
63/T9 Arresø (lake), Den.
187/J4 Arrey, NM,US
160/C2 Arriaga, Mex.
190/C1 Arriba, Co,US
105/F4 Ar Rifā'ī, Iraq
201/H2 Arrington, Va,US
187/H2 Arriola, Co,US
76/C1 Arriondas, Sp.
106/E4 Ar Riyāḍ (Riyadh) (cap.), SAr.
150/D2 Ar Riyān, Yem.
54/B4 Arrochar, Sc,UK
76/B3 Arronches, Port.
84/C2 Arrone, It.
84/B3 Arrone (riv.), It.
84/C3 Arrone (riv.), It.
86/B4 Arroscia (riv.), It.
79/G4 Arrou, Fr.
74/F3 Arroux (riv.), Fr.
204/C2 Arrowbear Lake, Ca,US
191/E4 Arrowhead (lake), Tx,US
194/E4 Arrowhead Nat'l Wild. Ref., ND,US
60/B1 Arrow, Lough (lake), Ire.
184/F2 Arrowrock (dam), Id,US
185/F2 Arrowrock (res.), Id,US
131/E3 Arrowsmith (pt.), Austl.
136/B3 Arrowsmith (peak), N.Z.
136/B4 Arrowtown, N.Z.
183/H2 Arrowwood, Ab,Can
172/D4 Arroyito, Arg.
76/B3 Arroyo de la Luz, Sp.
168/D3 Arroyo Grande, Bol.
186/B3 Arroyo Grande, Ca,US
190/B2 Arroyo Hondo, NM,US
190/B2 Arroyo Seco, NM,US
172/D4 Arrufó, Arg.
105/F4 Ar Rumaythah, Iraq
103/E3 Ar Ruṣayfah, Jor.
149/G3 Ar Ruṣayriṣ, Sudan
104/E3 Ar Ruṭbah, Iraq
106/F4 Ar Ruways, SAr.
62/C3 Års, Den.
105/H4 Arsanjān, Iran
109/L3 Arsen'yev, Rus.
150/A3 Ārsī (prov.), Eth.
87/E1 Arsiero, It.
95/L4 Arsk, Rus.
103/D1 Arslanköy, Turk.
64/F1 Ārslev, Den.
69/F5 Ars-sur-Moselle, Fr.
139/T11 Art (isl.), NCal.
150/B3 'Arta, Djib.
91/G3 Árta, Gre.
91/G3 Arta (gulf), Gre.
77/G3 Artá, Sp.
97/H5 Artashat, Arm.
158/E5 Arteaga, Mex.
159/E3 Arteaga, Mex.
76/A1 Arteijo, Sp.
109/L3 Artem, Rus.
161/F1 Artemisa, Cuba
97/J4 Artëm-Ostrov, Azer.
99/J3 Artëmovo, Ukr.
99/K3 Artemovsk, Ukr.
101/M4 Artemovskiy, Rus.
84/C4 Artena, It.
79/G4 Artenay, Fr.
72/B5 Artern, Ger.
204/B3 Artesia, Ca,US
200/C4 Artesia, Ms,US
190/B4 Artesia, NM,US
188/E3 Artesia Wells, Tx,US
81/E3 Arth, Swi.
196/B3 Arthabaska, Qu,Can
134/C3 Arthur (pt.), Austl.
132/C5 Arthur (riv.), Austl.
193/K4 Arthur, Il,US
194/F4 Arthur, ND,US
208/G6 Arthur (res.), Pa,US
201/H1 Arthur, WV,US
191/G4 Arthur City, Tx,US
199/G5 Arthurdale, WV,US
207/J9 Arthur Kill (str.), NJ, NY,US
136/B3 Arthur's (pass), N.Z.
136/B3 Arthurs Pass Nat'l Park, N.Z.
60/D5 Arthurstown, Ire.
95/N4 Arti, Rus.
173/E4 Artigas, Uru.
173/E3 Artigas (dept.), Uru.
97/G4 Artik, Arm.
86/D1 Artogne, It.
74/E1 Artois (hills), Fr.
68/A2 Artois (reg.), Fr.
68/B2 Artois, Collines de l' (hills), Fr.
104/D1 Artova, Turk.
98/E5 Artsiz, Ukr.
82/C5 Artuby (riv.), Fr.
171/J7 Artur Nogueira, Braz.
174/Q9 Arturo Merino Benítez (Santiago) (int'l arpt.), Chile
176/C4 Artux, China
104/E1 Artvin, Turk.
104/E1 Artvin (prov.), Turk.
130/D1 Aru (isls.), Indo.
153/F2 Aru, Zaire
153/G2 Arua, Ugan.
162/D4 Aruba (isl.), Neth.
142/B3 Arucas, Canl.
77/X16 Arucas, Canl.,Sp.
74/C5 Arudy, Fr.
171/K8 Arujá, Braz.
121/F1 Arun (riv.), China
121/F2 Arun (riv.), Nepal
59/F5 Arun (riv.), Eng,UK
121/J2 Arunachal Pradesh (state), India
59/F5 Arundel, Eng,UK
122/G4 Aruppukkottai, India
103/G7 'Arūrah, WBnk.
127/F3 Arus (cape), Indo.
151/B2 Arusha, Tanz.
151/B3 Arusha (prov.), Tanz.
151/B2 Arusha Chine, Tanz.
151/B2 Arusha Nat'l Park, Tanz.
139/L6 Arutua (atoll), FrPol.
122/H4 Aruvi (riv.), SrL.
153/F2 Aruwimi (riv.), Zaire
192/B4 Arvada, Co,US
185/K1 Arvada, Wy,US
60/C2 Arvagh, Ire.
82/C2 Arvan (riv.), Fr.
108/E2 Arvayheer, Mong.
80/C6 Arve (riv.), Fr.
61/F2 Arvidsjaur, Swe.
62/E2 Arvika, Swe.
186/C3 Arvin, Ca,US
83/C4 Arvo (lake), It.
83/C4 Arvo (riv.), It.
195/K4 Arvon (mt.), Mi,US
201/H2 Arvonia, Va,US
130/B1 Arwala, Indo.
141/X17 Aryānah, Tun.
141/X17 Aryānah (gov.), Tun.
114/A3 Arys', Kaz.
78/C5 Arz (riv.), Fr.
90/A2 Arzachena, It.
53/H3 Arzamas, Rus.
85/E6 Arzano, It.
70/A2 Arzbach, Ger.
71/F2 Arzberg, Ger.
67/G4 Arzen, Ger.
141/Q16 Arzew, Alg.
69/F3 Arzfeld, Ger.
97/H3 Arzgir, Rus.
87/E1 Arzignano, It.
81/G3 Arzl im Pitztal, Aus.
78/C5 Arzon, Fr.
76/A1 Arzúa, Sp.
69/E1 As, Belg.
71/F2 Aš, Czh.
62/D2 Ås, Nor.
154/C5 Asab, Namb.
145/G5 Asaba, Nga.
105/G3 Asadābād, Iran
144/D5 Asagny Nat'l Park, IvC.
124/B2 Asahan (riv.), Indo.
111/G3 Asahi, Japan
110/C3 Asahi (riv.), Japan
111/G2 Asahi-Bandai Nat'l Park, Japan
112/A4 Asahi-Bandi Nat'l Park, Japan
112/C2 Asahi-dake (mtn.), Japan
112/C2 Asahikawa, Japan
111/H7 Asaka, Japan
111/M9 Asake (riv.), Japan
150/B3 Asal, Djib.
150/B3 'Asal (mtn.), Djib.
150/B3 Asale, Eth.
105/H5 'Asalūyeh, Iran
145/E5 Asamankese, Gha.
111/F2 Asama-yama (mtn.), Japan
113/D4 Asan (bay), SKor.
145/E5 Asankrangwa, Gha.
121/F4 Asansol, India
118/C3 Āsāpur, India
111/F1 Asashi-dake (mtn.), Japan
139/H6 Asau, WSam.
146/C4 Asawanwah (well), Libya
150/B3 Āsayita, Eth.
69/G2 Asbach, Ger.
70/D5 Asbach-Bäumenheim, Ger.
95/P4 Asbest, Rus.
196/B3 Asbestos, Qu,Can
156/C3 Asbestos (mts.), SAfr.
150/B3 Āsbe Teferī, Eth.
193/J2 Asbury, Ia,US
207/D3 Asbury Park, NJ,US
83/B2 Ascea, It.
169/F4 Ascención, Bol.
159/J5 Ascención (bay), Mex.
174/E2 Ascensión, Arg.
162/D4 Ascension, NAnt.
140/A5 Ascension (isl.), StH.
85/D2 Ascensione, Monte dell' (peak), It.
71/G6 Aschach (riv.), Aus.
71/H6 Aschach an der Donau, Aus.
70/C3 Aschaffenburg, Ger.
71/F6 Aschau am Inn, Ger.
67/E5 Ascheberg, Ger.
67/E2 Aschendorf, Ger.
72/B4 Aschersleben, Ger.
84/B1 Asciano, It.
90/A1 Asco (riv.), Fr.
54/A5 Ascog, Sc,UK
85/D2 Ascoli Piceno, It.
85/D1 Ascoli Piceno (prov.), It.
85/F5 Ascoli Satriano, It.
81/E5 Ascona, Swi.
168/B2 Ascope, Peru
59/F4 Ascot, Eng,UK
172/B1 Ascotan (salt pan), Bol.
150/B2 Āseb, Eth.
150/B3 Āsebot, Eth.
62/F3 Aseda, Swe.
131/G1 Aseki, PNG
150/A4 Āsela, Eth.
61/F2 Åsele, Swe.
149/H4 Āsendabo, Eth.
67/G2 Asendorf, Ger.
67/G3 Asendorf, Ger.
93/G4 Asenovgrad, Bul.
62/B2 Åseral, Nor.
86/C3 Aserei, Monte (peak), It.
68/D5 Asfeld-la-Ville, Fr.
108/G2 Asgat, Mong.
59/G4 Ash, Eng,UK
145/F5 Asha, Nga.
59/E4 Ashampstead, Eng,UK
145/E5 Ashanti (reg.), Gha.
145/E5 Ashanti Uplands (reg.), Gha.
207/M8 Asharoken, NY,US
208/C3 Ashaway, RI,US
60/D3 Ashbourne, Ire.
57/G5 Ashbourne, Eng,UK
203/G2 Ashburn, Ga,US
132/C2 Ashburton (riv.), Austl
136/C3 Ashburton, N.Z.
58/C5 Ashburton, Eng,UK

132/C2 Ashburton Downs, Austl.
59/E1 Ashby (can.), Eng,UK
194/G4 Ashby, Mn,US
57/G6 Ashby-de-la-Zouch, Eng,UK
58/D3 Ashchurch, Eng,UK
182/D2 Ashcroft, BC,Can
191/G4 Ashdown, Ar,US
201/H3 Asheboro, NC,US
191/F3 Asher, Ok,US
194/E2 Ashern, Mb,Can
188/E3 Asherton, Tx,US
201/F3 Asheville, NC,US
191/J2 Ash Flat, Ar,US
135/D1 Ashford, Austl.
60/D3 Ashford, Ire.
53/M7 Ashford, Eng,UK
205/F2 Ashford, Al,US
208/B2 Ashford, Ct,US
59/F1 Ashfordby, Eng,UK
187/F3 Ash Fork, Az,US
197/R8 Ashgrove, On,Can
136/C3 Ashhurst, N.Z.
112/C2 Ashibetsu, Japan
57/G1 Ashington, Eng,UK
11/L10 Ashiya, Japan
110/C4 Ashizuri-misaki (cape), Japan
1/W17 Ashkal (lake), Tun.
105/J2 Ashkhabad (cap.), Trkm.
105/J2 Ashkhabad (int'l arpt.), Trkm.
146/B3 Ashkīdah, Libya
200/E4 Ashland, Al,US
190/E2 Ashland, Ks,US
201/F1 Ashland, Ky,US
202/B1 Ashland, La,US
208/C1 Ashland, Ma,US
196/C2 Ashland, Me,US
191/H1 Ashland, Mo,US
200/C3 Ashland, Ms,US
183/L5 Ashland, Mt,US
199/G3 Ashland, NY,US
208/E6 Ashland, Oh,US
208/E6 Ashland (co.), Oh,US
184/B2 Ashland, Or,US
206/B2 Ashland, Pa,US
188/E1 Ashland, Tx,US
195/J4 Ashland, Wi,US
200/D2 Ashland City, Tn,US
135/D1 Ashley, Austl.
193/K4 Ashley, Il,US
194/E4 Ashley, ND,US
206/C1 Ashley, Pa,US
208/A1 Ashley Falls, Ma,US
53/M6 Ashley Green, Eng,UK
130/A3 Ashmore (reef), Austl.
198/B5 Ashmore, Il,US
130/A3 Ashmore and Cartier Is. (terr.), Austl.
103/B4 Ashmūn, Egypt
182/D3 Ashnola Ind. Res., BC,Can
120/A3 Ashoknagar, India
112/C2 Ashoro, Japan
104/E4 Ash Shabakah, Iraq
103/E2 Ash Shamāl (gov.), Jor.
105/E4 Ash Shāmīyah, Iraq
107/G3 Ash Shāriqah, UAE
105/E3 Ash Sharqāt, Iraq
103/B4 Ash Sharqīyah (gov.), Egypt
105/F4 Ash Shaṭrah, Iraq
149/G2 Ash Shawal, Sudan
103/D4 Ash Shawbak, Jor.
106/D6 Ash Shaykh Sa'īd, Yem.
150/D2 Ash Shiḥr, Yem.
106/C4 Ash Shufayyah, SAr.
106/E3 Ash Shumlūl, SAr.
106/D5 Ash Shuqayq, SAr.
147/H3 Ash Shurayf, SAr.
118/C3 Ashta, India
198/F4 Ashtabula, Oh,US
208/G4 Ashtabula (co.), Oh,US
97/H4 Ashtarak, Arm.
53/N8 Ashtead, Eng,UK
118/C3 Ashti, India
105/G3 Āshtīān, Iran
156/C4 Ashton, SAfr.
185/H1 Ashton, Id,US
198/B4 Ashton, Il,US
192/E1 Ashton, SD,US
57/F5 Ashton-in-Makerfield, Eng,UK
57/F5 Ashton-under-Lyne, Eng,UK
196/A1 Ashuapmushuan (riv.), Qu,Can
200/D4 Ashville, Al,US
198/E5 Ashville, Oh,US
195/J4 Ashwabay (mt.), Wi,US
195/K5 Ashwaubenon, Wi,US
59/F2 Ashwell, Eng,UK
102/* Asia (cont.)
168/B4 Asia, Peru
87/E1 Asiago, It.
166/C2 Asidonhoppo, Sur.
63/L1 Asikkala, Fin.
141/L13 Asilah, Mor.
168/D4 Asillo, Peru
85/D4 Asina, It.
90/A2 Asinara (gulf), It.
90/A2 Asinara (isl.), It.
100/J4 Asino, Rus.
106/D5 'Asīr (mts.), SAr., Yemen
147/H5 Asis, Ras (cape), Sudan
104/E2 Aşkale, Turk.
57/E3 Askam in Furness, Eng,UK
99/G4 Askaniya-Nova, Ukr.
60/B4 Askeaton, Ire.
62/D2 Asker, Nor.
57/G4 Askern, Eng,UK
62/F2 Askersund, Swe.
200/B3 Askew, Ms,US
156/C2 Askham, SAfr.
62/D2 Askim, Nor.
62/D3 Askim, Swe.
91/G2 Askion (peak), Gre.
114/F1 Askiz, Rus.
207/K8 Askja (crater), Ice.
120/C1 Askot, India
64/E1 Askov, Den.
195/H4 Askov, Mn,US
149/H2 Āsmera, Eth.
62/F3 Asnen (lake), Swe.
53/T9 Asnières-sur-Oise, Fr.
53/S10 Asnières-sur-Seine, Fr.
86/D2 Asola, It.
87/E1 Asolo, It.
110/B4 Aso Nat'l Park, Japan
110/C3 Asosa, Eth.
110/B4 Aso-san (mtn.), Japan
106/C4 Asoteriba (peak), Sudan
147/H4 Asoteriba, Jabal (peak), Sudan
182/F4 Asotin, Wa,US
71/G6 Aspach, Aus.
57/E2 Aspatria, Eng,UK
77/E3 Aspe, Sp.
190/A1 Aspen, Co,US
184/B2 Aspen (lake), Or,US
103/B1 Aspendos (ruins), Turk.
182/D3 Aspen Grove, BC,Can
206/A5 Aspen Hill, Md,US
70/C5 Asperg, Ger.
188/D1 Aspermont, Tx,US
206/A4 Aspers, Pa,US
207/E1 Aspetuck (riv.), Ct,US
77/F1 Aspin, Col d' (pass), Fr.
105/E1 Aspindza, Geo.
136/B4 Aspiring (peak), N.Z.
82/B3 Aspres-sur-Buëch, Fr.
83/B6 Aspromonte (mts.), It.
91/H3 Aspropírgos, Gre.
197/G2 Aspy (bay), NS,Can
194/A1 Asquith, Sk,Can
142/C3 Assa, Mor.
143/G5 Assa Aguiene (peak), Alg.
144/C2 'Assâba, Massif de l' (reg.), Mrta.
104/D3 As Sabkhah, Syria
105/F3 As Sa'dīyah, Iraq
103/B5 Aş Şaff, Egypt
103/D4 Aş Şāfī, Jor.
149/F2 Aş Şafīyah, Sudan
142/B4 Assag, Uad (dry riv.), WSah.
104/E3 Aş Şāliḥīyah, Syria
105/G4 As Sālimīyah, Kuw.
106/E4 As Sālimīyah, SAr.
147/E2 As Sallūm, Egypt
105/F4 As Salmān, Iraq
103/D3 As Salṭ, Jor.
106/F4 As Salwá, SAr.
121/H2 Assam (state), India
105/F4 As Samāwah, Iraq
103/B4 As Santah, Egypt
145/G2 Assaouas, Niger
167/G4 Assaré, Braz.
191/F1 Assaria, Ks,US
103/D3 Aş Şarīḥ, Jor.
201/K1 Assateague I. Nat'l Seash., Md,US
141/W18 As Sawdā, Tun.
150/C2 As Şawma'ah, Yem.
68/D2 Asse, Belg.
155/F5 Assegaairivier (riv.), SAfr.
90/A3 Assemini, It.
66/D2 Assen, Neth.
68/C1 Assenede, Belg.
62/C4 Assens, Den.
62/D3 Assens, Den.
62/D3 Assentoft, Den.
69/E3 Assesse, Belg.
83/C5 Assi (riv.), It.
107/G4 As Sīb, Oman
146/C2 As Sidr, Libya
147/H4 As Sidr, SAr.
103/B4 As Sinbillāwayn, Egypt
194/B3 Assiniboia, Sk,Can
182/G2 Assiniboine (mtn.), BC,Can
194/D2 Assiniboine (riv.), Mb, Sk,Can
194/C2 Assiniboine Ind. Res., Sk,Can
170/C4 Assis, Braz.
170/B5 Assis Chateaubriand, Braz.
84/C1 Assisi, It.
71/F7 Assling, Ger.
86/C1 Asso, It.
85/D1 Asso (riv.), It.
152/B2 Assok-Ngoum, Gabon
140/K10 Assomada, CpV.
208/C2 Assonet, Ma,US
77/G1 Assou (riv.), Fr.
149/F4 As Sudd (reg.), Sudan
150/D2 As Sufāl, Yem.
149/G2 Aş Şufayyah, Sudan
143/H2 Aş Şukhayrah, Tun.
104/D3 As Sukhnah, Syria
149/G2 As Suki, Sudan
105/F3 As Sulaymānīyah, Iraq
105/F3 As Sulaymānīyah (gov.), Iraq
106/D3 As Sulaymī, SAr.
106/E4 As Sulayyil, SAr.
146/C2 As Sulṭān, Libya
149/E3 As Sumayḥ, Sudan
105/F5 Aş Şummān (mts.), SAr.
200/C1 Assumption, Il,US
104/E3 Aş Şuwār, Syria
103/E3 As Suwaydā', Syria
103/E3 As Suwaydā' (dist.), Syria
107/G4 As Suwayq, Oman
105/F3 Aş Şuwayrah, Iraq
103/C4 As Suways (gov.), Egypt
103/C5 As Suways (Suez), Egypt
121/H3 Astagram, Bang.
91/G3 Astakós, Gre.
97/J5 Astara, Azer.
105/G2 Āstārā, Iran
202/M6 Astatula, Fl,US
71/H6 Asten, Aus.
66/C6 Asten, Neth.
86/B3 Asti, It.
86/B3 Asti (prov.), It.
87/E1 Astico (riv.), It.
168/D4 Astillero, Peru
89/K3 Astipálaia, Gre.
89/K3 Astipálaia (isl.), Gre.
196/D2 Astle, NB,Can
171/P6 Astolfo Dutra, Braz.
59/E2 Aston, Eng,UK
58/D2 Aston on Clun, Eng,UK
170/C4 Astorga, Braz.
193/J3 Astoria, Il,US
207/K8 Astoria, NY,US
182/C4 Astoria, Or,US
62/E3 Åstorp, Swe.
174/D5 Astra, Arg.
53/H4 Astrakhan', Rus.
97/H3 Astrakhan Obl., Rus.
189/M9 Astrodome, Tx,US
84/B1 Astrone (riv.), It.
91/H4 Ástros, Gre.
189/M9 Astroworld, Tx,US
76/C1 Astudillo, Sp.
76/B1 Asturias, Principado de (aut. comm.), Sp.
59/E2 Astwood Bank, Eng,UK
111/L10 Asuka, Japan
111/N9 Asuke, Japan
169/E3 Asunción, Bol.
138/D3 Asuncion (isl.), NMar.
172/E3 Asunción (cap.), Par.
160/C2 Asunción Ixtaltepec, Mex.
159/F5 Asunción Nochixtlán, Mex.
173/E3 Asunción (Silvio Pettirossi) (int'l arpt.), Par.
62/F2 Asunden (lake), Swe.
169/E5 Asunta, Bol.
149/G5 Aswa, Ugan.
153/H2 Aswa (riv.), Ugan.
146/C3 Aswad, Al Harūj al (hills), Libya
147/G3 Aswān, Egypt
147/G4 Aswān (gov.), Egypt
147/G4 Aswan High (dam), Egypt
147/F3 Asyūṭ, Egypt
147/F3 Asyūṭ (gov.), Egypt
147/G2 Asyūṭī, Wādī al (dry riv.), Egypt
165/E4 Atabapo (riv.), Col., Ven.
104/B2 Atabey, Turk.
172/C2 Atacama (plat.), Arg.
172/B1 Atacama (des.), Chile
172/B3 Atacama (reg.), Chile
172/B1 Atacama (salt pan), Chile
164/B4 Atacames, Ecu.
145/F4 Atacora (range), Ben.
139/H5 Atafu (isl.), Tok.
145/F5 Atakpamé, Togo
171/F1 Atalaia, Braz.
168/D2 Atalaia do Norte, Braz.
91/H3 Atalándi, Gre.
168/C3 Atalaya, Peru
108/G1 Atamanovka, Rus.
157/H8 Atambohobe, Madg.
130/B2 Atambua, Indo.
111/F3 Atami, Japan
125/B5 Atap, Indo.
130/B2 Atapupu, Indo.
150/C2 'Ataq, Yem.
144/B1 Atar, Mrta.
76/D4 Atarfe, Sp.
159/E4 Atarjea, Mex.
120/C3 Atarra, India
108/D3 Atas Bogd (peak), Mong.
186/B3 Atascadero, Ca,US
189/E3 Atascosa, Tx,US
189/E3 Atascosa (riv.), Tx,US
114/B2 Atasu, Kaz.
104/D2 Atatürk (dam), Turk.
93/J5 Atatürk (int'l arpt.), Turk.
104/D2 Atatürk (res.), Turk.
130/B2 Atauro (isl.), Indo.
150/A3 Ātaya, Eth.
140/F3 Atbara (riv.), Eth., Sudan
149/G1 Atbara, Sudan
149/G1 'Atbarah, Nahr (riv.), Sudan
114/A1 Atbasar, Kaz.
202/C3 Atchafalaya (bay), La,US
189/J2 Atchafalaya (riv.), La,US
191/G1 Atchison, Ks,US
206/D4 Atco, NJ,US
145/E5 Atebubu, Gha.
76/E2 Ateca, Sp.
61/G1 Ateelva (riv.), Nor.
85/F6 Atella, It.
85/F6 Atella (riv.), It.
168/D4 Atén, Bol.
158/D4 Atengo (riv.), Mex.
85/D3 Aterno (riv.), It.
85/E3 Atessa, It.
206/C4 Atglen, Pa,US
62/C4 Ath, Belg.
178/E3 Athabasca (riv.), Ab,Can
178/E3 Athabasca (lake), Ab, Sk,Can
121/H3 Āthārabāri, Bang.
89/G4 Athār Şabrātah (ruins), Libya
146/D1 Athār Ţulmaythah (Ptolemaïs) (ruins), Libya
60/D2 Athboy, Ire.
60/A5 Athea, Ire.
184/D1 Athena, Or,US
207/J8 Athenia, NJ,US
60/B3 Athenry, Ire.
199/J2 Athens, On,Can
200/D3 Athens, Al,US
191/H3 Athens, Ar,US
201/F4 Athens, Ga,US
193/K4 Athens, Il,US
198/D3 Athens, Mi,US
199/K3 Athens, NY,US
198/E5 Athens, Oh,US
199/H4 Athens, Pa,US
200/E3 Athens, Tn,US
189/G1 Athens, Tx,US
201/G2 Athens, WV,US
91/H4 Athens (Athínai) (cap.), Gre.
59/E1 Atherstone, Eng,UK
134/B2 Atherton, Austl.
57/F4 Atherton, Eng,UK
118/E3 Athgarh, India
151/B2 Athi (riv.), Kenya
103/C2 Athienou, Cyp.
91/H4 Athínai (Athens), Gre.
91/L7 Athínai (Athens) (cap.), Gre.
151/B2 Athi River, Kenya
79/E3 Athis, Fr.
53/T10 Athis-Mons, Fr.
60/B2 Athleague, Ire.
60/C3 Athlone, Ire.
116/B5 Athok, Burma
136/B4 Athol, N.Z.
199/K3 Athol, Ma,US
54/C3 Atholl (forest), Sc,UK
196/D2 Atholville, NB,Can
91/J2 Áthos (peak), Gre.
60/D4 Athy, Ire.
148/C2 Ati, Chad
153/H2 Atiak, Ugan.
171/K8 Atibaia, Braz.
171/K7 Atibaia (riv.), Braz.
168/C5 Atico, Peru
76/D2 Atienza, Sp.
195/J3 Atikokan, On,Can
127/F3 Atinggola, Indo.
160/D3 Atitlán (lake), Guat.
139/K7 Atiu (isl.), Cookls.
159/Q9 Atizapan (arpt.), Mex.
101/R3 Atka, Rus.
177/D5 Atka, Ak,US
177/C5 Atka (isl.), Ak,US
97/H2 Atkarsk, Rus.
191/H3 Atkins, Ar,US
201/G2 Atkins, Va,US
177/M2 Atkinson (pt.), NW,Can
189/N9 Atkinson (isl.), Tx,US
159/F5 Atlacomulco de Fabela, Mex.
156/D2 Atlanta, SAfr.
200/E4 Atlanta, Ga,US
193/K3 Atlanta, Il,US
189/H2 Atlanta, La,US
198/D2 Atlanta, Mi,US
189/G1 Atlanta, Tx,US
201/M7 Atlanta Botan. Gdn., Ga,US
200/E4 Atlanta Hartsfield (int'l arpt.), Ga,US
200/E4 Atlanta Nav. Air Sta., Ga,US
50/G3 Atlantic (ocean)
201/G4 Atlantic (coastal pl.), US
193/G3 Atlantic, Ia,US
201/J3 Atlantic, NC,US
206/D5 Atlantic (co.), NJ,US
208/G4 Atlantic, Pa,US
185/J2 Atlantic (peak), Wy,US
203/H2 Atlantic Beach, Fl,US
207/E2 Atlantic Beach, NY,US
206/D5 Atlantic City, NJ,US
206/D5 Atlantic City (int'l arpt.), NJ,US
185/J2 Atlantic City, Wy,US
207/J10 Atlantic Highlands, NJ,US
167/D4 Atlántico (dept.), Col.
175/U12 Atlántida, Uru.
145/F5 Atlantique (prov.), Ben.
142/E2 Atlas (mts.), Afr.
205/K10 Atlas (peak), Ca,US
142/D2 Atlas, Moyen (mts.), Mor.
101/R4 Atlasovo, Rus.
143/E2 Atlas Saharien (mts.), Alg., Mor.
88/D3 Atlas, Tell (mts.), Alg.
159/M7 Atlazayanca, Mex.
177/M4 Atlin, BC,Can
177/M4 Atlin (lake), BC,Can
159/F5 Atlixco, Mex.
202/E2 Atmore, Al,US
182/B1 Atnarko (riv.), BC,Can
172/C2 Atocha, Bol.
191/F3 Atoka, Ok,US
191/F3 Atoka (res.), Ok,US
200/C3 Atoka, Tn,US
154/B1 Atome, Ang.
185/G2 Atomic City, Id,US
68/D2 Atomium, The, Belg.
153/F3 Atondo, Zaire
159/L6 Atotonilco el Grande, Mex.
142/B5 Atoui, Khatt (dry riv.), Mrta.
142/D5 Atouila, 'Erg (des.), Mali
160/B2 Atoyac (riv.), Mex.
177/G1 Atqasuk, Ak,US
121/G3 Atrai (riv.), Bang.
105/J2 Atrak (riv.), Iran
62/E3 Ätran (riv.), Swe.
164/B3 Atrato (riv.), Col.
120/B1 Atrauli, India
85/D2 Atri, It.
111/H7 Atsugi, Japan
111/N10 Atsumi, Japan
111/N10 Atsumi (pen.), Japan
103/D4 Aţ Ţafīlah, Jor.
106/D4 Aţ Ţā'if, SAr.
80/C4 Attalens, Swi.
103/E3 At Tall, Syria
200/D3 Attalla, Al,US
146/D3 Aţ Ţallāb, Libya
103/B4 At Tall al Kabīr, Egypt
146/D3 At Tamīmī, Libya
105/E3 At Ta'mīn (gov.), Iraq
123/D3 Attapu, Laos
203/F2 Attapulgus, Ga,US
188/C3 Attares, Mex.
179/H3 Attawapiskat, On,Can
179/H3 Attawapiskat (riv.), On,Can
208/C2 Attawaugan, Ct,US
196/B3 Attean (mtn.), Me,US
71/F6 Attel (riv.), Ger.
67/E6 Attendorn, Ger.
71/G7 Attersee (lake), Aus.
69/E4 Attert, Belg.
198/C4 Attica, In,US
191/E2 Attica, Ks,US
205/F5 Attica, Mi,US
198/E4 Attica, Oh,US
68/C5 Attichy, Fr.
87/E2 Attigliano, It.
68/D5 Attigny, Fr.
103/G7 'Attīl, WBnk.
122/F4 Attingal, India
208/C2 Attleboro, Ma,US
59/E2 Attleborough, Eng,UK
59/H2 Attleborough, Eng,UK
71/G6 Attnang-Puchheim, Aus.
189/G2 Attoyac (riv.), Tx,US
177/A5 Attu, Ak,US
177/A5 Attu (isl.), Ak,US
103/B5 Aţ Ţūr, Egypt
122/G3 Āttūr, India
103/D4 Aţ Ţūr, WBnk.
106/D6 At Turbah, Yem.
150/C2 At Turbah, Yem.
149/E2 Aţ Ţuwayshah, Sudan
104/E5 Aţ Ţuwayyah, SAr.
174/D2 Atuel (riv.), Arg.
142/B5 Atui, Uad (dry riv.), WSah.
164/B4 Atuntaqui, Ecu.
139/M5 Atuona, FrPol.
121/G3 Atura, Bang.
151/A1 Atura, Ugan.
62/G2 Åtvidaberg, Swe.
186/B2 Atwater, Ca,US
192/G1 Atwater, Mn,US
208/F5 Atwater, Oh,US
192/C3 Atwood, Co,US
190/D1 Atwood, Ks,US
208/F6 Atwood (lake), Oh,US
191/F3 Atwood, Ok,US
162/C2 Atwood (Samana) (cay), Bahm.
159/Q10 Atzcapotzalco, Mex.
81/F3 Au, Aus.
81/F3 Au, Swi.
165/E3 Auari (riv.), Braz.
161/E3 Auas, Hon.
161/E3 Auasbila, Hon.
154/C4 Aub, Namb.
130/B2 Aubá, Indo.
82/B6 Aubagne, Fr.
69/E4 Aubange, Belg.
68/D6 Aube (dept.), Fr.
80/A2 Aube (riv.), Fr.
74/F4 Aubenas, Fr.
79/G3 Aubergenville, Fr.
186/C2 Auberry, Ca,US
80/C4 Aubert, Mont (peak), Swi.
53/T10 Aubervilliers, Fr.
79/F3 Aube-sur-Rîle, Fr.
68/C6 Aubetin (riv.), Fr.
68/A5 Aubette (riv.), Fr.
68/A5 Aubevoye, Fr.
82/B4 Aubignon, Fr.
68/B3 Aubigny, Fr.
74/E3 Aubigny-sur-Nère, Fr.
74/E4 Aubin, Fr.
80/C5 Aubonne, Swi.
69/E5 Auboué, Fr.
74/E4 Aubrac (mts.), Fr.
191/J3 Aubrey, Ar,US
69/D3 Aubrives, Fr.
133/H5 Auburn, Austl.
200/E4 Auburn, Al,US
184/C4 Auburn, Ca,US
200/F3 Auburn, Ga,US
193/K4 Auburn, Il,US
198/D4 Auburn, In,US
191/G1 Auburn, Ks,US
200/D2 Auburn, Ky,US
208/C1 Auburn, Ma,US
196/B3 Auburn, Me,US
202/C2 Auburn, Ms,US
193/G3 Auburn, Ne,US
199/H3 Auburn, NY,US
206/B2 Auburn, Pa,US
205/C3 Auburn, Wa,US
202/M7 Auburndale, Fl,US
203/H3 Auburndale, Fl,US
205/F6 Auburn Hills, Mi,US
74/E4 Aubusson, Fr.
174/C3 Aucá Mahuida (peak), Arg.
63/K3 Auce, Lat.
74/D5 Auch, Fr.
119/G2 Auche, Burma
68/B3 Auchel, Fr.
54/D3 Auchenblae, Sc,UK
56/E2 Auchencairn, Sc,UK
145/G5 Auchi, Nga.
54/B6 Auchinleck, Sc,UK
54/C4 Auchterarder, Sc,UK
54/C4 Auchtermuchty, Sc,UK
68/B3 Auchy-lès-Hesdin, Fr.
203/G2 Aucilla (riv.), Fl,US
136/C2 Auckland, N.Z.
136/C2 Auckland (int'l arpt.), N.Z.
51/S8 Auckland (isls.), N.Z.
136/C2 Auckland (reg.), N.Z.
136/F6 Auckland Domain, N.Z.
74/E5 Aude (riv.), Fr.
195/L2 Auden, On,Can
68/D2 Auderghem, Belg.
196/B3 Audet, Qu,Can
80/C3 Audeux (riv.), Fr.
78/A4 Audierne, Fr.
78/A5 Audierne (bay), Fr.
80/C3 Audincourt, Fr.
57/F6 Audlem, Eng,UK
57/F5 Audley, Eng,UK
150/B4 Audo (range), Eth.
68/B2 Audruicq, Fr.
193/G3 Audubon, Ia,US
194/D4 Audubon Nat'l Wild. Ref., ND,US
69/E5 Audun-le-Roman, Fr.
69/E5 Audun-le-Tiche, Fr.
71/F1 Aue, Ger.
67/E2 Aue (riv.), Ger.
67/F3 Aue (riv.), Ger.
78/B4 Auen (riv.), Fr.
71/F1 Auerbach, Ger.
71/E3 Auerbach in der Oberpfalz, Ger.
81/G2 Auerberg (mtn.), Ger.
81/H5 Auer (Ora), It.
71/F2 Auersberg (peak), Ger.
70/E3 Aufess (riv.), Ger.
68/A4 Auffay, Fr.
134/B4 Augathella, Austl.
185/F2 Auger (falls), Id,US
56/A3 Augher, NI,UK
60/A4 Aughinish (isl.), Ire.
56/B3 Aughnacloy, NI,UK
60/D4 Aughrim, Ire.
198/D4 Auglaize (riv.), Oh,US
156/C3 Augrabies Falls Nat'l Park, SAfr.
156/C3 Augrabiesvalle (falls), SAfr.
198/E2 Au Gres, Mi,US
70/D6 Augsburg, Ger.
70/D6 Augsburg (Mühlhausen) (arpt.), Ger.
156/A2 Augub (peak), Namb.
132/B5 Augusta, Austl.
161/H4 Augusta (pt.), Col.
90/D4 Augusta, It.
90/D4 Augusta (gulf), It.
191/J3 Augusta, Ar,US
201/G4 Augusta, Ga,US
193/J3 Augusta, Il,US
191/F2 Augusta, Ks,US
196/C3 Augusta, Me,US
183/H4 Augusta, Mt,US
206/D1 Augusta, NJ,US
193/J1 Augusta, Wi,US
201/H1 Augusta, WV,US
67/F5 Augustdorf, Ger.
62/C4 Augustenborg, Den.
186/D4 Augustine Ind. Res., Ca,US
160/E3 Augusto César Sandino (int'l arpt.), Nic.
65/M2 Augustów, Pol.
128/C3 Augustus (isl.), Austl.
132/C3 Augustus (peak), Austl.
71/E5 Au in der Hallertau, Ger.
156/B2 Aukam, Namb.
123/B3 Auk Bok (isl.), Burma
185/F3 Auki, Sol.
201/J2 Aulander, NC,US
132/D2 Auld (lake), Austl.
54/C1 Auldearn, Sc,UK
77/M9 Aulencia (riv.), Sp.
81/F2 Aulendorf, Ger.
86/C4 Aulla, It.
53/T10 Aulnay-sous-Bois, Fr.
78/B4 Aulne (riv.), Fr.
195/G3 Aulneau (pen.), On,Can
68/C3 Aulnoye-Aymeries, Fr.
74/E4 Aulnat (Clermont-Ferrand) (int'l arpt.), Fr.
68/A3 Ault, Fr.
192/B3 Ault, Co,US
81/F4 Ault, Piz (peak), Swi.
72/B6 Auma, Ger.
72/B6 Auma (riv.), Ger.
68/A4 Aumale, Fr.
69/E5 Aumetz, Fr.
184/B1 Aumsville, Or,US
67/H1 Aumühle, Ger.
145/G4 Auna, Nga.
79/E2 Aunay-sur-Odon, Fr.
79/F5 Aune (riv.), Fr.
79/G4 Auneau, Fr.
68/B5 Aunette (riv.), Fr.
68/B5 Auneuil, Fr.
62/D3 Auning, Den.
154/C5 Auob (dry riv.), Namb.
156/C2 Auobrivier (dry riv.), SAfr.
82/C5 Aups, Fr.
124/D2 Aur (isl.), Malay.
138/G4 Aur (atoll), Mrsh.
206/C4 Aura, NJ,US
70/D4 Aurach, Ger.
70/D3 Aurach (riv.), Ger.
120/B2 Auraiya, India
120/E3 Aurangābād, India
120/A1 Aurangābād Saiyid, India
78/C5 Auray, Fr.
74/D5 Aureilhan, Fr.
193/G2 Aurelia, Ia,US
88/E4 Aurès (mts.), Alg.
67/E2 Aurich, Ger.
170/C4 Auriflama, Braz.
74/E4 Aurillac, Fr.
82/B6 Auriol, Fr.
87/G1 Aurisina, It.
62/B1 Aurland, Nor.
71/G6 Aurolzmünster, Aus.
167/G4 Aurora, Braz.
199/G3 Aurora, On,Can
165/G3 Aurora, Guy.
125/C2 Aurora, Phil.
125/C4 Aurora, Phil.
192/B4 Aurora, Co,US
205/P16 Aurora, Il,US
191/H2 Aurora, Mo,US
201/J3 Aurora, NC,US
192/E3 Aurora, Ne,US
186/C1 Aurora (ghost town), Nv,US
208/F5 Aurora, Oh,US
185/H4 Aurora, Ut,US
184/D4 Aurora Ghost Town, Nv,US
177/J3 Aurora Lodge, Ak,US
125/C2 Aurora Mem. Park, Phil.
134/A1 Aurukun Abor. Land, Austl.
85/D5 Aurunci (mts.), It.
156/B2 Aus, Namb.
87/G1 Ausa (riv.), It.
198/F3 Ausable (riv.), On,Can
198/E2 Au Sable (pt.), Mi,US
198/D2 Au Sable (riv.), Mi,US
142/B5 Ausert, WSah.
72/B3 Ausleben, Ger.
85/D5 Ausoni (mts.), It.
156/B3 Aussenkehr, Namb.
81/F3 Ausserrhoden (demi-canton), Swi.
74/E5 Aussillon, Fr.
62/B2 Aust-Agder (co.), Nor.
201/L7 Austell, Ga,US
73/A1 Austerlitz (Slavkov u Brna), Czh.
132/C3 Austin (lake), Austl.
194/E3 Austin, Mb,Can
178/G2 Austin (isl.), NW,Can
198/D5 Austin, In,US
200/D2 Austin, Ky,US
193/H2 Austin, Mn,US
184/E4 Austin, Nv,US
184/D1 Austin, Or,US
199/G4 Austin, Pa,US
189/F2 Austin, Tx,US
189/M9 Austin (bayou), Tx,US
208/G5 Austintown, Oh,US
189/G2 Austonio, Tx,US
128/* Australia (cont.)
182/C1 Australian, BC,Can
135/C3 Australian Alps (mts.), Austl.
135/D3 Australian Cap. Terr., Austl.
132/B5 Australind, Austl.
75/L3 Austria
61/P7 Austurhorn (pt.), Ice.
200/D4 Autaugaville, Al,US
166/B3 Autazes, Braz.
77/F1 Auterive, Fr.
68/B3 Authie (riv.), Fr.
79/E6 Authion (riv.), Fr.
79/F4 Authon-du-Perche, Fr.
158/D5 Autlán, Mex.
68/B5 Automne (riv.), Fr.
84/D4 Autore (peak), It.
68/C3 Autreppe, Belg.
74/F3 Autun, Fr.
130/C3 Auvergne, Austl.
74/E4 Auvergne (reg.), Fr.
74/E4 Auvergne (mts.), Fr.
53/S9 Auvers-sur-Oise, Fr.
74/D4 Auvézère (riv.), Fr.
74/E3 Auxerre, Fr.
68/B3 Auxi-le-Château, Fr.
80/B3 Auxonne, Fr.
198/E1 Aux Sables (riv.), On,Can
191/J1 Auxvasse, Mo,US
165/F3 Auyán-Tepuí (peak), Ven.
179/K2 Auyuittuq Nat'l Park, NW,Can
168/D4 Auzangate (peak), Peru
123/A1 Ava, Burma
193/K5 Ava, Il,US
191/H2 Ava, Mo,US
105/G3 Āvaj, Iran
74/E3 Avallon, Fr.
79/E4 Avaloirs, Mont de (mtn.), Fr.
197/L2 Avalon (pen.), Nf,Can
204/B4 Avalon, Ca,US
191/H1 Avalon, Mo,US
206/D5 Avalon, NJ,US
208/G6 Avalon, Pa,US
122/F3 Avanāshi, India
80/B3 Avanne-Aveney, Fr.
170/C4 Avaré, Braz.
139/K7 Avarua, N.Z.
105/M7 Avcilar, Turk.
99/J3 Avdeyevka, Ukr.
59/E4 Avebury, Eng,UK
59/E4 Avebury Stone Circle (ruins), Eng,UK
76/A2 Aveiro, Port.
76/A2 Aveiro (dist.), Port.
53/P7 Aveley, Eng,UK
68/C2 Avelgem, Belg.
85/F6 Avelino (prov.), It.
174/F2 Avellaneda, Arg.
85/E6 Avellino, It.
68/A4 Avelon (riv.), Fr.
186/B2 Avenal, Ca,US
80/D4 Avenches, Swi.
207/D2 Avenel, NJ,US
68/A6 Aver (riv.), Fr.
85/E6 Aversa, It.
182/G4 Avery, Id,US
202/C3 Avery Island, La,US
162/E4 Aves (isl.), Ven.
68/B3 Avesnes-le-Comte, Fr.
68/C3 Avesnes-sur-Helpe, Fr.
78/D5 Avessac, Fr.
62/G1 Avesta, Swe.
74/D4 Aveyron (riv.), Fr.
85/D3 Avezzano, It.
54/A4 Avich, Loch (lake), Sc,UK
54/C2 Aviemore, Sc,UK
82/D2 Avigliana, It.
85/F6 Avigliano, It.
82/A5 Avignon, Fr.
82/A5 Avignon (Caumont) (arpt.), Fr.
103/F7 Aviḥayil, Isr.
76/C2 Ávila de los Caballeros, Sp.
76/C1 Avilés, Sp.
87/D1 Avio, It.
68/B3 Avion, Fr.
197/J2 Aviron (pt.), Can
76/B3 Avis, Port.
206/A1 Avis, Pa,US
81/H5 Avisio (riv.), It.
76/B3 Aviz, Port.
68/D6 Avize, Fr.
62/C3 Avlum, Den.
135/B3 Avoca, Austl.
135/C4 Avoca, Austl.
56/B6 Avoca, Ire.
60/D4 Avoca (riv.), Ire.
193/G3 Avoca, Ia,US
199/H3 Avoca, NY,US
56/B1 Avoch, Sc,UK
79/F6 Avoine, Fr.
182/E2 Avola, BC,Can
90/D4 Avola, It.
132/C5 Avon (riv.), Austl.
74/E2 Avon, Fr.
58/D4 Avon (co.), Eng,UK
58/C6 Avon (riv.), Eng,UK
58/D4 Avon (riv.), Eng,UK
59/E4 Avon (riv.), Eng,UK
59/E5 Avon (riv.), Eng,UK
54/C2 Avon (riv.), Sc,UK
54/C5 Avon (riv.), Sc,UK
203/F2 Avon, Al,US
190/A1 Avon, Co,US
208/B2 Avon, Ct,US
193/J3 Avon, Il,US
208/C1 Avon, Ma,US
195/G5 Avon, Mn,US
191/J4 Avon, Ms,US
201/K3 Avon, NC,US
199/H3 Avon, NY,US
208/E5 Avon, Oh,US
60/D4 Avonbeg (riv.), Ire.
135/F2 Avondale, Austl.
187/F4 Avondale, Az,US
192/B4 Avondale, Co,US
206/C4 Avondale, Pa,US
133/H2 Avon Downs, Austl.
208/E4 Avon Lake, Oh,US
194/B2 Avonlea, Sk,Can
56/D6 Avonmore (riv.), Ire.
58/D4 Avonmouth, Eng,UK
202/M8 Avon Park, Fl,US
203/H4 Avon Park, Fl,US
202/N8 Avon Park Bomb. Ra., Fl,US
203/H4 Avon Park Bomb. Ra., Fl,US
132/C4 Avon Valley Nat'l Park, Austl.
54/B5 Avon Water (riv.), Sc,UK
78/D3 Avranches, Fr.
68/B4 Avre (riv.), Fr.
79/E2 Avre (riv.), Fr.
79/F3 Avre (riv.), Fr.
79/E5 Avrillé, Fr.
97/J5 Avrora, Azer.
118/D4 Āvupalli, India
152/B2 Awaé, Camr.
111/L10 Awaji, Japan
110/D3 Awaji (isl.), Japan
103/E3 A'waj, Nahr al (riv.), Syria
148/D3 Awakaba, CAfr.
69/E2 Awans, Belg.
136/C1 Awanui, N.Z.
150/C3 Āwarē, Eth.
150/B3 Āwash, Eth.
150/A3 Āwash Nat'l Park, Eth.
149/H3 Āwash Wenz (riv.), Eth.
154/B5 Awasibberge (peak), Namb.
145/E5 Awaso, Gha.
114/D3 Awat, China
136/C3 Awatere (riv.), N.Z.
146/B3 Awbārī, Libya
146/B3 Awbārī, Şaḥrā' (des.), Libya
60/B5 Awbeg (riv.), Ire.
150/C5 Awdheegle, Som.
54/A4 Awe, Loch (lake), Sc,UK
145/G5 Awgu, Nga.
150/A2 Āwira Wenz (riv.), Eth.
146/D2 Awjilah, Libya
145/G5 Awka, Nga.
193/F3 Awsīm, Egypt
62/F3 Axamo (int'l arpt.), Swe.
81/H3 Axams, Aus.
61/P6 Axarfjördhur (bay), Ice.
58/D4 Axbridge, Eng,UK
58/D4 Axe (riv.), Eng,UK
58/D5 Axe (riv.), Eng,UK
66/A6 Axel, Neth.
179/S7 Axel Heiberg (isl.), NW,Can
185/K3 Axial, Co,US
145/E5 Axim, Gha.
91/H2 Axios (riv.), Gre.
205/D2 Axis (dam), Wa,US
166/E4 Axixá de Goiás, Braz.
74/D5 Ax-les-Thermes, Fr.
58/D5 Axminster, Eng,UK
159/L8 Axochiapan, Mex.
203/G2 Axson, Ga,US
191/F1 Axtell, Ks,US
192/E3 Axtell, Ne,US
68/D5 Ay, Fr.
95/N5 Ay (riv.), Rus.
168/B2 Ayabaca, Peru
110/D3 Ayabe, Japan
174/F3 Ayacucho, Arg.
168/C4 Ayacucho, Peru
114/D2 Ayaguz, Kaz.
114/D2 Ayaguz (riv.), Kaz.
114/E4 Ayakkum (lake), China
111/M10 Ayama, Japan
144/E5 Ayamé I, Barrage d' (dam), IvC.
144/E5 Ayamé II, Barrage d' (dam), IvC.
76/B4 Ayamonte, Sp.
101/P4 Ayan, Rus.
104/C1 Ayancık, Turk.
165/G3 Ayanganna (peak), Guy.
145/G5 Ayangba, Nga.
101/S3 Ayanka, Rus.
164/C2 Ayapel, Col.
161/H5 Ayapel, Serranía (range), Col.
104/C1 Ayaş, Turk.
111/H7 Ayase, Japan
151/A1 Ayass (peak), Ugan.
168/D4 Ayaviri, Peru
107/J1 Āybak, Afg.
103/G7 'Aybāl, Jabal (Har Eval) (mtn.), WBnk.
97/J3 Aybas, Kaz.
104/D1 Aybastı, Turk.
114/A1 Aydabul, Kaz.
201/J3 Ayden, NC,US
104/A2 Aydın, Turk.
104/B2 Aydin (prov.), Turk.
103/C1 Aydıncık, Turk.
103/B1 Aydınkent, Turk.
105/N7 Aydınlı, Turk.
104/E1 Aydıntepe, Turk.
150/B3 Aydora, Eth.
97/L1 Aydyrlinskiy, Rus.
150/B3 Āyelu Terara (peak), Eth.
152/B3 Ayem, Gabon
80/D5 Ayer, Swi.
124/C2 Ayer Hitam, Malay.
199/K2 Ayer's Cliff, Qu,Can
133/F3 Ayers Rock (Uluru) (peak), Austl.
116/B5 Ayeyarwady (Irrawaddy) (div.), Burma
91/H3 Ayiá, Gre.
91/K3 Ayia Paraskeví, Gre.
91/K3 Ayiásos, Gre.
152/C2 Ayina (riv.), Afr.
91/J2 Ayios Athanásios, Gre.
91/J3 Ayios Evstrátios (isl.), Gre.
91/J5 Ayios Ioánnis, Ákra (cape), Gre.
91/K4 Ayios Kírikos, Gre.
91/H3 Ayios Konstandínos, Gre.
91/F3 Ayios Matthaíos, Gre.
91/J5 Ayios Nikólaos, Gre.
149/H2 Aykel, Eth.
101/M3 Aykhal, Rus.
59/F3 Aylesbury, Eng,UK
196/E3 Aylesford, NS,Can
59/G4 Aylesford, Eng,UK
59/H4 Aylesham, Eng,UK
76/D2 Ayllón, Sp.
178/F2 Aylmer (lake), NW,Can
198/F3 Aylmer, On,Can
183/N1 Aylsham, Sk,Can
59/H1 Aylsham, Eng,UK
168/C4 Ayna, Peru
141/W17 'Ayn Ad Darāhim, Tun.
104/D2 'Ayn al 'Arab, Syria
146/D1 'Ayn al Ghazālah, Libya
146/D3 'Ayn Ath Tha'lab, Libya
201/H4 Aynor, SC,US
106/D1 'Ayn, Ra's al, Syria
103/G8 'Aynūnah, SAr.
149/F3 Ayod, Sudan
120/D2 Ayodhyā, India
173/E3 Ayolas, Par.
101/S3 Ayon (isl.), Rus.
77/E3 Ayora, Sp.
145/F3 Ayorou, Niger
148/B5 Ayos, Camr.
159/F5 Ayotzintepec, Mex.
142/D4 'Ayoûn 'Abd el Mâlek (well), Mrta.
144/C2 'Ayoûn el 'Atroûs, Mrta.
134/B2 Ayr, Austl.
54/B6 Ayr, Sc,UK
54/B5 Ayr (riv.), Sc,UK
104/C2 Ayrancı, Turk.
56/D3 Ayre, Point of (pt.), Eng,UK
54/B6 Ayr, Heads of (pt.), Sc,UK
150/B3 Aysha, Eth.
57/H3 Ayton, Eng,UK
54/D5 Ayton, Sc,UK
149/H3 Aytony, Eth.
93/H4 Aytos, Bul.
74/C3 Aytré, Fr.
99/L4 Ayutinskiy, Rus.
158/D4 Ayutla, Mex.
123/C3 Ayutthaya (ruins), Thai.
91/K3 Ayvacık, Turk.
104/A2 Ayvalık, Turk.
69/E3 Aywaille, Belg.
122/B1 Azad Kashmir (terr.), Pak.
105/G3 Āzādshahr, Iran
77/F3 Azahar (coast), Sp.
111/M9 Azai, Japan
184/B2 Azalea, Or,US
205/E7 Azalia, Mi,US
120/D2 Azamgarh, India
168/D4 Azángaro, Peru
168/D4 Azángaro (riv.), Peru
143/H4 Azao (peak), Alg.
145/E2 Azaouad (reg.), Mali
145/G2 Azaouak, Vallée de l' (wadi), Mali, Niger
168/D5 Azapa, Chile
105/F2 Āzarān, Iran
105/F2 Āzarbāyjān-e Bākhtarī (gov.), Iran
105/F2 Āzarbāyjān-e Khāvarī (gov.), Iran
145/H4 Azare, Nga.
105/F2 Āzar Shahr, Iran
79/F6 Azay-le-Rideau, Fr.
103/E3 A'zāz, Syria
79/E5 Azé, Fr.
142/B5 Azefal, Galb (mts.), WSah.
142/B5 Azefal, Guelb (mts.), Mrta.
142/C2 Azemmour, Mor.
97/H4 Azerbaijan
149/H2 Āzezo, Eth.
122/E3 Azhikal, India
114/E1 Azhu-Tayga, Gora (peak), Rus.
142/D3 Azilal, Mor.
105/F2 Azizbekov, Arm.
104/D2 'Azīz, Jabal 'Abd al (mts.), Syria
189/F1 Azle, Tx,US
105/G3 Aznā, Iran
95/M5 Aznakayevo, Rus.
76/B4 Aznalcóllar, Sp.
164/B5 Azogues, Ecu.
77/R12 Azores (aut. reg.), Port.
77/R12 Azores (isls.), Port.
148/D3 Azoum, Bahr (dry riv.), Chad
142/D3 Azourki, Jebel (mtn.), Mor.
99/K4 Azov, Rus.
99/H4 Azov (sea), Rus., Ukr.
99/H5 Azovskoye, Ukr.
160/B2 Azoyú, Mex.
142/D2 Azrou, Mor.
187/F4 Aztec, Az,US
187/J2 Aztec, NM,US
187/H2 Aztec Ruins Nat'l Mon., NM,US
162/D3 Azua, DRep.
76/C3 Azuaga, Sp.
77/E2 Azuara, Sp.
164/B5 Azuay (prov.), Ecu.
111/M9 Azuchi, Japan
164/A3 Azueiro (pen.), Pan.
161/F5 Azuero (pen.), Pan.
172/B3 Azufre, Volcán del (vol.), Arg.
98/C5 Azuga, Rom.
174/F3 Azul, Arg.
172/B4 Azul (peak), Arg.
161/E4 Azul (mtn.), CR
159/H5 Azul (riv.), NAm.
168/B2 Azul, Cordillera (mts.), Peru
111/G2 Azuma-san (mtn.), Japan
111/F2 Azumaya-san (mtn.), Japan
148/D2 'Azūm, Wādī (dry riv.), Sudan
77/J1 Azur (coast), Fr.
75/G5 Azur, Côte d' (coast), Fr.
82/D5 Azur, Côte d' (reg.), Fr.
172/C1 Azurduy, Bol.
199/J2 Azure (mtn.), NY,US
204/C2 Azusa, Ca,US
141/V17 Azzaba, Alg.
103/G7 Az Zabābidah, WBnk.
103/E3 Az Zabadānī, Syria
103/D4 Az Zāhirīyah, WBnk.
87/D2 Azzano, It.
75/K4 Azzano Decimo, It.
86/C1 Azzano San Paolo, It.
103/B4 Az Zaqāzīq, Egypt
103/E3 Az Zarqā', Jor.
86/B1 Azzate, It.
146/B2 Az Zāwiyah, Libya
149/G1 Az Zaydāb, Sudan
150/B2 Az Zaydīyah, Yem.
106/D3 Az Zilfī, SAr.
105/F4 Az Zubayr, Iraq
103/G7 'Azzūn, WBnk.

B

117/E2 Ba (riv.), China
139/Y18 Ba, Fiji
54/B3 Bà (riv.), Sc,UK
123/E3 Ba (riv.), Viet.
130/A2 Baa, Indo.
139/U11 Baaba (isl.), NCal.
72/B4 Baalberge, Ger.
103/G8 Ba'al Ḥazor (Tall 'Asūr) (mtn.), WBnk.
135/D1 Baan Baa, Austl.
81/E3 Baar, Swi.
150/D5 Baarawe, Som.
150/D3 Baargaal, Som.
66/B6 Baarle-Hertog, Belg.
66/B6 Baarle-Nassau, Neth.
66/C4 Baarn, Neth.
108/D2 Baatsagaan, Mong.
107/J2 Baba (mts.), Afg.
93/F4 Baba (peak), Bul.
104/B1 Baba (pt.), Turk.
144/B3 Bababé, Mrta.
96/D4 Baba Burnu (pt.), Turk.
166/E4 Babaçulândia, Braz.
93/J3 Babadag, Rom.
154/B2 Babaera, Ang.
93/H5 Babaeski, Turk.
164/B5 Babahoyo, Ecu.
108/E3 Babai Gaxun, China
120/C1 Babai Khola (riv.), Nepal
91/K3 Babakale, Turk.
145/F4 Babana, Nga.
157/E3 Babanango, SAfr.
149/E3 Babanūsah, Sudan
130/C1 Babar (isl.), Indo.
130/C1 Babar (isls.), Indo.
124/C3 Babat, Indo.
151/A3 Babati, Tanz.
103/E1 Babatorun, Turk.
120/D3 Babatpur (int'l arpt.), India
94/G4 Babayevo, Rus.
183/H3 Babb, Mt,US
58/C5 Babbacombe (bay), Eng,UK
195/J4 Babbitt, Mn,US
184/D4 Babbitt, Nv,US
103/D3 B'abdā, Leb.
150/B2 Bab el Mandeb (str.), Afr., Asia
138/C4 Babelthuap (isl.), Palau
70/B3 Babenhausen, Ger.
70/D6 Babenhausen, Ger.
71/F6 Babensham, Ger.
120/C3 Baberu, India
124/B2 Babi (isl.), Indo.
96/A2 Babia Gora (peak), Pol.
116/D4 Babian (riv.), China
105/F3 Bābil (gov.), Iraq
120/B3 Babīna, India
134/B2 Babinda, Austl.
178/D3 Babine (riv.), BC,Can
105/H2 Bābol, Iran
73/B4 Bábolna, Hun.
105/H2 Bābol Sar, Iran
188/A3 Babonoyaba, Mex.
187/G5 Baboquivari (mts.), Az,US
148/B4 Baboua, CAfr.
202/M8 Babson Park, Fl,US
203/H4 Babson Park, Fl,US
141/M13 Bab Taza, Mor.
121/H4 Bābuganj, Bang.
145/H3 Babura, Nga.
125/C1 Babuyan (chan.), Phil.

# Babuya – Banī

125/C1 Babuyan (isl.), Phil.
125/C1 Babuyan (isls.), Phil.
105/F3 Babylon (ruins), Iraq
207/E2 Babylon, NY,US
150/C4 Bacaadweeyn, Som.
158/C3 Bacabachi, Mex.
166/B4 Bacabal, Braz.
167/E4 Bacabal, Braz.
158/C2 Bacadéhuachi, Mex.
166/D4 Bacajá (riv.), Braz.
159/H5 Bacalar, Mex.
160/D2 Bacalar (lag.), Mex.
127/G4 Bacan (isl.), Indo.
125/C1 Bacarra, Phil.
93/H2 Bacău, Rom.
93/H2 Bacău (co.), Rom.
123/D1 Bac Can, Viet.
80/C1 Baccarat, Fr.
87/F2 Bacchiglione (riv.), It.
123/D1 Bac Giang, Viet.
70/A2 Bacharach, Ger.
115/L8 Bacheng, China
120/B1 Bachhraon, India
158/D2 Bachíniva, Mex.
124/C1 Bachok, Malay.
114/C4 Bachu, China
178/G2 Back (riv.), NW,Can
206/B5 Back (riv.), Md,US
92/D3 Bačka (reg.), Yugo.
92/D3 Bačka Palanka, Yugo.
92/D3 Bačka Topola, Yugo.
196/D3 Back Bay, NB,Can
201/K2 Back Bay Nat'l Wild. Ref., Va,US
199/G5 Backbone (mtn.), Md, Wv,US
62/E2 Bäckefors, Swe.
70/C5 Backnang, Ger.
58/D4 Backwell, Eng,UK
123/D4 Bac Lieu, Viet.
123/D1 Bac Ninh, Viet.
125/C2 Baco (mt.), Phil.
158/C2 Bacoachi, Mex.
125/C3 Bacolod City, Phil.
125/E7 Bacoor, Phil.
123/D1 Bac Quang, Viet.
92/D2 Bácsalmás, Hun.
92/D2 Bács-Kiskun (co.), Hun.
73/D6 Bács-Tolna (co.), Hun.
59/H1 Bacton, Eng,UK
158/C3 Bácum, Mex.
57/F4 Bacup, Eng,UK
167/E3 Bacuri, Braz.
105/H3 Bād, Iran
192/D1 Bad (riv.), SD,US
71/F5 Bad Abbach, Ger.
73/B6 Badacsonytomaj, Hun.
122/E3 Badagara, India
119/H3 Badahe, China
108/E3 Badain Jarah (des.), China
101/L5 Badain Jaran (des.), China
169/F1 Badajós (lake), Braz.
76/B3 Badajoz, Sp.
77/L7 Badalona, Sp.
86/A5 Badalucco, It.
106/D2 Badanah, SAr.
113/A2 Badaohao, China
198/E3 Bad Axe, Mi,US
80/D2 Bad Bellingen, Ger.
67/E3 Badbergen, Ger.
70/B4 Bad Bergzabern, Ger.
72/B6 Bad Berka, Ger.
67/F6 Bad Berleberg, Ger.
71/E2 Bad Berneck, Ger.
72/B5 Bad Bibra, Ger.
72/B6 Bad Blankenburg, Ger.
70/D2 Bad Bocklet, Ger.
71/F2 Bad Brambach, Ger.
69/G2 Bad Breisig, Ger.
70/C2 Bad Brückenau, Ger.
70/C6 Bad Buchau, Ger.
70/B2 Bad Camberg, Ger.
197/G2 Baddeck, NS,Can
67/H4 Baddeckenstedt, Ger.
64/F1 Bad Doberan, Ger.
122/C2 Baddomalhi, Pak.
67/G5 Bad Driburg, Ger.
72/C4 Bad Düben, Ger.
70/B4 Bad Dürkheim, Ger.
72/C5 Bad Dürrenberg, Ger.
70/B6 Bad Dürrheim, Ger.
131/E1 Bade, Indo.
145/G4 Badeggi, Nga.
70/A2 Bad Ems, Ger.
73/A3 Baden, Aus.
81/E3 Baden, Swi.
208/G6 Baden, Pa,US
70/B5 Baden-Baden, Ger.
71/F7 Bad Endorf, Ger.
70/B5 Badener (peak), Ger.
54/B3 Badenoch (dist.), Sc,UK
80/D2 Badenweiler, Ger.
70/C6 Baden-Württemberg (state), Ger.
81/E1 Baden-Württemberg (state), Ger.
87/G2 Baderna, Cro.
72/A4 Badersleben, Ger.
67/F4 Bad Essen, Ger.
73/A4 Bad Fischau, Aus.
72/B5 Bad Frankenhausen, Ger.
72/E2 Bad Freienwalde, Ger.
67/H5 Bad Gandersheim, Ger.
75/K3 Badgastein, Aus.
197/J1 Badger, Nf,Can
192/C4 Badger (cr.), Co,US
194/F3 Badger, Mn,US
183/L5 Badger (peak), Mt,US
197/L1 Badger's Quay, Nf,Can
132/B4 Badgingarra Nat'l Park, Austl.
75/K3 Bad Goisern, Aus.
72/D6 Bad Gottleuba, Ger.
67/H5 Bad Grund, Ger.
71/H6 Bad Hall, Aus.
67/H5 Bad Harzburg, Ger.
81/H2 Bad Heilbrunn, Ger.
70/B5 Bad Herrenalb, Ger.
64/E3 Bad Hersfeld, Ger.
66/B4 Badhoevedorp, Neth.
75/K3 Bad Hofgastein, Aus.
70/B2 Bad Homburg vor der Höhe, Ger.
69/G2 Bad Honnef, Ger.
69/G2 Bad Hönningen, Ger.
87/E2 Badia Polesine, It.
81/F5 Badile, Pizzo (peak), It.
107/J4 Badīn, Pak.
201/G3 Badin, NC,US
201/G3 Badin (lake), NC,US
75/K3 Bad Ischl, Aus.
67/G5 Bad Karlshafen, Ger.
70/D2 Bad Kissingen, Ger.
72/B6 Bad Klosterlausnitz, Ger.
81/H2 Bad Kohlgrub, Ger.
70/C3 Bad König, Ger.
70/D2 Bad Königshofen, Ger.
72/B5 Bad Kösen, Ger.
72/C6 Bad Köstritz, Ger.
70/A3 Bad Kreuznach, Ger.
80/D2 Bad Krozingen, Ger.
194/C4 Badlands (uplands), ND,US
192/C2 Badlands (hills), SD,US
192/C2 Badlands Nat'l Park, SD,US
67/H6 Bad Langensalza, Ger.
72/B5 Bad Lauchstädt, Ger.
72/C5 Bad Lausick, Ger.
67/H5 Bad Lauterberg, Ger.
71/H5 Bad Leonfelden, Aus.
72/D4 Bad Liebenwerda, Ger.
70/B5 Bad Liebenzell, Ger.
67/F3 Bad Lippspringe, Ger.
69/G2 Bad Marienberg, Ger.
70/C4 Bad Mergentheim, Ger.
67/G4 Bad Munder am Deister, Ger.
69/G4 Bad Münster am Stein, Ger.
69/F2 Bad Münstereifel, Ger.
70/B2 Bad Nauheim, Ger.
67/G4 Bad Nenndorf, Ger.
69/G2 Bad Neuenahr-Ahrweiler, Ger.
70/D2 Bad Neustadt an der Saale, Ger.
191/H2 Bado, Mo,US
114/C5 Badoāb, India
67/F4 Bad Oeynhausen, Ger.
83/C5 Badolato Marina, It.
64/F2 Bad Oldesloe, Ger.
115/B5 Badong, China
80/C1 Badonviller, Fr.
70/C2 Bad Orb, Ger.
145/F5 Badou, Togo
92/D3 Badovinci, Yugo.
70/B6 Bad Peterstal-Griesbach, Ger.
157/E2 Bad Plaas, SAfr.
67/G5 Bad Pyrmont, Ger.
81/F3 Bad Ragaz, Swi.
105/F3 Badrah, Iraq
107/J3 Bādrāh, Pak.
70/C4 Bad Rappenau, Ger.
64/G5 Bad Reichenhall, Ger.
147/H4 Badr Ḩunayn, SAr.
195/J4 Bad River Ind. Res., Wi,US
72/E3 Bad Saarow-Pieskow, Ger.
67/H5 Bad Sachsa, Ger.
67/H4 Bad Salzdetfurth, Ger.
70/C1 Bad Salzschlirf, Ger.
67/F4 Bad Salzuflen, Ger.
64/F3 Bad Salzungen, Ger.
75/L3 Bad Sankt-Leonhard im Lavanttal, Aus.
67/F5 Bad Sassendorf, Ger.
71/G6 Bad Schallerbach, Aus.
72/C4 Bad Schmiedeberg, Ger.
70/C6 Bad Schussenried, Ger.
70/B2 Bad Schwalbach, Ger.
64/F2 Bad Schwartau, Ger.
64/F2 Bad Segeberg, Ger.
120/D3 Bādshāhpur, India
70/B2 Bad Söden am Taunus, Ger.
70/C2 Bad Soden-Salmünster, Ger.
67/G6 Bad Sooden-Allendorf, Ger.
72/B5 Bad Sulza, Ger.
72/A5 Bad Tennstedt, Ger.
81/H2 Bad Tölz, Ger.
116/E3 Badu, China
117/G3 Badu, China
117/H3 Badu, China
121/F3 Badua (riv.), India
118/D6 Badulla, SrL.
70/C6 Bad Urach, Ger.
121/G4 Bāduriā, India
70/B2 Bad Vilbel, Ger.
73/A4 Bad Vöslau, Aus.
81/F2 Bad Waldsee, Ger.
185/K2 Badwater (cr.), Wy,US
67/G6 Bad Wildungen, Ger.
72/B2 Bad Wilsnack, Ger.
70/C4 Bad Wimpfen, Ger.
71/G6 Bad Wimsbach-Neydharting, Aus.
70/D3 Bad Windsheim, Ger.
70/D6 Bad Wörishofen, Ger.
81/F2 Bad Wurzach, Ger.
71/H6 Bad Zell, Aus.
67/E2 Bad Zwischenahn, Ger.
182/B1 Baekaezo (riv.), BC,Can
76/C4 Baena, Sp.
170/D4 Baependi, Braz.
80/C2 Baerenkopf (mtn.), Fr.
69/F2 Baesweiler, Ger.
76/D4 Baeza, Sp.
145/H5 Bafang, Camr.
144/B3 Bafatá, GBis.
179/H1 Baffin (isl.), NW,Can
176/L2 Baffin (bay), NAm.
189/F4 Baffin (bay), Tx,US
189/N9 Baffle (pt.), Tx,US
148/A4 Bafia, Camr.
145/F4 Bafilo, Togo
144/D4 Bafing (riv.), Gui., IvC.
144/C3 Bafing (riv.), Gui., Mali
144/C3 Bafoulabé, Mali
145/H5 Bafoussam, Camr.
105/H4 Bāfq, Iran
104/C1 Bafra, Turk.
104/D1 Bafra Burnu (cape), Turk.
144/B2 Bafrechié (well), Mrta.
105/J4 Bāft, Iran
144/C5 Bafu, Libr.
153/F2 Bafwabalinga, Zaire
153/F2 Bafwabogbo, Zaire
153/F2 Bafwasende, Zaire
115/B3 Bag (salt lake), China
148/B2 Baga, Nga.
161/E4 Bagaces, CR
164/B3 Bagadó, Col.
120/E2 Bagaha, India
125/B4 Bagahak, Gunung (peak), Malay.
151/B3 Bagamoyo, Tanz.
108/D5 Bagan, China
125/D4 Baganga, Phil.
124/C2 Bagansiapiapi, Indo.
145/G3 Bagaroua, Niger
152/D3 Bagata, Zaire
82/C6 Bagaud (isl.), Fr.
99/L4 Bagayevskiy, Rus.
125/E6 Bagbag (cr.), Phil.
121/G3 Bāgbāri, Bang.
131/E3 Bagbiringula (pt.), Austl.
114/E3 Bagda (mts.), China
189/F5 Bagdad, Mex.
187/F3 Bagdad, Az,US
108/G1 Bagdarin, Rus.
173/F4 Bagé, Braz.
62/D4 Bagenkop, Den.
121/G4 Bāgerhāt, Bang.
99/J5 Bagerovo, Ukr.
125/C1 Baggao, Phil.
104/E2 Bağgöze, Turk.
185/K3 Baggs, Wy,US
58/B4 Baggy (pt.), Eng,UK
122/B2 Bāgh, Pak.
120/C3 Baghain (riv.), India
122/C2 Bāgha Purāna, India
105/F3 Baghdad (gov.), Iraq
105/H4 Baghdādābād, Iran
106/D2 Baghdad (Baghdād) (cap.), Iraq
90/C3 Bagheria, It.
105/J4 Bāghīn, Iran
107/J1 Baghlān, Afg.
120/A1 Bāghpat, India
105/J5 Bāghū, Iran
124/D3 Baginda (cape), Indo.
59/E2 Baginton (Coventry) (arpt.), Eng,UK
104/E2 Bağırpaşa (peak), Turk.
58/C3 Baglan, Wal,UK
195/G4 Bagley, Mn,US
120/D1 Bāglung, Nepal
121/E2 Bāgmati (riv.), India
120/E2 Bāgmati (zone), Nepal
62/C1 Bagn, Nor.
87/F4 Bagnacavallo, It.
83/B6 Bagnara Calabra, It.
86/B4 Bagnasco, It.
191/H1 Bagnell (dam), Mo,US
74/D5 Bagnères-de-Bigorre, Fr.
74/D5 Bagnères-de-Luchon, Fr.
53/S10 Bagneux, Fr.
86/D4 Bagni di Lucca, It.
84/C4 Bagni di Tivoli, It.
87/E5 Bagno a Ripoli, It.
84/A2 Bagno di Gavorrano, It.
87/E5 Bagno di Romagna, It.
79/E3 Bagnoles-de-l'Orne, Fr.
53/T10 Bagnolet, Fr.
85/E4 Bagnoli del Trigno, It.
85/F6 Bagnoli Irpino, It.
86/C2 Bagnolo Cremasco, It.
87/D3 Bagnolo in Piano, It.
86/D2 Bagnolo Mella, It.
87/D2 Bagnolo San Vito, It.
82/A4 Bagnols-sur-Cèze, Fr.
86/C4 Bagnone, It.
84/C2 Bagnoregio, It.
125/C3 Bago, Phil.
121/E3 Bagodar, India
144/D3 Bagoe (riv.), IvC., Mali
86/D1 Bagolino, It.
117/E3 Bagong, China
116/B5 Bago (Pegu) (div.), Burma
148/B2 Bagoroud (well), Chad
121/G2 Bāgrākot, India
63/J4 Bagrationovsk, Rus.
166/D3 Bagre, Braz.
168/B2 Bagua Grande, Peru
125/C1 Baguio, Phil.
148/C2 Baguirmi (reg.), Chad
124/C1 Bagun Serai, Malay.
149/H3 Bagusta, Eth.
191/G4 Bagwell, Tx,US
145/H2 Bagzane (peak), Niger
120/B2 Bāh, India
121/F2 Bahādurganj, India
120/D2 Bahādurganj, Nepal
120/A1 Bahādurgarh, India
121/F4 Bahaldā, India
162/B2 Bahamas
121/F4 Baharāgora, India
118/E3 Baharampur, India
124/C2 Bahau, Malay.
114/B6 Bahāwalnagar, Pak.
107/K3 Bahāwalpur, Pak.
104/D2 Bahçe, Turk.
105/E2 Bahçesaray, Turk.
121/F2 Bahera, India
120/B1 Baheri, India
151/A3 Bahi, Tanz.
151/A3 Bahi (swamp), Tanz.
171/E2 Bahía (state), Braz.
158/B3 Bahia Asunción, Mex.
174/E3 Bahía Blanca, Arg.
174/D5 Bahía Bustamante, Arg.
164/A5 Bahía de Caráquez, Ecu.
158/B2 Bahía de los Angeles, Mex.
118/D3 Bahía Honda, Cuba
160/E2 Bahía, Islas de la (isls.), Hon.
158/C2 Bahía Kino, Mex.
174/B4 Bahía Mansa, Chile
175/L8 Bahía Thetis, Arg.
158/B3 Bahía Tortugas, Mex.
149/H3 Bahir Dar, Eth.
120/B1 Bahjoi, India
107/G4 Bahlah, Oman
120/C2 Bahraich, India
106/F3 Bahrain
106/F3 Bahrain (gulf), Bahr., SAr.
140/E3 Baḩr al Arab (riv.), Sudan
105/E3 Baḩr al Milḩ (lake), Iraq
107/H3 Bahrām Chāh, Afg.
140/D4 Bahr Aouk (riv.), CAfr., Chad
147/F2 Baḩrīyah, Al Wāḩāt al (oasis), Egypt
107/H3 Bāhū Kalāt, Iran
115/C2 Bai (riv.), China
115/C4 Bai (riv.), China
92/F3 Baia de Aramă, Rom.
154/A3 Baía dos Tigres, Ang.
154/B2 Baia Farta, Ang.
93/F2 Baia Mare, Rom.
85/E6 Baiano, It.
166/D3 Baião, Braz.
93/F2 Baia Sprie, Rom.
172/E4 Baibiene, Arg.
148/B4 Baïbokoum, Chad
116/D3 Baicao (mts.), China
109/J2 Baicheng, China
114/D3 Baicheng, China
93/G3 Băicoi, Rom.
117/F3 Baidishi, China
151/C1 Baidoa (Baydhabo), Som.
115/D5 Baidong (lake), China
196/C1 Baie-Comeau, Qu,Can
196/C1 Baie-des-Bacons, Qu,Can
179/J3 Baie-du-Poste, Qu,Can
81/F2 Baienfurt, Ger.
70/B5 Baiersbronn, Ger.
70/E3 Baiersdorf, Ger.
196/E2 Baie-Sainte-Anne, NB,Can
196/B2 Baie-Saint-Paul, Qu,Can
196/D1 Baie-Trinité, Qu,Can
179/L4 Baie Verte, Nf,Can
117/F2 Baifusi, China
174/E2 Baigorrita, Arg.
115/H7 Baigou, China
115/G7 Baigou (riv.), China
120/C4 Baihar, India
115/C3 Baihua Shan (mtn.), China
105/E3 Ba'ījī, Iraq
115/G7 Baijian, China
51/Q3 Baikal (lake), Rus.
120/D4 Baikunthpur, India
164/D2 Bailadores, Ven.
57/G4 Baildon, Eng,UK
98/C5 Băile Govora, Rom.
92/F3 Băile Herculane, Rom.
76/D3 Bailén, Sp.
93/G3 Băile Olăneşti, Rom.
93/F3 Băileşti, Rom.
93/G2 Băile Tuşnad, Rom.
192/B4 Bailey, Co,US
201/H3 Bailey, NC,US
208/E6 Bailey Lakes, Oh,US
195/L5 Baileys Harbor, Wi,US
208/B2 Baileyville, Ct,US
117/F3 Bailicun, China
60/D2 Bailieborough, Ire.
55/H8 Bailivanish, Sc,UK
79/G4 Bailleau-le-Pin, Fr.
68/B2 Bailleul, Fr.
148/C3 Ba Illi, Chad
121/G3 Bailmān Diārkhāta, Bang.
108/F5 Bailong, China
108/E5 Bailong (riv.), China
115/C4 Bailu (riv.), China
154/B2 Bailundo, Ang.
108/E5 Baima, China
117/F3 Baimangying, China
108/F5 Baimianxia, China
131/G1 Baimuru, PNG
57/H5 Bain (riv.), Eng,UK
121/G1 Bainang, China
203/F2 Bainbridge, Ga,US
199/J3 Bainbridge, NY,US
198/E5 Bainbridge, Oh,US
206/B3 Bainbridge, Pa,US
205/B2 Bainbridge (isl.), Wa,US
206/B4 Bainbridge Nav. Trg. Sta., Md,US
78/D5 Bain-de-Bretagne, Fr.
114/E5 Baingoin, China
202/C2 Bains, La,US
80/C2 Bains-les-Bains, Fr.
82/C3 Bains, Sommet des (mtn.), Fr.
148/B4 Baipadgué, Chad
109/K2 Baiquan, China
114/D4 Bairab (lake), China
121/E2 Bairāgnia, India
177/F3 Baird (inlet), Ak,US
188/E1 Baird, Tx,US
138/G4 Bairiki (cap.), Kiri.
109/H3 Bairin Youqi, China
135/C3 Bairnsdale, Austl.
185/K2 Bairoil, Wy,US
103/E4 Bā'ir, Wādī (riv.), Jor.
79/E4 Bais, Fr.
125/C3 Bais, Phil.
74/D5 Baïse (riv.), Fr.
117/F5 Baisha, China
117/G4 Baisha, China
117/H3 Baisha, China
117/H2 Baishaguan, China
117/G2 Baishaling, China
117/F3 Baishan, China
117/H3 Baishe, China
117/H3 Baishi (peak), China
116/E1 Baishui, China
117/G2 Baishui, China
108/F5 Baishuijiang, China
63/K4 Baisogala, Lith.
117/H3 Baisong (pass), China
120/C1 Baitadi, Nepal
123/D2 Bai Thuong, Viet.
77/P10 Baixa de Banheira, Port.
171/E2 Baixa Grande, Braz.
115/C3 Baixiang, China
171/E3 Baixo Guandu, Braz.
113/B2 Baiyanggou, China
131/G1 Baiyer River, PNG
108/E4 Baiyin, China
116/C2 Baiyü, China
115/B3 Baiyu (mts.), China
117/H3 Baiyun, China
117/G4 Baiyun (int'l arpt.), China
117/G3 Baiyun (mtn.), China
175/J7 Baja (pt.), Chile
92/D2 Baja, Hun.
158/B2 Baja California (pen.), Mex.
204/C6 Baja California Norte (state), Mex.
158/B3 Baja California Sur (state), Mex.
141/W17 Bājah, Tun.
141/W17 Bājah (gov.), Tun.
188/D4 Baján, Mex.
120/C1 Bajāng, Nepal
73/A6 Bajánsenye, Hun.
158/B2 Baja, Punta (pt.), Mex.
127/F5 Bajawa, Indo.
105/J3 Bajestān, Iran
150/B2 Bājil, Yem.
109/J3 Bajilei, China
92/D4 Bajina Bašta, Yugo.
187/F5 Bajío del Alcalde, Mex.
121/H3 Bājitpur, Bang.
135/E1 Bajmba (peak), Austl.
92/D3 Bajmok, Yugo.
73/C4 Bajna, Hun.
161/F4 Bajo Boquete, Pan.
174/C5 Bajo de los Caracoles, Arg.
155/J2 Bajone (pt.), Moz.
174/B4 Bajo Palena, Chile
162/D3 Bajos de Haina, DRep.
91/G1 Bajram Curri, Alb.
120/C1 Bājura, Nepal
73/A6 Bak, Hun.
73/B4 Baka, Slvk.
148/C4 Bakaba, Chad
95/N5 Bakal, Rus.
148/D4 Bakala, CAfr.
152/D4 Bakali (riv.), Zaire
95/M5 Bakaly, Rus.
114/C2 Bakanas (riv.), Kaz.
148/D2 Bakaoré, Chad
75/L4 Bakar, Cro.
121/H4 Bākarganj, Bang.
144/A3 Bakau, Gam.
127/E3 Bakayan (peak), Indo.
66/C6 Bakel, Neth.
144/B3 Bakel, Sen.
178/G2 Baker (lake), NW,Can
175/J6 Baker (riv.), Chile
139/H4 Baker (isl.), PacUS
186/D3 Baker, Ca,US
202/E2 Baker, Fl,US
202/C2 Baker, La,US
194/B4 Baker, Mt,US
185/F4 Baker, Nv,US
191/E3 Baker (peak), Ok,US
184/E1 Baker, Or,US
182/D3 Baker (mt.), Wa,US
153/E2 Bakere, Zaire
200/E5 Baker Hill, Al,US
178/G2 Baker Lake, NW,Can
186/C3 Bakersfield, Ca,US
191/H2 Bakersfield, Mo,US
208/A2 Bakersville, Ct,US
201/F2 Bakersville, NC,US
57/G5 Bakewell, Eng,UK
97/L5 Bakharden, Trkm.
99/G5 Bakhchisaray, Ukr.
99/G2 Bakhmach, Ukr.
121/E2 Bakhra, India
105/F2 Bakhshāyesh, Iran
100/J3 Bakhta, Rus.
105/F3 Bākhtarān, Iran
105/F3 Bākhtarān (gov.), Iran
105/H4 Bakhtegān (lake), Iran
105/G4 Bakhtīārī & Chahār Maḩāll (gov.), Iran
121/E3 Bakhtiyārpur, India
165/G4 Bakhuis (mts.), Sur.
149/E4 Bakia, CAfr.
61/P6 Bakkaflói (bay), Ice.
104/B2 Baklan, Turk.
149/H3 Bako, Eth.
149/H4 Bako, Eth.
149/F5 Bakokandi (riv.), Zaire
73/B6 Bakony (mts.), Hun.
73/B5 Bakonybél, Hun.
73/C5 Bakonycsernye, Hun.
73/C5 Bakonysárkány, Hun.
73/B5 Bakonyszombathely, Hun.
153/H2 Bakora Corridor Game Rsv., Ugan.
145/G4 Bakori, Nga.
148/D4 Bakouma, CAfr.
152/C3 Bakoumba, Gabon
71/G2 Bakovský Potok (riv.), Czh.
144/C4 Bakoye (riv.), Gui., Mali
53/H4 Baku (cap.), Azer.
105/G1 Baku (int'l arpt.), Azer.
153/G2 Baku, Zaire
124/B2 Bakungan, Indo.
137/S Bakutis (coast), Ant.
153/E4 Bakwa-Kenge, Zaire
199/G2 Bala, On,Can
104/C2 Balâ, Turk.
56/E6 Bala, Wal,UK
127/E2 Balabac (str.), Malay., Phil.
125/B4 Balabac, Phil.
125/B4 Balabac (isl.), Phil.
107/K2 Bālā Bāgh, Afg.
103/E3 Ba'labakk, Leb.
94/H5 Balabanovo, Rus.
139/U12 Balabio (isl.), NCal.
105/F3 Balad, Iraq
108/E1 Balagansk, Rus.
120/C5 Bālāghāt, India
90/A1 Balagne (range), Fr.
125/E6 Balagtas, Phil.
77/F2 Balaguer, Sp.
124/C3 Balaiselasa, Indo.
74/C5 Balaïtous (mtn.), Fr.
155/G2 Balaka, Malw.
121/H4 Bālākāndi, Bang.
97/J4 Balakhany, Azer.
95/J4 Balakhna, Rus.
133/H5 Balaklava, Austl.
99/G5 Balaklava, Ukr.
99/J3 Balakleya, Ukr.
53/H3 Balakovo, Rus.
151/B1 Balal, Laga (dry riv.), Kenya
103/E3 Bal'amā, Jor.
125/B4 Balambangan (isl.), Malay.
107/H1 Bālā Morghab, Afg.
144/C4 Balan, Gui.
93/G2 Bălan, Rom.
159/H5 Balancán, Mex.
125/C2 Balanga, Phil.
152/D2 Balangala, Zaire
123/E3 Ba Lang An (cape), Viet.
86/A2 Balangero, It.
118/D3 Bālāngir, India
127/F4 Balantak, Indo.
168/B1 Balao, Ecu.
125/C1 Balaoan, Phil.
121/F4 Balarāmpur, India
53/H3 Balashov, Rus.
73/D3 Balassagyarmat, Hun.
73/B6 Balaton (lake), Hun.
193/G1 Balaton, Mn,US
73/C5 Balatonalmádi, Hun.
73/B6 Balatonfenyves, Hun.
73/B6 Balatonföldvár, Hun.
73/B6 Balatonfüred, Hun.
73/B6 Balatoni felvidek (hills), Hun.
73/B6 Balatonkeresztúr, Hun.
73/C6 Balatonszabadi, Hun.
73/B6 Balatonszárszó, Hun.
73/B6 Balatonszentgyörgy, Hun.
130/A2 Balaurin, Indo.
63/K4 Balbieriškis, Lith.
166/B3 Balbina (res.), Braz.
204/G8 Balboa, Ca,US
60/D2 Balbriggan, Ire.
150/C5 Balcad, Som.
174/F3 Balcarce, Arg.
194/C2 Balcarres, Sk,Can
56/E2 Balcary (pt.), Sc,UK
93/J4 Balchik, Bul.
188/L7 Balch Springs, Tx,US
136/B4 Balclutha, N.Z.
59/F4 Balcombe, Eng,UK
159/E2 Balcones (plat.), Tx,US
188/D3 Balcones Escarp-ment (plat.), Tx,US
132/C5 Bald (pt.), Austl.
201/G2 Bald (peak), Va,US
182/D4 Bald (mtn.), Wa,US
199/G5 Bald (mtn.), WV,US
206/A1 Bald Eagle Mtn. (ridge), Pa,US
194/E4 Baldhill (dam), ND,US
191/J3 Bald Knob, Ar,US
200/C2 Bald Knob (hill), Il,US
59/F3 Baldock, Eng,UK
63/L3 Baldone, Lat.
135/E1 Bald Rock Nat'l Park, Austl.
194/E3 Baldur, Mb,Can
203/H2 Baldwin, Fl,US
201/F3 Baldwin, Ga,US
202/C3 Baldwin, La,US
198/D3 Baldwin, Mi,US
194/D4 Baldwin, ND,US
207/L9 Baldwin, NY,US
208/H7 Baldwin, Pa,US
191/G1 Baldwin City, Ks,US
207/L9 Baldwin Harbour, NY,US
204/C2 Baldwin Park, Ca,US
199/H3 Baldwinsville, NY,US
200/C3 Baldwyn, Ms,US
194/D2 Baldy (mtn.), Mb,Can
187/H4 Baldy (peak), Az,US
183/K3 Baldy (mtn.), Mt,US
192/D3 Baldy (hill), Ne,US
160/D2 Baldy Beacon (mtn.), Belz.
87/G2 Bale, Cro.
150/B4 Balē (prov.), Eth.
77/F3 Baleares (Balearic) (isls.), Sp.
77/F3 Balearic (Baleares) (isls.), Sp.
171/F3 Baleia, Ponta da (pt.), Braz.
179/K3 Baleine (riv.), Qu,Can
179/J3 Baleine, Grande Rivière de la (riv.), Qu,Can
179/J3 Baleine, Petite Rivière de la (riv.), Qu,Can
150/A4 Bale Mtns. Nat'l Park, Eth.
69/E1 Balen, Belg.
125/C2 Baler, Phil.
81/F6 Balerna, Swi.
151/B1 Balesa (dry riv.), Kenya
118/E3 Baleshwar, India
108/H1 Baley, Rus.
145/F3 Baléyara, Niger
95/M4 Balezino, Rus.
182/F3 Balfour, BC,Can
156/E2 Balfour, SAfr.
54/B4 Balfron, Sc,UK
114/E3 Balguntay, China
150/D2 Balḩāf, Yem.
202/P8 Bal Harbour, Fl,US
150/B2 Balḫo, Djib.
145/H5 Bali, Camr.
118/B2 Bali, India
124/F4 Bali (isl.), Indo.
124/F5 Bali (prov.), Indo.
124/F4 Bali (sea), Indo.
124/F5 Bali (str.), Indo.
65/K3 Balice (int'l arpt.), Pol.
121/F4 Bāli Chak, India
113/C2 Balidianzi, China
131/E1 Baliem (riv.), Indo.
124/B2 Balige, Indo.
104/A2 Balıkesir, Turk.
104/A2 Balikesir (prov.), Turk.
96/C5 Balıkesir (prov.), Turk.
127/E4 Balikpapan, Indo.
124/C1 Balik Pulau, Malay.
124/D4 Balimbing, Indo.
125/B4 Balimbing, Phil.
131/F1 Balimo, PNG
116/E3 Baling, China
124/C1 Baling, Malay.
125/D3 Balingasag, Phil.
62/G2 Bälinge, Swe.
70/B6 Balingen, Ger.
183/L1 Baljennie, Sk,Can
66/C3 Balk, Neth.
52/F4 Balkan (mts.), Eur.
122/B1 Balkassar, Pak.
97/K4 Balkhan Obl., Trkm.
114/C2 Balkhash, Kaz.
114/B2 Balkhash (lake), Kaz.
182/G2 Ball (mtn.), Ab,Can
189/H2 Ball, La,US
60/A2 Balla, Ire.
132/D5 Balladonia, Austl.
60/D2 Ballagan (pt.), Ire.
60/B2 Ballaghaderreen, Ire.
61/F1 Ballangen, Nor.
79/F6 Ballan-Miré, Fr.
183/K5 Ballantine, Mt,US
56/C1 Ballantrae, Sc,UK
135/B3 Ballarat, Austl.
132/D4 Ballard (lake), Austl.
118/C4 Ballarpur, India
54/C2 Ballater, Sc,UK
56/D3 Ballaugh, IM,UK
144/C3 Ballé, Mali
172/B3 Ballenita (pt.), Chile
80/C4 Ballens, Swi.
72/B4 Ballenstedt, Ger.
137/L Balleny (isls.), Ant.
79/E2 Balleroy, Fr.
63/T9 Ballerup, Den.
174/E2 Ballesteros, Arg.
125/C1 Ballesteros, Phil.
200/E3 Ball Ground, Ga,US
120/E3 Ballia, India
132/C4 Ballidu, Austl.
135/E1 Ballina, Austl.
60/A1 Ballina, Ire.
60/B4 Ballina, Ire.
197/Q8 Ballinafad, On,Can
60/C4 Ballinakill, Ire.
55/H9 Ballinamallard, NI,UK
60/B3 Ballinasloe, Ire.
60/B6 Ballincollig, Ire.
56/B2 Ballinderry (riv.), NI,UK
60/B2 Ballindine, Ire.
60/B6 Ballineen, Ire.
60/B5 Ballingarry, Ire.
60/C4 Ballingarry, Ire.
188/E2 Ballinger, Tx,US
54/C4 Ballingry, Sc,UK
60/B2 Ballinlough, Ire.
54/C3 Ballinluig, Sc,UK
60/A2 Ballinrobe, Ire.
60/B2 Ballintober, Ire.
56/B1 Ballintoy, NI,UK
60/D4 Ballitore, Ire.
168/D5 Ballivián, Bol.
60/D2 Ballivor, Ire.
54/B2 Balloch, Sc,UK
54/B5 Balloch, Sc,UK
79/F4 Ballon, Fr.
80/C2 Ballon, Col du (pass), Fr.
80/C2 Ballon d'Alsace (mtn.), Fr.
80/C2 Ballon de Sevance (mtn.), Fr.
84/A2 Ballone (peak), It.
79/D5 Ballots, Fr.
208/C2 Ballouville, Ct,US
199/K3 Ballston Spa, NY,US
198/E4 Ballville, Oh,US
206/C3 Bally, Pa,US
60/D1 Ballybay, Ire.
60/A5 Ballybunnion, Ire.
60/D4 Ballycanew, Ire.
60/D4 Ballycarney, Ire.
56/C2 Ballycarry, NI,UK
55/G9 Ballycastle, Ire.
56/B1 Ballycastle, NI,UK
56/B2 Ballyclare, NI,UK
60/C1 Ballyconnell, Ire.
60/B6 Ballycotton, Ire.
60/C3 Ballycumber, Ire.
60/A6 Ballydehob, Ire.
60/A5 Ballyduff, Ire.
56/C2 Ballyeaston, NI,UK
60/B1 Ballyfarnan, Ire.
60/B2 Ballygar, Ire.
56/A3 Ballygawley, NI,UK
60/D5 Ballygeary, Ire.
56/C3 Ballygowan, NI,UK
60/C1 Ballyhaise, Ire.
56/C3 Ballyhalbert, NI,UK
60/B2 Ballyhaunis, Ire.
54/G10 Ballyheigue, Ire.
60/B5 Ballyhoura (mts.), Ire.
60/C2 Ballyjamesduff, Ire.
56/A1 Ballykelly, NI,UK
60/B5 Ballylanders, Ire.
56/A1 Ballyliffin, Ire.
60/A4 Ballylongford, Ire.
60/C2 Ballymahon, Ire.
60/A6 Ballymakeery, Ire.
56/B2 Ballymena, NI,UK
56/B2 Ballymena (dist.), NI,UK
56/B1 Ballymoney, NI,UK
56/B1 Ballymoney (dist.), NI,UK
60/C3 Ballymore, Ire.
60/D3 Ballymore Eustace, Ire.
60/B1 Ballymote, Ire.
60/C2 Ballynacargy, Ire.
60/C5 Ballynacourty (pt.), Ire.
56/C3 Ballynahinch, NI,UK
56/C2 Ballynure, NI,UK
60/B5 Ballyporeen, Ire.
56/C3 Ballyquintin (pt.), NI,UK
60/C4 Ballyragget, Ire.
60/C4 Ballyroan, Ire.
60/B1 Ballysadare, Ire.
55/G9 Ballyshannon, Ire.
60/D5 Ballyteige (bay), Ire.
56/C2 Ballywalter, NI,UK
174/C5 Balmaceda, Chile
175/J7 Balmaceda (peak), Chile
92/E2 Balmazújváros, Hun.
195/H2 Balmertown, On,Can
80/D5 Balmhorn (peak), Swi.
135/B3 Balmoral, Austl.
196/D2 Balmoral, NB,Can
155/F2 Balmoral, Zam.
54/C2 Balmoral Castle, Sc,UK
188/C2 Balmorhea, Tx,US
172/D4 Balnearia, Arg.
173/G3 Balneario Camboriú, Braz.
175/T12 Balneario Carras, Uru.
175/T12 Balneario Carrasco, Uru.
174/E3 Balneario Claromecó, Arg.
188/D3 Balneario de los Novillos Nat'l Park, Mex.
154/B2 Balombo, Ang.
134/C4 Balonne (riv.), Austl.
118/B2 Bālotra, India
115/B3 Balougou, China
135/B2 Balpunga, Austl.
120/D2 Balrāmpur, India
135/B2 Balranald, Austl.
93/G3 Balş, Rom.
59/E2 Balsall Common, Eng,UK
193/H1 Balsam Lake, Wi,US
168/B2 Balsapuerto, Peru
167/E4 Balsas, Braz.
167/E4 Balsas (riv.), Braz.
158/E5 Balsas (riv.), Mex.
159/M6 Balsas de Agua, Mex.
85/D4 Balsorano Nuovo, It.
63/R6 Bålsta, Swe.
80/D3 Balsthal, Swi.
98/E4 Balta, Ukr.
194/D3 Balta, ND,US
114/C5 Bāltal, India
76/C2 Baltanás, Sp.
173/E4 Baltasar Brum, Uru.
55/P12 Baltasound, Sc,UK
97/H1 Baltay, Rus.
62/H2 Baltic (sea), Eur.
65/K1 Baltic (spit), Pol., Rus.
208/F7 Baltic, Oh,US
94/H3 Baltic-Volga Waterway (can.), Rus.
103/B4 Balţīm, Egypt
60/A7 Baltimore, Ire.
206/B5 Baltimore, Md,US
206/B4 Baltimore (co.), Md,US
198/E5 Baltimore, Oh,US
206/B5 Baltimore Highlands-Lansdowne, Md,US
199/H5 Baltimore-Washington (int'l arpt.), Md,US
206/B5 Baltimore-Washington (int'l arpt.), Md,US
60/D4 Baltinglass, Ire.
63/H4 Baltiysk, Rus.
63/L4 Baltoji Vokė, Lith.
60/D2 Baltray, Ire.
67/E1 Baltrum (isl.), Ger.
107/H3 Baluchistan (reg.), Iran, Pak.
125/C2 Balud, Phil.
62/D3 Bælum, Den.
124/F4 Baluran Nat'l Park, Indo.
121/G3 Bālurghāt, India
105/J4 Balvard, Iran
67/E6 Balve, Ger.
63/M3 Balvi, Lat.
133/E2 Balwina Abor. Rsv., Austl.
104/A2 Balya, Turk.
97/J3 Balykshi, Kaz.
164/B5 Balzar, Ecu.
81/F3 Balzers, Lcht.
145/E3 Bam (prov.), Burk.
114/F5 Bam (lake), China
105/J4 Bam, Iran
109/J1 Bam, Rus.
148/B3 Bama, Nga.
195/J2 Bamaji (lake), On,Can
144/D3 Bamako (cap.), Mali
144/D3 Bamako (reg.), Mali
144/D3 Bamako (Senou) (int'l arpt.), Mali
152/D3 Bamania, Zaire
117/J2 Bamao, China
117/E3 Bama Yaozu Zizhixian, China
144/E2 Bamba, Mali
152/D2 Bamba, Zaire
152/C3 Bambama, Congo
161/E3 Bambana (riv.), Nic.
148/C3 Bambara, Chad
144/E3 Bambara Maoundé, Mali
140/E4 Bambari, CAfr.
70/D3 Bamberg, Ger.
201/G4 Bamberg, SC,US
57/F4 Bamber Ridge, Eng,UK
153/F2 Bambesa, Zaire
149/G3 Bambesi, Eth.
154/B2 Bambi, Ang.
153/F2 Bambili, Zaire
152/D3 Bambinga, Zaire
148/C5 Bambio, CAfr.
62/C2 Bamble, Nor.
132/D2 Bamboo Creek, Austl.
149/E4 Bambouti, CAfr.
148/B4 Bambouto (mts.), Camr.
149/G4 Bambu, Eth.
116/C2 Bamda, China
145/H5 Bamenda, Camr.
182/B3 Bamfield, BC,Can
192/B3 Bamforth Nat'l Wild. Ref., Wy,US
107/J2 Bāmiān, Afg.
117/G3 Bamian (mtn.), China
148/D4 Bamingui, CAfr.
148/C3 Bamingui (riv.), CAfr.
148/D3 Bamingui-Bangoran (pref.), CAfr.
148/C4 Bamingui-Bangoran Nat'l Park, CAfr.
148/C4 Bamingui-Gribingui Fauna Rsv., CAfr.
148/D4 Bamingui-Konkourou Fauna Rsv., CAfr.
70/B4 Bammental, Ger.
123/C3 Bamnet Narong, Thai.
158/C3 Bamoa, Mex.
120/B3 Bāmor Kalān, India
58/C5 Bampton, Eng,UK
107/H3 Bampūr (riv.), Iran
120/C3 Bamrauli (arpt.), India
131/F1 Bamu (riv.), PNG
130/D3 Bamyili, Austl.
138/F5 Banaba (isl.), Kiri.
167/G4 Banabuiu (res.), Braz.
175/G2 Bañado de Medina, Uru.
173/F4 Bañado de Rocha, Uru.
60/C3 Banagher, Ire.
151/A2 Banagi, Tanz.
125/C2 Banahao (mt.), Phil.
153/F2 Banalia, Zaire
144/C4 Banama, Gui.
144/D3 Banamba, Mali
144/B4 Banana (isls.), SLeo.
152/C4 Banana, Zaire
171/M7 Bananal, Braz.
170/C1 Bananal (isl.), Braz.
167/H4 Bananeiras, Braz.
121/H3 Banar (riv.), Bang.
121/H4 Bānaripāra, Bang.
93/H5 Banarlı, Turk.
118/B2 Banās (riv.), India
120/A2 Banas (riv.), India
147/G4 Banās, Ra's (pt.), Egypt
89/J1 Banat (reg.), Rom., Yugo.
92/E3 Banatsko Novo Selo, Yugo.
125/C1 Banaue, Phil.
150/C2 Bana, Wādī (dry riv.), Yem.
123/E3 Ban Ay Rieng, Viet.
104/B2 Banaz, Turk.
123/C2 Ban Ban, Laos
116/B2 Banbar, China
115/H6 Banbishan, China
123/C1 Ban Boun Tai, Laos
56/B3 Banbridge, NI,UK
56/B3 Banbridge (dist.), NI,UK
59/E2 Banbury, Eng,UK
144/B2 Banc d'Arguin Nat'l Park, Mrta.
86/A2 Banchette, It.
123/C2 Ban Chiang (ruins), Thai.
54/D2 Banchory, Sc,UK
161/F4 Banco (pt.), CR
199/H2 Bancroft, On,Can
189/H2 Bancroft, La,US
118/D2 Bāndā, India
120/B3 Banda, India
120/C3 Bāndā, India
127/H4 Banda (isls.), Indo.
130/B1 Banda (sea), Indo.
153/F1 Banda, Zaire
124/A1 Banda Aceh, Indo.
130/D1 Banda Elat, Indo.
124/B2 Bandahara (peak), Indo.
111/F1 Bandai-Asahi Nat'l Park, Japan
111/G2 Bandai-Asahi Nat'l Park, Japan
111/G2 Bandai-san (mtn.), Japan
152/C4 Bandakani, Zaire
144/D5 Bandama (riv.), IvC.
144/D4 Bandama Blanc (riv.), IvC.
144/D4 Bandama Rouge (riv.), IvC.
127/G4 Bandanaira, Indo.
123/B2 Ban Dan Lan Hoi, Thai.
105/J5 Bandar Abbas (int'l arpt.), Iran
116/B4 Bāndarban, Bang.
107/H3 Bandar Beheshtī (Chāh Behār), Iran
120/D4 Bandarchua, India
105/J5 Bandar-e 'Abbās, Iran
105/G2 Bandar-e Anzalī, Iran
105/G4 Bandar-e Būshehr, Iran
105/H5 Bandar-e Chārak, Iran
105/G4 Bandar-e Deylam, Iran
105/H2 Bandar-e Gaz, Iran
105/G2 Bandar-e Kīāshahr, Iran
105/H5 Bandar-e Kong, Iran
105/H5 Bandar-e Lengeh, Iran
105/G4 Bandar-e Māhshahr, Iran
105/H5 Bandar-e Maqām, Iran
107/F3 Bandar-e Moghūyeh, Iran
105/G4 Bandar-e Rīg, Iran
105/H2 Bandar-e Torkeman, Iran
125/A4 Bandar Seri Begawan (cap.), Bru.
155/G1 Bandawe, Malw.
76/B1 Bande, Sp.
171/K6 Bandeira do Sul, Braz.
170/B3 Bandeirantes, Braz.
170/C4 Bandeirantes, Braz.
171/E4 Bandeira, Pico da (peak), Braz.
157/H6 Bandeli, May.
187/J3 Bandelier Nat'l Mon., NM,US
172/D4 Bandera, Arg.
187/H3 Bandera (vol.), NM,US
188/E3 Bandera, Tx,US
188/B2 Banderas, Mex.
159/N7 Banderilla, Mex.
120/C4 Bandhavgarh Nat'l Park, India
62/D4 Bandholm, Den.
144/E3 Bandiagara, Mali
124/C4 Bandingagung, Indo.
120/E2 Bandīpur, Nepal
114/B5 Bandipura, India
122/F3 Bandipur Nat'l Park, India
93/H5 Bandırma, Turk.
93/J5 Bandirma (gulf), Turk.
152/B1 Bandjoun, Camr.
191/J2 Band Mill, Ar,US
82/B6 Bandol, Fr.
60/B6 Bandon, Ire.
60/B6 Bandon (riv.), Ire.
184/A2 Bandon, Or,US
119/J5 Ban Don, Viet.
123/C1 Ban Donkon, Laos
152/D3 Bandundu, Zaire
152/D4 Bandundu (pol. reg.), Zaire
124/D4 Bandung, Indo.
123/C2 Ban Dung, Thai.
132/D3 Bandya, Austl.
169/F5 Banegas, Bol.
105/F3 Bāneh, Iran
77/E3 Bañeres, Sp.
161/H1 Banes, Cuba
108/F5 Banfangzi, China
182/G2 Banff, Ab,Can
54/D1 Banff, Sc,UK
180/C1 Banff Nat'l Park, Ab, BC,Can.
144/D4 Banfora, Burk.
148/B4 Bang, CAfr.
122/C2 Banga, India
118/C5 Bangalore, India
134/D5 Bangalow, Austl.
148/A4 Bangangté, Camr.
121/G4 Bangaon, India
117/J5 Bangar, Phil.
120/C2 Bāngarmau, India
140/E4 Bangassou, CAfr.
127/E2 Bangau, Tanjong (cape), Malay.
153/F2 Bangazeno, Zaire
131/G1 Bangeta, Mount (peak), PNG
127/F4 Banggai (isls.), Indo.
114/C5 Banggong (lake), China
123/D2 Banghiang (riv.), Laos
124/F4 Bangil, Indo.
124/D3 Bangka (isl.), Indo.
124/D3 Bangka (str.), Indo.
124/F4 Bangkalan, Indo.
124/B2 Bangkaru (isl.), Indo.
124/C2 Bangkinang, Indo.
127/F3 Bangkir, Indo.
124/C3 Bangko, Indo.
123/C3 Bangkok (bight), Thai.
123/C3 Bangkok (int'l arpt.), Thai.
123/C3 Bangkok (Krung Thep) (cap.), Thai.
121/G4 Bangladesh
123/C5 Bang Lang (res.), Thai.
124/F5 Bangli, Indo.
116/C4 Bangma (mts.), China
123/C2 Bang Mun Nak, Thai.
194/C2 Bangor, Sk,Can
78/B6 Bangor, Fr.
56/C2 Bangor, NI,UK
56/D5 Bangor, Wal,UK
196/C3 Bangor, Me,US
196/C3 Bangor (int'l arpt.), Me,US
198/C3 Bangor, Mi,US
206/C2 Bangor, Pa,US
148/C3 Bangoran (riv.), CAfr.
148/C4 Bangoran-Bamingui Nat'l Park, CAfr.
57/F6 Bangor-is-y-Coed, Wal,UK
123/C3 Bang Phli, Thai.
121/F4 Bāngriposi, India
187/F2 Bangs (mt.), Az,US
188/E2 Bangs, Tx,US
123/B4 Bang Saphan, Thai.
153/E5 Bangu, Zaire
125/C1 Bangued, Phil.
140/D4 Bangui (cap.), CAfr.
148/C4 Bangui (int'l arpt.), CAfr.
152/B2 Bangui, EqG.
125/C1 Bangui, Phil.
124/B2 Bangunpurba, Indo.
123/C3 Bang Yai, Thai.
116/E3 Bangzha, China
103/B4 Banhā, Egypt
155/G4 Banhine Nat'l Park, Moz.
123/D2 Ban Hinkhan, Laos
123/B2 Ban Hong, Thai.
123/C2 Ban Houay Pamon, Laos
123/C1 Ban Houayxay, Laos
148/D4 Bani, CAfr.
162/D3 Baní, DRep.
144/D3 Bani (riv.), Mali
148/C5 Bania, CAfr.
121/H3 Baniachang, Bang.
144/C4 Banian, Gui.
145/F3 Bani-Bangou, Niger
162/D3 Bánica, DRep.
144/D3 Banifing (riv.), Burk., Mali
121/H4 Bānigrām, Bang.
107/L2 Banihāl (pass), India
142/D3 Bani, Jbel (mts.), Mor
145/F4 Banikoara, Ben.
147/F2 Banī Mazār, Egypt
150/B5 Banisa, Kenya
201/H2 Banister (riv.), Va,US
103/D4 Banī Suhaylah, Gaza

147/F2 **Banī Suwayf**, Egypt
147/F2 **Banī Suwayf** (gov.), Egypt
146/B2 **Bāni Walīd**, Libya
103/D2 **Bāniyās**, Syria
92/D3 **Banja Koviljača**, Yugo.
92/C3 **Banja Luka**, Bosn.
124/E4 **Banjar**, Indo.
126/D4 **Banjarmasin**, Indo.
123/B1 **Banjia**, China
117/F3 **Banjiang**, China
144/A3 **Banjul** (cap.), Gam.
97/J5 **Bank**, Azer.
121/F3 **Bānka**, India
130/D4 **Banka Banka**, Austl.
123/D3 **Ban Kadian**, Laos
123/B5 **Ban Kantang**, Thai.
123/B4 **Ban Kapong**, Thai.
144/E3 **Bankas**, Mali
119/J4 **Ban Kengkok**, Laos
117/H3 **Bankengting**, China
62/F3 **Bankeryd**, Swe.
54/C4 **Bankfoot**, Sc,UK
123/C1 **Ban Kha**, Laos
123/D3 **Ban Khampho**, Laos
54/D2 **Bankhead**, Sc,UK
200/D4 **Bankhead** (lake), Al,US
123/C4 **Ban Khlong Yai**, Thai.
123/B4 **Ban Khok Kloi**, Thai.
123/C5 **Ban Khuan Niang**, Thai.
121/E4 **Bānki**, India
145/F3 **Bankilare**, Niger
148/A4 **Bankim**, Camr.
135/B3 **Banks** (cape), Austl.
131/F2 **Banks** (isl.), Austl.
135/C4 **Banks** (str.), Austl.
178/C3 **Banks** (isl.), BC,Can
178/D1 **Banks** (isl.), NW,Can
136/C3 **Banks** (pen.), N.Z.
177/H4 **Banks** (pt.), Ak,US
200/E5 **Banks**, Al,US
182/E4 **Banks** (lake), Wa,US
138/F6 **Banks** (isls.), Van.
134/H8 **Bankstown**, Austl.
134/G8 **Bankstown** (arpt.), Austl.
123/B3 **Ban Kui Nua**, Thai.
121/F4 **Bānkurā**, India
91/H1 **Bankya**, Bul.
123/B3 **Ban Laem**, Thai.
119/H4 **Ban Len**, Laos
117/E4 **Banli**, China
123/D2 **Ban Loboy**, Laos
121/F3 **Banmankhi**, India
116/B3 **Banmauk**, Burma
123/E3 **Ban Mdrack**, Viet.
117/H3 **Banmian**, China
123/D2 **Ban Mong**, Viet.
123/D2 **Ban Muangsen**, Laos
60/D4 **Bann** (riv.), Ire.
56/B2 **Bann** (riv.), NI,UK
86/A3 **Banna** (riv.), It.
185/G1 **Bannack**, Mt,US
123/D2 **Ban Nakala**, Laos
78/B5 **Bannalec**, Fr.
123/D1 **Ban Na Mang**, Laos
123/C1 **Ban Nambak**, Laos
123/C5 **Bannang Sata**, Thai.
123/D2 **Ban Nape**, Laos
123/D2 **Ban Na Phao**, Laos
123/C1 **Ban Na Pho**, Laos
123/B4 **Ban Na San**, Thai.
201/F2 **Banner**, Ky,US
185/K1 **Banner**, Wy,US
186/D4 **Banning**, Ca,US
185/G1 **Bannock** (pass), Id,US
185/G2 **Bannock** (peak), Id,US
54/C4 **Bannockburn**, Sc,UK
54/C4 **Bannockburn Battlesite** (1314), Sc,UK
60/D5 **Bannow** (bay), Ire.
122/A1 **Bannu**, Pak.
82/B4 **Banon**, Fr.
168/B1 **Baños**, Ecu.
73/C2 **Bánovce nad Bebravou**, Slvk.
92/D3 **Banovići**, Bosn.
123/C4 **Ban Pak Phanang**, Thai.
123/C2 **Ban Panghai**, Laos
123/D2 **Ban Phaeng**, Thai.
123/C2 **Ban Phai**, Thai.
123/D3 **Ban Phon**, Laos
123/B3 **Banphot Phisai**, Thai.
115/B4 **Banpo** (ruins), China
123/B3 **Ban Pong**, Thai.
123/B3 **Ban Rai**, Thai.
123/C2 **Ban Saka**, Laos
121/G4 **Bansberia**, India
120/E3 **Bānsdīh**, India
60/B5 **Bansha**, Ire.
117/G3 **Banshi**, China
120/B3 **Bānsi**, India
120/D2 **Bānsi**, India
123/C2 **Ban Sieou**, Laos
121/G3 **Bansihāri**, India
65/H2 **Bansin**, Ger.
73/D2 **Banská Bystrica**, Slvk.
73/C3 **Banská Štiavnica**, Slvk.
93/F5 **Bansko**, Bul.
53/N8 **Banstead**, Eng,UK
118/B3 **Bānswāra**, India
123/C1 **Ban Ta Fa**, Laos
123/B2 **Ban Tak**, Thai.
196/D2 **Bantalor Game Ref.**, NB,Can
208/A2 **Bantam**, Ct,US
125/C3 **Bantayan**, Phil.
125/C3 **Bantayan** (isl.), Phil.
145/F4 **Banté**, Ben.
60/B5 **Banteer**, Ire.
124/F5 **Bantenan** (cape), Indo.
123/C2 **Ban Thabok**, Laos
116/E5 **Ban Tha Uthen**, Thai.
123/C2 **Ban Thieng**, Laos
123/B5 **Bantong Group** (isls.), Thai.
60/A6 **Bantry**, Ire.
60/A6 **Bantry** (bay), Ire.
123/D2 **Ban Tung**, Laos
76/C3 **Bañuelo** (mtn.), Sp.
122/D2 **Banūr**, India
123/C2 **Ban Woen**, Laos
123/C1 **Ban Xay**, Laos
123/D3 **Ban Xebang-Nouan**, Laos
117/F2 **Banxi**, China
124/A2 **Banyak** (isls.), Indo.
148/A4 **Banyo**, Camr.
77/G1 **Banyoles**, Sp.
123/B5 **Ban Yong Sata**, Thai.
124/F5 **Banyuwangi**, Indo.
124/F5 **Banyuwangi Selatan Nat'l Rsv.**, Indo.
131/G1 **Banz**, PNG
137/J **Banzare** (coast), Ant.
141/W17 **Banzart** (lake), Tun.
141/W17 **Banzart** (Bizerte), Tun.
115/B3 **Baode**, China
115/D3 **Baodi**, China
115/H7 **Baodi**, China
115/C3 **Baoding**, China
115/G7 **Baoding**, China
115/D4 **Baodugu** (mtn.), China
115/C4 **Baofeng**, China
116/E2 **Baoguangsi**, China
123/D1 **Bao Ha**, Viet.
108/F5 **Baoji**, China
119/J2 **Baojing**, China
115/B5 **Baokang**, China
123/D1 **Bao Lac**, Viet.
123/D4 **Bao Loc**, Viet.
148/B4 **Baoro**, CAfr.
161/J2 **Baoruco, Sierra de** (range), DRep.
115/E5 **Baoshan**, China
116/C3 **Baoshan**, China
117/J2 **Baoshan**, China
116/E3 **Baotian**, China
115/B2 **Baotou**, China
144/D4 **Baoulé** (riv.), IvC., Mali
144/C3 **Baoulé** (riv.), Mali
116/D2 **Baoxing**, China
117/G1 **Baoxinji**, China
115/D4 **Baoying**, China
118/D4 **Bāpatla**, India
68/B3 **Bapaume**, Fr.
206/C2 **Baptistown**, NJ,US
103/D3 **Bāqa el Gharbiyya**, Isr.
116/B1 **Baqên**, China
123/D4 **Ba Quan** (cape), Viet.
105/F3 **Ba'qūbah**, Iraq
172/B2 **Baquedano**, Chile
68/D5 **Bar** (riv.), Fr.
98/D3 **Bar**, Ukr.
92/D4 **Bar**, Yugo.
127/G4 **Bara**, Indo.
145/H4 **Bara**, Nga.
65/G1 **Bara**, Swe.
123/D4 **Ba Ra**, Viet.
126/E4 **Barabai**, Indo.
122/D1 **Barā Bangāhal**, India
120/C2 **Bāra Banki**, India
100/H4 **Barabinsk**, Rus.
193/K2 **Baraboo**, Wi,US
193/J2 **Baraboo** (riv.), Wi,US
76/D1 **Baracaldo**, Sp.
197/G3 **Barachois** (pt.), Can
196/E2 **Barachois**, NB,Can
196/E1 **Barachois**, Qu,Can
161/H1 **Baracoa**, Cuba
103/E3 **Baradá** (riv.), Syria
174/F2 **Baradero**, Arg.
135/D1 **BaradinOBe**, Austl.
120/E3 **Barāgaon**, India
151/B1 **Baragoi**, Kenya
161/G1 **Baraguá**, Cuba
164/D2 **Baragua**, Ven.
149/F2 **Bārah**, Sudan
162/D3 **Barahona**, DRep.
76/D2 **Barajas** (int'l arpt.), Sp.
92/E3 **Barajevo**, Yugo.
116/B3 **Barāk** (riv.), India
149/H1 **Baraka** (riv.), Sudan
153/G4 **Baraka**, Zaire
149/E3 **Barakah**, Sudan
121/F3 **Barākar** (riv.), India
107/J2 **Barakī Barak**, Afg.
134/C4 **Baralaba**, Austl.
122/D1 **Bārā Lācha La** (pass), India
126/D3 **Baram** (cape), Malay.
125/A4 **Baram** (riv.), Malay.
165/G3 **Barama** (riv.), Guy.
121/H2 **Barama**, India
165/G3 **Baramanni**, Guy.
118/B4 **Bārāmati**, India
165/F3 **Baramita**, Guy.
107/K2 **Baramula**, India
63/P4 **Baran'**, Bela.
118/C2 **Bāran**, India
153/F2 **Baranga**, Zaire
101/S3 **Baranikha**, Rus.
164/C2 **Baranoa**, Col.
85/D6 **Barano d'Ischia**, It.
177/L4 **Baranof** (isl.), Ak,US
96/C1 **Baranovichi**, Bela.
98/D2 **Baranovka**, Ukr.
92/C3 **Baranya** (co.), Hun.
171/E3 **Barão de Cocais**, Braz.
167/F4 **Barão de Grajaú**, Braz.
169/H5 **Barão de Melgaço**, Braz.
93/G2 **Baraolt**, Rom.
121/H3 **Barapani** (arpt.), India
69/E3 **Baraque de Fraiture** (hill), Belg.
125/D2 **Baras**, Phil.
121/G4 **Bārāsat**, India
130/B1 **Barat Daya** (isls.), Indo.
130/A2 **Barate**, Indo.
152/C4 **Baratier**, Congo
116/B3 **Barato**, India
121/E2 **Barauli**, India
120/A1 **Baraut**, India
164/C4 **Baraya**, Col.
170/E4 **Barbacena**, Braz.
164/B4 **Barbacoas**, Col.
167/O8 **Barbacoas**, Ven.
162/G4 **Barbados**
167/G4 **Barbalha**, Braz.
149/G1 **Barbar**, Sudan
93/H5 **Barbaros**, Turk.
142/A5 **Barbas** (cape), WSah.
77/F1 **Barbastro**, Sp.
76/C4 **Barbate de Franco**, Sp.
179/T6 **Barbeau** (peak), NW,Can
77/L6 **Barbera del Valles**, Sp.
82/B1 **Barberaz**, Fr.
87/E5 **Barberino di Mugello**, It.
157/E2 **Barberton**, SAfr.
208/F5 **Barberton**, Oh,US
74/C4 **Barbezieux-Saint-Hilaire**, Fr.
121/E3 **Bar Bigha**, India
121/E4 **Barbil**, India
57/F3 **Barbon**, Eng,UK
86/D5 **Barbona, Monte** (peak), It.
164/C3 **Barbosa**, Col.
201/H1 **Barboursville**, Va,US
200/F2 **Barbourville**, Ky,US
162/F3 **Barbuda** (isl.), Anti.
72/B4 **Barby**, Ger.
134/B3 **Barcaldine**, Austl.
54/A3 **Barcaldine**, Sc,UK
166/D3 **Barcarena**, Braz.
76/B3 **Barcarrota**, Sp.
89/J1 **Barcău** (riv.), Rom.
92/F2 **Barcaŭ** (riv.), Rom.
83/B6 **Barcellona Pozzo di Gotto**, It.
77/G2 **Barcelona**, Sp.
165/E2 **Barcelona**, Ven.
77/L7 **Barcelona-Prat** (int'l arpt.), Sp.
82/C4 **Barcelonnette**, Fr.
165/F5 **Barcelos**, Braz.
76/A2 **Barcelos**, Port.
65/J2 **Barcin**, Pol.
189/F2 **Barclay**, Tx,US
201/K2 **Barco**, NC,US
134/A4 **Barcoo** (riv.), Austl.
92/C3 **Barcs**, Hun.
65/L2 **Barczewo**, Pol.
186/E4 **Bard**, Ca,US
105/F1 **Barda**, Azer.
146/C4 **Bardagué, Enneri** (dry riv.), Chad
146/C4 **Bardaï**, Chad
174/C2 **Bardas Blancas**, Arg.
103/C4 **Bardawīl, Sabkhat al** (lag.), Egypt
65/L4 **Bardejov**, Slvk.
105/J3 **Bardeskan**, Iran
150/B5 **Bardheere**, Som.
86/C3 **Bardi**, It.
147/E2 **Bardīyah**, Libya
57/H5 **Bardney**, Eng,UK
118/B3 **Bārdoli**, India
87/D1 **Bardolino**, It.
82/C2 **Bardonecchia**, It.
207/K7 **Bardonia**, NY,US
204/B2 **Bardsdale**, Ca,US
56/D6 **Bardsey** (isl.), Wal,UK
200/E2 **Bardstown**, Ky,US
200/C2 **Bardwell**, Ky,US
189/F1 **Bardwell**, Tx,US
150/D3 **Bareeda**, Som.
86/B2 **Bareggio**, It.
120/B1 **Bareilly**, India
148/D2 **Barei, Wādī** (dry riv.), Sudan
120/B4 **Bareli**, India
135/C2 **Barellan**, Austl.
66/B5 **Barendrecht**, Neth.
79/F1 **Barentin**, Fr.
79/E3 **Barenton**, Fr.
51/L2 **Barents** (sea)
149/H2 **Barentu**, Eth.
81/E3 **Bäretswil**, Swi.
206/B3 **Bareville-Leacock-Leola**, Pa,US
78/D1 **Barfleur**, Fr.
78/D1 **Barfleur, Pointe de** (pt.), Fr.
114/D5 **Barga**, China
86/D4 **Barga**, It.
134/D4 **Bargara**, Austl.
118/D3 **Bargarh**, India
82/D3 **Barge**, It.
67/H1 **Bargfeld-Stegen**, Ger.
120/B4 **Bargi**, India
135/D2 **Bargo**, Austl.
58/C3 **Bargoed**, Wal,UK
67/H1 **Bargteheide**, Ger.
121/H4 **Bārguna**, Bang.
108/F1 **Barguzin** (riv.), Rus.
121/E3 **Bārh**, India
120/D2 **Barhaj**, India
120/D2 **Barhalganj**, India
135/C2 **Barham**, Austl.
121/F2 **Barhamjia**, Nepal
196/C3 **Bar Harbor**, Me,US
121/F3 **Barharwā**, India
121/E3 **Barhi**, India
59/G2 **Bar Hill**, Eng,UK
121/F3 **Barhiya**, India
120/A2 **Bāri**, India
90/E2 **Bari**, It.
85/G5 **Bari** (prov.), It.
152/D2 **Bari**, Zaire
151/A2 **Bariadi**, Tanz.
86/C1 **Bariano**, It.
87/E3 **Baricella**, It.
164/C3 **Barichara**, Col.
151/B2 **Baricho**, Kenya
147/H3 **Barīdī, Ra's** (pt.), SAr.
86/C3 **Barigazzo, Monte** (peak), It.
141/U18 **Barika**, Alg.
151/B4 **Barikiwa**, Tanz.
107/K1 **Barīkowt**, Afg.
85/F6 **Barile**, It.
188/C2 **Barilla Draw** (cr.), Tx,US
160/D3 **Barillas**, Guat.
165/G2 **Barima** (riv.), Guy., Ven.
165/F3 **Barima-Waini** (reg.), Guy.
164/D2 **Barinas**, Ven.
164/D2 **Barinas** (state), Ven.
182/D4 **Baring**, Wa,US
153/E3 **Baringa**, Zaire
153/E2 **Baringa I**, Zaire
152/D4 **Baringa-Twana**, Zaire
164/D2 **Barinitas**, Ven.
121/F5 **Baripāda**, India
170/C4 **Bariri**, Braz.
147/F3 **Bārīs**, Egypt
97/H4 **Barisakho**, Geo.
121/H4 **Barisāl**, Bang.
121/H4 **Barisāl** (dist.), Bang.
124/C3 **Barisan** (mts.), Indo.
90/A3 **Bari Sardo**, It.
85/D3 **Barisciano**, It.
126/D4 **Barito** (riv.), Indo.
172/C1 **Baritu Nat'l Park**, Arg.
82/C5 **Barjols**, Fr.
199/G2 **Bark** (lake), On,Can
195/J4 **Bark** (pt.), Wi,US
205/N13 **Bark** (riv.), Wi,US
121/E4 **Barka Kāna**, India
116/D2 **Barkam**, China
63/M3 **Barkava**, Lat.
133/M9 **Barker** (cr.), Austl.
197/T9 **Barker**, NY,US
189/G3 **Barker** (dam), Tx,US
189/G3 **Barker** (res.), Tx,US
144/B2 **Barkéwol el Abiod**, Mrta.
208/H5 **Barkeyville**, Pa,US
208/B1 **Barkhamsted** (res.), Ct,US
53/P7 **Barking & Dagenham** (bor.), Eng,UK
121/E3 **Barki Saria**, India
182/B3 **Barkley** (sound), BC,Can
200/C2 **Barkley** (dam), Ky,US
200/D2 **Barkley** (lake), Ky, Tn,US
131/D4 **Barkly** (tableland), Austl.
156/D3 **Barkly East**, SAfr.
128/E3 **Barkly Tablelands** (plat.), Austl.
156/D3 **Barkly West**, SAfr.
108/C3 **Barkol** (Barkol Kazak Zizhixian), China
114/F3 **Barkol Kazak Zizhixian** (Barkol), China
198/C2 **Bark River**, Mi,US
189/H1 **Barksdale A.F.B.**, La,US
57/F6 **Barlaston**, Eng,UK
57/G4 **Barlby**, Eng,UK
72/B3 **Barleben**, Ger.
69/E6 **Bar-le-Duc**, Fr.
132/C4 **Barlee** (lake), Austl.
132/B2 **Barlee** (range), Austl.
132/B2 **Barlee Range Nature Rsv.**, Austl.
85/G5 **Barletta**, It.
68/B3 **Barlin**, Fr.
65/H2 **Barlinek**, Pol.
191/G3 **Barling**, Ar,US
135/C2 **Barmedman**, Austl.
118/B2 **Barmer**, India
133/J5 **Barmera**, Austl.
58/B1 **Barmouth**, Wal,UK
67/G1 **Barmstedt**, Ger.
60/A3 **Barna**, Ire.
122/C2 **Barnāla**, India
191/E1 **Barnard**, Ks,US
57/G2 **Barnard Castle**, Eng,UK
114/D1 **Barnaul**, Rus.
92/B2 **Bärnbach**, Aus.
207/D4 **Barnegat**, NJ,US
207/D4 **Barnegat** (bay), NJ,US
207/D4 **Barnegat** (inlet), NJ,US
207/D4 **Barnegat Light**, NJ,US
195/J4 **Barnes**, Wi,US
199/G4 **Barnesboro**, Pa,US
200/E4 **Barnesville**, Ga,US
194/F4 **Barnesville**, Mn,US
53/N7 **Barnet**, Eng,UK
53/N7 **Barnet** (bor.), Eng,UK
199/K2 **Barnet**, Vt,US
66/C4 **Barneveld**, Neth.
78/D2 **Barneville-Carteret**, Fr.
203/G2 **Barney**, Ga,US
191/J1 **Barnhart**, Mo,US
159/E2 **Barnhart**, Tx,US
208/F7 **Barnhill**, Oh,US
121/H2 **Barni Hāt**, India
72/D2 **Barnim** (reg.), Ger.
57/F4 **Barnoldswick**, Eng,UK
191/F2 **Barnsdall**, Ok,US
57/G4 **Barnsley**, Eng,UK
196/B5 **Barnstable**, Ma,US
72/B5 **Barnstädt**, Ger.
58/B4 **Barnstaple**, Eng,UK
58/B4 **Barnstaple** (Bideford) (bay), Eng,UK
67/F3 **Barnstorf**, Ger.
58/E2 **Barnt Green**, Eng,UK
67/G5 **Barntrup**, Ger.
185/K2 **Barnum**, Wy,US
192/A2 **Bar Nunn**, Wy,US
183/H3 **Barnwell**, Ab,Can
201/G4 **Barnwell**, SC,US
144/C4 **Baro**, Gui.
145/G4 **Baro**, Nga.
118/B3 **Baroda**, India
120/B3 **Barodia Kalān**, India
191/G3 **Baron**, Ok,US
186/D4 **Barona Ranch Ind. Res.**, Ca,US
86/B1 **Barone, Monte** (peak), It.
108/D5 **Barong**, China
183/H3 **Barons**, Ab,Can
149/E4 **Baroua**, CAfr.
149/G3 **Baro Wenz** (riv.), Eth.
107/K1 **Barowghīl** (Khyber) (pass), Afg.
121/H2 **Barpeta**, India
146/B3 **Barqin**, Libya
198/E2 **Barques, Point Aux** (pt.), Mi,US
164/D2 **Barquisimeto**, Ven.
164/D2 **Barquisimeto** (int'l arpt.), Ven.
80/D1 **Barr**, Fr.
56/D1 **Barr**, Sc,UK
171/E1 **Barra**, Braz.
55/H8 **Barra** (isl.), Sc,UK
135/D1 **Barraba**, Austl.
170/C4 **Barra Bonita**, Braz.
121/G4 **Barrackpur**, India
161/F4 **Barra del Colorado Nat'l Park**, CR
161/F3 **Barra de Río Grande**, Nic.
170/A2 **Barra do Bugres**, Braz.
167/E4 **Barra do Corda**, Braz.
152/C5 **Barra do Cuanza**, Ang.
152/C5 **Barra do Dande**, Ang.
170/B2 **Barra do Garças**, Braz.
170/E4 **Barra do Piraí**, Braz.
173/G4 **Barra do Ribeiro**, Braz.
155/G4 **Barra Falsa, Ponta da** (pt.), Moz.
55/H8 **Barra Head** (pt.), Sc,UK
170/D4 **Barra Mansa**, Braz.
168/B2 **Barranca**, Peru
168/B3 **Barranca**, Peru
164/C3 **Barrancabermeja**, Col.
158/D3 **Barranca del Cobre Nat'l Park**, Mex.
164/C3 **Barranca de Upía**, Col.
174/C3 **Barrancas**, Arg.
172/E3 **Barrancas** (riv.), Arg.
174/C2 **Barrancas**, Chile
164/C2 **Barrancas**, Col.
165/F2 **Barrancas**, Ven.
164/C2 **Barranco de Loba**, Col.
76/B3 **Barrancos**, Port.
164/C2 **Barranquilla**, Col.
161/E3 **Barra Patuca**, Hon.
155/G4 **Barra, Ponta da** (pt.), Moz.
161/F4 **Barra Punta Gorda**, Nic.
167/F4 **Barras**, Braz.
164/C4 **Barras**, Col.
173/G3 **Barra Velha**, Braz.
208/B1 **Barre**, Ma,US
199/K2 **Barre**, Vt,US
174/C1 **Barreal**, Arg.
152/B3 **Barre de Portugais** (pt.), Gabon
171/E1 **Barreiras**, Braz.
166/B3 **Barreirinha**, Braz.
167/F3 **Barreirinhas**, Braz.
76/A3 **Barreiro**, Port.
167/F4 **Barreiros**, Braz.
82/C5 **Barrême**, Fr.
140/G7 **Barren** (isls.), Madg.
200/D2 **Barren** (riv.), Tn,US
157/G7 **Barren, Nosy** (isls.), Madg.
200/D2 **Barren River** (lake), Ky,US
208/B1 **Barre Plains**, Ma,US
169/E4 **Barrera**, Bol.
170/C4 **Barretos**, Braz.
189/G3 **Barrett**, Tx,US
178/E3 **Barrhead**, Ab,Can
54/B5 **Barrhead**, Sc,UK
56/D1 **Barrhill**, Sc,UK
199/G2 **Barrie**, On,Can
135/B1 **Barrier** (range), Austl.
205/P15 **Barrington**, Il,US
196/B4 **Barrington**, NH,US
208/C2 **Barrington**, RI,US
205/P15 **Barrington Hills**, Il,US
135/D1 **Barrington Tops** (peak), Austl.
135/D1 **Barrington Tops Nat'l Park**, Austl.
135/C1 **Barringun**, Austl.
167/F4 **Barro Duro**, Braz.
193/J1 **Barron**, Wi,US
195/J5 **Barronett**, Wi,US
134/B2 **Barron Gorge Nat'l Park**, Austl.
172/B3 **Barros Luco**, Chile
170/E4 **Barroso**, Braz.
162/F4 **Barrouallie**, StV.
132/B2 **Barrow** (isl.), Austl.
131/G3 **Barrow** (pt.), Austl.
178/G1 **Barrow** (str.), NW,Can
60/D5 **Barrow** (riv.), Ire.
177/G1 **Barrow**, Ak,US
177/G1 **Barrow** (pt.), Ak,US
57/H6 **Barrowby**, Eng,UK
133/G2 **Barrow Creek**, Austl.
57/F4 **Barrowford**, Eng,UK
57/E3 **Barrow-in-Furness**, Eng,UK
208/C2 **Barrowsville**, Ma,US
76/C1 **Barruelo de Santullán**, Sp.
58/C4 **Barry**, Wal,UK
187/F4 **Barry M. Goldwater Air Force Ra.**, Az,US
199/H2 **Barry's Bay**, On,Can
136/B3 **Barrytown**, N.Z.
97/L4 **Barsakel'mes** (salt pan), Uzb.
145/E3 **Barsalogho**, Burk.
107/L5 **Bārshi**, India
67/G4 **Barsinghausen**, Ger.
63/T8 **Bårslöv**, Swe.
67/E2 **Barssel**, Ger.
186/D3 **Barstow**, Ca,US
158/E2 **Barstow**, Tx,US
74/F2 **Bar-sur-Aube**, Fr.
74/F2 **Bar-sur-Seine**, Fr.
114/B4 **Bartang** (riv.), Taj.
80/D2 **Bartenheim**, Fr.
64/G1 **Barth**, Ger.
70/C5 **Bartholomä**, Ger.
81/F3 **Bartholomäberg**, Aus.
200/B4 **Bartholomew** (bayou), Ar, La,US
165/G3 **Bartica**, Guy.
93/L5 **Bartın**, Turk.
129/H3 **Bartle Frere** (peak), Austl.
191/G2 **Bartlesville**, Ok,US
205/P16 **Bartlett**, Il,US
192/E3 **Bartlett**, Ne,US
199/L2 **Bartlett**, NH,US
200/C3 **Bartlett**, Tn,US
189/F2 **Bartlett**, Tx,US
201/G2 **Bartley**, WV,US
161/G1 **Bartolomé Masó**, Cuba
155/G4 **Bartolomeu Dias**, Moz.
201/H1 **Barton**, Md,US
194/D3 **Barton**, ND,US
199/K2 **Barton**, Vt,US
59/F3 **Barton in the Clay**, Eng,UK
59/E5 **Barton on Sea**, Eng,UK
206/C1 **Bartonsville**, Pa,US
59/E1 **Barton under Needwood**, Eng,UK
57/H4 **Barton-upon-Humber**, Eng,UK
65/L1 **Bartoszyce**, Pol.
65/G2 **Bartow**, Ger.
202/M8 **Bartow**, Fl,US
203/H4 **Bartow**, Fl,US
168/B1 **Bartra Nuevo**, Peru
161/F4 **Barú** (vol.), Pan.
121/G4 **Bāruipur**, India
124/C2 **Baruman** (riv.), Indo.
126/B3 **Barumun** (riv.), Indo.
124/B2 **Barus**, Indo.
167/O7 **Baruta**, Ven.
72/D3 **Baruth**, Ger.
108/C2 **Baruun Huuray** (reg.), Mong.
108/G2 **Baruun-Urt**, Mong.
99/J3 **Barvenkovo**, Ukr.
184/A2 **Barview**, Or,US
118/C3 **Barwāha**, India
118/B3 **Barwāni**, India
120/B3 **Barwa Sāgar**, India
203/G2 **Barwick**, Ga,US
135/D1 **Barwon** (riv.), Austl.
65/J3 **Barycz** (riv.), Pol.
97/H1 **Barysh**, Rus.
98/F2 **Baryshevka**, Ukr.
86/C1 **Barzanò**, It.
144/D5 **Basa**, IvC.
87/G1 **Basaldella**, It.
152/D2 **Basankusu**, Zaire
76/D1 **Basauri**, Sp.
174/F2 **Basavilbaso**, Arg.
144/D4 **Basawa**, IvC.
125/C3 **Basay**, Phil.
196/E2 **Bas-Caraquet**, NB,Can
69/E4 **Bascharage**, Lux.
58/D1 **Baschurch**, Eng,UK
203/F2 **Bascom**, Fl,US
172/B4 **Bascuñan** (pt.), Chile
72/D2 **Basdorf**, Ger.
199/J3 **Baseball Hall of Fame**, NY,US
149/E4 **Basekpio**, Zaire
80/D2 **Basel**, Swi.
75/G3 **Basel/Mulhouse** (int'l arpt.), Fr.
81/H5 **Baselga di Pinè**, It.
85/E5 **Baselice**, It.
80/D3 **Baselland** (canton), Swi.
85/G6 **Basentello** (riv.), It.
83/C2 **Basento** (riv.), It.
183/H1 **Bashaw**, Ab,Can
156/E3 **Bashee** (riv.), SAfr.
117/J4 **Bashi** (chan.), Phil., Tai.
114/E1 **Bashkaus** (riv.), Rus.
95/M5 **Bashkir Aut. Rep.**, Rus.
97/G1 **Bashmakovo**, Rus.
105/G4 **Bāsht**, Iran
98/G4 **Bashtanka**, Ukr.
149/F2 **Ba'shūm**, Sudan
125/C4 **Basilan** (isl.), Phil.
125/C4 **Basilan** (peak), Phil.
125/C4 **Basilan** (str.), Phil.
59/G3 **Basildon**, Eng,UK
202/B2 **Basile**, La,US
86/C4 **Basilica di Fieschi**, It.
83/B2 **Basilicata** (reg.), It.
83/B5 **Basiluzzo** (isl.), It.
118/C3 **Bāsim**, India
183/H4 **Basin**, Mt,US
185/J1 **Basin**, Wy,US
59/E4 **Basingstoke**, Eng,UK
53/M8 **Basingstoke** (can.), Eng,UK
121/G4 **Basīrhāt**, India
103/D2 **Basīt, Ra's al** (pt.), Syria
92/B3 **Baška**, Cro.
196/C3 **Baskahegan** (lake), Me,US
105/F2 **Başkale**, Turk.
199/J1 **Baskatong** (res.), Qu,Can
130/A4 **Baskerville** (cape), Austl.
184/B1 **Baskett Slough Nat'l Wild. Ref.**, Or,US
104/D2 **Baskil**, Turk.
189/J1 **Baskin**, La,US
104/B2 **Başkomutan Nat'l Park**, Turk.
104/D2 **Başköy**, Turk.
104/B2 **Başmakçı**, Turk.
105/F2 **Bāsmenj**, Iran
120/A4 **Bāsoda**, India
151/A3 **Basodesh**, Tanz.
81/E5 **Basodino, Monte** (peak), It.
153/E2 **Basoko**, Zaire
122/C1 **Basoli**, India
152/E4 **Basongo**, Zaire
76/D1 **Basque Provinces** (aut. comm.), Sp.
80/D1 **Bas-Rhin** (dept.), Fr.
135/C3 **Bass** (str.), Austl.
139/L7 **Bass** (isls.), FrPol.
91/G4 **Bassae** (Vassés) (ruins), Gre.
183/H2 **Bassano**, Ab,Can
87/E1 **Bassano del Grappa**, It.
84/C3 **Bassano Romano**, It.
145/F4 **Bassari**, Togo
155/H4 **Bassas da India** (isl.), Reun.
175/S11 **Bassavilbaso**, Arg.
80/D3 **Bassecourt**, Swi.
116/B5 **Bassein**, Burma
116/B5 **Bassein** (riv.), Burma
118/B4 **Bassein**, India
148/D4 **Basse-Kotto** (pref.), CAfr.
69/E2 **Bassenge**, Belg.
69/G3 **Bassenheim**, Ger.
74/C2 **Basse-Normandie** (reg.), Fr.
82/B1 **Bassens**, Fr.
56/E2 **Bassenthwaite** (lake), Eng,UK
144/B3 **Basse Santa Su**, Gam.
162/F3 **Basse-Terre**, Guad.
162/F3 **Basse-Terre** (isl.), Guad.
162/F3 **Basseterre** (cap.), StK.
192/E2 **Bassett**, Ne,US
189/G1 **Bassett**, Tx,US
201/H2 **Bassett**, Va,US
196/C3 **Bass Harbor**, Me,US
144/D3 **Bassikounou**, Mrta.
196/F3 **Bass River**, NS,Can
54/D4 **Bass Rock** (isl.), Sc,UK
67/F3 **Bassum**, Ger.
195/J3 **Basswood** (lake), On,Can, Mn,US
62/E3 **Båstad**, Swe.
105/H5 **Bastak**, Iran
105/H2 **Basţām**, Iran
72/E6 **Bastei**, Ger.
90/A2 **Bastelicaccia**, Fr.
70/D2 **Bastheim**, Ger.
120/D2 **Bastī**, India
90/A1 **Bastia**, Fr.
84/C1 **Bastia**, It.
90/A1 **Bastia** (Poretta) (int'l arpt.), Fr.
69/E3 **Bastogne**, Belg.
170/C4 **Bastos**, Braz.
189/J1 **Bastrop**, La,US
189/F2 **Bastrop**, Tx,US
103/B4 **Basyūn**, Egypt
152/C4 **Bas-Zaïre** (pol. reg.), Zaire
152/B2 **Bata**, EqG.
125/C2 **Bataan** (mt.), Phil.
161/F1 **Batabanó** (gulf), Cuba
125/C1 **Batac**, Phil.
101/P3 **Batagay**, Rus.
93/G5 **Batak**, Bul.
126/D4 **Batakan**, Indo.
107/L2 **Batakūt**, India
122/C2 **Batāla**, India
167/F4 **Batalha**, Braz.
76/A3 **Batalha**, Port.
168/D5 **Batallas**, Bol.
97/M1 **Bataly**, Kaz.
153/F2 **Batama**, Zaire
97/L2 **Batamshinskiy**, Kaz.
138/B2 **Batan** (isls.), Phil.
116/C2 **Batang**, China
124/E4 **Batang**, Indo.
140/D4 **Batangafo**, CAfr.
125/C2 **Batangas**, Phil.
124/B2 **Batangtoru**, Indo.
127/H4 **Batanta** (mtn.), Indo.
118/B2 **Bātāru**, India
152/C4 **Bata-Siala**, Zaire
170/D4 **Batatais**, Braz.
202/C3 **Batataria** (bay), La,US
205/P16 **Batavia**, Il,US
199/G3 **Batavia**, NY,US
198/D5 **Batavia**, Oh,US
99/K4 **Bataysk**, Rus.
130/C3 **Batchelor**, Austl.
202/C2 **Batchelor**, La,US
198/D1 **Batchwana Bay**, On,Can
119/H5 **Batdambang**, Camb.
134/H9 **Bate** (bay), Austl.
152/C3 **Batéké** (plat.), Congo
194/A2 **Bateman**, Sk,Can
135/D2 **Batemans Bay**, Austl.
201/G4 **Batesburg**, SC,US
200/E4 **Batesville**, Al,US
191/J3 **Batesville**, Ar,US
198/D5 **Batesville**, In,US
200/C3 **Batesville**, Ms,US
188/E3 **Batesville**, Tx,US
201/H2 **Batesville**, Va,US
63/P2 **Batetskiy**, Rus.
131/D3 **Bath** (range), Austl.
196/D2 **Bath**, NB,Can
66/B6 **Bath**, Neth.
58/D4 **Bath**, Eng,UK
196/C4 **Bath**, Me,US
199/H3 **Bath**, NY,US
206/C2 **Bath**, Pa,US
148/C2 **Batha** (dry riv.), Chad
148/C2 **Batha** (pref.), Chad
148/C3 **Batha de Laïri** (dry riv.), Chad
199/G5 **Bath** (Berkeley Springs), WV,US
54/C5 **Bathgate**, Sc,UK
194/F3 **Bathgate**, ND,US
66/D4 **Bathmen**, Neth.
162/G4 **Bathsheba**, Bar.
200/C3 **Bath Springs**, Tn,US
135/D2 **Bathurst**, Austl.
130/C2 **Bathurst** (isl.), Austl.
196/E2 **Bathurst**, NB,Can
177/N1 **Bathurst** (cape), NW,Can
178/F2 **Bathurst** (inlet), NW,Can
179/R7 **Bathurst** (isl.), NW,Can
178/F2 **Bathurst Inlet**, NW,Can
150/B3 **Batī**, Eth.
151/B2 **Batian** (peak), Kenya
144/E4 **Batié**, Burk.
114/F2 **Batik** (mts.), China
106/E3 **Bāţin, Wādī al** (dry riv.), SAr.
204/C4 **Batiquitos** (lag.), Ca,US
196/A2 **Batiscan** (riv.), Qu,Can
105/H3 **Bāţlāq-e Gāv Khūnī** (marsh), Iran
57/G4 **Batley**, Eng,UK
135/D2 **Batlow**, Austl.
104/E2 **Batman**, Turk.
141/V18 **Batna**, Alg.
141/U18 **Batna** (wilaya), Alg.
92/E3 **Batočina**, Yugo.
155/E3 **Batoka**, Zam.
202/C2 **Baton Rouge** (cap.), La,US
158/D3 **Batopilas**, Mex.
122/C1 **Batoti**, India
148/B4 **Batouri**, Camr.
170/B2 **Batovi** (riv.), Braz.
103/D4 **Baţrā'** (Petra) (ruins), Jor.
61/J1 **Båtsfjord**, Nor.
103/G6 **Bat Shelomo**, Isr.
206/D4 **Batsto**, NJ,US
206/D4 **Batsto** (riv.), NJ,US
206/D4 **Batsto Hist. Vill.**, NJ,US
108/F2 **Batsümber**, Mong.
87/E2 **Battaglia Terme**, It.
121/H4 **Battali**, Bang.
67/F6 **Battenberg**, Ger.
51/M9 **Batterbee** (cape), Ant.
80/D3 **Bätterkinden**, Swi.
57/G3 **Battersby**, Eng,UK
53/N7 **Battersea**, Eng,UK
118/D6 **Batticaloa**, SrL.
122/H4 **Batticaloa** (dist.), SrL.
191/G3 **Battiest**, Ok,US
85/E6 **Battipaglia**, It.
183/J1 **Battle** (riv.), Ab,Can
59/G5 **Battle**, Eng,UK
201/J2 **Battleboro**, NC,US
193/G2 **Battle Creek**, Ia,US
198/D3 **Battle Creek**, Mi,US
192/F3 **Battle Creek**, Ne,US
191/H2 **Battlefield**, Mo,US
183/K1 **Battleford**, Sk,Can
195/G4 **Battle Lake**, Mn,US
184/E3 **Battle Mountain**, Nv,US
208/C2 **Battleship Cove**, Ma,US
189/M9 **Battleship Texas**, Tx,US
54/D3 **Battock** (mtn.), Sc,UK
92/E2 **Battonya**, Hun.
108/E2 **Battsengel**, Mong.
150/A4 **Batu** (peak), Eth.
127/E3 **Batu** (cape), Indo.
124/B3 **Batu** (isls.), Indo.
126/D3 **Batu** (bay), Malay.
126/D3 **Batu** (peak), Malay.
124/C2 **Batu Caves**, Malay.
174/Q9 **Batuco**, Chile
127/F4 **Batudaka** (isl.), Indo.
126/D3 **Batuensambang** (peak), Indo.
124/C1 **Batu Gajah**, Malay.
127/F4 **Batui**, Indo.
125/D4 **Batulaki**, Phil.
53/H4 **Batumi**, Geo.
97/G4 **Batumi** (int'l arpt.), Geo.
124/C2 **Batu Pahat**, Malay.
124/C1 **Batu Puteh** (peak), Malay.
124/D4 **Baturaja**, Indo.
99/G2 **Baturin**, Ukr.
95/P5 **Baturino**, Rus.
167/G4 **Baturité**, Braz.
124/D3 **Baturusa**, Indo.
124/C3 **Batusangkar**, Indo.
103/F7 **Bat Yam**, Isr.
95/K5 **Batyrevo**, Rus.
78/A3 **Batz** (isl.), Fr.
78/C6 **Batz-sur-Mer**, Fr.
125/C1 **Bauang**, Phil.
130/A1 **Baubau**, Indo.
145/H4 **Bauchi**, Nga.
145/H4 **Bauchi** (state), Nga.
78/B5 **Baud**, Fr.
195/G3 **Baudette**, Mn,US
164/B3 **Baudó** (mts.), Col.
164/B3 **Baudó** (riv.), Col.
161/G5 **Baudo, Serranía de** (range), Col.
79/E5 **Baugé**, Fr.
130/B2 **Baukau**, Indo.
179/L3 **Bauld** (cape), Nf,Can
80/C4 **Baulmes**, Swi.
145/F5 **Bauman** (peak), Togo
80/C3 **Baume-les-Dames**, Fr.
69/G4 **Baumholder**, Ger.
70/D3 **Baunach**, Ger.
70/D2 **Baunach** (riv.), Ger.
67/G6 **Baunatal**, Ger.
90/A2 **Baunei**, It.
125/D3 **Bauñgon**, Phil.
169/F4 **Baures**, Bol.
169/E4 **Baures** (riv.), Bol.
121/G4 **Bauria**, India
170/C4 **Baurú**, Braz.
63/L3 **Bauska**, Lat.
97/J3 **Bautino**, Kaz.
65/H3 **Bautzen**, Ger.
80/C3 **Bavans**, Fr.
71/E5 **Bavaria** (state), Ger.
75/J3 **Bavarian Alps** (mts.), Aus., Ger.
81/H3 **Bavarian Alps** (mts.), Aus., Ger.
68/C3 **Bavay**, Fr.
62/G2 **Båven** (lake), Swe.
86/B1 **Baveno**, It.
158/C2 **Baviácora**, Mex.
80/C2 **Bavilliers**, Fr.
158/C2 **Bavispe** (riv.), Mex.
95/M5 **Bavly**, Rus.
126/D4 **Bawan**, Indo.
120/A1 **Bawāna**, India
126/C4 **Bawang** (cape), Indo.
135/C3 **Baw Baw** (peak), Austl.
135/C3 **Baw Baw Nat'l Park**, Austl.
124/F4 **Bawean** (isl.), Indo.
145/E4 **Bawku**, Gha.
123/B2 **Bawlake**, Burma
183/H1 **Bawlf**, Ab,Can
115/H7 **Ba Xian**, China
117/F1 **Baxian**, China
119/J2 **Ba Xian**, China
108/C4 **Baxkorgan**, China
201/F5 **Baxley**, Ga,US
116/C2 **Baxoi**, China
195/G4 **Baxter**, Mn,US
191/G2 **Baxter Springs**, Ks,US
191/J3 **Bay**, Ar,US
193/K1 **Bay** (dam), Wi,US
161/G1 **Bayamo**, Cuba
162/E3 **Bayamón**, PR
109/K2 **Bayan**, China
127/E5 **Bayan**, Indo.
108/F2 **Bayan**, Mong.
114/C1 **Bayanaul**, Kaz.
108/G2 **Bayandelger**, Mong.
108/E1 **Bayangol**, Rus.
108/D5 **Bayan Har** (mts.), China
108/E2 **Bayanhongor**, Mong.
108/E3 **Bayanleg**, Mong.
108/E3 **Bayan Mod**, China
114/F2 **Bayannur**, Mong.
161/G4 **Bayano** (res.), Pan.
108/F3 **Bayan Obo**, China
108/E2 **Bayan-Ovoo**, Mong.
108/F3 **Bayan-Ovoo**, Mong.
109/J2 **Bayan Qagan**, China
108/G2 **Bayanterem**, Mong.
108/D2 **Bayan-Uul**, Mong.
193/G3 **Bayard**, Ia,US
192/C3 **Bayard**, Ne,US
187/H4 **Bayard**, NM,US
199/G5 **Bayard**, WV,US
104/C1 **Bayat**, Turk.
125/C3 **Bayawan**, Phil.
69/G3 **Baybach** (riv.), Ger.
125/D3 **Baybay**, Phil.
201/J3 **Bayboro**, NC,US
197/L2 **Bay Bulls**, Nf,Can
104/E1 **Bayburt**, Turk.
104/E1 **Bayburt** (prov.), Turk.
97/K3 **Baychunas**, Kaz.
99/M2 **Baychurovo**, Rus.
198/E3 **Bay City**, Mi,US
184/B1 **Bay City**, Or,US
189/G3 **Bay City**, Tx,US
193/H1 **Bay City**, Wi,US
100/G2 **Baydaratskaya** (bay), Rus.
197/L1 **Bay de Verde**, Nf,Can
150/B5 **Baydhabo** (Baidoa), Som.
108/D2 **Baydrag** (riv.), Mong.
80/A1 **Bayel**, Fr.
71/F5 **Bayerischer Wald** (hills), Ger.
71/G5 **Bayerischer Wald Nat'l Park**, Ger.
167/H4 **Bayeux**, Braz.
79/E2 **Bayeux**, Fr.
187/J2 **Bayfield**, Co,US
175/T11 **Baygorria, Artificial de** (res.), Uru.
106/E6 **Bayḩān al Qisāb**, Yem.
104/A2 **Bayındır**, Turk.
108/E1 **Baykal**, Rus.
108/F1 **Baykal** (lake), Rus.
101/L4 **Baykal** (mts.), Rus.
108/E1 **Baykal'sk**, Rus.
104/E2 **Baykan**, Turk.
95/N5 **Baykibashevo**, Rus.
100/K3 **Baykit**, Rus.
100/G5 **Baykonyr**, Kaz.
125/F7 **Bay, Laguna de** (lake), Phil.
195/H4 **Bay Lake**, Mn,US
197/K2 **Bay L'Argent**, Nf,Can
97/L1 **Baymak**, Rus.
198/D1 **Bay Mills Ind. Res.**, Mi,US
202/E2 **Bay Minette**, Al,US
182/G3 **Baynes Lake**, BC,Can
172/C3 **Bayo Grande** (peak), Arg.
125/C1 **Bayombong**, Phil.
80/C1 **Bayon**, Fr.
76/A1 **Bayona**, Sp.
202/K7 **Bayonet** (pt.), Fl,US
202/K7 **Bayonet Point**, Fl,US
203/G3 **Bayonet Point**, Fl,US
74/C5 **Bayonne**, Fr.
207/D2 **Bayonne**, NJ,US
202/C3 **Bayou Cane**, La,US
189/H1 **Bayou D'Arbonne** (lake), La,US
202/D2 **Bayou La Batre**, Al,US
189/J3 **Bayou Vista**, La,US
168/A2 **Bayóvar**, Peru
202/K6 **Bayport**, Fl,US
198/E3 **Bay Port**, Mi,US
195/Q6 **Bayport**, Mn,US
207/E2 **Bayport**, NY,US
107/H1 **Bayram-Ali**, Trkm.
93/H5 **Bayramıç**, Turk.
71/E3 **Bayreuth**, Ger.
207/J9 **Bay Ridge**, NY,US
197/L2 **Bay Roberts**, Nf,Can
103/D3 **Bayrūt** (Beirut) (cap.), Leb.
199/G2 **Bays** (lake), On,Can
197/G2 **Bay Saint Lawrence**, NS,Can
202/D2 **Bay Saint Louis**, Ms,US
77/E1 **Bayse** (riv.), Fr.
207/K8 **Bayside**, NY,US
200/C5 **Bay Springs**, Ms,US
200/C3 **Bay Springs** (lake), Ms,US
58/D1 **Bayston Hill**, Eng,UK
199/G2 **Baysville**, On,Can
132/K6 **Bayswater**, Austl.
150/B2 **Bayt al Faqīh**, Yem.
103/G8 **Bayt Fajjār**, WBnk.
103/D4 **Bayt Ḩānūn**, Gaza
103/D4 **Bayt Laḩm** (Bethlehem), WBnk.
189/G3 **Baytown**, Tx,US
103/G8 **Bayt Sāḩūr**, WBnk.
147/G5 **Bayudha** (des.), Sudan
124/C3 **Bayunglencir**, Indo.
136/D2 **Bay View**, N.Z.
208/F5 **Bay Village**, Oh,US
207/E2 **Bayville**, NY,US
186/B3 **Baywood-Los Osos**, Ca,US
146/B2 **Bayyal al Kabīr, Wādī** (dry riv.), Libya
114/A3 **Bayzhansay**, Kaz.
76/D4 **BazaOB**, Sp.
97/H4 **Bazardyuzyu, Gora** (peak), Rus.
105/F2 **Bāzargān**, Iran
95/L5 **Bazarnyye Mataki**, Rus.
97/J2 **Bazarshulan**, Kaz.
155/G4 **Bazaruto** (isl.), Moz.
74/C4 **Bazas**, Fr.
145/E4 **Bazèga** (prov.), Burk.
74/D5 **Bazet**, Fr.
116/E2 **Bazhong**, China
190/E1 **Bazine**, Ks,US
79/E5 **Bazouges**, Fr.
120/B1 **Bāzpur**, India
153/F2 **Bazuru**, Zaire
194/B4 **Beach**, ND,US
199/H2 **Beachburg**, On,Can
208/F6 **Beach City**, Oh,US
207/D4 **Beach Haven**, NJ,US
196/E3 **Beach Meadows**, NS,Can
135/B3 **Beachport**, Austl.
203/F2 **Beachton**, Ga,US
207/D4 **Beachwood**, NJ,US
208/F5 **Beachwood**, Oh,US
59/G5 **Beachy Head** (pt.), Eng,UK
58/C2 **Beacon** (hill), Wal,UK
199/K4 **Beacon**, NY,US
200/C3 **Beacon**, Tn,US
208/A3 **Beacon Falls**, Ct,US
203/F3 **Beacon Hill**, Fl,US
135/C4 **Beaconsfield**, Austl.
197/N7 **Beaconsfield**, Qu,Can
59/F3 **Beaconsfield**, Eng,UK
58/B5 **Beaford**, Eng,UK
130/C3 **Beagle** (gulf), Austl.
130/A4 **Beagle Bay Abor. Rsv.**, Austl.
130/A4 **Beagle Bay Mission**, Austl.
134/A4 **Beal** (mts.), Austl.
157/J6 **Bealanana**, Madg.
178/D4 **Beale** (cape), BC,Can
180/A2 **Beale** (cape), BC,Can.
182/B3 **Beale** (cape), BC,Can
184/C4 **Beale A.F.B.**, Ca,US
196/D3 **Beals**, Me,US
188/D1 **Beals** (cr.), Tx,US
82/C3 **Béal Traversier, Pic du** (peak), Fr.
58/D5 **Beaminster**, Eng,UK
157/H9 **Beampingaratra** (ridge), Madg.
197/S9 **Beamsville**, On,Can
100/C2 **Bear** (isl.), Nor.
177/K3 **Bear** (mt.), Ak,US
177/K2 **Bear** (mtn.), Ak,US
200/C3 **Bear** (cr.), Al,US
205/M10 **Bear** (cr.), Ca,US
184/C4 **Bear** (riv.), Ca,US
190/C2 **Bear** (cr.), Co, Ks,,US
208/A2 **Bear** (hill), Ct,US
208/A1 **Bear** (mtn.), Ct,US
206/C4 **Bear**, De,US
185/H2 **Bear** (lake), Id, Ut,US
185/H2 **Bear** (riv.), Id, Ut,US
200/C3 **Bear** (cr.), Ms,US
192/D3 **Bear** (hill), Ne,US
192/C2 **Bear** (mtn.), SD,US
188/K7 **Bear** (cr.), Tx,US
188/L7 **Bear** (cr.), Tx,US
189/M9 **Bear** (cr.), Tx,US
192/B3 **Bear** (cr.), Wy,US
60/A6 **Beara** (pen.), Ire.
200/E1 **Bear Branch**, In,US
200/D3 **Bear Creek**, Al,US
191/H4 **Bearden**, Ar,US
191/F3 **Bearden**, Ok,US
137/M **Beardmore** (glac.), Ant.
195/L3 **Beardmore**, On,Can
193/J3 **Beardstown**, Il,US
207/H7 **Bearfort** (mt.), NJ,US
198/C2 **Bear Lake**, Mi,US
185/H2 **Bear Lake Nat'l Wild. Ref.**, Id,US
192/B1 **Bear Lodge** (mts.), Wy,US
120/B4 **Bearma** (riv.), India
183/K3 **Bearpaw** (mts.), Mt,US
196/E3 **Bear River**, NS,Can
185/G3 **Bear River** (bay), Ut,US
185/G3 **Bear River Nat'l Wild. Ref.**, Ut,US
54/B5 **Bearsden**, Sc,UK
183/K1 **Bear, The** (hills), Sk,Can
185/H1 **Beartooth** (mts.), Mt, Wy,US
120/B3 **Beās** (riv.), India
122/D2 **Beās** (riv.), India
76/D1 **Beasain**, Sp.
76/D3 **Beas de Segura**, Sp.
162/D3 **Beata** (cape), DRep.
162/D3 **Beata** (isl.), DRep.
80/D4 **Beatenberg**, Swi.
131/E3 **Beatrice** (cape), Austl.
200/D5 **Beatrice**, Al,US
193/F3 **Beatrice**, Ne,US
155/F3 **Beatrice**, Zim.
191/F1 **Beattie**, Ks,US
54/C6 **Beattock**, Sc,UK
186/D2 **Beatty**, Nv,US
206/D2 **Beattystown**, NJ,US
200/F2 **Beattyville**, Ky,US
157/S15 **Beau Bassin**, Mrts.
82/A5 **Beaucaire**, Fr.
68/A4 **Beaucamps-le-Vieux**, Fr.
53/S9 **Beauchamp**, Fr.
82/A3 **Beauchastel**, Fr.
80/C3 **Beaucourt**, Fr.
134/D4 **Beaudesert**, Austl.
135/B3 **Beaufort**, Austl.
176/C2 **Beaufort** (sea), Can., US
82/C1 **Beaufort**, Fr.
82/C1 **Beaufort** (upland), Fr.
69/F4 **Beaufort**, Lux.
125/A4 **Beaufort**, Malay.
201/J3 **Beaufort**, NC,US
201/J3 **Beaufort** (inlet), NC,US
201/G4 **Beaufort**, SC,US
79/E6 **Beaufort-en-Vallée**, Fr.
201/G4 **Beaufort Marine Corps Air Base**, SC,US
156/C4 **Beaufort West**, SAfr.
79/G5 **Beaugency**, Fr.
199/K2 **Beauharnois**, Qu,Can
197/N7 **Beauharnois** (co.), Qu,Can
74/F4 **Beaujolais** (mts.), Fr.
59/E5 **Beaulieu**, Eng,UK
82/D5 **Beaulieu-sur-Mer**, Fr.
54/B2 **Beauly**, Sc,UK
54/B2 **Beauly** (firth), Sc,UK
54/B2 **Beauly** (riv.), Sc,UK
56/D5 **Beaumaris**, Wal,UK

# Beaum – Bertra

82/B4 **Beaumes-de-Venise,** Fr.
79/F2 **Beaumesnil,** Fr.
68/B3 **Beaumetz-les-Loges,** Fr.
68/D3 **Beaumont,** Belg.
183/H1 **Beaumont,** Ab,Can
78/D1 **Beaumont,** Fr.
204/D3 **Beaumont,** Ca,US
202/D2 **Beaumont,** Ms,US
189/G2 **Beaumont,** Tx,US
74/D5 **Beaumont-de-Lomagne,** Fr.
79/F2 **Beaumont-le-Roger,** Fr.
82/A3 **Beaumont-lès-Valence,** Fr.
53/S9 **Beaumont-sur-Oise,** Fr.
74/F3 **Beaune,** Fr.
79/E6 **Beaupréau,** Fr.
68/B3 **Beauquesne,** Fr.
69/D3 **Beauraing,** Belg.
68/A3 **Beaurainville,** Fr.
200/B5 **Beauregard,** Ms,US
82/B2 **Beaurepaire,** Fr.
68/C3 **Beaurevoir,** Fr.
194/F2 **Beauséjour,** Mb,Can
82/D5 **Beausoleil,** Fr.
187/H2 **Beautiful** (mtn.), NM,US
68/C4 **Beautor,** Fr.
68/B5 **Beauvais,** Fr.
68/B3 **Beauval,** Fr.
194/C2 **Beaver** (hills), Sk,Can
178/F3 **Beaver** (riv.), Sk,Can
178/D2 **Beaver** (riv.), Yk,Can
177/J2 **Beaver,** Ak,US
191/H2 **Beaver** (lake), Ar,US
192/D3 **Beaver** (cr.), Ks, Ne,US
202/B2 **Beaver,** La,US
198/D2 **Beaver** (isl.), Mi,US
183/L3 **Beaver** (cr.), Mt,US
194/B4 **Beaver** (cr.), Mt,ND,US
194/D4 **Beaver** (cr.), ND,US
192/E2 **Beaver** (cr.), Ne,US
198/E5 **Beaver,** Oh,US
190/D2 **Beaver,** Ok,US
190/D2 **Beaver** (riv.), Ok, Tx,US
208/G6 **Beaver,** Pa,US
208/G6 **Beaver** (co.), Pa,US
208/G6 **Beaver** (riv.), Pa,US
192/B2 **Beaver** (cr.), SD, Wy,US
190/E4 **Beaver** (cr.), Tx,US
185/G4 **Beaver,** Ut,US
185/G4 **Beaver** (riv.), Ut,US
182/B3 **Beaver,** Wa,US
193/K2 **Beaver** (dam), Wi,US
196/F3 **Beaverbank,** NS,Can
195/J4 **Beaver Bay,** Mn,US
192/E3 **Beaver City,** Ne,US
177/K3 **Beaver Creek,** Yk,Can
198/D5 **Beavercreek,** Oh,US
193/F3 **Beaver Crossing,** Ne,US
200/D2 **Beaver Dam,** Ky,US
201/J2 **Beaverdam,** Va,US
193/K2 **Beaver Dam,** Wi,US
193/J2 **Beaver Dam** (lake), Wi,US
182/E3 **Beaverdell,** BC,Can
208/G6 **Beaver Falls,** Pa,US
185/G1 **Beaverhead** (mts.), Id, Mt,US
185/G1 **Beaverhead** (riv.), Mt,US
183/H1 **Beaverhill** (lake), Ab,Can
206/C2 **Beaver Meadows,** Pa,US
206/A2 **Beaver Springs,** Pa,US
199/G2 **Beaverton,** On,Can
198/D3 **Beaverton,** Mi,US
184/B1 **Beaverton,** Or,US
206/A2 **Beavertown,** Pa,US
118/B2 **Beāwar,** India
189/F3 **Bebe,** Tx,US
148/C3 **Bébédjia,** Chad
170/C4 **Bebedouro,** Braz.
141/G3 **Beb el Mandeb** (str.), Afr., Asia
167/G4 **Beberibe,** Braz.
57/E5 **Bebington,** Eng,UK
148/C3 **Beboto,** Chad
148/C4 **Béboura III,** CAfr.
67/G7 **Bebra,** Ger.
73/C2 **Bebrava** (riv.), Slvk.
159/H4 **Becal,** Mex.
159/H5 **Becanchén,** Mex.
196/A2 **Bécancour,** Qu,Can
59/H2 **Beccles,** Eng,UK
92/E3 **Bečej,** Yugo.
76/B1 **Becerreá,** Sp.
143/E3 **Bechar,** Alg.
142/E3 **Bechar** (wilaya), Alg.
177/G4 **Becharof** (lake), Ak,US
177/G4 **Becharof Nat'l. Wild. Ref.,** Ak,US
70/D4 **Bechhofen,** Ger.
70/B3 **Bechtheim,** Ger.
71/H4 **Bechyně,** Czh.
195/G4 **Becida,** Mn,US
67/G2 **Beckdorf,** Ger.
53/N7 **Beckenham,** Eng,UK
81/E4 **Beckenried,** Swi.
200/C4 **Becker,** Ms,US
190/A3 **Becker,** NM,US
208/A1 **Becket,** Ma,US
69/F5 **Beckingen,** Ger.
57/H5 **Beckingham,** Eng,UK
201/G2 **Beckley,** WV,US
185/K1 **Beckton,** Wy,US
67/F5 **Beckum,** Ger.
189/G1 **Beckville,** Tx,US
184/C4 **Beckwourth,** Ca,US
93/G2 **Beclean,** Rom.
79/E6 **Bécon-les-Granits,** Fr.
80/D5 **Becs de Bosson** (peak), Swi.
57/G3 **Bedale,** Eng,UK
148/C4 **Bédaoyo,** Chad
74/E5 **Bédarieux,** Fr.
148/C3 **Bedaya,** Chad
66/D7 **Bedburg,** Ger.
66/D5 **Bedburg-Hau,** Ger.
53/C3 **Beddau,** Wal,UK
50/D5 **Beddgelert,** Wal,UK
149/H3 **Bedelē,** Eth.
63/D3 **Beder,** Den.
67/G1 **Bederkesa,** Ger.
150/B3 **Bedēsa,** Eth.
134/B1 **Bedford** (cape), Austl.
196/A3 **Bedford,** Qu,Can
156/D4 **Bedford,** SAfr.
59/F2 **Bedford,** Eng,UK
193/G3 **Bedford,** Ia,US
198/C5 **Bedford,** In,US
200/E1 **Bedford,** Ky,US
199/L3 **Bedford,** NH,US
208/F5 **Bedford,** Oh,US
199/G4 **Bedford,** Pa,US
188/K7 **Bedford,** Tx,US
201/H2 **Bedford,** Va,US
185/H2 **Bedford,** Wy,US
208/F5 **Bedford Heights,** Oh,US
207/E1 **Bedford Hills,** NY,US
59/G2 **Bedford Level** (reg.), Eng,UK
205/Q16 **Bedford Park,** Il,US
59/F2 **Bedfordshire** (co.), Eng,UK
189/G2 **Bedias,** Tx,US
148/C3 **Bédiondo,** Chad
57/G1 **Bedlington,** Eng,UK
53/M6 **Bedmond,** Eng,UK
82/B4 **Bédoin,** Fr.
124/C1 **Bedong,** Malay.
86/C4 **Bedonia,** It.
148/B2 **Bédouaram,** Niger
133/H3 **Bedourie,** Austl.
81/E5 **Bedretto,** Swi.
185/J4 **Bedrock,** Co,US
62/C3 **Bedsted,** Den.
66/D2 **Bedum,** Neth.
58/C3 **Bedwas,** Wal,UK
59/E2 **Bedworth,** Eng,UK
200/B3 **Beebe,** Ar,US
191/H3 **Bee Branch,** Ar,US
199/L2 **Beecher Falls,** Vt,US
192/C4 **Beecher Island,** Co,US
198/C5 **Beech Grove,** In,US
200/D3 **Beechgrove,** Tn,US
208/D1 **Beechwood,** Ma,US
135/C3 **Beechworth,** Austl.
183/L2 **Beechy,** Sk,Can
66/C5 **Beek,** Neth.
189/J1 **Beekman,** La,US
67/F5 **Beelen,** Ger.
190/D1 **Beeler,** Ks,US
72/C3 **Beelitz,** Ger.
134/D4 **Beenleigh,** Austl.
58/C5 **Beer,** Eng,UK
150/C3 **Beerato,** Som.
70/B3 **Beerfelden,** Ger.
58/C5 **Beer Head** (pt.), Eng,UK
103/D4 **Be'er Menuḥa,** Isr.
68/C1 **Beernem,** Belg.
103/D4 **Beersheba** (Be'er Sheva'), Isr.
103/D4 **Be'er Sheva'** (Beersheba), Isr.
103/F8 **Be'er Toviyya,** Isr.
69/D1 **Beerzel,** Belg.
66/D6 **Beesel,** Neth.
72/B4 **Beesenlaublingen,** Ger.
200/D2 **Bee Spring,** Ky,US
57/G6 **Beeston,** Eng,UK
72/B2 **Beetzendorf,** Ger.
72/C3 **Beetzsee** (lake), Ger.
189/F3 **Beeville,** Tx,US
153/E2 **Befale,** Zaire
157/G8 **Befandriana,** Madg.
157/J6 **Befandriana,** Madg.
157/H8 **Befasy,** Madg.
153/E2 **Befori,** Zaire
157/J7 **Beforona,** Madg.
157/H8 **Befotaka,** Madg.
157/J6 **Befotaka,** Madg.
135/D3 **Bega,** Austl.
67/F5 **Bega** (riv.), Ger.
121/H4 **Begamganj,** Bang.
120/B4 **Begamganj,** India
78/B3 **Bégard,** Fr.
97/K4 **Begarslan** (peak), Trkm.
92/E3 **Bega Veche** (riv.), Rom.
92/E3 **Begejci,** Yugo.
191/F3 **Beggs,** Ok,US
149/G3 **Bēgī,** Eth.
101/M2 **Begichev** (isl.), Rus.
56/B2 **Beg, Lough** (lake), NI,UK
62/C1 **Begna** (riv.), Nor.
63/N4 **Begoml',** Bela.
63/N2 **Begunitsy,** Rus.
121/F3 **Begusarai,** India
166/D1 **Béhague** (pt.), FrG.
126/B4 **Behala** (str.), Indo.
71/H6 **Behamberg,** Aus.
157/H9 **Behara,** Madg.
122/D2 **Behat,** India
105/G4 **Behbahān,** Iran
157/G8 **Beheloka,** Madg.
157/H7 **Behenjy,** Madg.
108/C4 **Behleg,** China
69/F5 **Behren-lès-Forbach,** Fr.
120/D1 **Behri** (riv.), Nepal
72/B6 **Behringen,** Ger.
105/H2 **Behshahr,** Iran
117/H2 **Bei** (mtn.), China
114/F3 **Bei** (mts.), China
117/F2 **Bei** (riv.), China
117/G3 **Bei** (riv.), China
109/K2 **Bei'an,** China
117/E1 **Beiba,** China
116/E2 **Beibei,** China
108/D4 **Beida** (riv.), China
113/A4 **Beidianzi,** China
71/F1 **Beierfeld,** Ger.
117/J3 **Beigantang** (isl.), Tai.
86/B4 **Beigua, Monte** (peak), It.
115/L8 **Beiguo,** China
117/F4 **Beihai,** China
115/D3 **Beijing** (cap.), China
115/H6 **Beijing** (prov.), China
115/D2 **Beijing Capital** (int'l arpt.), China
66/D3 **Beilen,** Neth.
117/G3 **Beiling,** China
117/F4 **Beiliu,** China
71/E4 **Beilngries,** Ger.
72/B4 **Beilrode,** Ger.
70/C4 **Beilstein,** Ger.
108/C5 **Beilu** (riv.), China
117/E4 **Beilun** (pass), China
148/B3 **Beinamar,** Chad
86/A2 **Beinasco,** It.
70/B3 **Beindersheim,** Ger.
54/B3 **Beinn a' Chuallaich** (mtn.), Sc,UK
54/C3 **Beinn a' Ghlò** (mtn.), Sc,UK
54/B2 **Beinn a' Mheadhoin, Loch** (lake), Sc,UK
54/A3 **Beinn Bhàn** (mtn.), Sc,UK
54/B4 **Beinn Bheula** (mtn.), Sc,UK
54/C2 **Beinn Bhrotain** (mtn.), Sc,UK
54/B4 **Beinn Bhuidhe** (mtn.), Sc,UK
54/B2 **Beinn Bhuidhe Mhór** (mtn.), Sc,UK
54/B1 **Beinn Dearg** (mtn.), Sc,UK
54/C3 **Beinn Dearg** (mtn.), Sc,UK
54/B4 **Beinn Dòrain** (mtn.), Sc,UK
54/A1 **Beinn Eighe** (mtn.), Sc,UK
54/B3 **Beinn Heasgarnich** (mtn.), Sc,UK
54/B3 **Beinn Mholach** (mtn.), Sc,UK
54/A4 **Beinn Mhór** (mtn.), Sc,UK
54/B1 **Beinn Tharsuinn** (mtn.), Sc,UK
80/E3 **Beinwil am See,** Swi.
115/E2 **Beipiao,** China
155/G3 **Beira,** Moz.
155/G3 **Beira** (int'l arpt.), Moz.
152/C5 **Beira Alta,** Ang.
117/F2 **Beirong,** China
115/C4 **Beiru** (riv.), China
103/D2 **Beirut** (int'l arpt.), Leb.
103/D3 **Beirut** (Bayrūt) (cap.), Leb.
183/H2 **Beiseker,** Ab,Can
117/F3 **Beishan,** China
155/F4 **Beitbridge,** Zim.
54/B5 **Beith,** Sc,UK
92/F2 **Beiuș,** Rom.
113/A2 **Beizhen,** China
76/B3 **Beja,** Port.
76/A4 **Beja** (dist.), Port.
141/T15 **Bejaïa,** Alg.
141/U17 **Bejaïa,** Alg.
141/T15 **Bejaïa** (wilaya), Alg.
141/U17 **Bejaïa** (wilaya), Alg.
76/C2 **Béjar,** Sp.
107/J3 **Bejhi** (riv.), Pak.
103/D3 **Bekaa** (Al Biqā') (val.), Leb.
124/D4 **Bekasi,** Indo.
97/K4 **Bekdash,** Trkm.
92/E2 **Békés,** Hun.
92/E2 **Békés** (co.), Hun.
92/E2 **Békéscsaba,** Hun.
104/B2 **Bekilli,** Turk.
157/H8 **Bekily,** Madg.
157/H9 **Bekitro,** Madg.
157/H7 **Bekodoka,** Madg.
150/A4 **Bek'ojī,** Eth.
157/H7 **Bekopaka,** Madg.
157/G8 **Bekoropoka,** Madg.
145/E5 **Bekwai,** Gha.
202/B2 **Bel,** La,US
118/B3 **Bela,** India
120/C3 **Belā,** India
107/J3 **Bela,** Pak.
73/C1 **Belá,** Slvk.
153/G2 **Bela,** Zaire
148/B2 **Belabérim** (well), Niger
148/B4 **Bélabo,** Camr.
92/E3 **Bela Crkva,** Yugo.
167/F3 **Bela Cruz,** Braz.
206/B4 **Bel Air,** Md,US
199/G5 **Bel Air-Cresaptown,** Md,US
191/F2 **Bel Aire,** Ks,US
133/M8 **Belair Rec. Park,** Austl.
206/B5 **Bel Air South,** Md,US
124/D4 **Belambanganumpu,** Indo.
120/D3 **Belan** (riv.), India
124/C1 **Belanak** (cape), Malay.
127/F3 **Belang,** Indo.
92/F4 **Bela Palanka,** Yugo.
71/H2 **Bělá pod Bezdězem,** Czh.
52/G3 **Belarus**
77/P10 **Belas,** Port.
154/C2 **Bela Vista,** Ang.
170/A4 **Bela Vista,** Braz.
155/G5 **Bela Vista,** Moz.
170/C3 **Bela Vista de Goiás,** Braz.
173/G2 **Bela Vista do Paraiso,** Braz.
124/B2 **Belawan,** Indo.
149/H3 **Belaya** (peak), Eth.
95/M5 **Belaya** (riv.), Rus.
99/L4 **Belaya Glina,** Rus.
99/L3 **Belaya Kalitva,** Rus.
99/G4 **Belaya Krinitsa,** Ukr.
98/F3 **Belaya Tserkov',** Ukr.
86/B3 **Belbo** (riv.), It.
65/K3 **Bełchatów,** Pol.
80/D2 **Belchen** (peak), Ger.
179/S7 **Belcher** (chan.), NW,Can
179/H3 **Belcher** (isls.), NW,Can
189/H1 **Belcher,** La,US
208/B1 **Belchertown,** Ma,US
77/E2 **Belchite,** Sp.
121/F4 **Belda,** India
121/G4 **Beldānga,** India
95/M5 **Belebey,** Rus.
73/B5 **Beled,** Hun.
150/C4 **Beled Weyne,** Som.
144/C5 **Belefuanai,** Libr.
148/B4 **Bélel,** Camr.
186/D3 **Belém,** Braz.
171/F1 **Belém de São Francisco,** Braz.
77/P10 **Belem Tower,** Port.
172/C3 **Belén,** Arg.
172/C2 **Belén** (riv.), Arg.
169/E5 **Belén,** Bol.
172/B1 **Belén,** Chile
103/C1 **Belen,** Turk.
103/E1 **Belen,** Turk.
172/E4 **Belén,** Uru.
190/A3 **Belen,** NM,US
175/S12 **Belén de Escobar,** Arg.
164/C3 **Belén de Umbría,** Col.
93/G4 **Belene,** Bul.
76/B1 **Belesar** (res.), Sp.
149/G3 **Beles Wenz** (riv.), Eth.
96/F1 **Belev,** Rus.
205/B2 **Belfair,** Wa,US
156/Q12 **Belfast,** SAfr.
56/C2 **Belfast,** NI,UK
56/C2 **Belfast** (dist.), NI,UK
56/C2 **Belfast** (inlet), NI,UK
196/C3 **Belfast,** Me,US
56/B2 **Belfast** (Aldergrove) (int'l arpt.), NI,UK
56/C2 **Belfast** (City) (int'l arpt.), NI,UK
56/C2 **Belfast Lough** (inlet), NI,UK
80/D4 **Belfaux,** Swi.
194/C4 **Belfield,** ND,US
149/G3 **Bēlfodiyo,** Eth.
54/E5 **Belford,** Eng,UK
80/C2 **Belfort,** Fr.
80/C2 **Belfort** (dept.), Fr.
197/Q8 **Belfountain,** On,Can
185/J1 **Belfry,** Mt,US
118/B4 **Belgaum,** India
72/D5 **Belgern,** Ger.
86/C2 **Belgioioso,** It.
64/C3 **Belgium**
53/G3 **Belgorod,** Rus.
98/F4 **Belgorod-Dnestrovskiy,** Ukr.
99/J2 **Belgorod Obl.,** Rus.
196/C3 **Belgrade,** Me,US
195/G5 **Belgrade,** Mn,US
191/J2 **Belgrade,** Mo,US
183/J5 **Belgrade,** Mt,US
92/E3 **Belgrade** (Beograd) (cap.), Yugo.
200/D3 **Belgreen,** Al,US
60/B1 **Belhavel** (lake), Ire.
201/J3 **Belhaven,** NC,US
145/H5 **Beli,** Nga.
91/G1 **Beli Drim** (riv.), Yugo.
92/E4 **Beli Drim** (riv), Yugo.
97/J4 **Belidzhi,** Rus.
92/D3 **Beli Manastir,** Cro.
152/C2 **Bélinga,** Gabon
201/H1 **Belington,** WV,US
97/G1 **Belinskiy,** Rus.
124/D3 **Belinyu,** Indo.
92/F4 **Beli Timok** (riv.), Yugo.
93/F5 **Belitsa,** Bul.
99/J3 **Belitskoye,** Ukr.
126/C4 **Belitung** (isl.), Indo.
160/D2 **Belize**
160/D2 **Belize** (int'l arpt.), Belz.
160/D2 **Belize** (riv.), Belz.
160/D2 **Belize City,** Belz.
166/C1 **Bélizon,** FrG.
92/E3 **Beljanica** (peak), Yugo.
191/G4 **Belk,** Tx,US
196/B4 **Belknap** (mtn.), NH,US
101/P2 **Bel'kovskiy** (isl.), Rus.
134/C4 **Bell,** Austl.
133/G5 **Bell** (pt.), Austl.
197/L2 **Bell** (isl.), Nf,Can
179/H2 **Bell** (pen.), NW,Can
179/J4 **Bell** (riv.), Qu,Can
69/G3 **Bell,** Ger.
131/F2 **Bell** (pt.), PNG
204/B3 **Bell,** Ca,US
203/G3 **Bell,** Fl,US
85/F6 **Bella,** It.
74/D3 **Bellac,** Fr.
82/C1 **Bellachat** (mtn.), Fr.
175/T11 **Bellaco,** Uru.
169/E3 **Bella Flor,** Bol.
56/B2 **Bellaghy,** NI,UK
81/F6 **Bellagio,** It.
198/D2 **Bellaire,** Mi,US
198/F4 **Bellaire,** Oh,US
189/M9 **Bellaire,** Tx,US
200/C4 **Bellamy,** Al,US
60/C2 **Bellananagh,** Ire.
81/F5 **Bellano,** It.
87/F4 **Bellaria,** It.
118/C4 **Bellary,** India
135/D1 **Bellata,** Austl.
172/C3 **Bella Vista,** Arg.
172/E4 **Bella Vista,** Arg.
169/F4 **Bella Vista,** Bol.
168/J7 **Bellavista,** Ecu.
90/A3 **Bellavista** (cape), It.
173/E2 **Bella Vista,** Par.
168/B2 **Bellavista,** Peru
191/G2 **Bella Vista,** Ar,US
205/G7 **Belle** (riv.), On,Can
205/G6 **Belle** (riv.), Mi,US
191/J1 **Belle,** Mo,US
201/G1 **Belle,** WV,US
202/K8 **Belleair,** Fl,US
203/G4 **Belleair,** Fl,US
202/K8 **Belleair Beach,** Fl,US
202/K8 **Belleair Bluffs,** Fl,US
161/H2 **Belle-Anse,** Haiti
68/C5 **Belleau,** Fr.
202/D3 **Belle Chasse,** La,US
82/B2 **Belledonne, Chaîne de** (range), Fr.
82/B2 **Belledonne, Grand Pic de** (peak), Fr.
56/B3 **Belleek,** NI,UK
200/C4 **Bellefontaine,** Ms,US
198/E4 **Bellefontaine,** Oh,US
191/H2 **Bellefonte,** Ar,US
206/C4 **Bellefonte,** De,US
199/H4 **Bellefonte,** Pa,US
194/C5 **Belle Fourche** (res.), ND,US
192/C1 **Belle Fourche,** SD,US
192/C1 **Belle Fourche** (riv.), SD, Wy,US
80/B5 **Bellegarde-sur-Valserine,** Fr.
203/H4 **Belle Glade,** Fl,US
206/A6 **Belle Haven,** Va,US
78/B6 **Belle-Ile** (isl.), Fr.
179/L3 **Belle Isle** (str.), Nf,Can
202/N7 **Belle Isle,** Fl,US
78/B3 **Belle-Isle-en-Terre,** Fr.
79/F4 **Bellême,** Fr.
70/D6 **Bellenberg,** Ger.
79/G1 **Bellencombre,** Fr.
134/B2 **Bellenden Ker Nat'l Park,** Austl.
197/K2 **Belleoram,** Nf,Can
206/D5 **Belleplain,** NJ,US
193/H3 **Belle Plaine,** Ia,US
191/F2 **Belle Plaine,** Ks,US
205/G7 **Belle River,** On,Can
74/E3 **Bellerive-sur-Allier,** Fr.
207/L9 **Bellerose,** NY,US
207/E2 **Belle Terre,** NY,US
68/C5 **Belleu,** Fr.
203/G3 **Belleview,** Fl,US
200/B2 **Belleview,** Mo,US
199/H2 **Belleville,** On,Can
191/H3 **Belleville,** Ar,US
193/K4 **Belleville,** Il,US
191/F1 **Belleville,** Ks,US
205/F7 **Belleville,** Mi,US
205/E7 **Belleville** (lake), Mi,US
199/E4 **Belleville,** Pa,US
69/E5 **Belleville-sur-Meuse,** Fr.
193/J2 **Bellevue,** Ia,US
206/B6 **Bellevue,** Md,US
193/G3 **Bellevue,** Ne,US
198/E4 **Bellevue,** Oh,US
208/G7 **Bellevue,** Pa,US
205/C2 **Bellevue,** Wa,US
198/C2 **Bellevue,** Wi,US
82/B1 **Belley,** Fr.
144/C5 **Belle Yella,** Libr.
204/B3 **Bellflower,** Ca,US
204/F8 **Bell Gardens,** Ca,US
80/B5 **Bellignat,** Fr.
62/D4 **Bellinge,** Den.
135/E1 **Bellingen,** Austl.
57/F1 **Bellingham,** Eng,UK
208/C1 **Bellingham,** Ma,US
194/F5 **Bellingham,** Mn,US
182/C3 **Bellingham,** Wa,US
202/D2 **Bellingrath Gardens,** Al,US
137/U **Bellingshausen** (sea), Ant.
139/K6 **Bellingshausen** (isl.), FrPol.
67/E2 **Bellingwolde,** Neth.
81/F5 **Bellinzona,** Swi.
196/D3 **Belliveau Cove,** NS,Can
85/E6 **Bellizzi,** It.
206/C4 **Bellmawr,** NJ,US
189/F2 **Bellmead,** Tx,US
207/E2 **Bellmore,** NY,US
164/C3 **Bello,** Col.
85/E5 **Bellona,** It.
138/F7 **Bellona** (reefs), NCal.
178/G1 **Bellot** (str.), NW,Can
199/K3 **Bellows Falls,** Vt,US
207/F2 **Bellport,** NY,US
54/D4 **Bell Rock** (Inchcape) (isl.), Sc,UK
200/C3 **Bells,** Tn,US
191/F4 **Bells,** Tx,US
54/B6 **Bellsbank,** Sc,UK
54/B5 **Bellshill,** Sc,UK
194/D1 **Bellsite,** Mb,Can
75/K3 **Belluno,** It.
87/E1 **Belluno** (prov.), It.
174/E2 **Bell Ville,** Arg.
156/B4 **Bellville,** SAfr.
203/H1 **Bellville,** Ga,US
208/E6 **Bellville,** Oh,US
189/F3 **Bellville,** Tx,US
80/E5 **Bellwald,** Swi.
183/H3 **Belly** (riv.), Ab,Can
67/F4 **Belm,** Ger.
207/D3 **Belmar,** NJ,US
76/C3 **Bélmez,** Sp.
193/H2 **Belmond,** Ia,US
196/F3 **Belmont,** NS,Can
205/K11 **Belmont,** Ca,US
202/B2 **Belmont,** La,US
208/C1 **Belmont,** Ma,US
200/C3 **Belmont,** Ms,US
183/K4 **Belmont,** Mt,US
201/G3 **Belmont,** NC,US
192/C2 **Belmont,** Ne,US
199/L3 **Belmont,** NH,US
199/G3 **Belmont,** NY,US
171/F2 **Belmonte,** Braz.
76/B2 **Belmonte,** Port.
76/D3 **Belmonte,** Sp.
160/D2 **Belmopan** (cap.), Belz.
55/G9 **Belmullet,** Ire.
157/H8 **Belo,** Madg.
171/E2 **Belo Campo,** Braz.
68/C2 **Beloeil,** Belg.
197/P6 **Beloeil,** Qu,Can
109/K1 **Belogorsk,** Rus.
99/H5 **Belogorsk,** Ukr.
92/F4 **Belogradchik,** Bul.
157/H9 **Beloha,** Madg.
170/E3 **Belo Horizonte,** Braz.
191/E1 **Beloit,** Ks,US
208/G6 **Beloit,** Oh,US
193/K2 **Beloit,** Wi,US
167/G5 **Belo Jardim,** Braz.
97/H4 **Belokany,** Azer.
148/B4 **Béloko,** CAfr.
99/K3 **Belokurakino,** Ukr.
94/G2 **Belomorsk,** Rus.
152/D3 **Belondo-Kundu,** Zaire
94/H5 **Beloomut,** Rus.
96/C1 **Beloozërsk,** Bela.
99/H2 **Belopol'ye,** Ukr.
76/D1 **Belorado,** Sp.
99/K5 **Belorechensk,** Rus.
104/C2 **Belören,** Turk.
53/J3 **Beloretsk,** Rus.
92/E4 **Beloševac,** Yugo.
93/H4 **Beloslav,** Bul.
157/H7 **Belo-Tsiribihina,** Madg.
93/G4 **Belovo,** Bul.
100/J4 **Belovo,** Rus.
99/K3 **Belovodsk,** Ukr.
94/H3 **Beloye** (lake), Rus.
94/H3 **Belozersk,** Rus.
95/Q5 **Belozërskoye,** Rus.
98/F3 **Belozor'ye,** Ukr.
75/G3 **Belp-Berne** (int'l arpt.), Swi.
57/G5 **Belper,** Eng,UK
198/F5 **Belpre,** Oh,US
121/E2 **Belsand,** India
57/G1 **Belsay,** Eng,UK
183/J4 **Belt,** Mt,US
166/C3 **Belterra,** Braz.
66/D3 **Belterwijde** (lake), Neth.
69/G3 **Beltheim,** Ger.
59/H1 **Belton,** Eng,UK
191/G1 **Belton,** Mo,US
201/F3 **Belton,** SC,US
189/F2 **Belton,** Tx,US
189/F2 **Belton** (lake), Tx,US
60/A2 **Beltra** (lake), Ire.
172/C3 **Beltrán,** Arg.
206/B5 **Beltsville,** Md,US
93/H2 **Bel'tsy,** Mol.
60/C1 **Belturbet,** Ire.
206/C2 **Beltzville** (lake), Pa,US
114/E2 **Belukha, Gora** (peak), Rus.
124/C2 **Belumut** (peak), Malay.
125/B4 **Beluran,** Malay.
73/C1 **Beluša,** Slvk.
205/K11 **Belvedere,** Ca,US
82/D3 **Belvédère du Cirque,** Fr.
83/B3 **Belvedere Marittimo,** It.
201/M7 **Belvedere Park,** Ga,US
83/C4 **Belvedere Spinello,** It.
193/K2 **Belvidere,** Il,US
206/C2 **Belvidere,** NJ,US
192/D2 **Belvidere,** SD,US
193/G1 **Belview,** Mn,US
197/Q8 **Belwood,** On,Can
134/B3 **Belyando** (riv.), Austl.
97/L2 **Belyayevka,** Rus.
98/F4 **Belyayevka,** Ukr.
96/E1 **Belynkovichi,** Bela.
100/G2 **Belyy** (isl.), Rus.
96/E1 **Belyye Berega,** Rus.
100/J4 **Belyy Yar,** Rus.
78/B5 **Belz,** Fr.
98/C2 **Belz,** Ukr.
72/C3 **Belzig,** Ger.
200/B4 **Belzoni,** Ms,US
191/G3 **Belzoni,** Ok,US
65/M3 **Bełżyce,** Pol.
148/C4 **Bémal,** CAfr.
157/J6 **Bemanevika,** Madg.
157/H7 **Bemaraha** (plat.), Madg.
157/H7 **Bemarivo** (riv.), Madg.
152/C4 **Bembe,** Ang.
145/F4 **Bembéréké,** Ben.
155/F3 **Bembezi** (riv.), Zim.
76/B1 **Bembibre,** Sp.
152/D5 **Bembo,** Ang.
135/D3 **Bemboka,** Austl.
59/E5 **Bembridge,** Eng,UK
155/F4 **Bemebesi,** Zim.
198/B5 **Bemelen,** Neth.
118/D3 **Bemetāra,** India
195/G4 **Bemidji,** Mn,US
194/F5 **Bemis,** SD,US
66/C5 **Bemmel,** Neth.
57/H3 **Bempton,** Eng,UK
195/G4 **Bena,** Mn,US
77/F1 **Benabarre,** Sp.
152/E4 **Bena-Bendi,** Zaire
153/E4 **Bena-Dibele,** Zaire
142/D2 **Benahmed,** Mor.
54/C1 **Ben Aigan** (hill), Sc,UK
54/B3 **Ben Alder** (mtn.), Sc,UK
135/C3 **Benalla,** Austl.
76/C4 **Benalmádena,** Sp.
183/G1 **Benalto,** Ab,Can
153/E4 **Bena-Makima,** Zaire
142/B5 **Ben Améra** (well), Mrta.
135/B2 **Benanee,** Austl.
121/G4 **Benāpol,** Bang.
120/D3 **Benares** (Vārānasi), India
76/C2 **Benavente,** Sp.
169/E4 **Benavides,** Bol.
189/E4 **Benavides,** Tx,US
54/C2 **Ben Avon** (mtn.), Sc,UK
56/B1 **Benbane Head** (pt.), NI,UK
55/H8 **Benbecula** (isl.), Sc,UK
133/H4 **Benbonyathe** (peak), Austl.
135/D3 **Ben Boyd Nat'l Park,** Austl.
60/C1 **Benbrack** (mtn.), Ire.
189/F1 **Benbrook,** Tx,US
189/F1 **Benbrook** (dam), Tx,US
188/K7 **Benbrook** (lake), Tx,US
56/B3 **Benburb,** NI,UK
189/F2 **Benchley,** Tx,US
54/C4 **Ben Chonzie** (mtn.), Sc,UK
54/C4 **Ben Cleuch** (mtn.), Sc,UK
54/A4 **Ben Cruachan** (mtn.), Sc,UK
132/C4 **Bencubbin,** Austl.
184/B1 **Bend,** Or,US
159/F2 **Bend,** Tx,US
124/E4 **Benda** (cape), Indo.
144/C5 **Bendaja,** Libr.
60/A4 **Ben Dash** (mtn.), Ire.
206/C5 **Ben Davis** (pt.), NJ,US
145/G5 **Bende,** Nga.
145/G5 **Bendel** (state), Nga.
177/F2 **Bendeleben** (mt.), Ak,US
135/D1 **Bendemeer,** Austl.
150/D3 **Bender Beyla,** Som.
150/D3 **Bender Cassim** (Bosaso), Som.
206/A4 **Bendersville,** Pa,US
93/J2 **Bendery,** Mol.
135/C3 **Bendigo,** Austl.
135/D3 **Bendoc,** Austl.
62/C4 **Bendorf,** Ger.
144/C4 **Bendugu,** SLeo.
144/C5 **Benduma,** Libr.
63/K3 **Bēne,** Lat.
103/F7 **Bene Beraq,** Isr.
179/L3 **Benedict** (mtn.), Nf,Can
81/H2 **Benediktbeuern,** Ger.
81/H2 **Benediktenwand** (peak), Ger.
167/F4 **Beneditinos,** Braz.
157/H8 **Benenitra,** Madg.
56/D1 **Beneraid** (hill), Sc,UK
71/H3 **Benešov,** Czh.
85/E5 **Benevento,** It.
85/E5 **Benevento** (prov.), It.
80/D1 **Benfeld,** Fr.
59/G3 **Benfleet,** Eng,UK
155/G3 **Benga,** Moz.
118/E4 **Bengal** (bay), Asia
148/B5 **Bengbis,** Camr.
115/D4 **Bengbu,** China
182/E4 **Benge,** Wa,US
146/D1 **Benghāzī,** Libya
84/H8 **Benghisa, Ponta Ta'** (pt.), Malta
123/D3 **Ben Giang,** Viet.
124/C2 **Bengkalis,** Indo.
124/C2 **Bengkalis** (isl.), Indo.
126/C3 **Bengkayang,** Indo.
124/C3 **Bengkulu,** Indo.
124/C4 **Bengkulu** (prov.), Indo.
152/C5 **Bengo** (bay), Ang.
152/C5 **Bengo** (prov.), Ang.
152/C5 **Bengo** (riv.), Ang.
194/B3 **Bengough,** Sk,Can
62/E2 **Bengtsfors,** Swe.
154/B2 **Benguela,** Ang.
154/B2 **Benguela** (dist.), Ang.
142/D2 **Benguerir,** Mor.
155/G4 **Benguerua** (isl.), Moz.
103/D3 **Ben Gurion** (int'l arpt.), Isr.
153/G5 **Bengweulu** (lake), Zam.
155/F1 **Bengweulu** (swamp), Zam.
55/J7 **Ben Hope** (mtn.), Sc,UK
169/E4 **Beni** (dept.), Bol.
169/E3 **Beni** (riv.), Bol.
120/D1 **Beni,** Nepal
153/G2 **Beni,** Zaire
143/E3 **Beni Abbes,** Alg.
77/F2 **Benicarló,** Sp.
205/K10 **Benicia,** Ca,US
77/E3 **Benidorm,** Sp.
77/E3 **Benifayó,** Sp.
77/E3 **Benigánim,** Sp.
54/B4 **Ben Ime** (mtn.), Sc,UK
142/D2 **Beni Mellal,** Mor.
145/F4 **Benin**
145/F5 **Benin** (bight), Ben., Nga.
146/D1 **Benina** (int'l arpt.), Libya
145/G5 **Benin City,** Nga.
143/E2 **Beni Ounif,** Alg.
77/F3 **Benisa,** Sp.
141/Q16 **Beni Saf,** Alg.
148/B3 **Benisheikh,** Nga.
142/E2 **Beni Tajit,** Mor.
194/D2 **Benito,** Mb,Can
158/E4 **Benito Juárez,** Mex.
174/B5 **Benjamin** (isl.), Chile
190/E4 **Benjamin,** Tx,US
168/D2 **Benjamin Constant,** Braz.
158/C2 **Benjamín Hill,** Mex.
112/B2 **Benkei-misaki** (cape), Japan
192/D3 **Benkelman,** Ne,US
54/B3 **Ben Lawers** (mtn.), Sc,UK
200/C1 **Benld,** Il,US
54/B4 **Ben Ledi** (mtn.), Sc,UK
56/D5 **Benllech,** Wal,UK
54/B4 **Ben Lomond** (mtn.), Sc,UK
186/A2 **Ben Lomond,** Ca,US
135/C4 **Ben Lomond Nat'l Park,** Austl.
54/B4 **Ben Lui** (mtn.), Sc,UK
54/C2 **Ben Macdui** (mtn.), Sc,UK
60/A1 **Benmore** (mtn.), Ire.
54/B4 **Ben More** (mtn.), Sc,UK
55/J7 **Ben More Assynt** (mtn.), Sc,UK
54/D2 **Bennachie** (hill), Sc,UK
56/C1 **Bennane Head** (pt.), Sc,UK
54/A6 **Bennan Head** (pt.), Sc,UK
202/D2 **Benndale,** Ms,US
67/H5 **Benneckenstein,** Ger.
177/M4 **Bennett,** BC,Can
101/R2 **Bennett** (isl.), Rus.
192/B4 **Bennett,** Co,US
190/A2 **Bennett** (peak), Co,US
190/C4 **Bennett,** NM,US
195/J4 **Bennett,** Wi,US
60/C4 **Bennettsbridge,** Ire.
201/H3 **Bennettsville,** SC,US
54/B3 **Ben Nevis** (mtn.), Sc,UK
144/B2 **Bennichchab,** Mrta.
185/H2 **Bennington,** Id,US
192/F4 **Bennington,** Ks,US
193/F3 **Bennington,** Ne,US
191/F3 **Bennington,** Ok,US
199/K3 **Bennington,** Vt,US
185/H3 **Bennion-Taylorsville,** Ut,US
78/A5 **Bénodet,** Fr.
191/J4 **Benoit,** Ms,US
124/C2 **Benom** (peak), Malay.
156/Q13 **Benoni,** SAfr.
157/J6 **Be, Nosy** (isl.), Madg.
148/B3 **Bénoué** (riv.), Chad
148/B3 **Bénoué Nat'l Park,** Camr.
148/C3 **Benoy,** Chad
123/D2 **Ben Quang,** Viet.
54/C2 **Ben Rinnes** (mtn.), Sc,UK
72/C3 **Bensdorf,** Ger.
205/Q16 **Bensenville,** Il,US
70/B3 **Bensheim,** Ger.
141/L14 **Ben Slimane,** Mor.
194/C3 **Benson,** Sk,Can
187/G5 **Benson,** Az,US
202/B2 **Benson,** La,US
195/G5 **Benson,** Mn,US
201/H3 **Benson,** NC,US
207/K9 **Bensonhurst,** NY,US
54/A3 **Ben Starav** (mtn.), Sc,UK
73/C5 **Benta** (riv.), Hun.
124/C1 **Benta Seberang,** Malay.
54/B2 **Ben Tee** (mtn.), Sc,UK
57/F3 **Bentham,** Eng,UK
67/E4 **Bentheim,** Ger.
116/E5 **Ben Thuy,** Viet.
144/B4 **Benti,** Gui.
154/B2 **Bentiaba,** Ang.
154/B2 **Bentiaba** (riv.), Ang.
131/E4 **Bentinck** (isl.), Austl.
54/C3 **Ben Tirran** (mtn.), Sc,UK
149/F3 **Bentiu,** Sudan
57/G4 **Bentley,** Eng,UK
194/E3 **Bentley,** ND,US
191/F3 **Bentley,** Ok,US
208/F5 **Bentleyville,** Oh,US
173/G4 **Bento Gonçalves,** Braz.
191/H3 **Benton,** Ar,US
193/K5 **Benton,** Il,US
200/C2 **Benton,** Ky,US
189/H1 **Benton,** La,US
200/C2 **Benton,** Mo,US
200/B4 **Benton,** Ms,US
206/B1 **Benton,** Pa,US
200/E3 **Benton,** Tn,US
124/C2 **Benton,** Malay.
198/C3 **Benton Harbor,** Mi,US
200/B4 **Bentonia,** Ms,US
183/J4 **Benton Lake Nat'l Wild. Ref.,** Mt,US
191/G2 **Bentonville,** Ar,US
201/H1 **Bentonville,** Va,US
123/D4 **Ben Tre,** Viet.
192/C4 **Bent's Old Fort Nat'l Hist. Site,** Co,US
126/D3 **Benua Martinus,** Indo.
145/G4 **Benue** (riv.), Nga.
145/G5 **Benue** (state), Nga.
54/B4 **Ben Vane** (mtn.), Sc,UK
54/B4 **Ben Vorlich** (mtn.), Sc,UK
54/C3 **Ben Vrackie** (mtn.), Sc,UK
189/G1 **Ben Wheeler,** Tx,US
54/B1 **Ben Wyvis** (mtn.), Sc,UK
113/B2 **Benxi,** China
113/C2 **Benxi,** China
142/E3 **Ben Zohra** (well), Alg.
125/D4 **Beo,** Indo.
92/D3 **Beočin,** Yugo.
127/J4 **Beoga,** Indo.
92/E3 **Beograd** (int'l arpt.), Yugo.
92/E3 **Beograd** (Belgrade) (cap.), Yugo.
120/C3 **Beohāri,** India
144/D5 **Béoumi,** IvC.
82/B3 **Béoux** (riv.), Fr.
184/E3 **Beowawe,** Nv,US
110/B4 **Beppu,** Japan
110/B4 **Beppu** (bay), Japan
162/F4 **Bequia** (isl.), StV.
167/E3 **Bequimão,** Braz.
121/G3 **Bera,** Bang.
56/A2 **Beragh,** NI,UK
157/H9 **Beraketa,** Madg.
157/J6 **Beramanja,** Madg.
124/C1 **Beras Basah** (cape), Malay.
120/A4 **Berasia,** India
91/F2 **Berat,** Alb.
127/E4 **Beratus** (peak), Indo.
71/E4 **Beratzhausen,** Ger.
127/H4 **Berau** (bay), Indo.
127/E3 **Berau** (riv.), Indo.
157/H7 **Beravina,** Madg.
81/F5 **Berbenno di Valtellina,** It.
150/C3 **Berbera,** Som.
140/D4 **Berberati,** CAfr.
165/G3 **Berbice** (riv.), Guy.
86/C3 **Berceto,** It.
68/D1 **Berchem,** Belg.
80/C4 **Bercher,** Swi.
71/E4 **Berching,** Ger.
97/L2 **Berchogur,** Kaz.
75/K3 **Berchtesgaden,** Ger.
75/K3 **Berchtesgaden Nat'l Park,** Ger.
68/A3 **Berck,** Fr.
189/F3 **Berclair,** Tx,US
150/C4 **Berdale,** Som.
98/E3 **Berdichev,** Ukr.
69/F4 **Berdorf,** Lux.
100/J4 **Berdsk,** Rus.
53/G4 **Berdyansk,** Ukr.
99/J4 **Berdyansk** (bay), Ukr.
148/C3 **Béré,** Chad
199/G5 **Berea,** Les.
193/K2 **Berea,** Ky,US
200/E2 **Berea,** Ky,US
208/F5 **Berea,** Oh,US
127/G3 **Berebere,** Indo.
98/C3 **Beregomet,** Ukr.
98/B3 **Beregovo,** Ukr.
86/C2 **Bereguardo,** It.
131/G2 **Bereina,** PNG
157/H8 **Bereketa,** Madg.
151/A3 **Bereku,** Tanz.
145/E5 **Berekum,** Gha.
172/B1 **Berenguela,** Bol.
147/G4 **Berenice** (ruins), Egypt
194/F1 **Berens** (isl.), Mb,Can
194/F1 **Berens River,** Mb,Can
157/H8 **Berenty,** Madg.
58/D5 **Bere Regis,** Eng,UK
196/E2 **Beresford,** NB,Can
193/F2 **Beresford,** SD,US
93/H2 **Berești,** Rom.
92/E2 **Berettyo** (riv.), Hun.
92/E2 **Berettyóújfalu,** Hun.
157/H7 **Berevo,** Madg.
96/C1 **Bereza,** Bela.
98/F2 **Berezan',** Ukr.
98/C3 **Berezhany,** Ukr.
94/H4 **Berezhnoye,** Rus.
96/D1 **Berezina** (riv.), Bela.
63/N5 **Berezino,** Bela.
94/J3 **Bereznik,** Rus.
53/J3 **Berezniki,** Rus.
98/F4 **Berezovka,** Ukr.
100/G3 **Berezovo,** Rus.
95/P4 **Berëzovskiy,** Rus.
109/L1 **Berezovyy,** Rus.
70/B5 **Berg,** Ger.
69/F4 **Berg,** Lux.
156/B4 **Berg** (riv.), SAfr.
81/F2 **Berg,** Swi.
72/C6 **Berga,** Ger.
104/A2 **Bergama,** Turk.
81/F6 **Bergamasque Alps** (mts.), It.
86/C1 **Bergamo,** It.
86/C1 **Bergamo** (prov.), It.
81/F2 **Bergatreute,** Ger.
71/G5 **Berg bei Rohrbach,** Aus.
72/B1 **Berge,** Ger.
67/H2 **Bergedorf,** Ger.
64/E2 **Bergen,** Ger.
67/G3 **Bergen,** Ger.
66/B3 **Bergen,** Neth.
62/A1 **Bergen,** Nor.
207/D1 **Bergen** (co.), NJ,US
66/B3 **Bergen aan Zee,** Neth.
67/G3 **Bergen-Belsen,** Ger.
166/C1 **Berg en Dal,** Sur.
207/E2 **Bergenfield,** NJ,US
66/B6 **Bergen op Zoom,** Neth.
74/D4 **Bergerac,** Fr.
79/H5 **Bergeresse** (riv.), Fr.
66/C6 **Bergeyk,** Neth.
72/D6 **Berggiesshübel,** Ger.
69/F2 **Bergheim,** Ger.
189/E3 **Bergheim,** Tx,US
208/G6 **Bergholz,** Oh,US
67/E6 **Bergisch Gladbach,** Ger.
67/E5 **Bergkamen,** Ger.
191/H2 **Bergman,** Ar,US
94/D2 **Bergnäset,** Swe.
67/E6 **Bergneustadt,** Ger.
64/F4 **Bergrheinfeld,** Ger.
62/H2 **Bergshamra,** Swe.
189/F2 **Bergstrom A.F.B.,** Tx,US
61/G2 **Bergsviken,** Swe..
70/D3 **Bergtheim,** Ger.
141/N13 **Berguent,** Mor.
68/B2 **Bergues,** Fr.
66/C2 **Bergum,** Neth.
66/D2 **Bergumermeer** (lake), Neth.
81/F4 **Bergün-Bravuogn,** Swi.
62/G1 **Bergviken** (lake), Swe.
72/C4 **Bergwitz,** Ger.
108/G2 **Berh,** Mong.
124/C3 **Berhala** (str.), Indo.
121/G3 **Berhampore,** India
118/D4 **Berhampur,** India
73/C5 **Berhida,** Hun.
124/D3 **Berikat** (cape), Indo.
176/A3 **Bering** (sea), NAm., Asia
101/S4 **Bering** (isl.), Rus.
177/E3 **Bering** (str.), Rus., Ak,US
69/E1 **Beringen,** Belg.
177/E2 **Bering Land Bridge Nat'l Prsv.,** Ak,US
101/T3 **Beringovskiy,** Rus.
190/A4 **Berino,** NM,US
99/G4 **Berislav,** Ukr.
124/C3 **Beritarikap** (cape), Indo.
76/D4 **Berja,** Sp.
141/N13 **Berkane,** Mor.
66/D4 **Berkel** (riv.), Ger.
66/B5 **Berkel,** Neth.
59/E3 **Berkeley,** Eng,UK
205/K11 **Berkeley,** Ca,US
206/D2 **Berkeley Heights,** NJ,US
201/M7 **Berkeley Lake,** Ga,US
199/G5 **Berkeley Springs** (Bath), WV,US
53/M6 **Berkhamsted,** Eng,UK
70/D6 **Berkheim,** Ger.
66/C3 **Berkhout,** Neth.
208/C2 **Berkley,** Ma,US
205/F6 **Berkley,** Mi,US
137/W **Berkner** (isl.), Ant.
93/F4 **Berkovitsa,** Bul.
206/C3 **Berks** (co.), Pa,US
59/E4 **Berkshire** (co.), Eng,UK
208/A3 **Berkshire,** Ct,US
208/A1 **Berkshire** (co.), Ma,US
208/A1 **Berkshire** (hills), Ma,US
59/E4 **Berkshire Downs** (uplands), Eng,UK
68/C3 **Berlaimont,** Fr.
76/D2 **Berlanga de Duero,** Sp.
68/C1 **Berlare,** Belg.
66/C5 **Berlicum,** Neth.
72/D2 **Berlin** (cap.), Ger.
72/D2 **Berlin** (state), Ger.
208/B2 **Berlin,** Ct,US
203/G2 **Berlin,** Ga,US
208/C1 **Berlin,** Ma,US
201/K1 **Berlin,** Md,US
199/L2 **Berlin,** NH,US
206/D4 **Berlin,** NJ,US
184/E4 **Berlin** (mtn.), Nv,US
208/F6 **Berlin,** Oh,US
208/G6 **Berlin** (res.), Oh,US
199/G5 **Berlin,** Pa,US
193/K2 **Berlin,** Wi,US
208/C6 **Berlin Center,** Oh,US
208/E5 **Berlin Heights,** Oh,US
72/D3 **Berlin** (Schönefeld) (int'l arpt.), Ger.
72/D2 **Berlin** (Tegel) (int'l arpt.), Ger.
72/D3 **Berlin** (Tempelhof) (arpt.), Ger.
137/V **Berlioz** (pt.), Ant.
135/D3 **Bermagui,** Austl.
174/D1 **Bermejo,** Arg.
172/D3 **Bermejo** (riv.), Arg.
172/E2 **Bermejo** (riv.), Arg.
172/D2 **Bermejo, Antiguo Cauce del** (riv.), Arg.
76/D1 **Bermeo,** Sp.
76/B2 **Bermillo de Sayago,** Sp.
176/L6 **Bermuda** (isl.), UK
206/A4 **Bermudian** (cr.), Pa,US
80/D3 **Bern** (canton), Swi.
80/D4 **Bern** (cap.), Swi.
173/E4 **Bernabé Rivera,** Uru.
168/A2 **Bernal,** Peru
83/C2 **Bernalda,** It.
190/A3 **Bernalillo,** NM,US
178/D1 **Bernard** (riv.), NW,Can
190/A3 **Bernardo,** NM,US
175/J7 **Bernardo O'Higgins Nat'l Park,** Chile
199/K3 **Bernardston,** Ma,US
206/D2 **Bernardsville,** NJ,US
80/E2 **Bernau,** Ger.
82/C2 **Bernaude, Roche** (mtn.), Fr.
79/F2 **Bernay,** Fr.
80/D4 **Bern-Belp** (int'l arpt.), Swi.
81/G2 **Bernbeuren,** Ger.
72/B4 **Bernburg,** Ger.
67/F2 **Berne** (riv.), Ger.
198/D4 **Berne,** In,US
80/D5 **Bernese Alps** (range), Swi.
53/S9 **Bernes-sur-Oise,** Fr.
73/A2 **Bernhardsthal,** Aus.
71/F4 **Bernhardswald,** Ger.
189/H1 **Bernice,** La,US
200/C2 **Bernie,** Mo,US
132/B3 **Bernier** (isl.), Austl.
178/G1 **Bernier** (bay), NW,Can
199/L1 **Bernierville,** Qu,Can
82/B2 **Bernin,** Fr.
81/F5 **Bernina** (mts.), It., Swi.
75/H3 **Bernina** (peak), Swi.
81/G5 **Bernina, Passo del** (pass), Swi.
81/F5 **Bernina, Piz** (peak), Swi.
68/C3 **Bernissart,** Belg.
69/G4 **Bernkastel-Kues,** Ger.
73/B3 **Bernolákovo,** Slvk.
71/F1 **Bernsbach,** Ger.
72/E5 **Bernsdorf,** Ger.
73/A5 **Bernstein,** Aus.
206/B3 **Bernville,** Pa,US
80/E3 **Beromünster,** Swi.
75/F5 **Béron** (riv.), Fr.
157/H8 **Beronono,** Madg.
157/H8 **Beroroha,** Madg.
71/H3 **Beroun,** Czh.
71/H3 **Berounka** (riv.), Czh.
92/F5 **Berovo,** Macd.
87/E3 **Berra,** It.
82/B6 **Berre** (lag.), Fr.
142/D2 **Berrechid,** Mor.
82/B6 **Berre-L'Étang,** Fr.
133/J5 **Berri,** Austl.
143/F2 **Berriane,** Alg.
135/C3 **Berridale,** Austl.
55/K7 **Berriedale,** Sc,UK
198/C4 **Berrien Springs,** Mi,US
58/C1 **Berriew,** Wal,UK
135/C2 **Berrigan,** Austl.
160/C2 **Berriozábal,** Mex.
175/T12 **Berrondo,** Uru.
174/D2 **Berrotarán,** Arg.
141/S15 **Berrouaghia,** Alg.
135/D2 **Berry,** Austl.
162/B1 **Berry** (isls.), Bahm.
197/G3 **Berry** (pt.), Can
183/J2 **Berry** (cr.), Ab,Can
88/D1 **Berry** (hist. reg.), Fr.
74/D3 **Berry** (reg.), Fr.
200/E1 **Berry,** Ky,US
79/G6 **Berry, Canal-du** (can.), Fr.
205/K9 **Berryessa** (lake), Ca,US
205/K9 **Berryessa** (peak), Ca,US
58/C6 **Berry Head** (pt.), Wal,UK
206/A2 **Berry Mountain** (ridge), Pa,US
191/G1 **Berryton,** Ks,US
201/J1 **Berryville,** Va,US
154/C5 **Berseba,** Namb.
67/E3 **Bersenbrück,** Ger.
98/E3 **釣Bershad',** Ukr.
72/D4 **Berste** (riv.), Ger.
95/L5 **Bersut,** Rus.
124/C1 **Bertam,** Malay.
195/G4 **Bertha,** Mn,US
199/K1 **Berthierville,** Qu,Can
194/D3 **Berthold,** ND,US
192/B3 **Berthoud,** Co,US
87/F4 **Bertinoro,** It.
87/G1 **Bertiolo,** It.
69/E3 **Bertogne,** Belg.
167/F4 **Bertolínia,** Braz.
148/B4 **Bertoua,** Camr.
189/E2 **Bertram,** Tx,US

130/B4 **Bertram, Mount** (peak), Austl.
175/J7 **Bertrand** (peak), Arg.
196/E2 **Bertrand,** NB,Can
69/E4 **Bertrix,** Belg.
68/C3 **Bertry,** Fr.
87/F3 **Bertuzzi, Valli** (lag.), It.
138/G5 **Beru** (isl.), Kiri.
124/C1 **Beruas,** Malay.
126/D3 **Beruit** (isl.), Malay.
54/D3 **Bervie Water** (riv.), Sc,UK
118/B2 **Berwa,** India
135/G5 **Berwick,** Austl.
196/E3 **Berwick,** NS,Can
196/B4 **Berwick,** Me,US
206/B1 **Berwick,** Pa,US
54/D5 **Berwick-upon-Tweed,** Eng,UK
56/E6 **Berwyn** (mts.), Wal,UK
205/Q16 **Berwyn,** Il,US
206/C3 **Berwyn-Devon,** Pa,US
187/F2 **Beryl,** Ut,US
92/C2 **Berzence,** Hun.
82/C4 **Bès** (riv.), Fr.
157/H7 **Besalampy,** Madg.
80/C3 **Besançon,** Fr.
148/B4 **Bésao,** Chad
130/A2 **Besar** (isl.), Indo.
127/E4 **Besar** (peak), Indo.
124/C2 **Besar** (peak), Malay.
74/E3 **Besbre** (riv.), Fr.
99/J2 **Besedino,** Rus.
124/C2 **Beserah,** Malay.
100/F6 **Beshahr,** Iran
63/N4 **Beshenkovichi,** Bela.
150/A3 **Beshlo Wenz** (riv.), Eth.
105/H4 **Beshneh,** Iran
130/B2 **Besikama,** Indo.
104/E2 **Beşiri,** Turk.
92/E3 **Beška,** Yugo.
65/K4 **Beskids** (mts.), Pol.
114/D2 **Beskol',** Kaz.
103/B1 **Beşkonak,** Turk.
97/H4 **Beslan,** Rus.
92/F4 **Besna Kobila** (peak), Yugo.
104/D2 **Besni,** Turk.
86/B1 **Besozzo,** It.
57/G4 **Bessacarr,** Eng,UK
53/S9 **Bessancourt,** Fr.
93/J2 **Bessarabia** (reg.), Mol.
93/J2 **Bessarabka,** Mol.
56/B3 **Bessbrook,** NI,UK
200/D4 **Bessemer,** Al,US
198/A1 **Bessemer,** Mi,US
205/D2 **Bessemer** (mtn.), Wa,US
208/G6 **Bessemer** (Walford), Pa,US
79/F5 **Bessé-sur-Braye,** Fr.
97/K3 **Besshoky, Gora** (peak), Kaz.
74/D3 **Bessines-sur-Gartempe,** Fr.
66/C6 **Best,** Neth.
159/E2 **Best,** Tx,US
72/D3 **Bestensee,** Ger.
114/B1 **Bestobe,** Kaz.
95/J3 **Bestuzhevo,** Rus.
67/F6 **Bestwig,** Ger.
130/D3 **Beswick,** Austl.
130/D3 **Beswick Abor. Land,** Austl.
60/D2 **Betaghstown,** Ire.
157/H7 **Betanantanana,** Madg.
167/K6 **Betania,** Col.
157/H9 **Betanty,** Madg.
172/C1 **Betanzos,** Bol.
76/A1 **Betanzos,** Sp.
148/B4 **Bétaré-Oya,** Camr.
150/A3 **Bete Hor,** Eth.
145/F4 **Bétérou,** Ben.
103/F8 **Bet Guvrin,** Isr.
141/M14 **Beth** (riv.), Mor.
156/Q13 **Bethal,** SAfr.
103/G6 **Beth Alpha Synagogue Nat'l Park,** Isr.
156/B2 **Bethanie,** Namb.
156/D2 **Bethanie,** SAfr.
199/G2 **Bethany,** On,Can
205/L11 **Bethany** (res.), Ca,US
208/B3 **Bethany,** Ct,US
193/K4 **Bethany,** Il,US
189/G1 **Bethany,** La,US
193/G3 **Bethany,** Mo,US
177/F3 **Bethel,** Ak,US
208/A3 **Bethel,** Ct,US
196/B3 **Bethel,** Me,US
191/G3 **Bethel,** Ok,US
206/B3 **Bethel,** Pa,US
199/K3 **Bethel,** Vt,US
191/F3 **Bethel Acres,** Ok,US
205/L10 **Bethel Island,** Ca,US
208/G7 **Bethel Park,** Pa,US
200/E2 **Bethelridge,** Ky,US
68/D5 **Bétheniville,** Fr.
68/D5 **Bétheny,** Fr.
56/D5 **Bethesda,** Wal,UK
206/A6 **Bethesda,** Md,US
68/B5 **Béthisy-Sainte-Pierre,** Fr.
156/E3 **Bethlehem,** SAfr.
208/A2 **Bethlehem,** Ct,US
206/C6 **Bethlehem,** Md,US
199/L2 **Bethlehem,** NH,US
206/C2 **Bethlehem,** Pa,US
206/C2 **Bethlehem-Allentown-Easton** (arpt.), Pa,US
103/D4 **Bethlehem** (Bayt Laḩm), WBnk.
80/C2 **Bethoncourt,** Fr.
142/D2 **Beth, Oued** (riv.), Mor.
207/E2 **Bethpage,** NY,US
156/D3 **Bethulie,** SAfr.
68/B2 **Béthune,** Fr.
68/A4 **Béthune** (riv.), Fr.
157/H8 **Betioky,** Madg.
133/J3 **Betoota,** Austl.
114/A2 **Betpak-Dala** (des.), Kaz.
157/H8 **Betroka,** Madg.
69/G6 **Betschdorf,** Fr.
103/D3 **Bet She'an,** Isr.
103/F8 **Bet Shemesh,** Isr.
196/C1 **Betsiamites,** Qu,Can
196/C1 **Betsiamites** (riv.), Qu,Can
196/C1 **Betsiamites Ind. Res.,** Qu,Can
196/C1 **Betsiamites, Pointe de** (pt.), Can
157/H7 **Betsiboka** (riv.), Madg.
195/L5 **Betsie** (pt.), Mi,US
201/F2 **Betsy Layne,** Ky,US
69/D6 **Bettancourt-la-Ferrée,** Fr.
146/C4 **Bette** (peak), Libya
69/F4 **Bettembourg,** Lux.
186/B3 **Betteravia,** Ca,US
206/B5 **Betterton,** Md,US
121/E2 **Bettiah,** India
80/D3 **Bettlach,** Swi.
177/H2 **Bettles,** Ak,US
84/B1 **Bettolle,** It.
78/D4 **Betton,** Fr.
120/A5 **Betūl,** India
167/K6 **Betulia,** Col.
66/C5 **Betuwe** (reg.), Neth.
120/B3 **Betwa** (riv.), India
56/E5 **Betws-y-Coed,** Wal,UK
69/G2 **Betzdorf,** Ger.
71/E3 **Betzenstein,** Ger.
152/C4 **Béu,** Ang.
135/B2 **Beulah,** Austl.
194/D2 **Beulah,** Mb,Can
192/B4 **Beulah,** Co,US
198/C2 **Beulah,** Mi,US
191/J4 **Beulah,** Ms,US
194/D4 **Beulah,** ND,US
205/P14 **Beulah** (lake), Wi,US
194/B5 **Beulah,** Wy,US
66/D3 **Beulakerwijde** (lake), Neth.
59/G4 **Beult** (riv.), Eng,UK
66/C5 **Beuningen,** Neth.
80/C3 **Beure,** Fr.
79/F2 **Beuvillers,** Fr.
79/G5 **Beuvron** (riv.), Fr.
53/U10 **Beuvronne** (riv.), Fr.
68/B2 **Beuvry,** Fr.
79/F2 **Beuzeville,** Fr.
84/C2 **Bevagna,** It.
67/H2 **Bevensen,** Ger.
195/K5 **Bevent,** Wi,US
67/E4 **Bever** (riv.), Ger.
82/D5 **Bévera** (riv.), Fr.
68/D1 **Beveren,** Belg.
81/F4 **Beverin, Piz** (peak), Swi.
132/C5 **Beverley,** Austl.
57/H4 **Beverley,** Eng,UK
198/F5 **Beverly,** Oh,US
201/H1 **Beverly,** WV,US
204/B2 **Beverly Hills,** Ca,US
205/F6 **Beverly Hills,** Mi,US
67/F2 **Beverstedt,** Ger.
67/G5 **Beverungen,** Ger.
66/B4 **Beverwijk,** Neth.
189/G2 **Bevil Oaks,** Tx,US
120/B3 **Bewār,** India
57/F1 **Bewcastle,** Eng,UK
199/G2 **Bewdley,** On,Can
58/D2 **Bewdley,** Eng,UK
59/G4 **Bewl Bridge** (res.), Eng,UK
80/D5 **Bex,** Swi.
69/G5 **Bexbach,** Ger.
59/G5 **Bexhill,** Eng,UK
57/F7 **Bexley** (bor.), Eng,UK
114/E4 **Bextograk,** China
93/H5 **Beyçayırı,** Turk.
93/K5 **Beycuma,** Turk.
93/J5 **Beykoz,** Turk.
144/C4 **Beyla,** Gui.
93/J5 **Beylerbeyi,** Turk.
105/N6 **Beylerbeyi Palace,** Turk.
150/B2 **Bēylul,** Eth.
69/E2 **Beyne-Heusay,** Belg.
97/K3 **Beyneu,** Kaz.
105/M6 **Beyoğlu,** Turk.
93/K5 **Beypazarı,** Turk.
122/E3 **Beypore,** India
122/F3 **Beypore** (riv.), India
104/B2 **Beyşehir,** Turk.
104/B2 **Beyşehir** (lake), Turk.
99/K4 **Beysug** (bay), Rus.
157/H8 **Bezaha,** Madg.
81/F3 **Bezau,** Aus.
92/D3 **Bezdan,** Yugo.
71/H1 **Bezděz** (peak), Czh.
71/H4 **Bezdrev** (lake), Czh.
94/H4 **Bezhetsk,** Rus.
97/H4 **Bezhta,** Rus.
74/F5 **Béziers,** Fr.
105/J2 **Bezmein,** Trkm.
120/D3 **Bhabua,** India
122/C1 **Bhadarwāh,** India
120/D4 **Bhadaur,** India
120/D3 **Bhadohī,** India
118/E3 **Bhadrak,** India
121/G2 **Bhadrapur,** Nepal
118/C5 **Bhadrāvati,** India
118/A3 **Bhadreswar,** India
121/F3 **Bhāgalpur,** India
122/B2 **Bhāi Pheru,** Pak.
121/G4 **Bhairab** (riv.), Bang.
121/H3 **Bhairab Bāzār,** Bang.
120/D2 **Bhairahawa,** Nepal
122/A2 **Bhakkar,** Pak.
122/D2 **Bhākra** (dam), India
121/E2 **Bhaktapur,** Nepal
121/H3 **Bhāluka,** Bang.
122/B1 **Bhalwāl,** Pak.
116/C3 **Bhamo,** Burma
118/B3 **Bhandāri,** India
120/B3 **Bhānder,** India
120/B4 **Bhānrer** (range), India
118/A3 **Bhanwār,** India
120/A2 **Bhāratpur,** India
120/E2 **Bharatpur,** Nepal
116/B3 **Bhareli** (riv.), India
121/E4 **Bharno,** India
118/B4 **Bharthana,** India
118/B3 **Bharuch,** India
120/A2 **Bhasāwar,** India
118/D3 **Bhātāpāra,** India
121/G4 **Bhātiāpāra Ghāt,** Bang.
122/C2 **Bhatinda,** India
118/B5 **Bhatkal,** India
121/G4 **Bhātpāra,** India
122/B1 **Bhaun,** Pak.
122/F3 **Bhavāni,** India
122/F3 **Bhavāni** (riv.), India
118/B3 **Bhavnagar,** India
122/B2 **Bhawāna,** Pak.
122/B2 **Bhawānigarh,** India
118/C3 **Bhawāni Mandi,** India
118/D4 **Bhawānipatna,** India
122/B1 **Bhera,** Pak.
121/G3 **Bheramara,** Bang.
120/C1 **Bheri** (zone), Nepal
122/C2 **Bhikkiwind Uttār,** India
121/E2 **Bhikna Thorī,** Nepal
118/D3 **Bhilai,** India
118/B2 **Bhīlwāra,** India
118/C4 **Bhīma** (riv.), India
118/D4 **Bhīmavaram,** India
121/E2 **Bhīmphedi,** Nepal
118/D4 **Bhimunipatnam,** India
120/B2 **Bhind,** India
120/B2 **Bhinga,** India
118/B3 **Bhīnmāl,** India
118/B4 **Bhiwandi,** India
121/F2 **Bhojpur,** Nepal
118/C3 **Bhokardan,** India
121/H4 **Bhola,** Bang.
120/B2 **Bhongaon,** India
120/A4 **Bhopāl,** India
120/A4 **Bhopal** (arpt.), India
118/B4 **Bhor,** India
54/A1 **Bhraoin, Loch** (lake), Sc,UK
118/E3 **Bhuban,** India
118/E3 **Bhubaneswar,** India
118/A3 **Bhūj,** India
120/A1 **Bhūkarherī,** India
123/B2 **Bhumibol** (dam), Thai.
118/C3 **Bhusawal,** India
121/G2 **Bhutan**
122/G3 **Bhuvanagiri,** India
114/F5 **Bi** (riv.), China
169/E2 **Biá** (riv.), Braz.
144/E5 **Bia** (riv.), Gui., IvC.
153/G2 **Biaboye,** Zaire
68/B3 **Biache-Saint-Vaast,** Fr.
152/A2 **Biafra** (bight), Afr.
127/J4 **Biak** (isl.), Indo.
65/M2 **Biała Podlaska,** Pol.
65/M3 **Biała Podlaska** (prov.), Pol.
65/L3 **Białobrzegi,** Pol.
65/J2 **Białogard,** Pol.
65/K4 **Białowieski Nat'l Park,** Pol.
65/M2 **Białystok,** Pol.
65/M2 **Białystok** (prov.), Pol.
75/J3 **Bianca** (peak), It.
90/D4 **Biancavilla,** It.
83/C6 **Bianco,** It.
85/D4 **Bianco** (peak), It.
86/B2 **Biandrate,** It.
86/B1 **Biandronno,** It.
148/D4 **Bianga,** CAfr.
144/D5 **Biankouma,** IvC.
116/E3 **Bianya,** China
116/E3 **Bianyang,** China
86/B2 **Bianze,** It.
153/F2 **Biaro,** Zaire
74/C5 **Biarritz,** Fr.
81/E5 **Biasca,** Swi.
147/F2 **Bibā,** Egypt
112/B2 **Bibai,** Japan
154/B2 **Bibala,** Ang.
152/B2 **Bibassé,** Gabon
86/D3 **Bibbiano,** It.
87/E5 **Bibbiena,** It.
148/B3 **Bibémi,** Camr.
70/B6 **Biberach,** Ger.
70/D6 **Biberach,** Ger.
70/C6 **Biberach an der Riss,** Ger.
80/D3 **Biberist,** Swi.
87/G1 **Bibione,** It.
121/H3 **Bibiyana** (riv.), Bang.
116/A3 **Bibiyana** (riv.), Bang., India
164/B5 **Biblián,** Ecu.
70/B3 **Biblis,** Ger.
196/C1 **Bic,** Qu,Can
171/E3 **Bicas,** Braz.
171/N6 **Bicas,** Braz.
93/H2 **Bicaz,** Rom.
85/F5 **Biccari,** It.
59/E3 **Bicester,** Eng,UK
149/G4 **Bichano,** Eth.
149/H3 **Bichena,** Eth.
135/D4 **Bicheno,** Austl.
120/C4 **Bichhia,** India
131/E3 **Bickerton** (isl.), Austl.
201/H1 **Bickle** (mtn.), WV,US
183/K2 **Bickleigh,** Sk,Can
182/D5 **Bickleton,** Wa,US
132/L7 **Bickley** (brook), Austl.
198/C5 **Bicknell,** In,US
185/H4 **Bicknell,** Ut,US
73/C5 **Bicske,** Hun.
145/G4 **Bida,** Nga.
125/B4 **Bidadari, Tanjong** (cape), Malay.
144/D5 **Bidaga** (rapids), IvC.
118/C4 **Bīdar,** India
107/K3 **Bīdāsar,** India
105/G4 **Bīd Boland,** Iran
196/B4 **Biddeford,** Me,US
66/C4 **Biddinghuizen,** Neth.
103/D3 **Biddiyā,** WBnk.
103/G8 **Biddū,** WBnk.
57/F5 **Biddulph,** Eng,UK
54/A3 **Bidean nam Bian** (mtn.), Sc,UK
58/B4 **Bideford,** Eng,UK
58/B4 **Bideford** (Barnstaple) (bay), Eng,UK
87/F4 **Bidente** (riv.), It.
59/E2 **Bidford on Avon,** Eng,UK
120/B2 **Bidhūna,** India
105/J3 **Bīdokht,** Iran
124/C1 **Bidor,** Malay.
123/E3 **Bi Doup** (peak), Viet.
77/E1 **Bidouze** (riv.), Fr.
150/A4 **Bidrē,** Eth.
154/C2 **Bié** (dist.), Ang.
154/C2 **Bié** (plat.), Ang.
184/C3 **Bieber,** Ca,US
70/B3 **Biebesheim am Rhein,** Ger.
65/M2 **Biebrza** (riv.), Pol.
72/B3 **Biederitz,** Ger.
153/F3 **Biega-Kahuzi Nat'l Park,** Zaire
80/D3 **Biel,** Swi.
65/J3 **Bielawa,** Pol.
54/D2 **Bieldside,** Sc,UK
67/F4 **Bielefeld,** Ger.
72/A5 **Bielen,** Ger.
179/J1 **Bieler** (lake), NW,Can
80/D3 **Bieler** (lake), Swi.
86/B1 **Biella,** It.
86/B1 **Biella** (prov.), It.
65/K4 **Bielsko** (prov.), Pol.
65/K4 **Bielsko-Biała,** Pol.
65/M2 **Bielsk Podlaski,** Pol.
67/H2 **Bienenbüttel,** Ger.
193/C3 **Bienfait,** Sk,Can
123/D4 **Bien Hoa,** Viet.
80/B5 **Bienne** (riv.), Fr.
86/D1 **Bienno,** It.
123/D1 **Bien Son,** Viet.
86/D5 **Bientina,** It.
166/C2 **Bienvenue,** FrG.
179/J3 **Bienville** (lake), Qu,Can
202/B1 **Bienville,** La,US
72/B4 **Biere,** Ger.
80/C4 **Bière,** Swi.
69/E2 **Bierset** (Liège) (int'l arpt.), Belg.
66/D2 **Bierum,** Neth.
65/J3 **Bierutów,** Pol.
66/B5 **Biesbosch** (reg.), Neth.
72/B2 **Biese** (riv.), Ger.
72/D2 **Biesenthal,** Ger.
80/B1 **Biesles,** Fr.
66/D5 **Biesme** (riv.), Fr.
70/C5 **Bietigheim,** Ger.
80/D5 **Bietschhorn** (peak), Swi.
69/E4 **Bièvre,** Belg.
53/S10 **Bièvre** (riv.), Fr.
53/S10 **Bièvres,** Fr.
85/E4 **Biferno** (riv.), It.
152/B3 **Bifoun,** Gabon
135/B2 **Big** (des.), Austl.
182/C2 **Big** (cr.), BC,Can
179/J2 **Big** (isl.), NW,Can
178/D1 **Big** (riv.), NW,Can
195/G3 **Big** (isl.), On,Can
191/J3 **Big** (cr.), Ar,US
201/M6 **Big** (cr.), Ga,US
192/D4 **Big** (cr.), Ks,US
205/E6 **Big** (lake), Mi,US
191/J1 **Big** (riv.), Mo,US
184/D3 **Big** (mtn.), Nv,US
189/M9 **Big** (cr.), Tx,US
201/H1 **Big** (mtn.), WV,US
93/H5 **Biga,** Turk.
104/B2 **Bigadiç,** Turk.
183/G4 **Big Arm,** Mt,US
196/D2 **Big Bald** (mtn.), NB,Can
183/J4 **Big Baldy** (mtn.), Mt,US
182/C2 **Big Bar Creek,** BC,Can
198/C2 **Big Bay de Noc** (bay), Mi,US
186/D3 **Big Bear City,** Ca,US
186/D3 **Big Bear Lake,** Ca,US
194/B3 **Big Beaver,** Sk,Can
183/J4 **Big Belt** (mts.), Mt,US
157/E2 **Big Bend,** Swaz.
192/E1 **Big Bend** (dam), SD,US
205/P14 **Big Bend,** Wi,US
188/C3 **Big Bend Nat'l Park,** Tx,US
200/B4 **Big Black** (riv.), Ms,US
191/F1 **Big Blue** (riv.), Ks,US
193/F3 **Big Blue** (riv.), Ks, Ne,US
192/F3 **Big Blue, West Fork** (riv.), Ne,US
189/F3 **Big Boggy Nat'l Wild. Ref.,** Tx,US
58/C6 **Bigbury** (bay), Eng,UK
191/G2 **Big Cabin,** Ok,US
188/C2 **Big Canyon** (cr.), Tx,US
186/C2 **Big Creek,** Ca,US
185/F1 **Big Creek,** Id,US
203/H4 **Big Cypress** (swamp), Fl,US
203/H4 **Big Cypress Nat'l Prsv.,** Fl,US
177/D2 **Big Diomede** (isl.), Rus.
193/K1 **Big Eau Pleine** (res.), Wi,US
195/K5 **Big Eddy** (falls), Wi,US
199/L2 **Bigelow** (mtn.), Me,US
195/H3 **Big Falls,** Mn,US
206/D1 **Big Flat** (brook), NJ,US
192/C2 **Big Foot** (pass), SD,US
189/E3 **Bigfoot,** Tx,US
195/H4 **Bigfork,** Mn,US
183/G3 **Bigfork,** Mt,US
135/D2 **Bigga,** Austl.
183/L1 **Biggar,** Sk,Can
54/C5 **Biggar,** Sc,UK
69/G1 **Biggasee** (lake), Ger.
130/B3 **Bigge** (isl.), Austl.
67/E6 **Bigge** (riv.), Ger.
134/D4 **Biggenden,** Austl.
191/J2 **Biggers,** Ar,US
67/E6 **Biggesee** (res.), Ger.
53/P8 **Biggin Hill,** Eng,UK
59/F2 **Biggleswade,** Eng,UK
184/C4 **Biggs,** Ca,US
188/A2 **Biggs Army Afld.,** Tx,US
185/G1 **Big Hole** (riv.), Mt,US
183/H5 **Big Hole Nat'l Bfld.,** Mt,US
183/L4 **Bighorn,** Mt,US
183/L5 **Bighorn** (riv.), Mt,US
185/J1 **Bighorn** (lake), Mt, Wy,US
185/K1 **Bighorn** (riv.), Mt, Wy,US
185/K1 **Big Horn,** Wy,US
185/K1 **Bighorn** (mts.), Wy,US
178/F4 **Bighorn** (riv.), Mt,Wy,US
185/J1 **Bighorn Canyon Nat'l Rec. Area,** Mt, Wy,US
162/C1 **Bight, The,** Bahm.
153/E2 **Bigi,** Zaire
199/J3 **Big Indian,** NY,US
188/D2 **Big Lake,** Tx,US
200/B3 **Big Lake Nat'l Wild. Ref.,** Ar,US
182/D1 **Big Lake Ranch,** BC,Can
206/A4 **Biglerville,** Pa,US
182/G2 **Big Lost** (riv.), Id,US
195/Q6 **Big Marine** (lake), Mn,US
193/K5 **Big Muddy** (riv.), Il,US
194/B3 **Big Muddy** (cr.), Mt,US
205/P14 **Big Muskego** (lake), Wi,US
193/F3 **Big Nemaha, North Fork** (riv.), Ne,US
144/A3 **Bignona,** Sen.
63/M4 **Bigosovo,** Bela.
186/C2 **Big Pine,** Ca,US
206/C1 **Big Pine** (hill), Pa,US
203/H5 **Big Pine Key,** Fl,US
204/C2 **Big Pines,** Ca,US
191/H2 **Big Piney,** Mo,US
191/H2 **Big Piney** (riv.), Mo,US
206/A4 **Big Pipe** (cr.), Md,US
208/E6 **Big Prairie,** Oh,US
198/C5 **Big Raccoon** (riv.), In,US
198/D3 **Big Rapids,** Mi,US
205/N16 **Big Rock,** Il,US
205/N16 **Big Rock** (cr.), Il,US
201/F2 **Big Rock,** Va,US
198/C2 **Big Sable** (pt.), Mi,US
190/C1 **Big Sandy** (cr.), Co,US
201/F1 **Big Sandy** (riv.), Ky, WV,US
183/J3 **Big Sandy,** Mt,US
200/C2 **Big Sandy** (riv.), Tn,US
185/J2 **Big Sandy,** Wy,US
185/J2 **Big Sandy** (riv.), Wy,US
203/G2 **Big Satilla** (cr.), Ga,US
195/G3 **Bigsby** (isl.), On,Can
193/F2 **Big Sioux** (riv.), Ia, SD,US
193/K1 **Big Smoky** (falls), Wi,US
200/E2 **Big South Fork Nat'l Rec. Area,** Ky, Tn,US
196/C3 **Big Spencer** (mtn.), Me,US
188/D1 **Big Spring,** Tx,US
194/F5 **Big Stone** (res.), Mn, SD,US
201/F2 **Big Stone Gap,** Va,US
194/F5 **Big Stone Nat'l Wild. Ref.,** Mn,US
200/B4 **Big Sunflower** (riv.), Ms,US
186/B2 **Big Sur,** Ca,US
202/A2 **Big Thicket Nat'l Prsv.,** Tx,US
192/B3 **Big Thompson** (riv.), Co,US
183/K5 **Big Timber,** Mt,US
178/H3 **Big Trout** (lake), On,Can
204/B2 **Big Tujunga** (canyon), Ca,US
183/H1 **Big Valley,** Ab,Can
188/E3 **Big Wells,** Tx,US
185/F2 **Big Wood** (riv.), Id,US
92/B3 **Bihać,** Yugo.
121/E3 **Bihār,** India
121/E3 **Bihār** (state), India
153/G3 **Biharamulo,** Tanz.
153/G3 **Biharamulo Game Rsv.,** Tanz.
121/F3 **Bihārīganj,** India
92/E2 **Biharkeresztes,** Hun.
92/F2 **Bihor** (co.), Rom.
68/A4 **Bihorel,** Fr.
112/D2 **Bihoro,** Japan
144/A4 **Bijagós** (arch.), GBis.
118/C4 **Bījāpur,** India
105/F3 **Bījār,** Iran
120/B3 **Bijāwar,** India
92/D3 **Bijeljina,** Bosn.
92/D4 **Bijelo Polje,** Yugo.
117/H3 **Bijia** (mtn.), China
116/C3 **Bijiang,** China
115/J7 **Bijiaquan,** China
116/E3 **Bijie,** China
121/H2 **Bijni,** India
120/B1 **Bijnor,** India
118/B2 **Bikampur,** India
118/B2 **Bīkaner,** India
138/G3 **Bikar** (atoll), Mrsh.
109/L2 **Bikin,** Rus.
109/M2 **Bikin** (riv.), Rus.
138/F3 **Bikini** (atoll), Mrsh.
155/F4 **Bikita,** Zim.
149/G3 **Bikori,** Sudan
152/D3 **Bikoro,** Zaire
120/E3 **Bikramganj,** India
154/B2 **Bikuar Nat'l Park,** Ang.
107/G4 **Bilād Manaḩ,** Oman
118/B2 **Bilāra,** India
120/B1 **Bilāri,** India
121/H2 **Bilāsipāra,** India
120/D1 **Bilāspur,** India
120/D4 **Bilāspur,** India
122/D2 **Bilāspur,** India
123/B3 **Bilauktaung** (range), Burma, Thai.
120/D1 **Bilauri,** Nepal
128/G5 **Bilba Morea Claypan** (lake), Austl.
76/D1 **Bilbao,** Sp.
103/B4 **Bilbays,** Egypt
92/D4 **Bileća,** Bosn.
104/B1 **Bilecik,** Turk.
93/K5 **Bilecik** (prov.), Turk.
103/G2 **Bīleh Savār,** Iran
73/B2 **Bílé Karpaty** (mts.), Czh.
65/M3 **Biłgoraj,** Pol.
120/C2 **Bilgrām,** India
120/C2 **Bilhaur,** India
153/F1 **Bili,** Zaire
148/D4 **Bili** (riv.), Zaire
101/S3 **Bilibino,** Rus.
155/G2 **Bilila,** Malw.
116/C5 **Bilin,** Burma
123/B2 **Bilin** (riv.), Burma
71/G1 **Bílina,** Czh.
71/G2 **Bílina** (riv.), Czh.
85/G6 **Bilioso** (riv.), It.
125/D3 **Biliran** (isl.), Phil.
145/H4 **Biliri,** Nga.
91/G2 **Bilisht,** Alb.
125/B4 **Bilit,** Malay.
113/B3 **Biliu** (riv.), China
192/B1 **Bill,** Wy,US
135/C2 **Billabong** (cr.), Austl.
144/C2 **Billaouār,** Mrta.
67/H1 **Bille** (riv.), Ger.
69/E5 **Billerbeck,** Ger.
74/C5 **Billère,** Fr.
196/B4 **Billerica,** Ma,US
59/G3 **Billericay,** Eng,UK
133/J5 **Billiat Consv. Park,** Austl.
70/C4 **Billigheim,** Ger.
130/B4 **Billiluna Abor. Land,** Austl.
57/F5 **Billinge,** Eng,UK
57/G2 **Billingham,** Eng,UK
183/K5 **Billings,** Mt,US
191/F2 **Billings,** Ok,US
62/E2 **Billingsfors,** Swe.
59/F4 **Billingshurst,** Eng,UK
102/K10 **Billiton** (isl.), Indo.
62/C4 **Billund,** Den.
62/C4 **Billund** (int'l arpt.), Den.
187/E3 **Bill Williams** (riv.), Az,US
146/B5 **Bilma,** Niger
149/H3 **Bīlo,** Eth.
134/C4 **Biloela,** Austl.
165/G4 **Biloku,** Guy.
202/D2 **Biloxi,** Ms,US
133/H3 **Bilpa Morea Claypan** (lake), Austl.
104/B4 **Bilqās Qism Awwal,** Egypt
120/B1 **Bilsi,** India
120/D2 **Bilthar,** India
66/C4 **Bilthoven,** Neth.
148/D2 **Biltine,** Chad
148/D2 **Biltine** (pref.), Chad
201/F2 **Biltmore,** Tn,US
69/E2 **Bilzen,** Belg.
127/E5 **Bima,** Indo.
135/D2 **Bimberi** (peak), Austl.
148/C4 **Bimbo,** CAfr.
162/B1 **Bimini** (isls.), Bahm.
82/B5 **Bimont, Barrage de** (dam), Fr.
71/F6 **Bina** (riv.), Ger.
73/C4 **Bíňa,** Slvk.
120/B3 **Bina-Etāwa,** India
135/D2 **Binalong,** Austl.
124/B2 **Binanga,** Indo.
141/X17 **Bin 'Arūs,** Tun.
141/X17 **Bin 'Arūs** (gov.), Tun.
126/D3 **Binatang,** Malay.
197/R9 **Binbrook,** On,Can
57/H5 **Binbrook,** Eng,UK
68/D3 **Binche,** Belg.
116/D3 **Binchuan,** China
135/D2 **Binda,** Austl.
108/G2 **Binder,** Mong.
148/B3 **Binder Foulbé,** Chad
120/C2 **Bindki,** India
132/C4 **Bindoon,** Austl.
125/C3 **Bindoy,** Phil.
152/D4 **Bindu,** Zaire
152/D4 **Bindungi,** Zaire
155/F3 **Bindura,** Zim.
77/F2 **Binéfar,** Sp.
59/F4 **Binfield,** Eng,UK
194/E4 **Binford,** ND,US
155/G3 **Binga** (mtn.), Moz.
155/E3 **Binga,** Zim.
135/D1 **Bingara,** Austl.
108/E4 **Bingcaowan,** China
70/A3 **Bingen,** Ger.
191/E3 **Binger,** Ok,US
144/E5 **Bingerville,** IvC.
57/H6 **Bingham,** Eng,UK
196/C3 **Bingham,** Me,US
199/J3 **Binghamton,** NY,US
146/B1 **Bin Ghashīr,** Libya
146/B3 **Bin Ghunaymah, Jabal** (mts.), Libya
57/G4 **Bingley,** Eng,UK
104/E2 **Bingöl,** Turk.
104/E2 **Bingöl** (prov.), Turk.
115/D4 **Binhai,** China
123/D4 **Binh Chanh,** Viet.
123/D4 **Binh Chau,** Viet.
116/B5 **Binhon** (peak), Burma
123/E3 **Binh Son,** Viet.
78/C3 **Binic,** Fr.
146/C4 **Bini Erdi** (well), Chad
77/G3 **Binisalem,** Sp.
124/B2 **Binjai,** Indo.
146/C2 **Bin Jawwād,** Libya
93/J5 **Binkılıç,** Turk.
144/C4 **Binkolo,** SLeo.
150/D3 **Binnah, Ras** (cape), Som.
135/D1 **Binnaway,** Austl.
80/D2 **Binningen,** Swi.
130/A1 **Binongko** (isl.), Indo.
143/H2 **Bin Qirdān,** Tun.
194/D2 **Binscarth,** Mb,Can
144/E2 **Bintagoungou,** Mali
124/E2 **Bintan** (isl.), Indo.
124/C1 **Bintang** (peak), Malay.
124/C1 **Bintang** (range), Malay.
144/B4 **Bintimodouya,** Gui.
103/D3 **Bint Jubayl,** Leb.
124/C4 **Bintuhan,** Indo.
103/F6 **Binyamina,** Isr.
117/F4 **Binyang,** China
145/G4 **Bin Yauri,** Nga.
152/C4 **Binza,** Zaire
115/D3 **Binzhou,** China
174/B3 **Bío-Bío** (reg.), Chile
174/B3 **Bío-Bío** (riv.), Chile
153/G2 **Biodi,** Zaire
92/B4 **Biograd,** Cro.
92/D4 **Biogradska Nat'l Park,** Yugo.
152/B2 **Bioko** (pol. reg.), EqG.
152/B2 **Bioko** (Fernando Po) (isl.), EqG.
186/B2 **Biola,** Ca,US
149/F5 **Biondi,** Zaire
142/C3 **Biougra,** Mor.
144/B4 **Bipoint** (Bissau) (int'l arpt.), GBis.
67/E3 **Bippen,** Ger.
118/C4 **Bīr,** India
109/L2 **Bira,** Rus.
148/C2 **Bir Abaya** (well), Chad
142/C4 **Bir Aïdiat** (well), Mrta.
146/B3 **Birāk,** Libya
146/B1 **Bi'r Al Ghanam,** Libya
150/D2 **Bi'r 'Alī,** Yem.
143/H2 **Bi'r 'Alī Bin Khalīfah,** Tun.
141/W17 **Bi'r Al Mashariqah,** Tun.
161/G1 **Birama** (pt.), Cuba
148/D3 **Birao,** CAfr.
121/F2 **Birātnagar,** Nepal
112/B4 **Biratori,** Japan
142/C4 **Bir Bel Guerdâne** (well), Mrta.
143/H4 **Bi'r Bu Kūsā** (well), Libya
178/E3 **Birch** (range), Ab,Can
194/E1 **Birch** (isl.), Mb,Can
183/H3 **Birch** (cr.), Mt,US
182/C3 **Birch Bay,** Wa,US
177/J2 **Birch Creek,** Ak,US
155/G3 **Birchenough Bridge,** Zim.
183/M1 **Birch Hills,** Sk,Can
135/B2 **Birchip,** Austl.
194/D1 **Birch River,** Mb,Can
191/J2 **Birch Tree,** Mo,US
193/J1 **Birchwood,** Wi,US
150/B4 **Bircot,** Eth.
137/X **Bird** (isl.), Austl.
191/F2 **Bird** (cr.), Ok,US
195/H3 **Bird Island,** Mn,US
129/K4 **Bird Islet** (isl.), Austl.
194/C2 **Bird Point,** Sk,Can
206/C3 **Birdsboro,** Pa,US
201/K2 **Birdsnest,** Va,US
135/D2 **Birds Rock** (peak), Austl.
133/H3 **Birdsville,** Austl.
194/D2 **Birdtail,** Mb,Can
130/D3 **Birdum,** Austl.
104/D2 **Birecik,** Turk.
143/G2 **Bir el Ater,** Alg.
142/D5 **Bir el Ksaïb** (well), Mali
107/G3 **Bīr-e 'Olyā,** Iran
124/B1 **Bireuen,** Indo.
121/G3 **Birganj,** Bang.
121/E2 **Bīrganj,** Nepal
170/C4 **Birigui,** Braz.
171/K8 **Biritiba-Mirim,** Braz.
100/F6 **Bīrjand,** Iran
107/G2 **Bīrjand,** Iran
104/B4 **Birkat Qārūn** (lake), Egypt
103/B5 **Birkat Qārūn** (lake), Egypt
144/B3 **Birkelane,** Sen.
70/B3 **Birkenau,** Ger.
138/G4 **Birkenebeu,** Kiri.
70/B5 **Birkenfeld,** Ger.
136/F6 **Birkenhead,** N.Z.
57/E5 **Birkenhead,** Eng,UK
69/G2 **Birken-Honigsessen,** Ger.
54/B5 **Birkenshaw,** Sc,UK
72/D2 **Birkenwerder,** Ger.
63/T9 **Birkerød,** Den.
84/H8 **Birkirkara,** Malta
81/H3 **Birkkarspitze** (peak), Aus.
93/H2 **Bîrlad,** Rom.
93/H2 **Bîrlad** (riv.), Rom.
98/D4 **Bîrlad** (riv.), Rom.
114/B3 **Birlik,** Kaz.
105/F2 **Birmay,** Azer.
59/E2 **Birmingham,** Eng,UK
59/E2 **Birmingham** (int'l arpt.), Eng,UK
200/D4 **Birmingham,** Al,US
205/F6 **Birmingham,** Mi,US
121/E4 **Birmitrapur,** India
142/C4 **Bir Mogreïn,** Mrta.
54/C3 **Birnam,** Sc,UK
195/K5 **Birnamwood,** Wi,US
183/L5 **Birney,** Mt,US
75/K3 **Birnhorn** (peak), Aus.
139/H5 **Birnie** (isl.), Kiri.
145/G4 **Birnin Gwari,** Nga.
145/G3 **Birnin Kebbi,** Nga.
145/G3 **Birni Nkonni,** Niger
145/H4 **Birnin Kudu,** Nga.
145/H3 **Biriniwa,** Nga.
109/L2 **Birobidzhan,** Rus.
143/E4 **Bir Ould Birni** (well), Alg.
142/E5 **Bîr Ounâne** (well), Mali
121/F2 **Bīrpur,** India
60/C3 **Birr,** Ire.
60/A2 **Birreencorragh** (mtn.), Ire.
130/D4 **Birrimbah,** Austl.
130/C4 **Birrindudu,** Austl.
135/D2 **Birriwa,** Austl.
80/D3 **Birs** (riv.), Swi.
80/D3 **Birse** (riv.), Swi.
148/C2 **Bir Sélia** (well), Chad
80/D2 **Birsfelden,** Swi.
95/M5 **Birsk,** Rus.
70/C2 **Birstein,** Ger.
63/L4 **Birštonas,** Lith.
141/M14 **Bir Tamtam,** Mor.
143/H4 **Bi'r Tegheri** (well), Libya
194/D2 **Birtle,** Mb,Can
108/C5 **Biru,** China
165/E3 **Biruaca,** Ven.
100/G5 **Biruni,** Uzb.
63/L3 **Biržai,** Lith.
103/G8 **Bi'r Zayt,** WBnk.
84/J8 **Birżebuġa,** Malta
142/E4 **Bir Zimla** (well), Alg.
143/H3 **Bi'r Zughrār** (well), Libya
93/F4 **Bis** (lake), Rom.
85/F5 **Bisaccia,** It.
148/B2 **Bisagana,** Nga.
111/M9 **Bisai,** Japan
120/B1 **Bīsalpur,** India
151/B1 **Bisa-Nadi Nat'l Rsv.,** Kenya
120/B1 **Bisauli,** India
187/H5 **Bisbee,** Az,US
194/E3 **Bisbee,** ND,US
74/C4 **Biscarrosse,** Fr.
74/C4 **Biscarrosse** (lag.), Fr.
74/B4 **Biscay** (bay), Eur.
162/A1 **Biscayne** (bay), Fl,US
202/P8 **Biscayne** (bay), Fl,US
203/H5 **Biscayne Nat'l Park,** Fl,US
90/E2 **Bisceglie,** It.
70/D3 **Bischberg,** Ger.
80/D1 **Bischheim,** Fr.
71/E2 **Bischofsgrün,** Ger.
70/B3 **Bischofsheim,** Ger.
70/D2 **Bischofsheim an der Rhön,** Ger.
75/K3 **Bischofshofen,** Aus.
72/E5 **Bischofswerda,** Ger.
81/F3 **Bischofszell,** Swi.
69/G6 **Bischwiller,** Fr.
137/V **Biscoe** (isls.), Ant.
201/H3 **Biscoe,** NC,US
200/B3 **Biscoe** (Fredonia), Ar,US
87/F5 **Biscubio** (riv.), It.
164/D2 **Biscucuy,** Ven.
153/E2 **Bisenge,** Zaire
85/G1 **Biševo** (isl.), Cro.
106/D4 **Bīshah** (dry riv.), SAr.
114/B3 **Bishkek** (cap.), Kyr.
121/F4 **Bishnupur,** India
156/D4 **Bisho,** SAfr.
186/C2 **Bishop,** Ca,US
205/E6 **Bishop** (int'l arpt.), Mi,US
189/F4 **Bishop,** Tx,US
57/G2 **Bishop Auckland,** Eng,UK
54/B5 **Bishopbriggs,** Sc,UK
208/G7 **Bishop-Cecil,** Pa,US
186/C2 **Bishop Ind. Res.,** Ca,US
58/D2 **Bishops Castle,** Eng,UK
58/D3 **Bishops Cleeve,** Eng,UK
197/K1 **Bishop's Falls,** Nf,Can
59/G3 **Bishop's Stortford,** Eng,UK
59/E5 **Bishops Waltham,** Eng,UK
54/B5 **Bishopton,** Sc,UK
201/G3 **Bishopville,** SC,US
57/H4 **Bishop Wilton,** Eng,UK
146/D4 **Bishrah, Ma'ṭan** (well), Libya
83/C3 **Bisignano,** It.
70/B6 **Bisingen,** Ger.
143/G2 **Biskra,** Alg.
141/T16 **Biskra** (wilaya), Alg.
141/U18 **Biskra** (wilaya), Alg.
65/L2 **Biskupiec,** Pol.
125/D3 **Bislig,** Phil.
197/R9 **Bismarck,** On,Can
138/D5 **Bismarck** (arch.), PNG
131/G1 **Bismarck** (range), PNG
131/G1 **Bismarck** (sea), PNG
191/H3 **Bismarck,** Ar,US
191/J2 **Bismarck,** Mo,US
194/D4 **Bismarck** (cap.), ND,US
72/B2 **Bismark,** Ger.
104/E2 **Bismil,** Turk.
161/F3 **Bismuna** (lag.), Nic.
153/G2 **Biso,** Ugan.
190/E1 **Bison,** Ks,US
192/C1 **Bison,** SD,US
94/C3 **Bispgarden,** Swe.
67/H2 **Bispingen,** Ger.
144/B4 **Bissau** (cap.), GBis.
144/B4 **Bissau** (Bipoint) (int'l arpt.), GBis.
145/H5 **Bissaula,** Nga.
67/F4 **Bissendorf,** Ger.
195/G2 **Bissett,** Mb,Can
151/C1 **Bissigh, Lach** (dry riv.), Som.
70/D5 **Bissingen,** Ger.
144/B3 **Bissora,** GBis.
86/B3 **Bistagno,** It.
93/G2 **Bistrița,** Rom.
98/C4 **Bistrița** (riv.), Rom.
93/G2 **Bistrița-Năsăud** (co.), Rom.
63/T9 **Bistrup,** Den.
120/C2 **Biswān,** India
164/D3 **Bita** (riv.), Col.
166/B1 **Bitagron,** Sur.
153/G4 **Bitale,** Tanz.
152/B2 **Bitam,** Gabon
69/F4 **Bitburg,** Ger.
69/G5 **Bitche,** Fr.
148/D2 **Bitéa, Ouadi** (dry riv.), Chad
118/B2 **Bithnok,** India
148/C3 **Bitkin,** Chad
104/E2 **Bitlis,** Turk.
104/E2 **Bitlis** (prov.), Turk.
92/E5 **Bitola,** Macd.
92/C5 **Bitonto,** It.
93/G2 **Bitrița** (riv.), Rom.
80/D2 **Bitschwiller,** Fr.
147/G2 **Bitter** (lakes), Egypt
185/J3 **Bitter** (cr.), Wy,US
185/J3 **Bitter Creek,** Wy,US
72/C4 **Bitterfeld,** Ger.
156/B3 **Bitterfontein,** SAfr.
190/B4 **Bitter Lake Nat'l Wild. Ref.,** NM,US
183/H1 **Bittern Lake,** Ab,Can
185/F1 **Bitterroot** (range), Id, Mt,US
90/A2 **Bitti,** It.
145/E4 **Bittou,** Burk.
127/G3 **Bitung,** Indo.
173/G3 **Bituruna,** Braz.
148/B3 **Biu,** Nga.
93/H2 **Bivolari,** Rom.
83/C6 **Bivongi,** It.
111/M9 **Biwa,** Japan
110/E3 **Biwa** (lake), Japan
191/J2 **Bixby,** Mo,US
191/G3 **Bixby,** Ok,US
149/H2 **Biyagundi,** Eth.
103/B4 **Biyalā,** Egypt
115/C4 **Biyang,** China
114/E1 **Biysk,** Rus.
197/N7 **Bizard** (isl.), Qu,Can
141/W17 **Bizerte** (Banzart), Tun.
61/M6 **Bjargtangar** (pt.), Ice.
62/E3 **Bjärnum,** Swe.
63/G9 **Bjärred,** Swe.
92/C3 **Bjelovar,** Cro.
61/F1 **Bjerkvik,** Nor.
62/C3 **Bjerringbro,** Den.
183/N1 **Bjorkdale,** Sk,Can
62/D2 **Bjørkelangen,** Nor.
62/G1 **Björklinge,** Swe.
63/S7 **Björknäs,** Swe.
62/A1 **Bjørnafjorden** (fjord), Nor.
179/S7 **Bjorne** (pen.), NW,Can
61/D3 **Bjugn,** Nor.
62/E3 **Bjuv,** Swe.
59/E1 **Blaby,** Eng,UK
92/E4 **Blace,** Yugo.
65/K3 **Błachownia,** Pol.
96/D4 **Black** (sea), Asia, Eur.
121/H2 **Black** (mts.), Bhu.
194/F2 **Black** (isl.), Mb,Can
195/K3 **Black** (bay), On,Can
195/M3 **Black** (riv.), On,Can
177/M3 **Black** (mtn.), Yk,Can
123/C1 **Black** (riv.), China
80/D2 **Black** (for.), Ger.
154/B5 **Black** (pt.), Namb.
136/D3 **Black** (pt.), N.Z.
58/A6 **Black** (pt.), Eng,UK
58/C3 **Black** (mtn.), Wal,UK
58/C3 **Black** (mts.), Wal,UK
200/B3 **Black** (riv.), Ar,US
182/G3 **Black** (mesa), Az,US
187/H4 **Black** (riv.), Az,US
205/L11 **Black** (hills), Ca,US
208/B3 **Black** (pt.), Ct,US
182/G4 **Black** (mtn.), Id,US
201/F2 **Black** (mtn.), Ky,US
202/C2 **Black** (riv.), La,US
198/D2 **Black** (lake), Mi,US
205/G5 **Black** (riv.), Mi,US
200/B3 **Black** (riv.), Mo,US
202/D2 **Black** (cr.), Ms,US
201/J3 **Black** (riv.), NC,US
187/J4 **Black** (range), NM,US
187/J4 **Black** (mesa), NM,US
208/E5 **Black** (riv.), Oh,US
190/C2 **Black** (mesa), Ok,US
206/B2 **Black** (cr.), Pa,US
201/H4 **Black** (riv.), SC,US
192/C1 **Black** (hills), SD, Wy,US
190/C3 **Black,** Tx,US
188/C3 **Black** (mtn.), Tx,US
188/D3 **Black** (mtn.), Tx,US
193/J1 **Black** (riv.), Wi,US
119/H3 **Black** (riv.), Viet.
54/D5 **Blackadder Water** (riv.), Sc,UK
134/B4 **Blackall,** Austl.
191/F2 **Black Bear** (cr.), Ok,US
203/H2 **Blackbeard I. Nat'l Wild. Ref.,** Ga,US
205/P16 **Blackberry** (cr.), Il,US
59/E3 **Black Bourton,** Eng,UK
57/F4 **Blackburn,** Eng,UK
54/C5 **Blackburn,** Sc,UK
191/H1 **Blackburn,** Mo,US
134/D4 **Blackbutt,** Austl.
184/B4 **Black Butte** (lake), Ca,US
187/F3 **Black Canyon City,** Az,US
185/K4 **Black Canyon of the Gunnison Nat'l Mon.,** Co,US
183/K3 **Black Coulee Nat'l Wild. Ref.,** Mt,US
54/B6 **Blackcraig** (hill), Sc,UK
193/K1 **Black Creek,** Wi,US
116/E4 **Black** (Da) (riv.), Viet.
123/C1 **Black** (Da) (riv.), Viet.
183/G2 **Black Diamond,** Ab,Can
205/C3 **Black Diamond,** Wa,US
59/F4 **Blackdown** (hill), Eng,UK
58/C5 **Blackdown** (hills), Eng,UK
134/C3 **Blackdown Tableland Nat'l Park,** Austl.
195/G4 **Blackduck,** Mn,US
208/E5 **Black, East Branch** (riv.), Oh,US
183/H1 **Blackfalds,** Ab,Can
185/G2 **Blackfoot,** Id,US
185/H2 **Blackfoot** (res.), Id,US
185/H2 **Blackfoot** (riv.), Id,US
183/H3 **Blackfoot,** Mt,US
183/H2 **Blackfoot Ind. Res.,** Ab,Can
183/H3 **Blackfoot Ind. Res.,** Mt,US
54/C4 **Blackford,** Sc,UK
192/B4 **Black Forest,** Co,US
70/B5 **Black Forest** (Schwarzwald) (uplands), Ger.
208/E6 **Black Fork** (riv.), Oh,US
191/G3 **Black Fork** (mtn.), Ok,US
191/G3 **Blackgum,** Ok,US
192/A3 **Blackhall** (mtn.), Wy,US
57/G2 **Blackhall Rocks,** Eng,UK
194/E4 **Black Hammer** (hill), ND,US
192/C1 **Black Hawk,** SD,US
60/A3 **Black Head** (pt.), Ire.
56/C2 **Black Head** (pt.), NI,UK
135/D2 **Blackheath,** Austl.
192/C1 **Black Hills** (caverns), SD,US
192/D1 **Black Horse,** SD,US
183/H2 **Blackie,** Ab,Can
54/B1 **Black Isle** (pen.), Sc,UK
190/E3 **Black Kettle Nat'l Grsld.,** Ok,US
189/B2 **Black Lake,** Qu,Can
191/H4 **Black Lake** (bayou), La,US
188/L7 **Blackland,** Tx,US
58/B6 **Blackmoor** (upland), Eng,UK
59/P6 **Blackmore,** Eng,UK
201/F3 **Black Mountain,** NC,US
134/B1 **Black Mountain Nat'l Park,** Austl.
185/G2 **Black Pine** (peak), Id,US
205/J10 **Black Point,** Ca,US
57/E4 **Blackpool,** Eng,UK
57/E4 **Blackpool** (arpt.), Eng,UK
154/B5 **Black Reef** (pt.), Namb.
161/G2 **Black River,** Jam.
198/E2 **Black River,** Mi,US
193/J1 **Black River Falls,** Wi,US
191/J2 **Black Rock,** Ar,US
184/D3 **Black Rock** (des.), Nv,US
207/G1 **Black Rock** (pt.), RI,US
57/F4 **Blackrod,** Eng,UK
201/G3 **Blacksburg,** SC,US
201/G2 **Blacksburg,** Va,US
98/E5 **Black Sea** (lowland), Ukr.
196/D3 **Blacks Harbour,** NB,Can
203/G2 **Blackshear,** Ga,US
203/G2 **Blackshear** (lake), Ga,US
60/D4 **Blackstairs** (mts.), Ire.
208/C1 **Blackstone,** Ma,US
208/C2 **Blackstone** (riv.), RI,US
201/H2 **Blackstone,** Va,US
195/K3 **Black Sturgeon** (riv.), On,Can
135/D1 **Black Sugarloaf** (peak), Austl.
134/G8 **Blacktown,** Austl.
196/E2 **Blackville,** NB,Can
201/G4 **Blackville,** SC,US
144/E4 **Black Volta** (riv.), Afr.
200/D4 **Black Warrior** (riv.), Al,US
200/D4 **Black Warrior, Locust Fork** (riv.), Al,US
200/D4 **Black Warrior, Mulberry Fork** (riv.), Al,US
134/C3 **Blackwater,** Austl.
60/D5 **Blackwater,** Ire.
60/C5 **Blackwater** (riv.), Ire.
60/D2 **Blackwater** (riv.), Ire.
59/G3 **Blackwater** (riv.), Eng,UK
56/B3 **Blackwater** (riv.), NI,UK
54/B3 **Blackwater** (res.), Sc,UK
202/L7 **Blackwater** (cr.), Fl,US
193/H4 **Blackwater** (riv.), Mo,US
201/J2 **Blackwater** (riv.), Va,US
190/C3 **Blackwater Draw** (stream), Tx,US
201/J1 **Blackwater Nat'l Wild. Ref.,** Md,US
191/F2 **Blackwell,** Ok,US
188/D1 **Blackwell,** Tx,US
208/E5 **Black, West Branch** (riv.), Oh,US
132/B5 **Blackwood** (riv.), Austl.
131/G1 **Blackwood** (cape), PNG
58/C3 **Blackwood,** Wal,UK
206/C4 **Blackwood,** NJ,US
66/C6 **Bladel,** Neth.
201/H3 **Bladenboro,** NC,US
206/B6 **Bladensburg,** Md,US
134/A3 **Bladensburg Nat'l Park,** Austl.
56/D2 **Bladnoch** (riv.), Sc,UK
194/A2 **Bladworth,** Sk,Can
56/E6 **Blaenau-Ffestiniog,** Wal,UK
58/C3 **Blaenavon,** Wal,UK
74/D5 **Blagnac,** Fr.
74/D5 **Blagnac** (Toulouse) (int'l arpt.), Fr.
69/E4 **Blagny,** Fr.
97/G3 **Blagodarniy,** Rus.
93/F4 **Blagoevgrad,** Bul.
109/K1 **Blagoveshchensk,** Rus.
78/D6 **Blain,** Fr.
196/D2 **Blaine,** Me,US
195/H5 **Blaine,** Mn,US
200/F2 **Blaine,** Tn,US
183/L1 **Blaine Lake,** Sk,Can
199/K2 **Blainville,** Qu,Can
79/E2 **Blainville-sur-Orne,** Fr.
193/F3 **Blair,** Ne,US
190/E3 **Blair,** Ok,US
206/C1 **Blair** (hill), Pa,US

193/J1 Blair, Wi,US
134/B3 Blair Athol, Austl.
54/C3 Blair Atholl, Sc,UK
54/C3 Blairgowrie, Sc,UK
183/G3 Blairmore, Ab,Can
184/C4 Blairsden, Ca,US
206/D2 Blairstown, NJ,US
200/F3 Blairsville, Ga,US
79/G3 Blaise (riv.), Fr.
80/A1 Blaise (riv.), Fr.
93/F2 Blaj, Rom.
146/B4 Blaka, Enneri (dry riv.), Niger
195/K3 Blake (pt.), Mi,US
203/F2 Blakely, Ga,US
199/J4 Blakely, Pa,US
191/H3 Blakely Mountain (dam), Ar,US
206/C1 Blakeslee, Pa,US
80/C3 Blamont, Fr.
82/C6 Blanc (cape), Fr.
75/G4 Blanc (mtn.), Fr.
140/A2 Blanc (cape), Mrta.
174/E3 Blanca (bay), Arg.
76/E3 Blanca, Sp.
77/E4 Blanca (coast), Sp.
187/K2 Blanca, Co,US
188/B2 Blanca (peak), Tx,US
158/B2 Blanca, Punta (pt.), Mex.
182/F3 Blanchard, Id,US
191/F3 Blanchard, Ok,US
60/D3 Blanchardstown, Ire.
193/K2 Blanchardville, Wi,US
133/G5 Blanche (cape), Austl.
132/D2 Blanche (lake), Austl.
133/H4 Blanche (lake), Austl.
82/C4 Blanche (riv.), Fr.
200/F1 Blanchester, Oh,US
165/F2 Blanchisseuse, Trin.
80/C6 Blanc, Mont (mtn.), Fr.
68/A2 Blanc Nez (cape), Fr.
172/B3 Blanco (riv.), Arg.
175/K6 Blanco (riv.), Arg.
169/F4 Blanco (riv.), Bol.
175/K8 Blanco (lake), Chile
174/C1 Blanco (riv.), Chile
161/E4 Blanco (cape), CR
156/C4 Blanco, SAfr.
187/J2 Blanco, NM,US
184/A2 Blanco (cape), Or,US
189/E2 Blanco, Tx,US
189/F3 Blanco (cr.), Tx,US
189/E2 Blanco (riv.), Tx,US
142/A5 Blanco (cape), WSah.
191/J1 Bland, Mo,US
201/G2 Bland, Va,US
208/B1 Blandford, Ma,US
58/D5 Blandford Forum, Eng,UK
187/H2 Blanding, Ut,US
77/G2 Blanes, Sp.
77/G1 Blanes, Serre de (mtn.), Fr.
124/B2 Blangkejeren, Indo.
124/B2 Blangpidie, Indo.
68/A4 Blangy-sur-Bresle, Fr.
65/G4 Blanice (riv.), Czh.
75/L2 Blanice (riv.), Czh.
68/C1 Blankenberge, Belg.
72/A4 Blankenburg, Ger.
67/G1 Blankenese, Ger.
72/D3 Blankenfelde, Ger.
69/F3 Blankenheim, Ger.
189/E2 Blanket, Tx,US
162/E5 Blanquilla (isl.), Ven.
65/J4 Blansko, Czh.
202/L7 Blanton, Fl,US
155/G2 Blantyre, Malw.
54/B5 Blantyre, Sc,UK
74/F3 Blanzy, Fr.
66/C4 Blaricum, Neth.
60/B6 Blarney, Ire.
60/B6 Blarney Castle and Stone, Ire.
81/E4 Blas, Piz (peak), Swi.
71/G4 Blatná, Czh.
92/C4 Blato, Cro.
80/D5 Blatten, Swi.
70/C6 Blau (riv.), Ger.
70/C6 Blaubeuren, Ger.
80/D2 Blauen (peak), Ger.
70/C6 Blaustein, Ger.
207/E1 Blauvelt, NY,US
73/B2 Blava (riv.), Slvk.
62/C4 Blåvands (pt.), Den.
64/E1 Blåvands Huk (pt.), Den.
78/B5 Blavet (riv.), Fr.
74/C4 Blaye, Fr.
78/C1 Blaye, The (Alderney) (arpt.), Chl,UK
135/D2 Blayney, Austl.
130/C3 Blaze (pt.), Austl.
67/H2 Bleckede, Ger.
92/B2 Bled, Slov.
62/C2 Blefjell (peak), Nor.
69/E2 Blégny, Belg.
68/C2 Bléharies, Belg.
92/B2 Bleiburg, Aus.
67/H6 Bleicherode, Ger.
81/G2 Bleick, Hohe (peak), Ger.
66/B4 Bleiswijk, Neth.
62/F3 Blekinge (co.), Swe.
68/B2 Blendecques, Fr.
67/G3 Blender, Ger.
198/F3 Blenheim, On,Can
136/C3 Blenheim, N.Z.
59/E3 Blenheim Palace, Eng,UK
69/F6 Blénod-lès-Pont-à-Mousson, Fr.
82/C4 Bléone (riv.), Fr.
84/C3 Blera, It.
82/D1 Blérancourt, Fr.
79/G6 Bléré, Fr.
66/D6 Blerick, Neth.
156/C4 Blesberg (peak), SAfr.
189/F3 Blessing, Tx,US
60/D3 Blessington, Ire.
53/N8 Bletchingley, Eng,UK
59/F2 Bletchley, Eng,UK
80/B4 Bletterans, Fr.
153/G2 Bleus (mts.), Zaire
191/H4 Blevins, Ar,US
59/E3 Blewbury, Eng,UK
188/D3 Blewett, Tx,US
180/D3 Blewett Falls (lake), NC,US
141/S15 Blida, Alg.
141/S15 Blida (wilaya), Alg.
57/G5 Blidworth, Eng,UK
71/E2 Blieloch-Stausee (res.), Ger.
69/G5 Blies (riv.), Fr.
69/G5 Blies (riv.), Ger.
69/G5 Bliesbruck, Fr.
69/G5 Blieskastel, Ger.
139/Y18 Bligh Water (sound), Fiji
125/D4 Blik (mt.), Phil.
182/E2 Blind Bay, BC,Can
198/E1 Blind River, On,Can
133/H4 Blinman, Austl.
144/D4 Blinndio, Mali
81/E5 Blinnenhorn (peak), Swi.
185/F2 Bliss, Id,US
185/F2 Bliss (dam), Id,US
196/D2 Blissfield, NB,Can
198/E4 Blissfield, Mi,US
124/F5 Blitar, Indo.
57/G6 Blithfield (res.), Eng,UK
145/F4 Blitta, Togo
137/L Blizzard (peak), Ant.
207/G1 Block (isl.), RI,US
208/C3 Block (isl.), RI,US
196/E3 Block House, NS,Can
208/C3 Block I. Coast Guard Sta., RI,US
208/C3 Block I. Nat'l Wild. Ref., RI,US
208/C3 Block Island (sound), US
208/C3 Block Island (arpt.), RI,US
208/C3 Block Island (New Shoreham), RI,US
80/D2 Blodelsheim, Fr.
66/B4 Bloemendaal, Neth.
156/D3 Bloemfontein, SAfr.
156/D2 Bloemhof, SAfr.
156/D2 Bloemhofdam (res.), SAfr.
79/G5 Blois, Fr.
66/C3 Blokker, Neth.
66/C3 Blokzijl, Neth.
67/E1 Blomberg, Ger.
67/G5 Blomberg, Ger.
62/G3 Blomstermåla, Swe.
80/C5 Blonay, Swi.
61/N6 Blönduós, Ice.
124/G5 Blongas, Indo.
183/H3 Blood Indian Res., Ab,Can
195/G2 Bloodvein (riv.), Mb,Can
195/G2 Bloodvein (riv.), On,Can
194/F2 Bloodvein River, Mb,Can
55/G9 Bloody Foreland (pt.), Ire.
189/G1 Bloomburg, Tx,US
193/J1 Bloomer, Wi,US
197/L1 Bloomfield, Nf,Can
208/B2 Bloomfield, Ct,US
193/H3 Bloomfield, Ia,US
198/C5 Bloomfield, In,US
200/C2 Bloomfield, Mo,US
183/M4 Bloomfield, Mt,US
207/D2 Bloomfield, NJ,US
187/J2 Bloomfield, NM,US
205/F6 Bloomfield Hills, Mi,US
134/B1 Bloomfield River Abor. Community, Austl.
202/L8 Bloomingdale, Fl,US
201/G4 Bloomingdale, Ga,US
205/P16 Bloomingdale, Il,US
207/H7 Bloomingdale, NJ,US
208/G7 Bloomingdale, Oh,US
189/F1 Blooming Grove, Tx,US
193/H2 Blooming Prairie, Mn,US
204/C2 Bloomington, Ca,US
185/H2 Bloomington, Id,US
193/K3 Bloomington, Il,US
198/C5 Bloomington, In,US
195/H5 Bloomington, Mn,US
189/F3 Bloomington, Tx,US
200/E2 Bloomington Springs, Tn,US
206/B1 Bloomsburg, Pa,US
206/C2 Bloomsbury, NJ,US
124/E4 Blora, Indo.
199/H4 Blossburg, Pa,US
80/D2 Blotzheim, Fr.
155/F4 Blouberg (peak), SAfr.
156/L10 Bloubergstrand, SAfr.
203/F2 Blountstown, Fl,US
200/D3 Blountsville, Al,US
201/F2 Blountville, Tn,US
71/G3 Blovice, Czh.
137/L Blowaway (peak), Ant.
201/G2 Blowing Rock, NC,US
59/E3 Bloxham, Eng,UK
58/E1 Bloxwich, Eng,UK
71/G2 Blšanka (riv.), Czh.
81/F3 Bludenz, Aus.
196/D2 Blue (mt.), Can
116/B4 Blue (mtn.), India
191/G3 Blue (mtn.), Ar,US
187/H4 Blue, Az,US
190/A1 Blue (riv.), Co,US
199/L2 Blue (mts.), Me,US
194/D4 Blue (hill), ND,US
196/B3 Blue (mtn.), NH,US
199/J3 Blue (mtn.), NY,US
191/F3 Blue (riv.), Ok,US
184/D1 Blue (mts.), Or, Wa,US
199/G4 Blue (hill), Pa,US
195/J5 Blue (hills), Wi,US
203/G2 Blue and Gray Museum, Ga,US
198/D5 Blue Ash, Oh,US
185/H3 Bluebell, Ut,US
203/H4 Blue Cypress (lake), Fl,US
193/G2 Blue Earth, Mn,US
193/G2 Blue Earth (riv.), Mn,US
191/H2 Blue Eye, Mo,US
201/G2 Bluefield, Va,US
201/G2 Bluefield, WV,US
161/F4 Bluefields, Nic.
161/F4 Bluefields (bay), Nic.
200/E1 Blue Grass (int'l arpt.), Ky,US
200/E2 Blue Grass-Lexington Army Dep., Ky,US
54/C1 Blue Head (pt.), Sc,UK
196/C3 Blue Hill, Me,US
192/E3 Blue Hill, Ne,US
205/Q16 Blue Island, Il,US
184/D2 Bluejoint (lake), Or,US
155/E2 Blue Lagoon Nat'l Park, Zam.
184/B3 Blue Lake, Ca,US
134/D4 Blue Lake Nat'l Park, Austl.
206/B3 Blue Marsh (lake), Pa,US
185/K4 Blue Mesa (dam), Co,US
190/A1 Blue Mesa (res.), Co,US
191/G1 Blue Mound, Ks,US
188/K7 Blue Mound, Tx,US
161/G2 Blue Mountain (peak), Jam.
200/C3 Blue Mountain, Ms,US
206/B3 Blue Mountain (ridge), Pa,US
199/J3 Blue Mountain Lake, NY,US
135/D2 Blue Mountains Nat'l Park, Austl.
131/D3 Blue Mud (bay), Austl.
149/G2 Blue Nile (riv.), Eth., Sudan
180/E2 Bluenose (lake), NW,Can
185/F1 Blue Nose (mtn.), Mt,US
191/F1 Blue Rapids, Ks,US
201/G2 Blue Ridge (mts.), US
200/E3 Blue Ridge, Ga,US
201/G2 Blue Ridge Pkwy., NC, Va,US
182/E1 Blue River, BC,Can
190/A1 Blue River, Co,US
184/B1 Blue River, Or,US
191/G1 Blue Springs, Mo,US
193/F3 Blue Springs, Ne,US
191/F2 Bluestem (lake), Ok,US
201/G2 Bluestone (lake), WV,US
187/J3 Bluewater, NM,US
134/C3 Bluff, Austl.
132/C5 Bluff (peak), Austl.
132/B3 Bluff (pt.), Austl.
136/B4 Bluff, N.Z.
201/J3 Bluff (pt.), NC,US
191/F2 Bluff (cr.), Ok, Ks,US
187/H2 Bluff, Ut,US
191/H4 Bluff City, Ar,US
191/F2 Bluff City, Ks,US
189/E1 Bluff Dale, Tx,US
130/B4 Bluff Face (range), Austl.
191/H3 Bluffton, Ar,US
198/D4 Bluffton, In,US
198/E4 Bluffton, Oh,US
189/F1 Blum, Tx,US
81/E2 Blumberg, Ger.
173/G3 Blumenau, Braz.
67/G2 Blumenthal, Ger.
80/D5 Blümlisalp (peak), Swi.
86/D1 Blumone, Cornone di (peak), It.
192/E1 Blunt, SD,US
182/D2 Blustry (mtn.), BC,Can
184/C2 Bly, Or,US
205/A1 Blyn, Wa,US
133/H5 Blyth, Austl.
57/G1 Blyth, Eng,UK
57/G5 Blyth, Eng,UK
59/H2 Blyth (riv.), Eng,UK
54/C5 Blyth Bridge, Sc,UK
57/F6 Blythe (riv.), Eng,UK
186/E4 Blythe, Ca,US
201/F4 Blythe, Ga,US
57/F6 Blythe Bridge, Eng,UK
205/G7 Blythewood, On,Can
200/C3 Blytheville, Ar,US
123/D4 B'nom M'hai (peak), Viet.
62/C2 Bø, Nor.
144/C5 Bo, SLeo.
125/C2 Boac, Phil.
160/E3 Boaco, Nic.
170/D4 Boa Esperança, Braz.
167/E4 Boa Esperança (res.), Braz.
115/C4 Bo'ai, China
144/C4 Boajibu, SLeo.
199/H4 Boalsburg, Pa,US
131/G1 Boana, PNG
127/G4 Boano (isl.), Indo.
166/B5 Boa Nova, Braz.
191/G3 Board Camp, Ar,US
198/G5 Boardman, Oh,US
184/D1 Boardman, Or,US
184/D1 Boardman Nav. Ra., Or,US
179/H2 Boas (riv.), NW,Can
167/G4 Boa Viagem, Braz.
166/A2 Boa Vista, Braz.
166/A2 Boa Vista (int'l arpt.), Braz.
140/K10 Boa Vista (isl.), CpV.
164/C3 Boavita, Col.
200/D3 Boaz, Al,US
73/B5 Boba, Hun.
135/C2 Bobadah, Austl.
117/F4 Bobai, China
141/G6 Bobaomby (cape), Madg.
72/C4 Bobbau, Ger.
118/D4 Bobbili, India
86/C3 Bobbio, It.
199/G2 Bobcaygeon, On,Can
153/F2 Bobenge, Zaire
70/B3 Bobenheim-Roxheim, Ger.
68/B6 Bobigny, Fr.
153/E2 Bobila, Zaire
70/D6 Bobingen, Ger.
70/C5 Böblingen, Ger.
144/D4 Bobo Dioulasso, Burk.
155/F4 Bobonong, Bots.
92/F4 Boboshevo, Bul.
92/D4 Bobotov Kuk (peak), Yugo.
92/F4 Bobovdol, Bul.
63/N4 Bobr, Bela.
65/H3 Bóbr (riv.), Pol.
73/A1 Bobrava (riv.), Czh.
98/G3 Bobrinets, Ukr.
92/C3 Bobrka, Ukr.
99/L2 Bobrov, Rus.
92/F8 Bobrovitsa, Ukr.
95/K3 Bobrovskoye, Rus.
96/D1 Bobruysk, Bela.
191/G4 Bob Sandlin (lake), Tx,US
149/G3 Bobuk, Sudan
162/D4 Bobures, Ven.
157/H8 Boby (peak), Madg.
164/D2 Boca de Aroa, Ven.
164/C2 Boca del Grita, Ven.
165/E2 Boca del Pao, Ven.
164/B3 Boca del Pepé, Col.
159/F5 Boca del Río, Mex.
169/E3 Boca do Acre, Braz.
203/G4 Boca Grande, Fl,US
167/F4 Bocaina, Braz.
171/M7 Bocaina (mts.), Braz.
77/E3 Bocairente, Sp.
170/E3 Bocaiúva, Braz.
144/D5 Bocanda, IvC.
148/B4 Bocaranga, CAfr.
181/K6 Boca Raton, Fl,US
202/P7 Boca Raton, Fl,US
203/H4 Boca Raton, Fl,US
161/E3 Bocay, Nic.
161/E3 Bocay (riv.), Nic.
83/C4 Bocchigliero, It.
155/F4 Bochem, SAfr.
160/C2 Bochil, Mex.
65/L4 Bochnia, Pol.
69/E1 Bocholt, Belg.
66/D5 Bocholt, Ger.
71/G2 Bochov, Czh.
67/E6 Bochum, Ger.
71/F1 Bockau, Ger.
67/H4 Bockenem, Ger.
69/H4 Bockenheim an der Weinstrasse, Ger.
67/F2 Bockhorn, Ger.
59/G3 Bocking, Eng,UK
152/B2 Bococo, EqG.
154/B2 Bocoio, Ang.
164/D2 Boconó, Ven.
69/D3 Bocq (riv.), Belg.
148/C4 Boda, CAfr.
62/F3 Bodafors, Swe.
135/D3 Bodalla, Austl.
101/M4 Bodaybo, Rus.
191/H4 Bodcau (cr.), Ar, La,,US
191/H4 Bodcaw, Ar,US
54/E2 Boddam, Sc,UK
132/C5 Boddington, Austl.
72/B4 Bode (riv.), Ger.
184/B4 Bodega (bay), Ca,US
66/B4 Bodegraven, Neth.
148/C1 Bodélé (reg.), Chad
61/G2 Boden, Swe.
70/B3 Bodenheim, Ger.
71/F6 Bodenkirchen, Ger.
71/G4 Bodenmais, Ger.
81/F2 Bodensee (Constance) (lake), Ger., Swi.
67/H3 Bodenteich, Ger.
60/B2 Boderg, Lough (lake), Ire.
145/G4 Bode-Sadu, Nga.
186/C3 Bodfish, Ca,US
118/C4 Bodhan, India
121/E3 Bodh Gaya, India
201/K3 Bodie (isl.), NC
122/F3 Bodināyakkanūr, India
199/H4 Bodines, Pa,US
81/E5 Bodio, Swi.
149/H4 Bodītī, Eth.
206/B5 Bodkin (pt.), Md,US
58/B6 Bodmin, Eng,UK
58/B5 Bodmin Moor (upland), Eng,UK
61/E2 Bodø, Nor.
167/G4 Bodocó, Braz.
108/C2 Bodonchiyn (riv.), Mong.
92/E1 Bodrog (riv.), Hun.
104/A2 Bodrum, Turk.
123/D4 Bo Duc, Viet.
92/E1 Bódvaszilas, Hun.
80/C5 Boëge, Fr.
156/A2 Boegoeberg (peak), Namb.
66/C5 Boekel, Neth.
153/E3 Boende, Zaire
189/E3 Boerne, Tx,US
200/B4 Boeuf (riv.), La,US
144/B4 Boffa, Gui.
153/G2 Boga, Zaire
151/B1 Bogal, Lach (dry riv.), Kenya
202/D2 Bogalusa, La,US
135/C1 Bogan (riv.), Austl.
145/E3 Bogandé, Burk.
135/C2 Bogan Gate, Austl.
148/C4 Bogangolo, CAfr.
134/B3 Bogantungan, Austl.
191/H1 Bogard, Mo,US
201/F4 Bogart, Ga,US
191/G4 Bogata, Tx,US
92/D3 Bogatić, Yugo.
97/J1 Bogatoye, Rus.
65/H3 Bogatynia, Pol.
97/J2 Bogatyrëvo, Kaz.
104/C1 Boğazkale-Alacahöyük Nat'l Park, Turk.
104/C1 Boğazkale-Alacahöyük Park, Turk.
104/C2 Boğazlıyan, Turk.
152/D2 Bogbonga, Zaire
114/E5 Bogcang (riv.), China
108/E2 Bogd, Mong.
108/B3 Bogda (mts.), China
108/B3 Bogda (peak), China
114/E3 Bogda Feng (peak), China
92/F5 Bogdanci, Macd.
97/G4 Bogdanovka, Geo.
71/F5 Bogen, Ger.
94/C1 Bogen, Nor.
156/A2 Bogenfels, Namb.
109/K2 Bogenli, China
62/D4 Bogense, Den.
201/G3 Boger City, NC,US
63/S7 Bogesundslandet (reg. park), Swe.
135/D1 Boggabilla, Austl.
135/D1 Boggabri, Austl.
60/A5 Boggeragh (mts.), Ire.
162/F3 Boggy (peak), Anti.
73/B6 Boglárlelle, Hun.
86/C4 Bogliasco, It.
202/D2 Bogne Homo (riv.), Ms,US
59/F5 Bognor Regis, Eng,UK
69/D4 Bogny-sur-Meuse, Fr.
148/B3 Bogo, Camr.
125/D3 Bogo, Phil.
99/H2 Bogodukhov, Ukr.
150/B4 Bogol Manyo, Eth.
135/C3 Bogong (peak), Austl.
135/C3 Bogong Nat'l Park, Austl.
124/D4 Bogor, Indo.
153/G2 Bogoro, Zaire
164/C3 Bogotá (cap.), Col.
167/L8 Bogotá (riv.), Col.
207/J8 Bogota, NJ,US
92/E5 Bogovinje, Macd.
121/G3 Bogra, Bang.
121/G3 Bogra (dist.), Bang.
56/E1 Bogrie (hill), Sc,UK
99/L3 Boguchar, Rus.
144/B2 Bogué, Mrta.
190/E1 Bogue, Ks,US
202/C2 Bogue Chitto (riv.), La,US
202/C2 Bogue Chitto, Ms,US
148/C4 Boguila, CAfr.
63/P4 Bogushëvsk, Bela.
98/F3 Boguslav, Ukr.
115/D3 Bohai (bay), China
115/E3 Bohai (str.), China
115/D3 Bo Hai (Chihli) (gulf), China
68/C4 Bohain-en-Vermandois, Fr.
71/G3 Bohemia (reg.), Czh.
71/G4 Bohemian Forest (uplands), Ger.
60/A5 Boherboy, Ire.
145/F5 Bohicon, Ben.
72/C5 Böhlen, Ger.
70/B4 Böhl-Iggelheim, Ger.
72/C5 Böhlitz-Ehrenberg, Ger.
67/G3 Böhme (riv.), Ger.
70/C5 Böhmenkirch, Ger.
67/F4 Bohmte, Ger.
205/P14 Bohners Lake, Wi,US
125/C3 Bohol (isl.), Phil.
125/C3 Bohol (str.), Phil.
92/C2 Böhönye, Hun.
116/E5 Bo Ho Su, Viet.
114/E3 Bohu, China
90/D2 Boiano, It.
196/D2 Boiestown, NB,Can
79/H5 Boigny-sur-Bionne, Fr.
206/A3 Boiling Springs, Pa,US
201/G3 Boiling Springs, SC,US
152/D3 Boimbo, Zaire
116/B4 Boinu (riv.), Burma, India
171/F2 Boipeba (isl.), Braz.
76/A1 Boiro, Sp.
170/C3 Bois (riv.), Braz.
197/K2 Bois (isl.), Nf,Can
198/D2 Bois Blanc (isl.), Mi,US
80/C4 Bois-d'Amont, Fr.
53/S10 Bois-d'Arcy, Fr.
197/N6 Bois-des-Filion, Qu,Can
184/E2 Boise (cap.), Id,US
184/F2 Boise (mts.), Id,US
184/E2 Boise (riv.), Id,US
190/C2 Boise City, Ok,US
68/A5 Bois-Guillaume, Fr.
194/D3 Boissevain, Mb,Can
201/G2 Boissevain, Va,US
53/S9 Boissy-l'Aillerie, Fr.
53/T10 Boissy-Saint-Léger, Fr.
67/H2 Boizenburg, Ger.
85/E5 Bojano, It.
125/C1 Bojeador (cape), Phil.
151/C1 Boji (plain), Kenya
73/B1 Bojkovice, Czh.
105/J2 Bojnūrd, Iran
124/E4 Bojonegoro, Indo.
145/G5 Boju, Nga.
145/H5 Boju Ega, Nga.
131/G1 Bok, PNG
152/D3 Bokala, Zaire
153/E2 Bokapo II, Zaire
118/E3 Bokaro Steel City, India
127/F3 Bokat, Indo.
153/E2 Bokata, Zaire
152/D3 Bokatola, Zaire
191/F3 Bokchito, Ok,US
144/B4 Boké, Gui.
144/B4 Boké (comm.), Gui.
153/E3 Bokele, Zaire
153/E2 Bokengo, Zaire
108/E1 Bokhan, Rus.
151/B1 Bokhol (plain), Kenya
62/A2 Boknafjorden (fjord), Nor.
152/C4 Boko, Congo
121/H3 Boko, India
114/D2 Boko, Kaz.
152/D2 Bokode, Zaire
151/B1 Bokol (peak), Kenya
127/J4 Bokondini, Indo.
148/C2 Bokoro, Chad
152/C4 Boko Songo, Congo
152/E3 Bokote, Zaire
123/B4 Bokpyin, Burma
156/E2 Boksburg, SAfr.
156/C2 Bokspits, Bots.
203/H4 Bok Tower, Fl,US
202/M8 Bok Tower Gdns., Fl,US
153/E3 Bokungu, Zaire
148/B2 Bol, Chad
148/C3 Bola, Bahr (dry riv.), Chad
144/B4 Bolama, GBis.
153/E2 Bolama, Zaire
107/J3 Bolān (pass), Pak.
158/E4 Bolaños, Mex.
76/D3 Bolaños de Calatrava, Sp.
93/H5 Bolayır, Turk.
79/F1 Bolbec, Fr.
193/G3 Bolckow, Mo,US
73/C6 Bölcske, Hun.
105/G4 Boldājī, Iran
93/H3 Boldeşti-Scăeni, Rom.
57/G2 Boldon, Eng,UK
114/D3 Bole, China
149/H3 Bole (int'l arpt.), Eth.
145/E4 Bole, Gha.
98/B3 Bolekhov, Ukr.
152/D3 Boleko, Zaire
130/A2 Boleng (peak), Indo.
191/H3 Boles, Ar,US
65/H3 Bolesł awiec, Pol.
191/F3 Boley, Ok,US
145/E4 Bolgatanga, Gha.
98/E5 Bolgrad, Ukr.
109/L2 Boli, China
153/E3 Bolia, Zaire
61/G2 Boliden, Swe.
200/C4 Boligee, Al,US
125/B1 Bolinao, Phil.
125/B1 Bolinao (cape), Phil.
189/G3 Boling, Tx,US
205/P16 Bolingbrook, Il,US
174/E3 Bolívar, Arg.
169/E4 Bolívar, Bol.
164/B3 Bolívar, Col.
164/C2 Bolívar (dept.), Col.
164/A4 Bolívar, Ecu.
164/B5 Bolívar (prov.), Ecu.
168/B2 Bolívar, Peru
191/H2 Bolivar, Mo,US
208/F6 Bolivar, Oh,US
200/C3 Bolivar, Tn,US
189/F1 Bolivar, Tx,US
189/G3 Bolivar (pen.), Tx,US
163/B2 Bolívar (peak), Ven.
165/E3 Bolívar (state), Ven.
165/F3 Bolívar, Cerro (mtn.), Ven.
164/D2 Bolívar, Pico (peak), Ven.
163/C4 Bolivia
201/H3 Bolivia, NC,US
96/F1 Bolkhov, Rus.
86/C1 Bollate, It.
69/F4 Bollendorf, Ger.
82/A4 Bollène, Fr.
80/D4 Bolligen, Swi.
57/F5 Bollin (riv.), Eng,UK
57/F5 Bollington, Eng,UK
63/S7 Bollmora, Swe.
62/G1 Bollnäs, Swe.
134/B5 Bollon, Austl.
76/B4 Bollullos Par del Condado, Sp.
62/E3 Bolmen (lake), Swe.
59/F5 Bolney, Eng,UK
97/H4 Bolnisi, Geo.
152/D3 Bolo, Zaire
152/D3 Bolobo, Zaire
87/E4 Bologna, It.
87/E3 Bologna (prov.), It.
80/B1 Bologne, Fr.
168/C2 Bolognesi, Peru
168/C3 Bolognesi, Peru
94/G4 Bologoye, Rus.
152/D2 Bolomba, Zaire
153/E3 Bolombo, Zaire
153/E3 Bolombo (riv.), Zaire
109/M2 Bolon', Rus.
109/M2 Bolon' (lake), Rus.
160/D2 Bolonchén de Rejón, Mex.
152/C5 Bolongongo, Ang.
154/B2 Bolonguera, Ang.
93/H2 Bolotino, Mol.
148/C3 Bolo-Vassako Nature Rsv., CAfr.
123/D3 Bolovens (plat.), Laos
168/D3 Bolpebra, Bol.
121/F4 Bolpur, India
84/B2 Bolsena, It.
84/B2 Bolsena (lake), It.
63/J4 Bol'shakovo, Rus.
99/H4 Bol'shaya Belozërka, Ukr.
65/N2 Bol'shaya Breëstovitsa, Bela.
97/J1 Bol'shaya Chernigovka, Rus.
97/J3 Bol'shaya Damba, Kaz.
97/K2 Bol'shaya Khobda (riv.), Kaz.
97/K1 Bol'shaya Kinel' (riv.), Rus.
95/P2 Bol'shaya Rogovaya (riv.), Rus.
95/M4 Bol'shaya Sosnova, Rus.
95/N2 Bol'shaya Synya (riv.), Rus.
109/L2 Bol'shaya Ussurka (riv.), Rus.
99/H4 Bol'shaya Znamenka, Ukr.
96/D1 Bol'shevik, Bela.
101/L2 Bol'shevik (isl.), Rus.
95/M2 Bol'shezemel'skaya (tundra), Rus.
100/F2 Bol'shoy Bolvanskiy Nos (pt.), Rus.
95/K5 Bol'shoye Boldino, Rus.
95/K5 Bol'shoye Nagatkino, Rus.
99/H2 Bol'shoye Soldatskoye, Rus.
97/H2 Bol'shoy Irgiz (riv.), Rus.
94/H3 Bol'shoy Kuganavolok, Rus.
101/Q2 Bol'shoy Lyakhovskiy (isl.), Rus.
95/N4 Bol'shoy Ut, Rus.
97/J2 Bol'shoy Uzen' (riv.), Kaz., Rus.
108/D1 Bol'shoy Yenisey (riv.), Rus.
199/G2 Bolsover, On,Can
57/G5 Bolsover, Eng,UK
66/C2 Bolsward, Neth.
77/F1 Boltaña, Sp.
58/C6 Bolt Head (pt.), Wal,UK
80/D4 Boltigen, Swi.
197/R8 Bolton, On,Can
57/F4 Bolton, Eng,UK
208/B2 Bolton, Ct,US
208/C1 Bolton, Ma,US
57/G4 Bolton Abbey, Eng,UK
93/K5 Bolu, Turk.
93/K5 Bolu (prov.), Turk.
61/M6 Bolungavik, Ice.
54/F11 Bolus Head (pt.), Ire.
104/B2 Bolvadin, Turk.
92/D3 Bóly, Hun.
93/H4 Bolyarovo, Bul.
81/H5 Bolzano (Bozen), It.
81/H4 Bolzano-Bozen (prov.), It.
152/C4 Boma, Zaire
135/D2 Bomaderry, Austl.
153/E2 Bomaneh, Zaire
154/B2 Bomba, Ang.
152/D2 Bombakabo, Zaire
135/D3 Bombala, Austl.
118/B4 Bombay, India
199/J5 Bombay Hook Nat'l Wild. Ref., De,US
206/C5 Bombay Hook Nat'l Wild. Ref., De,US
127/H4 Bomberai (pen.), Indo.
153/H2 Bombo, Ugan.
153/E2 Bomboma, Zaire
153/F2 Bombombi, Zaire
148/B2 Bomboyo, Chad
171/F1 Bom Conselho, Braz.
170/D3 Bom Despacho, Braz.
116/B2 Bomi, China
144/C5 Bomi, Libr.
153/F2 Bomili, Zaire
170/B3 Bom Jardim de Goiás, Braz.
170/D4 Bom Jardim de Minas, Braz.
152/C5 Bom Jesus, Ang.
167/E5 Bom Jesus, Braz.
167/H4 Bom Jesus, Braz.
171/E1 Bom Jesus da Gurguéia (mts.), Braz.
171/E2 Bom Jesus da Lapa, Braz.
170/C3 Bom Jesus de Goiás, Braz.
171/E4 Bom Jesus do Itabapoana, Braz.
171/K8 Bom Jesus dos Perdões, Braz.
67/G3 Bomlitz, Ger.
62/A2 Bømlo (isl.), Nor.
153/F2 Bomokandi (riv.), Zaire
152/D2 Bomongo, Zaire
170/D4 Bom Sucesso, Braz.
149/E4 Bomu (riv.), Zaire
90/B4 Bon (cape), Tun.
177/K3 Bona (mt.), Ak,US
105/J4 Bonāb, Iran
152/B1 Bonabéri, Camr.
81/F4 Bonaduz, Swi.
201/J2 Bon Air, Va,US
162/D4 Bonaire (isl.), NAnt.
135/E1 Bonalbo, Austl.
160/D2 Bonampak (ruins), Mex.
190/A1 Bonanza, Co,US
184/C2 Bonanza, Or,US
185/J3 Bonanza, Ut,US
182/D3 Bonanza (peak), Wa,US
162/D3 Bonao, DRep.
130/B3 Bonaparte (arch.), Austl.
182/D2 Bonaparte (riv.), BC,Can
182/E3 Bonaparte (mt.), Wa,US
177/F3 Bonasila (mtn.), Ak,US
196/E1 Bonaventure, Qu,Can
196/E1 Bonaventure (riv.), Qu,Can
197/L1 Bonavista, Nf,Can
197/L1 Bonavista (bay), Nf,Can
197/L1 Bonavista (cape), Nf,Can
190/B2 Boncarbo, Co,US
79/E4 Bonchamp-lès-Laval, Fr.
54/D6 Bonchester Bridge, Sc,UK
80/D3 Boncourt, Swi.
185/K4 Bond, Co,US
97/G1 Bondari, Rus.
87/E3 Bondeno, It.
134/H8 Bondi, Austl.
153/E2 Bondo, Zaire
125/C2 Bondoc (pen.), Phil.
144/E4 Bondoukou, IvC.
124/F4 Bondowoso, Indo.
208/B1 Bondsville, Ma,US
193/K1 Bonduel, Wi,US
127/F4 Bone (gulf), Indo.
127/F4 Bonebone, Indo.
85/E4 Bonefro, It.
194/E4 Bone Hill Nat'l Wild. Ref., ND,US
67/E5 Bönen, Ger.
74/D4 Bon-Encontre, Fr.
127/F5 Bonerate (isls.), Indo.
54/C4 Bo'ness, Sc,UK
192/E2 Bonesteel, SD,US
172/B3 Bonete (peak), Arg.
199/G1 Bonfield, On,Can
80/D3 Bonfol, Swi.
202/D2 Bonfouca, La,US
114/F5 Bong (lake), China
144/C5 Bong (co.), Libr.
144/C5 Bong (range), Libr.
154/C2 Bonga, Ang.
149/H4 Bonga, Eth.
125/C2 Bongabong, Phil.
121/H2 Bongaigaon, India
153/E2 Bongandanga, Zaire
127/E2 Bongao, Phil.
125/B4 Bonggaw, Phil.
125/B5 Bonggi (isl.), Indo.
126/E2 Bonggi (isl.), Malay.
127/F4 Bongka (riv.), Indo.
152/E2 Bongo, Zaire
153/E4 Bongo, Zaire
157/H7 Bongolava (uplands), Madg.
140/D3 Bongor, Chad
148/D3 Bongos, Massif des (plat.), CAfr.
148/D4 Bongou (riv.), CAfr.
144/D5 Bongouanou, IvC.
123/E3 Bong Son, Viet.
191/F4 Bonham, Tx,US
68/D1 Bonheiden, Belg.
54/B5 Bonhill, Sc,UK
80/D1 Bonhomme, Col du (pass), Fr.
145/E3 Boni, Mali
90/A2 Bonifacio, Fr.
90/A2 Bonifacio (str.), Fr., It.
203/F2 Bonifay, Fl,US
80/D4 Bönigen, Swi.
138/D2 Bonin (isls.), Japan
151/C2 Boni Nat'l Rsv., Kenya
187/H4 Bonita, Az,US
204/C5 Bonita, Ca,US
189/J1 Bonita, La,US
203/H4 Bonita Springs, Fl,US
170/A4 Bonito, Braz.
160/E3 Bonito (peak), Hon.
167/G4 Bonito de Santa Fé, Braz.
124/C3 Bonjol, Indo.
69/G2 Bonn, Ger.
75/G1 Bonn/Cologne (int'l arpt.), Ger.
81/E2 Bonndorf im Schwarzwald, Ger.
82/B3 Bonne (riv.), Fr.
201/H4 Bonneau, SC,US
53/S11 Bonnelles, Fr.
182/F3 Bonners Ferry, Id,US
80/C5 Bonne-sur-Ménoge, Fr.
194/F2 Bonnet (lake), Mb,Can
79/F4 Bonnétable, Fr.
200/B2 Bonne Terre, Mo,US
82/C4 Bonnette, Col de la (pass), Fr.
53/T10 Bonneuil-sur-Marne, Fr.
79/G4 Bonneval, Fr.
80/C5 Bonneville, Fr.
184/C1 Bonneville (dam), Or, Wa,US
205/C3 Bonney Lake, Wa,US
200/C1 Bonnie, Il,US
201/H3 Bonnie Doone, NC,US
68/A5 Bonnières-sur-Seine, Fr.
82/B5 Bonnieux, Fr.
70/C4 Bönnigheim, Ger.
145/G5 Bonny, Nga.
54/C5 Bonnybridge, Sc,UK
201/F2 Bonnyman, Ky,US
54/C5 Bonnyrigg, Sc,UK
178/E3 Bonnyville, Ab,Can
78/C5 Bono, Fr.
191/J3 Bono, Ar,US
90/A2 Bonorva, It.
204/C4 Bonsall, Ca,US
202/E2 Bon Secour, Al,US
202/E2 Bon Secour (bay), Al,US
80/C5 Bons-en-Chablais, Fr.
127/E3 Bontang, Indo.
156/C4 Bontberg (peak), SAfr.
156/C4 Bontebok Nat'l Park, SAfr.
127/E5 Bonthain, Indo.
144/B5 Bonthe, SLeo.
117/J5 Bontoc, Phil.
127/F5 Bontomatane, Indo.
189/H2 Bon Wier, Tx,US
145/E5 Bonyeri, Gha.
92/D2 Bonyhád, Hun.
137/J Bonzare (coast), Ant.
190/D2 Booker, Tx,US
201/H2 Booker T. Washington Nat'l Mon., Va,US
144/C4 Boola, Gui.
132/B2 Boolaloo, Austl.
135/C2 Booligal, Austl.
68/D1 Boom, Belg.
135/D1 Boomi, Austl.
190/B1 Boone, Co,US
193/H2 Boone, Ia,US
193/H2 Boone (riv.), Ia,US
201/G2 Boone, NC,US
201/F2 Boone (dam), Tn,US
191/H3 Booneville, Ar,US
200/F2 Booneville, Ky,US
200/C3 Booneville, Ms,US
199/F5 Boonsboro, Md,US
206/D2 Boonton, NJ,US
108/D2 Bööntsagaan (lake), Mong.
184/B4 Boonville, Ca,US
200/D1 Boonville, In,US
191/H1 Boonville, Mo,US
199/J3 Boonville, NY,US
169/E5 Boopi (riv.), Bol.
132/D4 Boorabbin Nat'l Park, Austl.
150/B3 Boorama, Som.
131/D4 Booroloola Abor. Land, Austl.
135/C1 Booroondara (peak), Austl.
135/C2 Booroorban, Austl.
135/D2 Boorowa, Austl.
68/A5 Boos, Fr.
70/D6 Boos, Ger.
64/F1 Boostedt, Ger.
191/H3 Booster, Ar,US
131/G2 Boot (reef), PNG
137/D Boothby (cape), Ant.
178/G1 Boothia (gulf), NW,Can
178/G1 Boothia (pen.), NW,Can
186/C2 Bootjack, Ca,US
57/E5 Bootle, Eng,UK
152/B3 Booué, Gabon
145/F5 Bopa, Ben.
70/D5 Bopfingen, Ger.
123/B3 Bo Phloi, Thai.
156/D2 Bophuthatswana (aut. rep.), SAfr.
153/E2 Bopili, Zaire
144/C5 Bopolu, Libr.
69/G3 Boppard, Ger.
135/C1 Boppy (peak), Austl.
171/E1 Boqueirão (hills), Braz.
172/D1 Boquerón (dept.), Par.
174/C4 Boquete (peak), Arg.
158/D3 Boquilla (res.), Mex.
188/C3 Boquillas del Carmen, Mex.
71/F3 Bor, Czh.
95/K4 Bor, Rus.
149/F4 Bor, Sudan
104/C2 Bor, Turk.
92/F3 Bor, Yugo.
139/K6 Bora Bora (isl.), FrPol.
123/C2 Borabu, Thai.
188/B2 Boracho (peak), Tx,US
185/G1 Borah (peak), Id,US
62/E3 Borås, Swe.
105/G4 Borāzjān, Iran
166/B4 Borba, Braz.
76/B3 Borba, Port.
86/B3 Borbera (riv.), It.
84/D2 Borbona, It.
74/D3 Borbonnais (hist. reg.), Fr.
86/B3 Borbore (riv.), It.
167/G4 Borborema (plat.), Braz.
92/E3 Borča, Yugo.
67/F5 Borchen, Ger.
137/M Borchgrevink (coast), Ant.
97/G4 Borçka, Turk.
66/D4 Borculo, Neth.
133/H5 Borda (cape), Austl.
171/K7 Borda da Mata, Braz.
74/C4 Bordeaux, Fr.
74/C4 Bordeaux (Merignac) (int'l arpt.), Fr.
189/J2 Bordelonville, La,US
132/C5 Borden, Austl.
179/R7 Borden (isl.), NW,Can
179/H2 Borden (pen.), NW,Can
196/F2 Borden, PE,Can
206/D3 Bordentown, NJ,US
54/C6 Borders (reg.), Sc,UK
135/B3 Bordertown, Austl.
86/A5 Bordighera, It.
141/T15 Bordj Bou Adderidj (wilaya), Alg.
141/T15 Bordj Bou Arreridj, Alg.
141/S15 Bordj el Kiffan, Alg.
142/E4 Bordj Flye Sainte-Marie, Alg.
141/S15 Bordj Manaïel, Alg.
143/F5 Bordj Moktar, Alg.
143/G3 Bordj Omar Driss, Alg.
59/F4 Bordon, Eng,UK
202/C3 Bordreaux (lake), La,US
150/A4 Borē, Eth.
144/E3 Boré, Mali
53/N7 Borehamwood, Eng,UK
86/D3 Boretto, It.
63/L1 Borgå (Porvoo), Fin.
61/N7 Borgarnes, Ice.
86/A2 Borgaro Torinese, It.
61/E2 Børgefjell Nat'l Park, Nor.
67/G5 Borgentreich, Ger.
67/E3 Börger, Ger.
66/D3 Borger, Neth.
190/D3 Borger, Tx,US
68/D1 Borgerhout, Belg.
77/F2 Borges Blanques, Sp.
86/C2 Borghetto Lodigiano, It.
86/B4 Borghetto Santo Spirito, It.
62/G3 Borgholm, Swe.
67/F4 Borgholzhausen, Ger.
67/E4 Borghorst, Ger.
83/C5 Borgia, It.
69/E2 Borgloon, Belg.
80/D5 Borgne (riv.), Swi.
202/D3 Borgne (lake), La,US
144/D4 Borgo (int'l arpt.), Burk.
90/A1 Borgo, Fr.
81/H5 Borgo, It.
86/D5 Borgo a Mozzano, It.
86/B3 Borgo d'Ale, It.
86/A1 Borgofranco d'Ivrea, It.
86/B1 Borgomanero, It.
86/C2 Borgonovo Val Tidone, It.
84/C5 Borgo Sabotino, It.
82/D4 Borgo San Dalmazzo, It.
87/E5 Borgo San Lorenzo, It.
86/D2 Borgosatollo, It.
86/B1 Borgosesia, It.
87/E4 Borgo Tossignano, It.
145/F4 Borgou (prov.), Ben.
86/C3 Borgo Val di Taro, It.
86/B2 Borgo Vercelli, It.
145/F4 Borgu Game Rsv., Nga.
62/B1 Borgund, Nor.
145/G5 Bori, Nga.
116/D5 Borikhan, Laos
96/F1 Borinskoye, Rus.
121/F3 Borio, India
98/B3 Borislav, Ukr.
53/H3 Borisoglebsk, Rus.
63/N4 Borisov, Bela.
99/J2 Borisovka, Rus.
98/F2 Borispol', Ukr.
98/F2 Borispol' (int'l arpt.), Ukr.
149/E4 Bo River, Sudan
157/H6 Boriziny, Madg.
168/B2 Borja, Peru
76/E2 Borja, Sp.
121/H2 Borjhar (arpt.), India
66/D5 Borken, Ger.
99/J3 Borki, Ukr.
62/C4 Børkop, Den.
148/C1 Borkou (reg.), Chad
148/C1 Borkou-Ennedi-Tibesti (pref.), Chad
66/D1 Borkum, Ger.
66/D1 Borkum (arpt.), Ger.
66/D1 Borkum (isl.), Ger.
151/B1 Bor, Lach (dry riv.), Kenya
62/F1 Borlänge, Swe.
82/C6 Bormes, Fr.
86/B4 Bormida, It.
86/B3 Bormida (riv.), It.
86/B3 Bormida di Millesimo (riv.), It.
86/B4 Bormida di Spigno (riv.), It.
81/G5 Bormio, It.
72/B3 Born, Ger.
66/C6 Born, Neth.
72/C5 Borna, Ger.
66/C2 Borndiep (chan.), Neth.
80/C6 Borne (riv.), Fr.
72/B4 Borne, Ger.
66/D4 Borne, Neth.
68/B5 Bornel, Fr.
68/D1 Bornem, Belg.
126/E3 Borneo (isl.), Asia
69/F2 Bornheim, Ger.
62/F4 Bornholm (co.), Den.
62/F4 Bornholm (isl.), Den.
65/H1 Bornholmsgat (chan.), Swe.
86/D1 Borno, It.
148/B2 Borno (state), Nga.
76/C4 Bornos, Sp.
67/H2 Börnsen, Ger.
148/B2 Bornu (plains), Nga.
149/E3 Boro (dry riv.), Sudan
124/E4 Borobudur (ruins), Indo.
100/K4 Borodino, Rus.
98/E4 Borodino, Ukr.
98/E2 Borodyanka, Ukr.
114/D3 Borohoro (mts.), China, Kaz.
144/E4 Boromo, Burk.
186/D3 Boron, Ca,US
125/D3 Borongan, Phil.
57/G3 Boroughbridge, Eng,UK
71/H5 Borovany, Czh.
94/G4 Borovichi, Rus.
114/D1 Borovlyanka, Rus.
93/G4 Borovo, Bul.
92/D3 Borovo, Cro.
96/F1 Borovsk, Rus.
95/Q4 Borovskiy, Rus.
95/Q5 Borovskoy, Kaz.
150/D3 Borraan, Som.
62/D2 Borre, Nor.
186/D4 Borrego Springs, Ca,US
60/D4 Borris, Ire.
60/C4 Borris in Ossory, Ire.
60/B4 Borrisokane, Ire.
60/C4 Borrisoleigh, Ire.
131/E4 Borroloola, Austl.
98/B4 Borşa, Rom.
98/C4 Borsec, Rom.
98/D3 Borshchëv, Ukr.
109/H1 Borshchovochnyy (mts.), Rus.
92/E1 Borsod-Abaúj-Zemplén (co.), Hun.
87/E1 Borso del Grappa, It.
66/A6 Borssele, Neth.
67/F3 Borstel, Ger.
114/E2 Bortala (riv.), China
74/E4 Bort-les-Orgues, Fr.
161/F4 Boruca, CR
105/G3 Borūjen, Iran
105/G3 Borūjerd, Iran
108/D3 Bor Ul (mts.), China
62/D4 Børup, Den.
105/E1 Borzhomi, Geo.
98/G2 Borzna, Ukr.
86/C4 Borzonasca, It.
73/C4 Börzsöny (mts.), Hun.
108/H1 Borzya, Rus.
90/A2 Bosa, It.
92/C3 Bosanska Dubica, Bosn.
92/C3 Bosanska Gradiška, Bosn.
92/C3 Bosanska Kostajnica, Bosn.
92/C3 Bosanska Krupa, Bosn.
92/D3 Bosanski Brod, Bosn.
92/C3 Bosanski Petrovac, Bosn.
92/D3 Bosanski Šamac, Bosn.
73/C2 Bošany, Slvk.
73/B4 Bősárkány, Hun.
150/D3 Bosaso (Bender Cassim), Som.
131/F1 Bosavi, Mount (peak), PNG
58/B5 Boscastle, Eng,UK
199/L3 Boscawen, NH,US
68/A4 Bosc-le-Hard, Fr.
84/C1 Bosco, It.
202/B1 Bosco, La,US
193/J2 Boscobel, Wi,US
87/F3 Bosco Mesola, It.
86/A2 Bosconero, It.
85/E6 Boscoreale, It.
85/E6 Boscotrecase, It.

116/E4 **Bose,** China
59/F5 **Bosham,** Eng,UK
109/N2 **Boshnyakovo,** Rus.
156/D3 **Boshof,** SAfr.
105/J3 **Boshrūyeh,** Iran
66/B4 **Boskoop,** Neth.
65/J4 **Boskovice,** Czh.
192/B3 **Bosler,** Wy,US
92/D3 **Bosna** (riv.), Bosn.
92/C3 **Bosnia and Hercegovina**
92/D3 **Bošnjaci,** Cro.
111/G3 **Bōsō** (pen.), Japan
152/D1 **Bosobolo,** Zaire
148/D4 **Bososama,** Zaire
93/J5 **Bosporus** (str.), Turk.
190/A3 **Bosque,** NM,US
190/A4 **Bosque del Apache Nat'l Wild. Ref.,** NM,US
190/A3 **Bosque Farms,** NM,US
175/K6 **Bosques Petrificados Nat. Mon.,** Arg.
191/J2 **Boss,** Mo,US
140/D4 **Bossangoa,** CAfr.
148/C4 **Bossembele,** CAfr.
148/C4 **Bossentélé,** CAfr.
189/H1 **Bossier City,** La,US
148/B2 **Bosso,** Niger
130/A4 **Bossut** (cape), Austl.
114/D4 **Bostan,** China
105/G4 **Bostān,** Iran
105/F2 **Bostānābād-e Bālā,** Iran
114/E3 **Bosten** (lake), China
57/H6 **Boston,** Eng,UK
191/H3 **Boston** (mts.), Ar, Ok,US
203/G2 **Boston,** Ga,US
208/C1 **Boston** (cap.), Ma,US
208/H7 **Boston,** Pa,US
191/G4 **Boston,** Tx,US
208/C1 **Boston Common,** Ma,US
208/F5 **Boston Heights,** Oh,US
203/H3 **Bostwick,** Fl,US
207/F1 **Bostwick** (pt.), NY,US
92/D3 **Bosut** (riv.), Cro.
198/C4 **Boswell,** In,US
81/E3 **Boswil,** Swi.
118/B3 **Botād,** India
134/H8 **Botany** (bay), Austl.
157/F2 **Botelerpunt** (pt.), SAfr.
171/K6 **Botelhos,** Braz.
123/C1 **Botene,** Laos
91/J1 **Botev** (peak), Bul.
93/F4 **Botevgrad,** Bul.
157/E2 **Bothaspas** (pass), SAfr.
156/D2 **Bothaville,** SAfr.
67/G2 **Bothel,** Ger.
57/E2 **Bothel,** Eng,UK
205/C2 **Bothell,** Wa,US
205/C2 **Bothell North-Alderwood Manor,** Wa,US
58/D5 **Bothenhampton,** Eng,UK
94/C3 **Bothnia** (gulf), Fin., Swe.
135/C4 **Bothwell,** Austl.
63/R7 **Botkyrka,** Swe.
154/D4 **Botletle** (riv.), Bots.
97/H4 **Botlikh,** Rus.
148/A5 **Bot Makak,** Camr.
98/D4 **Botoşani,** Rom.
93/H2 **Botoşani** (co.), Rom.
115/D3 **Botou,** China
123/D2 **Bo Trach,** Viet.
69/F3 **Botrange** (mtn.), Belg.
83/C5 **Botricello,** It.
156/L11 **Botrivier,** SAfr.
208/A3 **Botsford,** Ct,US
140/E7 **Botswana**
86/C1 **Bottanuco,** It.
83/C4 **Botte Donato** (peak), It.
57/H4 **Bottesford,** Eng,UK
57/H6 **Bottesford,** Eng,UK
86/D1 **Botticino,** It.
194/D3 **Bottineau,** ND,US
87/F2 **Bottrighe,** It.
66/D5 **Bottrop,** Ger.
170/C4 **Botucatu,** Braz.
197/K1 **Botwood,** Nf,Can
72/D2 **Bötzow,** Ger.
144/D4 **Bou** (riv.), IvC.
144/D5 **Bouaflé,** IvC.
144/D5 **Bouaké,** IvC.
148/C4 **Bouali,** CAfr.
152/D3 **Bouanga,** Congo
140/D4 **Bouar,** CAfr.
143/E2 **Bou Arfa,** Mor.
148/B3 **Bouba Ndjida Nat'l Park,** Camr.
71/G5 **Boubín** (peak), Czh.
82/B1 **Boubre** (riv.), Fr.
148/C4 **Bouca,** CAfr.
82/B6 **Bouc-Bel-Air,** Fr.
68/C3 **Bouchain,** Fr.
141/V17 **Bouchegouf,** Alg.
141/R16 **Bouchekif** (arpt.), Alg.
197/P6 **Boucherville,** Qu,Can
82/A5 **Bouches-du-Rhône** (dept.), Fr.
82/D3 **Bouchet** (mtn.), Fr.
144/C3 **Boucle du Baoulé Nat'l Park,** Mali
142/E3 **Boudenib,** Mor.
150/B4 **Boudi,** Eth.
145/E2 **Boû Djébéha** (well), Mali
80/C4 **Boudry,** Swi.
152/C3 **Bouenza** (pol. reg.), Congo
152/C3 **Bouenza** (riv.), Congo
141/S15 **Boufarik,** Alg.
53/S9 **Bouffémont,** Fr.
130/B3 **Bougainville** (cape), Austl.
134/B1 **Bougainville** (reef), Austl.
175/N7 **Bougainville** (cape), Falk.
138/E5 **Bougainville** (isl.), PNG
141/S15 **Bougara,** Alg.
141/V17 **Bougar'oûn** (cape), Alg.
144/D4 **Bougouni,** Mali
144/E4 **Bougouriba** (prov.), Burk.
143/F2 **Bougtob,** Alg.
74/C3 **Bouguenais,** Fr.
141/M13 **Bouhalla, Jebel** (mtn.), Mor.
141/V17 **Bou Hamdane** (riv.), Alg.
69/E4 **Bouillon,** Belg.
141/S15 **Bouira,** Alg.
141/S15 **Bouira** (wilaya), Alg.
141/S15 **Bou Ismaïl,** Alg.
142/C3 **Bou Izakarn,** Mor.
142/D2 **Boujad,** Mor.
141/R15 **Bou Kadir,** Alg.
141/M13 **Boukhalf** (Tangier) (int'l arpt.), Mor.
148/C5 **Boukoko,** CAfr.
145/F4 **Boukoumbé,** Ben.
142/D4 **Bou Laber** (well), Alg.
69/E4 **Boulaide,** Lux.
142/A5 **Boû Lanouâr,** Mrta.
142/C2 **Boulaouane,** Mor.
69/F5 **Boulay-Moselle,** Fr.
74/D4 **Boulazac,** Fr.
138/B8 **Boulder,** Austl.
192/B3 **Boulder,** Co,US
183/H4 **Boulder,** Mt,US
183/J4 **Boulder** (riv.), Mt,US
186/E3 **Boulder City,** Nv,US
186/A2 **Boulder Creek,** Ca,US
205/P16 **Boulder Hill,** Il,US
142/D2 **Boulemane,** Mor.
186/D4 **Boulevard,** Ca,US
145/E4 **Boulgo** (prov.), Burk.
133/H2 **Boulia,** Austl.
82/A2 **Boulieu-lès-Annonay,** Fr.
69/E5 **Bouligny,** Fr.
145/E3 **Boulkiemde** (prov.), Burk.
74/C3 **Boulogne** (riv.), Fr.
53/S10 **Boulogne-Billancourt,** Fr.
55/M11 **Boulogne-sur-Mer,** Fr.
59/H5 **Boulogne sur Mer,** Fr.
68/A2 **Boulogne-sur-Mer,** Fr.
79/F5 **Bouloire,** Fr.
145/E3 **Boulsa,** Burk.
57/F4 **Boulsworth** (hill), Eng,UK
142/D3 **Boumalne,** Mor.
152/C2 **Boumba** (riv.), Camr.
144/C2 **Boûmdeïd,** Mrta.
141/S15 **Boumerdas,** Alg.
141/S15 **Boumerdas** (wilaya), Alg.
77/F1 **Boumort** (mtn.), Sp.
144/E4 **Bouna,** IvC.
177/K3 **Boundary,** Yk,Can
186/C2 **Boundary** (peak), Nv,US
196/B3 **Boundary Bald** (mtn.), Me,US
133/J5 **Boundary Bend,** Austl.
195/J3 **Boundary Waters Canoe Wild. Area,** Mn,US
206/D2 **Bound Brook,** NJ,US
144/D4 **Boundiali,** IvC.
152/C3 **Boundji,** Congo
123/C1 **Boun Nua,** Laos
185/H3 **Bountiful,** Ut,US
51/T8 **Bounty** (isls.), N.Z.
152/C3 **Boupanda,** Congo
204/B1 **Bouquet** (canyon), Ca,US
204/B1 **Bouquet** (res.), Ca,US
138/F7 **Bourail,** NCal.
80/C3 **Bourbet, Rochers du** (mtn.), Fr.
193/J4 **Bourbeuse** (riv.), Mo,US
198/C4 **Bourbon,** In,US
191/J1 **Bourbon,** Mo,US
74/E3 **Bourbon-L'Archambault,** Fr.
88/D1 **Bourbonnais** (hist. reg.), Fr.
198/C4 **Bourbonnais,** Il,US
80/B2 **Bourbonne-les-Bains,** Fr.
68/B2 **Bourbourg,** Fr.
78/B4 **Bourbriac,** Fr.
141/L14 **Bou Regreg** (riv.), Mor.
141/M13 **Boureït,** Mor.
145/E2 **Bourem,** Mali
145/F2 **Bouressa** (wadi), Mali
202/C3 **Bourg,** La,US
79/F2 **Bourg-Achard,** Fr.
74/D4 **Bourganeuf,** Fr.
82/B2 **Bourg-de-Péage,** Fr.
80/B5 **Bourg-en-Bresse,** Fr.
74/E3 **Bourges,** Fr.
82/B1 **Bourget** (lake), Fr.
82/A3 **Bourg-lès-Valence,** Fr.
74/B3 **Bourgneuf** (bay), Fr.
68/D5 **Bourgogne,** Fr.
80/B3 **Bourgogne** (can.), Fr.
74/E3 **Bourgogne** (reg.), Fr.
82/B1 **Bourgoin-Jallieu,** Fr.
82/A4 **Bourg-Saint-Andéol,** Fr.
82/C1 **Bourg-Saint-Maurice,** Fr.
80/D6 **Bourg-Saint-Pierre,** Swi.
79/F2 **Bourgtheroulde-Infreville,** Fr.
79/F6 **Bourgueil,** Fr.
135/C1 **Bourke,** Austl.
80/B1 **Bourmont,** Fr.
82/B2 **Bourne** (riv.), Fr.
59/F1 **Bourne,** Eng,UK
53/M8 **Bourne** (riv.), Eng,UK
59/F3 **Bourne End,** Eng,UK
59/E5 **Bournemouth,** Eng,UK
59/E5 **Bournemouth** (arpt.), Eng,UK
59/E2 **Bournville,** Eng,UK
60/A5 **Bourn-Vincent Mem. Nat'l Park,** Ire.
192/D3 **Bourquim** (hill), Ne,US
69/F4 **Bourscheid,** Lux.
67/E3 **Bourtanger Moor** (reg.), Ger.
79/F3 **Bourth,** Fr.
59/E3 **Bourton on the Water,** Eng,UK
141/T16 **Bou Saâda,** Alg.
68/C2 **Bousbecque,** Fr.
187/E4 **Bouse,** Az,US
141/T15 **Bou Sellam, Oued** (riv.), Alg.
148/C3 **Bousso,** Chad
68/D3 **Boussois,** Fr.
145/E3 **Boussouma,** Burk.
144/B2 **Boutilimit,** Mrta.
132/B5 **Bouvard** (cape), Austl.
51/K8 **Bouvet** (isl.), Nor.
78/D6 **Bouvron,** Fr.
69/F6 **Bouxières-aux-Dames,** Fr.
69/G6 **Bouxwiller,** Fr.
145/G3 **Bouza,** Niger
79/D6 **Bouzille,** Fr.
69/F5 **Bouzonville,** Fr.
68/C5 **Bouzy,** Fr.
83/C6 **Bovalino,** It.
83/B7 **Bova Marina,** It.
86/D1 **Bovegno,** It.
67/G5 **Bovenden,** Ger.
66/C3 **Bovenkarspel,** Neth.
166/C2 **Boven Tapanahoni** (riv.), Sur.
66/D3 **Bovenwijde** (lake), Neth.
68/B4 **Boves,** Fr.
86/A4 **Boves,** It.
195/H4 **Bovey,** Mn,US
58/C5 **Bovey Tracey,** Eng,UK
86/D1 **Bovezzo,** It.
182/F4 **Bovill,** Id,US
190/C3 **Bovina,** Tx,US
53/M6 **Bovingdon,** Eng,UK
85/F5 **Bovino,** It.
105/G4 **Bovīr Aḩmadi and Kohkīlūyeh** (gov.), Iran
87/E2 **Bovolone,** It.
172/E4 **Bovril,** Arg.
183/H2 **Bow** (riv.), Ab,Can
192/E4 **Bow** (cr.), Ks,US
194/C3 **Bowbells,** ND,US
183/H2 **Bow City,** Ab,Can
192/E1 **Bowdle,** SD,US
183/L3 **Bowdoin Nat'l Wild. Ref.,** Mt,US
57/F5 **Bowdon,** Eng,UK
200/E4 **Bowdon,** Ga,US
194/E4 **Bowdon,** ND,US
174/D2 **Bowen,** Arg.
134/C3 **Bowen,** Austl.
182/C3 **Bowen Island,** BC,Can
66/C5 **Bowen Merwede** (can.), Neth.
206/C5 **Bowers Beach,** De,US
208/F7 **Bowerston,** Oh,US
57/G3 **Bowes,** Eng,UK
187/H4 **Bowie,** Az,US
206/B6 **Bowie,** Md,US
191/F4 **Bowie,** Tx,US
183/J3 **Bow Island,** Ab,Can
134/B2 **Bowling Green** (cape), Austl.
202/M8 **Bowling Green,** Fl,US
203/H4 **Bowling Green,** Fl,US
200/D2 **Bowling Green,** Ky,US
191/J1 **Bowling Green,** Mo,US
198/E4 **Bowling Green,** Oh,US
201/J1 **Bowling Green,** Va,US
134/B2 **Bowling Green Bay Nat'l Park,** Austl.
137/G **Bowman** (isl.), Ant.
182/D2 **Bowman** (mtn.), BC,Can
179/J2 **Bowman** (bay), NW,Can
201/F3 **Bowman,** Ga,US
194/C4 **Bowman,** ND,US
194/C5 **Bowman-Haley** (dam), ND,US
194/C4 **Bowman-Haley** (res.), ND,US
206/B3 **Bowmansdale,** Pa,US
206/C2 **Bowmanstown,** Pa,US
206/B3 **Bowmansville,** Pa,US
197/T8 **Bowmanville,** Nf,Can
55/H9 **Bowmore,** Sc,UK
57/E2 **Bowness-on-Solway,** Eng,UK
127/F4 **Bowokan** (isls.), Indo.
135/D2 **Bowral,** Austl.
191/F2 **Bowring,** Ok,US
130/B4 **Bow River Abor. Land,** Austl.
182/D1 **Bowron** (riv.), BC,Can
194/D1 **Bowsman,** Mb,Can
131/G1 **Bowutu** (mts.), PNG
154/E3 **Bowwood,** Zam.
70/C4 **Boxberg,** Ger.
192/B4 **Box Elder** (cr.), Co,US
183/J3 **Box Elder,** Mt,US
194/B5 **Box Elder** (riv.), Mt,US
192/C1 **Box Elder,** SD,US
192/C1 **Box Elder** (cr.), SD,US
185/L2 **Boxelder,** Wy,US
135/C3 **Box Hill,** Austl.
135/G5 **Box Hill,** Austl.
62/F2 **Boxholm,** Swe.
115/D3 **Boxing,** China
191/H3 **Boxley,** Ar,US
66/C5 **Boxmeer,** Neth.
108/H3 **Boxodoi,** China
200/E4 **Box Springs,** Ga,US
66/C5 **Boxtel,** Neth.
66/C2 **Boxum,** Neth.
104/C1 **Boyabat,** Turk.
152/D2 **Boyabo,** Zaire
164/C3 **Boyacá** (dept.), Col.
167/L7 **Boyaca** (dept.), Col.
105/M6 **Boyalik,** Turk.
132/B5 **Boyanup,** Austl.
98/F2 **Boyarka,** Ukr.
202/B2 **Boyce,** La,US
93/F4 **Boychinovtsi,** Bul.
189/F1 **Boyd,** Tx,US
191/J4 **Boydell,** Ar,US
135/D2 **Boyd-Konangra Nat'l Park,** Austl.
182/E3 **Boyds,** Wa,US
201/H2 **Boydton,** Va,US
115/C3 **Boye,** China
193/G2 **Boyer** (riv.), IA,US
192/C4 **Boyero,** Co,US
208/H5 **Boyers,** Pa,US
206/C3 **Boyertown,** Pa,US
183/M5 **Boyes,** Mt,US
201/J2 **Boykins,** Va,US
60/B2 **Boyle,** Ire.
200/B4 **Boyle,** Ms,US
208/C1 **Boylston,** Ma,US
60/D2 **Boyne** (riv.), Ire.
198/D2 **Boyne City,** Mi,US
198/D2 **Boyne Falls,** Mi,US
134/C3 **Boyne Island,** Austl.
191/G3 **Boynton,** Ok,US
202/P6 **Boynton Beach,** Fl,US
203/H4 **Boynton Beach,** Fl,US
185/J2 **Boysen** (dam), Wy,US
185/J2 **Boysen** (res.), Wy,US
172/D2 **Boyuibe,** Bol.
132/C5 **Boyup Brook,** Austl.
104/B1 **Boz** (pt.), Turk.
91/J3 **Bozcaada** (isl.), Gre.
91/K3 **Bozcaada,** Turk.
104/B2 **Bozdoğan,** Turk.
82/C2 **Bozel,** Fr.
183/J5 **Bozeman,** Mt,US
81/H5 **Bozen** (Bolzano), It.
117/F3 **Bozhai,** China
104/C2 **Bozkir,** Turk.
96/E4 **Bozkurt,** Turk.
206/B6 **Bozman,** Md,US
104/D2 **Bozova,** Turk.
104/B2 **Bozüyük,** Turk.
103/C1 **Bozyazı,** Turk.
86/D2 **Bozzolo,** It.
86/A3 **Bra,** It.
54/C3 **Braan** (riv.), Sc,UK
68/D2 **Brabant** (prov.), Belg.
59/G4 **Brabourne Lees,** Eng,UK
92/C4 **Brač** (isl.), Cro.
84/C3 **Bracciano,** It.
84/C3 **Bracciano** (lake), It.
199/G2 **Bracebridge,** On,Can
78/C5 **Brach,** Fr.
79/G5 **Bracieux,** Fr.
85/E6 **Bracigliano,** It.
94/B3 **Bräcke,** Swe.
67/H2 **Brackel,** Ger.
183/K3 **Bracken,** Sk,Can
70/C4 **Brackenheim,** Ger.
208/H6 **Brackenridge,** Pa,US
195/J5 **Brackett,** Wi,US
188/D3 **Brackettville,** Tx,US
59/E2 **Brackley,** Eng,UK
60/C3 **Bracknagh,** Ire.
59/F4 **Bracknell,** Eng,UK
67/F5 **Brackwede,** Ger.
173/G4 **Braço do Norte,** Braz.
170/C2 **Braço Menor do Araguaia** (riv.), Braz.
92/F2 **Brad,** Rom.
83/C2 **Bradano** (riv.), It.
56/D3 **Bradda Head** (pt.), IM,UK
194/D4 **Braddock,** ND,US
208/H7 **Braddock,** Pa,US
200/C3 **Braden,** Tn,US
203/G4 **Bradenton,** Fl,US
199/G2 **Bradford,** On,Can
57/G4 **Bradford,** Eng,UK
191/J3 **Bradford,** Ar,US
196/C3 **Bradford,** Me,US
198/D4 **Bradford,** Oh,US
199/G4 **Bradford,** Pa,US
208/C3 **Bradford,** RI,US
199/K3 **Bradford,** Vt,US
58/D4 **Bradford on Avon,** Eng,UK
59/E5 **Brading,** Eng,UK
191/H4 **Bradley,** Ar,US
186/B3 **Bradley,** Ca,US
208/B2 **Bradley** (int'l arpt.), Ct,US
198/C4 **Bradley,** Il,US
196/C3 **Bradley,** Me,US
201/F3 **Bradley,** SC,US
192/F1 **Bradley,** SD,US
195/K5 **Bradley,** Wi,US
207/D3 **Bradley Beach,** NJ,US
198/E4 **Bradner,** Oh,US
58/C5 **Bradninch,** Eng,UK
183/J3 **Brady,** Mt,US
192/D3 **Brady,** Ne,US
188/E2 **Brady,** Tx,US
188/E2 **Brady** (cr.), Tx,US
208/F5 **Brady Lake,** Oh,US
55/P12 **Brae,** Sc,UK
177/L3 **Braeburn,** Yk,Can
54/C2 **Braemar,** Sc,UK
54/C2 **Braemar** (dist.), Sc,UK
54/C2 **Braeriach** (mtn.), Sc,UK
132/D2 **Braeside,** Austl.
76/A2 **Braga,** Port.
76/A2 **Braga** (dist.), Port.
174/E2 **Bragado,** Arg.
167/E3 **Bragança,** Braz.
76/B2 **Bragança,** Port.
76/B2 **Bragança** (dist.), Port.
170/D4 **Bragança Paulista,** Braz.
183/G2 **Bragg Creek,** Ab,Can
191/G3 **Braggs,** Ok,US
98/F2 **Bragin,** Bela.
195/H5 **Braham,** Mn,US
116/C3 **Brahmakund,** India
121/H4 **Brāhmanbāria,** Bang.
119/F2 **Brahmaputra** (riv.), Asia
121/G1 **Brahmaputra** (Yarlung Zangbo) (riv.), China
56/D6 **Braich-y-Pwll** (pt.), Wal,UK
56/B2 **Braid** (riv.), NI,UK
198/B4 **Braidwood,** Il,US
93/H3 **Brăila,** Rom.
93/H3 **Brăila** (co.), Rom.
193/F3 **Brainard,** Ne,US
206/C2 **Brainards,** NJ,US
68/C5 **Braine,** Fr.
68/D2 **Braine-l'Alleud,** Belg.
68/D2 **Braine-le-Comte,** Belg.
195/G4 **Brainerd,** Mn,US
59/G3 **Braintree,** Eng,UK
208/D1 **Braintree,** Ma,US
130/D2 **Braithwaithe** (pt.), Austl.
156/C3 **Brak** (riv.), SAfr.
67/F2 **Brake,** Ger.
68/C2 **Brakel,** Belg.
67/G5 **Brakel,** Ger.
144/B2 **Brakna** (reg.), Mrta.
62/E2 **Brålanda,** Swe.
98/D5 **Brălia** (co.), Rom.
182/C2 **Bralorne,** BC,Can
74/E5 **Bram,** Fr.
197/R8 **Bramalea,** On,Can
191/F2 **Braman,** Ok,US
62/C4 **Bramdrupdam,** Den.
57/G4 **Bramhope,** Eng,UK
199/J3 **Bramley** (mtn.), NY,US
82/D4 **Bram, Monte** (peak), It.
199/G3 **Brampton,** On,Can
57/F2 **Brampton,** Eng,UK
198/C2 **Brampton,** Mi,US
67/E4 **Bramsche,** Ger.
67/F2 **Bramstedt,** Ger.
54/A1 **Bran** (riv.), Sc,UK
145/E5 **Branam,** Gha.
83/C7 **Brancaleone-Marina,** It.
183/M1 **Brancepeth,** Sk,Can
197/L2 **Branch,** Nf,Can
189/H2 **Branch,** La,US
195/H5 **Branch,** Mn,US
206/B2 **Branch Dale,** Pa,US
208/A3 **Branchville,** Ct,US
206/D1 **Branchville,** NJ,US
165/F5 **Branco** (riv.), Braz.
81/F3 **Brand,** Aus.
154/B4 **Brandberg** (peak), Namb.
62/D1 **Brandbu,** Nor.
62/C4 **Brande,** Den.
72/C3 **Brandenburg,** Ger.
72/D3 **Brandenburg** (state), Ger.
200/D2 **Brandenburg,** Ky,US
72/D6 **Brand-Erbisdorf,** Ger.
54/C1 **Branderburgh,** Sc,UK
54/A4 **Brander, Pass of** (pass), Sc,UK
57/H4 **Brandesburton,** Eng,UK
156/D3 **Brandfort,** SAfr.
72/C5 **Brandis,** Ger.
86/A2 **Brandizzo,** It.
194/E3 **Brandon,** Mb,Can
60/D4 **Brandon** (mtn.), Ire.
59/G2 **Brandon,** Eng,UK
190/C1 **Brandon,** Co,US
202/L8 **Brandon,** Fl,US
203/G4 **Brandon,** Fl,US
195/G5 **Brandon,** Mn,US
200/C4 **Brandon,** Ms,US
193/F2 **Brandon,** SD,US
199/K3 **Brandon,** Vt,US
174/F2 **Brandsen,** Arg.
191/J2 **Brandsville,** Mo,US
156/C3 **Brandvlei,** SAfr.
71/H2 **Brandýs nad Labem,** Czh.
206/C4 **Brandywine** (cr.), De, Pa,US
206/B6 **Brandywine,** Md,US
201/H1 **Brandywine,** WV,US
206/C3 **Brandywine, East Branch** (cr.), Pa,US
206/C4 **Brandywine, West Branch** (cr.), Pa,US
208/B3 **Branford,** Ct,US
203/G3 **Branford,** Fl,US
80/B4 **Branges,** Fr.
65/K1 **Braniewo,** Pol.
64/G5 **Brannenburg,** Ger.
59/E5 **Bransgore,** Eng,UK
197/Q9 **Brant** (co.), On,Can
207/D4 **Brant Beach,** NJ,US
198/F3 **Brantford,** On,Can
124/D4 **Branti,** Indo.
203/E2 **Brantley,** Al,US
193/J1 **Brantwood,** Wi,US
135/C4 **Branxholm,** Austl.
135/B3 **Branxholme,** Austl.
135/D2 **Branxton,** Austl.
54/D5 **Branxton,** Eng,UK
81/H5 **Branzoll** (Bronzolo), It.
197/G2 **Bras d'Or** (lake), NS,Can
191/J3 **Brasfield,** Ar,US
193/H3 **Brashear,** Mo,US
199/J2 **Brasher Falls-Winthrop,** NY,US
168/D3 **Brasiléia,** Braz.
170/D2 **Brasília** (cap.), Braz.
170/D3 **Brasília de Minas,** Braz.
170/C2 **Brasilia Nat'l Park,** Braz.
93/G3 **Braşov,** Rom.
93/G3 **Braşov** (co.), Rom.
145/G5 **Brass,** Nga.
66/B6 **Brasschaat,** Belg.
133/G2 **Brassey** (peak), Austl.
200/F3 **Brasstown Bald** (peak), Ga,US
62/D2 **Brastad,** Swe.
200/E4 **Braswell,** Ga,US
89/H2 **Brat** (isl.), Cro.
73/B3 **Bratislava** (cap.), Slvk.
73/B3 **Bratislava** (reg.), Slvk.
73/B3 **Bratislava** (Ivanka) (int'l arpt.), Slvk.
93/G4 **Bratsigovo,** Bul.
101/L4 **Bratsk,** Rus.
98/F4 **Bratskoye,** Ukr.
98/E3 **Bratslav,** Ukr.
199/K3 **Brattleboro,** Vt,US
92/D3 **Bratunac,** Bosn.
69/G3 **Braubach,** Ger.
161/F4 **Braulio Carrillo Nat'l Park,** CR
71/G6 **Braunau am Inn,** Aus.
70/B1 **Braunfels,** Ger.
67/H5 **Braunlage,** Ger.
81/E2 **Bräunlingen,** Ger.
72/B5 **Braunsbedra,** Ger.
67/H4 **Braunschweig** (arpt.), Ger.
67/H4 **Braunschweig** (Brunswick), Ger.
58/B4 **Braunton,** Eng,UK
175/K8 **Brava** (pt.), Chile
140/J11 **Brava** (isl.), CpV.
77/G2 **Brava** (coast), Sp.
175/T12 **Brava** (pt.), Uru.
198/F5 **Brave,** Pa,US
62/G2 **Bråviken** (inlet), Swe.
172/C1 **Bravo** (peak), Bol.
168/B2 **Bravo** (peak), Peru
164/C2 **Bravo** (riv.), Ven.
188/D3 **Bravo del Norte, Rio** (Rio Grande) (riv.), Mex.
186/E4 **Brawley,** Ca,US
179/J2 **Bray** (isl.), NW,Can
60/D3 **Bray,** Ire.
68/B1 **Bray-Dunes,** Fr.
79/F5 **Braye** (riv.), Fr.
56/B5 **Bray Head** (pt.), Ire.
191/H1 **Braymer,** Mo,US
68/B4 **Bray-sur-Somme,** Fr.
182/F1 **Brazeau** (mtn.), Ab,Can
182/F1 **Brazeau** (riv.), Ab,Can
80/B3 **Brazey-en-Plaine,** Fr.
163/D3 **Brazil**
163/E4 **Brazilian Highlands** (plat.), Braz.
165/E4 **Brazo Casiquare** (riv.), Ven.
171/L7 **Brazópolis,** Braz.
189/M9 **Brazoria** (co.), Tx,US
189/G3 **Brazoria Nat'l Wild. Ref.,** Tx,US
189/G3 **Brazos** (riv.), Tx,US
190/E4 **Brazos, Clear Fork** (riv.), Tx,US
190/D4 **Brazos, Double Mountain Fork** (riv.), Tx,US
190/D4 **Brazos, North Fork Double Mountain Fork** (riv.), Tx,US
190/D4 **Brazos, Salt Fork** (riv.), Tx,US
175/K7 **Brazo Sur** (riv.), Arg.
152/C4 **Brazzaville** (cap.), Congo
92/D3 **Brčko,** Bosn.
64/J2 **Brda** (riv.), Pol.
71/G3 **Brdy** (mts.), Czh.
204/C3 **Brea,** Ca,US
54/B4 **Breadalbane** (dist.), Sc,UK
182/D3 **Breakenridge** (mtn.), BC,Can
136/C1 **Bream** (pt.), N.Z.
58/D3 **Bream,** Eng,UK
54/E6 **Breamish** (riv.), Eng,UK
136/C2 **Bream Tail** (pt.), N.Z.
202/C2 **Breaux Bridge,** La,US
93/G3 **Breaza,** Rom.
86/B1 **Brebbia,** It.
124/E4 **Brebes,** Indo.
79/D3 **Brécey,** Fr.
79/H2 **Brêche** (riv.), Fr.
70/B2 **Brechen,** Ger.
54/D3 **Brechin,** Sc,UK
66/B6 **Brecht,** Belg.
192/A4 **Breckenridge,** Co,US
194/F4 **Breckenridge,** Mn,US
191/H1 **Breckenridge,** Mo,US
189/E1 **Breckenridge,** Tx,US
67/E6 **Breckerfeld,** Ger.
59/G2 **Breckland** (reg.), Eng,UK
175/K8 **Brecknock** (pen.), Chile
208/F5 **Brecksville,** Oh,US
73/A2 **Břeclav,** Czh.
58/C3 **Brecon,** Wal,UK
58/C3 **Brecon Beacons** (mts.), Wal,UK
58/C3 **Brecon Beacons Nat'l Park,** Wal,UK
82/C2 **Bréda** (riv.), Fr.
66/B5 **Breda,** Neth.
62/E3 **Bredaryd,** Swe.
156/C4 **Bredasdorp,** SAfr.
135/D2 **Bredbo,** Austl.
62/C4 **Bredebro,** Den.
68/B1 **Bredene,** Belg.
64/E1 **Bredstedt,** Ger.
69/E1 **Bree,** Belg.
156/B4 **Breë** (riv.), SAfr.
195/K5 **Breed,** Wi,US
200/C1 **Breese,** Il,US
66/B3 **Breezand,** Neth.
207/E2 **Breezy** (pt.), NY,US
195/G4 **Breezy Point,** Mn,US
81/E1 **Breg** (riv.), Ger.
81/F5 **Bregagno, Monte** (peak), It.
92/F5 **Bregalinca** (riv.), Macd.
91/H2 **Bregalnica** (riv.), Macd.
87/E1 **Breganze,** It.
81/F2 **Bregenz,** Aus.
81/F3 **Bregenzer Ache** (riv.), Aus.
92/F3 **Bregovo,** Bul.
78/D3 **Bréhal,** Fr.
78/C3 **Bréhat** (isl.), Fr.
72/C4 **Brehna,** Ger.
61/M6 **Breidhafjördhur** (bay), Ice.
81/F4 **Breil-Brigels,** Swi.
82/D5 **Breil-sur-Roya,** Fr.
80/D1 **Breisach,** Ger.
71/F7 **Breitbrunn am Chiemsee,** Ger.
71/G5 **Breitenauriegel** (peak), Ger.
69/G5 **Breitenbach,** Ger.
80/D3 **Breitenbach,** Swi.
71/E4 **Breitenbrunn,** Ger.
71/F2 **Breitenbrunn,** Ger.
67/H6 **Breitenworbis,** Ger.
80/D5 **Breithorn** (peak), Swi.
80/D6 **Breithorn** (peak), Swi., It.
72/C3 **Breitling** (lake), Ger.
170/C1 **Brejinho de Nazaré,** Braz.
167/F3 **Brejo,** Braz.
167/G4 **Brejo do Cruz,** Braz.
167/G4 **Brejo Santo,** Braz.
86/C1 **Brembate di Sopra,** It.
86/C1 **Brembilla,** It.
86/C2 **Brembio,** It.
86/C1 **Brembo** (riv.), It.
67/F2 **Bremen,** Ger.
67/F2 **Bremen** (int'l arpt.), Ger.
67/F1 **Bremen** (state), Ger.
67/F2 **Bremen** (state), Ger.
200/E4 **Bremen,** Ga,US
198/C4 **Bremen,** In,US
198/E5 **Bremen,** Oh,US
134/E7 **Bremer** (riv.), Austl.
67/F1 **Bremerhaven,** Ger.
67/F1 **Bremerhaven** (arpt.), Ger.
205/B2 **Bremerton,** Wa,US
67/G2 **Bremervörde,** Ger.
81/E3 **Bremgarten,** Swi.
80/D4 **Bremgarten bei Bern,** Swi.
62/A2 **Bremnes,** Nor.
189/F2 **Bremond,** Tx,US
70/D2 **Brend** (riv.), Ger.
205/E6 **Brendel** (lake), Mi,US
87/E2 **Brendola,** It.
58/C4 **Brendon** (hills), Eng,UK
189/F2 **Brenham,** Tx,US
56/E5 **Brenig, Llyn** (lake), Wal,UK
73/A4 **Brennbergbánya,** Hun.
80/B4 **Brenne** (riv.), Fr.
133/N9 **Brenner** (riv.), Austl.
81/H4 **Brenner** (Brennerpass) (pass), Aus.
81/E4 **Brenno** (riv.), Swi.
86/D1 **Breno,** It.
199/G1 **Brent,** On,Can
53/N7 **Brent** (bor.), Eng,UK
53/N7 **Brent** (res.), Eng,UK
53/N7 **Brent** (riv.), Eng,UK
200/D4 **Brent,** Al,US
87/F2 **Brenta** (riv.), It.
81/G5 **Brenta, Cima** (peak), It.
201/G2 **Brenton,** WV,US
53/P7 **Brentwood,** Eng,UK
205/L11 **Brentwood,** Ca,US
207/E2 **Brentwood,** NY,US
208/H7 **Brentwood,** Pa,US
200/D2 **Brentwood,** Tn,US
70/D5 **Brenz** (riv.), Ger.
86/D3 **Brescello,** It.
86/D1 **Brescia,** It.
86/D1 **Brescia** (prov.), It.
66/A6 **Breskens,** Neth.
189/F3 **Breslau,** Tx,US
68/A4 **Bresle** (riv.), Fr.
68/B5 **Bresles,** Fr.
82/C5 **Bresque** (riv.), Fr.
86/C2 **Bressana,** It.
75/J3 **Bressanone,** It.
55/P12 **Bressay** (isl.), Sc,UK
74/C3 **Bressuire,** Fr.
65/M2 **Brest,** Bela.
65/M2 **Brest** (int'l arpt.), Bela.
78/A4 **Brest,** Fr.
78/A4 **Brest** (Guipavas) (int'l arpt.), Fr.
65/M2 **Brest Obl.,** Bela.
78/A4 **Brest, Rade de** (har.), Fr.
78/C4 **Bretagne** (mts.), Fr.
78/D4 **Bretagne** (reg.), Fr.
157/R15 **Bretagne** (pt.), Reun.
168/C2 **Bretaña,** Peru
79/H1 **Breteuil,** Fr.
79/F3 **Breteuil-sur-Iton,** Fr.
68/B4 **Breteuil-sur-Noye,** Fr.
195/L5 **Brethren,** Mi,US
53/S11 **Brétigny-sur-Orge,** Fr.
183/G1 **Breton,** Ab,Can
202/D3 **Breton** (isl.), La,US
202/D3 **Breton** (sound), La,US
79/F4 **Bretoncelles,** Fr.
197/G2 **Breton Cove,** NS,Can
202/D3 **Breton Nat'l Wild. Ref.,** La,US
136/C1 **Brett** (cape), N.Z.
70/C4 **Brettach** (riv.), Ger.
79/F5 **Brette-les-Pins,** Fr.
70/B4 **Bretten,** Ger.
70/A3 **Bretzenheim,** Ger.
70/C3 **Breuberg,** Ger.
124/A1 **Breueh** (isl.), Indo.
66/C5 **Breugel,** Neth.
53/S11 **Breuillet,** Fr.
66/B4 **Breukelen,** Neth.
67/G6 **Breuna,** Ger.
80/B1 **Breuvannes-en-Bassigny,** Fr.
201/F3 **Brevard,** NC,US
166/D3 **Breves,** Braz.
177/E2 **Brevig Mission,** Ak,US
62/C2 **Brevik,** Nor.
63/S7 **Brevik,** Swe.
179/K2 **Brevoort** (isl.), NW,Can
135/C1 **Brewarrina,** Austl.
196/C3 **Brewer,** Me,US
193/K5 **Brewer,** Mo,US
199/H3 **Brewerton,** NY,US
144/C5 **Brewerville,** Libr.
58/D1 **Brewood,** Eng,UK
130/B3 **Brewster** (cape), Austl.
190/D1 **Brewster,** Ks,US
193/G2 **Brewster,** Mn,US
192/E3 **Brewster,** Ne,US
208/F6 **Brewster,** Oh,US
182/E3 **Brewster,** Wa,US
202/E2 **Brewton,** Al,US
156/Q13 **Breyten,** SAfr.
92/B3 **Brežice,** Slov.
143/F2 **Brezina,** Alg.
71/G3 **Březnice,** Czh.
92/F4 **Breznik,** Bul.
93/G3 **Brezoi,** Rom.
79/G3 **Brézolles,** Fr.
93/G4 **Brezovo,** Bul.
140/E4 **Bria,** CAfr.
75/G4 **Briançon,** Fr.
82/C3 **Briancon,** Fr.
58/C2 **Brianne, Lyn** (res.), Wal,UK
206/B1 **Briar Creek,** Pa,US
74/E3 **Briare,** Fr.
135/C2 **Bribbaree,** Austl.
82/C3 **Bric de Rubren** (mtn.), Fr.
190/D3 **Brice,** Tx,US
93/H1 **Brichany,** Mol.
207/D3 **Brick,** NJ,US
206/B3 **Brickerville,** Pa,US
53/M6 **Bricket Wood,** Eng,UK
78/D2 **Bricquebec,** Fr.
82/D3 **Bric Rosso** (peak), It.
193/H4 **Bridal Cave,** Mo,US
185/K5 **Bridal Veil** (falls), Co,US
60/B5 **Bride** (riv.), Ire.
56/D3 **Bride,** IM,UK
182/C2 **Bridge** (riv.), BC,Can
185/G2 **Bridge,** Id,US
189/H2 **Bridge City,** Tx,US
207/F2 **Bridgehampton,** NY,US
200/E2 **Bridgeman** (mtn.), Ky,US
58/C4 **Bridgend,** Wal,UK
54/C4 **Bridge of Allan,** Sc,UK
54/D2 **Bridge of Don,** Sc,UK
54/B5 **Bridge of Weir,** Sc,UK
186/C1 **Bridgeport,** Ca,US
208/A3 **Bridgeport,** Ct,US
198/C5 **Bridgeport,** Il,US
198/E3 **Bridgeport,** Mi,US
192/C3 **Bridgeport,** Ne,US
206/C4 **Bridgeport,** NJ,US
189/F1 **Bridgeport,** Tx,US
189/F1 **Bridgeport** (lake), Tx,US
182/E3 **Bridgeport,** Wa,US
201/G1 **Bridgeport,** WV,US
185/J1 **Bridger,** Mt,US
206/C5 **Bridgeton,** NJ,US
132/C5 **Bridgetown,** Austl.
162/G4 **Bridgetown** (cap.), Bar.
196/E3 **Bridgetown,** NS,Can
60/D5 **Bridgetown,** Ire.
198/D5 **Bridgetown,** Oh,US
196/E1 **Bridgeville,** Qu,Can
184/B3 **Bridgeville,** Ca,US
206/C6 **Bridgeville,** De,US
208/G7 **Bridgeville,** Pa,US
135/C4 **Bridgewater,** Austl.
196/E3 **Bridgewater,** NS,Can
208/A2 **Bridgewater,** Ct,US
208/D2 **Bridgewater,** Ma,US
201/H1 **Bridgewater,** Va,US
58/D1 **Bridgnorth,** Eng,UK
196/B3 **Bridgton,** Me,US
58/D4 **Bridgwater,** Eng,UK
58/C4 **Bridgwater** (bay), Eng,UK
57/H3 **Bridlington,** Eng,UK
57/H3 **Bridlington** (bay), Eng,UK
135/C4 **Bridport,** Austl.
58/D5 **Bridport,** Eng,UK
199/K3 **Bridport,** Vt,US
53/U10 **Brie** (reg.), Fr.
78/A4 **Briec,** Fr.
53/T10 **Brie-Comte-Robert,** Fr.
65/J3 **Brieg Brzeg,** Pol.
66/B5 **Brielle,** Neth.
207/D3 **Brielle,** NJ,US
80/E4 **Brienz,** Swi.
83/B2 **Brienza,** It.
80/D4 **Brienzersee** (lake), Swi.
196/D3 **Brier** (isl.), NS,Can
201/G4 **Brier** (cr.), Ga,US
199/H4 **Brier** (mtn.), Pa,US
205/C2 **Brier,** Wa,US
194/B2 **Briercrest,** Sk,Can
57/F4 **Brierfield,** Eng,UK
72/D2 **Brieselang,** Ger.
72/D5 **Brieske,** Ger.
69/E5 **Briey,** Fr.
75/G3 **Brig,** Swi.
81/E1 **Brigach** (riv.), Ger.
207/D5 **Brigantine,** NJ,US
57/H4 **Brigg,** Eng,UK
80/D5 **Brig-Glis,** Swi.
189/F2 **Briggs,** Tx,US
196/E2 **Briggs Corner,** NB,Can
185/G3 **Brigham City,** Ut,US
57/G4 **Brighouse,** Eng,UK
59/E5 **Brighstone,** Eng,UK
135/C3 **Bright,** Austl.
59/H3 **Brightlingsea,** Eng,UK
133/M9 **Brighton,** Austl.
199/H2 **Brighton,** On,Can
59/F5 **Brighton,** Eng,UK
192/B4 **Brighton,** Co,US
193/J4 **Brighton,** Il,US
205/E6 **Brighton,** Mi,US
200/C3 **Brighton,** Tn,US
205/P14 **Brighton,** Wi,US
54/C5 **Brightons,** Sc,UK
82/A1 **Brignais,** Fr.
78/A3 **Brignogan-Plage,** Fr.
82/C6 **Brignoles,** Fr.
122/G3 **Brihadeshwara Temple,** India
76/D2 **Brihuega,** Sp.
53/S11 **Briis-sous-Forges,** Fr.
87/G3 **Brijuni,** Cro.
144/A3 **Brikama,** Gam.
170/B4 **Brilhante** (riv.), Braz.
59/E3 **Brill,** Eng,UK
193/K1 **Brillion,** Wi,US
67/F6 **Brilon,** Ger.
208/B1 **Brimfield,** Ma,US
208/F5 **Brimfield,** Oh,US
57/G5 **Brimington,** Eng,UK
198/D1 **Brimley,** Mi,US
162/F3 **Brimstone Hill Nat'l Park,** StK.
91/E2 **Brindisi,** It.
191/J3 **Brinkley,** Ar,US
172/D4 **Brinkmann,** Arg.
191/H1 **Brinktown,** Mo,US
133/H5 **Brinkworth,** Austl.
58/E3 **Brinkworth,** Eng,UK
205/B2 **Brinnon,** Wa,US
203/F2 **Brinson,** Ga,US
202/P6 **Briny Breezes,** Fl,US
197/G2 **Brion** (isl.), Qu,Can
76/A1 **Brion,** Sp.
81/E5 **Brione,** Swi.
205/K11 **Briones** (res.), Ca,US
79/F2 **Brionne,** Fr.
79/E3 **Briouze,** Fr.
134/D4 **Brisbane,** Austl.
134/F6 **Brisbane** (int'l airpt.), Austl.
134/D4 **Brisbane** (int'l arpt.), Austl.
134/F6 **Brisbane** (riv.), Austl.
134/E6 **Brisbane For. Park,** Austl.
135/C3 **Brisbane Ranges Nat'l Park,** Austl.
135/D2 **Brisbane Waters Nat'l Park,** Austl.
182/F2 **Brisco,** BC,Can
87/E4 **Brisighella,** It.
79/E6 **Brissac-Quincé,** Fr.
81/E5 **Brissago,** Swi.
196/D2 **Bristol,** NB,Can.
199/H2 **Bristol,** Qu,Can
58/B4 **Bristol** (chan.), UK
58/D4 **Bristol,** Eng,UK
177/F4 **Bristol** (bay), Ak,US
186/E3 **Bristol** (dry lake), Ca,US
190/C1 **Bristol,** Co,US
208/B2 **Bristol,** Ct,US
203/F2 **Bristol,** Fl,US
203/G2 **Bristol,** Ga,US
208/C2 **Bristol** (co.), Ma,US
196/B4 **Bristol,** NH,US
206/D3 **Bristol,** Pa,US
208/C2 **Bristol,** RI,US
208/C2 **Bristol** (co.), RI,US
192/F1 **Bristol,** SD,US
201/F2 **Bristol,** Tn,US
188/L7 **Bristol,** Tx,US
199/K2 **Bristol,** Vt,US
58/D4 **Bristol** (Lulsgate) (int'l arpt.), Eng,UK
208/G5 **Bristolville,** Oh,US
191/F3 **Bristow,** Ok,US
170/C2 **Britânia,** Braz.
177/K2 **British** (mts.), Yk,Can, Ak,US
178/D3 **British Columbia** (prov.), Can.
179/S6 **British Empire** (range), NW,Can
102/G10 **British Indian Ocean Terr.**
53/N7 **British Museum,** Eng,UK
162/E3 **British Virgin Islands**
156/D2 **Brits,** SAfr.
156/C3 **Britstown,** SAfr.
193/H2 **Britt,** Ia,US
78/B4 **Brittany** (hist. reg.), Fr.
74/B2 **Brittany** (reg.), Fr.
192/F1 **Britton,** SD,US
188/K7 **Britton,** Tx,US
72/D2 **Britz,** Ger.
74/D4 **Brive-la-Gaillarde,** Fr.
74/E4 **Brives-Charensac,** Fr.
76/D1 **Briviesca,** Sp.
86/C1 **Brivio,** It.
78/D1 **Brix,** Fr.
58/C6 **Brixham,** Eng,UK
59/F2 **Brixworth,** Eng,UK
114/B3 **Brlik,** Kaz.
92/B2 **Brnik** (int'l arpt.), Yugo.
73/A1 **Brno,** Czh.
73/A1 **Brno** (Cernovice) (arpt.), Czh.
63/R6 **Bro,** Swe.
177/J3 **Broad** (pass), Ak,US
201/F4 **Broad** (riv.), Ga,US
201/G3 **Broad** (riv.), NC, SC,US
183/K1 **Broadacres,** Sk,Can
132/D4 **Broad Arrow,** Austl.
184/A2 **Broadbent,** Or,US
208/B2 **Broad Brook,** Ct,US
189/G2 **Broaddus,** Tx,US
135/C3 **Broadford,** Austl.
60/B5 **Broadford,** Ire.
206/C6 **Broadkill** (riv.), De,US
55/K9 **Broad Law** (mtn.), UK
54/C6 **Broad Law** (mtn.), Sc,UK
135/F5 **Broadmeadows,** Austl.
134/C3 **Broad Sound** (chan.), Austl.
59/H4 **Broadstairs,** Eng,UK
59/E5 **Broadstone,** Eng,UK
183/M5 **Broadus,** Mt,US
194/F2 **Broad Valley,** Mb,Can
183/K4 **Broadview,** Mt,US
208/F5 **Broadview Heights,** Oh,US
192/C3 **Broadwater,** Ne,US
135/E1 **Broadwater Nat'l Park,** Austl.
59/E2 **Broadway,** Eng,UK
59/E2 **Broadway** (hill), Eng,UK
206/C2 **Broadway,** NJ,US
201/H1 **Broadway,** Va,US
58/D5 **Broadwindsor,** Eng,UK
161/F1 **Broa, Ensenada de la** (bay), Cuba
62/F3 **Broby,** Swe.
80/D4 **Broc,** Swi.
63/K3 **Brocēni,** Lat.
178/F3 **Brochet,** Mb,Can
179/R7 **Brock** (isl.), NW,Can
183/K2 **Brock,** Sk,Can
67/H5 **Brocken** (peak), Ger.
59/E5 **Brockenhurst,** Eng,UK
183/H3 **Brocket,** Ab,Can
194/E3 **Brocket,** ND,US
132/C2 **Brockman** (peak), Austl.
199/H3 **Brockport,** NY,US
208/C1 **Brockton,** Ma,US
183/M3 **Brockton,** Mt,US
199/J2 **Brockville,** On,Can
199/G4 **Brockway,** Pa,US
199/G3 **Brocton,** NY,US
178/G1 **Brodeur** (pen.), NW,Can
206/C1 **Brodhead** (cr.), Pa,US
198/B3 **Brodhead,** Wi,US
206/C2 **Brodheadsville,** Pa,US
54/A5 **Brodick,** Sc,UK
65/K2 **Brodnica,** Pol.
98/C2 **Brody,** Ukr.
66/C4 **Broek in Waterland,** Neth.
66/B3 **Broek Op Langedijk,** Neth.
201/H3 **Brogden,** NC,US
79/F2 **Broglie,** Fr.
198/B2 **Brokaw,** Wi,US
135/D2 **Broken** (bay), Austl.
191/G2 **Broken Arrow,** Ok,US
187/J4 **Broken Back** (crater), NM,US
192/E3 **Broken Bow,** Ne,US
191/G3 **Broken Bow,** Ok,US
191/G3 **Broken Bow** (dam), Ok,US
191/G3 **Broken Bow** (lake), Ok,US
194/F2 **Brokenhead Ind. Res.,** Sk,Can
133/J4 **Broken Hill,** Austl.
190/B4 **Brokeoff** (mts.), NM,US
166/C1 **Brokopondo,** Sur.
166/C1 **Brokopondo** (dist.), Sur.
83/A6 **Brolo,** It.
72/A2 **Brome,** Ger.
53/P7 **Bromley,** Eng,UK
53/P7 **Bromley** (bor.), Eng,UK
155/F3 **Bromley,** Zim.
53/P7 **Bromley Common,** Eng,UK
63/R7 **Bromma,** Swe.
124/F4 **Bromo** (mtn.), Indo.
62/F3 **Bromölla,** Swe.
124/F5 **Bromo-Tengger-Semeru Nat'l Prsv.,** Indo.
58/D2 **Bromsgrove,** Eng,UK
67/F6 **Bromskirchen,** Ger.
58/D2 **Bromyard,** Eng,UK
82/A1 **Bron,** Fr.
191/G2 **Bronaugh,** Mo,US
63/T9 **Brøndby,** Den.
62/C3 **Brønderslev,** Den.
145/E5 **Brong-Ahafo** (reg.), Gha.
86/C2 **Broni,** It.
156/E2 **Bronkhorstspruit,** SAfr.
58/C3 **Bronllys,** Wal,UK
94/H5 **Bronnitsy,** Rus.
61/E2 **Brønnøysund,** Nor.
62/C4 **Brøns,** Den.
81/F3 **Bronschhofen,** Swi.
203/G3 **Bronson,** Fl,US
191/G2 **Bronson,** Ks,US
198/D4 **Bronson,** Mi,US
189/G2 **Bronson,** Tx,US
197/R9 **Bronte,** On,Can
90/D4 **Bronte,** It.
188/D2 **Bronte,** Tx,US
200/E5 **Bronwood,** Ga,US
207/K8 **Bronx** (co.), NY,US
207/K8 **Bronx** (riv.), NY,US
207/K8 **Bronxville,** NY,US
207/K8 **Bronx Zoo,** NY,US
81/H5 **Bronzolo** (Branzoll), It.
198/C4 **Brook,** In,US
194/E2 **Brookdale,** Can
201/G4 **Brookdale,** SC,US
189/H2 **Brookeland,** Tx,US
203/G3 **Brooker,** Fl,US
125/B3 **Brookes Point,** Phil.
196/F3 **Brookfield,** NS,Can
208/A3 **Brookfield,** Ct,US
205/Q16 **Brookfield,** Il,US
208/B1 **Brookfield,** Ma,US
191/H1 **Brookfield,** Mo,US
208/G5 **Brookfield,** Oh,US
199/K2 **Brookfield,** Vt,US
205/P13 **Brookfield,** Wi,US
190/B1 **Brook Forest,** Co,US
200/B5 **Brookhaven,** Ms,US
207/F2 **Brookhaven,** NY,US
184/A2 **Brookings,** Or,US
193/F1 **Brookings,** SD,US
201/G4 **Brooklet,** Ga,US
208/C1 **Brookline,** Ma,US
208/C2 **Brooklyn,** Ct,US
193/H3 **Brooklyn,** Ia,US
202/D2 **Brooklyn,** Ms,US
208/F5 **Brooklyn,** Oh,US
195/P6 **Brooklyn Center,** Mn,US
208/F5 **Brooklyn Heights,** Oh,US
207/K9 **Brooklyn** (Kings) (co.), NY,US
206/B5 **Brooklyn Park,** Md,US
195/H5 **Brooklyn Park,** Mn,US
53/N6 **Brookmans Park,** Eng,UK
201/H2 **Brookneal,** Va,US
195/H5 **Brook Park,** Mn,US
208/F5 **Brook Park,** Oh,US
183/J2 **Brooks,** Ab,Can
177/E2 **Brooks** (mtn.), Ak,US
177/F2 **Brooks** (range), Ak,US
205/K9 **Brooks,** Ca,US
184/B1 **Brooks,** Or,US
183/M1 **Brooksby,** Sk,Can
189/G3 **Brookshire,** Tx,US
206/C4 **Brookside,** De,US
198/C4 **Brookston,** In,US
195/H4 **Brookston,** Mn,US
202/L6 **Brooksville,** Fl,US
203/G3 **Brooksville,** Fl,US
200/E1 **Brooksville,** Ky,US
200/C4 **Brooksville,** Ms,US
132/C5 **Brookton,** Austl.
198/D5 **Brookville,** In,US
200/E1 **Brookville** (lake), In,US
207/L8 **Brookville,** NY,US
199/G4 **Brookville,** Pa,US
206/C4 **Broomall,** Pa,US
130/A4 **Broome,** Austl.
192/B4 **Broomfield,** Co,US
78/C4 **Broons,** Fr.

64/E1 **Brørup**, Den.
62/F4 **Brösarp**, Swe.
191/J2 **Broseley**, Mo,US
60/A5 **Brosna**, Ire.
60/C3 **Brosna** (riv.), Ire.
197/P7 **Brossard**, Qu,Can
170/C4 **Brotas**, Braz.
184/C2 **Brothers**, Or,US
57/H2 **Brotton**, Eng,UK
79/G4 **Brou**, Fr.
57/F2 **Brough**, Eng,UK
197/S8 **Brougham**, On,Can
55/N13 **Brough Head** (pt.), Sc,UK
56/B2 **Broughshane**, NI,UK
59/F2 **Broughton**, Eng,UK
54/C5 **Broughton**, Sc,UK
57/E3 **Broughton in Furness**, Eng,UK
179/K2 **Broughton Island**, NW,Can
59/G4 **Broughton Street**, Eng,UK
135/D2 **Broulee**, Austl.
148/C1 **Broulko** (well), Chad
202/C2 **Broussard**, La,US
80/A1 **Brousseval**, Fr.
66/A5 **Brouwersdam** (dam), Neth.
66/A5 **Brouwershaven**, Neth.
98/F2 **Brovary**, Ukr.
62/C3 **Brovst**, Den.
202/P7 **Broward** (co.), Fl,US
195/G4 **Browerville**, Mn,US
133/H5 **Brown** (peak), Austl.
133/G5 **Brown** (pt.), Austl.
183/J3 **Brown** (mt.), Mt,US
182/B4 **Brown** (pt.), Wa,US
198/E3 **Brown City**, Mi,US
58/D2 **Brown Clee** (hill), Eng,UK
198/C3 **Brown Deer**, Wi,US
202/B2 **Browndell**, Tx,US
188/C1 **Brownfield**, Tx,US
59/E1 **Brownhills**, Eng,UK
135/D2 **Browning**, Austl.
193/H3 **Browning**, Mo,US
183/H3 **Browning**, Mt,US
194/A2 **Brownlee**, Sk,Can
184/E1 **Brownlee** (dam), Id, Or,US
184/E1 **Brownlee** (res.), Id, Or,US
192/D2 **Brownlee**, Ne,US
200/D4 **Browns**, Al,US
198/C5 **Brownsburg**, In,US
59/E5 **Brownsea** (isl.), Eng,UK
206/D4 **Browns Mills**, NJ,US
185/J3 **Browns Park Nat'l Wild. Ref.**, Co,US
193/K4 **Brownstown**, Il,US
198/C5 **Brownstown**, In,US
194/F5 **Browns Valley**, Mn,US
200/D2 **Brownsville**, Ky,US
207/K9 **Brownsville**, NY,US
184/B1 **Brownsville**, Or,US
200/C3 **Brownsville**, Tn,US
189/F5 **Brownsville**, Tx,US
205/B2 **Brownsville**, Wa,US
196/C3 **Brownville**, Me,US
196/C3 **Brownville Junction**, Me,US
58/B5 **Brown Willy** (hill), Eng,UK
188/E2 **Brownwood**, Tx,US
188/E2 **Brownwood** (lake), Tx,US
53/N6 **Broxbourne**, Eng,UK
54/C5 **Broxburn**, Sc,UK
203/G2 **Broxton**, Ga,US
80/C4 **Broye** (riv.), Swi.
197/L2 **Broyle** (cape), Nf,Can
76/B3 **Brozas**, Sp.
68/B3 **Bruay-en-Artois**, Fr.
68/C3 **Bruay-sur-l'Escaut**, Fr.
132/C2 **Bruce** (peak), Austl.
183/H1 **Bruce**, Ab,Can
198/F2 **Bruce** (pen.), On,Can
193/J1 **Bruce**, Wi,US
195/K4 **Bruce Crossing**, Mi,US
198/F2 **Bruce Peninsula Nat'l Park**, On,Can
132/C4 **Bruce Rock**, Austl.
200/C2 **Bruceton**, Tn,US
189/F2 **Bruceville-Eddy**, Tx,US
80/D1 **Bruche** (riv.), Fr.
67/G3 **Bruchhausen-Vilsen**, Ger.
70/B2 **Bruchköbel**, Ger.
69/G5 **Bruchmühlbach-Miesau**, Ger.
70/B4 **Bruchsal**, Ger.
67/G5 **Brucht** (riv.), Ger.
72/C3 **Brück**, Ger.
75/K3 **Bruck an der Grossglockner-strasse**, Aus.
73/A3 **Bruck an der Leitha**, Aus.
75/L3 **Bruck an der Mur**, Aus.
71/F5 **Bruckberg**, Ger.
64/F5 **Bruckmühl**, Ger.
58/D4 **Brue** (riv.), Eng,UK
60/B5 **Bruff**, Ire.
62/C1 **Bruflat**, Nor.
68/C1 **Bruges** (Brugge), Belg.
80/D3 **Brügg**, Swi.
68/C1 **Brugge** (Bruges), Belg.
66/D6 **Brüggen**, Ger.
87/F1 **Brugnera**, It.
69/F2 **Brühl**, Ger.
201/F1 **Bruin**, Ky,US
208/H5 **Bruin**, Pa,US
66/B5 **Bruinisse**, Neth.
86/A2 **Bruino**, It.
154/C5 **Brukkaros** (peak), Namb.
195/J4 **Brule** (lake), Mn,US
195/J4 **Brule**, Wi,US
79/E5 **Brûlon**, Fr.
68/D4 **Brûly**, Belg.
171/E2 **Brumado**, Braz.
69/G6 **Brumath**, Fr.
66/D4 **Brummen**, Neth.
62/D1 **Brumunddal**, Nor.
90/A2 **Bruncu Spina** (peak), It.
59/H1 **Brundall**, Eng,UK
68/D4 **Brune** (riv.), Fr.
184/F2 **Bruneau** (riv.), Id,US
125/A4 **Brunei**
125/A4 **Brunei** (bay), Bru.
125/A5 **Brunei** (int'l arpt.), Bru.
77/M9 **Brunete**, Sp.
197/J2 **Brunette** (isl.), Nf,Can
61/E3 **Brunflo**, Swe.
189/E4 **Bruni**, Tx,US
75/J3 **Brunico**, It.
80/E4 **Brünigpass** (pass), Swi.
192/F3 **Bruning**, Ne,US
63/R6 **Brunna**, Swe.
73/A3 **Brunn am Gebirge**, Aus.
81/E4 **Brunnen**, Swi.
136/B3 **Brunner**, N.Z.
194/B1 **Bruno**, Sk,Can
53/T10 **Brunoy**, Fr.
67/G1 **Brunsbüttel**, Ger.
201/G4 **Brunson**, SC,US
69/E2 **Brunssum**, Neth.
80/D2 **Brunstatt**, Fr.
135/F5 **Brunswick**, Austl.
175/J8 **Brunswick** (pen.), Chile
203/H2 **Brunswick**, Ga,US
201/J1 **Brunswick**, Md,US
196/C4 **Brunswick**, Me,US
191/H1 **Brunswick**, Mo,US
208/F5 **Brunswick**, Oh,US
67/H4 **Brunswick** (Braunschweig), Ger.
134/D5 **Brunswick Heads**, Austl.
132/B5 **Brunswick Junction**, Austl.
196/C4 **Brunswick Nav. Air Sta.**, Me,US
60/B5 **Bruree**, Ire.
161/E3 **Brus** (lag.), Hon.
92/F4 **Brusartsi**, Bul.
85/E6 **Brusciano**, It.
95/J3 **Brusenets**, Rus.
183/L4 **Brusett**, Mt,US
194/E4 **Brush** (hill), ND,US
208/G6 **Brush** (cr.), Pa,US
188/L7 **Brushy** (cr.), Tx,US
189/F2 **Brushy** (cr.), Tx,US
189/G2 **Brushy Creek**, Tx,US
81/G5 **Brusio**, Swi.
173/G3 **Brusque**, Braz.
198/F3 **Brussels**, On,Can
193/L1 **Brussels**, Wi,US
68/D2 **Brussels** (Bruxelles) (cap.), Belg.
68/D2 **Brussels** (National) (int'l arpt.), Belg.
86/A1 **Brusson**, It.
135/C3 **Bruthen**, Austl.
58/D4 **Bruton**, Eng,UK
68/D2 **Bruxelles** (Brussels) (cap.), Belg.
80/C1 **Bruyères**, Fr.
53/S11 **Bruyères-le-Châtel**, Fr.
53/S9 **Bruyères-sur-Oise**, Fr.
78/D4 **Bruz**, Fr.
164/D2 **Bruzual**, Ven.
83/C6 **Bruzzano Zeffirio**, It.
137/U **Bryan** (coast), Ant.
133/H5 **Bryan** (peak), Austl.
198/D4 **Bryan**, Oh,US
189/F2 **Bryan**, Tx,US
99/K3 **Bryanka**, Ukr.
96/E1 **Bryansk**, Rus.
99/G1 **Bryansk Obl.**, Rus.
191/H3 **Bryant**, Ar,US
208/D1 **Bryantville**, Ma,US
187/F2 **Bryce Canyon**, Ut,US
187/F2 **Bryce Canyon Nat'l Park**, Ut,US
57/E5 **Brymbo**, Wal,UK
58/C2 **Bryn Brawd** (mtn.), Wal,UK
62/A2 **Bryne**, Nor.
58/C3 **Brynithel**, Wal,UK
58/C3 **Brynmawr**, Wal,UK
206/C3 **Bryn Mawr**, Pa,US
199/H2 **Bryson**, Qu,Can
189/E1 **Bryson**, Tx,US
201/F3 **Bryson City**, NC,US
99/K5 **Bryukhovetskaya**, Rus.
65/J3 **Brzeg Dolny**, Pol.
65/L4 **Brzesko**, Pol.
65/M4 **Brzozów**, Pol.
155/G2 **Bua** (riv.), Malw.
62/E3 **Bua**, Swe.
123/C3 **Bua Chum**, Thai.
138/E5 **Buala**, Sol.
126/D4 **Buang**, Indo.
127/F4 **Buapinang**, Indo.
124/C2 **Buatan**, Indo.
146/D2 **Bū Athlah** (well), Libya
131/E2 **Buaya** (riv.), Indo.
123/C3 **Bua Yai**, Thai.
144/B4 **Buba**, GBis.
153/G3 **Bubanza**, Buru.
144/B4 **Bubaque**, GBis.
80/D3 **Bubendorf**, Swi.
81/E3 **Bubikon**, Swi.
105/G4 **Būbiyan** (isl.), Kuw.
151/A3 **Bubu** (riv.), Tanz.
152/D2 **Buburu**, Zaire
155/F4 **Bubye** (riv.), Zim.
53/S10 **Buc**, Fr.
104/B2 **Bucak**, Turk.
103/C1 **Bucakkişla**, Turk.
164/C3 **Bucaramanga**, Col.
125/D3 **Bucas Grande** (isl.), Phil.
134/C3 **Bucasia**, Austl.
125/C1 **Bucay**, Phil.
130/A4 **Buccaneer** (arch.), Austl.
85/F6 **Buccino**, It.
77/P10 **Bucelas**, Port.
81/G1 **Buch**, Ger.
96/D2 **Bucha**, Ukr.
98/C3 **Buchach**, Ukr.
179/J1 **Buchan** (gulf), NW,Can
54/D1 **Buchan** (dist.), Sc,UK
194/C2 **Buchanan**, Sk,Can
144/C5 **Buchanan**, Libr.
200/E4 **Buchanan**, Ga,US
198/C4 **Buchanan**, Mi,US
194/E4 **Buchanan**, ND,US
189/E2 **Buchanan** (lake), Tx,US
201/H2 **Buchanan**, Va,US
189/E2 **Buchanan Dam**, Tx,US
205/K11 **Buchanan Field** (arpt.), Ca,US
55/L8 **Buchan Ness** (pt.), Sc,UK
197/J1 **Buchans**, Nf,Can
174/E2 **Buchardo**, Arg.
93/H3 **Bucharest** (București) (cap.), Rom.
71/F6 **Buchbach**, Ger.
70/C3 **Buchen**, Ger.
81/G2 **Buchenberg**, Ger.
153/H3 **Buchenzi**, Tanz.
69/G3 **Buchholz**, Ger.
67/G2 **Buchholz in der Nordheide**, Ger.
70/D6 **Buchloe**, Ger.
54/B4 **Buchlyvie**, Sc,UK
186/B3 **Buchon** (pt.), Ca,US
81/F3 **Buchs**, Swi.
68/A4 **Buchy**, Fr.
87/E6 **Bucine**, It.
202/D2 **Buckatunna**, Ms,US
202/D1 **Buckatunna** (cr.), Ms,US
72/C3 **Buckau** (riv.), Ger.
57/F3 **Buckden Pike** (mtn.), Eng,UK
67/G4 **Bückeburg**, Ger.
187/F4 **Buckeye**, Az,US
198/E5 **Buckeye Lake**, Oh,US
58/C6 **Buckfastleigh**, Eng,UK
199/L2 **Buckfield**, Me,US
201/G1 **Buckhannon**, WV,US
54/C4 **Buckhaven**, Sc,UK
189/F2 **Buckholts**, Tx,US
187/H4 **Buckhorn**, NM,US
53/P7 **Buckhurst Hill**, Eng,UK
54/D1 **Buckie**, Sc,UK
199/J2 **Buckingham**, Qu,Can
59/F3 **Buckingham**, Eng,UK
208/B2 **Buckingham**, Ct,US
201/H2 **Buckingham**, Va,US
53/N7 **Buckingham Palace**, Eng,UK
59/F3 **Buckinghamshire** (co.), Eng,UK
196/B2 **Buckland**, Qu,Can
177/F2 **Buckland**, Ak,US
130/B3 **Buckle** (head), Austl.
57/E5 **Buckley**, Wal,UK
198/B4 **Buckley**, Il,US
198/D2 **Buckley**, Mi,US
205/C3 **Buckley**, Wa,US
73/A4 **Bucklige Welt** (reg.), Aus.
190/E2 **Bucklin**, Ks,US
58/D2 **Bucknell**, Eng,UK
190/E1 **Buckner** (cr.), Ks,US
192/E4 **Buckner** (cr.), Ks,US
72/E2 **Buckow**, Ger.
198/C1 **Buckroe**, Mi,US
206/C3 **Bucks** (co.), Pa,US
54/D2 **Bucksburn**, Sc,UK
196/C3 **Bucksport**, Me,US
54/D2 **Buck, The** (mtn.), Sc,UK
73/B1 **Bučovice**, Czh.
152/C4 **Buco-Zau**, Ang.
68/B3 **Bucquoy**, Fr.
142/B4 **Bu Craa**, WSah.
196/E2 **Buctouche**, NB,Can
159/H4 **Buctzotz**, Mex.
98/D5 **București** (co.), Rom.
93/H3 **București** (Bucharest) (cap.), Rom.
68/C5 **Bucy-le-Long**, Fr.
198/E4 **Bucyrus**, Oh,US
189/F2 **Buda**, Tx,US
73/C4 **Budai hegy** (hill), Hun.
153/H2 **Budaka**, Ugan.
73/C4 **Budakeszi**, Hun.
96/D1 **Buda-Koshelëvo**, Bela.
73/C5 **Budaörs**, Hun.
73/D5 **Budapest** (cap.), Hun.
73/D4 **Budapest** (co.), Hun.
97/J2 **Budarino**, Kaz.
120/B1 **Budaun**, India
137/H **Budd** (coast), Ant.
205/B3 **Budd** (inlet), Wa,US
150/B4 **Buddi**, Eth.
206/D2 **Budd Lake**, NJ,US
54/D4 **Buddon Ness** (pt.), Sc,UK
90/A2 **Buddusò**, It.
150/B4 **Bude**, Eth.
58/B5 **Bude**, Eng,UK
58/B5 **Bude** (bay), Eng,UK
200/B5 **Bude**, Ms,US
66/C6 **Budel**, Neth.
64/E1 **Büdelsdorf**, Ger.
121/G4 **Budge-Budge**, India
120/A1 **Budhāna**, India
121/E2 **Budhanilantha**, Nepal
76/D2 **Budia**, Sp.
70/C2 **Büdingen**, Ger.
152/D2 **Budjala**, Zaire
58/C5 **Budleigh Salterton**, Eng,UK
63/Q2 **Budogoshch'**, Rus.
114/F4 **Budongquan**, China
87/E3 **Budrio**, It.
127/E4 **Budungbudung**, Indo.
92/D4 **Budva**, Yugo.
93/J2 **Budzhak** (reg.), Mol., Ukr.
152/B1 **Buea**, Camr.
82/B3 **Buëch** (riv.), Fr.
186/B3 **Buellton**, Ca,US
158/D4 **Buelna** (int'l arpt.), Mex.
206/D4 **Buena**, NJ,US
182/D4 **Buena**, Wa,US
174/D2 **Buena Esperanza**, Arg.
164/B5 **Buena Fe**, Ecu.
204/C3 **Buena Park**, Ca,US
164/B4 **Buenaventura**, Col.
158/D2 **Buenaventura**, Mex.
169/F5 **Buena Vista**, Bol.
194/B2 **Buena Vista**, Sk,Can
158/E5 **Buenavista**, Mex.
175/G2 **Buena Vista**, Uru.
186/C3 **Buena Vista** (dry lake), Ca,US
192/A4 **Buena Vista**, Co,US
200/E4 **Buena Vista**, Ga,US
201/H2 **Buena Vista**, Va,US
164/D3 **Buena Vista**, Ven.
174/B4 **Bueno** (riv.), Chile
171/K7 **Bueno Brandão**, Braz.
170/D3 **Buenópolis**, Braz.
174/F2 **Buenos Aires** (cap.), Arg.
174/C5 **Buenos Aires** (lake), Arg.
174/E3 **Buenos Aires** (prov.), Arg.
163/B7 **Buenos Aires** (lake), Arg., Chile
164/B4 **Buenos Aires**, Col.
164/D4 **Buenos Aires**, Col.
168/B2 **Buenos Aires**, Peru
165/E4 **Buenos Aires**, Ven.
175/S12 **Buenos Aires** (Jorge Newbery) (int'l arpt.), Arg.
175/S12 **Buenos Aires** (Ministro Pistarini) (int'l arpt.), Arg.
171/F2 **Buerarema**, Braz.
164/B4 **Buesaco**, Col.
80/C5 **Buet** (mtn.), Fr.
76/A1 **Bueu**, Sp.
135/C3 **Buffalo** (peak), Austl.
183/H1 **Buffalo** (lake), Ab,Can
157/E2 **Buffalo** (riv.), SAfr.
191/H2 **Buffalo** (riv.), Ar,US
191/G2 **Buffalo**, Ks,US
195/H5 **Buffalo**, Mn,US
193/G1 **Buffalo** (cr.), Mn,US
191/H2 **Buffalo**, Mo,US
199/G3 **Buffalo**, NY,US
190/E2 **Buffalo**, Ok,US
206/A2 **Buffalo** (cr.), Pa,US
206/A3 **Buffalo** (cr.), Pa,US
208/H6 **Buffalo** (cr.), Pa,US
201/G3 **Buffalo**, SC,US
192/C1 **Buffalo**, SD,US
200/D3 **Buffalo** (riv.), Tn,US
189/F2 **Buffalo**, Tx,US
201/G2 **Buffalo** (mtn.), Va,US
193/J1 **Buffalo**, Wi,US
201/G1 **Buffalo**, WV,US
185/K1 **Buffalo**, Wy,US
149/F3 **Buffalo Cape**, Sudan
193/H2 **Buffalo Center**, Ia,US
192/B4 **Buffalo Creek**, Co,US
192/C2 **Buffalo Gap**, SD,US
188/E1 **Buffalo Gap**, Tx,US
192/C2 **Buffalo Gap Nat'l Grsld.**, SD,US
205/Q15 **Buffalo Grove**, Il,US
194/E3 **Buffalo Lake Nat'l Wild. Ref.**, ND,US
190/C3 **Buffalo Lake Nat'l Wild. Ref.**, Tx,US
191/H2 **Buffalo Nat'l River**, Ar,US
135/B1 **Buffalo Riv. Overflow** (swamp), Austl.
151/B1 **Buffalo Springs Nat'l Rsv.**, Kenya
208/B2 **Buff Cap** (hill), Ct,US
156/B3 **Buffelsrivier** (dry riv.), SAfr.
202/M8 **Buffum** (lake), Fl,US
141/X17 **Bū Fīshah**, Tun.
200/E3 **Buford**, Ga,US
200/E3 **Buford** (dam), Ga,US
192/B3 **Buford**, Wy,US
93/G3 **Buftea**, Rom.
96/B1 **Bug** (riv.), Eur.
93/K2 **Bug** (estuary), Ukr.
164/B4 **Buga**, Col.
161/F4 **Bugaba**, Pan.
92/D2 **Bugac**, Hun.
153/H3 **Bugala** (isl.), Ugan.
164/B3 **Bugalagrande**, Col.
135/D1 **Bugaldie**, Austl.
74/E5 **Bugarach, Pic de** (peak), Fr.
153/G3 **Bugarama**, Rwa.
108/C2 **Bugat**, Mong.
153/G3 **Bugaza**, Zaire
59/E2 **Bugbrooke**, Eng,UK
93/H5 **Buğdaylı**, Turk.
97/K5 **Bugdayly**, Trkm.
124/E4 **Bugel** (pt.), Indo.
153/G3 **Bugene**, Tanz.
68/D1 **Buggenhout**, Belg.
153/H2 **Bugiri**, Ugan.
92/C3 **Bugojno**, Bosn.
153/H2 **Bugosa** (prov.), Ugan.
95/L1 **Bugrino**, Rus.
125/B3 **Bugsuk** (isl.), Phil.
95/M5 **Bugul'ma**, Rus.
97/K1 **Buguruslan**, Rus.
108/D4 **Buh** (riv.), China
104/D2 **Buhayrat al Asad** (lake), Syria
104/B4 **Buhayrat al Manzilah** (lake), Egypt
105/E3 **Buḩayrat ath Tharthār** (lake), Iraq
151/A2 **Buhemba**, Tanz.
155/F3 **Buhera**, Zim.
80/D2 **Buhl**, Fr.
81/E2 **Bühl**, Ger.
185/F2 **Buhl**, Id,US
70/C4 **Bühler** (riv.), Ger.
192/F4 **Buhler**, Ks,US
189/H2 **Buhler**, La,US
70/C5 **Bühlerzell**, Ger.
93/H2 **Buhuşi**, Rom.
145/E4 **Bui** (dam), Gha.
201/H3 **Buies Creek**, NC,US
145/E4 **Bui Gorge** (res.), Gha.
66/B4 **Buiksloot**, Neth.
58/C2 **Builth Wells**, Wal,UK
174/Q9 **Buin**, Chile
81/G4 **Buin, Piz** (peak), Swi.
95/K5 **Buinsk**, Rus.
95/L5 **Buinsk**, Rus.
171/F1 **Buique**, Braz.
142/B5 **Buir Ahmed** (well), WSah.
142/B5 **Buir Taiaret** (well), WSah.
82/B4 **Buis-les-Baronnies**, Fr.
154/C4 **Buitepos**, Namb.
76/C4 **Bujalance**, Sp.
92/E4 **Bujanovac**, Yugo.
87/G2 **Buje**, Cro.
93/H3 **Bujor**, Rom.
153/G3 **Bujumbura** (cap.), Buru.
153/G3 **Bujumbura** (int'l arpt.), Buru.
65/J2 **Buk**, Pol.
138/E5 **Buka** (isl.), PNG
108/H1 **Bukachacha**, Rus.
114/F4 **Bukadaban Feng** (peak), China
153/H3 **Bukakata**, Ugan.
153/F5 **Bukama**, Zaire
105/F2 **Būkān**, Iran
153/H3 **Bukasa** (isl.), Ugan.
153/G3 **Bukavu**, Zaire
151/A3 **Bukene**, Tanz.
123/C5 **Buket Bubat** (peak), Malay.
100/G6 **Bukhara**, Uzb.
93/F4 **Bukhovo**, Bul.
108/A2 **Bukhtarma** (riv.), Kaz.
151/A2 **Bukima**, Tanz.
124/D4 **Bukitkemuning**, Indo.
124/C1 **Bukit Mertajam**, Malay.
124/C3 **Bukittinggi**, Indo.
92/E1 **Bükki Nat'l Park**, Hun.
153/G3 **Bukoba**, Tanz.
151/A2 **Bukonyo**, Tanz.
114/D4 **Buksamaral**, China
126/B4 **Buku** (cape), Indo.
145/H4 **Bukuru**, Nga.
146/A3 **Bū Kūsa, Bi'r** (well), Libya
190/C4 **Bula**, Tx,US
152/C5 **Bula Atumba**, Ang.
125/E6 **Bulacan**, Phil.
81/E2 **Bülach**, Swi.
127/F4 **Bulagi**, Indo.
135/E2 **Bulahdelah**, Austl.
125/C2 **Bulalakao**, Phil.
125/C2 **Bulan**, Phil.
201/F2 **Bulan**, Ky,US
95/P4 **Bulanash**, Rus.
104/D1 **Bulancak**, Turk.
120/A1 **Bulandshahr**, India
104/E2 **Bulanık**, Turk.
127/F3 **Bulawa** (peak), Indo.
155/F4 **Bulawayo**, Zim.
155/F4 **Bulawayo** (int'l arpt.), Zim.
100/H4 **Bulayevo**, Kaz.
104/B2 **Buldan**, Turk.
168/B3 **Buldibuyo**, Peru
177/B5 **Buldir** (isl.), Ak,US
150/A4 **Bule**, Eth.
157/E2 **Bulembu**, Swaz.
108/C2 **Bulgan**, Mong.
108/E2 **Bulgan**, Mong.
108/C2 **Bulgan** (riv.), Mong.
93/G4 **Bulgaria**
93/H4 **Bŭlgarovo**, Bul.
83/B2 **Bulgheria** (peak), It.
134/A4 **Bulgroo**, Austl.
125/B3 **Bululuyan** (cape), Phil.
134/F7 **Bulimba** (cr.), Austl.
62/D4 **Bülk** (pt.), Ger.
149/H4 **Bulkʼī**, Eth.
59/E2 **Bulkington**, Eng,UK
182/G3 **Bull** (riv.), BC,Can
56/B1 **Bull** (pt.), NI,UK
203/H1 **Bull** (isl.), SC,US
69/F3 **Bullange**, Belg.
189/G1 **Bullard**, Tx,US
76/E3 **Bullas**, Sp.
150/C3 **Bullaxaar**, Som.
80/D4 **Bulle**, Swi.
135/C3 **Buller** (peak), Austl.
62/D4 **Bullerup**, Den.
132/C4 **Bullfinch**, Austl.
194/D5 **Bullhead**, SD,US
186/E3 **Bullhead City**, Az,US
69/F3 **Büllingen**, Belg.
53/R11 **Bullion**, Fr.
201/H2 **Bullock**, NC,US
134/A5 **Bulloo** (riv.), Austl.
135/B1 **Bulloo Downs**, Austl.
134/A5 **Bulloo Riv. Overflow** (swamp), Austl.
136/C3 **Bulls**, N.Z.
191/H2 **Bull Shoals**, Ar,US
191/H2 **Bull Shoals** (lake), Ar, Mo,US
187/F2 **Bull Valley** (mts.), Ut,US
184/E1 **Bully** (riv.), Or,US
68/B3 **Bully-les-Mines**, Fr.
108/D2 **Bulnayn** (mts.), Mong.
174/B3 **Bulnes**, Chile
131/G1 **Bulolo**, PNG
153/E4 **Bulongo**, Zaire
53/Q7 **Bulphan**, Eng,UK
156/D3 **Bultfontein**, SAfr.
125/D4 **Buluan**, Phil.
127/F5 **Bulukumba**, Indo.
152/D4 **Bulungu**, Zaire
153/E4 **Bulungu**, Zaire
153/H4 **Bulungwa**, Tanz.
152/C5 **Bumba**, Ang.
152/D4 **Bumba**, Zaire
153/E2 **Bumba**, Zaire
146/D1 **Bumbah, Khalīj al** (gulf), Libya
187/F3 **Bumble Bee**, Az,US
125/B4 **Bum Bum** (isl.), Malay.
144/C4 **Bumbuna**, SLeo.
116/C3 **Bumhpa** (peak), Burma
124/E4 **Bumiayu**, Indo.
121/H2 **Bum La** (pass), India
121/H2 **Bumthang**, Bhu.
121/H2 **Bumthang** (riv.), Bhu.
151/B1 **Buna**, Kenya
131/H2 **Buna**, PNG
189/H2 **Buna**, Tx,US
111/L9 **Bunaga-take** (peak), Japan
125/D3 **Bunawan**, Phil.
153/G3 **Bunazi**, Tanz.
132/B5 **Bunbury**, Austl.
193/H4 **Bunceton**, Mo,US
191/G3 **Bunch**, Ok,US
60/D4 **Bunclody**, Ire.
134/D4 **Bundaberg**, Austl.
135/D1 **Bundarra**, Austl.
67/E2 **Bünde**, Ger.
67/F4 **Bünde**, Ger.
118/C2 **Būndi**, India
131/G1 **Bundi**, PNG
55/G9 **Bundoran**, Ire.
121/E4 **Būndu**, India
125/D2 **Bunga** (pt.), Phil.
124/B3 **Bungalaut** (str.), Indo.
59/H2 **Bungay**, Eng,UK
135/D2 **Bungendore**, Austl.
189/E1 **Bunger**, Tx,US
123/C2 **Bung Kan**, Thai.
127/F4 **Bungku**, Indo.
152/C4 **Bungo**, Ang.
151/A1 **Bungoma**, Kenya
126/C3 **Bunguran** (isl.), Indo.
153/G2 **Bunia**, Zaire
63/T9 **Bunkeflo Strand**, Swe.
191/J2 **Bunker**, Mo,US
200/C1 **Bunker Hill**, Il,US
198/C4 **Bunker Hill**, In,US
199/G5 **Bunker Hill**, WV,US
189/M9 **Bunker Hill Village**, Tx,US
187/E2 **Bunkerville**, Nv,US
153/F5 **Bunkeya**, Zaire
202/B2 **Bunkie**, La,US
203/H3 **Bunnell**, Fl,US
66/C4 **Bunnik**, Neth.
77/E3 **Buñol**, Sp.
66/C4 **Bunschoten**, Neth.
123/D3 **Buntharik**, Thai.
59/F3 **Buntingford**, Eng,UK
157/E2 **Bunya**, Swaz.
151/A1 **Bunyala**, Kenya
134/C4 **Bunya Mountains Nat'l Park**, Austl.
104/C2 **Bünyan**, Turk.
189/E1 **Bunyan**, Tx,US
134/E6 **Bunya Park**, Austl.
125/B5 **Bunyu** (isl.), Indo.
81/E4 **Buochs**, Swi.
83/C6 **Buonamico** (riv.), It.
84/B1 **Buonconvento**, It.
123/E3 **Buon Me Thuot**, Viet.
123/E3 **Buon Mrong**, Viet.
131/F1 **Bupul**, Indo.
150/C4 **Buqde Caqable**, Som.
171/F1 **Buquim**, Braz.
151/B2 **Bura**, Kenya
149/E3 **Buram**, Sudan
114/D5 **Burang**, China
153/G2 **Buranga** (pass), Ugan.
97/K2 **Burannoye**, Rus.
87/F2 **Burano**, It.
87/F5 **Burano** (riv.), It.
140/G4 **Burao**, Som.
150/C3 **Burao** (Burco), Som.
202/D3 **Buras-Triumph**, La,US
125/D3 **Burauen**, Phil.
106/D3 **Buraydah**, SAr.
69/H2 **Burbach**, Ger.
204/B2 **Burbank**, Ca,US
205/Q16 **Burbank**, Il,US
208/F6 **Burbank**, Oh,US
182/E4 **Burbank**, Wa,US
204/F7 **Burbank-Glendale-Pasadena** (arpt.), Ca,US
68/B2 **Burbure**, Fr.
135/C2 **Burcher**, Austl.
150/C3 **Burco** (Burao), Som.
120/A3 **Burda**, India.
134/B3 **Burdekin** (riv.), Austl.
205/J10 **Burdell** (mtn.), Ca,US
191/F2 **Burden**, Ks,US
183/J3 **Burdett**, Ab,Can
190/E1 **Burdett**, Ks,US
192/E1 **Burdette**, SD,US
104/B2 **Burdur**, Turk.
104/B2 **Burdur** (lake), Turk.
104/B2 **Burdur** (prov.), Turk.
121/F4 **Burdwān**, India
149/G3 **Burē**, Eth.
149/H3 **Burē**, Eth.
59/H1 **Bure** (riv.), Eng,UK
67/F5 **Büren**, Ger.
66/C2 **Buren**, Neth.
66/C5 **Buren**, Neth.
80/D3 **Büren an der Aare**, Swi.
108/E2 **Bürengiyn** (mts.), Mong.
53/S10 **Bures-sur-Yvette**, Fr.
122/B2 **Būrewāla**, Pak.
109/L1 **Bureya** (mts.), Rus.
109/L1 **Bureya** (riv.), Rus.
198/F3 **Burford**, On,Can
59/E3 **Burford**, Eng,UK
103/C4 **Būr Fu'ād**, Egypt
62/C5 **Burg**, Ger.
62/D4 **Burg**, Ger.
64/E2 **Burg**, Ger.
72/B3 **Burg**, Ger.
72/E4 **Burg**, Ger.
93/H4 **Burgas**, Bul.
93/H4 **Burgas** (bay), Bul.
93/H4 **Burgas** (int'l arpt.), Bul.
91/K1 **Burgas** (prov.), Bul.
93/H4 **Burgas** (reg.), Bul.
70/D6 **Burgau**, Ger.
201/J3 **Burgaw**, NC,US
81/G2 **Burgberg im Allgäu**, Ger.
70/D4 **Burgbernheim**, Ger.
69/G3 **Burgbrohl**, Ger.
67/H4 **Burgdorf**, Ger.
80/D3 **Burgdorf**, Swi.
70/D3 **Burgebrach**, Ger.
72/B6 **Bürgel**, Ger.
73/A4 **Burgenland** (prov.), Aus.
197/J2 **Burgeo**, Nf,Can
156/D3 **Burgersdorp**, SAfr.
132/D4 **Burges** (peak), Austl.
178/C2 **Burgess** (mtn.), NW,Can
177/L2 **Burgess** (mtn.), Yk,Can
59/F5 **Burgess Hill**, Eng,UK
208/G7 **Burgettstown**, Pa,US
61/E2 **Burgfjället** (peak), Swe.
70/D3 **Burghaslach**, Ger.
71/F6 **Burghausen**, Ger.
54/C1 **Burghead**, Sc,UK
54/C1 **Burghead** (bay), Sc,UK
70/E5 **Burgheim**, Ger.
208/G5 **Burghill**, Oh,US
57/J5 **Burgh le Marsh**, Eng,UK
200/E2 **Burgin**, Ky,US
71/G6 **Burgkirchen**, Aus.
71/F6 **Burgkirchen an der Alz**, Ger.
70/E2 **Burgkunstadt**, Ger.
81/F2 **Bürglen**, Swi.
71/F4 **Burglengenfeld**, Ger.
67/F2 **Burglesum**, Ger.
159/F3 **Burgos**, Mex.
76/D1 **Burgos**, Sp.
70/C2 **Burgsinn**, Ger.
72/C6 **Burgstädt**, Ger.
81/H4 **Burgstall** (Postal), It.
67/E4 **Burgsteinfurt**, Ger.
62/H3 **Burgsvik**, Swe.
80/A3 **Burgundy** (hist. reg.), Fr.
74/F3 **Burgundy** (reg.), Fr.
67/G3 **Burgwedel**, Ger.
121/F4 **Burhābalang** (riv.), India
108/D4 **Burhan Budai** (mts.), China
104/A2 **Burhaniye**, Turk.
118/C3 **Burhānpur**, India
120/C4 **Burhar**, India
116/B3 **Burhi Dihing** (riv.), India
121/E3 **Burhi Gandak** (riv.), India
170/C4 **Buri**, Braz.
150/A2 **Buri** (pen.), Eth.
125/C2 **Burias** (isl.), Phil.
97/L2 **Buribay**, Rus.
161/F4 **Burica** (pen.), CR, Pan.
161/F4 **Burica** (pt.), Pan.
205/C3 **Burien**, Wa,US
197/K2 **Burin**, Nf,Can
197/K2 **Burin** (pen.), Nf,Can
123/C3 **Buriram**, Thai.
170/C4 **Buritama**, Braz.
167/F3 **Buriti**, Braz.
170/C3 **Buriti Alegre**, Braz.
167/F4 **Buriti Bravo**, Braz.
167/F3 **Buriti dos Lopes**, Braz.
170/D2 **Buritis**, Braz.
173/H1 **Buritizeiro**, Braz.
77/E3 **Burjasot**, Sp.
70/D2 **Burkardroth**, Ger.
72/E5 **Burkau**, Ger.
191/E3 **Burkburnett**, Tx,US
137/S **Burke** (isl.), Ant.
192/E2 **Burke**, SD,US
206/A6 **Burke**, Va,US
81/G4 **Bürkelkopf** (peak), Aus.
201/G2 **Burkes Garden**, Va,US
200/E2 **Burkesville**, Ky,US
131/E4 **Burketown**, Austl.
188/E2 **Burkett**, Tx,US
189/H2 **Burkeville**, Tx,US
201/H2 **Burkeville**, Va,US
72/C6 **Burkhardtsdorf**, Ger.
145/E3 **Burkina Faso**
199/G2 **Burk's Falls**, On,Can
70/C6 **Burladingen**, Ger.
189/F3 **Burleigh**, Tx,US
189/F1 **Burleson**, Tx,US
185/G2 **Burley**, Id,US
205/B3 **Burley**, Wa,US
97/K2 **Burli**, Kaz.
205/K11 **Burlingame**, Ca,US
191/G1 **Burlingame**, Ks,US
199/G3 **Burlington**, On,Can
192/C4 **Burlington**, Co,US
208/B2 **Burlington**, Ct,US
193/J3 **Burlington**, Ia,US
205/N15 **Burlington**, Il,US
193/G4 **Burlington**, Ks,US
200/E1 **Burlington**, Ky,US
196/C3 **Burlington**, Me,US
201/H2 **Burlington**, NC,US
194/D3 **Burlington**, ND,US
206/D3 **Burlington**, NJ,US
206/D4 **Burlington** (co.), NJ,US
191/E2 **Burlington**, Ok,US
199/K2 **Burlington**, Vt,US
182/C3 **Burlington**, Wa,US
205/P14 **Burlington**, Wi,US
193/G3 **Burlington Junction**, Mo,US
119/G2 **Burma** (Myanmar)
71/F7 **Bürmoos**, Aus.
200/C2 **Burna**, Ky,US
182/C3 **Burnaby**, BC,Can
93/K3 **Burnas** (lake), Ukr.
189/F3 **Burnell**, Tx,US
189/E2 **Burnet**, Tx,US
134/D4 **Burnett Heads**, Austl.
175/J8 **Burney** (peak), Chile
184/C3 **Burney**, Ca,US
184/C3 **Burney** (falls), Ca,US
191/F4 **Burneyville**, Ok,US
205/Q16 **Burnham**, Il,US
191/J2 **Burnham**, Mo,US
199/H4 **Burnham**, Pa,US
59/G3 **Burnham on Crouch**, Eng,UK
58/D4 **Burnham on Sea**, Eng,UK
135/C4 **Burnie-Somerset**, Austl.
57/F4 **Burnley**, Eng,UK
54/D5 **Burnmouth**, Sc,UK
135/B2 **Burns**, Austl.
185/K4 **Burns**, Co,US
184/D2 **Burns**, Or,US
190/E3 **Burns Flat**, Ok,US
178/E2 **Burnside** (riv.), NW,Can
166/B1 **Burnside**, Sur.
200/E2 **Burnside**, Ky,US
178/D3 **Burns Lake**, BC,Can
194/E4 **Burnstad**, ND,US
195/H5 **Burnsville**, Mn,US
200/C3 **Burnsville**, Ms,US
201/F3 **Burnsville**, NC,US
201/G1 **Burnsville**, WV,US
54/C4 **Burntisland**, Sc,UK
197/H2 **Burnt Islands**, Nf,Can
178/G3 **Burntwood** (riv.), Mb,Can
59/E1 **Burntwood**, Eng,UK
133/J5 **Buronga**, Austl.
86/B2 **Buronzo**, It.
196/D3 **Burpee Game Ref.**, NB,Can
103/G7 **Burqā**, WBnk.
108/B2 **Burqin**, China
108/B2 **Burqin** (riv.), China
103/G7 **Burqīn**, WBnk.
133/H5 **Burra**, Austl.
135/C2 **Burraboi**, Austl.
129/H6 **Burragorang** (lake), Austl.
133/H2 **Burramurra**, Austl.
91/G2 **Burrel**, Alb.
135/D2 **Burrendong** (res.), Austl.
135/D1 **Burren Junction**, Austl.
60/A3 **Burren, The** (reg.), Ire.
135/D2 **Burrewarra** (pt.), Austl.
77/E3 **Burriana**, Sp.
134/D5 **Burringbar**, Austl.
135/D2 **Burrinjuck** (res.), Austl.
187/F3 **Burro** (cr.), Az,US
191/E1 **Burr Oak**, Ks,US
166/B1 **Burroburro** (riv.), Guy.
158/E2 **Burro, Serranías del** (mts.), Mex.
134/A2 **Burrowes** (pt.), Austl.
56/D2 **Burrow Head** (pt.), Sc,UK
205/Q16 **Burr Ridge**, Il,US
134/D4 **Burrum Heads**, Austl.
134/D4 **Burrum River Nat'l Park**, Austl.
208/A2 **Burrville**, Ct,US
58/B3 **Burry** (inlet), Wal,UK
58/B3 **Burry Port**, Wal,UK
93/J5 **Bursa**, Turk.
93/J5 **Bursa** (prov.), Turk.
147/G3 **Būr Safājah**, Egypt
103/C4 **Būr Saʻīd** (gov.), Egypt
103/C4 **Būr Saʻīd** (Port Said), Egypt
67/E6 **Burscheid**, Ger.
57/F4 **Burscough Bridge**, Eng,UK
98/C3 **Burshtyn**, Ukr.
70/B3 **Bürstadt**, Ger.
183/K2 **Burstall**, Sk,Can
147/H5 **Būr Sūdān** (Port Sudan), Sudan
193/G2 **Burt**, Ia,US
198/E3 **Burt**, Mi,US
197/T9 **Burt**, NY,US
133/J5 **Burta**, Austl.
147/G2 **Būr Tawfīq**, Egypt
70/D6 **Burtenbach**, Ger.
182/F3 **Burton**, BC,Can
196/D3 **Burton**, NB,Can
59/E5 **Burton**, Eng,UK
201/F3 **Burton** (lake), Ga,US
205/E6 **Burton**, Mi,US
208/F5 **Burton**, Oh,US
201/G4 **Burton**, SC,US
189/F2 **Burton**, Tx,US
205/C3 **Burton**, Wa,US
59/F2 **Burton Latimer**, Eng,UK
59/E1 **Burton upon Trent**, Eng,UK
196/D2 **Burtts Corner**, NB,Can
127/G4 **Buru** (isl.), Indo.
103/B4 **Burullus, Buḩayrat al** (lag.), Egypt
150/D2 **Burūm**, Yem.
125/C2 **Buruncan** (pt.), Phil.
153/G3 **Burundi**
108/F2 **Burun Shibertuy** (peak), Rus.
153/G3 **Bururi**, Buru.
145/G5 **Burutu**, Nga.
177/L3 **Burwash Landing**, Yk,Can
59/G2 **Burwell**, Eng,UK
192/E3 **Burwell**, Ne,US
185/J2 **Burwell** (mt.), Wy,US
68/B5 **Bury**, Fr.
59/F5 **Bury**, Eng,UK
101/M4 **Buryat Aut. Rep.**, Rus.
99/G2 **Buryn'**, Ukr.
97/J3 **Burynshyk** (pt.), Kaz.
59/G2 **Bury Saint Edmunds**, Eng,UK
125/D4 **Busa** (mt.), Phil.
86/B3 **Busalla**, It.
153/F5 **Busanga**, Zaire
183/L5 **Busby**, Mt,US
86/A3 **Busca**, It.
202/L7 **Busch Gardens**, Fl,US
203/G3 **Busch Gardens**, Fl,US
201/J2 **Busch Gardens**, Va,US
153/H2 **Busembatia**, Ugan.
70/A4 **Busenberg**, Ger.
81/F5 **Buseno**, Swi.
56/B1 **Bush** (riv.), NI,UK
206/B5 **Bush** (riv.), Md,US
108/C2 **Büs Hayrhan** (peak), Mong.
105/G4 **Būshehr**, Iran
105/G4 **Būshehr** (gov.), Iran
114/D5 **Bushêngcaka**, China
53/M7 **Bushey**, Eng,UK
153/E4 **Bushimaie** (riv.), Zaire
206/C1 **Bushkill**, Pa,US
206/C1 **Bushkill** (falls), Pa,US
206/C1 **Bush Kill** (riv.), Pa,US
156/B3 **Bushmanland** (reg.), SAfr.
154/E4 **Bushman Pits**, Bots.
56/B1 **Bushmills**, NI,UK
202/L6 **Bushnell**, Fl,US
203/G3 **Bushnell**, Fl,US
193/J3 **Bushnell**, Il,US
191/E1 **Bushton**, Ks,US
151/A1 **Busia**, Kenya
68/C3 **Busigny**, Fr.
153/E2 **Businga**, Zaire
152/D3 **Busira** (riv.), Zaire
98/C3 **Busk**, Ukr.
62/C1 **Buskerud** (co.), Nor.
65/L3 **Busko-Zdrój**, Pol.
151/A1 **Busoga** (prov.), Ugan.
103/E3 **Buṣrá ash Shām**, Syria
132/B5 **Busselton**, Austl.
83/B2 **Bussento** (riv.), It.
149/E4 **Busseri** (riv.), Sudan
86/D3 **Busseto**, It.
80/B2 **Bussières-lès-Belmont**, Fr.
85/D3 **Bussi sul Tirino**, It.
87/D2 **Bussolengo**, It.
82/D2 **Bussoleno**, It.
66/C4 **Bussum**, Neth.
188/D4 **Bustamante**, Mex.
175/K7 **Bustamante** (pt.), Arg.
134/C4 **Bustard** (pt.), Austl.
93/G3 **Buşteni**, Rom.
86/B1 **Busto Arsizio**, It.
86/B1 **Busto Garolfo**, It.
153/E2 **Busu-Djanoa**, Zaire
152/E2 **Busu Kwanga**, Zaire
64/E1 **Büsum**, Ger.
152/E2 **Busu Melo**, Zaire
145/E4 **Busunu**, Gha.
152/D2 **Busu Yale**, Zaire
153/F2 **Buta**, Zaire
149/H3 **Butajīra**, Eth.
174/C3 **Buta Ranquil**, Arg.
153/G3 **Butare**, Rwa.
138/G4 **Butaritari** (isl.), Kiri.
133/H5 **Bute**, Austl.
182/B2 **Bute** (inlet), BC,Can
54/A5 **Bute** (isl.), Sc,UK
54/A5 **Bute** (sound), Sc,UK
108/E2 **Büteeliyn** (mts.), Mong.
151/B1 **Bute Helu**, Kenya
153/G2 **Butembo**, Zaire
69/F3 **Bütgenbach**, Belg.
156/E3 **Butha-Buthe**, Les.
86/D5 **Buti**, It.
153/G2 **Butiaba**, Ugan.
200/C4 **Butler**, Al,US
202/M7 **Butler** (lake), Fl,US
200/E4 **Butler**, Ga,US
198/D4 **Butler**, In,US
191/G1 **Butler**, Mo,US
207/H8 **Butler**, NJ,US
208/E6 **Butler**, Oh,US
208/H6 **Butler**, Pa,US
208/H6 **Butler** (co.), Pa,US
189/F2 **Butler**, Tx,US
60/C1 **Butlersbridge**, Ire.
92/D4 **Butmir** (int'l arpt.), Yugo.
201/H2 **Butner**, NC,US
130/A1 **Buton** (isl.), Indo.
53/S9 **Butry-sur-Oise**, Fr.
80/D4 **Bütschelegg** (peak), Swi.
81/F3 **Bütschwil**, Swi.
200/C4 **Buttahatchie** (riv.), Al, Ms,US
87/E2 **Buttapietra**, It.
184/C4 **Butte** (cr.), Ca,US
194/D4 **Butte**, ND,US
192/E2 **Butte**, Ne,US
70/B3 **Büttelborn**, Ger.
184/D1 **Butter** (cr.), Or,US
193/G2 **Butterfield**, Mn,US
201/H3 **Butters**, NC,US
124/C1 **Butterworth**, Malay.
156/E4 **Butterworth**, SAfr.
80/C4 **Buttes**, Swi.
183/H4 **Butte-Silver**, Mt,US
60/B5 **Buttevant**, Ire.
82/D2 **Buttigliera Alta**, It.
186/C3 **Buttonwillow**, Ca,US
87/G1 **Buttrio**, It.
72/B5 **Buttstädt**, Ger.
125/D3 **Butuan City**, Phil.
102/M10 **Butung** (isl.), Indo.
138/B5 **Butung** (isl.), Phil.
99/L2 **Buturlinovka**, Rus.
120/D2 **Butwal**, Nepal
70/B2 **Butzbach**, Ger.
64/F2 **Bützow**, Ger.
150/C3 **Buuhoodle**, Som.
150/C5 **Buulo Berde**, Som.
151/C2 **Buur Gaabo**, Som.
150/C5 **Buur Hakaba**, Som.
141/X17 **Bū 'Urqūb**, Tun.
153/H2 **Buvuma** (isl.), Ugan.
120/D3 **Buxar**, India
70/D7 **Buxheim**, Ger.
67/G2 **Buxtehude**, Ger.
57/G5 **Buxton**, Eng,UK
196/B4 **Buxton**, Me,US
94/J4 **Buy**, Rus.
195/H3 **Buyck**, Mn,US
97/H4 **Buynaksk**, Rus.
144/D5 **Buyo, Barrage de** (dam), IvC.
109/H2 **Buyr** (lake), Mong.
116/D4 **Buyuan** (riv.), China
93/J5 **Büyükada**, Turk.
105/N7 **Büyükada** (isl.), Turk.
91/K2 **Büyük Anafarta**, Turk.
104/D2 **Büyükarmutlu**, Turk.
93/J5 **Büyükçekmece**, Turk.
105/M6 **Büyükçekmece** (lake), Turk.
103/C1 **Büyükeceli**, Turk.
93/H5 **Büyükkarıştıran**, Turk.
109/N2 **Buyukly**, Rus.
89/L3 **Büyükmenderes** (riv.), Turk.
104/D2 **Büyükyurt**, Turk.
113/B2 **Buyun** (peak), China
151/B3 **Buyuni, Ras** (pt.), Tanz.
115/E2 **Buyun Shan** (peak), China
97/J3 **Buzachi** (pen.), Kaz.
89/K1 **Buzău** (riv.), Rom.
74/D3 **Buzançais**, Fr.
69/D5 **Buzancy**, Fr.
93/H3 **Buzău**, Rom.
93/H3 **Buzău** (co.), Rom.
93/H3 **Buzău** (riv.), Rom.
87/G2 **Buzet**, Cro.
155/G3 **Búzi** (riv.), Moz.
92/E3 **Buziaş**, Rom.
171/L8 **Búzios** (isl.), Braz.
73/B6 **Buzsák**, Hun.
53/J3 **Buzuluk**, Rus.
201/G3 **Buzzard Roost** (dam), SC,US
208/C3 **Buzzards** (bay), Ma,US
144/D4 **Bwandougou**, IvC.
152/D3 **Bwasa**, Zaire
60/B5 **Bweeng** (mtn.), Ire.
93/G4 **Byala**, Bul.
93/H4 **Byala**, Bul.
93/F4 **Byala Slatina**, Bul.
179/R7 **Byam Martin** (chan.), NW,Can
179/R7 **Byam Martin** (isl.), NW,Can
191/F3 **Byars**, Ok,US
65/J2 **Bydgoszcz**, Pol.
65/J2 **Bydgoszcz** (prov.), Pol.
183/H2 **Byemoor**, Ab,Can
190/E2 **Byers**, Ks,US
198/F5 **Byesville**, Oh,US
59/E2 **Byfield**, Eng,UK
53/M8 **Byfleet**, Eng,UK
132/L7 **Byford**, Austl.
62/B2 **Bygland**, Nor.
63/P5 **Bykhov**, Bela.
62/B2 **Bykle**, Nor.
97/H2 **Bykovo**, Rus.
101/N2 **Bykovskiy**, Rus.
187/G4 **Bylas**, Az,US
56/E5 **Bylchau**, Wal,UK
179/J1 **Bylot** (isl.), NW,Can
191/F3 **Byng**, Ok,US
198/F2 **Byng Inlet**, On,Can
206/B4 **Bynum** (run), Md,US
183/H4 **Bynum**, Mt,US
189/F2 **Bynum**, Tx,US
105/F2 **Byoyuk-Kirs** (peak), Azer.
207/E2 **Byram** (pt.), Ct,US
207/L7 **Byram** (riv.), Ct,US
200/B4 **Byram**, Ms,US
207/L7 **Byram** (lake), NY,US
207/E1 **Byram** (riv.), NY,US
137/U **Byrd** (cape), Ant.
137/L **Byrd** (glac.), Ant.
200/E2 **Byrdstown**, Tn,US
62/B2 **Byremo**, Nor.
135/C1 **Byrock**, Austl.
200/F4 **Byromville**, Ga,US
175/J6 **Byron** (isl.), Chile
205/L11 **Byron**, Ca,US
200/F4 **Byron**, Ga,US
193/K2 **Byron**, Il,US
135/E1 **Byron Bay**, Austl.
100/K2 **Byrranga** (mts.), Rus.
62/D3 **Byrum**, Den.
71/F2 **Bystice** (riv.), Czh.
65/K4 **Bystrá** (peak), Slvk.
71/H3 **Bystřice**, Czh.
101/N3 **Bytantay** (riv.), Rus.
73/C1 **Bytča, Veľ'ká**, Slvk.
65/K3 **Bytom**, Pol.
65/J1 **Bytów**, Pol.
105/M6 **Büyükçekmece**, Turk.
153/G3 **Byumba**, Rwa.

**C**

187/H1 **C** (can.), Co,US
123/D2 **Ca** (riv.), Viet.
173/E3 **Caacupé**, Par.
173/E3 **Caaguazú**, Par.
173/E2 **Caaguazú** (dept.), Par.
154/B2 **Caála**, Ang.
167/E5 **Caatingas** (reg.), Braz.
173/E3 **Caazapá**, Par.
173/E2 **Caazapá** (dept.), Par.
125/D3 **Cabadbaran**, Phil.
161/G1 **Cabaiguán**, Cuba
187/J4 **Caballo**, NM,US
187/J4 **Caballo** (res.), NM,US
168/D1 **Caballococha**, Peru
168/B3 **Cabana**, Peru
168/D4 **Cabanaconde**, Peru
76/C1 **Cabañaquinta**, Sp.
125/C2 **Cabanatuan City**, Phil.
58/C2 **Caban Coch** (res.), Wal,UK
77/F2 **Cabanes**, Sp.
196/C2 **Cabano**, Qu,Can
125/C1 **Cabarroquis**, Phil.
125/C3 **Cabatuan**, Phil.
167/H4 **Cabedelo**, Braz.
86/C3 **Cabella Ligure**, It.
74/E5 **Cabestany**, Fr.
76/C3 **Cabeza del Buey**, Sp.
168/B3 **Cabeza Lagarto** (pt.), Peru
187/F4 **Cabeza Prieta Nat'l Wild. Ref.**, Az,US
172/D1 **Cabezas**, Bol.
76/C1 **Cabezón de la Sal**, Sp.
174/E3 **Cabildo**, Arg.
164/D2 **Cabimas**, Ven.
152/C4 **Cabinda**, Ang.
152/B4 **Cabinda** (prov.), Ang.
182/G3 **Cabinet** (mts.), Mt,US
152/C5 **Cabiri**, Ang.
167/H5 **Cabo**, Braz.
174/D5 **Cabo Blanco**, Arg.
168/A2 **Cabo Blanco**, Peru
142/B4 **Cabo Bojador**, WSah.
175/L8 **Cabo de Hornos Nat'l Park**, Chile
155/H2 **Cabo Delgado** (prov.), Moz.
171/E4 **Cabo Frio**, Braz.
161/F3 **Cabo Gracias a Dios**, Nic.
179/J4 **Cabonga** (res.), Qu,Can
191/H2 **Cabool**, Mo,US
134/D4 **Caboolture**, Austl.
166/D2 **Cabo Orange Nat'l Park**, Braz.
155/G2 **Cabora Bassa** (dam), Moz.
155/F2 **Cabora Bassa** (lake), Moz.
197/H2 **Cabot** (str.), Nf, NS,Can
191/H3 **Cabot**, Ar,US
79/E2 **Cabourg**, Fr.
171/K6 **Cabo Verde**, Braz.

76/C4 Cabra, Sp.
172/C2 Cabra Corral (res.), Arg.
76/D4 Cabra de Santo Cristo, Sp.
162/D3 Cabral, DRep.
134/G8 Cabramatta, Austl.
90/A3 Cabras, It.
82/B3 Cabre, Col de (pass), Fr.
77/G3 Cabrera (isl.), Sp.
183/K2 Cabri, Sk,Can
76/E3 Cabriel (riv.), Sp.
82/B6 Cabriès, Fr.
186/D4 Cabrillo Nat'l Mon., Ca,US
82/C5 Cabris, Fr.
167/G5 Cabrobó, Braz.
165/E3 Cabruta, Ven.
164/D2 Cabudare, Ven.
125/C1 Cabugao, Phil.
187/H5 Cabullona, Mex.
164/D2 Cabure, Ven.
173/G3 Caçador, Braz.
92/E4 Čačak, Yugo.
154/B1 Cacala, Ang.
158/D4 Cacalotán, Mex.
171/L8 Caçapava, Braz.
173/F4 Caçapava do Sul, Braz.
201/H1 Cacapon (riv.), Va, WV,US
201/H1 Cacapon (mtn.), WV,US
90/A2 Caccia (cape), It.
85/G5 Caccia (peak), It.
83/C4 Caccuri, It.
173/F4 Cacequi, Braz.
170/A3 Cáceres, Braz.
164/C3 Cáceres, Col.
76/B3 Cáceres, Sp.
53/S10 Cachan, Fr.
174/Q10 Cachapoal (riv.), Chile
175/S13 Cachari, Arg.
191/J3 Cache (riv.), Ar,US
205/L9 Cache (cr.), Ca,US
205/L10 Cache (slough), Ca,US
185/G2 Cache (peak), Id,US
200/C2 Cache (riv.), Il,US
191/E3 Cache, Ok,US
182/D2 Cache Creek, BC,Can
192/B3 Cache la Poudre (riv.), Co,US
144/A3 Cacheu, GBis.
166/B4 Cachimbo (mts.), Braz.
154/C2 Cachingues, Ang.
165/E2 Cachipo, Ven.
173/G1 Cachoeira Alta, Braz.
171/L7 Cachoeira de Minas, Braz.
166/D3 Cachoeira do Arari, Braz.
173/F4 Cachoeira do Sul, Braz.
171/M7 Cachoeira Paulista, Braz.
171/P7 Cachoeiras de Macacu, Braz.
173/G4 Cachoeirinha, Braz.
171/E4 Cachoeiro de Itapemirim, Braz.
164/C4 Cachorras, Col.
172/B3 Cachos (pt.), Chile
73/B2 Čachtice, Slvk.
152/D5 Cacolo, Ang.
154/B2 Caconda, Ang.
171/K6 Caconde, Braz.
152/C4 Cacongo, Ang.
170/C3 Caçu, Braz.
152/C5 Cacuaco, Ang.
154/B2 Cacula, Ang.
154/B3 Caculuvar (riv.), Ang.
165/E3 Cacuri, Ven.
152/C5 Cacuso, Ang.
150/C3 Cadaadle, Som.
65/K4 Čadca, Slvk.
191/H3 Caddo (mts.), Ar,US
191/H3 Caddo (riv.), Ar,US
189/G1 Caddo (lake), La, Tx,US
191/F3 Caddo, Ok,US
189/E1 Caddo, Tx,US
189/F1 Caddo Mills, Tx,US
191/F4 Caddo Nat'l Grsld., Tx,US
191/H3 Caddo Valley, Ar,US
195/G3 Caddy Lake, Mb,Can
86/D3 Cadelbosco di Sopra, It.
81/F5 Cadelle, Monte (peak), It.
67/G1 Cadenberge, Ger.
82/B5 Cadenet, Fr.
58/C1 Cader Idris (mtn.), Wal,UK
191/J2 Cadet, Mo,US
133/G4 Cadibarrawirracanna (lake), Austl.
183/L3 Cadillac, Ab,Can
196/C3 Cadillac (mtn.), Me,US
198/D2 Cadillac, Mi,US
125/C3 Cadiz, Phil.
76/B4 Cádiz, Sp.
76/B4 Cádiz (gulf), Sp.
186/E3 Cadiz, Ca,US
186/E3 Cadiz (dry lake), Ca,US
200/D2 Cadiz, Ky,US
198/F4 Cadiz, Oh,US
59/E5 Cadnam, Eng,UK
183/J1 Cadogan, Ab,Can
70/D4 Cadolzburg, Ger.
182/F1 Cadomin, Ab,Can
195/J5 Cadott, Wi,US
87/D1 Cadria, Monte (peak), It.
82/C4 Caduc, Sommet du (mtn.), Fr.
201/F4 Cadwell, Ga,US
66/A6 Cadzand-Bad, Neth.
79/E2 Caen, Fr.
74/C2 Caen (har.), Fr.
87/F1 Caerano di San Marco, It.
58/D3 Caerleon, Wal,UK
56/D5 Caernafon Castle, Wal,UK
56/D5 Caernarfon, Wal,UK
56/D5 Caernarfon (bay), Wal,UK
58/C3 Caerphilly, Wal,UK
58/C1 Caersws, Wal,UK
199/G2 Caesarea, On,Can
103/F6 Caesarea Nat'l Park, Isr.
68/B2 Caëstre, Fr.
171/E3 Caeté, Braz.
171/E1 Cafarnaum, Braz.
86/A2 Cafasse, It.
172/C3 Cafayate, Arg.
125/C3 Cagayan (isls.), Phil.
125/C3 Cagayancillo, Phil.
125/D3 Cagayan de Oro City, Phil.
125/B4 Cagayan Sulu (isl.), Phil.
87/F5 Cagli, It.
90/A3 Cagliari, It.
90/A3 Cagliari (gulf), It.
85/F4 Cagnano Varano, It.
82/D5 Cagne (riv.), Fr.
82/D5 Cagnes-sur-Mer, Fr.
125/C1 Cagoyan (riv.), Phil.
125/C1 Cagua (mt.), Phil.
167/N7 Cagua, Ven.
164/C4 Caguán (riv.), Col.
162/E3 Caguas, PR
60/A6 Caha (mts.), Ire.
202/E1 Cahaba, Al,US
200/D4 Cahaba (riv.), Al,US
202/E1 Cahaba (ruins), Al,US
154/B3 Cahama, Ang.
60/C5 Caher, Ire.
60/A5 Caherbarnagh (mtn.), Ire.
60/B4 Caherconlish, Ire.
54/F11 Cahirsiveen (Cahirciveen), Ire.
193/J4 Cahokia, Il,US
187/H2 Cahone, Co,US
60/D4 Cahore (pt.), Ire.
74/D4 Cahors, Fr.
168/B2 Cahuapanas, Peru
186/D4 Cahuilla Ind. Res., Ca,US
164/D5 Cahuinari (riv.), Col.
161/F4 Cahuita (pt.), CR
161/F4 Cahuita Nat'l Park, CR
173/G3 Caí (riv.), Braz.
155/G3 Caia, Moz.
169/G4 Caiabis (mts.), Braz.
170/A1 Caiabis (uplands), Braz.
153/E5 Caianda, Ang.
170/B3 Caiapó (mts.), Braz.
170/C3 Caiapó (riv.), Braz.
170/C3 Caiapônia, Braz.
85/E5 Caiazzo, It.
161/G1 Caibarién, Cuba
167/H4 Caiçara, Braz.
165/F2 Caicara, Ven.
165/E3 Caicara de Orinoco, Ven.
167/K6 Caicedo, Col.
164/C3 Caicedonia, Col.
167/G4 Caicó, Braz.
161/H1 Caicos (passg.), Bahm., Trks.
162/C2 Caicos (isls.), Trks.
162/C2 Caicos Passage (chan.), Bahm., Trks.
171/K8 Caieiras, Braz.
153/E5 Caifuche, Ang.
168/D4 Cailloma, Peru
202/C3 Caillou (bay), La,US
68/A4 Cailly (riv.), Fr.
125/B2 Caiman (pt.), Phil.
154/B2 Caimbambo, Ang.
154/B2 Cainde, Ang.
172/C1 Caine (riv.), Bol.
108/E5 Cainnyigoin, China
193/H3 Cainsville, Mo,US
125/F6 Cainta, Phil.
123/D4 Cai Nuoc, Viet.
86/D4 Caio, Monte (peak), It.
152/C4 Caiongo, Ang.
86/B1 Cairate, It.
137/Y Caird (coast), Ant.
177/G3 Cairn (mtn.), Ak,US
199/G4 Cairnbrook, Pa,US
135/B3 Cairn Curran (dam), Austl.
54/B4 Cairndow, Sc,UK
54/C2 Cairn Gorm (mtn.), Sc,UK
54/C2 Cairngorm (mts), Sc,UK
55/K8 Cairngorm (mts.), Sc,UK
56/C2 Cairn Pat (hill), Sc,UK
54/C5 Cairnryan, Sc,UK
134/B2 Cairns, Austl.
134/B2 Cairns (int'l arpt.), Austl.
133/G2 Cairns (peak), Austl.
54/B6 Cairnsmore of Carsphairn (mtn.), Sc,UK
130/D5 Cairns, Mount (peak), Austl.
54/B6 Cairn Table (mtn.), Sc,UK
54/C2 Cairn Toul (mtn.), Sc,UK
103/B4 Cairo (int'l arpt.), Egypt
85/D4 Cairo (peak), It.
203/F2 Cairo, Ga,US
200/C2 Cairo, Il,US
191/H1 Cairo, Mo,US
192/E3 Cairo, Ne,US
103/B4 Cairo (Al Qāhirah) (cap.), Egypt
86/B4 Cairo Montenotte, It.
196/E2 Caissie (pt.), NB,Can
59/H1 Caister on Sea, Eng,UK
57/H5 Caistor, Eng,UK
197/R9 Caistor Centre, On,Can
197/R9 Caistorville, On,Can
154/B2 Caitou, Ang.
166/D3 Caiuana (bay), Braz.
154/C2 Caiundo, Ang.
117/H3 Caixi, China
172/C2 Caiza, Bol.
115/C5 Caizi (lake), China
164/B5 Cajabamba, Ecu.
168/B2 Cajabamba, Peru
168/B3 Cajacay, Peru
168/B2 Cajamarca, Peru
167/E3 Cajapió, Braz.
167/F3 Cajari, Braz.
168/B3 Cajatambo, Peru
167/F4 Cajazeiras, Braz.
164/B4 Cajibío, Col.
125/C2 Cajidiocan, Phil.
161/E1 Cajón (pt.), Cuba
204/C2 Cajon, Ca,US
204/C2 Cajon Junction, Ca,US
167/F3 Caju (isl.), Braz.
167/E4 Cajuapara (riv.), Braz.
172/C1 Cajuata, Bol.
104/B2 Çal, Turk.
145/H5 Calabar, Nga.
145/H5 Calabar (int'l arpt.), Nga.
204/B2 Calabasas, Ca,US
201/H4 Calabash, NC,US
165/E2 Calabozo, Ven.
83/B6 Calabrese, Appennino (mts.), It.
83/B6 Calabria Nat'l Park, It.
83/C4 Calabria Nat'l Park, It.
85/F6 Calabritto, It.
76/C4 Calaburras, Punta de (pt.), Sp.
77/F2 Calaceite, Sp.
168/D5 Calacoto, Bol.
90/A2 Cala d'Oliva, It.
92/F4 Calafat, Rom.
175/J7 Calafate, Arg.
125/C2 Calagua (isls.), Phil.
76/E1 Calahorra, Sp.
154/C3 Calai, Ang.
68/A2 Calais, Fr.
196/D3 Calais, Me,US
68/A2 Calais, Canal de (can.), Fr.
172/C2 Calalaste (mts.), Arg.
169/F3 Calama, Braz.
172/B2 Calama, Chile
164/C2 Calamar, Col.
164/C4 Calamar, Col.
172/B1 Calamarca, Bol.
152/C5 Calamba, Ang.
86/D5 Calambrone, It.
125/B2 Calamian (isls.), Phil.
76/E2 Calamocha, Sp.
76/B3 Calamonte, Sp.
192/E2 Calamus (riv.), Ne,US
92/F3 Călan, Rom.
76/B4 Calañas, Sp.
77/E2 Calanda, Sp.
124/A1 Calang, Indo.
90/A2 Calangianus, It.
125/C2 Calapan, Phil.
88/F3 Cala Piombo, Punta di (pt.), It.
184/B1 Calapooia (riv.), Or,US
93/H3 Călărași, Rom.
93/H3 Călărași (co.), Rom.
164/C3 Calarcá, Col.
76/E3 Calasparra, Sp.
76/E2 Calatayud, Sp.
76/E2 Calatorao, Sp.
72/D4 Calau, Ger.
125/C2 Calauag, Phil.
83/A6 Calavà (cape), It.
205/L12 Calaveras (res.), Ca,US
186/B1 Calaveras (riv.), Ca,US
125/C2 Calavite (cape), Phil.
125/C2 Calavite (mt.), Phil.
82/B5 Calavon (riv.), Fr.
125/C1 Calayan, Phil.
125/C1 Calayan (isl.), Phil.
125/D2 Calbayog City, Phil.
72/B4 Calbe, Ger.
67/H4 Calberlah, Ger.
125/D3 Calbiga, Phil.
174/B4 Calbuco, Chile
168/D4 Calca, Peru
167/H4 Calcanhar, Ponta do (pt.), Braz.
189/H3 Calcasieu (lake), La,US
189/H2 Calcasieu (riv.), La,US
164/A5 Calceta, Ecu.
172/D4 Calchaquí, Arg.
86/D5 Calci, It.
86/C1 Calcinate, It.
86/D2 Calcinato, It.
87/F5 Calcinelli, It.
86/C2 Calcio, It.
199/J2 Calcium, NY,US
166/D2 Calçoene, Braz.
121/G4 Calcutta, India
166/C1 Calcutta, Sur.
208/G6 Calcutta, Oh,US
81/H5 Caldaro (Kaltern), It.
171/K6 Caldas, Braz.
167/K6 Caldas, Col.
164/C3 Caldas (dept.), Col.
76/A3 Caldas da Rainha, Port.
170/C3 Caldas Novas, Braz.
57/E2 Caldbeck, Eng,UK
67/G6 Calden, Ger.
194/D2 Calder, Sk,Can
57/G4 Calder (riv.), Eng,UK
177/M4 Calder (mt.), Ak,US
172/B3 Caldera, Chile
142/A3 Caldera de Taburiente Nat'l Park, Canl.
87/E3 Calderara di Reno, It.
164/D2 Calderas, Ven.
54/C5 Caldercruix, Sc,UK
135/B5 Calderitas, Mex.
77/L6 Caldes de Montbui, Sp.
57/F2 Caldew (riv.), Eng,UK
58/D3 Caldicot, Wal,UK
87/E2 Caldiero, It.
105/E2 Çaldıran, Turk.
87/E1 Caldogno, It.
81/H6 Caldonazzo, It.
164/B4 Caldono, Col.
182/F4 Caldwell, Id,US
191/F2 Caldwell, Ks,US
207/H8 Caldwell, NJ,US
198/F5 Caldwell, Oh,US
189/F2 Caldwell, Tx,US
205/P14 Caldwell, Wi,US
58/B3 Caldy (isl.), Wal,UK
156/D3 Caledon (riv.), Les., SAfr.
156/B4 Caledon, SAfr.
197/R8 Caledon East, On,Can
183/E5 Caledonia (hills), NB,Can
196/E3 Caledonia, NS,Can
198/D3 Caledonia, Mi,US
193/J2 Caledonia, Mn,US
200/C4 Caledonia, Ms,US
198/E4 Caledonia, Oh,US
205/Q14 Caledonia, Wi,US
54/B2 Caledonian (can.), Sc,UK
77/G2 Calella, Sp.
134/C3 Calen, Austl.
90/A1 Calenzana, Fr.
87/E5 Calenzano, It.
200/D4 Calera, Al,US
191/F4 Calera, Ok,US
174/Q9 Calera de Tango, Chile
86/D3 Calestano, It.
161/H1 Caleta (pt.), Cuba
175/K8 Caleta Clarencia, Chile
158/E5 Caleta de Campos Chutla, Mex.
174/D5 Caleta Olivia, Arg.
174/Q10 Caletones, Chile
186/E4 Calexico, Ca,US
55/N13 Calfsound, Sc,UK
57/F3 Calf, The (mtn.), Eng,UK
183/G2 Calgary, Ab,Can
183/G2 Calgary (int'l arpt.), Ab,Can
192/B4 Calhan, Co,US
142/A2 Calheta, Madr.
77/S12 Calheta, Azor.,Port.
77/U15 Calheta, Madr.,Port.
200/D4 Calhoun, Al,US
200/E3 Calhoun, Ga,US
198/B5 Calhoun, Il,US
200/D2 Calhoun, Ky,US
191/H1 Calhoun, Mo,US
200/C4 Calhoun City, Ms,US
201/F3 Calhoun Falls, SC,US
164/B4 Cali, Col.
186/D3 Calico (ghost town), Ca,US
191/H2 Calico Rock, Ar,US
76/E4 Calida, Costa (coast), Sp.
186/E2 Caliente, Nv,US
206/D2 Califon, NJ,US
186/E5 California (gulf), Mex.
180/C4 California (state), US
204/C2 California (aqueduct), Ca,US
201/J1 California, Md,US
191/H1 California, Mo,US
199/G4 California, Pa,US
186/D3 California City, Ca,US
186/C3 California Hot Springs, Ca,US
172/C2 Calilegua, Arg.
172/C1 Calilegua Nat'l Park, Arg.
93/G3 Călimănești, Rom.
122/G3 Calimere (pt.), India
204/C2 Calimesa, Ca,US
172/B4 Calingasta, Arg.
191/H4 Calion, Ar,US
186/E4 Calipatria, Ca,US
205/J9 Calistoga, Ca,US
85/F6 Calitri, It.
197/P6 Calixa-Lavallée, Qu,Can
86/B4 Calizzano, It.
159/H4 Calkini, Mex.
104/B2 Çalköy, Turk.
189/H2 Call, Tx,US
133/J4 Callabonna (lake), Austl.
78/B4 Callac, Fr.
184/E4 Callaghan (mt.), Nv,US
188/E4 Callaghan, Tx,US
203/H2 Callahan, Fl,US
128/G5 Callahonna (lake), Austl.
168/D4 Callalli, Peru
60/C4 Callan, Ire.
54/B4 Callander, Sc,UK
66/B3 Callantsoog, Neth.
168/B4 Callao, Peru
185/G4 Callao, Ut,US
201/J2 Callao, Va,US
172/B1 Callapa, Bol.
60/B4 Callaun (mtn.), Ire.
203/F2 Callaway, Fl,US
194/G4 Callaway, Mn,US
174/Q9 Calle Larga, Chile
193/G2 Callender, Ia,US
82/C6 Callé-Rousse, Pointe de (pt.), Fr.
82/C5 Callian, Fr.
189/E3 Calliham, Tx,US
58/B6 Callington, Eng,UK
134/C4 Calliope, Austl.
189/H2 Call Junction, Tx,US
77/E3 Callosa de Ensarriá, Sp.
77/E3 Callosa de Segura, Sp.
78/B3 Callot (isl.), Fr.
183/H1 Calmar, Ab,Can
193/J2 Calmar, Ia,US
159/F4 Calnali, Mex.
58/D4 Calne, Eng,UK
86/C1 Calolziocorte, It.
154/B2 Calonga (riv.), Ang.
79/F2 Calonne (riv.), Fr.
68/B3 Calonne-Ricouart, Fr.
125/E6 Caloocan, Phil.
203/H4 Caloosahatchee (riv.), Fl,US
203/H4 Caloosahatchee Nat'l Wild. Ref., Fl,US
83/B2 Calore (riv.), It.
159/H4 Calotmul, Mex.
134/D4 Caloundra, Austl.
73/B4 Čalovo, Slvk.
77/F3 Calpe, Sp.
159/L7 Calpulálpan, Mex.
58/B6 Calstock, Eng,UK
90/D4 Caltagirone, It.
90/D4 Caltanissetta, It.
90/C4 Caltavuturo, It.
152/D5 Caluango, Ang.
152/D5 Calucinga, Ang.
154/C3 Calueque (dam), Ang.
74/F4 Caluire-et-Cuire, Fr.
152/C5 Calulo, Ang.
152/C5 Calumbo, Ang.
205/Q16 Calumet (riv.), Il,US
195/K4 Calumet, Mi,US
205/Q16 Calumet City, Il,US
205/Q16 Calumet Sag (chan.), Il,US
154/B2 Caluquembe, Ang.
86/A2 Caluso, It.
150/D3 Caluula, Som.
150/D3 Caluula, Raasiga (pt.), Som.
187/G4 Calva, Az,US
79/E3 Calvados (dept.), Fr.
203/F2 Calvary, Ga,US
83/B2 Calvello, It.
86/C2 Calvenzano, It.
197/L2 Calvert, Nf,Can
202/D2 Calvert, Al,US
189/F2 Calvert, Tx,US
200/C2 Calvert City, Ky,US
131/E4 Calvert Hills, Austl.
57/G5 Calverton, Eng,UK
206/B5 Calverton, Md,US
207/F2 Calverton, NY,US
90/A1 Calvi, Fr.
77/G3 Calvià, Sp.
85/D5 Calvilli (peak), It.
158/E4 Calvillo, Mex.
87/E4 Calvi, Monte (peak), It.
191/F3 Calvin, Ok,US
156/B3 Calvinia, SAfr.
85/E5 Calvi Risorta, It.
86/D2 Calvisano, It.
76/C2 Calvitero (mtn.), Sp.
85/F4 Calvo (peak), It.
72/B3 Calvörde, Ger.
70/B5 Calw, Ger.
76/D3 Calzada de Calatrava, Sp.
59/G2 Cam (riv.), Eng,UK
152/C5 Camabatela, Ang.
171/F2 Camaçari, Braz.
172/C2 Camacho, Bol.
158/E3 Camacho, Mex.
154/C2 Camacupa, Ang.
165/E2 Camaguán, Ven.
161/G1 Camagüey, Cuba
161/G1 Camagüey (arch.), Cuba
86/D5 Camaiore, It.
161/G1 Camajuaní, Cuba
152/D5 Camalengue, Ang.
171/F2 Camamu, Braz.
168/C5 Camaná, Peru
184/C4 Camanche (res.), Ca,US
193/J3 Camanche, Ia,US
171/K7 Camanducaia, Braz.
152/E5 Camanongue, Ang.
170/B3 Camapuã, Braz.
173/F3 Camaquã, Braz.
173/F3 Camaquã (riv.), Braz.
77/V15 Câmara de Lobos, Madr.,Port.
82/C6 Camarat (cape), Fr.
82/A4 Camaret-sur-Aigues, Fr.
78/A4 Camaret-sur-Mer, Fr.
172/C2 Camargo, Bol.
180/G7 Camargo, Mex.
76/D1 Camargo, Sp.
190/E2 Camargo, Ok,US
204/A2 Camarillo, Ca,US
76/A1 Camariñas, Sp.
161/E3 Camarón (cape), Hon.
188/D5 Camarón (riv.), Mex.
174/D5 Camarones, Arg.
174/D5 Camarones (bay), Arg.
172/B1 Camarones, Chile
76/B4 Camas, Sp.
182/F4 Camas (grsld.), Id,US
185/G1 Camas Nat'l Wild. Ref., Id,US
184/B2 Camas Valley, Or,US
167/G8 Camatagua, Ven.
167/G8 Camatagua (res.), Ven.
123/D4 Ca Mau, Viet.
123/D4 Ca Mau (cape), Viet.
152/D5 Camaxilo, Ang.
160/D3 Camayagua (mts.), Hon.
76/A1 Cambados, Sp.
170/C4 Cambará, Braz.
118/B3 Cambay, India
118/B3 Cambay (gulf), India
170/C4 Cambé, Braz.
59/F4 Camberley Frimley, Eng,UK
53/N7 Camberwell, Eng,UK
83/B3 Cambiano, It.
152/D5 Cambo (riv.), Ang.
152/D5 Cambo Camana, Ang.
123/D3 Cambodia
152/C5 Cambondo, Ang.
173/H3 Camboriú, Ponta do (pt.), Braz.
58/A6 Camborne, Eng,UK
68/C3 Cambrai, Fr.
186/B3 Cambria, Ca,US
58/C2 Cambrian (mts.), Wal,UK
130/C3 Cambridge (gulf), Austl.
161/G2 Cambridge, Jam.
136/C2 Cambridge, N.Z.
59/G2 Cambridge, Eng,UK
59/G2 Cambridge (int'l arpt.), Eng,UK
184/E1 Cambridge, Id,US
193/J3 Cambridge, Il,US
208/C1 Cambridge, Ma,US
201/J1 Cambridge, Md,US
195/H5 Cambridge, Mn,US
192/D3 Cambridge, Ne,US
199/K3 Cambridge, NY,US
198/F4 Cambridge, Oh,US
199/K2 Cambridge, Vt,US
178/F2 Cambridge Bay, NW,Can
198/D5 Cambridge City, In,US
198/F3 Cambridgeg, On,Can
199/E3 Cambridge-Narrows, NB,Can
59/G2 Cambridgeshire (co.), Eng,UK
198/F4 Cambridge Springs, Pa,US
77/F2 Cambrils, Sp.
170/D4 Cambuí, Braz.
153/E4 Cambulo, Ang.
170/D4 Cambuquira, Braz.
72/B5 Camburg, Ger.
54/B5 Cambuslang, Sc,UK
161/F5 Cambutal (mtn.), Pan.
135/D2 Camden, Austl.
130/A3 Camden (sound), Austl.
53/N7 Camden (bor.), Eng,UK
200/D5 Camden, Al,US
191/H4 Camden, Ar,US
206/C5 Camden, De,US
196/C3 Camden, Me,US
198/D4 Camden, Mi,US
201/J2 Camden, NC,US
206/C4 Camden, NJ,US
206/D4 Camden (co.), NJ,US
199/J3 Camden, NY,US
201/G3 Camden, SC,US
200/C2 Camden, Tn,US
189/G2 Camden, Tx,US
199/H2 Camden East, Can.
135/E1 Camden Haven, Austl.
191/H1 Camdenton, Mo,US
153/E5 Cameia, Ang.
153/E5 Cameia Nat'l Park, Ang.
58/B6 Camel (riv.), Eng,UK
206/C1 Camelback (mtn.), Pa,US
188/D5 Cameleón, Mex.
58/B5 Camelford, Eng,UK
136/C2 Camels Back (peak), N.Z.
87/G5 Camerano, It.
86/B2 Cameri, It.
84/D1 Camerino, It.
179/R7 Cameron (isl.), NW,Can
187/G3 Cameron, Az,US
192/B3 Cameron (peak), Co,US
202/B3 Cameron, La,US
191/G1 Cameron, Mo,US
185/H1 Cameron, Mt,US
189/F2 Cameron, Tx,US
195/J5 Cameron, Wi,US
124/C1 Cameron Highlands, Malay.
186/B1 Cameron Park, Ca,US
140/D4 Cameroon
148/A4 Cameroon Highlands (mts.), Camr., Nga.
83/B2 Camerota, It.
166/D3 Cametá, Braz.
188/L6 Camey, Tx,US
130/C4 Camfield, Austl.
85/D3 Camicia (peak), It.
68/A2 Camiers, Fr.
125/D3 Camiguin (isl.), Phil.
125/C2 Camiling, Phil.
203/F2 Camilla, Ga,US
174/E2 Camilo Aldao, Arg.
76/A2 Caminha, Port.
167/E3 Camiranga, Braz.
172/D2 Camiri, Bol.
87/E1 Camisano Vicentino, It.
153/E5 Camissombo, Ang.
104/C1 Çamlıdere, Turk.
104/C2 Çamlık Nat'l Park, Turk.
60/C2 Camlin (riv.), Ire.
103/D1 Çamlıyayla, Turk.
161/E3 Camoapa, Nic.
155/G4 Camo-Camo, Moz.
167/F3 Camocim, Braz.
86/C4 Camogli, It.
60/D4 Camolin, Ire.
68/B4 Camon, Fr.
133/H1 Camooweal, Austl.
166/C2 Camopi (riv.), FrG.
119/F6 Camorta (isl.), India
164/D3 Camoruco, Col.
125/D3 Camotes (sea), Phil.
85/F6 Campagna, It.
84/C4 Campagna di Roma (reg.), It.
87/F2 Campagna Lupia, It.
84/C3 Campagnano di Roma, It.
68/A3 Campagne, Fr.
87/D3 Campagnola Emilia, It.
173/E4 Campamento, Uru.
174/F2 Campana, Arg.
175/J7 Campana (isl.), Chile
174/C2 Campanario (peak), Arg.
76/C3 Campanario, Sp.
85/E6 Campanella (cape), It.
171/L6 Campanha, Braz.
198/C5 Camp Atterbury (mil. res.), In,US
136/C3 Campbell (cape), N.Z.
51/T8 Campbell (isl.), N.Z.
205/L12 Campbell, Ca,US
202/N7 Campbell, Fl,US
203/H3 Campbell, Fl,US
194/F4 Campbell, Mn,US
200/B2 Campbell, Mo,US
192/E3 Campbell, Ne,US
198/E4 Campbell (hill), Oh,US
189/G1 Campbell, Tx,US
199/H2 Campbellford, On,Can
122/B1 Campbellpore, Pak.
182/B2 Campbell River, BC,Can
199/H2 Campbell's Bay, Qu,Can
193/K2 Campbellsport, Wi,US
200/E2 Campbellsville, Ky,US
196/D2 Campbellton, NB,Can
203/F2 Campbellton, Fl,US
134/G9 Campbelltown, Austl.
135/C4 Campbell Town, Austl.
197/R9 Campbellville, On,Can
55/J9 Campbeltown, Sc,UK
203/G3 Camp Blanding (mil. res.), Fl,US
78/D6 Campbon, Fr.
191/G2 Camp Clark (mil. res.), Mo,US
197/S9 Campden, On,Can
159/F5 Campeche, Mex.
159/G4 Campeche (bay), Mex.
159/H5 Campeche (state), Mex.
84/C2 Campello sul Clitunno, It.
135/B3 Camperdown, Austl.
194/D2 Camperville, Mb,Can
171/K6 Campestre, Braz.
198/D2 Camp Grayling (mil. res.), Mi,US
123/D1 Cam Pha, Viet.
206/B3 Camp Hill, Pa,US
87/E5 Campi Bisenzio, It.
90/A3 Campidano (range), It.
84/A1 Campiglia Marittima, It.
60/D5 Campile, Ire.
76/E3 Campillo de Altobuey, Sp.
76/C4 Campillos, Sp.
170/B5 Campina da Lagoa, Braz.
167/H4 Campina Grande, Braz.
170/D4 Campinas, Braz.
170/C3 Campina Verde, Braz.
86/B1 Campione d'Italia, It.
191/H3 Camp Joseph T. Robinson, Ar,US
205/P14 Camp Lake, Wi,US
194/D4 Camp Lake Nat'l Wild. Ref., ND,US
201/J3 Camp Lejeune, NC,US
201/J3 Camp Lejeune Marine Base, NC,US
85/D2 Campli, It.
130/A2 Camplong, Indo.
186/C2 Camp Nelson, Ca,US
186/C2 Campo (int'l arpt.), Braz.
152/B2 Campo, Camr.
186/D4 Campo, Ca,US
164/C4 Campoalegre, Col.
85/E4 Campobasso, It.
85/E4 Campobasso (prov.), It.
196/D3 Campobello (isl.), NB,Can
170/D4 Campo Belo, Braz.
83/B6 Campo Calabro, It.
87/E2 Campodarsego, It.
76/D3 Campo de Criptana, Sp.
86/B1 Campo dei Fiori (peak), It.
164/C2 Campo de la Cruz, Col.
81/F5 Campodolcino, It.
173/F3 Campo Erê, Braz.
170/C3 Campo Florido, Braz.
171/E1 Campo Formoso, Braz.
87/D3 Campogalliano, It.
172/D3 Campo Gallo, Arg.
170/B4 Campo Grande, Braz.
186/D4 Campo Ind. Res., Ca,US
86/B3 Campo Ligure, It.
171/K8 Campo Limpo Paulista, Braz.
167/F4 Campo Maior, Braz.
76/B3 Campo Maior, Port.
86/B4 Campomorone, It.
76/B3 Campo Mourão, Braz.
87/F2 Campónogara, It.
172/C3 Campo Quijano, Arg.
83/C4 Campora San Giovanni, It.
167/G4 Campo Redondo, Braz.
86/A5 Camporosso, It.
168/B2 Camporredondo, Peru
76/C1 Camporredondo (res.), Sp.
152/B2 Campo Rsv., Camr.
171/E4 Campos, Braz.
163/D5 Campos (reg.), Braz.
87/E1 Camposampiero, It.
87/E3 Camposanto, It.
85/E5 Camposauro (peak), It.
172/D2 Campos Belos, Braz.
77/G3 Campos del Puerto, Sp.
170/D4 Campos do Jordão, Braz.
173/G3 Campos Novos, Braz.
167/F4 Campos Sales, Braz.
81/E5 Campo Tencia, Pizzo (peak), Swi.
87/D4 Campo Tizzoro, It.
85/D3 Campotosto (lake), It.
186/D4 Camp Pendleton (mil. res.), Ca,US
201/K2 Camp Pendleton, Va,US
204/C4 Camp Pendleton Marine Corps Base, Ca,US
195/G4 Camp Ripley (mil. res.), Mn,US
186/B3 Camp Roberts (mil. res.), Ca,US
202/D2 Camp Shelby, Ms,US
54/B4 Campsie Fells (hills), Sc,UK
206/B6 Camp Springs, Md,US
202/B2 Campti, La,US
201/F2 Campton, Ky,US
187/G3 Camp Verde, Az,US
187/G3 Camp Verde Ind. Res., Az,US
185/G3 Camp Williams (mil. res.), Ut,US
188/D3 Camp Wood, Tx,US
123/E4 Cam Ranh, Viet.
183/H1 Camrose, Ab,Can
123/D1 Cam Thuy, Viet.
84/B1 Camucia, It.
93/H5 Çan, Turk.
196/E2 Canaan (riv.), NB,Can
191/H3 Canaan, Ar,US
208/A1 Canaan, Ct,US
196/A4 Canaan, NH,US
208/A1 Canaan, NY,US
199/L2 Canaan, Vt,US
196/D2 Canaan Game Ref., NB,Can
166/B3 Canaçari (lake), Braz.
178/* Canada
174/E2 Cañada de Gómez, Arg.
169/F5 Cañada Larga, Bol.
175/S11 Cañada Nieto, Uru.
174/E2 Cañada Rosquín, Arg.
206/C1 Canadensis, Pa,US
191/F3 Canadian (riv.), US
190/D3 Canadian, Tx,US
175/K7 Cañadón de las Vacas, Arg.
174/C5 Cañadon Grande (mts.), Arg.
174/D5 Cañadón Seco, Arg.
164/D2 Canagua, Ven.
165/F3 Canaima Nat'l Park, Ven.
199/J3 Canajoharie, NY,US
93/H5 Çanakkale, Turk.
93/H5 Çanakkale (prov.), Turk.
139/U12 Canala, NCal.
87/E2 Canalbianco (riv.), It.
86/B3 Canale, It.
182/G2 Canal Flats, BC,Can
208/F6 Canal Fulton, Oh,US
174/F3 Canal No. 1 (can.), Arg.
174/F3 Canal No. 11 (can.), Arg.
175/F3 Canal No. 2 (riv.), Arg.
175/F3 Canal No. 5 (riv.), Arg.
174/F3 Canal No. 9 (can.), Arg.
203/H4 Canal Point, Fl,US
174/E2 Canals, Arg.
77/E3 Canals, Sp.
199/H3 Canandaigua, NY,US
158/C2 Cananea, Mex.
173/G2 Canaos (riv.), Braz.
168/B1 Cañar, Ecu.
164/B5 Cañar (prov.), Ecu.
205/G7 Canard (riv.), On,Can
161/F1 Canarreos (arch.), Cuba
207/K9 Canarsie, NY,US
77/X16 Canary Islands (aut. comm.), Sp.
161/E4 Cañas, CR
164/B3 Cañasgordas, Col.
86/D3 Canassa, It.
158/D3 Canatlán, Mex.
203/H3 Canaveral (cape), Fl,US
203/H3 Canaveral (pen.), Fl,US
203/H3 Canaveral Nat'l Seash., Fl,US
171/F2 Canavieiras, Braz.
135/C1 Canbelego, Austl.
135/D2 Canberra (arpt.), Austl.
135/D2 Canberra (cap.), Austl.
194/F5 Canby, Mn,US
184/B1 Canby, Or,US
78/D3 Cancale, Fr.
82/A2 Cance (riv.), Fr.
85/E5 Cancello-Arnone, It.
168/B2 Canchaque, Peru
68/A3 Canche (riv.), Fr.
159/J4 Cancún, Mex.
160/E1 Cancún, Mex.
159/J4 Cancun (int'l arpt.), Mex.
172/C3 Candado, Nevado del (peak), Arg.
168/D5 Candarave, Peru
104/A2 Çandarlı (gulf), Turk.
91/J3 Çandarlı (gulf), Turk.
76/B1 Candás, Sp.
76/C1 Candás, Sp.
79/D5 Candé, Fr.
171/F2 Candeias, Braz.
85/F5 Candela, It.
188/D4 Candela, Mex.
174/D2 Candelaria, Arg.
172/E1 Candelaria, Bol.
173/F4 Candelária, Braz.
159/H5 Candelaria, Mex.
159/H5 Candelaria (riv.), Mex.
85/F4 Candelaro (riv.), It.
76/C2 Candeleda, Sp.
135/D3 Candelo, Austl.
86/B1 Candelo, It.
197/N7 Candiac, Qu,Can
86/B2 Candia Lomellina, It.
167/E3 Cândido Mendes, Braz.
170/C4 Candido Mota, Braz.
126/D5 Canding (cape), Indo.
86/A3 Candiolo, It.
104/C2 Çandır, Turk.
201/M7 Candler-McAfee, Ga,US
208/A2 Candlewood (res.), Ct,US
207/D3 Candlewood, NJ,US
183/K1 Cando, Sk,Can
194/E3 Cando, ND,US
125/C1 Candon, Phil.
203/G2 Cane (cr.), Ga,US
187/F2 Cane Beds, Az,US
86/B1 Canegrate, It.
173/G4 Canela, Braz.
174/C1 Canela Baja, Chile
86/B3 Canelli, It.
175/F2 Canelones, Uru.
175/T12 Canelones (dept.), Uru.
170/B5 Canendeyú (dept.), Par.
173/F2 Canenoeyú (dept.), Par.
84/C3 Canepina, It.
159/E3 Caneros, Mex.
168/B4 Canete (riv.), Peru
76/E2 Cañete, Sp.
87/F1 Caneva, It.
191/G2 Caney, Ks,US
191/F2 Caney (riv.), Ks, Ok,US
191/F3 Caney, Ok,US
189/G3 Caney (cr.), Tx,US
200/D2 Caneyville, Ky,US
191/H4 Canfield, Ar,US
208/G5 Canfield, Oh,US
194/D4 Canfield Lake Nat'l Wild. Ref., ND,US
168/C4 Cangallo, Peru
154/C2 Cangamba, Ang.
152/D5 Cangandala, Ang.
76/A1 Cangas, Sp.
76/B1 Cangas de Narcea, Sp.
76/C1 Cangas de Onís, Sp.
124/D4 Cangkuang (cape), Indo.
154/C2 Cangoa, Ang.
156/C4 Cango Caves, SAfr.
154/D2 Cangombe, Ang.
154/C2 Cangonga, Ang.
117/H3 Cangqian, China
175/J7 Cangrejo (peak), Arg.
109/J1 Cangshan, China
115/D4 Cangshan, China
167/H4 Canguaretama, Braz.
173/F4 Canguçu, Braz.
154/C1 Cangumbe, Ang.
119/K3 Cangwu, China
119/G3 Cangyuan (Cangyuan Vazu Zizhixian), China
116/C4 Cangyuan Vazu Zizhixian, China
115/D3 Cangzhou, China
154/C3 Canhaua, Ang.
123/D1 Canh Cuoc (isl.), Viet.
154/B2 Canhoca, Ang.
167/G5 Canhotinho, Braz.
134/C4 Cania Gorge Nat'l Park, Austl.
179/K3 Caniapiscau (lake), Qu,Can
179/K3 Caniapiscau (riv.), Qu,Can
90/C4 Canicattì, It.
74/E5 Canigou, Pic de (peak), Fr.
104/C1 Canik (mts.), Turk.
76/D4 Caniles, Sp.
182/D2 Canim Lake, BC,Can
167/G4 Canindé, Braz.
167/F4 Canindé (riv.), Braz.
84/B3 Canino, It.
158/C3 Canipole, Mex.
207/H7 Canistear (res.), NJ,US
199/H3 Canisteo, NY,US
76/D4 Canjáyar, Sp.
166/B1 Canje (riv.), Guy.
190/A2 Canjilon, NM,US
150/C3 Cankhor, Som.
104/C1 Çankırı, Turk.
104/C1 Çankırı (prov.), Turk.
125/C3 Canlaon (vol.), Phil.
182/G2 Canmore, Ab,Can
55/H8 Canna (isl.), Sc,UK
122/E3 Cannanore, India
84/C2 Cannara, It.
85/G5 Canne (ruins), It.
201/F2 Cannel City, Ky,US
200/D2 Cannelton, In,US
69/F5 Canner (riv.), Fr.
81/E5 Cannero Riviera, It.
82/D5 Cannes, Fr.
83/A6 Canneto, It.
86/D2 Canneto sull'Oglio, It.
54/B2 Cannich, Sc,UK
54/B2 Cannich (riv.), Sc,UK
132/C4 Canning (peak), Austl.
132/L7 Canning (res.), Austl.
132/K7 Canning (riv.), Austl.
81/E5 Cannobio, It.
58/D1 Cannock, Eng,UK
190/C3 Cannon A.F.B., NM,US
194/D4 Cannon Ball, ND,US
194/D4 Cannonball (riv.), ND,US
182/C5 Cannon Beach, Or,US
208/A3 Cannondale, Ct,US
193/H1 Cannon Falls, Mn,US
134/C3 Cannonvale, Austl.
187/F2 Cannonville, Ut,US
135/D3 Cann River, Austl.
173/G4 Canoas, Braz.
135/D2 Canobolas (peaks), Austl.
202/E2 Canoe, Al,US
182/E1 Canoe River, BC,Can
204/E7 Canoga Park, Ca,US
164/D3 Caño Guaritico (riv.), Ven.
173/G3 Canoinhas, Braz.
57/F1 Canonbie, Sc,UK
208/C3 Canonchet, RI,US
187/J3 Cañoncito Ind. Res., NM,US
192/B4 Canon City, Co,US
160/C2 Cañon del Sumidero Nat'l Park, Mex.
159/M8 Cañon de Río Blanco Nat'l Park, Mex.
161/E4 Caño Negro Nat'l Wild. Ref., CR
190/A2 Canones, NM,US
187/J2 Cañon Largo (wash), Nv,US
198/F4 Canonsburg, Pa,US
203/G1 Canoochee (riv.), Ga,US
194/C2 Canora, Sk,Can
85/G5 Canosa di Puglia, It.
162/F4 Canouan (isl.), StV.
135/D2 Canowindra, Austl.
142/A5 Cansado, Mrta.
197/G3 Canso, NS,Can
197/G3 Canso (cape), NS,Can
168/B3 Canta, Peru
76/C1 Cantabria (aut. comm.), Sp.
88/B2 Cantabrica, Cordillera (range), Sp.
74/E4 Cantal (plat.), Fr.
76/D2 Cantalejo, Sp.
167/E3 Cantanhede, Braz.
76/A2 Cantanhede, Port.
165/E2 Cantaura, Ven.
79/G2 Canteleu, Fr.
134/H8 Canterbury, Austl.
136/B4 Canterbury (bight), N.Z.
136/C3 Canterbury (reg.), N.Z.
59/H4 Canterbury, Eng,UK
208/C2 Canterbury, Ct,US
59/H4 Canterbury Cathedral, Eng,UK
123/D4 Can Tho, Viet.
149/G4 Cantiere, Eth.
186/D3 Cantil, Ca,US
125/D3 Cantilan, Phil.
76/C4 Cantillana, Sp.
167/F5 Canto do Buriti, Braz.
208/B2 Canton, Ct,US
200/E3 Canton, Ga,US
193/J3 Canton, Il,US
191/F1 Canton, Ks,US
208/C1 Canton, Ma,US
205/E7 Canton, Mi,US
193/H1 Canton (riv.), Mn,US
193/J3 Canton, Mo,US
200/B4 Canton, Ms,US
201/F3 Canton, NC,US
206/C5 Canton, NJ,US
199/J2 Canton, NY,US
208/F6 Canton, Oh,US
191/E2 Canton, Ok,US
191/E2 Canton (lake), Ok,US
199/H4 Canton, Pa,US
192/F2 Canton, SD,US
189/G1 Canton, Tx,US
139/H5 Canton (Abariringa) (isl.), Kiri.
208/F6 Canton-Akron (reg. arpt.), Oh,US
117/G4 Canton (Guangzhou), China
76/D4 Cantoria, Sp.
86/C1 Cantù, It.
177/J3 Cantwell, Ak,US
174/F2 Cañuelas, Arg.
166/B4 Canumã (riv.), Braz.
135/B3 Canunda Nat'l Park, Austl.
169/E2 Canutama, Braz.
188/B4 Canutillo, Mex.
188/A2 Canutillo, Tx,US
59/G3 Canvey Island, Eng,UK
183/L1 Canwood, Sk,Can
79/F1 Cany-Barville, Fr.
195/H4 Canyon, Mn,US
183/J5 Canyon (mtn.), Mt,US
190/D3 Canyon, Tx,US
190/D4 Canyon, Tx,US
189/E3 Canyon (lake), Tx,US
185/H1 Canyon, Wy,US
184/D1 Canyon City, Or,US
180/E4 Canyon de Chelly Nat'l Mon., Az,US
187/H2 Canyon De Chelly Nat'l Mon., Az,US
183/J4 Canyon Ferry, Mt,US
189/E3 Canyon Lake, Tx,US
185/J4 Canyonlands Nat'l Park, Ut,US
184/B2 Canyonville, Or,US
86/C1 Canzo, It.
113/C2 Cao (riv.), China
123/D1 Cao Bang, Viet.
117/E3 Caodu (riv.), China
117/J2 Cao'e (riv.), China
113/C2 Caohecheng, China
113/C2 Caohekou, China
113/C2 Caohezhang, China
114/D3 Caohu, China
108/F5 Caojiawan, China
54/A3 Caol, Sc,UK
123/D4 Cao Lanh, Viet.
115/K8 Caoqiao, China
87/F1 Caorle, It.
86/C2 Caorso, It.
113/C1 Caoshi, China
115/C4 Cao Xian, China
125/B4 Cap (isl.), Phil.
192/D1 Capa, SD,US
205/G5 Capac, Mi,US
84/B3 Capalbio, It.
125/C2 Capalonga, Phil.
164/D3 Capanaparo (riv.), Ven.
167/E3 Capanema, Braz.
84/A2 Capanne (peak), It.
87/D5 Capannoli, It.
86/D5 Capannori, It.
170/C5 Capão Bonito, Braz.
173/G3 Capão Doce, Morro do (hill), Braz.
171/E4 Caparaó Nat'l Park, Braz.
76/A3 Caparica, Port.
164/D3 Caparo (riv.), Ven.
164/C3 Caparrapí, Col.
205/K9 Capay, Ca,US
74/C5 Capbreton, Fr.
196/D1 Cap-Chat, Qu,Can
82/D5 Cap d'Ail, Fr.
196/A2 Cap-de-la-Madeleine, Qu,Can
74/E4 Capdenac-Gare, Fr.
77/G3 Capdepera, Sp.
196/E1 Cap-des-Rosiers, Qu,Can
196/E3 Cap d'Or (cape), NS,Can
134/B3 Cape (riv.), Austl.
156/C3 Cape (prov.), SAfr.
132/D5 Cape Arid Nat'l Park, Austl.
135/D4 Cape Barren (isl.), Austl.
130/B3 Cape Bougainville Abor. Rsv., Austl.
197/G2 Cape Breton (highlands), NS,Can
197/G2 Cape Breton (isl.), NS,Can
179/K4 Cape Breton Highlands, NS,Can
197/G2 Cape Breton Highlands Nat'l Park, NS,Can
197/L2 Cape Broyle, Nf,Can
203/H3 Cape Canaveral A.F.B., Fl,US
201/J2 Cape Charles, Va,US
134/B2 Cape Cleveland Nat'l Park, Austl.
145/E5 Cape Coast, Gha.

# Châte – Chuku

203/G2 Chula, Ga,US
204/C5 Chula Vista, Ca,US
101/N4 Chul'man, Rus.
113/D5 Ch'ulp'o, SKor.
168/A2 Chulucanas, Peru
100/J4 Chulym (riv.), Rus.
114/E1 Chulyshman (riv.), Rus.
168/D4 Chuma, Bol.
107/L2 Chūmar, India
172/C4 Chumbicha, Arg.
93/G4 Chumerna (peak), Bul.
101/P4 Chumikan, Rus.
123/C2 Chum Phae, Thai.
123/B4 Chumphon, Thai.
123/C3 Chumsaeng, Thai.
113/E4 Chumunjin, SKor.
100/K4 Chuna (riv.), Rus.
117/J3 Chunan, Tai.
120/D3 Chunār, India
117/H3 Chunchi, China
113/D4 Ch'unch'ŏn, SKor.
202/D2 Chunchula, Al,US
113/D4 Ch'ungch'ong-Bukto (prov.), SKor.
113/D4 Ch'ungch'ŏng-Namdo (prov.), SKor.
113/D2 Chunggang, NKor.
117/J4 Chunghsingshintsun, Tai.
113/C3 Chunghwa, NKor.
113/D4 Ch'ungju, SKor.
113/D4 Ch'ungju-ho (lake), SKor.
113/C2 Ch'ungman (riv.), NKor.
113/E5 Ch'ungmu, SKor.
113/G6 Chungnang, SKor.
113/C3 Chūngsan, NKor.
153/G5 Chungu, Zam.
117/G1 Chunheji, China
159/H5 Chunhuhub, Mex.
122/B2 Chūniān, Pak.
200/C4 Chunky, Ms,US
122/G4 Chunnakam, SrL.
117/G4 Chunshui, China
101/L3 Chunya (riv.), Rus.
151/A4 Chunya, Tanz.
113/E4 Ch'unyang, SKor.
168/D4 Chupa, Peru
94/G2 Chupa, Rus.
168/C4 Chupaca, Peru
190/A3 Chupadera (mesa), NM,US
99/H2 Chupakhovka, Ukr.
95/K2 Chuprovo, Rus.
168/C4 Chuquibamba, Peru
172/B2 Chuquicamata, Chile
172/C1 Chuquichambi, Bol.
172/C1 Chuquichuqui, Bol.
172/C1 Chuquisaca (dept.), Bol.
81/F4 Chur, Swi.
116/B3 Churachandpur, India
168/C4 Churcampa, Peru
57/F4 Church, Eng,UK
194/D2 Churchbridge, Sk,Can
206/C5 Church Hill, Md,US
200/B5 Church Hill, Ms,US
135/C3 Churchill, Austl.
176/H4 Churchill (riv.), Can.
178/D3 Churchill (peak), BC,Can
178/G3 Churchill, Mb,Can
178/G3 Churchill (cape), Mb,Can
179/K3 Churchill (riv.), Nf,Can
178/F3 Churchill (lake), Sk,Can
200/E1 Churchill Downs, Ky,US
179/K3 Churchill Falls, Nf,Can
135/G5 Churchill Nat'l Park, Austl.
202/B2 Church Point, La,US
58/D1 Church Stretton, Eng,UK
206/B4 Churchville, Md,US
201/H1 Churchville, Va,US
121/E2 Churia Ghats (mts.), Nepal
168/B3 Churin, Peru
57/G6 Churnet (riv.), Eng,UK
118/B2 Churu, India
198/D4 Churubusco, In,US
164/D2 Churuguara, Ven.
159/E5 Churumuco de Morelos, Mex.
81/F4 Churwalden, Swi.
168/C4 Chuschi, Peru
114/C5 Chushul, India
95/N4 Chusovaya (riv.), Rus.
95/N4 Chusovoy, Rus.
196/C1 Chute-aux-Outardes, Qu,Can
152/B1 Chutes de Nachtigal, Camr.
99/H3 Chutovo, Ukr.
95/M4 Chutyr', Rus.
95/K5 Chuvash Aut. Rep., Rus.
188/B3 Chuviscar (riv.), Mex.
113/E4 Chuwang-san Nat'l Park, SKor.
116/D3 Chuxiong, China
108/B1 Chuya (riv.), Rus.
123/E3 Chu Yang Sin (peak), Viet.
117/H1 Chuzhou, China
111/M9 Chūzu, Japan
71/H5 Chvalšiny, Czh.
83/B3 Ciagola (peak), It.
124/E4 Ciamis, Indo.
84/C4 Ciampino, It.
84/C4 Ciampino (int'l arpt.), It.
124/D4 Cianjur, Indo.
124/D4 Cianjur, Indo.
170/B4 Cianorte, Braz.
124/D4 Cibatu, Indo.
187/G3 Cibecue, Az,US
186/E4 Cibola Nat'l Wild. Ref., Az, Ca,US
86/C4 Cicagna, It.
85/E6 Cicciano, It.
205/Q16 Cicero, Il,US
192/C2 Cicero (peak), SD,US
171/F1 Cicero Dantas, Braz.
90/C2 Cicero Nat'l Park, It.
92/E4 Čičevac, Yugo.
104/C1 Cide, Turk.
65/L2 Ciechanów, Pol.
65/K2 Ciechanów (prov.), Pol.
65/K2 Ciechocinek, Pol.
161/G1 Ciego de Ávila, Cuba
164/C2 Ciénaga, Col.
164/C2 Ciénaga de Oro, Col.
188/D5 Ciénega de Flores, Mex.
161/F1 Cienfuegos, Cuba
65/H3 Cieplice Śląskie Zdrój, Pol.
98/B3 Čierna, Slvk.
73/B3 Čierna voda (riv.), Slvk.
65/K4 Cieszyn, Pol.
76/E3 Cieza, Sp.
73/B3 Cífer, Slvk.
104/B2 Çifteler, Turk.
161/F1 Cifuentes, Cuba
76/D2 Cifuentes, Sp.
172/B3 Cifuncho, Chile
65/L4 Cigánd, Hun.
86/B2 Cigliano, It.
85/E4 Cigno (riv.), It.
76/D3 Cigüela (riv.), Sp.
104/C2 Cihanbeyli, Turk.
158/D5 Cihuatlán, Mex.
76/C3 Cijara (res.), Sp.
124/E4 Cijulang, Indo.
124/E4 Cilacap, Indo.
86/B2 Cilavegna, It.
105/E1 Çıldır, Turk.
105/E1 Çıldır (lake), Turk.
124/E4 Ciledug, Indo.
58/C2 Cilfaesty (hill), Wal,UK
76/B2 Cilleros, Sp.
186/E3 Cima, Ca,US
124/D4 Cimahi, Indo.
190/A1 Cimarron, Co,US
190/D2 Cimarron, Ks,US
191/E2 Cimarron (riv.), Ks, Ok,US
190/B2 Cimarron, NM,US
190/B2 Cimarron (cr.), NM,US
190/B2 Cimarron (range), NM,US
190/D2 Cimarron Nat'l Grsld., Ks,US
190/D2 Cimarron, North Fork (riv.), Co, Ks,US
84/C3 Cimino (peak), It.
87/D4 Cimone, Monte (peak), It.
92/F2 Cîmpeni, Rom.
93/F2 Cîmpia Turzii, Rom.
93/G3 Cîmpina, Rom.
93/G3 Cîmpulung, Rom.
93/G2 Cîmpulung Moldovenesc, Rom.
124/D4 Cina (cape), Indo.
104/E2 Çınar, Turk.
93/J5 Çınarcık, Turk.
164/D3 Cinaruco (riv.), Ven.
77/F1 Cinca (riv.), Sp.
92/C4 Cincar (peak), Bosn.
198/D5 Cincinnati, Oh,US
174/D4 Cinco Chañares, Arg.
174/C3 Cinco Saltos, Arg.
58/D3 Cinderford, Eng,UK
93/F3 Cindrelu (peak), Rom.
104/B2 Çine, Turk.
69/E3 Ciney, Belg.
86/D2 Cingia de'Botti, It.
87/G6 Cingoli, It.
86/C1 Cinisello Balsamo, It.
206/D4 Cinnaminson, NJ,US
79/F6 Cinq-Mars-la-Pile, Fr.
83/C6 Cinque Frondi, It.
160/C2 Cintalapa, Mex.
90/A1 Cinto (mtn.), Fr.
87/F1 Cinto Caomaggiore, It.
76/E1 Cintruénigo, Sp.
92/C4 Ćiovo (isl.), Cro.
124/E4 Cipatujah, Indo.
174/D3 Cipolletti, Arg.
167/K7 Circasia, Col.
84/D5 Circeo (peak), It.
84/D4 Circeo Nat'l Park, It.
177/K2 Circle, Ak,US
183/M4 Circle, Mt,US
177/K2 Circle Hot Springs, Ak,US
191/G1 Circleville, Ks,US
198/E5 Circleville, Oh,US
185/G4 Circleville, Ut,US
169/E5 Circuata, Bol.
124/E4 Cirebon, Indo.
124/E4 Ciremay (peak), Indo.
58/E3 Cirencester, Eng,UK
68/B5 Cires-lès-Mello, Fr.
86/A2 Ciriè, It.
83/D4 Cirò, It.
83/D4 Cirò Marina, It.
74/C4 Ciron (riv.), Fr.
124/D4 Ciruas, Indo.
86/C1 Cisano Bergamasco, It.
188/E1 Cisco, Tx,US
86/C1 Ciserano, It.
156/D4 Ciskei (aut. rep.), SAfr.
93/G3 Cisnădie, Rom.
200/C1 Cisne, Il,US
164/C3 Cisneros, Col.
174/B5 Cisnes (riv.), Chile
79/G6 Cisse (riv.), Fr.
198/C4 Cissna Park, Il,US
189/F3 Cistern, Tx,US
84/C4 Cisterna di Latina, It.
76/C1 Cistierna, Sp.
144/B4 Cité de Kassa, Gui.
159/M7 Citlaltépetl (vol.), Mex.
160/B2 Citlaltépetl (vol.), Mex.
203/G3 Citra, Fl,US
202/D2 Citronelle, Al,US
202/L6 Citrus (co.), Fl,US
156/B4 Citrusdal, SAfr.
205/M9 Citrus Heights, Ca,US
87/E1 Cittadella, It.
84/C2 Città della Pieve, It.
84/C4 Città del Vaticano (Vatican City)
87/F6 Città di Castello, It.
86/A2 Città di Torino (int'l arpt.), It.
84/C3 Cittaducale, It.
83/C6 Cittanova, It.
85/E2 Citta'Sant'Angelo, It.
86/B1 Cittiglio, It.
207/K8 City (isl.), NY,US
132/K6 City Beach, Austl.
56/C2 City (Belfast) (int'l arpt.), NI,UK
158/D4 Ciudad, Mex.
188/D3 Ciudad Acuna, Mex.
165/F2 Ciudad Bolívar, Ven.
164/D2 Ciudad Bolivia, Ven.
189/E4 Ciudad Camargo, Mex.
159/H5 Ciudad del Carmen, Mex.
173/F3 Ciudad del Este, Par.
188/B3 Ciudad Delicias, Mex.
159/F4 Ciudad del Maíz, Mex.
164/D2 Ciudad de Nutrias, Ven.
180/F7 Ciudad de Río Grande, Mex.
77/G3 Ciudadela, Sp.
165/F2 Ciudad Guayana, Ven.
158/D2 Ciudad Guerrero, Mex.
158/E5 Ciudad Guzmán, Mex.
159/E5 Ciudad Hidalgo, Mex.
188/A2 Ciudad Juárez, Mex.
158/E3 Ciudad Lerdo, Mex.
159/F4 Ciudad Madero, Mex.
159/F4 Ciudad Mante, Mex.
159/M8 Ciudad Mendoza, Mex.
188/E4 Ciudad Miguel Alemán, Mex.
158/D4 Ciudad Nat'l Park, Mex.
158/C3 Ciudad Obregón, Mex.
164/D2 Ciudad Ojeda, Ven.
165/F3 Ciudad Piar, Ven.
76/D3 Ciudad Real, Sp.
189/E5 Ciudad Río Bravo, Mex.
76/B2 Ciudad-Rodrigo, Sp.
159/M8 Ciudad Serdán, Mex.
159/F4 Ciudad Valles, Mex.
159/F4 Ciudad Victoria, Mex.
104/D1 Civa (pt.), Turk.
96/F4 Civa Burnu (pt.), Turk.
86/C1 Civate, It.
81/H5 Civezzano, It.
87/G1 Cividale del Friuli, It.
86/D1 Cividate Camuno, It.
84/C3 Civita Castellana, It.
85/D1 Civitanova Alta, It.
84/B3 Civitavecchia, It.
84/B2 Civitella (peak), It.
85/D2 Civitella del Tronto, It.
85/D4 Civitella Roveto, It.
74/D3 Civray, Fr.
79/G6 Civray-de-Touraine, Fr.
104/B2 Çivril, Turk.
115/L9 Cixi, China
115/C3 Ci Xian, China
80/B4 Cize, Fr.
104/E2 Cizre, Turk.
104/E2 Cizre (dam), Turk.
76/E1 Cizur, Sp.
184/E2 C.J. Strike (dam), Id,US
184/F2 C.J. Strike (res.), Id,US
184/B1 Clackamas (riv.), Or,US
54/C4 Clackmannan, Sc,UK
59/H3 Clacton on Sea, Eng,UK
58/C2 Claerwen (res.), Wal,UK
192/E4 Claflin, Ks,US
202/E2 Claiborne (dam), Al,US
189/H1 Claiborne (lake), La,US
206/B6 Claiborne, Md,US
78/C5 Claie (riv.), Fr.
74/D3 Clain (riv.), Fr.
178/E3 Claire (lake), Ab,Can
184/B3 Clair Engle (lake), Ca,US
189/E1 Clairette, Tx,US
202/L8 Clair Mel-Palm River, Fl,US
199/G4 Clairton, Pa,US
80/B4 Clairvaux-les-Lacs, Fr.
74/D3 Claise (riv.), Fr.
205/A2 Clallam (co.), Wa,US
182/B3 Clallam Bay, Wa,US
53/S10 Clamart, Fr.
74/E3 Clamecy, Fr.
183/J4 Clancy, Mt,US
194/F2 Clandeboye, Can
183/J1 Clandonald, Ab,Can
60/D3 Clane, Ire.
59/F5 Clanfield, Eng,UK
200/D4 Clanton, Al,US
194/E2 Clanwilliam, Mb,Can
156/B4 Clanwilliam, SAfr.
54/A5 Claonig, Sc,UK
82/D4 Clapier (mtn.), Fr.
82/C3 Clapier du Peyron (mtn.), Fr.
197/R9 Clappison's Corners, On,Can
174/F1 Clara, Arg.
174/D4 Clara (pt.), Arg.
60/C3 Clara, Ire.
202/D2 Clara, Ms,US
195/G5 Clara City, Mn,US
130/C3 Claravale, Austl.
60/B4 Clare (co.), Ire.
54/F10 Clare (isl.), Ire.
60/B3 Clare (riv.), Ire.
198/D3 Clare, Mi,US
82/D2 Clarée (riv.), Fr.
60/B3 Claregalway, Ire.
131/F3 Claremont (pt.), Austl.
204/C2 Claremont, Ca,US
199/K3 Claremont, NH,US
194/E5 Claremont, SD,US
191/G2 Claremore, Ok,US
60/B2 Claremorris, Ire.
135/E1 Clarence (riv.), Austl.
130/C3 Clarence (str.), Austl.
177/G3 Clarence (pt.), NW,Can
136/C3 Clarence, N.Z.
136/C3 Clarence (riv.), N.Z.
202/B2 Clarence, La,US
191/H1 Clarence, Mo,US
197/T9 Clarence, NY,US
191/J1 Clarence Cannon (dam), Mo,US
191/J1 Clarence Cannon Nat'l Wild. Ref., Mo,US
162/C2 Clarence Town, Bahm.
191/J3 Clarendon, Ar,US
190/D3 Clarendon, Tx,US
199/K3 Clarendon, Vt,US
197/L1 Clarenville, Nf,Can
183/H2 Claresholm, BC,Can
137/J Clarie (coast), Ant.
193/G3 Clarinda, Ia,US
198/F5 Clarington, Oh,US
158/B5 Clarion (isl.), Mex.
193/H2 Clarion, Ia,US
199/G4 Clarion, Pa,US
195/G4 Clarissa, Mn,US
198/F2 Clark (pt.), On,Can
207/H9 Clark, NJ,US
68/D5 Clark, Pa,US
206/B3 Clark (cr.), Pa,US
192/F1 Clark, SD,US
189/G2 Clark, Tx,US
182/D3 Clark (mtn.), Wa,US
185/J1 Clark, Wy,US
125/C2 Clark A.F.B., Phil.
185/G1 Clark Canyon (dam), Mt,US
185/G1 Clark Canyon (res.), Mt,US
187/F3 Clarkdale, Az,US
135/D4 Clarke (isl.), Austl.
134/B3 Clarke (range), Austl.
206/B4 Clarke (lake), Pa,US
201/F3 Clarkesville, Ga,US
194/G5 Clarkfield, Mn,US
182/F3 Clark Fork, Id,US
201/F4 Clark Hill (lake), Ga, SC,US
189/H1 Clarks, La,US
205/L10 Clarksburg, Ca,US
206/D3 Clarksburg, NJ,US
200/C3 Clarksburg, Tn,US
201/G1 Clarksburg, WV,US
200/B3 Clarksdale, Ms,US
196/E4 Clark's Harbour, NS,Can
201/F4 Clarks Hill, SC,US
201/F4 Clarks Hill (dam), SC,US
197/R8 Clarkson, On,Can
177/G4 Clarks Point, Ak,US
201/M7 Clarkston, Ga,US
205/F6 Clarkston, Mi,US
185/G3 Clarkston, Ut,US
182/F4 Clarkston, Wa,US
191/H3 Clarksville, Ar,US
193/H2 Clarksville, Ia,US
198/D4 Clarksville, In,US
200/D2 Clarksville, Tn,US
191/G4 Clarksville, Tx,US
201/H2 Clarksville, Va,US
200/C2 Clarkton, Mo,US
201/H3 Clarkton, NC,US
192/C3 Clarkville, Co,US
170/C2 Claro (riv.), Braz.
170/C3 Claro (riv.), Braz.
81/F5 Claro, Swi.
68/C3 Clary, Fr.
60/C6 Clashmore, Ire.
182/C4 Clatskanie, Or,US
56/D1 Clatteringshaws Loch (lake), Sc,UK
190/D3 Claude, Tx,US
170/D4 Cláudio, Braz.
56/A2 Claudy, NI,UK
190/B3 Claunch, NM,US
69/G5 Clausen, Ger.
67/H5 Clausthal-Zellerfeld, Ger.
125/D3 Claver, Phil.
125/C1 Claveria, Phil.
125/D3 Claveria, Phil.
194/A2 Clavet, Sk,Can
205/F6 Clawson, Mi,US
201/G4 Claxton, Ga,US
186/B1 Clay, Ca,US
200/D2 Clay, Ky,US
189/H1 Clay, La,US
201/G1 Clay, WV,US
194/B2 Claybank, Sk,Can
191/F1 Clay Center, Ks,US
192/E3 Clay Center, Ne,US
200/C1 Clay City, Il,US
198/C5 Clay City, In,US
200/F2 Clay City, Ky,US
57/G5 Clay Cross, Eng,UK
59/F2 Claydon, Eng,UK
53/U10 Claye-Souilly, Fr.
53/M7 Claygate, Eng,UK
203/F2 Clayhatchee, Al,US
56/D3 Clay Head (pt.), IM,UK
206/C4 Claymont, De,US
200/D4 Clay-Pinson-Chalkville, Al,US
187/G4 Claypool, Az,US
187/G3 Clay Springs, Az,US
205/E5 Clayton, Al,US
205/L11 Clayton, Ca,US
206/C5 Clayton, De,US
201/F3 Clayton, Ga,US
201/M7 Clayton (co.), Ga,US
185/F1 Clayton, Id,US
202/C2 Clayton, La,US
191/J1 Clayton, Mo,US
201/H3 Clayton, NC,US
206/C4 Clayton, NJ,US
190/C2 Clayton, NM,US
199/H2 Clayton, NY,US
191/G3 Clayton, Ok,US
57/F4 Clayton-le-Moors, Eng,UK
208/C2 Clayville, RI,US
175/S11 Clé (stream), Arg.
178/E3 Clear (range), Ab,Can
55/G11 Clear (cape), Ire.
187/G3 Clear (cr.), Az,US
184/B4 Clear (lake), Ca,US
184/C3 Clear (lake), Ca,US
190/B1 Clear (cr.), Co,US
189/M9 Clear (lake), Tx,US
185/K1 Clear (cr.), Wy,US
177/J4 Cleare (cape), Ak,US
201/F1 Clearfield, Ky,US
185/G3 Clearfield, Ut,US
159/E1 Clear Fork (riv.), Tx,US
184/B4 Clearlake, Ca,US
193/H2 Clear Lake, Ia,US
194/F5 Clear Lake, SD,US
193/H1 Clear Lake, Wi,US
184/C3 Clear Lake Nat'l Wild. Ref., Ca,US
184/B4 Clearlake Oaks, Ca,US
185/K1 Clearmont, Wy,US
182/G1 Clearwater (riv.), Ab,Can
182/D2 Clearwater, BC,Can
182/D2 Clearwater (riv.), BC,Can
203/G4 Clearwater, Fl,US
184/F1 Clearwater, Id,US
184/F1 Clearwater (mts.), Id,US
184/F1 Clearwater (riv.), Id,US
195/G4 Clearwater (riv.), Mn,US
200/B2 Clearwater (lake), Mo,US
182/B4 Clearwater, Wa,US
195/K5 Clearwater Lake, Wi,US
202/K8 Clearwater-Saint Petersburg (int'l arpt.), Fl,US
56/E2 Cleator Moor, Eng,UK
189/F1 Cleburne, Tx,US
79/E3 Clécy, Fr.
78/A4 Cléden-Cap-Sizun, Fr.
78/A3 Cléder, Fr.
182/D4 Cle Elum, Wa,US
57/H4 Cleethorpes, Eng,UK
58/D3 Cleeve (hill), Eng,UK
78/B4 Cléguérec, Fr.
133/M8 Cleland Rec. Area, Austl.
166/C2 Clément, FrG.
206/D4 Clementon, NJ,US
186/B1 Clements, Ca,US
196/E3 Clementsport, NS,Can
201/G2 Clemmons, NC,US
201/F3 Clemson, SC,US
201/G1 Clendenin, WV,US
188/E2 Cleo, Tx,US
58/D2 Cleobury Mortimer, Eng,UK
206/B3 Cleona, Pa,US
125/B3 Cleopatra Needle (mtn.), Phil.
191/E2 Cleo Springs, Ok,US
68/A4 Clères, Fr.
69/E3 Clerf (riv.), Belg., Lux.
82/A2 Clérieux, Fr.
134/B3 Clermont, Austl.
196/B2 Clermont, Qu,Can
68/B5 Clermont, Fr.
202/M6 Clermont, Fl,US
69/E5 Clermont-en-Argonne, Fr.
74/E4 Clermont-Ferrand (Aulnut) (int'l arpt.), Fr.
80/C3 Clerval, Fr.
69/F3 Clervaux, Lux.
79/G5 Cléry-Saint-André, Fr.
81/H5 Cles, It.
133/H5 Cleve, Austl.
58/D4 Clevedon, Eng,UK
134/B2 Cleveland (cape), Austl.
57/G2 Cleveland (co.), Eng,UK
57/G3 Cleveland (hills), Eng,UK
203/H4 Cleveland, Fl,US
200/F3 Cleveland, Ga,US
200/B4 Cleveland, Ms,US
183/K3 Cleveland, Mt,US
183/H3 Cleveland (mt.), Mt,US
194/E4 Cleveland, ND,US
190/B3 Cleveland, NM,US
208/F4 Cleveland, Oh,US
191/F2 Cleveland, Ok,US
201/F3 Cleveland, SC,US
200/E3 Cleveland, Tn,US
189/G2 Cleveland, Tx,US
185/H4 Cleveland, Ut,US
193/L2 Cleveland, Wi,US
208/F5 Cleveland Heights, Oh,US
208/F5 Cleveland-Hopkins (int'l arpt.), Oh,US
173/F3 Clevelândia, Braz.
166/D2 Clevelândia do Norte, Braz.
204/C3 Cleveland Nat'l For., Ca,US
60/A2 Clew (bay), Ire.
203/H4 Clewiston, Fl,US
68/B6 Clichy, Fr.
53/T10 Clichy-sous-Bois, Fr.
54/F10 Clifden, Ire.
187/H4 Cliff, NM,US
207/K8 Cliffside Park, NJ,US
207/J10 Cliffwood, NJ,US
58/D4 Clifton, Eng,UK
187/H4 Clifton, Az,US
185/J4 Clifton, Co,US
185/G2 Clifton, Id,US
198/C4 Clifton, Il,US
191/F1 Clifton, Ks,US
202/C2 Clifton, La,US
207/D2 Clifton, NJ,US
200/D3 Clifton, Tn,US
189/F2 Clifton, Tx,US
134/B2 Clifton Beach, Austl.
201/H2 Clifton Forge, Va,US
58/D2 Clifton upon Teme, Eng,UK
200/D2 Clifty, Ky,US
68/C5 Clignon (riv.), Fr.
183/K3 Climax, Sk,Can
192/A4 Climax, Co,US
203/F2 Climax, Ga,US
194/F4 Climax, Mn,US
188/L6 Climax, Tx,US
202/M8 Clinch (lake), Fl,US
201/F2 Clinch (riv.), Tn, Va,US
66/B6 Clinge, Neth.
72/A5 Clingen, Ger.
201/F3 Clingmans (mtn.), Tn,US
182/D2 Clinton, BC,Can
136/B4 Clinton, N.Z.
191/H3 Clinton, Ar,US
208/B3 Clinton, Ct,US
193/J3 Clinton, Ia,US
193/K3 Clinton, Il,US
198/C5 Clinton, In,US
193/G4 Clinton (lake), Ks,US
200/C2 Clinton, Ky,US
202/C2 Clinton, La,US
208/C1 Clinton, Ma,US
205/E6 Clinton, Mi,US
205/F6 Clinton (riv.), Mi,US
191/H1 Clinton, Mo,US
200/B4 Clinton, Ms,US
201/H3 Clinton, NC,US
206/D2 Clinton, NJ,US
207/H7 Clinton (res.), NJ,US
208/F6 Clinton, Oh,US
190/E3 Clinton, Ok,US
206/A1 Clinton (co.), Pa,US
201/G3 Clinton, SC,US
200/E2 Clinton, Tn,US
205/C2 Clinton, Wa,US
178/F2 Clinton-Colden (lake), NW,Can
178/B2 Clinton Creek, Yk,Can
205/G6 Clinton, Middle Branch (riv.), Mi,US
205/G6 Clinton, North Branch (riv.), Mi,US
206/B6 Clinton (Surratts-ville), Md,US
208/B3 Clintonville, Ct,US
208/H5 Clintonville, Pa,US
193/K1 Clintonville, Wi,US
54/D5 Clints Dod (hill), Sc,UK
201/F2 Clintwood, Va,US
203/F2 Clio, Al,US
198/E3 Clio, Mi,US
201/H3 Clio, SC,US
50/D5 Clipperton (isl.), Fr.
59/F2 Clipston, Eng,UK
182/C1 Clisbako (riv.), BC,Can
57/F4 Clitheroe, Eng,UK
84/C2 Clitunno (riv.), It.
136/D2 Clive, N.Z.
172/C1 Cliza, Bol.
183/K1 Cloan, Sk,Can
132/B2 Cloates (pt.), Austl.
156/D3 Clocolan, SAfr.
60/C4 Clogh, Ire.
60/C3 Cloghan, Ire.
60/C5 Clogheen, Ire.
55/H10 Clogher, Ire.
60/D2 Clogherhead, Ire.
56/B3 Clogher Head (pt.), Ire.
60/B3 Cloghjordan, Ire.
56/C3 Cloghy, NI,UK
78/B5 Clohars-Carnoët, Fr.
60/B6 Clonakilty, Ire.
60/B6 Clonakilty (bay), Ire.
60/C5 Clonaslee, Ire.
60/C3 Clonbullogue, Ire.
60/D4 Clondalkin, Ire.
60/D4 Clonegall, Ire.
60/C1 Clones, Ire.
60/B3 Clonfert, Ire.
56/A1 Clonmany, Ire.
60/C5 Clonmel, Ire.
60/C2 Clonmellon, Ire.
60/D5 Clonroche, Ire.
193/G1 Clontarf, Mn,US
60/C2 Cloone, Ire.
67/F3 Cloppenburg, Ger.
203/F2 Clopton, Al,US
195/H4 Cloquet, Mn,US
195/J4 Cloquet (riv.), Mn,US
196/E1 Cloridorme, Qu,Can
56/E1 Closeburn, Sc,UK
207/K8 Closter, NJ,US
185/K1 Cloud (peak), Wy,US
188/B1 Cloudcroft, NM,US
137/M Cloudmaker, The (peak), Ant.
177/G3 Cloudy (mtn.), Ak,US
191/G3 Cloudy, Ok,US
56/B2 Cloughmills, NI,UK
57/H3 Cloughton, Eng,UK
58/B4 Clovelly, Eng,UK
201/G3 Clover, SC,US
184/B4 Cloverdale, Ca,US
200/D1 Cloverdale, In,US
189/M9 Cloverleaf, Tx,US
201/H1 Clover Lick, WV,US
200/D2 Cloverport, Ky,US
186/C2 Clovis, Ca,US
190/C3 Clovis, NM,US
54/A3 Clovullin, Sc,UK
57/G5 Clowne, Eng,UK
79/G5 Cloyes-sur-le-Loir, Fr.
199/H2 Cloyne, On,Can
60/B6 Cloyne, Ire.
54/A2 Cluanie, Loch (lake), Sc,UK
93/F2 Cluj (co.), Rom.
93/F2 Cluj-Napoca, Rom.
58/C2 Clun, Eng,UK
58/B3 Clunderwen, Wal,UK
183/H2 Cluny, Ab,Can
80/C5 Cluses, Fr.
182/B1 Clusko (riv.), BC,Can
86/C1 Clusone, It.
176/J5 Clute, Tx,US
136/B4 Clutha (riv.), N.Z.
136/B4 Clutha-Central Otago (reg.), N.Z.
56/E5 Clwyd (co.), Wal,UK
57/F5 Clwyd (riv.), Wal,UK
57/E5 Clwydian (range), Wal,UK
58/C3 Clydach, Wal,UK
196/E4 Clyde (riv.), NS,Can
178/E3 Clyde, NW,Can
54/B5 Clyde (riv.), Sc,UK
191/F1 Clyde, Ks,US
194/E3 Clyde, ND,US
198/E4 Clyde, Oh,US
188/E1 Clyde, Tx,US
54/B5 Clydebank, Sc,UK
54/B6 Clyde, Firth of (inlet), Sc,UK
205/C2 Clyde Hill, Wa,US
54/C5 Clydesdale (val.), Sc,UK
55/K10 Clywd (riv.), Wal,UK
58/C2 Clywedog (riv.), Wal,UK
197/S8 CN Tower, On,Can
76/B2 Côa (riv.), Port.
186/D4 Coachella, Ca,US
186/E4 Coachella (can.), Ca,US
60/B6 Coachford, Ire.
56/B2 Coagh, NI,UK
188/D1 Coahoma, Tx,US
158/E5 Coahuayana, Mex.
158/E3 Coahuila (state), Mex.
188/C3 Coahuila de Zaragoza (state), Mex.
186/E2 Coal (val.), Nv,US
201/G2 Coal (mtn.), WV,US
201/G1 Coal (riv.), WV,US
54/C5 Coalburn, Sc,UK
193/K3 Coal City, Il,US
201/G2 Coal City, WV,US
183/H3 Coaldale, Ab,Can
187/K1 Coaldale, Co,US
184/E4 Coaldale, Nv,US
206/C2 Coaldale, Pa,US
191/F3 Coalgate, Ok,US
191/H1 Coal Hill, Ar,US
183/H3 Coalhurst, Ab,Can
186/B2 Coalinga, Ca,US
56/B2 Coalisland, NI,UK
185/K3 Coalmont, Co,US
200/E3 Coalmont, Tn,US
200/C1 Coalton, Il,US
198/E5 Coalton, Oh,US
59/E1 Coalville, Eng,UK
185/H3 Coalville, Ut,US
183/M5 Coalwood, Mt,US
171/F2 Coaraci, Braz.
169/F2 Coari, Braz.
169/E2 Coari (lake), Braz.
169/E2 Coari (riv.), Braz.
186/C2 Coarsegold, Ca,US
168/D4 Coasa, Peru
178/C2 Coast (mts.), Can.
151/B2 Coast (prov.), Kenya
180/B4 Coast (ranges), Ca,US
202/F2 Coastal (plain), Ga,US
136/B4 Coastal-North Otago (reg.), N.Z.
54/B5 Coatbridge, Sc,UK
160/B2 Coatecas Altas, Mex.
159/F5 Coatepec, Mex.
159/F5 Coatepec Harinas, Mex.
195/P7 Coates, Mn,US
206/C4 Coatesville, Pa,US
159/K8 Coatetelco, Mex.
196/B3 Coaticook, Qu,Can
200/C4 Coatopa, Al,US
179/H2 Coats (isl.), NW,Can
193/E2 Coats, Ks,US
137/Y Coats Land (reg.), Ant.
159/G5 Coatzacoalcos, Mex.
160/C2 Coatzacoalcos (riv.), Mex.
159/L8 Coatzingo, Mex.
159/M6 Coatzintla, Mex.
82/D2 Coazze, It.
159/J4 Coba (ruins), Mex.
76/B1 Coba de Serpe, Sierra de (mtn.), Sp.
208/B2 Cobalt, Ct,US
160/D3 Cobán, Guat.
135/C1 Cobar, Austl.
201/L6 Cobb (co.), Ga,US
199/H4 Cobb (hill), Pa,US
135/C3 Cobbadah, Austl.
135/D3 Cobberas (peak), Austl.
208/B1 Cobble Mtn. (res.), Ma,US
204/B1 Cobblestone (mtn.), Ca,US
201/F4 Cobbtown, Ga,US
135/B3 Cobden, Austl.
199/H2 Cobden, On,Can
200/C2 Cobden, Il,US
196/F3 Cobequid (mts.), NS,Can
60/B6 Cóbh, Ire.
53/M8 Cobham, Eng,UK
168/D3 Cobija, Bol.
199/J3 Cobleskill, NY,US
199/G2 Coboconk, On,Can
128/E2 Cobourg (pen.), Austl.
199/G3 Cobourg, On,Can
174/B3 Cobquecura, Chile
185/F3 Cobre, Nv,US
155/G2 Cóbuè, Moz.
135/F5 Coburg, Austl.
130/D2 Coburg (pen.), Austl.
70/D2 Coburg, Ger.
184/B1 Coburg, Or,US
199/L2 Coburn (mtn.), Me,US
164/B5 Coca, Ecu.
164/B5 Coca (riv.), Ecu.
168/D5 Cocachacra, Peru
167/F3 Cocal, Braz.
206/B3 Cocalico (cr.), Pa,US
168/D3 Cocama, Peru
172/C1 Cocapata, Bol.
81/G5 Coca, Pizzo di (peak), It.
86/C1 Coccaglio, It.
77/E3 Cocentaina, Sp.
172/C1 Cochabamba, Bol.
172/C1 Cochabamba (dept.), Bol.
165/F2 Coche (isl.), Ven.
69/G3 Cochem, Ger.
195/H2 Cochenour, On,Can
190/A1 Cochetopa (hills), Co,US
183/K1 Cochin, Sk,Can
122/F4 Cochin, India
122/F4 Cochin (arpt.), India
187/H4 Cochise, Az,US
208/C1 Cochituate, Ma,US
201/F4 Cochran, Ga,US
178/E3 Cochrane, Ab,Can
183/G2 Cochrane, Ab,Can
179/H4 Cochrane, On,Can
208/G4 Cochranton, Pa,US
72/B4 Cochstedt, Ger.
135/G5 Cockatoo, Austl.
133/J5 Cockburn, Austl.
130/D2 Cockburn (cape), Austl.
132/K7 Cockburn (sound), Austl.
198/E2 Cockburn (isl.), On,Can
175/J8 Cockburn (chan.), Chile
162/D2 Cockburn Harbour, Trks.
54/D5 Cockburnspath, Sc,UK
162/C1 Cockburn Town, Bahm.
54/D3 Cock Cairn (mtn.), Sc,UK
54/D5 Cockenzie, Sc,UK
57/E2 Cockermouth, Eng,UK
206/B5 Cockeysville, Md,US
188/L7 Cockrell Hill, Tx,US
156/D4 Cockscomb (peak), SAfr.
161/F4 Coclé del Norte, Pan.
161/G1 Coco (cay), Cuba
161/F3 Coco (riv.), Hon., Nic.
203/H3 Cocoa, Fl,US
152/B2 Cocobeach, Gabon
202/B2 Cocodrie (lake), La,US
187/F3 Coconino (plat.), Az,US
202/P7 Coconut Creek, Fl,US
186/E4 Cocopah Ind. Res., Az,US
135/C2 Cocoparra Nat'l Park, Austl.
167/K6 Cocorná, Col.
102/J11 Cocos (isls.), Austl.
170/D2 Côcos, Braz.
161/G4 Cocos (pt.), Pan.
83/C4 Cocuzzo (peak), It.
179/K3 Cod (isl.), Nf,Can
196/B4 Cod (cape), Ma,US
169/F1 Codajás, Braz.
57/G3 Cod Beck (riv.), Eng,UK
174/C2 Codegua, Chile
165/E2 Codera (cape), Ven.
194/A2 Coderre, Sk,Can
183/M1 Codette, Sk,Can
87/F3 Codigoro, It.
93/G3 Codlea, Rom.
167/F4 Codó, Braz.
86/C2 Codogno, It.
206/B4 Codorus (cr.), Pa,US
172/B1 Codpa, Chile
162/F3 Codrington, Anti.
87/F1 Codroipo, It.
197/H2 Codroy, Nf,Can
58/D1 Codsall, Eng,UK
192/D2 Cody, Ne,US
185/J1 Cody, Wy,US
201/F2 Coeburn, Va,US
174/B3 Coelemu, Chile
167/F4 Coelho Neto, Braz.
167/L7 Coello, Col.
134/A1 Coen, Austl.
166/B2 Coeroeni (Courantyne) (riv.), Sur.
67/E5 Coesfeld, Ger.
51/M6 Coëtivy (isl.), Sey.
182/F4 Coeur d'Alene, Id,US
182/F4 Coeur d'Alene (lake), Id,US
182/G4 Coeur d'Alene (mts.), Mt,US
182/F4 Coeur d'Alene Ind. Res., Id,US
66/D3 Coevorden, Neth.
191/G4 Coffee City, Tx,US
182/E4 Coffeepot (lake), Wa,US
200/C5 Coffeeville, Al,US
200/C5 Coffeeville (dam), Al,US
200/C4 Coffeeville, Ms,US
191/G2 Coffeyville, Ks,US
133/G5 Coffin Bay, Austl.
133/G5 Coffin Bay Nat'l Park, Austl.
135/E1 Coffs Harbour, Austl.
201/J2 Cofield, NC,US
159/F5 Cofre de Perote Nat'l Park, Mex.
93/J3 Cogealac, Rom.
59/G3 Coggeshall, Eng,UK
86/B1 Coggiola, It.
90/A2 Coghinas (lake), It.
74/C4 Cognac, Fr.
82/D1 Cogne, It.
82/B1 Cognin, Fr.
152/B2 Cogo, EqG.
86/B4 Cogoleto, It.
82/C6 Cogolin, Fr.
87/E1 Cogollo del Cengio, It.
76/D2 Cogolludo, Sp.
194/F4 Cogswell, ND,US
183/L4 Cohagen, Mt,US
206/C5 Cohansey (riv.), NJ,US
208/D1 Cohasset, Ma,US
199/H3 Cohocton, NY,US
199/K3 Cohoes, NY,US
172/C1 Cohoni, Bol.
135/C2 Cohuna, Austl.
132/L7 Cohunu Nat'l Park, Austl.
161/F5 Coiba (isl.), Pan.
175/K7 Coig (riv.), Arg.
79/G3 Coignières, Fr.
174/B5 Coihaique, Chile
174/C3 Coihueco, Chile
122/F3 Coimbatore, India
76/A2 Coimbra, Port.
76/A2 Coimbra (dist.), Port.
76/C4 Coín, Sp.
193/G3 Coin, Ia,US
77/P10 Coina (riv.), Port.
201/K2 Coinjock, NC,US
172/B1 Coipasa, Bol.
172/B1 Coipasa (salt pan), Bol.
74/F4 Coise (riv.), Fr.
164/D2 Cojedes (state), Ven.
164/A4 Cojimies, Ecu.
164/D2 Cojoro, Ven.
174/C5 Cojudo Blanco (peak), Arg.
160/D3 Cojutepeque, ESal.
92/E3 Čoka, Yugo.
195/E5 Cokato, Mn,US
200/D4 Coker, Al,US
185/H2 Cokeville, Wy,US
135/B3 Colac, Austl.
166/D3 Colares, Braz.
77/P10 Colares, Port.
168/B2 Colasay, Peru
171/E3 Colatina, Braz.
149/G3 Colba, Eth.
137/P Colbeck (cape), Ant.
191/F4 Colbert, Ok,US
72/B3 Colbitz, Ger.
72/B3 Colbitz-Letzlinger Heide (reg.), Ger.
199/H3 Colborne, On,Can
174/C2 Colbún, Chile
179/T7 Colburg (isl.), NW,Can
190/D1 Colby, Ks,US
205/B2 Colby, Wa,US
195/J5 Colby, Wi,US
168/D4 Colca (riv.), Peru
168/C4 Colcabamba, Peru
172/C2 Colchaqur (riv.), Arg.
205/G8 Colchester, On,Can
59/G3 Colchester, Eng,UK
208/B2 Colchester, Ct,US
193/J3 Colchester, Il,US
199/K2 Colchester, Vt,US
177/F4 Cold Bay, Ak,US
57/F2 Cold Fell (mtn.), Eng,UK
54/D5 Coldingham, Sc,UK
72/C5 Colditz, Ger.
196/F3 Coldspring (pt.), NS,Can
195/G5 Cold Spring, Mn,US
189/G2 Coldspring, Tx,US
207/M8 Cold Spring Harbor, NY,US
184/D1 Cold Springs Nat'l Wild. Ref., Or,US
182/E2 Coldstream, BC,Can
54/D5 Coldstream, Sc,UK
199/G2 Coldwater, On,Can
190/E2 Coldwater, Ks,US
198/D4 Coldwater, Mi,US
200/C3 Coldwater, Ms,US
200/C3 Coldwater (riv.), Ms,US
198/D4 Coldwater, Oh,US
190/D2 Coldwater (cr.), Ok, Tx,US
59/E3 Cole (riv.), Eng,UK
191/F3 Cole, Ok,US
135/C2 Coleambally, Austl.
208/A2 Colebrook, Ct,US
199/L2 Colebrook, NH,US
208/G4 Colebrook, Oh,US
191/H1 Cole Camp, Mo,US
58/D3 Coleford, Eng,UK
183/G3 Coleman, Ab,Can
202/L6 Coleman, Fl,US
203/F2 Coleman, Ga,US
198/D3 Coleman, Mi,US
191/F3 Coleman, Ok,US
188/E2 Coleman, Tx,US
188/E1 Coleman (lake), Tx,US
198/B2 Coleman, Wi,US
105/E2 Çölemerik, Turk.
157/E3 Colenso, SAfr.
135/B3 Coleraine, Austl.
56/B1 Coleraine, NI,UK
56/B1 Coleraine (dist.), NI,UK
195/H4 Coleraine, Mn,US
193/F2 Coleridge, Ne,US
122/G3 Coleroon (riv.), India
156/D3 Colesberg, SAfr.
59/E2 Coleshill, Eng,UK
206/A5 Colesville, Md,US
189/F3 Coleto Creek (res.), Tx,US
186/C1 Coleville, Ca,US
184/C4 Colfax, Ca,US
193/K3 Colfax, Il,US
198/C4 Colfax, In,US
202/B2 Colfax, La,US
194/F4 Colfax, ND,US
189/G1 Colfax, Tx,US
182/F4 Colfax, Wa,US
193/J1 Colfax, Wi,US
84/C1 Colfiorito, It.
179/S6 Colgate (cape), NW,Can
121/F3 Colgong, India
174/C5 Colhué Huapi (lake), Arg.
81/F5 Colico, It.
123/D2 Co Lieu, Viet.
133/J5 Colignan, Austl.
80/B5 Coligny, Fr.
156/D2 Coligny, SAfr.
66/A5 Colijnsplaat, Neth.
158/E5 Colima, Mex.
158/D5 Colima (state), Mex.
158/E5 Colima, Nevado de (peak), Mex.
174/C2 Colina, Chile
167/E4 Colinas, Braz.
170/C2 Colinas de Goiás, Braz.
76/D1 Colindres, Sp.
204/F7 Coliseum, Ca,US
63/Q1 Colkhov (riv.), Rus.
55/H8 Coll (isl.), Sc,UK
76/D2 Collado-Villalba, Sp.
86/D4 Collagna, It.
168/D5 Collana, Bol.
135/D1 Collarenebri, Austl.
185/K4 Collbran, Co,US
86/D5 Collecchio, It.
87/E6 Colle di Val d'Elsa, It.
155/F4 Colleen Bawn, Zim.
84/D4 Colleferro, It.
177/J3 College, Ak,US
201/M7 College Park, Ga,US
206/B6 College Park, Md,US
182/E4 College Place, Wa,US
193/G3 College Springs, Ia,US
189/F2 College Station, Tx,US
206/C3 Collegeville, Pa,US
86/C2 Collegno, It.
81/H4 Colle Isarco (Gossensass), It.
85/D4 Collelongo, It.
86/D5 Collesalvetti, It.
85/E5 Colle Sannita, It.
82/C3 Colle Sestriere, It.
85/E4 Colletorto, It.
188/K7 Colleyville, Tx,US
85/F6 Colliano, It.
85/E4 Colli a Volturno, It.
132/C5 Collie, Austl.
130/B4 Collier (bay), Austl.
132/C3 Collier (range), Austl.
57/G2 Collier Law (hill), Eng,UK
132/C3 Collier Range Nat'l Park, Austl.
208/G7 Colliers, WV,US
200/C3 Collierville, Tn,US
58/B6 Colliford (res.), Eng,UK
188/L6 Collin (co.), Tx,US
57/G4 Collingham, Eng,UK
198/F2 Collingwood, On,Can
136/C3 Collingwood, N.Z.
195/K2 Collins, On,Can
201/F4 Collins, Ga,US
191/H2 Collins, Mo,US
200/C5 Collins, Ms,US
183/J4 Collins, Mt,US
208/E5 Collins, Oh,US
200/E3 Collins (riv.), Tn,US
189/J1 Collinston, La,US
56/B5 Collinstown (Dublin) (int'l arpt.), Ire.
134/B3 Collinsville, Austl.
200/E3 Collinsville, Al,US
205/L10 Collinsville, Ca,US
208/B2 Collinsville, Ct,US
200/C4 Collinsville, Ms,US
191/G2 Collinsville, Ok,US
201/H2 Collinsville, Va,US
200/D3 Collinwood, Tn,US
141/V17 Collo, Alg.
80/C5 Collombey, Swi.
80/C5 Collonge-Bellerive, Swi.
80/B5 Collonges, Fr.
60/B1 Collooney, Ire.
172/C1 Collpa, Bol.
205/K11 Colma, Ca,US
193/F2 Colman, SD,US
80/D1 Colmar, Fr.
206/C3 Colmar, Pa,US
82/C4 Colmars, Fr.
70/D4 Colmberg, Ger.
76/C4 Colmenar, Sp.
76/D2 Colmenar de Oreja, Sp.
76/D2 Colmenar Viejo, Sp.
189/G2 Colmesneil, Tx,US
175/J7 Colmillo (cape), Chile
72/D6 Colmnitz, Ger.
56/D1 Colmonell, Sc,UK
79/E4 Colmont (riv.), Fr.
59/E3 Coln (riv.), Eng,UK
57/F4 Colne, Eng,UK
59/G3 Colne (riv.), Eng,UK
158/A2 Colnett, Punta (pt.), Mex.
53/N6 Colney Heath, Eng,UK
123/D1 Co Loa Citadel, Viet.
83/C2 Colobraro, It.
85/D2 Cologna Spiaggia, It.
87/E2 Cologna Veneta, It.
86/C1 Cologne, It.
195/N7 Cologne, Mn,US
206/D4 Cologne, NJ,US
69/G2 Cologne/Bonn (int'l arpt.), Ger.
69/F2 Cologne (Köln), Ger.
86/C1 Cologno Monzese, It.
193/K1 Coloma, Wi,US
79/E2 Colombelles, Fr.
53/S10 Colombes, Fr.
80/B1 Colombey-les-Belles, Fr.
80/A1 Colombey-les-Deux-Eglises, Fr.
164/C4 Colombia
188/E4 Colombia, Mex.
80/C4 Colombier, Swi.
86/D1 Colombine, Monte (peak), It.
82/C4 Colombis (mtn.), Fr.
173/G3 Colombo, Braz.
118/C6 Colombo (cap.), SrL.
86/A2 Colombo, Monte (peak), It.
74/D5 Colomiers, Fr.
160/D3 Colomoncagua, Hon.
174/E2 Colón, Arg.
174/F2 Colón, Arg.
161/F1 Colón, Cuba
161/E3 Colón (mts.), Hon.
159/E4 Colón, Mex.
161/G4 Colón, Pan.
175/G2 Colón, Uru.
185/K4 Colona, Co,US
168/A1 Colonche, Ecu.
120/C2 Colonelganj, India
138/C4 Colonia, Micro.
175/T12 Colonia (arpt.), Uru.
175/T12 Colonia (dept.), Uru.
207/D2 Colonia, NJ,US
174/E3 Colonia Barón, Arg.
172/E3 Colonia Benjamín Aceval, Par.
186/E4 Colonia Coahuila, Mex.
175/F2 Colonia Del Sacramento, Uru.
172/D4 Colonia Dora, Arg.
174/C3 Colonia Gobernador Ayala, Arg.
174/D3 Colonia Josefa, Arg.
174/C5 Colonia Las Heras, Arg.
173/E4 Colonia Lavalleja, Uru.
201/J1 Colonial Beach, Va,US
171/G1 Colônia Leopoldina, Braz.
201/J2 Colonial Heights, Va,US
201/J2 Colonial Nat'l Hist. Park, Va,US
206/B3 Colonial Park, Pa,US
188/A3 Colonia Nueva Delicias, Mex.
173/E2 Colonia Presidente Stroessner, Par.

175/S11 **Colonia San Javier,** Uru.
175/T12 **Colonia Valdense,** Uru.
174/D3 **Colonia Veinticinco de Mayo,** Arg.
173/F2 **Colonia Yby Yu,** Par.
153/E2 **Colon Koret,** Zaire
84/C4 **Colonna,** It.
194/B2 **Colonsay,** Sk,Can
55/H8 **Colonsay** (isl.), Sc,UK
191/G1 **Colony,** Ks,US
192/B1 **Colony,** Wy,US
189/E1 **Colony, The,** Tx,US
175/K7 **Colorado** (peak), Arg.
174/D3 **Colorado** (riv.), Arg.
170/C4 **Colorado,** Braz.
161/F4 **Colorado,** CR
180/D5 **Colorado** (riv.), Mex., US
186/E4 **Colorado** (riv.), NAm.
185/H4 **Colorado** (plat.), US
192/B4 **Colorado** (can.), Co,US
189/F2 **Colorado** (riv.), Tx,US
187/F2 **Colorado City,** Az,US
192/B5 **Colorado City,** Co,US
188/D1 **Colorado City,** Tx,US
185/J4 **Colorado Nat'l Mon.,** Co,US
186/E3 **Colorado Riv.** (aqueduct), Ca,US
186/E3 **Colorado Riv. Ind. Res.,** Az, Ca,US
172/C3 **Colorados** (marsh), Arg.
192/B4 **Colorado Springs,** Co,US
86/D3 **Colorno,** It.
82/B5 **Colostre** (riv.), Fr.
158/E4 **Colotlán,** Mex.
160/B2 **Colotlipa,** Mex.
198/F2 **Colpoys Bay,** On,Can
172/C1 **Colquechaca,** Bol.
172/C1 **Colquiri,** Bol.
203/F2 **Colquitt,** Ga,US
199/K3 **Colrain,** Ma,US
87/F1 **Col San Martino,** It.
160/D2 **Colson** (pt.), Belz.
183/L5 **Colstrip,** Mt,US
56/D1 **Colt** (hill), Sc,UK
174/C2 **Coltauco,** Chile
59/H1 **Coltishall,** Eng,UK
204/C2 **Colton,** Ca,US
185/H4 **Colton,** Ut,US
182/F4 **Colton,** Wa,US
207/D3 **Colts Neck,** NJ,US
163/D4 **Coluene** (riv.), Braz.
168/B1 **Columbe,** Ecu.
176/K1 **Columbia** (cape), Can.
182/F1 **Columbia** (mtn.), Ab,Can
179/T6 **Columbia** (cape), NW,Can
182/C5 **Columbia** (riv.), Can., US
203/F2 **Columbia,** Al,US
186/B1 **Columbia,** Ca,US
208/B2 **Columbia,** Ct,US
200/B1 **Columbia,** Il,US
200/E2 **Columbia,** Ky,US
202/B1 **Columbia,** La,US
206/B5 **Columbia,** Md,US
191/H1 **Columbia,** Mo,US
202/D2 **Columbia,** Ms,US
201/J3 **Columbia,** NC,US
206/C2 **Columbia,** NJ,US
206/B3 **Columbia,** Pa,US
201/G3 **Columbia,** SC,US
192/E1 **Columbia,** SD,US
200/D3 **Columbia,** Tn,US
182/E4 **Columbia** (plat.), Wa,US
198/D4 **Columbia City,** In,US
182/C5 **Columbia City,** Or,US
183/G3 **Columbia Falls,** Mt,US
195/P6 **Columbia Heights,** Mn,US
200/D4 **Columbiana,** Al,US
208/G6 **Columbiana,** Oh,US
208/G6 **Columbiana** (co.), Oh,US
182/E4 **Columbia Nat'l Wild. Ref.,** Wa,US
182/C4 **Columbian White Tailed Deer Nat'l Wild. Ref.,** Or,US
182/E2 **Columbia Reach** (lake), BC,Can
192/E1 **Columbia Road** (dam), SD,US
208/F5 **Columbia Station,** Oh,US
198/E3 **Columbiaville,** Mi,US
156/B4 **Columbine** (cape), SAfr.
185/K3 **Columbine,** Co,US
88/D3 **Columbretes** (isls.), Sp.
191/H4 **Columbus,** Ar,US
200/E4 **Columbus,** Ga,US
198/D5 **Columbus,** In,US
191/G2 **Columbus,** Ks,US
200/C4 **Columbus,** Ms,US
200/C4 **Columbus** (lake), Ms,US
183/K5 **Columbus,** Mt,US
201/F3 **Columbus,** NC,US
192/F3 **Columbus,** Ne,US
206/D3 **Columbus,** NJ,US
187/J5 **Columbus,** NM,US
184/D4 **Columbus** (salt marsh), Nv,US
198/E5 **Columbus,** Oh,US
189/F3 **Columbus,** Tx,US
193/K2 **Columbus,** Wi,US
200/C4 **Columbus A.F.B.,** Ms,US
198/D4 **Columbus Grove,** Oh,US
186/C1 **Columbus** (salt marsh), Nv,US
76/C1 **Colunga,** Sp.
172/B1 **Colupo, Cerro** (mtn.), Chile
184/B4 **Colusa,** Ca,US
184/B4 **Colusa Nat'l Wild. Ref.,** Ca,US
178/D2 **Colville** (lake), NW,Can
136/C2 **Colville** (cape), N.Z.
177/H2 **Colville** (riv.), Ak,US
182/F3 **Colville,** Wa,US
182/F3 **Colville** (riv.), Wa,US
183/E3 **Colville Ind. Res.,** Wa,US
205/B3 **Colvos** (passg.), Wa,US
58/D2 **Colwall,** Eng,UK
58/C4 **Colwinston,** Wal,UK
56/E5 **Colwyn Bay,** Wal,UK
87/F3 **Comacchio,** It.
75/K4 **Comacchio** (lag.), It.
87/F3 **Comacchio, Valli di** (lag.), It.
121/H1 **Comai,** China
158/E5 **Comala,** Mex.
159/G5 **Comalcalco,** Mex.
186/B1 **Comanche** (res.), Ca,US
192/B4 **Comanche** (cr.), Co,US
191/F3 **Comanche,** Ok,US
189/E2 **Comanche,** Tx,US
192/C5 **Comanche Nat'l Grsld.,** Co,US
175/K7 **Comandante Luis Piedrabuena,** Arg.
93/H2 **Comăneşti,** Rom.
172/C1 **Comarapa,** Bol.
150/C5 **Comar Gambon,** Som.
93/G3 **Comarnic,** Rom.
168/B3 **Comas,** Peru
168/C3 **Comas,** Peru
160/E3 **Comayagua,** Hon.
201/G4 **Combahee** (riv.), SC,US
172/B4 **Combarbalá,** Chile
80/B2 **Combeaufontaine,** Fr.
58/B4 **Combe Martin,** Eng,UK
205/G7 **Comber,** On,Can
56/C2 **Comber,** NI,UK
116/B5 **Combermere** (bay), Burma
193/K1 **Combined Locks,** Wi,US
69/E3 **Comblain-au-Pont,** Belg.
80/C6 **Combloux,** Fr.
78/D4 **Combourg,** Fr.
135/E1 **Comboyne,** Austl.
79/D5 **Combrée,** Fr.
78/C5 **Combs** (riv.), Fr.
201/F2 **Combs,** Ky,US
53/T11 **Combs-la-Ville,** Fr.
145/F5 **Comé,** Ben.
135/D1 **Come-by-Chance,** Austl.
169/F3 **Comemoração** (riv.), Braz.
162/D3 **Comendador,** DRep.
200/E4 **Comer,** Al,US
134/C4 **Comet** (riv.), Austl.
189/E3 **Comfort,** Tx,US
121/H4 **Comilla,** Bang.
121/H4 **Comilla** (dist.), Bang.
68/B2 **Comines,** Belg.
68/C2 **Comines,** Fr.
84/H7 **Comino** (isl.), Malta
160/C2 **Comitán,** Mex.
207/E2 **Commack,** NY,US
174/F3 **Commandante Nicanor Otamendi,** Arg.
74/E3 **Commentry,** Fr.
204/B2 **Commerce,** Ca,US
201/F3 **Commerce,** Ga,US
189/G1 **Commerce,** Tx,US
192/B4 **Commerce City,** Co,US
69/E6 **Commercy,** Fr.
166/C1 **Commewijne** (dist.), Sur.
194/F1 **Commissioner** (isl.), Mb,Can
179/H2 **Committee** (bay), NW,Can
195/K5 **Commonwealth,** Wi,US
114/B4 **Communism** (Kommunizma) (peak), Taj.
86/C1 **Como,** It.
81/F5 **Como** (lake), It.
86/C1 **Como** (prov.), It.
200/C3 **Como,** Ms,US
205/P14 **Como,** Wi,US
205/P14 **Como** (lake), Wi,US
174/D5 **Comodoro Rivadavia,** Arg.
144/D4 **Comoé** (prov.), Burk.
144/E4 **Comoé Nat'l Park,** IvC.
158/C3 **Comondú,** Mex.
122/F4 **Comorin** (cape), India
157/G5 **Comoros**
182/B3 **Comox,** BC,Can
152/B1 **Company,** Camr.
183/J2 **Compeer,** Ab,Can
68/B5 **Compiègne,** Fr.
85/F4 **Compomarino,** It.
158/D4 **Compostela,** Mex.
173/H2 **Comprida** (isl.), Braz.
82/C5 **Comps-sur-Artuby,** Fr.
204/B3 **Compton,** Ca,US
54/C4 **Comrie,** Sc,UK
198/D3 **Comstock,** Mi,US
188/D3 **Comstock,** Tx,US
85/D2 **Comunanza,** It.
165/E4 **Comunidad,** Ven.
121/H2 **Cona,** China
116/A2 **Co Nag** (lake), China
168/C4 **Conaica,** Peru
144/B4 **Conakry** (cap.), Gui.
144/B4 **Conakry** (comm.), Gui.
164/B5 **Conambo** (riv.), Ecu.
172/B4 **Conay,** Chile
182/D5 **Conboy Nat'l Wild. Ref.,** Wa,US
87/F5 **Conca** (riv.), It.
188/E3 **Concan,** Tx,US
78/B5 **Concarneau,** Fr.
170/C3 **Conceicão das Alagoas,** Braz.
171/E4 **Conceição de Macabu,** Braz.
166/D5 **Conceição do Araguaia,** Braz.
171/F1 **Conceição do Coité,** Braz.
171/E3 **Conceicão do Mato Dentro,** Braz.
171/L6 **Conceicão do Rio Verde,** Braz.
171/L7 **Conceicão dos Ouros,** Braz.
172/C3 **Concepción,** Arg.
172/E4 **Concepción,** Arg.
169/E3 **Concepción,** Bol.
169/F5 **Concepción,** Bol.
172/D1 **Concepción** (lake), Bol.
174/B3 **Concepción,** Chile
158/C3 **Concepción** (bay), Mex.
172/E2 **Concepción,** Par.
172/E1 **Concepción** (dept.), Par.
172/D3 **Concepción del Bermejo,** Arg.
159/E3 **Concepción del Oro,** Mex.
174/F2 **Concepción del Uruguay,** Arg.
158/C3 **Concepción, Punta** (pt.), Mex.
197/L2 **Conception** (bay), Nf,Can
154/B4 **Conception** (bay), Namb.
186/B3 **Conception** (pt.), Ca,US
86/D1 **Concesio,** It.
155/F3 **Concession,** Zim.
171/J7 **Conchal,** Braz.
190/B3 **Conchas** (lake), NM,US
53/U10 **Conches,** Fr.
79/F3 **Conches-en-Ouche,** Fr.
172/B2 **Conchi,** Chile
175/S12 **Conchillas,** Uru.
187/H3 **Concho,** Az,US
188/D2 **Concho** (riv.), Tx,US
188/B3 **Conchos** (riv.), Mex.
73/B4 **Conco** (riv.), Hun.
174/Q9 **Concón,** Chile
200/B3 **Concord,** Ar,US
205/K11 **Concord,** Ca,US
203/F2 **Concord,** Fl,US
200/C2 **Concord,** Mo,US
201/G3 **Concord,** NC,US
199/L3 **Concord,** NH,US
191/G4 **Concord,** Tx,US
201/H2 **Concord,** Va,US
205/N13 **Concord,** Wi,US
172/E4 **Concordia,** Arg.
173/F3 **Concórdia,** Braz.
167/K6 **Concordia,** Col.
158/D4 **Concordia,** Mex.
168/C2 **Concordia,** Peru
191/F1 **Concordia,** Ks,US
87/F1 **Concordia Sagittaria,** It.
87/D3 **Concordia sulla Secchia,** It.
208/C1 **Concord Museum,** Ma,US
160/D3 **Concuen** (riv.), Guat.
123/D2 **Con Cuong,** Viet.
161/G1 **Condado,** Cuba
129/J5 **Condamine** (riv.), Austl.
164/C5 **Condar,** Col.
171/F1 **Conde,** Braz.
192/E1 **Conde,** SD,US
68/C3 **Condé-sur-L'Escaut,** Fr.
79/E3 **Condé-sur-Noireau,** Fr.
79/F4 **Condé-sur-Sarthe,** Fr.
79/D2 **Condé-sur-Vire,** Fr.
171/E2 **Condeúba,** Braz.
86/D1 **Condino,** It.
135/C2 **Condobolin,** Austl.
74/D5 **Condom,** Fr.
134/C4 **Condomine** (riv.), Austl.
183/H4 **Condon,** Mt,US
184/C1 **Condon,** Or,US
183/G1 **Condor,** Ab,Can
82/D2 **Condove,** It.
82/A2 **Condrieu,** Fr.
64/C3 **Condroz** (plat.), Belg.
69/D3 **Condroz** (upland), Belg.
202/E2 **Conecuh** (riv.), Al,US
87/F1 **Conegliano,** It.
200/C4 **Conehatta,** Ms,US
187/J2 **Conejos** (riv.), Ca,US
190/A2 **Conejos,** Co,US
190/A2 **Conejos** (riv.), Co,US
199/G4 **Conemaugh** (riv.), Pa,US
174/E2 **Conesa,** Arg.
206/B3 **Conestoga** (riv.), Pa,US
158/D3 **Coneto de Comonfort,** Mex.
206/B3 **Conewago** (cr.), Pa,US
206/B4 **Conewago** (cr.), Pa,US
206/B3 **Conewago** (lake), Pa,US
207/K9 **Coney Island,** NY,US
170/E3 **Confins** (int'l arpt.), Braz.
69/E5 **Conflans-en-Jarnisy,** Fr.
53/S10 **Conflans-Sainte-Honorine,** Fr.
172/E2 **Confuso** (riv.), Par.
60/A2 **Cong,** Ire.
201/G4 **Congaree Swamp Nat'l Mon.,** SC,US
207/E1 **Congers,** NY,US
117/G4 **Conghua,** China
117/F3 **Congjiang,** China
57/F5 **Congleton,** Eng,UK
152/C3 **Congo**
140/D5 **Congo** (riv.), Afr.
152/C4 **Congo** (mts.), Ang.
167/G4 **Congo,** Braz.
171/K7 **Congonhal,** Braz.
173/J2 **Congonhas,** Braz.
170/D4 **Congonhas** (int'l arpt.), Braz.
140/E5 **Congo** (Zaire)
187/F3 **Congress,** Az,US
208/E6 **Congress,** Oh,US
78/B6 **Conguel, Pointe du** (pt.), Fr.
174/C3 **Conguillio Parque Nacional,** Chile
54/B4 **Conic** (hill), Sc,UK
174/C4 **Cónico** (peak), Arg.
174/C4 **Cónico, Nevado** (peak), Chile
79/G4 **Conie** (riv.), Fr.
76/B4 **Conil de la Frontera,** Sp.
57/H5 **Coningsby,** Eng,UK
57/G5 **Conisbrough,** Eng,UK
57/E3 **Coniston,** Eng,UK
57/E3 **Coniston Water** (lake), Eng,UK
201/M7 **Conley,** Ga,US
79/E4 **Conlie,** Fr.
56/C2 **Conlig,** NI,UK
179/J1 **Conn** (lake), NW,Can
60/A1 **Conn** (lake), Ire.
60/B2 **Connacht** (prov.), Ire.
57/E5 **Connah's Quay,** Wal,UK
68/C6 **Connantre,** Fr.
198/F4 **Conneaut,** Oh,US
208/G4 **Conneaut Lake,** Pa,US
199/L2 **Connecticut** (riv.), US
199/K4 **Connecticut** (state), US
199/H3 **Connecticut** (hill), NY,US
54/A4 **Connel,** Sc,UK
182/E4 **Connell,** Wa,US
199/G4 **Connellsville,** Pa,US
60/A2 **Connemara** (dist.), Ire.
55/G10 **Connemara Nat'l Park,** Ire.
125/C1 **Conner,** Phil.
79/F4 **Connerré,** Fr.
198/D5 **Connersville,** In,US
55/G9 **Conn, Lough** (lake), Ire.
208/G6 **Connoquenessing,** Pa,US
135/C2 **Conoble,** Austl.
164/B5 **Conocoto,** Ecu.
206/B3 **Conodoguinet** (cr.), Pa,US
175/K7 **Cono Grande** (peak), Arg.
54/B1 **Cononbridge,** Sc,UK
134/D4 **Conondale Nat'l Park,** Austl.
54/B1 **Conon, Falls of** (falls), Sc,UK
92/D3 **Čonoplja,** Yugo.
208/F6 **Conotton** (cr.), Oh,US
201/G3 **Conover,** NC,US
206/B4 **Conowingo** (dam), Md,US
74/E4 **Conques,** Fr.
183/L2 **Conquest,** Sk,Can
193/H2 **Conrad,** Ia,US
183/J3 **Conrad,** Mt,US
189/G2 **Conroe,** Tx,US
189/G2 **Conroe** (lake), Tx,US
87/E3 **Consandolo,** It.
207/F2 **Conscience Point Nat'l Wild. Ref.,** NY,US
69/F4 **Consdorf,** Lux.
170/E4 **Conselheiro Lafaiete,** Braz.
171/E3 **Conselheiro Pena,** Braz.
87/E3 **Conselice,** It.
87/E2 **Conselve,** It.
57/G2 **Consett,** Eng,UK
206/C3 **Conshohocken,** Pa,US
161/F1 **Consolación del Sur,** Cuba
123/D4 **Con Son** (isl.), Viet.
183/J1 **Consort,** Ab,Can
64/E5 **Constance** (lake), Eur.
88/F1 **Constance** (lake), Ger., Swi.
182/C4 **Constance** (mt.), Wa,US
81/F2 **Constance** (Bodensee) (lake), Ger., Swi.
162/F4 **Constant** (mtn.), Guad.
93/J3 **Constanţa,** Rom.
93/J3 **Constanţa** (co.), Rom.
77/F2 **Constantí,** Sp.
76/C4 **Constantina,** Sp.
141/V17 **Constantine,** Alg.
141/V17 **Constantine** (wilaya), Alg.
177/G4 **Constantine** (cape), Ak,US
162/D3 **Constanza,** DRep.
174/B2 **Constitución,** Chile
175/T11 **Constitución** (res.), Uru.
158/B2 **Constitución de 1857 Nat'l Park,** Mex.
201/M7 **Constitution,** Ga,US
76/D3 **Consuegra,** Sp.
183/K3 **Consul,** Sk,Can
121/F5 **Contai,** India
168/C2 **Contamana,** Peru
87/F2 **Contarina,** It.
171/E2 **Contas** (riv.), Braz.
170/D3 **Contegem,** Braz.
82/D5 **Contes,** Fr.
80/D5 **Conthey,** Swi.
84/C3 **Contigliano,** It.
68/B4 **Contigny,** Fr.
182/F1 **Continental** (ranges), Ab, BC,Can
187/G5 **Continental,** Az,US
160/E1 **Contoy** (isl.), Mex.
205/L11 **Contra Costa** (can.), Ca,US
205/L11 **Contra Costa** (co.), Ca,US
164/C3 **Contratación,** Col.
197/P6 **Contrecoeur,** Qu,Can
76/E3 **Contreras** (res.), Sp.
79/G6 **Contres,** Fr.
80/B1 **Contrexéville,** Fr.
177/J3 **Controller** (bay), Ak,US
174/B3 **Contulmo,** Chile
168/B2 **Contumazá,** Peru
85/F6 **Contursi Terme,** It.
69/G5 **Contwig,** Ger.
178/E2 **Contwoyto** (lake), NW,Can
68/B4 **Conty,** Fr.
164/C2 **Convención,** Col.
202/C2 **Convent,** La,US
84/C3 **Convento San Francesco,** It.
90/E2 **Conversano,** It.
202/B2 **Converse,** La,US
134/C3 **Conway** (cape), Austl.
191/H3 **Conway,** Ar,US
202/N6 **Conway,** Fl,US
198/D2 **Conway,** Mi,US
191/H2 **Conway,** Mo,US
199/L3 **Conway,** NH,US
208/G6 **Conway,** Pa,US
201/H4 **Conway,** SC,US
134/C3 **Conway Range Nat'l Park,** Austl.
191/F2 **Conway Springs,** Ks,US
56/E5 **Conway, Vale of** (val.), Wal,UK
56/E5 **Conwy,** Wal,UK
56/D5 **Conwy** (bay), Wal,UK
56/E5 **Conwy** (riv.), Wal,UK
200/E4 **Conyers,** Ga,US
206/B2 **Conyngham,** Pa,US
133/G4 **Coober Pedy,** Austl.
121/G2 **Cooch Behār,** India
134/F7 **Coochiemudlo** (isl.), Austl.
133/J4 **Coogee,** Austl.
133/F4 **Cook,** Austl.
175/K8 **Cook** (bay), Chile
136/B3 **Cook** (peak), N.Z.
136/C3 **Cook** (str.), N.Z.
177/H3 **Cook** (inlet), Ak,US
205/Q16 **Cook** (co.), Il,US
132/C5 **Cooke** (peak), Austl.
200/E2 **Cookeville,** Tn,US
156/D4 **Cookhouse,** SAfr.
137/L **Cook Ice Shelf,** Ant.
139/J6 **Cook Islands** (terr.), N.Z.
195/L5 **Cooks,** Mi,US
196/B3 **Cookshire,** Qu,Can
56/B2 **Cookstown,** NI,UK
56/B2 **Cookstown** (dist.), NI,UK
206/A5 **Cooksville,** Md,US
134/B1 **Cooktown,** Austl.
135/C1 **Coolabah,** Austl.
135/B3 **Coola Coola** (swamp), Austl.
134/B4 **Cooladdi,** Austl.
135/D1 **Coolah,** Austl.
135/C2 **Coolamon,** Austl.
60/B1 **Coolaney,** Ire.
135/E1 **Coolangatta,** Austl.
135/D1 **Coolatai,** Austl.
60/D2 **Cooley** (pt.), Ire.
132/D4 **Coolgardie,** Austl.
130/C3 **Coolibah,** Austl.
187/G4 **Coolidge,** Az,US
203/G2 **Coolidge,** Ga,US
189/F2 **Coolidge,** Tx,US
187/G4 **Coolidge Dam,** Az,US
134/D4 **Cooloola Nat'l Park,** Austl.
132/K7 **Cooloongup** (lake), Austl.
201/G1 **Coolville,** Oh,US
135/D3 **Cooma,** Austl.
60/A6 **Coomhola** (riv.), Ire.
205/N15 **Coon** (cr.), Il,US
205/G6 **Coon** (cr.), Mi,US
195/P6 **Coon** (riv.), Mn,US
135/D1 **Coonabarabran,** Austl.
135/A2 **Coonalpyn,** Austl.
135/D1 **Coonamble,** Austl.
132/D4 **Coonana Abor. Land,** Austl.
118/B5 **Coondapoor,** India
205/G6 **Coon, East Branch** (cr.), Mi,US
132/C2 **Coongan Abor. Land,** Austl.
122/F3 **Coonoor,** India
193/G3 **Coon Rapids,** Ia,US
195/H5 **Coon Rapids,** Mn,US
193/J2 **Coon Valley,** Wi,US
133/H4 **Cooper** (cr.), Austl.
182/F2 **Cooper** (mtn.), BC,Can
189/G1 **Cooper,** Tx,US
202/P7 **Cooper City,** Fl,US
206/C2 **Coopersburg,** Pa,US
194/E4 **Cooperstown,** ND,US
199/J3 **Cooperstown,** NY,US
133/G4 **Coorabie,** Austl.
132/C3 **Coordewandy** (peak), Austl.
135/A3 **Coorong Nat'l Park,** Austl.
132/C4 **Coorow,** Austl.
134/D4 **Cooroy,** Austl.
184/A2 **Coos** (bay), Or,US
200/D4 **Coosa** (riv.), Al, Ga,US
200/E3 **Coosa,** Ga,US
200/D4 **Coosada,** Al,US
200/E3 **Coosawattee** (riv.), Ga,US
184/A2 **Coos Bay,** Or,US
191/J2 **Coot** (mtn.), Mo,US
135/D2 **Cootamundra,** Austl.
60/C1 **Cootehill,** Ire.
168/D5 **Copacabana,** Bol.
164/C3 **Copacabana,** Col.
172/C1 **Copachuncho,** Bol.
174/C3 **Copahué** (vol.), Chile
160/C2 **Copainalá,** Mex.
208/A1 **Copake,** NY,US
160/B2 **Copala,** Mex.
159/F5 **Copalillo,** Mex.
182/B4 **Copalis Beach,** Wa,US
160/D3 **Copán** (ruins), Hon.
191/G2 **Copan,** Ok,US
189/F3 **Copano** (bay), Tx,US
76/E4 **Cope** (cape), Sp.
192/C4 **Cope,** Co,US
56/C2 **Copeland** (isl.), NI,UK
195/M5 **Copemish,** Mi,US
63/T9 **Copenhagen** (int'l arpt.), Den.
62/E4 **Copenhagen** (København) (cap.), Den.
167/L6 **Coper,** Col.
91/F2 **Copertino,** It.
135/D1 **Copeton** (dam), Austl.
188/L6 **Copeville,** Tx,US
207/E2 **Copiague,** NY,US
172/B3 **Copiapó,** Chile
172/B3 **Copiapó** (peak), Chile
172/B2 **Copiapó** (riv.), Chile
206/C2 **Coplay,** Pa,US
133/H4 **Copley,** Austl.
154/B2 **Coporolo,** Ang.
154/B2 **Coporolo** (riv.), Ang.
87/E3 **Copparo,** It.
188/K7 **Coppell,** Tx,US
166/B1 **Coppename** (riv.), Sur.
67/G4 **Coppenbrügge,** Ger.
178/B2 **Copper** (riv.), Ak,US
189/F2 **Copperas Cove,** Tx,US
155/E2 **Copperbelt** (prov.), Zam.
177/J3 **Copper Center,** Ak,US
194/D3 **Copperdahl** (hill), ND,US
200/E3 **Copperhill,** Tn,US
178/E2 **Coppermine,** NW,Can
178/E2 **Coppermine** (riv.), NW,Can
201/G2 **Copper Valley,** Va,US
80/C5 **Coppet,** Swi.
57/F4 **Coppull,** Eng,UK
93/G2 **Copşa Mică,** Rom.
114/E5 **Coqên,** China
57/F1 **Coquet** (riv.), Eng,UK
57/G1 **Coquet Dale** (val.), Eng,UK
184/A2 **Coquille,** Or,US
184/A2 **Coquille** (riv.), Or,US
172/B4 **Coquimbo,** Chile
172/B3 **Coquimbo** (reg.), Chile
182/C3 **Coquitlam,** BC,Can
185/J2 **Cora,** Wy,US
93/G4 **Corabia,** Rom.
170/D3 **Coração de Jesus,** Braz.
83/C4 **Corace** (riv.), It.
168/C4 **Coracora,** Peru
161/H2 **Corail,** Haiti
135/E1 **Coraki,** Austl.
129/k2 **Coral** (sea)
164/C2 **Corales del Rosario Nat'l Park,** Col.
203/H5 **Coral Gables,** Fl,US
179/H2 **Coral Harbour,** NW,Can
129/H3 **Coral Sea Is.** (terr.), Austl.
202/P7 **Coral Springs,** Fl,US
203/H4 **Coral Springs,** Fl,US
193/J3 **Coralville,** Ia,US
207/F2 **Coram,** NY,US
169/E5 **Corani,** Bol.
166/B1 **Corantijne** (Courantyne) (riv.), Sur.
172/C2 **Coranzulí,** Arg.
208/G6 **Coraopolis,** Pa,US
85/G5 **Corato,** It.
78/B4 **Coray,** Fr.
84/C2 **Corbara** (lake), It.
53/T11 **Corbeil-Essonnes,** Fr.
74/E2 **Corbeil-Essonnes,** Paris
173/F3 **Corbélia,** Braz.
141/T15 **Corbelin** (cape), Alg.
80/C2 **Corbenay,** Fr.
81/F5 **Corbet, Piz** (peak), Swi.
86/B2 **Corbetta,** It.
120/B1 **Corbett Nat'l Park,** India
68/B4 **Corbie,** Fr.
78/C2 **Corbière** (pt.), Chl,UK
74/E5 **Corbieres** (mts.), Fr.
200/E2 **Corbin,** Ky,US
206/D5 **Corbin City,** NJ,US
57/F2 **Corbridge,** Eng,UK
59/F2 **Corby,** Eng,UK
84/C3 **Corchiano,** It.
186/C2 **Corcoran,** Ca,US
195/N6 **Corcoran,** Mn,US
171/N7 **Corcovado** (mon.), Braz.
174/B4 **Corcovado** (gulf), Chile
174/B4 **Corcovado** (vol.), Chile
161/F4 **Corcovado Nat'l Park,** CR
191/J3 **Cord,** Ar,US
187/J3 **Cordata** (mesa), NM,US
208/C1 **Cordaville,** Ma,US
171/E4 **Cordeiro,** Braz.
200/F5 **Cordele,** Ga,US
189/F3 **Cordele,** Tx,US
205/K10 **Cordelia,** Ca,US
190/E3 **Cordell,** Ok,US
75/K4 **Cordenons,** It.
87/F1 **Cordignano,** It.
166/D4 **Cordilheiras** (mts.), Braz.
173/E2 **Cordillera** (dept.), Par.
164/B5 **Cordillera Central** (mts.), Col.
168/B2 **Cordillera Central** (mts.), Peru
125/C1 **Cordillera Central** (mts.), Phil.
164/C4 **Cordillera de los Picachos Nat'l Park,** Col.
133/J3 **Cordillo Downs,** Austl.
172/C4 **Córdoba,** Arg.
172/C3 **Córdoba** (mts.), Arg.
172/D3 **Córdoba** (prov.), Arg.
164/C2 **Córdoba** (dept.), Col.
159/F5 **Córdoba,** Mex.
76/C4 **Córdoba,** Sp.
172/C4 **Córdoba** (Pajas Blancas) (int'l arpt.), Arg.
168/C4 **Córdova,** Peru
177/J3 **Cordova,** Ak,US
177/J3 **Cordova** (peak), Ak,US
200/D4 **Cordova,** Al,US
206/C6 **Cordova,** Md,US
201/J3 **Core** (banks), NC,US
167/F3 **Coreaú,** Braz.
131/D4 **Corella** (lake), Austl.
76/E1 **Corella,** Sp.
167/G4 **Coremas,** Braz.
134/A3 **Corfield,** Austl.
89/H3 **Corfu** (isl.), Gre.
91/F3 **Corfu** (Kérkira) (isl.), Gre.
80/D3 **Corgémont,** Swi.
76/B1 **Corgo,** Sp.
84/C4 **Cori,** It.
76/B3 **Coria,** Sp.
76/B4 **Coria del Río,** Sp.
87/F5 **Coriano,** It.
170/D2 **Coribe,** Braz.
135/D2 **Coricudgy** (peak), Austl.
83/C3 **Corigliano Calabro,** It.
87/G5 **Corinaldo,** It.
131/E4 **Corinda,** Austl.
129/J3 **Coringa Islets** (isls.), Austl.
196/C3 **Corinna,** Me,US
191/G3 **Corinne,** Ok,US
52/F5 **Corinth,** Gre.
91/H3 **Corinth** (gulf), Gre.
200/C3 **Corinth,** Ms,US
199/K3 **Corinth,** NY,US
188/K6 **Corinth,** Tx,US
91/H4 **Corinth** (Kórinthos), Gre.
91/H4 **Corinth** (Kórinthos) (ruins), Gre.
170/D3 **Corinto,** Braz.
160/E3 **Corinto,** Nic.
168/D4 **Coripata,** Bol.
152/B2 **Corisco** (isl.), EqG.
152/B2 **Corisco** (bay), EqG., Gabon
76/A1 **Coristanco,** Sp.
170/A3 **Corixa Grande** (riv.), Braz.
60/B6 **Cork,** Ire.
60/B6 **Cork** (co.), Ire.
60/B6 **Cork** (har.), Ire.
60/B6 **Cork** (int'l arpt.), Ire.
203/H4 **Corkscrew** (swamp), Fl,US
90/C4 **Corleone,** It.
83/C2 **Corleto Perticara,** It.
93/H5 **Çorlu,** Turk.
79/F2 **Cormeilles,** Fr.
79/E2 **Cormelles,** Fr.
79/F6 **Cormery,** Fr.
87/G1 **Cormons,** It.
68/D5 **Cormontreuil,** Fr.
172/C2 **Cornaca,** Bol.
85/D4 **Cornacchia** (peak), It.
67/G6 **Cornberg,** Ger.
58/C1 **Corndon** (hill), Wal,UK
87/E1 **Cornedo Vicentino,** It.
201/F3 **Cornelia,** Ga,US
170/C4 **Cornélio Procópio,** Braz.
179/K2 **Cornelius Grinnel** (bay), NW,Can
204/B2 **Cornell,** Ca,US
198/B4 **Cornell,** Il,US
195/L5 **Cornell,** Mi,US
193/J1 **Cornell,** Wi,US
77/L7 **Cornella,** Sp.
135/C3 **Corner** (inlet), Austl.
197/J1 **Corner Brook,** Nf,Can
191/J3 **Cornerstone,** Ar,US
81/H6 **Cornetto** (peak), It.
87/E1 **Cornetto, Monte** (peak), It.
208/B3 **Cornfield** (pt.), Ct,US
187/H3 **Cornfields,** Az,US
54/D1 **Cornhill,** Sc,UK
84/A1 **Cornia** (riv.), It.
86/D4 **Corniglio,** It.
80/C2 **Cornimont,** Fr.
194/C3 **Corning,** Sk,Can
191/J2 **Corning,** Ar,US
184/B4 **Corning,** Ca,US
193/G3 **Corning,** Ia,US
191/F1 **Corning,** Ks,US
199/H3 **Corning,** NY,US
198/E5 **Corning,** Oh,US
134/B3 **Cornish** (cr.), Austl.
84/C2 **Corno** (peak), It.
87/D4 **Corno alle Scale** (peak), It.
86/D1 **Cornone di Blumone** (peak), It.
82/D3 **Cornour** (peak), It.
192/E2 **Corn Palace, The,** SD,US
175/L8 **Cornú** (peak), Arg.
195/J4 **Cornucopia,** Wi,US
87/F1 **Cornuda,** It.
190/B4 **Cornudas** (mts.), NM,US
188/B2 **Cornudas,** Tx,US
187/G3 **Cornville,** Az,US
179/S7 **Cornwall** (isl.), NW,Can
199/J2 **Cornwall,** On,Can
196/F2 **Cornwall,** PE,Can
55/J11 **Cornwall** (cape), Eng,UK
58/B6 **Cornwall** (co.), Eng,UK
208/A2 **Cornwall,** Ct,US
206/B3 **Cornwall,** Pa,US
179/S7 **Cornwallis** (isl.), NW,Can
203/H4 **Cornwell,** Fl,US
66/C2 **Cornwerd,** Neth.
133/H5 **Corny** (pt.), Austl.
164/D2 **Coro,** Ven.
140/J9 **Coroa** (mtn.), CpV.
167/E4 **Coroatá,** Braz.
172/B1 **Corocoro,** Bol.
60/A4 **Corofin,** Ire.
169/E5 **Coroico,** Bol.
170/D3 **Coromandel,** Braz.
118/D5 **Coromandel** (coast), India
136/C2 **Coromandel,** N.Z.
136/C2 **Coromandel** (pen.), N.Z.
125/C2 **Coron,** Phil.
125/C3 **Coron** (isl.), Phil.
204/C3 **Corona,** Ca,US
190/B3 **Corona,** NM,US
194/B3 **Coronach,** Sk,Can
204/G8 **Corona del Mar,** Ca,US
161/E4 **Coronado** (bay), CR
204/C5 **Coronado,** Ca,US
187/G5 **Coronado Nat'l Mon.,** Az,US
183/J1 **Coronation,** Ab,Can
178/E2 **Coronation** (gulf), NW,Can
157/E2 **Coronation Road,** SAfr.
174/E1 **Coronda,** Arg.
174/B3 **Coronel,** Chile
173/E3 **Coronel Bogado,** Par.
172/D2 **Coronel Cornejo,** Arg.
174/E3 **Coronel Dorrego,** Arg.
171/E3 **Coronel Fabriciano,** Braz.
174/D2 **Coronel Moldes,** Arg.
173/E3 **Coronel Oviedo,** Par.
174/E3 **Coronel Pringles,** Arg.
174/E3 **Coronel Suárez,** Arg.
175/F3 **Coronel Vidal,** Arg.
173/F3 **Coronel Vivida,** Braz.
168/B3 **Corongo,** Peru
166/B1 **Coronie** (dist.), Sur.
168/C4 **Coropuna** (peak), Peru
91/G2 **Çorovodë,** Alb.
160/D2 **Corozal,** Belz.
164/C2 **Corozal,** Col.
159/F4 **Corozal,** Mex.
165/E2 **Corozo Pando,** Ven.
54/A3 **Corpach,** Sc,UK
78/D5 **Corps-Nuds,** Fr.
173/F3 **Corpus,** Arg.
189/F4 **Corpus Christi,** Tx,US
189/F4 **Corpus Christi** (bay), Tx,US
189/F4 **Corpus Christi** (int'l arpt.), Tx,US
189/E3 **Corpus Christi** (lake), Tx,US
189/F4 **Corpus Christi Nav. Air Sta.,** Tx,US
172/C1 **Corque,** Bol.
174/B3 **Corral,** Chile
76/D3 **Corral de Almaguer,** Sp.
174/E2 **Corral de Bustos,** Arg.
77/Y16 **Corralejo,** Canl.,Sp.
164/C3 **Corrales,** Col.
190/A3 **Corrales,** NM,US
161/F1 **Corralillo,** Cuba
172/C4 **Corralitos** (peak), Arg.
135/B3 **Corrangamite** (lake), Austl.
80/C2 **Corre,** Fr.
174/E2 **Correa,** Arg.
161/F4 **Corredor,** CR
87/D3 **Correggio,** It.
170/D1 **Corrente,** Braz.
170/C3 **Corrente** (riv.), Braz.
170/E2 **Corrente** (riv.), Braz.
173/F1 **Correntes** (riv.), Braz.
155/G5 **Correntes, Cabo das** (cape), Moz.
60/A3 **Corrib, Lough** (lake), Ire.
85/D1 **Corridonia,** It.
54/A5 **Corrie,** Sc,UK
172/E3 **Corrientes,** Arg.
172/E3 **Corrientes** (prov.), Arg.
172/E3 **Corrientes** (riv.), Arg.
164/B3 **Corrientes** (cape), Col.
163/B2 **Corrientes** (pt.), Col.
161/E1 **Corrientes** (cape), Cuba
168/C1 **Corrientes** (riv.), Ecu., Peru
158/D4 **Corrientes, Cabo** (cape), Mex.
189/G2 **Corrigan,** Tx,US
132/C5 **Corrigin,** Austl.
58/C1 **Corris,** Wal,UK
165/G3 **Corriverton,** Guy.
199/G4 **Corry,** Pa,US
54/C2 **Corryhabbie** (mtn.), Sc,UK
135/C3 **Corryong,** Austl.
90/A1 **Corse** (cape), Fr.
90/A1 **Corse** (dept.), Fr.
75/H5 **Corse** (reg.), Fr.
54/B5 **Corse** (hill), Sc,UK
56/D1 **Corserine** (mtn.), Sc,UK
78/C3 **Corseul,** Fr.
56/C1 **Corsewall** (pt.), Sc,UK
58/D4 **Corsham,** Eng,UK
90/A1 **Corsica** (isl.), Fr.
192/E2 **Corsica,** SD,US
189/F1 **Corsicana,** Tx,US
86/C2 **Corsico,** It.
206/D5 **Corsons** (inlet), NJ,US
187/J3 **Cortada** (mesa), NM,US
80/C4 **Cortaillod,** Swi.
83/C5 **Cortale,** It.
187/G4 **Cortaro,** Az,US
90/A1 **Corte,** Fr.
76/B4 **Cortegana,** Sp.
86/C3 **Cortemaggiore,** It.
86/B3 **Cortemilia,** It.
125/D3 **Cortes,** Phil.
187/H2 **Cortez,** Co,US
75/K3 **Cortina d'Ampezzo,** It.
175/S12 **Cortines,** Arg.
198/B4 **Cortland,** Il,US
199/H3 **Cortland,** NY,US
208/G5 **Cortland,** Oh,US
84/B1 **Cortona,** It.
144/B4 **Corubal** (riv.), GBis.
76/A3 **Coruche,** Port.
97/G4 **Çoruh** (riv.), Turk.
104/C1 **Çorum,** Turk.
104/C1 **Çorum** (prov.), Turk.
170/A3 **Corumbá,** Braz.
170/C3 **Corumbá** (riv.), Braz.
171/F3 **Corumbaú** (pt.), Braz.
169/F4 **Corumbiara** (riv.), Braz.
205/H6 **Corunna,** On,Can
198/D3 **Corunna,** Mi,US
171/F1 **Coruripe,** Braz.
184/B1 **Corvallis,** Or,US
84/D3 **Corvaro,** It.
58/D2 **Corve** (riv.), Eng,UK
85/D3 **Corvo** (peak), It.
77/R12 **Corvo** (isl.), Azor.,Port.
57/E6 **Corwen,** Wal,UK
193/H3 **Corydon,** Ia,US
200/D1 **Corydon,** In,US
81/E5 **Corzoneso,** Swi.
172/D3 **Corzuela,** Arg.
158/D3 **Cosalá,** Mex.
159/G5 **Cosamaloapan,** Mex.
159/P8 **Cosamaloapan de Carpio,** Mex.
172/B1 **Cosapa,** Bol.
159/N7 **Cosautlán de Carvajal,** Mex.
169/D5 **Coscapa,** Bol.
84/C2 **Coscerno** (peak), It.
83/C3 **Coscile** (riv.), It.
159/M7 **Coscomatepec de Bravo,** Mex.
83/C4 **Cosenza,** It.
83/C4 **Cosenza** (prov.), It.
198/F4 **Coshocton,** Oh,US
208/E7 **Coshocton** (co.), Oh,US
160/E3 **Cosigüina** (pt.), Nic.
158/E4 **Cosío,** Mex.
76/D2 **Coslada,** Sp.
186/D4 **Cosmit Ind. Res.,** Ca,US
132/D3 **Cosmo Newberry Abor. Rsv.,** Austl.
171/J7 **Cosmópolis,** Braz.
74/E3 **Cosne-Cours-sur-Loire,** Fr.
74/E3 **Cosne d'Allier,** Fr.
159/N8 **Cosolapa,** Mex.
159/G5 **Cosoleacaque,** Mex.
76/B1 **Cospeito,** Sp.
172/C4 **Cosquín,** Arg.
153/E4 **Cossa,** Ang.
86/B1 **Cossato,** It.
79/E5 **Cossé-le-Vivien,** Fr.
79/G5 **Cosson** (riv.), Fr.
80/C4 **Cossonay,** Swi.
175/G2 **Costa Azul,** Uru.
87/E1 **Costabissara,** It.
77/G2 **Costa Brava** (int'l arpt.), Sp.
77/P10 **Costa da Caparica,** Port.
77/C4 **Costa del Sol** (coast), Sp.
87/E2 **Costa di Rovigo,** It.
77/P10 **Costa do Sol** (coast), Port.
86/C1 **Costa Masnaga,** It.
204/C3 **Costa Mesa,** Ca,US
161/F4 **Costa Rica**
168/D3 **Costa Rica,** Bol.
158/D3 **Costa Rica,** Mex.
90/A2 **Costa Smeralda** (int'l arpt.), It.
86/D1 **Costa Volpino,** It.
199/G4 **Costello,** Pa,US
192/C1 **Costello** (peak), SD,US
59/H1 **Costessey,** Eng,UK
93/G3 **Costeşti,** Rom.
86/B3 **Costigliole d'Asti,** It.
82/D3 **Costiglione Saluzzo,** It.
190/B2 **Costilla,** NM,US
205/M10 **Cosumnes** (riv.), Ca,US
72/C4 **Coswig,** Ger.
72/D5 **Coswig,** Ger.
168/C4 **Cotabambas,** Peru
125/D4 **Cotabato City,** Phil.
164/B4 **Cotacachi** (peak), Ecu.
169/E5 **Cotacajes** (riv.), Bol.
172/C2 **Cotagaita,** Bol.
168/C4 **Cotahuasi,** Peru
161/H4 **Cotatumbo** (riv.), Col., Ven.
192/E1 **Coteau des Prairies** (plat.), SD,US
199/J2 **Coteau-du-Lac,** Qu,Can
194/C3 **Coteau du Missouri** (plain), ND, SD,US
197/M7 **Coteau-Landing,** Qu,Can
202/C3 **Cote Blanche** (bay), La,US
82/D5 **Côte d'Azur** (reg.), Fr.
82/D5 **Côte d'Azur** (Nice) (int'l arpt.), Fr.
144/D5 **Côte d'Ivoire** (Ivory Coast)
80/A3 **Côte-d'Or** (dept.), Fr.
74/F3 **Côte d'Or** (uplands), Fr.
141/N13 **Côte du Rif** (Al Hoceima) (int'l arpt.), Mor.
142/E2 **Côte du Rif** (Al Hoceima) (int'l arpt.), Mor.
170/D2 **Cotegipe,** Braz.
78/D1 **Cotentin** (pen.), Fr.
85/D4 **Cotento** (peak), It.
199/K2 **Côte-Saint-Luc,** Qu,Can
78/B4 **Côtes-d'Armor** (dept.), Fr.
58/B3 **Cothi** (riv.), Wal,UK
171/K8 **Cotia,** Braz.
87/E4 **Cotignola,** It.
145/F5 **Cotonou,** Ben.
145/F5 **Cotonou** (int'l arpt.), Ben.
164/B5 **Cotopaxi** (prov.), Ecu.
164/B5 **Cotopaxi** (vol.), Ecu.
187/K1 **Cotopaxi,** Co,US
164/B5 **Cotopaxi Nat'l Park,** Ecu.
83/C4 **Cotronei,** It.
58/D4 **Cotswolds** (hills), Eng,UK
195/H5 **Cottage Grove,** Mn,U
184/B2 **Cottage Grove,** Or,U
201/G4 **Cottageville,** SC,US
205/G7 **Cottam,** On,Can
65/H3 **Cottbus,** Ger.
197/L1 **Cottel** (isl.), Nf,Can
59/G2 **Cottenham,** Eng,UK
191/H2 **Cotter,** Ar,US
82/C3 **Cottian Alps** (range), Fr., It.
166/C2 **Cottica,** Sur.
186/C2 **Cotto Center-Poplar,** Ca,US
195/H4 **Cotton,** Mn,US
189/N9 **Cotton** (lake), Tx,US
188/L7 **Cotton Bowl** (State Fair Park), Tx,US
203/F2 **Cottondale,** Fl,US
188/K6 **Cottondale,** Tx,US
191/J3 **Cotton Plant,** Ar,US
202/B2 **Cottonport,** La,US
200/E4 **Cottonton,** Al,US
189/H1 **Cotton Valley,** La,US
203/F2 **Cottonwood,** Al,US
187/F3 **Cottonwood,** Az,US
187/G3 **Cottonwood** (wash), Az,US
184/E1 **Cottonwood,** Id,US
191/F1 **Cottonwood** (riv.), Ks,US
193/G1 **Cottonwood,** Mn,US
193/G1 **Cottonwood** (riv.), Mn,US
189/F2 **Cottonwood,** Tx,US
188/B2 **Cottonwood** (cr.), Tx,US
185/J2 **Cottonwood** (cr.), Wy,US
191/F1 **Cottonwood Falls,** Ks,US
132/K6 **Cottsloe,** Austl.
162/D3 **Cotuí,** DRep.
188/E3 **Cotulla,** Tx,US
79/E5 **Couasnon** (riv.), Fr.
53/U10 **Coubert,** Fr.
74/C4 **Coubre, Pointe de la** (pt.), Fr.
191/J2 **Couch,** Mo,US
80/A3 **Couchey,** Fr.
189/H1 **Couchwood,** La,US
80/C5 **Cou, Col de** (pass), F
68/C5 **Coucy-le-Château-Auffrique,** Fr.
68/B1 **Coudekerque-Branche,** Fr.
199/G4 **Coudersport,** Pa,US
82/B5 **Coudoux,** Fr.
196/B2 **Coudres, Ile aux** (isl.), Qu,Can
78/D6 **Couëron,** Fr.
78/D4 **Couesnon** (riv.), Fr.
182/C4 **Cougar,** Wa,US
74/E5 **Couguille, Pic de** (peak), Fr.
79/F4 **Coulaines,** Fr.
182/E4 **Coulee City,** Wa,US
182/E4 **Coulee Dam,** Wa,US
182/E3 **Coulee Dam Nat'l Re Area,** Wa,US
137/M **Coulman** (isl.), Ant.
68/A2 **Coulogne,** Fr.
130/A4 **Coulomb** (pt.), Austl.
130/A4 **Coulomb Point Nat. Rsv.,** Austl.
68/C6 **Coulommiers,** Fr.
82/C5 **Coulomp** (riv.), Fr.
82/B5 **Coulon** (riv.), Fr.
199/H1 **Coulonge** (riv.), Qu,C
74/D4 **Coulounieix-Chamiers,** Fr.
53/N8 **Coulsdon,** Eng,UK
186/B2 **Coulterville,** Ca,US
200/C1 **Coulterville,** Il,US
60/C5 **Coumfea** (mtn.), Ire.
166/C1 **Counamama,** FrG.
200/C3 **Counce,** Tn,US
177/F3 **Council,** Ak,US
184/E1 **Council,** Id,US
193/G3 **Council Bluffs,** Ia,US
191/F1 **Council Grove,** Ks,US
182/F4 **Country Homes,** Wa,US
54/C3 **Coupar Angus,** Sc,UK
182/C3 **Coupeville,** Wa,US
53/U10 **Coupvray,** Fr.
165/G3 **Courantyne** (Corantijne) (riv.), Guy., Sur.
53/S10 **Courbevoie,** Fr.
68/D3 **Courcelles,** Belg.
69/F5 **Courcelles-Chaussy,** Fr.
68/A5 **Courcelles-sur-Seine,** Fr.
82/C2 **Courchevel** (arpt.), Fr
79/G5 **Cour-Cheverny,** Fr.
53/T11 **Courcouronnes,** Fr.
80/D3 **Courgenay,** Swi.
80/C6 **Courmayeur,** It.
74/E4 **Cournon-d'Auvergne,** Fr.
80/D3 **Courrendlin,** Swi.
80/D3 **Courroux,** Swi.
74/E5 **Coursan,** Fr.
79/E2 **Courseulles-sur-Mer,** Fr.
80/D3 **Courtelary,** Swi.
182/B3 **Courtenay,** BC,Can
194/E4 **Courtenay,** ND,US
80/D4 **Courtepin,** Swi.
82/A4 **Courthézon,** Fr.
197/T8 **Courtice,** On,Can
68/D6 **Courtisols,** Fr.
205/L10 **Courtland,** Ca,US
191/F1 **Courtland,** Ks,US
201/J2 **Courtland,** Va,US
60/B6 **Courtmacsherry,** Ire.
60/B6 **Courtmacsherry** (bay), Ire.
189/F2 **Courtney,** Tx,US
60/D4 **Courtown,** Ire.
68/C2 **Courtrai** (Kortrijk), Belg.
205/H6 **Courtright,** On,Can
53/T10 **Courtry,** Fr.
79/G4 **Courville-sur-Eure,** Fr
80/B4 **Cousance-du-Jura,** Fr
60/A6 **Cousane Gap** (pass), Ire.
202/B1 **Coushatta,** La,US
68/D3 **Cousolre,** Fr.
78/D2 **Coutances,** Fr.
183/L2 **Couteau** (hills), Sk,US
79/E3 **Couterne,** Fr.
166/D5 **Couto de Magalhaes,** Braz.
74/C4 **Coutras,** Fr.
183/J3 **Coutts,** Ab,Can
79/G3 **Couture-Boussey,** Fr.

165/F2 **Couva,** Trin.
80/C4 **Couvet,** Swi.
68/D3 **Couvin,** Belg.
74/D4 **Couzeix,** Fr.
77/P10 **Cova da Piedade,** Port.
76/C1 **Covadonga Nat'l Park,** Sp.
93/H3 **Covasna,** Rom.
92/G3 **Covasna** (co.), Rom.
145/F5 **Cové,** Ben.
54/B5 **Cove,** Sc,UK
191/G3 **Cove,** Ar,US
189/N9 **Cove,** Tx,US
201/G2 **Cove** (mtn.), WV,US
54/D2 **Cove Bay,** Sc,UK
201/F1 **Cove Gap,** WV,US
184/B4 **Covelo,** Ca,US
169/E4 **Covendo,** Bol.
207/L8 **Cove Neck,** NY,US
59/E2 **Coventry,** Eng,UK
59/E1 **Coventry** (can.), Eng,UK
208/B2 **Coventry,** Ct,US
59/E2 **Coventry** (Baginton) (arpt.), Eng,UK
105/M7 **Covered Market,** Turk.
201/H2 **Covesville,** Va,US
76/B2 **Covilhã,** Port.
204/C2 **Covina,** Ca,US
200/F4 **Covington,** Ga,US
198/C4 **Covington,** In,US
200/E1 **Covington,** Ky,US
202/C2 **Covington,** La,US
198/B1 **Covington,** Mi,US
198/D4 **Covington,** Oh,US
191/F2 **Covington,** Ok,US
189/F1 **Covington,** Tx,US
201/H2 **Covington,** Va,US
86/C2 **Covo,** It.
191/E1 **Cow** (cr.), Ks,US
184/B2 **Cow** (cr.), Or,US
54/A4 **Cowal** (dist.), Sc,UK
131/F2 **Cowal Creek Abor. Community,** Austl.
134/H8 **Cowan,** Austl.
132/D4 **Cowan** (lake), Austl.
200/D3 **Cowan,** Tn,US
133/J5 **Cowangie,** Austl.
196/A3 **Cowansville,** Qu,Can
132/B5 **Cowaramup,** Austl.
133/H4 **Coward Springs,** Austl.
133/H3 **Cowarie,** Austl.
192/C3 **Cowboy** (hill), Ne,US
58/C4 **Cowbridge,** Wal,UK
192/B2 **Cow Creek,** Wy,US
198/B5 **Cowden,** Il,US
54/C4 **Cowdenbeath,** Sc,UK
185/K3 **Cowdrey,** Co,US
200/F3 **Cowee** (mts.), NC,US
133/H5 **Cowell,** Austl.
59/E5 **Cowes,** Eng,UK
194/C2 **Cowessess Ind. Res.,** Sk,Can
201/L8 **Coweta** (co.), Ga,US
57/F2 **Cow Green** (res.), Eng,UK
189/E2 **Cowhouse** (cr.), Tx,US
182/B3 **Cowichan** (lake), BC,Can
54/C4 **Cowie,** Sc,UK
197/U10 **Cowlesville,** NY,US
183/G3 **Cowley,** Ab,Can
185/J1 **Cowley,** Wy,US
191/G3 **Cowlington,** Ok,US
135/C3 **Cowora,** Austl.
201/G3 **Cowpens Nat'l Bfld.,** SC,US
135/D2 **Cowra,** Austl.
159/F5 **Coxcotlán,** Mex.
57/G2 **Coxhoe,** Eng,UK
170/B3 **Coxim,** Braz.
170/B3 **Coxim** (riv.), Braz.
199/K3 **Coxsackie,** NY,US
116/A4 **Cox's Bāzār,** Bang.
197/H1 **Cox's Cove,** Nf,Can
198/F5 **Coxs Mills,** WV,US
200/D5 **Coy,** Al,US
174/Q10 **Coya,** Chile
144/B4 **Coyah,** Gui.
175/K7 **Coy Aike,** Arg.
188/B3 **Coyame,** Mex.
188/C2 **Coyanosa Draw** (cr.), Tx,US
172/B2 **Coya Sur,** Chile
53/T9 **Coye-la-Forêt,** Fr.
159/Q10 **Coyoacán,** Mex.
205/L12 **Coyote** (cr.), Ca,US
159/K7 **Coyotepec,** Mex.
159/E5 **Coyuca,** Mex.
160/A2 **Coyuca de Benítez,** Mex.
159/M6 **Coyutla,** Mex.
192/E3 **Cozad,** Ne,US
114/E5 **Cozhê,** China
160/E1 **Cozumel,** Mex.
159/J4 **Cozumel** (int'l arpt.), Mex.
160/E1 **Cozumel** (isl.), Mex.
193/K5 **Crab Orchard Nat'l Wild. Ref.,** Il,US
135/C4 **Cradle** (peak), Austl.
135/C4 **Cradle Mountain-Lake St. Clair Nat'l Park,** Austl.
156/D4 **Cradock,** SAfr.
208/G7 **Crafton,** Pa,US
196/A3 **Craftsbury,** Vt,US
177/K3 **Crag** (mtn.), Yk,Can
57/F3 **Crag** (hill), Eng,UK
177/M4 **Craig,** Ak,US
190/A1 **Craig,** Co,US
192/B3 **Craig** (mt.), Co,US
193/G3 **Craig,** Mo,US
183/J4 **Craig,** Mt,US
201/G1 **Craig** (cr.), Va,US
56/C2 **Craigavad,** NI,UK
56/B3 **Craigavon,** NI,UK
56/B3 **Craigavon** (dist.), NI,UK
208/G5 **Craig Beach,** Oh,US
54/C2 **Craigellachie,** Sc,UK
135/F5 **Craigieburn,** Austl.
201/H1 **Craigsville,** Va,US
201/G1 **Craigsville,** WV,US
194/B2 **Craik,** Sk,Can
54/D4 **Crail,** Sc,UK
70/D4 **Crailsheim,** Ger.
93/F3 **Craiova,** Rom.
81/E5 **Cramalina, Pizzo** (peak), Swi.
57/G1 **Cramlington,** Eng,UK
56/A1 **Crana** (riv.), Ire.
208/H5 **Cranberry,** Pa,US
58/D5 **Cranborne Chase** (for.), Eng,UK
135/C3 **Cranbourne,** Austl.
132/C5 **Cranbrook,** Austl.
182/G3 **Cranbrook,** BC,Can
59/G4 **Cranbrook,** Eng,UK
206/D3 **Cranbury,** NJ,US
194/D2 **Crandall,** Mb,Can
188/L7 **Crandall,** Tx,US
193/K1 **Crandon,** Wi,US
193/J3 **Crane** (lake), Il,US
191/H2 **Crane,** Mo,US
183/M4 **Crane,** Mt,US
188/C2 **Crane,** Tx,US
200/D3 **Crane Hill,** Al,US
195/H3 **Crane Lake,** Mn,US
200/D1 **Crane Nav. Weap. Support Ctr.,** In,US
207/E2 **Crane Neck** (pt.), NY,US
184/C2 **Crane Prairie** (res.), Or,US
194/E2 **Crane River,** Mb,Can
189/F2 **Cranfills Gap,** Tx,US
207/D2 **Cranford,** NJ,US
80/C6 **Cran-Gevrier,** Fr.
59/F4 **Cranleigh,** Eng,UK
208/C2 **Cranston,** RI,US
79/E5 **Craon,** Fr.
68/C5 **Craonne,** Fr.
82/A1 **Craponne,** Fr.
82/A5 **Craponne** (can.), Fr.
194/E3 **Crary,** ND,US
93/F2 **Crasna** (riv.), Rom.
55/L9 **Craster,** Eng,UK
184/B2 **Crater** (lake), Or,US
184/B2 **Crater** (peak), Or,US
184/B2 **Crater Lake Nat'l Park,** Or,US
185/G2 **Craters of the Moon Nat'l Mon.,** Id,US
167/F4 **Crateús,** Braz.
83/C3 **Crati** (riv.), It.
60/B4 **Cratloe,** Ire.
167/G4 **Crato,** Braz.
76/B3 **Crato,** Port.
189/H2 **Cravens,** La,US
170/D4 **Cravinhos,** Braz.
54/C6 **Crawford,** Sc,UK
185/K4 **Crawford,** Co,US
201/F4 **Crawford,** Ga,US
200/C4 **Crawford,** Ms,US
190/E3 **Crawford,** Ok,US
208/G4 **Crawford** (co.), Pa,US
189/F2 **Crawford,** Tx,US
182/F3 **Crawford Bay,** BC,Can
198/C4 **Crawfordsville,** In,US
203/F2 **Crawfordville,** Fl,US
201/F4 **Crawfordville,** Ga,US
72/A6 **Crawinkel,** Ger.
59/F4 **Crawley,** Eng,UK
53/P7 **Cray** (riv.), Eng,UK
53/P7 **Crayford,** Eng,UK
183/J4 **Crazy** (mts.), Mt,US
192/C2 **Crazy Horse,** SD,US
185/K1 **Crazy Woman** (cr.), Wy,US
206/A4 **Creagerstown,** Md,US
54/B3 **Creag Meagaidh** (mtn.), Sc,UK
193/K5 **Creal Springs,** Il,US
193/J1 **Cream,** Wi,US
206/B1 **Creasy** (Mifflinville), Pa,US
87/E2 **Creazzo,** It.
80/A5 **Crêches-sur-Saône,** Fr.
68/A3 **Crécy-en-Ponthieu,** Fr.
68/C4 **Crécy-sur-Serre,** Fr.
58/D2 **Credenhill,** Eng,UK
197/R8 **Credit** (riv.), On,Can
58/C5 **Crediton,** Eng,UK
178/F3 **Cree** (lake), Sk,Can
178/F3 **Cree** (riv.), Sk,Can
56/D2 **Cree** (riv.), Sc,UK
190/A2 **Creede,** Co,US
183/K3 **Creedman Coulee Nat'l Wild. Ref.,** Mt,US
189/F2 **Creedmoor,** Tx,US
158/D3 **Creel,** Mex.
194/C3 **Creelman,** Sk,Can
198/F2 **Creemore,** On,Can
56/D2 **Creetown,** Sc,UK
70/D4 **Creglingen,** Ger.
53/U10 **Crégy-lès-Meaux,** Fr.
69/F5 **Créhange,** Fr.
78/C3 **Créhen,** Fr.
178/F3 **Creighton,** Sk,Can
192/F2 **Creighton,** Ne,US
192/C1 **Creighton,** SD,US
197/G3 **Creignish,** NS,Can
68/B5 **Creil,** Fr.
86/C2 **Crema,** It.
82/B1 **Crémieu,** Fr.
67/H4 **Cremlingen,** Ger.
183/G2 **Cremona,** Ab,Can
86/D2 **Cremona,** It.
86/C2 **Cremona** (prov.), It.
200/B3 **Crenshaw,** Ms,US
202/D2 **Creola,** Al,US
189/H3 **Creole,** La,US
92/E3 **Crepaja,** Yugo.
166/B4 **Crepori** (riv.), Braz.
68/C4 **Crépy-en-Laonnois,** Fr.
68/B5 **Crépy-en-Valois,** Fr.
54/A3 **Creran, Loch** (inlet), Sc,UK
92/B3 **Cres,** Cro.
92/B3 **Cres** (isl.), Cro.
199/G5 **Cresaptown-Bel Air,** Md,US
192/E1 **Cresbard,** SD,US
203/H3 **Crescent** (lake), Fl,US
191/F3 **Crescent,** Ok,US
184/C2 **Crescent,** Or,US
184/A3 **Crescent City,** Ca,US
203/H3 **Crescent City,** Fl,US
117/F5 **Crescent Group** (isls.), China
86/B2 **Crescentino,** It.
184/C2 **Crescent Lake,** Or,US
192/C3 **Crescent Lake Nat'l Wild. Ref.,** Ne,US
193/H2 **Cresco,** Ia,US
206/C1 **Cresco,** Pa,US
87/E1 **Crespano del Grappa,** It.
87/E3 **Crespellano,** It.
68/C3 **Crespin,** Fr.
174/E2 **Crespo,** Arg.
207/K8 **Cresskill,** NJ,US
199/G4 **Cresson,** Pa,US
189/F1 **Cresson,** Tx,US
206/B2 **Cressona,** Pa,US
135/C4 **Cressy,** Austl.
82/B3 **Crest,** Fr.
190/A1 **Crested Butte,** Co,US
205/P16 **Crest Hill,** Il,US
204/C2 **Crestline,** Ca,US
198/E4 **Crestline,** Oh,US
182/F3 **Creston,** BC,Can
197/K2 **Creston,** Nf,Can
186/B3 **Creston,** Ca,US
193/G3 **Creston,** Ia,US
208/F6 **Creston,** Oh,US
187/K2 **Crestone,** Co,US
192/B5 **Crestone** (peak), Co,US
202/E2 **Crestview,** Fl,US
199/J5 **Crestwood Village,** NJ,US
57/G5 **Creswell,** Eng,UK
184/B2 **Creswell,** Or,US
131/D4 **Creswell Downs,** Austl.
135/B3 **Creswick,** Austl.
80/B5 **Crêt de la Neige** (mtn.), Fr.
80/B5 **Crêt du Nu** (mtn.), Fr.
82/C1 **Crêt du Rey** (mtn.), Fr.
91/J5 **Crete** (isl.), Gre.
91/J5 **Crete** (sea), Gre.
198/C4 **Crete,** Il,US
193/F3 **Crete,** Ne,US
53/T10 **Créteil,** Fr.
131/G1 **Cretin** (cape), PNG
54/B5 **Creuch** (hill), Sc,UK
77/G1 **Creus** (cape), Sp.
74/D3 **Creuse** (riv.), Fr.
71/E3 **Creussen,** Ger.
71/E3 **Creussen** (riv.), Ger.
69/F5 **Creutzwald-la-Croix,** Fr.
67/H6 **Creuzburg,** Ger.
86/B1 **Crevacuore,** It.
87/E3 **Crevalcore,** It.
68/B4 **Crèvecœur-le-Grand,** Fr.
77/E3 **Crevillente,** Sp.
81/E5 **Crevoladossola,** It.
57/F5 **Crewe,** Eng,UK
201/H2 **Crewe,** Va,US
58/D5 **Crewkerne,** Eng,UK
202/K7 **Crews** (lake), Fl,US
54/B4 **Crianlarich,** Sc,UK
135/C3 **Crib Point,** Austl.
56/D6 **Criccieth,** Wal,UK
83/C5 **Crichi,** It.
183/L3 **Crichton,** Sk,Can
173/G4 **Criciúma,** Braz.
201/G2 **Cricket,** NC,US
58/C3 **Crickhowell,** Wal,UK
59/E3 **Cricklade,** Eng,UK
54/C4 **Crieff,** Sc,UK
68/A3 **Criel-sur-Mer,** Fr.
56/E2 **Criffell** (hill), Eng,UK
92/B3 **Crikvenica,** Cro.
99/H5 **Crimean** (mts.), Ukr.
99/G5 **Crimean** (pen.), Ukr.
99/G5 **Crimean Obl.,** Ukr.
72/C6 **Crimmitschau,** Ger.
54/E1 **Crimond,** Sc,UK
192/B4 **Cripple Creek,** Co,US
79/F1 **Criquetot-l'Esneval,** Fr.
201/K2 **Crisfield,** Md,US
198/D1 **Crisp** (pt.), Mi,US
188/L7 **Crisp,** Tx,US
85/F5 **Crispiniano** (peak), It.
80/C4 **Crissier,** Swi.
173/F3 **Crissiumal,** Braz.
82/D3 **Crissolo,** It.
83/C3 **Crista d'Acri** (peak), It.
152/B3 **Cristal** (mts.), Gabon
170/C1 **Cristalândia,** Braz.
170/D3 **Cristalina,** Braz.
170/C2 **Cristalinho** (riv.), Braz.
171/L7 **Cristina,** Braz.
170/D1 **Cristino Castro,** Braz.
168/J7 **Cristóbal** (pt.), Ecu.
164/C2 **Cristóbal Colón** (peak), Col.
86/B4 **Cristoforo Colombo** (int'l arpt.), It.
92/F2 **Criștul Alb** (riv.), Rom.
93/G2 **Cristuru Secuiesc,** Rom.
89/J1 **Crișul Alb** (riv.), Rom.
92/E2 **Crișul Negru** (riv.), Rom.
98/B4 **Crișul Repede** (riv.), Rom.
193/K1 **Crivitz,** Wi,US
170/C2 **Crixás,** Braz.
170/C2 **Crixás-Açu** (riv.), Braz.
91/G2 **Crna Reka** (riv.), Macd.
92/B3 **Črnomelj,** Slov.
60/A2 **Croaghmoyle** (mtn.), Ire.
135/D3 **Croajingolong Nat'l Park,** Austl.
92/B3 **Croatia**
83/C4 **Crocchio** (riv.), It.
81/H5 **Croce, Monte** (peak), It.
81/H4 **Croce, Pico di** (peak), It.
196/A1 **Croche** (riv.), Qu,Can
80/C6 **Croche, Aiguille** (peak), Fr.
168/J7 **Crocker** (peak), Ecu.
126/E3 **Crocker** (mts.), Malay.
125/A4 **Crocker** (range), Malay.
193/H5 **Crocker,** Mo,US
56/E1 **Crocketford,** Sc,UK
205/K10 **Crockett,** Ca,US
189/G2 **Crockett,** Tx,US
200/C3 **Crockett Mills,** Tn,US
135/D2 **Crocodile** (pt.), Austl.
81/E5 **Crodo,** It.
200/D2 **Crofton,** Ky,US
206/B5 **Crofton,** Md,US
58/B3 **Crofty,** Wal,UK
60/D4 **Croghan** (mtn.), Ire.
60/A6 **Crohane** (mtn.), Ire.
82/B6 **Croisette** (cape), Fr.
78/C6 **Croisic** (har.), Fr.
78/C6 **Croisic, Pointe du** (pt.), Fr.
68/B3 **Croisilles,** Fr.
53/T10 **Croissy-Beaubourg,** Fr.
195/J3 **Croix** (lake), Mn,US
195/J3 **Croix** (lake), On,Can, Mn,US
80/B5 **Croix de la Serra, Col de la** (pass), Fr.
82/B3 **Croix Haute, Col de la** (pass), Fr.
82/D2 **Croix Rousse** (mtn.), Fr.
130/D2 **Croker** (isl.), Austl.
134/A1 **Croll Creek-Rokeby Nat'l Park,** Austl.
131/F3 **Croll-Rokeby Nat'l Park,** Austl.
54/B1 **Cromarty,** Sc,UK
54/B1 **Cromarty** (firth), Sc,UK
133/F3 **Crombie** (peak), Austl.
54/C2 **Cromdale,** Sc,UK
54/C2 **Cromdale** (hills), Sc,UK
194/D3 **Cromer,** Mb,Can
59/H1 **Cromer,** Eng,UK
64/A2 **Cromer,** Eng,UK
136/B4 **Cromwell,** N.Z.
200/C4 **Cromwell,** Al,US
208/B2 **Cromwell,** Ct,US
200/D2 **Cromwell,** Ky,US
191/F3 **Cromwell,** Ok,US
123/E3 **Crong A Na** (riv.), Viet.
134/H9 **Cronulla,** Austl.
57/G2 **Crook,** Eng,UK
162/C2 **Crooked** (isl.), Bahm.
203/F3 **Crooked** (isl.), Fl,US
202/M8 **Crooked** (lake), Fl,US
203/H4 **Crooked** (lake), Fl,US
190/D2 **Crooked** (cr.), Ks, Ok,US
184/C1 **Crooked** (riv.), Or,US
177/G3 **Crooked Creek,** Ak,US
161/H1 **Crooked Island** (passg.), Bahm.
162/C2 **Crooked Island Passage** (chan.), Bahm.
184/C1 **Crooked River Nat'l Grsld.,** Or,US
60/A7 **Crookhaven,** Ire.
193/F2 **Crooks,** SD,US
194/F4 **Crookston,** Mn,US
192/C1 **Crooks Tower** (peak), SD,US
60/B6 **Crookstown,** Ire.
198/E5 **Crooksville,** Oh,US
135/D2 **Crookwell,** Austl.
60/B4 **Croom,** Ire.
57/E5 **Crosby,** Eng,UK
195/H4 **Crosby,** Mn,US
202/C2 **Crosby,** Ms,US
194/C3 **Crosby,** ND,US
189/G3 **Crosby,** Tx,US
185/J2 **Crosby** (mt.), Wy,US
190/D4 **Crosbyton,** Tx,US
53/T10 **Crosne,** Fr.
145/H5 **Cross** (riv.), Camr., Nga.
154/B4 **Cross** (cape), Namb.
189/F2 **Cross,** Tx,US
201/G3 **Cross Anchor,** SC,US
203/G3 **Cross City,** Fl,US
191/J4 **Crossett,** Ar,US
57/F2 **Cross Fell** (mtn.), Eng,UK
183/G2 **Crossfield,** Ab,Can
54/C4 **Crossford,** Sc,UK
56/C3 **Crossgar,** NI,UK
58/C2 **Crossgates,** Wal,UK
60/B6 **Crosshaven,** Ire.
54/B6 **Crosshill,** Sc,UK
201/G3 **Cross Hill,** SC,US
54/B5 **Crosshouse,** Sc,UK
58/C3 **Crosskeys,** Wal,UK
195/G4 **Crosslake,** Mn,US
56/B3 **Crossmaglen,** NI,UK
56/E2 **Crossmichael,** Sc,UK
60/A1 **Crossmolina,** Ire.
188/E1 **Cross Plains,** Tx,US
193/K2 **Cross Plains,** Wi,US
145/H5 **Cross River** (state), Nga.
207/E1 **Cross River** (res.), NY,US
55/G9 **Crossroads,** Ire.
191/H4 **Cross Roads,** Ar,US
186/E3 **Cross Roads,** Ca,US
190/C4 **Crossroads,** NM,US
206/B4 **Cross Roads,** Pa,US
189/G1 **Cross Roads,** Tx,US
200/E3 **Crossville,** Al,US
200/C1 **Crossville,** Il,US
200/E3 **Crossville,** Tn,US
206/D3 **Crosswicks** (cr.), NJ,US
86/D3 **Crostolo** (riv.), It.
57/F4 **Croston,** Eng,UK
198/E3 **Croswell,** Mi,US
198/D5 **Crothersville,** In,US
188/C3 **Croton** (peak), Tx,US
83/D4 **Crotone,** It.
207/E1 **Croton-on-Hudson** (Croton-Harmon), NY,US
71/F1 **Crottendorf,** Ger.
59/G3 **Crouch** (riv.), Eng,UK
68/C5 **Crouy,** Fr.
68/C5 **Crouy-sur-Ourq,** Fr.
192/B3 **Crow** (cr.), Co,US
195/N6 **Crow** (riv.), Mn,US
192/E2 **Crow** (cr.), SD,US
192/C1 **Crow** (peak), SD,US
183/L5 **Crow Agency,** Mt,US
59/G4 **Crowborough,** Eng,UK
192/E1 **Crow Creek Ind. Res.,** SD,US
191/G3 **Crowder,** Ok,US
135/E1 **Crowdy Bay Nat'l Park,** Austl.
199/H2 **Crowe** (riv.), On,Can
190/E4 **Crowell,** Tx,US
185/J2 **Crowheart,** Wy,US
185/K1 **Crow Ind. Res.,** Mt,US
59/F1 **Crowland,** Eng,UK
57/H4 **Crowle,** Eng,UK
186/C2 **Crowley** (lake), Ca,US
202/B2 **Crowley,** La,US
188/K7 **Crowley,** Tx,US
200/B3 **Crowley's** (ridge), Ar,US
195/G5 **Crow, North Fork** (riv.), Mn,US
165/F2 **Crown Point** (int'l arpt.), Trin.
198/C4 **Crown Point,** In,US
187/H3 **Crownpoint,** NM,US
179/H1 **Crown Prince Frederik** (isl.), NW,Can
192/C1 **Crows Nest** (peak), SD,US
134/D4 **Crows Nest Falls Nat'l Park,** Austl.
195/G5 **Crow, South Fork** (riv.), Mn,US
59/F4 **Crowthorne,** Eng,UK
202/C1 **Crowville,** La,US
195/G4 **Crow Wing** (riv.), Mn,US
53/M7 **Croxley Green,** Eng,UK
134/A2 **Croydon,** Austl.
135/G5 **Croydon,** Austl.
53/N7 **Croydon,** Eng,UK
53/N7 **Croydon** (bor.), Eng,UK
206/D3 **Croydon,** Pa,US
51/M8 **Crozet** (isls.), FrAnt.
137/M **Crozier** (cape), Ant.
78/A4 **Crozon,** Fr.
54/A4 **Cruach Mhór** (mtn.), Sc,UK
54/A5 **Cruach nan Capull** (mtn.), Sc,UK
82/A3 **Cruas,** Fr.
168/D4 **Crucero,** Peru
161/G1 **Crucero Contramaestre,** Cuba
54/E2 **Cruden Bay,** Sc,UK
200/B4 **Cruger,** Ms,US
54/D3 **Cruick Water** (riv.), Sc,UK
159/F3 **Cruillas,** Mex.
200/C3 **Crum** (mtn.), Ms,US
56/B2 **Crumlin,** NI,UK
57/E2 **Crummock Water** (lake), Eng,UK
184/D2 **Crump** (lake), Or,US
200/C3 **Crump,** Tn,US
206/C5 **Crumpton,** Md,US
80/C5 **Cruseilles,** Fr.
60/B4 **Crusheen,** Ire.
69/E5 **Crusnes** (riv.), Fr.
161/G2 **Cruz** (cape), Cuba
174/E2 **Cruz Alta,** Arg.
173/F4 **Cruz Alta,** Braz.
77/P10 **Cruz Alta** (mtn.), Port.
172/C4 **Cruz del Eje,** Arg.
170/D4 **Cruzeiro,** Braz.
170/B4 **Cruzeiro do Oeste,** Braz.
168/C2 **Cruzeiro do Sul,** Braz.
167/G4 **Cruzeta,** Braz.
171/M6 **Cruzília,** Braz.
92/D3 **Crvenka,** Yugo.
57/E5 **Cryn-y-Brain** (mtn.), Wal,UK
195/P6 **Crystal,** Mn,US
187/H2 **Crystal,** NM,US
206/C1 **Crystal** (lake), Pa,US
184/D4 **Crystal Bay,** Nv,US
133/H5 **Crystal Brook,** Austl.
206/C2 **Crystal Cave,** Pa,US
194/E3 **Crystal City,** Mb,Can
188/E3 **Crystal City,** Tx,US
198/B1 **Crystal Falls,** Mi,US
201/H2 **Crystal Hill,** Va,US
208/B2 **Crystal Lake,** Ct,US
203/F2 **Crystal Lake,** Fl,US
205/P15 **Crystal Lake,** Il,US
203/G3 **Crystal River,** Fl,US
205/K11 **Crystal Springs** (res.), Ca,US
202/L7 **Crystal Springs,** Fl,US
200/B5 **Crystal Springs,** Ms,US
73/B5 **Csabrendek,** Hun.
73/C5 **Csákvár,** Hun.
73/B5 **Csángota-ér** (riv.), Hun.
92/F2 **Csenger,** Hun.
73/C5 **Csepel-sziget** (isl.), Hun.
73/A5 **Csepreg,** Hun.
73/D4 **Cserhát** (mts.), Hun.
73/A6 **Cserta** (riv.), Hun.
73/D4 **Csömör,** Hun.
92/E2 **Csongrád,** Hun.
92/E2 **Csongrád** (co.), Hun.
73/B4 **Csorna,** Hun.
73/A5 **Csórnoc-Herpenyő** (riv.), Hun.
92/E2 **Csorvás,** Hun.
73/C4 **Csóványos** (peak), Hun.
92/C2 **Csurgó,** Hun.
105/F3 **Ctesiphon** (ruins), Iraq
167/O7 **Cúa,** Ven.
174/C2 **Cuadro Nacional,** Arg.
160/B2 **Cuajinicuilapa,** Mex.
76/B2 **Cualedro,** Sp.
155/H2 **Cuamba,** Moz.
154/C2 **Cuanavale** (riv.), Ang.
154/D3 **Cuando** (riv.), Ang.
154/C2 **Cuando-Cubango** (dist.), Ang.
154/C3 **Cuangar,** Ang.
152/D4 **Cuango,** Ang.
152/D5 **Cuango,** Ang.
152/D5 **Cuango** (riv.), Ang.
152/C5 **Cuanza** (riv.), Ang.
152/C5 **Cuanza Norte** (prov.), Ang.
152/C5 **Cuanza Sul** (dist.), Ang.
173/E3 **Cuareim** (riv.), Bra., Uru.
175/G1 **Cuaró,** Uru.
77/E3 **Cuart de Poblet,** Sp.
174/D2 **Cuarto** (riv.), Arg.
154/C2 **Cuatir** (riv.), Ang.
158/E3 **Cuatrociénagas,** Mex.
172/D1 **Cuatro Ojos,** Bol.
158/D2 **Cuauhtémoc,** Mex.
158/E5 **Cuauhtémoc,** Mex.
159/L6 **Cuautepec de Hinojosa,** Mex.
159/Q9 **Cuautitlan,** Mex.
159/Q9 **Cuautitlan** (riv.), Mex.
159/K7 **Cuautitlán de Romero Rubio,** Mex.
160/B2 **Cuautla,** Mex.
159/F5 **Cuautla Morelos,** Mex.
161/F1 **Cuba**
76/B3 **Cuba,** Port.
202/D1 **Cuba,** Al,US
193/J3 **Cuba,** Il,US
191/F1 **Cuba,** Ks,US
191/J1 **Cuba,** Mo,US
190/A2 **Cuba,** NM,US
199/G3 **Cuba,** NY,US
193/J2 **Cuba City,** Wi,US
165/E2 **Cubagua** (isl.), Ven.
154/B2 **Cubal,** Ang.
154/B2 **Cubal** (riv.), Ang.
132/C5 **Cuballing,** Austl.
154/C3 **Cubango** (riv.), Ang.
173/H2 **Cubatão,** Braz.
167/G4 **Cubati,** Braz.
187/J3 **Cubero,** NM,US
104/C1 **Çubuk,** Turk.
204/C2 **Cucamonga** (Rancho Cucamonga), Ca,US
204/C2 **Cucamonga Wilderness,** Ca,US
87/F5 **Cuccurano,** It.
190/B2 **Cucharas** (riv.), Co,US
154/C2 **Cuchi,** Ang.
154/C2 **Cuchi** (riv.), Ang.
173/F5 **Cuchilla Caraguatá,** Uru.
187/J4 **Cuchillo,** NM,US
174/D3 **Cuchillo-Có,** Arg.
188/B3 **Cuchillo Parado,** Mex.
165/E3 **Cuchivero** (riv.), Ven.
160/D3 **Cuchumatanes, Sierra los** (range), Guat.
59/F4 **Cuckfield,** Eng,UK
59/G5 **Cuckmere** (riv.), Eng,UK
123/D1 **Cuc Phuong Nat'l Park,** Viet.
68/A3 **Cucq,** Fr.
165/E4 **Cucuí,** Braz.
164/C3 **Cúcuta,** Col.
160/D3 **Cucuyagua,** Hon.
204/F8 **Cudahy,** Ca,US
205/Q14 **Cudahy,** Wi,US
122/G3 **Cuddalore,** India
118/C5 **Cuddapah,** India
57/F5 **Cuddington,** Eng,UK
135/C3 **Cudgewa,** Austl.
76/B1 **Cudillero,** Sp.
80/D4 **Cudrefin,** Swi.
183/M1 **Cudworth,** Sk,Can
57/G4 **Cudworth,** Eng,UK
132/C3 **Cue,** Austl.
154/C2 **Cuebe** (riv.), Ang.
154/D2 **Cueio** (riv.), Ang.
154/C2 **Cueli** (riv.), Ang.
76/C2 **Cuéllar,** Sp.
164/B5 **Cuenca,** Ecu.
76/D2 **Cuenca,** Sp.
88/C2 **Cuenca** (mts.), Sp.
76/E2 **Cuenca** (range), Sp.
158/E3 **Cuencamé,** Mex.
159/E5 **Cueramo,** Mex.
159/F5 **Cuernavaca,** Mex.
189/F3 **Cuero,** Tx,US
82/C6 **Cuers,** Fr.
190/B3 **Cuervo,** NM,US
68/C3 **Cuesmes,** Belg.
188/B2 **Cuesta del Burro** (mts.), Tx,US
161/H1 **Cueto,** Cuba
164/D2 **Cueva de la Quebroda del Toro Nat'l Park,** Ven.
164/B4 **Cueva de los Guarcharos Nat'l Park,** Col.
76/E4 **Cuevas del Almanzora,** Sp.
77/F2 **Cuevas de Vinromá,** Sp.
186/D5 **Cuevitas,** Mex.
172/D2 **Cuevo,** Bol.
53/N6 **Cuffley,** Eng,UK
175/T12 **Cufré,** Uru.
93/F3 **Cugir,** Rom.
90/A2 **Cuglieri,** It.
74/D5 **Cugnaux-Vingtcasses,** Fr.
152/D4 **Cugo** (riv.), Ang.
73/B5 **Cuha** (riv.), Hun.
73/B4 **Cuhai-Bakony-ér** (riv.), Hun.
170/A2 **Cuiabá,** Braz.
170/A3 **Cuiabá** (riv.), Braz.
164/D2 **Cuicas,** Ven.
66/C5 **Cuijk,** Neth.
160/D3 **Cuilapa,** Guat.
60/C1 **Cuilcagh** (mtn.), Wal,UK
160/C3 **Cuilco** (riv.), Guat., Mex.
55/H8 **Cuillin** (sound), Sc,UK
152/D4 **Cuilo,** Ang.
152/C4 **Cuilo** (riv.), Ang.
152/D5 **Cuilo** (riv.), Ang.
152/C4 **Cuilo Pombo,** Ang.
154/B2 **Cuima,** Ang.
80/B4 **Cuisance** (riv.), Fr.
80/B5 **Cuiseaux,** Fr.
68/C5 **Cuise-la-Motte,** Fr.
80/B4 **Cuisery,** Fr.
167/G4 **Cuité,** Braz.
159/N8 **Cuitlahuac,** Mex.
154/C3 **Cuito** (riv.), Ang.
154/C2 **Cuito-Cuanavale,** Ang.
165/E5 **Cuiuni** (riv.), Braz.
117/G3 **Cuiwei** (mtn.), China
159/Q10 **Cujimalpa,** Mex.
92/F3 **Cujmir,** Rom.
124/D4 **Cukuh Batuberagam** (cape), Indo.
104/C2 **Çukur,** Turk.
105/E2 **Çukurca,** Turk.
123/E4 **Cu Lao** (isl.), Viet.
125/C3 **Culasi,** Phil.
192/D3 **Culbertson** (dam), Ne,US
135/C2 **Culcairn,** Austl.
56/A1 **Culdaff,** Ire.
56/A1 **Culdaff** (riv.), Ire.
168/B3 **Culebras,** Peru
66/C5 **Culemborg,** Neth.
135/C1 **Culgoa** (riv.), Austl.
158/D3 **Culiacán,** Mex.
125/B3 **Culion** (isl.), Phil.
125/C3 **Culion Res.,** Phil.
170/B2 **Culiseu** (riv.), Braz.
76/D4 **CúHar Baza,** Sp.
175/K8 **Cullen,** Arg.
54/D1 **Cullen,** Sc,UK
189/H1 **Cullen,** La,US
201/H2 **Cullen,** Va,US
60/A4 **Cullenagh** (riv.), Ire.
188/L6 **Culleoka,** Tx,US
77/E3 **Cullera,** Sp.
76/A1 **Culleredo,** Sp.
60/A2 **Cullin** (lake), Ire.
156/E2 **Cullinan,** SAfr.
200/D3 **Cullman,** Al,US
54/B2 **Culloden Battlesite** (1746), Sc,UK
200/C5 **Cullomburg,** Al,US
58/C5 **Cullompton,** Eng,UK
201/F3 **Cullowhee,** NC,US
80/C5 **Cully,** Swi.
56/B2 **Cullybackey,** NI,UK
205/D2 **Culmback** (dam), Wa,US
56/A1 **Culmore,** NI,UK
134/B5 **Culoga** (riv.), Austl.
80/B6 **Culoz,** Fr.
184/B2 **Culp Creek,** Or,US
201/J1 **Culpeper,** Va,US
172/C2 **Culpina,** Bol.
54/C4 **Culross,** Sc,UK
172/C1 **Culta,** Bol.
60/B3 **Cultra, Lough** (lake), Ire.
54/D2 **Cults,** Sc,UK
170/B2 **Culuene** (riv.), Braz.
132/E5 **Culver** (pt.), Austl.
198/C4 **Culver,** In,US
191/F1 **Culver,** Ks,US
195/H4 **Culver,** Mn,US
184/C1 **Culver,** Or,US
204/B2 **Culver City,** Ca,US
136/C3 **Culverden,** N.Z.
206/D1 **Culvers** (lake), NJ,US
167/E3 **Cumã** (bay), Braz.
165/E2 **Cumaná,** Ven.
82/B2 **Cumane** (riv.), Fr.
168/C3 **Cumaría,** Peru
168/B2 **Cumba,** Peru
164/B4 **Cumbal,** Col.
164/B4 **Cumbal, Nevado de** (peak), Col.
188/D5 **Cumberes de Monterrey Nat'l Park,** Mex.
182/B3 **Cumberland,** BC,Can
179/K2 **Cumberland** (pen.), NW,Can
179/K2 **Cumberland** (sound), NW,Can
200/E3 **Cumberland** (plat.), US
203/H2 **Cumberland** (isl.), Ga,US
201/F2 **Cumberland,** Ky,US
200/E2 **Cumberland** (lake), Ky,US
200/D2 **Cumberland** (riv.), Ky, Tn,US
199/G5 **Cumberland,** Md,US
206/C5 **Cumberland** (co.), NJ,US
206/A3 **Cumberland** (co.), Pa,US
201/H2 **Cumberland,** Va,US
205/D3 **Cumberland,** Wa,US
193/H1 **Cumberland,** Wi,US
201/F2 **Cumberland Gap Nat'l Hist. Park,** US
208/C2 **Cumberland Hill,** RI,US
203/H2 **Cumberland I. Nat'l Seash.,** Ga,US
54/C5 **Cumbernauld,** Sc,UK
152/C4 **Cumbi,** Ang.
172/B3 **Cumbre del Laudo** (peak), Arg.
187/J2 **Cumbres and Toltec Railroad,** Co,US
159/G5 **Cumbres Bastonal, Cerro** (mt.), Mex.
188/A3 **Cumbres de Majalca Nat'l Park,** Mex.
159/E3 **Cumbres de Monterrey Nat'l Park,** Mex.
57/F2 **Cumbria** (co.), Eng,UK
57/E3 **Cumbrian** (mts.), Eng,UK
118/C4 **Cumbum,** India
82/D3 **Cumiana,** It.
200/E3 **Cumming,** Ga,US
208/B1 **Cummington,** Ma,US
133/G5 **Cummins,** Austl.
135/D2 **Cumnock,** Austl.
54/B6 **Cumnock,** Sc,UK
158/C2 **Cumpas,** Mex.
104/C2 **Çumra,** Turk.
177/M5 **Cumshewa** (pt.), BC,Can
175/G1 **Cuñapirú,** Uru.
164/C4 **Cuñare,** Col.
165/E3 **Cunaviche,** Ven.
174/B3 **Cunco,** Chile
154/C2 **Cunde** (riv.), Ang.
132/D4 **Cundeelee Abor. Rsv.,** Austl.
132/C4 **Cunderdin,** Austl.
164/C3 **Cundinamarca** (dept.), Col.
159/G5 **Cunduacán,** Mex.
154/B3 **Cunene** (dist.), Ang.
154/C3 **Cunene** (dry riv.), Ang.
154/B3 **Cunene** (riv.), Ang.
86/A4 **Cuneo,** It.
86/A3 **Cuneo** (prov.), It.
189/G1 **Cuney,** Tx,US
123/E3 **Cung Son,** Viet.
170/D4 **Cunha,** Braz.
154/C2 **Cunhinga,** Ang.
154/C1 **Cunhinga** (riv.), Ang.
154/D2 **Cunjamba,** Ang.
134/B5 **Cunnamulla,** Austl.
191/E2 **Cunningham,** Ks,US
200/C2 **Cunningham,** Ky,US
191/G4 **Cunningham,** Tx,US
54/B5 **Cunninghame** (dist.), Sc,UK
61/H1 **Čuokkaraš'ša** (peak), Nor.
86/A2 **Cuorgnè,** It.
117/H2 **Cuozhen,** China
194/B2 **Cupar,** Sk,Can
54/C4 **Cupar,** Sc,UK
85/E3 **Cupello,** It.
205/K12 **Cupertino,** Ca,US
85/D1 **Cupra Marittima,** It.
87/G6 **Cupramontana,** It.
92/E4 **Ćuprija,** Yugo.
184/E1 **Cuprum,** Id,US
165/F3 **Cuquenán** (riv.), Ven.
158/E4 **Cuquío,** Mex.
171/F1 **Curaçá,** Braz.
162/D4 **Curaçao** (isl.), NAnt.
174/C3 **Curacautín,** Chile
174/Q9 **Curacaví,** Chile
168/D5 **Curahuara de Carangas,** Bol.
172/B1 **Curahuara de Pacajes,** Bol.
174/B3 **Curanilahue,** Chile
164/C5 **Curaray** (riv.), Ecu., Peru
160/E3 **Curaren,** Hon.
174/Q9 **Curaumilla** (pt.), Chile
92/F2 **Curcubăta** (peak), Rom.
74/E3 **Cure** (riv.), Fr.
185/K4 **Curecanti Nat'l Rec. Area,** Co,US
157/S15 **Curepipe,** Mrts.
174/B2 **Curepto,** Chile
169/G5 **Curiche Grande** (riv.), Bol.
174/C2 **Curicó,** Chile
170/D1 **Curimatá,** Braz.
83/C5 **Curinga,** It.
173/G3 **Curitiba,** Braz.
173/G3 **Curitibanos,** Braz.
185/G2 **Curlew Nat'l Grslds.,** Id,US
133/H4 **Curnamona,** Austl.
86/C1 **Curno,** It.
154/B3 **Curoca** (riv.), Ang.
86/B3 **Curone** (riv.), It.
60/D3 **Curragh, The,** Ire.
167/G4 **Currais Novos,** Braz.
166/D3 **Curralinho,** Braz.
140/K10 **Curral Velho,** CpV.
184/F4 **Currant,** Nv,US
184/F4 **Currant** (mtn.), Nv,US
133/J3 **Currawilla,** Austl.
162/B1 **Current,** Bahm.
191/J2 **Current** (riv.), Ar, Mo,US
200/B2 **Current, Jacks Fork** (riv.), Mo,US
135/B3 **Currie,** Austl.
54/C5 **Currie,** Sc,UK
201/J2 **Currituck,** NC,US
201/K2 **Currituck** (sound), NC,US
177/H3 **Curry,** Ak,US
93/G3 **Curtea de Argeş,** Rom.
92/E2 **Curtici,** Rom.
184/B2 **Curtin,** Or,US
173/E5 **Curtina,** Uru.
134/C3 **Curtis** (isl.), Austl.
138/H8 **Curtis** (isl.), N.Z.
76/A1 **Curtis,** Sp.
191/H4 **Curtis,** Ar,US
189/H1 **Curtis,** La,US
206/B6 **Curtis** (pt.), Md,US
166/D2 **Curuá** (isl.), Braz.
166/C3 **Curuá** (riv.), Braz.
166/C4 **Curuá** (riv.), Braz.
166/C3 **Curuá Una** (riv.), Braz.
166/E3 **Curuçá,** Braz.
168/C2 **Curuçú** (riv.), Braz.
173/F3 **Curuguaty,** Par.
161/E4 **Curú Nat'l Wild. Ref.,** CR
124/C3 **Curup,** Indo.
169/F4 **Cururú,** Bol.
167/E3 **Cururupu,** Braz.
172/E4 **Curuzú Cuatiá,** Arg.
170/D3 **Curvelo,** Braz.
199/G4 **Curwensville,** Pa,US
198/B1 **Curwood** (mt.), Mi,US
168/D4 **Cusco,** Peru
56/B1 **Cushendall,** NI,UK
56/B3 **Cusher** (riv.), NI,UK
54/D6 **Cushet Law** (mtn.), Eng,UK
191/F3 **Cushing,** Ok,US
189/G2 **Cushing,** Tx,US
191/J3 **Cushman,** Ar,US
208/B1 **Cushman,** Ma,US
182/F3 **Cusick,** Wa,US
86/D4 **Cusna, Monte** (peak), It.
154/B2 **Cussava** (riv.), Ang.
154/B2 **Cusse,** Ang.
74/E3 **Cusset,** Fr.
200/E4 **Cusseta,** Al,US
200/E4 **Cusseta,** Ga,US
183/L4 **Custer,** Mt,US
192/C2 **Custer,** SD,US
192/C1 **Custer** (peak), SD,US
190/E3 **Custer City,** Ok,US
69/F6 **Custines,** Fr.
167/G5 **Custódia,** Braz.
58/C5 **Cut** (hill), Eng,UK
189/G2 **Cut and Shoot,** Tx,US
154/C2 **Cutato,** Ang.
154/C1 **Cutato** (riv.), Ang.
154/C2 **Cutato** (riv.), Ang.
183/H3 **Cut Bank,** Mt,US
194/D3 **Cut Bank** (cr.), ND,US
207/F1 **Cutchogue,** NY,US
154/B2 **Cutenda,** Ang.
168/B2 **Cutervo,** Peru
200/E5 **Cuthbert,** Ga,US
183/K1 **Cut Knife,** Sk,Can
186/C2 **Cutler,** Ca,US
196/D3 **Cutler,** Me,US
203/H5 **Cutler Ridge,** Fl,US
202/C3 **Cut Off,** La,US
174/C3 **Cutral-Có,** Arg.
83/C4 **Cutro,** It.
118/E3 **Cuttack,** India
184/A3 **Cutten,** Ca,US
208/D3 **Cuttyhunk,** Ma,US
154/B2 **Cuvelai,** Ang.
152/C3 **Cuvette** (pol. reg.), Congo
132/B3 **Cuvier** (cape), Austl.
154/B1 **Cuvo** (riv.), Ang.
74/E5 **Cuxac-d'Aude,** Fr.
67/F1 **Cuxhaven,** Ger.
164/C5 **Cuyabeno,** Ecu.
208/F5 **Cuyahoga** (co.), Oh,US
208/F5 **Cuyahoga** (riv.), Oh,US
208/F5 **Cuyahoga Falls,** Oh,US
208/F5 **Cuyahoga Valley Nat'l Rec. Area,** Oh,US
186/C3 **Cuyama,** Ca,US
186/B3 **Cuyama** (riv.), Ca,US
186/D4 **Cuyapaipe Ind. Res.,** Ca,US
125/C3 **Cuyo,** Phil.
125/C3 **Cuyo** (isls.), Phil.
168/D4 **Cuyocuyo,** Peru
125/C3 **Cuyo East** (chan.), Phil.
125/C3 **Cuyo West** (chan.), Phil.
169/F4 **Cuyuchi,** Bol.
165/G3 **Cuyuni** (riv.), Guy., Ven.
165/F3 **Cuyuni-Mazaruni** (reg.), Guy.
168/D4 **Cuzco,** Peru
58/C3 **Cwm,** Wal,UK
58/C3 **Cwmafan,** Wal,UK
58/C3 **Cwmbran,** Wal,UK
192/D3 **C.W. McConaughy** (lake), Ne,US
153/G3 **Cyangugu,** Rwa.
91/J4 **Cyclades** (isls.), Gre.
194/B2 **Cymric,** Sk,Can
182/G1 **Cynthia,** Ab,Can
200/E1 **Cynthiana,** Ky,US
58/B3 **Cynwyl Elfed,** Wal,UK
183/J3 **Cypress** (hills), Ab, Sk,Can
200/D4 **Cypress,** Al,US
204/B3 **Cypress,** Ca,US
202/N7 **Cypress** (lake), Fl,US
189/G3 **Cypress,** Tx,US
189/M8 **Cypress** (cr.), Tx,US
203/H4 **Cypress Gardens,** Fl,US
103/C2 **Cyprus**
196/C2 **Cyr** (mtn.), Me,US
146/D2 **Cyrenaica** (reg.), Libya
146/D1 **Cyrene** (ruins), Libya
191/E3 **Cyril,** Ok,US
195/G5 **Cyrus,** Mn,US
68/C2 **Cysoing,** Fr.
58/B3 **Cywyn** (riv.), Wal,UK
73/C5 **Czákberény,** Hun.
65/J2 **Czaplinek,** Pol.
65/M2 **Czarna Biał ostocka,** Pol.
65/J2 **Czarne,** Pol.
65/J2 **Czarnków,** Pol.
65/H4 **Czech Republic**
65/K3 **Częstochowa,** Pol.
65/K3 **Czestochowa** (prov.), Pol.
65/J2 **Czł uchów,** Pol.

**D**

117/J2 **Da** (riv.), China
69/G2 **Daaden,** Ger.
109/J2 **Da'an,** China
115/B4 **Daba** (mts.), China
151/A4 **Dabaga,** Tanz.
145/G4 **Dabai,** Nga.
164/D2 **Dabajuro,** Ven.
144/D4 **Dabakala,** IvC.
73/D5 **Dabas,** Hun.
149/H2 **Dabat,** Eth.
104/C5 **Dabbāgh, Jabal** (mtn.), SAr.
164/B3 **Dabeiba,** Col.
117/H2 **Dabeibu,** China
123/B2 **Dabein,** Burma
72/D3 **Dabendorf,** Ger.
118/B3 **Dabhoi,** India
117/G2 **Dabie** (mts.), China
144/B4 **Dabissé Kayati,** Gui.
123/D1 **Da** (Black) (riv.), Viet.
69/G6 **Dabo,** Fr.
205/B2 **Dabob** (bay), Wa,US
109/K3 **Daboji,** China
144/C4 **Dabola,** Gui.
150/D4 **Daborow,** Som.
144/D5 **Dabou,** IvC.
145/E4 **Daboya,** Gha.
120/B3 **Dabra,** India
65/M2 **Dąbrowa Biał ostocka,** Pol.
65/K3 **Dąbrowa Górnicza,** Pol.
117/G3 **Dabu,** China
93/G4 **Dăbuleni,** Rom.
121/H4 **Dacca** (Dhākā) (cap.), Bang.
115/L8 **Dachang,** China
115/H7 **Dachang Huizu Zizhixian,** China
71/E6 **Dachau,** Ger.
117/G2 **Dacheng,** China
192/B3 **Dacono,** Co,US
123/D3 **Dac Sut,** Viet.
123/D3 **Dac To,** Viet.
200/F4 **Dacula,** Ga,US
166/B2 **Dadanawa,** Guy.
202/P8 **Dade** (co.), Fl,US
202/L7 **Dade City,** Fl,US
203/G3 **Dade City,** Fl,US
202/P8 **Dade-Metro Cultural Ctr.,** Fl,US
142/D3 **Dades, Oued** (riv.), Mor.
200/E4 **Dadeville,** Al,US
127/H4 **Dadi** (cape), Indo.
107/G3 **Dadnah,** UAE
123/E1 **Dadong,** China
118/B4 **Dadra & Nagar Haveli** (terr.), India
116/D2 **Dadu** (riv.), China
107/J3 **Dādu,** Pak.
118/D6 **Daduru** (riv.), SrL.
93/J3 **Dăeni,** Rom.
123/B4 **Daen Noi** (peak), Thai.
125/C2 **Daet,** Phil.
116/E3 **Dafang,** China
113/B1 **Dafanhe,** China
115/E4 **Dafeng,** China
116/D2 **Dafu,** China
118/C3 **Dag,** India
150/B4 **Dagaio,** Eth.
150/B4 **Daga Medo,** Eth.
144/B2 **Dagana,** Sen.
149/G3 **Daga Post,** Sudan
104/B2 **Dağardı,** Turk.
104/D2 **Dağbaşı,** Turk.
63/M3 **Dagda,** Lat.
152/E2 **Dage,** Zaire
97/H3 **Dagestan Aut. Rep.,** Rus.
97/J4 **Dagestanskiye Ogni,** Rus.
156/D4 **Daggaboersnek** (pass), SAfr.
188/C3 **Dagger** (mtn.), Tx,US
198/C2 **Daggett,** Mi,US
121/H1 **Daglung,** China
134/B2 **Dagmar Range Nat'l Park,** Austl.
80/B6 **Dagneux,** Fr.
108/D4 **Dagongcha,** China
115/H7 **Dagu,** China
116/D3 **Daguan,** China
116/E3 **Daguan,** China
134/E6 **D'Aguilar** (mtn.), Austl.
134/E6 **D'Aguilar** (range), Austl.
113/C1 **Dagujia,** China
109/K2 **Daguokui** (peak), China
125/C1 **Dagupan City,** Phil.
130/C4 **Daguragu Abor. Land,** Austl.
119/G2 **Dagxoi,** China
114/E5 **Dagzê** (lake), China
121/G1 **Dagzhuka,** China
115/C2 **Dahaituo Shan** (mtn.), China
150/A2 **Dahalak** (isl.), Eth.
102/D7 **Dahana** (des.), SAr.
118/B4 **Dāhānu,** India
118/A2 **Daharki,** Pak.
115/B2 **Dahei** (riv.), China
109/K2 **Daheiding** (peak), China
108/F5 **Dahekou,** China
115/G7 **Dahenan,** China
109/J2 **Da Hinggang** (mts.), China
150/B1 **Dahlak** (arch.), Eth.
69/F3 **Dahlem,** Ger.
72/D3 **Dahlem,** Ger.
72/D5 **Dahlen,** Ger.
67/H2 **Dahlenburg,** Ger.
200/C1 **Dahlgren,** Il,US
200/F3 **Dahlonega,** Ga,US
72/D4 **Dahme,** Ger.
72/D4 **Dahme** (riv.), Ger.
69/G5 **Dahn,** Ger.
123/D4 **Da Hoa,** Viet.
115/C5 **Dahong** (mtn.), China
114/C4 **Dahongliutan,** China
113/B2 **Dahongqi,** China
144/B3 **Dahra,** Sen.
72/A2 **Dähre,** Ger.
105/E2 **Dahūk,** Iraq
105/E2 **Dahūk** (gov.), Iraq
113/C2 **Dahuofang** (res.), China
113/B2 **Dahushan,** China
117/J2 **Dai** (isl.), China
115/C2 **Dai** (lake), China
130/C1 **Dai** (isl.), Indo.
111/M9 **Daian,** Japan
115/D3 **Daicheng,** China
111/G2 **Daigo,** Japan
123/B2 **Daik-u,** Burma
120/C1 **Dailekh,** Nepal
54/B6 **Dailly,** Sc,UK
123/E3 **Dai Loc,** Viet.
115/D3 **Daimiao,** China
76/D3 **Daimiel,** Sp.
189/G1 **Daingerfield,** Tx,US
116/C1 **Dainkognubma,** China
134/B2 **Daintree Nat'l Park,** Austl.
111/E3 **Daiō-zaki** (pt.), Japan
161/H2 **Daiquirí,** Cuba
122/A2 **Dāira Dīn Panāh,** Pak.
174/E3 **Daireaux,** Arg.
133/N8 **Dairy** (cr.), Austl.
195/H4 **Dairyland,** Wi,US
112/B3 **Dai-Segen-dake** (mtn.), Japan
110/C3 **Dai-sen** (mtn.), Japan
110/C2 **Daisen-Oki Nat'l Park,** Japan
110/C3 **Daisen-Oki Nat'l Park,** Japan
112/C2 **Daisetsuzan Nat'l Park,** Japan
191/H3 **Daisy,** Ar,US
201/F2 **Daisy,** Ky,US
191/G3 **Daisy,** Ok,US
200/E3 **Daisy-Soddy,** Tn,US
111/L10 **Daitō,** Japan
138/C2 **Daito** (isls.), Japan
115/C3 **Dai Xian,** China
117/H3 **Daiyun** (peak), China
162/D3 **Dajabón,** DRep.
133/H2 **Dajarra,** Austl.
119/K3 **Dajing,** China
108/C4 **Da Juh,** China

144/A3 **Dakar** (cap.), Sen.
144/A3 **Dakar** (reg.), Sen.
117/G3 **Dakeng**, China
150/B4 **Daketa Shet'** (dry riv.), Eth.
147/F3 **Dākhilah, Wāḩāt ad** (oasis), Egypt
121/H4 **Dakhin Shābāzpur** (isl.), Bang.
142/B5 **Dakhla**, WSah.
144/A1 **Dakhlet Nouadhibou** (reg.), Mrta.
123/D3 **Dak Nhe**, Viet.
145/G3 **Dakoro**, Niger
195/P7 **Dakota** (co.), Mn,US
193/G2 **Dakota City**, Ia,US
193/F2 **Dakota City**, Ne,US
92/E4 **Dakovica**, Yugo.
92/D3 **Dakovo**, Yugo.
137/A **Dakshin Gangotri**, Ant.
52/E2 **Dal** (riv.), Swe.
152/E5 **Dala**, Ang.
81/F3 **Dalaas**, Aus.
144/B4 **Dalaba**, Gui.
115/B2 **Dalad Qi**, China
108/H3 **Dalai** (salt lake), China
62/F1 **Dala-Järna**, Swe.
104/B2 **Dalaman**, Turk.
104/B2 **Dalaman** (int'l arpt.), Turk.
149/F3 **Dalāmī**, Sudan
108/E3 **Dalandzadgad**, Mong.
117/G4 **Dalangwan**, China
108/F2 **Dalanjargalan**, Mong.
114/D3 **Dalaoba**, China
62/E1 **Dalarna** (reg.), Swe.
63/S7 **Dalarö**, Swe.
123/E4 **Da Lat**, Viet.
61/Q6 **Dalatangi** (pt.), Ice.
54/A4 **Dalavich**, Sc,UK
56/E2 **Dalbeattie**, Sc,UK
134/C4 **Dalby**, Austl.
62/E4 **Dalby**, Swe.
147/F4 **Dal Cataract** (falls), Sudan
54/B1 **Dalcross** (Inverness) (int'l arpt.), Sc,UK
62/A1 **Dale**, Nor.
200/D1 **Dale**, In,US
201/G4 **Dale**, SC,US
189/F3 **Dale**, Tx,US
201/J1 **Dale City**, Va,US
200/E2 **Dale Hollow** (lake), Ky, Tn,US
66/D3 **Dalen**, Neth.
62/C2 **Dalen**, Nor.
156/Q13 **Daleside**, SAfr.
119/F3 **Daletme**, Burma
203/F2 **Daleville**, Al,US
66/D4 **Dalfsen**, Neth.
60/B2 **Dalgan** (riv.), Ire.
132/C3 **Dalgaranger** (peak), Austl.
190/C2 **Dalhart**, Tx,US
196/D1 **Dalhousie**, NB,Can
177/N1 **Dalhousie** (cape), NW,Can
122/C1 **Dalhousie**, India
115/B4 **Dali**, China
116/D3 **Dali**, China
115/B3 **Dali** (riv.), China
113/A3 **Dalian**, China
113/A3 **Dalian** (bay), China
113/A3 **Dalian** (int'l arpt.), China
108/E4 **Daliang**, China
76/D4 **Dalias**, Sp.
55/H8 **Daliburgh**, Sc,UK
105/F2 **Dalidag** (peak), Azer.
113/A2 **Daling** (riv.), China
113/D2 **Dalizi**, China
92/D3 **Dalj**, Cro.
54/C5 **Dalkeith**, Sc,UK
121/F3 **Dalkola**, India
177/M4 **Dall** (isl.), Ak,US
177/F3 **Dall** (lake), Ak,US
54/C1 **Dallas**, Sc,UK
200/E4 **Dallas**, Ga,US
184/B1 **Dallas**, Or,US
189/F1 **Dallas**, Tx,US
188/L7 **Dallas** (co.), Tx,US
193/J3 **Dallas City**, Il,US
188/K7 **Dallas-Fort Worth** (int'l arpt.), Tx,US
188/L7 **Dallas Love Field** (arpt.), Tx,US
193/H3 **Dallas-Melcher**, Ia,US
188/L7 **Dallas Nav. Air Sta.**, Tx,US
206/B4 **Dallastown**, Pa,US
193/H1 **Dalles of the Saint Croix, Mn,US**
182/D5 **Dallesport**, Wa,US
184/C1 **Dalles, The** (dam), Or,US
184/C1 **Dalles, The** (dam), Or, Wa,US
72/D2 **Dallgow**, Ger.
145/F3 **Dallol Bosso** (wadi), Mali, Niger
54/B4 **Dalmally**, Sc,UK
92/C4 **Dalmatia** (reg.), Cro.
206/B2 **Dalmatia**, Pa,US
95/P4 **Dalmatovo**, Rus.
54/B6 **Dalmellington**, Sc,UK
135/D3 **Dalmeny**, Austl.
86/C1 **Dalmine**, It.
109/M3 **Dal'negorsk**, Rus.
109/L2 **Dal'nerechensk**, Rus.
144/D5 **Daloa**, IvC.
150/B2 **Dalol**, Eth.
147/F4 **Dalqū**, Sudan
183/H2 **Dalroy**, Ab,Can
54/B5 **Dalry**, Sc,UK
134/B3 **Dalrymple** (lake), Austl.
54/B6 **Dalrymple**, Sc,UK
121/E3 **Dalsingh Sarai**, India
62/E3 **Dalsjöfors**, Swe.
62/E2 **Dals Långed**, Swe.
191/J2 **Dalton**, Ar,US
200/E3 **Dalton**, Ga,US
199/K3 **Dalton**, Ma,US
194/G4 **Dalton**, Mn,US
208/F6 **Dalton**, Oh,US
199/J4 **Dalton**, Pa,US
120/E3 **Daltonganj**, India
57/E3 **Dalton-in-Furness**, Eng,UK
108/E4 **Dalu**, China
121/G3 **Daluābāri**, Bang.
124/C2 **Daludalu**, Indo.
116/D4 **Daluo**, China
117/G4 **Daluo** (peak), China
125/C1 **Dalupiri** (isl.), Phil.
61/N6 **Dalvík**, Ice.
132/C4 **Dalwallinu**, Austl.
54/B3 **Dalwhinnie**, Sc,UK
188/K7 **Dalworthington Gardens**, Tx,US
130/C3 **Daly** (riv.), Austl.
178/H2 **Daly** (bay), NW,Can
205/K11 **Daly City**, Ca,US
130/C3 **Daly River**, Austl.
130/C3 **Daly River Abor. Land**, Austl.
130/C3 **Daly River Wild. Sanct.**, Austl.
132/D5 **Dalyup**, Austl.
130/D4 **Daly Waters**, Austl.
114/F5 **Dam** (riv.), China
145/H3 **Damagaram Takaya**, Niger
105/J5 **Damāgheh-ye Kūh** (pt.), Iran
107/K4 **Daman**, India
118/B3 **Damān**, India
118/B3 **Damān & Diu** (terr.), India
103/B4 **Damanhūr**, Egypt
171/H2 **Damao** (mtn.), China
130/C1 **Damar** (isl.), Indo.
148/C4 **Damara**, CAfr.
148/B2 **Damasak**, Nga.
103/E3 **Damascus** (int'l arpt.), Syria
191/H3 **Damascus**, Ar,US
203/F2 **Damascus**, Ga,US
206/A5 **Damascus**, Md,US
208/G6 **Damascus**, Oh,US
201/G2 **Damascus**, Va,US
103/E3 **Damascus** (Dimashq) (cap.), Syria
148/A3 **Damaturu**, Nga.
105/H3 **Damāvand**, Iran
105/H3 **Damāvand** (mtn.), Iran
117/G3 **Damaying**, China
152/C4 **Damba**, Ang.
80/D1 **Dambach-la-Ville**, Fr.
93/H5 **Dambaslar**, Turk.
116/B2 **Dāmbuk**, India
123/D4 **Dam Doi**, Viet.
161/H2 **Dame Marie**, Haiti
161/H2 **Dame Marie** (cape), Haiti
123/C1 **Damenglong**, China
59/E5 **Damerham**, Eng,UK
201/J1 **Dameron**, Md,US
149/E2 **Dam Gamad**, Sudan
105/H2 **Dāmghān**, Iran
103/B4 **Damietta** (Dumyāţ), Egypt
79/F4 **Damigni**, Fr.
115/C3 **Daming**, China
117/G3 **Daming**, China
117/F4 **Daming** (mtn.), China
113/B2 **Damintun**, China
69/D4 **Damion** (mtn.), Fr.
53/U9 **Dammartin-en-Goële**, Fr.
81/E4 **Dammastock** (peak), Swi.
68/C1 **Damme**, Belg.
67/F3 **Damme**, Ger.
121/F4 **Dāmodar** (riv.), India
120/B4 **Damoh**, India
189/G3 **Damon**, Tx,US
145/E4 **Damongo**, Gha.
80/B3 **Damparis**, Fr.
132/C2 **Dampier**, Austl.
132/C2 **Dampier** (arch.), Austl.
127/H4 **Dampier** (str.), Indo.
131/H1 **Dampier** (str.), PNG
130/A4 **Dampier Downs**, Austl.
53/R10 **Dampierre**, Fr.
80/B2 **Dampierre-sur-Salon**, Fr.
80/C3 **Damprichard**, Fr.
106/F5 **Damqawt**, Yem.
121/F1 **Damqog** (Marquan) (riv.), China
123/C4 **Damrei** (mts.), Camb.
66/D2 **Damsterdiep** (riv.), Neth.
117/H3 **Damuzhi** (mtn.), China
80/C3 **Damvant**, Swi.
79/G3 **Damville**, Fr.
69/E5 **Damvillers**, Fr.
66/D2 **Damwoude**, Neth.
114/F5 **Damxung**, China
115/B4 **Dan** (riv.), China
201/H2 **Dan** (riv.), NC,US
201/H2 **Dan** (riv.), Va,US
103/D4 **Dānā**, Jor.
120/D1 **Dāna**, Nepal
198/C5 **Dana**, In,US
150/B3 **Danakil** (reg.), Djib.
144/C5 **Danané**, IvC.
123/E2 **Da Nang**, Viet.
125/D3 **Danao**, Phil.
205/C4 **Dana Point**, Ca,US
116/D2 **Danba**, China
59/G3 **Danbury**, Eng,UK
208/A3 **Danbury**, Ct,US
201/G2 **Danbury**, NC,US
189/G3 **Danbury**, Tx,US
186/E3 **Danby** (dry lake), Ca,US
115/C4 **Dancheng**, China
194/E1 **Dancing** (pt.), Mb,Can
132/B4 **Dandaragan**, Austl.
152/C5 **Dande** (riv.), Ang.
120/C1 **Dandeldhura**, Nepal
135/G5 **Dandenong**, Austl.
135/G5 **Dandenong** (cr.), Austl.
135/G5 **Dandenong** (mt.), Austl.
54/C5 **Danderhall**, Sc,UK
63/S7 **Danderyd**, Swe.
152/D5 **Dando**, Ang.
113/C2 **Dandong**, China
115/F2 **Dandong** (arpt.), China
201/F2 **Dandridge**, Tn,US
57/F5 **Dane** (riv.), Eng,UK
196/D3 **Danforth**, Me,US
108/D4 **Dang** (riv.), China
150/B2 **Dangal**, Eth.
114/A4 **Dangara**, Taj.
117/J5 **Dangayos** (pt.), Phil.
152/C4 **Dange**, Ang.
145/G3 **Dange**, Nga.
152/C5 **Dange-ia-Menha**, Ang.
156/B4 **Danger** (pt.), SAfr.
133/H5 **Danggali Consv. Park**, Austl.
149/H3 **Dangila**, Eth.
115/L8 **Dangkou**, China
121/H2 **Dangme** (riv.), Bhu.
160/D2 **Dangriga**, Belz.
115/D4 **Dangshan**, China
115/D5 **Dangtu**, China
145/G4 **Dan Gulbi**, Nga.
149/H3 **Dangur**, Eth.
115/B5 **Dangyang**, China
157/E3 **Danhauser**, SAfr.
202/P7 **Dania**, Fl,US
154/D4 **Danieb** (dry riv.), Namb.
156/C3 **Danielskuil**, SAfr.
208/C2 **Danielson**, Ct,US
201/F3 **Danielsville**, Ga,US
206/C2 **Danielsville**, Pa,US
94/J4 **Danilov**, Rus.
115/B3 **Daning**, China
115/B4 **Danjiangkou**, China
115/B4 **Danjiangkou** (res.), China
80/C2 **Danjoutin**, Fr.
107/G4 **Ḑank**, Oman
120/A1 **Dankaur**, India
107/L2 **Dankhar Gompa**, India
96/F1 **Dankov**, Rus.
114/C3 **Dankova, Pik** (peak), Kyr.
116/D2 **Danleng**, China
160/E3 **Danlí**, Hon.
72/A3 **Danndorf**, Ger.
200/D4 **Dannelly** (res.), Al,US
62/G1 **Dannemora**, Swe.
199/K2 **Dannemora**, NY,US
72/B1 **Dannenberg**, Ger.
68/A2 **Dannes**, Fr.
136/D3 **Dannevirke**, N.Z.
144/E4 **Dano**, Burk.
123/C2 **Dan Sai**, Thai.
199/H3 **Dansville**, NY,US
202/D2 **Dantzler**, Ms,US
52/F4 **Danube** (riv.), Eur.
93/H3 **Danube, Borcea Branch** (riv.), Rom.
73/C5 **Danube** (Duna) (riv.), Hun.
73/B4 **Danube** (Dunaj) (riv.), Slvk.
93/J3 **Danube, Mouths of the** (delta), Rom.
93/J3 **Danube, Sfintu Gheorghe Branch** (riv.), Rom.
93/J3 **Danube, Sulina Branch** (riv.), Rom.
183/K4 **Danvers**, Mt,US
199/K2 **Danville**, Qu,Can
191/H3 **Danville**, Ar,US
205/L11 **Danville**, Ca,US
198/C4 **Danville**, Il,US
200/E2 **Danville**, Ky,US
208/E7 **Danville**, Oh,US
206/B2 **Danville**, Pa,US
201/H2 **Danville**, Va,US
199/K2 **Danville**, Vt,US
182/E3 **Danville**, Wa,US
117/F5 **Dan Xian**, China
116/D2 **Daocheng**, China
117/J2 **Daodou'ao**, China
77/Y17 **Daora**, WSah.
117/F4 **Daoshui**, China
109/L2 **Daotiandi**, China
144/E5 **Daoukro**, IvC.
142/D3 **Daoura, Oued ed** (dry riv.), Alg., Mor.
117/F3 **Dao Xian**, China
117/E2 **Daozhen**, China
125/D3 **Dapa**, Phil.
145/F4 **Dapaong**, Togo
202/E2 **Daphne**, Al,US
117/F2 **Dapingying**, China
125/C3 **Dapitan**, Phil.
123/E2 **Dapo**, China
117/F3 **Dapuzi**, China
108/D4 **Da Qaidam**, China
116/D4 **Daqiao**, China
117/H3 **Daqiao**, China
109/K2 **Daqing**, China
115/H7 **Daqing** (riv.), China
117/H3 **Daqiu**, China
107/H2 **Daqq-e Patargān** (lake), Afg., Iran
117/J2 **Daqu** (isl.), China
108/C3 **Daquanwan**, China
103/E3 **Dar'ā**, Syria
104/C3 **Dar'ā** (prov.), Syria
105/H4 **Dārāb**, Iran
122/A2 **Darāban**, Pak.
93/H1 **Darabani**, Rom.
125/C2 **Daraga**, Phil.
150/C3 **Daragodleh**, Som.
131/F1 **Darai** (hills), PNG
125/D3 **Daram**, Phil.
105/G3 **Dārān**, Iran
149/G2 **Dār 'Aqīl**, Sudan
108/G1 **Darasun**, Rus.
92/E4 **Daravica** (peak), Yugo.
123/E3 **Darāyyā**, Syria
149/G4 **Darbatto**, Eth.
63/J3 **Darbėnai**, Lith.
121/E2 **Darbhanga**, India
189/H1 **D'Arbonne Nat'l Wild. Ref.**, La,US
135/C3 **Darby**, Austl.
177/F3 **Darby** (cape), Ak,US
183/G4 **Darby**, Mt,US
206/C4 **Darby**, Pa,US
182/C2 **D'Arcy**, BC,Can
92/D3 **Darda**, Cro.
191/H3 **Dardanelle**, Ar,US
191/H3 **Dardanelle** (dam), Ar,US
93/H5 **Dardanelles** (str.), Turk.
135/G5 **Darebin** (cr.), Austl.
144/B2 **Dar el Barka**, Mrta.
142/D2 **Dar-el-Beida** (Casablanca), Mor.
104/D2 **Darende**, Turk.
53/P8 **Darent** (riv.), Eng,UK
105/J4 **Dār-e Rūd**, Iran
151/B3 **Dar es Salaam** (cap.), Tanz.
151/B3 **Dar es Salaam** (int'l arpt.), Tanz.
151/B3 **Dar es Salaam** (prov.), Tanz.
133/J5 **Dareton**, Austl.
182/D2 **Darfield**, BC,Can
86/D1 **Darfo**, It.
149/E2 **Darfur** (reg.), Sudan
56/B5 **Dargle** (riv.), Ire.
108/F2 **Darhan**, Mong.
108/F2 **Darhan** (peak), Mong.
108/G3 **Darhan Muminggan Lianheqi**, China
118/B3 **Dariāwad**, India
150/C3 **Darie Hills** (mts.), Som.
207/E1 **Darien**, Ct,US
203/G2 **Darien**, Ga,US
205/Q16 **Darien**, Il,US
161/G5 **Darién Nat'l Park**, Pan.
164/B2 **Darién, Serranía de** (range), Col., Pan.
108/G2 **Dariganga**, Mong.
161/G4 **Darién** (range), Pan.
105/G3 **Darjazīn**, Iran
121/G2 **Darjiling**, India
132/C5 **Darkan**, Austl.
108/D5 **Darlag**, China
132/L6 **Darling** (range), Austl.
133/J5 **Darling** (riv.), Austl.
156/B4 **Darling**, SAfr.
194/D3 **Darling** (lake), ND,US
134/C4 **Darling Downs** (ridge), Austl.
203/G4 **Darling Nat'l Wild. Ref.**, Fl,US
57/G2 **Darlington**, Eng,UK
198/C4 **Darlington**, In,US
206/B4 **Darlington**, Md,US
208/G6 **Darlington**, Pa,US
201/H3 **Darlington**, SC,US
193/J2 **Darlington**, Wi,US
135/C2 **Darlington Point**, Austl.
65/J1 **Darłowo**, Pol.
70/B3 **Darmstadt**, Ger.
200/D1 **Darmstadt**, In,US
146/D1 **Darnah**, Libya
141/W18 **Darnāya**, Tun.
68/A5 **Darnétal**, Fr.
80/C1 **Darney**, Fr.
135/B2 **Darnick**, Austl.
137/E **Darnley** (cape), Ant.
178/D2 **Darnley** (bay), NW,Can
76/E2 **Daroca**, Sp.
117/F3 **Darongjiang**, China
117/F2 **Darongtang**, China
57/G1 **Darras Hall**, Eng,UK
174/E3 **Darregueira**, Arg.
105/J2 **Darreh Gaz**, Iran
105/F3 **Darreh-ye Shahr**, Iran
182/D3 **Darrington**, Wa,US
148/D3 **Dar Rounga** (reg.), CAfr.
121/G4 **Dārsana**, Bang.
62/E4 **Darsser** (cape), Ger.
137/R **Dart** (cape), Ant.
58/C6 **Dart** (riv.), Eng,UK
53/P7 **Dartford**, Eng,UK
58/C6 **Dartington**, Eng,UK
58/C5 **Dartmoor** (upland), Eng,UK
58/C5 **Dartmoor Nat'l Park**, Eng,UK
135/C3 **Dartmouth** (dam), Austl.
135/C3 **Dartmouth** (res.), Austl.
196/F3 **Dartmouth**, NS,Can
58/C6 **Dartmouth**, Eng,UK
208/C2 **Dartmouth**, Ma,US
57/G4 **Darton**, Eng,UK
77/G3 **Dartuch** (cape), Sp.
131/F2 **Daru**, PNG
144/C5 **Daru**, SLeo.
127/G3 **Daruba**, Indo.
92/C3 **Daruvar**, Cro.
97/L4 **Darvaza**, Trkm.
125/B4 **Darvel** (bay), Malay.
54/B5 **Darvel**, Sc,UK
57/F4 **Darwen**, Eng,UK
155/F3 **Darwendale**, Zim.
130/C3 **Darwin**, Austl.
130/C3 **Darwin** (int'l arpt.), Austl.
174/B5 **Darwin** (bay), Chile
172/B3 **Darwin** (mts.), Chile
175/K8 **Darwin** (mts.), Chile
168/J6 **Darwin** (isl.), Ecu.
168/J7 **Darwin** (vol.), Ecu.
186/D2 **Darwin**, Ca,US
120/C2 **Daryābād**, India
107/H2 **Daryācheh-ye Sīstān** (lake), Iran
122/A2 **Darya Khan**, Pak.
105/J4 **Dārzīn**, Iran
109/K3 **Dashahe**, China
109/K3 **Dashanzui**, China
109/H3 **Dashengtang** (peak), China
115/B5 **Dashennongjia** (peak), China
150/A2 **Dashen Terara, Ras** (peak), Eth.
203/G2 **Dasher**, Ga,US
117/H2 **Dashi**, China
208/G6 **Dashields** (dam), Pa,US
97/H4 **Dashkesan**, Azer.
105/G4 **Dasht-e Āzādegān**, Iran
105/H3 **Dasht-e Kavīr** (des.), Iran
105/J4 **Dasht-e Lūt** (des.), Iran
107/H2 **Dasht-e Mārgow** (des.), Afg.
107/H3 **Dasht Kaur** (riv.), Pak.
145/E4 **Dasima**, Gha.
70/E6 **Dasing**, Ger.
122/C1 **Daska**, Pak.
145/F5 **Dassa-Zoumé**, Ben.
67/G5 **Dassel**, Ger.
195/G5 **Dassel**, Mn,US
67/H2 **Dassendorf**, Ger.
156/B4 **Dassen Island** (isl.), SAfr.
122/C2 **Dasūya**, India
126/E3 **Datadian**, Indo.
120/B1 **Dātāganj**, India
53/M7 **Datchet**, Eng,UK
123/D4 **Dat Do**, Viet.
123/B2 **Da Te**, Burma
112/B2 **Date**, Japan
187/F4 **Dateland**, Az,US
120/B3 **Datia**, India
117/F4 **Datian** (peak), China
187/J3 **Datil**, NM,US
108/E4 **Datong**, China
108/G3 **Datong**, China
115/C2 **Datong**, China
108/D4 **Datong** (mts.), China
108/D4 **Datong** (riv.), China
67/E5 **Datteln**, Ger.
118/B2 **Dattohar**, India
126/C3 **Datu** (cape), Malay.
124/C2 **Datuk** (cape), Indo.
122/A1 **Dāud Khel**, Pak.
63/L4 **Daugai**, Lith.
61/H4 **Daugava** (riv.), Lat.
63/L3 **Daugava** (riv.), Lat.
63/M4 **Daugavpils**, Lat.
204/B3 **Daugherty Field** (Long Beach) (arpt.), Ca,US
121/H4 **Daukādi**, Bang.
121/G4 **Daulatpur**, Bang.
164/B5 **Daule**, Ecu.
164/B5 **Daule** (riv.), Ecu.
69/F3 **Daun**, Ger.
123/B3 **Daung** (isl.), Burma
194/D2 **Dauphin**, Mb,Can
194/E2 **Dauphin** (lake), Mb,Can
194/E2 **Dauphin** (riv.), Mb,Can
197/G2 **Dauphin** (cape), NS,Can
206/B3 **Dauphin**, Pa,US
206/B3 **Dauphin** (co.), Pa,US
82/B3 **Dauphiné** (hist. reg.), Fr.
82/B4 **Dauphiné, Alpes du** (range), Fr.
202/D2 **Dauphin Island**, Al,US
145/H3 **Daura**, Nga.
118/C5 **Dāvangere**, India
125/D4 **Davao** (gulf), Phil.
125/D4 **Davao City**, Phil.
105/J2 **Dāvarzan**, Iran
150/C3 **Davegoriale**, Som.
156/Q13 **Davel**, SAfr.
196/A2 **Daveluyville**, Qu,Can
109/H1 **Davenda**, Rus.
133/F2 **Davenport** (peak), Austl.
133/G2 **Davenport** (range), Austl.
202/M7 **Davenport**, Fl,US
193/J3 **Davenport**, Ia,US
194/F4 **Davenport**, ND,US
192/F3 **Davenport**, Ne,US
191/F3 **Davenport**, Ok,US
182/E4 **Davenport**, Wa,US
59/E2 **Daventry**, Eng,UK
69/E3 **Daverdisse**, Belg.
82/A2 **Davézieux**, Fr.
179/T6 **Davgaard-Jensen** (reg.), Grld.
161/F4 **David**, Pan.
193/F3 **David City**, Ne,US
98/D1 **David-Gorodok**, Bela.
194/B2 **Davidson**, Sk,Can
191/G3 **Davidson**, Ar,US
205/K11 **Davidson** (mt.), Ca,US
201/G3 **Davidson**, NC,US
190/E3 **Davidson**, Ok,US
133/F3 **Davies** (peak), Austl.
189/F2 **Davilla**, Tx,US
54/D2 **Daviot**, Sc,UK
137/F **Davis** (sea), Ant.
137/F **Davis** (sta.), Ant.
183/M1 **Davis**, Sk,Can
176/M3 **Davis** (str.), NAm.
205/L9 **Davis**, Ca,US
205/E7 **Davis** (cr.), Mi,US
191/F3 **Davis**, Ok,US
199/G5 **Davis** (mt.), Pa,US
188/B2 **Davis** (mts.), Tx,US
201/H1 **Davis**, WV,US
201/F4 **Davisboro**, Ga,US
197/K2 **Davis Cove**, Nf,Can
184/C3 **Davis Creek**, Ca,US
186/E3 **Davis Dam**, Az,US
187/G4 **Davis-Monthan A.F.B.**, Az,US
205/E5 **Davison**, Mi,US
191/J2 **Davisville**, Mo,US
208/C2 **Davisville**, RI,US
95/M5 **Davlekanovo**, Rus.
144/D5 **Davo** (riv.), IvC.
81/F4 **Davos**, Swi.
108/C1 **Davst**, Mong.
113/B2 **Dawa**, China
117/F4 **Dawan**, China
117/H3 **Dawang** (mtn.), China
150/B4 **Dawa Wenz** (riv.), Eth.
114/E5 **Dawaxung**, China
115/D4 **Dawen** (riv.), China
58/C5 **Dawlish**, Eng,UK
106/D5 **Dawqah**, SAr.
134/C4 **Dawson** (riv.), Austl.
182/F2 **Dawson** (mtn.), BC,Can
178/C3 **Dawson**, Yk,Can
175/K8 **Dawson** (isl.), Chile
200/E5 **Dawson**, Ga,US
194/F5 **Dawson**, Mn,US
191/H2 **Dawson**, Mo,US
189/F2 **Dawson**, Tx,US
178/D3 **Dawson Creek**, BC,Can
200/D2 **Dawson Springs**, Ky,US
200/E3 **Dawsonville**, Ga,US
108/E5 **Dawu**, China
115/C5 **Dawu**, China
116/D2 **Dawu**, China
117/G2 **Dawu** (mtn.), China
117/G3 **Dawujiang**, China
117/E5 **Dawu Shan** (mtn.), China
106/G4 **Dawwah**, Oman
74/C5 **Dax**, Fr.
117/F2 **Daxian**, China
123/D1 **Daxin**, China
115/D3 **Daxing**, China
117/F3 **Daxing**, China
116/D2 **Daxue** (mts.), China
116/D2 **Daxue** (peak), China
117/F4 **Dayang**, China
113/B2 **Dayang** (riv.), China
124/B1 **Dayang Bunting** (isl.), Malay.
116/D3 **Dayao**, China
115/C5 **Daye**, China
116/D2 **Dayi**, China
113/D1 **Daying**, China
116/C3 **Daying** (riv.), China
135/C3 **Daylesford**, Austl.
186/D2 **Daylight** (pass), Ca,US
175/F1 **Daymán** (riv.), Uru.
149/E3 **Daym Zubayr**, Sudan
117/F2 **Dayong**, China
117/F3 **Dayong**, China
103/D4 **Dayr al Balaḩ**, Gaza
103/G7 **Dayr al Ghuşūn**, WBnk.
104/E3 **Dayr az Zawr**, Syria
104/E3 **Dayr Az Zawr** (prov.), Syria
103/G7 **Dayr Ballūţ**, WBnk.
103/G6 **Dayr Dibwān**, WBnk.
149/F2 **Dayr, Jabal ad-** (peak), Sudan
103/G7 **Dayr Sharaf**, WBnk.
147/F3 **Dayrūţ**, Egypt
183/H1 **Daysland**, Ab,Can
194/B2 **Day Star Ind. Res.**, Sk,Can
193/G2 **Dayton**, Ia,US
198/C4 **Dayton**, In,US
206/D3 **Dayton**, NJ,US
199/G3 **Dayton**, NY,US
198/D5 **Dayton**, Oh,US
184/B1 **Dayton**, Or,US
200/E3 **Dayton**, Tn,US
189/G2 **Dayton**, Tx,US
201/H1 **Dayton**, Va,US
182/F4 **Dayton**, Wa,US
185/K1 **Dayton**, Wy,US
203/H3 **Daytona Beach**, Fl,US
198/D5 **Dayton** (James M. Cox) (int'l arpt.), Oh,US
117/G3 **Dayu**, China
117/J3 **Dayu** (isl.), China
117/G2 **Dayuan**, China
117/G4 **Dayunwu** (mtn.), China
113/A2 **Dayushu**, China
194/E4 **Dazey**, ND,US
113/B3 **Dazhengjiatun**, China
117/E2 **Dazhu**, China
156/D3 **De Aar**, SAfr.
60/B4 **Dead** (riv.), Ire.
103/D4 **Dead** (sea), Isr., Jor.
203/F2 **Dead** (lake), Fl,US
177/J1 **Deadhorse**, Ak,US
132/C2 **Deadman** (peak), Austl.
185/H2 **Deadman** (mtn.), Wy,US
192/C1 **Deadwood**, SD,US
135/C3 **Deal** (isl.), Austl.
59/H4 **Deal**, Eng,UK
207/D3 **Deal**, NJ,US
206/B6 **Deale**, Md,US
201/K1 **Deal Island**, Md,US
182/B1 **Dean** (riv.), BC,Can
58/D3 **Dean, Forest of** (for.), Eng,UK
172/C4 **Deán Funes**, Arg.
132/C5 **Deanmill**, Austl.
189/F2 **Deanville**, Tx,US
205/F7 **Dearborn**, Mi,US
191/G1 **Dearborn**, Mo,US
205/F7 **Dearborn Heights**, Mi,US
201/F4 **Dearing**, Ga,US
57/G4 **Dearne**, Eng,UK
57/G4 **Dearne** (riv.), Eng,UK
182/F4 **Deary**, Id,US
177/N4 **Dease** (riv.), BC,Can
178/F2 **Dease** (str.), NW,Can
177/M4 **Dease Lake**, BC,Can
186/D2 **Death** (val.), Ca,US
186/D2 **Death Valley**, Ca,US
186/D2 **Death Valley Nat'l Mon.**, Ca, Nv,US
79/F2 **Deauville**, Fr.
105/F1 **Deavgay** (peak), Rus.
121/G4 **Debagrām**, India
148/A3 **Deba Habe**, Nga.
92/E5 **Debar**, Macd.
149/H2 **Debark'**, Eth.
203/H3 **De Bary**, Fl,US
177/G3 **Debauch** (mtn.), Ak,US
150/B2 **Debaysīma**, Eth.
183/L1 **Debden**, Sk,Can
93/G4 **Debelets**, Bul.
59/H2 **Deben** (riv.), Eng,UK
59/H2 **Debenham**, Eng,UK
189/G1 **De Berry**, Tx,US
196/F3 **Debert**, NS,Can
65/L3 **Dębica**, Pol.
121/H4 **Debīdwār**, Bang.
66/C4 **De Bilt**, Neth.
65/L3 **Dęblin**, Pol.
65/H2 **Dębno**, Pol.
177/J3 **Deborah** (mt.), Ak,US
150/A3 **Debra Zebit**, Eth.
150/A3 **Debre Birhan**, Eth.
92/E2 **Debrecen**, Hun.
149/H3 **Debre Lībanos Monastery**, Eth.
149/H3 **Debre Mark'os**, Eth.
150/A3 **Debre Sīna**, Eth.
149/H3 **Debre Tabor**, Eth.
149/H3 **Debre Werk'**, Eth.
149/G3 **Debre Zeyit**, Eth.
150/A3 **Debub**, Eth.
152/B1 **Debundscha** (pt.), Camr.
131/D4 **DeBurgh** (lake), Austl.
200/D3 **Decatur**, Al,US
200/E4 **Decatur**, Ga,US
193/K4 **Decatur**, Il,US
198/D4 **Decatur**, In,US
198/D3 **Decatur**, Mi,US
200/C4 **Decatur**, Ms,US
200/E3 **Decatur**, Tn,US
189/F1 **Decatur**, Tx,US
200/C3 **Decaturville**, Tn,US
74/E4 **Decazeville**, Fr.
118/C4 **Deccan** (plat.), India
116/D3 **Dechang**, China
121/H2 **Dechheling**, Bhu.
87/E3 **Decima**, It.
65/H3 **Děčín**, Czh.
82/A1 **Décines-Charpieu**, Fr.
72/E6 **Děčínský Sněžník** (peak), Czh.
74/E3 **Decize**, Fr.
192/A1 **Decker**, Mt,US
190/B1 **Deckers**, Co,US
198/E3 **Deckerville**, Mi,US
66/B2 **De Cocksdorp**, Neth.
83/C4 **Decollatura**, It.
193/J2 **Decorah**, Ia,US
191/F4 **De Cordova Bend** (dam), Tx,US
59/E3 **Deddington**, Eng,UK
72/A3 **Dedeleben**, Ger.
66/D3 **Dedemsvaart**, Neth.
208/C1 **Dedham**, Ma,US
196/C3 **Dedham**, Me,US
174/C5 **Dedo** (peak), Arg.
156/B4 **De Doorns**, SAfr.
156/L10 **De Doorns**, SAfr.
144/E3 **Dédougou**, Burk.
63/N3 **Dedovichi**, Rus.
109/K2 **Dedu**, China
155/G2 **Dedza**, Malw.
60/D2 **Dee** (riv.), Ire.
55/K10 **Dee** (riv.), Sc,UK
54/D2 **Dee** (riv.), Sc,UK
57/E5 **Dee** (riv.), Wal,UK
60/A1 **Deel** (riv.), Ire.
60/B5 **Deel** (riv.), Ire.
60/C2 **Deel** (riv.), Ire.
133/M8 **Deep** (cr.), Austl.
206/C6 **Deep** (cr.), De,US
201/H3 **Deep** (riv.), NC,US
196/E3 **Deep Brook**, NS,Can
182/C1 **Deep Creek Ind. Res.**, BC,Can
191/F3 **Deep Fork** (riv.), Ok,US
59/F1 **Deeping St. James**, Eng,UK
191/E3 **Deep Red** (cr.), Ok,US
199/H1 **Deep River**, On,Can
208/B3 **Deep River**, Ct,US
186/D2 **Deep Springs**, Ca,US
135/D1 **Deepwater**, Austl.
206/C5 **Deepwater** (pt.), De,US
191/H1 **Deepwater**, Mo,US
206/C4 **Deepwater**, NJ,US
194/F2 **Deer** (isl.), Mb,Can
60/A4 **Deer** (isl.), Ire.
206/B4 **Deer** (cr.), Md.,Pa,US
177/F5 **Deer** (isl.), Ak,US
200/B4 **Deer** (cr.), Ms,US
195/K5 **Deerbrook**, Wi,US
205/Q15 **Deerfield**, Il,US
199/K3 **Deerfield**, Ma,US
208/F5 **Deerfield**, Oh,US
202/P7 **Deerfield Beach**, Fl,US
203/H4 **Deerfield Beach**, Fl,US
177/F2 **Deering**, Ak,US
194/D3 **Deering**, ND,US
182/C5 **Deer Island**, Or,US
196/C3 **Deer Isle**, Me,US
197/J1 **Deer Lake**, Nf,Can
206/B2 **Deer Lake**, Pa,US
68/C2 **Deerlijk**, Belg.
183/H4 **Deer Lodge**, Mt,US
205/K9 **Deer Park**, Ca,US
205/P15 **Deer Park**, Il,US
206/B5 **Deer Park**, Md,US
207/E2 **Deer Park**, NY,US
189/M9 **Deer Park**, Tx,US
182/F4 **Deer Park**, Wa,US
195/H4 **Deer River**, Mn,US
195/L4 **Deerton**, Mi,US
195/H4 **Deerwood**, Mn,US
118/B3 **Deesa**, India
54/D2 **Deeside** (val.), Sc,UK
134/H8 **Dee Why**, Austl.
150/C3 **Deex Nugaaleed** (dry riv.), Som.
172/D1 **Defensores del Chaco Nat'l Park**, Par.
82/B6 **Déffend, Pointe du** (pt.), Fr.
198/D4 **Defiance**, Oh,US
207/K7 **DeForest** (lake), NY,US
198/B3 **De Forest**, Wi,US
203/E2 **De Funiak Springs**, Fl,US
56/E5 **Deganwy**, Wal,UK
148/B4 **de Gaulle**, CAfr.
116/C2 **Dêgê**, China
150/B3 **Degeh Bur**, Eth.
196/C2 **Dégelis**, Qu,Can
145/G5 **Degema**, Nga.
62/F2 **Degerfors**, Swe.
81/F3 **Degersheim**, Swi.
71/F5 **Deggendorf**, Ger.
70/C5 **Deggingen**, Ger.
86/B4 **Dego**, It.
149/H2 **Degoma**, Eth.
198/E4 **De Graff**, Oh,US
191/H3 **De Gray** (lake), Ar,US
132/C2 **De Grey**, Austl.
132/C2 **De Grey** (riv.), Austl.
99/L3 **Dĕgtevo**, Rus.
68/C1 **De Haan**, Belg.
105/H4 **Dehaj**, Iran
150/B2 **Dehalak Marine Nat'l Park**, Eth.
105/G4 **Dehdasht**, Iran
206/B3 **DeHart** (res.), Pa,US
105/H4 **Deh Bīd**, Iran
105/G4 **Deh Dasht**, Iran
105/G4 **Dehdez**, Iran
105/G3 **Deheq**, Iran
105/H4 **Deh-e Shīr**, Iran
105/F3 **Dehlorān**, Iran
107/L2 **Dehra Dūn**, India
120/E3 **Dehri**, India
117/H3 **Dehua**, China
109/K3 **Dehui**, China
70/B4 **Deidesheim**, Ger.
66/C5 **Deil**, Neth.
67/G1 **Deinste**, Ger.
68/C2 **Deinze**, Belg.
67/G4 **Deister** (mts.), Ger.
86/C4 **Deiva Marina**, It.
93/F2 **Dej**, Rom.
62/E2 **Deje**, Swe.
149/H3 **Dejen**, Eth.
117/F2 **Dejiang**, China
131/E1 **De Jongs** (cape), Indo.
201/M7 **Dekalb** (co.), Ga,US
193/K3 **De Kalb**, Il,US
205/N16 **De Kalb** (co.), Il,US
200/C4 **De Kalb**, Ms,US
91/L6 **Dekelia** (arpt.), Gre.
150/A2 **Dek'emhāre**, Eth.
153/E3 **Dekese**, Zaire
145/G5 **Dekina**, Nga.
203/G3 **Dekle Beach**, Fl,US
148/C4 **Dékoa**, CAfr.
66/B2 **De Koog**, Neth.
183/H2 **Delacour**, Ab,Can
202/D3 **Delacroix**, La,US
194/D3 **De Lacs** (riv.), ND,US
205/P13 **Delafield**, Wi,US
186/E2 **Delamar** (lake), Nv,US
203/H3 **De Land**, Fl,US
186/C3 **Delano**, Ca,US
195/N6 **Delano**, Mn,US
185/G4 **Delano** (peak), Ut,US
107/H2 **Delārām**, Afg.
156/D2 **Delareyville**, SAfr.
193/K3 **Delavan**, Il,US
205/N14 **Delavan**, Wi,US
205/N14 **Delavan** (lake), Wi,US
205/N14 **Delavan Lake**, Wi,US
206/C4 **Delaware** (riv.), US
181/L4 **Delaware** (state), US
206/C5 **Delaware** (bay), De, NJ,US
193/G4 **Delaware** (riv.), Ks,US
206/C2 **Delaware**, NJ,US
198/E4 **Delaware**, Oh,US
191/G2 **Delaware**, Ok,US
206/C4 **Delaware** (co.), Pa,US
188/B2 **Delaware** (mts.), Tx,US
206/C4 **Delaware City**, De,US
206/C2 **Delaware Water Gap** (pass), NJ, Pa,US
206/D1 **Delaware Water Gap Nat'l Rec. Area**, NJ, Pa,US
67/F5 **Delbrück**, Ger.
183/H1 **Delburne**, Ab,Can
174/D2 **Del Campillo**, Arg.
175/S12 **Del Carril**, Arg.
92/F5 **Delčevo**, Macd.
153/F5 **Delcommune** (res.), Zaire
66/D4 **Delden**, Neth.
204/C4 **Del Dios**, Ca,US
81/F5 **Delebio**, It.
135/D3 **Delegate**, Austl.
66/D2 **De Leijen** (lake), Neth.
80/D3 **Delémont**, Swi.
189/E1 **De Leon**, Tx,US
184/B4 **Delevan Nat'l Wild. Ref.**, Ca,US
66/B5 **Delft**, Neth.
122/G4 **Delft** (isl.), SrL.
66/D2 **Delfzijl**, Neth.
174/E4 **Delgada** (pt.), Arg.
184/A3 **Delgada** (pt.), Ca,US
155/J1 **Delgado, Cabo** (cape), Moz.
60/D3 **Delgany**, Ire.
108/D2 **Delger** (riv.), Mong.
108/E2 **Delgerhaan**, Mong.
108/E2 **Delgerhangay**, Mong.
149/H2 **Delgī**, Eth.
120/A1 **Delhi**, India
120/A1 **Delhi** (terr.), India
186/B2 **Delhi**, Ca,US
202/C1 **Delhi**, La,US
199/J3 **Delhi**, NY,US
148/B3 **Déli**, Chad
126/D4 **Delia**, Ab,Can
83/B6 **Delianuova**, It.
104/C2 **Delice**, Turk.
96/E5 **Delice** (riv.), Turk.
166/C1 **Délices**, FrG.
85/F5 **Deliceto**, It.
158/D2 **Delicias**, Mex.
164/C3 **Delicias**, Ven.
66/B5 **De Lier**, Neth.
191/H3 **Delight**, Ar,US
105/G3 **Delījān**, Iran
84/J8 **Delimara, Ponta Ta'** (pt.), Malta
108/D4 **Delingha**, China
196/B1 **Delisle**, Qu,Can
183/L2 **Delisle**, Sk,Can
72/C4 **Delitzsch**, Ger.
185/G1 **Dell**, Mt,US
188/B2 **Dell City**, Tx,US
67/E6 **Dellgen**, Ger.
193/F2 **Dell Rapids**, SD,US
208/F6 **Dellroy**, Oh,US
193/K2 **Dells, The** (reg.), Wi,US
195/Q6 **Dellwood**, Mn,US
141/S15 **Dellys**, Alg.
204/C5 **Del Mar**, Ca,US
201/K1 **Delmar**, De,US
183/K1 **Delmas**, Sk,Can
156/Q13 **Delmas**, SAfr.
69/F6 **Delme**, Fr.
67/F3 **Delme** (riv.), Ger.
67/F2 **Delmenhorst**, Ger.
171/F1 **Delmiro Gouveia**, Braz.
189/E4 **Delmita**, Tx,US
206/D5 **Delmont**, NJ,US
92/B3 **Delnice**, Cro.
190/A2 **Del Norte**, Co,US
135/C4 **Deloraine**, Austl.
194/D3 **Deloraine**, Mb,Can
196/G4 **Delphi**, In,US
91/H3 **Delphi** (Dhelfoí) (ruins), Gre.
191/F1 **Delphos**, Ks,US
198/D4 **Delphos**, Oh,US
156/D3 **Delportshoop**, SAfr.
205/M12 **Del Puerto** (cr.), Ca,US
206/D3 **Delran**, NJ,US
202/P7 **Delray Beach**, Fl,US
203/H4 **Delray Beach**, Fl,US
188/D3 **Del Rio**, Tx,US
61/F3 **Delsbo**, Swe.
197/N7 **Delson**, Qu,Can
182/C3 **Delta**, BC,Can
185/J4 **Delta**, Co,US
206/B4 **Delta**, Pa,US
185/G4 **Delta**, Ut,US
165/F2 **Delta Amacuro** (terr.), Ven.
191/J4 **Delta City**, Ms,US
175/T12 **Delta del Tigre**, Uru.
177/J3 **Delta Junction**, Ak,US
205/M11 **Delta-Mendota** (can.), Ca,US
202/D3 **Delta Nat'l Wild. Ref.**, La,US
198/D3 **Delton**, Mi,US
203/H3 **Deltona**, Fl,US
108/C2 **Delüün**, Mong.
204/C4 **De Luz**, Ca,US
174/E2 **Del Valle**, Arg.
205/L11 **Del Valle** (lake), Ca,US
60/C2 **Delvin**, Ire.
91/G3 **Delvinë**, Alb.
98/C3 **Delyatin**, Ukr.
95/M5 **Dēma** (riv.), Rus.
124/E4 **Demak**, Indo.
76/D1 **Demanda** (range), Sp.
177/K2 **Demarcation** (pt.), Ak,US
207/E2 **Demarest**, NJ,US
153/E4 **Demba**, Zaire
149/H3 **Dembech'a**, Eth.
157/H6 **Dembeni**, May.
149/H3 **Dembī**, Eth.
148/E4 **Dembia**, CAfr.
149/G3 **Dembī Dolo**, Eth.
115/C5 **Demchok**, India
66/C4 **De Meern**, Neth.
66/B7 **Demer** (riv.), Belg.
165/G3 **Demerara** (riv.), Guy.
165/G3 **Demerara-Mahaica** (reg.), Guy.
167/F4 **Demerval Lobão**, Braz.
80/A4 **Demigny**, Fr.
187/J4 **Deming**, NM,US
165/F4 **Demini** (riv.), Braz.
104/B2 **Demirci**, Turk.
104/C2 **Demirkazık** (peak), Turk.
104/C2 **Demirkent**, Turk.
93/H5 **Demirköy**, Turk.
93/J5 **Demirtaş**, Turk.
64/G2 **Demmin**, Ger.
83/A7 **Demone** (val.), It.
82/D4 **Demonte**, It.
200/D4 **Demopolis**, Al,US
198/C4 **Demotte**, In,US
124/C4 **Dempo** (peak), Indo.
132/D5 **Dempster** (pt.), Austl.
127/K4 **Demta**, Indo.
99/J3 **Demurino**, Ukr.
68/C3 **Denain**, Fr.
186/B2 **Denair**, Ca,US
150/B2 **Denakil** (reg.), Eth.
177/H3 **Denali Nat'l Park & Prsv.**, Ak,US
150/B4 **Denan**, Eth.
199/H2 **Denbigh**, On,Can
57/E5 **Denbigh**, Wal,UK
66/B2 **Den Burg**, Neth.
57/G4 **Denby Dale**, Eng,UK
123/C2 **Den Chai**, Thai.
144/D2 **Dendâra**, Mrta.
68/D2 **Dender** (riv.), Belg.
68/D2 **Denderleeuw**, Belg.
68/D1 **Dendermonde**, Belg.
155/F4 **Dendron**, SAfr.
66/D4 **Denekamp**, Neth.
115/C4 **Dengfeng**, China
117/G3 **Dengjiatang**, China
108/F3 **Dengkou**, China
116/B2 **Dêngqên**, China
117/G3 **Dengta**, China
115/C4 **Deng Xian**, China
132/B3 **Denham**, Austl.
132/B3 **Denham** (sound), Austl.
66/D4 **Den Ham**, Neth.
53/M7 **Denham**, Eng,UK
66/B3 **Den Helder**, Neth.
57/G4 **Denholme**, Eng,UK
77/F3 **Denia**, Sp.
135/C2 **Deniliquin**, Austl.
184/D3 **Denio**, Nv,US
177/H4 **Denison** (mt.), Ak,US
193/G2 **Denison**, Ia,US
191/G1 **Denison**, Ks,US
191/F4 **Denison** (dam), Ok,US
191/F4 **Denison**, Tx,US
104/B2 **Denizli**, Turk.
104/B2 **Denizli** (prov.), Turk.
71/E5 **Denkendorf**, Ger.
67/G4 **Denklingen**, Ger.
67/F5 **Denkmal-Hermanns** (arpt.), Ger.
137/G **Denman** (glac.), Ant.
135/D2 **Denman**, Austl.
62/C4 **Denmark**
132/C5 **Denmark**, Austl.
178/D3 **Denmark** (str.)
132/C5 **Denmark**, Austl.
193/J3 **Denmark**, Ia,US
201/G4 **Denmark**, SC,US
193/L1 **Denmark**, Wi,US
191/H3 **Dennard**, Ar,US
156/E2 **Dennilton**, SAfr.
208/F7 **Dennison**, Oh,US
206/D5 **Dennisville**, NJ,US
54/C4 **Denny**, Sc,UK
196/D3 **Dennysville**, Me,US
66/C3 **Den Oever**, Neth.
124/F5 **Denpasar**, Indo.
80/D5 **Dent Blanche** (peak), Swi.
82/C1 **Dent de Cons** (mtn.), Fr.
80/C4 **Dent de Lys** (peak), Swi.
80/D6 **Dent d'Hérens** (peak), It., Swi.
68/C2 **Dentergem**, Belg.
70/D4 **Dentlein am Forst**, Ger.
59/G5 **Denton**, Eng,UK
203/G2 **Denton**, Ga,US
206/C6 **Denton**, Md,US
183/K4 **Denton**, Mt,US
189/F1 **Denton**, Tx,US
188/K6 **Denton** (co.), Tx,US
191/F4 **Denton** (cr.), Tx,US
132/B5 **D'Entrecasteaux** (pt.), Austl.
138/D5 **D'Entrecasteaux** (isls.), PNG
80/C5 **Dents du Midi** (peak), Swi., It.
201/G3 **Dentsville**, SC,US
190/B1 **Denver** (cap.), Co,US
193/H2 **Denver**, Ia,US
206/B3 **Denver**, Pa,US
188/C1 **Denver City**, Tx,US
206/D2 **Denville**, NJ,US
183/K1 **Denzil**, Sk,Can
70/A6 **Denzlingen**, Ger.
120/A1 **Deoband**, India
118/D3 **Deogarh**, India
121/F3 **Deoghar**, India
120/B1 **Deoha** (riv.), India
118/B4 **Deolāli**, India
118/C2 **Deoli**, India
118/C3 **Deoli**, India
118/B2 **Deolia**, India
74/D3 **Déols**, Fr.
190/C2 **Deora**, Co,US
120/B4 **Deorī**, India
120/D2 **Deoria**, India
68/B1 **De Panne**, Belg.
66/C6 **De Peel** (reg.), Neth.
165/E1 **Dependencias Federales** (terr.), Ven.
193/K1 **De Pere**, Wi,US
197/T10 **Depew**, NY,US
191/F3 **Depew**, Ok,US
68/C2 **De Pinte**, Belg.
184/A1 **Depoe Bay**, Or,US
191/G4 **Deport**, Tx,US
199/J3 **Deposit**, NY,US
166/C1 **Dépôt Lézard**, FrG.
53/N7 **Deptford**, Eng,UK
101/P3 **Deputatskiy**, Rus.
200/E1 **Deputy**, In,US
116/C2 **Dêqên**, China
115/L9 **Deqing**, China
191/G3 **De Queen**, Ar,US
202/B2 **De Quincy**, La,US
153/G2 **Dera**, Zaire
122/A2 **Dera Ghāzi Khān**, Pak.
122/D2 **Dera Gopipur**, India
121/H3 **Derai**, Bang.
122/A2 **Dera Ismā'īl Khān**, Pak.
151/C1 **Dera, Lach** (dry riv.), Som.
150/A3 **Deramē Shet'** (riv.), Eth.
122/C1 **Derā Nānak**, India
98/D3 **Derazhnya**, Ukr.
149/H4 **Derba**, Eth.
53/H4 **Derbent**, Rus.
130/A4 **Derby**, Austl.
57/G6 **Derby**, Eng,UK
208/A3 **Derby**, Ct,US
191/F2 **Derby**, Ks,US
57/G6 **Derbyshire** (co.), Eng,UK
93/F3 **Đerdap Nat'l Park**, Yugo.
156/D2 **Derdepoort**, SAfr.
92/E2 **Derecske**, Hun.
93/H5 **Dereköy**, Turk.
105/M6 **Dereköy** (riv.), Turk.
108/F2 **Deren**, Mong.
80/D3 **Derendingen**, Swi.
150/A2 **Deresgē**, Eth.
97/J2 **Dergachi**, Rus.
99/J2 **Dergachi**, Ukr.
60/B4 **Derg, Lough** (lake), Ire.
202/B2 **De Ridder**, La,US
104/E2 **Derik**, Turk.
104/C2 **Derinkuyu**, Turk.
97/J2 **Derkul**, Kaz.
200/C4 **Derma**, Ms,US
191/J4 **Dermott**, Ar,US
69/G2 **Dernau**, Ger.
202/C3 **Dernieres** (isls.), La,US
78/D2 **Déroute** (str.), Fr.
74/B2 **Déroute** (passg.), Fr., Chl,UK
60/C2 **Derravaragh, Lough** (lake), Ire.
60/D4 **Derreen** (riv.), Ire.
60/D4 **Derry** (riv.), Ire.
199/L3 **Derry**, NH,US
187/J4 **Derry**, NM,US
56/C3 **Derryboy**, NI,UK
55/H9 **Derrylin**, NI,UK
60/C1 **Derrylin**, NI,UK
60/A6 **Derrynasaggart** (mts.), Ire.
59/G1 **Dersingham**, Eng,UK
149/H1 **Derudeb**, Sudan
84/C2 **Deruta**, It.
55/H8 **Dervaig**, Sc,UK
78/D5 **Derval**, Fr.
92/C3 **Derventa**, Bosn.
81/F5 **Dervio**, It.
56/B1 **Dervock**, NI,UK
135/C4 **Derwent** (riv.), Austl.
183/J1 **Derwent**, Ab,Can
57/F2 **Derwent** (res.), Eng,UK
57/E2 **Derwent** (riv.), Eng,UK
57/G5 **Derwent** (riv.), Eng,UK
57/H4 **Derwent** (riv.), Eng,UK
135/C4 **Derwent Bridge**, Austl.
56/E2 **Derwent Water** (lake), Eng,UK
114/A1 **Derzhavinsk**, Kaz.
174/D2 **Desaguadero** (riv.), Arg.
172/B1 **Desaguadero** (riv.), Bol.
168/D5 **Desaguadero**, Peru

159/Q9 **Desagüe, Gran Canal de** (can.), Mex.
202/C3 **Des Allemands**, La,US
202/C3 **Des Allemands** (lake), La,US
86/B2 **Desana**, It.
191/J3 **Des Arc**, Ar,US
191/J2 **Des Arc**, Mo,US
59/F2 **Desborough**, Eng,UK
174/C2 **Descabezado Grande** (vol.), Chile
170/D4 **Descalvado**, Braz.
160/E4 **Descartes** (pt.), CR
74/D3 **Descartes**, Fr.
184/C1 **Deschutes** (riv.), Or,US
184/C1 **Deschutes River Rec. Lands**, Or,US
161/H2 **Desdunes**, Haiti
150/A3 **Desē**, Eth.
174/D5 **Deseado** (riv.), Arg.
175/J8 **Deseado** (cape), Chile
175/L7 **Desengaño** (pt.), Arg.
86/D2 **Desenzano del Garda**, It.
185/G3 **Deseret Dep.** (mil. res.), Ut,US
199/H2 **Deseronto**, On,Can
199/H1 **Désert** (riv.), Qu,Can
186/E2 **Desert** (dry lake), Nv,US
184/D3 **Desert** (val.), Nv,US
77/V15 **Desertas** (isl.), Madr.,Port.
186/E4 **Desert Center**, Ca,US
186/D4 **Desert Hot Springs**, Ca,US
74/E3 **Désertines**, Fr.
186/E2 **Desert Nat'l Wild. Ref.**, Nv,US
115/B4 **Deshengpu**, China
198/E4 **Deshler**, Oh,US
172/C4 **Desiderio Tello**, Arg.
159/Q10 **Desierto de los Leones Nat'l Park**, Mex.
86/C1 **Desio**, It.
194/C3 **Des Lacs Nat'l Wild. Ref.**, ND,US
191/J2 **Desloge**, Mo,US
192/F1 **De Smet**, SD,US
193/H3 **Des Moines** (riv.), US
193/H3 **Des Moines** (cap.), Ia,US
193/H3 **Des Moines** (int'l arpt.), Ia,US
190/C2 **Des Moines**, NM,US
205/C3 **Des Moines**, Wa,US
193/G2 **Des Moines, East Fork** (riv.), Ia,US
96/D2 **Desna** (riv.), Rus., Ukr.
175/J8 **Desolación** (isl.), Chile
125/D3 **Desolation** (pt.), Phil.
156/D4 **Desolation, Valley of** (val.), SAfr.
195/K4 **Desor** (mt.), Mi,US
203/F2 **De Soto**, Ga,US
200/C2 **De Soto**, Il,US
191/J1 **De Soto**, Mo,US
202/D2 **De Soto**, Ms,US
189/F1 **DeSoto**, Tx,US
193/F3 **DeSoto Nat'l Wild. Ref.**, Ne,US
156/C4 **Despatch**, SAfr.
205/Q15 **Des Plaines**, Il,US
205/P16 **Des Plaines** (riv.), Il,US
145/F5 **Dessa**, Niger
72/C4 **Dessau**, Ger.
69/E1 **Dessel**, Belg.
80/C3 **Dessoubre** (riv.), Fr.
68/C1 **Destelbergen**, Belg.
167/G4 **Destêrro**, Braz.
203/E2 **Destin**, Fl,US
177/L3 **Destruction Bay**, Yk,Can
90/A2 **Desulo**, It.
68/A2 **Desvres**, Fr.
92/E3 **Deta**, Rom.
155/E3 **Dete**, Zim.
67/E2 **Detern**, Ger.
67/F5 **Detmold**, Ger.
195/L5 **Detour** (pt.), Mi,US
198/E2 **De Tour Village**, Mi,US
186/E3 **Detrital** (wash), Az,US
205/F7 **Detroit** (riv.), On,Can, Mi,US
205/F7 **Detroit**, Mi,US
184/B1 **Detroit**, Or,US
184/B1 **Detroit** (dam), Or,US
184/B1 **Detroit** (lake), Or,US
191/G4 **Detroit**, Tx,US
205/F7 **Detroit City** (int'l arpt.), Mi,US
198/C2 **Detroit Harbor**, Wi,US
194/G4 **Detroit Lakes**, Mn,US
205/F7 **Detroit Metro Wayne Co.** (int'l arpt.), Mi,US
70/D3 **Dettelbach**, Ger.
61/P6 **Dettifoss** (falls), Ice.
69/G6 **Dettwiller**, Fr.
123/D3 **Det Udom**, Thai.
135/D2 **Deua Nat'l Park**, Austl.
53/S10 **Deuil-la-Barre**, Fr.
68/B2 **Deûle** (riv.), Fr.
66/B6 **Deurne**, Belg.
66/C6 **Deurne**, Neth.
66/B6 **Deurne** (Antwerp) (int'l arpt.), Belg.
168/D4 **Deustua**, Peru
67/H2 **Deutsch Evern**, Ger.
73/A5 **Deutsch Kaltenbrunn**, Aus.
73/A4 **Deutschkreutz**, Aus.
75/L3 **Deutschlandsberg**, Aus.
73/A3 **Deutsch Wagram**, Aus.
197/N6 **Deux-Montagnes**, Qu,Can
197/M6 **Deux-Montagnes** (co.), Qu,Can
197/M7 **Deux Montagnes** (lake), Qu,Can
92/F3 **Deva**, Rom.
122/G4 **Devakottai**, India
191/J3 **De Valls Bluff**, Ar,US
92/E2 **Dévaványa**, Hun.
73/B5 **Devecser**, Hun.
104/E2 **Devegeçidi** (dam), Turk.
104/C2 **Develi**, Turk.
66/D4 **Deventer**, Neth.
54/D1 **Deveron** (riv.), Sc,UK
189/N9 **Devers, West Branch** (can.), Tx,US
200/B3 **De View** (bayou), Ar,US
69/D4 **Deville**, Fr.
202/B2 **Deville**, La,US
136/C3 **Devil River** (peak), N.Z.
166/C1 **Devil's** (isl.), FrG.
122/H4 **Devil's** (pt.), SrL.
194/E3 **Devils** (lake), ND,US
188/D2 **Devils** (riv.), Tx,US
60/C4 **Devilsbit** (mtn.), Ire.
54/C3 **Devil's Elbow** (pass), Sc,UK
185/J4 **Devil's Garden**, Ut,US
194/E3 **Devils Lake**, ND,US
177/M4 **Devils Paw** (mtn.), BC,Can, Ak,US
187/E3 **Devil's Playground** (des.), Ca,US
186/C2 **Devils Postpile Nat'l Mon.**, Ca,US
192/B1 **Devils Tower Nat'l Mon.**, Wy,US
93/G5 **Devin**, Bul.
189/E3 **Devine**, Tx,US
59/E4 **Devizes**, Eng,UK
92/H4 **Devnya**, Bul.
198/F5 **Devola**, Oh,US
91/G2 **Devoll** (riv.), Alb.
89/J2 **Devoll** (riv.), Alb.
183/H1 **Devon**, Ab,Can
179/S7 **Devon** (isl.), NW,Can
58/C5 **Devon** (co.), Eng,UK
54/C4 **Devon** (riv.), Sc,UK
206/C3 **Devon-Berwyn**, Pa,US
135/C4 **Devonport**, Austl.
136/F6 **Devonport**, N.Z.
204/C2 **Devore**, Ca,US
172/D4 **Devoto**, Arg.
190/C2 **Devoys** (peak), NM,US
93/K5 **Devrek**, Turk.
96/D4 **Devrek** (riv.), Turk.
96/E4 **Devrez** (riv.), Turk.
155/F3 **Devure** (riv.), Zim.
124/A2 **Dewa** (pt.), Indo.
112/B4 **Dewa** (mts.), Japan
191/G3 **Dewar**, Ok,US
118/C3 **Dewās**, India
183/J1 **Dewberry**, Ab,Can
156/D3 **Dewetsdorp**, SAfr.
187/F3 **Dewey**, Az,US
191/G2 **Dewey**, Ok,US
202/B2 **Deweyville**, Tx,US
66/D3 **De Wijk**, Neth.
183/G2 **De Winton**, Ab,Can
191/J3 **De Witt**, Ar,US
193/J3 **De Witt**, Ia,US
193/F3 **De Witt**, Ne,US
199/H3 **De Witt**, NY,US
57/G4 **Dewsbury**, Eng,UK
203/G1 **Dexter**, Ga,US
191/F2 **Dexter**, Ks,US
196/C3 **Dexter**, Me,US
200/C2 **Dexter**, Mo,US
190/B4 **Dexter**, NM,US
116/E2 **Deyang**, China
133/F4 **Dey-Dey** (lake), Austl.
105/J3 **Deyhūk**, Iran
105/G5 **Deyyer**, Iran
105/G3 **Dez** (riv.), Iran
105/G3 **Dezfūl**, Iran
177/E2 **Dezhneva, Mys** (pt.), Rus.
115/D3 **Dezhou**, China
156/L10 **D.F. Malan** (Cape Town) (int'l arpt.), SAfr.
121/E2 **Dhāding**, Nepal
147/G2 **Dhahab**, Egypt
106/C4 **Dhahabān**, SAr.
106/F3 **Dhahran**, SAr.
118/F3 **Dhākā** (cap.), Bang.
121/G4 **Dhākā** (dist.), Bang.
121/E2 **Dhāka**, India
121/H4 **Dhākā** (Dacca) (cap.), Bang.
121/H4 **Dhaleswari** (riv.), Bang.
116/B4 **Dhaleswari** (riv.), India
103/C2 **Dhali**, Cyp.
150/C2 **Dhamār**, Yem.
120/B1 **Dhāmpur**, India
118/D3 **Dhamtari**, India
122/C2 **Dhanaula**, India
120/B1 **Dhanaura**, India
121/F4 **Dhānbād**, India
120/C1 **Dhangarhi**, Nepal
121/F2 **Dhankuta**, Nepal
118/C3 **Dhār**, India
118/B3 **Dharampur**, India
121/F2 **Dharān Bāzār**, Nepal
122/F3 **Dhārāpuram**, India
120/C1 **Dharchula**, Nepal
118/B3 **Dhāri**, India
122/C2 **Dhāriwāl**, India
122/C1 **Dhār Khurd**, India
118/C5 **Dharmapuri**, India
118/C5 **Dharmavaram**, India
120/D4 **Dharmjaygarh**, India
122/C2 **Dharmkot**, India
122/D1 **Dharmsāla**, India
120/B3 **Dhasan** (riv.), India
120/D1 **Dhaulāgiri** (peak), Nepal
120/D1 **Dhaulāgiri** (zone), Nepal
120/B3 **Dhaura**, India
120/C2 **Dhaurahra**, India
118/B3 **Dhekiajuli**, India
91/H3 **Dhelfoí**, Gre.
91/H3 **Dhelfoí** (Delphi) (ruins), Gre.
91/G3 **Dhelvinákion**, Gre.
118/E3 **Dhenkānāl**, India
91/G3 **Dheskáti**, Gre.
80/A4 **Dheune** (riv.), Fr.
103/D4 **Dhībān**, Jor.
91/K2 **Dhidhimótikhon**, Gre.
150/B5 **Dhiinsoor**, Som.
91/K2 **Dhikaia**, Gre.
91/J4 **Dhílos** (ruins), Gre.
91/H4 **Dhimitsána**, Gre.
105/F4 **Dhī Qār** (gov.), Iraq
91/H3 **Dhírfis** (peak), Gre.
91/H3 **Dhístomon**, Gre.
155/F3 **Dhlo Dhlo** (ruins), Zim.
106/F5 **Dhofar** (reg.), Oman
91/G3 **Dhokímion**, Gre.
118/B3 **Dholka**, India
120/A2 **Dholpur**, India
91/H3 **Dhomokós**, Gre.
118/B4 **Dhond**, India
91/J4 **Dhonoúsa** (isl.), Gre.
118/B3 **Dhorāji**, India
120/D1 **Dhorpātan**, Nepal
91/J2 **Dhoxáton**, Gre.
91/J2 **Dhráma**, Gre.
69/F4 **Dhronbach** (riv.), Ger.
150/B2 **Dhubāb**, Yem.
121/G2 **Dhubri**, India
79/G5 **Dhuizon**, Fr.
118/B3 **Dhūlia**, India
121/F3 **Dhuliān**, India
122/B1 **Dhuliān**, Pak.
121/E2 **Dhulikhel**, Nepal
121/E2 **Dhungrebās**, Nepal
118/E2 **Dhupgāri**, India
122/C2 **Dhūri**, India
150/D3 **Dhuudo**, Som.
150/D3 **Dhuudo** (dry riv.), Som.
150/C4 **Dhuusamarreeb** (Dusa Marreb), Som.
91/J5 **Dia** (isl.), Gre.
82/D4 **Diable, Cime du** (peak), Fr.
177/H4 **Diablo** (mt.), Ak,US
205/L11 **Diablo** (mt.), Ca,US
205/L12 **Diablo** (range), Ca,US
188/B2 **Diablo** (mtn.), Tx,US
188/B2 **Diablo** (plat.), Tx,US
175/G2 **Diablo, Punta del** (pt.), Uru.
162/F4 **Diablotin** (peak), Dom.
171/K8 **Diadema**, Braz.
174/D5 **Diadema Argentina**, Arg.
144/A3 **Diaganiao**, Sen.
193/G3 **Diagonal**, Ia,US
172/B4 **Diaguitas**, Chile
144/B3 **Dialakoto**, Sen.
174/E2 **Diamante**, Arg.
174/D2 **Diamante** (riv.), Arg.
83/B3 **Diamante**, It.
133/J3 **Diamantina** (riv.), Austl.
171/E3 **Diamantina**, Braz.
171/E2 **Diamantina** (uplands), Braz.
133/J2 **Diamantina Lakes**, Austl.
170/A2 **Diamantino**, Braz.
135/G5 **Diamond** (cr.), Austl.
185/G1 **Diamond** (peak), Id,US
184/D2 **Diamond**, Or,US
184/B2 **Diamond** (peak), Or,US
204/G8 **Diamond Bar**, Ca,US
121/G4 **Diamond Harbour**, India
186/B1 **Diamond Springs**, Ca,US
116/D3 **Dian** (lake), China
62/D4 **Dianalund**, Den.
117/F4 **Dianbai**, China
116/D3 **Diancang** (mtn.), China
117/E2 **Dianjiang**, China
86/B5 **Diano Marina**, It.
170/D1 **Dianópolis**, Braz.
115/L8 **Dianshan** (lake), China
145/F3 **Diapaga**, Burk.
144/B3 **Diaroumé**, Sen.
206/D5 **Dias Creek**, NJ,US
81/F5 **Diavolezza** (peak), Swi.
191/J3 **Diaz**, Ar,US
120/B1 **Dibai**, India
153/E4 **Dibaya**, Zaire
152/D4 **Dibaya-Lubwe**, Zaire
137/J **Dibble Iceberg Tongue**, Ant.
148/B1 **Dibella** (well), Niger
156/C2 **Dibeng**, SAfr.
155/E4 **Dibete**, Bots.
120/B2 **Dibiāpur**, India
150/B3 **Dībīlē**, Eth.
147/F4 **Dibis, Bīr** (well), Egypt
189/G2 **Diboll**, Tx,US
118/B3 **Dibrugarh**, India
105/F3 **Dibs**, Iraq
207/G1 **Dickens** (pt.), RI,US
190/D4 **Dickens**, Tx,US
194/C4 **Dickinson**, ND,US
189/M9 **Dickinson**, Tx,US
189/M9 **Dickinson** (bayou), Tx,US
199/J2 **Dickinson Center**, NY,US
183/G1 **Dickson**, Ab,Can
191/F3 **Dickson**, Ok,US
200/D2 **Dickson**, Tn,US
87/E5 **Dicomano**, It.
66/D5 **Didam**, Neth.
59/E3 **Didcot**, Eng,UK
150/B2 **Didhav**, Eth.
144/C3 **Didiéni**, Mali
150/A2 **Didig Sala**, Eth.
149/G4 **Didinga** (hills), Sudan
183/G2 **Didsbury**, Ab,Can
107/K3 **Didwāna**, India
104/A2 **Didyma** (ruins), Turk.
82/B3 **Die**, Fr.
156/Q12 **Die Berg** (peak), SAfr.
69/G3 **Dieblich**, Ger.
144/E4 **Diébougou**, Burk.
70/B3 **Dieburg**, Ger.
72/D3 **Diedersdorf**, Ger.
183/L2 **Diefenbaker** (lake), Sk,Can
172/B3 **Diego de Almagro**, Chile
175/J7 **Diego de Almagro** (isl.), Chile
102/G10 **Diego Garcia** (isl.), Brln.
69/F4 **Diekirch**, Lux.
69/F4 **Diekirch** (dist.), Lux.
144/C3 **Diéma**, Mali
67/F5 **Diemel** (riv.), Ger.
66/B4 **Diemen**, Neth.
80/D4 **Diemtigen**, Swi.
123/C1 **Dien Bien Phu**, Viet.
123/D2 **Dien Chau**, Viet.
124/E4 **Dieng** (ruins), Indo.
123/E3 **Dien Khanh**, Viet.
69/E2 **Diepenbeek**, Belg.
66/D4 **Diepenveen**, Neth.
67/F3 **Diepholz**, Ger.
81/F3 **Diepoldsau**, Swi.
196/E2 **Dieppe**, NB,Can
68/A4 **Dieppe**, Fr.
69/G2 **Dierdorf**, Ger.
66/D4 **Dieren**, Neth.
191/G3 **Dierks**, Ar,US
70/D3 **Diespeck**, Ger.
81/H2 **Diessen am Ammersee**, Ger.
81/E2 **Diessenhofen**, Swi.
69/E2 **Diest**, Belg.
70/D6 **Dietenheim**, Ger.
70/D6 **Dietenhofen**, Ger.
198/B5 **Dieterich**, Il,US
70/D3 **Dietersheim**, Ger.
71/E4 **Dietfurt an der Altmühl**, Ger.
81/E3 **Dietikon**, Swi.
81/G2 **Dietmannsried**, Ger.
70/B2 **Dietzenbach**, Ger.
69/E5 **Dieue-sur-Meuse**, Fr.
82/B3 **Dieulefit**, Fr.
69/F6 **Dieulouard**, Fr.
69/F6 **Dieuze**, Fr.
63/L4 **Dievenišk̇es**, Lith.
66/D3 **Diever**, Neth.
70/B2 **Diez**, Ger.
151/C1 **Dif**, Kenya
148/B2 **Diffa**, Niger
145/H3 **Diffa** (dept.), Niger
69/E4 **Differdange**, Lux.
135/B3 **Difficult** (peak), Austl.
120/A2 **Dīg**, India
149/E4 **Digba**, Zaire
118/B3 **Digboi**, India
196/E3 **Digby**, NS,Can
196/D3 **Digby Neck** (pen.), NS,Can
149/G2 **Dighem**, Sudan
190/D1 **Dighton**, Ks,US
208/C2 **Dighton**, Ma,US
121/E3 **Dighwāra**, India
82/C4 **Digne**, Fr.
74/E3 **Digoin**, Fr.
105/E1 **Digor**, Turk.
97/H4 **Digora**, Rus.
125/D4 **Digos**, Phil.
118/C3 **Digras**, India
131/E1 **Digul** (riv.), Indo.
116/B2 **Dihang** (riv.), India
150/B4 **Dihun**, Eth.
68/D2 **Dijle** (Dyle) (riv.), Belg.
80/A3 **Dijon**, Fr.
148/C3 **Dik**, Chad
99/H3 **Dikan'ka**, Ukr.
150/B3 **Dikhil**, Djib.
103/B4 **Dikirnis**, Egypt
97/H4 **Diklosmta, Gora** (peak), Geo.
68/B1 **Diksmuide**, Belg.
100/J2 **Dikson**, Rus.
121/F2 **Diktel**, Nepal
148/B2 **Dikwa**, Nga.
149/H4 **Dī la**, Eth.
68/D2 **Dilbeek**, Belg.
104/A2 **Dilek Yarımadası Nat'l Park**, Turk.
130/B2 **Dili**, Indo.
123/E4 **Di Linh**, Viet.
97/H4 **Dilizhan**, Arm.
187/G3 **Dilkon**, Az,US
70/B1 **Dill** (riv.), Ger.
69/H2 **Dillenburg**, Ger.
193/F3 **Diller**, Ne,US
188/E3 **Dilley**, Tx,US
148/A2 **Dillia** (dry riv.), Niger
120/C1 **Dillikot**, Nepal
149/F2 **Dilling**, Sudan
69/F5 **Dillingen**, Ger.
70/D5 **Dillingen an der Donau**, Ger.
177/G4 **Dillingham**, Ak,US
185/G1 **Dillon**, Mt,US
201/H3 **Dillon**, SC,US
136/C3 **Dillon Cone** (peak), N.Z.
198/D4 **Dillonvale**, Oh,US
198/D5 **Dillsboro**, In,US
206/A3 **Dillsburg**, Pa,US
153/E5 **Dilolo**, Zaire
69/E1 **Dilsen**, Belg.
148/B4 **Dimako**, Camr.
116/B3 **Dimāpur**, India
81/G5 **Dimaro**, It.
104/D3 **Dimashq** (prov.), Syria
103/E3 **Dimashq** (Damascus) (cap.), Syria
125/C4 **Dimataling**, Phil.
156/D4 **Dimbaza**, SAfr.
153/E4 **Dimbelenge**, Zaire
144/D5 **Dimbokro**, IvC.
135/B3 **Dimboola**, Austl.
93/G3 **Dîmbovița** (co.), Rom.
134/B2 **Dimbulah**, Austl.
189/F2 **Dime Box**, Tx,US
101/P2 **Dimitrija Lapteva** (str.), Rus.
96/F2 **Dimitrov**, Ukr.
93/G4 **Dimitrovgrad**, Bul.
53/H3 **Dimitrovgrad**, Rus.
92/F4 **Dimitrovgrad**, Yugo.
148/A3 **Dimlang** (peak), Nga.
190/C3 **Dimmitt**, Tx,US
192/F2 **Dimock**, SD,US
103/D4 **Dimona**, Isr.
103/D4 **Dimona, Hare** (mtn.), Isr.
92/F4 **Dimovo**, Bul.
122/B1 **Dina**, Pak.
150/D3 **Dinach**, Som.
125/D3 **Dinagat**, Phil.
125/D3 **Dinagat** (isl.), Phil.
121/G3 **Dinājpur**, Bang.
121/G3 **Dinājpur** (dist.), Bang.
78/C4 **Dinan**, Fr.
122/C1 **Dīnānagar**, India
69/D3 **Dinant**, Belg.
104/B2 **Dinar**, Turk.
78/D3 **Dinard**, Fr.
78/C3 **Dinard** (Pleurtuit) (int'l arpt.), Fr.
91/E1 **Dinaric Alps** (range), Bosn., Cro.
58/B2 **Dinas** (pt.), Wal,UK
58/C4 **Dinas Powys**, Wal,UK
149/G2 **Dindar, Nahr Ad** (riv.), Sudan
149/G2 **Dinder Nat'l Park**, Sudan
149/G2 **Dinder Wenz** (riv.), Eth.
122/F3 **Dindigul**, India
145/H4 **Dindima**, Nga.
120/C4 **Dindori**, India
122/B1 **Dinga**, Pak.
117/F5 **Ding'an**, China
108/F4 **Dingbian**, China
121/G1 **Dinggyê**, China
117/G3 **Dingjiang**, China
109/J5 **Dingjiasuo**, China
54/F10 **Dingle**, Ire.
54/F10 **Dingle** (bay), Ire.
185/H2 **Dingle**, Id,US
206/D1 **Dingmans Ferry**, Pa,US
71/F5 **Dingolfing**, Ger.
125/C1 **Dingras**, Phil.
115/K8 **Dingshuzhen**, China
115/C4 **Dingtao**, China
144/C4 **Dinguiraye**, Gui.
177/G2 **Dingwall**, NS,Can
54/B1 **Dingwall**, Sc,UK
108/E4 **Dingxi**, China
115/C3 **Dingxiang**, China
115/G7 **Dingxing**, China
115/D4 **Dingyuan**, China
123/D1 **Dinh Lap**, Viet.
67/E5 **Dinkel** (riv.), Ger.
70/D4 **Dinkelsbühl**, Ger.
81/G1 **Dinkelscherben**, Ger.
67/F3 **Dinklage**, Ger.
187/G2 **Dinnebito** (wash), Az,US
202/K7 **Dinner** (pt.), Fl,US
57/G1 **Dinnington**, Eng,UK
156/D2 **Dinokana**, SAfr.
155/E4 **Dinokwe**, Bots.
185/J3 **Dinosaur**, Co,US
185/J3 **Dinosaur Nat'l Mon.**, Co, Ut,US
66/D5 **Dinslaken**, Ger.
66/B5 **Dintel Mark** (riv.), Neth.
66/B5 **Dintenloord**, Neth.
124/D4 **Dintiteladas**, Indo.
186/C2 **Dinuba**, Ca,US
201/J2 **Dinwiddie**, Va,US
66/D5 **Dinxperlo**, Neth.
144/D3 **Dioïla**, Mali
144/C4 **Diomandou**, Gui.
144/C4 **Dion** (riv.), Gui.
148/D1 **Diona** (well), Chad
73/C5 **Diósd**, Hun.
144/A3 **Dioulouloù**, Sen.
145/F3 **Dioundiou**, Niger
144/A3 **Diourbel**, Sen.
144/A3 **Diourbel** (reg.), Sen.
122/B2 **Dīpālpur**, Pak.
116/B3 **Diphu**, India
116/C2 **Diphu** (pass), India
107/J4 **Diplo**, Pak.
104/E2 **Dipni** (dam), Turk.
125/C3 **Dipolog**, Phil.
134/C3 **Dipperu Nat'l Park**, Austl.
70/C1 **Dipperz**, Ger.
72/D6 **Dippoldiswalde**, Ger.
161/H4 **Dique** (can.), Col.
107/K1 **Dīr**, Pak.
148/B2 **Dira** (well), Chad
121/J2 **Dirang Dzong**, India
144/E2 **Diré**, Mali
191/G4 **Direct**, Tx,US
131/F3 **Direction** (cape), Austl.
150/B3 **Dirē Dawa**, Eth.
152/D4 **Diriamba**, Nic.
154/D3 **Dirico**, Ang.
146/A2 **Dirj**, Libya
132/B3 **Dirk Hartog** (isl.), Austl.
146/B5 **Dirkou**, Niger
66/B5 **Dirksland**, Neth.
70/D7 **Dirlewang**, Ger.
135/D1 **Dirranbandi**, Austl.
54/D5 **Dirrington Great Law** (hill), Sc,UK
106/D5 **Dirs**, SAr.
185/H4 **Dirty Devil** (riv.), Ut,US
132/D2 **Disappointment** (lake), Austl.
139/L6 **Disappointment** (isls.), FrPol.
182/B4 **Disappointment** (cape), Wa,US
135/B3 **Discovery** (bay), Austl.
161/G2 **Discovery Bay**, Jam.
81/E4 **Disentis-Mustér**, Swi.
81/F5 **Disgrazi, Monte** (peak), It.
182/F4 **Dishman**, Wa,US
147/G3 **Dishnā**, Egypt
176/M3 **Disko** (isl.), Grld.
57/F5 **Disley**, Eng,UK
192/D3 **Dismal** (riv.), Ne,US
63/N4 **Disna**, Bela.
191/G2 **Disney**, Ok,US
204/C3 **Disneyland**, Ca,US
200/M7 **Disney Studios**, Fl,US
69/E2 **Dison**, Belg.
121/H2 **Dispur**, India
196/B3 **Disraëli**, Qu,Can
59/H2 **Diss**, Eng,UK
67/F4 **Dissen am Teutoburger Wald**, Ger.
56/E2 **Distington**, Eng,UK
206/B6 **District of Columbia** (cap.), US
164/C3 **Distrito Especial** (fed. dist.), Col.
175/S12 **Distrito Federal** (fed. dist.), Arg.
170/D2 **Distrito Federal** (fed. dist.), Braz.
159/F5 **Distrito Federal** (fed. dist.), Mex.
159/K7 **Distrito Federal** (fed. dist.), Mex.
165/E2 **Distrito Federal** (fed. dist.), Ven.
103/B4 **Disūq**, Egypt
115/L9 **Ditang**, China
59/F5 **Ditchling Beacon** (hill), Eng,UK
72/B4 **Ditfurt**, Ger.
90/D4 **Dittaino** (riv.), It.
70/D2 **Dittelbrunn**, Ger.
70/C5 **Ditzingen**, Ger.
118/B3 **Diu**, Damān and (terr.), India
92/D4 **Diva** (riv.), Yugo.
105/F3 **Dīvān Darreh**, Iran
78/D6 **Divatte** (riv.), Fr.
79/F4 **Dive** (riv.), Fr.
152/C3 **Divénié**, Congo
79/E2 **Dives** (riv.), Fr.
79/E2 **Dives-sur-Mer**, Fr.
78/D1 **Divette** (riv.), Fr.
105/G1 **Divichi**, Azer.
190/B1 **Divide**, Co,US
183/H5 **Divide**, Mt,US
206/C5 **Dividing Creek**, NJ,US
171/K6 **Divinolândia**, Braz.
170/D4 **Divinópolis**, Braz.
56/B2 **Divis** (mtn.), NI,UK
171/K6 **Divisa Nova**, Braz.
170/C3 **Divisões** (hills), Braz.
168/C2 **Divisor** (mts.), Braz.
100/K4 **Divnogorsk**, Rus.
97/G3 **Divnoye**, Rus.
144/D5 **Divo**, IvC.
80/C5 **Divonne-les-Bains**, Fr.
104/D2 **Divriği**, Turk.
153/E5 **Divuma**, Zaire
80/D5 **Dix** (lake), Swi.
145/E5 **Dixcove**, Gha.
196/B3 **Dixfield**, Me,US
203/G2 **Dixie**, Ga,US
185/F1 **Dixie**, Id,US
182/E4 **Dixie**, Wa,US
205/Q16 **Dixmoor**, Il,US
177/M4 **Dixon** (chan.), Ak,US
205/L10 **Dixon**, Ca,US
193/K3 **Dixon**, Il,US
200/D2 **Dixon**, Ky,US
191/H2 **Dixon**, Mo,US
183/G4 **Dixon**, Mt,US
190/B2 **Dixon**, NM,US
185/K3 **Dixon**, Wy,US
178/C3 **Dixon Entrance** (chan.), BC,Can, Ak,US
199/L2 **Dixville Notch**, NH,US
105/E2 **Diyadin**, Turk.
105/F3 **Diyālā** (gov.), Iraq
105/E2 **Diyarbakır**, Turk.
104/E2 **Diyarbakır** (prov.), Turk.
103/B4 **Diyarb Najm**, Egypt
152/B2 **Dizangué**, Camr.
117/F2 **Dizhuang**, China
148/B5 **Dja** (riv.), Camr.
152/C2 **Dja** (riv.), Camr., Congo
146/B4 **Djado**, Niger
146/B4 **Djado** (plat.), Niger
145/F5 **Djakotomé**, Ben.
143/G2 **Djamaa**, Alg.
153/F2 **Djamba**, Zaire
152/C3 **Djambala**, Congo
153/G2 **Djamu**, Zaire
143/H4 **Djanet**, Alg.
153/G2 **Dja Rsv.**, Camr.
148/C3 **Djébrène**, Chad
148/C2 **Djédaa**, Chad
143/F2 **Djedi, Oued** (dry riv.), Alg.
141/S16 **Djelfa**, Alg.
141/S16 **Djelfa** (wilaya), Alg.
149/E4 **Djema**, CAfr.
141/U17 **Djemila** (ruins), Alg.
144/D3 **Djénné**, Mali
148/B4 **Djerem** (riv.), Camr.
148/B2 **Djermaya**, Chad
145/E3 **Djibo**, Burk.
150/B2 **Djibouti**
150/B3 **Djibouti** (cap.), Djib.
144/C3 **Djiguéni**, Mrta.
144/D5 **Djiroutou**, IvC.
148/B4 **Djohong**, Camr.
152/C2 **Djouah** (riv.), Congo, Gabon
60/D3 **Djouce** (mtn.), Ire.
152/C3 **Djoué** (riv.), Congo
145/F4 **Djougou**, Ben.
148/B5 **Djoum**, Camr.
148/C2 **Djourab, Erg du** (des.), Chad
153/G2 **Djugu**, Zaire
61/P7 **Djúpivogur**, Ice.
200/C5 **D'Lo**, Ms,US
105/F1 **Dmanisi**, Geo.
99/G2 **Dmitriyevka**, Ukr.
99/H1 **Dmitriyev-L'govskiy**, Rus.
97/L2 **Dmitriyevskiy**, Kaz.
52/G3 **Dnepr** (riv.), Eur.
97/F4 **Dnepr** (estuary), Ukr.
99/H3 **Dneprodzerzhinsk**, Ukr.
99/H3 **Dneprodzerzhinsk** (res.), Ukr.
53/G4 **Dnepropetrovsk**, Ukr.
99/G3 **Dnepropetrovsk Obl.**, Ukr.
99/H4 **Dneprorudnoye**, Ukr.
96/D3 **Dnestr** (riv.), Eur.
93/J2 **Dnestrovsk**, Mol.
98/E4 **Dnestrovsk** (estuary), Ukr.
98/F2 **Dnieper** (lowland), Ukr.
98/E3 **Dnieper** (upland), Ukr.
63/N3 **Dno**, Rus.
108/E5 **Do** (riv.), China
145/E3 **Do** (lake), Mali
155/G3 **Doa**, Moz.
196/D2 **Doaktown**, NB,Can
157/J6 **Doany**, Madg.
140/D4 **Doba**, Chad
200/E4 **Dobbins A.F.B.**, Ga,US
207/E1 **Dobbs Ferry**, NY,US
133/J1 **Dobbyn**, Austl.
63/K3 **Dobele**, Lat.
72/D5 **Döbeln**, Ger.
127/H4 **Doberai** (pen.), Indo.
72/D4 **Doberlug-Kirchhain**, Ger.
65/H2 **Dobiegniew**, Pol.
130/D1 **Dobo**, Indo.
73/C4 **Dobogó-kő** (peak), Hun.
92/D3 **Doboj**, Bosn.
71/E2 **Döbra** (hill), Ger.
71/G3 **Dobřany**, Czh.
65/L2 **Dobre Miasto**, Pol.
99/L1 **Dobrinka**, Rus.
99/L2 **Dobrinka**, Rus.
71/H3 **Dobříš**, Czh.
98/B3 **Dobromil'**, Ukr.
99/J3 **Dobropol'ye**, Ukr.
73/A6 **Dobrovnik**, Slov.
93/H4 **Dobruja** (reg.), Bul., Rom.
98/F1 **Dobrush**, Bela.
95/N4 **Dobryanka**, Rus.
98/F1 **Dobryanka**, Ukr.
201/G2 **Dobson**, NC,US
121/G1 **Dobzha**, China
171/E3 **Doce** (riv.), Braz.
54/B4 **Dochart** (riv.), Sc,UK
133/F3 **Docker River**, Austl.
59/G1 **Docking**, Eng,UK
159/E4 **Doctor Arroyo**, Mex.
158/D2 **Doctor Belisario Domínguez**, Mex.
173/E3 **Doctor Cecilio Báez**, Par.
188/E5 **Doctor Coss**, Mex.
188/E5 **Doctor González**, Mex.
172/D2 **Doctor Pedro P. Peña**, Par.
92/F2 **Doctor Petru Groza**, Rom.
122/C1 **Doda**, India
122/F3 **Doda Betta** (mtn.), India
56/B5 **Dodder** (riv.), Ire.
53/P7 **Doddinghurst**, Eng,UK
89/K4 **Dodecanese** (isls.), Gre.
189/G2 **Dodge**, Tx,US
190/D2 **Dodge City**, Ks,US
204/F7 **Dodger Stadium**, Ca,US
198/B3 **Dodgeville**, Wi,US
58/B6 **Dodman** (pt.), Wal,UK
151/A4 **Dodola**, Eth.
151/A3 **Dodoma**, Tanz.
151/A3 **Dodoma** (prov.), Tanz.
91/G3 **Dodoni** (ruins), Gre.
151/C2 **Dodori Nat'l Rsv.**, Kenya
183/K2 **Dodsland**, Sk,Can
202/B1 **Dodson**, La,US
183/K3 **Dodson**, Mt,US
66/D4 **Doesburg**, Neth.
66/D5 **Doetinchem**, Neth.
127/G4 **Dofa**, Indo.
182/C2 **Dog** (riv.), BC,Can
194/E2 **Dog** (lake), Mb,Can
203/F3 **Dog** (isl.), Fl,US
114/E5 **Dogai Coring** (lake), China
104/B2 **Doğanbey**, Turk.
104/D1 **Doğankent** (riv.), Turk.
104/D2 **Doğanşar**, Turk.
104/D2 **Doğanşehir**, Turk.
104/C1 **Doğanyurt**, Turk.
104/B2 **Döğer**, Turk.
86/A3 **Dogliani**, It.
109/L4 **Dōgo** (isl.), Japan
110/C2 **Dōgo** (isl.), Japan
105/G4 **Do Gonbadān**, Iran
145/G3 **Dogondoutchi**, Niger
191/H2 **Dogpatch**, Ar,US
105/F2 **Doğubayazıt**, Turk.
104/D1 **Doğukaradeniz** (mts.), Turk.
102/E7 **Doha** (cap.), Qatar
106/F3 **Doha** (Ad Dawḩah) (cap.), Qatar
118/B3 **Dohad**, India
72/D6 **Dohna**, Ger.
120/D2 **Dohrīghāt**, India
123/B2 **Doi Inthanon Nat'l Park**, Thai.
123/B2 **Doi Khun Tan Nat'l Park**, Thai.
121/H1 **Doilungdêqên**, China
116/B3 **Doimara**, India
76/B1 **Doiras** (res.)
69/D3 **Doische**, Belg.
169/G4 **Dois Córregos**, Braz.
170/C4 **Dois Córregos**, Braz.
171/F2 **Dois de Julho** (int'l arpt.), Braz.
167/E1 **Dois Irmãos** (mts.), Braz.
170/C1 **Dois Irmãos de Goiás**, Braz.
123/B2 **Doi Suthep-Pui Nat'l Park**, Thai.
173/F3 **Dois Vizinhos**, Braz.
149/G2 **Doka**, Sudan
62/D1 **Dokka**, Nor.
66/D2 **Dokkum**, Neth.
66/C2 **Dokkumer Ee** (riv.), Neth.
63/M4 **Dokshitsy**, Bela.
71/H1 **Doksy**, Czh.
99/J4 **Dokuchayevsk**, Ukr.
186/E3 **Dolan Springs**, Az,US
196/A1 **Dolbeau**, Qu,Can
83/C3 **Dolcedorme, Serra** (peak), It.
78/D3 **Dol-de-Bretagne**, Fr.
80/B3 **Dôle**, Fr.
80/D6 **Dolent, Mont** (peak), Swi.
58/C1 **Dolgellau**, Wal,UK
118/B2 **Doli**, India
90/A3 **Dolianova**, It.
98/C3 **Dolina**, Ukr.
109/N2 **Dolinsk**, Rus.
99/G3 **Dolinskaya**, Ukr.
98/E4 **Dolinskoye**, Ukr.
93/F3 **Dolj** (co.), Rom.
54/C4 **Dollar**, Sc,UK
195/K4 **Dollar Bay**, Mi,US
183/K3 **Dollard**, Sk,Can
197/N7 **Dollard-des-Ormeaux**, Qu,Can
67/E2 **Dollard** (Dollart) (bay), Neth.
54/C5 **Dollar Law** (mtn.), Sc,UK
67/E2 **Dollart** (Dollard) (bay), Ger.
195/M4 **Dollarville**, Mi,US
64/D5 **Doller** (riv.), Fr.
72/E3 **Dollgen**, Ger.
72/C5 **Döllnitz**, Ger.
72/D5 **Döllnitz** (riv.), Ger.
70/E5 **Dollnstein**, Ger.
105/N6 **Dolmançe Palace**, Turk.
70/D1 **Dolmar** (peak), Ger.
92/C5 **Dolmen** (ruins), It.
92/E5 **Dolna Banjica**, Macd.
93/F4 **Dolna Banya**, Bul.
93/G4 **Dolní Dūbnik**, Bul.
73/A1 **Dolní Kounice**, Czh.
73/B2 **Dolnomoravský úval** (val.), Czh.
73/D1 **Dolný Kubín**, Slvk.
150/B4 **Dolo**, Eth.
127/E4 **Dolo**, Indo.
86/D4 **Dolo** (riv.), It.
144/C5 **Dololi**, Libr.
75/J3 **Dolomite Alps** (Alpi Dolomitiche) (range), It.
75/J3 **Dolomitiche, Alpi** (Dolomite Alps) (range), It.
82/A2 **Dolon** (riv.), Fr.
175/F3 **Dolores**, Arg.
168/D3 **Dolores**, Col.
160/D2 **Dolores**, Guat.
125/D2 **Dolores**, Phil.
77/E3 **Dolores**, Sp.
174/F2 **Dolores**, Uru.
187/H2 **Dolores**, Co,US
185/J4 **Dolores** (riv.), Co, Ut,US
164/D2 **Dolores**, Ven.
185/G4 **Dolores Hidalgo**, Mex.
175/N7 **Dolphin** (cape), Falk.
154/B5 **Dolphin** (pt.), Namb.
178/E1 **Dolphin and Union** (str.), NW,Can
57/F4 **Dolphinholme**, Eng,UK
92/A2 **Dölsach**, Aus.
58/B5 **Dolton**, Eng,UK
205/Q16 **Dolton**, Il,US
123/D2 **Do Luong**, Viet.
99/J4 **Dolzhanskaya**, Rus.
127/J4 **Dom** (peak), Indo.
80/D5 **Dom** (peak), Swi.
155/F3 **Doma**, Zim.
98/F4 **Domanevka**, Ukr.
104/B2 **Domaniç**, Turk.
170/B2 **Dom Aquino**, Braz.
121/G2 **Domār**, Bang.
120/D2 **Domariāganj**, India
155/G2 **Domasi**, Malw.
81/F4 **Domat-Ems**, Swi.
71/F4 **Domažlice**, Czh.
97/L2 **Dombarovskiy**, Rus.
75/G2 **Dombasle-sur-Meurthe**, Fr.
97/G4 **Dombay-Ul'gen, Gora** (peak), Geo.
154/B2 **Dombe Grande**, Ang.
80/B5 **Dombes** (reg.), Fr.
130/C3 **Dombey** (cape), Austl.
155/F3 **Domboshawa**, Zim.
92/D2 **Dombóvár**, Hun.
92/E1 **Dombrád**, Hun.
66/A5 **Domburg**, Neth.
166/C1 **Domburg**, Sur.
155/G4 **Dom Carlos** (pt.), Moz.
121/E3 **Domchānch**, India
186/E4 **Dome**, Az,US
137/J **Dome C** (sta.), Ant.
82/C4 **Dôme de Barrot** (mtn.), Fr.
82/C2 **Dôme de l'Arpont** (mtn.), Fr.
82/B2 **Domène**, Fr.
74/E3 **Domérat**, Fr.
187/F2 **Dome, The** (mtn.), Az,US
172/B4 **Domeyko**, Chile
172/B2 **Domeyko** (mts.), Chile
79/E3 **Domfront**, Fr.
172/E4 **Domínguez**, Arg.
162/F4 **Dominica**
162/D3 **Dominican Rep. Nat'l Park**, DRep.
162/D3 **Dominican Republic**
162/F4 **Dominica Passage** (chan.), West Indies
197/G2 **Dominion**, NS,Can
189/G1 **Domino**, Tx,US
153/E4 **Domiongo**, Zaire
72/B1 **Dömitz**, Ger.
80/C2 **Dommartin-lès-Remiremont**, Fr.
69/E6 **Dommartin-lès-Toul**, Fr.
121/H3 **Dommati**, India
69/E1 **Dommel** (riv.), Belg.
66/C6 **Dommel** (riv.), Belg., Neth.
72/C4 **Dommitzsch**, Ger.
72/C1 **Domnitz** (riv.), Ger.
123/D3 **Dom Noi** (res.), Thai.
150/C4 **Domo**, Eth.
94/H5 **Domodedovo** (int'l arpt.), Rus.
81/E5 **Domodossola**, It.
121/G2 **Domohāni**, India
157/H6 **Domoni**, Com.
53/S9 **Domont**, Fr.
73/C4 **Dömös**, Hun.
173/F4 **Dom Pedrito**, Braz.
167/E4 **Dom Pedro**, Braz.
127/E5 **Dompu**, Indo.
183/M1 **Domremy**, Sk,Can
80/B1 **Domrémy-la-Pucelle**, Fr.
73/D5 **Dömsöd**, Hun.
90/A3 **Domusnovas**, It.
174/C3 **Domuyo** (vol.), Arg.
134/C5 **Domvilk** (peak), Austl.
92/B2 **Domžale**, Slov.
130/C2 **Don** (cape), Austl.
78/D5 **Don** (riv.), Fr.
158/C3 **Don**, Mex.
99/L3 **Don** (ridge), Rus.
53/H4 **Don** (riv.), Rus.
57/G5 **Don** (riv.), Eng,UK
54/D2 **Don** (riv.), Sc,UK
155/G3 **Dona Ana**, Moz.
188/A1 **Doña Ana**, NM,US
60/D3 **Donabate**, Ire.
87/F2 **Donada**, It.
56/C2 **Donaghadee**, NI,UK
56/B2 **Donaghmore**, NI,UK
135/B3 **Donald**, Austl.
182/F2 **Donald**, BC,Can
191/H3 **Donaldson**, Ar,US
202/C2 **Donaldsonville**, La,US
203/F2 **Donalsonville**, Ga,US
76/B4 **Doñana Nat'l Park**, Sp.
74/E5 **Dona, Pic de la** (peak), Fr.
81/F4 **Donath**, Swi.
65/H4 **Donau** (Danube) (riv.), Aus., Ger.
81/E2 **Donaueschingen**, Ger.
70/D5 **Donauwörth**, Ger.
76/C3 **Don Benito**, Sp.
135/G5 **Doncaster**, Austl.
57/G4 **Doncaster**, Eng,UK
69/D4 **Donchery**, Fr.
152/C5 **Dondo**, Ang.
155/G3 **Dondo**, Moz.
153/E1 **Dondo**, Zaire
118/D6 **Dondra Head** (pt.), SrL.
93/H1 **Dondyushany**, Mol.
55/G9 **Donegal**, Ire.
55/G9 **Donegal** (bay), Ire.
56/A1 **Donegal** (co.), Ire.
60/B5 **Doneraile**, Ire.
99/L4 **Donets** (riv.), Rus., Ukr.
99/L3 **Donetsk**, Rus.
53/G4 **Donetsk**, Ukr.
99/J3 **Donetsk** (int'l arpt.), Ukr.
99/J4 **Donetsk Obl.**, Ukr.
116/E2 **Dong** (riv.), China
117/G4 **Dong** (riv.), China
119/G2 **Dong**, India
119/J5 **Dong** (riv.), Viet.
145/H5 **Donga** (riv.), Camr., Nga.
145/H5 **Donga**, Nga.
148/A4 **Donga** (riv.), Nga.
148/A4 **Dongai** (riv.), Camr.
132/B4 **Dongara**, Austl.
113/B2 **Dongbei** (plain), China
116/D3 **Dongchuan**, China
119/J3 **Dong Dang**, Viet.
115/E5 **Dongdongting Shan** (mtn.), China
115/D3 **Dong'e**, China
66/B5 **Dongen**, Neth.
78/C6 **Donges**, Fr.
117/F5 **Dongfang**, China
133/J5 **Donggali Consv. Park**, Austl.
113/C3 **Donggou**, China
117/G4 **Dongguan**, China
115/D3 **Dongguang**, China
113/D2 **Dong Ha**, Viet.
115/D4 **Donghai**, China
123/D2 **Donghen**, Laos
115/L8 **Donghezhen**, China
123/D2 **Dong Hoi**, Viet.
81/E5 **Dongio**, Swi.
117/G2 **Dongjia**, China
117/G2 **Dongjing** (riv.), China
113/B2 **Dongjingling**, China
117/H3 **Dongkeng**, China
121/G2 **Dongkya** (peak), India
117/G3 **Dongkyalong**, China
119/K3 **Dongli**, China
115/E2 **Dongliao** (riv.), China
114/E4 **Donglük**, China
123/D1 **Dongmen**, China
115/C4 **Dongming**, China
117/F4 **Dongnan** (mts.), China
123/D4 **Dong Noi** (riv.), Viet.
154/B2 **Dongo**, Ang.
81/F5 **Dongo**, It.
152/D2 **Dongo**, Zaire
153/E2 **Dongo**, Zaire
151/A3 **Dongobesh**, Tanz.
152/E2 **Dongo-Kuma**, Zaire
200/C2 **Dongola**, Il,US
152/D2 **Dongou**, Congo
115/D4 **Dongping**, China
115/D3 **Dongping** (lake), China
117/J2 **Dongshajiao**, China
115/L8 **Dongshan**, China
117/H4 **Dongshan** (isl.), China
117/G3 **Dongshao**, China
117/H4 **Dongsha** (Pratas) (isl.), China
115/B3 **Dongsheng**, China
115/E4 **Dongtai**, China
115/L9 **Dongtaio** (riv.), China
123/D2 **Dong Tau**, Viet.
117/G2 **Dongting** (lake), China
117/F2 **Dongtingxi**, China
154/B2 **Dongue**, Ang.
108/H2 **Dong Ujimqin Qi**, China
123/E1 **Dongxing**, China
115/D3 **Dongying**, China
108/E4 **Dongzhen**, China
115/D5 **Dongzhi**, China
174/Q10 **Donihue**, Chile
57/H6 **Donington**, Eng,UK
191/J2 **Doniphan**, Mo,US
92/E4 **Donji Komren**, Yugo.
178/C2 **Donjek** (riv.), Yk,Can
92/C3 **Donji Vakuf**, Bosn.
66/C5 **Donk**, Neth.
188/D4 **Don Martín**, Mex.
189/E4 **Donna**, Tx,US
86/A1 **Donnas**, It.
194/F5 **Donnelly**, Mn,US
184/C4 **Donner** (pass), Ca,US
70/A3 **Donnersberg** (peak), Ger.
184/D2 **Donner und Blitzen** (riv.), Or,US
132/B5 **Donnybrook**, Austl.
194/D3 **Donnybrook**, ND,US
80/D1 **Donon** (mtn.), Fr.
199/G4 **Donora**, Pa,US
84/A1 **Donoratico**, It.
186/B2 **Don Pedro** (res.), Ca,US
99/L4 **Donskoy**, Rus.
125/C2 **Donsol**, Phil.
78/D3 **Donville-les-Bains**, Fr.
116/B5 **Donyan** (riv.), Burma
70/C5 **Donzdorf**, Ger.
82/A4 **Donzère**, Fr.
74/E3 **Donzy**, Fr.
188/E2 **Doole**, Tx,US
132/C2 **Dooleena** (peak), Austl.
131/E4 **Doomadgee Abor. Community**, Austl.
131/E4 **Doomadgee Abor. Land**, Austl.
60/B4 **Doon**, Ire.
54/B6 **Doon** (riv.), Sc,UK
60/A4 **Doonbeg**, Ire.
60/A4 **Doonbeg** (riv.), Ire.
130/C3 **Doon Doon Abor. Land**, Austl.
177/H2 **Doonerak** (mt.), Ak,US
54/B6 **Doon, Loch** (lake), Sc,UK
202/D2 **Door** (pt.), La,US
195/L5 **Door** (pen.), Wi,US
66/C4 **Doorn**, Neth.
156/B3 **Doorn** (riv.), SAfr.
86/D1 **Doppo, Monte** (peak), It.
121/G1 **Doqên** (lake), China
132/D2 **Dora** (lake), Austl.
200/D4 **Dora**, Al,US
202/M6 **Dora** (lake), Fl,US
191/H2 **Dora**, Mo,US
190/C4 **Dora**, NM,US
86/A2 **Dora Baltea** (riv.), It.
77/F2 **Dorada** (coast), Sp.
82/D1 **Dora di Rhêmes** (riv.), It.
188/B4 **Dorado**, Mex.
107/K1 **Do Rāh** (pass), Afg.
114/B4 **Dorāh Ān** (pass), Pak.
75/G4 **Dora Riparia** (riv.), It.
201/M7 **Doraville**, Ga,US
196/E3 **Dorchester**, NB,Can
179/J2 **Dorchester** (cape), NW,Can
58/D5 **Dorchester**, Eng,UK
193/F5 **Dorchester**, Ne,US
206/D5 **Dorchester**, NJ,US
201/G4 **Dorchester**, SC,US
154/C4 **Dordabis**, Namb.
74/D4 **Dordogne** (riv.), Fr.
66/B5 **Dordrecht**, Neth.
156/D3 **Dordrecht**, SAfr.
74/F4 **Dore** (mts.), Fr.
74/E4 **Dore** (riv.), Fr.
54/B2 **Dores**, Sc,UK
170/D3 **Dores do Indaiá**, Braz.
71/F6 **Dorfen**, Ger.
71/F6 **Dorfen** (riv.), Ger.
90/A2 **Dorgali**, It.
108/C2 **Dörgön** (lake), Mong.
145/E3 **Dori**, Burk.
86/B4 **Doria**, It.
195/K3 **Dorion**, Can
199/J2 **Dorion**, Qu,Can
53/N8 **Dorking**, Eng,UK
80/D1 **Dorlisheim**, Fr.
66/D6 **Dormagen**, Ger.
68/C5 **Dormans**, Fr.
53/P8 **Dormans Land**, Eng,UK
208/G7 **Dormont**, Pa,US
80/D3 **Dornach**, Swi.
54/C2 **Dornbach Burn** (riv.), Sc,UK
81/F3 **Dornbirn**, Aus.
206/C2 **Dorney Park/Wildwater Kingdom**, Pa,US
70/B6 **Dornhan**, Ger.
72/B4 **Dornburg**, Ger.
86/B2 **Dorno**, It.
54/B1 **Dornoch**, Sc,UK
55/K8 **Dornoch Firth** (inlet), Sc,UK
70/C6 **Dornstadt**, Ger.
70/B6 **Dornstetten**, Ger.
145/E2 **Doro**, Mali
73/C4 **Dorog**, Hun.
94/G5 **Dorogobuzh**, Rus.
95/K2 **Dorogorskoye**, Rus.
93/H2 **Dorohoi**, Rom.
153/F2 **Doromo**, Zaire
82/C1 **Doron de Chaviere** (riv.), Fr.
206/D5 **Dorothy**, NJ,US
155/F3 **Dorowa Mining Lease**, Zim.
67/E3 **Dörpen**, Ger.
150/B2 **Dorra**, Djib.
191/E1 **Dorrance**, Ks,US
132/B3 **Dorre** (isl.), Austl.
59/E2 **Dorridge**, Eng,UK
135/E1 **Dorrigo**, Austl.
135/E1 **Dorrigo Nat'l Park**, Austl.
58/D1 **Dorrington**, Eng,UK
141/W17 **Dorsale** (mts.), Tun.
70/B2 **Dorsbach** (riv.), Ger.
58/D5 **Dorset** (co.), Eng,UK
66/D5 **Dorsten**, Ger.
80/B5 **Dortan**, Fr.
201/J2 **Dortches**, NC,US
67/E5 **Dortmund**, Ger.
67/E4 **Dortmund-Ems** (canal), Ger.
67/E5 **Dortmund** (Wickede) (int'l arpt.), Ger.
103/E1 **Dörtyol**, Turk.
67/F1 **Dorum**, Ger.

149/E4 **Doruma,** Zaire
197/N7 **Dorval,** Qu,Can
197/N7 **Dorval** (arpt.), Qu,Can
67/G3 **Dörverden,** Ger.
174/D5 **Dos Bahias** (cape), Arg.
187/H4 **Dos Cabezas,** Az,US
168/C2 **Dos de Mayo,** Peru
103/B1 **Döşemealtı,** Turk.
205/A2 **Dosewallips** (riv.), Wa,US
76/C4 **Dos Hermanas,** Sp.
111/H7 **Dōshi** (riv.), Japan
116/B3 **Dosing,** India
123/D1 **Do Son,** Viet.
186/B2 **Dos Palos,** Ca,US
93/G5 **Dospat,** Bul.
158/B2 **Dos Picachos, Cerro** (mt.), Mex.
174/D4 **Dos Pozos**
152/B2 **Dos Puntas** (cape), EqG.
164/C3 **Dos Quebradas,** Col.
172/B3 **Dos Reyes** (pt.), Chile
72/C2 **Dosse** (riv.), Ger.
145/F3 **Dosso,** Niger
145/F3 **Dosso** (dept.), Niger
87/F1 **Dosson,** It.
97/K3 **Dossor,** Kaz.
203/F2 **Dothan,** Al,US
177/K3 **Dot Lake,** Ak,US
67/F3 **Dötlingen,** Ger.
63/K4 **Dotnuva,** Lith.
81/E2 **Döttingen,** Swi.
182/C4 **Doty,** Wa,US
68/C3 **Douai,** Fr.
152/B1 **Douala,** Camr.
152/B1 **Douala** (int'l arpt.), Camr.
78/A4 **Douarnenez,** Fr.
78/A4 **Douarnenez** (bay), Fr.
134/D4 **Double Island** (pt.), Austl.
200/D3 **Double Springs,** Al,US
80/C4 **Doubs,** Fr.
80/C3 **Doubs** (dept.), Fr.
80/B4 **Doubs** (riv.), Fr.
130/B3 **Doubtful** (bay), Austl.
132/C5 **Doubtful Island** (bay), Austl.
136/C1 **Doubtless** (bay), N.Z.
189/G2 **Doucette,** Tx,US
68/C3 **Douchy-les-Mines,** Fr.
79/F1 **Doudeville,** Fr.
79/E6 **Doué-la-Fontaine,** Fr.
144/E3 **Douentza,** Mali
141/W17 **Dougga** (ruins), Tun.
191/G4 **Dougherty,** Tx,US
208/F7 **Doughty** (cr.), Oh,US
130/C3 **Douglas,** Austl.
156/C3 **Douglas,** SAfr.
56/D3 **Douglas,** IM,UK
54/C5 **Douglas,** Sc,UK
177/H4 **Douglas** (mt.), Ak,US
187/H5 **Douglas,** Az,US
203/G2 **Douglas,** Ga,US
201/L7 **Douglas** (co.), Ga,US
208/C1 **Douglas,** Ma,US
198/C3 **Douglas,** Mi,US
194/D4 **Douglas,** ND,US
201/F3 **Douglas** (lake), Tn,US
192/B2 **Douglas,** Wy,US
201/G3 **Douglas/Charlotte** (int'l arpt.), NC,US
182/D2 **Douglas Lake,** BC,Can
191/F2 **Douglass,** Ks,US
189/G2 **Douglass,** Tx,US
206/C3 **Douglassville,** Pa,US
196/E2 **Douglastown,** NB,Can
200/E4 **Douglasville,** Ga,US
201/L7 **Douglasville,** Ga,US
117/G1 **Dougou,** China
117/F3 **Doujiang,** China
152/B2 **Doula-Edéa Rsv.,** Camr.
80/B1 **Doulaincourt-Saucourt,** Fr.
68/B3 **Doullens,** Fr.
148/B4 **Doumé,** Camr.
148/B4 **Doumé** (riv.), Camr.
152/C3 **Doumé,** Gabon
55/N13 **Dounby,** Sc,UK
54/B4 **Doune,** Sc,UK
54/B4 **Doune** (mtn.), Sc,UK
71/G2 **Doupovské Hory** (mts.), Czh.
68/C3 **Dour,** Belg.
144/D3 **Doura,** Mali
170/C2 **Dourada** (uplands), Braz.
170/B4 **Dourados,** Braz.
170/B4 **Dourados** (riv.), Braz.
148/B3 **Dourbali,** Chad
53/S11 **Dourdan,** Fr.
74/E4 **Dourdou** (riv.), Fr.
148/D3 **Dourdoura,** Chad
142/E2 **Dourh, Jebel** (mtn.), Mor.
76/B2 **Douro** (riv.), Port.
88/B2 **Douro** (Duero) (riv.), Port.
78/B3 **Douron** (riv.), Fr.
205/P13 **Dousman,** Wi,US
80/C6 **Doussard,** Fr.
80/C5 **Douvaine,** Fr.
78/D2 **Douve** (riv.), Fr.
68/B2 **Douvrin,** Fr.
82/A2 **Doux** (riv.), Fr.
74/C4 **Douze** (riv.), Fr.
57/G6 **Dove** (riv.), Eng,UK
57/H3 **Dove** (riv.), Eng,UK
59/H2 **Dove** (riv.), Eng,UK
188/C3 **Dove** (mtn.), Tx,US
185/J5 **Dove Creek,** Co,US
135/C4 **Dover,** Austl.
132/E5 **Dover** (pt.), Austl.
68/A2 **Dover** (str.), Fr., UK*
59/H4 **Dover,** Eng,UK
191/H3 **Dover,** Ar,US
206/C5 **Dover** (cap.), De,US
202/L8 **Dover,** Fl,US
193/G4 **Dover,** Ks,US
208/C1 **Dover,** Ma,US
199/L3 **Dover,** NH,US
206/D2 **Dover,** NJ,US
208/F6 **Dover,** Oh,US
191/F3 **Dover,** Ok,US
206/B3 **Dover,** Pa,US
200/D2 **Dover,** Tn,US
206/C5 **Dover A.F.B.,** De,US
203/H2 **Dover Bluff,** Ga,US
196/C3 **Dover-Foxcroft,** Me,US
57/G6 **Doveridge,** Eng,UK
208/A2 **Dover Plains,** NY,US
96/D1 **Dovsk,** Bela.
191/G3 **Dow,** Ok,US
198/C4 **Dowagiac,** Mi,US
193/G3 **Dow City,** Ia,US
132/C4 **Dowerin,** Austl.
105/J2 **Dowghā'ī,** Iran
124/B2 **Dowi** (cape), Indo.
105/J4 **Dowlatābād,** Iran
183/J2 **Dowling,** Ab,Can
56/C3 **Down** (dist.), NI,UK
205/P16 **Downers Grove,** Il,US
204/B3 **Downey,** Ca,US
185/G2 **Downey,** Id,US
59/G1 **Downham Market,** Eng,UK
184/C4 **Downieville,** Ca,US
206/C3 **Downingtown,** Pa,US
56/C3 **Downpatrick,** NI,UK
191/E1 **Downs,** Ks,US
59/H4 **Downs, The** (harb.), Eng,UK
199/J3 **Downsville,** NY,US
59/E4 **Downton,** Eng,UK
193/H2 **Dows,** Ia,US
107/J1 **Dowshī,** Afg.
151/C1 **Doygaab,** Som.
184/C3 **Doyle,** Ca,US
208/F6 **Doylestown,** Oh,US
206/C3 **Doylestown,** Pa,US
190/A1 **Doyleville,** Co,US
110/C3 **Dōzen** (isl.), Japan
203/E2 **Dozier,** Al,US
79/E2 **Dozulé,** Fr.
142/C3 **Drâa** (cape), Mor.
142/D3 **Drâa, Hamada du** (plat.), Alg., Mor.
142/C3 **Drâa, Oued** (dry riv.), Alg., Mor.
82/B2 **Drac** (riv.), Fr.
170/C4 **Dracena,** Braz.
66/D2 **Drachten,** Neth.
93/G3 **Drăgănești-Olt,** Rom.
93/G3 **Drăgășani,** Rom.
92/F4 **Dragoman,** Bul.
165/F2 **Dragon's Mouth** (str.), Trin., Ven.
187/G4 **Dragoon,** Az,US
63/T9 **Dragør,** Den.
82/C5 **Draguignan,** Fr.
184/B2 **Drain,** Or,US
50/F8 **Drake** (passg.)
194/B2 **Drake,** Sk,Can
194/D4 **Drake,** ND,US
156/E3 **Drakensberg** (range), SAfr.
201/H2 **Drakes Branch,** Va,US
193/H3 **Drakesville,** Ia,US
153/G2 **Dramba,** Zaire
62/D2 **Drammen,** Nor.
82/C6 **Dramont, Cap du** (cape), Fr.
80/D5 **Drance** (riv.), Swi.
53/T10 **Drancy,** Fr.
62/C2 **Drangedal,** Nor.
80/C5 **Dranse** (riv.), Fr.
67/G6 **Dransfeld,** Ger.
56/B2 **Draperstown,** NI,UK
107/L2 **Drās,** India
75/L3 **Drau** (riv.), Aus.
92/C3 **Drava** (riv.), Eur.
68/B6 **Draveil,** Fr.
208/H7 **Dravosburg,** Pa,US
65/H2 **Drawa** (riv.), Pol.
65/H2 **Drawsko Pomorskie,** Pol.
194/F3 **Drayton,** ND,US
205/F6 **Drayton Plains,** Mi,US
182/G1 **Drayton Valley,** Ab,Can
72/E4 **Drebkau,** Ger.
54/B5 **Dreghorn,** Sc,UK
71/G5 **Dreiesselberg** (peak), Ger.
80/D2 **Dreisam** (riv.), Ger.
127/K4 **Drei Zinnen** (peak), PNG
67/E5 **Drensteinfurt,** Ger.
66/D3 **Drenthe** (prov.), Neth.
66/D3 **Drentse Hoofdvaart** (can.), Neth.
67/F3 **Drentwede,** Ger.
86/C2 **Dresano,** It.
198/E3 **Dresden,** On,Can
72/D5 **Dresden,** Ger.
72/D5 **Dresden** (arpt.), Ger.
198/E4 **Dresden,** Oh,US
200/C2 **Dresden,** Tn,US
193/H1 **Dresser,** Wi,US
68/A6 **Dreux,** Fr.
73/B1 **Dřevnice** (riv.), Czh.
200/B4 **Drew,** Ms,US
184/C2 **Drews** (res.), Or,US
184/D2 **Drewsey,** Or,US
191/G1 **Drexel,** Mo,US
189/F3 **Dreyer,** Tx,US
65/H2 **Drezdenko,** Pol.
66/C4 **Driebergen,** Neth.
69/H2 **Driedorf,** Ger.
206/C2 **Drifton-Woodside,** Pa,US
194/E4 **Drift Prairie** (grsld.), ND,US
185/H2 **Driggs,** Id,US
107/J4 **Drigh Road,** Pak.
60/A6 **Drimoleague,** Ire.
91/F2 **Drin** (gulf), Alb.
91/F1 **Drin** (riv.), Alb.
92/D3 **Drina** (riv.), Bosn., Yugo.
92/E5 **Drin i zi** (riv.), Alb.
189/E2 **Dripping Springs,** Tx,US
194/D4 **Driscoll,** ND,US
189/F4 **Driscoll,** Tx,US
189/H1 **Driskill** (mtn.), La,US
92/C4 **Drniš,** Cro.
87/D1 **Dro,** It.
62/D2 **Drøbak,** Nor.
92/F3 **Drobeta-Turnu Severin,** Rom.
67/G1 **Drochtersen,** Ger.
60/D2 **Drogheda,** Ire.
98/C1 **Drogichin,** Bela.
98/B3 **Drogobych,** Ukr.
60/D3 **Droichead Nuadh,** Ire.
58/D2 **Droitwich,** Eng,UK
93/H1 **Drokiya,** Mol.
69/G6 **Drolingen,** Fr.
67/E6 **Drolshagen,** Ger.
60/B1 **Dromahaire,** Ire.
82/B3 **Drôme** (dept.), Fr.
79/E2 **Drôme** (riv.), Fr.
60/B5 **Dromina,** Ire.
60/D2 **Dromiskin,** Ire.
56/A3 **Dromore** (riv.), Ire.
56/B3 **Dromore,** NI,UK
60/B1 **Dromore West,** Ire.
82/D4 **Dronero,** It.
57/G5 **Dronfield,** Eng,UK
54/B6 **Drongan,** Sc,UK
74/D4 **Dronne** (riv.), Fr.
66/C3 **Dronten,** Neth.
188/K6 **Drop,** Tx,US
74/D4 **Dropt** (riv.), Fr.
96/F1 **Droskovo,** Rus.
63/R7 **Drottingholm Palace,** Swe.
79/G4 **Droué,** Fr.
68/A6 **Drouette** (riv.), Fr.
72/C5 **Droyssig,** Ger.
86/A2 **Druento,** It.
201/M7 **Druid Hills,** Ga,US
201/J3 **Drum** (inlet), NC,US
56/C3 **Drumaness,** NI,UK
56/C2 **Drumbeg,** NI,UK
60/D2 **Drumcar,** Ire.
60/B5 **Drumcollogher,** Ire.
60/D2 **Drumcondra,** Ire.
183/H2 **Drumheller,** Ab,Can
60/B1 **Drumkeeran,** Ire.
60/D3 **Drumleck** (pt.), Ire.
60/C2 **Drumlish,** Ire.
134/B4 **Drummond** (peak), Austl.
133/G5 **Drummond** (pt.), Austl.
134/B4 **Drummond** (range), Austl.
196/D2 **Drummond,** NB,Can
185/H2 **Drummond,** Id,US
198/E1 **Drummond** (isl.), Mi,US
183/H4 **Drummond,** Mt,US
195/J4 **Drummond,** Wi,US
200/C3 **Drummonds,** Tn,US
196/A3 **Drummondville,** Qu,Can
56/D2 **Drummore,** Sc,UK
54/B2 **Drumnadrochit,** Sc,UK
56/A2 **Drumnakilly,** NI,UK
54/B3 **Drumochter, Pass of** (pass), Sc,UK
191/F3 **Drumright,** Ok,US
60/B1 **Drumshanbo,** Ire.
60/B2 **Drumsna,** Ire.
66/C5 **Drunen,** Neth.
194/F2 **Drunken** (pt.), Mb,Can
57/G1 **Druridge** (bay), Eng,UK
69/G6 **Drusenheim,** Fr.
63/K4 **Druskininkai,** Lith.
66/C5 **Druten,** Neth.
63/M4 **Druya,** Bela.
114/D2 **Druzhba,** Kaz.
99/G1 **Druzhba,** Ukr.
99/J3 **Druzhkovka,** Ukr.
92/C3 **Drvar,** Bosn.
65/K2 **Drwęca** (riv.), Pol.
205/M10 **Dry** (cr.), Ca,US
205/M9 **Dry** (cr.), Ca,US
194/E3 **Dry** (lake), ND,US
189/M9 **Dry** (cr.), Tx,US
185/J1 **Dry** (cr.), Wy,US
93/G4 **Dryanovo,** Bul.
190/C2 **Dry Cimarron** (riv.), US
177/K3 **Dry Creek,** Yk,Can
202/B2 **Dry Creek,** La,US
195/H3 **Dryden,** On,Can
205/F6 **Dryden,** Mi,US
199/H3 **Dryden,** NY,US
188/C2 **Dryden,** Tx,US
201/F2 **Dryden,** Va,US
192/B2 **Dry Fork** (cr.), Wy,US
58/C2 **Drygarn Fawr** (mtn.), Wal,UK
186/E2 **Dry Lake,** Nv,US
54/B4 **Drymen,** Sc,UK
189/H2 **Dry Prong,** La,US
200/E1 **Dry Ridge,** Ky,US
201/F1 **Dry Run,** Oh,US
130/B3 **Drysdale** (riv.), Austl.
130/B3 **Drysdale River Nat'l Park,** Austl.
203/G5 **Dry Tortugas** (keys), Fl,US
145/H5 **Dschang,** Camr.
115/B4 **Du** (riv.), China
58/B3 **Duad** (riv.), Wal,UK
134/C3 **Duaringa,** Austl.
162/D3 **Duarte** (peak), DRep.
204/G7 **Duarte,** Ca,US
104/C5 **Ḑubā,** SAr.
189/H1 **Dubach,** La,US
176/H3 **Dubawnt** (lake), Can.
178/F2 **Dubawnt** (lake), NW,Can
178/F2 **Dubawnt** (riv.), NW,Can
107/G3 **Dubayy,** UAE
135/D2 **Dubbo,** Austl.
153/G2 **Dubele,** Zaire
81/E3 **Dübendorf,** Swi.
72/C4 **Dübener Heide** (reg.), Ger.
72/D6 **Dubí,** Czh.
81/F5 **Dubino,** It.
60/D3 **Dublin** (bay), Ire.
60/D3 **Dublin** (cap.), Ire.
60/D3 **Dublin** (co.), Ire.
205/L11 **Dublin,** Ca,US
201/F4 **Dublin,** Ga,US
206/B4 **Dublin,** Md,US
198/E4 **Dublin,** Oh,US
206/C3 **Dublin,** Pa,US
189/E1 **Dublin,** Tx,US
201/G2 **Dublin,** Va,US
60/D3 **Dublin** (Collinstown) (int'l arpt.), Ire.
94/H4 **Dubna,** Rus.
73/C2 **Dubnica nad Váhom,** Slvk.
98/C2 **Dubno,** Ukr.
185/G1 **Dubois,** Id,US
199/G4 **Du Bois,** Pa,US
185/J2 **Dubois,** Wy,US
206/A1 **Duboistown,** Pa,US
93/J2 **Dubossary,** Mol.
93/J2 **Dubossary** (res.), Mol.
97/G2 **Dubovskiy,** Rus.
99/M4 **Dubovskoye,** Rus.
97/J1 **Dubovyy Umët,** Rus.
121/F4 **Dubra,** India
121/F4 **Dubrājpur,** India
144/B4 **Dubréka,** Gui.
98/D2 **Dubrovitsa,** Ukr.
96/E1 **Dubrovka,** Rus.
92/D4 **Dubrovnik,** Cro.
91/F1 **Dubrovnik** (int'l arpt.), Cro.
63/P4 **Dubrovno,** Bela.
148/D4 **Dubulu,** Zaire
193/J2 **Dubuque,** Ia,US
78/D3 **Ducey,** Fr.
71/G1 **Duchcov,** Czh.
185/H3 **Duchesne,** Ut,US
185/H3 **Duchesne** (riv.), Ut,US
133/H2 **Duchess,** Austl.
183/J2 **Duchess,** Ab,Can
139/N7 **Ducie** (isl.), Pitc.
50/C7 **Ducie** (isl.), UK
194/D2 **Duck** (mt.), Mb,Can
205/E6 **Duck** (lake), Mi,US
185/F4 **Duck** (cr.), Nv,US
200/D3 **Duck** (riv.), Tn,US
188/L7 **Duck** (cr.), Tx,US
205/A2 **Duckabush** (riv.), Wa,US
194/D1 **Duck Bay,** Mb,Can
200/C4 **Duck Hill,** Ms,US
183/L1 **Duck Lake,** Sk,Can
200/E3 **Ducktown,** Tn,US
184/E2 **Duck Valley Ind. Res.,** Or,US
184/F4 **Duckwater,** Nv,US
184/F4 **Duckwater Ind. Res.,** Nv,US
79/F2 **Duclair,** Fr.
123/D3 **Duc Lap,** Viet.
186/C3 **Ducor,** Ca,US
123/E3 **Duc Pho,** Viet.
123/D4 **Duc Phong,** Viet.
164/C4 **Duda** (riv.), Col.
57/E3 **Dudden** (riv.), Eng,UK
69/F5 **Dudelange,** Lux.
70/B4 **Dudenhofen,** Ger.
67/H5 **Duderstadt,** Ger.
120/D3 **Dūdhi,** India
121/F2 **Dudh Kosi** (riv.), Nepal
120/C1 **Dudhwa Nat'l Park,** India
174/E2 **Dudignac,** Arg.
80/D4 **Düdingen,** Swi.
100/J3 **Dudinka,** Rus.
58/D2 **Dudley,** Eng,UK
208/C1 **Dudley,** Ma,US
150/C4 **Dudub,** Eth.
73/B3 **Dudváh** (riv.), Slvk.
68/C1 **Dudzele,** Belg.
152/D4 **Due,** Zaire
144/D5 **Duékoué,** IvC.
76/C2 **Dueñas,** Sp.
191/G2 **Duenweg,** Mo,US
170/C1 **Dueré,** Braz.
76/C2 **Duero** (Douro) (riv.), Sp.
201/F3 **Due West,** SC,US
151/B2 **Dufaja** (dry riv.), Kenya
137/W **Dufek Massive** (mtn.), Ant.
138/F5 **Duff** (isl.), Sol.
68/D1 **Duffel,** Belg.
197/Q8 **Dufferin** (co.), On,Can
57/G6 **Duffield,** Eng,UK
197/Q9 **Duff's Corner,** On,Can
54/C2 **Dufftown,** Sc,UK
86/A1 **Dufour, Punta** (peak), It.
80/D6 **Dufourspitze** (peak), Swi.
121/H3 **Dugachhi,** Bang.
194/F3 **Dugald,** Mb,Can
153/F2 **Dugbia,** Zaire
202/B1 **Dugdemona** (riv.), La,US
198/C5 **Dugger,** In,US
92/B3 **Dugi Otok** (isl.), Cro.
69/E5 **Dugny-sur-Meuse,** Fr.
92/C3 **Dugo Selo,** Cro.
150/B3 **Dugu,** Eth.
185/G3 **Dugway,** Ut,US
185/G3 **Dugway Prov. Gnds.,** Ut,US
54/A2 **Duich, Loch** (inlet), Sc,UK
165/E4 **Duida** (peak), Ven.
165/E4 **Duida Marahuaca Nat'l Park,** Ven.
131/F3 **Duifken** (pt.), Austl.
67/G5 **Duingen,** Ger.
87/G1 **Duino,** It.
66/D6 **Duisburg,** Ger.
164/C3 **Duitama,** Col.
66/D5 **Duiven,** Neth.
151/C1 **Dujuuma,** Som.
150/A4 **Dukafulu,** Eth.
149/H2 **Dukambīya,** Eth.
191/H2 **Duke,** Mo,US
139/L7 **Duke of Gloucester** (isls.), FrPol.
54/B4 **Duke's** (pass), Sc,UK
208/D3 **Dukes** (co.), Ma,US
149/F4 **Duk Fadiat,** Sudan
106/F3 **Dukhān,** Qatar
65/L4 **Dukielska, Przełęcz** (Dukla) (pass), Pol.
65/L4 **Dukla** (Przełęcz Dukielska) (pass), Pol.
63/M4 **Dūkštas,** Lith.
148/D4 **Dula,** Zaire
202/C3 **Dulac,** La,US
108/D4 **Dulan,** China
172/D3 **Dulce** (riv.), Arg.
161/F4 **Dulce** (gulf), CR
190/A2 **Dulce,** NM,US
161/E3 **Dulce Nombre de Culmí,** Hon.
150/A2 **Dule,** Eth.
60/D2 **Duleek,** Ire.
93/H4 **Dŭlgopol,** Bul.
115/H7 **Duliu,** China
117/F3 **Duliu** (riv.), China
201/J1 **Dulles** (int'l arpt.), Va,US
199/H5 **Dulles** (Washington) (int'l arpt.), Va,US
122/A2 **Dullewāla,** Pak.
156/Q12 **Dullstroom,** SAfr.
67/E5 **Dülmen,** Ger.
54/C2 **Dulnain** (riv.), Sc,UK
116/B3 **Dulong** (pass), China
123/E4 **Du Long,** Viet.
93/H4 **Dulovo,** Bul.
125/C4 **Duluguin** (pt.), Phil.
201/M6 **Duluth,** Ga,US
195/H4 **Duluth,** Mn,US
58/C4 **Dulverton,** Eng,UK
103/E3 **Dūmā,** Syria
103/G7 **Dūmā,** WBnk.
125/C4 **Dumagasa** (pt.), Phil.
125/C3 **Dumaguete City,** Phil.
124/C2 **Dumai,** Indo.
125/C4 **Dumalinao,** Phil.
125/C3 **Dumanjug,** Phil.
125/B3 **Dumaran,** Phil.
125/B3 **Dumaran** (isl.), Phil.
135/D1 **Dumaresq** (riv.), Austl.
191/J4 **Dumas,** Ar,US
190/D3 **Dumas,** Tx,US
103/E3 **Ḑumayr,** Syria
54/B5 **Dumbarton,** Sc,UK
154/B1 **Dumbi,** Ang.
152/D4 **Dumbi,** Zaire
65/K4 **Ďumbier** (peak), Slvk.
132/C5 **Dumbleyung,** Austl.
148/A4 **Dumbo,** Camr.
93/G2 **Dumbrăveni,** Rom.
204/B2 **Dume** (pt.), Ca,US
117/H3 **Dumei,** China
56/E1 **Dumfries,** Sc,UK
54/C6 **Dumfries & Galloway** (reg.), Sc,UK
96/E1 **Duminichi,** Rus.
121/F3 **Dumka,** India
97/G4 **Dumlu,** Turk.
72/A2 **Dumme** (riv.), Ger.
72/B2 **Dumme** (riv.), Ger.
67/F3 **Dümmer** (lake), Ger.
179/J4 **Dumoine** (lake), Qu,Can
207/E2 **Dumont,** NJ,US
137/K **Dumont d'Urville,** Ant.
120/E3 **Dumraon,** India
121/F4 **Dumri,** India
103/B4 **Dumyāṭ** (gov.), Egypt
103/B4 **Dumyāṭ** (Damietta), Egypt
73/C5 **Duna** (Danube) (riv.), Hun.
73/C6 **Dunaföldvár,** Hun.
73/D5 **Dunaharaszti,** Hun.
73/B4 **Dunaj** (Danube) (riv.), Slvk.
65/L4 **Dunajec** (riv.), Pol.
73/B4 **Dunajská Streda,** Slvk.
73/D4 **Dunakeszi,** Hun.
73/B6 **Dunántúl** (reg.), Hun.
60/D2 **Dunany** (pt.), Ire.
73/C6 **Dunapataj,** Hun.
89/L1 **Dunării** (delta), Rom.
92/D2 **Dunaszekcso,** Hun.
73/D6 **Dunatetétlen,** Hun.
73/D5 **Duna-Tisza** (can.), Hun.
73/C6 **Dunaújváros,** Hun.
73/C6 **Dunavecse,** Hun.
73/D6 **Duna-Völgyi** (can.), Hun.
73/D5 **Duna-Völgyi-fő** (can.), Hun.
92/F4 **Dunavtsi,** Bul.
98/D3 **Dunayevtsy,** Ukr.
134/A2 **Dunbar,** Austl.
54/D5 **Dunbar,** Sc,UK
194/A2 **Dunblane,** Sk,Can
54/C4 **Dunblane,** Sc,UK
60/D3 **Dunboyne,** Ire.
182/C3 **Duncan,** BC,Can
187/H4 **Duncan,** Az,US
200/B3 **Duncan,** Ms,US
191/F3 **Duncan,** Ok,US
60/D5 **Duncannon,** Ire.
206/A3 **Duncannon,** Pa,US
55/K7 **Duncansby Head** (pt.), Sc,UK
189/F1 **Duncanville,** Tx,US
63/K3 **Dundaga,** Lat.
198/F2 **Dundalk,** On,Can
60/D2 **Dundalk,** Ire.
60/D2 **Dundalk** (bay), Ire.
206/B5 **Dundalk,** Md,US
132/D5 **Dundas** (lake), Austl.
130/C2 **Dundas** (str.), Austl.
179/R7 **Dundas** (pen.), NW,Can
197/R9 **Dundas,** On,Can
198/B5 **Dundas,** Il,US
198/E5 **Dundas,** Oh,US
157/E3 **Dundee,** SAfr.
54/D4 **Dundee,** Sc,UK
54/C4 **Dundee** (arpt.), Sc,UK
202/M7 **Dundee,** Fl,US
203/H3 **Dundee,** Fl,US
205/E8 **Dundee,** Mi,US
200/B3 **Dundee,** Ms,US
199/H3 **Dundee,** NY,US
190/E4 **Dundee,** Tx,US
54/B5 **Dundonald,** Sc,UK
56/C3 **Dundrum,** NI,UK
56/C3 **Dundrum** (bay), NI,UK
120/D2 **Dundwa** (range), Nepal
136/B4 **Dunedin,** N.Z.
202/K7 **Dunedin,** Fl,US
203/G3 **Dunedin,** Fl,US
135/D2 **Dunedoo,** Austl.
207/H9 **Dunellen,** NJ,US
184/A2 **Dunes City,** Or,US
55/H9 **Dunfanaghy,** Ire.
54/C4 **Dunfermline,** Sc,UK
135/D1 **Dungalear Station,** Austl.
198/F3 **Dungannon,** On,Can
56/B2 **Dungannon,** NI,UK
56/B3 **Dungannon** (dist.), NI,UK
118/B3 **Dungarpur,** India
60/C5 **Dungarvan,** Ire.
60/C5 **Dungarvan** (harb.), Ire.
71/F5 **Dungau** (reg.), Ger.
175/K8 **Dungeness** (pt.), Arg.
59/G5 **Dungeness** (pt.), Eng,UK
182/C3 **Dungeness,** Wa,US
56/B2 **Dungiven,** NI,UK
55/G9 **Dunglow,** Ire.
135/D2 **Dungog,** Austl.
153/G2 **Dungu,** Zaire
153/G2 **Dungu** (riv.), Zaire
199/K2 **Dunham,** Qu,Can
109/K3 **Dunhua,** China
108/C3 **Dunhuang,** China
54/C3 **Dunkeld,** Sc,UK
60/B3 **Dunkellin** (riv.), Ire.
68/B1 **Dunkerque** (Dunkirk), Fr.
58/C4 **Dunkery** (hill), Eng,UK
198/D4 **Dunkirk,** In,US
199/G3 **Dunkirk,** NY,US
68/B1 **Dunkirk** (Dunkerque), Fr.
182/C1 **Dunkley,** BC,Can
145/E5 **Dunkwa,** Gha.
60/D3 **Dún Laoghaire,** Ire.
193/G3 **Dunlap,** Ia,US
200/E3 **Dunlap,** Tn,US
60/D3 **Dunlavin,** Ire.
194/C2 **Dunleath,** Sk,Can
60/D2 **Dunleer,** Ire.
56/B2 **Dunloy,** NI,UK
60/A6 **Dunmanus** (bay), Ire.
60/A6 **Dunmanway,** Ire.
199/H1 **Dunmoine** (lake), Qu,Can
199/H1 **Dunmoine** (riv.), Qu,Can
60/B2 **Dunmore,** Ire.
199/J4 **Dunmore,** Pa,US
60/D5 **Dunmore East,** Ire.
56/B2 **Dunmurry,** NI,UK
189/J1 **Dunn,** La,US
201/H3 **Dunn,** NC,US
56/A2 **Dunnamanagh,** NI,UK
56/B2 **Dunnamore,** NI,UK
193/G2 **Dunnell,** Mn,US
203/G3 **Dunnellon,** Fl,US
80/D3 **Dünnern** (riv.), Swi.
55/N13 **Dunnet Head** (pt.), Sc,UK
54/C4 **Dunning,** Sc,UK
70/B6 **Dunningen,** Ger.
57/H4 **Dunnington,** Eng,UK
156/Q13 **Dunnottar,** SAfr.
201/J2 **Dunnsville,** Va,US
197/R10 **Dunnville,** On,Can
135/B3 **Dunolly,** Austl.
54/B5 **Dunoon,** Sc,UK
147/F5 **Dunqulah,** Sudan
106/C4 **Dunqunāb,** Sudan
56/D2 **Dunragit,** Sc,UK
54/C5 **Dun Rig** (mtn.), Sc,UK
54/D5 **Duns,** Sc,UK
132/B5 **Dunsborough,** Austl.
56/E1 **Dunscore,** Sc,UK
56/B1 **Dunseverick,** NI,UK
60/D3 **Dunshaughlin,** Ire.
184/B3 **Dunsmuir,** Ca,US
59/F3 **Dunstable,** Eng,UK
182/E1 **Dunster,** BC,Can
69/E5 **Dun-sur-Meuse,** Fr.
54/B5 **Duntocher,** Sc,UK
54/B6 **Dunure,** Sc,UK
197/L2 **Dunville,** Nf,Can
200/E4 **Dunwoody,** Ga,US
201/M7 **Dunwoody,** Ga,US
109/J1 **Duobukur** (riv.), China
116/E4 **Duojing,** China
108/H3 **Duolun,** China
205/P16 **Du Page** (co.), Il,US
205/P16 **Du Page** (riv.), Il,US
205/P16 **Du Page, East Branch** (riv.), Il,US
198/D5 **Dupont,** In,US
206/C1 **Dupont,** Pa,US
72/B1 **Dūpow,** Ger.
192/D1 **Dupree,** SD,US
132/B2 **Dupuy** (cape), Austl.
167/F4 **Duque Bacelar,** Braz.
171/E4 **Duque de Caxias,** Braz.
175/J7 **Duque de York** (isl.), Chile
208/H7 **Duquesne,** Pa,US
195/H4 **Duquette,** Mn,US
193/K4 **Du Quoin,** Il,US
103/D4 **Dūrā,** WBnk.
130/B4 **Durack** (range), Austl.
130/B4 **Durack** (riv.), Austl.
104/C1 **Durağan,** Turk.
103/D1 **Durak,** Turk.
190/B3 **Duran,** NM,US
82/B5 **Durance** (riv.), Fr.
198/E3 **Durand,** Mi,US
193/J1 **Durand,** Wi,US
158/D3 **Durango,** Mex.
188/B4 **Durango** (state), Mex.
76/D1 **Durango,** Sp.
187/J2 **Durango,** Co,US
132/C5 **Duranillin,** Austl.
200/C4 **Durant,** Ms,US
191/F4 **Durant,** Ok,US
175/F2 **Durazno,** Uru.
175/F2 **Durazno** (dept.), Uru.
157/E3 **Durban,** SAfr.
157/E3 **Durban** (Louis Botha) (int'l arpt.), SAfr.
156/L10 **Durbanville,** SAfr.
63/J3 **Durbe,** Lat.
80/C1 **Durbion** (riv.), Fr.
69/E3 **Durbuy,** Belg.
76/D4 **Dúrcal,** Sp.
92/C2 **Đurđevac,** Cro.
92/E3 **Đurđevo,** Yugo.
150/B3 **Durdur** (dry riv.), Som.
108/B2 **Düre,** China
107/J3 **Dureji,** Pak.
69/F2 **Düren,** Ger.
118/D3 **Durg,** India
121/F4 **Durgāpur,** India
121/G3 **Durgāpur,** India
66/C4 **Durgerdam,** Neth.
198/F2 **Durham,** On,Can
197/T8 **Durham** (co.), On,Can
57/G2 **Durham,** Eng,UK
57/F2 **Durham** (co.), Eng,UK
184/C4 **Durham,** Ca,US
208/B3 **Durham,** Ct,US
193/F4 **Durham,** Ks,US
193/J4 **Durham,** Mo,US
201/H3 **Durham,** NC,US
199/L3 **Durham,** NH,US
196/D2 **Durham Bridge,** NB,Can
133/J3 **Durham Downs,** Austl.
124/C2 **Duri,** Indo.
59/E5 **Durlston Head** (pt.), Eng,UK
106/E4 **Ḑurmā,** SAr.
68/D1 **Durme** (riv.), Belg.
92/D4 **Durmitor Nat'l Park,** Yugo.
142/B5 **Durnford** (pt.), WSah.
73/A3 **Dürnkrut,** Aus.
54/A5 **Duror,** Sc,UK
80/D3 **Dürrenroth,** Swi.
91/F2 **Durrës,** Alb.
59/E4 **Durrington,** Eng,UK
70/D6 **Dürrlauingen,** Ger.
60/C4 **Durrow,** Ire.
58/D3 **Dursley,** Eng,UK
104/B2 **Dursunbey,** Turk.
79/E5 **Durtal,** Fr.
149/F4 **Duru,** Zaire
148/C4 **Durugu,** Zaire
150/C3 **Durukhsi,** Eth.
105/M6 **Durusu,** Turk.
105/M6 **Durusu** (lake), Turk.
147/H1 **Duruz, Jabal ad** (mtn.), Syria
73/C3 **Ďur, Veľký,** Slvk.
127/J4 **D'Urville** (cape), Indo.
136/C3 **D'Urville** (isl.), N.Z.
150/C4 **Dusa Marreb** (Dhuusamarreeb), Som.
92/E4 **Dusanovo,** Yugo.
63/L4 **Dusetos,** Lith.
107/H1 **Dushak,** Trkm.
117/E3 **Dushan,** China
115/D2 **Du Shan** (peak), China
100/G6 **Dushanbe** (cap.), Taj.
97/H4 **Dusheti,** Geo.
117/E3 **Dushui** (riv.), China
136/A4 **Dusky** (sound), N.Z.
66/D6 **Düsseldorf,** Ger.
66/D6 **Düsseldorf** (int'l arpt.), Ger.
107/J1 **Dusti,** Taj.
191/F3 **Dustin,** Ok,US
65/J3 **Duszniki-Zdrój,** Pol.
182/F2 **Dutch** (cr.), BC,Can
57/H4 **Dutch** (riv.), Eng,UK
177/E5 **Dutch Harbor,** Ak,US
185/J3 **Dutch John,** Ut,US
206/B3 **Dutch Wonderland,** Pa,US
67/F4 **Düte** (riv.), Ger.
104/D2 **Dutluca,** Turk.
154/D5 **Dutlwe,** Bots.
156/L10 **Dutoitspiek** (peak), SAfr.
95/N3 **Dutovo,** Rus.
145/H4 **Dutse,** Nga.
145/H4 **Dutsen Wai,** Nga.
145/G3 **Dutsin-Ma,** Nga.
198/F3 **Dutton,** On,Can
183/J4 **Dutton,** Mt,US
185/G4 **Dutton** (mt.), Ut,US
145/F4 **Dutukpene,** Gha.
205/D2 **Duvall,** Wa,US
92/C4 **Duvno,** Bosn.
114/D4 **Düxanbibazar,** China
208/D1 **Duxbury,** Ma,US
117/H4 **Duxun,** China
117/E3 **Duyang,** China
117/E3 **Duyun,** China
143/H2 **Düz,** Tun.
93/K5 **Düzce,** Turk.
104/D2 **Düzici,** Turk.
93/G4 **Dve Mogili,** Bul.
94/H2 **Dvina** (bay), Rus.
95/K3 **Dvinskoy,** Rus.
71/H4 **Dvořiště** (lake), Czh.
73/B3 **Dvorníky,** Slvk.
73/C4 **Dvory nad Žitavou,** Slvk.
118/A3 **Dwārka,** India
121/F4 **Dwārkeswar** (riv.), India
198/B4 **Dwight,** Il,US
193/F4 **Dwight,** Ks,US
182/G4 **Dwoshak** (res.), Id,US
187/H4 **Dwyer** (Faywood), NM,US
56/D6 **Dwyfor** (riv.), Wal,UK
156/C4 **Dwyka** (riv.), SAfr.
96/E1 **Dyat'kovo,** Rus.
96/C1 **Dyatlovo,** Bela.
62/D3 **Dybvad,** Den.
195/L5 **Dyckesville,** Wi,US
179/K2 **Dyer** (cape), NW,Can
175/J7 **Dyer** (cape), Chile
198/C4 **Dyer,** In,US
186/C2 **Dyer,** Nv,US
200/C2 **Dyer,** Tn,US
200/C2 **Dyersburg,** Tn,US
193/J2 **Dyersville,** Ia,US
200/B3 **Dyess,** Ar,US
188/E1 **Dyess A.F.B.,** Tx,US
58/B3 **Dyfed** (co.), Wal,UK
56/D6 **Dyffryn,** Wal,UK
58/C1 **Dyfi** (riv.), Wal,UK
73/A2 **Dyje** (riv.), Czh.
131/H2 **Dyke Ackland** (bay), PNG
97/G4 **Dykh-tau, Gora** (peak), Rus.
64/C3 **Dyle** (riv.), Belg.
68/D2 **Dyle** (Dijle) (riv.), Belg.
71/F3 **Dyleň** (peak), Czh.
65/K2 **Dylewska** (peak), Pol.
94/C5 **Dylewska Gora** (peak), Pol.
59/G4 **Dymchurch,** Eng,UK
98/F2 **Dymer,** Ukr.
134/C3 **Dysart,** Austl.
194/B2 **Dysart,** Sk,Can
193/H2 **Dysart,** Ia,US
156/C4 **Dysseldorp,** SAfr.
97/H4 **Dyul'tydag, Gora** (peak), Rus.
95/M5 **Dyurtyuli,** Rus.
155/G2 **Dzalanyama** (range), Malw., Moz.
157/J6 **Dzamandzar,** Madg.
157/H6 **Dzaoudzi** (cap.), May.
157/H6 **Dzaoudzi** (int'l arpt.), May.
108/C2 **Dzavhan** (riv.), Mong.
99/J4 **Dzenzik** (pt.), Ukr.
96/F3 **Dzenzik, Mys** (pt.), Ukr.
108/C2 **Dzereg,** Mong.
63/M5 **Dzerzhinsk,** Bela.
53/H3 **Dzerzhinsk,** Rus.
98/D2 **Dzerzhinsk,** Ukr.
99/J3 **Dzerzhinsk,** Ukr.
114/B3 **Dzhalal-Abad,** Kyr.
109/J1 **Dzhalinda,** Rus.
97/K2 **Dzhambeyty,** Kaz.
114/B3 **Dzhambul,** Kaz.
97/K4 **Dzhanga,** Trkm.
99/H5 **Dzhankoy,** Ukr.
97/H2 **Dzhanybek,** Kaz.
99/G4 **Dzharylgach** (gulf), Ukr.
93/G5 **Dzhebel,** Bul.
97/H5 **Dzhebrail,** Azer.
105/F2 **Dzhermuk,** Arm.
97/M1 **Dzhetygara,** Kaz.
114/A2 **Dzhezkazgan,** Kaz.
114/B4 **Dzhirgatal',** Taj.
100/G5 **Dzhizak,** Uzb.
99/K5 **Dzhubga,** Rus.
101/P4 **Dzhugdzhur** (range), Rus.
97/H5 **Dzhul'fa,** Azer.
100/G5 **Dzhusaly,** Kaz.
65/L2 **Działdowo,** Pol.
159/H5 **Dzibalchén,** Mex.
159/H4 **Dzibilchaltún** (ruins), Mex.
159/H4 **Dzidzantún,** Mex.
65/J3 **Dzierżoniów,** Pol.
159/H4 **Dzitbalché,** Mex.
108/B3 **Dzungarian** (basin), China
114/D3 **Dzungarian Gate** (pass), China
108/G3 **Dzüünbayan,** Mong.
108/E2 **Dzüünbayan-Ulaan,** Mong.
114/F2 **Dzüüngovĭ,** Mong.
108/D2 **Dzüünhangay,** Mong.
108/F2 **Dzüünharaa,** Mong.
108/F2 **Dzuunmod,** Mong.

**E**

192/C4 **Eads,** Co,US
195/H5 **Eagan,** Mn,US
195/P7 **Eagan,** Mn,US
187/H3 **Eagar,** Az,US
179/L3 **Eagle** (riv.), Nf,Can
195/H3 **Eagle** (lake), On,Can
183/K2 **Eagle** (cr.), Sk,Can
183/K1 **Eagle** (hills), Sk,Can
60/A5 **Eagle** (mtn.), Ire.
177/K3 **Eagle,** Ak,US
184/C3 **Eagle** (lake), Ca,US
186/E4 **Eagle** (mts.), Ca,US
186/C1 **Eagle** (peak), Ca,US
185/K4 **Eagle,** Co,US
185/K4 **Eagle** (riv.), Co,US
184/E2 **Eagle,** Id,US
200/E1 **Eagle** (cr.), Ky,US
195/J4 **Eagle** (mtn.), Mn,US
193/F3 **Eagle,** Ne,US
190/B4 **Eagle** (cr.), NM,US
208/G5 **Eagle** (cr.), Oh,US
188/B2 **Eagle** (peak), Tx,US
189/N9 **Eagle** (pt.), Tx,US
205/P14 **Eagle,** Wi,US
205/P14 **Eagle** (lake), Wi,US
185/H1 **Eagle** (peak), Wy,US
195/G4 **Eagle Bend,** Mn,US
186/D3 **Eagle Crags** (mtn.), Ca,US
193/H2 **Eagle Grove,** Ia,US
202/M8 **Eagle Lake,** Fl,US
196/C2 **Eagle Lake,** Me,US
189/F3 **Eagle Lake,** Tx,US
191/H4 **Eagle Mills,** Ar,US
188/K7 **Eagle Mtn.** (lake), Tx,US
188/D3 **Eagle Pass,** Tx,US
184/B2 **Eagle Point,** Or,US
195/K5 **Eagle River,** Wi,US
201/H2 **Eagle Rock,** Va,US
57/E1 **Eaglesfield,** Sc,UK
54/B5 **Eaglesham,** Sc,UK
191/G3 **Eagleton,** Ar,US
191/G3 **Eagletown,** Ok,US
184/C3 **Eagleville,** Ca,US
193/H3 **Eagleville,** Mo,US
130/A2 **Eahun,** Indo.
200/C3 **Eaker A.F.B.,** Ar,US
191/E3 **Eakly,** Ok,US
53/M7 **Ealing** (bor.), Eng,UK
57/F4 **Earby,** Eng,UK
195/H2 **Ear Falls,** On,Can
59/G2 **Earith,** Eng,UK
191/J3 **Earle,** Ar,US
207/D3 **Earle Nav. Weap. Ctr.,** NJ,US
194/B2 **Earl Grey,** Sk,Can
186/C3 **Earlimart,** Ca,US
193/G3 **Earling,** Ia,US
200/D2 **Earlington,** Ky,US
59/F2 **Earls Barton,** Eng,UK
191/F3 **Earlsboro,** Ok,US
59/G3 **Earls Colne,** Eng,UK
54/D4 **Earlsferry,** Sc,UK
54/B4 **Earl's Seat** (mtn.), Sc,UK
54/D5 **Earlston,** Sc,UK
59/H2 **Earl Stonham,** Eng,UK
196/F3 **Earltown,** NS,Can
193/J2 **Earlville,** Ia,US
193/K3 **Earlville,** Il,US
193/G2 **Early,** Ia,US
188/E2 **Early,** Tx,US
54/C4 **Earn** (riv.), Sc,UK
54/B4 **Earn, Loch** (lake), Sc,UK
136/B4 **Earnslaw** (peak), N.Z.
186/E3 **Earp,** Ca,US
57/G2 **Easington,** Eng,UK
57/G3 **Easingwold,** Eng,UK
60/B1 **Easky,** Ire.
201/F3 **Easley,** SC,US
132/D4 **East** (mt.), Austl.
132/D4 **East** (peak), Austl.
197/G2 **East** (pt.), PE,Can
136/D2 **East** (cape), N.Z.
177/B6 **East** (cape), Ak,US
186/E4 **East** (mesa), Ca,US
203/H5 **East** (cape), Fl,US
202/D3 **East** (bay), La,US
208/D1 **East** (pt.), Ma,US
206/C5 **East** (pt.), NJ,US
207/L9 **East** (bay), NY,US
207/K9 **East** (riv.), NY,US
189/G3 **East** (bay), Tx,US
205/C3 **East** (passg.), Wa,US
202/D2 **Eastabuchie,** Ms,US
130/D3 **East Alligator** (riv.), Austl.
59/G2 **East Anglia** (reg.), Eng,UK
196/B3 **East Angus,** Qu,Can
182/F2 **East Arrow Park,** BC,Can
130/C3 **East Baines** (riv.), Austl.
206/C2 **East Bangor,** Pa,US
53/N7 **East Barnet,** Eng,UK
165/G4 **East Berbice-Corentyne** (reg.), Guy.
165/G3 **East Berbice-Coronie** (reg.), Guy.
59/H3 **East Bergholt,** Eng,UK
208/B2 **East Berlin,** Ct,US
206/B4 **East Berlin,** Pa,US
200/E2 **East Bernstadt,** Ky,US
206/B1 **East Berwick,** Pa,US
195/H5 **East Bethel,** Mn,US
192/B4 **East Bijou** (cr.), Co,US
59/G5 **Eastbourne,** Eng,UK
199/G4 **East Brady,** Pa,US
202/E2 **East Brewton,** Al,US
208/D1 **East Bridgewater,** Ma,US
208/B1 **East Brookfield,** Ma,US
206/D3 **East Brunswick,** NJ,US
208/H6 **East Butler,** Pa,US
191/E3 **East Cache** (cr.), Ok,US
162/D2 **East Caicos** (isl.), Trks.
54/C5 **East Calder,** Sc,UK
191/H4 **East Camden,** Ar,US
208/A1 **East Canaan,** Ct,US
208/F6 **East Canton,** Oh,US
185/H4 **East Carbon,** Ut,US
57/G1 **East Chevington,** Eng,UK
205/R16 **East Chicago,** In,US
117/J3 **East China** (sea), China
53/M8 **East Clandon,** Eng,UK
208/F4 **East Claridon,** Oh,US
58/B3 **East Cleddau** (riv.), Wal,UK
208/F4 **East Cleveland,** Oh,US
183/H2 **East Coulee,** Ab,Can
58/C5 **East Dart** (riv.), Eng,UK
59/G1 **East Dereham,** Eng,UK
205/G7 **East Detroit** (East Pointe), Mi,US
201/J3 **East Dismal** (swamp), NC,US
208/C1 **East Douglas,** Ma,US
201/F4 **East Dublin,** Ga,US
183/K3 **Eastend,** Sk,Can
139/Q7 **Easter** (isl.), Chile
154/B5 **Easter** (pt.), Namb.
197/H2 **Eastern** (pt.), Nf,Can
145/E5 **Eastern** (reg.), Gha.
151/B1 **Eastern** (prov.), Kenya
144/C4 **Eastern** (prov.), SLeo.
122/H4 **Eastern** (prov.), SrL.
149/G2 **Eastern** (reg.), Sudan
153/H2 **Eastern** (prov.), Ugan.
57/H4 **Eastern** (plain), Eng,UK
206/B6 **Eastern** (bay), Md,US
155/F2 **Eastern** (prov.), Zam.
110/A4 **Eastern Channel** (str.), Japan
131/G2 **Eastern Fields** (reef), PNG
118/C5 **Eastern Ghats** (mts.), India
122/F4 **Eastern Ghats** (uplands), India
131/G1 **Eastern Highlands** (prov.), PNG
206/B5 **Eastern Neck I. Nat'l Wild. Ref.,** Md,US
108/D1 **Eastern Sayan** (mts.), Rus.
100/K4 **Eastern Sayans** (mts.), Rus.
175/N8 **East Falkland** (isl.), Falk.
163/D7 **East Falkland** (isl.), U.K.
196/B5 **East Falmouth,** Ma,US
207/M9 **East Farmingdale,** NY,US
68/C2 **East Flanders** (prov.), Belg.
201/F3 **East Flat Rock,** NC,US
208/B2 **Eastford,** Ct,US
208/C1 **East Foxboro,** Ma,US
208/D2 **East Freetown,** Ma,US
67/E1 **East Frisian** (isls.), Ger.
184/E4 **Eastgate,** Nv,US
183/H3 **East Glacier Park,** Mt,US
59/F1 **East Glen** (riv.), Eng,UK
208/B2 **East Granby,** Ct,US
198/D3 **East Grand Rapids,** Mi,US
206/C3 **East Greenville,** Pa,US
208/C2 **East Greenwich,** RI,US
200/E4 **East Griffin,** Ga,US
59/F4 **East Grinstead,** Eng,UK
195/G4 **East Gull Lake,** Mn,US
208/B3 **East Haddam,** Ct,US
196/C5 **Eastham,** Ma,US
208/B2 **East Hampton,** Ct,US
208/B1 **Easthampton,** Ma,US
207/F2 **East Hampton,** NY,US
207/F2 **East Hampton** (arpt.), NY,US
208/B2 **East Hartford,** Ct,US
208/B2 **East Hartland,** Ct,US
208/B3 **East Haven,** Ct,US
183/J4 **East Helena,** Mt,US
205/C2 **East Hill-Meridian,** Wa,US
207/L8 **East Hills,** NY,US
202/B1 **East Hodge,** La,US
53/M8 **East Horsley,** Eng,UK
198/D2 **East Jordan,** Mi,US
100/J5 **East Kazakhstan Obl.,** Kaz.
54/B5 **East Kilbride,** Sc,UK
208/C2 **East Killingly,** Ct,US
109/K4 **East Korea** (bay), NKor.
113/D3 **East Korea** (Tongjosŏn) (bay), NKor.
189/E1 **Eastland,** Tx,US
198/D3 **East Lansing,** Mi,US
186/E2 **East Las Vegas,** Nv,US
57/G6 **East Leake,** Eng,UK
208/A1 **East Lee,** Ma,US
59/E5 **Eastleigh,** Eng,UK
59/E5 **Eastleigh** (Southampton) (int'l arpt.), Eng,UK
54/D5 **East Linton,** Sc,UK
208/G6 **East Liverpool,** Oh,US
156/D4 **East London,** SAfr.
208/B1 **East Longmeadow,** Ma,US
204/F7 **East Los Angeles,** Ca,US
208/B3 **East Lyme,** Ct,US
196/D3 **East Machias,** Me,US
176/K4 **Eastmain** (riv.), Can.
179/J3 **Eastmain** (riv.), Qu,Can
201/F4 **Eastman,** Ga,US
193/J2 **Eastman,** Wi,US
201/G3 **East Marion,** NC,US
207/E2 **East Meadow,** NY,US
57/G6 **East Midlands** (int'l arpt.), Eng,UK
185/H3 **East Millcreek,** Ut,US
196/C3 **East Millinocket,** Me,US
186/E3 **East Mojave Nat'l Scenic Area,** Ca,US
53/M7 **East Molesey,** Eng,UK
199/K2 **East Montpelier,** Vt,US
207/F2 **East Moriches,** NY,US
208/A2 **East Morris,** Ct,US
203/H4 **East Naples,** Fl,US
207/J8 **East Newark,** NJ,US
193/G3 **East Nishnabotna** (riv.), Ia,US
193/G3 **East Nodaway** (riv.), Ia,US
207/E2 **East Northport,** NY,US
182/C4 **East Olympia,** Wa,US
58/D5 **Easton,** Eng,UK
186/C2 **Easton,** Ca,US
208/A3 **Easton,** Ct,US
207/E1 **Easton** (res.), Ct,US
202/B2 **Easton,** La,US
208/C1 **Easton,** Ma,US
206/B6 **Easton,** Md,US
196/D2 **Easton,** Me,US
191/G1 **Easton,** Mo,US
206/C2 **Easton,** Pa,US
189/G1 **Easton,** Tx,US
206/C2 **Easton-Bethlehem-Allentown** (arpt.), Pa,US
207/D2 **East Orange,** NJ,US
208/A1 **East Otis,** Ma,US
203/H3 **East Palatka,** Fl,US
208/G6 **East Palestine,** Oh,US
207/F2 **East Patchogue,** NY,US
206/B3 **East Petersburg,** Pa,US
200/E4 **East Point,** Ga,US
202/B1 **East Point,** La,US
205/G7 **East Pointe** (East Detroit), Mi,US
196/D3 **Eastport,** Me,US
207/F2 **Eastport,** NY,US
205/B2 **East Port Orchard,** Wa,US
200/C2 **East Prairie,** Mo,US
206/B4 **East Prospect,** Pa,US
208/C2 **East Providence,** RI,US
208/C2 **East Putnam,** Ct,US
184/C4 **East Quincy-Quincy,** Ca,US
199/K4 **East Quogue,** NY,US
57/H5 **East Retford,** Eng,UK
200/E3 **East Ridge,** Tn,US
57/E2 **Eastriggs,** Sc,UK
207/K8 **East River** (str.), NY,US
208/F6 **East Rochester,** Oh,US
207/L9 **East Rockaway,** NY,US
201/H3 **East Rockingham,** NC,US
207/J8 **East Rutherford,** NJ,US
59/H4 **Eastry,** Eng,UK
200/B1 **East Saint Louis,** Il,US
101/S2 **East Siberian** (sea), Rus.
206/C1 **East Side,** Pa,US
182/C3 **Eastsound,** Wa,US
208/F6 **East Sparta,** Oh,US
201/G3 **East Spencer,** NC,US
206/C2 **East Stroudsburg,** Pa,US
59/G5 **East Sussex** (co.), Eng,UK
198/E2 **East Tawas,** Mi,US

189/G1 East Texas Oil Museum, Tx,US
185/J2 East Thermopolis, Wy,US
58/B4 East the Water, Eng,UK
202/C3 East Timbalier I. Nat'l Wild. Ref., La,US
202/N7 East Tohopekaliga (lake), Fl,US
205/P14 East Troy, Wi,US
201/K2 Eastville, Va,US
186/C1 East Walker (riv.), Ca, Nv,US
208/D2 East Wareham, Ma,US
54/C4 East Wemyss, Sc,UK
182/D4 East Wenatchee, Wa,US
206/D3 East Windsor, NJ,US
208/B2 East Windsor Hill, Ct,US
59/F5 East Wittering, Eng,UK
57/G6 Eastwood, Eng,UK
208/C2 East Woodstock, Ct,US
197/S8 East York, On,Can
59/E2 Eatington, Eng,UK
192/B3 Eaton, Co,US
198/D4 Eaton, In,US
198/D5 Eaton, Oh,US
208/E5 Eaton Estates, Oh,US
183/K2 Eatonia, Sk,Can
198/D3 Eaton Rapids, Mi,US
207/E2 Eatons Neck (pt.), NY,US
59/F2 Eaton Socon, Eng,UK
201/F4 Eatonton, Ga,US
207/D3 Eatontown, NJ,US
202/N6 Eatonville, Fl,US
182/C4 Eatonville, Wa,US
57/H5 Eau (riv.), Eng,UK
53/S10 Eaubonne, Fr.
179/J3 Eau Claire (lake), Qu,Can
208/H5 Eau Claire, Pa,US
193/J1 Eau Claire, Wi,US
193/J1 Eau Claire (riv.), Wi,US
68/A4 Eaulne (riv.), Fr.
138/D4 Eauripik (isl.), Micr.
74/D5 Eauze, Fr.
148/D5 Ebalo (riv.), Zaire
59/E4 Ebble (riv.), Eng,UK
58/C3 Ebbw Vale, Wal,UK
152/B2 Ebebiyin, EqG.
167/K6 Ebéjico, Col.
67/H6 Ebeleben, Ger.
62/D3 Ebeltoft, Den.
73/A4 Ebenfurth, Aus.
198/C1 Eben Junction, Mi,US
199/G4 Ebensburg, Pa,US
75/K3 Ebensee, Aus.
70/B4 Eberbach, Ger.
73/A3 Ebergassing, Aus.
67/H5 Ebergötzen, Ger.
70/E3 Ebermannstadt, Ger.
70/D2 Ebern, Ger.
70/A3 Ebernburg, Ger.
70/C5 Ebersbach an der Fils, Ger.
71/E6 Ebersberg, Ger.
71/G6 Eberschwang, Aus.
80/D1 Ebersheim, Fr.
72/D2 Eberswalde-Finow, Ger.
112/B2 Ebetsu, Japan
119/H2 Ebian, China
111/H7 Ebina, Japan
70/C6 Ebingen, Ger.
114/D3 Ebinur (lake), China
81/F3 Ebnat-Kappel, Swi.
144/D3 Ebo (lake), Mali
153/E2 Ebola (riv.), Zaire
85/F6 Eboli, It.
148/A5 Ebolowa, Camr.
138/F4 Ebon (isl.), Mrsh.
154/B4 Ebony, Namb.
201/J2 Ebony, Va,US
152/B2 Eboro, Gabon
70/D3 Ebrach, Ger.
73/A4 Ebreichsdorf, Aus.
77/F2 Ebro (riv.), Sp.
195/G4 Ebro, Mn,US
82/B3 Ebron (riv.), Fr.
67/H2 Ebstorf, Ger.
159/F5 Ecatepec de Morelos, Mex.
57/E1 Ecclefechan, Sc,UK
57/F5 Eccles, Eng,UK
201/G2 Eccles, WV,US
57/F6 Eccleshall, Eng,UK
93/H5 Eceabat, Turk.
125/C1 Echague, Phil.
80/C4 Echallens, Swi.
161/F4 Echandi (mtn.), CR
168/C4 Echarate, Peru
70/C6 Echaz (riv.), Ger.
145/H3 Eché Fadadinga (wadi), Niger
117/G2 Echeng, China
111/M9 Echigawa, Japan
71/E6 Eching, Ger.
82/B2 Echirolles, Fr.
97/H4 Echmiadzin, Arm.
202/B2 Echo, La,US
207/H7 Echo (lake), NJ,US
184/D1 Echo, Or,US
198/D1 Echo Bay, Can.
178/E2 Echo Bay, NW,Can
200/D2 Echols, Ky,US
66/C6 Echt, Neth.
70/C5 Echterdingen (Stuttgart) (int'l arpt.), Ger.
69/F4 Echternach, Lux.
135/C3 Echuca, Austl.
133/M9 Echunga (cr.), Austl.
70/B2 Echzell, Ger.
76/C4 Ecija, Sp.
92/E3 Ečka, Yugo.
72/B5 Eckartsberga, Ger.
64/E1 Eckernförde, Ger.
63/H1 Eckerö, Fin.
63/H1 Eckerö (isl.), Fin.
58/D2 Eckington, Eng,UK
183/G1 Eckville, Ab,Can
200/D4 Eclectic, Al,US
179/H1 Eclipse (sound), NW,Can
79/F5 Ecommoy, Fr.
208/G6 Economy, Pa,US
205/F7 Ecorse, Mi,US
205/F7 Ecorse (riv.), Mi,US
68/A5 Ecos, Fr.
79/E3 Ecouché, Fr.
53/T9 Ecouen, Fr.
79/F3 Ecouves, Signal d' (peak), Fr.
75/G4 Ecrins Nat'l Park, Fr.
82/C3 Ecrins Nat'l Park, Fr.
88/E1 Ecrins Nat'l Park, Fr.
69/E6 Ecrouves, Fr.
200/C3 Ecru, Ms,US
163/B3 Ecuador
80/C4 Ecublens, Swi.
150/B2 Ed, Eth.
62/D2 Ed, Swe.
183/K1 Edam, Sk,Can
66/C3 Edam, Neth.
122/F3 Edapalli, India
55/N13 Eday (isl.), Sc,UK
104/A2 Edcemit (gulf), Turk.
142/B4 Edchera, WSah.
72/B4 Edderitz, Ger.
54/B1 Edderton, Sc,UK
54/C5 Eddleston, Sc,UK
182/F3 Eddy (peak), Id,US
189/F2 Eddy-Bruceville, Tx,US
135/D4 Eddystone (pt.), Austl.
194/E2 Eddystone, Mb,Can
58/B6 Eddystone Rocks (isl.), Eng,UK
193/H3 Eddyville, Ia,US
200/C2 Eddyville, Ky,US
66/C4 Ede, Neth.
145/G5 Ede, Nga.
152/B2 Edéa, Camr.
68/D1 Edegem, Belg.
143/G4 Edehin Ouarene (des.), Alg.
173/G1 Edéia, Braz.
92/E1 Edelény, Hun.
67/H4 Edemissen, Ger.
135/D3 Eden, Austl.
194/E2 Eden, Mb,Can
164/B5 Edén, Ecu.
57/F2 Eden (riv.), Eng,UK
54/D4 Eden (riv.), Sc,UK
187/H4 Eden, Az,US
201/K1 Eden, Md,US
201/H2 Eden, NC,US
188/E2 Eden, Tx,US
185/J2 Eden, Wy,US
53/P8 Edenbridge, Eng,UK
156/D3 Edenburg, SAfr.
136/B4 Edendale, N.Z.
157/E3 Edendale, SAfr.
60/C3 Edenderry, Ire.
135/B3 Edenhope, Austl.
70/B4 Edenkoben, Ger.
197/Q8 Eden Mills, On,Can
195/H5 Eden Prairie, Mn,US
195/P7 Eden Prairie, Mn,US
57/F2 Edenside (vall.), Eng,UK
201/J2 Edenton, NC,US
194/B2 Edenwold, Sk,Can
67/F6 Eder (riv.), Ger.
67/G6 Eder (riv.), Ger.
67/F6 Eder-Stausee (res.), Ger.
67/E2 Edewecht, Ger.
132/D2 Edgar (peak), Austl.
183/K5 Edgar, Mt,US
192/F3 Edgar, Ne,US
195/K5 Edgar, Wi,US
202/C2 Edgard, La,US
191/J2 Edgar Springs, Mo,US
196/B5 Edgartown, Ma,US
59/E2 Edgbaston, Eng,UK
100/C2 Edge (isl.), Sval.
188/K7 Edgecliff, Tx,US
177/L4 Edgecumbe (cape), Ak,US
202/B1 Edgefield, La,US
201/G4 Edgefield, SC,US
194/E4 Edgeley, ND,US
179/K2 Edgell (isl.), NW,Can
206/B5 Edgemere, Md,US
192/C2 Edgemont, SD,US
183/J1 Edgerton, Ab,Can
195/G5 Edgerton, Mn,US
198/D4 Edgerton, Oh,US
198/B3 Edgerton, Wi,US
182/F2 Edgewater, BC,Can
203/H3 Edgewater, Fl,US
206/D3 Edgewater Park, NJ,US
202/N7 Edgewood, Fl,US
193/K4 Edgewood, Il,US
206/B5 Edgewood, Md,US
190/A3 Edgewood, NM,US
206/B2 Edgewood, Pa,US
191/G4 Edgewood, Tx,US
206/B5 Edgewood Arsenal (mil. res.), Md,US
205/C3 Edgewood-North Hill, Wa,US
208/G6 Edgeworth, Pa,US
58/D1 Edgmond, Eng,UK
53/N7 Edgware, Eng,UK
91/H2 Edhessa, Gre.
136/B4 Edievale, N.Z.
144/C5 Edina, Libr.
195/H5 Edina, Mn,US
195/P7 Edina, Mn,US
193/H3 Edina, Mo,US
198/F4 Edinboro, Pa,US
200/C4 Edinburg, Ms,US
194/F3 Edinburg, ND,US
208/G5 Edinburg, Pa,US
189/E4 Edinburg, Tx,US
201/H1 Edinburg, Va,US
54/C5 Edinburgh, Sc,UK
198/D5 Edinburgh, In,US
54/C5 Edinburgh (Turnhouse) (int'l arpt.), Sc,UK
155/G2 Edingeni, Malw.
93/H5 Edirne, Turk.
104/A1 Edirne (prov.), Turk.
93/H5 Edirne (prov.), Turk.
186/C3 Edison, Ca,US
192/B4 Edison, Co,US
203/F2 Edison, Ga,US
206/D2 Edison, NJ,US
207/J8 Edison Nat'l Hist. Site, NJ,US
201/G4 Edisto, SC,US
201/G4 Edisto (isl.), SC,US
201/G4 Edisto (riv.), SC,US
201/G4 Edisto Island, SC,US
201/G4 Edisto, North Fork (riv.), SC,US
201/G4 Edisto, South Fork (riv.), SC,US
133/H5 Edithburgh, Austl.
182/E1 Edith Cavell (mtn.), Ab,Can
143/H4 Edjeleh, Alg.
145/F2 Edjérir (wadi), Mali
191/F3 Edmond, Ok,US
205/C2 Edmonds, Wa,US
166/C1 Edmondt, FrG.
134/B2 Edmonton, Austl.
176/F4 Edmonton, Can.
178/E3 Edmonton (cap.), Ab,Can
183/H1 Edmonton (cap.), Ab,Can
183/H1 Edmonton (int'l arpt.), Ab,Can
53/N7 Edmonton, Eng,UK
200/E2 Edmonton, Ky,US
198/D3 Edmore, Mi,US
194/E3 Edmore, ND,US
134/B2 Edmund Kennedy Nat'l Park, Austl.
196/C2 Edmundston, NB,Can
191/G2 Edna, Ks,US
189/F3 Edna, Tx,US
177/M4 Edna Bay, Ak,US
111/H7 Edo (riv.), Japan
81/G5 Edolo, It.
189/G1 Edom, Tx,US
104/A2 Edremit, Turk.
96/C5 Edremit (gulf), Turk.
62/F1 Edsbyn, Swe.
182/F1 Edson, Ab,Can
174/D2 Eduardo Castex, Arg.
167/H4 Eduardo Gomes, Braz.
166/A3 Eduardo Gomes (int'l arpt.), Braz.
133/F2 Edward (peak), Austl.
195/K3 Edward (isl.), On,Can
153/G3 Edward (lake), Ugan., Zaire
134/A1 Edward River Abor. Community, Austl.
193/J3 Edwards (riv.), Il,US
200/B4 Edwards, Ms,US
199/J2 Edwards, NY,US
188/D2 Edwards (plat.), Tx,US
186/C3 Edwards A.F.B., Ca,US
193/K4 Edwardsville, Il,US
206/C1 Edwardsville, Pa,US
137/P Edward VII (pen.), Ant.
137/D Edward VIII (bay), Ant.
203/F2 Edwin, Al,US
54/D3 Edzell, Sc,UK
159/H5 Edzná (ruins), Mex.
66/D4 Eefde, Neth.
177/F3 Eek, Ak,US
68/C1 Eeklo, Belg.
184/B4 Eel (riv.), Ca,US
200/D1 Eel (riv.), In,US
66/D2 Eelde-Paterswolde, Neth.
184/B3 Eel, South Fork (riv.), Ca,US
66/C4 Eem (riv.), Neth.
66/D2 Eems (Ems) (riv.), Neth.
66/D2 Eemshaven (har.), Neth.
66/D2 Eemskanaal (can.), Neth.
66/C6 Eersel, Neth.
138/F6 Efate (isl.), Van.
71/H6 Eferding, Aus.
195/H4 Effie, Mn,US
193/J2 Effigy Mounds Nat'l Mon., Ia,US
197/S9 Effingham, On,Can
53/M8 Effingham, Eng,UK
193/K4 Effingham, Il,US
191/G1 Effingham, Ks,US
206/C2 Effort, Pa,US
104/C1 Eflâni, Turk.
131/G2 Efogi, PNG
93/J3 Eforie, Rom.
80/D2 Efringen-Kirchen, Ger.
58/C1 Efyrnwy, Lyn (lake), Wal,UK
56/E6 Efyrnwy, Llyn (lake), Wal,UK
90/C3 Egadi (isls.), It.
70/D5 Egan (riv.), Ger.
188/K7 Egan, Tx,US
175/T11 Egaña, Uru.
145/G4 Egbe, Nga.
153/F2 Egbunda, Zaire
177/G4 Egegik, Ak,US
194/E3 Egeland, ND,US
72/B4 Egeln, Ger.
71/F2 Eger (riv.), Ger.
92/E2 Eger, Hun.
62/B2 Egersund, Nor.
73/A6 Egervár, Hun.
73/B6 Eger-víz (riv.), Hun.
62/D4 Egeskov, Den.
67/H2 Egestorf, Ger.
81/F3 Egg, Aus.
81/E3 Egg, Swi.
64/E1 Eggebek, Ger.
67/F5 Eggegebirge (ridge), Ger.
71/F6 Eggelsberg, Aus.
75/L2 Eggenburg, Aus.
73/A4 Eggendorf, Aus.
71/F6 Eggenfelden, Ger.
70/B4 Eggenstein-Leopoldshafen, Ger.
62/F5 Eggesin, Ger.
206/D4 Egg Harbor City, NJ,US
206/C5 Egg Island (pt.), NJ,US
80/D4 Eggiwil, Swi.
135/B3 Egg Lagoon, Austl.
59/G3 Egglescliffe, Eng,UK
57/G2 Eggleston, Eng,UK
71/F7 Eggstätt, Ger.
53/M7 Egham, Eng,UK
69/D2 Eghezée, Belg.
61/P6 Egilsstadhir, Ice.
184/B2 Egito, Ang.
108/E1 Egiyn (riv.), Mong.
74/E4 Egletons, Fr.
202/E2 Eglin A.F.B., Fl,US
56/A1 Eglinton (Londonderry) (int'l arpt.), NI,UK
179/R7 Eglinton (isl.), NW,Can
56/A1 Eglinton, NI,UK
81/E2 Eglisau, Swi.
58/C4 Eglwys Brewis, Wal,UK
53/S11 Égly, Fr.
66/B3 Egmond aan Zee, Neth.
196/E2 Egmont (bay), PE,Can
196/E2 Egmont (cape), PE,Can
136/C2 Egmont (cape), N.Z.
136/C2 Egmont (peak), N.Z.
202/K8 Egmont (key), Fl,US
203/G4 Egmont Key Nat'l Wild. Ref., Fl,US
81/F2 Egnach, Swi.
81/H5 Egna (Neumarkt), It.
185/J5 Egnar, Co,US
152/B3 Egoumbi, Gabon
121/F5 Egra, India
56/E3 Egremont, Eng,UK
104/B2 Eğridir, Turk.
104/B2 Eğridir (lake), Turk.
62/C4 Egtved, Den.
170/D2 Eguas (riv.), Braz.
147/F3 Egypt
202/L7 Egypt Lake, Fl,US
145/G5 Eha Amufu, Nga.
70/D3 Ehebach (riv.), Ger.
70/E5 Ehekirchen, Ger.
110/C4 Ehime (pref.), Japan
70/D4 Ehingen, Ger.
81/F1 Ehingen, Ger.
72/B3 Ehle (riv.), Ger.
80/D1 Ehn (riv.), Fr.
186/E4 Ehrenberg, Az,US
72/C6 Ehrenfriedersdorf, Ger.
201/G4 Ehrhardt, SC,US
70/B1 Ehringshausen, Ger.
81/G3 Ehrwald, Aus.
139/L5 Eiao (isl.), FrPol.
76/D1 Eibar, Sp.
70/D3 Eibelstadt, Ger.
71/F1 Eibenstock, Ger.
66/D4 Eibergen, Neth.
70/B3 Eich, Ger.
69/G6 Eichel (riv.), Fr.
70/E6 Eichenau, Ger.
70/C3 Eichenbühl, Ger.
71/F5 Eichendorf, Ger.
70/C2 Eichenzell, Ger.
70/E5 Eichstätt, Ger.
72/D3 Eichwalde, Ger.
67/H3 Eicklingen, Ger.
67/G1 Eidelstedt, Ger.
62/B1 Eidfjord, Nor.
134/C4 Eidsvold, Austl.
62/D1 Eidsvoll, Nor.
69/F3 Eifel (plat.), Ger.
64/D4 Eifel (upland), Ger.
155/F3 Eiffel Flats, Zim.
53/S10 Eiffel Tower, Fr.
111/M9 Eigenji, Japan
80/D4 Eiger (peak), Swi.
197/F3 Eigg (mtn.), NS,Can
55/H8 Eigg (isl.), Sc,UK
118/B6 Eight Degree (chan.), India, Mald.
185/G1 Eighteenmile (peak), Id,US
137/T Eights (coast), Ant.
130/A4 Eighty Mile (beach), Austl.
66/B2 Eijerlandse Gat (chan.), Neth.
69/E2 Eijsden, Neth.
62/A1 Eikelandsosen, Nor.
135/C3 Eildon, Austl.
135/C3 Eildon (lake), Austl.
72/C5 Eilenburg, Ger.
165/G4 Eilerts de Haan (mts.), Sur.
54/A3 Eil, Loch (inlet), Sc,UK
62/D1 Eina, Nor.
134/A2 Einasleigh (riv.), Austl.
67/G5 Einbeck, Ger.
66/C6 Eindhoven, Neth.
66/C6 Eindhoven (int'l arpt.), Neth.
72/B4 Eine (riv.), Ger.
72/C6 Einsiedel, Ger.
81/E3 Einsiedeln, Swi.
69/F6 Einville-au-Jard, Fr.
168/D2 Eirunepé, Braz.
154/C5 Eirup, Namb.
81/H4 Eisack (Isarco) (riv.), It.
69/E4 Eisch (riv.), Lux.
154/D4 Eiseb (dry riv.), Bots., Namb.
67/H7 Eisenach, Ger.
70/B3 Eisenberg, Ger.
75/L3 Eisenerz, Aus.
182/G2 Eisenhower (mtn.), Ab,Can
206/A4 Eisenhower Nat'l Hist. Site, Pa,US
65/H2 Eisenhüttenstadt, Ger.
73/A4 Eisenstadt, Aus.
69/G2 Eiserfeld, Ger.
70/D2 Eisfeld, Ger.
63/L4 Eišiškės, Lith.
72/B4 Eisleben, Ger.
69/G3 Eitelborn, Ger.
67/F3 Eiter (riv.), Ger.
69/G2 Eitorf, Ger.
71/E6 Eitting, Ger.
77/E1 Ejea de los Caballeros, Sp.
157/H9 Ejeda, Madg.
164/D2 Ejido, Ven.
158/C3 Ejido Insurgentes, Mex.
188/D4 Ejido Nadadores, Mex.
109/J3 Ejin Horo Qi, China
108/E3 Ejin Qi, China
145/G5 Ejule, Nga.
145/E5 Ejura, Gha.
160/B2 Ejutla, Mex.
183/M5 Ekalaka, Mt,US
145/H5 Ekang, Nga.
152/C2 Ekata, Gabon
62/E3 Ekeby, Swe.
61/G4 Ekenäs, Fin.
94/D4 Ekenäs, Fin.
63/K2 Ekenäs (Tammisaari), Fin.
66/B6 Ekeren, Belg.
63/R7 Ekerö, Swe.
63/R7 Ekerön (isl.), Swe.
145/G5 Eket, Nga.
136/C3 Eketahuna, N.Z.
97/J2 Ekhínos, Gre.
114/C1 Ekibastuz, Kaz.
109/L1 Ekimchan, Rus.
121/E3 Ekma, India
153/E2 Ekoko, Zaire
153/F3 Ekoli, Zaire
145/H5 Ekondo Titi, Camr.
145/G5 Ekpoma, Nga.
62/F3 Eksjö, Swe.
177/G4 Ekuk, Ak,US
153/E3 Ekuku, Zaire
153/E2 Ekukula, Zaire
179/H3 Ekwan (riv.), On,Can
155/G1 Ekwendeni, Malw.
177/G4 Ekwok, Ak,US
116/C5 Ela, Burma
142/B5 El Aargub, WSah.
142/B5 El Aatf (reg.), WSah.
174/C3 El Abanico, Chile
143/F2 El Abiodh Sidi Chrikh, Alg.
150/C4 Ēl Ābrēd, Eth.
144/C2 El 'Acâba (reg.), Mrta.
141/S15 El Affroun, Alg.
188/B4 El Águila, Mex.
182/C2 Elaho (riv.), BC,Can
191/J3 Elaine, Ar,US
141/N13 El Aïoun, Mor.
188/E4 El Álamo, Mex.
143/G2 El Alia, Alg.
165/F2 El Almacén, Ven.
172/B1 El Alto (int'l arpt.), Bol.
168/A2 El Alto, Peru
164/D2 El Amparo de Apure, Ven.
106/B3 El Amra (Abydos) (ruins), Egypt
58/C2 Elan (riv.), Wal,UK
53/R10 Élancourt, Fr.
155/E5 Elands (riv.), SAfr.
156/Q12 Elandsrivier (riv.), SAfr.
164/A5 El Anegado, Ecu.
151/B2 Elangata Wuas, Kenya
141/V18 El Aouinet, Alg.
76/C4 El Arahal, Sp.
144/D2 El Arhlaf (well), Mrta.
143/E2 El Aricha, Alg.
134/B2 El Arish, Austl.
152/B2 Elarmilon, Gabon
174/C2 El Arrayán, Chile
91/H3 Elassón, Gre.
76/D1 El Astillero, Sp.
103/D5 Elat, Isr.
147/G2 Elat (int'l arpt.), Isr.
103/D5 Elat (int'l arpt.), Isr.
91/H3 Elátia, Gre.
138/D4 Elato (isl.), Micr.
145/F5 Elavagnon, Togo
167/G7 El Avila Nat'l Park, Ven.
104/D2 Elazığ, Turk.
104/D2 Elazığ (prov.), Turk.
172/B4 El Azufre, Paso (pass), Chile
84/A2 Elba (isl.), It.
203/E2 Elba, Al,US
164/C3 El Bagre, Col.
109/M1 El'ban, Rus.
164/C2 El Banco, Col.
76/B1 El Barco, Sp.
76/C2 El Barco de Ávila, Sp.
159/F3 El Barretal, Mex.
91/G2 Elbasan, Alb.
164/D2 El Baúl, Ven.
143/F2 El Bayadh, Alg.
143/F2 El Bayadh (wilaya), Alg.
70/A1 Elbbach (riv.), Ger.
64/E2 Elbe (riv.), Ger.
72/B3 Elbe-Havel (can.), Ger.
71/H2 Elbe (Labe) (riv.), Czh.
151/C1 El Ben, Kenya
185/K4 Elbert (mt.), Co,US
190/A1 Elbert (mtn.), Co,US
188/E1 Elbert, Tx,US
201/F3 Elberton, Ga,US
67/H2 Elbe-Seitenkanal (can.), Ger.
79/G2 Elbeuf, Fr.
81/G3 Elbigenalp, Aus.
72/A4 Elbingerode, Ger.
104/D2 Elbistan, Turk.
65/K1 Elbląg, Pol.
65/K2 Elbląg (prov.), Pol.
174/C4 El Bolsón, Arg.
76/D3 El Bonillo, Sp.
142/D2 El Borouj, Mor.
182/G2 Elbow (riv.), Ab,Can
194/A2 Elbow, Sk,Can
194/G5 Elbow Lake, Mn,US
53/H4 El'brus (peak), Rus.
97/G4 El'brus, Gora (peak), Rus.
105/G2 Elbruz (mts.), Iran
66/C4 Elburg, Neth.
76/D2 El Burgo de Osma, Sp.
151/A2 Elburgon, Kenya
205/P16 Elburn, Il,US
106/E1 Elburz (mts.), Iran
174/C4 El Caín, Arg.
160/E3 El Cajón (res.), Hon.
204/D5 El Cajon, Ca,US
165/F3 El Callao, Ven.
189/F3 El Campo, Tx,US
188/C5 El Cantabro, Mex.
188/B2 El Capitan (peak), Tx,US
169/E4 El Carmen, Bol.
169/F4 El Carmen, Bol.
174/B3 El Carmen, Chile
164/B3 El Carmen, Col.
168/B4 El Carmen, Peru
165/E4 El Carmen, Ven.
164/C2 El Carmen de Bolívar, Col.
188/A3 El Carrizalillo, Mex.
165/F3 El Casabe, Ven.
77/N8 El Casar de Talamanca, Sp.
160/D2 El Cayo, Belz.
186/E4 El Centro, Ca,US
186/E4 El Centro Nav. Air Facility, Ca,US
161/J2 El Cercado, DRep.
175/K7 El Cerrito, Arg.
164/B4 El Cerrito, Col.
205/K11 El Cerrito, Ca,US
172/D1 El Cerro, Bol.
162/F5 El Cerro del Aripo (mtn.), Trin.
164/D2 El Cerrón (peak), Ven.
161/H4 El César (dept.), Col.
164/C2 El César (dept.), Col.
131/D2 Elcho (isl.), Austl.
193/K1 Elcho, Wi,US
174/C3 El Chocón (res.), Arg.
172/D2 El Chorro, Arg.
164/C3 El Cocuy, Col.
164/C3 El Cocuy Nat'l Park, Col.
167/L7 El Colegio, Col.
172/E3 El Colorado, Arg.
175/K8 El Cóndor, Arg.
159/H5 El Corozal, Mex.
188/D4 El Cuarenta, Mex.
174/C3 El Cuy, Arg.
205/B3 Eld (inlet), Wa,US
77/E3 Elda, Sp.
151/A1 Eldama Ravine, Kenya
64/G2 Elde (riv.), Ger.
72/B1 Eldena, Ger.
150/C3 El Der (dry riv.), Som.
150/B4 El Dere, Eth.
206/B5 Eldersburg, Md,US
186/D4 El Descanso, Mex.
164/C2 El Difícil, Col.
101/P3 El'dikan, Rus.
104/C1 Eldivan, Turk.
140/B2 El Djouf (des.), Afr.
142/D5 El Djouf (des.), Afr.
144/C1 El Djouf (des.), Mrta.
193/H3 Eldon, Ia,US
191/H1 Eldon, Mo,US
205/A2 Eldon, Wa,US
193/H2 Eldora, Ia,US
206/D5 Eldora, NJ,US
173/F3 Eldorado, Arg.
173/F2 Eldorado, Braz.
173/G3 Eldorado, Braz.
164/C3 Eldorado (int'l arpt.), Col.
158/D3 El Dorado, Mex.
191/H4 El Dorado, Ar,US
200/C2 Eldorado, Il,US
191/F2 El Dorado, Ks,US
191/F2 El Dorado (lake), Ks,US
190/E3 Eldorado, Ok,US
188/D2 Eldorado, Tx,US
165/F3 El Dorado, Ven.
191/G2 El Dorado Springs, Mo,US
151/A1 Eldoret, Kenya
200/D4 Eldridge, Al,US
193/J3 Eldridge, Ia,US
201/G1 Eleanor, WV,US
188/D4 El Ébano, Mex.
190/E3 Electra, Tx,US
82/B5 Électricité de France (can.), Fr.
205/C4 Electron, Wa,US
167/K7 El Eden (arpt.), Col.
91/L6 Elefsis (arpt.), Gre.
142/D4 El Eglab (plat.), Alg.
63/K3 Eleja, Lat.
92/E2 Elek, Hun.
63/L4 Elektrénai, Lith.
53/G3 Elektrostal', Rus.
145/G5 Elele, Nga.
164/D2 El Empedrado, Ven.
174/D2 Elena, Arg.
93/G4 Elena, Bul.
137/W Elephant (isl.), Ant.
148/C4 Eléphant (rapids), CAfr.
196/B3 Elephant (mtn.), Me,US
188/C2 Elephant (mtn.), Tx,US
187/J4 Elephant Butte, NM,US
187/J4 Elephant Butte (res.), NM,US
167/F4 Elesbão Veloso, Braz.
77/M8 El Escorial, Sp.
105/E2 Eleşkirt, Turk.
76/C2 El Espinar, Sp.
141/U17 El Eulma, Alg.
162/B1 Eleuthera (isl.), Bahm.
200/B2 Eleven Point (riv.), Ar,US
191/J2 Eleven Point (riv.), Ar, Mo,US
91/H3 Elevsis, Gre.
91/L6 Elevsis, Gre.
91/J2 Elevtheroúpolis, Gre.
186/E4 El Faro, Mex.
76/A1 El Ferrol, Sp.
202/K7 Elfers, Fl,US
203/G3 Elfers, Fl,US
70/C2 Elfershausen, Ger.
177/L4 Elfin Cove, Ak,US
197/R9 Elfrida, On,Can
187/H5 Elfrida, Az,US
194/C2 Elfros, Sk,Can
158/C3 El Fuerte, Mex.
103/F6 El Fureidis, Isr.
149/G3 El Galhak, Sudan
172/C3 El Galpón, Arg.
81/E3 Elgg, Swi.
194/D3 Elgin, Can
54/C1 Elgin, Sc,UK
187/G5 Elgin, Az,US
205/P15 Elgin, Il,US
191/F2 Elgin, Ks,US
194/D4 Elgin, ND,US
186/E2 Elgin, Nv,US
191/E3 Elgin, Ok,US
184/E1 Elgin, Or,US
201/G3 Elgin, SC,US
200/C2 Elgin, Tn,US
189/F2 Elgin, Tx,US
76/D1 Elgóibar, Sp.
143/F3 El Golea, Alg.
160/D3 El Golfete (lake), Guat.
205/K11 El Granada, Ca,US
165/F2 El Guachara Nat'l Park, Ven.
188/C3 El Guaje, Mex.
167/P7 El Guapo, Ven.
149/G2 El Gulut, Eth.
142/C2 El Had Harrara, Mor.
141/M14 El Hajeb, Mor.
141/T16 El Ham (riv.), Alg.
142/D4 El Hank (escarp.), Afr.
164/A2 El Harino, Pan.
143/E4 El Harta (well), Alg.
159/F4 El Higo, Mex.
190/C4 Elida, NM,US
198/D4 Elida, Oh,US
54/D4 Elie, Sc,UK
153/F3 Elila, Zaire
153/F3 Elila (riv.), Zaire
156/B4 Elim, SAfr.
177/F3 Elim, Ak,US
63/M1 Elimäki, Fin.
188/D3 El Infante, Mex.
59/E5 Eling, Eng,UK
196/B4 Eliot, Me,US
153/E3 Elipa, Zaire
63/N1 Elisenvaara, Rus.
167/F5 Eliseu Martins, Braz.
53/H4 Elista, Rus.
133/M8 Elizabeth, Austl.
196/D2 Elizabeth (mtn.), NB,Can
156/A2 Elizabeth (bay), Namb.
190/B1 Elizabeth, Co,US
201/L7 Elizabeth, Ga,US
189/H2 Elizabeth, La,US
196/B5 Elizabeth (isl.), Ma,US
208/D3 Elizabeth (isls.), Ma,US
194/F4 Elizabeth, Mn,US
207/D2 Elizabeth, NJ,US
188/K6 Elizabeth, Tx,US
201/H2 Elizabeth, WV,US
132/K7 Elizabethan Village, Austl.
201/J2 Elizabeth City, NC,US
201/F2 Elizabethton, Tn,US
200/C2 Elizabethtown, Il,US
198/D5 Elizabethtown, In,US
200/E2 Elizabethtown, Ky,US
201/H3 Elizabethtown, NC,US
199/K2 Elizabethtown, NY,US
206/B3 Elizabethtown, Pa,US
206/B2 Elizabethville, Pa,US
76/E1 Elizondo, Sp.
142/C2 El Jadida, Mor.
185/K4 El Jebel, Co,US
182/G2 Elk (riv.), BC,Can
65/M2 Ełk, Pol.
200/D3 Elk (riv.), Al, Tn,US
205/L10 Elk (slough), Ca,US
190/A1 Elk (mts.), Co,US
191/F2 Elk (riv.), Ks,US
206/C5 Elk (riv.), Md,US
190/E3 Elk (cr.), Ok,US
182/F5 Elk (mtn.), Or,US
199/J4 Elk (hill), Pa,US
192/C1 Elk (cr.), SD,US
200/D3 Elk (ridge), Tn,US
201/G1 Elk (riv.), WV,US
192/A3 Elk (mtn.), Wy,US
193/J2 Elkader, Ia,US
142/D2 El Kbab, Mor.
184/F1 Elk City, Id,US
191/G2 Elk City, Ks,US
191/G2 Elk City (dam), Ks,US
190/E3 Elk City, Ok,US
184/B4 Elk Creek, Ca,US
193/F3 Elk Creek, Ne,US
142/D2 El Kelaa des Srarhna, Mor.
69/G2 Elkenroth, Ger.
150/B4 Ēl Kerē, Eth.
182/G2 Elkford, BC,Can
205/M10 Elk Grove, Ca,US
205/Q15 Elk Grove Village, Il,US
198/D4 Elkhart, In,US
190/D2 Elkhart, Ks,US
189/G2 Elkhart, Tx,US
144/C2 El Khatt (depr.), Mrta.
142/C5 El Khatt (escarp.), Mrta.
142/E5 El Khnâchîch (escarp.), Mali
194/D3 Elkhorn, Mb,Can
193/F3 Elkhorn (riv.), Ne,US
205/N14 Elkhorn, Wi,US
93/H4 Elkhovo, Bul.
201/G2 Elkin, NC,US
201/H1 Elkins, WV,US
178/E3 Elk Island Nat'l Park, Ab,Can
183/H1 Elk Island Nat'l Park, Ab,Can
199/H4 Elkland, Pa,US
206/C4 Elk Mills, Md,US
185/K3 Elk Mountain, Wy,US
182/G3 Elko, BC,Can
184/F3 Elko, Nv,US
150/C4 Ēl K'oran, Eth.
193/F2 Elk Point, SD,US
198/D2 Elk Rapids, Mi,US
206/B5 Elk Ridge, Md,US
195/H5 Elk River, Mn,US
141/V17 El Kroub, Alg.
141/T15 El Kseur, Alg.
158/D1 Elk Silver, NM,US
185/J3 Elk Springs, Co,US
200/D2 Elkton, Ky,US
206/C4 Elkton, Md,US
200/D3 Elkton, Tn,US
201/H1 Elkton, Va,US
200/E2 Elk Valley, Tn,US
201/G1 Elkview, WV,US
183/J3 Elkwater, Ab,Can
177/J3 Ellamar, Ak,US
57/G4 Elland, Eng,UK
200/E4 Ellaville, Ga,US
78/B5 Ellé (riv.), Fr.
69/F2 Elle (riv.), Ger.
71/F2 Ellefeld, Ger.
179/R7 Ellef Ringnes (isl.), NW,Can
150/A5 Ēl Lēh, Eth.
57/E2 Ellen (riv.), Eng,UK
185/H4 Ellen (mt.), Ut,US
70/D4 Ellenberg, Ger.
130/B4 Ellendale, Austl.
206/C6 Ellendale, De,US
194/E4 Ellendale, ND,US
182/D4 Ellensburg, Wa,US
203/G4 Ellenton, Fl,US
203/G2 Ellenton, Ga,US
199/J4 Ellenville, NY,US
201/M7 Ellenwood, Ga,US
67/H5 Eller (riv.), Ger.
69/G4 Ellerbach (riv.), Ger.
201/H3 Ellerbe, NC,US
86/A4 Ellero (riv.), It.
196/F2 Ellerslie, PE,Can
200/E4 Ellerslie, Ga,US
189/J3 Ellerslie, La,US
135/D3 Ellery (peak), Austl.
179/T6 Ellesmere (isl.), NW,Can
179/T6 Ellesmere I. Nat'l Park, NW,Can
57/F5 Ellesmere Port, Eng,UK
198/C5 Ellettsville, In,US
68/C2 Ellezelles, Belg.
78/B4 Elliant, Fr.
174/Q9 El Libertador General Bernardo O'Higgins (reg.), Chile
178/F2 Ellice (riv.), NW,Can
206/B5 Ellicott City, Md,US
200/E3 Ellijay, Ga,US
208/B2 Ellington, Ct,US
191/J2 Ellington, Mo,US
91/H4 Ellinikón (int'l arpt.), Gre.
91/L7 Ellinikón (int'l arpt.), Gre.
191/E1 Ellinwood, Ks,US
156/D3 Elliot, SAfr.
135/H5 Elliot (key), Fl,US
198/E1 Elliot Lake, On,Can
133/H4 Elliot Price Consv. Park, Austl.
130/D4 Elliott, Austl.
193/G3 Elliott, Ia,US
201/G3 Elliott, SC,US
201/H1 Elliott (peak), Va,US
185/F1 Ellis, Id,US
190/E1 Ellis, Ks,US
207/J9 Ellis (isl.), NY,US
188/L7 Ellis (co.), Tx,US
198/C2 Ellison Bay, Wi,US
155/E4 Ellisras, SAfr.
133/G5 Elliston, Austl.
183/H4 Elliston, Mt,US
200/C5 Ellisville, Ms,US
161/G4 El Llano, Pan.
54/D2 Ellon, Sc,UK
201/G4 Elloree, SC,US
57/H4 Elloughton, Eng,UK
67/H5 Ellrich, Ger.
191/J2 Ellsinore, Mo,US
137/T Ellsworth (mts.), Ant.
191/E1 Ellsworth, Ks,US
196/C3 Ellsworth, Me,US
193/H1 Ellsworth, Wi,US
192/C1 Ellsworth A.F.B., SD,US
137/U Ellsworth Land (reg.), Ant.
70/D5 Ellwangen, Ger.
208/G6 Ellwood City, Pa,US
81/F4 Elm, Swi.
192/E1 Elm (riv.), ND, SD,US
195/E5 Elm (lake), SD,US
194/E5 Elm (riv.), SD,US
193/H2 Elma, Ia,US
197/T10 Elma, NY,US
104/C2 Elmadağ, Turk.
143/E5 El Mahia (reg.), Mali
174/C4 El Maitén, Arg.
103/A1 Elmalı, Turk.
150/B4 El Mallaile, Eth.
187/H3 El Malpais Nat'l Mon., NM,US
165/F3 El Manteco, Ven.
174/Q9 El Manzanito, Chile
174/Q10 El Manzano, Chile
158/B2 El Marmol, Mex.
90/A3 Elmas (int'l arpt.), It.
77/L7 El Masnou, Sp.
201/J3 Elm City, NC,US
194/F3 Elm Creek, Mb,Can
192/E3 Elm Creek, Ne,US
150/B4 El Medera, Eth.
202/B2 Elmer, La,US
193/H4 Elmer, Mo,US
206/C4 Elmer, NJ,US
148/C2 El Messir (well), Chad
189/N9 Elmgrove (pt.), Tx,US
205/P13 Elm Grove, Wi,US
205/Q16 Elmhurst, Il,US
165/F3 El Miamo, Ven.
141/V17 El Milia, Alg.
145/E5 Elmina, Gha.
199/H3 Elmira, NY,US
184/B1 Elmira, Or,US
204/C1 El Mirage, Ca,US
204/C1 El Mirage (dry lake), Ca,US
186/D3 El Mirage (lake), Ca,US
199/H3 Elmira Heights, NY,US
168/D5 El Misti (vol.), Peru
183/G4 Elmo, Mt,US
169/E4 El Mojar, Bol.
77/N8 El Molar, Sp.
207/E2 Elmont, NY,US
77/L6 El Montcau (peak), Sp.
204/B2 El Monte, Ca,US
207/J9 Elmora, NJ,US
135/C3 Elmore, Austl.
193/G2 Elmore, Mn,US
191/F3 Elmore City, Ok,US
188/B3 El Morreon, Mex.
174/C1 El Morrito (pt.), Chile
187/H3 El Morro, NM,US
142/C5 El Mrâyer (well), Mrta.
144/C2 El Mreyyé (reg.), Mrta.
196/F3 Elmsdale, NS,Can
196/E2 Elmsdale, PE,Can
207/K7 Elmsford, NY,US
67/G1 Elmshorn, Ger.
70/A4 Elmstein, Ger.
59/G2 Elmswell, Eng,UK
158/C3 El Muerto, Mex.
199/G2 Elmvale, On,Can
208/D1 Elmwood, Ma,US
193/F3 Elmwood, Ne,US
190/D2 Elmwood, Ok,US
205/Q16 Elmwood Park, Il,US
207/D2 Elmwood Park, NJ,US
205/Q14 Elmwood Park, Wi,US
142/D4 El Mzereb (well), Mali
158/C3 El Naranjo, Mex.
158/D4 El Nayar, Mex.
74/E5 Elne, Fr.
160/E3 El Negrito, Hon.
174/C2 El Nevado (peak), Arg.
125/B3 El Nido, Phil.
186/B2 El Nido, Ca,US
198/C5 Elnora, In,US
171/L6 Elói Mendes, Braz.
174/Q10 El Olivar Alto, Chile
201/H2 Elon College, NC,US
198/F3 Elora, On,Can
200/D3 Elora, Tn,US
78/A4 Elorn (riv.), Fr.
168/A1 El Oro (prov.), Ecu.
174/E2 Elortondo, Arg.
164/D3 Elorza, Ven.
166/A1 El Oso, Ven.
143/G2 El Oued, Alg.
143/G2 El Oued (wilaya), Alg.
134/H8 Elouera Bushland Rsv., Austl.
184/C1 Elowah (falls), Or,US
187/G4 Eloy, Az,US
164/B5 Eloy Alfaro, Ecu.
80/C1 Éloyes, Fr.
172/D2 El Palmar, Bol.
159/N8 El Palmar, Mex.
165/F3 El Palmar, Ven.
174/F1 El Palmar Nat'l Park, Arg.
158/D3 El Palmito, Mex.
165/E2 El Pao, Ven.
165/F2 El Pao, Ven.
164/C4 El Paraíso, Col.
160/E3 El Paraíso, Hon.
77/N8 El Pardo, Sp.
198/B4 El Paso, Il,US
188/A2 El Paso, Tx,US
188/A2 El Paso (int'l arpt.), Tx,US
186/B3 El Paso de Robles (Paso Robles), Ca,US
158/D1 El Paso Gap, NM,US
188/B3 El Pastor, Mex.
164/C4 El Pato, Col.
159/E3 El Pequeño, Mex.
169/E4 El Perú, Bol.
60/B2 Elphin, Ire.
194/D2 Elphinstone, Mb,Can
169/E4 El Pilar, Bol.
165/F2 El Pilar, Ven.
172/D3 El Pintado, Arg.
172/C3 El Piquete, Arg.
118/D6 Elpitiya, SrL.
159/J5 El Placer, Mex.
174/C2 El Plumerillo (Mendoza) (int'l arpt.), Arg.
186/C2 El Portal, Ca,US
188/B2 El Porvenir, Mex.
161/G4 El Porvenir, Pan.
190/B3 El Porvenir, NM,US
164/D3 El Porvenir, Ven.
159/E3 El Potosí, Mex.
160/A1 El Potosí Nat'l Park, Mex.
77/G2 El Prat de Llobregat, Sp.
168/K7 El Progreso, Ecu.
160/D3 El Progreso, Guat.
160/E3 El Progreso, Hon.
172/C2 El Puente, Bol.
76/B4 El Puerto de Santa María, Sp.
164/B4 El Pun, Ecu.
172/C3 El Quebrachal, Arg.
158/D4 El Quelite, Mex.
172/B3 Elqui (riv.), Chile
174/Q9 El Quisco, Chile
167/N8 El Rastro, Ven.
188/D3 El Remolino, Mex.
191/F3 El Reno, Ok,US
172/C2 El Rey Nat'l Park, Arg.
204/A2 El Rio, Ca,US
202/P7 El Rio (can.), Fl,US
203/H4 El Rio (can.), Fl,US
190/A2 El Rito, NM,US
161/F4 El Roble, Pan.
200/D4 Elrod, Al,US
165/E2 El Roque, Ven.
183/K2 Elrose, Sk,Can
201/J3 Elroy, NC,US
193/J2 Elroy, Wi,US
177/L3 Elsa, Yk,Can
87/E5 Elsa (riv.), It.
76/B2 Elsa (res.), Sp.
76/C1 Elsa (riv.), Sp.
189/F4 Elsa, Tx,US
188/E4 El Sabinal Nat'l Park, Mex.
193/J4 Elsah, Il,US
175/L7 El Salado, Arg.
167/K7 El Salado, Col.
158/D3 El Salado, Mex.
160/D3 El Salvador
161/H1 El Salvador, Cuba
160/D3 El Salvador (int'l arpt.), ESal.
159/E3 El Salvador, Mex.
164/D3 El Samán de Apure, Ven.
188/A3 El Sauz, Mex.
188/D4 El Sauz, Mex.
191/J1 Elsberry, Mo,US
67/G2 Elsdorf, Ger.
67/F4 Else (riv.), Ger.
204/B3 El Segundo, Ca,US
162/D3 El Seibo, DRep.
114/F4 Elsen (lake), China
70/C3 Elsenfeld, Ger.
70/B4 Elsenz (riv.), Ger.
191/H2 Elsey, Mo,US
67/F2 Elsfleth, Ger.
147/F4 El Shab (well), Egypt
198/D3 Elsie, Mi,US
204/C3 Elsinore (lake), Ca,US
185/G4 Elsinore, Ut,US
69/E2 Elsloo, Neth.
206/C4 Elsmere, De,US
164/D3 El Socorro, Col.
158/B2 El Socorro, Mex.
174/C5 El Sombrero, Arg.
165/E2 El Sombrero, Ven.
174/C2 El Sosneado, Arg.
66/C5 Elst, Neth.
72/D2 Elstal, Ger.
59/F4 Elstead, Eng,UK
72/C4 Elster, Ger.
72/C5 Elster (riv.), Ger.
71/F1 Elsterberg, Ger.
72/D5 Elsterwerda, Ger.
72/E5 Elstra, Ger.
174/Q9 El Tabo, Chile
159/F4 El Tajín (ruins), Mex.
172/C3 El Tala, Arg.
164/C3 El Tama Nat'l Park, Ven.
164/B5 El Tambo, Ecu.
141/W17 El Tarf, Alg.
141/V17 El Tarf (gov.), Alg.
130/A2 Eltari (int'l arpt.), Indo.
76/B1 El Teleno (mtn.), Sp.
159/F3 El Temascal, Mex.
159/L7 El Tepozteco Nat'l Park, Mex.
136/C2 Eltham, N.Z.
53/P7 Eltham, Eng,UK
76/C2 El Tiemblo, Sp.
165/E2 El Tigre, Ven.
70/D3 Eltmann, Ger.
164/D2 El Tocuyo, Ven.
97/H2 El'ton (lake), Rus.
202/B2 Elton, La,US
193/K1 Elton, Wi,US
182/E4 Eltopia, Wa,US
204/C3 El Toro, Ca,US
189/F3 El Toro, Tx,US
165/F2 El Toro, Ven.
172/B4 El Tránsito, Chile
172/D5 El Trébol, Arg.
188/B3 El Trece, Mex.
164/B5 El Triunfo, Ecu.
158/C4 El Triunfo, Mex.
165/F2 El Tucuche (peak), Trin.
188/A4 El Tule, Mex.
188/D3 El Tule, Mex.
164/D3 El Tuparro Nat'l Park, Col.
70/B2 Eltville am Rhein, Ger.
118/D4 Elūru, India
63/M2 Elva, Est.
187/J2 El Vado, NM,US
161/F4 El Valle, Pan.
103/D1 Elvanlı, Turk.
76/B3 Elvas, Port.
78/C5 Elven, Fr.
188/D4 El Venado, Mex.
161/F4 El Venado (isl.), Nic.
62/D1 Elverum, Nor.
164/C3 El Viejo, Col.
160/E3 El Viejo, Nic.
164/D2 El Vigía, Ven.
164/D1 El Vinculo, Ven.
200/B2 Elvins, Mo,US
132/C2 Elvire (peak), Austl.
86/B2 Elvo (riv.), It.
174/Q9 El Volcán, Chile
188/C3 El Volcán, Mex.
151/C1 El Wak, Kenya
183/J3 Elwell (lake), Mt,US
198/D4 Elwood, In,US
192/E3 Elwood, Ne,US
206/D4 Elwood-Magnolia, NJ,US
56/E5 Elwy (riv.), Wal,UK
72/A5 Elxleben, Ger.
59/G2 Ely, Eng,UK
195/J4 Ely, Mn,US
185/F4 Ely, Nv,US
164/D3 El Yagual, Ven.
103/F7 Elyashiv, Isr.
59/G2 Ely, Isle of (reg.), Eng,UK
164/C3 El Yopal, Col.
208/E5 Elyria, Oh,US
206/B2 Elysburg, Pa,US
204/F7 Elysian Park, Ca,US
162/E3 El Yunque (mtn.), PR
70/B2 Elz, Ger.
80/D1 Elz (riv.), Ger.
70/B6 Elzach, Ger.
69/G3 Elzbach (riv.), Ger.
67/G4 Elze, Ger.
175/K7 El Zurdo, Arg.
105/H2 Emāmshahr, Iran
107/G1 Emām Taqī, Iran
62/F3 Emån (riv.), Swe.
170/B3 Emas Nat'l Park, Braz.
97/K3 Emba, Kaz.
97/K3 Emba (riv.), Kaz.
172/C2 Embarcación, Arg.
198/C5 Embarras (riv.), Il,US
195/H4 Embarrass, Mn,US
198/B2 Embarrass, Wi,US
112/B1 Embetsu, Japan
168/D3 Embira (riv.), Braz.
152/D2 Embondo, Zaire
170/D3 Emborcação (res.), Braz.
81/E3 Embrach, Swi.
82/C3 Embrun, Fr.

67/H2 **Embsen**, Ger.
151/B2 **Embu**, Kenya
171/K8 **Embu-Guaçu**, Braz.
67/E2 **Emden**, Ger.
193/K3 **Emden**, Il,US
116/D2 **Emei**, China
116/D2 **Emei** (peak), China
135/G5 **Emerald**, Austl.
130/A4 **Emeriau** (pt.), Austl.
194/F3 **Emerson**, Mb,Can
191/H4 **Emerson**, Ar,US
207/J8 **Emerson**, NJ,US
190/C2 **Emery** (peak), NM,US
192/F2 **Emery**, SD,US
185/H4 **Emery**, Ut,US
205/G7 **Emeryville**, On,Can
205/K11 **Emeryville**, Ca,US
104/B2 **Emet**, Turk.
182/F4 **Emida**, Id,US
185/H1 **Emigrant**, Mt,US
185/H1 **Emigrant** (peak), Mt,US
206/B3 **Emigsville**, Pa,US
158/E3 **Emiliano Zapata**, Mex.
86/D4 **Emilia-Romagna** (reg.), It.
82/D1 **Emilius** (peak), It.
86/A1 **Emilius, Monte** (peak), It.
114/D2 **Emin**, China
114/D2 **Emin** (riv.), China
191/J2 **Eminence**, Mo,US
93/H4 **Emine, Nos** (cape), Bul.
104/B2 **Emirdağ**, Turk.
104/C2 **Emirgazi**, Turk.
153/G3 **Emir Pasha** (gulf), Tanz.
146/C4 **Emissi, Tarso** (peak), Chad
135/C4 **Emita**, Austl.
157/E2 **Emlembe** (peak), Swaz.
208/H5 **Emlenton**, Pa,US
66/D3 **Emlichheim**, Ger.
165/H4 **Emma** (riv.), Sur.
62/F3 **Emmaboda**, Swe.
63/K2 **Emmaste**, Est.
206/C2 **Emmaus**, Pa,US
80/D4 **Emme** (riv.), Swi.
66/C3 **Emmeloord**, Neth.
66/D3 **Emmen**, Neth.
81/E3 **Emmenbrücke**, Swi.
80/D1 **Emmendingen**, Ger.
80/D3 **Emmental** (vall.), Swi.
67/G5 **Emmer** (riv.), Ger.
67/E5 **Emmerbach** (riv.), Ger.
66/E3 **Emmer-Compascuum**, Neth.
66/D5 **Emmerich**, Ger.
134/B4 **Emmet**, Austl.
191/H4 **Emmet**, Ar,US
193/G2 **Emmetsburg**, Ia,US
184/E2 **Emmett**, Id,US
205/G6 **Emmett**, Mi,US
81/E2 **Emmingen-Liptingen**, Ger.
206/A4 **Emmitsburg**, Md,US
177/F3 **Emmonak**, Ak,US
185/H3 **Emmons** (mt.), Ut,US
59/G1 **Emneth**, Eng,UK
92/E2 **Emőd**, Hun.
189/G1 **Emory**, Tx,US
188/C3 **Emory** (peak), Tx,US
80/C5 **Emosson** (lake), Swi.
158/C3 **Empalme**, Mex.
157/E3 **Empangeni**, SAfr.
172/E3 **Empedrado**, Arg.
174/B2 **Empedrado**, Chile
201/F4 **Empire**, Ga,US
198/C2 **Empire**, Mi,US
208/G6 **Empire**, Oh,US
87/D5 **Empoli**, It.
191/F1 **Emporia**, Ks,US
201/J2 **Emporia**, Va,US
199/G4 **Emporium**, Pa,US
105/J3 **'Emrānī**, Iran
66/D2 **Ems** (riv.), Ger.
64/D2 **Ems** (riv.), Ger., Neth.
67/E4 **Emsbüren**, Ger.
67/E4 **Emsdetten**, Ger.
66/D2 **Ems** (Eems) (riv.), Neth.
67/E2 **Ems-Jade** (can.), Ger.
70/D3 **Emskirchen**, Ger.
67/E3 **Emsland** (reg.), Ger.
67/F3 **Emstek**, Ger.
109/K3 **Emu**, China
63/M2 **Emumägi** (hill), Est.
134/C3 **Emu Park**, Austl.
109/J1 **Emur** (riv.), China
56/B3 **Emyvale**, Ire.
111/E3 **Ena**, Japan
151/A2 **Enangiperi**, Kenya
127/J4 **Enarotali**, Indo.
185/K3 **Encampment**, Wy,US
158/B2 **Encantada, Cerro de la** (mtn.), Mex.
158/B3 **Encantado, Cerro** (mt.), Mex.
158/E4 **Encarnación**, Mex.
173/F3 **Encarnación**, Par.
144/E5 **Enchi**, Gha.
188/E3 **Encinal**, Tx,US
204/C4 **Encinitas**, Ca,US
204/E7 **Encino**, Ca,US
189/E4 **Encino**, Tx,US
164/C3 **Enciso**, Col.
164/D4 **Enciso**, Col.
174/D2 **Encón**, Arg.
164/C2 **Encontrados**, Ven.
135/A2 **Encounter** (bay), Austl.
173/F4 **Encruzilhada do Sul**, Braz.
92/E1 **Encs**, Hun.
151/B2 **Endau** (peak), Kenya
130/A2 **Ende**, Indo.
130/A2 **Ende** (isl.), Indo.
131/F2 **Endeavour** (str.), Austl.
194/C1 **Endeavour**, Sk,Can
134/B1 **Endeavour River Nat'l Park**, Austl.
151/A1 **Endebess**, Kenya
139/H5 **Enderbury** (isl.), Kiri.
182/E2 **Enderby**, BC,Can
137/D **Enderby Land** (reg.), Ant.
194/F4 **Enderlin**, ND,US
199/H3 **Endicott**, NY,US
182/F4 **Endicott**, Wa,US
80/D1 **Endingen**, Ger.
82/C5 **Endre** (riv.), Fr.
199/H3 **Endwell** (Hooper), NY,US
130/D2 **Endyalgourt** (isl.), Austl.
168/C3 **Ene** (riv.), Peru
132/B4 **Eneabba**, Austl.
62/D2 **Enebakk**, Nor.
99/K5 **Enem**, Rus.
114/C3 **Energeticheskiy**, Kaz.
97/L2 **Energetik**, Rus.
73/B4 **Enese**, Hun.
138/F3 **Enewetak** (atoll), Mrsh.
51/S5 **Enewetak** (isl.), Mrsh.
91/K2 **Enez**, Turk.
196/F3 **Enfield**, NS,Can
53/N7 **Enfield**, Eng,UK
53/N7 **Enfield** (bor.), Eng,UK
208/B2 **Enfield**, Ct,US
200/C1 **Enfield**, Il,US
196/C3 **Enfield**, Me,US
201/J2 **Enfield**, NC,US
199/K3 **Enfield**, NH,US
131/F1 **Enga** (prov.), PNG
198/D1 **Engadine**, Mi,US
102/M8 **Engaño** (cape), Phil.
112/C1 **Engaru**, Japan
151/B2 **Engaruka** (basin), Tanz.
151/B3 **Engassumet**, Tanz.
156/E3 **Engcobo**, SAfr.
81/E4 **Engelberg**, Swi.
73/A3 **Engelhartstetten**, Aus.
71/G5 **Engelhartszell**, Aus.
53/H3 **Engel's**, Rus.
72/C5 **Engelsdorf**, Ger.
69/G2 **Engelskirchen**, Ger.
66/D2 **Engelsmanplaat** (isl.), Neth.
81/E2 **Engen**, Ger.
171/N7 **Engenheiro Paulo de Froutin**, Braz.
67/F4 **Enger**, Ger.
71/H6 **Engerwitzdorf**, Aus.
126/B5 **Enggano** (isl.), Indo.
149/H1 **Enghershatu** (peak), Eth.
68/D2 **Enghien**, Belg.
81/F4 **Engi**, Swi.
55/K10 **England**, UK
191/J3 **England**, Ar,US
202/B2 **England A.F.B.**, La,US
187/J4 **Engle**, NM,US
68/C3 **Englefontaine**, Fr.
194/F4 **Englevale**, ND,US
203/G4 **Englewood**, Fl,US
207/E2 **Englewood**, NJ,US
207/K8 **Englewood Cliffs**, NJ,US
137/V **English** (coast), Ant.
195/H2 **English** (riv.), On,Can
74/B2 **English** (chan.), Eur.
200/D1 **English**, In,US
177/H4 **English Bay**, Ak,US
121/G3 **English Bāzār**, India
131/E2 **English Companys, The** (isls.), Austl.
206/D5 **English Creek**, NJ,US
197/K2 **English Harbour West**, Nf,Can
195/J3 **English River**, On,Can
207/D3 **Englishtown**, NJ,US
152/B2 **Engong**, Gabon
155/G1 **Engucwini**, Malw.
77/E3 **Enguera**, Sp.
63/K3 **Engure**, Lat.
103/G6 **'En Harod**, Isr.
200/C3 **Enid** (lake), Ms,US
191/F2 **Enid**, Ok,US
203/G2 **Enigma**, Ga,US
112/B2 **Eniwa**, Japan
201/F3 **Enka**, NC,US
70/A4 **Enkenbach-Alsenborn**, Ger.
66/C3 **Enkhuizen**, Neth.
69/G4 **Enkirch**, Ger.
62/G2 **Enköping**, Swe.
208/G7 **Enlow-Imperial**, Pa,US
90/D4 **Enna**, It.
148/D1 **Ennedi** (plat.), Chad
60/C3 **Ennell, Lough** (lake), Ire.
148/C2 **Ennē, Ouadi** (dry riv.), Chad
67/E6 **Ennepe** (riv.), Ger.
67/E6 **Ennepetal**, Ger.
53/S9 **Ennery**, Fr.
135/C1 **Enngonia**, Austl.
192/C1 **Enning**, SD,US
67/F5 **Enningerloh**, Ger.
60/B4 **Ennis**, Ire.
185/H1 **Ennis**, Mt,US
189/F1 **Ennis**, Tx,US
60/D4 **Enniscorthy**, Ire.
60/D3 **Enniskerry**, Ire.
55/H9 **Enniskillen**, NI,UK
199/G2 **Ennismore**, Can.
60/A4 **Ennistimon**, Ire.
71/H6 **Enns**, Aus.
92/A2 **Enns** (riv.), Aus.
82/B4 **Ennuye** (riv.), Fr.
187/F2 **Enoch**, Ut,US
190/C4 **Enochs**, Tx,US
134/E6 **Enoggera** (res.), Austl.
191/H3 **Enola**, Ar,US
206/B3 **Enola**, Pa,US
208/G6 **Enon** (Enon Valley), Pa,US
61/G1 **Enontekiö**, Fin.
208/G6 **Enon Valley** (Enon), Pa,US
201/G3 **Enoree**, SC,US
201/G3 **Enoree** (riv.), SC,US
196/A3 **Enosburg Falls**, Vt,US
117/G4 **Enping**, China
188/D4 **Enramadas**, Mex.
127/E4 **Enrekang**, Indo.
54/B2 **Enrick** (riv.), Sc,UK
175/S11 **Enrique Carbó**, Arg.
162/D3 **Enriquillo**, DRep.
66/D4 **Enschede**, Neth.
71/E4 **Ensdorf**, Ger.
67/E6 **Ense**, Ger.
175/T12 **Ensenada**, Arg.
186/D5 **Ensenada**, Mex.
69/G5 **Ensheim** (arpt.), Ger.
115/B5 **Enshi**, China
198/C2 **Ensign**, Mi,US
80/D2 **Ensisheim**, Fr.
202/E2 **Ensley**, Fl,US
153/H2 **Entebbe**, Ugan.
153/H2 **Entebbe** (int'l arpt.), Ugan.
71/F3 **Entenbühl** (peak), Ger.
199/H2 **Enterprise**, On,Can
203/F2 **Enterprise**, Al,US
191/F1 **Enterprise**, Ks,US
202/C2 **Enterprise**, La,US
200/C4 **Enterprise**, Ms,US
191/G3 **Enterprise**, Ok,US
184/E1 **Enterprise**, Or,US
182/D4 **Entiat**, Wa,US
80/E4 **Entlebuch**, Swi.
82/A5 **Entraigues-sur-Sorges**, Fr.
79/E5 **Entrammes**, Fr.
182/F1 **Entrance**, Ab,Can
135/D2 **Entrance, The**, Austl.
82/B2 **Entre-deux-Guiers**, Fr.
174/B4 **Entre Lagos**, Chile
174/F2 **Entre Ríos** (prov.), Arg.
172/C2 **Entre Ríos**, Bol.
166/C4 **Entre Rios**, Braz.
155/H2 **Entre-Rios**, Moz.
160/E3 **Entre Ríos, Cordillera** (range), Hon.
170/D4 **Entre Rios de Minas**, Braz.
82/C5 **Entrevaux**, Fr.
175/K8 **Entre Vientos**, Chile
76/A3 **Entroncamento**, Port.
197/G2 **Entry** (isl.), Qu,Can
182/G1 **Entwistle**, Ab,Can
80/D1 **Entzheim**, Fr.
75/G2 **Entzheim** (Strasbourg) (int'l arpt.), Fr.
80/D1 **Entzheim** (Strasbourg) (int'l arpt.), Fr.
130/D1 **Enu** (isl.), Indo.
145/G5 **Enugu**, Nga.
145/G5 **Enugu Ngwo**, Nga.
205/D3 **Enumclaw**, Wa,US
111/N10 **Enushū** (sea), Japan
68/A4 **Envermeu**, Fr.
167/K6 **Envigado**, Col.
168/D2 **Envira**, Braz.
153/F3 **Enyamba**, Zaire
116/E2 **Enyang**, China
152/D2 **Enyellé**, Congo
73/C6 **Enying**, Hun.
70/C5 **Enz** (riv.), Ger.
86/D4 **Enza** (riv.), It.
111/F3 **Enzan**, Japan
69/F4 **Enzbach** (riv.), Ger.
73/A3 **Enzersdorf an der Fischa**, Aus.
73/A4 **Enzesfeld**, Aus.
70/B5 **Enzklösterle**, Ger.
188/D2 **Eola**, Tx,US
191/J1 **Eolia**, Mo,US
79/F2 **Epaignes**, Fr.
80/C4 **Epalinges**, Swi.
91/J5 **Epáno Arkhánai**, Gre.
91/H2 **Epanomí**, Gre.
202/M7 **EPCOT Ctr.**, Fl,US
66/C4 **Epe**, Neth.
145/F5 **Epe**, Nga.
68/C3 **Épehy**, Fr.
152/D2 **Epéna**, Congo
133/G2 **Epenarra**, Austl.
68/C5 **Épernay**, Fr.
68/A6 **Épernon**, Fr.
80/D1 **Epfig**, Fr.
89/K3 **Ephesus** (ruins), Turk.
185/H4 **Ephraim**, Ut,US
195/L5 **Ephraim**, Wi,US
206/B3 **Ephrata**, Pa,US
182/E4 **Ephrata**, Wa,US
138/F6 **Epi** (isl.), Van.
91/H4 **Epidaurus** (Epídharros) (ruins), Gre.
89/J3 **Epidaurus** (Epídhavros) (ruins), Gre.
91/H4 **Epídhavros** (Epidaurus) (ruins), Gre.
82/C2 **Épierre**, Fr.
80/C1 **Épinal**, Fr.
80/C1 **Épinal** (Mirecourt) (arpt.), Fr.
53/S10 **Épinay-sur-Orge**, Fr.
53/S10 **Épinay-sur-Seine**, Fr.
165/G3 **Epira**, Guy.
91/G3 **Epirus** (reg.), Gre.
103/C2 **Episkopi**, Cyp.
85/D6 **Epomeo** (vol.), It.
79/G2 **Epone**, Fr.
69/F5 **Eppelborn**, Ger.
69/G5 **Eppenbrunn**, Ger.
68/C4 **Eppeville**, Fr.
134/H8 **Epping**, Austl.
53/P6 **Epping**, Eng,UK
53/P7 **Epping** (for.), Eng,UK
70/B4 **Eppingen**, Ger.
134/B3 **Epping Forest Nat'l Park**, Austl.
70/D6 **Eppishausen**, Ger.
189/J1 **Epps**, La,US
183/M5 **Epsie**, Mt,US
53/N8 **Epsom**, Eng,UK
59/F4 **Epsom and Ewell**, Eng,UK
79/G2 **Epte** (riv.), Fr.
154/C4 **Epukiro**, Namb.
154/C4 **Epukiro** (dry riv.), Namb.
153/G2 **Epulu** (riv.), Zaire
154/B3 **Epupa** (falls), Ang.
57/H4 **Epworth**, Eng,UK
200/E3 **Epworth**, Ga,US
193/J2 **Epworth**, Ia,US
105/H4 **Eqlīd**, Iran
153/E2 **Equateur** (pol. reg.), Zaire
148/D5 **Equateur** (reg.), Zaire
152/B2 **Equatorial Guinea**
78/D1 **Équeurdreville-Hainneville**, Fr.
59/H5 **Équihen Plage**, Fr.
68/A2 **Équihen-Plage**, Fr.
154/B2 **Equimina**, Ang.
116/C3 **Er** (lake), China
78/B3 **Er** (isls.), Fr.
87/D5 **Era** (riv.), It.
131/G1 **Era** (riv.), PNG
87/F1 **Eraclea**, It.
83/C2 **Eraclea** (ruins), It.
90/C4 **Eraclea Minoa** (ruins), It.
90/E2 **Eraclea Minoa** (ruins), It.
53/S9 **Éragny**, Fr.
125/B3 **Eran**, Phil.
160/D3 **Erandique**, Hon.
202/B3 **Erath**, La,US
131/G1 **Erave**, PNG
131/G1 **Erave** (riv.), PNG
118/D6 **Eravur**, SrL.
123/B3 **Erawan Nat'l Park**, Thai.
86/C1 **Erba**, It.
104/D1 **Erbaa**, Turk.
70/C3 **Erbach**, Ger.
71/F3 **Erbendorf**, Ger.
64/D4 **Erbeskopf** (peak), Ger.
103/C2 **Ercan** (int'l arpt.), Cyp.
78/D5 **Ercé-en-Lamée**, Fr.
105/E2 **Erçek**, Turk.
105/E2 **Erçek** (lake), Turk.
174/B3 **Ercilla**, Chile
105/E2 **Erciş**, Turk.
104/C2 **Erciyes** (peak), Turk.
68/C3 **Erclin** (riv.), Fr.
73/C5 **Ercsi**, Hun.
73/C5 **Érd**, Hun.
113/E1 **Erdao** (riv.), China
72/B5 **Erdeborn**, Ger.
93/H5 **Erdek**, Turk.
93/H5 **Erdek** (gulf), Turk.
103/D1 **Erdemli**, Turk.
108/G3 **Erdene**, Mong.
108/E2 **Erdenedalay**, Mong.
108/E2 **Erdenet**, Mong.
78/B5 **Erdeven**, Fr.
146/D5 **Erdi-Ma** (plat.), Chad
148/D1 **Erdi-Ma** (upland), Chad
71/E6 **Erding**, Ger.
78/D6 **Erdre** (riv.), Fr.
70/E6 **Erdweg**, Ger.
137/M **Erebus** (vol.), Ant.
173/F3 **Erechim**, Braz.
108/G2 **Ereen Davaanï** (mts.), Mong.
93/K5 **Ereğli**, Turk.
127/F4 **Ereke**, Indo.
84/C1 **Eremo delle Carceri**, It.
87/E5 **Eremo di Camaldoli**, It.
114/D3 **Erenhaberga** (mts.), China
108/G3 **Erenhot**, China
93/K5 **Erenler**, Turk.
104/E2 **Erentepe**, Turk.
165/H5 **Erepecu** (lake), Braz.
150/B3 **Ērer Shet'** (dry riv.), Eth.
76/C2 **Eresma** (riv.), Sp.
91/H3 **Erétria**, Gre.
97/H4 **Erevan** (int'l arpt.), Arm.
69/E3 **Érezée**, Belg.
70/C3 **Erfa** (riv.), Ger.
142/D3 **Erfoud**, Mor.
88/B5 **Erfoud**, Mor.
69/F1 **Erft** (riv.), Ger.
69/F2 **Erftstadt**, Ger.
72/B6 **Erfurt**, Ger.
72/A6 **Erfurt** (arpt.), Ger.
104/D2 **Ergani**, Turk.
93/H5 **Ergene Nehri** (riv.), Turk.
63/L3 **Ērgļi**, Lat.
78/A4 **Ergué-Gabéric**, Fr.
148/C3 **Erguig, Bahr** (riv.), Chad
109/H1 **Ergun** (riv.), China, Rus.
109/J1 **Ergun Youqi**, China
109/J1 **Ergun Zuoqi**, China
194/F4 **Erhard**, Mn,US
117/J4 **Erhlin**, Tai.
113/C2 **Erhulai**, China
149/H1 **Eriba**, Sudan
66/D3 **Erica**, Neth.
90/C3 **Erice**, It.
76/A3 **Ericeira**, Port.
54/B3 **Ericht** (riv.), Sc,UK
54/C3 **Ericht** (riv.), Sc,UK
54/B3 **Ericht, Loch** (lake), Sc,UK
190/E3 **Erick**, Ok,US
194/E2 **Erickson**, Can
195/H3 **Ericsburg**, Mn,US
198/F3 **Erie** (lake), Can., US
191/G2 **Erie**, Ks,US
197/T9 **Erie** (can.), NY,US
197/T10 **Erie** (co.), NY,US
208/H5 **Erie** (co.), Oh,US
198/F3 **Erie**, Pa,US
198/F3 **Erie** (int'l arpt.), Pa,US
208/H4 **Erie Nat'l Wild. Ref.**, Pa,US
150/C3 **Erigabo** (Ceerigaabo), Som.
194/E2 **Eriksdale**, Mb,Can
62/F3 **Eriksmalå**, Swe.
138/F4 **Erikub** (atoll), Mrsh.
153/H2 **Erima**, Ugan.
91/G4 **Erímanthos** (peak), Gre.
112/C2 **Erimo**, Japan
112/C3 **Erimo-misaki** (cape), Japan
197/Q8 **Erin**, On,Can
200/D2 **Erin**, Tn,US
189/H2 **Erin**, Tx,US
91/H3 **Erithraí**, Gre.
150/A1 **Eritrea** (prov.), Eth.
106/C5 **Eritrea** (reg.), Eth.
149/H1 **Eritrea** (Ērta) (reg.), Eth.
66/D6 **Erkelenz**, Ger.
63/H1 **Erken** (isl.), Swe.
70/D6 **Erkheim**, Ger.
60/C4 **Erkina** (riv.), Ire.
72/D3 **Erkner**, Ger.
66/D6 **Erkrath**, Ger.
80/D3 **Erlach**, Swi.
205/B2 **Erlands Point-Kitsap Lake**, Wa,US
116/D2 **Erlang** (peak), China
70/E3 **Erlangen**, Ger.
198/D5 **Erlanger**, Ky,US
71/G5 **Erlau** (riv.), Ger.
133/G3 **Erldunda**, Austl.
70/B4 **Erlenbach** (riv.), Ger.
80/D4 **Erlenbach**, Swi.
70/C3 **Erlenbach am Main**, Ger.
70/C3 **Erlenbach bei Marktheidenfeld**, Ger.
191/H4 **Erling** (lake), Ar,US
80/D3 **Erlinsbach**, Swi.
109/K2 **Erlongshan**, China
115/F2 **Erlongshan** (res.), China
58/C6 **Erme** (riv.), Eng,UK
66/C4 **Ermelo**, Neth.
156/Q13 **Ermelo**, SAfr.
103/C1 **Ermenek**, Turk.
103/C1 **Ermenek** (riv.), Turk.
53/U9 **Ermenonville**, Fr.
130/B2 **Ermera**, Indo.
135/C2 **Ermeran Station**, Austl.
183/H1 **Ermineskin Ind. Res.**, Ab,Can
91/H4 **Ermióni**, Gre.
53/S10 **Ermont**, Fr.
91/J4 **Ermoúpolis**, Gre.
70/C6 **Erms** (riv.), Ger.
133/G3 **Ernabella**, Austl.
122/F4 **Ernākulam**, India
69/H2 **Erndtebrück**, Ger.
79/E4 **Ernée**, Fr.
74/C2 **Ernée** (riv.), Fr.
55/H9 **Erne, Lower Lough** (lake), NI,UK
164/C2 **Ernesto Cortissoz** (int'l arpt.), Col.
60/C1 **Erne, Upper Lough** (lake), NI,UK
73/A2 **Ernstbrunn**, Aus.
71/H6 **Ernsthofen**, Aus.
122/F3 **Erode**, India
70/D6 **Erolzheim**, Ger.
134/A4 **Eromanga**, Austl.
202/B1 **Eros**, La,US
135/D2 **Erowal Bay**, Austl.
68/C2 **Erpe**, Belg.
69/G2 **Erpel**, Ger.
113/C2 **Erpengdianzi**, China
108/C3 **Erpu**, China
68/D3 **Erquelinnes**, Belg.
78/C3 **Erquy**, Fr.
142/D3 **Er Rachidīa**, Mor.
142/E3 **Er Raoui, 'Erg** (des.), Alg.
155/H3 **Errego**, Moz.
141/M13 **Er Rif** (mts.), Mor.
55/G9 **Errigal** (mtn.), Ire.
52/C3 **Erris** (pt.), Ire.
54/G9 **Erris Head** (pt.), Ire.
86/B4 **Erro** (riv.), It.
54/B3 **Errochty, Loch** (lake), Sc,UK
54/C4 **Errol**, Sc,UK
196/B3 **Errol**, NH,US
138/F6 **Erromango** (isl.), Van.
81/F4 **Err, Piz d'** (peak), Swi.
67/H4 **Erse** (riv.), Ger.
91/G2 **Ersekë**, Alb.
117/H2 **Ershibadu**, China
183/H1 **Erskine**, Ab,Can
194/F4 **Erskine**, Mn,US
80/D1 **Erstein**, Fr.
81/E4 **Erstfeld**, Swi.
149/H1 **Ērta** (Eritrea) (reg.), Eth.
114/D3 **Ertai**, China
99/L2 **Ertil'**, Rus.
70/C6 **Ertingen**, Ger.
108/B2 **Ertix** (riv.), China
68/C1 **Ertvelde**, Belg.
104/E2 **Eruh**, Turk.
154/C4 **Erundu**, Namb.
173/F5 **Erval**, Braz.
173/G3 **Erval d'Oeste**, Braz.
171/E4 **Ervália**, Braz.
185/K2 **Ervay**, Wy,US
201/H3 **Erwin**, NC,US
201/F2 **Erwin**, Tn,US
67/F5 **Erwitte**, Ger.
116/C3 **Eryuan**, China
91/F2 **Erzen** (riv.), Alb.
64/G3 **Erzgebirge** (Krušné Hory) (mts.), Czh., Ger.
72/D6 **Erzgebirge** (Krušné Hory) (mts.), Czh., Ger.
71/F2 **Erzgebirge** (Krušné Hory) (mts.), Ger.
70/B3 **Erzhausen**, Ger.
114/G1 **Erzin**, Rus.
104/D2 **Erzincan**, Turk.
104/D2 **Erzincan** (prov.), Turk.
104/E2 **Erzurum**, Turk.
104/E1 **Erzurum** (prov.), Turk.
138/D5 **Esa'ala**, PNG
153/E3 **Esambo**, Zaire
112/B3 **Esan-misaki** (cape), Japan
83/C3 **Esaro** (riv.), It.
112/B3 **Esashi**, Japan
112/B4 **Esashi**, Japan
112/C1 **Esashi**, Japan
104/D1 **Esbiye**, Turk.
62/C4 **Esbjerg**, Den.
62/C4 **Esbjerg** (int'l arpt.), Den.
53/U10 **Esbly**, Fr.
63/L1 **Esbo** (Espoo), Fin.
191/E1 **Esbon**, Ks,US
187/J3 **Escabosa**, NM,US
167/H5 **Escada**, Braz.
187/F2 **Escalante** (des.), Tx, Ut,US
187/G2 **Escalante**, Ut,US
185/G4 **Escalante** (des.), Ut,US
187/G2 **Escalante** (riv.), Ut,US
158/D3 **Escalón**, Mex.
184/C5 **Escalon**, Ca,US
76/C2 **Escalona**, Sp.
203/E2 **Escambia** (riv.), Fl,US
82/C6 **Escampobariou** (pt.), Fr.
198/C2 **Escanaba**, Mi,US
195/L4 **Escanaba** (riv.), Mi,US
198/C1 **Escanaba** (riv.), Mi,US
125/C1 **Escarpada** (pt.), Phil.
202/D2 **Escatawpa** (riv.), Ms,US
68/C3 **Escaudain**, Fr.
74/E1 **Escaut** (riv.), Belg.
64/B3 **Escaut** (riv.), Belg., Fr.
68/C3 **Escaut** (riv.), Fr.
69/E6 **Esch** (riv.), Fr.
70/B6 **Eschach** (riv.), Ger.
81/E1 **Eschach** (riv.), Ger.
81/G2 **Eschach** (riv.), Ger.
80/D1 **Eschau**, Fr.
67/H3 **Eschede**, Ger.
81/F3 **Eschen**, Lcht.
70/C5 **Eschenbach**, Ger.
71/E3 **Eschenbach in der Oberpfalz**, Ger.
67/G5 **Eschershausen**, Ger.
68/B5 **Esches** (riv.), Fr.
70/A4 **Eschkopf** (mt.), Ger.
80/D4 **Escholzmatt**, Swi.
69/E5 **Esch-sur-Alzette**, Lux.
69/E4 **Esch-sur-Sure**, Lux.
67/H6 **Eschwege**, Ger.
69/F2 **Eschweiler**, Ger.
188/E4 **Escobares**, Tx,US
188/D5 **Escobedo** (int'l arpt.), Mex.
168/D4 **Escoma**, Bol.
204/C4 **Escondido**, Ca,US
204/C4 **Escondido** (cr.), Ca,US
196/C1 **Escoumins**, Qu,Can
82/A3 **Escoutay** (riv.), Fr.
165/E3 **Escudillas**, Ven.
158/D4 **Escuinapa**, Mex.
160/D3 **Escuintla**, Guat.
160/C3 **Escuintla**, Mex.
196/E2 **Escuminac** (pt.), NB,Can
103/G6 **Esdraelon, Plain of** (plain), Isr.
148/A5 **Eséka**, Camr.
104/C1 **Esenboga** (int'l arpt.), Turk.
104/D2 **Esence** (peak), Turk.
67/E1 **Esens**, Ger.
77/F1 **Esera** (riv.), Sp.
105/G3 **Eşfahān**, Iran
105/H3 **Eşfahān** (gov.), Iran
107/H3 **Esfandak**, Iran
105/J2 **Esfarāyen**, Iran
105/G3 **Esfarvarīn**, Iran
58/C1 **Esgair Ddu** (mtn.), Wal,UK
57/G2 **Esh**, Eng,UK
55/P12 **Esha Ness** (pt.), Sc,UK
116/D3 **Eshan Yizu Zizhixian**, China
53/M7 **Esher**, Eng,UK
153/F4 **Eshimba**, Zaire
157/E3 **Eshowe**, SAfr.
105/G3 **Eshtehārd**, Iran
57/G2 **Esh Winning**, Eng,UK
87/G5 **Esina** (riv.), It.
86/D1 **Esine**, It.
84/C1 **Esino** (riv.), It.
157/H9 **Esira**, Madg.
57/E2 **Esk** (riv.), Eng,UK
57/H3 **Esk** (riv.), Eng,UK
55/K9 **Esk** (riv.), Sc,UK
54/C6 **Eskdale** (val.), Sc,UK
57/E1 **Eskdale** (val.), Sc,UK
61/Q6 **Eskifjördhur**, Ice.
104/C2 **Eskil**, Turk.
62/G2 **Eskilstuna**, Swe.
104/D2 **Eskimalatya**, Turk.
177/M2 **Eskimo** (lakes), NW,Can
178/G2 **Eskimo Point**, NW,Can
104/C1 **Eskipazar**, Turk.
104/B2 **Eskişehir**, Turk.
104/B2 **Eskişehir** (prov.), Turk.
96/D5 **Eskişehir** (prov.), Turk.
195/H4 **Esko**, Mn,US
191/F1 **Eskridge**, Ks,US
76/C1 **Esla** (riv.), Sp.
105/F3 **Eslāmābād**, Iran
105/G2 **Eslāmābād**, Iran
67/F6 **Eslohe**, Ger.
62/E4 **Eslöv**, Swe.
104/B2 **Eşme**, Turk.
161/G1 **Esmeralda**, Cuba
164/B4 **Esmeraldas**, Ecu.
164/B4 **Esmeraldas** (prov.), Ecu.
194/E3 **Esmond**, ND,US
201/H2 **Esmont**, Va,US
172/C2 **Esmoraca**, Bol.
69/E2 **Esneux**, Belg.
164/D1 **Espada** (pt.), Col.
107/H3 **Espakeh**, Iran
74/E4 **Espalion**, Fr.
198/F1 **Espanola**, On,Can
168/K7 **Española** (isl.), Ecu.
190/A3 **Española**, NM,US
77/K6 **Esparreguera**, Sp.
160/E3 **Esparta**, Hon.
205/K9 **Esparto**, Ca,US
76/C4 **Espejo**, Sp.
67/F4 **Espelkamp**, Ger.
167/H4 **Esperança**, Braz.
132/D5 **Esperance**, Austl.
132/D5 **Esperance** (bay), Austl.
169/F5 **Esperancita**, Bol.
167/F3 **Esperantina**, Braz.
167/E4 **Esperantinópolis**, Braz.
175/K7 **Esperanza**, Arg.
162/D3 **Esperanza**, DRep.
158/C3 **Esperanza**, Mex.
159/M8 **Esperanza**, Mex.
168/D3 **Esperanza**, Peru
175/T11 **Esperanza**, Uru.
165/E4 **Esperanza**, Ven.
85/D5 **Esperia**, It.
76/A3 **Espichel** (cape), Port.
164/C3 **Espinal**, Col.
159/M6 **Espinal**, Mex.
168/D4 **Espinar**, Peru
171/E4 **Espinhaço** (mts.), Braz.
172/J1 **Espinhaço** (mts.), Braz.
163/E4 **Espinhaço** (range), Braz.
76/A2 **Espinho**, Port.
172/E3 **Espinillo**, Arg.
175/F2 **Espinillo** (pt.), Uru.
171/E2 **Espinosa**, Braz.
171/E3 **Espirito Santo** (state), Braz.
171/K7 **Espírito Santo do Pinhal**, Braz.
160/E2 **Espíritu Santo** (bay), Mex.
158/C3 **Espíritu Santo** (isl.), Mex.
125/D2 **Espiritu Santo** (cape), Phil.
138/F6 **Espiritu Santo** (isl.), Van.
159/H4 **Espita**, Mex.
171/F1 **Esplanada**, Braz.
77/E2 **Espluga de Francolí**, Sp.
77/L7 **Espluges**, Sp.
63/L1 **Espoo** (Esbo), Fin.
76/A2 **Esposende**, Port.
196/C1 **Esprit-Saint**, Qu,Can
155/G4 **Espungabera**, Moz.
206/B1 **Espy**, Pa,US
174/C4 **Esquel**, Arg.
182/C3 **Esquimalt**, BC,Can
172/E4 **Esquina**, Arg.
63/T8 **Esrum Sø** (lake), Den.
142/C3 **Essaouira**, Mor.
152/B1 **Essé**, Camr.
67/G5 **Esse** (riv.), Ger.
66/B6 **Essen**, Belg.
66/E6 **Essen**, Ger.
71/F5 **Essenbach**, Ger.
135/F5 **Essendon**, Austl.
132/D3 **Essendon** (peak), Austl.
69/H4 **Essenheim**, Ger.
141/Q16 **Es Senia** (int'l arpt.), Alg.
165/G3 **Essequibo** (riv.), Guy.
166/B1 **Essequibo** (riv.), Guy.
165/G3 **Essequibo Island-West Demerara** (reg.), Guy.
205/G7 **Essex**, On,Can
205/G7 **Essex** (co.), On,Can
53/P6 **Essex** (co.), Eng,UK
186/E3 **Essex**, Ca,US
208/B3 **Essex**, Ct,US
193/G3 **Essex**, Ia,US
206/B5 **Essex**, Md,US
183/H3 **Essex**, Mt,US
207/D2 **Essex** (co.), NJ,US
207/H8 **Essex** (co.), NJ,US
199/K2 **Essex**, Vt,US
207/H8 **Essex Fells**, NJ,US
199/K2 **Essex Junction**, Vt,US
198/E3 **Essexville**, Mi,US
201/F2 **Essie**, Ky,US
70/C5 **Esslingen**, Ger.
101/R4 **Esso**, Rus.
68/C5 **Essômes-sur-Marne**, Fr.
53/S11 **Essonne** (dept.), Fr.
53/T11 **Essonne** (riv.), Fr.
148/B5 **Est** (prov.), Camr.
152/C2 **Est** (prov.), Camr.
80/C1 **Est** (can.), Fr.
184/B1 **Estacada**, Or,US
158/B1 **Estación Coatiuila**, Mex.
175/L8 **Estados** (isl.), Arg.
105/H4 **Eşţahbān**, Iran
68/B2 **Estaires**, Fr.
171/F1 **Estância**, Braz.
190/A3 **Estancia**, NM,US
175/L8 **Estancia La Carmen**, Arg.
175/L8 **Estancia La Sera**, Arg.
159/G5 **Estancia Macaya**, Mex.
159/F4 **Estancia Tamuín**, Mex.
172/D3 **Estanislao del Campo**, Arg.
172/C2 **Estarca**, Bol.
77/F1 **Estats, Pico de** (peak), Sp.
80/C4 **Estavayer-le-Lac**, Swi.
157/E3 **Estcourt**, SAfr.
67/G2 **Este** (riv.), Ger.
87/E2 **Este**, It.
173/G4 **Esteio**, Braz.
160/E3 **Estelí**, Nic.
76/D1 **Estella**, Sp.
204/C3 **Estelle** (mtn.), Ca,US
193/F1 **Estelline**, SD,US
190/D3 **Estelline**, Tx,US
206/D5 **Estell Manor** (Risley), NJ,US
162/D3 **Este Nat'l Park**, DRep.
76/C4 **Estepa**, Sp.
76/C4 **Estepona**, Sp.
163/D6 **Este, Punta de**, Uru.
177/J3 **Ester**, Ak,US
82/C6 **Esterel** (upland), Fr.
194/C2 **Esterhazy**, Sk,Can
152/B2 **Esterias** (cape), Gabon
68/C6 **Esternay**, Fr.
71/G5 **Esternberg**, Aus.
186/B3 **Estero** (pt.), Ca,US
75/G5 **Estéron** (riv.), Fr.
82/D5 **Esteron** (riv.), Fr.
67/E3 **Esterwegen**, Ger.
192/B3 **Estes Park**, Co,US
194/C3 **Estevan**, Sk,Can
193/G2 **Estherville**, Ia,US
201/G4 **Estill**, SC,US
200/D3 **Estill Springs**, Tn,US
68/D3 **Estinnes-Au-Mont**, Belg.
203/F2 **Esto**, Fl,US
183/K2 **Eston**, Sk,Can
57/G2 **Eston**, Eng,UK
63/L2 **Estonia**
76/A3 **Estoril**, Port.
76/A3 **Estrala** (range), Port.
205/F8 **Estral Beach**, Mi,US
68/B5 **Estrées-Saint-Denis**, Fr.
173/G4 **Estrêla**, Braz.
76/B2 **Estrela, Serra da** (mtn.), Port.
76/A3 **Estrela, Serra da** (range), Port.
158/B2 **Estrella, Punta** (pt.), Mex.
88/B3 **Estremadura** (reg.), Sp.
76/B3 **Estremoz**, Port.
166/D5 **Estrondo** (mts.), Braz.
170/C1 **Estrondo** (uplands), Braz.
152/B3 **Esturaire** (prov.), Gabon
153/E2 **Esumba** (isl.), Zaire
79/F6 **Esvres**, Fr.
73/C4 **Esztergom**, Hun.
78/C3 **Étables-sur-Mer**, Fr.
133/H4 **Etadunna**, Austl.
120/B2 **Etah**, India
69/E5 **Etain**, Fr.
154/B3 **Etaka** (dry riv.), Namb.
138/E4 **Etal** (isl.), Micr.
54/D5 **Etal**, Eng,UK
69/E4 **Étalle**, Belg.
79/H4 **Étampes**, Fr.
68/A2 **Étaples**, Fr.
120/B2 **Etāwah**, India
158/C3 **Etchojoa**, Mex.
73/C4 **Ete**, Hun.
152/B3 **Etéké**, Gabon
78/B5 **Étel**, Fr.
78/B5 **Etel, Rivière d'** (riv.), Fr.
152/B2 **Etembue**, EqG.
69/E4 **Ethe**, Belg.
191/J3 **Ethel**, Ar,US
194/D2 **Ethelbert**, Mb,Can
132/D2 **Ethel Creek**, Austl.
185/J2 **Ethete**, Wy,US
140/F4 **Ethiopia**
149/G3 **Ethiopian** (plat.), Eth.
150/A2 **Ethiopian** (plat.), Eth.
200/D3 **Ethridge**, Tn,US
111/M9 **Eti** (riv.), Japan
93/H6 **Etili**, Turk.
152/A1 **Etinan**, Nga.
53/T11 **Étiolles**, Fr.
154/B4 **Etiro**, Namb.
80/C1 **Étival-Clairefontaine**, Fr.
54/A4 **Etive, Loch** (inlet), Sc,UK
184/B3 **Etna**, Ca,US
208/H6 **Etna**, Pa,US
90/D4 **Etna, Monte** (Mount Etna) (vol.), It.
89/G3 **Etna, Mount** (vol.), It.
90/D4 **Etna, Mount** (Monte Etna) (vol.), It.
62/A2 **Etne**, Nor.
197/R8 **Etobicoke**, On,Can
153/F5 **Étoile**, Zaire
82/A3 **Étoile-sur-Rhône**, Fr.
177/E3 **Etolin** (str.), Ak,US
200/E3 **Eton**, Ga,US
112/E1 **Etorofu** (isl.), Rus.
154/B3 **Etosha Nat'l Park**, Namb.
153/C3 **Etosha Pan** (salt pan), Namb.
152/C3 **Etoumbi**, Congo
200/E3 **Etowah** (riv.), Ga,US
201/F3 **Etowah**, NC,US
200/E3 **Etowah**, Tn,US
79/H4 **Étréchy**, Fr.
68/A5 **Étrépagny**, Fr.
79/F1 **Étretat**, Fr.
93/G4 **Etropole**, Bul.
80/D6 **Etroubles**, It.
174/E2 **Etruria**, Arg.
81/G4 **Etsch** (Adige) (riv.), It.
111/F2 **Etsu-Joshin Kogen Nat'l Park**, Japan
103/F7 **Et Taiyiba**, Isr.
69/F4 **Ettelbruck**, Lux.
80/D1 **Ettenheim**, Ger.
66/B5 **Etten-Leur**, Neth.
68/D2 **Etterbeek**, Belg.
206/B3 **Etters** (Goldsboro), Pa,US
103/F7 **Et Tīra**, Isr.
70/B5 **Ettlingen**, Ger.
54/C6 **Ettrick**, Sc,UK
193/J1 **Ettrick**, Wi,US
54/C6 **Ettrick Pen** (mtn.), Sc,UK
54/C5 **Ettrick Water** (riv.), Sc,UK
70/D6 **Ettringen**, Ger.
183/J3 **Etzikom Coulee** (cr.), Ab,Can
68/A3 **Eu**, Fr.
139/H7 **Eua** (isl.), Tonga
135/C2 **Euabalong**, Austl.
134/B2 **Eubenangee Swamp Nat'l Park**, Austl.
182/C1 **Euchiniko** (riv.), BC,Can
133/F4 **Eucla Motel**, Austl.
208/F4 **Euclid**, Oh,US
171/F1 **Euclides da Cuhna**, Braz.
129/H7 **Eucumbene** (lake), Austl.
191/J4 **Eudora**, Ar,US
135/A2 **Eudunda**, Austl.
200/E5 **Eufaula**, Al,US
191/G3 **Eufaula**, Ok,US
191/G3 **Eufaula** (dam), Ok,US
191/G3 **Eufaula** (lake), Ok,US
71/G7 **Eugendorf**, Aus.
184/B1 **Eugene**, Or,US
158/B3 **Eugenia, Punta** (pt.), Mex.
135/D2 **Eugowra**, Austl.
200/E3 **Euharlee**, Ga,US
188/K7 **Euless**, Tx,US
134/B5 **Eulo**, Austl.
203/H2 **Eulonia**, Ga,US
76/B1 **Eume** (lake), Sp.
135/D1 **Eumungerie**, Austl.
134/C3 **Eungella Nat'l Park**, Austl.
202/B2 **Eunice**, La,US
190/C4 **Eunice**, NM,US
69/F2 **Eupen**, Belg.
102/D6 **Euphrates** (riv.), Asia
106/D2 **Euphrates** (riv.), Iraq
105/F4 **Euphrates** (riv.), Iraq, Syria
96/F5 **Euphrates** (riv.), Turk.
200/C4 **Eupora**, Ms,US
63/K1 **Eura**, Fin.
63/J1 **Eurajoki**, Fin.
68/A5 **Eure** (dept.), Fr.
79/F2 **Eure** (dept.), Fr.
68/A5 **Eure** (riv.), Fr.
79/G2 **Eure** (riv.), Fr.
79/G3 **Eure** (riv.), Fr.
79/G4 **Eure** (riv.), Fr.
68/A6 **Eure-et-Loir** (dept.), Fr.
79/G4 **Eure-et-Loir** (dept.), Fr.
179/S6 **Eureka**, NW,Can
179/S7 **Eureka** (sound), NW,Can
184/A3 **Eureka**, Ca,US
185/K5 **Eureka**, Co,US
193/K3 **Eureka**, Il,US
191/F2 **Eureka**, Ks,US
182/G3 **Eureka**, Mt,US
184/F4 **Eureka**, Nv,US
189/F1 **Eureka**, Tx,US
185/G4 **Eureka**, Ut,US
182/E4 **Eureka**, Wa,US
191/H2 **Eureka Springs**, Ar,US
135/C3 **Euroa**, Austl.
68/B6 **Eurodisney**, Fr.
80/C1 **Euron** (riv.), Fr.
152/B2 **Europa** (pt.), EqG.
141/M12 **Europa** (pt.), Gib.
140/F7 **Europa** (isl.), Reu.
155/J4 **Europa** (isl.), Reun.
81/H3 **Europabrücke**, Aus.
52/* **Europe** (cont.)
66/B5 **Europoort**, Neth.
69/F2 **Euskirchen**, Ger.
70/C3 **Eussenheim**, Ger.
203/H3 **Eustis**, Fl,US
196/B3 **Eustis**, Me,US
133/J5 **Euston**, Austl.
200/D4 **Eutaw**, Al,US
64/F1 **Eutin**, Ger.
155/G1 **Eutini**, Malw.
69/E6 **Euville**, Fr.
57/F4 **Euxton**, Eng,UK
189/J2 **Eva**, La,US
189/G2 **Evadale**, Tx,US
130/D4 **Eva Downs**, Austl.
156/E2 **Evander**, SAfr.
179/H2 **Evans** (str.), NW,Can
192/B3 **Evans**, Co,US
192/B4 **Evans** (mt.), Co,US
201/F4 **Evans**, Ga,US
202/B2 **Evans**, La,US
201/G1 **Evans**, WV,US
182/G1 **Evansburg**, Ab,Can
208/G6 **Evans City**, Pa,US
135/E1 **Evans Head**, Austl.
205/Q15 **Evanston**, Il,US
185/H3 **Evanston**, Wy,US
191/G3 **Evansville**, Ar,US
200/C1 **Evansville**, Il,US
200/D2 **Evansville**, In,US
195/G4 **Evansville**, Mn,US
198/B3 **Evansville**, Wi,US
192/A2 **Evansville**, Wy,US
189/E2 **Evant**, Tx,US
54/B1 **Evanton**, Sc,UK
198/D3 **Evart**, Mi,US
201/F2 **Evarts**, Ky,US
156/D2 **Evaton**, SAfr.
105/H5 **Evaz**, Iran
78/C5 **Evel** (riv.), Fr.
195/H4 **Eveleth**, Mn,US
191/J2 **Evening Shade**, Ar,US
101/L3 **Evenki Aut. Okr.**, Rus.
59/E3 **Evenlode** (riv.), Eng,UK
101/R3 **Evensk**, Rus.
61/F1 **Evenskjer**, Nor.
200/E3 **Evensville**, Tn,US
103/F7 **Even Yehuda**, Isr.
135/D3 **Everard** (cape), Austl.
133/G4 **Everard** (lake), Austl.
133/G3 **Everard** (peak), Austl.
58/D4 **Evercreech**, Eng,UK
191/G1 **Everest**, Ks,US
102/H7 **Everest, Mount** (mtn.), Nepal
118/E2 **Everest, Mount** (Qomolangma) (peak), China
121/F1 **Everest, Mount** (Sagarmatha) (mtn.), China, Nepal
203/H2 **Everett**, Ga,US
208/C1 **Everett**, Ma,US
208/A1 **Everett** (mt.), Ma,US
199/G4 **Everett**, Pa,US
205/C2 **Everett**, Wa,US
68/C1 **Evergem**, Belg.
203/H5 **Everglades City**, Fl,US
203/H5 **Everglades Nat'l Park**, Fl,US
162/A1 **Everglades, The** (swamp), Fl,US
202/P7 **Everglades, The** (swamp), Fl,US
203/H5 **Everglades, The** (swamp), Fl,US
202/E2 **Evergreen**, Al,US
205/Q16 **Evergreen Park**, Il,US
188/K7 **Everman**, Tx,US
59/F3 **Eversholt**, Eng,UK
182/C3 **Everson**, Wa,US
67/E5 **Everswinkel**, Ger.
198/D5 **Everton**, In,US
191/H2 **Everton**, Mo,US
59/E2 **Evesham**, Eng,UK
80/C5 **Évian-les-Bains**, Fr.
152/B2 **Evinayong**, EqG.
91/G3 **Évinos** (riv.), Gre.
62/B2 **Evje**, Nor.
80/D5 **Evolène**, Swi.
76/B3 **Évora**, Port.
76/A3 **Évora** (dist.), Port.
79/D6 **Evre** (riv.), Fr.
79/E4 **Evre** (riv.), Fr.
79/E2 **Évrecy**, Fr.
68/A5 **Évreux**, Fr.
79/E4 **Évron**, Fr.
91/H4 **Evrótas** (riv.), Gre.
53/T11 **Évry**, Fr.
91/H3 **Évvoia** (gulf), Gre.
89/K3 **Évvoia** (isl.), Gre.
91/H3 **Évvoia** (isl.), Gre.
91/H3 **Evxinoúpolis**, Gre.
206/C4 **Ewan**, NJ,US
133/G2 **Ewaninga**, Austl.
161/G2 **Ewarton**, Jam.
53/N7 **Ewell**, Eng,UK
201/J2 **Ewell**, Md,US
109/H2 **Ewenkizu Zizhiqi**, China
200/F1 **Ewing**, Ky,US
193/J3 **Ewing**, Mo,US
192/E2 **Ewing**, Ne,US
206/D3 **Ewing**, NJ,US
152/C3 **Ewo**, Congo
169/E4 **Exaltación**, Bol.
91/H2 **Exaplátanos**, Gre.
202/E2 **Excel**, Al,US
193/H4 **Excello**, Mo,US
191/G1 **Excelsior Springs**, Mo,US
177/L4 **Excursion Inlet**, Ak,US
58/C5 **Exe** (riv.), Eng,UK
195/J5 **Exeland**, Wi,US
198/F3 **Exeter**, On,Can
58/C5 **Exeter**, Eng,UK
58/C5 **Exeter** (arpt.), Eng,UK
186/C2 **Exeter**, Ca,US
191/H2 **Exeter**, Mo,US
192/F3 **Exeter**, Ne,US
199/L3 **Exeter**, NH,US
206/C1 **Exeter**, Pa,US
208/C2 **Exeter**, RI,US
80/C3 **Exincourt**, Fr.
193/G3 **Exira**, Ia,US
58/C5 **Exminster**, Eng,UK
58/C4 **Exmoor** (upland), Eng,UK
55/K11 **Exmoor Nat'l Park**, Eng,UK
58/C4 **Exmoor Nat'l Park** Eng, Eng,UK
201/K2 **Exmore**, Va,US
132/B2 **Exmouth**, Austl.
132/B2 **Exmouth** (gulf), Austl.
175/J7 **Exmouth** (pen.), Chile
58/C5 **Exmouth**, Eng,UK
200/E4 **Experiment**, Ga,US
197/J1 **Exploits** (riv.), Nf,Can
182/C3 **Extension**, BC,Can
202/C2 **Extension**, La,US
171/K7 **Extrema**, Braz.
76/B3 **Extremadura** (aut. comm.), Sp.
148/B3 **Extrême-Nord** (prov.), Camr.
167/G4 **Exu**, Braz.
162/B1 **Exuma** (sound), Bahm.
70/B6 **Eyach** (riv.), Ger.
81/E1 **Eyach** (riv.), Ger.
177/J3 **Eyak**, Ak,US
57/G5 **Eyam**, Eng,UK
153/E3 **Eyangu**, Zaire
151/A2 **Eyasi** (lake), Tanz.
70/C5 **Eyb** (riv.), Ger.
62/C2 **Eydehamn**, Nor.
59/H2 **Eye**, Eng,UK
59/F1 **Eye** (brook), Eng,UK
54/D5 **Eyemouth**, Sc,UK
82/B5 **Eyguières**, Fr.
150/D4 **Eyl**, Som.
103/G8 **Eyn Hemed Nat'l Park**, Isr.
53/P7 **Eynsford**, Eng,UK
82/A5 **Eyragues**, Fr.
132/E5 **Eyre**, Austl.
137/C7 **Eyre** (lake), Austl.
133/G5 **Eyre** (pen.), Austl.
60/B3 **Eyrecourt**, Ire.
133/H4 **Eyre North** (lake), Austl.
133/H4 **Eyre South** (lake), Austl.
82/A3 **Eyrieux** (riv.), Fr.
72/C5 **Eythra**, Ger.
105/M6 **Eyüp**, Turk.
105/M6 **Eyüp Mosque**, Turk.
53/T9 **Ézanville**, Fr.
160/B1 **Ezequiel Montes**, Mex
91/K3 **Ezine**, Turk.
68/A6 **Ézy-sur-Eure**, Fr.
189/F3 **Ezzell**, Tx,US

## F

139/L6 **Faaa**, FrPol.
139/X15 **Faaa** (Papeete) (int'l arpt.), FrPol.
150/B5 **Faafaxdhuun**, Som.
87/D3 **Fabbrico**, It.
188/A2 **Fabens**, Tx,US
76/B1 **Fabero**, Sp.
62/D4 **Fåborg**, Den.
87/F6 **Fabriano**, It.
84/C3 **Fabrica di Roma**, It.
114/C3 **Fabrichnyy**, Kaz.
83/C6 **Fabrizia**, It.
183/J1 **Fabyan**, Ab,Can
164/C3 **Facatativá**, Col.
68/C2 **Faches-Thumesnil**, Fr.
145/H2 **Fachi**, Niger
174/C5 **Facundo**, Arg.
148/D1 **Fada**, Chad
148/A2 **Fadadinga, Éché** (dry riv.), Niger
54/A1 **Fada, Lochan** (lake), Sc,UK
145/F3 **Fada-N'Gourma**, Burk.
104/E3 **Fadghamī**, Syria
144/C4 **Fadugu**, SLeo.
87/E4 **Faenza**, It.
84/B2 **Faete** (peak), It.
148/C4 **Fafa** (riv.), CAfr.
76/A2 **Fafe**, Port.
150/C4 **Fafen Shet'** (dry riv.), Eth.
139/S9 **Fagali** (Apia) (int'l arpt.), WSam.
93/G3 **Făgăraş**, Rom.
62/F2 **Fagersta**, Swe.
87/E4 **Faggiola, Monte** (peak), It.

145/H4 **Faggo**, Nga.
72/C1 **Fäglitz** (riv.), Ger.
175/L8 **Fagnano** (lake), Arg.
83/C3 **Fagnano Castello**, It.
68/D6 **Fagnières**, Fr.
144/D2 **Faguibine** (lake), Mali
166/C4 **Fagundes**, Braz.
72/D5 **Fahna** (riv.), Ger.
71/E6 **Fahrenzhausen**, Ger.
77/S12 **Faial** (isl.), Azor.,Port.
85/E6 **Faiano**, It.
141/W18 **Fā'id**, Tun.
81/E5 **Faido**, Swi.
149/H4 **Faille**, Eth.
57/F4 **Failsworth**, Eng,UK
69/E6 **Fains-Véel**, Fr.
55/P13 **Fair** (isl.), Sc,UK
177/J3 **Fairbanks**, Ak,US
187/G5 **Fairbanks**, Az,US
189/H1 **Fairbanks**, La,US
201/H3 **Fair Bluff**, NC,US
198/D5 **Fairborn**, Oh,US
200/E4 **Fairburn**, Ga,US
201/L7 **Fairburn**, Ga,US
192/C2 **Fairburn**, SD,US
193/K3 **Fairbury**, Il,US
193/F3 **Fairbury**, Ne,US
182/F4 **Fairchild A.F.B.**, Wa,US
191/J2 **Fairdealing**, Mo,US
194/B3 **Fairfax**, Mb,Can
205/J11 **Fairfax**, Ca,US
193/G3 **Fairfax**, Mo,US
200/F1 **Fairfax**, Oh,US
191/F2 **Fairfax**, Ok,US
201/G4 **Fairfax**, SC,US
192/E2 **Fairfax**, SD,US
206/A6 **Fairfax**, Va,US
206/A6 **Fairfax** (co.), Va,US
199/K2 **Fairfax**, Vt,US
205/C3 **Fairfax**, Wa,US
134/G8 **Fairfield**, Austl.
205/K10 **Fairfield**, Ca,US
207/E1 **Fairfield**, Ct,US
208/A3 **Fairfield** (co.), Ct,US
193/J3 **Fairfield**, Ia,US
185/F2 **Fairfield**, Id,US
200/C1 **Fairfield**, Il,US
196/C3 **Fairfield**, Me,US
183/J4 **Fairfield**, Mt,US
201/J3 **Fairfield**, NC,US
192/E3 **Fairfield**, Ne,US
207/H8 **Fairfield**, NJ,US
198/D5 **Fairfield**, Oh,US
206/A4 **Fairfield**, Pa,US
189/F2 **Fairfield**, Tx,US
201/H2 **Fairfield**, Va,US
199/K2 **Fairfield**, Vt,US
182/F4 **Fairfield**, Wa,US
191/H3 **Fairfield Bay**, Ar,US
194/E2 **Fairford**, Mb,Can
59/E3 **Fairford**, Eng,UK
198/E3 **Fairgrove**, Mi,US
191/H2 **Fair Grove**, Mo,US
208/D2 **Fairhaven**, Ma,US
205/G6 **Fair Haven**, Mi,US
199/H3 **Fair Haven**, NY,US
199/K3 **Fair Haven**, Vt,US
56/B1 **Fair Head** (pt.), NI,UK
206/C4 **Fair Hill**, Md,US
202/E2 **Fairhope**, Al,US
55/P13 **Fair Isle** (isl.), Sc,UK
200/E1 **Fairland**, In,US
206/B5 **Fairland**, Md,US
191/G2 **Fairland**, Ok,US
207/D2 **Fair Lawn**, NJ,US
208/F5 **Fairlawn**, Oh,US
201/G2 **Fairlawn**, Va,US
206/B5 **Fairlee**, Md,US
206/D3 **Fairless Hills**, Pa,US
136/B4 **Fairlie**, N.Z.
54/B5 **Fairlie**, Sc,UK
194/D3 **Fairlight**, Sk,Can
59/G5 **Fairlight**, Eng,UK
186/B2 **Fairmead**, Ca,US
193/G2 **Fairmont**, Mn,US
193/F3 **Fairmont**, Ne,US
201/H3 **Fairmont**, NC,US
201/G1 **Fairmont**, WV,US
182/G2 **Fairmont Hot Springs**, BC,Can
200/E3 **Fairmount**, Ga,US
194/F4 **Fairmount**, ND,US
199/H3 **Fairmount**, NY,US
205/M9 **Fair Oaks**, Ca,US
201/L7 **Fair Oaks**, Ga,US
198/C3 **Fair Plain**, Mi,US
201/G2 **Fairplains**, NC,US
190/B1 **Fairplay**, Co,US
200/E2 **Fairplay**, Ky,US
191/H2 **Fair Play**, Mo,US
194/C5 **Fairpoint**, SD,US
198/F4 **Fairport Harbor**, Oh,US
206/C5 **Fairton**, NJ,US
196/E3 **Fairvale**, NB,Can
178/E3 **Fairview**, Ab,Can
200/E3 **Fairview**, Ga,US
191/G1 **Fairview**, Ks,US
202/C2 **Fairview**, La,US
198/D2 **Fairview**, Mi,US
191/G2 **Fairview**, Mo,US
194/B4 **Fairview**, Mt,US
207/K8 **Fairview**, NJ,US
191/F2 **Fairview**, Ok,US
200/D3 **Fairview**, Tn,US
190/D4 **Fairview**, Tx,US
155/G3 **Fairview** (peak), Zim.
198/C5 **Fairview Park**, In,US
208/F5 **Fairview Park**, Oh,US
177/L4 **Fairweather** (cape), Ak,US
177/L4 **Fairweather** (mt.), BC,Can, Ak,US
122/B2 **Faisalabad**, Pak.
201/H3 **Faison**, NC,US
91/J5 **Faistós** (ruins), Gre.
120/D2 **Faizābād**, India
162/E3 **Fajardo**, PR
139/M6 **Fakahina** (isl.), FrPol.
139/H5 **Fakaofo** (isl.), Tok.
139/L6 **Fakarava** (atoll), FrPol.
59/G1 **Fakenham**, Eng,UK
127/H4 **Fakfak**, Indo.
152/B1 **Fako** (peak), Camr.
62/E4 **Fakse**, Den.
62/E4 **Fakse** (bay), Den.
64/G1 **Fakse Bugt** (bay), Den.
62/E4 **Fakse Ladeplads**, Den.
123/C2 **Fak Tha**, Thai.
115/E2 **Faku**, China
58/B6 **Fal** (riv.), Eng,UK
144/C4 **Falaba**, SLeo.
79/E3 **Falaise**, Fr.
144/C3 **Falaise de Tambaoura** (escarp.), Mali
145/G2 **Falaise de Tiguidit** (escarp.), Niger
121/G2 **Fālākāta**, India
116/B4 **Falam**, Burma
103/G7 **Falāmah**, WBnk.
167/L6 **Falan**, Col.
91/H3 **Fálanna**, Gre.
85/D5 **Falciano del Massico**, It.
93/J2 **Fălciu**, Rom.
141/Q16 **Falcon** (cape), Alg.
188/E4 **Falcon** (int'l res.), Mex., Tx,US
188/E4 **Falcon** (dam), Tx,US
164/D2 **Falcón** (state), Ven.
87/G5 **Falconara** (arpt.), It.
87/G5 **Falconara Marittima**, It.
83/B6 **Falcone**, It.
199/G3 **Falconer**, NY,US
195/G3 **Falcon Lake**, Mb,Can
144/C3 **Falémé** (riv.), Afr.
139/S9 **Faleolo**, WSam.
139/R9 **Faleolo** (Apia) (int'l arpt.), WSam.
93/H2 **Faleshty**, Mol.
189/E4 **Falfurrias**, Tx,US
144/B4 **Falissadé**, Gui.
72/D2 **Falkenberg**, Ger.
72/D4 **Falkenberg**, Ger.
62/E3 **Falkenberg**, Swe.
59/H2 **Falkenham**, Eng,UK
72/D2 **Falkensee**, Ger.
71/F2 **Falkenstein**, Ger.
54/C5 **Falkirk**, Sc,UK
175/M8 **Falkland** (sound), Falk.
54/C4 **Falkland**, Sc,UK
175/M8 **Falkland** (Malvinas) (isls.), UK
62/E2 **Falköping**, Swe.
200/D3 **Falkville**, Al,US
191/F2 **Fall** (riv.), Ks,US
204/C4 **Fallbrook**, Ca,US
205/D2 **Fall City**, Wa,US
193/J1 **Fall Creek**, Wi,US
80/D6 **Fallere, Monte** (peak), It.
67/G3 **Fallingbostel**, Ger.
183/M4 **Fallon**, Mt,US
184/D4 **Fallon**, Nv,US
184/D4 **Fallon Ind. Res.**, Nv,US
191/F2 **Fall River**, Ks,US
208/C2 **Fall River**, Ma,US
198/B3 **Fall River**, Wi,US
206/A6 **Falls Church**, Va,US
193/G3 **Falls City**, Ne,US
184/B1 **Falls City**, Or,US
189/E3 **Falls City**, Tx,US
199/G4 **Falls Creek**, Pa,US
201/H2 **Falls Lake** (res.), NC,US
200/D2 **Falls of Rough**, Ky,US
206/B4 **Fallston**, Md,US
208/A2 **Falls Village**, Ct,US
145/F3 **Falmey**, Niger
162/F3 **Falmouth**, Anti.
196/E3 **Falmouth**, NS,Can
58/A6 **Falmouth**, Eng,UK
58/A6 **Falmouth** (bay), Eng,UK
200/E1 **Falmouth**, Ky,US
199/L4 **Falmouth**, Ma,US
198/D2 **Falmouth**, Mi,US
201/J1 **Falmouth**, VA,US
130/A4 **False Cape Bossut** (cape), Austl.
131/F2 **False Orford Ness** (cape), Austl.
177/F5 **False Pass**, Ak,US
62/C4 **Falshöft** (pt.), Ger.
161/J2 **Falso** (cape), DRep.
161/F3 **Falso** (cape), Hon.
158/C4 **Falso, Cabo** (cape), Mex.
175/K8 **Falso Cabo de Hornos** (cape), Chile
62/E4 **Falster** (isl.), Den.
87/E5 **Falterona, Monte** (peak), It.
93/H2 **Fălticeni**, Rom.
62/F1 **Falun**, Swe.
103/C2 **Famagusta**, Cyp.
103/C2 **Famagusta** (bay), Cyp.
103/C2 **Famagusta** (dist.), Cyp.
172/C3 **Famaillá**, Arg.
149/G3 **Famakah**, Sudan
105/G3 **Fāmanīn**, Iran
172/C4 **Famatina**, Arg.
69/F5 **Fameck**, Fr.
69/E3 **Famenne** (reg.), Belg.
195/G2 **Family** (lake), Mb,Can
186/C3 **Famoso**, Ca,US
144/D3 **Fana**, Mali
62/A1 **Fana**, Nor.
115/D5 **Fanchang**, China
200/C2 **Fancy Farm**, Ky,US
141/G7 **Fandriana**, Madg.
60/D2 **Fane** (riv.), Ire.
123/B2 **Fang**, Thai.
149/F3 **Fangak**, Sudan
144/C4 **Fangamandou**, Gui.
139/L6 **Fangatau** (isl.), FrPol.
139/L7 **Fangataufa** (isl.), FrPol.
115/C4 **Fangcheng**, China
123/E1 **Fangcheng**, China
119/J3 **Fangcheng Gezu Zizhixian**, China
117/H3 **Fangdao**, China
117/E2 **Fangdou** (mts.), China
109/J3 **Fangjiatun**, China
117/J4 **Fangliao**, Tai.
115/B3 **Fangshan**, China
115/G7 **Fangshan**, China
117/G2 **Fangxi**, China
115/B4 **Fang Xian**, China
157/H8 **Fanirìa**, Madg.
117/F3 **Fanjing** (peak), China
54/A1 **Fannich, Loch** (lake), Sc,UK
202/M7 **Fannie** (lake), Fl,US
200/C4 **Fannin**, Ms,US
189/F3 **Fannin**, Tx,US
139/K4 **Fanning** (Tabuaeran) (isl.), Kiri.
62/C4 **Fanø** (isl.), Den.
87/G5 **Fano**, It.
117/J3 **Fanshan**, China
191/G3 **Fanshawe**, Ok,US
115/C3 **Fanshi**, China
123/C1 **Fan Si Pan** (peak), Viet.
207/H9 **Fanwood**, NJ,US
103/G7 **Faqqū'ah**, WBnk.
103/B4 **Fāqūs**, Egypt
103/B4 **Farafangana**, Madg.
157/J8 ...

156/B2 **Farāfirah**, Wāḥāt al (oasis), Egypt
100/G6 **Farāh**, Afg.
107/H2 **Farāh** (riv.), Afg.
103/G7 **Fa'rah, Wādī** (dry riv.), WBnk.
84/C3 **Fara in Sabina**, It.
144/D3 **Farako**, Mali
186/A2 **Farallon** (isls.), Ca,US
165/E2 **Farallon Centinela** (isl.), Ven.
138/D3 **Farallon de Medinilla** (isl.), NMar.
138/D2 **Farallon de Pajaros** (isl.), NMar.
164/B4 **Farallones de Cali Nat'l Park**, Col.
184/B5 **Farallon Nat'l Wild. Ref.**, Ca,US
144/D3 **Faramana**, Burk.
144/C4 **Faranah**, Gui.
144/C4 **Faranah** (comm.), Gui.
86/B1 **Fara Novarese**, It.
157/H8 **Faraony** (riv.), Madg.
102/C8 **Farasan** (isls.), SAr.
150/B1 **Farasān** (isls.), SAr.
138/D4 **Faraulep** (isl.), Micr.
191/J1 **Farber**, Mo,US
68/D3 **Farciennes**, Belg.
79/F5 **Fare** (riv.), Fr.
59/E5 **Fareham**, Eng,UK
74/D2 **Fare, Hill of** (hill), Sc,UK
174/Q9 **Farellones**, Chile
68/C6 **Faremoutiers**, Fr.
63/R7 **Farentuna**, Swe.
136/C3 **Farewell** (cape), N.Z.
177/H3 **Farewell**, Ak,US
84/C3 **Fara Filiorum Petri**, It.
62/D2 **Färgelanda**, Swe.
203/G2 **Fargo**, Ga,US
194/F4 **Fargo**, ND,US
190/E2 **Fargo**, Ok,US
193/H1 **Faribault**, Mn,US
120/A1 **Farīdābād**, India
122/C2 **Farīdkot**, India
120/A1 **Farīdnagar**, India
121/G4 **Farīdpur**, Bang.
121/G4 **Farīdpur** (dist.), Bang.
120/B1 **Farīdpur**, India
154/B4 **Farilhao** (cape), Namb.
144/B3 **Farim**, GBis.
193/K4 **Farina**, Il,US
191/H3 **Farindale**, Ar,US
59/E3 **Faringdon**, Eng,UK
103/B4 **Fāriskūr**, Egypt
150/A3 **Farit, Amba** (peak), Eth.
193/J2 **Farley**, Ia,US
190/B2 **Farley**, NM,US
191/G2 **Farlington**, Ks,US
198/B4 **Farmer City**, Il,US
188/L7 **Farmers Branch**, Tx,US
198/C5 **Farmersburg**, In,US
189/F3 **Farmersville**, Ca,US
188/L6 **Farmersville**, Tx,US
189/H1 **Farmerville**, La,US
207/D3 **Farmingdale**, NJ,US
207/M9 **Farmingdale**, NY,US
198/D2 **Farmington**, Ar,US
208/B2 **Farmington**, Ct,US
206/C6 **Farmington**, De,US
193/J3 **Farmington**, Il,US
196/B3 **Farmington**, Me,US
205/F7 **Farmington**, Mi,US
195/H5 **Farmington**, Mn,US
191/J1 **Farmington**, Mo,US
199/L3 **Farmington**, NH,US
187/H2 **Farmington**, NM,US
185/H3 **Farmington**, Ut,US
182/F4 **Farmington**, Wa,US
205/F7 **Farmington Hills**, Mi,US
144/B4 **Farmoréya**, Gui.
201/J3 **Farmville**, NC,US
201/H2 **Farmville**, Va,US
73/C3 **Farnádska voda** (riv.), Slvk.
59/F4 **Farnborough**, Eng,UK
55/L9 **Farne** (isls.), Eng,UK
84/B2 **Farnese**, It.
182/F2 **Farnham** (mtn.), BC,Can
59/F4 **Farnham**, Eng,UK
182/F3 **Farnham** (peak), Id,US
53/P7 **Farningham**, Eng,UK
72/B5 **Farnstädt**, Ger.
57/F4 **Farnworth**, Eng,UK
166/B3 **Faro**, Braz.
178/C2 **Faro**, Yk,Can
148/B4 **Faro** (riv.), Chad
76/B4 **Faro**, Port.
76/A4 **Faro** (dist.), Port.
76/B4 **Faro** (int'l arpt.), Port.
52/D2 **Faroe** (isls.), Den.
61/F4 **Fårön** (isl.), Swe.
148/B3 **Faro Nat'l Park**, Camr.
63/H3 **Fårösund**, Swe.
132/B2 **Farquhar** (cape), Austl.
141/H5 **Farquhar** (isls.), Sey.
200/E3 **Farragut**, Tn,US
60/A5 **Farranfore** (arpt.), Ire.
54/B2 **Farrar** (riv.), Sc,UK
105/H4 **Farrāshband**, Iran
208/G5 **Farrell**, Pa,US
207/K9 **Far Rockaway**, NY,US
105/G3 **Farrokh Shahr**, Iran
173/G4 **Farroupilha**, Braz.
120/B2 **Farrukhābād**, India
120/A1 **Farrukhnagar**, India
105/H4 **Fars** (gov.), Iran
91/H3 **Fársala**, Gre.
105/G3 **Fārsān**, Iran
62/C3 **Farsø**, Den.
62/B2 **Farsund**, Nor.
106/F5 **Fartak, Ra's** (pt.), Yem.
170/C4 **Fartura**, Braz.
63/T9 **Farum**, Den.
176/N4 **Farvel** (cape), Grld.
137/T **Farwell** (isl.), Ant.
190/C3 **Farwell**, Tx,US
105/H4 **Fasā**, Iran
90/E2 **Fasano**, It.
103/C1 **Faşıkan** (pass), Turk.
103/D3 **Fassala-Néré**, Mrta.
67/H3 **Fassberg**, Ger.
54/D5 **Fast Castle** (pt.), Sc,UK
98/E2 **Fastov**, Ukr.
127/H4 **Fatagar Tuting** (cape), Indo.
122/B1 **Fatahjang**, Pak.
51/T6 **Fataka** (isl.), Sol.
188/L7 **Fate**, Tx,US
73/B4 **Fatehābād**, India
122/C2 **Fatehgarh Chūriān**, India
118/B2 **Fatehpur**, India
120/B2 **Fatehpur**, India
120/C2 **Fatehpur**, India
120/C3 **Fatehpur**, India
122/B2 **Fatehpur**, Pak.
85/D5 **Fate, Monte delle** (peak), It.
99/H1 **Fatëzh**, Rus.
198/F2 **Fathom Five Nat'l Marine Park**, On,Can
144/B3 **Fatick**, Sen.
144/A3 **Fatick** (reg.), Sen.

121/H4 **Fatikchhari**, Bang.
76/A3 **Fátima**, Port.
170/B4 **Fátima do Sul**, Braz.
106/C4 **Fāṭimah** (dry riv.), SAr.
144/B3 **Fatoto**, Gam.
73/C2 **Fatra, Veľká** (mts.), Slvk.
104/D1 **Fatsa**, Turk.
139/M6 **Fatu Hiva** (isl.), FrPol.
152/D4 **Fatunda**, Zaire
80/C5 **Faucille, Col de la** (pass), Fr.
80/B1 **Faucilles** (mts.), Fr.
56/A2 **Faughan** (riv.), NI,UK
86/D5 **Fauglia**, It.
54/C5 **Fauldhouse**, Sc,UK
191/G4 **Faulkner**, Tx,US
192/E1 **Faulkton**, SD,US
69/F5 **Faulquemont**, Fr.
132/B3 **Faure** (isl.), Austl.
93/H3 **Făurei**, Rom.
82/C3 **Faurio, Roche** (mtn.), Fr.
61/E2 **Fauske**, Nor.
79/F1 **Fauville-en-Caux**, Fr.
69/E4 **Fauvillers**, Belg.
87/F6 **Favalto, Monte** (peak), It.
90/C4 **Favara**, It.
80/D1 **Fave** (riv.), Fr.
82/C1 **Faverges**, Fr.
80/C2 **Faverney**, Fr.
59/G4 **Faversham**, Eng,UK
90/C4 **Favignana**, It.
152/C4 **Favre**, Congo
86/A2 **Favria**, It.
146/D2 **Fawākhir, Ḥussayyāt al** (well), Libya
59/E5 **Fawley**, Eng,UK
178/H3 **Fawn** (riv.), On,Can
206/B4 **Fawn Grove**, Pa,US
145/E5 **Fawumang**, Gha.
61/M7 **Faxaflói** (bay), Ice.
170/C4 **Faxinal**, Braz.
148/C1 **Faya-Largeau**, Chad
104/E5 **Fayd**, SAr.
82/C5 **Fayence**, Fr.
200/D4 **Fayette**, Al,US
201/L8 **Fayette** (co.), Ga,US
193/J2 **Fayette**, Ia,US
191/H1 **Fayette**, Mo,US
200/B5 **Fayette**, Ms,US
198/C2 **Fayette Hist. Townsite**, Mi,US
191/G2 **Fayetteville**, Ar,US
200/E4 **Fayetteville**, Ga,US
201/H3 **Fayetteville**, NC,US
200/F1 **Fayetteville**, Oh,US
199/H5 **Fayetteville**, Pa,US
200/D3 **Fayetteville**, Tn,US
189/F3 **Fayetteville**, Tx,US
201/G1 **Fayetteville**, WV,US
80/B2 **Fayl-Billot**, Fr.
187/H4 **Faywood** (Dwyer), NM,US
87/G3 **Fažana**, Cro.
145/F4 **Fazao** (mts.), Gha., Togo
145/F4 **Fazao Nat'l Park**, Togo
170/C3 **Fazenda Nova**, Braz.
122/C2 **Fāzilka**, India
142/B5 **Fdérik**, Mrta.
60/B4 **Feakle**, Ire.
199/H5 **Feale** (riv.), Ire.
201/J4 **Fear** (cape), NC,US
55/K8 **Fearn, Hill of** (hill), Sc,UK
206/D3 **Feasterville-Trevose**, Pa,US
184/C4 **Feather** (falls), Ca,US
184/C4 **Feather** (riv.), Ca,US
184/C4 **Feather, Middle Fork** (riv.), Ca,US
184/C4 **Feather, North Fork** (riv.), Ca,US
136/J9 **Featherston**, N.Z.
57/G4 **Featherstone**, Eng,UK
155/F3 **Featherstone**, Zim.
79/F1 **Fécamp**, Fr.
80/D1 **Fecht** (riv.), Fr.
122/A1 **Fed. Admin. Tribal Areas** (terr.), Pak.
172/E4 **Federación**, Arg.
195/G4 **Federal Dam**, Mn,US
207/K9 **Federal Hall Nat'l Mem.**, NY,US
201/K1 **Federalsburg**, Md,US
205/C3 **Federal Way**, Wa,US
70/C6 **Federsee** (lake), Ger.
150/B3 **Fedīs**, Eth.
62/A1 **Fedje**, Nor.
95/P5 **Fedorovka**, Kaz.
97/J2 **Fedorovka**, Rus.
99/J2 **Fedorovka**, Rus.
97/K4 **Fëdorovka**, Rus.
201/F2 **Fedscreek**, Ky,US
56/A2 **Feeny**, NI,UK
150/C4 **Feerfeer**, Som.
78/C5 **Fegréac**, Fr.
92/F2 **Fehérgyarmat**, Hun.
64/F1 **Fehmarn** (isl.), Ger.
64/F1 **Fehmarn Belt** (str.), Ger., Den.
72/C2 **Fehrbellin**, Ger.
115/D4 **Fei** (riv.), China
171/E4 **Feia** (lake), Braz.
115/D3 **Feicheng**, China
115/D5 **Feidong**, China
68/C3 **Feignies**, Fr.
115/D4 **Fei Huang** (riv.), China
136/C3 **Feilding**, N.Z.
80/A5 **Feillans**, Fr.
76/A2 **Feira**, Port.
171/F2 **Feira de Santana**, Braz.
75/L3 **Feistritz** (riv.), Aus.
115/D5 **Feixi**, China
115/D4 **Fei Xian**, China
73/C5 **Fejér** (co.), Hun.
62/D4 **Fejø** (isl.), Den.
104/C2 **Feke**, Turk.
92/D3 **Feketić**, Yugo.
77/G3 **Felanitx**, Sp.
198/C2 **Felch**, Mi,US
81/H2 **Feldafing**, Ger.
71/H6 **Feldkirchen**, Aus.
81/H2 **Feldkirchen**, Aus.
71/H6 **Feldkirchen an der Donau**, Aus.
75/L3 **Feldkirchen bei Graz**, Aus.
75/L3 **Feldkirchen in Kärnten**, Aus.
86/A2 **Feletto**, It.
87/G1 **Feletto Umberto**, It.
173/E3 **Feliciano** (riv.), Arg.
198/D5 **Felicity**, Oh,US
86/D3 **Felino**, It.
159/H5 **Felipe Carillo Puerto**, Mex.
190/B4 **Felix** (riv.), NM,US
155/F3 **Felixburg**, Zim.
73/A4 **Felixdorf**, Aus.
170/D3 **Felixlândia**, Braz.
59/H3 **Felixstowe**, Eng,UK
188/B2 **Félix U. Gómez**, Mex.
86/B3 **Felizzano**, It.
69/F4 **Fell**, Ger.
70/C5 **Fellbach**, Ger.
57/G2 **Felling**, Eng,UK
186/C3 **Fellows**, Ca,US
203/H4 **Fellsmere**, Fl,US
67/G6 **Felsberg**, Ger.
81/F4 **Felsberg**, Swi.
189/H1 **Felsenthal**, Ar,US
191/H4 **Felsenthal Nat'l Wild. Ref.**, Ar,US
73/A6 **Felső-válicka** (riv.), Hun.
190/C2 **Felt**, Ok,US
53/M7 **Feltham**, Eng,UK
186/A2 **Felton**, Ca,US
206/C5 **Felton**, De,US
194/F4 **Felton**, Mn,US
206/B4 **Felton**, Pa,US
59/G2 **Feltwell**, Eng,UK
84/D2 **Fema** (peak), It.
62/D4 **Femø** (isl.), Den.
115/C4 **Fen** (riv.), China
80/B3 **Fénay**, Fr.
195/K5 **Fence**, Wi,US
187/H3 **Fence Lake**, NM,US
149/G3 **Fencho**, Eth.
121/H3 **Fenchuganj**, Bang.
76/A1 **Fene**, Sp.
199/G2 **Fenelon Falls**, On,Can
103/D1 **Fener** (pt.), Turk.
69/G6 **Fénétrange**, Fr.
91/J2 **Fengári** (peak), Gre.
113/C2 **Fengcheng**, China
117/G3 **Fengchuihudie** (peak), China
117/G2 **Fengding** (mtn.), China
108/F5 **Fenggang**, China
117/E3 **Fenghuang**, China
115/B5 **Fengjie**, China
115/B3 **Fengjie**, China
117/G2 **Fengkou**, China
117/E2 **Fengle**, China
117/H3 **Fengle**, China
115/D5 **Fengle** (riv.), China
117/J4 **Fenglin**, Tai.
108/G5 **Fenglingdu**, China
115/D3 **Fengnan**, China
115/D2 **Fengning**, China
116/C3 **Fengqing**, China
115/C4 **Fengqiu**, China
115/D3 **Fengrun**, China
109/H3 **Fengshan**, China
117/E3 **Fengshan**, China
119/J3 **Fengshan**, China
117/G3 **Fengshuba** (res.), China
109/J1 **Fengshui** (peak), China
115/H7 **Fengtai**, China
117/G3 **Fengtian**, China
108/F5 **Feng Xian**, China
115/D4 **Feng Xian**, China
115/E5 **Fengxian**, China
108/F5 **Fengxiang**, China
115/B3 **Fengyang**, China
115/D4 **Fengyang**, China
115/C2 **Fengzhen**, China
108/F5 **Fengzhou**, China
121/H4 **Feni**, Bang.
177/C5 **Fenimore** (passg.), Ak,US
186/E3 **Fenner**, Ca,US
193/J2 **Fennimore**, Wi,US
198/C3 **Fennville**, Mi,US
157/H7 **Fenoarivo**, Madg.
157/J7 **Fenoarivo Atsinanana**, Madg.
117/H3 **Fenshui** (pass), China
117/H4 **Fenshui Guan** (pass), China
117/F2 **Fenshuizhen**, China
62/D4 **Fensmark**, Den.
71/F4 **Fensterbach** (riv.), Ger.
59/G2 **Fens, The** (reg.), Eng,UK
202/B2 **Fenton**, La,US
205/E6 **Fenton**, Mi,US
205/E6 **Fenton** (lake), Mi,US
201/G1 **Fenwick**, WV,US
115/B3 **Fenxi**, China
99/H5 **Feodosiya**, Ukr.
91/K2 **Férai**, Gre.
60/C3 **Ferbane**, Ire.
72/B3 **Ferchland**, Ger.
200/D1 **Ferdinand**, In,US
65/G2 **Ferdinandshof**, Ger.
105/J3 **Ferdows**, Iran
68/C6 **Fère-Champenoise**, Fr.
68/C5 **Fère-en-Tardenois**, Fr.
84/C2 **Ferentillo**, It.
85/D4 **Ferentino**, It.
84/C3 **Ferento** (ruins), It.
105/G3 **Fereydūn Shahr**, Iran
114/B3 **Fergana**, Uzb.
198/F3 **Fergus**, On,Can
60/B4 **Fergus** (riv.), Ire.
194/F4 **Fergus Falls**, Mn,US
178/F2 **Ferguson** (lake), NW,Can
200/E2 **Ferguson**, Ky,US
73/D5 **Ferihegy** (int'l arpt.), Hun.
144/D4 **Ferkéssédougou**, IvC.
144/B3 **Ferlo, Vallée du** (wadi), Sen.
56/A3 **Fermanagh** (dist.), NI,UK
78/D1 **Fermanville**, Fr.
199/J1 **Ferme-Neuve**, Qu,Can
197/L2 **Fermeuse**, Nf,Can
87/F5 **Fermignano**, It.
204/F8 **Fermin** (pt.), Ca,US
205/P16 **Fermi Nat'l Accelerator Lab.**, Il,US
85/D1 **Fermo**, It.
76/B2 **Fermoselle**, Sp.
60/B5 **Fermoy**, Ire.
172/D3 **Fernández**, Arg.
159/F4 **Fernández**, Mex.
168/J7 **Fernandina** (isl.), Ecu.
203/H2 **Fernandina Beach**, Fl,US
172/E3 **Fernando de la Mora**, Par.
163/F3 **Fernando de Noronha** (isls.), Braz.
152/B2 **Fernando Po** (Bioko) (isl.), EqG.
170/C4 **Fernandópolis**, Braz.
76/C4 **Fernán-Núñez**, Sp.
184/A3 **Ferndale**, Ca,US
206/B5 **Ferndale**, Md,US
205/F7 **Ferndale**, Mi,US

199/G4 **Ferndale**, Pa,US
182/C3 **Ferndale**, Wa,US
59/E5 **Ferndown**, Eng,UK
54/C2 **Ferness**, Sc,UK
80/C5 **Ferney-Voltaire**, Fr.
182/G3 **Fernie**, BC,Can
184/D3 **Fernley**, Nv,US
81/G3 **Fernpass** (pass), Aus.
184/B1 **Fern Ridge** (lake), Or,US
60/D4 **Ferns**, Ire.
135/G5 **Ferntree Gully Nat'l Park**, Austl.
182/F4 **Fernwood**, Id,US
202/C2 **Fernwood**, Ms,US
122/E3 **Feroke**, India
202/C3 **Fer, Point au** (pt.), La,US
189/J3 **Fer, Pointe au** (pt.), La,US
83/C2 **Ferrandina**, It.
87/E3 **Ferrara**, It.
87/E3 **Ferrara** (prov.), It.
82/D5 **Ferrat** (cape), Fr.
76/B3 **Ferreira do Alentejo**, Port.
166/D2 **Ferreira Gomes**, Braz.
191/G4 **Ferrell's Bridge** (dam), Tx,US
184/A2 **Ferrelo** (cape), Or,US
168/B2 **Ferreñafe**, Peru
74/C4 **Ferret** (cape), Fr.
80/D3 **Ferrette**, Fr.
202/C2 **Ferriday**, La,US
86/C3 **Ferriere**, It.
68/D3 **Ferrière-la-Grande**, Fr.
69/E3 **Ferrières**, Belg.
188/L7 **Ferris**, Tx,US
199/K2 **Ferrisburg**, Vt,US
185/H4 **Ferron**, Ut,US
201/G2 **Ferrum**, Va,US
54/D3 **Ferryden**, Sc,UK
59/G5 **Ferryfield** (Lydd) (int'l arpt.), Eng,UK
57/G2 **Ferryhill**, Eng,UK
197/L2 **Ferryland**, Nf,Can
202/E2 **Ferry Pass**, Fl,US
58/B3 **Ferryside**, Wal,UK
95/N5 **Fershampenuaz**, Rus.
194/F4 **Fertile**, Mn,US
172/C3 **Fértil, Valle** (val.), Arg.
75/M3 **Fertő** (Neusiedler See) (lake), Aus., Hun.
73/A4 **Fertőszentmiklós**, Hun.
66/C2 **Ferwerd**, Neth.
141/M13 **Fès**, Mor.
80/C2 **Fesches-le-Châtel**, Fr.
152/D4 **Feshi**, Zaire
54/C2 **Feshie** (riv.), Sc,UK
194/E4 **Fessenden**, ND,US
80/D2 **Fessenheim**, Fr.
133/M8 **Festival Centre**, Austl.
191/J1 **Festus**, Mo,US
53/M8 **Fetcham**, Eng,UK
93/H3 **Fetești**, Rom.
55/P12 **Fethaland** (pt.), Sc,UK
60/C5 **Fethard**, Ire.
104/B2 **Fethiye**, Turk.
53/R10 **Feucherolles**, Fr.
70/E4 **Feucht**, Ger.
70/D4 **Feuchtwangen**, Ger.
179/J3 **Feuilles** (lake), Qu,Can
179/J3 **Feuilles, Rivière aux** (riv.), Qu,Can
68/A4 **Feuquières**, Fr.
68/A3 **Feuquières-en-Vimeu**, Fr.
74/F4 **Feurs**, Fr.
103/E1 **Fevzipaşa**, Turk.
206/C1 **F. E. Walter** (res.), Pa,US
192/B3 **F. E. Warren A.F.B.**, Wy,US
107/K1 **Feyzābād**, Afg.
82/A1 **Feyzin**, Fr.
141/M14 **Fez** (Saiss) (int'l arpt.), Mor.
42/A3 **Fezzan** (reg.), Libya
146/B4 **Fezzane** (well), Niger
56/E6 **Ffestiniog**, Wal,UK
157/H8 **Fianarantsoa**, Madg.
157/H8 **Fianarantsoa** (prov.), Madg.
84/C3 **Fiano Romano**, It.
84/D1 **Fiastrone** (riv.), It.
87/E3 **Ficarolo**, It.
149/H3 **Fichē**, Eth.
71/F2 **Fichtelberg** (peak), Ger.
71/E2 **Fichtelgebirge** (mts.), Ger.
71/E3 **Fichtelnaab** (riv.), Ger.
156/D3 **Ficksburg**, SAfr.
84/C2 **Ficulle**, It.
86/D3 **Fidenza**, It.
144/C4 **Fié** (riv.), Gui., Mali
55/N13 **Fiedrik**, Sc,UK
130/D3 **Field** (isl.), Austl.
141/G7 **Field** (riv.), Austl.
182/F1 **Field**, BC,Can
198/F1 **Field**, On,Can
193/J4 **Fieldon**, Il,US
202/B2 **Fields**, La,US
184/D2 **Fields**, Or,US
72/C3 **Fiener Bruch** (marsh), Ger.
93/G3 **Fieni**, Rom.
91/F2 **Fier**, Alb.
80/B6 **Fier** (riv.), Fr.
91/G1 **Fierzë** (lake), Alb.
81/E5 **Fiesch**, Swi.
87/F5 **Fiesole**, It.
87/E3 **Fiesso Umbertiano**, It.
54/D4 **Fife** (reg.), Sc,UK
205/C3 **Fife**, Wa,US
54/D4 **Fife Ness** (pt.), Sc,UK
135/C2 **Fifield**, Austl.
147/G5 **Fifth Cataract** (falls), Sudan
191/H3 **Fiftysix**, Ar,US
141/Q16 **Figalo** (cape), Alg.
90/A2 **Figari**, Fr.
74/E4 **Figeac**, Fr.
133/G2 **Figg** (peak), Austl.
87/E5 **Figline Valdarno**, It.
155/F4 **Figtree**, Zim.
76/A2 **Figueira da Foz**, Port.
77/G1 **Figueres**, Sp.
143/E2 **Figuig**, Mor.
148/B3 **Figuil**, Camr.
157/G8 **Fiherenana** (riv.), Madg.
143/H2 **Fijāl, Shaṭṭ al** (dry lake), Tun.
138/G6 **Fiji**
150/B3 **Fīk'**, Eth.
155/F4 **Filabusi**, Zim.
167/E4 **Filadélfia**, Braz.
164/C3 **Filadelfia**, Col.
83/C5 **Filadelfia**, It.
172/D2 **Filadelfia**, Par.
86/C4 **Filattiera**, It.
137/X **Filchner Ice Shelf**, Ant.
183/M2 **File** (hills), Sk,Can
185/F2 **Filer**, Id,US
57/H3 **Filey**, Eng,UK
57/H3 **Filey** (bay), Eng,UK
91/H3 **Filí**, Gre.
91/L6 **Filí**, Gre.
93/F3 **Filiași**, Rom.
91/G3 **Filiatai**, Gre.
91/G4 **Filiatrá**, Gre.
83/A5 **Filicudi** (isl.), It.
80/C6 **Filière** (riv.), Fr.
145/F3 **Filingué**, Niger
91/G3 **Filippiás**, Gre.
91/J2 **Filippoi** (ruins), Gre.
62/F2 **Filipstad**, Swe.
81/F4 **Filisur**, Swi.
194/C3 **Fillmore**, Sk,Can
204/B2 **Fillmore**, Ca,US
193/G3 **Fillmore**, Mo,US
185/G4 **Fillmore**, Ut,US
139/S9 **Filo** (peak), WSam.
159/H5 **Filomena Mata**, Mex.
91/J4 **Filótion**, Gre.
87/G6 **Filottrano**, It.
70/C5 **Fils** (riv.), Ger.
67/E2 **Filsum**, Ger.
58/D3 **Filton**, Eng,UK
150/B4 **Fī Itu**, Eth.
137/Z **Fimbul Ice Shelf**, Ant.
152/D3 **Fimi** (riv.), Zaire
87/E3 **Finale Emilia**, It.
86/B4 **Finale Ligure**, It.
76/D4 **Fiñana**, Sp.
144/C3 **Fina Rsv.**, Mali
201/H2 **Fincastle**, Va,US
183/L4 **Finch**, Mt,US
134/C3 **Finch Hatton**, Austl.
53/N7 **Finchley**, Eng,UK
69/F4 **Findel** (Luxembourg) (int'l arpt.), Lux.
54/C1 **Findhorn**, Sc,UK
54/C1 **Findhorn** (riv.), Sc,UK
177/L2 **Findlay** (mtn.), Yk,Can
198/B5 **Findlay**, Il,US
198/E4 **Findlay**, Oh,US
54/D1 **Findochty**, Sc,UK
206/C2 **Finesville**, NJ,US
135/D4 **Fingal**, Austl.
194/F4 **Fingal**, ND,US
199/H3 **Finger** (lakes), NY,US
200/C3 **Finger**, Tn,US
155/F2 **Fingoè**, Moz.
80/C5 **Finhaut**, Swi.
74/E4 **Finiels, Sommet de** (peak), Fr.
103/B1 **Finike**, Turk.
78/A4 **Finistère** (dept.), Fr.
76/A1 **Finisterre**, Sp.
76/A1 **Finisterre** (cape), Sp.
133/G3 **Finke** (riv.), Austl.
133/G3 **Finke Gorge Nat'l Park**, Austl.
75/K3 **Finkenstein**, Aus.
67/G1 **Finkenwerder**, Ger.
206/B5 **Finksburg**, Md,US
61/H2 **Finland**
63/L2 **Finland** (gulf), Eur.
195/J4 **Finland**, Mn,US
167/K7 **Finlandia**, Col.
178/D3 **Finlay** (riv.), BC,Can
188/B2 **Finlay** (mts.), Tx,US
195/H4 **Finlayson**, Mn,US
62/C3 **Fjerritslev**, Den.
135/C2 **Finley**, Austl.
194/F4 **Finley**, ND,US
191/G3 **Finley**, Ok,US
200/C2 **Finley**, Tn,US
182/E4 **Finley**, Wa,US
184/B1 **Finley Nat'l Wild. Ref.**, Or,US
55/H9 **Finn** (riv.), Ire.
72/B5 **Finne** (ridge), Ger.
183/H2 **Finnegan**, Ab,Can
67/E6 **Finnentrop**, Ger.
205/C2 **Finn Hill-Inglewood**, Wa,US
134/B1 **Finnigan, Mount** (peak), Austl.
133/G5 **Finniss** (cape), Austl.
131/G1 **Finnisterre** (range), PNG
61/G1 **Finnmark** (co.), Nor.
85/D2 **Fino** (riv.), It.
86/C1 **Fino Mornasco**, It.
72/D2 **Finowfurt**, Ger.
72/D2 **Finowkanal** (can.), Ger.
107/G4 **Fins**, Oman
131/G1 **Finschhafen**, PNG
71/E6 **Finsing**, Ger.
62/F2 **Finspång**, Swe.
80/E4 **Finsteraarhorn** (peak), Swi.
72/D4 **Finsterwalde**, Ger.
55/N13 **Finstown**, Sc,UK
63/H1 **Finström**, Fin.
67/G2 **Fintel**, Ger.
56/A3 **Fintona**, NI,UK
80/D5 **Fionnay**, Swi.
54/A1 **Fionn Loch** (lake), Sc,UK
84/B3 **Fiora** (riv.), It.
87/D3 **Fiorano**, It.
136/A4 **Fiordland Nat'l Park**, N.Z.
86/C3 **Fiorenzuola d'Arda**, It.
85/D2 **Fiori, Monte de** (peak), It.
157/H7 **Firavahana**, Madg.
205/B3 **Fircrest**, Wa,US
186/B2 **Firebaugh**, Ca,US
207/E2 **Fire Island Nat'l Seash.**, NY,US
87/E5 **Firenze** (prov.), It.
87/E5 **Firenze** (Florence), It.
87/E4 **Firenzuola**, It.
192/E1 **Firesteel** (cr.), SD,US
192/B3 **Firestone**, Co,US
174/E2 **Firmat**, Arg.
74/E4 **Firmi**, Fr.
170/C3 **Firminópolis**, Braz.
74/F4 **Firminy**, Fr.
83/C3 **Firmo**, It.
120/B2 **Fīrozābād**, India
122/C2 **Fīrozpur**, India
147/G3 **First Cataract** (falls), Egypt
185/G2 **Firth**, Id,US
105/H4 **Fīrūzābād**, Iran
105/H3 **Fīrūz Kūh**, Iran
105/J2 **Firyuza**, Trkm.
73/A3 **Fischa** (riv.), Aus.
70/D6 **Fischach**, Ger.
73/A3 **Fischamend**, Aus.
75/L3 **Fischbacher** (mts.), Aus.
67/G2 **Fischbek**, Ger.
81/G3 **Fischen im Allgäu**, Ger.
155/F2 **Fisenge**, Zam.
154/C5 **Fish** (riv.), Namb.
156/C3 **Fish** (riv.), SAfr.
57/G2 **Fishburn**, Eng,UK
186/C2 **Fish Camp**, Ca,US
137/E **Fisher** (glac.), Ant.
133/F4 **Fisher**, Austl.
182/G3 **Fisher** (mtn.), BC,Can
195/F2 **Fisher** (bay), Mb,Can
179/H2 **Fisher** (str.), NW,Can
191/J3 **Fisher**, Ar,US
193/K3 **Fisher**, Il,US
202/B2 **Fisher**, La,US
194/F4 **Fisher**, Mn,US
201/H1 **Fisher**, WV,US
194/F2 **Fisher Bay**, Mb,Can
194/F2 **Fisher Branch**, Mb,Can
134/F6 **Fisherman** (isl.), Austl.
201/K2 **Fishermans I. Nat'l Wild. Ref.**, Va,US
188/D2 **Fisher, O. C.** (lake), Tx,US
208/C3 **Fishers** (isl.), NY,US
201/H1 **Fishersville**, Va,US
58/B3 **Fishguard**, Wal,UK
195/G1 **Fishing** (lake), Mb,Can
201/J2 **Fishing** (cr.), NC,US
206/A1 **Fishing** (cr.), Pa,US
206/B1 **Fishing** (cr.), Pa,US
96/F4 **Fisht, Gora** (peak), Rus.
57/J6 **Fishtoft**, Eng,UK
191/J2 **Fisk**, Mo,US
208/B1 **Fiskdale**, Ma,US
183/K2 **Fiske**, Sk,Can
208/C2 **Fiskeville**, RI,US
63/S7 **Fisksätra**, Swe.
68/C5 **Fismes**, Fr.
199/L3 **Fitchburg**, Ma,US
193/K2 **Fitchburg**, Wi,US
55/P13 **Fitful Head** (pt.), Sc,UK
62/A2 **Fitjar**, Nor.
200/B4 **Fitler**, Ms,US
139/S8 **Fito** (peak), WSam.
63/R7 **Fittja**, Swe.
177/L2 **Fitton** (mtn.), Yk,Can
168/D3 **Fitzcarrald**, Peru
203/G2 **Fitzgerald**, Ga,US
132/C5 **Fitzgerald Riv. Nat'l Park**, Austl.
191/F3 **Fitzhugh**, Ok,US
174/D5 **Fitzroy**, Arg.
175/J7 **Fitzroy** (peak), Arg.
134/C3 **Fitzroy** (riv.), Austl.
175/N7 **Fitzroy**, Falk.
130/B4 **Fitzroy Crossing**, Austl.
179/R7 **Fitzwilliam** (str.), NW,Can
198/F2 **Fitzwilliam** (isl.), On,Can
84/D4 **Fiuggi**, It.
85/F6 **Fiumarella** (riv.), It.
83/C4 **Fiumenica** (riv.), It.
87/F1 **Fiume Veneto**, It.
84/C4 **Fiumicino**, It.
196/E3 **Five Islands**, NS,Can
185/J2 **Fivemile** (cr.), Wy,US
56/A3 **Fivemiletown**, NI,UK
54/A2 **Five Sisters** (mtn.), Sc,UK
86/D4 **Fivizzano**, It.
153/G4 **Fizi**, Zaire
97/H5 **Fizuli**, Azer.
62/A1 **Fjell**, Nor.
62/C3 **Fjerritslev**, Den.
62/F2 **Fjugesta**, Swe.
62/C1 **Flå**, Nor.
70/D4 **Flachslanden**, Ger.
69/F5 **Flack**, Fr.
59/F3 **Flackwell Heath**, Eng,UK
70/D1 **Fladungen**, Ger.
192/C4 **Flagler**, Co,US
203/H3 **Flagler Beach**, Fl,US
202/P6 **Flagler Museum**, Fl,US
200/E2 **Flagpole** (mtn.), Tn,US
187/G3 **Flagstaff**, Az,US
196/B3 **Flagstaff** (lake), Me,US
184/D2 **Flagstaff** (lake), Or,US
62/B1 **Flåm**, Nor.
78/D1 **Flamanville**, Fr.
193/J1 **Flambeau** (riv.), Wi,US
197/R9 **Flamborough**, On,Can
57/H3 **Flamborough**, Eng,UK
57/H3 **Flamborough Head** (pt.), Eng,UK
72/C3 **Fläming** (hills), Ger.
185/J3 **Flaming Gorge** (dam), Ut,US
185/J3 **Flaming Gorge** (res.), Wy.,Ut, US
185/J3 **Flaming Gorge Nat'l Rec. Area**, Ut, Wy,US
178/F4 **Flaming Gorge Nat'l Rec. Area**, Wy,US
203/H5 **Flamingo**, Fl,US
164/D1 **Flamingo Field** (int'l arpt.), NAnt.
195/H1 **Flanagan** (riv.), On,Can
68/B2 **Flanders** (reg.), Belg., Fr.
207/F2 **Flanders**, NY,US
167/L7 **Flandes**, Col.
193/F1 **Flandreau**, SD,US
192/F1 **Flasher**, ND,US
136/A4 **Flat** (peak), N.Z.
197/H1 **Flat Bay**, Nf,Can
207/K9 **Flatbush**, NY,US
177/L3 **Flat Creek**, Yk,Can
183/G3 **Flathead** (riv.), BC,Can
183/H3 **Flathead** (range), Mt,US
183/G4 **Flathead Ind. Res.**, Mt,US
183/H3 **Flathead, Middle Fork** (riv.), Mt,US
183/H4 **Flathead, South Fork** (riv.), Mt,US
58/C4 **Flat Holm** (isl.), Eng,UK
185/G1 **Flatiron** (mtn.), Id,US
189/F3 **Flatonia**, Tx,US
191/J2 **Flat River**, Mo,US
205/F7 **Flat Rock**, Mi,US
201/G2 **Flat Rock**, NC,US
134/B1 **Flattery** (cape), Austl.
182/B3 **Flattery** (cape), Wa,US
185/K4 **Flat Tops, The** (mts.), Co,US
183/K4 **Flatwillow** (cr.), Mt,US
201/F1 **Flatwoods**, Ky,US
202/B2 **Flatwoods**, La,US
164/B5 **Flavio Alfaro**, Ecu.
81/F3 **Flawil**, Swi.
183/K2 **Flaxcombe**, Sk,Can
80/D2 **Flaxlanden**, Fr.
82/C5 **Flayosc**, Fr.
183/J1 **Fleet**, Ab,Can
59/F4 **Fleet**, Eng,UK
57/E4 **Fleetwood**, Eng,UK
206/C3 **Fleetwood**, Pa,US
62/B2 **Flekkefjord**, Nor.
194/D2 **Fleming**, Sk,Can
192/C3 **Fleming**, Co,US
201/F2 **Fleming-Neon**, Ky,US
200/F1 **Flemingsburg**, Ky,US
191/H2 **Flemington**, Mo,US
206/D2 **Flemington**, NJ,US
135/F5 **Flemington Racecourse**, Austl.
62/G2 **Flen**, Swe.
64/E1 **Flensburg**, Ger.
86/D2 **Flero**, It.
69/E2 **Fleron**, Belg.
79/E3 **Flers**, Fr.
60/A5 **Flesk** (riv.), Ire.
62/A1 **Flesland** (int'l arpt.), Nor.
198/E2 **Fletcher** (lake), Mi,US
201/F3 **Fletcher**, NC,US
191/E3 **Fletcher**, Ok,US
80/D5 **Fletschhorn** (peak), Swi.
74/D5 **Fleurance**, Fr.
80/C4 **Fleurier**, Swi.
68/D3 **Fleurus**, Belg.
79/G5 **Fleury-les-Aubrais**, Fr.
79/G2 **Fleury-sur-Andelle**, Fr.
79/E2 **Fleury-sur-Orne**, Fr.
64/C2 **Flevoland** (polders), Neth.
66/C4 **Flevoland** (prov.), Neth.
81/G3 **Flexenpass** (pass), Aus.
70/C2 **Flieden**, Ger.
70/C2 **Flieden** (riv.), Ger.
81/G3 **Fliess**, Aus.
72/D4 **Fliess** (riv.), Ger.
72/C4 **Flieth** (riv.), Ger.
56/E2 **Flimby**, Eng,UK
81/F4 **Flims**, Swi.
132/B5 **Flinders** (bay), Austl.
133/G5 **Flinders** (isl.), Austl.
133/H5 **Flinders** (ranges), Austl.
134/C2 **Flinders** (reefs), Austl.
134/A2 **Flinders** (riv.), Austl.
133/H5 **Flinders Chase Nat'l Park**, Austl.
133/H4 **Flinders Ranges Nat'l Park**, Austl.
68/C3 **Flines-lez-Raches**, Fr.
178/F3 **Flin Flon**, Mb,Can
179/J2 **Flint** (lake), NW,Can
139/K6 **Flint** (isl.), Kiri.
57/E5 **Flint**, Wal,UK
200/D3 **Flint** (riv.), Al, Tn,US
200/E4 **Flint** (riv.), Ga,US
201/M7 **Flint** (riv.), Ga,US
203/F2 **Flint** (riv.), Ga,US
191/F2 **Flint** (hills), Ks,US
205/E5 **Flint**, Mi,US
62/D4 **Flintbek**, Ger.
200/D3 **Flint City**, Al,US
191/G1 **Flint Hills Nat'l Wild. Ref.**, Ks,US
199/H2 **Flinton**, On,Can
204/B2 **Flintridge-La Cañada**, Ca,US
205/F6 **Flint, South Branch** (riv.), Mi,US
201/M8 **Flippen**, Ga,US
62/E1 **Flisa**, Nor.
59/F3 **Flitwick**, Eng,UK
77/F2 **Flix**, Sp.
68/B3 **Flixecourt**, Fr.
69/G4 **Flize**, Fr.
189/G2 **Flo**, Tx,US
159/Q10 **Floating Gardens**, Mex.
62/E2 **Floby**, Swe.
62/E3 **Floda**, Swe.
54/D5 **Flodden**, Eng,UK
67/F1 **Flögelner See** (lake), Ger.
72/D6 **Flöha**, Ger.
72/D6 **Flöha** (riv.), Ger.
69/G4 **Floing**, Fr.
202/E2 **Flomaton**, Al,US
70/B3 **Flonheim**, Ger.
132/C2 **Flora** (peak), Austl.
125/C1 **Flora**, Phil.
193/K4 **Flora**, Il,US
125/C4 **Flora**, In,US
189/H2 **Flora**, La,US
200/B4 **Flora**, Ms,US
182/D3 **Flora** (mtn.), Wa,US
191/J3 **Floral**, Ar,US
203/E2 **Florala**, Al,US
202/L6 **Floral City**, Fl,US
203/G3 **Floral City**, Fl,US
207/E2 **Floral Park**, NY,US
69/F5 **Florange**, Fr.
167/G4 **Florânia**, Braz.
131/E4 **Floraville**, Austl.
187/J4 **Flora Vista**, NM,US
69/D3 **Floreffe**, Belg.
52/E4 **Florence**, It.
200/D3 **Florence**, Al,US
191/J4 **Florence**, Ar,US
187/G4 **Florence**, Az,US
192/B4 **Florence**, Co,US
191/F1 **Florence**, Ks,US
198/D5 **Florence**, Ky,US
200/B4 **Florence**, Ms,US
183/G4 **Florence**, Mt,US
184/A2 **Florence**, Or,US
201/H3 **Florence**, SC,US
194/F5 **Florence**, SD,US
189/F2 **Florence**, Tx,US
198/B2 **Florence**, Wi,US
87/E5 **Florence** (Firenze), It.
204/F8 **Florence-Graham**, Ca,US
187/G4 **Florence Junction**, Az,US
194/D4 **Florence Lake Nat'l Wild. Ref.**, ND,US
196/D2 **Florenceville**, NB,Can
172/E4 **Florencia**, Arg.
164/C4 **Florencia**, Col.
68/D3 **Florennes**, Belg.
174/D4 **Florentino Ameghino**, Arg.
195/H4 **Florenton**, Mn,US
69/E4 **Florenville**, Belg.
174/E3 **Flores** (riv.), Arg.
167/G4 **Flores**, Braz.
160/D2 **Flores**, Guat.
125/E5 **Flores** (isl.), Indo.
130/A1 **Flores** (sea), Indo.
77/R12 **Flores** (isl.), Azor.,Port.
175/T11 **Flores** (dept.), Uru.
167/F4 **Flores do Piauí**, Braz.
93/J2 **Floreshty**, Mol.
167/G5 **Floresta**, Braz.
189/E3 **Floresville**, Tx,US
206/D2 **Florham Park**, NJ,US
167/F4 **Floriano**, Braz.
173/G3 **Florianópolis**, Braz.
168/D4 **Florida**, Bol.

164/B4 Florida, Col.
161/G1 Florida, Cuba
162/A1 Florida (str.), Cuba, Fl,US
160/D3 Florida, Hon.
176/J7 Florida (str.), NAm.
168/B2 Florida, Peru
175/F2 Florida, Uru.
175/F2 Florida (dept.), Uru.
203/F2 Florida (state), US
203/H5 Florida (bay), Fl,US
203/H5 Florida (cape), Fl,US
203/H5 Florida (keys), Fl,US
207/D1 Florida, NY,US
164/C3 Floridablanca, Col.
203/H5 Florida City, Fl,US
175/L7 Florida Negra, Arg.
203/G3 Florida's Silver Springs, Fl,US
90/D4 Floridia, It.
202/B2 Florien, La,US
205/M10 Florin, Ca,US
91/G2 Flórina, Gre.
191/J1 Florissant, Mo,US
190/B1 Florissant Fossil Beds Nat'l Mon., Co,US
61/C3 Florø, Nor.
70/C2 Flörsbachtal, Ger.
70/B2 Flörsheim am Main, Ger.
70/B3 Flörsheim-Dalsheim, Ger.
70/B2 Florstadt, Ger.
71/F3 Flossenbürg, Ger.
200/F4 Flovilla, Ga,US
188/K6 Flower Mound, Tx,US
201/L7 Floyd, Ga,US
193/F2 Floyd (riv.), Ia,US
190/C3 Floyd, NM,US
201/G2 Floyd, Va,US
190/D4 Floydada, Tx,US
81/G4 Fluchthorn (peak), Aus.
81/F4 Flüelapass (pass), Swi.
81/E4 Flüelen, Swi.
66/C3 Fluessen (lake), Neth.
78/D4 Fluine (riv.), Fr.
90/A3 Flumendosa (riv.), It.
81/F3 Flums, Swi.
198/E3 Flushing, Mi,US
207/K8 Flushing, NY,US
66/A6 Flushing (Vlissingen), Neth.
188/D1 Fluvanna, Tx,US
131/F2 Fly (riv.), PNG
137/T Flying Fish (cape), Ant.
190/B4 Flying H, NM,US
131/F2 Fly River (delta), PNG
61/P6 Fnjóská (riv.), Ice.
194/C2 Foam Lake, Sk,Can
190/E4 Foard City, Tx,US
92/D4 Foča, Bosn.
54/C1 Fochabers, Sc,UK
156/P13 Fochville, SAfr.
75/K4 Foci del Po, It.
64/E1 Fockbek, Ger.
93/H3 Focşani, Rom.
79/H6 Foëcy, Fr.
130/C3 Fog (bay), Austl.
119/K3 Fogang, China
143/F4 Foggaret ez Zoua, Alg.
85/F5 Foggia, It.
85/F5 Foggia (prov.), It.
127/G4 Fogi, Indo.
87/F5 Foglia (riv.), It.
84/C5 Fogliano (lake), It.
86/A2 Foglizzo, It.
63/J2 Föglö (isl.), Fin.
140/J10 Fogo (isl.), CpV.
75/L3 Fohnsdorf, Aus.
64/E1 Föhr (isl.), Ger.
69/F4 Föhren, Ger.
84/B1 Foiano della Chiana, It.
74/D5 Foix, Fr.
96/E1 Fokino, Rus.
62/B1 Folarskardnuten (peak), Nor.
61/D2 Folda (fjord), Nor.
92/E2 Földeák, Hun.
91/J4 Folégandros (isl.), Gre.
68/C4 Folembray, Fr.
179/J2 Foley (isl.), NW,Can
203/G2 Foley, Fl,US
195/H5 Foley, Mn,US
191/J1 Foley, Mo,US
87/E1 Folgaria, It.
84/C2 Foligno, It.
59/H4 Folkestone, Eng,UK
203/G2 Folkston, Ga,US
208/G7 Follansbee, WV,US
189/G3 Follets (isl.), Tx,US
83/C3 Follone (riv.), It.
84/A2 Follonica, It.
84/A2 Follonica (gulf), It.
201/H4 Folly Beach, SC,US
69/F5 Folschviller, Fr.
186/B1 Folsom, Ca,US
184/C4 Folsom (lake), Ca,US
206/D4 Folsom, NJ,US
93/J3 Folteşti, Rom.
157/G6 Fomboni, Com.
167/M7 Fómeque, Col.
97/G3 Fomin, Rus.
199/J3 Fonda, NY,US
82/C3 Fond de Peinin, Pic du (peak), Fr.
178/F3 Fond du Lac, Sk,Can
178/F3 Fond du Lac (riv.), Sk,Can
193/K2 Fond du Lac, Wi,US
195/H4 Fond du Lac Ind. Res., Mn,US
79/F6 Fondettes, Fr.
85/D5 Fondi, It.
85/F4 Fondi (lake), It.
81/H5 Fondo, It.
138/G5 Fongafale (cap.), Tuv.
61/D3 Fongen (peak), Nor.
144/B3 Fongolanbi, Sen.
90/A2 Fonni, It.
76/B1 Fonsagrada, Sp.
164/C2 Fonseca, Col.
160/E3 Fonseca (gulf), NAm.
82/B2 Fontaine, Fr.
74/E2 Fontainebleau, Fr.
80/A3 Fontaine-lès-Dijon, Fr.
80/C2 Fontaine-lès-Luxeuil, Fr.
68/D3 Fontaine-L'Evêque, Belg.
204/C2 Fontana, Ca,US
191/G1 Fontana, Ks,US
200/F3 Fontana (dam), NC,US
200/F3 Fontana (lake), NC,US
85/F5 Fontanarosa, It.
90/D4 Fontanarossa (int'l arpt.), It.
86/C2 Fontanella, It.
86/D3 Fontanellato, It.
193/G3 Fontanelle, Ia,US
87/E1 Fontaniva, It.
165/E5 Fonte Boa, Braz.
80/D3 Fontenais, Swi.
74/C3 Fontenay-le-Comte, Fr.
53/S10 Fontenay-le-Fleury, Fr.
79/E2 Fontenay-le-Marmion, Fr.
53/S11 Fontenay-les-Briis, Fr.
53/T10 Fontenay-sous-Bois, Fr.
53/U10 Fontenay-Trésigny, Fr.
185/H2 Fontenelle (dam), Wy,US
185/H2 Fontenelle (res.), Wy,US
167/L7 Fontibón, Col.
69/F5 Fontoy, Fr.
82/C3 Font Sancte, Pic de la (peak), Fr.
61/P6 Fontur (pt.), Ice.
82/B6 Fontvieille, Fr.
73/B6 Fonyód, Hun.
182/F1 Foothills, Ab,Can
135/F5 Footscray, Austl.
108/F5 Foping, China
177/H3 Foraker (mt.), Ak,US
69/F5 Forbach, Fr.
70/B5 Forbach, Ger.
135/D2 Forbes, Austl.
182/F2 Forbes (mtn.), Ab,Can
136/A4 Forbes (peak), N.Z.
194/F5 Forbes, ND,US
121/F2 Forbesganj, India
145/G5 Forcados, Nga.
82/B5 Forcalquier, Fr.
76/A1 Forcarey, Sp.
70/E3 Forchheim, Ger.
73/A4 Forchtenstein, Aus.
196/D4 Forchu (cape), NS,Can
80/D5 Forclaz, Col de la (pass), Swi.
130/C3 Ford (cape), Austl.
54/D5 Ford, Eng,UK
205/E7 Ford (lake), Mi,US
195/L4 Ford (riv.), Mi,US
130/D1 Fordate (isl.), Indo.
186/C3 Ford City, Ca,US
199/G4 Ford City, Pa,US
72/B4 Forderstedt, Ger.
207/K8 Fordham, NY,US
59/E5 Fordingbridge, Eng,UK
202/G2 Fordoche, La,US
207/D2 Fords, NJ,US
135/C1 Ford's Bridge, Austl.
182/C4 Fords Prairie, Wa,US
200/D2 Fordsville, Ky,US
194/F3 Fordville, ND,US
191/H4 Fordyce, Ar,US
144/B4 Forécariah, Gui.
58/C4 Foreland (pt.), Eng,UK
59/E5 Foreland, The (pt.), Eng,UK
183/J3 Foremost, Ab,Can
59/H4 Foreness (pt.), Eng,UK
85/F6 Forenza, It.
198/F3 Forest, On,Can
189/J1 Forest, La,US
200/C4 Forest, Ms,US
194/F3 Forest (riv.), ND,US
193/H4 Forest, Oh,US
189/G2 Forest, Tx,US
201/H4 Forestbrook, SC,US
183/H1 Forestburg, Ab,Can
202/N6 Forest City, Fl,US
193/H2 Forest City, Ia,US
201/G3 Forest City, NC,US
199/J4 Forest City, Pa,US
184/C4 Foresthill, Ca,US
206/B4 Forest Hill, Md,US
189/F1 Forest Hill, Tx,US
201/G2 Forest Hill, WV,US
207/K9 Forest Hills, NY,US
200/D2 Forest Hills, Tn,US
135/D4 Forestier (cape), Austl.
195/H5 Forest Lake, Mn,US
195/H5 Foreston, Mn,US
201/M7 Forest Park, Ga,US
199/J3 Forestport, NY,US
130/B3 Forest River Abor. Rsv., Austl.
196/C1 Forestville, Qu,Can
206/B6 Forestville, Md,US
199/G3 Forestville, NY,US
193/L1 Forestville, Wi,US
78/B5 Forêt (bay), Fr.
150/B3 Forêt du Day Nat'l Park, Djib.
74/F4 Forez (mts.), Fr.
54/D3 Forfar, Sc,UK
183/L2 Forgan, Sk,Can
190/D2 Forgan, Ok,US
53/S11 Forges-les-Bains, Fr.
68/A4 Forges-les-Eaux, Fr.
81/G2 Forggensee (lake), Ger.
196/E1 Forillon Nat'l Park, Qu,Can
85/E6 Forino, It.
85/D6 Forio, It.
200/C3 Forked Deer, North Fork (riv.), Tn,US
200/C3 Forked Deer, South Fork (riv.), Tn,US
189/H3 Forked Island, La,US
207/D4 Forked River, NJ,US
56/B3 Forkill, NI,UK
200/D4 Forkland, Al,US
194/D2 Fork River, Mb,Can
182/B4 Forks, Wa,US
87/F4 Forlì, It.
87/F4 Forlì (prov.), It.
87/F4 Forlimpopoli, It.
194/F4 Forman, ND,US
54/D2 Formartine (dist.), Sc,UK
81/E5 Formazza, It.
57/E4 Formby, Eng,UK
57/E4 Formby (pt.), Eng,UK
84/C3 Formello, It.
77/F3 Formentera (isl.), Sp.
77/G3 Formentor, Cabo de (cape), Sp.
68/A4 Formerie, Fr.
85/D5 Formia, It.
170/D4 Formiga, Braz.
87/D3 Formigine, It.
87/E3 Formignana, It.
172/E3 Formosa, Arg.
172/E2 Formosa (prov.), Arg.
170/D2 Formosa, Braz.
169/H4 Formosa (mts.), Braz.
170/B1 Formosa (uplands), Braz.
144/A4 Formosa (isl.), GBis.
156/C4 Formosa (peak), SAfr.
191/H3 Formosa, Ar,US
170/C2 Formoso, Braz.
170/C1 Formoso (riv.), Braz.
170/D2 Formoso (riv.), Braz.
87/E5 Fornacelle, It.
83/B7 Fornaci, It.
86/D4 Fornaci di Barga, It.
62/D3 Fornæs (cape), Den.
62/D2 Fornebu (int'l arpt.), Nor.
188/L7 Forney, Tx,US
86/A2 Forno Canavese, It.
63/P2 Fornosovo, Rus.
86/D3 Fornovo di Taro, It.
85/E3 Foro (riv.), It.
148/D2 Foro Burunga, Sudan
99/G5 Foros, Ukr.
172/D3 Forres, Arg.
54/C1 Forres, Sc,UK
133/F4 Forrest, Austl.
191/J3 Forrest City, Ar,US
130/B3 Forrest River Mission, Austl.
194/E3 Forrest Station, Mb,Can
188/D1 Forsan, Tx,US
62/B2 Forsand, Nor.
134/A2 Forsayth, Austl.
62/E2 Forshaga, Swe.
63/K1 Forssa, Fin.
135/E2 Forster, Austl.
71/E6 Forstern, Ger.
134/A3 Forsyth (range), Austl.
200/F4 Forsyth, Ga,US
191/H2 Forsyth, Mo,US
183/L4 Forsyth, Mt,US
207/D5 Forsythe Nat'l Wild. Ref., NJ,US
107/K3 Fort Abbās, Pak.
194/E4 Fort Abercrombie, ND,US
179/H3 Fort Albany, On,Can
169/E3 Fortaleza, Bol.
169/E4 Fortaleza, Bol.
167/G3 Fortaleza, Braz.
167/E4 Fortaleza dos Nogueiras, Braz.
175/G2 Fortaleza Santa Teresa, Uru.
198/D5 Fort Ancient, Oh,US
187/H2 Fort Apache, Az,US
187/G3 Fort Apache Ind. Res., Az,US
201/J1 Fort A.P. Hill (mil. res.), Va,US
199/G5 Fort Ashby, WV,US
198/B3 Fort Atkinson, Wi,US
54/B2 Fort Augustus, Sc,UK
156/D4 Fort Beaufort, SAfr.
196/E3 Fort Beauséjour Nat'l Hist. Park, NB,Can
189/E1 Fort Belknap, Tx,US
183/K3 Fort Belknap Ind. Res., Mt,US
206/A6 Fort Belvoir (mil. res.), Va,US
189/M9 Fort Bend (co.), Tx,US
198/C5 Fort Benjamin Harrison, In,US
200/E4 Fort Benning (mil. res.), Ga,US
200/E4 Fort Benning South, Ga,US
183/J4 Fort Benton, Mt,US
194/C4 Fort Berthold Ind. Res., ND,US
184/C3 Fort Bidwell, Ca,US
187/J4 Fort Bliss (mil. res.), NM, Tx,US
187/H4 Fort Bowie Nat'l Hist. Site, Az,US
184/B4 Fort Bragg, Ca,US
201/H3 Fort Bragg (mil. res.), NC,US
200/D1 Fort Branch, In,US
185/H3 Fort Bridger, Wy,US
194/C4 Fort Buford Hist. Site, ND,US
200/D2 Fort Campbell (mil. res.), Ky, Tn,US
192/B4 Fort Carson, Co,US
191/G3 Fort Chaffee, Ar,US
199/K2 Fort Chambly Nat'l Hist. Park, Qu,Can
179/K3 Fort-Chimo (Kuujjuaq), Qu,Can
178/E3 Fort Chipewyan, Ab,Can
194/D4 Fort Clark Hist. Site, ND,US
192/B3 Fort Collins, Co,US
202/D2 Fort Conde, Al,US
200/D4 Fort Davis, Al,US
188/C2 Fort Davis, Tx,US
188/C2 Fort Davis Nat'l Hist. Site, Tx,US
69/E5 Fort de Douaumont, Fr.
187/G2 Fort Defiance, Az,US
162/F4 Fort-de-France, Mart.
124/C3 Fort de Kock, Indo.
200/D5 Fort Deposit, Al,US
162/F4 Fort Desaix, Mart.
202/K8 Fort DeSoto Park, Fl,US
203/G4 Fort DeSoto Park, Fl,US
69/E5 Fort de Vaux, Fr.
206/D3 Fort Dix (mil. res.), NJ,US
193/G2 Fort Dodge, Ia,US
193/G2 Fort Dodge Hist. Museum, Ia,US
200/D2 Fort Donelson Nat'l Bfld., Tn,US
199/J2 Fort Drum (mil. res.), NY,US
185/J3 Fort Duchesne, Ut,US
153/E5 Forte Cameia, Ang.
86/D5 Forte dei Marmi, It.
199/K3 Fort Edward, NY,US
152/D4 Forte República, Ang.
197/T10 Fort Erie, On,Can
132/C2 Fortescue (riv.), Austl.
206/C5 Fortescue, NJ,US
196/D2 Fort Fairfield, Me,US
195/H3 Fort Frances, On,Can
178/D2 Fort Franklin, NW,Can
203/H2 Fort Fredrica Nat'l Mon., Ga,US
202/D2 Fort Gaines, Al,US
200/E3 Fort Gaines, Ga,US
190/B2 Fort Garland, Co,US
159/F2 Fort Gates, Tx,US
201/F1 Fort Gay, WV,US
197/S9 Fort George, On,Can
179/J3 Fort-George (Chisasibi), Qu,Can
199/G3 Fort George Nat'l Hist. Park, On,Can
191/G3 Fort Gibson, Ok,US
191/G2 Fort Gibson (lake), Ok,US
201/M7 Fort Gillem, Ga,US
178/D2 Fort Good Hope, NW,Can
201/F4 Fort Gordon (mil. res.), Ga,US
187/H4 Fort Grant, Az,US
202/M8 Fort Green, Fl,US
60/D5 Forth (mtn.), Ire.
54/C5 Forth, Sc,UK
54/D4 Forth (inlet), Sc,UK
54/C4 Forth (riv.), Sc,UK
185/G2 Fort Hall, Id,US
185/G2 Fort Hall Ind. Res., Id,US
207/D2 Fort Hamilton, NY,US
207/D3 Fort Hancock, NJ,US
188/B2 Fort Hancock, Tx,US
54/B4 Forth, Carse of (plain), Sc,UK
199/H2 Fort Henry, On,Can
55/K8 Forth, Firth of (inlet), Sc,UK
189/F2 Fort Hood, Tx,US
206/B5 Fort Howard, Md,US
187/G5 Fort Huachuca (mil. res.), Az,US
186/B3 Fort Hunter Liggett (mil. res.), Ca,US
172/D2 Fortín Avalos Sánchez, Par.
172/D2 Fortín Capitán Escobar, Par.
172/E2 Fortín Carlos Antonio López, Par.
172/E2 Fortín Casanillo, Par.
172/E2 Fortín Coronel Bogado, Par.
172/E1 Fortín Coronel Sánchez, Par.
159/N8 Fortín de las Flores, Mex.
186/C2 Fort Independence Ind. Res., Ca,US
206/B3 Fort Indiantown Gap (mil. res.), Pa,US
172/E2 Fortín Florida, Par.
172/E3 Fortín General Bruguez, Par.
172/E2 Fortín Guaraní, Par.
172/D2 Fortín Hernandarias, Par.
172/D2 Fortín Infante Rivarola, Par.
172/E2 Fortín Isla Poi, Par.
172/E1 Fortín Mutum, Bol.
172/D1 Fortín Palmar de las Islas, Par.
172/E2 Fortín Presidente Ayala, Par.
172/E3 Fortín Teniente Esteban Martínez, Par.
172/D2 Fortín Teniente Gabino Mendoza, Par.
172/D2 Fortín Teniente Juan E. López, Par.
172/D2 Fortín Teniente Primero Ramiro Espínola, Par.
174/D3 Fortín Uno, Arg.
172/E2 Fortín Zalazar, Par.
186/D3 Fort Irwin (mil. res.), Ca,US
201/G3 Fort Jackson (mil. res.), SC,US
203/G5 Fort Jefferson Nat'l Mon., Fl,US
151/B3 Fort Jesus, Kenya
196/C2 Fort Kent, Me,US
200/E2 Fort Knox (mil. res.), Ky,US
192/B2 Fort Laramie (can.), Wy,US
192/B2 Fort Laramie Nat'l Hist. Site, Wy,US
190/E1 Fort Larned Nat'l Hist. Site, Ks,US
162/A1 Fort Lauderdale, Fl,US
203/H4 Fort Lauderdale, Fl,US
202/P7 Fort Lauderdale-Hollywood (int'l arpt.), Fl,US
203/H4 Fort Lauderdale-Hollywood (int'l arpt.), Fl,US
201/G3 Fort Lawn, SC,US
191/G1 Fort Leavenworth (mil. res.), Ks,US
207/E2 Fort Lee, NJ,US
199/K2 Fort Lennox Nat'l Hist. Park, Qu,Can
191/H2 Fort Leonard Wood, Mo,US
200/A2 Fort Leonard Wood (mil. res.), Mo,US
205/B3 Fort Lewis, Wa,US
178/D2 Fort Liard, NW,Can
161/J2 Fort Liberté, Haiti
199/H5 Fort Loudon, Pa,US
192/B3 Fort Lupton, Co,US
192/C4 Fort Lyon (can.), Co,US
198/D2 Fort Mackinac, Mi,US
183/H3 Fort Macleod, Ab,Can
193/J3 Fort Madison, Ia,US
68/A3 Fort-Mahon-Plage, Fr.
205/F7 Fort Malden Nat'l Hist. Park, On.,Can
194/D4 Fort Mandan Hist. Site, ND,US
68/B1 Fort-Mardyck, Fr.
203/H3 Fort Matanzas Nat'l Mon., Fl,US
200/E4 Fort McClellan (mil. res.), Al,US
203/H3 Fort McCoy, Fl,US
193/J1 Fort McCoy, Wi,US
184/E3 Fort McDermitt Ind. Res., Or.,Nv,US
206/B5 Fort McHenry Nat'l Mon. & Hist. Site, Md,US
178/E3 Fort McMurray, Ab,Can
177/M2 Fort McPherson, NW,Can
201/M7 Fort McPherson, Ga,US
203/H4 Fort Meade, Fl,US
206/B5 Fort Meade (mil. res.), Md,US
198/D2 Fort Michilimac kinac, Mi,US
201/G3 Fort Mill, SC,US
183/G4 Fort Missoula, Mt,US
186/E3 Fort Mojave Ind. Res., Az, Ca,US
207/D3 Fort Monmouth, NJ,US
201/J2 Fort Monroe, Va,US
202/D2 Fort Morgan, Al,US
192/C3 Fort Morgan, Co,US
201/G4 Fort Motte, SC,US
201/H4 Fort Moultrie, SC,US
203/H4 Fort Myers, Fl,US
178/D3 Fort Nelson, BC,Can
178/D3 Fort Nelson (riv.), BC,Can
192/D2 Fort Niobrara Nat'l Wild. Ref., Ne,US
178/D2 Fort Norman, NW,Can
57/F4 Forton, Eng,UK
186/B2 Fort Ord, Ca,US
85/F4 Fortore (riv.), It.
200/E3 Fort Payne, Al,US
183/L3 Fort Peck, Mt,US
183/L4 Fort Peck (dam), Mt,US
183/L4 Fort Peck (lake), Mt,US
183/M3 Fort Peck Ind. Res., Mt,US
194/B3 Fort Peck Ind. Res., Mt,US
188/E1 Fort Phantom Hill, Tx,US
201/J2 Fort Pickett (mil. res.), Va,US
203/H4 Fort Pierce, Fl,US
192/D1 Fort Pierre Nat'l Grsld., SD,US
199/J3 Fort Plain, NY,US
202/B2 Fort Polk (mil. res.), La,US
153/G2 Fort Portal, Ugan.
178/E2 Fort Providence, NW,Can
201/G4 Fort Pulaski Nat'l Mon., Ga,US
194/C2 Fort Qu'Appelle, Sk,Can
188/B2 Fort Quitman (ruins), Tx,US
201/K3 Fort Raleigh Nat'l Hist. Site, NC,US
192/E2 Fort Randall (dam), SD,US
194/F4 Fort Ransom Hist. Site, ND,US
178/E2 Fort Resolution, NW,Can
185/J1 Fortress (mtn.), Wy,US
197/G3 Fortress of Louisbourg Nat'l Hist. Park, NS,Can
194/D4 Fort Rice Hist. Site, ND,US
193/F4 Fort Riley, Ks,US
191/F1 Fort Riley (mil. res.), Ks,US
195/G4 Fort Ripley, Mn,US
155/F4 Fort Rixon, Zim.
184/C2 Fort Rock, Or,US
54/B1 Fortrose, Sc,UK
184/B4 Fort Ross, Ca,US
203/F2 Fort Rucker (mil. res.), Al,US
178/D3 Fort Saint James, BC,Can
178/D3 Fort Saint John, BC,Can
178/E3 Fort Saskatchewan, Ab,Can
191/G2 Fort Scott, Ks,US
191/G2 Fort Scott Nat'l Hist. Site, Ks,US
194/E4 Fort Seward Hist. Site, ND,US
201/H1 Fort Seybert, WV,US
198/D4 Fort Shawnee, Oh,US
97/J3 Fort-Shevchenko, Kaz.
191/E3 Fort Sill (mil. res.), Ok,US
178/D2 Fort Simpson, NW,Can
178/E2 Fort Smith, NW,Can
191/G3 Fort Smith, Ar,US
185/K1 Fort Smith, Mt,US
191/G3 Fort Smith Nat'l Hist. Site, Ar,US
199/J3 Fort Stanwix Nat'l Mon., NY,US
201/G5 Fort Stewart, Ga,US
201/G4 Fort Stewart (mil. res.), Ga,US
188/C2 Fort Stockton, Tx,US
190/B3 Fort Sumner, NM,US
201/H4 Fort Sumter Nat'l Mon., SC,US
187/H4 Fort Thomas, Az,US
198/D5 Fort Thomas, Ky,US
207/E2 Fort Tilden, NY,US
194/E4 Fort Totten, ND,US
194/E4 Fort Totten Ind. Res., ND,US
191/G3 Fort Towson, Ok,US
174/D2 Fortuna, Arg.
167/E4 Fortuna, Braz.
184/A3 Fortuna, Ca,US
191/H1 Fortuna, Mo,US
194/C3 Fortuna, ND,US
177/F3 Fortuna Ledge, Ak,US
197/K2 Fortune, Nf,Can
197/K2 Fortune (bay), Nf,Can
162/C2 Fortune (Long Cay) (cay), Bahm.
58/D5 Fortuneswell, Eng,UK
183/M1 Fort Union Trading Post Nat'l Hist. Site, Mt,US
200/F4 Fort Valley, Ga,US
184/B1 Fort Vancouver Nat'l Hist. Site, Or,US
178/E3 Fort Vermilion, Ab,Can
198/D5 Fortville, In,US
207/D2 Fort Wadsworth, NY,US
202/E2 Fort Walton Beach, Fl,US
185/J2 Fort Washakie, Wy,US
206/A6 Fort Washington Park, Md,US
198/D4 Fort Wayne, In,US
199/J2 Fort Wellington Nat'l Hist. Park, Can.
203/G3 Fort White, Fl,US
54/A3 Fort William, Sc,UK
187/H3 Fort Wingate, NM,US
187/H3 Fort Wingate (mil. res.), NM,US
189/E1 Fort Wolters, Tx,US
191/E4 Fort Wolters (mil. res.), Tx,US
189/F1 Fort Worth, Tx,US
188/K7 Fort Worth-Dallas (int'l arpt.), Tx,US
188/K7 Fort Worth Museum of Science and History, Tx,US
194/D4 Fort Yates, ND,US
206/C1 Forty Fort, Pa,US
198/E2 Forty Mile (pt.), Mi,US
186/D2 Fortymile (wash), Nv,US
134/B2 Forty Mile Scrub Nat'l Park, Austl.
177/J2 Fort Yukon, Ak,US
186/E4 Fort Yuma Ind. Res., Ca,US
105/H5 Forūr (isl.), Iran
82/A6 Fos (gulf), Fr.
167/M7 Fosca, Col.
117/G4 Foshan, China
179/S7 Fosheim (pen.), NW,Can
145/E5 Foso, Gha.
57/G3 Foss (riv.), Eng,UK
85/E3 Fossacesia, It.
83/A5 Fossa di Felci (mtn.), It.
87/F1 Fossalta di Piave, It.
87/F1 Fossalta di Portogruaro, It.
86/A3 Fossano, It.
84/C1 Fossato di Vico, It.
53/T9 Fosses, Fr.
69/D3 Fosses-la-Ville, Belg.
184/C1 Fossil, Or,US
185/H3 Fossil Butte Nat'l Mon., Wy,US
87/F2 Fossò, It.
87/F5 Fossombrone, It.
194/C1 Fosston, Sk,Can
195/G4 Fosston, Mn,US
82/A6 Fos-sur-Mer, Fr.
135/C3 Foster, Austl.
191/G1 Foster, Mo,US
184/B1 Foster, Or,US
188/C1 Foster, Tx,US
198/C2 Foster City, Mi,US
198/E4 Fostoria, Oh,US
73/D4 Fót, Hun.
117/H3 Fotan, China
148/B2 Fotokol, Camr.
79/G1 Foucarmont, Fr.
80/B3 Foucherans, Fr.
78/A5 Fouesnant, Fr.
69/E6 Foug, Fr.
152/B3 Fougamou, Gabon
78/D4 Fougères, Fr.
80/C2 Fougerolles, Fr.
68/B4 Fouilloy, Fr.
181/H4 Fouke, Ar,US
106/C4 Foul (bay), Egypt
122/H4 Foul (pt.), SrL.
55/N12 Foula (isl.), Sc,UK
59/G3 Foulness (isl.), Eng,UK
59/G3 Foulness (pt.), Eng,UK
57/H4 Foulness (riv.), Eng,UK
59/H1 Foulsham, Eng,UK
136/B3 Foulwind (cape), N.Z.
145/H5 Foumban, Camr.
148/A4 Foumbot, Camr.
157/G5 Foumbouni, Com.
142/C3 Foum el Hassane, Mor.
142/D3 Foum Zguid, Mor.
144/A3 Foundiougne, Sen.
190/B1 Fountain, Co,US
192/B4 Fountain (cr.), Co,US
203/F2 Fountain, Fl,US
195/N6 Fountain (lake), Mn,US
185/H4 Fountain Green, Ut,US
206/C2 Fountain Hill, Pa,US
187/G4 Fountain Hills, Az,US
201/F3 Fountain Inn, SC,US
200/E2 Fountain Run, Ky,US
57/G3 Fountains Abbey, Eng,UK
204/C3 Fountain Valley, Ca,US
82/A3 Fourchambault, Fr.
191/H3 Fourche La Fave (riv.), Ar,US
130/C2 Fourcroy (cape), Austl.
182/F4 Four Lakes, Wa,US
59/E4 Four Marks, Eng,UK
68/D4 Fourmies, Fr.
192/A2 Fourmile (peak), Wy,US
190/B4 Fourmile Draw (cr.), NM,US
177/D5 Four Mountains (isls.), Ak,US
157/R15 Fournaise, Piton de la (peak), Reun.
82/C2 Fourneaux, Fr.
82/A5 Fourques, Fr.
195/K4 Fourteen Mile (pt.), Mi,US
147/G5 Fourth Cataract (falls), Sudan
144/B4 Fouta Djallon (reg.), Gha.
136/A4 Foveaux (str.), N.Z.
58/B6 Fowey, Eng,UK
58/B6 Fowey (riv.), Eng,UK
186/C2 Fowler, Ca,US
192/B4 Fowler, Co,US
198/C4 Fowler, In,US
198/D3 Fowler, Mi,US
133/J4 Fowlers Gap, Austl.
200/C3 Fowlkes, Tn,US
105/G2 Fowman, Iran
177/M3 Fox (mtn.), Yk,Can
177/E5 Fox (isls.), Ak,US
191/H5 Fox, Ar,US
193/J3 Fox (riv.), Ia, Mo,US
205/P15 Fox (lake), Il,US
205/P16 Fox (riv.), Il,US
193/K3 Fox (riv.), Il, Wi,US
195/L5 Fox, Mi,US
191/F3 Fox, Ok,US
184/D1 Fox, Or,US
205/B3 Fox (isl.), Wa,US
205/P14 Fox (riv.), Wi,US
208/C1 Foxboro, Ma,US
208/H5 Foxburg, Pa,US
208/H6 Fox Chapel, Pa,US
196/C3 Foxcroft-Dover, Me,US
179/J2 Foxe (basin), NW,Can
179/H2 Foxe (chan.), NW,Can
179/J2 Foxe (pen.), NW,Can
62/D2 Foxen (lake), Swe.
60/A2 Foxford, Ire.
136/B3 Fox Glacier, N.Z.
197/L2 Fox Harbour, Nf,Can
205/P15 Fox Lake, Il,US
185/K3 Foxpark, Wy,US
205/P15 Fox River Grove, Il,US
59/G2 Foxton, Eng,UK
193/K2 Fox Valley, Sk,Can
54/B2 Foyers, Sc,UK
56/A2 Foyle (riv.), NI,UK
56/A1 Foyle, Lough (inlet), Ire., NI,UK
60/A4 Foynes, Ire.
76/B1 Foz, Sp.
168/C3 Foz do Breu, Braz.
154/A3 Foz do Cunene, Ang.
173/F3 Foz do Iguaçu, Braz.
206/B2 Frackville, Pa,US
77/F2 Fraga, Sp.
161/G1 Fragosa (cay), Cuba
173/G3 Fraiburgo, Braz.
175/G2 Fraile Muerto, Uru.
172/C2 Fraile Pintado, Arg.
80/B3 Fraisans, Fr.
80/D1 Fraize, Fr.
68/C3 Frameries, Belg.
208/C1 Framingham, Ma,US
59/H2 Framlingham, Eng,UK
70/C2 Frammersbach, Ger.
170/D4 Franca, Braz.
85/E3 Francavilla al Mare, It.
83/B7 Francavilla di Sicilia, It.
91/E2 Francavilla Fontana, It.
83/C2 Francavilla in Sinni, It.
74/D3 France
53/T9 France, Pays de (plain), Fr.
74/E5 France, Roc de (mtn.), Fr.
178/C2 Frances (lake), Yk,Can
161/E1 Francés (cape), Cuba
161/F1 Frances (cape), Cuba
198/C4 Francesville, In,US
152/C3 Franceville, Gabon
80/C3 Franche-Comté (hist. reg.), Fr.
80/B2 Franche-Comté (reg.), Fr.
175/T11 Francia, Uru.
194/C2 Francis, Sk,Can
191/F3 Francis, Ok,US
185/H3 Francis, Ut,US
192/E2 Francis Case (lake), SD,US
171/N6 Francisco de Assis (arpt.), Braz.
168/C1 Francisco de Orellana, Peru
159/H5 Francisco Escárcega, Mex.
158/E3 Francisco I. Madero, Mex.
188/B3 Francisco Portillo, Mex.
155/E4 Francistown, Bots.
155/E4 Francistown (int'l arpt.), Bots.
171/K8 Franco da Rocha, Braz.
87/E3 Francolino, It.
199/L2 Franconia, NH,US
53/S10 Franconville, Fr.
66/C2 Franeker, Neth.
80/B5 Frangy, Fr.
191/E4 Frankell, Tx,US
67/F6 Frankenau, Ger.
72/D6 Frankenberg, Ger.
67/F6 Frankenberg-Eder, Ger.
71/G6 Frankenburg am Hausruck, Aus.
70/D4 Frankenhöhe (mts.), Ger.
71/G7 Frankenmarkt, Aus.
198/E3 Frankenmuth, Mi,US
70/B3 Frankenthal, Ger.
71/E2 Franken Wald (for.), Ger.
199/H2 Frankford, On,Can
201/K1 Frankford, De,US
156/E2 Frankfort, SAfr.
198/C4 Frankfort, In,US
191/F1 Frankfort, Ks,US
200/E1 Frankfort (cap.), Ky,US
198/C2 Frankfort, Mi,US
198/E5 Frankfort, Oh,US
208/G7 Frankfort Springs, Pa,US
65/H2 Frankfurt, Ger.
70/B2 Frankfurt (int'l arpt.), Ger.
70/B2 Frankfurt am Main, Ger.
132/D5 Frank Hann Nat'l Park, Austl.
70/E3 Fränkische Alb (mts.), Ger.
70/D4 Fränkische Rezat (riv.), Ger.
70/C2 Fränkische Saale (riv.), Ger.
70/E2 Fränkische Schweiz (reg.), Ger.
135/C3 Frankland (cape), Austl.
137/M Franklin (isl.), Ant.
177/N1 Franklin (bay), NW,Can
178/D2 Franklin (mts.), NW,Can
199/K2 Franklin, Qu,Can
177/G1 Franklin (pt.), Ak,US
187/H4 Franklin, Az,US
208/B2 Franklin, Ct,US
200/E4 Franklin, Ga,US
185/H2 Franklin, Id,US
198/C5 Franklin, In,US
191/G2 Franklin, Ks,US
200/D2 Franklin, Ky,US
202/C3 Franklin, La,US
208/C1 Franklin, Ma,US
205/F6 Franklin, Mi,US
201/F3 Franklin, NC,US
192/E3 Franklin, Ne,US
199/L3 Franklin, NH,US
206/D1 Franklin, NJ,US
198/D5 Franklin, Oh,US
208/H5 Franklin, Pa,US
200/D3 Franklin, Tn,US
189/F2 Franklin, Tx,US
201/J2 Franklin, Va,US
205/P14 Franklin, Wi,US
201/H1 Franklin, WV,US
182/E3 Franklin D. Roosevelt (res.), Wa,US
198/B4 Franklin Grove, Il,US
196/C4 Franklin I. Nat'l Wild. Ref., Me,US
207/D1 Franklin Lakes, NJ,US
135/C4 Franklin-Lower Gordon Wild Rivers Nat'l Park, Austl.
206/D1 Franklin Mineral Museum, NJ,US
205/Q16 Franklin Park, Il,US
208/G6 Franklin Park, Pa,US
207/E2 Franklin Square, NY,US
202/C2 Franklinton, La,US
201/H2 Franklinton, NC,US
199/G3 Franklinville, NY,US
189/G1 Frankston, Tx,US
205/Q14 Franksville, Wi,US
200/C5 Frankville, Al,US
80/B3 Franois, Fr.
196/D1 Franquelin, Qu,Can
79/F1 Franqueville-Saint-Pierre, Fr.
156/L10 Franschhoek, SAfr.
154/B4 Fransfontein, Namb.
173/F3 Fransisco Beltrão, Braz.
171/K8 Fransisco Morato, Braz.
171/E3 Fransisco Sá, Braz.
94/C3 Fränsta, Swe.
71/F2 Františkovy Lázně, Czh.
64/G1 Franzburg, Ger.
100/F2 Franz Josef Land (arch.), Rus.
84/C4 Frascati, It.
83/C3 Frascineto, It.
134/D4 Fraser (isl.), Austl.
132/C3 Fraser (peak), Austl.
182/D3 Fraser (riv.), BC,Can
205/G6 Fraser, Mi,US
156/C3 Fraserburg, SAfr.
54/D1 Fraserburgh, Sc,UK
135/C3 Fraser Nat'l Park, Austl.
136/D2 Frasertown, N.Z.
199/G2 Fraserville, On,Can
194/F2 Fraserwood, Mb,Can
80/C4 Frasne, Fr.
68/D2 Frasnes-Lez-Gosselies, Belg.
87/E2 Frassine (riv.), It.
87/D2 Frassino, It.
85/E5 Frasso Telesino, It.
81/F3 Frastanz, Aus.
87/F5 Frati, Monte dei (peak), It.
81/E2 Frauenfeld, Swi.
73/A4 Frauenkirchen, Aus.
71/F6 Fraunberg, Ger.
188/D5 Fraustro, Mex.
174/F2 Fray Bentos, Uru.
172/B3 Fray Jorge Nat'l Park, Chile
175/U12 Fray Marcos, Uru.
195/G4 Frazee, Mn,US
130/A4 Frazier Downs Abor. Land, Austl.
186/C3 Frazier Park, Ca,US
69/F2 Frechen, Ger.
128/A5 Frecinet (estuary), Austl.
70/B4 Freckenfeld, Ger.
156/E3 Fred (peak), SAfr.
189/G2 Fred, Tx,US
63/T9 Fredensborg, Den.
193/H1 Frederic, Wi,US
64/E1 Frederica, Den.
206/C5 Frederica, De,US
62/C4 Fredericia, Den.
129/J4 Frederick (reef), Austl.
199/H5 Frederick, Md,US
206/A5 Frederick (co.), Md,US
190/E3 Frederick, Ok,US
192/E1 Frederick, SD,US
193/H2 Fredericksburg, Ia,US
208/F6 Fredericksburg, Oh,US
206/B3 Fredericksburg, Pa,US
189/E2 Fredericksburg, Tx,US
201/J1 Fredericksburg, Va,US
201/J1 Fredericksburg & Spotsylvania Nat'l Mil. Park, Va,US
135/E1 Frederickton, Austl.
191/J2 Fredericktown, Mo,US
208/E7 Fredericktown, Oh,US
173/F3 Frederico Westphalen, Braz.
196/D3 Fredericton (cap.), NB,Can
196/D3 Fredericton Junction, NB,Can
62/C3 Frederiks, Den.
63/T9 Frederiksberg, Den.
63/T9 Frederiksborg (co.), Den.
62/E4 Frederiksborg Castle, Den.
62/D3 Frederikshavn, Den.
63/T9 Frederikssund, Den.
162/E3 Frederiksted, USVI
166/B2 Frederik Willem IV (falls), Sur.
72/D3 Fredersdorf bei Berlin, Ger.
167/K6 Fredonia, Col.
187/F2 Fredonia, Az,US
191/G2 Fredonia, Ks,US
194/E4 Fredonia, ND,US
199/G3 Fredonia, NY,US
208/G5 Fredonia, Pa,US
198/C3 Fredonia, Wi,US
200/B3 Fredonia (Biscoe), Ar,US
62/F1 Fredriksberg, Swe.
62/D2 Fredrikstad, Nor.
191/J1 Freeburg, Mo,US
206/B2 Freeburg, Pa,US
186/B2 Freedom, Ca,US
190/E2 Freedom, Ok,US
208/G6 Freedom, Pa,US
185/H2 Freedom, Wy,US
207/D3 Freehold, NJ,US
186/C1 Freel (peak), Ca,US
206/B4 Freeland, Md,US
206/C1 Freeland, Pa,US
205/B1 Freeland, Wa,US
133/G2 Freeling (peak), Austl.
133/H4 Freeling Heights (peak), Austl.
197/Q9 Freelton, On,Can
192/F2 Freeman, SD,US
206/C2 Freemansburg, Pa,US
162/B1 Freeport, Bahm.
203/E2 Freeport, Fl,US
193/K2 Freeport, Il,US
196/C4 Freeport, Me,US
207/E2 Freeport, NY,US
208/H6 Freeport, Pa,US
189/G3 Freeport, Tx,US
189/E4 Freer, Tx,US
144/B4 Freetown (cap.), SLeo.
198/C5 Freetown, In,US
144/B4 Freetown (Lungi) (int'l arpt.), SLeo.
184/D1 Freewater-Milton, Or,US
76/B3 Fregenal de la Sierra, Sp.
84/C4 Fregene, It.
78/C3 Fréhel (cape), Fr.
64/G3 Freib (riv.), Ger.
72/D6 Freiberg, Ger.
64/G3 Freiberger Mulde (riv.), Ger.
80/D2 Freiburg, Ger.
81/E3 Freienbach, Swi.
72/D4 Freienhufen, Ger.
79/D5 Freigné, Fr.
71/E3 Freihung, Ger.
171/E3 Frei Inocêncio, Braz.
71/F7 Freilassing, Ger.
70/B4 Freinsheim, Ger.
174/B3 Freire, Chile
172/B4 Freirina, Chile
69/G4 Freisen, Ger.
71/E6 Freising, Ger.
71/H6 Freistadt, Aus.
72/D6 Freital, Ger.
76/B2 Freixo de Espada à Cinta, Port.
74/E5 Frejorgues (Montpellier) (int'l arpt.), Fr.
82/C6 Fréjus, Fr.
82/C6 Fréjus (gulf), Fr.
62/A1 Frekhaug, Nor.
132/K7 Fremantle, Austl.
70/D5 Fremdingen, Ger.
58/B4 Fremington, Eng,UK
186/B2 Fremont, Ca,US
193/H3 Fremont, Ia,US
198/D4 Fremont, In,US
198/D3 Fremont, Mi,US
201/J3 Fremont, NC,US
193/F3 Fremont, Ne,US
198/E4 Fremont, Oh,US
185/H4 Fremont, Ut,US
185/G3 Fremont (isl.), Ut,US
185/H4 Fremont (riv.), Ut,US
187/G1 Fremont (riv.), Ut,US
185/J2 Fremont (lake), Wy,US
185/J2 Fremont (peak), Wy,US
198/F1 French (riv.), On,Can
206/C3 French (cr.), Pa,US
201/F3 French Broad (riv.), NC, Tn,US
200/F2 Frenchburg, Ky,US
200/C4 French Camp, Ms,US
206/C3 French Creek St. Park, Pa,US
139/J2 French Frigate (shoals), Hi,US
184/D2 Frenchglen, Or,US
166/C2 French Guiana (dpcy.), Fr.
200/D1 French Lick, In,US
183/K3 Frenchman (riv.), Sk,Can, Mt,US
192/C3 Frenchman (cr.), Co, Ne,US
197/S8 Frenchman's (bay), On,Can
135/C4 Frenchmans Cap (peak), Austl.
60/B2 Frenchpark, Ire.
139/M6 French Polynesia (terr.), Fr.
198/F1 French River, On,Can
195/J4 French River, Mn,US
183/G4 Frenchtown, Mt,US
206/C2 Frenchtown, NJ,US
206/C5 Frenchville, Me,US
141/R16 Frenda, Alg.
82/C2 Frêne, Pic du (peak), Fr.
53/S9 Frépillon, Fr.
67/E4 Freren, Ger.
69/F5 Frescaty (Metz) (arpt.), Fr.
166/D4 Fresco (riv.), Braz.
144/D5 Fresco, IvC.
60/C4 Freshford, Ire.
197/L2 Freshwater, Nf,Can
59/E5 Freshwater, Eng,UK
174/B4 Fresia, Chile
79/F4 Fresnay-sur-Sarthe, Fr.
53/S10 Fresnes, Fr.
69/E5 Fresnes-en-Woëvre, Fr.
158/E4 Fresnillo, Mex.
167/K6 Fresno, Col.
186/C2 Fresno, Ca,US
186/B2 Fresno (riv.), Ca,US
183/J3 Fresno (res.), Mt,US
189/M9 Fresno, Tx,US
68/C4 Fresnoy-le-Grand, Fr.
68/A3 Fressenneville, Fr.
80/C2 Fresse-sur-Moselle, Fr.
63/R6 Frestaby, Swe.
85/E3 Fretani (mts.), It.
68/C2 Fretin, Fr.
54/C3 Freuchie, Loch (lake), Sc,UK
69/G2 Freudenberg, Ger.
70/C3 Freudenberg, Ger.
70/B6 Freudenstadt, Ger.
68/B3 Frévent, Fr.
131/D4 Frewena, Austl.
199/G3 Frewsburg, NY,US
72/B5 Freyburg, Ger.
132/B3 Freycinet (har.), Austl.
135/D4 Freycinet Nat'l Park, Austl.
69/F5 Freyming-Merlebach, Fr.
172/D4 Freyre, Arg.
71/E4 Freystadt, Ger.
119/G5 Freyung, Ger.
144/B4 Fria, Gui.
154/B3 Fria (cape), Namb.
186/C2 Friant, Ca,US
186/C2 Friant (dam), Ca,US
186/C3 Friant-Kern (can.), Ca,US
200/B3 Friars Point, Ms,US
172/C4 Frías, Arg.
168/B2 Frías, Peru
80/D4 Fribourg, Swi.
80/D4 Fribourg (canton), Swi.
80/E2 Frick, Swi.
70/D3 Frickenhausen am Main, Ger.
182/C3 Friday Harbor, Wa,US
70/B6 Fridingen an der Donau, Ger.
195/P6 Fridley, Mn,US
71/F7 Fridolfing, Ger.
72/D5 Frieberger Mulde (riv.), Ger.
70/B2 Friedberg, Ger.
70/D6 Friedberg, Ger.
67/E2 Friedeburg, Ger.
199/G4 Friedens, Pa,US
72/C4 Friedersdorf, Ger.
67/G6 Friedland, Ger.
70/B2 Friedrichsdorf, Ger.
81/F2 Friedrichshafen, Ger.
81/F2 Friedrichshafen (arpt.), Ger.
64/E1 Friedrichstadt, Ger.
69/G5 Friedrichsthal, Ger.
72/D2 Friedrichsthal, Ger.
67/F7 Frielendorf, Ger.
190/D1 Friend, Ks,US
193/F3 Friend, Ne,US
191/H3 Friendship, Ar,US
200/C3 Friendship, Tn,US
193/K2 Friendship, Wi,US
189/G3 Friendswood, Tx,US
189/H1 Frierson, La,US
72/C2 Friesack, Ger.
69/G2 Friesenhagen, Ger.
70/A6 Friesenheim, Ger.
66/C2 Friesland (prov.), Neth
67/E2 Friesoythe, Ger.
85/E6 Frignano, It.
80/D6 Frignicourt, Fr.
144/B4 Friguiagbé, Gui.
59/F4 Frimley, Eng,UK
59/H3 Frinton, Eng,UK
50/G7 Frio (cape), Braz.
189/E3 Frio (riv.), Tx,US
54/D3 Friockheim, Sc,UK
190/C3 Frio Draw (stream), NM, Tx,US

76/B1 Friol, Sp.
190/C3 Friona, Tx,US
69/F4 Frisange, Lux.
192/A4 Frisco, Co,US
208/G6 Frisco, Pa,US
188/L6 Frisco, Tx,US
202/E2 Frisco City, Al,US
208/A1 Frissel (mt.), Ct,US
62/E3 Fristad, Swe.
190/D3 Fritch, Tx,US
62/E3 Fritsla, Swe.
67/G6 Fritzlar, Ger.
75/K3 Friuli-Venezia Giulia (reg.), It.
59/H6 Friville Escarbotin, Fr.
68/A3 Friville-Escarbotin, Fr.
56/E2 Frizington, Eng,UK
179/K2 Frobisher (bay), NW,Can
57/F5 Frodsham, Eng,UK
200/E2 Frogue, Ky,US
61/D3 Frohavet (bay), Nor.
75/L3 Frohnleiten, Aus.
183/M3 Froid, Mt,US
68/D3 Froid-chapelle, Belg.
80/C2 Froideconche, Fr.
79/H1 Froissy, Fr.
62/C2 Froland, Nor.
99/M3 Frolovo, Rus.
185/J1 Fromberg, Mt,US
133/J4 Frome (lake), Austl.
133/H4 Frome (riv.), Austl.
58/D4 Frome, Eng,UK
58/D2 Frome (riv.), Eng,UK
58/D5 Frome (riv.), Eng,UK
80/B1 Froncles, Fr.
192/B3 Front (range), Co,US
152/D4 Fronteira, Ang.
76/B3 Fronteira, Port.
82/C1 Frontenex, Fr.
71/F5 Frontenhausen, Ger.
159/E3 Frontera, Mex.
159/G5 Frontera, Mex.
160/C3 Frontera Comalapa, Mex.
158/C2 Fronteras, Mex.
183/K3 Frontier, Sk,Can
194/F4 Frontier, ND,US
188/E3 Frontier Times Museum, Tx,US
74/E5 Frontignan, Fr.
74/D5 Fronton, Fr.
201/H1 Front Royal, Va,US
81/G5 Frosinone, It.
85/D5 Frosinone (prov.), It.
61/E3 Frösö, Swe.
85/E4 Frosolone, It.
137/J Frost (glac.), Ant.
189/F1 Frost, Tx,US
199/G5 Frostburg, Md,US
202/M8 Frostproof, Fl,US
203/H4 Frostproof, Fl,US
80/C2 Frotey-lès-Vesoul, Fr.
69/F6 Frouard, Fr.
62/F2 Frövi, Swe.
60/B6 Frower (pt.), Ire.
61/D3 Frøya (isl.), Nor.
179/H2 Frozen (str.), NW,Can
68/B2 Fruges, Fr.
89/G1 Fruili (reg.), It.
87/F1 Fruili-Venezia Giulia (reg.), It.
202/D2 Fruitdale, Al,US
197/R9 Fruitland, On,Can
184/E1 Fruitland, Id,US
201/K1 Fruitland, Md,US
182/F3 Fruitvale, BC,Can
182/D4 Fruitvale, Wa,US
99/H5 Frunzenskoye, Ukr.
98/E4 Frunzovka, Ukr.
89/H1 Fruška Gora (mts.), Cro., Yugo.
92/D3 Fruška Gora Nat'l Park, Yugo.
170/C4 Frutal, Braz.
80/D4 Frutigen, Swi.
174/B4 Frutillar, Chile
65/K4 Frýdek-Místek, Czh.
195/B3 Fryeburg, Me,US
115/C5 Fu (riv.), China
117/H3 Fu'an, China
152/C4 Fubo, Ang.
87/D5 Fucecchio, It.
142/B5 Fuch, WSah.
115/D3 Fucheng, China
64/E3 Fuchskaute (peak), Ger.
69/H2 Fuchskauten (peak), Ger.
110/C3 Fuchū, Japan
117/H2 Fuchun, China
115/D5 Fuchun (riv.), China
117/H4 Fude, China
127/H3 Fudi (mtn.), Indo.
117/J3 Fuding, China
76/C4 Fuengirola, Sp.
76/D2 Fuenlabrada, Sp.
76/C2 Fuensalida, Sp.
77/N8 Fuente, Sp.
77/E4 Fuente-Álamo, Sp.
76/B3 Fuente de Cantos, Sp.
76/B3 Fuente del Maestre, Sp.
76/C2 Fuentelapeña, Sp.
76/C3 Fuente Obejuna, Sp.
76/E1 Fuenterrabía, Sp.
76/C2 Fuentesaúco, Sp.
76/C4 Fuentes de Andalucía, Sp.
76/B2 Fuentes de Oñoro, Sp.
158/C3 Fuerte (riv.), Mex.
77/F2 Fuerte Olimpo, Par.
142/B3 Fuerteventura (isl.), Canl.,Sp.
117/H3 Fufang, China
125/C1 Fuga (isl.), Phil.
62/D4 Fuglebjerg, Den.
119/G2 Fugong, China
115/C4 Fugou, China
108/B2 Fuhai, China
67/H1 Fuhlsbüttel (Hamburg) (int'l arpt.), Ger.
72/B4 Fuhne (riv.), Ger.
67/H4 Fuhse (riv.), Ger.
111/F3 Fuji, Japan
111/F3 Fuji (riv.), Japan
117/H3 Fujian (prov.), China
111/F3 Fujieda, Japan
111/F3 Fuji-Hakone-Izu Nat'l Park, Japan
111/L10 Fujiidera, Japan
111/H7 Fujimi, Japan
111/H7 Fujino, Japan
111/F3 Fujinomiya, Japan
111/F2 Fujioka, Japan
111/F3 Fujisawa, Japan
111/J7 Fujishiro, Japan
111/M9 Fujiwara, Japan
111/F3 Fujiyama (mtn.), Japan
111/F3 Fujiyoshida, Japan
112/C2 Fukagawa, Japan
114/E3 Fukang, China
110/D3 Fukuchiyama, Japan
110/A4 Fukue, Japan
110/A4 Fukue (arpt.), Japan
110/A4 Fukue (isl.), Japan
110/E2 Fukui, Japan
110/E3 Fukui (pref.), Japan
110/B4 Fukuoka, Japan
110/B4 Fukuoka (int'l arpt.), Japan
110/B4 Fukuoka (pref.), Japan
111/E3 Fukuroi, Japan
137/C Fukushima (peak), Ant.
112/B3 Fukushima, Japan
111/F2 Fukushima (pref.), Japan
110/C3 Fukuyama, Japan
144/B4 Fulacunda, GBis.
107/J2 Fūlādī (mtn.), Afg.
59/G2 Fulbourn, Eng,UK
191/G4 Fulbright, Tx,US
70/C1 Fulda, Ger.
70/C1 Fulda (riv.), Ger.
193/G2 Fulda, Mn,US
57/G4 Fulford, Eng,UK
117/E2 Fuling, China
162/F5 Fullarton, Trin.
204/C3 Fullerton, Ca,US
189/H2 Fullerton, La,US
192/F3 Fullerton, Ne,US
206/C2 Fullerton (Whitehall), Pa,US
80/D5 Fully, Swi.
81/H3 Fulpmes, Aus.
197/R9 Fulton, On,Can
200/D5 Fulton, Al,US
191/H4 Fulton, Ar,US
201/M7 Fulton (co.), Ga,US
191/G1 Fulton, Ks,US
200/C2 Fulton, Ky,US
191/J1 Fulton, Mo,US
200/C3 Fulton, Ms,US
199/H3 Fulton, NY,US
189/F3 Fulton, Tx,US
200/D4 Fultondale, Al,US
62/E1 Fulufjället (peak), Swe.
117/F3 Fuluo, China
57/F4 Fulwood, Eng,UK
87/F5 Fumaiolo, Monte (peak), It.
69/D4 Fumay, Fr.
74/D4 Fumel, Fr.
116/D3 Fumin, China
111/H7 Funabashi, Japan
138/G5 Funafuti (isl.), Tuv.
115/C4 Funan, China
142/A2 Funchal, Madr.
142/A2 Funchal (int'l arpt.), Madr., Port.
77/V15 Funchal, Madr.,Port.
164/C2 Fundación, Col.
76/B2 Fundão, Port.
196/D3 Fundy (bay), NB, NS,Can
196/E3 Fundy Nat'l Park, NB,Can
155/G4 Funhalouro, Moz.
115/D4 Funing, China
116/E4 Funing, China
60/B5 Funshion (riv.), Ire.
145/E4 Funsi, Gha.
203/G2 Funston, Ga,US
145/G4 Funtua, Nga.
167/L7 Funza, Col.
81/G4 Fuorn (Ofenpass) (pass), Swi.
115/C3 Fuping, China
115/L8 Fuqiao, China
119/J2 Fuquan, China
113/C2 Fur (riv.), China
80/B6 Furan (riv.), Fr.
155/G2 Furancungo, Moz.
112/C2 Furano, Japan
83/B7 Furci Siculo, It.
82/B2 Fure (riv.), Fr.
63/T9 Furesø (lake), Den.
70/A3 Fürfeld, Ger.
94/J4 Furmanov, Rus.
97/J2 Furmanovo, Kaz.
55/J8 Furnace, UK
54/A4 Furnace, Sc,UK
83/B6 Furnari, It.
170/D4 Furnas (res.), Braz.
135/C4 Furneaux Group (isls.), Austl.
67/G3 Fürstenau, Ger.
72/D1 Fürstenberg, Ger.
92/C2 Fürstenfeld, Aus.
70/E6 Fürstenfeldbruck, Ger.
72/E3 Fürstenwalde, Ger.
70/D4 Fürth, Ger.
71/F5 Furth, Ger.
75/J2 Fürth, Ger.
71/F4 Furth im Wald, Ger.
70/B6 Furtwangen im Schwarzwald, Ger.
62/F1 Furudal, Swe.
112/B4 Furukawa, Japan
179/H2 Fury and Hecla (str.), NW,Can
164/C3 Fusagasugá, Col.
115/B4 Fushan, China
115/E3 Fushan, China
117/F3 Fushi, China
117/H3 Fushi, China
117/H3 Fushu, China
113/B2 Fushun, China
116/E2 Fushun, China
113/B2 Fushuncheng, China
87/E4 Fusignano, It.
81/E5 Fusio, Swi.
111/M9 Fuso, Japan
113/D1 Fusong, China
111/H7 Fussa, Japan
81/G2 Füssen, Ger.
123/D1 Fusui, China
174/C4 Futaleufú, Chile
111/M10 Futami, Japan
92/D3 Futog, Yugo.
174/B4 Futrono, Chile
111/F3 Futtsu, Japan
138/H6 Futuna (isl.), Wall.
103/B4 Fuwah, Egypt
115/B3 Fu Xian, China
116/D3 Fuxian (lake), China
113/A1 Fuxin, China
117/E2 Fuxing, China
113/A1 Fuxin Monggolzu Zizhixian, China
108/H5 Fuyang, China
115/C4 Fuyang, China
117/H4 Fuyang, China
117/F3 Fuyi (riv.), China
109/J2 Fuyu, China
116/E3 Fuyuan, China
108/B2 Fuyun, China
65/L5 Füzesabony, Hun.
117/H3 Fuzhou, China
113/A3 Fuzhoucheng, China
153/E4 Fwamba, Zaire
200/E3 Fyffe, Al,US
53/P6 Fyfield, Eng,UK
62/D4 Fyn (co.), Den.
61/D5 Fyn (isl.), Den.
54/A4 Fyne, Loch (inlet), Sc,UK
62/C2 Fyresdal, Nor.
63/R6 Fysingen (lake), Swe.
54/D2 Fyvie, Sc,UK

## G

145/E4 Ga, Gha.
150/C4 Gaalkacyo (Galcaio), Som.
66/D5 Gaanderen, Neth.
66/C2 Gaast, Neth.
197/G3 Gabarus, NS,Can
197/G3 Gabarus (cape), NS,Can
74/C5 Gabas (riv.), Fr.
184/E4 Gabbs, Nv,US
73/B4 Gabčíkovo, Slvk.
152/C5 Gabela, Ang.
143/H2 Gabes (gulf), Tun.
152/D4 Gabia, Zaire
87/F5 Gabicce Mare, It.
136/D2 Gable End (pt.), N.Z.
70/D6 Gablingen, Ger.
73/A3 Gablitz, Aus.
152/B3 Gabon
152/B2 Gabon (estuary), Gabon
154/E5 Gaborone (cap.), Bots.
154/E5 Gaborone (Sir Seretse Khama) (int'l arpt.), Bots.
149/E3 Gabras, Sudan
60/A6 Gabriel (mtn.), Ire.
93/G4 Gabrovo, Bul.
86/A1 Gaby, It.
79/F3 Gacé, Fr.
105/G4 Gachsārān, Iran
194/E4 Gackle, ND,US
92/D4 Gacko, Bosn.
118/C4 Gadag-Betgeri, India
120/B4 Gādarwāra, India
81/E4 Gadmen, Swi.
97/H5 Gadrut, Azer.
200/D3 Gadsden, Al,US
186/E4 Gadsden, Az,US
63/T9 Gadstrup, Den.
99/H2 Gadyach, Ukr.
155/F3 Gadzema, Zim.
148/C4 Gadzi, CAfr.
93/G3 Găeşti, Rom.
85/D5 Gaeta, It.
85/D5 Gaeta (gulf), It.
121/H3 Gafargaon, Bang.
201/G3 Gaffney, SC,US
148/B3 Gagal, Chad
145/H3 Gagarawa, Nga.
94/G5 Gagarin, Rus.
187/H4 Gage, NM,US
190/E2 Gage, Ok,US
196/D3 Gagetown, NB,Can
198/E3 Gagetown, Mi,US
70/B5 Gaggenau, Ger.
86/C2 Gaggiano, It.
87/D4 Gaggio Montano, It.
86/B1 Gaglianico, It.
144/D5 Gagnoa, IvC.
179/K3 Gagnon, Qu,Can
53/T10 Gagny, Fr.
96/G4 Gagra, Geo.
122/D2 Gagret, India
198/E4 Gahanna, Oh,US
120/D3 Gahmar, India
144/C5 Gahnpa, Libr.
121/G3 Gaibandha, Bang.
81/G3 Gaichtpass (pass), Aus.
108/D4 Gaidain'goinba, China
92/A2 Gail (riv.), Aus.
188/D1 Gail, Tx,US
70/C5 Gaildorf, Ger.
74/D5 Gaillac, Fr.
208/B3 Gaillard (lake), Ct,US
68/A4 Gaillefontaine, Fr.
68/A5 Gaillon, Fr.
75/K3 Gailtaler Alps (mts.), Aus.
174/D4 Gaiman, Arg.
71/E5 Gaimersheim, Ger.
200/E2 Gainesboro, Tn,US
200/C4 Gainesville, Al,US
203/G3 Gainesville, Fl,US
200/F3 Gainesville, Ga,US
191/H2 Gainesville, Mo,US
191/F4 Gainesville, Tx,US
57/G2 Gainford, Eng,UK
79/F1 Gainneville, Fr.
194/D3 Gainsborough, Sk,Can
57/H5 Gainsborough, Eng,UK
133/G4 Gairdner (lake), Austl.
155/G3 Gairezi (riv.), Zim.
54/C2 Gairn (riv.), Sc,UK
81/F3 Gais, Swi.
206/A5 Gaithersburg, Md,US
113/B2 Gai Xian, China
63/L3 Gaizina (peak), Lat.
94/E4 Gaizina Kalns (hill), Lat.
73/A3 Gajary, Slvk.
122/B3 Gājol, India
156/C2 Gakarosa (peak), SAfr.
145/H5 Gakem, Nga.
177/J3 Gakona, Ak,US
121/G1 Gala, China
172/C3 Galan (peak), Arg.
151/B2 Galana (riv.), Kenya
105/H2 Galand, Iran
152/B4 Galanga, Ang.
152/C2 Galangue, Ang.
73/B3 Galanta, Slvk.
76/D2 Galapagar, Sp.
168/J6 Galápagos (isls.), Ecu.
168/J7 Galápagos (prov.), Ecu.
168/J7 Galápagos Nat'l Park, Ecu.
122/C1 Galār, India
54/D5 Galashiels, Sc,UK
93/J3 Galați, Rom.
93/H3 Galați (co.), Rom.
93/D5 Galati Mamertino, It.
91/F2 Galatina, It.
91/G2 Galatiní, Gre.
91/H2 Galátista, Gre.
91/F2 Galatone, It.
83/C6 Galatro, It.
82/A2 Galaure (riv.), Fr.
201/G2 Galax, Va,US
91/H3 Galaxídhiou, Gre.
60/B5 Galbally, Ire.
86/C1 Galbiate, It.
141/G4 Galcaio, Som.
150/C4 Galcaio (Gaalkacyo), Som.
142/B3 Gáldar, Canl.
158/D2 Galeana, Mex.
158/E3 Galeana, Mex.
127/G3 Galela, Indo.
177/G3 Galena, Ak,US
185/F2 Galena (peak), Id,US
193/J2 Galena, Il,US
191/G2 Galena, Ks,US
206/C5 Galena, Md,US
191/H2 Galena, Mo,US
182/F2 Galena Bay, BC,Can
189/M9 Galena Park, Tx,US
165/F2 Galeota (pt.), Trin.
174/B3 Galera (pt.), Chile
164/A4 Galera (pt.), Ecu.
162/F5 Galera (pt.), Trin.
193/J3 Galesburg, Il,US
199/H4 Galeton, Pa,US
60/A5 Galey (riv.), Ire.
56/B2 Galgorm, NI,UK
97/G4 Gali, Geo.
82/C2 Galibier, Col du (pass), Fr.
94/J4 Galich, Rus.
65/L3 Galicia (reg.), Pol., Ukr.
76/A1 Galicia (aut. comm.), Sp.
88/B2 Galicia (reg.), Sp.
92/E5 Galičica Nat'l Park, Macd.
122/B1 Gali Jāgīr, Pak.
105/H2 Galīkash, Iran
103/D3 Galilee, Sea of (Tiberias) (lake), Isr.
75/J5 Galileo Galilei (G. Galilei) (int'l arpt.), It.
86/D5 Galileo Galilei (G. Galilei) (int'l arpt.), It.
148/B4 Galim, Camr.
81/F3 Galinakopf (peak), Aus.
152/C5 Galinda, Ang.
198/E4 Galion, Oh,US
187/G4 Galiuro (mts.), Az,US
131/D3 Galiwinku, Austl.
55/H7 Gallan Head (pt.), Sc,UK
86/B1 Gallarate, It.
79/G3 Gallardon, Fr.
193/H4 Gallatin, Mo,US
185/H1 Gallatin (riv.), Mt, Wy,US
200/D2 Gallatin, Tn,US
183/J5 Gallatin Gateway, Mt,US
200/C3 Gallaway, Tn,US
118/D6 Galle, SrL.
175/K7 Gallegos (riv.), Arg.
172/B3 Galleguillos, Chile
60/B6 Galley Head (pt.), Ire.
202/C3 Galliano, La,US
86/B2 Galliate, It.
88/D4 Gallicano, It.
190/A2 Gallina, NM,US
164/D1 Gallinas (pt.), Col.
190/B3 Gallinas, NM,US
187/J3 Gallinas (mts.), NM,US
190/B3 Gallinas (riv.), NM,US
202/E1 Gallion, Al,US
91/E2 Gallipoli, It.
93/H5 Gallipoli (pen.), Turk.
93/H5 Gallipoli (Gelibolu), Turk.
201/F1 Gallipolis, Oh,US
61/G2 Gällivare, Swe.
71/H6 Gallneukirchen, Aus.
90/C3 Gallo (cape), It.
81/G4 Gallo (lake), It.
195/K5 Galloway, Wi,US
56/D2 Galloway, Mull of (pt.), Sc,UK
71/G6 Gallspach, Aus.
187/H3 Gallup, NM,US
76/E2 Gallur, Sp.
53/R10 Gally (riv.), Fr.
103/F8 Gal'on, Isr.
134/H8 Galston, Austl.
54/B5 Galston, Sc,UK
108/D2 Galt, Mong.
205/M10 Galt, Ca,US
62/C3 Galten, Den.
60/B5 Galty (mts.), Ire.
60/B5 Galtymore (mtn.), Ire.
108/E2 Galuut, Mong.
193/J3 Galva, Il,US
191/F1 Galva, Ks,US
174/B3 Galvarino, Chile
189/G3 Galveston, Tx,US
189/G3 Galveston (bay), Tx,US
189/M9 Galveston (co.), Tx,US
189/G3 Galveston (isl.), Tx,US
174/E2 Gálvez, Arg.
76/C3 Gálvez, Sp.
60/A3 Galway, Ire.
60/A3 Galway (bay), Ire.
60/B3 Galway (co.), Ire.
60/B3 Galway (Carnmore) (arpt.), Ire.
87/E2 Galzignano, It.
123/D1 Gam (riv.), Viet.
68/A4 Gamaches, Fr.
156/C2 Gamagara (dry riv.), SAfr.
111/E3 Gamagōri, Japan
164/C2 Gamarra, Col.
125/D2 Gamay, Phil.
121/G1 Gamba, China
152/B3 Gamba, Gabon
153/F4 Gamba, Zaire
145/E4 Gambaga, Gha.
145/E4 Gambaga Scarp (escarp.), Gha., Togo
124/C2 Gambang, Malay.
86/D2 Gambara, It.
118/A2 Gambat, Pak.
85/E5 Gambatesa, It.
149/G3 Gambēla, Eth.
177/D3 Gambell, Ak,US
149/G3 Gambella Nat'l Park, Eth.
87/E2 Gambellara, It.
206/B5 Gamber, Md,US
87/F4 Gambettola, It.
144/B3 Gambia
140/A3 Gambia (riv.), Afr.
144/A3 Gambia (riv.), Gam.
144/B3 Gambie (riv.), Gui., Sen.
130/C2 Gambier (cape), Austl.
139/M7 Gambier (isls.), FrPol.
208/E7 Gambier, Oh,US
164/C3 Gámbita, Col.
148/D4 Gambo, CAfr.
197/K1 Gambo, Nf,Can
86/B2 Gambolò, It.
152/C3 Gamboma, Congo
148/B4 Gamboula, CAfr.
167/H5 Gameleira, Braz.
187/H3 Gamerco, NM,US
201/G3 Gamewell, NC,US
65/H5 Gaming, Aus.
156/C4 Gamka (riv.), SAfr.
156/B3 Gamkab (dry riv.), Namb.
61/G3 Gamlakaleby (Kokkola), Fin.
62/G3 Gamleby, Swe.
59/F2 Gamlingay, Eng,UK
94/D2 Gammelstad, Swe.
70/C6 Gammertingen, Ger.
133/H4 Gammon Ranges Nat'l Park, Austl.
111/M9 Gamo, Japan
149/H4 Gamo Gofa (reg.), Eth.
71/G7 Gampern, Aus.
65/G5 Gamsfeld (peak), Aus.
116/C2 Gamtog, China
149/H4 Gamud (peak), Eth.
117/G2 Gan (riv.), China
74/C5 Gan, Fr.
187/H3 Ganado, Az,US
189/F3 Ganado, Tx,US
199/H2 Gananoque, On,Can
105/G4 Ganāveh, Iran
117/E3 Ganbashao, China
123/E2 Gancheng, China
154/B2 Ganda, Ang.
153/E4 Gandajika, Zaire
121/E2 Gandak (riv.), India
120/D1 Gandaki (zone), Nepal
125/D2 Gandara, Phil.
154/C1 Gandarinha, Ang.
79/F5 Gandelin (riv.), Fr.
197/K1 Gander, Nf,Can
197/K1 Gander (lake), Nf,Can
67/F2 Ganderkesee, Ger.
77/F2 Gandesa, Sp.
118/B3 Gāndhīdhām, India
118/B3 Gandhinagar, India
118/B3 Gāndhi Sāgar (res.), India
77/E3 Gandia, Sp.
86/C1 Gandino, It.
121/E1 Gandisê (mts.), China
153/G3 Gandjo, Zaire
171/F4 Gandoca-Manzanillo Nat'l Wild. Ref., CR
185/G4 Gandy, Ut,US
121/E1 Ganesh (mtn.), China
118/C2 Ganeshganj, India
114/F4 Gang, China
121/G3 Ganga (Ganges) (riv.), Asia
148/D5 Gangala-Na-Bodio, Zaire
174/C4 Gan Gan, Arg.
120/A2 Gangāpur, India
145/H3 Gangara, Niger
121/G3 Gangārāmpur, India
121/G5 Gānga Sāgar, India
116/B4 Gangaw, Burma
108/E4 Gangca, China
121/E2 Gangdisê (mts.), China
67/F5 Gangelt, Ger.
182/C3 Ganges, BC,Can
74/E5 Ganges, Fr.
121/G3 Ganges (Ganga) (riv.), Asia
118/E3 Ganges, Mouths of the (delta), Bang., India
90/D4 Gangi, It.
71/F6 Gangkofen, Ger.
152/C5 Gango (riv.), Ang.
120/A1 Gangoh, India
182/C2 Gang Ranch, BC,Can
121/G2 Gangtok, India
117/H3 Gangtou, China
103/G7 Gan Hashlosha Nat'l Park, Isr.
120/B2 Ganj Dundwara, India
113/A3 Ganjingzi, China
63/T9 Ganløse, Den.
119/H2 Ganluo, China
109/J2 Gannan, China
74/E3 Gannat, Fr.
185/J2 Gannett (peak), Wy,US
192/E1 Gann Valley, SD,US
115/B3 Ganquan, China
156/B4 Gansbaai, SAfr.
73/A3 Gänserndorf, Aus.
114/F4 Gansu (prov.), China
130/A4 Gantheaume (pt.), Austl.
80/D4 Gantrisch (peak), Swi.
96/C1 Gantsevichi, Bela.
203/E2 Gantt, Al,US
201/F3 Gantt, SC,US
125/B3 Gantung (mt.), Phil.
115/F3 Ganxitang, China
148/A3 Ganye, Nga.
156/D2 Ganyesa, SAfr.
115/D4 Ganyu, China
97/J3 Ganyushkino, Kaz.
117/G3 Ganzhou, China
64/G2 Ganzlin, Ger.
145/E3 Ganzourgou (prov.), Burk.
117/G3 Gao (mtn.), China
145/E2 Gao, Mali
145/E2 Gao (reg.), Mali
145/E3 Gao, Niger
153/G2 Gao, Zaire
117/G3 Gao'an, China
117/G3 Gaobei, China
115/C3 Gaocheng, China
115/D5 Gaochun, China
117/J2 Gaojian, China
108/E4 Gaolan, China
117/G4 Gaolan (isl.), China
116/C3 Gaoligong (mts.), China
113/A4 Gaoling, China
115/D3 Gaomi, China
117/F3 Gaomutang, China
115/L8 Gaoping, China
115/L8 Gaoqiao, China
115/D3 Gaoqing, China
117/F2 Gaoqitou, China
54/A3 Gaor Bheinn or Gulvain (mtn.), Sc,UK
108/D4 Gaotai, China
115/D3 Gaotang, China
117/H3 Gaotian, China
144/E4 Gaoua, Burk.
144/B4 Gaoual, Gui.
116/E2 Gao Xian, China
117/G3 Gaoxingxu, China
115/C3 Gaoyang, China
115/C3 Gaoyi, China
115/D4 Gaoyou, China
115/D4 Gaoyou (lake), China
117/F4 Gaozhou, China
82/C3 Gap, Fr.
206/B4 Gap, Pa,US
82/B6 Gapeau (riv.), Fr.
201/G2 Gap Mills, WV,US
135/B1 Gap, The, Austl.
60/C5 Gap, The (pass), Ire.
114/C5 Gar, China
108/D5 Gar (riv.), China
150/D4 Garacad, Som.
161/G4 Garachiné, Pan.
161/G4 Garachiné (pt.), Pan.
135/D1 Garah, Austl.
121/G4 Garai (riv.), Bang.
131/G1 Garaina, PNG
142/A3 Garajonay Nat'l Park, Canl.
144/D4 Garalo, Mali
60/B2 Gara, Lough (lake), Ire.
153/G1 Garamba Nat'l Park, Zaire
150/B3 Gara Muleta (peak), Eth.
79/G3 Garancières, Fr.
145/E4 Garango, Burk.
171/F1 Garanhuns, Braz.
131/E4 Garawa-Waanyi Abor. Land, Austl.
148/D3 Garba, CAfr.
150/B5 Garbahaarrey, Som.
151/B1 Garba Tula, Kenya
191/F2 Garber, Ok,US
184/B3 Garberville, Ca,US
64/E2 Garbsen, Ger.
170/C4 Garça, Braz.
170/B3 Garças (riv.), Braz.
53/S10 Garches, Fr.
71/F6 Garching an der Alz, Ger.
190/B2 Garcia, Co,US
76/C3 Garcia de Sota (res.), Sp.
82/A4 Gard (dept.), Fr.
74/F5 Gard (riv.), Fr.
87/D1 Garda, It.
86/D1 Garda (lake), It.
97/H4 Gardabani, Geo.
82/B6 Gardanne, Fr.
194/F3 Gardar, ND,US
141/V17 Garde, Cap de (cape), Alg.
72/B2 Gardelegen, Ger.
132/K7 Garden (isl.), Austl.
198/E1 Garden (riv.), On,Can
195/L5 Garden, Mi,US
198/D2 Garden (isl.), Mi,US
195/L5 Garden (pen.), Mi,US
204/B3 Gardena, Ca,US
201/G4 Garden City, Ga,US
184/E2 Garden City, Id,US
190/D2 Garden City, Ks,US
205/F7 Garden City, Mi,US
191/G1 Garden City, Mo,US
207/E2 Garden City, NY,US
194/F5 Garden City, SD,US
201/H4 Garden City Beach, SC,US
207/L9 Garden City Park, NY,US
200/D4 Gardendale, Al,US
204/C3 Garden Grove, Ca,US
193/H3 Garden Grove, Ia,US
121/G4 Garden Reach, India
207/D3 Garden State Arts Ctr., NJ,US
54/D1 Gardenstown, Sc,UK
194/F3 Gardenton, Mb,Can
184/F1 Garden Valley, Id,US
206/A1 Garden View, Pa,US
107/J2 Gardēz, Afg.
122/C2 Gardhīwāla, India
203/H2 Gardi, Ga,US
194/A2 Gardiner (dam), Sk,Can
196/C3 Gardiner, Me,US
185/H1 Gardiner, Mt,US
184/A2 Gardiner, Or,US
205/B1 Gardiner, Wa,US
207/F1 Gardiners (bay), NY,US
207/F1 Gardiners (isl.), NY,US
208/B2 Gardner (lake), Ct,US
203/H4 Gardner, Fl,US
191/G1 Gardner, Ks,US
199/L3 Gardner, Ma,US
196/D3 Gardner (lake), Me,US
196/C2 Gardner (mtn.), Me,US
182/D3 Gardner (mtn.), Wa,US
139/H5 Gardner (Nukumororo) (isl.), Kiri.
86/D1 Gardone val Trompia, It.
73/C5 Gárdony, Hun.
54/B4 Gare Loch (inlet), Sc,UK
54/B4 Garelochhead, Sc,UK
86/B4 Garessio, It.
143/G4 Garet el Djenoun (peak), Alg.
202/M8 Garfield (lake), Fl,US
201/F4 Garfield, Ga,US
190/E1 Garfield, Ks,US
183/L5 Garfield (peak), Mt,US
207/D2 Garfield, NJ,US
187/J4 Garfield, NM,US
189/F2 Garfield, Tx,US
182/F4 Garfield, Wa,US
208/F5 Garfield Heights, Oh,US
57/G4 Garforth, Eng,UK
91/G4 Gargaliánoi, Gre.
74/D4 Gargan (mtn.), Fr.
85/F4 Gargano (plat.), It.
79/G2 Gargenville, Fr.
53/T10 Garges-lès-Gonesse, Fr.
87/D1 Gargnano, It.
57/F4 Gargrave, Eng,UK
63/J4 Gargždai, Lith.
120/B4 Garhākotā, India
121/F4 Garhbeta, India
120/C4 Garhi, India
122/A1 Garh Mahārāja, Pak.
120/B1 Garhmuktesar, India
122/B2 Garhshankar, India
173/G4 Garibaldi, Braz.
182/C3 Garibaldi, BC,Can
184/B1 Garibaldi, Or,US
156/B3 Garies, SAfr.
85/D5 Garigliano (riv.), It.
83/C4 Gariglione (peak), It.
54/D2 Garioch (dist.), Sc,UK
151/B2 Garissa, Kenya
120/B1 Garjia, India
194/D2 Garland, Mb,Can
191/G2 Garland, Ks,US
196/C3 Garland, Me,US
201/H3 Garland, NC,US
189/F1 Garland, Tx,US
202/D1 Garlandville, Ms,US
86/B2 Garlasco, It.
63/K4 Garliava, Lith.
56/D2 Garlieston, Sc,UK
72/B1 Garlin, Ger.
105/J2 Garmeh, Iran
81/H3 Garmisch-Partenkirchen, Ger.
54/C1 Garmouth, Sc,UK
105/H3 Garmsār, Iran
183/K4 Garneill, Mt,US
193/H2 Garner, Ia,US
201/H3 Garner, NC,US
208/A1 Garnet (hill), Ma,US
155/F2 Garneton, Zam.
191/G1 Garnett, Ks,US
201/G4 Garnett, SC,US
197/K2 Garnish, Nf,Can
135/B2 Garnpung (lake), Austl.
63/S6 Garnsviken (lake), Swe.
74/D4 Garonne (riv.), Fr.
141/G4 Garoowe, Som.
173/G4 Garopaba, Braz.
145/E2 Garou (lake), Mali
148/B3 Garoua, Camr.
148/B3 Garoua (int'l arpt.), Camr.
148/B4 Garoua Boulaï, Camr.
62/F2 Garphyttan, Swe.
77/K7 Garraf (range), Sp.
56/D6 Garreg, Wal,UK
67/F3 Garrel, Ger.
193/F2 Garretson, SD,US
198/D4 Garrett, In,US
189/F1 Garrett, Tx,US
192/B2 Garrett, Wy,US
208/F5 Garrettsville, Oh,US
201/F1 Garrison, Ky,US
195/H4 Garrison, Mn,US
191/H2 Garrison, Mo,US
183/H4 Garrison, Mt,US
194/D4 Garrison, ND,US
194/D4 Garrison (dam), ND,US
189/G2 Garrison, Tx,US
185/F4 Garrison, Ut,US
56/C1 Garron (pt.), NI,UK
76/B3 Garrovillas, Sp.
179/H2 Garry (bay), NW,Can
178/F2 Garry (lake), NW,Can
54/A2 Garry (riv.), Sc,UK
54/B3 Garry (riv.), Sc,UK
54/B2 Garry, Loch (lake), Sc,UK
183/L5 Garryowen, Mt,US
71/F6 Gars am Inn, Ger.
75/L2 Gars am Kamp, Aus.
151/C2 Garsen, Kenya
57/F4 Garstang, Eng,UK
71/H6 Garsten, Aus.
67/H6 Garte (riv.), Ger.
74/D3 Gartempe (riv.), Fr.
58/C2 Garth, Wal,UK
54/B4 Gartmore, Sc,UK
70/B5 Gärtringen, Ger.
124/D4 Garut, Indo.
56/B2 Garvagh, NI,UK
120/D3 Garwa, India
65/L3 Garwolin, Pol.
207/H9 Garwood, NJ,US
189/F3 Garwood, Tx,US
205/R16 Gary, In,US
193/F1 Gary, SD,US
189/G1 Gary, Tx,US
201/G2 Gary, WV,US
114/D5 Garyarsa, China
116/C2 Garyi, China
202/C2 Garyville, La,US
62/E4 Garz, Ger.
72/C1 Garz, Ger.
188/E5 Garza González, Mex.
116/D2 Garzê, China
164/C4 Garzón, Col.
114/F4 Gas (lake), China
121/G2 Gasa, Bhu.
61/P6 Gæsafjöll (peak), Ice.
125/C2 Gasan, Phil.
105/H2 Gasan-Kuli, Trkm.
81/G4 Gaschurn, Aus.
198/D4 Gas City, In,US
200/B1 Gasconade (riv.), Mo,US
74/C5 Gascony (reg.), Fr.
132/C3 Gascoyne (peak), Austl.
132/C3 Gascoyne (riv.), Austl.
132/B3 Gascoyne Junction, Austl.
149/H2 Gash (dry riv.), Eth.
148/A4 Gashaka, Nga.
116/B2 Gasheng, India
145/H3 Gashua, Nga.
68/A5 Gasny, Fr.
126/C4 Gaspar (riv.), Indo.
182/C2 Gaspard (riv.), BC,Can
196/E1 Gaspé, Qu,Can
196/E1 Gaspé (bay), Qu,Can
196/E1 Gaspé (pen.), Qu,Can
196/E1 Gaspé, Cap de (cape), Qu,Can
83/C5 Gasperina, It.
203/G4 Gasparilla (isl.), Fl,US
71/G6 Gaspoltshofen, Aus.
197/T9 Gasport, NY,US
99/H5 Gaspra, Ukr.
112/B4 Gas-san (mtn.), Japan
86/A2 Gassino Torinese, It.
145/H4 Gassol, Nga.
191/H2 Gassville, Ar,US
201/J2 Gaston, NC,US
201/H2 Gaston (lake), NC, Va,US
184/B1 Gaston, Or,US
201/G4 Gaston, SC,US
201/G3 Gastonia, NC,US
188/L7 Gastonia, Tx,US
91/G4 Gastoúni, Gre.
174/C3 Gastre, Arg.
103/F8 Gat, Isr.
103/C2 Gata (cape), Cyp.
76/B2 Gata (range), Sp.
76/D4 Gata, Cabo de (cape), Sp.
77/F3 Gata de Gorgos, Sp.
63/P2 Gatchina, Rus.
190/D2 Gate, Ok,US
201/F2 Gate City, Va,US
56/D2 Gatehouse-of-Fleet, Sc,UK
184/B1 Gates, Or,US
178/F1 Gateshead (isl.), NW,Can
57/G2 Gateshead, Eng,UK
153/F4 Gates of Hell (Portes d'Enfer), Zaire
177/H2 Gates of the Arctic Nat'l Pk. & Prsv., Ak,US
201/J2 Gatesville, NC,US
189/F2 Gatesville, Tx,US
185/J4 Gateway, Co,US
184/C1 Gateway, Or,US
200/B1 Gateway Arch Nat'l Hist. Site (Jefferson Nat'l Expansion Mem.), Mo,US
207/E3 Gateway Nat'l Rec. Area, NJ, NY,US
207/E2 Gateway Nat'l Rec. Area, NY,US
201/H2 Gathright (dam), Va,US
155/F4 Gaths Mine, Zim.
172/B2 Gatico, Chile
74/C3 Gâtine (hills), Fr.
199/J2 Gatineau, Qu,Can
199/J1 Gatineau (riv.), Qu,Can
201/F3 Gatlinburg, Tn,US
72/D3 Gatow, Ger.
73/A3 Gattendorf, Aus.
78/D1 Gatteville-le-Phare, Fr.
86/B1 Gattianara, It.
134/D4 Gatton, Austl.
161/G4 Gatun (dam), Pan.
161/G4 Gatún (lake), Pan.
105/G3 Gatvand, Iran
53/N8 Gatwick (London) (int'l arpt.), Eng,UK
70/B3 Gau Algesheim, Ger.
69/H4 Gau-Bickelheim, Ger.
70/B3 Gau Bischofsheim, Ger.
68/C4 Gauchy, Fr.
76/C4 Gaucín, Sp.
105/J2 Gaudan, Trkm.
121/H2 Gauhāti, India
63/L3 Gauja (riv.), Lat.
63/M3 Gaujiena, Lat.
70/D3 Gaukönigshofen, Ger.
201/G1 Gauley (riv.), WV,US
57/G2 Gaunless (riv.), Eng,UK
70/B3 Gau Odernheim, Ger.
54/B3 Gaur (riv.), Sc,UK
121/G2 Gauripur, India
121/F2 Gauri Sankar (mtn.), Nepal
121/H4 Gaurnadi, Bang.
189/F2 Gause, Tx,US
62/C2 Gausta (peak), Nor.
71/E6 Gauting, Ger.
63/L3 Gauya Nat'l Park, Lat.
77/G2 Gavà, Sp.
77/K7 Gava, Sp.
86/D1 Gavardo, It.
107/H3 Gavāter, Iran
105/H5 Gāvbandī, Iran
91/J5 Gávdhos (isl.), Gre.
76/E1 Gave de Pau (riv.), Fr.
68/C2 Gavere, Belg.
105/F2 Gāvgān, Iran
86/B3 Gavi, It.
76/B3 Gavião, Port.
192/F2 Gavins Point (dam), SD,US
186/B3 Gaviota, Ca,US
86/B1 Gavirate, It.
62/G1 Gävle, Swe.
62/G1 Gävleborg (co.), Swe.
78/D3 Gavray, Fr.
116/C3 Gawai, Burma
73/A3 Gaweinstal, Aus.
133/H5 Gawler, Austl.
133/G5 Gawler (ranges), Austl.
145/E5 Gawso, Gha.
108/D3 Gaxun (lake), China
97/L2 Gay, Rus.
201/G1 Gay (mtn.), WV,US
109/K3 Gaya (riv.), China
121/E3 Gayā, India
145/F4 Gaya, Niger
148/C3 Gayam, Chad
153/G3 Gayaza, Ugan.
208/D3 Gay Head, Ma,US
199/L4 Gay Head (pt.), Ma,US
208/D3 Gay Head (pt.), Ma,US
121/H2 Gaylegphug, Bhu.
190/E1 Gaylord, Ks,US
198/D2 Gaylord, Mi,US
193/G1 Gaylord, Mn,US
208/A2 Gaylordsville, Ct,US
134/C4 Gayndah, Austl.
95/M3 Gayny, Rus.
98/E3 Gaysin, Ukr.
193/J2 Gays Mills, Wi,US
192/F2 Gayville, SD,US
98/E3 Gayvoron, Ukr.
105/G3 Gaz, Iran
104/C4 Gaza, Gaza
155/G4 Gaza (prov.), Moz.
100/G5 Gaz-Achak, Trkm.
103/D4 Gaza (Ghazzah), Gaza
145/G3 Gazaoua, Niger
103/C4 Gaza Strip
103/D4 Gaza Strip (occ. zone)
184/B3 Gazelle, Ca,US
103/E1 Gaziantep, Turk.
103/E1 Gaziantep (prov.), Turk.
93/H5 Gaziköy, Turk.
109/H1 Gazimur (riv.), Rus.
103/C1 Gazipaşa, Turk.
80/D1 Gazon de Faing (peak), Fr.
86/C1 Gazzaniga, It.
148/D4 Gbadolite, Zaire
144/B5 Gbangbatok, SLeo.
144/C5 Gbarnga, Libr.
73/B2 Gbely, Slvk.
145/H5 Gboko, Nga.
145/G5 Gbongan, Nga.
65/K1 Gdańsk, Pol.
65/K1 Gdańsk (prov.), Pol.
65/K1 Gdańsk (gulf), Pol., Rus.
94/C5 Gdańsk (gulf), Pol., Rus.
63/M2 Gdov, Rus.
65/K1 Gdynia, Pol.
115/D5 Ge (lake), China
54/A3 Geal Charn (mtn.), Sc,UK
54/C2 Geal Charn (mtn.), Sc,UK
196/D3 Geary, NB,Can
191/E3 Geary, Ok,US
60/C3 Geashill, Ire.
208/F5 Geauga (co.), Oh,US
70/D1 Gebaberg (peak), Ger.
191/G1 Gebaur-Richards A.F.B., Mo,US
149/G3 Geba Wenz (riv.), Eth.
127/G3 Gebe (isl.), Indo.
147/H4 Gebeit Mine, Sudan
72/A5 Gebesee, Ger.
69/G2 Gebhardshain, Ger.
150/B3 Gebilu, Eth.
103/B1 Gebiz, Turk.
67/H6 Gebra-Hainleite, Ger.
149/H3 Gebre Guracha, Eth.
93/J5 Gebze, Turk.
124/D4 Gede (peak), Indo.
151/C2 Gede, Kenya
103/F8 Gedera, Isr.
70/C2 Gedern, Ger.
151/C2 Gede Ruins Nat'l Mon., Kenya
105/E2 Gedikbulak, Turk.
104/D2 Gedikler, Turk.
69/D4 Gedinne, Belg.
104/B2 Gediz, Turk.
104/A2 Gediz (riv.), Turk.
150/C4 Gedlegubē, Eth.
149/H3 Gēdo, Eth.
62/D4 Gedser, Den.
62/D4 Gedser (cape), Den.
62/C3 Gedsted, Den.
69/E1 Geel, Belg.
135/C3 Geelong, Austl.
132/B4 Geelvink (chan.), Austl.
67/E3 Geeste, Ger.
67/F2 Geeste (riv.), Ger.
67/F1 Geestemünde, Ger.
67/H2 Geesthacht, Ger.
135/C4 Geeveston, Austl.
71/E2 Gefrees, Ger.
150/B2 Gegeya Shet' (dry riv.), Eth.
114/D5 Gê'gyai, China
67/F3 Gehrde, Ger.
67/G4 Gehrden, Ger.
72/B6 Gehren, Ger.
148/A2 Geidam, Nga.
58/C2 Geifas (mtn.), Wal,UK
149/G3 Geigar, Sudan
81/G3 Geige, Hohe (peak), Aus.
195/K2 Geikie (isl.), On,Can
178/F3 Geikie (riv.), Sk,Can
130/B4 Geikie Gorge Nat'l Park, Austl.
69/F2 Geilenkirchen, Ger.
62/C1 Geilo, Nor.
111/M10 Geinō, Japan
71/F5 Geiselhöring, Ger.
70/D3 Geiselwind, Ger.
71/E5 Geisenfeld, Ger.
71/F6 Geisenhausen, Ger.
70/A3 Geisenheim, Ger.
70/B6 Geislingen, Ger.
70/C5 Geislingen an der Steige, Ger.
199/G4 Geistown, Pa,US
153/H3 Geita, Tanz.
72/C5 Geithain, Ger.
116/D4 Gejiu, China
117/H3 Gekeng, China
149/F4 Gel (riv.), Sudan
90/D4 Gela, It.
90/D4 Gela (gulf), It.
150/C4 Geladī, Eth.
151/B2 Gelai (peak), Tanz.
124/C1 Gelang (cape), Malay.
82/D4 Gélas, Cime du (peak), Fr.
81/E5 Gelato (mtn.), It.
66/C4 Gelderland (prov.), Neth.
66/C5 Geldermalsen, Neth.
66/D5 Geldern, Ger.
70/D2 Geldersheim, Ger.
66/C6 Geldrop, Neth.
69/E2 Geleen, Neth.
150/B3 Gelemso, Eth.
72/C6 Gelenau, Ger.
104/B2 Gelendost, Turk.
99/K5 Gelendzhik, Rus.
93/H5 Gelibolu (Gallipoli), Turk.
96/C4 Gelibolu Yarımadası Nat'l Park, Turk.
149/H3 Gelīla, Eth.
105/E2 Gelincik (peak), Turk.
126/D4 Gelinggang, Indo.
58/C3 Gelligaer, Wal,UK
70/C2 Gelnhausen, Ger.
66/E5 Gelsenkirchen, Ger.
70/E6 Geltendorf, Ger.
80/D3 Gelterkinden, Swi.
64/E1 Gelting, Ger.
124/C2 Gemas, Malay.
69/D2 Gembloux, Belg.
131/G1 Gembogl, PNG
145/H5 Gembu, Nga.
152/D2 Gemena, Zaire
82/B6 Gémenos, Fr.
66/C5 Gemert, Neth.
93/J5 Gemlik, Turk.
93/J5 Gemlik (gulf), Turk.
75/K3 Gemona del Friuli, It.
156/C2 Gemsbok-Kalahari Nat'l Park, SAfr.
154/D5 Gemsbok Nat'l Park, Bots.
177/G3 Gemuk (mtn.), Ak,US
70/C2 Gemünden am Main, Ger.
109/J1 Gen (riv.), China
156/L11 Genadendal, SAfr.
150/B4 Genalē Wenz (riv.), Eth.
68/D2 Genappe, Belg.
90/A3 Genargentu (mts.), It.
80/A6 Genay, Fr.
84/C4 Genazzano, It.
104/E2 Genç, Turk.
66/D5 Gendringen, Neth.
66/C5 Gendt, Neth.
66/D3 Genemuiden, Neth.
186/D4 General Abelardo L. Rodriguez (int'l arpt.), Mex.
174/D3 General Acha, Arg.
168/D2 General Alfredo Vasquez Cobo (int'l arpt.), Col.
174/D2 General Alvear, Arg.
174/E3 General Alvear, Arg.
174/E2 General Arenales, Arg.
173/E3 General Artigas, Par.
174/F2 General Belgrano, Arg.
188/E5 General Bravo, Mex.
174/E2 General Cabrera, Arg.
174/F1 General Campos, Arg.
170/B2 General Carneiro, Braz.
174/B5 General Carrera (lake), Chile
159/E3 General Cepeda, Mex.
174/D4 General Conesa, Arg.
174/E2 General Deheza, Arg.
208/C1 General Edward Lawrence Logan (int'l arpt.), Ma,US
174/D3 General Enrique Godoy, Arg.
172/D2 General Eugenio A. Garay, Par.
174/F2 General Galarza, Arg.
186/C2 General Grant Grove (Kings Canyon Nat'l Park), Ca,US
207/K8 General Grant Nat'l Mem., NY,US
165/E2 General José Antonio Anzoategui (int'l arpt.), Ven.
172/E3 General José de San Martín, Arg.
159/F5 General Juan Alvarez, Mex.
160/B2 General Juan Álvarez Nat'l Park, Mex.
175/F3 General Juan Madariaga, Arg.

172/B1 General Lagos, Chile
175/S12 General Las Heras, Arg.
175/T13 General Lavalle, Arg.
172/C4 General Manuel Belgrano (peak), Arg.
172/C3 General Martín Miguel De Güemes, Arg.
205/Q14 General Mitchell (int'l arpt.), Wi,US
175/S12 General Paz, Arg.
174/E2 General Pico, Arg.
174/E2 General Pinto, Arg.
174/D3 General Roca, Arg.
172/D1 General Saavedra, Bol.
167/G4 General Sampaio, Braz.
175/S12 General San Martín, Arg.
165/F2 General Santiago Marino (int'l arpt.), Ven.
125/D4 General Santos, Phil.
186/C2 General Sherman Tree (Kings Canyon Nat'l Park), Ca,US
159/F3 General Terán, Mex.
93/J4 General-Toshevo, Bul.
188/E4 General Treviño, Mex.
188/A3 General Trías, Mex.
125/E7 General Trias, Phil.
174/E2 General Viamonte, Arg.
188/B3 General Villalobas (arpt.), Mex.
174/E2 General Villegas, Arg.
81/F6 Generoso, Monte (peak), Swi.
182/F4 Genesee, Id,US
205/P14 Genesee, Wi,US
205/P14 Genesee Depot, Wi,US
191/E1 Geneseo, Ks,US
199/H3 Geneseo, NY,US
205/E6 Genessee (co.), Mi,US
199/G3 Genessee (riv.), NY,US
150/A3 Genet, Eth.
80/C5 Geneva (int'l arpt.), Swi.
203/F2 Geneva, Al,US
185/H2 Geneva, Id,US
205/P16 Geneva, Il,US
198/D4 Geneva, In,US
192/F3 Geneva, Ne,US
199/H3 Geneva, NY,US
198/F4 Geneva, Oh,US
208/G4 Geneva, Pa,US
189/H2 Geneva, Tx,US
205/P14 Geneva (lake), Wi,US
80/C5 Geneva (Genève), Swi.
80/C5 Geneva (Léman) (lake), Fr., Swi.
80/C5 Genève (canton), Swi.
80/C5 Genève (Geneva), Swi.
117/E3 Gengding (mtn.), China
70/B6 Gengenbach, Ger.
117/G4 Genglou, China
116/C4 Gengma Daizu Vazu Zizhixian, China
113/B2 Gengzhuang, China
99/H4 Genichesk, Ukr.
76/C4 Genil (riv.), Sp.
79/G6 Genillé, Fr.
69/E2 Genk, Belg.
80/B3 Genlis, Fr.
70/D6 Gennach (riv.), Ger.
66/C5 Gennep, Neth.
53/S10 Gennevilliers, Fr.
52/D4 Genoa, It.
193/K2 Genoa, Il,US
192/F3 Genoa, Ne,US
198/E4 Genoa, Oh,US
205/P15 Genoa City, Wi,US
86/B4 Genoa (Genova), It.
185/H4 Genola, Ut,US
167/K7 Génova, Col.
86/B4 Genova (gulf), It.
86/C4 Genova (prov.), It.
86/B4 Genova (Genoa), It.
168/K6 Genovesa (isl.), Ecu.
70/A3 Gensingen, Ger.
68/C1 Gent-Brugge (can.), Belg.
124/D4 Genteng (cape), Indo.
68/C1 Gent (Ghent), Belg.
72/C3 Genthin, Ger.
126/C3 Genting, Indo.
63/T9 Gentofte, Den.
191/G2 Gentry, Ar,US
68/D2 Genval, Belg.
85/G6 Genzano di Lucania, It.
84/C4 Genzano di Roma, It.
132/B5 Geographe (bay), Austl.
132/B3 Geographe (chan.), Austl.
194/D3 Geographical Center of North America, ND,US
192/E4 Geographical Center of the 48 Contiguous States, Ks,US
192/C1 Geographical Center of United States, SD,US
97/H4 Geokchay, Azer.
105/J2 Geok-Tepe, Trkm.
132/D2 George (lake), Austl.
134/C3 George (pt.), Austl.
179/K3 George (riv.), Qu,Can
156/C4 George, SAfr.
153/G3 George (lake), Ugan.
203/H3 George (lake), Fl,US
193/F2 George, Ia,US
199/K3 George (lake), NY,US
182/E4 George, Wa,US
100/E1 George Land (isl.), Rus.
70/E4 Georgensmünd, Ger.
198/C5 George Rogers Clark Nat'l Hist. Park, In,US
134/G9 Georges (riv.), Austl.
128/G3 Georgetown, Austl.
129/H8 George Town, Austl.
134/A2 Georgetown, Austl.
135/C4 George Town, Austl.
162/C2 George Town, Bahm.
197/R8 Georgetown, On,Can
197/F2 Georgetown, PE,Can
161/F2 George Town, Cay.
144/B3 Georgetown, Gam.
165/G3 Georgetown (cap.), Guy.
124/C1 Georgetown, Malay.
162/F4 Georgetown, StV.
192/B4 Georgetown, Co,US
208/A3 Georgetown, Ct,US
201/K1 Georgetown, De,US
203/H3 Georgetown, Fl,US
203/F2 Georgetown, Ga,US
203/H2 Georgetown, Ga,US
185/H2 Georgetown, Id,US
198/C5 Georgetown, Il,US
200/E1 Georgetown, Ky,US
202/B2 Georgetown, La,US
198/E5 Georgetown, Oh,US
201/H4 Georgetown, SC,US
189/F2 Georgetown, Tx,US
137/L George V (coast), Ant.
137/V George VI (sound), Ant.
200/E4 George, Walter F. (res.), Al, Ga,US
201/J1 George Washington Birthplace Nat'l Mon., Va,US
191/G2 George Washington Carver Nat'l Mon., Mo,US
189/E3 George West, Tx,US
97/G4 Georgia
182/B3 Georgia (strait), BC,Can
181/K5 Georgia (state), US
203/G2 Georgia Agrirama, Ga,US
199/K2 Georgia Center, Vt,US
201/M7 Georgia Dome, Ga,US
198/F2 Georgian (bay), On,Can
202/E2 Georgiana, Al,US
203/H3 Georgiana, Fl,US
198/F2 Georgian Bay Is. Nat'l Park, On,Can
133/H2 Georgina (riv.), Austl.
93/H4 Georgi Traykov, Bul.
67/F4 Georgsmarienhütte, Ger.
72/C6 Gera, Ger.
72/A6 Gera (riv.), Ger.
68/C2 Geraardsbergen, Belg.
172/G2 Geral (mts.), Braz.
194/D2 Gerald, Sk,Can
200/B1 Gerald, Mo,US
163/E3 Geral de Goiás (range), Braz.
136/B4 Geraldine, N.Z.
183/J4 Geraldine, Mt,US
132/B4 Geraldton, Austl.
195/L3 Geraldton, On,Can
80/C1 Gérardmer, Fr.
73/A3 Gerasdorf bei Wien, Aus.
105/H5 Gerāsh, Iran
184/C2 Gerber (res.), Or,US
80/C1 Gerbéviller, Fr.
74/F4 Gerbier de Jonc (mtn.), Fr.
72/B4 Gerbstedt, Ger.
67/H3 Gerdau (riv.), Ger.
177/H3 Gerdine (mt.), Ak,US
82/A2 Gère (riv.), Fr.
73/C4 Gerecse (mts.), Hun.
73/C4 Gerecse (peak), Hun.
93/L5 Gerede, Turk.
107/H2 Gereshk, Afg.
81/H2 Geretsried, Ger.
76/D4 Gérgal, Sp.
104/D2 Gerger, Turk.
131/G1 Gerhards (cape), PNG
124/C1 Gerik, Malay.
192/C3 Gering, Ne,US
72/C5 Geringswalde, Ger.
184/D3 Gerlach, Nv,US
65/L4 Gerlachovský Štít (peak), Slvk.
80/D3 Gerlafingen, Swi.
208/G7 Germano, Oh,US
206/A5 Germantown, Md,US
200/C3 Germantown, Tn,US
193/K2 Germantown, Wi,US
64/E3 Germany
71/E6 Germering, Ger.
70/B4 Germersheim, Ger.
198/D1 Germfask, Mi,US
81/E6 Germinaga, It.
156/E2 Germiston, SAfr.
70/B5 Gernsbach, Ger.
71/E2 Geroldsgrün, Ger.
71/E6 Gerolsbach, Ger.
69/F3 Gerolstein, Ger.
70/D3 Gerolzhofen, Ger.
77/G2 Gerona (Girona), Sp.
187/G4 Geronimo, Az,US
77/E1 Ger, Pic du (peak), Fr.
68/D3 Gerpinnes, Belg.
53/M7 Gerrards Cross, Eng,UK
81/E5 Gerra (Verzasca), Swi.
135/D2 Gerringong, Austl.
74/D5 Gers (riv.), Fr.
81/E4 Gersau, Swi.
70/C2 Gersfeld, Ger.
69/G5 Gersheim, Ger.
70/B3 Gerspenz (riv.), Ger.
70/E5 Gerstetten, Ger.
80/D1 Gerstheim, Fr.
70/D6 Gersthofen, Ger.
67/H7 Gerstungen, Ger.
184/B1 Gervais, Or,US
82/B3 Gervanne (riv.), Fr.
175/G2 Gervasio, Uru.
72/B3 Gerwisch, Ger.
114/D5 Gêrzê, China
104/C1 Gerze, Turk.
66/E5 Gescher, Ger.
67/F5 Geseke, Ger.
151/D1 Gesira, Som.
69/D4 Gespunsart, Fr.
70/D6 Gessertshausen, Ger.
82/D4 Gesso (riv.), It.
85/F5 Gesualdo, It.
69/E3 Gesves, Belg.
63/H1 Geta, Fin.
76/D2 Getafe, Sp.
115/B5 Getai, China
69/E2 Gete (riv.), Belg.
62/E3 Getinge, Swe.
64/E1 Gettorf, Ger.
206/A4 Gettysburg, Pa,US
192/E1 Gettysburg, SD,US
206/A4 Gettysburg Nat'l Mil. Park, Pa,US
173/F3 Getúlio Vargas, Braz.
137/S Getz Ice Shelf, Ant.
191/F2 Geuda Springs, Ks,US
69/E2 Geul (riv.), Belg., Neth.
124/B1 Geureudong (peak), Indo.
135/D2 Geurie, Austl.
105/E2 Gevaş, Turk.
67/E6 Gevelsberg, Ger.
92/F5 Gevgelija, Macd.
150/B3 Gewanē, Eth.
80/C5 Gex, Fr.
71/F1 Geyer, Ger.
70/C3 Geyersberg (peak), Ger.
91/K3 Geyikli, Turk.
104/D2 Geyiksuyu, Turk.
156/D2 Geysdorp, SAfr.
157/H6 Geyser (reef), Madg.
93/K5 Geyve, Turk.
114/B4 Gez (riv.), China
86/D5 G. Galilei (Galileo Galilei) (int'l arpt.), It.
103/E3 Ghabāghib, Syria
149/F3 Ghābat al 'Arab, Sudan
146/A2 Ghadāmis, Libya
146/B3 Ghaddūwah, Libya
147/G3 Ghadir, Bi'r (well), Egypt
122/D2 Ghaggar (riv.), India
120/E2 Ghaghara (Goghra) (riv.), India
121/E4 Ghāghra, India
145/E4 Ghana
107/K3 Ghantiāli, India
154/D4 Ghanzi, Bots.
154/D4 Ghanzi (dist.), Bots.
141/W17 Ghār Ad Dimā', Tun.
120/A1 Gharaunda, India
147/F5 Gharb Binna, Sudan
88/F4 Gharbī, Jazīrat al (isl.), Tun.
143/F2 Ghardaïa, Alg.
143/F3 Ghardaïa (wilaya), Alg.
120/D4 Gharghoda, India
105/G3 Gharqābād, Iran
143/G2 Gharsah, Shaţţ al (salt lake), Tun.
146/B1 Gharyān, Libya
146/A3 Ghāt, Libya
121/F4 Ghātāl, India
120/C2 Ghātampur, India
121/F4 Ghātsīla, India
150/D2 Ghayl Bā Wazīr, Yem.
148/C2 Ghazal, Bahr el (riv.), Chad
141/P13 Ghazaouet, Alg.
120/A1 Ghaziābād, India
120/C3 Ghāzīpur, India
120/D3 Ghāzīpur, India
107/J2 Ghaznī, Afg.
103/D4 Ghazzah (Gaza), Gaza
86/D2 Ghedi, It.
195/H4 Gheen, Mn,US
86/B1 Ghemme, It.
108/G2 Ghengis Khan Wall (ruins), Mong.
68/C1 Ghent (Gent), Belg.
93/H2 Gheorghe Gheorghiu-Dej, Rom.
93/G2 Gheorgheni, Rom.
93/F2 Gherla, Rom.
118/B2 Gheura, India
90/A2 Ghilarza, It.
174/C5 Ghio (lake), Arg.
143/H2 Ghirārah, Khalij Bū (gulf), Tun.
86/C1 Ghisalba, It.
90/A1 Ghisonaccia, Fr.
189/F2 Gholson, Tx,US
107/J4 Ghora Bāri, Pak.
120/D1 Ghorāi, Nepal
186/D2 Ghost Town, Nv,US
118/A2 Ghotki, Pak.
121/F3 Ghugri (riv.), India
121/G2 Ghum, India
106/D5 Ghurayrah, SAr.
107/H2 Ghūriān, Afg.
146/A2 Ghuzayyil, Bi'r al (well), Libya
146/C2 Ghuzayyil, Sabkhat (salt marsh), Libya
99/L5 Giaginskaya, Rus.
123/D1 Gia Lam (int'l arpt.), Viet.
123/D4 Gia Nghia, Viet.
84/B3 Giannutri (isl.), It.
156/E3 Giant's Castle (peak), SAfr.
56/B1 Giant's Causeway, NI,UK
124/F5 Gianyar, Indo.
123/D4 Gia Rai, Viet.
90/D4 Giarre, It.
82/D2 Giaveno, It.
123/E3 Gia Vuc, Viet.
150/A2 Giba'i Shet' (riv.), Eth.
192/E3 Gibbon, Ne,US
185/G1 Gibbonsville, Id,US
130/B4 Gibb River, Austl.
206/C4 Gibbstown, NJ,US
154/C5 Gibeon, Namb.
79/E2 Giberville, Fr.
149/H4 Gībē Shet' (riv.), Eth.
149/H3 Gībē Wenz (riv.), Eth.
80/D4 Gibloux, Mont (peak), Swi.
76/B4 Gibraleón, Sp.
197/S8 Gibraltar (pt.), On,Can
76/B4 Gibraltar (str.), Mor., Sp.
76/C4 Gibraltar, UK
76/C4 Gibraltar (dpcy.), UK
55/M10 Gibraltar (pt.), UK
204/A1 Gibraltar (res.), Ca,US
205/F7 Gibraltar, Mi,US
135/E1 Gibraltar Range Nat'l Park, Austl.
189/H1 Gibsland, La,US
132/D5 Gibson, Austl.
132/E2 Gibson (des.), Austl.
201/F4 Gibson, Ga,US
201/H3 Gibson, NC,US
198/E4 Gibsonburg, Oh,US
193/K3 Gibson City, Il,US
132/E3 Gibson Desert Nat. Rsv., Austl.
202/M7 Gibsonia, Fl,US
208/H6 Gibsonia, Pa,US
182/C3 Gibsons, BC,Can
202/L8 Gibsonton, Fl,US
149/G3 Gīdamī, Eth.
122/C2 Giddarbāha, India
189/F2 Giddings, Tx,US
202/L6 Giddon (lake), Fl,US
200/C2 Gideon, Mo,US
103/C4 Gidi (Mamarr al Jady) (pass), Egypt
148/B3 Gidjibo, Camr.
149/H4 Gidollē, Eth.
73/B3 Gidra (riv.), Slvk.
70/C3 Giebelstadt, Ger.
67/H5 Gieboldehausen, Ger.
63/L4 Giedraičiai, Lith.
74/E3 Gien, Fr.
70/D5 Giengen an der Brenz, Ger.
82/C6 Giens, Fr.
82/C6 Giens, Presqu'île de (pen.), Fr.
82/A1 Gier (riv.), Fr.
72/B4 Giersleben, Ger.
80/E4 Giessbachfälle (falls), Swi.
80/D1 Giessen (riv.), Fr.
70/B1 Giessen, Ger.
66/B5 Giessendam, Neth.
66/D2 Gieten, Neth.
66/D3 Giethoorn, Neth.
68/B6 Gif, Fr.
105/J2 Gīfān, Iran
83/C6 Giffone, It.
179/H1 Gifford (riv.), NW,Can
54/D5 Gifford, Sc,UK
203/H4 Gifford, Fl,US
198/B4 Gifford, Il,US
201/G4 Gifford, SC,US
182/D5 Gifford (peak), Wa,US
80/C5 Giffre (riv.), Fr.
67/H4 Gifhorn, Ger.
53/S10 Gif-sur-Yvette, Fr.
111/E3 Gifu, Japan
111/E3 Gifu (pref.), Japan
99/L4 Gigant, Rus.
158/C3 Giganta, Sierra de la (mts.), Mex.
164/C4 Gigante, Col.
160/E4 Gigante (pt.), Nic.
57/F3 Giggleswick, Eng,UK
205/B3 Gig Harbor, Wa,US
84/A3 Giglio (isl.), It.
84/A3 Giglio Porto, It.
77/G1 Gignac, Fr.
76/C1 Gijón, Sp.
153/G3 Gikongoro, Rwa.
158/B1 Gila (riv.), Az,,NM,US
187/F4 Gila (des.), Az,US
187/H4 Gila (mts.), Az,US
180/D5 Gila (riv.), Az,US
187/F4 Gila (riv.), Az, NM,US
187/H4 Gila, NM,US
187/F4 Gila Bend, Az,US
187/F4 Gila Bend Ind. Res., Az,US
187/H4 Gila Cliff Dwellings Nat'l Mon., NM,US
105/G2 Gīlān (gov.), Iran
105/F3 Gīlān-e Gharb, Iran
187/F4 Gila River Ind. Res., Az,US
57/H4 Gilberdyke Newport, Eng,UK
134/A2 Gilbert (riv.), Austl.
182/B2 Gilbert (mtn.), BC,Can
138/G5 Gilbert (isls.), Kiri.
187/G4 Gilbert, Az,US
193/H2 Gilbert, Ia,US
202/C1 Gilbert, La,US
185/H3 Gilbert (peak), Ut,US
200/C5 Gilbertown, Al,US
194/D2 Gilbert Plains, Mb,Can
205/P15 Gilberts, Il,US
170/D1 Gilbués, Braz.
194/F3 Gilby, ND,US
70/E6 Gilching, Ger.
189/G3 Gilchrist, Tx,US
174/C2 Gil de Vilches Nat'l Park, Chile
155/H3 Gilé, Moz.
208/B2 Gilead, Ct,US
58/C3 Gilfach Goch, Wal,UK
56/B3 Gilford, NI,UK
199/L3 Gilford, NH,US
207/D4 Gilford Park, NJ,US
135/D1 Gilgandra, Austl.
151/B2 Gilgil, Kenya
107/K1 Gilgit, Pak.
114/B4 Gilgit (riv.), Pak.
135/C2 Gilgunnia, Austl.
124/F5 Gilimanuk, Indo.
199/K3 Gill, Ma,US
178/G3 Gillam, Mb,Can
63/T8 Gilleleje, Den.
133/H5 Gilles (lake), Austl.
193/K4 Gillespie, Il,US
191/J3 Gillett, Ar,US
189/F3 Gillett, Tx,US
193/K1 Gillett, Wi,US
185/L1 Gillette, Wy,US
80/C3 Gilley, Fr.
191/H4 Gilliam, La,US
58/D4 Gillingham, Eng,UK
59/G4 Gillingham, Eng,UK
60/B1 Gill, Lough (lake), Ire.
80/C5 Gilly, Swi.
198/C4 Gilman, Il,US
195/J5 Gilman, Wi,US
193/H3 Gilman City, Mo,US
204/D3 Gilman Hot Springs, Ca,US
189/G1 Gilmer, Tx,US
185/G1 Gilmore, Id,US
149/G4 Gīlo Wenz (riv.), Eth.
107/K1 Gilqit (riv.), Pak.
186/B2 Gilroy, Ca,US
131/F1 Giluwe (peak), PNG
109/K1 Gilyuy (riv.), Rus.
66/B5 Gilze, Neth.
149/G3 Gīmbī, Eth.
80/C4 Gimel, Swi.
162/F4 Gimie (mtn.), StL.
83/C5 Gimigliano, It.
194/F2 Gimli, Mb,Can
62/H1 Gimo, Swe.
77/F1 Gimone (riv.), Fr.
111/M9 Ginan, Japan
150/A3 Gīnch'ī, Eth.
150/A2 Gīnda, Eth.
69/E2 Gingelom, Belg.
149/H4 Gingero, Eth.
132/B4 Gingin, Austl.
134/C4 Gin Gin, Austl.
157/E3 Gingindlovu, SAfr.
125/D3 Gingoog, Phil.
65/G1 Gingst, Ger.
150/B4 Gīnīr, Eth.
66/B5 Ginneken, Neth.
90/E2 Ginosa, It.
112/J7 Ginowan, Japan
76/B1 Ginzo de Limia, Sp.
140/G4 Giohar, Som.
150/C5 Giohar (Jawhar), Som.
83/B2 Gioi, It.
83/B5 Gioia (gulf), It.
85/D4 Gioia dei Marsi, It.
90/E2 Gioia del Colle, It.
83/B6 Gioia Tauro, It.
83/C6 Gioiosa Ionica, It.
83/A6 Gioiosa Marea, It.
81/E5 Giornico, Swi.
91/J3 Gioūra (isl.), Gre.
81/G4 Gioveretto (peak), It.
87/E5 Giovi, Monte (peak), It.
59/G2 Gipping (riv.), Eng,UK
191/J2 Gipsy, Mo,US
152/C4 Girard, Congo
193/K4 Girard, Il,US
191/G2 Girard, Ks,US
208/G5 Girard, Oh,US
198/F3 Girard, Pa,US
164/C3 Girardot, Col.
167/K6 Girardota, Col.
196/A1 Girardville, Qu,Can
206/B2 Girardville, Pa,US
82/D4 Giraud (mtn.), Fr.
154/B2 Giraul (riv.), Ang.
154/B2 Giraul de Cima, Ang.
69/E5 Giraumont, Fr.
150/B3 Girawa, Eth.
54/D2 Girdle Head (pt.), Sc,UK
55/K8 Girdle Ness (pt.), Sc,UK
104/D1 Giresun, Turk.
104/D1 Giresun (prov.), Turk.
86/B1 Girgnasco, It.
152/D2 Giri (riv.), Zaire
121/F3 Gīrīdīh, India
83/C5 Girifalco, It.
135/C1 Girilambone, Austl.
53/N7 Girling (res.), Eng,UK
80/C2 Giromagny, Fr.
164/C3 Giron, Col.
164/B5 Girón, Ecu.
52/D4 Girona, Sp.
77/G2 Girona (Gerona), Sp.
80/B1 Gironcourt-sur-Vraine, Fr.
74/C4 Gironde (riv.), Fr.
77/F1 Gironella, Sp.
135/D1 Girraween Nat'l Park, Austl.
59/G2 Girton, Eng,UK
134/B2 Giru, Austl.
173/F4 Giruá, Braz.
56/D1 Girvan, Sc,UK
56/D1 Girvan, Water of (riv.), Sc,UK
188/C2 Girvin, Tx,US
136/D2 Gisborne, N.Z.
153/G3 Gisenyi, Rwa.
62/E3 Gislaved, Swe.
68/A5 Gisors, Fr.
85/E3 Gissi, It.
68/B1 Gistel, Belg.
62/D3 Gistrup, Den.
153/G3 Gitarama, Rwa.
153/G3 Gitega, Buru.
94/B2 Gittsfjället (peak), Swe.
107/K4 Giu (isl.), India
81/F5 Giubiasco, Swi.
85/E6 Giugliano in Campania, It.
84/C4 Giulianello, It.
85/D2 Giulianova, It.
93/H3 Giurgeni, Rom.
93/G4 Giurgiu, Rom.
93/G3 Giurgiu (co.), Rom.
86/C1 Giussano, It.
103/F7 Giv'atayim, Isr.
103/F8 Giv'at Brenner, Isr.
103/F7 Giv'at Hayyim, Isr.
62/C4 Give, Den.
69/D3 Givet, Fr.
82/A1 Givors, Fr.
80/C5 Givrine, Col de la (pass), Swi.
68/D3 Givry, Belg.
69/D6 Givry-en-Argonne, Fr.
145/G4 Giwa, Nga.
155/F4 Giyani, SAfr.
149/H3 Giyon, Eth.
103/B5 Giza, The Pyramids of (Ahrāmāt al Jīzah), Egypt
101/R3 Gizhiga (bay), Rus.
138/E5 Gizo, Sol.
65/L1 Giżycko, Pol.
83/C5 Gizzeria, It.
62/D1 Gjerdrum, Nor.
62/D3 Gjerlev, Den.
62/C2 Gjerstad, Nor.
91/G2 Gjirokastër, Alb.
178/G2 Gjoa Haven, NW,Can
62/D1 Gjøvik, Nor.
91/F2 Gjuhëzës, Kep i (cape), Alb.
69/E2 Glabbeek, Belg.
197/H2 Glace Bay, NS,Can
182/F2 Glacier, BC,Can
182/D3 Glacier (peak), Wa,US
178/C3 Glacier Bay Nat'l Park, Ak,US
177/L4 Glacier Bay Nat'l Park & Prsv., Ak,US
182/F2 Glacier Nat'l Park, BC,Can
183/H3 Glacier Nat'l Park, Mt,US
66/D5 Gladbeck, Ger.
193/H2 Gladbrook, Ia,US
201/G2 Glade Spring, Va,US
189/G1 Gladewater, Tx,US
63/T9 Gladsakse, Den.
182/F3 Gladsheim (peak), BC,Can
133/H5 Gladstone, Austl.
194/E2 Gladstone, Mb,Can
198/C2 Gladstone, Mi,US
194/C4 Gladstone, ND,US
206/D2 Gladstone-Peapack, NJ,US
198/D3 Gladwin, Mi,US
201/H2 Gladys, Va,US
62/D2 Glafsfjorden (lake), Swe.
57/H3 Glaisdale, Eng,UK
52/E2 Glåma (riv.), Nor.
62/D1 Glama (riv.), Nor.
183/L2 Glamis, Sk,Can
54/D3 Glamis, Sc,UK
186/E4 Glamis, Ca,US
62/D4 Glamsbjerg, Den.
69/G4 Glan (riv.), Ger.
125/D4 Glan, Phil.
58/C3 Glanamman, Wal,UK
60/A5 Glanaruddery (mts.), Ire.
200/B5 Glancy, Ms,US
68/D4 Gland (riv.), Fr.
80/C5 Gland, Swi.
82/C2 Glandon (riv.), Fr.
60/A6 Glandore, Ire.
67/F4 Glandorf, Ger.
60/B5 Glanworth, Ire.
81/E3 Glärnisch (range), Swi.
81/F3 Glarus, Swi.
81/F4 Glarus (canton), Swi.
81/E4 Glarus (mts.), Swi.
75/H3 Glarus Alps (range), Swi.
58/C2 Glasbury, Wal,UK
191/F1 Glasco, Ks,US
54/B5 Glasgow, Sc,UK
206/C4 Glasgow, De,US
200/E2 Glasgow, Ky,US
183/L3 Glasgow, Mt,US
201/H2 Glasgow, Va,US
54/B5 Glasgow (Abbotsinch) (int'l arpt.), Sc,UK
54/B5 Glasgow (Prestwick) (int'l arpt.), Sc,UK
70/B2 Glashütten, Ger.
183/K1 Glaslyn, Sk,Can
56/D6 Glaslyn (riv.), Wal,UK
54/C3 Glas Maol (mtn.), Sc,UK
56/D3 Glass (riv.), IM,UK
54/B2 Glass (riv.), Sc,UK
191/E2 Glass (mts.), Ok,US
188/C2 Glass (mts.), Tx,US
206/C4 Glassboro, NJ,US
54/B1 Glass, Loch (lake), Sc,UK
206/B6 Glassmanor-Oxon Hill, Md,US
208/H7 Glassport, Pa,US
58/D4 Glastonbury, Eng,UK
208/B2 Glastonbury, Ct,US
70/B6 Glatt (riv.), Ger.
81/E2 Glatt (riv.), Swi.
81/E2 Glattfelden, Swi.
72/C6 Glauchau, Ger.
93/H4 Glavinitsa, Bul.
145/F5 Glazoué, Ben.
53/J3 Glazov, Rus.
200/C2 Gleason, Tn,US
198/B2 Gleason, Wi,US
99/K4 Glebovka, Rus.
187/H5 Gleeson, Az,US
183/H2 Gleichen, Ab,Can
92/B2 Gleisdorf, Aus.
70/C5 Glems (riv.), Ger.
59/G2 Glemsford, Eng,UK
57/H6 Glen (riv.), Eng,UK
195/H4 Glen, Mn,US
185/G1 Glen, Mt,US
187/G2 Glen (canyon), Tx, Ut,US
135/C3 Glenaladale Nat'l Park, Austl.
200/B4 Glen Allan, Ms,US
201/J2 Glen Allen, Va,US
74/A3 Glenan (isls.), Fr.
78/B5 Glénan (isls.), Fr.
195/M5 Glen Arbor, Mi,US
56/C2 Glenarm, NI,UK
56/C2 Glenarm (riv.), NI,UK
194/C2 Glenavon, Sk,Can
136/B4 Glenavy, N.Z.
56/B2 Glenavy, NI,UK
135/D2 Glenbawn (dam), Austl.
194/E3 Glenboro, Mb,Can
134/G8 Glenbrook, Austl.
184/D4 Glenbrook, Nv,US
194/D3 Glenburn, ND,US
206/B5 Glen Burnie, Md,US
183/L1 Glenbush, Sk,Can
187/G2 Glen Canyon (dam), Az,US
187/G2 Glen Canyon Nat'l Rec. Area, Az, Ut,US
56/E1 Glencaple, Sc,UK
155/F3 Glenclova, Zim.
198/F3 Glencoe, On,Can
157/E3 Glencoe, SAfr.
54/A3 Glencoe, Sc,UK
54/B3 Glen Coe (pass), Sc,UK
205/Q15 Glencoe, Il,US
195/G5 Glencoe, Mn,US
191/F2 Glencoe, Ok,US
207/E2 Glen Cove, NY,US
188/E2 Glen Cove, Tx,US
194/D5 Glencross, SD,US
187/F4 Glendale, Az,US
204/B2 Glendale, Ca,US
200/E2 Glendale, Ky,US
208/A1 Glendale, Ma,US
193/H3 Glendale, Mo,US
186/E2 Glendale, Nv,US
208/C2 Glendale, RI,US
189/G2 Glendale, Tx,US
187/F2 Glendale, Ut,US
198/C3 Glendale, Wi,US
155/F3 Glendale, Zim.
204/F7 Glendale-Burbank-Pasadena (arpt.), Ca,US
205/P16 Glendale Heights, Il,US
134/C3 Glenden, Austl.
183/M4 Glendive, Mt,US
192/B2 Glendo, Wy,US
192/B2 Glendo (dam), Wy,US
192/B2 Glendo (res.), Wy,US
201/H3 Glendon, NC,US
204/C2 Glendora, Ca,US
56/B1 Glendun (riv.), NI,UK
60/D4 Glenealy, Ire.
206/A6 Glen Echo, Md,US
136/F6 Glen Eden, N.Z.
191/E1 Glen Elder, Ks,US
133/M8 Glenelg, Austl.
135/B3 Glenelg (riv.), Austl.
55/J8 Glenelg, UK
206/B5 Glenelg, Md,US
194/E2 Glenella, Mb,Can
56/A2 Glenelly (riv.), NI,UK
199/J3 Glenfield, NY,US
189/F3 Glen Flora, Tx,US
206/D2 Glen Gardner, NJ,US
60/A6 Glengarriff, Ire.
132/C3 Glengarry (range), Austl.
135/D1 Glen Innes, Austl.
56/D2 Glenluce, Sc,UK
206/B1 Glen Lyon, Pa,US
207/D1 Glenmere (lake), NY,US
208/E6 Glenmont, Oh,US
206/A5 Glenmont-Wheaton, Md,US
54/B2 Glen Mòr (val.), Sc,UK
202/B2 Glenmora, La,US
134/C4 Glenmorgan, Austl.
177/J3 Glennallen, Ak,US
60/B2 Glennamaddy, Ire.
188/L7 Glenn Heights, Tx,US
185/F2 Glenns Ferry, Id,US
186/C3 Glennville, Ca,US
201/G5 Glennville, Ga,US
206/C4 Glenolden, Pa,US
182/C4 Glenoma, Wa,US
177/M4 Glenora, BC,Can
134/H8 Glenorie, Austl.
133/H2 Glenormiston, Austl.
191/F3 Glenpool, Ok,US
207/J8 Glen Ridge, NJ,US
190/C3 Glenrio, NM,US
207/D2 Glen Rock, NJ,US
206/B4 Glen Rock, Pa,US
185/L2 Glenrock, Wy,US
189/F1 Glen Rose, Tx,US
54/C4 Glenrothes, Sc,UK
199/K3 Glens Falls, NY,US
56/B2 Glenshane (pass), NI,UK
206/C3 Glenside, Pa,US
55/G9 Glenties, Ire.
56/D1 Glentrool, Sc,UK
194/A3 Glentworth, Sk,Can
194/D4 Glen Ullin, ND,US
55/H9 Glenveagh Nat'l Park, Ire.
205/Q15 Glenview, Il,US
205/Q15 Glenview Nav. Air Sta., Il,US
60/B5 Glenville, Ire.
193/H2 Glenville, Mn,US
201/G1 Glenville, WV,US
197/R8 Glen Williams, On,Can
208/F5 Glenwillow, Oh,US
183/H3 Glenwood, Ab,Can
203/E2 Glenwood, Al,US
191/H3 Glenwood, Ar,US
201/F4 Glenwood, Ga,US
193/G3 Glenwood, Ia,US
195/G5 Glenwood, Mn,US
206/D1 Glenwood, NJ,US
187/H4 Glenwood, NM,US
185/H4 Glenwood, Ut,US
195/H5 Glenwood City, Wi,US
190/A1 Glenwood Springs, Co,US
54/A2 Gleouraich (mtn.), Sc,UK
183/K2 Glidden, Sk,Can
193/G2 Glidden, Ia,US
72/C3 Glienicke, Ger.
91/L7 Glifáhda, Gre.
62/F3 Glimåkra, Swe.
92/C3 Glina, Cro.
67/H1 Glinde, Ger.
72/C3 Glindow, Ger.
61/D3 Glittertinden (peak), Nor.
65/K3 Gliwice, Pol.
187/G4 Globe, Az,US
99/G3 Globino, Ukr.
81/G4 Glockturm (peak), Aus.
93/H2 Glodyany, Mol.
65/H5 Gloggnitz, Aus.
65/J3 Głogów, Pol.
65/J3 Głogówek, Pol.
70/E6 Glonn (riv.), Ger.
161/G1 Gloria (bay), Cuba
157/H5 Glorieuses, Iles (isls.), Reun.
134/E6 Glorious (mtn.), Austl.
177/D3 Glory of Russia (cape), Ak,US
57/G5 Glossop, Eng,UK
189/H1 Gloster, La,US
202/C2 Gloster, Ms,US
63/T9 Glostrup, Den.
72/B4 Glöthe, Ger.
97/H1 Glotovka, Rus.
135/D2 Gloucester, Austl.
199/J2 Gloucester, On,Can
58/D3 Gloucester, Eng,UK
199/L3 Gloucester, Ma,US
206/C4 Gloucester (co.), NJ,US
201/J2 Gloucester C. H. (Gloucester), Va,US
206/C4 Gloucester City, NJ,US
201/J2 Gloucester (Gloucester C. H.), Va,US
201/J2 Gloucester Point, Va,US
58/D3 Gloucestershire (co.), Eng,UK
58/D3 Gloucester, Vale of (val.), Eng,UK
131/H1 Glouster, PNG
198/E5 Glouster, Oh,US
60/B6 Glouthane, Ire.
197/J1 Glover (isl.), Nf,Can
191/G3 Glover, Ok,US
160/E2 Glovers (reef), Belz.
199/J3 Gloversville, NY,US
197/K1 Glovertown, Nf,Can
65/K3 Głowno, Pol.
65/J3 Głubczyce, Pol.
99/L3 Glubokiy, Rus.
63/M4 Glubokoye, Bela.
114/D1 Glubokoye, Kaz.
65/J3 Głuchołazy, Pol.
64/E1 Glücksburg, Ger.
67/G1 Glückstadt, Ger.
99/G2 Glukhov, Ukr.
63/T9 Glumslöv, Swe.
98/C3 Glybokaya, Ukr.
60/D2 Glyde (riv.), Ire.
58/C3 Glyncorrwg, Wal,UK
206/B5 Glyndon, Md,US
194/F4 Glyndon, Mn,US
62/C3 Glyngøre, Den.
56/C2 Glynn, NI,UK
58/C3 Glyn Neath, Wal,UK
65/H4 Gmünd, Aus.
71/G7 Gmunden, Aus.
208/F7 Gnadenhutten, Oh,US
145/E3 Gnagna (prov.), Burk.
67/G2 Gnarrenburg, Ger.
96/D1 Gnezdovo, Rus.
63/H5 Gniew, Pol.
65/J2 Gniezno, Pol.
98/E3 Gnivan', Ukr.
92/E4 Gnjilane, Yugo.
58/D1 Gnosall, Eng,UK
132/C5 Gnowangerup, Austl.
110/C3 Gō (riv.), Japan
118/B4 Goa (state), India
156/B2 Goageb, Namb.
121/H2 Goālpāra, India
121/F4 Goāltor, India
188/C2 Goat (mtn.), Tx,US
54/A5 Goat Fell (mtn.), Sc,UK
57/H3 Goathland, Eng,UK
182/D1 Goat River, BC,Can
150/A4 Goba, Eth.
155/G5 Goba, Moz.
154/B4 Gobabeb, Namb.
154/C4 Gobabis, Namb.
174/F2 Gobernador Castro, Arg.
174/C5 Gobernador Costa, Arg.
172/D4 Gobernador Crespo, Arg.
174/D3 Gobernador Duval, Arg.
175/K7 Gobernador Gregores, Arg.
173/E4 Gobernador Ingeniero Valetín Virasoro, Arg.
175/S11 Gobernador Mansilla, Arg.
108/E3 Gobi (des.), China, Mong.
120/E5 Gobindpur, India
71/G6 Göblberg (peak), Aus.
110/D4 Gobō, Japan
57/E6 Gobowen, Eng,UK
206/C4 G. O. Carlson/Chester (co. arpt.), Pa,US
66/D5 Goch, Ger.
156/B2 Gochas, Namb.
70/D2 Gochsheim, Ger.
123/D4 Go Cong, Viet.
73/D4 Göd, Hun.
150/B4 Goda, Eth.
121/G3 Godāgāri, Bang.
59/F4 Godalming, Eng,UK
123/D4 Go Dau Ha, Viet.
118/D4 Godāvari (riv.), India
196/D1 Godbout, Qu,Can
121/F3 Goddā, India
150/B4 Godē, Eth.
92/F3 Godeanu (peak), Rom.
91/H1 Godech, Bul.
198/F3 Goderich, On,Can
79/F1 Goderville, Fr.
193/J4 Godfrey, Il,US
118/B3 Godhra, India
150/C4 Godinlabe, Som.
69/D3 Godinne, Belg.
188/K7 Godley, Tx,US
59/F2 Godmanchester, Eng,UK
127/F4 Godo (mtn.), Indo.
111/M9 Gōdo, Japan
92/D2 Gödöllő, Hun.
58/A6 Godolphin Cross, Eng,UK
174/C2 Godoy Cruz, Arg.
178/G3 Gods (lake), Mb,Can
178/G3 Gods (riv.), Mb,Can
179/H2 Gods Mercy (bay), NW,Can
53/N8 Godstone, Eng,UK
176/M3 Godthåb (Nuuk), Grld.
114/C4 Godwin-Austen (K2) (peak), China, Pak.
66/A5 Goerce, Neth.
66/A6 Goes, Neth.
191/F1 Goessel, Ks,US
198/D1 Goetzville, Mi,US
191/G1 Goff, Ks,US
199/L3 Goffstown, NH,US
97/G3 Gofitskoye, Rus.
195/K4 Gogebic (lake), Mi,US
195/J4 Gogebic (range), Mi,US
81/G1 Göggingen, Ger.
120/E2 Goghra (Ghaghara) (riv.), India
63/M1 Gogland (isl.), Rus.
130/B4 Gogo, Austl.
149/G4 Gogo, Eth.
157/H9 Gogogogo, Madg.
145/F4 Gogounou, Ben.
118/D2 Gogra (riv.), India
149/F3 Gogrial, Sudan
120/B2 Gohad, India
120/A1 Gohāna, India
120/A4 Goharganj, India
149/H3 Goha Ts'iyon, Eth.
67/G3 Gohbach (riv.), Ger.
167/H4 Goiana, Braz.
170/C3 Goiandira, Braz.
170/C2 Goianésia, Braz.
170/C3 Goiânia, Braz.
167/H4 Goianinha, Braz.
170/C3 Goianira, Braz.
170/C2 Goiás, Braz.
170/C2 Goiás (state), Braz.
170/D1 Goiás, Serra Geral de (uplands), Braz.
170/C3 Goiatuba, Braz.
54/B4 Goil, Loch (inlet), Sc,UK
116/C2 Goinsargoin, China
170/B5 Goio-Erê, Braz.
66/C5 Goirle, Neth.
76/A2 Góis, Port.
87/D2 Goito, It.
149/H3 Gojam (prov.), Eth.
149/H4 Gojeb Wenz (riv.), Eth.
110/D3 Gojō, Japan
112/B4 Gojōme, Japan
122/B2 Gojra, Pak.
96/E4 Gok (riv.), Turk.
110/B4 Gokase (riv.), Japan
111/M9 Gokashō, Japan
93/G5 Gökçeada (isl.), Turk.
93/L5 Gökçebey, Turk.
148/B3 Gokoro-Mozogo Nat'l Park, Camr.
103/C1 Göksu (riv.), Turk.
104/D2 Göksun, Turk.
123/B1 Gokteik, Burma
103/C1 Göktepe, Turk.
155/F3 Gokwe, Zim.
62/C1 Gol, Nor.
121/E4 Gola, India
120/C1 Gola Gokarannāth, India
103/D3 Golan Heights (reg.), Syria
121/J3 Golāpganj, Bang.
86/B1 Golasecca, It.
98/G4 Golaya Pristan', Ukr.
104/C2 Gölbaşı, Turk.
104/D2 Gölbaşı, Turk.
80/C1 Golbey, Fr.
57/F5 Golborne, Eng,UK
200/C2 Golconda, Il,US
93/J5 Gölcük, Turk.
182/G3 Gold (cr.), BC,Can
79/E2 Gold (beach), Fr.
205/B2 Gold (mtn.), Wa,US
81/F3 Goldach, Swi.
65/M1 Gołdap, Pol.
70/C3 Goldbach, Ger.
72/A4 Goldbach (riv.), Ger.
205/D2 Gold Bar, Wa,US
184/A2 Gold Beach, Or,US
72/B2 Goldbeck, Ger.
64/G2 Goldberg, Ger.
182/C2 Gold Bridge, BC,Can
134/D4 Gold Coast, Austl.
145/E5 Gold Coast (reg.), Gha.
182/F2 Golden, BC,Can
60/B5 Golden, Ire.
136/C3 Golden (bay), N.Z.
192/B4 Golden, Co,US
190/A3 Golden, NM,US
202/P8 Golden Beach, Fl,US
191/G2 Golden City, Mo,US
182/D5 Goldendale, Wa,US
72/A5 Goldene Aue (reg.), Ger.
205/J11 Golden Gate (chan.), Ca,US
203/H4 Golden Gate, Fl,US
156/E3 Golden Gate Highlands Nat'l Park, SAfr.
205/J11 Golden Gate Nat'l Rec. Area, Ca,US
199/H2 Golden Lake Ind. Res., Can.
183/K2 Golden Prairie, Sk,Can
202/N6 Goldenrod, Fl,US
185/G3 Golden Spike Nat'l Hist. Site, Ut,US
67/F3 Goldenstedt, Ger.
122/C2 Golden Temple, India
60/B4 Golden Vale (plain), Ire.
195/P6 Golden Valley, Mn,US
155/F3 Golden Valley, Zim.
193/H2 Goldfield, Ia,US
186/D2 Goldfield, Nv,US
184/B2 Gold Hill, Or,US
71/E2 Goldkronach, Ger.
70/D1 Goldlauter, Ger.
202/B1 Goldonna, La,US
186/D2 Gold Point, Nv,US
206/C5 Goldsboro, Md,US
201/J3 Goldsboro, NC,US
188/E1 Goldsboro, Tx,US
206/B3 Goldsboro (Etters), Pa,US
132/C2 Goldsworthy, Austl.
189/E2 Goldthwaite, Tx,US
104/E1 Göle, Turk.
65/H2 Goleniów, Pol.
186/C3 Goleta, Ca,US
161/F4 Golfito Nat'l Wild. Ref., CR
90/A2 Golfo Aranci, It.
186/E5 Golfo Santa Clara, Mex.
135/B2 Gol Gol, Austl.
103/A1 Gölhisar, Turk.
189/F3 Goliad, Tx,US
189/F2 Golinda, Tx,US
104/D1 Gölköy, Turk.
70/D3 Gollach (riv.), Ger.
73/A3 Göllersdorf, Aus.
70/B3 Göllheim, Ger.
104/A2 Gölmarmara, Turk.
108/C4 Golmud, China
98/C2 Goloby, Ukr.
150/B3 Gololcha, Eth.
155/G2 Golomoti Station, Malw.
94/J5 Golovanovo, Rus.
177/F3 Golovin, Ak,US
94/J5 Golovino, Rus.
112/D2 Golovnina Gora (mt.), Rus.
112/D2 Golovnino, Rus.
105/G3 Golpāyegān, Iran
93/K5 Gölpazarı, Turk.
73/A4 Gols, Aus.
63/M4 Gol'shany, Bela.
72/D4 Golssen, Ger.
191/E2 Goltry, Ok,US
206/C5 Golts, Md,US
65/K2 Golub-Dobrzyń, Pol.
92/D4 Golubovci (int'l arpt.), Yugo.
152/C5 Golungo Alto, Ang.
194/C4 Golva, ND,US
93/H4 Golyama Kamchiya (riv.), Bul.
93/G5 Golyama Syutkya (peak), Bul.
93/G5 Golyam Perelik (peak), Bul.
72/C3 Golzow, Ger.
153/G3 Goma, Zaire
153/G3 Goma (int'l arpt.), Zaire
125/B4 Gomantong Caves, Malay.
70/C6 Gomaringen, Ger.
120/D2 Gomati (riv.), India
153/G2 Gombari, Zaire
152/C4 Gombe, Ang.
145/H4 Gombe, Nga.
153/G4 Gombe (riv.), Tanz.
152/C4 Gombe-Matadi, Zaire
153/G4 Gombe Nat'l Park, Tanz.
98/F1 Gomel', Bela.
98/E2 Gomel' Obl., Bela.
142/A4 Gomera (isl.), Canl.
53/S10 Gometz-le-Châtel, Fr.
188/B2 Gomez (peak), Tx,US
158/D2 Gómez Farías, Mex.
159/E3 Gómez Farías, Mex.
159/F4 Gómez Farías, Mex.
158/E3 Gómez Palacio, Mex.
105/H2 Gomīshān, Iran
72/B3 Gommern, Ger.
114/E5 Gomo, China
121/F4 Gomoh, India
81/F3 Goms, Swi.
80/E5 Goms (val.), Swi.
59/F4 Gomshall, Eng,UK
131/H2 Gona, PNG
105/J3 Gonābād, Iran
161/H2 Gonaïves, Haiti
155/F4 Gonarezhou Nat'l Park, Zim.
161/H2 Gonâve (gulf), Haiti
161/H2 Gonâve (isl.), Haiti
105/H2 Gonbad-e Qābūs, Iran
92/E1 Gönc, Hun.
167/E4 Gonçalves Dias, Braz.
82/B2 Goncelin, Fr.
120/C2 Gondā, India
118/B3 Gondal, India
149/H2 Gonder, Eth.
150/A2 Gonder (prov.), Eth.
149/H2 Gonder (reg.), Eth.
118/D3 Gondia, India
196/E3 Gondola Point, NB,Can
76/A2 Gondomar, Port.
76/A1 Gondomar, Sp.
80/B1 Gondrecourt-le-Château, Fr.
69/E6 Gondreville, Fr.
93/H5 Gönen, Turk.
53/T10 Gonesse, Fr.
82/C6 Gonfaron, Fr.
79/F2 Gonfreville-l'Orcher, Fr.
117/E4 Gong'an, China
117/F3 Gong'an, China
119/F2 Gongbo'gyamda, China
113/B2 Gongchangling, China
117/F4 Gongche, China
116/D2 Gongga (peak), China
121/H1 Gonggar, China
117/F4 Gongguan, China
108/E4 Gonghe, China
114/D3 Gongliu, China
152/D4 Gongo, Zaire
145/H4 Gongola (riv.), Nga.
145/H4 Gongola (state), Nga.
135/C1 Gongolgon, Austl.
117/G4 Gongping, China
119/G2 Gongshan Drungzu Nuzu Zizhixian, China
117/G2 Gongtian, China
116/D3 Gongwang (mts.), China
117/G3 Gongxi, China
115/C4 Gong Xian, China
115/F2 Gongzhuling, China
175/F2 Goñi, Uru.
151/B3 Gonja, Tanz.
116/C2 Gonjo, China
91/H3 Gónnoi, Gre.
112/B3 Gonohe, Japan
156/D4 Gonubie, SAfr.
195/G4 Gonvick, Mn,US
73/B4 Gönyű, Hun.
92/C2 Gonyű, Hun.
87/D3 Gonzaga, It.
125/C1 Gonzaga, Phil.
186/B2 Gonzales, Ca,US
202/C2 Gonzales, La,US
189/F3 Gonzales, Tx,US
164/C2 González, Col.
159/F4 González, Mex.
202/E2 Gonzalez, Fl,US
151/C2 Goobweyn, Som.
201/J2 Goochland, Va,US

137/J Goodenough (cape), Ant.
188/D2 Goodfellow A.F.B., Tx,US
198/D2 Good Hart, Mi,US
154/E5 Goodhope, Bots.
156/B4 Good Hope, Cape of, SAfr.
185/F2 Gooding, Id,US
203/H5 Goodland, Fl,US
190/D1 Goodland, Ks,US
191/G2 Goodman, Mo,US
198/B2 Goodman, Wi,US
134/E7 Goodna, Austl.
177/F4 Goodnews Bay, Ak,US
135/C1 Goodooga, Austl.
205/E6 Goodrich, Mi,US
194/D4 Goodrich, ND,US
189/G2 Goodrich, Tx,US
194/G3 Goodridge, Mn,US
194/C2 Good Spirit (lake), Sk,Can
186/E3 Goodsprings, Nv,US
193/G1 Good Thunder, Mn,US
193/J1 Goodview, Mn,US
200/D4 Goodwater, Al,US
190/D2 Goodwell, Ok,US
58/B3 Goodwick, Wal,UK
191/J3 Goodwin, Ar,US
156/B4 Goodwood, SAfr.
66/C4 Gooimeer (lake), Neth.
57/H4 Goole, Eng,UK
135/C2 Goolgowi, Austl.
135/D2 Gooloogong, Austl.
135/A2 Goolwa, Austl.
132/C4 Goomalling, Austl.
135/C1 Goombalie, Austl.
134/D4 Goombungee, Austl.
135/D1 Goondiwindi, Austl.
132/D4 Goongarrie Nat'l Park, Austl.
66/D4 Goor, Neth.
184/C3 Goose (lake), Ca, Or,US
206/C5 Goose (pt.), De,US
185/G2 Goose (cr.), Id,US
194/F4 Goose (riv.), ND,US
50/F3 Goose Bay, Can.
179/K3 Goose Bay-Happy Valley, Nf,Can
185/J1 Gooseberry (cr.), Wy,US
201/G4 Goose Creek, SC,US
175/N7 Goose Green, Falk.
57/F5 Goostrey, Eng,UK
121/G4 Gopālganj, Bang.
120/E2 Gopālganj, India
121/G3 Gopālpur, Bang.
120/D3 Gopat (riv.), India
122/F3 Gopichettipālaiyam, India
70/C5 Göppingen, Ger.
123/D4 Go Quao, Viet.
65/J3 Góra, Pol.
97/H5 Goradiz, Azer.
65/L3 Góra Kalwaria, Pol.
120/C4 Gorakhpur, India
120/D2 Gorakhpur, India
120/A3 Goras, India
92/D4 Goražde, Bosn.
175/S12 Gorchs, Arg.
184/F1 Gorda (pt.), Cuba
161/F3 Gorda (pt.), Nic.
161/F4 Gorda (pt.), Nic.
82/B5 Gordes, Fr.
104/B2 Gördes, Turk.
81/E5 Gordevio, Swi.
96/D1 Gordeyevka, Rus.
148/D3 Gordil, CAfr.
62/C4 Gørding, Den.
200/D4 Gordo, Al,US
81/E5 Gordola, Swi.
135/C4 Gordon, Austl.
135/C4 Gordon (lake), Austl.
54/D5 Gordon, Sc,UK
203/F2 Gordon, Al,US
201/F4 Gordon, Ga,US
192/D2 Gordon (cr.), Ne,US
130/C4 Gordon Downs, Austl.
194/B2 Gordon Ind. Res., Sk,Can
156/L11 Gordon's Bay, SAfr.
201/H1 Gordonsville, Va,US
134/B2 Gordonvale, Austl.
148/C4 Goré, Chad
149/G3 Gorē, Eth.
136/B4 Gore, N.Z.
59/G1 Gore (pt.), Eng,UK
177/H4 Gore (pt.), Ak,US
199/J3 Gore (mtn.), NY,US
201/H1 Gore, Va,US
198/E2 Gore Bay, On,Can
54/C5 Gorebridge, Sc,UK
185/F1 Goree, Tx,US
104/D1 Görele, Turk.
60/D4 Goresbridge, Ire.
200/C2 Goreville, Il,US
60/D4 Gorey, Ire.
78/C2 Gorey, Chl,UK
105/H2 Gorgān, Iran
105/H2 Gorgān (riv.), Iran
69/F4 Gorge du Loup, Lux.
82/C5 Gorges du Verdon, Fr.
142/D2 Gorges du Ziz, Mor.
144/B3 Gorgol (reg.), Mrta.
144/B2 Gorgol (riv.), Mrta.
86/C6 Gorgona (isl.), It.
86/C1 Gorgonzola, It.
149/H2 Gorgora, Eth.
192/E4 Gorham, Ks,US
196/B4 Gorham, Me,US
199/L2 Gorham, NH,US
97/H4 Gori, Geo.
66/B5 Gorinchem, Neth.
59/E3 Goring, Eng,UK
59/F5 Goring by Sea, Eng,UK
97/H5 Goris, Arm.
87/G1 Gorizia, It.
87/G1 Gorizia (prov.), It.
93/F3 Gorj (co.), Rom.
96/D1 Gorki, Bela.
94/J4 Gor'kiy (res.), Rus.
95/K4 Gor'kiy (Nizhniy Novgorod), Rus.
65/L4 Gorlice, Pol.
65/H3 Görlitz, Ger.
58/C2 Gorllwyn (mtn.), Wal,UK
72/B1 Gorlosen, Ger.
53/G4 Gorlovka, Ukr.
186/C3 Gorman, Ca,US
189/E1 Gorman, Tx,US
60/D2 Gormanston, Ire.
120/B2 Gormī, India
197/S8 Gormley, On,Can
93/G4 Gorna Oryakhovitsa, Bul.
80/D6 Gorner (glac.), It., Swi.
92/E3 Gornji Milanovac, Yugo.
92/C4 Gornji Vakuf, Bosn.
100/J4 Gorno-Altay Aut. Obl., Rus.
114/E1 Gorno-Altaysk, Rus.
100/H6 Gorno-Badakhstan Aut. Obl., Taj.
95/N4 Gornozavodsk, Rus.
96/F1 Gornyak, Rus.
99/J3 Gornyak, Ukr.
99/L3 Gornyatskiy, Rus.
109/L3 Gornyy, Rus.
97/H2 Gornyy Balykley, Rus.
109/H1 Gornyy Zerentuy, Rus.
150/B4 Goro, Eth.
87/F3 Goro, It.
149/H3 Goroch'an (peak), Eth.
98/C3 Gorodënka, Ukr.
95/J4 Gorodets, Rus.
98/F3 Gorodishche, Ukr.
98/F2 Gorodnya, Ukr.
63/N4 Gorodok, Bela.
98/B3 Gorodok, Ukr.
98/D3 Gorodok, Ukr.
99/L4 Gorodovikovsk, Rus.
127/G4 Gorogoro, Indo.
131/G1 Goroka, PNG
98/C2 Gorokhov, Ukr.
145/E3 Gorom Gorom, Burk.
155/F3 Goromonzi, Zim.
127/H4 Gorong (isl.), Indo.
155/G3 Gorongosa, Serra da (peak), Moz.
155/G3 Gorongoza, Moz.
155/G3 Gorongoza Nat'l Park, Moz.
127/F3 Gorontalo, Indo.
145/G3 Goronyo, Nga.
87/F3 Goro, Po di (riv.), It.
66/D3 Gorredijk, Neth.
105/G4 Gorreh, Iran
79/E4 Gorron, Fr.
58/B3 Gorseinon, Wal,UK
99/K2 Gorshechnoye, Rus.
99/K3 Gorskoye, Ukr.
66/D4 Gorssel, Neth.
205/B2 Gorst, Wa,US
60/B3 Gort, Ire.
60/B2 Gorteen, Ire.
56/A2 Gortin, NI,UK
189/H2 Gorum, La,US
80/E2 Görwihl, Ger.
99/K5 Goryachiy Klyuch, Rus.
98/D1 Goryn' (riv.), Bela., Ukr.
85/D2 Gorzano (peak), It.
72/C4 Görzig, Ger.
72/C3 Görzke, Ger.
65/H2 Gorzów (prov.), Pol.
65/H2 Gorzów Wielkopolski, Pol.
150/C3 Gos, Eth.
120/D2 Gosainganj, India
81/E4 Göschenen, Swi.
110/D3 Gōse, Japan
72/B5 Goseck, Ger.
111/F2 Gosen, Japan
57/G2 Gosforth, Eng,UK
98/D2 Goshcha, Ukr.
197/G3 Goshen, NS,Can
208/A2 Goshen, Ct,US
198/D4 Goshen, In,US
208/B1 Goshen, Ma,US
206/D5 Goshen, NJ,US
199/J4 Goshen, NY,US
185/H4 Goshen, Ut,US
192/B3 Goshen Hole (lowland), SD, Wy,US
112/B3 Goshogawara, Japan
185/F3 Goshute (dry lake), Nv,US
185/F3 Goshute (val.), Nv,US
185/F3 Goshute Ind. Res., Nv, Ut,US
67/H5 Goslar, Ger.
200/C3 Gosnell, Ar,US
92/B3 Gospić, Cro.
59/E5 Gosport, Eng,UK
202/E2 Gosport, Al,US
200/D1 Gosport, In,US
144/A3 Gossas, Sen.
81/F3 Gossau, Swi.
81/H4 Gossenass (Colle Isarco), It.
70/A4 Gossersweiler-Stein, Ger.
72/C6 Gössnitz, Ger.
97/M2 Gostepriimnyy, Rus.
63/N2 Gostilitsy, Rus.
99/J2 Gostishchevo, Rus.
92/E5 Gostivar, Macd.
98/F2 Gostomel', Ukr.
65/J3 Gostyń, Pol.
65/K2 Gostynin, Pol.
150/B3 Gota, Eth.
62/G2 Göta (riv.), Swe.
62/E3 Götaland (reg.), Swe.
190/E3 Gotebo, Ok,US
62/D3 Göteborg, Swe.
62/D2 Göteborg och Bohus (co.), Swe.
148/A4 Gotel (mts.), Camr., Nga.
111/F3 Gotemba, Japan
62/E2 Götene, Swe.
67/H7 Gotha, Ger.
145/F3 Gothèye, Niger
62/G3 Gotland (co.), Swe.
62/G3 Gotland (isl.), Swe.
110/A4 Gotō (isls.), Japan
93/F5 Gotse Delchev, Bul.
63/H2 Gotska Sandön (isl.), Swe.
63/H2 Gotska Sandön Nat'l Park, Swe.
110/C3 Gōtsu, Japan
80/D1 Gottenheim, Ger.
67/G5 Göttingen, Ger.
81/E2 Gottmadingen, Ger.
86/D2 Gottolengo, It.
81/F3 Götzis, Aus.
78/B4 Gouarec, Fr.
113/A2 Goubangzi, China
66/B4 Gouda, Neth.
156/B4 Gouda, SAfr.
144/B3 Goudiry, Sen.
145/H3 Goudoumaria, Niger
78/A4 Gouesnou, Fr.
78/A4 Gouessant (riv.), Fr.
78/C4 Gouet (riv.), Fr.
50/J8 Gough (isl.), StH.
201/F4 Gough, Ga,US
179/J4 Gouin (res.), Qu,Can
198/D1 Goulais (pt.), On,Can
198/D1 Goulais (riv.), On,Can
135/D2 Goulburn, Austl.
128/E2 Goulburn (isls.), Austl.
135/D2 Goulburn (riv.), Austl.
137/P Gould (coast), Ant.
132/C3 Gould (peak), Austl.
191/J4 Gould, Ar,US
190/E3 Gould, Ok,US
188/E2 Gouldbusk, Tx,US
195/M4 Gould City, Mi,US
197/L2 Goulds, Nf,Can
196/C3 Gouldsboro, Me,US
206/C1 Gouldsboro, Pa,US
183/L2 Gouldtown, Sk,Can
148/B2 Goulfey, Camr.
142/C3 Goulimine, Mor.
142/D3 Goulmima, Mor.
117/F4 Goulou (mts.), China
116/E3 Goulou (peak), China
144/D3 Goumbou, Mali
91/H2 Gouménissa, Gre.
144/E2 Goundam, Mali
148/C3 Goundi, Chad
148/B3 Gounou Gaya, Chad
144/B3 Gouraye, Mrta.
145/E3 Gourcy, Burk.
74/D4 Gourdon, Fr.
145/H3 Gouré, Niger
78/B4 Gourin, Fr.
156/C4 Gourits (riv.), SAfr.
145/F3 Gourma (prov.), Burk.
145/F3 Gourma (reg.), Burk.
145/E2 Gourma-Rharous, Mali
68/A5 Gournay-en-Bray, Fr.
146/C5 Gouro, Chad
54/B5 Gourock, Sc,UK
53/T9 Goussainville, Fr.
171/E3 Gouvêa, Braz.
76/B2 Gouveia, Port.
199/J2 Gouverneur, NY,US
68/B5 Gouvieux, Fr.
69/E3 Gouvy, Belg.
162/F4 Gouyave, Gren.
194/B2 Govan, Sk,Can
120/A2 Govardhan, India
190/D1 Gove, Ks,US
98/C3 Goverla (peak), Ukr.
167/E4 Governador Archer, Braz.
173/G3 Governador Celso Ramos, Braz.
167/G4 Governador Dix-Sept Rosado, Braz.
167/E4 Governador Eugênio Barros, Braz.
171/E3 Governador Valadares, Braz.
195/K4 Government (peak), Mi,US
192/C1 Government (hill), SD,US
192/B3 Government (peak), Wy,US
184/C1 Government Camp, Or,US
125/D4 Governor Generoso, Phil.
207/J9 Governors (isl.), NY,US
162/B1 Governors Harbour, Bahm.
108/D3 Govĭ Altayn (mts.), Mong.
120/C3 Govindgarh, India
122/D2 Govind Sāgar (res.), India
199/G3 Gowanda, NY,US
107/H3 Gowd-e-Zereh (lake), Afg.
58/B3 Gower (pen.), Wal,UK
191/G1 Gower, Mo,US
105/J4 Gowk, Iran
60/C2 Gowna, Lough (lake), Ire.
60/C4 Gowran, Ire.
193/G2 Gowrie, Ia,US
54/C4 Gowrie, Carse of (plain), Sc,UK
135/C4 Gowrie Park, Austl.
57/H4 Goxhill, Eng,UK
172/E4 Goya, Arg.
74/A4 Goyen (riv.), Fr.
168/B3 Goyllarisquizga, Peru
93/K5 Göynük, Turk.
57/F5 Goyt (riv.), Eng,UK
99/K5 Goytkhskiy (pass), Rus.
111/M9 Gozaisho-yama (peak), Japan
148/D2 Goz Beïda, Chad
104/D2 Gözeli, Turk.
114/D4 Gozha (lake), China
84/H7 Gozo (isl.), Malta
148/D4 Gozobangi (rapids), CAfr.
148/D3 Goz Sassulko (dune), CAfr.
86/B1 Gozzano, It.
156/D4 Graaff-Reinet, SAfr.
66/D4 Graafschap (reg.), Neth.
66/B6 Graauw, Neth.
70/D6 Graben, Ger.
156/B2 Graberberg (peak), Namb.
156/L11 Grabouw, SAfr.
64/F2 Grabow, Ger.
81/F3 Grabs, Swi.
167/E4 Graça Aranha, Braz.
92/B3 Gračac, Cro.
92/D3 Gračanica, Bosn.
185/H2 Grace, Id,US
194/E4 Grace City, ND,US
79/F2 Grace, Côte de (coast), Fr.
199/H1 Gracefield, Qu,Can
134/C3 Gracemere, Austl.
191/E3 Gracemont, Ok,US
203/F2 Graceville, Fl,US
194/F5 Graceville, Mn,US
80/D5 Grächen, Swi.
99/M5 Grachëvka, Rus.
97/J2 Grachev Kust, Rus.
160/D3 Gracias, Hon.
161/F3 Gracias a Dios (cape), Nic.
77/S12 Graciosa (isl.), Azor.,Port.
92/D3 Gradačac, Bosn.
166/D4 Gradaús, Braz.
87/G1 Gradisca d'Isonzo, It.
99/G3 Gradizhsk, Ukr.
87/G1 Grado, It.
76/B1 Grado, Sp.
203/E2 Grady, Al,US
191/J3 Grady, Ar,US
190/C3 Grady, NM,US
191/F3 Grady, Ok,US
193/G2 Graettinger, Ia,US
71/E6 Gräfelfing, Ger.
71/G5 Grafenau, Ger.
70/E3 Gräfenberg, Ger.
72/C4 Gräfenhainichen, Ger.
70/D3 Gräfenrheinfeld, Ger.
72/A6 Gräfenroda, Ger.
72/A5 Gräfentonna, Ger.
71/E3 Grafenwöhr, Ger.
86/C2 Graffignana, It.
59/F2 Grafham Water (lake), Eng,UK
72/B6 Gräfinau-Angstedt, Ger.
71/E6 Grafing bei München, Ger.
62/C1 Gråfjell (peak), Nor.
189/E1 Graford, Tx,US
70/E6 Grafrath, Ger.
135/E1 Grafton, Austl.
134/B2 Grafton (pass.), Austl.
196/D2 Grafton, NB,Can
191/J1 Grafton, Il,US
208/C1 Grafton, Ma,US
194/F3 Grafton, ND,US
208/E5 Grafton, Oh,US
198/C3 Grafton, Wi,US
201/G1 Grafton, WV,US
85/E6 Gragnano, It.
178/C3 Graham (isl.), BC,Can
179/S7 Graham (isl.), NW,Can
195/J3 Graham, On,Can
187/H4 Graham (mt.), Az,US
203/G3 Graham, Fl,US
196/C3 Graham (lake), Me,US
201/H2 Graham, NC,US
191/F3 Graham, Ok,US
189/E1 Graham, Tx,US
205/C3 Graham, Wa,US
100/G1 Graham Bell (isl.), Rus.
194/E2 Grahamdale, Mb,Can
204/F8 Graham-Florence, Ca,US
137/V Graham Land (reg.), Ant.
156/D4 Grahamstown, SAfr.
199/J4 Grahamsville, NY,US
88/E1 Graian (mts.), Fr., It.
82/C1 Graian Alps (range), Fr., It.
60/D4 Graiguenamanagh, Ire.
59/G4 Grain, Eng,UK
81/H3 Grainau, Ger.
144/C5 Grain Coast (reg.), Libr.
190/D1 Grainfield, Ks,US
124/F5 Grajagan, Indo.
167/E4 Grajaú, Braz.
167/E4 Grajaú (riv.), Braz.
65/M2 Grajewo, Pol.
62/C4 Gram, Den.
92/F4 Gramada, Bul.
71/H6 Gramastetten, Aus.
74/D4 Gramat, Fr.
74/D4 Gramat (plat.), Fr.
72/B5 Gramme (riv.), Ger.
82/D5 Grammont, Mont (mtn.), Fr.
54/B3 Grampian (mts.), Sc,UK
54/D2 Grampian (reg.), Sc,UK
135/B3 Grampians Nat'l Park, Austl.
135/B3 Grampians, The (mts.), Austl.
66/D3 Gramsbergen, Neth.
91/G2 Gramsh, Alb.
72/E1 Gramzow, Ger.
62/D1 Gran, Nor.
82/D4 Grana (riv.), It.
164/C4 Granada, Col.
160/E4 Granada, Nic.
76/D4 Granada, Sp.
190/C1 Granada, Co,US
142/A3 Granadilla de Abona, Canl.
158/C2 Granados, Mex.
175/K7 Gran Altiplanicie Central (plat.), Arg.
60/C2 Granard, Ire.
87/E3 Granarolo dell'Emilia, It.
175/K7 Gran Bajo de San Julián (val.), Arg.
174/C5 Gran Bajo Oriental (val.), Arg.
189/F1 Granbury, Tx,US
189/E1 Granbury (lake), Tx,US
182/E3 Granby (riv.), BC,Can
196/A3 Granby, Qu,Can
192/B3 Granby, Co,US
192/B3 Granby (lake), Co,US
208/B1 Granby, Ma,US
191/G2 Granby, Mo,US
142/B4 Gran Canaria (int'l arpt.), Canl.
142/B4 Gran Canaria (isl.), Canl.
172/D2 Gran Chaco (reg.), Arg., Par.
168/B3 Gran Chavín (dept.), Peru
196/E2 Grand (lake), NB,Can
197/J1 Grand (lake), Nf,Can
197/T9 Grand (isl.), On,Can
198/F2 Grand (riv.), On,Can
179/J3 Grand (riv.), Qu,Can
115/D4 Grand (can.), China
56/B5 Grand (can.), Ire.
151/B2 Grand (falls), Kenya
200/B3 Grand (prairie), Ar,US
187/F2 Grand (canyon), Az,US
187/F3 Grand (canyon), Az,US
193/H4 Grand (riv.), Ia, Mo,US
202/B3 Grand (lake), La,US
202/C3 Grand (lake), La,US
195/L4 Grand (isl.), Mi,US
198/E2 Grand (lake), Mi,US
198/C3 Grand (riv.), Mi,US
197/T9 Grand (isl.), NY,US
198/D4 Grand (lake), Oh,US
208/G5 Grand (riv.), Oh,US
192/D1 Grand (riv.), SD,US
144/E5 Grand Aféri, IvC.
80/D2 Grand Alsace (can.), Fr.
82/C1 Grand Arc (mtn.), Fr.
166/D5 Grandaús (mts.), Braz.
162/B1 Grand Bahama (isl.), Bahm.
197/K2 Grand Bank, Nf,Can
144/C5 Grand Bassa (co.), Libr.
144/E5 Grand-Bassam, IvC.
196/D3 Grand Bay, NB,Can
202/D2 Grand Bay, Al,US
191/H4 Grand Bayou, La,US
82/C4 Grand Bérard (mtn.), Fr.
205/E6 Grand Blanc, Mi,US
78/C6 Grand Brière (swamp), Fr.
199/H2 Grand Calumet (isl.), Qu,Can
79/D2 Grandcamp-Maisy, Fr.
202/B1 Grand Cane, La,US
187/F2 Grand Canyon, Az,US
187/F2 Grand Canyon Nat'l Park, Az,US
144/C5 Grand Cape Mount (co.), Libr.
161/F2 Grand Cayman (isl.), Cay.
178/E3 Grand Centre, Ab,Can
144/C5 Grand Cess, Libr.
80/C2 Grand-Charmont, Fr.
189/H3 Grand Chenier, La,US
80/B6 Grand Colombier (mtn.), Fr.
80/D6 Grand Combin (peak), Swi.
182/E4 Grand Coulee, Wa,US
182/E4 Grand Coulee (dam), Wa,US
80/C4 Grandcour, Swi.
79/G2 Grand-Couronne, Fr.
80/C2 Grand Drumont (mtn.), Fr.
175/K7 Grande (bay), Arg.
175/K8 Grande (riv.), Arg.
172/D1 Grande (riv.), Bol.
170/B4 Grande (isl.), Braz.
171/N8 Grande (isl.), Braz.
166/C3 Grande (lake), Braz.
166/A2 Grande (mts.), Braz.
167/F4 Grande (mts.), Braz.
170/D1 Grande (riv.), Braz.
170/D4 Grande (riv.), Braz.
172/B3 Grande (pt.), Chile
160/D3 Grande (riv.), Guat.
85/D3 Grande (peak), It.
159/Q9 Grande (riv.), Mex.
161/G4 Grande (pt.), Pan.
175/T11 Grande (stream), Uru.
190/C2 Grande (mtn.), NM,US
196/A2 Grande-Anse, Qu,Can
193/G3 Grand, East Fork (riv.), Ia, Mo,US
82/C3 Grande Autane (mtn.), Fr.
178/E3 Grande Cache, Ab,Can
196/E1 Grande-Cascapédia, Qu,Can
82/C2 Grande Casse, Pointe de la (peak), Fr.
157/G5 Grande Comore (isl.), Com.
90/C1 Grande, Corno (peak), It.
166/C3 Grande de Curuaí (lake), Braz.
166/D3 Grande de Gurupá (isl.), Braz.
166/A3 Grande de Manacapuru, Braz.
165/F5 Grande de Manacapuru (lake), Braz.
161/E3 Grande de Matagalpa (riv.), Nic.
80/D5 Grande Dixence, Barrage de la (dam), Swi.
197/G2 Grande-Entrée, Qu,Can
83/D2 Grande, Mare (bay), It.
90/C4 Grande, Monte (peak), It.
194/F3 Grande Pointe, Mb,Can
178/E3 Grande Prairie, Ab,Can
78/D5 Grande-Res-de-Vioreau (res.), Fr.
146/B5 Grand Erg de Bilma (des.), Niger
143/E3 Grand Erg Occidental (des.), Alg.
143/G3 Grand Erg Oriental (des.), Alg., Tun.
176/G7 Grande, Rio (riv.), US, Mex.
196/E1 Grande-Rivière, Qu,Can
162/C3 Grande Rivière du Nord, Haiti
184/E1 Grande Ronde (riv.), Or, Wa,US
82/C2 Grande Rousses (range), Fr.
161/H2 Grande Saline, Haiti
82/D1 Grande Sassière, Aiguille de la (peak), Fr.
82/C4 Grande Séolane (mtn.), Fr.
186/E4 Gran Desierto (des.), Mex.
80/D6 Grandes Jorasses (peak), It.
68/B1 Grande-Synthe, Fr.
162/F3 Grande-Terre (isl.), Guad.
196/E1 Grande-Vallée, Qu,Can
82/D1 Grand Eyvia (riv.), It.
196/D2 Grand Falls, NB,Can
197/K1 Grand Falls, Nf,Can
158/E2 Grandfalls, Tx,US
191/E3 Grandfield, Ok,US
182/E3 Grand Forks, BC,Can
194/F4 Grand Forks, ND,US
194/F4 Grand Forks A.F.B., ND,US
68/B2 Grand-Fort-Philippe, Fr.
78/D5 Grand-Fougeray, Fr.
68/B5 Grandfresnoy, Fr.
82/C2 Grand Galibier (mtn.), Fr.
161/H2 Grand Goâve, Haiti
199/J3 Grand Gorge, NY,US
196/D3 Grand Harbour, NB,Can
198/C3 Grand Haven, Mi,US
191/J2 Grandin, Mo,US
192/E3 Grand Island, Ne,US
202/D3 Grand Isle, La,US
199/K2 Grand Isle, Vt,US
144/D5 Grand Jide (co.), Libr.
185/J4 Grand Junction, Co,US
200/C3 Grand Junction, Tn,US
144/D5 Grand-Lahou, IvC.
196/D3 Grand Manan (isl.), NB,Can
194/F2 Grand Marais, Mb,Can
198/D1 Grand Marais, Mi,US
195/J4 Grand Marais, Mn,US
68/C6 Grand Marin (riv.), Fr.
198/B3 Grand Marsh, Wi,US
193/H2 Grand Meadow, Mn,US
196/A2 Grand-Mère, Qu,Can
78/C5 Grand Mont, Pointe du (pt.), Fr.
80/C5 Grand Mont Ruan (mtn.), Fr.
182/C4 Grand Mound, Wa,US
80/D5 Grand Muveran (peak), Swi.
194/C5 Grand, North Fork (riv.), SD,US
76/A3 Grândola, Port.
82/C4 Grand Parpaillon (mtn.), Fr.
82/B2 Grand Pic de Belledonne (peak), Fr.
145/F5 Grand-Popo, Ben.
195/K4 Grand Portage, Mn,US
195/J3 Grand Portage Ind. Res., Mn,US
195/K4 Grand Portage Nat'l Mon., Mn,US
198/C3 Grand Portal (pt.), Mi,US
188/L7 Grand Prairie, Tx,US
69/D5 Grandpré, Fr.
196/E3 Grand Pré Nat'l Hist. Park, NS,Can
82/D3 Grand Queyron (mtn.), Fr.
198/D3 Grand Rapids, Mi,US
195/L5 Grand Rapids (dam), Mi,US
195/H4 Grand Rapids, Mn,US
194/E4 Grand Rapids, ND,US
82/A5 Grand Rhône (riv.), Fr.
192/C1 Grand River Nat'l Grsld., SD,US
184/B1 Grand Ronde, Or,US
182/F4 Grand Ronde (riv.), Or,US
78/C2 Grand Russel (chan.), Chl,UK
189/G1 Grand Saline, Tx,US
166/C1 Grand Santi, FrG.
80/C4 Grandson, Swi.
192/C1 Grand, South Fork (riv.), SD,US
80/C4 Grand Taureau (mtn.), Fr.
185/H2 Grand Teton (peak), Wy,US
185/H2 Grand Teton Nat'l Park, Wy,US
193/K5 Grand Tower, Il,US
198/D2 Grand Traverse (bay), Mi,US
162/D2 Grand Turk, Trks.
53/M6 Grand Union (can.), Eng,UK
197/Q8 Grand Valley, On,Can
82/B3 Grand Veymont (mtn.), Fr.
194/D2 Grandview, Mb,Can
184/E2 Grand View, Id,US
201/E1 Grandview, Oh,US
189/F1 Grandview, Tx,US
182/E4 Grandview, Wa,US
199/G4 Grandview Park, Pa,US
191/F1 Grandview Plaza, Ks,US
80/C2 Grandvillars, Fr.
198/D3 Grandville, Mi,US
68/A4 Grandvilliers, Fr.
82/A3 Grane, Fr.
174/C2 Graneros, Chile
62/E1 Granfjället (peak), Swe.
133/M8 Grange, Austl.
60/B2 Grange (riv.), Ire.
57/F3 Grange, Eng,UK
80/C5 Grange, Mont de (mtn.), Fr.
54/C4 Grangemouth, Sc,UK
177/L3 Granger (mtn.), Yk,Can
193/K2 Granger, In,US
189/F2 Granger, Tx,US
182/D4 Granger, Wa,US
62/F1 Grängesberg, Swe.
80/C1 Granges-sur-Vologne, Fr.
184/E1 Grangeville, Id,US
82/B2 Granier (mtn.), Fr.
82/B2 Granier, Col du (pass), Fr.
192/A4 Granite, Co,US
182/G4 Granite (peak), Id,US
182/G5 Granite (peak), Id,US
183/J4 Granite (mtn.), Mt,US
185/G1 Granite (peak), Mt,US
185/J1 Granite (peak), Mt,US
191/E3 Granite, Ok,US
185/K1 Granite (pass), Wy,US
182/B2 Granite Bay, BC,Can
192/B3 Granite Canon, Wy,US
200/B1 Granite City, Il,US
195/G5 Granite Falls, Mn,US
189/E2 Granite Shoals, Tx,US
191/J2 Graniteville, Mo,US
136/B3 Granity, N.Z.
167/F3 Granja, Braz.
174/D5 Gran Laguna Salada (lake), Arg.
191/G3 Grannis, Ar,US
77/G2 Granollers, Sp.
77/L6 Granollers, Sp.
86/A1 Gran Paradiso Nat'l Park, It.
161/H2 Gran Piedra (hill), Cuba
75/J3 Gran Pilastro (peak), It.
187/J3 Gran Quivira, NM,US
82/B5 Grans, Fr.
165/F3 Gran Sabana, La (plain), Ven.
85/D3 Gran Sasso d'Italia (mts.), It.
72/C5 Granschütz, Ger.
72/D1 Gransee, Ger.
200/D3 Grant, Al,US
190/B1 Grant, Co,US
198/D3 Grant, Mi,US
185/G1 Grant, Mt,US
192/D3 Grant, Ne,US
184/D4 Grant (mt.), Nv,US
184/F4 Grant (range), Nv,US
77/Y16 Gran Tarajal, Canl.,Sp.
193/G3 Grant City, Mo,US
57/H6 Grantham, Eng,UK
195/J5 Granton, Wi,US
54/C2 Grantown-on-Spey, Sc,UK
201/M7 Grant Park, Ga,US
187/J3 Grants, NM,US
201/J3 Grantsboro, NC,US
193/H1 Grantsburg, Wi,US
183/G4 Grantsdale, Mt,US
184/B2 Grants Pass, Or,US
201/G1 Grantsville, WV,US
200/E4 Grantville, Ga,US
168/B2 Gran Vilaya, Peru
178/F3 Granville (lake), Mb,Can
78/D3 Granville, Fr.
193/K3 Granville, Il,US
208/B1 Granville, Ma,US
199/K3 Granville, NY,US
196/E3 Granville Ferry, NS,Can
189/G2 Grapeland, Tx,US
205/B3 Grapeview, Wa,US
205/B3 Grapeview-Allyn, Wa,US
191/H3 Grapevine, Ar,US
189/F1 Grapevine, Tx,US
188/K6 Grapevine (lake), Tx,US
67/F2 Grasberg, Ger.
71/E6 Grasbrunn, Ger.
70/B3 Grasellenbach, Ger.
157/E2 Graskop, SAfr.
182/G3 Grasmere, BC,Can
156/P13 Grasmere, SAfr.
57/E3 Grasmere, Eng,UK
62/H1 Gräsö (isl.), Swe.
206/B6 Grasonville, Md,US
205/P15 Grass (lake), Il,US
85/G6 Grassano, It.
185/J2 Grass Creek, Wy,US
82/C5 Grasse, Fr.
197/R9 Grassie, On,Can
87/E5 Grassina, It.
57/G3 Grassington, Eng,UK
194/A3 Grasslands Nat'l Park, Sk,Can
183/K4 Grass Range, Mt,US
184/C4 Grass Valley, Ca,US
135/C4 Grassy, Austl.
203/H5 Grassy (key), Fl,US
201/G1 Grassy (mtn.), WV,US
194/C4 Grassy Butte, ND,US
183/J3 Grassy Lake, Ab,Can
63/T8 Græsted, Den.
62/E2 Grästorp, Swe.
197/L1 Grates (pt.), Nf,Can
197/L1 Grates Cove, Nf,Can
92/B2 Gratkorn, Aus.
206/B2 Gratz, Pa,US
168/A2 Grau (dept.), Peru
81/F4 Graubünden (canton), Swi.
74/E5 Graulhet, Fr.
72/D6 Graupa, Ger.
77/F1 Graus, Sp.
66/C5 Grave, Neth.
81/F5 Gravedona, It.
194/A3 Gravelbourg, Sk,Can
195/L5 Gravel I. Nat'l Wild. Ref., Wi,US
68/B2 Gravelines, Fr.
86/B1 Gravellona Toce, It.
191/H3 Gravelly, Ar,US
155/F4 Gravelotte, SAfr.
199/G2 Gravenhurst, On,Can
70/B2 Grävenwiesbach, Ger.
192/D1 Grave of Sitting Bull, SD,US
53/Q7 Gravesend, Eng,UK
82/A5 Graveson, Fr.
68/A5 Gravigny, Fr.
85/G6 Gravina (riv.), It.
85/G6 Gravina di Puglia, It.
161/H2 Gravois, Pointe à (pt.), Haiti
80/B3 Gray, Fr.
201/F4 Gray, Ga,US
200/E2 Gray, Ky,US
196/B4 Gray, Me,US
184/B2 Grayback (mtn.), Or,US
182/B4 Grayland, Wa,US
177/F3 Grayling, Ak,US
198/D2 Grayling, Mi,US
53/P7 Grays, Eng,UK
185/H2 Grays (lake), Id,US
182/B4 Grays (har.), Wa,US
205/P15 Grayslake, Il,US
201/F1 Grayson, Ky,US
202/B1 Grayson, La,US
200/D4 Graysville, Al,US
200/D1 Grayville, Il,US
75/L3 Graz, Aus.
76/C4 Grazalema, Sp.
85/E5 Grazzanise, It.
62/D2 Greåker, Nor.
82/B6 Gréasque, Fr.
135/C4 Great (lake), Austl.
60/B6 Great (isl.), Ire.
50/E3 Great (lakes), NAm.
184/E3 Great (basin), US
192/D2 Great (plains), US
183/J4 Great (falls), Mt,US
196/B4 Great (bay), NH,US
206/D5 Great (bay), NJ,US
207/J8 Great (falls), NJ,US
162/B1 Great Abaco (isl.), Bahm.
206/D3 Great Adventure/Six Flags, NJ,US
65/L5 Great Alföld (plain), Hun.
205/L12 Great America, Ca,US
205/Q15 Great America (Six Flags), Il,US
132/E5 Great Australian (bight), Austl.
162/B1 Great Bahama (bank), Bahm.
59/F2 Great Barford, Eng,UK
134/B1 Great Barrier (reef), Austl.
136/C2 Great Barrier (isl.), N.Z.
134/B2 Great Barrier Reef Marine Park, Austl.
208/A1 Great Barrington, Ma,US
59/G2 Great Barton, Eng,UK
180/D4 Great Basin Nat'l Park, Nv,US
185/F4 Great Basin Nat'l Park, Nv,US
186/E1 Great Basin Nat'l Park, Nv,US
178/D2 Great Bear (lake), NW,Can
191/E1 Great Bend, Ks,US
199/J2 Great Bend, NY,US
103/C4 Great Bitter (lake), Egypt
53/M8 Great Bookham, Eng,UK
156/C3 Great Brak (riv.), SAfr.
55/L9 Great Britain (isl.), UK
206/D5 Great Cedar (swamp), NJ,US
51/P5 Great Coco (isl.), Burma
59/G2 Great Cornard, Eng,UK
54/B5 Great Cumbrae (isl.), Sc,UK
201/J2 Great Dismal Swamp Nat'l Wild. Ref., NC, Va,US
185/J2 Great Divide (basin), Wy,US
135/C2 Great Dividing (range), Austl.
57/H4 Great Driffield, Eng,UK
59/G3 Great Dunmow, Eng,UK
206/D5 Great Egg (har.), NJ,US
206/D4 Great Egg Harbor (riv.), NJ,US
145/F5 Greater Accra (reg.), Gha.
176/J8 Greater Antilles (isls.), NAm.
97/L3 Greater Barsuki (des.), Kaz.
199/G3 Greater Buffalo (int'l arpt.), NY,US
200/E1 Greater Cincinnati (int'l arpt.), Oh,US
53/P7 Greater London (co.), Eng,UK
57/F5 Greater Manchester (co.), Eng,UK
208/G7 Greater Pittsburgh (int'l arpt.), Pa,US
199/H3 Greater Rochester (int'l arpt.), NY,US
126/C4 Greater Sunda (isls.), Indo.
187/G5 Greaterville, Az,US
136/C1 Great Exhibition (bay), N.Z.
162/C2 Great Exuma (isl.), Bahm.
194/F2 Great Falls, Mb,Can
183/J4 Great Falls, Mt,US
201/G3 Great Falls, SC,US
156/D4 Great Fish (pt.), SAfr.
156/D4 Great Fish (riv.), SAfr.
206/D1 Great Gorge/Vernon Valley & Action Park, NJ,US
59/F2 Great Gransden, Eng,UK
162/B1 Great Guana (cay), Bahm.
57/G2 Greatham, Eng,UK
57/F4 Great Harwood, Eng,UK
102/G6 Great Himalaya (range), Asia
162/C2 Great Inagua (isl.), Bahm.
118/A2 Great Indian (des.), India, Pak.
156/C3 Great Karoo (reg.), SAfr.
156/D4 Great Kei (riv.), SAfr.
193/L2 Great Lakes Nav. Trg. Ctr., Il,US
205/Q15 Great Lakes Nav. Trg. Ctr., Il,US
58/D2 Great Malvern, Eng,UK
198/D4 Great Miami (riv.), Oh,US
59/E3 Great Milton, Eng,UK
197/J2 Great Miquelon (isl.), StP.
58/B5 Great Mis Tor (hill), Eng,UK
196/C3 Great Moose (lake), Me,US
124/B2 Great Mosque (Masjid Raya), Indo.
207/E2 Great Neck, NY,US
119/F6 Great Nicobar (isl.), India
59/G1 Great Ouse (riv.), Eng,UK
135/C4 Great Oyster (bay), Austl.
207/F2 Great Peconic (bay), NY,US
201/H4 Great Pee Dee (riv.), SC,US
207/H8 Great Piece Meadows, NJ,US
153/G4 Great Rift (val.), Afr.
151/A3 Great Ruaha (riv.), Tanz.
199/J3 Great Sacandaga (lake), NY,US
80/D6 Great Saint Bernard (pass), Swi., It.
162/B1 Great Sale (cay), Bahm.
185/G3 Great Salt (lake), Ut,US
185/G3 Great Salt Lake (des.), Ut,US
191/E2 Great Salt Plains (lake), Ok,US
183/K2 Great Sand (hills), Sk,Can
190/B2 Great Sand Dunes Nat'l Mon., Co,US
146/E2 Great Sand Sea (des.), Egypt, Libya
132/D2 Great Sandy (des.), Austl.
134/D4 Great Sandy Nat'l Park, Austl.
144/B4 Great Scarcies (riv.), Gui., SLeo.
59/G2 Great Shelford, Eng,UK
57/G3 Great Shunner Fell (mtn.), Eng,UK
178/E2 Great Slave (lake), NW,Can
200/F3 Great Smoky Mts. Nat'l Park, NC, Tn,US
207/E2 Great South (bay), NY,US
59/G4 Great Stour (riv.), Eng,UK
206/D2 Great Swamp Nat'l Wild. Ref., NJ,US
123/B3 Great Tenasserim (riv.), Burma
58/B5 Great Torrington, Eng,UK
133/F3 Great Victoria (des.), Austl.
133/E4 Great Victoria Des. Nat. Rsv., Austl.
196/F3 Great Village, NS,Can
115/B3 Great Wall (ruins), China
53/P7 Great Warley, Eng,UK
196/D3 Great Wass (isl.), Me,US
135/C4 Great Western Tiers (mts.), Austl.
203/H5 Great White Heron Nat'l Wild. Ref., Fl,US
156/B4 Great Winterhoek (peak), SAfr.
58/D2 Great Witley, Eng,UK
59/H1 Great Yarmouth, Eng,UK
64/A2 Great Yarmouth, Eng,UK
105/E2 Great Zab (riv.), Iraq
155/F4 Great Zimbabwe (ruins), Zim.
70/C2 Grebenhain, Ger.
98/G2 Grebënka, Ukr.
98/F3 Grebënki, Ukr.
67/G6 Grebenstein, Ger.
145/H2 Grébon (peak), Niger
103/D2 Greco (cape), Cyp.
175/F2 Greco, Uru.
85/D4 Greco, Monte (peak), It.
71/E6 Greding, Ger.
76/C2 Gredos (range), Sp.
79/D6 Grée (riv.), Fr.
91/G3 Greece
192/B3 Greeley, Co,US
191/G1 Greeley, Ks,US
192/E3 Greeley Center (Greeley), Ne,US
192/E3 Greeley (Greeley Center), Ne,US
201/H4 Greeleyville, SC,US
179/S6 Greely (fjord), NW,Can
135/D3 Green (cape), Austl.
203/H3 Green (swamp), Fl,US
193/K2 Green (riv.), Il,US
200/D2 Green (riv.), Ky,US
196/B3 Green (mtn.), Me,US
195/K4 Green, Mi,US
195/P6 Green (lake), Mn,US
201/H3 Green (swamp), NC,US
184/B2 Green, Or,US
208/C2 Green (st. arpt.), RI,US
189/F3 Green, Tx,US
185/H4 Green (riv.), Ut,US
199/K3 Green (mts.), Vt,US
205/D3 Green (riv.), Wa,US
195/L5 Green (bay), Wi,US
198/B3 Green (lake), Wi,US
178/E4 Green (riv.), Wy,US
186/C3 Greenacres, Ca,US
203/H4 Greenacres City, Fl,US
193/K1 Green Bay, Wi,US
195/L5 Green Bay Nat'l Wild. Ref., Wi,US
201/J1 Greenbelt, Md,US
206/B6 Greenbelt Park, Md,US
185/J3 Green, Blacks Fork (riv.), Wy,US
191/H3 Greenbrier, Ar,US
201/H1 Greenbrier (riv.), WV,US
208/D1 Greenbush, Ma,US
196/C3 Greenbush, Me,US
194/F3 Greenbush, Mn,US
132/C5 Greenbushes, Austl.
56/B1 Greencastle, Ire.
198/C5 Greencastle, In,US
193/H3 Greencastle, Mo,US
199/H5 Greencastle, Pa,US
193/H3 Green City, Mo,US
203/H3 Green Cove Springs, Fl,US
206/D5 Green Creek, NJ,US
205/Q14 Greendale, Wi,US
193/H2 Greene, Ia,US
196/B3 Greene, Me,US
199/J3 Greene, NY,US
208/C2 Greene, RI,US
201/F2 Greeneville, Tn,US
196/E3 Greenfield, NS,Can
186/B2 Greenfield, Ca,US
193/G3 Greenfield, Ia,US
200/B1 Greenfield, Il,US
198/D5 Greenfield, In,US
199/K3 Greenfield, Ma,US
191/H2 Greenfield, Mo,US
198/E5 Greenfield, Oh,US
200/C2 Greenfield, Tn,US
205/P14 Greenfield, Wi,US
197/P7 Greenfield Park, Qu,Can
208/G6 Greenford, Oh,US
191/H2 Green Forest, Ar,US
206/B5 Green Haven, Md,US
200/D2 Green Hill, Tn,US
56/C2 Greenisland, NI,UK
189/F3 Green Lake, Tx,US
193/K2 Green Lake, Wi,US
50/G2 Greenland (dpcy.), Den.
176/R2 Greenland (sea), NAm.
195/K4 Greenland, Mi,US
176/N2 Greenland (Kalaallit Nunaat), Den.
206/C3 Green Lane (res.), Pa,US
54/D5 Greenlaw, Sc,UK
191/F1 Greenleaf, Ks,US
54/C6 Green Lowther (mtn.), Sc,UK
206/B4 Greenmount, Md,US
54/B5 Greenock, Sc,UK
60/D1 Greenore, Ire.
60/D5 Greenore (pt.), Ire.
132/B4 Greenough (riv.), Austl.
177/K2 Greenough (mt.), Ak,US
184/B1 Green Peter (lake), Or,US
200/D4 Green Pond, Al,US
206/D1 Green Pond, NJ,US
207/H8 Green Pond (lake), NJ,US
207/F1 Greenport, NY,US
191/H1 Green Ridge, Mo,US
197/S8 Green River, On,Can
127/K4 Green River, PNG
200/E2 Green River (hill), Ky,US
200/E2 Green River (lake), Ky,US
185/H4 Green River, Ut,US
185/J3 Green River, Wy,US
187/H3 Greens (peak), Az,US
189/M9 Greens (bayou), Tx,US
200/D4 Greensboro, Al,US
203/F2 Greensboro, Fl,US
201/F4 Greensboro, Ga,US
206/C6 Greensboro, Md,US
201/H2 Greensboro, NC,US
198/D5 Greensburg, In,US
190/E2 Greensburg, Ks,US
200/E2 Greensburg, Ky,US
202/C2 Greensburg, La,US
208/F6 Greensburg, Pa,US
197/L1 Greenspond, Nf,Can
198/E4 Green Springs, Oh,US
183/K2 Greenstreet, Sk,Can
198/G3 Greensville, On,Can
193/H3 Greentop, Mo,US
208/F6 Greentown, Oh,US
198/B5 Greenup, Il,US
201/F1 Greenup, Ky,US
134/B2 Greenvale, Austl.
187/G5 Green Valley, Az,US
204/B1 Green Valley, Ca,US
206/A5 Green Valley, Md,US
204/C2 Green Valley Lake, Ca,US
207/H9 Green Village, NJ,US
144/C5 Greenville, Libr.
200/D5 Greenville, Al,US
184/C3 Greenville, Ca,US
203/G2 Greenville, Fl,US
200/E4 Greenville, Ga,US

193/K4 Greenville, Il,US
200/D2 Greenville, Ky,US
196/C3 Greenville, Me,US
198/D3 Greenville, Mi,US
191/J2 Greenville, Mo,US
200/B4 Greenville, Ms,US
201/J3 Greenville, NC,US
198/D4 Greenville, Oh,US
208/G5 Greenville, Pa,US
208/C2 Greenville, RI,US
201/F3 Greenville, SC,US
189/F1 Greenville, Tx,US
185/G4 Greenville, Ut,US
196/C3 Greenville Junction, Me,US
205/D3 Greenwater (riv.), Wa,US
183/N1 Greenwater Lake, Sk,Can
135/D2 Greenwell Point, Austl.
53/P7 Greenwich (bor.), Eng,UK
199/K4 Greenwich, Ct,US
207/L8 Greenwich (pt.), Ct,US
199/K3 Greenwich, NY,US
208/E5 Greenwich, Oh,US
53/P7 Greenwich Observatory, Eng,UK
207/K9 Greenwich Village, NY,US
197/S8 Greenwood, On,Can
191/G3 Greenwood, Ar,US
206/C6 Greenwood, De,US
203/F2 Greenwood, Fl,US
198/C5 Greenwood, In,US
200/B4 Greenwood, Ms,US
207/D1 Greenwood (lake), NJ, NY,US
201/F3 Greenwood, SC,US
201/F3 Greenwood (lake), SC,US
207/D1 Greenwood Lake, NY,US
192/B4 Greenwood Village, Co,US
187/H3 Greer, Az,US
208/E6 Greer, Oh,US
201/F3 Greer, SC,US
191/H3 Greers Ferry, Ar,US
191/J3 Greers Ferry (dam), Ar,US
191/H3 Greers Ferry (lake), Ar,US
60/D4 Greese (riv.), Ire.
191/H3 Greeson (lake), Ar,US
66/D6 Grefrath, Ger.
153/G3 Gregoire Kayibanda (Kigali) (int'l arpt.), Rwa.
168/D2 Gregório (riv.), Braz.
133/E2 Gregory (lake), Austl.
133/H4 Gregory (lake), Austl.
134/A2 Gregory (range), Austl.
131/E4 Gregory (riv.), Austl.
200/F3 Gregory (peak), NC,US
192/E2 Gregory, SD,US
132/E2 Gregory Lake Abor. Land, Austl.
72/D1 Greiffenberg, Ger.
65/G1 Greifswald, Ger.
65/G1 Greifswalder Bodden (bay), Ger.
198/D2 Greilickville, Mi,US
92/B2 Greimberg (peak), Aus.
72/C6 Greiz, Ger.
94/H1 Gremikha, Rus.
95/N4 Gremyachinsk, Rus.
62/D3 Grenå, Den.
162/F5 Grenada
200/C4 Grenada, Ms,US
200/C4 Grenada (lake), Ms,US
74/D5 Grenade-sur-Garonne, Fr.
68/B3 Grenay, Fr.
80/D3 Grenchen, Swi.
135/D2 Grenfell, Austl.
194/C2 Grenfell, Sk,Can
82/B2 Grenoble, Fr.
82/B2 Grenoble (Saint Geoirs) (arpt.), Fr.
191/F2 Grenola, Ks,US
194/C3 Grenora, ND,US
131/F2 Grenville (cape), Austl.
80/D2 Grenzach-Wyhlen, Ger.
82/B5 Gréoux-les-Bains, Fr.
72/C4 Greppin, Ger.
184/B1 Gresham, Or,US
124/F4 Gresik, Indo.
61/E2 Gressåmoen Nat'l Park, Nor.
82/D1 Gressan, It.
82/B3 Gresse (riv.), Fr.
84/A2 Gresseto (prov.), It.
203/G1 Gresston, Ga,US
57/E2 Greta (riv.), Eng,UK
57/F3 Greta (riv.), Eng,UK
135/C4 Gretna, Austl.
57/E2 Gretna, Sc,UK
203/F2 Gretna, Fl,US
202/C3 Gretna, La,US
201/H2 Gretna, Va,US
59/F1 Gretton, Eng,UK
70/D3 Grettstadt, Ger.
53/U10 Gretz-Armainvilliers, Fr.
72/A5 Greussen, Ger.
63/T9 Greve, Den.
87/E5 Greve (riv.), It.
87/E5 Greve in Chianti, It.
66/B5 Grevelingendam (dam), Neth.
67/E4 Greven, Ger.
91/G2 Grevená, Gre.
66/D6 Grevenbroich, Ger.
69/F4 Grevenmacher, Lux.
69/F4 Grevenmacher (dist.), Lux.
64/F2 Grevesmühlen, Ger.
66/A5 Grevlingen (chan.), Neth.
131/E3 Grey (cape), Austl.
133/J4 Grey (range), Austl.
197/J2 Grey (riv.), Nf,Can
56/C2 Grey (pt.), NI,UK
56/C2 Grey Abbey, NI,UK
185/J1 Greybull, Wy,US
185/J1 Greybull (riv.), Wy,US
183/K5 Greycliff, Mt,US
177/L3 Grey Hunter (peak), Yk,Can
156/E2 Greylingstad, SAfr.
199/K3 Greylock (mt.), Ma,US
136/B3 Greymouth, N.Z.
134/B2 Grey Peaks Nat'l Park, Austl.
197/J2 Grey River, Nf,Can
57/F2 Greystoke, Eng,UK
60/D3 Greystones, Ire.
136/J9 Greytown, N.Z.
157/E3 Greytown, SAfr.
69/D2 Grez-Doiceau, Belg.
87/E1 Grezzana, It.
99/L2 Gribanovskiy, Rus.
58/B6 Gribbin (pt.), Eng,UK
148/C4 Gribingui (pref.), CAfr.
148/C4 Gribingui (riv.), CAfr.
148/C4 Gribingui-Bamingui Fauna Rsv., CAfr.
184/C4 Gridley, Ca,US
193/K3 Gridley, Il,US
191/G1 Gridley, Ks,US
81/E5 Gridone (Monte Limidario) (peak), It.
81/E3 Griefensee (lake), Swi.
66/C2 Griend (isl.), Neth.
81/H3 Gries am Brenner, Aus.
70/B3 Griesheim, Ger.
71/G6 Grieskirchen, Aus.
81/H3 Griesskogel (peak), Aus.
71/F7 Griesstätt, Ger.
194/C3 Griffin, Sk,Can
202/M6 Griffin (lake), Fl,US
200/E4 Griffin, Ga,US
199/J3 Griffiss A.F.B., NY,US
135/C2 Griffith, Austl.
205/R16 Griffith, In,US
204/F7 Griffith Park, Ca,US
191/J3 Griffithville, Ar,US
201/J3 Grifton, NC,US
190/C2 Griggs, Ok,US
86/C1 Grigna (peak), It.
82/A4 Grignan, Fr.
87/E2 Grignano Polesine, It.
82/C1 Grignon, Fr.
68/B6 Grigny, Fr.
82/A1 Grigny, Fr.
93/J2 Grigoriopol', Mol.
94/H5 Grigor'yevskoye, Rus.
160/C2 Grijalva (riv.), Mex.
66/D2 Grijpskerk, Neth.
82/A4 Grillon, Fr.
135/C4 Grim (cape), Austl.
83/C4 Grimaldi, It.
148/D4 Grimari, CAfr.
82/C6 Grimaud, Fr.
82/C6 Grimaud (riv.), Fr.
98/D3 Grimaylov, Ukr.
69/D2 Grimbergen, Belg.
201/J3 Grimesland, NC,US
80/D5 Grimisuat, Swi.
58/D2 Grimley, Eng,UK
72/C5 Grimma, Ger.
64/G1 Grimmen, Ger.
72/D2 Grimnitzsee (lake), Ger.
197/R9 Grimsby, On,Can
57/H4 Grimsby, Eng,UK
81/E4 Grimselpass (pass), Swi.
61/N6 Grimsey (isl.), Ice.
200/E2 Grimsley, Tn,US
62/C2 Grimstad, Nor.
61/M7 Grindavík, Ice.
80/E4 Grindelwald, Swi.
62/C4 Grindsted, Den.
179/S7 Grinnel (pen.), NW,Can
193/H3 Grinnell, Ia,US
92/B2 Grintavec (peak), Slov.
156/E3 Griqualand East (reg.), SAfr.
156/C2 Griqualand West (reg.), SAfr.
156/C3 Griquatown, SAfr.
179/S7 Grise Fiord, NW,Can
68/A2 Gris Nez (cape), Fr.
83/B3 Grisolia, It.
63/H1 Grisslehamn, Swe.
198/C4 Grissom A.F.B., In,US
193/G3 Griswold, Ia,US
53/U10 Grisy-Suisnes, Fr.
148/C4 Grivaï Pamia, CAfr.
205/K10 Grizzly (bay), Ca,US
182/F4 Grizzly (mtn.), Id,US
186/B1 Grizzly Flats, Ca,US
92/C3 Grmeč (mtn.), Bosn.
167/F3 Groaíras, Braz.
69/D1 Grobbendonk, Belg.
72/D3 Gröben, Ger.
71/E6 Gröbenzell, Ger.
72/C5 Gröbers, Ger.
63/J3 Grobiņa, Lat.
156/E2 Groblersdal, SAfr.
156/C3 Groblershoop, SAfr.
72/B4 Grobzig, Ger.
72/D5 Gröditz, Ger.
65/J3 Grodków, Pol.
63/K5 Grodno, Bela.
63/L5 Grodno Obl., Bela.
65/J2 Grodzisk Wielkopolski, Pol.
63/N5 Grodzyanka, Bela.
66/D4 Groenlo, Neth.
189/F2 Groesbeck, Tx,US
66/C5 Groesbeek, Neth.
72/C5 Groitzsch, Ger.
78/B5 Groix, Fr.
78/B5 Groix (isl.), Fr.
65/L3 Grójec, Pol.
64/F1 Grömitz, Ger.
86/C1 Gromo, It.
66/E4 Gronau, Ger.
135/C2 Grong Grong, Austl.
66/D2 Groningen, Neth.
66/D2 Groningen (prov.), Neth.
166/C1 Groningen, Sur.
81/H5 Gronlait (peak), It.
183/M1 Gronlid, Sk,Can
81/F5 Grono, Swi.
190/D3 Groom, Tx,US
156/C4 Groot (riv.), SAfr.
154/B4 Grootberg (peak), Namb.
156/Q13 Grootdraaidam (res.), SAfr.
128/F2 Groote Eylandt (isl.), Austl.
131/E3 Groote Eylandt (isl.), Austl.
66/D2 Grootegast, Neth.
154/C3 Grootfontein, Namb.
155/E4 Grootgeluk, SAfr.
154/C4 Groot Kleeberg (mts.), Namb.
155/F4 Groot-Letabarivier (riv.), SAfr.
156/D2 Groot-Marico, SAfr.
155/E5 Groot Marico (riv.), SAfr.
156/D2 Groot-Marico (riv.), SAfr.
156/C3 Grootvloer (salt pan), SAfr.
154/C4 Groot Waterberg (mts.), Namb.
86/C2 Gropello Cairoli, It.
69/G5 Grosbliederstroff, Fr.
81/G5 Grosio, It.
162/F4 Gros Islet, StL.
179/L4 Gros Morne (mtn.), Nf,Can
196/E1 Gros-Morne, Qu,Can
197/J1 Gros Morne Nat'l Park, Nf,Can
74/F3 Grosne (riv.), Fr.
78/C2 Grosnez (pt.), Chl,UK
166/D2 Grossa (pt.), Braz.
70/D6 Grossaitingen, Ger.
67/G6 Grossalmerode, Ger.
154/C4 Gross Barmen, Namb.
72/D3 Grossbeeren, Ger.
70/B3 Gross Bieberau, Ger.
70/C5 Grossbottwar, Ger.
70/E1 Grossbreitenbach, Ger.
67/E3 Grosse Aa (riv.), Ger.
72/B3 Grosse Graben (riv.), Ger.
205/F7 Grosse Ile, Mi,US
205/F7 Grosse Ile (isl.), Mi,US
71/F5 Grosse Laber (riv.), Ger.
70/C6 Grosse Lauter (riv.), Ger.
71/G6 Grosse Mühl (riv.), Aus.
156/A2 Grosse Münzenberg (peak), Namb.
67/H6 Grossengottern, Ger.
72/D5 Grossenhain, Ger.
69/G2 Grosse Nister (riv.), Ger.
67/F3 Grossenkneten, Ger.
70/C1 Grossenlüder, Ger.
62/C4 Grossenwiehe, Ger.
73/A3 Gross-Enzersdorf, Aus.
205/G7 Grosse Pointe, Mi,US
205/G7 Grosse Pointe Farms, Mi,US
205/G7 Grosse Pointe Park, Mi,US
205/G7 Grosse Pointe Shores, Mi,US
205/G7 Grosse Pointe Woods, Mi,US
80/D5 Grosser Aletsch (glac.), Swi.
71/G4 Grosser Arber (peak), Ger.
67/G3 Grosser Aue (riv.), Ger.
72/A6 Grosser Beer-Berg (peak), Ger.
75/L3 Grosser Bösenstein (peak), Aus.
81/G3 Grosser Daumen (peak), Ger.
70/B2 Grosser Feldberg (peak), Ger.
70/D2 Grosser Gleichberg (peak), Ger.
70/B6 Grosser Heuberg (mts.), Ger.
67/F1 Grosser Knechtsand (isl.), Ger.
72/E4 Grosser Mochowsee (lake), Ger.
72/D5 Grosse Röder (riv.), Ger.
71/H6 Grosse Rodl (riv.), Aus.
65/H4 Grosser Peilstein (peak), Aus.
72/C3 Grosser Plessower (lake), Ger.
75/L3 Grosser Priel (peak), Aus.
65/H5 Grosser Pyhrgas (peak), Aus.
71/G5 Grosser Rachel (peak), Ger.
72/C3 Grosser Seddiner (lake), Ger.
72/D3 Grosser Selchower (lake), Ger.
72/D1 Grosser Stechlinsee (lake), Ger.
72/E5 Grosser Stockteich (lake), Ger.
196/D3 Grosses Coques, NS,Can
67/E2 Grosses Meer (lake), Ger.
92/A2 Grosses Wiesbachhorn (peak), Aus.
84/B2 Grosseto, It.
84/A2 Grosseto, Formiche di (rock), It.
72/A5 Grossfurra, Ger.
70/B3 Grossgerau, Ger.
72/D3 Grossglienicke, Ger.
75/K3 Grossglockner (peak), Aus.
67/H1 Grosshansdorf, Ger.
72/D6 Grossharthmannsdorf, Ger.
70/C3 Grossheubach, Ger.
72/B5 Grosskayna, Ger.
72/C5 Grosskorbetha, Ger.
69/G3 Grossmaischeid, Ger.
72/B5 Grossmonra, Ger.
75/H5 Grosso (cape), Fr.
67/H3 Gross Oesingen, Ger.
72/B4 Grossörner, Ger.
167/G4 Grossos, Braz.
73/A5 Grosspetersdorf, Aus.
72/B4 Grossquenstedt, Ger.
72/E4 Grossräschen, Ger.
72/E5 Grossröhrsdorf, Ger.
72/B4 Grossrosenburg, Ger.
69/F5 Grossrosseln, Ger.
72/D2 Gross Schönebeck, Ger.
65/H4 Grosssiegharts, Aus.
154/B4 Gross Spitzkoppe (peak), Namb.
72/A3 Gross Twülpstedt, Ger.
70/B3 Gross Umstadt, Ger.
70/C3 Grosswallstadt, Ger.
80/E3 Grosswangen, Swi.
73/A4 Grosswarasdorf, Aus.
70/B3 Gross-Zimmern, Ger.
92/B3 Grosuplje, Slov.
206/C2 Grosvenor Dale, Ct,US
185/H2 Gros Ventre (riv.), Wy,US
69/E2 Grote Gete (riv.), Belg.
69/D1 Grote Nete (riv.), Belg.
208/B3 Groton, Ct,US
199/H3 Groton, NY,US
192/E1 Groton, SD,US
208/B3 Groton-New London (arpt.), Ct,US
84/C4 Grottaferrata, It.
87/G1 Grotta Gigante, It.
90/E2 Grottaglie, It.
85/F5 Grottaminarda, It.
85/D2 Grottammare, It.
69/E3 Grotte de Han, Belg.
84/B2 Grotte di Castro, It.
83/C6 Grotteria, It.
84/C2 Grotte Santo Stefano, It.
77/E1 Grottes de Bétharram, Fr.
182/D4 Grotto, Wa,US
201/H1 Grottoes, Va,US
85/G6 Grottole, It.
193/G2 Grotto of the Redemption, Ia,US
78/D3 Grouin, Pointe du (pt.), Fr.
142/D2 Grou, Oued (riv.), Mor.
185/G3 Grouse Creek, Ut,US
66/C2 Grouw, Neth.
59/E3 Grove, Eng,UK
206/B5 Grove (pt.), Md,US
191/G2 Grove, Ok,US
188/L7 Grove (cr.), Tx,US
198/E5 Grove City, Oh,US
208/G5 Grove City, Pa,US
200/D5 Grove Hill, Al,US
186/B2 Groveland, Ca,US
202/M6 Groveland, Fl,US
192/B3 Grover, Co,US
185/H4 Grover, Ut,US
185/H2 Grover, Wy,US
186/B3 Grover City, Ca,US
206/D3 Groverville-Yardville, NJ,US
189/H3 Groves, Tx,US
196/B3 Groveton, NH,US
189/G2 Groveton, Tx,US
206/A6 Groveton, Va,US
187/F4 Growler (wash), Az,US
97/H4 Groznyy (int'l arpt.), Rus.
53/H4 Groznyy, Rus.
191/J3 Grubbs, Ar,US
79/F1 Gruchet-le-Valasse, Fr.
93/H4 Grudovo, Bul.
65/K2 Grudziądz, Pol.
196/B2 Grues, Ile aux (isl.), Qu,Can
86/A2 Grugliasco, It.
190/C3 Grulla Nat'l Wild. Ref., NM,US
83/B2 Grumentum (ruins), It.
151/A2 Grumeti (riv.), Tanz.
85/E6 Grumo Nevano, It.
62/E2 Grums, Swe.
72/C6 Grüna, Ger.
156/B2 Grünau, Namb.
71/G7 Grünau im Almtal, Aus.
71/F2 Grünbach, Ger.
70/C2 Gründau, Ger.
82/C3 Grun de Saint-Maurice (mtn.), Fr.
201/F2 Grundy, Va,US
193/H2 Grundy Center, Ia,US
57/E2 Grune (pt.), Eng,UK
72/D3 Grünheide, Ger.
70/C3 Grünsfeld, Ger.
70/B3 Grünstadt, Ger.
194/F3 Grunthal, Mb,Can
71/E6 Grünwald, Ger.
190/D2 Gruver, Tx,US
80/D4 Gruyère (lake), Swi.
80/D4 Gruyères, Swi.
63/K3 Gruzdžiai, Lith.
63/P2 Gryady, Rus.
96/F1 Gryazi, Rus.
94/J4 Gryazovets, Rus.
62/F1 Grycksbo, Swe.
65/H2 Gryfice, Pol.
65/H2 Gryfino, Pol.
195/G3 Grygla, Mn,US
80/D5 Gryon, Swi.
71/G7 Gschwandt, Aus.
70/C5 Gschwend, Ger.
80/D5 Gstaad, Swi.
80/D5 Gsteig, Swi.
117/H3 Gu (mtn.), China
121/E4 Gua, India
174/B4 Guabun (pt.), Chile
164/C3 Guaca, Col.
164/D4 Guacamayo, Col.
161/G1 Guacanayabo (gulf), Cuba
164/E2 Guacara, Ven.
164/B4 Guacarí, Col.
165/E2 Guacharo Nat'l Park, Ven.
172/C3 Guachipas, Arg.
158/D3 Guachochi, Mex.
161/F4 Guácimo, CR
171/E4 Guaçuí, Braz.
158/E4 Guadalajara, Mex.
76/D2 Guadalajara, Sp.
88/B3 Guadalquivir (riv.), Sp.
138/E6 Guadalcanal (isl.), Sol.
76/C3 Guadalcanal, Sp.
76/E4 Guadalentín (riv.), Sp.
76/D3 Guadalimar (riv.), Sp.
74/B8 Guadalix (riv.), Sp.
77/E2 Guadalope (riv.), Sp.
76/D4 Guadalquivir (riv.), Sp.
172/C1 Guadalupe, Bol.
172/C2 Guadalupe, Bol.
167/F4 Guadalupe, Braz.
164/C4 Guadalupe, Col.
158/D3 Guadalupe, Mex.
158/E4 Guadalupe, Mex.
188/D3 Guadalupe, Mex.
188/D4 Guadalupe, Mex.
176/E7 Guadalupe (isl.), Mex.
159/Q9 Guadalupe (res.), Mex.
161/G4 Guadalupe, Pan.
168/B2 Guadalupe, Peru
168/C4 Guadalupe, Peru
76/C3 Guadalupe, Sp.
76/C3 Guadalupe (range), Sp.
186/B3 Guadalupe, Ca,US
190/B4 Guadalupe (mts.), NM, Tx,US
188/B2 Guadalupe (peak), Tx,US
190/B5 Guadalupe (peak), Tx,US
189/F3 Guadalupe (riv.), Tx,US
188/A2 Guadalupe Bravos, Mex.
188/B2 Guadalupe Mts. Nat'l Park, Tx,US
158/D3 Guadalupe Victoria, Mex.
159/M7 Guadalupe Victoria, Mex.
158/D3 Guadalupe y Calvo, Mex.
190/B2 Guadalupita, NM,US
76/C2 Guadarrama, Sp.
77/M8 Guadarrama (mts.), Sp.
77/M8 Guadarrama (pass), Sp.
76/C2 Guadarrama (range), Sp.
76/C3 Guadarrama (riv.), Sp.
164/D2 Guadarrama, Ven.
162/F3 Guadeloupe (dept.), Fr.
176/L8 Guadeloupe (isl.), Fr.
162/F3 Guadeloupe Nat'l Park, Guad.
162/F3 Guadeloupe Passage (chan.), NAm.
159/Q9 Guadelupe, Basilica of, Mex.
76/C3 Guadiana (riv.), Sp.
76/B4 Guadiana (riv.), Sp., Port.
76/D4 Guadiana Menor (riv.), Sp.
76/D4 Guadix, Sp.
164/C3 Guaduas, Col.
174/B4 Guafo (chan.), Chile
174/B4 Guafo (isl.), Chile
201/F2 Guage, Ky,US
164/B5 Guagua Pichincha (peak), Ecu.
173/G4 Guaíba, Braz.
161/G1 Guaicanamar, Cuba
162/F5 Guaico, Trin.
161/G1 Guáimaro, Cuba
165/F3 Guaina, Ven.
164/D4 Guainía (comm.), Col.
164/D4 Guainía (riv.), Col., Ven.
165/F3 Guaiquinima (peak), Ven.
170/C4 Guaíra, Braz.
173/F3 Guaíra, Braz.
173/G2 Guaíra, Braz.
173/E2 Guairá (dept.), Par.
174/B4 Guaiteca (isl.), Chile
169/E3 Guajará-Mirim, Braz.
161/H4 Guajira (pen.), Col.
164/D1 Guajira (pen.), Col., Ven.
164/B5 Gualaceo, Ecu.
160/E3 Gualaco, Hon.
184/B4 Gualala, Ca,US
160/D3 Gualán, Guat.
168/B1 Gualaquiza, Ecu.
84/C1 Gualdo Tadino, It.
174/F2 Gualeguay, Arg.
174/F2 Gualeguay (riv.), Arg.
174/F2 Gualeguaychú, Arg.
174/D4 Gualicho (val.), Arg.
172/B1 Guallatiri (vol.), Chile
138/D3 Guam (isl.), PacUS
167/E3 Guamá (riv.), Braz.
164/C2 Guamal, Col.
174/B5 Guamblin (isl.), Chile
168/B1 Guamote, Ecu.
158/D3 Guamuchil, Mex.
124/C1 Gua Musang, Malay.
115/D3 Gu'an, China
115/H7 Gu'an, China
161/F1 Guanabacoa, Cuba
171/N7 Guanabara (bay), Braz.
158/D3 Guanacevi, Mex.
161/E1 Guanahacabibes (gulf), Cuba
161/E1 Guanahacabibes (pen.), Cuba
160/E2 Guanaja, Hon.
160/E2 Guanaja (isl.), Hon.
161/F1 Guanajay, Cuba
159/E4 Guanajuato, Mex.
159/E4 Guanajuato (state), Mex.
159/E4 Guanajuato-Leon (int'l arpt.), Mex.
165/F3 Guanajuña, Ven.
171/E2 Guanambi, Braz.
165/E2 Guanape, Ven.
164/D2 Guanare, Ven.
164/D2 Guanare (riv.), Ven.
164/D2 Guanarito, Ven.
165/E3 Guanay (peak), Ven.
117/G3 Guanbei, China
117/H3 Guanbei, China
115/C3 Guancen Shan (mtn.), China
117/G3 Guanchao, China
172/B4 Guandacol, Arg.
115/B3 Guandi Shan (mtn.), China
115/B5 Guandu, China
117/F2 Guandu, China
161/E1 Guane, Cuba
108/F5 Guanfangpu, China
117/H3 Guangchang, China
115/D5 Guangde, China
117/G3 Guangdong (prov.), China
116/E2 Guangfu, China
117/G4 Guanghai, China
115/C3 Guangling, China
113/B3 Guanglu (isl.), China
116/D3 Guangmao (mtn.), China
117/H2 Guangming (peak), China
115/D5 Guangming Ding (peak), China
116/E3 Guangnan, China
115/C3 Guangping, China
117/H3 Guangping, China
115/D3 Guangrao, China
115/C4 Guangshan, China
117/G2 Guangshui, China
117/F4 Guangxi Zhuangzu Zizhiqu (aut. reg.), China
116/E1 Guangyuan, China
117/H3 Guangze, China
119/K3 Guangzhou, China
117/G4 Guangzhou (Canton), China
171/E3 Guanhães, Braz.
165/F3 Guanipa (riv.), Ven.
117/F2 Guanmian (mts.), China
115/C4 Guannan, China
184/D2 Guano (lake), Or,US
113/C2 Guanshui, China
161/H1 Guantánamo, Cuba
161/H2 Guantánamo Bay U.S. Nav. Base, Cuba
115/C3 Guantao, China
115/G6 Guanting (res.), China
164/B5 Guanujo, Ecu.
108/E5 Guan Xian, China
115/C3 Guan Xian, China
116/D2 Guan Xian, China
108/E5 Guanyinqiao, China
115/D4 Guanyun, China
117/F2 Guanzhou, China
164/B3 Guapa, Col.
164/B4 Guapi, Col.
173/G1 Guapó, Braz.
173/G4 Guaporé, Braz.
169/F4 Guaporé (riv.), Braz.
172/B1 Guaqui, Bol.
77/E1 Guara (peak), Sp.
167/H4 Guarabira, Braz.
170/C4 Guaraci, Braz.
167/F4 Guaraciaba do Norte, Braz.
170/C1 Guaraí, Braz.
164/B5 Guaranda, Ecu.
171/N6 Guarani, Braz.
171/E4 Guarapari, Braz.
173/G3 Guarapuava, Braz.
171/N6 Guararé, Braz.
170/C4 Guararapes, Braz.
167/H5 Guararapes (int'l arpt.), Braz.
171/K8 Guararema, Braz.
171/F3 Guaratinga, Braz.
170/D4 Guaratinguetá, Braz.
173/G3 Guaratuba, Braz.
168/D4 Guarayos, Bol.
124/C1 Guar Chempedak, Malay.
85/D4 Guarcino, It.
76/B2 Guarda, Port.
76/B2 Guarda (dist.), Port.
77/E3 Guardamar del Segura, Sp.
86/C2 Guardamiglio, It.
167/N8 Guardatinajas, Ven.
83/C6 Guardavalle, It.
84/C2 Guardea, It.
81/H4 Guardia Alta (peak), It.
85/E3 Guardiagrele, It.
174/E4 Guardia Mitre, Arg.
85/E5 Guardia Sanframondi, It.
76/B3 Guareña, Sp.
167/O7 Guarenas, Ven.
131/G2 Guari, PNG
170/C4 Guariba, Braz.
166/A5 Guaribe (riv.), Braz.
161/H1 Guarico (pt.), Cuba
165/E2 Guárico (res.), Ven.
167/N8 Guárico (res.), Ven.
165/E2 Guárico (riv.), Ven.
165/E2 Guárico (state), Ven.
165/E2 Guárico (state), Ven.
167/L7 Guarinó (riv.), Col.
165/E2 Guariquito-Aguaro Nat'l Park, Ven.
167/K6 Guarne, Col.
171/K9 Guarujá, Braz.
171/K9 Guarujá, Braz.
170/D4 Guarulhos, Braz.
171/K8 Guarulhos (int'l arpt.), Braz.
161/F5 Guarumal, Pan.
158/C3 Guasave, Mex.
167/M7 Guasca, Col.
164/D3 Guasdualito, Ven.
161/G1 Guasimal, Cuba
165/F3 Guasipati, Ven.
86/D3 Guastalla, It.
167/K6 Guatapé, Col.
160/D3 Guatemala
160/D3 Guatemala (cap.), Guat.
164/C3 Guateque, Col.
167/O7 Guatire, Ven.
172/B4 Guatulame, Chile
164/C4 Guaviare (comm.), Col.
164/D4 Guaviare (riv.), Col.
170/D4 Guaxupé, Braz.
165/E4 Guayabal, Ven.
167/L7 Guayabal de Síquima, Col.
164/C4 Guayabero (riv.), Col.
161/G1 Guayabo (cay), Cuba
159/F4 Guayalejo (riv.), Mex.
162/E3 Guayama, PR
160/E3 Guayape (riv.), Hon.
164/B5 Guayaquil, Ecu.
164/A5 Guayaquil (gulf), Ecu.
169/E3 Guayaramerín, Bol.
164/C4 Guayas (riv.), Col.
164/B5 Guayas, Ecu.
164/A5 Guayas (prov.), Ecu.
172/C1 Guayatayoc (lake), Arg.
172/E2 Guaycurú (riv.), Arg.
158/C3 Guaymas, Mex.
149/G3 Guba, Eth.
95/N4 Gubakha, Rus.
87/F6 Gubbio, It.
65/H3 Guben, Ger.
145/H4 Gubi, Nga.
65/H3 Gubin, Pol.
99/J2 Gubkin, Rus.
115/B4 Gucheng, China
115/C3 Gucheng, China
116/E1 Gucheng, China
117/F1 Gucheng, China
108/E2 Guchin-Us, Mong.
122/F3 Güdalür, India
122/F4 Güdalür, India
77/E2 Gúdar (range), Sp.
97/G4 Gudauta, Geo.
62/D3 Gudenå (riv.), Den.
67/G6 Gudensberg, Ger.
97/H4 Gudermes, Rus.
118/D4 Gudivāda, India
149/H4 Gudo (peak), Eth.
117/E3 Gudong, China
117/G4 Gudou (peak), China
67/H1 Gudow, Ger.
93/L5 Güdül, Turk.
118/C5 Güdūr, India
80/D2 Guebwiller, Fr.
76/D1 Guecho, Sp.
144/C4 Guéckédou, Gui.
148/C2 Guédi (peak), Chad
144/B1 Guelb Azefal (mts.), Mrta.
142/C5 Guelb er Rîchât (peak), Mrta.
148/B3 Guéléngdeng, Chad
141/V17 Guelma, Alg.
141/V17 Guelma (gov.), Alg.
198/F3 Guelph, On,Can
142/B4 Guelta Zemmur, WSah.
143/G2 Guemar, Alg.
78/D5 Guémené-Penfao, Fr.
78/B4 Guémené-sur-Scorff, Fr.
159/F4 Güémez, Mex.
69/F5 Guénange, Fr.
78/C6 Guenrolet, Fr.
78/C5 Guer, Fr.
148/C3 Guéra (pref.), Chad
142/A5 Güera, WSah.
175/K7 Güer Aike, Arg.
148/C3 Guéra, Massif de (peak), Chad
76/D6 Guérande, Fr.
143/G2 Guerara, Alg.
141/N13 Guercif, Mor.
148/D2 Guéréda, Chad
74/D3 Guéret, Fr.
142/A5 Guerguerat, WSah.
145/F4 Guérin Kouka, Togo
76/D1 Guernica y Luno, Sp.
194/B2 Guernsey, Sk,Can
78/C2 Guernsey (isl.), UK
78/C2 Guernsey (int'l arpt.), Chl,UK
74/B2 Guernsey (isl.), Chl,UK
192/B2 Guernsey, Wy,US
144/C2 Guérou, Mrta.
189/E4 Guerra, Tx,US
188/D3 Guerrero, Mex.
159/E5 Guerrero (state), Mex.
143/E3 Guerzim, Alg.
74/F3 Gueugnon, Fr.
68/C5 Gueux, Fr.
189/H2 Gueydan, La,US
145/H3 Guézaoua, Niger
149/H4 Gugē (peak), Eth.
105/G3 Güged, Iran
80/D4 Guggisberg, Swi.
87/E3 Gugielmo Marconi (int'l arpt.), It.
89/F1 Gugielmo Marconi (int'l arpt.), It.
70/B4 Güglingen, Ger.
85/E4 Guglionesi, It.
150/A3 Gugu (peak), Eth.
130/D3 Guguan (isl.), NMar.
150/C4 Guguraqu, Eth.
117/H2 Guhe, China
117/F4 Gui (riv.), China
77/X16 Guía de Isora, Sp.
163/C2 Guiana (plat.), SAm.
163/C2 Guiana Highlands (mts.), SAm.
144/D5 Guibéroua, IvC.
156/B2 Guibes, Namb.
78/D5 Guichen, Fr.
115/D5 Guichi, China
160/C2 Guichicovi, Mex.
175/F2 Guichón, Uru.
145/G3 Guidan-Roumji, Niger
148/C3 Guidari, Chad
148/B3 Guidder, Camr.
78/B5 Guidel, Fr.
148/B3 Guidiguis, Camr.
144/B3 Guidimaka (reg.), Mrta.
145/H3 Guidimouni, Niger
119/J2 Guiding, China
86/D2 Guidizzolo, It.
119/K2 Guidong, China
84/C4 Guidonia, It.
82/B1 Guiers (riv.), Fr.
144/D5 Guiglo, IvC.
78/D5 Guignen, Fr.
53/U11 Guignes, Fr.
68/C5 Guignicourt, Fr.
164/E2 Güigüe, Ven.
125/E6 Guiguinto, Phil.
125/C3 Guihulñgan, Phil.
155/G5 Guija, Moz.
76/C2 Guijuelo, Sp.
82/C3 Guil (riv.), Fr.
132/B4 Guilderton, Austl.
53/M8 Guildford, Eng,UK
199/L2 Guildhall, Vt,US
78/A4 Guilers, Fr.
208/B3 Guilford, Ct,US
196/C3 Guilford, Me,US
199/J3 Guilford, NY,US
201/H2 Guilford C. H. Nat'l Mil. Park, NC,US
82/A3 Guilherand, Fr.
117/F3 Guilin, China
117/F3 Guilin (int'l arpt.), China
117/F3 Guiling, China
82/C3 Guillaume (mtn.), Fr.
179/J3 Guillaume-Delisle (lake), Qu,Can
82/C4 Guillaumes, Fr.
76/B4 Guillena, Sp.
82/C3 Guillestre, Fr.
58/C1 Guilsfield, Wal,UK
78/A5 Guilvinec, Fr.
167/E3 Guimarães, Braz.
76/A2 Guimarães, Port.
173/H1 Guimarânia, Braz.
125/C3 Guimaras (isl.), Phil.
125/D2 Guimba, Phil.
148/B4 Guimbiri (peak), Camr.
115/D4 Guimeng Ding (mtn.), China
200/D4 Guin, Al,US
108/E4 Guinan, China
54/A1 Guinard (riv.), Sc,UK
125/D3 Guindulman, Phil.
144/C4 Guinea
144/A4 Guinea (gulf), Afr.
144/B3 Guinea-Bissau
68/A2 Guînes, Fr.
78/B3 Guingamp, Fr.
144/B3 Guingan, Gui.
144/B3 Guinguinéo, Sen.
125/C2 Guintinguintin (mt.), Phil.
160/E4 Guiones (pt.), CR
78/A4 Guipavas, Fr.
78/A4 Guipavas (Brest) (int'l arpt.), Fr.
117/F4 Guiping, China
170/B3 Guiratinga, Braz.
142/E3 Guir, Hamada du (plat.), Alg., Mor.
148/B3 Guiri, Camr.
165/F2 Güiria, Ven.
143/E2 Guir, Oued (riv.), Alg., Mor.
166/D1 Guisanbourg, FrG.
57/G2 Guisborough, Eng,UK
68/C4 Guiscard, Fr.
78/B4 Guiscriff, Fr.
68/C4 Guise, Fr.
57/G4 Guiseley, Eng,UK
78/A3 Guissény, Fr.
76/B1 Guitiriz, Sp.
144/D5 Guitri, IvC.
125/D3 Guiuan, Phil.
116/D2 Guixi, China
117/H4 Gui Xian, China
116/E3 Guiyang, China
117/G3 Guiyang, China
116/E3 Guizhou (prov.), China
74/C4 Gujan-Mestras, Fr.
118/B3 Gujarāt (state), India
122/B1 Gūjar Khān, Pak.
148/A3 Gujba, Nga.
122/C1 Gujrānwāla, Pak.
122/C1 Gujrāt, Pak.
99/K3 Gukovo, Rus.
108/E4 Gulang, China
120/A1 Gulaothi, India
135/D1 Gulargambone, Austl.
120/C1 Gularia, Nepal
118/C4 Gulbarga, India
63/M3 Gulbene, Lat.
69/G3 Guldenbach (riv.), Ger.
150/B4 Guldima, Eth.
103/E1 Güldüzü, Turk.
117/H4 Guleitou, China
62/A1 Gulen, Nor.
131/G1 Gulf (prov.), PNG
189/E4 Gulf (coast. pl.), Tx,US
203/G3 Gulf Hammock (swamp), Fl,US
202/E2 Gulf Is. Nat'l Seash., Al, Ms,US
203/G4 Gulfport, Fl,US
202/D2 Gulfport, Ms,US
202/E2 Gulf Shores, Al,US
202/P7 Gulf Stream, Fl,US
120/B3 Gulganj, India
135/D2 Gulgong, Austl.
100/G5 Gulistan, Uzb.
109/J2 Guliya (peak), China
177/J3 Gulkana, Ak,US
99/L5 Gul'kevichi, Rus.
183/H1 Gull (lake), Ab,Can
195/K3 Gull (riv.), On,Can
56/B2 Gulladuff, NI,UK
54/D4 Gullane, Sc,UK
54/D4 Gullane Head (pt.), Sc,UK
195/K3 Gull Bay, On,Can
195/K3 Gull Bay Ind. Res., On,Can
197/L2 Gull Island (pt.), Nf,Can
198/C2 Gulliver, Mi,US
183/K2 Gull Lake, Sk,Can
62/F2 Gullspång, Swe.
104/B2 Güllükdağı (Termessos) Nat'l Park, Turk.
114/B5 Gulmarg, India
103/C1 Gülnar, Turk.
69/E2 Gulpen, Neth.
72/C2 Gülper (lake), Ger.
91/K3 Gülpınar, Turk.
104/C2 Gülşehir, Turk.
153/H2 Gulu, Ugan.
93/G4 Gülübovo, Bul.
149/H2 Guluy, Eth.
93/G4 Gulyantsi, Bul.
99/J4 Gulyaypole, Ukr.
120/D1 Gum, Nepal
122/A2 Gumal (riv.), Pak.
154/D3 Gumare, Bots.
149/F3 Gumbiel, Sudan
151/A4 Gumbiro, Tanz.
69/G6 Gumbrechtshoffen, Fr.
145/H3 Gumel, Nga.
121/E4 Gumia, India
131/G1 Gumine, PNG
121/E4 Gumla, India
111/F2 Gumma (pref.), Japan
67/E6 Gummersbach, Ger.
145/G3 Gummi, Nga.
73/A3 Gumpoldskirchen, Aus.
121/H4 Gumti (riv.), India
96/E4 Gümüşhacıköy, Turk.
104/D1 Gümüşhane, Turk.
104/D1 Gümüşhane (prov.), Turk.
93/K5 Gümüşova, Turk.
149/H3 Guna (peak), Eth.
120/A3 Guna, India
150/A3 Guna Terara (peak), Eth.
189/F1 Gun Barrel City, Tx,US
135/C2 Gunbower, Austl.
116/B2 Güncang, China
135/D2 Gundagai, Austl.
70/A6 Gundelfingen, Ger.
70/D5 Gundelfingen an der Donau, Ger.
70/C4 Gundelsheim, Ger.
69/H4 Gundersheim, Ger.
69/G6 Gundershoffen, Fr.
153/E2 Gundji, Zaire
122/F3 Gundlupet, India
103/C1 Gündoğmuş, Turk.
104/B2 Güney, Turk.
104/D2 Güneydogu Toroslar (mts.), Turk.
154/C4 Gunib (dry riv.), Namb.
97/H4 Gunib, Rus.
92/D3 Gunja, Cro.
187/F2 Gunlock, Ut,US
120/B1 Gunnaur, India
62/G3 Gunnebo, Swe.
135/D1 Gunnedah, Austl.
135/D2 Gunning, Austl.
190/A1 Gunnison, Co,US
190/A1 Gunnison (riv.), Co,US
191/J4 Gunnison, Ms,US
185/H4 Gunnison, Ut,US
133/H1 Gunpowder, Austl.
206/B5 Gunpowder (riv.), Md,US
71/G6 Gunskirchen, Aus.
114/B4 Gunt (riv.), Taj.
191/F4 Gunter, Tx,US
200/D4 Gunter A.F.B., Al,US
70/B3 Guntersblum, Ger.
200/D3 Guntersville, Al,US
200/D3 Guntersville (dam), Al,US
200/D3 Guntersville (lake), Al,US
194/F2 Gunton, Mb,Can
200/C3 Guntown, Ms,US
73/A3 Guntramsdorf, Aus.
118/D4 Guntūr, India
124/B2 Gunung Leuser Nat'l Park, Indo.
125/A5 Gunung Mulu Nat'l Park, Malay.
124/B2 Gunungsitoli, Indo.
124/D4 Gunungsugih, Indo.
124/B2 Gunungtua, Indo.
70/D6 Günz (riv.), Ger.
70/D6 Günzburg, Ger.
70/D4 Gunzenhausen, Ger.
115/C4 Guo (riv.), China
117/J2 Guoju, China
115/D4 Guoyang, China
149/H3 Gurage (peak), Eth.
93/G2 Gura Humorului, Rom.
107/K2 Gurais, India
108/B2 Gurbantünggut (des.), China
122/C1 Gurdāspur, India
191/H4 Gurdon, Ar,US
97/H4 Gurdzhaani, Geo.
148/E2 Gurgei (peak), Sudan
104/D1 Gürgentepe, Turk.
167/E5 Gurguéia (riv.), Braz.
150/B4 Guri, Eth.
165/F3 Guri (res.), Ven.
130/C2 Gurig Nat'l Park, Austl.
75/L3 Gurk (riv.), Aus.
121/E2 Gurkha, Nepal
93/G4 Gurkovo, Bul.
75/K3 Gurkthaler (mts.), Aus.
135/D1 Gurley, Austl.
200/D3 Gurley, Al,US
201/H3 Gurley, SC,US
205/Q15 Gurnee, Il,US
196/B4 Gurnet (pt.), Ma,US
195/J4 Gurney, Wi,US
155/G3 Guro, Moz.
104/E2 Güroymak, Turk.
105/E2 Gürpınar, Turk.
105/M7 Gürpinar, Turk.
120/B3 Gursarai, India
109/M1 Gurskoye, Rus.
93/J5 Gürsu, Turk.
150/B3 Gursum, Eth.
127/G3 Guruapin, Indo.
122/C2 Guru Har Sahāi, India
124/C1 Gurun, Malay.
104/D2 Gürün, Turk.
168/D3 Gurupá, Braz.
170/C1 Gurupi, Braz.
167/E3 Gurupi (cape), Braz.
166/D4 Gurupi (mts.), Braz.
167/E3 Gurupi (riv.), Braz.
118/B3 Guru Sikhar (mtn.), India
155/F3 Guruve, Zim.
108/G2 Gurvandzagal, Mong.
97/J3 Gur'yev, Kaz.
97/J3 Guryev (int'l arpt.), Kaz.
97/J3 Gur'yev Obl., Kaz.
99/H5 Gurzuf, Ukr.
145/G3 Gusau, Nga.
72/B3 Güsen, Ger.
63/K4 Gusev, Rus.
113/B3 Gushan, China
115/C4 Gushi, China
145/E4 Gushiago, Gha.
112/J7 Gushikawa, Japan
117/G4 Gushui, China
92/D4 Gusinje, Yugo.
101/L4 Gusinoozërsk, Rus.
121/F4 Guskhara, India
94/J5 Gus'-Khrustal'nyy, Rus.
90/A3 Guspini, It.
73/A5 Güssing, Aus.
86/D3 Gussola, It.
63/S7 Gustausberg, Swe.
162/F3 Gustavia, Guad.
159/Q10 Gustavo A. Marrero, Mex.
189/E4 Gustavo Díaz Ordaz, Mex.
187/F5 Gustavo Sotelo, Mex.
177/L4 Gustavus, Ak,US
72/B4 Güsten, Ger.
69/F4 Gusterath, Ger.
186/B2 Gustine, Ca,US
189/E2 Gustine, Tx,US
64/G2 Güstrow, Ger.
62/G2 Gusum, Swe.
98/D3 Gusyatin, Ukr.
116/B2 Gutang, China
71/H6 Gutau, Aus.
67/F5 Gütersloh, Ger.
200/E2 Guthrie, Ky,US
191/F3 Guthrie, Ok,US
193/G3 Guthrie Center, Ia,US
117/H3 Gutian, China
159/F4 Gutiérrez Zamora, Mex.
159/M6 Gutiérrez Zamora, Mex.
117/G3 Guting, China
81/E4 Guttannen, Swi.
193/J2 Guttenberg, Ia,US
207/J8 Guttenberg, NJ,US
81/F2 Guttingen, Swi.
61/E3 Gutulia Nat'l Park, Nor.
67/G6 Guxhagen, Ger.
108/G4 Guxian, China
115/B3 Guxian, China
117/G3 Guxian, China
191/H3 Guy, Ar,US
189/G3 Guy, Tx,US
165/G3 Guyana
53/S10 Guyancourt, Fr.
201/F1 Guyandotte (riv.), WV,US
115/B2 Guyang, China
74/C4 Guyenne (reg.), Fr.
135/E1 Guy Fawkes River Nat'l Park, Austl.
59/G1 Guyhirn, Eng,UK
149/G3 Guyī, Eth.
190/D2 Guymon, Ok,US
116/C3 Guyong, China
201/F3 Guyot (mt.), NC,US
78/D3 Guyoult (riv.), Fr.
135/D1 Guyra, Austl.
197/G3 Guysborough, NS,Can
201/G4 Guyton, Ga,US
108/F4 Guyuan, China
108/H3 Guyuan, China
103/B1 Güzelbağ, Turk.
103/B1 Güzelsu, Turk.
119/J2 Guzhang, China
115/D4 Guzhen, China
187/J5 Guzmán, Mex.
158/D2 Guzman (lake), Mex.
187/J5 Guzman, Laguna di (lake), Mex.
63/J4 Gvardeysk, Rus.
99/H5 Gvardeyskoye, Ukr.
116/B5 Gwa, Burma
155/E3 Gwaai, Zim.
135/D1 Gwabegar, Austl.
145/G3 Gwadabawa, Nga.
107/H3 Gwādar, Pak.
155/E3 Gwai (riv.), Zim.
120/B2 Gwalior, India
120/B2 Gwalior (arpt.), India
155/F4 Gwanda, Zim.
135/D2 Gwandalan, Austl.
145/G4 Gwarzo, Nga.
59/F1 Gwash (riv.), Eng,UK
58/C2 Gwaunceste (mtn.), Wal,UK
65/J2 Gwda (riv.), Pol.
58/A6 Gweek, Eng,UK
155/E3 Gwembe, Zam.
58/D3 Gwent (co.), Wal,UK
57/E5 Gwersyllt, Wal,UK
155/F3 Gweru, Zim.
198/C1 Gwinn, Mi,US
194/F4 Gwinner, ND,US
201/M7 Gwinnett (co.), Ga,US
148/B3 Gwoza, Nga.
135/D1 Gwydir (riv.), Austl.
56/D5 Gwynedd (co.), Wal,UK
80/B3 Gy, Fr.
119/F2 Gyaca, China
73/D5 Gyál, Hun.
121/E1 Gya La (Lajing) (pass), China, Nepal
97/H4 Gyandzhe, Azer.
114/E5 Gyangrang, China
121/G1 Gyangzê, China
108/D4 Gyaring, China
109/D5 Gyaring (lake), China
145/F5 Gyasikan, Gha.
100/H2 Gyda (pen.), Rus.
116/B2 Gyêmdong, China
121/H2 Gyetsa, Bhu.

67/G2 **Gyhum,** Ger.
121/E1 **Gyirong,** China
62/D4 **Gyldenløveshøj** (peak), Den.
134/D4 **Gympie,** Austl.
116/B5 **Gyobingauk,** Burma
92/E2 **Gyoma,** Hun.
73/B6 **Gyöngös** (riv.), Hun.
92/D2 **Gyöngyös,** Hun.
73/A5 **Gyöngyös** (riv.), Hun.
92/D2 **Gyonk,** Hun.
73/B4 **Győr,** Hun.
73/B4 **Győr-Sopron** (co.), Hun.
73/B4 **Győrújbarát,** Hun.
185/K4 **Gypsum,** Co,US
191/F1 **Gypsum,** Ks,US
194/E2 **Gypsumville,** Mb,Can
182/F3 **Gypsy** (peak), Wa,US
92/E2 **Gyula,** Hun.
84/J8 **Gżira,** Malta

## H

121/G2 **Ha,** Bhu.
68/D2 **Haacht,** Belg.
71/H6 **Haag,** Aus.
71/G6 **Haag am Hausruck,** Aus.
71/E6 **Haag an der Amper,** Ger.
71/F6 **Haag in Oberbayern,** Ger.
66/D4 **Haaksbergen,** Neth.
68/D2 **Haaltert,** Belg.
66/A5 **Haamstede,** Neth.
66/E6 **Haan,** Ger.
139/H6 **Ha'apai Group** (isls.), Tonga
61/H2 **Haapavesi,** Fin.
63/K2 **Haapsalu,** Est.
71/E6 **Haar,** Ger.
70/A4 **Haardt** (mts.), Ger.
66/B4 **Haarlem,** Neth.
136/B3 **Haast,** N.Z.
136/B4 **Haast** (pass), N.Z.
133/F2 **Haast Bluff,** Austl.
133/F2 **Haasts Bluff Abor. Land,** Austl.
107/J3 **Hab** (riv.), Pak.
108/B2 **Habahe,** China
71/F2 **Habartov,** Czh.
151/B1 **Habaswein,** Kenya
69/E4 **Habay,** Belg.
151/C1 **Habay,** Som.
150/C2 **Ḩabbān,** Yem.
105/E3 **Ḩabbānīyah,** Iraq
81/H3 **Habicht** (peak), Aus.
121/H3 **Habiganj,** Bang.
111/L10 **Habikino,** Japan
112/D2 **Habomai** (isls.), Rus.
112/B1 **Haboro,** Japan
121/G4 **Hābra,** India
80/D2 **Habsheim,** Fr.
165/F3 **Hacha** (falls), Ven.
67/F3 **Hache** (riv.), Ger.
69/G2 **Hachenburg,** Ger.
109/N5 **Hachijō** (isl.), Japan
112/B3 **Hachimantai-Towada Nat'l Park,** Japan
112/A3 **Hachimori,** Japan
112/B3 **Hachinohe,** Japan
111/F3 **Hachiōji,** Japan
187/H5 **Hachita,** NM,US
104/C2 **Hacıbektaş,** Turk.
204/C3 **Hacienda Heights,** Ca,US
104/C2 **Hacılar,** Turk.
133/H4 **Hack** (peak), Austl.
187/F3 **Hackberry,** Az,US
190/D1 **Hackberry** (cr.), Ks,US
202/B3 **Hackberry,** La,US
195/G4 **Hackensack,** Mn,US
207/D2 **Hackensack,** NJ,US
207/J8 **Hackensack** (riv.), NJ, NY,US
201/G1 **Hacker Valley,** WV,US
60/D4 **Hacketstown,** Ire.
206/D2 **Hackettstown,** NJ,US
200/D3 **Hackleburg,** Al,US
53/N7 **Hackney** (bor.), Eng,UK
123/D1 **Ha Coi,** Viet.
114/D3 **Hadadong,** China
122/B1 **Hadāli,** Pak.
70/B2 **Hadamar,** Ger.
111/F3 **Hadano,** Japan
106/C4 **Hadarba** (cape), Sudan
147/H4 **Hadarba, Ras** (cape), Sudan
148/C2 **Haddad, Ouadi** (dry riv.), Chad
208/B3 **Haddam,** Ct,US
59/F3 **Haddenham,** Eng,UK
54/D5 **Haddington,** Sc,UK
201/F2 **Haddix,** Ky,US
201/F4 **Haddock,** Ga,US
206/C4 **Haddonfield,** NJ,US
206/C4 **Haddon** (Westmont), NJ,US
107/G4 **Ḩadd, Ra's al** (pt.), Oman
145/H3 **Hadejia,** Nga.
145/H3 **Hadejia** (riv.), Nga.
67/F1 **Hadelner** (can.), Ger.
103/D3 **Ḩadera,** Isr.
62/C4 **Haderslev,** Den.
150/D2 **Hadhramaut** (reg.), Yem.
102/E8 **Hadībоh,** Yem.
103/C1 **Hadım,** Turk.
148/D3 **Hadjer Bandala,** Chad
92/E2 **Hadjú-Bihar** (co.), Hun.
178/F1 **Hadley** (bay), NW,Can
208/B1 **Hadley,** Ma,US
53/Q8 **Hadlow,** Eng,UK
208/B3 **Hadlyme,** Ct,US
113/D5 **Hadong,** SKor.
121/H4 **Hadrāibāri,** India
73/A2 **Hadres,** Aus.
57/F1 **Hadrian's Wall** (ruins), Eng,UK
61/E1 **Hadselfjorden** (fjord), Nor.
62/D3 **Hadsten,** Den.
62/D3 **Hadsund,** Den.
113/C3 **Haeju,** NKor.
113/C4 **Haeju** (bay), NKor.
180/S9 **Haena** (pt.), Hi,US
113/D5 **Haenam,** SKor.
155/F4 **Haenertsburg,** SAfr.
109/K3 **Haengyŏng-ni,** NKor.
105/F4 **Ḩafar al Bāţin,** SAr.
183/L1 **Hafford,** Sk,Can
104/D2 **Hafik,** Turk.
122/B1 **Hāfizābād,** Pak.
116/B3 **Hāflong,** India
61/N7 **Hafnarfjördhur,** Ice.
61/P7 **Hafnarhreppur,** Ice.
106/E3 **Ḩafr al Bātin,** SAr.
105/G4 **Haft Gel,** Iran
141/H3 **Hafun** (pt.), Som.
150/D3 **Hafun, Ras** (pt.), Som.
201/G4 **Hagan,** Ga,US
189/G1 **Hagansport,** Tx,US
191/H3 **Hagarville,** Ar,US
71/F5 **Hagelstadt,** Ger.
177/F4 **Hagemeister** (isl.), Ak,US
67/E6 **Hagen,** Ger.
67/E4 **Hagen am Teutoburger Wald,** Ger.
67/F2 **Hagen im Bremischen,** Ger.
64/F2 **Hagenow,** Ger.
149/H3 **Hāgere Hiywet,** Eth.
150/A4 **Hāgere Selam,** Eth.
185/F2 **Hagerman,** Id,US
190/B4 **Hagerman,** NM,US
185/F2 **Hagerman Fossil Beds Nat'l Mon.,** Id,US
198/D5 **Hagerstown,** In,US
199/H5 **Hagerstown,** Md,US
74/C5 **Hagetmau,** Fr.
62/E1 **Hagfors,** Swe.
183/H4 **Haggin** (mt.), Mt,US
110/B3 **Hagi,** Japan
123/D1 **Ha Giang,** Viet.
58/D2 **Hagley,** Eng,UK
81/F2 **Hagnau am Bodensee,** Ger.
69/F5 **Hagondange,** Fr.
60/A4 **Hags Head** (pt.), Ire.
183/L1 **Hague,** Sk,Can
194/E4 **Hague,** ND,US
199/K3 **Hague,** NY,US
74/C2 **Hague, Cap de la** (cape), Fr.
69/G6 **Haguenau,** Fr.
66/B4 **Hague, The** ('s-Gravenhage) (cap.), Neth.
77/Y17 **Hagunía,** WSah.
157/G5 **Hahaia,** Com.
138/D2 **Hahashima** (isl.), Jap.
157/G5 **Hahaya** (int'l arpt.), Com.
203/G2 **Hahira,** Ga,US
67/H6 **Hahle** (riv.), Ger.
133/M9 **Hahndorf,** Austl.
69/G3 **Hahnenbach** (riv.), Ger.
70/B2 **Hahnstätten,** Ger.
115/D3 **Hai** (riv.), China
115/E4 **Hai'an,** China
117/F4 **Hai'an,** China
111/L10 **Haibara,** Japan
113/B2 **Haicheng,** China
71/E3 **Haidenaab** (riv.), Ger.
71/H6 **Haidershofen,** Aus.
115/H7 **Haidian,** China
123/D1 **Hai Duong,** Viet.
103/D3 **Haifa** (dist.), Isr.
103/D3 **Haifa** (Ḩefa), Isr.
117/G4 **Haifeng,** China
69/H2 **Haiger,** Ger.
70/B6 **Haigerloch,** Ger.
192/D3 **Haigler,** Ne,US
123/D1 **Hai Hau,** Viet.
117/F4 **Haikang,** China
117/F4 **Haikou,** China
117/J2 **Haikou,** China
117/F4 **Haikou** (int'l arpt.), China
180/T10 **Haiku-Pauwela,** Hi,US
104/E5 **Ḩā'il,** SAr.
116/B3 **Hailākāndi,** India
109/H2 **Hailar,** China
109/J2 **Hailar** (riv.), China
189/H1 **Haile,** La,US
185/F2 **Hailey,** Id,US
179/J4 **Haileybury,** On,Can
117/F4 **Hailing** (isl.), China
59/G5 **Hailsham,** Eng,UK
183/K4 **Hailstone Nat'l Wild. Ref.,** Mt,US
109/K2 **Hailun,** China
115/E5 **Haimen,** China
81/G3 **Haiming,** Aus.
71/F6 **Haiming,** Ger.
67/F6 **Haina,** Ger.
117/F5 **Hainan** (isl.), China
117/F5 **Hainan** (prov.), China
117/F4 **Hainan** (str.), China
68/B2 **Hainaut** (prov.), Belg.
70/C1 **Hainburg,** Ger.
73/A3 **Hainburg an der Donau,** Aus.
177/L4 **Haines,** Ak,US
184/E1 **Haines,** Or,US
203/H3 **Haines City,** Fl,US
177/L3 **Haines Junction,** Yk,Can
205/P15 **Hainesville,** Il,US
206/D1 **Hainesville,** NJ,US
189/G1 **Hainesville,** Tx,US
64/F3 **Hainich** (hill), Ger.
67/H6 **Hainich** (mts.), Ger.
72/D6 **Hainichen,** Ger.
115/L9 **Haining,** China
72/A5 **Hainleite** (mts.), Ger.
72/C6 **Hainsberg,** Ger.
123/D1 **Haiphong** (Hai Phong), Viet.
117/H3 **Haitan** (isl.), China
161/H2 **Haiti**
117/F5 **Haitou,** China
123/E2 **Hai Van** (pass), Viet.
119/K3 **Haixia** (str.), China
115/D3 **Haixing,** China
108/E4 **Haiyan,** China
115/L9 **Haiyan,** China
119/K3 **Haiyan,** China
115/E3 **Haiyang,** China
113/B3 **Haiyang** (isl.), China
108/F4 **Haiyuan,** China
115/D4 **Haizhou** (bay), China
71/F2 **Háj** (peak), Czh.
73/B5 **Hajagos** (riv.), Hun.
65/L5 **Hajdú-Bihar** (co.), Hun.
92/E2 **Hajdúboszormény,** Hun.
92/E2 **Hajdúdorog,** Hun.
92/E2 **Hajdúhadház,** Hun.
92/E2 **Hajdúnánás,** Hun.
92/E2 **Hajdúszoboszló,** Hun.
90/A5 **Ḩājib Al 'Uyūn,** Tun.
121/H4 **Hājīganj,** Bang.
111/F1 **Hajiki-zaki** (pt.), Japan
121/E3 **Hājīpur,** India
149/G2 **Ḩajj 'Abd Allāh,** Sudan
150/B2 **Ḩajjah,** Yem.
105/H4 **Ḩājjīābād,** Iran
65/M2 **Hajnówka,** Pol.
121/H2 **Hājo,** India
92/D2 **Hajós,** Hun.
116/B4 **Haka,** Burma
139/L5 **Hakahau,** Fr.Pol.
133/G3 **Hakee** (peak), Austl.
61/H3 **Häkin-Pyhä Nat'l Park,** Fin.
105/E2 **Hakkâri** (prov.), Turk.
110/D3 **Hakken-san** (mtn.), Japan
103/D1 **Hakkıbey,** Turk.
112/B3 **Hakkōda-san** (mtn.), Japan
112/B3 **Hakodate,** Japan
111/H7 **Hakone,** Japan
111/H8 **Hakone-Fuji-Izu Nat'l Park,** Japan
154/C4 **Hakosberge** (mts.), Namb.
111/E2 **Hakui,** Japan
111/M10 **Hakusan,** Japan
111/E2 **Haku-san** (mtn.), Japan
111/E2 **Hakusan Nat'l Park,** Japan
107/J3 **Hāla,** Pak.
104/D3 **Ḩalab** (prov.), Syria
103/E1 **Ḩalab** (Aleppo), Syria
105/F3 **Ḩalabjah,** Iraq
159/M6 **Halachó,** Mex.
115/H7 **Halagang,** China
147/H4 **Ḩalā'ib,** Sudan
180/T10 **Halawa,** Hi,US
72/B4 **Halberstadt,** Ger.
194/C3 **Halbrite,** Sk,Can
73/A4 **Halbturn,** Aus.
125/C2 **Halcon** (mt.), Phil.
62/D2 **Halden,** Nor.
72/B3 **Haldensleben,** Ger.
81/G2 **Haldenwang,** Ger.
121/G4 **Haldia,** India
121/G2 **Haldībāri,** India
121/G4 **Haldībunia,** Bang.
197/R10 **Haldimand,** On,Can
197/Q10 **Haldimand-Norfolk** (co.), On,Can
108/G2 **Haldzan,** Mong.
174/E3 **Hale,** Arg.
132/C3 **Hale** (peak), Austl.
151/B3 **Hale,** Tanz.
57/F5 **Hale,** Eng,UK
191/H1 **Hale,** Mo,US
180/T10 **Haleakala Nat'l Park,** Hi,US
190/D3 **Hale Center,** Tx,US
207/J8 **Haledon,** NJ,US
69/E2 **Halen,** Belg.
205/P14 **Hales Corners,** Wi,US
58/D2 **Halesowen,** Eng,UK
59/H2 **Halesworth,** Eng,UK
194/C5 **Haley-Bowman** (dam), ND,US
194/C4 **Haley-Bowman** (res.), ND,US
200/D3 **Haleyville,** Al,US
149/G2 **Halfa Aj Jadīda,** Sudan
144/E5 **Half Assini,** Gha.
183/K5 **Halfbreed Nat'l Wild. Ref.,** Mt,US
206/A3 **Half Falls** (mtn.), Pa,US
71/F7 **Halfing,** Ger.
201/J3 **Half Moon,** NC,US
182/C3 **Halfmoon Bay,** BC,Can
205/K12 **Half Moon Bay,** Ca,US
134/C3 **Half Tide Beach,** Austl.
199/H5 **Halfway,** Md,US
191/H2 **Halfway,** Mo,US
184/E1 **Halfway,** Or,US
103/D4 **Ḩalḩūl,** WBnk.
199/G2 **Haliburton,** On,Can
199/H2 **Haliburton** (hills), On,Can
134/B2 **Halifax,** Austl.
131/G4 **Halifax** (bay), Austl.
196/F3 **Halifax** (int'l arpt.), Can
196/F3 **Halifax** (cap.), NS,Can
57/G4 **Halifax,** Eng,UK
208/D2 **Halifax,** Ma,US
201/J2 **Halifax,** NC,US
206/B3 **Halifax,** Pa,US
201/H2 **Halifax,** Va,US
63/K1 **Halikko,** Fin.
105/J4 **Halīl** (riv.), Iran
91/K3 **Halileli,** Turk.
124/D4 **Halim Perdana Kusuma** (int'l arpt.), Indo.
108/D2 **Haliun,** Mong.
63/M2 **Haljala,** Est.
63/T9 **Häljarp,** Swe.
177/H1 **Halkett** (cape), Ak,US
135/C2 **Hall,** Austl.
130/B3 **Hall** (pt.), Austl.
179/K2 **Hall** (pen.), NW,Can
138/E4 **Hall** (isls.), Micr.
177/D3 **Hall** (isl.), Ak,US
183/H4 **Hall,** Mt,US
55/K7 **Halladale** (riv.), Sc,UK
182/E1 **Hallam** (peak), BC,Can
206/B3 **Hallam** (Hellam), Pa,US
62/E3 **Halland** (co.), Swe.
202/P8 **Hallandale,** Fl,US
109/K5 **Halla-san** (mtn.), SKor.
179/H2 **Hall Beach,** NW,Can
62/G2 **Hällbybrunn,** Swe.
68/D2 **Halle,** Belg.
67/F4 **Halle,** Ger.
72/B5 **Halle,** Ger.
184/F3 **Halleck,** Nv,US
61/E4 **Hällefors,** Swe.
62/G2 **Hälleforsnäs,** Swe.
75/K3 **Hallein,** Aus.
67/F6 **Hallenberg,** Ger.
68/A4 **Hallencourt,** Fr.
72/B5 **Halle-Neustadt,** Ger.
71/E5 **Hallertau** (reg.), Ger.
137/M **Hallett** (cape), Ant.
189/F3 **Hallettsville,** Tx,US
194/C4 **Halliday,** ND,US
62/C1 **Hallingdalselvi** (riv.), Nor.
81/H3 **Hall in Tirol,** Aus.
194/F3 **Hallock,** Mn,US
196/C3 **Hallowell,** Me,US
191/F3 **Hall Park,** Ok,US
200/C3 **Halls,** Tn,US
62/F2 **Hallsberg,** Swe.
130/B4 **Halls Creek,** Austl.
63/R7 **Hallsfjärden** (lake), Swe.
70/D3 **Hallstadt,** Ger.
62/G2 **Hallstahammar,** Swe.
62/H1 **Hallstavik,** Swe.
189/H1 **Hall Summit,** La,US
189/G1 **Hallsville,** Tx,US
64/B4 **Hallu** (riv.), Fr.
68/B3 **Hallue** (riv.), Fr.
68/C2 **Halluin,** Fr.
66/C2 **Hallum,** Neth.
71/G7 **Hallwang,** Aus.
80/E3 **Hallwilersee** (lake), Swi.
113/E5 **Hallyŏ Haesang Nat'l Park,** SKor.
110/A3 **Hallyŏ Haesong Nat'l Park,** SKor.
127/G3 **Halmahera** (isl.), Indo.
127/G4 **Halmahera** (sea), Indo.
102/M9 **Halmshera** (isl.), Indo.
62/E3 **Halmstad,** Swe.
90/B4 **Ḩalq al Wādī,** Tun.
62/D3 **Hals,** Den.
184/B1 **Halsey,** Or,US
62/E3 **Hälsingborg,** Swe.
59/G3 **Halstead,** Eng,UK
191/F1 **Halstead,** Ks,US
66/B5 **Halsteren,** Neth.
108/C4 **Haltang** (riv.), China
61/D3 **Haltdalen,** Nor.
57/H4 **Haltemprice,** Eng,UK
67/E5 **Haltern,** Ger.
188/K7 **Haltom City,** Tx,US
197/R8 **Halton** (co.), On,Can
197/R8 **Halton Hills,** On,Can
57/F2 **Haltwhistle,** Eng,UK
121/F4 **Haludpukhur,** India
67/E6 **Halver,** Ger.
67/E3 **Halverder Aa** (riv.), Ger.
148/B3 **Ham,** Chad
68/C4 **Ham,** Fr.
110/C3 **Hamada,** Japan
105/G3 **Hamadān,** Iran
105/G3 **Hamadān** (gov.), Iran
103/E2 **Ḩamāh,** Syria
104/D3 **Ḩamāh** (prov.), Syria
111/M10 **Hamajima,** Japan
111/E3 **Hamakita,** Japan
103/E1 **Hamam,** Turk.
111/E3 **Hamamatsu,** Japan
112/D2 **Hamanaka,** Japan
62/D1 **Hamar,** Nor.
147/G3 **Ḩamāţah, Jabal** (mtn.), Egypt
112/C1 **Hamatombetsu,** Japan
118/D6 **Hambantota,** SrL.
67/F2 **Hambergen,** Ger.
59/E5 **Hamble,** Eng,UK
57/G3 **Hambleton** (hills), Eng,UK
67/G3 **Hambühren,** Ger.
67/G1 **Hamburg,** Ger.
67/H1 **Hamburg** (state), Ger.
191/J4 **Hamburg,** Ar,US
193/G3 **Hamburg,** Ia,US
206/D1 **Hamburg,** NJ,US
199/G3 **Hamburg,** NY,US
206/C2 **Hamburg,** Pa,US
67/H1 **Hamburg** (Fuhlsbüttel) (int'l arpt.), Ger.
78/D3 **Hambye,** Fr.
106/D5 **Ḩamḑah,** SAr.
106/D5 **Ḩamdānah,** SAr.
208/B3 **Hamden,** Ct,US
199/J3 **Hamden,** NY,US
198/E5 **Hamden,** Oh,US
147/H3 **Ḩamḑ, Wādī al** (dry riv.), SAr.
63/K1 **Häme** (prov.), Fin.
63/K1 **Hämeenkyrö,** Fin.
63/L1 **Hämeenlinna,** Fin.
132/B3 **Hamelin,** Austl.
132/B3 **Hamelin Pool** (bay), Austl.
67/G4 **Hameln,** Ger.
150/B4 **Hamero Hadad,** Eth.
132/C2 **Hamersley** (range), Austl.
132/C2 **Hamersley Range Nat'l Park,** Austl.
198/E5 **Hamersville,** Oh,US
59/H3 **Hamford Water** (inlet), Eng,UK
113/E2 **Hamgyŏng** (mts.), NKor.
113/D2 **Hamgyŏng-Namdo** (prov.), NKor.
113/D3 **Hamhŭng,** NKor.
113/D3 **Hamhŭng-Si,** NKor.
108/C3 **Hami,** China
105/G4 **Ḩamīdīyeh,** Iran
125/D4 **Hamiguitan** (mt.), Phil.
192/E2 **Hamill,** SD,US
135/B3 **Hamilton,** Austl.
179/L3 **Hamilton** (inlet), Nf,Can
199/G3 **Hamilton,** On,Can
197/R9 **Hamilton** (har.), On,Can
136/C2 **Hamilton,** N.Z.
54/B5 **Hamilton,** Sc,UK
200/D3 **Hamilton,** Al,US
205/L12 **Hamilton** (mt.), Ca,US
185/K3 **Hamilton,** Co,US
202/M7 **Hamilton** (lake), Fl,US
200/E4 **Hamilton,** Ga,US
191/F2 **Hamilton,** Ks,US
198/C3 **Hamilton,** Mi,US
191/H1 **Hamilton,** Mo,US
183/G4 **Hamilton,** Mt,US
199/J3 **Hamilton,** NY,US
199/J3 **Hamilton** (mtn.), NY,US
198/D5 **Hamilton,** Oh,US
208/C2 **Hamilton,** RI,US
189/E2 **Hamilton,** Tx,US
207/K8 **Hamilton Grange Mem.,** NY,US
206/D3 **Hamilton Square-Mercerville,** NJ,US
197/Q9 **Hamilton-Wentworth** (co.), On,Can
146/D2 **Ḩamīm, Wādī al** (dry riv.), Libya
63/M1 **Hamina,** Fin.
194/D2 **Hamiota,** Mb,Can
120/C3 **Hamīrpur,** India
122/D2 **Hamīrpur,** India
113/D3 **Hamju,** NKor.
195/H5 **Ham Lake,** Mn,US
201/H3 **Hamlet,** NC,US
188/D1 **Hamlin,** Tx,US
201/F1 **Hamlin,** WV,US
67/E5 **Hamm,** Ger.
69/G2 **Hamm,** Ger.
70/B3 **Hamm,** Ger.
141/V17 **Hamma-Bouziane,** Alg.
90/B4 **Ḩammām Al Anf,** Tun.
141/X17 **Ḩammāmāt, Khalīj al** (gulf), Tun.
142/C5 **Hammami** (reg.), Mrta.
141/Q16 **Hamman, Oued el** (riv.), Alg.
156/E2 **Hammanskraal,** SAfr.
63/H1 **Hammarland,** Fin.
62/E2 **Hammarön** (isl.), Swe.
94/C3 **Hammarstrand,** Swe.
68/D1 **Hamme,** Belg.
67/F2 **Hamme** (riv.), Ger.
62/C3 **Hammel,** Den.
70/C2 **Hammelburg,** Ger.
206/B3 **Hammer** (cr.), Pa,US
61/G1 **Hammerfest,** Nor.
72/D3 **Hammer Fliess** (riv.), Ger.
62/F4 **Hammershus,** Den.
53/N7 **Hammersmith & Fulham** (bor.), Eng,UK
184/F2 **Hammett,** Id,US
66/D5 **Hamminkeln,** Ger.
190/E3 **Hammon,** Ok,US
208/B3 **Hammonasset** (pt.), Ct,US
205/R16 **Hammond,** In,US
202/C2 **Hammond,** La,US
183/M5 **Hammond,** Mt,US
53/N6 **Hammond Street,** Eng,UK
208/G6 **Hammondsville,** Oh,US
206/D4 **Hammonton,** NJ,US
55/P12 **Hamnavoe,** Sc,UK
61/F1 **Hamnvik,** Nor.
69/E3 **Hamois,** Belg.
152/C4 **Hamon,** Congo
69/E1 **Hamont-Achel,** Belg.
144/C3 **Hamoud,** Mrta.
136/B4 **Hampden,** N.Z.
208/B1 **Hampden,** Ma,US
208/B1 **Hampden** (co.), Ma,US
196/C3 **Hampden,** Me,US
194/E3 **Hampden,** ND,US
201/H2 **Hampden Sydney,** Va,US
59/E4 **Hampshire** (co.), Eng,UK
205/N15 **Hampshire,** Il,US
208/B1 **Hampshire** (co.), Ma,US
59/E4 **Hampshire Downs** (hills), Eng,UK
53/N7 **Hampstead,** Eng,UK
206/B4 **Hampstead,** Md,US
196/E3 **Hampton,** NB,Can
191/H4 **Hampton,** Ar,US
208/B2 **Hampton,** Ct,US
203/G3 **Hampton,** Fl,US
193/H2 **Hampton,** Ia,US
199/L3 **Hampton,** NH,US
184/C2 **Hampton,** Or,US
206/A4 **Hampton,** Pa,US
201/G4 **Hampton,** SC,US
201/F2 **Hampton,** Tn,US
201/J2 **Hampton,** Va,US
207/F2 **Hampton Bays,** NY,US
53/M7 **Hampton Court,** Eng,UK
206/B5 **Hampton Nat'l Hist. Site,** Md,US
135/G6 **Hampton Park,** Austl.
201/J2 **Hampton Roads** (estuary), Va,US
113/D5 **Hamp'yŏng,** SKor.
146/A2 **Ḩamrā, Al Ḩamādah al** (upland), Libya
142/C4 **Hamra, Saguia el** (dry riv.), WSah.
149/E2 **Ḩamrat ash Shaykh,** Sudan
156/B3 **Ham River,** Namb.
69/F5 **Ham-sous-Varsberg,** Fr.
196/B3 **Ham-Sud,** Qu,Can
205/F7 **Hamtramck,** Mi,US
127/J4 **Hamuku,** Indo.
111/H7 **Hamura,** Japan
113/D5 **Hamyang,** SKor.
113/D4 **Hamyŏl,** SKor.
113/E2 **Hamyŏng-Bukto** (prov.), NKor.
115/C5 **Han** (riv.), China
113/D4 **Han** (riv.), SKor.
120/C5 **Hana** (riv.), India
180/U10 **Hana,** Hi,US
201/G4 **Hanahan,** SC,US
150/B2 **Hanainef,** Eth.
147/H3 **Ḩanak,** SAr.
105/E1 **Hanak,** Turk.
112/B4 **Hanamaki,** Japan
180/U11 **Hanamalo** (pt.), Hi,US
109/M5 **Hanamatsu,** Japan
150/C4 **Hanan,** Eth.
151/A3 **Hanang** (peak), Tanz.
70/B2 **Hanau,** Ger.
112/B3 **Hanawa,** Japan
200/D3 **Hanceville,** Al,US
115/C5 **Hanchuan,** China
202/M8 **Hancock** (lake), Fl,US
199/G5 **Hancock,** Md,US
196/C3 **Hancock,** Me,US
195/K4 **Hancock,** Mi,US
194/G5 **Hancock,** Mn,US
199/J4 **Hancock,** NY,US
193/K1 **Hancock,** Wi,US
208/G6 **Hancock** (co.), WV,US
206/C4 **Hancocks Bridge,** NJ,US
208/A1 **Hancock Shaker Vill.,** Ma,US
199/H3 **Hancock** (Syracuse) (int'l arpt.), NY,US
111/M10 **Handa,** Japan
113/D2 **Handae-ri,** NKor.
115/C3 **Handan,** China
114/B5 **Handawor,** India
183/K1 **Handel,** Sk,Can
67/G2 **Handeloh,** Ger.
63/S7 **Handen,** Swe.
151/B3 **Handeni,** Tanz.
62/C4 **Handewitt,** Ger.
120/D3 **Handiā,** India
73/C2 **Handlová,** Slvk.
194/C3 **Handsworth,** Sk,Can
59/E1 **Handsworth,** Eng,UK
111/H7 **Haneda** (int'l arpt.), Japan
186/C2 **Hanford,** Ca,US
182/E4 **Hanford Site,** Wa,US
108/D2 **Hangayn** (mts.), Mong.
115/B3 **Hanggin Qi,** China
201/G2 **Hanging Rock** (mtn.), NC,US
58/C5 **Hangingstone** (hill), Eng,UK
156/L11 **Hangklip** (cape), SAfr.
182/F4 **Hangman** (cr.), Id, Wa,US
61/G4 **Hangö,** Fin.
63/K2 **Hangö** (Hanko), Fin.
115/H7 **Hangu,** China
122/A1 **Hangu,** Pak.
115/L9 **Hangzhou,** China
115/E5 **Hangzhou** (bay), China
108/C2 **Hanhöhiy** (mts.), Mong.
104/E2 **Hani,** Turk.
150/B2 **Ḩanīsh al Kabīr** (isl.), Yem.
154/B2 **Hanja** (riv.), Ang.
126/D4 **Hanjalipan,** Indo.
117/H3 **Hanjiang,** China
67/H3 **Hankensbüttel,** Ger.
156/D4 **Hankey,** SAfr.
194/F4 **Hankinson,** ND,US
63/L1 **Hanko** (Hangö), Fin.
114/C5 **Hanle,** India
194/A2 **Hanley,** Sk,Can
136/C3 **Hanmer,** N.Z.
183/J2 **Hanna,** Ab,Can
202/B2 **Hanna,** La,US
185/K3 **Hanna,** Wy,US
194/E4 **Hannaford,** ND,US
194/E3 **Hannah,** ND,US
200/E4 **Hannahs Mill,** Ga,US
111/L10 **Hannan,** Japan
193/J4 **Hannibal,** Mo,US
199/H3 **Hannibal,** NY,US
198/F5 **Hannibal,** Oh,US
130/B3 **Hann, Mount** (peak), Austl.
111/H7 **Hannō,** Japan
67/G4 **Hannover,** Ger.
67/G4 **Hannover** (int'l arpt.), Ger.
69/E2 **Hannut,** Belg.
62/F4 **Hanöbukten** (bay), Swe.
123/D1 **Hanoi** (Ha Noi) (cap.), Viet.
198/F2 **Hanover,** On,Can
175/J7 **Hanover** (isl.), Chile
156/D3 **Hanover,** SAfr.
193/J2 **Hanover,** Il,US
200/E1 **Hanover,** In,US
191/F1 **Hanover,** Ks,US
208/D1 **Hanover,** Ma,US
195/N6 **Hanover,** Mn,US
199/K3 **Hanover,** NH,US
206/B4 **Hanover,** Pa,US
201/J2 **Hanover,** Va,US
205/P16 **Hanover Park,** Il,US
208/G6 **Hanoverton,** Oh,US
73/A4 **Hanság** (reg.), Hun.
73/B4 **Hansági** (can.), Hun.
196/B4 **Hanscom A.F.B.,** Ma,US
121/F3 **Hānsdiha,** India
204/B2 **Hansen** (dam), Ca,US
185/F2 **Hansen,** Id,US
204/F7 **Hansen Dam Rec. Area,** Ca,US
115/D5 **Hanshan,** China
118/C2 **Hānsi,** India
193/G1 **Hanska** (lake), Mn,US
136/E3 **Hanson** (bay), N.Z.
208/D1 **Hanson,** Ma,US
67/H2 **Hanstedt,** Ger.
62/C3 **Hanstholm,** Den.
190/E1 **Hanston,** Ks,US
205/B2 **Hansville,** Wa,US
114/D3 **Hantengri Feng** (peak), China
197/L1 **Hant's Harbour,** Nf,Can
196/E3 **Hantsport,** NS,Can
179/J2 **Hantzsch** (riv.), NW,Can
118/B2 **Hanumāngarh,** India
108/E2 **Hanuy** (riv.), Mong.
135/C2 **Hanwood,** Austl.
116/D2 **Hanyuan,** China
152/C5 **Hanza,** Ang.
108/F5 **Hanzhong,** China
139/L6 **Hao** (atoll), FrPol.
50/B6 **Hao** (isl.), FrPol.
117/G3 **Haoshan,** China
148/D1 **Haouach, Ouadi** (dry riv.), Chad
61/H2 **Haparanda,** Swe.
113/E5 **Hapch'ŏn,** SKor.
201/M7 **Hapeville,** Ga,US
184/B3 **Happy Camp,** Ca,US
187/G3 **Happy Jack,** Az,US
202/D3 **Happy Jack,** La,US
133/M9 **Happy Valley** (res.), Austl.
179/K3 **Happy Valley-Goose Bay,** Nf,Can
113/D4 **Haptŏk,** SKor.
120/A1 **Hāpur,** India
103/D5 **Ḩaql,** SAr.
168/C4 **Haquira,** Peru
108/D4 **Har** (lake), China
108/C2 **Har** (lake), Mong.
108/F2 **Haraa** (riv.), Mong.
106/E4 **Ḩaraḑ,** SAr.
150/B1 **Ḩaraḑ,** Yem.
106/D5 **Ḩarajah,** SAr.
111/G2 **Haramachi,** Japan
122/B2 **Harappa** (ruins), Pak.
155/F3 **Harare** (cap.), Zim.
155/F3 **Harare** (int'l arpt.), Zim.
146/D3 **Ḩarash, Bi'r al** (well), Libya
108/F2 **Har-Ayag,** Mong.
108/F2 **Har-Ayrag,** Mong.
148/C2 **Haraz,** Chad
148/D3 **Haraze-Mangueigne,** Chad
144/C5 **Harbel,** Libr.
206/C6 **Harbeson,** De,US
109/K2 **Harbin,** China
103/E1 **Harbiye,** Turk.
68/B4 **Harbonnières,** Fr.
62/C3 **Harboøre,** Den.
198/E3 **Harbor Beach,** Mi,US
204/F8 **Harbor City,** Ca,US
198/D2 **Harbor Springs,** Mi,US
197/K2 **Harbour Breton,** Nf,Can
197/L2 **Harbour Grace,** Nf,Can
197/L2 **Harbour Main,** Nf,Can
67/G2 **Harburg,** Ger.
70/D5 **Harburg,** Ger.
59/E2 **Harbury,** Eng,UK
62/D4 **Hårby,** Den.
81/F3 **Hard,** Aus.
120/A4 **Hardā,** India
62/B1 **Hardangervidda Nat'l Park,** Nor.
154/C5 **Hardap** (dam), Namb.
67/H3 **Hardau** (riv.), Ger.
200/E4 **Hardaway,** Al,US
202/M8 **Hardee** (co.), Fl,US
201/G4 **Hardeeville,** SC,US
67/G5 **Hardegsen,** Ger.
68/A2 **Hardelot-Plage,** Fr.
66/D3 **Hardenberg,** Neth.
191/F3 **Harden City,** Ok,US
66/C4 **Harderwijk,** Neth.
70/C3 **Hardheim,** Ger.
193/J4 **Hardin,** Il,US
200/C2 **Hardin,** Ky,US
183/L5 **Hardin,** Mt,US
189/G2 **Hardin,** Tx,US
157/E3 **Harding,** SAfr.
200/E4 **Harding** (lake), Al,US
200/E4 **Harding** (lake), Ga,US
200/D2 **Hardinsburg,** Ky,US
183/J1 **Hardisty,** Ab,Can
120/C2 **Hardoi,** India
187/H3 **Hardscrabble** (wash), Az,US
191/E2 **Hardtner,** Ks,US
107/L3 **Hardwār,** India
208/B1 **Hardwick,** Ma,US
201/F4 **Hardwick-Midway,** Ga,US
196/B2 **Hardwood** (mtn.), Me,US
175/K8 **Hardy** (pen.), Chile
191/J2 **Hardy,** Ar,US
192/F3 **Hardy,** Ne,US
197/K1 **Hare Bay,** Nf,Can
68/C2 **Harelbeke,** Belg.
67/E3 **Haren,** Ger.
66/D2 **Haren,** Neth.
150/B3 **Hārer,** Eth.
150/B3 **Hārergē** (prov.), Eth.
103/G7 **Har Eval** (Jabal 'Aybāl) (mtn.), WBnk.
150/B3 **Harewa,** Eth.
79/F2 **Harfleur,** Fr.
206/B4 **Harford** (co.), Md,US
199/J4 **Harford,** Pa,US
150/B4 **Hargele,** Eth.
69/G4 **Hargesheim,** Ger.
150/C3 **Hargeysa,** Som.
150/C3 **Hargeysa** (int'l arpt.), Som.
93/G2 **Harghita** (co.), Rom.
93/G2 **Harghita** (peak), Rom.
150/A2 **Hargīgo,** Eth.
108/E2 **Harhorin,** Mong.
63/K2 **Hari** (str.), Est.
124/C3 **Hari** (riv.), Indo.
150/C2 **Ḩarīb,** Yem.
154/C5 **Haribes,** Namb.
118/C5 **Harihar,** India
120/E3 **Hariharganj,** India
122/C2 **Harīke,** India
103/E1 **Ḩārim,** Syria
110/D3 **Harima** (sound), Japan
103/D3 **Ḩarīmā,** Jor.
53/N7 **Haringey** (bor.), Eng,UK
121/G4 **Haringhāta** (riv.), Bang.
66/B5 **Haringvliet** (chan.), Neth.
66/B5 **Haringvlietdam** (dam), Neth.
122/F4 **Haripād,** India
107/H2 **Harīrūd** (riv.), Afg.
102/F6 **Harirud** (riv.), Asia
103/G7 **Ḩāris,** WBnk.
118/C3 **Harisal,** India
63/K1 **Harjavalta,** Fin.
189/F2 **Harker Heights,** Tx,US
193/G3 **Harlan,** Ia,US
201/F2 **Harlan,** Ky,US
192/E3 **Harlan Co.** (dam), Ne,US
192/E3 **Harlan Co.** (lake), Ne,US
56/D6 **Harlech,** Wal,UK
201/F4 **Harlem,** Ga,US
183/K3 **Harlem,** Mt,US
207/K8 **Harlem,** NY,US
208/F6 **Harlem Springs,** Oh,US
59/H2 **Harleston,** Eng,UK
189/G1 **Harleton,** Tx,US
201/G4 **Harleyville,** SC,US
66/C2 **Harlingen,** Neth.
189/F4 **Harlingen,** Tx,US
59/F3 **Harlington,** Eng,UK
53/P6 **Harlow,** Eng,UK
194/E3 **Harlow,** ND,US
183/K4 **Harlowton,** Mt,US
73/A3 **Harmannsdorf,** Aus.
66/B4 **Harmelen,** Neth.
147/G1 **Har Meron** (mtn.), Isr.
193/H2 **Harmony,** Mn,US
208/G6 **Harmony,** Pa,US
208/C2 **Harmony,** RI,US
120/E2 **Harnātānr,** India
68/B3 **Harnes,** Fr.
206/A4 **Harney,** Md,US
184/D2 **Harney** (lake), Or,US
184/D2 **Harney** (val.), Or,US
180/F3 **Harney** (peak), SD,US
121/H4 **Harni,** Bang.
122/A1 **Harnoli,** Pak.
61/F3 **Härnösand,** Swe.
109/J2 **Har Nur,** China
76/D1 **Haro,** Sp.
158/C3 **Haro, Cabo** (pt.), Mex.
204/B1 **Harold,** Ca,US
59/F3 **Harpenden,** Eng,UK
177/L3 **Harper** (mtn.), Yk,Can
144/D5 **Harper,** Libr.
136/B3 **Harper** (pass), N.Z.
177/K3 **Harper** (mt.), Ak,US
186/D3 **Harper** (lake), Ca,US
191/E2 **Harper,** Ks,US
184/E2 **Harper,** Or,US
188/E2 **Harper,** Tx,US
205/B2 **Harper,** Wa,US
199/H5 **Harpers Ferry Nat'l Hist. Park,** WV,US
200/D4 **Harpersville,** Al,US
202/D1 **Harperville,** Ms,US
205/G7 **Harper Woods,** Mi,US
200/D2 **Harpeth** (riv.), Tn,US
67/F3 **Harpstedt,** Ger.
109/H3 **Harqin Qi,** China
115/D2 **Harqin Zuoyi Monggolzu Zizhixian,** China
150/D2 **Ḩarrah,** Yem.
120/B4 **Harrai,** India
104/D2 **Harran,** Turk.
191/H4 **Harrell,** Ar,US
179/J4 **Harricana** (riv.), Qu,Can
203/H2 **Harrietts Bluff,** Ga,US
207/D1 **Harriman,** NY,US
200/E3 **Harriman,** Tn,US
207/D1 **Harriman St. Park,** NY,US
135/E1 **Harrington,** Austl.
206/C6 **Harrington,** De,US
196/D3 **Harrington,** Me,US
207/K8 **Harrington Park,** NJ,US
133/G4 **Harris** (lake), Austl.
133/F3 **Harris** (peak), Austl.
183/L2 **Harris,** Sk,Can
55/H8 **Harris** (reg.), Sc,UK
203/G3 **Harris** (lake), Fl,US
195/L5 **Harris,** Mi,US
201/H3 **Harris** (lake), NC,US
200/E2 **Harris** (mtn.), Tn,US
189/M9 **Harris** (co.), Tx,US
191/J3 **Harrisburg,** Ar,US
200/C2 **Harrisburg,** Il,US
184/B1 **Harrisburg,** Or,US
206/B3 **Harrisburg,** Pa,US
206/B3 **Harrisburg** (int'l arpt.), Pa,US
64/E1 **Harrislee,** Ger.
156/E3 **Harrismith,** SAfr.
179/L3 **Harrison** (cape), Nf,Can
177/H1 **Harrison** (bay), Ak,US
191/H2 **Harrison,** Ar,US
201/F4 **Harrison,** Ga,US
182/F4 **Harrison,** Id,US
198/D2 **Harrison,** Mi,US
192/C2 **Harrison,** Ne,US
207/J9 **Harrison,** NJ,US
207/E2 **Harrison,** NY,US
198/D5 **Harrison,** Oh,US
208/F7 **Harrison** (co.), Oh,US
200/E3 **Harrison,** Tn,US
202/C2 **Harrisonburg,** La,US
201/H1 **Harrisonburg,** Va,US
191/G1 **Harrisonville,** Mo,US
198/F3 **Harriston,** On,Can
200/B5 **Harriston,** Ms,US
193/K4 **Harristown,** Il,US
198/E2 **Harrisville,** Mi,US
200/B5 **Harrisville,** Ms,US
208/G5 **Harrisville,** Pa,US
208/C2 **Harrisville,** RI,US
201/G1 **Harrisville,** WV,US
198/C5 **Harrodsburg,** In,US
200/E2 **Harrodsburg,** Ky,US
57/G4 **Harrogate,** Eng,UK
200/F2 **Harrogate-Shawnee,** Tn,US
190/E3 **Harrold,** Tx,US
135/B3 **Harrow,** Austl.
205/G7 **Harrow,** On,Can
53/N7 **Harrow,** Eng,UK
53/M7 **Harrow** (bor.), Eng,UK
191/H1 **Harry S Truman** (dam), Mo,US
191/H1 **Harry S Truman** (res.), Mo,US
191/G1 **Harry S Truman Nat'l Hist. Site,** Mo,US
67/G2 **Harsefeld,** Ger.
67/F5 **Harsewinkel,** Ger.
66/C4 **Harskamp,** Neth.
72/B4 **Harsleben,** Ger.
205/G6 **Harson's Island,** Mi,US
118/B2 **Harsor,** India
61/F1 **Harstad,** Nor.
178/C2 **Hart** (riv.), Yk,Can
198/C3 **Hart,** Mi,US
207/K8 **Hart** (isl.), NY,US
184/C2 **Hart** (lake), Or,US
184/D2 **Hart** (mtn.), Or,US
190/C3 **Hart,** Tx,US
156/C3 **Hartbeesrivier** (dry riv.), SAfr.
194/D1 **Harte** (mtn.), Mb,Can
62/B1 **Hårteigen** (peak), Nor.
66/B5 **Hartelkanaal** (can.), Neth.
54/C6 **Hart Fell** (mtn.), Sc,UK
144/C5 **Hartford,** Libr.
203/F2 **Hartford,** Al,US
208/B2 **Hartford,** Ct,US
208/B2 **Hartford** (co.), Ct,US
191/G1 **Hartford,** Ks,US
200/D2 **Hartford,** Ky,US
206/D4 **Hartford,** NJ,US
196/A4 **Hartford,** Vt,US
198/B3 **Hartford,** Wi,US
198/D4 **Hartford City,** In,US
72/C5 **Hartha,** Ger.
72/D6 **Hartha,** Ger.
80/D2 **Hartheim,** Ger.
54/C5 **Harthill,** Sc,UK
193/F2 **Hartington,** Ne,US
196/D2 **Hartland,** NB,Can
58/B5 **Hartland,** Eng,UK
58/B4 **Hartland** (pt.), Eng,UK
205/E6 **Hartland,** Mi,US
199/K3 **Hartland,** Vt,US
58/D2 **Hartlebury,** Eng,UK
57/G2 **Hartlepool,** Eng,UK
206/A2 **Hartleton,** Pa,US
53/P7 **Hartley,** Eng,UK
193/G2 **Hartley,** Ia,US
177/N5 **Hartley Bay,** BC,Can
206/C5 **Hartly,** De,US
154/B3 **Hartmannberge** (mts.), Namb.
72/C6 **Hartmannsdorf,** Ger.
130/B4 **Hart, Mount** (peak), Austl.
184/D2 **Hart Mtn. Nat'l Antelope Ref.,** Or,US
194/D3 **Hartney,** Mb,Can
156/D3 **Harts** (riv.), SAfr.
201/F1 **Harts,** WV,US
207/E1 **Hartsdale,** NY,US
200/D3 **Hartselle,** Al,US
200/E4 **Hartsfield Atlanta** (int'l arpt.), Ga,US
59/E1 **Hartshill,** Eng,UK
191/J2 **Hartshorn,** Mo,US
191/G3 **Hartshorne,** Ok,US
133/G2 **Harts Range,** Austl.
205/B3 **Hartstene** (isl.), Wa,US
208/G4 **Hartstown,** Pa,US
201/G3 **Hartsville,** SC,US
200/D2 **Hartsville,** Tn,US
191/H2 **Hartville,** Mo,US
208/F6 **Hartville,** Oh,US
201/F3 **Hartwell,** Ga,US
201/F3 **Hartwell** (dam), Ga,US
201/F3 **Hartwell** (lake), Ga, SC,US
135/C4 **Hartz Mtn. Nat'l Park,** Austl.
69/G6 **Hartzviller,** Fr.
127/E3 **Harun** (peak), Indo.
107/K3 **Hārūnābād,** Pak.
125/A4 **Harun, Bukit** (peak), Indo.
114/F2 **Har Us** (lake), Mong.
108/D2 **Har-Us** (riv.), Mong.
107/H2 **Hārūt** (riv.), Afg.
205/N15 **Harvard,** Il,US
199/L3 **Harvard,** Ma,US
192/E3 **Harvard,** Ne,US
200/D3 **Harvest,** Al,US
132/B5 **Harvey,** Austl.
196/E3 **Harvey,** NB,Can
205/Q16 **Harvey,** Il,US
198/C1 **Harvey,** Mi,US
194/E4 **Harvey,** ND,US
206/B1 **Harveys** (lake), Pa,US
59/H3 **Harwich,** Eng,UK
208/A2 **Harwinton,** Ct,US
194/F4 **Harwood,** ND,US
57/G5 **Harworth,** Eng,UK
120/A1 **Haryana** (state), India
67/H5 **Harz** (mts.), Ger.
72/B4 **Harzgerode,** Ger.
104/C2 **Hasan** (peak), Turk.
104/E2 **Hasankeyf,** Turk.
120/B1 **Hasanpur,** India
207/D2 **Hasbrouck Heights,** NJ,US
120/D4 **Hasdo** (riv.), India
67/E3 **Hase** (riv.), Ger.
70/D1 **Hasel** (riv.), Ger.
67/E3 **Haselünne,** Ger.
80/D3 **Hasenmalt** (mtn.), Swi.
111/M9 **Hashima,** Japan
110/D3 **Hashimoto,** Japan
105/G3 **Hashtgerd,** Iran
142/C4 **Hasi el Farsía** (well), WSah.
107/K3 **Hāsilpur,** Pak.
191/H3 **Haskell,** Ar,US
191/G3 **Haskell,** Ok,US
188/E1 **Haskell,** Tx,US
71/H5 **Haslach an der Mühl,** Aus.
70/B6 **Haslach im Kinzigtal,** Ger.
80/D3 **Hasle bei Burgdorf,** Swi.
59/F4 **Haslemere,** Eng,UK
205/F6 **Hasler** (cr.), Mi,US
188/K7 **Haslet,** Tx,US
198/D3 **Haslett,** Mi,US
57/F4 **Haslingden,** Eng,UK
57/F5 **Haslington,** Eng,UK
67/G1 **Hasloh,** Ger.
121/H3 **Hāsmāi,** Bang.
68/C3 **Haspres,** Fr.
103/E1 **Hassa,** Turk.
118/C5 **Hassan,** India
142/B4 **Hassan** (Laayoune) (int'l arpt.), WSah.
187/F3 **Hassayampa** (riv.), Az,US
70/D2 **Hassberge** (hills), Ger.
189/E2 **Hasse,** Tx,US
179/S7 **Hassel** (sound), NW,Can
67/G3 **Hassel,** Ger.
72/A4 **Hasselfelde,** Ger.
69/E2 **Hasselt,** Belg.
66/D3 **Hasselt,** Neth.
70/D2 **Hassfurt,** Ger.
141/S16 **Hassi Bahbah,** Alg.
143/F3 **Hassi bou Zid** (well), Alg.
143/F3 **Hassi Cheïkh** (well), Alg.
143/G3 **Hassi el Hadjar** (well), Alg.
143/H4 **Hassi el Mislane** (well), Alg.
143/G2 **Hassi er Rebib** (well), Alg.
143/F3 **Hassi Fahl** (well), Alg.
143/F3 **Hassi Inifel** (well), Alg.
143/F3 **Hassi Izi** (well), Alg.
143/F3 **Hassi Khanem** (well), Alg.
143/E3 **Hassi Massine** (well), Alg.
143/G3 **Hassi Messaoud,** Alg.
143/F3 **Hassi Mouïna** (well), Alg.
143/G4 **Hassi Tabelbalet** (well), Alg.
72/D5 **Hasslau,** Ger.
72/D1 **Hassleben,** Ger.
62/E3 **Hässleholm,** Swe.
62/G2 **Hasslo** (int'l arpt.), Swe.
70/B4 **Hassloch,** Ger.
67/G4 **Haste,** Ger.
135/C3 **Hastings,** Austl.
136/D2 **Hastings,** N.Z.
144/B4 **Hastings,** SLeo.
55/M11 **Hastings,** UK
59/G5 **Hastings,** Eng,UK
203/H3 **Hastings,** Fl,US
198/D3 **Hastings,** Mi,US
195/H5 **Hastings,** Mn,US
195/H5 **Hastings** (dam), Mn,US
192/E3 **Hastings,** Ne,US
199/G4 **Hastings,** Pa,US
59/G5 **Hastings Battlesite,** Eng,UK
207/E1 **Hastings-on-Hudson,** NY,US
111/H7 **Hasuda,** Japan
61/G1 **Hasvik,** Nor.
190/C1 **Haswell,** Co,US
143/H3 **Ḩasy Iferfes** (well), Libya
143/H4 **Ḩasy In 'Agiuel** (well), Libya
143/H4 **Ḩasy Suis** (well), Libya
143/H4 **Ḩasy Timenocalin** (well), Libya
184/C3 **Hat** (mtn.), Ca,US
141/W18 **Ḩaţab** (riv.), Tun.
203/H3 **Hatachineha** (lake), Fl,US
111/M9 **Hatashō,** Japan
103/E1 **Hatay** (prov.), Turk.
206/C3 **Hatboro,** Pa,US
187/J4 **Hatch,** NM,US
187/F2 **Hatch,** Ut,US
123/B5 **Hat Chao Mai Nat'l Park,** Thai.
200/E4 **Hatchechubbee,** Al,US
175/J7 **Hatcher** (peak), Arg.
133/G2 **Hatches Creek,** Austl.
200/C3 **Hatchie** (riv.), Ms, Tn,US
200/C3 **Hatchie Nat'l Wild. Ref.,** Tn,US
202/M7 **Hatchineha** (lake), Fl,US
92/F3 **Haţeg,** Rom.
135/B2 **Hatfield,** Austl.
53/N6 **Hatfield,** Eng,UK
191/G3 **Hatfield,** Ar,US
208/B1 **Hatfield,** Ma,US
206/C3 **Hatfield,** Pa,US
108/E1 **Hatgal,** Mong.
121/E4 **Hāt Gāmāria,** India
121/H4 **Hāthāzāri,** Bang.
135/E1 **Hat Head,** Austl.
135/E1 **Hat Head Nat'l Park,** Austl.
57/G5 **Hathersage,** Eng,UK
120/B2 **Hāthras,** India
121/H4 **Hātia** (isl.), Bang.
121/H4 **Hātia** (riv.), Bang.
106/C4 **Ḩāţibah, Ra's** (pt.), SAr.
123/D4 **Ha Tien,** Viet.
123/D2 **Ha Tinh,** Viet.
195/K5 **Hatley,** Wi,US
123/B5 **Hat Nai Yang Nat'l Park,** Thai.
164/D3 **Hato Corozal,** Col.
111/H7 **Hatogaya,** Japan
162/D3 **Hato Mayor,** DRep.
111/H7 **Hatoyama,** Japan
120/B3 **Hatta,** India
133/J5 **Hattah-Kulkyne Nat'l Park,** Austl.
124/D4 **Hatta-Sukarno** (int'l arpt.), Indo.
66/D4 **Hattem,** Neth.
69/G6 **Hatten,** Fr.
67/F2 **Hatten,** Ger.
201/K3 **Hatteras,** NC,US
201/K3 **Hatteras** (cape), NC,US
201/K3 **Hatteras** (isl.), NC,US
70/B2 **Hattersheim am Mein,** Ger.

202/D2 Hattiesburg, Ms,US
160/D2 Hattieville, Belz.
67/E6 Hattingen, Ger.
183/K2 Hatton, Sk,Can
57/G6 Hatton, Eng,UK
54/E2 Hatton, Sc,UK
200/D3 Hatton, Al,US
194/F4 Hatton, ND,US
187/F1 Hatton, Ut,US
63/L1 Hattula, Fin.
92/D2 Hatvan, Hun.
123/C5 Hat Yai, Thai.
123/C5 Hat Yai (int'l arpt.), Thai.
70/B4 Hatzenbühl, Ger.
67/F6 Hatzfeld, Ger.
123/E3 Hau Bon, Viet.
68/B2 Haubourdin, Fr.
200/D1 Haubstadt, In,US
150/C3 Haud (reg.), Eth.
62/B2 Hauge, Nor.
195/J5 Haugen, Wi,US
62/A2 Haugesund, Nor.
189/H1 Haughton, La,US
123/D4 Hau Giang (riv.), Viet.
73/A2 Haugsdorf, Aus.
62/B2 Haukeligrend, Nor.
61/H2 Haukipudas, Fin.
70/C1 Haune (riv.), Ger.
71/F7 Haunsberg (peak), Aus.
70/D6 Haunstetten, Ger.
207/E2 Hauppauge, NY,US
136/F6 Hauraki (gulf), N.Z.
62/A1 Haus, Nor.
70/B6 Hausach, Ger.
63/L1 Hausjärvi, Fin.
77/E1 Hauskoa (mtn.), Fr.
81/F4 Hausstock (peak), Swi.
142/D3 Haut Atlas (mts.), Mor.
80/B1 Haute-Marne (dept.), Fr.
149/E4 Haute-Mbomou (pref.), CAfr.
79/G1 Haute-Normandie (reg.), Fr.
179/K4 Hauterive, Qu,Can
82/C3 Hautes-Alpes (dept.), Fr.
148/B4 Haute-Sangha (pref.), CAfr.
80/B2 Haute-Saône (dept.), Fr.
80/C5 Haute-Savoie (dept.), Fr.
69/E3 Hautes Fagnes (uplands), Belg., Ger.
80/B6 Hauteville-Lompnes, Fr.
196/C3 Haut, Isle au (isl.), Me,US
148/D4 Haut-Kotto (pref.), CAfr.
68/C3 Hautmont, Fr.
80/B1 Hautmont, Côte de (hill), Fr.
152/C3 Haut-Ogooué (prov.), Gabon
80/D2 Haut-Rhin (dept.), Fr.
53/S10 Hauts-de-Seine (dept.), Fr.
143/E2 Hauts Plateaux (plat.), Alg., Mor.
153/F2 Haut-Zaïre (reg.), Zaire
180/T10 Hauula, Hi,US
203/F2 Havana, Fl,US
193/J3 Havana, Il,US
194/F5 Havana, ND,US
161/F1 Havana (La Habana) (cap.), Cuba
139/V13 Havannah (chan.), NCal.
59/F5 Havant, Eng,UK
186/E3 Havasu (lake), Az, Ca,US
186/E3 Havasu Nat'l Wild. Ref., Az, Ca,US
187/F2 Havasupai Ind. Res., Az,US
62/H3 Havdhem, Swe.
62/E4 Havdrup, Den.
72/C2 Havel (can.), Ger.
72/C2 Havel (riv.), Ger.
69/E3 Havelange, Belg.
72/C2 Havelberg, Ger.
72/C2 Havelland (reg.), Ger.
72/C2 Havelländischer Grosser Hauptkanal (can.), Ger.
72/C2 Havelländisches Luch (marsh), Ger.
196/E3 Havelock, NB,Can
199/H2 Havelock, On,Can
136/C3 Havelock, N.Z.
201/J3 Havelock, NC,US
136/D2 Havelock North, N.Z.
66/D3 Havelte, Neth.
191/F2 Haven, Ks,US
59/G3 Havengore (isl.), Eng,UK
58/B3 Haverfordwest, Wal,UK
59/G2 Haverhill, Eng,UK
199/L3 Haverhill, Ma,US
199/K2 Haverhill, NH,US
53/P7 Havering (bor.), Eng,UK
207/E1 Haverstraw, NY,US
190/E2 Haviland, Ks,US
105/G2 Ḩavīq, Iran
65/K4 Havířov, Czh.
67/E5 Havixbeck, Ger.
65/H4 Havlíčkův Brod, Czh.
62/C4 Havneby, Den.
78/D6 Hâvre (riv.), Fr.
183/K3 Havre, Mt,US
79/F1 Havre-Antifer (harb.), Fr.
197/G2 Havre-Aubert, Qu,Can
206/B4 Havre de Grace, Md,US
183/K3 Havre North, Mt,US
179/K3 Havre-Saint-Pierre, Qu,Can
93/H5 Havsa, Turk.
104/C1 Havza, Turk.
200/E3 Haw (peak), NC,US
201/H2 Haw (riv.), NC,US
180/S10 Hawaii (state), US
180/U11 Hawaii (isl.), Hi,US
139/H2 Hawaiian (isls.), Hi,US
204/F8 Hawaiian Gardens, Ca,US
180/U11 Hawaii Volcanoes Nat'l Park, Hi,US
105/G4 Ḩawallī, Kuw.
136/C3 Hawarden, N.Z.
57/E5 Hawarden, Wal,UK
193/F2 Hawarden, Ia,US
150/C4 Hawd (reg.), Som.
136/B4 Hawea (lake), N.Z.
136/C2 Hawera, N.Z.
57/F3 Hawes, Eng,UK
200/D2 Hawesville, Ky,US
57/F2 Haweswater (res.), Eng,UK
180/U10 Hawi, Hi,US
54/D6 Hawick, Sc,UK
135/E2 Hawke (cape), Austl.
136/D2 Hawke (bay), N.Z.
133/H4 Hawker, Austl.
136/D2 Hawkes' Bay (reg.), N.Z.
130/D2 Hawkesbury (pt.), Austl.
134/G8 Hawkesbury (riv.), Austl.
179/J4 Hawkesbury, On,Can
136/D2 Hawke's Valley (reg.), N.Z.
184/D4 Hawkins (peak), Ca,US
193/J1 Hawkins, Wi,US
201/F4 Hawkinsville, Ga,US
200/B1 Hawk Point, Mo,US
201/G3 Hawksbill (mtn.), NC,US
201/H1 Hawksbill (mtn.), Va,US
135/E2 Hawks Nest, Austl.
162/C1 Hawks Nest (pt.), Bahm.
194/E4 Hawks Nest (peak), ND,US
192/C5 Hawley, Co,US
194/F4 Hawley, Mn,US
199/J4 Hawley, Pa,US
188/E1 Hawley, Tx,US
208/A3 Hawleyville, Ct,US
143/H2 Ḩawmat As Sūq, Tun.
207/K8 Haworth, NJ,US
191/G4 Haworth, Ok,US
105/F4 Hawr al Ḩammār (lake), Iraq
103/B4 Ḩawsh 'Īsá, Egypt
156/B4 Hawston, SAfr.
204/B3 Hawthorne, Ca,US
203/G3 Hawthorne, Fl,US
207/J8 Hawthorne, NJ,US
184/D4 Hawthorne, Nv,US
207/E1 Hawthorne, NY,US
189/G2 Hawthorne, Tx,US
184/D4 Hawthorne Amm. Dep., Nv,US
205/P15 Hawthorn Woods, Il,US
103/D3 Ḩawwārah, Jor.
150/A2 Ḩawzēn, Eth.
57/G3 Haxby, Eng,UK
192/D3 Haxtun, Co,US
135/C2 Hay, Austl.
130/C3 Hay (cape), Austl.
134/C3 Hay (pt.), Austl.
133/H3 Hay (riv.), Austl.
178/E3 Hay (riv.), Ab,Can
182/F4 Hay, Wa,US
112/B4 Hayachine-san (mtn.), Japan
111/H7 Hayama, Japan
69/F5 Hayange, Fr.
149/F3 Haybān, Sudan
149/F3 Haybān (peak), Sudan
69/D3 Haybes, Fr.
177/F2 Haycock, Ak,US
187/G4 Hayden, Az,US
185/K3 Hayden, Co,US
182/F4 Hayden, Id,US
187/F4 Hayden-Rhodes (aqueduct), Az,US
208/B1 Haydenville, Ma,US
57/F5 Haydock, Eng,UK
57/G5 Haydon Bridge, Eng,UK
178/G3 Hayes (riv.), Mb,Can
178/G2 Hayes (riv.), NW,Can
179/T7 Hayes (pen.), Grld.
53/M7 Hayes, Eng,UK
177/J3 Hayes (mt.), Ak,US
192/D1 Hayes, SD,US
195/K5 Hayes, Wi,US
200/F3 Hayesville, NC,US
208/E6 Hayesville, Oh,US
184/B3 Hayfork, Ca,US
70/C6 Hayingen, Ger.
58/A6 Hayle, Eng,UK
58/A6 Hayle (riv.), Eng,UK
59/F5 Hayling (isl.), Eng,UK
203/G2 Haylow, Ga,US
104/C2 Haymana, Turk.
191/J3 Haynes, Ar,US
195/C4 Haynes, ND,US
189/H1 Haynesville, La,US
200/D4 Hayneville, Al,US
150/D2 Haynin, Yem.
58/C2 Hay on Wye, Wal,UK
93/H5 Hayrabolu, Turk.
178/E2 Hay River, NW,Can
183/J2 Hays, Ab,Can
191/F1 Hays, Ks,US
183/K4 Hays, Mt,US
146/B2 Hayshah, Sabkhat al (salt marsh), Libya
192/C2 Hay Springs, Ne,US
195/K2 Haystack (mtn.), On,Can
200/D1 Haysville, In,US
191/F2 Haysville, Ks,US
200/C2 Hayti, Mo,US
193/F1 Hayti, SD,US
205/K11 Hayward, Ca,US
195/J4 Hayward, Wi,US
59/F5 Haywards Heath, Eng,UK
191/G3 Haywood, Ok,US
147/C3 Hayyirah, Qarārat al (depr.), Libya
105/J4 Hazār (mtn.), Iran
201/F2 Hazard, Ky,US
208/B2 Hazardville, Ct,US
121/E4 Hazāribāg, India
68/B2 Hazebrouck, Fr.
200/C2 Hazel, Ky,US
194/F5 Hazel, SD,US
196/D2 Hazeldean, NB,Can
182/C5 Hazel Dell, Wa,US
200/D3 Hazel Green, Al,US
57/F5 Hazel Grove, Eng,UK
197/G3 Hazel Hill, NS,Can
198/B2 Hazelhurst, Wi,US
191/F2 Hazel Park, Mi,US
191/E2 Hazelton, Ks,US
194/D4 Hazelton, ND,US
185/K1 Hazelton (peak), Wy,US
179/R7 Hazen (str.), NW,Can
177/E3 Hazen (bay), Ak,US
191/J3 Hazen, Ar,US
194/D4 Hazen, ND,US
184/D4 Hazen, Nv,US
183/L3 Hazenmore, Sk,Can
66/B4 Hazerswoude-Dorp, Neth.
121/H4 Hāzipur, Bang.
201/F5 Hazlehurst, Ga,US
200/B5 Hazlehurst, Ms,US
59/F3 Hazlemere, Eng,UK
183/K2 Hazlet, Sk,Can
207/D3 Hazlet, NJ,US
206/C2 Hazleton, Pa,US
133/F2 Hazlett (lake), Austl.
111/N10 Hazu, Japan
117/G3 He (riv.), China
59/G1 Heacham, Eng,UK
59/G4 Headcorn, Eng,UK
60/A3 Headford, Ire.
57/G4 Headingley, Eng,UK
203/F2 Headland, Al,US
155/G3 Headlands, Zim.
197/K2 Head of Bay d'Espoir-Milltown, Nf,Can
196/F3 Head of Jeddore, NS,Can
196/F3 Head of Saint Margarets Bay, NS,Can
182/G4 Headquarters, Id,US
198/B2 Heafford Junction, Wi,US
184/B4 Healdsburg, Ca,US
191/F3 Healdton, Ok,US
135/G5 Healesville, Austl.
177/J3 Healy, Ak,US
190/D1 Healy, Ks,US
57/G6 Heanor, Eng,UK
155/F4 Heany Junction, Zim.
51/P8 Heard (isl.), Austl.
189/F2 Hearne, Tx,US
137/V Hearst (isl.), Ant.
179/H4 Hearst, On,Can
194/C4 Heart (riv.), ND,US
194/D4 Heart Butte (dam), ND,US
54/D5 Heart Law (hill), Sc,UK
197/L2 Heart's Delight, Nf,Can
183/K1 Hearts Hill, Sk,Can
179/K4 Heath (pt.), Qu,Can
188/L7 Heath, Tx,US
135/C3 Heathcote, Austl.
134/G9 Heathcote Nat'l Park, Austl.
197/H1 Heatherton, Nf,Can
59/G5 Heathfield, Eng,UK
53/M7 Heathrow (London) (int'l arpt.), Eng,UK
201/J2 Heathsville, Va,US
189/E4 Hebbronville, Tx,US
196/E3 Hebbs Cross, NS,Can
57/F4 Hebden Bridge, Eng,UK
115/G6 Hebei (prov.), China
135/C1 Hebel, Austl.
187/G3 Heber, Az,US
186/E4 Heber, Ca,US
185/H3 Heber City, Ut,US
191/H3 Heber Springs, Ar,US
202/C1 Hebert, La,US
71/E6 Hebertshausen, Ger.
185/H1 Hebgen (dam), Mt,US
185/H1 Hebgen (lake), Mt,US
115/C4 Hebi, China
184/B1 Hebo, Or,US
52/C3 Hebrides (isls.), Sc,UK
55/H8 Hebrides (sea), Sc,UK
55/H8 Hebrides, Inner (isls.), Sc,UK
55/G8 Hebrides, Outer (isls.), Sc,UK
196/D4 Hebron, NS,Can
208/B2 Hebron, Ct,US
205/P15 Hebron, Il,US
198/C4 Hebron, In,US
194/C4 Hebron, ND,US
192/F3 Hebron, Ne,US
188/L6 Hebron, Tx,US
103/D4 Hebron (Al Khalīl), WBnk.
62/G2 Heby, Swe.
176/D4 Hecate (str.), Can.
177/M5 Hecate (str.), BC,Can
159/H4 Hecelchakán, Mex.
117/F3 Hechi, China
70/B6 Hechingen, Ger.
69/E1 Hechtel, Belg.
67/G1 Hechthausen, Ger.
116/E2 Hechuan, China
57/H6 Heckington, Eng,UK
72/B4 Hecklingen, Ger.
194/F2 Hecla (isl.), Mb,Can
192/E1 Hecla, SD,US
179/R7 Hecla and Griper (bay), NW,Can
136/J8 Hector (mt.), N.Z.
191/H3 Hector, Ar,US
193/G1 Hector, Mn,US
117/H2 Hecun, China
62/C2 Heddal, Nor.
78/D4 Hédé, Fr.
66/C5 Hedel, Neth.
62/F1 Hedemora, Swe.
62/C4 Hedensted, Den.
117/F4 Hedi (res.), China
190/D3 Hedley, Tx,US
62/D1 Hedmark (co.), Nor.
112/K7 Hedo-misaki (cape), Japan
57/H4 Hedon, Eng,UK
193/H3 Hedrick, Ia,US
189/M9 Hedwig Village, Tx,US
67/E3 Heede, Ger.
67/E4 Heek, Ger.
66/B3 Heemskerk, Neth.
66/B4 Heemstede, Neth.
66/D4 Heerde, Neth.
66/C3 Heerenveen, Neth.
66/B3 Heerhugowaard, Neth.
69/E2 Heerlen, Neth.
69/E2 Heers, Belg.
66/C5 Heesch, Neth.
67/G2 Heeslingen, Ger.
66/C6 Heeze, Neth.
103/D3 Hefa (Haifa), Isr.
115/D5 Hefei, China
115/B5 Hefeng Tujiazu Zizhixian, China
200/E4 Heflin, Al,US
189/H1 Heflin, La,US
109/L2 Hegang, China
75/H3 Hegau (mts.), Ger.
81/E2 Hegau (reg.), Ger.
80/D2 Hégenheim, Fr.
62/C1 Heggenes, Nor.
111/L10 Heguri, Japan
73/B4 Hegyeshalom, Hun.
73/A5 Hegykőzség, Hun.
123/B1 Heho, Burma
108/D4 Hei (riv.), China
112/B4 Hei (riv.), Japan
115/B3 Heicha Shan (mtn.), China
108/E4 Heichongtan, China
64/E1 Heide, Ger.
70/E4 Heideck, Ger.
135/G5 Heidelberg, Austl.
70/B4 Heidelberg, Ger.
156/D4 Heidelberg, SAfr.
156/E2 Heidelberg, SAfr.
200/C5 Heidelberg, Ms,US
66/D5 Heiden, Ger.
81/F3 Heiden, Swi.
72/D6 Heidenau, Ger.
70/D4 Heidenheim, Ger.
70/D5 Heidenheim, Ger.
75/L2 Heidenreichstein, Aus.
69/E4 Heiderscheid, Lux.
70/C2 Heigenbrücken, Ger.
109/K1 Heihe, China
64/F1 Heikendorf, Ger.
156/D2 Heilbron, SAfr.
70/C4 Heilbronn, Ger.
70/D4 Heilbronn, Ger.
81/F2 Heiligenberg, Ger.
75/K3 Heiligenblut, Aus.
64/F1 Heiligenhafen, Ger.
66/D6 Heiligenhaus, Ger.
67/H6 Heiligenstadt, Ger.
109/L2 Heilong (riv.), China
101/N5 Heilong (Amur) (riv.), China
66/B3 Heiloo, Neth.
70/D4 Heilsbronn, Ger.
61/N7 Heimaey (isl.), Ice.
69/F2 Heimbach, Ger.
80/D4 Heimberg, Swi.
70/B5 Heimsheim, Ger.
66/D4 Heino, Neth.
63/M1 Heinola, Fin.
66/D6 Heinsberg, Ger.
113/B2 Heishan, China
183/H1 Heisler, Ab,Can
80/D2 Heitersheim, Ger.
115/C3 Heituo Shan (mtn.), China
111/M9 Heiwa, Japan
108/F4 Hejialiang, China
115/D3 Hejian, China
117/F4 Hejiang, China
115/B4 Hejin, China
114/E3 Hejing, China
108/D4 Heka, China
68/D2 Hekelgem, Belg.
104/D2 Hekimhan, Turk.
111/M10 Hekinan, Japan
61/N7 Hekla (vol.), Ice.
108/G5 Hekou, China
119/H3 Hekou (Hekou Yaozu Zizhixian), China
116/D4 Hekou Yaozu Zizhixian, China
119/H3 Hekou Yaozu Zizhixian (Hekou), China
65/K1 Hel, Pol.
70/F4 Helan (mts.), China
72/A5 Helbe (riv.), Ger.
72/B4 Helbra, Ger.
69/E1 Helchteren, Belg.
70/D2 Heldburg, Ger.
66/D6 Helden, Neth.
72/B5 Heldrungen, Ger.
200/F3 Helen, Ga,US
132/L6 Helena (brook), Austl.
191/J3 Helena, Ar,US
184/B3 Helena, Ca,US
201/F4 Helena, Ga,US
183/H4 Helena, Mt,US
191/E2 Helena, Ok,US
201/G3 Helena, SC,US
54/B4 Helensburgh, Sc,UK
130/D4 Helen Springs, Austl.
136/C2 Helensville, N.Z.
103/F8 Ḩelez, Isr.
62/F3 Helgasjön (lake), Swe.
64/D1 Helgoländer Bucht (bay), Ger.
67/F1 Helgolander Bucht (bay), Ger.
171/L7 Heliodora, Braz.
62/E3 Heliport (int'l arpt.), Swe.
117/H2 Helixi, China
206/B3 Hellam (Hallam), Pa,US
57/F8 Hellebæk, Den.
105/G4 Ḩelleh (riv.), Iran
66/D4 Hellendoorn, Neth.
69/F3 Hellenthal, Ger.
206/C2 Hellertown, Pa,US
66/B5 Hellevoetsluis, Neth.
148/C3 Hélibongo, Chad
76/E3 Hellín, Sp.
184/E1 Hells (canyon), Id, Or,US
184/E1 Hells Canyon (dam), Id, Or,US
184/F1 Hells Canyon Nat'l Rec. Area, Id, Or,US
151/B2 Hell's Gate Nat'l Park, Kenya
183/G5 Hells Half Acre (mtn.), Id,US
107/H2 Helmand (riv.), Afg.
102/F7 Helmand (riv.), Afg., Iran
71/E2 Helmbrechts, Ger.
72/B5 Helme (riv.), Ger.
154/C5 Helmeringhausen, Namb.
177/K2 Helmet (mtn.), Ak,US
207/H10 Helmetta, NJ,US
66/C6 Helmond, Neth.
57/G3 Helmsley, Eng,UK
70/C3 Helmstadt, Ger.
72/B3 Helmstedt, Ger.
183/H4 Helmville, Mt,US
109/K3 Helong, China
185/H4 Helper, Ut,US
71/G6 Helpfau-Uttendorf, Aus.
57/F5 Helsby, Eng,UK
80/E5 Helsenhorn (peak), Swi.
63/T8 Helsingborg, Swe.
63/T8 Helsinge, Den.
63/L1 Helsingfors (Helsinki) (cap.), Fin.
63/T8 Helsingør, Den.
52/F2 Helsinki (cap.), Fin.
63/L1 Helsinki (Helsingfors) (cap.), Fin.
63/L1 Helsinki-Vantaa (int'l arpt.), Fin.
58/A6 Helston, Eng,UK
201/F2 Helton, Ky,US
117/F3 Helukou, China
172/D4 Helvecia, Arg.
61/G3 Helvetinjärven Nat'l Park, Fin.
60/C5 Helvick (pt.), Ire.
68/C2 Hem, Fr.
68/B2 Hem (riv.), Fr.
183/J2 Hemaruka, Ab,Can
71/E4 Hemau, Ger.
53/M6 Hemel Hempstead, Eng,UK
67/F2 Hemelingen, Ger.
67/E6 Hemer, Ger.
204/D3 Hemet, Ca,US
196/E3 Hemford, NS,Can
192/C2 Hemingford, Ne,US
201/H4 Hemingway, SC,US
67/G4 Hemmingen, Ger.
67/G1 Hemmoor, Ger.
189/H2 Hemphill, Tx,US
207/E2 Hempstead, NY,US
207/L8 Hempstead (har.), NY,US
189/F2 Hempstead, Tx,US
200/E3 Hemp Top (peak), Ga,US
59/H1 Hemsby, Eng,UK
62/H3 Hemse, Swe.
62/C1 Hemsedal, Nor.
57/G4 Hemsworth, Eng,UK
200/E3 Henagar, Al,US
115/B4 Henan (prov.), China
62/D2 Henån, Swe.
78/C3 Hénanbihen, Fr.
76/D2 Henares (riv.), Sp.
112/A3 Henashi-zaki (pt.), Japan
133/G3 Henbury, Austl.
74/C5 Hendaye, Fr.
93/K5 Hendek, Turk.
174/E3 Henderson, Arg.
136/F6 Henderson, N.Z.
139/N7 Henderson (isl.), Pitc.
200/D2 Henderson, Ky,US
189/J2 Henderson, La,US
206/C5 Henderson, Md,US
201/H2 Henderson, NC,US
192/F3 Henderson, Ne,US
186/E2 Henderson, Nv,US
199/H3 Henderson, NY,US
200/C3 Henderson, Tn,US
189/G1 Henderson, Tx,US
205/B3 Henderson (bay), Wa,US
201/F3 Hendersonville, NC,US
200/D2 Hendersonville, Tn,US
53/N7 Hendon, Eng,UK
193/F1 Hendricks, Mn,US
201/H1 Hendricks, WV,US
66/B5 Hendrik-Ido-Ambacht, Neth.
166/B1 Hendrik Top (peak), Sur.
156/D3 Hendrik Verwoerdam (res.), SAfr.
156/Q13 Hendrina, SAfr.
182/D1 Hendrix Lake, BC,Can
59/F5 Henfield, Eng,UK
115/L8 Heng (isl.), China
117/G3 Heng (peak), China
116/D3 Heng (riv.), China
131/G1 Henganofi, PNG
113/B1 Hengdaohe, China
119/K2 Hengdong, China
116/C2 Hengduan (mts.), China
66/D4 Hengelo, Neth.
71/G5 Hengersberg, Ger.
117/F1 Hengkou, China
115/B4 Hengshan, China
108/F4 Hengshan, China
119/K2 Hengshan, China
115/C3 Heng Shan (mtn.), China
115/C3 Hengshui, China
154/B1 Hengue, Ang.
117/J2 Hengxi, China
117/F4 Heng Xian, China
117/G3 Hengyang, China
68/B3 Hénin-Beaumont, Fr.
133/M8 Henley Beach, Austl.
59/F3 Henley on Thames, Eng,UK
206/C6 Henlopen (cape), De,US
206/C6 Henlopen Acres, De,US
59/E2 Henley in Arden, Eng,UK
62/C4 Henne, Den.
78/B5 Hennebont, Fr.
69/G2 Hennef, Ger.
156/D2 Hennenman, SAfr.
193/K3 Hennepin, Il,US
193/J3 Hennepin (can.), Il,US
195/N6 Hennepin (co.), Mn,US
191/F3 Hennepin, Ok,US
191/F2 Hennessey, Ok,US
72/D2 Hennigsdorf, Ger.
196/B4 Henniker, NH,US
195/G4 Henning, Mn,US
200/C3 Henning, Tn,US
69/E2 Henri-Chapelle, Belg.
191/E4 Henrietta, Tx,US
179/H3 Henrietta Maria (cape), On,Can
187/G2 Henrieville, Ut,US
165/E2 Henri Pittier Nat'l Park, Ven.
177/M5 Henry (cape), BC,Can
201/F4 Henry (co.), Ga,US
193/K3 Henry, Il,US
192/D2 Henry, Ne,US
192/F1 Henry, SD,US
185/H4 Henry (mts.), Ut,US
201/H2 Henry, Va,US
201/J2 Henry (cape), Va,US
191/G3 Henryetta, Ok,US
205/F7 Henry Ford Museum & Greenfield Vill., Mi,US
200/E1 Henryville, In,US
206/C1 Henryville, Pa,US
198/F3 Hensall, On,Can
68/C3 Hensies, Belg.
194/D4 Hensler, ND,US
191/H3 Hensley, Ar,US
154/B4 Hentiesbaai, Namb.
108/F2 Hentiyn (mts.), Mong.
135/C2 Henty, Austl.
116/B5 Henzada, Burma
183/L1 Hepburn, Sk,Can
117/H4 Heping, China
191/G2 Hepler, Ks,US
70/B3 Heppenheim an der Bergstrasse, Ger.
184/D1 Heppner, Or,US
117/F4 Hepu, China
115/K8 Heqiao, China
116/D3 Heqing, China
115/B3 Hequ, China
61/N6 Heraðsvötn (riv.), Ice.
186/B1 Herald, Ca,US
107/H2 Herāt, Afg.
77/F7 Hérault (riv.), Fr.
82/B2 Herbasse (riv.), Fr.
78/D5 Herbault, Fr.
134/B2 Herbert (riv.), Austl.
183/L2 Herbert, Sk,Can
131/G1 Herbert (peak), PNG
202/E2 Herbert, Al,US
193/J3 Herbert Hoover Nat'l Hist. Site, Ia,US
134/B2 Herberton, Austl.
134/B2 Herbert River (falls), Austl.
134/B2 Herbert River Falls Nat'l Park, Austl.
69/E4 Herbeumont, Belg.
78/C6 Herbignac, Fr.
53/S10 Herblay, Fr.
80/D1 Herbolzheim, Ger.
70/D5 Herbrechtingen, Ger.
72/A5 Herbsleben, Ger.
70/C1 Herbstein, Ger.
92/D4 Hercegnovi, Yugo.
173/G3 Hercílio Luz (int'l arpt.), Braz.
85/E6 Herculaneum (ruins), It.
205/K10 Hercules, Ca,US
67/E6 Herdecke, Ger.
69/G2 Herdorf, Ger.
161/E4 Heredia, CR
58/D2 Hereford, Eng,UK
187/G5 Hereford, Az,US
206/B4 Hereford, Md,US
206/D5 Hereford (inlet), NJ,US
206/C3 Hereford, Pa,US
192/C1 Hereford, SD,US
190/C3 Hereford, Tx,US
58/D2 Hereford & Worcester (co.), Eng,UK
139/L6 Hereheretue (isl.), FrPol.
93/J5 Hereke, Turk.
76/C3 Herencia, Sp.
73/B5 Herend, Hun.
69/D1 Herentals, Belg.
138/B3 Heretaniwha (pt.), N.Z.
67/F4 Herford, Ger.
81/E4 Hergiswil, Swi.
78/D6 Héric, Fr.
80/C2 Héricourt, Fr.
80/C3 Hérimoncourt, Fr.
72/A5 Heringen, Ger.
191/F1 Herington, Ks,US
182/B2 Heriot Bay, BC,Can
105/F2 Herīs, Iran
81/F3 Herisau, Swi.
69/E2 Herk (riv.), Belg.
69/E2 Herk-de-Stad, Belg.
199/J3 Herkimer, NY,US
108/G2 Herlen (riv.), Mong.
67/H6 Herleshausen, Ger.
63/T9 Herlev, Den.
184/C3 Herlong, Ca,US
78/C2 Herm (isl.), UK
195/K4 Herman, Mi,US
193/F1 Herman, Mn,US
208/H6 Herman, Pa,US
55/P12 Herma Ness (pt.), Sc,UK
193/J4 Hermann, Mo,US
133/G2 Hermannsburg, Austl.
67/H3 Hermannsburg, Ger.
133/G2 Hermannsburg Abor. Land, Austl.
67/F5 Hermanns-Denkmal (arpt.), Ger.
62/B1 Hermansverk, Nor.
198/C2 Hermansville, Mi,US
156/B4 Hermanus, SAfr.
200/B5 Hermanville, Ms,US
69/G5 Hermersberg, Ger.
68/B5 Hermes, Fr.
69/F4 Hermeskeil, Ger.
135/C1 Hermidale, Austl.
184/D1 Hermiston, Or,US
197/J2 Hermitage (bay), Nf,Can
191/H4 Hermitage, Ar,US
191/H2 Hermitage, Mo,US
208/G5 Hermitage, Pa,US
200/E2 Hermitage Springs, Tn,US
136/B3 Hermitage, The, N.Z.
190/D4 Hermleigh, Tx,US
103/D3 Hermon (mtn.), Leb., Syria
196/C3 Hermon, Me,US
199/J2 Hermon, NY,US
192/C2 Hermosa, SD,US
204/B3 Hermosa Beach, Ca,US
158/C2 Hermosillo, Mex.
172/D3 Hermoso Campo, Arg.
72/B6 Hermsdorf, Ger.
72/D2 Hermsdorf, Ger.
173/F3 Hernandarias, Par.
158/E4 Hernández, Mex.
190/A2 Hernandez, NM,US
174/E2 Hernando, Arg.
202/K6 Hernando (co.), Fl,US
200/C3 Hernando, Ms,US
76/E1 Hernani, Sp.
192/D4 Herndon, Ks,US
206/B2 Herndon, Pa,US
68/D2 Herne, Belg.
67/E5 Herne, Ger.
59/H4 Herne Bay, Eng,UK
62/C3 Herning, Den.
103/G8 Herodian (ruins), WBnk.
103/G8 Herodion Nat'l Park, WBnk.
158/B2 Heroica Caborca, Mex.
187/G5 Heroica Nogales, Mex.
70/E3 Heroldsberg, Ger.
196/D1 Heron (isl.), NB,Can
187/J2 Heron (lake), NM,US
195/L3 Heron Bay, On,Can
117/F2 Herong, China
193/G2 Heron Lake, Mn,US
79/E2 Hérouville-Saint-Clair, Fr.
70/D1 Herpf (riv.), Ger.
62/C2 Herre, Nor.
194/D5 Herreid, SD,US
70/B5 Herrenberg, Ger.
76/C4 Herrera, Sp.
76/C3 Herrera del Duque, Sp.
76/C1 Herrera de Pisuerga, Sp.
159/J5 Herrero (pt.), Mex.
62/D2 Herrestad, Swe.
135/C4 Herrick, Austl.
200/C1 Herrick, Il,US
70/D4 Herrieden, Ger.
200/C2 Herrin, Il,US
69/G6 Herrlisheim, Fr.
62/E2 Herrljunga, Swe.
81/H2 Herrsching am Ammersee, Ger.
74/D5 Hers (riv.), Fr.
71/E3 Hersbruck, Ger.
70/A1 Herschbach, Ger.
67/E6 Herscheid, Ger.
183/K2 Herschel, Sk,Can
177/L2 Herschel, Yk,Can
193/K3 Herscher, Il,US
78/C5 Hersé (mtn.), Fr.
69/D1 Herselt, Belg.
206/B3 Hershey, Pa,US
206/B3 Hersheypark, Pa,US
172/D4 Hersilia, Arg.
69/E2 Herstal, Belg.
59/G5 Herstmonceux, Eng,UK
67/E5 Herten, Ger.
59/F3 Hertford, Eng,UK
201/J2 Hertford, NC,US
53/N6 Hertfordshire (co.), Eng,UK
76/C2 Hervás, Sp.
67/E2 Herve, Belg.
167/K6 Herveo, Col.
134/D4 Hervey (bay), Austl.
134/D4 Hervey Bay, Austl.
66/D5 Herwen, Neth.
70/B4 Herxheim bei Landau, Ger.
72/D4 Herzberg, Ger.
67/H5 Herzberg am Harz, Ger.
67/F5 Herzebrock-Clarholz, Ger.
68/C2 Herzele, Belg.
67/E3 Herzlake, Ger.
103/F7 Herzliyya, Isr.
70/D3 Herzogenaurach, Ger.
80/D3 Herzogenbuchsee, Swi.
92/B1 Herzogenburg, Aus.
69/F2 Herzogenrath, Ger.
121/E4 Hesādi, India
69/D3 Hesbaye (plat.), Belg.
68/B3 Hesdin, Fr.
67/E2 Hesel, Ger.
117/F4 Heshan, China
117/G2 Heshengqiao, China
108/F4 Heshui, China
115/C3 Heshun, China
80/D2 Hésingue, Fr.
69/F4 Hesperange, Lux.
204/C2 Hesperia, Ca,US
198/C3 Hesperia, Mi,US
187/H2 Hesperus, Co,US
177/M3 Hess (riv.), Yk,Can
67/G6 Hesse (state), Ger.
67/F5 Hessel (riv.), Ger.
198/D1 Hessel, Mi,US
67/H4 Hessen, Ger.
67/G5 Hessisch Lichtenau, Ger.
67/G4 Hessisch Oldendorf, Ger.
57/H4 Hessle, Eng,UK
191/F1 Hesston, Ks,US
57/E5 Heswall, Eng,UK
205/L11 Hetch Hetchy (aqueduct), Ca,US
70/B3 Hettenleidelheim, Ger.
194/C4 Hettinger, ND,US
57/G2 Hetton-le-Hole, Eng,UK
72/B4 Hettstedt, Ger.
69/F4 Hetzerath, Ger.
70/C5 Heubach, Ger.
67/E5 Heubach (riv.), Ger.
70/B1 Heuchelheim, Ger.
72/A4 Heudeber, Ger.
65/H5 Heukuppe (peak), Aus.
66/C5 Heusden, Neth.
69/E1 Heusden-Zolder, Belg.
70/B2 Heusenstamm, Ger.
69/F5 Heusweiler, Ger.
199/J2 Heuvelton, NY,US
79/F1 Hève, Cap de la (cape), Fr.
69/D2 Heverlee, Belg.
92/E2 Heves, Hun.
65/L5 Heves (co.), Hun.
73/B6 Hévíz, Hun.
73/A2 Hevlín, Czh.
207/D1 Hewitt, NJ,US
189/F2 Hewitt, Tx,US
183/L3 Hewitt Lake Nat'l Wild. Ref., Mt,US
207/L9 Hewlett, NY,US
207/E2 Hewlett (pt.), NY,US
81/G3 Hexenkopf (peak), Aus.
57/F2 Hexham, Eng,UK
117/F2 Hexi, China
115/D5 He Xian, China
117/F3 He Xian, China
109/H3 Hexigten, China
109/H3 Hexigten Qi, China
156/L10 Hex River (mts.), SAfr.
156/L10 Hex River (pass), SAfr.
188/E2 Hext, Tx,US
105/N7 Heybeli (isl.), Turk.
185/G2 Heyburn, Id,US
82/B1 Heyrieux, Fr.
57/F3 Heysham, Eng,UK
66/C6 Heythuysen, Neth.
117/G4 Heyuan, China
135/B3 Heywood, Austl.
57/F4 Heywood, Eng,UK
193/K3 Heyworth, Il,US
57/C4 Heze, China
116/E3 Hezhang, China
181/K6 Hialeah, Fl,US
203/H5 Hialeah, Fl,US
202/P8 Hialeah Gardens, Fl,US
200/F3 Hiawassee, Ga,US
193/J2 Hiawatha, Ia,US
191/G1 Hiawatha, Ks,US
195/L4 Hiawatha, Mi,US
199/G2 Hiawatha Ind. Res., On,Can
195/H4 Hibbing, Mn,US
135/C4 Hibbs (pt.), Austl.
161/F1 Hicacos (pt.), Cuba
177/M4 Hickman (mtn.), BC,Can
200/C2 Hickman, Ky,US
193/F3 Hickman, Ne,US
205/Q16 Hickory (cr.), Il,US
200/C4 Hickory, Ms,US
201/G3 Hickory, NC,US
201/G3 Hickory (lake), NC,US
188/K6 Hickory (cr.), Tx,US
200/D3 Hickory Flat, Ms,US
191/J3 Hickory Ridge, Ar,US
206/C1 Hickory Run St. Park, Pa,US
207/E2 Hicksville, NY,US
198/D4 Hicksville, Oh,US
189/H1 Hico, La,US
189/E2 Hico, Tx,US
111/E3 Hida (riv.), Japan
105/G2 Hīdaj, Iran
111/H7 Hidaka, Japan
112/C2 Hidaka, Japan
112/C2 Hidaka (mts.), Japan
110/D4 Hidaka (riv.), Japan
159/E3 Hidalgo, Mex.
159/F3 Hidalgo, Mex.
160/B1 Hidalgo (state), Mex.
189/E4 Hidalgo, Tx,US
67/F4 Hiddenhausen, Ger.
204/B2 Hidden Hills, Ca,US
167/F4 Hidrolândia, Braz.
170/C3 Hidrolândia, Braz.
170/C2 Hidrolina, Braz.
175/J6 Hielo Norte, Campo de (glac.), Chile
175/J7 Hielo Sur, Campo de (glac.), Chile
138/F7 Hienghène, NCal.
104/B2 Hierapolis (ruins), Turk.
79/E5 Hière (riv.), Fr.
142/A4 Hierro (isl.), Canl.
77/W17 Hierro (isl.), Canl.,Sp.
174/C2 Hierro Viejo, Chile
67/E2 Hieve (lake), Ger.
111/H7 Higashikurume, Japan
111/H7 Higashimurayama, Japan
111/G1 Higashine, Japan
111/L10 Higashi-Ōsaka, Japan
111/K10 Higashiura, Japan
111/H7 Higashiyamato, Japan
111/L10 Higashiyoshino, Japan
191/H1 Higbee, Mo,US
208/B3 Higganum, Ct,US
198/D2 Higgins (lake), Mi,US
198/D2 Higgins Lake, Mi,US
193/H4 Higginsville, Mo,US
184/B2 High (isl.), Mi,US
184/C1 High (des.), Or,US
206/C1 High (hill), Pa,US
59/F2 Higham Ferrers, Eng,UK
58/D4 Highbridge, Eng,UK
206/D2 High Bridge, NJ,US
132/C5 High Bury, Austl.
192/D3 High Butler (lake), Ne,US
201/G2 High Eagle (peak), NC,US
189/G3 High Island, Tx,US
201/F2 High Knob (peak), Va,US
201/G2 High Knob (peak), Va,US
54/B2 Highland (reg.), Sc,UK
204/C2 Highland, Ca,US
182/A1 Highland (pt.), Fl,US
205/R16 Highland, In,US
193/G4 Highland, Ks,US
186/E2 Highland (peak), Nv,US
202/P7 Highland Beach, Fl,US
206/B6 Highland Beach, Md,US
202/M8 Highland City, Fl,US
206/D1 Highland Lakes, NJ,US
205/Q15 Highland Park, Il,US
205/F7 Highland Park, Mi,US
206/D3 Highland Park, NJ,US
199/H4 Highland Park, Pa,US
188/L7 Highland Park, Tx,US
202/M8 Highlands (co.), Fl,US
201/F3 Highlands, NC,US
207/E3 Highlands, NJ,US
189/G3 Highlands, Tx,US
208/N9 Highlands (res.), Tx,US
178/E3 High Level, Ab,Can
58/D2 Highley, Eng,UK
192/E1 Highmore, SD,US
125/C2 High Park (mtn.), Phil.
201/G3 High Point, NC,US
206/D1 High Point (mtn.), NJ,US
206/D1 High Point St. Park, NJ,US
178/E3 High Prairie, Ab,Can
191/J1 High Ridge, Mo,US
183/H2 High River, Ab,Can
201/G3 High Rock (lake), NC,US
206/B3 Highspire, Pa,US
203/G3 High Springs, Fl,US
57/F3 High Street (mtn.), Eng,UK
57/E4 Hightown, Eng,UK
206/D3 Hightstown, NJ,US
58/B5 High Willhays (hill), Eng,UK
205/Q15 Highwood, Il,US
183/J4 Highwood, Mt,US
183/J4 Highwood Baldy (mtn.), Mt,US
59/E3 Highworth, Eng,UK
59/F3 High Wycombe, Eng,UK
187/G4 Higley, Az,US
167/O7 Higuerote, Ven.
185/G2 Higüey, DRep.
103/B4 Hihyā, Egypt
61/J3 Hiidenportin Nat'l Park, Fin.
63/K2 Hiiumaa (isl.), Est.
77/E2 Híjar, Sp.
106/C3 Hijāz, Jabal al (mts.), SAr.
147/H3 Ḩijāz, Jabal al (mts.), SAr.
180/B4 Hiji, Japan
174/Q9 Hijuelas de Conchali, Chile
111/L9 Hikami, Japan
186/E2 Hiko, Nv,US
110/E3 Hikone, Japan
139/L6 Hikueru (atoll), FrPol.
50/B6 Hikueru (isl.), FrPol.
136/C1 Hikurangi, N.Z.
136/D2 Hikurangi (peak), N.Z.
130/B1 Hila, Indo.
146/D1 Hilāl, Ra's al (pt.), Libya
198/B2 Hilbert, Wi,US
194/E2 Hilbre, Mb,Can
69/H2 Hilchenbach, Ger.
188/E4 Hilda, Tx,US
187/F2 Hildale, Ut,US
70/D2 Hildburghausen, Ger.
190/C2 Hildebrand, Or,US
196/F3 Hilden, NS,Can
66/D6 Hilden, Ger.
70/D1 Hilders, Ger.
67/G4 Hildesheim, Ger.
195/J5 Hiles, Wi,US
183/K4 Hilger, Mt,US
67/G3 Hilgermissen, Ger.
206/B3 Hill (isl.), Pa,US
185/J4 Hill (cr.), Ut,US
162/G4 Hillaby (mtn.), Bar.
185/G3 Hill Air Force Ra., Ut,US
137/L Hillary (coast), Ant.
207/J7 Hillburn, NY,US
190/E1 Hill City, Ks,US
192/C2 Hill City, SD,US
191/F4 Hill City, Tx,US
207/D1 Hillcrest, NY,US
202/M8 Hillcrest Heights, Fl,US
67/F4 Hille, Ger.
66/B4 Hillegom, Neth.
135/D2 Hill End, Austl.
62/E4 Hillerød, Den.
69/F3 Hillesheim, Ger.
56/B2 Hillhall, NI,UK
121/G3 Hilli, Bang.
203/H2 Hilliard, Fl,US
199/H3 Hillier, Can.
53/M7 Hillingdon (bor.), Eng,UK
54/C1 Hill of Fearn, Sc,UK
55/K8 Hill of Fearn, Sc,UK
193/F2 Hills, Mn,US
203/H4 Hillsboro (can.), Fl,US
193/K4 Hillsboro, Il,US
191/F1 Hillsboro, Ks,US
206/C6 Hillsboro, Md,US
191/J1 Hillsboro, Mo,US
200/C4 Hillsboro, Ms,US
194/F4 Hillsboro, ND,US
187/J4 Hillsboro, NM,US
198/E5 Hillsboro, Oh,US
184/B1 Hillsboro, Or,US
189/F1 Hillsboro, Tx,US
193/J2 Hillsboro, Wi,US
202/P7 Hillsboro Beach, Fl,US
196/B4 Hillsboro (Hillsborough), NH,US
134/C3 Hillsborough (chan.), Austl.
196/E3 Hillsborough, NB,Can
196/F2 Hillsborough (bay), PE,Can
56/B3 Hillsborough, NI,UK
205/K11 Hillsborough, Ca,US
202/L8 Hillsborough (bay), Fl,US
202/L8 Hillsborough (co.), Fl,US
202/L7 Hillsborough (riv.), Fl,US
201/H2 Hillsborough, NC,US
206/D3 Hillsborough, NJ,US
196/B4 Hillsborough (Hillsboro), NH,US
197/Q8 Hillsburgh, On,Can
184/B2 Hills Creek (res.), Or,US
199/G2 Hillsdale, On,Can
191/G1 Hillsdale (lake), Ks,US
198/D4 Hillsdale, Mi,US
207/D1 Hillsdale, NJ,US
208/A1 Hillsdale, NY,US
199/H4 Hillsgrove, Pa,US
54/D3 Hillside, Sc,UK
187/F3 Hillside, Az,US
187/G1 Hillside, Co,US
207/D2 Hillside, NJ,US
200/B4 Hillside Nat'l Wild. Ref., Ms,US
195/M3 Hillsport, On,Can
183/H3 Hill Spring, Ab,Can
135/C2 Hillston, Austl.
208/G5 Hillsville, Pa,US
201/G2 Hillsville, Va,US
55/P12 Hillswick, Sc,UK
201/G4 Hilltonia, Ga,US
56/B3 Hilltown, NI,UK
200/E1 Hillview, Ky,US
186/B2 Hilmar-Irwin, Ca,US
180/U11 Hilo, Hi,US
125/D3 Hilonghilong (mt.), Phil.
70/E4 Hilpoltstein, Ger.
57/E3 Hilpsford (pt.), Eng,UK
121/E3 Hilsa, India
184/B3 Hilt, Ca,US
80/D4 Hilterfingen, Swi.
203/F2 Hilton, Ga,US
199/H3 Hilton, NY,US
203/H1 Hilton Head (isl.), SC,US
201/G4 Hilton Head Island, SC,US
66/C6 Hilvarenbeek, Neth.
66/C4 Hilversum, Neth.
81/E2 Hilzingen, Ger.
200/F2 Hima, Ky,US
122/D2 Himachal Pradesh (state), India
122/G6 Himalaya, Great (range), Asia
121/E1 Himālchuli (mtn.), Nepal
125/C3 Himamaylan, Phil.
61/G2 Himanka, Fin.
91/F2 Himarë, Alb.
73/A3 Himberg, Aus.
149/H2 Himbirti, Eth.
110/D3 Himeji, Japan
110/D3 Himeji Castle, Japan
111/E2 Himi, Japan
67/G1 Himmelpforten, Ger.
149/H2 Himora, Eth.
103/E2 Ḩimş, Syria
104/D3 Ḩimş (prov.), Syria
125/D3 Hinatuan, Phil.
200/E3 Hinch (mtn.), Tn,US
161/H2 Hinche, Haiti
129/H3 Hinchinbrook (isl.), Austl.
177/J3 Hinchinbrook (chan.), Ak,US
134/B2 Hinchinbrook I. Nat'l Park, Austl.
59/E1 Hinckley, Eng,UK
198/B4 Hinckley, Il,US
208/F5 Hinckley, Oh,US
185/G4 Hinckley, Ut,US
133/G5 Hincks Consv. Park, Austl.
152/C4 Hinda, Congo
120/A1 Hindan (riv.), India
120/A2 Hindaun, India
81/G3 Hindelang, Ger.
66/C3 Hindeloopen, Neth.
57/H2 Hinderwell, Eng,UK
57/F4 Hindley, Eng,UK
201/F2 Hindman, Ky,US
135/B2 Hindmarsh (lake), Austl.
136/B4 Hinds, N.Z.
107/J1 Hindu Kush (mts.), Afg., Pak.
118/C5 Hindupur, India
199/K2 Hinesburg, Vt,US
202/B2 Hineston, La,US
201/G5 Hinesville, Ga,US
118/C3 Hinganghāt, India
208/D1 Hingham, Ma,US
107/J3 Hingol (riv.), Pak.
118/C4 Hingoli, India
107/J3 Hingorja, Pak.
122/H4 Hingurakgoda, SrL.
104/E2 Hınıs, Turk.
111/M9 Hino, Japan
111/M9 Hino (riv.), Japan
111/H7 Hinode, Japan
111/H7 Hinohara, Japan

76/C3 **Hinojosa del Duque,** Sp.
110/C3 **Hino-misaki** (cape), Japan
205/Q16 **Hinsdale,** Il,US
208/A1 **Hinsdale,** Ma,US
199/K3 **Hinsdale,** NH,US
57/F6 **Hinstock,** Eng,UK
67/E2 **Hinte,** Ger.
81/F4 **Hinterrhein** (riv.), Swi.
81/H3 **Hinterriss,** Aus.
81/F3 **Hinterrugg** (peak), Swi.
69/G5 **Hinterweidenthal,** Ger.
182/F1 **Hinton,** Ab,Can
191/E3 **Hinton,** Ok,US
201/G2 **Hinton,** WV,US
202/D2 **Hintonville,** Ms,US
125/D3 **Hinunangan,** Phil.
81/E3 **Hinwil,** Swi.
188/D5 **Hipólito,** Mex.
66/B3 **Hippolytushoef,** Neth.
57/G3 **Hipswell,** Eng,UK
111/L9 **Hira** (mts.), Japan
110/A4 **Hirado,** Japan
110/D3 **Hirakata,** Japan
118/D3 **Hirakud** (res.), India
201/L7 **Hiram,** Ga,US
196/B4 **Hiram,** Me,US
208/F5 **Hiram,** Oh,US
151/B2 **Hiraman** (dry riv.), Kenya
120/B4 **Hiran** (riv.), India
112/B3 **Hiranai,** Japan
120/B3 **Hīrāpur,** India
112/H8 **Hirara,** Japan
110/C3 **Hirata,** Japan
111/H7 **Hiratsuka,** Japan
104/C2 **Hirfanlı** (dam), Turk.
93/H2 **Hîrlău,** Rom.
150/B3 **Hīrna,** Eth.
112/C2 **Hiro'o,** Japan
112/B3 **Hirosaki,** Japan
110/C3 **Hiroshima,** Japan
110/C3 **Hiroshima** (arpt.), Japan
110/C3 **Hiroshima** (pref.), Japan
70/E3 **Hirschaid,** Ger.
71/E3 **Hirschau,** Ger.
70/B4 **Hirschhorn,** Ger.
68/D4 **Hirson,** Fr.
93/H3 **Hîrşova,** Rom.
62/C3 **Hirtshals,** Den.
58/C3 **Hirwaun,** Wal,UK
110/E3 **Hisai,** Japan
118/C2 **Hisār,** India
104/B2 **Hisarcık,** Turk.
103/D4 **Ḩisbān,** Jor.
200/E2 **Hiseville,** Ky,US
108/E2 **Hishig-Öndör,** Mong.
150/C1 **Ḩişn al 'Abr,** Yem.
162/C2 **Hispaniola** (isl.), DRep., Haiti
202/E2 **Historic Pensacola Vill.,** Fl,US
121/E3 **Hisua,** India
105/E3 **Hīt,** Iraq
111/G2 **Hitachi,** Japan
111/G2 **Hitachi-ōta,** Japan
194/C3 **Hitchcock,** Sk,Can
191/E3 **Hitchcock,** Ok,US
192/E1 **Hitchcock,** SD,US
189/M9 **Hitchcock,** Tx,US
59/F3 **Hitchin,** Eng,UK
201/F1 **Hitchins,** Ky,US
110/B4 **Hitoyoshi,** Japan
61/C3 **Hitra** (isl.), Nor.
63/T8 **Hittarp,** Swe.
194/F4 **Hitterdal,** Mn,US
81/F3 **Hittisau,** Aus.
72/B1 **Hitzacker,** Ger.
81/E3 **Hitzkirch,** Swi.
139/M5 **Hiva Oa** (isl.), FrPol.
200/C5 **Hiwannee,** Ms,US
200/F3 **Hiwassee** (lake), NC,US
200/E3 **Hiwassee** (riv.), NC, Tn,US
182/C1 **Hixon,** BC,Can
111/L9 **Hiyoshi,** Japan
104/E2 **Hizan,** Turk.
62/F2 **Hjälmaren** (lake), Swe.
94/B2 **Hjartfjellet** (peak), Nor.
63/U9 **Hjärup,** Swe.
62/A1 **Hjellestad,** Nor.
62/B2 **Hjelmeland,** Nor.
62/C3 **Hjerm,** Den.
62/F2 **Hjo,** Swe.
62/C3 **Hjørring,** Den.
123/B1 **Hka** (riv.), Burma
116/C2 **Hkakabo** (peak), Burma
157/E3 **Hlabisa,** SAfr.
157/E2 **Hlatikulu,** Swaz.
123/B2 **Hlegu,** Burma
73/B3 **Hlohovec,** Slvk.
157/E3 **Hlokozi,** SAfr.
71/H4 **Hluboká nad Vltava,** Czh.
157/F3 **Hluhluwe,** SAfr.
134/G8 **Hmas-Nirimba,** Austl.
116/C5 **Hmawbi,** Burma
116/B4 **Hmunpui,** India
145/F5 **Ho,** Gha.
123/D1 **Hoa Bin,** Viet.
123/E4 **Hoa Da,** Viet.
183/G1 **Hoadley,** Ab,Can
123/C1 **Hoang Lien** (mts.), Viet.
154/B3 **Hoanib** (dry riv.), Namb.
179/K2 **Hoare** (bay), NW,Can
154/B3 **Hoarusib** (dry riv.), Namb.
185/H2 **Hoback** (peak), Wy,US
154/C3 **Hoba Meteorite,** Namb.
111/G2 **Hobara,** Japan
135/C4 **Hobart,** Austl.
135/C4 **Hobart** (int'l arpt.), Austl.
190/E3 **Hobart,** Ok,US
205/D3 **Hobart,** Wa,US
194/E4 **Hobart Lake Nat'l Wild. Ref.,** ND,US
137/Q **Hobbs** (coast), Ant.
190/C4 **Hobbs,** NM,US
203/H4 **Hobe Sound Nat'l Wild. Ref.,** Fl,US
68/D1 **Hoboken,** Belg.
207/D2 **Hoboken,** NJ,US
108/B2 **Hoboksar,** China
114/E2 **Hoboksar Monggol Zizhixian** (Hoboksar), China
62/C3 **Hobro,** Den.
136/C2 **Hobson** (peak), N.Z.
183/K4 **Hobson,** Mt,US
201/J3 **Hobucken,** NC,US
150/D4 **Hobyo,** Som.
93/K5 **Hocaköy,** Turk.
92/A2 **Hochalmspitze** (peak), Aus.
70/C3 **Höchberg,** Ger.
71/F6 **Hochburg,** Aus.
70/C6 **Hochdorf,** Ger.
194/F3 **Hochfeld,** Mb,Can
154/C4 **Hochfeld,** Namb.
69/G6 **Hochfelden,** Fr.
81/F3 **Hochfinsler** (peak), Swi.
81/G3 **Hochgrat** (peak), Ger.
70/B2 **Hochheim am Main,** Ger.
123/D4 **Ho Chi Minh City** (Saigon), Viet.
116/E4 **Ho Chi Minh Mausoleum,** Viet.
75/K3 **Hochkönig** (peak), Aus.
113/E2 **Hŏch'ŏn,** NKor.
113/D2 **Hŏch'ŏn** (riv.), NKor.
75/L3 **Hochschwab** (peak), Aus.
69/G3 **Hochsimmer** (peak), Ger.
70/A4 **Hochspeyer,** Ger.
81/F3 **Höchst,** Aus.
70/E2 **Hochstadt am Main,** Ger.
70/D3 **Höchstadt an der Aisch,** Ger.
70/D5 **Hochstädt an der Donau,** Ger.
69/G4 **Hochstetten-Dhaun,** Ger.
70/B3 **Höchst im Odenwald,** Ger.
81/G3 **Hochvogel** (peak), Aus.
81/F4 **Hochwang** (peak), Swi.
70/B4 **Hockenheim,** Ger.
206/C4 **Hockessin,** De,US
201/F1 **Hocking** (riv.), Oh,US
59/G3 **Hockley,** Eng,UK
79/D2 **Hoc, Pointe du** (pt.), Fr.
120/A2 **Hodal,** India
57/F4 **Hodder** (riv.), Eng,UK
53/N6 **Hoddesdon,** Eng,UK
67/G3 **Hodenhagen,** Ger.
196/D2 **Hodgdon,** Me,US
202/B1 **Hodge,** La,US
200/E2 **Hodgenville,** Ky,US
197/K1 **Hodges** (hill), Nf,Can
204/C4 **Hodges** (lake), Ca,US
183/M4 **Hodges,** Mt,US
190/E4 **Hodges,** Tx,US
197/L1 **Hodge's Cove,** Nf,Can
183/L2 **Hodgeville,** Sk,Can
130/D3 **Hodgson** (riv.), Austl.
194/F2 **Hodgson,** Mb,Can
144/C2 **Hodh** (reg.), Mrta.
103/F7 **Hod HaSharon,** Isr.
144/D2 **Hodh ech Chargui** (reg.), Mrta.
144/C2 **Hodh El Gharbi** (reg.), Mrta.
92/E2 **Hódmezovásárhely,** Hun.
150/C3 **Hodmo** (dry riv.), Som.
141/T16 **Hodna, Chott el** (dry lake), Alg.
57/F6 **Hodnet,** Eng,UK
73/B2 **Hodonín,** Czh.
78/C6 **Hoedic** (isl.), Fr.
157/E2 **Hoedspruit,** SAfr.
69/E2 **Hoegnel** (riv.), Belg.
190/B2 **Hoehne,** Co,US
66/A6 **Hoek,** Neth.
66/B5 **Hoekse Waard** (polder), Neth.
66/B5 **Hoek van Holland,** Neth.
69/G6 **Hoenheim,** Fr.
69/E2 **Hoensbroek,** Neth.
69/G6 **Hoerdt,** Fr.
69/E2 **Hoeselt,** Belg.
66/C4 **Hoevelaken,** Neth.
66/B5 **Hoeven,** Neth.
113/D3 **Hoeyang,** NKor.
61/J1 **Hoeybuktmoen** (int'l arpt.), Nor.
151/A1 **Hoeys Bridge,** Kenya
71/E2 **Hof,** Ger.
70/C1 **Hofbieber,** Ger.
61/N6 **Höfdhakaupstadhur,** Ice.
184/C3 **Hoffman** (mt.), Ca,US
194/G5 **Hoffman,** Mn,US
205/P15 **Hoffman Estates,** Il,US
154/C4 **Hoffnung,** Namb.
67/G6 **Hofgeismar,** Ger.
70/D2 **Hofheim in Unterfranken,** Ger.
156/D3 **Hofmeyr,** SAfr.
115/B3 **Hofong Qagan** (salt lake), China
62/G1 **Hofors,** Swe.
61/P6 **Hofsá** (riv.), Ice.
61/N7 **Hofsjökull** (glac.), Ice.
110/B3 **Hōfu,** Japan
201/K2 **Hog** (isl.), Va,US
200/E4 **Hogansville,** Ga,US
133/H2 **Hogarth** (peak), Austl.
192/C3 **Hogback** (mtn.), Ne,US
201/F3 **Hogback** (mtn.), SC,US
183/K3 **Hogeland,** Mt,US
66/C4 **Hoge Veluwe Nat'l Park,** Neth.
151/B3 **Hogoro,** Tanz.
92/D2 **Hogyész,** Hun.
67/G6 **Hohegrass** (peak), Ger.
73/A2 **Hohenau an der March,** Aus.
71/E6 **Hohenbrunn,** Ger.
81/F3 **Hohenems,** Aus.
67/H4 **Hohenhameln,** Ger.
72/C6 **Hohenleuben,** Ger.
71/F6 **Hohenlinden,** Ger.
62/C5 **Hohenlockstedt,** Ger.
70/C4 **Hohenloher Ebene** (plain), Ger.
72/C5 **Hohenmölsen,** Ger.
81/H2 **Hohenpeissenberg,** Ger.
70/D2 **Hohenroth,** Ger.
72/C3 **Hohenseeden,** Ger.
72/D4 **Hohenseefeld,** Ger.
72/C6 **Hohenstein-Ernstthal,** Ger.
81/E2 **Hohentengen,** Ger.
72/C4 **Hohenthurm,** Ger.
200/D3 **Hohenwald,** Tn,US
71/E1 **Hohenwarte-Stausee** (res.), Ger.
62/C4 **Hohenwestedt,** Ger.
75/K3 **Hoher Dachstein** (peak), Aus.
75/K3 **Hohe Tauern** (mts.), Aus.
75/K3 **Hohe Tauern Nat'l Park,** Aus.
80/D4 **Hohgant** (peak), Swi.
115/B2 **Hohhot,** China
69/G2 **Höhn,** Ger.
80/D1 **Hohneck** (mtn.), Fr.
72/B5 **Höhnstedt,** Ger.
67/H2 **Hohnstorf,** Ger.
149/H1 **Hoho,** Eth.
187/G4 **Hohokam Pima Nat'l Mon.,** Az,US
69/G3 **Höhr-Grenzhausen,** Ger.
114/F4 **Hoh Sai** (lake), China
114/F4 **Hoh Xil** (lake), China
114/E4 **Hoh Xil** (mts.), China
123/E3 **Hoi An,** Viet.
153/G2 **Hoima,** Ugan.
191/E1 **Hoisington,** Ks,US
108/D4 **Hoit Taria,** China
123/D1 **Hoi Xuan,** Viet.
62/D4 **Højby,** Den.
62/C4 **Højer,** Den.
110/C4 **Hōjō,** Japan
136/C1 **Hokianga** (har.), N.Z.
136/B3 **Hokitika,** N.Z.
112/C2 **Hokkaidō** (dept.), Japan
112/B2 **Hokkaidō** (isl.), Japan
62/C2 **Hokksund,** Nor.
105/J2 **Ḩokmābād,** Iran
111/G2 **Hokota,** Japan
111/K10 **Hokudan,** Japan
111/M9 **Hokusei,** Japan
62/C1 **Hol,** Nor.
151/C2 **Hola,** Kenya
168/D3 **Holanda,** Bol.
62/D4 **Holbaek,** Den.
57/J6 **Holbeach,** Eng,UK
135/C2 **Holbrook,** Austl.
59/H3 **Holbrook,** Eng,UK
187/G3 **Holbrook,** Az,US
208/C1 **Holbrook,** Ma,US
199/K4 **Holbrook,** NY,US
192/D4 **Holcomb,** Ks,US
195/J5 **Holcombe,** Wi,US
183/H1 **Holden,** Ab,Can
208/C1 **Holden,** Ma,US
196/C3 **Holden,** Me,US
191/H1 **Holden,** Mo,US
201/F2 **Holden,** WV,US
191/F3 **Holdenville,** Ok,US
57/H4 **Holderness** (pen.), Eng,UK
196/B4 **Holderness,** NH,US
194/B2 **Holdfast,** Sk,Can
195/G5 **Holdingford,** Mn,US
67/F3 **Holdorf,** Ger.
192/E3 **Holdrege,** Ne,US
62/D4 **Holeby,** Den.
161/G1 **Holguín,** Cuba
73/B2 **Holíč,** Slvk.
202/K7 **Holiday,** Fl,US
205/P15 **Holiday Hills,** Il,US
177/G3 **Holitna** (riv.), Ak,US
62/E1 **Höljes,** Swe.
191/H3 **Holla Bend Nat'l Wild. Ref.,** Ar,US
73/A2 **Hollabrunn,** Aus.
200/C3 **Holladay,** Tn,US
208/B1 **Holland,** Ma,US
206/B6 **Holland** (pt.), Md,US
198/C3 **Holland,** Mi,US
189/F2 **Holland,** Tx,US
200/B4 **Hollandale,** Ms,US
199/J3 **Holland Patent,** NY,US
66/B4 **Hollandse IJssel** (riv.), Neth.
55/N13 **Hollandstoun,** Sc,UK
72/B5 **Holleben,** Ger.
67/G2 **Hollenstedt,** Ger.
59/H2 **Hollesley,** Eng,UK
70/E3 **Hollfeld,** Ger.
191/E4 **Holliday,** Tx,US
199/G4 **Hollidaysburg,** Pa,US
201/H2 **Hollins,** Va,US
177/M4 **Hollis,** Ak,US
190/E3 **Hollis,** Ok,US
132/B2 **Hollister** (peak), Austl.
186/B2 **Hollister,** Ca,US
191/H2 **Hollister,** Mo,US
201/J2 **Hollister,** NC,US
208/C1 **Holliston,** Ma,US
69/E2 **Hollogne-aux-Pierres,** Belg.
63/L1 **Hollola,** Fin.
190/A4 **Holloman A.F.B.,** NM,US
66/C2 **Hollum,** Neth.
62/E4 **Höllviksnäs,** Swe.
192/C4 **Holly,** Co,US
205/E6 **Holly,** Mi,US
205/B2 **Holly,** Wa,US
200/B4 **Holly Bluff,** Ms,US
191/J3 **Holly Grove,** Ar,US
203/H3 **Holly Hill,** Fl,US
201/G4 **Holly Hill,** SC,US
201/J3 **Holly Ridge,** NC,US
66/C4 **Hollysloot,** Neth.
200/C3 **Holly Springs,** Ms,US
191/H3 **Hollywood,** Ar,US
204/F7 **Hollywood,** Ca,US
203/H4 **Hollywood,** Fl,US
201/G4 **Hollywood,** SC,US
204/F7 **Hollywood Bowl,** Ca,US
202/P7 **Hollywood-Fort Lauderdale** (int'l arpt.), Fl,US
203/H4 **Hollywood-Fort Lauderdale** (int'l arpt.), Fl,US
189/E3 **Hollywood Park,** Tx,US
67/G1 **Holm,** Ger.
178/E1 **Holman,** NW,Can
190/B2 **Holman,** NM,US
61/N6 **Hólmavík,** Ice.
207/D3 **Holmdel,** NJ,US
193/J2 **Holmen,** Wi,US
134/C2 **Holmes** (reefs), Austl.
182/E1 **Holmes** (riv.), BC,Can
208/F6 **Holmes** (co.), Oh,US
57/F5 **Holmes Chapel,** Eng,UK
53/N8 **Holmesdale** (val.), Eng,UK
62/D2 **Holmestrand,** Nor.
208/F6 **Holmesville,** Oh,US
57/H4 **Holme upon Spalding Moor,** Eng,UK
57/G4 **Holmfirth,** Eng,UK
54/B6 **Holmhead,** Sc,UK
137/C **Holm-Lützow** (bay), Ant.
61/G3 **Holmsund,** Swe.
103/D3 **Ḩolon,** Isr.
156/B2 **Holoog,** Namb.
62/C3 **Holstebro,** Den.
193/G2 **Holstein,** Ia,US
300/F2 **Holston** (riv.), Tn,US
201/F2 **Holston, North Fork** (riv.), Va,US
201/F2 **Holston Ordnance Works,** Tn,US
201/G2 **Holston, South Fork** (riv.), Va, Tn,US
58/B5 **Holsworthy,** Eng,UK
59/H1 **Holt,** Eng,UK
200/D4 **Holt,** Al,US
205/M11 **Holt,** Ca,US
202/E2 **Holt,** Fl,US
198/D3 **Holt,** Mi,US
191/G1 **Holt,** Mo,US
72/A4 **Holtemme** (riv.), Ger.
66/D4 **Holten,** Neth.
67/E2 **Holtland,** Ger.
191/G1 **Holton,** Ks,US
191/H1 **Holts Summit,** Mo,US
207/E2 **Holtsville,** NY,US
196/D2 **Holtville,** NB,Can
186/E4 **Holtville,** Ca,US
66/C2 **Holwerd,** Neth.
54/A5 **Holy** (isl.), Sc,UK
56/D5 **Holy** (isl.), Wal,UK
60/C4 **Holycross,** Ire.
177/G3 **Holy Cross,** Ak,US
185/K4 **Holy Cross, Mount of the** (mt.), Co,US
56/D5 **Holyhead,** Wal,UK
56/D5 **Holyhead** (mtn.), Wal,UK
54/E5 **Holy** (Lindisfarne) (isl.), Eng,UK
192/C3 **Holyoke,** Co,US
208/B1 **Holyoke,** Ma,US
197/L2 **Holyrood,** Nf,Can
191/E1 **Holyrood,** Ks,US
200/E4 **Holy Trinity,** Al,US
57/E5 **Holywell,** Wal,UK
56/C2 **Holywood,** NI,UK
72/C5 **Holzhausen,** Ger.
64/F5 **Holzkirchen,** Ger.
67/G5 **Holzminden,** Ger.
67/E6 **Holzwickede,** Ger.
156/B3 **Hom** (dry riv.), Namb.
151/A2 **Homa** (peak), Kenya
151/A2 **Homa Bay,** Kenya
182/B2 **Homathko** (riv.), BC,Can
66/D6 **Homberg,** Ger.
67/G6 **Homberg,** Ger.
145/E3 **Hombori,** Mali
145/E3 **Hombori Tondo** (peak), Mali
69/F5 **Hombourg-Haut,** Fr.
69/G5 **Homburg,** Ger.
179/K2 **Home** (bay), NW,Can
69/E5 **Homécourt,** Fr.
134/B2 **Home Hill,** Austl.
190/A2 **Homelake,** Co,US
204/C3 **Homeland,** Ca,US
203/G2 **Homeland,** Ga,US
177/H4 **Homer,** Ak,US
201/F3 **Homer,** Ga,US
189/H1 **Homer,** La,US
198/D3 **Homer,** Mi,US
199/H3 **Homer,** NY,US
203/G2 **Homerville,** Ga,US
183/H5 **Homestake** (pass), Mt,US
134/B3 **Homestead,** Austl.
203/H5 **Homestead,** Fl,US
208/H7 **Homestead,** Pa,US
203/H5 **Homestead A.F.B.,** Fl,US
193/F3 **Homestead Nat'l Mon.,** Ne,US
184/C4 **Homewood,** Ca,US
205/Q16 **Homewood,** Il,US
208/F6 **Homeworth,** Oh,US
149/H2 **Homib** (dry riv.), Eth.
106/C5 **Homib** (riv.), Eth.
62/A2 **Hommersåk,** Nor.
202/C2 **Homochitto** (riv.), Ms,US
155/G4 **Homoíne,** Moz.
125/D3 **Homonhon** (isl.), Phil.
203/G3 **Homosassa,** Fl,US
202/K6 **Homosassa** (bay), Fl,US
203/G3 **Homosassa Springs,** Fl,US
203/G3 **Homosassa Springs Nat. World,** Fl,US
159/H4 **Homún,** Mex.
191/G3 **Hon,** Ar,US
180/U11 **Honaunau-Napoopoo,** Hi,US
118/B5 **Honāvar,** India
112/C2 **Honbetsu,** Japan
123/D4 **Hon Chong,** Viet.
164/C3 **Honda,** Col.
58/C3 **Honddu** (riv.), Wal,UK
156/B3 **Hondeklipbaai,** SAfr.
160/D2 **Hondo** (riv.), Belz., Mex.
110/B4 **Hondo,** Japan
205/L12 **Hondo** (arroyo), Ca,US
190/B4 **Hondo,** NM,US
190/B4 **Hondo** (riv.), NM,US
188/E3 **Hondo,** Tx,US
188/E3 **Hondo** (cr.), Tx,US
159/Q9 **Hondo de Tepotzotlán** (riv.), Mex.
68/B2 **Hondschoote,** Fr.
64/D2 **Hondsrug** (hills), Neth.
66/D3 **Hondsrug** (reg.), Neth.
160/E3 **Honduras**
160/D2 **Honduras** (gulf), NAm.
201/F3 **Honea Path,** SC,US
62/D1 **Hønefoss,** Nor.
199/J4 **Honesdale,** Pa,US
159/L6 **Honey,** Mex.
184/C3 **Honey** (lake), Ca,US
205/P14 **Honey** (cr.), Wi,US
59/E2 **Honeybourne,** Eng,UK
206/C3 **Honey Brook,** Pa,US
205/P14 **Honey Creek,** Wi,US
191/G4 **Honey Grove,** Tx,US
185/G3 **Honeyville,** Ut,US
79/F2 **Honfleur,** Fr.
117/G2 **Hong** (lake), China
115/C4 **Hong** (riv.), China
113/E1 **Hongam-nodongjagu,** NKor.
115/C5 **Hong'an,** China
113/B2 **Hongchang,** China
113/D4 **Hongch'ŏn,** SKor.
117/F4 **Hongdu,** China
119/J2 **Hongdu** (riv.), China
123/D1 **Hong Gai,** Viet.
108/C4 **Honggouzi,** China
116/E3 **Hongguo,** China
115/C5 **Honghu,** China
117/F3 **Hongjiang,** China
117/G4 **Hong Kong** (int'l arpt.), HK
117/G4 **Hong Kong** (dpcy.), UK
138/A2 **Hong Kong** (dpcy.), UK
117/H3 **Honglai,** China
115/B3 **Hongliu** (riv.), China
108/C3 **Hongliuhe,** China
108/D3 **Hongliuquan,** China
117/H3 **Honglu,** China
117/H2 **Hongmiao** (mtn.), China
113/B2 **Hongqi,** China
117/J2 **Hongqiao,** China
115/E5 **Hongqiao** (int'l arpt.), China
123/E2 **Hongqizhen,** China
123/C1 **Hong** (Red) (riv.), Viet.
80/D5 **Hongrin** (lake), Swi.
117/H3 **Hongshan** (mtn.), China
114/D2 **Hongshanzui,** China
117/E4 **Hongshui** (riv.), China
113/D4 **Hongsŏng,** SKor.
115/C3 **Hongtao Shan** (mtn.), China
117/H3 **Hongtian,** China
115/B3 **Hongtong,** China
179/K4 **Honguedo** (passg.), Qu,Can
196/E1 **Honguedo** (str.), Qu,Can
113/D2 **Hongwŏn,** NKor.
116/D2 **Hongya,** China
115/B5 **Hongyan,** China
117/H4 **Hongyang,** China
108/E5 **Hongyuan,** China
115/D4 **Hongze,** China
115/D4 **Hongze** (lake), China
138/E5 **Honiara** (cap.), Sol.
58/C5 **Honiton,** Eng,UK
112/B4 **Honjō,** Japan
61/H1 **Honningsvåg,** Nor.
62/D3 **Hönö,** Swe.
191/G3 **Honobia,** Ok,US
180/T10 **Honolulu,** Hi,US
180/T10 **Honolulu** (int'l arpt.), Hi,US
200/D5 **Honoraville,** Al,US
72/D2 **Hönow,** Ger.
123/D4 **Hon Quan,** Viet.
101/Q6 **Honshu** (isl.), Japan
109/M5 **Honshū** (isl.), Japan
111/E3 **Honshu** (isl.), Japan
112/B3 **Honshū** (isl.), Japan
51/S4 **Honshu** (isl.), Japan
73/D3 **Hontianske Nemce,** Slvk.
132/C5 **Hood** (pt.), Austl.
131/G2 **Hood** (pt.), PNG
205/L10 **Hood,** Ca,US
205/J10 **Hood** (mtn.), Ca,US
188/K7 **Hood** (co.), Tx,US
205/B2 **Hood** (can.), Wa,US
184/C1 **Hood, Mount** (mtn.), Or,US
184/C1 **Hood River,** Or,US
66/B4 **Hoofddorp,** Neth.
66/C6 **Hoogeloon,** Neth.
66/B6 **Hoogerheide,** Neth.
66/D3 **Hoogeveen,** Neth.
66/D3 **Hoogeveense Vaart** (can.), Neth.
66/D2 **Hoogezand,** Neth.
121/G4 **Hooghly** (riv.), India
121/G4 **Hooghly-Chinsura,** India
66/C3 **Hoogkarspel,** Neth.
68/C2 **Hooglede,** Belg.
66/B6 **Hoogstraten,** Belg.
66/B5 **Hoogvliet,** Neth.
134/C3 **Hook** (isl.), Austl.
59/F4 **Hook,** Eng,UK
180/U11 **Hookena,** Hi,US
190/D2 **Hooker,** Ok,US
130/C4 **Hooker Creek,** Austl.
130/C4 **Hooker Creek Abor. Land,** Austl.
60/D5 **Hook Head** (pt.), Ire.
199/L3 **Hooksett,** NH,US
177/L4 **Hoonah,** Ak,US
184/B3 **Hoopa,** Ca,US
184/B3 **Hoopa Valley Ind. Res.,** Ca,US
190/B2 **Hooper,** Co,US
193/F3 **Hooper,** Ne,US
177/E3 **Hooper Bay,** Ak,US
199/H3 **Hooper** (Endwell), NY,US
198/C4 **Hoopeston,** Il,US
194/F3 **Hoople,** ND,US
156/D2 **Hoopstad,** SAfr.
62/E4 **Höör,** Swe.
66/C3 **Hoorn,** Neth.
66/C3 **Hoornse Hop** (bay), Neth.
199/K3 **Hoosick Falls,** NY,US
186/E2 **Hoover** (dam), Az,US
192/C1 **Hoover,** SD,US
201/F2 **Hoover** (mtn.), WV,US
104/E1 **Hopa,** Turk.
206/D2 **Hopatcong,** NJ,US
206/D2 **Hopatcong** (lake), NJ,US
132/D5 **Hope** (lake), Austl.
182/D3 **Hope,** BC,Can
57/E5 **Hope,** Wal,UK
177/J3 **Hope,** Ak,US
191/H4 **Hope,** Ar,US
198/D5 **Hope,** In,US
191/F1 **Hope,** Ks,US
194/F4 **Hope,** ND,US
206/D2 **Hope,** NJ,US
190/B4 **Hope,** NM,US
208/C2 **Hope,** RI,US
189/F3 **Hope,** Tx,US
179/K3 **Hopedale,** Nf,Can
208/C1 **Hopedale,** Ma,US
208/G7 **Hopedale,** Oh,US
159/H5 **Hopelchén,** Mex.
54/C1 **Hopeman,** Sc,UK
201/H3 **Hope Mills,** NC,US
179/K2 **Hopes Advance** (cape), Qu,Can
58/C6 **Hope's Nose** (pt.), Eng,UK
132/D5 **Hopetoun,** Austl.
162/B1 **Hope Town,** Bahm.
156/D3 **Hopetown,** SAfr.
58/D2 **Hope under Dinmore,** Eng,UK
134/B1 **Hope Vale Abor. Community,** Austl.
134/B1 **Hope Vale Abor. Land,** Austl.
208/C2 **Hope Valley,** RI,US
197/F3 **Hopewell,** NS,Can
206/D3 **Hopewell,** NJ,US
201/J2 **Hopewell,** Va,US
196/E3 **Hopewell Cape,** NB,Can
206/C3 **Hopewell Furnace Nat'l Hist. Site,** Pa,US
187/G2 **Hopi Ind. Res.,** Az,US
116/C3 **Hopin,** Burma
78/A4 **Hôpital-Camfrout,** Fr.
133/F3 **Hopkins** (lake), Austl.
135/B3 **Hopkins** (riv.), Austl.
195/P7 **Hopkins,** Mn,US
193/G3 **Hopkins,** Mo,US
200/D2 **Hopkinsville,** Ky,US
208/C1 **Hopkinton,** Ma,US
196/B4 **Hopkinton,** NH,US
208/C3 **Hopkinton,** RI,US
67/F6 **Hoppecke** (riv.), Ger.
204/B2 **Hopper Mtn. Nat'l Wild. Ref.,** Ca,US
69/G4 **Hoppstädten-Weiersbach,** Ger.
67/E4 **Hopsten,** Ger.
182/C4 **Hoquiam,** Wa,US
108/E4 **Hor,** China
177/J2 **Horace** (mtn.), Ak,US
190/D1 **Horace,** Ks,US
194/F4 **Horace,** ND,US
111/L9 **Hōrai-san** (peak), Japan
104/E1 **Horasan,** Turk.
191/G4 **Horatio,** Ar,US
71/G4 **Horažďovice,** Czh.
70/B6 **Horb am Neckar,** Ger.
103/D3 **Ḩorbat Qesari** (ruins), Isr.
80/D1 **Horbourg-Wihr,** Fr.
81/F2 **Hörbranz,** Aus.
57/G4 **Horbury,** Eng,UK
188/B3 **Horcasitas,** Mex.
76/D2 **Horche,** Sp.
161/F4 **Horconcitos,** Pan.
172/C2 **Horcones** (riv.), Arg.
62/A1 **Hordaland** (co.), Nor.
57/G2 **Horden,** Eng,UK
70/B4 **Hördt,** Ger.
93/G3 **Horezu,** Rom.
70/D6 **Horgau,** Ger.
81/E3 **Horgen,** Swi.
108/F3 **Hörh** (peak), Mong.
51/S6 **Horiara** (cap.), Sol.
193/K2 **Horicon,** Wi,US
198/B3 **Horicon Nat'l Wild. Ref.,** Mi,US
115/B2 **Horinger,** China
173/F3 **Horizontina,** Braz.
53/N8 **Horley,** Eng,UK
137/R **Horlick Ice Stream,** Ant.
162/E3 **Hormigüeros,** PR
105/H5 **Hormozgān** (gov.), Iran
105/H5 **Hormūd-e Mīr Khūnd,** Iran
107/G3 **Hormuz** (str.), Asia
105/H5 **Hormuz** (str.), Iran, Oman
75/L2 **Horn,** Aus.
163/C8 **Horn** (cape), Chile
61/M6 **Horn** (pt.), Ice.
202/D2 **Horn** (isl.), Ms,US
76/C4 **Hornachuelos,** Sp.
65/L4 **Hornád** (riv.), Slvk.
73/C2 **Horná Štubňa,** Slvk.
61/E2 **Hornavan** (lake), Swe.
69/G5 **Hornbach,** Ger.
67/F5 **Horn-Bad Meinberg,** Ger.
63/T8 **Hornbæk,** Den.
182/F1 **Hornbeck,** Ab,Can
202/B2 **Hornbeck,** La,US
70/B6 **Hornberg,** Ger.
67/H4 **Hornburg,** Ger.
197/R8 **Hornby,** On,Can
136/C3 **Hornby,** N.Z.
182/B3 **Hornby Island,** BC,Can
57/H5 **Horncastle,** Eng,UK
53/P7 **Hornchurch,** Eng,UK
62/G1 **Horndal,** Swe.
67/G2 **Horneburg,** Ger.
199/H3 **Hornell,** NY,US
200/B2 **Hornersville,** Mo,US
73/B3 **Horné Saliby,** Slvk.
175/L8 **Horn** (Hornos) (cape), Chile
71/G3 **Horní Bříza,** Czh.
70/B5 **Hornisgrinde** (peak), Ger.
71/F2 **Horní Slavkov,** Czh.
186/B2 **Hornitos,** Ca,US
200/B3 **Horn Lake,** Ms,US
175/L8 **Hornos** (Horn), Cabo de (cape), Chile
68/A4 **Hornoy-le-Bourg,** Fr.
134/H8 **Hornsby,** Austl.
57/H4 **Hornsea,** Eng,UK
62/D3 **Hornslet,** Den.
62/C4 **Hörnum** (cape), Ger.
64/E1 **Hornum Odde** (cape), Ger.
112/C2 **Horoshiri-dake** (mtn.), Japan
71/G3 **Hořovice,** Czh.
136/C3 **Horowhenua** (reg.), N.Z.
115/E1 **Horqin Youyi Zhongqi,** China
115/E2 **Horqin Zuoyi Houqi,** China
115/E1 **Horqin Zuoyi Zhongqi,** China
173/E2 **Horqueta,** Par.
58/B6 **Horrabridge,** Eng,UK
116/A2 **Horru,** China
71/H6 **Hörsching,** Aus.
190/C1 **Horse** (cr.), Co,US
188/C2 **Horse** (mtn.), Tx,US
192/B3 **Horse** (cr.), Wy,US
200/E2 **Horse Cave,** Ky,US
192/B3 **Horse Creek,** Wy,US
182/D1 **Horsefly,** BC,Can
182/D1 **Horsefly** (lake), BC,Can
182/D1 **Horsefly** (riv.), BC,Can
199/H3 **Horseheads,** NY,US
62/C4 **Horsens,** Den.
203/G3 **Horseshoe Beach,** Fl,US
191/J2 **Horseshoe Bend,** Ar,US
184/E2 **Horseshoe Bend,** Id,US
200/E4 **Horseshoe Bend Nat'l Mil. Park,** Al,US
199/G5 **Horse Shoe Run,** WV,US
182/F2 **Horsethief** (cr.), BC,Can
59/H3 **Horsey** (isl.), Eng,UK
57/G4 **Horsforth,** Eng,UK
135/B3 **Horsham,** Austl.
59/F4 **Horsham,** Eng,UK
206/C3 **Horsham,** Pa,US
62/G1 **Horslandet** (pen.), Swe.
71/F3 **Horšovský Týn,** Czh.
62/D5 **Horst,** Ger.
66/D6 **Horst,** Neth.
67/E4 **Hörstel,** Ger.
67/E4 **Horstmar,** Ger.
77/S12 **Horta,** Azor.,Port.
77/N9 **Hortaleza,** Sp.
62/D2 **Horten,** Nor.
203/H2 **Hortense,** Ga,US
80/B2 **Hortes,** Fr.
92/E2 **Hortobágyi Nat'l Park,** Hun.
177/N2 **Horton** (riv.), NW,Can
191/G1 **Horton,** Ks,US
191/G2 **Horton,** Mo,US
207/F1 **Horton** (pt.), NY,US
53/P7 **Horton Kirby,** Eng,UK
62/C4 **Høruphav,** Den.
71/H4 **Horusický Rybník** (lake), Czh.
62/D4 **Hørve,** Den.
103/D4 **Ḩorvot 'Avedat** (ruins), Isr.
103/F6 **Ḩorvot Dor,** Isr.
103/D4 **Ḩorvot Meẓada** (Masada) (ruins), Isr.
81/E3 **Horw,** Swi.
57/F4 **Horwich,** Eng,UK
149/H4 **Hosa'ina,** Eth.
70/C2 **Hösbach,** Ger.
72/E5 **Hosena,** Ger.
70/C2 **Hosenfeld,** Ger.
146/D4 **Hosenofu** (well), Libya
148/B3 **Hoséré Vokré** (peak), Camr.
203/F2 **Hosford,** Fl,US
107/H3 **Hoshāb,** Pak.
120/A4 **Hoshangābād,** India
122/C2 **Hoshiārpur,** India
69/F3 **Hosingen,** Lux.
182/G3 **Hosmer,** BC,Can
192/E1 **Hosmer,** SD,US
81/E4 **Hospental,** Swi.
118/C4 **Hospet,** India
174/Q9 **Hospital,** Chile
60/B5 **Hospital,** Ire.
189/H1 **Hosston,** La,US
73/B5 **Hosszúpereszteg,** Hun.
175/K8 **Hoste** (isl.), Chile
55/P12 **Hoswick,** Sc,UK
123/B2 **Hot,** Thai.
111/E2 **Hotaka,** Japan
111/E2 **Hotaka-dake** (mtn.), Japan
114/C4 **Hotan,** China
114/D4 **Hotan** (riv.), China
156/C2 **Hotazel,** SAfr.
185/K4 **Hotchkiss,** Co,US
208/A2 **Hotchkissville,** Ct,US
184/E4 **Hot Creek** (range), Nv,US
187/G3 **Hotevilla,** Az,US
130/C3 **Hotham** (cape), Austl.
127/H4 **Hoti,** Indo.
108/E2 **Hotont,** Mong.
192/C2 **Hot Springs,** SD,US
191/H3 **Hot Springs Nat'l Park,** Ar,US
192/A3 **Hot Sulphur Springs,** Co,US
178/E2 **Hottah** (lake), NW,Can
156/A2 **Hottentot** (bay), Namb.
154/B5 **Hottentots** (pt.), Namb.
69/E3 **Hotton,** Belg.
117/E2 **Hou** (riv.), China
123/C1 **Houamuang,** Laos
78/C6 **Houat** (isl.), Fr.
116/E3 **Houchang,** China
187/H3 **Houck,** Az,US
68/B3 **Houdain,** Fr.
68/A6 **Houdan,** Fr.
144/D4 **Houet** (prov.), Burk.
69/E3 **Houffalize,** Belg.
195/K4 **Houghton,** Mi,US
198/D2 **Houghton** (lake), Mi,US
195/K4 **Houghton** (pt.), Mi,US
199/G3 **Houghton,** NY,US
194/E5 **Houghton,** SD,US
192/E1 **Houghton** (dam), SD,US
198/D2 **Houghton Lake,** Mi,US
57/G2 **Houghton-le-Spring,** Eng,UK
53/S10 **Houilles,** Fr.
79/E2 **Houlgate,** Fr.
196/D2 **Houlton,** Me,US
195/Q6 **Houlton,** Wi,US
115/B4 **Houma,** China
202/C3 **Houma,** La,US
144/E4 **Houndé,** Burk.
53/M7 **Hounslow** (bor.), Eng,UK
68/B2 **Houplines,** Fr.
136/C2 **Houraki** (gulf), N.Z.
59/H6 **Hourdel** (pt.), Fr.
68/A3 **Hourdel, Pointe du** (pt.), Fr.
54/A2 **Hourn, Loch** (inlet), Sc,UK
74/C4 **Hourtin,** Fr.
208/A3 **Housatonic** (riv.), Ct,US
208/A1 **Housatonic,** Ma,US
180/D4 **House** (range), Ut,US
57/F1 **Housesteads Roman Fort,** Eng,UK
80/D1 **Houssen,** Fr.
177/J3 **Houston,** Ak,US
206/C6 **Houston,** De,US
203/G2 **Houston,** Fl,US
193/J2 **Houston,** Mn,US
191/J2 **Houston,** Mo,US
200/C4 **Houston,** Ms,US
189/G3 **Houston,** Tx,US
189/G2 **Houston** (lake), Tx,US
189/N9 **Houston** (pt.), Tx,US
191/H1 **Houstonia,** Mo,US
189/G3 **Houston Intercontinental** (int'l arpt.), Tx,US
189/M9 **Houston Ship** (chan.), Tx,US
156/L11 **Houtbaai,** SAfr.
66/C4 **Houten,** Neth.
69/E1 **Houthalen,** Belg.
68/B2 **Houthulst,** Belg.
128/A5 **Houtman Abrolhos** (isls.), Austl.
132/B4 **Houtman Abrolhos** (rocks), Austl.
66/C3 **Houtribdijk** (dam), Neth.
63/J1 **Houtskär** (isl.), Fin.
69/E3 **Houyet,** Belg.
113/B2 **Houyingzi,** China
108/F5 **Houzhenzi,** China
62/D1 **Hov,** Nor.
62/F2 **Hova,** Swe.
108/C2 **Hovd,** Mong.
63/T9 **Hove** (riv.), Den.
59/F5 **Hove,** Eng,UK
67/F5 **Hövelhof,** Ger.
192/E1 **Hoven,** SD,US
187/H2 **Hovenweep Nat'l Mon.,** Co,US
59/H1 **Hoveton,** Eng,UK
62/E1 **Hovfjället** (peak), Swe.
57/H3 **Hovingham,** Eng,UK
195/K4 **Hovland,** Mn,US
62/F3 **Hovmantorp,** Swe.
108/E1 **Hövsgöl** (lake), Mong.
62/F2 **Hovsta,** Swe.
148/D2 **Howa, Ouadi** (dry riv.), Chad
134/D4 **Howard,** Austl.
131/D2 **Howard** (isl.), Austl.
196/E2 **Howard,** NB,Can
177/H2 **Howard** (hill), Ak,US
177/G2 **Howard** (pass), Ak,US
192/B4 **Howard,** Co,US
191/F2 **Howard,** Ks,US
206/B5 **Howard** (co.), Md,US
208/E7 **Howard,** Oh,US
192/F1 **Howard,** SD,US
193/K1 **Howard,** Wi,US
207/K9 **Howard Beach,** NY,US
198/D3 **Howard City,** Mi,US
205/D3 **Howard Hanson** (dam), Wa,US
205/D3 **Howard Hanson** (res.), Wa,US
193/G1 **Howard Lake,** Mn,US
184/B2 **Howard Prairie** (lake), Or,US
188/D2 **Howards** (cr.), Tx,US
198/C3 **Howards Grove,** Wi,US
149/E1 **Howar, Wādī** (dry riv.), Sudan
57/H4 **Howden,** Eng,UK
135/D3 **Howe** (cape), Austl.
182/C3 **Howe** (sound), BC,Can
191/G3 **Howe,** Ok,US
191/F4 **Howe,** Tx,US
199/J3 **Howe Caverns,** NY,US
198/E3 **Howell,** Mi,US
207/D3 **Howell,** NJ,US
136/F6 **Howick,** N.Z.
157/E3 **Howick,** SAfr.
202/D2 **Howison,** Ms,US
139/H4 **Howland** (isl.), PacUS
196/C3 **Howland,** Me,US
197/J1 **Howley,** Nf,Can
55/H8 **Howmore,** Sc,UK
121/G4 **Howrah,** India
182/F2 **Howser,** BC,Can
191/J2 **Hoxie,** Ar,US
190/D1 **Hoxie,** Ks,US
64/E3 **Höxter,** Ger.
114/E3 **Hoxud,** China
55/N13 **Hoy** (isl.), Sc,UK
67/G3 **Hoya,** Ger.
62/B1 **Høyanger,** Nor.
65/H3 **Hoyerswerda,** Ger.
57/E5 **Hoylake,** Eng,UK
57/G5 **Hoyland Nether,** Eng,UK
77/N8 **Hoyo-de Manzanares,** Sp.
76/B2 **Hoyos,** Sp.
69/E3 **Hoyoux** (riv.), Belg.
196/D3 **Hoyt,** NB,Can
191/G1 **Hoyt,** Ks,US
183/M4 **Hoyt,** Mt,US
191/G3 **Hoyt,** Ok,US
108/E2 **Hoyt Tamir** (riv.), Mong.
111/M9 **Hozumi,** Japan
71/G3 **Hracholusky, Údolní nádrž** (res.), Czh.
65/H3 **Hradec Králové,** Czh.
71/G2 **Hradiště** (peak), Czh.
71/F2 **Hranice,** Czh.
92/D4 **Hrasnica,** Bosn.
92/B2 **Hrastnik,** Slov.
87/G1 **Hrastovlje,** Slov.
71/G2 **Hřivice,** Czh.
61/M6 **Hrolleifsborg** (peak), Ice.
73/C4 **Hron** (riv.), Slvk.
65/J3 **Hronov,** Czh.
65/M3 **Hrubieszów,** Pol.
65/J3 **Hrubý Jeseník** (mts.), Czh.
73/A2 **Hrušovany nad Jevĭsovkou,** Czh.
61/P6 **Hrútafjöll** (peak), Ice.
119/G3 **Hsenwi,** Burma
116/C4 **Hsi-hseng,** Burma
117/J3 **Hsinchu,** Tai.
123/B1 **Hsipaw,** Burma
117/J4 **Hsiukulan** (mtn.), Tai.
117/J3 **Hsüeh** (peak), Tai.
119/G2 **Htawgaw,** Burma
108/G5 **Hua** (peak), China
154/B3 **Huab** (dry riv.), Namb.
169/F4 **Huacaraje,** Bol.
172/D2 **Huacareta,** Bol.
172/D2 **Huacaya,** Bol.
172/B1 **Huachacalla,** Bol.
117/G3 **Huacheng,** China
169/F4 **Huachi,** Bol.
108/F4 **Huachi,** China
168/B3 **Huacho,** Peru
168/C3 **Huachón,** Peru
109/L2 **Huachuan,** China
187/G5 **Huachuca** (mts.), Az,US
187/G5 **Huachuca City,** Az,US
168/B3 **Huacrachuco,** Peru
108/G3 **Huade,** China
109/K3 **Huadian,** China
113/C2 **Huadianzi,** China
117/J2 **Huading** (mtn.), China
123/B3 **Hua Hin,** Thai.
139/K6 **Huahine** (isl.), FrPol.
115/C4 **Huai** (riv.), China
115/D4 **Huai'an,** China
108/H5 **Huaibei,** China
115/C4 **Huaibin,** China
117/F3 **Huaihua,** China
117/G4 **Huaiji,** China
115/C2 **Huailai,** China
115/D4 **Huainan,** China
115/D5 **Huaining,** China
115/C3 **Huairen,** China
115/D2 **Huairou,** China
115/C4 **Huaiyang,** China
115/D4 **Huaiyin,** China
123/B5 **Huai Yot,** Thai.
115/D4 **Huaiyuan,** China
158/D4 **Huajicori,** Mex.
159/F5 **Huajuapan de León,** Mex.
174/C2 **Hualañé,** Chile
187/F3 **Hualapai** (mts.), Az,US
187/F3 **Hualapai** (peak), Az,US
187/F3 **Hualapai Ind. Res.,** Az,US
172/C3 **Hualfín,** Arg.
168/B2 **Hualgayoc,** Peru
117/J4 **Hualien,** Tai.
168/C4 **Hualla,** Peru
168/B2 **Huallaga** (riv.), Peru
168/B3 **Huallanca,** Peru
168/B2 **Huamachuco,** Peru
168/B3 **Huamantanga,** Peru
159/F5 **Huamantla,** Mex.
154/B2 **Huambo,** Ang.
154/B2 **Huambo** (dist.), Ang.
168/B2 **Huambos,** Peru
160/C2 **Huamelula,** Mex.
159/F5 **Huamuxtitlán,** Mex.
117/G2 **Huan** (riv.), China
109/L2 **Huanan,** China
172/B2 **Huanaqui,** Bol.
169/E4 **Huanay,** Bol.
168/D4 **Huancané,** Peru
168/C4 **Huancapi,** Peru
168/B3 **Huancaspata,** Peru
168/C4 **Huancavelica,** Peru
168/B3 **Huancaybamba,** Peru
168/C4 **Huancayo,** Peru
172/C2 **Huanchaca** (peak), Bol.
115/D4 **Huang** (riv.), China
123/C2 **Huang** (riv.), Laos, Thai.
116/E1 **Huangbayi,** China
117/H3 **Huangbei,** China
115/C4 **Huangchuan,** China
117/F3 **Huangcun,** China
115/C5 **Huanggang,** China
117/H3 **Huanggang** (peak), China
115/D3 **Huanghua,** China
113/B2 **Huanghuadian,** China
117/H2 **Huangjinbu,** China
116/E2 **Huangjinggou,** China
117/H3 **Huangjinkenggang** (mtn.), China
115/K8 **Huangli,** China
115/B4 **Huangling,** China
117/F5 **Huangliu,** China
115/B4 **Huanglong,** China
117/G3 **Huanglong,** China
115/B4 **Huanglongtan,** China
117/H3 **Huangmao** (peak), China
115/C5 **Huangmei,** China
108/F5 **Huangniupu,** China
115/C5 **Huangpi,** China
119/J2 **Huangping,** China
115/C2 **Huangqi** (lake), China
115/D5 **Huangshan,** China
115/C5 **Huangshi,** China
117/H3 **Huangshidu,** China
115/C5 **Huangtang** (lake), China
117/F3 **Huangtianpu,** China
115/B4 **Huangtu** (plat.), China
117/F2 **Huangtudian,** China
174/E3 **Huanguelén,** Arg.
115/L9 **Huangwan,** China
115/D3 **Huang** (Yellow) (riv.), China
115/B4 **Huangyunpu,** China
117/H2 **Huangzhai,** China
117/G2 **Huangzhan,** China
108/E4 **Huangzhong,** China
116/D3 **Huaning,** China
119/J3 **Huanjiang,** China
113/C2 **Huanren,** China
168/C4 **Huanta,** Peru
115/D3 **Huantai,** China
168/B3 **Huántar,** Peru
168/B3 **Huánuco,** Peru
172/C1 **Huanuni,** Bol.
117/G3 **Huanxi,** China
108/F4 **Huan Xian,** China
161/E3 **Huapi** (mts.), Nic.
116/D3 **Huaping,** China
108/F5 **Huaqiaozhen,** China
159/F5 **Huaquechula,** Mex.
168/A1 **Huaquillas,** Ecu.
172/B1 **Huara,** Chile
168/B3 **Huaral,** Peru
168/B3 **Huaráz,** Peru
172/C1 **Huari,** Bol.
168/B3 **Huari,** Peru
168/C3 **Huaricolca,** Peru
168/D5 **Huarina,** Bol.
168/B3 **Huarmey,** Peru
168/B4 **Huarochirí,** Peru
168/C4 **Huarocondo,** Peru
168/C3 **Huasahuasi,** Peru
123/C4 **Hua Sai,** Thai.
168/B3 **Huascarán** (peak), Peru
168/B3 **Huascaran Nat'l Park,** Peru
172/B3 **Huasco** (riv.), Chile
115/B4 **Hua Shan** (peak), China
117/G3 **Huashi,** China
117/G3 **Huashi** (mts.), China
158/C3 **Huatabampo,** Mex.
113/A2 **Huatong,** China
169/E4 **Huatunas** (lake), Bol.
160/B2 **Huatusco,** Mex.
159/F5 **Huatuxco,** Mex.
159/N7 **Huatuxco de Chicuellar,** Mex.
159/F4 **Huauchinango,** Mex.
168/B3 **Huaura,** Peru
160/B2 **Huautla,** Mex.
159/F5 **Huautla de Jiménez,** Mex.
115/C4 **Hua Xian,** China
117/J2 **Huayang,** China
108/F5 **Huayangzhen,** China
116/E2 **Huaying,** China
168/B3 **Huaylas,** Peru
168/B3 **Huayllay,** Peru
168/C4 **Huaypata,** Peru
113/D1 **Huayuan,** China
117/G2 **Huayuan,** China
119/J2 **Huayuan,** China
108/E4 **Huazhaizi,** China
119/K3 **Huazhou,** China
113/B2 **Huazi,** China
202/D2 **Hub,** Ms,US
177/L3 **Hubbard** (mt.), Ak,US, Yk,Can
194/C2 **Hubbard,** Sk,Can
193/H2 **Hubbard,** Ia,US
198/E2 **Hubbard** (lake), Mi,US
208/G5 **Hubbard,** Oh,US
184/B1 **Hubbard,** Or,US
189/F2 **Hubbard,** Tx,US
188/E1 **Hubbard Creek** (res.), Tx,US
196/E3 **Hubbards,** NS,Can
187/H3 **Hubbell Trading Post Nat'l Hist. Site,** Az,US
115/C5 **Hubei** (prov.), China
115/B4 **Hubei Kou** (pass), China
198/D5 **Huber Heights,** Oh,US
118/C4 **Hubli-Dhārwār,** India
73/D1 **Hubová,** Slvk.
113/D2 **Huch'ang,** NKor.
66/D6 **Hückelhoven,** Ger.
67/E6 **Hückeswagen,** Ger.
57/G5 **Hucknall Torkard,** Eng,UK
68/A2 **Hucqueliers,** Fr.
115/L8 **Hudai,** China
57/G4 **Huddersfield,** Eng,UK
63/R7 **Huddinge,** Swe.
67/F2 **Hude,** Ger.

62/G1 **Hudiksvall,** Swe.
137/L **Hudson** (cape), Ant.
179/H2 **Hudson** (bay), Can.
176/K3 **Hudson** (str.), Can.
179/J2 **Hudson** (str.), NW, Qu,Can
195/H2 **Hudson,** On,Can
197/M7 **Hudson,** Qu,Can
207/J9 **Hudson** (riv.), US
203/G3 **Hudson,** Fl,US
198/B4 **Hudson,** Il,US
208/C1 **Hudson,** Ma,US
196/C3 **Hudson,** Me,US
198/D4 **Hudson,** Mi,US
201/G3 **Hudson,** NC,US
199/L3 **Hudson,** NH,US
207/J9 **Hudson** (co.), NJ,US
207/E1 **Hudson** (riv.), NJ, NY,US
199/K3 **Hudson,** NY,US
199/J3 **Hudson** (riv.), NY,US
208/F5 **Hudson,** Oh,US
191/G2 **Hudson** (lake), Ok,US
189/G2 **Hudson,** Tx,US
193/H1 **Hudson,** Wi,US
178/F3 **Hudson Bay,** Sk,Can
199/K3 **Hudson Falls,** NY,US
188/K7 **Hudson Oaks,** Tx,US
178/D3 **Hudson's Hope,** BC,Can
123/D2 **Hue,** Viet.
190/A4 **Hueco** (mts.), NM, Tx,US
188/B2 **Hueco** (mts.), Tx,US
92/F2 **Huedin,** Rom.
160/D3 **Huehuetenango,** Guat.
159/L6 **Huehuetla,** Mex.
159/L8 **Huehuetlán el Chico,** Mex.
158/D3 **Huejotitán,** Mex.
159/L7 **Huejotzingo,** Mex.
158/E4 **Huejuquilla el Alto,** Mex.
159/F4 **Huejutla,** Mex.
160/B1 **Huejutla de Reyes,** Mex.
78/B4 **Huelgoat,** Fr.
76/D4 **Huelma,** Sp.
76/B4 **Huelva,** Sp.
76/B3 **Huelva** (riv.), Sp.
174/B4 **Huequi** (vol.), Chile
76/E4 **Huercal-Overa,** Sp.
192/B5 **Huerfano** (cr.), Co,US
190/B2 **Huerfano** (riv.), Co,US
77/E1 **Huesca,** Sp.
76/D4 **Huéscar,** Sp.
174/F3 **Huesos** (riv.), Arg.
159/E5 **Huetamo,** Mex.
76/D2 **Huete,** Sp.
160/C2 **Hueyapan de Ocampo,** Mex.
81/E2 **Hüfingen,** Ger.
201/H4 **Huger,** SC,US
134/B3 **Hughenden,** Austl.
183/J1 **Hughenden,** Ab,Can
174/E2 **Hughes,** Arg.
133/F4 **Hughes,** Austl.
177/H2 **Hughes,** Ak,US
191/J3 **Hughes,** Ar,US
189/G1 **Hughes Springs,** Tx,US
206/B1 **Hughesville,** Pa,US
186/B2 **Hughson,** Ca,US
55/H12 **Hugh Town,** UK
81/H2 **Huglfing,** Ger.
118/E3 **Hugli** (riv.), India
192/C4 **Hugo,** Co,US
195/Q6 **Hugo,** Mn,US
191/G3 **Hugo,** Ok,US
191/G3 **Hugo** (dam), Ok,US
191/G3 **Hugo** (lake), Ok,US
190/D2 **Hugoton,** Ks,US
115/C3 **Huguan,** China
117/J2 **Hui** (mtn.), China
108/H2 **Hui** (riv.), China
156/B2 **Huib-Hock** (plat.), Namb.
159/K6 **Huichapan,** Mex.
113/D2 **Hŭich'ŏn,** NKor.
154/B2 **Huíla** (dist.), Ang.
154/B2 **Huíla** (plat.), Ang.
164/C4 **Huila** (dept.), Col.
164/C4 **Huila, Nevado del** (peak), Col.
119/H2 **Huili,** China
159/G5 **Huimanguillo,** Mex.
115/D3 **Huimin,** China
109/K3 **Huinan,** China
174/D2 **Huinca Renancó,** Arg.
108/F4 **Huining,** China
113/D2 **Hŭisaek-pong** (mtn.), NKor.
115/E5 **Hui Shan** (mtn.), China
119/J2 **Huishui,** China
79/F4 **Huisne** (riv.), Fr.
79/G5 **Huisseau-sur-Cosson,** Fr.
66/C5 **Huissen,** Neth.
119/J2 **Huitong,** China
63/K1 **Huittinen,** Fin.
159/M7 **Huitzilan,** Mex.
159/F5 **Huitzuco,** Mex.
159/K8 **Huitzuco de los Figueroa,** Mex.
115/C4 **Hui Xian,** China
160/C3 **Huixtla,** Mex.
116/D3 **Huize,** China
66/C4 **Huizen,** Neth.
117/G4 **Huizhou,** China
108/E2 **Hujirt,** Mong.
122/B2 **Hujra,** Pak.
113/C5 **Hŭksan** (arch.), SKor.
154/D4 **Hukuntsi,** Bots.
191/F2 **Hulah** (dam), Ok,US
191/F2 **Hulah** (lake), Ok,US
109/K2 **Hulan,** China
108/K2 **Hulan** (riv.), China
198/D1 **Hulbert,** Mi,US
191/G3 **Hulbert,** Ok,US
108/F2 **Huld,** Mong.
192/B1 **Hulett,** Wy,US
199/J2 **Hull,** Qu,Can
57/H4 **Hull,** Eng,UK
57/H4 **Hull** (riv.), Eng,UK
193/F2 **Hull,** Ia,US
208/D1 **Hull,** Ma,US
67/F4 **Hüllhorst,** Ger.
63/K2 **Hullo,** Est.
139/H5 **Hull** (Orona) (isl.), Kiri.
66/B6 **Hulst,** Neth.
62/F3 **Hultsfred,** Swe.
115/B3 **Hulu** (riv.), China
108/H2 **Hulun** (lake), China
103/B5 **Ḩulwān,** Egypt
109/K1 **Huma,** China
109/K1 **Huma** (riv.), China
172/C2 **Humahuaca,** Arg.
169/E3 **Humaitá,** Bol.
169/F2 **Humaitá,** Braz.
172/E3 **Humaitá,** Par.
156/D4 **Humansdorp,** SAfr.
191/H2 **Humansville,** Mo,US
168/C4 **Humay,** Peru
154/B3 **Humbe,** Ang.
197/J1 **Humber** (riv.), Nf,Can
197/S8 **Humber** (bay), On,Can
197/R8 **Humber** (riv.), On,Can
57/H4 **Humber** (riv.), Eng,UK
57/H4 **Humberside** (arpt.), Eng,UK
57/H4 **Humberside** (co.), Eng,UK
57/H4 **Humberston,** Eng,UK
167/F3 **Humberto de Campos,** Braz.
189/G3 **Humble,** Tx,US
158/E1 **Humble City,** NM,US
194/B1 **Humboldt,** Sk,Can
161/G5 **Humboldt** (bay), Col.
138/F7 **Humboldt** (peak), NCal.
187/F3 **Humboldt,** Az,US
184/A3 **Humboldt** (bay), Ca,US
193/G2 **Humboldt,** Ia,US
191/G2 **Humboldt,** Ks,US
194/F3 **Humboldt,** Mn,US
193/G3 **Humboldt,** Ne,US
184/D3 **Humboldt** (lake), Nv,US
184/D3 **Humboldt** (riv.), Nv,US
184/D3 **Humboldt** (riv.), Nv, Ut,US
200/C3 **Humboldt,** Tn,US
184/F3 **Humboldt, North Fork** (riv.), Nv,US
135/C2 **Hume** (lake), Austl.
107/G3 **Hūmedān,** Iran
65/L4 **Humenné,** Slvk.
193/H3 **Humeston,** Ia,US
174/E2 **Humida** (plain), Arg.
63/T9 **Humlebæk,** Den.
62/C3 **Humlum,** Den.
206/B3 **Hummelstown,** Pa,US
206/B2 **Hummels Wharf,** Pa,US
191/J3 **Humnoke,** Ar,US
199/G2 **Humphrey,** On,Can
177/K2 **Humphrey** (pt.), Ak,US
191/J3 **Humphrey,** Ar,US
192/F3 **Humphrey,** Ne,US
187/G3 **Humphreys** (peak), Az,US
186/C2 **Humphreys** (mt.), Ca,US
130/C3 **Humpty Doo,** Austl.
57/F1 **Humshaugh,** Eng,UK
113/C2 **Hun** (riv.), China
146/B2 **Hūn,** Libya
61/N6 **Húnaflói** (bay), Ice.
117/F2 **Hunan** (prov.), China
109/L3 **Hunchun,** China
122/B2 **Hundewāli,** Pak.
198/F5 **Hundred,** WV,US
70/A2 **Hundsangen,** Ger.
92/F3 **Hunedoara,** Rom.
92/F2 **Hunedoara** (co.), Rom.
81/E3 **Hünenberg,** Swi.
64/E3 **Hünfeld,** Ger.
73/D4 **Hungaroring,** Hun.
92/D2 **Hungary**
70/B2 **Hungen,** Ger.
135/C1 **Hungerford,** Austl.
59/E4 **Hungerford,** Eng,UK
113/E4 **Hŭnghae,** SKor.
113/D3 **Hŭngnam,** NKor.
113/D3 **Hŭngnyŏng-nodongjagu,** NKor.
182/G4 **Hungry** (peak), Id,US
183/G3 **Hungry Horse** (dam), Mt,US
154/C2 **Hungulo,** Ang.
108/C2 **Hüngüy** (riv.), Mong.
123/D1 **Hung Yen,** Viet.
113/D2 **Hunjiang,** China
145/G4 **Hunkui,** Nga.
57/H3 **Hunmanby,** Eng,UK
62/D2 **Hunnebostrand,** Swe.
191/F2 **Hunnewell,** Ks,US
66/C6 **Hunsel,** Neth.
69/G1 **Hunspatch,** Fr.
64/D4 **Hunsrück** (mts.), Ger.
69/G4 **Hunsrück** (plat.), Ger.
59/G1 **Hunstanton,** Eng,UK
185/K1 **Hunt** (mtn.), Wy,US
67/F2 **Hunte** (riv.), Ger.
135/C4 **Hunter** (isl.), Austl.
135/D2 **Hunter** (riv.), Austl.
177/H3 **Hunter** (mt.), Ak,US
189/H2 **Hunter,** La,US
194/F4 **Hunter,** ND,US
199/J3 **Hunter** (mtn.), NY,US
189/E3 **Hunter,** Tx,US
203/H1 **Hunter Army Afld.,** Ga,US
206/D2 **Hunterdon** (co.), NJ,US
182/E3 **Hunters,** Wa,US
189/M9 **Hunters Creek Village,** Tx,US
201/G3 **Huntersville,** NC,US
136/C2 **Hunterville,** N.Z.
200/D1 **Huntingburg,** In,US
199/J2 **Huntingdon,** Qu,Can
59/F2 **Huntingdon,** Eng,UK
199/G4 **Huntingdon,** Pa,US
200/C2 **Huntingdon,** Tn,US
57/G4 **Huntington,** Eng,UK
198/D4 **Huntington,** In,US
208/B1 **Huntington,** Ma,US
207/E2 **Huntington,** NY,US
207/M8 **Huntington** (bay), NY,US
184/E1 **Huntington,** Or,US
206/B1 **Huntington** (cr.), Pa,US
189/G2 **Huntington,** Tx,US
201/F1 **Huntington,** WV,US
207/M8 **Huntington Bay,** NY,US
204/C3 **Huntington Beach,** Ca,US
204/B3 **Huntington Park,** Ca,US
207/M8 **Huntington Station,** NY,US
205/F7 **Huntington Woods,** Mi,US
200/D3 **Huntland,** Tn,US
205/P15 **Huntley,** Il,US
136/C2 **Huntly,** N.Z.
54/D2 **Huntly,** Sc,UK
177/M4 **Hunts Inlet,** BC,Can
205/C2 **Hunts Point,** Wa,US
199/G2 **Huntsville,** On,Can
200/D3 **Huntsville,** Al,US
191/H2 **Huntsville,** Ar,US
191/H1 **Huntsville,** Mo,US
206/B1 **Huntsville** (res.), Pa,US
200/E2 **Huntsville,** Tn,US
189/G2 **Huntsville,** Tx,US
182/E4 **Huntsville,** Wa,US
159/H4 **Hunucmá,** Mex.
66/D5 **Hünxe,** Ger.
115/C3 **Hunyuan,** China
117/H2 **Huo** (mtn.), China
114/D3 **Huocheng,** China
115/C4 **Huojia,** China
109/H2 **Huolin Gol,** China
109/K2 **Huolongmen,** China
117/E2 **Huolupu,** China
131/G1 **Huon** (gulf), PNG
131/G1 **Huon** (pen.), PNG
123/D2 **Huong Hoa,** Viet.
123/D2 **Huong Khe,** Viet.
123/D2 **Huong Son,** Viet.
119/J4 **Huong Thuy,** Viet.
135/C4 **Huonville,** Austl.
115/D4 **Huoqiu,** China
115/D5 **Huoshan,** China
115/B3 **Huo Shan** (mtn.), China
117/H3 **Huotong,** China
115/B3 **Huo Xian,** China
106/E3 **Ḩuraymilā,** SAr.
73/C4 **Hurbanovo,** Slvk.
198/F2 **Hurd** (cape), On,Can
62/D1 **Hurdal,** Nor.
150/D3 **Hurdiyo,** Som.
201/H2 **Hurdle Mills,** NC,US
53/S11 **Hurepoix** (reg.), Fr.
115/E2 **Hure Qi,** China
202/D2 **Hurley,** Ms,US
187/H4 **Hurley,** NM,US
199/J4 **Hurley,** NY,US
195/J4 **Hurley,** Wi,US
54/B5 **Hurlford,** Sc,UK
201/K1 **Hurlock,** Md,US
179/H4 **Huron** (lake), Can., US
186/B2 **Huron,** Ca,US
195/K4 **Huron** (bay), Mi,US
195/K4 **Huron** (mts.), Mi,US
205/G6 **Huron** (pt.), Mi,US
205/F7 **Huron** (riv.), Mi,US
208/E5 **Huron,** Oh,US
208/E5 **Huron** (co.), Oh,US
208/E5 **Huron** (riv.), Oh,US
198/E2 **Huron** (lake), On,Can, Mi,US
192/E1 **Huron,** SD,US
195/K4 **Huron Is. Nat'l Wild. Ref.,** Mi,US
195/L4 **Huron Mountain,** Mi,US
202/E2 **Hurricane,** Al,US
187/F2 **Hurricane** (cliffs), Az,US
194/E3 **Hurricane** (lake), ND,US
187/F2 **Hurricane,** Ut,US
201/F1 **Hurricane,** WV,US
188/K7 **Hurst,** Tx,US
59/F5 **Hurstpierpoint,** Eng,UK
68/D4 **Hurtaut** (riv.), Fr.
69/F2 **Hürth,** Ger.
200/E4 **Hurtsboro,** Al,US
136/C3 **Hurunui** (riv.), N.Z.
62/C3 **Hurup,** Den.
150/A3 **Huruta,** Eth.
57/G3 **Hurworth,** Eng,UK
120/E3 **Husainābād,** India
121/H3 **Husainpur,** Bang.
61/P6 **Húsavík,** Ice.
59/E2 **Husbands Bosworth,** Eng,UK
117/H2 **Hushan,** China
205/Q14 **Husher,** Wi,US
117/H3 **Hushi,** China
93/J2 **Huşi,** Rom.
135/D2 **Huskisson,** Austl.
177/G2 **Huslia,** Ak,US
62/A2 **Husnes,** Nor.
183/H2 **Hussar,** Ab,Can
69/E5 **Hussigny-Godbrange,** Fr.
193/K2 **Hustisford,** Wi,US
73/A2 **Hustopeče,** Czh.
64/E1 **Husum,** Ger.
61/F3 **Husum,** Swe.
108/E2 **Hutag,** Mong.
124/C2 **Hutanopan,** Indo.
188/L7 **Hutchins,** Tx,US
203/H5 **Hutchinson** (isl.), Fl,US
191/F1 **Hutchinson,** Ks,US
195/G5 **Hutchinson,** Mn,US
150/B1 **Ḩūth,** Yem.
116/D3 **Hutiaoxia,** China
200/D1 **Hutsonville,** Il,US
136/J9 **Hutt** (riv.), N.Z.
191/H4 **Huttig,** Ar,US
70/C6 **Hüttisheim,** Ger.
70/D5 **Hüttlingen,** Ger.
57/J5 **Huttoft,** Eng,UK
134/C4 **Hutton** (peak), Austl.
53/Q7 **Hutton,** Eng,UK
57/H4 **Hutton Cranswick,** Eng,UK
192/B3 **Hutton Lake Nat'l Wild. Ref.,** Wy,US
57/G3 **Hutton Rudby,** Eng,UK
197/R8 **Huttonville,** On,Can
80/D3 **Huttwil,** Swi.
108/B3 **Hutubi,** China
115/C3 **Hutuo** (riv.), China
77/H1 **Huveane** (riv.), Fr.
82/B5 **Huveane** (riv.), Fr.
103/G7 **Ḩuwwārah,** WBnk.
117/G3 **Huxi,** China
115/B4 **Hu Xian,** China
193/H3 **Huxley,** Ia,US
202/B2 **Huxley,** Tx,US
69/E2 **Huy,** Belg.
57/F5 **Huyton-with-Roby,** Eng,UK
105/G4 **Hūzgān,** Iran
115/L9 **Huzhou,** China
61/N6 **Hvammstangi,** Ice.
61/P7 **Hvannadalshnúkur** (peak), Ice.
92/C4 **Hvar,** Cro.
92/C4 **Hvar** (isl.), Cro.
62/C4 **Hvide Sande,** Den.
63/T9 **Hvidovre,** Den.
61/N7 **Hvítá** (riv.), Ice.
61/N7 **Hvolsvöllur,** Ice.
113/D3 **Hwach'ŏn,** SKor.
113/E2 **Hwadae,** NKor.
155/E3 **Hwange,** Zim.
155/E3 **Hwange** (Wankie) Nat'l Park, Zim.
113/D3 **Hwanghae-Bukto** (prov.), NKor.
113/C3 **Hwanghae-Namdo** (prov.), NKor.
113/C3 **Hwangju,** NKor.
113/D3 **Hwangju** (riv.), NKor.
113/D2 **Hwap'yŏng,** NKor.
113/D5 **Hwasun,** SKor.
113/E5 **Hwayang,** SKor.
174/B5 **Hyades** (peak), Chile
182/D4 **Hyak,** Wa,US
113/D2 **Hyangsan,** NKor.
108/C2 **Hyargas,** Mong.
108/C2 **Hyargas** (lake), Mong.
206/A5 **Hyattstown,** Md,US
206/B6 **Hyattsville,** Md,US
201/H2 **Hyco** (res.), NC,US
177/M4 **Hydaburg,** Ak,US
136/B4 **Hyde,** N.Z.
57/F5 **Hyde,** Eng,UK
132/C5 **Hyden,** Austl.
201/F2 **Hyden,** Ky,US
53/N7 **Hyde Park,** Eng,UK
199/K4 **Hyde Park,** NY,US
196/A3 **Hyde Park,** Vt,US
177/M4 **Hyder,** Ak,US
118/C4 **Hyderābād,** India
107/J3 **Hyderābād,** Pak.
184/A3 **Hydesville,** Ca,US
82/C6 **Hyères,** Fr.
82/C6 **Hyères** (har.), Fr.
82/C6 **Hyères** (isls.), Fr.
78/B4 **Hyères** (riv.), Fr.
113/E2 **Hyesan,** NKor.
178/D2 **Hyland** (riv.), Yk,Can
62/A1 **Hyllestad,** Nor.
62/E3 **Hyltebruk,** Swe.
201/F2 **Hylton** (hill), Ky,US
110/D3 **Hyōgo** (pref.), Japan
113/G6 **Hyŏndŭngsan** (mt.), SKor.
110/D3 **Hyō-no-sen** (mtn.), Japan
202/P6 **Hypoluxo,** Fl,US
148/D4 **Hyrra Banda,** CAfr.
185/H3 **Hyrum,** Ut,US
183/L4 **Hysham,** Mt,US
135/C4 **Hythe,** Austl.
59/E5 **Hythe,** Eng,UK
59/H4 **Hythe,** Eng,UK
200/D3 **Hytop,** Al,US
110/B4 **Hyūga,** Japan
63/L1 **Hyvinkää,** Fin.

## I

150/B4 **Iabalo,** Eth.
170/C4 **Iacanga,** Braz.
168/D3 **Iaco** (riv.), Braz., Peru
171/E2 **Iaçu,** Braz.
92/A2 **Iâf di Montasio** (peak), It.
157/H8 **Iakora,** Madg.
131/F1 **Ialibu,** PNG
98/D5 **Ialomiţa** (co.), Rom.
93/H3 **Ialomiţa** (riv.), Rom.
157/H8 **Ianakafy,** Madg.
157/H8 **Ianapera,** Madg.
93/H2 **Iaşi,** Rom.
93/H2 **Iaşi** (co.), Rom.
91/J2 **Iasmos,** Gre.
202/B2 **Iatt** (lake), La,US
125/B2 **Iba,** Phil.
145/F5 **Ibadan,** Nga.
164/C3 **Ibagué,** Col.
167/K7 **Ibagué** (arpt.), Col.
170/C4 **Ibaiti,** Braz.
125/C3 **Ibajay,** Phil.
153/G3 **Ibanda,** Ugan.
161/E3 **Ibans** (lag.), Hon.
185/G3 **Ibapah,** Ut,US
185/G4 **Ibapah** (peak), Ut,US
92/E4 **Ibar** (riv.), Yugo.
110/C3 **Ibara,** Japan
111/L10 **Ibaraki,** Japan
111/F2 **Ibaraki** (pref.), Japan
164/B4 **Ibarra,** Ecu.
172/E3 **Ibarreta,** Arg.
150/C2 **Ibb,** Yem.
149/F4 **Ibba** (riv.), Sudan
67/E4 **Ibbenbüren,** Ger.
145/F2 **Ibdekhene** (wadi), Mali
152/D2 **Ibenga** (riv.), Congo
172/E3 **Iberá** (marsh), Arg.
168/C2 **Iberia,** Peru
168/D3 **Iberia,** Peru
191/H1 **Iberia,** Mo,US
76/D2 **Ibérico, Sistema** (range), Sp.
199/K2 **Iberville,** Qu,Can
145/G4 **Ibeto,** Nga.
110/E3 **Ibi** (riv.), Japan
145/H4 **Ibi,** Nga.
77/E3 **Ibi,** Sp.
167/F3 **Ibiapada** (mts.), Braz.
167/F3 **Ibiapina,** Braz.
171/F2 **Ibicaraí,** Braz.
173/F3 **Ibicuí** (riv.), Braz.
174/F2 **Ibicuy,** Arg.
171/F1 **Ibimirim,** Braz.
173/F3 **Ibirapuitã** (riv.), Braz.
173/F4 **Ibirubá,** Braz.
170/C4 **Ibitinga,** Braz.
171/J8 **Ibiúna,** Braz.
77/F3 **Ibiza,** Sp.
77/F3 **Ibiza** (isl.), Sp.
167/G5 **Ibo,** Braz.
110/D3 **Ibo** (riv.), Japan
155/J2 **Ibo,** Moz.
153/G3 **Ibondo,** Zaire
145/F5 **Iboro,** Nga.
171/E2 **Ibotirama,** Braz.
152/B3 **Iboundji** (peak), Gabon
107/G4 **Ibrā',** Oman
148/E3 **Ibrah, Wādī** (dry riv.), Sudan
65/L4 **Ibrány,** Hun.
107/G4 **'Ibrī,** Oman
93/H5 **İbriktepe,** Turk.
103/B5 **Ibshawāy,** Egypt
59/E1 **Ibstock,** Eng,UK
127/G3 **Ibu,** Indo.
127/G3 **Ibu** (mtn.), Indo.
111/M9 **Ibuki,** Japan
111/M9 **Ibuki-yama** (peak), Japan
124/F5 **Ibus** (cape), Indo.
163/C3 **Içá** (riv.), Braz.
168/D1 **Iça** (riv.), Braz.
168/C4 **Ica,** Peru
165/F3 **Icabarú,** Ven.
165/E4 **Içana,** Braz.
164/D4 **Içana** (riv.), Braz., Col.
172/C4 **Icaño,** Arg.
173/F2 **Icaraíma,** Braz.
78/C2 **Icart** (pt.), Chl,UK
167/E3 **Icatu,** Braz.
103/C1 **İçel** (prov.), Turk.
61/N7 **Iceland**
118/B4 **Ichalkaranji,** India
121/G3 **Ichāmati** (riv.), Bang.
118/D4 **Ichchāpuram,** India
70/D6 **Ichenhausen,** Ger.
145/G5 **Icheu,** Nga.
120/A4 **Ichhāwar,** India
111/J7 **Ichihara,** Japan
111/L9 **Ichijima,** Japan
111/H7 **Ichikawa,** Japan
169/E5 **Ichilo** (riv.), Bol.
112/B3 **Ichinohe,** Japan
110/E3 **Ichinomiya,** Japan
112/B4 **Ichinoseki,** Japan
111/M10 **Ichishi,** Japan
98/G2 **Ichnya,** Ukr.
172/C1 **Ichoca,** Bol.
113/D3 **Ich'ŏn,** NKor.
113/D4 **Ich'ŏn,** SKor.
68/C1 **Ichtegem,** Belg.
72/A6 **Ichterhausen,** Ger.
172/B1 **Ichuña,** Peru
206/A3 **Ickesburg,** Pa,US
167/G4 **Icó,** Braz.
142/A3 **Icod de los Vinos,** Canl.,Sp.
157/G5 **Iconi,** Com.
157/G5 **Iconi** (int'l arpt.), Com.
164/C3 **Icononzo,** Col.
177/K4 **Icy** (bay), Ak,US
177/F1 **Icy** (cape), Ak,US
177/L4 **Icy** (str.), Ak,US
191/G4 **Idabel,** Ok,US
150/B4 **Idabo,** Eth.
193/G2 **Ida Grove,** Ia,US
145/G5 **Idah,** Nga.
180/C3 **Idaho** (state), US
184/F2 **Idaho City,** Id,US
185/G2 **Idaho Falls,** Id,US
185/G2 **Idaho Nat'l Eng. Lab.,** Id,US
190/C1 **Idalia,** Co,US
190/D4 **Idalou,** Tx,US
76/B3 **Idanha-a-Nova,** Port.
122/F3 **Idāppādi,** India
118/B3 **Idar,** India
69/G4 **Idarkopf** (peak), Ger.
69/G4 **Idar-Oberstein,** Ger.
198/C4 **Idaville,** In,US
206/A3 **Idaville,** Pa,US
111/L10 **Ide,** Japan
200/E4 **Ideal,** Ga,US
94/G2 **Idel',** Rus.
143/G5 **Ideles,** Alg.
108/D2 **Ider,** Mong.
108/D2 **Ider** (riv.), Mong.
200/E3 **Ider,** Al,US
147/G3 **Idfū,** Egypt
91/J5 **Ídhi** (peak), Gre.
91/H4 **Ídhra,** Gre.
124/B1 **Idi,** Indo.
87/E3 **Idice** (riv.), It.
104/E2 **Idil,** Turk.
152/D4 **Idiofa,** Zaire
145/F5 **Idiroko,** Nga.
153/G3 **Idjwe** (isl.), Zaire
103/B4 **Idkū,** Egypt
57/H5 **Idle** (riv.), Eng,UK
103/E2 **Idlib,** Syria
103/E2 **Idlib** (dist.), Syria
103/D4 **Idnah,** WBnk.
103/F8 **Idnah,** WBnk.
92/B3 **Idrija,** Slov.
141/M13 **Idriss I** (dam), Mor.
141/M13 **Idriss I** (res.), Mor.
63/N3 **Idritsa,** Rus.
86/D1 **Idro** (lake), It.
70/B2 **Idstein,** Ger.
186/D4 **Idyllwild-Pine Cove,** Ca,US
112/J7 **Ie** (isl.), Japan
63/L3 **Iecava,** Lat.
152/C4 **Iema,** Ang.
68/B2 **Ieper,** Belg.
91/J5 **Ierápetra,** Gre.
91/H2 **Ierissós,** Gre.
87/F1 **Iesolo,** It.
151/B4 **Ifakara,** Tanz.
145/G5 **Ifaki,** Nga.
138/D4 **Ifalik** (isl.), Micr.
157/H8 **Ifanadiana,** Madg.
145/G5 **Ife,** Nga.
81/G3 **Ifen, Hoher** (peak), Ger., Aus.
146/A2 **Iferfes, Hasy** (well), Libya
145/H2 **Iferouâne,** Niger
81/H2 **Iffeldorf,** Ger.
70/B5 **Iffezheim,** Ger.
145/G5 **Ifon,** Nga.
143/F5 **Iforas, Adrar des** (mts.), Alg., Mali
142/D2 **Ifrane,** Mor.
79/E2 **Ifs,** Fr.
111/M10 **Iga,** Japan
111/M10 **Iga** (riv.), Japan
92/C2 **Igal,** Hun.
151/A3 **Igalula,** Tanz.
153/H2 **Iganga,** Ugan.
164/C5 **Igara Paraná** (riv.), Col.
170/D4 **Igarapava,** Braz.
167/E3 **Igarapé Açu,** Braz.
169/E1 **Igarapé Água Preta** (riv.), Braz.
167/E4 **Igarapé Grande,** Braz.
166/D3 **Igarapé-Miri,** Braz.
167/H4 **Igarassu,** Braz.
171/K8 **Igaratá,** Braz.
100/J3 **Igarka,** Rus.
145/G5 **Igarra,** Nga.
173/F3 **Igatimí,** Par.
118/B4 **Igatpuri,** India
151/A4 **Igawa,** Tanz.
145/G4 **Igbetti,** Nga.
145/F4 **Igboho,** Nga.
142/C3 **Igdet** (peak), Mor.
105/F2 **Iğdır,** Turk.
69/F4 **Igel,** Ger.
62/G1 **Iggesund,** Swe.
53/P8 **Ightham,** Eng,UK
177/H2 **Igikpak** (mt.), Ak,US
81/F4 **Igis,** Swi.
177/G4 **Igiugig,** Ak,US
90/A3 **Iglesias,** It.
143/E3 **Igli,** Alg.
70/D6 **Igling,** Ger.
95/N5 **Iglino,** Rus.
179/H2 **Igloolik,** NW,Can
195/J3 **Ignace,** On,Can
205/J10 **Ignacio,** Ca,US
187/J2 **Ignacio,** Co,US
159/P8 **Ignacio de la Llave,** Mex.
160/C2 **Ignacio Ramírez,** Mex.
159/F4 **Ignacio Zaragoza,** Mex.
63/M4 **Ignalina,** Lith.
93/H5 **İğneada,** Turk.
93/J5 **İğneada** (cape), Turk.
80/C1 **Igney,** Fr.
80/A2 **Ignon** (riv.), Fr.
53/S10 **Igny,** Fr.
151/A2 **Igombe,** Tanz.
153/H4 **Igombe** (riv.), Tanz.
94/G5 **Igorevskaya,** Rus.
208/A3 **Igor I. Sikorsky Mem.** (arpt.), Ct,US
91/G3 **Igoumenítsa,** Gre.
95/M4 **Igra,** Rus.
171/F1 **Igreja Nova,** Braz.
100/G3 **Igrim,** Rus.
173/F2 **Iguaçu Nat'l Park,** Braz.
171/E2 **Iguaí,** Braz.
160/B2 **Iguala,** Mex.
77/F2 **Igualada,** Sp.
159/F5 **Iguala de la Independencia,** Mex.
170/D5 **Iguape,** Braz.
170/C5 **Iguape** (stream), Braz.
170/B4 **Iguatemi** (riv.), Braz.
167/G4 **Iguatu,** Braz.
173/F3 **Iguazú** (int'l arpt.), Arg.
163/D5 **Iguazú Falls,** Braz.
173/F2 **Iguazu Nat'l Park,** Arg.
152/B3 **Iguéla,** Gabon
142/C4 **Iguetti, Sebkhet** (dry lake), Mrta.
151/A3 **Igugunu,** Tanz.
142/D4 **Iguidi, 'Erg** (des.), Alg., Mrta.
157/J6 **Iharana,** Madg.
112/J7 **Iheya** (isl.), Japan
108/F2 **Ihhayrhan,** Mong.
145/G5 **Ihiala,** Nga.
157/H8 **Ihosy,** Madg.
157/G8 **Ihotry** (lake), Madg.
104/B2 **Ihsaniye,** Turk.
131/G1 **Ihu,** PNG
168/B3 **Ihuari,** Peru
145/G5 **Ihuo,** Nga.
61/H2 **Ii,** Fin.
100/C3 **Ii** (riv.), Fin.
111/E3 **Iida,** Japan
150/D4 **Iidaan,** Som.
111/F2 **Iide-san** (mtn.), Japan
94/E2 **Iijoki** (riv.), Fin.
111/M10 **Iinan,** Japan
63/M2 **Iisaku,** Est.
61/H3 **Iisalmi,** Fin.
111/M10 **Iitaka,** Japan
63/M1 **Iitti,** Fin.
111/F2 **Iiyama,** Japan
110/B4 **Iizuka,** Japan
151/C2 **Ijara,** Kenya
145/G5 **Ijebu Ijesha,** Nga.
145/F5 **Ijebu Ode,** Nga.
142/B5 **Ijill** (peak), Mrta.
142/B5 **Ijill, Sebkhet** (dry lake), Mrta.
66/C2 **IJlst,** Neth.
66/C4 **IJmeer** (bay), Neth.
66/B4 **IJmuiden,** Neth.
144/B2 **Ijnaoun** (well), Mrta.
61/H2 **Ijoki** (riv.), Fin.
142/D5 **Ijoubbane, 'Erg** (des.), Mali
66/C4 **IJssel** (riv.), Neth.
66/C3 **IJsselmeer** (lake), Neth.
66/C2 **IJsselmeer** (Afsluitdijk) (dam), Neth.
66/C3 **IJsselmuiden,** Neth.
66/C4 **IJsselstein,** Neth.
173/F4 **Ijuí,** Braz.
173/F3 **Ijuí** (riv.), Braz.
110/B5 **Ijūin,** Japan
66/A6 **IJzendijke,** Neth.
68/B2 **Ijzer** (riv.), Belg.
95/M5 **Ik** (riv.), Rus.
157/H7 **Ikahavo** (plat.), Madg.
157/H8 **Ikalamavony,** Madg.
153/E3 **Ikali,** Zaire
153/G4 **Ikamba,** Tanz.
153/E3 **Ikanda Nord,** Zaire
145/H5 **Ikang,** Nga.
145/G5 **Ikare,** Nga.
91/J4 **Ikaría** (isl.), Gre.
151/A3 **Ikasi,** Tanz.
62/C3 **Ikast,** Den.
110/C3 **Ikeda,** Japan
145/F5 **Ikeja,** Nga.
153/E3 **Ikela,** Zaire
152/D2 **Ikelemba,** Congo
152/D2 **Ikelemba** (riv.), Zaire
145/G5 **Ikem,** Nga.
111/M10 **Ikenokoya-yama** (peak), Japan
145/G5 **Ikere,** Nga.
93/F4 **Ikhtiman,** Bul.
110/A4 **Iki** (arpt.), Japan
110/A4 **Iki** (chan.), Japan
110/A4 **Iki** (isl.), Japan
97/H3 **Iki-Burul,** Rus.
145/G5 **Ikire,** Nga.
145/G5 **Ikirun,** Nga.
104/C2 **İkizce,** Turk.
104/E1 **İkizdere,** Turk.
145/G5 **Ikole,** Nga.
145/H5 **Ikom,** Nga.
111/L10 **Ikoma,** Japan
151/A2 **Ikoma,** Tanz.
157/H8 **Ikongo,** Madg.
157/H7 **Ikopa** (riv.), Madg.
145/F5 **Ikorodu,** Nga.
145/G5 **Ikot Ekpene,** Nga.
145/H5 **Ikot Okpora,** Nga.
153/F3 **Ikozi,** Zaire
151/A3 **Ikungi,** Tanz.
151/A3 **Ikungu,** Tanz.
110/D3 **Ikuno,** Japan
73/A4 **Ikva** (riv.), Hun.
168/D5 **Ilabaya,** Peru
153/G4 **Ilagala,** Tanz.
125/C1 **Ilagan,** Phil.
122/G4 **Ilaiyānkudi,** India
157/H8 **Ilaka,** Madg.
157/J7 **Ilaka,** Madg.
105/F3 **Īlām,** Iran
105/F3 **Īlām** (gov.), Iran
121/F2 **Ilam,** Nepal
121/F4 **Ilām Bāzār,** India
117/J3 **Ilan,** Tai.
151/A3 **Ilangali,** Tanz.
81/F4 **Ilanz,** Swi.
145/G4 **Ila Orangun,** Nga.
145/F5 **Ilaro,** Nga.
73/C2 **Ilava,** Slvk.
168/D5 **Ilave,** Peru
65/K2 **Iława,** Pol.
149/F1 **'Ilay,** Sudan
87/E5 **Il Castello, Monte** (peak), It.
58/D4 **Ilchester,** Eng,UK
178/F3 **Ile-à-la-Crosse,** Sk,Can
153/E4 **Ilebo,** Zaire
74/E2 **Ile-de-France** (reg.), Fr.
53/T9 **Ile-de-France** (prov.), Fr.
197/N6 **Ile-de-Montréal** (co.), Qu,Can
197/N6 **Ile-Jésus** (co.), Qu,Can
97/K2 **Ilek** (riv.), Kaz., Rus.
97/K2 **Ilek,** Rus.
60/A6 **Ilen** (riv.), Ire.
197/N7 **Ile-Perrot,** Qu,Can
144/E5 **Iles Ehotilés Nat'l Park,** IvC.
145/G5 **Ilesha,** Nga.
72/A4 **Ilfeld,** Ger.
190/B3 **Ilfeld,** NM,US
80/D4 **Ilfis** (riv.), Swi.
53/P7 **Ilford,** Eng,UK
134/B3 **Ilfracombe,** Austl.
58/B4 **Ilfracombe,** Eng,UK
96/E4 **Ilgaz,** Turk.
104/C1 **Ilğazdağı Nat'l Park,** Turk.
104/B2 **Ilgın,** Turk.
170/D4 **Ilhabela,** Braz.
171/M8 **Ilha Grande** (bay), Braz.
170/C3 **Ilha Solteira** (res.), Braz.
76/A2 **Ílhavo,** Port.
72/B3 **Ilhe** (riv.), Ger.
154/B4 **Ilhea** (pt.), Namb.
171/F2 **Ilhéus,** Braz.
114/C3 **Ili** (riv.), China, Kaz.
177/H4 **Iliamna,** Ak,US
177/G4 **Iliamna** (lake), Ak,US
177/H3 **Iliamna** (vol.), Ak,US
104/D2 **İliç,** Turk.
104/E2 **Ilıca,** Turk.
93/K2 **Il'ichevsk,** Ukr.
170/D4 **Ilicínea,** Braz.
192/C3 **Iliff,** Co,US
125/C3 **Iligan** (bay), Phil.
125/D3 **Iligan City,** Phil.
92/D4 **Ilijaš,** Bosn.
164/B5 **Iliniza** (peak), Ecu.
109/N2 **Il'inskiy,** Rus.
95/K4 **Il'inskoye,** Rus.
130/B2 **Iliomar,** Indo.
92/B3 **Ilirska Bistrica,** Slov.
104/E2 **Ilisu** (res.), Turk.
93/H6 **Ilium** (Troy) (ruins), Turk.
57/G6 **Ilkeston,** Eng,UK
105/F2 **Īlkhchī,** Iran
57/G4 **Ilkley,** Eng,UK
81/F3 **Ill** (riv.), Aus.
80/D1 **Ill** (riv.), Fr.
135/C2 **Illabo,** Austl.
76/D2 **Illana,** Sp.
174/C1 **Illapel,** Chile
87/E1 **Illasi** (riv.), It.
133/G3 **Illbillee** (peak), Austl.
97/H5 **Il'Ichëvsk,** Azer.
78/D4 **Ille** (riv.), Fr.
78/D4 **Ille-el-Rance, Canal-d'** (can.), Fr.
78/D4 **Ille-et-Vilaine** (dept.), Fr.
145/G3 **Illela,** Nga.
145/G3 **Illéla,** Niger
70/D6 **Iller** (riv.), Ger.
183/K3 **Illerbrun,** Sk,Can
70/D6 **Illertissen,** Ger.
76/D2 **Illescas,** Sp.
78/D4 **Illet** (riv.), Fr.
79/G4 **Illiers-Combray,** Fr.
150/D4 **Illigh, Ras** (pt.), Som.
172/C1 **Illimani** (peak), Bol.
69/G5 **Illingen,** Ger.
181/J4 **Illinois** (state), US
184/B2 **Illinois** (riv.), Ca, Or,US
193/J4 **Illinois** (riv.), Il,US
143/H4 **Illizi,** Alg.
143/G4 **Illizi** (wilaya), Alg.
80/D1 **Illkirch-Graffenstaden,** Fr.
81/F2 **Illmensee,** Ger.
73/A4 **Illmitz,** Aus.
81/E3 **Illnau,** Swi.
58/A6 **Illogan,** Eng,UK
76/D4 **Illora,** Sp.
157/E3 **Illovo,** SAfr.
145/G5 **Illushi,** Nga.
131/E3 **Illyungmadja** (pt.), Austl.
80/D2 **Illzach,** Fr.
71/E5 **Ilm** (riv.), Ger.
61/G3 **Ilmajoki,** Fin.
67/G5 **Ilme** (riv.), Ger.
94/F4 **Il'men'** (lake), Rus.
72/A6 **Ilmenau,** Ger.
67/H2 **Ilmenau** (riv.), Ger.
58/D5 **Ilminster,** Eng,UK
168/D5 **Ilo,** Peru
145/G5 **Ilobu,** Nga.
174/B2 **Iloca,** Chile
125/C3 **Iloilo City,** Phil.
151/A3 **Ilongero,** Tanz.
145/G4 **Ilorin,** Nga.
99/K4 **Ilovaysk,** Ukr.
99/M3 **Ilovlya,** Rus.
97/H2 **Ilovlya** (riv.), Rus.
66/B4 **Ilpendam,** Neth.
101/S4 **Il'pyrskiy,** Rus.
67/H4 **Ilse** (riv.), Ger.
67/H4 **Ilsede,** Ger.
67/H5 **Ilsenburg,** Ger.
70/C4 **Ilsfeld,** Ger.
70/C4 **Ilshofen,** Ger.
99/K5 **Il'skiy,** Rus.
149/G4 **Īlubabor** (reg.), Eth.
63/M4 **Ilūkste,** Lat.
182/B4 **Ilwaco,** Wa,US
130/B1 **Ilwaki,** Indo.
105/J1 **Il'yaly,** Trkm.
93/H5 **Ilyas** (pt.), Turk.
95/N3 **Ilych** (riv.), Rus.
71/G5 **Ilz** (riv.), Ger.
110/C3 **Imabari,** Japan
111/F2 **Imaichi,** Japan
157/H8 **Imaloto** (riv.), Madg.
104/C2 **İmamoğlu,** Turk.
94/F2 **Imandra** (lake), Rus.
157/H9 **Imanombo,** Madg.
110/A4 **Imari,** Japan
149/G4 **Imatong** (mts.), Sudan
63/N1 **Imatra,** Fin.
110/E3 **Imazu,** Japan
111/J7 **Imba,** Japan
164/B4 **Imbabura** (prov.), Ecu.
166/A1 **Imbaimadai,** Guy.
173/G4 **Imbituba,** Braz.
184/E1 **Imbler,** Or,US
97/K5 **Imeni 26 Bakinskikh Komissarov,** Trkm.
107/H1 **Imeni Chapayeva,** Trkm.
99/H2 **Imeni Karla Libknekhta,** Rus.
157/J7 **Imerimandroso,** Madg.
152/D2 **Imese,** Zaire
150/B4 **Īmī,** Eth.
142/C3 **Imi n'Tanout,** Mor.
97/J5 **Imishli,** Azer.
91/L7 **Imittós** (mt.), Gre.
113/C5 **Imja** (isl.), SKor.
113/D3 **Imjin** (riv.), NKor., SKor.
184/D3 **Imlay,** Nv,US
205/F5 **Imlay City,** Mi,US
81/E2 **Immendingen,** Ger.
67/G6 **Immenhausen,** Ger.
81/F2 **Immenstaad am Bodensee,** Ger.
81/G2 **Immenstadt im Allgäu,** Ger.
57/H4 **Immingham,** Eng,UK
203/H4 **Immokalee,** Fl,US
184/E1 **Imnaha,** Or,US
184/E1 **Imnaha** (riv.), Or,US
177/J2 **Imnavait** (mtn.), Ak,US
145/G5 **Imo** (state), Nga.
87/E4 **Imola,** It.
127/K4 **Imonda,** PNG
142/D2 **Imouzzer des Marmoucha,** Mor.
167/E4 **Imperatriz,** Braz.
86/B5 **Imperia,** It.
86/A5 **Imperia** (prov.), It.
194/B2 **Imperial,** Sk,Can
168/B4 **Imperial,** Peru
186/E4 **Imperial** (dam), Az,US
186/E4 **Imperial** (res.), Az, Ca,US
186/E4 **Imperial,** Ca,US
186/E4 **Imperial** (val.), Ca,US
192/D3 **Imperial,** Ne,US
188/C2 **Imperial,** Tx,US
204/C5 **Imperial Beach,** Ca,US
208/G7 **Imperial-Enlow,** Pa,US
186/E4 **Imperial Nat'l Wild. Ref.,** Az, Ca,US
111/H7 **Imperial Palace,** Japan
86/A5 **Impero** (riv.), It.
152/D2 **Impfondo,** Congo
116/B3 **Imphāl,** India
74/E3 **Imphy,** Fr.
172/C2 **Impora,** Bol.
87/E5 **Impruneta,** It.
154/B2 **Impulo,** Ang.
93/J5 **İmrali** (isl.), Turk.
104/D2 **İmranlı,** Turk.
93/G5 **İmroz,** Turk.
113/D5 **Imshil,** SKor.
81/G3 **Imst,** Aus.
158/C2 **Imuris,** Mex.
125/E7 **Imus,** Phil.
125/E7 **Imus** (riv.), Phil.
154/D3 **Imusho,** Zam.
111/E3 **Ina,** Japan
111/L10 **Ina** (riv.), Japan
65/H2 **Ina** (riv.), Pol.
125/D3 **Inabanga,** Phil.
111/M9 **Inabe,** Japan
137/E **Inaccessability, Pole of,** Ant.
111/L10 **Inagawa,** Japan
111/H7 **Inagi,** Japan
167/G5 **Inajá,** Braz.
186/D4 **Inaja Ind. Res.,** Ca,US
168/D4 **Inambari,** Peru
168/D4 **Inambari** (riv.), Peru
143/H3 **I-n-Amenas,** Alg.
143/G5 **I-n-Amguel,** Alg.
111/K10 **Inami,** Japan
136/C3 **Inangahua Junction,** N.Z.
127/H4 **Inanwatan,** Indo.
141/M13 **Inaouene** (riv.), Mor.
168/D3 **Iñapari,** Peru
61/H1 **Inari** (lake), Fin.
93/G2 **Inău** (peak), Rom.
111/G2 **Inawashiro** (lake), Japan
143/H5 **I-n-Azaoua** (dry riv.), Niger
111/M9 **Inazawa,** Japan
168/D4 **Inca** (dept.), Peru
77/G3 **Inca,** Sp.
172/C3 **Incahuasi,** Arg.
172/B3 **Incahuasi, Cerro de** (peak), Chile
103/C1 **İncekum** (pt.), Turk.
145/F2 **I-n-Chaouâg** (wadi), Mali
54/D4 **Inchcape** (Bell Rock) (isl.), Sc,UK
182/E3 **Inchelium,** Wa,US
68/A3 **Incheville,** Fr.
60/A6 **Inchigeelagh,** Ire.
54/B5 **Inchinnan,** Sc,UK
144/B2 **Inchiri** (reg.), Mrta.
54/C4 **Inchkeith** (isl.), Sc,UK
55/J7 **Inchnadamph,** Sc,UK
113/D4 **Inch'ŏn,** SKor.
113/D4 **Inch'ŏn-Jikhalsi,** SKor.
155/G3 **Inchope,** Moz.
104/A2 **İncirliova,** Turk.
87/E5 **Incisa in Val d'Arno,** It.
155/G5 **Incomati** (riv.), Moz.
171/K7 **Inconfidentes,** Braz.
143/E5 **I-n-Dagouber** (well), Mali
170/D4 **Indaiatuba,** Braz.
125/C4 **Indanan,** Phil.
149/H2 **Inda Silasē,** Eth.
116/C4 **Indaw,** Burma
116/B3 **Indawgyi** (lake), Burma
69/F2 **Inde** (riv.), Ger.
188/B5 **Indé,** Mex.
69/F2 **Inden,** Ger.
160/D2 **Independence,** Belz.
186/C2 **Independence,** Ca,US
193/J2 **Independence,** Ia,US
191/G2 **Independence,** Ks,US
200/E1 **Independence,** Ky,US
202/C2 **Independence,** La,US
191/G1 **Independence,** Mo,US
184/E3 **Independence** (mts.), Nv,US
184/B1 **Independence,** Or,US
188/C2 **Independence** (cr.), Tx,US
201/G2 **Independence,** Va,US
206/C4 **Independence Nat'l Hist. Park,** Pa,US
172/C1 **Independencia,** Bol.
167/F4 **Independência,** Braz.
170/B2 **Independencia,** Braz.
168/B4 **Independencia,** Peru
97/J2 **Inder** (lake), Kaz.
124/C3 **Inderapura** (cape), Indo.
97/J2 **Inderborskiy,** Kaz.
205/D2 **Index,** Wa,US
118/C3 **India**
51/N6 **Indian** (ocean)
201/M7 **Indian** (cr.), Ga,US
195/L4 **Indian** (lake), Mi,US
192/D2 **Indian** (hill), Ne,US
181/J4 **Indiana** (state), US
199/G4 **Indiana,** Pa,US
205/R16 **Indiana Dunes Nat'l Lakesh.,** In,US
198/C5 **Indianapolis,** In,US
198/C5 **Indianapolis** (int'l arpt.), In,US
198/C5 **Indianapolis Motor Speedway,** In,US
197/G2 **Indian Brook,** NS,Can
159/H5 **Indian Church,** Belz.
206/B3 **Indian Echo Caverns,** Pa,US
203/H3 **Indian Harbour Beach,** Fl,US
194/C2 **Indian Head,** Sk,Can
199/J3 **Indian Lake,** NY,US
203/G2 **Indianola,** Ga,US
193/H3 **Indianola,** Ia,US
200/B4 **Indianola,** Ms,US
189/F3 **Indianola,** Tx,US
205/B2 **Indianola,** Wa,US
188/E2 **Indian Pictographs,** Tx,US
198/D2 **Indian River,** Mi,US
202/K8 **Indian Rocks Beach,** Fl,US
203/G4 **Indian Rocks Beach,** Fl,US
200/F4 **Indian Springs,** Ga,U
186/E2 **Indian Springs,** Nv,U
203/H4 **Indiantown,** Fl,US
201/G2 **Indian Valley,** Va,US
187/G3 **Indian Wells,** Az,US
170/C3 **Indiaporã,** Braz.
87/E6 **Indicatore,** It.
95/L2 **Indiga,** Rus.
101/Q3 **Indigirka** (riv.), Rus.
92/E3 **Indija,** Yugo.
186/D4 **Indio,** Ca,US
120/A1 **Indira Gandhi** (int'l arpt.), India
123/C1 **Indochina** (reg.), Asi
127/E4 **Indonesia**
134/E6 **Indooroopilly,** Austl.
118/C3 **Indore,** India
124/C3 **Indragiri** (riv.), Indo.
124/E4 **Indramayu,** Indo.
124/E4 **Indramayu** (cape), Indo.
124/C3 **Indrapura,** Indo.
118/D4 **Indrāvati** (riv.), India
79/G6 **Indre** (dept.), Fr.
79/F6 **Indre** (riv.), Fr.
62/A1 **Indre Arna,** Nor.
79/F5 **Indre-et-Loire** (dept. Fr.
79/F6 **Indrois** (riv.), Fr.
154/C2 **Indungo,** Ang.
86/B1 **Induno Olona,** It.
102/F7 **Indus** (riv.), Asia
107/J4 **Indus, Mouths of the** (delta), Pak.
208/G6 **Industry,** Pa,US
189/F3 **Industry,** Tx,US
143/G5 **In Ebeggi** (well), Alg
104/C1 **İnebolu,** Turk.
93/H5 **İnece,** Turk.
93/H5 **İnecek,** Turk.
145/E1 **I-n-Echaï** (well), Ma
143/H4 **Inedbirenne** (int'l arpt.), Alg.
104/B1 **İnegöl,** Turk.
143/G4 **I-n-Eker,** Alg.
92/E2 **Ineu,** Rom.
201/F2 **Inez,** Ky,US
189/F3 **Inez,** Tx,US
142/C3 **Inezgane,** Mor.
142/C3 **Inezgane** (Agadir) (in arpt.), Mor.
143/H5 **In Ezzane** (well), Alg
146/A4 **In Ezzane** (well), Algeria
156/C4 **Infanta** (cape), SAfr.
152/A2 **Infante dom Henriqu** SaoT.
144/C3 **I-n-Farba,** Mrta.
158/E5 **Infiernillo** (res.), Me
76/C1 **Infiesto,** Sp.
167/H4 **Ingá,** Braz.
145/G2 **I-n-Gall,** Niger
191/H4 **Ingalls,** Ar,US
195/L5 **Ingalls,** Mi,US
153/E3 **Inganda,** Zaire
164/B5 **Ingapirca,** Ecu.
63/S7 **Ingarö,** Swe.
63/S7 **Ingarö** (isl.), Swe.
153/F2 **Ingasu,** Zaire
53/Q7 **Ingatestone,** Eng,UK
68/C2 **Ingelmunster,** Belg.
152/D3 **Ingende,** Zaire
172/D2 **Ingeniero Guillermo N. Juárez,** Arg.
174/C2 **Ingeniero Gustavo André,** Arg.
174/C4 **Ingeniero Jacobacc** Arg.
174/D2 **Ingeniero Luiggi,** Ar
142/B4 **Ingenio,** Canl.,Sp.
80/D1 **Ingersheim,** Fr.
198/F3 **Ingersoll,** On,Can
108/E3 **Inggen,** China
134/B2 **Ingham,** Austl.
134/G8 **Ingleburn,** Austl.
70/B2 **Ingleheim,** Ger.
199/J2 **Ingleside,** On,Can
206/C5 **Ingleside,** Md,US
57/G2 **Ingleton,** Eng,UK
134/C5 **Inglewood,** Austl.
135/B3 **Inglewood,** Austl.
197/R8 **Inglewood,** On,Can
136/C2 **Inglewood,** N.Z.
204/B3 **Inglewood,** Ca,US
205/C2 **Inglewood-Finn Hil** Wa,US
203/G3 **Inglis,** Fl,US
108/G1 **Ingoda** (riv.), Rus.
57/J5 **Ingoldmells,** Eng,UK
71/E5 **Ingolstadt,** Ger.
183/L4 **Ingomar,** Mt,US
197/G2 **Ingonish,** NS,Can
197/G2 **Ingonish Beach,** NS,Can
200/C1 **Ingraham,** Il,US
208/G7 **Ingram,** Pa,US
188/E2 **Ingram,** Tx,US
79/E6 **Ingrandes,** Fr.
53/Q7 **Ingrave,** Eng,UK
172/D2 **Ingre,** Bol.
79/G5 **Ingré,** Fr.
137/E **Ingrid Christianson** (coast), Ant.
145/G2 **I-n-Guezzâm,** Alg.
93/L2 **Ingulets,** Ukr.
99/G4 **Ingulets,** Ukr.
99/G3 **Ingulets** (riv.), Ukr.
97/G4 **Inguri** (riv.), Geo.
157/E2 **Ingwavuma,** SAfr.
69/G6 **Ingwiller,** Fr.
153/E5 **Inhacalunga,** Ang.
155/G4 **Inhambane,** Moz.
155/G4 **Inhambane** (prov.), Moz.
155/G3 **Inhaminga,** Moz.
171/E3 **Inhapim,** Braz.
155/G5 **Inharrime,** Moz.
155/G4 **Inhassoro,** Moz.
152/C4 **Inhuca,** Ang.
167/F4 **Inhuma,** Braz.
170/C3 **Inhumas,** Braz.
76/E3 **Iniesta,** Sp.
166/C2 **Inini,** FrG.
166/C2 **Inini** (riv.), FrG.
164/D4 **Inírida** (riv.), Col.
60/B6 **Inishannon,** Ire.
54/F10 **Inishbofin** (isl.), Ire.
60/A6 **Inishcarra** (res.), Ire
60/A1 **Inishcrone,** Ire.
60/A3 **Inishmaan** (arpt.), Ir
60/A3 **Inishmeer** (arpt.), Ire
56/A1 **Inishowen** (pen.), Ir
56/B1 **Inishowen Head** (pt Ire.
60/C5 **Inistioge,** Ire.
110/A1 **Inje,** SKor.
149/H3 **Injibara,** Eth.
134/C4 **Injune,** Austl.

J

156/D4 Jansenville, SAfr.
156/Q13 Jan Smuts (Johannesburg) (int'l arpt.), SAfr.
170/D2 Januária, Braz.
103/C5 Janūb Sīnā' (gov.), Egypt
79/G4 Janville, Fr.
78/D5 Janzé, Fr.
146/B1 Janzūr, Libya
118/C3 Jaora, India
109/M4 Japan
109/L4 Japan (sea), Asia
111/E3 Japanese Alps (range), Japan
111/E2 Japanese Alps Nat'l Park, Japan
168/C2 Japiim, Braz.
169/E1 Japura (riv.), Braz.
161/G5 Jaqué, Pan.
162/D3 Jarabacoa, DRep.
104/D2 Jarābulus, Syria
106/D5 Jarad, SAr.
170/C2 Jaraguá, Braz.
76/C2 Jaraíz de la Vera, Sp.
187/J3 Jarales, NM,US
174/D5 Jaramillo, Arg.
76/C2 Jarandilla de la Vera, Sp.
122/B2 Jarānwāla, Pak.
103/D3 Jarash, Jor.
143/H2 Jarbah, Jazīrat (isl.), Tun.
184/F3 Jarbidge, Nv,US
62/G1 Järbo, Swe.
146/D1 Jardas al 'Abīd, Libya
167/G4 Jardim, Braz.
170/A4 Jardim, Braz.
167/G4 Jardim do Seridó, Braz.
164/C3 Jardín, Col.
191/G4 Jardin, Tx,US
173/F3 Jardín América, Arg.
131/F3 Jardine (riv.), Austl.
131/F2 Jardine River Nat'l Park, Austl.
161/G1 Jardines de la Reina (arch.), Cuba
63/R7 Jarfalla, Swe.
108/D2 Jargalant, Mong.
108/E2 Jargalant, Mong.
79/H5 Jargeau, Fr.
166/C2 Jari (riv.), Braz.
121/F4 Jaridih, India
88/F4 Jarīd, Shaţţ al (dry lake), Tun.
143/H2 Jarjīs, Tun.
65/G2 Jarmen, Ger.
62/G2 Järna, Swe.
69/E5 Jarny, Fr.
125/D3 Jaro, Phil.
65/J3 Jarocin, Pol.
120/A4 Jarod, India
65/H3 Jaroměř, Czh.
65/M3 Jarosław, Pol.
187/K2 Jaroso, Co,US
201/J2 Jarratt, Va,US
206/B4 Jarrettsville, Md,US
57/G2 Jarrow, Eng,UK
123/C2 Jars (plain), Laos
116/D5 Jars, Plain of (plain), Laos
108/F4 Jartai, China
115/E1 Jarud Qi, China
63/L2 Järva-Jaani, Est.
63/L2 Järvakandi, Est.
63/L1 Järvenpää, Fin.
69/F6 Jarville-la-Malgrange, Fr.
139/J5 Jarvis (isl.), PacUS
201/K2 Jarvisburg, NC,US
62/G1 Järvsö, Swe.
120/E4 Jashpurnagar, India
121/F3 Jasidih, India
124/C2 Jasin, Malay.
107/G3 Jāsk, Iran
65/L4 Jasło, Pol.
198/C5 Jasonville, In,US
182/E1 Jasper, Ab,Can
200/D4 Jasper, Al,US
191/H2 Jasper, Ar,US
203/G2 Jasper, Fl,US
200/E3 Jasper, Ga,US
200/D1 Jasper, In,US
193/F2 Jasper, Mn,US
191/G2 Jasper, Mo,US
200/E3 Jasper, Tn,US
189/H2 Jasper, Tx,US
182/E1 Jasper Nat'l Park, Ab,Can
120/B1 Jaspur, India
70/C2 Jassa (riv.), Ger.
92/B3 Jastrebarsko, Cro.
65/J2 Jastrowie, Pol.
65/K4 Jastrzębie Zdroj, Pol.
120/B2 Jaswantnagar, India
92/E2 Jászapáti, Hun.
92/D2 Jászárokszállás, Hun.
92/D2 Jászberény, Hun.
92/E2 Jászladány, Hun.
92/E2 Jász-Nagykun-Szolnok (co.), Hun.
170/C3 Jataí, Braz.
166/B3 Jatapu (riv.), Braz.
120/B3 Jatāra, India
160/D2 Jataté (riv.), Mex.
167/G4 Jati, Braz.
107/J4 Jāti, Pak.
124/E4 Jatibarang, Indo.
161/G1 Jatibonico, Cuba
77/E3 Játiva, Sp.
142/B4 Jat, Uad el (dry riv.), WSah.
170/C4 Jaú, Braz.
169/F1 Jaú (riv.), Braz.
165/E5 Jauaperi (riv.), Braz.
165/F5 Jauaperi (riv.), Braz.
166/C3 Jauaru (mts.), Braz.
165/F3 Jaua Sarisarinama Nat'l Park, Ven.
130/A4 Jaubert (cape), Austl.
78/B3 Jaudy (riv.), Fr.
122/B1 Jauharābād, Pak.
168/C3 Jauja, Peru
159/F4 Jaumave, Mex.
80/D4 Jaun, Swi.
74/D3 Jaunay-Clan, Fr.
63/L3 Jaunjelgava, Lat.
80/D4 Jaunpass (pass), Swi.
63/M3 Jaunpiebalga, Lat.
63/K3 Jaunpils, Lat.
120/D3 Jaunpur, India
170/A2 Jauru (riv.), Braz.
82/C5 Jausiers, Fr.
124/D4 Java (isl.), Indo.
124/E4 Java (sea), Indo.
168/C2 Javari (riv.), Braz.
77/F3 Jávea, Sp.
175/J6 Javier (isl.), Chile
173/E4 Javier de Viana, Uru.
73/D3 Javorie (mt.), Slvk.
73/B2 Javořina, Veľká (peak), Slvk.
71/G2 Javornice (riv.), Czh.
71/G4 Javorník (peak), Czh.
71/H3 Javorová Skála (peak), Czh.
79/E4 Javron-les-Chapelles, Fr.
124/D4 Jawa Barat (prov.), Indo.
122/D2 Jawāla Mukhi, India
124/E4 Jawa Tengah (prov.), Indo.
124/F4 Jawa Timur (prov.), Indo.
150/C5 Jawhar (Giohar), Som.
126/C4 Jawi, Indo.
65/J3 Jawor, Pol.
202/E2 Jay, Fl,US
196/B3 Jay, Me,US
191/G2 Jay, Ok,US
199/K2 Jay (peak), Vt,US
127/J4 Jaya (peak), Indo.
168/B2 Jayanca, Peru
127/K4 Jayapura, Indo.
121/H4 Jaydebpur, Bang.
121/F2 Jaynagar, India
121/G4 Jaynagar, India
188/D1 Jayton, Tx,US
59/H3 Jaywick, Eng,UK
106/D5 Jazā'ir Farasān (isls.), SAr.
190/D1 J. B. Thomas (lake), Tx,US
194/D3 J. Clark Sayler Nat'l Wild. Ref., ND,US
186/E3 Jean, Nv,US
189/E1 Jean, Tx,US
202/C3 Jeanerette, La,US
202/C3 Jean Lafitte, La,US
145/G4 Jebba, Nga.
168/B2 Jeberos, Peru
62/C3 Jebjerg, Den.
124/D3 Jebus, Indo.
54/D6 Jedburgh, Sc,UK
65/L4 Jedlicze, Pol.
65/L3 Jędrzejów, Pol.
54/D6 Jed Water (riv.), Sc,UK
72/B1 Jeetze (riv.), Ger.
193/G1 Jeffers, Mn,US
185/H1 Jeffers, Mt,US
200/D4 Jefferson, Al,US
190/B1 Jefferson, Co,US
201/F3 Jefferson, Ga,US
193/G2 Jefferson, Ia,US
185/G1 Jefferson (riv.), Mt,US
201/G2 Jefferson, NC,US
184/E4 Jefferson (mtn.), Nv,US
199/J3 Jefferson, NY,US
198/F4 Jefferson, Oh,US
208/G7 Jefferson (co.), Oh,US
184/B1 Jefferson, Or,US
184/C1 Jefferson (mtn.), Or,US
189/G1 Jefferson, Tx,US
201/J2 Jefferson, Va,US
205/B2 Jefferson (co.), Wa,US
193/K2 Jefferson, Wi,US
205/N14 Jefferson (co.), Wi,US
193/H4 Jefferson City, Mo,US
191/H1 Jefferson City (cap.), Mo,US
201/F2 Jefferson City, Tn,US
200/B1 Jefferson Nat'l Expansion Mem. (Gateway Arch Nat'l Hist. Site), Mo,US
201/F4 Jeffersonville, Ga,US
200/E1 Jeffersonville, In,US
200/F2 Jeffersonville, Ky,US
201/G2 Jeffrey, WV,US
185/K2 Jeffrey City, Wy,US
197/H1 Jeffrey's, Nf,Can
156/D4 Jeffreys Bay, SAfr.
145/G3 Jega, Nga.
80/D3 Jegenstorf, Swi.
71/G2 Jehličná (mt.), Czh.
174/B5 Jeinemeni (peak), Chile
173/E2 Jejui Guazú (riv.), Par.
63/L3 Jēkabpils, Lat.
203/H2 Jekyll (isl.), Ga,US
65/J3 Jelcz-Laskowice, Pol.
73/C3 Jelence, Slvk.
65/H3 Jelenia Góra, Pol.
65/H3 Jelenia Góra (prov.), Pol.
118/E2 Jelep (pass), China
63/K3 Jelgava, Lat.
124/C1 Jeli, Malay.
73/B3 Jelka, Slvk.
200/E2 Jellico, Tn,US
195/L3 Jellicoe, On,Can
192/A3 Jelm, Wy,US
105/F3 Jelow Gīr, Iran
85/E4 Jelsi, It.
142/C2 Jemaa Sahim, Mor.
124/D2 Jemaja (isl.), Malay.
124/C2 Jemaluang, Malay.
68/C3 Jemappes, Belg.
148/D3 Jema Shet' (riv.), Eth.
124/F5 Jember, Indo.
151/B3 Jembiani, Tanz.
187/J3 Jemez (mts.), NM,US
187/J3 Jemez (riv.), NM,US
187/J3 Jemez Ind. Res., NM,US
190/A3 Jemez Pueblo, NM,US
190/A3 Jemez Springs, NM,US
108/B2 Jeminay, China
200/D4 Jemison, Al,US
127/E4 Jempang (riv.), Indo.
147/G3 Jemsa, Egypt
72/B6 Jena, Ger.
202/B2 Jena, La,US
81/F4 Jenaz, Swi.
73/B3 Jenbach, Aus.
127/E5 Jeneponto, Indo.
70/D7 Jengen, Ger.
121/G4 Jenidah, Bang.
198/D3 Jenison, Mi,US
201/F2 Jenkins, Ky,US
206/C3 Jenkintown, Pa,US
191/G2 Jenks, Ok,US
73/A6 Jennersdorf, Aus.
203/G2 Jennings, Fl,US
190/D1 Jennings, Ks,US
202/B2 Jennings, La,US
166/C1 Jenny, Sur.
178/F2 Jenny Lind (isl.), NW,Can
185/J3 Jensen, Ut,US
203/H4 Jensen Beach, Fl,US
179/H2 Jens Munk (isl.), NW,Can
124/E4 Jepara, Indo.
175/S12 Jeppener, Arg.
168/B2 Jequetepeque, Peru
171/E2 Jequié, Braz.
170/D3 Jequitaí, Braz.
171/E3 Jequitinhonha, Braz.
171/F2 Jequitinhonha (riv.), Braz.
141/N13 Jerada, Mor.
124/C2 Jerantut, Malay.
130/D1 Jerdera, Indo.
159/E4 Jerécuaro, Mex.
161/H2 Jérémie, Haiti
171/F1 Jeremoabo, Braz.
150/B3 Jerer Shet' (dry riv.), Eth.
158/E4 Jerez, Mex.
76/B4 Jerez de la Frontera, Sp.
76/B3 Jerez de los Caballeros, Sp.
134/B3 Jericho, Austl.
207/E2 Jericho, NY,US
103/D4 Jericho (Arīḩā), WBnk.
72/C3 Jerichow, Ger.
167/G4 Jericó, Braz.
164/C3 Jericó, Col.
191/G2 Jerico Springs, Mo,US
135/C2 Jerilderie, Austl.
208/C2 Jerimoth (hill), RI,US
189/E1 Jermyn, Tx,US
191/J4 Jerome, Ar,US
187/F3 Jerome, Az,US
185/F2 Jerome, Id,US
208/E6 Jerome Fork (riv.), Oh,US
208/E6 Jeromesville, Oh,US
132/C5 Jerramungup, Austl.
78/C2 Jersey (isl.), ChI,UK
207/D2 Jersey City, NJ,US
207/H8 Jersey City (res.), NJ,US
206/A1 Jersey Shore, Pa,US
78/C2 Jersey (States) (int'l arpt.), ChI,UK
189/G3 Jersey Village, Tx,US
193/J4 Jerseyville, Il,US
124/C1 Jerteh, Malay.
167/F4 Jerumenha, Braz.
106/B2 Jerusalem, Isr.
103/F8 Jerusalem (dist.), Isr.
191/H3 Jerusalem, Ar,US
103/G8 Jerusalem (arpt.), WBnk.
103/G8 Jerusalem Walls Nat'l Park, Isr.
103/D4 Jerusalem (Yerushalayim) (cap.), Isr.
182/C2 Jervis (inlet), BC,Can
135/D2 Jervis Bay, Austl.
90/A3 Jerzu, It.
67/G6 Jesberg, Ger.
92/B2 Jesenice, Slov.
71/F2 Jesenice, Udolní nádrž (res.), Czh.
87/G5 Jesi, It.
72/C4 Jessen, Ger.
62/D1 Jessheim, Nor.
191/H3 Jessieville, Ar,US
72/C4 Jessnitz, Ger.
121/G4 Jessore, Bang.
121/G4 Jessore (dist.), Bang.
202/N6 Jessup (lake), Fl,US
203/H3 Jessup (lake), Fl,US
171/J7 Jesuânia, Braz.
203/H2 Jesup, Ga,US
197/N6 Jésus (isl.), Qu,Can
173/F3 Jesús, Par.
190/E2 Jesus (mt.), Ks,US
159/G5 Jesús Carranza, Mex.
172/B1 Jesús de Machaca, Bol.
172/C4 Jesús María, Arg.
167/M6 Jesús María, Col.
161/G1 Jesús Menéndez, Cuba
191/E2 Jet, Ok,US
144/A4 Jeta (isl.), GBis.
190/E1 Jetmore, Ks,US
118/B3 Jetpur, India
81/G1 Jettingen-Scheppach, Ger.
72/E1 Jetzendorf, Ger.
79/E6 Jeu (riv.), Fr.
68/D3 Jeumont, Fr.
64/E1 Jevenstedt, Ger.
62/F1 Jever, Ger.
73/A2 Jevišovka (riv.), Czh.
62/D1 Jevnaker, Nor.
120/A1 Jewar, India
192/C2 Jewel Cave Nat'l Mon., SD,US
191/E1 Jewell, Ks,US
193/H2 Jewell Junction, Ia,US
208/F7 Jewett, Oh,US
189/F2 Jewett, Tx,US
208/C2 Jewett City, Ct,US
118/D4 Jeypore, India
91/F1 Jezerce (peak), Alb.
71/G4 Jezerní Stěna (peak), Czh.
65/K2 Jeziorak (lake), Pol.
121/F3 Jhā Jhā, India
121/A3 Jhajjar, India
121/G4 Jhālakāti, Bang.
118/C3 Jhālawār, India
121/E4 Jhalida, India
107/J3 Jhal Jhao, Pak.
120/B1 Jhālū, India
122/B2 Jhang Sadar, Pak.
121/F2 Jhanjhārpur, India
120/B3 Jhānsi, India
121/F2 Jhāpa, Nepal
121/F4 Jhārgrām, India
121/F4 Jharia, India
120/E5 Jhārsuguda, India
122/B1 Jhawāriān, Pak.
122/B1 Jhelum (riv.), India, Pak.
122/B1 Jhelum, Pak.
121/G4 Jhenida, Bang.
122/B2 Jhumra, Pak.
116/B1 Ji (riv.), China
115/L8 Jiading, China
121/G3 Jiāganj, India
119/K2 Jiahe, China
108/F5 Jialing (riv.), China
115/C4 Jialu (riv.), China
109/L2 Jiamusi, China
113/D2 Ji'an, China
117/G3 Ji'an, China
117/F4 Jian (riv.), China
117/H3 Jian (riv.), China
109/H3 Jianchang, China
113/C2 Jianchang, China
115/D2 Jianchang, China
116/E2 Jiancheng, China
123/E1 Jiang (riv.), China
119/J2 Jiang'an, China
116/C3 Jiangao (mtn.), China
116/D4 Jiangcheng Hanizu Yizu Zizhixian (Jiangcheng), China
119/H3 Jiangcheng (Jiangcheng Hanizu Yizu Zizhixian), China
116/D3 Jiangchuan, China
115/D4 Jiangdu, China
117/F3 Jianghua Yaozu Zizhixian, China
109/H3 Jiangjiadian, China
116/E2 Jiangjin, China
108/G5 Jiangjunhe, China
114/F3 Jiangjunmiao, China
113/A3 Jiangjunshi, China
108/D3 Jiangjuntai, China
117/F2 Jiangkou, China
117/G3 Jiangkou, China
117/J2 Jiangkou, China
108/F5 Jiangkouzhen, China
117/F2 Jiangkouzhen, China
115/C5 Jiangling, China
117/G4 Jiangmen, China
116/E2 Jiangmenchang, China
115/D5 Jiangning, China
115/D4 Jiangsu (prov.), China
117/G3 Jiangwan, China
117/G3 Jiangxi (prov.), China
115/B4 Jiang Xian, China
117/H1 Jiangxiang, China
117/F2 Jiangya, China
115/E5 Jiangyin, China
117/F3 Jiangyong, China
116/E2 Jiangyou, China
119/J2 Jianhe, China
115/D4 Jianhu, China
115/C5 Jianli, China
117/H3 Jian'ou, China
109/H3 Jianping, China
115/B5 Jianshi, China
116/D4 Jianshui, China
117/H3 Jianyang, China
116/D1 Jiaochangba, China
115/C3 Jiaocheng, China
109/K3 Jiaohe, China
117/J2 Jiaojiang, China
115/C3 Jiaokou, China
109/J3 Jiaolai (riv.), China
115/D4 Jiaonan, China
117/J2 Jiaotou, China
115/C4 Jiaozuo, China
115/K8 Jiapu, China
115/D4 Jiashan, China
115/L9 Jiashan, China
114/C4 Jiashi, China
115/B3 Jia Xian, China
115/D4 Jiaxiang, China
115/L9 Jiaxing, China
117/F3 Jiaya, China
109/L2 Jiayin, China
116/E3 Jiayou, China
115/C5 Jiayu, China
108/D4 Jiayuguan, China
117/H4 Jiazi, China
145/G3 Jibiya, Nga.
164/D4 Jibóia, Braz.
93/F2 Jibou, Rom.
107/G4 Jibsh, Ra's (pt.), Oman
190/A2 Jicarilla Apache Ind. Res., NM,US
159/N8 Jicaro, Mex.
161/F5 Jicarón (isl.), Pan.
65/H3 Jičín, Czh.
159/F5 Jico, Mex.
150/C3 Jidali (dry riv.), Som.
147/H4 Jiddah, SAr.
119/F2 Jido, India
109/L2 Jidong, China
117/G3 Jiehualong, China
117/G4 Jieshi, China
108/F4 Jieshipu, China
115/C4 Jieshou, China
115/B3 Jiexiu, China
117/H4 Jieyang, China
63/L4 Jieznas, Lith.
103/G8 Jifnā, WBnk.
149/H3 Jiga, Eth.
132/D2 Jigalong Abor. Land, Austl.
202/C1 Jigger, La,US
184/F3 Jiggs, Nv,US
161/G1 Jiguaní, Cuba
113/C1 Jiguanshan, China
108/E5 Jigzhi, China
65/H4 Jihlava, Czh.
73/A1 Jihlava (riv.), Czh.
71/H4 Jihočeský (reg.), Czh.
73/A2 Jihomoravský (reg.), Czh.
150/C4 Jiiqley, Som.
141/U17 Jijel (gov.), Alg.
93/H2 Jijia (riv.), Rom.
150/B3 Jijiga, Eth.
77/E3 Jijona, Sp.
149/G3 Jikawo, Eth.
147/E4 Jilfal Kabīr, Hadabat al (upland), Egypt
65/J4 Jilhava (riv.), Czh.
114/E2 Jili (lake), China
151/C1 Jilib, Som.
109/K3 Jilin, China
113/D1 Jilin (prov.), China
109/J1 Jiliu (riv.), China
77/E2 Jiloca (riv.), Sp.
159/F5 Jilotepec de Abasolo, Mex.
71/H3 Jílové u Prahy, Czh.
149/H4 Jīma, Eth.
161/J2 Jimaní, DRep.
153/E5 Jimbe, Ang.
93/E3 Jimbolia, Rom.
134/D4 Jimboomba, Austl.
117/H3 Jimei, China
76/C4 Jimena de la Frontera, Sp.
158/D3 Jiménez, Mex.
188/D3 Jiménez, Mex.
117/F2 Jimingsi, China
149/G3 Jimmeza, Sudan
200/E4 Jimmy Carter Nat'l Hist. Site, Ga,US
115/E3 Jimo, China
108/B3 Jimsar, China
206/C2 Jim Thorpe, Pa,US
158/E3 Jimulco, Mex.
203/F2 Jim Woodruff (dam), Fl,US
117/G2 Jin (riv.), China
117/H3 Jin (riv.), China
115/D3 Jinan, China
117/H2 Jin'an, China
51/Q4 Jinan, China
108/E4 Jinchang, China
113/A2 Jincheng, China
115/C4 Jincheng, China
116/D1 Jinchuan, China
115/C3 Jinci Temple, China
118/E2 Jīnd, India
135/D3 Jindabyne, Austl.
135/D3 Jindabyne (dam), Austl.
65/H4 Jindřichův Hradec, Czh.
117/E2 Jinfo (mtn.), China
108/D4 Jinfosi, China
115/B4 Jing (riv.), China
115/B3 Jingbian, China
115/D5 Jingde, China
117/H2 Jingdezhen, China
119/H3 Jingdong, China
135/C2 Jingellic, Austl.
117/G3 Jinggangshan, China
116/D4 Jinggu, China
115/D3 Jinghai, China
113/B4 Jinghaiwei, China
114/D3 Jinghe, China
116/D4 Jinghong, China
115/E4 Jingjiang, China
115/B3 Jingle, China
115/C5 Jingmen, China
108/F4 Jingning, China
116/D3 Jingping (mts.), China
115/C5 Jingshan, China
108/E4 Jingtai, China
116/E4 Jingxi, China
115/D5 Jing Xian, China
117/F3 Jing Xian, China
108/G4 Jingyou, China
113/D1 Jingyu, China
108/E4 Jingyuan, China
115/D4 Jinhu, China
117/H2 Jinhua, China
108/H4 Jining, China
115/C2 Jining, China
115/D4 Jining, China
153/H2 Jinja, Ugan.
124/C2 Jinjang, Malay.
117/E4 Jinjie, China
149/H4 Jinka, Eth.
119/H2 Jinkouhe, China
117/G3 Jinlansi, China
117/H3 Jinmen (isl.), China
160/E3 Jinotega, Nic.
160/E4 Jinotepe, Nic.
116/D4 Jinping, China
117/F3 Jinping, China
115/B4 Jinqian (riv.), China
117/H2 Jinsha, China
119/J2 Jinsha, China
115/E5 Jinshan, China
115/L9 Jinshanwei, China
116/D3 Jinsha (Yangtze) (riv.), China
119/K2 Jinshi, China
108/F5 Jinshui, China
115/D5 Jintan, China
117/G2 Jintang, China
125/C2 Jintotolo (chan.), Phil.
118/C4 Jintūr, India
115/E4 Jinxi, China
117/H3 Jinxi, China
113/A3 Jin Xian, China
115/C3 Jin Xian, China
115/D3 Jinxiang, China
119/K3 Jinxiu Yaozu Zizhixian, China
117/J2 Jinyun, China
115/C5 Jinzhai, China
115/E2 Jinzhou, China
113/A3 Jinzhou (bay), China
169/F2 Ji-Paraná, Braz.
169/F3 Jiparaná (riv.), Braz.
164/A5 Jipijapa, Ecu.
158/E5 Jiquilpan de Juárez, Mex.
159/Q9 Jiquipilco, Mex.
149/H4 Jīrēn, Eth.
147/F3 Jirgā, Egypt
108/H3 Jirin Gol, China
71/G2 Jirkov, Czh.
105/J4 Jīroft, Iran
115/B4 Jishan, China
117/F2 Jishou, China
103/E2 Jisr ash Shughūr, Syria
117/G3 Jitan, China
124/C1 Jitra, Malay.
93/F4 Jiu (riv.), Rom.
117/E2 Jiucheng, China
116/D2 Jiuding (mtn.), China
117/H4 Jiudongshan, China
117/H3 Jiufeng, China
117/G2 Jiugong (mtn.), China
117/H2 Jiuhua (mtn.), China
115/C5 Jiujiang, China
117/G3 Jiulianshan, China
117/G2 Jiuling (mts.), China
116/D2 Jiulong, China
113/B4 Jiurongcheng, China
109/K3 Jiutai, China
117/F4 Jiutang, China
117/J2 Jiuwan (mts.), China
117/F3 Jiuxincheng, China
108/F5 Jiuyongshou, China
115/K9 Jiuyuhang, China
109/K1 Jiuzhan, China
107/H3 Jīwani, Pak.
109/L2 Jixi, China
117/H2 Jixi, China
109/H3 Ji Xian, China
115/B2 Jixian, China
115/C4 Ji Xian, China
115/D2 Ji Xian, China
115/D3 Jiyang, China
117/G3 Jiyuan, China
147/F2 Jizah, Pyramids of (ruins), Egypt
150/B1 Jīzān, SAr.
115/C3 Jize, China
71/H2 Jizera (riv.), Czh.
147/H3 Jizl, Wādī al (dry riv.), SAr.
110/C3 Jizō-zaki (pt.), Japan
116/D3 Jizu (mtn.), China
106/F5 Jiz', Wādī al (dry riv.), Yem.
173/G3 Joaçaba, Braz.
72/D2 Joachimsthal, Ger.
159/N8 Joachín, Mex.
171/E3 Joaíma, Braz.
144/A3 Joal, Sen.
166/D3 Joana Peres, Braz.
201/G3 Joanna, SC,US
167/H4 João Câmara, Braz.
167/E4 João Lisboa, Braz.
171/E3 João Monlevade, Braz.
167/H4 João Pessoa, Braz.
170/D3 João Pinheiro, Braz.
173/G2 Joaquim Távora, Braz.
189/G2 Joaquin, Tx,US
175/T12 Joaquín Suárez, Uru.
172/C3 Joaquín V. González, Arg.
161/G1 Jobabo, Cuba
201/F3 Jocassee (dam), SC,US
70/B4 Jockgrim, Ger.
160/E3 Jocón, Hon.
76/D4 Jódar, Sp.
118/B2 Jodhpur, India
69/D2 Jodoigne, Belg.
61/J3 Joensuu, Fin.
188/L7 Joe Pool (lake), Tx,US
111/F2 Jōetsu, Japan
69/F5 Joeuf, Fr.
121/F2 Jogbani, India
63/M2 Jõgeva, Est.
196/E3 Joggins, NS,Can
105/J5 Joghdān, Iran
156/E2 Johannesburg, SAfr.
186/D3 Johannesburg, Ca,US
156/Q13 Johannesburg (Jan Smuts) (int'l arpt.), SAfr.
71/F2 Johanngeorgenstadt, Ger.
120/C4 Johilla (riv.), India
184/D1 John Day, Or,US
184/C1 John Day (dam), Or,US
184/C1 John Day (riv.), Or,US
184/C1 John Day Fossil Beds Nat'l Mon., Or,US
184/D1 John Day, Middle Fork (riv.), Or,US
184/D1 John Day, North Fork (riv.), Or,US
207/E2 John F. Kennedy (int'l arpt.), NY,US
132/C4 John Forrest Nat'l Park, Austl.
201/H2 John H. Kerr (dam), Va,US
190/C1 John Martin (res.), Co,US
55/K7 John O'Groats, Sc,UK
191/G1 John Redmond (res.), Ks,US
54/D3 Johnshaven, Sc,UK
139/J3 Johnson (atoll), PacUS
190/D2 Johnson, Ks,US
197/T9 Johnson (cr.), NY,US
188/K7 Johnson (co.), Tx,US
199/K2 Johnson, Vt,US
192/B2 Johnson (mtn.), Wy,US
206/D2 Johnsonburg, NJ,US
199/G4 Johnsonburg, Pa,US
199/J3 Johnson City, NY,US
201/F2 Johnson City, Tn,US
189/E2 Johnson City, Tx,US
186/C3 Johnsondale, Ca,US
188/D2 Johnson Draw (cr.), Tx,US
194/E4 Johnson Lake Nat'l Wild. Ref., ND,US
177/M3 Johnsons Crossing, Yk,Can
136/H9 Johnsonville, N.Z.
201/H4 Johnsonville, SC,US
132/D5 Johnston (lake), Austl.
58/B3 Johnston, Wal,UK
193/H3 Johnston, Ia,US
201/G4 Johnston, SC,US
153/G5 Johnston (falls), Zam.
200/C2 Johnston City, Il,US
54/B5 Johnstone, Sc,UK
199/J2 Johnstown, On,Can
60/C4 Johnstown, Ire.
199/J3 Johnstown, NY,US
198/E4 Johnstown, Oh,US
199/G4 Johnstown, Pa,US
206/A4 Johnsville, Md,US
204/C3 John Wayne/Orange Co. (int'l arpt.), Ca,US
124/C2 Johor (riv.), Malay.
124/C2 Johor (state), Malay.
124/C2 Johor Baharu, Malay.
71/G1 Jöhstadt, Ger.
74/E3 Joigny, Fr.
200/B3 Joiner, Ar,US
173/G3 Joinville, Braz.
137/W Joinville (isl.), Ant.
80/B1 Joinville, Fr.
159/F5 Jojutla, Mex.
159/K8 Jojutla de Juárez, Mex.
149/G3 Jokau, Sudan
63/K1 Jokioinen, Fin.
61/F2 Jokkmokk, Swe.
61/P6 Jökulsárgljúfur Nat'l Park, Ice.
87/E3 Jolanda di Savoia, It.
105/F2 Jolfā, Iran
205/P16 Joliet, Il,US
183/K5 Joliet, Mt,US
198/B4 Joliet Army Amm. Dep., Il,US
199/K1 Joliette, Qu,Can
189/F2 Jollyville, Tx,US
125/C4 Jolo, Phil.
125/C4 Jolo (isl.), Phil.
63/H1 Jomala, Fin.
125/C2 Jomalig (isl.), Phil.
124/F4 Jombang, Indo.
152/D5 Jombo (riv.), Ang.
116/C2 Jomda, China
151/B2 Jomo Kenyatta (int'l arpt.), Kenya
120/D1 Jomosom, Nepal
151/A2 Jomu, Tanz.
81/E3 Jona, Swi.
159/L8 Jonacatepec
63/L4 Jonava, Lith.
68/C5 Jonchery-sur-Vesle, Fr.
179/S7 Jones (sound), NW,Can
200/D4 Jones, Al,US
189/J1 Jones, La,US
207/L9 Jones (inlet), NY,US
206/A2 Jones (mtn.), Pa,US
207/L9 Jones Beach St. Park, NY,US
191/J3 Jonesboro, Ar,US
201/M7 Jonesboro, Ga,US
200/C2 Jonesboro, Il,US
198/D4 Jonesboro, In,US
202/B1 Jonesboro, La,US
56/B3 Jonesborough, NI,UK
201/F2 Jonesborough, Tn,US
196/E4 Jones-Harbour (pt.), NS,Can
196/D3 Jonesport, Me,US
200/B3 Jonestown, Ms,US
206/B3 Jonestown, Pa,US
198/D4 Jonesville, Mi,US
201/G2 Jonesville, NC,US
149/F4 Jonglei, Sudan
63/L3 Joniškelis, Lith.
63/K3 Joniškis, Lith.
62/F3 Jönköping, Swe.
62/F3 Jönköping (co.), Swe.
196/B1 Jonquière, Qu,Can
82/A4 Jonquières, Fr.
159/G5 Jonuta, Mex.
74/C4 Jonzac, Fr.
132/K6 Joondalup (lake), Austl.
191/G2 Joplin, Mo,US
183/J3 Joplin, Mt,US
202/C3 Joppa, Il,US
206/B5 Joppa (Joppatowne), Md,US
206/B5 Joppatowne (Joppa), Md,US
120/A2 Jora, India
103/D4 Jordan
103/D4 Jordan, Asia
197/S9 Jordan, On,Can
184/E2 Jordan (cr.), Or,Id,US
106/C2 Jordan (riv.), Jor.
200/D4 Jordan (dam), Al,US
200/D4 Jordan (lake), Al,US
183/L4 Jordan, Mt,US
201/H3 Jordan (lake), NC,US
206/C2 Jordan (cr.), Pa,US
185/H3 Jordan (riv.), Ut,US
197/S9 Jordan Station, On,Can
184/E2 Jordan Valley, Or,US
63/S7 Jordbro, Swe.
175/J7 Jorge (cape), Chile
168/B4 Jorge Chavez (int'l arpt.), Peru
175/S12 Jorge Newbery (Buenos Aires) (int'l arpt.), Arg.
116/B3 Jorhāt, India
120/C1 Joriāpāni, Nepal
67/G1 Jork, Ger.
187/J4 Jornada del Muerto (vall.), NM,US
62/B2 Jørpeland, Nor.
145/H4 Jos, Nga.
145/H4 Jos (plat.), Nga.
125/D4 Jose Abad Santos, Phil.
169/E4 José Agustín Palacios, Bol.
175/G2 José Batlle y Ordóñez, Uru.
173/G2 José Bonifacio, Braz.
159/N7 José Cardel, Mex.
167/F4 José de Freitas, Braz.
175/F2 José Enrique Rodó, Uru.
164/D2 Josefa Camejo (int'l arpt.), Ven.
174/E3 José María Blanco, Arg.
164/C3 José María Cordova (int'l arpt.), Col.
161/F1 José Martí (int'l arpt.), Cuba
125/C2 Jose Pañganiban, Phil.
175/G2 José Pedro Varela, Uru.
184/E1 Joseph, Or,US
185/G4 Joseph, Ut,US
130/C3 Joseph Bonaparte (gulf), Austl.
187/G3 Joseph City, Az,US
188/L6 Josephine, Tx,US
111/F2 Joshin-Etsu Kogen Nat'l Park, Japan
121/F5 Joshipur, India
208/B3 Joshua (pt.), Ct,US
189/F1 Joshua, Tx,US
186/D3 Joshua Tree, Ca,US
186/D4 Joshua Tree Nat'l Mon., Ca,US
78/C5 Josselin, Fr.
62/C1 Jotunheimen Nat'l Park, Nor.
79/E4 Jouanne (riv.), Fr.
68/C6 Jouarre, Fr.
79/F6 Joué-lès-Tours, Fr.
78/D6 Joué-sur-Erdre, Fr.
134/B2 Jourama Falls Nat'l Park, Austl.
189/E3 Jourdanton, Tx,US
66/C3 Joure, Neth.
63/N1 Joutseno, Fin.
61/H2 Joutsijärvi, Fin.
80/C4 Joux (lake), Fr.
79/G3 Jouy, Fr.
53/S10 Jouy-en-Josas, Fr.
53/S9 Jouy-le-Moutier, Fr.
68/C6 Jouy-sur-Morin, Fr.
161/F1 Jovellanos, Cuba
82/C2 Jovet (mtn.), Fr.
105/J2 Joveyn (riv.), Iran
121/J3 Jowai, India
105/J3 Jow Khvāh, Iran
105/G3 Jowsheqān-e Qālī, Iran
177/M3 Joy (mtn.), Yk,Can
202/B2 Joyce, La,US
60/A2 Joyce's Country (dist.), Ire.
111/L10 Jōyō, Japan
112/B2 Jozankei Spa, Japan
204/E7 J. Paul Getty Museum, Ca,US
200/D2 J. P. Priest (lake), Tn,US
144/A2 Jreïda, Mrta.
117/F2 Ju (riv.), China
158/E3 Juan Aldama, Mex.
172/C3 Juan Bautista Alberdi, Arg.
115/C4 Juancheng, China
124/F4 Juanda (int'l arpt.), Indo.
182/B3 Juan de Fuca (str.), BC,Can, Wa,US
162/D3 Juan de Herrera, DRep.
157/G7 Juan de Nova, Reun.
174/F3 Juan Fernández, Arg.
163/A6 Juan Fernández (isls.), Chile
165/F2 Juangriego, Ven.
175/T11 Juan Jackson, Uru.
174/E2 Juan José Paso, Arg.
168/B2 Juanjuí, Peru
175/T12 Juan L. Lacaze, Uru.
161/E4 Juan Santamaria (int'l arpt.), CR
174/F3 Juárez, Arg.
158/C2 Juarez, Mex.
159/E3 Juárez, Mex.
188/D4 Juárez, Mex.
159/F5 Juárez (int'l arpt.), Mex.
159/K7 Juárez (int'l arpt.), Mex.
186/D4 Juarez, Sierra de (mts.), Mex.
145/E5 Juaso, Gha.
170/D4 Juatinga, Ponta de (pt.), Braz.
167/G4 Juàzeirinho, Braz.
171/E1 Juazeiro, Braz.
167/G4 Juazeiro do Norte, Braz.
144/C5 Juazohn, Libr.
149/F4 Juba, Sudan
104/E4 Jubbah, SAr.
150/B5 Jubba, Webi (riv.), Som.
151/C1 Jubba, Webi (riv.), Som.
64/E1 Jübek, Ger.
168/B1 Jubones (riv.), Ecu.
77/Y17 Juby (cape), Mor.
76/D3 Júcar (riv.), Sp.
167/G4 Jucás, Braz.
66/D6 Jüchen, Ger.
158/E4 Juchipila, Mex.
159/N7 Juchique de Ferrer, Mex.
160/C2 Juchitán, Mex.
167/G4 Jucurutu, Braz.
194/E4 Jud, ND,US
62/A2 Judaberg, Nor.
103/G8 Judaea (reg.), WBnk.
161/E4 Judas (pt.), CR
75/L3 Judenburg, Aus.
116/C3 Judian, China
183/K4 Judith (mts.), Mt,US
183/K4 Judith Gap, Mt,US
194/D4 Judson, ND,US
191/J3 Judsonia, Ar,US
62/D4 Juelsminde, Den.
78/C4 Jugon-les-Lacs, Fr.
150/B1 Juḩā, SAr.
147/F3 Juhaynah, Egypt
171/F1 Juicai (mtn.), China
161/E3 Juigalpa, Nic.
53/U9 Juilly, Fr.
117/H2 Juilong (mtn.), China
79/H4 Juine (riv.), Fr.
117/J4 Juishui, Tai.
66/E1 Juist, Ger.
66/E1 Juist (arpt.), Ger.
66/D1 Juist (isl.), Ger.
171/E4 Juiz de Fora, Braz.
117/H3 Juizhen, China
80/B5 Jujurieux, Fr.
172/C1 Jujuy (prov.), Arg.
71/F6 Julbach, Ger.
168/B3 Julcán, Peru
192/C3 Julesburg, Co,US
168/D5 Juli, Peru
168/D4 Juliaca, Peru
133/J2 Julia Creek, Austl.
182/F4 Juliaetta, Id,US
186/D4 Julian, Ca,US
202/M7 Juliana (lake), Fl,US
75/K3 Julian Alps (mts.), It., Slov.
166/B2 Juliana Top (peak), Sur.
69/F2 Jülich, Ger.
81/F5 Julierpass (pass)
189/M9 Juliff, Tx,US
188/B3 Julimes, Mex.
173/F4 Júlio de Castilhos, Braz.
206/D3 Juliustown, NJ,US
78/D3 Julouville, Fr.
122/C2 Jullundur, India
115/C3 Julu, China
115/C3 Juma (riv.), China
116/C1 Jumanggoin, China
168/B2 Jumbilla, Peru
155/F3 Jumbo, Zim.
79/F2 Jumièges, Fr.
76/E3 Jumilla, Sp.
141/W17 Jūmīn (riv.), Tun.
63/L2 Juminda (pt.), Est.
120/D1 Jumla, Nepal
67/E2 Jümme (riv.), Ger.
112/B4 Jūmonji, Japan
195/J5 Jump (riv.), Wi,US
200/C3 Jumpertown, Ms,US
201/G2 Jumping Branch, WV,US
117/G2 Jun (mtn.), China
118/B3 Jūnāgadh, India
115/D4 Junan, China
174/C2 Juncal (peak), Arg., Chile
183/H4 Junction (mtn.), Mt,US
188/E2 Junction, Tx,US
185/G4 Junction, Ut,US
191/H4 Junction City, Ar,US
191/F1 Junction City, Ks,US
200/E2 Junction City, Ky,US
189/H1 Junction City, La,US
191/J2 Junction City, Mo,US
184/B1 Junction City, Or,US
195/K5 Junction City, Wi,US
134/A4 Jundah, Austl.
170/D4 Jundiaí, Braz.
115/H6 Jundu (mts.), China
141/W17 Jundūbah, Tun.
141/W17 Jundūbah (gov.), Tun.
177/M4 Juneau (cap.), Ak,US
193/K2 Juneau, Wi,US
77/F2 Juneda, Sp.
135/C2 Junee, Austl.
186/C2 June Lake, Ca,US
115/B3 Jungar Qi, China
80/D4 Jungfrau (peak), Swi.
80/D4 Jungfraujoch, Swi.
63/S7 Jungfrufjärden (bay), Swe.
126/C3 Jungkat, Indo.
189/J3 Jungle Gardens, La,US
69/F4 Junglinster, Lux.
149/F4 Jungoley, Qanat (can.), Sudan
192/E3 Juniata, Ne,US
206/A2 Juniata (co.), Pa,US
206/A2 Juniata (riv.), Pa,US
92/E4 Junik, Yugo.
174/C2 Junín, Arg.
174/E2 Junín, Arg.
164/B4 Junín, Ecu.
164/A5 Junín, Ecu.
168/C3 Junín, Peru
201/H1 Junior, WV,US
196/D2 Juniper, NB,Can
185/J3 Juniper (mtn.), Co,US
200/E4 Juniper, Ga,US
204/C2 Juniper Hills, Ca,US
186/B2 Junipero Serra (peak), Ca,US
68/D5 Juniville, Fr.
103/D3 Jūnīyah, Leb.
115/C3 Junji Guan (pass), China
117/H3 Junkou, China
116/E2 Junlian, China
79/E2 Juno (beach), Fr.
200/E3 Juno, Ga,US
188/D2 Juno, Tx,US
203/H4 Juno Beach, Fl,US
117/H2 Junpu, China
61/F3 Junsele, Swe.
172/B4 Juntas, Chile
108/D5 Ju'nyungoin, China
63/L3 Juodupė, Lith.
171/E3 Juparanã (lake), Braz.
173/G1 Jupiá (res.), Braz.
196/F1 Jupiter (riv.), Qu,Can
203/H4 Jupiter, Fl,US
205/A2 Jupiter (mt.), Wa,US
170/D5 Juquiá, Braz.
171/J8 Juquitiba, Braz.
149/F3 Jur (riv.), Sudan
80/C4 Jura (mts.), Eur.
80/B4 Jura (dept.), Fr.
80/D3 Jura (canton), Swi.
55/H9 Jura (isl.), Sc,UK
55/J9 Jura (sound), Sc,UK
164/B3 Juradó, Col.
74/C5 Jurançon, Fr.
63/K4 Jurbarkas, Lith.
68/C2 Jurbise, Belg.
56/D3 Jurby Head (pt.), IM,UK
132/B4 Jurien, Austl.
63/K3 Jūrmala, Lat.
124/C2 Jurong, Sing.
73/B3 Jur pri Bratislave, Slvk.
165/E5 Juruá (riv.), Braz.
169/E2 Juruá (riv.), Braz.
169/G4 Juruena, Braz.
169/G3 Juruena (riv.), Braz.
166/B3 Juruti, Braz.
61/G3 Jurva, Fin.
117/F4 Jushi, China
111/M9 Jushiyama, Japan
117/H3 Jushui, China
177/M5 Juskatla, BC,Can
80/B2 Jussey, Fr.
68/C4 Jussy, Fr.
80/C5 Jussy, Swi.
201/G2 Justice, WV,US
188/D1 Justiceburg, Tx,US
189/F1 Justin, Tx,US
174/D2 Justo Daract, Arg.
208/F6 Justus, Oh,US
168/D2 Jutaí, Braz.
169/D2 Jutaí (riv.), Braz.
72/D4 Jüterbog, Ger.
160/D3 Jutiapa, Guat.
160/E3 Juticalpa, Hon.
61/D4 Jutland (pen.), Den.
206/D2 Jutland, NJ,US
61/H3 Juva, Fin.
161/K7 Juventud (Pinos) (is Cuba
79/D4 Juvigné, Fr.
79/E3 Juvigny-sous-Andaine, Fr.
53/T10 Juvisy-sur-Orge, Fr.
115/D4 Ju Xian, China
115/D4 Juye, China
105/H4 Jūyom, Iran
115/C5 Juzhang (riv.), China
92/E4 Južna Morava (riv.), Yugo.
154/E5 Jwaneng, Bots.
62/D4 Jyderup, Den.
63/T9 Jyllinge, Den.
61/H3 Jyväskylä, Fin.

## K

114/C4 K2 (Godwin-Austin) (mtn.), China, Pak.
113/C3 Ka (isl.), NKor.
153/H2 Kaabong, Ugan.
107/G1 Kaakhka, Trkm.
180/S10 Kaala (peak), Hi,US
180/U11 Kaalualu, Hi,US
156/C3 Kaap (plat.), SAfr.
157/E2 Kaapmuiden, SAfr.
63/K1 Kaarina, Fin.
66/D5 Kaarst, Ger.
144/C4 Kaba, Gui.
92/E2 Kaba, Hun.
131/E1 Kaba, Indo.
121/G4 Kabadak (riv.), Ban
130/A1 Kabaena (isl.), Indo.
159/H4 Kabah (ruins), Mex.
144/C4 Kabala, SLeo.
153/G3 Kabale, Ugan.
153/G2 Kabalega (falls), Ug
153/G2 Kabalega Nat'l Par Ugan.
153/F4 Kabalo, Zaire
153/F5 Kabamba (lake), Zaire
153/F4 Kabambare, Zaire
153/F4 Kabango, Zaire
124/B2 Kabanjahe, Indo.
125/C3 Kabankalan, Phil.
97/G4 Kabardin-Balkar A Rep., Rus.
99/J5 Kabardinka, Rus.
153/G3 Kabare, Zaire
146/A2 Kābāw, Libya
145/G5 Kabba, Nga.
122/F3 Kabbani (riv.), India
153/G4 Kabeke, Zaire
153/E4 Kabelekese, Zaire
153/H2 Kaberamaido, Ugar
153/F3 Kabeta, Zaire
195/H3 Kabetogama (lake), Mn,US
153/F4 Kabeya Maji, Zaire
73/B5 Kab-hegy (peak), H
150/A3 Kabī, Eth.
123/C3 Kabin Buri, Thai.
153/F4 Kabinda, Zaire
141/V17 Kabir (riv.), Alg.
146/C2 Kabīr, As Sabkh al (salt marsh), Liby
104/F3 Kabīr Kūh (mts.), S
122/A2 Kabīrwāla, Pak.
90/A5 Kabīyah (lag.), Tun.
148/E2 Kabkābīyah, Sudar
93/H4 Kableshkovo, Bul.
148/C4 Kabo, CAfr.
153/G4 Kabobo, Zaire
127/H4 Kabolaa, Indo.
107/J2 Kābol (Kābul) (cap.), Afg.
154/E2 Kabompo, Zam.
154/D2 Kabompo (riv.), Zan
126/D3 Kabong, Malay.
153/F4 Kabongo, Zaire
120/C3 Kabrai, India
102/F6 Kābul (cap.), Afg.
107/J2 Kabul (riv.), Afg.
107/J2 Kābul (Kābol) (cap.), Afg.
155/F2 Kabunda, Zaire
125/D5 Kaburuang (isl.), Inc
149/G1 Kabūshīyah, Sudan
155/F2 Kabwe, Zam.
92/E4 Kačanik, Yugo.
63/K4 Kačergine, Lith.
155/F2 Kachalola, Zam.
177/H4 Kachemak, Ak,US
177/H4 Kachemak (bay), Ak,US
145/G4 Kachia, Nga.
154/E3 Kachikau, Bots.
116/C3 Kachin (state), Bur
114/C1 Kachiry, Kaz.
108/F1 Kachug, Rus.
104/E1 Kaçkar (peak), Turk
123/B2 Kada, Burma
122/F4 Kadaianallur, India
151/A1 Kadam (peak), Uga
123/B3 Kadan (isl.), Burma
71/G2 Kadaň, Czh.
138/G6 Kadavu (isl.), Fiji
109/H1 Kadaya, Rus.
148/B5 Kadéï (riv.), Camr., CAfr.
127/F5 Kadesa, Indo.
144/D4 Kadiana, Mali
105/N7 Kadıköy, Turk.
93/H5 Kadıköy, Turk.
153/F5 Kadilo, Zaire

133/H5 Kadina, Austl.
104/C2 Kadınhanı, Turk.
145/E3 Kadiogo (prov.), Burk.
144/D4 Kadiolo, Mali
118/C5 Kadiri, India
104/D2 Kadirli, Turk.
104/C2 Kadışehri, Turk.
192/D2 Kadoka, SD,US
111/L10 Kadoma, Japan
155/F3 Kadoma, Zim.
116/B6 Kadônkani, Burma
97/H1 Kadoshkino, Rus.
63/M2 Kadrina, Est.
145/G4 Kaduna, Nga.
145/G4 Kaduna (riv.), Nga.
145/G4 Kaduna (state), Nga.
149/F3 Kāduqli, Sudan
97/H5 Kadzharan, Arm.
95/M2 Kadzherom, Rus.
113/C3 Kaech'ŏn, NKor.
144/B2 Kaédi, Mrta.
113/D2 Kaehwa-ri, NKor.
148/B3 Kaélé, Camr.
123/C2 Kaeng Khlo, Thai.
123/B3 Kaeng Krachan Nat'l Park, Thai.
113/D4 Kaep'ung, NKor.
113/D3 Kaesŏng, NKor.
113/D4 Kaesŏng-Si, NKor.
104/D4 Kāf, SAr.
153/E5 Kafakumba, Zaire
53/H5 Kafan, Arm.
145/H4 Kafanchan, Nga.
107/J2 Kafar Jar Ghar (mts.), Afg.
156/D4 Kaffraria (reg.), SAfr.
144/B3 Kaffrine, Sen.
148/E3 Kafia Kingi, Sudan
91/J3 Kafirévs, Akra (cape), Gre.
103/B4 Kafr ad Dawwār, Egypt
103/B4 Kafr ash Shaykh, Egypt
103/B4 Kafr ash Shaykh (gov.), Egypt
103/B4 Kafr az Zayyāt, Egypt
103/G7 Kafr Qarʽ, Isr.
103/F7 Kafr Qāsim, Isr.
153/G2 Kafu (riv.), Ugan.
155/E1 Kafubu (riv.), Zaire
155/F2 Kafue, Zam.
155/F2 Kafue (dam), Zam.
155/F2 Kafue (riv.), Zam.
155/E2 Kafue Flats (swamp), Zam.
154/E2 Kafue Nat'l Park, Zam.
155/G1 Kafukule, Malw.
153/G5 Kafulwe, Zam.
110/E2 Kaga, Japan
131/G1 Kagamuga (int'l arpt.), PNG
100/G6 Kagan, Uzb.
108/E4 Kagang, China
98/F3 Kagarlyk, Ukr.
110/D3 Kagawa (pref.), Japan
152/D5 Kagendala Nat'l Park, Ang.
153/G3 Kagera (riv.), Afr.
63/U8 Kågeröd, Swe.
93/J5 Kağıthane, Turk.
105/M6 Kağıthane (riv.), Turk.
105/E1 Kağızman, Turk.
149/F2 Kagmar, Sudan
110/B5 Kagoshima, Japan
110/B5 Kagoshima (bay), Japan
110/B5 Kagoshima (int'l arpt.), Japan
110/B5 Kagoshima (pref.), Japan
131/F1 Kagua, PNG
93/J3 Kagul, Mol.
150/B3 K'aha, Eth.
151/A2 Kahama, Tanz.
126/D4 Kahayan (riv.), Indo.
151/B2 Kahe, Tanz.
152/D4 Kahemba, Zaire
151/B4 Kahindi, Tanz.
180/T10 Kahiu (pt.), Hi,US
72/B6 Kahla, Ger.
108/D1 Kahmsara (riv.), Rus.
122/C2 Kāhna, Pak.
144/C5 Kahnple, Libr.
105/J5 Kahnūj, Iran
144/C5 Kahnwia, Libr.
193/J3 Kahoka, Mo,US
180/U11 Kahoolawe (isl.), Hi,US
180/T10 Kahoolawe (isl.), Hi,US
61/G1 Kahperusvaara (peak), Fin.
104/D2 Kahramanmaraş, Turk.
104/D2 Kahraman Maraş (prov.), Turk.
107/K3 Kahror Pakka, Pak.
104/D2 Kâhta, Turk.
180/T10 Kahuku, Hi,US
180/T10 Kahuku (pt.), Hi,US
180/T10 Kahului, Hi,US
153/F3 Kahuzi-Biega Nat'l Park, Zaire
130/D1 Kai (isls.), Indo.
145/F4 Kaiama, Nga.
131/G1 Kaiapit, PNG
136/C3 Kaiapoi, N.Z.
187/F2 Kaibab (plat.), Az, Ut,US
187/F2 Kaibab Ind. Res., Az,US
111/L9 Kaibara, Japan
130/D1 Kai Besar (isl.), Indo.
187/G2 Kaibito, Az,US
187/G2 Kaibito (plat.), Az, Ut,US
114/E3 Kaidu (riv.), China
165/G3 Kaieteur (falls), Guy.
165/G3 Kaieteur Nat'l Park, Guy.
108/G5 Kaifeng, China
110/D4 Kaifu, Japan
112/C4 Kaigan-Rikuchū Nat'l Park, Japan
120/D1 Kāigaon, Nepal
117/E2 Kaijiang, China
130/D1 Kai Kecil (isl.), Indo.
136/C3 Kaikoura, N.Z.
144/C4 Kailahun, SLeo.
121/J3 Kailāshahar, India
117/E3 Kaili, China
115/E4 Kailu, China
180/T10 Kailua, Hi,US
180/U11 Kailua, Hi,US
127/H4 Kaimana, Indo.
108/D5 Kaimar, China
152/C4 Kai Mbaku, Zaire
120/B2 Kaimganj, India
120/C3 Kaimur (range), India
63/K2 Käina, Est.
156/B2 Kainab (dry riv.), Namb.
92/B2 Kainach (riv.), Aus.
110/D3 Kainan, Japan
131/G1 Kainantu, PNG
155/E2 Kaindu, Zam.
145/G4 Kainji (dam), Nga.
145/G4 Kainji (lake), Nga.
91/G3 Kainoúryion, Gre.
131/G1 Kaintiba, PNG
136/C2 Kaipara (har.), N.Z.
136/F6 Kaipara (riv.), N.Z.
187/G2 Kaiparowits (plat.), Ut,US
115/J7 Kaiping, China
120/A1 Kairāna, India
134/B2 Kairi, Austl.
131/G2 Kairuku, PNG
111/H7 Kaisei, Japan
80/D4 Kaiseregg (peak), Swi.
69/G3 Kaisersesch, Ger.
69/G5 Kaiserslautern, Ger.
80/D1 Kaiserstuhl (peak), Ger.
70/D5 Kaisheim, Ger.
63/L4 Kaišiadorys, Lith.
124/D3 Kait (cape), Indo.
136/C1 Kaitaia, N.Z.
136/B4 Kaitangata, N.Z.
133/G2 Kaitej Abor. Land, Austl.
114/C6 Kaithal, India
151/A2 Kaiti, Tanz.
180/T10 Kaiwi (chan.), Hi,US
119/J2 Kaiyang, China
109/J3 Kaiyuan, China
115/F2 Kaiyuan, China
116/D4 Kaiyuan, China
111/M9 Kaizu, Japan
111/L10 Kaizuka, Japan
52/F2 Kajaani, Fin.
133/J2 Kajabbi, Austl.
127/F5 Kajang, Indo.
124/C2 Kajang, Malay.
124/D2 Kajang (peak), Malay.
151/B2 Kajiado, Kenya
113/E5 Kaji-san (mtn.), SKor.
149/F5 Kajo-Kaji, Sudan
145/G4 Kajuru, Nga.
149/G3 Kākā, Sudan
61/G3 Kakaanpää, Fin.
195/K3 Kakabeka Falls, On,Can
148/B1 Kakada (well), Chad
130/D3 Kakadu Nat'l Park, Austl.
156/C3 Kakamas, SAfr.
151/A1 Kakamega, Kenya
111/E3 Kakamigahara, Japan
92/D3 Kakanj, Bosn.
144/C5 Kakata, Libr.
121/G5 Kākdwīp, India
177/M4 Kake, Ak,US
177/M4 Kaketsa (mtn.), BC,Can
105/J3 Kākhk, Iran
99/G4 Kakhovka, Ukr.
99/G4 Kakhovka (res.), Ukr.
155/F2 Kakielo, Zaire
118/D4 Kākināda, India
153/H2 Kakiri, Ugan.
111/L9 Kako (riv.), Japan
154/D2 Kakonga, Zam.
153/G3 Kakonko, Tanz.
120/C2 Kākori, India
120/B2 Kakrāla, India
144/B4 Kakrima (riv.), Gui.
177/K1 Kaktovik, Ak,US
118/B2 Kaku, India
111/G2 Kakuda, Japan
151/A1 Kakuma, Kenya
155/F2 Kakumbi, Zam.
153/E4 Kakuna, Zaire
112/B4 Kakunodate, Japan
145/G4 Kakuri, Nga.
153/G3 Kakuto, Ugan.
151/B2 Kakya, Kenya
122/H4 Kala (riv.), SrL.
141/X18 Kalaa-Kebia, Tun.
179/L1 Kalaallit Nunaat (Greenland), Den.
122/A1 Kālābāgh, Pak.
130/B2 Kalabahi, Indo.
125/B4 Kalabakan, Malay.
154/D2 Kalabo, Zam.
116/B5 Kalabyin, Burma
99/L2 Kalach, Rus.
105/G2 Kalā Chāy, Iran
100/H4 Kalachinsk, Rus.
99/M3 Kalach-na-Donu, Rus.
119/F3 Kaladan (riv.), Burma
199/H2 Kaladar, On,Can
180/U11 Ka Lae (cape), Hi,US
120/B1 Kālāgarh, India
154/D4 Kalahari (des.), Afr.
156/C2 Kalahari-Gemsbok Nat'l Park, SAfr.
180/S10 Kalaheo, Hi,US
121/H2 Kālāigaon, India
107/H1 Kala-I-Mor, Trkm.
121/E2 Kalaiya, Nepal
101/M4 Kalakan, Rus.
145/F4 Kalalé, Ben.
105/H2 Kalāleh, Iran
182/B4 Kalaloch, Wa,US
107/K1 Kalām, Pak.
182/C4 Kalama, Wa,US
91/L7 Kalamáki, Gre.
148/B2 Kalamaloué Nat'l Park, Camr.
155/E4 Kalamare, Bots.
91/H2 Kalamariá, Gre.
91/H4 Kalamáta, Gre.
198/D3 Kalamazoo, Mi,US
198/D3 Kalamazoo (riv.), Mi,US
99/G5 Kalamitsk (bay), Ukr.
91/G3 Kalampáka, Gre.
99/G4 Kalanchak, Ukr.
157/J6 Kalandy, Madg.
151/A3 Kalangali, Tanz.
108/H1 Kalanguy, Rus.
146/D3 Kalanshiyū ar Ramlī al Kabīr, Sarīr (des.), Libya
146/D3 Kalanshiyū, Sarīr (des.), Libya
180/U11 Kalaoa, Hi,US
130/A1 Kalaotoa (isl.), Indo.
93/J2 Kalarash, Mol.
121/G4 Kalaroa, Bang.
118/B2 Kālasar, India
123/C2 Kalasin, Thai.
107/J3 Kalāt, Pak.
180/T10 Kalaupapa, Hi,US
91/H3 Kalávrita, Gre.
116/C4 Kalaw, Burma
107/G3 Kalbā, UAE
134/D4 Kalbar, Austl.
132/B3 Kalbarri, Austl.
132/B3 Kalbarri Nat'l Park, Austl.
72/B2 Kalbe, Ger.
141/X18 Kalbīyah (lake), Tun.
61/N7 Kaldakvísl (riv.), Ice.
104/B2 Kale, Turk.
104/C1 Kalecik, Turk.
182/E3 Kaleden, BC,Can
130/A1 Kaledupa (isl.), Indo.
67/H5 Kalefeld, Ger.
153/G3 Kalehe, Zaire
153/F4 Kalema, Zaire
153/G4 Kalemie, Zaire
153/G4 Kalemie (int'l arpt.), Zaire
116/B4 Kalemyo, Burma
153/E5 Kalenda, Zaire
154/E1 Kalene Hill, Zam.
105/J2 Kāl-e Shūr (riv.), Iran
65/K3 Kalety, Pol.
198/C2 Kaleva, Mi,US
94/F2 Kalevala, Rus.
116/B4 Kalewa, Burma
155/E2 Kaleya, Zam.
138/B8 Kalgoorlie, Austl.
132/D4 Kalgoorlie-Boulder, Austl.
63/R7 Kalhall, Swe.
120/B2 Kali (riv.), India
121/H4 Kālia, Bang.
121/H3 Kāliākair, Bang.
93/J4 Kaliakra, Nos (pt.), Bul.
124/D4 Kalianda, Indo.
125/C3 Kalibo, Phil.
198/D4 Kalida, Oh,US
120/D2 Kāli Gandaki (riv.), Nepal
121/G4 Kālīganj, Bang.
118/C5 Kaligiri, India
120/C1 Kālikot, Nepal
153/F3 Kalima, Zaire
118/D4 Kalimala, India
126/D4 Kalimantan (reg.), Indo.
89/K3 Kálimnos, Gre.
89/K3 Kálimnos (isl.), Gre.
121/G2 Kālimpong, India
63/J4 Kaliningrad, Rus.
94/H5 Kaliningrad, Rus.
63/H4 Kaliningrad (lag.), Rus.
63/J4 Kaliningrad Obl., Rus.
105/F1 Kalinino, Arm.
99/K5 Kalinino, Rus.
97/H2 Kalininsk, Rus.
144/C4 Kalinko, Gui.
98/E1 Kalinkovichi, Bela.
99/H2 Kalinovka, Rus.
98/E3 Kalinovka, Ukr.
153/H2 Kaliro, Ugan.
150/D3 Kalis, Som.
153/G3 Kalisizo, Ugan.
183/G3 Kalispell, Mt,US
182/F3 Kalispell Ind. Res., Wa,US
65/K3 Kalisz, Pol.
65/J3 Kalisz (prov.), Pol.
153/G4 Kaliua, Tanz.
61/G2 Kalix, Swe.
61/G2 Kalixälv (riv.), Swe.
121/G3 Kāliyāganj, India
122/D2 Kālka, India
130/C4 Kalkaringi, Austl.
198/D2 Kalkaska, Mi,US
154/C4 Kalkfeld, Namb.
154/D4 Kalkfontein, Bots.
154/C5 Kalkhügel, Namb.
121/H4 Kālkini, Bang.
154/C5 Kalkrand, Namb.
122/G3 Kallakkurichichi, India
122/B1 Kallar Kahār, Pak.
63/M2 Kallaste, Est.
71/G6 Kallham, Aus.
122/F4 Kallidaikurichchi, India
62/F3 Kallinge, Swe.
62/F3 Kallinge (int'l arpt.), Swe.
91/L7 Kallithea, Gre.
61/E3 Kallsjön (lake), Swe.
145/G3 Kalmalo, Nga.
62/G3 Kalmar, Swe.
62/G3 Kalmar (co.), Swe.
62/G3 Kalmar (int'l arpt.), Swe.
62/G3 Kalmarsund (sound), Swe.
70/B4 Kalmit (mtn.), Ger.
66/B6 Kalmthout, Belg.
99/M4 Kalmyk Aut. Rep., Rus.
97/J2 Kalmykovo, Kaz.
121/G4 Kālna, India
120/D4 Kalnai, India
63/K3 Kalnciems, Lat.
121/H3 Kalni (riv.), Bang.
99/L4 Kalnibolotskaya, Rus.
92/D2 Kalocsa, Hun.
91/J1 Kalofer, Bul.
180/T10 Kalohi (chan.), Hi,US
92/F5 Kalokhórion, Gre.
153/F4 Kaloko, Zaire
118/B3 Kālol, India
153/F3 Kalole, Zaire
154/D2 Kalombo, Zam.
155/E3 Kalomo, Zam.
193/J3 Kalona, Ia,US
125/D4 Kalongan, Indo.
153/H2 Kalongo, Ugan.
149/F3 Kaloqi, Sudan
122/F3 Kalpatta, India
120/B2 Kālpi, India
114/C3 Kalpin, China
122/G4 Kalpitiya, SrL.
75/L3 Kalsdorf bei Graz, Aus.
177/G3 Kaltag, Ak,US
95/M5 Kaltasy, Rus.
81/F3 Kaltbrunn, Swi.
64/E2 Kaltenkirchen, Ger.
70/D1 Kaltennordheim, Ger.
81/H5 Kaltern (Caldaro), It.
145/H4 Kaltungo, Nga.
118/D6 Kalu (riv.), SrL.
94/H5 Kaluga, Rus.
94/G5 Kaluga Obl., Rus.
127/E4 Kaluku, Indo.
155/F2 Kalulushi, Zam.
130/B3 Kalumburu Abor. Rsv., Austl.
130/B3 Kalumburu Mission, Austl.
124/C2 Kalumpang, Malay.
62/D4 Kalundborg, Den.
153/G3 Kalungu, Ugan.
153/G5 Kalungwishi (riv.), Zam.
122/A1 Kalūr Kot, Pak.
98/C3 Kalush, Ukr.
118/C6 Kalutara, SrL.
63/K4 Kalvarija, Lith.
155/F2 Kalwelwe, Zam.
118/B4 Kalyān, India
94/H4 Kalyazin, Rus.
116/B5 Kama, Burma
95/M4 Kama (res.), Rus.
53/J3 Kama (riv.), Rus.
153/F3 Kama, Zaire
153/G3 Kamachumu, Tanz.
111/J7 Kamagaya, Japan
112/B4 Kamaishi, Japan
63/L4 Kamajai, Lith.
121/E4 Kāmākhyānagar, India
180/T10 Kamakou (peak), Hi,US
111/H7 Kamakura, Japan
166/A1 Kamakusa, Guy.
144/B4 Kamakwie, SLeo.
153/G4 Kamalampaka, Tanz.
122/B2 Kamālia, Pak.
180/T10 Kamalo, Hi,US
120/A2 Kāman, India
104/C2 Kaman, Turk.
153/G3 Kamande, Zaire
144/E2 Kamango (lake), Mali
153/G2 Kamango, Zaire
154/B3 Kamanjab, Namb.
153/G3 Kamanyola, Zaire
150/B2 Kamaran (isl.), Yem.
165/F3 Kamarang, Guy.
118/C4 Kāmāreddi, India
118/E3 Kāmārhāti, India
165/G3 Kamaria (falls), Guy.
185/H3 Kamas, Ut,US
120/C3 Kamāsin, India
155/E3 Kamativi, Zim.
145/G3 Kamba, Nga.
132/D4 Kambalda, Austl.
122/F4 Kambam, India
152/D4 Kamba-Poko, Zaire
118/A2 Kambar, Pak.
153/E4 Kambaswana, Zaire
144/B4 Kambia, SLeo.
130/B2 Kambing (isl.), Indo.
63/M2 Kambja, Est.
153/F5 Kambove, Zaire
127/F4 Kambuno (peak), Indo.
101/R4 Kamchatka (pen.), Rus.
101/R4 Kamchatka Obl., Rus.
93/H4 Kamchiya (riv.), Bul.
89/K2 Kamchiya, Luda (riv.), Bul.
184/D1 Kamela, Or,US
67/E5 Kamen, Ger.
153/F4 Kamena, Zaire
153/F4 Kamende, Zaire
65/M2 Kamenets, Bela.
98/D3 Kamenets-Podol'skiy, Ukr.
73/C4 Kamenička, Slvk.
92/A3 Kamenjak, Rt (cape), Cro.
97/J2 Kamenka, Kaz.
93/J1 Kamenka, Mol.
109/M3 Kamenka, Rus.
95/K2 Kamenka, Rus.
96/F2 Kamenka, Rus.
97/H1 Kamenka, Rus.
99/K2 Kamenka, Rus.
98/G3 Kamenka, Ukr.
98/C2 Kamenka-Bugskaya, Ukr.
99/H4 Kamenka-Dneprovskaya, Ukr.
98/C2 Kamen'-Kashirskiy, Ukr.
114/D1 Kamen'-na-Obi, Rus.
63/N1 Kamennogorsk, Rus.
99/L5 Kamennomostskaya, Rus.
93/H4 Kameno, Bul.
99/L4 Kamenolomni, Rus.
101/S3 Kamenskoye, Rus.
99/L3 Kamensk-Shakhtinskiy, Rus.
95/P4 Kamensk-Ural'skiy, Rus.
72/E5 Kamenz, Ger.
110/D3 Kameoka, Japan
127/H4 Kameri, Indo.
54/A5 Kames, Sc,UK
111/M10 Kameyama, Japan
111/J7 Kami, Japan
182/F4 Kamiah, Id,US
65/H2 Kamień Pomorski, Pol.
156/B3 Kamieskroon, SAfr.
111/H7 Kamifukuoka, Japan
110/A4 Kamigotō (arpt.), Japan
112/B3 Kamiisco, Japan
111/M9 Kamiishizu, Japan
153/E4 Kamiji, Zaire
112/C2 Kamikawa, Japan
180/U11 Kamilo (pt.), Hi,US
153/F5 Kamina, Zaire
111/G1 Kaminoyama, Japan
177/H4 Kamishak (bay), Ak,US
110/B5 Kamiyaku, Japan
121/F3 Kamla (riv.), India
182/D2 Kamloops, BC,Can
123/C4 Kamlot, Camb.
111/L10 Kammaki, Japan
70/D6 Kammlach (riv.), Ger.
92/B2 Kamnik, Slov.
97/H4 Kamo, Arm.
111/F2 Kamo, Japan
111/J7 Kamo (riv.), Japan
111/G3 Kamogawa, Japan
110/D3 Kamojima, Japan
122/C2 Kāmoke, Pak.
153/E4 Kamonia, Zaire
75/L2 Kamp (riv.), Aus.
153/H2 Kampala (cap.), Ugan.
125/D4 Kampalili (mtn.), Phil.
124/C2 Kampar (riv.), Indo.
124/C1 Kampar, Malay.
69/G3 Kamp-Bornhofen, Ger.
64/E1 Kampen, Ger.
66/C3 Kampen, Neth.
153/F3 Kampene, Zaire
123/B2 Kamphaeng Phet, Thai.
123/B2 Kamphaeng Phet (ruins), Thai.
65/L2 Kampinoski Nat'l Park, Pol.
66/D6 Kamp-Lintfort, Ger.
113/E5 Kamp'o, SKor.
123/D4 Kampong Cham, Camb.
123/D3 Kampong Chhnang, Camb.
123/C5 Kampong Kadok, Malay.
123/D3 Kampong Khleang, Camb.
124/C1 Kampong Kuala Besut, Malay.
124/C1 Kampong Lalok, Malay.
124/C1 Kampong Raja, Malay.
123/C4 Kampong Saom, Camb.
123/C4 Kampong Saom (bay), Camb.
124/C2 Kampong Sedenak, Malay.
124/D2 Kampong Sedili Kechil, Malay.
123/D4 Kampong Spoe, Camb.
127/E2 Kampong Tampasis, Malay.
125/B4 Kampong Telupid, Malay.
123/D3 Kampong Thum, Camb.
123/D4 Kampong Trabek, Camb.
123/D4 Kampot, Camb.
144/E3 Kampti, Burk.
127/H4 Kamrau (bay), Indo.
194/D2 Kamsack, Sk,Can
144/B4 Kamsar, Gui.
72/B6 Kamsdorf, Ger.
95/L5 Kamskoye Ust'ye, Rus.
151/C1 Kamsuuma, Som.
152/D4 Kamtsha (riv.), Zaire
122/G4 Kamudi, India
112/B2 Kamui-misaki (cape), Japan
161/F4 Kámuk (mtn.), CR
153/H2 Kamuli, Ugan.
153/E4 Kamwandu, Zaire
105/F3 Kāmyārān, Iran
99/J4 Kamyshevatskaya, Rus.
53/H3 Kamyshin, Rus.
95/M5 Kamyshla, Rus.
97/K1 Kamyshla, Rus.
95/P4 Kamyshlov, Rus.
99/J4 Kamysh-Zarya, Ukr.
97/J3 Kamyzyak, Rus.
179/J3 Kanaaupscow (riv.), Qu,Can
187/F2 Kanab (plat.), Az,US
187/F2 Kanab (cr.), Az, Ut,US
187/F2 Kanab, Ut,US
177/C6 Kanaga (isl.), Ak,US
177/C6 Kanaga (vol.), Ak,US
111/F3 Kanagawa (pref.), Japan
111/H7 Kanagawa (pref.), Japan
179/K3 Kanairiktok (riv.), Nf,Can
127/H4 Kanaka, Indo.
111/L10 Kanan, Japan
153/E4 Kananga, Zaire
120/C4 Kanaoudi, India
187/F2 Kanarraville, Ut,US
53/H3 Kanash, Rus.
199/J2 Kanata, On,Can
197/N7 Kanawake Ind. Res., Qu,Can
193/H2 Kanawha, Ia,US
201/F1 Kanawha (riv.), WV,US
111/E2 Kanazawa, Japan
153/G3 Kanazi, Tanz.
119/G3 Kanbalu, Burma
123/B3 Kanchanaburi, Thai.
123/B4 Kanchanadit, Thai.
118/E2 Kānchenjunga (mtn.), Nepal
118/C5 Kānchīpuram, India
121/G4 Kanchrāpārā, India
153/E4 Kanda-Kanda, Zaire
94/G2 Kandalaksha, Rus.
61/K2 Kandalaksha (gulf), Rus.
94/G2 Kandalaksha (gulf), Rus.
152/D4 Kandale, Zaire
124/B2 Kandang, Indo.
124/E4 Kandanghaur, Indo.
91/H5 Kándanos, Gre.
63/K3 Kandava, Lat.
139/Y18 Kandavu Passage (chan.), Fiji
70/B4 Kandel, Ger.
70/B6 Kandel (peak), Ger.
131/F1 Kandep, PNG
80/D4 Kander (riv.), Swi.
80/D2 Kandern, Ger.
80/D5 Kandersteg, Swi.
107/J3 Kandhkot, Pak.
120/A1 Kāndhla, India
145/F4 Kandi, Ben.
121/G4 Kāndi, India
127/F3 Kandi (cape), Indo.
153/G2 Kandi, Zaire
93/K5 Kandıra, Turk.
135/D2 Kandos, Austl.
107/J3 Kandrāch, Pak.
157/H7 Kandreho, Madg.
95/M5 Kandry, Rus.
118/C4 Kandukūr, India
118/D6 Kandy, SrL.
179/T7 Kane (bay), NW,Can
193/J4 Kane, Il,US
205/P16 Kane (co.), Il,US
199/G4 Kane, Pa,US
148/B2 Kanem (pref.), Chad
180/T10 Kaneohe, Hi,US
98/F3 Kanev, Ukr.
98/F2 Kanev (res.), Ukr.
205/N16 Kaneville, Il,US
94/H2 Kanëvka, Rus.
99/K4 Kanevskaya, Rus.
112/B4 Kaneyama, Japan
154/D4 Kang, Bots.
121/G5 Kanga (riv.), Bang.
151/B3 Kanga, Tanz.
153/G2 Kanga, Zaire
144/C4 Kangaba, Mali
104/D2 Kangal, Turk.
105/H5 Kangān, Iran
105/J5 Kangān, Iran
132/C2 Kangan Abor. Land, Austl.
124/C1 Kangar, Malay.
144/C4 Kangaré, Mali
133/G5 Kangaroo (isl.), Austl.
165/G3 Kangaruma, Guy.
63/L1 Kangasala, Fin.
105/F3 Kangāvar, Iran
108/G3 Kangbao, China
116/D2 Kangding, China
124/F4 Kangean (isl.), Indo.
124/F4 Kangean (isls.), Indo.
149/G4 Kangen (riv.), Sudan
152/D5 Kangendala Nat'l Park, Ang.
113/D2 Kanggye, NKor.
113/D4 Kanggyŏng, SKor.
113/D4 Kanghwa, SKor.
113/D4 Kanghwa (isl.), SKor.
149/E3 Kangi, Sudan
179/K3 Kangiqsualujjuaq, Qu,Can
179/J2 Kangiqsujuaq, Qu,Can
179/J2 Kangirsuk, Qu,Can
113/D5 Kangjin, SKor.
124/C2 Kangkar Dohol, Malay.
121/G1 Kangmar, China
113/C3 Kangnam, NKor.
113/C2 Kangnam (mts.), NKor.
113/G6 Kangnam, SKor.
113/E4 Kangnŭng, SKor.
113/C4 Kangnyŏng, NKor.
152/B2 Kango, Gabon
151/B2 Kangondi, Kenya
115/E2 Kangping, China
122/D1 Kāngra, India
114/D5 Kangrinboqê Feng (peak), China
113/C3 Kangsŏ, NKor.
113/F6 Kangsŏ, SKor.
116/B3 Kangto (peak), China
152/C4 Kangu, Zaire
113/D3 Kangwŏn-do (prov.), NKor.
113/E4 Kangwŏn-do (prov.), SKor.
114/C4 Kangxiwar, China
118/C3 Kanhān (riv.), India
120/C4 Kanha Nat'l Park, India
116/B4 Kani, Burma
144/D4 Kani, IvC.
111/N9 Kani, Japan
153/F4 Kaniama, Zaire
111/M9 Kanie, Japan
95/K2 Kanin (pen.), Rus.
151/B2 Kaningo, Kenya
94/J1 Kanin Nos, Rus.
52/H2 Kanin Nos (pt.), Rus.
135/B3 Kaniva, Austl.
122/F4 Kanjirapalli, India
92/E2 Kanjiža, Yugo.
198/C4 Kankakee, Il,US
198/C4 Kankakee (riv.), Il, In,US
144/C4 Kankan, Gui.
144/C4 Kankan (comm.), Gui.
118/D3 Kānker, India
122/H4 Kankesanturai, SrL.
144/C3 Kankossa, Mrta.
117/J2 Kanmen, China
110/C3 Kanmuri-yama (mtn.), Japan
201/G3 Kannapolis, NC,US
120/B2 Kannauj, India
122/F4 Kanniyākumāri, India
111/H7 Kannon-zaki (pt.), Japan
61/G3 Kannus, Fin.
145/H4 Kano, Nga.
145/H3 Kano (state), Nga.
155/F2 Kanona, Zam.
156/C3 Kanoneiland, SAfr.
110/C3 Kan'onji, Japan
191/E1 Kanopolis, Ks,US
192/E4 Kanopolis (lake), Ks,US
185/G4 Kanosh, Ut,US
207/H7 Kanouse (mtn.), NJ,US
154/C4 Kano Vlei, Namb.
126/D3 Kanowit, Malay.
110/B5 Kanoya, Japan
120/C2 Kānpur, India
120/C2 Kanpur (arpt.), India
151/B2 Kansarokana (dry riv.), Kenya
181/G4 Kansas (state), US
200/D4 Kansas, Al,US
198/C5 Kansas, Il,US
193/F4 Kansas (riv.), Ks,US
191/G1 Kansas City, Ks,US
191/G1 Kansas City, Mo,US
191/G1 Kansas City (int'l arpt.), Mo,US
191/F1 Kansas Cosmosphere & Space Ctr., Ks,US
205/P14 Kansasville, Wi,US
153/F5 Kansenia, Zaire
100/K4 Kansk, Rus.
113/E3 Kansŏng, SKor.
114/B3 Kant, Kyr.
118/D3 Kantābānji, India
145/F3 Kantchari, Burk.
145/F4 Kanté, Togo
99/K3 Kantemirovka, Rus.
120/B1 Kānth, India
123/D3 Kantharalak, Thai.
111/F2 Kantō (prov.), Japan
159/J4 Kantunilkín, Mex.
60/B5 Kanturk, Ire.
166/A2 Kanuku (mts.), Braz., Guy.
111/F2 Kanuma, Japan
177/H2 Kanuti Nat'l Wild. Ref., Ak,US
145/E4 Kanyanga, Gha.
154/E5 Kanye, Bots.
154/E2 Kanyilombi, Zam.
123/B2 Kanyutkwin, Burma
153/F5 Kanzenze, Zaire
113/E3 Kanzi, China
123/D3 Kaoh Nhek, Camb.
117/J4 Kaohsiung, Tai.
117/J4 Kaohsiung (int'l arpt.), Tai.
154/C4 Kaokoveld (reg.), Namb.
144/A3 Kaolack, Sen.
144/B3 Kaolack (reg.), Sen.
99/H3 Kaolinovo, Bul.
154/E2 Kaoma, Zam.
153/G5 Kaongweshi (riv.), Zam.
146/C5 Kaortchi (well), Chad
146/D5 Kaouar (oasis), Niger
123/B3 Kapa, Burma
180/S9 Kapaa, Hi,US
180/U11 Kapaahu, Hi,US
180/U10 Kapaau, Hi,US
136/J8 Kapakapuni (mtn.), N.Z.
155/F2 Kapalala, Zam.
125/D4 Kapalong, Phil.
153/E4 Kapambwe, Zaire
153/E5 Kapanga, Zaire
92/E4 Kapaonik (mts.), Yugo.
114/C3 Kapchagay, Kaz.
114/C3 Kapchagay (res.), Kaz.
151/A1 Kapchorwa, Ugan.
151/B1 Kapedo, Kenya
66/B6 Kapellen, Belg.
151/A1 Kapenguria, Kenya
155/F2 Kapengwe, Zam.
75/L3 Kapfenberg, Aus.
93/H5 Kapıdağı (pen.), Turk.
138/E4 Kapingamarangi (isl.), Micr.
155/F2 Kapiri Mposhi, Zam.
179/H3 Kapiskau (riv.), On,Can
202/B3 Kaplan, La,US
71/H5 Kaplice, Czh.
123/B4 Kapoe, Thai.
149/G4 Kapoeta, Sudan
153/G4 Kapona, Zaire
91/G1 Kaponik (upland), Yugo.
151/A4 Kaporo, Malw.
73/C6 Kapos (riv.), Hun.
92/C2 Kaposvár, Hun.
205/C4 Kapowsin, Wa,US
62/D1 Kapp, Nor.
64/E1 Kappeln, Ger.
70/B5 Kappelrodeck, Ger.
81/G3 Kappl, Aus.
151/A1 Kapsabet, Kenya
113/E2 Kapsan, NKor.
63/K4 Kapsukas, Lith.
73/B5 Káptalanfa, Hun.
126/C4 Kapuas (riv.), Indo.
126/D3 Kapuas Hulu (mts.), Indo., Malay.
133/H5 Kapunda, Austl.
118/B2 Kapūria, India
122/C2 Kapūrthala, India
179/H4 Kapuskasing, On,Can
153/G5 Kaputa, Zam.
73/B4 Kapuvár, Hun.
105/F2 Kapydzhik (peak), Azer.
97/H5 Kapydzhik, Gora (peak), Azer.
113/D4 Kap'yŏng, SKor.
95/Q1 Kara, Rus.
95/Q1 Kara (riv.), Rus.
53/J1 Kara (sea), Rus.
104/C2 Karaali, Turk.
114/B4 Karaart, Taj.
114/B3 Kara-Balta, Kyr.
97/K2 Karabau, Kaz.
93/H5 Karabiğa, Turk.
97/K4 Kara-Bogaz-Gol, Trkm.
97/K4 Kara-Bogaz-Gol (gulf), Trkm.
127/H4 Karabra (riv.), Indo.
97/H4 Karabudakhkent, Rus.
104/C1 Karabük, Turk.
100/K4 Karabula, Rus.
97/H4 Karabulak, Rus.
93/J5 Karaburun, Turk.
97/M2 Karabutak, Kaz.
104/D2 Karaca (peak), Turk.
104/B1 Karacabey, Turk.
93/H5 Karacadağ, Turk.
93/J5 Karacaköy, Turk.
103/C1 Karaçal (peak), Turk.
93/H5 Karacaoğlan, Turk.
97/J5 Karachala, Azer.
99/L5 Karachay-Cherkass Aut. Obl., Rus.
96/E1 Karachev, Rus.
107/J4 Karāchi, Pak.
73/B6 Karád, Hun.
118/B4 Karād, India
93/K5 Karadere, Turk.
114/B2 Karaganda, Kaz.
114/C2 Karagayly, Kaz.
102/R4 Karaginskiy (isl.), Rus.
114/E1 Karagoš (peak), Rus.
95/N5 Karaidel'skiy, Rus.
122/G3 Kāraikkudi, India
104/C2 Karaisalı, Turk.
122/G4 Karaitivu (isl.), SrL.
105/G3 Karaj, Iran
124/C2 Karak, Malay.
97/L5 Kara-Kala, Trkm.
97/L3 Karakalpak Aut. Rep., Uzb.
114/C4 Karakax (riv.), China
104/D2 Karakaya (dam), Turk.
104/D2 Karakeçi, Turk.
125/D4 Karakelong (isl.), Indo.
108/E3 Karakhoto (ruins), China
104/E2 Karakoçan, Turk.
114/C4 Karakoram (range), Asia
107/L1 Karakoram (pass), India
114/C4 Karakoram (pass), India
150/A3 Kara K'orē, Eth.
144/C3 Karakoro (riv.), Mali, Mrta.
107/L1 Karakorum (pass), China
108/E2 Karakorum (ruins), Mong.
105/E2 Karaköse, Turk.
104/E2 Karaköy, Turk.
114/B3 Kara-Kul', Kyr.
114/B4 Karakul' (lake), Taj.
100/G6 Karakul', Uzb.
97/L5 Karakumy (des.), Trkm.
154/C3 Karakuwisa, Namb.
97/K4 Karakyon, Gora (peak), Trkm.
107/H1 Karakyr (peak), Trkm.
127/E4 Karam (riv.), Indo.
108/B2 Karamagay, China
104/C2 Karaman, Turk.
103/C1 Karaman (prov.), Turk.
104/B2 Karamanlı, Turk.
114/D2 Karamay, China
153/G3 Karambi, Tanz.
136/C3 Karamea, N.Z.
136/B3 Karamea (bight), N.Z.
107/H1 Karamet-Niyaz, Trkm.
114/E4 Karamiran, China
114/D4 Karamiran (riv.), China
114/E4 Karamiran Shankou (pass), China
151/A1 Karamoja (prov.), Ugan.
93/J5 Karamürsel, Turk.
63/N3 Karamyshevo, Rus.
119/G4 Karan (state), Burma
124/F5 Karangasem, Indo.
101/S4 Karanginskiy (bay), Rus.
101/S4 Karanginskiy (isl.), Rus.
118/C3 Kāranja, India
123/B2 Karan (Kayin) (state), Burma
93/H4 Karapelit, Bul.
104/C2 Karapınar, Turk.
149/G2 Karari, Sudan
165/G3 Karasabai, Guy.
110/A3 Kara-saki (pt.), Japan
93/L5 Karaşar, Turk.
156/B3 Karasburg, Namb.
61/H1 Karasjok, Nor.
111/M10 Karasu, Japan
93/K5 Karasu, Turk.
114/C1 Karasuk, Rus.
161/F3 Karatá (lag.), Nic.
114/C2 Karatal (riv.), Kaz.
103/D1 Karataş, Turk.
114/B3 Karatau, Kaz.
114/A3 Karatau (mts.), Kaz.
123/B4 Karathuri, Burma
97/K2 Karatobe, Kaz.
97/K3 Karaton, Kaz.
121/G3 Karatoya (riv.), Bang.
110/A4 Karatsu, Japan
120/A2 Karauli, India
104/E1 Karaurgan, Turk.
91/G3 Karáva (peak), Gre.
114/B3 Karavan, Kyr.
124/D4 Karawang, Indo.
96/F4 Karayaka, Turk.
104/E2 Karayazı, Turk.
114/B2 Karazhal, Kaz.
147/G5 Karbalā', Iraq
105/F3 Karbalā', Iraq
105/E3 Karbalā' (gov.), Iraq
70/B2 Karben, Ger.
92/E2 Karcag, Hun.
91/K3 Kardhámila, Gre.
91/G3 Kardhítsa, Gre.
91/G3 Kardhitsomagoúla, Gre.
63/K2 Kärdla, Est.
73/A5 Kardos-ér (riv.), Hun.
121/E3 Kareha (riv.), India
120/B4 Karelī, India
100/D3 Karelian Aut. Rep., Rus.
153/G4 Karema, Tanz.
108/H1 Karenga (riv.), Rus.
120/B3 Karera, India
61/G1 Karesuando, Swe.
142/D4 Karêt (reg.), Mrta.
63/M2 Kärevere, Est.
97/K2 Kargala, Rus.
100/J4 Kargasok, Rus.
104/C1 Kargı, Turk.
94/H3 Kargopol', Rus.
120/B2 Karhal, India
63/K1 Karhijärvi (lake), Fin.
145/H4 Kari, Nga.
91/G3 Kariá, Gre.
141/M13 Karia Ba Mohammed, Mor.
91/J2 Kariaí, Gre.
157/H8 Karianga, Madg.
155/F3 Kariba (dam), Zam.
155/E3 Kariba (lake), Zam., Zim.
155/F3 Kariba, Zim.
112/A2 Kariba-yama (mtn.), Japan
154/B4 Karibib, Namb.
153/G2 Karibumba, Zaire
122/G3 Karikal, India
145/F3 Karimama, Ben.
126/C4 Karimata (isl.), Indo.
126/C4 Karimata (str.), Indo.
118/C4 Karīmnagar, India
131/G1 Karimui, PNG
150/C3 Karin, Som.
150/D3 Karin, Som.
62/E4 Karise, Den.
153/G3 Karisimbi (vol.), Zaire
91/J3 Káristos, Gre.
111/M10 Kariya, Japan
150/D3 Karkaar (mts.), Som.
118/B5 Kārkal, India
138/D5 Karkar (isl.), PNG
100/H5 Karkaralinsk, Kaz.
99/G5 Karkinitsk (gulf), Ukr.
63/L1 Karkkila, Fin.
103/G7 Karkur, Isr.
114/B4 Karla Marksa, Pik (peak), Taj.
192/E2 Karl E. Mundt Nat'l Wild. Ref., SD,US
62/G1 Karlholmsbruk, Swe.
65/H1 Karlino, Pol.
104/E2 Karlıova, Turk.
99/K3 Karlo-Libknekhtovsk, Ukr.
92/B3 Karlovac, Slov.
99/H3 Karlovka, Ukr.
93/G4 Karlovo, Bul.
71/F2 Karlovy Vary, Czh.
71/F2 Karlovy Vary (arpt.), Czh.
70/B4 Karlsdorf-Neuthard, Ger.
71/E6 Karlsfeld, Ger.
62/F3 Karlshamn, Swe.
70/E5 Karlshuld, Ger.
62/F2 Karlskoga, Swe.
71/E5 Karlskron, Ger.
62/F3 Karlskrona, Swe.
63/T9 Karlslunde Strand, Den.
70/B4 Karlsruhe, Ger.
194/D3 Karlsruhe, ND,US
62/E2 Karlstad, Swe.
194/F3 Karlstad, Mn,US
70/C3 Karlstadt, Ger.
70/C2 Karlstein am Main, Ger.
177/H4 Karluk, Ak,US
147/F5 Karmah, Sudan
118/C4 Karmāla, India
121/F3 Karmatānr, India
103/D3 Karmel, Har (Mount Carmel) (mtn.), Isr.
120/A1 Karnāl, India
120/C1 Karnali (riv.), Nepal
120/C1 Karnali (zone), Nepal
120/C1 Karnali (riv.), Tibet
121/H4 Karnaphuli (res.), Bang.
122/F3 Karnataka (state), India
189/F3 Karnes City, Tx,US
93/H4 Karnobat, Bul.
92/A2 Kärnten (prov.), Aus.
148/C3 Karo, Chad
155/F3 Karoi, Zim.
125/C4 Karomatan, Phil.
151/A4 Karonga, Malw.
156/C4 Karoo Nat'l Park, SAfr.
135/A2 Karoonda, Austl.
122/A2 Karor, Pak.
149/H1 Karora, Sudan
127/E5 Karoso (cape), Indo.
133/J5 Karpakora, Austl.
89/K4 Kárpathos, Gre.
89/K4 Kárpathos (isl.), Gre.
98/C3 Karpatskiy Nat'l Park, Ukr.
91/G3 Karpenísion, Gre.
95/K3 Karpogory, Rus.
132/C2 Karratha, Austl.
156/M11 Kars (riv.), SAfr.
105/E1 Kars, Turk.
104/E1 Kars (prov.), Turk.
97/G4 Kars (riv.), Turk.
61/H3 Kärsämäki, Fin.
104/C2 Karsantı, Turk.
63/M3 Kārsava, Lat.
72/B5 Karsdorf, Ger.
100/G6 Karshi, Uzb.
72/B1 Karstädt, Ger.
97/M1 Kartaly, Rus.
122/C2 Kartārpur, India
72/C2 Karthane (riv.), Ger.
93/L3 Kartinitsk (gulf), Ukr.
153/F4 Kartushi, Zaire
65/K1 Kartuzy, Pol.
135/D2 Karuah, Austl.
153/H2 Karuma (falls), Ugan.
134/A2 Karumba, Austl.
105/G4 Kārūn (riv.), Iran
130/B4 Karunjie, Austl.
62/C3 Karup, Den.
122/G3 Karūr, India
153/F3 Karushe, Zaire
190/C1 Karval, Co,US
65/K4 Karviná, Czh.
118/B5 Karwar, India
108/G1 Karymskoye, Rus.
61/D4 Kås, Den.
148/E2 Kas, Sudan
103/A1 Kaş, Turk.
177/M4 Kasaan, Ak,US
111/L10 Kasagi, Japan
121/F4 Kāsai (riv.), India
110/D3 Kasai, Japan
152/D3 Kasai (riv.), Zaire
153/E4 Kasai-Occidental (pol. reg.), Zaire
153/E3 Kasai-Oriental (pol. reg.), Zaire
153/E5 Kasaji, Zaire
153/G5 Kasakalawe, Zam.
155/E2 Kasalu, Zam.
111/G2 Kasama, Japan
153/G5 Kasama, Zam.
111/M9 Kasamatsu, Japan
154/E3 Kasane, Bots.
153/G5 Kasanga, Tanz.
154/E3 Kasanga (falls), Zam.
152/C4 Kasangulu, Zaire
155/F2 Kasanka Nat'l Park, Zam.
110/C3 Kasaoka, Japan
118/C5 Kāsaragod, India
147/H5 Kasar, Ras (cape), Sudan
111/M10 Kasartori-yama (peak), Japan
178/F2 Kasba (lake), NW,Can
142/D2 Kasba Tadla, Mor.
110/B5 Kaseda, Japan
155/E1 Kaseke, Zaire
151/B4 Kasembe, Tanz.
154/E2 Kasempa, Zam.
153/G5 Kasenga, Zaire
153/G2 Kasenyi, Zaire
153/G2 Kasese, Ugan.
153/F3 Kasese, Zaire
123/C3 Kaset Wisai, Thai.
120/B2 Kāsganj, India
195/J3 Kashabowie, On,Can
107/H1 Kashaf (riv.), Iran
105/G3 Kāshān, Iran
99/L3 Kashary, Rus.
114/C4 Kashi, China
111/L10 Kashiba, Japan
153/G5 Kashiba, Zam.
110/D3 Kashihara, Japan
110/B4 Kashima, Japan
111/G3 Kashima, Japan
94/H4 Kashin, Rus.
120/B1 Kāshīpur, India
111/H7 Kashiwa, Japan
111/L10 Kashiwara, Japan
111/F2 Kashiwazaki, Japan
105/J3 Kāshmar, Iran
122/C1 Kashmīr, Jammu and (state), India
118/A2 Kashmor, Pak.
105/J2 Kashof (riv.), Iran
153/G3 Kashofu, Zaire
120/D2 Kasia, India
153/E5 Kasidiji (riv.), Zaire
151/B2 Kasigau (peak), Kenya
177/F3 Kasigluk, Ak,US
177/H3 Kasilof, Ak,US
94/J5 Kasimov, Rus.
153/G2 Kasindi, Zaire
153/F4 Kasinge, Zaire
127/G4 Kasiruta (isl.), Indo.
127/H4 Kasiui (isl.), Indo.
155/G2 Kasiya, Malw.
193/K4 Kaskaskia (riv.), Il,US
63/N2 Kas'kovo, Rus.
182/F3 Kaslo, BC,Can
127/J4 Kasonaweja, Indo.
126/D4 Kasongan, Indo.
153/F4 Kasongo, Zaire
152/D4 Kasongo-Lunda, Zaire
153/F4 Kasonguele, Zaire
89/K4 Kásos (isl.), Gre.
97/H4 Kaspi, Geo.
93/H4 Kaspichan, Bul.
97/H4 Kaspiysk, Rus.
97/H3 Kaspiyskiy, Rus.
149/H2 Kassala, Sudan
91/H3 Kassándra (pen.), Gre.
91/H2 Kassándria, Gre.
67/G6 Kassel, Ger.
165/G4 Kassikaityu (riv.), Guy.
193/H1 Kasson, Mn,US
104/C1 Kastamonu, Turk.
104/C1 Kastamonu (prov.), Turk.
91/K2 Kastanéai, Gre.
69/G3 Kastellaun, Ger.
91/J5 Kastéllion, Gre.
92/C4 Kaštel Stari, Cro.
92/C4 Kaštel Sućurac, Cro.
69/D1 Kasterlee, Belg.
71/E4 Kastl, Ger.
91/G2 Kastoría, Gre.
99/K2 Kastornoye, Rus.
91/G3 Kastrakíou (lake), Gre.
62/E4 Kastrup (int'l arpt.), Den.
111/L9 Kasuga, Japan
111/E3 Kasugai, Japan
124/D4 Kasui, Indo.
111/F3 Kasukabe, Japan
153/F3 Kasuku (riv.), Zaire
153/G4 Kasulu, Tanz.
111/G2 Kasumiga (lake), Japan
155/G2 Kasungu, Malw.
155/G2 Kasungu Nat'l Park, Malw.
155/G2 Kasupe, Malw.
122/C2 Kasūr, Pak.
154/E3 Kataba, Zam.
148/A2 Katagum (riv.), Nga.
196/C3 Katahdin (mtn.), Me,US
153/F3 Katako-Kombe, Zaire
91/G4 Katákolon, Gre.
153/G3 Katale, Zaire
153/G3 Katana, Zaire
153/E4 Katanda, Zaire
153/G3 Katanda, Zaire
140/E5 Katanga (reg.), Zaire
153/F5 Katanga (Shaba) (pol. reg.), Zaire
120/B4 Katangi, India
132/C5 Katanning, Austl.
111/L10 Katano, Japan
153/F3 Katanti, Zaire
120/C1 Katarniān Ghāt, India
91/G4 Katastárion, Gre.
153/G4 Katavi Nat'l Park, Tanz.
119/F6 Katchall (isl.), India
153/E4 Katea, Zaire
153/F4 Katea, Zaire
153/H3 Katebo, Ugan.
188/E2 Katemcy, Tx,US
153/G4 Katenga, Zaire
91/H2 Katerini, Gre.
151/A3 Katesh, Tanz.
177/M4 Kates Needle (mtn.), Ak,US
155/G2 Katete, Malw.
155/G2 Katete, Zam.

120/D4 Katghora, India
116/C3 Katha, Burma
130/D3 Katherine, Austl.
130/D3 Katherine (riv.), Austl.
186/E3 Katherine, Az,US
130/D3 Katherine Gorge Nat'l Park, Austl.
120/B1 Kāthgodām, India
107/K4 Kathiawar (pen.), India
133/G2 Kathleen (peak), Austl.
202/L7 Kathleen, Fl,US
203/G1 Kathleen, Ga,US
121/E2 Kāthmāndu (cap.), Nepal
194/F4 Kathryn, ND,US
122/C1 Kathua, India
144/C3 Kati, Mali
144/D3 Katiéna, Mali
121/F3 Katihār, India
121/F3 Kātikund, India
144/D4 Katiola, IvC.
149/F3 Katla, Sudan
67/H5 Katlenburg-Lindau, Ger.
114/E4 Katma, China
177/H4 Katmai (vol.), Ak,US
177/G4 Katmai Nat'l Park & Prsv., Ak,US
91/G3 Káto Akhaía, Gre.
153/G4 Katoba, Tanz.
91/G3 Katokhí, Gre.
153/E4 Katombe, Zaire
207/E1 Katonah, NY,US
91/H2 Káto Nevrokópion, Gre.
153/G2 Katonga (riv.), Ugan.
135/D2 Katoomba, Austl.
91/G3 Katoúna, Gre.
65/K3 Katowice, Pol.
65/K3 Katowice (prov.), Pol.
120/C3 Katra, India
122/C1 Katra, India
121/F4 Kātrās, India
97/H2 Katrichev, Rus.
147/G2 Katrīnah, Jabal (Mount Catherine) (mnt), Egypt
106/B3 Katrīnah, Jabal (Mount Catherine) (mtn.), Egypt
147/G2 Katrīnah, Jabal (Mount Catherine) (mtn.), Egypt
62/G2 Katrineholm, Swe.
54/B4 Katrine, Loch (lake), Sc,UK
157/H6 Katsepe, Madg.
153/F4 Katshi, Zaire
91/G3 Katsikás, Gre.
145/G3 Katsina, Nga.
145/G3 Katsina (state), Nga.
145/H5 Katsina Ala (riv.), Camr., Nga.
145/H5 Katsina Ala, Nga.
111/L9 Katsura (riv.), Japan
110/D3 Katsuragi, Japan
111/L10 Katsuragi-san (peak), Japan
111/G2 Katsuta, Japan
111/G3 Katsuura, Japan
110/E2 Katsuyama, Japan
62/D3 Kattegat (str.), Den., Swe.
145/E4 Katua, Gha.
149/F2 Katul (mtn.), Sudan
155/G1 Katumbi, Malw.
114/E1 Katun' (riv.), Rus.
114/E1 Katun'chuya (riv.), Rus.
154/E3 Katundu, Zam.
121/F3 Kātūria, India
155/F1 Katuta Kampemba, Zam.
121/G4 Kātwa, India
153/G2 Katwa, Zaire
153/G3 Katwe, Ugan.
66/B4 Katwijk aan Zee, Neth.
70/B4 Katzenbach (riv.), Ger.
70/C4 Katzenbuckel (peak), Ger.
70/A2 Katzenelnbogen, Ger.
70/E2 Katzhütte, Ger.
69/F3 Katzwinkel, Ger.
180/S10 Kauai (chan.), Hi,US
139/K2 Kauai (isl.), Hi,US
180/S9 Kauai (isl.), Hi,US
154/D3 Kaudum (dry riv.), Namb.
154/D3 Kaudum Game Park, Namb.
81/G2 Kaufbeuren, Ger.
70/D6 Kaufering, Ger.
189/F1 Kaufman, Tx,US
188/L7 Kaufman (co.), Tx,US
67/G6 Kaufungen, Ger.
63/L3 Kauhajoki, Fin.
61/G3 Kauhanevan-Pohjankankaan Nat'l Park, Fin.
61/G3 Kauhava, Fin.
180/U10 Kauhola (pt.), Hi,US
180/U10 Kauiki Head (pt.), Hi,US
193/K1 Kaukauna, Wi,US
154/B3 Kaukaveld (mts.), Namb.
139/L6 Kaukura (atoll), FrPol.
180/R9 Kaulakahi (chan.), Hi,US
155/F2 Kaulashishi (hill), Zam.
71/E1 Kaulsdorf, Ger.
180/T10 Kaumalapau, Hi,US
153/F5 Kaumba, Zaire
180/U11 Kauna (pt.), Hi,US
180/T10 Kaunakakai, Hi,US
63/K4 Kaunas, Lith.
63/K4 Kaunas (int'l arpt.), Lith.
65/M1 Kaunas (int'l arpt.), Lith.
63/L4 Kaunas (res.), Lith.
145/G3 Kaura Namoda, Nga.
151/B1 Kauro, Kenya
93/J2 Kaushany, Mol.
61/G1 Kautokeino, Nor.
63/K1 Kauttua, Fin.
123/B4 Kau-ye (isl.), Burma
92/F5 Kavadarci, Macd.
91/F2 Kavajë, Alb.
104/E2 Kavakbaşı, Turk.
91/J2 Kavála, Gre.
109/M3 Kavalerovo, Rus.
118/C5 Kāvali, India
138/C4 Kavangel (isls.), Palau
154/C3 Kavango (riv.), Namb.
105/H4 Kavār, Iran
181/B5 Kavaratti, India
93/J4 Kavarna, Bul.
63/L4 Kavarskas, Lith.
138/E5 Kavieng, PNG
154/E3 Kavimba, Bots.
105/H4 Kavīr-e Bāfq (salt depr.), Iran
105/J3 Kavīr-e Namak (salt depr.), Iran
63/U9 Kävlinge, Swe.
166/C1 Kaw, FrG.
191/F2 Kaw (dam), Ok,US
191/F2 Kaw (lake), Ok,US
116/C5 Kawa, Burma
147/F5 Kawa (ruins), Sudan
112/B4 Kawabe, Japan
111/J7 Kawachi, Japan
111/L10 Kawachi-Nagano, Japan
111/M10 Kawage, Japan
111/F3 Kawagoe, Japan
111/H7 Kawagoe, Japan
111/M9 Kawagoe, Japan
111/F3 Kawaguchi, Japan
180/R10 Kawaihoa (pt.), Hi,US
180/S9 Kawaikini (peak), Hi,US
149/F4 Kawajena, Sudan
111/H7 Kawajima, Japan
111/L10 Kawakami, Japan
111/G2 Kawamata, Japan
153/G5 Kawambwa, Zam.
154/E2 Kawana, Zam.
111/L10 Kawanishi, Japan
120/C4 Kawardha, India
199/G2 Kawartha (lakes), On,Can
111/F3 Kawasaki, Japan
111/M9 Kawashima, Japan
191/F2 Kaw City, Ok,US
136/D2 Kawerau, N.Z.
136/C2 Kawhia, N.Z.
124/F4 Kawi (mtn.), Indo.
186/D2 Kawich (peak), Nv,US
127/E5 Kawinda, Indo.
150/B2 Kawkabān, Yem.
116/C5 Kawkareik, Burma
116/B4 Kawlin, Burma
123/B2 Kawludo, Burma
147/G3 Kawm Umbū, Egypt
123/B3 Kawsaing, Burma
123/B4 Kawthaung, Burma
114/D3 Kax (riv.), China
114/C3 Kaxgar (riv.), China
177/L2 Kay (pt.), Yk,Can
95/M4 Kay, Rus.
145/E4 Kaya, Burk.
113/E5 Kaya, SKor.
104/C2 Kayadibi, Turk.
148/B4 Kayagangiri (peak), CAfr.
123/B2 Kayah (state), Burma
122/G4 Kāyalpatnam, India
155/E2 Kayamba (hills), Zam.
127/E3 Kayan (riv.), Indo.
144/B3 Kayanga (riv.), Sen.
122/F4 Kāyankulam, India
144/A3 Kayar, Sen.
127/F4 Kayasa, Indo.
113/D4 Kaya-san (mtn.), SKor.
113/E5 Kaya-san Nat'l Park, SKor.
122/F4 Kayattār, India
185/K2 Kaycee, Wy,US
153/E5 Kayembe-Mukulu, Zaire
187/G2 Kayenta, Az,US
144/C3 Kayes, Mali
144/C3 Kayes (reg.), Mali
123/B2 Kayin (Karan) (state), Burma
69/F5 Kayl, Lux.
93/K5 Kaymaz, Turk.
72/C6 Kayna, Ger.
93/J5 Kaynarca, Turk.
93/K5 Kaynaşlı, Turk.
127/G3 Kayoa (isl.), Indo.
97/H2 Kaysatskoye, Rus.
166/B2 Kayser (mts.), Sur.
104/E2 Kayser (dam), Turk.
104/C2 Kayseri, Turk.
104/C2 Kayseri (prov.), Turk.
80/D1 Kaysersberg, Fr.
185/H3 Kaysville, Ut,US
133/G2 Kaytej Abor. Land, Austl.
124/D3 Kayuagung, Indo.
194/B3 Kayville, Sk,Can
100/J3 Kayyerkan, Rus.
99/M2 Kazachka, Rus.
99/J2 Kazach'ya Lopan', Ukr.
97/H4 Kazakh, Azer.
114/B2 Kazakh (uplands), Kaz.
100/G5 Kazakhstan
178/F2 Kazan (riv.), NW,Can
53/H3 Kazan', Rus.
95/L5 Kazan (int'l arpt.), Rus.
103/C1 Kazancı, Turk.
97/K5 Kazandzhik, Trkm.
99/G4 Kazanka, Ukr.
104/D1 Kazanlı, Turk.
93/G4 Kazanlŭk, Bul.
99/L3 Kazanskaya, Rus.
99/L5 Kazanskaya, Rus.
99/H5 Kazantip (cape), Ukr.
98/E3 Kazatin, Ukr.
145/H3 Kazaure, Nga.
97/H4 Kazbegi, Geo.
97/H4 Kazbek (peak), Geo.
105/G4 Kāzerūn, Iran
95/L3 Kazhim, Rus.
97/J4 Kazi-Magomed, Azer.
65/L3 Kazimierza Wielka, Pol.
104/C2 Kâzımkarabekir, Turk.
92/E1 Kazincbarcika, Hun.
116/B3 Kaziranga Nat'l Park, India
153/E5 Kaziza, Zaire
63/K4 Kazlų Rūda, Lith.
97/J2 Kaztalovka, Kaz.
154/E3 Kazuma Pan Nat'l Park, Zim.
153/E4 Kazumba, Zaire
112/B3 Kazuno, Japan
97/L5 Kazy, Trkm.
71/G4 Kdyně, Czh.
91/J4 Kéa, Gre.
91/J4 Kéa (isl.), Gre.
180/U11 Keaau, Hi,US
189/H1 Keachi, La,US
58/B3 Keady, NI,UK
180/T11 Keahole (pt.), Hi,US
187/G3 Keams Canyon, Az,US
180/T10 Keanapapa (pt.), Hi,US
207/D3 Keansburg, NJ,US
199/G2 Kearney, On,Can
192/E3 Kearney, Ne,US
56/C3 Kearny (pt.), NI,UK
187/G4 Kearny, Az,US
207/D2 Kearny, NJ,US
205/E5 Kearsley (cr.), Mi,US
191/F1 Keats, Ks,US
200/E2 Keavy, Ky,US
180/T10 Keawakapu, Hi,US
180/U11 Keawekaheka (pt.), Hi,US
104/D2 Keban, Turk.
104/D2 Keban (dam), Turk.
144/A3 Kébémer, Sen.
61/F2 Kebnekaise (peak), Swe.
150/C4 K'ebri Dehar, Eth.
124/E4 Kebumen, Indo.
92/D2 Kecel, Hun.
104/B2 Keçiborlu, Turk.
92/D2 Kecskemét, Hun.
97/H4 Kedabek, Azer.
124/C1 Kedah (state), Malay.
63/K4 Kėdainiai, Lith.
69/F5 Kédange-sur Canner, Fr.
196/D2 Kedgwick, NB,Can
196/D2 Kedgwick Game Ref., NB,Can
124/F4 Kediri, Indo.
109/K2 Kedong, China
144/B3 Kédougou, Sen.
65/K3 Kędzierzyn-Koźle, Pol.
182/D2 Keefers, BC,Can
205/F6 Keego Harbor, Mi,US
178/D2 Keele (riv.), NW,Can
178/C2 Keele (peak), Yk,Can
194/B2 Keeler, Sk,Can
186/D2 Keeler, Ca,US
117/J3 Keelung, Tai.
54/D3 Keen (mtn.), Sc,UK
186/C3 Keene, Ca,US
199/K3 Keene, NH,US
189/F1 Keene, Tx,US
146/C5 Ké, Enneri (dry riv.), Chad
135/D1 Keepit (dam), Austl.
130/C3 Keep River Nat'l Park, Austl.
134/A1 Keer-weer (cape), Austl.
194/D2 Keeseekoose Ind. Res., Sk,Can
156/B2 Keetmanshoop, Namb.
195/G3 Keewatin, On,Can
195/H4 Keewatin, Mn,US
135/C2 Keewong, Austl.
149/H4 Kefa (reg.), Eth.
91/G3 Kefallinía (isl.), Gre.
130/B2 Kefamenanu, Indo.
103/F7 Kefar Sava, Isr.
103/F7 Kefar Vitkin, Isr.
145/G4 Keffi, Nga.
145/H3 Keffin Hausa, Nga.
61/M7 Keflavík, Ice.
61/M7 Keflavík (int'l arpt.), Ice.
149/H2 K'eftya, Eth.
119/J5 Ke Ga (cape), Viet.
118/D6 Kegalla, SrL.
57/G6 Kegworth, Eng,UK
69/G6 Kehl, Ger.
63/L2 Kehra, Est.
80/D4 Kehrsatz, Swi.
123/B1 Ke-hsi Mānsām, Burma
57/G4 Keighley, Eng,UK
111/L9 Keihoku, Japan
63/L2 Keila, Est.
135/F5 Keilor, Austl.
60/A6 Keimaneigh (pass), Ire.
156/C3 Keimoes, SAfr.
153/F3 Keisha, Zaire
145/G3 Keïta, Niger
148/C3 Kéita, Bahr (riv.), Chad
135/B3 Keith, Austl.
130/C2 Keith (cape), Austl.
54/D1 Keith, Sc,UK
182/D1 Keithley Creek, BC,Can
189/H1 Keithville, La,US
184/B1 Keizer, Or,US
196/E3 Kejimkujik Nat'l Park, NS,Can
180/S10 Kekaha, Hi,US
92/D2 Kékes (peak), Hun.
150/C4 K'elafo, Eth.
115/B3 Kelan, China
120/A2 Kelān Devī, India
127/G4 Kelang (isl.), Indo.
124/C2 Kelang, Malay.
124/C1 Kelantan (riv.), Malay.
124/C1 Kelantan (state), Malay.
105/F1 Kel'badzhar, Azer.
69/F3 Kelberg, Ger.
72/B5 Kelbra, Ger.
91/G2 Këlcyrë, Alb.
145/H3 Kélé-Kélé, Niger
149/G4 Kelem, Eth.
96/D5 Keles, Turk.
71/E5 Kelheim, Ger.
127/J4 Kelila, Indo.
105/G3 Kelīshād, Iran
70/D2 Kelkheim, Ger.
104/D1 Kelkit, Turk.
104/D1 Kelkit (riv.), Turk.
69/F4 Kell, Ger.
152/C3 Kellé, Congo
66/D5 Kellen, Ger.
62/D4 Kellenhusen, Ger.
178/D2 Keller (lake), NW,Can
204/C2 Keller (peak), Ca,US
189/F1 Keller, Tx,US
132/C4 Kellerberrin, Austl.
190/D3 Kellerville, Tx,US
178/D1 Kellett (cape), NW,Can
198/E4 Kelleys (isl.), Oh,US
194/C2 Kelliher, Sk,Can
195/G4 Kelliher, Mn,US
193/H3 Kellogg, Ia,US
182/F4 Kellogg, Id,US
56/B2 Kells, NI,UK
189/E3 Kelly A.F.B., Tx,US
195/H4 Kelly Lake, Mn,US
194/F4 Kellys Slough Nat'l Wild. Ref., ND,US
63/K4 Kelmė, Lith.
98/D3 Kel'mentsy, Ukr.
140/D4 Kélo, Chad
182/E3 Kelowna, BC,Can
57/F5 Kelsall, Eng,UK
58/A6 Kelsey Head (pt.), UK
184/B4 Kelseyville, Ca,US
194/D3 Kelso, Sk,Can
54/D5 Kelso, Sc,UK
186/E3 Kelso, Ca,US
182/C4 Kelso, Wa,US
70/B2 Kelsterbach, Ger.
117/F4 Kelu, China
124/C2 Keluang, Malay.
59/G3 Kelvedon, Eng,UK
195/K3 Kelvin (isl.), On,Can
194/C1 Kelvington, Sk,Can
120/A3 Kelwāra, India
150/D3 Kelyexeed, Som.
94/G2 Kem', Rus.
94/G2 Kem' (riv.), Rus.
125/A4 Kemabong, Malay.
144/D3 Ké Macina, Mali
104/D2 Kemah, Turk.
189/M9 Kemah, Tx,US
104/D2 Kemaliye, Turk.
104/E1 Kemalpaşa, Turk.
124/C1 Kemasik, Malay.
148/C3 Kémata I, Chad
81/H3 Kematen in Tirol, Aus.
148/D4 Kembé, CAfr.
72/C4 Kemberg, Ger.
58/D3 Kemble, Eng,UK
149/H3 Kembolcha, Eth.
80/D2 Kembs, Fr.
92/E1 Kemecse, Hun.
126/D3 Kemena (riv.), Malay.
73/C3 Kemence, Hun.
103/B1 Kemer, Turk.
105/M6 Kemerburgaz, Turk.
104/C2 Kemerhisar, Turk.
100/J4 Kemerovo, Rus.
61/H2 Kemi, Fin.
61/H2 Kemijärvi, Fin.
61/H2 Kemijoki (riv.), Fin.
68/B2 Kemmel, Belg.
185/H3 Kemmerer, Wy,US
71/E3 Kemnath, Ger.
54/D2 Kemnay, Sc,UK
148/C4 Kémo-Gribingui (pref.), CAfr.
137/W Kemp (pen.), Ant.
191/F4 Kemp, Ok,US
189/F1 Kemp, Tx,US
190/E4 Kemp (lake), Tx,US
144/D3 Kemparana, Mali
61/H2 Kempele, Fin.
66/D6 Kempen, Ger.
69/G3 Kempenich, Ger.
66/C6 Kempenland (reg.), Belg.
66/B6 Kempisch (can.), Belg.
135/E1 Kempsey, Austl.
195/K5 Kempster, Wi,US
59/F2 Kempston, Eng,UK
81/G2 Kempten, Ger.
135/C4 Kempton, Austl.
156/E2 Kempton Park, SAfr.
206/A5 Kemptown, Md,US
199/J2 Kemptville, On,Can
120/B1 Kemri, India
127/E3 Kemul (peak), Indo.
120/C3 Ken (riv.), India
143/E3 Kenadsa, Alg.
177/H3 Kenai, Ak,US
177/H3 Kenai Fjords Nat'l Park, Ak,US
177/H3 Kenai Nat'l Wild. Ref., Ak,US
149/G4 Kenamuke (swamp), Sudan
201/J3 Kenansville, NC,US
194/A2 Kenaston, Sk,Can
201/H2 Kenbridge, Va,US
124/E4 Kendal, Indo.
57/F3 Kendal, Eng,UK
135/E1 Kendall, Austl.
202/P8 Kendall, Fl,US
203/H5 Kendall, Fl,US
205/P16 Kendall (co.), Il,US
206/D3 Kendall Park, NJ,US
198/D4 Kendallville, In,US
127/F4 Kendari, Indo.
91/J2 Kéndavros, Gre.
148/C3 Kèndégué, Chad
66/D5 Kendel (riv.), Neth., Ger.
189/G3 Kendleton, Tx,US
118/E3 Kendrāpāra, India
187/G3 Kendrick (peak), Az,US
203/G3 Kendrick, Fl,US
182/F4 Kendrick, Id,US
151/A2 Kendu Bay, Kenya
196/C3 Kenduskeag, Me,US
144/D4 Kénédougou (prov.), Burk.
189/F3 Kenedy, Tx,US
195/K4 Keneenaw (pen.), Mi,US
189/G2 Kenefick, Tx,US
194/D5 Kenel, SD,US
144/C5 Kenema, SLeo.
192/E3 Kenesaw, Ne,US
116/E5 Keng Deng, Laos
152/C4 Kenge, Zaire
152/D4 Kenge, Zaire
123/B1 Keng Hkam, Burma
123/B1 Kēng Tung, Burma
156/C3 Kenhardt, SAfr.
206/C3 Kenhorst, Pa,US
144/C3 Kéniéba, Mali
144/C3 Kénié-Baoulé Rsv., Mali
59/E2 Kenilworth, Eng,UK
207/H9 Kenilworth, NJ,US
185/H4 Kenilworth, Ut,US
125/B4 Keningau, Malay.
141/L3 Kenitra, Mor.
115/D3 Kenli, China
56/D1 Ken, Loch (lake), Sc,UK
201/H3 Kenly, NC,US
60/A6 Kenmare, Ire.
60/A6 Kenmare (riv.), Ire.
194/D3 Kenmare, ND,US
134/C4 Kenmore, Austl.
54/C3 Kenmore, Sc,UK
197/T10 Kenmore, NY,US
205/C2 Kenmore, Wa,US
129/K4 Kenn (reef), Austl.
69/F4 Kenn, Ger.
190/C4 Kenna, NM,US
192/A3 Kennaday (peak), Wy,US
189/G2 Kennard, Tx,US
196/C3 Kennebec (riv.), Me,US
192/E2 Kennebec, SD,US
196/B4 Kennebunk, Me,US
188/K7 Kennedale, Tx,US
132/B3 Kennedy (range), Austl.
179/T6 Kennedy (chan.), NW,Can
194/C2 Kennedy, Sk,Can
177/K4 Kennedy (str.), Ak,US
200/D4 Kennedy, Al,US
194/F3 Kennedy, Mn,US
207/E2 Kennedy, John F. (int'l arpt.)
203/H3 Kennedy Space Ctr., Fl,US
206/C5 Kennedyville, Md,US
81/F3 Kennelbach, Aus.
66/B4 Kennemerduinen Nat'l Park, Neth.
202/C3 Kenner, La,US
201/L6 Kennesaw, Ga,US
200/E4 Kennesaw Mtn. Nat'l Bfld. Park, Ga,US
201/L7 Kennesaw Mtn. Nat'l Bfld. Park, Ga,US
58/D4 Kennet (can.), Eng,UK
59/E4 Kennet (riv.), Eng,UK
202/K8 Kenneth City, Fl,US
200/B2 Kennett, Mo,US
206/C4 Kennett Square, Pa,US
182/E4 Kennewick, Wa,US
195/M2 Kenogami (riv.), On,Can
177/L3 Keno Hill, Yk,Can
195/G3 Kenora, On,Can
205/Q14 Kenosha, Wi,US
205/P14 Kenosha (co.), Wi,US
194/E4 Kensal, ND,US
191/J3 Kensett, Ar,US
207/K7 Kensico (res.), NY,US
196/F2 Kensington, PE,Can
208/B2 Kensington, Ct,US
190/E1 Kensington, Ks,US
195/G5 Kensington, Mn,US
208/G6 Kensington, Oh,US
53/N7 Kensington & Chelsea (bor.), Eng,UK
152/C3 Kenstsèle, Congo
178/F2 Kent (pen.), NW,Can
205/H7 Kent (co.), On,Can
53/P8 Kent (co.), Eng,UK
57/F3 Kent (riv.), Eng,UK
208/A2 Kent, Ct,US
206/C5 Kent (co.), De,US
206/C5 Kent (co.), Md,US
206/B6 Kent (isl.), Md,US
206/B6 Kent (pt.), Md,US
205/E6 Kent (lake), Mi,US
208/F5 Kent, Oh,US
184/C1 Kent, Or,US
208/C2 Kent (co.), RI,US
158/D2 Kent, Tx,US
205/C3 Kent, Wa,US
114/A3 Kentau, Kaz.
135/C3 Kent Group (isls.), Austl.
117/J4 Kenting Nat'l Park, Tai.
198/C4 Kentland, In,US
194/D3 Kenton, Mb,Can
206/C5 Kenton, De,US
198/B1 Kenton, Mi,US
198/E4 Kenton, Oh,US
190/C2 Kenton, Ok,US
200/C2 Kenton, Tn,US
200/E2 Kentucky (state), US
200/C2 Kentucky (dam), Ky,US
200/E1 Kentucky (riv.), Ky,US
200/C2 Kentucky (lake), Ky, Tn,US
201/F2 Kentucky, Middle Fork (riv.), Ky,US
200/F2 Kentucky, North Fork (riv.), Ky,US
59/G4 Kent, Vale of (val.), Eng,UK
196/E3 Kentville, NS,Can
202/C2 Kentwood, La,US
198/D3 Kentwood, Mi,US
194/D2 Kenville, Mb,Can
206/D2 Kenvil-Succasunna, NJ,US
56/D1 Ken, Water of (riv.), Sc,UK
201/M7 Kenwood, Ga,US
140/F4 Kenya
193/H1 Kenyon, Mn,US
208/C3 Kenyon, RI,US
111/H7 Ken-zaki (pt.), Japan
80/D1 Kenzingen, Ger.
193/J3 Keokuk, Ia,US
183/H2 Keoma, Ab,Can
120/C4 Keonchi, India
118/E3 Keonjhar, India
193/J3 Keosauqua, Ia,US
193/J3 Keota, Ia,US
201/F3 Keowee (dam), SC,US
201/F3 Keowee (lake), SC,US
94/G2 Kepa, Rus.
124/C3 Kepahiang, Indo.
131/E1 Kepi, Indo.
92/D5 Kep i Rodonit (cape), Alb.
65/J3 Kępno, Pol.
134/C3 Keppel Sands, Austl.
104/B2 Kepsut, Turk.
122/F3 Kerala (state), India
135/B2 Kerang, Austl.
145/F4 Kéran Nat'l Park, Togo
149/H4 Keranyu, Eth.
91/H4 Keratéa, Gre.
99/J5 Kerch' (str.), Rus., Ukr.
53/G4 Kerch', Ukr.
99/H5 Kerch' (pen.), Ukr.
145/F2 Kerchouel, Mali
78/B6 Kerdonis, Pointe de (pt.), Fr.
131/G1 Kerema, PNG
182/E3 Keremeos, BC,Can
104/C1 Kerempe (pt.), Turk.
96/E4 Kerempe Burnu (pt.), Turk.
149/H2 Keren, Eth.
189/F1 Kerens, Tx,US
94/G2 Keret', Rus.
94/G2 Keret' (lake), Rus.
144/A3 Kerewan, Gam.
51/N8 Kerguélen (isl.), FrAnt.
199/J4 Kerhonkson, NY,US
151/A2 Kericho, Kenya
149/G2 Keri Kera, Sudan
136/C1 Kerikeri (cape), N.Z.
124/C3 Kerinci (peak), Indo.
151/B1 Kerio (dry riv.), Kenya
151/A1 Kerio Valley Nat'l Rsv., Kenya
114/D4 Keriya (riv.), China
114/D4 Keriya Shankou (pass), China
73/A6 Kerka (riv.), Hun.
66/C5 Kerkdriel, Neth.
149/H1 Kerkebet, Eth.
66/D6 Kerken, Ger.
195/G5 Kerkhoven, Mn,US
100/G6 Kerki, Trkm.
91/H2 Kerkinis (lake), Gre.
91/F3 Kérkira (Corfu), Gre.
91/F3 Kérkira (Corfu) (isl.), Gre.
69/F2 Kerkrade, Neth.
66/C5 Kerkwijk, Neth.
191/H3 Kerlin, Ar,US
78/A3 Kerlouan, Fr.
138/G7 Kermadec (isls.), N.Z.
105/J4 Kermān, Iran
105/J4 Kermān (gov.), Iran
186/B2 Kerman, Ca,US
93/H4 Kermen, Bul.
188/C2 Kermit, Tx,US
186/C3 Kern (riv.), Ca,US
201/G2 Kernersville, NC,US
186/C3 Kern-Friant (can.), Ca,US
81/E4 Kerns, Swi.
186/C3 Kernville, Ca,US
124/C1 Keroh, Malay.
91/F3 Kéros (isl.), Gre.
145/F4 Kérou, Ben.
144/C4 Kérouané, Gui.
131/G1 Kerowagi, PNG
69/F2 Kerpen, Ger.
183/G4 Kerr (dam), Mt,US
201/H2 Kerr, John H. (res.), NC, Va,US
183/K2 Kerrobert, Sk,Can
191/G3 Kerr, Robert S. (lake), Ok,US
188/E2 Kerrville, Tx,US
60/A5 Kerry (co.), Ire.
58/C2 Kerry, Wal,UK
150/B3 K'ersa, Eth.
199/G4 Kersey, Pa,US
182/C1 Kersley, BC,Can
141/N13 Kert (riv.), Mor.
108/G2 Kerulen (riv.), China, Mong.
78/B5 Kervignac, Fr.
143/E3 Kerzaz, Alg.
69/H4 Kerzenheim, Ger.
80/D4 Kerzers, Swi.
121/G4 Kesabpur, Bang.
93/H5 Keşan, Turk.
81/F4 Kesch, Piz (peak), Swi.
112/B4 Kesen'numa, Japan
59/H2 Kesgrave, Eng,UK
109/K2 Keshan, China
193/K1 Keshena, Wi,US
195/K5 Keshena (falls), Wi,US
118/B3 Keshod, India
104/C2 Keskin, Turk.
61/H3 Keski-Suomi (prov.), Fin.
70/D5 Kesselbach (riv.), Ger.
59/H2 Kessingland, Eng,UK
104/B1 Kestel, Turk.
94/F2 Kesten'ga, Rus.
66/C5 Kesteren, Neth.
57/E2 Keswick, Eng,UK
73/B6 Keszthely, Hun.
73/B6 Keszthelyi hegy (hill), Hun.
100/J4 Ket' (riv.), Rus.
145/F5 Keta, Gha.
100/K2 Keta (riv.), Rus.
124/D4 Ketapang, Indo.
124/D3 Ketaun, Indo.
177/M4 Ketchikan, Ak,US
185/F2 Ketchum, Id,US
148/B4 Kété, Camr.
145/E5 Kete Krachi, Gha.
66/C3 Ketelmeer (lake), Neth.
145/F5 Kétou, Ben.
65/L1 Kętrzyn, Pol.
70/B4 Ketsch, Ger.
152/C2 Ketta, Congo
59/F2 Kettering, Eng,UK
198/D5 Kettering, Oh,US
182/E3 Kettle (riv.), BC,Can, Wa,US
198/E3 Kettle (pt.), On,Can
195/H4 Kettle (riv.), Mn,US
182/E3 Kettle Falls, Wa,US
186/C2 Kettleman City, Ca,US
205/P14 Kettle Moraine St. Park, Wi,US
195/H4 Kettle River, Mn,US
182/E3 Kettle River (range), Wa,US
57/F3 Kettlewell, Eng,UK
72/C3 Ketzin, Ger.
124/A1 Ketudeunom, Indo.
199/H3 Keuka (lake), NY,US
199/H3 Keuka Park, NY,US
66/B4 Keukenhof, Neth.
144/A2 Keur Massène, Mrta.
61/H3 Keuruu, Fin.
145/F5 Kévé, Togo
66/D3 Kevelaer, Ger.
183/J3 Kevin, Mt,US
162/C2 Kew, Trks.
193/K3 Kewanee, Il,US
198/C4 Kewanna, In,US
198/B3 Kewaskum, Wi,US
193/L1 Kewaunee, Wi,US
195/K4 Keweenaw (bay), Mi,US
195/L4 Keweenaw (pt.), Mi,US
53/N7 Kew Gardens, Eng,UK
149/H4 K'ey Āfer, Eth.
192/E2 Keya Paha (riv.), Ne, SD,US
202/P8 Key Biscayne, Fl,US
186/B2 Keyes, Ca,US
114/D3 Keyi, China
194/C2 Key Ind. Res., The, Sk,Can
203/H5 Key Largo, Fl,US
203/H5 Key Largo (key), Fl,US
130/C3 Keyling (inlet), Austl.
60/B1 Key, Lough (lake), Ire.
206/A4 Keymar, Md,US
58/D4 Keynsham, Eng,UK
207/D3 Keyport, NJ,US
205/B2 Keyport, Wa,US
201/H1 Keyser, WV,US
202/K7 Keystone (lake), Fl,US
191/F2 Keystone (dam), Ok,US
191/F2 Keystone (lake), Ok,US
203/G3 Keystone Heights, Fl,US
201/H2 Keysville, Va,US
191/H1 Keytesville, Mo,US
105/G3 Keytū, Iran
203/H5 Key West, Fl,US
203/H5 Key West (int'l arpt.), Fl,US
203/G5 Key West Nat'l Wild. Ref., Fl,US
203/H5 Key West Nav. Air Sta., Fl,US
57/G6 Keyworth, Eng,UK
155/F4 Kezi, Zim.
65/L4 Kežmarok, Slvk.
154/D5 Kgalagadi (dist.), Bots.
154/E5 Kgatleng (dist.), Bots.
154/D4 Kgwebe (hills), Bots.
150/C3 Khaanziir, Ras (cape), Som.
95/M2 Khabarikha, Rus.
109/M2 Khabarovsk, Rus.
97/J4 Khachmas, Azer.
149/E3 Khadari, Wādī Al (dry riv.), Sudan
116/B5 Khadaungnge (peak), Burma
99/K5 Khadyzhensk, Rus.
106/E3 Khafjī, Ra's al, SAr.
121/F3 Khagaria, India
121/H4 Khagrāchari, Bang.
120/A2 Khair, India
120/C2 Khairābād, India
107/J3 Khairpur, Pak.
97/G4 Khaishi, Geo.
121/F3 Khajuri, India
154/D5 Khakhea, Bots.
91/H3 Khalándrion, Gre.
120/D2 Khalīlābād, India
105/G2 Khalkhāl, Iran
91/H2 Khalkhidhikhí (pen.), Gre.
91/H2 Khalkidhón, Gre.
91/H3 Khalkís, Gre.
107/G4 Khalūf, Oman
108/E1 Khamar-Daban (mts.), Rus.
120/C4 Khamaria, India
107/J4 Khambaliya, India
118/C3 Khāmgaon, India
106/D5 Khamīs Mushayt, SAr.
123/D2 Khamkeut, Laos
123/D3 Kham Khuan Kaeo, Thai.
118/D4 Khammam, India
150/B2 Khamr, Yem.
154/B4 Khan (dry riv.), Namb.
107/J1 Khānābād, Afg.
103/E3 Khān Abū Shāmāt, Syria
105/F3 Khānaqīn, Iraq
105/H2 Khān Behbīn, Iran
121/F2 Khāndbāri, Nepal
118/C3 Khandwa, India
101/P3 Khandyga, Rus.
122/A2 Khānewāl, Pak.
122/B2 Khāngāh Dogrān, Pak.
91/J5 Khaniá, Gre.
109/L3 Khanka (lake), Rus.
120/A3 Khānkar, India
108/E1 Khankh, Mong.
97/H4 Khanlar, Azer.
122/D2 Khanna, India
95/P2 Khanovey, Rus.
107/K3 Khānpur, Pak.
103/E2 Khān Shaykhūn, Syria
99/K5 Khanskaya, Rus.
114/B3 Khantau, Kaz.
100/G3 Khanty-Mansiysk, Rus.
100/G3 Khanty-Mansiysk Aut. Okr., Rus.
103/D4 Khān Yūnus, Gaza
123/C3 Khao Chamao-Khao Wong Nat'l Park, Thai.
123/C3 Khao Khitchakut Nat'l Park, Thai.
123/B3 Khao Laem (res.), Thai.
123/B3 Khao Sam Roi Yot Nat'l Park, Thai.
123/C3 Khao Wong-Khao Chamao Nat'l Park, Thai.
123/C3 Khao Yai Nat'l Park, Thai.
108/G2 Khapcheranga, Rus.
97/H3 Kharabali, Rus.
121/F3 Kharagpur, India
121/F4 Kharagpur, India
122/A1 Kharak, Pak.
107/J3 Khārān, Pak.
105/H3 Kharānoq, Iran
121/F4 Kharar, India
122/D2 Kharar, India
103/D4 Kharās, WBnk.
118/B2 Kharbara, India
103/G8 Kharbatā, WBnk.
118/C3 Khargon, India
122/B1 Khāriān, Pak.
147/F3 Khārijah, Al Wāḥāt al (oasis), Egypt
147/G3 Kharīt, Wādī al (dry riv.), Egypt
105/G4 Khārk (isl.), Iran
53/G4 Khar'kov, Ukr.
99/J3 Kharkov (int'l arpt.), Ukr.
99/H3 Khar'kov Obl., Ukr.
94/H1 Kharlovka, Rus.
93/G5 Kharmanli, Bul.
94/J4 Kharovsk, Rus.
141/M13 Kharrour (riv.), Mor.
120/D5 Kharsia, India
149/G2 Khartoum (int'l arpt.), Sudan
149/G1 Khartoum (reg.), Sudan
149/G2 Khartoum (Al Khurṭūm) (cap.), Sudan
149/G2 Khartoum North (Al Khurṭūm Baḥrī), Sudan
151/A2 Kharumwa, Tanz.
105/J2 Kharv-e 'Olyā, Iran
109/L3 Khasan, Rus.
97/H4 Khasavyurt, Rus.
105/J3 Khāsf, Iran
107/H2 Khāsh (riv.), Afg.
107/H3 Khāsh, Iran
149/G2 Khashm al Qirbah, Sudan
97/G4 Khashuri, Geo.
121/H3 Khasi (hills), India
93/G5 Khaskovo, Bul.
93/G5 Khaskovo (reg.), Bul.
101/L2 Khatanga, Rus.
101/L2 Khatanga (gulf), Rus.
101/L2 Khatanga (riv.), Rus.
120/A1 Khatauli, India
120/A4 Khātegaon, India
120/B1 Khatīma, India
103/C4 Khatmia (pass), Egypt
121/F4 Khātra, India
122/B1 Khaur, Pak.
107/J4 Khāvda, India
106/E6 Khawrah, Yem.
107/G3 Khawr Fakkān, UAE
106/D5 Khay', SAr.
147/H3 Khaybar, SAr.
107/G3 Khaymah, Ra's al, UAE
105/F3 Khazzān Darbandīkhān (res.), Iraq
105/F3 Khazzān Dūkān (res.), Iraq
149/G2 Khazzān Jabal Al Awliyā (White Nile) (dam), Sudan
120/A1 Khekra, India
97/G4 Khelvachauri, Geo.
141/S15 Khemis el Khechna, Alg.
141/S15 Khemis Miliana, Alg.
141/L14 Khemisset, Mor.
122/C2 Khem Karan, India
123/D2 Khemmarat, Thai.
141/V18 Khenchela, Alg.
143/G2 Khenchela (wilaya), Alg.
142/D2 Khenifra, Mor.
105/H4 Kherāmeh, Iran
120/C2 Kheri, India
120/A2 Kheria (arpt.), India
105/G4 Khersān (riv.), Iran
98/G4 Kherson, Ukr.
98/G4 Kherson (int'l arpt.), Ukr.
99/G5 Khersonesskiy (cape), Ukr.
99/H4 Kherson Obl., Ukr.
123/D2 Khe Sanh, Viet.
105/J3 Khezrī, Iran
63/N1 Khiitola, Rus.
108/G1 Khilok, Rus.
108/F1 Khilok (riv.), Rus.
91/K3 Khíos, Gre.
91/J3 Khíos (isl.), Gre.
121/F4 Khirpai, India
93/G4 Khisarya, Bul.
105/F1 Khiv, Rus.
100/G5 Khiva, Uzb.
93/H4 Khlebarovo, Bul.
93/K1 Khlevnoye, Rus.
123/B2 Khlong Khlung, Thai.
123/C3 Khlung, Thai.
98/D3 Khmel'nik, Ukr.
98/D3 Khmel'nitskiy, Ukr.
98/D3 Khmel'nitskiy Obl., Ukr.
97/G4 Khobi, Geo.
98/C3 Khodorov, Ukr.
95/M1 Khodovarikha, Rus.
100/F5 Khodzheyli, Uzb.
107/J2 Khojak (pass), Pak.
123/C3 Khok Samrong, Thai.
122/D1 Khoksar, India
107/J1 Kholm, Afg.
63/P3 Kholm, Rus.
94/J2 Kholmogorskaya, Rus.
94/J2 Kholmogory, Rus.
109/N2 Kholmsk, Rus.
155/G2 Kholombidzo (falls), Malw.
108/E1 Kholtoson, Rus.
105/G2 Khomām, Iran
154/C4 Khomas Hochland (mts.), Namb.
105/G3 Khomeyn, Iran
105/G3 Khomeynī shahr, Iran
99/H2 Khomutovka, Rus.
123/D3 Khong Chiam, Thai.
105/H5 Khonj, Iran
123/C2 Khon Kaen, Thai.
101/Q3 Khonuu, Rus.
99/M2 Khopër (riv.), Rus.
109/L2 Khor, Rus.
109/M2 Khor (riv.), Rus.
150/B2 Khor Angar, Djib.
105/J3 Khorāsān (gov.), Iran
91/J5 Khóra Sfakíon, Gre.
95/N2 Khoreyver, Rus.
108/F1 Khorinsk, Rus.
89/K3 Khorion, Gre.
154/B4 Khorixas, Namb.
151/C1 Khorof Harar, Kenya
114/B4 Khorog, Taj.
109/L3 Khorol', Rus.
99/G3 Khorol, Ukr.
105/G3 Khorramābād, Iran
105/G4 Khorramshahr, Iran
123/C2 Kho Sawai (plat.), Thai.
97/H3 Khosheutovo, Rus.
105/G4 Khosrowābād, Iran
105/F2 Khosrowshahr, Iran
98/D3 Khotin, Ukr.
94/H4 Khot'kovo, Rus.
177/G3 Khotol (mtn.), Ak,US
142/D2 Khouribga, Mor.
114/F1 Khovu-Aksy, Rus.
121/H3 Khowai, India
107/J2 Khowst, Afg.
98/E2 Khoyniki, Bela.
99/L2 Khrenovoye, Rus.
119/F3 Khreum, Burma
91/J2 Khrisoúpolis, Gre.
98/E3 Khristinovka, Ukr.
97/L2 Khromtau, Kaz.
91/J5 Khrysi (isl.), Gre.
123/C2 Khûan Ubon Ratana (res.), Thai.
97/H4 Khuchni, Rus.
97/J4 Khudat, Azer.
122/B2 Khudiān, Pak.
154/E4 Khudumelapye, Bots.
114/A3 Khudzhand, Taj.
106/D4 Khuff, SAr.
154/D5 Khuis, Bots.
123/D3 Khu Khan, Thai.
121/G4 Khulna, Bang.
121/G4 Khulna (dist.), Bang.
97/G4 Khulo, Geo.
107/L1 Khūnjerāb (pass), Pak.
121/E4 Khunti, India
123/B2 Khun Yuam, Thai.
120/B3 Khurai, India
118/E3 Khurda, India
120/A1 Khurja, India
105/J3 Khūsf, Iran
122/B1 Khushāb, Pak.
98/B3 Khust, Ukr.
120/C1 Khūtār, India
146/C2 Khuwaymah, Thimād al (well), Libya
149/F2 Khuwayy, Sudan
116/B3 Khūzami, India
107/J3 Khuzdār, Pak.
105/G4 Khūzestān (gov.), Iran
105/G4 Khūzestan, Jolgeh-ye (plain), Iran
109/L3 Khvalynka, Rus.
105/G3 Khvonsār, Iran
105/H3 Khvor, Iran
105/G4 Khvormūj, Iran
97/J1 Khvorostyanka, Rus.
105/F2 Khvoy, Iran
114/B5 Khyber (pass), Afg., Pak.
97/J4 Khyrdalan, Azer.
138/E5 Kia, Sol.
135/D2 Kiama, Austl.
152/D4 Kiama, Zaire
125/D4 Kiamba, Phil.
153/G4 Kiambi, Zaire
191/G3 Kiamichi (mts.), Ok,US
191/G3 Kiamichi (riv.), Ok,US
177/F2 Kiana, Ak,US
125/C1 Kiangan, Phil.
157/H7 Kiangara, Madg.
157/H8 Kianjavato, Madg.
91/H3 Kiáton, Gre.
62/C3 Kibæk, Den.
152/C4 Kibala, Ang.
153/G2 Kibali (riv.), Zaire
153/F4 Kibamba, Zaire
153/G4 Kibanga, Zaire
152/C3 Kibangou, Congo
107/L2 Kibar, India
151/A2 Kibara, Tanz.
151/A4 Kibau, Tanz.
125/D4 Kibawe, Phil.
151/B3 Kibaya, Tanz.
201/F4 Kibbee, Ga,US
57/G2 Kibblesworth, Eng,UK
151/B3 Kiberege, Tanz.
61/J1 Kibergneset (pt.), Nor.
145/E5 Kibi, Gha.
151/A2 Kibigori, Kenya
151/B3 Kibindu, Tanz.
152/D4 Kibinga, Zaire
151/B3 Kibiti, Tanz.
145/H4 Kibiya, Nga.
153/G2 Kiboga, Ugan.
151/B2 Kiboko, Kenya
153/F3 Kibombo Rive, Zaire
153/G3 Kibondo, Tanz.
151/B2 Kibongoto, Tanz.
150/A4 Kibre Mengist, Eth.
93/K5 Kıbrısçık, Turk.
153/G3 Kibungo, Rwa.
153/G2 Kibuye, Rwa.
153/G4 Kibwesa, Tanz.
151/B2 Kibwezi, Kenya
92/E5 Kičevo, Macd.
120/B1 Kichha, India
193/J2 Kickapoo (riv.), Wi,US
191/G1 Kickapoo Ind. Res., Ks,US
60/A6 Kid (mtn.), Ire.
145/F2 Kidal, Mali
127/G2 Kidapawan, Phil.
58/D2 Kidderminster, Eng,UK
153/H2 Kidepo Valley Nat'l Park, Ugan.
151/B3 Kidete, Tanz.
144/B3 Kidira, Sen.
136/D2 Kidnappers (cape), N.Z.
151/B3 Kidodi, Tanz.
208/F6 Kidron, Oh,US
57/F5 Kidsgrove, Eng,UK
151/B3 Kidugallo, Tanz.
58/B3 Kidwelly, Wal,UK
64/F1 Kiel (bay), Den., Ger.
64/F1 Kiel, Ger.
193/K2 Kiel, Wi,US
65/L3 Kielce, Pol.
65/L3 Kielce (prov.), Pol.
57/F1 Kielder, Eng,UK
57/F1 Kielder (res.), Eng,UK
66/B6 Kieldrecht, Belg.
144/E3 Kiémbara, Burk.
153/F5 Kiembe, Zaire
123/D1 Kien An, Viet.
123/D4 Kien Duc, Viet.
153/F5 Kienge, Zaire
123/D4 Kien Thanh, Viet.
67/E6 Kierspe, Ger.
193/H2 Kiester, Mn,US
138/E5 Kieta, PNG
98/F2 Kiev (Kiyev) (cap.), Ukr.
98/E2 Kiev Obl., Ukr.
144/C2 Kiffa, Mrta.
91/L6 Kifisiá, Gre.
105/F3 Kifrī, Iraq
153/F4 Kifusa, Zaire
152/D4 Kifwanzondo, Zaire
153/G3 Kigali (cap.), Rwa.
153/G3 Kigali (Gregoire Kayibanda) (int'l arpt.), Rwa.
151/A3 Kiganga, Tanz.
104/E2 Kiğı, Turk.
153/G4 Kigoma, Tanz.
153/G4 Kigoma (pol. reg.), Tanz.
113/E4 Kigye, SKor.
180/T10 Kihei, Hi,US
63/L2 Kihnu (isl.), Est.
180/U11 Kiholo, Hi,US
63/J1 Kihti (str.), Fin.
151/B4 Kihundo, Tanz.
151/B3 Kihurio, Tanz.
110/D4 Kii (chan.), Japan
110/D4 Kii (mts.), Japan
114/D3 Kiines (riv.), China
113/E5 Kijang, SKor.
151/B3 Kijungu, Tanz.
112/L6 Kikai (isl.), Japan
153/G3 Kikarara, Ugan.
180/R9 Kikepa (pt.), Hi,US
177/H2 Kikiktat (mtn.), Ak,US
92/E3 Kikinda, Yugo.
107/H3 Kikki, Pak.
135/C2 Kikoira, Austl.
151/A3 Kikombo, Tanz.
112/B3 Kikonai, Japan
131/G1 Kikori, PNG
186/F4 Kikori (riv.), PNG
152/D4 Kikwit, Zaire
62/E2 Kil, Swe.
61/G2 Kilafors, Swe.
151/B2 Kilaguni, Kenya
122/G4 Kilakarai, India
151/A2 Kilalo, Tanz.
160/E3 Kilambe (mtn.), Nic.
122/D1 Kilār, India
180/S9 Kilauea, Hi,US
54/B5 Kilbarchan, Sc,UK
60/C3 Kilbeggan, Ire.
60/D2 Kilberry, Ire.
54/B5 Kilbirnie, Sc,UK
189/J1 Kilbourne, La,US
54/A6 Kilbrannan (sound), Sc,UK
197/L2 Kilbride, Nf,Can
197/R9 Kilbride, On,Can
55/H8 Kilchoan, Sc,UK
113/E2 Kilchu, NKor.
60/D3 Kilcock, Ire.
60/A3 Kilcolgan (pt.), Ire.
60/B3 Kilconnell, Ire.
60/D3 Kilcoole, Ire.
60/C3 Kilcormac, Ire.
134/D4 Kilcoy, Austl.
54/B5 Kilcreggan, Sc,UK
60/B3 Kilcrow (riv.), Ire.
60/D3 Kilcullen, Ire.
196/F2 Kildare (cape), PE,Can
60/D3 Kildare, Ire.
60/D3 Kildare (co.), Ire.
189/G1 Kildare, Tx,US
205/P15 Kildeer, Il,US
61/K1 Kil'din (isl.), Rus.
155/F3 Kildonan, Zim.
60/B5 Kildorrery, Ire.
153/G2 Kilembe, Ugan.
152/D4 Kilembe, Zaire
60/A4 Kilfenora, Ire.
60/B5 Kilfinnane, Ire.
60/A6 Kilgarvan, Ire.
185/H1 Kilgore, Id,US
189/G1 Kilgore, Tx,US
151/A2 Kilgoris, Kenya
57/H3 Kilham, Eng,UK
179/R7 Kilian (isl.), NW,Can
151/B2 Kilifi, Kenya
122/F4 Kilikollūr, India
151/B2 Kilimanjaro (int'l arpt.), Tanz.
151/B2 Kilimanjaro (mtn.), Tanz.
151/B2 Kilimanjaro (prov.), Tanz.
151/B2 Kilimanjaro Nat'l Park, Tanz.
151/A3 Kilimatinde, Tanz.
93/K5 Kilimli, Turk.
151/B3 Kilindoni, Tanz.
63/L2 Kilingi-Nõmme, Est.
122/H4 Kilinochchi, SrL.
122/H4 Kilinochchi (dist.), SrL.
103/E1 Kilis, Turk.
98/E5 Kiliya, Ukr.
60/A4 Kilkee, Ire.
56/B3 Kilkeel, NI,UK

60/B2 Kilkelly, Ire.
60/C4 Kilkenny, Ire.
60/C4 Kilkenny (co.), Ire.
91/H2 Kilkís, Gre.
60/B4 Kilkishen, Ire.
134/D4 Kilkivan, Austl.
60/D3 Kill, Ire.
60/A4 Killadysert, Ire.
60/A1 Killala, Ire.
60/A1 Killala (bay), Ire.
60/B4 Killaloe, Ire.
199/H2 Killaloe Station, On,Can
183/J1 Killam, Ab,Can
57/G5 Killamarsh, Eng,UK
134/H8 Killara, Austl.
135/E1 Killarney, Austl.
194/E3 Killarney, Mb,Can
60/A5 Killarney, Ire.
60/C1 Killashandra, Ire.
60/B5 Killavullen, Ire.
208/F7 Killbuck, Oh,US
208/F6 Killbuck (cr.), Oh,US
194/A3 Killdeer, Sk,Can
194/C4 Killdeer, ND,US
194/C4 Killdeer Bfld., ND,US
201/K2 Kill Devil Hills, NC,US
60/C6 Killeagh, Ire.
54/B4 Killearn, Sc,UK
189/F2 Killeen, Tx,US
200/D3 Killen, Al,US
60/C4 Killenaule, Ire.
202/C2 Killian, La,US
54/C3 Killiecrankie (pass), Sc,UK
54/B4 Killin, Sc,UK
60/A4 Killinaboy, Ire.
56/C3 Killinchy, NI,UK
179/K2 Killinek (isl.), NW,Can
199/K3 Killington (peak), Vt,US
208/B3 Killingworth, Ct,US
91/G4 Killíni, Gre.
91/H4 Killíni (peak), Gre.
56/C3 Killough, NI,UK
60/C2 Killucan, Ire.
207/K8 Kill Van Kull (str.), NJ, NY,US
55/G9 Killybegs, Ire.
56/A2 Killyclogher, NI,UK
56/C3 Killyleagh, NI,UK
60/D3 Kilmacanoge, Ire.
54/B5 Kilmacolm, Sc,UK
60/C5 Kilmacow, Ire.
60/C5 Kilmacthomas, Ire.
60/C5 Kilmaganny, Ire.
60/B5 Kilmallock, Ire.
54/B5 Kilmarnock, Sc,UK
201/J2 Kilmarnock, Va,US
58/B5 Kilmar Tor (hill), Eng,UK
54/B5 Kilmaurs, Sc,UK
60/C5 Kilmeadan, Ire.
60/D4 Kilmichael (pt.), Ire.
60/A4 Kilmihill, Ire.
135/C3 Kilmore, Austl.
60/D5 Kilmore Quay, Ire.
60/A4 Kilmurry, Ire.
60/C2 Kilnaleck, Ire.
55/J8 Kilninver, Sc,UK
153/G2 Kilo, Zaire
151/B4 Kilombero (riv.), Tanz.
153/F3 Kilometre 28, Zaire
153/G2 Kilomines, Zaire
151/B3 Kilosa, Tanz.
61/G1 Kilpisjärvi, Fin.
56/B1 Kilraghts, NI,UK
56/B2 Kilrea, NI,UK
54/D4 Kilrenny, Sc,UK
60/A4 Kilrush, Ire.
60/C5 Kilsheelan, Ire.
54/B5 Kilsyth, Sc,UK
60/B2 Kiltamagh, Ire.
153/G5 Kilwa, Zaire
153/G5 Kilwa (isl.), Zam.
151/B4 Kilwa Kivinje, Tanz.
151/B4 Kilwa Masoko, Tanz.
56/C2 Kilwaughter, NI,UK
54/B5 Kilwinning, Sc,UK
60/B5 Kilworth, Ire.
190/C2 Kim, Co,US
131/E1 Kimaan, Indo.
151/A2 Kimali, Tanz.
151/B3 Kimamba, Tanz.
133/H5 Kimba, Austl.
152/C3 Kimba, Congo
192/C3 Kimball, Ne,US
138/E5 Kimbe, PNG
134/B2 Kimberley (cape), Austl.
130/B4 Kimberley (plat.), Austl.
182/G3 Kimberley, BC,Can
156/D3 Kimberley, SAfr.
185/F2 Kimberly, Id,US
184/D1 Kimberly, Or,US
113/E2 Kimch'aek, NKor.
113/E4 Kimch'ŏn, SKor.
113/E5 Kimhae, SKor.
113/E5 Kimhae (int'l arpt.), SKor.
91/J3 Kími, Gre.
91/H2 Kímina, Gre.
63/K1 Kimito (isl.), Fin.
111/F3 Kimitsu, Japan
113/D5 Kimje, SKor.
91/J2 Kimméria, Gre.
91/J4 Kímolos (isl.), Gre.
152/C4 Kimongo, Congo
151/A1 Kimoset, Kenya
61/J3 Kimovaara, Rus.
96/F1 Kimovsk, Rus.
153/F4 Kimpanga, Zaire
152/C4 Kimpese, Zaire
113/D4 Kimp'o, SKor.
113/D4 Kimp'o (int'l arpt.), SKor.
94/H4 Kimry, Rus.
127/E2 Kinabalu (peak), Malay.
125/B4 Kinabalu, Gunung (peak), Malay.
125/B4 Kinabalu Nat'l Park, Malay.
127/E2 Kinabatangan (riv.), Malay.
133/J5 Kinalung, Austl.
151/B3 Kinango, Kenya
124/B3 Kinapat (cape), Indo.
203/F2 Kinard, Fl,US
201/G3 Kinards, SC,US
125/B4 Kinarut, Malay.
182/E1 Kinbasket (lake), BC,Can
55/K7 Kinbrace, Sc,UK
183/L3 Kincaid, Sk,Can
191/G1 Kincaid, Ks,US
198/F2 Kincardine, On,Can
54/C4 Kincardine, Sc,UK
203/F1 Kinchafoonee (cr.), Ga,US
133/J5 Kinchega Nat'l Park, Austl.
177/N4 Kincolith, BC,Can
54/C2 Kincraig, Sc,UK
73/C5 Kincsesbánya, Hun.
153/F5 Kinda, Zaire
152/E4 Kindambi, Zaire
75/L3 Kindberg, Aus.
72/B5 Kindelbrück, Ger.
152/D4 Kindembe, Zaire
202/B2 Kinder, La,US
57/G5 Kinder Scout (mtn.), Eng,UK
183/K2 Kindersley, Sk,Can
144/B4 Kindia, Gui.
144/B4 Kindia (comm.), Gui.
71/E5 Kinding, Ger.
194/F4 Kindred, ND,US
69/G5 Kindsbach, Ger.
153/F3 Kindu, Zaire
97/J1 Kinel', Rus.
53/H3 Kineshma, Rus.
59/E2 Kineton, Eng,UK
135/C3 King (isl.), Austl.
132/C5 King (lake), Austl.
134/B4 King (peak), Austl.
130/A4 King (sound), Austl.
177/N4 King (mtn.), BC,Can
177/K3 King (peak), Yk,Can
201/G2 King, NC,US
199/G4 King (hill), Pa,US
158/E2 King (mtn.), Tx,US
205/D2 King (co.), Wa,US
147/H4 King Abdul Aziz (int'l arpt.), SAr.
201/J2 King And Queen C. H., Va,US
152/C4 Kinganga, Zaire
134/C4 Kingaroy, Austl.
198/B2 King-Chain O' Lakes, Wi,US
179/R7 King Christian (isl.), NW,Can
176/P3 King Christian IX Land (reg.), Grld.
176/Q2 King Christian X Land (reg.), Grld.
197/R8 King City, On,Can
186/B2 King City, Ca,US
193/G3 King City, Mo,US
177/F4 King Cove, Ak,US
196/B3 Kingfield, Me,US
191/F3 Kingfisher, Ok,US
176/N3 King Frederik VI Coast (reg.), Grld.
176/Q2 King Frederik VIII Land (reg.), Grld.
182/G2 King George (mtn.), BC,Can
139/L6 King George (isl.), FrPol.
201/J1 King George, Va,US
53/N7 King George's (res.), Eng,UK
54/C4 Kinghorn, Sc,UK
63/N2 Kingisepp, Rus.
135/C3 Kinglake Nat'l Park, Austl.
135/G5 Kinglake Nat'l Park, Austl.
130/B4 King Leopold (ranges), Austl.
139/J4 Kingman (reef), PacUS
187/E3 Kingman, Az,US
191/E2 Kingman, Ks,US
206/C3 King of Prussia, Pa,US
153/F3 Kingombe, Zaire
133/G4 Kingoonyah, Austl.
184/A3 King Range Nat'l Consv. Area, Ca,US
186/C2 Kings (riv.), Ca,US
200/B4 Kings, Ms,US
188/L7 Kings (cr.), Tx,US
185/H3 Kings (peak), Ut,US
177/G4 King Salmon, Ak,US
184/C4 Kings Beach, Ca,US
58/C6 Kingsbridge, Eng,UK
207/K9 Kings (Brooklyn) (co.), NY,US
186/C2 Kingsburg, Ca,US
189/F3 Kingsbury, Tx,US
186/C2 Kings Canyon Nat'l Park, Ca,US
59/E4 Kingsclere, Eng,UK
59/F1 King's Cliffe, Eng,UK
133/H5 Kingscote, Austl.
60/D2 Kingscourt, Ire.
190/E2 Kingsdown, Ks,US
198/B2 Kingsford, Mi,US
134/H8 Kingsford Smith-Sydney (int'l arpt.), Austl.
198/D5 Kings Island, Oh,US
58/D2 Kingsland, Eng,UK
191/H4 Kingsland, Ar,US
203/H2 Kingsland, Ga,US
189/E2 Kingsland, Tx,US
53/M6 Kings Langley, Eng,UK
193/G2 Kingsley, Ia,US
198/D2 Kingsley, Mi,US
192/D3 Kingsley (dam), Ne,US
59/G1 King's Lynn, Eng,UK
201/G3 Kings Mountain, NC,US
201/G3 Kings Mtn. Nat'l Mil. Park, SC,US
132/K6 Kings Park, Austl.
207/L8 Kings Point, NY,US
201/F2 Kingsport, Tn,US
54/C4 King's Seat (hill), Sc,UK
59/E2 Kings Sutton, Eng,UK
58/C5 Kingsteignton, Eng,UK
135/C4 Kingston, Austl.
199/H2 Kingston, On,Can
161/G2 Kingston (cap.), Jam.
138/F7 Kingston, Norfl.
202/B1 Kingston, La,US
208/D2 Kingston, Ma,US
191/G1 Kingston, Mo,US
187/J4 Kingston, NM,US
199/K4 Kingston, NY,US
201/F1 Kingston, Oh,US
191/F4 Kingston, Ok,US
206/C1 Kingston, Pa,US
208/C3 Kingston, RI,US
200/E3 Kingston, Tn,US
205/C2 Kingston, Wa,US
135/A3 Kingston S.E., Austl.
200/D2 Kingston Springs, Tn,US
59/F4 Kingston upon Thames, Eng,UK
53/N7 Kingston upon Thames (bor.), Eng,UK
135/D1 Kingstown, Austl.
162/F4 Kingstown (cap.), StV.
201/H4 Kingstree, SC,US
147/G3 Kings, Valley of the (val.), Egypt
205/G7 Kingsville, On,Can
206/B5 Kingsville, Md,US
189/F4 Kingsville, Tx,US
189/F4 Kingsville Nav. Air Sta., Tx,US
58/C6 Kingswear, UK
58/D2 Kingswinford, Eng,UK
58/D4 Kingswood, Eng,UK
200/D2 Kingswood, Ky,US
103/D3 King Ţalāl (dam), Jor.
58/D2 Kington, Eng,UK
152/D4 Kingushi, Zaire
54/B2 Kingussie, Sc,UK
178/G2 King William (isl.), NW,Can
201/J2 King William, Va,US
156/D4 King William's Town, SAfr.
189/M8 Kingwood, Tx,US
201/H1 Kingwood, WV,US
153/G5 Kiniama, Zaire
152/D4 Kiniati, Zaire
104/A2 Kınık, Turk.
183/M1 Kinistino Ind. Res., Sk,Can
177/L4 Kinkaid (mtn.), Ak,US
200/C2 Kinkaid (lake), Il,US
152/C4 Kinkala, Congo
110/D3 Kinki (prov.), Japan
144/B4 Kinkon, Chutes de (falls), Gui.
152/C4 Kinkosi, Zaire
54/A1 Kinlochewe, Sc,UK
54/B3 Kinlochleven, Sc,UK
54/B3 Kinloch Rannoch, Sc,UK
54/C1 Kinloss, Sc,UK
56/E5 Kinmel, Wal,UK
193/K4 Kinmundy, Il,US
62/E3 Kinna, Swe.
54/D1 Kinnairds Head (pt.), Sc,UK
60/C3 Kinnegad, Ire.
206/D2 Kinnelon, NJ,US
207/H8 Kinnelon (lake), NJ,US
103/F8 Kinneret-Negev Conduit, Isr.
201/F1 Kinnikinnick, Oh,US
60/C3 Kinnitty, Ire.
122/H4 Kinniya, SrL.
110/D3 Kino (riv.), Japan
69/E1 Kinrooi, Belg.
54/C4 Kinross, Sc,UK
71/F4 Kinsach (riv.), Ger.
197/S8 Kinsale, On,Can
60/B6 Kinsale, Ire.
60/B6 Kinsale (harb.), Ire.
62/B1 Kinsarvik, Nor.
183/M4 Kinsey, Mt,US
152/C4 Kinshasa (cap.), Zaire
152/C4 Kinshasa (pol. reg.), Zaire
190/E2 Kinsley, Ks,US
208/G5 Kinsman, Oh,US
203/E2 Kinston, Al,US
201/J3 Kinston, NC,US
191/G3 Kinta, Ok,US
145/E4 Kintampo, Gha.
151/A3 Kintinku, Tanz.
206/C2 Kintnersville, Pa,US
54/D2 Kintore, Sc,UK
55/J9 Kintyre (pen.), Sc,UK
194/E4 Kintyre, ND,US
56/C1 Kintyre, Mull of (pt.), Sc,UK
80/D1 Kintzheim, Fr.
111/F2 Kinu (riv.), Japan
60/B3 Kinvarra, Ire.
195/F1 Kinwow (bay), Mb,Can
151/A3 Kinyangiri, Tanz.
149/G5 Kinyeti (peak), Sudan
70/B6 Kinzig (riv.), Ger.
70/C2 Kinzig (riv.), Ger.
151/A3 Kiomboi, Tanz.
192/B4 Kiowa, Co,US
192/B4 Kiowa (cr.), Co,US
192/B3 Kiowa (peak), Co,US
191/E2 Kiowa, Ks,US
191/G3 Kiowa, Ok,US
190/D2 Kiowa (cr.), Ok, Tx,US
190/B2 Kiowa Nat'l Grsld., NM,US
180/T10 Kipahulu, Hi,US
153/F4 Kipange, Zaire
91/G4 Kiparissía, Gre.
91/G4 Kiparissía (gulf), Gre.
199/G1 Kipawa, Qu,Can
199/G1 Kipawa (lake), Qu,Can
63/N2 Kipen', Rus.
93/J2 Kipercheny, Mol.
153/G4 Kipili, Tanz.
155/F2 Kipilingu, Zaire
151/C2 Kipini, Kenya
151/A1 Kipkarren (riv.), Kenya
194/C2 Kipling, Sk,Can
177/F4 Kipnuk, Ak,US
80/D5 Kippel, Swi.
54/B4 Kippen, Sc,UK
197/H1 Kippens, Nf,Can
60/D3 Kippure (mtn.), Ire.
208/E5 Kipton, Oh,US
155/E1 Kipushi, Zaire
111/N10 Kira, Japan
138/F6 Kirakira, Sol.
157/H7 Kiranomena, Madg.
122/G3 Kīranūr, India
91/H3 Kira Panayía (isl.), Gre.
120/B1 Kīratpur, India
148/B3 Kirawa, Nga.
93/H5 Kirazlı, Turk.
63/K2 Kirbla, Est.
191/H3 Kirby, Ar,US
183/L5 Kirby, Mt,US
189/H2 Kirbyville, Tx,US
91/K2 Kırcasalih, Turk.
69/G4 Kirchberg, Ger.
71/F1 Kirchberg, Ger.
72/C6 Kirchberg, Ger.
80/D3 Kirchberg, Swi.
70/D6 Kirchberg an der Iller, Ger.
70/C4 Kirchberg an der Jagst, Ger.
67/F3 Kirchdorf, Ger.
69/G2 Kirchen, Ger.
71/E2 Kirchenlamitz, Ger.
71/E3 Kirchenthumbach, Ger.
70/D6 Kirchheim, Ger.
70/B3 Kirchheimbolanden, Ger.
70/C5 Kirchheim unter Teck, Ger.
67/F6 Kirchhundem, Ger.
67/F4 Kirchlengern, Ger.
67/G3 Kirchlinteln, Ger.
72/C3 Kirchmöser, Ger.
73/A5 Kirchschlag in der Buckligen Welt, Aus.
81/H2 Kirchsee (lake), Ger.
71/E6 Kirchseeon, Ger.
71/F6 Kirchweidach, Ger.
70/A7 Kirchzarten, Ger.
70/C3 Kirchzell, Ger.
56/C3 Kircubbin, NI,UK
56/D2 Kircudbright (bay), Sc,UK
101/L4 Kirensk, Rus.
114/B3 Kirgizskiy (mts.), Kyr.
100/F5 Kirgiz Steppe (grsld.), Kaz., Rus.
152/D3 Kiri, Zaire
91/H3 Kiriákion, Gre.
138/H5 Kiribati
104/E1 Kırık, Turk.
103/E1 Kırıkhan, Turk.
104/C2 Kırıkkale, Turk.
104/C2 Kirikkale (prov.), Turk.
108/C3 Kirikkuduk, China
94/H4 Kirillov, Rus.
99/H4 Kirillovka, Ukr.
63/Q2 Kirishi, Rus.
110/B5 Kirishima-Yaku Nat'l Park, Japan
110/B5 Kirishima-yama (mtn.), Japan
139/K4 Kiritimati (Christmas) (isl.), Kiri.
104/A2 Kırkağaç, Turk.
57/G4 Kirkburton, Eng,UK
57/F5 Kirkby, Eng,UK
57/G5 Kirkby in Ashfield, Eng,UK
57/F3 Kirkby Lonsdale, Eng,UK
57/H3 Kirkbymoorside, Eng,UK
57/F3 Kirkby Stephen, Eng,UK
54/C4 Kirkcaldy, Sc,UK
56/C2 Kirkcolm, Sc,UK
54/C6 Kirkconnel, Sc,UK
56/D2 Kirkcowan, Sc,UK
56/D2 Kirkcudbright, Sc,UK
118/B4 Kirkee, India
62/E1 Kirkenær, Nor.
61/J1 Kirkenes, Nor.
57/F4 Kirkham, Eng,UK
54/B2 Kirkhill, Sc,UK
56/D2 Kirkinner, Sc,UK
54/B5 Kirkintilloch, Sc,UK
63/L1 Kirkkonummi (Kyrkslätt), Fin.
197/N7 Kirkland, Qu,Can
54/C6 Kirkland (hill), Sc,UK
187/F3 Kirkland, Az,US
198/B3 Kirkland, Il,US
205/C2 Kirkland, Wa,US
179/H4 Kirkland Lake, On,Can
104/A2 Kırklar (peak), Turk.
93/H5 Kırklareli, Turk.
93/H5 Kırklareli (prov.), Turk.
54/C5 Kirkliston, Sc,UK
56/D3 Kirkmichael, IM,UK
54/C5 Kirkmuirhill, Sc,UK
93/L2 Kirkovgrad Obl., Ukr.
57/F3 Kirkstone (pass), Eng,UK
193/H3 Kirksville, Mo,US
54/C3 Kirkton of Glenisla, Sc,UK
105/F3 Kirkūk, Iraq
55/N13 Kirkwall, Sc,UK
156/D4 Kirkwood, SAfr.
206/C4 Kirkwood, De,US
69/G4 Kirn, Ger.
151/B3 Kirongwe, Tanz.
151/A4 Kiropa, Tanz.
96/E1 Kirov, Rus.
53/H4 Kirovakan, Arm.
95/P4 Kirovgrad, Rus.
95/P5 Kirovo, Rus.
95/L4 Kirovo-Chepetsk, Rus.
98/G3 Kirovograd, Ukr.
98/F3 Kirovograd Obl., Ukr.
96/D1 Kirovsk, Bela.
63/P2 Kirovsk, Rus.
107/H1 Kirovsk, Trkm.
99/K3 Kirovsk, Ukr.
100/H5 Kirovskiy, Kaz.
97/J3 Kirovskiy, Rus.
99/H5 Kirovskoye, Ukr.
99/K3 Kirovskoye, Ukr.
183/J2 Kirriemuir, Ab,Can
54/D3 Kirriemuir, Sc,UK
70/B4 Kirrweiler, Ger.
95/M4 Kirs, Rus.
53/H3 Kirsanov, Rus.
104/C2 Kırşehir, Turk.
104/C2 Kirsehir (prov.), Turk.
187/H2 Kirtland, NM,US
190/A3 Kirtland A.F.B., NM,US
192/B2 Kirtley, Wy,US
57/H6 Kirton, Eng,UK
57/H5 Kirton in Lindsey, Eng,UK
61/G2 Kiruna, Swe.
153/F3 Kirundu, Zaire
208/F4 Kirwan (res.), Oh,US
192/E4 Kirwin, Ks,US
192/E4 Kirwin (res.), Ks,US
190/E1 Kirwin Nat'l Wild. Ref., Ks,US
192/E4 Kirwin Nat'l Wild. Ref., Ks,US
95/K5 Kirya, Rus.
111/F2 Kiryū, Japan
62/F3 Kisa, Swe.
112/A4 Kisakata, Japan
153/F2 Kisangani, Zaire
153/F2 Kisangani (int'l arpt.), Zaire
152/C4 Kisantu, Zaire
130/B1 Kisar (isl.), Indo.
124/B2 Kisaran, Indo.
151/B3 Kisarawe, Tanz.
111/F3 Kisarazu, Japan
151/B3 Kisauni (Zanzibar) (int'l arpt.), Tanz.
198/C1 K.I. Sawyer A.F.B., Mi,US
73/C5 Kisbér, Hun.
194/C3 Kisbey, Sk,Can
100/J4 Kiselevsk, Rus.
152/D4 Kisenda, Zaire
153/E5 Kisenge, Zaire
151/A2 Kisessa, Tanz.
105/H5 Kīsh, Iran
105/H5 Kīsh (isl.), Iran
153/G3 Kishanda, Tanz.
121/F2 Kishanganj, India
118/B2 Kishangarh, India
120/A2 Kishangarh, India
145/F4 Kishi, Nga.
93/J2 Kishinëv (cap.), Mol.
93/J2 Kishinev (int'l arpt.), Mol.
112/D2 Kishiro-Shitsugen Nat'l Park, Japan
110/D3 Kishiwada, Japan
121/G3 Kishoreganj, Bang.
121/H3 Kishorganj, Bang.
122/C1 Kishtwar, India
205/N15 Kishwaukee (riv.), Il,US
153/G3 Kisi, Zaire
151/A3 Kisigo (riv.), Tanz.
151/A2 Kisii, Kenya
151/B3 Kisiju, Tanz.
151/B3 Kisiwani, Tanz.
177/B6 Kiska (isl.), Ak,US
177/B5 Kiska (vol.), Ak,US
196/A2 Kiskissink, Qu,Can
73/B6 Kis Koppány (riv.), Hun.
73/D6 Kiskőrös, Hun.
92/D2 Kiskunfélegyháza, Hun.
92/D2 Kiskunhalas, Hun.
73/D5 Kiskunlacháza, Hun.
92/D2 Kiskunmajsa, Hun.
73/D6 Kiskunsági (can.), Hun.
73/D5 Kiskunsági Nat'l Park, Hun.
53/H4 Kislovodsk, Rus.
151/C2 Kismaayo (Chisimayu), Som.
111/E3 Kiso (riv.), Japan
111/M9 Kisogawa, Japan
153/G3 Kisoro, Ugan.
111/M9 Kisozaki, Japan
41/W18 Kisrah, Tun.
91/H5 Kíssamos, Gre.
191/H2 Kissee Mills, Mo,US
144/C4 Kissidougou, Gui.
202/N7 Kissimmee, Fl,US
203/H3 Kissimmee, Fl,US
202/N8 Kissimmee (lake), Fl,US
203/H4 Kissimmee (lake), Fl,US
203/H4 Kissimmee (riv.), Fl,US
70/D6 Kissing, Ger.
81/F2 Kisslegg, Ger.
147/E4 Kissū, Jabal (peak), Sudan
144/B4 Kissy, SLeo.
92/E2 Kisújszállás, Hun.
151/A2 Kisumu, Kenya
92/F1 Kisvárda, Hun.
151/B4 Kiswere, Tanz.
111/G2 Kita (inlet), Japan
144/C3 Kita, Mali
100/G6 Kitab, Uzb.
111/M9 Kitagata, Japan
111/G2 Kita-Ibaraki, Japan
112/B4 Kitakami, Japan
112/B4 Kitakami (mts.), Japan
111/F2 Kitakata, Japan
110/B4 Kitakyūshū, Japan
110/B4 Kitakyūshū (arpt.), Japan
151/A1 Kitale, Kenya
112/C2 Kitami, Japan
112/C1 Kitami (mts.), Japan
111/H6 Kitamoto, Japan
151/B4 Kitangari, Tanz.
151/A3 Kitangiri (lake), Tanz.
192/C4 Kit Carson, Co,US
198/F3 Kitchener, On,Can
201/F4 Kite, Ga,US
61/J3 Kitee, Fin.
153/G4 Kitendwe, Zaire
153/F4 Kitengo, Zaire
153/H2 Kitgum, Ugan.
91/H4 Kíthira, Gre.
91/H4 Kíthira (isl.), Gre.
91/J4 Kíthnos, Gre.
91/J4 Kíthnos (isl.), Gre.
120/A1 Kithor, India
178/D3 Kitimat, BC,Can
177/M5 Kitkatla, BC,Can
152/C4 Kitomesa, Zaire
205/B3 Kitsap (co.), Wa,US
205/B2 Kitsap Lake-Erlands Point, Wa,US
183/J1 Kitscoty, Ab,Can
98/C3 Kitsman', Ukr.
199/G4 Kittanning, Pa,US
206/C1 Kittatinny (mts.), NJ, Pa,US
196/B4 Kittery, Me,US
187/G4 Kitt Peak Nat'l Observatory, Az,US
73/B3 Kittsee, Aus.
201/K2 Kitty Hawk, NC,US
153/F4 Kitu, Zaire
151/B2 Kitui, Kenya
131/G1 Kitumala (pt.), PNG
151/B2 Kitumbeine (peak), Tanz.
151/B4 Kitumbini, Tanz.
151/A3 Kitunda, Tanz.
151/C4 Kitunguli, Tanz.
155/F2 Kitwe, Zam.
75/K3 Kitzbühel, Aus.
70/D3 Kitzingen, Ger.
72/C5 Kitzscher, Ger.
151/C2 Kiunga, Kenya
131/F1 Kiunga, PNG
151/C2 Kiunga Marine Nat'l Rsv., Kenya
61/H3 Kiuruvesi, Fin.
151/B3 Kiuyu, Ras (pt.), Tanz.
177/F2 Kivalina, Ak,US
61/H2 Kivalo (mts.), Fin.
98/C2 Kivertsy, Ukr.
63/M1 Kivijärvi (lake), Fin.
63/M2 Kiviõli, Est.
63/L2 Kivi-Vigala, Est.
153/G3 Kivu (lake), Rwa., Zaire
153/F3 Kivu (pol. reg.), Zaire
131/F2 Kiwai (isl.), PNG
151/A4 Kiwira, Tanz.
98/F2 Kiyev (res.), Ukr.
114/B1 Kiyevka, Kaz.
99/M4 Kiyevka, Rus.
98/F2 Kiyev (Kiev) (cap.), Ukr.
93/J5 Kıyıköy, Turk.
111/H7 Kiyokawa, Japan
111/H7 Kiyose, Japan
111/M9 Kiyosu, Japan
152/D5 Kizamba, Zaire
53/J3 Kizel, Rus.
95/K3 Kizëma, Rus.
105/G2 Kizhaba, Azer.
114/B4 Kizil (riv.), China
103/A1 Kızılcadağ, Turk.
104/C1 Kızılcahamam, Turk.
104/B2 Kızıldag Nat'l Park, Turk.
104/B2 Kızılhisar, Turk.
104/C1 Kızılırmak (riv.), Turk.
104/C2 Kızılören, Turk.
97/L1 Kizil'skoye, Rus.
104/E2 Kızıltepe, Turk.
103/C1 Kızılyaka, Turk.
151/B4 Kizimbani, Tanz.
151/B3 Kizimkazi, Tanz.
53/H4 Kizlyar, Rus.
111/L10 Kizu, Japan
110/E3 Kizu (riv.), Japan
112/B3 Kizukuri, Japan
97/L5 Kizyl-Arvat, Trkm.
97/K5 Kizyl-Kaya, Trkm.
97/K5 Kizyl-Su, Trkm.
94/C1 Kjerkestinden (peak), Nor.
62/C2 Kjevik (int'l arpt.), Nor.
61/E2 Kjølen (Kölen) (mts.), Nor., Swe.
71/G3 Klabava (riv.), Czh.
73/C2 Kl'ačno, Slvk.
92/D3 Kladanj, Bosn.
131/E2 Kladar, Indo.
71/H2 Kladno, Czh.
92/F3 Kladovo, Yugo.
123/C3 Klaeng, Thai.
75/L3 Klagenfurt, Aus.
187/H3 Klagetoh, Az,US
63/J4 Klaipėda, Lith.
73/C2 Kl'ak (peak), Slvk.
124/F4 Klakah, Indo.
184/A3 Klamath, Ca,US
185/B2 Klamath (mts.), Ca, Or,US
184/B3 Klamath (riv.), Ca, Or,US
184/C2 Klamath Falls, Or,US
184/C2 Klamath For. Nat'l Wild. Ref., Or,US
100/B3 Klar (riv.), Swe.
61/E3 Klarälven (riv.), Swe.
62/D3 Klarup, Den.
157/E2 Klaserie, SAfr.
71/G2 Klášterec nad Ohří, Czh.
124/E4 Klaten, Indo.
71/G4 Klatovy, Czh.
81/F3 Klaus, Aus.
81/H4 Klausen (Chiusa), It.
81/E4 Klausenpass (pass), Swi.
177/M4 Klawock, Ak,US
177/L3 Klaza (mtn.), Yk,Can
66/E3 Klazienaveen, Neth.
182/B2 Kleena Kleene, BC,Can
69/G5 Kleinblittersdorf, Ger.
197/R8 Kleinburg, On,Can
72/D4 Kleine Elster (riv.), Ger.
80/E4 Kleine Emme (riv.), Swi.
69/E2 Kleine Gete (riv.), Belg.
71/F5 Kleine Laber (riv.), Ger.
66/B6 Kleine Nete (riv.), Belg.
70/C3 Kleinheubach, Ger.
156/B2 Klein Karas, Namb.
155/F4 Klein-Letabarivier (riv.), SAfr.
80/D3 Kleinlützel, Swi.
72/D3 Kleinmachnow, Ger.
156/L11 Kleinmond, SAfr.
156/Q12 Kleinolifants (riv.), SAfr.
70/C3 Kleinrinderfeld, Ger.
156/B3 Kleinsee, SAfr.
154/B4 Klein Spitzkoppe (peak), Namb.
156/B3 Klein Vaaldoorn, Namb.
70/C3 Kleinwallstadt, Ger.
70/B3 Kleinwinternheim, Ger.
193/H2 Klemme, Ia,US
62/A2 Kleppe, Nor.
62/A1 Kleppestø, Nor.
156/D2 Klerksdorp, SAfr.
98/D2 Klesov, Ukr.
71/H5 Klet' (peak), Czh.
96/E1 Kletnya, Rus.
99/M3 Kletskiy, Rus.
72/D4 Klettwitz, Ger.
66/D5 Kleve, Ger.
63/N5 Klichev, Bela.
109/H1 Klichka, Rus.
182/D5 Klickitat, Wa,US
72/C2 Klietz, Ger.
96/D1 Klimovichi, Bela.
98/G1 Klimovo, Rus.
92/E4 Klina, Yugo.
182/B2 Klinaklini (riv.), BC,Can
125/D4 Kling, Phil.
70/C3 Klingenberg am Main, Ger.
70/B4 Klingenmünster, Ger.
71/F2 Klingenthal, Ger.
71/F2 Klínovec (peak), Czh.
62/H3 Klintehamn, Swe.
96/E1 Klintsy, Rus.
156/E2 Klip (riv.), SAfr.
62/E3 Klippan, Swe.
156/D4 Klipplaat, SAfr.
93/G4 Klisura, Bul.
62/C3 Klitmøller, Den.
92/D3 Kljajićevo, Yugo.
92/C3 Ključ, Bosn.
65/K2 Kłodawa, Pol.
65/J3 Kłodzko, Pol.
62/D2 Klokkarstua, Nor.
187/G4 Klondyke, Az,US
81/E3 Klöntalersee (lake), Swi.
66/B6 Kloosterzande, Neth.
64/G1 Kloster, Ger.
67/F3 Klosterbach (riv.), Ger.
72/D2 Klosterfelde, Ger.
70/D6 Klosterlechfeld, Ger.
72/B4 Klostermansfeld, Ger.
73/A3 Klosterneuburg, Aus.
81/F4 Klosters, Swi.
75/L3 Klosterwappen (peak), Aus.
81/E3 Kloten, Swi.
116/C5 Klothuhta Zayat, Burma
72/B2 Klötze, Ger.
177/L3 Kluane, Yk,Can
177/K3 Kluane Nat'l Park, Yk,Can
65/K3 Kluczbork, Pol.
177/L3 Klukshu, Yk,Can
177/L4 Klukwan, Ak,US
66/B5 Klundert, Neth.
67/E3 Klüstenkanal (can.), Ger.
95/M5 Klyavlino, Rus.
94/J4 Klyaz'ma (riv.), Rus.
101/S4 Klyuchevskaya (peak), Rus.
101/S4 Klyuchi, Rus.
193/J1 Knapp (hill), Wi,US
182/C4 Knappa, Or,US
62/E3 Knäred, Swe.
57/G3 Knaresborough, Eng,UK
59/F3 Knebworth, Eng,UK
183/H2 Kneehills (cr.), Ab,Can
70/D3 Knetzgau, Ger.
93/G4 Knezha, Bul.
194/C4 Knife (riv.), ND,US
194/D4 Knife River Ind. Vill. Nat'l Hist. Site, ND,US
182/B2 Knight (inlet), BC,Can
58/C2 Knighton, Wal,UK
205/L11 Knightsen, Ca,US
92/C3 Knin, Cro.
188/E3 Knippa, Tx,US
75/L3 Knittelfeld, Aus.
70/B4 Knittlingen, Ger.
62/G2 Knivsta, Swe.
71/H5 Knížecí Stolec (peak), Czh.
71/F3 Knížecí Strom (peak), Czh.
92/F4 Knjaževac, Yugo.
132/C5 Knob (cape), Austl.
125/C2 Knob (peak), Phil.
132/B4 Knobby (pt.), Austl.
191/J2 Knobel, Ar,US
54/D1 Knoch (hill), Sc,UK
60/B2 Knock, Ire.
60/C6 Knockadoon Head (pt.), Ire.
60/B1 Knockalongy (mtn.), Ire.
60/C5 Knockanaffrin (mtn.), Ire.
60/A6 Knockboy (mtn.), Ire.
56/B2 Knockcloghrim, NI,UK
60/A6 Knockeirke (mtn.), Ire.
56/B1 Knocklayd (mtn.), NI,UK
60/B5 Knocklong, Ire.
60/C5 Knockmealdown (mtn.), Ire.
60/B5 Knockmealdown (mts.), Ire.
60/A5 Knocknagashel, Ire.
60/B5 Knockshanahullion (mtn.), Ire.
68/C1 Knokke-Heist, Belg.
154/B5 Knoll (pt.), Namb.
62/D3 Knøsen (peak), Den.
62/E4 Knösen (pt.), Swe.
91/J5 Knosós (Knossos) (ruins), Gre.
91/J5 Knossos (Knosós) (ruins), Gre.
188/D1 Knott, Tx,US
57/F4 Knott End, Eng,UK
57/G4 Knottingley, Eng,UK
204/G8 Knott's Berry Farm, Ca,US
201/K2 Knotts Island, NC,US
196/A3 Knowlton, Qu,Can
137/G Knox (coast), Ant.
135/G5 Knox, Austl.
177/M4 Knox (cape), BC,Can
198/C4 Knox, In,US
194/E3 Knox, ND,US
208/E7 Knox (co.), Oh,US
208/E6 Knox (lake), Oh,US
199/G4 Knox, Pa,US
188/E1 Knox City, Tx,US
200/F4 Knoxville, Ga,US
193/H3 Knoxville, Ia,US
202/C2 Knoxville, Ms,US
200/F3 Knoxville, Tn,US
57/F5 Knutsford, Eng,UK
156/C4 Knysna, SAfr.
109/M2 Ko (peak), Rus.
180/T10 Koali, Hi,US
154/D4 Koanaka (hills), Bots.
151/B3 Koani, Tanz.
120/E3 Koāth, India
124/D3 Koba, Indo.
144/B3 Koba-Niokolo Nat'l Park, Sen.
150/B2 Kobar Sink (depr.), Eth.
110/B5 Kobayashi, Japan
110/D3 Kōbe, Japan
99/H3 Kobelyaki, Ukr.
63/T9 København (co.), Den.
62/E4 København (Copenhagen) (cap.), Den.
144/C3 Kobenni, Mrta.
69/G3 Kobern-Gondorf, Ger.
127/G4 Kobipato (peak), Indo.
81/F3 Koblach, Aus.
69/G3 Koblenz, Ger.
81/E2 Koblenz, Swi.
150/A2 K'obo, Eth.
149/G4 Kobowan (swamp), Sudan
94/G4 Kobozha, Rus.
95/L3 Kobra, Rus.
65/N2 Kobrin, Bela.
130/D1 Kobroor (isl.), Indo.
113/D5 Kobu, SKor.
177/G2 Kobuk, Ak,US
177/G2 Kobuk (riv.), Ak,US
177/G2 Kobuk Valley Nat'l Park, Ak,US
97/G4 Kobuleti, Geo.
111/F3 Kobushi-ga-take (mtn.), Japan
73/A2 Kobylí, Czh.
71/H3 Kocába (riv.), Czh.
93/J5 Kocaeli (prov.), Turk.
104/D2 Koçalı, Turk.
92/F5 Kočani, Macd.
105/E2 Kocapınar, Turk.
92/B3 Kočevje, Slov.
179/J2 Koch (isl.), NW,Can
113/D5 Koch'ang, SKor.
81/H2 Kochel am See, Ger.
81/H2 Kochelsee (lake), Ger.
95/J3 Kochen'ga, Rus.
70/C4 Kocher (riv.), Ger.
92/F4 Kocherinovo, Bul.
97/G1 Kochetovka, Rus.
95/M4 Kochevo, Rus.
110/C4 Kōchi, Japan
110/C4 Kōchi (arpt.), Japan
110/C4 Kōchi (pref.), Japan
95/P2 Kochmes, Rus.
72/C4 Kochstedt, Ger.
97/H3 Kochubey, Rus.
99/L5 Kochubeyevskoye, Rus.
121/H2 Kochugaon, India
118/D4 Kodala, India
121/E2 Kodari, Nepal
121/E3 Kodarmā, India
177/H4 Kodiak, Ak,US
177/H4 Kodiak (isl.), Ak,US
177/H4 Kodiak Nat'l Wild. Ref., Ak,US
118/B3 Kodinār, India
73/B5 Kodó (riv.), Hun.
149/G3 Kodok, Sudan
112/B3 Kodomari, Japan
93/H2 Kodry (hills), Mol.
93/J1 Kodyma, Ukr.
68/B1 Koekelare, Belg.
120/D3 Koel (riv.), India
69/F5 Koenigsmacker, Fr.
154/C5 Koes, Namb.
113/D4 Koesan, SKor.
165/G4 Koetari (riv.), Guy., Sur.
187/F4 Kofa (mts.), Az,US
187/E4 Kofa Nat'l Wild. Ref., Az,US
93/H5 Kofçaz, Turk.
150/A4 Kofelē, Eth.
156/D3 Koffiefontein, SAfr.
127/G4 Kofiau (isl.), Indo.
145/E5 Koforidua, Gha.
111/F3 Kōfu, Japan
114/D3 Koga, China
111/F2 Koga, Japan
153/H4 Koga, Tanz.
111/H7 Koganei, Japan
62/E4 Køge, Den.
62/E4 Køge Bugt (bay), Den.
144/B4 Kogon (riv.), Gui.
113/D5 Kŏgum (isl.), SKor.
122/A1 Kohāt, Pak.
63/L2 Kohila, Est.
116/B3 Kohīma, India
105/G4 Kohkīlūyeh and Bovīr Aḩmadi (gov.), Iran
198/C3 Kohler, Wi,US
187/G3 Kohls Ranch, Az,US
71/H5 Kohout (peak), Czh.
63/M2 Kohtla-Järve, Est.
113/D5 Kohŭng, SKor.
159/H5 Kohunlich (ruins), Mex.
154/B5 Koichab (dry riv.), Namb.
156/A2 Koichab (dry riv.), Namb.
177/K3 Koidern, Yk,Can
144/C4 Koidu, SLeo.
63/L2 Koigi, Est.
119/F6 Koihoa, India
120/D2 Koilābās, Nepal
93/F5 Koímisis, Gre.
144/C4 Koindu, SLeo.
111/H7 Koito (riv.), Japan
151/B2 Koito, Kenya
63/M3 Koiva (riv.), Est.
113/E5 Kŏje (isl.), SKor.
132/C5 Kojonup, Austl.
65/L4 Kojšovská Hol'a (peak), Slvk.
123/B1 Kok (riv.), Burma
150/A3 K'ok'a (lake), Eth.
111/M10 Kōka, Japan
150/A3 K'ok'a Gidib (dam), Eth.
111/J7 Kokai (riv.), Japan
114/B3 Kokand, Uzb.
63/J2 Kökar (isl.), Fin.
127/H4 Kokas, Indo.
114/A1 Kokchetav, Kaz.
63/J1 Kokemäenjoki (riv.), Fin.
63/N4 Kokhanovo, Bela.
177/H4 Kokhonak, Ak,US
52/F2 Kokkola, Fin.
61/G3 Kokkola (Gamlakaleby), Fin.
63/L3 Koknese, Lat.
145/G4 Koko, Nga.
145/G5 Koko, Nga.
131/G2 Kokoda, PNG
144/C3 Kokofata, Mali
153/G2 Kokola, Zaire
198/C4 Kokomo, In,US
127/J4 Kokonau, Indo.
154/D5 Kokong, Bots.
121/H2 Kokrajhar, India
177/H3 Kokrines, Ak,US
113/D3 Koksan, NKor.
114/C3 Kokshaal-Tau (mts.), Kyr.
68/B1 Koksijde, Belg.
179/K3 Koksoak (riv.), Qu,Can
99/L3 Koksovyy, Rus.
156/E3 Kokstad, SAfr.
110/B5 Kokubu, Japan
109/H1 Kokuy, Rus.
131/G1 Kol, PNG
130/D1 Kola (isl.), Indo.
94/H1 Kola (pen.), Rus.
94/G1 Kola (riv.), Rus.
122/F4 Kolachel, India
144/C4 Kolahun, Libr.
127/F4 Kolaka, Indo.
118/C5 Kolār, India
120/A3 Kolāras, India
73/C4 Kolárovo, Slvk.
92/D4 Kolašin, Yugo.
62/G2 Kolbäck, Swe.
130/B2 Kolbano, Indo.
64/G5 Kolbermoor, Ger.
151/C2 Kolbio, Kenya
148/D2 Kolbus, Sudan
65/L3 Kolbuszowa, Pol.
144/B3 Kolda, Sen.
144/B3 Kolda (reg.), Sen.
62/C4 Kolding, Den.
153/F2 Kole, Zaire
121/E4 Kolebira, India
61/E2 Kölen (Kjølen) (mts.), Nor., Swe.
144/B4 Kolenté, Gui.
138/C5 Kolepom (isl.), Indo.
94/G2 Kolezhma, Rus.
63/L2 Kolgaküla, Est.
63/N2 Kolgompya (cape), Rus.
95/K1 Kolguyev (isl.), Rus.
118/B4 Kolhāpur, India
144/B3 Koliba (riv.), Gui.
177/G4 Koliganek, Ak,US
65/H3 Kolĭn, Czh.
144/B4 Koliya, Gui.
63/K3 Kolka, Lat.
63/K3 Kolkasrags (pt.), Lat.
107/J1 Kolkhozabad, Taj.
71/F5 Kollbach (riv.), Ger.
72/B5 Kölleda, Ger.
71/F4 Kollnburg, Ger.
66/D2 Kollum, Neth.
156/A2 Kolmanskop, Namb.
66/D7 Köln (Cologne), Ger.
65/L2 Kolno, Pol.
96/A1 Koło, Pol.
151/A3 Kolo, Tanz.
180/S10 Koloa, Hi,US
65/H1 Kołobrzeg, Pol.
148/B3 Kolofata, Camr.
95/K4 Kologriv, Rus.
73/B1 Kolojedka (riv.), Czh.
144/C3 Kolokani, Mali
150/B4 Kololo, Eth.
53/G3 Kolomna, Rus.
98/C3 Kolomyya, Ukr.
144/D4 Kolondiéba, Mali
144/D3 Kolongotomo, Mali
138/E4 Kolonia (cap.), Micr.
118/C6 Kolonnawa, SrL.
116/B3 Kolosib, India
144/D3 Kolossa (riv.), Mali
100/J4 Kolpashevo, Rus.
63/P2 Kolpino, Rus.
99/J1 Kolpny, Rus.
98/F2 Kolpyta, Ukr.
62/F2 Kolsva, Swe.
92/E3 Kolubara (riv.), Yugo
65/K3 Koluszki, Pol.
114/A1 Koluton (riv.), Kaz.
95/N2 Kolva (riv.), Rus.
61/D2 Kolvereid, Nor.
153/F5 Kolwezi, Zaire
101/R2 Kolyma (lowland), Rus.
101/R3 Kolyma (range), Rus.
101/R3 Kolyma (riv.), Rus.
97/H1 Kolyshley, Rus.
92/F4 Kom (peak), Bul.
152/C2 Kom (riv.), Camr., Gabon
123/B3 Koma, Burma
111/H7 Koma (riv.), Japan
92/E2 Komádi, Hun.
148/A2 Komadugu Gana (riv.), Nga.
145/H3 Komadugu Yobé (riv.), Nga.
111/H7 Komae, Japan
111/E3 Komagane, Japan
111/M9 Komaki, Japan
111/E3 Komaki (arpt.), Japan
153/G2 Komanda, Zaire
101/S4 Komandorskiye (isls.), Rus.
99/H1 Komarichi, Rus.
98/F2 Komarin, Bela.
73/C4 Komárno, Slvk.
73/C4 Komárom, Hun.
92/D2 Komárom-Esztergom (co.), Hun.
157/E2 Komatipoort, SAfr.
156/R12 Komatirivier (riv.), SAfr.
110/E2 Komatsu, Japan
110/E2 Komatsu (int'l arpt.), Japan
110/D4 Komatsushima, Japan
153/E2 Komba, Zaire
154/C3 Kombat, Namb.
153/F4 Kombe, Zaire
145/E3 Kombissiri, Burk.
151/A2 Kome (isl.), Tanz.
153/H3 Kome (isl.), Tanz.
153/H3 Kome (isl.), Ugan.
87/G1 Komen, Slov.
124/D3 Komering (riv.), Indo.
95/L2 Komi Aut. Rep., Rus.
95/M3 Komi-Permyak Aut. Okr., Rus.
73/C3 Komjatice, Slvk.
92/D2 Komló, Hun.
156/L11 Kommetjie, SAfr.
63/P2 Kommunar, Rus.
53/G4 Kommunarsk, Ukr.
114/B4 Kommunizma (Communism) (peak), Taj.
131/F1 Komo, PNG
127/E5 Komodo (isl.), Indo.
127/E5 Komodo I. Nat'l Park, Indo.
144/C4 Komodougou, Gui.
144/E5 Komoé (riv.), IvC.
152/C3 Komono, Congo
110/E3 Komono, Japan
131/E2 Komoran (isl.), Indo.
91/J2 Komotiní, Gre.
156/D3 Kompasberg (peak), SAfr.
131/F1 Kompiam, PNG
93/J2 Komrat, Mol.
101/L1 Komsomolets (isl.), Rus.
97/K3 Komsomol'skiy, Kaz.
95/K5 Komsomol'skiy, Rus.
95/P2 Komsomol'skiy, Rus.
97/H3 Komsomol'skiy, Rus.
109/M1 Komsomol'sk-na-Amure, Rus.
97/H2 Komsomol'skoye, Rus.
99/G3 Komsomol'skoye, Ukr.
99/J3 Komsomol'skoye, Ukr.
99/K4 Komsomol'skoye, Ukr.
154/C3 Komukanti, Namb.
91/K3 Kömür (pt.), Turk.
99/G2 Komyshnya, Ukr.
114/A2 Kon (riv.), Kaz.
144/D5 Konabonou, IvC.
94/H4 Konakovo, Rus.
11/M10 Kōnan, Japan
111/M9 Kōnan, Japan
135/D2 Konangra-Boyd Nat'l Park, Austl.
121/E4 Konār (res.), India
121/E4 Konār (riv.), India
107/H3 Konārak, Iran
107/K2 Konar-e Khāş, Afg.
191/F3 Konawa, Ok,US
127/F4 Konaweha (riv.), Indo.
111/L10 Konda, Japan
108/G1 Konda (riv.), Rus.
118/D4 Kondagaon, India
152/B4 Kondé Sounga, Congo
132/C5 Kondinin, Austl.
151/A3 Kondoa, Tanz.
94/G3 Kondopoga, Rus.
107/J1 Kondūz, Afg.
138/F7 Koné, NCal.
94/J3 Konetsgor'ye, Rus.
123/C4 Kong (isl.), Camb.
144/D4 Kong, IvC.
123/D3 Kong (riv.), Laos
130/D1 Kongapatalabata, Indo.
148/D4 Kongbo, CAfr.
177/F4 Kongiganak, Ak,US
113/D4 Kongju, SKor.
149/G4 Kong Kong (riv.), Sudan
123/B2 Kong Krailat, Thai.
115/D4 Kong Miao, China
113/F6 Kongnŭng (riv.), SKor.
154/D3 Kongola, Namb.
153/F4 Kongolo, Zaire
149/F4 Kongor, Sudan
145/E3 Kongoussi, Burk.
111/L10 Kongō-zan (peak), Japan
62/C2 Kongsberg, Nor.
62/E1 Kongsvinger, Nor.
116/E2 Kongtan, China
152/C2 Kongué, Chutes de (falls), Gabon
114/C4 Kongur Shan (peak), China
151/B3 Kongwa, Tanz.
65/K3 Koniecpol, Pol.
70/D2 Königsberg in Bayern, Ger.
70/B5 Königsberg-Stein, Ger.
70/D5 Königsbronn, Ger.
72/D5 Königsbrück, Ger.
70/D6 Königsbrunn, Ger.
81/G2 Königschlösser, Ger.
81/H2 Königsdorf, Ger.
72/B6 Königsee, Ger.

# König – Kvern

70/B6 Königsfeld im Schwarzwald, Ger.
67/H4 Königslutter am Elm, Ger.
72/E6 Konigstein, Ger.
70/B2 Königstein im Taunus, Ger.
69/G2 Königswinter, Ger.
72/D3 Königs Wusterhausen, Ger.
65/K2 Konin, Pol.
65/K2 Konin (prov.), Pol.
144/C4 Konindou, Gui.
91/G3 Konispol, Alb.
91/G2 Kónitsa, Gre.
80/D4 Köniz, Swi.
92/C4 Konjic, Bosn.
154/C5 Konkeip (dry riv.), Namb.
156/B2 Konkiep, Namb.
156/B2 Konkiep (dry riv.), Namb.
155/E2 Konkola, Zam.
145/E4 Konkori, Gha.
144/B4 Konkouré (riv.), Gui.
148/D4 Konkourou-Bamingui Fauna Rsv., CAfr.
72/B4 Könnern, Ger.
61/H3 Konnevesi, Fin.
144/D3 Konobougou, Mali
80/D4 Konolfingen, Swi.
94/J3 Konosha, Rus.
99/G2 Konotop, Ukr.
123/E3 Kon Plong, Viet.
114/E3 Konqi (riv.), China
112/D2 Konsen (plat.), Japan
65/L3 Końskie, Pol.
149/H4 Konso, Eth.
65/L2 Konstancin-Jeziorna, Pol.
99/H3 Konstantinovka, Ukr.
99/H4 Konstantinovka, Ukr.
99/J3 Konstantinovka, Ukr.
99/L4 Konstantinovsk, Rus.
65/K3 Konstantynów Łódzki, Pol.
81/F2 Konstanz, Ger.
145/G4 Kontagora, Nga.
148/B4 Kontcha, Camr.
94/J4 Konteyevo, Rus.
68/D1 Kontich, Belg.
61/J3 Kontiolahti, Fin.
123/E3 Kon Tum, Viet.
93/K5 Konuralp, Turk.
73/B4 Kóny, Hun.
104/C2 Konya, Turk.
103/C1 Konya (prov.), Turk.
69/F4 Konz, Ger.
151/B2 Konza, Kenya
182/G3 Koocenusa (lake), Mt,US
66/B4 Koog aan de Zaan, Neth.
130/C3 Koolpinyah, Austl.
132/C4 Koolyanobbing, Austl.
135/C2 Koondrook, Austl.
63/L2 Koonga, Est.
133/G4 Koonibba, Austl.
198/C4 Koontz Lake, In,US
135/D2 Koorawatha, Austl.
132/C4 Koorda, Austl.
63/M2 Koosa, Est.
185/H4 Koosharem, Ut,US
182/G4 Kooskia, Id,US
182/F3 Kootenai Nat'l Wild. Ref., Id,US
182/F3 Kootenay (lake), BC,Can
182/G2 Kootenay (riv.), BC,Can
182/F2 Kootenay Nat'l Park, BC,Can
135/D1 Kootingal, Austl.
104/E1 Kop (pass), Turk.
120/D2 Kopāganj, India
131/F1 Kopaigo, PNG
118/B4 Kopargaon, India
145/F4 Kopargo, Ben.
61/N7 Kópavogur, Ice.
144/D5 Kope (peak), IvC.
72/D3 Köpenick, Ger.
87/G1 Koper, Slov.
62/A2 Kopervik, Nor.
95/P5 Kopeysk, Rus.
96/G4 Kop Gecidi (pass), Turk.
153/E2 Kopia, Zaire
116/B3 Kopili (riv.), India
62/G2 Köping, Swe.
91/F1 Koplik, Alb.
130/A2 Kopondei (cape), Indo.
63/N2 Koporskiy (bay), Rus.
62/D1 Koppang, Nor.
62/F2 Kopparberg, Swe.
62/E1 Kopparberg (co.), Swe.
208/G6 Koppel, Pa,US
109/M2 Koppi (riv.), Rus.
156/D2 Koppies, SAfr.
92/C2 Koprivnica, Cro.
93/G4 Koprivshtitsa, Bul.
103/B1 Köprü (riv.), Turk.
103/C1 Köprülü, Turk.
104/B2 Köprülü Kanyon Nat'l Park, Turk.
98/F2 Kopti, Ukr.
113/C2 Kop'ung, NKor.
63/P4 Kopys', Bela.
105/H4 Kor (riv.), Iran
120/C2 Kora, India
111/M9 Kōra, Japan
91/G2 Korab (peak), Alb.
71/G4 Koráb (peak), Czh.
96/G1 Korablino, Rus.
150/C4 K'orahē, Eth.
110/C3 Korakuen Garden, Japan
179/K3 Koraluk (riv.), Nf,Can
114/E4 Koramlik, China
75/L4 Korana (riv.), Bosn., Cro.
151/B2 Kora Nat'l Park, Kenya
118/D4 Koraput, India
120/D4 Korba, India
67/F6 Korbach, Ger.
150/A2 K'orbeta, Eth.
124/C1 Korbu (peak), Malay.
91/G2 Korçë, Alb.
92/C4 Korčula, Cro.
92/C4 Korčula (isl.), Cro.
90/E1 Korčulanski (chan.), Cro.
92/C4 Korčulanski (chan.), Cro.
69/F4 Kordel, Ger.
105/F3 Kordestān (gov.), Iran
105/H2 Kord Küy, Iran
149/F2 Kordofan (reg.), Sudan
113/B3 Korea (bay), China, NKor.
110/A4 Korea (str.), Japan, SKor.
113/D4 Korean Folk Vill., SKor.
113/D2 Korea, North
113/D4 Korea, South
150/A2 Korem, Eth.
99/K5 Korenovsk, Rus.
98/D2 Korets, Ukr.
101/S3 Korf, Rus.
104/D1 Korgan, Turk.
114/D3 Korgas, China
144/D4 Korhogo, IvC.
127/J4 Korido, Indo.
144/E3 Korienzé, Mali
127/J4 Korim, Indo.
91/H2 Korinós, Gre.
91/H4 Korinthos (Corinth), Gre.
91/H4 Kórinthos (Corinth) (ruins), Gre.
73/B5 Kőris-hegy (peak), Hun.
72/C2 Köritz, Ger.
111/G2 Kōriyama, Japan
146/B4 Korizo, Passe de (pass), Chad
95/P5 Korkino, Rus.
101/R3 Korkodon (riv.), Rus.
103/B1 Korkuteli, Turk.
114/E3 Korla, China
103/C2 Kormakiti (cape), Cyp.
73/A5 Körmend, Hun.
92/B4 Kornat (isl.), Cro.
67/H6 Körner, Ger.
93/J2 Korneshty, Mol.
73/A3 Korneuburg, Aus.
192/C4 Kornman, Co,US
75/L5 Kornot (isl.), Cro.
70/C5 Korntal-Münchingen, Ger.
70/C5 Kornwestheim, Ger.
139/Z18 Koro (isl.), Fiji
138/G6 Koro (sea), Fiji
144/D4 Koro, IvC.
144/E3 Koro, Mali
131/F1 Koroba, PNG
99/J2 Korocha, Rus.
93/K5 Köroğlu (peak), Turk.
151/B3 Korogwe, Tanz.
135/B3 Koroit, Austl.
96/B2 Korolëvo, Ukr.
127/G2 Koronadal, Phil.
91/H2 Korónia (lake), Gre.
65/J2 Koronowo, Pol.
91/L7 Koropí, Gre.
138/C4 Koror (cap.), Palau
92/E2 Körös (riv.), Hun.
98/E2 Korosten', Ukr.
98/E2 Korostyshev, Ukr.
95/P1 Korotaikha (riv.), Rus.
148/C1 Koro Toro, Chad
177/D5 Korovin (vol.), Ak,US
97/K1 Korovino, Rus.
63/J1 Korpo, Fin.
109/N2 Korsakov, Rus.
66/D6 Korschenbroich, Ger.
62/D4 Korsør, Den.
98/F3 Korsun'-Shevchenkovskiy, Ukr.
65/L1 Korsze, Pol.
68/C1 Kortemark, Belg.
69/E2 Kortenaken, Belg.
68/D2 Kortenberg, Belg.
69/E2 Kortessem, Belg.
114/E2 Korti Linchang, China
68/C2 Kortrijk, Belg.
94/J4 Kortsevo, Rus.
145/H5 Korup Nat'l Park, Camr.
102/R3 Koryak (range), Rus.
101/S3 Koryak Aut. Okr., Rus.
95/K3 Koryazhma, Rus.
111/L10 Kōryō, Japan
113/E5 Koryŏng, SKor.
98/G2 Koryukovka, Ukr.
89/K3 Kós, Gre.
89/K3 Kós (isl.), Gre.
111/E3 Kosai, Japan
110/A3 Ko-saki (pt.), Japan
123/C3 Ko Samut Nat'l Park, Thai.
113/D3 Kosan, NKor.
96/F1 Kosaya Gora, Rus.
71/E5 Kösching, Ger.
65/J2 Kościan, Pol.
65/J1 Kościerzyna, Pol.
135/D3 Kosciusko (peak), Austl.
200/C4 Kosciusko, Ms,US
135/D3 Kosciusko Nat'l Park, Austl.
63/L2 Kose, Est.
104/D1 Köse, Turk.
111/M10 Kosei, Japan
147/F4 Kosha, Sudan
111/F3 Koshigaya, Japan
112/K5 Koshiki (isl.), Japan
107/H2 Koshk, Afg.
97/K3 Koshkar, Kaz.
191/J2 Koshkonong, Mo,US
193/K2 Koshkonong (lake), Wi,US
120/A2 Kosi, India
121/F2 Kosi (riv.), India
121/F4 Kosi (zone), Nepal
65/L4 Košice, Slvk.
118/C4 Kosigi, India
104/B2 Koskinoú, Gre.
95/L3 Koslan, Rus.
114/C2 Kosoba, Gora (peak), Kaz.
113/E3 Kosŏng, NKor.
113/E5 Kosŏng, SKor.
98/C3 Kosov, Ukr.
92/E4 Kosovo (aut. reg.), Yugo.
92/E4 Kosovo Polje, Yugo.
91/G1 Kosovska Kamenica, Yugo.
92/E4 Kosovska Mitrovica, Yugo.
71/F3 Kosový (riv.), Czh.
138/F4 Kosrae (isl.), Micr.
189/F2 Kosse, Tx,US
144/D3 Kossi (prov.), Burk.
144/D5 Kossou (lake), IvC.
144/D5 Kossou, Barrage de (dam), IvC.
62/F3 Kosta, Swe.
71/H3 Kostelec nad Černými Lesy, Czh.
156/D2 Koster, SAfr.
93/F4 Kostinbrod, Bul.
73/B2 Kostol'any, Vel'ké, Slvk.
94/F2 Kostomuksha, Kaz.
98/D2 Kostopol', Ukr.
53/H3 Kostroma, Rus.
94/J4 Kostroma (riv.), Rus.
94/J4 Kostroma Obl., Rus.
65/H2 Kostrzyn, Pol.
65/J2 Kostrzyn, Pol.
96/E1 Kostyukovichi, Bela.
95/N4 Kos'va (riv.), Rus.
95/N2 Kos'yu, Rus.
95/N2 Kos'yu (riv.), Rus.
65/J1 Koszalin, Pol.
65/H2 Koszalin (prov.), Pol.
73/A5 Kőszeg, Hun.
118/C2 Kota, India
120/D4 Kota, India
111/N10 Kōta, Japan
124/D4 Kotaagung, Indo.
124/C1 Kota Baharu, Malay.
124/C3 Kotabaru, Indo.
125/B4 Kota Belud, Malay.
126/D4 Kotabesi, Indo.
124/D4 Kotabumi, Indo.
127/F3 Kotabunan, Indo.
124/D3 Kotadaik, Indo.
122/A2 Kot Addu, Pak.
122/F3 Kotagiri, India
124/D4 Kotajawa, Indo.
125/B4 Kota Kinabalu, Malay.
125/B4 Kota Kinabalu (int'l arpt.), Malay.
118/D4 Kotapād, India
124/C2 Kotapinang, Indo.
124/C2 Kotatengah, Indo.
124/C2 Kota Tinggi, Malay.
120/B1 Kotdwāra, India
93/H4 Kotel, Bul.
95/L4 Kotel'nich, Rus.
99/M4 Kotel'nikovo, Rus.
101/P2 Kotel'nyy (isl.), Rus.
99/H2 Kotel'va, Ukr.
122/C2 Kot Fateh, India
122/D2 Kotgarh, India
72/B4 Köthen, Ger.
153/H2 Kotido, Ugan.
63/M1 Kotka, Fin.
122/C2 Kot Kapūra, India
122/D1 Kotla, India
53/H2 Kotlas, Rus.
122/B1 Kotli, Pak.
177/F3 Kotlik, Ak,US
63/N2 Kotly, Rus.
111/M9 Kotō, Japan
145/E5 Kotoka (int'l arpt.), Gha.
145/G4 Koton Karifi, Nga.
92/D4 Kotor, Yugo.
92/C3 Kotor Varoš, Bosn.
97/H2 Kotovo, Rus.
93/J2 Kotovsk, Mol.
97/G1 Kotovsk, Rus.
98/E4 Kotovsk, Ukr.
107/J3 Kotri, Pak.
121/G4 Kotrung-Uttarpara, India
121/B1 Kot Sārang, Pak.
118/D4 Kottagūdem, India
122/F4 Kottai Malai (mtn.), India
122/G3 Kottāmpatti, India
122/F3 Kottayam, India
118/C6 Kotte, SrL.
73/A4 Kottingbrunn, Aus.
148/D4 Kotto (riv.), CAfr.
101/L3 Kotuy (riv.), Rus.
177/F2 Kotzebue, Ak,US
177/E2 Kotzebue (sound), Ak,US
72/B5 Kötzschen, Ger.
71/F4 Kötzting, Ger.
145/F4 Kouandé, Ben.
148/C4 Kouango, CAfr.
148/C2 Kouba Olanga, Chad
144/C4 Koubia, Gui.
196/E2 Kouchibouguac (bay), NB,Can
196/E2 Kouchibouguac Nat'l Park, NB,Can
145/E3 Koudougou, Burk.
91/J5 Koufonísion (isl.), Gre.
177/E2 Kougarok (mtn.), Ak,US
152/B2 Kougoulé, Gabon
117/J4 Kouhu, Tai.
152/B4 Kouilou (pol. reg.), Congo
152/C4 Kouilou (riv.), Congo
179/J2 Koukdjuak (riv.), NW,Can
148/C4 Kouki, CAfr.
148/D4 Koukourou, CAfr.
152/C3 Koula-Moutou, Gabon
144/C4 Koulé, Gui.
144/D3 Koulikoro, Mali
145/F3 Koulou, Niger
144/B3 Koulountou (riv.), Gui., Sen.
148/B3 Koum, Camr.
138/F7 Koumac, NCal.
134/C3 Koumala, Austl.
152/B2 Koumameyong, Gabon
144/D4 Koumandougou, Gui.
144/D4 Koumantou, Mali
144/D4 Koumban, Gui.
144/B4 Koumbia, Gui.
144/D3 Koumbi Saleh (ruins), Mrta.
140/D4 Koumra, Chad
144/B3 Koundara, Gui.
148/B4 Koundé, CAfr.
144/C3 Koundian, Mali
144/C4 Koundou, Gui.
144/B3 Koungheul, Sen.
148/C3 Kouno, Chad
114/C2 Kounradskiy, Kaz.
189/G2 Kountze, Tx,US
145/H5 Koupé (peak), Camr.
145/E3 Koupéla, Burk.
144/B4 Kouraïa Konkouré, Gui.
145/E3 Kouritenga (prov.), Burk.
166/C1 Kourou, FrG.
144/C3 Kouroba, Mali
144/C3 Kouroussa, Gui.
144/D3 Koury, Mali
148/B2 Kousseri, Camr.
146/C5 Koussi, Emi (peak), Chad
144/D3 Koutiala, Mali
144/D4 Kouto, IvC.
198/C4 Kouts, In,US
63/M1 Kouvola, Fin.
152/D3 Kouyou (riv.), Congo
92/E3 Kovačevac, Yugo.
92/E3 Kovačica, Yugo.
104/B2 Kovada Gölü Nat'l Park, Turk.
122/F4 Kovalam, India
104/D1 Kovans, Turk.
94/G2 Kovda, Rus.
94/F2 Kovdor, Rus.
94/F2 Kovdozero (lake), Rus.
98/C2 Kovel', Ukr.
92/E3 Kovilj, Yugo.
122/F4 Kovilpatti, India
94/J4 Kovrov, Rus.
118/C5 Kovūr, India
97/G1 Kovylkino, Rus.
134/A1 Kowanyama Abor. Community, Austl.
153/F3 Kowe, Zaire
107/J1 Kowkcheh (riv.), Afg.
107/H2 Kowl-e Namaksār (lake), Afg., Iran
117/G4 Kowloon, HK
113/D3 Kowŏn, NKor.
107/J2 Kowt-e 'Ashrow, Afg.
114/D4 Koxlax, China
144/C5 Koyama, Gui.
110/B5 Kōyama, Japan
93/G4 Koynare, Bul.
177/F3 Koyuk, Ak,US
177/G3 Koyukuk, Ak,US
177/H2 Koyukuk (riv.), Ak,US
177/G2 Koyukuk Nat'l Wild. Ref., Ak,US
177/H2 Koyukuk, North Fork (riv.), Ak,US
177/H2 Koyukuk, South Fork (riv.), Ak,US
111/N10 Kozakai, Japan
104/C2 Kozaklı, Turk.
104/C2 Kozan, Turk.
91/G2 Kozáni, Gre.
92/C3 Kozara Nat'l Park, Bosn.
73/C3 Kozárovce, Slvk.
99/G3 Kozel'shchina, Ukr.
96/E1 Kozel'sk, Rus.
73/B5 Kőzépső-Hajag (peak), Hun.
95/L4 Kozha, Rus.
122/E3 Kozhikode, India
94/H3 Kozhozero (lake), Rus.
95/N2 Kozhva, Rus.
95/M2 Kozhva (riv.), Rus.
65/L3 Kozienice, Pol.
93/F4 Kozloduy, Bul.
94/H4 Kozlovo, Rus.
93/K5 Kozlu, Turk.
104/E2 Kozluk, Turk.
65/J3 Koźmin, Pol.
95/L3 Koz'mino, Rus.
93/F4 Koznitsa (peak), Bul.
98/C3 Kozova, Ukr.
65/H3 Kożuchów, Pol.
145/G4 Kpagouda, Togo
145/F5 Kpalimé, Togo
145/F5 Kpandu, Gha.
145/F5 Kpémé, Togo
123/B4 Kra (isth.), Burma, Thai.
156/D3 Kraai (riv.), SAfr.
156/L10 Kraaifontein, SAfr.
66/B6 Krabbendijke, Neth.
123/B4 Krabi, Thai.
123/B4 Kra Buri, Thai.
123/D3 Kracheh, Camb.
124/E4 Kragan, Indo.
62/C2 Kragerø, Nor.
92/E3 Kragujevac, Yugo.
71/F6 Kraiburg am Inn, Ger.
70/B4 Kraichbach (riv.), Ger.
70/B4 Kraichgau (reg.), Ger.
71/E6 Krailling, Ger.
124/D4 Krakatau (Krakatoa) (vol.), Indo.
124/D4 Krakatoa (Krakatau) (vol.), Indo.
123/D3 Krakor, Camb.
65/K3 Kraków, Pol.
65/K3 Kraków (prov.), Pol.
198/B2 Krakow, Wi,US
123/C3 Kralanh, Camb.
162/D4 Kralendijk, NAnt.
92/E4 Kraljevo, Yugo.
71/G3 Kralovice, Czh.
71/H2 Kralupy nad Vltavou, Czh.
53/G4 Kramatorsk, Ukr.
194/D3 Kramer, ND,US
61/F3 Kramfors, Swe.
66/B5 Krammer (chan.), Neth.
91/G3 Kranéa Elassónos, Gre.
81/H3 Kranebitten (int'l arpt.), Aus.
89/F1 Kranebitten (int'l arpt.), Aus.
66/D5 Kranenburg, Ger.
72/B6 Kranichfeld, Ger.
91/H4 Kranídhion, Gre.
92/B2 Kranj, Slov.
157/E3 Kranskop, SAfr.
154/B4 Kranzberg, Namb.
65/J3 Krapkowice, Pol.
98/D3 Krasilov, Ukr.
63/M4 Krāslava, Lat.
71/F2 Kraslice, Czh.
94/J5 Krasnaya Gorbatka, Rus.
96/C1 Krasnaya Sloboda, Bela.
65/M3 Kraśnik, Pol.
65/M3 Kraśnik Fabryczny, Pol.
95/N5 Krasninsk, Rus.
97/H2 Krasnoarmeysk, Rus.
99/J3 Krasnoarmeysk, Ukr.
99/K5 Krasnoarmeyskaya, Rus.
99/M4 Krasnoarmeyskiy, Rus.
95/K3 Krasnoborsk, Rus.
53/G4 Krasnodar, Rus.
99/K5 Krasnodar (int'l arpt.), Rus.
99/K5 Krasnodar Kray, Rus.
99/K3 Krasnodon, Ukr.
99/K3 Krasnogorovka, Ukr.
96/F1 Krasnogorsk, Rus.
99/K3 Krasnograd, Ukr.
99/L5 Krasnogvardeyskoye, Rus.
99/H5 Krasnogvardeyskoye, Ukr.
109/H1 Krasnokamensk, Rus.
95/M4 Krasnokamsk, Rus.
95/M5 Krasnokholmskiy, Rus.
99/K2 Krasnolesnyy, Rus.
99/J3 Krasnooskol'skoye (res.), Ukr.
99/J3 Krasnopavlovka, Ukr.
99/G5 Krasnoperekopsk, Ukr.
99/H2 Krasnopol'ye, Ukr.
94/H2 Krasnoshchel'ye, Rus.
97/G1 Krasnoslobodsk, Rus.
97/H2 Krasnoslobodsk, Rus.
100/G4 Krasnotur'insk, Rus.
95/N4 Krasnoufimsk, Rus.
95/P4 Krasnoural'sk, Rus.
95/N4 Krasnovishersk, Rus.
97/K5 Krasnovodsk, Trkm.
97/K4 Krasnovodsk (int'l arpt.), Trkm.
105/H1 Krasnowodsk (int'l arpt.), Trkm.
100/K4 Krasnoyarsk, Rus.
97/L2 Krasnoyarskiy, Rus.
63/M4 Krasnoye, Bela.
93/J2 Krasnoye, Mol.
99/K2 Krasnoye, Rus.
98/C3 Krasnoye, Ukr.
65/M3 Krasnystaw, Pol.
105/F2 Krasnyy Bazar, Azer.
108/F1 Krasnyy Chikoy, Rus.
98/E4 Krasnyye Okny, Ukr.
97/J1 Krasnyy Gulyay, Rus.
97/K2 Krasnyy Kholm, Rus.
95/N5 Krasnyy Klyuch, Rus.
97/H2 Krasnyy Kut, Rus.
99/J3 Krasnyy Liman, Ukr.
99/K3 Krasnyy Luch, Ukr.
95/Q5 Krasnyy Oktyabr', Rus.
99/L4 Krasnyy Sulin, Rus.
97/H2 Krasnyy Yar, Rus.
97/J1 Krasnyy Yar, Rus.
97/J3 Krasnyy Yar, Rus.
92/F4 Kratovo, Macd.
70/C4 Krautheim, Ger.
123/C4 Kravanh (mts.), Camb.
124/D4 Krawang, Indo.
97/H4 Kraynovka, Rus.
63/K4 Kražiai, Lith.
142/D5 Kreb en Nâga (escarp.), Mali, Mrta.
94/H3 Krechetovo, Rus.
63/P2 Krechevitsy, Rus.
70/D2 Kreck (riv.), Ger.
66/D6 Krefeld, Ger.
67/G5 Kreiensen, Ger.
91/G3 Kremastón (lake), Gre.
71/G4 Křemelna (riv.), Czh.
99/G3 Kremenchug, Ukr.
99/G3 Kremenchug (res.), Ukr.
98/C2 Kremenets, Ukr.
99/K3 Kremennaya, Ukr.
183/J3 Kremlin, Mt,US
72/D2 Kremmen, Ger.
185/K3 Kremmling, Co,US
73/C2 Kremnica, Slvk.
72/D4 Kremnitz (riv.), Ger.
67/G1 Krempe, Ger.
75/L2 Krems an der Donau, Aus.
71/H6 Kremsmünster, Aus.
71/G6 Krenglbach, Aus.
206/C2 Kresgeville, Pa,US
93/F5 Kresna, Bul.
190/D3 Kress, Tx,US
81/F2 Kressbronn am Bodensee, Ger.
101/T3 Kresta (gulf), Rus.
91/G2 Kréstena, Gre.
94/H5 Kresty, Rus.
63/J4 Kretinga, Lith.
69/F2 Kreuzau, Ger.
70/C2 Kreuzberg (peak), Ger.
81/F2 Kreuzlingen, Swi.
69/G2 Kreuztal, Ger.
70/C3 Kreuzwertheim, Ger.
91/H2 Kría Vrísi, Gre.
152/B2 Kribi, Camr.
96/D1 Krichev, Bela.
190/C3 Krider, NM,US
72/C5 Kriebitzsch, Ger.
75/L3 Krieglach, Aus.
81/E3 Kriens, Swi.
112/B1 Kril'on, Rus.
112/B1 Kril'on (pen.), Rus.
109/N2 Kril'on, Mys (cape), Rus.
148/B3 Krim-Krim, Chad
66/B5 Krimpen aan de IJssel, Neth.
109/H3 Krinichki, Ukr.
93/G5 Krinídhes, Gre.
89/J4 Kriós (cape), Gre.
118/D4 Krishna (riv.), India
118/C5 Krishnagiri, India
121/H2 Krishnai, India
121/G4 Krishnanagar, India
121/G3 Krishnapur, India
62/G3 Kristdala, Swe.
62/B2 Kristiansand, Nor.
62/F3 Kristianstad, Swe.
62/E3 Kristianstad (co.), Swe.
62/F4 Kristianstad (int'l arpt.), Swe.
61/C3 Kristiansund, Nor.
62/F2 Kristinehamn, Swe.
92/F4 Kriva Palanka, Macd.
63/M4 Krivichi, Bela.
98/F4 Krivoye Ozero, Ukr.
99/G4 Krivoy Rog, Ukr.
95/L3 Krivushevo, Rus.
92/B3 Krk, Cro.
92/B3 Krk (isl.), Cro.
92/C3 Krka (riv.), Cro.
65/J3 Krnov, Czh.
155/F5 Krokodil (riv.), SAfr.
155/E5 Krokodilrivier (riv.), SAfr.
61/E3 Krokom, Swe.
91/G2 Krókos, Gre.
66/C4 Kröller Müller Museum, Neth.
99/G2 Krolovets, Ukr.
72/B6 Krölpa, Ger.
65/J4 Kroměříž, Czh.
96/E1 Kromy, Rus.
71/E2 Kronach, Ger.
194/B2 Kronau, Sk,Can
70/B2 Kronberg im Taunus, Ger.
123/C4 Krong Kaoh Kong, Camb.
123/D4 Krong Keb, Camb.
62/F3 Kronoberg (co.), Swe.
63/N2 Kronshtadt, Rus.
71/H6 Kronstorf, Aus.
134/C4 Kroombit Tops Nat'l Park, Austl.
156/D2 Kroonstad, SAfr.
95/N5 Kropachevo, Rus.
53/H4 Kropotkin, Rus.
62/C4 Kropp, Ger.
72/B4 Kroppenstedt, Ger.
65/L4 Krosno, Pol.
65/L4 Krosno (prov.), Pol.
65/H2 Krosno Odrzańskie, Pol.
72/B6 Krossen, Ger.
72/C5 Krostitz, Ger.
65/J3 Krotoszyn, Pol.
95/L5 Krotovka, Rus.
81/G3 Krottenkopf, Grat (peak), Aus.
202/C2 Krotz Springs, La,US
91/J5 Krousón, Gre.
69/G4 Kröv, Ger.
92/B3 Krško, Slov.
73/D3 Krtíš (riv.), Slvk.
73/D3 Krtíš, Veľký, Slvk.
67/G1 Kruckau (riv.), Ger.
155/F4 Kruger Nat'l Park, SAfr.
157/E2 Kruger Nat'l Park, SAfr.
156/P13 Krugersdorp, SAfr.
95/N5 Kruglitsa, Gora (peak), Rus.
177/A5 Krugloi (pt.), Ak,US
124/C4 Krui, Indo.
66/B6 Kruibeke, Belg.
154/C4 Kruin, Namb.
66/B6 Kruiningen, Neth.
156/D4 Kruisfontein, SAfr.
92/D5 Krujë, Alb.
63/M4 Krulevshchina, Bela.
189/F1 Krum, Tx,US
70/D6 Krumbach, Ger.
73/A4 Krumbach Markt, Aus.
81/F3 Krummenau, Swi.
93/G5 Krumovgrad, Bul.
81/H3 Krün, Ger.
123/C3 Krung Thep (Bangkok) (cap.), Thai.
73/D3 Krupina, Slvk.
73/D3 Krupinica (riv.), Slvk.
72/D6 Krupka, Czh.
62/C4 Kruså, Den.
177/F2 Krusenstern (cape), Ak,US
92/E4 Kruševac, Yugo.
92/E5 Kruševo, Macd.
71/F2 Krušné Hory (Erzgebirge) (mts.), Czh., Ger.
65/K2 Kruszwica, Pol.
95/P5 Krutoyarskiy, Rus.
177/L4 Kruzof (isl.), Ak,US
99/K4 Krylovskaya, Rus.
99/K5 Krymsk, Rus.
65/L4 Krynica, Pol.
98/E3 Kryzhopol', Ukr.
65/M3 Krzna (riv.), Pol.
65/J2 Krzyż, Pol.
141/S16 Ksar el Boukhari, Alg.
141/M13 Ksar el Kebir, Mor.
143/F2 Ksel, Djebel (mtn.), Alg.
109/H1 Ksen'yevka, Rus.
99/J2 Kshenskiy, Rus.
103/C2 Ktima, Cyp.
124/B1 Kuah, Malay.
115/D4 Kuai (riv.), China
125/A4 Kuala Belait, Bru.
124/C1 Kuala Berang, Malay.
124/C1 Kuala Dungun, Malay.
124/C1 Kuala Kangsar, Malay.
124/C2 Kuala Kelawang, Malay.
124/C1 Kuala Kerai, Malay.
124/C2 Kuala Kubu Baharu, Malay.
124/C1 Kuala Kurau, Malay.
124/B1 Kualalangsa, Indo.
124/C1 Kuala Lipis, Malay.
124/C2 Kuala Lumpur (cap.), Malay.
124/C2 Kuala Lumpur (int'l arpt.), Malay.
124/C3 Kualamandah, Indo.
124/C2 Kuala Pahang, Malay.
125/A4 Kuala Penyu, Malay.
124/C2 Kuala Pilah, Malay.
180/T10 Kualapuu, Hi,US
124/C2 Kuala Rompin, Malay.
124/C2 Kuala Selangor, Malay.
124/B1 Kualasimpang, Indo.
124/C1 Kuala Terengganu, Malay.
124/C3 Kualatungkal, Indo.
125/B4 Kuamut, Malay.
117/J4 Kuan (peak), Tai.
115/D2 Kuancheng, China
113/C2 Kuandian, China
124/C2 Kuantan, Malay.
53/H4 Kuba, Azer.
99/J5 Kuban' (riv.), Rus.
99/K5 Kubano-Priazov (plain), Rus.
104/E3 Kubaysah, Iraq
148/D3 Kubbum, Sudan
94/H4 Kubenskoye (lake), Rus.
110/C4 Kubokawa, Japan
93/H4 Kubrat, Bul.
126/E3 Kubumesaai, Indo.
124/F5 Kubutambahan, Indo.
92/E3 Kučevo, Yugo.
121/F4 Kuchaiburi, India
81/G3 Kuchen (peak), Aus.
70/C5 Kuchen, Ger.
126/C3 Kuchinarai, Thai.
126/D3 Kuching, Malay.
112/L6 Kuchino (isl.), Japan
75/K3 Kuchl, Aus.
107/H2 Kūchnay Darvīshān, Afg.
91/F2 Kuçovë, Alb.
105/M6 Küçükçekmece (lake), Turk.
91/K3 Küçükkuyu, Turk.
126/D3 Kuda, Indo.
110/D3 Kudamatsu, Japan
145/G4 Kudan, Nga.
114/B4 Kudara, Taj.
125/B4 Kudat, Malay.
130/D1 Kudene, Indo.
63/K4 Kudirkos-Naumiestis, Lith.
122/G4 Kudremalai (pt.), SrL.
124/E4 Kudus, Indo.
53/J3 Kudymkar, Rus.
146/D3 Kufrah (oasis), Libya
103/D3 Kufrinjah, Jor.
75/K3 Kufstein, Aus.
97/L1 Kugarchi, Rus.
70/B4 Kuhardt, Ger.
70/E6 Kühbach, Ger.
105/F3 Kūhdasht, Iran
105/J5 Kūhestak, Iran
61/J2 Kuhmo, Fin.
63/L1 Kuhmoinen, Fin.
105/H3 Kūhpāyeh, Iran
72/D1 Kuhzer (lake), Ger.
161/E3 Kuikuinita, Nic.
66/D3 Kuinder of Tjonger (riv.), Neth.
154/B4 Kuiseb (dry riv.), Namb.
117/F4 Kuishan (mtn.), China
117/G4 Kuitan, China
154/C2 Kuito, Ang.
177/M4 Kuiu (isl.), Ak,US
63/K2 Kuivastu, Est.
113/D3 Kujang, NKor.
145/E5 Kujani Game Rsv., Gha.
65/K2 Kujawy (reg.), Pol.
112/B3 Kuji, Japan
110/B4 Kujū-san (mtn.), Japan
161/E3 Kukalaya (riv.), Nic.
148/B2 Kukawa, Nga.
116/C3 Kuke (riv.), China
91/G1 Kukës, Alb.
111/F2 Kuki, Japan
131/G2 Kukipi, PNG
111/J7 Kukizaki, Japan
63/L1 Kukkia (lake), Fin.
73/A5 Kukmirn, Aus.
95/L4 Kukmor, Rus.
95/N4 Kukushtan, Rus.
105/H5 Kūl (riv.), Iran
92/F4 Kula, Bul.
104/B2 Kula, Turk.
92/D3 Kula, Yugo.
122/A2 Kulachi, Pak.
97/J2 Kulagino, Kaz.
124/C2 Kulai, Malay.
106/D4 Kulākh, SAr.
151/B1 Kulal (peak), Kenya
97/J3 Kulaly (isl.), Kaz.
97/K4 Kulandag (mts.), Trkm.
121/J3 Kularua, Bang.
122/G4 Kulasekharapatnam, India
97/G4 Kulashi, Geo.
63/J3 Kuldīga, Lat.
154/D4 Kule, Bots.
94/J5 Kulebaki, Rus.
123/D3 Kulen, Camb.
150/B3 Kulen Shet' (dry riv.), Eth.
122/C1 Kulgām, India
133/G3 Kulgera, Austl.
97/L1 Kulgunino, Rus.
98/F2 Kulikovka, Ukr.
124/C1 Kulim, Malay.
132/C5 Kulin, Austl.
122/G3 Kulittalai, India
133/J5 Kulkyne-Hattah Nat'l Park, Austl.
63/L2 Kullamaa, Est.
62/E3 Kullen (cape), Swe.
107/L2 Kullu, India
194/E4 Kulm, ND,US
148/D2 Kulma, Wādī (dry riv.), Sudan
71/E2 Kulmbach, Ger.
94/J3 Kuloy, Rus.
95/J2 Kuloy, Rus.
95/J2 Kuloy (riv.), Rus.
120/B3 Kulpahār, India
206/B2 Kulpmont, Pa,US
206/C3 Kulpsville, Pa,US
97/K3 Kul'sary, Kaz.
70/C3 Külsheim, Ger.
121/H2 Kulsi (riv.), Bang.
121/F4 Kulti, India
122/D2 Kulu, India
104/C2 Kulu, Turk.
100/H4 Kulunda, Rus.
114/C1 Kulunda (lake), Rus.
114/D1 Kulunda (riv.), Rus.
114/C1 Kulunda Steppe (grsld.), Kaz., Rus.
107/J1 Kulyab, Taj.
113/D4 Kŭm (riv.), SKor.
53/H4 Kuma (riv.), Rus.
111/F2 Kumagaya, Japan
121/G2 Kumai, India
112/A2 Kumaishi, Japan
97/M2 Kumak, Rus.
165/G4 Kumaka, Guy.
110/B4 Kumamoto, Japan
110/B4 Kumamoto (int'l arpt.), Japan
110/B4 Kumamoto (pref.), Japan
110/E4 Kumano, Japan
110/D4 Kumano (riv.), Japan
92/E4 Kumanovo, Macd.
110/E3 Kumano-Yoshino Nat'l Park, Japan
121/G4 Kumār (riv.), Bang.
136/B3 Kumara, N.Z.
121/F4 Kumardubhi, India
121/G4 Kumārkhāli, Bang.
145/E5 Kumasi, Gha.
111/L10 Kumatori, Japan
53/H4 Kumayri, Arm.
145/H5 Kumba, Camr.
122/G3 Kumbakonam, India
131/F2 Kumbe, Indo.
134/C4 Kumbia, Austl.
148/A4 Kumbo, Camr.
113/D4 Kŭmch'ŏn, SKor.
97/K5 Kum-Dag, Trkm.
112/J7 Kumé (isl.), Japan
53/J3 Kumertau, Rus.
113/D3 Kŭmgang, NKor.
113/E3 Kumgang-san (mtn.), NKor.
122/D2 Kumhārsain, India
113/E5 Kŭmho (riv.), SKor.
113/D3 Kŭmhwa, SKor.
113/E4 Kumi, SKor.
153/H2 Kumi, Ugan.
111/L10 Kumiyama, Japan
116/C3 Kumjawng (pass), India
93/H6 Kumkale, Turk.
93/J5 Kumköy, Turk.
62/F2 Kumla, Swe.
103/B1 Kumluca, Turk.
71/E4 Kümmersbruck, Ger.
52/F2 Kumo (riv.), Fin.
145/H4 Kumo, Nga.
116/C3 Kumon (range), Burma
113/D4 Kŭmsan, SKor.
113/D3 Kŭmsanp'o, NKor.
153/G3 Kumsenga, Tanz.
118/C3 Kumta, India
180/U11 Kumukahi (cape), Hi,US
131/F1 Kumurkek, Indo.
99/M3 Kumylzhenskaya, Rus.
184/E2 Kuna, Id,US
112/E2 Kunashiri (isl.), Rus.
120/B3 Kūnch, India
120/E1 Kunchha, Nepal
63/M2 Kunda, Est.
120/C3 Kunda, India
122/F4 Kundara, India
120/B1 Kundarkhi, India
120/D2 Kundauli, India
153/F5 Kundelunga (mts.), Zaire
153/F5 Kundelungu Nat'l Park, Zaire
122/A1 Kundiān, Pak.
131/G1 Kundiawa, PNG
118/B3 Kundla, India
95/P5 Kundravy, Rus.
151/B3 Kunduchi, Tanz.
124/C2 Kundur (isl.), Indo.
154/B3 Kunene (riv.), Namb.
62/D3 Kungälv, Swe.
97/L4 Kungrad, Uzb.
63/R7 Kungsängen, Swe.
63/R7 Kungsangen (int'l arpt.), Swe.
62/E3 Kungsbacka, Swe.
62/D2 Kungshamn, Swe.
152/D2 Kungu, Zaire
153/G5 Kungu, Zam.
53/J3 Kungur, Rus.
151/A4 Kungutas, Tanz.
123/B2 Kungyangon, Burma
92/E2 Kunhegyes, Hun.
116/C4 Kunhing, Burma
110/B4 Kunimi-dake (mtn.), Japan
124/E4 Kuningan, Indo.
111/H7 Kunitachi, Japan
107/L1 Kunjirap (pass), China
114/C4 Kunjirap Daban (pass), China
206/C2 Kunkletown, Pa,US
102/H6 Kunlan (mts.), China
119/G3 Kunlong, Burma
114/C4 Kunlun (mts.), China
117/F4 Kunlun (pass), China
92/E2 Kunmadaras, Hun.
116/D3 Kunming, China
116/D3 Kunming (int'l arpt.), China
130/B3 Kunmunya Abor. Rsv., Austl.
122/E3 Kunnamangalam, India
122/F3 Kunnamkulam, India
73/B1 Kunovice, Czh.
113/D5 Kunsan, SKor.
115/E5 Kunshan, China
92/E2 Kunszentmárton, Hun.
73/D5 Kunszentmiklós, Hun.
144/B3 Kuntaur, Gam.
153/E3 Kuntshankoie, Zaire
120/A3 Kunu (riv.), India
130/C3 Kununurra, Austl.
120/A2 Kunwāri (riv.), India
113/E4 Kunwi, SKor.
145/H3 Kunya, Nga.
63/P3 Kun'ya, Rus.
113/A4 Kunyu (mtn.), China
115/E3 Kunyu Shan (mtn.), China
70/C1 Künzell, Ger.
149/H3 K'unzila, Eth.
152/D3 Kunzulu, Zaire
71/G5 Kunžvartské (pass), Czh.
117/J2 Kuocang (peak), China
63/L1 Kuohijärvi (lake), Fin.
94/F2 Kuolayarvi, Rus.
63/M1 Kuolimo (lake), Fin.
61/H3 Kuopio, Fin.
61/H3 Kuopio (prov.), Fin.
131/G1 Kup, PNG
92/B3 Kupa (riv.), Cro., Slov.
130/A2 Kupang, Indo.
131/G1 Kuper (range), PNG
131/H2 Kupiano, PNG
100/H4 Kupino, Rus.
63/L4 Kupiškis, Lith.
70/B5 Kuppenheim, Ger.
177/M4 Kupreanof (isl.), Ak,US
99/J3 Kupyansk, Ukr.
99/J3 Kupyansk-Uzlovoy, Ukr.
101/M5 Kuqa, China
109/L1 Kur (riv.), Rus.
97/J5 Kura (riv.), Azer., Geo.
97/H4 Kurakh, Rus.
99/J4 Kurakhovo, Ukr.
97/H1 Kurakino, Rus.
122/D2 Kūrālī, India
111/L9 Kurama-yama (peak), Japan
110/C3 Kurashiki, Japan
120/D4 Kurasia, India
147/F5 Kuraymah, Sudan
110/C3 Kurayoshi, Japan
114/D2 Kurchum, Kaz.
105/E2 Kurdistan (reg.), Asia
93/G5 Kŭrdzhali, Bul.
91/J2 Kŭrdzhali (res.), Bul.
110/C3 Kure, Japan
104/C1 Küre, Turk.
104/C1 Küre (mts.), Turk.
138/H2 Kure (isl.), Hi,US
120/D2 Kurebhār, India
63/K2 Kuressaare, Est.
100/K3 Kureyka (riv.), Rus.
97/P5 Kurgan, Rus.
99/L5 Kurganinsk, Rus.
99/J5 Kurgan Obl., Rus.
107/J1 Kurgan-Tyube, Taj.
120/A2 Kurgaon, India
113/G6 Kuri, SKor.
138/G4 Kuria (isl.), Kiri.
106/G5 Kuria Muria (isls.), Oman
121/G3 Kurīgrām, Bang.
112/B4 Kurikoma-yama (mtn.), Japan
101/Q5 Kuril (isls.), Rus.
97/J2 Kurilovka, Rus.
153/H2 Kuril'sk, Rus.
134/H8 Ku-Ring-Gai Nat'l Park, Austl.
154/C3 Kuring Kuru, Namb.
122/F3 Kurinjippādi, India
161/E3 Kurinwas (riv.), Nic.
112/B3 Kurisawa, Japan
112/B2 Kuriyama, Japan
103/C1 Kürkçü, Turk.
113/N1 Kurkiyoki, Rus.
116/C4 Kurla, India
94/J5 Kurlovskiy, Rus.
149/G3 Kurmuk, Sudan
118/C4 Kurnool, India
113/F7 Kuro, SKor.
112/C4 Kurodashō, Japan
112/B3 Kuroishi, Japan
111/G2 Kuroiso, Japan
194/C2 Kuroki, Sk,Can
108/G1 Kurort-Darasun, Rus.
71/F2 Kurort Oberwiesenthal, Ger.
111/M10 Kuroso-yama (peak), Japan
136/B4 Kurow, N.Z.
135/D2 Kurrajong, Austl.
122/A1 Kurram (riv.), Pak.
135/D2 Kurri Kurri, Austl.
134/H8 Kurrimine Beach, Austl.
99/M5 Kursavka, Rus.
63/K4 Kuršėnai, Lith.
122/G2 Kurseong, India
53/G3 Kursk, Rus.
63/J4 Kurskiy (lag.), Rus.
99/H2 Kursk Obl., Rus.
92/E4 Kuršumlija, Yugo.
104/C1 Kurşunlu, Turk.
104/E2 Kurtalan, Turk.
105/J5 Kurtamysh, Rus.
67/E6 Kürten, Ger.
149/F1 Kurtī, Sudan
105/M7 Kurtköy, Turk.
121/H2 Kuru (riv.), Bhu.
149/E3 Kuru (riv.), Sudan
104/B2 Kuruca (pass), Turk.
104/D2 Kuruçay, Turk.
97/G4 Kuruçay (riv.), Turk.
114/E3 Kuruktag (mts.), China
156/C2 Kuruman, SAfr.
156/C2 Kurumanrivier (dry riv.), SAfr.
110/B4 Kurume, Japan
108/G1 Kurumkan, Rus.
133/G2 Kurundi, Austl.
118/D6 Kurunegala, SrL.
165/G3 Kurupukari, Guy.
147/F4 Kurur, Jabal (peak), Sudan
134/E6 Kurwongbah (lake), Austl.
95/N3 Kur'ya, Rus.
113/D5 Kurye, SKor.
113/C3 Kuryong (riv.), NKor.
113/E5 Kuryongp'o-ri, SKor.
104/A2 Kuşadası, Turk.
97/M1 Kusakan, Kaz.
97/J4 Kusary, Azer.
123/C2 Ku Sathan (peak), Thai.
111/L9 Kusatsu, Japan
111/M9 Kusatsu, Japan
104/B1 Kuş Cenneti Nat'l Park, Turk.
89/L2 Kuş Cenneti Nat'l Park, Turk.
69/G4 Kusel, Ger.
107/K4 Kushālgarh, India
99/K4 Kushchevskaya, Rus.
145/G4 Kusheriki, Nga.
111/M10 Kushida (riv.), Japan
111/N9 Kushihara, Japan
110/B5 Kushikino, Japan
110/B5 Kushima, Japan
110/D4 Kushimoto, Japan
112/D2 Kushiro, Japan
112/D2 Kushiro (riv.), Japan
107/H1 Kushka, Trkm.
100/G4 Kushmurun, Kaz.
95/Q5 Kushmurun (lake), Kaz.
122/D1 Kushol, India
121/G4 Kushtia, Bang.
121/G4 Kushtia (dist.), Bang.
108/F4 Kushui (riv.), China
97/J2 Kushum (riv.), Kaz.
121/H3 Kusiyara (riv.), Bang.
177/F4 Kuskokwim (bay), Ak,US
177/G3 Kuskokwim (mts.), Ak,US
177/F3 Kuskokwim (riv.), Ak,US
177/H3 Kuskokwim, North Fork (riv.), Ak,US
177/H3 Kuskokwim, South Fork (riv.), Ak,US
120/D1 Kusma, Nepal
81/E3 Küsnacht, Swi.
113/C3 Kusŏng, NKor.
112/C2 Kussharo (lake), Japan
81/E3 Küssnacht am Rigi, Swi.
97/M1 Kustanay, Kaz.
97/M1 Kustanay (int'l arpt.), Kaz.
97/M2 Kustanay Obl., Kaz.
97/G1 Kustarevka, Rus.
70/C5 Kusterdingen, Ger.
149/G2 Kūstī, Sudan
111/M10 Kusu, Japan
123/D2 Kusuman, Thai.
123/C4 Kut (isl.), Thai.
145/G4 Kuta, Nga.
124/B2 Kutacane, Indo.
104/B2 Kütahya, Turk.
104/B2 Kütahya (prov.), Turk.
99/K5 Kutais, Rus.
53/H4 Kutaisi, Geo.
97/G4 Kutaisi (int'l arpt.), Geo.
118/A3 Kutch (gulf), India
118/A3 Kutch (reg.), India
112/B2 Kutchan, Japan
112/C1 Kutcharo (lake), Japan
107/J4 Kutch, Rann of (swamp), India, Pak.
67/G2 Kutenholz, Ger.
145/G4 Kutiwenji, Nga.
105/F1 Kutkashen, Azer.
65/H4 Kutná Hora, Czh.
65/K2 Kutno, Pol.
154/D4 Kutse Game Rsv., Bots.
111/L9 Kutsuki, Japan
80/E3 Küttigen, Swi.
152/D3 Kutu, Zaire
108/E1 Kutulik, Rus.
151/C1 Kutulo, Lagh (dry riv.), Kenya
149/E2 Kutum, Sudan
153/E3 Kutu-Owanga, Zaire
73/B2 Kúty, Slvk.
81/G1 Kutzenhausen, Ger.
206/C2 Kutztown, Pa,US
178/E1 Kuujjua (riv.), NW,Can
179/K3 Kuujjuaq (Fort-Chimo), Qu,Can
179/J3 Kuujjuarapik, Qu,Can
97/K4 Kuuli-Mayak, Trkm.
61/J2 Kuusamo, Fin.
63/M1 Kuusankoski, Fin.
63/M2 Kuutse (hill), Est.
94/E4 Kuutse Mägi (hill), Est
97/L2 Kuvandyk, Rus.
154/C2 Kuvango, Ang.
105/F4 Kuwait
105/F4 Kuwait (int'l arpt.), Kuw.
105/F4 Kuwait (Al Kuwayt) (cap.), Kuw.
120/D2 Kuwānā (riv.), India
110/E3 Kuwana, Japan
95/L5 Kuybyshev, Rus.
53/H3 Kuybyshev (res.), Rus.
98/F4 Kuybyshevka, Ukr.
95/Q5 Kuybyshevskiy, Kaz.
115/B3 Kuye (riv.), China
105/F2 Küysanjaq, Iraq
108/C3 Küysu, China
94/F2 Kuyto (lake), Rus.
114/E3 Kuytun, China
114/D2 Kuytun (riv.), China
165/G4 Kuyuwini (riv.), Guy.
172/F4 Kuzhittura, India
177/E2 Kuzitrin (riv.), Ak,US
63/P1 Kuz'molovskiy, Rus.
97/H1 Kuznetsk, Rus.
94/H2 Kuzomen', Rus.
97/H1 Kuzovatovo, Rus.
103/D1 Kuzucubelen, Turk.
112/B3 Kuzumaki, Japan
61/F1 Kvaløy (isl.), Nor.
97/H4 Kvareli, Geo.
92/B3 Kvarnerić (chan.), Cro.
62/D4 Kværndrup, Den.
92/B3 Kvarner (chan.), Cro.
75/L4 Kvarnerić (chan.), Cro
61/C3 Kvernberget (arpt.), Nor.

61/E2 Kvigtinden (peak), Nor.
62/B2 Kvinesdal, Nor.
62/B2 Kvinnherad, Nor.
152/D3 Kwa (riv.), Zaire
69/E1 Kwaadmechelen, Belg.
113/G7 Kwach'ŏn, SKor.
113/C3 Kwail, NKor.
123/B3 Kwai, River (bridge), Thai.
138/F4 Kwajelein (atoll), Mrsh.
149/F3 Kwajok, Sudan
166/C1 Kwakoegron, Sur.
113/C3 Kwaksan, NKor.
165/G3 Kwakwani, Guy.
151/B3 Kwale, Kenya
145/G4 Kwali, Nga.
157/E3 KwaMashu, SAfr.
145/E4 Kwamen Kwesi, Gha.
152/D3 Kwamouth, Zaire
151/A3 Kwa Mtoro, Tanz.
156/Q12 Kwandebele (homeland), SAfr.
154/D3 Kwando (riv.), Bots., Namb.
113/D4 Kwangch'ŏn, SKor.
113/D5 Kwangju, SKor.
113/G7 Kwangju, SKor.
113/D5 Kwangju-Jikhalsi, SKor.
140/D5 Kwango (riv.), Ang., Zaire
113/F7 Kwangsan (mtn.), SKor.
151/B3 Kwangwazi, Tanz.
113/D5 Kwangyang, SKor.
153/H2 Kwania (res.), Ugan.
113/D5 Kwansan, SKor.
145/G4 Kwara (state), Nga.
151/A3 Kwaraha (peak), Tanz.
145/G3 Kwatarkwashi, Nga.
155/F3 Kwekwe, Zim.
154/E4 Kweneng (dist.), Bots.
152/D4 Kwenge (riv.), Zaire
177/F3 Kwethluk, Ak,US
65/K2 Kwidzyn, Pol.
177/F4 Kwigillingok, Ak,US
150/A2 Kwīha, Eth.
131/G2 Kwikila, PNG
152/D4 Kwilu (riv.), Zaire
132/B5 Kwinana, Austl.
166/B2 Kwitara (riv.), Guy.
148/C3 Kyabé, Chad
135/C3 Kyabram, Austl.
123/B2 Kyaikkami, Burma
123/B2 Kyaikpi, Burma
123/B2 Kyaiktiyo Pagoda, Burma
116/C5 Kyaikto, Burma
123/B2 Kya-in Seikkyi, Burma
153/G3 Kyaka, Tanz.
108/F1 Kyakhta, Rus.
135/B2 Kyalite, Austl.
133/G5 Kyancutta, Austl.
116/B5 Kyangin, Burma
123/D2 Ky Anh, Viet.
112/J7 Kyan-zaki (cape), Japan
94/G3 Kyargozero, Rus.
123/B2 Kyaukki, Burma
116/C4 Kyaukme, Burma
116/B4 Kyaukpadaung, Burma
116/B5 Kyaukpyu, Burma
116/C4 Kyaukse, Burma
116/B5 Kyaunggon, Burma
63/K4 Kybartai, Lith.
153/G2 Kyegegwa, Ugan.
122/D1 Kyelang, India
153/G2 Kyenjojo, Ugan.
113/D4 Kyeryong-san Nat'l Park, SKor.
116/C5 Kyidaunggan, Burma
108/E4 Kyikug, China
116/B4 Kyindwe, Burma
73/B1 Kyjov, Czh.
183/K2 Kyle, Sk,Can
54/B5 Kyle (dist.), Sc,UK
192/C2 Kyle, SD,US
189/F3 Kyle, Tx,US
194/C2 Kylemore, Sk,Can
155/F4 Kyle Nat'l Park, Zim.
69/F3 Kyll (riv.), Ger.
69/F3 Kyllburg, Ger.
59/F2 Kym (riv.), Eng,UK
63/M1 Kymi (prov.), Fin.
63/M1 Kymijoki (riv.), Fin.
118/C3 Kymore, India
95/N4 Kyn, Rus.
135/C3 Kyneton, Austl.
71/F2 Kynšperk nad Ohří, Czh.
133/J2 Kynuna, Austl.
151/A1 Kyoga (res.), Ugan.
110/D3 Kyōga-misaki (cape), Japan
135/E1 Kyogle, Austl.
111/F3 Kyonan, Japan
113/G7 Kyŏngan, SKor.
113/F6 Kyongbok Palace, SKor.
113/C4 Kyŏnggi (bay), SKor.
113/D4 Kyŏnggi-do (prov.), SKor.
113/E5 Kyŏngju, SKor.
113/E5 Kyŏngju Nat'l Park, SKor.
113/E5 Kyŏngsan, SKor.
113/E4 Kyŏngsang-bukto (prov.), SKor.
113/E5 Kyŏngsang-namdo (prov.), SKor.
113/E2 Kyŏngsŏng, NKor.
116/B5 Kyŏnkadun, Burma
110/D3 Kyōto, Japan
110/D3 Kyōto (pref.), Japan
111/L10 Kyōto Imperial Palace, Japan
103/C2 Kyrenia, Cyp.
103/C2 Kyrenia (dist.), Cyp.
114/B3 Kyrgyzstan
72/C2 Kyritz, Ger.
63/L1 Kyrkslätt (Kirkkonummi), Fin.
63/K1 Kyrösjärvi (lake), Fin.
95/N2 Kyrta, Rus.
97/J2 Kyrykuduk, Kaz.
95/P5 Kyshtym, Rus.
116/E5 Ky Son, Viet.
103/C2 Kythrea, Cyp.
95/N4 Kytlym, Rus.
116/B4 Kyunhla, Burma
105/G1 Kyurdamir, Azer.
110/B5 Kyūshū (isl.), Japan
110/B4 Kyūshū (mts.), Japan
110/B4 Kyūshū (prov.), Japan
92/F4 Kyustendil, Bul.
101/N2 Kyusyur, Rus.
119/F4 Kywebwe, Burma
114/F1 Kyzyl, Rus.
100/G5 Kyzylkum (des.), Kaz.,Uzb.
100/G5 Kzyl-Orda, Kaz.
100/H4 Kzyltu, Kaz.

L

73/A2 Laa an der Thaya, Aus.
71/E4 Laaber, Ger.
64/G2 Laage, Ger.
161/H4 La Aguja, Cabo de (pt.), Col.
71/G7 Laakirchen, Aus.
76/B4 La Algaba, Sp.
76/E2 La Almunia de Doña Godina, Sp.
161/F4 La Amistad Int'l Park, CR
159/N7 La Antigua Veracruz, Mex.
174/B3 La Araucanía (reg.), Chile
68/C1 Laarne, Belg.
150/C3 Laas Caanood, Som.
158/D2 La Ascensión, Mex.
150/C3 Laas Dhaareed, Som.
81/G4 Laas (Lasa), It.
150/D3 Laas Qoray, Som.
174/D3 La Asturiana, Arg.
165/F2 La Asunción, Ven.
67/G4 Laatzen, Ger.
160/D3 La Aurora (int'l arpt.), Guat.
81/F4 Laax, Swi.
142/B4 Laayoune, WSah.
142/B4 Laayoune (Hassan) (int'l arpt.), WSah.
188/C3 La Babia, Mex.
202/C3 Labadieville, La,US
196/B1 La Baie, Qu,Can
76/A1 La Baña, Sp.
76/C1 La Bañeza, Sp.
126/D3 Labang, Malay.
158/E4 La Barca, Mex.
185/H2 La Barge, Wy,US
175/G2 La Barra, Uru.
79/F3 La Barre-en-Ouche, Fr.
60/A4 Labasheeda, Ire.
125/C3 Labason, Phil.
68/B2 La Bassée, Fr.
82/C1 La Bâthie, Fr.
82/C3 La Bâtie-Neuve, Fr.
73/C4 Lábatlan, Hun.
78/C6 La Baule-Escoublac, Fr.
79/F4 La Bazoge, Fr.
80/C4 L'Abbaye, Swi.
84/B2 Labbro (peak), It.
65/H3 Labe (riv.), Czh.
144/B4 Labé, Gui.
144/B4 Labé (comm.), Gui.
71/H2 Labe (Elbe) (riv.), Czh.
199/J1 Labelle, Qu,Can
203/H4 La Belle, Fl,US
71/F5 Laberweinting, Ger.
125/B4 Labian, Tanjong (cape), Malay.
92/B3 Labin, Cro.
99/L5 Labinsk, Rus.
124/C2 Labis, Malay.
77/G2 La Bisbal, Sp.
165/E2 La Blanquilla (isl.), Ven.
159/H4 Labná (ruins), Mex.
125/C2 Labo, Phil.
79/G3 La Bonneville, Fr.
79/F3 La Bonneville-sur-Iton, Fr.
174/E2 Laborde, Arg.
65/L4 Laborec (riv.), Slvk.
127/F4 Labota, Indo.
172/E4 Labougle, Arg.
74/C4 Labouheyre, Fr.
174/E2 Laboulaye, Arg.
179/M4 Labrador (sea), Can.
179/K3 Labrador (reg.), Nf,Can
179/K3 Labrador City, Nf,Can
169/E2 Lábrea, Braz.
80/C2 La Bresse, Fr.
196/C1 Labrieville, Qu,Can
80/D1 La Broque, Fr.
194/F3 La Broquerie, Mb,Can
74/E5 Labruguière, Fr.
69/E5 Labry, Fr.
125/A4 Labuan (terr.), Malay.
124/D4 Labuhan, Indo.
127/E5 Labuhanbajo, Indo.
124/C2 Labuhanbilik, Indo.
124/B2 Labuhanhaji, Indo.
124/D4 Labuhanmaringgai, Indo.
124/B2 Labuhanruku, Indo.
125/B5 Labuk (bay), Malay.
127/E2 Labuk (riv.), Malay.
92/E5 Labuništa, Macd.
71/F4 Labutta, Burma
100/G3 Labytnangi, Rus.
91/F2 Laç, Alb.
148/B2 Lac (pref.), Chad
188/D3 La Cabecera, Mex.
183/K2 Lacadena, Sk,Can
197/P7 Lacadie, Qu,Can
142/A3 La Caldera de Taburiente Nat'l Park, Canl.,Sp.
174/C2 La Calera, Chile
167/M7 La Calera, Col.
197/N6 Lac-Alouette, Qu,Can
158/E3 La Campana, Mex.
76/C4 La Campana, Sp.
174/C2 La Campana Nat'l Park, Chile
204/B2 La Cañada-Flintridge, Ca,US
74/C4 Lacanau-Océan, Fr.
165/F2 La Canoa, Ven.
160/D2 Lacantum (riv.), Mex.
68/C4 La Capelle-en-Thiérache, Fr.
174/E2 La Carlota, Arg.
76/C4 La Carlota, Sp.
175/L8 La Carmen, Arg.
76/D3 La Carolina, Sp.
202/B2 Lacassine Nat'l Wild. Ref., La,US
159/Q9 La Catedral (mt.), Mex.
67/E5 Lacaune, Fr.
196/D1 Lac-au-Saumon, Qu,Can
196/A2 Lac-aux-Sables, Qu,Can
196/A1 Lac-Bouchette, Qu,Can
118/B5 Laccadive (sea), India
86/C2 Lacchiarella, It.
80/D5 Lacco Ameno, It.
195/J5 Lac Court Oreilles Ind. Res., Wi,US
196/C2 Lac-des-Aigles, Qu,Can
196/B3 Lac-Drolet, Qu,Can
194/F2 Lac du Bonnet, Mb,Can
199/J1 Lac-du-Cerf, Qu,Can
198/B2 Lac du Flambeau, Wi,US
195/K4 Lac du Flambeau Ind. Res., Wi,US
85/F5 Lacedonia, It.
196/A2 Lac-Édouard, Qu,Can
160/E3 La Ceiba, Hon.
160/E3 La Ceiba (int'l arpt.), Hon.
164/D3 La Ceiba, Ven.
167/K6 La Ceja, Col.
53/S10 La Celle-Saint-Cloud, Fr.
200/C2 La Center, Ky,US
135/A3 Lacepede (bay), Austl.
155/G3 Lacerdónia, Moz.
81/G4 Laces (Latsch), It.
196/B2 Lac-Etchemin, Qu,Can
191/J4 Lacey, Ar,US
205/B3 Lacey, Wa,US
94/H3 Lacha (lake), Rus.
129/H6 Lachan (riv.), Austl.
68/A5 Lachapelle-aux-Pots, Fr.
80/A5 La Chapelle-de-Guinchay, Fr.
78/C6 La Chapelle-des-Marais, Fr.
82/C3 La Chapelle-en-Valgodemard, Fr.
74/F2 La Chapelle-St-Luc, Fr.
78/D6 La Chapelle-sur-Erdre, Fr.
79/F5 La Chartres-sur-le-Loir, Fr.
79/G5 La Chaussée-Saint-Victor, Fr.
80/C3 La Chaux-de-Fonds, Swi.
82/B4 La Chavière, Montagne de (mtn.), Fr.
168/B3 Lachay (pt.), Peru
81/E3 Lachen, Swi.
197/N6 Lachenaie, Qu,Can
67/H3 Lachendorf, Ger.
82/C5 Lachens (riv.), Fr.
120/A2 Lachhmangarh, India
122/A1 Lāchi, Pak.
197/N7 Lachine, Qu,Can
164/D2 La Chinita (int'l arpt.), Ven.
135/C2 Lachlan (riv.), Austl.
164/C5 La Chorrera, Col.
161/G4 La Chorrera, Pan.
67/H3 Lachte (riv.), Ger.
121/G2 Lachung, India
199/J2 Lachute, Qu,Can
190/A3 La Cienega, NM,US
76/A1 La Ciñiza, Sp.
82/B6 La Ciotat, Fr.
199/G3 Lackawanna, NY,US
206/C1 Lackawanna (co.), Pa,US
189/E3 Lackland A.F.B., Tx,US
62/E2 Läckö, Swe.
178/E3 Lac La Biche, Ab,Can
182/D2 Lac La Hache, BC,Can
178/E2 Lac la Martre, NW,Can
130/B2 Laclubar, Indo.
80/C6 La Clusaz, Fr.
196/B3 Lac-Mégantic, Qu,Can
117/J5 Lacob ti-Duyong (mt.), Phil.
172/C3 La Cocha, Arg.
58/D4 Lacock, Eng,UK
82/D5 La Colle-sur-Loup, Fr.
159/F3 La Coma, Mex.
184/B1 Lacomb, Or,US
183/H1 Lacombe, Ab,Can
202/D2 Lacombe, La,US
193/K3 Lacon, Il,US
159/Q9 La Concepción (res.), Mex.
160/E4 La Concepción, Nic.
161/F4 La Concepción, Pan.
164/D2 La Concepción, Ven.
160/C2 La Concordia, Mex.
199/L3 Laconia, NH,US
203/G3 Lacoochee, Fl,US
175/G2 La Coronilla, Uru.
76/A1 La Coruña, Sp.
82/B2 La Côte-Saint-André, Fr.
53/T10 La Courneuve, Fr.
74/D4 La Couronne, Fr.
183/L3 Lac Pelletier, Sk,Can
193/F1 Lac qui Parle (lake), Mn,US
82/C6 La Crau, Fr.
74/C3 La Crèche, Fr.
192/D2 Lacreek Nat'l Wild. Ref., SD,US
204/B2 La Crescenta-Montrose, Ca,US
172/D4 La Criolla, Arg.
196/A2 La Croche, Qu,Can
68/B5 Lacroix-Saint-Ouen, Fr.
130/C3 Lacross (isl.), Austl.
190/E1 La Crosse, Ks,US
201/H2 La Crosse, Va,US
193/J2 La Crosse, Wi,US
174/Q9 La Cruz, Chile
164/B4 La Cruz, Col.
160/E4 La Cruz, CR
158/D3 La Cruz, Mex.
158/D3 La Cruz, Mex.
175/F2 La Cruz, Uru.
196/B2 Lac-Saint-Charles, Qu,Can
195/H2 Lac Seul, On,Can
123/D1 Lac Son, Viet.
126/C1 Lac Thien, Viet.
175/G2 La Cuchilla, Uru.
188/C3 La Cuesta, Mex.
168/J7 La Cumbre (vol.), Ecu.
191/G1 La Cygne, Ks,US
189/F2 Lacy-Lakeview, Tx,US
107/L2 Ladakh (mts.), Pak., India
170/A3 Ladário, Braz.
67/E4 Ladbergen, Ger.
54/C2 Ladder (hills), Sc,UK
190/D1 Ladder (cr.), Co, Ks,US
135/B3 Laddon (riv.), Austl.
191/J3 Laddonia, Mo,US
65/J3 Lądek-Zdrój, Pol.
73/A2 Ladendorf, Aus.
184/B2 Ladera Heights, Ca,US
156/C4 Ladismith, SAfr.
84/C4 Ladispoli, It.
149/F4 Lado, Sudan
63/P1 Ladoga (lake), Rus.
80/C5 La Dôle (peak), Swi.
81/E4 La Dorada, Col.
196/A1 La Doré, Qu,Can
174/D2 La Dormida, Arg.
99/K5 Ladozhskaya, Rus.
63/P1 Ladozhskoye Ozero, Rus.
175/J8 Ladrillero (mtn.), Chile
161/G1 Ladrillo (pt.), Cuba
201/G4 Ladson, SC,US
88/D1 La Durande (mtn.), Fr.
94/G3 Ladva-Vetka, Rus.
54/B5 Lady (isl.), Sc,UK
54/C4 Ladybank, Sc,UK
135/D4 Lady Barron, Austl.
57/G5 Ladybower (res.), Eng,UK
156/D3 Ladybrand, SAfr.
123/D4 Lady Chua Xu, Temple of, Viet.
194/C1 Lady Lake, Sk,Can
203/H3 Lady Lake, Fl,US
182/C3 Ladysmith, BC,Can
157/E3 Ladysmith, SAfr.
193/J1 Ladysmith, Wi,US
159/H5 Ladyville, Belz.
98/E3 Ladyzhin, Ukr.
138/F4 Lae (isl.), Mrsh.
131/G1 Lae, PNG
123/C2 Lae, Thai.
169/E4 La Embocada, Bol.
67/E4 Laer, Ger.
172/E3 La Escondida, Arg.
159/F3 La Escondida, Mex.
165/E4 La Esmeralda, Ven.
62/D3 Laesø (isl.), Den.
174/C4 La Esperanza, Arg.
169/E4 La Esperanza, Bol.
169/E4 La Esperanza, Bol.
169/F5 La Esperanza, Bol.
160/D3 La Esperanza, Hon.
165/F2 La Esperanza, Ven.
160/E3 La Esperanza, Sierra (range), Hon.
76/B1 La Estaca de Bares, Punta de (cape), Sp.
175/T12 La Estanzuela, Uru.
76/A1 La Estrada, Sp.
174/Q10 La Estrella, Chile
172/C4 La Falda, Arg.
82/B5 La Fare-les-Oliviers, Fr.
82/C6 La Farlède, Fr.
200/E4 Lafayette, Al,US
205/K11 Lafayette, Ca,US
192/B4 Lafayette, Co,US
200/E3 La Fayette, Ga,US
198/C4 Lafayette, In,US
202/B2 Lafayette, La,US
196/B3 Lafayette (mt.), NH,US
206/D1 Lafayette, NJ,US
184/B1 Lafayette, Or,US
200/D2 Lafayette, Tn,US
191/J2 Lafe, Ar,US
68/C4 La Fère, Fr.
79/E3 La Ferrière-aux-Étangs, Fr.
79/F4 La Ferte-Bernard, Fr.
68/C6 La Ferté-Gaucher, Fr.
79/G6 La Ferté-Imbault, Fr.
79/E3 La Ferté-Macé, Fr.
68/C5 La Ferté-Milon, Fr.
68/C6 La Ferté-sous-Jouarre, Fr.
79/G5 La Ferté-St-Aubin, Fr.
79/F3 La Ferté-Vidame, Fr.
145/H4 Lafia, Nga.
145/G4 Lafiagi, Nga.
202/C3 Lafitte, La,US
194/A3 Lafleche, Sk,Can
79/E5 La Flèche, Fr.
75/L3 Lafnitz (riv.), Aus.
200/E2 La Follette, Tn,US
197/M6 Lafontaine, Qu,Can
198/D4 La Fontaine, In,US
75/G4 La Font Sancte, Pic de (peak), Fr.
202/C3 Lafourche (bayou), La,US
172/D4 La Francia, Arg.
164/C2 La Fria, Ven.
119/F6 Lāfūl, India
85/D2 Laga (mts.), It.
149/H5 Laga Balal (riv.), Kenya
196/E2 Lagacéville, NB,Can
78/C5 La Gacilly, Fr.
173/H1 Lagamar, Braz.
62/E3 Lagan, Swe.
62/E3 Lagan (riv.), Swe.
56/B3 Lagan (riv.), NI,UK
82/A4 La Gard-Adhémar, Fr.
82/C6 La Garde, Fr.
82/C6 La Garde-Freinet, Fr.
53/S10 La Garenne-Colombes, Fr.
87/D2 Lagarina (val.), It.
187/J2 La Garita, Co,US
190/A2 La Garita (mts.), Co,US
77/L6 La Garriga, Sp.
171/F1 Lagarto, Braz.
125/C1 Lagawe, Phil.
153/G2 Lagbo, Zaire
148/B3 Lagdo (lake), Camr.
148/B3 Lagdo, Barrage de (dam), Camr.
67/F5 Lage, Ger.
62/C1 Lågen (riv.), Nor.
62/D1 Lågen (riv.), Nor.
173/G3 Lages, Braz.
66/B4 Lage Vaart (can.), Neth.
54/B2 Laggan, Sc,UK
54/B3 Laggan, Loch (lake), Sc,UK
150/A5 Lagh Bogal (dry riv.), Kenya
150/A5 Lagh Bor (dry riv.), Kenya
143/F2 Laghouat, Alg.
143/F2 Laghouat (wilaya), Alg.
150/B5 Lagh Sure (dry riv.), Kenya
60/C5 Laghtnafrankee (mtn.), Ire.
76/E3 La Gineta, Sp.
78/D1 La Glacerie, Fr.
164/C2 La Gloria, Col.
189/E4 La Gloria, Tx,US
80/B6 Lagnieu, Fr.
53/U9 Lagny-le-Sec, Fr.
53/U10 Lagny-sur-Marne, Fr.
83/C4 Lago, It.
76/A4 Lagoa, Port.
170/D4 Lagoa da Prata, Braz.
170/D3 Lagoa Formosa, Braz.
164/B4 Lago Agrio (Nueva Loja), Ecu.
173/G4 Lagoa Vermelha, Braz.
175/K7 Lago Cardiel, Arg.
167/E4 Lago da Pedra, Braz.
160/D3 Lago de Atitlán Nat'l Park, Guat.
97/H4 Lagodekhi, Geo.
81/E5 Lago Gelato, Pizzo di (peak), It.
83/B2 Lagonegro, It.
166/D2 Lago Piratuba Bio. Rsv., Braz.
175/K6 Lago Posadas, Arg.
174/C4 Lago Puelo Nat'l Park, Arg.
74/C3 Lagord, Fr.
145/F5 Lagos, Nga.
145/F5 Lagos (state), Nga.
76/A4 Lagos, Port.
87/F3 Lagosanto, It.
158/E4 Lagos de Moreno, Mex.
174/C5 Lago Verde, Chile
175/J7 Lago Viedma, Arg.
176/K4 La Grande (riv.), Can.
184/D1 La Grande, Or,US
82/B2 La Grande Moucherolle (mtn.), Fr.
82/C3 La Grande Ruine (mtn.), Fr.
130/A4 La Grange, Austl.
200/E4 La Grange, Ga,US
198/D4 Lagrange, In,US
200/E1 La Grange, Ky,US
196/C3 Lagrange, Me,US
193/J3 La Grange, Mo,US
201/J3 La Grange, NC,US
208/E5 Lagrange, Oh,US
189/F3 La Grange, Tx,US
192/B3 La Grange, Wy,US
165/F3 La Gran Sabana (plain), Ven.
82/C2 La Grave, Fr.
161/J4 La Grita, Ven.
191/J3 La Grue (bayou), Ar,US
196/B3 La Guadeloupe, Qu,Can
167/O7 La Guaira, Ven.
164/C2 La Guajira (dept.), Col.
172/C4 La Guardia, Arg.
172/D1 La Guardia, Bol.
74/B5 Laguardia, Sp.
76/A2 La Guardia, Sp.
76/D1 Laguardia, Sp.
207/E2 La Guardia (int'l arpt.), NY,US
78/D5 La Guerche-de-Bretagne, Fr.
174/D3 La Guerra (peak), Arg.
173/G4 Laguna, Braz.
186/E4 Laguna (dam), Az,US
205/M10 Laguna (cr.), Ca,US
186/D4 Laguna (mts.), Ca,US
187/J3 Laguna, NM,US
189/F4 Laguna Atascosa Nat'l Wild. Ref., Tx,US
204/C3 Laguna Beach, Ca,US
203/F2 Laguna Beach, Fl,US
174/C3 Laguna Blanca Nat'l Park, Arg.
158/B2 Laguna Chapala, Mex.
76/C2 Laguna de Duero, Sp.
165/E2 Laguna de la Restinga Nat'l Park, Ven.
174/C3 Laguna del Laja Nat'l Park, Chile
174/D4 Laguna Grande, Arg.
175/K7 Laguna Grande, Arg.
204/C3 Laguna Hills, Ca,US
187/J3 Laguna Ind. Res., NM,US
174/E1 Laguna Larga, Arg.
172/B2 Lagunas, Chile
168/B2 Lagunas, Peru
168/C2 Lagunas, Peru
186/E4 Laguna Salada (dry lake), Mex.
174/B5 Laguna San Rafael Nat'l Park, Chile
160/B2 Lagunas de Chacahua Nat'l Park, Mex.
174/Q9 Laguna Verde, Chile
172/D3 Laguna Yema, Arg.
81/H4 Lagundo (Algund), It.
164/D2 Lagunetas, Ven.
172/D1 Lagunillas, Bol.
174/Q9 Lagunillas, Chile
158/D4 Lagunillas, Mex.
164/D2 Lagunillas, Ven.
161/E3 Laguntara (lag.), Hon.
113/C2 Lagushao, China
161/F1 La Habana (Havana) (cap.), Cuba
204/C3 La Habra, Ca,US
125/B4 Lahad Datu, Malay.
123/C3 Lahan Sai, Thai.
120/B2 Lahār, India
191/G2 La Harpe, Ks,US
120/C2 Lāharpur, India
124/C3 Lahat, Indo.
196/D3 La Have (riv.), NS,Can
78/D3 La Haye-du-Puits, Fr.
78/D3 La Haye-Pesnel, Fr.
121/E2 Laheria Sarāi, India
124/B2 Lahewa, Indo.
172/B4 La Higuera, Chile
150/C2 Laḩij, Yem.
105/G2 Lāhījān, Iran
64/E3 Lahn (riv.), Ger.
67/G3 Lahnstein, Ger.
62/E3 Laholm, Swe.
62/E3 Laholmsbukten (bay), Swe.
191/E2 Lahoma, Ok,US
205/K12 La Honda, Ca,US
184/D4 Lahontan (dam), Nv,US
184/D4 Lahontan (res.), Nv,US
122/C2 Lahore, Pak.
122/C2 Lahore (int'l arpt.), Pak.
165/F2 La Horqueta, Ven.
165/F3 La Horqueta, Ven.
169/E4 La Horquilla, Bol.
70/A6 Lahr, Ger.
105/F2 Lāhrūd, Iran
63/L1 Lahti, Fin.
168/A2 La Huaca, Peru
159/E5 La Huacana, Mex.
158/D5 La Huerta, Mex.
140/D4 Laï, Chad
131/F1 Laiagam, PNG
115/D4 Lai'an, China
87/D6 Laiatico, It.
119/J3 Laibin, China
123/C1 Lai Chau, Viet.
70/C6 Laichingen, Ger.
54/B3 Laidon, Loch (lake), Sc,UK
180/T10 Laie, Hi,US
115/B5 Laifeng, China
79/F3 L'Aigle, Fr.
82/B6 L'Aigle, Cap de (cape), Fr.
86/B5 Laigueglia, It.
143/E2 L'Aiguille, Cap de (cape), Alg.
61/G3 Laihia, Fin.
123/B1 Lai-hka, Burma
79/G5 Lailly-en-Val, Fr.
86/C1 Lainate, It.
156/C4 Laingsburg, SAfr.
61/G2 Lainioälven (riv.), Swe.
183/L1 Laird, Sk,Can
124/C3 Lais, Indo.
125/D4 Lais, Phil.
151/B1 Laisamis, Kenya
95/L5 Laishevo, Rus.
115/C3 Laishui, China
94/C2 Laisvall, Swe.
63/J1 Laitila, Fin.
81/H5 Laives (Leifers), It.
115/D3 Laiwu, China
115/E3 Laixi, China
115/E3 Laiyang, China
115/C3 Laiyuan, China
115/D3 Laizhou (bay), China
174/C3 Laja (lake), Chile
168/B2 La Jalca, Peru
190/B2 La Jara, Co,US
190/A2 La Jara, NM,US
168/B2 Lajas, Peru
75/J5 Lajatico, It.
82/C4 La Javie, Fr.
171/E1 Laje, Braz.
173/G4 Lajeado, Braz.
171/F1 Lajedo, Braz.
167/G4 Lajes, Braz.
77/S12 Lajes (int'l arpt.), Azor.,Port.
77/S12 Lajes do Pico, Azor.,Port.
121/E1 Lajing (Gya La) (pass), China, Nepal
186/D4 La Jolla Ind. Res., Ca,US
194/B2 Lajord, Sk,Can
92/D2 Lajosmizse, Hun.
172/C1 La Joya, Bol.
158/D3 La Joya, Mex.
168/D5 La Joya, Peru
164/B5 La Joya de los Sachas, Ecu.
187/E4 La Joyita, Mex.
116/B3 Lāju, India
192/C5 La Junta, Co,US
144/D3 Lakamané, Mali
157/J7 Lakato, Madg.
205/J9 Lake (co.), Ca,US
202/M6 Lake (co.), Fl,US
205/P15 Lake (co.), Il,US
205/R16 Lake (co.), In,US
185/G4 Lake (cr.), Nv, Ut,US
208/F4 Lake (co.), Oh,US
208/E5 Lake (plain), Oh,US
203/H3 Lake Alfred, Fl,US
194/E3 Lake Alice Nat'l Wild. Ref., ND,US
194/B3 Lake Alma, Sk,Can
186/B1 Lake Alpine, Ca,US
133/F3 Lake Amadeus Abor. Land, Austl.
192/E2 Lake Andes, SD,US
192/E2 Lake Andes Nat'l Wild. Ref., SD,US
195/M5 Lake Ann, Mi,US
204/C2 Lake Arrowhead, Ca,US
202/B2 Lake Arthur, La,US
190/B4 Lake Arthur, NM,US
160/D3 Lake Atitlán Nat'l Park, Guat.
205/P15 Lake Barrington, Il,US
205/P14 Lake Beulah, Wi,US
205/Q15 Lake Bluff, Il,US
135/B2 Lake Boga, Austl.
151/B1 Lake Bogoria Nat'l Rsv., Kenya
135/B3 Lake Bolac, Austl.
202/M7 Lake Buena Vista, Fl,US
203/G2 Lake Butler, Fl,US
135/C2 Lake Cargelligo, Austl.
205/P15 Lake Catherine, Il,US
202/B2 Lake Charles, La,US
182/E3 Lake Chelan (dam), Wa,US
182/D3 Lake Chelan Nat'l Rec. Area, Wa,US
183/G3 Lake City, Ar,US
184/C3 Lake City, Ca,US
190/A1 Lake City, Co,US
203/G2 Lake City, Fl,US
201/M7 Lake City, Ga,US
193/G2 Lake City, Ia,US
198/D2 Lake City, Mi,US
193/H1 Lake City, Mn,US
198/F3 Lake City, Pa,US
201/H4 Lake City, SC,US
194/F5 Lake City, SD,US
200/E2 Lake City, Tn,US
178/A2 Lake Clark Nat'l Park, Ak,US
177/H3 Lake Clark Nat'l Park & Prsv., Ak,US
182/B3 Lake Cowichan, BC,Can
193/G1 Lake Crystal, Mn,US
188/K6 Lake Dallas, Tx,US
193/K2 Lake Delton, Wi,US
57/E2 Lake District Nat'l Park, Eng,UK
195/Q7 Lake Elmo, Mn,US
204/C3 Lake Elsinore, Ca,US
133/H4 Lake Eyre Nat'l Park, Austl.
205/E6 Lake Fenton, Mi,US
199/G2 Lakefield, On,Can
193/G2 Lakefield, Mn,US
134/B1 Lakefield Nat'l Park, Austl.
205/Q15 Lake Forest, Il,US
205/C2 Lake Forest Park, Wa,US
184/E1 Lake Fork, Id,US
208/E6 Lake Fork (riv.), Oh,US
189/G1 Lake Fork (res.), Tx,US
185/H3 Lake Fork (riv.), Ut,US
205/P14 Lake Geneva, Wi,US
190/B1 Lake George, Co,US
198/D3 Lake George, Mi,US
199/K3 Lake George, NY,US
194/E4 Lake George Nat'l Wild. Ref., ND,US
132/C5 Lake Grace, Austl.
191/H3 Lake Hamilton, Ar,US
179/K2 Lake Harbour, NW,Can
186/E3 Lake Havasu City, Az,US
203/H3 Lake Helen, Fl,US
188/E3 Lakehills, Tx,US
186/C3 Lake Hughes, Ca,US
207/D3 Lakehurst, NJ,US
207/D3 Lakehurst Nav. Air Eng. Ctr., NJ,US
194/E4 Lake Ilo Nat'l Wild. Ref., ND,US
205/P15 Lake in the Hills, Il,US
186/C3 Lake Isabella, Ca,US
200/C2 Lake Isom Nat'l Wild. Ref., Tn,US
189/G3 Lake Jackson, Tx,US
202/M6 Lake Jem, Fl,US
132/C5 Lake King, Austl.
181/K6 Lakeland, Fl,US
203/H3 Lakeland, Fl,US
203/G2 Lakeland, Ga,US
202/C2 Lakeland, La,US
195/Q7 Lakeland, Mn,US
204/C3 Lakeland Village, Ca,US
195/M5 Lake Leelanau, Mi,US
194/B1 Lake Lenore, Sk,Can
195/K4 Lake Linden, Mi,US
193/G4 Lake Lotawana, Mo,US
182/F2 Lake Louise, Ab,Can
133/F2 Lake Mackay Abor. Land, Austl.
132/B3 Lake Macleod, Austl.
155/G2 Lake Malawi Nat'l Park, Malw.
151/A2 Lake Manyara Nat'l Park, Tanz.
202/N6 Lake Mary, Fl,US
183/K4 Lake Mason Nat'l Wild. Ref., Mt,US
153/G3 Lake Mburo Nat'l Park, Ugan.
183/H3 Lake McDonald, Mt,US
186/E2 Lake Mead Nat'l Rec. Area, Az, Nv,US
190/D3 Lake Meredith Nat'l Rec. Area, Tx,US
91/G2 Lake Mikri Prespa Nat'l Park, Gre.
193/H2 Lake Mills, Ia,US
198/B3 Lake Mills, Wi,US
177/H3 Lake Minchumina, Ak,US
206/D1 Lake Mohawk, NJ,US
202/N6 Lake Monroe, Fl,US
187/G3 Lake Montezuma, Az,US
205/P15 Lakemoor, Il,US
208/F5 Lakemore, Oh,US
131/F1 Lake Murray, PNG
151/B2 Lake Nakuru Nat'l Park, Kenya
133/H2 Lake Nash, Austl.
194/D4 Lake Nettie Nat'l Wild. Ref., ND,US
59/G2 Lakenheath, Eng,UK
198/D3 Lake Odessa, Mi,US
193/H4 Lake of the Ozarks (res.), Mo,US
195/G3 Lake of the Woods (lake), On,Can, Mn,US
205/F6 Lake Orion, Mi,US
184/B1 Lake Oswego, Or,US
203/G3 Lake Panasoffkee, Fl,US
202/P6 Lake Park, Fl,US
203/G2 Lake Park, Ga,US
193/G2 Lake Park, Ia,US
194/F4 Lake Park, Mn,US
204/C3 Lake Perris St. Rec. Area, Ca,US
203/H4 Lake Placid, Fl,US
199/K2 Lake Placid, NY,US
199/J3 Lake Pleasant, NY,US
184/B4 Lakeport, Ca,US
189/G1 Lakeport, Tx,US
192/F1 Lake Preston, SD,US
189/J1 Lake Providence, La,US
207/E2 Lake Ronkonkoma, NY,US
135/C4 Lake Saint Clair-Cradle Mountain Nat'l Park, Austl.
195/Q7 Lake Saint Croix Beach, Mn,US
135/D3 Lakes Entrance, Austl.
61/H1 Lakesfjorden (fjord), Nor.
206/B5 Lake Shore, Md,US
195/G4 Lake Shore, Mn,US
204/D5 Lakeside, Ca,US
183/G3 Lakeside, Mt,US
192/C2 Lakeside, Ne,US
184/A2 Lakeside, Or,US
185/G3 Lakeside, Ut,US
201/J2 Lakeside, Va,US
187/H3 Lakeside-Pinetop, Az,US
135/C3 Lakes Nat'l Park, The, Austl.
205/R16 Lake Station, In,US
205/C1 Lake Stevens, Wa,US
207/L8 Lake Success, NY,US
190/D3 Lake Tanglewood, Tx,US
183/K3 Lake Thibadeau Nat'l Wild. Ref., Mt,US
195/K5 Lake Tomahawk, Wi,US
185/H3 Laketown, Ut,US
201/F3 Lake Toxaway, NC,US
191/H2 Lakeview, Ar,US
191/J3 Lake View, Ar,US
204/C3 Lakeview, Ca,US
200/E3 Lakeview, Ga,US
193/G2 Lake View, Ia,US
198/D3 Lakeview, Mi,US
185/H1 Lakeview, Mt,US
184/C2 Lakeview, Or,US
190/D3 Lakeview, Tx,US
205/P15 Lake Villa, Il,US
191/J4 Lake Village, Ar,US
208/D2 Lakeville, Ma,US
205/F6 Lakeville (lake), Mi,US
195/H5 Lakeville, Mn,US
195/P7 Lakeville, Mn,US
201/H3 Lake Waccamaw, NC,US
203/H4 Lake Wales, Fl,US
132/D3 Lake Way, Austl.
189/F2 Lakeway, Tx,US
204/B3 Lakewood, Ca,US
192/B4 Lakewood, Co,US
203/E2 Lakewood, Fl,US
205/P15 Lakewood, Il,US
207/D3 Lakewood, NJ,US
190/B4 Lakewood, NM,US
199/G3 Lakewood, NY,US
208/F5 Lakewood, Oh,US
182/C3 Lakewood, Wa,US
193/K1 Lakewood, Wi,US
203/H3 Lake Woodruff Nat'l Wild. Ref., Fl,US
202/P6 Lake Worth, Fl,US
203/H4 Lake Worth, Fl,US
189/F2 Lakewview-Lacy, Tx,US
194/C3 Lake Zahl Nat'l Wild. Ref., ND,US
205/P15 Lake Zurich, Il,US
94/F3 Lakhdenpokh'ya, Rus.
63/L2 Lakhemaaskiy Nat'l Park, Est.
120/C2 Lakhīmpur, India
120/B4 Lakhnādon, India
118/A3 Lakhpat, India
98/D1 Lakhva, Bela.
61/N7 Laki (vol.), Ice.
190/D2 Lakin, Ks,US
122/A1 Lakki, Pak.
89/K3 Lakkion, Gre.
91/H4 Lakonía (gulf), Gre.
130/C2 Lakor (isl.), Indo.
144/D5 Lakota, IvC.
194/E3 Lakota, ND,US
118/B5 Lakshadweep (isls.), India
118/B6 Lakshadweep (terr.), India
121/H4 Lākshām, Bang.
121/H4 Lakshmipur, Bang.
125/C4 Lala, Phil.
151/A2 Lalago, Tanz.
142/A3 La Laguna, Canl.,Sp.
172/B4 La Laja, Arg.
159/F4 La Laja, Mex.
105/G3 Lālajīn, Iran
122/B1 Lāla Mūsa, Pak.
157/H8 Lalana (riv.), Madg.
124/D3 Lalang (riv.), Indo.
93/H5 Lālapaşa, Turk.
152/B2 Lalara, Gabon
120/C3 Lalauli, India
82/D2 L'Albaron (mtn.), Fr.
121/E2 Lālbhitti, Nepal
172/E3 La Leonesa, Arg.
121/E3 Lālganj, India
121/G3 Lālgola, India
105/G3 Lālī, Iran
122/B2 Lāliān, Pak.
150/A2 Lalībela, Eth.
164/A5 La Libertad, Ecu.
160/D2 La Libertad, Guat.
160/E3 La Libertad, Hon.
174/C2 La Ligua, Chile
130/B1 Laliki, Indo.
109/K3 Lalin (riv.), China
76/A1 Lalín, Sp.
74/D4 Lalinde, Fr.
76/C4 La Línea de la Concepción, Sp.
120/B3 Lalitpur, India
121/E2 Lalitpur (Pātan), Nepal
77/L6 La Llagosta, Sp.
132/C2 Lalla Rookh Abor. Land, Austl.
82/C4 L'Allier, Montagne de (mtn.), Fr.
121/G3 Lālmanir Hāt, Bang.
174/E4 La Lobería, Arg.
178/F3 La Loche, Sk,Can
86/A3 La Loggia, It.
82/C6 La Londe-les-Maures, Fr.
79/G4 La Loupe, Fr.
68/D3 La Louvière, Belg.
121/G3 Lālpur, Bang.
76/C4 La Luisiana, Sp.
188/D4 La Luz, Mex.
190/B4 La Luz, NM,US
76/B4 La Luz, Costa de (coast), Sp.
149/F4 Lalyo, Sudan
119/F3 Lāma, Bang.
56/D1 Lamachan (mtn.), Sc,UK
74/E3 La Machine, Fr.
90/A2 La Maddalena, It.
68/C2 La Madeleine, Fr.
187/J2 La Madera, NM,US
119/G2 Lamadi, China
188/D4 Lamadrid, Mex.
125/B4 Lamag, Malay.
145/F4 Lama-Kara, Togo
130/A2 Lamakera, Indo.
196/B2 La Malbaie, Qu,Can
197/K2 Lamaline, Nf,Can
160/D2 Lamanai (ruins), Belz.
89/C3 La Mancha (reg.), Sp.
126/D4 Lamandau (riv.), Indo.
191/H3 Lamar, Ar,US
192/C4 Lamar, Co,US
191/G2 Lamar, Mo,US
199/H4 Lamar, Pa,US
201/G3 Lamar, SC,US
80/B1 Lamarche, Fr.
80/B3 Lamarche-sur-Saône, Fr.
165/F2 La Margarita, Ven.
174/D3 Lamarque, Arg.
189/G3 La Marque, Tx,US
178/E2 La Martre (lake), NW,Can
160/E3 La Masica, Hon.
82/A3 Lamastre, Fr.
196/A2 La Maurice Nat'l Park, Qu,Can
181/M2 La Mauricie Nat'l Park, Qu,Can
107/L2 Lāmayūrū, India
71/G6 Lambach, Aus.
78/C4 Lamballe, Fr.
172/E3 Lambaré, Par.
152/B3 Lambaréné, Gabon
170/D4 Lambari, Braz.
138/G6 Lambasa, Fiji
60/D3 Lambay (isl.), Ire.
168/B2 Lambayeque, Peru
56/B3 Lambeg, NI,UK
144/C3 Lambé Koba (riv.), Mali
137/E Lambert (glac.), Ant.
200/B3 Lambert, Ms,US
193/G1 Lamberton, Mn,US
208/H5 Lamberton-Chess (arpt.), Pa,US
191/J1 Lambert-Saint Louis (int'l arpt.), Mo,US
200/B1 Lambert-Saint Louis (int'l arpt.), Mo,US
156/B4 Lambert's Bay, SAfr.
198/E4 Lambertville, Mi,US
206/D3 Lambertville, NJ,US
82/B5 Lambesc, Fr.
53/N7 Lambeth (bor.), Eng,UK
59/E3 Lambourn, Eng,UK
168/C4 Lambrama, Peru
70/B4 Lambrecht, Ger.
83/B2 Lambro (riv.), It.
86/C2 Lambro (riv.), It.
201/G2 Lambsburg, Va,US
70/B3 Lambsheim, Ger.
205/H6 Lambton (co.), On,Can
196/B3 Lambton, Qu,Can
183/L5 Lame Deer, Mt,US
76/B2 Lamego, Port.
82/C2 La Meije (mtn.), Fr.
79/E6 La Ménitré, Fr.
164/C4 La Mensura (peak), Col.
196/E2 Lamèque, NB,Can
76/B1 La Merca, Sp.
172/C4 La Merced, Arg.
172/C2 La Merced, Bol.
168/C3 La Merced, Peru
74/F3 La Mère Boitier, Signal de (mtn.), Fr.
133/J5 Lameroo, Austl.
167/L7 La Mesa, Col.
160/E3 La Mesa (int'l arpt.), Hon.
159/F3 La Mesa, Mex.
204/C5 La Mesa, Ca,US
190/A4 La Mesa, NM,US
188/D1 Lamesa, Tx,US
164/D2 La Mesa, Ven.
91/H3 Lamía, Gre.
191/H1 Lamine (riv.), Mo,US
206/D2 Lamington (riv.), NJ,US
134/D5 Lamington Nat'l Park, Austl.
204/B3 La Mirada, Ca,US
158/C2 La Misa, Mex.
125/C4 Lamitan, Phil.
54/A5 Lamlash, Sc,UK
54/D5 Lammermuir (hills), Sc,UK
62/F3 Lammhult, Swe.
63/L1 Lammi, Fin.
182/D1 Lamming Mills, BC,Can
184/F3 Lamoille, Nv,US
193/J3 La Moine (riv.), Il,US
125/C2 Lamon (bay), Phil.
182/E4 Lamona, Wa,US
75/J4 Lamone (riv.), It.
124/F4 Lamongan, Indo.
193/H3 Lamoni, Ia,US
85/D4 La Monna (peak), It.
186/C3 Lamont, Ca,US
203/G2 Lamont, Fl,US
191/F2 Lamont, Ok,US
168/C3 La Montaña (reg.), Peru
191/H1 La Monte, Mo,US
77/K7 La Morella (peak), Sp.
188/C3 La Morita, Mex.
53/T9 Lamorlaye, Fr.
188/C3 La Mota (mtn.), Tx,US
138/D4 Lamotrek (isl.), Micr.
78/C4 La Motte, Fr.
79/H5 Lamotte-Beuvron, Fr.
82/B3 La Motte-d'Aveillans, Fr.
82/C4 La Motte-du-Caire, Fr.
82/B1 La Motte-Servolex, Fr.
194/E4 LaMoure, ND,US
174/Q9 Lampa, Chile
168/D4 Lampa, Peru
123/B2 Lampang, Thai.
123/C2 Lam Pao (res.), Thai.
189/E2 Lampasas, Tx,US
189/E2 Lampasas (riv.), Tx,US
78/A4 Lampaul-Plouarzel, Fr.
188/D4 Lampazos de Naranjo, Mex.
191/H2 Lampe, Mo,US
90/C5 Lampedusa, It.
70/B3 Lampertheim, Ger.
58/B2 Lampeter, Wal,UK
206/B4 Lampeter, Pa,US
58/B3 Lamphey, Wal,UK
123/B2 Lamphun, Thai.
194/C3 Lampman, Sk,Can
87/D5 Lamporecchio, It.
195/J5 Lampson, Wi,US
124/D4 Lampung (prov.), Indo.
67/G1 Lamstedt, Ger.
151/C2 Lamu, Kenya
151/C2 Lamu (isl.), Kenya
168/B2 Lamud, Peru
161/F4 La Muerte, Cerro (mtn.), CR
188/B3 La Mula, Mex.
82/B3 La Mure, Fr.
153/H2 Lamwo (peak), Ugan.
187/K3 Lamy, NM,US
117/J4 Lan (isl.), Tai.
81/H4 Lana, It.
139/K2 Lanai (isl.), Hi,US
180/T10 Lanai (isl.), Hi,US
180/T10 Lanaihale (peak), Hi,US
69/E2 Lanaken, Belg.
125/D4 Lanao (lake), Phil.
77/F3 La Nao, Cabo de (cape), Sp.
103/C2 Lanarca (dist.), Cyp.
160/C2 Lana, Río de la (riv.), Mex.
54/C5 Lanark, Sc,UK
193/K2 Lanark, Il,US
188/A2 Lanark, NM,US
125/B4 Lanas Village, Malay.
116/E3 Lanba, China
123/B4 Lanbi (isl.), Burma
108/D5 Lancang (riv.), China
116/C4 Lancang Lahuzu Zizhixian, China
119/G3 Lancang Lahuzu Zizhixian (Lancang), China
119/G3 Lancang (Lancang Lahuzu Zizhixian), China
57/F4 Lancashire (co.), Eng,UK
57/F4 Lancashire (plain), Eng,UK
179/H1 Lancaster (sound), NW,Can
57/F3 Lancaster, Eng,UK
186/C3 Lancaster, Ca,US
200/E2 Lancaster, Ky,US
208/C1 Lancaster, Ma,US
194/F3 Lancaster, Mn,US
193/H3 Lancaster, Mo,US
199/L2 Lancaster, NH,US
197/T10 Lancaster, NY,US
198/E5 Lancaster, Oh,US
206/B3 Lancaster, Pa,US
206/B3 Lancaster (arpt.), Pa,US
206/B4 Lancaster (co.), Pa,US
201/G3 Lancaster, SC,US
189/F1 Lancaster, Tx,US
201/J2 Lancaster, Va,US
193/J2 Lancaster, Wi,US
192/B2 Lance (cr.), Wy,US
82/C1 Lancebranlette (mtn.), Fr.
192/B2 Lance Creek, Wy,US
132/B4 Lancelin, Austl.
183/K2 Lancer, Sk,Can
57/G2 Lanchester, Eng,UK
97/G4 Lanchkhuti, Geo.
85/E3 Lanciano, It.
174/B3 Lanco, Chile
82/B5 Lançon-Provence, Fr.
65/M3 Łańcut, Pol.
80/C5 Lancy, Swi.
71/F5 Landau an der Isar, Ger.

70/B4 **Landau in der Pfalz**, Ger.
200/C2 **Land Between the Lakes Rec. Area**, Ky, Tn,US
81/G3 **Landeck**, Aus.
78/A3 **Landéda**, Fr.
69/E2 **Landen**, Belg.
70/B4 **Landenburg**, Ger.
133/G2 **Lander** (riv.), Austl.
185/J2 **Lander**, Wy,US
78/A4 **Landerneau**, Fr.
74/C4 **Landes** (reg.), Fr.
67/G3 **Landesbergen**, Ger.
74/B3 **Landes de Lanvaux** (reg.), Fr.
183/K1 **Landis**, Sk,Can
206/A3 **Landisburg**, Pa,US
206/B3 **Landis Valley Museum**, Pa,US
206/B3 **Landisville-Salunga**, Pa,US
78/A3 **Landivisiau**, Fr.
79/D4 **Landivy**, Fr.
67/G1 **Land Kehdingen** (reg.), Ger.
202/L7 **Land O'Lakes**, Fl,US
198/B1 **Land O'Lakes**, Wi,US
68/C3 **Landrecies**, Fr.
86/C2 **Landriano**, It.
167/F4 **Landri Sales**, Braz.
201/F3 **Landrum**, SC,US
70/D6 **Landsberg**, Ger.
134/B3 **Landsborough** (cr.), Austl.
58/A6 **Land's End** (pt.), Eng,UK
80/D2 **Landser**, Fr.
71/F5 **Landshut**, Ger.
62/E4 **Landskrona**, Swe.
66/B4 **Landsmeer**, Neth.
69/G5 **Landstuhl**, Ger.
62/E3 **Landvetter** (int'l arpt.), Swe.
152/D2 **Landza**, Congo
79/F6 **Lane** (riv.), Fr.
174/C3 **La Negra**, Arg.
57/F2 **Lanercost**, Eng,UK
60/C2 **Lanesborough**, Ire.
191/G4 **Lanesport**, Ar,US
78/B5 **Lanester**, Fr.
200/E4 **Lanett**, Al,US
80/D3 **La Neuveville**, Swi.
194/B3 **Lang**, Can
183/M3 **Lang**, Sk,Can
117/J2 **Lang** (mtn.), China
91/H2 **Langadhás**, Gre.
91/H4 **Langádhia**, Gre.
150/A4 **Langano** (lake), Eth.
127/F4 **Langara**, Indo.
54/D3 **Lang Craig** (pt.), Sc,UK
183/H2 **Langdon**, Ab,Can
194/E3 **Langdon**, ND,US
74/E4 **Langeac**, Fr.
79/F6 **Langeais**, Fr.
156/B4 **Langebaanweg**, SAfr.
156/C3 **Langeberg** (mts.), SAfr.
156/L10 **Langeberg** (mts.), SAfr.
148/H1 **Langeb, Khawr** (dry riv.), Sudan
62/D4 **Langeland** (isl.), Den.
208/G7 **Langeloth**, Pa,US
67/H5 **Langelsheim**, Ger.
67/F1 **Langen**, Ger.
70/D5 **Langenaltheim**, Ger.
81/F2 **Langenargen**, Ger.
70/D6 **Langenau**, Ger.
71/E6 **Langenbach**, Ger.
67/E6 **Langenberg**, Ger.
194/D2 **Langenburg**, Sk,Can
72/B5 **Langendorf**, Ger.
72/B5 **Langeneichstädt**, Ger.
81/G3 **Längenfeld**, Aus.
66/D6 **Langenfeld**, Ger.
67/G4 **Langenhagen**, Ger.
64/E1 **Langenhorn**, Ger.
65/H4 **Langenlois**, Aus.
71/E6 **Langenpreising**, Ger.
70/C2 **Langenselbold**, Ger.
71/H6 **Langenstein**, Aus.
80/D3 **Langenthal**, Swi.
75/L3 **Langenwang**, Aus.
70/D4 **Langenzenn**, Ger.
73/A3 **Langenzersdorf**, Aus.
67/E1 **Langeoog**, Ger.
67/E1 **Langeoog** (isl.), Ger.
100/H3 **Langepas**, Rus.
70/D6 **Langerringen**, Ger.
62/D4 **Langeskov**, Den.
62/C2 **Langesund**, Nor.
80/D3 **Langeten** (riv.), Swi.
115/D3 **Langfang**, China
192/F1 **Langford**, SD,US
70/D4 **Langfurth**, Ger.
124/C2 **Langgam**, Indo.
124/B2 **Langgapayung**, Indo.
108/C6 **Langgar**, China
183/L1 **Langham**, Sk,Can
59/F1 **Langham**, Eng,UK
86/D3 **Langhirano**, It.
57/F1 **Langholm**, Sc,UK
206/D3 **Langhorne**, Pa,US
61/N7 **Langjökull** (glac.), Ice.
124/B1 **Langkawi** (isl.), Malay.
119/G6 **Langkawi** (isl.), Thai.
123/B4 **Lang Kha Tuk** (peak), Thai.
125/B4 **Langkon**, Malay.
53/M7 **Langley**, Eng,UK
205/C1 **Langley**, Wa,US
201/J2 **Langley A.F.B.**, Va,US
184/A2 **Langlois**, Or,US
80/D4 **Langnau im Emmental**, Swi.
59/G5 **Langney** (pt.), UK
74/E4 **Langogne**, Fr.
61/E1 **Langøya** (isl.), Nor.
114/C5 **Langqên** (riv.), China
71/F5 **Langquaid**, Ger.
80/B2 **Langres**, Fr.
80/B2 **Langres, Plateau de** (plat.), Fr.
114/C4 **Langru**, China
79/E2 **Langrune-sur-Mer**, Fr.
124/B1 **Langsa**, Indo.
62/G1 **Langshyttan**, Swe.
123/D1 **Lang Son**, Viet.
197/S8 **Langstaff**, On,Can
191/F3 **Langston**, Ok,US
123/B4 **Lang Suan**, Thai.
117/F2 **Langtang**, China
145/H4 **Langtang**, Nga.
121/E1 **Langtang Lirung** (mtn.), Nepal
121/E1 **Langtang Nat'l Park**, Nepal
113/C2 **Langtou**, China
188/D3 **Langtry**, Tx,US
77/G1 **Languedoc** (hist. reg.), Fr.
82/A4 **Languedoc-Roussillon** (reg.), Fr.
78/C4 **Langueux**, Fr.
78/B5 **Languidic**, Fr.
191/J3 **L'Anguille** (riv.), Ar,US
67/G3 **Langwedel**, Ger.
81/G1 **Langweid am Lech**, Ger.
81/F4 **Langwies**, Swi.
115/D5 **Langxi**, China
115/C3 **Langya Shan** (mtn.), China
206/B6 **Lanham-Seabrook**, Md,US
194/B2 **Lanigan**, Sk,Can
183/M1 **Lanigan** (riv.), Sk,Can
174/C3 **Lanín** (vol.), Chile
174/C3 **Lanín Nat'l Park**, Arg.
121/G2 **Lankāpāra Hāt**, India
194/F3 **Lankin**, ND,US
117/G4 **Lankou**, China
168/D4 **Lanlacuni Bajo**, Peru
78/B3 **Lanmeur**, Fr.
78/B5 **Lann-Bihoué** (Lorient) (arpt.), Fr.
74/D5 **Lannemezan**, Fr.
74/D5 **Lannemezan** (plat.), Fr.
58/A6 **Lanner**, Eng,UK
78/A3 **Lannilis**, Fr.
78/B3 **Lannion**, Fr.
78/B3 **Lannion** (bay), Fr.
78/B3 **Lannion** (Servel) (arpt.), Fr.
199/J1 **L'Annonciation**, Qu,Can
158/D4 **La Noria**, Mex.
53/S11 **La Norville**, Fr.
78/C4 **Lanouée**, Fr.
82/B3 **Lans** (mts.), Fr.
123/B2 **Lan Sang Nat'l Park**, Thai.
206/C3 **Lansdale**, Pa,US
199/H2 **Lansdowne**, On,Can
120/B1 **Lansdowne**, India
206/C4 **Lansdowne**, Pa,US
206/B5 **Lansdowne-Baltimore Highlands**, Md,US
195/K4 **L'Anse Ind. Res.**, Mi,US
194/D3 **Lansford**, ND,US
206/C2 **Lansford**, Pa,US
117/G3 **Lanshan**, China
177/M3 **Lansing**, Yk,Can
193/J2 **Lansing**, Ia,US
205/Q16 **Lansing**, Il,US
198/D3 **Lansing** (cap.), Mi,US
82/C2 **Lanslebourg-Mont-Cenis**, Fr.
123/B5 **Lanta** (isl.), Thai.
202/P6 **Lantana**, Fl,US
117/G4 **Lantang**, China
80/C2 **Lanterne** (riv.), Fr.
82/D5 **Lantosque**, Fr.
123/C1 **Lantouy**, Laos
194/D5 **Lantry**, SD,US
196/F3 **Lantz**, NS,Can
182/B3 **Lantzville**, BC,Can
175/S12 **Lanús**, Arg.
90/A3 **Lanusei**, It.
84/C4 **Lanuvio**, It.
125/D3 **Lanuza**, Phil.
78/C4 **Lanvallay**, Fr.
78/C5 **Lanvaux** (uplands), Fr.
78/A4 **Lanvéoc**, Fr.
109/K2 **Lanxi**, China
117/H2 **Lanxi**, China
172/C1 **Lanza**, Bol.
85/E6 **Lanzara**, It.
142/B3 **Lanzarote** (isl.), Canl., Sp.
142/B3 **Lanzarote** (int'l arpt.), Canl.,Sp.
73/A4 **Lanzenkirchen**, Aus.
73/A2 **Lanžhot**, Czh.
108/E4 **Lanzhou**, China
81/F6 **Lanzo d'Intelvi**, It.
86/A2 **Lanzo Torinese**, It.
113/D2 **Lao** (mts.), China
109/J4 **Lao** (peak), China
116/C2 **Lao** (riv.), China
83/B3 **Lao** (riv.), It.
125/C1 **Laoag**, Phil.
113/B2 **Laobian**, China
123/D1 **Lao Cai**, Viet.
108/F5 **Laocheng**, China
117/G2 **Laodao** (riv.), China
109/K1 **Laodaodian**, China
123/C1 **Lao Fu Chai**, Laos
117/G2 **Laoguanzui**, China
109/H3 **Laoha** (riv.), China
115/B4 **Laohekou**, China
113/A3 **Laohutun**, China
60/C4 **Laois** (Leix) (co.), Ire.
115/B4 **Laojun Shan** (mtn.), China
172/B3 **La Ola**, Chile
113/D2 **Laoling**, China
68/C4 **Laon**, Fr.
165/E2 **La Orchila** (isl.), Ven.
142/A3 **La Orotava**, Canl.
168/C3 **La Oroya**, Peru
123/C2 **Laos**
115/E3 **Laoshan**, China
115/E3 **Lao Shan** (peak), China
109/J4 **Laotie** (mtn.), China
115/E3 **Laotie Shan** (mtn.), China
113/C2 **Laotuding** (peak), China
115/F2 **Laotuding Shan** (peak), China
141/M13 **Laou** (riv.), Mor.
77/G1 **Laouzas, Barrage de** (dam), Fr.
173/G3 **Lapa**, Braz.
145/G4 **Lapai**, Nga.
188/D3 **La Palestina**, Mex.
142/A3 **La Palma** (isl.), Canl., Sp.
164/C3 **La Palma**, Col.
158/D3 **La Palma**, Mex.
161/G4 **La Palma**, Pan.
77/X16 **La Palma** (arpt.), Canl.,Sp.
175/G2 **La Paloma**, Uru.
82/A4 **Lapalud**, Fr.
174/D3 **La Pampa** (prov.), Arg.
172/D4 **La Para**, Arg.
165/F3 **La Paragua**, Ven.
76/B4 **La Parra** (int'l arpt.), Sp.
175/K8 **Lapataia**, Arg.
174/D2 **La Paz**, Arg.
172/B1 **La Paz** (cap.), Bol.
168/D4 **La Paz** (dept.), Bol.
164/C3 **La Paz**, Col.
160/E3 **La Paz**, Hon.
158/C3 **La Paz**, Mex.
158/C3 **La Paz** (bay), Mex.
125/D3 **La Paz**, Phil.
175/F2 **La Paz**, Uru.
199/J2 **La Pêche**, Qu,Can
164/D5 **La Pedrera**, Col.
94/F3 **Lapeenranta**, Fin.
205/F5 **Lapeer**, Mi,US
205/F6 **Lapeer** (co.), Mi,US
167/L6 **La Peña**, Col.
161/F4 **La Peña**, Pan.
82/B6 **La Penne-sur-Huveaune**, Fr.
188/B3 **La Perla**, Mex.
112/B1 **La Perouse** (str.), Japan, Rus.
80/D1 **La Petite-Raon**, Fr.
200/D5 **Lapine**, Al,US
184/C2 **La Pine**, Or,US
61/H3 **Lapinlahti**, Fin.
103/C2 **Lapithos**, Cyp.
202/C2 **La Place**, La,US
61/F1 **Lapland** (reg.), Eur.
192/D1 **La Plant**, SD,US
175/F2 **La Plata**, Arg.
175/T12 **La Plata** (arpt.), Arg.
164/C4 **La Plata**, Col.
187/H2 **La Plata** (riv.), Co, NM,US
201/J1 **La Plata**, Md,US
193/J3 **La Plata**, Mo,US
163/D6 **La Plata, Río de** (riv.), Arg., Uru.
68/D3 **La Plate Taile, Barrage de** (dam), Belg.
77/F1 **La Pobla de Lillet**, Sp.
196/B2 **La Pocatière**, Qu,Can
197/H2 **La Poile**, Nf,Can
185/J3 **Lapoint**, Ut,US
76/C1 **La Pola de Gordón**, Sp.
79/E6 **La Pommeraye**, Fr.
192/B3 **Laporte**, Co,US
198/C4 **La Porte**, In,US
189/H4 **Laporte**, Pa,US
189/G3 **La Porte**, Tx,US
193/H2 **La Porte City**, Ia,US
186/D4 **La Posta Ind. Res.**, Ca,US
109/N1 **Lapotina** (mtn.), Rus.
92/E3 **Lapovo**, Yugo.
158/B3 **La Poza**, Mex.
63/N1 **Lappeenranta**, Fin.
71/F4 **Lappersdorf**, Ger.
61/H2 **Lappi** (prov.), Fin.
197/N7 **La Prairie**, Qu,Can
197/N7 **Laprarie** (co.), Qu,Can
188/E3 **La Pryor**, Tx,US
104/A1 **Lâpseki**, Turk.
101/N2 **Laptev** (sea), Rus.
61/G3 **Lapua**, Fin.
77/G3 **La Puebla**, Sp.
76/D3 **La Puebla de Almoradiel**, Sp.
76/C4 **La Puebla de Cazalla**, Sp.
76/B4 **La Puebla del Río**, Sp.
76/C3 **La Puebla de Montalbán**, Sp.
204/C2 **La Puente**, Ca,US
107/K3 **Lapundra**, India
164/A5 **La Puntilla** (pt.), Ecu.
158/E3 **La Purísima**, Mex.
93/J2 **Lapushna**, Mol.
65/M2 **Ł apy**, Pol.
147/F4 **Laqiyat al Arba'īn**, Sudan
164/D2 **La Quebrada**, Ven.
79/G3 **La-Queue-lès-Yvelines**, Fr.
191/H2 **Laquey**, Mo,US
172/C2 **La Quiaca**, Arg.
85/D3 **L'Aquila**, It.
85/D3 **L'Aquila** (prov.), It.
105/H5 **Lār**, Iran
135/C3 **Lara**, Austl.
164/D2 **Lara** (state), Ven.
76/A1 **Laracha**, Sp.
141/L13 **Larache**, Mor.
60/D2 **Laracor**, Ire.
82/B4 **Laragne-Montéglin**, Fr.
105/J5 **Lārak** (isl.), Iran
76/C4 **La Rambla**, Sp.
192/B3 **Laramie** (riv.), Co, Wy,US
180/E3 **Laramie**, Wy,US
192/B3 **Laramie**, Wy,US
192/A2 **Laramie** (mts.), Wy,US
192/B2 **Laramie** (peak), Wy,US
173/F3 **Laranjeiras do Sul**, Braz.
130/A2 **Larantuka**, Indo.
130/C1 **Larat**, Indo.
130/D1 **Larat** (isl.), Indo.
77/G1 **La Ravièqe, Barrage de** (dam), Fr.
82/B3 **La Ravoire**, Fr.
141/S15 **Larba**, Alg.
82/C4 **Larche, Col de** (pass), Fr.
207/K8 **Larchmont**, NY,US
77/E1 **Larcis** (riv.), Fr.
74/B2 **L'Arcouest, Pointe de** (pt.), Fr.
78/B3 **L'Arcouest, Pointe de** (pt.), Fr.
62/B1 **Lærdalsøyri**, Nor.
82/C6 **Lardier** (cape), Fr.
79/H3 **Lardy**, Fr.
168/B3 **Laredo**, Peru
76/D1 **Laredo**, Sp.
193/H3 **Laredo**, Mo,US
183/K3 **Laredo**, Mt,US
188/E4 **Laredo**, Tx,US
188/E4 **Laredo** (int'l arpt.), Tx,US
174/D3 **La Reforma**, Arg.
66/C4 **Laren**, Neth.
168/C4 **Lares**, Peru
189/F4 **Larga** (lake), Tx,US
82/C3 **L'Argentière-la-Bessée**, Fr.
82/B4 **Largne** (riv.), Fr.
161/F1 **Largo** (cay), Cuba
54/D4 **Largo** (bay), Sc,UK
203/G4 **Largo**, Fl,US
203/H5 **Largo** (key), Fl,US
206/B6 **Largo**, Md,US
187/H3 **Largo** (cr.), NM,US
54/B5 **Largs**, Sc,UK
80/D2 **Largue** (riv.), Fr.
76/E1 **La Rhune** (mtn.), Fr.
127/F4 **Lariang** (riv.), Indo.
84/C4 **Lariano**, It.
76/C4 **La Rinconada**, Sp.
85/E4 **Larino**, It.
172/C4 **La Rioja**, Arg.
172/C3 **La Rioja** (prov.), Arg.
76/D1 **La Rioja** (aut. comm.), Sp.
91/H3 **Lárisa**, Gre.
59/G2 **Lark** (riv.), Eng,UK
107/J3 **Lārkāna**, Pak.
54/C5 **Larkhall**, Sc,UK
197/H1 **Lark Harbour**, Nf,Can
59/E4 **Larkhill**, Eng,UK
205/J11 **Larkspur**, Ca,US
192/B4 **Larkspur**, Co,US
78/B5 **Larmor-Plage**, Fr.
103/C2 **Larnaca**, Cyp.
103/C2 **Larnaca** (int'l arpt.), Cyp.
56/C2 **Larne**, NI,UK
56/C2 **Larne** (dist.), NI,UK
190/E1 **Larned**, Ks,US
56/C2 **Larne Lough** (inlet), NI,UK
76/C1 **La Robla**, Sp.
80/D4 **La Roche**, Swi.
78/C6 **La Roche-Bernard**, Fr.
82/A3 **La Roche-de-Glun**, Fr.
82/C3 **La Roche-de-Rame**, Fr.
69/E3 **La Roche-en-Ardenne**, Belg.
74/C3 **La Rochelle**, Fr.
78/A4 **La Roche-Maurice**, Fr.
80/C5 **La Roche-sur-Foron**, Fr.
74/C3 **La Roche-sur-Yon**, Fr.
69/F4 **Larochette**, Lux.
76/D3 **La Roda**, Sp.
162/D3 **La Romana**, DRep.
178/F3 **La Ronge**, Sk,Can
178/F3 **La Ronge** (lake), Sk,Can
153/G2 **Laropi**, Ugan.
82/B5 **La Roque-d'Anthéron**, Fr.
74/D5 **Laroque-d'Olmes**, Fr.
202/C3 **Larose**, La,US
188/D3 **La Rosita**, Mex.
87/D5 **La Rotta**, It.
160/C2 **Larrainzar**, Mex.
160/E3 **Larreynaga**, Nic.
130/D3 **Larrimah**, Austl.
174/F2 **Larroque**, Arg.
206/A1 **Larrys** (cr.), Pa,US
197/G3 **Larry's River**, NS,Can
178/G1 **Larsen** (sound), NW,Can
177/H4 **Larsen Bay**, Ak,US
137/V **Larsen Ice Shelf**, Ant.
137/C **Larsen-Riiser** (pen.), Ant.
137/Y **Larsen-Riiser Ice Shelf**, Ant.
183/L3 **Larslan**, Mt,US
189/J2 **Larto**, La,US
64/A3 **L'Artois, Collines de** (hills), Fr.
76/B1 **La Rúa**, Sp.
186/D4 **La Rumorosa**, Mex.
74/C5 **Laruns**, Fr.
62/D2 **Larvik**, Nor.
167/G7 **La Sabana**, Ven.
130/A1 **Lasahau**, Indo.
185/J4 **La Sal**, Ut,US
185/J4 **La Sal** (mts.), Ut,US
81/G4 **Lasa** (Laas), It.
194/F3 **La Salle**, Can
199/K2 **La Salle**, Can.
197/N7 **La Salle**, Qu,Can
82/C3 **La Salle**, Fr.
192/B3 **La Salle**, Co,US
193/K3 **La Salle**, Il,US
87/F1 **La Salute di Livenza**, It.
126/E3 **Lasan**, Indo.
116/B3 **Lasanbāri**, India
192/C4 **Las Animas**, Co,US
175/K8 **La Sara**, Arg.
80/C4 **La Sarraz**, Swi.
181/L2 **La Sarre**, Qu,Can
79/F2 **La Saussaye**, Fr.
82/C6 **La Sauvette** (mtn.), Fr.
165/E1 **Las Aves** (isls.), Ven.
174/C4 **Las Bayas**, Arg.
158/D4 **Las Bayas**, Mex.
71/H6 **Lasberg**, Aus.
172/B3 **Las Bombas**, Chile
165/E3 **Las Bonitas**, Ven.
172/D3 **Las Breñas**, Arg.
76/C4 **Las Cabezas de San Juan**, Sp.
174/C2 **Las Cabras**, Chile
188/D4 **Las Cabras**, Mex.
175/G2 **Lascano**, Uru.
172/C2 **Lascar** (vol.), Chile
190/B2 **Lascar**, Co,US
159/E3 **Las Carboneras**, Mex.
172/B4 **Las Casuarinas**, Arg.
159/G5 **Las Choapas**, Mex.
190/A4 **Las Cruces**, NM,US
188/A1 **Las Cruces** (int'l arpt.), NM,US
188/C4 **Las Delicias**, Mex.
124/E4 **Lasem**, Indo.
172/B4 **La Serena**, Chile
82/B3 **La Servelle** (mtn.), Fr.
77/F1 **La Seu d'Urgell**, Sp.
188/C3 **Las Eutimias**, Mex.
82/B6 **La Seyne-sur-Mer**, Fr.
174/F3 **Las Flores**, Arg.
188/D4 **Las Golondrinas**, Mex.
183/K1 **Lashburn**, Sk,Can
164/C4 **Las Hermosas Nat'l Park**, Col.
174/D2 **Las Higueras**, Arg.
126/C4 **Lashio**, Burma
107/H2 **Lashkar Gāh**, Afg.
95/L5 **Lashmanka**, Rus.
124/B2 **Lasia** (isl.), Indo.
161/G1 **La Sierpe**, Cuba
83/C4 **La Sila** (mts.), It.
175/J8 **La Silueta** (peak), Chile
164/C4 **Las Juntas**, Col.
174/C3 **Las Lajas**, Arg.
174/C3 **Las Lajas** (peak), Arg.
165/E3 **Las Lajitas**, Ven.
168/A2 **Las Lomas**, Peru
172/D3 **Las Lomitas**, Arg.
160/D2 **Las Margaritas**, Mex.
161/E1 **Las Martinas**, Cuba
161/J2 **Las Matas de Farfán**, DRep.
165/E2 **Las Mercedes**, Ven.
164/D3 **Las Montañitas**, Ven.
125/D2 **Las Navas**, Phil.
68/D2 **Lasne-Chapelle-Saint-Lambert**, Belg.
158/D3 **Las Nieves**, Mex.
76/D3 **La Solana**, Sp.
127/F4 **Lasolo** (riv.), Indo.
68/B4 **La Somme, Canal de** (can.), Fr.
74/D3 **La Souterraine**, Fr.
186/D4 **Las Palmas** (riv.), Mex.
161/F4 **Las Palmas**, Pan.
174/C2 **Las Palmas de Cocalán Nat'l Park**, Chile
140/A2 **Las Palmas de Gran Canaria**, Canl.,Sp.
187/J5 **Las Palomas**, Mex.
169/E4 **Las Pampitas**, Bol.
172/D5 **Las Parejas**, Arg.
76/D3 **Las Pedroñeras**, Sp.
174/E2 **Las Perdices**, Arg.
169/E4 **Las Petas**, Bol.
169/G5 **Las Petas**, Bol.
86/C4 **La Spezia**, It.
86/C4 **La Spezia** (prov.), It.
168/D4 **Las Piedras**, Peru
175/F2 **Las Piedras**, Uru.
164/C2 **Las Piedras**, Ven.
165/F2 **Las Piedras**, Ven.
125/E6 **Las Piñas**, Phil.
175/F2 **Las Pipinas**, Arg.
174/D4 **Las Plumas**, Arg.
174/E2 **Las Rosas**, Arg.
77/N9 **Las Rozas**, Sp.
79/E4 **Lassay-les-Châteaux**, Fr.
73/A3 **Lassee**, Aus.
184/C3 **Lassen** (peak), Ca,US
184/C3 **Lassen Volcanic Nat'l Park**, Ca,US
137/V **Lassiter** (coast), Ant.
199/K2 **L'Assomption**, Qu,Can
197/N6 **L'Assomption** (co.), Qu,Can
197/P6 **L'Assomption** (riv.), Qu,Can
54/C5 **Lasswade**, Sc,UK
161/F5 **Las Tablas**, Pan.
187/J2 **Las Tablas**, NM,US
76/D3 **Las Tablas de Daimiel Nat'l Park**, Sp.
172/B3 **Lastarria** (vol.), Chile
183/M2 **Last Mountain** (lake), Sk,Can
172/B4 **Las Tórtolas** (peak), Chile
172/E4 **Las Toscas**, Arg.
173/F5 **Las Toscas**, Uru.
152/C3 **Lastoursville**, Gabon
92/C4 **Lastovo**, Cro.
92/C4 **Lastovo** (isl.), Cro.
92/C4 **Lastovski** (chan.), Cro.
87/E5 **Lastra a Signa**, It.
165/E3 **Las Trincheras**, Ven.
67/E3 **Lastrup**, Ger.
161/G1 **Las Tunas**, Cuba
82/B2 **La Sûre** (mtn.), Fr.
79/F5 **La Suze-sur-Sarthe**, Fr.
158/C2 **Las Varas**, Mex.
158/D4 **Las Varas**, Mex.
174/E1 **Las Varillas**, Arg.
190/B3 **Las Vegas**, NM,US
186/E2 **Las Vegas**, Nv,US
190/B3 **Las Vegas Nat'l Wild. Ref.**, NM,US
168/D5 **Las Yaras**, Peru
138/F6 **Lata**, Sol.
179/L3 **La Tabatière**, Qu,Can
164/B5 **Latacunga**, Ecu.
137/U **Latady** (isl.), Ant.
121/H4 **Latākhola**, Bang.
106/C1 **Latakia**, Syria
103/D2 **Latakia** (Al Lādhiqīyah), Syria
145/F4 **L'Atakora** (prov.), Ben.
167/K7 **La Tebaida**, Col.
121/E4 **Lātehār**, India
81/H5 **Latemar** (peak), It.
196/B1 **Laterrière**, Qu,Can
90/E2 **Laterza**, It.
74/C4 **La Teste-de-Buch**, Fr.
80/C6 **La Tête à l'Ane** (peak), Fr.
189/G2 **Latexo**, Tx,US
191/F2 **Latham**, Ks,US
79/F6 **Lathan** (riv.), Fr.
205/M11 **Lathrop**, Ca,US
191/G1 **Lathrop**, Mo,US
82/C1 **La Thuile**, It.
160/E3 **La Tigra Nat'l Park**, Hon.
53/M7 **Latimer**, Eng,UK
193/H2 **Latimer**, Ia,US
84/C5 **Latina**, It.
84/D5 **Latina** (prov.), It.
84/C4 **Latina Scalo**, It.
87/G1 **Latisana**, It.
89/G2 **Latium** (reg.), It.
73/B4 **Latja** (riv.), Hun.
83/C1 **Lato** (riv.), It.
174/D2 **La Toma**, Arg.
186/C2 **Laton**, Ca,US
65/L4 **Latorica** (riv.), Slvk.
165/E2 **La Tortuga** (isl.), Ven.
130/A4 **Latouche Treville** (cape), Austl.
82/B5 **La Tour-d'Aigues**, Fr.
80/C5 **La Tour-de-Peilz**, Swi.
80/D4 **La Tour-de-Trême**, Swi.
82/B1 **La Tour-du-Pin**, Fr.
182/C5 **Latourell** (falls), Or,US
174/D2 **La Tranca**, Arg.
74/C4 **La Tremblade**, Fr.
172/C3 **La Trinidad**, Arg.
125/C1 **La Trinidad**, Phil.
160/C2 **La Trinitaria**, Mex.
82/D5 **La Trinité**, Fr.
196/C1 **La Trinité-des-Monts**, Qu,Can
78/C4 **La Trinité-Porhoët**, Fr.
78/B5 **La Trinité-sur-Mer**, Fr.
135/C4 **Latrobe**, Austl.
135/C3 **Latrobe** (peak), Austl.
135/C3 **Latrobe** (riv.), Austl.
164/B5 **La Troncal**, Ecu.
83/C2 **Latronico**, It.
172/B3 **La Troya** (riv.), Arg.
81/G4 **Latsch** (Laces), It.
74/E5 **Lattes**, Fr.
207/L8 **Lattingtown**, NY,US
196/A2 **La Tuque**, Qu,Can
118/C4 **Lātūr**, India
78/C6 **La Turballe**, Fr.
63/L3 **Latvia**
123/B3 **Lat Yao**, Thai.
95/L2 **Lat'yuga**, Rus.
145/H4 **Lau**, Nga.
70/B1 **Laubach**, Ger.
72/E5 **Laubusch**, Ger.
172/B1 **Lauca Nat'l Park**, Chile
75/G3 **Lauch** (riv.), Fr.
81/F1 **Lauchert** (riv.), Ger.
72/D5 **Lauchhammer**, Ger.
70/D5 **Lauchheim**, Ger.
70/C3 **Lauda-Königshofen**, Ger.
194/D3 **Lauder**, Mb,Can
54/D5 **Lauder**, Sc,UK
200/C4 **Lauderdale**, Ms,US
205/N14 **Lauderdale** (lakes), Wi,US
202/P7 **Lauderdale-by-the-Sea**, Fl,US
202/P7 **Lauderdale Lakes**, Fl,US
202/P7 **Lauderhill**, Fl,US
82/A4 **Laudun**, Fr.
67/G2 **Lauenbrück**, Ger.
67/H2 **Lauenburg**, Ger.
80/D5 **Lauenen**, Swi.
70/D2 **Lauer** (riv.), Ger.
70/E3 **Lauf**, Ger.
70/C2 **Laufach**, Ger.
71/F7 **Laufen**, Ger.
80/D3 **Laufen**, Swi.
80/E2 **Laufenburg**, Swi.
70/C4 **Lauffen am Neckar**, Ger.
58/B3 **Laugharne**, Wal,UK
133/G2 **Laughlen** (peak), Austl.
186/E3 **Laughlin**, Nv,US
188/D3 **Laughlin A.F.B.**, Tx,US
138/H6 **Lau Group** (isls.), Fiji
61/G3 **Lauhanvuoren Nat'l Park**, Fin.
116/C3 **Lauhkaung**, Burma
70/D5 **Lauingen**, Ger.
61/H3 **Laukaa**, Fin.
63/K4 **Laukuva**, Lith.
135/C4 **Launceston**, Austl.
58/B5 **Launceston**, Eng,UK
60/A5 **Laune** (riv.), Ire.
53/U9 **Launette** (riv.), Fr.
123/B3 **Launglon**, Burma
169/F4 **La Unión**, Bol.
174/B4 **La Unión**, Chile
164/B4 **La Unión**, Col.
160/E3 **La Unión**, ESal.
159/E5 **La Unión**, Mex.
168/A2 **La Unión**, Peru
168/B3 **La Unión**, Peru
77/E4 **La Unión**, Sp.
187/J5 **La Unión**, NM,US
164/E2 **La Unión**, Ven.
180/U11 **Laupahoehoe**, Hi,US
80/D4 **Laupen**, Swi.
80/D4 **Lauperswil**, Swi.
70/C6 **Laupheim**, Ger.
82/C4 **L'Aupillon** (mtn.), Fr.
131/G3 **Laura**, Austl.
133/H5 **Laura**, Austl.
194/A2 **Laura**, Sk,Can
81/E5 **Laurasca, Cima della** (peak), It.
165/E3 **La Urbana**, Ven.
83/C6 **Laureana di Borrello**, It.
201/K1 **Laurel**, De,US
203/G4 **Laurel**, Fl,US
200/E1 **Laurel**, In,US
206/B5 **Laurel**, Md,US
200/C5 **Laurel**, Ms,US
183/K5 **Laurel**, Mt,US
193/F2 **Laurel**, Ne,US
201/J2 **Laurel**, Va,US
201/G4 **Laurel Bay**, SC,US
206/C3 **Laureldale**, Pa,US
202/E2 **Laurel Hill**, Fl,US
206/C4 **Laurel Springs**, NJ,US
206/A2 **Laurelton**, Pa,US
56/B3 **Laurelvale**, NI,UK
207/D3 **Laurence Harbor**, NJ,US
54/D3 **Laurencekirk**, Sc,UK
193/G2 **Laurens**, Ia,US
201/F3 **Laurens**, SC,US
198/E1 **Laurentian** (plat.), Can
197/N6 **Laurentides**, Qu,Can
83/B2 **Laurenzana**, It.
83/C4 **Laurenzana** (riv.), It.
83/B2 **Lauria**, It.
194/E2 **Laurier**, Mb,Can
199/L1 **Laurier-Station**, Qu,Can
56/D2 **Laurieston**, Sc,UK
201/H3 **Laurinburg**, NC,US
82/B5 **Lauris**, Fr.
195/K4 **Laurium**, Mi,US
120/E2 **Lauriya Nandangarh**, India
85/E6 **Lauro**, It.
83/C3 **Lauropoli**, It.
80/C4 **Lausanne**, Swi.
70/E2 **Lauscha**, Ger.
127/E4 **Laut** (isl.), Indo.
72/E5 **Lauta**, Ger.
174/B3 **Lautaro**, Chile
130/B2 **Lautem**, Indo.
75/H2 **Lauter** (riv.), Fr.
69/G5 **Lauter** (riv.), Fr., Ger.
70/C5 **Lauter** (riv.), Ger.
71/E4 **Lauterach** (riv.), Ger.
64/E3 **Lauterbach**, Ger.
70/E2 **Lauterbach** (riv.), Ger.
69/H6 **Lauterburg**, Ger.
80/D4 **Lauterbrunnen**, Swi.
69/G4 **Lauterecken**, Ger.
138/G6 **Lautoka**, Fiji
62/D2 **Lauve**, Nor.
66/D2 **Lauwers** (chan.), Neth.
66/D2 **Lauwersmeer** (lake), Neth.
184/C3 **Lava Beds Nat'l Mon.**, Ca,US
202/D1 **Lavaca**, Al,US
189/F3 **Lavaca** (bay), Tx,US
189/F3 **Lavaca** (riv.), Tx,US
86/C4 **Lavagna**, It.
86/C4 **Lavagna** (riv.), It.
185/G2 **Lava Hot Springs**, Id,US
199/K2 **Laval**, Qu,Can
79/E4 **Laval**, Fr.
199/G5 **La Vale**, Md,US
82/B6 **La Valette-du-Var**, Fr.
175/G2 **Lavalleja** (dept.), Uru.
207/D4 **Lavallette**, NJ,US
80/B2 **La Vallinot**, Fr.
105/H5 **Lāvān** (isl.), Iran
82/C2 **La Vanoise** (upland), Fr.
82/C2 **La Vanoise Nat'l Park**, Fr.
80/B5 **Lavans-lès-Saint-Claude**, Fr.
75/L3 **Lavant** (riv.), Aus.
174/B3 **Lavapié** (pt.), Chile
157/H8 **Lavaraty**, Madg.
63/K2 **Lavassaare**, Est.
77/F1 **Lavaur**, Fr.
76/C1 **La Vecilla de Curveño**, Sp.
167/L7 **La Vega**, Col.
162/D3 **La Vega**, DRep.
164/C1 **La Vela, Cabo de** (pt.), Col.
74/D5 **Lavelanet**, Fr.
85/F5 **Lavello**, It.
86/B1 **Lavena**, It.
86/B1 **Laveno**, It.
158/C3 **La Ventana**, Mex.
200/D2 **La Vergne**, Tn,US
187/F2 **La Verkin**, Ut,US
87/E5 **La Verna**, It.
204/C2 **La Verne**, Ca,US
190/E2 **Laverne**, Ok,US
189/E3 **La Vernia**, Tx,US
53/R10 **La Verrière**, Fr.
132/D4 **Laverton**, Austl.
80/D5 **Lavey**, Swi.
87/E3 **Lavezzola**, It.
158/E3 **La Víbora**, Mex.
164/B4 **La Victoria**, Col.
164/D3 **La Victoria**, Ven.
165/E2 **La Victoria**, Ven.
79/F3 **La Vieille-Lyre**, Fr.
167/K8 **La Vieja** (riv.), Col.
62/A1 **Lavik**, Nor.
79/F6 **La Ville-aux-Dames**, Fr.
196/E2 **Laville**, NB,Can
183/K4 **Lavina**, Mt,US
87/E4 **Lavino** (riv.), It.
167/K7 **La Virginia**, Col.
81/H5 **Lavis**, It.
188/L6 **Lavon**, Tx,US
189/F1 **Lavon** (dam), Tx,US
188/L6 **Lavon** (lake), Tx,US
201/F3 **Lavonia**, Ga,US
76/A2 **Lavos**, Port.
82/A3 **La Voulte-sur-Rhône**, Fr.
170/D4 **Lavras**, Braz.
167/G4 **Lavras da Mangabeira**, Braz.
91/J4 **Lávrion**, Gre.
155/F2 **Lavushi Manda Nat'l Park**, Zam.
166/C1 **Lawa** (riv.), FrG., Sur.
116/C5 **Lawabauk**, Burma
124/F4 **Lawang**, Indo.
69/G6 **La Wantzenau**, Fr.
107/K1 **Lawarai** (pass), Pak.
120/A1 **Lāwar Khās**, India
125/A4 **Lawas**, Malay.
150/C2 **Lawdar**, Yem.
184/D2 **Lawen**, Or,US
126/D3 **Lawit** (mtn.), Indo.
124/C1 **Lawit** (peak), Malay.
123/B1 **Lawksawk**, Burma
197/K2 **Lawn**, Nf,Can
188/E1 **Lawn**, Tx,US
204/B3 **Lawndale**, Ca,US
131/E4 **Lawn Hill**, Austl.
177/M5 **Lawnhill**, BC,Can
131/E4 **Lawn Hill Nat'l Park**, Austl.
105/E4 **Lawqah**, SAr.
144/E4 **Lawra**, Gha.
136/B4 **Lawrence**, N.Z.
198/C5 **Lawrence**, In,US
191/G1 **Lawrence**, Ks,US
199/L3 **Lawrence**, Ma,US
192/E3 **Lawrence**, Ne,US
207/E2 **Lawrence**, NY,US
208/G5 **Lawrence** (co.), Pa,US
188/L7 **Lawrence**, Tx,US
198/D5 **Lawrenceburg**, In,US
200/D3 **Lawrenceburg**, Tn,US
198/F3 **Lawrence Park**, Pa,US
196/D3 **Lawrence Station**, NB,Can
56/B3 **Lawrencetown**, NI,UK
200/F4 **Lawrenceville**, Ga,US
198/C5 **Lawrenceville**, Il,US
206/D3 **Lawrenceville**, NJ,US
201/J2 **Lawrenceville**, Va,US
194/A2 **Lawson**, Sk,Can
191/H4 **Lawson**, Ar,US
191/G1 **Lawson**, Mo,US
203/G2 **Lawtey**, Fl,US
191/E3 **Lawton**, Ok,US
124/E4 **Lawu** (peak), Indo.
104/C4 **Lawz, Jabal al** (mtn.), SAr.
147/G2 **Lawz, Jabal al** (mtn.), SAr.
203/G2 **Lax**, Ga,US
62/F2 **Laxa**, Swe.
56/D3 **Laxey**, IM,UK
69/F6 **Laxou**, Fr.
74/C3 **Lay** (riv.), Fr.
95/N2 **Laya** (riv.), Rus.
127/F4 **Layar** (cape), Indo.
139/H2 **Laycan** (isl.), Hi,US
82/B4 **Laye** (riv.), Fr.
150/D2 **Layjūn**, Yem.
106/E4 **Laylā**, SAr.
105/F3 **Laylān**, Iraq
79/E6 **Layon** (riv.), Fr.
69/F6 **Lay-Saint-Christophe**, Fr.
203/H5 **Layton**, Fl,US
206/D1 **Layton**, NJ,US
185/H3 **Layton**, Ut,US
184/B4 **Laytonville**, Ca,US
60/D2 **Laytown**, Ire.
101/Q4 **Lazarev**, Rus.
92/E3 **Lazarevac**, Yugo.
186/E5 **Lázaro Cárdenas**, Mex.
63/K4 **Lazdijai**, Lith.
125/C3 **Lazi**, Phil.
85/D2 **Lazio** (reg.), It.
87/D1 **Lazise**, It.
101/P3 **Lazo**, Rus.
57/F2 **Lazonby**, Eng,UK
98/E4 **Lazovsk**, Mol.
83/B7 **Lazzaro**, It.
86/C3 **Lazzaro, Monte** (peak), It.
59/F3 **Lea** (riv.), Eng,UK
123/C3 **Leach**, Camb.
59/E3 **Leach** (riv.), Eng,UK
206/B3 **Leacock-Leola-Bareville**, Pa,US
196/C3 **Lead** (mtn.), Me,US
192/C1 **Lead**, SD,US
188/E2 **Leaday**, Tx,US
182/B4 **Leadbetter** (pt.), Wa,US
57/H5 **Leadenham**, Eng,UK
183/K2 **Leader**, Sk,Can
54/D5 **Leader Water** (riv.), Sc,UK
191/H2 **Lead Hill**, Ar,US
58/D2 **Leadon** (riv.), Eng,UK
192/A4 **Leadville**, Co,US
202/D2 **Leaf**, Ms,US
202/D2 **Leaf** (riv.), Ms,US
135/B2 **Leaghur** (lake), Austl.
189/G3 **League City**, Tx,US
201/F4 **Leah**, Ga,US
202/D2 **Leakesville**, Ms,US
188/E3 **Leakey**, Tx,US
53/N7 **Lea** (Lee) (riv.), Eng,UK
154/D2 **Lealui**, Zam.
59/E2 **Leam** (riv.), Eng,UK
205/G7 **Leamington**, On,Can
185/G4 **Leamington**, Ut,US
117/H2 **Le'an** (riv.), China
132/B4 **Leander** (pt.), Austl.
189/F2 **Leander**, Tx,US
173/F3 **Leandro N. Alem**, Arg.
60/A5 **Leane** (lake), Ire.
98/C5 **Leaota** (peak), Rom.
132/B2 **Learmonth**, Austl.
203/F2 **Leary**, Ga,US
191/J1 **Leasburg**, Mo,US
183/L1 **Leask**, Sk,Can
53/N8 **Leatherhead**, Eng,UK
68/D3 **L'Eau d'Heure** (riv.), Belg.
68/D3 **L'Eau d'Heure, Barrage de** (dam), Belg.
191/G1 **Leavenworth**, Ks,US
182/D4 **Leavenworth**, Wa,US
208/G5 **Leavittsburg**, Oh,US
65/J1 **Ł eba**, Pol.
69/F5 **Lebach**, Ger.
125/D4 **Lebak**, Phil.
182/C4 **Lebam**, Wa,US
152/B3 **Lébamba**, Gabon
92/E4 **Lebane**, Yugo.
152/C2 **Lébango**, Congo
103/D3 **Lebanon**
103/D3 **Lebanon** (mts.), Leb.
187/H2 **Lebanon**, Co,US
208/B2 **Lebanon**, Ct,US
198/C4 **Lebanon**, In,US
191/E1 **Lebanon**, Ks,US
200/E2 **Lebanon**, Ky,US
191/H2 **Lebanon**, Mo,US
199/K3 **Lebanon**, NH,US
206/D2 **Lebanon**, NJ,US
198/D5 **Lebanon**, Oh,US
191/F4 **Lebanon**, Ok,US
184/B1 **Lebanon**, Or,US
206/B3 **Lebanon**, Pa,US
206/B3 **Lebanon** (co.), Pa,US
200/D2 **Lebanon**, Tn,US
201/F2 **Lebanon**, Va,US
200/E2 **Lebanon Junction**, Ky,US
206/C5 **Lebanon-Rising Sun**, De,US
69/F5 **Le Ban-Saint-Martin**, Fr.
68/D2 **Lebbeke**, Belg.
202/C2 **Lebeau**, La,US
82/B6 **Le Beausset**, Fr.
186/C3 **Lebec**, Ca,US
99/H2 **Lebedin**, Ukr.
101/N4 **Lebedinyy**, Rus.
95/H5 **Lebedyan'**, Rus.
141/M13 **Lebene** (riv.), Mor.
73/B4 **Lébény**, Hun.
196/C1 **Le Bic**, Qu,Can
72/C4 **Lebien**, Ger.
152/C3 **Lébiga**, Congo
74/D3 **Le Blanc**, Fr.
53/T10 **Le Blanc-Mesnil**, Fr.
191/G1 **Lebo**, Ks,US
155/F5 **Lebombo** (mts.), Moz., SAfr.
78/C5 **Le Bono**, Fr.
65/J1 **Lębork**, Pol.
82/C2 **Le Bourg-d'Oisans**, Fr.
82/B1 **Le Bourget-du-Lac**, Fr.
53/T10 **Le Bourget** (Paris) (arpt.), Fr.
156/Q12 **Lebowa** (homeland), SAfr.
157/E2 **Lebowakgomo**, SAfr.
80/C4 **Le Brassus**, Swi.
74/F3 **Le Breuil**, Fr.
76/B4 **Lebrija**, Sp.
76/A2 **Leça da Palmeira**, Port.
82/D5 **Le Cannet**, Fr.
82/C6 **Le Cannet-des-Maures**, Fr.
68/C3 **Le Cateau**, Fr.
91/F2 **Lecce**, It.
85/D4 **Lecce nei Marsi**, It.
86/C1 **Lecci** (lake), It.
86/C1 **Lecco**, It.
193/H1 **Le Center**, Mn,US
81/G3 **Lech**, Aus.
81/G1 **Lech** (riv.), Aus., Ger.
80/D5 **Le Châble**, Swi.
119/K2 **Lechang**, China
80/D3 **Le Chasseral** (peak), Swi.
80/C4 **Le Chasseron** (peak), Swi.
81/G2 **Lechbruck**, Ger.
161/G1 **Leche** (lag.), Cuba
53/S10 **Le Chesnay**, Fr.
69/D4 **Le Chesne**, Fr.
80/C5 **Le Cheval Blanc** (mtn.), Fr.
82/C2 **Le Cheval Noir** (mtn.), Fr.
74/F4 **Le Cheylard**, Fr.
59/E3 **Lechlade**, Eng,UK
81/G3 **Lechtaler Alps** (mts.), Aus.
64/E1 **Leck**, Ger.
60/A3 **Leckavrea** (mtn.), Ire.
193/J3 **Le Claire**, Ia,US
202/B2 **Lecompte**, La,US
152/C3 **Léconi**, Gabon
78/A4 **Le Conquet**, Fr.
75/J5 **Le Cornate** (peak), It.
79/G4 **Le Coudray**, Fr.
77/G1 **Le Crès**, Fr.
74/F3 **Le Creusot**, Fr.
78/C6 **Le Croisic**, Fr.
68/A3 **Le Crotoy**, Fr.
74/D5 **Lectoure**, Fr.
65/M3 **Ł eczna**, Pol.
67/E2 **Leda** (riv.), Ger.
124/C2 **Ledang** (peak), Malay.
58/D2 **Ledbury**, Eng,UK
68/C2 **Lede**, Belg.
68/C2 **Ledegem**, Belg.
76/C2 **Ledesma**, Sp.
132/B4 **Ledge Point**, Austl.
183/J3 **Ledger**, Mt,US
152/D3 **Lediba**, Zaire
152/C5 **Lêdo** (cape), Ang.
117/F5 **Ledong**, China
87/D1 **Ledro** (lake), It.
183/H1 **Leduc**, Ab,Can
82/B4 **Le Duffre** (mtn.), Fr.
81/F5 **Ledu, Pizzo** (peak), It.
60/B6 **Lee** (riv.), Ire.
203/G2 **Lee**, Fl,US
208/A1 **Lee**, Ma,US
196/C3 **Lee**, Me,US
206/B1 **Lee** (mtn.), Pa,US
195/G4 **Leech** (lake), Mn,US
195/G4 **Leech Lake Ind. Res.**, Mn,US
191/G3 **Lee Creek**, Ar,US
183/G1 **Leedale**, Ab,Can
190/E3 **Leedey**, Ok,US
57/G4 **Leeds**, Eng,UK
200/D4 **Leeds**, Al,US
194/E3 **Leeds**, ND,US
187/F2 **Leeds**, Ut,US
57/G4 **Leeds and Bradford** (int'l arpt.), Eng,UK
57/G4 **Leeds and Liverpool** (can.), Eng,UK
206/D5 **Leeds Point**, NJ,US
72/D2 **Leegebruch**, Ger.
66/D2 **Leek**, Neth.
57/F5 **Leek**, Eng,UK
53/N7 **Lee** (Lea) (riv.), Eng,UK
132/B4 **Leeman**, Austl.
67/E2 **Leer**, Ger.
66/C5 **Leerdam**, Neth.
66/C4 **Leersum**, Neth.
203/H3 **Leesburg**, Fl,US
203/F2 **Leesburg**, Ga,US
206/D5 **Leesburg**, NJ,US
201/J1 **Leesburg**, Va,US
200/E4 **Lees Crossing**, Ga,US
67/G3 **Leese**, Ger.
206/C3 **Leesport**, Pa,US
191/G1 **Lees Summit**, Mo,US
136/C3 **Leeston**, N.Z.
202/B2 **Leesville**, La,US
208/F7 **Leesville** (dam), Oh,US
208/F7 **Leesville** (res.), Oh,US
201/H2 **Leesville** (dam), Va,US
201/H2 **Leesville** (lake), Va,US
135/C2 **Leeton**, Austl.
208/G6 **Leetonia**, Oh,US
208/G6 **Leetsdale**, Pa,US
156/L10 **Leeu** (riv.), SAfr.
156/D2 **Leeudoringstad**, SAfr.
66/C2 **Leeuwarden**, Neth.
132/B5 **Leeuwin** (cape), Austl.
132/B5 **Leeuwin-Naturaliste Nat'l Park**, Austl.
202/C3 **Leeville**, La,US
186/C2 **Lee Vining**, Ca,US
162/F3 **Leeward Islands** (isls.), West Indies
78/B4 **Le Faouët**, Fr.
78/B3 **Leff** (riv.), Fr.
86/C1 **Leffe**, It.
152/C3 **Léfini** (riv.), Congo
152/C3 **Léfini Rsv.**, Congo
103/C2 **Lefka**, Cyp.
145/H5 **Lefo** (peak), Camr.
78/A3 **Le Folgoët**, Fr.
194/C4 **Lefor**, ND,US
132/D4 **Lefroy** (lake), Austl.
201/G1 **Left Hand**, WV,US
135/C4 **Legana**, Austl.
76/D2 **Leganés**, Sp.
81/G2 **Legau**, Ger.
125/C2 **Legazpi**, Phil.
76/D1 **Legazpia**, Sp.
135/C4 **Legges Tor** (peak), Austl.
65/L2 **Legionowo**, Pol.
69/E4 **Léglise**, Belg.
87/E2 **Legnago**, It.
86/B1 **Legnano**, It.
87/E2 **Legnaro**, It.
65/J3 **Legnica**, Pol.
65/H3 **Legnica** (prov.), Pol.
81/F5 **Legnone, Monte** (peak), It.
206/A4 **Le Gore**, Md,US
196/E2 **Le Goulet**, NB,Can
80/C5 **Le Grammont** (peak), Swi.
82/C1 **Le Grand** (mtn.), Fr.
186/B2 **Le Grand**, Ca,US
80/D2 **Le Grand Ballon** (mtn.), Fr.
82/C4 **Le Grand Coyer** (mtn.), Fr.
132/D5 **Le Grande** (cape), Austl.
79/F5 **Le Grand-Lucé**, Fr.
79/G2 **Le Grand-Quevilly**, Fr.
74/F5 **Le Grau-du-Roi**, Fr.
86/C4 **Le Grazie**, It.
78/B3 **Léguer** (riv.), Fr.
114/C5 **Leh**, India
79/F2 **Le Havre**, Fr.
72/B6 **Lehesten**, Ger.
185/H3 **Lehi**, Ut,US
191/F3 **Lehigh**, Ok,US
206/C2 **Lehigh** (co.), Pa,US
206/C2 **Lehigh** (riv.), Pa,US
203/H4 **Lehigh Acres**, Fl,US
206/C2 **Lehighton**, Pa,US
60/A4 **Lehinch**, Ire.
72/C3 **Lehnin**, Ger.
78/C4 **Léhon**, Fr.
79/G1 **Le Houlme**, Fr.
194/E4 **Lehr**, ND,US
70/D4 **Lehrberg**, Ger.
67/G4 **Lehrte**, Ger.
154/D4 **Lehututu**, Bots.
117/G3 **Lei** (riv.), China
84/B3 **Leia** (riv.), It.
122/A2 **Leiah**, Pak.
71/F5 **Leiblfing**, Ger.
75/L3 **Leibnitz**, Aus.
119/J2 **Leibo**, China
72/D3 **Leibsch**, Ger.
59/E1 **Leicester**, Eng,UK
208/C1 **Leicester**, Ma,US
59/E1 **Leicestershire** (co.), Eng,UK
133/H2 **Leichhardt** (dam), Austl.
131/E4 **Leichhardt** (falls), Austl.
134/B3 **Leichhardt** (range), Austl.
128/F3 **Leichhardt** (riv.), Austl.
131/E4 **Leichhardt** (riv.), Austl.
66/E6 **Leichlingen**, Ger.
66/B4 **Leiden**, Neth.
66/B4 **Leiderdorp**, Neth.
66/B4 **Leidschendam**, Neth.
66/A7 **Leie** (riv.), Belg.
81/H5 **Leifers** (Laives), It.
53/N8 **Leigh**, Eng,UK
53/P8 **Leigh**, Eng,UK
133/H4 **Leigh Creek**, Austl.
60/D4 **Leighlinbridge**, Ire.
59/F3 **Leighton Buzzard**, Eng,UK
117/F3 **Leigong** (mtn.), China
117/G2 **Leihe**, China
168/B2 **Leimebamba**, Peru
70/B4 **Leimersheim**, Ger.
70/C5 **Lein** (riv.), Ger.
183/L2 **Leinan**, Sk,Can
67/G5 **Leine** (riv.), Ger.
67/H6 **Leinefelde**, Ger.
70/C5 **Leinfelden-Echterdingen**, Ger.
132/D3 **Leinster**, Austl.
60/D4 **Leinster** (mtn.), Ire.
60/C3 **Leinster** (prov.), Ire.
58/D2 **Leintwardine**, Eng,UK
70/D6 **Leipheim**, Ger.
206/C5 **Leipsic**, De,US
206/C5 **Leipsic** (riv.), De,US
198/E4 **Leipsic**, Oh,US
72/C5 **Leipzig**, Ger.
72/C5 **Leipzig** (reg.), Ger.
68/D2 **Leir** (riv.), Belg.
62/C1 **Leira**, Nor.
76/A3 **Leiria**, Port.
76/A3 **Leiria** (dist.), Port.
62/A2 **Leirvik**, Nor.
63/K2 **Leisi**, Est.
133/F2 **Leisler** (peak), Austl.
72/C5 **Leisnig**, Ger.
59/H2 **Leiston cum Sizewell**, Eng,UK
203/H5 **Leisure City**, Fl,US
200/D2 **Leitchfield**, Ky,US

185/K1 **Leiter**, Wy,US
59/F4 **Leith** (hill), Eng,UK
54/C5 **Leith**, Sc,UK
73/A3 **Leitha** (riv.), Aus.
73/A4 **Leithagebirge** (mts.), Aus.
60/B2 **Leitrim**, Ire.
60/C2 **Leitrim** (co.), Ire.
72/B3 **Leitzkau**, Ger.
60/C4 **Leix** (Laois) (co.), Ire.
60/D3 **Leixlip**, Ire.
117/G3 **Leiyang**, China
115/B4 **Leiyuanzhen**, China
117/F4 **Leizhou** (pen.), China
63/M3 **Lejasciems**, Lat.
63/K4 **Lejpalingis**, Lith.
64/C3 **Lek**, Neth.
66/B5 **Lek** (riv.), Neth.
152/C3 **Lékana**, Congo
91/G4 **Lekhainá**, Gre.
144/C2 **Lekhcheb**, Mrta.
66/B5 **Lekkerkerk**, Neth.
145/G5 **Lekki** (lag.), Nga.
152/C2 **Lékoli-Pandaka Animal Rsv.**, Congo
152/C3 **Lekóti** (riv.), Congo
152/C3 **Lékoumou** (pol. reg.), Congo
62/F1 **Leksands-Noret**, Swe.
94/F3 **Leksozero** (lake), Rus.
150/A4 **Leku**, Eth.
127/G3 **Lelai** (cape), Indo.
193/K3 **Leland**, Il,US
198/D2 **Leland**, Mi,US
200/B4 **Leland**, Ms,US
201/H3 **Leland**, NC,US
80/D3 **Le Landeron**, Swi.
62/E2 **Lelång** (lake), Swe.
82/C4 **Le Lauzet-Ubaye**, Fr.
82/C6 **Le Lavandou**, Fr.
98/E2 **Lel'chitsy**, Bela.
174/C4 **Leleque**, Arg.
190/D3 **Lelia Lake**, Tx,US
115/D3 **Leling**, China
127/H4 **Lelintah**, Indo.
79/E5 **Le Lion-d'Angers**, Fr.
80/C3 **Le Locle**, Swi.
130/A2 **Lelogama**, Indo.
78/D6 **Le Loroux-Bottereau**, Fr.
138/F4 **Lelu**, Micro.
82/C6 **Le Luc**, Fr.
79/F5 **Le Lude**, Fr.
166/C1 **Lelydorp**, Sur.
66/C3 **Lelystad**, Neth.
62/C3 **Lem**, Den.
175/L8 **Le Maire** (str.), Arg.
81/E5 **Lema, Monte** (peak), It.
80/C5 **Léman** (Geneva) (lake), Fr., Swi.
79/F5 **Le Mans**, Fr.
193/F2 **Le Mars**, Ia,US
150/B4 **Lema Shilindi**, Eth.
69/G5 **Lembach**, Fr.
194/C2 **Lemberg**, Sk,Can
69/G5 **Lemberg**, Ger.
70/B6 **Lemberg** (peak), Ger.
81/E1 **Lemberg** (peak), Ger.
124/B1 **Lembu** (peak), Indo.
170/D4 **Leme**, Braz.
53/T11 **Le Mée-sur-Seine**, Fr.
79/F4 **Le Mêle-sur-Sarthe**, Fr.
61/H1 **Lemenjoen Nat'l Park**, Fin.
79/F3 **Le Merlerault**, Fr.
97/H2 **Lemeshkino**, Rus.
68/A5 **Le Mesnil-Esnard**, Fr.
53/S10 **Le Mesnil-le-Roi**, Fr.
53/R10 **Le Mesnil-Saint-Denis**, Fr.
68/D6 **Le Mesnil-sur-Oger**, Fr.
67/F4 **Lemgo**, Ger.
185/G1 **Lemhi**, Id,US
185/G1 **Lemhi** (range), Id,US
190/A3 **Lemitar**, NM,US
63/J1 **Lemland**, Fin.
63/H2 **Lemland** (isl.), Fin.
66/C3 **Lemmer**, Neth.
187/G4 **Lemmon** (mt.), Az,US
194/C5 **Lemmon**, SD,US
79/E2 **Le Molay-Littry**, Fr.
80/C5 **Le Môle** (mtn.), Fr.
82/C3 **Le Monêtier-les-Bains**, Fr.
204/C5 **Lemon Grove**, Ca,US
201/H3 **Lemon Springs**, NC,US
78/D3 **Le-Mont-Saint-Michel**, Fr.
186/C2 **Lemoore**, Ca,US
186/B2 **Lemoore Nav. Air Sta.**, Ca,US
80/C4 **Le Morond** (mtn.), Fr.
74/E4 **Le Moure de la Gardille** (mtn.), Fr.
82/C3 **Le Mourre Froid** (mtn.), Fr.
192/D3 **Lemoyne**, Ne,US
160/D3 **Lempa** (riv.), NAm.
63/K1 **Lempäälä**, Fin.
74/E4 **Lempdes**, Fr.
116/B4 **Lemro** (riv.), Burma
142/B4 **Lemsid**, WSah.
92/B5 **Le Murge** (mts.), It.
90/E2 **Le Murge** (upland), It.
82/C6 **Le Muy**, Fr.
95/P2 **Lemva** (riv.), Rus.
62/C3 **Lemvig**, Den.
67/F2 **Lemwerder**, Ger.
116/B5 **Lemyethna**, Burma
194/E3 **Lena**, Mb,Can
62/D1 **Lena**, Nor.
108/F1 **Lena** (riv.), Rus.
193/K2 **Lena**, Il,US
202/B2 **Lena**, La,US
192/D3 **Lena**, Ne,US
201/G4 **Lena**, SC,US
193/K1 **Lena**, Wi,US
206/D5 **Lenape** (lake), NJ,US
167/F3 **Lençóis Maranhenses Nat'l Park**, Braz.
170/C4 **Lençóis Paulista**, Braz.
73/A6 **Lendava** (riv.), Slov.
94/F3 **Lendery**, Rus.
87/E2 **Lendinara**, It.
60/C2 **Lene, Lough** (lake), Ire.
79/F2 **Le Neuborg**, Fr.
71/F6 **Lengdorf**, Ger.
153/F4 **Lenge**, Zaire
67/H4 **Lengede**, Ger.
71/F1 **Lengenfeld**, Ger.
67/E4 **Lengerich**, Ger.
124/C1 **Lenggong**, Malay.
81/H2 **Lenggries**, Ger.
108/C4 **Lenghu**, China
80/D3 **Lengnau**, Swi.
117/F3 **Lengshuijiang**, China
117/F3 **Lengshuitan**, China
172/B4 **Lengua de Vaca** (pt.), Chile
152/C2 **Lengué** (Namobessie) (riv.), Congo
155/G3 **Lengwe Nat'l Park**, Malw.
73/B6 **Lengyeltóti**, Hun.
113/B2 **Lengzipu**, China
206/C2 **Lenhartsville**, Pa,US
149/H4 **Lenia**, Eth.
99/H3 **Lenina** (lake), Ukr.
114/B4 **Lenina, Pik** (peak), Kyr.
94/F4 **Leningrad** (Saint Petersburg), Rus.
137/L **Leningradskaya**, Ant.
99/K4 **Leningradskaya**, Rus.
177/B2 **Leningradskiy**, Rus.
99/H5 **Lenino**, Ukr.
114/D1 **Leninogorsk**, Kaz.
95/M5 **Leninogorsk**, Rus.
95/M4 **Leninsk**, Rus.
96/F1 **Leninskiy**, Rus.
100/J4 **Leninsk-Kuznetskiy**, Rus.
97/L2 **Leninskoye**, Kaz.
109/L2 **Leninskoye**, Rus.
92/E2 **Leninváros**, Hun.
80/D5 **Lenk**, Swi.
53/H5 **Lenkoran'**, Azer.
67/E6 **Lenne** (riv.), Ger.
67/F6 **Lennestadt**, Ger.
70/C5 **Lenningen**, Ger.
175/L8 **Lennox** (isl.), Chile
54/B5 **Lennox** (hills), Sc,UK
204/F8 **Lennox**, Ca,US
193/F2 **Lennox**, SD,US
54/B5 **Lennoxtown**, Sc,UK
196/B3 **Lennoxville**, Qu,Can
86/D2 **Leno**, It.
201/G3 **Lenoir**, NC,US
200/E3 **Lenoir City**, Tn,US
80/C4 **Le Noirmont** (mtn.), Fr.
80/C3 **Le Noirmont**, Swi.
80/C5 **Le Noirmont** (peak), Swi.
85/D5 **Lenola**, It.
190/D1 **Lenora**, Ks,US
194/D3 **Lenore**, Mb,Can
183/M1 **Lenore** (lake), Sk,Can
68/C3 **Le Nouvion-en-Thiérache**, Fr.
203/G2 **Lenox**, Ga,US
193/G3 **Lenox**, Ia,US
208/A1 **Lenox**, Ma,US
208/A1 **Lenox Dale**, Ma,US
68/C2 **Lens**, Belg.
68/B3 **Lens**, Fr.
80/D5 **Lens**, Swi.
64/F1 **Lensahn**, Ger.
101/M3 **Lensk**, Rus.
194/D1 **Lenswood**, Mb,Can
66/C5 **Lent**, Neth.
97/G4 **Lentekhi**, Geo.
73/A6 **Lenti**, Hun.
71/E5 **Lenting**, Ger.
63/L4 **Lentvaris**, Lith.
61/F1 **Lenvik**, Nor.
186/D3 **Lenwood**, Ca,US
123/B4 **Lenya**, Burma
54/B4 **Leny, Pass of** (pass), Sc,UK
80/E3 **Lenzburg**, Swi.
72/B1 **Lenzen**, Ger.
71/G7 **Lenzing**, Aus.
80/E2 **Lenzkirch**, Ger.
145/E4 **Léo**, Burk.
75/L3 **Leoben**, Aus.
68/B2 **Leoberghe**, Fr.
73/A4 **Leobersdorf**, Aus.
87/E1 **Leogra** (riv.), It.
127/F3 **Leok**, Indo.
191/H3 **Leola**, Ar,US
192/E1 **Leola**, SD,US
206/B3 **Leola-Leacock-Bareville**, Pa,US
58/D2 **Leominster**, Eng,UK
199/L3 **Leominster**, Ma,US
74/C4 **Leon** (lag.), Fr.
159/E4 **León**, Mex.
158/C3 **León** (int'l arpt.), Mex.
160/E3 **León**, Nic.
76/C1 **León**, Sp.
193/H3 **Leon**, Ia,US
191/F4 **Leon**, Ok,US
189/E2 **Leon** (riv.), Tx,US
189/G2 **Leona**, Tx,US
188/E3 **Leona** (riv.), Tx,US
205/F6 **Leonard**, Mi,US
194/F4 **Leonard**, ND,US
189/F1 **Leonard**, Tx,US
207/J10 **Leonardo**, NJ,US
84/C4 **Leonardo da Vinci** (int'l arpt.), It.
201/J1 **Leonardtown**, Md,US
154/C4 **Leonardville**, Namb.
191/F1 **Leonardville**, Ks,US
204/B1 **Leona Valley**, Ca,US
70/C5 **Leonberg**, Ger.
71/H6 **Leonding**, Aus.
139/H6 **Leone**, ASam.
80/E5 **Leone, Monte** (peak), It.
174/E2 **Leones**, Arg.
84/C2 **Leonessa**, It.
90/D4 **Leonforte**, It.
135/C3 **Leongatha**, Austl.
159/E4 **León-Guanajuato** (int'l arpt.), Mex.
207/K8 **Leonia**, NJ,US
91/H4 **Leonídhion**, Gre.
172/B3 **León Muerto** (mtn.), Chile
132/D4 **Leonora**, Austl.
159/F2 **Leon Valley**, Tx,US
137/F **Leopold and Astrid** (coast), Ant.
171/P6 **Leopoldina**, Braz.
68/C1 **Leopoldkanaal** (can.), Belg.
69/E1 **Leopoldsburg**, Belg.
73/A3 **Leopoldsdorf im Marchfelde**, Aus.
67/F4 **Leopoldshöhe**, Ger.
193/F2 **Leota**, Mn,US
190/D1 **Leoti**, Ks,US
93/J2 **Leovo**, Mol.
160/D3 **Lepaera**, Hon.
78/B6 **Le Palais**, Fr.
74/D4 **Le Palais-sur-Vienne**, Fr.
82/C6 **Le Palyvestre** (Toulon/Hyères) (arpt.), Fr.
80/C1 **Lépanges-sur-Vologne**, Fr.
200/B3 **Lepanto**, Ar,US
124/D3 **Lepar** (isl.), Indo.
74/D4 **Le Passage**, Fr.
76/B4 **Lepe**, Sp.
82/A2 **Le Péage-de-Roussillon**, Fr.
53/S10 **Le Pecq**, Fr.
63/N4 **Lepel'**, Bela.
78/D6 **Le Pellerin**, Fr.
91/G3 **Lepenoú**, Gre.
92/F3 **Lepenski Vir**, Yugo.
79/G3 **Le-Perray-en-Yvelines**, Fr.
80/D2 **Le Petit Ballon** (mtn.), Fr.
79/G2 **Le Petit-Couronne**, Fr.
79/G2 **Le Petit-Quevilly**, Fr.
154/E4 **Lephepe**, Bots.
154/B2 **Lepi**, Ang.
117/H2 **Leping**, China
84/C4 **Lepini** (mts.), It.
196/A3 **L'Épiphanie**, Qu,Can
53/U9 **Le Plessis-Belleville**, Fr.
53/T10 **Le Plessis-Trévise**, Fr.
82/B1 **Le Pont-de-Beauvoisin**, Fr.
82/B2 **Le Pont-de-Claix**, Fr.
82/A5 **Le Pontet**, Fr.
88/F1 **Lepontine** (mts.), It., Swi.
81/E5 **Lepontine Alps** (mts.), It., Swi.
157/R15 **Le Port**, Reun.
68/A2 **Le Portel**, Fr.
78/C6 **Le Pouliguen**, Fr.
82/A3 **Le Pouzin**, Fr.
61/H3 **Leppävirta**, Fin.
82/C6 **Le Pradet**, Fr.
196/D3 **Lepreau** (pt.), NB,Can
196/D3 **Lepreau Game Ref.**, NB,Can
73/C6 **Lepsény**, Hun.
114/C2 **Lepsy**, Kaz.
114/C2 **Lepsy** (riv.), Kaz.
146/B1 **Leptis Magna** (ruins), Libya
91/H2 **Leptokariá**, Gre.
77/F1 **Le Puech** (mtn.), Fr.
74/E4 **Le Puy**, Fr.
169/E5 **Leque**, Bol.
172/B2 **Lequena**, Chile
172/C1 **Lequepalca**, Bol.
68/C3 **Le Quesnoy**, Fr.
196/E3 **Lequille**, NS,Can
191/G3 **Lequire**, Ok,US
82/D2 **Lera** (peak), It.
144/D4 **Léraba** (riv.), Burk., IvC.
53/T10 **Le Raincy**, Fr.
86/A2 **Lera, Monte** (peak), It.
82/C2 **Le Rateau** (mtn.), Fr.
90/C4 **Lercara Friddi**, It.
159/P8 **Lerdo de Tejada**, Mex.
148/B3 **Léré**, Chad
144/D3 **Léré**, Mali
145/H4 **Lere**, Nga.
78/A4 **Le Relecq-Kerhuon**, Fr.
156/E3 **Leribe**, Les.
86/C4 **Lerici**, It.
164/D4 **Lérida**, Col.
77/F2 **Lérida** (Lleida), Sp.
97/J5 **Lerik**, Azer.
76/E1 **Lerín**, Sp.
82/D5 **Lérins** (isls.), Fr.
159/H5 **Lerma**, Mex.
159/K7 **Lerma** (riv.), Mex.
76/D1 **Lerma**, Sp.
81/G3 **Lermoos**, Aus.
198/B5 **Lerna**, Il,US
82/C2 **Le Rocher Blanc** (mtn.), Fr.
69/E6 **Lérouville**, Fr.
187/G3 **Leroux** (wash), Az,US
156/D3 **Le Rouxdam, P. K.** (res.), SAfr.
82/B6 **Le Rove**, Fr.
194/B2 **Leroy**, Sk,Can
202/E2 **Leroy**, Al,US
193/K3 **Le Roy**, Il,US
191/G1 **Le Roy**, Ks,US
193/H2 **Le Roy**, Mn,US
194/F3 **Leroy**, ND,US
189/F2 **Leroy**, Tx,US
62/E3 **Lerum**, Swe.
80/C3 **Le Russey**, Fr.
55/P12 **Lerwick**, Sc,UK
197/N7 **Léry**, Qu,Can
86/B1 **Lesa**, It.
82/B1 **Les Abrets**, Fr.
78/B5 **Les Alignements de Carnac**, Fr.
68/A5 **Les Andelys**, Fr.
82/A5 **Les Angles**, Fr.
79/F3 **Le Sap**, Fr.
82/C6 **Les Arcs**, Fr.
82/B1 **Les Avenières**, Fr.
82/C1 **Les Bauges** (upland), Fr.
80/C3 **Les Bois**, Swi.
80/D3 **Les Breuleux**, Swi.
82/D5 **L'Escarène**, Fr.
161/H2 **Les Cayes**, Haiti
197/M7 **Les Cèdres**, Qu,Can
53/R10 **Les Clayes-sous-Bois**, Fr.
80/C6 **Les Contamines-Montjoie**, Fr.
80/D5 **Les Diablerets** (range), Swi.
83/C4 **Lese** (riv.), It.
82/B2 **Les Échelles**, Fr.
96/G4 **Leselidze**, Geo.
80/D5 **Le Sépey**, Swi.
151/A1 **Leseru**, Kenya
196/C1 **Les Escoumins**, Qu,Can
79/G3 **Les-Essarts-le-Roi**, Fr.
80/C5 **Les Gets**, Fr.
116/D2 **Leshan**, China
80/D5 **Les Haudères**, Swi.
69/D4 **Les Hautes-Rivières**, Fr.
74/C3 **Les Herbiers**, Fr.
95/K2 **Leshukonskoye**, Rus.
53/T10 **Lésigny**, Fr.
86/C3 **Lesima, Monte** (peak), It.
85/F4 **Lesina**, It.
85/F4 **Lesina** (lake), It.
69/E5 **Les Islettes**, Fr.
61/D3 **Lesja**, Nor.
62/F2 **Lesjöfors**, Swe.
65/M4 **Lesko**, Pol.
92/E4 **Leskovac**, Yugo.
91/G2 **Leskovik**, Alb.
54/C4 **Leslie**, Sc,UK
191/H3 **Leslie**, Ar,US
200/E5 **Leslie**, Ga,US
198/D3 **Leslie**, Mi,US
53/T10 **Les Lilas**, Fr.
54/C5 **Lesmahagow**, Sc,UK
82/B4 **Les Mées**, Fr.
78/C3 **Les Minquiers** (isls.), Chl,UK
53/S10 **Les Molières**, Fr.
82/C4 **Les Monges** (mtn.), Fr.
80/D5 **Les Mosses**, Swi.
68/A6 **Les Mureaux**, Fr.
78/A3 **Lesneven**, Fr.
92/D3 **Lešnica**, Yugo.
95/M4 **Lesnoy**, Rus.
109/N2 **Lesogorsk**, Rus.
109/L2 **Lesopil'noye**, Rus.
82/C3 **Les Orres**, Fr.
100/K4 **Lesosibirsk**, Rus.
156/D3 **Lesotho**
109/L2 **Lesozavodsk**, Rus.
74/C4 **Lesparre-Médoc**, Fr.
82/B6 **Les Pennes-Mirabeau**, Fr.
78/D1 **Les Pieux**, Fr.
77/G1 **L'Espinouse, Sommet de** (peak), Fr.
79/E6 **Les Ponts-de-Cé**, Fr.
80/C4 **Les Ponts-de-Martel**, Swi.
68/C2 **Lesquin** (Lille) (int'l arpt.), Fr.
79/E6 **Les Rosiers**, Fr.
80/C5 **Les Rousses**, Fr.
74/C3 **Les Sables-d'Olonne**, Fr.
141/V17 **Les Salines** (int'l arpt.), Alg.
78/D2 **Lessay**, Fr.
69/E4 **Lesse** (riv.), Belg.
62/F3 **Lessebo**, Swe.
78/B3 **Les Sept** (isls.), Fr.
162/E3 **Lesser Antilles** (isls.), NAm.
105/E1 **Lesser Kavkaz** (mts.), Arm., Geo.
97/G4 **Lesser Kavkaz** (mts.), Eur.
178/E3 **Lesser Slave** (lake), Ab,Can
127/E5 **Lesser Sunda** (isls.), Indo.
68/C2 **Lessines**, Belg.
189/J2 **Lessley**, Ms,US
69/E5 **L'Est, Canal de** (can.), Fr.
191/J2 **Lesterville**, Mo,US
78/D6 **Les Touches**, Fr.
80/C4 **Le Suchet** (peak), Swi.
193/H1 **Le Sueur**, Mn,US
68/B6 **Les Ulis**, Fr.
126/D3 **Lesung** (peak), Indo.
80/C4 **Les Verrières**, Swi.
91/J3 **Lésvos** (isl.), Gre.
56/C2 **Leswalt**, Sc,UK
65/J3 **Leszno**, Pol.
65/J3 **Leszno** (prov.), Pol.
155/F4 **Letaba**, SAfr.
157/R15 **Le Tampon**, Reun.
197/G2 **L'Étang-du-Nord**, Qu,Can
53/S10 **L'Étang-la-Ville**, Fr.
196/B2 **L'Étape**, Qu,Can
92/E2 **Létavértes**, Hun.
192/E2 **Letcher**, SD,US
59/F3 **Letchworth**, Eng,UK
84/E4 **Lete** (riv.), It.
84/D1 **Letegge** (peak), It.
82/A3 **Le Teil**, Fr.
54/D3 **Letham**, Sc,UK
183/H3 **Lethbridge**, Ab,Can
197/L1 **Lethbridge**, Nf,Can
67/F2 **Lethe** (riv.), Ger.
79/F4 **Le Theil-sur-Huisne**, Fr.
165/G4 **Lethem**, Guy.
80/C1 **Le Tholy**, Fr.
82/B5 **Le Thor**, Fr.
79/F2 **Le Thuit-Signol**, Fr.
130/B2 **Leti** (isl.), Indo.
130/B2 **Leti** (isls.), Indo.
98/D3 **Letichev**, Ukr.
168/D2 **Leticia**, Col.
115/D3 **Leting**, China
80/D5 **L'Etivaz**, Swi.
95/L4 **Letka**, Rus.
154/E4 **Letlhakane**, Bots.
154/E5 **Letlhakeng**, Bots.
93/G4 **Letnitsa**, Bul.
68/B3 **L'Étoile**, Fr.
124/D2 **Letong**, Indo.
59/H5 **Le Touquet Paris Plage**, Fr.
68/A2 **Le Touquet-Paris-Plage**, Fr.
82/B2 **Le Touvet**, Fr.
116/B5 **Letpadan**, Burma
79/F2 **Le Trait**, Fr.
82/B4 **Le Tréboux** (mtn.), Fr.
82/C1 **Le Trélod** (mtn.), Fr.
68/A3 **Le Tréport**, Fr.
65/H2 **Letschin**, Ger.
123/B4 **Letsôk-Aw** (isl.), Burma
135/B2 **Lette**, Austl.
55/H9 **Letterkenny**, Ire.
199/H4 **Letterkenny Army Dep.**, Pa,US
85/E3 **Lettomanoppello**, It.
72/B3 **Letzlingen**, Ger.
72/C6 **Leubnitz**, Ger.
202/N6 **Leu Botan. Gardens**, Fl,US
91/F3 **Leuca**, It.
74/E5 **Leucate**, Fr.
54/D4 **Leuchars**, Sc,UK
80/D5 **Leuk**, Swi.
80/D5 **Leukerbad**, Swi.
70/B1 **Leun**, Ger.
72/C5 **Leuna**, Ger.
187/G3 **Leupp**, Az,US
55/H7 **Leurbost**, Sc,UK
66/C4 **Leusden-Zuid**, Neth.
124/B2 **Leuser** (peak), Indo.
70/D4 **Leutershausen**, Ger.
81/G2 **Leutkirch im Allgäu**, Ger.
69/D2 **Leuven** (Louvain), Belg.
68/C2 **Leuze-en-Hainaut**, Belg.
91/H3 **Levádhia**, Gre.
82/C6 **Le Val**, Fr.
80/C2 **Le Val-d'Ajol**, Fr.
53/S10 **Levallois-Perret**, Fr.
61/D3 **Levanger**, Nor.
82/C6 **Levant** (isl.), Fr.
86/C4 **Levante** (coast), It.
86/C4 **Levanto**, It.
73/B2 **Leváre, Vel'ke**, Slvk.
68/A5 **Le Vaudreuil**, Fr.
174/B5 **Level** (isl.), Chile
206/B4 **Level**, Md,US
190/C4 **Levelland**, Tx,US
202/P7 **Level No. 33** (can.), Fl,US
177/G4 **Levelock**, Ak,US
157/F2 **Leven** (pt.), SAfr.
57/H4 **Leven**, Eng,UK
57/F3 **Leven** (riv.), Eng,UK
57/G3 **Leven** (riv.), Eng,UK
54/D4 **Leven**, Sc,UK
54/C4 **Leven** (riv.), Sc,UK
54/A3 **Leven, Loch** (inlet), Sc,UK
54/C4 **Leven, Loch** (lake), Sc,UK
82/D5 **Levens**, Fr.
81/E5 **Leventina** (Prato), It.
130/A4 **Leveque** (cape), Austl.
170/C1 **Lever** (riv.), Braz.
55/H8 **Leverburgh**, UK
208/B1 **Leverett**, Ma,US
198/D2 **Levering**, Mi,US
66/D6 **Leverkusen**, Ger.
79/G4 **Lèves**, Fr.
53/S10 **Le Vésinet**, Fr.
73/C3 **Levice**, Slvk.
81/H5 **Levico Terme**, It.
80/C4 **Levier**, Fr.
74/E5 **Le Vigan**, Fr.
136/C3 **Levin**, N.Z.
179/J4 **Lévis**, Qu,Can
53/R10 **Lévis-Saint-Nom**, Fr.
207/E2 **Levittown**, NY,US
206/D3 **Levittown**, Pa,US
91/G3 **Levkás**, Gre.
91/G3 **Levkás** (isl.), Gre.
91/G3 **Levkímmi**, Gre.
95/L2 **Levkinskaya**, Rus.
89/J3 **Levkós** (isl.), Gre.
65/L4 **Levoča**, Slvk.
142/A5 **Lévrier** (bay), Mrta.
93/G4 **Levski**, Bul.
138/G6 **Levuka**, Fiji
78/D1 **Lévy** (cape), Fr.
203/G3 **Levy** (lake), Fl,US
192/C3 **Lewellen**, Ne,US
59/G5 **Lewes**, Eng,UK
206/C6 **Lewes**, De,US
65/J3 **Lewin Brzeski**, Pol.
197/H1 **Lewis** (hill), Nf,Can
136/C3 **Lewis** (pass), N.Z.
55/H7 **Lewis** (isl.), Sc,UK
187/H2 **Lewis**, Co,US
193/G3 **Lewis**, Ia,US
190/E2 **Lewis**, Ks,US
183/H3 **Lewis** (range), Mt,US
192/F2 **Lewis & Clark** (lake), NE, SD,US
182/C4 **Lewis and Clark Nat'l Wild. Ref.**, Wa,US
200/D2 **Lewisburg**, Ky,US
206/B2 **Lewisburg**, Pa,US
200/D3 **Lewisburg**, Tn,US
201/G2 **Lewisburg**, WV,US
55/H7 **Lewis, Butt of** (prom.), Sc,UK
53/N7 **Lewisham** (bor.), Eng,UK
200/D2 **Lewisport**, Ky,US
200/D3 **Lewis Smith** (lake), Al,US
182/F4 **Lewiston**, Id,US
196/B3 **Lewiston**, Me,US
197/S9 **Lewiston**, NY,US
185/H3 **Lewiston**, Ut,US
201/J2 **Lewiston Woodville**, NC,US
193/J3 **Lewistown**, Il,US
183/K4 **Lewistown**, Mt,US
199/H4 **Lewistown**, Pa,US
191/H4 **Lewisville**, Ar,US
189/F1 **Lewisville**, Tx,US
188/L7 **Lewisville** (lake), Tx,US
130/A2 **Lewotobi** (peak), Indo.
194/B3 **Lewvan**, Sk,Can
191/J3 **Lexa**, Ar,US
201/F4 **Lexington**, Ga,US
193/K3 **Lexington**, Il,US
200/E1 **Lexington**, Ky,US
208/C1 **Lexington**, Ma,US
191/H1 **Lexington**, Mo,US
200/B4 **Lexington**, Ms,US
201/G3 **Lexington**, NC,US
192/E3 **Lexington**, Ne,US
198/E4 **Lexington**, Oh,US
191/F3 **Lexington**, Ok,US
184/D1 **Lexington**, Or,US
201/G4 **Lexington**, SC,US
200/C3 **Lexington**, Tn,US
189/F2 **Lexington**, Tx,US
201/H2 **Lexington**, Va,US
200/E2 **Lexington-Blue Grass Army Dep.**, Ky,US
201/J1 **Lexington Park**, Md,US
57/G3 **Leyburn**, Eng,UK
116/E3 **Leye**, China
57/F4 **Leyland**, Eng,UK
59/G4 **Leysdown**, UK
80/D5 **Leysin**, Swi.
82/B1 **Leysse** (riv.), Fr.
125/D3 **Leyte**, Phil.
125/D3 **Leyte** (gulf), Phil.
125/D3 **Leyte** (isl.), Phil.
53/N7 **Leyton**, Eng,UK
80/D5 **Leytron**, Swi.
82/A4 **Lez** (riv.), Fr.
65/M3 **Leżajsk**, Pol.
175/T12 **Lezama**, Arg.
165/E2 **Lezama**, Ven.
82/B5 **Lèze** (riv.), Fr.
91/F2 **Lezhë**, Alb.
116/E2 **Lezhi**, China
74/E5 **Lézignan-Corbières**, Fr.
76/D3 **Lezuza**, Sp.
99/H2 **L'gov**, Rus.
121/F1 **Lhagoi Kangri** (mtn.), China
54/C1 **Lhanbyrd**, Sc,UK
116/B2 **Lhari**, China
121/H1 **Lhasa**, China
116/A2 **Lhasa** (int'l arpt.), China
121/H1 **Lhasa** (riv.), China
116/C2 **Lhatog**, China
121/F1 **Lhazê**, China
78/D4 **L'Hermitage**, Fr.
124/A1 **Lhokkruet**, Indo.
124/B1 **Lhokseumawe**, Indo.
124/B1 **Lhoksukon**, Indo.
116/C2 **Lhorong**, China
88/D2 **L'Hospitalet**, Sp.
77/G2 **L'Hospitalet de Llobregat**, Sp.
121/H1 **Lhozhag**, China
79/E4 **L'Huisserie**, Fr.
121/G2 **Lhuntsi**, Bhu.
119/G2 **Lhünzê**, China
116/A2 **Lhünzhub**, China
115/B5 **Li** (riv.), China
115/C4 **Li** (riv.), China
117/F3 **Li** (riv.), China
123/B2 **Li**, Thai.
116/E3 **Lian** (riv.), China
117/G3 **Lian** (riv.), China
117/H3 **Liancheng**, China
68/B5 **Liancourt**, Fr.
110/B2 **Liancourt** (rocks), Japan, SKor.
127/G4 **Liang**, Indo.
115/C2 **Liangcheng**, China
117/G3 **Liangcun**, China
117/F4 **Liangdong**, China
117/F2 **Lianghekou**, China
113/B2 **Liangjia**, China
113/A3 **Liangjiadian**, China
126/D3 **Liangpran** (peak), Indo.
115/D4 **Liang Shan** (mtn.), China
113/C2 **Liangshui**, China
108/F5 **Liangting**, China
116/D3 **Liangwan** (mts.), Laos
115/B3 **Liangzhen**, China
115/C5 **Liangzi** (lake), China
119/K2 **Lianhua**, China
117/G4 **Lianhua** (mts.), China
117/H3 **Lianjiang**, China
117/G3 **Liannan Yaozu Zizhixian**, China
117/G3 **Lianping**, China
117/H3 **Lianpu**, China
113/B2 **Lianshanguan**, China
115/D4 **Lianshui**, China
115/L8 **Liantang**, China
117/F3 **Liantang**, China
123/E1 **Liantang**, China
117/G3 **Lian Xian**, China
117/G2 **Lianyun** (peak), China
115/D4 **Lianyungang**, China
113/A2 **Liao** (riv.), China
115/C3 **Liaocheng**, China
113/A2 **Liaodong** (gulf), China
113/B3 **Liaodong** (pen.), China
108/C3 **Liaodun**, China
113/B2 **Liaoning** (prov.), China
113/B2 **Liaoyang**, China
115/F2 **Liaoyuan**, China
113/B2 **Liaozhong**, China
107/K3 **Liāquatpur**, Pak.
178/D2 **Liard** (riv.), NW,Can
124/D3 **Liat** (isl.), Indo.
125/C3 **Libacao**, Phil.
120/D1 **Libānggaon**, Nepal
167/K7 **Líbano**, Col.
194/F2 **Libau**, Mb,Can
182/G3 **Libby**, Mt,US
182/G3 **Libby** (dam), Mt,US
71/H2 **Liběchovka** (riv.), Czh.
152/D2 **Libenge**, Zaire
190/D2 **Liberal**, Ks,US
191/G2 **Liberal**, Mo,US
174/C2 **Liberatador General Bernardo O'Higgins** (reg.), Chile
68/C3 **Libercourt**, Fr.
171/M7 **Liberdade**, Braz.
170/B1 **Liberdade** (riv.), Braz.
65/H3 **Liberec**, Czh.
85/E3 **Liberi** (arpt.), It.
144/C5 **Liberia**
161/E4 **Liberia**, CR
159/H5 **Libertad**, Belz.
160/D2 **Libertad**, Belz.
175/F2 **Libertad**, Uru.
164/D2 **Libertad**, Ven.
167/O8 **Libertad de Orituco**, Ven.
172/C2 **Libertador General San Martín**, Arg.
194/B2 **Liberty**, Sk,Can
193/J4 **Liberty**, Il,US
198/D5 **Liberty**, In,US
200/E2 **Liberty**, Ky,US
206/B5 **Liberty** (res.), Md,US
191/G1 **Liberty**, Mo,US
202/C2 **Liberty**, Ms,US
201/H3 **Liberty**, NC,US
199/J4 **Liberty**, NY,US
191/F4 **Liberty**, Ok,US
189/G2 **Liberty**, Tx,US
189/H2 **Liberty**, Tx,US
189/N9 **Liberty** (co.), Tx,US
206/B4 **Liberty Grove**, Md,US
203/E2 **Libertyville**, Al,US
205/Q15 **Libertyville**, Il,US
69/E4 **Libin**, Belg.
125/C2 **Libmanan**, Phil.
117/E3 **Libo**, China
127/G4 **Libobo** (cape), Indo.
71/G2 **Liboc** (riv.), Czh.
71/H2 **Libochovice**, Czh.
153/E2 **Liboko**, Zaire
125/C2 **Libon**, Phil.
91/G2 **Librazhd**, Alb.
159/M7 **Libres**, Mex.
152/B2 **Libreville** (cap.), Gabon
152/B2 **Libreville** (int'l arpt.), Gabon
117/F4 **Libu**, China
146/C2 **Libya**
146/D3 **Libyan** (des.), Egypt, Libya
146/D2 **Libyan** (plat.), Egypt, Libya
174/C2 **Licantén**, Chile
90/C4 **Licata**, It.
86/D4 **Licciana Nardi**, It.
104/E2 **Lice**, Turk.
70/B1 **Lich**, Ger.
115/C3 **Licheng**, China
59/E1 **Lichfield**, Eng,UK
155/G2 **Lichinga**, Moz.
155/G2 **Lichinga** (plat.), Moz.
67/F5 **Lichtenau**, Ger.
70/B5 **Lichtenau**, Ger.
70/D4 **Lichtenau**, Ger.
72/D2 **Lichtenberg**, Ger.
156/D2 **Lichtenburg**, SAfr.
70/E2 **Lichtenfels**, Ger.
72/D3 **Lichtenrade**, Ger.
81/F3 **Lichtensteig**, Swi.
72/C6 **Lichtenstein**, Ger.
72/C6 **Lichtentanne**, Ger.
66/D5 **Lichtenvoorde**, Neth.
72/D3 **Lichterfelde**, Ger.
68/C1 **Lichtervelde**, Belg.
117/F2 **Lichuan**, China
117/H3 **Lichuan**, China
200/E1 **Licking** (riv.), Ky,US
191/J2 **Licking**, Mo,US
205/L12 **Lick Observatory**, Ca,US
90/D2 **Licosa** (cape), It.
83/A2 **Licosa** (pt.), It.
68/A2 **Licques**, Fr.
155/H2 **Licungo** (riv.), Moz.
63/L5 **Lida**, Bela.
113/B4 **Lidao**, China
57/F1 **Liddell Water** (riv.), Sc,UK
80/D6 **Liddes**, Swi.
179/R7 **Liddon** (gulf), NW,Can
194/F4 **Lidgerwood**, ND,US
91/H3 **Lidhoríkion**, Gre.
71/H2 **Lidice**, Czh.
62/H2 **Lidingö**, Swe.
62/E2 **Lidköping**, Swe.
59/F2 **Lidlington**, Eng,UK
87/F2 **Lido**, It.
145/F3 **Lido**, Niger
87/F1 **Lido di Iesolo**, It.
84/C4 **Lido di Ostia**, It.
65/K2 **Lidzbark**, Pol.
65/L1 **Lidzbark Warmiński**, Pol.
78/C4 **Lié** (riv.), Fr.
71/H5 **Liebenau**, Aus.
67/G6 **Liebenau**, Ger.
156/E2 **Liebenbergsvlei** (riv.), SAfr.
190/E1 **Liebenthal**, Ks,US
72/D2 **Liebenwalde**, Ger.
72/C5 **Liebertwolkwitz**, Ger.
133/F2 **Liebig** (peak), Austl.
158/B3 **Liebre** (bay), Mex.
81/F3 **Liechtenstein**
68/D2 **Liedekerke**, Belg.
69/E2 **Liège**, Belg.
69/E3 **Liège** (prov.), Belg.
69/E2 **Liège** (Bierset) (int'l arpt.), Belg.
61/J3 **Lieksa**, Fin.
63/L3 **Lielvarde**, Lat.
66/C5 **Lienden**, Neth.
67/E4 **Lienen**, Ger.
75/K3 **Lienz**, Aus.
63/J3 **Liepāja**, Lat.
63/M3 **Liepna**, Lat.
68/D1 **Lier**, Belg.
69/E3 **Lierneux**, Belg.
74/E1 **Lies** (riv.), Belg.
69/F3 **Lieser** (riv.), Ger.
63/K1 **Liesjärven Nat'l Park**, Fin.
68/C4 **Liesse**, Fr.
80/D3 **Liestal**, Swi.
63/K1 **Lieto**, Fin.
79/F2 **Lieurey**, Fr.
68/B3 **Liévin**, Fr.
199/J1 **Lièvre** (riv.), Qu,Can
196/C2 **Lièvres, Ile aux** (isl.), Qu,Can
80/B2 **Liez** (lake), Fr.
75/L3 **Liezen**, Aus.
153/E2 **Lifake**, Zaire
130/B2 **Lifau**, Indo.
60/D3 **Liffey** (riv.), Ire.
80/B1 **Liffol-le-Grand**, Fr.
55/H9 **Lifford**, Ire.
78/D4 **Liffré**, Fr.
139/V12 **Lifou** (isl.), NCal.
152/C3 **Lifouta**, Gabon
58/B5 **Lifton**, Eng,UK
151/A4 **Liganga**, Tanz.
127/F1 **Ligao**, Phil.
63/L3 **Līgatne**, Lat.
203/F3 **Lighthouse** (pt.), Fl,US
202/P7 **Lighthouse Point**, Fl,US
135/C1 **Lightning Ridge**, Austl.
87/G1 **Lignano Sabbiadoro**, It.
194/C3 **Lignite**, ND,US
69/E6 **Ligny-en-Barrois**, Fr.
81/F5 **Ligoncio, Pizzo** (peak), It.
155/H2 **Ligonha** (riv.), Moz.
198/D4 **Ligonier**, In,US
91/H4 **Ligoúrion**, Gre.
86/B3 **Ligure** (mts.), It.
75/H4 **Ligure** (range), It.
86/C4 **Liguria** (reg.), It.
75/H5 **Ligurian** (sea), Eur.
86/B5 **Ligurian** (sea), It.
129/J3 **Lihou** (reef), Austl.
180/S10 **Lihue**, Hi,US
63/K2 **Lihula**, Est.
119/H2 **Lijiang** (Lijiang Naxizu Zizhixian), China
119/H2 **Lijiang Naxizu Zizhixian** (Lijiang), China
115/D3 **Lijin**, China
117/H2 **Liju** (mtn.), China
153/F5 **Likasi**, Zaire
153/E2 **Likati**, Zaire
182/D1 **Likely**, BC,Can
94/G4 **Likhoslavl'**, Rus.
99/L3 **Likhovskoy**, Rus.
153/E2 **Likimi**, Zaire
155/G2 **Likoma** (isl.), Malw.
153/E3 **Likoto**, Zaire
152/D2 **Likouala** (pol. reg.), Congo
152/C2 **Likouala** (riv.), Congo
152/D2 **Likouala aux Herbes** (riv.), Congo
152/D3 **Likouala Mossaka** (riv.), Congo
126/C3 **Liku**, Indo.
153/E3 **Lilanga**, Zaire
200/C2 **Lilbourn**, Mo,US
201/M7 **Lilburn**, Ga,US
90/A1 **L'Ile-Rousse**, Fr.
53/T10 **L'Ile-Saint-Denis**, Fr.
67/F2 **Lilienthal**, Ger.
119/K2 **Liling**, China
122/B1 **Lilla**, Pak.
62/E2 **Lilla Edet**, Swe.
69/D1 **Lille**, Belg.
68/C2 **Lille**, Fr.
62/C4 **Lille Bælt** (chan.), Den.
79/F1 **Lillebonne**, Fr.
62/D1 **Lillehammer**, Nor.
68/C2 **Lille** (Lesquin) (int'l arpt.), Fr.
63/T9 **Lillerød**, Den.
68/B2 **Lillers**, Fr.
62/C2 **Lillesand**, Nor.
62/D2 **Lillestrøm**, Nor.
188/K7 **Lillian**, Tx,US
189/H1 **Lillie**, La,US
137/L **Lillie Marleen Hütte**, Ant.
54/D5 **Lilliesleaf**, Sc,UK
201/H3 **Lillington**, NC,US
205/A3 **Lilliwaup**, Wa,US
76/D3 **Lillo**, Sp.
182/C2 **Lillooet**, BC,Can
182/C2 **Lillooet** (riv.), BC,Can
155/G2 **Lilongwe** (cap.), Malw.
125/C3 **Liloy**, Phil.
200/E2 **Lily**, Ky,US
195/K5 **Lily**, Wi,US
135/C3 **Lilydale**, Austl.
92/D4 **Lim** (riv.), Yugo.
175/S12 **Lima**, Arg.
173/E2 **Lima**, Par.
168/B4 **Lima** (cap.), Peru
168/B3 **Lima** (dept.), Peru
76/A2 **Lima** (riv.), Port.
195/J4 **Lima** (mtn.), Mn,US
185/G1 **Lima**, Mt,US
185/G1 **Lima** (res.), Mt,US
199/H3 **Lima**, NY,US
198/D4 **Lima**, Oh,US
174/Q9 **Limache**, Chile
81/E5 **Limadario, Monte** (Gridone) (peak), It.
171/N6 **Lima Duarte**, Braz.
172/C2 **Limal**, Bol.
124/E4 **Liman** (peak), Indo.
97/H3 **Liman**, Rus.
65/L4 **Limanowa**, Pol.
103/C2 **Limassol**, Cyp.
103/C2 **Limassol** (dist.), Cyp.
56/B1 **Limavady**, NI,UK
56/A2 **Limavady** (dist.), NI,UK
208/F6 **Limaville**, Oh,US
174/C4 **Limay** (riv.), Arg.
68/A6 **Limay**, Fr.
174/D3 **Limay Mahuida**, Arg.
70/C4 **Limbach**, Ger.
72/C6 **Limbach-Oberfrohna**, Ger.
125/A4 **Limbang** (riv.), Malay.
168/D4 **Limbani**, Peru
90/A2 **Limbara** (peak), It.
63/L3 **Limbaži**, Lat.
118/B3 **Limbdi**, India
152/B1 **Limbe**, Camr.
161/H2 **Limbé**, Haiti
155/G2 **Limbe**, Malw.
86/C1 **Limbiate**, It.
69/E2 **Limbourg**, Belg.
125/B4 **Limbuak**, Malay.
130/C4 **Limbunya**, Austl.
69/E2 **Limburg** (prov.), Belg.
69/E1 **Limburg** (prov.), Neth.
70/B2 **Limburg an der Lahn**, Ger.
70/B4 **Limburgerhof**, Ger.
62/E1 **Limedsforsen**, Swe.
197/R8 **Limehouse**, On,Can
53/T10 **Limeil-Brévannes**, Fr.
170/D4 **Limeira**, Braz.
54/C4 **Limekilns**, Sc,UK
87/E2 **Limena**, It.
91/J2 **Limenária**, Gre.
194/A3 **Limerick**, Sk,Can
60/B4 **Limerick**, Ire.
60/B5 **Limerick** (co.), Ire.
208/A2 **Lime Rock**, Ct,US
191/H3 **Limestone**, Ar,US
196/D2 **Limestone**, Me,US
185/J1 **Limestone**, Mt,US
189/F2 **Limestone** (lake), Tx,US
177/G3 **Lime Village**, Ak,US
62/C3 **Limfjorden** (chan.), Den.
76/B2 **Limia** (riv.), Sp.
199/L3 **Limington**, Me,US
87/D5 **Limite**, It.
131/D3 **Limmen** (bight), Austl.
131/E3 **Limmen Bight** (riv.), Austl.
91/H3 **Límni**, Gre.
91/J3 **Límnos** (isl.), Gre.
167/H4 **Limoeiro**, Braz.
167/G4 **Limoeiro do Norte**, Braz.
74/D4 **Limoges**, Fr.
74/D4 **Limogne** (plat.), Fr.
161/F4 **Limón**, CR
161/E3 **Limón**, Hon.
192/C4 **Limon**, Co,US
86/A4 **Limone Piemonte**, It.
87/D1 **Limone sul Garda**, It.
169/E4 **Limoquije**, Bol.
53/S11 **Limours**, Fr.
74/D4 **Limousin** (mts.), Fr.
74/D4 **Limousin** (reg.), Fr.
74/E5 **Limoux**, Fr.
155/G4 **Limpopo** (riv.), Afr.
53/P8 **Limpsfield**, Eng,UK
117/F3 **Limu**, China
117/F5 **Limu** (mtn.), China
154/D2 **Limulunga**, Zam.
151/B2 **Limuru**, Kenya
105/E4 **Līnah**, SAr.
94/F1 **Linakhamari**, Rus.
125/C4 **Linao** (pt.), Phil.
125/B3 **Linapacan** (isl.), Phil.
81/G4 **Linard, Piz** (peak), Swi.
174/C2 **Linares**, Chile
159/F3 **Linares**, Mex.
76/D3 **Linares**, Sp.
91/J3 **Linariá**, Gre.
84/B3 **Linaro** (cape), It.
86/C2 **Linate** (int'l arpt.), It.
116/D4 **Lincang**, China
185/K2 **Linch**, Wy,US
115/C3 **Lincheng**, China
117/H3 **Linchuan**, China
174/E2 **Lincoln**, Arg.
179/T6 **Lincoln** (sea), NW,Can
197/S9 **Lincoln**, On,Can
57/H5 **Lincoln**, Eng,UK
184/C4 **Lincoln**, Ca,US
206/C6 **Lincoln**, De,US
193/K3 **Lincoln**, Il,US
191/E1 **Lincoln**, Ks,US
208/C1 **Lincoln**, Ma,US
196/C3 **Lincoln**, Me,US
194/D4 **Lincoln**, ND,US
193/F3 **Lincoln** (cap.), Ne,US
196/B3 **Lincoln**, NH,US
190/B4 **Lincoln**, NM,US
206/B3 **Lincoln**, Pa,US
189/F2 **Lincoln**, Tx,US
184/A1 **Lincoln Beach**, Or,US
200/D1 **Lincoln Boyhood Nat'l Mem.**, In,US
199/G4 **Lincoln Caverns**, Pa,US
192/E4 **Lincoln Center** (Lincoln), Ks,US
184/A1 **Lincoln City**, Or,US
57/H5 **Lincoln Heath** (woodl.), Eng,UK
208/E6 **Lincoln Heights**, Oh,US
193/K4 **Lincoln Home Nat'l Hist. Site**, Il,US
192/E4 **Lincoln** (Lincoln Center), Ks,US
133/G5 **Lincoln Nat'l Park**, Austl.
192/B4 **Lincoln Park**, Co,US
200/E4 **Lincoln Park**, Ga,US
205/F7 **Lincoln Park**, Mi,US
207/D2 **Lincoln Park**, NJ,US
188/L6 **Lincoln Park**, Tx,US
57/H5 **Lincolnshire** (co.), Eng,UK
57/H5 **Lincolnshire Wolds** (grsld.), Eng,UK
201/F4 **Lincolnton**, Ga,US
201/G3 **Lincolnton**, NC,US
193/F4 **Lincolnville**, Ks,US
207/D3 **Lincroft**, NJ,US
90/A2 **L'Incudine, Mont** (mtn.), Fr.
62/C3 **Lind**, Den.
184/C4 **Linda**, Ca,US
200/E3 **Lindale**, Ga,US
189/G1 **Lindale**, Tx,US
81/F2 **Lindau**, Ger.
81/E3 **Lindau**, Swi.
204/C5 **Lindberg Field-San Diego** (int'l arpt.), Ca,US
66/D3 **Linde** (riv.), Neth.
134/C3 **Lindeman** (isl.), Austl.
70/B1 **Linden**, Ger.
165/G3 **Linden**, Guy.
200/D4 **Linden**, Al,US
187/G3 **Linden**, Az,US
186/B1 **Linden**, Ca,US
198/C4 **Linden**, In,US
205/E6 **Linden**, Mi,US
207/D2 **Linden**, NJ,US
200/D3 **Linden**, Tn,US
189/G1 **Linden**, Tx,US
205/G7 **Linden Beach**, On,Can
81/F2 **Lindenberg im Allgäu**, Ger.
70/B3 **Lindenfels**, Ger.
205/P15 **Lindenhurst**, Il,US
207/E2 **Lindenhurst**, NY,US
72/C5 **Lindenthal**, Ger.
206/D4 **Lindenwold**, NJ,US
67/E3 **Lindern**, Ger.
62/F2 **Lindesberg**, Swe.
62/B2 **Lindesnes**, Nor.
62/B3 **Lindesnes** (cape), Nor.
62/C4 **Lindewitt**, Ger.
89/L3 **Líndhos** (ruins), Gre.
151/B4 **Lindi**, Tanz.
151/B4 **Lindi** (prov.), Tanz.
155/H1 **Lindi** (reg.), Tanz.
153/F2 **Lindi** (riv.), Zaire
109/J2 **Lindian**, China
54/E5 **Lindisfarne** (Holy) (isl.), Eng,UK
67/E6 **Lindlar**, Ger.
156/D2 **Lindley**, SAfr.
135/D3 **Lind Nat'l Park**, Austl.
62/E3 **Lindome**, Swe.
192/C4 **Lindon**, Co,US
185/H3 **Lindon**, Ut,US
72/C2 **Lindow**, Ger.
187/J2 **Lindrith**, NM,US
132/F3 **Lindsay** (mt.), Austl.
132/C5 **Lindsay** (peak), Austl.
199/G2 **Lindsay**, On,Can
186/C2 **Lindsay**, Ca,US
183/M4 **Lindsay**, Mt,US
191/F3 **Lindsay**, Ok,US
191/F1 **Lindsborg**, Ks,US
62/G3 **Lindsdal**, Swe.
195/H5 **Lindstrom**, Mn,US
139/K4 **Line** (isls.), Kiri.
206/B4 **Lineboro**, Md,US
206/B2 **Line Mountain** (ridge), Pa,US
200/E4 **Lineville**, Al,US
193/H3 **Lineville**, Ia,US
115/B3 **Linfen**, China
54/A2 **Ling** (riv.), Sc,UK
124/D3 **Linga** (isl.), Indo.
206/A5 **Linganore** (cr.), Md,US
117/F5 **Lingao**, China
125/C1 **Lingayen**, Phil.
125/C1 **Lingayen** (gulf), Phil.
115/B4 **Lingbao**, China
115/D4 **Lingbi**, China
115/C4 **Lingchuan**, China
66/C5 **Linge** (riv.), Neth.
154/D2 **Lingelengenda**, Zam.
67/E3 **Lingen**, Ger.
53/N8 **Lingfield**, Eng,UK
124/D2 **Lingga** (isls.), Indo.
115/L9 **Linghu**, China
192/B2 **Lingle**, Wy,US
206/B3 **Linglestown**, Pa,US
117/E4 **Lingma**, China
69/G6 **Lingolsheim**, Fr.
153/E2 **Lingomo**, Zaire
115/C3 **Lingqiu**, China
115/C3 **Lingshan**, China
117/F4 **Lingshan**, China
115/B3 **Lingshi**, China
117/F5 **Lingshui**, China
117/H3 **Lingtou**, China
144/B3 **Linguère**, Sen.
153/E2 **Lingunda**, Zaire
108/F4 **Lingwu**, China
117/J3 **Lingxi**, China
108/H4 **Ling Xian**, China
115/D3 **Ling Xian**, China
119/K2 **Ling Xian**, China
115/E5 **Lingyang Shan** (mtn.), China
115/L8 **Lingyen Shan** (mtn.), China
115/E5 **Lingyin Si**, China
115/D2 **Lingyuan**, China
119/J3 **Lingyun**, China
117/J2 **Linhai**, China
115/A2 **Linhe**, China
196/B2 **Linière**, Qu,Can
113/D2 **Linjiang**, China
62/F2 **Linköping**, Swe.
63/K3 **Linkuva**, Lith.
54/C5 **Linlithgow**, Sc,UK
115/C3 **Linliu Shan** (mtn.), China
81/E3 **Linmat** (riv.), Swi.
191/F1 **Linn**, Ks,US
191/J1 **Linn**, Mo,US
159/F3 **Linn**, Tx,US
61/J3 **Linnansaaren Nat'l Park**, Fin.
191/H1 **Linn Creek**, Mo,US
208/F5 **Linndale**, Oh,US
193/H4 **Linneus**, Mo,US
58/A3 **Linney Head** (pt.), Wal,UK
54/A3 **Linnhe, Loch** (inlet), Sc,UK
69/F2 **Linnich**, Ger.
206/B2 **Linntown**, Pa,US
195/H5 **Lino Lakes**, Mn,US
195/P6 **Lino Lakes**, Mn,US
90/C5 **Linosa**, It.
149/E4 **Linqasi**, Sudan
115/C3 **Linqing**, China
115/D3 **Linqu**, China
115/C4 **Linquan**, China
115/C4 **Linru**, China
170/C4 **Lins**, Braz.
144/B4 **Linsan**, Gui.
66/B4 **Linschoten**, Neth.
115/D4 **Linshu**, China
108/D4 **Linshui**, China
161/G2 **Linstead**, Jam.
157/H9 **Linta** (riv.), Madg.
81/E4 **Linth** (riv.), Swi.
81/F4 **Linthal**, Swi.
194/C1 **Lintlaw**, Sk,Can
59/G2 **Linton**, Eng,UK
198/C5 **Linton**, In,US
194/D4 **Linton**, ND,US
189/H1 **Linville**, La,US
57/H5 **Linwood**, Eng,UK
208/C1 **Linwood**, Ma,US
198/E3 **Linwood**, Mi,US
119/K2 **Linwu**, China
115/C3 **Linxi**, China
108/E4 **Linxia**, China
115/C3 **Lin Xian**, China

154/D3 Linyanti (swamp), Bots., Namb.
115/B4 Linyi, China
115/D3 Linyi, China
115/D4 Linyi, China
115/C4 Linying, China
71/H6 Linz, Aus.
71/H6 Linz (int'l arpt.), Aus.
69/G2 Linz am Rhein, Ger.
108/E4 Linze, China
115/C3 Linzhang, China
155/H2 Lioma, Moz.
82/A6 Lion (gulf), Fr.
203/H4 Lion Country Safari, Fl,US
85/F6 Lioni, It.
52/D4 Lions (gulf), Fr.
155/F3 Lions Den, Zim.
198/F2 Lion's Head, On,Can
79/E2 Lion-sur-Mer, Fr.
130/B1 Lioppa, Indo.
148/D4 Lioto, CAfr.
63/P4 Liozno, Bela.
83/A6 Lipari, It.
83/A6 Lipari (isl.), It.
83/A5 Lipari (isls.), It.
83/A5 Lipari, Eolie o (Lipari) (isls.), It.
124/C3 Lipatkain, Indo.
61/J3 Liperi, Fin.
53/G3 Lipetsk, Rus.
96/F1 Lipetsk (int'l arpt.), Rus.
99/K1 Lipetsk Obl., Rus.
172/C1 Lipez (mts.), Bol.
172/C1 Lipez (riv.), Bol.
59/F4 Liphook, Eng,UK
94/H3 Lipin Bor, Rus.
117/F3 Liping, China
93/H1 Lipkany, Mol.
92/E4 Lipljan, Yugo.
75/L2 Lipno (res.), Czh.
65/K2 Lipno, Pol.
71/H5 Lipno, Údolní nádrž (res.), Czh.
155/H3 Lipobane (pt.), Moz.
155/G1 Lipoche, Moz.
86/C1 Lipomo, It.
92/E2 Lipova, Rom.
98/E3 Lipovets, Ukr.
66/E5 Lippe (riv.), Ger.
67/F5 Lippetal, Ger.
67/F5 Lippstadt, Ger.
98/A2 Lipsko, Pol.
194/C2 Lipton, Sk,Can
73/D2 Liptovská Lúžna, Slvk.
65/K4 Liptovský Mikuláš, Slvk.
135/C3 Liptrap (cape), Austl.
117/F3 Lipu, China
83/D4 Lipuda (riv.), It.
114/D5 Lipu La (pass), India
114/D5 Lipu Lehk Shankou (pass), China
153/H2 Lira, Ugan.
152/D3 Liranga, Congo
155/G2 Lirangwe, Malw.
168/C4 Lircay, Peru
79/D6 Liré, Fr.
85/D4 Liri (riv.), It.
77/E3 Liria, Sp.
81/F5 Liro (riv.), It.
125/D5 Lirung, Indo.
97/M1 Lisakovsk, Kaz.
153/E2 Lisala, Zaire
77/P10 Lisboa (dist.), Port.
76/A3 Lisboa (int'l arpt.), Port.
76/A3 Lisboa (Lisbon) (cap.), Port.
52/C5 Lisbon (cap.), Port.
76/A3 Lisbon (dist.), Port.
77/P10 Lisbon (int'l arpt.), Port.
189/H1 Lisbon, La,US
206/A5 Lisbon, Md,US
196/B3 Lisbon, Me,US
194/F4 Lisbon, ND,US
196/L2 Lisbon, NH,US
208/G6 Lisbon, Oh,US
196/B4 Lisbon Falls, Me,US
76/A3 Lisbon (Lisboa) (cap.), Port.
56/B2 Lisburn, NI,UK
56/B3 Lisburn (dist.), NI,UK
177/E2 Lisburne (cape), Ak,US
60/B5 Liscarroll, Ire.
197/F3 Liscomb Game Sanct, NS,Can
60/A3 Lisdoonvarna, Ire.
62/D3 Liseleje, Den.
115/B4 Li Shan (mtn.), China
116/D3 Lishe (riv.), China
115/F2 Lishu, China
117/H2 Lishui, China
139/H2 Lisianski (isl.), Hi,US
99/K3 Lisichansk, Ukr.
79/F2 Lisieux, Fr.
63/P1 Lisiy Nos, Rus.
58/B6 Liskeard, Eng,UK
53/G3 Liski, Rus.
205/P16 Lisle, Il,US
53/S9 L'Isle-Adam, Fr.
68/B5 L'Isle-Adam, Fr.
74/D5 L'Isle-en-Dodon, Fr.
82/B5 L'Isle-sur-la-Sorgue, Fr.
80/C3 L'Isle-sur-le-Doubs, Fr.
74/D5 L'Isle-sur-Tarn, Fr.
196/B2 L'Islet, Qu,Can
196/C1 L'Isle-Verte, Qu,Can
202/D1 Lisman, Al,US
135/E1 Lismore, Austl.
60/C5 Lismore, Ire.
56/B3 Lisnacree, NI,UK
60/C1 Lisnaskea, NI,UK
71/H4 Lišov, Czh.
92/C2 Lispeszentadorján, Hun.
59/F4 Liss, Eng,UK
66/B4 Lisse, Neth.
53/T11 Lisses, Fr.
64/E1 List, Ger.
67/E6 Lister (riv.), Ger.
198/F3 Listowel, On,Can
60/A5 Listowel, Ire.
108/E1 Listvyanka, Rus.
116/D2 Litang, China
116/D2 Litang (riv.), China
103/D3 Līṭānī (riv.), Leb.
166/C2 Litani (riv.), Sur., FrG.
73/A1 Litava (riv.), Czh.
71/G3 Litavka (riv.), Czh.
130/C3 Litchfield, Austl.
208/A2 Litchfield, Ct,US
208/A2 Litchfield (co.), Ct,US
193/K4 Litchfield, Il,US
198/D3 Litchfield, Mi,US
195/G5 Litchfield, Mn,US
192/E3 Litchfield, Ne,US
208/E5 Litchfield, Oh,US
194/E4 Litchville, ND,US
155/F2 Liteta, Zam.
66/C5 Lith, Neth.
57/F5 Litherland, Eng,UK
135/D2 Lithgow, Austl.
201/L7 Lithia Springs, Ga,US
201/M7 Lithonia, Ga,US
63/K4 Lithuania
92/B2 Litija, Slov.
98/E3 Litin, Ukr.
121/F3 Litipāra, India
206/B3 Lititz, Pa,US
71/H1 Litoměřice, Czh.
151/B4 Litoo, Tanz.
109/M2 Litovko, Rus.
63/M4 Litovskiy Nat'l Park, Lith.
134/D4 Littabella Nat'l Park, Austl.
81/E3 Littau, Swi.
200/C2 Little (riv.), Ar, Mo,US
203/G2 Little (riv.), Ga,US
202/C3 Little (lake), La,US
189/H2 Little (riv.), La,US
201/H3 Little (riv.), NC,US
191/F3 Little (riv.), Ok,US
191/G4 Little (riv.), Ok,US
201/F3 Little (mtn.), SC,US
189/F2 Little (riv.), Tx,US
73/A5 Little Alföld (plain), Hun.
185/J3 Little America, Wy,US
119/F5 Little Andaman (isl.), India
191/F1 Little Arkansas (riv.), Ks,US
190/D1 Little Beaver (cr.), Co, Ks,US
208/G6 Little Beaver, Middle Fork (riv.), Oh,US
208/G6 Little Beaver, North Fork (riv.), Oh,US
208/G6 Little Beaver, West Fork (riv.), Oh,US
53/N6 Little Berkhamstead, Eng,UK
185/K1 Little Bighorn (riv.), Mt, Wy,US
183/L5 Little Big Horn Nat'l Mon., Mt,US
201/G1 Little Birch, WV,US
103/C4 Little Bitter (lake), Egypt
192/F3 Little Blue (riv.), Ks, Ne,US
57/F4 Littleborough, Eng,UK
183/H2 Little Bow (riv.), Ab,Can
205/Q16 Little Calumet (riv.), Il,US
197/L1 Little Catalina, Nf,Can
161/F2 Little Cayman (isl.), Cay.
53/M7 Little Chalfont, Eng,UK
193/K1 Little Chute, Wi,US
187/G3 Little Colorado (riv.), Az,US
208/C2 Little Compton, RI,US
206/C5 Little Creek, De,US
54/B5 Little Cumbrae (isl.), Sc,UK
198/F2 Little Current, On,Can
189/M8 Little Cypress (cr.), Tx,US
58/C5 Little Dart (riv.), Eng,UK
184/C2 Little Deschutes (riv.), Or,US
135/B3 Little Desert Nat'l Park, Austl.
177/E2 Little Diomede (isl.), Ak,US
207/D4 Little Egg (har.), NJ,US
189/F1 Little Elm, Tx,US
195/G5 Little Falls, Mn,US
207/J8 Little Falls, NJ,US
182/F4 Little Falls (dam), Wa,US
207/J8 Little Ferry, NJ,US
187/F2 Littlefield, Az,US
190/C4 Littlefield, Tx,US
206/B1 Little Fishing (cr.), Pa,US
195/H3 Littlefork, Mn,US
182/D2 Little Fort, BC,Can
148/B3 Little Gombi, Nga.
195/G1 Little Grand Rapids, Mb,Can
59/F5 Littlehampton, Eng,UK
197/L1 Little Heart's Ease, Nf,Can
162/C2 Little Inagua (isl.), Bahm.
201/G1 Little Kanawha (riv.), WV,US
156/C4 Little Karoo (reg.), SAfr.
186/D3 Little Lake, Ca,US
198/C1 Little Lake, Mi,US
206/C2 Little Lehigh (riv.), Pa,US
202/L8 Little Manatee (riv.), Fl,US
202/L8 Little Manatee, South Fork (riv.), Fl,US
195/J4 Little Marais, Mn,US
192/A2 Little Medicine Bow (riv.), Wy,US
55/H8 Little Minch (sound), Sc,UK
197/J2 Little Miquelon (isl.), StP,Fr.
194/C5 Little Missouri (riv.), US
191/H3 Little Missouri (riv.), Ar,US
194/C4 Little Missouri Nat'l Grsld., ND,US
199/J3 Little Moose (mtn.), NY,US
194/C3 Little Muddy (riv.), ND,US
206/B1 Little Muncy (cr.), Pa,US
207/K8 Little Neck (bay), NY,US
193/F3 Little Nemaha (riv.), Ne,US
119/F6 Little Nicobar (isl.), India
201/F4 Little Ocmulgee (riv.), Ga,US
59/G2 Little Ouse (riv.), Eng,UK
133/M8 Little Para (res.), Austl.
133/M8 Little Para (riv.), Austl.
206/B5 Little Pawtuxent (riv.), Md,US
202/M8 Little Payne (cr.), Fl,US
207/F2 Little Peconic (bay), NY,US
201/H3 Little Pee Dee (riv.), SC,US
182/F3 Little Pend Oreille Nat'l Wild. Ref., Wa,US
195/L3 Little Pic (riv.), On,Can
183/K1 Little Pine & Lucky Man Ind. Res., Ab,Can
201/F3 Little Pisgah (mtn.), NC,US
59/G2 Littleport, Eng,UK
192/B1 Little Powder (riv.), Mt, Wy,US
205/N14 Little Prairie, Wi,US
191/J3 Little Red (riv.), Ar,US
182/B3 Little River, BC,Can
136/C3 Little River, N.Z.
191/E1 Little River, Ks,US
201/H4 Little River, SC,US
181/H5 Little Rock (cap.), Ar,US
191/H3 Little Rock (cap.), Ar,US
204/C1 Littlerock, Ca,US
205/N16 Little Rock (cr.), Il,US
195/G5 Little Rock, Mn,US
182/C4 Littlerock, Wa,US
191/H3 Little Rock A.F.B., Ar,US
160/D2 Little Rocky (pt.), Belz.
196/C2 Little Russell (mtn.), Me,US
198/C3 Little Sable (pt.), Mi,US
203/F3 Little Saint George (isl.), Fl,US
177/L3 Little Salmon, Yk,Can
78/C2 Little Sark (isl.), Chl,UK
144/B4 Little Scarcies (riv.), Gui., SLeo.
206/C2 Little Schuylkill (riv.), Pa,US
208/G5 Little Shenango (riv.), Pa,US
193/G2 Little Sioux (riv.), Ia,US
193/F2 Little Sioux, West Fork (riv.), Ia,US
177/B5 Little Sitkin (isl.), Ak,US
185/J3 Little Snake (riv.), Co, Wy,US
59/G4 Little Stour (riv.), Eng,UK
206/A4 Littlestown, Pa,US
59/F2 Little Stukeley, Eng,UK
195/K5 Little Suamico, Wi,US
206/B3 Little Swatara (cr.), Pa,US
200/E4 Little Tallapoosa (riv.), Al, Ga,US
60/C4 Littleton, Ire.
192/B4 Littleton, Co,US
196/D2 Littleton, Me,US
199/L2 Littleton, NH,US
199/G3 Little Valley, NY,US
200/C1 Little Wabash (riv.), Il,US
200/C1 Little Wabash, Skillet Fork (riv.), Il,US
192/D2 Little White (riv.), SD,US
191/E4 Little Wichita (riv.), Tx,US
191/E4 Little Wichita, North Fork (riv.), Tx,US
185/J2 Little Wind (riv.), Wy,US
185/F2 Little Wood (riv.), Id,US
105/E3 Little Zab (riv.), Iraq
152/B1 Littoral (prov.), Camr.
71/G1 Litvínov, Czh.
113/C1 Liu (riv.), China
108/F5 Liuba, China
117/G3 Liuche, China
117/F4 Liuchen, China
119/J3 Liucheng, China
117/H2 Liudongqiao, China
109/J5 Liuduo, China
113/C1 Liuhe, China
117/J2 Liuheng (isl.), China
123/E1 Liujing, China
117/H2 Liukou, China
117/J4 Liukuei, Tai.
151/A4 Liuli, Tanz.
115/B3 Liulin, China
117/G3 Liushi, China
114/F3 Liushuquan, China
154/D2 Liuwa Plain Nat'l Park, Zam.
117/G4 Liuxi (riv.), China
119/K2 Liuyang, China
117/G2 Liuyang (riv.), China
117/F3 Liuzhou, China
117/G2 Liuzigang, China
87/G2 Livade, Cro.
91/H2 Livádhion, Gre.
91/H3 Livanátai, Gre.
63/M3 Līvāni, Lat.
79/F3 Livarot, Fr.
177/J2 Livengood, Ak,US
87/F1 Livenza (riv.), It.
163/C2 Live Oak, Ca,US
203/G2 Live Oak, Fl,US
69/F6 Liverdun, Fr.
205/L11 Livermore, Ca,US
192/B3 Livermore, Co,US
193/G2 Livermore, Ia,US
200/D2 Livermore, Ky,US
199/L2 Livermore, Me,US
188/B2 Livermore (mt.), Tx,US
196/B3 Livermore Falls, Me,US
134/G8 Liverpool, Austl.
196/E3 Liverpool, NS,Can
177/M2 Liverpool (bay), NW,Can
179/J1 Liverpool (cape), NW,Can
57/F5 Liverpool, Eng,UK
57/E5 Liverpool (bay), Eng,UK
206/B2 Liverpool, Pa,US
189/M9 Liverpool, Tx,US
57/F5 Liverpool (Speke) (int'l arpt.), Eng,UK
57/H2 Liverton, Eng,UK
82/B2 Livet-et-Gavet, Fr.
81/G4 Livigno, It.
160/D3 Livingston, Guat.
54/C5 Livingston, Sc,UK
200/C4 Livingston, Al,US
186/B2 Livingston, Ca,US
202/M8 Livingston (lake), Fl,US
200/E2 Livingston, Ky,US
202/C2 Livingston, La,US
205/E6 Livingston (co.), Mi,US
183/J5 Livingston, Mt,US
207/D2 Livingston, NJ,US
200/E2 Livingston, Tn,US
189/G2 Livingston, Tx,US
189/G2 Livingston (lake), Tx,US
183/G2 Livingstone (range), Ab,Can
152/C4 Livingstone (falls), Zaire
154/E3 Livingstone, Zam.
155/F2 Livingstone Mem., Zam.
155/G1 Livingstonia, Malw.
199/J4 Livingston Manor, NY,US
92/C4 Livno, Bosn.
96/F1 Livny, Rus.
61/H2 Livojoki (riv.), Fin.
202/C2 Livonia, La,US
205/F7 Livonia, Mi,US
199/H3 Livonia, NY,US
86/D5 Livorno, It.
84/A2 Livorno (prov.), It.
86/D6 Livorno (prov.), It.
86/B2 Livorno Ferraris, It.
171/E2 Livramento do Brumado, Braz.
82/A3 Livron-sur-Drôme, Fr.
68/B6 Livry-Gargan, Fr.
182/B2 Liwa, Chad
124/D4 Liwa, Indo.
151/B4 Liwale, Tanz.
149/G4 Liwan, Sudan
155/G2 Liwonde, Malw.
155/G2 Liwonde Nat'l Park, Malw.
117/F2 Li Xian, China
115/D4 Lixin, China
60/A5 Lixnaw, Ire.
91/G3 Lixoúrion, Gre.
115/D5 Liyang, China
117/F3 Liyong, China
58/A7 Lizard, Eng,UK
58/A7 Lizard (pt.), Eng,UK
194/D2 Lizard Point Ind. Res., Sk,Can
58/A6 Lizard, The (pen.), Eng,UK
200/F4 Lizella, Ga,US
113/B3 Lizifang, China
116/D2 Liziping, China
68/C5 Lizy-sur-Ourcq, Fr.
92/E4 Ljubic, Yugo.
92/C3 Ljubija, Bosn.
94/B3 Ljubinje, Bosn.
92/B2 Ljubljana (cap.), Slov.
92/C4 Ljubuški, Cro.
61/F3 Ljungan (riv.), Swe.
62/E3 Ljungby, Swe.
62/F2 Ljungsbro, Swe.
62/D2 Ljungskile, Swe.
94/C3 Ljusdal, Swe.
62/G1 Ljusnan (riv.), Swe.
62/G1 Ljusne, Swe.
62/H2 Ljustero (isl.), Swe.
142/C3 Lkst, Jebel (mtn.), Mor.
74/E5 Llabanere (Perpignan) (int'l arpt.), Fr.
174/C2 Llaillay, Chile
174/C3 Llaima (vol.), Chile
172/C1 Llallagua, Bol.
168/D4 Llalli, Peru
58/B2 Llanarth, Wal,UK
56/D5 Llanberis, Wal,UK
56/D5 Llanberis, Pass of (pass), Wal,UK
174/C2 Llancañelo (lake), Arg.
58/C3 Llandeilo, Wal,UK
58/D3 Llandogo, Wal,UK
58/C3 Llandovery, Wal,UK
56/E6 Llandrillo, Wal,UK
58/C2 Llandrindod Wells, Wal,UK
56/E5 Llandudno, Wal,UK
58/C3 Llandybie, Wal,UK
58/B2 Llandyssul, Wal,UK
58/B3 Llanelli, Wal,UK
56/E6 Llanelltyd, Wal,UK
56/D6 Llanenddwyn, Wal,UK
56/D5 Llanerchymedd, Wal,UK
76/C1 Llanes, Sp.
58/C1 Llanfair Caereinion, Wal,UK
56/E5 Llanfairfechan, Wal,UK
56/D5 Llanfair-Pwllgwyngyll, Wal,UK
58/C1 Llanfyllin, Wal,UK
58/C2 Llangammarch Wells, Wal,UK
58/C3 Llangattock, Wal,UK
57/E6 Llangollen, Wal,UK
58/C2 Llangurig, Wal,UK
58/C2 Llanidloes, Wal,UK
56/D5 Llanllyfni, Wal,UK
58/B3 Llannon, Wal,UK
190/B2 Llano, NM,US
189/E2 Llano, Tx,US
188/E2 Llano (riv.), Tx,US
152/C2 Llano Blanco, Mex.
190/C4 Llano Estacado (plain), NM, Tx,US
58/B2 Llanon, Wal,UK
163/C2 Llanos (plain), Col.
164/D3 Llanos (plain), Col., Ven.
163/C2 Llanos (plain), Ven.
174/B4 Llanquihue (lake), Chile
57/E5 Llanrhaeadr, Wal,UK
58/B2 Llanrhystyd, Wal,UK
58/A3 Llanrian, Wal,UK
56/E5 Llanrwst, Wal,UK
58/D3 Llanthony, Wal,UK
58/C3 Llantrisant, Wal,UK
58/C4 Llantwit Major, Wal,UK
56/E6 Llanuwchllyn, Wal,UK
58/C1 Llanwnog, Wal,UK
58/C1 Llanwrtyd Wells, Wal,UK
168/B3 Llata, Peru
190/A2 Llaves, NM,US
57/E5 Llay, Wal,UK
58/C2 Lledrod, Wal,UK
52/D4 Lleida, Sp.
77/F2 Lleida (Lérida), Sp.
159/F4 Llera de Canales, Mex.
76/B3 Llerena, Sp.
56/D6 Lleyn (pen.), Wal,UK
172/B1 Llica, Bol.
174/B3 Llico, Chile
77/H1 Llivia, Sp.
77/F1 Llobregat (riv.), Sp.
77/D1 Llodio, Sp.
125/D3 Llorente, Phil.
77/G2 Lloret de Mar, Sp.
207/E2 Lloyd (pt.), NY,US
207/E2 Lloyd Harbor, NY,US
178/F3 Lloydminster, Ab, Sk,Can
183/K1 Lloydminster, Ab, Sk,Can
197/J1 Lloyds (riv.), Nf,Can
77/G3 Lluchmayor, Sp.
172/B3 Llullaillaco (peak), Arg.
172/B3 Llullaillaco (vol.), Chile
58/C3 Llynfi (riv.), Wal,UK
116/E4 Lo (riv.), Viet.
172/B1 Loa (riv.), Chile
185/H4 Loa, Ut,US
170/B4 Loanda, Braz.
152/B3 Loanda, Gabon
152/D4 Loange (riv.), Zaire
152/C4 Loango Buele, Zaire
54/C5 Loanhead, Sc,UK
86/B4 Loano, It.
77/N8 Loaoya (can.), Sp.
153/G3 Loashi, Zaire
95/K2 Lobanskaya, Rus.
158/E4 Lobatos, Mex.
154/E5 Lobatse, Bots.
152/D1 Lobaya (riv.), CAfr.
148/C4 Lobaye (pref.), CAfr.
148/C5 Lobaye (riv.), CAfr.
68/D3 Lobbes, Belg.
72/B4 Löbejün, Ger.
200/D3 Lobelville, Tn,US
71/E2 Lobenstein, Ger.
133/M8 Lobenthal, Austl.
174/F3 Loberia, Arg.
82/B3 L'Obiou (mtn.), Fr.
154/B2 Lobito, Ang.
168/A2 Lobitos, Peru
127/H4 Lobo, Indo.
144/D5 Lobo (riv.), IvC.
188/B2 Lobo, Tx,US
174/F2 Lobos, Arg.
172/B2 Lobos (pt.), Chile
172/B4 Lobos (pt.), Chile
174/B2 Lobos, Punta de (pt.), Chile
72/C3 Loburg, Ger.
78/C5 Loc (riv.), Fr.
86/A2 Locana, It.
81/E5 Locarno, Swi.
54/B3 Lochaber (dist.), Sc,UK
56/D2 Lochans, Sc,UK
56/E1 Locharbriggs, Sc,UK
81/F2 Lochau, Aus.
54/A4 Lochawe, Sc,UK
55/H8 Lochboisdale, Sc,UK
192/B3 Lochbuie, Co,US
54/B4 Lochearnhead, Sc,UK
66/D4 Lochem, Neth.
54/B2 Lochend, Sc,UK
74/D3 Loches, Fr.
54/C4 Lochgelly, Sc,UK
54/A4 Lochgilphead, Sc,UK
54/B4 Lochgoilhead, Sc,UK
202/N6 Loch Haven Center, Fl,US
157/E2 Lochiel, SAfr.
54/C2 Lochindorb (lake), Sc,UK
155/E2 Lochinvar Nat'l Park, Zam.
55/J7 Lochinver, Sc,UK
56/E1 Lochmaben, Sc,UK
55/H8 Lochmaddy, Sc,UK
65/L2 Łochów, Pol.
54/A5 Lochranza, Sc,UK
206/B5 Loch Raven (res.), Md,US
68/C1 Lochristi, Belg.
182/G4 Lochsa (riv.), Id,US
54/B5 Lochwinnoch, Sc,UK
54/B3 Lochy (riv.), Sc,UK
54/B3 Lochy, Loch (lake), Sc,UK
133/G5 Lock, Austl.
133/H5 Lock #3 (dam), Austl.
133/J5 Lock #5 (dam), Austl.
133/J5 Lock #6 (dam), Austl.
205/L10 Locke, Ca,US
188/B2 Locke (mt.), Tx,US
186/B1 Lockeford, Ca,US
73/A5 Lockenhaus, Aus.
196/E4 Lockeport, NS,Can
57/E1 Lockerbie, Sc,UK
191/G4 Lockesburg, Ar,US
188/C1 Lockettville, Tx,US
135/C2 Lockhart, Austl.
202/N6 Lockhart, Fl,US
189/F3 Lockhart, Tx,US
134/A1 Lockhart Abor. Land, Austl.
131/F3 Lockhart River Abor. Community, Austl.
199/H4 Lock Haven, Pa,US
135/C3 Lockington, Austl.
190/D3 Lockney, Tx,US
72/B1 Löcknitz (riv.), Ger.
194/F2 Lockport, Mb,Can
205/P16 Lockport, Il,US
202/C3 Lockport, La,US
199/G3 Lockport, NY,US
194/B2 Lockwood, Sk,Can
53/N7 Lockwood (res.), Eng,UK
78/C5 Locmariaquer, Fr.
78/C4 Locminé, Fr.
123/D4 Loc Ninh, Viet.
191/F3 Loco, Ok,US
78/B5 Locoal-Mendon, Fr.
190/C4 Loco Hills, NM,US
68/B2 Locon, Fr.
85/F5 Locone (riv.), It.
78/B3 Locquirec, Fr.
83/C6 Locri, It.
83/C6 Locri Epizefiri (ruins), It.
78/A4 Locronan, Fr.
78/A5 Loctudy, Fr.
168/D5 Locumba, Peru
193/H3 Locust (cr.), Mo,US
191/G2 Locust Grove, Ok,US
103/F8 Lod, Isr.
192/D2 Lodan (cr.), Ne,US
63/U9 Lodde (riv.), Swe.
63/U9 Löddeköpinge, Swe.
129/G7 Loddon (riv.), Austl.
59/H1 Loddon, Eng,UK
64/A2 Loddon, Eng,UK
59/E4 Loddon (riv.), Eng,UK
71/H2 Lodenice (riv.), Czh.
74/E5 Lodève, Fr.
94/G3 Lodeynoye Pole, Rus.
183/J3 Lodge (cr.), Ab, Can, Mt,US
185/K1 Lodge Grass, Mt,US
182/G1 Lodgepole, Ab,Can
183/K3 Lodge Pole, Mt,US
192/B3 Lodgepole (cr.), Ne, Wy,US
192/C1 Lodgepole, SD,US
86/C2 Lodi, It.
205/M10 Lodi, Ca,US
191/J2 Lodi, Mo,US
207/D2 Lodi, NJ,US
208/E5 Lodi, Oh,US
189/G1 Lodi, Tx,US
198/B3 Lodi, Wi,US
153/E4 Lodi, Zaire
86/C2 Lodi Vecchio, It.
153/E3 Lodja, Zaire
76/D1 Lodosa, Sp.
81/E5 Lodrino, Swi.
151/A1 Lodwar, Kenya
65/K3 Łódź, Pol.
65/K3 Łódź (prov.), Pol.
77/N9 Loeches, Sp.
123/C2 Loei, Thai.
66/C4 Loenen, Neth.
153/F4 Loengo, Zaire
156/B3 Loeriesfontein, SAfr.
144/C5 Lofa (co.), Libr.
144/C5 Lofa (riv.), Libr.
81/E2 Löffingen, Ger.
153/E2 Lofonda, Zaire
61/D2 Lofoten (isls.), Nor.
57/H2 Loftus, Eng,UK
133/M8 Lofty (mtn.), Austl.
132/C3 Lofty (range), Austl.
135/C4 Lofty (range), Austl.
145/F3 Loga, Niger
134/F7 Logan, Austl.
196/D1 Logan (mtn.), Qu,Can
177/K3 Logan (mtn.), Yk,Can
193/G3 Logan, Ia,US
190/E1 Logan, Ks,US
193/F2 Logan (cr.), Ks,US
208/C1 Logan (int'l arpt.), Ma,US
183/H3 Logan (pass), Mt,US
190/C3 Logan, NM,US
198/E5 Logan, Oh,US
185/H3 Logan, Ut,US
182/D3 Logan (mt.), Wa,US
201/G2 Logan, WV,US
186/E2 Logandale, Nv,US
182/D2 Logan Lake, BC,Can
200/D4 Logan Martin (dam), Al,US
200/D4 Logan Martin (lake), Al,US
56/D2 Logan, Mull of (pt.), Sc,UK
198/C4 Logansport, In,US
202/B2 Logansport, La,US
206/A1 Loganton, Pa,US
200/F4 Loganville, Ga,US
206/B4 Loganville, Pa,US
92/B3 Logatec, Slov.
152/C4 Loge (riv.), Ang.
196/E2 Loggieville, NB,Can
148/B3 Logone (riv.), Camr., Chad
148/B3 Logone Birni, Camr.
148/B3 Logone-Occidental (pref.), Chad
148/B4 Logone Occidental (riv.), Chad
148/C3 Logone-Oriental (pref.), Chad
148/C3 Logone Oriental (riv.), Chad
76/D1 Logroño, Sp.
76/C3 Logrosán, Sp.
62/C3 Løgstør, Den.
62/D3 Løgten, Den.
62/D4 Lohals, Den.
121/E4 Lohārdaga, India
156/C3 Lohatlha, SAfr.
118/B2 Lohāwat, India
70/B1 Löheberg, Ger.
67/G6 Lohfelden, Ger.
63/L1 Lohja, Fin.
63/K1 Lohjanjärvi (lake), Fin.
193/H4 Lohman, Mo,US
69/G2 Lohmar, Ger.
188/E2 Lohn, Tx,US
64/E2 Lohne, Ger.
67/F3 Löhne, Ger.
127/F4 Loholoho, Indo.
70/C3 Lohr, Ger.
87/E4 Loiano, It.
174/Q10 Loica, Chile
116/C5 Loi-kaw, Burma
153/E3 Loile (riv.), Zaire
116/C4 Loi Lun (range), Burma
63/K1 Loimaa, Fin.
74/E2 Loing (riv.), Fr.
79/E5 Loir (riv.), Fr.
82/A2 Loire (dept.), Fr.
78/C6 Loire (riv.), Fr.
78/D5 Loire-Atlantique (dept.), Fr.
79/G5 Loiret (dept.), Fr.
79/E5 Loir-et-Cher (dept.), Fr.
79/E4 Loiron, Fr.
69/E5 Loisin (riv.), Fr.
116/C4 Loi Song (mtn.), Burma
151/A2 Loita (hills), Kenya
168/B2 Loja, Ecu.
168/B2 Loja (prov.), Ecu.
76/C4 Loja, Sp.
62/C4 Løjt Kirkeby, Den.
149/F4 Loka, Sudan
153/F3 Lokandu, Zaire
105/H1 Lokbatan, Azer.
68/D1 Lokeren, Belg.
99/G2 Lokhvitsa, Ukr.
151/A1 Lokichar, Kenya
149/G4 Lokichokio, Kenya
149/G4 Lokitaung, Kenya
61/H2 Lokka, Fin.
62/C3 Løkken, Den.
63/P3 Loknya, Rus.
145/G5 Loko, Nga.
153/E3 Lokofe, Zaire
145/G5 Lokoja, Nga.
152/D3 Lokolama, Zaire
153/E3 Lokolia, Zaire
152/D3 Lokolo (riv.), Zaire
157/H8 Lokomby, Madg.
148/B5 Lokomo, Camr.
151/A1 Lokopo, Ugan.
151/B1 Lokori, Kenya
152/D3 Lokoro (riv.), Zaire
92/E2 Lőkösháza, Hun.
73/D4 Lokos-patak (riv.), Hun.
145/F5 Lokossa, Ben.
96/E1 Lokot', Rus.
179/K2 Loks (isl.), NW,Can
63/L2 Loksa, Est.
151/A1 Lokwakangole, Kenya
144/C5 Lola, Gui.
200/C2 Lola, Ky,US
153/H2 Lolelia, Ugan.
151/A2 Lolgorien, Kenya
153/E2 Lolingo, Zaire
151/A2 Loliondo, Tanz.
189/F3 Lolita, Tx,US
151/B2 Lolkisale, Tanz.
62/D4 Lolland (isl.), Den.
70/B3 Lollar, Ger.
152/C3 Lolo (riv.), Gabon
183/G4 Lolo, Mt,US
153/E2 Lolo, Zaire
153/F3 Lolo, Zaire
148/A5 Lolodorf, Camr.
159/F4 Lolotla, Mex.
138/G5 Lolua, Tuv.
151/A1 Lolui (isl.), Ugan.
92/F4 Lom, Bul.
148/B4 Lom (riv.), Camr.
71/G3 Lom (hill), Czh.
61/D3 Lom, Nor.
144/C4 Loma (mts.), Gui., SLeo.
204/C5 Loma (pt.), Ca,US
183/J4 Loma, Mt,US
169/E3 Loma Alta, Bol.
188/D3 Loma Alta, Tx,US
159/G5 Loma Bonita, Mex.
204/C2 Loma Linda, Ca,US
144/C4 Loma Mansa (peak), SLeo.
153/F3 Lomami (riv.), Zaire
174/E3 Loma Negra, Arg.
168/C4 Lomas, Peru
174/E3 Lomas del Real, Mex.
175/S12 Lomas de Zamora, Arg.
86/C1 Lomazzo, It.
154/D2 Lomba (riv.), Ang.
205/P16 Lombard, Il,US
166/D2 Lombarda (mts.), Braz.
86/D2 Lombardy (reg.), It.
152/D5 Lombe, Ang.
130/A1 Lombe, Indo.
130/A2 Lomblem (isl.), Indo.
127/F5 Lomblen (isl.), Indo.
102/L10 Lomboc (isl.), Indo.
127/E5 Lombok, Indo.
124/F5 Lombok (isl.), Indo.
124/F5 Lombok (str.), Indo.
152/C4 Lombolo, Congo
145/F5 Lomé (cap.), Togo
145/F5 Lomé (int'l arpt.), Togo
153/E3 Lomela, Zaire
153/E3 Lomela (riv.), Zaire
86/B2 Lomello, It.
189/E2 Lometa, Tx,US
148/B5 Lomié, Camr.
193/K2 Lomira, Wi,US
204/B3 Lomita, Ca,US
62/E4 Lomma, Swe.
63/T9 Lommabukten (bay), Swe.
72/D5 Lommatzsch, Ger.
74/E1 Lomme, Fr.
69/E1 Lommel, Belg.
71/G4 Lomnice (riv.), Czh.
71/H4 Lomnice nad Lužnicí, Czh.
183/H2 Lomond, Ab,Can
54/C4 Lomond (hills), Sc,UK
54/B4 Lomond, Loch (lake), Sc,UK
87/E4 Lomone (riv.), It.
63/N2 Lomonosov, Rus.
127/E5 Lompobatang (peak), Indo.
186/B3 Lompoc, Ca,US
123/C2 Lom Sak, Thai.
65/M2 Łomża, Pol.
65/M2 Łomża (prov.), Pol.
118/B4 Lonāvale, India
174/B3 Loncoche, Chile
174/C3 Loncopué, Arg.
68/D2 Londerzeel, Belg.
151/A2 Londiani, Kenya
68/A4 Londinières, Fr.
198/F3 London, On,Can
161/F3 London (reef), Nic.
53/N7 London, Eng,UK
59/F3 London (cap.), Eng,UK
186/C2 London, Ca,US
200/E2 London, Ky,US
198/E5 London, Oh,US
188/E2 London, Tx,US
186/E3 London Bridge, Az,US
53/N7 London, City of (bor.), Eng,UK
53/N6 London Colney, Eng,UK
130/B3 Londonderry (cape), Austl.
175/J8 Londonderry (isl.), Chile
56/A2 Londonderry, NI,UK
56/A2 Londonderry (dist.), NI,UK
196/B4 Londonderry, NH,US
56/A1 Londonderry (Eglinton) (arpt.), IN,UK
53/N8 London (Gatwick) (int'l arpt.), Eng,UK
53/M7 London (Heathrow) (int'l arpt.), Eng,UK
59/G3 London (Stansted) (int'l arpt.), Eng,UK
172/C3 Londres, Arg.
170/C4 Londrina, Braz.
154/B2 Londuimbali, Ang.
70/D5 Lone (riv.), Ger.
184/E4 Lone (mtn.), Nv,US
192/C1 Lone (mtn.), SD,US
182/D2 Lone Butte, BC,Can
186/C2 Lone Pine, Ca,US
202/B2 Lonepine, La,US
186/C2 Lone Pine Ind. Res., Ca,US
134/E7 Lone Pine Sanct., Austl.
183/K1 Lone Rock, Sk,Can
134/C4 Lonesome Nat'l Park, Austl.
202/C2 Lone Star, La,US
189/G1 Lone Star, Tx,US
144/C3 Lonétou, Mali
190/E3 Lone Wolf, Ok,US
162/C2 Long (cay), Bahm.
162/C2 Long (isl.), Bahm.
197/K2 Long (isl.), Nf,Can
196/D3 Long (isl.), NS,Can
195/L3 Long (lake), On,Can
198/F3 Long (pt.), On,Can
194/D3 Long (lake), Sk,Can
77/F1 Long (peak), Fr.
60/A6 Long (isl.), Ire.
131/G1 Long (isl.), PNG
101/T2 Long (str.), Rus.
123/B2 Long, Thai.
58/C1 Long (mtn.), UK
177/G3 Long, Ak,US
202/K8 Long (key), Fl,US
203/H5 Long (key), Fl,US
208/D2 Long (pond), Ma,US
196/C2 Long (lake), Me,US
198/E2 Long (lake), Mi,US
195/K4 Long (pt.), Mi,US
194/D4 Long (lake), ND,US
199/J2 Long (lake), NY,US
207/E2 Long (isl.), NY,US
182/C4 Long (isl.), Wa,US
195/J5 Long (lake), Wi,US
195/K5 Long (lake), Wi,US
154/C2 Longa, Ang.
152/C5 Longa (riv.), Ang.
154/C2 Longa (riv.), Ang.
167/F3 Longá (riv.), Braz.
119/J3 Long'an, China
87/E2 Longare, It.
174/C2 Longaví, Chile
197/S10 Long Beach, On,Can
204/B3 Long Beach, Ca,US
198/C4 Long Beach, In,US
202/D2 Long Beach, Ms,US
201/J4 Long Beach, NC,US
207/D4 Long Beach (isl.), NJ,US
207/E2 Long Beach, NY,US
182/B4 Long Beach, Wa,US
182/B4 Long Beach (pen.), Wa,US
204/B3 Long Beach (Daugherty Field) (arpt.), Ca,US
204/F8 Long Beach Nav. Shipyard, Ca,US
57/G1 Longbenton, Eng,UK
125/B5 Longberang, Indo.
127/E3 Longbia, Indo.
203/G4 Longboat Key, Fl,US
126/E3 Longboh, Indo.
207/E3 Long Branch, NJ,US
205/B3 Longbranch, Wa,US
59/E2 Long Buckby, Eng,UK
69/E3 Longchamps, Belg.
116/E2 Longchang, China
123/D1 Long Chau, Viet.
117/G3 Longchuan, China
117/G3 Longchuan (riv.), China
54/E6 Long Crag (hill), Eng,UK
184/D1 Long Creek, Or,US
59/F3 Long Crendon, Eng,UK
191/E2 Longdale, Ok,US
108/F4 Longde, China
53/N7 Long Ditton, Eng,UK
117/F2 Longdongping, China
57/G6 Long Eaton, Eng,UK
69/E5 Longeau (riv.), Fr.
199/J4 Long Eddy, NY,US
79/F4 Longeuve (riv.), Fr.
69/E6 Longeville-en-Barrois, Fr.
69/F5 Longeville-lès-Metz, Fr.
69/F5 Longeville-lès-Saint-Avold, Fr.
196/B3 Longfellow (mts.), Me,US
53/P7 Longfield, Eng,UK
135/C4 Longford, Austl.
60/C2 Longford, Ire.
117/H3 Longgang, China
205/Q15 Long Grove, Il,US
116/E4 Longguang, China
117/F5 Longgun, China
208/A3 Long Hill, Ct,US
115/D2 Longhua, China
117/F3 Longhua (pass), China
117/F3 Longhui, China
151/B2 Longido, Tanz.
207/L8 Long Island (sound), US
208/B3 Long Island (sound), Ct,US
207/E2 Long Island (sound), Ct, NY,US
190/E1 Long Island, Ks,US
207/E2 Long Island, Mac Arthur (arpt.), NY,US
109/J2 Longjiang, China
116/E3 Longjie, China
53/S10 Longjumeau, Fr.
127/E3 Long Ketiok, Indo.
115/E3 Longkou, China
195/L3 Longlac, On,Can
199/J3 Long Lake, NY,US
192/E1 Long Lake, SD,US
195/L3 Long Lake Ind. Res., On,Can
194/E4 Long Lake Nat'l Wild. Ref., ND,US
191/H2 Long Lane, Mo,US
58/D4 Longleat House, Eng,UK
125/A5 Long Lelang, Malay.
119/J2 Longli, China
54/A2 Long, Loch (inlet), Sc,UK
54/B4 Long, Loch (inlet), Sc,UK
208/B1 Longmeadow, Ma,US
115/C4 Longmen, China
116/D3 Longmen, China
115/B4 Longmen Shan (mtn.), China
115/C4 Longmen Shiyao, China
192/B3 Longmont, Co,US
58/D1 Long Mynd, The (hill), Eng,UK
117/G3 Longnan, China
207/E1 Long Neck (pt.), Ct,US
54/D5 Longniddry, Sc,UK
57/G5 Longnor, Eng,UK
79/F3 Longny-au-Perche, Fr.
152/D2 Longo, Congo
83/C4 Longobucco, It.
154/B2 Longonjo, Ang.
151/B2 Longonot (peak), Kenya
123/D4 Long Phu, Viet.
194/E3 Long Plain Ind. Res., Sk,Can
197/G3 Long Point, NS,Can
198/F3 Long Point Beach, On,Can
196/B3 Long Pond, Me,US
53/S11 Longpont-sur-Orge, Fr.
206/D5 Longport, NJ,US
195/G5 Long Prairie, Mn,US
68/A3 Longpré-les-Corps-Saints, Fr.
117/H2 Longquan, China
197/H2 Long Range (mts.), Nf,Can
134/B3 Longreach, Austl.
116/D1 Longriba, China
57/F4 Longridge, Eng,UK
192/B3 Longs (peak), Co,US
125/A4 Long Semado, Malay.
117/F2 Longshan, China
108/E4 Longshou (mts.), China
202/B1 Longstreet, La,US
57/J6 Long Sutton, Eng,UK
117/F4 Longtan, China
191/F2 Longton, Ks,US
57/F2 Longtown, Eng,UK
68/B4 Longueau, Fr.
68/B5 Longueil-Annel, Fr.
79/E6 Longué-Jumelles, Fr.
68/B2 Longuenesse, Fr.
199/K2 Longueuil, Qu,Can
69/E5 Longuyon, Fr.
206/D2 Long Valley, NJ,US
80/B3 Longvic, Fr.
183/G2 Longview, Ab,Can
200/C4 Longview, Ms,US
189/G1 Longview, Tx,US
182/C4 Longview, Wa,US
202/B2 Longville, La,US
117/G4 Longwo, China
202/N6 Longwood, Fl,US
201/H3 Longwood, NC,US
206/C4 Longwood Gardens, Pa,US
188/D1 Longworth, Tx,US
69/E4 Longwy, Fr.
108/E4 Longxi, China
108/F5 Long Xian, China
117/G3 Longxingshi, China
123/D4 Long Xuyen, Viet.
117/H3 Longyan, China
100/B2 Longyearbyen, Sval.
117/H2 Longyou, China
123/D1 Longzhou, China
120/A1 Loni, India
87/E2 Lonigo, It.
67/E3 Löningen, Ger.
116/C3 Lonkin, Burma
66/D4 Lonneker, Neth.
191/J3 Lonoke, Ar,US
174/E3 Lonquimay, Arg.
74/C5 Lons, Fr.
62/F3 Lönsboda, Swe.
80/B4 Lons-le-Saunier, Fr.
116/C3 Lonton, Burma
69/E2 Lontzen, Belg.
80/D5 Lonza (riv.), Swi.
125/C2 Looc, Phil.
58/B6 Looe, Eng,UK
58/B6 Looe (isl.), Eng,UK
200/D1 Loogootee, In,US
134/B1 Lookout (pt.), Austl.
182/G4 Lookout (mtn.), Id,US
201/J1 Lookout (pt.), Md,US
198/E2 Lookout (pt.), Mi,US
201/J3 Lookout (cape), NC,U
184/B1 Lookout (cape), Or,U
151/A2 Loolmalasin (peak), Tanz.
130/B4 Looma, Austl.
184/C4 Loomis, Ca,US
182/E3 Loomis, Wa,US
182/F3 Loon Lake, Wa,US
66/C5 Loon op Zand, Neth.
188/C1 Loop, Tx,US
54/G10 Loop Head (pt.), Ire.
182/D1 Loos, BC,Can
68/C2 Loos, Fr.
193/J4 Loose Creek, Mo,US
114/F3 Lop (lake), China
157/H8 Lopary, Madg.
97/H4 Lopatin, Rus.
96/F1 Lopatinskiy, Rus.
101/R4 Lopatka (cape), Rus.
95/P4 Lopatkovo, Rus.
149/G4 Lopaye, Sudan
123/C3 Lop Buri, Thai.
188/E4 Lopeno, Tx,US
78/A4 Loperhet, Fr.
152/B3 Lopez (cape), Gabon
125/C2 Lopez, Phil.
186/B2 Lopez (pt.), Ca,US
66/B5 Lopik, Neth.
153/E2 Lopori (riv.), Zaire
61/G1 Lopphavet (bay), Nor
63/L1 Loppi, Fin.
97/H2 Lopukhovka, Rus.
95/M3 Lopydino, Rus.
133/G4 Lora (cr.), Austl.
107/J3 Lora (riv.), Pak.
76/C4 Lora del Río, Sp.
107/J3 Lora, Hāmūn-i- (lake), Pak.
208/E5 Lorain, Oh,US
208/E5 Lorain (co.), Oh,US
188/D1 Loraine, Tx,US
107/J2 Loralai, Pak.
77/E4 Lorca, Sp.
70/A2 Lorch, Ger.
70/C5 Lorch, Ger.
105/G4 Lordegān, Iran
129/K6 Lord Howe (isl.), Aus
187/H4 Lordsburg, NM,US
194/D3 Lords Lake Nat'l Wil Ref., ND,US
208/G5 Lordstown, Oh,US
130/B2 Loré, Indo.
69/G3 Lorelei, Ger.
170/D4 Lorena, Braz.
189/F2 Lorena, Tx,US
138/D5 Lorengau, PNG
62/D2 Lørenskog, Nor.
127/J5 Lorentz (riv.), Indo.
66/C2 Lorentzsluizen (dam), Neth.
190/D4 Lorenzo, Tx,US
175/F2 Lorenzo Geyres, Uru.
87/F2 Loreo, It.
105/G3 Lorestān (gov.), Iran
169/E4 Loreto, Bol.
167/E4 Loreto, Braz.
168/D1 Loreto, Col.
164/B5 Loreto, Ecu.
87/G6 Loreto, It.
173/E2 Loreto, Par.
85/D3 Loreto Aprutino, It.
194/F3 Lorette, Mb,Can
82/A1 Lorette, Fr.
196/B2 Loretteville, Qu,Can
200/E2 Loretto, Ky,US
200/D3 Loretto, Tn,US
82/C6 Lorgues, Fr.
151/B1 Lorian (swamp), Ken
164/C2 Lorica, Col.
78/B5 Lorient, Fr.
141/N13 L'Oriental (reg.), Mor
78/B5 Lorient (Lann-Bihoue) (arpt.), Fr.
199/J2 L'Orignal, On,Can
178/G2 Lorillard (riv.), NW,Can
92/D2 Lorinci, Hun.
183/L3 Loring, Mt,US
82/A3 Loriol-sur-Drôme, Fr.
201/H3 Loris, SC,US
189/J2 Lorman, Ms,US
200/E5 Lorman, Ms,US
135/B3 Lorne, Austl.
197/R8 Lorne Park, On,Can
55/H8 Lorn, Firth of (inlet), Sc,UK
87/E5 Loro Ciuffenna, It.
151/A1 Lorosuk (peak), Ken
69/G6 Lorquin, Fr.
80/D2 Lörrach, Ger.
69/F6 Lorrain (plat.), Fr.
197/N6 Lorraine, Qu,Can
64/D4 Lorraine (plat.), Fr.
69/F5 Lorraine (reg.), Fr.
191/E1 Lorraine, Ks,US
60/B3 Lorrha, Ire.
70/B3 Lorsch, Ger.
57/F2 Lorton, Eng,UK
208/A6 Lorton, Va,US
151/B1 Loruk, Kenya
67/E3 Lorup, Ger.

151/B1 Losai Nat'l Rsv., Kenya
204/B3 Los Alamitos, Ca,US
188/D3 Los Álamos, Mex.
186/B3 Los Alamos, Ca,US
190/A3 Los Alamos, NM,US
190/B3 Los Alamos, NM,US
188/E4 Los Aldamas, Mex.
174/C4 Los Alerces Nat'l Park, Arg.
186/E4 Los Algodones, Mex.
172/C4 Los Altos, Arg.
205/K12 Los Altos, Ca,US
160/D3 Los Amates, Guat.
174/C2 Los Andes, Chile
164/B4 Los Andes, Col.
174/B3 Los Ángeles, Chile
204/B2 Los Angeles, Ca,US
204/B1 Los Angeles (aqueduct), Ca,US
204/B2 Los Angeles (co.), Ca,US
204/B3 Los Angeles (int'l arpt.), Ca,US
204/F8 Los Angeles (int'l arpt.), Ca,US
204/F8 Los Angeles (riv.), Ca,US
204/F8 Los Angeles Outer (har.), Ca,US
168/C4 Los Aquijes, Peru
159/F4 Los Aztecas, Mex.
186/B2 Los Banos, Ca,US
76/C4 Los Barrios, Sp.
158/C3 Los Burros, Mex.
175/S12 Los Cardales, Arg.
172/C2 Los Cardoñes Nat'l Park, Arg.
165/F2 Los Castillos, Ven.
175/T12 Los Cerrillos, Uru.
172/E4 Los Charrúas, Arg.
190/A3 Los Chaves, NM,US
163/B7 Los Chonos (arch.), Chile
174/D2 Los Cóndores, Arg.
76/C1 Los Corrales de Buelna, Sp.
186/D4 Los Coyotes Ind. Res., Ca,US
169/E4 Los Cusis, Bol.
158/C4 Los Frailes, Mex.
189/F4 Los Fresnos, Tx,US
186/B2 Los Gatos, Ca,US
175/J7 Los Glaciares Nat'l Park, Arg.
162/D3 Los Haitises Nat'l Park, DRep.
69/F4 Losheim, Ger.
188/E5 Los Herreras, Mex.
99/H4 Loshkarëvka, Ukr.
63/N4 Loshnitsa, Bela.
158/C3 Los Hornos, Mex.
65/M2 Łosice, Pol.
161/F1 Los Indios (can.), Cuba
75/L4 Lošinj (isl.), Cro.
89/G1 Lošinj (isl.), Cro.
92/B3 Lošinj (isl.), Cro.
98/F2 Losinovka, Ukr.
164/B3 Los Katios Nat'l Park, Col.
151/B1 Loskiria (peak), Kenya
174/B3 Los Lagos, Chile
174/B4 Los Lagos (reg.), Chile
168/C4 Los Libertadores-Wari (dept.), Peru
142/A3 Los Llanos de Aridane, Canl.
77/X16 Los Llanos de Aridane, Canl.,Sp.
190/A3 Los Lunas, NM,US
159/F4 Los Mármoles Nat'l Park, Mex.
174/C4 Los Menucos, Arg.
158/C3 Los Mochis, Mex.
184/B3 Los Molinos, Ca,US
174/C5 Los Monos, Arg.
174/B4 Los Muermos, Chile
76/C3 Los Navalmorales, Sp.
76/C3 Los Navalucillos, Sp.
80/B3 Losne, Fr.
167/K7 Los Nevados Nat'l Park, Col.
188/E4 Los Nogales, Mex.
186/B3 Los Olivos, Ca,US
189/E4 Los Olmos (cr.), Tx,US
81/E5 Losone, Swi.
168/A2 Los Órganos, Peru
164/B3 Los Orquídeas Nat'l Park, Col.
186/B3 Los Osos-Baywood, Ca,US
204/A1 Los Padres Nat'l For., Ca,US
76/C4 Los Palacios y Villafranca, Sp.
186/D4 Los Palmas (riv.), Mex.
130/B2 Los Palos, Indo.
175/J8 Los Pingüinos Nat'l Park, Chile
190/A2 Los Pinos (riv.), Co,US
188/D3 Los Pintos, Mex.
158/C4 Los Planes, Mex.
158/C2 Los Pocitos, Mex.
187/J3 Los Ranchos de Albuquerque, NM,US
158/E5 Los Reyes, Mex.
174/Q9 Los Riecillos, Chile
164/B5 Los Ríos (prov.), Ecu.
165/E2 Los Roques (isls.), Ven.
72/B5 Lossa (riv.), Ger.
161/F5 Los Santos, Pan.
76/B3 Los Santos de Maimona, Sp.
174/B3 Los Sauces, Chile
188/B4 Los Sauces, Mex.
70/B6 Lossburg, Ger.
66/E4 Losser, Neth.
54/C1 Lossie (riv.), Sc,UK
54/C1 Lossiemouth, Sc,UK
71/F1 Lössnitz, Ger.
151/B3 Lossoganeu (hill), Tanz.
184/C2 Lost (riv.), Ca.,Or,US
202/C3 Lost (lake), La,US
81/F5 Lostallo, Swi.
174/C5 Los Tamariscos, Arg.
164/D2 Los Taques, Ven.
201/F2 Lost Creek, Ky,US
184/B2 Lost Creek (res.), Or,US
198/F5 Lost Creek, WV,US
190/C4 Lost Draw (cr.), Tx,US
172/D4 Los Telares, Arg.
165/E2 Los Teques, Ven.
165/F2 Los Testigos (isls.), Ven.
186/C3 Lost Hills, Ca,US
185/G1 Lost River (range), Id,US
206/C2 Lost River Caverns, Pa,US
191/F1 Lost Springs, Ks,US
58/B6 Lostwithiel, Eng,UK
194/C3 Lostwood Nat'l Wild. Ref., ND,US
172/B3 Los Vientos, Chile
174/C1 Los Vilos, Chile
76/D3 Los Yébenes, Sp.
74/D4 Lot (riv.), Fr.
152/E4 Lot (riv.), Fr.
174/B3 Lota, Chile
62/D1 Løten, Nor.
107/G1 Lotfābād, Trkm.
153/H2 Lothaa, Ugan.
54/C5 Lothian (reg.), Sc,UK
149/G4 Lotikipi (plain), Kenya
153/E3 Loto, Zaire
149/G4 Lotogipi (swamp), Kenya
152/D3 Lotoi (riv.), Zaire
155/E4 Lotsane (dry riv.), Bots.
189/F2 Lott, Tx,US
67/E4 Lotte, Ger.
149/G4 Lotuke (peak), Sudan
152/D3 Lotumbe, Zaire
184/C4 Lotus, Ca,US
115/B5 Lou (riv.), China
123/C1 Louang Namtha, Laos
152/C4 Louango (Shiloango) (riv.), Congo
123/C2 Louangphrabang, Laos
191/H4 Louann, Ar,US
152/C4 Loubomo, Congo
72/D6 Loučná (peak), Czh.
78/C4 Loudéac, Fr.
117/F3 Loudi, China
152/C4 Loudima, Congo
200/E3 Loudon, Tn,US
199/K3 Loudonville, NY,US
208/E6 Loudonville, Oh,US
74/D3 Loudun, Fr.
79/E5 Loué, Fr.
80/B3 Loue (riv.), Fr.
152/C3 Louessé (riv.), Congo
197/G1 L'Ouest, Pointe de (pt.), Qu,Can
79/E6 Louet (riv.), Fr.
115/B3 Loufan, China
144/A3 Louga, Sen.
144/B3 Louga (reg.), Sen.
57/G6 Loughborough, Eng,UK
56/B3 Loughbrickland, NI,UK
179/R7 Lougheed (isl.), NW,Can
56/B3 Loughgall, NI,UK
202/M7 Loughman, Fl,US
60/B3 Loughrea, Ire.
53/P7 Loughton, Eng,UK
80/B4 Louhans, Fr.
157/E2 Louieville, SAfr.
200/C4 Louin, Ms,US
152/C4 Louingi, Congo
202/M7 Louisa (lake), Fl,US
201/F1 Louisa, Ky,US
201/H1 Louisa, Va,US
157/E3 Louis Botha (Durban) (int'l arpt.), SAfr.
197/H3 Louisbourg, NS,Can
191/G1 Louisburg, Ks,US
201/H2 Louisburg, NC,US
182/D2 Louis Creek, BC,Can
197/G3 Louisdale, NS,Can
189/F3 Louise, Tx,US
196/A2 Louiseville, Qu,Can
138/E6 Louisiade (arch.), PNG
181/H5 Louisiana (state), US
202/B3 Louisiana (pt.), La,US
191/J1 Louisiana, Mo,US
155/F4 Louis Trichardt, SAfr.
200/E5 Louisville, Al,US
190/B1 Louisville, Co,US
201/F4 Louisville, Ga,US
193/K4 Louisville, Il,US
200/E1 Louisville, Ky,US
200/C4 Louisville, Ms,US
193/F3 Louisville, Ne,US
208/F6 Louisville, Oh,US
179/J3 Louis XIV (pt.), Qu,Can
94/G2 Loukhi, Rus.
141/M13 Loukkos (riv.), Mor.
153/G2 Loukouo, Congo
76/A4 Loulé, Port.
152/B1 Loum, Camr.
71/G2 Louny, Czh.
82/C5 Loup (riv.), Fr.
192/E3 Loup (riv.), Ne,US
192/E3 Loup City, Ne,US
56/B2 Loup, The, NI,UK
68/C3 Lourches, Fr.
53/U10 L'Ourcq (can.), Fr.
197/H1 Lourdes, Nf,Can
74/C5 Lourdes, Fr.
74/D5 Lourdes/Tarbes (int'l arpt.), Fr.
77/P10 Loures, Port.
76/A3 Louriçal, Port.
76/A3 Lourinhã, Port.
79/H5 Loury, Fr.
76/A3 Lousã, Port.
77/P10 Lousa, Port.
117/E2 Loushan (pass), China
152/C4 Loutété, Congo
135/C1 Louth, Austl.
60/D2 Louth, Ire.
60/D2 Louth (co.), Ire.
57/H5 Louth, Eng,UK
91/H3 Loutrá Aidhipsoú, Gre.
91/H4 Loutrákion, Gre.
77/E1 Louts (riv.), Fr.
69/D2 Louvain (Leuven), Belg.
200/E4 Louvale, Ga,US
171/K8 Louveira, Braz.
79/E4 Louverné, Fr.
82/A5 Louviers, Fr.
192/B4 Louviers, Co,US
79/D4 Louvigné-du-Désert, Fr.
53/T9 Louvres, Fr.
68/C3 Louvroil, Fr.
68/B2 Lovaart (can.), Belg.
73/C5 Lovasberény, Hun.
94/F4 Lovat' (riv.), Bela., Rus.
63/P3 Lovat' (riv.), Rus.
92/D3 Lovćenac, Yugo.
92/D4 Lovćen Nat'l Park, Yugo.
93/G4 Lovech, Bul.
91/J1 Lovech (prov.), Bul.
93/G4 Lovech (reg.), Bul.
201/M8 Lovejoy, Ga,US
189/G2 Lovelady, Tx,US
192/B3 Loveland, Co,US
185/J1 Lovell, Wy,US
184/D3 Lovelock, Nv,US
206/B5 Love Point, Md,US
86/D1 Lovere, It.
183/K2 Loverna, Sk,Can
193/K2 Loves Park, Il,US
193/H3 Lovilia, Ia,US
190/B4 Loving, NM,US
201/H2 Lovingston, Va,US
190/C4 Lovington, NM,US
76/A2 Lovios, Sp.
63/M1 Lovisa, Fin.
65/J5 Lövő, Hun.
73/A5 Lövő, Hun.
92/C2 Lovo, Hun.
63/R7 Lovön (isl.), Swe.
71/H1 Lovosice, Czh.
94/G2 Lovozero (lake), Rus.
152/C4 Lóvua, Ang.
179/H2 Low (cape), NW,Can
184/C2 Low (des.), Or,US
153/F3 Lowa (riv.), Zaire
140/E5 Lowa (riv.), Zaire
159/E2 Lowake, Tx,US
57/H6 Lowdham, Eng,UK
190/D1 Lowe, Ks,US
194/F3 Lowe Farm, Mb,Can
191/G2 Lowell, Ar,US
182/G4 Lowell, Id,US
184/E2 Lowell (lake), Id,US
198/C4 Lowell, In,US
195/J3 Lowell, Ma,US
198/F5 Lowell, Oh,US
184/B2 Lowell, Or,US
187/G3 Lowell Observatory, Az,US
208/G5 Lowellville, Oh,US
156/B2 Löwen (dry riv.), Namb.
70/C4 Löwenstein, Ger.
184/D3 Lower (lake), Ca,US
198/D1 Lower (falls), Mi,US
207/J9 Lower (bay), NY,US
205/D3 Lower (dam), Wa,US
185/H1 Lower (falls), Wy,US
195/G2 Lower Arrow (lake), BC,Can
73/A2 Lower Austria (prov.), Aus.
59/E2 Lower Brailes, Eng,UK
192/E1 Lower Brule Ind. Res., SD,US
208/H6 Lower Burrell, Pa,US
81/G4 Lower Engadine (vall.), Swi.
120/B2 Lower Ganges (can.), India
135/B8 Lower Glenelg Nat'l Park, Austl.
135/C4 Lower Gordon-Franklin Wild Rivers Nat'l Park, Austl.
187/E2 Lower Granite (gorge), Az,US
59/E3 Lower Heyford, Eng,UK
136/C3 Lower Hutt, N.Z.
177/F3 Lower Kalskag, Ak,US
184/C3 Lower Klamath (lake), Ca,US
184/C2 Lower Klamath Nat'l Wild. Ref., Ca, Or,US
55/H9 Lower Lough Erne (lake), NI,UK
185/H1 Lower Mesa (falls), Id,US
182/E4 Lower Monumental (dam), Wa,US
53/P6 Lower Nazeing, Eng,UK
204/D5 Lower Otay (lake), Ca,US
200/D5 Lower Peach Tree, Al,US
195/G4 Lower Red (lake), Mn,US
205/E7 Lower Rouge (riv.), Mi,US
67/G3 Lower Saxony (state), Ger.
193/G1 Lower Sioux Ind. Res., Mn,US
203/G3 Lower Suwannee Nat'l Wild. Ref., Fl,US
93/J3 Lower Trajan's (wall), Mol., Ukr.
98/E5 Lower Trajan's Wall (ruins), Mol., Ukr.
100/K3 Lower Tunguska (riv.), Rus.
193/K4 Lower Wabash (riv.), Il,US
196/E4 Lower Wedgeport, NS,Can
196/E4 Lower West Pubnico, NS,Can
202/M7 Lowery (lake), Fl,US
155/F2 Lower Zambezi Nat'l Park, Zam.
59/H2 Lowestoft, Eng,UK
64/A2 Lowestoft, Eng,UK
186/D2 Lowest Point in the United States (Death Valley), Ca,US
54/E5 Lowick, Eng,UK
65/K2 Łowicz, Pol.
184/F1 Lowman, Id,US
201/H2 Lowmoor, Va,US
202/E1 Lowndesboro, Al,US
191/H1 Lowry City, Mo,US
56/E1 Lowther (hills), Sc,UK
197/R9 Lowville, On,Can
199/J3 Lowville, NY,US
202/P6 Loxahatchee, Fl,US
202/P6 Loxahatchee Nat'l Wild. Ref., Fl,US
203/H4 Loxahatchee Nat'l Wild. Ref., Fl,US
202/P8 Loxahatchee Slough (swamp), Fl,US
160/B3 Loxicha, Mex.
67/F2 Loxstedt, Ger.
133/J5 Loxton, Austl.
156/C3 Loxton, SAfr.
133/J5 Loxton North, Austl.
151/A3 Loya, Tanz.
193/J1 Loyal, Wi,US
201/F2 Loyall, Ky,US
184/C4 Loyalton, Ca,US
206/B2 Loyalton, Pa,US
139/V12 Loyalty (isls.), NCal.
78/C5 Loyat, Fr.
80/B6 Loyettes, Fr.
98/F2 Loyev, Bela.
54/A2 Loyne, Loch (lake), Sc,UK
95/M4 Loyno, Rus.
153/H2 Loyoro, Ugan.
206/A3 Loysville, Pa,US
92/D3 Loznica, Yugo.
93/H4 Loznitsa, Bul.
99/J3 Lozovaya, Ukr.
93/G2 Lozovik, Yugo.
95/L3 Lozym, Rus.
117/G2 Lu (peak), China
115/C5 Lu (riv.), China
117/J4 Lü (isl.), Tai.
148/C5 Lua (riv.), Zaire
155/H3 Luabo, Moz.
155/E3 Luacano, Ang.
153/E4 Luachimo, Ang.
153/E5 Luachimo (riv.), Ang., Zaire
153/E4 Luaco, Ang.
152/D2 Lua Dekere (riv.), Zaire
124/B3 Luaha-sibuha, Indo.
155/G3 Luala (riv.), Moz.
153/F3 Lualaba (riv.), Zaire
153/E2 Luale, Zaire
152/C4 Luali, Zaire
115/J6 Luam (riv.), China
153/F4 Luama (riv.), Zaire
180/T10 Lua Makika (crater), Hi,US
154/E2 Luampa, Zam.
154/E2 Luampa (riv.), Zam.
115/D5 Lu'an, China
115/D2 Luan (riv.), China
161/G2 Luana (pt.), Jam.
117/F4 Luancheng, China
115/B4 Luanchuan, China
76/C1 Luanco, Sp.
152/C5 Luanda (cap.), Ang.
152/C5 Luanda (prov.), Ang.
151/A1 Luanda, Kenya
152/D5 Luando, Ang.
152/D5 Luando (riv.), Ang.
152/D5 Luando Nature Rsv., Ang.
123/C5 Luang (lag.), Thai.
123/B4 Luang (peak), Thai.
123/C2 Luang Prabang (range), Laos
152/D5 Luangue, Ang.
152/D4 Luangue (riv.), Ang.
154/D2 Luanguinga (riv.), Ang., Zam.
155/F2 Luangwa (riv.), Moz., Zam.
153/H5 Luangwa (riv.), Zam.
153/G5 Luangwe (riv.), Zam.
108/C5 Luanhaizi, China
153/F5 Luano (int'l arpt.), Zaire
115/D2 Luanping, China
155/F2 Luanshya, Zam.
115/D3 Luan Xian, China
153/E5 Luao, Ang.
153/E5 Luao (riv.), Ang.
155/F1 Luapula (riv.), Zaire, Zam.
153/G5 Luapula (prov.), Zam.
76/B1 Luarca, Sp.
153/E5 Luashi, Zaire
155/F2 Luatize (riv.), Moz.
153/E5 Luau (riv.), Ang.
152/B2 Luba, EqG.
160/D2 Lubaantun (ruins), Belz.
65/M3 Lubaczów, Pol.
152/D5 Lubalo, Ang.
65/H3 Lubań, Pol.
63/M3 Lubāna, Lat.
125/C2 Lubang, Phil.
125/B2 Lubang (isl.), Phil.
154/B2 Lubango, Ang.
153/F3 Lubango, Zaire
153/G5 Lubansenshi (riv.), Zam.
153/F4 Lubao, Zaire
65/M3 Lubartów, Pol.
65/K2 Lubawa, Pol.
67/F4 Lübbecke, Ger.
69/D2 Lubbeek, Belg.
72/D4 Lübben, Ger.
72/D4 Lübbenau, Ger.
72/D1 Lübbesee (lake), Ger.
190/D4 Lubbock, Tx,US
196/D3 Lubec, Me,US
64/F2 Lübeck, Ger.
201/G1 Lubeck, WV,US
153/F4 Lubefu, Zaire
153/F4 Lubefu (riv.), Zaire
65/M3 Lubelska (upland), Pol.
97/K2 Lubenka, Kaz.
153/G3 Lubero, Zaire
153/G3 Lubero (riv.), Zaire
82/B5 Lubéron (ridge), Fr.
153/E4 Lubi (riv.), Zaire
65/K2 Lubień Kujawski, Pol.
153/G4 Lubika, Zaire
153/E5 Lubilash (riv.), Zaire
65/J3 Lubin, Pol.
65/M3 Lublin, Pol.
65/M3 Lublin (prov.), Pol.
65/K3 Lubliniec, Pol.
63/M3 Lubmin, Ger.
54/B4 Lubnaig, Loch (lake), Sc,UK
99/G2 Lubny, Ukr.
65/J2 Luboń, Pol.
153/F3 Lubongola, Zaire
76/D4 Lubrín, Sp.
65/H3 Lubsko, Pol.
125/C1 Lubuagan, Phil.
153/F4 Lububu, Zaire
153/F5 Lubudi, Zaire
153/E4 Lubudi (riv.), Zaire
153/F5 Lubudi (riv.), Zaire
153/F4 Lubue (riv.), Zaire
124/C3 Lubuklinggau, Indo.
124/B2 Lubukpakam, Indo.
124/C2 Lubuksikaping, Indo.
153/F5 Lubumbashi, Zaire
153/F4 Lubunda, Zaire
153/F3 Lubutu, Zaire
155/F1 Lubwe, Zam.
152/C5 Lucala, Ang.
152/C5 Lucala (riv.), Ang.
198/F3 Lucan, On,Can
60/D3 Lucan, Ire.
123/D1 Luc An Chau, Viet.
177/K3 Lucania (mtn.), Yk,Can
85/F6 Lucano, Appennino (mts.), It.
108/D4 Lücaoshan, China
153/E5 Lucapa, Ang.
191/E1 Lucas, Ks,US
208/E6 Lucas, Oh,US
188/L6 Lucas, Tx,US
174/F2 Lucas González, Arg.
198/E5 Lucasville, Oh,US
86/D5 Lucca, It.
86/D5 Lucca (prov.), It.
90/A1 Lucciana, Fr.
79/G4 Lucé, Fr.
56/D2 Luce (bay), Sc,UK
189/M8 Luce (bayou), Tx,US
202/D2 Lucedale, Ms,US
170/C4 Lucélia, Braz.
125/C2 Lucena, Phil.
76/C4 Lucena, Sp.
76/E2 Lucena del Cid, Sp.
82/B3 Luc-en-Diois, Fr.
65/K4 Lučenec, Slvk.
80/C4 Lucens, Swi.
85/F4 Lucera, It.
168/D4 Lucerna, Peru
204/C1 Lucerne (lake), Ca,US
182/D3 Lucerne, Wa,US
185/J2 Lucerne, Wy,US
81/E3 Lucerne (Luzern) (canton), Swi.
186/D3 Lucerne Valley, Ca,US
81/E3 Lucerne (Vierwaldstättensee) (lake), Swi.
190/A4 Lucero (lake), NM,US
187/J4 Lucero (lake), NM,US
187/J3 Lucero (mesa), NM,US
116/D3 Luchang, China
109/L2 Luchegorsk, Rus.
115/C3 Lucheng, China
116/E3 Lucheng, China
79/F5 Luché-Pringé, Fr.
155/G2 Lucheringo (riv.), Moz.
72/B2 Lüchow, Ger.
119/K3 Luchuan, China
116/D4 Lüchun, China
186/B2 Lucia, Ca,US
166/B2 Lucie (riv.), Sur.
203/F2 Lucile, Ga,US
135/B3 Lucindale, Austl.
154/B2 Lucira, Ang.
154/B2 Luciras (bay), Ang.
85/E4 Lucito, It.
193/H1 Luck, Wi,US
72/C5 Lucka, Ger.
72/D4 Luckau, Ger.
121/F3 Luckeesarai, India
72/C5 Luckenau, Ger.
72/D3 Luckenwalde, Ger.
178/F3 Lucknow, On,Can
120/C2 Lucknow, India
120/C2 Lucknow (arpt.), India
202/B1 Lucky, La,US
183/L2 Lucky Lake, Sk,Can
184/E2 Lucky Peak (dam), Id,US
85/D4 Luco dei Marsi, It.
81/E4 Lucomagno, Passo del (pass), Swi.
108/G5 Lücongpo, China
161/H1 Lucrecia (cape), Cuba
87/F5 Lucrezia, It.
79/E2 Luc-sur-Mer, Fr.
152/C4 Lucunga, Ang.
154/D2 Lucusse, Ang.
133/H2 Lucy Creek, Austl.
65/M3 Łuków, Pol.
93/H4 Luda Kamchiya (riv.), Bul.
194/E4 Ludden, ND,US
190/D1 Ludell, Ks,US
67/E6 Lüdenscheid, Ger.
156/A2 Lüderitz, Namb.
118/C2 Ludesar, India
81/F3 Ludesch, Aus.
59/E4 Ludgershall, Eng,UK
122/C2 Ludhiāna, India
119/H2 Ludian, China
116/D2 Luding, China
67/E5 Ludinghausen, Ger.
198/C3 Ludington, Mi,US
58/D2 Ludlow, Eng,UK
186/D3 Ludlow, Ca,US
208/B1 Ludlow, Ma,US
199/G4 Ludlow, Pa,US
194/C5 Ludlow, SD,US
199/K3 Ludlow, Vt,US
93/G3 Ludogorie (reg.), Bul.
203/H2 Ludowici, Ga,US
93/G2 Luduș, Rom.
62/F1 Ludvika, Swe.
71/E4 Ludwigs (can.), Ger.
70/C5 Ludwigsburg, Ger.
72/D3 Ludwigsfelde, Ger.
70/B4 Ludwigshafen, Ger.
64/F2 Ludwigslust, Ger.
71/E2 Ludwigsstadt, Ger.
63/M3 Ludza, Lat.
135/D2 Lue, Austl.
153/E5 Luebo, Zaire
188/E1 Lueders, Tx,US
153/F3 Lueki, Zaire
153/E5 Luemba (riv.), Ang., Zaire
153/E5 Luemba, Zaire
154/D1 Luembe (riv.), Ang.
153/F5 Luembi (riv.), Zaire
154/C1 Luena, Ang.
154/D2 Luena (riv.), Ang., Zam.
153/F5 Luena, Zaire
154/E2 Luena Flats (swamp), Zam.
154/D3 Luengue (riv.), Ang.
155/G3 Luenha (riv.), Moz.
82/C5 Luens, Col de (pass), Fr.
153/E4 Lueta (riv.), Zaire
108/F5 Lüeyang, China
117/H3 Lufeng, China
117/G4 Lufeng, China
152/C4 Lufico, Ang.
153/F4 Lufira (riv.), Zaire
189/G2 Lufkin, Tx,US
152/C4 Lufu, Zaire
154/E2 Lufupa (riv.), Zam.
63/N2 Luga, Rus.
63/N2 Luga (bay), Rus.
63/N2 Luga (riv.), Rus.
153/G2 Luga, Zaire
86/C3 Lugagnano Val d'Arda, It.
81/E6 Lugano (lake), It., Swi.
81/E6 Lugano, Swi.
53/G4 Lugansk, Ukr.
99/K3 Lugansk (int'l arpt.), Ukr.
99/K3 Lugansk Obl., Ukr.
138/F6 Luganville, Van.
151/B2 Lugards (falls), Kenya
72/C6 Lugau, Ger.
92/E3 Lugavčina, Yugo.
153/H2 Lugazi, Ugan.
67/G5 Lügde, Ger.
155/H3 Lugela, Moz.
155/H2 Lugenda (riv.), Moz.
55/K10 Lugg (riv.), UK
58/D2 Lugg (riv.), Eng,UK
98/E2 Luginy, Ukr.
60/D4 Lugnaquillia (mtn.), Ire.
87/E4 Lugo, It.
76/B1 Lugo, Sp.
76/B1 Lugo (prov.), Sp.
87/E1 Lugo di Vicenza, It.
201/G3 Lugoff, SC,US
153/H2 Lugogo (riv.), Ugan.
92/E3 Lugoj, Rom.
114/B3 Lugovoy, Kaz.
97/H2 Lugovskoye, Rus.
80/C5 Lugrin, Fr.
116/D2 Lugu, China
153/F3 Lugulu (riv.), Zaire
153/F3 Lugunga (peak), Tanz.
151/B4 Luguruka, Tanz.
73/B1 Luhačovice, Czh.
115/D4 Luhe, China
67/H2 Lühe (riv.), Ger.
71/F3 Lühe (riv.), Ger.
71/F3 Lühe-Wildenau, Ger.
116/C3 Luhit (riv.), India
151/B3 Luhombero (peak), Tanz.
117/G3 Luhongshi, China
151/A2 Luhumbo, Tanz.
116/D2 Luhuo, China
154/D2 Lui (riv.), Zam.
153/E5 Luia, Ang.
154/D2 Luia (riv.), Ang.
155/G2 Luia (riv.), Moz.
155/G3 Luia (riv.), Moz.
154/D3 Luiana, Ang.
154/D3 Luiana (riv.), Ang.
54/B1 Luichart, Loch (lake), Sc,UK
113/D2 Luidaogou, China
152/D4 Luie (riv.), Zaire
87/F4 Luigi Ridolfi (arpt.), It.
153/E4 Luilaka (riv.), Zaire
153/E4 Luilu (riv.), Zaire
81/E6 Luino, It.
79/G4 Luisant, Fr.
167/F3 Luís Correia, Braz.
167/E3 Luís Domingues, Braz.
153/F5 Luishia, Zaire
158/E4 Luis Moya, Mex.
137/X Luitpold (coast), Ant.
153/E4 Luiza, Zaire
174/D2 Luján, Arg.
115/D5 Lujiang, China
73/C1 Lúka (peak), Slvk.
187/H2 Lukachukai, Az,US
73/A5 Lukácsháza, Hun.
152/C4 Lukala (riv.), Ang., Zaire
152/D4 Lukala (riv.), Zaire
155/E2 Lukanga (swamp), Zam.
92/D3 Lukavac, Bosn.
132/C3 Luke (peak), Austl.
187/F4 Luke A.F.B., Az,US
152/D3 Lukenie (riv.), Zaire
187/F5 Lukeville, Az,US
96/F1 Lukhovitsy, Rus.
93/G5 Lūki, Bul.
152/C4 Luki, Zaire
152/D3 Lukolela, Zaire
153/F4 Lukolela, Zaire
117/G2 Lukoupu, China
93/G4 Lukovit, Bul.
65/M3 Łuków, Pol.
95/K5 Lukoyanov, Rus.
153/F4 Lukuga (riv.), Zaire
152/C4 Lukula, Zaire
153/G4 Lukulu, Zam.
153/G5 Lukulu (riv.), Zam.
139/E4 Lukunor (isl.), Micr.
155/F2 Lukusashi (riv.), Zam.
155/G2 Lukusuzi Nat'l Park, Zam.
120/A3 Lukwasa, India
153/G5 Lukwesa, Zam.
189/H2 Lula, La,US
100/B3 Lule (riv.), Swe.
61/G2 Luleå, Swe.
61/G2 Luleälv (riv.), Swe.
93/H5 Lüleburgaz, Turk.
172/C3 Lules, Arg.
119/H2 Luliang, China
122/C2 Luliāni, Pak.
153/G4 Lulimba, Zaire
189/F3 Luling, Tx,US
115/B4 Luling Guan (pass), China
115/D3 Lulong, China
152/D2 Lulonga, Zaire
152/D2 Lulonga (riv.), Zaire
58/D4 Lulsgate (Bristol) (int'l arpt.), Eng,UK
138/G5 Lulua, Tuv.
153/E4 Lulua (riv.), Zaire
149/F4 Luluba, Sudan
154/D2 Lumai, Ang.
114/D5 Lumajamgdong (lake), China
124/F5 Lumajang, Indo.
153/G5 Lumangwe (falls), Zam.
154/D2 Lumbala Kaquengue, Ang.
154/D2 Lumbala N'guimbo, Ang.
154/D3 Lumbe (riv.), Zam.
201/H3 Lumber (riv.), NC, SC,US
201/F5 Lumber City, Ga,US
202/D2 Lumberton, Ms,US
201/H3 Lumberton, NC,US
206/D4 Lumberton, NJ,US
187/J2 Lumberton, NM,US
189/G2 Lumberton, Tx,US
120/D2 Lumbini (zone), Nepal
125/B4 Lumbis, Indo.
155/J2 Lumbo, Moz.
94/J2 Lumbovka, Rus.
76/B2 Lumbrales, Sp.
81/F4 Lumbrein, Swi.
68/B2 Lumbres, Fr.
182/E4 Lumby, BC,Can
116/B3 Lumding, India
153/E5 Lumeje, Ang.
171/M6 Luminárias, Braz.
69/E2 Lummen, Belg.
182/C3 Lummi Ind. Res., Wa,US
63/J1 Lumparland, Fin.
123/D3 Lumphat, Camb.
200/E4 Lumpkin, Ga,US
194/B2 Lumsden, Can
183/M2 Lumsden, Sk,Can
136/B4 Lumsden, N.Z.
54/D2 Lumsden, Sc,UK
115/L8 Lumu, China
124/B2 Lumut, Indo.
124/D3 Lumut (cape), Indo.
124/C1 Lumut, Malay.
125/C1 Luna, Phil.
204/C2 Luna (mtn.), Ca,US
187/H4 Luna, NM,US
154/D2 Lunache, Ang.
168/B4 Lunahuaná, Peru
116/D3 Lunan (mts.), China
186/E1 Lunar (crater), Nv,US
184/F4 Lunar Crater, Nv,US
79/F5 Lunay, Fr.
54/C4 Luncarty, Sc,UK
182/B3 Lund, BC,Can
62/E4 Lund, Swe.
185/F4 Lund, Nv,US
185/G4 Lund, Ut,US
153/D5 Lunda Norte (prov.), Ang.
194/E2 Lundar, Mb,Can
154/D1 Lunda Sul (dist.), Ang.
153/E5 Lunda Sul (prov.), Ang.
155/G2 Lundazi, Zam.
183/G3 Lundbreck, Ab,Can
62/D4 Lundby, Den.
191/J3 Lundell, Ar,US
155/F4 Lundi (riv.), Zim.
155/G1 Lundu, Zam.
58/B4 Lundy (isl.), Eng,UK
67/F2 Lune (riv.), Ger.
57/F2 Lune (riv.), Eng,UK
57/F3 Lune (riv.), Eng,UK
67/H2 Lüneburg, Ger.
67/G2 Lüneburger Heide (reg.), Ger.
74/F5 Lunel, Fr.
67/E5 Lünen, Ger.
196/E3 Lunenburg, NS,Can
196/B3 Lunenburg, Vt,US
79/F1 Luneray, Fr.
67/F2 Lunestedt, Ger.
60/B2 Lung (riv.), Ire.
154/E2 Lunga (riv.), Zam.
151/B3 Lunga-Lunga, Kenya
114/D5 Lungdo, China
80/E4 Lungern, Swi.
144/B4 Lungi, SLeo.
144/B4 Lungi (Freetown) (int'l arpt.), SLeo.
116/B4 Lunglei, India
83/C3 Lungro, It.
121/G1 Lungsang, China
121/H4 Lungthung, India
116/B4 Lungtian, India
154/C2 Lungue-Bungo (riv.), Ang.
154/D2 Lungwebungu (riv.), Zam.
118/B3 Luni (riv.), India
98/D1 Luninets, Bela.
184/D4 Luning, Nv,US
97/H1 Lunino, Rus.
189/H2 Lunita, La,US
67/E4 Lünne, Ger.
114/D3 Luntai, China
155/G2 Lunzu, Malw.
115/B3 Luo (riv.), China
115/B4 Luo (riv.), China
115/B4 Luo (riv.), China
109/L2 Luobei, China
117/H3 Luobo (mtn.), China
114/E4 Luobuzhuang, China
117/F3 Luocheng, China
116/E3 Luodian, China
117/F4 Luoding, China
117/G4 Luofu (peak), China
117/H3 Luohan (mtn.), China
115/C4 Luohe, China
119/K3 Luojing, China
115/D4 Luoma (lake), China
117/F5 Luonan, China
123/C1 Luong (mts.), Viet.
153/G5 Luongo (riv.), Zam.
115/B4 Luoning, China
116/E3 Luoping, China
117/H3 Luoqiao, China
117/F3 Luoqing (riv.), China
115/C4 Luoshan, China
117/F2 Luoshuikan, China
115/C5 Luotian, China
117/F4 Luoxu, China
115/C4 Luoyang, China
117/F3 Luoyang, China
115/B3 Luoyukou, China
152/C4 Luozi, Zaire
151/A4 Lupa Market, Tanz.
155/E3 Lupane, Zim.
116/E3 Lupanshui, China
153/F5 L'Upemba Nat'l Park, Zaire
98/B5 Lupeni, Rom.
154/C2 Lupire, Ang.
151/B4 Lupiro, Tanz.
125/D4 Lupon, Phil.
187/H3 Lupton, Az,US
153/E4 Luputa, Zaire
84/H8 Luqa (int'l arpt.), Malta
108/E5 Luqu, China
116/D3 Luquan, China
152/D5 Luquembo, Ang.
107/J2 Lūrah (riv.), Afg.
203/G2 Luraville, Fl,US
68/A6 Luray, Fr.
191/E1 Luray, Ks,US
201/H1 Luray, Va,US
80/C2 Lure, Fr.
82/B4 Lure (ridge), Fr.
56/B3 Lurgan, NI,UK
75/H5 Luri, Fr.
172/C1 Luribay, Bol.
168/B4 Lurín, Peru
155/J2 Lúrio, Moz.
155/H2 Lúrio (riv.), Moz.
92/A2 Lurnfeld, Aus.
61/E2 Lurøy, Nor.
191/H3 Lurton, Ar,US
153/G3 Lusahunga, Tanz.
155/F2 Lusaka (cap.), Zam.
155/F2 Lusaka (int'l arpt.), Zam.
155/F2 Lusaka (prov.), Zam.
153/F4 Lusambo, Zaire
153/E4 Lusambo, Zaire
153/F4 Lusangi, Zaire
183/K1 Luseland, Sk,Can
155/F2 Lusemfwa (riv.), Zam.
71/G5 Lusen (peak), Ger.
153/G5 Lusenga Nat'l Park, Zam.
115/C4 Lushan, China
115/D3 Lu Shan (mtn.), China
115/C5 Lu Shan (peak), China
115/B4 Lushi, China
152/D4 Lushiko (riv.), Zaire
130/B4 Lush, Mount (peak), Austl.
91/F2 Lushnje, Alb.
151/B3 Lushoto, Tanz.
116/C3 Lushui, China
109/J4 Lüshun, China
60/D2 Lusk, Ire.
192/B2 Lusk, Wy,US
154/B2 Luso, Ang.
54/B4 Luss, Sc,UK
81/F3 Lustenau, Aus.
183/M3 Lustre, Mt,US
117/G3 Lutang, China
154/D2 Lutembo (riv.), Ang.
186/B1 Luther (pass), Ca,US
198/D2 Luther, Mi,US
191/F3 Luther, Ok,US
188/D1 Luther, Tx,US
80/D3 Luthern, Swi.
200/E4 Luthersville, Ga,US
206/B5 Lutherville, Md,US
154/D4 Lutike, Bots.
66/D1 Lütjehorn (isl.), Ger.
62/D4 Lütjenburg, Ger.
59/F3 Luton, Eng,UK
59/F3 Luton (int'l arpt.), Eng,UK
125/A4 Lutong, Malay.
80/C5 Lutry, Swi.
195/J4 Lutsen, Mn,US
153/F4 Lutshi, Zaire
152/D4 Lutshima, Zaire
152/D4 Lutshima (riv.), Zaire
98/C2 Lutsk, Ukr.
67/F5 Lutter (riv.), Ger.
80/D2 Lutterbach, Fr.
99/K3 Lutugino, Ukr.
81/F3 Lutz (riv.), Aus.
202/L7 Lutz, Fl,US
203/G3 Lutz, Fl,US
72/C5 Lützen, Ger.
137/C Lützow-Holm (bay), Ant.
150/D3 Luud, Waadi (dry riv.), Som.
63/M1 Luumäki, Fin.
150/B5 Luuq, Som.
152/D5 Luvalo, Ang.
203/E2 Luverne, Al,US
193/F2 Luverne, Mn,US
153/F4 Luvidjo (riv.), Zaire
152/C4 Luvo, Ang.
94/F2 Luvozero, Rus.
152/C4 Luvu, Zaire
153/G4 Luvua (riv.), Zaire
151/B4 Luwegu (riv.), Tanz.
155/F2 Luwembe, Zam.
153/H2 Luwero, Ugan.
153/G5 Luwingu, Zam.
80/A4 Lux, Fr.
200/C4 Luxapallila (cr.), Al, Ms,US
69/E4 Luxembourg
69/E4 Luxembourg (prov.), Belg.
69/F4 Luxembourg (cap.), Lux.
69/F4 Luxembourg (dist.), Lux.
69/F4 Luxembourg (Findel) (int'l arpt.), Lux.
193/L1 Luxemburg, Wi,US
80/C2 Luxeuil-les-Bains, Fr.
116/C3 Luxi, China
116/D3 Luxi, China
119/K2 Luxi, China
119/J2 Lu Xian, China
152/D5 Luxico (riv.), Ang.
117/G2 Luxikou, China
140/F2 Luxor, Egypt
147/G3 Luxor (int'l arpt.), Egypt
200/C3 Luxora, Ar,US
147/G3 Luxor (Al Uqşur), Egypt
115/L8 Luxu, China
117/F4 Luxu, China
74/C5 Luy (riv.), Fr.
113/A2 Lüyang, China
115/B3 Luya Shan (mtn.), China
82/C3 Luye (riv.), Fr.
115/C4 Luyi, China
79/F6 Luynes, Fr.
170/D3 Luz, Braz.
95/K3 Luza, Rus.
95/L3 Luza (riv.), Rus.
81/F4 Luzein, Swi.
80/E3 Luzern (canton), Swi.
206/B1 Luzerne (co.), Pa,US
81/E3 Luzern (Lucerne), Swi.
119/J3 Luzhai, China
116/E3 Luzhi, China
116/D3 Lüzhi (riv.), China
116/E2 Luzhou, China
170/D3 Luziânia, Braz.
73/C3 Lužianky, Slvk.
167/F3 Luzilândia, Braz.
153/H2 Luzinga, Ugan.
71/H4 Lužnice (riv.), Czh.
75/L2 Luznice (riv.), Czh.
138/B2 Luzon (str.)
125/C1 Luzon (isl.), Phil.
125/B2 Luzon (sea), Phil.
87/D3 Luzzara, It.
83/C4 Luzzi, It.
98/C3 L'viv, Ukr.
98/B2 L'viv Obl., Ukr.
153/H2 Lwala (peak), Ugan.
153/G5 Lwena Mission, Zam.
123/C1 Lwi (riv.), Burma
63/N2 Lyady, Rus.
96/C1 Lyakhovichi, Bela.
153/G3 Lyantonde, Ugan.
95/P3 Lyapin (riv.), Rus.
94/F3 Lyaskelya, Rus.
93/G4 Lyaskovets, Bul.
72/D1 Lychen, Ger.
61/F2 Lycksele, Swe.
206/A1 Lycoming (co.), Pa,US
206/B1 Lycoming-Williamsport (co. arpt.), Pa,US
59/G5 Lydd, Eng,UK
137/Y Lyddan (isl.), Ant.
59/G5 Lydd (Ferryfield) (int'l arpt.), Eng,UK
157/E2 Lydenburg, SAfr.
202/C3 Lydia, La,US
58/D3 Lydney, Eng,UK
182/F2 Lyell (mtn.), BC,Can
133/F2 Lyell Brown (peak), Austl.
189/F4 Lyford, Tx,US
206/B2 Lykens, Pa,US
193/H2 Lyle, Mn,US
182/D5 Lyle, Wa,US
200/D3 Lyles, Tn,US
194/D3 Lyleton, Mb,Can
202/D2 Lyman, Ms,US
201/F3 Lyman, SC,US
185/H4 Lyman, Ut,US
185/H3 Lyman, Wy,US
58/C5 Lyme (bay), Eng,UK
58/D5 Lyme Regis, Eng,UK
59/E5 Lymington, Eng,UK
57/F5 Lymm, Eng,UK
65/L1 Łyna (riv.), Pol.
56/D5 Lynas (pt.), Wal,UK
207/E2 Lynbrook, NY,US
206/B5 Lynch, Md,US
192/E2 Lynch, Ne,US
191/H2 Lynchburg, Mo,US
200/B3 Lynchburg, Ms,US
200/F1 Lynchburg, Oh,US
200/D3 Lynchburg, Tn,US
201/H2 Lynchburg, Va,US
201/G3 Lynches (riv.), SC,US
201/H2 Lynch Station, Va,US
134/B2 Lynd, Austl.
134/A2 Lynd (riv.), Austl.
182/C3 Lynden, Wa,US
133/H4 Lyndhurst, Austl.
59/E5 Lyndhurst, Eng,UK
207/D2 Lyndhurst, NJ,US
208/F4 Lyndhurst, Oh,US
132/B2 Lyndon, Austl.
191/G1 Lyndon, Ks,US
196/A3 Lyndon, Vt,US
189/E2 Lyndon B. Johnson (lake), Tx,US
188/K6 Lyndon B. Johnson Nat'l Grsld., Tx,US
189/E2 Lyndon B. Johnson Nat'l Hist. Park, Tx,US
189/G3 Lyndon B. Johnson Space Ctr., Tx,US
199/G3 Lyndonville, NY,US
199/K2 Lyndonville, Vt,US
208/H6 Lyndora, Pa,US
57/F1 Lyne (riv.), Eng,UK
55/N13 Lyness, Sc,UK
63/T9 Lyngby-Tårbæk, Den.
62/B2 Lyngdal, Nor.
63/T9 Lynge, Den.
61/G1 Lyngen (fjord), Nor.
200/D3 Lynn, Al,US
191/J2 Lynn, Ar,US
199/L3 Lynn, Ma,US
203/F2 Lynn Haven, Fl,US
178/F3 Lynn Lake, Mb,Can
205/C2 Lynnwood, Wa,US
58/C4 Lynton, Eng,UK
63/M4 Lyntupy, Bela.
204/B3 Lynwood, Ca,US
178/F2 Lynx (lake), NW,Can
82/A1 Lyon, Fr.
54/B3 Lyon (riv.), Sc,UK
190/C1 Lyon (can.), Co,US
200/B3 Lyon, Ms,US
199/K2 Lyon (mtn.), NY,US
54/B3 Lyon, Loch (lake), Sc,UK
82/B2 Lyonne (riv.), Fr.
132/C2 Lyons (riv.), Austl.
201/F4 Lyons, Ga,US
198/C5 Lyons, In,US
191/E1 Lyons, Ks,US
199/H3 Lyons, NY,US
205/P14 Lyons, Wi,US
82/B1 Lyon (Satolas) (int'l arpt.), Fr.
199/J3 Lyons Falls, NY,US
79/G2 Lyons-la-Forêt, Fr.
208/A3 Lyons Plain, Ct,US
58/C4 Lype (hill), Eng,UK
138/E5 Lyra (reef), PNG
74/E1 Lys (riv.), Belg., Fr.
68/B2 Lys (riv.), Fr.
86/A1 Lys (riv.), It.
65/K4 Lysá (peak), Czh.
62/D2 Lysaker, Nor.
71/H2 Lysá nad Labem, Czh.
73/C1 Lysá pod Makytou, Slvk.
63/M4 Lysaya (hill), Bela.
94/E5 Lysaya, Gora (hill), Bela.
62/D2 Lysekil, Swe.
65/L3 Łysica (peak), Pol.
71/F2 Lysina (peak), Czh.
185/K2 Lysite, Wy,US
68/C2 Lys-lez-Lannoy, Fr.
80/D3 Lyss, Swi.
62/D3 Lystrup, Den.
53/J3 Lys'va, Rus.
97/H2 Lysyye Gory, Rus.
58/D5 Lytchett Matravers, Eng,UK
57/E4 Lytham Saint Anne's, Eng,UK
204/C2 Lytle (cr.), Ca,US
189/E3 Lytle, Tx,US
204/C2 Lytle Creek, Ca,US
136/C3 Lyttelton, N.Z.
182/D2 Lytton, BC,Can
96/D1 Lyuban', Bela.
98/D3 Lyubar, Ukr.
97/F2 Lyubech, Ukr.
96/F1 Lyubertsy, Rus.
98/C2 Lyubeshov, Ukr.
93/H5 Lyubimets, Bul.
98/C2 Lyuboml', Ukr.
99/H3 Lyubotin, Ukr.
96/E1 Lyudinovo, Rus.
58/C3 Lywd (riv.), Wal,UK

## M

123/C1 Ma (riv.), Laos, Viet.
103/D3 Ma'alot, Isr.
152/B2 Ma'an, Camr.
115/L9 Ma'an, China
103/D4 Ma'ān, Jor.
103/E5 Ma'ān (gov.), Jor.
94/F2 Maanselkä (mts.), Fin.
115/D5 Ma'anshan, China
63/L2 Maardu, Est.
66/C6 Maarheeze, Neth.
103/E2 Ma'arrat an Nu'mān, Syria
66/C4 Maarssen, Neth.
64/D3 Maas (riv.), Eur.
66/C6 Maasbracht, Neth.
66/D6 Maasbree, Neth.
69/E1 Maaseik, Belg.
125/D3 Maasin, Phil.
69/E2 Maasmechelen, Belg.
66/B5 Maassluis, Neth.
155/F4 Maasstroom, SAfr.
66/C5 Maastricht, Neth.
69/E2 Maastricht (int'l arpt.), Neth.
155/G4 Maave, Moz.
103/G6 Ma'ayan Harod Nat'l Park, Isr.
127/G3 Maba, Indo.
154/D3 Mababe (depr.), Bots.
125/D3 Mabaho (mtn.), Phil.
125/C2 Mabalacat, Phil.
155/G4 Mabalane, Moz.
189/F1 Mabank, Tx,US
165/G2 Mabaruma, Guy.
117/G2 Mabating, China
112/B3 Mabechi (riv.), Japan
193/J2 Mabel, Mn,US
200/C4 Maben, Ms,US
119/H2 Mabian, China
201/H1 Mabie, WV,US
125/C3 Mabinay, Phil.
125/D3 Mabini, Phil.
57/J5 Mablethorpe, Eng,UK
201/L7 Mableton, Ga,US
156/E2 Mabopane, SAfr.
155/G4 Mabote, Moz.
197/G2 Mabou, NS,Can
145/E2 Mabroûk, Mali
182/E4 Mabton, Wa,US
155/H3 Mabu (peak), Moz.
154/D5 Mabuasehube Game Rsv., Bots.
152/C5 Mabubas, Ang.
151/A2 Mabuki, Tanz.
154/E5 Mabuli, Bots.
174/B5 Macá (peak), Chile
174/E3 Macachín, Arg.
171/E4 Macaé, Braz.
76/D4 Macael, Sp.
167/H4 Macaíba, Braz.
155/G2 Macaloge, Moz.
76/B3 Mação, Port.
117/G4 Macao (Macau) (cap.), Macau
117/G4 Macao (Macau) (dpcy.), Port.
166/D2 Macapá, Braz.
168/B2 Macará, Ecu.
164/C3 Macaravita, Col.
165/F2 Macareo Santo Niño, Ven.
168/D4 Macari, Peru
135/B3 Macarthur, Austl.
207/E2 MacArthur/Long Island (arpt.), NY,US
164/B5 Macas, Ecu.
167/G4 Macau, Braz.
138/H7 Macauley (isl.), N.Z.

117/G4 **Macau** (Macao) (cap.), Macau
117/G4 **Macau** (Macao) (dpcy.), Port.
164/C4 **Macaya** (riv.), Col.
161/H2 **Macaya, Pic de** (peak), Haiti
193/J3 **MacBride** (lake), Ia,US
81/E5 **Maccagno,** It.
196/E3 **Maccan,** NS,Can
84/C4 **Maccarese,** It.
203/G2 **Macclenny,** Fl,US
57/F5 **Macclesfield,** Eng,UK
57/F5 **Macclesfield** (can.), Eng,UK
156/D3 **Macdhui** (peak), SAfr.
195/K3 **Macdiarmid,** On,Can
202/L8 **MacDill A.F.B.,** Fl,US
203/G4 **MacDill A.F.B.,** Fl,US
133/F2 **Macdonald** (lake), Austl.
183/H4 **MacDonald** (pass), Mt,US
133/G2 **MacDonell** (ranges), Austl.
195/H1 **MacDowell** (riv.), On,Can
54/D1 **Macduff,** Sc,UK
76/B1 **Maceda,** Sp.
91/G2 **Macedonia**
91/G2 **Macedonia** (reg.), Gre.
91/G2 **Macedonia** (reg.), Gre., Macd.
191/H4 **Macedonia,** Ar,US
208/F5 **Macedonia,** Oh,US
171/G1 **Maceió,** Braz.
167/G4 **Maceió** (pt.), Braz.
144/C4 **Macenta,** Gui.
85/D1 **Macerata,** It.
87/G6 **Macerata** (prov.), It.
196/D3 **Maces Bay,** NB,Can
137/E **Macey** (peak), Ant.
198/F5 **Macfarlan,** WV,US
133/H5 **Macfarlane** (lake), Austl.
60/A6 **Macgillycuddy's Reeks** (mts.), Ire.
194/E3 **MacGregor,** Mb,Can
172/C1 **Macha,** Bol.
172/C1 **Machacamarca,** Bol.
156/D3 **Machache** (peak), Les.
164/B5 **Machachi,** Ecu.
171/L6 **Machado,** Braz.
161/H4 **Machado, Ciénaga de** (lake), Col.
156/Q12 **Machadodorp,** SAfr.
172/D3 **Machagai,** Arg.
155/G4 **Machaíla,** Moz.
151/B2 **Machakos,** Kenya
168/B1 **Machala,** Ecu.
174/C2 **Machalí,** Chile
164/A5 **Machalilla Nat'l Park,** Ecu.
124/C1 **Machang,** Malay.
155/G4 **Machanga,** Moz.
160/D2 **Machaquilá** (riv.), Guat.
172/D2 **Machareti,** Bol.
56/D2 **Machars, The** (pen.), Sc,UK
133/H3 **Machattie** (lake), Austl.
155/G4 **Machaze,** Moz.
74/C3 **Machecoul,** Fr.
164/C2 **Machedo** (lake), Col.
155/F3 **Macheke,** Zim.
99/M2 **Machekha,** Rus.
155/F4 **Machemma** (ruins), SAfr.
58/C3 **Machen,** Wal,UK
115/C5 **Macheng,** China
193/K2 **Machesney Park,** Il,US
122/D2 **Māchhīwāra,** India
120/D3 **Machhlīshahr,** India
108/F5 **Machi,** China
196/D3 **Machias,** Me,US
199/G3 **Machias,** NY,US
196/D3 **Machiasport,** Me,US
76/D1 **Machichaco** (cape), Sp.
77/V15 **Machico,** Madr.,Port.
111/H7 **Machida,** Japan
154/E3 **Machili** (riv.), Zam.
118/D4 **Machilipatnam,** India
164/C2 **Machiques,** Ven.
188/D3 **Macho,** Mex.
190/B4 **Macho, Arroyo del** (cr.), NM,US
154/E3 **Machobani,** Zam.
71/H1 **Machovo Jezero** (res.), Czh.
168/C4 **Machu Picchu** (ruins), Peru
169/E4 **Machupo** (riv.), Bol.
58/C1 **Machynlleth,** Wal,UK
174/F2 **Maciá,** Arg.
155/G5 **Macia,** Moz.
174/E2 **Maciel,** Arg.
93/J3 **Măcin,** Rom.
144/D3 **Macina** (reg.), Mali
135/D1 **Macintyre** (riv.), Austl.
185/J4 **Mack,** Co,US
134/C3 **Mackay,** Austl.
133/F2 **Mackay** (lake), Austl.
185/G2 **Mackay,** Id,US
137/E **MacKenzie** (bay), Ant.
134/C3 **Mackenzie** (riv.), Austl.
178/D3 **Mackenzie,** BC,Can
178/C2 **Mackenzie** (mts.), NW,Can
177/N2 **Mackenzie** (riv.), NW,Can
179/C2 **Mackenzie** (bay), NW, Yk,Can
179/R7 **Mackenzie King** (isl.), NW,Can
182/C1 **Mackin** (riv.), BC,Can
198/D2 **Mackinac** (str.), Mi,US
193/K3 **Mackinaw** (riv.), Il,US
198/D2 **Mackinaw City,** Mi,US
136/A4 **Mackinnon** (pass), N.Z.
151/B2 **Mackinnon Road,** Kenya
183/K1 **Macklin,** Sk,Can
134/B2 **Macknade,** Austl.
201/G1 **Macksburg,** Oh,US
191/H2 **Macks Creek,** Mo,US
135/E1 **Macksville,** Austl.
190/E2 **Macksville,** Ks,US
135/E1 **Maclean,** Austl.
156/E3 **Maclear,** SAfr.
134/F7 **Macleay** (isl.), Austl.
132/B3 **Macleod** (lake), Austl.
177/L3 **Macmillan** (riv.), Yk,Can
194/D2 **MacNutt,** Sk,Can
193/J3 **Macomb,** Il,US
205/G6 **Macomb** (co.), Mi,US
90/A2 **Macomer,** It.
155/J2 **Macomia,** Moz.
80/A5 **Mâcon,** Fr.
191/J4 **Macon** (bayou), Ar, La,US
200/F4 **Macon,** Ga,US
198/B5 **Macon,** Il,US
205/E7 **Macon** (cr.), Mi,US
191/H1 **Macon,** Mo,US
200/C4 **Macon,** Ms,US
80/B1 **Maconcourt,** Fr.
155/H1 **Macondes** (plat.), Moz.
154/D2 **Macondo,** Ang.
154/D2 **Macondo** (riv.), Ang.
205/E7 **Macon, North Branch** (cr.), Mi,US
56/B1 **Macosquin,** NI,UK
76/C2 **Macotera,** Sp.
194/C3 **Macoun,** Sk,Can
193/J4 **Macoupin** (cr.), Il,US
166/C1 **Macouria,** FrG.
155/G4 **Macovane** (pt.), Moz.
135/C4 **Macquarie** (har.), Austl.
51/S8 **Macquarie** (isl.), Austl.
135/C1 **Macquarie** (riv.), Austl.
135/C4 **Macquarie** (riv.), Austl.
129/G8 **Macquarie Harbour** (bay), Austl.
137/D **Mac-Robertson Land** (reg.), Ant.
60/B6 **Macroom,** Ire.
194/A2 **Macrorie,** Sk,Can
199/G2 **MacTier,** On,Can
160/D3 **Macuelizo,** Hon.
169/E2 **Macuim** (riv.), Braz.
164/D1 **Macuira Nat'l Park,** Col.
168/B1 **Macuma** (riv.), Ecu.
133/H3 **Macumba** (riv.), Austl.
206/C2 **Macungie,** Pa,US
168/D4 **Macusani,** Peru
159/G5 **Macuspana,** Mex.
158/C3 **Macuzari** (res.), Mex.
193/F2 **Macy,** Ne,US
184/B3 **Mad** (riv.), Ca,US
103/D4 **Ma'dabā,** Jor.
148/B3 **Madagali,** Nga.
157/H8 **Madagascar**
104/D5 **Madā'in Şāliḩ,** SAr.
146/B4 **Madama,** Niger
197/G3 **Madame** (isl.), NS,Can
93/G5 **Madan,** Bul.
118/C5 **Madanapalle,** India
131/G1 **Madang,** PNG
131/G1 **Madang** (int'l arpt.), PNG
131/G1 **Madang** (prov.), PNG
143/H2 **Madanīyīn,** Tun.
143/H2 **Madanīyīn** (gov.), Tun.
108/F5 **Madao,** China
145/G3 **Madaoua,** Niger
92/D2 **Madaras,** Hun.
121/G2 **Mādāri Hāt,** India
121/H4 **Mādārīpur,** Bang.
145/G3 **Madarounfa,** Niger
116/C5 **Madauk,** Burma
199/H2 **Madawaska** (riv.), On,Can
196/C2 **Madawaska,** Me,US
150/C5 **Madaxmaroodi,** Som.
123/B1 **Madaya,** Burma
95/K5 **Madayevo,** Rus.
196/B5 **Maddaket,** Ma,US
85/E5 **Maddaloni,** It.
161/G4 **Madden** (dam), Pan.
200/C4 **Madden,** Ms,US
194/E4 **Maddock,** ND,US
66/B5 **Made,** Neth.
149/F4 **Madeir,** Sudan
166/B4 **Madeira** (riv.), Braz.
77/V15 **Madeira** (isl.), Madr., Port.
77/U14 **Madeira** (aut. reg.), Port.
202/K8 **Madeira Beach,** Fl,US
182/B3 **Madeira Park,** BC,Can
169/F3 **Madeirinha** (riv.), Braz.
81/G3 **Mädelegabel** (peak), Ger., Aus.
196/E1 **Madeleine** (riv.), Qu,Can
193/G1 **Madelia,** Mn,US
184/C3 **Madeline,** Ca,US
195/J4 **Madeline** (isl.), Wi,US
104/D2 **Maden,** Turk.
81/F3 **Mäder,** Aus.
169/E3 **Madera** (riv.), Bol.
158/C2 **Madera,** Mex.
161/E4 **Madera** (vol.), Nic.
186/B2 **Madera,** Ca,US
158/E2 **Madera** (mtn.), Tx,US
187/G5 **Madera Canyon,** Az,US
121/F3 **Madhipura,** India
121/F2 **Madhubani,** India
121/G4 **Madhumati** (riv.), Bang.
121/F3 **Madhupur,** India
121/F2 **Mādhura,** India
121/E2 **Madhwāpur,** India
120/B4 **Madhya Pradesh** (state), India
151/A2 **Madiany,** Kenya
156/D2 **Madibogo,** SAfr.
151/A4 **Madibura,** Tanz.
169/E4 **Madidi** (riv.), Bol.
108/G4 **Madihui,** China
156/D2 **Madikwe,** SAfr.
191/F3 **Madill,** Ok,US
152/C4 **Madimba,** Zaire
146/D1 **Madīnat al Abyār,** Libya
150/C2 **Madīnat ash Sha'b,** Yem.
104/D3 **Madīnat ath Thawrah,** Syria
152/B1 **Madingo,** Congo
152/B4 **Madingo-Kayes,** Congo
152/C4 **Madingou,** Congo
153/H2 **Madi Opei,** Ugan.
157/H7 **Madirovalo,** Madg.
183/K2 **Madison,** Sk,Can
200/D3 **Madison,** Al,US
200/B3 **Madison,** Ar,US
205/L9 **Madison,** Ca,US
208/B3 **Madison,** Ct,US
203/G2 **Madison,** Fl,US
201/F4 **Madison,** Ga,US
200/E1 **Madison,** In,US
191/F1 **Madison,** Ks,US
196/C3 **Madison,** Me,US
194/F5 **Madison,** Mn,US
191/H1 **Madison,** Mo,US
200/B4 **Madison,** Ms,US
183/J5 **Madison** (riv.), Mt,US
192/F3 **Madison,** Ne,US
206/D2 **Madison,** NJ,US
198/F4 **Madison,** Oh,US
193/F1 **Madison,** SD,US
201/H1 **Madison,** Va,US
193/K2 **Madison** (cap.), Wi,US
201/G1 **Madison,** WV,US
208/F6 **Madisonburg,** Oh,US
205/F6 **Madison Heights,** Mi,US
201/H2 **Madison Heights,** Va,US
200/D2 **Madisonville,** Ky,US
202/C2 **Madisonville,** La,US
200/E3 **Madisonville,** Tn,US
189/G2 **Madisonville,** Tx,US
124/E4 **Madiun,** Indo.
152/C2 **Madjngo,** Gabon
199/H2 **Madoc,** On,Can
151/B1 **Mado Gali, Laga** (dry riv.), Kenya
151/B1 **Mado Gashi,** Kenya
108/D5 **Madoi,** China
80/C1 **Madon** (riv.), Fr.
63/M3 **Madona,** Lat.
82/D5 **Madone d'Utelle** (mtn.), Fr.
119/K3 **Madong,** China
108/F4 **Madongchuan,** China
90/C4 **Madonie Nebrodi** (mts.), It.
81/G5 **Madonna di Campiglio,** It.
107/G5 **Madrakah, Ra's al** (pt.), Oman
118/D5 **Madras,** India
184/C1 **Madras,** Or,US
159/F3 **Madre** (bay), Mex.
125/C1 **Madre** (mts.), Phil.
189/F4 **Madre** (lag.), Tx,US
169/F5 **Madrecitas,** Bol.
171/M6 **Madre de Deus de Minas,** Braz.
168/D4 **Madre de Dios** (riv.), Bol., Peru
175/J7 **Madre de Dios** (isl.), Chile
159/E5 **Madre del Sur, Sierra** (mts.), Mex.
158/C2 **Madre Occidental, Sierra** (mts.), Mex.
188/C3 **Madre Oriental, Sierra** (mts.), Mex.
74/E5 **Madrès** (mtn.), Fr.
160/C3 **Madre, Sierra** (mts.), Mex.
125/C1 **Madre, Sierra** (mts.), Phil.
164/C3 **Madrid,** Col.
76/C2 **Madrid** (aut. comm.), Sp.
76/D2 **Madrid** (cap.), Sp.
193/H3 **Madrid,** Ia,US
76/D3 **Madridejos,** Sp.
168/D4 **Madrigal,** Peru
76/C2 **Madrigal de las Altas Torres,** Sp.
76/C3 **Madrigalejo,** Sp.
81/F4 **Madrisahorn** (peak), Swi.
76/C3 **Madroñera,** Sp.
195/H2 **Madsen,** On,Can
152/C4 **Maduda,** Zaire
118/D4 **Madugula,** India
151/A2 **Madukani,** Tanz.
122/F3 **Madukkarai,** India
132/E4 **Madura,** Austl.
124/F4 **Madura** (isl.), Indo.
122/G4 **Madurai,** India
122/G4 **Madurai** (arpt.), India
93/G5 **Madzharovo,** Bul.
111/F2 **Maebashi,** Japan
123/B1 **Mae Chan,** Thai.
123/C2 **Mae Charim,** Thai.
123/B2 **Mae Hong Son,** Thai.
77/F2 **Maella,** Sp.
113/D3 **Maengsan,** NKor.
84/D4 **Maenza,** It.
123/B2 **Mae Ping Nat'l Park,** Thai.
113/E4 **Maep'o,** SKor.
123/B2 **Mae Ramat,** Thai.
87/F1 **Maerne,** It.
123/B1 **Mae Sai,** Thai.
123/B2 **Mae Sariang,** Thai.
185/J3 **Maeser,** Ut,US
123/B2 **Mae Sot,** Thai.
58/C3 **Maesteg,** Wal,UK
161/G2 **Maestra, Sierra** (range), Cuba
123/B2 **Mae Taeng,** Thai.
123/B2 **Mae Tho** (peak), Thai.
157/H7 **Maevatanana,** Madg.
138/F6 **Maewo** (isl.), Van.
123/B2 **Mae Ya** (mtn.), Thai.
194/D1 **Mafeking,** Mb,Can
156/D3 **Mafeteng,** Les.
69/E3 **Maffe,** Belg.
135/C3 **Maffra,** Austl.
151/B4 **Mafia** (chan.), Tanz.
141/G5 **Mafia** (isl.), Tanz.
156/D2 **Mafikeng,** SAfr.
174/B3 **Māfil,** Chile
144/C4 **Mafou** (riv.), Gui.
173/G3 **Mafra,** Braz.
76/A3 **Mafra,** Port.
155/F3 **Mafungabusi** (plat.), Zim.
101/R4 **Magadan,** Rus.
151/B2 **Magadi,** Kenya
81/E5 **Magadino,** Swi.
167/F3 **Magalhães de Almeida,** Braz.
184/C4 **Magalia,** Ca,US
156/P12 **Magalies Berg** (range), SAfr.
156/P12 **Magaliesburg,** SAfr.
125/C2 **Magallanes,** Phil.
175/K8 **Magallanes** (Magellan) (str.), Arg., Chile
175/K8 **Magallanes y Antártica Chilena** (reg.), Chile
148/D4 **Magamba,** CAfr.
164/C2 **Magangué,** Col.
125/D4 **Maganoy,** Phil.
103/C1 **Mağara,** Turk.
145/H3 **Magaria,** Niger
131/H2 **Magarida,** PNG
125/C1 **Magat** (riv.), Phil.
191/H3 **Magazine,** Ar,US
191/H3 **Magazine** (mtn.), Ar,US
109/K1 **Magdagachi,** Rus.
197/F2 **Magdalen** (isls.), Qu,Can
175/T12 **Magdalena,** Arg.
169/E4 **Magdalena,** Bol.
161/H4 **Magdalena** (dept.), Col.
167/L7 **Magdalena** (riv.), Col.
158/C2 **Magdalena,** Mex.
187/J3 **Magdalena,** NM,US
127/E3 **Magdalena, Gunung** (peak), Malay.
72/B3 **Magdeburg,** Ger.
72/B3 **Magdeburger Börde** (plain), Ger.
129/J3 **Magdelaine** (cays), Austl.
80/D2 **Magden,** Swi.
171/N7 **Magé,** Braz.
200/C5 **Magee,** Ms,US
56/C2 **Magee, Island** (pen.), NI,UK
124/E4 **Magelang,** Indo.
175/K8 **Magellan** (Magallanes) (str.), Arg., Chile
132/C5 **Magenta** (lake), Austl.
68/C5 **Magenta,** Fr.
86/B2 **Magenta,** It.
61/H1 **Magerøya** (isl.), Nor.
124/E4 **Magetan,** Indo.
81/E5 **Maggia,** Swi.
81/E5 **Maggia** (riv.), Swi.
87/E6 **Maggio, Monte** (peak), It.
86/C3 **Maggiorasca, Monte** (peak), It.
84/C2 **Maggiore** (peak), It.
85/E5 **Maggiore** (peak), It.
81/E6 **Maggiore** (lake), It., Swi.
87/E5 **Maggiore, Monte** (peak), It.
147/F2 **Maghāghah,** Egypt
144/B3 **Maghama,** Mrta.
120/D2 **Maghar,** India
60/B4 **Maghera** (mtn.), Ire.
56/B2 **Maghera,** NI,UK
56/B2 **Magherafelt,** NI,UK
56/B2 **Magherafelt** (dist.), NI,UK
141/W18 **Maghīla, Jabal** (peak), Tun.
141/P13 **Maghnia,** Alg.
88/C4 **Maghrib, Al** (reg.), Alg., Mor.
57/F4 **Maghull,** Eng,UK
185/F2 **Magic** (res.), Id,US
202/M7 **Magic Kingdom,** Fl,US
56/B1 **Magilligan,** NI,UK
56/B1 **Magilligan** (pt.), NI,UK
84/C1 **Magione,** It.
92/D3 **Maglaj,** Bosn.
85/D3 **Magliano de'Marsi,** It.
84/C3 **Magliano Sabina,** It.
92/D4 **Maglić** (peak), Yugo.
91/F2 **Maglie,** It.
74/D3 **Magnac-Laval,** Fr.
121/H5 **Magnāma,** Bang.
199/G2 **Magnetawan,** On,Can
198/F2 **Magnetawan** (riv.), On,Can
134/B2 **Magnetic** (pass.), Austl.
134/B2 **Magnetic I. Nat'l Park,** Austl.
95/N5 **Magnitka,** Rus.
95/N5 **Magnitogorsk,** Rus.
95/N5 **Magnitogorsk** (int'l arpt.), Rus.
191/H4 **Magnolia,** Ar,US
206/C5 **Magnolia,** De,US
202/C2 **Magnolia,** Ms,US
189/G2 **Magnolia,** Tx,US
206/D4 **Magnolia-Elwood,** NJ,US
68/A5 **Magny-en-Vexin,** Fr.
53/S10 **Magny-les-Hameaux,** Fr.
155/F2 **Mágoè,** Moz.
196/A3 **Magog,** Qu,Can
149/H4 **Mago Nat'l Park,** Eth.
58/D3 **Magor,** Wal,UK
155/E3 **Magoye,** Zam.
86/C4 **Magra** (riv.), It.
183/H3 **Magrath,** Ab,Can
87/D3 **Magreta,** It.
125/D3 **Magsaysay,** Phil.
123/D1 **Maguan,** China
166/D3 **Maguarinho** (cape), Braz.
155/G5 **Magude,** Moz.
140/E4 **Maguerite** (peak), Zaire
87/D1 **Magugnano,** It.
121/G4 **Māgura,** Bang.
116/B4 **Magwe,** Burma
116/B5 **Magwe** (div.), Burma
73/C6 **Magyarkeszi,** Hun.
116/B4 **Magyichaung,** Burma
105/F2 **Mahābād,** Iran
120/C1 **Mahābārat** (range), Nepal
157/H7 **Mahabe,** Madg.
157/H8 **Mahabo,** Madg.
157/H7 **Mahaboboka,** Madg.
118/B4 **Mahād,** India
150/C5 **Mahadday Weyn,** Som.
120/B4 **Mahadeo** (range), India
139/X15 **Mahaena,** FrPol.
121/F3 **Mahāgama,** India
153/G2 **Mahagi,** Zaire
153/G2 **Mahagi-Port,** Zaire
165/G3 **Mahaica,** Guy.
165/G3 **Mahaica-Berbice** (reg.), Guy.
165/G3 **Mahaicony Village,** Guy.
157/H6 **Mahajamba** (bay), Madg.
157/H7 **Mahajamba** (riv.), Madg.
141/G6 **Mahajanga,** Madg.
157/H6 **Mahajanga** (prov.), Madg.
157/H7 **Mahajilo** (riv.), Madg.
120/C1 **Maha Kali** (riv.), India
120/C1 **Mahakali** (zone), Nepal
127/E3 **Mahakam** (riv.), Indo.
155/E4 **Mahalapye,** Bots.
105/G3 **Maḩallāt,** Iran
122/D2 **Mahalpur,** India
120/D4 **Māhān** (riv.), India
105/J4 **Māhān,** Iran
118/D3 **Mahānadī** (riv.), India
121/F3 **Mahananda** (riv.), India
144/D4 **Mahandiabani** (riv.), IvC.
151/A4 **Mahanje,** Tanz.
157/J7 **Mahanoro,** Madg.
206/B2 **Mahanoy** (cr.), Pa,US
206/B2 **Mahanoy City,** Pa,US
206/B2 **Mahantango** (cr.), Pa,US
206/B2 **Mahantango Mtn.** (ridge), Pa,US
109/K3 **Mahao,** China
120/D2 **Mahārājganj,** India
121/E2 **Mahārājganj,** India
118/C2 **Mahārajpur,** India
118/B4 **Mahārāshtra** (state), India
118/D3 **Mahāsamund,** India
123/C2 **Maha Sarakham,** Thai.
157/H8 **Mahasoabe,** Madg.
121/G3 **Mahāsthān** (ruin), Bang.
157/H7 **Mahavavy** (riv.), Madg.
120/B1 **Mahawa** (riv.), India
122/H4 **Mahaweli** (riv.), SrL.
116/E5 **Mahaxai,** Laos
157/H8 **Mahazoarivo,** Madg.
157/H7 **Mahazoma,** Madg.
118/C4 **Mahbubnagar,** India
106/D4 **Mahd adh Dhahab,** SAr.
165/G3 **Mahdia,** Guy.
107/L2 **Mahe,** India
122/E3 **Mahe,** India
141/H5 **Mahé** (isl.), Sey.
157/S15 **Mahébourg,** Mrts.
151/B4 **Mahenge,** Tanz.
136/B4 **Maheno,** N.Z.
121/G4 **Mahespur,** Bang.
108/E4 **Mahezhen,** China
120/B2 **Mahgawān,** India
136/D2 **Mahia** (pen.), N.Z.
121/F4 **Mahīshādal,** India
157/H7 **Mahitsy,** Madg.
116/B4 **Mahlaing,** Burma
80/D1 **Mahlberg,** Ger.
143/G2 **Mahmel, Djebel** (mtn.), Alg.
120/C2 **Mahmūdābād,** India
107/J1 **Maḩmūd-e 'Erāqī,** Afg.
104/B2 **Mahmudiye,** Turk.
194/G4 **Mahnomen,** Mn,US
120/B3 **Mahoba,** India
198/B4 **Mahomet,** Il,US
60/C5 **Mahon** (riv.), Ire.
77/H3 **Mahón,** Sp.
196/E3 **Mahone Bay,** NS,Can
208/G6 **Mahoning** (co.), Oh,US
208/G5 **Mahoning** (riv.), Oh, Pa,US
120/B3 **Mahroni,** India
195/Q6 **Mahtomedi,** Mn,US
108/D4 **Mahuanggou,** China
180/U10 **Mahukona,** Hi,US
116/B3 **Mahur,** India
155/F3 **Mahusekwa,** Zim.
151/B4 **Mahuta,** Tanz.
118/B3 **Mahuva,** India
120/A2 **Mahwah,** India
207/D1 **Mahwah,** NJ,US
76/A2 **Maia,** Port.
134/E6 **Maiala Nat'l Park,** Austl.
77/F2 **Maials,** Sp.
138/G4 **Maiana** (isl.), Kiri.
139/W15 **Maiao** (isl.), FrPol.
164/C2 **Maicao,** Col.
80/C3 **Maîche,** Fr.
165/H5 **Maicuru** (riv.), Braz.
83/C5 **Maida,** It.
206/C2 **Maiden** (cr.), Pa,US
59/F3 **Maidenhead,** Eng,UK
58/D5 **Maiden Newton,** Eng,UK
54/B6 **Maidens,** Sc,UK
127/G3 **Maidi,** Indo.
205/G7 **Maidstone,** On,Can
183/K1 **Maidstone,** Sk,Can
59/G4 **Maidstone,** Eng,UK
148/B3 **Maiduguri,** Nga.
153/G2 **Maie,** Zaire
81/F3 **Maienfeld,** Swi.
83/C5 **Maierato,** It.
145/H3 **Maigatari,** Nga.
68/B4 **Maignelay-Montigny,** Fr.
60/B4 **Maigue** (riv.), Ire.
120/C3 **Maihar,** India
110/E3 **Maihara,** Japan
121/H4 **Maijdi,** Bang.
120/C4 **Maikala** (range), India
153/F3 **Maiko** (riv.), Zaire
153/F3 **Maiko Nat'l Park,** Zaire
130/D1 **Maikoor** (riv.), Indo.
148/C3 **Maikoro,** Chad
120/C1 **Mailāni,** India
68/D6 **Mailly-le-Camp,** Fr.
107/K3 **Mailsi,** Pak.
124/B2 **Maimoon Palace** (Istana Maimoon), Indo.
198/F2 **Main** (chan.), On,Can
70/B2 **Main** (riv.), Ger.
56/B2 **Main** (riv.), NI,UK
197/H3 **Main-à-Dieu,** NS,Can
121/G2 **Maināguri,** India
128/G6 **Main Barrier** (range), Austl.
70/D3 **Mainbernheim,** Ger.
183/L2 **Main Centre,** Sk,Can
53/U11 **Maincy,** Fr.
152/D3 **Mai-Ndombe** (lake), Zaire
70/E4 **Main-Donau** (can.), Ger.
79/E4 **Maine** (hills), Fr.
79/E4 **Maine** (hist. reg.), Fr.
79/E6 **Maine** (riv.), Fr.
60/A5 **Maine** (riv.), Ire.
196/C4 **Maine** (gulf), US
196/B3 **Maine** (state), US
79/E6 **Maine-et-Loire** (dept.), Fr.
148/B2 **Maïné-Soroa,** Niger
119/G2 **Maingkwan,** Burma
116/B4 **Maingnyaung,** Burma
70/C4 **Mainhardt,** Ger.
70/B2 **Mainhausen,** Ger.
125/D3 **Mainit,** Phil.
116/C2 **Mainkung,** China
55/N13 **Mainland** (isl.), Sc,UK
55/P12 **Mainland** (isl.), Sc,UK
116/B2 **Mainling,** China
130/D3 **Mainoru,** Austl.
120/B2 **Mainpurī,** India
134/C5 **Main Range Nat'l Park,** Austl.
70/D3 **Mainstockheim,** Ger.
79/G3 **Maintenon,** Fr.
157/H7 **Maintirano,** Madg.
197/J1 **Main Top Sail** (mtn.), Nf,Can
79/G4 **Mainvilliers,** Fr.
70/B3 **Mainz,** Ger.
140/K10 **Maio** (isl.), CpV.
85/E6 **Maiori,** It.
174/R10 **Maipo** (vol.), Arg., Chile
174/Q9 **Maipo** (riv.), Chile
174/F3 **Maipú,** Arg.
174/C2 **Maipú,** Chile
165/E2 **Maiquetía,** Ven.
86/A3 **Maira** (riv.), It.
172/D1 **Mairana,** Bol.
171/E1 **Mairi,** Braz.
171/K8 **Mairiporã,** Braz.
120/E2 **Mairwa,** India
70/E6 **Maisach,** Ger.
161/H2 **Mais Gate** (int'l arpt.), Haiti
63/L4 **Maišiagala,** Lith.
116/A4 **Maiskhāl,** Bang.
153/H3 **Maisome** (isl.), Tanz.
53/T10 **Maisons-Alfort,** Fr.
53/S10 **Maisons-Laffitte,** Fr.
155/E4 **Maitengwe,** Bots.
121/F4 **Maithon** (res.), India
133/H5 **Maitland,** Austl.
135/D2 **Maitland,** Austl.
196/F3 **Maitland,** NS,Can
199/J2 **Maitland,** On,Can
198/F3 **Maitland** (riv.), On,Can
202/N6 **Maitland,** Fl,US
125/D4 **Maitum,** Phil.
161/F3 **Maiz Grande** (isl.), Nic.
114/F6 **Maizhokunggar,** China
69/F5 **Maizières-lès-Metz,** Fr.
161/F3 **Maiz Pequeña** (isl.), Nic.
110/D3 **Maizuru,** Japan
77/N9 **Majadahonda,** Sp.
91/G2 **Maja e Zezë** (peak), Alb.
164/C2 **Majagual,** Col.
124/E4 **Majalengka,** Indo.
141/W17 **Majardah** (mts.), Alg., Tun.
141/W17 **Majardah** (riv.), Tun.
92/E3 **Majdanpek,** Yugo.
146/B3 **Majdūl,** Libya
127/E4 **Majene,** Indo.
120/C3 **Majhgawān,** India
149/G4 **Majī,** Eth.
115/D3 **Majia** (riv.), China
119/K3 **Majiang,** China
151/A2 **Maji Moto,** Tanz.
122/C2 **Majītha,** India
81/F5 **Majolapass** (pass), Swi.
166/C2 **Majoli,** Sur.
183/K2 **Major,** Sk,Can
188/C2 **Major** (peak), Tx,US
171/L6 **Major Brigadeird Trompowsky** (arpt.), Braz.
77/G3 **Majorca** (Mallorca) (isl.), Sp.
149/E2 **Majrūr, Wādī** (dry riv.), Sudan
116/B3 **Mājuli,** India
92/D3 **Majur,** Yugo.
138/G4 **Majuro** (atoll), Mrsh.
138/G4 **Majuro** (cap.), Mrsh.
152/C3 **Makabana,** Congo
148/A5 **Makak,** Camr.
154/D4 **Makalamabedi,** Bots.
121/F2 **Makālu** (peak), China, Nepal
151/A4 **Makampi,** Tanz.
114/D2 **Makanchi,** Kaz.
156/E2 **Makapaanstad,** SAfr.
136/J9 **Makara** (riv.), N.Z.
148/B2 **Makari,** Camr.
194/D2 **Makaroff,** Mb,Can
109/N2 **Makarov,** Rus.
92/C4 **Makarska,** Cro.
95/J4 **Makar'yev,** Rus.
153/G5 **Makasa,** Zam.
126/E4 **Makassar** (str.), Indo.
97/K3 **Makat,** Kaz.
139/L6 **Makatea** (isl.), FrPol.
125/F6 **Makati,** Phil.
116/C3 **Makaw,** Burma
180/T10 **Makawao,** Hi,US
152/D3 **Makaya,** Zaire
157/H8 **Makay, Massif** (plat.), Madg.
139/L6 **Makemo** (atoll), FrPol.
180/T10 **Makena,** Hi,US
144/B4 **Makeni,** SLeo.
53/G4 **Makeyevka,** Ukr.
154/E4 **Makgadikgadi Pans** (salt pans), Bots.
154/E4 **Makgadikgadi Pans Game Rsv.,** Bots.
53/H4 **Makhachkala,** Rus.
97/J3 **Makhambet,** Kaz.
122/B2 **Makhdūmpur,** Pak.
105/F4 **Makhfar al Busayyah,** Iraq
105/E3 **Makhmūr,** Iraq
95/P4 **Makhnëvo,** Rus.
147/H2 **Makhrūq, Wādī al** (dry riv.), Jor.
127/G3 **Makian** (isl.), Indo.
153/G2 **Makilimbo,** Zaire
138/G4 **Makin** (isl.), Kiri.
194/E2 **Makinak,** Mb,Can
114/B1 **Makinsk,** Kaz.
106/C4 **Makkah** (Mecca), SAr.
179/L3 **Makkovik,** Nf,Can
66/C2 **Makkum,** Neth.
92/E2 **Makó,** Hun.
153/G2 **Makofi,** Zaire
152/C2 **Makokou,** Gabon
151/A4 **Makonde,** Tanz.
151/B4 **Makonde** (plat.), Tanz.
151/A4 **Makongolosi,** Tanz.
136/D2 **Makorako** (peak), N.Z.
153/G3 **Makota,** Ugan.
152/C2 **Makoua,** Congo
65/L2 **Maków Mazowiecki,** Pol.
91/H3 **Makrakómi,** Gre.
107/G4 **Makran** (coast), Iran, Pak.
107/H3 **Makran** (reg.), Iran, Pak.
107/K3 **Makrāna,** India
91/H2 **Makrokhórion,** Gre.
97/J1 **Maksimovka,** Rus.
120/A3 **Maksudangarh,** India
93/H5 **Maksutlu,** Turk.
142/C5 **Makteïr** (reg.), Mrta.
105/F2 **Mākū,** Iran
151/A4 **Makumbako,** Tanz.
153/E4 **Makumbi,** Zaire
117/H4 **Makung,** Tai.
154/E3 **Makunka,** Zam.
110/B5 **Makurazaki,** Japan
145/H5 **Makurdi,** Nga.
177/E5 **Makushin** (vol.), Ak,US
151/A1 **Makutano,** Kenya
151/B2 **Makuyuni,** Tanz.
121/E2 **Makwānpur Garhi,** Nepal
155/F3 **Makwiro,** Zim.
144/B2 **Mal,** Mrta.
62/C2 **Mæl,** Nor.
148/C4 **Mala,** CAfr.
160/E4 **Mala** (pt.), CR
161/G5 **Mala** (pt.), Pan.
168/B4 **Mala,** Peru
94/C2 **Mala,** Swe.
125/D4 **Malabang,** Phil.
118/B5 **Malabar** (coast), India
203/H3 **Malabar,** Fl,US
122/E3 **Malabar Coast** (reg.), India
76/G5 **Malabata** (pt.), Mor.
87/E3 **Malabergo,** It.
152/B2 **Malabo** (cap.), EqG.
125/E6 **Malabon,** Phil.
175/T12 **Mal Abrigo,** Uru.
125/B3 **Malabuñgan,** Phil.
171/E3 **Malacacheta,** Braz.
125/F6 **Malacanang Palace,** Phil.
123/B5 **Malacca** (str.), Malay., Thai.
73/B3 **Malacky,** Slvk.
185/G2 **Malad** (riv.), Id, Ut,US
185/G2 **Malad City,** Id,US
81/F4 **Maladers,** Swi.
152/D4 **Maladi-Mukedi,** Zaire
73/C1 **Malá Fatra** (mts.), Slvk.
76/C4 **Málaga,** Sp.
76/C4 **Málaga** (int'l arpt.), Sp.
204/F8 **Malaga** (cove), Ca,US
206/C4 **Malaga,** NJ,US
190/B4 **Malaga,** NM,US
153/G4 **Malagarasi,** Tanz.
153/G4 **Malagarasi** (riv.), Tanz.
76/D3 **Malagón,** Sp.
161/G1 **Malagueta** (bay), Cuba
60/D3 **Malahide,** Ire.
157/H8 **Malaimbandy,** Madg.
138/F5 **Malaita** (isl.), Sol.
149/F3 **Malakāl,** Sudan
118/D4 **Malakangiri,** India
120/A2 **Mālākhera,** India
189/F1 **Malakoff,** Tx,US
122/B1 **Malakwāl,** Pak.
131/G2 **Malalaua,** PNG
174/B3 **Malalhue,** Chile
164/C2 **Malambo,** Col.
124/F4 **Malang,** Indo.
140/D5 **Malange,** Ang.
121/E2 **Malangwa,** Nepal
152/D5 **Malanje,** Ang.
154/C1 **Malanje** (dist.), Ang.
152/D5 **Malanje** (prov.), Ang.
81/F4 **Malans,** Swi.
78/C5 **Malansac,** Fr.
145/F4 **Malanville,** Ben.
125/D4 **Malapatan,** Phil.
122/F3 **Malappuram,** India
107/H3 **Malār,** Pak.
63/R7 **Mälaren** (lake), Swe.
174/C2 **Malargüe,** Arg.
127/E5 **Malasoro** (pt.), Indo.
174/D5 **Malaspina,** Arg.
104/D2 **Malatya,** Turk.
104/D2 **Malatya** (prov.), Turk.
82/B4 **Malaucène,** Fr.
79/G1 **Malaunay,** Fr.
122/C2 **Malaut,** India
125/B4 **Malawali** (isl.), Malay.
140/F6 **Malawi**
155/G2 **Malawi** (Nyasa) (lake), Afr.
123/B5 **Malay** (pen.), Malay.
124/C1 **Malaya** (reg.), Malay.
102/K9 **Malaya** (state), Malay.
99/H4 **Malaya Belozërka,** Ukr.
98/G2 **Malaya Devitsa,** Ukr.
63/Q2 **Malaya Vishera,** Rus.
98/F3 **Malaya Viska,** Ukr.
125/D3 **Malaybalay,** Phil.
105/G3 **Malāyer,** Iran
126/C2 **Malaysia**
95/L2 **Malazemel'skaya** (tundra), Rus.
104/E2 **Malazgirt,** Turk.
196/B2 **Malbaie** (riv.), Qu,Can
145/G3 **Malbaza-Usine,** Niger
133/J2 **Malbon,** Austl.
65/K1 **Malbork,** Pol.
172/D4 **Malbrán,** Arg.
74/D5 **Malcaras, Pic de** (peak), Fr.
87/D1 **Malcesine,** It.
64/G2 **Malchin,** Ger.
108/C2 **Malchin,** Mong.
133/M8 **Malcolm** (cr.), Austl.
87/F2 **Malcontenta,** It.
68/C1 **Maldegem,** Belg.
139/K5 **Malden** (isl.), Kiri.
208/C1 **Malden,** Ma,US
200/C2 **Malden,** Mo,US
182/F4 **Malden,** Wa,US
118/B6 **Maldive** (isls.), Mald.
102/G9 **Maldives**
135/C3 **Maldon,** Austl.
59/G3 **Maldon,** Eng,UK
175/G2 **Maldonado,** Uru.
175/G2 **Maldonado** (dept.), Uru.
102/G9 **Male** (cap.), Mald.
51/N5 **Male** (isl.), Mald.
91/H4 **Maléa, Ákra** (cape), Gre.
152/C4 **Malebo** (Stanley) (pool), Congo, Zaire
118/B3 **Mālegaon,** India
149/F4 **Malek,** Sudan
73/B3 **Malé Karpaty** (mts.), Slvk.
105/F2 **Malek Kandī,** Iran
138/F6 **Malekula** (isl.), Van.
153/F5 **Malemba-Nkulu,** Zaire
74/D4 **Malemort-sur-Corrèze,** Fr.
64/F1 **Malente,** Ger.
134/D4 **Maleny,** Austl.
86/C2 **Maleo,** It.
122/C2 **Māler Kotla,** India
91/H3 **Malesina,** Gre.
78/C5 **Malestroit,** Fr.
200/C3 **Malesus,** Tn,US
83/A5 **Malfa,** It.
151/B1 **Malgis** (dry riv.), Kenya
97/H4 **Malgobek,** Rus.
77/G2 **Malgrat de Mar,** Sp.
86/C1 **Malgrate,** It.
149/E2 **Malha Wells,** Sudan
184/D2 **Malheur** (lake), Or,US
184/E2 **Malheur** (riv.), Or,US
157/S14 **Malheureux** (cape), Mrts.
184/D2 **Malheur Nat'l Wild. Ref.,** Or,US
140/B3 **Mali**
123/B3 **Mali** (isl.), Burma
144/B3 **Mali,** Gui.
153/F3 **Mali,** Zaire
91/J5 **Mália,** Gre.
108/F4 **Malian** (riv.), China
108/E3 **Malianjing,** China
204/B2 **Malibu,** Ca,US
79/E5 **Malicorne-sur-Sarthe,** Fr.
142/E4 **Maligat Barani** (well), Alg.
120/C2 **Malīhābād,** India
82/C4 **Malijai,** Fr.
126/D4 **Maliku,** Indo.
127/F4 **Maliku,** Indo.
62/F3 **Målilla,** Swe.
92/B3 **Mali Lošinj,** Cro.
172/B4 **Malimán de Abajo,** Arg.
124/C1 **Malim Nawar,** Malay.
117/F3 **Malin,** China
56/A1 **Malin,** Ire.
98/E2 **Malin,** Ukr.
184/C2 **Malin,** Or,US
73/A3 **Malina** (riv.), Slvk.
125/B5 **Malinau,** Indo.
125/C3 **Malindang** (mtn.), Phil.
151/C2 **Malindi,** Kenya
68/D1 **Malines** (Mechelen), Belg.
152/C3 **Malinga,** Gabon
115/C3 **Maling Guan** (pass), China
124/D4 **Malingping,** Indo.
55/H9 **Malin Head** (pt.), Ire.
114/E1 **Malinovka,** Rus.
99/M2 **Malinovka,** Rus.
82/D4 **Malinvern** (mtn.), Fr.
151/B4 **Malinyi,** Tanz.
157/H8 **Malio** (riv.), Madg.
123/D1 **Malipo,** China
107/J4 **Malīr Cantonment,** Pak.
82/A3 **Malissard,** Fr.
125/D4 **Malita,** Phil.
143/H2 **Malītah,** Tun.
123/B4 **Maliwun,** Burma
150/B4 **Malka Mari Nat'l Park,** Kenya
93/H5 **Malkara,** Turk.
93/H5 **Malko Tŭrnovo,** Bul.
135/D3 **Mallacoota,** Austl.
55/J8 **Mallaig,** Sc,UK
145/H3 **Mallammaduri,** Nga.
120/C2 **Mallānwān,** India
141/W17 **Mallāq** (riv.), Tun.
88/F3 **Mallaq, Wādī** (riv.), Tun.
63/K1 **Mallasvesi** (lake), Fin.
147/F3 **Mallawī,** Egypt
133/J5 **Mallee Cliffs Nat'l Park,** Austl.
76/E2 **Mallén,** Sp.
80/D3 **Malleray,** Swi.
81/F5 **Mallero** (riv.), It.
71/F5 **Mallersdorf-Pfaffenberg,** Ger.
81/G4 **Malles** (Mals), It.
174/B5 **Mallín Grande,** Chile
174/Q10 **Malloa,** Chile
77/G3 **Mallorca** (Majorca) (isl.), Sp.
203/G3 **Mallory** (swamp), Fl,US
60/B5 **Mallow,** Ire.
56/B2 **Mallusk,** Ire.
166/C1 **Malmanoury,** FrG.
61/G2 **Malmberget,** Swe.
69/F3 **Malmédy,** Belg.
156/B4 **Malmesbury,** SAfr.
58/D3 **Malmesbury,** Eng,UK
62/G2 **Malmköping,** Swe.
62/E4 **Malmö,** Swe.
62/E4 **Malmöhus** (co.), Swe.
162/D4 **Malmok** (peak), NAnt.
62/F2 **Malmslätt,** Swe.
183/J4 **Malmstrom A.F.B.,** Mt,US
95/L4 **Malmyzh,** Rus.
86/B1 **Malnate,** It.
87/E1 **Malo,** It.
182/E3 **Malo,** Wa,US
99/J1 **Maloarkhangel'sk,** Rus.
166/C4 **Maloca,** Braz.
138/G4 **Maloelap** (atoll), Mrsh.
125/E6 **Malolos,** Phil.
155/G2 **Malombe** (lake), Malw.
86/A2 **Malone** (riv.), It.
203/F2 **Malone,** Fl,US
199/J2 **Malone,** NY,US
189/F2 **Malone,** Tx,US
116/D3 **Malong,** China
153/E4 **Malonga,** Zaire
153/E5 **Malonga,** Zaire
153/G5 **Malonje** (peak), Tanz.
81/G5 **Malonno,** It.
65/L3 **Mał opolska** (upland), Pol.
65/N3 **Malorita,** Bela.
61/C3 **Måløy,** Nor.
94/H5 **Maloyaroslavets,** Rus.
190/A4 **Malpais, The** (lava flow), NM,US
76/B3 **Malpartida de Cáceres,** Sp.
76/B3 **Malpartida de Plasencia,** Sp.
57/F5 **Malpas,** Eng,UK
163/A2 **Malpelo** (isl.), Col.
86/B1 **Malpensa** (int'l arpt.), It.
196/F2 **Malpeque** (bay), PE,Can
76/A1 **Malpica,** Sp.
71/H5 **Malsch** (riv.), Aus.
70/B5 **Malsch,** Ger.
71/H5 **Malše** (riv.), Czh.
81/G4 **Mals** (Malles), It.
84/H8 **Malta**
167/G4 **Malta,** Braz.
63/M3 **Malta,** Lat.
84/H7 **Malta** (chan.), Malta
84/H8 **Malta** (isl.), Malta
185/G2 **Malta,** Id,US
183/L3 **Malta,** Mt,US
198/F5 **Malta,** Oh,US
154/C5 **Maltahöhe,** Namb.
148/B2 **Maltam,** Camr.
57/G2 **Maltby,** Eng,UK
57/G5 **Maltby,** Eng,UK
136/C3 **Malte Brun** (peak), N.Z.
104/B1 **Maltepe,** Turk.
80/E3 **Malters,** Swi.
197/R8 **Malton,** On,Can
57/H3 **Malton,** Eng,UK
108/F5 **Malu,** China
130/C1 **Maluku** (prov.), Indo.
152/C4 **Maluku,** Zaire
153/F3 **Malumba,** Zaire
62/E1 **Malung,** Swe.
125/C4 **Maluso,** Phil.
149/G3 **Malūt,** Sudan
81/E5 **Malvaglia,** Swi.
118/B4 **Malvan,** India
77/P10 **Malveira,** Port.
135/G5 **Malvern,** Austl.
203/F2 **Malvern,** Al,US
191/H3 **Malvern,** Ar,US
193/G3 **Malvern,** Ia,US
208/F6 **Malvern,** Oh,US
206/C3 **Malvern,** Pa,US
207/L9 **Malverne,** NY,US
58/D2 **Malvern** (Great Malvern), Eng,UK
175/M8 **Malvinas, Islas** (Falkland Is.), UK
175/M8 **Malvinas, Islas** (Falkland Islands) (dpcy.), UK
72/E4 **Malxe** (riv.), Ger.
73/B3 **Malý Dunaj** (riv.), Slvk
95/P4 **Malysheva,** Rus.
97/J2 **Malyy Uzen'** (riv.), Ka
108/D1 **Malyy Yenisey** (riv.), Rus.
69/F6 **Malzéville,** Fr.
101/M4 **Mama,** Rus.
167/H4 **Mamanguape,** Braz.
207/E2 **Mamaroneck,** NY,US
103/C4 **Mamarr al Jady** (Gidi (pass), Egypt
103/C4 **Mamarr Mitlah** (Mitla (pass), Egypt
155/E3 **Mamba,** Zam.
125/D3 **Mambajao,** Phil.
151/A3 **Mambali,** Tanz.
131/G2 **Mambare** (riv.), PNG
153/G2 **Mambasa,** Zaire
127/J4 **Mamberamo** (riv.), Indo.
152/D2 **Mambéré** (riv.), CAfr.
104/D2 **Mambij,** Syria
152/C2 **Mambili** (riv.), Congo
144/B4 **Mambiya,** Gui.
173/F3 **Mamborê,** Braz.
154/E3 **Mambova,** Zam.
151/C2 **Mambrui,** Kenya
153/F2 **Mambunga,** Zaire
125/C2 **Mamburao,** Phil.
97/J4 **Mamedkala,** Rus.
69/F4 **Mamer,** Lux.
79/F4 **Mamers,** Fr.
68/B2 **Mametz,** Fr.
145/H5 **Mamfé,** Camr.
80/C3 **Mamirolle,** Fr.
95/R5 **Mamlyutka,** Kaz.
70/E6 **Mammendorf,** Ger.
71/F5 **Mamming,** Ger.
83/C6 **Mammola,** It.
187/G4 **Mammoth,** Az,US
200/D2 **Mammoth Cave Nat'l Park,** Ky,US
186/C2 **Mammoth Lakes,** Ca,US
192/C2 **Mammoth Site,** SD,US
191/J2 **Mammoth Spring,** Ar,US
63/H4 **Mamonovo,** Rus.
169/E3 **Mamore** (riv.), Bol., Braz.
144/B4 **Mamou,** Gui.
202/B2 **Mamou,** La,US
157/H6 **Mamoutzou,** May.
157/H7 **Mampikony,** Madg.
152/D2 **Mampoko,** Zaire
145/E5 **Mampong,** Gha.
63/J4 **Mamry** (lake), Pol.
127/E4 **Mamuju,** Indo.
188/D4 **Mamulique,** Mex.
105/G3 **Ma'mūnīyeh,** Iran
154/D4 **Mamuno,** Bots.
169/G1 **Mamuru** (riv.), Braz.
151/B3 **Mamwera** (peak), Tanz.
115/C5 **Man** (riv.), China
144/D5 **Man,** IvC.
55/J9 **Man** (isl.), UK
166/C1 **Mana,** FrG.
165/H3 **Mana** (riv.), FrG.
136/H9 **Mana** (isl.), N.Z.
164/A5 **Manabí** (prov.), Ecu.
160/D3 **Manabique, Punta de** (pt.), Hon.
166/A3 **Manacapuru,** Braz.
166/A3 **Manacapuru** (lake), Braz.
58/A6 **Manacle** (pt.), UK
77/G3 **Manacor,** Sp.
127/F3 **Manado,** Indo.
68/D3 **Manage,** Belg.
160/E3 **Managua** (cap.), Nic.
160/E3 **Managua** (lake), Nic.
207/D4 **Manahawkin,** NJ,US
136/C2 **Manaia,** N.Z.
157/J7 **Manakambahiny,** Madg.
141/G7 **Manakara,** Madg.
150/B2 **Manākhah,** Yem.
206/D3 **Manalapan,** NJ,US
122/D1 **Manāli,** India
106/F3 **Manama** (Al Manāmah) (cap.), Bahr.
122/G4 **Mānāmadurai,** India
157/H7 **Manambaho** (riv.), Madg.
157/H8 **Manandantanana** (riv.), Madg.
141/G6 **Mananara,** Madg.
157/H8 **Mananara** (riv.), Madg
157/J7 **Mananara** (riv.), Madg
157/H7 **Manandaza,** Madg.
157/H8 **Manandona,** Madg.
120/E1 **Manangbhot,** Nepal
141/G7 **Mananjary,** Madg.
157/H8 **Mananjary** (riv.), Madg.
144/D4 **Manankoro,** Mali
122/F3 **Mānantavādi,** India
157/H9 **Manantenina,** Madg.
175/K8 **Manantiales,** Chile
167/O8 **Manapire** (riv.), Ven.
155/F2 **Mana Pools Nat'l Park,** Zim.
122/G3 **Manappārai,** India
157/H7 **Manarantsandry,** Madg.
86/C4 **Manara, Punta** (pt.), It
114/E3 **Manas,** China
114/D2 **Manas** (lake), China
114/E3 **Manas** (riv.), China
121/H2 **Manās** (riv.), India
150/B5 **Manas,** Som.
121/E1 **Manāslu** (mtn.), Nepa
207/D3 **Manasquan,** NJ,US
207/D3 **Manasquan** (riv.), NJ,US
190/B2 **Manassa,** Co,US
201/J1 **Manassas,** Va,US
201/J1 **Manassas Nat'l Bfld. Park,** Va,US
91/G1 **Manastir Dečani,** Yugo.
91/G1 **Manastir Gračanica,** Yugo.
91/G1 **Manastir Sopoćani,** Yugo.
130/B2 **Manatang,** Indo.
202/L8 **Manatee** (co.), Fl,US
203/G4 **Manatee** (lake), Fl,US

111/H7 **Manatsuru**, Japan
130/B2 **Manatuto**, Indo.
131/G2 **Manau**, PNG
123/B3 **Manaung**, Burma
166/A3 **Manaus**, Braz.
103/B1 **Manavgat**, Turk.
193/K1 **Manawa**, Wi,US
118/C3 **Manāwar**, India
136/D3 **Manawatu** (reg.), N.Z.
125/D4 **Manay**, Phil.
168/D4 **Mañazo**, Peru
111/H7 **Manazuru-misaki** (cape), Japan
121/F4 **Mānbāzār**, India
56/D3 **Man, Calf of** (isl.), IM,UK
80/B2 **Mance** (riv.), Fr.
198/D2 **Mancelona**, Mi,US
76/D4 **Mancha Real**, Sp.
208/C1 **Manchaug**, Ma,US
78/D2 **Manche** (dept.), Fr.
115/C3 **Mancheng**, China
118/C4 **Mancherāl**, India
134/E6 **Manchester** (lake), Austl.
57/F5 **Manchester**, Eng,UK
200/D4 **Manchester**, Al,US
208/B2 **Manchester**, Ct,US
200/E4 **Manchester**, Ga,US
193/J2 **Manchester**, Ia,US
191/J1 **Manchester**, Il,US
200/F2 **Manchester**, Ky,US
206/B4 **Manchester**, Md,US
198/D3 **Manchester**, Mi,US
199/L3 **Manchester**, NH,US
200/F1 **Manchester**, Oh,US
191/E2 **Manchester**, Ok,US
206/B3 **Manchester**, Pa,US
200/D3 **Manchester**, Tn,US
199/K3 **Manchester**, Vt,US
205/B2 **Manchester**, Wa,US
57/F5 **Manchester** (Ringway) (int'l arpt.), Eng,UK
113/B2 **Manchuria** (reg.), China
84/B2 **Manciano**, It.
69/E5 **Mancieulles**, Fr.
168/A2 **Máncora**, Peru
187/H2 **Mancos**, Co,US
187/H2 **Mancos** (riv.), Co,US
120/D4 **Mand** (riv.), India
105/H4 **Mand** (riv.), Iran
107/H3 **Mand**, Pak.
121/G3 **Mānda**, Bang.
148/C3 **Manda**, Chad
149/E3 **Manda** (peak), Sudan
153/H4 **Manda**, Tanz.
153/H5 **Manda**, Tanz.
157/H8 **Mandabe**, Madg.
170/C4 **Mandaguari**, Braz.
118/B3 **Mandal**, India
62/B2 **Mandal**, Nor.
127/K4 **Mandala** (peak), Indo.
116/C4 **Mandalay**, Burma
123/A1 **Mandalay** (div.), Burma
116/C4 **Mandalay Palace**, Burma
101/L5 **Mandalgovĭ**, Mong.
105/F3 **Mandalī**, Iraq
108/E3 **Mandal-Ovoo**, Mong.
125/E6 **Mandaluyong**, Phil.
194/D4 **Mandan**, ND,US
148/C3 **Manda Nat'l Park**, Chad
115/D4 **Mandang Shan** (mtn.), China
122/G4 **Mandapam**, India
148/B3 **Mandara** (mts.), Camr., CAfr.
127/F5 **Mandasavu** (peak), Indo.
83/C4 **Mandatoriccio**, It.
125/C3 **Mandaue**, Phil.
120/B1 **Mandāwar**, India
82/C5 **Mandelieu-la-Napoule**, Fr.
86/C1 **Mandello del Lario**, It.
150/B5 **Mandera**, Kenya
151/B3 **Mandera**, Tanz.
69/F3 **Manderscheid**, Ger.
185/K1 **Manderson**, Wy,US
80/C3 **Mandeure**, Fr.
161/G2 **Mandeville**, Jam.
202/C2 **Mandeville**, La,US
122/D2 **Māndi**, India
157/J7 **Mandialaza**, Madg.
144/C4 **Mandiana**, Gui.
122/B2 **Mandi Būrewāla**, Pak.
155/G3 **Mandié**, Moz.
155/G2 **Mandimba**, Moz.
127/G4 **Mandiola** (isl.), Indo.
121/E4 **Mandira** (res.), India
122/B2 **Mandi Sādiqganj**, Pak.
153/G4 **Mandje**, Zaire
152/B3 **Mandji**, Gabon
120/C4 **Mandla**, India
62/C4 **Mandø** (isl.), Den.
145/G4 **Mando**, Nga.
152/B2 **Mandoc** (falls), EqG.
98/B3 **Mándok**, Hun.
157/H7 **Mandoto**, Madg.
91/H3 **Mandoúdhion**, Gre.
145/F4 **Mandouri**, Togo
91/L6 **Mándra**, Gre.
157/H9 **Mandrare** (riv.), Madg.
157/J6 **Mandritsara**, Madg.
157/H8 **Mandronarivo**, Madg.
157/H8 **Mandrosonoro**, Madg.
118/C3 **Mandsaur**, India
126/D4 **Mandumai**, Indo.
132/B5 **Mandurah**, Austl.
91/E2 **Manduria**, It.
118/A3 **Māndvi**, India
118/C5 **Mandya**, India
82/B5 **Mane**, Fr.
120/D1 **Mane** (pass), Nepal
59/G2 **Manea**, Eng,UK
120/D4 **Manendragarh**, India
145/H5 **Manéngouba, Massif du** (peak), Camr.
121/E3 **Maner**, India
86/D2 **Manerbio**, It.
98/C2 **Manevichi**, Ukr.
104/B5 **Manfalūt**, Egypt
194/E4 **Manfred**, ND,US
85/F4 **Manfredonia**, It.
85/G4 **Manfredonia** (gulf), It.
115/B4 **Mang** (riv.), China
170/E2 **Manga**, Braz.
145/E4 **Manga**, Burk.
148/B2 **Manga** (reg.), Chad, Niger
170/D1 **Mangabeiras** (hills), Braz.
152/C4 **Manga Grande**, Ang.
152/D4 **Mangai**, Zaire
139/K7 **Mangaia** (isl.), CookIs.
136/C2 **Mangakino**, N.Z.
121/J2 **Mangaldai**, India
125/C1 **Mangaldan**, Phil.
93/J4 **Mangalia**, Rom.
151/B3 **Mangalisa** (peak), Tanz.
148/C2 **Mangalmé**, Chad
118/B5 **Mangalore**, India
157/H7 **Mangamila**, Madg.
153/E2 **Mangania**, Zaire
125/D5 **Mangarang**, Indo.
171/M7 **Mangaratiba**, Braz.
139/M7 **Mangareva** (isl.), FrPol.
136/C2 **Mangaweka**, N.Z.
117/E3 **Mangchang**, China
144/B4 **Mange**, SLeo.
148/D3 **Mangeigne**, Chad
152/C4 **Mangembo**, Zaire
121/G2 **Mangen**, India
62/A1 **Manger**, Nor.
60/A6 **Mangerton** (mtn.), Ire.
202/C1 **Mangham**, La,US
116/B4 **Mangin** (range), Burma
97/K4 **Mangistauz Obl.**, Kaz.
127/E3 **Mangkalihat** (cape), Indo.
122/B1 **Mangla**, Pak.
122/B1 **Mangla** (dam), Pak.
122/B1 **Mangla** (res.), Pak.
168/A1 **Manglaralto**, Ecu.
164/B4 **Manglares** (pt.), Col.
120/A1 **Manglaur**, India
132/K7 **Mangles** (bay), Austl.
108/C4 **Mangnai**, China
145/F4 **Mango**, Togo
202/L8 **Mango**, Fl,US
155/G2 **Mangoche**, Malw.
157/H8 **Mangoky** (riv.), Madg.
127/G4 **Mangole** (isl.), Indo.
153/F3 **Mangombe**, Zaire
136/C1 **Mangonui**, N.Z.
157/J7 **Mangoro** (riv.), Madg.
58/D4 **Mangotsfield**, Eng,UK
118/B3 **Māngrol**, India
76/B2 **Mangualde**, Port.
175/G2 **Mangueira** (lake), Braz.
152/B3 **Manguéné**, Gabon
146/B4 **Mangueni** (plat.), Niger
109/J1 **Mangui**, China
190/E3 **Mangum**, Ok,US
153/G2 **Manguredjipa**, Zaire
155/F4 **Mangwe**, Zim.
113/C3 **Man'gyŏngdae**, NKor.
97/J4 **Mangyshlak**, Kaz.
97/J3 **Mangyshlak** (pen.), Kaz.
97/K4 **Mangyshlak** (plat.), Kaz.
108/C2 **Manhan**, Mong.
207/L8 **Manhasset**, NY,US
207/L8 **Manhasset** (bay), NY,US
191/F1 **Manhattan**, Ks,US
183/J5 **Manhattan**, Mt,US
184/E4 **Manhattan**, Nv,US
207/J9 **Manhattan** (isl.), NY,US
204/B3 **Manhattan Beach**, Ca,US
69/E3 **Manhay**, Belg.
206/B3 **Manheim**, Pa,US
155/G5 **Manhiça**, Moz.
123/B1 **Man Hpang**, Burma
171/E4 **Manhuaçu**, Braz.
171/E4 **Manhumirim**, Braz.
91/H4 **Máni** (pen.), Gre.
157/H7 **Mania** (riv.), Madg.
155/G2 **Maniamba**, Moz.
152/C4 **Manianga**, Zaire
120/C4 **Maniāri** (riv.), India
155/G3 **Manica**, Moz.
155/G3 **Manica** (prov.), Moz.
155/F3 **Manicaland** (prov.), Zim.
196/C1 **Manic-Deux** (dam), Qu,Can
166/A4 **Manicoré**, Braz.
166/A4 **Manicoré** (riv.), Braz.
179/K3 **Manicouagan** (res.), Qu,Can
179/K3 **Manicouagan** (riv.), Qu,Can
134/C3 **Manifold** (cape), Austl.
116/C2 **Maniganggo**, China
194/F2 **Manigotagan**, Mb,Can
121/F3 **Manihāri**, India
139/L6 **Manihi** (isl.), FrPol.
139/J6 **Manihiki** (isl.), CookIs.
121/G3 **Manikarchar**, India
121/G4 **Mānikganj**, Bang.
125/C2 **Manila** (bay), Phil.
125/C2 **Manila** (cap.), Phil.
200/B3 **Manila**, Ar,US
185/J3 **Manila**, Ut,US
135/D1 **Manilla**, Austl.
193/G3 **Manilla**, Ia,US
144/D3 **Manimpé**, Mali
165/E3 **Maniña**, Ven.
157/J7 **Maningory** (riv.), Madg.
130/D3 **Maningrida**, Austl.
124/C3 **Maninjau** (lake), Indo.
127/G4 **Manipa** (str.), Indo.
120/D4 **Manipat** (hills), India
116/B3 **Manipur** (state), India
104/A2 **Manisa**, Turk.
104/B2 **Manisa** (prov.), Turk.
88/C3 **Manises**, Sp.
56/D3 **Man, Isle of** (isl.), UK
198/C2 **Manistee**, Mi,US
198/C2 **Manistique**, Mi,US
198/D1 **Manistique** (lake), Mi,US
183/K1 **Manito** (lake), Sk,Can
193/K3 **Manito**, Il,US
178/F3 **Manitoba** (prov.), Can.
194/E2 **Manitoba** (lake), Mb,Can
195/L4 **Manitou** (isl.), Mi,US
190/E3 **Manitou**, Ok,US
198/E2 **Manitoulin** (isl.), On,Can
192/B4 **Manitou Springs**, Co,US
195/M3 **Manitouwadge**, On,Can
198/F2 **Manitowaning**, On,Can
195/J4 **Manitowish**, Wi,US
193/L1 **Manitowoc**, Wi,US
170/B1 **Manitsauá-Missu** (riv.), Braz.
199/J1 **Maniwaki**, Qu,Can
199/H1 **Maniwaki Ind. Res.**, Qu,Can
164/C3 **Manizales**, Col.
157/H8 **Manja**, Madg.
155/G5 **Manjacaze**, Moz.
157/J7 **Manjakandriana**, Madg.
122/F3 **Manjeri**, India
113/D2 **Manjiang**, China
105/G2 **Manjīl**, Iran
132/C5 **Manjimup**, Austl.
118/C4 **Manjlegaon**, India
107/L5 **Mānjra** (riv.), India
191/E1 **Mankato**, Ks,US
193/H1 **Mankato**, Mn,US
155/F5 **Mankayane**, Swaz.
122/A2 **Mankera**, Pak.
148/A4 **Manki II**, Camr.
148/B4 **Mankim**, Camr.
144/D4 **Mankono**, IvC.
183/L3 **Mankota**, Sk,Can
122/H4 **Mankulam**, SrL.
108/F3 **Manlay**, Mong.
177/H2 **Manley Hot Springs**, Ak,US
199/J3 **Manlius**, NY,US
76/D2 **Manlleu**, Sp.
134/H8 **Manly**, Austl.
193/H2 **Manly**, Ia,US
118/B3 **Manmād**, India
117/J5 **Manmanoc** (mtn.), Phil.
123/B4 **Man Mia** (peak), Thai.
116/C3 **Mān Ming**, Burma
124/C4 **Manna**, Indo.
133/J5 **Mannahill**, Austl.
122/G4 **Mannar** (gulf), India, SrL.
122/G4 **Mannar**, SrL.
122/H4 **Mannar** (dist.), SrL.
122/G4 **Mannar** (isl.), SrL.
122/G3 **Mannārgudi**, India
81/E3 **Männedorf**, Swi.
73/A4 **Mannersdorf am Leithagebirge**, Aus.
73/A5 **Mannersdorf an der Rabnitz**, Aus.
156/C4 **Mannetjiesberg** (peak), SAfr.
191/F2 **Mannford**, Ok,US
70/B4 **Mannheim**, Ger.
70/B4 **Mannheim** (Neu-Ostheim) (arpt.), Ger.
178/E3 **Manning**, Ab,Can
179/Q7 **Manning** (cape), NW,Can
191/H3 **Manning**, Ar,US
193/G3 **Manning**, Ia,US
192/D4 **Manning**, Ks,US
194/C4 **Manning**, ND,US
201/G4 **Manning**, SC,US
182/D3 **Manning Park**, BC,Can
201/G1 **Mannington**, WV,US
206/C4 **Mannington Meadow** (lake), NJ,US
59/H3 **Manningtree**, Eng,UK
80/D4 **Männlifluh** (peak), Swi.
199/H3 **Mannsville**, NY,US
90/A2 **Mannu** (riv.), It.
90/A3 **Mannu** (riv.), It.
133/H5 **Mannum**, Austl.
183/J1 **Mannville**, Ab,Can
144/C5 **Mano** (riv.), Libr., SLeo.
169/E3 **Manoa**, Bol.
177/G4 **Manokotak**, Ak,US
138/C5 **Manokwari**, Indo.
157/G8 **Manombo**, Madg.
157/J7 **Manompana**, Madg.
153/F4 **Manono**, Zaire
153/F4 **Manonwa**, Zaire
85/E3 **Manoppello**, It.
203/G2 **Manor**, Ga,US
189/F2 **Manor**, Tx,US
55/G9 **Manor Hamilton**, Ire.
207/F2 **Manorville**, NY,US
82/B5 **Manosque**, Fr.
113/D2 **Manp'o**, NKor.
139/H5 **Manra** (Sydney) (isl.), Kiri.
77/F2 **Manresa**, Sp.
155/F1 **Mansa**, Zam.
144/B3 **Mansa Konko**, Gam.
125/C2 **Mansalay**, Phil.
119/G3 **Mān Sam**, Burma
179/H2 **Mansel** (isl.), NW,Can
72/B4 **Mansfeld**, Ger.
135/C3 **Mansfield**, Austl.
57/G5 **Mansfield**, Eng,UK
191/G3 **Mansfield**, Ar,US
198/B4 **Mansfield**, Il,US
202/B1 **Mansfield**, La,US
208/C1 **Mansfield**, Ma,US
208/E6 **Mansfield**, Oh,US
199/H4 **Mansfield**, Pa,US
192/E1 **Mansfield**, SD,US
189/F1 **Mansfield**, Tx,US
189/F2 **Mansfield** (dam), Tx,US
199/K2 **Mansfield** (mtn.), Vt,US
182/E4 **Mansfield**, Wa,US
208/B2 **Mansfield Hollow** (dam), Ct,US
208/E6 **Mansfield Lahm** (mun. arpt.), Oh,US
57/G5 **Mansfield Woodhouse**, Eng,UK
119/G3 **Mān Si**, Burma
76/C1 **Mansilla de las Mulas**, Sp.
144/B3 **Mansôa**, GBis.
193/G2 **Manson**, Ia,US
202/B2 **Mansura**, La,US
164/A5 **Manta**, Ecu.
86/A3 **Manta**, It.
200/C3 **Mantachie**, Ms,US
121/H3 **Mantala**, Bang.
125/B3 **Mantalingajan** (mtn.), Phil.
152/E3 **Mantantale**, Zaire
151/A2 **Mantare**, Tanz.
183/K2 **Mantario**, Sk,Can
168/C3 **Mantaro** (riv.), Peru
186/B2 **Manteca**, Ca,US
164/D3 **Mantecal**, Ven.
165/E3 **Mantecal**, Ven.
200/C4 **Mantee**, Ms,US
76/B2 **Manteigas**, Port.
171/E3 **Mantena**, Braz.
198/C4 **Manteno**, Il,US
201/K3 **Manteo**, NC,US
190/D2 **Manter**, Ks,US
68/A6 **Mantes-la-Jolie**, Fr.
68/A6 **Mantes-la-Ville**, Fr.
116/C3 **Mān Tha**, Burma
118/C4 **Manthani**, India
185/H4 **Manti**, Ut,US
170/D4 **Mantiqueira** (mts.), Braz.
198/D2 **Manton**, Mi,US
208/C2 **Manton**, RI,US
62/F2 **Mantorp**, Swe.
193/H1 **Mantorville**, Mn,US
172/B2 **Mantos Blancos**, Chile
115/C3 **Mantou Shan** (mtn.), China
87/D2 **Mantova**, It.
86/D2 **Mantova** (prov.), It.
63/L1 **Mäntsalä**, Fin.
161/E1 **Mantua**, Cuba
206/C4 **Mantua**, NJ,US
208/F5 **Mantua**, Oh,US
95/K4 **Manturovo**, Rus.
63/M1 **Mäntyharju**, Fin.
63/J1 **Mäntyluoto**, Fin.
121/H3 **Manu** (riv.), Bang.
168/D4 **Manú**, Peru
168/D3 **Manu** (riv.), Peru
139/J6 **Manua** (isls.), ASam.
139/K6 **Manuae** (atoll), CookIs.
170/C1 **Manuel Alves da Natividade** (riv.), Braz.
188/B3 **Manuel Benavides**, Mex.
187/H3 **Manuelito**, NM,US
105/J5 **Manūjān**, Iran
124/E4 **Manuk** (riv.), Indo.
125/C3 **Manukan**, Phil.
136/C2 **Manukau**, N.Z.
136/F7 **Manukau** (har.), N.Z.
60/A2 **Manulla**, Ire.
130/D1 **Manumbai** (riv.), Indo.
206/D5 **Manumuskin** (riv.), NJ,US
168/C3 **Manú Nat'l Park**, Peru
168/D3 **Manuripe** (riv.), Bol., Peru
169/E3 **Manuripe Heath Amazonica Nat'l Rsv.**, Bol.
138/D5 **Manus** (isl.), PNG
136/D2 **Manutuke**, N.Z.
194/F3 **Manvel**, ND,US
189/M9 **Manvel**, Tx,US
206/D2 **Manville**, NJ,US
192/B2 **Manville**, Wy,US
116/C3 **Mān Wein**, Burma
202/B2 **Many**, La,US
155/F3 **Manyame** (riv.), Zim.
152/C4 **Manyanga**, Congo
151/A2 **Manyara** (lake), Tanz.
183/J3 **Manyberries**, Ab,Can
99/L4 **Manych** (riv.), Rus.
99/M4 **Manych-Gudilo** (lake), Rus.
187/H2 **Many Farms**, Az,US
151/A3 **Manyoni**, Tanz.
122/A1 **Manzai**, Pak.
174/C3 **Manzanar**, Chile
167/K6 **Manzanares**, Col.
76/D3 **Manzanares**, Sp.
77/N8 **Manzanares** (riv.), Sp.
161/G1 **Manzanillo**, Cuba
158/D5 **Manzanillo**, Mex.
158/D5 **Manzanillo** (int'l arpt.), Mex.
161/F4 **Manzanillo-Gandoca Nat'l Wild. Ref.**, CR
182/C5 **Manzanita**, Or,US
186/D4 **Manzanita Ind. Res.**, Ca,US
87/G1 **Manzano**, It.
187/J3 **Manzano**, NM,US
190/A3 **Manzano** (peak), NM,US
190/C1 **Manzanola**, Co,US
153/G4 **Manzanza**, Zaire
109/H2 **Manzhouli**, China
84/C3 **Manziana**, It.
80/A5 **Manziat**, Fr.
147/G2 **Manzilah, Buḩayat al** (lake), Egypt
141/X17 **Manzil Bū Zalafah**, Tun.
157/E2 **Manzini**, Swaz.
157/E2 **Manzini** (Matsapa) (int'l arpt.), Swaz.
148/B2 **Mao**, Chad
162/D3 **Mao**, DRep.
119/J2 **Maoba**, China
117/F1 **Maobaguan**, China
113/C2 **Maodianzi**, China
116/D1 **Mao'ergai**, China
108/F4 **Maojing**, China
127/J4 **Maoke** (mts.), Indo.
117/F4 **Maoming**, China
108/D4 **Maoniushan**, China
115/H6 **Maoshan**, China
116/B3 **Mao Songsang**, India
108/F5 **Maotian**, China
116/D3 **Maotou** (peak), China
116/D2 **Maowen Qiangzu Zizhixian**, China
117/H3 **Maoyang**, China
115/H7 **Maozhou**, China
155/F4 **Mapai**, Moz.
114/D5 **Mapam** (lake), China
127/F4 **Mapane**, Indo.
160/C3 **Mapastepec**, Mex.
131/E1 **Mapi** (riv.), Indo.
127/J4 **Mapia**, Indo.
158/E3 **Mapimí**, Mex.
158/D3 **Mapimí** (depr.), Mex.
165/E3 **Mapire**, Ven.
169/D4 **Mapiri**, Bol.
169/E3 **Mapiri**, Bol.
197/R8 **Maple**, On,Can
187/H4 **Maple** (peak), Az,US
193/G2 **Maple** (riv.), Ia,US
183/K3 **Maple Creek**, Sk,Can
197/N7 **Maple Grove**, Qu,Can
195/H5 **Maple Grove**, Mn,US
195/P6 **Maple Grove**, Mn,US
208/F5 **Maple Heights**, Oh,US
191/F1 **Maple Hill**, Ks,US
205/N16 **Maple Park**, Il,US
198/D3 **Maple Rapids**, Mi,US
182/C3 **Maple Ridge**, BC,Can
194/E4 **Maple River Nat'l Wild. Ref.**, ND,US
191/J2 **Maples**, Mo,US
206/D4 **Maple Shade**, NJ,US
200/D4 **Maplesville**, Al,US
193/G2 **Mapleton**, Ia,US
196/C2 **Mapleton**, Me,US
193/H2 **Mapleton**, Mn,US
184/B1 **Mapleton**, Or,US
185/H3 **Mapleton**, Ut,US
205/C3 **Maple Valley**, Wa,US
208/C2 **Mapleville**, RI,US
195/P6 **Maplewood**, Mn,US
207/D2 **Maplewood**, NJ,US
198/C2 **Maplewood**, Wi,US
113/F6 **Map'o**, SKor.
131/F2 **Mapoon Abor. Rsv.**, Austl.
131/F2 **Mapoon Mission Sta.**, Austl.
164/D3 **Maporal**, Ven.
201/K2 **Mappsville**, Va,US
165/G5 **Mapuera** (riv.), Braz.
157/E3 **Mapumolo**, SAfr.
118/B4 **Mapusa**, India
157/F2 **Maputa**, SAfr.
155/G5 **Maputo** (cap.), Moz.
155/G5 **Maputo** (int'l arpt.), Moz.
155/G5 **Maputo** (prov.), Moz.
155/G5 **Maputo** (riv.), Moz.
147/H5 **Maqdam, Ras** (cape), Sudan
108/D5 **Maqên**, China
104/C4 **Maqnā**, SAr.
107/J2 **Maqor**, Afg.
114/D5 **Maquan** (riv.), China
152/C4 **Maquela do Zombo**, Ang.
196/E1 **Maquereau, Pointe au** (pt.), Qu,Can
174/C4 **Maquinchao**, Arg.
193/J2 **Maquoketa**, Ia,US
193/J2 **Maquoketa** (riv.), Ia,US
193/J2 **Maquoketa, North Fork** (riv.), Ia,US
173/G2 **Mar** (mts.), Braz.
116/D1 **Mar** (riv.), China
54/D2 **Mar** (dist.), Sc,UK
182/E2 **Mara**, BC,Can
166/B1 **Mara**, Guy.
153/H3 **Mara** (pol. reg.), Tanz.
151/A2 **Mara** (prov.), Tanz.
151/A2 **Mara** (riv.), Tanz.
166/D4 **Marabá**, Braz.
166/D2 **Maracá** (isl.), Braz.
164/D2 **Maracaibo**, Ven.
161/J4 **Maracaibo** (lake), Ven.
170/B4 **Maracaju**, Braz.
172/F1 **Maracaju** (mts.), Braz.
167/E3 **Maracanã**, Braz.
166/C3 **Maracanaquará** (plat.), Braz.
171/E2 **Maracás**, Braz.
165/E2 **Maracay**, Ven.
167/N7 **Maracay** (arpt.), Ven.
76/D4 **Maracena**, Sp.
146/C2 **Marādah**, Libya
145/G3 **Maradi**, Niger
145/G3 **Maradi** (dept.), Niger
105/F2 **Marāgheh**, Iran
120/B2 **Mārahra**, India
165/E4 **Marahuaca** (peak), Ven.
125/C1 **Maraira** (pt.), Phil.
191/G1 **Marais des Cygnes** (riv.), Ks, Mo,US
166/D3 **Marajó** (bay), Braz.
166/D3 **Marajó** (isl.), Braz.
151/B1 **Maralal**, Kenya
151/B1 **Maralal Nat'l Sanct.**, Kenya
148/C4 **Marali**, CAfr.
97/G4 **Maralik**, Arm.
133/F4 **Maralinga-Tjarutja Abor. Land**, Austl.
125/D4 **Maramag**, Phil.
171/N8 **Marambaia** (isl.), Braz.
191/J2 **Maramee** (riv.), Mo,US
144/B4 **Marampa**, SLeo.
93/F2 **Maramureş** (co.), Rom.
124/C2 **Maran**, Malay.
187/G4 **Marana**, Az,US
105/F2 **Marand**, Iran
145/G2 **Marandet**, Niger
124/C1 **Marang**, Malay.
168/D4 **Marangani**, Peru
167/G3 **Maranguape**, Braz.
170/C2 **Maranhão** (riv.), Braz.
170/D1 **Maranhão** (state), Braz.
87/G1 **Marano** (lag.), It.
134/C4 **Maranoa** (riv.), Austl.
85/E6 **Marano di Napoli**, It.
87/G1 **Marano Lagunare**, It.
168/C2 **Marañon** (riv.), Peru
87/D4 **Marano sul Panaro**, It.
87/E1 **Marano Vicentino**, It.
74/C3 **Marans**, Fr.
144/D5 **Maraoue Nat'l Park**, IvC.
166/E3 **Marapanim**, Braz.
124/C3 **Marapi** (peak), Indo.
124/D3 **Maras** (peak), Indo.
93/H3 **Mărăşeşti**, Rom.
83/B3 **Maratea**, It.
195/L3 **Marathon**, On,Can
91/H3 **Marathón**, Gre.
91/M6 **Marathon** (arpt.), Gre.
203/H5 **Marathon**, Fl,US
199/H3 **Marathon**, NY,US
188/C2 **Marathon**, Tx,US
198/B2 **Marathon City**, Wi,US
173/F4 **Marau**, Braz.
122/B1 **Marauliānwāla**, Pak.
173/F3 **Maravilha**, Braz.
169/E3 **Maravillas**, Bol.
188/C3 **Maravillas** (cr.), Tx,US
146/D1 **Marāwah**, Libya
131/G1 **Marawaka**, PNG
125/D3 **Marawi**, Phil.
147/F5 **Marawī**, Sudan
172/C4 **Marayes**, Arg.
58/A6 **Marazion**, Eng,UK
80/D4 **Marbach**, Swi.
70/C5 **Marbach am Neckar**, Ger.
69/F6 **Marbache**, Fr.
76/C4 **Marbella**, Sp.
187/G2 **Marble** (canyon), Az,US
200/F3 **Marble**, NC,US
132/C2 **Marble Bar**, Austl.
187/G2 **Marble Canyon**, Az,US
189/E2 **Marble Falls**, Tx,US
156/E2 **Marble Hall**, SAfr.
200/C2 **Marble Hill**, Mo,US
182/D3 **Marblemount**, Wa,US
196/B3 **Marbleton**, Qu,Can
185/H2 **Marbleton**, Wy,US
64/E3 **Marburg**, Ger.
206/B4 **Marburg** (lake), Pa,US
200/D4 **Marbury**, Al,US
73/B4 **Marcal** (riv.), Hun.
92/C2 **Marcali**, Hun.
86/B2 **Marcallo**, It.
168/D4 **Marcapata**, Peru
154/A3 **Marca, Ponta da** (pt.), Ang.
183/L1 **Marcelin**, Sk,Can
191/H1 **Marceline**, Mo,US
173/G3 **Marcelino Ramos**, Braz.
191/J3 **Marcella**, Ar,US
84/C3 **Marcellina**, It.
198/D3 **Marcellus**, Mi,US
59/G1 **March**, Eng,UK
204/C3 **March A.F.B.**, Ca,US
136/J9 **Marchant** (mtn.), N.Z.
152/C4 **Marche**, Congo
74/D3 **Marche** (mts.), Fr.
87/F5 **Marche** (reg.), It.
69/E3 **Marche-en-Famenne**, Belg.
73/A3 **Marchegg**, Aus.
168/J6 **Marchena** (isl.), Ecu.
76/C4 **Marchena**, Sp.
86/D1 **Marcheno**, It.
89/G2 **Marches** (reg.), It.
83/C4 **Marchesato** (val.), It.
73/A3 **Marchfeld** (reg.), Aus.
68/C3 **Marchiennes-Ville**, Fr.
69/E3 **Marchin**, Belg.
131/E2 **Marchinbar** (isl.), Austl.
172/D3 **Mar Chiquita** (lake), Arg.
73/A3 **March** (Morava) (riv.), Aus.
71/H6 **Marchtrenk**, Aus.
194/D2 **Marchwell**, Sk,Can
84/A2 **Marciana Marina**, It.
85/E5 **Marcianise**, It.
80/B3 **Marcilly-sur-Tille**, Fr.
68/A2 **Marck**, Fr.
80/D1 **Marckolsheim**, Fr.
167/F3 **Marco**, Braz.
203/H5 **Marco**, Fl,US
203/H5 **Marco** (isl.), Fl,US
68/C3 **Marcoing**, Fr.
184/B1 **Marcola**, Or,US
87/F1 **Marcon**, It.
168/C4 **Marcona**, Peru
182/G2 **Marconi** (mtn.), BC,Can
83/C2 **Marconia**, It.
87/F1 **Marco Polo** (Venice) (int'l arpt.), It.
174/E2 **Marcos Juárez**, Arg.
182/C1 **Marcosli** (riv.), BC,Can
68/C2 **Marcq-en-Baroeul**, Fr.
193/G2 **Marcus**, Ia,US
177/J3 **Marcus Baker** (mtn.), Ak,US
199/K2 **Marcy** (mtn.), NY,US
97/H4 **Mardakert**, Azer.
107/K2 **Mardān**, Pak.
175/F3 **Mar del Plata**, Arg.
59/G4 **Marden**, Eng,UK
68/C5 **Mardeuil**, Fr.
104/E2 **Mardin**, Turk.
104/E2 **Mardin** (prov.), Turk.
139/W12 **Maré** (isl.), NCal.
87/F5 **Marecchia** (riv.), It.
170/B5 **Marechal Candido Rondon**, Braz.
171/G1 **Marechal Deodoro**, Braz.
134/B2 **Mareeba**, Austl.
54/A1 **Maree, Loch** (lake), Sc,UK
57/H5 **Mareham le Fen**, Eng,UK
127/F4 **Marek**, Indo.
84/B2 **Maremma** (reg.), It.
144/C3 **Maréna**, Mali
183/K2 **Marengo**, Sk,Can
193/H3 **Marengo**, Ia,US
205/N15 **Marengo**, Il,US
200/D1 **Marengo**, In,US
195/J4 **Marengo**, Wi,US
195/K4 **Marenisco**, Mi,US
74/C4 **Marennes**, Fr.
154/C3 **Mareolaboom**, Namb.
157/H8 **Marerano**, Madg.
59/G5 **Maresfield**, Eng,UK
188/B2 **Marfa**, Tx,US
135/C2 **Marfield**, Austl.
97/J3 **Marfino**, Rus.
122/B1 **Margalla Hills Nat'l Park**, Pak.
58/C3 **Margam**, Wal,UK
99/H4 **Marganets**, Ukr.
118/B4 **Margao**, India
197/G2 **Margaree**, NS,Can
197/G2 **Margaree Valley**, NS,Can
132/C2 **Margaret** (peak), Austl.
130/B4 **Margaret** (riv.), Austl.
190/E3 **Margaret**, Tx,US
132/B5 **Margaret River**, Austl.
204/C4 **Margarita** (peak), Ca,US
165/F2 **Margarita** (isl.), Ven.
91/G3 **Margarítion**, Gre.
157/E3 **Margate**, SAfr.
59/H4 **Margate**, Eng,UK
202/P7 **Margate**, Fl,US
206/D5 **Margate City**, NJ,US
74/E4 **Margeride** (mts.), Fr.
130/B2 **Margeta** (cape), Indo.
153/G2 **Margherita** (peak), Zaire
85/G5 **Margherita di Savoia**, It.
92/F2 **Marghita**, Rom.
114/B3 **Margilan**, Uzb.
68/B5 **Margny-lès-Compiègne**, Fr.
194/C2 **Margo**, Sk,Can
114/E5 **Margog Caka** (lake), China
125/C4 **Margosatubig**, Phil.
69/E2 **Margraten**, Neth.
137/V **Marguerite** (bay), Ant.
182/C1 **Marguerite**, BC,Can
121/H1 **Margyang**, China
73/B2 **Marhat** (peak), Slvk.
167/H4 **Mari**, Braz.
131/F2 **Mari**, PNG
131/D3 **Maria** (isl.), Austl.
135/D4 **Maria** (peak), Austl.
196/E1 **Maria**, Qu,Can
139/K7 **Maria** (isl.), FrPol.
125/C2 **Maria Aurora**, Phil.
158/D4 **María Cleófas** (isl.), Mex.
171/L7 **Maria da Fé**, Braz.
120/D3 **Mariāhū**, India
135/D4 **Maria I. Nat'l Park**, Austl.
174/E1 **Maria Juana**, Arg.
151/B2 **Mariakani**, Kenya
68/B1 **Mariakerke**, Belg.
170/C4 **Marialva**, Braz.
158/D4 **María Madre** (isl.), Mex.
158/D4 **María Magdalena** (isl.), Mex.
134/C3 **Marian**, Austl.
161/F1 **Marianao**, Cuba
191/J3 **Marianna**, Ar,US
203/F2 **Marianna**, Fl,US
86/C1 **Mariano Comense**, It.
172/E4 **Mariano I. Loza**, Arg.
71/F3 **Mariánské Lázně**, Czh.
157/H6 **Mariarano**, Madg.
183/H3 **Marias, Dry Fork** (riv.), Mt,US
161/F5 **Mariato** (pt.), Pan.
136/C1 **Maria van Diemen** (cape), N.Z.
150/C2 **Ma'rib**, Yem.
62/D4 **Maribo**, Den.
92/B2 **Maribor**, Slov.
171/P7 **Maricá**, Braz.
187/F4 **Maricopa**, Az,US
187/F4 **Maricopa** (mts.), Az,US
186/C3 **Maricopa**, Ca,US
187/F4 **Maricopa Ak Chin Ind. Res.**, Az,US
149/F4 **Marīdī**, Sudan
165/E5 **Marié** (riv.), Braz.
137/S **Marie Byrd Land** (reg.), Ant.
162/F4 **Marie-Galante** (isl.), Guad.
63/H1 **Mariehamn**, Fin.
63/H1 **Mariehamn** (int'l arpt.), Fin.
63/U9 **Marieholm**, Swe.
161/F1 **Mariel**, Cuba
72/D6 **Marienberg**, Ger.
68/D3 **Marienbourg**, Belg.
166/C1 **Mariënburg**, Sur.
72/D3 **Marienfelde**, Ger.
67/E1 **Marienhafe**, Ger.
67/E6 **Marienheide**, Ger.
154/C5 **Mariental**, Namb.
199/G4 **Marienville**, Pa,US
62/E2 **Mariestad**, Swe.
200/E4 **Marietta**, Ga,US
201/L7 **Marietta**, Ga,US
194/F5 **Marietta**, Mn,US
200/C3 **Marietta**, Ms,US
198/F5 **Marietta**, Oh,US
191/F4 **Marietta**, Ok,US
206/B3 **Marietta**, Pa,US
194/C2 **Marieval**, Sk,Can
151/A1 **Marigat**, Kenya
85/E6 **Marigliano**, It.
82/B6 **Marignane**, Fr.
78/D2 **Marigny**, Fr.
162/F4 **Marigot**, Dom.
162/F3 **Marigot**, Fr.
125/D3 **Marihatag**, Phil.
125/F6 **Marikina**, Phil.
125/F6 **Marikina** (riv.), Phil.
125/E6 **Marilao**, Phil.
170/C4 **Marília**, Braz.
173/F3 **Mariluz**, Braz.
188/D5 **Marín**, Mex.
76/A1 **Marín**, Sp.
205/J10 **Marin** (co.), Ca,US
83/B3 **Marina**, It.
186/B2 **Marina**, Ca,US
204/B3 **Marina del Rey**, Ca,US
204/F8 **Marina del Rey** (har.), Ca,US
86/B5 **Marina di Andora**, It.
83/B3 **Marina di Camerota**, It.
86/D4 **Marina di Carrara**, It.
83/C4 **Marina di Fuscaldo**, It.
83/C2 **Marina di Ginosa**, It.
83/C6 **Marina di Gioiosa Ionica**, It.
84/A2 **Marina di Grosseto**, It.
86/D4 **Marina di Massa**, It.
87/G5 **Marina di Montemarciano**, It.
86/D5 **Marina di Pisa**, It.
87/F4 **Marina di Ravenna**, It.
83/C3 **Marina di Schiavonea**, It.
85/E3 **Marina di Vasto**, It.
63/N5 **Mar'ina Gorka**, Bela.
125/C2 **Marinduque** (isl.), Phil.
200/C1 **Marine**, Il,US
205/G6 **Marine City**, Mi,US
186/D3 **Marine Corps Logistics Base**, Ca,US
133/M8 **Marineland**, Austl.
203/H3 **Marineland of Florida**, Fl,US
151/C2 **Marine Nat'l Rsv.**, Kenya
80/D3 **Marin-Epagnier**, Swi.
53/R9 **Marines**, Fr.
193/L1 **Marinette**, Wi,US
205/K10 **Marine World Africa USA**, Ca,US
170/C4 **Maringá**, Braz.
153/E2 **Maringa** (riv.), Zaire
202/C2 **Maringouin**, La,US
155/G3 **Marínguè**, Moz.
76/A3 **Marinha Grande**, Port.
76/A2 **Marinhas**, Port.
99/J4 **Mar'inka**, Ukr.
84/C4 **Marino**, It.
129/J3 **Marion** (reef), Austl.
200/D4 **Marion**, Al,US
200/B3 **Marion**, Ar,US
208/B2 **Marion**, Ct,US
202/M7 **Marion** (cr.), Fl,US
203/H4 **Marion** (lake), Fl,US
193/J2 **Marion**, Ia,US
193/K5 **Marion**, Il,US
198/D4 **Marion**, In,US
191/F1 **Marion**, Ks,US
191/F1 **Marion** (lake), Ks,US
200/C2 **Marion**, Ky,US
189/H1 **Marion**, La,US
208/D2 **Marion**, Ma,US
198/D2 **Marion**, Mi,US
202/D1 **Marion**, Ms,US
201/F3 **Marion**, NC,US
194/E4 **Marion**, ND,US
198/E4 **Marion**, Oh,US
201/H3 **Marion**, SC,US
201/G4 **Marion** (lake), SC,US
193/F2 **Marion**, SD,US
201/G2 **Marion**, Va,US
193/K1 **Marion**, Wi,US
197/G3 **Marion Bridge**, NS,Can
200/D4 **Marion Junction**, Al,US
191/H2 **Marionville**, Mo,US
166/D2 **Maripa**, FrG.
165/E3 **Maripa**, Ven.
166/C2 **Maripasoula**, FrG.
186/C2 **Mariposa**, Ca,US
186/C2 **Mariposa** (grove), Ca,US
167/L6 **Mariquita**, Col.
172/D2 **Mariscal Estigarribia**, Par.
164/B5 **Mariscal Sucre** (int'l arpt.), Ecu.
193/K4 **Marissa**, Il,US
143/H2 **Mārith**, Tun.
82/D4 **Maritime Alps** (range), Fr., It.
93/G4 **Maritsa** (riv.), Bul.
96/C4 **Maritsa** (riv.), Bul., Turk.
53/G4 **Mariupol'**, Ukr.
99/J4 **Mariupol** (int'l arpt.), Ukr.
95/K4 **Mariy Aut. Rep.**, Rus.
63/L2 **Märjamaa**, Est.
103/D3 **Marj 'Uyūn**, Leb.
66/B6 **Mark** (riv.), Belg.
187/F2 **Markagunt** (plat.), Ut,US
108/B2 **Markakol** (lake), Kaz.
116/C2 **Markam**, China
151/D1 **Marka** (Merca), Som.
62/E3 **Markaryd**, Swe.
105/G3 **Markazī** (gov.), Iran
198/F2 **Markdale**, On,Can
81/F2 **Markdorf**, Ger.
191/J3 **Marked Tree**, Ar,US
66/C4 **Marken** (isl.), Neth.
66/C4 **Markerwaard** (polder), Neth.
193/K2 **Markesan**, Wi,US
59/E1 **Market Bosworth**, Eng,UK
59/F1 **Market Deeping**, Eng,UK
57/F6 **Market Drayton**, Eng,UK
59/F2 **Market Harborough**, Eng,UK
56/B3 **Markethill**, NI,UK
57/H5 **Market Rasen**, Eng,UK
57/H4 **Market Weighton**, Eng,UK
70/C5 **Markgroningen**, Ger.
114/C5 **Markha**, India
179/J2 **Markham** (bay), NW,Can
199/G3 **Markham**, On,Can
131/G1 **Markham** (riv.), PNG
189/F3 **Markham**, Tx,US
65/L2 **Marki**, Pol.
54/C4 **Markinch**, Sc,UK
114/C4 **Markit**, China
72/C5 **Markkleeberg**, Ger.
198/D4 **Markle**, In,US
186/C1 **Markleeville**, Ca,US
66/C3 **Marknesse**, Neth.
71/F2 **Markneukirchen**, Ger.
91/L7 **Markópoulon**, Gre.
148/C4 **Markounda**, CAfr.
108/E1 **Markova**, Rus.
92/E3 **Markovac**, Yugo.
99/K3 **Markovka**, Ukr.
101/T3 **Markovo**, Rus.
145/F3 **Markoye**, Burk.
72/C5 **Markranstädt**, Ger.
97/H2 **Marks**, Rus.
200/B3 **Marks**, Ms,US
202/B2 **Marksville**, La,US
70/D3 **Markt Bibart**, Ger.
70/D3 **Marktbreit**, Ger.
70/D4 **Markt Erlbach**, Ger.
70/C3 **Marktheidenfeld**, Ger.
71/E6 **Markt Indersdorf**, Ger.
71/F6 **Marktl**, Ger.
81/G2 **Marktoberdorf**, Ger.
71/F3 **Marktredwitz**, Ger.
81/G2 **Markt Rettenbach**, Ger.
71/E6 **Markt Schwaben**, Ger.
191/J1 **Mark Twain** (lake), Mo,US
193/J3 **Mark Twain Nat'l Wild. Ref.**, Il, Ia,US
193/J4 **Mark Twain Nat'l Wild. Ref.**, Il, Mo,US
67/E5 **Marl**, Ger.
133/G3 **Marla**, Austl.
182/F1 **Marlboro**, Ab,Can
207/D3 **Marlboro**, NJ,US
134/C3 **Marlborough**, Austl.
136/C3 **Marlborough** (reg.), N.Z.
59/E4 **Marlborough**, Eng,UK
208/B2 **Marlborough**, Ct,US
208/C1 **Marlborough**, Ma,US
68/C4 **Marle**, Fr.
81/H4 **Marlengo** (Marling), It.
69/G6 **Marlenheim**, Fr.
68/B3 **Marles-les-Mines**, Fr.
198/E3 **Marlette**, Mi,US
189/F2 **Marlin**, Tx,US
81/H4 **Marling** (Marlengo), It.
201/G1 **Marlinton**, WV,US
64/G1 **Marlow**, Ger.
59/F3 **Marlow**, Eng,UK
201/G4 **Marlow**, Ga,US
191/F3 **Marlow**, Ok,US
206/D4 **Marlton**, NJ,US
68/C3 **Marly**, Fr.
53/T9 **Marly-la-Ville**, Fr.
53/S10 **Marly-le-Roi**, Fr.
69/F5 **Marly-sur-Seille**, Fr.
201/H3 **Mar-Mac**, NC,US
191/J2 **Marmaduke**, Ar,US
74/D4 **Marmande**, Fr.
93/H5 **Marmara**, Turk.
93/H5 **Marmara** (isl.), Turk.
53/F4 **Marmara** (sea), Turk.
93/H5 **Marmaraereğlisi**, Turk.
104/B2 **Marmaris**, Turk.
194/C4 **Marmarth**, ND,US
166/A4 **Marmelos** (riv.), Braz.
201/G1 **Marmet**, WV,US
132/D4 **Marmion** (lake), Austl.
195/J3 **Marmion** (lake), On,Can
87/D2 **Marmirolo**, It.
75/J3 **Marmolada** (peak), It.
76/C3 **Marmolejo**, Sp.
169/F2 **Marmoles** (riv.), Braz.
81/F5 **Marmontana, Monte** (peak), It.
199/H2 **Marmora**, On,Can
206/D5 **Marmora**, NJ,US
182/G4 **Marmot** (peak), Mt,US
69/G6 **Marmoutier**, Fr.
80/B3 **Marnay**, Fr.
80/C5 **Marnaz**, Fr.
68/C6 **Marne** (dept.), Fr.
53/U10 **Marne** (riv.), Fr.
64/E2 **Marne**, Ger.
80/B3 **Marne à la Saône** (can.), Fr.
69/D6 **Marne au Rhin, Canal de la** (can.), Fr.
97/H4 **Marneuli**, Geo.
58/D5 **Marnhull**, Eng,UK
148/C3 **Maro**, Chad
139/H2 **Maro** (reef), Hi,US
193/K3 **Maroa**, Il,US
165/E4 **Maroa**, Ven.
157/J6 **Maroantsetra**, Madg.
146/C5 **Maro, Enneri** (dry riv.), Chad
157/H8 **Marofandilia**, Madg.
139/L6 **Marokau** (atoll), FrPol.
141/G7 **Marolambo**, Madg.
70/D2 **Maroldsweisach**, Ger.
53/S11 **Marolles-en-Hurepoix**, Fr.
79/G2 **Maromme**, Fr.
157/J6 **Maromokotro** (peak), Madg.
155/F3 **Marondera**, Zim.
86/D1 **Marone**, It.
165/H3 **Maroni** (riv.), FrG., Sur.
134/D4 **Maroochydore-Mooloolaba**, Austl.
185/K4 **Maroon** (peak), Co,US
161/G2 **Maroon Town**, Jam.
157/H8 **Maropaika**, Madg.
87/E1 **Marostica**, It.
157/J7 **Marotandrano**, Madg.
87/G5 **Marotta**, It.
148/B3 **Maroua**, Camr.
166/C2 **Marouini** (riv.), FrG.
165/H4 **Marouni** (riv.), FrG.
157/J6 **Marovato**, Madg.
141/G6 **Marovoay**, Madg.
165/H3 **Marowijne** (dist.), Sur.
69/G5 **Marpingen**, Ger.
57/F5 **Marple**, Eng,UK
108/D5 **Marqên Gangri** (peak), China
191/J2 **Marquand**, Mo,US
121/F1 **Marquan** (Damqog) (riv.), China
156/D3 **Marquard**, SAfr.
138/D8 **Marquarie** (riv.), Austl.
139/M5 **Marquesas** (isls.), FrPol.
203/G5 **Marquesas** (keys), Fl,US
167/K6 **Marquetalia**, Col.
194/F2 **Marquette**, Mb,Can
191/F1 **Marquette**, Ks,US
198/C1 **Marquette**, Mi,US
189/F2 **Marquez**, Tx,US
194/B2 **Marquis**, Sk,Can
68/A2 **Marquise**, Fr.
155/G5 **Marracuene**, Moz.
87/E4 **Marradi**, It.
148/E2 **Marrah** (peak), Sudan
148/E2 **Marrah, Jabal** (mts.), Sudan
142/D3 **Marrakech**, Mor.
142/C3 **Marrakech** (Menara) (int'l arpt.), Mor.
135/C4 **Marrawah**, Austl.
133/H4 **Marree**, Austl.
155/G3 **Marromeu**, Moz.
200/E2 **Marrowbone**, Ky,US
155/H2 **Marrupa**, Moz.
208/G6 **Mars**, Pa,US
146/C2 **Marsá al Burayqah**, Libya
141/N13 **Marsa Ben Mehidi**, Alg.
151/B1 **Marsabit**, Kenya
150/A5 **Marsabit Nat'l Rsv.**, Kenya
90/C4 **Marsala**, It.
147/E2 **Marsá Matrūh**, Egypt
103/B5 **Marsá Maţrūḩ** (gov.), Egypt
147/F2 **Marsá Matrūh** (gov.), Egypt
53/U10 **Marsange** (riv.), Fr.
80/A3 **Marsannay-la-Côte**, Fr.
67/F6 **Marsberg**, Ger.
84/C2 **Marsciano**, It.
135/C2 **Marsden**, Austl.
183/K1 **Marsden**, Sk,Can
57/G4 **Marsden**, Eng,UK
66/B3 **Marsdiep** (chan.), Neth.
82/B6 **Marseille**, Fr.
82/A5 **Marseille au Rhône** (can.), Fr.
79/G2 **Marseille-en-Beauvaisis**, Fr.
82/B6 **Marseille** (Provence) (int'l arpt.), Fr.
193/K3 **Marseilles**, Il,US
167/K7 **Marsella**, Col.
170/D4 **Mar, Serro do** (cliffs), Braz.
189/J3 **Marsh** (isl.), La,US
199/G5 **Marsh** (mtn.), Md,US
205/F7 **Marsh** (cr.), Mi,US
206/A4 **Marsh** (cr.), Pa,US
185/J3 **Marsh** (peak), Ut,US
133/H2 **Marshall** (riv.), Austl.
144/C5 **Marshall**, Libr.
191/H3 **Marshall**, Ar,US
198/C5 **Marshall**, Il,US
198/D3 **Marshall**, Mi,US
193/G1 **Marshall**, Mn,US
191/H1 **Marshall**, Mo,US
201/F3 **Marshall**, NC,US
191/F2 **Marshall**, Ok,US
189/G1 **Marshall**, Tx,US
201/H1 **Marshall** (mtn.), Va,US
138/G3 **Marshall Islands**
206/C4 **Marshallton**, De,US
193/H2 **Marshalltown**, Ia,US
200/F4 **Marshallville**, Ga,US
208/F6 **Marshallville**, Oh,US
208/D1 **Marshfield**, Ma,US
191/H2 **Marshfield**, Mo,US
193/J1 **Marshfield**, Wi,US
208/D1 **Marshfield Hills**, Ma,US
59/E3 **Marsh Gibbon**, Eng,UK
162/B1 **Marsh Harbour**, Bahm.
196/D2 **Mars Hill**, Me,US
201/F3 **Mars Hill**, NC,US
206/C6 **Marshyhope** (cr.), De, Md,US
83/B2 **Marsico Nuovo**, It.
57/G2 **Marske-by-the-Sea**, Eng,UK
192/C2 **Marsland**, Ne,US
86/A1 **Mars, Monte** (peak), It.
62/G2 **Märsta**, Swe.
200/C2 **Marston**, Mo,US
120/E1 **Marsyandi** (riv.), Nepal
84/B2 **Marta**, It.
84/B3 **Marta** (riv.), It.
123/B2 **Martaban**, Burma
123/B2 **Martaban** (gulf), Burma
84/C2 **Martano** (peak), It.
148/B4 **Martap**, Camr.
124/D4 **Martapura**, Indo.
126/D4 **Martapura**, Indo.
69/E4 **Martelange**, Belg.
186/B1 **Martell**, Ca,US
87/F1 **Martellago**, It.
195/M2 **Marten Falls Ind. Res.**, Can
194/A1 **Martensville**, Sk,Can
67/G3 **Martfeld**, Ger.
201/F1 **Martha**, Ky,US
190/E3 **Martha**, Ok,US
208/D3 **Martha's Vineyard** (isl.), Ma,US
84/C3 **Martignano** (lake), It.
79/E4 **Martigné**, Fr.
78/D5 **Martigné-Ferchaud**, Fr.
80/D5 **Martigny**, Swi.
80/B1 **Martigny-les-Bains**, Fr.
82/B6 **Martigues**, Fr.
137/S **Martin** (pen.), Ant.
73/C1 **Martin**, Slvk.
200/E4 **Martin** (dam), Al,US
200/E4 **Martin** (lake), Al,US
202/B1 **Martin**, La,US
198/D3 **Martin**, Mi,US
195/L5 **Martin** (isl.), Mi,US
194/D4 **Martin**, ND,US
192/D2 **Martin**, SD,US
200/C2 **Martin**, Tn,US
90/E2 **Martina Franca**, It.

136/J9 **Martinborough,** N.Z.
175/S12 **Martín Chico,** Uru.
189/F3 **Martindale,** Tx,US
86/C1 **Martinengo,** It.
159/F4 **Martínez,** Mex.
205/K10 **Martinez,** Ca,US
201/F4 **Martinez,** Ga,US
159/M6 **Martínez de la Torre,** Mex.
172/C2 **Martínez del Tineo,** Arg.
162/F4 **Martinique** (isl.), Fr.
162/F4 **Martinique Passage** (chan.), West Indies
200/E4 **Martin Luther King, Jr. Nat'l Hist. Site,** Ga,US
91/H3 **Martínon,** Gre.
167/F3 **Martinópole,** Braz.
167/G4 **Martins,** Braz.
199/J3 **Martinsburg,** NY,US
199/G4 **Martinsburg,** Pa,US
201/J1 **Martinsburg,** WV,US
206/C2 **Martins Creek,** Pa,US
198/F4 **Martins Ferry,** Oh,US
85/D2 **Martinsicuro,** It.
191/G4 **Martins Mills,** Tx,US
200/D1 **Martinsville,** Il,US
198/C5 **Martinsville,** In,US
202/C2 **Martinsville,** Ms,US
206/D2 **Martinsville,** NJ,US
201/H2 **Martinsville,** Va,US
50/H7 **Martin Vaz** (isls.), Braz.
58/D2 **Martley,** Eng,UK
58/D5 **Martock,** Eng,UK
62/D4 **Martofte,** Den.
136/C3 **Marton,** N.Z.
77/F2 **Martorell,** Sp.
76/D4 **Martos,** Sp.
73/C4 **Martovce,** Slvk.
74/D5 **Martres-Tolosane,** Fr.
146/D1 **Martūba,** Libya
97/L2 **Martuk,** Kaz.
97/H4 **Martuni,** Arm.
192/E2 **Marty,** SD,US
97/J2 **Martynovo,** Kaz.
145/G3 **Maru,** Nga.
125/A4 **Marudi,** Malay.
110/C3 **Marugame,** Japan
171/F1 **Maruim,** Braz.
111/F2 **Maruko,** Japan
167/K6 **Marulanda,** Col.
66/D2 **Marum,** Neth.
151/B4 **Marumba,** Tanz.
201/J1 **Marumsco Nat'l Wild. Ref.,** Va,US
153/G5 **Marungu** (mts.), Zaire
110/E2 **Maruoka,** Japan
139/M7 **Marutea** (isl.), FrPol.
111/H7 **Maruyama,** Japan
105/H4 **Marv Dasht,** Iran
187/H2 **Marvel,** Co,US
200/B3 **Marvell,** Ar,US
194/F5 **Marvin,** SD,US
185/H4 **Marvine** (mtn.), Ut,US
183/J1 **Marwayne,** Ab,Can
70/D5 **Marxheim,** Ger.
134/D4 **Mary** (riv.), Austl.
107/H1 **Mary,** Trkm.
202/C2 **Mary** (lake), Ms,US
105/G3 **Maryānaj,** Iran
114/C4 **Maryang,** China
132/B2 **Mary Anne** (passg.), Austl.
134/D4 **Maryborough,** Austl.
135/B3 **Maryborough,** Austl.
156/C3 **Marydale,** SAfr.
206/C5 **Marydel,** Md,US
202/E2 **Mary Esther,** Fl,US
194/D3 **Maryfield,** Sk,Can
133/J2 **Mary Kathleen,** Austl.
54/D3 **Marykirk,** Sc,UK
144/C5 **Maryland** (co.), Libr.
181/C4 **Maryland** (state), US
206/B5 **Maryland City,** Md,US
155/F3 **Maryland Junction,** Zim.
206/B4 **Maryland Line,** Md,US
188/D1 **Maryneal,** Tx,US
56/E2 **Maryport,** Eng,UK
197/K2 **Marystown,** Nf,Can
185/G4 **Marysvale,** Ut,US
184/C4 **Marysville,** Ca,US
191/F1 **Marysville,** Ks,US
205/H6 **Marysville,** Mi,US
183/H4 **Marysville,** Mt,US
198/E4 **Marysville,** Oh,US
206/B3 **Marysville,** Pa,US
205/C1 **Marysville,** Wa,US
134/D5 **Maryvale,** Austl.
193/G3 **Maryville,** Mo,US
200/F3 **Maryville,** Tn,US
87/E4 **Marzabotto,** It.
85/F6 **Marzano** (peak), It.
164/B3 **Marzo** (pt.), Col.
159/F3 **Marzo, 18 de,** Mex.
146/B3 **Marzūq,** Libya
143/H4 **Marzūq, Ḩamadāt** (plat.), Libya
146/B3 **Marzūq, Hamādat** (upland), Libya
146/B3 **Marzūq, Şaḩrā** (des.), Libya
151/B1 **Masabit Nat'l Rsv.,** Kenya
103/D4 **Masada** (H̱orvot Meẕada) (ruins), Isr.
150/C3 **Masagan** (dry riv.), Som.
151/A2 **Masai Mara Nat'l Rsv.,** Kenya
151/B3 **Masai Steppe** (grsld.), Tanz.
153/G3 **Masaka,** Ugan.
124/F4 **Masalembu Besar** (isl.), Indo.
97/J5 **Masally,** Azer.
77/E3 **Masamagrell,** Sp.
127/F4 **Masamba,** Indo.
113/E5 **Masan,** SKor.
153/E3 **Masanga,** Zaire
153/G4 **Masangwe** (hill), Tanz.
202/L7 **Masaryktown,** Fl,US
151/B4 **Masasi,** Tanz.
172/D1 **Masaví,** Bol.
160/E4 **Masaya,** Nic.
125/C2 **Masbate,** Phil.
141/R16 **Mascara,** Alg.
141/R16 **Mascara** (wilaya), Alg.
157/S15 **Mascarene** (isls.), Mrts., Reun.
85/F6 **Maschito,** It.
200/F2 **Mascot,** Tn,US
158/D4 **Mascota,** Mex.
202/M6 **Mascotte,** Fl,US
203/H3 **Mascotte,** Fl,US
197/N6 **Mascouche,** Qu,Can
153/F4 **Mase,** Zaire
130/C2 **Masela** (isl.), Indo.
70/C6 **Maselheim,** Ger.
87/E2 **Maserà di Padova,** It.
153/G3 **Masereka,** Zaire
156/D3 **Maseru** (cap.), Les.
156/D3 **Maseru** (Moshoeshoe) (int'l arpt.), Les.
80/D2 **Masevaux,** Fr.
62/A1 **Masfjorden,** Nor.
117/H3 **Masha,** China
155/F4 **Mashaba,** Zim.
102/E6 **Mashad,** Iran
153/E4 **Mashala,** Zaire
57/G3 **Masham,** Eng,UK
119/J3 **Mashan,** China
99/H3 **Mashevka,** Ukr.
107/G1 **Mashhad,** Iran
112/B2 **Mashike,** Japan
105/J4 **Mashīz,** Iran
107/H3 **Māshkel, Hāmūn-i-** (lake), Pak.
107/H3 **Māshkīd** (riv.), Iran
155/F3 **Mashonaland Central** (prov.), Zim.
155/F3 **Mashonaland East** (prov.), Zim.
155/F3 **Mashonaland West** (prov.), Zim.
97/J4 **Mashtaga,** Azer.
103/B4 **Mashtūl as Sūq,** Egypt
112/D2 **Mashū** (lake), Japan
158/C3 **Masiaca,** Mex.
76/A1 **Maside,** Sp.
150/D2 **Masīlah, Wādī al** (dry riv.), Yem.
97/L1 **Masim** (peak), Rus.
153/G2 **Masindi,** Ugan.
153/H2 **Masindi Port,** Ugan.
125/B2 **Masinloc,** Phil.
107/G5 **Masira** (gulf), Oman
102/E7 **Masira** (isl.), Oman
107/G4 **Maşīrah** (isl.), Oman
97/H5 **Masis,** Arm.
168/C3 **Masisea,** Peru
153/G3 **Masisi,** Zaire
105/G4 **Masjed-e Soleymān,** Iran
124/B2 **Masjid Raya** (Great Mosque), Indo.
160/D2 **Maskall,** Belz.
159/H5 **Maskalls,** Belz.
150/B3 **Maskan, Ras** (cape), Som.
142/D2 **Masker, Jebel** (mtn.), Mor.
107/G4 **Maskin,** Oman
60/A2 **Mask, Lough** (lake), Ire.
107/G3 **Maskūtān,** Iran
63/R7 **Måsnaren** (lake), Swe.
157/J6 **Masoala** (cape), Madg.
157/J6 **Masoala** (pen.), Madg.
157/H7 **Masoarivo,** Madg.
193/K4 **Mason,** Il,US
198/D3 **Mason,** Mi,US
184/D4 **Mason,** Nv,US
198/D5 **Mason,** Oh,US
191/F3 **Mason,** Ok,US
188/E2 **Mason,** Tx,US
205/A3 **Mason** (co.), Wa,US
205/A3 **Mason** (lake), Wa,US
198/E5 **Mason,** WV,US
201/J3 **Masonboro,** NC,US
193/H2 **Mason City,** Ia,US
193/K3 **Mason City,** Il,US
86/B3 **Masone,** It.
199/G5 **Masontown,** Pa,US
200/D2 **Masonville,** Ky,US
77/X17 **Maspalomas,** Canl.,Sp.
77/K6 **Masquefa,** Sp.
121/E2 **Masrakh,** India
86/D4 **Massa,** It.
86/D4 **Massa-Carrara** (prov.), It.
181/B3 **Massachusetts** (state), US
208/D1 **Massachusetts** (bay), Ma,US
86/D5 **Massaciuccoli** (lake), It.
87/E3 **Massa Finalese,** It.
87/F3 **Massa Fiscaglia,** It.
90/E2 **Massafra,** It.
148/B2 **Massaguet,** Chad
148/B2 **Massakory,** Chad
87/E4 **Massa Lombarda,** It.
85/E6 **Massa Lubrense,** It.
84/A1 **Massa Marittima,** It.
84/C2 **Massa Martana,** It.
99/H5 **Massandra,** Ukr.
155/G4 **Massangena,** Moz.
167/F3 **Massapê,** Braz.
207/E2 **Massapequa,** NY,US
207/M9 **Massapequa Park,** NY,US
86/D5 **Massarosa,** It.
70/D2 **Massbach,** Ger.
199/J2 **Massena,** NY,US
148/C3 **Massenya,** Chad
177/M5 **Masset,** BC,Can
179/S7 **Massey** (sound), NW,Can
198/E1 **Massey,** On,Can
206/C5 **Massey,** Md,US
153/E5 **Massibi,** Ang.
74/E4 **Massif Central** (plat.), Fr.
144/D4 **Massigui,** Mali
208/F6 **Massillon,** Oh,US
155/G4 **Massinga,** Moz.
155/G4 **Massingir,** Moz.
137/G **Masson** (isl.), Ant.
53/S10 **Massy,** Fr.
147/H4 **Mastābah,** SAr.
182/G4 **Mastadon** (mtn.), Id,US
136/C3 **Masterton,** N.Z.
66/B5 **Mastgat** (chan.), Neth.
207/F2 **Mastic,** NY,US
207/F2 **Mastic Beach,** NY,US
71/H3 **Mastnik** (riv.), Czh.
107/J3 **Mastung,** Pak.
147/H4 **Mastūrah,** SAr.
146/B3 **Mastūtah, Bi'r al** (well), Libya
110/B3 **Masuda,** Japan
151/B4 **Masuguru,** Tanz.
124/C3 **Masurai** (peak), Indo.
208/G5 **Masury,** Oh,US
155/F4 **Masvingo,** Zim.
155/F4 **Masvingo** (prov.), Zim.
151/A2 **Maswa Game Rsv.,** Tanz.
103/E2 **Maşyāf,** Syria
91/F2 **Mat** (riv.), Alb.
153/E4 **Mata,** Zaire
155/E3 **Matabeleland North** (prov.), Zim.
155/F4 **Matabeleland South** (prov.), Zim.
121/G2 **Mātābhānga,** India
130/B2 **Mata Bia** (peak), Indo.
164/D3 **Mata de Guanábana,** Ven.
152/C4 **Matadi** (Gombe), Zaire
148/C1 **Mataga** (well), Chad
160/E3 **Matagalpa,** Nic.
161/E3 **Matagalpa, Rio Grande de** (riv.), Nic.
189/G3 **Matagorda,** Tx,US
189/F3 **Matagorda** (bay), Tx,US
189/F3 **Matagorda** (isl.), Tx,US
189/G3 **Matagorda** (pen.), Tx,US
171/F1 **Mata Grande,** Braz.
124/D2 **Matak** (isl.), Indo.
154/B2 **Matala,** Ang.
118/D6 **Matale,** SrL.
144/B3 **Matam,** Sen.
156/C2 **Mata Mata,** SAfr.
153/E4 **Matamba,** Zaire
145/H3 **Mataméye,** Niger
199/J4 **Matamoras,** Pa,US
158/E3 **Matamoros,** Mex.
189/F5 **Matamoros,** Mex.
174/C1 **Matancilla,** Chile
158/C3 **Matancita,** Mex.
155/F1 **Matanda,** Zam.
151/B4 **Matandu** (riv.), Tanz.
176/L5 **Matane,** Can.
196/D1 **Matane,** Qu,Can
196/D1 **Matane** (riv.), Qu,Can
157/H8 **Matanga,** Madg.
161/F1 **Matanzas,** Cuba
170/C4 **Matão,** Braz.
158/C2 **Matape** (riv.), Mex.
196/D2 **Matapédia,** Qu,Can
165/F2 **Mata, Punta de,** Ven.
174/C2 **Mataquito** (riv.), Chile
106/C6 **Matara** (ruins), Egypt
150/A2 **Matara,** Eth.
118/D6 **Matara,** SrL.
124/G5 **Mataram,** Indo.
91/G3 **Mataránga,** Gre.
168/C5 **Matarani,** Peru
130/D3 **Mataranka,** Austl.
77/G2 **Mataró,** Sp.
156/E3 **Matatiele,** SAfr.
139/L7 **Mataura,** FrPol.
136/B4 **Mataura,** N.Z.
136/B4 **Mataura** (riv.), N.Z.
138/H6 **Mata Utu,** Wall.
136/D2 **Matawai,** N.Z.
207/D3 **Matawan,** NJ,US
196/A2 **Matawin** (riv.), Qu,Can
97/L3 **Matay,** Kaz.
164/C3 **Matecana** (int'l arpt.), Col.
169/F4 **Mateguá,** Bol.
159/E4 **Matehuala,** Mex.
155/F4 **Mateke** (hills), Zim.
173/F3 **Matelândia,** Braz.
84/D1 **Matelica,** It.
90/E2 **Matera,** It.
83/C2 **Matera** (prov.), It.
145/F4 **Matéri,** Ben.
85/E5 **Matese** (lake), It.
85/E4 **Matese** (mts.), It.
92/F2 **Mátészalka,** Hun.
154/E3 **Matetsi,** Zim.
80/C3 **Mathay,** Fr.
121/G4 **Mathbaria,** Bang.
151/A1 **Matheniko Game Rsv.,** Ugan.
194/F2 **Matheson Island,** Mb,Can
151/B1 **Mathew's** (peak), Kenya
204/C3 **Mathews** (lake), Ca,US
202/C3 **Mathews,** La,US
201/J2 **Mathews,** Va,US
86/A2 **Mathi,** It.
189/F3 **Mathis,** Tx,US
188/D2 **Mathis Field** (arpt.), Tx,US
200/C4 **Mathiston,** Ms,US
135/C2 **Mathoura,** Austl.
120/A2 **Mathurā,** India
125/D4 **Mati,** Phil.
171/E4 **Matias Barbosa,** Braz.
167/F3 **Matias Olímpio,** Braz.
160/C2 **Matías Romero,** Mex.
78/C3 **Matignon,** Fr.
161/E3 **Matíguas,** Nic.
204/A2 **Matilija** (dam), Ca,US
151/A4 **Matimbuka,** Tanz.
167/E4 **Matinha,** Braz.
207/E2 **Matinicock** (pt.), NY,US
196/C4 **Matinicus,** Me,US
164/D3 **Matiyuri** (riv.), Ven.
120/B4 **Matkuli,** India
121/G4 **Mātla** (riv.), India
57/G5 **Matlock,** Eng,UK
143/H2 **Maţmāţah,** Tun.
155/F4 **Matobo** (Matopos) Nat'l Park, Zim.
167/F4 **Matões,** Braz.
169/G4 **Mato Grosso,** Braz.
170/A2 **Mato Grosso** (plat.), Braz.
169/G4 **Mato Grosso** (state), Braz.
170/B4 **Mato Grosso do Sul** (state), Braz.
163/D4 **Mato Grosso, Planalto de** (plat.), Braz.
155/G5 **Matolo-Rio,** Moz.
148/A5 **Matomb,** Camr.
151/B3 **Matombo,** Tanz.
155/F4 **Matopos,** Zim.
155/F4 **Matopos** (Matobo) Nat'l Park, Zim.
76/A2 **Matosinhos,** Port.
166/C1 **Matoury,** FrG.
152/B3 **Matouti** (pt.), Gabon
171/E2 **Mato Verde,** Braz.
107/G4 **Maţraḩ,** Oman
81/H3 **Matrei am Brenner,** Aus.
75/K3 **Matrei in Osttirol,** Aus.
167/H5 **Matriz de Camaragibe,** Braz.
156/B4 **Matroosberg** (peak), SAfr.
63/K2 **Matsalu** (str.), Est.
157/E2 **Matsapa** (Manzini) (int'l arpt.), Swaz.
157/H8 **Matsiatra** (riv.), Madg.
157/J6 **Matsoandakana,** Madg.
182/C3 **Matsqui,** BC,Can
111/L10 **Matsubara,** Japan
111/H7 **Matsubushi,** Japan
111/H7 **Matsuda,** Japan
111/H7 **Matsudo,** Japan
110/C3 **Matsue,** Japan
112/B3 **Matsumae,** Japan
111/E2 **Matsumoto,** Japan
111/E2 **Matsumoto** (arpt.), Japan
110/E3 **Matsusaka,** Japan
111/G1 **Matsushima,** Japan
110/E2 **Matsutō,** Japan
110/C4 **Matsuyama,** Japan
110/C4 **Matsuyama** (arpt.), Japan
81/F4 **Matt,** Swi.
201/J3 **Mattamuskeet** (lake), NC,US
201/J3 **Mattamuskeet Nat'l Wild. Ref.,** NC,US
122/F4 **Mattancherry Palace,** India
208/D2 **Mattapoisett,** Ma,US
201/J2 **Mattaponi** (riv.), Va,US
81/H6 **Mattarello,** It.
199/G1 **Mattawa,** On,Can
182/E4 **Mattawa,** Wa,US
196/C3 **Mattawamkeag,** Me,US
80/D6 **Matterhorn** (peak), It., Swi.
73/A4 **Mattersburg,** Aus.
80/D5 **Mattertal** (val.), Swi.
205/Q16 **Matteson,** Il,US
136/J9 **Matthews** (mtn.), N.Z.
177/H2 **Matthews** (mtn.), Ak,US
200/C2 **Matthews,** Mo,US
201/G3 **Matthews,** NC,US
162/C2 **Matthew Town,** Bahm.
202/M7 **Mattie** (lake), Fl,US
71/G6 **Mattig** (riv.), Aus.
71/G6 **Mattighofen,** Aus.
85/G4 **Mattinata,** It.
207/F2 **Mattituck,** NY,US
80/E5 **Mattmarksee** (lake), Swi.
110/E2 **Mattō,** Japan
56/B4 **Mattock** (riv.), Ire.
193/K4 **Mattoon,** Il,US
195/K5 **Mattoon,** Wi,US
71/G7 **Mattsee,** Aus.
121/H3 **Mātua,** Bang.
168/B3 **Matucana,** Peru
199/J2 **Matumbla** (mtn.), NY,US
155/G3 **Matundwe** (range), Malw., Moz.
165/F2 **Maturín,** Ven.
155/F3 **Matusadona Nat'l Park,** Zim.
125/D4 **Matutum** (mtn.), Phil.
99/K4 **Matveyev Kurgan,** Rus.
73/A3 **Matzen,** Aus.
165/G3 **Maú** (riv.), Guy., Ven.
120/C3 **Mau,** India
120/C4 **Mau,** India
151/A2 **Mau** (peak), Kenya
155/H2 **Maúa,** Moz.
120/C3 **Mau Aimma,** India
68/D4 **Maubert-Fontaine,** Fr.
68/C3 **Maubeuge,** Fr.
116/B5 **Ma-ubin,** Burma
74/D5 **Maubourguet,** Fr.
54/B5 **Mauchline,** Sc,UK
132/B2 **Maud** (pt.), Austl.
54/D1 **Maud,** Sc,UK
191/F3 **Maud,** Ok,US
189/G1 **Maud,** Tx,US
120/C3 **Maudaha,** India
135/C2 **Maude,** Austl.
183/J4 **Maudlow,** Mt,US
155/G5 **Mau-é-Ele,** Moz.
71/G6 **Mauerkirchen,** Aus.
166/B3 **Maués,** Braz.
166/B4 **Maués Açu** (riv.), Braz.
138/D3 **Maug** (isls.), NMar.
120/C3 **Mauganj,** India
56/D3 **Maughold,** IM,UK
56/D3 **Maughold Head** (pt.), IM,UK
74/F5 **Mauguio,** Fr.
60/B4 **Mauherslieve** (mtn.), Ire.
139/K2 **Maui** (isl.), Hi,US
95/P5 **Mauk,** Rus.
139/K7 **Mauke** (isl.), CookIs.
116/B4 **Maukkadaw,** Burma
70/B5 **Maulbronn,** Ger.
68/A6 **Mauldre** (riv.), Fr.
174/B2 **Maule** (reg.), Chile
174/C1 **Maule** (riv.), Chile
79/G2 **Maule,** Fr.
74/C3 **Mauléon,** Fr.
174/B4 **Maullín,** Chile
121/H3 **Maulvi Bāzār,** Bang.
120/D3 **Mau** (Maunath Bhanjan), India
198/E4 **Maumee,** Oh,US
198/D4 **Maumee** (riv.), Oh,US
130/A2 **Maumere,** Indo.
60/A2 **Maumtrasna** (mtn.), Ire.
154/D3 **Maun,** Bots.
154/D3 **Maun** (int'l arpt.), Bots.
180/U11 **Mauna Kea** (peak), Hi,US
180/U11 **Mauna Loa** (peak), Hi,US
120/D3 **Maunath Bhanjan** (Mau), India
155/E4 **Maunatlala,** Bots.
136/C2 **Maungaturoto,** N.Z.
116/B4 **Maungdaw,** Burma
78/D1 **Maupertus** (Cherbourg) (int'l arpt.), Fr.
139/K6 **Maupiti** (isl.), FrPol.
122/C2 **Maur,** India
81/E3 **Maur,** Swi.
120/B3 **Mau Rānīpur,** India
120/C2 **Maurāwān,** India
53/S10 **Maurecourt,** Fr.
68/A6 **Maurepas,** Fr.
202/C2 **Maurepas** (lake), La,US
82/C6 **Maures** (mts.), Fr.
74/E4 **Mauriac,** Fr.
133/F4 **Maurice** (lake), Austl.
206/C5 **Maurice** (riv.), NJ,US
143/F5 **Maurice Cortier** (ruins), Alg.
206/D5 **Mauricetown,** NJ,US
189/H2 **Mauriceville,** Tx,US
179/J4 **Mauricie Nat'l Park,** Qu,Can
82/C2 **Maurienne** (val.), Fr.
170/C3 **Maurilândia,** Braz.
192/C1 **Maurine,** SD,US
140/A3 **Mauritania**
167/G4 **Mauriti,** Braz.
157/S15 **Mauritius**
85/E4 **Mauro** (peak), It.
78/C4 **Mauron,** Fr.
151/B3 **Maurui,** Tanz.
200/C3 **Maury City,** Tn,US
193/J2 **Mauston,** Wi,US
71/H6 **Mauthausen,** Aus.
80/D6 **Mauvoisin, Barrage de** (dam), Swi.
122/F4 **Māvelikara,** India
187/H4 **Maverick,** Az,US
168/D3 **Mavila,** Peru
154/D2 **Mavinga,** Ang.
130/A3 **Mavis** (reef), Austl.
91/H3 **Mavrommátion,** Gre.
92/E5 **Mavrovo Nat'l Park,** Macd.
155/F3 **Mavuradonha** (mts.), Zim.
201/J3 **Maw** (pt.), NC,US
153/F2 **Mawa,** Zaire
124/C2 **Mawai,** Malay.
120/A1 **Mawāna Khurd,** India
152/D4 **Mawanga,** Zaire
130/A1 **Mawasangka,** Indo.
123/B4 **Maw Daung** (pass), Thai.
117/E3 **Mawei,** China
116/C3 **Mawhun,** Burma
153/F2 **Mawiwi,** Zaire
150/C2 **Māwiyah,** Yem.
116/C4 **Mawkmai,** Burma
116/B4 **Mawlaik,** Burma
121/H3 **Mawliba,** India
119/G3 **Mawlu,** Burma
121/H3 **Mawphlang,** India
150/B2 **Mawshij,** Yem.
137/E **Mawson,** Ant.
137/D **Mawson** (coast), Ant.
194/D4 **Max,** ND,US
182/B3 **Maxah Ind. Res.,** Wa,US
167/H4 **Maxaranguape,** Braz.
159/H4 **Maxcanú,** Mex.
69/F6 **Maxéville,** Fr.
71/F4 **Maxhütte-Haidhof,** Ger.
189/H2 **Maxie,** La,US
202/D2 **Maxie,** Ms,US
155/G4 **Maxixe,** Moz.
201/G2 **Max Meadows,** Va,US
201/H3 **Maxton,** NC,US
183/H4 **Maxville,** Mt,US
190/B2 **Maxwell,** NM,US
200/D4 **Maxwell A.F.B.,** Al,US
190/B2 **Maxwell Nat'l Wild. Ref.,** NM,US
134/A3 **Maxwelton,** Austl.
54/D4 **May** (isl.), Sc,UK
181/M4 **May** (cape), NJ,US
188/E2 **May,** Tx,US
160/D2 **Maya** (mts.), Belz., Guat.
126/C4 **Maya** (isl.), Indo.
101/P4 **Maya** (riv.), Rus.
160/D2 **Maya Beach,** Belz.
162/C2 **Mayaguana** (isl.), Bahm.
161/H1 **Mayaguana** (passg.), Bahm.
162/C2 **Mayaguana Passage** (chan.), Bahm.
162/E3 **Mayagüez,** PR
145/G3 **Mayahi,** Niger
97/G4 **Mayakovskiy,** Geo.
107/K1 **Mayakovskogo** (peak), Taj.
114/B4 **Mayakovskogo, Pik** (peak), Taj.
152/D4 **Mayala,** Zaire
152/C3 **Mayama,** Congo
152/C4 **Maya Maya** (int'l arpt.), Congo
152/D4 **Mayamba,** Zaire
105/H2 **Mayāmey,** Iran
108/F5 **Mayan,** China
119/J2 **Mayang,** China
116/B3 **Mayāng Imphāl,** India
161/H1 **Mayarí,** Cuba
111/L10 **Maya-san** (peak), Japan
205/E7 **Maybee,** Mi,US
185/J3 **Maybell,** Co,US
54/B6 **Maybole,** Sc,UK
150/A2 **Maych'ew,** Eth.
105/F3 **Maydān,** Iraq
150/C3 **Maydh,** Som.
150/B1 **Maydī,** Yem.
125/D3 **Maydolong,** Phil.
152/C2 **Mayébout,** Gabon
69/G3 **Mayen,** Ger.
79/E4 **Mayenne,** Fr.
79/E4 **Mayenne** (dept.), Fr.
79/E3 **Mayenne** (riv.), Fr.
187/F3 **Mayer,** Az,US
195/N7 **Mayer,** Mn,US
200/B4 **Mayersville,** Ms,US
201/G4 **Mayesville,** SC,US
79/F5 **Mayet,** Fr.
191/G1 **Mayetta,** Ks,US
150/C2 **Mayfa'ah,** Yem.
183/L1 **Mayfair,** Sk,Can
54/C5 **Mayfield,** Sc,UK
200/C2 **Mayfield,** Ky,US
185/H4 **Mayfield,** Ut,US
208/F4 **Mayfield Heights,** Oh,US
190/B4 **Mayhill,** NM,US
114/C1 **Maykain,** Kaz.
53/H4 **Maykop,** Rus.
59/G3 **Mayland,** Eng,UK
183/L1 **Maymont,** Sk,Can
116/C4 **Maymyo,** Burma
97/H1 **Mayna,** Rus.
189/J2 **Mayna,** La,US
121/H4 **Maynāmati,** Bang.
191/J2 **Maynard,** Ar,US
208/C1 **Maynard,** Ma,US
200/F2 **Maynardville,** Tn,US
199/H2 **Maynooth,** On,Can
60/D3 **Maynooth,** Ire.
174/C5 **Mayo** (riv.), Arg.
177/L3 **Mayo,** Yk,Can
60/A2 **Mayo,** Ire.
60/A2 **Mayo** (co.), Ire.
158/C3 **Mayo** (riv.), Mex.
203/G2 **Mayo,** Fl,US
206/B6 **Mayo,** Md,US
201/H2 **Mayo** (res.), NC,US
148/B3 **Mayo Belwa,** Nga.
148/B3 **Mayo-Kébbi** (pref.), Chad
148/B3 **Mayo Kébi** (riv.), CAfr., Chad
152/C3 **Mayoko,** Congo
169/E4 **Mayo Mayo,** Bol.
125/C2 **Mayon** (vol.), Phil.
148/B3 **Mayo Oulo,** Camr.
76/D1 **Mayor** (cape), Sp.
172/D1 **Mayor Pablo Lagerenza,** Par.
140/G6 **Mayotte** (isl.), Fr.
157/H6 **Mayotte** (terr.), Fr.
192/A2 **Mayoworth,** Wy,US
125/C1 **Mayoyao,** Phil.
189/F1 **Maypearl,** Tx,US
161/G2 **May Pen,** Jam.
203/H2 **Mayport Nav. Air Sta.,** Fl,US
105/F4 **Maysān** (gov.), Iraq
109/K1 **Mayskiy,** Rus.
97/H4 **Mayskiy,** Rus.
99/L4 **Mayskiy,** Rus.
206/D5 **Mays Landing,** NJ,US
200/F1 **Mays Lick,** Ky,US
200/F1 **Maysville,** Ky,US
193/G4 **Maysville,** Mo,US
191/F3 **Maysville,** Ok,US
103/G7 **Maythalūn,** WBnk.
155/F1 **Mayuka,** Zam.
152/B3 **Mayumba,** Gabon
122/G3 **Mayuram,** India
194/F4 **Mayville,** ND,US
199/G3 **Mayville,** NY,US
184/C1 **Mayville,** Or,US
193/K2 **Mayville,** Wi,US
204/F8 **Maywood,** Ca,US
205/Q16 **Maywood,** Il,US
193/J4 **Maywood,** Mo,US
192/D3 **Maywood,** Ne,US
207/J8 **Maywood,** NJ,US
155/E2 **Mazabuka,** Zam.
166/D3 **Mazagão,** Braz.
182/D3 **Mazama,** Wa,US
74/E5 **Mazamet,** Fr.
82/B4 **Mazan,** Fr.
168/C1 **Mazán,** Peru
105/H2 **Māzandarān** (gov.), Iran
159/E3 **Mazapil,** Mex.
90/C4 **Mazara** (val.), It.
90/C4 **Mazara del Vallo,** It.
107/J1 **Mazār-e Sharīf,** Afg.
76/A1 **Mazaricos,** Sp.
76/E4 **Mazarrón,** Sp.
114/D4 **Mazartag,** China
165/G3 **Mazaruni** (riv.), Guy.
158/C2 **Mazatán,** Mex.
160/D3 **Mazatenango,** Guat.
158/D4 **Mazatlán,** Mex.
187/G3 **Mazatzal** (mts.), Az,US
187/G3 **Mazatzal** (peak), Az,US
79/E6 **Mazé,** Fr.
63/K3 **Mažeikiai,** Lith.
194/A3 **Mazenod,** Sk,Can
134/B3 **Mazeppa Nat'l Park,** Austl.
56/B3 **Mazetown,** NI,UK
104/D2 **Mazgirt,** Turk.
191/G2 **Mazie,** Ok,US
104/D2 **Mazıkıran** (pass), Turk.
152/D4 **Mazinda,** Zaire
68/B3 **Mazingarbe,** Fr.
152/D4 **Mazingu,** Zaire
63/K3 **Mazirbe,** Lat.
168/D5 **Mazocruz,** Peru
155/G3 **Mazoe** (riv.), Moz.
155/F3 **Mazoe,** Zim.
193/K2 **Mazomanie,** Wi,US
153/F4 **Mazomeno,** Zaire
198/B4 **Mazon,** Il,US
108/D3 **Mazong** (peak), China
155/F3 **Mazowe** (riv.), Zim.
63/L3 **Mazsalaca,** Lat.
155/F4 **Mazunga,** Zim.
65/L2 **Mazury** (reg.), Pol.
146/D2 **Māzūz, Ma'ţan** (well), Libya
155/E3 **Mbabala,** Zam.
153/G5 **Mbabala** (isl.), Zam.
157/E2 **Mbabane** (cap.), Swaz.
148/B4 **Mbabo** (peak), Camr.
144/B3 **Mbacké,** Sen.
148/C4 **Mbaére** (riv.), CAfr.
144/B2 **Mbagne,** Mrta.
144/D5 **Mbahiakro,** IvC.
152/D2 **Mbaïki,** CAfr.
148/B4 **Mbakaou,** Camr.
148/B4 **Mbakaou** (lake), Camr.
148/B4 **Mbakaou, Barrage de** (dam), Camr.
153/G5 **Mbala,** Zam.
155/F4 **Mbalabala,** Zim.
152/C2 **Mbalam,** Camr.
151/B2 **Mbalambala,** Kenya
153/H2 **Mbale,** Ugan.
152/D3 **Mbali,** Zaire
152/D3 **Mbali-Iboma,** Zaire
148/A5 **Mbalmayo,** Camr.
145/H5 **Mbam** (riv.), Camr.
151/A4 **Mbamba Bay,** Tanz.
148/A4 **Mbam, Massif du** (peak), Camr.
148/A5 **Mbam Minkoum** (peak), Camr.
152/D2 **Mbandaka,** Zaire
148/A4 **Mbandjok,** Camr.
148/B5 **Mbang,** Camr.
152/B1 **Mbanga,** Camr.
152/B3 **Mbanio** (lag.), Gabon
152/C4 **Mbanza Congo,** Ang.
151/B4 **Mbaranganda** (riv.), Tanz.
151/B4 **Mbarangandu,** Tanz.
153/G3 **Mbarara,** Ugan.
148/D4 **Mbari** (riv.), CAfr.
148/C5 **Mbata,** CAfr.
148/B4 **Mbé,** Camr.
139/Y18 **Mbengga** (isl.), Fiji
155/F4 **Mberengwa,** Zim.
153/G5 **Mbereshi Mission,** Zam.
151/A4 **Mbeya,** Tanz.
151/A4 **Mbeya** (peak), Tanz.
153/H4 **Mbeya** (pol. reg.), Tanz.
151/A3 **Mbeya** (prov.), Tanz.
151/A4 **Mbeya** (range), Tanz.
155/G1 **Mbeya,** Zam.
152/B3 **M'Bigou,** Gabon
148/D4 **Mbii,** CAfr.
152/C3 **Mbinda,** Congo
144/D4 **Mbingué,** IvC.
152/B2 **Mbini,** EqG.
152/B2 **Mbini** (riv.), EqG.
153/G4 **Mbirira,** Tanz.
153/G3 **Mbirizi,** Ugan.
155/F4 **Mbizi,** Zim.
151/A3 **Mbogo,** Tanz.
149/E4 **Mboki,** CAfr.
153/G3 **Mboko,** Zaire
155/F2 **Mboloma,** Zam.
152/C3 **Mbomo,** Congo
148/D4 **Mbomou** (pref.), CAfr.
149/E4 **Mbomou** (riv.), CAfr.
152/B2 **Mbonda** (pt.), EqG.
144/A3 **Mboro,** Sen.
127/F5 **Mborong,** Indo.
152/B1 **Mbouda,** Camr.
148/C4 **Mboula,** CAfr.
144/B3 **Mboune, Vallée du** (wadi), Sen.
152/C3 **Mbouomo,** Congo
144/A3 **M'Bour,** Sen.
144/B2 **M'Bout,** Mrta.
148/C4 **Mbres,** CAfr.
153/E4 **Mbuji-Mayi,** Zaire
151/A2 **Mbulu,** Tanz.
172/E4 **Mburucuya,** Arg.
151/B2 **Mbuvu,** Kenya
173/E3 **Mbuyapey,** Par.
155/G2 **Mbuzi,** Zam.
151/B4 **Mbwemburu** (riv.), Tanz.
151/A3 **Mbwikwe,** Tanz.
196/D3 **McAdam,** NB,Can
206/C2 **McAdoo,** Pa,US
190/D4 **McAdoo,** Tx,US
206/D1 **McAfee,** NJ,US
201/M7 **McAfee-Candler,** Ga,US
191/G3 **McAlester,** Ok,US
190/C3 **McAlister,** NM,US
206/A2 **McAlisterville,** Pa,US
189/E4 **McAllen,** Tx,US
201/F2 **McAndrews,** Ky,US
198/E5 **McArthur,** Oh,US
199/H2 **McArthur Mills,** Can.
198/D2 **McBain,** Mi,US
201/G4 **McBean,** Ga,US
201/G3 **McBee,** SC,US
182/D1 **McBride,** BC,Can
191/F4 **McBride,** Ok,US
183/M3 **McCabe,** Mt,US
184/E1 **McCall,** Id,US
200/B5 **McCall Creek,** Ms,US
188/C2 **McCamey,** Tx,US
185/G2 **McCammon,** Id,US
186/E2 **McCarran** (int'l arpt.), Nv,US
177/K3 **McCarthy,** Ak,US
154/D5 **McCarthy's Rust,** Bots.
195/K5 **McCaslin** (mtn.), Wi,US
188/D1 **McCaulley,** Tx,US
200/E3 **McCaysville,** Ga,US
205/C3 **McChord A.F.B.,** Wa,US
189/F2 **McClanahan,** Tx,US
190/C1 **McClave,** Co,US
190/D3 **McClellan** (cr.), Tx,US
205/M9 **McClellan A.F.B.,** Ca,US
201/H4 **McClellanville,** SC,US
184/B3 **McCloud** (riv.), Ca,US
200/C2 **McClure,** Il,US
206/A2 **McClure,** Pa,US
194/D4 **McClusky,** ND,US
201/H3 **McColl,** SC,US
202/C2 **McComb,** Ms,US
198/E4 **McComb,** Oh,US
192/D3 **McConaughy, C.W.** (lake), Ne,US
200/C2 **McConnell,** Tn,US
191/F2 **McConnell A.F.B.,** Ks,US
199/H5 **McConnellsburg,** Pa,US
198/F5 **McConnelsville,** Oh,US
192/D3 **McCook,** Ne,US
189/E4 **McCook,** Tx,US
183/L3 **McCord,** Sk,Can
201/F4 **McCormick,** SC,US
196/E3 **McCoy** (pt.), NB,Can
190/E1 **McCracken,** Ks,US
191/J3 **McCrory,** Ar,US
205/P15 **McCullom Lake,** Il,US
202/E2 **McCullough,** Al,US
191/G2 **McCune,** Ks,US
191/G3 **McCurtain,** Ok,US
189/F2 **McDade,** Tx,US
206/B6 **McDaniel,** Md,US
202/E2 **McDavid,** Fl,US
184/E3 **McDermitt,** Nv,US
51/N8 **McDonald** (isls.), Austl.
177/F3 **McDonald** (mtn.), Ak,US
190/C4 **McDonald,** NM,US
208/G5 **McDonald,** Oh,US
208/G7 **McDonald,** Pa,US
188/B2 **McDonald Observatory,** Tx,US
133/H5 **McDonnell** (peak), Austl.
200/E4 **McDonough,** Ga,US
201/M8 **McDonough,** Ga,US
177/L2 **McDougall** (pass), NW, Yk,Can
206/A1 **McElhattan,** Pa,US
200/D2 **McEwen,** Tn,US
189/G3 **McFadden Nat'l Wild. Ref.,** Tx,US
186/C3 **McFarland,** Ca,US
195/L4 **McFarland,** Mi,US
198/B3 **McFarland,** Wi,US
187/H3 **McGaffey,** NM,US
183/K2 **McGee,** Sk,Can
191/G3 **McGee Creek** (lake), Ok,US
200/B4 **McGehee,** Ar,US
200/F3 **McGhee Tyson** (int'l arpt.), Tn,US
185/F4 **McGill,** Nv,US
177/G3 **McGrath,** Ak,US
195/H4 **McGrath,** Mn,US
199/H3 **McGraw,** NY,US
196/D2 **McGraw Brook,** NB,Can
205/G7 **McGregor,** On,Can
195/H4 **McGregor,** Mn,US
194/C3 **McGregor,** ND,US
189/F2 **McGregor,** Tx,US
206/D3 **McGuire A.F.B.,** NJ,US
205/P15 **McHenry,** Il,US
205/N15 **McHenry** (co.), Il,US
200/D2 **McHenry,** Ky,US
202/D2 **McHenry,** Ms,US
151/B4 **Mchinga,** Tanz.
155/G2 **Mchinji,** Malw.
202/D2 **McIntosh,** Al,US
194/G4 **McIntosh,** Mn,US
190/A3 **McIntosh,** NM,US
192/D1 **McIntosh,** SD,US
191/G1 **McIvern** (lake), Ks,US
182/E5 **McKay Creek Nat'l Wild. Ref.,** Or,US
139/H5 **McKean** (isl.), Kiri.
179/K2 **McKeand** (riv.), NW,Can
200/F2 **McKee,** Ky,US
206/D5 **McKee City,** NJ,US
208/H7 **McKeesport,** Pa,US
208/G7 **McKees Rocks,** Pa,US
198/G2 **McKellar,** On,Can
202/E2 **McKenzie,** Al,US
184/B1 **McKenzie** (riv.), Or,US
200/C2 **McKenzie,** Tn,US
133/J2 **McKinlay,** Austl.
177/H3 **McKinley** (mtn.), Ak,US
177/J3 **McKinley Park,** Ak,US
184/A3 **McKinleyville,** Ca,US
191/G4 **McKinney** (bayou), La, Tx,US
189/F1 **McKinney,** Tx,US
188/C3 **McKinney** (mtn.), Tx,US
186/C3 **McKittrick,** Ca,US
202/D2 **McLain,** Ms,US
133/G2 **McLaren Creek Abor. Land,** Austl.
192/D1 **McLaughlin,** SD,US
193/K3 **McLean,** Il,US
196/C2 **McLean** (mtn.), Me,US
190/D3 **McLean,** Tx,US
206/A6 **McLean,** Va,US
200/C1 **McLeansboro,** Il,US
128/A4 **McLeod** (lake), Austl.
182/F1 **McLeod** (riv.), Ab,Can
178/E2 **McLeod** (bay), NW,Can
178/F1 **M'Clintock** (chan.), NW,Can
184/B2 **McLoughlin** (mtn.), Or,US
182/D2 **McLure,** BC,Can
178/E1 **M'Clure** (str.), NW,Can
191/F3 **McMillan,** Ok,US
184/B1 **McMinnville,** Or,US
200/E3 **McMinnville,** Tn,US
195/G3 **McMunn,** Mb,Can
137/M **McMurdo,** Ant.
191/H4 **McNab,** Ar,US
196/D2 **McNamee,** NB,Can
187/H3 **McNary,** Az,US
184/D1 **McNary** (dam), Or,US
182/E4 **McNary Nat'l Wild. Ref.,** Wa,US
195/K5 **McNaughton,** Wi,US
187/H5 **McNeal,** Az,US
191/H4 **McNeil,** Ar,US
205/B3 **McNeil** (isl.), Wa,US
202/D2 **McNeill,** Ms,US
155/G2 **Mcocha,** Malw.
187/H2 **McPhee** (res.), Co,US
191/F1 **McPherson,** Ks,US
189/E3 **McQueeney,** Tx,US
191/J3 **McRae,** Ar,US
201/F4 **McRae,** Ga,US
201/F2 **McRoberts,** Ky,US
206/A4 **McSherrystown,** Pa,US
194/E4 **McVille,** ND,US
200/D5 **McWilliams,** Al,US
151/A3 **Mdabulo,** Tanz.
151/A3 **Mdaburo,** Tanz.
151/A4 **Mdandu,** Tanz.
108/E5 **Mê** (riv.), China
194/B1 **Meacham,** Sk,Can
186/E2 **Mead** (lake), Az, Nv,US
193/F3 **Mead,** Ne,US
177/G2 **Meade** (riv.), Ak,US
190/D2 **Meade,** Ks,US
192/C1 **Meadow,** SD,US
188/C1 **Meadow,** Tx,US
185/G4 **Meadow,** Ut,US
178/F3 **Meadow Lake,** Sk,Can
195/H4 **Meadowlands,** Mn,US
207/J8 **Meadowlands Sports Complex,** NJ,US
184/E1 **Meadows,** Id,US
206/B6 **Meadows,** Md,US
197/R8 **Meadowvale,** On,Can
184/C4 **Meadow Valley,** Ca,US
186/E2 **Meadow Valley** (wash), Nv,US
184/C4 **Meadow Vista,** Ca,US
191/H1 **Meadville,** Mo,US
200/B5 **Meadville,** Ms,US
198/F4 **Meadville,** Pa,US
198/F2 **Meaford,** On,Can
112/C2 **Me-akan-dake** (mtn.), Japan
60/A6 **Mealagh** (riv.), Ire.
76/A2 **Mealhada,** Port.
54/B3 **Meall a' Bhuiridh** (mtn.), Sc,UK
54/B3 **Meall Buidhe** (mtn.), Sc,UK
54/C3 **Meall Dearg** (mtn.), Sc,UK
54/B2 **Meall Dubh** (mtn.), Sc,UK
54/C4 **Meall nam Fuaran** (mtn.), Sc,UK
54/C3 **Meall Tairneachan** (mtn.), Sc,UK
208/G5 **Meander Creek** (res.), Oh,US
167/E4 **Mearim** (riv.), Braz.
54/D3 **Mearns, Howe of the** (dist.), Sc,UK
59/E1 **Measham,** Eng,UK
177/F2 **Meat** (mtn.), Ak,US
60/D2 **Meath** (co.), Ire.
183/M1 **Meath Park,** Sk,Can
68/B4 **Méaulte,** Fr.
53/U10 **Meaux,** Fr.
201/H2 **Mebane,** NC,US
152/B3 **Mebenda** (peak), Gabon
152/C4 **Mebridege** (riv.), Ang.
124/F5 **Mebulu** (cape), Indo.
159/M6 **Mecapalapa,** Mex.
186/D4 **Mecca,** Ca,US
106/C4 **Mecca** (Makkah), SAr.
198/E4 **Mechanicsburg,** Oh,US
206/A3 **Mechanicsburg,** Pa,US
206/B3 **Mechanicsburg Nav. Supply Dep.,** Pa,US
201/J2 **Mechanicsville,** Va,US
202/C3 **Mechant** (lake), La,US
150/B3 **Mechara,** Eth.
68/D1 **Mechelen** (Malines), Belg.
143/E2 **Mecheria,** Alg.
121/F2 **Mechi** (zone), Nepal
148/B2 **Méchiméré,** Chad
93/H5 **Mecidiye,** Turk.
104/C1 **Mecitözü,** Turk.
81/F2 **Meckenbeuren,** Ger.
69/G2 **Meckenheim,** Ger.
62/D4 **Mecklenburg** (bay), Ger.
64/F1 **Mecklenburger Bucht** (bay), Ger.
155/H2 **Meconta,** Moz.
172/C2 **Mecoya,** Bol.
89/H1 **Mecsek** (mts.), Hun.
155/H2 **Mecuburi** (riv.), Moz.
155/J2 **Mecúfi,** Moz.
155/G2 **Mecuia** (peak), Moz.
155/H2 **Mecula,** Moz.
86/C1 **Meda,** It.
118/C4 **Medak,** India
124/B2 **Medan,** Indo.
124/C2 **Medang** (cape), Indo.
174/E3 **Médanos,** Arg.
175/L7 **Medanosa** (pt.), Arg.
164/D2 **Medanos de Coro Nat'l Park,** Ven.
198/C4 **Medaryville,** In,US
59/F1 **Medbourne,** Eng,UK
141/S15 **Médéa** (wilaya), Alg.
67/F6 **Medebach,** Ger.
171/E3 **Medeiros Neto,** Braz.
164/C3 **Medellín,** Col.
86/B2 **Mede Lomellina,** It.
81/E4 **Medel, Piz** (peak), Swi.
66/C3 **Medemblik,** Neth.
57/G5 **Meden** (riv.), Eng,UK
144/B2 **Mederdra,** Mrta.
86/D3 **Medesano,** It.
82/C6 **Mèdes, Cap de** (cape), Fr.
104/C2 **Medetsiz** (peak), Turk
208/C1 **Medfield,** Ma,US
208/C1 **Medford,** Ma,US
207/F2 **Medford,** NY,US
191/F2 **Medford,** Ok,US
184/B2 **Medford,** Or,US
193/J1 **Medford,** Wi,US
206/D4 **Medford Lakes,** NJ,US
93/J3 **Medgidia,** Rom.
149/F4 **Medi,** Sudan
206/C4 **Media,** Pa,US
174/C1 **Media Agua,** Arg.
173/F3 **Medianeira,** Braz.
193/J3 **Mediapolis,** Ia,US
93/G2 **Mediaş,** Rom.
182/F4 **Medical Lake,** Wa,US
87/E4 **Medicina,** It.
183/G1 **Medicine** (riv.), Ab,Can
193/H3 **Medicine** (cr.), Mo,US
183/M3 **Medicine** (lake), Mt,US
192/D3 **Medicine** (cr.), Ne,US
192/D2 **Medicine** (cr.), SD,US
185/K3 **Medicine Bow** (mts.), Co, Wy,US
185/K3 **Medicine Bow,** Wy,US
192/A3 **Medicine Bow** (peak), Wy,US
185/K2 **Medicine Bow** (riv.), Wy,US
183/J2 **Medicine Hat,** Ab,Can
194/E5 **Medicine Knoll** (cr.), SD,US
183/M3 **Medicine Lake,** Mt,US
183/M3 **Medicine Lake Nat'l Wild. Ref.,** Mt,US
191/E2 **Medicine Lodge,** Ks,US
190/E2 **Medicine Lodge** (riv.), Ks, Ok,US
194/G3 **Medika,** Mb,Can
164/C3 **Medina,** Col.
147/H3 **Medina** (int'l arpt.), SAr.
59/E5 **Medina** (riv.), Eng,UK
195/N7 **Medina,** Mn,US
194/E4 **Medina,** ND,US
199/G3 **Medina,** NY,US
208/F5 **Medina,** Oh,US
208/F5 **Medina** (co.), Oh,US
200/C3 **Medina,** Tn,US
188/E3 **Medina,** Tx,US
189/E3 **Medina** (riv.), Tx,US
205/C2 **Medina,** Wa,US
106/C4 **Medina** (Al Madīnah), SAr.
76/D2 **Medinaceli,** Sp.
76/C2 **Medina del Campo,** Sp.
76/D1 **Medina de Pomar,** Sp.
76/C2 **Medina de Rioseco,** Sp.
144/B3 **Médina Gonassé,** Sen.
76/C4 **Medina-Sidonia,** Sp.
63/L4 **Medininkai,** Lith.
121/F4 **Medinipur,** India
189/F3 **Medio** (cr.), Tx,US
164/C5 **Mediodía,** Col.
142/D2 **Mediouna,** Mor.
51/K4 **Mediterranean** (sea)
153/F2 **Medje,** Zaire
97/L2 **Mednogorsk,** Rus.
116/B2 **Mêdog,** China
86/D2 **Medole,** It.
87/E3 **Medolla,** It.
200/B1 **Medora,** Il,US
198/C5 **Medora,** In,US
194/C4 **Medora,** ND,US
152/B2 **Médouneu,** Gabon
149/H1 **Medruriet,** Eth.
183/K1 **Medstead,** Sk,Can
99/M3 **Medveditsa** (riv.), Rus.
97/H2 **Medveditsa, Gora** (riv.), Rus.
99/K5 **Medvedovskaya,** Rus.
99/J2 **Medvënka,** Rus.
101/S2 **Medvezh'i** (isls.), Rus.
94/G3 **Medvezh'yegorsk,** Rus.
92/B2 **Medvode,** Slov.
53/P8 **Medway** (riv.), Eng,UK
208/C1 **Medway,** Ma,US
196/C3 **Medway,** Me,US
94/G5 **Medyn',** Rus.
98/A3 **Medzilaborce,** Slvk.
132/C3 **Meekatharra,** Austl.
185/K3 **Meeker,** Co,US
197/J1 **Meelpaeg** (lake), Nf,Can
66/B6 **Meer,** Belg.
72/C6 **Meerane,** Ger.
67/G3 **Meerbach** (riv.), Ger.
66/D6 **Meerbusch,** Ger.
69/E1 **Meerhout,** Belg.
81/F2 **Meersburg,** Ger.
69/E2 **Meerssen,** Neth.
120/A1 **Meerut,** India
59/E1 **Meese** (riv.), Eng,UK
185/J1 **Meeteetse,** Wy,US
69/E1 **Meeuwen,** Belg.
149/H4 **Mēga,** Eth.
127/H4 **Mega,** Indo.
124/C4 **Mega** (isl.), Indo.
91/G3 **Megála Kalívia,** Gre.
91/H2 **Megáli Panayía,** Gre.
150/B4 **Megalo,** Eth.
104/A2 **Megálon Khoríon,** Gre.
91/H4 **Megalópolis,** Gre.
99/H5 **Meganom** (cape), Ukr.
196/B3 **Megantic** (mtn.), Qu,Can
91/H3 **Mégara,** Gre.
189/E1 **Megargel,** Tx,US
80/C6 **Megève,** Fr.
150/A3 **Megezez** (peak), Eth.
121/H3 **Meghalaya** (state), India
121/H4 **Meghna** (riv.), Bang.
103/G6 **Megiddo,** Isr.
103/G6 **Megiddo** (ruins), Isr.
103/A1 **Megista** (isl.), Gre.
63/Q1 **Megrega,** Rus.
105/F2 **Megri,** Arm.
155/F4 **Meguzalala,** Moz.
69/E2 **Mehaigne** (riv.), Belg.
150/A3 **Mehal Mēda,** Eth.
61/H1 **Mehamn,** Nor.
132/C2 **Meharry** (mtn.), Austl.
141/R16 **Mehdia,** Alg.
105/H3 **Mehdīshahr,** Iran
67/G1 **Mehe** (riv.), Ger.
98/B5 **Mehedinţi** (co.), Rom.
121/G4 **Meherpur,** Bang.
201/H2 **Meherrin** (riv.), NC, Va,US
63/M2 **Mehikoorma,** Est.

118/C3 **Mehkar**, India
70/A4 **Mehlingen**, Ger.
120/D2 **Mehndāwal**, India
105/G3 **Mehrabad** (Tehrān) (int'l arpt.), Iran
105/F2 **Mehrabān**, Iran
105/H5 **Mehrān** (riv.), Iran
69/F4 **Mehring**, Ger.
105/H4 **Mehrīz**, Iran
71/G6 **Mehrnbach**, Aus.
118/B3 **Mehsāna**, India
117/G4 **Mei** (riv.), China
151/A3 **Meia Meia**, Tanz.
173/G1 **Meia Ponte** (riv.), Braz.
148/B4 **Meidougou**, Camr.
148/B4 **Meiganga**, Camr.
179/R6 **Meighen** (isl.), NW,Can
54/C3 **Meigle**, Sc,UK
203/F2 **Meigs**, Ga,US
119/H2 **Meigu**, China
109/K3 **Meihekou**, China
54/B4 **Meikle Bin** (mtn.), Sc,UK
54/D5 **Meikle Says Law** (mtn.), Sc,UK
117/H3 **Meikou**, China
116/B4 **Meiktila**, Burma
81/E3 **Meilen**, Swi.
67/H4 **Meine**, Ger.
67/H4 **Meinersen**, Ger.
204/A2 **Meiners Oaks**, Ca,US
67/E6 **Meinerzhagen**, Ger.
70/D1 **Meiningen**, Ger.
80/E4 **Meiringen**, Swi.
69/G4 **Meisenheim**, Ger.
116/D2 **Meishan**, China
117/H3 **Meishan**, China
115/C5 **Meishan** (res.), China
117/H3 **Meishuikeng**, China
72/D5 **Meissen**, Ger.
67/G6 **Meissner** (peak), Ger.
117/G3 **Meitian**, China
70/D5 **Meitingen**, Ger.
111/M10 **Meiwa**, Japan
69/E4 **Meix-devant-Virton**, Belg.
117/H3 **Meizhou**, China
87/E2 **Mejaniga**, It.
142/D5 **Mejaouda** (well), Mrta.
172/B2 **Mejillones**, Chile
152/C2 **Mekambo**, Gabon
150/A3 **Mekane Selam**, Eth.
150/A2 **Mek'elē**, Eth.
144/A3 **Mékhé**, Sen.
150/A3 **Mek'ī**, Eth.
146/B2 **Mekili**, Libya
194/F3 **Mekinock**, ND,US
141/M14 **Meknès**, Mor.
145/F5 **Meko**, Nga.
123/D4 **Mekong** (riv.), Asia
127/F4 **Mekongga** (peak), Indo.
116/D4 **Mekong** (Lancang) (riv.), China
123/D4 **Mekong, Mouths of the** (delta), Viet.
177/E3 **Mekoryuk**, Ak,US
124/E2 **Melaka**, Malay.
124/E2 **Melaka** (state), Malay.
85/F6 **Melandro** (riv.), It.
138/E5 **Melanesia** (reg.)
122/F4 **Melappālaiyam**, India
126/D4 **Melawi** (riv.), Indo.
67/H2 **Melbeck**, Ger.
59/G2 **Melbourn**, Eng,UK
135/C3 **Melbourne**, Austl.
178/F2 **Melbourne** (isl.), NW,Can
57/G6 **Melbourne**, Eng,UK
191/J2 **Melbourne**, Ar,US
203/H3 **Melbourne**, Fl,US
61/E1 **Melbu**, Nor.
194/E4 **Melby** (hills), ND,US
193/H3 **Melcher-Dallas**, Ia,US
174/B5 **Melchor** (isl.), Chile
160/D2 **Melchor de Mencos**, Guat.
188/D4 **Melchor Múzquiz**, Mex.
188/E4 **Melchor Ocampo**, Mex.
58/D5 **Melcombe Regis**, Eng,UK
87/F4 **Meldola**, It.
64/E1 **Meldorf**, Ger.
194/F2 **Meleb**, Mb,Can
86/B5 **Mele, Capo** (cape), It.
86/C2 **Melegnano**, It.
92/E3 **Melenci**, Yugo.
94/J5 **Melenki**, Rus.
78/D4 **Melesse**, Fr.
97/K1 **Meleuz**, Rus.
179/J3 **Mélèzes** (riv.), Qu,Can
81/E5 **Melezza** (riv.), It.
85/D4 **Melfa** (riv.), It.
148/C3 **Melfi**, Chad
85/F6 **Melfi**, It.
183/M1 **Melfort**, Sk,Can
76/A1 **Melgaço**, Port.
167/L7 **Melgar**, Col.
76/C1 **Melgar de Fernamental**, Sp.
61/D3 **Melhus**, Nor.
70/B3 **Melibocus** (peak), Ger.
83/C6 **Melicucco**, It.
86/B1 **Melide**, Swi.
91/G4 **Meligalás**, Gre.
92/F5 **Meliki**, Gre.
151/B2 **Melili** (peak), Kenya
141/N13 **Melilla**, Sp.
174/B5 **Melimoyu** (peak), Chile
174/B4 **Melinca**, Chile
174/Q9 **Melipilla**, Chile
80/C2 **Mélisey**, Fr.
83/D4 **Melissa**, It.
91/F3 **Melissano**, It.
194/D3 **Melita**, Mb,Can
143/H2 **Melita** (int'l arpt.), Tun.
83/B6 **Melito** (riv.), It.
83/B7 **Melito di Porto Salvo**, It.
53/G4 **Melitopol'**, Ukr.
206/B5 **Melitota**, Md,US
75/L2 **Melk**, Aus.
150/A4 **Melka Guba**, Eth.
150/B4 **Melka Meri**, Eth.
73/A3 **Melkasa**, Eth.
156/L10 **Melkbosstrand**, SAfr.
58/D4 **Melksham**, Eng,UK
86/D2 **Mella** (riv.), It.
62/E2 **Mellan Fryken** (lake), Swe.
68/C2 **Melle**, Belg.
67/F4 **Melle**, Ger.
141/W17 **Mellègue** (riv.), Alg.
62/E2 **Mellerud**, Swe.
192/E1 **Mellette**, SD,US
76/B1 **Mellid**, Sp.
84/H8 **Mellieħa**, Malta
57/F3 **Melling**, Eng,UK
81/E3 **Mellingen**, Swi.
129/K3 **Mellish** (reef), Austl.
149/E2 **Mellit**, Sudan
175/J7 **Mellizo Sur** (peak), Chile
70/D2 **Mellrichstadt**, Ger.
67/F1 **Mellum** (isl.), Ger.
157/E3 **Melmoth**, SAfr.
93/F5 **Melnik**, Bul.
71/H2 **Mělník**, Czh.
98/D3 **Mel'nitsa-Podol'skaya**, Ukr.
175/G2 **Melo**, Uru.
197/N7 **Melocheville**, Qu,Can
127/F5 **Melolo**, Indo.
145/H5 **Mélong**, Camr.
143/G2 **Melrhir, Chott** (salt lake), Alg.
135/C2 **Melrose**, Austl.
54/D5 **Melrose**, Sc,UK
202/B2 **Melrose**, La,US
206/B4 **Melrose**, Md,US
195/G5 **Melrose**, Mn,US
190/C3 **Melrose**, NM,US
193/J1 **Melrose**, Wi,US
54/D5 **Melrose Abbey**, Sc,UK
190/C3 **Melrose Bomb. Ra.**, NM,US
205/Q16 **Melrose Park**, Il,US
81/F3 **Mels**, Swi.
183/L4 **Melstone**, Mt,US
67/G6 **Melsungen**, Ger.
57/G4 **Meltham**, Eng,UK
135/C3 **Melton**, Austl.
57/H6 **Melton Mowbray**, Eng,UK
155/H3 **Melúli** (riv.), Moz.
53/T11 **Melun**, Fr.
154/C3 **Melunga**, Ang.
122/G3 **Melūr**, India
191/G1 **Melvern**, Ks,US
191/G1 **Melvern** (lake), Ks,US
132/K7 **Melville**, Austl.
131/E3 **Melville** (bay), Austl.
134/B1 **Melville** (cape), Austl.
130/C2 **Melville** (isl.), Austl.
179/L3 **Melville** (lake), Nf,Can
179/R7 **Melville** (isl.), NW,Can
179/H2 **Melville** (pen.), NW,Can
194/C2 **Melville**, Sk,Can
125/B4 **Melville** (cape), Phil.
202/C2 **Melville**, La,US
183/K4 **Melville**, Mt,US
207/E2 **Melville**, NY,US
208/C2 **Melville**, RI,US
200/C5 **Melvin**, Al,US
159/F2 **Melvin**, Tx,US
205/F7 **Melvindale**, Mi,US
92/D2 **Mélykút**, Hun.
86/C2 **Melzo**, It.
91/F2 **Memaliaj**, Alb.
114/D5 **Mêmar** (lake), China
121/G4 **Memāri**, India
155/J2 **Memba**, Moz.
126/C4 **Membalong**, Indo.
79/F4 **Même** (riv.), Fr.
66/D1 **Memmert** (isl.), Ger.
81/G2 **Memmingen**, Ger.
123/D4 **Memot**, Camb.
103/B5 **Memphis** (ruins), Egypt
205/G6 **Memphis**, Mi,US
193/H3 **Memphis**, Mo,US
200/B3 **Memphis**, Tn,US
200/C3 **Memphis** (int'l arpt.), Tn,US
190/D3 **Memphis**, Tx,US
200/C3 **Memphis Nav. Air Sta.**, Tn,US
196/A3 **Memphrémagog** (lake), Qu,Can
199/K2 **Memphremagog** (res.), Can., US
150/A4 **Mena**, Eth.
130/B2 **Mena**, Indo.
144/D3 **Mèna**, Mali
98/G2 **Mena**, Ukr.
191/G3 **Mena**, Ar,US
175/T11 **Menafra**, Uru.
81/F5 **Menaggio**, It.
195/G4 **Menahga**, Mn,US
56/D5 **Menai** (str.), Wal,UK
56/D5 **Menai Bridge**, Wal,UK
145/F3 **Ménaka**, Mali
66/C3 **Menaldum**, Neth.
185/H2 **Menan**, Id,US
127/F4 **Menanga**, Indo.
142/C3 **Menara** (Marrakech) (int'l arpt.), Mor.
157/H9 **Menarandra** (riv.), Madg.
76/C3 **Menasalbas**, Sp.
193/K1 **Menasha**, Wi,US
157/H7 **Menavava** (riv.), Madg.
149/E2 **Menawashei**, Sudan
174/C4 **Mencué**, Arg.
126/D4 **Mendawai** (riv.), Indo.
74/E4 **Mende**, Fr.
150/A4 **Mendebo** (mts.), Eth.
67/E6 **Menden**, Ger.
177/E4 **Mendenhall** (cape), Ak,US
200/C5 **Mendenhall**, Ms,US
171/N7 **Mendes**, Braz.
168/B1 **Méndez**, Ecu.
159/F3 **Méndez**, Mex.
183/K2 **Mendham**, Sk,Can
206/D2 **Mendham**, NJ,US
149/G3 **Mendī**, Eth.
131/F1 **Mendi**, PNG
83/C4 **Mendicino**, It.
69/G3 **Mendig**, Ger.
58/D4 **Mendip** (hills), Eng,UK
184/B4 **Mendocino**, Ca,US
180/B3 **Mendocino** (cape), Ca,US
184/B4 **Mendocino** (pass), Ca,US
124/C2 **Mendol** (isl.), Indo.
208/C1 **Mendon**, Ma,US
198/D3 **Mendon**, Mi,US
191/H1 **Mendon**, Mo,US
135/D1 **Mendooran**, Austl.
186/B2 **Mendota**, Ca,US
193/K3 **Mendota**, Il,US
195/P7 **Mendota**, Mn,US
205/M11 **Mendota-Delta** (can.), Ca,US
195/P7 **Mendota Heights**, Mn,US
174/C2 **Mendoza**, Arg.
174/C2 **Mendoza** (prov.), Arg.
161/E1 **Mendoza**, Cuba
168/B2 **Mendoza**, Peru
175/T12 **Mendoza**, Uru.
174/C2 **Mendoza** (El Plumerillo) (int'l arpt.), Arg.
157/H9 **Mendrare** (riv.), Madg.
81/E6 **Mendrisio**, Swi.
92/F3 **Menedinți** (co.), Rom.
86/C3 **Menegosa, Monte** (peak), It.
164/D2 **Mene Grande**, Ven.
104/A2 **Menemen**, Turk.
208/D3 **Menemsha**, Ma,US
68/C2 **Menen**, Belg.
151/B2 **Menengai** (crater), Kenya
108/H2 **Menengiyn** (plain), Mong.
78/A4 **Menez Hom** (mtn.), Fr.
90/C4 **Menfi**, It.
115/D4 **Mengcheng**, China
70/C6 **Mengen**, Ger.
93/L5 **Mengen**, Turk.
70/E2 **Mengersgereuth-Hämmern**, Ger.
70/B1 **Mengerskirchen**, Ger.
75/L3 **Mengeš**, Slov.
124/D4 **Menggala**, Indo.
125/B4 **Menggatal**, Malay.
123/C1 **Menghai**, China
76/D4 **Mengíbar**, Sp.
71/F5 **Mengkofen**, Ger.
123/C1 **Mengla**, China
116/C4 **Menglian Daizu Lahuzu Vazu Zizhixian**, China
115/D4 **Menglianggu** (mtn.), China
123/C1 **Mengman**, China
117/F3 **Mengshan**, China
115/C4 **Meng Xian**, China
123/C1 **Mengxing**, China
115/D4 **Mengyin**, China
116/D4 **Mengzi**, China
68/A5 **Ménilles**, Fr.
133/J5 **Menindee**, Austl.
133/J5 **Menindee** (dam), Austl.
133/J5 **Menindee** (lake), Austl.
135/A2 **Meningie**, Austl.
200/E3 **Menlo**, Ga,US
174/B5 **Menlolat** (peak), Chile
205/K12 **Menlo Park**, Ca,US
207/H9 **Menlo Park**, NJ,US
53/T11 **Mennecy**, Fr.
79/G6 **Mennetou-sur-Cher**, Fr.
172/E1 **Mennonite Colonies**, Par.
194/D4 **Menoken Ind. Vill. Hist. Site**, ND,US
198/C2 **Menominee**, Mi,US
198/C2 **Menominee** (riv.), Mi, Wi,US
193/K1 **Menominee Ind. Res.**, Wi,US
193/K2 **Menomonee Falls**, Wi,US
193/J1 **Menomonie**, Wi,US
154/C2 **Menongue**, Ang.
77/H3 **Menorca** (int'l arpt.), Sp.
77/H3 **Menorca** (Minorca) (isl.), Sp.
84/C3 **Mentana**, It.
177/K3 **Mentasta Lake**, Ak,US
124/B3 **Mentawai** (isls.), Indo.
124/B3 **Mentawai** (str.), Indo.
124/C2 **Mentekab**, Malay.
67/H6 **Menteroda**, Ger.
80/C6 **Menthon-St-Bernard**, Fr.
187/H3 **Mentmore**, NM,US
82/D5 **Menton**, Fr.
204/C2 **Mentone**, Ca,US
198/C4 **Mentone**, In,US
188/C2 **Mentone**, Tx,US
194/F4 **Mentor**, Mn,US
198/F4 **Mentor**, Oh,US
115/H7 **Mentougou**, China
80/C4 **Mentue** (riv.), Swi.
53/R9 **Menucourt**, Fr.
131/G1 **Menyamya**, PNG
127/E3 **Menyapa** (peak), Indo.
108/E4 **Menyuan**, China
141/W17 **Menzel Bourguiba**, Tun.
177/M3 **Menzie** (mtn.), Yk,Can
132/D4 **Menzies**, Austl.
80/E3 **Menziken**, Swi.
81/E3 **Menzingen**, Swi.
80/E3 **Menznau**, Swi.
87/F1 **Meolo**, It.
59/E5 **Meon** (riv.), Eng,UK
53/Q7 **Meopham**, Eng,UK
188/B3 **Meoqui**, Mex.
127/H4 **Meos Waar** (isl.), Indo.
183/K1 **Meota**, Sk,Can
82/B4 **Meouge** (riv.), Fr.
152/C4 **Mepala**, Ang.
97/G4 **Mepistskaro** (peak), Geo.
66/D3 **Meppel**, Neth.
67/E3 **Meppen**, Ger.
77/E2 **Mequinenzo** (res.), Sp.
193/L2 **Mequon**, Wi,US
79/G5 **Mer**, Fr.
81/F5 **Mera** (riv.), It., Swi.
124/D4 **Merak**, Indo.
191/J2 **Meramec** (riv.), Mo,US
81/H4 **Merano**, It.
197/K2 **Merasheen** (isl.), Nf,Can
126/D4 **Meratus** (mts.), Indo.
131/F2 **Merauke**, Indo.
131/F1 **Merauke** (riv.), Indo.
133/J5 **Merbein**, Austl.
164/B4 **Mercaderes**, Col.
151/D1 **Merca** (Marka), Som.
82/C4 **Mercantour Nat'l Park**, Fr.
87/F5 **Mercatello sul Metauro**, It.
85/E6 **Mercato**, It.
85/E6 **Mercato San Severino**, It.
87/F5 **Mercato Saraceno**, It.
186/B2 **Merced**, Ca,US
186/C2 **Merced** (grove), Ca,US
186/C2 **Merced** (peak), Ca,US
186/B2 **Merced** (riv.), Ca,US
174/C1 **Mercedario** (peak), Arg.
172/E4 **Mercedes**, Arg.
174/D2 **Mercedes**, Arg.
174/F2 **Mercedes**, Arg.
175/F2 **Mercedes**, Uru.
189/F4 **Mercedes**, Tx,US
136/C2 **Mercer**, N.Z.
193/H3 **Mercer**, Mo,US
206/D3 **Mercer** (co.), NJ,US
206/D3 **Mercer** (co. arpt.), NJ,US
208/G5 **Mercer**, Pa,US
208/G5 **Mercer** (co.), Pa,US
205/C2 **Mercer** (isl.), Wa,US
205/C2 **Mercer Island**, Wa,US
199/H5 **Mercersburg**, Pa,US
206/D3 **Mercerville-Hamilton Square**, NJ,US
68/D2 **Merchtem**, Belg.
197/N7 **Mercier**, Qu,Can
104/E2 **Mercimekkale**, Turk.
85/E6 **Mercogliano**, It.
186/E2 **Mercury**, Nv,US
188/E2 **Mercury**, Tx,US
179/K2 **Mercy** (cape), Yk,Can
69/E5 **Mercy-le-Bas**, Fr.
74/E5 **Merdellou** (mtn.), Fr.
78/D2 **Merdere** (riv.), Fr.
79/E4 **Merdereau** (riv.), Fr.
78/C4 **Merdrignac**, Fr.
68/C2 **Mere**, Belg.
58/D4 **Mere**, Eng,UK
79/H6 **Méreau**, Fr.
150/A2 **Mereb Shet'** (dry riv.), Eth.
149/H2 **Mereb Wenz** (dry riv.), Eth.
175/M8 **Meredith** (cape), Falk.
190/C1 **Meredith** (lake), Co,US
199/L3 **Meredith**, NH,US
190/D3 **Meredith** (lake), Tx,US
193/J4 **Meredosia**, Il,US
193/J4 **Meredosia Nat'l Wild. Ref.**, Il,US
150/C5 **Mereeg**, Som.
99/J3 **Merefa**, Ukr.
68/C2 **Merelbeke**, Belg.
70/B1 **Merenberg**, Ger.
158/C2 **Meresichic**, Mex.
123/D3 **Mereuch**, Camb.
79/H4 **Méréville**, Fr.
53/Q8 **Mereworth**, Eng,UK
109/J2 **Mergel** (riv.), China
81/E6 **Mergozzo**, It.
123/B3 **Mergui**, Burma
123/B4 **Mergui** (arch.), Burma
93/H5 **Meriç**, Turk.
89/K2 **Meriç** (riv.), Turk.
93/G4 **Merichleri**, Bul.
68/B3 **Méricourt**, Fr.
159/H4 **Mérida**, Mex.
76/B3 **Mérida**, Sp.
164/D2 **Mérida**, Ven.
164/D3 **Mérida** (mts.), Ven.
164/D2 **Mérida** (state), Ven.
208/B2 **Meriden**, Ct,US
192/B3 **Meriden**, Wy,US
203/H2 **Meridian**, Ga,US
184/E2 **Meridian**, Id,US
200/C4 **Meridian**, Ms,US
191/F3 **Meridian**, Ok,US
208/H6 **Meridian**, Pa,US
189/F2 **Meridian**, Tx,US
205/C2 **Meridian-East Hill**, Wa,US
200/C4 **Meridian Nav. Air Sta.**, Ms,US
202/D1 **Meridian Station**, Ms,US
200/D3 **Meridianville**, Al,US
74/C4 **Mérignac**, Fr.
74/C4 **Mérignac** (Bordeaux) (int'l arpt.), Fr.
151/B1 **Merille, Laga** (dry riv.), Kenya
135/D3 **Merimbula**, Austl.
134/C3 **Merinda**, Austl.
70/D6 **Mering**, Ger.
148/B3 **Meringa**, Nga.
151/D1 **Merin Gubai**, Som.
192/C3 **Merino**, Co,US
175/F2 **Merinos**, Uru.
92/F2 **Mérk**, Hun.
188/D1 **Merkel**, Tx,US
70/D4 **Merkendorf**, Ger.
63/L4 **Merkinė**, Lith.
68/D1 **Merksem**, Belg.
66/B6 **Merksplas**, Belg.
131/H1 **Merkus** (cape), PNG
124/C2 **Merlimau**, Malay.
68/A3 **Merlimont**, Fr.
174/D2 **Merlo**, Arg.
149/G1 **Meroe** (ruins), Sudan
86/C1 **Merone**, It.
103/D3 **Meron, Har** (mtn.), Isr.
143/G2 **Merouane, Chott** (salt lake), Alg.
132/C4 **Merredin**, Austl.
135/F5 **Merri** (cr.), Austl.
187/G3 **Merriam** (crater), Az,US
55/J9 **Merrick** (mtn.), UK
207/E2 **Merrick**, NY,US
199/J2 **Merrickville**, On,Can
192/E2 **Merricourt**, ND,US
184/C2 **Merrill**, Or,US
193/K1 **Merrill**, Wi,US
205/Q16 **Merrill C. Meigs** (arpt.), Il,US
206/C2 **Merrill Creek** (res.), NJ,US
198/C4 **Merrillville**, In,US
199/L3 **Merrimack**, NH,US
196/B4 **Merrimack** (riv.), NH,US
192/D2 **Merriman**, Ne,US
58/D5 **Merriott**, Eng,UK
182/D2 **Merritt**, BC,Can
203/H3 **Merritt** (isl.), Fl,US
192/D2 **Merritt** (dam), Ne,US
192/D2 **Merritt** (res.), Ne,US
203/H3 **Merritt Island**, Fl,US
203/H3 **Merritt Island Nat'l Wild. Ref.**, Fl,US
135/D2 **Merriwa**, Austl.
135/C2 **Merriwagga**, Austl.
195/K4 **Merriweather**, Mi,US
189/J1 **Mer Rouge**, La,US
203/F2 **Merrow**, Ct,US
202/B2 **Merryville**, La,US
106/D6 **Mersa Fatma**, Eth.
150/B2 **Mersa Fatma**, Eth.
150/A1 **Mersa Gulbub**, Eth.
149/H1 **Mersa Tek'lay**, Eth.
69/F4 **Mersch**, Lux.
84/B1 **Merse** (riv.), It.
54/D5 **Merse** (dist.), Sc,UK
72/C5 **Merseburg**, Ger.
57/F5 **Mersey** (riv.), Eng,UK
57/F5 **Merseyside** (co.), Eng,UK
103/D1 **Mersin**, Turk.
124/C2 **Mersing**, Malay.
150/C4 **Mersin Galgalo**, Eth.
68/A3 **Mers-les-Bains**, Fr.
63/K3 **Mērsrags**, Lat.
53/N8 **Merstham**, Eng,UK
69/F5 **Merten**, Fr.
189/F1 **Mertens**, Tx,US
69/F4 **Mertert**, Lux.
69/F4 **Mertesdorf**, Ger.
58/C3 **Merthyr Tydfil**, Wal,UK
76/B4 **Mértola**, Port.
53/N7 **Merton** (bor.), Eng,UK
149/H3 **Mertule Maryam**, Eth.
137/K **Mertz** (glac.), Ant.
188/D2 **Mertzon**, Tx,US
69/G6 **Mertzwiller**, Fr.
68/B5 **Méru**, Fr.
151/B1 **Meru**, Kenya
151/B2 **Meru** (peak), Tanz.
124/F5 **Meru Betiri Nat'l Prsv.**, Indo.
151/B1 **Meru Nat'l Park**, Kenya
167/F3 **Meruoca**, Braz.
68/B2 **Merville**, Fr.
183/K1 **Mervin**, Sk,Can
118/B2 **Merwa**, India
66/C5 **Merwedekanaal** (can.), Neth.
53/S9 **Méry-sur-Oise**, Fr.
67/E4 **Merzen**, Ger.
69/F2 **Merzenich**, Ger.
104/C1 **Merzifon**, Turk.
69/F5 **Merzig**, Ger.
175/K7 **Mesa** (peak), Arg.
177/G3 **Mesa** (mtn.), Ak,US
187/G4 **Mesa**, Az,US
185/J4 **Mesa**, Co,US
190/B4 **Mesa**, NM,US
195/H4 **Mesabi** (range), Mn,US
146/A3 **Mesach Mellet** (hills), Libya
91/E2 **Mesagne**, It.
91/J5 **Mesarás** (gulf), Gre.
187/H2 **Mesa Verde Nat'l Park**, Co,US
188/B1 **Mescalero**, NM,US
190/C4 **Mescalero** (ridge), NM,US
190/B4 **Mescalero** (sands), NM,US
190/B4 **Mescalero Apache Ind. Res.**, NM,US
67/F6 **Meschede**, Ger.
87/F5 **Mescolino, Monte** (peak), It.
86/C4 **Mesco, Punta di** (pt.), It.
149/H2 **Mesfinto**, Eth.
95/L3 **Meshchura**, Rus.
105/F2 **Meshgīn Shahr**, Iran
149/F3 **Meshra'ar Raqq**, Sudan
198/D2 **Mesick**, Mi,US
187/J4 **Mesilla**, NM,US
83/B6 **Mesima** (riv.), It.
190/B2 **Mesita**, Co,US
187/J3 **Mesita**, NM,US
124/D4 **Mesiu**, Indo.
79/E5 **Meslay-du-Maine**, Fr.
81/F5 **Mesocco**, Swi.
87/F3 **Mesola**, It.
91/G3 **Mesolóngion**, Gre.
157/J8 **Mesomeloka**, Madg.
174/F2 **Mesopotamia** (reg.), Arg.
105/E3 **Mesopotamia** (reg.), Iraq
208/G5 **Mesopotamia**, Oh,US
83/C4 **Mesoraca**, It.
70/C3 **Mespelbrunn**, Ger.
78/C6 **Mesquer**, Fr.
187/J4 **Mesquite**, NM,US
187/E2 **Mesquite**, Nv,US
189/F1 **Mesquite**, Tx,US
142/E2 **Mesrouh, Jebel** (mtn.), Mor.
143/F2 **Messaad**, Alg.
78/D5 **Messac**, Fr.
155/H1 **Messalo** (riv.), Moz.
148/B5 **Messaména**, Camr.
69/E4 **Messancy**, Belg.
79/E3 **Messei-St-Gervais**, Fr.
70/B3 **Messel**, Ger.
175/J7 **Messier** (chan.), Chile
83/B6 **Messina**, It.
83/B6 **Messina** (prov.), It.
83/B6 **Messina** (str.), It.
155/F4 **Messina**, SAfr.
199/H1 **Messines**, Qu,Can
155/G4 **Messinge** (riv.), Moz.
91/H4 **Messíni**, Gre.
91/H4 **Messíni** (gulf), Gre.
70/C7 **Messkirch**, Ger.
70/B6 **Messstetten**, Ger.
154/B4 **Messum Crater** (peak), Namb.
53/U10 **Messy**, Fr.
93/F5 **Mesta** (riv.), Bul.
97/G4 **Mestia**, Geo.
71/F3 **Město**, Czh.
87/F2 **Mestre**, It.
87/E2 **Mestrino**, It.
96/F4 **Mesudiye**, Turk.
151/B3 **Mesumba** (peak), Tanz.
144/C5 **Mesurado** (cape), Libr.
164/C4 **Meta** (dept.), Col.
164/D3 **Meta** (riv.), Col., Ven.
85/E6 **Meta**, It.
196/B1 **Metabetchouan**, Qu,Can
196/B2 **Métabetchouane** (riv.), Qu,Can
155/J2 **Metacáua** (pt.), Moz.
150/A3 **Metahāra**, Eth.
179/K2 **Meta Incognita** (pen.), NW,Can
202/C3 **Metairie**, La,US
182/F5 **Metaline Falls**, Wa,US
87/D6 **Metallifere** (mts.), It.
205/F6 **Metamora**, Mi,US
172/C3 **Metán**, Arg.
155/G2 **Metangula**, Moz.
82/C2 **Metaponto**, It.
83/C2 **Metapontum** (ruins), It.
87/F5 **Metauro** (riv.), It.
199/J2 **Metcalfe**, On,Can
191/J4 **Metcalfe**, Ms,US
196/D3 **Meteghan**, NS,Can
196/D3 **Meteghan River**, NS,Can
67/E4 **Metelen**, Ger.
149/H2 **Metema**, Eth.
187/G3 **Meteor** (crater), Az,US
91/G3 **Metéora**, Gre.
57/H5 **Metheringham**, Eng,UK
54/C4 **Methil**, Sc,UK
54/D2 **Methlick**, Sc,UK
91/G4 **Methóni**, Gre.
182/D3 **Methow** (riv.), Wa,US
130/B3 **Methuen** (peak), Austl.
199/L3 **Methuen**, Ma,US
136/B3 **Methven**, N.Z.
54/C4 **Methven**, Sc,UK
164/C4 **Metica** (riv.), Col.
183/J1 **Metiskow**, Ab,Can
92/C4 **Metković**, Cro.
160/B2 **Metlatonoc**
143/F2 **Metlili Chaamba**, Alg.
92/B2 **Metnitz**, Aus.
200/B3 **Meto** (bayou), Ar,US
155/H2 **Metoro**, Moz.
83/C6 **Metramo** (riv.), It.
124/D4 **Metro**, Indo.
202/P8 **Metro-Dade Cultural Ctr.**, Fl,US
200/C2 **Metropolis**, Il,US
205/K11 **Metropolitan Oakland** (int'l arpt.), Ca,US
197/S8 **Metro Toronto Zoo**, On,Can
202/P8 **Metrozoo**, Fl,US
203/H5 **Metrozoo**, Fl,US
91/G3 **Métsovon**, Gre.
205/Q15 **Mettawa**, Il,US
71/F6 **Mettenheim**, Ger.
201/F4 **Metter**, Ga,US
69/D3 **Mettet**, Belg.
67/E4 **Mettingen**, Ger.
69/F5 **Mettlach**, Ger.
68/C2 **Mettler**, Ca,US
71/G6 **Mettmach**, Aus.
66/D6 **Mettmann**, Ger.
122/F3 **Mettupālaiyam**, India
122/F3 **Mettūr**, India
149/G3 **Metu**, Eth.
207/D2 **Metuchen**, NJ,US
103/D3 **Metulla**, Isr.
69/F5 **Metz**, Fr.
191/G2 **Metz**, Mo,US
69/F5 **Metz** (Frescaty) (arpt.), Fr.
70/C5 **Metzingen**, Ger.
159/F4 **Metztitlán**, Mex.
78/C4 **Meu** (riv.), Fr.
53/S10 **Meudon**, Fr.
70/A2 **Meudt**, Ger.
124/B1 **Meulaboh**, Indo.
79/G2 **Meulan**, Fr.
68/C2 **Meulebeke**, Belg.
79/G5 **Meung-sur-Loire**, Fr.
80/C1 **Meurthe** (riv.), Fr.
69/E6 **Meurthe-et-Moselle** (dept.), Fr.
69/E3 **Meuse** (riv.), Belg., Fr.
68/E6 **Meuse** (dept.), Fr.
74/F2 **Meuse** (uplands), Fr.
69/E5 **Meuse, Cotes de** (uplands), Fr.
72/C5 **Meuselwitz**, Ger.
79/F3 **Meuvette** (riv.), Fr.
80/A3 **Meuzin** (riv.), Fr.
103/G8 **Mevasseret Ziyyon**, Isr.
57/G5 **Mexborough**, Eng,UK
158/D4 **Mexcaltitán**, Mex.
189/F2 **Mexia**, Tx,US
166/D2 **Mexiana** (isl.), Braz.
186/E4 **Mexicali**, Mex.
187/H2 **Mexican Hat**, Ut,US
187/H3 **Mexican Springs**, NM,US
176/G7 **Mexico**
159/E5 **Mexico** (state), Mex.
176/H7 **Mexico** (gulf), NAm.
198/C4 **Mexico**, In,US
196/B3 **Mexico**, Me,US
191/J1 **Mexico**, Mo,US
199/H3 **Mexico**, NY,US
199/H3 **Mexico** (bay), NY,US
206/A2 **Mexico**, Pa,US
203/F3 **Mexico Beach**, Fl,US
159/K7 **Mexico City** (cap.), Mex.
80/B6 **Meximieux**, Fr.
105/H3 **Meybod**, Iran
125/F6 **Meycauayan**, Phil.
105/H4 **Meydān-e Gel** (lake), Iran
72/E1 **Meyenburg**, Ger.
177/M4 **Meyers Chuck**, Ak,US
199/G5 **Meyersdale**, Pa,US
208/F6 **Meyers Lake**, Oh,US
156/Q13 **Meyerton**, SAfr.
82/B2 **Meylan**, Fr.
107/H1 **Meymaneh**, Afg.
152/B2 **Méyo Kyé**, Gabon
82/B5 **Meyrargues**, Fr.
80/C5 **Meyrin**, Swi.
80/C5 **Meythet**, Fr.
80/C6 **Meythet** (Annecy) (arpt.), Fr.
82/B1 **Meyzieu**, Fr.
103/D4 **Mezada, Horvot** (Masada) (ruins), Isr.
116/B5 **Mezaligon**, Burma
93/F4 **Mezdra**, Bul.
74/E5 **Mèze**, Fr.
82/C5 **Mézel**, Fr.
95/K2 **Mezen'**, Rus.
94/J2 **Mezen'** (bay), Rus.
53/H2 **Mezen'** (riv.), Rus.
97/F4 **Mezha** (riv.), Rus.
100/J4 **Mezhdurechensk**, Rus.
100/G4 **Mezhdurechenskiy**, Rus.
100/E2 **Mezhdusharskiy** (isl.), Rus.
99/J3 **Mezhevaya**, Ukr.
98/B3 **Mezhgor'ye**, Ukr.
79/E2 **Mézidon-Canon**, Fr.
92/E2 **Mezőberény**, Hun.
73/C6 **Mezőfalva**, Hun.
73/C6 **Mezőföld** (range), Hun.
92/E2 **Mezőkovácsháza**, Hun.
92/E2 **Mezőkövesd**, Hun.
73/C6 **Mezőszilas**, Hun.
92/E2 **Mezőtúr**, Hun.
158/B2 **Mezquital**, Mex.
158/C3 **Mezquital**, Mex.
158/D4 **Mezquital**, Mex.
158/E4 **Mezquitic**, Mex.
81/G5 **Mezzana, Cima** (peak), It.
81/H5 **Mezzocorona**, It.
87/F3 **Mezzogoro**, It.
81/H5 **Mezzolombardo**, It.
151/A1 **Mfangano** (isl.), Ugan.
152/B2 **Mfou**, Camr.
154/E3 **Mfuwe**, Zam.
63/P2 **Mga**, Rus.
109/N1 **Mgachi**, Rus.
151/B3 **Mgambo**, Tanz.
151/B2 **Mgeta**, Tanz.
151/B4 **Mgeta**, Tanz.
151/A3 **Mgori**, Tanz.
142/D3 **M'goun** (peak), Mor.
54/B2 **Mhòr, Loch** (lake), Sc,UK
118/C3 **Mhow**, India
195/L5 **Mhunze**, Tanz.
113/D3 **Mi** (riv.), China
160/B2 **Miahuatlán**, Mex.
76/C3 **Miajadas**, Sp.
148/C3 **Miaméré**, CAfr.
194/E3 **Miami**, Mb,Can
186/G4 **Miami**, Az,US
162/A1 **Miami**, Fl,US
202/P8 **Miami**, Fl,US
203/H5 **Miami**, Fl,US
203/H4 **Miami** (can.), Fl,US
202/P8 **Miami** (int'l arpt.), Fl,US
203/H5 **Miami** (int'l arpt.), Fl,US
200/E1 **Miami** (riv.), Oh,US
191/G2 **Miami**, Ok,US
190/D3 **Miami**, Tx,US
181/K6 **Miami Beach**, Fl,US
202/P8 **Miami Beach**, Fl,US
203/H5 **Miami Beach**, Fl,US
198/D5 **Miamisburg**, Oh,US
202/P8 **Miami Shores**, Fl,US
202/P8 **Miami Springs**, Fl,US
120/A3 **Miāna**, India
108/D4 **Miancaowan**, China
122/B2 **Miān Channūn**, Pak.
115/B4 **Mianchi**, China
105/J2 **Mīāndasht**, Iran
105/F2 **Mīāndoāb**, Iran
157/H7 **Miandrivazo**, Madg.
105/F2 **Mīāneh**, Iran
117/H4 **Mianhu**, China
122/B1 **Miāni**, Pak.
116/D2 **Mianmian** (mts.), China
116/D2 **Mianning**, China
207/E1 **Mianus** (riv.), Ct,US
122/A1 **Miānwāli**, Pak.
116/E2 **Mianyang**, China
116/E2 **Mianzhu**, China
116/C3 **Miāo**, India
115/E3 **Miaodao** (isls.), China
117/F3 **Miao'er** (peak), China
115/H6 **Miaofeng Shan** (mtn.), China
117/F2 **Miaoshi**, China
157/H7 **Miarinarivo**, Madg.
157/J7 **Miarinarivo**, Madg.
157/G8 **Miary**, Madg.
95/P5 **Miass**, Rus.
95/Q5 **Miass** (riv.), Rus.
65/J2 **Miastko**, Pol.
168/B1 **Miazal**, Ecu.
152/D3 **Mibenge**, Zaire
147/G5 **Miberika**, Sudan
182/E1 **Mica Creek**, BC,Can
203/G3 **Micanopy**, Fl,US
164/B4 **Micay**, Col.
203/H4 **Micco**, Fl,US
203/F2 **Miccosukee**, Fl,US
203/H4 **Miccosukee Ind. Res.**, Fl,US
65/L4 **Michalovce**, Slvk.
197/G3 **Michaud** (pt.), NS,Can
135/D2 **Michelago**, Austl.
71/E3 **Michelfeld**, Ger.
177/K2 **Michelson** (mtn.), Ak,US
70/C3 **Michelstadt**, Ger.
72/D3 **Michendorf**, Ger.
162/D3 **Miches**, DRep.
200/C3 **Michie**, Tn,US
198/B1 **Michigamme**, Mi,US
195/K4 **Michigamme** (lake), Mi,US
195/K4 **Michigamme** (riv.), Mi,US
198/C3 **Michigan** (lake), US
181/J2 **Michigan** (state), US
194/E3 **Michigan**, ND,US
198/D3 **Michigan Center**, Mi,US
198/C4 **Michigan City**, In,US
200/C3 **Michigan City**, Ms,US
198/E2 **Michigan Is. Nat'l Wild. Ref.**, Mi,US
195/L5 **Michigan Potawatomi Ind. Res.**, Mi,US
195/M4 **Michipicoten** (isl.), On,Can
159/E5 **Michoacan** (state), Mex.
93/H4 **Michurin**, Bul.
53/H3 **Michurinsk**, Rus.
57/F2 **Mickle Fell** (mtn.), Eng,UK
57/F2 **Mickleton**, Eng,UK
206/C4 **Mickleton**, NJ,US
161/E3 **Mico** (riv.), Nic.
152/C4 **Miconje**, Ang.
162/F4 **Micoud**, StL.
138/E3 **Micronesia** (reg.)
138/D4 **Micronesia, Fed. States of**
126/C3 **Midai**, Indo.
145/G2 **Midal** (well), Niger
194/C3 **Midale**, Sk,Can
141/N13 **Midar**, Mor.
66/A6 **Middelburg**, Neth.
156/D3 **Middelburg**, SAfr.
157/E2 **Middelburg**, SAfr.
64/E1 **Middelfart**, Den.
66/B5 **Middelharnis**, Neth.
68/B1 **Middelkerke**, Belg.
66/C3 **Middenmeer**, Neth.
197/K1 **Middle** (ridge), Nf,Can
184/C3 **Middle** (lake), Ca,US
205/M11 **Middle** (riv.), Ca,US
193/G3 **Middle** (riv.), Ia,US
207/L9 **Middle** (bay), NY,US
206/A2 **Middle** (cr.), Pa,US
201/H1 **Middle** (riv.), Va,US
201/G1 **Middle** (mtn.), WV,US
119/F5 **Middle Andaman** (isl.), India
208/D2 **Middleboro**, Ma,US
201/G1 **Middlebourne**, WV,US
208/F6 **Middlebranch**, Oh,US
195/G3 **Middlebro**, Mb,Can
203/H2 **Middleburg**, Fl,US
206/A4 **Middleburg**, Md,US
206/A2 **Middleburg**, Pa,US
199/J3 **Middleburgh**, NY,US
208/F5 **Middleburg Heights**, Oh,US
208/A2 **Middlebury**, Ct,US
198/D4 **Middlebury**, In,US
199/K2 **Middlebury**, Vt,US
162/D2 **Middle Caicos** (isl.), Trks.
188/D2 **Middle Concho** (riv.), Tx,US
193/H3 **Middle Fabius** (riv.), Mo,US
208/B2 **Middlefield**, Ct,US
208/A1 **Middlefield**, Ma,US
208/F5 **Middlefield**, Oh,US
208/B2 **Middle Haddam**, Ct,US
57/G3 **Middleham**, Eng,UK
195/L5 **Middle Inlet**, Wi,US
183/M1 **Middle Lake**, Sk,Can
192/D3 **Middle Loup** (riv.), Ne,US
136/B4 **Middlemarch**, N.Z.
134/C3 **Middlemount**, Austl.
190/D3 **Middle Pease** (riv.), Tx,US
197/U9 **Middleport**, NY,US
198/E5 **Middleport**, Oh,US
206/B2 **Middleport**, Pa,US
193/G3 **Middle Raccoon** (riv.), Ia,US
206/B5 **Middle River**, Md,US
194/F3 **Middle River**, Mn,US
205/F7 **Middle Rouge** (riv.), Mi,US
200/F2 **Middlesboro**, Ky,US
57/G2 **Middlesbrough**, Eng,UK
59/F4 **Middlesex** (reg.), Eng,UK
208/B2 **Middlesex** (co.), Ct,US
208/C1 **Middlesex** (co.), Ma,US
201/H3 **Middlesex**, NC,US
206/D2 **Middlesex**, NJ,US
206/D3 **Middlesex** (co.), NJ,US
196/A3 **Middlesex**, Vt,US
184/B1 **Middle Sister** (mtn.), Or,US
196/F3 **Middle Stewiacke**, NS,Can
133/H5 **Middleton**, Austl.
196/E3 **Middleton**, NS,Can
57/F4 **Middleton**, Eng,UK
184/E2 **Middleton**, Id,US
200/C3 **Middleton**, Tn,US
198/B3 **Middleton**, Wi,US
59/E2 **Middleton Cheney**, Eng,UK
57/F2 **Middleton-in-Teesdale**, Eng,UK
56/B3 **Middletown**, NI,UK
205/J9 **Middletown**, Ca,US
208/B2 **Middletown**, Ct,US
206/C5 **Middletown**, De,US
198/D4 **Middletown**, In,US
207/D3 **Middletown**, NJ,US
199/J4 **Middletown**, NY,US
198/D5 **Middletown**, Oh,US
206/B3 **Middletown**, Pa,US
208/C3 **Middletown**, RI,US
201/H1 **Middletown**, Va,US
198/D3 **Middleville**, Mi,US
57/F5 **Middlewich**, Eng,UK
196/E3 **Middlewood**, NS,Can
184/C4 **Middle Yuba** (riv.), Ca,US
142/D2 **Midelt**, Mor.
58/C3 **Mid Glamorgan** (co.), Wal,UK
59/F5 **Midhurst**, Eng,UK
74/D5 **Midi** (can.), Fr.
74/D4 **Midi-Pyrénées** (reg.), Fr.
201/F1 **Midkiff**, WV,US
132/L6 **Midland**, Austl.
199/G2 **Midland**, On,Can
198/D3 **Midland**, Mi,US
184/C2 **Midland**, Or,US
208/G6 **Midland**, Pa,US
192/D1 **Midland**, SD,US
188/C2 **Midland**, Tx,US
188/C2 **Midland** (int'l arpt.), Tx,US
205/C3 **Midland**, Wa,US
61/F3 **Midlanda** (int'l arpt.), Swe.
203/F2 **Midland City**, Al,US
207/J8 **Midland Park**, NJ,US
155/F3 **Midlands** (prov.), Zim.
60/B6 **Midleton**, Ire.
205/Q16 **Midlothian**, Il,US
189/F1 **Midlothian**, Tx,US
67/F1 **Midlum**, Ger.
200/B4 **Midnight**, Ms,US
128/G6 **Midona** (lake), Austl.
157/H8 **Midongy Atsimo**, Madg.
74/C5 **Midou** (riv.), Fr.
125/D4 **Midsayap**, Phil.
58/D4 **Midsomer Norton**, Eng,UK
119/H2 **Midu**, China
208/F7 **Midvale**, Oh,US
201/F4 **Midville**, Ga,US
182/E3 **Midway**, BC,Can
138/H2 **Midway** (isls.), PacUS
200/E4 **Midway**, Al,US
206/C6 **Midway**, De,US
203/F2 **Midway**, Fl,US
201/G5 **Midway**, Ga,US
200/E1 **Midway**, Ky,US
202/B2 **Midway**, La,US
192/E2 **Midway**, Ne,US
188/B1 **Midway**, NM,US
189/G2 **Midway**, Tx,US
205/Q16 **Midway** (Chicago) (arpt.), Il,US
201/F4 **Midway-Hardwick**, Ga,US
135/C4 **Midway Point-Sorell**, Austl.
185/K2 **Midwest**, Wy,US
191/F3 **Midwest City**, Ok,US
104/C5 **Midyan** (reg.), SAr.
104/E2 **Midyat**, Turk.
55/P12 **Mid Yell**, Sc,UK
96/B4 **Midzhur** (peak), Bul.
92/F4 **Midžor** (peak), Yugo.
110/B4 **Mie**, Japan
110/E3 **Mie** (pref.), Japan
65/H2 **Międzychód**, Pol.
65/J3 **Międzylesie**, Pol.
65/M3 **Międzyrzec Podlaski**, Pol.
65/H2 **Międzyrzecz**, Pol.
65/H2 **Międzyzdroje**, Pol.
70/A2 **Miehlen**, Ger.
152/C2 **Miéle I**, Congo
188/E4 **Mier**, Mex.
93/G2 **Miercurea Ciuc**, Rom.
76/C1 **Mieres**, Sp.
75/J3 **Miesbach**, Ger.
150/B3 **Mī'ēso**, Eth.
72/B3 **Mieste**, Ger.
208/E6 **Mifflin**, Oh,US
206/A2 **Mifflin**, Pa,US
206/A2 **Mifflinburg**, Pa,US
206/A2 **Mifflintown**, Pa,US
206/B1 **Mifflinville** (Creasy), Pa,US
156/D2 **Migdol**, SAfr.
74/E3 **Mignennes**, Fr.
86/D5 **Migliarino**, It.
86/B3 **Mignanego**, It.
85/D5 **Mignano Monte Lungo**, It.
80/C4 **Mignovillard**, Fr.
151/A2 **Migori**, Kenya
151/A2 **Migori** (riv.), Kenya
158/C4 **Migriño**, Mex.
159/N8 **Miguel Alemán** (res.), Mex.
167/F4 **Miguel Alves**, Braz.
158/E3 **Miguel Auza**, Mex.
171/E1 **Miguel Calmon**, Braz.
175/T12 **Miguelete**, Uru.
159/Q10 **Miguel Hidalgo**, Mex.
158/E4 **Miguel Hidalgo** (int'l arpt.), Mex.
158/C3 **Miguel Hidalgo** (res.), Mex.
170/C4 **Miguelópolis**, Braz.
171/N7 **Miguel Pereira**, Braz.
174/E3 **Miguel Riglos**, Arg.
76/D3 **Miguelturra**, Sp.
113/D4 **Migŭm**, SKor.
104/B2 **Mihalıççık**, Turk.
110/D3 **Mihama**, Japan
110/C3 **Mihara**, Japan
111/G2 **Miharu**, Japan
122/H4 **Mihintale** (ruins), SrL.
107/J3 **Mihrābpur**, Pak.
77/E2 **Mijares** (riv.), Sp.
76/C4 **Mijas**, Sp.
150/D2 **Mijdāḥah**, Yem.
66/B4 **Mijdrecht**, Neth.
112/B2 **Mikasa**, Japan
98/D1 **Mikashevichi**, Bela.
111/N10 **Mikawa** (bay), Japan
111/N9 **Mikawa-Mino** (mts.), Japan
153/F5 **Mikengere**, Zaire
151/B3 **Mikese**, Tanz.
97/G4 **Mikha Tskhakaya**, Geo.
96/F1 **Mikhaylov**, Rus.
93/F4 **Mikhaylovgrad**, Bul.
92/F4 **Mikhaylovgrad** (reg.), Bul.
99/M2 **Mikhaylovka**, Rus.
99/H4 **Mikhaylovka**, Ukr.
95/N4 **Mikhaylovsk**, Rus.
103/F7 **Mikhmoret**, Isr.
94/H5 **Mikhnëvo**, Rus.
111/K10 **Miki**, Japan
91/H4 **Mikinai**, Gre.
91/H4 **Mikinai** (Mycenae) (ruins), Gre.
151/C4 **Mikindani**, Tanz.
184/C1 **Mikkalo**, Or,US
61/H3 **Mikkeli**, Fin.
63/L1 **Mikkeli** (prov.), Fin.
152/B2 **Mikomeseng**, EqG.
91/J4 **Míkonos**, Gre.
91/J4 **Míkonos** (isl.), Gre.
153/E4 **Mikope**, Zaire
91/G2 **Mikrí Prespa** (lake), Gre.
98/C3 **Mikulintsy**, Ukr.
73/A2 **Mikulov**, Czh.
111/M10 **Mikuma**, Japan
151/B3 **Mikumi**, Tanz.
151/B3 **Mikumi Nat'l Park**, Tanz.
95/L3 **Mikun'**, Rus.
110/E2 **Mikuni**, Japan
111/F2 **Mikuni-tōge** (pass), Japan
141/U17 **Mila** (gov.), Alg.
195/H5 **Milaca**, Mn,US
167/G4 **Milagres**, Braz.
164/B5 **Milagro**, Ecu.
120/B1 **Milak**, India
120/A2 **Milakpur**, India
189/H2 **Milam**, Tx,US
52/D4 **Milan**, It.
201/F4 **Milan**, Ga,US
200/E1 **Milan**, In,US
194/G5 **Milan**, Mn,US
193/H3 **Milan**, Mo,US
196/B3 **Milan**, NH,US
187/J3 **Milan**, NM,US
198/E4 **Milan**, Oh,US
200/C3 **Milan**, Tn,US
152/D5 **Milando**, Ang.
135/A2 **Milang**, Austl.
155/G3 **Milange**, Moz.
86/C2 **Milan** (Milano), It.
86/C2 **Milano** (prov.), It.
189/F2 **Milano**, Tx,US
86/C2 **Milano** (Milan), It.
104/A2 **Milas**, Turk.
89/K3 **Milâs**, Turk.
83/B6 **Milazzo**, It.
83/B6 **Milazzo** (gulf), It.
83/B6 **Milazzo, Capo di** (cape), It.
194/F5 **Milbank**, SD,US
58/D5 **Milborne Port**, Eng,UK
192/E3 **Milburn**, Ne,US
191/F3 **Milburn**, Ok,US
72/B2 **Milde** (riv.), Ger.
183/L2 **Milden**, Sk,Can
59/G2 **Mildenhall**, Eng,UK
183/M4 **Mildred**, Mt,US
133/J5 **Mildura**, Austl.
116/D3 **Mile**, China
150/B3 **Mīlē**, Eth.
135/F5 **Milepa**, Tanz.
134/C4 **Miles**, Austl.
188/D2 **Miles**, Tx,US
199/H4 **Milesburg**, Pa,US
183/M4 **Miles City**, Mt,US
71/G1 **Milešovka** (peak), Czh.
194/B3 **Milestone**, Sk,Can
83/C5 **Mileto**, It.
85/E5 **Miletto, Monte** (peak), It.
71/H4 **Milevsko**, Czh.
150/B3 **Mīlē Wenz** (riv.), Eth.
60/B4 **Milford**, Ire.
59/F4 **Milford**, Eng,UK
56/B3 **Milford**, NI,UK
208/A3 **Milford**, Ct,US
206/C6 **Milford**, De,US
203/F2 **Milford**, Ga,US
193/G2 **Milford**, Ia,US
198/C4 **Milford**, Il,US
191/F1 **Milford**, Ks,US
191/F1 **Milford** (lake), Ks,US
208/C1 **Milford**, Ma,US
196/C3 **Milford**, Me,US
205/E6 **Milford**, Mi,US
193/F3 **Milford**, Ne,US
199/L3 **Milford**, NH,US
206/C2 **Milford**, NJ,US
206/D1 **Milford**, PA,US
189/F1 **Milford**, Tx,US
185/G4 **Milford**, Ut,US
58/A3 **Milford Haven**, Wal,UK
58/A3 **Milford Haven** (inlet), Wal,UK
59/E5 **Milford on Sea**, Eng,UK
196/F3 **Milford Station**, NS,Can
146/C2 **Milh, Sabkhat al** (salt marsh), Libya
138/G4 **Mili** (atoll), Mrsh.
84/A1 **Milia** (riv.), It.
65/J3 **Milicz**, Pol.
130/C2 **Milikapiti**, Austl.
180/S10 **Mililani Town**, Hi,US
130/D3 **Milingimbi Mission**, Austl.
193/J2 **Military** (ridge), Wi,US
183/F4 **Milk** (riv.), Can., US
59/E4 **Milk** (hill), Eng,UK
183/H3 **Milk River**, Ab,Can

137/G Mill (isl.), Ant.
179/J2 Mill (isl.), NW,Can
66/C5 Mill, Neth.
205/G5 Mill (cr.), Mi,US
208/F7 Mill (cr.), Oh,US
206/B3 Mill (cr.), Pa,US
134/B2 Millaa Millaa, Austl.
74/E4 Millau, Fr.
182/C3 Mill Bay, BC,Can
192/E2 Millboro, SD,US
201/H2 Millboro, Va,US
205/K11 Millbrae, Ca,US
133/M8 Millbrook (res.), Austl.
199/G2 Millbrook, On,Can
58/B6 Millbrook, Eng,UK
200/D4 Millbrook, Al,US
207/H9 Millburn, NJ,US
185/H3 Millburne, Wy,US
208/C1 Millbury, Ma,US
184/B1 Mill City, Or,US
191/F3 Mill Creek, Ok,US
208/B2 Milldale, Ct,US
201/F4 Milledgeville, Ga,US
193/K3 Milledgeville, Il,US
200/C3 Milledgeville, Tn,US
197/N6 Mille Iles (riv.), Qu,Can
195/J3 Mille Lacs (lake), On,Can
195/H4 Mille Lacs (lake), Mn,US
195/H4 Mille Lacs Ind. Res., Mn,US
201/G4 Millen, Ga,US
187/G5 Miller (peak), Az,US
192/E1 Miller, SD,US
189/E4 Miller (int'l arpt.), Tx,US
189/N9 Miller (pt.), Tx,US
191/G4 Miller Grove, Tx,US
99/L3 Millerovo, Rus.
208/F6 Millersburg, Oh,US
184/B1 Millersburg, Or,US
206/B2 Millersburg, Pa,US
188/E1 Millers Creek (res.), Tx,US
202/E1 Millers Ferry, Al,US
200/D4 Millers Ferry (dam), Al,US
206/A2 Millerstown, Pa,US
188/E2 Millersview, Tx,US
206/B4 Millersville, Pa,US
186/C2 Millerton (lake), Ca,US
208/A2 Millerton, NY,US
197/J1 Millertown, Nf,Can
195/G4 Millerville, Mn,US
86/B4 Millesimo, It.
183/H1 Millet, Ab,Can
188/E3 Millett, Tx,US
56/C1 Milleur (pt.), Sc,UK
74/D4 Millevaches (plat.), Fr.
197/R9 Millgrove, On,Can
135/B3 Millicent, Austl.
202/E2 Milligan, Fl,US
197/S8 Milliken, On,Can
192/B3 Milliken, Co,US
191/J4 Millikin, La,US
66/D5 Millingen aan de Rijn, Neth.
206/C5 Millington, Md,US
200/C3 Millington, Tn,US
196/C2 Millinocket, Me,US
208/C1 Millis, Ma,US
56/C2 Millisle, NI,UK
134/C4 Millmerran, Austl.
206/A2 Millmont, Pa,US
207/L8 Mill Neck, NY,US
57/E3 Millom, Eng,UK
54/B5 Millport, Sc,UK
200/C4 Millport, Al,US
208/A1 Mill River, Ma,US
200/C5 Millry, Al,US
190/B2 Mills, NM,US
185/K2 Mills, Wy,US
201/K1 Millsboro, De,US
200/C1 Mill Shoals, Il,US
191/J2 Mill Spring, Mo,US
207/F1 Millstone (pt.), Ct,US
206/D3 Millstone (riv.), NJ,US
201/G1 Millstone, WV,US
132/C2 Millstream-Chichester Nat'l Park, Austl.
60/A5 Millstreet, Ire.
135/D2 Millthorpe, Austl.
57/F3 Millthrop, Eng,UK
200/D1 Milltown, In,US
207/H10 Milltown, NJ,US
197/K2 Milltown-Head of Bay d'Espoir, Nf,Can
60/A4 Milltown Malbay, Ire.
133/J1 Millungera, Austl.
208/H7 Millvale, Pa,US
205/J11 Mill Valley, Ca,US
196/E3 Mill Village, NS,Can
208/C1 Millville, Ma,US
206/C5 Millville, NJ,US
198/D5 Millville, Oh,US
206/B1 Millville, Pa,US
191/H4 Millwood (dam), Ar,US
191/G4 Millwood (lake), Ar,US
203/G2 Millwood, Ga,US
201/G1 Millwood, WV,US
206/D5 Milmay, NJ,US
138/E5 Milne (bay), PNG
54/B5 Milngavie, Sc,UK
194/F4 Milnor, ND,US
57/F4 Milnrow, Eng,UK
144/C4 Milo (riv.), Gui.
193/H3 Milo, Ia,US
196/C3 Milo, Me,US
180/U11 Milolii, Hi,US
91/J4 Milos, Gre.
91/J4 Milos (isl.), Gre.
72/C2 Milow, Ger.
133/J4 Milpa, Austl.
159/Q10 Milpa Alta, Mex.
133/J4 Milparinka, Austl.
158/C3 Milpillas, Mex.
205/L12 Milpitas, Ca,US
200/E1 Milroy, In,US
199/H4 Milroy, Pa,US
70/C1 Milseburg (peak), Ger.
201/N7 Milstead, Ga,US
70/C3 Miltenberg, Ger.
135/D2 Milton, Austl.
199/G3 Milton, On,Can
136/B4 Milton, N.Z.
57/F2 Milton, Eng,UK
59/G4 Milton, Eng,UK
208/A2 Milton, Ct,US
206/C6 Milton, De,US
202/E2 Milton, Fl,US
193/H3 Milton, Ia,US
191/J1 Milton, Il,US
208/C1 Milton, Ma,US
194/E3 Milton, ND,US
199/L3 Milton, NH,US
208/F5 Milton (res.), Oh,US
206/B1 Milton, Pa,US
199/K2 Milton, Vt,US
205/C3 Milton, Wa,US
193/K2 Milton, Wi,US
195/G4 Miltona, Mn,US
184/D1 Milton-Freewater, Or,US
197/R8 Milton Heights, On,Can
59/F2 Milton Keynes, Eng,UK
54/D3 Milton Ness (pt.), Sc,UK
54/B5 Milton of Campsie, Sc,UK
191/F1 Miltonvale, Ks,US
55/G10 Miltown Malbay, Ire.
117/G2 Miluo (riv.), China
198/F3 Milverton, On,Can
58/C4 Milverton, Eng,UK
205/Q13 Milwaukee, Wi,US
205/Q14 Milwaukee (co.), Wi,US
70/D2 Milz (riv.), Ger.
187/J4 Mimbres, NM,US
187/J4 Mimbres (riv.), NM,US
110/B4 Mimi (riv.), Japan
74/C4 Mimizan, Fr.
112/B3 Mimmaya, Japan
152/B3 Mimongo, Gabon
116/D2 Min (riv.), China
117/H3 Min (riv.), China
141/R16 Mina (riv.), Alg.
188/D4 Mina, Mex.
184/D4 Mina, Nv,US
105/J5 Mīnāb, Iran
174/D1 Mina Clavero, Arg.
170/C2 Minaçu, Braz.
127/F3 Minahasa (pen.), Indo.
195/G3 Minaki, On,Can
111/M10 Minakuchi, Japan
110/B4 Minamata, Japan
111/F3 Minami-Alps Nat'l Park, Japan
111/M10 Minamichita, Japan
138/D2 Minamiiō (isl.), Japan
112/B3 Minamikayabe, Japan
138/E2 Minami-Tori-Shima (isl.), Japan
111/L10 Minamiyamashiro, Japan
172/C2 Mina Pirquitas, Arg.
161/G1 Minas, Cuba
164/B5 Minas (peak), Ecu.
124/C2 Minas, Indo.
175/G2 Minas, Uru.
175/G2 Minas de Corrales, Uru.
161/F1 Minas de Matahambre, Cuba
76/B4 Minas de Riotinto, Sp.
170/D3 Minas Gerais (state), Braz.
105/G4 Mīnā' Su'ūd, Kuw.
159/G5 Minatitlán, Mex.
116/B4 Minbu, Burma
116/B4 Minbya, Burma
174/C1 Mincha, Chile
122/B2 Minchinābād, Pak.
58/D3 Minchinhampton, Eng,UK
174/B4 Minchinmávida (vol.), Chile
55/H8 Minch, The (sound), Sc,UK
87/D2 Mincino (riv.), It.
191/F3 Minco, Ok,US
125/C4 Mindanao (isl.), Phil.
125/C3 Mindanao (sea), Phil.
70/D6 Mindel (riv.), Ger.
70/D6 Mindelheim, Ger.
140/J10 Mindelo, CpV.
198/E2 Mindemoya, On,Can
199/G2 Minden, On,Can
67/F4 Minden, Ger.
189/H1 Minden, La,US
192/E3 Minden, Ne,US
184/D4 Minden, Nv,US
189/G1 Minden, Tx,US
185/G1 Minden City, Mi,US
189/B3 Mindif, Camr.
123/F1 Mindiptana, Indo.
125/C3 Mindoro (isl.), Phil.
125/C2 Mindoro (str.), Phil.
152/C4 Mindouli, Congo
95/N5 Mindyak, Rus.
195/H3 Mine Centre, On,Can
60/C5 Mine Head (pt.), Ire.
58/C4 Minehead, Eng,UK
170/B3 Mineiros, Braz.
191/J1 Mineola, Mo,US
207/E2 Mineola, NY,US
189/G1 Mineola, Tx,US
200/C2 Miner, Mo,US
185/H1 Miner, Mt,US
189/F3 Mineral, Tx,US
182/C4 Mineral, Wa,US
208/F6 Mineral City, Oh,US
159/L6 Mineral del Monte, Mex.
97/G3 Mineral'nye Vody, Rus.
97/G3 Mineralnyye Vody (int'l arpt.), Rus.
200/B2 Mineral Point, Mo,US
193/J2 Mineral Point, Wi,US
191/H4 Mineral Springs, Ar,US
188/E1 Mineral Wells, Tx,US
201/G1 Mineralwells, WV,US
87/E2 Minerbe, It.
75/H5 Minerbio (pt.), Fr.
87/E3 Minerbio, It.
206/B2 Minersville, Pa,US
185/G4 Minersville, Ut,US
208/F6 Minerva, Oh,US
85/G5 Minervino Murge, It.
199/H3 Minetto, NY,US
199/K2 Mineville-Witherbee, NY,US
70/B4 Minfeld, Ger.
114/D4 Minfeng, China
115/C3 Ming (riv.), China
153/F5 Minga, Zaire
148/D4 Minga, CAfr.
107/K2 Mingāora, Pak.
83/B2 Mingardo (riv.), It.
53/H4 Mingechaur, Azer.
97/H4 Mingechaur (res.), Azer.
132/B4 Mingenew, Austl.
116/B4 Mingin, Burma
76/E3 Minglanilla, Sp.
152/C3 Mingo, Congo
190/D1 Mingo, Ks,US
208/G7 Mingo Junction, Oh,US
191/J2 Mingo Nat'l Wild. Ref., Mo,US
152/C2 Mingouli, Chutes de (falls), Gabon
151/B4 Mingoyo, Tanz.
116/D2 Mingshan, China
108/D3 Mingshui, China
109/K2 Mingshui, China
123/A1 Mingun, Ancient City of (ruins), Burma
115/L8 Minhang, China
108/E4 Minhe, China
116/B5 Minhla, Burma
76/B1 Minho (riv.), Sp.
118/B2 Miniāri, India
148/C3 Minia-Siniaka Fauna Rsv., Chad
185/G2 Minidoka (dam), Id,US
185/G2 Minidoka Nat'l Wild. Rec., Id,US
132/D4 Minigwal (lake), Austl.
132/B2 Minilya, Austl.
194/D2 Miniota, Mb,Can
175/S12 Ministro Pistarini (Buenos Aires) (int'l arpt.), Arg.
194/D1 Minitonas, Mb,Can
131/G1 Minj, PNG
149/F4 Minkamman, Sudan
152/C2 Minkébé, Montagne de (peak), Gabon
114/B3 Min-Kush, Kyr.
133/H5 Minlaton, Austl.
108/E4 Minle, China
145/G4 Minna, Nga.
191/F1 Minneapolis, Ks,US
195/H5 Minneapolis, Mn,US
195/P7 Minneapolis, Mn,US
195/H5 Minneapolis-Saint Paul (Wold Chamberlain) (int'l arpt.), Mn,US
194/E2 Minnedosa, Mb,Can
202/M7 Minnehaha (lake), Fl,US
193/H1 Minnehaha (falls), Mn,US
195/P7 Minnehaha (falls), Mn,US
202/M6 Minneola, Fl,US
202/M6 Minneola (lake), Fl,US
190/D2 Minneola, Ks,US
193/G1 Minneota, Mn,US
192/B4 Minnequa (can.), Co,US
181/G2 Minnesota (state), US
194/F5 Minnesota (riv.), Mn, SD,US
195/P7 Minnesota Zoo and Gardens, Mn,US
195/H5 Minnetonka, Mn,US
195/P7 Minnetonka, Mn,US
195/N7 Minnetonka (lake), Mn,US
193/G1 Minnewaska (lake), Mn,US
56/D2 Minnigaff, Sc,UK
133/G5 Minnipa, Austl.
195/J2 Minnis (lake), On,Can
195/H2 Minnitaki (lake), On,Can
111/E3 Mino, Japan
88/B2 Miño (riv.), Port., Sp.
76/A1 Miño, Sp.
111/F3 Minobu, Japan
198/B2 Minocqua, Wi,US
111/N9 Mino-Mikawa (mts.), Japan
193/K3 Minonk, Il,US
111/L10 Mino'o, Japan
111/L10 Mino'o (riv.), Japan
52/D5 Minorca (isl.), Sp.
77/G3 Minorca (Menorca) (isl.), Sp.
85/E6 Minori, It.
208/D1 Minot, Ma,US
194/D3 Minot, ND,US
194/D3 Minot A.F.B., ND,US
108/E4 Minqin, China
117/H3 Minqing, China
115/C4 Minquan, China
67/F1 Minsener Oog (isl.), Ger.
63/M5 Minsk (cap.), Bela.
63/M5 Minsk (int'l arpt.), Bela.
65/L2 Mińsk Mazowiecki, Pol.
63/M4 Minsk Obl., Bela.
59/G4 Minster, Eng,UK
198/D4 Minster, Oh,US
148/B4 Minta, Camr.
114/B4 Mintaka (pass), China
200/D4 Minter, Al,US
201/G3 Mint Hill, NC,US
54/E1 Mintlaw, Sc,UK
196/D2 Minto, NB,Can
178/E1 Minto (inlet), NW,Can
177/L3 Minto, Yk,Can
177/J2 Minto, Ak,US
194/F3 Minto, ND,US
148/B5 Mintom II, Camr.
194/B3 Minton, Sk,Can
190/A1 Minturn, Co,US
85/D5 Minturnae (ruins), It.
85/D5 Minturno, It.
105/H2 Mīnūdasht, Iran
103/B4 Minūf, Egypt
100/K4 Minusinsk, Rus.
81/E5 Minusio, Swi.
116/C2 Minutang, India
152/C2 Minvoul, Gabon
106/E5 Minwakh, Yem.
108/E5 Min Xian, China
117/F3 Minxiao, China
103/B4 Minyā al Qamḥ, Egypt
95/N5 Min'yar, Rus.
135/B3 Minyip, Austl.
198/D2 Mio, Mi,US
82/A1 Mions, Fr.
63/M4 Miory, Bela.
116/B2 Mipi, India
114/E3 Miquan, China
95/P5 Mir, Rus.
197/G3 Mira (riv.), NS,Can
164/B4 Mira (riv.), Col., Ecu.
76/A2 Mira, Port.
76/A4 Mira (riv.), Port.
189/H1 Mira, La,US
193/J2 Mirabel, Qu,Can
197/M6 Mirabel (int'l arpt.), Qu,Can
85/E5 Mirabella Eclano, It.
87/E3 Mirabello, It.
171/E4 Miracema, Braz.
163/E3 Miracema do Norte, Braz.
86/C2 Miradolo Terme, It.
167/E4 Mirador, Braz.
174/C4 Mirador (pass), Chile
164/C3 Miraflores, Col.
164/C4 Miraflores, Col.
168/B3 Miraflores, Peru
161/H2 Miragoâne, Haiti
118/B4 Miraj, India
204/C2 Mira Loma, Ca,US
172/D4 Miramar, Arg.
174/F3 Miramar, Arg.
136/H9 Miramar, N.Z.
204/C5 Miramar, Ca,US
202/P8 Miramar, Fl,US
87/F4 Miramare (arpt.), It.
204/C5 Miramar Nav. Air Sta., Ca,US
82/B5 Miramas, Fr.
91/J5 Mirambéllou (gulf), Gre.
196/E2 Miramichi (bay), NB,Can
196/E2 Miramichi-Nelson, NB,Can
74/D4 Miramont-de-Guyenne, Fr.
204/A2 Mira Monte, Ca,US
122/A2 Mīrān, Pak.
170/A4 Miranda, Braz.
170/A3 Miranda (riv.), Braz.
85/E4 Miranda, It.
194/E5 Miranda, SD,US
165/E2 Miranda (state), Ven.
76/D1 Miranda de Ebro, Sp.
76/A2 Miranda do Corvo, Port.
76/B2 Miranda do Douro, Port.
74/D5 Mirande, Fr.
76/B2 Mirandela, Port.
170/C3 Mirandiba, Braz.
188/E4 Mirando City, Tx,US
87/E3 Mirandola, It.
170/C4 Mirandópolis, Braz.
87/F2 Mirano, It.
170/C1 Miranorte, Braz.
120/A1 Mīrānpur, India
170/C4 Mirassol, Braz.
87/F2 Mira Taglio, It.
161/E4 Miravalles (vol.), CR
76/B1 Miravalles (mtn.), Sp.
97/H4 Mir-Bashir, Azer.
107/F5 Mirbāţ, Oman
161/H2 Mirebalais, Haiti
80/B3 Mirebeau-sur-Bèze, Fr.
80/C1 Mirecourt, Fr.
80/C1 Mirecourt (Épinal) (arpt.), Fr.
149/E3 Mireigha, Sudan
57/G4 Mirfield, Eng,UK
99/G3 Mirgorod, Ukr.
125/A4 Miri, Malay.
134/C4 Miriam Vale, Austl.
173/G1 Mirim (lake), Braz., Uru.
164/D2 Mirimire, Ven.
91/J3 Mirina, Gre.
172/E3 Miriñay (riv.), Arg.
172/E3 Mirinzal, Braz.
164/D5 Miritiparaná (riv.), Col.
107/H3 Mīrjāveh, Iran
87/G2 Mirna (riv.), Cro.
137/G Mirnyy, Ant.
101/M3 Mirnyy, Rus.
98/F3 Mironovka, Ukr.
64/G2 Mirow, Ger.
122/B1 Mīrpur, Pak.
145/H3 Mirria, Niger
183/H1 Mirror, Ab,Can
206/D4 Mirror (lake), NJ,US
114/E3 Mirsali, China
121/H4 Mīrsarāi, Bang.
122/C1 Mirthal, India
83/C3 Mirto, It.
91/H4 Mirtóön (sea), Gre.
113/E5 Miryang, SKor.
97/H4 Mirzaani, Geo.
121/H3 Mirzāpur, Bang.
120/D3 Mirzāpur, India
87/G5 Misa (riv.), It.
153/G1 Misa, Zaire
147/E4 Misāha, Bīr (well), Egypt
110/D3 Misaki, Japan
87/F5 Misano Adriatico, It.
159/F5 Misantla, Mex.
151/B3 Misasa, Tanz.
112/B3 Misawa, Japan
85/E5 Miscano (riv.), It.
73/A5 Mischendorf, Aus.
196/E2 Miscou (isl.), NB,Can
196/E1 Miscou (pt.), NB,Can
196/E2 Miscou Centre, NB,Can
83/C2 Misegna (riv.), It.
202/B3 Misere (lake), La,US
107/K1 Misgār, Pak.
105/G4 Mish'āb, Ra's (pt.), SAr.
168/C3 Mishagua, Peru
109/L2 Mishan, China
208/D2 Mishaum (pt.), Ma,US
198/C4 Mishawaka, In,US
177/F2 Misheguk (mtn.), Ak,US
198/C2 Mishicot, Wi,US
111/F3 Mishima, Japan
95/M5 Mishkino, Rus.
90/C3 Misilmeri, It.
158/B2 Misión de San Fernando, Mex.
173/F2 Misiones (mts.), Arg.
173/F2 Misiones (prov.), Arg.
173/E2 Misiones (dept.), Par.
161/F3 Miskitos (cay), Nic.
92/E1 Miskolc, Hun.
146/A3 Mislane, Hassi el (well), Algeria
149/G1 Mismār, Sudan
111/M10 Misono, Japan
127/H4 Misool (isl.), Indo.
195/J4 Misquah (hills), Mn,US
146/B1 Miṣrātah, Libya
147/B1 Miṣrātah, Ras (pt.), Libya
167/G4 Missão Velha, Braz.
78/C6 Missillac, Fr.
179/H3 Missinaibi (riv.), On,Can
182/C3 Mission, BC,Can
204/C5 Mission (bay), Ca,US
191/G2 Mission (mtn.), Ok,US
184/D1 Mission, Or,US
189/E4 Mission, Tx,US
134/B2 Mission Beach, Austl.
189/M9 Mission Bend, Tx,US
204/C4 Mission Ind. Res., Ca,US
194/D5 Mission Ridge, SD,US
204/C3 Mission Viejo, Ca,US
202/D2 Missisippi Sandhill Crane Nat'l Wild. Ref., Ms,US
198/E1 Mississagi (riv.), On,Can
199/G3 Mississauga, On,Can
132/D5 Mississippi (pt.), Austl.
181/H5 Mississippi (state), US
202/C2 Mississippi (riv.), La,US
202/D3 Mississippi (delta), Ms,US
202/D2 Mississippi (sound), Ms,US
199/H2 Mississippi Station, On,Can
138/C5 Missol (isl.), Indo.
183/H4 Missoula, Mt,US
191/J1 Missouri (riv.), US
181/H4 Missouri (state), US
189/G3 Missouri City, Tx,US
194/A2 Missouri Coteau (hills), Sk,Can
194/C4 Missouri Slope, ND,US
193/G3 Missouri Valley, Ia,US
151/A2 Missungwi, Tanz.
182/C5 Mist, Or,US
134/B3 Mistake (cr.), Austl.
130/C4 Mistake Creek, Austl.
197/L2 Mistaken (pt.), Nf,Can
196/A1 Mistassini, Qu,Can
179/J3 Mistassini (lake), Qu,Can
183/N1 Mistatim, Sk,Can
73/A2 Mistelbach an der Zaya, Aus.
59/H3 Mistley, Eng,UK
91/H4 Mistrás (ruins), Gre.
90/D4 Mistretta, It.
177/M4 Misty Fjords Nat'l Mon., Ak,US
111/G1 Misugi, Japan
155/F2 Miswa, Zam.
111/H7 Mitake, Japan
111/N9 Mitake, Japan
158/D4 Mita, Punta de (pt.), Mex.
164/D2 Mitare, Ven.
149/H1 Mitatib, Sudan
133/M9 Mitcham, Austl.
58/D3 Mitcheldean, Eng,UK
134/B4 Mitchell, Austl.
131/D3 Mitchell (riv.), Austl.
134/A1 Mitchell (riv.), Austl.
200/D4 Mitchell (dam), Al,US
200/D4 Mitchell (lake), Al,US
191/H2 Mitchell, Ar,US
198/C5 Mitchell, In,US
201/F3 Mitchell (mtn.), NC,US
184/C1 Mitchell, Or,US
192/E2 Mitchell, SD,US
134/A1 Mitchell & Alice Rivers Nat'l Park, Austl.
205/H7 Mitchell Bay, On,Can
191/J4 Mitchellville, Ar,US
60/B5 Mitchelstown, Ire.
103/B4 Mīt Ghamr, Egypt
118/B2 Mithankot, Pak.
121/G3 Mithapukur, Bang.
107/J4 Mithi, Pak.
91/K3 Mithimna, Gre.
139/K6 Mitiaro (isl.), Cookls.
91/K3 Mitilini, Gre.
160/B2 Mitla (ruins), Mex.
103/C4 Mitla (Mamarr Mitlah) (pass), Egypt
111/G2 Mito, Japan
152/B2 Mitra (peak), EqG.
175/L8 Mitre (pen.), Arg.
136/C3 Mitre (peak), N.Z.
188/C2 Mitre (peak), Tx,US
99/K3 Mitrofanovka, Rus.
53/T10 Mitry-Mory, Fr.
157/G5 Mitsamiouli, Com.
153/G2 Mitshibu, Zaire
157/H7 Mitsinjo, Madg.
157/J6 Mitsio, Nosy (isl.), Madg.
150/A2 Mits'iwa, Eth.
111/M10 Mitsue, Japan
111/F2 Mitsukaidō, Japan
111/F2 Mitsuke, Japan
135/D2 Mittagong, Austl.
81/F3 Mittagspitze (peak), Aus.
81/G3 Mittelberg, Aus.
67/F4 Mittelland (can.), Ger.
67/E3 Mittelradde (riv.), Ger.
81/H3 Mittenwald, Ger.
72/D1 Mittenwalde, Ger.
75/K3 Mittersill, Aus.
71/F3 Mitterteich, Ger.
144/B4 Mitti, Gui.
71/E6 Mittlere-Isar (can.), Ger.
72/C6 Mittweida, Ger.
64/G3 Mittweide, Ger.
164/D4 Mitú, Col.
164/D4 Mituas, Col.
153/G4 Mitumba (mts.), Zaire
117/G2 Mituosi, China
153/F5 Mitwaba, Zaire
70/E2 Mitwitz, Ger.
153/H2 Mityana, Ugan.
152/B2 Mitzic, Gabon
111/H7 Miura, Japan
111/H7 Miura (pen.), Japan
160/D3 Mixco Viejo (ruins), Guat.
115/C4 Mi Xian, China
159/F4 Mixquiahuala, Mex.
160/B2 Mixteco (riv.), Mex.
111/M10 Miya (riv.), Japan
111/M10 Miyagawa, Japan
111/G1 Miyagi (pref.), Japan
112/B4 Miyako, Japan
112/H8 Miyako (isls.), Japan
110/B5 Miyakonojō, Japan
97/K2 Miyaly, Kaz.
111/L9 Miyama, Japan
110/B5 Miyanojō, Japan
111/H6 Miyashiro, Japan
110/B5 Miyazaki, Japan
110/B5 Miyazaki (arpt.), Japan
110/B4 Miyazaki (pref.), Japan
110/D3 Miyazu, Japan
119/H2 Miyi, China
110/D3 Miyoshi, Japan
115/D2 Miyun, China
115/D2 Miyun (res.), China
146/B2 Mizdah, Libya
56/B6 Mizen Head (pt.), Ire.
93/H3 Mizil, Rom.
93/F4 Miziya, Bul.
98/D2 Mizoch, Ukr.
116/B4 Mizoram (state), India
194/B5 Mizpah (cr.), Mt,US
206/D5 Mizpah, NJ,US
104/C4 Mizpe Ramon, Isr.
172/C1 Mizque, Bol.
111/E3 Mizunami, Japan
112/B4 Mizusawa, Japan
62/F2 Mjölby, Swe.
62/D2 Mjøndalen, Nor.
62/E3 Mjörn (lake), Swe.
62/D1 Mjøsa (lake), Nor.
151/A3 Mkalama, Tanz.
151/B3 Mkata, Tanz.
151/B3 Mkata (plain), Tanz.
151/B3 Mkoani, Tanz.
151/B3 Mkokotoni, Tanz.
151/B3 Mkomazi Game Rsv., Tanz.
153/G4 Mkombo (riv.), Tanz.
151/B3 Mkondoa (riv.), Tanz.
142/D3 Mkorn, Jebel (mtn.), Mor.
151/B3 Mkumbi, Ras (pt.), Tanz.
155/F2 Mkushi, Zam.
155/F2 Mkushi (riv.), Zam.
157/F2 Mkuze, SAfr.
157/F2 Mkuze (riv.), SAfr.
71/H2 Mladá Boleslav, Czh.
71/H3 Mladá Vožice, Czh.
92/E3 Mladenovac, Yugo.
153/G4 Mlala (hills), Tanz.
65/L2 Mława, Pol.
92/C4 Mljet (isl.), Cro.
90/E1 Mljet (isl.), Cro.
92/C4 Mljet Nat'l Park, Cro.
155/G2 Mlolo, Zam.
156/D2 Mmabatho, SAfr.
155/E4 Mmadinare, Bots.
155/E4 Mmamabula, Bots.
154/E5 Mmathethe, Bots.
151/C2 Mnazini, Kenya
71/H3 Mníšek, Czh.
151/A4 Mnyera (riv.), Tanz.
61/E2 Mo, Nor.
161/H1 Moa, Cuba
130/B2 Moa (isl.), Indo.
144/C5 Moa (riv.), Libr., SLeo.
151/B3 Moa, Tanz.
185/J4 Moab, Ut,US
152/B3 Moabi, Gabon
138/H6 Moala Group (isls.), Fiji
135/C1 Moama, Austl.
135/C3 Moama, Austl.
155/G5 Moamba, Moz.
76/A1 Moaña, Sp.
152/C3 Moanda, Gabon
186/E2 Moapa, Nv,US
186/E2 Moapa (peak), Nv,US
186/E2 Moapa River Ind. Res., Nv,US
60/C3 Moate, Ire.
105/G3 Mobārakeh, Iran
148/D4 Mobaye, CAfr.
190/D3 Mobeetie, Tx,US
191/H1 Moberly, Mo,US
202/D2 Mobile, Al,US
202/D2 Mobile (bay), Al,US
202/D2 Mobile (pt.), Al,US
192/D1 Mobridge, SD,US
162/D3 Moca, DRep.
73/C4 Moča, Slvk.
103/C1 Moca (pass), Turk.
164/B5 Mocache, Ecu.
166/D3 Mocajuba, Braz.
155/J2 Moçambique, Moz.
206/B1 Mocanaqua, Pa,US
187/F2 Moccasin, Az,US
116/E4 Moc Chau, Viet.
150/B2 Mocha, Yem.
168/B3 Moche, Peru
165/E2 Mochima Nat'l Park, Ven.
123/D4 Moc Hoa, Viet.
154/E5 Mochudi, Bots.
168/B2 Mochumí, Peru
155/J1 Mocímboa da Praia, Moz.
92/D2 Mociu, Rom.
62/E3 Möckeln (lake), Swe.
72/B3 Möckern, Ger.
62/F1 Mockfjärd, Swe.
70/C4 Möckmühl, Ger.
201/G3 Mocksville, NC,US
76/D4 Moclín, Sp.
182/B4 Moclips, Wa,US
164/B4 Mocoa, Col.
170/D4 Mococa, Braz.
154/B2 Môco, Morro de (peak), Ang.
172/E4 Mocoretá, Arg.
158/D3 Mocorito, Mex.
158/C2 Moctezuma, Mex.
158/D2 Moctezuma, Mex.
159/E4 Moctezuma, Mex.
155/H3 Mocuba, Moz.
82/C2 Modane, Fr.
118/B3 Modāsa, India
58/C6 Modbury, Eng,UK
156/D3 Modderrivier (riv.), SAfr.
60/B6 Model Village, Ire.
87/D3 Modena, It.
87/D4 Modena (prov.), It.
185/G4 Modena, Ut,US
75/G2 Moder (riv.), Fr., Ger.
186/B2 Modesto, Ca,US
90/D4 Modica, It.
87/E4 Modigliana, It.
153/E2 Modjamboli, Zaire
204/C3 Modjeska, Ca,US
148/B1 Modjigo (reg.), Niger
73/A3 Mödling, Aus.
201/F4 Modoc, SC,US
184/C3 Modoc Nat'l Wild. Ref., Ca,US
73/B3 Modra, Slvk.
92/D3 Modriča, Bosn.
73/D3 Modrý Kameň, Slvk.
123/E3 Mo Duc, Viet.
90/E2 Modugno, It.
135/C3 Moe, Austl.
156/A2 Moeb (bay), Namb.
136/C2 Moehau (hill), N.Z.
78/B5 Moëlan-sur-Mer, Fr.
57/E5 Moel Fammau (mtn.), Wal,UK
57/E6 Moel Fferna (mtn.), Wal,UK
58/C1 Moelfre (mtn.), UK
58/C2 Moel Hywel (mtn.), Wal,UK
57/E6 Moel Sych (mtn.), Wal,UK
62/D1 Moelv, Nor.
58/C2 Moel y Llyn (mtn.), Wal,UK
138/E4 Moen, Micr.
166/C1 Moengo, Sur.
187/G2 Moenkapi (wash), Az,US
187/G2 Moenkopi, Az,US
139/K7 Moerai, FrPol.
66/C5 Moerbeke, Belg.
66/B5 Moerdijk, Neth.
136/C1 Moerewa, N.Z.
66/D6 Moers, Ger.
68/C1 Moervaart (can.), Belg.
81/F5 Moesa (riv.), Swi.
68/C3 Moeuvres, Fr.
136/B4 Moffat (peak), N.Z.
54/C6 Moffat, Sc,UK
192/B5 Moffat, Co,US
194/D4 Moffit, ND,US
122/C2 Moga, India
150/C5 Mogadishu (Muqdisho) (cap.), Som.
208/F5 Mogadore, Oh,US
76/B2 Mogadouro, Port.
152/D2 Mogalo, Zaire
112/B4 Mogami, Japan
111/G2 Mogami (riv.), Japan
155/E4 Mogapinyana, Bots.
116/C3 Mogaung, Burma
77/L6 Mogent (riv.), Sp.
70/C5 Mögglingen, Ger.
170/D4 Mogi das Cruzes, Braz.
149/H4 Mogige, Eth.
170/D4 Mogi-Guaçu, Braz.
63/P5 Mogilëv, Bela.
96/D1 Mogilev (int'l arpt.), Bela.
96/D1 Mogilev Obl., Bela.
98/D3 Mogilev-Podol'skiy, Ukr.
135/D1 Mogil Mogil, Austl.
65/J2 Mogilno, Pol.
171/J7 Mogi-Mirim, Braz.
155/J2 Mogincual, Moz.
87/D3 Mogliano, It.
85/D1 Mogliano, It.
87/F1 Mogliano Veneto, It.
172/B4 Mogna, Arg.
109/H1 Mogocha, Rus.
149/F3 Mogogh, Sudan
116/C4 Mogok, Burma
187/G3 Mogollon (plat.), Az,US
187/G3 Mogollon (rim), Az,US
187/H4 Mogollon, NM,US
187/H4 Mogollon (mts.), NM,US
155/E4 Mogolrivier (riv.), SAfr.
90/A3 Mogoro, It.
175/F3 Mogotes (pt.), Arg.
151/A2 Mogotio, Kenya
160/E3 Mogotón (peak), Nic.
108/F1 Mogoytuy, Rus.
120/D3 Mogra Bādshāhpur, India
76/B4 Moguer, Sp.
108/G1 Mogzon, Rus.
92/D3 Mohács, Hun.
156/D3 Mohales Hoek, Les.
194/D3 Mohall, ND,US
141/N13 Mohamed V (dam), Mor.
141/N13 Mohamed V (res.), Mor.
142/D2 Mohamed V (Casablanca) (int'l arpt.), Mor.
105/J3 Moḥammadābād, Iran
141/R16 Mohammadia, Alg.
141/L14 Mohammedia, Mor.
121/E3 Mohana (riv.), India
121/H3 Mohanganj, Bang.
120/D3 Mohaniā, India
186/E3 Mohave (lake), Az, Nv,US
195/K4 Mohawk, Mi,US
206/D1 Mohawk (lake), NJ,US
199/J3 Mohawk (riv.), NY,US
208/F6 Mohawk (lake), Oh,US
62/F3 Moheda, Swe.
208/B3 Mohegan, Ct,US
157/G6 Mohéli (isl.), Com.
154/D3 Mohembo, Bots.
60/A4 Moher, Cliffs of, Ire.
177/E3 Mohican (cape), Ak,US
208/E7 Mohican (riv.), Oh,US
60/C2 Mohill, Ire.
80/D2 Möhlin, Swi.
72/C6 Mohlsdorf, Ger.
67/F6 Möhne (riv.), Ger.
67/F6 Möhnestausee (res.), Ger.
206/C3 Mohnton, Pa,US
119/G3 Mohnyin, Burma
168/D4 Moho, Peru
151/B4 Mohoro, Tanz.
206/C3 Mohrsville, Pa,US
151/B3 Moi (int'l arpt.), Kenya
62/B2 Moi, Nor.
85/E5 Moiano, It.
87/D6 Moie, It.
114/D5 Moincêr, China
93/H2 Moinești, Rom.
114/A3 Moinkum (des.), Kaz.
145/E5 Moinsi (hills), Gha.
199/H2 Moira (riv.), On,Can
82/B2 Moirans, Fr.
80/B5 Moirans-en-Montagne, Fr.
63/L2 Mõisaküla, Est.
78/D5 Moisdon-la-Rivière, Fr.
179/K3 Moisie (riv.), Qu,Can
68/B4 Moislains, Fr.
74/D4 Moissac, Fr.
148/C3 Moïssala, Chad
77/Q10 Moita, Port.
165/E3 Moitaco, Ven.
76/E4 Mojácar, Sp.
186/C3 Mojave, Ca,US
204/C1 Mojave (des.), Ca,US
204/C1 Mojave (riv.), Ca,US
116/D4 Mojiang Hanizu Zizhixian, China
171/K7 Moji-Guaçu (riv.), Braz.
92/D4 Mojkovac, Yugo.
172/C2 Mojo, Bol.
150/A3 Mojo, Eth.
172/C1 Mojocoya, Bol.
124/F4 Mojokerto, Indo.
168/D4 Mojos, Bol.
169/E4 Mojos (plain), Bol.
166/D3 Moju, Braz.
166/D3 Moju (riv.), Braz.
111/F2 Mōka, Japan
121/E3 Mokameh, India
205/M11 Mokelumne (aqueduct), Ca,US
205/M10 Mokelumne (riv.), Ca,US
205/Q16 Mokena, Il,US
156/E3 Mokhotlong, Les.
96/F1 Mokhovoye, Rus.
138/F4 Mokil (isl.), Micr.
123/B3 Mokochu (peak), Thai.
116/B3 Mokokchūng, India
148/B3 Mokolo, Camr.
152/D2 Mokolo, Zaire
113/D5 Mokp'o, SKor.
92/E3 Mokrin, Yugo.
97/G1 Moksha (riv.), Rus.
180/S10 Mokuleia, Hi,US
153/E2 Mokumbusu, Zaire
145/G4 Mokwa, Nga.
69/E1 Mol, Belg.
92/E3 Mol, Yugo.
90/E2 Mola di Bari, It.
184/B1 Molalla, Or,US
91/H4 Moláoi, Gre.
82/B1 Molard Noir (mtn.), Fr.
86/B3 Molare, It.
160/E1 Molas (pt.), Mex.
92/B3 Molat (isl.), Cro.
76/E3 Molatón (mtn.), Sp.
67/E3 Molbergen, Ger.
57/E5 Mold, Wal,UK
93/H2 Moldavia (reg.), Rom.
93/G2 Moldavian Carpathians (range), Rom.
61/C3 Molde, Nor.
98/D4 Moldova
93/H2 Moldova (riv.), Rom.
92/E3 Moldova Nouă, Rom.
93/G3 Moldoveanu (peak), Rom.
82/C6 Môle (riv.), Fr.
53/M7 Mole (riv.), Eng,UK
153/G3 Mole, Zaire
161/H2 Môle, Cap du (cape), Haiti
145/E4 Mole Game Rsv., Gha.
148/D4 Molegbe, Zaire
193/K1 Mole Lake Ind. Res., Wi,US
200/E4 Molena, Ga,US
154/E5 Molepolole, Bots.
161/H2 Môle St. Nicolas, Haiti
63/L4 Molėtai, Lith.
90/E2 Molfetta, It.
127/F3 Molibagu, Indo.
115/F2 Molihong Shan (peak), China
174/C2 Molina, Chile
76/E2 Molina, Sp.
76/E3 Molina de Segura, Sp.
193/J3 Moline, Il,US
191/F2 Moline, Ks,US
87/E3 Molinella, It.
82/C3 Molines-en-Queyras, Fr.
69/E4 Molinfaing, Belg.
76/D3 Molinicos, Sp.
202/E2 Molino, Fl,US
159/L7 Molino de Flores Nat'l Park, Mex.
153/G5 Moliro, Zaire
85/E4 Molise (reg.), It.
83/B2 Moliterno, It.
62/E2 Molkom, Swe.
75/K3 Möll (riv.), Aus.
105/G1 Mollakend, Azer.
61/D5 Møllebjerg (peak), Den.
168/C5 Mollendo, Peru
80/C4 Mollendruz, Col du (pass), Swi.
77/F2 Mollerussa, Sp.
174/C2 Molles (pt.), Chile
175/F2 Molles, Uru.
77/L6 Mollet del Vallès, Sp.
77/L7 Mollins de Rei, Sp.
81/F3 Mollis, Swi.
64/F2 Mölln, Ger.
201/J2 Mollusk, Va,US
62/E3 Mölndal, Swe.
62/E3 Mölnlycke, Swe.
116/C4 Molo, Burma
151/A2 Molo, Kenya
99/H4 Molochansk, Ukr.
83/C6 Molochio, It.
99/H4 Molochnoye (lake), Ukr.
155/H2 Molócue (riv.), Moz.
63/M4 Molodechno, Bela.
137/D Molodezhnaya, Ant.
99/K3 Molodogvardeysk, Ukr.
94/H4 Mologa (riv.), Rus.
180/T10 Molokai (isl.), Hi,US
94/H4 Molokovo, Rus.
95/L4 Moloma (riv.), Rus.
135/D2 Molong, Austl.
154/D5 Molopo (dry riv.), Bots.
140/E7 Molopo (riv.), Bots., SAfr.
156/C2 Molopoivier (dry riv.), SAfr.
91/H3 Mólos, Gre.
152/C2 Moloundou, Camr.
80/D1 Molsheim, Fr.
156/D3 Molteno, SAfr.
130/C1 Molu (isl.), Indo.
127/G4 Molucca (sea), Indo.
127/G4 Moluccas (isls.), Indo.
81/G5 Molveno, It.
81/G5 Molveno (lake), It.
155/H3 Moma, Moz.
153/E3 Moma, Zaire
153/F2 Mombango II, Zaire
151/B3 Mombasa, Kenya
112/C1 Mombetsu, Japan
112/C2 Mombetsu, Japan
151/B3 Mombo, Tanz.
152/D3 Momboyo (riv.), Zaire
70/C2 Mömbris, Ger.
93/G5 Momchilgrad, Bul.
198/C4 Momence, Il,US
127/H4 Momfafa (cape), Indo.
68/D3 Momignies, Belg.
70/C3 Mömlingen, Ger.
86/B1 Momo, It.
112/B3 Momoishi, Japan
164/C2 Mompós, Col.
152/D3 Mompoto, Zaire
123/B2 Mon, Burma
116/B4 Mon (riv.), Burma
116/C5 Mon (state), Burma
62/E4 Møn (isl.), Den.
176/L8 Mona (chan.), NAm.
162/E3 Mona (isl.), PR
208/G6 Monaca, Pa,US
82/D5 Monaco
82/D5 Monaco (cap.), Mona.
54/B2 Monadhliath (mts.), Sc,UK
196/A4 Monadnock (mtn.), NH,US
155/H3 Monaepa (pt.), Moz.
165/F2 Monagas (state), Ven.
60/D1 Monaghan, Ire.
60/D1 Monaghan (co.), Ire.
161/F5 Monagrillo, Pan.
161/F4 Monagrillo (ruins), Pan.
188/C2 Monahans, Tx,US
194/E4 Monango, ND,US
162/D3 Mona Passage (chan.), West Indies
155/J2 Monapo, Moz.
152/D5 Mona Quimbundo, Ang.
183/J4 Monarch, Mt,US
54/A2 Monar, Loch (lake), Sc,UK
182/E2 Monashee (mts.), BC,Can
83/C6 Monasterace, It.
60/C3 Monasterevin, Ire.
148/A4 Monatélé, Camr.
134/H8 Mona Vale, Austl.
77/E3 Moncada, Sp.
86/A3 Moncalieri, It.
86/B2 Moncalvo, It.
167/E3 Monção, Braz.
76/D2 Moncayo (range), Sp
80/E4 Mönch (peak), Swi.
94/G2 Monchegorsk, Rus.
66/D6 Mönchengladbach, Ger.
73/A4 Mönchhof, Aus.
76/A4 Monchique, Port.
76/A4 Monchique (range), Port.
201/G4 Moncks Corner, SC,U
188/D4 Monclova, Mex.
78/C4 Moncontour, Fr.
196/E2 Moncton, NB,Can
76/A2 Mondego (cape), Po
76/A2 Mondego (riv.), Port.
76/D2 Mondéjar, Sp.
79/E2 Mondeville, Fr.
153/E2 Mondimbi, Zaire
148/B2 Mondo, Chad
151/A3 Mondo, Tanz.
87/G5 Mondolfo, It.
76/B1 Mondoñedo, Sp.
69/F5 Mondorf-les-Bains, Lux.
86/A4 Mondovì, It.
193/J1 Mondovi, Wi,US
82/A4 Mondragon, Fr.
76/D1 Mondragón, Sp.
85/D5 Mondragone, It.
71/G7 Mondsee, Aus.
71/G7 Mondsee (lake), Aus
151/B2 Monduli, Tanz.
108/E1 Mondy, Rus.
86/C4 Moneglia, It.
91/H4 Monemvasía, Gre.
187/J2 Monero, NM,US
174/E3 Mones Cazón, Arg.
199/G4 Monessen, Pa,US
76/B3 Monesterio, Sp.
185/K2 Moneta, Wy,US
191/H2 Monett, Mo,US
191/J3 Monette, Ar,US
60/C4 Moneygall, Ire.
56/C2 Money Head (pt.), Sc,UK
56/B2 Moneymore, NI,UK
56/C2 Moneyreagh, NI,UK
87/G1 Monfalcone, It.
86/B3 Monferrato (reg.), It.
76/B3 Monforte, Port.
76/B1 Monforte, Sp.
83/B6 Monforte San Giorgi It.
151/B4 Monga, Tanz.
153/E1 Monga, Zaire
171/K9 Mongaguá, Braz.
153/E2 Mongala (riv.), Zaire
149/F4 Mongalla, Sudan
153/F2 Mongandjo, Zaire
121/H2 Mongar, Bhu.
199/J3 Mongaup (mtn.), NY,US
123/D1 Mong Cai, Viet.
132/C4 Mongers (lake), Aust
113/C3 Monggümp'o, NKor.
123/B1 Möng Hang, Burma
87/E4 Monghidoro, It.
123/B1 Möng Hpāyak, Burm
123/B1 Möng Hsat, Burma
116/C4 Möng Hsu, Burma
121/F3 Monghyr, India
116/C4 Möng Küng, Burma
123/B1 Möng Long, Burma
123/B2 Möng Mau, Burma
116/C4 Möng Nai, Burma
148/C2 Mongo, Chad
144/C4 Mongo (riv.), Gui., SLeo.
108/D2 Mongolia
152/B2 Mongomo, EqG.
148/D2 Mongororo, Chad
148/C5 Mongoumba, CAfr.
152/B3 Mongoungou, Gabon
123/B1 Möng Pan, Burma
116/C4 Möng Pawn, Burma
123/B1 Möng Ping, Burma
123/B1 Möng Tōn, Burma
123/B1 Möng Tüm, Burma
154/D2 Mongu, Zam.
144/B2 Mônguel, Mrta.
116/C4 Möng Yai, Burma
116/C4 Möng Yang, Burma
116/D4 Möng Yawng, Burma
116/C4 Möng Yu, Burma
196/C4 Monhegan (isl.), Me,US
66/D6 Monheim, Ger.
70/D5 Monheim, Ger.
114/F2 Mönh Hayrhan Uul (peak), Mong.
108/E1 Mönh Sarĭdag (peak), Mong.
116/E3 Moni, China
103/C2 Moni, Cyp.
56/E1 Moniaive, Sc,UK
195/K5 Monico, Wi,US
153/G2 Monietu, Zaire
54/D4 Monifieth, Sc,UK
164/C3 Moniquirá, Col.
77/K6 Monistrol de Montserrat, Sp.
74/F4 Monistrol-sur-Loire, Fr.
184/E4 Monitor (mts.), Nv,US
182/D4 Monitor, Wa,US
60/B3 Monivea, Ire.
125/D4 Monkayo, Phil.
155/G2 Monkey Bay, Malw.
202/P8 Monkey Jungle, Fl,US
133/K9 Monkey Mia, Austl.
160/D2 Monkey River, Belz.
65/M2 Mońki, Pol.
153/E3 Monkoto, Zaire
206/B5 Monks (isl.), Md,US
199/K2 Monkton, Vt,US
58/D3 Monmouth, Eng,UK
193/J3 Monmouth, Il,US
196/B3 Monmouth, Me,US
207/D3 Monmouth (co.), NJ,US
184/B1 Monmouth, Or,US
207/E3 Monmouth Beach, NJ,US
206/D3 Monmouth Junction, NJ,US
58/D2 Monnow (riv.), UK
79/E6 Monnaie, Fr.
66/C4 Monnickendam, Neth.
145/F5 Mono (prov.), Ben.
161/F4 Mono (pt.), Nic.
145/F5 Mono (riv.), Togo
204/A1 Mono (cr.), Ca,US
186/C1 Mono (lake), Ca,US

206/A4 Monocacy (riv.), Md, Pa,US
199/H5 Monocacy Nat'l Btfld., Md,US
196/B5 Monomoy Nat'l Wild. Ref., Ma,US
198/C4 Monon, In,US
193/J2 Monona, Ia,US
198/F5 Monongah, WV,US
198/G5 Monongahela (riv.), Pa, WV,US
90/E2 Monopoli, It.
92/D2 Monor, Hun.
197/R8 Mono Road, On,Can
77/E3 Monóvar, Sp.
76/E2 Monreal del Campo, Sp.
90/C3 Monreale, It.
208/A3 Monroe, Ct,US
202/N6 Monroe (lake), Fl,US
200/F4 Monroe, Ga,US
193/H3 Monroe, Ia,US
198/D4 Monroe, In,US
200/D1 Monroe (lake), In,US
189/H1 Monroe, La,US
198/E4 Monroe, Mi,US
205/E7 Monroe (co.), Mi,US
201/G3 Monroe, NC,US
207/D1 Monroe, NY,US
206/C1 Monroe (co.), Pa,US
185/G4 Monroe, Ut,US
185/G4 Monroe (peak), Ut,US
205/D2 Monroe, Wa,US
193/K2 Monroe, Wi,US
200/D1 Monroe City, In,US
191/J1 Monroe City, Mo,US
202/E2 Monroeville, Al,US
198/D4 Monroeville, In,US
206/C4 Monroeville, NJ,US
208/H7 Monroeville, Pa,US
144/C5 Monrovia (cap.), Libr.
204/C2 Monrovia, Ca,US
144/C5 Monrovia (Roberts) (int'l arpt.), Libr.
68/C3 Mons, Belg.
76/B2 Monsanto, Port.
69/F2 Monschau, Ger.
127/F4 Monse, Indo.
168/B2 Monsefú, Peru
87/E2 Monselice, It.
167/F4 Monsenhor Hipólito, Braz.
167/F4 Monsenhor Tabosa, Braz.
207/D1 Monsey, NY,US
70/B3 Monsheim, Ger.
208/B1 Monson, Ma,US
196/C3 Monson, Me,US
66/B4 Monster, Neth.
62/G3 Mönsteras, Swe.
87/D5 Monsummano Terme, It.
86/A3 Montà, It.
70/A2 Montabaur, Ger.
81/F3 Montafon (val.), Aus.
87/E2 Montagnana, It.
157/J6 Montagne d'Ambre Nat'l Park, Madg.
148/B4 Montagne de Nganha (peak), Camr.
53/U9 Montagny-Sainte-Félicité, Fr.
156/C4 Montagu, SAfr.
130/B3 Montague (sound), Austl.
197/F2 Montague, PE,Can
177/L3 Montague (isl.), Ak,US
186/E5 Montague (isl.), Mex.
177/J4 Montague (isl.), Ak,US
177/J4 Montague (str.), Ak,US
184/B3 Montague, Ca,US
199/K3 Montague, Ma,US
198/C3 Montague, Mi,US
206/D1 Montague, NJ,US
191/F4 Montague, Tx,US
74/C3 Montaigu, Fr.
87/D5 Montaione, It.
189/G2 Montalba, Tx,US
77/E2 Montalbán, Sp.
83/B6 Montalbano Elicona, It.
83/C2 Montalbano Jonico, It.
84/B1 Montalcino, It.
87/D3 Montale, It.
87/E5 Montale, It.
80/B6 Montalieu-Vercieu, Fr.
83/B6 Montalto (peak), It.
84/D3 Montalto di Castro, It.
83/C4 Montalto Uffugo, It.
76/B3 Montalvão, Port.
204/A2 Montalvo, Ca,US
163/B3 Montaña (for.), Peru
80/D5 Montana, Swi.
180/D2 Montana (state), US
168/C1 Montaña, La (reg.), Peru
76/B3 Montánchez, Sp.
171/E3 Montanha, Braz.
205/J11 Montara, Ca,US
76/A3 Montargil, Port.
74/E3 Montargis, Fr.
68/B5 Montataire, Fr.
78/C4 Montauban, Fr.
77/F1 Montaud, Pic de (peak), Fr.
207/G1 Montauk, NY,US
207/G1 Montauk (pt.), NY,US
74/F3 Montbard, Fr.
79/F6 Montbazon, Fr.
80/C2 Montbéliard, Fr.
189/N9 Mont Belvieu, Tx,US
77/F2 Montblanc, Sp.
77/L7 Montcada i Reixac, Sp.
201/G2 Montcalm, WV,US
196/C2 Mont-Carmel, Qu,Can
74/F3 Montceau-les-Mines, Fr.
82/C2 Mont-Cenis (lake), Fr.
82/C2 Mont Cenis, Col du (pass), Fr.
204/C2 Montclair, Ca,US
207/J8 Montclair, NJ,US
68/D4 Montcornet, Fr.
74/C5 Mont-de-Marsan, Fr.
68/B4 Montdidier, Fr.
79/F5 Montdoubleau, Fr.
83/B3 Montea (peak), It.
172/D1 Monteagudo, Bol.
160/B2 Monte Albán (ruins), Mex.
166/C3 Monte Alegre, Braz.
167/H4 Monte Alegre, Braz.
170/D2 Monte Alegre de Goiás, Braz.
76/E3 Montealegre del Castillo, Sp.
170/C3 Monte Alegre de Minas, Braz.
167/E5 Monte Alegre do Piauí, Braz.
170/C4 Monte Alto, Braz.
189/F4 Monte Alto, Tx,US
171/E2 Monte Azul, Braz.
132/B2 Montebello (isls.), Austl.
167/K6 Montebello, Col.
204/B2 Montebello, Ca,US
83/B7 Montebello Ionico, It.
87/E2 Montebello Vicentino, It.
87/F1 Montebelluna, It.
154/B2 Monte Bello, Ang.
78/D2 Montebourg, Fr.
86/C3 Montebruno, It.
85/F5 Montecalvo Irpino, It.
173/F3 Montecarlo, Arg.
82/D5 Monte-Carlo, Mona.
170/D3 Monte Carmelo, Braz.
164/D2 Monte Carmelo, Ven.
172/E4 Monte Caseros, Arg.
87/G6 Montecassiano, It.
87/D5 Montecatini Terme, It.
86/D3 Montecavolo, It.
87/F5 Montecchio, It.
87/E1 Montecchio Magiore, It.
86/B2 Montechiaro d'Asti, It.
85/E4 Montecilfone, It.
204/A2 Montecito, Ca,US
174/D2 Monte Comán, Arg.
84/C4 Montecompatri, It.
85/E6 Montecorvino Rovella, It.
83/C2 Monte Cotugno (lake), It.
162/D3 Monte Cristi, DRep.
169/F4 Monte Cristo, Bol.
84/A3 Montecristo (isl.), It.
160/D3 Montecristo Nat'l Park, ESal.
85/E6 Monte di Procida, It.
166/C3 Monte Dourado, Braz.
160/E3 Monte el Chile (mtn.), Hon.
85/E6 Montefalcione, It.
84/C2 Montefalco, It.
85/F5 Montefalcone di Val Fortore, It.
85/E4 Montefalcone nel Sannio, It.
87/F5 Montefeltro (reg.), It.
84/C2 Montefiascone, It.
87/E2 Monteforte D'Alpone, It.
85/E6 Monteforte Irpino, It.
76/C4 Montefrío, Sp.
85/D1 Montegiorgio, It.
161/G2 Montego Bay, Jam.
85/D1 Montegranaro, It.
87/E2 Montegrotto Terme, It.
76/B2 Montehermoso, Sp.
167/G4 Monteiro, Braz.
130/C4 Montejinnie, Austl.
83/B2 Monte la Spina (peak), It.
77/P10 Montelavar, Port.
175/K7 Monte León, Arg.
84/C3 Montelibretti, It.
82/A3 Montélimar, Fr.
172/E2 Monte Lindo (riv.), Arg.
172/E1 Montelindo (riv.), Par.
188/D3 Montell, Tx,US
85/F6 Montella, It.
76/C4 Montellano, Sp.
185/F3 Montello, Nv,US
193/K2 Montello, Wi,US
87/E5 Montelupo Fiorentino, It.
86/B3 Montemagno, It.
174/E2 Monte Maíz, Arg.
87/G5 Montemarciano, It.
174/D5 Montemayor (plat.), Arg.
85/E5 Montemiletto, It.
85/F5 Montemilone, It.
159/F3 Montemorelos, Mex.
76/A3 Montemor-o-Novo, Port.
76/A2 Montemor-o-Velho, Port.
76/A2 Montemuro (mtn.), Port.
83/B2 Montemurro, It.
79/E4 Montenay, Fr.
74/C4 Montendre, Fr.
173/G4 Montenegro, Braz.
174/Q9 Montenegro, Chile
167/K7 Montenegro, Col.
92/D4 Montenegro (rep.), Yugo.
83/C4 Montenero (peak), It.
85/E4 Montenero di Bisaccia, It.
64/B5 Montenoison, Butte de (mtn.), Fr.
171/F3 Monte Pascoal Nat'l Park, Braz.
172/B4 Monte Patria, Chile
162/D3 Monte Plata, DRep.
155/H2 Montepuez, Moz.
155/J2 Montepuez (riv.), Moz.
84/B1 Montepulciano, It.
172/D3 Monte Quemado, Arg.
74/E2 Montereau-faut-Yonne, Fr.
186/B2 Monterey, Ca,US
186/A2 Monterey (bay), Ca,US
189/J2 Monterey, La,US
208/A1 Monterey, Ma,US
200/E2 Monterey, Tn,US
201/H1 Monterey, Va,US
204/B2 Monterey Park, Ca,US
164/C2 Montería, Col.
172/D1 Montero, Bol.
85/E4 Monteroduni, It.
84/B3 Monteroni d'Arbia, It.
172/C3 Monteros, Arg.
80/D6 Monte Rosa (mtn.), It., Swi.
81/G4 Monterosso (peak), It.
86/C4 Monterosso al Mare, It.
83/C5 Monterosso Calabro, It.
84/C3 Monterotondo, It.
159/E3 Monterrey, Mex.
76/B2 Monterrey, Sp.
175/K7 Montes (pt.), Arg.
167/E4 Montes Altos, Braz.
85/D5 Monte San Biagio, It.
83/B2 Monte San Giacomo, It.
182/C4 Montesano, Wa,US
83/B2 Montesano sulla Marcellana, It.
85/F4 Monte Sant'Angelo, It.
85/E5 Montesarchio, It.
83/C1 Montescaglioso, It.
170/E3 Montes Claros, Braz.
87/D4 Montese, It.
85/E2 Montesilvano Marina, It.
87/E5 Montespertoli, It.
53/S10 Montesson, Fr.
85/D1 Monte Urano, It.
82/B4 Monteux, Fr.
200/D4 Montevallo, Al,US
87/E5 Montevarchi, It.
169/D3 Monte Verde, Bol.
175/F2 Montevideo (cap.), Uru.
175/T12 Montevideo (dept.), Uru.
195/G5 Montevideo, Mn,US
185/G2 Monteview, Id,US
192/A5 Monte Vista, Co,US
190/A2 Monte Vista Nat'l Wild. Ref., Co,US
53/U10 Montévrain, Fr.
205/L10 Montezuma (slough), Ca,US
200/E4 Montezuma, Ga,US
193/H3 Montezuma, Ia,US
198/C5 Montezuma, In,US
190/D2 Montezuma, Ks,US
190/B3 Montezuma, NM,US
187/H2 Montezuma (cr.), Ut,US
187/G3 Montezuma Castle Nat'l Mon., Az,US
187/H2 Montezuma Creek, Ut,US
69/E5 Montfaucon, Fr.
53/T10 Montfermeil, Fr.
80/B3 Montferrand-le-Château, Fr.
66/B4 Montfoort, Neth.
78/D4 Montfort, Fr.
68/A6 Montfort-l'Amaury, Fr.
79/F2 Montfort-sur-Risle, Fr.
152/B3 Mont Fouri Rsv., Congo, Gabon
82/A5 Montfrin, Fr.
82/C3 Montgenèvre, Fr.
82/C3 Montgenèvre, Col de (pass), Fr.
53/T10 Montgeron, Fr.
58/C1 Montgomery, Wal,UK
200/D4 Montgomery (cap.), Al,US
201/G5 Montgomery, Ga,US
205/P16 Montgomery, Il,US
202/B2 Montgomery, La,US
206/A5 Montgomery (co.), Md,US
206/B1 Montgomery, Pa,US
206/C3 Montgomery (co.), Pa,US
208/G6 Montgomery (dam), Pa,US
189/G2 Montgomery, Tx,US
189/M8 Montgomery (co.), Tx,US
201/G1 Montgomery, WV,US
191/J1 Montgomery City, Mo,US
206/A5 Montgomery Village, Md,US
206/C3 Montgomeryville, Pa,US
74/E5 Montgrand (mtn.), Fr.
187/G4 Monthan-Davis A.F.B., Az,US
69/D4 Monthermé, Fr.
80/C5 Monthey, Swi.
80/B1 Monthureux-sur-Saône, Fr.
53/U9 Monthyon, Fr.
86/C2 Monticelli d'Ongina, It.
86/D3 Monticelli Terme, It.
191/J4 Monticello, Ar,US
205/K9 Monticello (dam), Ca,US
203/G2 Monticello, Fl,US
200/F4 Monticello, Ga,US
193/J2 Monticello, Ia,US
193/K3 Monticello, Il,US
198/C4 Monticello, In,US
200/E2 Monticello, Ky,US
189/J1 Monticello, La,US
196/D2 Monticello, Me,US
193/J3 Monticello, Mo,US
200/B5 Monticello, Ms,US
187/J4 Monticello, NM,US
199/J4 Monticello, NY,US
185/J5 Monticello, Ut,US
201/H2 Monticello, Va,US
87/E1 Monticello Conte Otto, It.
86/D2 Montichiari, It.
80/A1 Montier-en-Der, Fr.
68/B3 Montigny-en-Gohelle, Fr.
53/S10 Montigny-le-Bretonneux, Fr.
80/B1 Montigny-le-Roi, Fr.
53/S10 Montigny-lès-Cormeilles, Fr.
69/F5 Montigny-les-Metz, Fr.
75/G2 Montigny-lès-Metz, Fr.
68/D3 Montigny-le-Tilleul, Belg.
76/A3 Montijo, Port.
76/B3 Montijo, Sp.
76/C4 Montilla, Sp.
79/F1 Montivilliers, Fr.
196/C1 Mont-Joli, Qu,Can
199/J1 Mont-Laurier, Qu,Can
80/C3 Montlebon, Fr.
53/S11 Montlhéry, Fr.
196/E1 Mont-Louis, Qu,Can
79/F6 Montlouis-sur-Loire, Fr.
74/E3 Montluçon, Fr.
80/B6 Montluel, Fr.
196/B2 Montmagny, Qu,Can
194/C2 Montmartre, Sk,Can
69/E4 Montmédy, Fr.
82/C2 Montmélian, Fr.
80/A5 Montmerle-sur-Saône, Fr.
82/A3 Montmeyran, Fr.
68/C6 Montmirail, Fr.
53/S10 Montmorency, Fr.
74/D3 Montmorillon, Fr.
80/B4 Montmorot, Fr.
183/L1 Mont Nebo, Sk,Can
134/C4 Monto, Austl.
86/C2 Montodine, It.
78/C6 Montoir-de-Bretagne, Fr.
79/F5 Montoire-sur-le-Loir, Fr.
69/F5 Montois-la-Montagne, Fr.
87/F4 Montone (riv.), It.
87/D5 Montopoli, It.
85/D2 Montorio al Vomano, It.
87/E2 Montorio Veronese, It.
76/C3 Montoro, Sp.
158/D3 Montoros, Mex.
206/B1 Montour (co.), Pa,US
206/B2 Montour (ridge), Pa,US
199/H3 Montour Falls, NY,US
206/B1 Montoursville, Pa,US
144/D5 Mont Peko Nat'l Park, IvC.
161/G2 Montpelier, Jam.
185/H2 Montpelier, Id,US
198/D4 Montpelier, In,US
200/C4 Montpelier, Ms,US
194/E4 Montpelier, ND,US
198/D4 Montpelier, Oh,US
199/K2 Montpelier (cap.), Vt,US
199/J2 Montpellier, Qu,Can
74/E5 Montpellier, Fr.
74/E5 Montpellier (Frejorgues) (int'l arpt.), Fr.
79/G5 Mont-près-Chambord, Fr.
199/K2 Montréal, Qu,Can
80/B5 Montréal, Fr.
197/N6 Montréal-Est, Qu,Can
197/N6 Montréal-Nord, Qu,Can
74/D5 Montréjeau, Fr.
68/A3 Montreuil, Fr.
79/E5 Montreuil-Juigné, Fr.
80/C5 Montreux, Swi.
80/C2 Montreux-Château, Fr.
79/D6 Montrevault, Fr.
80/B5 Montrevel-en-Bresse, Fr.
79/G6 Montrichard, Fr.
80/C4 Montricher, Swi.
54/D3 Montrose, Sc,UK
200/B4 Montrose, Ar,US
185/K4 Montrose, Co,US
198/E3 Montrose, Mi,US
195/N6 Montrose, Mn,US
191/G1 Montrose (lake), Mo,US
199/J4 Montrose, Pa,US
54/D3 Montrose Basin (lag.), Sc,UK
204/B2 Montrose-La Crescenta, Ca,US
201/J1 Montross, Va,US
53/S10 Montrouge, Fr.
197/N6 Mont-Royal, Qu,Can
74/C3 Montreuil-Bellay, Fr.
53/U10 Montry, Fr.
79/F6 Monts, Fr.
79/G2 Mont-Saint-Aignan, Fr.
197/P6 Mont-Saint-Hilaire, Qu,Can
78/D3 Mont-Saint-Michel, Fr.
78/D3 Mont-Saint-Michel (bay), Fr.
144/D4 Mont Sangbé Nat'l Park, IvC.
77/L6 Montseny Nat'l Park, Sp.
144/C5 Montserrado (co.), Libr.
77/F2 Montserrat (mtn.), Sp.
162/F3 Montserrat (isl.), UK
166/C1 Montsinéry, FrG.
53/S9 Montsoult, Fr.
80/B4 Mont-sous-Vaudrey, Fr.
196/D1 Monts, Pointe des (pt.), Qu,Can
69/E4 Mont-St-Martin, Fr.
79/E4 Montsûrs, Fr.
172/B3 Monturaqui, Chile
207/J7 Montvale, NJ,US
202/M6 Montverde, Fl,US
206/D2 Montville, NJ,US
208/F4 Montville, Oh,US
187/H2 Monument (val.), Az, Ut,US
192/B4 Monument, Co,US
190/D1 Monument (rocks), Ks,US
184/D1 Monument, Or,US
188/C1 Monument Draw (cr.), NM, Tx,US
192/D4 Monument Rocks, Ks,US
187/G2 Monument Valley Navajo Tribal Park, Az, Ut,US
153/E2 Monveda, Zaire
116/B4 Monywa, Burma
86/C1 Monza, It.
155/E3 Monze, Zam.
69/G4 Monzingen, Ger.
168/B3 Monzón, Peru
77/F2 Monzón, Sp.
208/B2 Moodus, Ct,US
191/J2 Moody, Mo,US
189/F2 Moody, Tx,US
191/G2 Moodys, Ok,US
157/E3 Mooirivier, SAfr.
66/C5 Mook, Neth.
155/E4 Mookane, Bots.
156/P13 Mool (riv.), SAfr.
132/C3 Mooloo Downs, Austl.
134/D4 Mooloolaba-Maroochydore, Austl.
201/G1 Moomaw (lake), WV,US
60/C5 Mooncoin, Ire.
134/C4 Moonie, Austl.
133/H5 Moonta, Austl.
132/C4 Moora, Austl.
135/G5 Moorabbin, Austl.
194/B5 Moorcroft, Wy,US
132/C4 Moore (lake), Austl.
197/S8 Moore (pt.), On,Can
185/G2 Moore, Id,US
183/K4 Moore, Mt,US
191/F3 Moore, Ok,US
185/H4 Moore, Ut,US
139/K6 Moorea (isl.), FrPol.
201/H1 Moorefield, WV,US
203/H4 Moore Haven, Fl,US
190/E2 Mooreland, Ok,US
70/E6 Moorenweis, Ger.
132/B4 Moore River Nat'l Park, Austl.
162/B1 Moore's (isl.), Bahm.
201/H3 Moores Creek Nat'l Bfld., NC,US
206/D4 Moorestown, NJ,US
198/C5 Mooresville, In,US
201/G3 Mooresville, NC,US
194/F4 Mooreton, ND,US
205/H6 Mooretown, On,Can
54/C5 Moorfoot (hills), Sc,UK
194/F4 Moorhead, Mn,US
189/F2 Mooringsport, La,US
135/B2 Moorook, Austl.
204/B2 Moorpark, Ca,US
156/B4 Moorreesburg, SAfr.
68/C2 Moorslede, Belg.
71/E6 Moosburg, Ger.
194/F2 Moose (isl.), Mb,Can
194/C3 Moose (mtn.), Sk,Can
196/B3 Moose (riv.), Me,US
195/J4 Moose (mtn.), Mn,US
177/J3 Moose Creek, Ak,US
196/C3 Moosehead (lake), Me,US
177/H3 Mooseheart (mtn.), Ak,US
205/P16 Mooseheart, Il,US
182/C1 Moose Heights, BC,Can
194/E2 Moosehorn, Mb,Can
196/D3 Moosehorn Nat'l Wild. Res., Me,US
194/B2 Moose Jaw, Sk,Can
177/J3 Moose Pass, Ak,US
183/N1 Moose Range, Sk,Can
199/L2 Moosilauke, Mount (mtn.), NH,US
71/E6 Moosinning, Ger.
194/D2 Moosomin, Sk,Can
179/H3 Moosonee, On,Can
80/D3 Moosseedorf, Swi.
71/F5 Moosthenning, Ger.
208/C2 Moosup, Ct,US
155/G3 Mopeia, Moz.
154/E4 Mopipi, Bots.
144/D3 Mopti, Mali
144/E3 Mopti (reg.), Mali
168/D5 Moquegua, Peru
168/D4 Moquegua-Tacna-Puno (dept.), Peru
172/B1 Moquegua-Tacna-Puno (reg.), Peru
175/S12 Moquehuá, Arg.
73/C5 Mór, Hun.
121/F4 Mor (riv.), India
148/B3 Mora, Camr.
76/A3 Mora, Port.
76/D3 Mora, Sp.
62/F1 Mora, Swe.
189/H2 Mora, La,US
195/H5 Mora, Mn,US
190/B3 Mora, NM,US
190/B3 Mora (riv.), NM,US
91/F1 Morača (riv.), Yugo.
120/B1 Morādābād, India
167/G4 Morada Nova, Braz.
77/E2 Mora de Rubielos, Sp.
174/C2 Morado Nat'l Park, Chile
157/H7 Morafenobe, Madg.
65/K2 Morąg, Pol.
205/K11 Moraga, Ca,US
92/D2 Mórahalom, Hun.
53/R10 Morainvilliers, Fr.
76/D3 Moral de Calatrava, Sp.
174/B5 Moraleda (chan.), Chile
76/B2 Moraleja, Sp.
160/D3 Morales, Guat.
141/G6 Moramanga, Madg.
191/G2 Moran, Ks,US
188/E1 Moran, Tx,US
185/H2 Moran, Wy,US
134/C3 Moranbah, Austl.
139/M7 Morane (isl.), FrPol.
53/T10 Morangis, Fr.
79/E5 Morannes, Fr.
83/C3 Morano Calabro, It.
161/G2 Morant Bay, Jam.
157/J7 Morarano Chrome, Madg.
55/J8 Morar, Loch (lake), Sc,UK
80/D4 Morat (lake), Swi.
76/D2 Morata de Tajuña, Sp.
76/E3 Moratalla, Sp.
65/J4 Morava (riv.), Czh.
91/G1 Morava (riv.), Yugo.
73/B2 Morava (March) (riv.), Slvk.
105/H2 Morāveh Tappeh, Iran
73/A1 Moravia (reg.), Czh.
193/H3 Moravia, Ia,US
199/H3 Moravia, NY,US
189/F3 Moravia, Tx,US
201/G2 Moravian Falls, NC,US
65/J4 Moravská Třebová, Czh.
65/H4 Moravské Budějovice, Czh.
73/B2 Moravské Lieskové, Slvk.
73/B1 Moravský Písek, Czh.
132/C4 Morawa, Austl.
163/D2 Morawhanna, Guy.
130/C3 Moray (range), Austl.
52/C3 Moray (bay), Sc,UK
54/C1 Moray (firth), Sc,UK
69/G4 Morbach, Ger.
68/B2 Morbecque, Fr.
81/F5 Morbegno, It.
80/C4 Morbier, Fr.
78/B5 Morbihan (dept.), Fr.
78/C5 Morbihan (gulf), Fr.
81/F6 Morbio Inferiore, Swi.
73/A4 Mörbisch am See, Aus.
62/G3 Mörbylånga, Swe.
74/C4 Morcenx, Fr.
87/F5 Morciano di Romagna, It.
80/C5 Morclan, Pic de (mtn.), Fr.
80/C5 Morclan, Pic de (peak), Fr.
85/E5 Morcone, It.
78/D4 Mordelles, Fr.
194/E3 Morden, Mb,Can
53/N7 Morden, Eng,UK
135/G6 Mordialloc, Austl.
99/L1 Mordovo, Rus.
94/H5 Mordves, Rus.
97/G1 Mordvian Aut. Rep., Rus.
135/B3 Morea, Austl.
192/C1 Moreau (riv.), SD,US
192/C1 Moreau, North Fork (riv.), SD,US
192/C1 Moreau, South Fork (riv.), SD,US
54/D5 Morebattle, Sc,UK
57/F3 Morecambe, Eng,UK
57/E3 Morecambe (bay), Eng,UK
135/D1 Moree, Austl.
79/G5 Morée, Fr.
131/F2 Morehead, PNG
201/F1 Morehead, Ky,US
201/J3 Morehead City, NC,US
200/C2 Morehouse, Mo,US
80/E5 Mörel, Swi.
185/G2 Moreland, Id,US
159/E5 Morelia, Mex.
197/F2 Morell, PE,Can
134/A3 Morella, Austl.
77/E2 Morella, Sp.
188/D3 Morelos, Mex.
160/B2 Morelos (state), Mex.
154/D3 Moremi Wild. Rsv., Bots.
120/B2 Morena, India
76/C3 Morena (range), Sp.
187/H4 Morenci, Az,US
198/D4 Morenci, Mi,US
93/G3 Moreni, Rom.
169/E3 Moreno, Bol.
158/C2 Moreno, Mex.
88/B3 Moreno (mts.), Sp.
204/C3 Moreno Valley, Ca,US
61/C3 Møre og Romsdal (co.), Nor.
178/C3 Moresby (isl.), BC,Can
82/B1 Morestel, Fr.
134/F6 Moreton (bay), Austl.
134/D4 Moreton (cape), Austl.
134/D4 Moreton (isl.), Austl.
53/P6 Moreton, Eng,UK
58/C5 Moretonhampstead, Eng,UK
59/E3 Moreton in Marsh, Eng,UK
134/D4 Moreton Island Nat'l Park, Austl.
86/A3 Moretta, It.
68/B4 Moreuil, Fr.
95/N2 Moreyu (riv.), Rus.
80/C4 Morez, Fr.
133/H5 Morgan, Austl.
207/F1 Morgan (pt.), Ct,US
203/F2 Morgan, Ga,US
189/F1 Morgan, Tx,US
185/H3 Morgan, Ut,US
199/K2 Morgan, Vt,US
200/B4 Morgan Brake Nat'l Wild. Ref., Ms,US
202/C3 Morgan City, La,US
200/D2 Morganfield, Ky,US
186/B2 Morgan Hill, Ca,US
164/E3 Morganito, Ven.
90/D4 Morgantina (ruins), It.
200/E3 Morganton, Ga,US
201/G3 Morganton, NC,US
198/C5 Morgantown, In,US
200/D2 Morgantown, Ky,US
206/C3 Morgantown, Pa,US
198/G5 Morgantown, WV,US
191/F1 Morganville, Ks,US
202/C2 Morganza, La,US
74/E3 Morge (riv.), Fr.
156/Q13 Morgenzon, SAfr.
80/C4 Morges, Swi.
82/D1 Morgex, It.
107/H1 Morghāb (riv.), Afg.
80/C5 Morgins, Pas de (pass), Fr., Swi.
62/G2 Morgongåva, Swe.
82/C3 Morgon, Pic de (peak), Fr.
174/B3 Morguilla (pt.), Chile
69/F6 Morhange, Fr.
121/E3 Morhar (riv.), India
108/C3 Mori, China
87/D1 Mori, It.
112/B2 Mori, Japan
133/M8 Morialta Consv. Park, Austl.
190/A3 Moriarty, NM,US
144/C4 Moribaya, Gui.
164/D3 Morichal, Col.
164/D4 Morichal, Col.
84/C3 Moricone, It.
54/B1 Morie, Loch (lake), Sc,UK
82/A5 Morières-lès-Avignon, Fr.
79/H4 Morigny-Champigny, Fr.
111/L10 Moriguchi, Japan
156/D3 Morija, Les.
71/F3 Mori Kazak Zizhixian (Mori), China
109/J2 Morin Dawa, China
67/G5 Moringen, Ger.
112/B4 Morioka, Japan
135/D2 Morisset, Austl.
54/B2 Moriston (riv.), Sc,UK
111/H7 Moriya, Japan
110/D3 Moriyama, Japan
78/B3 Morlaix, Fr.
78/B3 Morlaix (bay), Fr.
190/D1 Morland, Ks,US
68/D3 Morlanwelz, Belg.
70/B3 Mörlenbach, Ger.
57/G4 Morley, Eng,UK
200/E2 Morley, Tn,US
83/B3 Mormanno, It.
185/F1 Mormon (mtn.), Id,US
186/E2 Mormon (mts.), Nv,US
186/E2 Mormon (peak), Nv,US
54/D1 Mormond (hill), Sc,UK
187/G3 Mormon Lake, Az,US
118/B4 Mormugao, India
82/A1 Mornant, Fr.
134/F6 Morningside, Austl.
60/B5 Morningstar (riv.), Ire.
193/J3 Morning Sun, Ia,US
131/E4 Mornington (isl.), Austl.
175/J7 Mornington (isl.), Chile
60/D2 Mornington, Ire.
70/E5 Mörnsheim, Ger.
85/E3 Moro (riv.), It.
107/J3 Moro, Pak.
124/C4 Moro (gulf), Phil.
191/J3 Moro, Ar,US
191/H4 Moro (cr.), Ar,US
184/C1 Moro, Or,US
131/G1 Morobe, PNG
131/G1 Morobe (prov.), PNG
198/C4 Morocco, In,US
160/E3 Morocelí, Hon.
169/E5 Morochata, Bol.
168/B3 Morococha, Peru
151/B3 Morogoro, Tanz.
151/B3 Morogoro (prov.), Tanz.
135/C3 Moroka-Wonnangatta Nat'l Park, Austl.
156/C2 Morokweng, SAfr.
159/E4 Moroleón, Mex.
157/G8 Morombe, Madg.
174/F2 Morón, Arg.
161/G1 Morón, Cuba
108/E2 Mörön, Mong.
164/D2 Morón, Ven.
168/B1 Morona, Ecu.
168/B1 Morona (riv.), Ecu., Peru
168/B1 Morona-Santiago (prov.), Ecu.
157/H8 Morondava (riv.), Madg.
157/H8 Morondava, Madg.
76/C4 Morón de la Frontera, Sp.
144/D4 Morondo, IvC.
186/D4 Morongo Ind. Res., Ca,US
186/D3 Morongo Valley, Ca,US
157/G5 Moroni (cap.), Com.
185/H4 Moroni, Ut,US
127/G3 Morotai (isl.), Indo.
127/G3 Morotai (str.), Indo.
151/A1 Moroto, Ugan.
151/A1 Moroto (peak), Ugan.
111/H7 Moroyama, Japan
99/L3 Morozovsk, Rus.
171/E1 Morpará, Braz.
57/G1 Morpeth, Eng,UK
103/C2 Morphou, Cyp.
103/C2 Morphou (bay), Cyp.
66/C3 Morra (lake), Neth.
193/G4 Morrill, Ks,US
191/H3 Morrilton, Ar,US
183/H2 Morrin, Ab,Can
167/F3 Morrinhos, Braz.
170/C3 Morrinhos, Braz.
133/F3 Morris (peak), Austl.
194/F3 Morris, Mb,Can
194/F3 Morris (riv.), Mb,Can
204/C2 Morris (res.), Ca,US
208/A2 Morris, Ct,US
193/K3 Morris, Il,US
194/G5 Morris, Mn,US
206/D2 Morris (co.), NJ,US
199/J3 Morris, NY,US
191/G3 Morris, Ok,US
199/J2 Morrisburg, On,Can
176/P1 Morris Jesup (cape), Grld.
193/K3 Morrison, Il,US
191/F2 Morrison, Ok,US
200/E3 Morrison, Tn,US
193/K4 Morrisonville, Il,US
206/D2 Morris Plains, NJ,US
189/E1 Morris Sheppard (dam), Tx,US
197/Q9 Morriston, On,Can
58/C3 Morriston, Wal,UK
187/F4 Morristown, Az,US
206/D2 Morristown, NJ,US
199/J2 Morristown, NY,US
194/D5 Morristown, SD,US
201/F2 Morristown, Tn,US
196/A3 Morristown, Vt,US
206/D2 Morristown Nat'l Mil. Park, NJ,US
196/A3 Morrisville, Me,US
199/J3 Morrisville, NY,US
206/D3 Morrisville, Pa,US
134/A2 Morr Morr Abor. Land, Austl.
172/B2 Morro (pt.), Chile
170/C4 Morro Agudo, Braz.
186/B3 Morro Bay, Ca,US
167/N8 Morrocoyes, Ven.
164/D2 Morrocoy Nat'l Park, Ven.
161/F5 Morro de Puercos (pt.), Pan.
171/E1 Morro do Chapéu, Braz.
85/D3 Morrone (peak), It.
168/A2 Mórrope, Peru
168/B2 Morropón, Peru
159/F5 Morro, Punta del (pt.), Mex.
167/E3 Morros, Braz.
161/G4 Morrosquillo (gulf), Col.
87/G6 Morrovalle, It.
200/E4 Morrow, Ga,US
201/M7 Morrow, Ga,US
202/B2 Morrow, La,US
62/F3 Mörrum, Swe.
155/G3 Morrumbala, Moz.
155/G4 Morrumbene, Moz.
62/C3 Mørs (isl.), Den.
53/T11 Morsang-sur-Orge, Fr.
69/F5 Morsbach, Fr.
69/G2 Morsbach, Ger.
80/D2 Morschwiller-le-Bas, Fr.
183/L2 Morse, Sk,Can
202/B2 Morse, La,US
195/J4 Morse, Wi,US
192/B3 Morse (cr.), Wy,US
53/H3 Morshansk, Rus.
97/J3 Morskoy (isl.), Kaz.
67/G3 Morsum, Ger.
80/C1 Mortagne (riv.), Fr.
79/F3 Mortagne-au-Perche, Fr.
74/C3 Mortagne-sur-Sèvre, Fr.
79/E3 Mortain, Fr.
86/B2 Mortara, It.
80/B3 Morte (riv.), Fr.
58/B4 Morte (pt.), UK
80/C3 Morteau, Fr.
87/G1 Mortegliano, It.
83/B6 Mortelle, It.
172/D4 Morteros, Arg.
170/C2 Mortes (riv.), Braz.
59/E4 Mortimer, Eng,UK
58/D2 Mortimers Cross, Eng,UK
194/A2 Mortlach, Sk,Can
135/B3 Mortlake, Austl.
200/C4 Morton, Ms,US
190/C4 Morton, Tx,US
182/C4 Morton, Wa,US
205/Q15 Morton Grove, Il,US
135/D2 Morton Nat'l Park, Austl.
207/F1 Morton Nat'l Wild. Ref., NY,US
79/F3 Mortrée, Fr.
68/D1 Mortsel, Belg.
135/C2 Morundah, Austl.
171/K7 Morungaba, Braz.
135/D2 Moruya, Austl.
74/E3 Morvan (plat.), Fr.
134/B4 Morven, Austl.
136/B4 Morven, N.Z.
54/C2 Morven (mtn.), Sc,UK
203/G2 Morven, Ga,US
118/B3 Morvi, India
80/C2 Morvillars, Fr.
200/D5 Morvin, Al,US
135/C3 Morwell, Austl.
80/C5 Morzine, Fr.
76/A1 Mos, Sp.
70/C4 Mosbach, Ger.
183/L4 Mosby, Mt,US
77/P10 Moscavide, Port.
85/D2 Mosciano Sant'Angelo, It.
94/G5 Moscow (upland), Rus.
191/J3 Moscow, Ar,US
182/F4 Moscow, Id,US
190/D2 Moscow, Ks,US
196/C3 Moscow, Me,US
200/C3 Moscow, Tn,US
94/H5 Moscow (Moskva) (cap.), Rus.
94/H5 Moscow Obl., Rus.
137/H Moscow U. Ice Shelf, Ant.
69/F4 Mosel (riv.), Ger.
154/E5 Moselebe (dry riv.), Bots.
68/F5 Moselle (dept.), Fr.
69/F5 Moselle (riv.), Fr.
80/C2 Moselotte (riv.), Fr.
197/G3 Moser River, NS,Can
182/E4 Moses (lake), Wa,US
182/E4 Moses Lake, Wa,US
155/E4 Mosetse, Bots.
95/K2 Moseyevo, Rus.
61/N7 Mosfellsbær, Ice.
136/B4 Mosgiel, N.Z.
156/C2 Moshaweng (dry riv.), SAfr.
63/M2 Moshchnyy (isl.), Rus.
117/F2 Moshi, China
151/B2 Moshi, Tanz.
156/D3 Moshoeshoe (Maseru) (int'l arpt.), Les.
154/E5 Moshupa, Bots.
95/M2 Mosh'yuga, Rus.
72/C4 Mosigkau, Ger.
65/J2 Mosina, Pol.
193/K1 Mosinee, Wi,US
95/N4 Mosino, Rus.
154/E3 Mosi-oa-Tunya Nat'l Park, Zam.
154/E3 Mosi-oa-Tunya (Victoria) (falls), Zam.
153/E2 Mosite, Zaire
61/E2 Mosjøen, Nor.
97/M1 Moskalëvka, Kaz.
94/G5 Moskva (riv.), Rus.
94/H5 Moskva (Moscow) (cap.), Rus.
182/B2 Mosley (riv.), BC,Can
97/G1 Mosolovo, Rus.
154/E5 Mosomane, Bots.
73/B4 Mosoni-Duna (riv.), Hun.
73/B4 Mosonmagyaróvár, Hun.
114/E3 Mosouwan, China
96/F3 Mospino, Ukr.
164/B4 Mosquera, Col.
190/C3 Mosquero, NM,US
161/E3 Mosquitia (reg.), Hon.
161/G4 Mosquito (pt.), Pan.
186/E3 Mosquito (dry lake), Ca,US
193/G3 Mosquito (cr.), Ia,US
208/G5 Mosquito Creek (res.), Oh,US
161/F4 Mosquitos (gulf), Pan.
161/E4 Mosquitos, Costa de (reg.), Nic.
62/D2 Moss, Nor.
152/D3 Mossaka, Congo
194/B3 Mossbank, Sk,Can
205/K11 Moss Beach, Ca,US
202/B2 Moss Bluff, La,US
156/C4 Mosselbaai, SAfr.
152/C3 Mossendjo, Congo
80/D5 Mosses, Col des (pass), Swi.
135/C2 Mossgiel, Austl.
144/E4 Mossi Highlands (upland), Burk.
70/C6 Mössingen, Ger.
186/B2 Moss Landing, Ca,US
57/F4 Mossley, Eng,UK
56/C2 Mossley, NI,UK
134/B2 Mossman, Austl.
167/G4 Mossoró, Braz.
202/D2 Moss Point, Ms,US
56/B1 Moss-side, NI,UK
155/J2 Mossuril, Moz.
135/D2 Moss Vale, Austl.
203/E2 Mossy Head, Fl,US
182/C4 Mossyrock, Wa,US
71/G1 Most, Czh.
141/R16 Mostaganem, Alg.
141/R15 Mostaganem (wilaya), Alg.
92/C4 Mostar, Bosn.
173/G4 Mostardas, Braz.
98/B3 Mostiska, Ukr.
99/K3 Mostki, Ukr.
76/D2 Móstoles, Sp.
99/L5 Mostovskoy, Rus.
60/C2 Mostrim, Ire.
65/N2 Mosty, Bela.
125/B4 Mostyn, Malay.
57/E5 Mostyn, Wal,UK
105/E2 Mosul (Al Mawşil), Iraq
62/B2 Møsvatnet (lake), Nor.
149/H3 Mot'a, Eth.
172/D1 Motacucito, Bol.
76/D3 Mota del Cuervo, Sp.
160/D3 Motagua (riv.), Guat.
62/F2 Motala, Swe.
118/D4 Moter, India
160/D2 Mother (pt.), Belz.
54/C5 Motherwell, Sc,UK
113/B2 Motian (mtn.), China
115/E2 Motian Ling (mtn.), China
121/E2 Motīhāri, India
76/E3 Motilla del Palancar, Sp.
195/G4 Motley, Mn,US
155/E4 Motloutse, Bots.
155/E4 Motloutse (riv.), Bots.
153/G2 Moto, Zaire
112/J7 Motobu, Japan
63/Q2 Motokhovo, Rus.
154/D5 Motokwe, Bots.
65/N2 Motol', Bela.
83/B2 Motola (peak), It.
111/G2 Motomiya, Japan
111/J7 Motono, Japan
61/K1 Motovskiy (gulf), Rus.
87/G2 Motovun, Cro.
112/B4 Motoyoshi, Japan
160/C3 Motozintla de Mendoza, Mex.
76/D4 Motril, Sp.
112/A2 Motsuta-misaki (cape), Japan
194/C4 Mott, ND,US
87/F1 Motta di Livenza, It.
86/B1 Mottarone (peak), It.
83/B6 Motta San Giovanni, It.
86/B2 Motta Visconti, It.
136/C3 Motueka, N.Z.
159/H4 Motul de Felipe Carrillo Puerto, Mex.
168/B2 Motupe, Peru
136/F6 Motutapu (isl.), N.Z.
100/K4 Motygino, Rus.
152/B2 Mouanko, Camr.
82/C5 Mouans-Sarteux, Fr.
80/B4 Mouchard, Fr.
161/J1 Mouchoir (passg.), Trks.
91/J3 Moúdhros, Gre.
144/B2 Moudjéria, Mrta.
80/C4 Moudon, Swi.
82/D5 Mougins, Fr.
144/B2 Mougris (well), Mrta.
144/E3 Mouhoun (prov.), Burk.
152/B3 Mouila, Gabon
108/F5 Moujiaba, China
148/D4 Mouka, CAfr.
152/C3 Moukoumbi, Gabon
135/C2 Moulamein, Austl.
135/C2 Moulamein (riv.), Austl.
141/M13 Moulay Idriss, Mor.
141/M13 Moulay Yakoub, Mor.
179/R7 Mould Bay, NW,Can
57/F5 Mouldsworth, Eng,UK
74/E3 Moulins, Fr.
116/C5 Moulmein, Burma
141/N13 Moulouya (riv.), Mor.
142/D2 Moulouya, Oued (riv.), Mor.
59/G2 Moulton, Eng,UK
200/D3 Moulton, Al,US
193/H3 Moulton, Ia,US
189/F3 Moulton, Tx,US
199/L3 Moultonboro, NH,US
203/G2 Moultrie, Ga,US
201/G4 Moultrie (lake), SC,US
195/N7 Mound, Mn,US
200/B4 Mound Bayou, Ms,US
200/C2 Mound City, Il,US
191/G1 Mound City, Ks,US
193/G3 Mound City, Mo,US
192/D1 Mound City, SD,US
198/E5 Mound City Group Nat'l Mon., Oh,US
140/D4 Moundou, Chad
191/F1 Moundridge, Ks,US
200/C2 Mounds, Il,US
191/F3 Mounds, Ok,US
193/K2 Mounds, Cave Of The, Wi,US
195/P6 Mounds View, Mn,US
198/F5 Moundsville, WV,US
200/D4 Moundville, Al,US
191/G2 Moundville, Mo,US
123/C3 Moung Roessei, Camb.
123/D3 Mounlapamok, Laos
77/E1 Moun Né (mtn.), Fr.
134/B3 Mount Aberdeen Nat'l Park, Austl.
118/B3 Mount Abu, India
178/D2 Mountain (riv.), NW,Can
194/E3 Mountain, ND,US
206/A3 Mountain (cr.), Pa,US
188/K7 Mountain (cr.), Tx,US
193/K1 Mountain, Wi,US
190/A3 Mountainair, NM,US
58/C3 Mountain Ash, Wal,UK
200/D4 Mountain Brook, Al,US
191/G3 Mountainburg, Ar,US
184/F3 Mountain City, Nv,US
201/G2 Mountain City, Tn,US
188/L7 Mountain Creek (lake), Tx,US
199/H2 Mountain Grove, On,Can
191/H2 Mountain Grove, Mo,US
191/H2 Mountain Home, Ar,US
184/F2 Mountain Home, Id,US
206/C1 Mountainhome, Pa,US
185/H3 Mountain Home, Ut,US
193/G2 Mountain Lake, Mn,US
199/G5 Mountain Lake Park, Md,US
207/H8 Mountain Lakes, NJ,US
149/F4 Mountain Nile (riv.), Sudan
182/F1 Mountain Park, Ab,Can
201/M7 Mountain Park, Ga,US
191/H3 Mountain Pine, Ar,US
177/M4 Mountain Point, Ak,US
201/F3 Mountain Rest, SC,US
207/H9 Mountainside, NJ,US
206/C1 Mountain Top, Pa,US
183/H3 Mountain View, Ab,Can
191/H3 Mountain View, Ar,US
205/K12 Mountain View, Ca,US
180/U11 Mountain View, Hi,US
191/J2 Mountain View, Mo,US
191/E3 Mountain View, Ok,US
185/H3 Mountain View, Wy,US
177/F3 Mountain Village, Ak,US
156/D4 Mountain Zebra Nat'l Park, SAfr.
206/A5 Mount Airy, Md,US
201/G2 Mount Airy, NC,US
199/G2 Mount Albert, On,Can
133/G2 Mount Allan Abor. Land, Austl.
184/B1 Mount Angel, Or,US
125/D4 Mount Apo Nat'l Park, Phil.
125/C2 Mount Arayat Nat'l Park, Phil.
133/J4 Mount Arrowsmith, Austl.
136/B4 Mount Aspiring Nat'l Park, N.Z.
156/E3 Mount Ayliff, SAfr.
193/G3 Mount Ayr, Ia,US
182/D3 Mount Baker Nat'l Rec. Area, Wa,US
205/D3 Mount Baker-Snoqualmie Nat'l For., Wa,US
204/C2 Mount Baldy, Ca,US
144/C5 Mount Barclay, Libr.
132/C5 Mount Barker, Austl.
135/A2 Mount Barker, Austl.
133/G2 Mount Barkly Abor. Land, Austl.
134/C5 Mount Barney Nat'l Park, Austl.
135/C3 Mount Beauty, Austl.
60/B3 Mount Bellew Bridge, Ire.
133/M9 Mount Bold (res.), Austl.
135/C3 Mount Buffalo Nat'l Park, Austl.
200/D1 Mount Carmel, Il,US
206/B2 Mount Carmel, Pa,US
187/F2 Mount Carmel, Ut,US
193/K2 Mount Carroll, Il,US
133/G3 Mount Cavenagh, Austl.
201/G1 Mount Clare, WV,US
205/G6 Mount Clemens, Mi,US
136/B3 Mount Cook Nat'l Park, N.Z.
134/E6 Mount Coot'tha, Austl.

112/B2 Naganuma, Japan
111/F2 Nagaoka, Japan
110/D3 Nagaokakyō, Japan
122/G3 Nagappattinam, India
120/A2 Nagar, India
111/J7 Nagara, Japan
111/E3 Nagara (riv.), Japan
121/G4 Nagarbāri, Bang.
111/H7 Nagareyama, Japan
118/B4 Nagar Haveli, Dadrak (terr.), India
118/C4 Nāgārjuna Sāgar (res.), India
118/B3 Nagar Pārkar, Pak.
120/D3 Nagar Untāri, India
121/H1 Nagarzê, China
177/M5 Nagas (pt.), BC,Can
110/A4 Nagasaki, Japan
110/A4 Nagasaki (int'l arpt.), Japan
110/A4 Nagasaki (pref.), Japan
110/A4 Nagasaki Peace Park, Japan
111/M9 Nagashima, Japan
110/B3 Nagato, Japan
118/B2 Nāgaur, India
118/C3 Nāgda, India
66/C3 Nagele, Neth.
122/F4 Nāgercoil, India
120/B1 Nagīna, India
107/K1 Nagir, Pak.
149/G4 Nagishot, Sudan
60/B5 Nagles (mts.), Ire.
112/J7 Nago, Japan
120/C3 Nāgod, India
70/B5 Nagold, Ger.
99/K4 Nagol'no-Tarasovka, Ukr.
153/H2 Nagongera, Ugan.
114/F2 Nagoonnuur, Mong.
97/H5 Nagorno-Karabakh Aut. Obl., Azer.
101/N4 Nagornyy, Rus.
95/L4 Nagorsk, Rus.
153/F2 Nagosira, Zaire
87/D1 Nago-Torbole, It.
111/E3 Nagoya, Japan
111/M9 Nagoya Castle, Japan
102/G7 Nāgpur, India
114/C6 Nāgpur, India
118/C3 Nāgpur, India
116/B2 Nagqu, China
108/C5 Nagqu (riv.), China
201/K3 Nags Head, NC,US
63/J1 Nagu, Fin.
162/D3 Nagua, DRep.
111/H7 Naguri, Japan
92/C2 Nagyatád, Hun.
92/D2 Nagybatony, Hun.
92/E1 Nagyhalász, Hun.
73/C4 Nagyigmánd, Hun.
92/E2 Nagykálló, Hun.
92/C2 Nagykanizsa, Hun.
92/D2 Nagykáta, Hun.
92/D2 Nagykőrös, Hun.
92/E1 Nagy-Milic (peak), Hun.
73/B5 Nagysimonyi, Hun.
112/J7 Naha, Japan
126/D3 Nahabuan, Indo.
122/D2 Nāhan, India
178/D2 Nahanni Nat'l Park, NW,Can
208/D1 Nahant, Ma,US
103/D3 Nahariyya, Isr.
138/D2 Nahashima (isls.), Japan
182/C2 Nahatlatch (riv.), BC,Can
105/G3 Nahāvand, Iran
69/G4 Nahe (riv.), Ger.
103/G8 Naḥḥālīn, WBnk.
145/E4 Nahouri (prov.), Burk.
72/B2 Nahrstedt, Ger.
174/B3 Nahuelbuta Nat'l Park, Chile
163/B7 Nahuel Huapí (lake), Arg.
174/C4 Nahuel Huapí (lake), Arg.
174/C4 Nahuel Huapí Nat'l Park, Arg.
174/B3 Nahuentúe, Chile
203/H2 Nahunta, Ga,US
158/D3 Naica, Mex.
194/B1 Naicam, Sk,Can
67/D7 Naiguatá, Ven.
121/G4 Naihāti, India
108/C4 Naij Gol (riv.), China
108/C4 Naij Tal, China
110/C3 Naikai-Seto Nat'l Park, Japan
130/A2 Naikliu, Indo.
71/E2 Naila, Ger.
58/D4 Nailsea, Eng,UK
58/D3 Nailsworth, Eng,UK
149/G2 Na'ima, Sudan
115/E2 Naiman Qi, China
176/L4 Nain, Can.
179/K3 Nain, Nf,Can
105/H3 Nā'īn, Iran
120/B1 Naini Tal, India
120/C4 Nainpur, India
74/D3 Naintré, Fr.
54/C1 Nairn, Sc,UK
54/B2 Nairn (riv.), Sc,UK
133/M9 Nairne, Austl.
133/M9 Nairne (cr.), Austl.
151/B2 Nairobi (cap.), Kenya
151/B2 Nairobi Nat'l Park, Kenya
149/G4 Naita (peak), Eth.
151/B2 Naivasha, Kenya
69/E6 Naives-Rosières, Fr.
105/G3 Najafābād, Iran
120/A1 Najafgarh, India
104/E5 Najd (des.), SAr.
76/D1 Nájera, Sp.
120/B1 Najībābād, India
113/D5 Naju, SKor.
111/K9 Naka, Japan
110/D4 Naka (riv.), Japan
111/G2 Naka (riv.), Japan
123/D2 Na Kae, Thai.
111/H7 Nakai, Japan
111/F1 Nakajō, Japan
180/T10 Nakalele (pt.), Hi,US
111/G2 Nakaminato, Japan
110/C4 Nakamura, Japan
111/F2 Nakano, Japan
110/C3 Nakano (lake), Japan
112/B3 Nakasato, Japan
112/D2 Nakashibetsu, Japan
153/H2 Nakasongola, Ugan.
110/B5 Nakatane, Japan
110/B4 Nakatsu, Japan
111/E3 Nakatsugawa, Japan
149/H1 Nak'fa, Eth.
53/H5 Nakhichevan', Azer.
97/H5 Nakhichevan Aut. Rep., Azer.
105/F2 Nakhichevan Aut. Rep. (prov.), Azer.
109/L3 Nakhodka, Rus.
123/C3 Nakhon Nayok, Thai.
123/C3 Nakhon Pathom, Thai.
123/D2 Nakhon Phanom, Thai.
123/C3 Nakhon Ratchasima, Thai.
123/C3 Nakhon Sawan, Thai.
123/B4 Nakhon Si Thammarat, Thai.
123/C2 Nakhon Thai, Thai.
107/J4 Nakhtarāna, India
153/H2 Nakifuma, Ugan.
195/L2 Nakina, On,Can
63/J1 Nakkila, Fin.
65/J2 Nakľo nad Notecią, Pol.
177/G4 Naknek, Ak,US
122/C2 Nakodar, India
153/H5 Nakonde, Zam.
145/E4 Nakong, Gha.
156/B3 Nakop, Namb.
113/E3 Naksan-sa, SKor.
62/D4 Nakskov, Den.
113/E4 Naktong, SKor.
113/E5 Naktong (riv.), SKor.
151/B2 Nakuru, Kenya
182/F2 Nakusp, BC,Can
107/J3 Nāl (riv.), Pak.
116/E3 Nalao, China
108/F2 Nalayh, Mong.
155/G5 Naláźi, Moz.
69/F5 Nalbach, Ger.
121/H2 Nalbāri, India
135/D3 Nalbaugh Nat'l Park, Austl.
53/H4 Nal'chik, Rus.
97/G4 Nalchik (int'l arpt.), Rus.
123/C2 Nale, Laos
118/C4 Nalgonda, India
121/F3 Nalhāti, India
121/H3 Nalitābāri, Bang.
118/A3 Naliya, India
93/K5 Nallıhan, Turk.
76/B1 Nalón (riv.), Sp.
116/C3 Nalong, Burma
146/A2 Nālūt, Libya
116/A2 Nam (lake), China
113/D3 Nam (riv.), NKor.
113/D5 Nam (riv.), SKor.
154/B3 Namacunde, Ang.
155/H3 Namacurra, Moz.
155/G2 Namadzi, Malw.
120/D2 Namāi, Nepal
105/G3 Namak (lake), Iran
122/G3 Nāmakkal, India
107/G2 Namakzār-e Shadād (salt dep.), Iran
124/D3 Namang, Indo.
151/B2 Namanga, Kenya
113/B3 Namangan, Uzb.
113/G7 Namansansong Prov. Park, SKor.
153/G4 Namanyere, Tanz.
155/H2 Namapa, Moz.
151/B4 Namaputa, Tanz.
156/B3 Namaqualand (reg.), SAfr.
144/B3 Namari, Sen.
127/J4 Namaripi (cape), Indo.
155/H2 Namarrói, Moz.
153/H2 Namasagali, Ugan.
138/E5 Namatanai, PNG
151/B4 Nambanje, Tanz.
190/B3 Nambe, NM,US
69/G4 Nambern, Ger.
134/D4 Nambour, Austl.
152/C5 Nambuangongo, Ang.
135/E1 Nambucca Heads, Austl.
132/B4 Nambung Nat'l Park, Austl.
123/D4 Nam Can, Viet.
116/A2 Namco, China
123/C1 Nam Cum, Viet.
113/E2 Namdae (riv.), NKor.
61/D2 Namdalseid, Nor.
123/D1 Nam Dinh, Viet.
63/S7 Nämdöfjärden (sound), Swe.
195/J4 Namekagon (riv.), Wi,US
145/E3 Namentenga (prov.), Burk.
111/E2 Namerikawa, Japan
155/H2 Nametil, Moz.
195/L3 Namewaminikan (riv.), On,Can
113/D5 Namhae, SKor.
113/D5 Namhae (isl.), SKor.
124/C1 Nami, Malay.
154/B5 Namib (des.), Namb.
154/B2 Namibe, Ang.
154/B2 Namibe (dist.), Ang.
154/B2 Namibe (int'l arpt.), Ang.
140/D7 Namibia
154/B4 Namib-Naukluft Park, Namb.
111/G2 Namie, Japan
111/F2 Namioka, Japan
158/D2 Namiquipa, Mex.
155/G2 Namitete, Malw.
120/D1 Namja (pass), Nepal
116/B2 Namjagbarwa (peak), China
123/B1 Namlan, Burma
121/G1 Namling, China
81/G3 Namloser Wetterspitze (peak), Aus.
123/C2 Nam Nao Nat'l Park, Thai.
123/B4 Namnoi (peak), Burma
152/C2 Namobessie (Lengué) (riv.), Congo
135/D1 Namoi (riv.), Austl.
138/E4 Namonuito (isl.), Micr.
138/F4 Namorik (isl.), Mrsh.
157/J8 Namorona, Madg.
184/E2 Nampa, Id,US
144/D3 Nampala, Mali
123/C2 Nam Pat, Thai.
123/C2 Nam Phong, Thai.
113/C3 Namp'o, NKor.
155/H2 Nampula, Moz.
155/H2 Nampula (prov.), Moz.
113/D5 Namp'yŏng, SKor.
127/G4 Namrole, Indo.
116/B3 Nāmrup, India
123/B1 Namsang, Burma
113/D2 Namsa-ri, NKor.
114/D6 Namsê Shankou (pass), China
61/D2 Namsos, Nor.
123/B2 Nam Tok Mae Surin Nat'l Park, Thai.
138/F4 Namu (atoll), Mrsh.
155/H2 Namúli, Serra (mts.), Moz.
123/C2 Nam Un (res.), Thai.
155/H2 Namuno, Moz.
69/D3 Namur, Belg.
69/D3 Namur (prov.), Belg.
154/C3 Namutoni, Namb.
155/E2 Namwala, Zam.
113/D5 Namwŏn, SKor.
65/J3 Namysłów, Pol.
117/G3 Nan (mts.), China
116/E1 Nan (riv.), China
117/F1 Nan (riv.), China
123/C2 Nan, Thai.
123/C2 Nan (riv.), Thai.
148/G4 Nanaam, Khawr (dry riv.), Sudan
148/C4 Nana Barya (riv.), CAfr., Chad
148/C4 Nana Barya Fauna Rsv., CAfr.
159/L7 Nanacamilpa, Mex.
153/E5 Nana Candundo, Ang.
112/B3 Nanae, Japan
200/D4 Nanafalia, Al,US
182/C3 Nanaimo, BC,Can
113/E2 Nanam, NKor.
148/B4 Nana-Mambéré (pref.), CAfr.
134/D4 Nanango, Austl.
117/H4 Nan'ao, China
111/E2 Nanao, Japan
120/A1 Nanauta, India
168/C1 Nanay (riv.), Peru
115/L8 Nanbaozhen, China
174/C2 Nancagua, Chile
109/K2 Nancha, China
117/G2 Nanchang, China
116/E2 Nanchong, China
117/E2 Nanchuan, China
69/F6 Nancy, Fr.
160/E4 Nandaime, Nic.
119/J3 Nandan, China
117/G2 Nandashan, China
118/C4 Nānded, India
155/F4 Nandi Mill, Zim.
116/C4 Nanding (riv.), China
152/D5 Nandonge, Ang.
69/E3 Nandrin, Belg.
117/F4 Nandu, China
117/F5 Nandu (riv.), China
118/B3 Nandurbār, India
53/T11 Nandy, Fr.
118/C4 Nandyāl, India
113/B2 Nanfen, China
117/H3 Nanfeng, China
117/J4 Nang (isl.), Phil.
148/B4 Nanga-Eboko, Camr.
127/F5 Nangalili, Indo.
126/D4 Nangamahap, Indo.
126/D3 Nangamentebah, Indo.
107/K1 Nanga Parbat (mtn.), Pak.
126/D4 Nangapinoh, Indo.
155/J2 Nangata (pt.), Moz.
123/B4 Nangin, Burma
113/D2 Nangnim, NKor.
113/D2 Nangnim (mts.), NKor.
113/D2 Nangong, China
121/F1 Nangpa (pass), Nepal
121/F1 Nangpula (pass), China
116/C1 Nangqên, China
123/C3 Nang Rong, Thai.
125/C3 Nangtud (mt.), Phil.
151/B2 Nangua, Tanz.
113/A3 Nanguanling, China
135/B3 Nangwarry, Austl.
116/B2 Nang Xian, China
117/J4 Nanhai, Tai.
113/A4 Nanhuang, China
115/E5 Nanhui, China
154/D2 Nanikelako, Zam.
117/F4 Nanjiangkou, China
116/D3 Nanjian Yizu Zizhixian, China
115/D4 Nanjing, China
116/C4 Nanka (riv.), Burma, China
122/B2 Nankāna Sāhib, Pak.
110/D4 Nanki (arpt.), Japan
110/C4 Nankoku, Japan
117/H3 Nankou, China
154/C3 Nankova, Ang.
116/D4 Nanlan (riv.), Burma, China
115/C3 Nanle, China
115/D4 Nanling, China
112/D2 Nanliqiao, China
117/F4 Nanliu (riv.), China
109/K3 Nanlou (peak), China
112/D3 Nannestad, Nor.
132/C3 Nannine, Austl.
117/F4 Nanning, China
111/M9 Nannō, Japan
132/B5 Nannup, Austl.
60/D2 Nanny (riv.), Ire.
116/E3 Nanpan (riv.), China
120/C2 Nānpāra, India
115/D3 Nanpi, China
117/H3 Nanping, China
115/J7 Nanpu, China
111/M10 Nansei, Japan
112/H8 Nansei Shoto (Ryukyu) (isls.), Japan
201/J2 Nansemond Nat'l Wild. Ref., Va,US
179/S6 Nansen (sound), NW,Can
117/H3 Nansheng, China
121/K2 Nansio, Tanz.
82/B6 Nans-les-Pins, Fr.
79/G5 Nant (riv.), Fr.
113/B2 Nantai, China
111/F2 Nantai-san (mtn.), Japan
53/S10 Nanterre, Fr.
78/D6 Nantes, Fr.
78/B4 Nantes à Brest (can.), Fr.
74/C3 Nantes (Château Bougon) (int'l arpt.), Fr.
53/U9 Nanteuil-le-Haudouin, Fr.
68/B6 Nanteuil-lès-Meaux, Fr.
117/H3 Nantian, China
117/J2 Nantian, China
198/F3 Nanticoke, On,Can
206/B1 Nanticoke, Pa,US
54/A4 Nant, Loch (lake), Sc,UK
183/H2 Nanton, Ab,Can
115/E4 Nantong, China
80/B5 Nantua, Fr.
196/B5 Nantucket, Ma,US
196/C5 Nantucket (isl.), Ma,US
196/B5 Nantucket (sound), Ma,US
196/B5 Nantucket Nat'l Wild. Ref., Ma,US
155/H2 Nantúpi, Moz.
57/F5 Nantwich, Eng,UK
58/C3 Nantyglo, Wal,UK
199/G4 Nanty-Glo, Pa,US
207/D1 Nanuet, NY,US
139/Z18 Nanuku (chan.), Fiji
138/G5 Nanumanga (isl.), Tuv.
138/G5 Nanumea (isl.), Tuv.
171/E3 Nanuque, Braz.
115/C4 Nanwon (res.), China
117/H3 Nanwutai (mtn.), China
116/E2 Nanxi, China
115/L8 Nanxiang, China
108/F5 Nanxing, China
115/L9 Nanxun, China
151/B4 Nanyamba, Tanz.
108/G5 Nanyang, China
115/D4 Nanyang, China
115/D4 Nanyang (lake), China
117/G3 Nanyue, China
151/B1 Nanyuki, Kenya
113/C2 Nanzamu, China
115/B5 Nanzhang, China
115/C4 Nanzhao, China
179/J3 Naococane (lake), Qu,Can
121/G3 Naogaon, Bang.
118/A3 Naokot, Pak.
109/L2 Naoli (riv.), China
159/N7 Naolinco de Victoria, Mex.
173/F4 Não-Me-Toque, Braz.
154/C4 Naos, Namb.
144/D5 Naoua (falls), IvC.
91/H2 Náousa, Gre.
91/J4 Náousa, Gre.
117/F4 Naozhou (isl.), China
205/K10 Napa, Ca,US
205/K10 Napa (co.), Ca,US
205/K10 Napa (riv.), Ca,US
205/K10 Napa (val.), Ca,US
73/B1 Napajedla, Czh.
205/K10 Napa Junction, Ca,US
151/A1 Napak (peak), Ugan.
177/F3 Napakiak, Ak,US
199/H2 Napanee, On,Can
177/F3 Napaskiak, Ak,US
147/F5 Napata (ruins), Sudan
182/C4 Napavine, Wa,US
205/P16 Naperville, Il,US
80/D4 Napf (peak), Swi.
127/J4 Napido, Indo.
131/D2 Napier (pt.), Austl.
136/D2 Napier, N.Z.
156/L11 Napier, SAfr.
130/B3 Napier Broome (bay), Austl.
130/C4 Napier, Mount (peak), Austl.
197/N7 Napierville (co.), Qu,Can
194/D3 Napinka, Mb,Can
203/H4 Naples, Fl,US
182/F3 Naples, Id,US
196/B4 Naples, Me,US
199/H3 Naples, NY,US
189/G1 Naples, Tx,US
185/J3 Naples, Ut,US
85/E6 Naples (Napoli), It.
203/H4 Naples Park, Fl,US
119/J3 Napo, China
164/B5 Napo (prov.), Ecu.
164/C5 Napo (riv.), Ecu., Peru
168/C1 Napo (riv.), Peru
198/D3 Napoleon, Mi,US
194/E4 Napoleon, ND,US
198/D4 Napoleon, Oh,US
202/C3 Napoleonville, La,US
85/E4 Napoletano, Appennino (mts.), It.
85/E6 Napoli (gulf), It.
85/E6 Napoli (prov.), It.
85/E6 Napoli (Naples), It.
82/C5 Napoule (gulf), Fr.
133/J3 Nappa Merrie, Austl.
198/C4 Nappanee, In,US
133/G2 Napperby, Austl.
59/E2 Napton on the Hill, Eng,UK
139/L6 Napuka (isl.), FrPol.
150/C2 Naqīl Sumārah (pass), Yem.
110/D3 Nara, Japan
110/D3 Nara (pref.), Japan
144/D3 Nara, Mali
107/J4 Nāra (riv.), Pak.
206/C6 Naraberth, Pa,US
135/C3 Naracoopa, Austl.
135/B3 Naracoorte, Austl.
132/C4 Naradhan, Austl.
124/D2 Narail, Bang.
120/C3 Naraini, India
114/D5 Nara Logna (pass), Nepal
182/E3 Naramata, BC,Can
114/F2 Naranbulag, Mong.
164/B5 Naranjal, Ecu.
159/H5 Naranjal, Mex.
168/B1 Naranjito, Ecu.
159/E3 Naranjo, Mex.
172/E1 Naranjos, Bol.
105/G3 Narāq, Iran
118/D4 Narasannapeta, India
111/J7 Narashino, Japan
114/D3 Narat, China
123/C5 Narathiwat, Thai.
190/C3 Nara Visa, NM,US
121/H4 Nārāyanganj, Bang.
120/C4 Nārāyanganj, India
120/D2 Narayani (riv.), Nepal
121/E2 Nārāyani (zone), Nepal
118/C4 Nārāyanpet, India
58/B3 Narberth, Wal,UK
74/E5 Narbonne, Fr.
76/B1 Narcea (riv.), Sp.
91/F2 Nardò, It.
167/L6 Nare, Col.
58/B6 Nare (pt.), UK
134/G9 Narellan, Austl.
132/C5 Narembeen, Austl.
144/C3 Naréna, Mali
179/T7 Nares (str.), Can., Grld.
65/L2 Narew (riv.), Pol.
161/G4 Narganá, Pan.
118/B3 Nargol, India
154/C5 Narib, Namb.
157/H6 Narinda, Madg.
157/H6 Narinda (bay), Madg.
167/K6 Nariño, Col.
164/B4 Nariño (dept.), Col.
111/G3 Narita (int'l arpt.), Japan
175/K8 Nariz (peak), Chile
192/F4 Narka, Ks,US
121/E2 Narkatiāganj, India
120/A4 Narmada (riv.), India
97/G4 Narman, Turk.
84/C2 Narni, It.
84/C2 Narni Scalo, It.
63/M4 Naroch', Bela.
53/K2 Narodnaya (peak), Rus.
151/A2 Narok, Kenya
151/B2 Naro Moru, Kenya
76/A1 Narón, Sp.
135/D3 Narooma, Austl.
98/E2 Narovlya, Bela.
122/C1 Nārowāl, Pak.
61/G3 Närpes, Fin.
125/B3 Narra, Phil.
135/D1 Narrabri, Austl.
208/C2 Narragansett (bay), RI,US
208/C3 Narragansett Pier, RI,US
135/C2 Narrandera, Austl.
132/C5 Narrogin, Austl.
135/D2 Narromine, Austl.
191/H3 Narrows (dam), Ar,US
201/G2 Narrows, Va,US
207/J9 Narrows, The (str.), NJ,US
120/B4 Narsimhapur, India
120/A4 Narsingarh, India
121/H4 Narsingdi, Bang.
121/H4 Narsinghdi, Bang.
82/C6 Nartuby (riv.), Fr.
156/B2 Narubis, Namb.
95/K5 Naruksovo, Rus.
151/B4 Narungombe, Tanz.
110/D3 Naruto, Japan
62/N3 Narva, Est.
63/M2 Narva (bay), Est., Rus.
63/M2 Narva (res.), Est., Rus.
63/M2 Narva (riv.), Est., Rus.
125/C1 Narvacan, Phil.
63/N2 Narva-Jõesuu, Est.
61/F1 Narvik, Nor.
53/J2 Nar'yan-Mar, Rus.
114/C3 Naryn, Kyr.
114/B3 Naryn (riv.), Kyr.
97/H3 Naryn Khuduk, Rus.
86/A3 Narzole, It.
145/G4 Nasarawa, Nga.
103/E2 Naṣarī'yah, Jabal an (mts.), Syria
202/D2 NASA Test Ctr., Ms,US
187/J4 NASA Test Facility, NM,US
93/G2 Năsăud, Rom.
201/K2 NASA Wallops Flight Ctr., Va,US
174/D2 Naschel, Arg.
187/H2 Naschitti, NM,US
54/A1 Na Sealga, Loch (lake), Sc,UK
136/B4 Naseby, N.Z.
182/C4 Naselle, Wa,US
59/F3 Nash, Eng,UK
58/C4 Nash (pt.), Wal,UK
191/E2 Nash, Ok,US
191/G3 Nashoba, Ok,US
193/H2 Nashua, Ia,US
183/L3 Nashua, Mt,US
199/L3 Nashua, NH,US
191/H4 Nashville, Ar,US
203/G2 Nashville, Ga,US
193/K4 Nashville, Il,US
198/C5 Nashville, In,US
198/D3 Nashville, Mi,US
201/J3 Nashville, NC,US
200/D2 Nashville, Tn,US
200/D2 Nashville (int'l arpt.), Tn,US
92/D3 Našice, Cro.
65/L2 Nasielsk, Pol.
63/K1 Nasijärvi (lake), Fin.
118/B4 Nāsik, India
130/A2 Nasikonis (cape), Indo.
149/G3 Nāṣir, Sudan
118/B2 Nasīrābād, India
107/J3 Nasīrābād, Pak.
83/A6 Naso, It.
125/C3 Naso (pt.), Phil.
200/C1 Nason, Il,US
200/C2 Nasonville, RI,US
139/Z17 Nasorolevu (peak), Fiji
97/J4 Nasosnyy, Azer.
120/E3 Nāsriganj, India
177/N4 Nass (riv.), BC,Can
70/D2 Nassach (riv.), Ger.
162/B1 Nassau (cap.), Bahm.
175/L8 Nassau (bay), Chile
139/J6 Nassau (isl.), Cookls.
70/A2 Nassau, Ger.
206/C6 Nassau, De,US
203/H2 Nassau (sound), Fl,US
207/E2 Nassau (co.), NY,US
189/M9 Nassau Bay, Tx,US
201/K2 Nassawadox, Va,US
147/G4 Nasser (lake), Egypt
81/G3 Nassereith, Aus.
144/E4 Nassian, IvC.
62/F3 Nässjö, Swe.
69/E3 Nassogne, Belg.
145/F4 Nassoukou, Ben.
179/J3 Nastapoka (isls.), NW,Can
70/A2 Nastätten, Ger.
63/K1 Nastola, Fin.
62/D4 Næstved, Den.
111/F2 Nasu-dake (mtn.), Japan
125/C2 Nasugbu, Phil.
73/D4 Naszály (peak), Hun.
116/C5 Nat (peak), Burma
155/E4 Nata, Bots.
164/A2 Natá, Pan.
164/C4 Natagaima, Col.
167/H4 Natal, Braz.
124/B2 Natal, Indo.
157/E3 Natal (prov.), SAfr.
202/C3 Natalbany, La,US
189/E3 Natalia, Tx,US
173/E3 Natalicio Talavera, Par.
122/C3 Naṭanz, Iran
122/G3 Nataraja Temple, India
111/L9 Natashō, Japan
179/K3 Natashquan (riv.), Qu,Can
202/B2 Natchez, La,US
181/H5 Natchez, Ms,US
189/J2 Natchez, Ms,US
200/B5 Natchez, Ms,US
200/B5 Natchez Trace Pkwy., US
202/B2 Natchitoches, La,US
81/H5 Naters, Swi.
139/Z17 Natewa (bay), Fiji
201/H2 Nathalie, Va,US
208/B2 Nathan Hale St. Mon., Ct,US
118/B3 Nāthdwāra, India
155/G3 Nathenje, Malw.
192/A4 Nathrop, Co,US
208/C1 Natick, Ma,US
159/E3 Natillas, Mex.
135/B3 Natimuk, Austl.
206/B5 National Agriculture Research Ctr., Md,US
206/B5 National Aquarium, Md,US
91/L6 National Archaeological Museum, Gre.
190/A3 National Atomic Museum, NM,US
183/G4 National Bison Range, Mt,US
68/D2 National (Brussels) (int'l arpt.), Belg.
131/G2 National Cap. Dist. (prov.), PNG
204/C5 National City, Ca,US
59/E2 National Exhibition Centre, Eng,UK
206/A5 National Institutes of Health, Md,US
203/H5 National Key Deer Ref., Fl,US
195/L4 National Mine, Mi,US
136/H9 National Museum, N.Z.
206/B5 National Security Agency, Md,US
154/B4 National West Coast Rec. Area, Namb.
145/F4 Natitingou, Ben.
170/D1 Natividade, Braz.
123/B3 Natkyizin, Burma
103/D4 Natl, Jor.
190/E1 Natoma, Ks,US
121/G3 Nator, Bang.
151/A2 Natron (lake), Tanz.
208/H6 Natrona Heights, Pa,US
122/G3 Nattam, India
119/G4 Nattaung (peak), Burma
71/G6 Natternbach, Aus.
70/D5 Nattheim, Ger.
62/F3 Nättraby, Swe.
126/C3 Natuna (isls.), Indo.
189/E3 Natural Bridge Caverns, Tx,US
187/G2 Natural Bridges Nat'l Mon., Ut,US
132/B5 Naturaliste (cape), Austl.
132/B3 Naturaliste (chan.), Austl.
132/B5 Naturaliste-Leeuwin Nat'l Park, Austl.
188/K7 Nature Ctr., Tx,US
185/J4 Naturita, Co,US
81/G4 Naturns (Naturno), It.
81/G4 Naturno (Naturns), It.
198/D1 Naubinway, Mi,US
159/K7 Naucalpan de Juárez, Mex.
159/Q10 Naucalpan de Morelos, Mex.
74/E4 Naucelle, Fr.
81/G4 Nauders, Aus.
156/E3 Naudesnek (pass), SAfr.
72/C2 Nauen, Ger.
121/F3 Naugachhia, India
121/G4 Naugaon Sādāt, India
208/A3 Naugatuck, Ct,US
208/A2 Naugatuck (riv.), Ct,US
159/M7 Nauhcampatépetl (vol.), Mex.
70/B3 Nauheim, Ger.
63/L4 Naujamiestis, Lith.
125/C2 Naujan, Phil.
63/K3 Naujoji-Akmenė, Lith.
156/A2 Naukluft-Namib Game Rsv., Namb.
154/B4 Nauklult-Namib Park, Namb.
67/G6 Naumburg, Ger.
123/B2 Naunggala, Burma
116/C5 Naunglon, Burma
72/C5 Naunhof, Ger.
69/G3 Nauort, Ger.
103/D4 Nā'ūr, Jor.
138/F5 Nauru
122/C1 Nāushahra, India
108/F1 Naushki, Rus.
139/Y18 Nausori (Suva) (int'l arpt.), Fiji
168/C2 Nauta, Peru
159/N6 Nautla, Mex.
200/D4 Nauvoo, Al,US
193/J3 Nauvoo, Il,US
188/D3 Nava, Mex.
77/N8 Navacarrada (pass), Sp.
86/A4 Nava, Colle di (pass), It.
76/C2 Nava del Rey, Sp.
187/H3 Navajo, Az,US
190/A2 Navajo (peak), Co,US
187/J2 Navajo (lake), Co, NM,US
190/A2 Navajo (riv.), Co, NM,US
183/M3 Navajo, Mt,US
187/J2 Navajo (dam), NM,US
187/G2 Navajo Nat'l Mon., Az,US
125/D3 Naval, Phil.
180/T10 Naval Bomb. Ra., Hi,US
77/M9 Navalcarnero, Sp.
76/C3 Navalmoral de la Mata, Sp.
186/C3 Naval Petro. Rsv., Ca,US
203/H2 Naval Support Submarine Base, Ga,US
76/C3 Navalvillar de Pela, Sp.
56/B4 Navan, Ire.
101/T3 Navarin (cape), Rus.
175/L8 Navarino (isl.), Chile
76/D1 Navarre (aut. comm.), Sp.
88/C2 Navarre (reg.), Sp.
208/F6 Navarre, Oh,US
174/F2 Navarro, Arg.
184/B4 Navarro, Ca,US
77/F2 Navas, Sp.
76/D3 Navas de San Juan, Sp.
189/F2 Navasota, Tx,US
189/F2 Navasota (riv.), Tx,US
161/H2 Navassa (isl.), USVI
58/A6 Navax (pt.), UK
86/D1 Nave, It.
80/C2 Navenne, Fr.
76/B1 Navia, Sp.
76/B1 Navia (riv.), Sp.
174/D2 Navidad, Chile
189/F3 Navidad (riv.), Tx,US
170/B4 Naviraí, Braz.
96/E1 Navlya, Rus.
188/L6 Navo, Tx,US
93/J3 Năvodari, Rom.
100/G5 Navoi, Uzb.
158/C3 Navojoa, Mex.
158/D3 Navolato, Mex.
125/E6 Navotas, Phil.
91/G3 Návpaktos, Gre.
91/H4 Návplion, Gre.
145/E4 Navrongo, Gha.
118/B3 Navsāri, India
179/H1 Navy Board (inlet), NW,Can
205/B2 Navy Yard City, Wa,US
121/G3 Nawābganj, Bang.
118/D2 Nawābganj, India
120/B1 Nawābganj, India
107/J3 Nawābshāh, Pak.
121/E3 Nawāda, India
122/A1 Nawān Jandānwāla, Pak.
122/C1 Nawānshahr, India
122/D2 Nawāshahr, India
116/C4 Nawnghkio, Burma
123/B1 Nawngleng, Burma
107/G5 Nawş, Ra's (pt.), Oman
119/J2 Naxi, China
91/J4 Náxos, Gre.
91/J4 Náxos (isl.), Gre.
164/B4 Naya, Col.
158/D4 Nayarit (state), Mex.
105/H5 Nāy Band, Iran
105/J3 Nāy Band, Iran
59/G3 Nayland, Eng,UK
191/J2 Naylor, Mo,US
119/J2 Nayong, China
112/C1 Nayoro, Japan
108/B2 Nayramadlīn (peak), Mong.
114/E2 Nayramadlīn Orgil (peak), Mong.
195/G4 Naytahwaush, Mn,US
155/G2 Nayuci, Malw.
114/B4 Nayzatash, Pereval (pass), Taj.
166/E4 Nazaré, Braz.
76/A3 Nazaré, Port.
167/H4 Nazaré da Mata, Braz.
167/F4 Nazaré do Piauí, Braz.
171/K8 Nazaré Paulista, Braz.
68/C2 Nazareth, Belg.
206/C2 Nazareth, Pa,US
103/D3 Nazareth (Nazerat), Isr.
158/D3 Nazas, Mex.
158/D3 Nazas (riv.), Mex.
168/C4 Nazca, Peru
168/C4 Nazca Lines, Peru
112/K6 Naze, Japan
79/F6 Nazelles-Négron, Fr.
103/D3 Nazerat (Nazareth), Isr.
59/H3 Naze, The (pt.), Eng,UK
104/B2 Nazilli, Turk.
121/H4 Nāzir Hāt, Bang.
182/C1 Nazko (riv.), BC,Can
97/H4 Nazran', Rus.
150/A3 Nazrēt, Eth.
107/G4 Nazwá, Oman
100/H4 Nazyvayevsk, Rus.
154/D3 Ncamasere (dry riv.), Bots.
155/E2 Nchanga, Zam.
153/G5 Nchelenge, Zam.
155/G2 Ncheu, Malw.
155/G2 Nchisi, Malw.
154/D4 Ncojane, Bots.
159/H5 N.C.P. Nueva Coahuila, Mex.
155/F2 Ndabala, Zam.
151/A3 Ndala, Tanz.
152/C5 Ndalatando, Ang.
145/F4 Ndali, Ben.
148/D3 Ndele, CAfr.
148/B4 Ndélélé, Camr.
152/B3 Ndendé, Gabon
151/A4 Ndengu, Tanz.
138/F6 Ndeni (isl.), Sol.
151/B2 Ndethya-Ngai Nat'l Rsv., Kenya
144/A2 Ndiago, Mrta.
148/A4 Ndikiniméki, Camr.
148/B4 Ndim, CAfr.
140/D3 N'Djamena (cap.), Chad
148/B2 N'Djamena (int'l arpt.), Chad
152/C4 N'djili (int'l arpt.), Zaire
152/B3 N'Djolé, Gabon
152/B3 Ndogo (lag.), Gabon
155/F2 Ndola, Zam.
151/B2 Ndolo Corner, Kenya
153/E4 Ndombi, Zaire
145/H5 Ndop, Camr.
152/B2 Ndouaniang, Gabon
144/D5 Ndouci, IvC.
152/B3 Ndougou, Gabon
144/B2 Ndrhamcha, Sebkha de (dry lake), Mrta.
148/D4 Ndu, Zaire
151/A3 Nduguti, Tanz.
151/A3 Nduli, Tanz.
151/B4 Ndumbwe, Tanz.
151/B3 Ndungu, Tanz.
74/C4 Né (riv.), Fr.
91/J5 Néa Alikarnassós, Gre.
91/H3 Néa Ankhíalos, Gre.
91/H3 Néa Artáki, Gre.
56/B2 Neagh, Lough (lake), NI,UK
182/B3 Neah Bay, Wa,US
89/J3 Néa Ionía, Gre.
91/H3 Néa Ionía, Gre.
96/B5 Néa Ionía, Gre.
91/H2 Néa Kallikrátia, Gre.
91/H4 Néa Kíos, Gre.
133/F3 Neale (lake), Austl.
91/H2 Néa Mikhanióna, Gre.
91/H2 Néa Moudhaniá, Gre.
93/H2 Neamţ (co.), Rom.
91/G3 Néa Péramos, Gre.
91/G2 Neápolis, Gre.
91/H2 Neápolis, Gre.
91/J5 Neápolis, Gre.
91/H2 Néa Potídhaia, Gre.
177/A6 Near (isls.), Ak,US
58/C3 Neath, Wal,UK
58/C3 Neath (riv.), Wal,UK
91/H2 Néa Triglia, Gre.
91/K2 Néa Víssa, Gre.
206/B6 Neavitt, Md,US
91/H2 Néa Zíkhni, Gre.
56/D3 Neb (riv.), IM,UK
153/G2 Nebbi, Ugan.
81/G3 Nebel-Horn (peak), Ger.
80/D3 Nebikon, Swi.
82/D3 Nebin (peak), It.
198/D1 Nebish (isl.), Mi,US
97/K5 Nebit-Dag, Trkm.
165/E4 Neblina, Pico da (peak), Braz.
134/E6 Nebo (mtn.), Austl.
157/E2 Nebo, SAfr.
191/J1 Nebo, Il,US
189/H2 Nebo, La,US
191/H2 Nebo, Mo,US
185/H4 Nebo (mt.), Ut,US
72/B5 Nebra, Ger.
192/D3 Nebraska (state), US
193/G3 Nebraska City, Ne,US
90/C4 Nebrodi, Madonie (mts.), It.
193/J1 Necedah, Wi,US
193/J1 Necedah Nat'l Wild. Ref., Wi,US
178/D3 Nechako (riv.), BC,Can
98/F4 Nechayannoye, Ukr.
194/F3 Neche, ND,US
189/G2 Neches, Tx,US
189/G2 Neches (riv.), Tx,US
149/H4 Nechisar Nat'l Park, Eth.
71/G2 Nechranice, Údolní nádrž (res.), Czh.
70/B4 Neckar (riv.), Ger.
70/B4 Neckargemünd, Ger.
70/B4 Neckarsteinach, Ger.
70/C4 Neckarsulm, Ger.
139/J2 Necker (isl.), Hi,US
174/F3 Necochea, Arg.
164/B2 Necoclí, Col.
84/C3 Necropoli (ruins), It.
76/A1 Neda, Sp.
73/B3 Neded, Slvk.
91/J2 Nedelino, Bul.
92/C2 Nedelišće, Cro.
189/H3 Nederland, Tx,US
66/C6 Nederweert, Neth.
132/K6 Nedlands, Austl.
121/H1 Nêdong, China
122/F4 Nedumangād, India
66/D4 Neede, Neth.
202/D2 Needham, Al,US
208/C1 Needham, Ma,US
59/H2 Needham Market, Eng,UK
59/F2 Needingworth, Eng,UK
185/J1 Needle (mtn.), Wy,US
182/E3 Needles, BC,Can
136/C2 Needles (pt.), N.Z.
186/E3 Needles, Ca,US
59/E5 Needles, The (seastacks), UK
189/G3 Needville, Tx,US
200/D4 Neely Henry (lake), Al,US
191/J2 Neelyville, Mo,US
172/E2 Neembucú (dept.), Par.
193/K1 Neenah, Wi,US
194/E2 Neepawa, Mb,Can
132/K6 Neerabup Nat'l Park, Austl.
69/E1 Neerpelt, Belg.
124/C2 Nee Soon, Sing.
67/H2 Neetze, Ger.
67/H2 Neetze (riv.), Ger.
150/A2 Nefasit, Eth.
150/A3 Nefas Mewch'a, Eth.
69/F2 Neffelbach (riv.), Ger.
143/G2 Neftah, Tun.
97/J5 Neftechala, Azer.
99/K5 Neftegorsk, Rus.
53/J3 Neftekamsk, Rus.
97/H3 Neftekumsk, Rus.
102/C7 Nefud (des.), SAr.
56/D6 Nefyn, Wal,UK
144/C3 Négala, Mali
155/F2 Nega Nega, Zam.
124/F5 Negara, Indo.
195/L4 Negaunee, Mi,US
150/A4 Negēlē, Eth.
124/C2 Negeri Sembilan (state), Malay.
103/D4 Negev (reg.), Isr.
103/F8 Negev-Kinneret Conduit, Isr.
93/G3 Negoiu (peak), Rom.
155/H1 Negomano, Moz.
118/C6 Negombo, SrL.
63/M5 Negoreloye, Bela.
92/F3 Negotin, Yugo.
92/F5 Negotino, Macd.
160/D2 Negra (pt.), Belz.
168/A2 Negra (pt.), Peru
187/J3 Negra (mesa), NM,US
119/F4 Negrais (cape), Burma
87/D1 Negrar, It.
202/B2 Negreet, La,US
76/A1 Negreira, Sp.
172/B1 Negreiros, Chile
93/H2 Negreşti, Rom.
161/G2 Negril, Jam.
172/B1 Negrillos, Bol.
143/G2 Negrine, Alg.
168/A2 Negritos, Peru
174/C3 Negro (peak), Arg.
172/E2 Negro (riv.), Arg.
174/D3 Negro (riv.), Arg.
169/F4 Negro (riv.), Bol.
170/A3 Negro (riv.), Braz.
172/E2 Negro (riv.), Par.
163/C3 Negro (riv.), SAm.
175/F2 Negro (riv.), Uru., Braz.
175/T11 Negro, Arroyo (stream), Uru.
125/C3 Negros (isl.), Phil.
196/E2 Neguac, NB,Can
182/C5 Nehalem (riv.), Or,US
107/G2 Nehbandān, Iran
67/E6 Neheim-Hüsten, Ger.
120/B1 Nehtaur, India
139/H6 Neiafu, Tonga
162/D3 Neiba, DRep.
161/J2 Neiba, Sierra de (range), DRep.
157/R15 Neiges, Piton des (peak), Reun.
183/J4 Neihart, Mt,US
115/C4 Neihuang, China
116/E2 Neijiang, China
183/K1 Neilburg, Sk,Can
193/J1 Neillsville, Wi,US
193/J1 Neillsville (hill), Wi,US
195/J5 Neillsville (hills), Wi,US
197/G2 Neil's Harbour, NS,Can
54/B5 Neilston, Sc,UK
108/G3 Nei Monggol (plat.), China
154/B4 Neineis, Namb.
115/C3 Neiqiu, China
167/K6 Neira, Col.
164/C4 Neiva, Col.
115/B4 Neixiang, China
178/G3 Nejanilini (lake), Mb,Can
160/C2 Nejapa, Mex.
71/F2 Nejdek, Czh.
149/G3 Nejo, Eth.
103/E1 Nejrab (int'l arpt.), Syria
105/H2 Nekā, Iran
153/G2 Nekalagba, Zaire
149/H3 Nek'emtē, Eth.
99/L2 Nekhayevskiy, Rus.
193/K1 Nekoosa, Wi,US
97/H2 Nekrasovo, Rus.
62/F4 Neksø, Den.
76/B2 Nelas, Port.
94/G4 Nelidovo, Rus.
192/E3 Neligh, Ne,US
208/E7 Nellie, Oh,US
200/C4 Nellieburg, Ms,US
122/G3 Nellikkuppam, India
70/C5 Nellingen, Ger.
186/D2 Nellis Air Force Ra., Nv,US
118/C5 Nellore, India
172/D4 Nelson, Arg.
135/B3 Nelson (cape), Austl.
176/H4 Nelson (riv.), Can.
182/F3 Nelson, BC,Can
175/J7 Nelson (str.), Chile
136/C3 Nelson, N.Z.
131/H2 Nelson (cape), PNG
57/F4 Nelson, Eng,UK
58/C3 Nelson, Wal,UK
177/F3 Nelson (isl.), Ak,US
187/F3 Nelson, Az,US
191/H1 Nelson, Mo,US
192/E3 Nelson, Ne,US
186/E3 Nelson, Nv,US
135/E2 Nelson Bay, Austl.
136/C3 Nelson Bays (reg.), N.Z.
178/D3 Nelson Forks, BC,Can
177/F4 Nelson Lagoon, Ak,US
136/C3 Nelson Lakes Nat'l Park, N.Z.
196/E2 Nelson-Miramichi, NB,Can
198/E5 Nelsonville, Oh,US
157/E2 Nelspruit, SAfr.
144/D2 Néma, Mrta.
144/D2 Néma, Dhar (hills), Mrta.
193/G3 Nemaha, Ne,US
63/K4 Neman, Rus.
63/K4 Neman (Nemunas) (riv.), Eur.
130/A2 Nembrala, Indo.
86/C1 Nembro, It.
91/H4 Neméa, Gre.
63/L4 Nemenčinė, Lith.
84/C4 Nemi, It.
135/D1 Nemingha, Austl.
93/H2 Nemira (peak), Rom.
98/B2 Nemirov, Ukr.
98/E3 Nemirov, Ukr.
167/M6 Nemocón, Col.
109/J2 Nemor (riv.), China
74/E2 Nemours, Fr.
73/C2 Nemšová, Slvk.
63/K4 Nemunas (Neman) (riv.), Eur.
112/D2 Nemuro, Japan
112/D2 Nemuro (pen.), Japan
112/D2 Nemuro (str.), Japan, Rus.
109/J2 Nen (riv.), China
60/B4 Nenagh, Ire.
177/J3 Nenana, Ak,US
124/C2 Nenasi, Malay.
80/D5 Nendaz, Swi.
59/G1 Nene (riv.), Eng,UK
95/M2 Nenets Aut. Okr., Rus.
109/K2 Nenjiang, China
70/A2 Nentershausen, Ger.
81/F3 Nenzing, Aus.
191/G2 Neodesha, Ks,US
193/K4 Neoga, Il,US
193/G3 Neola, Ia,US
185/H3 Neola, Ut,US
201/F2 Neon-Fleming, Ky,US
91/H2 Néon Petritsion, Gre.
193/K1 Neopit, Wi,US
120/B1 Neoria Husainpur, India
191/G2 Neosho (riv.), Ks, Ok,US
191/G2 Neosho, Mo,US
193/G4 Neosho Falls, Ks,US
91/H2 Néos Marmarás, Gre.
93/F5 Néos Skopós, Gre.
77/F1 Néouville, Pic de (peak), Fr.
159/Q10 Neo Volcanica, Cordillera (range), Mex.
120/D1 Nepal (ctry.)
120/C1 Nepālganj, Nepal
121/F2 Nepāltār, Nepal
118/D3 Nepanagar, India
134/G8 Nepean (riv.), Austl.
199/J2 Nepean, Can.
168/B3 Nepeña, Peru
205/F5 Nepessina (lake), Mi,US
185/H4 Nephi, Ut,US
60/A1 Nephin (mtn.), Ire.
60/A1 Nephin Beg (mtn.), Ire.
60/A2 Nephin Beg (range), Ire.
84/C3 Nepi, It.
196/E2 Nepisiguit (bay), NB,Can
196/D2 Nepisiguit (riv.), NB,Can
153/G2 Nepoko (riv.), Zaire
170/D4 Nepomuceno, Braz.
71/G4 Nepomuk, Czh.
207/D3 Neptune City, NJ,US
84/C3 Nera (riv.), It.
74/D4 Nérac, Fr.
71/H2 Neratovice, Czh.
108/H1 Nercha (riv.), Rus.
108/H1 Nerchinsk, Rus.
94/J4 Nerekhta, Rus.
70/D5 Neresheim, Ger.
63/L4 Nereta, Lat.
85/D2 Nereto, It.
92/D4 Neretva (riv.), Bosn., Cro.
63/J4 Neringa, Lith.
63/L4 Neris (riv.), Lith.
76/D4 Nerja, Sp.
168/A2 Nérmete (pt.), Peru
91/J5 Nerokoúros, Gre.
87/F5 Nerone, Monte (peak), It.
170/C3 Nerópolis, Braz.
76/D3 Nerpio, Sp.
70/D6 Nersingen, Ger.
76/B4 Nerva, Sp.
87/F1 Nervesa della Battaglia, It.
86/C4 Nervi, It.
82/D5 Nervia (riv.), It.

86/A5 **Nèrvia** (riv.), It.
86/B1 **Nerviano**, It.
101/N4 **Neryungri**, Rus.
66/C2 **Nes**, Neth.
62/C1 **Nes**, Nor.
62/C1 **Nesbyen**, Nor.
206/C1 **Nescopeck** (cr.), Pa,US
96/C4 **Nesebūr**, Bul.
206/C3 **Neshaminy** (cr.), Pa,US
208/G5 **Neshannock** (cr.), Pa,US
61/06 **Neskaupstadhur**, Ice.
68/B4 **Nesle**, Fr.
53/S9 **Nesles-la-Vallée**, Fr.
182/E3 **Nespelem**, Wa,US
82/B4 **Nesque** (riv.), Fr.
206/C2 **Nesquehoning**, Pa,US
54/B2 **Ness** (riv.), Sc,UK
190/E1 **Ness City**, Ks,US
67/H6 **Nesse** (riv.), Ger.
177/M4 **Nesselrode** (mt.), Ak,US
81/G2 **Nesselwang**, Ger.
81/F3 **Nesslau**, Swi.
54/B2 **Ness, Loch** (lake), Sc,UK
65/M3 **Nesterov**, Ukr.
97/K1 **Nesterovka**, Rus.
57/E5 **Neston**, Eng,UK
84/C1 **Nestore** (riv.), It.
195/H3 **Nestor Falls**, On,Can
91/G2 **Nestórion**, Gre.
91/J2 **Néstos** (riv.), Gre.
73/C4 **Nesvady**, Slvk.
96/C1 **Nesvizh**, Bela.
103/F8 **Nes Ziyyona**, Isr.
195/K4 **Net** (riv.), Mi,US
103/D3 **Netanya**, Isr.
120/E4 **Netarhāt**, India
184/B1 **Netarts**, Or,US
191/G1 **Netawaka**, Ks,US
206/D2 **Netcong**, NJ,US
67/G5 **Nethe** (riv.), Ger.
58/D3 **Netherend**, Eng,UK
183/K2 **Netherhill**, Sk,Can
66/B5 **Netherlands**
162/D5 **Netherlands Antilles** (isls.), Neth.
54/C2 **Nethy Bridge**, Sc,UK
98/D2 **Netishin**, Ukr.
59/E5 **Netley**, Eng,UK
83/C4 **Neto** (riv.), It.
71/H4 **Netolice**, Czh.
69/H2 **Netphen**, Ger.
121/H3 **Netrakona**, Bang.
81/F3 **Netstal**, Swi.
66/D6 **Nette** (riv.), Ger.
67/H5 **Nette** (riv.), Ger.
69/G3 **Nettebach** (riv.), Ger.
69/F3 **Nettersheim**, Ger.
66/D6 **Nettetal**, Ger.
179/J2 **Nettilling** (lake), NW,Can
195/H3 **Nett Lake**, Mn,US
195/H3 **Nett Lake Ind. Res.**, Mn,US
57/H5 **Nettleham**, Eng,UK
200/C3 **Nettleton**, Ms,US
84/C5 **Nettuno**, It.
71/E6 **Neubiberg**, Ger.
65/G2 **Neubrandenburg**, Ger.
70/C3 **Neubrunn**, Ger.
70/B5 **Neubulach**, Ger.
70/B5 **Neuburg**, Ger.
70/E5 **Neuburg an der Donau**, Ger.
70/D6 **Neuburg an der Kammel**, Ger.
80/C4 **Neuchâtel**, Swi.
80/C4 **Neuchâtel** (canton), Swi.
80/C4 **Neuchâtel** (lake), Swi.
67/H2 **Neu Darchau**, Ger.
194/C2 **Neudorf**, Sk,Can
73/A4 **Neudörfl**, Aus.
72/B1 **Neue Elde** (riv.), Ger.
72/C2 **Neue Jäglitz** (riv.), Ger.
70/B5 **Neuenbürg**, Ger.
80/D2 **Neuenburg am Rhein**, Ger.
70/D4 **Neuendettelsau**, Ger.
64/G1 **Neuendorf**, Ger.
72/D3 **Neuendorfer** (lake), Ger.
72/D2 **Neuenhagen**, Ger.
66/D4 **Neuenhaus**, Ger.
67/E4 **Neuenkirchen**, Ger.
67/F3 **Neuenkirchen**, Ger.
67/E6 **Neuenrade**, Ger.
70/C4 **Neuenstadt am Kocher**, Ger.
70/C4 **Neuenstein**, Ger.
69/F3 **Neuerburg**, Ger.
71/E6 **Neufahrn bei Freising**, Ger.
80/D1 **Neuf-Brisach**, Fr.
69/E4 **Neufchâteau**, Belg.
80/B1 **Neufchâteau**, Fr.
68/A2 **Neufchâtel**, Fr.
68/A4 **Neufchâtel-en-Bray**, Fr.
73/A4 **Neufeld an der Leitha**, Aus.
69/D4 **Neufmanil**, Fr.
81/G2 **Neugablonz**, Ger.
72/D4 **Neugraben** (riv.), Ger.
71/G6 **Neuhaus am Inn**, Ger.
70/E1 **Neuhaus am Rennweg**, Ger.
70/A2 **Neuhäusel**, Ger.
81/E2 **Neuhausen am Rheinfall**, Swi.
70/E2 **Neuhaus-Schierschnitz**, Ger.
154/C4 **Neu Heusis**, Namb.
70/C2 **Neuhof**, Ger.
70/D4 **Neuhof an der Zenn**, Ger.
70/B4 **Neuhofen**, Ger.
71/H6 **Neuhofen an der Krems**, Aus.
79/F5 **Neuillé-Pont-Pierre**, Fr.
68/B5 **Neuilly-en-Thelle**, Fr.
80/B2 **Neuilly-l'Évêque**, Fr.
68/C5 **Neuilly-St-Front**, Fr.
53/T10 **Neuilly-sur-Marne**, Fr.
53/S10 **Neuilly-sur-Seine**, Fr.
70/B2 **Neu-Isenburg**, Ger.
72/B1 **Neu Kaliss**, Ger.
64/E1 **Neukirchen**, Ger.
72/C6 **Neukirchen**, Ger.
71/G6 **Neukirchen an der Vöckla**, Aus.
71/G5 **Neukirchen vorm Wald**, Ger.
72/B5 **Neumark**, Ger.
71/G7 **Neumarkt am Wallersee**, Aus.
81/H5 **Neumarkt** (Egna), It.
71/H6 **Neumarkt im Mühlkreis**, Aus.
71/E4 **Neumarkt in der Oberpfalz**, Ger.
71/F6 **Neumarkt-Sankt Veit**, Ger.
64/E1 **Neumünster**, Ger.
79/G5 **Neung-sur-Beuvron**, Fr.
81/E2 **Neunkirch**, Swi.
73/A4 **Neunkirchen**, Aus.
69/G5 **Neunkirchen**, Ger.
69/H2 **Neunkirchen**, Ger.
69/G2 **Neunkirchen-Seelscheid**, Ger.
70/B4 **Neu-Ostheim** (Mannheim) (arpt.), Ger.
70/B4 **Neupotz**, Ger.
174/C3 **Neuquén**, Arg.
174/C3 **Neuquén** (prov.), Arg.
174/C3 **Neuquén** (riv.), Arg.
72/C2 **Neuruppin**, Ger.
70/D6 **Neusäss**, Ger.
201/J3 **Neuse** (riv.), NC,US
92/C2 **Neuseider** (lake), Aus.
73/A4 **Neusiedl am See**, Aus.
65/J5 **Neusiedler** (lake), Aus.
73/A4 **Neusiedler See** (Fertő) (lake), Aus., Hun.
66/D6 **Neuss**, Ger.
64/G2 **Neustadt**, Ger.
69/G2 **Neustadt**, Ger.
72/B6 **Neustadt**, Ger.
72/C2 **Neustadt**, Ger.
67/G4 **Neustadt am Rübenberge**, Ger.
70/D3 **Neustadt an der Aisch**, Ger.
71/E5 **Neustadt an der Donau**, Ger.
71/F3 **Neustadt an der Waldnaab**, Ger.
70/B4 **Neustadt an der Weinstrasse**, Ger.
70/E2 **Neustadt bei Coburg**, Ger.
64/F1 **Neustadt in Holstein**, Ger.
81/H3 **Neustift im Stubaital**, Aus.
64/G2 **Neustrelitz**, Ger.
71/F5 **Neutraubling**, Ger.
72/E2 **Neutrebbin**, Ger.
70/D6 **Neu-Ulm**, Ger.
74/G2 **Neuves-Maisons**, Fr.
74/E4 **Neuvic**, Fr.
79/H4 **Neuville-aux-Bois**, Fr.
80/A6 **Neuville-sur-Saône**, Fr.
79/F4 **Neuville-sur-Sarthe**, Fr.
79/F5 **Neuvy-le-Roi**, Fr.
67/F1 **Neuwerk** (isl.), Ger.
69/G3 **Neuwied**, Ger.
65/H2 **Neuzelle**, Ger.
72/D3 **Neu Zittau**, Ger.
63/P2 **Neva** (riv.), Rus.
76/D4 **Nevada** (mts.), Sp.
180/C4 **Nevada** (state), US
193/H2 **Nevada**, Ia,US
191/G2 **Nevada**, Mo,US
188/L6 **Nevada**, Tx,US
184/C4 **Nevada City**, Ca,US
164/C4 **Nevada del Huila Nat'l Park**, Col.
186/D2 **Nevada Test Site**, Nv,US
159/K7 **Nevado de Toluca Nat'l Park**, Mex.
174/C2 **Nevado, Sierra del** (mts.), Arg.
63/N3 **Nevel'**, Rus.
68/C1 **Nevele**, Belg.
109/N2 **Nevel'sk**, Rus.
109/J1 **Never**, Rus.
74/E3 **Nevers**, Fr.
135/C1 **Nevertire**, Austl.
92/D4 **Nevesinje**, Bosn.
183/L3 **Neville**, Sk,Can
99/L5 **Nevinnomyssk**, Rus.
162/F3 **Nevis** (isl.), StK.
162/F3 **Nevis** (peak), StK.
195/G4 **Nevis**, Mn,US
87/F5 **Nevola** (riv.), It.
104/C2 **Nevşehir**, Turk.
104/C2 **Nevşehir** (prov.), Turk.
167/F4 **New** (riv.), Guy.
59/E5 **New** (for.), Eng,UK
187/F4 **New** (riv.), Az,US
201/J3 **New** (riv.), NC,US
201/G1 **New** (riv.), Va, WV,US
56/E2 **New Abbey**, Sc,UK
151/B4 **Newala**, Tanz.
200/E1 **New Albany**, In,US
200/C3 **New Albany**, Ms,US
195/K5 **Newald**, Wi,US
59/E4 **New Alresford**, Eng,UK
165/G3 **New Amsterdam**, Guy.
57/H5 **New Ancholme** (riv.), Eng,UK
135/C1 **New Angledool**, Austl.
191/J3 **Newark**, Ar,US
205/K11 **Newark**, Ca,US
206/C4 **Newark**, De,US
198/B4 **Newark**, Il,US
207/D2 **Newark**, NJ,US
207/J9 **Newark** (bay), NJ,US
207/J9 **Newark** (int'l arpt.), NJ,US
199/H3 **Newark**, NY,US
198/E4 **Newark**, Oh,US
188/K6 **Newark**, Tx,US
57/H5 **Newark-on-Trent**, Eng,UK
199/H3 **Newark Valley**, NY,US
193/K4 **New Athens**, Il,US
195/G5 **New Auburn**, Mn,US
193/J1 **New Auburn**, Wi,US
202/D2 **New Augusta**, Ms,US
198/D3 **Newaygo**, Mi,US
205/G6 **New Baltimore**, Mi,US
208/G6 **New Beaver**, Pa,US
208/D2 **New Bedford**, Ma,US
208/D2 **New Bedford** (mun. arpt.), Ma,US
208/G5 **New Bedford**, Pa,US
199/J3 **New Berlin**, NY,US
206/B2 **New Berlin**, Pa,US
205/P14 **New Berlin**, Wi,US
206/C3 **New Berlinville**, Pa,US
201/J3 **New Bern**, NC,US
200/C2 **Newbern**, Tn,US
203/G3 **Newberry**, Fl,US
198/D1 **Newberry**, Mi,US
201/G3 **Newberry**, SC,US
199/G4 **New Bethlehem**, Pa,US
57/G1 **Newbiggin-by-the-Sea**, Eng,UK
60/C1 **Newbliss**, Ire.
191/H1 **New Bloomfield**, Mo,US
206/A3 **New Bloomfield**, Pa,US
201/F1 **New Boston**, Oh,US
191/G4 **New Boston**, Tx,US
208/B1 **New Braintree**, Ma,US
189/E3 **New Braunfels**, Tx,US
198/D4 **New Bremen**, Oh,US
58/C2 **Newbridge on Wye**, Wal,UK
195/P6 **New Brighton**, Mn,US
208/G6 **New Brighton**, Pa,US
131/H1 **New Britain** (isl.), PNG
208/B2 **New Britain**, Ct,US
206/C3 **New Britain**, Pa,US
196/D2 **New Brunswick** (prov.), Can
206/D3 **New Brunswick**, NJ,US
198/C4 **New Buffalo**, Mi,US
206/B3 **New Buffalo**, Pa,US
56/A2 **New Buildings**, NI,UK
191/J2 **Newburg**, Ar,US
194/D3 **Newburg**, ND,US
54/C4 **Newburgh**, Sc,UK
54/E2 **Newburgh**, Sc,UK
199/J4 **Newburgh**, NY,US
208/F5 **Newburgh Heights**, Oh,US
57/G2 **Newburn**, Eng,UK
200/C2 **New Burnside**, Il,US
59/E4 **Newbury**, Eng,UK
196/A3 **Newbury**, Vt,US
145/G4 **New Bussa**, Nga.
57/F3 **Newby Bridge**, Eng,UK
138/F6 **New Caledonia** (terr.), Fr.
139/U12 **New Caledonia** (isl.), NCal.
207/E1 **New Canaan**, Ct,US
196/E1 **New Carlisle**, Qu,Can
88/C3 **New Castile** (reg.), Sp.
135/D2 **Newcastle**, Austl.
196/E2 **Newcastle**, NB,Can
199/G3 **Newcastle**, On,Can
56/B5 **Newcastle**, Ire.
60/A5 **Newcastle**, Ire.
60/D3 **Newcastle**, Ire.
157/E2 **Newcastle**, SAfr.
57/G1 **Newcastle** (int'l arpt.), Eng,UK
56/C3 **Newcastle**, NI,UK
206/C4 **New Castle**, De,US
206/C5 **New Castle** (co.), De,US
198/D5 **New Castle**, In,US
191/F3 **Newcastle**, Ok,US
208/G5 **New Castle**, Pa,US
189/E1 **Newcastle**, Tx,US
187/F2 **Newcastle**, Ut,US
201/G2 **New Castle**, Va,US
192/B2 **Newcastle**, Wy,US
58/B2 **Newcastle Emlyn**, Wal,UK
57/F1 **Newcastleton**, Sc,UK
57/F5 **Newcastle-under-Lyme**, Eng,UK
57/G2 **Newcastle upon Tyne**, Eng,UK
130/D4 **Newcastle Waters**, Austl.
205/R16 **New Chicago**, In,US
207/E1 **New City**, NY,US
206/B1 **New Columbia**, Pa,US
206/B1 **New Columbus**, Pa,US
187/H2 **Newcomb**, NM,US
198/F4 **Newcomerstown**, Oh,US
200/C2 **New Concord**, Ky,US
198/F5 **New Concord**, Oh,US
208/G6 **New Cumberland** (dam), Oh,US
206/B3 **New Cumberland**, Pa,US
208/G6 **New Cumberland**, WV,US
54/B6 **New Cumnock**, Sc,UK
183/H3 **New Dayton**, Ab,Can
190/D4 **New Deal**, Tx,US
54/D2 **New Deer**, Sc,UK
135/C3 **Newdegate**, Austl.
120/A1 **New Delhi** (cap.), India
182/F3 **New Denver**, BC,Can
53/N8 **Newdigate**, Eng,UK
207/J9 **New Dorp**, NY,US
191/H4 **New Edinburg**, Ar,US
193/F1 **New Effington**, SD,US
206/D3 **New Egypt**, NJ,US
69/F4 **Newel**, Ger.
134/B2 **Newell**, Austl.
193/G2 **Newell**, Ia,US
192/C1 **Newell**, SD,US
208/G6 **Newell**, WV,US
201/G4 **New Ellenton**, SC,US
202/C1 **Newellton**, La,US
194/C4 **New England**, ND,US
135/E1 **New England Nat'l Park**, Austl.
177/F4 **Newenham** (cape), Ak,US
58/D3 **Newent**, Eng,UK
189/J3 **New Era**, La,US
186/B2 **New Exchequer** (dam), Ca,US
208/A3 **New Fairfield**, Ct,US
199/G3 **Newfane**, NY,US
199/K3 **Newfane**, Vt,US
206/C4 **Newfield**, NJ,US
200/B1 **New Florence**, Mo,US
179/K3 **Newfoundland** (prov.), Can.
179/L4 **Newfoundland** (isl.), Nf,Can
206/D1 **Newfoundland**, NJ,US
206/C1 **Newfoundland**, Pa,US
185/G3 **Newfoundland Evaporation Basin**, Ut,US
191/H1 **New Franklin**, Mo,US
206/B4 **New Freedom**, Pa,US
206/B1 **New Galilee**, Pa,US
56/D1 **New Galloway**, Sc,UK
138/E5 **New Georgia** (isls.), Sol.
138/E5 **New Georgia** (sound), Sol.
196/E3 **New Germany**, NS,Can
196/F3 **New Glasgow**, NS,Can
197/N6 **New Glasgow**, Qu,Can
196/B4 **New Gloucester**, Me,US
206/D4 **New Gretna**, NJ,US
138/C5 **New Guinea** (isl.), Indo., PNG
189/G3 **Newgulf**, Tx,US
182/D3 **Newhalem**, Wa,US
177/H4 **Newhalen**, Ak,US
53/P7 **Newham** (bor.), Eng,UK
199/L3 **New Hampshire** (state), US
193/H2 **New Hampton**, Ia,US
138/D5 **New Hanover** (isl.), PNG
157/E3 **New Hanover**, SAfr.
197/G3 **New Harbour**, NS,Can
200/D1 **New Harmony**, In,US
187/F2 **New Harmony**, Ut,US
208/B2 **New Hartford**, Ct,US
59/F5 **Newhaven**, Eng,UK
208/B3 **New Haven**, Ct,US
208/B3 **New Haven** (co.), Ct,US
200/C2 **New Haven**, Il,US
198/D4 **New Haven**, In,US
200/E2 **New Haven**, Ky,US
205/G6 **New Haven**, Mi,US
200/B1 **New Haven**, Mo,US
201/G1 **New Haven**, WV,US
192/B1 **New Haven**, Wy,US
208/B3 **New Haven-Tweed** (arpt.), Ct,US
138/F6 **New Hebrides** (isls.), Van.
200/C5 **New Hebron**, Ms,US
186/B1 **New Hogan** (dam), Ca,US
206/B3 **New Holland**, Pa,US
193/K2 **New Holstein**, Wi,US
188/D1 **New Home**, Tx,US
200/D3 **New Hope**, Al,US
191/H3 **Newhope**, Ar,US
200/C4 **New Hope**, Ms,US
201/H3 **New Hope**, NC,US
201/J3 **New Hope**, NC,US
206/D3 **New Hope**, Pa,US
188/L6 **New Hope**, Tx,US
194/C4 **New Hradec**, ND,US
207/L9 **New Hyde Park**, NY,US
202/C2 **New Iberia**, La,US
59/G5 **Newick**, Eng,UK
208/B2 **Newington**, Ct,US
201/G4 **Newington**, Ga,US
138/E5 **New Ireland** (isl.), PNG
206/D3 **New Jersey** (state), US
200/D2 **New Johnsonville**, Tn,US
208/H6 **New Kensington**, Pa,US
201/J2 **New Kent**, Va,US
191/F2 **Newkirk**, Ok,US
201/G2 **Newland**, NC,US
208/G5 **New Lebanon**, Pa,US
194/D4 **New Leipzig**, ND,US
205/Q16 **New Lenox**, Il,US
198/E5 **New Lexington**, Oh,US
191/F3 **New Lima**, Ok,US
190/D3 **Newlin**, Tx,US
206/D4 **New Lisbon**, NJ,US
193/J2 **New Lisbon**, Wi,US
179/J4 **New Liskeard**, On,Can
202/B2 **Newllano**, La,US
208/B3 **New London**, Ct,US
208/B2 **New London** (co.), Ct,US
195/G5 **New London**, Mn,US
191/J1 **New London**, Mo,US
189/G1 **New London**, Tx,US
198/B2 **New London**, Wi,US
208/B3 **New London-Groton** (arpt.), Ct,US
208/B3 **New London Submarine Base**, Ct,US
198/G2 **New Lowell**, On,Can
208/G4 **New Lyme**, Oh,US
58/A6 **Newlyn**, Eng,UK
200/C2 **New Madrid**, Mo,US
54/C5 **Newmains**, Sc,UK
132/C2 **Newman**, Austl.
132/C2 **Newman** (peak), Austl.
186/B2 **Newman**, Ca,US
198/C5 **Newman**, Il,US
194/F4 **Newman**, ND,US
158/D1 **Newman**, NM,US
208/G6 **New Manchester**, WV,US
192/F3 **Newman Grove**, Ne,US
134/F6 **Newmarket**, Austl.
199/G2 **Newmarket**, On,Can
60/A5 **Newmarket**, Ire.
136/F6 **Newmarket**, N.Z.
59/G2 **Newmarket**, Eng,UK
200/D3 **New Market**, Al,US
193/G3 **New Market**, Ia,US
206/A5 **New Market**, Md,US
199/L3 **Newmarket**, NH,US
201/H1 **New Market**, Va,US
60/B4 **Newmarket on Fergus**, Ire.
208/A1 **New Marlborough**, Ma,US
198/F5 **New Martinsville**, WV,US
184/E1 **New Meadows**, Id,US
180/E5 **New Mexico** (state), US
208/G6 **New Middletown**, Oh,US
208/A2 **New Milford**, Ct,US
207/D2 **New Milford**, NJ,US
54/D1 **Newmill**, Sc,UK
57/F5 **New Mills**, Eng,UK
200/E4 **Newnan**, Ga,US
203/G3 **Newnans** (lake), Fl,US
58/D3 **Newnham**, Eng,UK
132/C4 **New Norcia**, Austl.
135/C4 **New Norfolk**, Austl.
183/H1 **New Norway**, Ab,Can
202/C3 **New Orleans**, La,US
202/C3 **New Orleans** (int'l arpt.), La,US
206/A4 **New Oxford**, Pa,US
199/J4 **New Paltz**, NY,US
198/D4 **New Paris**, In,US
200/D1 **New Pekin** (Pekin), In,US
208/F7 **New Philadelphia**, Oh,US
206/B2 **New Philadelphia**, Pa,US
184/C3 **New Pine Creek**, Or,US
54/D1 **New Pitsligo**, Sc,UK
136/C2 **New Plymouth**, N.Z.
184/E2 **New Plymouth**, Id,US
196/E1 **Newport**, Qu,Can
60/A2 **Newport**, Ire.
60/B4 **Newport**, Ire.
57/F6 **Newport**, Eng,UK
59/E5 **Newport**, Eng,UK
58/B2 **Newport**, Wal,UK
58/D3 **Newport**, Wal,UK
191/J3 **Newport**, Ar,US
204/C3 **Newport** (bay), Ca,US
206/C4 **Newport**, De,US
198/C5 **Newport**, In,US
200/E1 **Newport**, Ky,US
196/C3 **Newport**, Me,US
195/P7 **Newport**, Mn,US
201/J3 **Newport**, NC,US
199/K3 **Newport**, NH,US
206/C5 **Newport**, NJ,US
199/J3 **Newport**, NY,US
184/A1 **Newport**, Or,US
206/A3 **Newport**, Pa,US
208/C3 **Newport**, RI,US
208/C2 **Newport** (co.), RI,US
201/F3 **Newport**, Tn,US
199/K2 **Newport**, Vt,US
182/F3 **Newport**, Wa,US
204/C3 **Newport Beach**, Ca,US
206/C5 **Newport Meadows** (lake), NJ,US
201/J2 **Newport News**, Va,US
54/D4 **Newport-on-Tay**, Sc,UK
59/F2 **Newport Pagnell**, Eng,UK
202/K7 **New Port Richey**, Fl,US
203/G3 **New Port Richey**, Fl,US
193/H1 **New Prague**, Mn,US
208/A2 **New Preston**, Ct,US
162/B1 **New Providence** (isl.), Bahm.
206/D2 **New Providence**, NJ,US
58/A6 **Newquay**, Eng,UK
58/B2 **New Quay**, Wal,UK
58/A6 **Newquay Civil** (arpt.), UK
58/C2 **New Radnor**, Wal,UK
196/E1 **New Richmond**, Qu,Can
200/E1 **New Richmond**, Oh,US
193/H1 **New Richmond**, Wi,US
201/G2 **New River Gorge Nat'l Riv.**, WV,US
202/C2 **New Roads**, La,US
207/E2 **New Rochelle**, NY,US
194/E4 **New Rockford**, ND,US
59/G5 **New Romney**, Eng,UK
196/E3 **New Ross**, NS,Can
60/D5 **New Ross**, Ire.
57/G5 **New Rossington**, Eng,UK
130/C4 **Newry**, Austl.
56/B3 **Newry**, NI,UK
56/B3 **Newry** (can.), NI,UK
194/D4 **New Salem**, ND,US
183/H1 **New Sarepta**, Ab,Can
137/Z **New Schwabenland** (reg.), Ant.
54/C4 **New Scone**, Sc,UK
145/G4 **New Shagunnu**, Nga.
193/H3 **New Sharon**, Ia,US
208/C3 **New Shoreham** (Block Island), RI,US
207/D3 **New Shrewsbury** (Tinton Falls), NJ,US
101/P2 **New Siberian** (isls.), Rus.
203/H3 **New Smyrna Beach**, Fl,US
135/C1 **New South Wales** (state), Austl.
198/E5 **New Straitsville**, Oh,US
193/G4 **New Strawn** (Strawn), Ks,US
177/G4 **New Stuyahok**, Ak,US
189/G2 **New Summerfield**, Tx,US
196/C2 **New Sweden**, Me,US
200/F2 **New Tazewell**, Tn,US
177/F3 **Newtok**, Ak,US
58/D2 **Newton**, Eng,UK
57/E1 **Newton**, Sc,UK
203/F2 **Newton**, Ga,US
201/N8 **Newton** (co.), Ga,US
193/H3 **Newton**, Ia,US
198/B5 **Newton**, Il,US
191/F1 **Newton**, Ks,US
208/C1 **Newton**, Ma,US
200/C4 **Newton**, Ms,US
201/G3 **Newton**, NC,US
206/D1 **Newton**, NJ,US
189/H2 **Newton**, Tx,US
185/H3 **Newton**, Ut,US
58/C5 **Newton Abbot**, Eng,UK
57/G2 **Newton Aycliffe**, Eng,UK
199/J2 **Newton Falls**, NY,US
208/G5 **Newton Falls**, Oh,US
58/B6 **Newton Ferrers**, Eng,UK
54/C5 **Newtongrange**, Sc,UK
57/F5 **Newton-le-Willows**, Eng,UK
54/B5 **Newton Mearns**, Sc,UK
54/B2 **Newtonmore**, Sc,UK
57/G1 **Newton on the Moor**, Eng,UK
56/D2 **Newton Stewart**, Sc,UK
54/D5 **Newton Tors** (hill), Eng,UK
206/D4 **Newtonville**, NJ,US
135/B3 **Newtown**, Austl.
60/B5 **Newtown**, Ire.
58/C1 **Newtown**, Wal,UK
208/A3 **Newtown**, Ct,US
193/H3 **Newtown**, Mo,US
194/C4 **New Town**, ND,US
206/D3 **Newtown**, Pa,US
56/C2 **Newtownabbey**, NI,UK
56/C2 **Newtownards**, NI,UK
55/H9 **Newtownbutler**, NI,UK
60/C1 **Newtownbutler**, NI,UK
60/C2 **Newtown Forbes**, Ire.
56/B3 **Newtownhamilton**, NI,UK
60/D3 **Newtown Mount Kennedy**, Ire.
54/D5 **Newtown Saint Boswells**, Sc,UK
60/A5 **Newtown Sandes**, Ire.
206/C4 **Newtown Square**, Pa,US
56/A2 **Newtownstewart**, NI,UK
58/C3 **New Tredegar**, Wal,UK
206/C2 **New Tripoli**, Pa,US
54/C3 **Newtyle**, Sc,UK
193/G1 **New Ulm**, Mn,US
189/F3 **New Ulm**, Tx,US
200/F1 **New Vienna**, Oh,US
203/F2 **Newville**, Al,US
193/H3 **New Virginia**, Ia,US
198/E4 **New Washington**, Oh,US
197/G2 **New Waterford**, NS,Can
208/G6 **New Waterford**, Oh,US
182/C3 **New Westminster**, BC,Can
198/C5 **New Whiteland**, In,US
208/G5 **New Wilmington**, Pa,US
206/A4 **New Windsor**, Md,US
199/J3 **New York** (state), US
207/K9 **New York**, NY,US
207/K8 **New York** (co.), NY,US
195/G4 **New York Mills**, Mn,US
136/* **New Zealand**
137/L **New Zealand** (peak), Ant.
111/L10 **Neyagawa**, Japan
58/B3 **Neyland**, Wal,UK
105/H4 **Neyrīz**, Iran
105/J2 **Neyshābūr**, Iran
95/P4 **Neyva** (riv.), Rus.
122/G3 **Neyveli**, India
122/F4 **Neyyāttinkara**, India
78/D1 **Nez de Jobourg** (pt.), Fr.
98/F2 **Nezhin**, Ukr.
97/G3 **Nezlobnaya**, Rus.
182/F4 **Nezperce**, Id,US
182/F4 **Nez Perce Ind. Res.**, Id,US
202/B2 **Nezpique** (bayou), La,US
71/G3 **Nezvěstice**, Czh.
126/C3 **Ngabang**, Indo.
152/D3 **Ngabé**, Congo
130/D1 **Ngabordamlu** (cape), Indo.
155/G3 **Ngabu**, Malw.
155/E2 **Ngabwe**, Zam.
151/B4 **Ngaga**, Tanz.
136/B3 **Ngahere**, N.Z.
151/B2 **Ngai-Ndethya Nat'l Rsv.**, Kenya
148/B2 **Ngala**, Nga.
125/D5 **Ngalipaeng**, Indo.
127/F6 **Ngalu**, Indo.
148/C3 **Ngama**, Chad
136/J8 **Ngamanu Bird Sanct.**, N.Z.
148/A4 **Ngambé**, Camr.
154/E3 **Ngambwe** (rapids), Zam.
116/C2 **Ngamda**, China
154/D4 **Ngami** (lake), Bots.
154/D3 **Ngamiland** (dist.), Bots.
121/F1 **Ngamring**, China
151/A4 **Nganda** (peak), Malw.
151/C2 **Ngangerabeli** (plain), Kenya
114/D5 **Ngangla Ringco** (lake), China
152/C5 **N'gangula**, Ang.
114/E5 **Nganguzê** (lake), China
148/B4 **Nganha Montagne de** (peak), Camr.
123/B2 **Ngao**, Thai.
148/B4 **Ngaoundal**, Camr.
148/B4 **Ngaoundéré**, Camr.
136/B4 **Ngapara**, N.Z.
153/G3 **Ngara**, Tanz.
124/D4 **Ngaras**, Indo.
135/B2 **Ngarkat Consv. Park**, Austl.
133/F2 **Ngarti Abor. Land**, Austl.
136/C2 **Ngaruawahia**, N.Z.
136/D2 **Ngatapa**, N.Z.
116/B5 **Ngathaingyaung**, Burma
138/E4 **Ngatik** (atoll), Micr.
138/B5 **Ngato**, Camr.
139/Z18 **Ngau** (isl.), Fiji
136/C2 **Ngauruhoe** (vol.), N.Z.
124/E4 **Ngawi**, Indo.
148/D3 **Ngaya-Yata Fauna Rsv.**, CAfr.
152/D2 **Ngele**, Zaire
151/B3 **Ngerengere**, Tanz.
123/D2 **Nghia Dan**, Viet.
123/D1 **Nghia Lo**, Viet.
152/C4 **Ngidinga**, Zaire
151/A2 **Ngiro, Ewaso** (riv.), Kenya
151/B1 **Ng'iro, Ewaso** (riv.), Kenya
154/B3 **Ngiva**, Ang.
152/C3 **Ngo**, Congo
123/E4 **Ngoan Muc** (pass), Viet.
119/J4 **Ngoc Linh** (peak), Viet.
127/G3 **Ngofakiaha**, Indo.
151/A2 **Ngogwa**, Tanz.
148/B5 **Ngoïla**, Camr.
152/C2 **Ngoko** (riv.), Camr., Congo
148/D4 **Ngolo, Chutes de** (falls), CAfr.
152/B2 **Ngom** (falls), EqG.
155/F4 **Ngomahuru**, Zim.
148/A5 **Ngomedzap**, Camr.
151/C2 **Ngomeni, Ras** (cape), Kenya
151/B2 **Ngong**, Kenya
154/D3 **Ngonye** (falls), Zam.
114/E5 **Ngoqumaima**, China
153/H2 **Ngora**, Ugan.
109/D5 **Ngoring** (lake), China
151/A2 **Ngorongoro Consv. Area**, Tanz.
148/C5 **Ngoto**, CAfr.
156/N12 **Ngotwane** (riv.), SAfr.
148/A5 **Ngoulemakong**, Camr.
152/B3 **Ngounié** (prov.), Gabon
152/B3 **Ngounié** (riv.), Gabon
152/D2 **Ngoura**, Chad
148/B2 **Ngouri**, Chad
148/B2 **Ngourti**, Niger
148/C1 **N'Goutchei** (well), Chad
149/E4 **Ngouyo**, CAfr.
151/A3 **Ngoywa**, Tanz.
153/G3 **Ngozi**, Buru.
151/A2 **Ngudu**, Tanz.
148/B4 **Nguélémendouka**, Camr.
148/B2 **Nguigmi**, Niger
130/C2 **Nguiu**, Austl.
130/D3 **Ngukurr**, Austl.
138/C4 **Ngulu** (isl.), Micr.
123/C2 **Ngum** (riv.), Laos
151/B4 **Ngumbe Sukani, Ras** (pt.), Tanz.
155/F4 **Ngundu Halt**, Zim.
151/A2 **Ngunga**, Tanz.
152/C5 **Ngunza**, Ang.
124/F5 **Ngurah Rai** (int'l arpt.), Indo.
145/H3 **Nguru**, Nga.
151/B3 **Nguru** (mts.), Tanz.
145/H5 **Nguti**, Camr.
123/D1 **Nguyen Binh**, Viet.
116/C5 **Ngwedaung**, Burma
157/E2 **Ngwenya** (peak), Swaz.
155/F2 **Ngwerere**, Zam.
166/B3 **Nhamundá**, Braz.
166/B3 **Nhamundá** (riv.), Braz.
170/C4 **Nhandeara**, Braz.
155/G3 **Nhandugue** (riv.), Moz.
152/C5 **Nhangue-ia-Pepe**, Ang.
152/D5 **Nharêa**, Ang.
123/E3 **Nha Trang**, Viet.
152/C5 **Nhia** (riv.), Ang.
135/B3 **Nhill**, Austl.
157/E2 **Nhlangano**, Swaz.
123/D1 **Nho Quan**, Viet.
131/E3 **Nhulunbuy**, Austl.
153/F3 **Niabembe**, Zaire
144/E3 **Niafounké**, Mali
197/S9 **Niagara** (co.), On,Can
197/S9 **Niagara** (riv.), Can., US
197/T9 **Niagara** (co.), NY,US
198/C2 **Niagara**, Wi,US
193/H2 **Niagara Cave**, Mn,US
199/G3 **Niagara Falls**, On,Can
199/G3 **Niagara Falls**, NY,US
197/S9 **Niagara-on-the-Lake**, On,Can
144/C3 **Niagassola**, Gui.
144/D4 **Niakaramandougou**, IvC.
145/F3 **Niamey** (cap.), Niger
145/F3 **Niamey** (dept.), Niger
145/F3 **Niamey** (int'l arpt.), Niger
145/F4 **Niamtougou**, Togo
144/C4 **Niandan** (riv.), Gui.
153/F2 **Niangara**, Zaire
144/E3 **Niangay** (lake), Mali
144/D4 **Niangoloko**, Burk.
191/H2 **Niangua**, Mo,US
191/H2 **Niangua** (riv.), Mo,US
115/C3 **Niangzi Guan** (pass), China
153/F2 **Nia-Nia**, Zaire
208/B3 **Niantic**, Ct,US
152/C3 **Niari** (pol. reg.), Congo
152/C3 **Niari** (riv.), Congo
124/B2 **Nias** (isl.), Indo.
155/H2 **Niassa** (prov.), Moz.
41/W17 **Nibbar**, Tun.
185/H3 **Nibley**, Ut,US
124/C1 **Nibong Tebal**, Malay.
63/J3 **Nīca**, Lat.
161/E3 **Nicaragua**
161/E4 **Nicaragua** (lake), Nic.
83/C5 **Nicastro-Sambiase**, It.
196/C3 **Nicatous** (lake), Me,US
82/D5 **Nice**, Fr.
82/D5 **Nice** (Côte d'Azur) (int'l arpt.), Fr.
203/E2 **Niceville**, Fl,US
86/A3 **Nichelino**, It.
115/L9 **Nicheng**, China
110/B5 **Nichinan**, Japan
120/D2 **Nichlaul**, India
161/F1 **Nicholas** (chan.), Bahm., Cuba
200/E2 **Nicholasville**, Ky,US
203/G2 **Nicholls**, Ga,US
162/B1 **Nicholls Town**, Bahm.
202/L8 **Nichols**, Fl,US
201/H3 **Nichols**, SC,US
130/C4 **Nicholson**, Austl.
132/C3 **Nicholson** (range), Austl.
131/E4 **Nicholson** (riv.), Austl.
201/F2 **Nickelsville**, Va,US
166/B1 **Nickerie** (dist.), Sur.
166/B1 **Nickerie** (riv.), Sur.
132/C2 **Nickol** (bay), Austl.
119/F6 **Nicobar** (isls.), India
119/F6 **Nicobar, Car** (isl.), India
182/D2 **Nicola Mameet Ind. Res.**, BC,Can
196/A2 **Nicolet**, Qu,Can
193/G1 **Nicollet**, Mn,US
207/E2 **Nicolls** (pt.), NY,US
103/C2 **Nicosia** (cap.), Cyp.
103/C2 **Nicosia** (dist.), Cyp.
90/D4 **Nicosia**, It.
83/B5 **Nicotera**, It.
161/E4 **Nicoya**, CR
161/E4 **Nicoya** (gulf), CR
161/E4 **Nicoya** (pen.), CR
196/D2 **Nictau**, NB,Can
196/E3 **Nictaux**, NS,Can
80/D3 **Nidau**, Swi.
57/G4 **Nidd** (riv.), Eng,UK
70/C2 **Nidda**, Ger.
70/B2 **Nidda** (riv.), Ger.
70/B2 **Niddatal**, Ger.
70/C2 **Nidder** (riv.), Ger.
69/F2 **Nideggen**, Ger.
69/G6 **Niderviller**, Fr.
116/E3 **Nidong**, China
81/E4 **Nidwalden** (demi-canton), Swi.
65/L2 **Nidzica**, Pol.
64/E1 **Niebüll**, Ger.
75/G2 **Nied** (riv.), Fr.
69/F5 **Nied** (riv.), Ger.
67/G6 **Niedenstein**, Ger.
69/F4 **Niederanven**, Lux.
72/D5 **Niederau**, Ger.
80/D3 **Niederbipp**, Swi.
69/G6 **Niederbronn-les-Bains**, Fr.
75/K3 **Niedere Tauern** (mts.), Aus.
69/G2 **Niederfischbach**, Ger.
81/E3 **Niederhasli**, Swi.
72/D4 **Niederlausitz** (reg.), Ger.
70/B2 **Niedernhausen**, Ger.
69/H4 **Nieder-Olm**, Ger.
67/E1 **Niedersächsisches Wattenmeer Nat'l Park**, Ger.
72/A4 **Niedersachswerfen**, Ger.
70/C4 **Niederstetten**, Ger.
70/D5 **Niederstotzingen**, Ger.
81/F3 **Niederurnen**, Swi.
92/B1 **Niederösterreich** (prov.), Aus.
70/D2 **Niederwerrn**, Ger.
72/D6 **Niederwiesa**, Ger.
71/F5 **Niederwinkling**, Ger.
69/F2 **Niederzier**, Ger.
69/G3 **Niederzissen**, Ger.
152/B2 **Niefang**, EqG.
70/B5 **Niefern-Öschelbronn**, Ger.
65/L2 **Niegocin** (lake), Pol.
67/G5 **Nieheim**, Ger.
144/D4 **Niélé**, IvC.
148/B4 **Niem**, CAfr.
153/G4 **Niemba**, Zaire
72/C3 **Niemegk**, Ger.
65/J3 **Niemodlin**, Pol.
67/G3 **Nienburg**, Ger.
144/D5 **Niénokoué** (peak), IvC.
72/C3 **Nieplitz** (riv.), Ger.
68/B2 **Nieppe**, Fr.
144/B3 **Niéri Ko** (riv.), Sen.
66/D5 **Niers** (riv.), Ger.
70/B3 **Nierstein**, Ger.
123/D4 **Niet Ban Tinh Xa**, Viet.
166/C1 **Nieuw-Amsterdam**, Sur.
66/D5 **Nieuw-Bergen**, Neth.
66/D3 **Nieuw-Buinen**, Neth.
66/C4 **Nieuwegein**, Neth.
66/B4 **Nieuwendam**, Neth.
66/D2 **Nieuwe Pekela**, Neth.
66/B5 **Nieuwerkerk aan de IJssel**, Neth.
67/E2 **Nieuweschans**, Neth.
66/B4 **Nieuwkoop**, Neth.
130/D1 **Nieuw Krai Ker**, Indo.
66/D3 **Nieuwleusen**, Neth.
66/C4 **Nieuw-Loosdrecht**, Neth.
166/B1 **Nieuw-Nickerie**, Sur.
156/B3 **Nieuwoudtville**, SAfr.
68/B1 **Nieuwpoort**, Belg.
68/B1 **Nieuwpoort-Bad**, Belg.
66/D3 **Nieuw-Schoonebeek**, Neth.
66/B5 **Nieuw-Vossemeer**, Neth.
169/E4 **Nieve**, Bol.
104/C2 **Niğde**, Turk.
104/C2 **Niğde** (prov.), Turk.
156/E2 **Nigel**, SAfr.
156/Q13 **Nigel**, SAfr.
140/C3 **Niger**
145/G5 **Niger** (riv.), Afr.
145/G4 **Niger** (state), Nga.
140/C4 **Nigeria**
145/G5 **Niger, Mouths of the** (delta), Nga.
54/B1 **Nigg** (bay), Sc,UK
136/B4 **Nightcaps**, N.Z.
182/E3 **Nighthawk**, Wa,US
177/F3 **Nightmute**, Ak,US
76/A1 **Nigrán**, Sp.
91/H2 **Nigríta**, Gre.
139/J2 **Nihoa** (isl.), Hi,US
111/G2 **Nihonmatsu**, Japan
120/B1 **Nihtaur**, India
111/F3 **Nii** (isl.), Japan
111/F2 **Niigata**, Japan
111/F2 **Niigata** (int'l arpt.), Japan
111/F2 **Niigata** (pref.), Japan
110/C4 **Niihama**, Japan
180/R10 **Niihau** (isl.), Hi,US
112/C2 **Niikappu** (riv.), Japan
110/C3 **Niimi**, Japan
111/F2 **Niitsu**, Japan
111/H7 **Niiza**, Japan
76/D4 **Níjar**, Sp.
66/C4 **Nijkerk**, Neth.
68/D1 **Nijlen**, Belg.
66/C5 **Nijmegen**, Neth.
66/D4 **Nijverdal**, Neth.
91/H3 **Nikaia**, Gre.
94/F1 **Nikel'**, Rus.
97/L2 **Nikel'tau**, Kaz.
130/B2 **Nikiniki**, Indo.
177/H3 **Nikishka**, Ak,US
91/J2 **Nikisiani**, Gre.
99/K2 **Nikitovka**, Rus.
73/A4 **Nikitsch**, Aus.
145/F4 **Nikki**, Ben.
111/F2 **Nikkō**, Japan
111/F2 **Nikkō Nat'l Park**, Japan
75/L3 **Niklasdorf**, Aus.
93/L2 **Nikolaev** (int'l arpt.), Ukr.
93/G4 **Nikolaevo**, Bul.
177/H3 **Nikolai**, Ak,US
98/B3 **Nikolayev**, Ukr.
98/G4 **Nikolayev**, Ukr.
97/H1 **Nikolayevka**, Rus.
98/F4 **Nikolayevka**, Ukr.
99/G5 **Nikolayevka**, Ukr.
99/J3 **Nikolayevka**, Ukr.
63/N2 **Nikolayevo**, Rus.
98/F4 **Nikolayev Obl.**, Ukr.
97/H2 **Nikolayevsk**, Rus.
101/Q4 **Nikolayevsk-na-Amure**, Rus.
97/H1 **Nikol'sk**, Rus.
177/E5 **Nikolski**, Ak,US
94/H4 **Nikol'skiy Torzhok**, Rus.
101/S4 **Nikol'skoye**, Rus.
97/F3 **Nikol'skoye**, Rus.
153/G5 **Nikonga** (riv.), Tanz.
94/H3 **Nikonova Gora**, Rus.
93/G4 **Nikopol**, Bul.
53/G4 **Nikopol'**, Ukr.
104/D1 **Niksar**, Turk.
107/H3 **Nīkshahr**, Iran
92/D4 **Nikšić**, Yugo.
138/G5 **Nikunau** (isl.), Kiri.
130/C1 **Nila** (isl.), Indo.
186/E4 **Niland**, Ca,US
122/H4 **Nilaveli**, SrL.
103/B4 **Nile** (delta), Egypt
140/F2 **Nile** (riv.), Egypt, Sudan
153/G2 **Nile** (prov.), Ugan.
103/B4 **Nile, Damietta Branch** (riv.), Egypt
103/B4 **Nile, Rosetta Branch** (riv.), Egypt
205/Q15 **Niles**, Il,US
198/C4 **Niles**, Mi,US
208/G5 **Niles**, Oh,US
122/F3 **Nilgiri** (hills), India
103/G8 **Nīlīn**, WBnk.
167/L7 **Nilo**, Col.
171/N7 **Nilópolis**, Braz.
121/G3 **Nilphāmāri**, Bang.
61/J3 **Nilsiä**, Fin.
69/F5 **Nilvange**, Fr.
118/B3 **Nīmach**, India
118/B2 **Nīmāj**, India
109/L1 **Niman** (riv.), Rus.
144/C5 **Nimba** (peak), IvC.
144/C5 **Nimba** (co.), Libr.
74/F5 **Nîmes**, Fr.
208/F6 **Nimishillen** (cr.), Oh,US
182/B1 **Nimpo Lake**, BC,Can
137/L **Nimrod** (glac.), Ant.
136/B4 **Nimrod** (peak), N.Z.
69/F4 **Nimsbach** (riv.), Ger.
107/L2 **Nimu**, India
149/G5 **Nimule**, Sudan
149/F5 **Nimule Nat'l Park**, Sudan
92/B3 **Nin**, Cro.
190/C2 **Ninaview**, Co,US
104/E3 **Nīnawá** (gov.), Iraq
183/G4 **Ninepipe Nat'l Wild. Ref.**, Mt,US
188/C3 **Nine Point** (mesa), Tx,US
136/C1 **Ninety Mile** (beach), N.Z.
201/F3 **Ninety Six**, SC,US
201/F3 **Ninety Six Nat'l Hist. Site**, SC,US
105/E2 **Nineveh** (ruins), Iraq
84/C4 **Ninfa** (ruins), It.
174/D4 **Ninfas** (pt.), Arg.
109/K3 **Ning'an**, China
117/J2 **Ningbo**, China
131/F1 **Ningerum**, PNG
117/G3 **Ninggang**, China
117/H2 **Ningguo**, China
115/H7 **Ninghe**, China
115/C3 **Ningjin**, China
115/D3 **Ningjin**, China
116/C2 **Ningjing** (mts.), China
116/D3 **Ninglang Yizu Zizhixian**, China
115/C4 **Ningling**, China
117/E4 **Ningmeng**, China
123/D1 **Ningming**, China
115/C3 **Ningwu**, China
115/B3 **Ningxia Huizu Zizhiqu** (aut. reg.), China
116/D3 **Ningyang**, China
119/K2 **Ningyuan**, China
123/D1 **Ninh Binh**, Viet.
123/E3 **Ninh Hoa**, Viet.
78/C4 **Ninian** (riv.), Fr.
208/C3 **Ninigret Nat'l Wild. Ref.**, RI,US
177/H3 **Ninilchik**, Ak,US
138/D5 **Niningo** (isl.), PNG
191/F2 **Ninnescah** (riv.), Ks,US
191/E2 **Ninnescah, North Fork** (riv.), Ks,US
191/E2 **Ninnescah, South Fork** (riv.), Ks,US
137/K **Ninnis** (glac.), Ant.
125/C2 **Nino Aquino** (int'l arpt.), Phil.
112/B3 **Ninohe**, Japan
111/H7 **Ninomiya**, Japan
68/D2 **Ninove**, Belg.
125/F7 **Ninoy Aquino** (int'l arpt.), Phil.
170/B4 **Nioaque**, Braz.
170/A4 **Nioaque** (riv.), Braz.
192/E2 **Niobrara**, Ne,US
192/E2 **Niobrara** (riv.), Ne, Wy,US
144/B3 **Niokolo Koba**, Sen.
144/B3 **Niokolo-Koba Nat'l Park**, Sen.
116/B3 **Nioku**, India
148/B4 **Niong** (peak), Camr.
144/D3 **Niono**, Mali
144/C4 **Nionsamoridougou**, Gui.
144/B3 **Nioro-du-Rip**, Sen.
144/C3 **Nioro du Sahel**, Mali
74/C3 **Niort**, Fr.
157/G6 **Nioumachoua**, Com.
131/F1 **Nipa**, PNG
178/F3 **Nipawin**, Sk,Can
161/H1 **Nipe** (bay), Cuba
154/C3 **Nipele** (dry riv.), Namb.
195/K3 **Nipigon**, On,Can
195/K3 **Nipigon** (bay), On,Can
195/K3 **Nipigon** (lake), On,Can
195/K3 **Nipigon** (riv.), On,Can
179/J4 **Nipissing** (lake), On,Can
199/G1 **Nipissing** (riv.), On,Can
186/B3 **Nipomo**, Ca,US
205/P15 **Nippersink** (cr.), Il,US
186/E3 **Nipton**, Ca,US
174/C3 **Ñiquén**, Chile
161/G1 **Niquero**, Cuba
105/F2 **Nīr**, Iran
111/F3 **Nirasaki**, Japan
174/C5 **Ñireguao**, Chile
134/H8 **Nirimba-Hmas**, Austl.
118/C4 **Nirmal**, India
121/F2 **Nirmāli**, India
92/E4 **Niš**, Yugo.
92/E4 **Niš** (int'l arpt.), Yugo.
76/B3 **Nisa**, Port.
105/F4 **Nişāb**, SAr.
150/C2 **Nişāb**, Yem.
91/H1 **Nišava** (riv.), Yugo.
90/D4 **Niscemi**, It.
111/M9 **Nishiharu**, Japan
111/L9 **Nishiki**, Japan
110/C3 **Nishiki** (riv.), Japan
111/L10 **Nishinomiya**, Japan
110/B5 **Nishino'omote**, Japan
111/E3 **Nishio**, Japan
110/D3 **Nishiwaki**, Japan
65/M3 **Nisko**, Pol.
194/C5 **Nisland**, SD,US
98/E4 **Nisporeny**, Mol.
205/B3 **Nisqually**, Wa,US
205/B3 **Nisqually** (riv.), Wa,US
205/B3 **Nisqually Ind. Res.**, Wa,US
205/B3 **Nisqually Nat'l Wild. Ref.**, Wa,US
205/B3 **Nisqually Reach** (str.), Wa,US
138/E5 **Nissan** (isl.), PNG
62/E3 **Nissan** (riv.), Swe.
77/G1 **Nissan-lez-Enserune**, Fr.
62/C2 **Nisser** (lake), Nor.
111/N9 **Nisshin**, Japan
62/C3 **Nissum** (bay), Den.
195/G4 **Nisswa**, Mn,US
171/E4 **Niterói**, Braz.
56/E1 **Nith** (riv.), Sc,UK
56/E1 **Nithsdale** (vall.), Sc,UK
114/C5 **Niti** (pass), India
130/B2 **Nitibe**, Indo.
182/G1 **Niton Junction**, Ab,Can
73/C3 **Nitra**, Slvk.
73/C4 **Nitra** (riv.), Slvk.
73/C2 **Nitrica** (riv.), Slvk.
95/P4 **Nitsa** (riv.), Rus.
62/D1 **Nittedal**, Nor.
69/F4 **Nittel**, Ger.
71/F4 **Nittenau**, Ger.
139/H6 **Niuafo'ou** (isl.), Tonga
139/H6 **Niuatoputapu Group** (isls.), Tonga
114/F4 **Niubiziliang**, China

117/E3 Niuchang, China
139/J7 Niue (terr.), N.Z.
138/G6 Niulakita (isl.), Tuv.
116/D3 Niulan (riv.), China
113/C2 Niumaowu, China
126/C3 Niut (peak), Indo.
138/G5 Niutau (isl.), Tuv.
117/J2 Niutou (isl.), China
117/H2 Niutou (mtn.), China
117/F1 Niutoudian, China
130/A2 Niuwudu (cape), Indo.
113/B2 Niuxintai, China
113/B2 Niuzhuang, China
63/T9 Nivå, Den.
63/T9 Nivå (bay), Den.
68/D2 Nivelles, Belg.
74/E3 Nivernais (hills), Fr.
194/F3 Niverville, Mb,Can
199/K3 Niverville, NY,US
192/B3 Niwot, Co,US
191/H2 Nixa, Mo,US
116/C3 Nixi, China
184/D4 Nixon, Nv,US
189/F3 Nixon, Tx,US
114/D4 Niya (riv.), China
110/C4 Niyodo (riv.), Japan
76/B3 Niza, Port.
118/C4 Nizāmābād, India
95/K4 Nizhegorod Obl., Rus.
95/M4 Nizhnekama (res.), Rus.
95/L5 Nizhnekamsk, Rus.
101/K4 Nizhneudinsk, Rus.
100/H3 Nizhnevartovsk, Rus.
101/P2 Nizhneyansk, Rus.
97/H2 Nizhniy Baskunchak, Rus.
99/M3 Nizhniy Chir, Rus.
99/L2 Nizhniy Kislyay, Rus.
97/G1 Nizhniy Lomov, Rus.
95/K4 Nizhniy Novgorod (Gor'kiy), Rus.
95/N4 Nizhniy Tagil, Rus.
95/K4 Nizhniy Yenangsk, Rus.
95/K2 Nizhnyaya Pesha, Rus.
95/N4 Nizhnyaya Tura, Rus.
95/M3 Nizhnyaya Voch', Rus.
104/D2 Nizip, Turk.
73/D2 Nízké Tatry (mts.), Slvk.
65/K4 Nízke Tatry Nat'l Park, Slvk.
83/B7 Nizza di Sicilia, It.
86/B3 Nizza Monferrato, It.
61/M7 Njarðvík, Ice.
151/A4 Njombe, Tanz.
151/A3 Njombe (riv.), Tanz.
151/A2 Njoro, Kenya
148/A4 Nkambe, Camr.
157/E3 Nkandla, SAfr.
152/C4 Nkayi, Congo
152/C3 Nkeni (riv.), Congo
155/G1 Nkhata Bay, Malw.
155/G2 Nkhotakota, Malw.
145/H5 Nkogam, Massif du (peak), Camr.
145/H5 Nkomfap, Nga.
152/B3 Nkomi (lag.), Gabon
153/G4 Nkondwe, Tanz.
145/H5 N'Kongsamba, Camr.
144/D4 Nkourala, Mali
148/B5 Nkout (peak), Camr.
151/A3 Nkululu (riv.), Tanz.
153/G2 Nkusi (riv.), Ugan.
116/C3 Nmai (riv.), Burma
145/G5 Nnewi, Nga.
68/B5 Noailles, Fr.
121/H4 Noākhāli, Bang.
121/H4 Noākhāli (dist.), Bang.
87/F1 Noale, It.
121/E4 Noāmundi, India
196/A5 Noank, Ct,US
177/F2 Noatak, Ak,US
177/F2 Noatak (riv.), Ak,US
177/F2 Noatak Nat'l Prsv., Ak,US
60/D2 Nobber, Ire.
110/B4 Nobeoka, Japan
191/F3 Noble, Ok,US
183/H3 Nobleford, Ab,Can
208/G7 Noblestown-Sturgeon, Pa,US
198/C4 Noblesville, In,US
197/R8 Nobleton, On,Can
202/L6 Nobleton, Fl,US
164/A5 Noboa, Ecu.
112/B2 Noboribetsu, Japan
170/A2 Nobres, Braz.
203/H4 Nocatee, Fl,US
133/J3 Noccundra, Austl.
81/G5 Noce (riv.), It.
83/B3 Noce (riv.), It.
85/E5 Nocelleto, It.
85/E6 Nocera Inferiore, It.
85/E6 Nocera Superiore, It.
83/C4 Nocera Tirinese, It.
84/C1 Nocera Umbra, It.
86/D3 Noceto, It.
160/B2 Nochixtlán, Mex.
92/C5 Noci, It.
206/C3 Nockamixon St. Park, Pa,US
191/F4 Nocona, Tx,US
111/H7 Noda, Japan
193/G3 Nodaway (riv.), Mo,US
63/T9 Nødebo, Den.
200/D3 Nodgrass (hill), Tn,US
141/P13 Noé (cape), Alg.
191/G2 Noel, Mo,US
191/E2 Noel, Ok,US
198/F1 Noelville, On,Can
174/E2 Noetinger, Arg.
68/B3 Noeux-les-Mines, Fr.
159/M8 Nogales, Mex.
187/G5 Nogales, Az,US
149/H2 Nogara, Eth.
87/E2 Nogara, It.
74/C5 Nogaro, Fr.
63/H4 Nogat (riv.), Pol.
110/B4 Nogata, Japan
80/B1 Nogent, Fr.
68/C6 Nogent-l'Artaud, Fr.
68/A6 Nogent-le-Roi, Fr.
79/F4 Nogent-le-Rotrou, Fr.
53/T10 Nogent-sur-Marne, Fr.
68/B5 Nogent-sur-Oise, Fr.
74/E2 Nogent-sur-Seine, Fr.
94/H5 Noginsk, Rus.
101/Q4 Nogliki, Rus.
134/B4 Nogoa (riv.), Austl.
113/D5 Nogodan-san (mtn.), SKor.
108/C2 Nogoonuur, Mong.
174/F2 Nogoyá, Arg.
73/D4 Nógrád (co.), Hun.
77/F1 Noguera Pallarosa (riv.), Sp.
113/E4 Nogwak-san (mtn.), SKor.
118/B2 Nohar, India
112/B3 Noheji, Japan
69/G4 Nohfelden, Ger.
160/E2 Nohkú (pt.), Mex.
109/K5 Nohwa, SKor.
80/C2 Noidans-lès-Vesoul, Fr.
199/H1 Noire (riv.), Qu,Can
79/E3 Noireau (riv.), Fr.
78/B4 Noires (mts.), Fr.
74/B3 Noirmoutier (isl.), Fr.
68/B6 Noisiel, Fr.
53/T10 Noisy-le-Grand, Fr.
53/S10 Noisy-le-Roi, Fr.
68/B6 Noisy-le-Sec, Fr.
111/F3 Nojima-zaki (pt.), Japan
154/D3 Nokaneng, Bots.
107/G1 Nokhur, Trkm.
63/K1 Nokia, Fin.
127/F4 Nokilalaki (peak), Indo.
107/H3 Nok Kundi, Pak.
194/B2 Nokomis, Sk,Can
193/K4 Nokomis, Il,US
148/B2 Nokou, Chad
148/C5 Nola, CAfr.
85/E6 Nola, It.
188/K7 Nolan (riv.), Tx,US
159/F2 Nolanville, Tx,US
86/A2 Nole, It.
200/D3 Nolensville, Tn,US
86/B4 Noli, It.
86/B4 Noli, Capo di (cape), It.
201/F2 Nolichucky (riv.), Tn,US
200/D2 Nolin River (lake), Ky,US
95/L4 Nolinsk, Rus.
203/F2 Noma, Fl,US
131/F1 Nomad, PNG
135/D2 Nomadgi Nat'l Park, Austl.
208/D3 Nomans Land (isl.), Ma,US
208/D3 Nomans Land I. Nat'l Wild. Ref., Ma,US
158/D4 Nombre de Dios, Mex.
160/E3 Nombre de Dios, Cordillera (range), Hon.
95/L2 Nomburg, Rus.
177/E3 Nome, Ak,US
177/F3 Nome (cape), Ak,US
69/F6 Noméxy, Fr.
80/C1 Nomexy, Fr.
108/F3 Nomgon, Mong.
110/B5 Nomo-misaki (cape), Japan
110/A4 Nomo-zaki (pt.), Japan
108/D2 Nömrög, Mong.
154/C5 Nomtsas, Namb.
178/F2 Nonacho (lake), NW,Can
68/A6 Nonancourt, Fr.
87/E3 Nonantola, It.
177/H4 Nondalton, Ak,US
151/A3 Nondwa, Tanz.
86/A3 None, It.
68/B5 Nonette (riv.), Fr.
115/F1 Nong'an, China
123/C2 Nong Bua Lamphu, Thai.
123/B3 Nong Chang, Thai.
153/E3 Nongempulu, Zaire
152/D3 Nongenturi, Zaire
123/D2 Nong Han (res.), Thai.
123/C2 Nong Het, Laos
123/C2 Nong Khai, Thai.
157/E2 Nongoma, SAfr.
123/C2 Nong Pet, Laos
123/C3 Nong Phai, Thai.
121/H3 Nongstoin, India
154/B4 Nonidas, Namb.
72/C5 Nonnewitz, Ger.
69/F4 Nonnweiler, Ger.
158/D3 Nonoava, Mex.
172/C4 Nonogasta, Arg.
138/G5 Nonouti (atoll), Kiri.
115/E5 Nonri (isl.), China
113/D4 Nonsan, SKor.
123/C3 Non Sung, Thai.
74/D4 Nontron, Fr.
182/C3 Nooksack, Wa,US
194/C3 Noonan, ND,US
189/G1 Noonday, Tx,US
130/B4 Noonkanbah Abor. Land, Austl.
66/A5 Noordbeveland (isl.), Neth.
66/B3 Noorderhaaks (isl.), Neth.
66/B3 Noordhollandsch (can.), Neth.
156/B3 Noordoewer, Namb.
66/C3 Noordoostpolder (polder), Neth.
66/B4 Noordwijk aan Zee, Neth.
66/B4 Noordwijkerhout, Neth.
66/B4 Noordzeekanaal (can.), Neth.
63/J1 Noormarkku, Fin.
177/F2 Noorvik, Ak,US
134/D4 Noosa-Tewantin, Austl.
152/C4 Nóqui, Ang.
109/L1 Nora (riv.), Rus.
62/F2 Nora, Swe.
201/F2 Nora, Va,US
105/F1 Nor Achin, Arm.
125/D4 Norala, Phil.
176/K5 Noranda-Rouyn, Can.
133/J2 Noranside, Austl.
144/C4 Norassouba, Gui.
62/F1 Norberg, Swe.
175/S12 Norberto de la Riestra, Arg.
191/H1 Norborne, Mo,US
190/D1 Norcatur, Ks,US
84/B3 Norchia (ruins), It.
84/D2 Norcia, It.
204/C3 Norco, Ca,US
201/M7 Norcross, Ga,US
148/B3 Nord (prov.), Camr.
197/M6 Nord (riv.), Qu,Can
68/C3 Nord (dept.), Fr.
62/C4 Nordborg, Den.
62/D4 Nordby, Den.
68/B3 Nord, Canal du (can.), Fr.
67/E1 Norddeich, Ger.
182/F1 Nordegg, Ab,Can
182/G1 Nordegg (riv.), Ab,Can
77/T13 Nordela (int'l arpt.), Azor.,Port.
67/E1 Norden, Ger.
67/F2 Nordenham, Ger.
100/K2 Nordenskjöld (arch.), Rus.
67/E1 Norderney, Ger.
67/E1 Norderney (arpt.), Ger.
67/E1 Norderney (isl.), Ger.
67/G1 Norderstedt, Ger.
153/E4 Nordeste, Ang.
61/C3 Nordfjordeid, Nor.
72/B3 Nordgermersleben, Ger.
72/A4 Nordhausen, Ger.
189/F3 Nordheim, Tx,US
67/F1 Nordholz, Ger.
67/E4 Nordhorn, Ger.
80/D1 Nordhouse, Fr.
62/C3 Nordjylland (co.), Den.
61/H1 Nordkapp (North) (cape), Nor.
61/H1 Nordkinn (pt.), Nor.
67/E5 Nordkirchen, Ger.
61/E2 Nordland (co.), Nor.
205/B1 Nordland, Wa,US
70/D5 Nördlingen, Ger.
61/F3 Nordmaling, Swe.
152/B3 Nord-Nyanga Rsv., Congo, Gabon
67/G1 Nord-Ostee (can.), Ger.
148/A4 Nord-Ouest (prov.), Camr.
141/M13 Nord Ouest (reg.), Mor.
68/A3 Nord-Pas-de-Calais (reg.), Fr.
67/E3 Nord-Radde (riv.), Ger.
67/E3 Nord-Sud (can.), Ger.
135/D2 Nords Wharf, Austl.
61/E2 Nord-Trøndelag (co.), Nor.
67/E4 Nordwalde, Ger.
60/C4 Nore (riv.), Ire.
74/E5 Nore, Pic de (peak), Fr.
62/C1 Noresund, Nor.
129/M5 Norfolk (isl.), Austl.
135/C4 Norfolk (peak), Austl.
59/G1 Norfolk (co.), Eng,UK
191/H2 Norfolk (dam), Ar,US
208/A2 Norfolk, Ct,US
208/C1 Norfolk, Ma,US
208/C1 Norfolk (co.), Ma,US
192/F2 Norfolk, Ne,US
199/J2 Norfolk, NY,US
201/J2 Norfolk, Va,US
59/H1 Norfolk Broads (swamp), Eng,UK
201/J2 Norfolk Navy Base, Va,US
66/D2 Norg, Neth.
201/J2 Norge, Va,US
62/B1 Norheimsund, Nor.
189/F4 Norias, Tx,US
111/E2 Norikura-dake (mtn.), Japan
100/J3 Noril'sk, Rus.
199/G2 Norland, On,Can
202/P8 Norland, Fl,US
201/H2 Norlina, NC,US
84/C4 Norma, It.
193/K3 Normal, Il,US
134/A2 Norman (riv.), Austl.
191/H3 Norman, Ar,US
201/G3 Norman (lake), NC,US
191/F3 Norman, Ok,US
134/B1 Normanby, Austl.
138/E6 Normanby (isl.), PNG
195/P7 Normandale Japanese Garden, Mn,US
79/E3 Normandie, Collines de (hills), Fr.
196/A1 Normandin, Qu,Can
79/E2 Normandy (hist. reg.), Fr.
188/D3 Normandy, Tx,US
188/D3 Normandy Beach, NJ,US
205/C3 Normandy Park, Wa,US
189/F2 Norman, Tx,US
161/G2 Norman Manley (int'l arpt.), Jam.
203/G2 Norman Park, Ga,US
208/A1 Norman Rockwell Museum, Ma,US
197/L2 Norman's Cove, Nf,Can
134/A2 Normanton, Austl.
57/G4 Normanton, Eng,UK
178/D2 Norman Wells, NW,Can
132/C5 Nornalup-Walpole Nat'l Park, Austl.
168/B2 Nororiental de Marañon (dept.), Peru
156/B3 Norotshama (peak), Namb.
194/C2 Norquay, Sk,Can
174/C4 Ñorquincó, Arg.
63/R6 Norra Björkfjärden (bay), Swe.
63/S6 Norra Ljusterö (isl.), Swe.
61/F2 Norrbotten (co.), Swe.
76/B1 Norrea (riv.), Sp.
62/D4 Nørre Alslev, Den.
62/C4 Nørre Nebel, Den.
68/B2 Norrent-Fontes, Fr.
62/C3 Nørre Vorupør, Den.
205/Q16 Norridge, Il,US
196/C3 Norridgewock, Me,US
200/E2 Norris, Tn,US
200/F2 Norris (lake), Tn,US
200/C2 Norris City, Il,US
206/C3 Norristown, Pa,US
62/G2 Norrköping, Swe.
61/F2 Norrland (reg.), Swe.
62/G1 Norrsundet, Swe.
63/H2 Norrtälje, Swe.
63/R7 Norrviken (lake), Swe.
62/C3 Nors, Den.
132/D5 Norseman, Austl.
61/F2 Norsjö, Swe.
138/F6 Norsup, Van.
174/E4 Norte (pt.), Arg.
175/F3 Norte (pt.), Arg.
166/D3 Norte (chan.), Braz.
169/G3 Norte (mts.), Braz.
166/D2 Norte, Cabo do (cape), Braz.
175/J6 Norte, Campo de Hielo (glacier), Chile
164/C2 Norte de Santander (dept.), Col.
170/A2 Nortelândia, Braz.
142/A3 Norte Los Rodeos (int'l arpt.), Canl.,Sp.
77/X16 Norte Los Rodeos (int'l arpt.), Canl.,Sp.
67/G5 Nörten-Hardenberg, Ger.
132/B4 North (pt.), Austl.
135/C3 North (pt.), Austl.
135/C4 North (pt.), Austl.
197/G2 North (cape), NS,Can
198/E1 North (chan.), On,Can
196/F2 North (cape), PEI,Can
60/A3 North (sound), Ire.
149/G4 North (isl.), Kenya
136/C1 North (cape), N.Z.
136/C2 North (isl.), N.Z.
56/C1 North (chan.), UK
52/D3 North (sea), UK
55/N13 North (sound), Sc,UK
177/D5 North (cape), Ak,US
177/F3 North (peak), Ak,US
206/B5 North (pt.), Md,US
196/C3 North (bay), Me,US
198/E2 North (pt.), Mi,US
201/G4 North, SC,US
188/L7 North (lake), Tx,US
199/K3 North Adams, Ma,US
92/D4 North Albanian Alps (mts.), Alb., Yugo.
57/G3 Northallerton, Eng,UK
132/C4 Northam, Austl.
58/B4 Northam, Eng,UK
176/* North America (cont.)
208/B1 North Amherst, Ma,US
132/B4 Northampton, Austl.
59/F2 Northampton, Eng,UK
59/E2 Northampton (uplands), Eng,UK
208/B1 Northampton, Ma,US
206/C2 Northampton, Pa,US
206/C2 Northampton (co.), Pa,US
59/F2 Northamptonshire (co.), Eng,UK
119/F5 North Andaman (isl.), India
201/J2 North Anna (riv.), Va,US
207/J8 North Arlington, NJ,US
201/M7 North Atlanta, Ga,US
50/H3 North Atlantic (ocean)
208/C2 North Attleboro, Ma,US
201/G4 North Augusta, SC,US
179/K3 North Aulatsivik (isl.), Nf,Can
205/P16 North Aurora, Il,US
53/N6 Northaw, Eng,UK
207/M9 North Babylon, NY,US
182/F3 North Baldy (mtn.), Wa,US
54/A3 North Ballachulish, Sc,UK
198/E4 North Baltimore, Oh,US
56/D3 North Barrule (mtn.), IM,UK
183/K1 North Battleford, Sk,Can
199/G1 North Bay, On,Can
205/Q14 North Bay, Wi,US
206/B6 North Beach, Md,US
207/D4 North Beach Haven, NJ,US
198/B3 North Bend, BC,Can
182/D3 North Bend, BC,Can
184/A2 North Bend, Or,US
199/H4 North Bend, Pa,US
205/D3 North Bend, Wa,US
207/D2 North Bergen, NJ,US
54/D4 North Berwick, Sc,UK
208/G5 North Bloomfield, Oh,US
208/C1 Northborough, Ma,US
189/F2 North Bosque (riv.), Tx,US
135/C1 North Bourke, Austl.
66/C5 North Brabant (prov.), Neth.
206/D2 North Branch, NJ,US
208/B3 North Branford, Ct,US
208/C1 Northbridge, Ma,US
205/Q15 Northbrook, Il,US
208/B1 North Brookfield, Ma,US
206/D3 North Brunswick, NJ,US
153/G2 North Buganda (prov.), Ugan.
162/D2 North Caicos (isl.), Trks.
207/H8 North Caldwell, NJ,US
191/E3 North Canadian (riv.), Ok,US
208/B2 North Canton, Ct,US
208/F6 North Canton, Oh,US
206/D6 North Cape May, NJ,US
178/G3 North Caribou (lake), On,Can
201/G3 North Carolina (state), US
208/D2 North Carver, Ma,US
182/D3 North Cascades Nat'l Park, Wa,US
122/H4 North Central (prov.), SrL.
159/F1 North Central (plain), Tx,US
201/H4 North Charleston, SC,US
205/Q15 North Chicago, Il,US
132/C5 Northcliffe, Austl.
208/D1 North Cohasset, Ma,US
57/H5 North Collingham, Eng,UK
199/G3 North Collins, NY,US
188/D2 North Concho (riv.), Tx,US
136/F6 Northcote, N.Z.
182/C3 North Cowichan, BC,Can
191/J4 North Crossett, Ar,US
194/D4 North Dakota (state), US
132/B5 North Dandalup, Austl.
201/M7 North Decatur, Ga,US
58/D5 North Dorset Downs (uplands), Eng,UK
56/C2 North Down (dist.), NI,UK
59/F4 North Downs (hills), Eng,UK
201/M7 North Druid Hills, Ga,US
192/D1 North Eagle Butte, SD,US
134/C3 North East (pt.), Austl.
162/C2 Northeast (pt.), Bahm.
155/E4 North-East (dist.), Bots.
161/G2 Northeast (pt.), Jam.
177/E3 Northeast (cape), Ak,US
206/C4 North East, Md,US
199/G3 North East, Pa,US
196/C3 North East Carry, Me,US
151/B1 North Eastern (prov.), Kenya
100/C2 Northeast Land (isl.), Sval.
162/B1 North East Providence (chan.), Bahm.
186/D3 North Edwards, Ca,US
208/A1 North Egremont, Ma,US
67/G5 Northeim, Ger.
59/G1 North Elmham, Eng,UK
193/H3 North English, Ia,US
191/F2 North Enid, Ok,US
131/F2 North Entrance (inlet), PNG
145/E4 Northern (reg.), Gha.
103/D3 Northern (dist.), Isr.
155/G1 Northern (reg.), Malw.
131/G2 Northern (prov.), PNG
144/B4 Northern (prov.), SLeo.
122/H4 Northern (prov.), SrL.
149/F1 Northern (reg.), Sudan
153/H2 Northern (prov.), Ugan.
155/F1 Northern (prov.), Zam.
114/B4 Northern Areas (terr.), Pak.
183/L5 Northern Cheyenne Ind. Res., Mt,US
139/J6 Northern Cook (isls.), Cookls.
52/H2 Northern Dvina (riv.), Rus.
55/H9 Northern Ireland, UK
195/J3 Northern Light (lake), On,Can
138/D3 Northern Marianas, US
131/F2 Northern Peninsula Abor. Rsv., Austl.
100/G3 Northern Sos'va (riv.), Rus.
91/J3 Northern Sporades (isls.), Gre.
128/E3 Northern Territory (terr.), Austl.
95/N3 Northern Ural (mts.), Rus.
95/K4 Northern Uval (hills), Rus.
177/K2 Northern Yukon Nat'l Park, Yk,Can
54/C5 North Esk (riv.), Sc,UK
54/D3 North Esk (riv.), Sc,UK
193/H3 North Fabius (riv.), Ia, Mo,US
208/A2 Northfield, Ct,US
193/H1 Northfield, Mn,US
199/L3 Northfield, NH,US
208/F5 Northfield, Oh,US
190/D3 Northfield, Tx,US
199/K2 Northfield, Vt,US
53/P7 Northfleet, Eng,UK
59/G1 North Fond du Lac, Wi,US
59/H4 North Foreland (pt.), Eng,UK
186/C2 North Fork, Ca,US
185/G1 North Fork, Id,US
191/G4 North Fork (cr.), Tx,US
198/F5 North Fork Village, Oh,US
203/H4 North Fort Myers, Fl,US
198/D2 North Fox (isl.), Mi,US
64/E1 North Frisian (isls.), Den., Ger.
76/C4 North Front (int'l arpt.), Gib.
194/C3 Northgate, Sk,Can
121/H2 North Gauhāti, India
130/D2 North Goulburn (isl.), Austl.
208/B2 North Granby, Ct,US
208/C2 North Grosvenor Dale, Ct,US
208/B1 North Hadley, Ma,US
207/J8 North Haledon, NJ,US
208/D1 North Hanover, Ma,US
201/J3 North Harlowe, NC,US
208/B1 North Hatfield, Ma,US
121/H4 North Hātia (isl.), Bang.
208/B3 North Haven, Ct,US
196/C3 North Haven, Me,US
196/D3 North Head, NB,Can
199/K2 North Hero, Vt,US
205/M9 North Highlands, Ca,US
205/C3 North Hill-Edgewood, Wa,US
202/B1 North Hodge, La,US
66/B3 North Holland (prov.), Neth.
204/F7 North Hollywood, Ca,US
151/B1 North Horr, Kenya
195/Q7 North Hudson, Wi,US
203/H4 North Hutchinson (isl.), Fl,US
57/H5 North Hykeham, Eng,UK
208/F6 North Industry, Oh,US
198/C4 North Judson, In,US
95/Q5 North Kazakhstan Obl., Rus.
194/C4 North Killdeer (mtn.), ND,US
198/F4 North Kingsville, Oh,US
151/B2 North Kitui Nat'l Rsv., Kenya
113/D2 North Korea
116/B3 North Lakhimpur, India
136/C1 Northland (reg.), N.Z.
186/E2 North Las Vegas, Nv,US
208/F6 North Lawrence, Oh,US
208/G6 North Lima, Oh,US
207/M9 North Lindenhurst, NY,US
191/H3 North Little Rock, Ar,US
185/H3 North Logan, Ut,US
204/F8 North Long Beach, Ca,US
192/D2 North Loup (riv.), Ne,US
155/G1 North Luangwa Nat'l Park, Zam.
198/F4 North Madison, Oh,US
176/G2 North Magnetic Pole, NAm.
198/D4 North Manchester, In,US
195/M5 North Manitou, Mi,US
198/C2 North Manitou (isl.), Mi,US
208/D1 North Marshfield, Ma,US
202/P8 North Miami, Fl,US
202/P8 North Miami Beach, Fl,US
208/D2 North Middleboro, Ma,US
55/H8 North Minch (The Minch) (sound), Sc,UK
206/B1 North Mtn. (ridge), Pa,US
198/C3 North Muskegon, Mi,US
201/H4 North Myrtle Beach, SC,US
202/P7 North New River (can.), Fl,US
191/F1 North Newton, Ks,US
61/H1 North (Nordkapp) (cape), Nor.
185/H3 North Ogden, Ut,US
208/F5 North Olmsted, Oh,US
97/G4 North Ossetian Aut. Rep., Rus.
138/F3 North Pacific (ocean)
202/P6 North Palm Beach, Fl,US
190/D3 North Pease (riv.), Tx,US
197/S9 North Pelham, On,Can
208/D1 North Pembroke, Ma,US
130/C3 North Peron (isl.), Austl.
58/C4 North Petherton, Eng,UK
134/E6 North Pine (riv.), Austl.
206/D2 North Plainfield, NJ,US
192/D3 North Platte, Ne,US
192/C3 North Platte Nat'l Wild. Ref., Ne,US
208/D2 North Plymouth, Ma,US
177/J3 North Pole, Ak,US
200/D4 Northport, Al,US
203/G4 North Port, Fl,US
198/D2 Northport, Mi,US
182/E3 Northport, Wa,US
194/C3 North Portal, Sk,Can
207/E2 Northport (Old Northport), NY,US
206/A5 North Potomac, Md,US
184/E1 North Powder, Or,US
205/P14 North Prairie, Wi,US
208/C2 North Providence, RI,US
205/C3 North Puyallup, Wa,US
193/G2 North Raccoon (riv.), Ia,US
202/K8 North Redington Beach, Fl,US
64/E3 North Rhine-Westphalia (state), Ger.
188/K7 North Richland Hills, Tx,US
204/E7 Northridge, Ca,US
208/E5 North Ridgeville, Oh,US
187/F2 North Rim, Az,US
55/N13 North Ronaldsay (isl.), Sc,UK
208/F5 North Royalton, Oh,US
189/F2 Northrup, Tx,US
196/F2 North Rustico, PE,Can
182/C3 North Saanich, BC,Can
184/B1 North Santiam (riv.), Or,US
178/E3 North Saskatchewan (riv.), Can
208/D1 North Scituate, Ma,US
208/C2 North Scituate, RI,US
57/G2 North Shields, Eng,UK
100/K2 North Siberian (plain), Rus.
184/C1 North Sister (peak), Or,US
193/H3 North Skunk (riv.), Ia,US
57/J5 North Somercotes, Eng,UK
195/H1 North Spirit Lake, On,Can
208/C3 North Stonington, Ct,US
195/P6 North St. Paul, Mn,US
134/D4 North Stradbroke (isl.), Austl.
199/L2 North Stratford, NH,US
191/G4 North Sulphur (riv.), Tx,US
208/C2 North Swansea, Ma,US
197/G2 North Sydney, NS,Can
136/C2 North Taranaki (bight), N.Z.
207/E1 North Tarrytown, NY,US
198/C5 North Terre Haute, In,US
182/E1 North Thompson (riv.), BC,Can
57/H5 North Thoresby, Eng,UK
59/E4 North Tidworth, Eng,UK
55/H7 North Tolsta, Sc,UK
199/G3 North Tonawanda, NY,US
200/B3 North Tunica, Ms,US
195/K4 North Twin (lake), Wi,US
57/F1 North Tyne (riv.), Eng,UK
55/H8 North Uist (isl.), Sc,UK
181/P2 Northumberland (str.), NB, PE,Can
196/F2 Northumberland (str.), Qu,Can
57/F1 Northumberland (co.), Eng,UK
196/B3 Northumberland, NH,US
206/B2 Northumberland, Pa,US
206/B2 Northumberland (co.), Pa,US
57/F1 Northumberland Nat'l Park, Eng,UK
184/B2 North Umpqua (riv.), Or,US
207/E1 Northvale, NJ,US
207/L9 North Valley Stream, NY,US
178/D4 North Vancouver, BC,Can
198/D5 North Vernon, In,US
208/A2 Northville, Ct,US
205/F7 Northville, Mi,US
199/J3 Northville, NY,US
192/E1 Northville, SD,US
206/C3 North Wales, Pa,US
59/H1 North Walsham, Eng,UK
64/A2 North Walsham, Eng,UK
177/K3 Northway, Ak,US
53/P6 North Weald Bassett, Eng,UK
132/B2 North West (cape), Austl.
161/G2 Northwest (pt.), Jam.
203/H5 Northwest (cape), Fl,US
122/H4 North Western (prov.), SrL.
154/E2 North-Western (prov.), Zam.
114/B4 Northwest Frontier (prov.), Pak.
197/K1 Northwest Gander (riv.), Nf,Can
54/A2 North West Highlands (mts.), Sc,UK
162/B1 North West Providence (chan.), Bahm.
178/E2 Northwest Territories (terr.), Can.
57/H5 North Wheatley, Eng,UK
57/F5 Northwich, Eng,UK
190/D4 North Wichita (riv.), Tx,US
206/D5 North Wildwood, NJ,US
201/G2 North Wilkesboro, NC,US
208/A3 North Wilton, Ct,US
199/L3 North Windham, Me,US
57/G5 North Wingfield, Eng,UK
193/H2 Northwood, Ia,US
194/F4 Northwood, ND,US
208/C2 North Woodstock, Ct,US
197/S8 North York, On,Can
57/H3 North York Moors Nat'l Park, Eng,UK
57/G3 North Yorkshire (co.), Eng,UK
196/E3 Norton, NB,Can
177/F3 Norton (bay), Ak,US
177/E3 Norton (sound), Ak,US
190/E1 Norton, Ks,US
208/C2 Norton, Ma,US
208/F5 Norton, Oh,US
188/D2 Norton, Tx,US
201/F2 Norton, Va,US
201/H1 Norton, WV,US
155/F3 Norton, Zim.
57/F6 Norton Bridge, Eng,UK
198/G3 Norton Shores, Mi,US
200/D2 Nortonville, Ky,US
64/E1 Nortorf, Ger.
78/D6 Nort-sur-Erdre, Fr.
197/R8 Norval, On,Can
137/Z Norvegia (cape), Ant.
69/F2 Nörvenich, Ger.
204/B3 Norwalk, Ca,US
207/E1 Norwalk, Ct,US
207/M7 Norwalk (riv.), Ct,US
198/E4 Norwalk, Oh,US
193/J2 Norwalk, Wi,US
61/B3 Norway
196/B3 Norway, Me,US
198/C2 Norway, Mi,US
178/G3 Norway House, Mb,Can
179/S7 Norwegian (bay), NW,Can
52/C2 Norwegian (sea), Eur.
208/D1 Norwell, Ma,US
198/F3 Norwich, On,Can
59/H1 Norwich, Eng,UK
59/H1 Norwich (int'l arpt.), Eng,UK
208/B2 Norwich, Ct,US
191/F2 Norwich, Ks,US
199/J3 Norwich, NY,US
199/K3 Norwich, Vt,US
185/J4 Norwood, Co,US
202/C2 Norwood, La,US
208/C1 Norwood, Ma,US
195/N7 Norwood, Mn,US
201/G3 Norwood, NC,US
207/E2 Norwood, NJ,US
199/J2 Norwood, NY,US
198/D5 Norwood, Oh,US
112/D2 Nosappu-misaki (cape), Japan
183/J1 Nose (hill), Ab,Can
111/L10 Nose, Japan
89/K2 Nos Emine (cape), Bul.
112/B1 Noshappu-misaki (cape), Japan
107/K1 Noshaq (mtn.), Pak.
112/B3 Noshiro, Japan
93/H4 Nos Maslen Nos (pt.), Bul.
126/E2 Nosong (cape), Malay.
113/D5 Nosŏng, SKor.
125/A4 Nosong, Tanjong (cape), Malay.
154/D5 Nosop (dry riv.), Bots.
95/K4 Nosovaya, Rus.
98/F2 Nosovka, Ukr.
107/G3 Noşratābād, Iran
171/F1 Nossa Senhora da Glória, Braz.
169/G4 Nossa Senhora do Livramento, Braz.
62/E2 Nossebro, Swe.
72/D5 Nossen, Ger.
55/K7 Noss Head (pt.), Sc,UK
154/C4 Nossob (dry riv.), Namb.
156/C2 Nossobrivier (dry riv.), SAfr.
144/D3 Nossombougou, Mali
157/J8 Nosy-Varika, Madg.
73/B5 Noszlop, Hun.
85/D2 Notaresco, It.
200/E4 Notasulga, Al,US
175/J7 Notch (cape), Chile
65/J2 Notec (riv.), Pol.
90/D4 Noto, It.
90/D4 Noto (gulf), It.
90/D4 Noto (val.), It.
111/E2 Noto (pen.), Japan
90/D4 Noto Antica (ruins), It.
62/C2 Notodden, Nor.
111/M9 Notogawa, Japan
112/C1 Notoro (lake), Japan
179/L4 Notre Dame (bay), Nf,Can
196/C2 Notre Dame (mts.), Qu,Can
53/T10 Notre Dame, Fr.
79/G2 Notre-Dame-de-Bondeville, Fr.
79/F2 Notre-Dame-de-Gravenchon, Fr.
199/J2 Notre-Dame-de-la-Salette, Qu,Can
197/N7 Notre-Dame-de-l'Ile-Perrot, Qu,Can
194/E3 Notre-Dame-de-Lourdes, Mb,Can
196/B2 Notre-Dame-des-Monts, Qu,Can
196/C2 Notre-Dame-du-Lac, Qu,Can
145/F5 Notsé, Togo
133/G5 Nott (peak), Austl.
198/F2 Nottawasaga (bay), On,Can
179/J3 Nottaway (riv.), Qu,Can
62/D2 Nøtterøy, Nor.
179/H2 Nottingham (isl.), NW,Can
157/E3 Nottingham, SAfr.
57/G6 Nottingham, Eng,UK
57/H5 Nottinghamshire (co.), Eng,UK
201/H2 Nottoway, Va,US
201/J2 Nottoway (riv.), Va,US
202/C2 Nottoway Plantation, La,US
67/E5 Nottuln, Ger.
183/L3 Notukeu (riv.), Sk,Can
152/D2 Nouabalé (riv.), Congo
142/A5 Nouadhibou, Mrta.
142/A5 Nouadhibou (int'l arpt.), Mrta.
144/B2 Nouakchott (cap.), Mrta.
144/B2 Nouakchott (int'l arpt.), Mrta.
144/A2 Nouâmghâr, Mrta.
79/F5 Nouan-le-Fuzelier, Fr.
77/F1 Noue (riv.), Fr.
139/V13 Nouméa (cap.), NCal.
139/V13 Nouméa (Tontouta) (int'l arpt.), NCal.
144/E3 Nouna, Burk.
156/D3 Noupoort, SAfr.
68/A3 Nouvion, Fr.
69/D4 Nouvion-sur-Meuse, Fr.
69/D4 Nouzonville, Fr.
73/A6 Nova, Hun.
208/E5 Nova, Oh,US
170/B4 Nova Andradina, Braz.
73/C3 Nová Baňa, Slvk.
170/B2 Nova Brasilândia, Braz.
152/C4 Nova Caipemba, Ang.
93/F3 Novaci, Rom.
167/H4 Nova Cruz, Braz.
73/C2 Nová Dubnica, Slvk.
87/F5 Novafeltria, It.
171/E4 Nova Friburgo, Braz.
152/D5 Nova Gaia, Ang.
87/G1 Nova Gorica, Slov.
92/C3 Nova Gradiška, Cro.
170/C4 Nova Granada, Braz.
171/E4 Nova Iguaçu, Braz.
73/C2 Nováky, Slvk.
144/B3 Nova Lamego, GBis.
81/H5 Nova Levante (Welshnofen), It.
125/F6 Novaliches (res.), Phil.
170/E3 Nova Lima, Braz.
170/B4 Nova Loudrina, Braz.
155/G3 Nova Lusitânia, Moz.
155/G4 Nova Mambone, Moz.
167/G4 Nova Olinda, Braz.
166/B3 Nova Olinda do Norte, Braz.
92/E3 Nova Pazova, Yugo.
173/G4 Nova Prata, Braz.
86/B2 Novara, It.
86/B1 Novara (prov.), It.
167/F4 Nova Russas, Braz.
196/E3 Nova Scotia (prov.), Can
140/J11 Nova Sintra, CpV.
83/C2 Nova Siri Scalo, It.
155/G4 Nova Sofala, Moz.
81/F5 Novate Mezzola, It.
167/E3 Nova Timboteua, Braz.
205/J10 Novato, Ca,US
92/D4 Nova Varoš, Yugo.
170/B2 Nova Xavantina, Braz.
99/K3 Novaya Astrakhan', Ukr.
98/F2 Novaya Basan', Ukr.
98/E2 Novaya Borovaya, Ukr.
101/L4 Novaya Igirma, Rus.
98/E5 Novaya Ivanovka, Ukr.
99/G4 Novaya Kakhovka, Ukr.
99/L2 Novaya Kalitva, Rus.
97/J2 Novaya Kazanka, Kaz.
63/Q1 Novaya Ladoga, Rus.
99/G4 Novaya Maluksa, Rus.
99/G4 Novaya Mayachka, Ukr.
98/F4 Novaya Odessa, Ukr.
99/G3 Novaya Praga, Ukr.
101/R2 Novaya Sibir' (isl.), Rus.
98/D3 Novaya Ushitsa, Ukr.
99/K2 Novaya Usman', Rus.
99/H3 Novaya Vodolaga, Ukr.
100/E2 Novaya Zemlya (isl.), Rus.
93/H4 Nova Zagora, Bul.
87/E1 Nove, It.
71/H5 Nové Hrady, Czh.
77/E3 Novelda, Sp.
87/D3 Novellara, It.
65/J4 Nové Mesto nad Váhom, Slvk.
73/B2 Nové Mĕsto nad Váhom, Slvk.
73/A1 Nové Mlýny, Vodny nadrź (lake), Czh.
87/F1 Noventa di Piave, It.
87/E2 Noventa Vicentina, It.
82/A5 Noves, Fr.
71/F2 Nové Sedlo, Czh.
71/G2 Nové Strašeci, Czh.
73/C4 Nové Zámky, Slvk.
63/P2 Novgorod, Rus.
63/N3 Novgorodka, Rus.
98/G3 Novgorodka, Ukr.
63/P2 Novgorod Obl., Rus.
99/G2 Novgorod-Severskiy, Ukr.
99/J3 Novgorodskoye, Ukr.
205/F7 Novi, Mi,US
92/E3 Novi Banovci, Yugo.
92/E3 Novi Bečej, Yugo.
188/E2 Novice, Tx,US
87/D3 Novi di Modena, It.
87/G2 Novigrad, Cro.
93/F4 Novi Iskŭr, Bul.
109/N2 Novikovo, Rus.
86/B3 Novi Ligure, It.
80/C3 Novillars, Fr.
158/D4 Novillero, Mex.
193/H3 Novinger, Mo,US
93/H4 Novi Pazar, Bul.
92/E4 Novi Pazar, Yugo.
92/D3 Novi Sad, Yugo.
164/B3 Nóvita, Col.
92/B3 Novi Vinodolski, Cro.
170/B2 Novo (riv.), Braz.
171/N6 Novo (riv.), Braz.
97/K2 Novoalekseyevka, Kaz.
99/H4 Novoalekseyevka, Ukr.
97/H4 Novo Alexeyevka (int'l arpt.), Geo.
100/J4 Novoaltaysk, Rus.
99/M2 Novoanninskiy, Rus.
166/A4 Novo Aripuanã, Braz.
99/K4 Novoazovsk, Ukr.
95/N5 Novobelokatay, Rus.
97/J3 Novobogatinskoye, Kaz.
99/H4 Novobogdanovka, Ukr.
95/K4 Novocheboksarsk, Rus.
53/H4 Novocherkassk, Rus.
97/J1 Novodevich'ye, Rus.
99/K3 Novodruzhesk, Ukr.
94/G5 Novodugino, Rus.
98/D2 Novograd-Volynskiy, Ukr.
99/J3 Novogrodovka, Ukr.
63/L5 Novogrudok, Bela.
173/G4 Novo Hamburgo, Braz.
170/C4 Novo Horizonte, Braz.
71/H5 Novohradské Hory (mts.), Czh.
63/M3 Novoizborsk, Rus.
100/G5 Novokazalinsk, Kaz.
99/L2 Novokhopërskiy, Rus.
99/L5 Novokubansk, Rus.
97/J1 Novokuybyshevsk, Rus.
100/J4 Novokuznetsk, Rus.
63/P1 Novoladozhskiy (can.), Rus.
137/A Novolazarevskaya, Ant.
63/N4 Novolukoml', Bela.
92/B3 Novo Mesto, Slov.
92/E3 Novo Miloševo, Yugo.
99/K4 Novominskaya, Rus.
98/F3 Novomirgorod, Ukr.
100/D4 Novomoskovsk, Rus.
99/H3 Novomoskovsk, Ukr.
99/H4 Novonikolayevka, Ukr.
99/M2 Novonikolayevskiy, Rus.
108/E1 Novonukutskiy, Rus.
167/F4 Novo Oriente, Braz.
99/H3 Novopokrovka, Ukr.
99/L5 Novopokrovskaya, Rus.
63/N4 Novopolotsk, Bela.
99/G4 Novorontsovka, Ukr.
53/G4 Novorossiysk, Rus.
97/L2 Novorossiyskoye, Kaz.
63/N3 Novorzhev, Rus.
98/D3 Novoselitsa, Ukr.
99/G5 Novosëlovskoye, Ukr.
97/K1 Novosergiyevka, Rus.
99/K4 Novoshakhtinsk, Rus.
100/J4 Novosibirsk, Rus.
96/F1 Novosil', Rus.
99/K2 Novosil'skoye, Rus.
95/P5 Novosineglazovskiy, Rus.
63/P3 Novosokol'niki, Rus.
63/J4 Novostroyevo, Rus.
99/K5 Novo-Titarovskaya, Rus.
53/J3 Novotroitsk, Rus.
99/H4 Novotroitskoye, Ukr.
98/F3 Novoukrainka, Ukr.
97/J1 Novoul'yanovsk, Rus.
97/J2 Novouzensk, Rus.
98/C2 Novovolynsk, Ukr.
99/K2 Novovoronezhskiy, Rus.
95/L4 Novovyatsk, Rus.
99/H1 Novoyamskoye, Rus.
94/E5 Novoyel'nya, Bela.
96/D1 Novozybkov, Rus.
92/C3 Novska, Cro.
65/K4 Nový Jičín, Czh.
98/G4 Novyy Bug, Ukr.
98/E2 Novyye Belokorovichi, Ukr.
99/H3 Novyye Sanzhary, Ukr.
99/J2 Novyy Oskol, Rus.
100/H3 Novyy Port, Rus.
98/C3 Novyy Rozdol, Ukr.
99/H5 Novyy Svet, Ukr.
95/Q4 Novyy Tap, Rus.
100/H3 Novyy Urengoy, Rus.
97/K4 Novyy Uzen', Kaz.
65/L3 Nowa Dęba, Pol.
65/J3 Nowa Ruda, Pol.
65/M3 Nowa Sarzyna, Pol.
65/H3 Nowa Sól, Pol.
191/G2 Nowata, Ok,US
65/K2 Nowe, Pol.
65/K2 Nowe Miasto Lubawskie, Pol.
60/A6 Nowen (mtn.), Ire.
135/D1 Nowendoc, Austl.
119/F2 Nowgong, India
120/B3 Nowgong, India
177/H3 Nowitna (riv.), Ak,US
177/H3 Nowitna Nat'l Wild. Ref., Ak,US
65/H2 Nowogard, Pol.
185/K2 Nowood (cr.), Wy,US
135/D2 Nowra, Austl.
107/K2 Nowshera, Pak.
65/K1 Nowy Dwór Gdański, Pol.
65/L4 Nowy Sącz, Pol.
65/L4 Nowy Sącz (prov.), Pol.
65/K1 Nowy Staw, Pol.
65/L4 Nowy Targ, Pol.
65/J2 Nowy Tomyśl, Pol.
200/C4 Noxapater, Ms,US
182/G4 Noxon, Mt,US
200/C4 Noxubee (riv.), Al, Ms,US
200/C4 Noxubee Nat'l Wild. Ref., Ms,US
76/A1 Noya, Sp.
100/H3 Noyabr'sk, Rus.
78/C4 Noyal-Pontivy, Fr.
78/D4 Noyal-sur-Vilaine, Fr.
79/F5 Noyant, Fr.
79/E5 Noyant-la-Gravoyère, Fr.
68/B5 Noye (riv.), Fr.
79/F5 Noyers-sur-Sarthe, Fr.
79/G6 Noyers-sur-Cher, Fr.

122/F3 **Noyil** (riv.), India
68/C4 **Noyon**, Fr.
78/D5 **Nozay**, Fr.
152/C3 **Nsah**, Congo
152/C2 **Nsak**, Gabon
155/G3 **Nsanje**, Malw.
145/E5 **Nsawam**, Gha.
157/F3 **Nseleni**, SAfr.
152/B2 **Nsoc**, EqG.
152/D3 **Nsondia**, Zaire
116/C3 **Nsopzup**, Burma
145/G5 **Nsukka**, Nga.
153/G5 **Nsumbu Nat'l Park**, Zam.
145/E5 **Nsuta**, Gha.
152/B2 **Ntem** (riv.), Afr.
144/B2 **Nterguent**, Mrta.
153/G2 **Ntoroko**, Ugan.
152/B2 **Ntoum**, Gabon
148/A4 **Ntui**, Camr.
153/E4 **Ntulume**, Zaire
153/G3 **Ntungamo**, Ugan.
153/G2 **Ntusi**, Ugan.
154/E4 **Ntwetwe Pan** (salt pan), Bots.
116/C3 **Nu** (mts.), China
108/D5 **Nu** (riv.), China
124/C2 **Nuang** (peak), Malay.
206/C1 **Nuangola**, Pa,US
117/H2 **Nuanshui**, China
149/F3 **Nūbah, Jibāl An** (mts.), Sudan
116/B2 **Nubgang** (pass), China
147/G4 **Nubian** (des.), Sudan
92/F2 **Nucet**, Rom.
185/J4 **Nucla**, Co,US
70/D2 **Nüdlingen**, Ger.
189/F4 **Nueces** (riv.), Tx,US
178/G2 **Nueltin** (lake), NW,Can
66/C6 **Nuenen**, Neth.
115/E2 **Nü'er** (riv.), China
168/C2 **Nueva Alejandría**, Peru
172/D1 **Nueva Asunción** (dept.), Par.
188/E4 **Nueva Ciudad Guerrero**, Mex.
160/D2 **Nueva Coahuila Nat'l Cap. Park**, Mex.
160/D3 **Nueva Concepción**, Guat.
174/D2 **Nueva Constitución**, Arg.
165/E2 **Nueva Esparta** (state), Ven.
172/D3 **Nueva Esperanza**, Arg.
164/D2 **Nueva Florida**, Ven.
173/E2 **Nueva Germania**, Par.
161/F1 **Nueva Gerona**, Cuba
175/F2 **Nueva Helvecia**, Uru.
174/B3 **Nueva Imperial**, Chile
164/B4 **Nueva Loja** (Lago Agrio), Ecu.
174/C5 **Nueva Lubecka**, Arg.
160/D3 **Nueva Ocotepéque**, Hon.
175/S11 **Nueva Palmira**, Uru.
159/N8 **Nueva Patria**, Mex.
188/D4 **Nueva Rosita**, Mex.
174/E2 **Nueve de Julio**, Arg.
161/G1 **Nuevitas**, Cuba
174/D4 **Nuevo** (gulf), Arg.
204/C3 **Nuevo**, Ca,US
175/S11 **Nuevo Berlin**, Uru.
158/D2 **Nuevo Casas Grandes**, Mex.
161/F4 **Nuevo Chagres**, Pan.
158/D3 **Nuevo Ideal**, Mex.
188/E4 **Nuevo Laredo**, Mex.
186/E4 **Nuevo León**, Mex.
159/F3 **Nuevo León** (state), Mex.
169/E3 **Nuevo Mundo**, Bol.
175/S11 **Nuevo Palmira**, Uru.
189/F4 **Nuevo Progresso**, Mex.
164/C5 **Nuevo Rocafuerte**, Ecu.
81/F4 **Nufenen**, Swi.
81/E5 **Nufenenpass** (pass), Swi.
150/D3 **Nugaaleed** (val.), Som.
190/E4 **Nugent**, Tx,US
136/B4 **Nugget** (pt.), N.Z.
138/E5 **Nuguria** (isls.), PNG
139/J2 **Nuhau** (isl.), Hi,US
67/F6 **Nuhne** (riv.), Ger.
138/G5 **Nui** (isl.), Tuv.
177/H1 **Nuiqsut**, Ak,US
80/A3 **Nuits-St-Georges**, Fr.
111/N10 **Nukata**, Japan
177/F4 **Nuklunek** (mtn.), Ak,US
139/H7 **Nuku'alofa** (cap.), Tonga
138/G5 **Nukufetau** (isl.), Tuv.
139/L5 **Nuku Hiva** (isl.), FrPol.
138/H5 **Nukulaelae** (isl.), Tuv.
138/F5 **Nukumanu** (atoll), PNG
139/H5 **Nukumororo** (Gardner) (isl.), Kiri.
139/H5 **Nukunonu** (isl.), Tok.
138/E4 **Nukuoro** (isl.), Micr.
100/F5 **Nukus**, Uzb.
139/M6 **Nukutavake** (isl.), FrPol.
177/G3 **Nulato**, Ak,US
77/E3 **Nules**, Sp.
132/D2 **Nullagine**, Austl.
133/F4 **Nullarbor**, Austl.
132/E5 **Nullarbor** (plain), Austl.
133/F4 **Nullarbor Nat'l Park**, Austl.
148/B3 **Numan**, Nga.
66/B5 **Numansdorp**, Neth.
111/F2 **Numata**, Japan
149/E4 **Numatinna** (riv.), Sudan
111/F3 **Numazu**, Japan
196/C2 **Number Nine** (mtn.), Me,US
153/G3 **Numbi**, Zaire
69/G2 **Nümbrecht**, Ger.
131/D3 **Numbulwar**, Austl.
127/H4 **Numfoor** (isl.), Indo.
63/K1 **Nummi**, Fin.
135/C3 **Numurkah**, Austl.
177/F3 **Nunapitchuk**, Ak,US
135/G5 **Nunawading**, Austl.
164/C3 **Nunchia**, Col.
72/D5 **Nünchritz**, Ger.
199/H3 **Nunda**, NY,US
135/D1 **Nundle**, Austl.
59/E1 **Nuneaton**, Eng,UK
132/C4 **Nungarin**, Austl.
135/D3 **Nungatta Nat'l Park**, Austl.
113/D3 **Nüng-ni**, NKor.
155/H2 **Nungo**, Moz.
153/H3 **Nungwe**, Tanz.
177/E4 **Nunivak** (isl.), Ak,US
191/G3 **Nunley**, Ar,US
200/D3 **Nunnelly**, Tn,US
80/D3 **Nunningen**, Swi.
168/D4 **Nuñoa**, Peru
66/C4 **Nunspeet**, Neth.
57/G2 **Nunthorpe**, Eng,UK
125/B4 **Nunukan**, Indo.
109/J1 **Nuomin** (riv.), China
144/C5 **Nuon** (riv.), IvC., Libr.
90/A2 **Nuoro**, It.
150/C2 **Nuqūb**, Yem.
164/B3 **Nuquí**, Col.
114/D4 **Nur**, China
103/E1 **Nur** (mts.), Turk.
114/B2 **Nura** (riv.), Kaz.
105/G4 **Nūrābād**, Iran
100/G5 **Nurata**, Uzb.
69/F3 **Nürburgring**, Ger.
86/C3 **Nure** (riv.), It.
206/B2 **Nuremberg**, Pa,US
104/D2 **Nurhak**, Turk.
158/C2 **Nuri**, Mex.
147/F5 **Nuri** (ruins), Sudan
84/D3 **Nuria** (peak), It.
133/H5 **Nuriootpa**, Austl.
107/L2 **Nūrla**, India
95/L5 **Nurlat**, Rus.
122/C2 **Nūrmahal**, India
63/L1 **Nurmijärvi**, Fin.
70/E4 **Nürnberg**, Ger.
70/E4 **Nürnberg** (int'l arpt.), Ger.
120/B1 **Nūrpur**, India
135/C1 **Nurri** (peak), Austl.
189/F3 **Nursery**, Tx,US
70/C5 **Nürtingen**, Ger.
86/A1 **Nus**, It.
124/F5 **Nusa Barung Nat'l Rsv.**, Indo.
150/C2 **Nūsah**, Yem.
116/C2 **Nu** (Salween) (riv.), China
130/A2 **Nusa Tenggara Timur** (prov.), Indo.
104/D2 **Nusaybin**, Turk.
105/G3 **Nūshābād**, Iran
177/G4 **Nushagak** (riv.), Ak,US
107/J3 **Nushki**, Pak.
54/C5 **Nutberry** (hill), Sc,UK
69/E2 **Nuth**, Neth.
72/C4 **Nuthe** (riv.), Ger.
72/D3 **Nuthe** (riv.), Ger.
72/D3 **Nuthe-Graben** (riv.), Ger.
194/C1 **Nut Lake Ind. Res.**, Sk,Can
207/D2 **Nutley**, NJ,US
187/H4 **Nutrioso**, Az,US
196/F3 **Nuttby** (mtn.), NS,Can
130/D3 **Nutwood Downs**, Austl.
176/M3 **Nuuk** (Godthåb), Grld.
139/X15 **Nuupere** (pt.), FrPol.
86/B1 **Nuvolento**, It.
120/D1 **Nuwākot**, Nepal
147/G2 **Nuwaybi'**, Egypt
156/L10 **Nuy** (riv.), SAfr.
155/G3 **Nuza** (peak), Zim.
81/F3 **Nüziders**, Aus.
148/A4 **Nwa**, Camr.
154/E3 **Nxai Pan** (salt pan), Bots.
154/E3 **Nxai Pan Nat'l Park**, Bots.
154/D3 **Nxaunxau**, Bots.
104/D5 **Nyaake**, Libr.
132/C5 **Nyabing**, Austl.
153/G3 **Nyabisindu**, Rwa.
207/E1 **Nyack**, NY,US
153/G3 **Nya-Ghezi**, Zaire
133/J5 **Nyah**, Austl.
151/A3 **Nyahua**, Tanz.
151/B1 **Nyahururu Falls**, Kenya
135/B2 **Nyah West**, Austl.
116/B2 **Nyainqêntanglha** (mts.), China
114/F5 **Nyainqêntanglha Feng** (peak), China
116/B1 **Nyainrong**, China
151/A2 **Nyakabindi**, Tanz.
153/G3 **Nyakanyasi**, Tanz.
155/G1 **Nyaka Nat'l Park**, Malw.
145/E5 **Nyakrom**, Gha.
95/P3 **Nyaksimvol'**, Rus.
154/D2 **Nyakulenga**, Zam.
149/E2 **Nyala**, Sudan
121/E1 **Nyalam**, China
151/A2 **Nyalikungu**, Tanz.
155/F3 **Nyamandhlovu**, Zim.
155/G3 **Nyamapande**, Zim.
151/A2 **Nyambiti**, Tanz.
143/D3 **Nyamina**, Mali
149/F3 **Nyamlell**, Sudan
151/B4 **Nyamtumbo**, Tanz.
94/J3 **Nyandoma**, Rus.
121/G1 **Nyang** (riv.), China
152/B3 **Nyanga** (riv.), Congo, Gabon
152/B3 **Nyanga**, Gabon
152/B3 **Nyanga** (prov.), Gabon
152/B3 **Nyanga-Nord Rsv.**, Congo, Gabon
155/G3 **Nyangui** (peak), Zim.
155/G3 **Nyanyadzi**, Zim.
151/A2 **Nyanza** (prov.), Kenya
153/G4 **Nyanza-Lac**, Buru.
151/B3 **Nyanzwa**, Tanz.
140/F6 **Nyasa** (Malawi) (lake), Afr.
123/B2 **Nyaunglebin**, Burma
95/N4 **Nyazepetrovsk**, Rus.
155/G3 **Nyazura**, Zim.
62/E1 **Nybergsund**, Nor.
64/F1 **Nyborg**, Den.
61/J1 **Nyborg**, Nor.
62/F3 **Nybro**, Swe.
121/H1 **Nyêmo**, China
145/E5 **Nyenasi**, Gha.
73/C4 **Nyergesújfalu**, Hun.
151/B2 **Nyeri**, Kenya
149/G3 **Nyerol**, Sudan
116/D1 **Nyikog** (riv.), China
114/E5 **Nyima**, China
155/F2 **Nyimba**, Zam.
92/F2 **Nyírábrány**, Hun.
65/L5 **Nyíradony**, Hun.
92/F2 **Nyírbátor**, Hun.
92/E2 **Nyíregyháza**, Hun.
92/F2 **Nyírmada**, Hun.
151/B1 **Nyiru** (peak), Kenya
62/C3 **Nykøbing**, Den.
62/D4 **Nykøbing**, Den.
62/G2 **Nyköping**, Swe.
63/R7 **Nykvarn**, Swe.
57/C5 **Nylrivier** (riv.), SAfr.
156/E2 **Nylstroom**, SAfr.
135/C2 **Nymagee**, Austl.
62/G2 **Nynäshamn**, Swe.
135/C1 **Nyngan**, Austl.
114/C5 **Nyoma Rap**, India
80/C5 **Nyon**, Swi.
148/A5 **Nyong** (riv.), Camr.
82/B4 **Nyons**, Fr.
71/G3 **Nýřany**, Czh.
95/N3 **Nyrob**, Rus.
71/G4 **Nýrsko**, Czh.
71/G4 **Nýrsko, Údolní nádrž** (res.), Czh.
65/J3 **Nysa**, Pol.
184/E2 **Nyssa**, Or,US
62/D4 **Nysted**, Den.
112/A4 **Nyūdō-zaki** (pt.), Japan
94/F2 **Nyuk** (lake), Rus.
95/K3 **Nyukhcha**, Rus.
95/K3 **Nyuksenitsa**, Rus.
95/K3 **Nyúl**, Hun.
153/G4 **Nyunzu**, Zaire
101/M3 **Nyurba**, Rus.
95/L3 **Nyuvchim**, Rus.
111/E2 **Nyūzen**, Japan
151/A3 **Nzega**, Tanz.
144/C5 **Nzérékoré**, Gui.
144/C4 **Nzérékoré** (comm.), Gui.
148/D4 **Nzeret**, Zaire
152/C4 **N'zeto**, Ang.
144/D5 **Nzi** (riv.), IvC.

**O**

112/A3 **Ō** (isl.), Japan
59/E1 **Oadby**, Eng,UK
194/D4 **Oahe** (res.), ND, SD,US
192/D1 **Oahe** (dam), SD,US
139/K2 **Oahu** (isl.), Hi,US
180/S10 **Oahu** (isl.), Hi,US
194/F3 **Oakbank**, Mb,Can
196/B5 **Oak Bluffs**, Ma,US
194/D2 **Oakburn**, Mb,Can
185/K3 **Oak Creek**, Co,US
205/Q14 **Oak Creek**, Wi,US
186/B2 **Oakdale**, Ca,US
208/B3 **Oakdale**, Ct,US
202/B2 **Oakdale**, La,US
208/C1 **Oakdale**, Ma,US
195/G7 **Oakdale**, Mn,US
208/G7 **Oakdale**, Pa,US
194/E4 **Oakes**, ND,US
182/F4 **Oakesdale**, Wa,US
134/C4 **Oakey**, Austl.
196/C2 **Oakfield**, Me,US
205/Q16 **Oak Forest**, Il,US
191/H2 **Oak Grove**, Ar,US
185/K4 **Oak Grove**, Co,US
200/D2 **Oak Grove**, Ky,US
189/J1 **Oak Grove**, La,US
200/D2 **Oak Grove**, Tn,US
200/B2 **Oak Grove Heights**, Ar,US
59/F1 **Oakham**, Eng,UK
208/B1 **Oakham**, Ma,US
198/E4 **Oak Harbor**, Oh,US
182/C3 **Oak Harbor**, Wa,US
203/H3 **Oak Hill**, Fl,US
198/C2 **Oak Hill**, Mi,US
198/E5 **Oak Hill**, Oh,US
200/D2 **Oak Hill**, Tn,US
201/G2 **Oak Hill**, WV,US
186/C2 **Oakhurst**, Ca,US
208/G2 **Oakhurst**, Ok,US
191/F2 **Oakhurst**, Ok,US
194/D3 **Oak Lake**, Mb,Can
205/K11 **Oakland**, Ca,US
202/M6 **Oakland**, Fl,US
198/B5 **Oakland**, Il,US
206/B5 **Oakland**, Md,US
196/C3 **Oakland**, Me,US
205/F6 **Oakland** (co.), Mi,US
205/F6 **Oakland** (lake), Mi,US
191/H2 **Oakland**, Mo,US
193/F3 **Oakland**, Ne,US
207/D1 **Oakland**, NJ,US
184/B2 **Oakland**, Or,US
199/J4 **Oakland**, Pa,US
205/A3 **Oakland** (bay), Wa,US
200/D1 **Oakland City**, In,US
202/P7 **Oakland Park**, Fl,US
135/C2 **Oaklands**, Austl.
205/Q16 **Oak Lawn**, Il,US
59/E3 **Oakley**, Eng,UK
59/E2 **Oakley**, Eng,UK
205/L11 **Oakley**, Ca,US
185/G2 **Oakley**, Id,US
190/D1 **Oakley**, Ks,US
200/B4 **Oakley**, Ms,US
185/H3 **Oakley**, Ut,US
208/H6 **Oakmont**, Pa,US
132/D2 **Oakover** (riv.), Austl.
201/F4 **Oak Park**, Ga,US
205/Q16 **Oak Park**, Il,US
205/F7 **Oak Park**, Mi,US
191/J4 **Oak Ridge**, La,US
206/D1 **Oak Ridge**, NJ,US
200/E2 **Oak Ridge**, Tn,US
197/S8 **Oak Ridges**, On,Can
194/D2 **Oak River**, Mb,Can
58/D3 **Oaksey**, Eng,UK
204/B1 **Oaks, The**, Ca,US
198/C5 **Oaktown**, In,US
204/A2 **Oak View**, Ca,US
194/F3 **Oakville**, Mb,Can
199/G3 **Oakville**, On,Can
208/A2 **Oakville**, Ct,US
191/J1 **Oakville**, Mo,US
200/F3 **Oakwood**, Ga,US
189/G2 **Oakwood**, Tx,US
201/F2 **Oakwood**, Va,US
205/P15 **Oakwood Hills**, Il,US
136/B4 **Oamaru**, N.Z.
55/H9 **Oa, Mull of** (pt.), Sc,UK
157/G6 **Oani**, Com.
204/B2 **Oat** (mtn.), Ca,US
204/E7 **Oat** (mtn.), Ca,US
135/C4 **Oatlands**, Austl.
186/E3 **Oatman**, Az,US
160/B2 **Oaxaca**, Mex.
160/B2 **Oaxaca** (state), Mex.
176/H8 **Oaxaca de Juárez**, Mex.
100/H3 **Ob'** (gulf), Rus.
114/D1 **Ob'** (riv.), Rus.
138/F6 **Oba** (isl.), Van.
148/A4 **Obala**, Camr.
188/D4 **Oballos**, Mex.
110/D3 **Obama**, Japan
145/H5 **Oban** (hills), Camr., Nga.
136/B4 **Oban**, N.Z.
55/J8 **Oban**, Sc,UK
112/B4 **Obanazawa**, Japan
167/K7 **Obando**, Col.
111/N9 **Obara**, Japan
111/M10 **Obata**, Japan
153/F3 **Obaya**, Zaire
182/F1 **Obed**, Ab,Can
63/L4 **Obelia**, Lith.
136/B4 **Obelisk** (peak), N.Z.
173/F3 **Oberá**, Arg.
81/E4 **Oberalppass** (pass), Swi.
81/E4 **Oberalpstock** (peak), Swi.
81/H2 **Oberammergau**, Ger.
70/D4 **Oberasbach**, Ger.
81/H2 **Oberau**, Ger.
69/G6 **Oberbetschdorf**, Fr.
80/D3 **Oberburg**, Swi.
70/B4 **Oberderdingen**, Ger.
80/D4 **Oberdiessbach**, Swi.
71/E6 **Oberding**, Ger.
80/D3 **Oberdorf**, Swi.
67/H6 **Oberdorla**, Ger.
70/D2 **Oberelsbach**, Ger.
80/E3 **Oberentfelden**, Swi.
81/E3 **Oberglatt**, Swi.
81/G2 **Obergünzburg**, Ger.
71/E6 **Oberhaching**, Ger.
66/D6 **Oberhausen**, Ger.
70/B5 **Oberkirch**, Ger.
70/D5 **Oberkochen**, Ger.
71/E2 **Oberkotzau**, Ger.
72/D5 **Oberlausitz** (reg.), Ger.
190/D1 **Oberlin**, Ks,US
202/B2 **Oberlin**, La,US
208/E5 **Oberlin**, Oh,US
72/C6 **Oberlungwitz**, Ger.
80/D1 **Obernai**, Fr.
70/C3 **Obernburg am Main**, Ger.
70/B6 **Oberndorf am Neckar**, Ger.
71/F7 **Oberndorf bei Salzburg**, Aus.
71/H6 **Oberneukirchen**, Aus.
67/G4 **Obernkirchen**, Ger.
69/H4 **Ober-Olm**, Ger.
135/D2 **Oberon**, Austl.
71/F3 **Oberpfälzer Wald** (for.), Ger.
73/A5 **Oberpullendorf**, Aus.
70/B3 **Ober Ramstadt**, Ger.
81/E3 **Oberrieden**, Swi.
81/F3 **Oberriet**, Swi.
72/B5 **Oberröblingen**, Ger.
81/F4 **Obersaxen**, Swi.
71/E6 **Oberschleissheim**, Ger.
71/F5 **Oberschneiding**, Ger.
73/A5 **Oberschützen**, Aus.
81/E3 **Obersiggenthal**, Swi.
81/E2 **Oberstammheim**, Swi.
81/G3 **Oberstaufen**, Ger.
81/G3 **Oberstdorf**, Ger.
69/G4 **Oberthal**, Ger.
71/G7 **Obertrum am See**, Aus.
70/B2 **Obertshausen**, Ger.
72/D1 **Oberückersee** (lake), Ger.
70/B2 **Oberursel**, Ger.
81/F3 **Oberuzwil**, Swi.
71/F4 **Oberviechtach**, Ger.
81/E4 **Oberwald**, Swi.
73/A5 **Oberwart**, Aus.
72/B6 **Oberweissbach**, Ger.
70/A2 **Oberwesel**, Ger.
80/D4 **Oberwil**, Swi.
75/L3 **Oberwölz**, Aus.
81/E3 **Obfelden**, Swi.
72/B5 **Obhausen**, Ger.
127/G4 **Obi** (isl.), Indo.
127/G4 **Obi** (isls.), Indo.
127/G4 **Obi** (str.), Indo.
145/G5 **Obiaruku**, Nga.
166/C3 **Óbidos**, Braz.
76/A3 **Óbidos**, Port.
112/C2 **Obihiro**, Japan
92/E4 **Obilić**, Yugo.
71/F7 **Obing**, Ger.
200/C2 **Obion**, Tn,US
200/C2 **Obion** (riv.), Tn,US
112/B1 **Obira**, Japan
99/H4 **Obitochnaya** (bay), Ukr.
111/J7 **Obitsu** (riv.), Japan
99/M3 **Oblivskaya**, Rus.
198/C5 **Oblong**, Il,US
123/B2 **Ob Luang Gorge**, Thai.
109/L2 **Obluch'ye**, Rus.
94/H5 **Obninsk**, Rus.
149/E4 **Obo**, CAfr.
108/B4 **Obo**, China
153/F3 **Obokote**, Zaire
114/F4 **Obo Liang**, China
145/G5 **Obolo**, Nga.
65/J2 **Oborniki**, Pol.
65/J3 **Oborniki Śląskie**, Pol.
152/C3 **Obouya**, Congo
99/J2 **Oboyan'**, Rus.
94/J3 **Obozerskiy**, Rus.
65/J2 **Obra** (riv.), Pol.
92/E3 **Obrenovac**, Yugo.
92/E4 **Obrež**, Yugo.
184/B2 **O'Brien**, Or,US
67/E4 **O'Briensbridge**, Ire.
70/C3 **Obrigheim**, Ger.
71/G7 **Obtrumer See** (lake), Aus.
111/M10 **Ōbu**, Japan
145/E5 **Obuasi**, Gha.
145/H5 **Obubra**, Nga.
145/H5 **Obudu**, Nga.
98/F2 **Obukhov**, Ukr.
131/G1 **Obura**, PNG
81/E4 **Obwalden** (demi-canton), Swi.
93/H4 **Obzor**, Bul.
203/G3 **Ocala**, Fl,US
158/C2 **Ocampo**, Mex.
158/E3 **Ocampo**, Mex.
159/F4 **Ocampo**, Mex.
164/C2 **Ocaña**, Col.
76/D3 **Ocaña**, Sp.
74/C5 **Occabe, Sommet d'** (peak), Fr.
86/B1 **Occhieppo Inferiore**, It.
86/B1 **Occhieppo Superiore**, It.
87/E3 **Occhiobello**, It.
85/E4 **Occhito** (lake), It.
172/B1 **Occidental, Cordillera** (range), Chile, Peru
164/B3 **Occidental, Cordillera** (range), Col., Ecu.
168/B2 **Occidental, Cordillera** (range), Ecu., Peru
86/B2 **Occimiano**, It.
177/L4 **Ocean** (cape), Ak,US
203/H4 **Ocean** (can.), Fl,US
206/D4 **Ocean** (co.), NJ,US
201/G2 **Oceana**, WV,US
201/J2 **Oceana Nav. Air Sta.**, Va,US
207/E2 **Ocean Beach**, NY,US
201/K1 **Ocean City**, Md,US
206/D5 **Ocean City**, NJ,US
178/D3 **Ocean Falls**, BC,Can
207/D4 **Ocean Gate**, NJ,US
208/C2 **Ocean Grove**, Ma,US
207/D3 **Ocean Grove**, NJ,US
138/* **Oceania**
186/B3 **Oceano**, Ca,US
182/B4 **Ocean Park**, Wa,US
201/K1 **Ocean Pines**, Md,US
202/P6 **Ocean Ridge**, Fl,US
204/C4 **Oceanside**, Ca,US
207/E2 **Oceanside**, NY,US
201/K1 **Ocean View**, De,US
206/D5 **Ocean View**, NJ,US
206/D5 **Oceanville**, NJ,US
123/D4 **Oc-Eo, Ancient City of** (ruins), Viet.
188/D2 **O. C. Fisher** (lake), Tx,US
98/F4 **Ochakov**, Ukr.
97/G4 **Ochamchira**, Geo.
194/C2 **Ochapowace Ind. Res.**, Sk,Can
191/G2 **Ochelata**, Ok,US
182/G1 **O'Chiese Ind. Res.**, Ab,Can
112/D2 **Ochiishi-misaki** (cape), Japan
54/C4 **Ochil** (hills), Sc,UK
203/F2 **Ochlocknee**, Ga,US
203/F2 **Ochlockonee** (riv.), Fl,US
145/G5 **Ochobo**, Nga.
203/H5 **Ochopee**, Fl,US
70/D3 **Ochsenfurt**, Ger.
70/C6 **Ochsenhausen**, Ger.
81/F3 **Ochsenkopf** (peak), Aus.
69/G3 **Ochtendung**, Ger.
67/E4 **Ochtrup**, Ger.
67/F2 **Ochtum** (riv.), Ger.
203/G2 **Ocilla**, Ga,US
59/E3 **Ock** (riv.), Eng,UK
62/G1 **Ockelbo**, Swe.
70/A3 **Ockenheim**, Ger.
203/H2 **Ocklawaha**, Fl,US
201/F5 **Ocmulgee** (riv.), Ga,US
201/F4 **Ocmulgee Nat'l Mon.**, Ga,US
93/F2 **Ocna Mureș**, Rom.
93/G3 **Ocna Sibiului**, Rom.
93/G3 **Ocnele Mari**, Rom.
202/M6 **Ocoee**, Fl,US
203/H3 **Ocoee**, Fl,US
168/C5 **Ocoña**, Peru
168/C4 **Ocoña** (riv.), Peru
201/F4 **Oconee** (lake), Ga,US
201/F4 **Oconee** (riv.), Ga,US
198/B3 **Oconomowoc**, Wi,US
193/L1 **Oconto**, Wi,US
195/K5 **Oconto** (riv.), Wi,US
198/B2 **Oconto** (riv.), Wi,US
193/K1 **Oconto Falls**, Wi,US
162/D3 **Ocos** (bay), DRep.
160/C2 **Ocosingo**, Mex.
182/B4 **Ocosta**, Wa,US
160/E3 **Ocotal**, Nic.
160/B2 **Ocotlán de Morelos**, Mex.
201/K3 **Ocracoke**, NC,US
168/B3 **Ocros**, Peru
206/B4 **Octararo** (cr.), Pa,US
74/C2 **Octeville**, Fr.
78/F1 **Octeville-sur-Mer**, Fr.
101/L1 **October Revolution** (isl.), Rus.
167/N7 **Ocumare de la Costa**, Ven.
165/E2 **Ocumare del Tuy**, Ven.
172/C1 **Ocurí**, Bol.
145/E5 **Oda**, Gha.
110/C3 **Oda**, Japan
106/C4 **Oda** (peak), Sudan
61/P7 **Ódádhahraun** (lava flow), Ice.
113/E2 **Ŏdaejin**, NKor.
113/E4 **Odaesan Nat'l Park**, SKor.
111/M10 **Ōdai**, Japan
110/E3 **Ōdaigahara-san** (mtn.), Japan
147/H4 **Oda, Jabal** (peak), Sudan
63/T8 **Ödåkra**, Swe.
195/J4 **Odanah**, Wi,US
112/B3 **Ōdate**, Japan
111/F3 **Odawara**, Japan
62/B1 **Odda**, Nor.
62/D4 **Odder**, Den.
150/B4 **Oddur** (Xuddur), Som.
193/G2 **Odebolt**, Ia,US
67/F6 **Odeborn** (riv.), Ger.
198/B4 **Odell**, Il,US
182/D5 **Odell**, Or,US
190/E3 **Odell**, Tx,US
72/D6 **Odelzhausen**, Ger.
189/F4 **Odem**, Tx,US
76/A4 **Odemira**, Port.
104/A2 **Ödemiş**, Turk.
156/D2 **Odendaalsrus**, SAfr.
62/D4 **Odense**, Den.
62/D4 **Odense** (int'l arpt.), Den.
67/E6 **Odenthal**, Ger.
206/B5 **Odenton**, Md,US
72/E2 **Oderberg**, Ger.
72/E2 **Oderbruch** (marsh), Ger.
82/C2 **Oderen**, Fr.
65/H2 **Oderhaff** (lag.), Ger., Pol.
72/D2 **Oder-Havel** (can.), Ger.
65/H2 **Oder** (Odra) (riv.), Ger., Pol.
72/D3 **Oder-Spree** (can.), Ger.
87/F1 **Oderzo**, It.
98/F4 **Odessa**, Ukr.
206/C5 **Odessa**, De,US
202/K7 **Odessa**, Fl,US
194/F5 **Odessa**, Mn,US
199/H3 **Odessa**, NY,US
188/C2 **Odessa**, Tx,US
182/E4 **Odessa**, Wa,US
206/C5 **Odessa, Hist. Homes of**, De,US
188/C2 **Odessa Meteor** (crater), Tx,US
98/E4 **Odessa Obl.**, Ukr.
78/B4 **Odet** (riv.), Fr.
144/D4 **Odienné**, IvC.
182/E2 **Odin** (mtn.), BC,Can
200/C1 **Odin**, Il,US
191/E1 **Odin**, Ks,US
94/H5 **Odintsovo**, Rus.
125/C2 **Odiongan**, Phil.
77/P10 **Odivelas**, Port.
93/H3 **Odobești**, Rom.
79/E2 **Odon** (riv.), Fr.
198/C5 **Odon**, In,US
123/D4 **Odongk**, Camb.
188/D1 **O'Donnell**, Tx,US
197/L2 **O'Donnells**, Nf,Can
66/D3 **Odoorn**, Neth.
98/C4 **Odorheiu**, Rom.
93/G2 **Odorheiu Secuiesc**, Rom.
65/H2 **Odra** (Oder) (riv.), Ger., Pol.
203/G2 **Odum**, Ga,US
92/D3 **Odžaci**, Yugo.
152/C2 **Odzala Nat'l Park**, Congo
155/G3 **Odzi**, Zim.
155/G3 **Odzi** (riv.), Zim.
152/B3 **Odziba**, Congo
111/L9 **Ōe**, Japan
72/A3 **Oebisfelde**, Ger.
72/D6 **Oederan**, Ger.
66/B4 **Oegstgeest**, Neth.
167/F4 **Oeiras**, Braz.
67/F5 **Oelde**, Ger.
166/C2 **Oelemari** (riv.), Sur.
192/C2 **Oelrichs**, SD,US
72/D6 **Oelsa**, Ger.
71/F2 **Oelsnitz**, Ger.
193/J2 **Oelwein**, Ia,US
139/M7 **Oeno** (isl.), Pitc.,UK
130/D3 **Oenpelli**, Austl.
80/D3 **Oensingen**, Swi.
67/E5 **Oer-Erkenschwick**, Ger.
70/D2 **Oerlenbach**, Ger.
69/E4 **Oesling** (mts.), Lux.
66/B6 **Oesterdam** (dam), Neth.
70/B3 **Oestrich-Winkel**, Ger.
91/H3 **Oeta Nat'l Park**, Gre.
81/G3 **Oetz**, Aus.
104/E1 **Of**, Turk.
200/C4 **Ofahoma**, Ms,US
194/B4 **O'Fallon** (cr.), Mt,US
85/F5 **Ofanto** (riv.), It.
103/D4 **Ofaqim**, Isr.
81/E5 **Ofenhorn** (Punta d'Arbola) (peak), Swi.
81/G4 **Ofenpass** (Fuorn) (pass), Swi.
145/G4 **Offa**, Nga.
60/C3 **Offaly** (co.), Ire.
86/C2 **Offanengo**, It.
80/C2 **Offement**, Fr.
70/B2 **Offenbach**, Ger.
70/A6 **Offenburg**, Ger.
192/E5 **Offerle**, Ks,US
203/G2 **Offerman**, Ga,US
85/D2 **Offida**, It.
70/D6 **Offingen**, Ger.
152/B3 **Offoué** (riv.), Gabon
152/B3 **Offoué Integrated Rsv.**, Gabon
79/F1 **Offranville**, Fr.
70/B3 **Offstein**, Ger.
193/G3 **Offutt A.F.B.**, Ne,US
75/F1 **Oftersheim**, Ger.
75/G3 **Oftringen**, Swi.
112/B4 **Ōfunato**, Japan
112/A4 **Oga**, Japan
112/A4 **Oga** (pen.), Japan
112/B4 **Ogachi**, Japan
150/B4 **Ogadēn** (reg.), Eth.
110/E3 **Ōgaki**, Japan
192/D3 **Ogallala**, Ne,US
138/D2 **Ogasawara**, Japan
112/A3 **Ogata**, Japan
112/B4 **Ogatsu**, Japan
112/B3 **Ogawara** (lake), Japan
145/G4 **Ogbomosho**, Nga.
191/G4 **Ogden**, Ar,US
193/G2 **Ogden**, Ia,US
191/F1 **Ogden**, Ks,US
185/H3 **Ogden**, Ut,US
206/D1 **Ogdensburg**, NJ,US
199/J2 **Ogdensburg**, NY,US
201/G4 **Ogeechee** (riv.), Ga,US
194/B3 **Ogema**, Sk,Can
86/C1 **Oggiono**, It.
111/F2 **Ogi**, Japan
179/H4 **Ogidaki** (mtn.), Can.
156/E2 **Ogies**, SAfr.
177/L3 **Ogilvie** (mts.), Yk,Can
178/C2 **Ogilvie** (riv.), Yk,Can
195/H5 **Ogilvie**, Mn,US
192/C2 **Oglala**, SD,US
192/C2 **Oglala Nat'l Grsld.**, Ne,US
97/K5 **Oglanly**, Trkm.
193/K3 **Oglesby**, Il,US
159/F2 **Oglesby**, Tx,US
200/E4 **Oglethorpe**, Ga,US
86/D2 **Oglio** (riv.), It.
134/C3 **Ogmore**, Austl.
58/C4 **Ogmore by Sea**, Wal,UK
80/B3 **Ognon** (riv.), Fr.
127/F3 **Ogoamas** (peak), Indo.
109/L1 **Ogodzha**, Rus.
145/H5 **Ogoja**, Nga.
152/B3 **Ogooué** (riv.), Congo, Gabon
152/C2 **Ogooué-Ivindo** (prov.), Gabon
152/C3 **Ogooué-Lolo** (prov.), Gabon
152/B3 **Ogooué-Maritime** (prov.), Gabon
94/G3 **Ogorelyshi**, Rus.
111/H7 **Ogose**, Japan
93/F4 **Ogosta** (riv.), Bul.
149/E2 **Ogr**, Sudan
63/L3 **Ogre**, Lat.
111/M9 **Oguchi**, Japan
92/B3 **Ogulin**, Cro.
145/F5 **Ogun** (riv.), Nga.
145/F5 **Ogun** (state), Nga.
97/K5 **Ogurchinskiy** (isl.), Trkm.
145/G5 **Ogurugu**, Nga.
104/D2 **Oğuz**, Turk.
145/G5 **Ogwashi Uku**, Nga.
145/G5 **Ohafia**, Nga.
136/A4 **Ohai**, N.Z.
136/C2 **Ohakune**, N.Z.
143/H3 **Ohanet**, Alg.
134/G8 **O'Hares** (cr.), Austl.
112/B3 **Ōhata**, Japan
136/B4 **Ohau** (lake), N.Z.
67/E2 **Ohe** (riv.), Ger.
67/E2 **Ohey**, Belg.
175/J7 **O'Higgins** (lake), Chile
208/G7 **Ohio** (riv.), US
181/K3 **Ohio** (state), US
190/C3 **Ohio**, Co,US
198/E4 **Ohio Caverns**, Oh,US
208/G6 **Ohioville**, Pa,US
71/G7 **Ohlsdorf**, Aus.
81/H2 **Ohlstadt**, Ger.
70/C1 **Ohm** (riv.), Ger.
57/F1 **Oh Me Edge** (hill), Eng,UK
201/F4 **Ohoopee** (riv.), Ga,US
154/B3 **Ohopoho**, Namb.
72/A6 **Ohrdruf**, Ger.
65/H3 **Ohře** (riv.), Czh.
71/H2 **Ohře** (riv.), Czh.
72/B3 **Ohre** (riv.), Ger.
92/E5 **Ohrid** (lake), Alb., Macd.
92/E5 **Ohrid**, Macd.
157/E2 **Ohrigstad**, SAfr.
136/C2 **Ohura**, N.Z.
116/C2 **Oi** (riv.), China
111/H7 **Ōi**, Japan
111/F3 **Ōi** (riv.), Japan
166/C2 **Oiapoque**, Braz.
54/B2 **Oich, Loch** (lake), Sc,UK
77/P10 **Oieiras**, Port.
121/J1 **Oiga**, China
68/B3 **Oignies**, Fr.
80/B5 **Oignin** (riv.), Fr.
208/H4 **Oil** (cr.), Pa,US
190/C4 **Oil Center**, NM,US
189/H1 **Oil City**, La,US
208/H5 **Oil City**, Pa,US
186/C3 **Oildale**, Ca,US
183/J3 **Oilmont**, Mt,US
91/H3 **Oinófita**, Gre.
91/H3 **Oinoí**, Gre.
78/D3 **Oir** (riv.), Fr.
66/C5 **Oirschot**, Neth.
53/T9 **Oise** (dept.), Fr.
53/S9 **Oise** (riv.), Fr.
68/C5 **Oise à l'Aisne, Canal de** (can.), Fr.
68/A4 **Oisemont**, Fr.
111/H7 **Ōiso**, Japan
79/G2 **Oissel**, Fr.
66/C5 **Oisterwijk**, Neth.
68/C3 **Oisy-le-Verger**, Fr.
110/B4 **Ōita**, Japan
110/B4 **Ōita** (arpt.), Japan
110/B4 **Ōita** (pref.), Japan
110/B4 **Ōita** (riv.), Japan
121/G1 **Oiyug**, China
204/A2 **Ojai**, Ca,US
65/K3 **Ojcowski Nat'l Park**, Pol.
61/G2 **Ojebyn**, Swe.
111/L10 **Ōji**, Japan
188/B3 **Ojinaga**, Mex.
111/F2 **Ojiya**, Japan
158/E4 **Ojocaliente**, Mex.
190/A2 **Ojo Caliente**, NM,US
188/A3 **Ojo de Laguna**, Mex.
158/B3 **Ojo de Liebre** (lag.), Mex.
161/G2 **Ojo del Toro** (peak), Cuba
172/B3 **Ojos del Salado** (peak), Arg.
163/C5 **Ojos del Salado** (peak), Chile
186/D5 **Ojos Negros**, Mex.
76/E2 **Ojos Negros**, Sp.
197/M7 **Oka**, Qu,Can
152/C3 **Oka**, Congo
145/G5 **Oka**, Nga.
53/H3 **Oka** (riv.), Rus.
131/E2 **Okaba**, Indo.
154/C4 **Okahandja**, Namb.
202/M6 **Okahumpka**, Fl,US
136/C1 **Okaihau**, N.Z.
197/M6 **Oka Ind. Res.**, Qu,Can
179/K3 **Okak** (isl.), Nf,Can
148/A4 **Okala**, Camr.
182/E2 **Okanagan** (lake), BC,Can
182/D3 **Okanagan** (range), BC,Can
182/E3 **Okanagan Falls**, BC,Can
152/B3 **Okanda Nat'l Park**, Gabon
152/B2 **Okano** (riv.), Gabon
182/E3 **Okanogan**, Wa,US
182/E3 **Okanogan** (riv.), Wa,US
131/G1 **Okapa**, PNG
154/C4 **Okaputa**, Namb.
122/B2 **Okāra**, Pak.
191/F3 **Okarche**, Ok,US
105/H2 **Okarem**, Trkm.
154/B3 **Okatana**, Namb.
202/D1 **Okatibbee** (lake), Ms,US
136/C2 **Okato**, N.Z.
154/C3 **Okaukuejo**, Namb.
154/D3 **Okavango** (riv.), Afr.
154/D3 **Okavango Delta** (reg.), Bots.
110/B4 **Ōkawa**, Japan
200/C1 **Okawville**, Il,US
191/G3 **Okay**, Ok,US
111/F2 **Okaya**, Japan
110/C3 **Okayama**, Japan
110/C3 **Okayama** (pref.), Japan
111/E3 **Okazaki**, Japan
154/C4 **Okazize**, Namb.
113/D4 **Okch'ŏn**, SKor.
205/L2 **Okęcie** (int'l arpt.), Pol.
203/H4 **Okeechobee**, Fl,US
203/H4 **Okeechobee** (lake), Fl,US
191/E2 **Okeene**, Ok,US
203/G2 **Okefenokee** (swamp), Ga,US
203/G2 **Okefenokee Heritage Ctr.**, Ga,US
203/G2 **Okefenokee Nat'l Wild. Ref.**, Ga,US
111/H7 **Okegawa**, Japan
58/C5 **Okehampton**, Eng,UK
145/F4 **Oke Iho**, Nga.
191/F3 **Okemah**, Ok,US
58/B5 **Okement** (riv.), Eng,UK
198/D3 **Okemos**, Mi,US
145/G5 **Okene**, Nga.
67/H4 **Oker** (riv.), Ger.
145/G5 **Okerembete**, Nga.
191/F2 **Okesa**, Ok,US
193/F4 **Oketo**, Ks,US
101/Q4 **Okha**, Rus.
121/F2 **Okhaldhunga**, Nepal
91/J3 **Ókhi** (peak), Gre.
101/Q4 **Okhotsk** (sea), Japan, Rus.
101/Q4 **Okhotsk**, Rus.
110/C2 **Oki** (arpt.), Japan
110/C2 **Oki** (isls.), Japan
110/C2 **Oki-Daisen Nat'l Park**, Japan
156/B3 **Okiep**, SAfr.
112/K7 **Okinawa** (isl.), Japan
112/J7 **Okinawa** (isls.), Japan
112/J8 **Okinawa** (pref.), Japan
112/K7 **Okinoerabu** (isl.), Japan
138/C2 **Okino-Tori-Shima** (Parece Vela) (isl.), Japan
145/G5 **Okitipupa**, Nga.
119/G4 **Okkan**, Burma
113/D5 **Okku**, SKor.
191/F3 **Oklahoma** (state), US
191/F3 **Oklahoma City** (cap.), Ok,US
191/G3 **Oklahoma High Top** (mtn.), Ok,US
190/E3 **Oklaunion**, Tx,US
203/H3 **Oklawaha** (riv.), Fl,US
191/G3 **Okmulgee**, Ok,US
93/H1 **Oknitsa**, Mol.
145/G5 **Oko**, Nga.
193/G2 **Okobaji** (lakes), Ia,US
192/D1 **Okobojo** (cr.), SD,US
151/A1 **Okok** (riv.), Ugan.
200/C3 **Okolona**, Ms,US
154/B3 **Okondeka**, Namb.
152/C3 **Okondja**, Gabon
112/C1 **Okoppe**, Japan
183/H2 **Okotoks**, Ab,Can
140/E6 **Okovango** (riv.), Afr.
147/G4 **Oko, Wādī** (dry riv.), Sudan
152/C3 **Okoyo**, Congo
62/C4 **Oksbøl**, Den.
95/M2 **Oksino**, Rus.
61/E2 **Oksskolten** (peak), Nor.
191/G3 **Oktaha**, Ok,US
97/H4 **Oktemberyan**, Arm.
123/B2 **Oktwin**, Burma
97/L2 **Oktyabr'sk**, Kaz.
97/J1 **Oktyabr'sk**, Rus.
108/A2 **Oktyabr'skiy**, Kaz.
109/K1 **Oktyabr'skiy**, Rus.
94/J3 **Oktyabr'skiy**, Rus.
95/M5 **Oktyabr'skiy**, Rus.
97/G3 **Oktyabr'skiy**, Rus.
97/K1 **Oktyabr'skiy**, Rus.
97/K1 **Oktyabr'skoye**, Rus.
99/H5 **Oktyabr'skoye**, Ukr.
110/B4 **Ōkuchi**, Japan
94/G4 **Okulovka**, Rus.
95/M2 **Okunev Nos**, Rus.
112/A2 **Okushiri**, Japan
112/A2 **Okushiri** (isl.), Japan
145/F4 **Okuta**, Nga.
111/H7 **Okutama**, Japan
154/D4 **Okwa** (dry riv.), Bots.
101/R4 **Ola**, Rus.
191/H3 **Ola**, Ar,US
201/M8 **Ola**, Ga,US
184/E1 **Ola**, Id,US
61/N6 **Ólafsfjördhur**, Ice.
61/M7 **Ólafsvík**, Ice.
63/K3 **Olaine**, Lat.
205/B3 **Olalla**, Wa,US
186/C2 **Olancha**, Ca,US
186/C2 **Olancha** (peak), Ca,US
160/E3 **Olanchito**, Hon.
62/G3 **Öland** (isl.), Swe.
62/G3 **Ölands norra udde** (pt.), Swe.
62/G3 **Ölands södra udde** (pt.), Swe.
82/C3 **Olan, Pic d'** (peak), Fr.
80/D2 **Olanto** (riv.), It.
133/J5 **Olary**, Austl.
185/K4 **Olathe**, Co,US
191/G1 **Olathe**, Ks,US
191/G1 **Olathe Nav. Air Sta.**, Ks,US
174/E3 **Olavarría**, Arg.
65/J3 **Oława**, Pol.
67/F5 **Ölbach** (riv.), Ger.
187/G4 **Olberg**, Az,US
72/D6 **Olbernhau**, Ger.
90/A2 **Olbia**, It.
81/H1 **Olching**, Ger.
199/G3 **Olcott**, NY,US
205/L11 **Old** (riv.), Ca,US
189/N9 **Old** (riv.), Tx,US
161/G1 **Old Bahama** (chan.), Bahm., Cuba
182/E3 **Old Baldy** (mtn.), Wa,US
135/E1 **Old Bar**, Austl.
59/G2 **Old Bedford** (can.), Eng,UK
207/M8 **Old Bethpage**, NY,US
207/D3 **Old Bridge**, NJ,US
88/B2 **Old Castile** (reg.), Sp.
60/C2 **Oldcastle**, Ire.
103/G8 **Old City**, Isr.
177/L2 **Old Crow**, Yk,Can
151/A2 **Oldeani**, Tanz.
151/A2 **Oldeani** (peak), Tanz.
66/C4 **Oldebroek**, Neth.
66/C3 **Oldemarkt**, Neth.
191/J2 **Olden**, Mo,US
189/E1 **Olden**, Tx,US
64/F1 **Oldenburg**, Ger.
67/F2 **Oldenburg**, Ger.
198/D5 **Oldenburg**, In,US
70/B3 **Oldenwald** (for.), Ger.
66/D4 **Oldenzaal**, Neth.
185/H1 **Old Faithful**, Wy,US
207/E2 **Old Field** (pt.), NY,US
199/J3 **Old Forge**, NY,US
199/J3 **Old Forge**, Pa,US
199/G3 **Old Fort Niagara**, NY,US
57/F4 **Oldham**, Eng,UK
177/H4 **Old Harbor**, Ak,US
200/D2 **Old Hickory** (lake), Tn,US
72/B5 **Oldisleben**, Ger.
60/C4 **Oldleighlin**, Ire.
208/B3 **Old Lyme**, Ct,US
183/G3 **Oldman** (riv.), Ab,Can
56/E3 **Old Man of Coolston, The** (mtn.), Eng,UK
55/N13 **Old Man of Hoy**, Sc,UK
206/C4 **Oldmans** (cr.), NJ,US
54/D2 **Oldmeldrum**, Sc,UK
205/Q15 **Old Mill Creek**, Il,US
208/C3 **Old Mystic**, Ct,US
59/F2 **Old Nene** (riv.), Eng,UK
207/E2 **Old Northport** (Northport), NY,US
151/B2 **Ol-Doinyo Sabuk Nat'l Park**, Kenya
67/F1 **Oldoog** (isl.), Ger.
197/L1 **Old Perlican**, Nf,Can
66/B4 **Old Rhine** (riv.), Neth.
183/G2 **Olds**, Ab,Can
208/B3 **Old Saybrook**, Ct,US
200/C2 **Old Shawneetown**, Il,US
202/K7 **Oldsmar**, Fl,US
199/L2 **Old Speck** (mtn.), Me,US
208/B1 **Old Sturbridge Village**, Ma,US
202/K8 **Old Tampa** (bay), Fl,US
207/K7 **Old Tappan**, NJ,US
203/G3 **Old Town**, Fl,US
196/C3 **Old Town**, Me,US
151/A2 **Olduvai** (gorge), Tanz.
206/D2 **Oldwick**, NJ,US
53/M7 **Old Windsor**, Eng,UK
194/A2 **Old Wives** (lake), Sk,Can
199/G3 **Olean**, NY,US
196/E2 **O'Leary**, PE,Can
65/M1 **Olecko**, Pol.
86/B1 **Oleggio**, It.
76/B3 **Oleiros**, Port.
76/A1 **Oleiros**, Sp.
101/N4 **Olekma** (riv.), Rus.
101/N3 **Olëkminsk**, Rus.
205/B2 **Olele** (pt.), Wa,US
165/H4 **Olemari** (riv.), Sur.
62/A2 **Ølen**, Nor.
94/G1 **Olenegorsk**, Rus.
101/M3 **Olënek**, Rus.
101/N2 **Olenek** (bay), Rus.
101/N2 **Olenëk** (riv.), Rus.
94/G2 **Olenitsa**, Rus.
99/J4 **Olenovka**, Ukr.
198/E4 **Olentangy** (riv.), Oh,US
114/B1 **Olenty** (riv.), Kaz.
74/C4 **Oléron** (isl.), Fr.
77/K6 **Olesa de Montserrat**, Sp.
98/C3 **Olesko**, Ukr.
65/J3 **Oleśnica**, Pol.
65/K3 **Olesno**, Pol.
84/D4 **Olevano Romano**, It.
98/D2 **Olevsk**, Ukr.
206/C3 **Oley**, Pa,US
67/E5 **Olfen**, Ger.
133/F3 **Olga** (peak), Austl.
109/M3 **Ol'ga**, Rus.
86/C1 **Olginate**, It.
99/K5 **Ol'ginka**, Rus.
108/B2 **Olgiy**, Mong.
62/C4 **Ølgod**, Den.
76/B4 **Olhão**, Port.
171/F1 **Olho d'Água das Flores**, Braz.
75/L4 **Olib** (isl.), Cro.
90/A2 **Oliena**, It.
154/C4 **Olifants** (dry riv.), Namb.
156/B3 **Olifants** (riv.), SAfr.
156/P12 **Olifantshoek**, SAfr.
156/E2 **Olifantsrivier** (riv.), SAfr.
138/D4 **Olimarao** (isl.), Micr.
91/G4 **Olimbía** (Olympia) (ruins), Gre.
89/K4 **Ólimbos**, Gre.
91/H2 **Ólimbos** (Mount Olympus) (peak), Gre.
170/C4 **Olímpia**, Braz.
104/B2 **Olimpos Beydağları Nat'l Park**, Turk.
159/F5 **Olinalá**, Mex.
167/H5 **Olinda**, Braz.
155/H3 **Olinda** (pt.), Moz.
184/B3 **Olinda**, Ca,US
171/F1 **Olindina**, Braz.
95/M5 **Olinskiy**, Rus.
174/E2 **Oliva**, Arg.
77/E3 **Oliva**, Sp.
76/B3 **Oliva de la Frontera**, Sp.
76/A3 **Olivais**, Port.
172/B4 **Olivares, Cerro de** (peak), Chile
183/M5 **Olive**, Mt,US
200/C2 **Olive Branch**, Il,US
200/C3 **Olive Branch**, Ms,US
201/F1 **Olive Hill**, Ky,US
184/C4 **Olivehurst**, Ca,US
170/D4 **Oliveira**, Braz.
76/B3 **Olivenza**, Sp.
182/E3 **Oliver**, BC,Can
203/F1 **Oliver** (dam), Al,US
200/E4 **Oliver** (lake), Al, Ga,US
188/K6 **Oliver** (cr.), Tx,US
195/H4 **Oliver**, Wi,US
174/E2 **Oliveros**, Arg.
200/E2 **Oliver Springs**, Tn,US
79/G5 **Olivet**, Fr.
192/F2 **Olivet**, SD,US
195/G5 **Olivia**, Mn,US
81/E4 **Olivone**, Swi.
99/K2 **Ol'khovatka**, Rus.
202/B2 **Olla**, La,US
168/D4 **Ollachea**, Peru
172/B2 **Ollagüe** (vol.), Bol.
53/S11 **Ollainville**, Fr.
77/E3 **Olleria**, Sp.
168/B3 **Olleros**, Peru
194/B4 **Ollie**, Mt,US
82/B6 **Ollioules**, Fr.
80/D5 **Ollon**, Swi.
122/F3 **Ollūr**, India
76/C2 **Olmedo**, Sp.
151/A2 **Olmesutye**, Kenya
190/E1 **Olmitz**, Ks,US
168/B2 **Olmos**, Peru
208/F5 **Olmsted Falls**, Oh,US
174/Q9 **Olmué**, Chile
59/F2 **Olney**, Eng,UK
198/B5 **Olney**, Il,US
206/A5 **Olney**, Md,US
183/G3 **Olney**, Mt,US
189/E1 **Olney**, Tx,US
62/F3 **Olofström**, Swe.
151/B2 **Oloitokitok**, Kenya
65/J4 **Olomouc**, Czh.
63/Q1 **Olonets**, Rus.
125/C2 **Olongapo**, Phil.
74/C3 **Olonne-sur-Mer**, Fr.
151/B2 **Olorgasailie Nat'l Mon.**, Kenya
74/C5 **Oloron-Sainte-Marie**, Fr.
145/F5 **Olorunda**, Nga.
77/G1 **Olot**, Sp.
108/H1 **Olovyannaya**, Rus.
101/S3 **Oloy** (range), Rus.
67/E6 **Olpe**, Ger.
193/F4 **Olpe**, Ks,US
73/B1 **Olšava** (riv.), Czh.
67/F6 **Olsberg**, Ger.
191/F1 **Olsburg**, Ks,US
63/P4 **Ol'sha**, Rus.
98/F3 **Ol'shanka**, Ukr.
99/H2 **Ol'shany**, Ukr.
66/D4 **Olst**, Neth.
62/E4 **Ølstykke**, Den.
65/L2 **Olsztyn**, Pol.
65/L2 **Olsztyn** (prov.), Pol.
65/L2 **Olsztynek**, Pol.
93/G3 **Olt** (co.), Rom.
93/G4 **Olt** (riv.), Rom.
172/C4 **Olta**, Arg.
174/C4 **Olte** (mts.), Arg.
80/D3 **Olten**, Swi.
93/H3 **Oltenița**, Rom.
93/F3 **Olteț** (riv.), Rom.
190/C3 **Olton**, Tx,US
86/C1 **Oltre il Colle**, It.
104/E1 **Oltu**, Turk.
104/E1 **Oltu** (riv.), Turk.
117/J4 **Oluanpi**, Tai.
117/J4 **Oluan Pi** (cape), Tai.
145/G5 **Oluku**, Nga.
104/E1 **Olur**, Turk.
190/E3 **Olustee**, Ok,US
125/C4 **Olutanga** (isl.), Phil.
72/B3 **Olvenstedt**, Ger.

76/C4 Olvera, Sp.
82/B5 Olympe (mtn.), Fr.
205/B3 Olympia (cap.), Wa,US
202/P8 Olympia Heights, Fl,US
91/G4 Olympia (Olimbía) (ruins), Gre.
205/A2 Olympic (mts.), Wa,US
133/H4 Olympic Dam, Austl.
205/A1 Olympic Game Farm, Wa,US
205/A2 Olympic Nat'l For., Wa,US
182/B3 Olympic Nat'l Park, Wa,US
182/C4 Olympic Nat'l Park, Wa,US
103/C2 Olympus (mtn.), Cyp.
182/C4 Olympus (mtn.), Wa,US
91/H2 Olympus, Mount (Olimbos) (peak), Gre.
91/H2 Olympus Nat'l Park, Gre.
101/S3 Olyutorskiy (bay), Rus.
114/D5 Oma, China
112/B3 Ōma, Japan
95/K2 Oma (riv.), Rus.
200/B5 Oma, Ms,US
111/E2 Ōmachi, Japan
111/F3 Ōmae-zaki (pt.), Japan
112/B4 Ōmagari, Japan
56/A2 Omagh, NI,UK
56/A2 Omagh (dist.), NI,UK
168/C2 Omaguas, Peru
79/E2 Omaha (beach), Fr.
191/H2 Omaha, Ar,US
200/E4 Omaha, Ga,US
193/G3 Omaha, Ne,US
189/G1 Omaha, Tx,US
193/F2 Omaha Ind. Res., Ne,US
182/E3 Omak, Wa,US
122/G3 Omalūr, India
107/G4 Oman
107/G4 Oman (gulf), Asia
161/G4 Omar Torrijos Herrera (int'l arpt.), Pan.
154/B4 Omaruru, Namb.
154/B4 Omaruru (dry riv.), Namb.
168/B4 Omas, Peru
154/C3 Omatako (dry riv.), Namb.
168/D5 Omate, Peru
112/B3 Ōma-zaki (pt.), Japan
130/B2 Ombai (str.), Indo.
154/B3 Ombalantu, Namb.
148/C4 Ombella-Mpoko (pref.), CAfr.
58/D2 Ombersley, Eng,UK
148/A4 Ombessa, Camr.
154/B3 Ombombo, Namb.
152/B3 Omboué, Gabon
84/B2 Ombrone (riv.), It.
114/E5 Ombu, China
175/T11 Ombúes de Lavalle, Uru.
175/T11 Ombúes de Oribe, Uru.
149/G2 Omdurman (Umm Durmān), Sudan
111/H7 Ōme, Japan
60/D1 Omeath, Ire.
203/G2 Omega, Ga,US
86/B1 Omegna, It.
135/C3 Omeo, Austl.
104/E2 Ömerli, Turk.
104/B1 Ömerli (dam), Turk.
105/N7 Ömerli (res.), Turk.
160/E4 Ometepe (isl.), Nic.
160/B2 Ometepec, Mex.
149/H2 Om Hājer, Eth.
111/M9 Ōmi, Japan
111/M9 Ōmihachiman, Japan
90/E1 Omiš, Cro.
154/C4 Omitara, Namb.
160/B2 Omitlán (riv.), Mex.
111/G2 Ōmiya, Japan
177/M4 Ommaney (cape), Ak,US
66/D3 Ommen, Neth.
108/F2 Ömnödelger, Mong.
108/C2 Ömnögovĭ, Mong.
90/A2 Omodeo (lake), It.
145/G5 Omoko, Nga.
102/D3 Omolon (riv.), Rus.
149/G4 Omo Nat'l Park, Eth.
112/B4 Omono (riv.), Japan
149/H4 Omo Wenz (riv.), Eth.
199/H2 Ompah, On,Can
193/K1 Omro, Wi,US
100/H4 Omsk, Rus.
101/R3 Omsukchan, Rus.
112/C1 Ōmu, Japan
145/G4 Omu Aran, Nga.
153/G2 Omugo, Ugan.
93/G3 Omul (peak), Rom.
145/G5 Omuo, Nga.
110/A4 Ōmura, Japan
93/H4 Omurtag, Bul.
110/B4 Ōmuta, Japan
95/M4 Omutninsk, Rus.
153/F3 Onadikondo, Zaire
191/F1 Onaga, Ks,US
111/G1 Onagawa, Japan
194/E5 Onaka, SD,US
193/J2 Onalaska (lake), Mn, Wi,US
189/G2 Onalaska, Tx,US
182/C4 Onalaska, Wa,US
193/J2 Onalaska, Wi,US
195/H4 Onamia, Mn,US
201/K2 Onancock, Va,US
194/D2 Onanole, Mb,Can
198/F1 Onaping (lake), On,Can
198/B4 Onarga, Il,US
158/D2 Oñate, Mex.
76/D1 Oñate, Sp.
193/F2 Onawa, Ia,US
182/F4 Onaway, Id,US
198/D2 Onaway, Mi,US
174/E1 Oncativo, Arg.
56/D3 Onchan, IM,UK
154/B3 Oncócua, Ang.
77/E3 Onda, Sp.
154/C3 Ondangua, Namb.
65/L4 Ondava (riv.), Slvk.
120/A3 Onder, India
145/G5 Ondo, Nga.
145/G5 Ondo (state), Nga.
108/D2 Öndörhaan, Mong.
108/C2 Öndorhangay, Mong.
154/B3 Ondorushu (falls), Ang., Namb.
87/E1 Oné, It.
203/G4 Oneco, Fl,US
183/J3 Onefour, Ab,Can
94/H3 Onega, Rus.
94/H2 Onega (bay), Rus.
94/G3 Onega (lake), Rus.
94/H2 Onega (pen.), Rus.
94/H3 Onega (riv.), Rus.
182/D1 One Hundred and Fifty Mile House, BC,Can
182/D2 One Hundred Mile House, BC,Can
136/F6 Onehunga, N.Z.
199/J3 Oneida, NY,US
199/J3 Oneida (lake), NY,US
206/B2 Oneida, Pa,US
200/E2 Oneida, Tn,US
193/K1 Oneida Ind. Res., Wi,US
192/E2 O'Neill, Ne,US
193/H2 Onekama, Mi,US
200/D4 Oneonta, Al,US
199/J3 Oneonta, NY,US
136/F6 One Tree Hill, N.Z.
80/C5 Onex, Swi.
154/B3 Ongenga, Namb.
153/F4 Ongeri, Zaire
108/E2 Ongiyn (riv.), Mong.
113/C4 Ongjin, NKor.
151/B2 Ongobit, Kenya
118/D4 Ongole, India
69/D3 Onhaye, Belg.
116/C5 Onhne, Burma
97/G4 Oni, Geo.
192/D1 Onida, SD,US
77/E3 Onil, Sp.
157/G8 Onilahy (riv.), Madg.
145/G5 Onitsha, Nga.
157/H7 Onive (riv.), Madg.
113/C3 Onjŏng, NKor.
133/M8 Onkaparinga (riv.), Austl.
201/K2 Onley, Va,US
68/C3 Onnaing, Fr.
58/D2 Onny (riv.), Eng,UK
110/D3 Ono, Japan
110/E3 Ōno, Japan
110/B4 Onoda, Japan
136/J9 Onoke (lake), N.Z.
108/F1 Onokhoy, Rus.
110/C3 Onomichi, Japan
108/G2 Onon, Mong.
108/G1 Onon (riv.), Mong., Rus.
165/E2 Onoto, Ven.
138/G5 Onotoa (isl.), Kiri.
183/G1 Onoway, Ab,Can
156/L11 Onrus, SAfr.
132/B2 Onslow, Austl.
66/E2 Onstwedde, Neth.
111/E3 Ontake-san (mtn.), Japan
178/H3 Ontario (prov.), Can.
199/G2 Ontario (lake), Can., US
204/C2 Ontario, Ca,US
204/C2 Ontario (int'l arpt.), Ca,US
184/E1 Ontario, Or,US
206/C3 Ontelaunee (lake), Pa,US
77/E3 Onteniente, Sp.
195/K4 Ontonagon, Mi,US
195/K4 Ontonagon Ind. Res., Mi,US
138/F5 Ontong Java (isl.), Sol.
166/C1 Onverwacht, Sur.
189/J1 Onward, Ms,US
200/B4 Onward, Ms,US
113/D4 Onyang, SKor.
186/C3 Onyx, Ca,US
164/C3 Onzaga, Col.
79/G6 Onzain, Fr.
152/C5 Onzo (riv.), Ang.
130/A4 Oobagooma, Austl.
133/G3 Oodnadatta, Austl.
150/C3 Ood Weyne, Som.
60/B4 Oola, Ire.
133/F4 Ooldea, Austl.
198/C5 Oolitic, In,US
191/G2 Oologah, Ok,US
191/G2 Oologah (lake), Ok,US
66/B5 Ooltgensplaat, Neth.
177/M5 Oona River, BC,Can
200/E3 Oostanaula (riv.), Ga,US
66/A6 Oostburg, Neth.
193/L2 Oostburg, Wi,US
66/C4 Oostelijk Flevoland (polder), Neth.
68/B1 Oostende (Ostend), Belg.
66/C5 Oosterbeek, Neth.
66/C2 Oosterend, Neth.
66/B5 Oosterhout, Neth.
66/A5 Oosterschelde (chan.), Neth.
64/B3 Oosterschelde (estuary), Neth.
66/A5 Oosterscheldedam (dam), Neth.
66/D3 Oosterwolde, Neth.
68/C2 Oosterzele, Belg.
68/C1 Oostkamp, Belg.
66/D2 Oostmahorn, Neth.
66/C4 Oostvaarderplassen (lake), Neth.
66/C2 Oost-Vlieland, Neth.
66/B5 Oostvoorne, Neth.
66/B4 Oostzaan, Neth.
122/F3 Ootacamund, India
66/D4 Ootmarsum, Neth.
156/D2 Otse, Bots.
93/H4 Opaka, Bul.
192/C1 Opal, SD,US
153/F3 Opala, Zaire
65/J2 Opalenica, Pol.
202/P8 Opa-Locka, Fl,US
134/A3 Opalton, Austl.
149/G5 Opari, Sudan
95/L4 Oparino, Rus.
92/B3 Opatija, Cro.
65/L3 Opatów, Pol.
65/J4 Opava, Czh.
200/E4 Opelika, Al,US
202/B2 Opelousas, La,US
199/G2 Opéongo (lake), On,Can
86/C2 Opera, It.
70/C6 Öpfingen, Ger.
69/E1 Opglabbeek, Belg.
183/L3 Opheim, Mt,US
177/G3 Ophir, Ak,US
185/K5 Ophir, Co,US
184/A2 Ophir, Or,US
132/C2 Ophthalmia (range), Austl.
145/G5 Opi, Nga.
159/H4 Opichén, Mex.
127/G4 Opin, Indo.
66/D6 Opladen, Ger.
66/C5 Oploo, Neth.
66/B3 Opmeer, Neth.
145/G5 Opobo, Nga.
63/N3 Opochka, Rus.
65/L3 Opoczno, Pol.
158/C2 Opodepe, Mex.
65/J3 Opole, Pol.
65/J3 Opole (prov.), Pol.
65/L3 Opole Lubelskie, Pol.
191/G2 Opolis, Ks,US
97/K3 Opornyy, Kaz.
99/H3 Oposhnya, Ukr.
136/D2 Opotiki, N.Z.
92/E3 Opovo, Yugo.
203/E2 Opp, Al,US
61/D3 Oppdal, Nor.
87/E2 Oppeano, It.
70/B6 Oppenau, Ger.
70/B3 Oppenheim, Ger.
85/F6 Oppido Lucano, It.
83/B6 Oppido Mamertina, It.
62/C1 Oppland (co.), Nor.
182/F4 Opportunity, Wa,US
190/D2 Optima (lake), Ok,US
190/D2 Optima Nat'l Wild. Ref., Ok,US
136/C1 Opua, N.Z.
68/D2 Opwijk, Belg.
193/J3 Oquawka, Il,US
158/D3 Ora (riv.), Mex.
81/H5 Ora (Auer), It.
187/G4 Oracle, Az,US
201/K3 Oracoke (isl.), NC,US
92/E2 Oradea, Rom.
207/J8 Oradell, NJ,US
207/J8 Oradell (res.), NJ,US
92/E4 Orahovac, Yugo.
92/C3 Orahovica, Cro.
120/B3 Orai, India
187/G2 Oraibi (wash), Az,US
80/B4 Orain (riv.), Fr.
82/B5 Oraison, Fr.
141/Q16 Oran, Alg.
141/Q16 Oran (wilaya), Alg.
200/C2 Oran, Mo,US
113/E2 Orang, NKor.
113/E2 Orang (riv.), NKor.
156/B3 Orange (riv.), Afr.
135/D2 Orange, Austl.
166/D1 Orange (cape), Braz.
82/A4 Orange, Fr.
166/C2 Orange (mts.), Sur.
204/G8 Orange, Ca,US
204/C3 Orange (co.), Ca,US
208/A3 Orange, Ct,US
203/F2 Orange, Fl,US
202/M6 Orange (co.), Fl,US
207/D2 Orange, NJ,US
206/D1 Orange (co.), NY,US
189/H2 Orange, Tx,US
201/H1 Orange, Va,US
202/E2 Orange Beach, Al,US
207/K7 Orangeburg, NY,US
201/G4 Orangeburg, SC,US
203/H3 Orange City, Fl,US
193/F2 Orange City, Ia,US
204/C3 Orange Co./John Wayne (int'l arpt.), Ca,US
186/C2 Orange Cove, Ca,US
156/D3 Orange Free State (prov.), SAfr.
202/D2 Orange Grove, Ms,US
203/H2 Orange Park, Fl,US
203/H3 Orange Springs, Fl,US
186/B1 Orangevale, Ca,US
198/F3 Orangeville, On,Can
208/C5 Orangeville, Oh,US
206/B1 Orangeville, Pa,US
160/D2 Orange Walk, Belz.
144/A4 Orango (isl.), GBis.
72/C4 Oranienbaum, Ger.
72/D2 Oranienburg, Ger.
66/D3 Oranjekanaal (can.), Neth.
156/B3 Oranjemund, Namb.
162/D4 Oranjestad, Aru.
162/F3 Oranjestad, NAnt.
60/B3 Oranmore, Ire.
127/H4 Oransbari, Indo.
141/Q16 Oran, Sebkha d' (lake), Alg.
154/E4 Orapa, Bots.
103/D3 Or 'Aqiva, Isr.
125/D2 Oras, Phil.
93/F3 Orăştie, Rom.
73/D1 Orava (riv.), Slvk.
193/K5 Oraville, Il,US
92/E3 Oraviţa, Rom.
74/E5 Orb (riv.), Fr.
86/B3 Orba (riv.), It.
86/A2 Orbassano, It.
80/C4 Orbe, Swi.
80/C4 Orbe (riv.), Swi.
79/F2 Orbec-en-Auge, Fr.
84/B3 Orbetello, It.
80/D1 Orbey, Fr.
76/C1 Orbigo (riv.), Sp.
79/F2 Orbiquet (riv.), Fr.
135/D3 Orbost, Austl.
62/G1 Örbyhus, Swe.
182/C3 Orcas (isl.), Wa,US
76/D3 Orcera, Sp.
80/B3 Orchamps, Fr.
80/C3 Orchamps-Vennes, Fr.
205/F6 Orchard (lake), Mi,US
185/K4 Orchard City, Co,US
183/G4 Orchard Homes, Mt,US
205/F6 Orchard Lake Village, Mi,US
185/J4 Orchard Mesa, Co,US
182/E3 Orchards, Wa,US
192/B3 Orchard Valley, Wy,US
68/C3 Orchies, Fr.
54/B4 Orchy (riv.), Sc,UK
84/B2 Orcia (riv.), It.
87/F5 Orciano di Pesaro, It.
82/C3 Orcières, Fr.
84/A2 Orco (riv.), It.
168/C4 Orcopampa, Peru
74/F3 Or, Côte d' (uplands), Fr.
168/C3 Orcotuna, Peru
186/B3 Orcutt, Ca,US
130/C3 Ord (riv.), Austl.
192/E3 Ord, Ne,US
158/D4 Ordaz (int'l arpt.), Mex.
74/B1 Ordenes, Sp.
187/F2 Orderville, Ut,US
77/F1 Ordesa y Monte Perdido Nat'l Park, Sp.
130/B4 Ord, Mount (peak), Austl.
85/F5 Ordona, It.
115/B3 Ordos (des.), China
130/C4 Ord River, Austl.
104/D1 Ordu, Turk.
104/D1 Ordu (prov.), Turk.
97/H5 Ordubad, Azer.
192/C4 Ordway, Co,US
105/F1 Ordzhonikidze, Azer.
97/H3 Ordzhonikidze, Kaz.
99/H4 Ordzhonikidze, Ukr.
99/J5 Ordzhonikidze, Ukr.
145/G5 Ore, Nga.
165/G3 Orealla, Guy.
184/D3 Oreana, Nv,US
184/D4 Oreana (peak), Nv,US
62/F2 Örebro, Swe.
62/F2 Örebro (co.), Swe.
62/F2 Örebro (int'l arpt.), Swe.
189/G1 Ore City, Tx,US
180/B3 Oregon (state), US
193/K2 Oregon, Il,US
193/G4 Oregon, Mo,US
201/K3 Oregon (inlet), NC,US
198/E4 Oregon, Oh,US
184/B2 Oregon Caves Nat'l Mon., Or,US
184/B1 Oregon City, Or,US
184/A2 Oregon Dunes Nat'l Rec. Area, Or,US
192/B2 Oregon Trail Ruts, Wy,US
62/H1 Öregrund, Swe.
99/H4 Orekhov, Ukr.
63/P4 Orekhovsk, Bela.
96/F1 Orël, Rus.
96/E2 Orel' (riv.), Ukr.
168/C2 Orellana, Peru
76/C3 Orellana la Vieja, Sp.
96/F1 Orel Obl., Rus.
185/H3 Orem, Ut,US
53/J3 Orenburg, Rus.
97/K2 Orenburg (int'l arpt.), Rus.
97/K1 Orenburg Obl., Rus.
104/B2 Örencik, Turk.
76/B1 Orense, Sp.
91/K2 Orestiás, Gre.
62/E4 Øresund (sound), Den., Swe.
136/B4 Oreti (riv.), N.Z.
189/H2 Oretta, La,US
136/C2 Orewa, N.Z.
135/C4 Orford, Austl.
59/H2 Orford, Eng,UK
199/K3 Orford, NH,US
59/H2 Orford Ness (pt.), UK
190/A4 Organ, NM,US
190/A4 Organ (mts.), NM,US
166/C1 Organabo, FrG.
187/F4 Organ Pipe Cactus Nat'l Mon., Az,US
171/P7 Órgãos (mts.), Braz.
76/D3 Orgaz, Sp.
53/T11 Orge (riv.), Fr.
80/B4 Orgelet, Fr.
79/G4 Orgères-en-Beauce, Fr.
53/R10 Orgeval, Fr.
93/J2 Orgeyev, Mol.
90/A2 Orgosolo, It.
96/D5 Orhaneli, Turk.
93/J5 Orhangazi, Turk.
108/F2 Orhon (riv.), Mong.
74/C5 Orhy, Pic d' (peak), Fr.
76/D4 Oria, Sp.
184/A3 Orick, Ca,US
60/D2 Oriel (mtn.), Ire.
193/G3 Orient, Ia,US
207/F1 Orient (pt.), NY,US
159/M7 Oriental, Mex.
201/J3 Oriental, NC,US
172/C1 Oriental, Cordillera (range), Bol.
168/B2 Oriental, Cordillera (range), Bol., Peru
161/H5 Oriental, Cordillera (range), Col.
164/B5 Oriental, Cordillera (range), Col., Ecu.
174/E3 Oriente, Arg.
68/C4 Origny-Sainte-Benoîte, Fr.
77/E3 Orihuela, Sp.
199/G2 Orillia, On,Can
63/L1 Orimattila, Fin.
192/B2 Orin, Wy,US
205/K11 Orinda, Ca,US
172/C1 Orinoca, Bol.
165/F2 Orinoco (riv.), Col., Ven.
165/F2 Orinoco (delta), Ven.
86/C1 Orio al Serio (int'l arpt.), It.
83/C2 Oriolo, It.
84/C3 Oriolo Romano, It.
125/C2 Orion, Phil.
193/J3 Orion, Il,US
205/F6 Orion (lake), Mi,US
121/E5 Orissa (state), India
63/K2 Orissaare, Est.
121/F5 Orissa Coast (can.), India
90/A3 Oristano, It.
90/A3 Oristano (gulf), It.
145/F5 Orita Eruwa, Nga.
167/G8 Orituco (riv.), Ven.
84/B4 Oriva, Wy,US
63/L1 Orivesi, Fin.
166/C3 Oriximiná, Braz.
159/M8 Orizaba, Mex.
159/K6 Orizabita, Mex.
170/C3 Orizona, Braz.
92/D4 Orjen (peak), Yugo.
76/D4 Orjiva, Sp.
67/F6 Orke (riv.), Ger.
62/E3 Orkelljunga, Swe.
91/H3 Orkhomenós, Gre.
183/L3 Orkney, Sk,Can
156/D2 Orkney, SAfr.
55/N13 Orkney (isls.), Sc,UK
76/B6 Orla (riv.), Ger.
188/C2 Orla, Tx,US
72/B6 Orlamünde, Ger.
196/C3 Orland, Me,US
170/D4 Orlândia, Braz.
181/K6 Orlando, Fl,US
202/N6 Orlando, Fl,US
203/H3 Orlando, Fl,US
203/H3 Orlando (int'l arpt.), Fl,US
201/G1 Orlando, WV,US
83/B6 Orlando, Capo d' (cape), It.
205/Q16 Orland Park, Il,US
63/R7 Orlången (lake), Swe.
173/G4 Orleães, Braz.
79/G5 Orléanais (hist. reg.), Fr.
196/B2 Orléans (isl.), Qu,Can
79/G5 Orléans, Fr.
184/B3 Orleans, Ca,US
196/C5 Orleans, Ma,US
192/E3 Orleans, Ne,US
199/K2 Orleans, Vt,US
71/H3 Orlík, Údolní nádrž (res.), Czh.
65/K4 Orlová, Czh.
97/G3 Orlovskiy, Rus.
99/M4 Orlovskiy, Rus.
145/G5 Orlu, Nga.
53/T10 Orly, Fr.
53/T10 Orly (Paris) (int'l arpt.), Fr.
192/C1 Orman (dam), SD,US
93/K5 Ormanlı, Turk.
107/H3 Ormāra, Pak.
86/A4 Ormea, It.
79/G5 Ormes, Fr.
79/F4 Ormes (riv.), Fr.
91/H2 Ormília, Gre.
194/B3 Ormiston, Sk,Can
54/D5 Ormiston, Sc,UK
125/D3 Ormoc City, Phil.
203/H3 Ormond Beach, Fl,US
203/H3 Ormond-by-the-Sea, Fl,US
80/C4 Or, Mont d' (mtn.), Fr.
57/F4 Ormskirk, Eng,UK
199/K2 Ormstown, Qu,Can
74/F2 Ornain (riv.), Fr.
80/C3 Ornans, Fr.
86/B1 Ornavasso, It.
79/F3 Orne (dept.), Fr.
69/F5 Orne (riv.), Fr.
79/E2 Orne (riv.), Fr.
61/E2 Ørnes, Nor.
65/L1 Orneta, Pol.
61/F3 Örnsköldsvik, Swe.
113/D2 Oro, NKor.
169/F4 Orobayaya, Bol.
81/F5 Orobie, Alpi (range), It.
167/G5 Orocó, Braz.
164/D3 Orocué, Col.
144/D4 Orodara, Burk.
77/E1 Oroel (peak), Sp.
182/F4 Orofino, Id,US
204/C1 Oro Grande, Ca,US
184/F1 Orogrande, Id,US
190/A4 Orogrande, NM,US
139/L6 Orohena (peak), FrPol.
172/C2 Oro Ingenio, Bol.
87/E1 Orolo (riv.), It.
138/E4 Oroluk (isl.), Micr.
196/D3 Oromocto, NB,Can
90/A1 Oro, Monte d' (mtn.), Fr.
82/A2 Oron (riv.), Fr.
145/H5 Oron, Nga.
134/E1 Orona (isl.), Kiri.
136/H9 Orongorongo (riv.), N.Z.
80/C4 Oron-la-Ville, Swi.
196/C3 Orono, Me,US
166/B2 Oronoque (riv.), Guy.
103/E2 Orontes (riv.), Asia
76/C3 Oropesa, Sp.
151/A1 Oropoi, Kenya
109/J1 Oroqen Zizhiqi, China
125/C3 Oroquieta, Phil.
167/G4 Orós, Braz.
167/G4 Orós (res.), Braz.
90/A2 Orosei, It.
90/A2 Orosei (gulf), It.
92/E2 Orosháza, Hun.
186/C2 Orosi, Ca,US
73/C5 Oroszlány, Hun.
101/R3 Orotukan, Rus.
184/E3 Orovada, Nv,US
187/G4 Oro Valley, Az,US
184/C4 Oroville, Ca,US
184/C4 Oroville (lake), Ca,US
182/E3 Oroville, Wa,US
57/F3 Orpington, Eng,UK
80/D3 Orpund, Swi.
195/H3 Orr, Mn,US
62/F3 Orrefors, Swe.
57/F4 Orrell, Eng,UK
193/G4 Orrick, Mo,US
54/B2 Orrin (res.), Sc,UK
54/B2 Orrin (riv.), Sc,UK
196/C3 Orrington, Me,US
90/A3 Orroli, It.
133/H5 Orroroo, Austl.
206/A4 Orrtanna, Pa,US
200/D4 Orrville, Al,US
208/F6 Orrville, Oh,US
53/T9 Orry-la-Ville, Fr.
62/F1 Orsa, Swe.
87/F1 Orsago, It.
85/F5 Orsara di Puglia, It.
53/S10 Orsay, Fr.
53/Q7 Orsett, Eng,UK
63/P4 Orsha, Bela.
82/D3 Orsiera (peak), It.
53/J3 Orsk, Rus.
85/E6 Orso, Capo d' (cape), It.
85/E3 Orsogna, It.
80/C4 Orsonnens, Swi.
92/F3 Orşova, Rom.
61/C3 Ørsta, Nor.
62/G2 Örsundsbro, Swe.
86/B1 Orta (lake), It.
104/C1 Orta, Turk.
104/B2 Ortaca, Turk.
104/C1 Ortaköy, Turk.
104/C2 Ortaköy, Turk.
85/F5 Orta Nova, It.
84/C3 Orte, It.
87/E4 Orte (riv.), It.
164/C4 Ortega, Col.
76/B1 Ortegal (cape), Sp.
70/C2 Ortenberg, Ger.
84/C3 Orte Scalo, It.
73/A3 Orth an der Donau, Aus.
74/C5 Orthez, Fr.
81/F5 Ortigara, Monte (peak), It.
76/B1 Ortigueira, Sp.
205/C3 Orting, Wa,US
188/B3 Ortiz, Mex.
190/A2 Ortiz, Co,US
167/N8 Ortiz, Ven.
81/G4 Ortles (peak), It.
81/G5 Ortles (mts.), It., Swi.
169/E3 Ortón (riv.), Bol.
109/H2 Ortón (riv.), China
85/E3 Ortona, It.
203/H4 Ortona, Fl,US
205/F6 Ortonville, Mi,US
194/F5 Ortonville, Mn,US
114/C3 Orto-Tokoy, Kyr.
72/D5 Ortrand, Ger.
67/H3 Örtze (riv.), Ger.
105/F2 Orūmīyeh, Iran
168/D4 Orurillo, Peru
172/C1 Oruro, Bol.
172/C1 Oruro (dept.), Bol.
62/D2 Orust (isl.), Swe.
78/D5 Orvault, Fr.
84/C2 Orvieto, It.
137/V Orville (coast), Ant.
59/H2 Orwell (riv.), Eng,UK
208/G4 Orwell, Oh,US
199/K3 Orwell, Vt,US
206/B2 Orwigsburg, Pa,US
206/B2 Orwin-Reinerton-Muir, Pa,US
108/H2 Orxon (riv.), China
93/F4 Oryakhovo, Bul.
103/F7 Or Yehuda, Isr.
98/G3 Orzhitsa, Ukr.
86/C2 Orzinuovi, It.
65/L2 Orzysz, Pol.
62/A1 Os, Nor.
161/F4 Osa (pen.), CR
95/M4 Osa, Rus.
194/C3 Osage, Sk,Can
193/H2 Osage, Ia,US
191/H1 Osage (riv.), Ks, Mo,US
195/G4 Osage, Mn,US
189/F2 Osage, Tx,US
192/B2 Osage, Wy,US
191/H1 Osage Beach, Mo,US
191/G1 Osage City, Ks,US
110/D3 Ōsaka, Japan
111/L10 Ōsaka (bay), Japan
111/L10 Ōsaka (int'l arpt.), Japan
110/D3 Ōsaka (pref.), Japan
111/L10 Ōsaka Castle, Japan
195/G5 Osakis, Mn,US
193/G1 Osakis (lake), Mn,US
113/D4 Osan, SKor.
170/D4 Osasco, Braz.
193/G4 Osawatomie, Ks,US
177/E3 Osborn (mt.), Ak,US
191/E1 Osborne, Ks,US
69/F4 Osburg, Ger.
182/G4 Osburn, Id,US
62/E3 Osby, Swe.
166/C2 Oscar, FrG.
191/F4 Oscar, Ok,US
200/C3 Osceola, Ar,US
202/N7 Osceola (co.), Fl,US
193/H3 Osceola, Ia,US
193/G4 Osceola, Mo,US
192/F3 Osceola, Ne,US
199/H4 Osceola, Pa,US
193/H1 Osceola, Wi,US
72/D5 Oschatz, Ger.
72/B3 Oschersleben, Ger.
90/A2 Oschiri, It.
190/A4 Oscura (mts.), NM,US
67/G1 Osdorf, Ger.
85/E3 Osento (riv.), It.
200/E1 Osgood, In,US
199/J2 Osgoode, On,Can
114/B3 Osh, Kyr.
154/B3 Oshakati, Namb.
112/B2 Oshamambe, Japan
199/G3 Oshawa, On,Can
112/B4 Oshika (pen.), Japan
154/B3 Oshikango, Namb.
111/F3 Ōshima (arpt.), Japan
112/A2 Oshima (pen.), Japan
154/C3 Oshivelo, Namb.
192/C3 Oshkosh, Ne,US
193/K1 Oshkosh, Wi,US
63/L4 Oshmyany, Bela.
105/F2 Oshnovīyeh, Iran
145/G5 Oshogbo, Nga.
152/D3 Oshwe, Zaire
92/D3 Osijek, Cro.
87/G6 Osimo, It.
86/C1 Osio Sotto, It.
92/E3 Osipaonica, Yugo.
99/J4 Osipenko, Ukr.
96/D1 Osipovichi, Bela.
154/C4 Osire, Namb.
193/G3 Oskaloosa, Ia,US
62/G3 Oskarshamn, Swe.
62/E3 Oskarström, Swe.
99/J3 Oskol (riv.), Rus., Ukr.
73/A1 Oslava (riv.), Czh.
73/A1 Oslavany, Czh.
62/D2 Oslo (cap.), Nor.
194/F3 Oslo, Mn,US
62/D2 Oslofjord (fjord), Nor.
118/C4 Osmānābād, India
104/C1 Osmancık, Turk.
93/K5 Osmaneli, Turk.
103/E1 Osmaniye, Turk.
63/N2 Os'mino, Rus.
194/E3 Osnabrock, ND,US
199/J2 Osnabruck, On,Can
67/F4 Osnabrück, Ger.
64/D2 Osnabrück/Münster (int'l arpt.), Ger.
195/J2 Osnaburgh (lake), On,Can
195/J2 Osnaburgh House, On,Can
53/S9 Osny, Fr.
205/M11 Oso (mt.), Ca,US
182/D3 Oso, Wa,US
153/G3 Oso (riv.), Zaire
81/E5 Osogna, Swi.
154/C4 Osona, Namb.
173/G4 Osório, Braz.
174/B4 Osorno, Chile
76/C1 Osorno, Sp.
182/E3 Osoyoos, BC,Can
182/E3 Osoyoos Ind. Res., BC,Can
86/A5 Ospedaletti, It.
87/E2 Ospedaletto Euganeo, It.
86/D1 Ospitaletto, It.
134/B1 Osprey (reef), Austl.
66/C5 Oss, Neth.
135/C4 Ossa (peak), Austl.
91/H3 Ossa (mtn.), Gre.
76/B3 Ossa (range), Port.
203/H2 Ossabaw (isl.), Ga,US
201/G5 Ossabaw (sound), Ga,US
203/H2 Ossabaw I. Heritage Prsv., Ga,US
145/G5 Osse (riv.), Nga.
74/D5 Osséja, Fr.
193/J1 Osseo, Wi,US
57/G4 Ossett, Eng,UK
90/A2 Ossi, It.
198/D4 Ossian, In,US
198/E2 Ossineke, Mi,US
207/E1 Ossining, NY,US
199/L3 Ossipee, NH,US
101/S4 Ossora, Rus.
94/G4 Ostashkov, Rus.
67/E4 Ostbevern, Ger.
67/G1 Oste (riv.), Ger.
203/H3 Osteen, Fl,US
87/E3 Ostellato, It.
67/G1 Osten, Ger.
68/B1 Ostend (Oostende), Belg.
94/G5 Oster, Rus.
98/F2 Oster, Ukr.
72/B2 Osterburg, Ger.
70/C4 Osterburken, Ger.
62/G1 Österbybruk, Swe.
62/F3 Österbymo, Swe.
67/F4 Ostercappeln, Ger.
62/E1 Österdalälven (riv.), Swe.
66/D1 Osterems (chan.), Neth.
72/B5 Osterfeld, Ger.
62/F2 Östergötland (co.), Swe.
71/G5 Osterhofen, Ger.
67/F2 Osterholz-Scharmbeck, Ger.
87/E4 Osteria Grande, It.
71/F6 Ostermiething, Aus.
72/C4 Osternienburg, Ger.
67/H5 Osterode, Ger.
64/F3 Osterode am Harz, Ger.
61/E3 Östersund, Swe.
62/G1 Östervåla, Swe.
196/B5 Osterville, Ma,US
72/B3 Osterweddingen, Ger.
72/A4 Osterwieck, Ger.
70/C5 Ostfildern, Ger.
62/D2 Østfold (co.), Nor.
67/E2 Ostfriesland (reg.), Ger.
62/H1 Östhammar, Swe.
80/D1 Ostheim, Fr.
70/D2 Ostheim vor der Rhön, Ger.
70/B3 Osthofen, Ger.
84/C4 Ostia Antica, It.
84/C4 Ostia Antica (ruins), It.
86/D2 Ostiano, It.
87/E2 Ostiglia, It.
160/E4 Ostional Nat'l Wild. Ref., CR
87/G5 Ostra, It.
81/F2 Ostrach (riv.), Ger.
62/E2 Östra Silen (lake), Swe.
65/K4 Ostrava, Czh.
87/G5 Ostra Vetere, It.
73/D2 Ostredok (peak), Slvk.
67/E2 Ostrhauderfehn, Ger.
68/C3 Ostricourt, Fr.
70/B4 Ostringen, Ger.
92/D4 Ostri Rt (cape), Yugo.
65/K2 Ostróda, Pol.
98/D2 Ostrog, Ukr.
99/K2 Ostrogozhsk, Rus.
65/L2 Ostrołęka, Pol.
65/L2 Ostrołęka (prov.), Pol.
95/N5 Ostrolenka, Rus.
63/M4 Ostroshitskiy Gorodok, Bela.
71/F2 Ostrov, Czh.
63/N3 Ostrov, Rus.
63/L4 Ostrovets, Bela.
94/J4 Ostrovskoye, Rus.
73/B3 Ostrov Žitný, Vel'ký (isl.), Slvk.
65/L3 Ostrowiec Świętokrzyski, Pol.
65/L2 Ostrów Mazowiecka, Pol.
65/J3 Ostrów Wielkopolski, Pol.
63/L5 Ostryna, Bela.
65/J3 Ostrzeszów, Pol.
62/E4 Ostseebad Binz, Ger.
65/G1 Ostseebad Göhren, Ger.
64/G1 Ostseebad Prerow, Ger.
67/H1 Oststeinbek, Ger.
160/C2 Ostuacan, Mex.
90/E2 Ostuni, It.
182/E4 O'Sullivan (dam), Wa,US
91/G2 Osum (riv.), Alb.
93/G4 Osŭm (riv.), Bul.
110/B5 Ōsumi (isls.), Japan
110/B5 Ōsumi (pen.), Japan
110/B5 Ōsumi (str.), Japan
76/C4 Osuna, Sp.
151/A2 Osupuga (peak), Kenya
170/C4 Osvaldo Cruz, Braz.
57/G3 Oswaldkirk, Eng,UK
57/F4 Oswaldtwistle, Eng,UK
199/J2 Oswegatchie, NY,US
199/J2 Oswegatchie (riv.), NY,US
205/P16 Oswego, Il,US
191/G2 Oswego, Ks,US
206/D4 Oswego (riv.), NJ,US
199/H3 Oswego, NY,US
199/H3 Oswego (riv.), NY,US
57/E6 Oswestry, Eng,UK
65/K3 Oświęcim, Pol.
202/C2 Osyka, Ms,US
110/F2 Ōta, Japan
110/C3 Ōta (riv.), Japan
136/F6 Otahuhu, N.Z.
110/C3 Otake, Japan
111/G3 Otaki, Japan
136/C3 Otaki, N.Z.
111/G2 Otakine-yama (mtn.), Japan
167/L6 Otanche, Col.
112/B2 Otaru, Japan
195/M3 Otasawiam (riv.), On,Can
136/A4 Otautau, N.Z.
71/H4 Otava (riv.), Czh.
164/B4 Otavalo, Ecu.
154/C3 Otavi, Namb.
111/G2 Ōtawara, Japan
204/C5 Otay, Ca,US
154/B3 Otchinjau, Ang.
130/D4 O. T. Downs, Austl.
199/J3 Otego, NY,US
92/F3 Oţelu Roşu, Rom.
136/B4 Otematata, N.Z.
139/L6 Otepa, FrPol.
63/M2 Otepää, Est.
76/B1 Otero de Rey, Sp.
158/C3 Oteros (riv.), Mex.
108/D2 Otgon, Mong.
108/D2 Otgon Tenger (peak), Mong.
182/E4 Othello, Wa,US
53/U9 Othis, Fr.
91/F3 Othonoí (isl.), Gre.
145/F4 Oti (riv.), Gui.
158/D3 Otinapa, Mex.
154/B3 Otinhungwa, Namb.
136/B3 Otira, N.Z.
191/E1 Otis, Ks,US
202/B1 Otis, La,US
208/A1 Otis (res.), Ma,US
188/B1 Otis, NM,US
196/B5 Otis Air Nat'l Guard Base, Ma,US
154/C4 Otjihajavara, Namb.
154/C3 Otjikondo, Namb.
154/B4 Otjimbingue, Namb.
154/C4 Otjinene, Namb.
154/C4 Otjiwarongo, Namb.
154/B4 Otjohorongo, Namb.
154/B3 Otjokavare, Namb.
154/C4 Otjosondjou (dry riv.), Namb.
154/C4 Otjosondu, Namb.
57/G4 Otley, Eng,UK
92/B3 Otočac, Cro.
112/C2 Otofuke, Japan
114/A3 Otog Qi, China
108/F4 Otog Qianqi, China
92/D3 Otok, Cro.
93/H3 Otopeni (int'l arpt.), Rom.
136/C2 Otorohanga, N.Z.
195/J2 Otoskwin (riv.), On,Can
111/N10 Otowa, Japan
62/B2 Otra (riv.), Nor.
99/L5 Otradnaya, Rus.
63/P2 Otradnoye, Rus.
97/J1 Otradnyy, Rus.
91/F2 Otranto (str.), Alb., It.
91/F2 Otranto, It.
73/B1 Otrokovice, Czh.
198/D3 Otsego, Mi,US
110/D3 Ōtsu, Japan
112/B4 Ōtsuchi, Japan
145/F5 Otta, Nga.
61/D3 Otta, Nor.
85/E6 Ottaviano, It.
179/H3 Ottawa (isls.), NW,Can
199/J2 Ottawa (cap.), On,Can
199/J2 Ottawa (int'l arpt.), On,Can
193/K3 Ottawa, Il,US
191/G1 Ottawa, Ks,US
198/D4 Ottawa, Oh,US
198/E4 Ottawa Hills, Oh,US
198/E4 Ottawa Nat'l Wild. Ref., Oh,US
199/H2 Ottawa (Outaouais) (riv.), On, Qu,Can
72/D5 Ottendorf-Okrilla, Ger.
71/H6 Ottensheim, Aus.
58/C5 Otter (riv.), Eng,UK
192/A1 Otter, Mt,US
208/G5 Otter (cr.), Pa,US
199/K3 Otter (riv.), Vt,US
69/G5 Otterbach, Ger.
198/C4 Otterbein, In,US
67/G2 Otterberg, Ger.
57/F1 Otterburn, Eng,UK
194/F3 Otterburne, Mb,Can
185/H4 Otter Creek (res.), Ut,US
66/C4 Otterlo, Neth.
67/F1 Otterndorf, Ger.
67/G2 Ottersberg, Ger.
53/M7 Ottershaw, Eng,UK
195/G4 Ottertail, Mn,US
195/G4 Otter Tail (lake), Mn,US
194/F4 Otter Tail (riv.), Mn,US
58/C5 Ottery Saint Mary, Eng,UK
73/B4 Ottevény, Hun.
194/C2 Otthon, Sk,Can
68/D2 Ottignies-Louvain-La-Neuve, Belg.
70/D5 Öttingen im Bayern, Ger.
80/D2 Ottmarsheim, Fr.
81/G2 Ottobeuren, Ger.
71/E6 Ottobrunn, Ger.
86/C3 Ottone, It.
156/D2 Ottosdal, SAfr.
206/C3 Ottsville, Pa,US
193/H3 Ottumwa, Ia,US
69/G5 Ottweiler, Ger.
145/G5 Otukpa, Nga.
159/L7 Otumba de Gómez Farías, Mex.
172/E1 Otuquis (swamp), Bol.
145/H5 Oturkpo, Nga.
168/B2 Otuzco, Peru
135/B3 Otway (cape), Austl.
175/J8 Otway (bay), Chile
175/K8 Otway (sound), Chile
135/B3 Otway Nat'l Park, Austl.
200/D1 Otwell, In,US
65/L2 Otwock, Pol.
98/C3 Otynya, Ukr.
81/G4 Ötztal Alps (mts.), Aus., It.
81/G3 Ötztaler Ache (riv.), Aus.
112/B4 Ou (mts.), Japan
123/C1 Ou (riv.), Laos
191/H3 Ouachita (lake), Ar,US
191/H4 Ouachita (riv.), Ar, La,US
191/G3 Ouachita (mts.), Ar, Ok,US
142/C5 Ouadane, Mrta.
148/D3 Ouadda, CAfr.
148/D2 Ouaddaï (pref.), Chad
148/C2 Ouaddaï (reg.), Chad
148/B2 Ouad Nâga, Mrta.
145/E3 Ouagadougou (cap.), Burk.
145/E3 Ouagadougou (int'l arpt.), Burk.
148/C1 Ouahazeïne (well), Chad
145/E3 Ouahigouya, Burk.
148/D4 Ouaka (pref.), CAfr.
148/D4 Ouaka (riv.), CAfr.
144/D2 Oualâta, Mrta.
144/D2 Oualâta, Dhar (hills), Mrta.
144/C3 Oualia, Mali
142/C2 Oualidia, Mor.
145/F3 Ouallam, Niger
166/D1 Ouanary, FrG.
148/D3 Ouanda Djallé, CAfr.
148/C4 Ouandago, CAfr.
148/D3 Ouandja, CAfr.
148/D3 Ouandjia-Vakaga Fauna Rsv., CAfr.
148/D4 Ouango, CAfr.
74/E3 Ouanne (riv.), Fr.
166/C2 Ouaqui, FrG.
166/C2 Ouaqui (riv.), FrG.
149/E4 Ouara (riv.), CAfr.
142/C5 Ouarane (reg.), Mrta.
199/K1 Ouareau (riv.), Qu,Can
145/F4 Ouargaye, Burk.
143/G3 Ouargla, Alg.
143/G3 Ouargla (wilaya), Alg.
142/C3 Ouarkziz, Jebel (mts.), Alg., Mor.
142/D3 Ouarzazate, Mor.
142/D3 Ouarzazate (int'l arpt.), Mor.
141/S16 Ouassel, Nahr (riv.), Alg.
145/F3 Ouatagouna, Mali
148/C5 Oubangi (Ubangi) (riv.), Afr.
148/C4 Oubangui (riv.), CAfr.
145/E3 Oubritenga (prov.), Burk.
80/B3 Ouche (riv.), Fr.
79/G5 Oucques, Fr.
111/L10 Ōuda, Japan
145/E3 Oudalan (prov.), Burk.
66/B5 Oud-Beijerland, Neth.
66/A5 Ouddorp, Neth.
66/D5 Oude IJssel (riv.), Neth.
68/C2 Oudenaarde, Belg.
66/B5 Oudenbosch, Neth.
68/B1 Oudenburg, Belg.
66/E2 Oude Pekela, Neth.
66/B2 Oudeschild, Neth.
66/B5 Oude-Tonge, Neth.
66/D2 Oude Westereems (chan.), Neth.
79/E5 Oudon (riv.), Fr.
117/F3 Oudong, China
156/C4 Oudtshoorn, SAfr.
66/B6 Oud-Turnhout, Belg.
140/B2 Oued Dráa (riv.), Mor.
144/E2 Oued el Hadjar (well), Mali
141/R16 Oued Rhiou, Alg.
142/D2 Oued Zem, Mor.
144/D4 Ouéléssébougou, Mali
145/F5 Ouémé (prov.), Ben.
145/F4 Ouémé (riv.), Ben.
139/V13 Ouen (isl.), NCal.
141/W18 Ouenza, Alg.
141/M13 Ouerrha (riv.), Mor.
74/A2 Ouessant (isl.), Fr.
145/F4 Ouessè, Ben.
152/D2 Ouesso, Congo
152/D2 Ouesso (int'l arpt.), Congo
148/A4 Ouest (prov.), Camr.
161/H1 Ouest (pt.), Haiti
161/H2 Ouest (pt.), Haiti
141/M13 Ouezzane, Mor.
60/A3 Oughterard, Ire.
60/C2 Oughter, Lough (lake), Ire.
148/C4 Ouham (pref.), CAfr.
148/C3 Ouham (riv.), CAfr., Chad
148/C4 Ouham-Pendé (pref.), CAfr.
68/C5 Ouichy-le-Château, Fr.
145/F5 Ouidah, Ben.
79/E2 Ouistreham, Fr.
144/D2 Oujaf, Mrta.
141/P13 Oujda, Mor.
141/P13 Oujda (Angads) (int'l arpt.), Mor.
144/B1 Oujeft, Mrta.
142/C3 Oulad Teïma, Mor.
61/J2 Oulangan Nat'l Park, Fin.
144/C3 Ould Yenjé, Mrta.
82/B4 Oule (riv.), Fr.
143/G2 Ouled Djellal, Alg.
82/A1 Oullins, Fr.
142/D2 Oulmes, Mor.
133/H5 Oulnina (peak), Austl.
148/D3 Oulou, Bahr (riv.), CAfr.
61/H2 Oulu, Fin.
61/H2 Oulu (prov.), Fin.
61/H2 Oulujärvi (lake), Fin.
82/C2 Oulx, It.
148/D2 Oum Chalouba, Chad
144/D5 Oumé, IvC.
141/V18 Oum El Bouaghi, Alg.
141/V18 Oum El Bouaghi (wilaya), Alg.
142/D2 Oum er Rbia, Oued (riv.), Mor.
148/C2 Oum Hadjer, Chad
142/C5 Oumm ed Droûs Guebli, Sebkhet (dry lake), Mrta.
142/C4 Oumm ed Droûs Telli, Sebkhet (dry lake), Mrta.
142/C3 Ounara, Mor.
94/E2 Ounasjoki (riv.), Fin.
59/F2 Oundle, Eng,UK
194/C3 Oungre, Sk,Can
146/D5 OuniangaKebir, Chad
146/D5 Ounianga-Sérir, Chad
148/C4 Ouogo, CAfr.
69/E2 Oupeye, Belg.
69/E4 Our (riv.), Belg.
69/F4 Our (riv.), Eur.
185/K4 Ouray, Co,US
192/A4 Ouray (peak), Co,US
185/J3 Ouray, Ut,US
80/A2 Ource (riv.), Fr.
68/C5 Ourcq (riv.), Fr.
61/H1 Øure Anarjokka Nat'l Park, Nor.
61/F1 Øure Dividal Nat'l Park, Nor.
167/E3 Ourém, Braz.
146/C4 Ouri, Chad
167/F4 Ouricuri, Braz.
170/C4 Ourinhos, Braz.
76/A4 Ourique, Port.
167/G5 Ouro Branco, Braz.
145/H5 Ourofane, Niger
171/K7 Ouro Fino, Braz.
144/D3 Ouro Modi, Mali
155/G5 Ouro, Ponta do (pt.), Moz.
171/E4 Ouro Preto, Braz.
80/A4 Ouroux-sur-Saône, Fr.
69/E3 Ourthe (riv.), Belg.
69/E3 Ourthe Occidentale (riv.), Belg.
69/E3 Ourthe Oriental (riv.), Belg.
141/M13 Ourtzarh, Mor.
79/F1 Ourville-en-Caux, Fr.
135/C4 Ouse, Austl.
57/H4 Ouse (riv.), Eng,UK
59/G5 Ouse (riv.), Eng,UK
57/G3 Ouse (riv.), Eng,UK
203/G2 Ousley, Ga,US
144/A3 Oussouye, Sen.
78/C5 Oust (riv.), Fr.
77/Q11 Outão, Port.
199/H2 Outaouais (Ottawa) (riv.), Qu,Can
79/F4 Outarville, Fr.
144/D2 Outeïd Arkas (well), Mali
55/G8 Outer Hebrides (isls.), Sc,UK
186/C4 Outer Santa Barbara (passg.), Ca,US
76/A1 Outes, Sp.
154/C4 Outjo, Namb.
194/A2 Outlook, Sk,Can
183/M3 Outlook, Mt,US
68/A2 Outreau, Fr.
197/N6 Outremont, Qu,Can
139/V12 Ouvéa (isl.), NCal.
139/V12 Ouvéa (lag.), NCal.
82/A4 Ouvèze (riv.), Fr.
133/J5 Ouyen, Austl.
148/B1 Ouzou Bézédinga (well), Niger
177/H4 Ouzinkie, Ak,US
79/G5 Ouzouer-le-Marché, Fr.
104/C1 Ovacık, Turk.
104/D2 Ovacık, Turk.
86/B3 Ovada, It.
139/Y18 Ovalau (isl.), Fiji
172/B4 Ovalle, Chile
152/C2 Ovan, Gabon
165/E3 Ovana (peak), Ven.
183/H4 Ovando, Mt,US

76/A2 **Ovar**, Port.
172/C3 **Ovejaria** (peak), Arg.
69/G2 **Overath**, Ger.
193/G4 **Overbrook**, Ks,US
191/F3 **Overbrook**, Ok,US
66/B5 **Overflakkee** (isl.), Neth.
200/B4 **Overflow Nat'l Wild. Ref.**, Ar,US
187/G3 **Overgaard**, Az,US
61/D2 **Overhalla**, Nor.
68/D2 **Overijse**, Belg.
66/D3 **Overijssel** (prov.), Neth.
66/D4 **Overijssels** (can.), Neth.
61/G2 **Överkalix**, Swe.
191/G1 **Overland Park**, Ks,US
206/B5 **Overlea**, Md,US
66/C5 **Overloon**, Neth.
174/C5 **Overo** (peak), Arg.
69/E1 **Overpelt**, Belg.
59/E1 **Overseal**, Eng,UK
59/H1 **Overstrand**, Eng,UK
59/E4 **Overton**, Eng,UK
57/F6 **Overton**, Wal,UK
186/E2 **Overton**, Nv,US
189/G1 **Overton**, Tx,US
61/G2 **Övertorneå**, Swe.
62/G3 **Överum**, Swe.
202/D2 **Ovett**, Ms,US
199/H3 **Ovid**, NY,US
98/F4 **Ovidiopol'**, Ukr.
76/C1 **Oviedo**, Sp.
63/J3 **Oviši**, Lat.
60/D4 **Ovoca**, Ire.
62/B1 **Øvre Årdal**, Nor.
62/E1 **Övre Fryken** (lake), Swe.
61/J1 **Øvre Pasvik Nat'l Park**, Nor.
62/B2 **Øvre Sirdal**, Nor.
91/G3 **Ovriá**, Gre.
98/E2 **Ovruch**, Ukr.
136/B4 **Owaka**, N.Z.
153/E3 **Owama**, Zaire
152/C3 **Owando**, Congo
112/B3 **Ōwani**, Japan
111/N9 **Owariasahi**, Japan
110/E3 **Owase**, Japan
202/E2 **Owassa**, Al,US
206/D1 **Owassa** (lake), NJ,US
191/G2 **Owasso**, Ok,US
193/H1 **Owatonna**, Mn,US
199/H3 **Owego**, NY,US
60/C3 **Owel, Lough** (lake), Ire.
133/H5 **Owen**, Austl.
70/C5 **Owen**, Ger.
136/C3 **Owen** (peak), N.Z.
193/J1 **Owen**, Wi,US
152/B2 **Owendo**, Gabon
153/H2 **Owen Falls** (dam), Ugan.
136/E4 **Owenga**, N.Z.
60/A1 **Oweniny** (riv.), Ire.
56/A2 **Owenkillew** (riv.), NI,UK
161/F2 **Owen Roberts** (int'l arpt.), Cay.
186/D2 **Owens** (dry lake), Ca,US
186/D3 **Owens** (peak), Ca,US
186/C2 **Owens** (riv.), Ca,US
190/D4 **Owens**, Tx,US
200/D2 **Owensboro**, Ky,US
198/C5 **Owensburg**, In,US
200/D3 **Owens Cross Roads**, Al,US
198/F2 **Owen Sound**, On,Can
131/G1 **Owen Stanley** (range), PNG
200/D1 **Owensville**, In,US
191/J1 **Owensville**, Mo,US
200/E1 **Owenton**, Ky,US
145/G5 **Owerri**, Nga.
81/F2 **Owingen**, Ger.
206/B6 **Owings**, Md,US
206/B5 **Owings Mills**, Md,US
200/F1 **Owingsville**, Ky,US
185/J2 **Owl Creek** (mts.), Wy,US
145/G5 **Owo**, Nga.
198/D3 **Owosso**, Mi,US
105/F3 **Owrāmān**, Iran
145/G5 **Owutu**, Nga.
184/E2 **Owyhee** (riv.), US
184/E2 **Owyhee** (mts.), Id, Or,US
184/E3 **Owyhee**, Nv,US
184/E2 **Owyhee** (dam), Or,US
184/E2 **Owyhee, South Fork** (riv.), Id, Nv,US
106/E1 **Owzan** (riv.), Iran
168/C3 **Oxapampa**, Peru
194/C3 **Oxbow**, Sk,Can
205/F6 **Oxbow** (lake), Mi,US
62/G2 **Oxelösund**, Swe.
196/F3 **Oxford**, NS,Can
136/C3 **Oxford**, N.Z.
59/E3 **Oxford**, Eng,UK
59/E3 **Oxford** (can.), Eng,UK
200/E4 **Oxford**, Al,US
191/J2 **Oxford**, Ar,US
208/A3 **Oxford**, Ct,US
198/C4 **Oxford**, In,US
191/F2 **Oxford**, Ks,US
208/C1 **Oxford**, Ma,US
196/B3 **Oxford**, Me,US
205/F6 **Oxford**, Mi,US
200/C3 **Oxford**, Ms,US
201/H2 **Oxford**, NC,US
192/E3 **Oxford**, Ne,US
199/J3 **Oxford**, NY,US
198/D5 **Oxford**, Oh,US
206/C4 **Oxford**, Pa,US
59/E3 **Oxfordshire** (co.), Eng,UK
53/M7 **Oxhey**, Eng,UK
62/E4 **Oxie**, Swe.
159/H4 **Oxkutzcab**, Mex.
135/C2 **Oxley**, Austl.
134/E7 **Oxley** (cr.), Austl.
204/A2 **Oxnard**, Ca,US
204/A2 **Oxnard** (arpt.), Ca,US
204/A2 **Oxnard Beach**, Ca,US
206/A6 **Oxon Hill Farm**, Md,US
206/B6 **Oxon Hill-Glassmanor**, Md,US
53/M8 **Oxshott**, Eng,UK
60/B1 **Ox** (Slieve Gamph) (mts.), Ire.
53/N8 **Oxted**, Eng,UK
54/D5 **Oxton**, Sc,UK
126/D3 **Oya**, Malay.
111/E2 **Oyabe**, Japan
182/E2 **Oyama**, BC,Can
111/F2 **Oyama**, Japan
111/M10 **Ōyamada**, Japan
111/L10 **Ōyamazaki**, Japan
163/D2 **Oyapock** (riv.), Braz., FrG.
166/C2 **Oyapock** (riv.), Braz.,FrG.
152/B2 **Oyem**, Gabon
183/J2 **Oyen**, Ab,Can
68/B2 **Oye-Plage**, Fr.
62/D1 **Øyer**, Nor.
146/C5 **Oyé Yeska** (well), Chad
55/J7 **Oykell** (riv.), Sc,UK
195/G4 **Oylen**, Mn,US
101/Q3 **Oymyakon**, Rus.
152/C3 **Oyo**, Congo
145/F5 **Oyo**, Nga.
145/F4 **Oyo** (state), Nga.
111/L10 **Ōyodo**, Japan
110/B5 **Ōyodo** (riv.), Japan
168/B3 **Oyón**, Peru
80/B5 **Oyonnax**, Fr.
189/G3 **Oyster** (cr.), Tx,US
207/E2 **Oyster Bay**, NY,US
207/L8 **Oyster Bay** (har.), NY,US
207/L8 **Oyster Bay Cove**, NY,US
207/E2 **Oyster Bay Nat'l Wild. Ref.**, NY,US
114/B3 **Oy-Tal**, Kyr.
67/G2 **Oyten**, Ger.
151/A2 **Oyugis**, Kenya
105/E2 **Özalp**, Turk.
125/C3 **Ozamiz City**, Phil.
79/G4 **Ozanne** (riv.), Fr.
96/D1 **Ozarichi**, Bela.
191/G2 **Ozark** (plat.), US
203/F2 **Ozark**, Al,US
191/H3 **Ozark**, Ar,US
191/H2 **Ozark** (mts.), Ar,US
191/H2 **Ozark**, Mo,US
191/J2 **Ozark Nat'l Scenic Rivwy.**, Mo,US
191/H1 **Ozarks, Lake of the** (res.), Mo,US
98/A2 **Ożarów**, Pol.
193/G4 **Ozawkie**, Ks,US
92/E1 **Ózd**, Hun.
101/R4 **Ozernovskiy**, Rus.
101/S4 **Ozernoy** (cape), Rus.
97/J2 **Ozernoye**, Rus.
97/M2 **Ozërnyy**, Rus.
109/N2 **Ozerskiy**, Rus.
63/L5 **Ozëry**, Bela.
182/B3 **Ozette** (lake), Wa,US
182/B3 **Ozette Ind. Res.**, Wa,US
94/H5 **Ozherel'ye**, Rus.
90/A2 **Ozieri**, It.
65/K3 **Ozimek**, Pol.
104/C2 **Özkonak**, Turk.
53/U10 **Ozoir-la-Ferrière**, Fr.
202/K7 **Ozona**, Fl,US
188/D2 **Ozona**, Tx,US
154/C4 **Ozondjacheberg** (peak), Namb.
191/H3 **Ozone**, Ar,US
207/K9 **Ozone Park**, NY,US
73/C6 **Ozora**, Hun.
65/K3 **Ozorków**, Pol.
53/U11 **Ozouer-le-Voulgis**, Fr.
110/C4 **Ōzu**, Japan
159/F4 **Ozuluama**, Mex.
159/L7 **Ozumba de Alzate**, Mex.
97/G4 **Ozurgeti**, Geo.
87/E4 **Ozzano dell'Emilia**, It.

## P

176/N3 **Paamiut**, Grld.
116/C5 **Pa-an**, Burma
70/E5 **Paar** (riv.), Ger.
156/B4 **Paarl**, SAfr.
63/T8 **Påarp**, Swe.
180/U10 **Paauilo**, Hi,US
113/E2 **P'abal-li**, NKor.
124/F4 **Pabean**, Indo.
65/K3 **Pabianice**, Pol.
183/G4 **Pablo Nat'l Wild. Ref.**, Mt,US
121/G4 **Pābna**, Bang.
121/G3 **Pābna** (dist.), Bang.
63/L4 **Pabradė**, Lith.
78/B3 **Pabu**, Fr.
169/E3 **Pacaás Novos** (mts.), Braz.
169/F3 **Pacaás Novos Nat'l Park**, Braz.
166/D3 **Pacajá** (riv.), Braz.
167/G4 **Pacajus**, Braz.
156/C4 **Pacaltsdorp**, SAfr.
165/F4 **Pacaraimã** (mts.), Braz., Ven.
168/B2 **Pacasmayo**, Peru
167/G3 **Pacatuba**, Braz.
168/C2 **Pacaya Samiria Nat'l Rsv.**, Peru
168/C3 **Paccha**, Peru
78/D4 **Pacé**, Fr.
202/E2 **Pace**, Fl,US
90/C4 **Paceco**, It.
83/B6 **Pace del Mela**, It.
168/B4 **Pachacamac**, Peru
168/C4 **Pachaconas**, Peru
168/C4 **Pachamarca** (riv.), Peru
208/C2 **Pachaug** (pond), Ct,US
158/C2 **Pacheco**, Mex.
186/B2 **Pacheco** (pass), Ca,US
97/G1 **Pachelma**, Rus.
120/A3 **Pachhār**, India
90/D4 **Pachino**, It.
168/C3 **Pachitea** (riv.), Peru
168/B2 **Pachiza**, Peru
120/B4 **Pachmarhī**, India
167/L6 **Pacho**, Col.
160/B1 **Pachuca**, Mex.
159/F4 **Pachuca de Soto**, Mex.
153/G2 **Pachwa**, Ugan.
50/B4 **Pacific** (ocean)
182/B2 **Pacific** (ranges ), BC,Can
205/C3 **Pacific**, Wa,US
205/K11 **Pacifica**, Ca,US
182/B4 **Pacific Beach**, Wa,US
184/B1 **Pacific City**, Or,US
186/B2 **Pacific Grove**, Ca,US
204/B2 **Pacifico** (mtn.), Ca,US
204/E7 **Pacific Palisades**, Ca,US
182/B3 **Pacific Rim Nat'l Park**, BC,Can
124/F4 **Pacinan** (cape), Indo.
124/E5 **Pacitan**, Indo.
164/D4 **Pacoa**, Col.
77/P10 **Paço de Arcos**, Port.
201/G3 **Pacolet** (riv.), SC,US
167/K6 **Pácora**, Col.
166/C3 **Pacoval**, Braz.
73/B6 **Pacsa**, Hun.
68/A5 **Pacy-sur-Eure**, Fr.
125/D4 **Padada**, Phil.
122/D1 **Padam**, India
118/D3 **Padampur**, India
124/C3 **Padang**, Indo.
124/C2 **Padang** (isl.), Indo.
124/D4 **Padangcermin**, Indo.
124/C2 **Padang Endau**, Malay.
124/C3 **Padangpanjang**, Indo.
124/B2 **Padangsidempuan**, Indo.
124/A1 **Padangtigi**, Indo.
94/G3 **Padany**, Rus.
125/A4 **Padas** (riv.), Malay.
116/B5 **Padaung**, Burma
172/C2 **Padcaya**, Bol.
53/N7 **Paddington**, Eng,UK
205/P14 **Paddock Lake**, Wi,US
59/G4 **Paddock Wood**, Eng,UK
201/G1 **Paden City**, WV,US
67/F5 **Paderborn**, Ger.
67/F5 **Paderborn** (arpt.), Ger.
87/F1 **Paderno**, It.
153/H2 **Padibe**, Ugan.
107/J3 **Pad Īdan**, Pak.
57/F4 **Padiham**, Eng,UK
172/C1 **Padilla**, Bol.
159/F3 **Padilla**, Mex.
92/E3 **Padina**, Yugo.
61/E2 **Padjelanta Nat'l Park**, Swe.
122/F4 **Padmanābhapuram**, India
87/E2 **Padova** (prov.), It.
87/E2 **Padova** (Padua), It.
152/C4 **Padrão, Ponta do** (pt.), Ang.
120/D2 **Padrauna**, India
189/F4 **Padre** (isl.), Tx,US
170/C2 **Padre Bernardo**, Braz.
189/F4 **Padre Island Nat'l Seash.**, Tx,US
76/A1 **Padrón**, Sp.
156/D4 **Padrone**, (cape), SAfr.
118/B2 **Pādru**, India
58/B5 **Padstow**, Eng,UK
87/E2 **Padua** (Padova), It.
200/C2 **Paducah**, Ky,US
190/D3 **Paducah**, Tx,US
76/D4 **Padul**, Sp.
83/B2 **Padula**, It.
85/E5 **Paduli**, It.
113/D4 **Paech'ŏn**, NKor.
113/E2 **Paegam**, NKor.
113/D2 **Paeksan-ni**, NKor.
113/E4 **Paektŏk-san** (mtn.), SKor.
113/E2 **Paektu-San** (mtn.), NKor.
113/C4 **Paengnyŏng** (isl.), SKor.
136/C2 **Paeroa**, N.Z.
87/F1 **Paese**, It.
83/B2 **Paestum** (ruins), It.
164/C3 **Páez**, Col.
164/C4 **Páez**, Col.
155/F4 **Pafúri**, Moz.
92/B3 **Pag**, Cro.
92/B3 **Pag** (isl.), Cro.
125/C4 **Pagadian**, Phil.
124/E3 **Pagai Selatan** (isl.), Indo.
124/C3 **Pagai Utara** (isl.), Indo.
116/B4 **Pagan**, Burma
138/D3 **Pagan** (isl.), NMar.
172/B4 **Pagancillo**, Arg.
85/E6 **Pagani**, It.
85/D3 **Paganica**, It.
84/B2 **Paganico**, It.
124/C4 **Pagaralam**, Indo.
126/D4 **Pagatan**, Indo.
123/B3 **Pagawyun**, Burma
187/G2 **Page**, Az,US
194/F4 **Page**, ND,US
191/G3 **Page**, Ok,US
63/J4 **Pagėgiai**, Lith.
201/G3 **Pageland**, SC,US
153/H2 **Pager** (riv.), Ugan.
124/D3 **Pagerdewa**, Indo.
121/H3 **Pāgla**, Bang.
84/B2 **Paglia** (riv.), It.
85/E3 **Paglieta**, It.
69/F6 **Pagny-dur-Moselle**, Fr.
185/K3 **Pagoda** (peak), Co,US
125/A4 **Pagon, Bukit** (mtn.), Malay.
139/H6 **Pago Pago** (cap.), ASam.
139/T10 **Pago Pago** (int'l arpt.), ASam.
190/A2 **Pagosa Springs**, Co,US
121/G2 **Pagri**, China
187/J3 **Paguate**, NM,US
195/M3 **Pagwachuan** (riv.), On,Can
195/M2 **Pagwa River**, On,Can
180/U11 **Pahala**, Hi,US
124/C2 **Pahang** (riv.), Malay.
124/C2 **Pahang** (state), Malay.
136/C3 **Pahaoa** (riv.), N.Z.
161/F3 **Páhara** (lag.), Nic.
120/C3 **Pahāri Buzurg**, India
120/B1 **Pahāsu**, India
136/C3 **Pahiatua**, N.Z.
119/F5 **Pahlagaon**, India
203/H4 **Pahokee**, Fl,US
186/E2 **Pahranagat Nat'l Wild. Ref.**, Nv,US
184/D3 **Pah-Rum** (peak), Nv,US
186/E2 **Pahrump**, Nv,US
159/L6 **Pahuatlán de Valle**, Mex.
186/D2 **Pahute** (mesa), Nv,US
115/C5 **Pai** (lake), China
180/T10 **Paia**, Hi,US
91/L7 **Paiania**, Gre.
186/B2 **Paicines**, Ca,US
63/L2 **Paide**, Est.
58/C6 **Paignton**, Eng,UK
168/B2 **Paiján**, Peru
63/L1 **Päijänne** (lake), Fin.
121/E1 **Paikü** (lake), China
174/D4 **Pailemán**, Arg.
123/C3 **Pailin**, Camb.
180/T10 **Pailolo** (chan.), Hi,US
78/C6 **Paimboeuf**, Fr.
167/L6 **Paime**, Col.
63/K1 **Paimio**, Fin.
124/C3 **Painan**, Indo.
174/C2 **Paine**, Chile
175/J7 **Paine** (peak), Chile
198/F4 **Painesville**, Oh,US
58/C2 **Painscastle**, Wal,UK
195/K4 **Paint** (riv.), Mi,US
198/E5 **Paint** (riv.), Oh,US
201/G2 **Paint Bank**, Va,US
187/G2 **Painted** (des.), Az,US
187/F4 **Painted Rock** (res.), Az,US
188/E2 **Paint Rock**, Tx,US
201/F2 **Paintsville**, Ky,US
164/C3 **Paipa**, Col.
198/F2 **Paisley**, On,Can
54/B5 **Paisley**, Sc,UK
184/C2 **Paisley**, Or,US
168/A2 **Paita**, Peru
118/C4 **Paithan**, India
61/G2 **Pajala**, Swe.
164/A5 **Paján**, Ecu.
172/C4 **Pajas Blancas** (Córdoba) (int'l arpt.), Arg.
65/K3 **Pajęczno**, Pol.
161/F4 **Pajonal Abajo**, Pan.
136/F7 **Pakakura**, N.Z.
124/C2 **Pakanbaru**, Indo.
165/F3 **Pakaraima** (mts.), Guy.
136/C3 **Pakawau**, N.Z.
123/C1 **Pak Ban**, Laos
123/C2 **Pak Beng**, Laos
113/C3 **Pakch'ŏn**, NKor.
123/C3 **Pak Chong**, Thai.
135/G6 **Pakenham**, Austl.
175/J7 **Pakenham** (cape), Chile
91/J5 **Pákhnes** (peak), Gre.
107/H3 **Pakistan**
92/B3 **Paklenica Nat'l Park**, Cro.
116/B4 **Pakokku**, Burma
183/J3 **Pakowki** (lake), Ab,Can
122/B2 **Pākpattan**, Pak.
119/H6 **Pak Phanang**, Thai.
92/C3 **Pakrac**, Cro.
63/K4 **Pakruojis**, Lith.
73/C6 **Paks**, Hun.
121/G3 **Paksey**, Bang.
123/C3 **Pak Thong Chai**, Thai.
127/F4 **Pakue**, Indo.
153/G2 **Pakwach**, Ugan.
123/D3 **Pakxe**, Laos
204/C4 **Pala**, Ca,US
77/N9 **Palacio Real**, Sp.
189/F3 **Palacios**, Tx,US
82/B2 **Paladru** (lake), Fr.
77/G2 **Palafrugell**, Sp.
90/D4 **Palagonia**, It.
85/G3 **Palagruža** (isls.), Cro.
122/F4 **Palai**, India
204/C4 **Pala Ind. Res.**, Ca,US
91/F3 **Palaiokastritsa**, Gre.
91/G3 **Pálairos**, Gre.
79/E4 **Palais** (riv.), Fr.
53/S10 **Palaiseau**, Fr.
118/D4 **Pālakolla**, India
155/F4 **Palalarivier** (riv.), SAfr.
91/H3 **Palamás**, Gre.
77/G2 **Palamós**, Sp.
101/R4 **Palana**, Rus.
125/C1 **Palanan**, Phil.
125/C1 **Palanan** (mtn.), Phil.
125/C1 **Palanan** (pt.), Phil.
125/C2 **Palanas**, Phil.
168/B2 **Palanda**, Ecu.
63/J4 **Palanga**, Lith.
126/D4 **Palangkaraya**, Indo.
118/B3 **Pālanpur**, India
83/C3 **Palanuda** (peak), It.
180/T10 **Palaoa** (pt.), Hi,US
155/E4 **Palapye**, Bots.
118/C5 **Palar** (riv.), India
127/F3 **Palasa**, Indo.
121/H2 **Palāsbāri**, India
76/B1 **Palas de Rey**, Sp.
85/E4 **Palata**, It.
205/P15 **Palatine**, Il,US
101/R3 **Palatka**, Rus.
203/H3 **Palatka**, Fl,US
114/D2 **Palattsy**, Kaz.
188/D4 **Palau**, Mex.
138/C4 **Palau** (terr.), US
123/B3 **Palauk**, Burma
123/B3 **Palaw**, Burma
125/B3 **Palawan** (chan.), Phil.
125/B3 **Palawan** (isl.), Phil.
172/B1 **Palaya**, Bol.
125/C2 **Palayan**, Phil.
122/F4 **Pālayankottai**, India
90/D4 **Palazzolo Acreide**, It.
87/G1 **Palazzolo dello Stella**, It.
85/F6 **Palazzo San Gervasio**, It.
169/E5 **Palca**, Bol.
190/E1 **Palco**, Ks,US
63/L2 **Paldiski**, Est.
121/E1 **Pāldor** (mtn.), Nepal
127/F3 **Paleleh**, Indo.
124/D3 **Palembang**, Indo.
186/E4 **Palen** (dry lake), Ca,US
174/C4 **Palena**, Chile
174/B4 **Palena** (riv.), Chile
85/E4 **Palena**, It.
76/C1 **Palencia**, Sp.
159/H5 **Palenque**, Mex.
159/H5 **Palenque Nat'l Park**, Mex.
83/C4 **Paleparto** (peak), It.
197/R9 **Palermo**, On,Can
90/C3 **Palermo**, It.
184/C4 **Palermo**, Ca,US
194/C3 **Palermo**, ND,US
206/D5 **Palermo**, NJ,US
90/E2 **Palese** (int'l arpt.), It.
172/B2 **Palestina**, Chile
167/K6 **Palestina**, Col.
200/B3 **Palestine**, Ar,US
198/C5 **Palestine**, Il,US
189/G2 **Palestine**, Tx,US
189/G1 **Palestine** (lake), Tx,US
84/C4 **Palestrina**, It.
86/B2 **Palestro**, It.
107/K5 **Pālghar**, India
122/F3 **Pālghāt**, India
113/D5 **P'algong-san** (mtn.), SKor.
113/E4 **P'algong-san** (mtn.), SKor.
132/B2 **Palgrave** (peak), Austl.
154/B4 **Palgrave** (pt.), Namb.
120/C3 **Palhāna**, India
167/G4 **Palhano**, Braz.
173/G3 **Palhoça**, Braz.
118/B2 **Pāli**, India
118/D3 **Pāli**, India
120/D4 **Pāli**, India
175/K8 **Pali Aike Nat'l Park**, Chile
120/C1 **Paliā Kalān**, India
84/D4 **Paliano**, It.
92/D2 **Palić**, Yugo.
84/C4 **Palidoro**, It.
127/F4 **Palima**, Indo.
83/B2 **Palinuro**, It.
83/B2 **Palinuro** (cape), It.
91/H3 **Palioúrion, Ákra** (cape), Gre.
195/H4 **Palisade**, Mn,US
185/H2 **Palisades**, Id,US
185/H2 **Palisades** (dam), Id,US
207/K8 **Palisades** (bluff), NJ,US
207/K7 **Palisades**, NY,US
207/J7 **Palisades Intst. Park**, NJ,US
207/D1 **Palisades Intst. Park**, NY,US
207/E2 **Palisades Park**, NJ,US
69/E4 **Paliseul**, Belg.
118/B3 **Pālitāna**, India
63/K2 **Palivere**, Est.
118/B3 **Pāliyād**, India
159/G5 **Palizada**, Mex.
92/C3 **Paljenik** (peak), Bosn.
122/G4 **Palk** (str.), India, SrL.
122/G4 **Palk** (bay), SrL.
81/G4 **Palla Bianca** (Weisskugel) (mtn.), It.
135/D1 **Pallamallawa**, Austl.
85/E3 **Pallano** (peak), It.
169/E3 **Pallar**, Bol.
134/B2 **Pallarenda**, Austl.
168/B3 **Pallasca**, Peru
60/B4 **Pallas Grean**, Ire.
60/B4 **Pallaskenry**, Ire.
61/H1 **Pallas-Ounastunturin Nat'l Park**, Fin.
97/H2 **Pallasovka**, Rus.
61/H1 **Pallastunturi** (peak), Fin.
153/H2 **Pallisa**, Ugan.
136/C3 **Palliser** (cape), N.Z.
131/G4 **Palm** (isls.), Austl.
170/D2 **Palma** (riv.), Braz.
155/J1 **Palma**, Moz.
77/G3 **Palma**, Sp.
85/E6 **Palma Campania**, It.
167/G4 **Palmácia**, Braz.
76/C4 **Palma del Río**, Sp.
90/C4 **Palma di Montechiaro**, It.
77/G3 **Palma Mallorca** (int'l arpt.), Sp.
87/G1 **Palmanova**, It.
161/H4 **Palmar** (riv.), Ven.
171/G1 **Palmares**, Braz.
171/G1 **Palmares** (arpt.), Braz.
169/F5 **Palmarito**, Bol.
164/D3 **Palmarito**, Ven.
84/C6 **Palmarola** (isl.), It.
173/G3 **Palmas**, Braz.
144/D5 **Palmas** (cape), Libr.
161/H1 **Palma Soriano**, Cuba
203/H3 **Palm Bay**, Fl,US
134/H8 **Palm Beach**, Austl.
202/P6 **Palm Beach**, Fl,US
202/P6 **Palm Beach** (co.), Fl,US
203/H4 **Palm Beach** (int'l arpt.), Fl,US
202/P6 **Palm Beach Gardens**, Fl,US
203/H4 **Palm Beach Gardens**, Fl,US
202/P6 **Palm Beach Shores**, Fl,US
204/C5 **Palm City**, Ca,US
203/H4 **Palm City**, Fl,US
204/B1 **Palmdale**, Ca,US
186/D4 **Palm Desert**, Ca,US
173/G3 **Palmeira**, Braz.
140/K10 **Palmeira**, CpV.
173/F3 **Palmeira das Missões**, Braz.
171/F1 **Palmeira dos Índios**, Braz.
167/F4 **Palmeirais**, Braz.
170/D2 **Palmeiras** (riv.), Braz.
170/C3 **Palmeiras de Goiás**, Braz.
167/G5 **Palmeirina**, Braz.
152/C5 **Palmeirinhas, Ponta deas** (pt.), Ang.
77/Q10 **Palmela**, Port.
137/V **Palmer** (arch.), Ant.
194/A3 **Palmer**, Sk,Can
177/J3 **Palmer**, Ak,US
191/F1 **Palmer**, Ks,US
208/B1 **Palmer**, Ma,US
189/F1 **Palmer**, Tx,US
205/D3 **Palmer**, Wa,US
192/B4 **Palmer Lake**, Co,US
137/V **Palmer Land** (reg.), Ant.
199/H2 **Palmer Rapids**, On,Can
134/C3 **Palmerston** (cape), Austl.
198/F3 **Palmerston**, On,Can
139/J6 **Palmerston** (atoll), CookIs.
136/B4 **Palmerston**, N.Z.
134/B2 **Palmerston Nat'l Park**, Austl.
136/C3 **Palmerston North**, N.Z.
206/C2 **Palmerton**, Pa,US
134/B1 **Palmerville**, Austl.
203/G4 **Palmetto**, Fl,US
189/F3 **Palmetto Bend** (dam), Tx,US
203/G3 **Palm Harbor**, Fl,US
83/B6 **Palmi**, It.
174/C2 **Palmilla**, Chile
161/F1 **Palmillas** (pt.), Cuba
159/F4 **Palmillas**, Mex.
164/B4 **Palmira**, Col.
134/B2 **Palm Island Abor. Settlement**, Austl.
173/G2 **Palmital**, Braz.
175/F2 **Palmitas**, Uru.
173/F3 **Palmitos**, Braz.
202/L8 **Palm River-Claire Mel**, Fl,US
186/D4 **Palm Springs**, Ca,US
139/J4 **Palmyra** (isl.), PacUS
104/D3 **Palmyra** (ruins), Syria
200/D1 **Palmyra**, In,US
198/E4 **Palmyra**, Mi,US
193/J4 **Palmyra**, Mo,US
199/H3 **Palmyra**, NY,US
206/B3 **Palmyra**, Pa,US
201/H2 **Palmyra**, Va,US
205/N14 **Palmyra**, Wi,US
118/E3 **Palmyras** (pt.), India
56/E2 **Palnackie**, Sc,UK
122/F3 **Palni**, India
122/F3 **Palni** (hills), India
125/D3 **Palo**, Phil.
205/K12 **Palo Alto**, Ca,US
206/B2 **Palo Alto**, Pa,US
189/F4 **Palo Alto Bfld. Nat'l Hist. Site**, Tx,US
158/C3 **Palo Bola**, Mex.
190/D2 **Palo Duro** (cr.), Ok, Tx,US
190/D3 **Palo Duro** (canyon), Tx,US
190/C3 **Palo Duro** (cr.), Tx,US
126/C3 **Paloh**, Indo.
149/G3 **Paloich**, Sudan
84/C3 **Palombara Sabina**, It.
172/D1 **Palometas**, Bol.
165/H4 **Palomeu** (riv.), Sur.
75/J4 **Palon** (peak), It.
187/H5 **Paloncillo** (mts.), Az, NM,US
87/E1 **Palon, Cima** (peak), It.
189/E1 **Palo Pinto**, Tx,US
172/E3 **Palo Santo**, Arg.
172/D2 **Palos Blancos**, Bol.
77/E4 **Palos, Cabo de** (cape), Sp.
86/C1 **Palosco**, It.
76/B4 **Palos de la Frontera**, Sp.
205/Q16 **Palos Hills**, Il,US
204/F8 **Palos Verdes** (hills), Ca,US
204/F8 **Palos Verdes** (pt.), Ca,US
204/B3 **Palos Verdes Estates**, Ca,US
182/F4 **Palouse**, Wa,US
186/E4 **Palo Verde**, Ca,US
161/E4 **Palo Verde Nat'l Park**, CR
120/D2 **Pālpa**, Nepal
168/C4 **Palpa**, Peru
172/C3 **Palpalá**, Arg.
127/G4 **Palpetu** (cape), Indo.
61/H2 **Paltamo**, Fin.
127/E4 **Palu**, Indo.
130/A2 **Palu** (isl.), Indo.
104/D2 **Palu**, Turk.
125/C2 **Paluan**, Phil.
83/C3 **Paludi**, It.
120/A1 **Palwal**, India
145/F4 **Pama**, Burk.
172/B4 **Pama**, Chile
126/C3 **Pamangkat**, Indo.
124/D4 **Pamanukan** (cape), Indo.
164/D5 **Pamar**, Col.
145/H4 **Pambeguwa**, Nga.
135/D3 **Pambula**, Austl.
124/F4 **Pamekasan**, Indo.
124/D4 **Pameungpeuk**, Indo.
120/D5 **Pāmgarh**, India
73/A4 **Pamhagen**, Aus.
74/D5 **Pamiers**, Fr.
114/B4 **Pamir** (riv.), Afg., Taj.
114/B4 **Pamir** (reg.), China, Taj.
201/J3 **Pamlico** (riv.), NC,US
201/J3 **Pamlico** (sound), NC,US
165/E4 **Pamoni**, Ven.
190/D3 **Pampa**, Tx,US
168/C4 **Pampachiri**, Peru
168/C4 **Pampacolca**, Peru
172/E3 **Pampa del Indio**, Arg.
172/D3 **Pampa de los Guanacos**, Arg.
172/C3 **Pampa de los Salinas** (salt flat), Arg.
172/C1 **Pampa Grande**, Bol.
127/F4 **Pampanua**, Indo.
163/C6 **Pampas** (reg.), Arg.
168/B3 **Pampas**, Peru
168/C4 **Pampas**, Peru
168/C4 **Pampas** (riv.), Peru
76/B2 **Pampilhosa da Serra**, Port.
201/H4 **Pamplico**, SC,US
164/C3 **Pamplona**, Col.
76/E1 **Pamplona**, Sp.
170/E3 **Pampulha** (int'l arpt.), Braz.
107/K2 **Pāmpur**, India
93/K5 **Pamukova**, Turk.
201/J2 **Pamunkey Ind. Res.**, Va,US
152/C3 **Pana**, Gabon
193/K4 **Pana**, Il,US
159/H4 **Panabá**, Mex.
125/D4 **Panabo**, Phil.
186/E2 **Panaca**, Nv,US
172/C1 **Panacachi**, Bol.
203/F2 **Panacea**, Fl,US
118/C6 **Panadura**, SrL.
120/B4 **Pānāgar**, India
93/G4 **Panagyurishte**, Bul.
124/D4 **Panaitan** (isl.), Indo.
118/B4 **Pānāji**, India
161/F4 **Panama**
161/G4 **Panamá** (bay), Pan.
161/F4 **Panama** (can.), Pan.
161/G4 **Panamá** (cap.), Pan.
161/G4 **Panama** (gulf), Pan.
161/G4 **Panama** (isth.), Pan.
191/G3 **Panama**, Ok,US
203/F2 **Panama City**, Fl,US
164/B2 **Panamá Viejo** (ruins), Pan.
173/F4 **Panambi**, Braz.
186/D2 **Panamint** (range), Ca,US
168/C3 **Panao**, Peru
125/D3 **Panaon** (isl.), Phil.
83/B5 **Panarea** (isl.), It.
87/E3 **Panaro** (riv.), It.
124/F4 **Panarukan**, Indo.
202/L6 **Panasoffkee** (lake), Fl,US
125/C3 **Panay** (gulf), Phil.
125/C3 **Panay** (isl.), Phil.
184/E4 **Pancake** (range), Nv,US
92/E3 **Pančevo**, Yugo.
121/G2 **Panchagarh**, Bang.
124/D2 **Panchor**, Malay.
121/G4 **Pānchur**, India
92/E4 **Pančicev vrh** (peak), Yugo.
121/F4 **Pancilet** (res.), India
93/H3 **Panciu**, Rom.
155/G5 **Panda**, Moz.
153/F5 **Panda**, Zaire
152/C2 **Pandaka-Lékoli Animal Rsv.**, Congo
122/E3 **Pandalayini**, India
188/D2 **Pandale**, Tx,US
154/E3 **Pandamatenga**, Bots.
125/C3 **Pandan**, Phil.
125/D2 **Pandan**, Phil.
120/C4 **Pandaria**, India
172/C2 **Pan de Azúcar**, Bol.
175/G2 **Pan de Azúcar**, Uru.
172/B2 **Pan de Azúcar Nat'l Park**, Chile
124/D4 **Pandeglang**, Indo.
63/L3 **Pandėlys**, Lith.
118/C4 **Pandharpur**, India
133/H3 **Pandie Pandie**, Austl.
86/C2 **Pandino**, It.
169/E3 **Pando** (dept.), Bol.
175/G2 **Pando**, Uru.
122/D2 **Pāndoh**, India
131/G2 **Pandora** (passg.), PNG
62/C3 **Pandrup**, Den.
121/H2 **Pandu**, India
121/G4 **Pandua**, India
169/E5 **Panduro**, Bol.
167/G5 **Panelas**, Braz.
63/L4 **Panevėžys**, Lith.
114/D3 **Panfilov**, Kaz.
99/M2 **Panfilovo**, Rus.
116/C4 **Pang** (riv.), Burma
139/H7 **Pangai**, Tonga
91/J2 **Pangaíon** (peak), Gre.
152/C3 **Pangala**, Congo
124/E4 **Pangandaran**, Indo.
151/B3 **Pangani**, Tanz.
151/B3 **Pangani** (riv.), Tanz.
59/E4 **Pangbourne**, Eng,UK
200/B3 **Pangburn**, Ar,US
153/F3 **Pangi**, Zaire
131/G1 **Pangia**, PNG
115/G6 **Pangjiabu**, China
127/E4 **Pangkajene**, Indo.
124/B1 **Pangkalanberandan**, Indo.
126/D4 **Pangkalanpembuang**, Indo.
124/B1 **Pangkalansusu**, Indo.
127/F4 **Pangkalaseang** (cape), Indo.
123/C1 **Pang Kalom**, Laos
124/D3 **Pangkalpinang**, Indo.
116/C4 **Pang Long**, Burma
179/K2 **Pangnirtung**, NW,Can
124/D4 **Pangrango-Mount Gede Nat'l Park**, Indo.
116/C3 **Pangsau** (pass), India
174/B3 **Panguipulli**, Chile
187/F2 **Panguitch**, Ut,US
144/C4 **Panguma**, SLeo.
124/B2 **Pangururan**, Indo.
125/C4 **Pangutaran**, Phil.
125/C4 **Pangutaran** (isl.), Phil.
125/B4 **Pangutaran** (isls.), Phil.
113/D3 **P'an'gyo**, NKor.
190/D3 **Panhandle**, Tx,US
127/J4 **Paniai** (lake), Indo.
153/E4 **Pania-Mutombo**, Zaire
180/R10 **Paniau** (peak), Hi,US
84/C1 **Panicale**, It.
138/F7 **Panié** (peak), NCal.
121/G4 **Pānihāti**, India
120/A1 **Pānīpat**, India
125/C3 **Panitan**, Phil.
124/D4 **Panjang**, Indo.
122/D2 **Panjgraon**, India
107/H3 **Panjgūr**, Pak.
107/K1 **Panj** (Pyandzh) (riv.), Afg., Taj.
105/F3 **Panjwīn**, Iraq
72/D2 **Panke** (riv.), Ger.
72/D2 **Pankow**, Ger.
145/H4 **Pankshin**, Nga.
113/D4 **P'anmunjŏm**, NKor.
113/D4 **P'anmun-ŭp**, NKor.
120/C3 **Panna**, India
132/C2 **Pannawonica**, Austl.
134/F7 **Pannikin** (isl.), Austl.
73/B4 **Pannonhalma Vasútállomás**, Hun.
103/C2 **Pano Lefkara**, Cyp.
103/C2 **Pano Panayia**, Cyp.
103/C2 **Pano Platres**, Cyp.
193/G3 **Panora**, Ia,US
170/C4 **Panorama**, Braz.
91/H2 **Panórama**, Gre.
122/G3 **Panruti**, India
113/B2 **Panshan**, China
109/K3 **Panshi**, China
117/F2 **Panshizhen**, China
121/F4 **Pānskura**, India
57/E6 **Pant**, Eng,UK
59/G3 **Pant** (riv.), Eng,UK
124/C1 **Pantai Remis**, Malay.
187/G4 **Pantano** (wash), Az,US
130/A2 **Pantar** (isl.), Indo.
201/J3 **Pantego**, NC,US
188/K7 **Pantego**, Tx,US
90/B4 **Pantelleria**, It.
90/B4 **Pantelleria** (isl.), It.
130/B2 **Pante Makasar**, Indo.
119/F3 **Pantha**, Burma
201/M7 **Panthersville**, Ga,US
200/B4 **Panther Swamp Nat'l Wild. Ref.**, Ms,US
124/C2 **Panti**, Indo.
86/C2 **Pantigliate**, It.
130/B4 **Pantijan Abor. Land**, Austl.
53/T10 **Pantin**, Fr.
164/C5 **Pantoja**, Peru
76/B1 **Pantón**, Sp.
125/D4 **Pantukan**, Phil.
152/D3 **Panu**, Zaire
159/F4 **Pánuco**, Mex.
159/F4 **Panuco** (riv.), Mex.
160/B1 **Pánuco** (riv.), Mex.
124/B2 **Panyabungan**, Indo.
145/H4 **Panyam**, Nga.
116/D3 **Panzhihua**, China
160/D3 **Panzós**, Guat.
167/N8 **Pao** (riv.), Ven.
171/F1 **Pão de Açúcar**, Braz.
83/C4 **Paola**, It.
84/J8 **Paola**, Malta
191/G1 **Paola**, Ks,US
200/D1 **Paoli**, In,US
191/F3 **Paoli**, Ok,US
206/C3 **Paoli**, Pa,US
190/A1 **Paonia**, Co,US
122/D2 **Paonta**, India
148/C4 **Paoua**, CAfr.
123/C3 **Paoy Pet**, Camb.
113/B1 **Paozi**, China
113/C2 **Paoziyan**, China
114/B3 **Pap**, Uzb.
73/B5 **Pápa**, Hun.
160/E4 **Papagayo** (gulf), CR
187/F4 **Papago Ind. Res.**, Az,US
180/U11 **Papaikou**, Hi,US
83/B2 **Papa, Monte de** (peak), It.
122/G3 **Papanāsam**, India
159/F4 **Papantla**, Mex.
159/M6 **Papantla de Olarte**, Mex.
168/C2 **Papaplaya**, Peru
125/A4 **Papar**, Malay.
139/X15 **Papara**, FrPol.
136/F6 **Papatoetoe**, N.Z.
55/N13 **Papa Westray** (isl.), Sc,UK
139/L6 **Papeete**, FrPol.
139/X15 **Papeete** (cap.), FrPol.
139/X15 **Papeete** (Faaa) (int'l arpt.), FrPol.
67/E2 **Papenburg**, Ger.
66/B5 **Papendrecht**, Neth.
139/X15 **Papenoo**, FrPol.
139/X15 **Papetoai**, FrPol.
103/C2 **Paphos**, Cyp.
103/C2 **Paphos** (dist.), Cyp.
63/K3 **Papilė**, Lith.
193/F3 **Papillion**, Ne,US
199/J2 **Papineauville**, Qu,Can
89/J2 **Papingut** (peak), Alb.
91/G2 **Papingut, Maj'e** (peak), Alb.
127/H4 **Papisoi** (cape), Indo.
149/F4 **Papiu**, Sudan
73/B5 **Papod** (peak), Hun.
172/B3 **Paposo**, Chile
70/D5 **Pappenheim**, Ger.
73/C1 **Papradno**, Slvk.
60/A5 **Paps, The** (mtn.), Ire.
131/G2 **Papua** (gulf), PNG
138/D5 **Papua New Guinea**
174/C2 **Papudo**, Chile
123/B2 **Papun**, Burma
133/F2 **Papunya**, Austl.
161/E4 **Paquera**, CR
166/D3 **Pará** (riv.), Braz.
170/D3 **Pará** (riv.), Braz.
166/C3 **Pará** (state), Braz.
166/C1 **Para** (dist.), Sur.
165/E3 **Pará** (falls), Ven.
132/C2 **Paraburdoo**, Austl.
125/C2 **Paracale**, Phil.
171/N7 **Paracambi**, Braz.
168/B4 **Paracas** (pen.), Peru
168/B4 **Paracas Nat'l Rsv.**, Peru
170/D3 **Paracatu**, Braz.
170/D3 **Paracatu** (riv.), Braz.
117/F5 **Paracel** (isls.), China
102/N7 **Parace Vela** (Okino-Tori-Shima) (isl.), Japan
133/H4 **Parachilna**, Austl.
185/J4 **Parachute**, Co,US
92/E4 **Paraćin**, Yugo.
77/N8 **Paracuellos**, Sp.
167/G3 **Paracuru**, Braz.
170/D3 **Pará de Minas**, Braz.
165/G4 **Para de Oeste** (riv.), Braz.
104/B2 **Paradhísion** (int'l arpt.), Gre.
118/E3 **Paradip**, India
197/L2 **Paradise**, Nf,Can
166/B1 **Paradise**, Guy.
187/H5 **Paradise**, Az,US
184/C4 **Paradise**, Ca,US
190/E1 **Paradise**, Ks,US
198/D1 **Paradise**, Mi,US
182/G4 **Paradise**, Mt,US
186/E2 **Paradise**, Nv,US
206/B3 **Paradise**, Pa,US
189/F1 **Paradise**, Tx,US
190/A3 **Paradise Hills**, NM,US
183/J1 **Paradise Valley**, Ab,Can
187/G4 **Paradise Valley**, Az,US
185/J4 **Paradox**, Co,US
133/M8 **Parafield** (arpt.), Austl.
98/G2 **Parafiyevka**, Ukr.
167/E3 **Paragominas**, Braz.
187/F2 **Paragonah**, Ut,US
191/J2 **Paragould**, Ar,US
169/F4 **Paraguá** (riv.), Bol.
165/F3 **Paragua** (riv.), Ven.
170/D4 **Paraguaçu**, Braz.
171/E2 **Paraguaçu** (riv.), Braz.
170/C4 **Paraguaçu Paulista**, Braz.
169/G4 **Paraguai** (riv.), Braz.
164/D2 **Paraguaipoa**, Ven.
164/D1 **Paraguaná** (pen.), Ven.
173/E3 **Paraguarí**, Par.
173/E2 **Paraguari** (dept.), Par.
172/D1 **Paraguay**
170/A4 **Paraguay** (riv.), Arg., Par.
163/E5 **Paraíba** (riv.), Braz.
167/G4 **Paraíba** (state), Braz.
171/N7 **Paraíba do Sul**, Braz.
171/L8 **Paraíba do Sul** (riv.), Braz.
167/E4 **Paraibano**, Braz.
171/L8 **Paraibuna** (riv.), Braz.
171/N6 **Paraibuna** (riv.), Braz.
170/D1 **Paraim** (riv.), Braz.
63/K1 **Parainen** (Pargas), Fin.
161/F4 **Paraíso**, CR
159/G5 **Paraíso**, Mex.
170/B4 **Paraiso do Norte**, Braz.
170/C1 **Paraíso do Norte de Goiás**, Braz.
171/K7 **Paraisópolis**, Braz.
145/F4 **Parakou**, Ben.
131/F2 **Parama** (isl.), PNG
122/G4 **Paramagudi**, India
166/C1 **Paramaribo** (cap.), Sur.
166/C1 **Paramaribo** (dist.), Sur.
167/F4 **Parambu**, Braz.
164/C3 **Paramillo** (peak), Col.
164/B3 **Paramillo Nat'l Park**, Col.
171/E2 **Paramirim**, Braz.
171/E2 **Paramirim** (riv.), Braz.
91/G3 **Paramithía**, Gre.
167/G4 **Paramoti**, Braz.
204/B3 **Paramount**, Ca,US
207/D2 **Paramus**, NJ,US
101/R4 **Paramushir** (isl.), Rus.
174/E1 **Paraná**, Arg.
174/E2 **Paraná** (riv.), Arg.
170/D2 **Paranã**, Braz.
170/B4 **Paranã** (riv.), Braz.
170/D2 **Paranã** (riv.), Braz.
170/B4 **Paraná** (state), Braz.
173/G3 **Paranaguá**, Braz.
173/G2 **Paranaguá** (bay), Braz.
170/C3 **Paranaíba**, Braz.
170/D3 **Paranaíba** (riv.), Braz.
175/S11 **Paraná Ibicuy** (riv.), Arg.
173/G1 **Paranaíbo** (riv.), Braz.
166/A4 **Paraná Madeirinha** (riv.), Braz.
173/G1 **Paranapanema** (riv.), Braz.
172/G2 **Paranapiacaba** (mts.), Braz.
125/E6 **Parañaque**, Phil.
163/D4 **Paranatinga** (riv.), Braz.
166/B3 **Paraná Urariá** (riv.), Braz.
170/B4 **Paranavai**, Braz.
125/C4 **Parang**, Phil.
122/H4 **Parangi** (riv.), SrL.
170/D3 **Paraopeba**, Braz.
170/D3 **Paraopeba** (riv.), Braz.
167/N8 **Parapara**, Ven.
136/C3 **Paraparaumu**, N.Z.
172/D1 **Parapetí** (riv.), Bol.
188/E4 **Parás**, Mex.
120/D2 **Parāsi**, Nepal
120/B4 **Parāsia**, India
135/B2 **Para Station**, Austl.
171/M8 **Parati**, Braz.
86/C1 **Paratico**, It.
171/E2 **Paratinga**, Braz.
171/L8 **Paratinga** (riv.), Braz.
170/C3 **Paraúna**, Braz.
83/C5 **Paravati**, It.
122/F4 **Paravūr**, India
53/T10 **Paray-Vieille-Poste**, Fr.
167/H4 **Paràzinho**, Braz.
120/A4 **Pārbati** (riv.), India
121/G3 **Pārbatipur**, Bang.
118/C4 **Parbhani**, India
79/F6 **Parçay-Meslay**, Fr.
79/E5 **Parcé-sur-Sarthe**, Fr.
64/F2 **Parchim**, Ger.
65/M3 **Parczew**, Pol.
103/D3 **Pardes Ḩanna**, Isr.
103/F7 **Pardes Ḩanna-Kardur**, Isr.
118/B3 **Pārdi**, India
114/E5 **Parding**, China
170/B4 **Pardo** (riv.), Braz.
170/D4 **Pardo** (riv.), Braz.
171/E2 **Pardo** (riv.), Braz.
132/C2 **Pardoo**, Austl.
65/H3 **Pardubice**, Czh.
124/F4 **Pare**, Indo.
151/B2 **Pare** (mts.), Tanz.
169/F4 **Parecis** (mts.), Braz.
77/P10 **Parede**, Port.
76/C1 **Paredes de Nava**, Sp.
160/C2 **Paredón**, Mex.
188/D5 **Paredón**, Mex.
174/C2 **Paredones**, Chile
167/G4 **Parelhas**, Braz.
74/C4 **Parempuyre**, Fr.
118/C4 **Parenda**, India
83/C4 **Parenti**, It.
74/C4 **Parentis-en-Born**, Fr.
127/E4 **Parepare**, Indo.
174/D2 **Parera**, Arg.
77/L6 **Parets del Vallès**, Sp.
72/B3 **Parey**, Ger.
91/G3 **Párga**, Gre.
63/K1 **Pargas** (Parainen), Fin.
69/D6 **Pargny-sur-Saulx**, Fr.
63/P1 **Pargolovo**, Rus.
172/C1 **Paria**, Bol.
165/F2 **Paria** (gulf), Trin., Ven.
187/G2 **Paria** (riv.), Az, Ut,US
168/B3 **Pariacoto**, Peru
165/E2 **Pariaguán**, Ven.
124/C3 **Pariaman**, Indo.
96/D1 **Parichi**, Bela.
127/F4 **Parigi**, Indo.
79/F5 **Parigné-l'Évêque**, Fr.
79/D3 **Parigny**, Fr.
165/F4 **Parima** (riv.), Braz.
165/E4 **Parima** (mts.), Braz., Ven.
172/B1 **Parinacota** (peak), Chile
168/C2 **Parinari**, Peru
168/A2 **Pariñas** (pt.), Peru
135/B2 **Paringa**, Austl.
98/F3 **Parîngu Mare, Vîrful** (peak), Rom.
166/B3 **Parintins**, Braz.
198/F3 **Paris**, Can.
53/T10 **Paris**, Fr.
68/B6 **Paris** (cap.), Fr.
191/H3 **Paris**, Ar,US
185/H2 **Paris**, Id,US
198/C5 **Paris**, Il,US
200/E1 **Paris**, Ky,US
196/B3 **Paris**, Me,US
191/H1 **Paris**, Mo,US
200/C3 **Paris**, Ms,US
200/C2 **Paris**, Tn,US
191/G4 **Paris**, Tx,US
68/B5 **Paris** (Charles de Gaulle) (int'l arpt.), Fr.
199/J2 **Parishville**, NY,US
74/E2 **Paris** (Orly) (int'l arpt.), Fr.
161/F4 **Parita** (bay), Pan.
185/K3 **Park** (range), Co,US
194/F3 **Park** (riv.), ND,US
194/A2 **Parkbeg**, Sk,Can
207/K8 **Parkchester**, NY,US
205/Q15 **Park City**, Il,US
191/F2 **Park City**, Ks,US
200/D2 **Park City**, Ky,US
183/K5 **Park City**, Mt,US
196/F2 **Parkdale**, PE,Can
189/J1 **Parkdale**, Ar,US
184/C1 **Parkdale**, Or,US
131/E4 **Parker** (pt.), Austl.
186/E3 **Parker**, Az,US
192/B4 **Parker**, Co,US
202/M7 **Parker** (lake), Fl,US
191/G1 **Parker**, Ks,US
208/H5 **Parker**, Pa,US
193/F2 **Parker**, SD,US
192/C2 **Parker** (peak), SD,US
189/F1 **Parker**, Tx,US
188/K7 **Parker** (co.), Tx,US
187/E3 **Parker Dam**, Ca,US
196/B4 **Parker River Nat'l Wild. Ref.**, Ma,NH,US
193/H2 **Parkersburg**, Ia,US
198/B5 **Parkersburg**, Il,US
201/G1 **Parkersburg**, WV,US
197/K2 **Parker's Cove**, Nf,Can
195/G4 **Parkers Prairie**, Mn,US
135/D2 **Parkes**, Austl.
206/C4 **Parkesburg**, Pa,US
59/H3 **Parkeston**, Eng,UK
195/J5 **Park Falls**, Wi,US
198/C4 **Park Forest**, Il,US
56/B2 **Parkgate**, NI,UK
58/A5 **Park Head** (pt.), UK
198/F3 **Parkhill**, On,Can
191/G3 **Park Hill**, Ok,US
59/E5 **Parkhurst**, Eng,UK
191/J3 **Parkin**, Ar,US
205/C3 **Parkland**, Wa,US
194/D3 **Parkman**, Sk,Can
196/C3 **Parkman**, Me,US
208/F5 **Parkman**, Oh,US
195/G4 **Park Rapids**, Mn,US
205/Q15 **Park Ridge**, Il,US
207/D1 **Park Ridge**, NJ,US
194/F3 **Park River**, ND,US
191/H3 **Parks**, Ar,US
183/L1 **Parkside**, Sk,Can
206/C4 **Parkside**, Pa,US
201/K2 **Parksley**, Va,US
71/F5 **Parkstetten**, Ger.
192/F2 **Parkston**, SD,US
182/B3 **Parksville**, BC,Can
201/F4 **Parksville**, SC,US
206/B4 **Parkton**, Md,US
201/H3 **Parkton**, NC,US
185/G3 **Park Valley**, Ut,US
193/J3 **Park View**, Ia,US
206/B5 **Parkville**, Md,US
206/B4 **Parkville**, Pa,US
205/L9 **Parkway-Sacramento**, Ca,US
201/H3 **Parkwood**, NC,US
76/D2 **Parla**, Sp.

118/D4 Parlakhemundi, India
193/F1 Parle, Lac qui (lake), Mn,US
118/C4 Parli, India
136/H9 Parliament Buildings, N.Z.
186/C2 Parlier, Ca,US
190/A1 Parlin, Co,US
86/D3 Parma, It.
86/D3 Parma (prov.), It.
86/D3 Parma (riv.), It.
184/E2 Parma, Id,US
200/C2 Parma, Mo,US
208/F5 Parma, Oh,US
208/F5 Parma Heights, Oh,US
53/S9 Parmain, Fr.
192/D2 Parmelee, SD,US
170/D1 Parnaguá, Braz.
167/F3 Parnaíba, Braz.
167/F4 Parnaíba (riv.), Braz.
167/G5 Parnamirim, Braz.
167/F4 Parnarama, Braz.
91/H3 Parnassós (peak), Gre.
91/H3 Parnassos Nat'l Park, Gre.
136/C3 Parnassus, N.Z.
133/H5 Parndana, Austl.
73/A4 Parndorf, Aus.
136/F6 Parnell, N.Z.
190/D3 Parnell, Tx,US
91/H3 Párnis (peak), Gre.
91/H4 Párnon (mts.), Gre.
63/L2 Pärnu, Est.
63/L2 Pärnu (bay), Est.
63/L2 Pärnu-Jaagupi, Est.
121/G2 Paro, Bhu.
113/D3 P'aro-ho (lake), SKor.
74/E2 Paron, Fr.
87/D2 Parona di Valpolicella, It.
135/C1 Paroo (riv.), Austl.
91/J4 Páros, Gre.
91/J4 Páros (isl.), Gre.
156/B4 Parow, SAfr.
187/F2 Parowan, Ut,US
81/F4 Parpan, Swi.
82/C2 Parrachée (mtn.), Fr.
174/C3 Parral, Chile
208/F6 Parral, Oh,US
134/H8 Parramatta, Austl.
201/K2 Parramore (isl.), Va,US
158/E3 Parras de la Fuente, Mex.
58/D4 Parrett (riv.), Eng,UK
200/D4 Parrish, Al,US
202/L8 Parrish, Fl,US
201/G4 Parris Island, SC,US
201/G4 Parris Island Marine Base, SC,US
161/E4 Parrita, CR
188/A3 Parrita, Mex.
202/P8 Parrot Jungle, Fl,US
200/E5 Parrott, Ga,US
196/E3 Parrsboro, NS,Can
155/E4 Parr's Halt, Bots.
179/H2 Parry (bay), NW,Can
178/F1 Parry (chan.), NW,Can
179/R7 Parry (isls.), NW,Can
198/F2 Parry Sound, On,Can
72/A2 Parsau, Ger.
71/E4 Parsberg, Ger.
81/G3 Parseierspitze (peak), Aus.
194/C4 Parshall, ND,US
206/D2 Parsippany, NJ,US
207/H8 Parsippany-Troy Hills, NJ,US
182/F2 Parson, BC,Can
130/D3 Parsons (range), Austl.
191/G2 Parsons, Ks,US
201/F3 Parsons (mtn.), SC,US
200/C3 Parsons, Tn,US
201/H1 Parsons, WV,US
130/D3 Parsons, Mount (peak), Austl.
72/E2 Parsteiner (lake), Ger.
145/F4 Partago, Ben.
94/C2 Pårtefjället (peak), Swe.
70/C2 Partenstein, Ger.
72/C5 Parthe (riv.), Ger.
74/C3 Parthenay, Fr.
62/E3 Partille, Swe.
90/C3 Partinico, It.
109/L3 Partizansk, Rus.
73/C2 Partizánske, Slvk.
191/E2 Partridge, Ks,US
60/A2 Partry (mts.), Ire.
118/C4 Partūr, India
166/C3 Paru (riv.), Braz.
166/B3 Paru de Oeste (riv.), Braz.
122/F3 Parūr, India
168/D4 Paruro, Peru
118/D4 Pārvathīpuram, India
57/G5 Parwich, Eng,UK
114/D5 Paryang, China
156/D2 Parys, SAfr.
197/J1 Pasadena, Nf,Can
204/B2 Pasadena, Ca,US
202/L7 Pasadena (lake), Fl,US
206/B5 Pasadena, Md,US
189/G3 Pasadena, Tx,US
204/F7 Pasadena-Burbank-Glendale (arpt.), Ca,US
164/A5 Pasado (cape), Ecu.
168/B1 Pasaje, Ecu.
123/C3 Pa Sak (riv.), Thai.
124/C2 Pasaman (peak), Indo.
120/D4 Pasān, India
97/H4 Pasanauri, Geo.
124/C3 Pasarbantal, Indo.
124/C3 Pasarkuok, Indo.
124/B2 Pasarsorkam, Indo.
130/A1 Pasarwajo, Indo.
123/B2 Pasawng, Burma
125/C2 Pasay City, Phil.
202/D2 Pascagoula, Ms,US
202/D2 Pascagoula (riv.), Ms,US
93/H2 Paşcani, Rom.
71/H6 Pasching, Aus.
202/L6 Pasco (co.), Fl,US
182/E4 Pasco, Wa,US
208/C2 Pascoag, RI,US
168/B3 Pasco, Cerro de, Peru
175/J7 Pascua (riv.), Chile
168/B1 Pascuales, Ecu.
68/A3 Pas-de-Calais (dept.), Fr.
68/B3 Pas-en-Artois, Fr.
97/G1 Pashkovo, Rus.
99/K5 Pashkovskiy, Rus.
87/G1 Pasian di Prato, It.
87/F1 Pasiano, It.
125/C2 Pasig, Phil.
116/B2 Pāsighāt, India
104/E2 Pasinler, Turk.
160/D2 Pasión, Río de la (riv.), Guat.
124/C1 Pasir Mas, Malay.
124/C1 Pasir Puteh, Malay.
65/K1 Pasłęk, Pol.
65/L2 Pasłęka (riv.), Pol.
132/D5 Pasley (cape), Austl.
92/B4 Pašman (isl.), Cro.
107/H3 Pasni, Pak.
174/C4 Paso de Indios, Arg.
172/E3 Paso de la Patria, Arg.
175/G1 Paso del Cerro, Uru.
159/N8 Paso del Macho, Mex.
173/E4 Paso de los Libres, Arg.
175/T11 Paso de los Toros, Uru.
174/C2 Paso del Planchón (peak), Chile
159/F5 Paso de Ovejas, Mex.
172/E3 Paso de Patria, Par.
174/C4 Paso Flores, Arg.
167/O8 Paso Real, Ven.
186/B3 Paso Robles (El Paso de Robles), Ca,US
196/E1 Paspébiac, Qu,Can
122/C1 Pasrūr, Pak.
177/M3 Pass (peak), Yk,Can
196/C3 Passadumkeag (mtn.), Me,US
60/D5 Passage East, Ire.
203/G4 Passage Key Nat'l Wild. Ref., Fl,US
167/F4 Passagem Franca, Braz.
60/B6 Passage West, Ire.
207/D2 Passaic, NJ,US
207/H7 Passaic (co.), NJ,US
207/D2 Passaic (riv.), NJ,US
193/G3 Passais-la-Conception, Fr.
171/M7 Passa Quatro, Braz.
71/G5 Passau, Ger.
202/D2 Pass Christian, Ms,US
68/C2 Passendale, Belg.
90/D4 Passero (pt.), It.
125/C3 Passi, Phil.
84/C1 Passignano sul Trasimeno, It.
86/D1 Passirano, It.
84/C3 Passo Corese, It.
173/F4 Passo Fundo, Braz.
173/F2 Passo Fundo (res.), Braz.
87/G1 Passons, It.
145/E3 Passoré (prov.), Burk.
173/F3 Passo Real (res.), Braz.
170/D4 Passos, Braz.
80/D3 Passwang (peak), Swi.
75/G4 Passy, Fr.
164/B5 Pastaza (prov.), Ecu.
168/B2 Pastaza (riv.), Ecu., Peru
63/J5 Pastek (riv.), Pol.
178/F3 Pas, The, Mb,Can
164/B4 Pasto, Col.
177/F3 Pastol (bay), Ak,US
187/H2 Pastora (peak), Az,US
76/B1 Pastoriza, Sp.
167/E4 Pastos Bons, Braz.
190/B3 Pastura, NM,US
125/C1 Pasuquin, Phil.
124/F4 Pasuruan, Indo.
63/L3 Pasvalys, Lith.
92/D2 Pásztó, Hun.
168/D4 Pata, Bol.
148/D3 Pata, CAfr.
172/C1 Patacamaya, Bol.
125/C3 Patag Nat'l Park, Phil.
174/D4 Patagonia (reg.), Arg.
187/G5 Patagonia, Az,US
124/C4 Patah (peak), Indo.
118/B3 Pātan, India
120/B4 Pātan, India
120/C1 Pātan, Nepal
170/A3 Patanal Matogrossense Nat'l Park, Braz.
127/G3 Patani, Indo.
145/G5 Patani, Nga.
121/E2 Pātan (Lalitpur), Nepal
196/D1 Patapédia (riv.), Qu,Can
206/B4 Patapsco, Md,US
206/B5 Patapsco (riv.), Md,US
206/B4 Patapsco, North Branch (riv.), Md,US
120/A1 Pataudi, India
79/G4 Patay, Fr.
168/B2 Pataz, Peru
133/J5 Patchewollock, Austl.
207/E2 Patchogue, NY,US
58/D3 Patchway, Eng,UK
151/C2 Pate (isl.), Kenya
136/C2 Patea, N.Z.
145/G4 Pategi, Nga.
57/G3 Pateley Bridge, Eng,UK
121/H4 Patenga, Bang.
121/H4 Patenga (arpt.), Bang.
87/E3 Paterna, Sp.
92/A2 Paternion, Aus.
85/D3 Paterno, It.
90/D4 Paternò, It.
182/E3 Pateros, Wa,US
207/D2 Paterson, NJ,US
120/D4 Pathalgaon, India
122/F4 Pathanāmthitta, India
122/C1 Pathānkot, India
121/G4 Pātharghāta, Bang.
121/E2 Patharkot, Nepal
185/K2 Pathfinder (dam), Wy,US
185/K2 Pathfinder (res.), Wy,US
185/K2 Pathfinder Nat'l Wild. Ref., Wy,US
123/B4 Pathiu, Thai.
183/M1 Pathlow, Sk,Can
124/E4 Pati, Indo.
130/B2 Pati, Indo.
164/B4 Patía, Col.
164/B4 Patía (riv.), Col.
122/D2 Patiāla, India
125/C4 Patikul, Phil.
121/G3 Pātiram, India
121/H4 Patiya, Bang.
114/E4 Patkaglik, China
121/E3 Patna, India
121/E3 Patna (arpt.), India
54/B6 Patna, Sc,UK
125/C2 Patnanongan (isl.), Phil.
125/C3 Patnongon, Phil.
105/E2 Patnos, Turk.
173/F3 Pato Branco, Braz.
200/D1 Patoka, In,US
200/D1 Patoka (lake), In,US
200/D1 Patoka (riv.), In,US
91/F2 Patos, Alb.
167/G4 Patos, Braz.
173/G3 Patos (lag.), Braz., Uru.
170/D3 Patos de Minas, Braz.
172/C4 Patquía, Arg.
91/G3 Pátrai, Gre.
91/G3 Patrai (gulf), Gre.
121/F4 Pātrasāer, India
121/E4 Patrātu, India
133/F2 Patricia (peak), Austl.
183/J2 Patricia, Ab,Can
188/C1 Patricia, Tx,US
130/C5 Patricia, Mount (peak), Austl.
175/J7 Patricio Lynch (isl.), Chile
203/H3 Patrick A.F.B., Fl,US
201/G2 Patrick Springs, Va,US
57/H4 Patrington, Eng,UK
170/D3 Patrocínio, Braz.
189/H2 Patroon, Tx,US
203/E2 Patsaliga (cr.), Al,US
81/H3 Patscherkofel (peak), Aus.
123/C5 Pattani, Thai.
123/C3 Pattaya, Thai.
196/C3 Patten, Me,US
67/G4 Pattensen, Ger.
191/J3 Patterson, Ar,US
186/B2 Patterson, Ca,US
203/G2 Patterson, Ga,US
202/C3 Patterson, La,US
191/J2 Patterson, Mo,US
122/C2 Patti, India
83/A6 Patti, It.
83/B6 Patti (gulf), It.
94/E2 Pattijoki, Fin.
58/D1 Pattingham, Eng,UK
200/B5 Pattison, Ms,US
122/B2 Pattoki, Pak.
199/G4 Patton, Pa,US
193/G3 Pattonsburg, Mo,US
122/G3 Pattukkottai, India
177/N4 Pattullo (mtn.), BC,Can
167/G4 Patu, Braz.
118/F3 Patuākhāli, Bang.
121/H4 Patuākhāli, Bang.
121/H4 Patuākhāli (dist.), Bang.
160/E3 Patuca (mts.), Hon.
161/E3 Patuca (pt.), Hon.
161/E3 Patuca (riv.), Hon.
124/D4 Patuha (peak), Indo.
92/F3 Pătulele, Rom.
206/B6 Patuxent (riv.), Md,US
206/B5 Patuxent Nat'l Wild. Ref., Md,US
206/A5 Patuxent River St. Park, Md,US
73/C4 Páty, Hun.
159/E5 Pátzcuaro, Mex.
74/C5 Pau, Fr.
168/C4 Paucarbamba, Peru
168/C3 Paucartambo, Peru
168/D4 Paucartambo, Peru
167/G4 Pau dos Ferros, Braz.
74/C4 Pauillac, Fr.
195/G1 Pauingassi, Can
169/E2 Pauini, Braz.
169/D2 Pauini (riv.), Braz.
116/B5 Pauksa (peak), Burma
123/B2 Pauktaw, Burma
161/E3 Paulaya (riv.), Hon.
198/E2 Paul B. Wurtsmith A.F.B., Mi,US
187/F3 Paulden, Az,US
201/L7 Paulding (co.), Ga,US
200/C4 Paulding, Ms,US
198/D4 Paulding, Oh,US
184/D1 Paulina, Or,US
182/E1 Pauline (mtn.), BC,Can
191/G1 Pauline, Ks,US
171/J7 Paulínia, Braz.
206/D1 Paulins (kill), NJ,US
166/C1 Paul Isnard, FrG.
167/H4 Paulista, Braz.
167/F5 Paulistana, Braz.
193/G2 Paullina, Ia,US
86/C2 Paullo, It.
171/F1 Paulo Afonso, Braz.
171/F1 Paulo Afonso Nat'l Park, Braz.
167/E4 Paulo Ramos, Braz.
157/E2 Paulpietersburg, SAfr.
206/C4 Paulsboro, NJ,US
199/J2 Paul Smiths, NY,US
191/F3 Pauls Valley, Ok,US
58/D4 Paulton, Eng,UK
204/D3 Pauma Valley, Ca,US
167/M6 Pauna, Col.
116/B5 Paungde, Burma
121/C5 Pauri, India
171/E1 Pausa, Peru
74/C5 Pau (Uzein) (int'l arpt.), Fr.
185/G4 Pavant (range), Ut,US
171/E3 Pavão, Braz.
105/F3 Pāveh, Iran
91/J1 Pavel Banya, Bul.
86/C2 Pavia, It.
86/C2 Pavia (prov.), It.
74/D5 Pavie, Fr.
182/D2 Pavilion, BC,Can
185/J2 Pavillion, Wy,US
79/F1 Pavilly, Fr.
63/J3 Pāvilosta, Lat.
95/K4 Pavino, Rus.
93/G4 Pavlikeni, Bul.
114/C1 Pavlodar, Kaz.
177/F4 Pavlof (vol.), Ak,US
99/H3 Pavlograd, Ukr.
94/J5 Pavlovo, Rus.
63/P2 Pavlovsk, Rus.
112/E2 Pavlovsk, Rus.
99/K4 Pavlovskaya, Rus.
73/A2 Pavlovské vrchy (mts.), Czh.
95/P5 Pavlovskiy, Kaz.
99/G3 Pavlysh, Ukr.
203/G2 Pavo, Ga,US
164/C4 Pavón, Col.
86/A2 Pavone Canavese, It.
86/D2 Pavone del Mella, It.
87/D4 Pavullo nel Frignano, It.
63/N2 Pavy, Rus.
153/F2 Pawa, Zaire
126/D4 Pawan (riv.), Indo.
120/C1 Pawāyan, India
208/C3 Pawcatuck, Ct,US
148/A4 Pawé (peak), Camr.
191/F2 Pawhuska, Ok,US
145/E4 Pawia, Gha.
116/C4 Pawn (riv.), Burma
192/C3 Pawnee (buttes), Co,US
193/K4 Pawnee, Il,US
191/F2 Pawnee (riv.), Ks,US
191/F2 Pawnee, Ok,US
193/F3 Pawnee City, Ne,US
192/F4 Pawnee Indian Vill., Ks,US
192/B3 Pawnee Nat'l Grsld., Co,US
190/E1 Pawnee Rock, Ks,US
198/D3 Paw Paw, Mi,US
198/C3 Paw Paw Lake, Mi,US
208/C2 Pawtucket, RI,US
206/B5 Pawtuxent (riv.), Md,US
91/F3 Paxoí (isl.), Gre.
91/G3 Paxoí (Yáios), Gre.
177/J3 Paxson, Ak,US
135/D2 Paxton, Austl.
203/E2 Paxton, Fl,US
198/B4 Paxton, Il,US
208/C1 Paxton, Ma,US
191/G5 Paxton, Tx,US
94/G3 Pay, Rus.
123/B2 Payagyi, Burma
127/G3 Payaheislam, Indo.
124/C3 Payakumbuh, Indo.
174/C3 Payén, Altiplanicie del (plat.), Arg.
80/C4 Payerne, Swi.
184/E1 Payette, Id,US
184/E1 Payette (riv.), Id,US
184/E1 Payette, North Fork (riv.), Id,US
184/F1 Payette, South Fork (riv.), Id,US
95/P1 Pay-Khoy (mts.), Rus.
179/J3 Payne (lake), Qu,Can
202/M8 Payne (cr.), Fl,US
132/C4 Paynes Find, Austl.
135/C3 Paynesville, Austl.
195/G5 Paynesville, Mn,US
183/K1 Paynton, Sk,Can
175/F2 Paysandú, Uru.
175/S11 Paysandú (arpt.), Uru.
172/E3 Paysandú (dept.), Uru.
175/S11 Paysandú (int'l arpt.), Uru.
53/T9 Pays de France (plain), Fr.
74/C3 Pays de la Loire (reg.), Fr.
78/D5 Pays-de-la-Loire (reg.), Fr.
79/E4 Pays de la Loire (reg.), Fr.
79/F5 Pays-de-la-Loire (reg.), Fr.
74/D2 Pays du Caux (reg.), Fr.
187/G3 Payson, Az,US
193/J4 Payson, Il,US
185/H3 Payson, Ut,US
174/C3 Payún (peak), Arg.
160/D3 Paz (riv.), ESal., Guat.
105/G4 Pāzanān, Iran
104/D1 Pazar, Turk.
104/D2 Pazarcık, Turk.
93/G4 Pazardzhik, Bul.
96/D5 Pazaryeri, Turk.
164/D3 Paz de Ariporo, Col.
164/C3 Paz del Río, Col.
87/G2 Pazin, Cro.
203/E2 Pea (riv.), Al,US
173/F2 Peabiru, Braz.
191/F1 Peabody, Ks,US
199/L3 Peabody, Ma,US
178/E3 Peace (riv.), Ab,Can
202/M8 Peace (riv.), Fl,US
203/H4 Peace (riv.), Fl,US
110/C3 Peace Mem. Park, Japan
176/F4 Peace River, Can.
178/E3 Peace River, Ab,Can
191/J2 Peace Valley, Mo,US
208/C3 Peace-Wakefield, RI,US
182/E3 Peachland, BC,Can
187/F3 Peach Springs, Az,US
201/M7 Peachtree (cr.), Ga,US
200/E4 Peachtree City, Ga,US
132/D5 Peak Charles Nat'l Park, Austl.
57/G5 Peak District Nat'l Park, Eng,UK
196/C2 Peaked (mtn.), Me,US
60/A6 Peakeen (mtn.), Ire.
132/C3 Peak Hill, Austl.
135/D2 Peak Hill, Austl.
201/G2 Peak, The (peak), NC,US
76/D4 Peal de Becerro, Sp.
185/J4 Peale (mtn.), Ut,US
206/D2 Peapack-Gladstone, NJ,US
204/C1 Pearblossom, Ca,US
187/H5 Pearce, Az,US
191/G2 Pea Ridge, Ar,US
201/G2 Pearisburg, Va,US
202/C2 Pearl (riv.), La, Ms,US
200/B4 Pearl, Ms,US
159/F2 Pearl, Tx,US
204/B1 Pearland, Ca,US
189/G3 Pearland, Tx,US
139/H2 Pearl and Hermes (reef), Hi,US
205/G6 Pearl Beach, Mi,US
193/K2 Pearl City, Il,US
117/G4 Pearl River (est.), China, HK
207/D1 Pearl River, NY,US
188/E3 Pearsall, Tx,US
199/G3 Pearson (int'l arpt.), On,Can
203/G2 Pearson, Ga,US
156/D4 Pearston, SAfr.
179/R7 Peary (chan.), NW,Can
195/H5 Pease, Mn,US
190/E3 Pease (riv.), Tx,US
78/C5 Péaule, Fr.
155/H3 Pebane, Moz.
168/D1 Pebas, Peru
153/E4 Pebeengu, Zaire
59/E2 Pebworth, Eng,UK
92/E4 Peć, Yugo.
189/E2 Pecan (bayou), Tx,US
124/E4 Pecangakan, Indo.
202/B3 Pecan Island, La,US
193/J2 Pecatonica (riv.), Il, Wi,US
81/E5 Peccia, Swi.
87/D5 Peccioli, It.
204/C4 Pechanga Ind. Res., Ca,US
77/G1 Pech de Guillaument (mtn.), Fr.
93/H3 Pechea, Rom.
94/F1 Pechenga, Rus.
99/J3 Pechenegi (res.), Ukr.
53/J2 Pechora, Rus.
95/M1 Pechora (bay), Rus.
53/J2 Pechora (riv.), Rus.
63/M3 Pechory, Rus.
92/E2 Pecica, Rom.
191/F2 Peckham, Ok,US
206/C1 Pecks (pond), Pa,US
82/C2 Peclet, Aiguille de (peak), Fr.
207/F2 Peconic (riv.), NY,US
83/C5 Pecoraro (peak), It.
180/F5 Pecos (riv.), NM, Tx,US
188/C2 Pecos, Tx,US
68/C2 Pecq, Belg.
68/C3 Pecquencourt, Fr.
92/D2 Pécs, Hun.
83/C4 Pedace, It.
161/F5 Pedasí, Pan.
85/D1 Pedaso, It.
135/C4 Pedder (lake), Austl.
156/D4 Peddie, SAfr.
87/D2 Pedemonte, It.
161/E4 Pedernal (pt.), Nic.
172/B2 Pedernales (salt pan), Chile
162/D3 Pedernales, DRep.
158/D2 Pedernales, Mex.
188/E2 Pedernales (riv.), Tx,US
165/F2 Pedernales, Ven.
170/C4 Pederneiras, Braz.
133/G3 Pedirka, Austl.
182/F1 Pedley, Ab,Can
204/C3 Pedley, Ca,US
171/E3 Pedra Azul, Braz.
152/C4 Pedra do Feitiço, Ang.
140/K10 Pedra Lume, CpV.
171/L7 Pedralva, Braz.
164/D2 Pedregal, Ven.
77/F3 Pedreguer, Sp.
171/K7 Pedreira, Braz.
167/F4 Pedreiras, Braz.
158/E3 Pedriceña, Mex.
206/C4 Pedricktown, NJ,US
118/D6 Pedro (pt.), SrL.
192/C1 Pedro, SD,US
170/C1 Pedro Afonso, Braz.
159/H5 Pedro Antonio Santos, Mex.
167/G4 Pedro Avelino, Braz.
177/H4 Pedro Bay, Ak,US
161/F1 Pedro Betancourt, Cuba
164/A5 Pedro Carbo, Ecu.
164/D4 Pedro Chico, Col.
170/B3 Pedro Gomes, Braz.
165/E4 Pedro II (isl.), Braz.
173/F2 Pedro Juan Caballero, Par.
170/D3 Pedro Leopoldo, Braz.
173/E4 Pedro Luro, Arg.
159/F4 Pedro Montoya, Mex.
172/B3 Pedro Montt, Chile
173/F4 Pedro Osório, Braz.
172/E4 Pedro R. Fernández, Arg.
167/F4 Pedro Segundo, Braz.
54/C5 Peebles, Sc,UK
198/E5 Peebles, Oh,US
132/B2 Peedamulla Abor. Land, Austl.
201/G3 Pee Dee (riv.), NC,US
201/G3 Pee Dee Nat'l Wild. Ref., NC,US
207/E1 Peekskill, NY,US
132/B3 Peel (inlet), Austl.
134/F6 Peel (isl.), Austl.
178/C1 Peel (sound), NW,Can
197/R8 Peel (co.), On,Can
56/D3 Peel, IM,UK
122/F3 Peelamedu (arpt.), India
57/F1 Peel Fell (mtn.), Eng,UK
182/C4 Pe Ell, Wa,US
188/L7 Peeltown, Tx,US
62/E5 Peene (riv.), Ger.
69/E1 Peer, Belg.
183/M3 Peerless, Mt,US
182/G1 Peers, Ab,Can
192/C3 Peetz, Co,US
136/C3 Pegasus (bay), N.Z.
72/C5 Pegau, Ger.
86/B4 Pegli, It.
84/C2 Peglia (peak), It.
83/B2 Peglio (riv.), It.
71/E3 Pegnitz, Ger.
71/E3 Pegnitz (riv.), Ger.
77/E3 Pego, Sp.
87/D3 Pegognaga, It.
72/C5 Pegomas, Fr.
57/G1 Pegswood, Eng,UK
116/C5 Pegu, Burma
116/B4 Pegu (mts.), Burma
116/C5 Pegu (riv.), Burma
116/B5 Pegu (Bago) (div.), Burma
194/F2 Peguis Ind. Res., Sk,Can
59/H4 Pegwell (bay), Eng,UK
93/H5 Pehlivanköy, Turk.
145/F4 Péhonko, Ben.
174/E2 Pehuajó, Arg.
174/C2 Pehuenche (pass), Chile
183/H3 Peigan Ind. Res., Ab,Can
108/G4 Peijiachuankou, China
115/B3 Peijiachuonkou, China
117/J4 Peikang, Tai.
75/F5 Peillac, Fr.
117/J4 Peinanchu (mtn.), Tai.
172/B2 Peine, Chile
67/H4 Peine, Ger.
63/M2 Peipus (lake), Est., Rus.
81/H2 Peissenberg, Ger.
117/J4 Peitawu (peak), Tai.
81/G2 Peiting, Ger.
170/C2 Peixe, Braz.
170/C2 Peixe (riv.), Braz.
170/C4 Peixe (riv.), Braz.
171/N6 Peixe (riv.), Braz.
115/D4 Pei Xian, China
172/B4 Pejerreyes, Chile
124/E4 Pekalongan, Indo.
124/C2 Pekan, Malay.
126/B3 Pekan Nanas, Malay.
124/B3 Pekanbaru, Indo.
193/K3 Pekin, Il,US
200/D1 Pekin (New Pekin), In,US
124/D4 Pelabuhanratu, Indo.
124/D4 Pelabuhanratu (bay), Indo.
174/C5 Pelada (plain), Arg.
90/C5 Pelagie (isls.), It.
200/C4 Pelahatchie, Ms,US
126/D4 Pelaihari, Indo.
124/C2 Pelalawan, Indo.
82/C4 Pelat (mtn.), Fr.
92/F3 Peleaga (peak), Rom.
96/B3 Peleaga, Vîrful (peak), Rom.
101/M4 Peleduy, Rus.
162/F4 Pelée (isl.), On,Can
179/H4 Pelee (pt.), On,Can
162/F4 Pelée (mtn.), Mart.
174/D10 Pelequén, Chile
134/A2 Pelham, Austl.
197/S9 Pelham, On,Can
200/D4 Pelham, Al,US
203/F2 Pelham, Ga,US
208/B1 Pelham, Ma,US
207/K8 Pelham, NY,US
207/K8 Pelham Bay Park, NY,US
207/K8 Pelham Manor, NY,US
65/H4 Pelhřimov, Czh.
194/D1 Pelican (lake), Mb,Can
154/B4 Pelican (pt.), SAfr.
177/L4 Pelican, Ak,US
202/B2 Pelican, La,US
195/N6 Pelican (lake), Mn,US
189/N9 Pelican (isl.), Tx,US
203/H4 Pelican I. Nat'l Wild. Ref., Fl,US
194/F4 Pelican Rapids, Mn,US
144/A4 Pelindă, Ponta de (pt.), GBis.
82/B5 Pélissanne, Fr.
92/E5 Pelister (peak), Macd.
92/E5 Pelister Nat'l Park, Macd.
92/C4 Pelješac (pen.), Cro.
195/K4 Pelkie, Mi,US
91/H2 Pélla, Gre.
91/H2 Pélla (ruins), Gre.
193/H3 Pella, Ia,US
83/B6 Pelloro, Punta di (pt.), It.
200/D4 Pell City, Al,US
174/E3 Pellegrini, Arg.
83/C3 Pellegrino (peak), It.
87/F2 Pellestrina, It.
82/D3 Pellice (riv.), It.
205/P14 Pell Lake, Wi,US
61/H2 Pello, Swe.
198/D2 Pellston, Mi,US
178/H2 Pelly (bay), NW,Can
177/M3 Pelly (riv.), Yk,Can
178/H2 Pelly Bay, NW,Can
177/L3 Pelly Crossing, Yk,Can
91/G3 Pelopónnisos (reg.), Gre.
83/B7 Peloritani (mts.), It.
173/F4 Pelotas, Braz.
173/G2 Pelotas (riv.), Braz.
65/K2 Pelplin, Pol.
191/H3 Pelsor, Ar,US
202/C3 Pelto (lake), La,US
82/C3 Pelvoux, Fr.
82/C3 Pelvoux (mtn.), Fr.
82/C3 Pelvoux (upland), Fr.
124/E4 Pemalang, Indo.
127/F4 Pemali (cape), Indo.
130/A1 Pemali (cape), Indo.
124/B2 Pematangsiantar, Indo.
155/J2 Pemba, Moz.
141/G5 Pemba (isl.), Tanz.
151/B3 Pemba (prov.), Tanz.
155/E3 Pemba, Zam.
132/C5 Pemberton, Austl.
182/C2 Pemberton, BC,Can
206/D4 Pemberton, NJ,US
182/G1 Pembina (riv.), Ab,Can
194/E3 Pembina (hills), Mb,Can
194/E3 Pembina (riv.), Mb, Can, Mt,US
194/F3 Pembina, ND,US
194/E3 Pembina Hist. Site, ND,US
195/L5 Pembine, Wi,US
199/H2 Pembroke, On,Can
58/B3 Pembroke, Wal,UK
201/G4 Pembroke, Ga,US
200/D2 Pembroke, Ky,US
208/D1 Pembroke, Ma,US
196/D3 Pembroke, Me,US
201/H3 Pembroke, NC,US
196/B4 Pembroke, NH,US
201/G2 Pembroke, Va,US
58/B3 Pembroke Dock, Wal,UK
203/H5 Pembroke Pines, Fl,US
55/J11 Pembrokeshire Coast Nat'l Park, Wal,UK
53/P8 Pembury, Eng,UK
195/L5 Pemebonwon (dam), Mi,US
195/L5 Pemenee (falls), Wi,US
174/B3 Pemuco, Chile
161/F4 Peña Blanca (mtn.), Pan.
76/A2 Penafiel, Port.
76/C2 Peñafiel, Sp.
174/Q9 Peñaflor, Chile
174/G4 Peña Forte, Braz.
76/D2 Peñalara (mtn.), Sp.
167/E3 Penalva, Braz.
76/B2 Penamacor, Port.
130/D1 Penambulai (isl.), Indo.
125/B4 Penampang, Malay.
124/C2 Penang (int'l arpt.), Malay.
170/C4 Penápolis, Braz.
76/C2 Peñaranda de Bracamonte, Sp.
206/C2 Pen Argyl, Pa,US
77/E2 Peñarroya (mtn.), Sp.
76/C3 Peñarroya-Pueblonuevo, Sp.
58/C4 Penarth, Wal,UK
175/L8 Peñas (cape), Arg.
168/D5 Peñas, Bol.
76/C1 Peñas (cape), Sp.
190/B4 Peñasco (riv.), NM,US
175/J6 Penas, Golfo de (gulf), Chile
174/C2 Pencahue, Chile
120/B5 Pench (riv.), India
174/B3 Penco, Chile
148/C4 Pendé (riv.), CAfr.
91/L6 Pendelikón (mtn.), Gre.
144/C4 Pendembu, SLeo.
167/G4 Pendências, Braz.
130/A4 Pender (bay), Austl.
193/F2 Pender, Ne,US
130/A4 Pender Bay Abor. Land, Austl.
105/N7 Pendik, Turk.
145/F4 Pendjari (riv.), Ben., Burk.
145/F4 Pendjari Nat'l Park, Ben.
57/F4 Pendle (hill), Eng,UK
198/D5 Pendleton, In,US
184/D1 Pendleton, Or,US
127/F4 Pendolo, Indo.
123/C4 Pendopo, Indo.
182/F3 Pend Oreille (riv.), Id, Wa,US
182/F3 Pend Oreille (lake), Id,US
182/F3 Pend Oreille (mtn.), Id,US
183/H3 Pendroy, Mt,US
76/A2 Peneda-Gerês Nat'l Park, Port.
171/F1 Penedo, Braz.
58/C1 Penegoes, Wal,UK
153/G4 Pene-Mende, Zaire
198/G2 Penetanguishene, On,Can
118/C4 Penganga (riv.), India
124/F5 Pengastulan, Indo.
157/E2 Penge, SAfr.
53/N7 Penge, Eng,UK
153/F4 Penge, Zaire
115/K9 Penggong, China
117/H3 Penghu, China
117/H4 Penghu (isl.), Tai.
115/E3 Penglai, China
116/E2 Penglaizhen, China
135/C4 Penguin, Austl.
116/D2 Peng Xian, China
173/G3 Penha, Braz.
155/G3 Penhalonga, Zim.
78/A4 Penhir, Pointe de (pt.), Fr.
183/H1 Penhold, Ab,Can
76/C4 Penibético, Sistema (range), Sp.
86/C3 Penice, Monte (peak), It.
76/A3 Peniche, Port.
54/C5 Penicuik, Sc,UK
124/F5 Penida (isl.), Indo.
72/C6 Penig, Ger.
199/H3 Peninsula (pt.), NY,US
208/F5 Peninsula, Oh,US
165/F2 Península de Paria Nat'l Park, Ven.
77/F2 Peñíscola, Sp.
172/B4 Peñita, Chile
167/E5 Penitentes (mts.), Braz.
159/E4 Pénjamo, Mex.
58/D1 Penkridge, Eng,UK
56/E5 Penmaenmawr, Wal,UK
78/A5 Penmarch, Fr.
78/A5 Penmarc'h, Pointe de (pt.), Fr.
194/E3 Penn, ND,US
84/C1 Penna (peak), It.
196/F3 Pennant (pt.), NS,Can
183/K2 Pennant, Sk,Can
85/E3 Penna, Punta della (cape), It.
182/D3 Pennask (mtn.), BC,Can
85/D3 Penne, It.
92/C5 Penne (pt.), It.
185/H5 Pennell (mtn.), Ut,US
118/C5 Penner (riv.), India
203/H3 Penney Farms, Fl,US
206/C2 Penn Forest (res.), Pa,US
208/H7 Penn Hills, Pa,US
196/D2 Penniac, NB,Can
80/D6 Pennine Alps (mts.), It., Swi.
57/F2 Pennine Chain (range), Eng,UK
200/C4 Pennington, Al,US
196/C2 Pennington (mtn.), Me,US
206/D3 Pennington, NJ,US
201/F2 Pennington Gap, Va,US
84/C1 Pennino (peak), It.
206/A2 Penns (cr.), Pa,US
206/C4 Pennsauken, NJ,US
198/F5 Pennsboro, WV,US
206/C3 Pennsburg, Pa,US
206/A2 Penns Creek (mtn.), Pa,US
206/C4 Penns Grove, NJ,US
206/D3 Penns Park, Pa,US
206/C4 Pennsville, NJ,US
199/G4 Pennsylvania (state), US
199/H3 Pennsylvania (hill), NY,US
179/S7 Penny (str.), NW,Can
199/H3 Penn Yan, NY,US
206/C3 Pennypack (cr.), Pa,US
196/C3 Penobscot (bay), Me,US
196/C3 Penobscot (riv.), Me,US
196/C3 Penobscot Ind. Res., Me,US
167/K6 Peñol, Col.
167/K6 Peñol (res.), Col.
135/B3 Penola, Austl.
158/D3 Peñón Blanco, Mex.
133/G4 Penong, Austl.
161/F4 Penonomé, Pan.
56/E1 Penpont, Sc,UK
56/D5 Penrhyn Mawr (pt.), Wal,UK
56/D6 Penrhyn Mawr (pt.), Wal,UK
139/K5 Penrhyn (Tongareva) (isl.), Cookls.
134/G8 Penrith, Austl.
57/F2 Penrith, Eng,UK
192/B4 Penrose, Co,US
58/A6 Penryn, Eng,UK
137/X Pensacola (mts.), Ant.
202/E2 Pensacola, Fl,US
203/E2 Pensacola (bay), Fl,US
191/G2 Pensacola (dam), Ok,US
202/E2 Pensacola Nav. Air Sta., Fl,US
202/E2 Pensacola Village, Historic, Fl,US
169/F4 Pensamiento, Bol.
194/B2 Pense, Sk,Can
135/B3 Penshurst, Austl.
53/P8 Penshurst, Eng,UK
125/B4 Pensiangan, Malay.
58/B5 Pensilva, Eng,UK
167/K6 Pensilvania, Col.
206/A6 Pentagon, Va,US
138/F6 Pentecost (isl.), Van.
167/G3 Pentecoste, Braz.
93/H3 Penteleu (peak), Rom.
80/C4 Penthalaz, Swi.
182/E3 Penticton, BC,Can
182/E3 Penticton Ind. Res., BC,Can
58/B5 Pentire (pt.), UK
134/B3 Pentland, Austl.
54/C5 Pentland (hills), Sc,UK
55/N13 Pentland Firth (inlet), Sc,UK
198/C3 Pentwater, Mi,US
58/B3 Pentyrch, Wal,UK
174/C2 Peñuelas Nat'l Park, Chile
78/B3 Penvénan, Fr.
123/B2 Penwegon, Burma
158/E2 Penwell, Tx,US
58/A6 Penwith (pen.), Eng,UK
57/E6 Pen-y-Cae, Wal,UK
57/F3 Pen-y-Ghent (mtn.), Eng,UK
56/E5 Pen-y-Gogarth (pt.), Wal,UK
58/C2 Pen y Gurnos (mtn.), Wal,UK
53/H3 Penza, Rus.
194/B2 Penzance, Sk,Can
58/A6 Penzance, Eng,UK
97/G1 Penza Obl., Rus.
81/H2 Penzberg, Ger.
78/B3 Penzé (riv.), Fr.
101/S3 Penzhina (bay), Rus.
101/S3 Penzhina (riv.), Rus.
70/D6 Penzing, Ger.
64/G2 Penzlin, Ger.
187/F4 Peoria, Az,US
193/K3 Peoria, Il,US
159/E4 Peotillos, Mex.
161/F1 Pepe (cape), Cuba
180/U11 Pepeekeo, Hi,US
180/U11 Pepeekeo (pt.), Hi,US
144/B4 Pepel, SLeo.
193/H1 Pepin (lake), Mn, Wi,US
193/H1 Pepin, Wi,US
69/E2 Pepinster, Belg.
208/F5 Pepper Pike, Oh,US
91/F2 Peqin, Alb.
195/K4 Pequaming, Mi,US
207/D2 Pequannock, NJ,US
206/B4 Pequea (cr.), Pa,US
206/D2 Pequest (riv.), NJ,US
195/G4 Pequot Lakes, Mn,US
129/G2 Pera (head), Austl.
124/D3 Perabumulih, Indo.
165/F3 Perai-tepuí, Ven.
124/C1 Perak (riv.), Malay.
124/C1 Perak (state), Malay.
77/M9 Perales (riv.), Sp.
76/E1 Peralta, Sp.
175/T11 Peralta, Uru.
187/J3 Peralta, NM,US
91/J5 Pérama, Gre.
122/G3 Perambalūr, India
196/E1 Percé, Qu,Can
80/C6 Percée, Pointe (peak), Fr.
79/F3 Perche (hills), Fr.
73/A3 Perchtoldsdorf, Aus.
189/G2 Percilla, Tx,US
132/E2 Percival (lakes), Austl.
190/C2 Percival, Sk,Can
134/C3 Percy (isls.), Austl.
79/D3 Percy, Fr.
193/K4 Percy, Il,US
156/Q13 Perdekop, SAfr.
91/G3 Pérdhika, Gre.
77/F1 Perdido (mtn.), Sp.
202/E2 Perdido, Al,US
170/D4 Perdões, Braz.
183/L1 Perdue, Sk,Can
98/B3 Perechin, Ukr.
134/D4 Peregian Beach, Austl.
98/C3 Pereginsko, Ukr.
164/C3 Pereira, Col.
170/C4 Pereira Barreto, Braz.
167/G4 Pereiro, Braz.
77/F2 Perelló, Sp.
97/J2 Peremětnoye, Kaz.
96/F1 Peremyshl', Rus.
98/C3 Peremyshlyany, Ukr.
132/C4 Perenjori, Austl.
99/H2 Peresechnaya, Ukr.
99/H3 Pereshchepino, Ukr.
94/H4 Pereslavl'-Zalesskiy, Rus.
87/E5 Peretola (int'l arpt.), It.
97/K2 Perevolotskiy, Rus.
109/M2 Pereyaslavka, Rus.
98/F2 Pereyaslav-Khmel'nitskiy, Ukr.
71/H6 Perg, Aus.
174/E2 Pergamino, Arg.
104/A2 Pergamum (ruins), Turk.
81/H5 Pergine Valsugana, It.
87/F5 Pergola, It.
195/G4 Perham, Mn,US
92/E2 Periam, Rom.
179/J3 Péribonca (riv.), Qu,Can
172/C3 Perico, Arg.
161/F1 Perico, Cuba
158/D3 Pericos, Mex.
158/D4 Pericos, Mex.
187/G4 Peridot, Az,US
78/D2 Périers, Fr.
183/N1 Périgord, Sk,Can
74/D4 Périgueux, Fr.
164/C2 Perijá, Sierra de (mts.), Col., Ven.
106/D6 Perim (isl.), Yem.
167/E3 Peri-Mirim, Braz.
124/C1 Peringat, Malay.
73/A5 Perint (riv.), Hun.
91/J3 Peristéra (isl.), Gre.
91/L6 Peristéri, Gre.
174/C5 Perito Moreno, Arg.
175/K6 Perito Moreno Nat'l Park, Arg.
122/F3 Periyakulam, India
122/F3 Periyar (riv.), India
122/F4 Periyar Wild. Sanct., India
206/C3 Perkasie, Pa,US
73/C5 Perkáta, Hun.
201/G4 Perkins, Ga,US
198/C2 Perkins, Mi,US
191/F3 Perkins, Ok,US
202/D2 Perkinston, Ms,US
206/C3 Perkiomen (cr.), Pa,US
69/F5 Perl, Ger.
161/F3 Perlas (lag.), Nic.
161/F3 Perlas (pt.), Nic.
161/G4 Perlas (arch.), Pan.
72/B1 Perleberg, Ger.
92/E3 Perlez, Yugo.
124/B1 Perlis (state), Malay.
53/J3 Perm', Rus.
91/G2 Përmet, Alb.
188/C2 Permian Basin Petrol. Museum, Tx,US
95/M4 Perm' Obl., Rus.
167/G5 Pernambuco (state), Braz.
86/B2 Pernate, It.
191/F3 Pernell, Ok,US
82/B4 Pernes-les-Fontaines, Fr.
92/F4 Pernik, Bul.
63/K1 Perniö, Fin.
132/B3 Peron (pen.), Austl.
68/B4 Péronne, Fr.
82/D3 Perosa Argentina, It.
159/F5 Perote, Mex.
200/E5 Perote, Al,US
80/B6 Pérouges, Fr.
74/E5 Perpignan, Fr.
74/E5 Perpignan (Llabanere) (int'l arpt.), Fr.
58/A6 Perranporth, UK
68/A5 Perriers-sur-Andelle, Fr.
80/B4 Perrigny, Fr.
189/E1 Perrin, Tx,US
203/H5 Perrine, Fl,US
204/C3 Perris, Ca,US
204/C3 Perris (res.), Ca,US
190/B3 Perro, Laguna del (lake), NM,US
82/C2 Perron des Encombres (mtn.), Fr.
161/G1 Perros (bay), Cuba
78/B3 Perros-Guirec, Fr.
197/N7 Perrot (isl.), Qu,Can
178/F2 Perry (riv.), NW,Can
203/G2 Perry, Fl,US
200/F4 Perry, Ga,US
193/G3 Perry, Ia,US
191/G1 Perry (lake), Ks,US
196/D3 Perry, Me,US
191/J1 Perry, Mo,US
199/G3 Perry, NY,US
191/F2 Perry, Ok,US
206/A3 Perry (co.), Pa,US
206/B5 Perry Hall, Md,US
208/F6 Perry Heights, Oh,US
206/B5 Perryman, Md,US
198/E4 Perrysburg, Oh,US
208/E6 Perrysville, Oh,US
190/D2 Perryton, Tx,US
191/H4 Perrytown, Ar,US
177/G4 Perryville, Ak,US
191/H3 Perryville, Ar,US
200/E2 Perryville, Ky,US
206/B4 Perryville, Md,US
193/K5 Perryville, Mo,US
200/C3 Perryville, Tn,US
53/S9 Persan, Fr.
106/F3 Persepolis (ruins), Iran
169/F4 Perseverancia, Bol.
63/R7 Pershagen, Swe.
58/D2 Pershore, Eng,UK
98/D2 Pershotravnevoye, Ukr.
98/D2 Pershotravnevoye, Ukr.
99/J4 Pershotravnevoye, Ukr.
106/E3 Persian (gulf), Asia
62/E3 Perstorp, Swe.
124/C2 Pertandangan (cape), Indo.
104/D2 Pertek, Turk.
132/B4 Perth, Austl.
132/K6 Perth (int'l arpt.), Austl.
199/H2 Perth, On,Can
54/C4 Perth, Sc,UK
191/F2 Perth, Ks,US
207/D2 Perth Amboy, NJ,US
196/D2 Perth-Andover, NB,Can
132/K6 Perth Zoo, Austl.
149/H1 Pertokar, Eth.
82/B5 Pertuis, Fr.
74/C3 Pertuis Breton (inlet), Fr.
90/A2 Pertusato (cape), Fr.
168/C3 Peru
193/K3 Peru, Il,US
198/C4 Peru, In,US
192/F3 Peru, Ks,US
196/B3 Peru, Me,US
193/G3 Peru, Ne,US
92/D4 Perućačko (lake), Bosn.
84/C1 Perugia, It.
84/C1 Perugia (prov.), It.
170/D5 Peruíbe, Braz.
122/F3 Perumpāvūr, India
93/G4 Perushtitsa, Bul.
68/C2 Péruwelz, Belg.
104/E2 Pervari, Turk.
95/J5 Pervomaysk, Rus.
98/F3 Pervomaysk, Ukr.
108/H1 Pervomayskiy, Rus.
97/G1 Pervomayskiy, Rus.
99/J3 Pervomayskiy, Ukr.
97/J2 Pervomayskoye, Rus.
97/G2 Pervomayskoye, Rus.
97/H2 Pervomayskoye, Rus.
99/L3 Pervomayskoye, Rus.
99/G5 Pervomayskoye, Ukr.
95/N4 Pervoural'sk, Rus.
69/D2 Perwez, Belg.
80/D3 Péry, Swi.
87/E5 Pesa (riv.), It.
124/D4 Pesagi (peak), Indo.
87/F5 Pesaro, It.
87/F5 Pesaro e Urbino (prov.), It.
186/A2 Pescadero, Ca,US
186/A2 Pescadero (pt.), Ca,US
117/H4 Pescadore (chan.), Tai.
117/H4 Pescadores (arch.), Tai.
87/D2 Pescantina, It.
85/E3 Pescara, It.
85/D3 Pescara (prov.), It.
85/E3 Pescara (riv.), It.
85/D4 Pescasseroli, It.
99/K3 Peschanka, Ukr.
99/L4 Peschanokopskoye, Rus.
97/J4 Peschanyy, Mys (cape), Kaz.
85/G4 Peschici, It.
87/D5 Pescia, It.
85/D3 Pescina, It.
85/E4 Pescocostanzo, It.
85/F6 Pescopagano, It.
80/C4 Peseux, Swi.
95/L2 Pesha (riv.), Rus.
107/K2 Peshāwar, Pak.
91/G2 Peshkopi, Alb.
93/G4 Peshtera, Bul.
193/L1 Peshtigo, Wi,US
195/L5 Peshtigo (riv.), Wi,US
94/H5 Peski, Rus.
95/M4 Peskovka, Rus.
98/E2 Peskovka, Ukr.
80/B3 Pesmes, Fr.
63/P1 Pesochnyy, Rus.
76/B2 Peso da Régua, Port.
167/G5 Pesqueira, Braz.
188/D5 Pesquería (riv.), Mex.
74/C4 Pessac, Fr.
72/C2 Pessin, Ger.
74/D5 Pessons, Pic dels (peak), And.
73/D5 Pest (co.), Hun.
94/G4 Pestovo, Rus.
85/E3 Petacciato, It.
103/D3 Petah Tiqwa, Isr.
202/D2 Petal, Ms,US
91/J4 Petalión (gulf), Gre.
205/J10 Petaluma, Ca,US
205/J10 Petaluma (riv.), Ca,US
69/E4 Pétange, Lux.
121/E4 Petārbār, India
165/E2 Petare, Ven.
91/G3 Pétas, Gre.
158/D3 Petatlán (riv.), Mex.
155/F2 Petauke, Zam.

199/H2 Petawawa, On,Can
198/G2 Petawawa (riv.), On,Can
159/H5 Petcacab, Mex.
160/D2 Peten Itzá (lake), Guat.
193/J1 Petenwell (dam), Wi,US
193/K1 Petenwell (lake), Wi,US
133/H5 Peterborough, Austl.
199/G2 Peterborough, On,Can
59/F1 Peterborough, Eng,UK
54/D2 Peterculter, Sc,UK
54/E2 Peterhead, Sc,UK
137/T Peter I (isl.), Ant.
50/E9 Peter I (isl.), Nor.
57/G2 Peterlee, Eng,UK
202/E2 Peterman, Al,US
133/F3 Petermann Abor. Land, Austl.
174/C2 Peteroa (vol.), Arg.
178/F3 Peter Pond (lake), Sk,Can
206/B3 Peters (mtn.), Pa,US
70/D4 Petersaurach, Ger.
70/C1 Petersberg, Ger.
177/M4 Petersburg, Ak,US
193/K3 Petersburg, Il,US
200/D1 Petersburg, In,US
194/E3 Petersburg, ND,US
190/D4 Petersburg, Tx,US
201/J2 Petersburg, Va,US
201/H1 Petersburg, WV,US
201/J2 Petersburg Nat'l Bfld., Va,US
194/F2 Petersfield, Mb,Can
59/F5 Petersfield, Eng,UK
67/F4 Petershagen, Ger.
71/E6 Petershausen, Ger.
200/D3 Petersville-Underwood, Al,US
92/E1 Pétervására, Hun.
197/K1 Peterview, Nf,Can
73/C5 Pétfürdő, Hun.
83/C4 Petilia Policastro, It.
161/H2 Pétionville, Haiti
82/B3 Petit Buëch (riv.), Fr.
196/E1 Petit-Cap, Qu,Can
196/E3 Petitcodiac, NB,Can
197/G3 Petit-de-Grat, NS,Can
196/D1 Petite-Matane, Qu,Can
161/H2 Petite Rivière de l'Artibonite, Haiti
69/F5 Petite-Rosselle, Fr.
161/H2 Petit Goâve, Haiti
191/G3 Petit Jean (riv.), Ar,US
152/B3 Petit Loango Nat'l Park, Gabon
196/D3 Petit Manan Nat'l Wild. Ref., Me,US
68/C6 Petit Marin (riv.), Fr.
179/K3 Petit Mécatina (riv.), Qu,Can
82/C2 Petit Mont Blanc (mtn.), Fr.
68/C6 Petit Morin (riv.), Fr.
199/J1 Petit Nation (riv.), Qu,Can
80/B4 Petit-Noir, Fr.
53/S9 Petit Rosne (riv.), Fr.
196/B1 Petit-Saguenay, Qu,Can
82/C1 Petit Saint-Bernard, Col du (pass), Fr.
61/J3 Petkeljärven Nat'l Park, Fin.
118/B3 Petlād, India
159/F5 Petlalcingo, Mex.
159/H4 Peto, Mex.
174/C2 Petorca, Chile
198/D2 Petoskey, Mi,US
101/M2 Petra (isls.), Rus.
103/D4 Petra (Baṭrā') (ruins), Jor.
147/G2 Petra (Baṭrā') (ruins), Jor.
199/H3 Petre (pt.), On,Can
77/E3 Petrel, Sp.
85/D5 Petrella (peak), It.
85/E4 Petrella Tifernina, It.
95/N3 Petretsovo, Rus.
203/E2 Petrey, Al,US
93/F5 Petrich, Bul.
187/H3 Petrified Forest Nat'l Park, Az,US
98/E1 Petrikov, Bela.
99/H3 Petrikovka, Ukr.
93/F3 Petrila, Rom.
85/D1 Petritoli, It.
63/N2 Petrodvorets, Rus.
93/F4 Petrokhanski Prokhod (pass), Bul.
171/F1 Petrolândia, Braz.
198/E3 Petrolia, On,Can
208/H5 Petrolia, Pa,US
191/E3 Petrolia, Tx,US
171/E1 Petrolina, Braz.
83/C4 Petronà, It.
99/J3 Petropavlovka, Ukr.
100/G4 Petropavlovsk, Kaz.
101/R4 Petropavlovsk-Kamchatskiy, Rus.
97/H3 Petropavlovskoye, Rus.
171/E4 Petrópolis, Braz.
200/E2 Petros, Tn,US
93/F3 Petroşani, Rom.
85/D4 Petroso (peak), It.
73/B2 Petrov, Czh.
92/D3 Petrovaradin, Yugo.
98/F4 Petrovka, Ukr.
97/H1 Petrovsk, Rus.
99/J5 Petrovskaya, Rus.
99/K3 Petrovskiy Yam, Rus.
97/L1 Petrovskoye, Rus.
99/K3 Petrovskoye, Ukr.
108/F1 Petrovsk-Zabaykal'skiy, Rus.
94/G3 Petrozavodsk, Rus.
63/P1 Petrozavodsk Obl., Rus.
156/D3 Petrusburg, SAfr.
156/E2 Petrus Steyn, SAfr.
156/D3 Petrusville, SAfr.
71/H7 Pettenbach, Aus.
57/F2 Petterill (riv.), Eng,UK
194/E4 Pettibone, ND,US
191/H3 Pettigrew, Ar,US
83/C4 Pettinascura (peak), It.
189/F3 Pettus, Tx,US
94/H5 Petushki, Rus.
59/F5 Petworth, Eng,UK
92/A2 Petzeck (peak), Aus.
71/G6 Peuerbach, Aus.
124/B1 Peuetsagoe (mtn.), Indo.
177/G4 Peulik (mtn.), Ak,US
174/C2 Peumo, Chile
124/B1 Peureulak, Indo.
124/B1 Peusangan (pt.), Indo.
101/T3 Pevek, Rus.
191/J1 Pevely, Mo,US
59/G5 Pevensey, Eng,UK
205/P13 Pewaukee, Wi,US
205/P13 Pewaukee (lake), Wi,US
59/E4 Pewsey, Eng,UK
103/C2 Peyia, Cyp.
105/G3 Peyk, Iran
82/C5 Peymeinade, Fr.
74/C5 Peyrehorade, Fr.
82/B5 Peyrolles-en-Provence, Fr.
82/B4 Peyruis, Fr.
95/K2 Peza (riv.), Rus.
74/E5 Pézenas, Fr.
73/B3 Pezinok, Slvk.
122/A1 Pezu, Pak.
70/D6 Pfaffenhausen, Ger.
70/D6 Pfaffenhofen an der Ilm, Ger.
81/G1 Pfaffenhofen an der Roth, Ger.
69/G6 Pfaffenhoffen, Fr.
81/E3 Pfäffikon, Swi.
71/F6 Pfaffing, Ger.
80/D3 Pfaffnau, Swi.
73/A3 Pfaffstätten, Aus.
71/F4 Pfahl (ridge), Ger.
69/G5 Pfälzer Wald (for.), Ger.
70/B5 Pfalzgrafenweiler, Ger.
71/F6 Pfarrkirchen, Ger.
71/F5 Pfatter, Ger.
71/E5 Pfeffenhausen, Ger.
71/E5 Pfettrach (riv.), Ger.
67/G6 Pfieffe (riv.), Ger.
70/B5 Pfinztal, Ger.
189/F2 Pflugerville, Tx,US
70/B5 Pforzheim, Ger.
71/F4 Pfreimd, Ger.
71/F3 Pfreimd (riv.), Ger.
70/B3 Pfrimm (riv.), Ger.
70/C6 Pfronstetten, Ger.
81/G2 Pfronten, Ger.
81/G4 Pfroslkopf (peak), Aus.
81/F2 Pfullendorf, Ger.
81/G4 Pfunds, Aus.
70/B3 Pfungstadt, Ger.
122/C2 Phagwāra, India
123/C1 Phak (riv.), Laos
155/F4 Phalaborwa, SAfr.
120/A1 Phalauda, India
68/C2 Phalempin, Fr.
122/B1 Phālia, Pak.
200/B4 Phalia (bayou), Ms,US
118/B2 Phalodi, India
155/G2 Phalombe, Malw.
69/G6 Phalsbourg, Fr.
123/B2 Phan, Thai.
123/C3 Phanat Nikhom, Thai.
123/B4 Phangan (isl.), Thai.
123/C3 Phang Hoei (range), Thai.
123/B4 Phangnga, Thai.
123/B4 Phanom, Thai.
123/C3 Phanom Dongrak (mts.), Camb., Thai.
123/E4 Phan Rang, Viet.
123/E4 Phan Thiet, Viet.
121/F2 Phāphlu, Nepal
189/E4 Pharr, Tx,US
116/E4 Phat Diem, Viet.
123/C5 Phatthalung, Thai.
123/C2 Phaya Fo (peak), Thai.
123/B2 Phayao, Thai.
194/C2 Pheasant (hills), Sk,Can
204/C2 Phelan, Ca,US
201/J3 Phelps (lake), NC,US
198/B1 Phelps, Wi,US
200/E4 Phenix City, Al,US
156/C2 Phepane (dry riv.), SAfr.
123/B3 Phet Buri, Thai.
123/C2 Phetchabun, Thai.
123/D3 Phiafai, Laos
123/D3 Phibun Mangsahan, Thai.
123/C2 Phichai, Thai.
123/C2 Phichit, Thai.
121/F2 Phidim, Nepal
200/C4 Philadelphia, Ms,US
199/J4 Philadelphia, NY,US
206/C4 Philadelphia, Pa,US
206/C4 Philadelphia (int'l arpt.), Pa,US
106/B4 Philae (ruins), Egypt
200/D3 Phil Campbell, Al,US
192/D1 Philip, SD,US
200/B4 Philipp, Ms,US
68/D3 Philippeville, Belg.
201/G1 Philippi, WV,US
138/B3 Philippine (sea), Asia
125/* Philippines
70/B4 Philippsburg, Ger.
183/H4 Philipsburg, Mt,US
199/G4 Philipsburg, Pa,US
66/B5 Philipsdam (dam), Neth.
60/C3 Philipstown, Ire.
156/D3 Philipstown, SAfr.
122/C2 Phillaur, India
196/B3 Phillips, Me,US
193/J1 Phillips, Wi,US
182/B2 Phillips Arm, BC,Can
203/G2 Phillipsburg, Ga,US
190/E1 Phillipsburg, Ks,US
191/H2 Phillipsburg, Mo,US
206/C2 Phillipsburg, NJ,US
184/B4 Philo, Ca,US
185/J4 Philomath, Or,US
200/D2 Philpot, Ky,US
123/C3 Phimai, Thai.
123/C3 Phimai (ruins), Thai.
196/C4 Phippsburg, Me,US
123/C2 Phitsanulok, Thai.
123/D4 Phnom Penh (Phnum Penh) (cap.), Camb.
123/D4 Phnum Penh (int'l arpt.), Camb.
123/D4 Phnum Penh (Phnom Penh) (cap.), Camb.
123/D3 Phnum Tbeng Meanchey, Camb.
123/C5 Pho (pt.), Thai.
139/H5 Phoenix (isls.), Kiri.
180/D5 Phoenix, Az,US
187/F4 Phoenix (cap.), Az,US
201/G2 Phoenix (mtn.), NC,US
184/B2 Phoenix, Or,US
60/D3 Phoenix Park, Ire.
139/H5 Phoenix (Rawaki) (isl.), Kiri.
206/C3 Phoenixville, Pa,US
123/C3 Phon, Thai.
123/C1 Phongsali, Laos
123/C2 Phon Phisai, Thai.
123/C2 Phon Thong, Thai.
123/C2 Phou Bia (peak), Laos
123/D2 Phou Huatt (peak), Viet.
123/C2 Phou Khoun, Laos
123/C1 Phou Loi (peak), Laos
123/D2 Phou Xai Lai Leng (peak), Laos
123/C2 Phrae, Thai.
123/C3 Phra Nakhon Si Ayutthaya, Thai.
123/C3 Phra Phutthabat, Thai.
123/B4 Phra Thong (isl.), Thai.
123/B4 Phsar Ream, Camb.
123/D2 Phuc Loi, Viet.
116/E4 Phuc Yen, Viet.
123/C2 Phu Hin Rong Kla Nat'l Park, Thai.
123/E4 Phu Hoi, Viet.
123/B5 Phuket, Thai.
123/B5 Phuket (isl.), Thai.
123/C2 Phu Kradung, Thai.
123/C2 Phu Kradung Nat'l Park, Thai.
118/D3 Phulabāni, India
122/B1 Phularwan, Pak.
121/G3 Phulbāri, Bang.
121/H3 Phulbāri, India
116/B4 Phuldungsei, India
123/D2 Phu Loc, Viet.
120/D3 Phūlpur, India
121/G4 Phultala, Bang.
123/D1 Phu Luong, Viet.
123/D1 Phu Luong (peak), Viet.
123/D1 Phu Ly, Viet.
123/D4 Phumi Banam, Camb.
123/D3 Phumi Chhlong, Camb.
123/D3 Phumi Chhuk, Camb.
123/C4 Phumi Choan, Camb.
123/D3 Phumi Kampong Putrea Chas, Camb.
123/D3 Phumi Kampong Trabek, Camb.
123/C3 Phumi Kouk Kduoch, Camb.
123/D4 Phumi Krek, Camb.
123/D3 Phumi Labang Siek, Camb.
123/D3 Phumi Mlu Prey, Camb.
123/D3 Phumi O Pou, Camb.
123/D3 Phumi Phang, Camb.
123/D3 Phumi Phsar, Camb.
123/D3 Phumi Phsa Romeas, Camb.
123/D3 Phumi Prek Kak, Camb.
123/D3 Phumi Prek Preah, Camb.
123/C3 Phumi Samraong, Camb.
123/D3 Phumi Spoe Tbong, Camb.
123/D3 Phumi Sre Ta Chan, Camb.
123/C3 Phumi Ta Krei, Camb.
123/C3 Phumi Thma Pok, Camb.
123/C3 Phumi Toek Sok, Camb.
123/C4 Phumi Veal Renh, Camb.
123/E3 Phu My, Viet.
123/E3 Phu Nhon, Viet.
121/G2 Phuntsholing, Bhu.
123/D2 Phu Phan Nat'l Park, Thai.
123/C4 Phu Quoc, Viet.
123/C4 Phu Quoc (isl.), Viet.
123/D4 Phu Rieng, Viet.
123/C2 Phu Rua Nat'l Park, Thai.
123/D1 Phu Tho, Viet.
123/C3 Phutthaisong, Thai.
123/D2 Phu Vang, Viet.
115/D4 Pi (riv.), China
153/F2 Pia, Zaire
171/F1 Piaçabuçu, Braz.
86/C2 Piacenza, It.
86/C3 Piacenza (prov.), It.
165/F2 Piacoa, Ven.
86/D2 Piadena, It.
83/B2 Piaggine, It.
84/B2 Piancastagnaio, It.
87/F6 Pian di Serra (peak), It.
85/E3 Pianella, It.
86/C3 Pianello val Tidone, It.
86/A2 Pianezza, It.
87/F6 Piangipane, It.
113/B2 Pianling, China
85/E6 Piano di Sorrento, It.
87/E4 Pianoro, It.
84/A2 Pianosa (isl.), It.
85/F3 Pianosa (isl.), It.
84/B2 Piansano, It.
151/A1 Pian-Upe Game Rsv., Ugan.
117/F3 Piaoli, China
194/B2 Piapot Ind. Res., Sk,Can
165/F2 Piarco (int'l arpt.), Trin.
86/A3 Piasco, It.
65/L2 Piaseczno, Pol.
93/H2 Piatra Neamţ, Rom.
167/F5 Piauí (riv.), Braz.
167/F4 Piauí (state), Braz.
87/F1 Piave (riv.), It.
86/D1 Piazza, It.
86/D4 Piazza al Serchio, It.
90/D4 Piazza Armerina, It.
86/C1 Piazza Brembana, It.
81/G5 Piazzi, Cima de' (peak), It.
87/E1 Piazzola sul Brenta, It.
149/G3 Pibor (riv.), Eth., Sudan
149/G4 Pibor Post, Sudan
195/L3 Pic (isl.), On,Can
195/L3 Pic (riv.), On,Can
172/B2 Pica, Chile
187/G4 Picacho, Az,US
190/B4 Picacho, NM,US
53/T9 Picardie (prov.), Fr.
68/A4 Picardie (reg.), Fr.
79/H1 Picardy (hist. reg.), Fr.
68/B4 Picardy (reg.), Fr.
206/D2 Picatinny Arsenal (mil. res.), NJ,US
78/D2 Picauville, Fr.
202/D2 Picayune, Ms,US
90/E2 Piccolo (lag.), It.
85/E6 Picentino (riv.), It.
85/F6 Picerno, It.
160/D2 Pich, Mex.
168/D5 Pichacani, Peru
172/C2 Pichanal, Arg.
191/G2 Picher, Ok,US
174/C2 Pichidangui, Chile
174/C2 Pichidegua, Chile
174/C2 Pichilemu, Chile
158/C3 Pichilingue, Mex.
164/B5 Pichincha, Ecu.
164/B4 Pichincha (prov.), Ecu.
97/G1 Pichkiryayevo, Rus.
71/G6 Pichl bei Wels, Aus.
120/B3 Pichor, India
160/C2 Pichucalco, Mex.
200/C4 Pickens, Ms,US
191/G3 Pickens, Ok,US
201/F3 Pickens, SC,US
199/G3 Pickering, On,Can
57/H3 Pickering, Eng,UK
57/H3 Pickering, Vale of (val.), Eng,UK
198/D1 Pickford, Mi,US
195/J2 Pickle Lake, On,Can
189/G1 Pickton, Tx,US
200/C3 Pickwick (dam), Tn,US
200/C3 Pickwick (lake), Tn,US
200/C3 Pickwick Dam, Tn,US
134/B2 Picnic Bay, Austl.
77/S12 Pico (isl.), Azor.,Port.
165/E4 Pico da Neblina Nat'l Park, Braz.
159/M7 Pico de Orizaba Nat'l Park, Mex.
174/D5 Pico de Salamanca, Arg.
204/B3 Pico Rivera, Ca,US
167/F4 Picos, Braz.
168/B2 Picota, Peru
174/D5 Pico Truncado, Arg.
68/B4 Picquigny, Fr.
133/G5 Picraman (lake), Austl.
168/B2 Picsi, Peru
199/H3 Picton, On,Can
136/C3 Picton, N.Z.
197/F3 Pictou, NS,Can
197/F3 Pictou (isl.), NS,Can
184/D1 Picture (gorge), Or,US
183/H3 Picture Butte, Ab,Can
198/C1 Pictured Rocks Nat'l Lakesh., Mi,US
184/C2 Picture Rock (pass), Or,US
206/B1 Picture Rocks, Pa,US
167/G4 Picuí, Braz.
187/K2 Picuris Ind. Res., NM,US
189/F2 Pidcoke, Tx,US
58/D5 Piddle (riv.), Eng,UK
153/F4 Pidi, Zaire
118/D6 Pidurutagala (peak), SrL.
195/K3 Pie (isl.), On,Can
171/M6 Piedade do Rio Grande, Braz.
164/C3 Piedecuesta, Col.
84/C2 Piediluco (lake), It.
85/E1 Piedimulera, It.
86/B2 Piedmont (reg.), It.
201/G3 Piedmont (plat.), US
200/E4 Piedmont, Al,US
205/K11 Piedmont, Ca,US
191/J2 Piedmont, Mo,US
191/F3 Piedmont, Ok,US
201/F3 Piedmont, SC,US
192/C1 Piedmont, SD,US
200/F4 Piedmont Nat'l Wild. Ref., Ga,US
186/C2 Piedra, Ca,US
76/C3 Piedrabuena, Sp.
164/D2 Piedra Grande, Ven.
76/C2 Piedrahita, Sp.
175/F2 Piedras (pt.), Arg.
167/L7 Piedras, Col.
168/D3 Piedras (riv.), Peru
175/T11 Piedras Coloradas, Uru.
159/N8 Piedras Negras, Mex.
188/D3 Piedras Negras, Mex.
173/E5 Piedra Sola, Uru.
174/E2 Piedritas, Arg.
188/C3 Piedritas, Mex.
65/K3 Piekary Śląskie, Pol.
156/B4 Piekenierskloof (pass), SAfr.
61/H3 Pieksämäki, Fin.
94/E3 Pieksamaki, Fin.
61/J3 Pielinen (lake), Fin.
65/L4 Pieniński Nat'l Park, Pol.
69/E5 Piennes, Fr.
65/H3 Pieńsk, Pol.
77/K6 Piera, Sp.
192/B3 Pierce, Co,US
202/M8 Pierce, Fl,US
202/M8 Pierce (lake), Fl,US
182/G4 Pierce, Id,US
192/F2 Pierce, Ne,US
205/C3 Pierce (co.), Wa,US
195/Q7 Pierce (co.), Wi,US
191/G2 Pierce City, Mo,US
190/D2 Pierceville, Ks,US
87/G1 Pieris, It.
207/K7 Piermont, NY,US
55/N13 Pierowall, Sc,UK
192/F1 Pierpont, SD,US
202/B2 Pierre (bayou), La,US
200/B4 Pierre (bayou), Ms,US
192/D1 Pierre, SD,US
80/B4 Pierre-de-Bresse, Fr.
82/C6 Pierrefeu-du-Var, Fr.
53/T10 Pierrefitte-sur-Seine, Fr.
199/K2 Pierrefonds, Qu,Can
68/C5 Pierrefonds, Fr.
80/C3 Pierrefontaine-les-Varans, Fr.
82/A4 Pierrelatte, Fr.
53/S9 Pierrelaye, Fr.
202/C3 Pierre Part, La,US
68/A6 Pierres, Fr.
82/B5 Pierrevert, Fr.
68/C5 Pierry, Fr.
203/H3 Pierson, Fl,US
73/B2 Piešt'any, Slvk.
73/B2 Piešt'any (arpt.), Slvk.
73/A4 Piesting (riv.), Aus.
80/D3 Pieterlen, Swi.
157/E3 Pietermaritzburg, SAfr.
155/F4 Pietersburg, SAfr.
187/H3 Pie Town, NM,US
85/E4 Pietracatella, It.
83/B2 Pietra del Pertusillo (lake), It.
85/F6 Pietragalla, It.
86/B4 Pietra Ligure, It.
87/F6 Pietralunga, It.
85/E5 Pietramelara, It.
85/F4 Pietramontecorvino, It.
167/O8 Pietra, Punta de (res.), Ven.
86/D5 Pietrasanta, It.
85/E5 Pietravairano, It.
86/A5 Pietravecchia, Monte (peak), It.
157/E2 Piet Retief, SAfr.
93/G2 Pietrosul (peak), Rom.
96/C3 Pietrosul, Vîrful (peak), Rom.
86/B2 Pieve del Cairo, It.
87/E3 Pieve di Cento, It.
87/F1 Pieve di Soligo, It.
86/A4 Pieve di Teco, It.
86/C2 Pieve Emanuele, It.
86/C4 Pieve Ligure, It.
86/D4 Pievepelago, It.
86/C2 Pieve Porto Morone, It.
87/F5 Pieve Santo Stefano, It.
81/E6 Pieve Vergonte, It.
183/H1 Pigeon (lake), Ab,Can
198/E3 Pigeon, Mi,US
195/J3 Pigeon (riv.), On,Can, Mn,US
200/B2 Piggott, Ar,US
157/E2 Piggs Peak, Swaz.
84/D4 Piglio, It.
86/A5 Pigna, It.
85/E5 Pignataro Maggiore, It.
85/F6 Pignola, It.
161/F1 Pigs (bay), Cuba
145/E4 Pigu, Gha.
174/E3 Pigüé, Arg.
120/C2 Pihāni, India
167/K7 Pijáo, Col.
160/C3 Pijijiapan, Mex.
66/B4 Pijnacker, Neth.
160/E3 Pijol (peak), Hon.
206/C1 Pike (co.), Pa,US
138/D4 Pikelot (isl.), Micr.
180/E4 Pikes (peak), Co,US
190/B1 Pikes (pk.), Co,US
206/B1 Pikes Creek (res.), Pa,US
206/B5 Pikesville, Md,US
156/B4 Piketberg, SAfr.
198/E5 Piketon, Oh,US
201/F2 Pikeville, Ky,US
200/E3 Pikeville, Tn,US
125/D4 Pikit, Phil.
113/B3 Pikou, China
175/S13 Pila, Arg.
65/J2 Piła, Pol.
65/J2 Piła (prov.), Pol.
172/E2 Pilagá (riv.), Arg.
154/E5 Pilane, Bots.
156/P12 Pilanesberg (range), SAfr.
171/E1 Pilão Arcado, Braz.
174/E1 Pilar, Arg.
171/G1 Pilar, Braz.
172/E3 Pilar, Par.
127/F1 Pilar, Phil.
80/E4 Pilatus (peak), Swi.
172/C1 Pilaya (riv.), Bol.
205/D1 Pilchuck (riv.), Wa,US
172/E2 Pilcomayo (riv.), SAm.
53/P7 Pilgrims Hatch, Eng,UK
125/C2 Pili, Phil.
120/B1 Pīlībhīt, India
96/B2 Pilica (riv.), Pol.
91/H3 Pilion (peak), Gre.
92/D2 Pilis, Hun.
73/C4 Pilis (mts.), Hun.
73/C4 Pilis (peak), Hun.
73/C4 Piliscsaba, Hun.
73/C4 Pilisvörösvár, Hun.
120/A1 Pilkhua, India
135/C4 Pillar (cape), Austl.
57/E2 Pillar (mtn.), Eng,UK
205/K12 Pillar (pt.), Ca,US
182/B3 Pillar (pt.), Wa,US
135/D1 Pilliga, Austl.
80/D5 Pillon, Col du (pass), Swi.
206/B2 Pillow, Pa,US
82/B6 Pilon du Roi (mtn.), Fr.
91/G4 Pilos, Gre.
182/G5 Pilot (mtn.), Id,US
200/E2 Pilot (mtn.), Tn,US
194/B2 Pilot Butte, Sk,Can
191/H1 Pilot Grove, Mo,US
188/L6 Pilot Grove (cr.), Tx,US
191/J2 Pilot Knob, Mo,US
186/D1 Pilot Knob (peak), Nv,US
194/E3 Pilot Mound, Mb,Can
201/G2 Pilot Mountain, NC,US
177/G4 Pilot Point, Ak,US
189/F1 Pilot Point, Tx,US
184/D1 Pilot Rock, Or,US
177/F3 Pilot Station, Ak,US
202/D3 Pilottown, La,US
71/G3 Pilsen (Plzeň), Czh.
81/H3 Pilsensee (lake), Ger.
71/F5 Pilsting, Ger.
63/J3 Piltene, Lat.
60/C5 Piltown, Ire.
97/K1 Pilyugino, Rus.
187/H4 Pima, Az,US
152/D3 Pimamga-Moke, Zaire
169/F3 Pimenta Bueno, Braz.
127/F3 Pimpi, Indo.
118/B4 Pimpri-Chinchwad, India
161/G5 Piña (pt.), Pan.
77/G3 Pina, Sp.
117/E2 Pinacate, Cerro (mtn.), Mex.
175/J7 Pináculo (peak), Arg.
187/H4 Pinaleno (mts.), Az,US
125/C2 Pinamalayan, Phil.
175/F3 Pinamar, Arg.
123/B5 Pinang (cape), Malay.
126/A2 Pinang (isl.), Malay.
125/B4 Pinangah, Malay.
104/D2 Pınarbaşı, Turk.
161/F1 Pinar del Río, Cuba
93/H5 Pinarhisar, Turk.
168/B1 Piñas, Ecu.
125/C2 Pinatubo, Mount (vol.), Phil.
194/G2 Pinawa, Mb,Can
57/H6 Pinchbeck, Eng,UK
183/H3 Pincher Creek, Ab,Can
198/E3 Pinckney, Mi,US
193/K4 Pinckneyville, Il,US
198/E3 Pinconning, Mi,US
92/E2 Pincota, Rom.
197/N7 Pincourt, Qu,Can
65/L3 Pińczów, Pol.
152/C5 Pinda, Ang.
191/H2 Pindall, Ar,US
171/L7 Pindamonhangaba, Braz.
167/E4 Pindaré (riv.), Braz.
167/E4 Pindaré-Mirim, Braz.
122/B1 Pind Dādan Khān, Pak.
122/B1 Pindi Gheb, Pak.
131/G1 Pindiu, PNG
171/E1 Pindobaçu, Braz.
166/D3 Pindobal, Braz.
91/G3 Pindos Nat'l Park, Gre.
91/G2 Pindus (mts.), Gre.
118/B3 Pindwāra, India
197/L2 Pine (cape), Nf,Can
187/G3 Pine, Az,US
190/B1 Pine, Co,US
203/G4 Pine (isl.), Fl,US
203/G3 Pine (pt.), Fl,US
185/F2 Pine, Id,US
205/G6 Pine (riv.), Mi,US
191/J2 Pine, Mo,US
203/C2 Pine (hills), Ms,US
194/B4 Pine (hills), Mt,US
192/C2 Pine (ridge), Ne,US
199/H4 Pine (riv.), Pa,US
189/G1 Pine, Tx,US
188/C3 Pine (mtn.), Tx,US
200/D5 Pine Apple, Al,US
206/D4 Pine Barrens (reg.), NJ,US
207/D4 Pine Beach, NJ,US
191/H3 Pine Bluff, Ar,US
201/H3 Pinebluff, NC,US
191/H3 Pine Bluff Arsenal, Ar,US
199/J4 Pine Bush, NY,US
202/N7 Pine Castle, Fl,US
195/H5 Pine City, Mn,US
207/H7 Pinecliff (lake), NJ,US
186/D4 Pine-Cove-Idyllwild, Ca,US
130/C3 Pine Creek, Austl.
207/E1 Pine Creek (pt.), Ct,US
194/G3 Pinecreek, Mn,US
191/G3 Pine Creek (lake), Ok,US
77/G2 Pineda de Mar, Sp.
187/G3 Pinedale, Az,US
186/C2 Pinedale, Ca,US
185/J2 Pinedale, Wy,US
194/F2 Pine Dock, Mb,Can
194/F2 Pine Falls, Mb,Can
186/C2 Pine Flat (res.), Ca,US
94/J2 Pinega, Rus.
94/J2 Pinega (riv.), Rus.
202/C2 Pine Grove, La,US
206/B2 Pine Grove, Pa,US
200/D5 Pine Hill, Al,US
206/D4 Pine Hill, NJ,US
202/M8 Pine Hills, Fl,US
200/F4 Pinehurst, Ga,US
182/F4 Pinehurst, Id,US
201/H3 Pinehurst, NC,US
189/G2 Pinehurst, Tx,US
137/T Pine Island (bay), Ant.
193/H1 Pine Island, Mn,US
203/G4 Pine Island Nat'l Wild. Ref., Fl,US
200/E2 Pine Knot, Ky,US
203/G4 Pineland, Fl,US
201/G4 Pineland, SC,US
189/H2 Pineland, Tx,US
156/L10 Pinelands, SAfr.
200/D4 Pine Level, Al,US
202/K8 Pinellas (co.), Fl,US
202/K8 Pinellas (pt.), Fl,US
203/G4 Pinellas Park, Fl,US
190/B4 Pine Lodge, NM,US
208/B2 Pine Meadow, Ct,US
189/G1 Pine Mills, Tx,US
178/E2 Pine Point, NW,Can
202/B2 Pine Prairie, La,US
175/F2 Piñera, Uru.
192/C2 Pine Ridge, SD,US
192/C2 Pine Ridge Ind. Res., SD,US
194/D2 Pine River, Mb,Can
195/G4 Pine River, Mn,US
82/D3 Pinerolo, It.
207/D2 Pines (lake), NJ,US
183/G4 Pinesdale, Mt,US
189/G1 Pines, Lake O'The (lake), Tx,US
205/G6 Pine, South Branch (riv.), Mi,US
188/B2 Pine Springs, Tx,US
198/D1 Pine Stump Junction, Mi,US
183/M4 Pine, The (hills), Mt,US
85/E2 Pineto, It.
187/H3 Pinetop-Lakeside, Az,US
201/J3 Pinetops, NC,US
157/E3 Pinetown, SAfr.
203/G2 Pinetta, Fl,US
74/D4 Pineuilh, Fr.
186/D4 Pine Valley, Ca,US
187/F2 Pine Valley, Ut,US
201/F4 Pineview, Ga,US
200/F2 Pineville, Ky,US
202/B2 Pineville, La,US
191/G2 Pineville, Mo,US
201/G3 Pineville, NC,US
201/G4 Pineville, SC,US
201/G2 Pineville, WV,US
191/H3 Piney, Ar,US
203/F2 Piney (isl.), Fl,US
201/J3 Piney Green, NC,US
201/J1 Piney Point, Md,US
189/M9 Piney Point Village, Tx,US
201/H2 Piney River, Va,US
200/C4 Piney Woods, Ms,US
123/B2 Ping (riv.), Thai.
116/D4 Pingbian Miaozu Zizhixian, China
117/E2 Pingchang, China
117/J1 Pingchao, China
115/C3 Pingding, China
115/D4 Pingdingshan, China
138/F4 Pingelap (isl.), Micr.
132/C5 Pingelly, Austl.
123/D1 Ping'erguan, China
117/E3 Pingfa, China
115/D2 Pinggu, China
119/J3 Pingguo, China
117/G4 Pinghai, China
117/H3 Pinghai, China
115/L9 Pinghu, China
117/G2 Pingjing (pass), China
115/C5 Pingjing Guan (pass), China
117/E2 Pingjinpu, China
117/F3 Pingle, China
115/B4 Pinglu, China
115/C3 Pinglu, China
119/K3 Pingnan, China
117/G4 Pingnan, China
185/G2 Pingree, Id,US
117/G4 Pingsha, China
115/C3 Pingshan, China
117/G3 Pingshi, China
115/C3 Pingshun, China
119/J2 Pingtang, China
108/F5 Pingtou, China
117/J4 Pingtung, Tai.
115/L9 Pingwang, China
115/C3 Pingxiang, China
116/E4 Pingxiang, China
117/G3 Pingxiang, China
115/C3 Pingxing Guan (pass), China
109/J4 Pingyang, China
115/C3 Pingyao, China
115/D4 Pingyi, China
115/D3 Pingyin, China
123/E1 Pingyin, China
117/F3 Pingyong, China
115/C4 Pingyu, China
115/D3 Pingyuan, China
170/D4 Pinhal, Braz.
77/Q10 Pinhal Novo, Port.
167/E3 Pinheiro, Braz.
173/F4 Pinheiro Machado, Braz.
171/E3 Pinheiros, Braz.
76/B2 Pinhel, Port.
203/G2 Pinhook (swamp), Fl,US
169/E2 Pinhuã (riv.), Braz.
124/B2 Pini (isl.), Indo.
91/G3 Piniós (riv.), Gre.
91/G4 Piniós (riv.), Gre.
132/K6 Pinjar (lake), Austl.
132/B5 Pinjarra, Austl.
73/A5 Pinka (riv.), Aus.
73/A5 Pinkafeld, Aus.
133/G5 Pinkawillinie Consv. Park, Austl.
66/C2 Pinkegat (chan.), Neth.
201/J3 Pink Hill, NC,US
119/G3 Pinlebu, Burma
186/B2 Pinnacles Nat'l Mon., Ca,US
182/E2 Pinnacles, The (mtn.), BC,Can
133/J5 Pinnaroo, Austl.
67/G1 Pinnau (riv.), Ger.
67/G1 Pinneberg, Ger.
174/C3 Pino Hachado, Paso de (pass), Arg.
205/K10 Pinole, Ca,US
187/G2 Pinon, Az,US
190/B1 Pinon, Co,US
190/B4 Piñon, NM,US
204/C2 Pinon Hills, Ca,US
201/G4 Pinopolis, SC,US
201/H4 Pinopolis (dam), SC,US
159/E4 Pinos, Mex.
186/C3 Pinos (mtn.), Ca,US
161/F1 Pinos (Juventad) (isl.), Cuba
77/E3 Pinoso, Sp.
76/D4 Pinos-Puente, Sp.
160/B2 Pinotepa Nacional, Mex.
127/E4 Pinrang, Indo.
139/V13 Pins (isl.), NCal.
138/F7 Pins, Ile des (isl.), NCal.
98/D1 Pinsk, Bela.
98/C2 Pinsk (marsh), Bela., Ukr.
200/D4 Pinson-Clay-Chalkville, Al,US
198/F3 Pins, Point aux (pt.), On,Can
168/J6 Pinta (isl.), Ecu.
190/B3 Pintada Arroyo (cr.), NM,US
175/T11 Pintado, Uru.
172/B2 Pintados, Chile
174/C3 Pinto, Chile
77/N9 Pinto, Sp.
187/F2 Pintura, Ut,US
125/D3 Pintuyan, Phil.
81/G5 Pinzolo, It.
87/F5 Piobbico, It.
186/E2 Pioche, Nv,US
82/A4 Piolenc, Fr.
85/D2 Piomba (riv.), It.
84/A2 Piombino, It.
84/A2 Piombino (chan.), It.
87/F1 Piombino Dese, It.
189/J1 Pioneer, La,US
185/G1 Pioneer (mts.), Mt,US
132/L7 Pioneer World, Austl.
100/J2 Pioner (isl.), Rus.
51/L1 Pionerskiy, Rus.
65/L3 Pionki, Pol.
136/C2 Piopio, N.Z.
199/L2 Piopolis, Qu,Can
169/F1 Piorini (lake), Braz.
169/F1 Piorini (riv.), Braz.
86/A3 Piossasco, It.
86/B3 Piota (riv.), It.
65/K3 Piotrków (prov.), Pol.
65/K3 Piotrków Trybunalski, Pol.
87/F2 Piove di Sacco, It.
87/E1 Piovene-Rocchette, It.
167/E3 Pio XII, Braz.
172/C3 Pipanaco (salt pan), Arg.
118/B2 Pīpār, India
120/B4 Pipariā, India
206/C3 Pipersville, Pa,US
200/C3 Piperton, Tn,US
187/F2 Pipe Spring Nat'l Mon., Az,US
194/E4 Pipestem (cr.), ND,US
194/D3 Pipestone, Mb,Can
194/D3 Pipestone (cr.), Mb, Sk,Can
195/J1 Pipestone (riv.), On,Can
193/F1 Pipestone, Mn,US
193/F1 Pipestone Nat'l Mon., Mn,US
122/A1 Piplān, Pak.
179/J4 Pipmuacan (res.), Qu,Can
132/C2 Pippingarra Abor. Land, Austl.
120/D3 Pipra, India
120/D2 Pipraich, India
78/D5 Pipriac, Fr.
114/D3 Piqanlik, China
193/G5 Piqua, Ks,US
198/D4 Piqua, Oh,US
167/G4 Piquet Carneiro, Braz.
171/L7 Piquete, Braz.
170/B3 Piquiri (riv.), Braz.
173/F2 Piquiri (riv.), Braz.
170/C3 Piracanjuba, Braz.
166/D3 Piracaua, Braz.
170/D4 Piracicaba, Braz.
167/F3 Piracuruca, Braz.
113/C2 Pirae-bong (mtn.), NKor.
171/N7 Piraí, Braz.
170/C5 Piraí do Sul, Braz.
91/H4 Piraiévs, Gre.
170/C4 Piraju, Braz.
170/C4 Pirajuí, Braz.
175/J7 Pirámide (peak), Chile
87/G1 Piran, Slov.
172/E3 Piranè, Arg.
171/E4 Piranga (riv.), Braz.
170/C3 Piranhas, Braz.
170/B4 Piranhas (riv.), Braz.
167/E3 Pirapemas, Braz.
170/D3 Pirapora, Braz.
175/G2 Pirarajá, Uru.
170/D4 Pirássununga, Braz.
173/F3 Piratini (riv.), Braz.
169/E5 Piray (riv.), Bol.
174/C1 Pircas (peak), Arg.
170/C2 Pirenópolis, Braz.
170/C3 Pires do Rio, Braz.
121/G3 Pīrganj, Bang.
91/G4 Pírgos, Gre.
91/J5 Pírgos, Gre.
152/C5 Piri, Ang.
78/C6 Piriac-sur-Mer, Fr.
175/G2 Piriápolis, Uru.
173/E3 Piribebuy, Par.
131/E1 Pirimapun, Indo.
93/F5 Pirin (mtn.), Bul.
93/F5 Pirin (mts.), Bul.
91/H2 Pirin (peak), Bul.
93/F5 Pirin Nat'l Park, Bul.
167/F4 Piripiri, Braz.
171/E1 Piritiba, Braz.
164/D2 Píritu, Ven.
63/K1 Pirkkala, Fin.
63/K1 Pirkkala-Tampere (int'l arpt.), Fin.
122/B2 Pīr Mahal, Pak.
69/G5 Pirmasens, Ger.
72/D6 Pirna, Ger.
120/E3 Piro, India
121/G4 Pirojpur, Bang.
136/C2 Pirongia (peak), N.Z.
92/F4 Pirot, Yugo.
122/C1 Pīr Panjal (range), India
167/H4 Pirpirituba, Braz.
161/G5 Pirre (mtn.), Pan.
120/B3 Pirthīpur, India
204/B2 Piru, Ca,US
204/B1 Piru (cr.), Ca,US
204/B2 Piru (lake), Ca,US
98/G2 Piryatin, Ukr.
91/J3 Piryíon, Gre.
86/D5 Pisa, It.
87/D6 Pisa (prov.), It.
168/D4 Pisac, Peru
172/B1 Pisagua, Chile
86/D4 Pisanino, Monte (peak), It.
127/E2 Pisau, Tanjong (cape), Malay.
164/C3 Pisba Nat'l Park, Col.
206/B6 Piscataway, Md,US
206/D2 Piscataway, NJ,US
168/B4 Pisco, Peru
168/C4 Pisco (riv.), Peru
168/B3 Piscobamba, Peru
71/H4 Písek, Czh.
71/H3 Písek (peak), Czh.
194/F3 Pisek, ND,US
136/B4 Pisgah (peak), N.Z.
200/E3 Pisgah, Al,US
198/D5 Pisgah, Oh,US
114/C4 Pishan, China
107/H3 Pīshīn, Iran
107/J2 Pishīn, Pak.
95/K4 Pishnur, Rus.
105/G3 Pīshvā, Iran
92/C3 Piskavica, Bosn.
99/H3 Pis'mennoye, Ukr.
186/B3 Pismo Beach, Ca,US
81/G4 Pisoc, Piz (peak), Swi.
169/F4 Piso Firme, Bol.
86/D1 Pisogne, It.
84/C4 Pisoniano, It.
145/E3 Pissila, Burk.
172/B3 Pissis (peak), Arg.
68/B4 Pissy, Fr.
205/P15 Pistakee (lake), Il,US
83/C2 Pisticci, It.
87/D5 Pistoia, It.
87/D5 Pistoia (prov.), It.
184/A2 Pistol River, Or,US
76/C1 Pisuerga (riv.), Sp.
65/L2 Pisz, Pol.
184/B3 Pit (riv.), Ca,US
144/B4 Pita, Gui.
164/B4 Pitalito, Col.
170/C5 Pitanga, Braz.
139/N7 Pitcairn (isl.), Pitc.
208/H7 Pitcairn, Pa,US
139/N7 Pitcairn Islands (terr.), UK
61/G2 Piteå, Swe.
61/F2 Piteälv (riv.), Swe.
93/G3 Piteşti, Rom.
91/K2 Pithion, Gre.
79/H4 Pithiviers, Fr.
202/K7 Pithlachascotee (riv.), Fl,US
120/C1 Pithoragarh, India
84/B2 Pitigliano, It.
167/H4 Pitimbu, Braz.
158/C2 Pitiquito, Mex.
133/F3 Pitjantjatjara Abor. Lands, Austl.
177/F3 Pitkas Point, Ak,US
185/K4 Pitkin, Co,US
202/B2 Pitkin, La,US
54/C3 Pitlochry, Sc,UK
206/C4 Pitman, NJ,US
54/D2 Pitmedden, Sc,UK
148/B3 Pitoa, Camr.
125/C2 Pitogo, Phil.
92/C3 Pitomača, Cro.
68/A5 Pîtres, Fr.
174/B3 Pitrufquén, Chile
155/E4 Pitsane, Bots.
134/H8 Pitt (lake), Austl.
182/C3 Pitt (riv.), BC,Can
136/E4 Pitt (isl.), N.Z.
136/E4 Pitt (str.), N.Z.
195/G3 Pitt, Mn,US
73/A4 Pitten, Aus.
73/A4 Pitten (riv.), Aus.
54/D4 Pittenweem, Sc,UK
161/F4 Pittier (mtn.), CR
203/G2 Pitts, Ga,US
200/C4 Pittsboro, Ms,US
201/H3 Pittsboro, NC,US
205/L10 Pittsburg, Ca,US
191/G2 Pittsburg, Ks,US
191/H2 Pittsburg, Mo,US
199/L2 Pittsburg, NH,US
191/G3 Pittsburg, Ok,US
189/G1 Pittsburg, Tx,US
208/H7 Pittsburgh, Pa,US
193/J4 Pittsfield, Il,US
208/A1 Pittsfield, Ma,US
196/C3 Pittsfield, Me,US
199/K3 Pittsford, Vt,US
206/C1 Pittston, Pa,US
206/D2 Pittstown, NJ,US
201/H2 Pittsville, Va,US
134/C4 Pittsworth, Austl.
81/G3 Pitzbach (riv.), Aus.
170/D4 Piũí, Braz.
87/E3 Piumazzo, It.
168/A2 Piura, Peru
185/G4 Piute (res.), Ut,US
120/D1 Piuthān, Nepal
91/F1 Piva (riv.), Yugo.
109/M1 Pivan', Rus.
99/J3 Pivdennoye, Ukr.
164/C2 Pivijay, Col.
92/D4 Pivsko (lake), Yugo.
116/D2 Pi Xian, China
186/C3 Pixley, Ca,US
159/H5 Pixoyal, Mex.
168/D5 Pizacoma, Peru
76/C4 Pizarra, Sp.
95/K4 Pizhma (riv.), Rus.
81/F4 Pizol (peak), Swi.
86/C2 Pizzighettone, It.
83/C5 Pizzo, It.
85/D3 Pizzoli, It.
84/C3 Pizzuto (peak), It.
78/A4 Plabennec, Fr.
160/D2 Placentia (pt.), Belz.
197/L2 Placentia, Nf,Can
197/K2 Placentia (bay), Nf,Can
204/C3 Placentia, Ca,US
160/E2 Placer, Mex.
125/D3 Placer, Phil.
205/M9 Placer (co.), Ca,US
186/B1 Placerville, Ca,US
185/J4 Placerville, Co,US
161/G1 Placetas, Cuba
93/G4 Plachkovtsi, Bul.
169/E3 Plácido de Castro, Braz.
172/B2 Placilla de Caracoles, Chile
190/A3 Placitas, NM,US
187/J3 Placitas (Placita), NM,US
80/D4 Plaffeien, Swi.
69/G3 Plaidt, Ger.
53/T9 Plailly, Fr.
123/C3 Plai Mat (riv.), Thai.
189/H1 Plain Dealing, La,US
80/C1 Plaine (riv.), Fr.
191/H4 Plainfield, Ar,US
208/C2 Plainfield, Ct,US
205/P16 Plainfield, Il,US
198/C5 Plainfield, In,US
196/A4 Plainfield, NH,US
206/D2 Plainfield, NJ,US
193/K1 Plainfield, Wi,US
200/B4 Plain (Richland), Ms,US
200/E4 Plains, Ga,US
190/D2 Plains, Ks,US
182/G4 Plains, Mt,US
206/C1 Plains, Pa,US
188/C1 Plains, Tx,US
206/D3 Plainsboro, NJ,US
201/F1 Plains, The, Oh,US
191/H3 Plainview, Ar,US
193/H1 Plainview, Mn,US
192/F2 Plainview, Ne,US
207/E2 Plainview, NY,US
190/D3 Plainview, Tx,US
208/B2 Plainville, Ct,US
190/E1 Plainville, Ks,US
208/C1 Plainville, Ma,US
198/D3 Plainwell, Mi,US
53/R10 Plaisir, Fr.
124/D3 Plaju, Indo.
127/E5 Plampang, Indo.
162/C2 Plana (cays), Bahm.
71/F3 Planá, Czh.
186/B2 Planada, Ca,US
174/Q9 Planchada, Chile
80/C2 Plancher-Bas, Fr.
80/C2 Plancher-les-Mines, Fr.
78/C3 Plancoët, Fr.
82/C6 Plan-de-la-Tour, Fr.
92/E3 Plandište, Yugo.
72/C3 Plane (riv.), Ger.
99/H5 Planerskoye, Ukr.
164/C2 Planeta Rica, Col.
202/P8 Planet Ocean, Fl,US
71/G4 Plánice, Czh.
81/F3 Planken, Lcht.
193/F2 Plankinton, SD,US
80/C5 Plan-les-Ouates, Swi.
205/N16 Plano, Il,US
189/F1 Plano, Tx,US
203/H4 Plantation, Fl,US
203/H5 Plantation Key, Fl,US
203/G3 Plant City, Fl,US
200/C3 Plantersville, Ms,US
202/C2 Plaquemine, La,US
76/B2 Plasencia, Sp.
95/P5 Plast, Rus.
196/D2 Plaster Rock, NB,Can
196/D2 Plaster Rock-Renous Game Ref., NB,Can
109/M3 Plastun, Rus.
71/G3 Plasy, Czh.
175/F2 Plata (riv.), Arg.
165/F4 Platanal, Ven.
90/C4 Platani (riv.), It.
85/F6 Platano (riv.), It.
175/T12 Plata, Río de la (est.), Arg.,Uru.
197/G2 Plateau, NS,Can
145/H4 Plateau (state), Nga.
152/C3 Plateaux (pol. reg.), Congo
68/D3 Plate Taille, Barrage de la (dam), Belg.
91/H2 Plati, Gre.
83/C6 Plati, It.
177/F4 Platinum, Ak,US
99/K5 Platnirovskaya, Rus.
164/C2 Plato, Col.
180/F3 Platte (riv.), US
193/G4 Platte (riv.), Ia, Mo,US
192/E2 Platte, SD,US
191/G1 Platte City, Mo,US
192/B3 Platteville, Co,US
193/J2 Platteville, Wi,US
71/F5 Plattling, Ger.
191/G1 Plattsburg, Mo,US
199/K2 Plattsburgh, NY,US
199/K2 Plattsburgh A.F.B., NY,US
193/G3 Plattsmouth, Ne,US
72/A6 Plaue, Ger.
72/C3 Plaue, Ger.
72/D6 Plaue, Ger.
72/F2 Plauen, Ger.
72/C3 Plauer (lake), Ger.
92/D4 Plav, Yugo.
73/B2 Plavecký Mikuláš, Slvk.
63/L3 Pļaviņas, Lat.
81/G4 Plavna Dadaint, Piz (peak), Swi.
96/F1 Plavsk, Rus.
160/E3 Playa de los Muertos (ruins), Hon.
189/F5 Playa General Lauro Villar, Mex.
158/C2 Playa Noriega (lake), Mex.
164/A5 Playas, Ecu.
187/H5 Playas (lake), NM,US
159/G5 Playa Vicente, Mex.
123/E3 Play Cu (Pleiku), Viet.
189/G3 Pleak, Tx,US
196/D3 Pleasant (mtn.), NB,Can
197/G2 Pleasant Bay, NS,Can
183/M1 Pleasantdale, Sk,Can
185/H3 Pleasant Grove, Ut,US

205/K11 Pleasant Hill, Ca,US
202/B2 Pleasant Hill, La,US
191/G1 Pleasant Hill, Mo,US
208/E6 Pleasant Hill (dam), Oh,US
208/E6 Pleasant Hill (res.), Oh,US
206/B5 Pleasant Hills, Md,US
208/H7 Pleasant Hills, Pa,US
191/H2 Pleasant Hope, Mo,US
205/L11 Pleasanton, Ca,US
191/G1 Pleasanton, Ks,US
192/E3 Pleasanton, Ne,US
187/H4 Pleasanton, NM,US
189/E3 Pleasanton, Tx,US
136/B4 Pleasant Point, N.Z.
196/D3 Pleasant Point Ind. Res., Me,US
205/Q14 Pleasant Prairie, Wi,US
208/B2 Pleasant Valley, Ct,US
159/E1 Pleasant Valley, Tx,US
200/D2 Pleasant View, Tn,US
185/H3 Pleasant View, Ut,US
193/H3 Pleasantville, Ia,US
206/D5 Pleasantville, NJ,US
207/E1 Pleasantville, NY,US
199/G4 Pleasantville, Pa,US
200/D3 Pleasantville, Tn,US
200/E1 Pleasure Ridge Park, Ky,US
74/E4 Pléaux, Fr.
78/D5 Pléchâtel, Fr.
71/G5 Plechý (Plöcken-stein) (peak), Czh., Ger.
78/C4 Plédran, Fr.
123/D3 Plei Doch, Viet.
123/E3 Pleiku (Play Cu), Viet.
78/D3 Pleine-Fougères, Fr.
70/D4 Pleinfeld, Ger.
72/C5 Pleisse (riv.), Ger.
78/C5 Plélan-le-Grand, Fr.
78/C4 Plélan-le-Petit, Fr.
78/C4 Plémet, Fr.
78/C3 Pléneuf-Val-André, Fr.
93/F3 Plenița, Rom.
135/G5 Plenty (riv.), Austl.
183/K2 Plenty, Sk,Can
136/D2 Plenty (bay), N.Z.
183/M3 Plentywood, Mt,US
124/D4 Plered, Indo.
78/C3 Plérin, Fr.
78/C5 Plescop, Fr.
94/J3 Plesetsk, Rus.
63/M4 Pleshchenitsy, Bela.
71/F2 Plesná (riv.), Czh.
92/C3 Pleso (int'l arpt.), Yugo.
72/D5 Plessa, Ger.
78/D5 Plessé, Fr.
196/B2 Plessisville, Qu,Can
78/C4 Plestan, Fr.
78/B3 Plestin-les-Grèves, Fr.
65/J3 Pleszew, Pol.
67/E6 Plettenberg, Ger.
78/B3 Pleubian, Fr.
78/C3 Pleurtuit, Fr.
78/C3 Pleurtuit (Dinard) (int'l arpt.), Fr.
93/G4 Pleven, Bul.
183/M4 Plevna, Mt,US
78/B4 Pleyben, Fr.
78/B4 Pleyber-Christ, Fr.
144/D5 Plibo, Libr.
73/D3 Pliešovce, Slvk.
93/H4 Pliska, Bul.
92/B3 Plitvice Lakes Nat'l Park, Cro.
75/L4 Plitvička Jezera Nat'l Park, Cro.
92/D4 Pljevlja, Yugo.
80/D1 Plobsheim, Fr.
92/B4 Ploča, Rt (pt.), Yugo.
92/C4 Ploče, Cro.
65/K2 Płock, Pol.
65/K2 Płock (prov.), Pol.
71/G5 Plöckenstein (Plechý) (peak), Ger.
92/C4 Pločno (peak), Bosn.
68/B2 Ploegsteert, Belg.
78/B5 Ploemeur, Fr.
78/C5 Ploërmel, Fr.
78/C4 Ploeuc-sur-Lié, Fr.
78/A5 Plogastel-Saint-Germain, Fr.
78/A4 Plogoff, Fr.
93/H3 Ploiești, Rom.
91/K3 Plomárion, Gre.
69/E2 Plombières, Belg.
80/C2 Plombières-les-Bains, Fr.
80/A3 Plombières-lès-Dijon, Fr.
64/F1 Plön, Ger.
78/A5 Plonéour-Lanvern, Fr.
65/L2 Płońsk, Pol.
78/B3 Plouagat, Fr.
78/B5 Plouay, Fr.
78/C3 Ploubalay, Fr.
78/B3 Ploubazlanec, Fr.
65/H3 Ploučnice (riv.), Czh.
78/A3 Ploudalmézeau, Fr.
78/A3 Ploudaniel, Fr.
78/A3 Plouescat, Fr.
78/C4 Ploufragan, Fr.
78/B3 Plougasnou, Fr.
78/A4 Plougastel-Daoulas, Fr.
78/B3 Plougonven, Fr.
78/C4 Plouguenast, Fr.
78/A3 Plouguerneau, Fr.
78/B4 Plouguernével, Fr.
78/B3 Plouguiel, Fr.
78/C3 Plouha, Fr.
78/A4 Plouhinec, Fr.
78/A3 Plouider, Fr.
78/B3 Plouigneau, Fr.
78/B3 Ploumagoar, Fr.
78/A3 Plounéour-Trez, Fr.
78/B4 Plouray, Fr.
78/B3 Plourin-lès-Morlaix, Fr.
78/A3 Plouvorn, Fr.
78/A4 Plouzané, Fr.
78/A3 Plouzévéde, Fr.
93/G4 Plovdiv, Bul.
93/G5 Plovdiv (reg.), Bul.
193/K1 Plover, Wi,US
78/A5 Plozévet, Fr.
78/A5 Pluguffan, Fr.
78/A5 Pluguffan (Quimper) (int'l arpt.), Fr.
207/F1 Plum (isl.), NY,US
208/H7 Plum, Pa,US
194/E2 Plumas, Mb,Can
78/C4 Plumaugat, Fr.
56/A2 Plumbridge, NI,UK
193/H1 Plum City, Wi,US
194/F3 Plum Coulee, Mb,Can
191/H3 Plumerville, Ar,US
189/G2 Plum Grove, Tx,US
78/C4 Plumieux, Fr.
182/F4 Plummer, Id,US
132/E4 Plumridge Lakes Nat. Rsv., Austl.
206/C3 Plumsteadville, Pa,US
155/E4 Plumtree, Zim.
63/J4 Plungė, Lith.
184/D2 Plush, Or,US
78/B5 Pluvigner, Fr.
162/F3 Plymouth, Monts.
58/B6 Plymouth, Eng,UK
58/B6 Plymouth (arpt.), Eng,UK
58/B6 Plymouth (sound), Eng,UK
186/B1 Plymouth, Ca,US
202/M6 Plymouth, Fl,US
193/J3 Plymouth, Il,US
198/C4 Plymouth, In,US
208/D2 Plymouth, Ma,US
208/D2 Plymouth (co.), Ma,US
195/H5 Plymouth, Mn,US
201/J3 Plymouth, NC,US
193/F3 Plymouth, Ne,US
199/L3 Plymouth, NH,US
198/E4 Plymouth, Oh,US
206/C1 Plymouth, Pa,US
193/L2 Plymouth, Wi,US
208/D2 Plymouth Rock, Ma,US
208/D2 Plympton, Ma,US
58/C2 Plynlimon (mtn.), UK
71/G3 Plzeň (Pilsen), Czh.
65/J2 Pniewy, Pol.
145/E4 Pô, Burk.
87/F3 Po (delta), It.
87/E3 Po (riv.), It.
86/C2 Po (val.), It.
171/K8 Poá, Braz.
165/E2 Poa (riv.), Ven.
144/C5 Poabli, Libr.
135/C4 Poatina, Austl.
145/F5 Pobé, Ben.
114/D3 Pobedy, Pik (peak), Kyr.
65/J2 Pobiedziska, Pol.
77/F1 Pobla de Segur, Sp.
175/G2 Poblado Blanquillo, Uru.
201/G1 Poca, WV,US
182/F1 Pocahontas, Ab,Can
191/J2 Pocahontas, Ar,US
193/G2 Pocahontas, Ia,US
200/C1 Pocahontas, Il,US
167/E4 Poção de Pedra, Braz.
194/D5 Pocasse Nat'l Wild. Ref., SD,US
191/F3 Pocasset, Ok,US
185/G2 Pocatello, Id,US
98/C2 Pochayev, Ukr.
96/E1 Pochep, Rus.
94/G5 Pochinok, Rus.
113/E2 Poch'ŏn, NKor.
113/D4 P'och'ŏn, SKor.
99/G5 Pochtovoye, Ukr.
160/B3 Pochutla, Mex.
167/G4 Pocinhos, Braz.
158/C2 Pocito Casas, Mex.
72/D6 Pockau, Ger.
71/G6 Pöcking, Ger.
81/H2 Pöcking, Ger.
138/E6 Pocklington (reef), PNG
57/H4 Pocklington, Eng,UK
172/C1 Pocoata, Bol.
171/E2 Poções, Braz.
171/L6 Poço Fundo, Braz.
201/K1 Pocomoke City, Md,US
172/C1 Pocona, Bol.
172/B1 Poconchile, Chile
170/A3 Poconé, Braz.
206/C1 Pocono (cr.), Pa,US
206/C1 Pocono (lake), Pa,US
206/C1 Pocono (mts.), Pa,US
206/C1 Pocono Lake, Pa,US
206/C1 Pocono Pines, Pa,US
170/D4 Poços de Caldas, Braz.
171/K6 Poços de Caldas (arpt.), Braz.
172/C1 Pocpo, Bol.
161/F4 Pocrí, Pan.
118/C5 Podalakūr, India
63/P3 Podberez'ye, Rus.
71/G2 Podbořany, Czh.
94/G4 Podborov'ye, Rus.
95/N3 Podcher'ye, Rus.
65/K3 Poddębice, Pol.
63/P3 Poddor'ye, Rus.
86/C3 Podenzano, It.
99/K2 Podgorenskiy, Rus.
99/H3 Podgorodnoye, Ukr.
87/F3 Po di Goro (riv.), It.
87/F2 Po di Venezia (riv.), It.
87/E3 Po di Volano (riv.), It.
65/M3 Podlasie (reg.), Pol.
98/B2 Podlaska (prov.), Pol.
94/H5 Podol'sk, Rus.
144/B2 Podor, Sen.
94/G3 Podporozh'ye, Rus.
92/C3 Podravska Slatina, Cro.
92/E4 Podujevo, Yugo.
73/B3 Podunajské Biskupice, Slvk.
98/D3 Podvolochisk, Ukr.
93/H3 Poenari Burchi, Rom.
156/B3 Pofadder, SAfr.
87/E6 Poggibonsi, It.
85/F4 Poggio Imperiale, It.
87/E6 Poggiola, It.
85/E6 Poggiomarino, It.
84/C3 Poggio Mirteto, It.
84/C3 Poggio Moiano, It.
87/E3 Poggio Renatico, It.
87/E3 Poggio Rusco, It.
152/D4 Pogoso, Zaire
91/G2 Pogradec, Alb.
109/L3 Pogranichnyy, Rus.
98/E3 Pogrebishche, Ukr.
177/F5 Pogromni (vol.), Ak,US
97/K1 Pogromnoye, Rus.
127/F4 Poh, Indo.
180/U11 Pohakuloa (mil. res.), Hi,US
113/E4 P'ohang, SKor.
113/E2 P'oha-ri, NKor.
206/C2 Pohatcong (cr.), NJ,US
94/D3 Pohjankankaan-Kauhanevan Nat'l Park, Fin.
61/G3 Pohjanmaa (reg.), Fin.
138/E4 Pohnpei (isl.), Micr.
180/U11 Pohoiki, Hi,US
116/E4 Pohong, China
206/C2 Pohopoco (cr.), Pa,US
206/C2 Pohopoco Mtn. (ridge), Pa,US
73/A2 Pohořelice, Czh.
98/B6 Poiana Mare, Rom.
71/E6 Poing, Ger.
137/H Poinsett (cape), Ant.
178/E2 Point (lake), NW,Can
191/H4 Point, La,US
202/D3 Point a la Hache, La,US
202/C3 Point au Fer (isl.), La,US
177/M4 Point Baker, Ak,US
189/G2 Point Blank, Tx,US
189/F3 Point Comfort, Tx,US
196/D1 Pointe-à-la-Croix, Qu,Can
162/F3 Pointe-à-Pitre, Guad.
161/H2 Pointe à Raquette, Haiti
198/F2 Pointe au Baril Station, On,Can
196/B2 Pointe-au-Pic, Qu,Can
196/C1 Pointe-aux-Outardes, Qu,Can
197/N6 Pointe-aux-Trembles, Qu,Can
197/N6 Pointe-Calumet, Qu,Can
197/N7 Pointe-Claire, Qu,Can
195/G2 Pointe du Bois, Mb,Can
196/E2 Pointe-du-Chêne, NB,Can
205/H6 Point Edward, On,Can
152/B4 Pointe Noir (int'l arpt.), Congo
152/B4 Pointe-Noire, Congo
196/E2 Pointe-Verte, NB,Can
162/F5 Point Fortin, Trin.
177/E2 Point Hope, Ak,US
199/L4 Point Judith, RI,US
208/C3 Point Judith C.G. Sta., RI,US
197/K2 Point Lance, Nf,Can
177/F2 Point Lay, Ak,US
135/E1 Point Lookout (peak), Austl.
199/G5 Point Marion, Pa,US
204/A2 Point Mugo Nav. Air Sta., Ca,US
204/A2 Point Mugo St. Park, Ca,US
122/H4 Point Pedro, SrL.
198/E4 Point Pelee Nat'l Park, On,Can
205/G8 Point Pelee Nat'l Park, On,Can
207/D3 Point Pleasant, NJ,US
206/C3 Point Pleasant, Pa,US
201/F1 Point Pleasant, WV,US
207/D3 Point Pleasant Beach, NJ,US
186/A1 Point Reyes Nat'l Seash., Ca,US
182/C3 Point Roberts, Wa,US
82/C1 Point-Saint-Bernard, Col du (pass), Fr.
165/F1 Point Salines (int'l arpt.), Gren.
132/E4 Point Salvation Abor. Rsv., Austl.
208/G7 Point St. Park, Pa,US
86/A3 Poirino, It.
185/K2 Poison (cr.), Wy,US
199/J1 Poisson Blanc (res.), Qu,Can
132/C1 Poissonier (pt.), Austl.
132/C1 Poissonnier (pt.), Austl.
53/S10 Poissy, Fr.
74/D3 Poitiers, Fr.
74/C3 Poitou (hist. reg.), Fr.
74/C3 Poitou-Charentes (reg.), Fr.
68/A4 Poix-de-Picardie, Fr.
68/D4 Poix-Terron, Fr.
172/C1 Pojo, Bol.
63/K1 Pojo, Fin.
187/J3 Pojoaque, NM,US
61/J3 Pojois-Karjala (prov.), Fin.
118/B2 Pokaran, India
135/D1 Pokataroo, Austl.
195/H4 Pokegama (lake), Mn,US
120/D1 Pokhara, Nepal
97/K1 Pokhvistnevo, Rus.
123/E4 Po Klong Garai Cham Towers, Viet.
153/F2 Poko, Zaire
97/K2 Pokrovka, Rus.
101/N3 Pokrovsk, Rus.
96/F1 Pokrovskoye, Rus.
99/K4 Pokrovskoye, Rus.
99/J4 Pokrovskoye, Ukr.
99/K3 Pokrovskoye, Ukr.
63/P3 Pola, Rus.
71/H2 Polabská Nížina (reg.), Czh.
187/G3 Polacca, Az,US
187/G3 Polacca (wash), Az,US
92/C4 Polače, Cro.
76/C1 Pola de Laviana, Sp.
76/C1 Pola de Lena, Sp.
76/C1 Pola de Siero, Sp.
107/H3 Polān, Iran
96/A2 Pol'ana (peak), Slvk.
175/T11 Polanco del Yi, Uru.
65/K2 Poland
196/B3 Poland, Me,US
199/J3 Poland, NY,US
208/G5 Poland, Oh,US
65/L3 Połaniec, Pol.
95/P2 Polar Urals (mts.), Rus.
104/C2 Polatlı, Turk.
69/G3 Polch, Ger.
65/J2 Połczyn-Zdrój, Pol.
107/J1 Pol-e-Khomri, Afg.
105/H2 Pol-e Sefīd, Iran
87/E3 Polesella, It.
87/E2 Polesine (reg.), It.
98/E2 Polesskoye, Ukr.
59/E1 Polesworth, Eng,UK
96/D1 Poles'ye, Bela.
95/P4 Polevskoy, Rus.
105/F3 Pol-e Zahāb, Iran
92/E2 Polgár, Hun.
73/C5 Polgárdi, Hun.
113/D5 Pŏlgyo, SKor.
148/B3 Poli, Camr.
91/J4 Políaigos (isl.), Gre.
83/B2 Policastro (gulf), It.
65/H2 Police, Pol.
83/C2 Policoro, It.
80/B4 Poligny, Fr.
91/H2 Políkastron, Gre.
91/H2 Políkhni, Gre.
91/K3 Polikhnítos, Gre.
125/C2 Polillo (isl.), Phil.
125/C2 Polillo (isls.), Phil.
125/C2 Polillo (str.), Phil.
103/C2 Polis, Cyp.
83/C6 Polistena, It.
91/H2 Políyiros, Gre.
92/B2 Polje, Slov.
202/M8 Polk (co.), Fl,US
192/F3 Polk, Ne,US
208/E6 Polk, Oh,US
208/H5 Polk, Pa,US
202/M7 Polk City, Fl,US
65/J3 Polkowice, Pol.
200/C4 Polkville, Ms,US
201/G3 Polkville, NC,US
85/F6 Polla, It.
122/F3 Pollāchi, India
72/B4 Polleben, Ger.
77/G3 Pollensa, Sp.
85/D1 Pollenza, It.
83/C3 Pollino (peak), It.
184/E1 Pollock, Id,US
202/B2 Pollock, La,US
194/D5 Pollock, SD,US
186/B1 Pollock Pines, Ca,US
183/J2 Pollockville, Ab,Can
193/K3 Polo, Il,US
191/G1 Polo, Mo,US
160/D3 Polochic (riv.), Guat.
99/J4 Pologi, Ukr.
125/D4 Polomolok, Phil.
124/B2 Polonia (int'l arpt.), Indo.
175/G2 Polonia (cape), Uru.
195/K5 Polonia, Wi,US
122/H5 Polonnaruwa, SrL.
122/H4 Polonnaruwa (dist.), SrL.
98/D2 Polonnoye, Ukr.
63/N4 Polotsk, Bela.
58/B6 Polperro, Eng,UK
93/G4 Polski Trŭmbesh, Bul.
183/G4 Polson, Mt,US
99/H3 Poltava, Ukr.
99/G3 Poltava Obl., Ukr.
63/L2 Põltsamaa, Est.
71/H5 Poluška (peak), Czh.
63/M2 Põlva, Est.
187/J3 Polvadera, NM,US
174/R9 Polvaredas, Arg.
94/F3 Polvijärvi, Fin.
94/G1 Polyarnyy, Rus.
139/J3 Polynesia (reg.)
87/D6 Pomarance, It.
201/G3 Pomaria, SC,US
83/C1 Pomarico, It.
73/D4 Pomáz, Hun.
171/E4 Pomba (riv.), Braz.
167/G4 Pombal, Braz.
76/A3 Pombal, Port.
140/J9 Pombas, CpV.
65/H2 Pomerania (reg.), Pol.
65/H1 Pomeranian (bay), Ger., Pol.
187/G5 Pomerene, Az,US
173/G3 Pomerode, Braz.
165/G3 Pomeroon-Supernaam (reg.), Guy.
56/B2 Pomeroy, NI,UK
198/E5 Pomeroy, Oh,US
182/F4 Pomeroy, Wa,US
84/C4 Pomezia, It.
208/C2 Pomfret, Ct,US
85/E6 Pomigliano d'Arco, It.
138/E5 Pomio, PNG
193/G1 Pomme de Terre (riv.), Mn,US
191/H2 Pomme de Terre (riv.), Mo,US
70/D3 Pommersfelden, Ger.
156/A2 Pomona, Namb.
204/C2 Pomona, Ca,US
191/G1 Pomona, Ks,US
191/G1 Pomona (lake), Ks,US
206/B5 Pomona, Md,US
200/B2 Pomona, Mo,US
206/D5 Pomona, NJ,US
93/H4 Pomorie, Bul.
103/C2 Pomos (pt.), Cyp.
98/F3 Pomoshnaya, Ukr.
95/M3 Pomozdino, Rus.
203/H4 Pompano Beach, Fl,US
85/E6 Pompei, It.
85/E6 Pompei (ruins), It.
170/C4 Pompéia, Braz.
170/D3 Pompeu, Braz.
69/F6 Pompey, Fr.
183/L5 Pompeys Pillar, Mt,US
86/C2 Pompiano, It.
207/H8 Pompton (lakes), NJ,US
207/H8 Pompton (riv.), NJ,US
207/D1 Pompton Lakes, NJ,US
145/E4 Pô Nat'l Park, Burk.
193/F2 Ponca, Ne,US
192/E2 Ponca (cr.), Ne, SD,US
191/F2 Ponca City, Ok,US
86/D2 Poncarale, It.
162/E3 Ponce, PR
203/F2 Ponce de Leon, Fl,US
203/H3 Ponce Inlet, Fl,US
192/A4 Poncha Springs, Co,US
202/C2 Ponchatoula, La,US
80/B5 Poncin, Fr.
130/B3 Pond (cape), Austl.
179/J1 Pond (inlet), NW,Can
190/B1 Pond (cr.), Co,US
208/A3 Pond (pt.), Ct,US
200/D2 Pond (riv.), Ky,US
191/F2 Pond Creek, Ok,US
189/F1 Ponder, Tx,US
182/F3 Ponderay, Id,US
190/A3 Ponderosa, NM,US
122/G3 Pondicherry, India
122/G3 Pondicherry (terr.), India
179/J1 Pond Inlet, NW,Can
195/G3 Ponemah, Mn,US
86/B5 Ponente (coast), It.
76/B1 Ponferrada, Sp.
170/C4 Pongaí, Braz.
113/D5 Pongdong, SKor.
113/E4 Ponghwa, SKor.
123/C3 Pong Nam Ron, Thai.
149/E4 Pongo (riv.), Sudan
157/E2 Pongolo (riv.), SAfr.
113/C3 Pongsan, NKor.
122/D1 Pongunagu, India
151/B3 Pongwe, Tanz.
144/E4 Poni (prov.), Burk.
65/M3 Poniatowa, Pol.
122/G3 Ponnaiyar (riv.), India
122/E3 Ponnani, India
183/H1 Ponoka, Ab,Can
97/K1 Ponomarevka, Rus.
124/E4 Ponorogo, Indo.
94/J2 Ponoy, Rus.
94/H2 Ponoy (riv.), Rus.
127/F4 Ponrang, Indo.
74/C4 Pons, Fr.
86/D5 Ponsacco, It.
136/F6 Ponsonby, N.Z.
68/D3 Pont-à-Celles, Belg.
77/S12 Ponta da Pico (mtn.), Azor.,Port.
77/T13 Ponta Delgada, Azor.,Port.
166/D3 Ponta de Pedras, Braz.
167/H4 Ponta do Calcanhar (pt.), Braz.
77/U15 Ponta do Sol, Madr.,Port.
173/G3 Ponta Grossa, Braz.
68/C2 Pont-à-Marcq, Fr.
69/F6 Pont-à-Mousson, Fr.
170/B4 Ponta Porã, Braz.
58/C3 Pontardawe, Wal,UK
58/B3 Pontardulais, Wal,UK
80/C4 Pontarlier, Fr.
87/E5 Pontassieve, It.
79/F2 Pont-Audemer, Fr.
53/T10 Pontault-Combault, Fr.
78/B5 Pont-Aven, Fr.
86/A2 Pont Canavese, It.
53/U10 Pontcarré, Fr.
82/C2 Pontcharra, Fr.
202/C2 Pontchartrain (lake), La,US
78/C6 Pontchâteau, Fr.
78/A4 Pont-Croix, Fr.
80/B5 Pont-d'Ain, Fr.
78/A4 Pont-de-Buis-lès-Quimerch, Fr.
82/B1 Pont-de-Chéruy, Fr.
68/A5 Pont-de-l'Arche, Fr.
80/C3 Pont-de-Roide, Fr.
80/A5 Pont-de-Vaux, Fr.
80/A5 Pont-de-Veyle, Fr.
74/E4 Pont-du-Château, Fr.
170/D2 Ponte Alta do Bom Jesus, Braz.
170/D1 Ponte Alta do Norte, Braz.
87/D5 Ponte Buggianese, It.
85/E6 Pontecagnano, It.
85/D5 Pontecorvo, It.
86/B3 Pontecurone, It.
86/C3 Ponte dell'Olio, It.
86/D5 Pontedera, It.
76/A3 Ponte de Sor, Port.
81/G5 Ponte di Legno, It.
87/F1 Ponte di Piave, It.
76/A2 Ponte do Lima, Port.
57/G4 Pontefract, Eng,UK
183/L3 Ponteix, Sk,Can
86/C1 Ponte Lambro, It.
57/G1 Ponteland, Eng,UK
85/E5 Pontelandolfo, It.
87/F2 Pontelongo, It.
171/E4 Ponte Nova, Braz.
86/C3 Pontenure, It.
58/C2 Ponterwyd, Wal,UK
87/E2 Ponte San Nicolò, It.
58/D1 Pontesbury, Eng,UK
169/G4 Pontes e Lacerda, Braz.
86/B2 Pontestura, It.
86/B1 Ponte Tresa, It.
125/C3 Pontevedra, Phil.
76/A1 Pontevedra, Sp.
82/A1 Pont-Évêque, Fr.
86/D2 Pontevico, It.
79/G4 Pontgouin, Fr.
79/D2 Pont-Hébert, Fr.
193/K3 Pontiac, Il,US
205/F6 Pontiac, Mi,US
205/F6 Pontiac (lake), Mi,US
191/H2 Pontiac, Mo,US
126/C4 Pontianak, Indo.
124/C2 Pontian Kechil, Malay.
84/D5 Pontinia, It.
78/C4 Pontivy, Fr.
78/A5 Pont-l'Abbé, Fr.
79/F2 Pont-l'Évêque, Fr.
79/G6 Pontlevoy, Fr.
166/B5 Ponto da Divisão, Braz.
53/S9 Pontoise, Fr.
78/D3 Pontorson, Fr.
200/C3 Pontotoc, Ms,US
191/F3 Pontotoc, Ok,US
188/E2 Pontotoc, Tx,US
68/B5 Pontpoint, Fr.
86/C4 Pontremoli, It.
68/A3 Pont-Remy, Fr.
81/F5 Pontresina, Swi.
58/C2 Pontrhydfendigaid, Wal,UK
183/M1 Pontrilas, Sk,Can
58/D3 Pontrilas, Eng,UK
68/B5 Pont-Sainte Maxence, Fr.
74/F4 Pont-Saint-Esprit, Fr.
82/A4 Pont-Saint-Esprit, Fr.
86/A1 Pont-Saint-Martin, It.
78/B5 Pont-Scorff, Fr.
79/F5 Pontvallain, Fr.
58/B3 Pontyates, Wal,UK
58/C3 Pontyclun, Wal,UK
58/C3 Pont y Cymmer, Wal,UK
199/G2 Pontypool, On,Can
58/C3 Pontypool, Wal,UK
58/C3 Pontypridd, Wal,UK
136/D4 Ponui (isl.), N.Z.
183/J5 Pony, Mt,US
119/G2 Ponyo, Burma
84/C6 Ponza, It.
84/C6 Ponza (isl.), It.
84/C6 Ponziane (isls.), It.
152/C3 Pool (pol. reg.), Congo
58/E5 Poole, Eng,UK
59/E5 Poole (bay), Eng,UK
55/J8 Poolewe, Sc,UK
118/B4 Poona, India
133/J5 Pooncarie, Austl.
132/C3 Poondarrie (peak), Austl.
133/F3 Poondinna (peak), Austl.
172/C1 Poopó, Bol.
172/C1 Poopó (lake), Bol.
194/B2 Poor Man Ind. Res., Sk,Can
63/K2 Põõsapää Neem (pt.), Est.
207/F2 Poosepatuck Ind. Res., NY,US
116/B4 Popa (peak), Burma
99/K3 Popasnaya, Ukr.
164/B4 Popayán, Col.
201/H3 Pope A.F.B., NC,US
98/E3 Popel'nya, Ukr.
68/B2 Poperinge, Belg.
158/C2 Popigochic (riv.), Mex.
135/B2 Popilta (lake), Austl.
93/H3 Popina, Bul.
135/B2 Popio (lake), Austl.
195/G1 Poplar (riv.), Mb, On,Can
206/B6 Poplar (isl.), Md,US
194/B3 Poplar, Mt,US
194/B3 Poplar (riv.), Sk,Can, Mt,US
191/J2 Poplar Bluff, Mo,US
186/C2 Poplar-Cotton Center, Ca,US
182/F2 Poplar Creek, BC,Can
194/F2 Poplarfield, Mb,Can
195/G1 Poplar Hill, On,Can
201/G3 Poplar Tent, NC,US
202/D2 Poplarville, Ms,US
183/M3 Poplar, West Fork (riv.), Sk,Can, Mt,US
85/D3 Popoli, It.
131/H2 Popondetta, PNG
93/H4 Popovo, Bul.
71/E4 Poppberg (peak), Ger.
66/C6 Poppel, Belg.
70/C2 Poppenhausen, Ger.
70/D2 Poppenhausen, Ger.
87/E5 Poppi, It.
65/L4 Poprad, Slvk.
65/L4 Poprad (riv.), Slvk.
113/D3 Pŏptong, NKor.
208/B3 Poquonock Bridge, Ct,US
201/J2 Poquoson, Va,US
167/F4 Poranga, Braz.
136/D3 Porangahau, N.Z.
170/C2 Porangatu, Braz.
118/A3 Porbandar, India
86/D5 Porcari, It.
164/C3 Porce (riv.), Col.
87/F1 Porcia, It.
172/C1 Porco, Bol.
76/C4 Porcuna, Sp.
194/C2 Porcupine (hills), Mb, Sk,Can
183/L3 Porcupine (cr.), Mt,US
192/C2 Porcupine, SD,US
177/K2 Porcupine (riv.), Yk,Can, Ak,US
134/B3 Porcupine Gorge Nat'l Park, Austl.
194/C1 Porcupine Plain, Sk,Can
87/F1 Pordenone, It.
87/F1 Pordenone (prov.), It.
78/C3 Pordic, Fr.
93/G4 Pordim, Bul.
164/D3 Pore, Col.
87/G2 Poreč, Cro.
170/C4 Porecatu, Braz.
63/L5 Porech'ye, Bela.
95/K5 Poretskoye, Rus.
90/A1 Poretta (Bastia) (int'l arpt.), Fr.
131/F1 Porgera, PNG
63/J1 Pori, Fin.
63/J1 Pori (int'l arpt.), Fin.
136/C3 Porirua, N.Z.
136/H9 Porirua (har.), N.Z.
63/N3 Porkhov, Rus.
165/F2 Porlamar, Ven.
81/F5 Porlezza, It.
58/C4 Porlock, Eng,UK
134/A1 Pormpuraaw Abor. Land, Austl.
74/B3 Pornic, Fr.
78/C6 Pornichet, Fr.
83/B5 Poro (peak), It.
109/N2 Poronaysk, Rus.
172/C4 Porongo (peak), Arg.
132/C5 Porongurup Nat'l Park, Austl.
91/H4 Póros, Gre.
95/M3 Porozhsk, Rus.
137/J Porpoise (bay), Ant.
82/C6 Porquerolles (isl.), Fr.
80/D3 Porrentruy, Swi.
87/D4 Porretta Terme, It.
76/A1 Porriño, Sp.
61/H1 Porsangen (fjord), Nor.
62/C2 Porsgrunn, Nor.
78/A3 Porspoder, Fr.
104/B2 Porsuk (riv.), Turk.
169/F5 Portachuelo, Bol.
133/M8 Port Adelaide, Austl.
56/B3 Portadown, NI,UK
56/C3 Portaferry, NI,UK
195/E2 Portage (bay), Mb,Can
196/C2 Portage, Me,US
198/D3 Portage, Mi,US
195/K4 Portage (lake), Mi,US
195/L5 Portage (pt.), Mi,US
208/F5 Portage (co.), Oh,US
208/F6 Portage (lakes), Oh,US
199/G4 Portage, Pa,US
193/K2 Portage, Wi,US
199/H2 Portage-du-Fort, Can.
208/F5 Portage Lakes, Oh,US
194/E3 Portage la Prairie, Mb,Can
200/C2 Portageville, Mo,US
187/H5 Portal, Az,US
201/G4 Portal, Ga,US
194/C3 Portal, ND,US
182/B3 Port Alberni, BC,Can
135/C3 Port Albert, Austl.
76/B3 Portalegre, Port.
76/B3 Portalegre (dist.), Port.
190/C3 Portales, NM,US
177/M4 Port Alexander, Ak,US
156/D4 Port Alfred, SAfr.
199/G4 Port Allegany, Pa,US
202/C2 Port Allen, La,US
182/C3 Port Angeles, Wa,US
161/G2 Port Antonio, Jam.
54/A3 Port Appin, Sc,UK
189/F4 Port Aransas, Tx,US
60/C3 Portarlington, Ire.
189/H3 Port Arthur, Tx,US
55/H9 Port Askaig, Sc,UK
133/H5 Port Augusta, Austl.
197/H1 Port au Port (bay), Nf,Can
197/H1 Port au Port (pen.), Nf,Can
161/H2 Port-au-Prince (cap.), Haiti
198/E2 Port Austin, Mi,US
56/C3 Portavogie, NI,UK
67/F4 Porta Westfalica, Ger.
78/D2 Portbail, Fr.
54/A5 Port Bannatyne, Sc,UK
202/C2 Port Barre, La,US
119/F5 Port Blair, India
205/B2 Port Blakely, Wa,US
197/K1 Port Blandford, Nf,Can
189/G3 Port Bolivar, Tx,US
77/G1 Portbou, Sp.
144/E5 Port-Bouët, IvC.
144/E5 Port Bouet (Abidjan) (int'l arpt.), IvC.
79/E4 Port-Brillet, Fr.
133/H5 Port Broughton, Austl.
179/K2 Port Burwell, Qu,Can
121/G4 Port Canning, India
206/B2 Port Carbon, Pa,US
199/G2 Port Carling, On,Can
179/K3 Port-Cartier, Qu,Can
136/B4 Port Chalmers, N.Z.
203/G4 Port Charlotte, Fl,US
59/E5 Portchester, UK
207/E2 Port Chester, NY,US
177/M5 Port Clements, BC,Can
198/E4 Port Clinton, Oh,US
206/B2 Port Clinton, Pa,US
199/G3 Port Colborne, On,Can
198/E5 Port Columbus (int'l arpt.), Oh,US
197/R8 Port Credit, On,Can
82/C6 Port-Cros Nat'l, Fr.
197/T8 Port Darlington, On,Can
135/C4 Port Davey (har.), Austl.
82/A6 Port-de-Bouc, Fr.
161/H2 Port-de-Paix, Haiti
206/B4 Port Deposit, Md,US
124/C2 Port Dickson, Malay.
205/B1 Port Discovery (bay), Wa,US
134/B2 Port Douglas, Austl.
202/D3 Port Eads, La,US
177/M4 Port Edward, BC,Can
193/K1 Port Edwards, Wi,US
167/G4 Porteiras, Braz.
166/D3 Portel, Braz.
196/E2 Port Elgin, NB,Can
198/F2 Port Elgin, On,Can
156/D4 Port Elizabeth, SAfr.
162/F4 Port Elizabeth, StV.
206/D5 Port Elizabeth, NJ,US
55/H9 Port Ellen, Sc,UK
172/D4 Porteña, Arg.
79/E2 Port-en-Bessin-Huppain, Fr.
196/B4 Porter, Me,US
191/G3 Porter, Ok,US
189/M8 Porter, Tx,US
200/F4 Porterdale, Ga,US
56/D3 Port Erin, IM,UK
206/C1 Porters (lake), Pa,US
196/F3 Porters Lake, NS,Can
208/G6 Portersville, Pa,US
156/L10 Porterville, SAfr.
186/C2 Porterville, Ca,US
153/F4 Portes d'Enfer (Gates of Hell), Zaire
82/A3 Portes-lès-Valence, Fr.
161/J3 Portete (bay), Col.
74/D5 Portet-sur-Garonne, Fr.
58/B3 Port Eynon, Wal,UK
58/B3 Port Eynon (pt.), Wal,UK
172/B3 Portezuelo del León Muerto (mtn.), Arg.
172/B3 Portezuelo de Socompa (pass), Chile
135/B3 Port Fairy, Austl.
205/B2 Port Gamble, Wa,US
205/B2 Port Gamble Ind. Res., Wa,US
152/B3 Port-Gentil, Gabon
200/B5 Port Gibson, Ms,US
54/B5 Port Glasgow, Sc,UK
56/B2 Portglenone, NI,UK
54/C1 Portgordon, Sc,UK
177/H4 Port Graham, Ak,US
58/C3 Porth, Wal,UK
145/G5 Port Harcourt, Nga.
145/G5 Port Harcourt (int'l arpt.), Nga.
178/D3 Port Hardy, BC,Can
197/G3 Port Hawkesbury, NS,Can
58/C4 Porthcawl, Wal,UK
132/C2 Port Hedland, Austl.
132/C2 Port Hedland (int'l arpt.), Austl.
177/G4 Port Heiden, Ak,US
182/F3 Porthill, Id,US
58/A6 Porthleven, Eng,UK
56/D6 Porthmadog, Wal,UK
197/G2 Port Hood, NS,Can
199/G3 Port Hope, On,Can
198/E3 Port Hope, Mi,US
175/N7 Port Howard, Falk.
204/A2 Port Hueneme, Ca,US
205/H6 Port Huron, Mi,US
85/E6 Portici, It.
97/J5 Port Il'ich, Azer.
174/Q9 Portillo, Chile
76/A4 Portimão, Port.
58/B5 Port Isaac, Eng,UK
58/B5 Port Isaac (bay), Eng,UK
189/F4 Port Isabel, Tx,US
58/D4 Portishead, Eng,UK
207/E2 Port Jefferson, NY,US
206/D1 Port Jervis, NY,US
130/C3 Port Keats, Austl.
133/G5 Port Kenny, Austl.
54/D1 Portknockie, Sc,UK
205/G6 Port Lambton, On,Can
135/B3 Portland, Austl.
135/D2 Portland, Austl.
135/C4 Portland (cape), Austl.
199/H2 Portland, On,Can
161/G2 Portland (pt.), Jam.
136/C1 Portland, N.Z.
58/D6 Portland (pt.), Eng,UK
191/J4 Portland, Ar,US
177/N4 Portland (inlet), BC,Can, Ak,US
208/B2 Portland, Ct,US
203/E2 Portland, Fl,US
198/D4 Portland, In,US
196/B4 Portland, Me,US
194/F4 Portland, ND,US
184/B1 Portland, Or,US
184/B1 Portland (int'l arpt.), Or,US
200/D2 Portland, Tn,US
189/F4 Portland, Tx,US
55/K11 Portland, Bill of (pt.), Eng,UK
58/D5 Portland, Isle of (pen.), Eng,UK
199/L3 Portland Jetport (int'l arpt.), Me,US
74/E5 Port-la-Nouvelle, Fr.
60/C3 Portlaoise, Ire.
189/F3 Port Lavaca, Tx,US
60/C5 Portlaw, Ire.
54/D2 Portlethen, Sc,UK
199/J3 Port Leyden, NY,US
133/G5 Port Lincoln, Austl.
177/H4 Port Lions, Ak,US
131/G2 Portlock (reef), PNG
144/B4 Port Loko, SLeo.
78/B5 Port-Louis, Fr.
162/F3 Port-Louis, Guad.
157/S15 Port Louis (cap.), Mrts.
205/B2 Port Ludlow, Wa,US
135/B3 Port MacDonnell, Austl.
135/E1 Port Macquarie, Austl.
205/B2 Port Madison Ind. Res., Wa,US
54/C1 Portmahomack, Sc,UK
161/G2 Port Maria, Jam.
60/D3 Portmarnock, Ire.
199/G2 Port McNicoll, On,Can
196/E3 Port Medway, NS,Can
179/K4 Port-Menier, Qu,Can
207/J10 Port Monmouth, NJ,US
161/G2 Portmore, Jam.
131/G2 Port Moresby (cap.), PNG
189/H3 Port Neches, Tx,US
196/C1 Portneuf (riv.), Qu,Can
136/H9 Port Nicholson (inlet), N.Z.
156/B3 Port Nolloth, SAfr.
206/C5 Port Norris, NJ,US
167/F3 Pôrto, Braz.
90/A1 Porto (gulf), Fr.
76/A2 Porto, Port.
76/A2 Porto (dist.), Port.
76/A2 Porto (int'l arpt.), Port.
173/G4 Pôrto Alegre, Braz.
152/C5 Porto Amboim, Ang.
154/B1 Porto Amboim (bay), Ang.
84/A2 Porto Azzurro, It.
161/G4 Portobelo Nat'l Park, Pan.
171/G1 Pôrto Calvo, Braz.
85/F4 Portocannone, It.
86/B1 Porto Ceresio, It.
87/G6 Portocivitanova, It.
189/F3 Port O'Conner, Tx,US
171/F1 Pôrto da Fôlha, Braz.
76/A3 Porto de Mós, Port.
166/C3 Porto de Moz, Braz.
167/H5 Pôrto de Pedras, Braz.
90/C4 Porto Empedocle, It.
84/B3 Porto Ercole, It.
169/G4 Porto Esperança, Braz.
170/D4 Pôrto Feliz, Braz.
84/A2 Portoferraio, It.
170/D4 Pôrto Ferreira, Braz.
86/C4 Portofino, It.
55/H7 Port of Ness, Sc,UK
167/E4 Porto Franco, Braz.
162/F5 Port-of-Spain (cap.) Trin.
87/F3 Porto Garibaldi, It.
144/B4 Porto Gole, GBis.
87/F1 Portogruaro, It.
140/K10 Porto Inglês, CpV.
184/C4 Portola, Ca,US
87/E3 Portomaggiore, It.
142/A2 Porto Moniz, Madr.
170/B2 Porto Moroco, Braz.
170/A4 Porto Murtinho, Braz.
170/C1 Porto Nacional, Braz.
145/F5 Porto-Novo (cap.), Ben.
140/J9 Porto Novo, CpV.
122/G3 Portonovo, India
166/C2 Porto Poet, Braz.
87/G6 Porto Potenza Picena, It.
203/H3 Port Orange, Fl,US
205/B2 Port Orchard, Wa,US
87/G6 Porto Recanati, It.
184/A2 Port Orford, Or,US
152/C4 Porto Rico, Ang.
170/B4 Pôrto Rico, Braz.
87/G1 Portorož, Slov.
85/D1 Porto San Giorgio, It.
85/D1 Porto Sant'Elpidio, It.
142/A2 Porto Santo (isl.), Madr.,Port.
84/B3 Porto Santo Stefano, It.
171/F3 Porto Seguro, Braz.
87/F3 Porto Tolle, It.
90/A2 Porto Torres, It.
173/G3 Porto União, Braz.
86/B1 Porto Valtravaglia, It.
90/A2 Porto-Vecchio, Fr.
169/F3 Porto Velho, Braz.
86/C4 Portovenere, It.
164/A5 Portoviejo, Ecu.
56/C2 Portpatrick, Sc,UK
206/C4 Port Penn, De,US
135/C3 Port Phillip (bay), Austl.
133/H5 Port Pirie, Austl.
207/H9 Port Reading, NJ,US
55/H8 Portree, Sc,UK
182/B3 Port Renfrew, BC,Can
206/D4 Port Republic, NJ,US
197/L1 Port Rexton, Nf,Can
202/K7 Port Richey, Fl,US
207/J9 Port Richmond, NY,US
60/B4 Portroe, Ire.
198/F3 Port Rowan, On,Can
206/A2 Port Royal, Pa,US
201/G4 Port Royal, SC,US
201/G4 Port Royal (sound), SC,US
56/B1 Portrush, NI,UK
104/C4 Port Said, Egypt
103/C4 Port Said (Būr Sa'īd), Egypt
203/F3 Port Saint Joe, Fl,US
156/E3 Port Saint Johns, SAfr.
82/A6 Port-Saint-Louis-du-Rhône, Fr.
203/H4 Port Saint Lucie, Fl,US
56/D3 Port Saint Mary, IM,UK
175/N7 Port San Carlos, Falk.
125/C4 Port Santa Maria, Phil.
59/E5 Portsea (isl.), Eng,UK
54/D5 Port Seton, Sc,UK
199/G2 Port Severn, On,Can
157/E3 Port Shepstone, SAfr.
177/M4 Port Simpson, BC,Can
59/F5 Portslade by Sea, Eng,UK
162/F4 Portsmouth, Dom.
59/E5 Portsmouth, Eng,UK
201/K3 Portsmouth (isl.), NC,US
199/L3 Portsmouth, NH,US
201/F1 Portsmouth, Oh,US
208/C2 Portsmouth, RI,US
201/J2 Portsmouth, Va,US
54/D1 Portsoy, Sc,UK
198/F3 Port Stanley, On,Can
135/E2 Port Stephens (bay), Austl.
175/M8 Port Stephens, Falk.
56/B1 Portstewart, NI,UK
106/C5 Port Sudan, Sudan
147/H5 Port Sudan (Būr Sūdān), Sudan
202/D3 Port Sulphur, La,US
80/C2 Port-sur-Saône, Fr.
58/C3 Port Talbot, Wal,UK
182/C3 Port Townsend, Wa,US
76/A3 Portugal
172/C2 Portugalete, Bol.
76/D1 Portugalete, Sp.
164/D2 Portuguesa (riv.), Ven.
164/D2 Portuguesa (state), Ven.
204/F8 Portuguese Bend, Ca,US
60/B3 Portumna, Ire.
197/L1 Port Union, Nf,Can
74/E5 Port-Vendres, Fr.
133/H5 Port Victoria, Austl.
133/H5 Port Wakefield, Austl.
207/E2 Port Washington, NY,US
208/F7 Port Washington, Oh,US
193/L2 Port Washington, Wi,US
124/C1 Port Weld, Malay.
201/G4 Port Wentworth, Ga,US
56/D2 Port William, Sc,UK
196/E3 Port Williams, NS,Can
195/J4 Port Wing, Wi,US
191/G3 Porum, Ok,US
168/D3 Porvenir, Bol.
169/F4 Porvenir, Bol.
175/K8 Porvenir, Chile
168/C2 Porvenir, Peru
175/T11 Porvenir, Uru.
63/L1 Porvoo (Borgä), Fin.
69/G2 Porz, Ger.
76/C3 Porzuna, Sp.
90/A2 Posada, It.
173/F3 Posadas, Arg.
76/C4 Posadas, Sp.
92/C3 Posavina (val.), Bosn., Cro.
81/G5 Poschiavo, Swi.
200/D1 Poseyville, In,US
91/F2 Poshnjë, Alb.
105/H3 Posht-e Bādām, Iran
61/J2 Posio, Fin.
85/E6 Positano, It.
127/F4 Poso, Indo.
127/F4 Poso (lake), Indo.
186/C3 Poso (cr.), Ca,US
105/E1 Posof, Turk.
113/D5 Posŏng, SKor.
113/D5 Posŏng (bay), SKor.
113/D5 Posŏng (riv.), SKor.
164/A5 Posorja, Ecu.
114/D1 Pospelikha, Rus.
170/D2 Posse, Braz.
148/C4 Possel, CAfr.
205/C2 Possession (pt.), Wa,US
205/C2 Possession (sound), Wa,US
72/B6 Pössneck, Ger.
191/E4 Possum Kingdom (lake), Tx,US
188/D1 Post, Tx,US
81/H4 Postal (Burgstall), It.
63/M4 Postavy, Bela.
156/C3 Postmasburg, SAfr.
191/E4 Postoak, Tx,US
92/B3 Postojna, Slov.
71/G2 Postolprty, Czh.
186/E4 Poston, Az,US
172/D1 Postrervalle, Bol.
193/J2 Postville, Ia,US
182/G4 Pot (mtn.), Id,US
127/F5 Pota, Indo.
121/H1 Potala Palace, China
91/H5 Potamós, Gre.
166/B1 Potaro (riv.), Guy.
165/G3 Potaro-Siparuni (reg.), Guy.
193/F4 Potawatami Ind. Res., Ks,US
198/C2 Potawatomie Ind. Res., Mi,US
198/B2 Potawatomie Ind. Res., Wi,US
191/G1 Potawatomi Ind. Res., Ks,US
193/K1 Potawatomi Ind. Res., Wi,US
156/D2 Potchefstroom, SAfr.
191/G3 Poteau, Ok,US
189/E3 Poteet, Tx,US
167/G4 Potengi, Braz.
85/F6 Potenza, It.
85/F6 Potenza (prov.), It.
84/C1 Potenza (riv.), It.
87/G6 Potenza Picena, It.
76/C1 Potes, Sp.
155/F5 Potgietersrus, SAfr.
189/E3 Poth, Tx,US
182/E4 Potholes (res.), Wa,US
167/F4 Poti (riv.), Braz.
53/H4 Poti, Geo.
87/E6 Poti, Alpe di (peak), It.
79/E3 Potigny, Fr.
145/H4 Potiskum, Nga.
182/F4 Potlatch, Id,US
201/J1 Potomac (riv.), US
198/C4 Potomac, Il,US
206/A5 Potomac, Md,US
144/C5 Potoru, SLeo.
172/C1 Potosí, Bol.
172/C1 Potosí (dept.), Bol.
180/F7 Potosí, Mex.
191/J2 Potosi, Mo,US
186/E3 Potosi (mtn.), Nv,US
188/E1 Potosi, Tx,US
172/B3 Potrerillos, Chile
186/D4 Potrero, Ca,US
172/B4 Potro, Cerro el (peak), Arg., Chile
72/D3 Potsdam, Ger.
199/J2 Potsdam, NY,US
73/A4 Pottendorf, Aus.
71/E3 Pottenstein, Ger.
192/C3 Potter, Ne,US
208/C3 Potter Hill, RI,US
53/N6 Potters Bar, Eng,UK
59/F2 Potterspury, Eng,UK
191/H2 Pottersville, Mo,US
70/E5 Pöttmes, Ger.
59/F2 Potton, Eng,UK
191/F4 Pottsboro, Tx,US
200/C3 Potts Camp, Ms,US
206/C3 Pottstown, Pa,US
206/B2 Pottsville, Pa,US
118/D6 Pottuvil, SrL.
191/F2 Potwin, Ks,US
79/D5 Pouancé, Fr.
72/C4 Pouch, Ger.
197/L2 Pouch Cove, Nf,Can
199/K4 Poughkeepsie, NY,US
80/B3 Pouilley-les-Vignes, Fr.
78/B6 Poulains, Pointe de (pt.), Fr.
203/G2 Poulan, Ga,US
60/D3 Poulaphouca (res.), Ire.
78/A5 Pouldreuzic, Fr.
205/B2 Poulsbo, Wa,US
57/G5 Poulter (riv.), Eng,UK
199/K3 Poultney, Vt,US
57/F4 Poulton-le-Fylde, Eng,UK
152/B2 Pouma, Camr.
113/D4 Poŭn, SKor.
201/F2 Pound, Va,US
198/B2 Pound, Wi,US
152/B3 Pounga-Nganda, Gabon
123/D2 Poungthak, Laos
144/E4 Poura, Burk.

82/C1 Pourri (mtn.), Fr.
69/E4 Pouru-Saint-Rémy, Fr.
170/D4 Pouso Alegre, Braz.
148/B3 Pouss, Camr.
123/C3 Pouthisat, Camb.
123/C3 Pouthisat (riv.), Camb.
74/C3 Pouzauges, Fr.
73/C1 Považská Bystrica, Slvk.
73/B2 Povážský Inovec (mts.), Slvk.
87/D2 Povegliano Veronese, It.
94/G3 Povenets, Rus.
83/B6 Poverello (mtn.), It.
86/D3 Poviglio, It.
76/A2 Póvoa de Varzim, Port.
99/M2 Povorino, Rus.
109/L3 Povorotnyy, Mys (cape), Rus.
179/J2 Povungnituk, Qu,Can
179/J2 Povungnituk (riv.), Qu,Can
199/G1 Powassan, On,Can
204/C5 Poway, Ca,US
185/L1 Powder (riv.), Mt, Wy,US
184/E1 Powder (riv.), Or,US
190/A1 Powderhorn, Co,US
191/G4 Powderly, Tx,US
185/K2 Powder, North Fork (riv.), Wy,US
185/K2 Powder River, Wy,US
185/K1 Powder River (pass), Wy,US
185/K2 Powder, South Fork (riv.), Wy,US
201/L7 Powder Springs, Ga,US
183/M5 Powderville, Mt,US
162/B1 Powell (pt.), Bahm.
187/G2 Powell (lake), Az, Ut,US
206/B3 Powell (cr.), Pa,US
200/E2 Powell, Tn,US
201/F2 Powell (riv.), Tn, Va,US
201/G1 Powell (mtn.), WV,US
185/J1 Powell, Wy,US
182/B3 Powell River, BC,Can
201/G1 Powellton, WV,US
193/J4 Power, Mt,US
197/S9 Power (res.), NY,US
60/B6 Power Head (pt.), Ire.
198/C2 Powers, Mi,US
184/A2 Powers, Or,US
205/P14 Powers (lake), Wi,US
194/C3 Powers Lake, ND,US
198/F5 Powhatan Point, Oh,US
58/C2 Powys (co.), Wal,UK
58/C1 Powys, Vale (vall.), Wal,UK
170/B2 Poxoréo, Braz.
170/B3 Poxoreu (riv.), Braz.
117/G2 Poyang (lake), China
193/K1 Poygan (lake), Wi,US
193/K2 Poynette, Wi,US
189/G1 Poynor, Tx,US
57/F5 Poynton, Eng,UK
76/A1 Poyo, Sp.
73/A2 Poysdorf, Aus.
198/B2 Poy Sippi, Wi,US
104/C2 Pozantı, Turk.
92/E3 Požarevac, Yugo.
159/F4 Poza Rica, Mex.
92/E4 Požega, Yugo.
95/N4 Pozhva, Rus.
65/J2 Poznań, Pol.
65/J2 Poznań (prov.), Pol.
76/D4 Pozo Alcón, Sp.
172/B2 Pozo Almonte, Chile
76/C3 Pozoblanco, Sp.
172/E2 Pozo Colorado, Par.
174/E2 Pozo del Molle, Arg.
169/F5 Pozo del Tigre, Bol.
172/C3 Pozo Hondo, Arg.
76/E3 Pozohondo, Sp.
77/N9 Pozuelo de Alarcón, Sp.
172/C1 Pozuelos (lake), Arg.
165/E2 Pozuelos, Ven.
168/C3 Pozuzo, Peru
87/D3 Pozza, It.
90/D4 Pozzallo, It.
85/E4 Pozzilli, It.
86/B3 Pozzolo Formigaro, It.
84/D2 Pozzoni (peak), It.
87/E2 Pozzonovo, It.
85/E6 Pozzuoli, It.
84/B1 Pozzuolo, It.
65/K2 Prabuty, Pol.
123/B4 Pracham Hiang (pt.), Thai.
71/H4 Prachatice, Czh.
123/C3 Prachin Buri, Thai.
123/C3 Prachin Buri (riv.), Thai.
123/B4 Prachuap Khiri Khan, Thai.
81/G4 Prad am Stilfserjoch (Prato allo Stelvio), It.
65/J3 Praděd (peak), Czh.
164/B4 Pradera, Col.
74/E5 Prades, Fr.
171/F3 Prado, Braz.
204/C3 Prado (dam), Ca,US
76/C4 Prado del Rey, Sp.
204/C3 Prado Flood Control Basin, Ca,US
81/E4 Pragelpass (pass), Swi.
191/F3 Prague, Ok,US
71/H2 Prague (Praha) (cap.), Czh.
71/H2 Prague (Ruzyně) (int'l arpt.), Czh.
71/G3 Praha (peak), Czh.
71/H2 Praha (reg.), Czh.
71/H2 Praha (Prague) (cap.), Czh.
93/G3 Prahova (co.), Rom.
140/K11 Praia (cap.), CpV.
140/K11 Praia (int'l arpt.), CpV.
83/B3 Praia a Mare, It.
77/S12 Praia de Victória, Azor.,Port.
171/K9 Praia Grande, Braz.
166/C3 Prainha, Braz.
169/F2 Prainha, Braz.
134/B3 Prairie, Austl.
192/E3 Prairie (cr.), Ne,US
192/C1 Prairie City, SD,US
192/D4 Prairie Dog (cr.), Ks,US
180/F5 Prairie Dog Town Fork (riv.), Ok, Tx,US
193/J2 Prairie du Chien, Wi,US
195/J5 Prairie Farm, Wi,US
205/P15 Prairie Grove, Il,US
195/H5 Prairie Island Ind. Res., Mn,US
200/C4 Prairie Point, Ms,US
197/N6 Prairies (riv.), Qu,Can
189/G2 Prairie View, Tx,US
189/F1 Prairieville, Tx,US
123/C3 Prakhon Chai, Thai.
86/D2 Pralboino, It.
82/C2 Pralognan-la-Vanoise, Fr.
86/B1 Pralungo, It.
71/G6 Pram (riv.), Aus.
124/E4 Prambanan (ruins), Indo.
62/E4 Pramort, Ger.
123/B3 Pran Buri, Thai.
123/B3 Pran Buri (res.), Thai.
145/E5 Prang, Gha.
80/C5 Prangins, Swi.
118/D4 Prānhita (riv.), India
124/B2 Prapat, Indo.
123/D3 Prasat Preah Vihear, Camb.
97/H3 Praskoveya, Rus.
62/E4 Præstø, Den.
65/K3 Praszka, Pol.
167/G4 Prata, Braz.
87/F1 Prata di Pordenone, It.
85/E6 Prata di Principato Ultra, It.
167/F4 Prata do Piauí, Braz.
87/E6 Pratantico, It.
117/H4 Pratas (reef), China
117/H4 Pratas (Dongsha) (isl.), China
72/C4 Pratau, Ger.
77/L7 Prat-Barcelona (int'l arpt.), Sp.
81/F4 Prätigau (vall.), Swi.
87/E5 Prato, It.
81/G4 Prato allo Stelvio (Prad am Stilfserjoch), It.
85/D3 Pratola Peligna, It.
81/E5 Prato (Leventina), Swi.
87/E5 Pratomagno (mts.), It.
83/B2 Prato Perillo, It.
87/E5 Pratovecchio, It.
175/J7 Pratt (isl.), Chile
191/E2 Pratt, Ks,US
80/D2 Pratteln, Swi.
191/H3 Prattsville, Ar,US
199/J3 Prattsville, NY,US
200/D4 Prattville, Al,US
80/B2 Prauthoy, Fr.
95/J4 Pravdinsk, Rus.
93/F4 Pravets, Bul.
76/B1 Pravia, Sp.
55/K11 Prawle (pt.), Eng,UK
188/B2 Praxedis G. Guerrero, Mex.
124/G5 Praya, Indo.
82/B2 Préalpes (upland), Fr.
79/E5 Précigné, Fr.
68/B5 Précy-sur-Oise, Fr.
87/E4 Predappio, It.
75/J3 Predazzo, It.
93/G3 Predeal, Rom.
86/B3 Predosa, It.
194/C2 Preeceville, Sk,Can
79/E4 Pré-en-Pail, Fr.
57/F6 Prees, Eng,UK
57/F4 Preesall, Eng,UK
64/F1 Preetz, Ger.
92/E5 Pregolya (riv.), Rus.
164/D2 Pregonero, Ven.
63/M3 Preiļi, Lat.
123/D4 Prek Pouthi, Camb.
183/K2 Prelate, Sk,Can
81/F5 Premana, It.
74/E3 Prémery, Fr.
77/L7 Premiá de Mar, Sp.
72/C2 Premnitz, Ger.
189/E4 Premont, Tx,US
91/G2 Prenjas, Alb.
193/J1 Prentice, Wi,US
202/D2 Prentiss, Ms,US
65/G2 Prenzlau, Ger.
109/L3 Preobrazheniye, Rus.
65/J4 Přerov, Czh.
80/C6 Pré-Saint-Didier, It.
75/J3 Presanella (peak), It.
81/G5 Presanella, Cima (peak), It.
57/F5 Prescot, Eng,UK
199/J2 Prescott, On,Can
191/H4 Prescott, Ar,US
187/F3 Prescott, Az,US
193/G3 Prescott, Ia,US
191/G1 Prescott, Ks,US
195/G7 Prescott, Wi,US
187/F3 Prescott Valley, Az,US
73/C3 Prešov, Slvk.
73/C2 Presel'any, Slvk.
92/E4 Preševo, Yugo.
172/D3 Presidencia Roque Sáenz Peña, Arg.
170/C4 Presidente Bernardes, Braz.
167/E4 Presidente Dutra, Braz.
170/B4 Presidente Epitácio, Braz.
172/E1 Presidente Hayes (dept.), Par.
170/C4 Presidente Prudente, Braz.
174/B5 Presidente Ríos (lake), Chile
170/C4 Presidente Venceslau, Braz.
206/D4 Presidential Lake Estates, NJ,US
158/D4 Presidio (riv.), Mex.
188/B3 Presidio, Tx,US
189/F3 Presidio La Bahia, Tx,US
93/H4 Preslav, Bul.
53/U10 Presles-en-Brie, Fr.
81/G6 Presolana, Pizzo della (peak), It.
86/D1 Presolana, Pizzo della (peak), It.
65/L4 Prešov, Slvk.
91/G2 Prespa (lake), Eur.
196/C2 Presque Isle, Me,US
198/E2 Presque Isle, Mi,US
195/L4 Presque Isle (pt.), Mi,US
195/K4 Presque Isle, Wi,US
201/J2 Presquile Nat'l Wild. Ref., Va,US
71/E3 Pressath, Ger.
73/A3 Pressbaum, Aus.
57/E5 Prestatyn, Wal,UK
145/E5 Prestea, Gha.
58/D2 Presteigne, Wal,UK
62/D1 Prestfoss, Nor.
71/G3 Přeštice, Czh.
135/G5 Preston, Austl.
132/C2 Preston (cape), Austl.
57/F4 Preston, Eng,UK
58/D5 Preston, Eng,UK
54/D5 Preston, Sc,UK
200/E4 Preston, Ga,US
193/J2 Preston, Ia,US
185/H2 Preston, Id,US
191/E2 Preston, Ks,US
206/C6 Preston, Md,US
193/H2 Preston, Mn,US
200/C4 Preston, Ms,US
185/F4 Preston, Nv,US
191/G3 Preston, Ok,US
205/D2 Preston, Wa,US
54/D5 Prestonpans, Sc,UK
201/F2 Prestonsburg, Ky,US
57/F4 Prestwich, Eng,UK
54/B6 Prestwick, Sc,UK
59/F3 Prestwood, Eng,UK
170/D1 Prêto (riv.), Braz.
170/D3 Prêto (riv.), Braz.
169/F2 Prêto do Igapó-Açu (riv.), Braz.
156/E2 Pretoria (cap.), SAfr.
157/E2 Pretoriuskop, SAfr.
72/C4 Prettin, Ger.
206/B4 Pretty Boy (res.), Md,US
191/E2 Pretty Prairie, Ks,US
194/D4 Pretty Rock Nat'l Wild. Ref., ND,US
72/C4 Pretzsch, Ger.
67/F4 Preussisch Oldendorf, Ger.
92/B2 Prevalje, Slov.
91/G3 Préveza, Gre.
199/J2 Prévost, Qu,Can
187/H3 Prewitt, NM,US
119/J5 Prey Veng, Camb.
109/H1 Priargunsk, Rus.
99/J4 Priazov (upland), Ukr.
99/H4 Priazovskoye, Ukr.
177/D4 Pribilof (isls.), Ak,US
92/D4 Priboj, Yugo.
71/H3 Příbram, Czh.
196/C1 Price, Qu,Can
206/C5 Price, Md,US
191/F5 Price (falls), Ok,US
185/H4 Price, Ut,US
185/H4 Price (riv.), Ut,US
202/C2 Pricedale, Ms,US
202/D2 Prichard, Al,US
70/D3 Prichsenstadt, Ger.
189/E2 Priddy, Tx,US
203/G2 Pridgen, Ga,US
76/D2 Priego, Sp.
76/C4 Priego de Córdoba, Sp.
63/J3 Priekule, Lat.
63/J4 Priekulė, Lith.
63/K4 Prienai, Lith.
156/C3 Prieska, SAfr.
182/F3 Priest (lake), Id,US
184/D2 Priest (riv.), Id,US
182/E4 Priest Rapids (dam), Wa,US
182/F3 Priest River, Id,US
76/C1 Prieta (mtn.), Sp.
190/A3 Prieta (mesa), NM,US
73/C2 Prievidza, Slvk.
72/C1 Prignitz (reg.), Ger.
92/C3 Prijedor, Bosn.
92/D4 Prijepolje, Yugo.
97/H3 Prikaspian (plain), Kaz., Rus.
99/J2 Prikolotnoye, Ukr.
97/H3 Prikumsk, Rus.
97/H3 Prikumskiy, Rus.
92/E5 Prilep, Mcd.
80/C4 Prilly, Swi.
98/G2 Priluki, Ukr.
196/E3 Prim (pt.), NS,Can
196/F2 Prim (pt.), PE,Can
191/H3 Prim, Ar,US
84/C4 Prima Porta, It.
167/E3 Primavera, Braz.
206/C6 Prime Hook Nat'l Wild. Ref., De,US
167/F3 Primeira Cruz, Braz.
172/D3 Primero (riv.), Arg.
175/J7 Primero (cape), Chile
59/E1 Primethorpe, Eng,UK
192/B3 Primghar, Ia,US
97/J4 Primorsk, Azer.
63/J4 Primorsk, Rus.
63/N1 Primorsk, Rus.
97/H2 Primorsk, Rus.
99/H5 Primorskiy, Ukr.
101/P5 Primorskiy Kray, Rus.
99/J4 Primorsko-Akhtarsk, Rus.
99/K4 Primorsko-Akhtarsk, Rus.
98/F5 Primorskoye, Ukr.
99/J4 Primorskoye, Ukr.
69/F5 Prims (riv.), Ger.
183/K1 Prince, Sk,Can
178/E1 Prince Albert (pen.), NW,Can
178/E1 Prince Albert (sound), NW,Can
183/M1 Prince Albert, Sk,Can
156/C4 Prince Albert, SAfr.
178/F3 Prince Albert Nat'l Park, Sk,Can
178/D1 Prince Alfred (cape), NW,Can
179/J2 Prince Charles (isl.), NW,Can
176/L5 Prince Edward (isl.), Can.
51/L8 Prince Edward (isls.), SAfr.
196/F2 Prince Edward Island (prov.), Can
196/F2 Prince Edward Island Nat'l Park, PE,Can
201/J1 Prince Frederick, Md,US
178/D3 Prince George, BC,Can
201/J2 Prince George, Va,US
206/B6 Prince Georges (co.), Md,US
179/R7 Prince Gustav Adolf (sea), NW,Can
137/C Prince Harold (coast), Ant.
178/G1 Prince Leopold (isl.), NW,Can
66/C2 Princenhof (lake), Neth.
131/F2 Prince of Wales (isl.), Austl.
178/G1 Prince of Wales (isl.), NW,Can
178/E1 Prince of Wales (str.), NW,Can
177/M4 Prince of Wales (isl.), Ak,US
137/C Prince Olav (coast), Ant.
179/R7 Prince Patrick (isl.), NW,Can
178/G1 Prince Regent (inlet), NW,Can
130/B3 Prince Regent Nat. Rsv., Austl.
177/M4 Prince Rupert, BC,Can
167/G4 Princesa Isabel, Braz.
198/C5 Princes Lake, In,US
59/F3 Princes Risborough, Eng,UK
201/K1 Princess Anne, Md,US
137/A Princess Astrid (coast), Ant.
131/F3 Princess Charlotte (bay), Austl.
179/S6 Princess Margaret (range), NW,Can
137/Z Princess Martha (coast), Ant.
137/B Princess Ragnhild (coast), Ant.
178/D3 Princess Royal (isl.), BC,Can
162/F5 Princes Town, Trin.
193/K3 Princeton, Il,US
200/D1 Princeton, In,US
191/G1 Princeton, Ks,US
200/D2 Princeton, Ky,US
189/H1 Princeton, La,US
208/C1 Princeton, Ma,US
196/D3 Princeton, Me,US
198/C1 Princeton, Mi,US
193/H1 Princeton, Mn,US
193/H3 Princeton, Mo,US
206/D3 Princeton, NJ,US
189/F1 Princeton, Tx,US
201/G2 Princeton, WV,US
206/D3 Princeton Junction, NJ,US
180/S9 Princeville, Hi,US
193/K3 Princeville, Il,US
196/D3 Prince William, NB,Can
177/J3 Prince William (sound), Ak,US
73/A6 Principális (can.), Hun.
152/A2 Príncipe (isl.), SaoT.
177/K3 Prindle (vol.), Ak,US
184/C1 Prineville, Or,US
184/C1 Prineville (res.), Or,US
192/C2 Pringle, SD,US
190/D3 Pringle, Tx,US
69/C6 Pringy, Fr.
195/G5 Prinsburg, Mn,US
68/B5 Prinsenbeek, Neth.
66/C2 Prinses Margriet (can.), Neth.
161/F3 Prinzapolka, Nic.
161/E3 Prinzapolka (riv.), Nic.
90/D4 Priolo di Gargallo, It.
76/A1 Prior (cape), Sp.
84/D2 Priore (peak), It.
89/G2 Priore, Monte (peak), It.
193/H1 Prior Lake, Mn,US
195/P7 Prior Lake, Mn,US
195/H5 Prior Lake Ind. Res., Mn,US
114/D2 Priozernyy, Kaz.
63/P1 Priozersk, Rus.
98/E2 Pripyat' (riv.), Bela., Ukr.
98/F2 Pripyat', Ukr.
67/G1 Prisdorf, Ger.
97/J5 Prishib, Azer.
99/J2 Pristen', Rus.
92/E4 Priština, Yugo.
190/C2 Pritchett, Co,US
70/D6 Prittriching, Ger.
72/B3 Pritzerbe, Ger.
72/C1 Pritzwalk, Ger.
82/A3 Privas, Fr.
84/D5 Priverno, It.
95/P4 Privokzal'nyy, Rus.
97/H2 Privolzhskiy, Rus.
97/J1 Privolzh'ye, Rus.
97/G3 Priyutnoye, Rus.
97/K3 Priyutovo, Rus.
92/C4 Prizren, Yugo.
92/C3 Prnjavor, Bosn.
92/D3 Prnjavor, Yugo.
92/B5 Probištip, Mcd.
124/F4 Probolinggo, Indo.
71/E1 Probstzella, Ger.
85/E6 Procida, It.
191/G3 Proctor, Ok,US
189/E2 Proctor, Tx,US
189/E1 Proctor (lake), Tx,US
198/F5 Proctor, WV,US
118/C5 Proddatūr, India
76/B3 Proença-a-Nova, Port.
159/M7 Profesor Rafael Ramírez, Mex.
69/D3 Profondeville, Belg.
208/F6 Pro Football Hall of Fame, Oh,US
160/D1 Progreso, Mex.
188/D4 Progreso, Mex.
161/F4 Progreso, Pan.
175/T11 Progreso, Uru.
159/K6 Progreso de Obregon, Mex.
109/K2 Progress, Rus.
87/E3 Progresso, It.
97/H4 Prokhladnyy, Rus.
95/P5 Prokhorovka, Rus.
114/E1 Prokop'yevsk, Rus.
92/E4 Prokuplje, Yugo.
99/L4 Proletarsk, Rus.
99/L2 Proletarskiy, Rus.
116/B5 Prome, Burma
206/C1 Promised Land (lake), Pa,US
170/C4 Promissão, Braz.
170/C4 Promissão (res.), Braz.
185/G3 Promontory, Ut,US
97/H3 Promyslovoye, Rus.
171/F1 Propriá, Braz.
90/A2 Propriano, Fr.
92/B3 Prorva, Kaz.
87/G1 Prosecco, It.
72/D5 Prösen, Ger.
134/C3 Proserpine, Austl.
95/J2 Prosna (riv.), Pol.
91/H2 Prosotsáni, Gre.
133/M8 Prospect, Austl.
208/B2 Prospect, Ct,US
184/B2 Prospect, Or,US
208/G6 Prospect, Pa,US
177/L3 Prospector (mtn.), Yk,Can
207/J8 Prospect Park, NJ,US
199/G4 Prospect Park, Pa,US
188/L6 Prosper, Tx,US
125/D3 Prosperidad, Phil.
201/G3 Prosperity, SC,US
201/G2 Prosperity, WV,US
60/D3 Prosperous, Ire.
182/E4 Prosser, Wa,US
65/J4 Prostějov, Czh.
134/C4 Proston, Austl.
65/L3 Prószowice, Pol.
190/E2 Protection, Ks,US
71/H4 Protivín, Czh.
94/H5 Protvino, Rus.
93/H4 Provadiya, Bul.
202/B2 Provencal, La,US
88/E2 Provence (hist. reg.), Fr.
75/G5 Provence (mts.), Fr.
82/C5 Provence (range), Fr.
82/B5 Provence (reg.), Fr.
82/B3 Provence-Alpes-Côte d'Azur (reg.), Fr.
75/G4 Provence-Alpes-Côte d'Azur (reg.), Fr.
82/B6 Provence (Marseille) (int'l arpt.), Fr.
136/A4 Providence (cape), N.Z.
200/D4 Providence, Al,US
186/E3 Providence (mts.), Ca,US
200/D2 Providence, Ky,US
208/C2 Providence, RI,US
208/C2 Providence (co.), RI,US
185/H3 Providence, Ut,US
198/E2 Providence Bay, On,Can
169/F3 Providência (mts.), Braz.
161/F3 Providencia (isl.), Col.
162/C2 Providenciales (isl.), Trks.
177/D3 Provideniya, Rus.
196/B4 Provincetown, Ma,US
74/E2 Provins, Fr.
185/H3 Provo, Ut,US
185/H3 Provo (riv.), Ut,US
77/T13 Provoação, Azor.,Port.
183/J1 Provost, Ab,Can
92/C4 Prozor, Bosn.
173/G3 Prudentópolis, Braz.
57/G2 Prudhoe, Eng,UK
177/J1 Prudhoe (bay), Ak,US
177/J1 Prudhoe Bay, Ak,US
65/J3 Prudnik, Pol.
99/J2 Prudyanka, Ukr.
191/F2 Prue, Ok,US
69/F3 Prüm (riv.), Ger.
186/B2 Prunedale, Ca,US
90/A2 Prunelli-di-Fiumorbo, Fr.
65/K1 Pruszcz Gdański, Pol.
65/L2 Pruszków, Pol.
93/J2 Prut (riv.), Eur.
81/G3 Prutz, Aus.
65/N2 Pruzhany, Bela.
137/F Prydz (bay), Ant.
183/K5 Pryor, Mt,US
185/J1 Pryor (cr.), Mt,US
191/G2 Pryor (Creek), Ok,US
65/L2 Przasnysz, Pol.
65/H3 Przemków, Pol.
65/M4 Przemyśl, Pol.
65/M4 Przemyśl (prov.), Pol.
65/M3 Przeworsk, Pol.
114/C3 Przheval'sk, Kyr.
94/C5 Przyladek Rozewie (cape), Pol.
65/L3 Przysucha, Pol.
91/H3 Psakhná, Gre.
91/G3 Psará (isl.), Gre.
91/G4 Psárion, Gre.
99/L5 Psebay, Rus.
99/G3 Psël (riv.), Rus., Ukr.
94/F4 Pskov (lake), Est., Rus.
63/N3 Pskov, Rus.
63/N3 Pskov Obl., Rus.
71/H2 Pšovka (riv.), Czh.
65/K4 Pszczyna, Pol.
63/M5 Ptich' (riv.), Bela.
91/G2 Ptolemaís, Gre.
146/D1 Ptolemaïs (Ăthār Ţulmaythah) (ruins), Libya
92/B2 Ptuj, Slov.
123/C2 Pua, Thai.
116/E3 Pu'an, China
113/D5 Puan, SKor.
174/Q9 Puangue, Chile
117/F4 Pubei, China
168/C1 Puca Barranca, Peru
168/B2 Pucacaca, Peru
168/C3 Pucallpa, Peru
172/C1 Pucara, Bol.
168/B1 Pucará, Ecu.
168/B2 Pucará, Peru
168/D4 Pucará, Peru
172/B1 Pucarani, Bol.
168/D1 Pucaurco, Peru
205/G7 Puce, On,Can
115/B4 Pucheng, China
113/D4 Puch'ŏn, SKor.
173/C1 Púchov, Slvk.
174/Q9 Puchuncaví, Chile
93/G3 Pucioasa, Rom.
65/K1 Puck, Pol.
60/B4 Puckaun, Ire.
193/K2 Puckaway (lake), Wi,US
59/G3 Puckeridge, Eng,UK
200/C4 Puckett, Ms,US
71/H6 Pucking, Aus.
174/C3 Pucón, Chile
113/C4 Pudae (riv.), NKor.
94/H3 Pudasjärvi, Fin.
61/H2 Pudasjärvi, Fin.
58/D5 Puddletown, Eng,UK
95/M4 Pudem, Rus.
69/G2 Puderbach, Ger.
156/D2 Pudimoe, SAfr.
94/H3 Pudozh, Rus.
57/G4 Pudsey, Eng,UK
116/D3 Pudu (riv.), China
122/G3 Pudukkottai, India
159/F5 Puebla, Mex.
159/F5 Puebla (state), Mex.
76/C3 Puebla de Alcocer, Sp.
76/D4 Puebla de Don Fadrique, Sp.
76/B3 Puebla de la Calzada, Sp.
76/A1 Puebla del Caramiñal, Sp.
76/B1 Puebla de Sanabria, Sp.
76/B1 Puebla de Trives, Sp.
159/L7 Puebla de Zaragoza, Mex.
164/C2 Pueblito, Col.
159/L8 Pueblo (state), Mex.
192/B4 Pueblo, Co,US
192/B4 Pueblo Army Dep., Co,US
187/K2 Pueblo de Taos Ind. Res., NM,US
160/E3 Pueblo Nuevo, Nic.
164/D2 Pueblo Nuevo, Ven.
160/D3 Pueblo Nuevo Tiquisate, Guat.
192/B4 Pueblo West, Co,US
174/D3 Puelches, Arg.
174/D3 Puelén, Arg.
204/G8 Puente (hills), Ca,US
174/C2 Puente Alto, Chile
76/A1 Puenteareas, Sp.
76/A1 Puente Caldelas, Sp.
76/A1 Puente-Ceso, Sp.
159/K8 Puente de Ixtla, Mex.
174/C2 Puente del Inca, Arg.
76/A1 Puentedeume, Sp.
76/C4 Puente-Genil, Sp.
164/C3 Puente Nacional, Col.
168/B3 Puente Piedra, Peru
76/B1 Puentes de García Rodríguez, Sp.
169/E4 Puerta, Bol.
180/R10 Pueo (pt.), Hi,US
116/D4 Pu'er, China
187/H3 Puerco (riv.), Az, NM,US
172/E2 Puerto Abente, Par.
168/D4 Puerto Acosta, Bol.
174/B5 Puerto Aguirre, Chile
174/B5 Puerto Aisén, Chile
169/F4 Puerto Alegre, Bol.
169/E4 Puerto Almacen, Bol.
168/B2 Puerto América, Peru
164/C4 Puerto Argentina, Col.
161/F4 Puerto Armuelles, Pan.
169/F4 Puerto Arturo, Bol.
175/K8 Puerto Arturo, Chile
164/C5 Puerto Arturo, Peru
164/B4 Puerto Asís, Col.
165/E3 Puerto Ayacucho, Ven.
168/J7 Puerto Ayora, Ecu.
172/E2 Puerto Bahía Negra, Par.
169/E4 Puerto Ballivián, Bol.
168/K7 Puerto Baquerizo Moreno, Ecu.
160/D3 Puerto Barrios, Guat.
168/C3 Puerto Bermúdez, Peru
164/C3 Puerto Berrío, Col.
167/L6 Puerto Berrío (arpt.), Col.
174/B5 Puerto Bertrand, Chile
168/C4 Puerto Caballas, Peru
164/D2 Puerto Cabello, Ven.
167/M7 Puerto Cabello (arpt.), Ven.
161/F3 Puerto Cabezas, Nic.
169/E4 Puerto Calvimonte, Bol.
169/E4 Puerto Canoa, Bol.
164/D5 Puerto Carranza, Col.
165/E3 Puerto Carreño, Col.
172/E2 Puerto Casado, Par.
174/B5 Puerto Chacabuco, Chile
174/B5 Puerto Cisnes, Chile
175/K7 Puerto Coig, Arg.
172/E2 Puerto Colón, Par.
161/F4 Puerto Cortés, CR
158/C3 Puerto Cortés, Mex.
164/D2 Puerto Cumarebo, Ven.
142/A3 Puerto de la Cruz, Canl.
158/B2 Puerto de La Libertad, Mex.
142/B3 Puerto del Rosario, Canl.
76/A1 Puerto del Son, Sp.
174/D5 Puerto Deseado, Arg.
164/C4 Puerto El Carmen, Ecu.
164/B2 Puerto Escondido, Col.
160/B3 Puerto Escondido, Mex.
173/F3 Puerto Esperanza, Arg.
172/E2 Puerto Esperanza, Par.
172/E2 Puerto Fonciere, Par.
169/F4 Puerto Frey, Bol.
172/E1 Puerto General Busch, Bol.
169/E3 Puerto General Ovando, Bol.
169/E5 Puerto Grether, Bol.
174/B5 Puerto Guadal, Chile
175/L8 Puerto Harberton, Arg.
168/D4 Puerto Heath, Bol.
164/C4 Puerto Huitoto, Col.
173/F3 Puerto Iguazú, Arg.
168/C3 Puerto Inca, Peru
174/C5 Puerto Ingeniero Ibáñez, Chile
164/E4 Puerto Inírida, Col.
172/E1 Puerto Isabel, Bol.
168/B1 Puerto José Pardo, Peru
165/E2 Puerto La Cruz, Ven.
172/E2 Puerto Leda, Par.
168/D4 Puerto Leguía, Peru
164/C5 Puerto Leguízamo, Col.
169/E4 Puerto Leigue, Bol.
161/F3 Puerto Lempira, Hon.
76/C3 Puertollano, Sp.
174/D4 Puerto Lobos, Arg.
158/B2 Puerto Lobos, Mex.
164/C3 Puerto López, Col.
164/D2 Puerto López, Col.
76/E4 Puerto Lumbreras, Sp.
164/C5 Puerto Madero, Mex.
174/D4 Puerto Madryn, Arg.
168/D4 Puerto Maldonado, Peru
169/E5 Puerto Mamoré, Bol.
172/E2 Puerto María, Par.
164/C4 Puerto Mercedes, Col.
172/E2 Puerto Mihanovich, Par.
174/B4 Puerto Montt, Chile
160/E3 Puerto Morazán, Nic.
160/E1 Puerto Morelos, Mex.
168/B3 Puerto Morín, Peru
164/B3 Puerto Mutis, Col.
174/B5 Puerto Napo, Ecu.
175/J7 Puerto Natales, Chile
161/L6 Puerto Niño, Col.
164/C3 Puerto Nuevo, Chile
164/D3 Puerto Nuevo, Col.
161/G4 Puerto Obaldía, Pan.
168/C3 Puerto Ocopa, Peru
167/L6 Puerto Olaya, Col.
161/G1 Puerto Padre, Cuba
165/E3 Puerto Páez, Ven.
169/E4 Puerto Pando, Bol.
169/E5 Puerto Patiño, Bol.
158/B2 Puerto Peñasco, Mex.
172/E2 Puerto Pinasco, Par.
173/F3 Puerto Piray, Arg.
165/E2 Puerto Píritu, Ven.
164/C4 Puerto Pizarro, Col.
162/D3 Puerto Plata, DRep.
168/D3 Puerto Portillo, Peru
168/C3 Puerto Prado, Peru
175/J7 Puerto Prat, Chile
125/B3 Puerto Princesa, Phil.
174/B5 Puerto Puyuguapi, Chile
174/B4 Puerto Quellón, Chile
169/E3 Puerto Rapirrán, Bol.
76/B4 Puerto Real, Sp.
169/E3 Puerto Rico, Bol.
164/C4 Puerto Rico, Col.
162/E3 Puerto Rico (trench), PR
162/E3 Puerto Rico (commonwealth), US
189/E4 Puerto Rico, Tx,US
164/D3 Puerto Rondón, Col.
175/S11 Puerto Ruiz, Arg.
174/B3 Puerto Saavedra, Chile
164/C4 Puerto Saíz, Col.
167/L6 Puerto Salgar, Col.
169/E4 Puerto Salinas, Bol.
172/E2 Puerto Sastre, Par.
169/F4 Puerto Saucedo, Bol.
76/C4 Puerto Serrano, Sp.
169/E4 Puerto Siles, Bol.
172/E1 Puerto Suárez, Bol.
168/B3 Puerto Supe, Peru
173/E2 Puerto Tacurú Pytá, Par.
168/D4 Puerto Tahuantinsuyo, Peru
164/B4 Puerto Tejada, Col.
164/C5 Puerto Toledo, Col.
169/E5 Puerto Torno, Bol.
168/B1 Puerto Tunigrama, Peru
158/D4 Puerto Vallarta, Mex.
174/B4 Puerto Varas, Chile
169/E4 Puerto Vargas, Bol.
169/F5 Puerto Velarde, Bol.
168/C3 Puerto Victoria, Peru
161/E4 Puerto Viejo, CR
168/J7 Puerto Villamil, Ecu.
169/E5 Puerto Villarroel, Bol.
169/F4 Puerto Villazón, Bol.
168/C2 Puerto Wilches, Col.
175/L8 Puerto Williams, Chile
175/K8 Puerto Yartou, Chile
172/D1 Puesto de Pailas, Bol.
174/C5 Pueyrredón (lake), Arg.
56/D5 Puffin (isl.), Wal,UK
97/J1 Pugachev, Rus.
151/A3 Puge, Tanz.
124/F4 Puger, Indo.
182/C4 Puget (sound), Wa,US
82/C6 Puget-sur-Argens, Fr.
82/C5 Puget-Théniers, Fr.
82/C6 Puget-Ville, Fr.
85/F4 Puglia (reg.), It.
196/F3 Pugwash, NS,Can
63/M2 Puhja, Est.
77/F1 Puigcerdà, Sp.
74/E5 Puigmal (mtn.), Fr.
77/G1 Puigsacalm (mtn.), Sp.
168/D4 Puina, Bol.
144/C5 Pujehun, SLeo.
116/D2 Pujiang, China
164/B5 Pujilí, Ecu.
113/D2 Pujŏn (lake), NKor.
124/D4 Pujut (cape), Indo.
136/B3 Pukaki (lake), N.Z.
180/T10 Pukalani, Hi,US
113/F6 Puk'ansan (mtn.), SKor.
113/D4 Puk'an-san Nat'l Park, SKor.
139/J6 Pukapuka (isl.), Cookls.
139/M6 Puka Puka (isl.), FrPol.
139/M6 Pukarua (isl.), FrPol.
195/M3 Pukaskwa Nat'l Park, On,Can
113/D3 Pukch'ang, NKor.
113/C2 Pukchin, NKor.
113/E2 Pukch'ŏng, NKor.
113/E2 Pukdae (riv.), NKor.
91/F1 Pukë, Alb.
113/D4 Pukhan (riv.), NKor., SKor.
63/N5 Pukhovichi, Bela.
120/B2 Pukhrāyān, India
136/B2 Pukoo, Hi,US
117/H3 Pukou, China
92/E4 Pukovac, Yugo.
113/E2 Pukp'ot'ae-san (mtn.), NKor.
94/J3 Puksoozero, Rus.
130/A2 Pukuatu (cape), Indo.
87/G3 Pula, Cro.
172/C2 Pulacayo, Bol.
113/A3 Pulandian (bay), China
172/E1 Pulanduta (pt.), Phil.
125/D3 Pulangi (riv.), Phil.
138/D4 Pulap (isl.), Micr.
202/D1 Pulaski, Ms,US
199/H3 Pulaski, NY,US
208/G5 Pulaski, Pa,US
200/D3 Pulaski, Tn,US
201/G2 Pulaski, Va,US
193/K1 Pulaski, Wi,US
131/E1 Pulau (riv.), Indo.
124/C3 Pulaukijang, Indo.
124/B1 Pulau Pinang (state), Malay.
65/L3 Puławy, Pol.
59/F5 Pulborough, Eng,UK
66/D7 Pulheim, Ger.
167/L7 Puli, Col.
127/G3 Pulisan (cape), Indo.
122/F4 Puliyangudi, India
73/A2 Pulkau (riv.), Aus.
63/P2 Pulkovo (int'l arpt.), Rus.
81/H1 Pullach im Isartal, Ger.
198/C3 Pullman, Mi,US
182/F4 Pullman, Wa,US
80/C5 Pully, Swi.
125/C1 Pulog (mtn.), Phil.
72/D5 Pulsen, Ger.
72/E5 Pulsnitz, Ger.
72/D5 Pulsnitz (riv.), Ger.
65/L2 Pułtusk, Pol.
114/D4 Pulu, China
104/D2 Pülümür, Turk.
138/D4 Puluwat (isl.), Micr.
80/D2 Pulversheim, Fr.
114/B5 Pulwama, India
121/F1 Pum (riv.), China
121/H1 Puma (lake), China
151/A3 Puma, Tanz.
194/B5 Pumpkin (cr.), Mt,US
58/C2 Pumpsaint, Wal,UK
188/D3 Pumpville, Tx,US
121/H2 Pumu (pass), China
172/C1 Puna, Bol.
164/A5 Puna (isl.), Ecu.
139/X15 Punaauia, FrPol.
136/B3 Punakaiki, N.Z.
121/G2 Punākha, Bhu.
122/F4 Punalūr, India
172/C1 Punata, Bol.
122/C1 Punch, India
122/C1 Punch (riv.), India
182/C1 Punchaw, BC,Can
121/G1 Püncogling, China
155/F4 Punda Marie-Ruskamp, SAfr.
120/A1 Pündri, India
126/B3 Punggai (cape), Malay.
113/E4 P'unggi, SKor.
201/J3 Pungo (riv.), NC,US
155/G3 Púngoè (riv.), Moz.
201/J3 Pungo Nat'l Wild. Ref., NC,US
201/K2 Pungoteague, Va,US
113/E2 P'ungsan, NKor.
113/E2 P'ungsŏ, NKor.
155/G3 Pungwe (falls), Zim.
153/F3 Punia, Zaire
172/B3 Punilla (mts.), Chile
172/B3 Punitaqui, Chile
122/C2 Punjab (state), India
122/B2 Punjab (plains), Pak.
122/B2 Punjab (prov.), Pak.
122/G4 Punkudutivu (isl.), SrL.
168/D4 Puno, Peru
121/E3 Punpun (riv.), India
204/A2 Punta, Ca,US
158/B3 Punta Abreojos, Mex.
159/J5 Punta Allen, Mex.
174/E3 Punta Alta, Arg.
175/K8 Punta Arenas, Chile
186/D5 Punta Banda, Cabo (cape), Mex.
164/D2 Punta Cardón, Ven.
81/E5 Punta d'Arbola (Ofenhorn) (peak), It.
168/D5 Punta de Bombón, Peru
172/B4 Punta de Díaz, Chile
163/D6 Punta de Este, Uru.
175/G2 Punta del Este, Uru.
175/G2 Punta del Este (Capitán Curbelo) (int'l arpt.), Uru.
160/D2 Punta Gorda, Belz.
161/F4 Punta Gorda (bay), Nic.
184/A3 Punta Gorda (pt.), Ca,US
203/G4 Punta Gorda, Fl,US
87/F4 Punta Marina, It.
172/B2 Punta Negra, Salar de (salt pan), Chile
187/F5 Punta Peñasco, Mex.
90/D3 Punta Raisi (int'l arpt.), It.
161/E4 Puntarenas, CR
186/D5 Punta San Tomás (pt.), Mex.
175/T11 Puntas de Maciel, Uru.
76/B4 Punta Umbría, Sp.
199/G4 Punxsutawney, Pa,US
157/S15 Puobe d'Or, Mrts.
180/S10 Puolo (pt.), Hi,US
164/B4 Pupiales, Col.
168/D4 Pupuya (peak), Bol.
115/C5 Puqi, China
119/K3 Puqian, China
168/C4 Puquio, Peru
162/D5 Puquios, Chile
100/H3 Pur (riv.), Rus.
120/A3 Pura, India
164/B4 Puracé (vol.), Col.
164/B4 Puracé Nat'l Park, Col.
120/C1 Pūranpur, India
131/G1 Purari (riv.), PNG
73/A4 Purbach am Neusiedler See, Aus.
58/D5 Purbeck, Isle of (pen.), Eng,UK
124/E4 Purbolinggo, Indo.
182/F2 Purcell (mts.), BC,Can
191/F3 Purcell, Ok,US
182/D4 Purcell (mtn.), Wa,US
193/H4 Purdin, Mo,US
199/H2 Purdy, On,Can
191/H2 Purdy, Mo,US
201/J2 Purdy, Va,US
164/D5 Puré (riv.), Col.
130/A1 Pure, Indo.
174/B3 Purén, Chile
190/C2 Purgatorie (riv.), Co,US
70/D6 Pürgen, Ger.
75/L2 Purgstall an der Erlauf, Aus.
118/D3 Purī, India
164/C4 Purificación, Col.
63/L2 Purikari (pt.), Est.
73/A3 Purkersdorf, Aus.
53/N8 Purley, Eng,UK
66/B3 Purmerend, Neth.
118/C4 Pūrna, India
118/C3 Pūrna (riv.), India
121/F3 Purnia, India
59/E3 Purton, Eng,UK
159/E4 Puruándiro de Calderón, Mex.
164/D5 Puruê (riv.), Braz.
165/E3 Puruey, Ven.
121/F4 Purūlia, India
165/E4 Puruname, Ven.
165/F3 Puruni (riv.), Guy.
169/F2 Purús (riv.), Braz.
118/D4 Purushottampur, India
131/F2 Purutu (isl.), PNG
202/D2 Purvis, Ms,US
93/G4 Pŭrvomay, Bul.
120/C2 Purwa, India
124/D4 Purwakarta, Indo.
124/E4 Purwodadi, Indo.
124/E4 Purwokerto, Indo.
124/E4 Purworejo, Indo.
200/C2 Puryear, Tn,US
113/E1 Puryŏng, NKor.
118/C4 Pusad, India
113/E5 Pusan, SKor.
113/E5 Pusan-Jikhalsi, SKor.
110/A3 Pusan-jikhalsi (prov.), SKor.
124/B1 Pusat Gayo (mts.), Indo.
70/D3 Puschendorf, Ger.
96/F1 Pushchino, Rus.
63/P2 Pushkin, Rus.
97/J5 Pushkino, Azer.
97/H3 Pushkino, Rus.
63/N3 Pushkinskiye Gory, Rus.
200/C4 Pushmataha, Al,US
92/E2 Püspökladány, Hun.
79/G4 Pussay, Fr.
63/M2 Püssi, Est.
98/B3 Pustomyty, Ukr.
98/E1 Pustoshka, Rus.
159/H5 Pustunich, Mex.
145/E4 Pusuga, Gha.
121/G4 Pusur (riv.), Bang.
73/C5 Pusztaszabolcs, Hun.
153/G5 Puta, Zam.
174/C2 Putaendo, Chile
205/L9 Putah (cr.), Ca,US
117/J4 Putai, Tai.
172/C1 Putana (vol.), Chile
79/E3 Putanges-Pont-Écrepin, Fr.
116/C3 Putao, Burma
117/F3 Putaoxu, China
136/C2 Putaruru, N.Z.
121/G3 Puthia, Bang.
122/H4 Puthukkudiyiruppu, SrL.
117/G2 Putian, China
98/C4 Putila, Ukr.
168/D4 Putina, Peru
126/D4 Puting (cape), Indo.
108/A2 Putintsevo, Kaz.
99/G2 Putivl', Ukr.
160/B2 Putla, Mex.
72/C1 Putlitz, Ger.
202/D1 Putnam, Al,US
208/C2 Putnam, Ct,US
191/E3 Putnam, Ok,US
188/E1 Putnam, Tx,US
208/A3 Putnam Lake, NY,US
203/F2 Putney, Ga,US
194/E5 Putney, SD,US
199/K3 Putney, Vt,US
164/C4 Putomayo (inten.), Col.
100/K3 Putorana (mts.), Rus.
174/C4 Putrachoique (peak), Arg.
172/B1 Putre, Chile
122/G4 Puttalam, SrL.
122/G4 Puttalam (dist.), SrL.
68/D1 Putte, Belg.
69/F5 Puttelange-aux-Lacs, Fr.
66/C4 Putten, Neth.
66/B5 Putten (isl.), Neth.
64/F1 Puttgarden, Ger.
71/E3 Puttlach (riv.), Ger.
69/F5 Püttlingen, Ger.
144/C5 Putu (range), Libr.
164/C5 Putumayo (riv.), SAm.
126/D3 Putussibau, Indo.
180/U11 Puuanahulu, Hi,US
180/T10 Puuiki, Hi,US
180/T10 Puu Kukui (peak), Hi,US
63/M1 Puula (lake), Fin.
63/M2 Puurmani, Est.
68/D1 Puurs, Belg.
180/R10 Puuwai, Hi,US
116/D3 Puwei, China
117/H3 Puxi, China
115/B3 Pu Xian, China
200/B2 Puxico, Mo,US
205/C3 Puyallup, Wa,US
205/C3 Puyallup (riv.), Wa,US
205/C3 Puyallup Ind. Res., Wa,US
115/C4 Puyang, China
74/E4 Puy de Barbier (peak), Fr.
74/E4 Puy de Sancy (peak), Fr.
190/A3 Puye (cliff dwelling), NM,US
187/J3 Puye (cliff dwellings), NM,US
174/B4 Puyehue (lake), Chile
174/B4 Puyehue (vol.), Chile
174/B4 Puyehué Nat'l Park, Chile
74/E5 Puylaurens, Fr.
74/D5 Puymorens, Col de (pass), Fr.
164/B5 Puyo, Ecu.
113/D4 Puyŏ, SKor.
82/C3 Puy-Saint-Vincent, Fr.
136/A4 Puysegur (pt.), N.Z.
113/E2 Puyun, NKor.
77/G3 Puzal, Sp.
151/B3 Pwani (prov.), Tanz.
113/C3 P'warwŏn, NKor.
153/G5 Pweto, Zaire
56/D6 Pwllheli, Wal,UK
94/H2 Pyalitsa, Rus.
94/G3 Pyal'ma, Rus.
116/B5 Pyamalaw (riv.), Burma
107/J1 Pyandzh, Taj.
107/K1 Pyandzh (Panj) (riv.), Afg., Taj.
94/F2 Pyaozero (lake), Rus.
119/G4 Pyapon, Burma
100/J2 Pyasina (riv.), Rus.
97/G3 Pyatigorsk, Rus.
99/G3 Pyatikhatki, Ukr.
136/B4 Pye (hill), N.Z.
74/F4 Pyfara (mtn.), Fr.
61/H3 Pyhä-Häkin Nat'l Park, Fin.
61/H3 Pyhäjärvi, Fin.
63/K1 Pyhäjärvi (lake), Fin.
63/M1 Pyhäjärvi (lake), Fin.
61/H2 Pyhäntä, Fin.
61/H2 Pyhätunturi (peak), Fin.
63/M1 Pyhtää, Fin.
116/B4 Pyinmana, Burma
116/C5 Pyinmana, Burma
58/C3 Pyle, Wal,UK
208/G4 Pymatuning (res.), Oh,US
113/C3 Pyŏksŏng, NKor.
113/D2 Pyŏkdong, NKor.
113/C2 P'yŏngan-Bukto (prov.), NKor.
113/C3 P'yŏngan-Namdo (prov.), NKor.
113/D4 P'yŏngch'ang, SKor.
113/D3 P'yŏngch'ŏn, NKor.
113/D3 P'yŏnggang, NKor.
113/E4 P'yŏnghae, SKor.
113/D2 P'yŏngnamjin, NKor.
113/C3 P'yŏngsan, NKor.
113/C3 P'yŏngsong, NKor.
113/D4 Pyŏngt'aek, SKor.
113/C3 P'yŏngwŏn, NKor.
113/C3 P'yŏngyang (cap.), NKor.
113/C3 P'yŏngyang (int'l arpt.), NKor.
113/C3 P'yŏngyang-Si, NKor.
113/D5 Pyŏnsanbando Nat'l Park, SKor.
177/M4 Pyramid (mtn.), BC,Can
204/B1 Pyramid (lake), Ca,US
185/G1 Pyramid (peak), Id,US
198/D2 Pyramid (pt.), Mi,US
184/D4 Pyramid (lake), Nv,US
192/A2 Pyramid (peak), Wy,US
184/D3 Pyramid Lake Ind. Res., Nv,US
77/E1 Pyrenees (range), Eur.
74/C5 Pyrénées Occidentales Nat'l Park, Fr.
65/H2 Pyrzyce, Pol.
95/K4 Pyshchug, Rus.

95/Q4 Pyshma (riv.), Rus.
63/M3 Pytalovo, Rus.
116/C5 Pyu, Burma
123/B2 Pyuntaza, Burma

Q

103/E4 Qā'al Jafr (salt pan), Jor.
179/T7 Qaanaaq, Grld.
103/D3 Qabalān, WBnk.
103/D3 Qabātiyah, WBnk.
143/H2 Qābis, Tun.
143/H2 Qābis (gov.), Tun.
150/D1 Qabr Hūd, Yem.
156/E3 Qachas Nek, Les.
146/D2 Qadd al Qamḩ, Abyār (well), Libya
122/C2 Qādiān, India
103/F7 Qadima, Isr.
122/A2 Qādirpur Rān, Pak.
105/H2 Qa'emshahr, Iran
107/G2 Qā'en, Iran
91/G1 Qafa e Malit (pass), Alb.
146/B2 Qāf, Bi'r al (well), Libya
103/G7 Qaffīn, WBnk.
143/H2 Qafşah, Tun.
143/H2 Qafşah (gov.), Tun.
109/J2 Qagan (lake), China
114/E3 Qagannur, China
115/C2 Qahar Youyi Qianqi, China
108/C4 Qaidam (basin), China
149/G2 Qala'an Naḩl, Sudan
103/F7 Qalansuwa, Isr.
141/X17 Qal'at Al Andalus, Tun.
141/W18 Qal'at Aş Şanam, Tun.
106/D5 Qal'at Bīshah, SAr.
105/F2 Qal'at Dīzah, Iraq
105/F4 Qal'at Sukkar, Iraq
107/G3 Qal'eh-ye Deh-e Bārez, Iran
149/H2 Qallābāt, Sudan
103/D4 Qallīn, Egypt
103/D3 Qalqīlyah, WBnk.
103/D4 Qalyūb, Egypt
106/F5 Qamar, Ghubbat al (bay), Yem.
102/J6 Qamdo, China
146/D2 Qamīnis, Libya
84/H8 Qammieħ, Ras il- (pt.), Malta
103/D3 Qānā, Leb.
104/E5 Qanā, SAr.
103/G7 Qanah, Wādī (dry riv.), WBnk.
107/J2 Qandahār, Afg.
150/D3 Qandala, Som.
141/W17 Qanţarat Al Faḩş, Tun.
176/N3 Qaqortoq, Grld.
104/E4 Qārah, SAr.
114/C4 Qarak, China
105/F2 Qarāmqū (riv.), Iran
141/W17 Qar'at al Ashkal (lake), Tun.
150/D3 Qardho, Som.
105/G3 Qareh Chāy (riv.), Iran
105/F2 Qareh Sū (riv.), Iran
105/F2 Qareh Zīā' od Dīn, Iran
146/D2 Qarn, Wādī al (dry riv.), Libya
114/F4 Qarqan (riv.), China
89/F4 Qarqannah, Juzur (isls.), Tun.
89/J2 Qarrit (pass), Alb.
91/G2 Qarrit, Qaf'e (pass), Alb.
90/B4 Qarţājannah (ruins), Tun.
147/F2 Qārūn, Birkat (lake), Egypt
146/B2 Qaryat abu Nujaym, Libya
146/B2 Qaryat Abū Qurayn, Libya
146/D2 Qaryat az Zuwaytīnah, Libya
146/E2 Qaşr al Jady, Libya
104/E3 Qaşr al Khubbāz, Iraq
107/H3 Qaşr-e Qand, Iran
105/F3 Qaşr-e Shīrīn, Iran
147/E3 Qaşr Farāfirah, Egypt
141/X18 Qaşr Hallāl, Tun.
150/C2 Qa'ţabah, Yem.
103/E3 Qaţanā, Syria
106/F3 Qatar
147/E2 Qattara (depr.), Egypt
103/E2 Qaţţīnah (lake), Syria
149/G1 Qawz Abū Dulū (dunes), Sudan
149/G1 Qawz Rajab, Sudan
114/D3 Qaxi, China
149/G3 Qaysān, Sudan
116/B2 Qayū, China
105/E3 Qayyārah, Iraq
118/A2 Qāzi Ahmad, Pak.
100/F6 Qazvīn, Iran
102/D6 Qazvīn, Iran
105/G2 Qazvīn, Iran
103/F8 Qedma, Isr.
91/F2 Qendrevica (peak), Alb.
179/L2 Qeqertarsuaq, Grld.
105/J5 Qeshm, Iran
105/H5 Qeshm (isl.), Iran
105/G2 Qeydār, Iran
106/E1 Qezel (riv.), Iran
105/F2 Qezel Owzan (riv.), Iran
119/J2 Qi (riv.), China
115/D4 Qian (can.), China
113/B2 Qian (mts.), China
113/B2 Qian (peak), China
115/D5 Qian (riv.), China
117/F2 Qian (riv.), China
109/J3 Qian'an, China
117/H3 Qianban, China
117/J2 Qiancun, China
117/H3 Qiange, China
117/G2 Qianjiang, China
116/D2 Qianning, China
115/L9 Qianqing, China
115/D5 Qianqiu Guan (pass), China
115/E2 Qian Shan (peak), China
114/D2 Qianshanlaoba, China
109/H3 Qianxi, China
117/G2 Qiaodong, China
116/D3 Qiaojia, China
123/C1 Qiaomaidi, China
117/G2 Qiaoshe, China
115/L9 Qiaosi, China
117/F3 Qiaotouhe, China
117/F4 Qiaoxu, China
143/H2 Qibilī, Tun.
143/H2 Qibilī (gov.), Tun.
103/G8 Qibyā, WBnk.
113/D2 Qidaogou, China
109/J5 Qidong, China
108/D5 Qidukou, China
114/E4 Qiemo, China
115/B5 Qifeng Guan (pass), China
117/G3 Qigong, China
115/D3 Qihe, China
109/H4 Qikou, China
122/C1 Qila Dīdār Singh, Pak.
108/D4 Qilian (mts.), China
108/D4 Qilian (peak), China
113/A2 Qilihe, China
117/G3 Qiling, China
108/C3 Qilizhen, China
103/G8 Qilt, Wādī (dry riv.), WBnk.
114/F4 Qimantag (mts.), China
115/D5 Qimen, China
115/B4 Qin (mts.), China
115/C4 Qin (riv.), China
147/G3 Qinā, Egypt
147/G3 Qinā (gov.), Egypt
147/G3 Qinā, Wādī (dry riv.), Egypt
117/F2 Qing (riv.), China
109/K2 Qing'an, China
113/B2 Qingchengzi, China
115/E3 Qingdao, China
113/A2 Qingduizi, China
115/C4 Qingfeng, China
116/E2 Qingfu, China
109/K2 Qinggang, China
108/D4 Qinghai (lake), China
108/D4 Qinghai (mts.), China
116/B1 Qinghai (prov.), China
115/C3 Qinghe, China
113/C2 Qinghecheng, China
113/A2 Qinghemen, China
117/H2 Qinghua, China
117/G2 Qingjiang, China
115/D2 Qinglong, China
117/F2 Qingping, China
117/F4 Qingping, China
115/E5 Qingpu, China
117/G2 Qingshan, China
116/D2 Qingshen, China
108/E4 Qingshizui, China
117/F3 Qingshui (riv.), China
115/B3 Qingshuihe, China
114/E3 Qingshuihezi, China
116/C3 Qingshuilang (mts.), China
117/F3 Qingxi, China
115/D5 Qingyang, China
117/H2 Qingyang, China
113/C1 Qingyuan, China
117/G4 Qingyuan, China
119/K3 Qingyuan, China
117/G4 Qingyuan (mts.), China
115/D3 Qingyun, China
109/H4 Qingzhou, China
115/D3 Qinhuangdao, China
115/C4 Qinshui, China
115/C5 Qinyang, China
115/C5 Qinyuan, China
117/F4 Qinzhou, China
119/K4 Qionghai, China
116/D2 Qionglai, China
116/D2 Qionglai (mts.), China
119/K4 Qiongshan, China
123/E2 Qiongzhong, China
116/E1 Qipan (pass), China
109/J2 Qiqihar, China
108/D3 Qiquanhu, China
105/H4 Qīr, Iran
114/D4 Qira, China
103/D3 Qiryat Ata, Isr.
103/D3 Qiryat Bialik, Isr.
103/D4 Qiryat Gat, Isr.
103/F8 Qiryat Mal'akhi, Isr.
103/D3 Qiryat Shemona, Isr.
103/D3 Qiryat Yam, Isr.
117/F4 Qisha, China
150/D2 Qishn, Yem.
115/B3 Qishuyan, China
108/B3 Qitai, China
109/L2 Qitaihe, China
117/G3 Qitian (mtn.), China
113/B2 Qiumuzhuang, China
115/E3 Qixia, China
115/C4 Qi Xian, China
116/E3 Qixing (pass), China
109/J2 Qixing (riv.), China
109/K2 Qixingpao, China
117/H2 Qixitian, China
109/K1 Qizhan, China
105/G3 Qom, Iran
105/G3 Qom (riv.), Iran
116/B2 Qomo, China
118/E2 Qomolangma (Everest) (peak), China
105/G3 Qomsheh, Iran
107/J1 Qondūz (riv.), Afg.
121/H1 Qonggyai, China
84/H8 Qormi, Malta
105/F3 Qorveh, Iran
105/G3 Qorveh, Iran
151/D1 Qoryooley, Som.
105/G3 Qoţbābād, Iran
105/J5 Qoţbābād, Iran
107/G3 Qoţbābād, Iran
105/F2 Qoţūr, Iran
117/F2 Qu (riv.), China
117/H2 Qu (riv.), China
208/B1 Quabbin (res.), Ma,US
208/C2 Quaddick, Ct,US
59/F3 Quainton, Eng,UK
132/C5 Quairading, Austl.
67/E3 Quakenbrück, Ger.
208/B3 Quaker Hill, Ct,US
206/C3 Quakertown, Pa,US
85/E6 Qualiano, It.
182/B3 Qualicum Beach, BC,Can
195/H5 Quamba, Mn,US
135/B2 Quambatook, Austl.
135/C1 Quambone, Austl.
108/H5 Quan (riv.), China
190/E3 Quanah, Tx,US
115/B4 Quanbao Shan (mtn.), China
123/E3 Quang Ngai, Viet.
115/L9 Quangongting, China
123/D2 Quang Trach, Viet.
123/D2 Quang Tri, Viet.
115/D4 Quanjiao, China
201/J1 Quantico Marine Corps Res., Va,US
58/C4 Quantocks (hills), Eng,UK
113/D1 Quanyang, China
117/F3 Quanzhou, China
117/H3 Quanzhou, China
119/K2 Quanzhou, China
191/G2 Quapaw, Ok,US
180/E1 Qu'Appelle (riv.), Mb, Sk,Can
194/C2 Qu'Appelle (riv.), Mb, Sk,Can
194/C2 Qu'Appelle, Sk,Can
183/L2 Qu'Appelle (dam), Sk,Can
179/K2 Quaqtaq, Qu,Can
173/E4 Quaraí, Braz.
68/C3 Quaregnon, Belg.
126/E4 Quarles (mts.), Indo.
86/B1 Quarona, It.
87/D5 Quarrata, It.
206/B4 Quarryville, Pa,US
87/F1 Quarto d'Altino, It.
152/C5 Quarto de Fevereiro (int'l arpt.), Ang.
90/A3 Quartu Sant'Elena, It.
186/E4 Quartz (peak), Ca,US
204/B1 Quartz Hill, Ca,US
186/E4 Quartzsite, Az,US
157/S15 Quatre Bornes, Mrts.
81/G4 Quattervals (peak), Swi.
190/C3 Quay, NM,US
90/A4 Quballāt, Tun.
105/J2 Qūchān, Iran
135/D2 Queanbeyan, Austl.
179/J3 Québec (prov.), Can.
196/B2 Québec, Qu,Can
196/B2 Québec (int'l arpt.), Qu,Can
171/M7 Quebra-Cangalha (mts.), Braz.
175/F1 Quebracho, Uru.
172/C2 Quechisla, Bol.
159/M8 Quecholac, Mex.
174/B4 Quedal (pt.), Chile
58/D3 Quedgeley, Eng,UK
72/B4 Quedlinburg, Ger.
103/E4 Queen Alia (int'l arpt.), Jor.
206/C6 Queen Anne, Md,US
206/C5 Queen Annes (co.), Md,US
182/B2 Queen Bess (mtn.), BC,Can
59/G4 Queenborough, UK
176/D4 Queen Charlotte (isls.), Can.
177/M5 Queen Charlotte, BC,Can
178/C3 Queen Charlotte (sound), BC,Can
189/G1 Queen City, Tx,US
187/G4 Queen Creek, Az,US
179/R7 Queen Elizabeth (isls.), NW,Can
137/G Queen Mary (coast), Ant.
53/M7 Queen Mary (res.), Eng,UK
204/F8 Queen Mary/Spruce Goose, Ca,US
137/P Queen Maud (mts.), Ant.
178/F2 Queen Maud (gulf), NW,Can
137/Z Queen Maud Land (reg.), Ant.
130/C3 Queens (chan.), Austl.
179/S7 Queens (chan.), NW,Can
56/E1 Queensberry (mtn.), Sc,UK
57/G4 Queensbury, Eng,UK
57/E5 Queensferry, Wal,UK
134/B3 Queensland (state), Austl.
197/S9 Queenston, On,Can
135/C4 Queenstown, Austl.
165/G3 Queenstown, Guy.
156/D3 Queenstown, SAfr.
206/B6 Queenstown, Md,US
132/D4 Queen Victoria Spring Nat. Rsv., Austl.
71/A4 Queich (riv.), Ger.
69/H5 Queich (riv.), Ger.
69/G5 Queidersbach, Ger.
174/B4 Queilén, Chile
166/D3 Queimada (isl.), Braz.
171/F1 Queimadas, Braz.
152/D5 Quela, Ang.
79/E5 Quelaines, Fr.
155/F2 Quelimane, Moz.
76/A3 Queluz, Port.
188/D3 Quemado, Tx,US
161/H1 Quemado, Punta del (pt.), Cuba
154/C2 Quembo (riv.), Ang.
182/E3 Quemú Quemú, Arg.
59/E3 Quenington, Eng,UK
161/E4 Quepos, CR
174/F3 Quequén, Arg.
174/F3 Quequén Grande (riv.), Arg.
86/D5 Querceta, It.
168/A2 Querecotillo, Peru
159/E4 Querétaro, Mex.
159/F4 Querétaro (state), Mex.
72/B5 Querfurt, Ger.
87/E1 Quero, It.
158/C2 Querobabi, Mex.
170/D2 Querqueville, Fr.
161/E4 Quesada, CR
76/D4 Quesada, Sp.
115/C4 Queshan, China
182/D1 Quesnel, BC,Can
182/D1 Quesnel (lake), BC,Can
182/D1 Quesnel (riv.), BC,Can
68/C2 Quesnoy-sur-Deûle, Fr.
123/E3 Que Son, Viet.
78/C4 Quessoy, Fr.
190/B2 Questa, NM,US
78/C5 Questembert, Fr.
167/M7 Quetame, Col.
80/B3 Quetigny, Fr.
107/J2 Quetta, Pak.
78/D1 Quettehou, Fr.
202/B2 Queue de Tortue (bayou), La,US
174/B5 Queulat Nat'l Park, Chile
154/B1 Queve Cangombe, Ang.
164/B5 Quevedo (riv.), Ecu.
78/B5 Quéven, Fr.
78/C4 Quévert, Fr.
160/D3 Quezaltenango, Guat.
125/B3 Quezon, Phil.
125/D4 Quezon, Phil.
127/E2 Quezon, Phil.
125/C2 Quezon City, Phil.
125/C2 Quezon Nat'l Park, Phil.
104/E5 Qufār, SAr.
115/D4 Qufu, China
152/C5 Quibala, Ang.
152/C5 Quibaxe, Ang.
164/B3 Quibdó, Col.
78/B6 Quiberon, Fr.
78/B5 Quiberon (bay), Fr.
78/B5 Quiberon (pen.), Fr.
146/A1 Quibilī (gov.), Tun.
152/C4 Quibocolo, Ang.
164/D2 Quíbor, Ven.
168/C4 Quicacha, Peru
152/C5 Quiçama Nat'l Park, Ang.
67/G1 Quickborn, Ger.
152/C5 Quicombo, Ang.
174/B3 Quidico, Chile
69/G5 Quierschied, Ger.
80/B3 Quigney, Fr.
187/F4 Quijotoa, Az,US
174/B3 Quilaco, Chile
174/B4 Quilán (cape), Chile
122/E3 Quilāndi, India
168/C5 Quilca, Peru
205/B2 Quilcene, Wa,US
154/B2 Quilengues, Ang.
182/B4 Quileute Ind. Res., Wa,US
86/B4 Quiliano, It.
174/Q9 Quilicura, Chile
174/C2 Quilimarí, Chile
172/C4 Quilino, Arg.
194/B1 Quill (lakes), Sk,Can
168/C4 Quillabamba, Peru
172/C1 Quillacas, Bol.
172/C1 Quillacollo, Bol.
174/B4 Quillagua (pt.), Chile
74/E5 Quillan, Fr.
79/F2 Quillebeuf-sur-Seine, Fr.
174/C3 Quilleco, Chile
194/B1 Quill Lake, Sk,Can
174/C2 Quillota, Chile
168/B4 Quilmaná, Peru
172/C3 Quilmes (peak), Arg.
152/C5 Quilombo dos Dembos, Ang.
122/F4 Quilon, India
134/B4 Quilpie, Austl.
174/C2 Quilpué, Chile
60/A4 Quilty, Ire.
152/C4 Quimbata, Ang.
152/D4 Quimbele, Ang.
172/C1 Quime, Bol.
172/D3 Quimilí, Arg.
172/D1 Quimome (riv.), Bol.
78/A4 Quimper, Fr.
78/B5 Quimperlé, Fr.
78/A5 Quimper (Pluguffan) (int'l arpt.), Fr.
60/B4 Quin, Ire.
182/C4 Quinault (riv.), Wa,US
182/B4 Quinault Ind. Res., Wa,US
201/H3 Quinby, SC,US
168/D4 Quince Mil, Peru
80/C2 Quincey, Fr.
203/F2 Quincy, Fl,US
193/J4 Quincy, Il,US
208/C1 Quincy, Ma,US
198/D4 Quincy, Mi,US
182/E4 Quincy, Wa,US
184/C4 Quincy-East Quincy, Ca,US
53/T10 Quincy-sous-Sénart, Fr.
68/B6 Quincy-Voisins, Fr.
167/K8 Quindío (dept.), Col.
208/C2 Quinebaug (riv.), Ct,US
174/D2 Quines, Arg.
177/F4 Quinhagak, Ak,US
123/E3 Qui Nhon, Viet.
189/F1 Quinlan, Tx,US
184/D3 Quinn (riv.), Nv,US
208/B3 Quinnipiac (riv.), Ct,US
208/C1 Quinsigamond (res.), Ma,US
76/C3 Quintana de la Serena, Sp.
76/D3 Quintanar de la Orden, Sp.
76/E3 Quintanar del Rey, Sp.
160/D2 Quintana Roo (state), Mex.
174/Q9 Quintay, Chile
199/H2 Quinte (bay), On,Can
190/D1 Quinter, Ks,US
174/Q9 Quintero, Chile
78/C4 Quintin, Fr.
174/D2 Quinto (riv.), Arg.
77/E2 Quinto, Sp.
81/E4 Quinto, Swi.
87/F1 Quinto di Treviso, It.
87/E2 Quinto di Valpantena, It.
206/C4 Quinton, NJ,US
191/G3 Quinton, Ok,US
201/G1 Quinwood, WV,US
86/D2 Quinzano d'Oglio, It.
152/C4 Quinzau, Ang.
155/J1 Quionga, Moz.
167/G5 Quipapá, Braz.
154/B2 Quipungo, Ang.
164/D3 Quirey, Col.
174/B3 Quirihue, Chile
151/C4 Quirimba (arch.), Moz.
155/J1 Quirimba (isls.), Moz.
135/D1 Quirindi, Austl.
170/C3 Quirinópolis, Braz.
165/F2 Quiriquire, Ven.
172/D1 Quiroga, Bol.
76/B1 Quiroga, Sp.
172/D1 Quirusillas, Bol.
168/B3 Quiruvilca, Peru
196/E3 Quispamsis, NB,Can
155/J2 Quissanga, Moz.
155/G5 Quissico, Moz.
87/D2 Quistello, It.
152/D5 Quitapa, Ang.
190/D3 Quitaque, Tx,US
154/B3 Quiteve, Ang.
172/D3 Quitilipi, Arg.
203/G2 Quitman, Ga,US
189/H1 Quitman, La,US
200/C4 Quitman, Ms,US
189/G1 Quitman, Tx,US
164/B5 Quito (cap.), Ecu.
187/F5 Quitovac, Mex.
174/B3 Quitratúe, Chile
192/E4 Quivira Nat'l Wild. Ref., Ks,US
191/E1 Quivira Nat'l Wild. Ref., Ks,US
167/G4 Quixadá, Braz.
167/G4 Quixeramobim, Braz.
167/G4 Quixeré, Braz.
152/C5 Quizenga, Ang.
117/G3 Qujiang, China
117/F4 Qujie, China
116/D3 Qujing, China
90/B4 Qulaybīyah, Tun.
117/E4 Quli, China
191/J2 Qulin, Mo,US
108/C4 Qumar (riv.), China
108/C5 Qumarrabdün, China
156/E3 Qumbu, SAfr.
207/F2 Quogue, NY,US
178/G2 Quoich (riv.), NW,Can
54/A2 Quoich, Loch (lake), Sc,UK
56/C3 Quoile (riv.), NI,UK
156/B4 Quoin (pt.), SAfr.
133/H5 Quorn, Austl.
90/B4 Quranbālīyah, Tun.
107/G4 Qurayyāt, Oman
90/B4 Qurbah, Tun.
103/E2 Qurnat as Sawdā' (mtn.), Leb.
147/G3 Qūş, Egypt
146/D2 Quşayr ad Daffah (ruins), Libya
105/F2 Qūshchī, Iran
105/H3 Qūsheh, Iran
121/J1 Qusum, China
90/B5 Quşūr As Sāf, Tun.
156/D3 Quthing, Les.
117/G1 Quwan, China
115/B4 Quwo, China
117/F4 Quwu (mts.), China
121/H1 Qūxū, China
115/C3 Quyang, China
123/C1 Quynh Nhai, Viet.
115/C3 Quzhou, China
117/H2 Quzhou, China
92/D5 Qyteti Stalin, Alb.

R

71/G6 Raab, Aus.
75/L3 Raab (riv.), Aus.
75/L3 Raabs an der Thaya, Aus.
134/G8 Raaf-Richmond, Austl.
61/H2 Raahe, Fin.
66/D4 Raalte, Neth.
66/B5 Raamsdonk, Neth.
63/T9 Rāān (riv.), Swe.
103/F7 Ra'ananna, Isr.
179/S7 Raanes (pen.), NW,Can
124/F4 Raas (isl.), Indo.
63/L2 Raasiku, Est.
151/C2 Raas Jumbo, Som.
92/B3 Rab, Cro.
92/B3 Rab (isl.), Cro.
73/B4 Rába (riv.), Hun.
73/A6 Rábafüzes, Hun.
73/A5 Rábahidvég, Hun.
151/B2 Rabai, Kenya
149/G2 Rabak, Sudan
77/F1 Rabastens, Fr.
84/H8 Rabat, Malta
141/L13 Rabat (cap.), Mor.
141/L13 Rabat (Salé) (int'l arpt.), Mor.
84/H7 Rabat (Victoria), Malta
138/E5 Rabaul, PNG
87/F4 Rabbi (riv.), It.
192/C1 Rabbit (cr.), SD,US
190/C2 Rabbit Ear (mtn.), NM,US
185/K3 Rabbit Ears (pass), Co,US
185/K3 Rabbit Ears (peak), Co,US
183/L1 Rabbit Lake, Sk,Can
73/B4 Rábca (can.), Hun.
72/C2 Räbel, Ger.
121/F2 Rabgala (pass), China
147/H3 Rābigh, SAr.
140/K10 Rabil, CpV.
160/D3 Rabinal, Guat.
81/F4 Rabiusa (riv.), Swi.
65/K4 Rabka, Pol.
118/C4 Rabkavi, India
73/A4 Rabnitz (riv.), Aus.
94/G2 Rabocheostrovsk, Rus.
197/T8 Raby (pt.), On,Can
146/D3 Rabyānah, Şaḩrā' (des.), Libya
86/A3 Racconigi, It.
202/K6 Raccoon (pt.), Fl,US
203/G3 Raccoon (pt.), Fl,US
202/C3 Raccoon (pt.), La,US
198/E5 Raccoon (riv.), Oh,US
208/C6 Raccoon (cr.), Pa,US
179/L4 Race (cape), Nf,Can
202/C3 Raceland, La,US
196/B4 Rachel Carson Nat'l Wild. Ref., Me,US
123/D4 Rach Gia, Viet.
123/D4 Rach Gia (bay), Viet.
65/K3 Racibórz, Pol.
205/Q14 Racine, Wi,US
205/P14 Racine (co.), Wi,US
80/C3 Racine, Mont (peak), Swi.
73/C5 Ráckeve, Hun.
191/J1 Racola, Mo,US
174/D5 Rada Tilly, Arg.
92/F3 Rădăuţi, Rom.
71/G3 Radbuza (riv.), Czh.
99/L3 Radchenskoye, Rus.
200/E2 Radcliff, Ky,US
57/F4 Radcliffe, Eng,UK
57/G6 Radcliffe on Trent, Eng,UK
67/F4 Raddestorf, Ger.
72/D5 Radeberg, Ger.
72/D5 Radebeul, Ger.
71/G3 Radeč (peak), Czh.
72/C4 Radegast, Ger.
98/C2 Radekhov, Ukr.
92/A2 Radenthein, Aus.
183/J4 Radersburg, Mt,US
67/E6 Radevormwald, Ger.
201/G2 Radford, Va,US
118/B3 Rādhanpur, India
141/X17 Rādis, Tun.
183/L1 Radisson, Sk,Can
193/J1 Radisson, Wi,US
133/J5 Radium Hill, Austl.
182/F2 Radium Hot Springs, BC,Can
187/J4 Radium Springs, NM,US
53/N6 Radlett, Eng,UK
93/G4 Radnevo, Bul.
71/G3 Radnice, Czh.
81/E2 Radolfzell, Ger.
65/L3 Radom, Pol.
65/L3 Radom (prov.), Pol.
92/F4 Radomir, Bul.
65/K3 Radomsko, Pol.
98/E2 Radomyshl', Ukr.
92/F5 Radoviš, Macd.
92/B2 Radovljica, Slov.
62/A1 Radøy (isl.), Nor.
75/K3 Radstadt, Aus.
58/D4 Radstock, Eng,UK
63/L4 Radun', Bela.
63/K4 Radviliškis, Lith.
194/B3 Radville, Sk,Can
147/H3 Raḑwá, Jabal (mtn.), SAr.
58/C3 Radyr, Wal,UK
65/K2 Radziejów, Pol.
65/L2 Radzymin, Pol.
65/M3 Radzyń Podlaski, Pol.
179/H3 Rae (isth.), NW,Can
178/E2 Rae (riv.), NW,Can
120/C2 Rāe Bareli, India
178/E2 Rae-Edzo, NW,Can
201/H3 Raeford, NC,US
69/F2 Raeren, Belg.
66/D5 Raesfeld, Ger.
132/D4 Raeside (lake), Austl.
136/C2 Raetihi, N.Z.
113/A2 Raeyang (riv.), China
172/D4 Rafaela, Arg.
164/C2 Rafael Nunez (int'l arpt.), Col.
103/D4 Rafaḩ, Gaza
148/D4 Rafai, CAfr.
105/E4 Rafḩā', SAr.
103/G7 Rafīdīyah, WBnk.
121/E3 Rafiganj, India
91/J3 Rafina, Gre.
91/M6 Rafina, Gre.
141/X17 Rafrāf, Tun.
105/J4 Rafsanjān, Iran
130/B4 Raft (pt.), Austl.
185/G2 Raft (riv.), Id, Ut,US
81/E2 Rafz, Swi.
149/E3 Raga, Sudan
125/D4 Ragang (mtn.), Phil.
125/C2 Ragay (gulf), Phil.
132/D5 Ragged (peak), Austl.
175/J8 Ragged (pt.), Chile
196/C4 Ragged (isl.), Me,US
56/A1 Raghtin More (mtn.), Ire.
120/A3 Rāghugarh, India
121/F4 Raghunāthpur, India
58/D3 Raglan, Wal,UK
200/D4 Ragland, Al,US
61/E2 Rago Nat'l Park, Nor.
53/P8 Ragstone (range), Eng,UK
72/C4 Raguhn, Ger.
97/G3 Raguli, Rus.
90/D4 Ragusa, It.
108/E5 Ra'gyagoinba, China
148/D3 Rahad al Bardī, Sudan
149/G2 Rahad, Nahr Ar (riv.), Sudan
145/H4 Rahama, Nga.
60/C3 Rahan, Ire.
120/B4 Rāhatgarh, India
67/F4 Rahden, Ger.
122/B1 Rahīmyār Khān, Pak.
151/B1 Rahole Nat'l Rsv., Kenya
62/D1 Råholt, Nor.
122/D2 Rāhon, India
136/C2 Rahotu, N.Z.
118/B4 Rāhuri, India
207/D2 Rahway, NJ,US
79/F3 Rai, Fr.
85/D3 Raiano, It.
139/K6 Raiatea (isl.), FrPol.
118/C4 Raichūr, India
192/D2 Raiders (hill), SD,US
121/G3 Raiganj, India
120/D5 Raigarh, India
130/A2 Raijua (isl.), Indo.
122/E4 Raikera, India
206/E4 Railroad, Pa,US
204/C3 Railroad Canyon (res.), Ca,US
70/D5 Rain, Ger.
71/H5 Rainbach im Mühlkreis, Aus.
135/B2 Rainbow, Austl.
204/C4 Rainbow, Ca,US
134/D4 Rainbow Beach, Austl.
187/G2 Rainbow Bridge Nat'l Mon., Ut,US
200/D4 Rainbow City, Al,US
201/G2 Rainelle, WV,US
57/F4 Rainford, Eng,UK
53/P7 Rainham, Eng,UK
182/C4 Rainier, Or,US
182/D4 Rainier (mtn.), Wa,US
125/D4 Rainis, Indo.
200/E3 Rainsville, Al,US
193/H3 Rainsville, NM,US
57/G5 Rainworth, Eng,UK
195/H3 Rainy (riv.), On, Mn,Can
195/H3 Rainy (lake), On,Can, Mn,US
195/H3 Rainy, Big Fork (riv.), Mn,US
195/H4 Rainy, Little Fork (riv.), Mn,US
195/G3 Rainy River, On,Can
102/H7 Raipur, India
121/E5 Rāipur, India
120/B3 Raipur, India
139/L6 Rairoa (atoll), FrPol.
147/H4 Ra'īs, SAr.
64/F1 Raisdorf, Ger.
205/E8 Raisin (riv.), Mi,US
61/G3 Raisio, Fin.
68/C3 Raismes, Fr.
195/K3 Raith, On,Can
139/L7 Raivavae (isl.), FrPol.
122/C2 Rāiwind, Pak.
124/B2 Raja (pt.), Indo.
124/D4 Rajabasa (peak), Indo.
118/D4 Rājahmundry, India
118/C4 Rājampet, India
126/D3 Rajang (riv.), Malay.
107/K3 Rājanpur, Pak.
122/C1 Rājaori, India
122/F4 Rājapālaiyam, India
118/B4 Rājāpur, India
120/C3 Rājāpur, India
118/B2 Rājasthan (state), India
121/E3 Rajauli, India
118/B2 Rājawas, India
121/G4 Rājbāri, Bang.
121/F2 Rājbirāj, Nepal
73/C1 Rajčianka (riv.), Slvk.
73/C1 Rajec, Slvk.
121/G3 Rājendraganj, Bang.
121/E4 Rāj Gāngpur, India
107/L3 Rajgarh, India
118/C3 Rājgarh, India
120/A2 Rājgarh, India
121/E3 Rājgir, India
73/A1 Rajhrad, Czh.
73/B4 Rajka, Hun.
118/B3 Rājkot, India
121/F3 Rājmahāl, India
121/F3 Rājmahal (hills), India
118/D3 Rāj-Nāndagaon, India
121/G4 Rājpur, India
122/D2 Rājpura, India
121/G3 Rājshāhi, Bang.
121/G3 Rājshāhi (dist.), Bang.
118/B3 Rājula, India
121/F1 Raka, China
121/F1 Raka (riv.), China
139/J5 Rakahanga (isl.), Cookls.
136/B3 Rakaia, N.Z.
136/B3 Rakaia (riv.), N.Z.
92/E1 Rakamaz, Hun.
107/K1 Rakaposhi (mtn.), Pak.
116/B5 Rakhine (state), Burma
98/E3 Rakhny Lesovyye, Ukr.
98/C3 Rakhov, Ukr.
107/H3 Rakhshān (riv.), Pak.
136/F6 Rakino (isl.), N.Z.
138/G6 Rakiraki, Fiji
99/H2 Rakitnoye, Rus.
98/F3 Rakitnoye, Ukr.
63/M2 Rakke, Est.
62/D2 Rakkestad, Nor.
154/E4 Rakops, Bots.
73/D5 Rakos-patak (riv.), Hun.
71/G2 Rakovnicky Potok (riv.), Czh.
71/G2 Rakovník, Czh.
93/G4 Rakovski, Bul.
63/M2 Rakvere, Est.
151/A2 Rakwaro, Kenya
71/H2 Rakytka (riv.), Czh.
87/E2 Raldon, It.
200/C4 Raleigh, Ms,US
201/H3 Raleigh (cap.), NC,US
194/D4 Raleigh, ND,US
201/H3 Raleigh-Durham (int'l arpt.), NC,US
138/F4 Ralik Chain (arch.), Mrsh.
69/F4 Ralingen, Ger.
190/D4 Ralls, Tx,US
195/L4 Ralph, Mi,US
183/J2 Ralston, Ab,Can
199/H4 Ralston, Pa,US
185/J1 Ralston, Wy,US
161/E3 Rama, Nic.
143/H2 Ramādah, Tun.
150/B2 Ramādah, Yem.
187/H3 Ramah, NM,US
187/H3 Ramah Navajo Ind. Res., NM,US
199/G2 Rama Ind. Res., On,Can
170/D2 Ramalho (ridge), Braz.
103/D4 Rām Allāh, WBnk.
122/G4 Ramanāthapuram, India
122/G4 Ramanathaswamy Temple, India
207/H7 Ramapo (mts.), NJ,US
207/J7 Ramapo (riv.), NJ, NY,US
118/B4 Ramas (cape), India
103/D3 Ramat Gan, Isr.
103/F7 Ramat HaSharon, Isr.
154/E5 Ramatlabama, Bots.
82/C6 Ramatuelle, Fr.
72/B4 Ramberg (peak), Ger.
80/C1 Rambervillers, Fr.
139/Z17 Rambi (isl.), Fiji
124/F5 Rambipuji, Indo.
68/A6 Rambouillet, Fr.
58/B6 Rame (pt.), UK
197/J2 Ramea, Nf,Can
121/F2 Rāmechhāp, Nepal
200/D4 Ramer, Al,US
120/C1 Rāmeshwar, India
122/G4 Rāmeswaram, India
120/B1 Rāmgangā (riv.), India
121/E4 Rāmgarh, Bang.
121/E4 Rāmgarh, India
60/C6 Ram Head (pt.), Ire.
105/G4 Rāmhormoz, Iran
105/H2 Rāmīān, Iran
130/D3 Ramingining, Austl.
188/D4 Ramírez, Mex.
150/B3 Ramīs Shet' (riv.), Eth.
80/D3 Ramiswil, Swi.
121/F4 Rāmjībanpur, India
103/D4 Ramla, Isr.
63/T8 Ramløse, Den.
150/B2 Ramlu (peak), Eth.
62/C3 Ramme, Den.
103/D5 Ramm, Jabal (mtn.), Jor.
103/G8 Rammūn, WBnk.
120/B1 Rāmnagar, India
120/C3 Rāmnagar, India
120/D3 Rāmnagar, India
122/C1 Rāmnagar, India
62/G2 Ramnäs, Swe.
155/E4 Ramokgwebana, Bots.
99/K2 Ramon', Rus.
190/B3 Ramon, NM,US
186/D4 Ramona, Ca,US
191/G2 Ramona, Ok,US
80/C2 Ramonchamp, Fr.
103/D4 Ramon, Har (mtn.), Isr.
104/C4 Ramon, Har (mtn.), Isr.
60/C2 Ramor, Lough (lake), Ire.
159/E3 Ramos Arizpe, Mex.
81/G4 Ramosch, Swi.
154/E5 Ramotswa, Bots.
121/G4 Rāmpāl, Bang.
177/H2 Rampart, Ak,US
192/B4 Rampart (range), Co,US
118/B3 Rāmpur, India
120/B1 Rāmpur, India
122/D2 Rāmpur, India
118/C2 Rampura, India
122/C2 Rāmpura Mandi, India
121/F3 Rāmpur Hāt, India
116/B5 Ramree (isl.), Burma
120/C2 Rāmsanehī ghāt, India
118/B2 Ramsar, India
106/F1 Ramsar (Sakht Sar), Iran
195/K4 Ramsay, Mi,US
183/H5 Ramsay, Mt,US
57/F4 Ramsbottom, Eng,UK
59/E4 Ramsbury, Eng,UK
81/E2 Ramsen, Swi.
201/H3 Ramseur, NC,US
59/F2 Ramsey, Eng,UK
56/D3 Ramsey, IM,UK
56/D3 Ramsey (bay), IM,UK
58/A3 Ramsey (isl.), Wal,UK
193/K4 Ramsey, Il,US
193/H1 Ramsey (co.), Mn,US
207/J7 Ramsey, NJ,US
59/H4 Ramsgate, Eng,UK
105/G4 Rāmshīr, Iran
69/G5 Ramstein-Miesenbach, Ger.
150/B5 Ramu, Kenya
131/G1 Ramu (riv.), PNG
63/L4 Ramygala, Lith.
121/G4 Rānāghāt, India
126/C3 Ranai, Indo.
125/B4 Ranau, Malay.
200/E4 Ranburne, Al,US
174/C2 Rancagua, Chile
78/C4 Rance (riv.), Fr.
164/C2 Rancheria (riv.), Col.
185/K1 Ranchester, Wy,US
121/E4 Rānchī, India
121/E4 Ranchi (arpt.), India
205/M9 Rancho Cordova, Ca,US
204/C2 Rancho Cucamonga (Cucamonga), Ca,US
188/D4 Rancho Mezquitosa, Mex.
186/D4 Rancho Mirage, Ca,US
204/B3 Rancho Palos Verdes, Ca,US
174/F2 Ranchos, Arg.
204/C4 Rancho Santa Fe, Ca,US
190/B2 Ranchos De Taos, NM,US
174/B4 Ranco (lake), Chile
206/D3 Rancocas, NJ,US
174/D2 Rancul, Arg.
82/B5 Rancure (riv.), Fr.
150/B3 Randa, Djib.
62/A2 Randaberg, Nor.
195/G4 Randall, Mn,US
206/B5 Randallstown, Md,US
56/B2 Randalstown, NI,UK
90/D4 Randazzo, It.
156/P13 Randburg, SAfr.
81/E2 Randen, Hoher (peak), Ger.
62/D3 Randers, Den.
152/B3 Randi II, Gabon
201/H3 Randleman, NC,US
191/E3 Randlett, Ok,US
185/J3 Randlett, Ut,US
187/G4 Randolph, Az,US
208/C1 Randolph, Ma,US
193/F2 Randolph, Ne,US
206/D2 Randolph, NJ,US
208/F5 Randolph, Oh,US
185/H3 Randolph, Ut,US
199/K3 Randolph, Vt,US
198/B3 Randolph, Wi,US
197/L1 Random (isl.), Nf,Can
79/F3 Randonnai, Fr.
72/E1 Randow (riv.), Ger.
127/J4 Randowaya, Indo.
186/D3 Randsburg, Ca,US
62/D1 Randsfjorden (lake), Nor.
134/H8 Randwick, Austl.
61/G2 Råneå, Swe.
144/B3 Ranérou, Sen.
79/E3 Rânes, Fr.
121/F3 Rāneswar, India
136/B4 Ranfurly, N.Z.
123/C2 Rang (peak), Thai.
123/C5 Rangae, Thai.
116/B4 Rangāmāti, Bang.
122/G3 Ranganathaswamy Temple, India
116/B3 Rangāpāra, India
127/E4 Rangasa (cape), Indo.
68/A3 Rang-du-Fliers, Fr.
196/B3 Rangeley, Me,US
185/J3 Rangely, Co,US
200/E3 Ranger, NC,US
189/E1 Ranger, Tx,US
155/F3 Range, The, Zim.
121/H2 Rangia, India
136/C3 Rangiora, N.Z.
139/L6 Rangiroa (atoll), FrPol.
124/D4 Rangkasbitung, Indo.
116/C5 Rangoon (div.), Burma
116/C5 Rangoon (Yangon) (cap.), Burma
121/G3 Rangpur, Bang.
121/G3 Rangpur (dist.), Bang.
118/C5 Rānībennur, India
195/H3 Ranier, Mn,US
120/D2 Rānīganj, India
121/E3 Rānīganj, India
121/F2 Rānīganj, India
121/F4 Rānīganj, India
120/B1 Rānīkhet, India
120/B3 Rānīpur, India
120/D3 Rāni Tāl, India
107/K3 Ranjitpura, India
133/H2 Ranken (riv.), Austl.
198/C4 Rankin, Il,US
188/D2 Rankin, Tx,US
178/G2 Rankin Inlet, NW,Can
135/C2 Rankins Springs, Austl.
81/F3 Rankweil, Aus.
54/B3 Rannoch, Loch (lake), Sc,UK
145/H4 Rano, Nga.
157/H8 Ranohira, Madg.
157/H8 Ranomafana, Madg.
123/B4 Ranong, Thai.
157/H8 Ranotsara, Madg.
174/C3 Ranquil del Norte, Arg.
69/G3 Ransbach-Baumbach, Ger.
127/H4 Ransiki, Indo.
190/E1 Ransom, Ks,US
197/T9 Ransomville, NY,US
201/J1 Ranson, WV,US
69/E1 Ranst, Belg.
70/B2 Ranstadt, Ger.
157/J6 Rantabe, Madg.
124/C2 Rantaukampar, Indo.
124/C3 Rantaupanjang, Indo.
124/B2 Rantauprapat, Indo.
127/F4 Rantekombola (peak), Indo.
68/B5 Rantigny, Fr.
103/G7 Rantīs, WBnk.
198/B4 Rantoul, Il,US
61/H2 Rantsila, Fin.
123/D2 Rao Co (peak), Laos
80/C1 Raon-l'Étape, Fr.
138/H7 Raoul (isl.), N.Z.
115/C3 Raoyang, China
139/L7 Rapa (isl.), FrPol.
86/C4 Rapallo, It.
174/Q9 Rapel, Chile
174/Q10 Rapel (lake), Chile
183/K5 Rapelje, Mt,US
174/B5 Raper, Cabo (cape), Chile
201/H2 Raphine, Va,US
192/C1 Rapid (cr.), SD,US
133/H5 Rapid Bay, Austl.
194/D2 Rapid City, Mb,Can
198/D2 Rapid City, Mi,US
192/C1 Rapid City, SD,US
196/A2 Rapide-Blanc, Qu,Can
85/D4 Rapido (riv.), It.
198/C2 Rapid River, Mi,US
63/M2 Räpina, Est.
63/L2 Rapla, Est.
84/B1 Rapolano Terme, It.
85/F6 Rapolla, It.
201/J2 Rappahannock (riv.), Va,US
72/A4 Rappbode Stausee (res.), Ger.
120/D2 Rapti (riv.), India
120/D1 Rāpti (zone), Nepal
169/E4 Rápulo (riv.), Bol.
120/D1 Rara Nat'l Park, Nepal
206/D2 Raritan (riv.), NJ,US
207/D3 Raritan (bay), NJ, NY,US
206/D2 Raritan, North Branch (riv.), NJ,US
206/D2 Raritan, South Branch (riv.), NJ,US
80/D5 Raron, Swi.
139/J7 Rarotonga (isl.), Cookls.
174/E4 Rasa (pt.), Arg.
146/A1 Ra's Ajdīr, Libya
104/E2 Ra's al 'Ayn, Syria
141/X17 Ra's Al Jabal, Tun.
105/G4 Ra's al Khafjī, SAr.
105/H5 Ra's al Khaymah, UAE
105/H5 Ras Al Khaymah (int'l arpt.), UAE
103/D5 Ra's An Naqb, Jor.
71/F1 Raschau, Ger.
63/K4 Raseiniai, Lith.
141/Q16 Rās el Ma, Alg.
144/D2 Rās el Mâ, Mali
141/T16 Rās el Oued, Alg.
106/B3 Ra's Gharib, Egypt
147/G2 Ra's Gharib, Egypt
149/F3 Rashād, Sudan
56/B2 Rasharkin, NI,UK
103/D3 Rashayya, Leb.
103/B4 Rashīd (Rosetta), Egypt
105/G2 Rasht, Iran
122/G3 Rāsipuram, India
123/D3 Rasi Salai, Thai.
107/H3 Rāsk, Iran
92/E4 Raška, Yugo.
118/B2 Rāsla, India
178/G2 Rasmussen (basin), NW,Can
77/P10 Raso (cape), Port.
132/E4 Rason (lake), Austl.
120/D3 Rasrā, India
87/E5 Rassina, It.
97/G1 Rasskazovo, Rus.
97/K2 Rassypnaya, Rus.
70/B5 Rastatt, Ger.
67/F2 Rastede, Ger.
72/B5 Rastenberg, Ger.
177/B6 Rat (isls.), Ak,US
124/D4 Rata (cape), Indo.
127/F3 Ratahan, Indo.
118/B2 Ratangarh, India
120/D4 Ratanpur, India
123/B3 Rat Buri, Thai.
189/G2 Ratcliff, Tx,US
120/B3 Rāth, India
60/D3 Rathangan, Ire.
193/H3 Rathbun (lake), Ia,US
60/D3 Rathcoole, Ire.
60/B5 Rathcormack, Ire.
60/C4 Rathdowney, Ire.
60/D4 Rathdrum, Ire.
182/F4 Rathdrum, Id,US
116/B4 Rathedaung, Burma
72/C2 Rathenow, Ger.
56/B3 Rathfriland, NI,UK
60/C5 Rathgormuck, Ire.
60/B4 Rathkeale, Ire.
56/B1 Rathlin (isl.), NI,UK
56/B1 Rathlin (sound), NI,UK
60/B5 Rathluirc, Ire.
60/A5 Rathmore, Ire.
60/D3 Rathmore, Ire.
60/D4 Rathnew, Ire.
60/C2 Rathowen, Ire.
60/D4 Rathvilly, Ire.
60/C3 Rathwire, Ire.
114/C6 Ratia, India
138/F4 Ratik Chain (arch.), Mrsh.
66/D6 Ratingen, Ger.
92/C3 Ratkovo, Yugo.
118/C3 Ratlām, India
118/B4 Ratnāgiri, India
118/D6 Ratnapura, SrL.
92/C2 Ratno, Ukr.
60/D3 Ratoath, Ire.
190/B2 Raton, NM,US
190/B2 Raton (pass), NM,US
123/C5 Rattaphum, Thai.
190/E2 Rattle Snake (cr.), Ks,US
192/E4 Rattlesnake (cr.), Ks,US
54/C3 Rattray, Sc,UK
62/F1 Rättvik, Swe.
64/F2 Ratzeburg, Ger.
124/C2 Rau, Indo.
124/C2 Raub, Malay.
77/F3 Rauch, Arg.
195/H4 Rauch, Mn,US
61/P6 Raudhinūpur (pt.), Ice.
61/P6 Raufarhöfn, Ice.
62/D1 Raufoss, Nor.
70/D3 Rauhe Ebrach (riv.), Ger.
71/E3 Rauher Kulm (hill), Ger.
171/E4 Raul Soares, Braz.
61/G3 Rauma, Fin.
63/L3 Rauna, Lat.
59/F2 Raunds, Eng,UK
124/F5 Raung (peak), Indo.
136/C2 Raupehu (vol.), N.Z.
121/E4 Raurkela, India
121/F1 Rausa Garhi, Nepal
112/D1 Rausu, Japan
63/N1 Rautjärvi, Fin.
121/H4 Rauzan, Bang.
90/C4 Ravanusa, It.
105/J4 Rāvar, Iran
87/E3 Ravarino, It.
98/B2 Rava-Russkaya, Ukr.
68/C6 Ravels, Belg.
201/G2 Raven, Va,US
199/K3 Ravena, NY,US
184/C3 Ravendale, Ca,US
57/E3 Ravenglass, Eng,UK
87/F4 Ravenna, It.
87/E4 Ravenna (prov.), It.
204/B2 Ravenna, Ca,US
200/F2 Ravenna, Ky,US
198/D3 Ravenna, Mi,US
193/F3 Ravenna, Ne,US
208/F5 Ravenna, Oh,US
208/F5 Ravenna Arsenal, Oh,US
81/F2 Ravensburg, Ger.
205/D3 Ravensdale, Wa,US
57/G5 Ravenshead, Eng,UK
134/B2 Ravenshoe, Austl.
132/D5 Ravensthorpe, Austl.
201/G1 Ravenswood, WV,US
60/D5 Raven, The (pt.), Ire.
122/B2 Rāvi (riv.), India, Pak.
92/B2 Ravne na Koroškem, Slov.
107/H1 Ravnina, Trkm.
104/E3 Rāwah, Iraq
139/H5 Rawaki (Phoenix) (isl.), Kiri.
122/B1 Rāwalpindi, Pak.
122/B1 Rawalpindi/Islamabad (int'l arpt.), Pak.
65/L3 Rawa Mazowiecka, Pol.
199/K1 Rawdon, Qu,Can

136/C1 Rawene, N.Z.
106/D5 Rawḩah, SAr.
65/J3 Rawicz, Pol.
187/G4 Rawley Wash (dry riv.), Az,US
132/E4 Rawlinna, Austl.
185/K3 Rawlins, Wy,US
133/E3 Rawlinson (peak), Austl.
57/G5 Rawmarsh, Eng,UK
174/D4 Rawson, Arg.
57/F4 Rawtenstall, Eng,UK
116/C2 Rawu, China
121/E2 Raxaul Bazar, India
197/H2 Ray (cape), Nf,Can
194/C3 Ray, ND,US
126/D4 Raya (peak), Indo.
118/C5 Rāyadrug, India
118/D4 Rāyagada, India
203/H2 Raybon, Ga,US
109/K2 Raychikhinsk, Rus.
105/J4 Rāyen, Iran
95/M5 Rayevskiy, Rus.
188/L7 Ray Hubbard (lake), Tx,US
59/G3 Rayleigh, Eng,UK
183/H3 Raymond, Ab,Can
186/C2 Raymond, Ca,US
193/K4 Raymond, Il,US
196/B4 Raymond, Me,US
195/G5 Raymond, Mn,US
200/B4 Raymond, Ms,US
182/C4 Raymond, Wa,US
205/P14 Raymond, Wi,US
200/B2 Raymondville, Mo,US
199/J2 Raymondville, NY,US
189/F4 Raymondville, Tx,US
194/B2 Raymore, Sk,Can
191/G1 Raymore, Mo,US
202/B2 Rayne, La,US
208/C2 Raynham, Ma,US
208/C2 Raynham Center, Ma,US
159/F4 Rayón, Mex.
159/E3 Rayones, Mex.
123/C3 Rayong, Thai.
159/E5 Rayón Nat'l Park, Mex.
189/F1 Ray Roberts (lake), Tx,US
106/F5 Raysūt, Oman
189/J1 Rayville, La,US
105/G3 Razan, Iran
97/H4 Razdan, Arm.
98/F4 Razdel'naya, Ukr.
99/G5 Razdol'noye, Ukr.
93/J3 Razelm (lake), Rom.
93/H4 Razgrad, Bul.
91/K1 Razgrad (reg.), Bul.
93/F5 Razlog, Bul.
78/A4 Raz, Pointe du (pt.), Fr.
99/J2 Razumnoye, Rus.
74/C3 Ré (isl.), Fr.
58/D2 Rea (riv.), Eng,UK
196/C3 Readfield, Me,US
59/F4 Reading, Eng,UK
191/G1 Reading, Ks,US
198/D4 Reading, Mi,US
198/D5 Reading, Oh,US
206/C3 Reading, Pa,US
206/C3 Reading/Carl A. Spaatz Field (reg. arpt.), Pa,US
200/B4 Readland, Ar,US
194/B3 Readlyn, Sk,Can
191/J1 Readsville, Mo,US
189/F2 Reagan, Tx,US
168/C3 Real, Cordillera (mts.), Bol., Peru
175/T12 Real de San Carlos, Uru.
174/D2 Realicó, Arg.
189/E4 Realitos, Tx,US
82/C6 Réal Martin (riv.), Fr.
60/B3 Rea, Lough (lake), Ire.
81/E4 Realp, Swi.
206/B3 Reamstown, Pa,US
123/C3 Reang Kesei, Camb.
139/M6 Reao (isl.), FrPol.
68/C6 Rebais, Fr.
132/D4 Rebecca (lake), Austl.
201/F5 Rebecca, Ga,US
88/E4 Rebib, Hassi er (well), Alg.
65/K1 Rębiechowo (int'l arpt.), Pol.
81/F3 Rebstein, Swi.
112/B1 Rebun, Japan
112/B1 Rebun (isl.), Japan
112/B1 Rebun-Rishiri-Sarobetsu Nat'l Park, Japan
87/G6 Recanati, It.
83/B2 Recanello (riv.), It.
86/C4 Recco, It.
132/E5 Recherche (arch.), Austl.
69/F6 Réchicourt-le-Château, Fr.
98/F1 Rechitsa, Bela.
73/A5 Rechnitz, Aus.
80/D4 Rechthalten, Swi.
167/H5 Recife, Braz.
156/D4 Recife (cape), SAfr.
67/E4 Recke, Ger.
80/E5 Reckingen, Swi.
67/E5 Recklinghausen, Ger.
64/G2 Recknitz (riv.), Ger.
80/C3 Réclère, Swi.
123/B2 Reclining Buddha (Shwethalyaung) (ruins), Burma
185/L1 Recluse, Wy,US
87/E1 Recoaro Terme, It.
172/E4 Reconquista, Arg.
80/D3 Reconvilier, Swi.
172/C4 Recreo, Arg.
172/D4 Recreo, Arg.
191/J2 Rector, Ar,US
168/B3 Recuay, Peru
106/C4 Red (sea), Afr., Asia
194/F3 Red (riv.), Mb,Can
197/K2 Red (isl.), Nf,Can
116/D4 Red (riv.), China, Viet.
56/B1 Red (bay), NI,UK
181/H5 Red (riv.), US
190/E2 Red (hills), Ks,US
202/D2 Red (cr.), Ms,US
65/K1 Reda, Pol.
201/M7 Redan, Ga,US
124/C1 Redang (isl.), Malay.
69/E4 Redange-sur-Attert, Lux.
207/D3 Red Bank, NJ,US
201/G4 Red Bank, SC,US
200/E3 Red Bank, Tn,US
200/C3 Red Bay, Al,US
203/F2 Red Bay, Fl,US
183/L1 Redberry (lake), Sk,Can
182/C1 Red Bluff, BC,Can
184/B3 Red Bluff, Ca,US
190/C5 Red Bluff (res.), NM, Tx,US
200/E2 Red Boiling Springs, Tn,US
59/F3 Redbourn, Eng,UK
53/P7 Redbridge (bor.), Eng,UK
193/K4 Red Bud, Il,US
195/G4 Redby, Mn,US
57/G2 Redcar, Eng,UK
183/J2 Redcliff, Ab,Can
190/A1 Red Cliff, Co,US
155/F3 Redcliff, Zim.
134/F6 Redcliffe, Austl.
132/D4 Redcliffe (peak), Austl.
195/J4 Red Cliff Ind. Res., Wi,US
133/J5 Red Cliffs, Austl.
192/E3 Red Cloud, Ne,US
199/H3 Red Creek, NY,US
176/F4 Red Deer, Can.
183/H1 Red Deer, Ab,Can
183/J2 Red Deer (riv.), Ab,Can
183/N1 Red Deer (riv.), Sk,Can
206/C6 Redden, De,US
156/D3 Reddersburg, SAfr.
177/G3 Red Devil, Ak,US
203/G3 Reddick, Fl,US
184/B3 Redding, Ca,US
208/A3 Redding, Ct,US
201/H1 Reddish (mtn.), WV,US
59/E2 Redditch, Eng,UK
57/F1 Rede (riv.), Eng,UK
190/E3 Red, Elm Fork (riv.), Ok, Tx,US
166/D5 Redenção, Braz.
170/D1 Redenção do Gurguéia, Braz.
192/B3 Red Feather Lakes, Co,US
191/H3 Redfield, Ar,US
192/E1 Redfield, SD,US
189/N9 Red Fish (isl.), Tx,US
205/F7 Redford, Mi,US
191/J2 Redford, Mo,US
188/B3 Redford, Tx,US
189/E4 Red Gate, Tx,US
198/B2 Redgranite, Wi,US
53/N8 Redhill, Eng,UK
180/T10 Red Hill (peak), Hi,US
206/C3 Red Hill, Pa,US
201/H2 Red Hill-Patrick Henry Nat'l Mem., Va,US
81/G5 Re di Castello, Monte (peak), It.
92/C2 Rédics, Hun.
192/C1 Redig, SD,US
197/J1 Red Indian (lake), Nf,Can
69/G6 Réding, Fr.
202/K8 Redington Beach, Fl,US
198/D4 Redkey, In,US
94/H4 Redkino, Rus.
195/H2 Red Lake, On,Can
195/G4 Red Lake, Mn,US
195/G3 Red Lake (riv.), Mn,US
194/F4 Red Lake Falls, Mn,US
195/G3 Red Lake Ind. Res., Mn,US
195/H3 Red Lake Road, On,Can
206/A5 Redland, Md,US
134/F7 Redland Bay, Austl.
204/C2 Redlands, Ca,US
185/J4 Redlands, Co,US
202/E2 Red Level, Al,US
64/G2 Redlin, Ger.
206/C4 Red Lion, De,US
206/B4 Red Lion, Pa,US
185/J1 Red Lodge, Mt,US
193/F4 Redmond (res.), Ks,US
184/C1 Redmond, Or,US
185/H4 Redmond, Ut,US
205/C2 Redmond, Wa,US
186/D3 Red Mountain, Ca,US
70/D4 Rednitz (riv.), Ger.
190/E3 Red, North Fork (riv.), Ok, Tx,US
201/M7 Red Oak, Ga,US
193/G3 Red Oak, Ia,US
188/L7 Red Oak, Tx,US
188/L7 Red Oak (cr.), Tx,US
78/C5 Redon, Fr.
76/A1 Redondela, Sp.
165/F4 Redondo (peak), Braz.
76/B3 Redondo, Port.
190/A3 Redondo (peak), NM,US
205/C3 Redondo, Wa,US
204/B3 Redondo Beach, Ca,US
177/H3 Redoubt (vol.), Ak,US
183/K1 Red Pheasant Ind. Res., Sk,Can
190/D3 Red, Prairie Dog Town Fork (riv.), Tx,US
194/F4 Red River (val.), Mn, ND,US
191/G4 Red River Army Dep., Tx,US
194/F4 Red River of the North (riv.), Mn, ND,US
195/K3 Red Rock, Can
193/H3 Red Rock (lake), Ia,US
187/H4 Redrock, NM,US
189/F3 Red Rock, Tx,US
187/G2 Red Rock (plat.), Ut,US
185/H1 Red Rock Lakes Nat'l Wild. Ref., Mt,US
133/E5 Red Rocks (pt.), Austl.
58/A6 Redruth, Eng,UK
190/D3 Red, Salt Fork (riv.), Ok, Tx,US
192/D1 Red Scaffold, SD,US
147/H4 Red Sea (hills), Sudan
192/C2 Red Shirt, SD,US
201/H3 Red Springs, NC,US
178/D2 Redstone (riv.), NW,Can
185/K4 Redstone, Co,US
192/E1 Redstone (cr.), SD,US
200/D3 Redstone Arsenal, Al,US
185/J4 Redvale, Co,US
194/D3 Redvers, Sk,Can
145/E4 Red Volta (riv.), Burk., Gui.
183/M4 Redwater (riv.), Mt,US
184/B3 Redway, Ca,US
192/D3 Red Willow (cr.), Ne,US
192/D3 Red Willow (dam), Ne,US
192/B5 Red Wing, Co,US
193/H1 Red Wing, Mn,US
193/G1 Redwood (riv.), Mn,US
205/K12 Redwood City, Ca,US
193/G1 Redwood Falls, Mn,US
184/A3 Redwood Nat'l Park, Ca,US
200/D3 Reece City, Al,US
191/J4 Reed, Ar,US
196/C3 Reed, Me,US
196/C2 Reed (mtn.), Me,US
190/E3 Reed, Ok,US
198/D3 Reed City, Mi,US
194/C4 Reeder, ND,US
59/H1 Reedham, Eng,UK
186/C2 Reedley, Ca,US
206/D5 Reeds (bay), NJ,US
193/J2 Reedsburg, Wi,US
191/H2 Reeds Spring, Mo,US
135/B3 Reedy (cr.), Austl.
202/M7 Reedy (cr.), Fl,US
202/N8 Reedy (lake), Fl,US
159/J5 Reef (pt.), Belz.
138/F6 Reef (isls.), Sol.
136/B3 Reefton, N.Z.
200/C2 Reelfoot Lake Nat'l Wild. Ref., Tn,US
60/B2 Ree, Lough (lake), Ire.
59/H1 Reepham, Eng,UK
66/D5 Rees, Ger.
198/E3 Reese, Mi,US
178/E5 Reese (riv.), Nv,US
180/C4 Reese (riv), Nv,US
184/E4 Reese (riv.), Nv,US
67/G2 Reessum, Ger.
66/D3 Reest (riv.), Neth.
57/G3 Reeth, Eng,UK
66/B4 Reeuwijk, Neth.
104/D2 Refahiye, Turk.
200/C4 Reform, Al,US
159/H5 Reforma, Mex.
189/F3 Refugio, Tx,US
174/Q9 Refugio lo Valdés, Chile
65/H2 Rega (riv.), Pol.
71/G5 Regen, Ger.
71/F4 Regen (riv.), Ger.
171/F3 Regência, Pontal de (pt.), Braz.
167/F4 Regeneração, Braz.
71/F4 Regensburg, Ger.
81/E3 Regensdorf, Swi.
71/F4 Regenstauf, Ger.
194/C4 Regent, ND,US
134/H8 Regents Park, Austl.
53/N7 Regent's Park, Eng,UK
143/F4 Reggane, Alg.
66/D4 Regge (riv.), Neth.
87/E5 Reggello, It.
202/D3 Reggio, La,US
83/B6 Reggio di Calabria, It.
83/B6 Reggio di Calabria (prov.), It.
87/D3 Reggiolo, It.
86/D3 Reggio nell'Emilia, It.
86/D3 Reggio nell'Emilia (prov.), It.
93/G2 Reghin, Rom.
183/M2 Regina (cap.), Sk,Can
166/C1 Régina, FrG.
187/J2 Regina, NM,US
194/B2 Regina Beach, Sk,Can
72/C5 Regis-Breitingen, Ger.
170/D5 Registro, Braz.
70/D3 Regnitz (riv.), Ger.
81/F5 Regoledo, It.
76/B3 Reguengosde Monsaraz, Port.
194/B3 Regway, Sk,Can
71/F2 Rehau, Ger.
67/G4 Rehburg-Loccum, Ger.
72/D2 Rehfelde, Ger.
120/B4 Rehlī, India
70/D6 Rehling, Ger.
69/F5 Rehlingen-Siersburg, Ger.
154/C4 Rehoboth, Namb.
208/C2 Rehoboth, Ma,US
187/H3 Rehoboth, NM,US
206/C6 Rehoboth Beach, De,US
69/E5 Réhon, Fr.
103/F8 Rehovot, Isr.
206/B3 Rehrersburg, Pa,US
70/D3 Reiche Ebrach (riv.), Ger.
70/B2 Reichelsheim, Ger.
70/B3 Reichelsheim, Ger.
71/F1 Reichenbach, Ger.
80/D4 Reichenbach im Kandertal, Swi.
69/G5 Reichenbach-Steegen, Ger.
70/C3 Reichenberg, Ger.
71/E6 Reichertshausen, Ger.
69/G2 Reichshof, Ger.
69/G6 Reichshoffen, Fr.
69/G6 Reichstett, Fr.
133/F4 Reid, Austl.
80/D3 Reiden, Swi.
200/C2 Reidland, Ky,US
201/F4 Reidsville, Ga,US
201/H2 Reidsville, NC,US
53/N8 Reigate, Eng,UK
80/C5 Reignier, Fr.
192/C3 Reilly (hill), Ne,US
68/D5 Reims, Fr.
68/D5 Reims, Cathédrale de, Fr.
68/D5 Reims (Champagne) (arpt.), Fr.
175/J7 Reina Adelaida (arch.), Chile
164/D1 Reina Beatrix (int'l arpt.), Aru.
80/D3 Reinach, Swi.
80/E3 Reinach, Swi.
193/H2 Reinbeck, Ia,US
67/H1 Reinbek, Ger.
194/F1 Reindeer (isl.), Mb,Can
178/F3 Reindeer (lake), Mb,Sk,Can
206/B2 Reinerton-Orwin-Muir, Pa,US
70/B3 Reinheim, Ger.
194/F3 Reinland, Mb,Can
76/C1 Reinosa, Sp.
72/C4 Reinsdorf, Ger.
69/F4 Reinsfeld, Ger.
71/F6 Reischach, Ger.
69/F4 Reisdorf, Lux.
61/G1 Reisduoddarhal'di (peak), Nor.
70/B1 Reiskirchen, Ger.
71/F5 Reissingerbach (riv.), Ger.
206/B5 Reisterstown, Md,US
66/D2 Reitdiep (riv.), Neth.
156/E2 Reitz, SAfr.
149/F4 Rejaf, Sudan
159/H4 Rejon (int'l arpt.), Mex.
178/F2 Reliance, NW,Can
192/E2 Reliance, SD,US
141/R16 Relizane, Alg.
158/D3 Rellano, Mex.
67/G1 Rellingen, Ger.
69/G2 Remagen, Ger.
79/F4 Rémalard, Fr.
169/F4 Remanso, Bol.
171/E1 Remanso, Braz.
87/G1 Remanzacco, It.
53/S11 Remarde (riv.), Fr.
133/H5 Remarkable (peak), Austl.
124/E4 Rembang, Indo.
124/C2 Rembau, Malay.
141/Q16 Remchi, Alg.
161/F4 Remedios, Pan.
195/H4 Remer, Mn,US
203/G2 Remerton, Ga,US
69/F4 Remich, Lux.
69/E2 Remicourt, Belg.
198/C4 Remington, In,US
166/C1 Rémire, FrG.
80/C1 Remiremont, Fr.
200/D4 Remlap, Al,US
67/H4 Remlingen, Ger.
97/G3 Remontnoye, Rus.
70/C5 Rems (riv.), Ger.
67/E6 Remscheid, Ger.
193/G2 Remsen, Ia,US
199/J3 Remsen, NY,US
68/B5 Rémy, Fr.
115/B5 Ren (riv.), China
62/D1 Rena, Nor.
82/B2 Renage, Fr.
191/J3 Rena Lara, Ms,US
80/C3 Renan, Swi.
79/D5 Renazé, Fr.
87/E3 Renazzo, It.
174/C2 Renca, Chile
63/L3 Rencēni, Lat.
70/A5 Rench (riv.), Ger.
70/B5 Renchen, Ger.
197/K2 Rencontre East, Nf,Can
200/C1 Rend (lake), Il,US
63/K3 Renda, Lat.
83/C4 Rende, It.
69/E3 Rendeux, Belg.
64/E1 Rendsburg, Ger.
80/C4 Renens, Swi.
197/L2 Renews-Cappahayden, Nf,Can
199/H2 Renfrew, On,Can
54/B5 Renfrew, Sc,UK
208/H6 Renfrew, Pa,US
124/C2 Rengam, Malay.
124/C3 Rengat, Indo.
174/C2 Rengo, Chile
69/G3 Rengsdorf, Ger.
119/K2 Renhua, China
116/E3 Renhuai, China
98/E5 Reni, Ukr.
66/C5 Renkum, Neth.
133/J5 Renmark, Austl.
138/F6 Rennell (isl.), Sol.
69/H2 Rennerod, Ger.
70/E5 Rennertshofen, Ger.
78/D4 Rennes, Fr.
78/D4 Rennes (Saint Jacques) (int'l arpt.), Fr.
195/G3 Rennie, Mb,Can
70/B5 Renningen, Ger.
87/F3 Reno (riv.), It.
184/D4 Reno, Nv,US
189/F1 Reno, Tx,US
156/C3 Renoster (riv.), SAfr.
156/D2 Renoster (riv.), SAfr.
196/D2 Renous-Plaster Rock Game Ref., NB,Can
199/H4 Renovo, Pa,US
115/D3 Renqiu, China
117/E2 Renshizhen, China
117/H3 Renshou, China
198/C4 Rensselaer, In,US
76/E1 Rentería, Sp.
54/B5 Renton, Sc,UK
205/C3 Renton, Wa,US
201/F4 Rentz, Ga,US
195/G5 Renville, Mn,US
194/D1 Renwer, Mb,Can
68/D4 Renwez, Fr.
145/E3 Réo, Burk.
127/F5 Reo, Indo.
120/E3 Reoti, India
73/B4 Répce (riv.), Hun.
73/B5 Répcelak, Hun.
161/H4 Repelón, Col.
199/K2 Repentigny, Qu,Can
63/N1 Repino, Rus.
98/F2 Repki, Ukr.
80/A5 Replonges, Fr.
57/G6 Repton, Eng,UK
191/F1 Republic, Ks,US
198/C1 Republic, Mi,US
191/H2 Republic, Mo,US
207/E2 Republic (arpt.), NY,US
182/E3 Republic, Wa,US
193/F4 Republican (riv.), Ks, Ne,US
192/C4 Republican, South Fork (riv.), Co, Ks,US
134/C3 Repulse (bay), Austl.
179/H2 Repulse Bay, NW,Can
165/G4 Repununi (riv.), Guy.
99/K2 Rep'yëvka, Rus.
168/C2 Requena, Peru
77/E3 Requena, Sp.
174/C2 Requiñoa, Chile
166/A1 Rera, Braz.
167/F4 Reriutuba, Braz.
104/D1 Reşadiye, Turk.
63/S7 Resarö (isl.), Swe.
81/G4 Reschen (Resia), It.
81/G4 Reschensee (Resia) (lake), It.
174/B5 Rescue (pt.), Chile
204/E7 Reseda, Ca,US
92/E5 Resen, Macd.
171/M7 Resende, Braz.
76/B2 Resende, Port.
194/C1 Reserve, Sk,Can
187/H4 Reserve, NM,US
195/J5 Reserve, Wi,US
99/H3 Reshetilovka, Ukr.
81/G4 Resia, Passo di (pass), It.
81/G4 Resia (Reschen), It.
81/G4 Resia (Reschensee) (lake), It.
172/E3 Resistencia, Arg.
92/E3 Reşiţa, Rom.
176/H2 Resolute, Can.
178/G1 Resolute, NW,Can
179/K2 Resolution (isl.), NW,Can
58/C3 Resolven, Wal,UK
76/C1 Respenda de la Peña, Sp.
171/E3 Resplendor, Braz.
155/G5 Ressano Garcia, Moz.
68/B4 Ressons-sur-Matz, Fr.
79/F6 Restigné, Fr.
196/D2 Restigouche (riv.), NB,Can
194/D3 Reston, Mb,Can
206/A6 Reston, Va,US
205/C2 Restoration (pt.), Wa,US
65/L1 Reszel, Pol.
160/D3 Retalhuleu, Guat.
68/D4 Rethel, Fr.
67/G3 Rethem, Ger.
91/J5 Réthimnon, Gre.
69/E1 Retie, Belg.
78/D5 Retiers, Fr.
92/F3 Retrezap Nat'l Park, Rom.
73/D4 Rétság, Hun.
81/G2 Rettenberg, Ger.
75/L2 Retz, Aus.
72/C5 Reuden, Ger.
79/F6 Reugny, Fr.
157/R15 Réunion (dpcy.), Fr.
77/F2 Reus, Sp.
66/C6 Reusel, Neth.
81/E3 Reuss (riv.), Swi.
64/G2 Reuterstadt Stavenhagen, Ger.
70/C6 Reutlingen, Ger.
94/H5 Reutov, Rus.
81/G3 Reutte, Aus.
103/F8 Revadim, Isr.
94/G2 Revda, Rus.
95/N4 Revda, Rus.
186/D2 Reveille (peak), Nv,US
53/T10 Reveillon (riv.), Fr.
74/D5 Revel, Fr.
182/E2 Revelstoke, BC,Can
159/F4 Reventadero, Mex.
168/A2 Reventazón, Peru
83/C4 Reventino (peak), It.
183/K1 Revenue, Sk,Can
87/E2 Revere, It.
208/C1 Revere, Ma,US
134/H8 Revesby, Austl.
73/B6 Révfülöp, Hun.
69/D6 Revigny-sur-Ornain, Fr.
158/B5 Revillagigedo (isls.), Mex.
78/D1 Réville, Fr.
194/F5 Revillo, SD,US
68/D4 Revin, Fr.
114/B4 Revolyutsii, Pik (peak), Taj.
61/G1 Revsbotn (fjord), Nor.
155/G2 Revúboè (riv.), Moz.
73/D1 Revúca (riv.), Slvk.
155/G3 Revuè (riv.), Moz.
165/G4 Rewa (riv.), Guy.
120/C3 Rewa, India
120/A1 Rewāri, India
177/J3 Rex (mtn.), Ak,US
185/H2 Rexburg, Id,US
190/D1 Rexford, Ks,US
182/G3 Rexford, Mt,US
68/B2 Rexpoëde, Fr.
196/E2 Rexton, NB,Can
161/G4 Rey (isl.), Pan.
148/B3 Rey Bouba, Camr.
191/J3 Reydell, Ar,US
59/H2 Reydon, Eng,UK
169/E4 Reyes, Bol.
159/M6 Reyes de Vallarta, Mex.
103/E1 Reyhanlı, Turk.
52/A2 Reykjanestá (cape), Ice.
61/N7 Reykjavík (cap.), Ice.
61/N7 Reykjavík (int'l arpt.), Ice.
172/D4 Reynaldo Cullen, Arg.
200/E4 Reynolds, Ga,US
191/J2 Reynolds, Mo,US
198/E5 Reynoldsburg, Oh,US
189/E4 Reynosa, Mex.
82/C5 Reyran (riv.), Fr.
80/B5 Reyssouze (riv.), Fr.
78/D6 Rezé, Fr.
63/M3 Rēzekne, Lat.
93/J2 Rezina, Mol.
86/D1 Rezzato, It.
81/F5 Rhaetian Alps (mts.), It., Swi.
142/C5 Rhallamane (reg.), Mrta.
142/C4 Rhallamane, Sebkhet de (dry lake), Mrta.
194/C4 Rhame, ND,US
88/D4 Rharbi, Zahrez (dry lake), Alg.
142/D3 Rhart, Jebel (mtn.), Mor.
81/F3 Rhätikon (mts.), Aus., Swi.
142/D3 Rhat, Jebel (mtn.), Mor.
58/C2 Rhayader, Wal,UK
67/F5 Rheda-Wiedenbrück, Ger.
66/D5 Rhede, Ger.
67/E2 Rhede, Ger.
66/D5 Rheden, Neth.
59/F2 Rhee (Cam) (riv.), Eng,UK
194/C2 Rhein, Sk,Can
81/E2 Rheinau, Swi.
69/F2 Rheinbach, Ger.
66/D5 Rheinberg, Ger.
69/G2 Rheinbreitbach, Ger.
69/G3 Rheinbrohl, Ger.
67/E4 Rheine, Ger.
81/E2 Rheinfall, Swi.
80/D2 Rheinfelden, Ger.
64/D3 Rhein (Rhine) (riv.), Eur.
72/C1 Rheinsberg, Ger.
81/F5 Rheinwaldhorn (peak), Swi.
142/D3 Rhemiles (well), Alg.
66/C5 Rhenen, Neth.
142/D3 Rheris, Oued (dry riv.), Mor.
72/C2 Rhin (riv.), Ger.
80/D1 Rhinau, Fr.
199/K4 Rhinebeck, NY,US
67/E5 Rhine-Herne (can.), Ger.
183/L2 Rhineland, Sk,Can
193/J4 Rhineland, Mo,US
193/K1 Rhinelander, Wi,US
69/F3 Rhineland-Palatinate (state), Ger.
64/D3 Rhine (Rhein) (riv.), Eur.
72/C2 Rhinkanal (can.), Ger.
72/C2 Rhinluch (marsh), Ger.
55/H9 Rhinns (pt.), Sc,UK
153/G2 Rhino Camp, Ugan.
72/C2 Rhinow, Ger.
64/D4 Rhin (Rhine) (riv.), Fr.
141/R16 Rhiou (riv.), Alg.
142/C3 Rhir (cape), Mor.
69/D3 Rhisnes, Belg.
58/C1 Rhiw (riv.), Wal,UK
86/C1 Rho, It.
60/C3 Rhode, Ire.
208/C2 Rhode (isl.), RI,US
208/C2 Rhode Island (state), US
208/C3 Rhode Island (sound), RI,US
187/F4 Rhodes-Hayden (aqueduct), Az,US
104/B2 Rhodes (Rōdhos), Gre.
89/L3 Rhodes (Ródhos), Gre.
89/K3 Rhodes (Ródhos) (isl.), Gre.
93/F4 Rhodope (mts.), Bul.
188/K6 Rhome, Tx,US
70/D1 Rhön (mts.), Ger.
58/C3 Rhondda, Wal,UK
82/A1 Rhône (dept.), Fr.
74/F4 Rhône (riv.), Fr., Swi.
81/E4 Rhone (glac.), Swi.
80/B3 Rhône au Rhin (can.), Fr.
68/C3 Rhonelle (riv.), Fr.
57/E6 Rhosllanerchrugog, Wal,UK
58/B3 Rhossili, Wal,UK
56/E5 Rhuddlan, Wal,UK
55/H8 Rhum (isl.), Sc,UK
67/H5 Rhume (riv.), Ger.
141/V17 Rhumel (riv.), Alg.
78/C6 Rhuys (pen.), Fr.
58/C2 Rhyddhywel (mtn.), Wal,UK
58/B2 Rhydowen, Wal,UK
56/E5 Rhyl, Wal,UK
58/C3 Rhymney, Wal,UK
54/D2 Rhynie, Sc,UK
186/D2 Rhyolite, Nv,US
152/B2 Riaba, EqG.
83/C6 Riace, It.
167/E4 Riachão, Braz.
170/D1 Riachão das Neves, Braz.
171/F1 Riachão do Jacuípe, Braz.
171/E2 Riacho de Santana, Braz.
167/H4 Riachuelo, Braz.
175/T12 Riachuelo, Uru.
78/D6 Riaillé, Fr.
204/C2 Rialto, Ca,US
149/F3 Riangnom, Sudan
76/A1 Rianjo, Sp.
84/C3 Riano, It.
76/C1 Riaño, Sp.
78/B5 Riantec, Fr.
122/C1 Riāsi, India
124/C2 Riau (isls.), Indo.
124/C2 Riau (prov.), Indo.
76/D2 Riaza, Sp.
193/K1 Rib (mtn.), Wi,US
76/A1 Ribadavia, Sp.
76/B1 Ribadeo, Sp.
76/C1 Ribadesella, Sp.
157/H8 Riban'i Manamby (mts.), Madg.
170/B4 Ribas do Rio Pardo, Braz.
155/H2 Ribauè, Moz.
57/F4 Ribble (riv.), Eng,UK
57/F4 Ribblesdale (vall.), Eng,UK
62/C4 Ribe, Den.
62/C4 Ribe (co.), Den.
80/D1 Ribeauvillé, Fr.
68/B4 Ribécourt-Dreslincourt, Fr.
140/J10 Ribeira Brava, CpV.
142/A2 Ribeira Brava, Madr.
76/B2 Ribeira de Pena, Port.
171/F1 Ribeira do Pombal, Braz.
77/T13 Ribeira Grande, Azor.
140/J9 Ribeira Grande, CpV.
171/G1 Ribeirão, Braz.
170/D4 Ribeirão Preto, Braz.
167/E4 Ribeiro Gonçalves, Braz.
68/C4 Ribemont, Fr.
90/C4 Ribera, It.
190/B3 Ribera, NM,US
169/E3 Riberalta, Bol.
193/J1 Rib Lake, Wi,US
64/G1 Ribnitz-Damgarten, Ger.
84/B2 Ribolla, It.
183/J1 Ribstone, Ab,Can
183/J1 Ribstone (cr.), Ab,Can
71/H3 Říčany u Prahy, Czh.
164/B4 Ricaurte, Col.
85/E5 Riccia, It.
87/F5 Riccione, It.
86/C4 Ricco'del Golfo, It.
199/G2 Rice (lake), On,Can
186/E3 Rice, Ca,US
195/G5 Rice, Mn,US
189/F1 Rice, Tx,US
182/E3 Rice, Wa,US
203/H2 Riceboro, Ga,US
193/J1 Rice Lake, Wi,US
195/H4 Rice Lake Nat'l Wild. Res., Mn,US
193/H2 Riceville, Ia,US
198/F2 Rich (cape), On,Can
142/D2 Rich, Mor.
191/G3 Rich (mtn.), Ar,US
201/F3 Richard B. Russell (dam), SC,US
178/C2 Richards (isl.), NW,Can
191/G2 Richards, Mo,US
157/F3 Richard's Bay, SAfr.
191/G1 Richards-Gebaur A.F.B., Mo,US
198/D1 Richards Landing, On,Can
196/B3 Richardson (lakes), Me,US
189/F1 Richardson, Tx,US
144/B2 Richard Toll, Sen.
194/C4 Richardton, ND,US
206/C3 Richboro, Pa,US
201/G2 Rich Creek, Va,US
132/C5 Riche (cape), Austl.
66/C2 Richel (isl.), Neth.
197/P7 Richelieu, Qu,Can
199/K2 Richelieu (riv.), Qu,Can
183/M4 Richey, Mt,US
185/F2 Richfield, Id,US
195/P7 Richfield, Mn,US
208/F5 Richfield, Oh,US
206/A2 Richfield, Pa,US
185/G4 Richfield, Ut,US
199/K2 Richford, Vt,US
186/C3 Richgrove, Ca,US
56/B3 Richhill, NI,UK
191/G1 Rich Hill, Mo,US
196/E2 Richibucto, NB,Can
200/E4 Richland, Ga,US
191/H2 Richland, Mo,US
202/C1 Richland, Ms,US
206/D5 Richland, NJ,US
208/E6 Richland (co.), Oh,US
206/B3 Richland, Pa,US
189/F2 Richland, Tx,US
182/E4 Richland, Wa,US
201/F3 Richland Balsam (peak), NC,US
193/J2 Richland Center, Wi,US
189/F2 Richland Creek (res.), Tx,US
188/K7 Richland Hills, Tx,US
200/B4 Richland (Plain), Ms,US
201/J3 Richlands, NC,US
201/G2 Richlands, Va,US
188/E2 Richland Springs, Tx,US
206/C3 Richlandtown, Pa,US
134/A3 Richmond, Austl.
135/D2 Richmond, Austl.
182/C3 Richmond, BC,Can
196/A3 Richmond, Qu,Can
136/C3 Richmond, N.Z.
156/C3 Richmond, SAfr.
157/E3 Richmond, SAfr.
57/G3 Richmond, Eng,UK
191/G4 Richmond, Ar,US
205/K11 Richmond, Ca,US
205/P15 Richmond, Il,US
198/D5 Richmond, In,US
191/G1 Richmond, Ks,US
200/E2 Richmond, Ky,US
202/C1 Richmond, La,US
208/A1 Richmond, Ma,US
205/G6 Richmond, Mi,US
195/G5 Richmond, Mn,US
191/H1 Richmond, Mo,US
208/G7 Richmond, Oh,US
189/G3 Richmond, Tx,US
185/H3 Richmond, Ut,US
201/J2 Richmond (cap.), Va,US
199/K2 Richmond, Vt,US
205/C2 Richmond Beach-Innis Arden, Wa,US
198/E5 Richmond Dale, Oh,US
202/P8 Richmond Heights, Fl,US
208/F4 Richmond Heights, Oh,US
199/G3 Richmond Hill, On,Can
201/G5 Richmond Hill, Ga,US
201/J2 Richmond Nat'l Bfld. Park, Va,US
134/G8 Richmond-Raaf, Austl.
207/D2 Richmond (Staten Island) (co.), NY,US
207/J9 Richmond Town, NY,US
53/N7 Richmond upon Thames (bor.), Eng,UK
199/J3 Richmondville, NY,US
183/K2 Richmound, Sk,Can
201/J2 Rich Square, NC,US
81/E3 Richterswil, Swi.
192/B3 Richthofen (mtn.), Co,US
202/D2 Richton, Ms,US
193/L3 Richton Park, Il,US
199/J2 Richville, NY,US
80/D2 Richwiller, Fr.
189/H1 Richwood, La,US
198/E4 Richwood, Oh,US
189/G3 Richwood, Tx,US
201/G1 Richwood, WV,US
191/J1 Richwoods, Mo,US
80/D2 Rickenbach, Ger.
198/E5 Rickenbacker Air Nat'l Guard Base, Oh,US
200/E2 Rickman, Tn,US
53/M7 Rickmansworth, Eng,UK
76/E2 Ricla, Sp.
187/H2 Rico, Co,US
92/E1 Ricse, Hun.
150/C2 Ridā', Yem.
66/B5 Ridderkerk, Neth.
184/E2 Riddle, Id,US
184/B2 Riddle, Or,US
199/H2 Rideau (lake), On,Can
199/J2 Rideau (riv.), On,Can
194/B5 Ridge, Mt,US
186/D3 Ridgecrest, Ca,US
202/C2 Ridgecrest, La,US
198/C5 Ridge Farm, Il,US
208/A3 Ridgefield, Ct,US
207/J8 Ridgefield, NJ,US
182/C5 Ridgefield, Wa,US
182/C5 Ridgefield Nat'l Wild. Ref., Wa,US
207/J8 Ridgefield Park, NJ,US
200/B4 Ridgeland, Ms,US
201/G4 Ridgeland, SC,US
206/C6 Ridgely, Md,US
200/C2 Ridgely, Tn,US
203/G3 Ridge Manor, Fl,US
201/G4 Ridge Spring, SC,US
198/F3 Ridgetown, On,Can
201/G4 Ridgeville, SC,US
193/H3 Ridgeway, Mo,US
201/H2 Ridgeway, Va,US
207/D2 Ridgewood, NJ,US
207/K9 Ridgewood, NY,US
185/K4 Ridgway, Co,US
199/G4 Ridgway, Pa,US
194/D2 Riding (mtn.), Mb,Can
57/G2 Riding Mill, Eng,UK
178/F3 Riding Mtn. Nat'l Park, Mb,Can
194/D2 Riding Mtn. Nat'l Park, Mb,Can
54/D6 Ridlees Cairn (hill), Eng,UK
206/C4 Ridley (cr.), Pa,US
164/D3 Riecito (riv.), Col., Ven.
78/B5 Riec-sur-Belon, Fr.
67/F3 Riede, Ger.
71/E5 Riedenburg, Ger.
71/G6 Ried im Innkreis, Aus.
71/H6 Ried im Traunkreis, Aus.
80/D2 Riedisheim, Fr.
70/C6 Riedlingen, Ger.
69/F5 Riegelsberg, Ger.
206/C2 Riegelsville, Pa,US
81/H2 Riegsee (lake), Ger.
80/D2 Riehen, Swi.
71/E6 Riem (Munich) (int'l arpt.), Ger.
69/E2 Riemst, Belg.
70/C2 Rieneck, Ger.
200/C3 Rienzi, Ms,US
72/D5 Riesa, Ger.
69/G5 Rieschweiler-Mühlbach, Ger.
175/J8 Riesco (isl.), Chile
87/E1 Riese Pio X, It.
156/D3 Riet (riv.), SAfr.
63/J4 Rietavas, Lith.
67/F5 Rietberg, Ger.
156/C4 Rietbron, SAfr.
154/D4 Rietfontein (dry riv.), Bots., Namb.
154/D4 Rietfontein, Namb.
84/C3 Rieti, It.
84/C3 Rieti (prov.), It.
72/C3 Rietzer (lake), Ger.
57/G3 Rievaulx, Eng,UK
82/C5 Riez, Fr.
88/B4 Rif, Er (mts.), Mor.
182/C4 Riffe (lake), Wa,US
185/K4 Rifle, Co,US
61/N6 Rifsnes (pt.), Ice.
151/A1 Rift Valley (prov.), Kenya
63/K3 Riga (gulf), Est., Lat.
145/G4 Rigacikun, Nga.
63/L3 Riga (Rīga) (cap.), Lat.
185/H2 Rigby, Id,US
107/H2 Rīgestan (reg.), Afg.
184/E1 Riggins, Id,US
80/D4 Riggisberg, Swi.
81/E3 Rigi (peak), Swi.
84/C3 Rignano Flaminio, It.
85/F4 Rignano Garganico, It.
87/E5 Rignano sull'Arno, It.
179/L3 Rigolet, Nf,Can
148/B2 Rig Rig, Chad
54/C5 Rigside, Sc,UK
63/K2 Riguldi, Est.
120/D3 Rihand (dam), India
120/D4 Rihand (riv.), India
120/D3 Rihand Sāgar (res.), India
63/L1 Riihimäki, Fin.
137/C Riiser-Larsen (pen.), Ant.
137/Y Riiser-Larsen Ice Shelf, Ant.
61/J2 Riisitunturin Nat'l Park, Fin.
92/B3 Rijeka, Cro.
66/B5 Rijen, Neth.
66/B4 Rijnsburg, Neth.
66/B5 Rijsbergen, Neth.
66/D4 Rijssen, Neth.
66/B4 Rijswijk, Neth.
207/K8 Rikers (isl.), NY,US
139/M7 Rikitea, FrPol.
112/C4 Rikuchū-Kaigan Nat'l Park, Japan
112/B4 Rikuzentakata, Japan
93/F4 Rila, Bul.
93/F4 Rila (mts.), Bul.
191/F1 Riley, Ks,US
184/D2 Riley, Or,US
196/D2 Riley Brook, NB,Can
80/A6 Rillieux-la-Pape, Fr.
187/G4 Rillito, Az,US
91/H1 Rilski Manastir, Bul.
139/K7 Rimatara (isl.), FrPol.
65/L4 Rimavská Sobota, Slvk.
106/D3 Rīma, Wādi (dry riv.), SAr.
70/B3 Rimbach, Ger.
183/G1 Rimbey, Ab,Can
148/C2 Rimé, Ouadi (dry riv.), Chad
199/G4 Rimersburg, Pa,US
62/F2 Rimforsa, Swe.
87/F4 Rimini, It.
93/H3 Rîmnicu Sărat, Rom.
93/G3 Rîmnicu Vîlcea, Rom.
68/D4 Rimogne, Fr.
196/C1 Rimouski, Qu,Can
196/C1 Rimouski (riv.), Qu,Can
196/C1 Rimouski-Est, Qu,Can
70/C3 Rimpar, Ger.
80/D5 Rimpfischhorn (peak), Swi.
136/H9 Rimutaka (range), N.Z.
136/J9 Rimutaka Forest Park, N.Z.
91/F2 Rinas (int'l arpt.), Alb.
121/G1 Rinbung, China
108/D1 Rinchinlhümbe, Mong.
71/G5 Rinchnach, Ger.
172/C3 Rincón (peak), Arg.
172/C1 Rincón (salt pan), Chile
161/F4 Rincón (pt.), Pan.
175/G2 Rincón, Uru.
187/G4 Rincon (peak), Az,US
201/G4 Rincon, Ga,US
187/J4 Rincon, NM,US
172/C2 Rinconada, Arg.
76/C4 Rincón de la Victoria, Sp.
161/E4 Rincón de la Vieja Nat'l Park, CR
158/E4 Rincón de Romos, Mex.
199/K3 Rindge, NH,US
63/S7 Rindö (isl.), Swe.
135/C4 Ringarooma, Austl.
60/B6 Ringaskiddy, Ire.
56/C3 Ringboy (pt.), NI,UK
62/D1 Ringebu, Nor.
81/F4 Ringelspitz (peak), Swi.
200/E3 Ringgold, Ga,US
202/B1 Ringgold, La,US
145/H3 Ringim, Nga.
62/C3 Ringkøbing, Den.
62/B3 Ringkøbing (co.), Den.
62/B3 Ringkøbing Fjord (lag.), Den.
183/J4 Ringling, Mt,US
191/F3 Ringling, Ok,US
203/G4 Ringling Museum, Fl,US
59/G5 Ringmer, Eng,UK
206/D3 Ringoes, NJ,US
191/G3 Ringold, Ok,US
56/B1 Ringsend, NI,UK
62/D4 Ringsted, Den.
206/B2 Ringtown, Pa,US
66/B4 Ringvaart (can.), Neth.
61/F1 Ringvassøy (isl.), Nor.
57/F5 Ringway (Manchester) (int'l arpt.), Eng,UK
133/G2 Ringwood, Austl.
59/E5 Ringwood, Eng,UK
207/D1 Ringwood, NJ,US
207/J7 Ringwood St. Park, NJ,US
91/J4 Rínia (isl.), Gre.
174/B3 Riñihue, Chile
56/C2 Rinns, The (pen.), Sc,UK
67/G4 Rinteln, Ger.
68/A2 Rinxent, Fr.
202/D2 Rio, La,US
168/B2 Río Abiseo Nat'l Park, Peru
173/G3 Rio Azul, Braz.
164/B5 Riobamba, Ecu.
168/D5 Río Blanco, Bol.
174/Q9 Río Blanco, Chile
160/B2 Río Blanco, Mex.
185/K4 Rio Blanco, Co,US
171/P7 Rio Bonito, Braz.
170/B4 Rio Branco, Braz.
175/G2 Rio Branco, Uru.
173/G3 Rio Branco do Sul, Braz.
170/B4 Rio Brilhante, Braz.
174/B4 Río Bueno, Chile
161/G1 Río Cauto, Cuba
172/C4 Río Ceballos, Arg.
175/K7 Río Chico, Arg.
175/T12 Riochuelo, Uru.
174/C2 Río Clarillo Nat'l Park, Chile
169/G5 Rio Claro, Braz.
170/D4 Rio Claro, Braz.
162/F5 Rio Claro, Trin.
174/D3 Río Colorado, Arg.
174/D2 Río Cuarto, Arg.
171/E2 Rio de Contas, Braz.
171/E4 Rio de Janeiro, Braz.
171/E4 Rio de Janeiro (state), Braz.
184/A3 Rio Dell, Ca,US
173/G3 Rio do Sul, Braz.
160/D3 Río Dulce Nat'l Park, Guat.
77/Q10 Rio Frio, Port.
175/K7 Río Gallegos, Arg.
175/L8 Río Grande, Arg.
173/F5 Rio Grande, Braz.
158/E4 Río Grande, Mex.
180/G6 Rio Grande (riv.), Mex. US
190/A2 Rio Grande (can.), Co,US
206/D5 Rio Grande, NJ,US
201/F1 Rio Grande, Oh,US
159/F3 Rio Grande (plain), Tx,US
189/E4 Rio Grande City, Tx,US
171/K8 Rio Grande da Serra, Braz.
167/G4 Rio Grande do Norte (state), Braz.
167/F4 Rio Grande do Piauí, Braz.
173/F3 Rio Grande do Sul (state), Braz.
189/F4 Rio Grande Valley (int'l arpt.), Tx,US
188/C3 Rio Grande Village, Tx,US
164/C2 Riohacha, Col.
161/F4 Río Hato, Pan.
159/F3 Rio Hondo, Tx,US
168/B2 Rioja, Peru
166/A3 Rio Jaú Nat'l Park, Braz.
159/H4 Río Lagartos, Mex.
171/G1 Rio Largo, Braz.
87/E4 Riolo Terme, It.
74/E4 Riom, Fr.
86/C4 Riomaggiore, It.
76/A3 Rio Maior, Port.
84/A2 Rio Marina, It.
174/C5 Río Mayo, Arg.
74/E4 Riom-ès-Montagne, Fr.
152/B2 Rio Muni (pol. reg.), EqG.
182/F3 Riondel, BC,Can
74/C5 Rion-des-Landes, Fr.
173/G3 Rio Negrinho, Braz.
174/C4 Río Negro (prov.), Arg.
173/E1 Rio Negro, Braz.
173/F1 Rio Negro, Braz.
174/B4 Río Negro, Chile
164/C3 Rionegro, Col.
175/T11 Río Negro (dept.), Uru.
175/F2 Río Negro (res.), Uru.
85/F6 Rionero in Vulture, It.
85/E4 Rionero Sannitico, It.
173/F4 Rio Pardo, Braz.
172/E2 Río Pilcomayo Nat'l Park, Arg.
190/A3 Rio Rancho, NM,US
171/F1 Rio Real, Braz.
74/F3 Riorges, Fr.
76/B2 Ríos, Sp.
172/C3 Río Salago, Desagües del (swamp), Arg.
87/D3 Rio Saliceto, It.
172/C3 Río Salvage (marsh), Arg.
174/E1 Río Segundo, Arg.
174/B5 Río Simpson Nat'l Park, Chile
164/B3 Riosucio, Col.
164/C3 Riosucio, Col.
175/S11 Río Tala, Arg.
174/D2 Río Tercero, Arg.
164/B5 Río Tigre, Ecu.
167/H4 Rio Tinto, Braz.
82/B6 Riou (isl.), Fr.
170/C3 Rio Verde, Braz.
175/K8 Río Verde, Chile
159/F4 Ríoverde, Mex.
170/B3 Rio Verde de Mato Grosso, Braz.
205/L10 Rio Vista, Ca,US
189/F1 Rio Vista, Tx,US
80/C3 Rioz, Fr.
169/E2 Riozinho (riv.), Braz.
85/E4 Ripalimosano, It.
84/A2 Ripalti, Punta dei (pt.), It.
92/E3 Ripanj, Yugo.
86/D6 Riparbella, It.
84/C3 Ripa Sottile (lake), It.
85/D2 Ripatransone, It.
53/M8 Ripley, Eng,UK
186/E4 Ripley, Ca,US
200/C3 Ripley, Ms,US
200/F1 Ripley, Oh,US
191/F2 Ripley, Ok,US
200/C3 Ripley, Tn,US
201/G1 Ripley, WV,US
77/G1 Ripoll, Sp.
77/L6 Ripoll (riv.), Sp.
77/L6 Ripollet, Sp.
199/J2 Ripon, Qu,Can
57/G3 Ripon, Eng,UK
186/B2 Ripon, Ca,US
193/K2 Ripon, Wi,US
90/D4 Riposto, It.
196/D3 Ripples, NB,Can
199/H5 Rippon, WV,US
57/G4 Ripponden, Eng,UK
207/L7 Rippowam (riv.), Ct,US
120/D2 Riri Bāzār, Nepal
167/K6 Risaralda, Col.
164/C2 Risaralda (dept.), Col.
153/F3 Risasi, Zaire
58/C3 Risca, Wal,UK
112/B1 Rishiri, Japan
112/B1 Rishiri (isl.), Japan
112/B1 Rishiri-Rebun-Sarobetsu Nat'l Park, Japan
103/D4 Rishon LeZiyyon, Isr.
188/E1 Rising Star, Tx,US

198/D5 **Rising Sun,** In,US
206/B4 **Rising Sun,** Md,US
206/C5 **Rising Sun-Lebanon,** De,US
182/C2 **Riske Creek,** BC,Can
79/F2 **Risle** (riv.), Fr.
206/D5 **Risley** (Estell Manor), NJ,US
92/B3 **Risnjak** (peak), Cro.
92/B3 **Risnjak Nat'l Park,** Cro.
93/G3 **Rîşnov,** Rom.
191/H4 **Rison,** Ar,US
62/C2 **Risør,** Nor.
53/T11 **Ris-Orangis,** Fr.
82/C3 **Risoul,** Fr.
81/F1 **Riss** (riv.), Ger.
80/C5 **Risse** (riv.), Fr.
63/L2 **Risti,** Est.
63/M1 **Ristiina,** Fin.
190/C1 **Rita Blanca** (cr.), Tx,US
190/C2 **Rita Blanca Nat'l Grsld.,** Ok, Tx,US
164/C3 **Ritacuba** (peak), Col.
138/C2 **Ritaiō** (isl.), Japan
156/D3 **Ritchie,** SAfr.
187/H3 **Rito** (cr.), NM,US
87/E5 **Ritoio, Monte** (peak), It.
67/F2 **Ritterhude,** Ger.
208/F6 **Rittman,** Oh,US
111/L9 **Rittō,** Japan
182/E4 **Ritzville,** Wa,US
87/D1 **Riva,** It.
172/B4 **Rivadavia,** Arg.
172/D3 **Rivadavia,** Arg.
174/E2 **Rivadavia,** Arg.
82/B2 **Rival** (riv.), Fr.
86/A5 **Riva Ligure,** It.
86/D2 **Rivalta,** It.
86/C3 **Rivanazzano,** It.
201/H2 **Rivanna** (riv.), Va,US
158/D2 **Riva Palacio,** Mex.
86/A3 **Riva Pressơ Chieri,** It.
86/A2 **Rivara,** It.
86/A2 **Rivarolo Canavese,** It.
86/D2 **Rivarolo Mantovano,** It.
160/E4 **Rivas,** Nic.
81/E6 **Riva San Vitale,** Swi.
105/J3 **Rīvash,** Iran
82/A1 **Rive-de-Gier,** Fr.
174/E3 **Rivera,** Arg.
174/B5 **Rivera** (isl.), Chile
81/E5 **Rivera,** Swi.
173/F4 **Rivera,** Uru.
173/F3 **Rivera** (dept.), Uru.
186/B2 **Riverbank,** Ca,US
197/G3 **River Bourgeois,** NS,Can
144/C5 **River Cess,** Libr.
186/C2 **Riverdale,** Ca,US
200/E4 **Riverdale,** Ga,US
194/D4 **Riverdale,** ND,US
207/H8 **Riverdale,** NJ,US
207/K8 **Riverdale,** NY,US
197/G3 **River Denys,** NS,Can
207/J8 **River Edge,** NJ,US
202/E2 **River Falls,** Al,US
193/H1 **River Falls,** Wi,US
86/C3 **Rivergaro,** It.
207/F2 **Riverhead,** NY,US
196/E3 **River Hébert,** NS,Can
194/A2 **Riverhurst,** Sk,Can
129/H7 **Riverina** (reg.), Austl.
196/F3 **River John,** NS,Can
188/K7 **River Oaks,** Tx,US
196/E3 **Riverport,** NS,Can
205/F7 **River Rouge,** Mi,US
194/D2 **Rivers,** Mb,Can
145/G5 **Rivers** (state), Nga.
156/C4 **Riversdale,** SAfr.
204/C3 **Riverside,** Ca,US
204/C3 **Riverside** (co.), Ca,US
192/B3 **Riverside** (can.), Co,US
206/D3 **Riverside,** NJ,US
184/D2 **Riverside,** Or,US
206/B2 **Riverside,** Pa,US
189/G2 **Riverside,** Tx,US
185/K3 **Riverside,** Wy,US
196/E3 **Riverside-Albert,** NB,Can
134/G8 **Riverstone,** Austl.
60/B1 **Riverstown,** Ire.
60/B6 **Riverstown,** Ire.
133/H5 **Riverton,** Austl.
194/F2 **Riverton,** Can
197/F3 **Riverton,** NS,Can
136/A4 **Riverton,** N.Z.
185/H3 **Riverton,** Ut,US
199/G5 **Riverton,** Va,US
185/J2 **Riverton,** Wy,US
207/J8 **River Vale,** NJ,US
196/E2 **Riverview,** NB,Can
202/L8 **Riverview,** Fl,US
205/F7 **Riverview,** Mi,US
205/Q15 **Riverwoods,** Il,US
68/A4 **Rivery,** Fr.
82/B2 **Rives,** Fr.
186/E3 **Riviera,** Az,US
189/F4 **Riviera,** Tx,US
203/H4 **Riviera Beach,** Fl,US
206/B5 **Riviera Beach,** Md,US
196/A2 **Rivière-à-Pierre,** Qu,Can
196/E1 **Rivière-au-Renard,** Qu,Can
196/C2 **Rivière-Bleue,** Qu,Can
196/C2 **Rivière-du-Loup,** Qu,Can
196/B1 **Rivière-Éternité,** Qu,Can
156/L11 **Riviersonder-endreeks** (mts.), SAfr.
87/G1 **Rivignano,** It.
86/A2 **Rivoli,** It.
86/C2 **Rivolta d'Adda,** It.
68/D2 **Rixensart,** Belg.
199/G4 **Rixford,** Pa,US
80/D2 **Rixheim,** Fr.
1[illegible]/E4 **Riyadh** (Ar Riyāḑ) (cap.), SAr.
103/E3 **Rīyāq,** Leb.
125/C2 **Rizal,** Phil.
125/E6 **Rizal Park,** Phil.
104/E1 **Rize,** Turk.
104/E1 **Rize** (prov.), Turk.
115/D4 **Rizhao,** China
103/D2 **Rizokarpasso,** Cyp.
83/B6 **Rizziconi,** It.
83/D5 **Rizzuto** (cape), It.
62/C2 **Rjukan,** Nor.
144/B2 **Rkîz,** Mrta.
144/B2 **Rkîz** (lake), Mrta.
62/D1 **Roa,** Nor.
76/D2 **Roa,** Sp.
59/F2 **Roade,** Eng,UK
54/D3 **Roadside,** Sc,UK
162/E3 **Road Town** (cap.), BVI
185/J4 **Roan** (plat.), Co, Ut,US
57/F1 **Roan Fell** (hill), Sc,UK
201/F2 **Roan High** (peak), NC,US
74/F3 **Roanne,** Fr.
82/B3 **Roanne** (riv.), Fr.
200/E4 **Roanoke,** Al,US
201/J3 **Roanoke** (riv.), NC, Va,US
207/F2 **Roanoke** (pt.), NY,US
188/K6 **Roanoke,** Tx,US
201/H2 **Roanoke,** Va,US
201/J2 **Roanoke Rapids,** NC,US
189/G2 **Roans Prairie,** Tx,US
206/B2 **Roaring** (cr.), Pa,US
199/H4 **Roaring Branch,** Pa,US
190/A1 **Roaring Fork** (riv.), Co,US
190/D4 **Roaring Springs,** Tx,US
160/E2 **Roatán,** Hon.
160/E2 **Roatán** (isl.), Hon.
200/D2 **Robards,** Ky,US
86/A2 **Robassomero,** It.
105/J3 **Robāţ-e Khān,** Iran
105/J3 **Robāţ-e Sang,** Iran
105/G3 **Robāţ Karīm,** Iran
182/F1 **Robb,** Ab,Can
86/C1 **Robbiate,** It.
135/C4 **Robbins** (isl.), Austl.
201/H3 **Robbins,** NC,US
196/D3 **Robbinston,** Me,US
200/F3 **Robbinsville,** NC,US
86/B2 **Robbio,** It.
135/A3 **Robe,** Austl.
133/J4 **Robe** (peak), Austl.
150/A4 **Robē,** Eth.
150/B4 **Robē,** Eth.
60/A2 **Robe** (riv.), Ire.
86/B1 **Robecchetto con Induno,** It.
86/D2 **Robecco d'Oglia,** It.
62/E4 **Röbel,** Ger.
201/J3 **Robersonville,** NC,US
80/B5 **Robert** (mtn.), Fr.
200/E4 **Roberta,** Ga,US
69/E6 **Robert-Espagne,** Fr.
188/D2 **Robert Lee,** Tx,US
164/B4 **Roberto Payán,** Col.
198/E2 **Roberts** (cape), On,Can
177/E4 **Roberts** (mtn.), Ak,US
185/G2 **Roberts,** Id,US
198/B4 **Roberts,** Il,US
185/J1 **Roberts,** Mt,US
59/G5 **Robertsbridge,** Eng,UK
182/C3 **Roberts Creek,** BC,Can
184/E4 **Roberts Creek** (mtn.), Nv,US
61/G2 **Robertsfors,** Swe.
120/D3 **Robertsganj,** India
191/G3 **Robert S. Kerr** (lake), Ok,US
144/C5 **Roberts** (Monrovia) (int'l arpt.), Libr.
156/B4 **Robertson,** SAfr.
185/H3 **Robertson,** Wy,US
144/C5 **Robertsport,** Libr.
60/D3 **Robertstown,** Ire.
208/F6 **Robertsville,** Oh,US
196/A1 **Roberval,** Qu,Can
206/B3 **Robesonia,** Pa,US
86/A4 **Robilante,** It.
201/G2 **Robinette-Amhertsdale,** WV,US
57/H3 **Robin Hood's Bay,** Eng,UK
201/F4 **Robins A.F.B.,** Ga,US
132/C3 **Robinson** (ranges), Austl.
198/C5 **Robinson,** Il,US
182/G3 **Robinson** (mtn.), Mt,US
189/F2 **Robinson,** Tx,US
205/C3 **Robinson** (pt.), Wa,US
163/B6 **Robinson Crusoe** (isl.), Chile
134/C4 **Robinson Gorge Nat'l Park,** Austl.
131/E4 **Robinson River,** Austl.
131/H2 **Robinson River,** PNG
131/E4 **Robinson River Abor. Land,** Austl.
200/D4 **Robinson Springs,** Al,US
133/J5 **Robinvale,** Austl.
82/B5 **Robion,** Fr.
187/J4 **Robledo** (mtn.), NM,US
164/C2 **Robles,** Col.
178/F3 **Roblin,** Mb,Can
72/B5 **Röblingen am See,** Ger.
172/E1 **Roboré,** Bol.
183/K3 **Robsart,** Sk,Can
182/E1 **Robson** (mtn.), BC,Can
189/F4 **Robstown,** Tx,US
191/H2 **Roby,** Mo,US
188/D1 **Roby,** Tx,US
76/A3 **Roca, Cabo da** (cape), Port.
164/A5 **Rocafuerte,** Ecu.
74/D4 **Rocamadour,** Fr.
194/D2 **Rocanville,** Sk,Can
158/B5 **Roca Partida** (isl.), Mex.
159/G5 **Roca Partida, Punta** (pt.), Mex.
167/H3 **Rocas** (isls.), Braz.
83/C4 **Roccabernarda,** It.
86/D2 **Roccabianca,** It.
83/B2 **Roccadaspide,** It.
85/D3 **Rocca di Mezzo,** It.
83/D4 **Rocca di Neto,** It.
84/C4 **Rocca di Papa,** It.
84/D4 **Roccagorga,** It.
83/C2 **Rocca Imperiale,** It.
83/B7 **Roccalumera,** It.
85/E4 **Roccamandolfi,** It.
85/D5 **Roccamonfina,** It.
83/C2 **Roccanova,** It.
85/E6 **Roccarainola,** It.
84/C3 **Rocca Romana, Monte di** (peak), It.
87/E4 **Rocca San Casciano,** It.
85/D4 **Roccasecca,** It.
84/B2 **Roccastrada,** It.
86/A4 **Roccavione,** It.
83/C6 **Roccella Ionica,** It.
83/C5 **Roccelletta del Vescovo di Squillace** (ruins), It.
85/F5 **Rocchetta Sant'Antonio,** It.
82/D2 **Rocciamelone** (peak), It.
74/E5 **Roc de France** (mtn.), Fr.
80/D1 **Roc du Haut du Faite** (mtn.), Fr.
175/G2 **Rocha,** Uru.
175/G2 **Rocha** (dept.), Uru.
166/C1 **Rochambeau** (int'l arpt.), FrG.
57/F4 **Rochdale,** Eng,UK
80/C5 **Roche,** Swi.
58/B6 **Roche,** Eng,UK
82/C3 **Rocheaire, Pic de** (peak), Fr.
82/C3 **Rochebrune, Pic de** (peak), Fr.
79/F6 **Rochecorbon,** Fr.
69/E3 **Rochefort,** Belg.
74/C4 **Rochefort,** Fr.
78/C5 **Rochefort-en-Terre,** Fr.
79/E6 **Rochefort-sur-Loire,** Fr.
80/C3 **Roche-lez-Beaupré,** Fr.
201/F5 **Rochelle,** Ga,US
193/K3 **Rochelle,** Il,US
188/E2 **Rochelle,** Tx,US
207/J8 **Rochelle Park,** NJ,US
82/A3 **Rochemaure,** Fr.
82/B4 **Rocher-Garaux** (mtn.), Fr.
77/J1 **Roches Blanches** (mtn.), Fr.
135/C3 **Rochester,** Austl.
59/G4 **Rochester,** Eng,UK
193/K4 **Rochester,** Il,US
198/C4 **Rochester,** In,US
200/D2 **Rochester,** Ky,US
208/D2 **Rochester,** Ma,US
205/F6 **Rochester,** Mi,US
193/H1 **Rochester,** Mn,US
199/L3 **Rochester,** NH,US
199/H3 **Rochester,** NY,US
208/E5 **Rochester,** Oh,US
208/G6 **Rochester,** Pa,US
199/K3 **Rochester,** Vt,US
205/P14 **Rochester,** Wi,US
205/F6 **Rochester Hills,** Mi,US
59/G3 **Rochford,** Eng,UK
60/C3 **Rochfortbridge,** Ire.
72/C5 **Rochlitz,** Ger.
190/B3 **Rociada,** NM,US
183/L3 **Rock** (cr.), Sk,Can, Mt,US
193/F2 **Rock** (riv.), Ia, Mn,US
193/K3 **Rock** (riv.), Il, Wi,US
208/D2 **Rock,** Ma,US
198/C1 **Rock,** Mi,US
194/E3 **Rock** (lake), ND,US
184/E3 **Rock** (cr.), Nv,US
184/C1 **Rock** (cr.), Or,US
192/F2 **Rock** (cr.), SD,US
182/F4 **Rock** (cr.), Wa,US
192/A3 **Rock** (cr.), Wy,US
206/D2 **Rockaway,** NJ,US
207/H8 **Rockaway** (riv.), NJ,US
207/K9 **Rockaway** (inlet), NY,US
207/K9 **Rockaway** (pt.), NY,US
184/B1 **Rockaway Beach** (Rockaway), Or,US
207/K9 **Rockaway Park,** NY,US
184/B1 **Rockaway** (Rockaway Beach), Or,US
203/F2 **Rock Bluff,** Fl,US
201/G1 **Rock Cave,** WV,US
60/C1 **Rockcorry,** Ire.
177/L3 **Rock Creek,** Yk,Can
193/H1 **Rock Creek,** Mn,US
134/H8 **Rockdale,** Austl.
201/M7 **Rockdale** (co.), Ga,US
205/P16 **Rockdale,** Il,US
189/F2 **Rockdale,** Tx,US
137/R **Rockefeller** (plat.), Ant.
69/G4 **Rockenhausen,** Ger.
188/L7 **Rockett,** Tx,US
193/K3 **Rock Falls,** Il,US
193/J1 **Rock Falls,** Wi,US
200/D2 **Rockfield,** Ky,US
200/D4 **Rockford,** Al,US
193/K2 **Rockford,** Il,US
198/D4 **Rockford,** Oh,US
182/F4 **Rockford,** Wa,US
196/B3 **Rock Forest,** Qu,Can
194/B3 **Rockglen,** Sk,Can
206/B2 **Rock Glen,** Pa,US
206/B5 **Rock Hall,** Md,US
134/C3 **Rockhampton,** Austl.
130/D4 **Rockhampton Downs,** Austl.
201/G3 **Rock Hill,** SC,US
188/L6 **Rockhill,** Tx,US
132/B5 **Rockingham,** Austl.
201/H3 **Rockingham,** NC,US
199/K3 **Rockingham,** Vt,US
193/J3 **Rock Island,** Il,US
189/F3 **Rock Island,** Tx,US
199/J2 **Rockland,** On,Can
185/G2 **Rockland,** Id,US
208/D1 **Rockland,** Ma,US
196/C3 **Rockland,** Me,US
207/D1 **Rockland** (co.), NY,US
189/G2 **Rockland,** Tx,US
207/K7 **Rockland Lake,** NY,US
135/B3 **Rocklands** (res.), Austl.
203/H3 **Rockledge,** Fl,US
206/C3 **Rockledge,** Pa,US
184/C4 **Rocklin,** Ca,US
200/E3 **Rockmart,** Ga,US
200/E4 **Rock Mills,** Al,US
191/H3 **Rockport,** Ar,US
184/B4 **Rockport,** Ca,US
200/D2 **Rockport,** In,US
200/D2 **Rockport,** Ky,US
193/G3 **Rock Port,** Mo,US
202/C2 **Rockport,** Ms,US
189/F3 **Rockport,** Tx,US
182/D3 **Rockport,** Wa,US
193/F2 **Rock Rapids,** Ia,US
185/L3 **Rock River,** Wy,US
136/C3 **Rocks** (pt.), N.Z.
206/B4 **Rocks,** Md,US
162/B1 **Rock Sound,** Bahm.
183/L4 **Rock Springs,** Mt,US
188/D2 **Rocksprings,** Tx,US
185/J3 **Rock Springs,** Wy,US
165/G3 **Rockstone,** Guy.
135/C2 **Rock, The,** Austl.
198/B3 **Rockton,** Il,US
192/B4 **Rockvale,** Co,US
193/F2 **Rock Valley,** Ia,US
196/D4 **Rockville,** NS,Can
198/C5 **Rockville,** In,US
206/A5 **Rockville,** Md,US
208/C2 **Rockville,** RI,US
187/F2 **Rockville,** Ut,US
207/E2 **Rockville Centre,** NY,US
189/F1 **Rockwall,** Tx,US
188/L7 **Rockwall** (co.), Tx,US
193/H2 **Rockwell,** Ia,US
208/F5 **Rockwell** (lake), Oh,US
193/G2 **Rockwell City,** Ia,US
197/Q8 **Rockwood,** On,Can
196/C3 **Rockwood,** Me,US
200/E3 **Rockwood,** Tn,US
159/F2 **Rockwood,** Tx,US
130/C2 **Rocky** (pt.), Austl.
160/D2 **Rocky** (pt.), Belz.
176/E4 **Rocky** (mts.), NAm.
154/B3 **Rocky** (pt.), Namb.
200/F2 **Rocky** (mtn.), Ky,US
201/G3 **Rocky** (riv.), NC,US
188/B1 **Rocky** (dam), NM,US
207/F1 **Rocky** (pt.), NY,US
190/E3 **Rocky,** Ok,US
183/K3 **Rocky Boys Ind. Res.,** Mt,US
135/C4 **Rocky Cape Nat'l Park,** Austl.
183/H2 **Rockyford,** Ab,Can
192/C4 **Rocky Ford,** Co,US
201/G4 **Rocky Ford,** Ga,US
198/E5 **Rocky Fork** (lake), Oh,US
208/B2 **Rocky Hill,** Ct,US
198/E1 **Rocky Island** (lake), On,Can
191/H1 **Rocky Mount,** Mo,US
201/J3 **Rocky Mount,** NC,US
201/H2 **Rocky Mount,** Va,US
190/B1 **Rocky Mountain Arsenal,** Co,US
182/G1 **Rocky Mountain House,** Ab,Can
180/E3 **Rocky Mountain Nat'l Park,** US
192/A3 **Rocky Mountain Nat'l Park,** Co,US
201/J3 **Rocky Point,** NC,US
207/F2 **Rocky Point,** NY,US
192/B1 **Rockypoint,** Wy,US
182/D4 **Rocky Reach** (dam), Wa,US
208/F5 **Rocky River,** Oh,US
208/F5 **Rocky, West Branch** (riv.), Oh,US
68/D4 **Rocroi,** Fr.
72/B6 **Roda** (riv.), Ger.
71/E2 **Rodach** (riv.), Ger.
70/D2 **Rodach bei Coburg,** Ger.
69/G5 **Rodalben,** Ger.
201/K3 **Rodanthe,** NC,US
190/B2 **Rodarte,** NM,US
62/C1 **Rødberg,** Nor.
62/D4 **Rødbyhavn,** Den.
62/C4 **Rødding,** Den.
58/D1 **Roden** (riv.), Eng,UK
70/C2 **Rodenbach,** Ger.
158/D3 **Rodeo,** Mex.
205/K10 **Rodeo,** Ca,US
187/H5 **Rodeo,** NM,US
72/D5 **Röderau,** Ger.
201/G2 **Roderfield,** WV,US
70/B3 **Rödermark,** Ger.
189/H1 **Rodessa,** La,US
71/F1 **Rodewisch,** Ger.
74/E4 **Rodez,** Fr.
91/H2 **Rodholívos,** Gre.
89/L3 **Ródhos** (ruins), Gre.
89/L3 **Ródhos** (Rhodes), Gre.
89/K3 **Ródhos** (Rhodes) (isl.), Gre.
85/F4 **Rodi Garganico,** It.
86/D2 **Rodigo,** It.
71/F4 **Roding,** Ger.
53/P7 **Roding** (riv.), Eng,UK
133/G3 **Rodinga** (peak), Austl.
67/F4 **Rödinghausen,** Ger.
99/J3 **Rodinskoye,** Ukr.
72/C4 **Rodleben,** Ger.
136/C2 **Rodney** (cape), N.Z.
191/J5 **Rodney,** Ms,US
92/C4 **Rodoč,** Bosn.
91/F2 **Rodonit, Kep i** (cape), Alb.
63/T9 **Rødovre,** Den.
167/F4 **Rodrigues,** Braz.
51/N6 **Rodrigues** (isl.), Mrts.
175/T12 **Rodríguez,** Uru.
62/E4 **Rødvig,** Den.
56/B2 **Roe** (riv.), NI,UK
132/C2 **Roebourne,** Austl.
130/A4 **Roebuck** (bay), Austl.
201/G3 **Roebuck,** SC,US
130/A4 **Roebuck Plains,** Austl.
155/F5 **Roedtan,** SAfr.
81/H5 **Roen** (peak), It.
66/D6 **Roer** (riv.), Neth.
66/C6 **Roermond,** Neth.
68/C2 **Roeselare,** Belg.
205/D2 **Roesiger** (lake), Wa,US
179/H2 **Roes Welcome** (sound), NW,Can
191/F3 **Roff,** Ok,US
83/B2 **Rofrano,** It.
92/C4 **Rogač,** Cro.
96/D1 **Rogachev,** Bela.
99/K2 **Rogachëvka,** Rus.
169/E4 **Rogagua** (lake), Bol.
62/A2 **Rogaland** (co.), Nor.
92/B2 **Rogaška Slatina,** Slov.
92/D4 **Rogatica,** Bosn.
98/C3 **Rogatin,** Ukr.
72/B3 **Rogätz,** Ger.
182/F2 **Rogers,** BC,Can
191/G2 **Rogers,** Ar,US
208/C2 **Rogers,** Ct,US
189/H2 **Rogers,** La,US
194/E4 **Rogers,** ND,US
208/G6 **Rogers,** Oh,US
189/F2 **Rogers,** Tx,US
201/G2 **Rogers** (mtn.), Va,US
198/E2 **Rogers City,** Mi,US
196/E2 **Rogersville,** NB,Can
200/D3 **Rogersville,** Al,US
191/H2 **Rogersville,** Mo,US
201/F2 **Rogersville,** Tn,US
208/C2 **Roger Williams Nat'l Mem.,** RI,US
83/C3 **Roggiano Gravina,** It.
80/D3 **Roggwil,** Swi.
90/A1 **Rogliano,** Fr.
83/C4 **Rogliano,** It.
87/D6 **Roglio** (riv.), It.
82/B6 **Rognac,** Fr.
61/E2 **Rognan,** Nor.
72/B1 **Rögnitz** (riv.), Ger.
80/B1 **Rognon** (riv.), Fr.
82/A5 **Rognonas,** Fr.
145/G4 **Rogo,** Nga.
169/E4 **Rogoaguado** (lake), Bol.
65/J2 **Rogoźno,** Pol.
184/A2 **Rogue** (riv.), Or,US
184/B2 **Rogue River,** Or,US
149/F4 **Rohl** (riv.), Sudan
186/A1 **Rohnert Park,** Ca,US
71/E5 **Rohr,** Ger.
73/A4 **Rohrbach bei Mattersburg,** Aus.
69/G5 **Rohrbach-lès-Bitche,** Fr.
72/B2 **Rohrberg,** Ger.
107/J3 **Rohri,** Pak.
71/E6 **Röhrmoos,** Ger.
120/A1 **Rohtak,** India
120/D3 **Rohtās,** India
191/J4 **Rohwer,** Ar,US
86/A5 **Roia** (riv.), It.
123/C2 **Roi Et,** Thai.
82/A2 **Roiffieux,** Fr.
63/L1 **Roine** (lake), Fin.
68/C4 **Roisel,** Fr.
53/T10 **Roissy,** Fr.
53/T9 **Roissy-en-France,** Fr.
72/C4 **Roitzsch,** Ger.
63/K3 **Roja,** Lat.
174/E2 **Rojas,** Arg.
159/F4 **Rojo, Cabo** (cape), Mex.
162/E3 **Rojo, Cabo** (cape), PR
151/B2 **Roka,** Kenya
124/C2 **Rokan,** Indo.
124/C2 **Rokan** (riv.), Indo.
134/A1 **Rokeby-Croll Creek Nat'l Park,** Austl.
144/C4 **Rokel** (riv.), SLeo.
63/L4 **Rokiškis,** Lith.
98/D2 **Rokitnoye,** Ukr.
112/B3 **Rokkasho,** Japan
111/L10 **Rokkō-san** (peak), Japan
124/C3 **Rokot** (cape), Indo.
71/G3 **Rokycany,** Czh.
73/A1 **Rokytná** (riv.), Czh.
80/B2 **Rolampont,** Fr.
194/F3 **Roland,** Mb,Can
193/H2 **Roland,** Ia,US
170/C4 **Rolândia,** Braz.
71/F2 **Rolava** (riv.), Czh.
62/B2 **Røldal,** Nor.
66/D3 **Rolde,** Neth.
194/E3 **Rolette,** ND,US
193/G2 **Rolfe,** Ia,US
187/F4 **Roll,** Az,US
191/J2 **Rolla,** Mo,US
194/E3 **Rolla,** ND,US
157/E2 **Rolle,** SAfr.
80/C5 **Rolle,** Swi.
205/B2 **Rollingbay,** Wa,US
200/B4 **Rolling Fork,** Ms,US
183/J2 **Rolling Hills,** Ab,Can
204/F8 **Rolling Hills Estates,** Ca,US
205/P15 **Rolling Meadows,** Il,US
190/D4 **Rolling Prairies** (plains), Tx,US
87/D3 **Rolo,** It.
153/H2 **Rom** (peak), Ugan.
134/C4 **Roma,** Austl.
84/C4 **Roma** (prov.), It.
62/H3 **Roma,** Swe.
188/E4 **Roma,** Tx,US
87/E4 **Romagna** (reg.), It.
86/B1 **Romagnano Sesia,** It.
74/E4 **Romagnat,** Fr.
69/E5 **Romagne-sous-Montfaucon,** Fr.
201/H4 **Romain** (cape), SC,US
179/K3 **Romaine** (riv.), Qu,Can
80/B2 **Romaine** (riv.), Fr.
93/F4 **Roman,** Bul.
93/H2 **Roman,** Rom.
82/C2 **Romanche** (riv.), Fr.
130/B1 **Romang** (isl.), Indo.
130/B1 **Romang** (str.), Indo.
93/F3 **Romania**
99/H5 **Roman Kosh** (peak), Ukr.
161/G1 **Romano** (cay), Cuba
203/H5 **Romano** (cape), Fl,US
86/A2 **Romano Canavese,** It.
87/E1 **Romano d'Ezzelino,** It.
86/C1 **Romano di Lombardia,** It.
108/G1 **Romanovka,** Rus.
97/H2 **Romanovka,** Rus.
87/G1 **Romans d'Isonzo,** It.
81/F2 **Romanshorn,** Swi.
82/B2 **Romans-sur-Isère,** Fr.
177/E3 **Romanzof** (cape), Ak,US
84/C4 **Roma** (Rome) (cap.), It.
97/H2 **Romashki,** Rus.
69/F5 **Rombas,** Fr.
125/C2 **Romblon,** Phil.
200/E3 **Rome,** Ga,US
193/K3 **Rome,** Il,US
199/J3 **Rome,** NY,US
184/E2 **Rome,** Or,US
199/H4 **Rome,** Pa,US
205/N14 **Rome,** Wi,US
80/B4 **Romenay,** Fr.
187/K2 **Romeo,** Co,US
205/F6 **Romeo,** Mi,US
205/P16 **Romeoville,** Il,US
190/C3 **Romero,** Tx,US
84/C4 **Rome** (Roma) (cap.), It.
190/B3 **Romeroville,** NM,US
53/P7 **Romford,** Eng,UK
70/D2 **Römhild,** Ger.
78/D4 **Romillé,** Fr.
68/A5 **Romilly-sur-Andelle,** Fr.
74/E2 **Romilly-sur-Seine,** Fr.
142/D2 **Rommani,** Mor.
66/D6 **Rommerskirchen,** Ger.
201/H1 **Romney,** WV,US
59/G4 **Romney Marsh** (reg.), Eng,UK
99/G2 **Romny,** Ukr.
62/C4 **Rømø** (isl.), Den.
99/G3 **Romodan,** Ukr.
97/H1 **Romodanovo,** Rus.
204/C3 **Romoland,** Ca,US
80/C4 **Romont,** Swi.
79/G6 **Romorantin-Lanthenay,** Fr.
59/E5 **Romsey,** Eng,UK
62/D2 **Rømskog,** Nor.
205/F7 **Romulus,** Mi,US
81/E3 **Ron** (riv.), Swi.
123/D2 **Ron,** Viet.
116/E5 **Ron** (cape), Viet.
56/D3 **Ronaldsway** (Isle of Man) (arpt.), IM,UK
183/G4 **Ronan,** Mt,US
82/A3 **Ronbion** (riv.), Fr.
87/F1 **Roncade,** It.
173/F3 **Roncador,** Braz.
170/B2 **Roncador** (uplands), Braz.
201/G2 **Ronceverte,** WV,US
80/C2 **Ronchamp,** Fr.
87/G1 **Ronchi dei Legionari,** It.
87/G1 **Ronchi dei Legionari** (int'l arpt.), It.
84/C3 **Ronciglione,** It.
87/F4 **Ronco** (riv.), It.
87/E2 **Ronco All'Adige,** It.
87/D2 **Roncoferraro,** It.
86/B3 **Ronco Scrivia,** It.
68/C2 **Roncq,** Fr.
76/C4 **Ronda,** Sp.
61/D3 **Rondane Nat'l Park,** Nor.
191/J3 **Rondo,** Ar,US
166/A5 **Rondônia** (state), Braz.
170/B3 **Rondonópolis,** Braz.
107/L1 **Rondu,** Pak.
117/F3 **Rong** (riv.), China
117/F3 **Rong'an,** China
116/E2 **Rongchang,** China
113/B4 **Rongcheng,** China
115/C3 **Rongcheng,** China
138/F3 **Rongelap** (atoll), Mrsh.
138/F3 **Rongerik** (atoll), Mrsh.
117/F3 **Rongjiang,** China
117/G2 **Rongjiawan,** China
117/H2 **Rongkou,** China
123/C2 **Rong Kwang,** Thai.
119/J2 **Rongshui Miaozu Zizhixian,** China
63/M2 **Rõngu,** Est.
119/K3 **Rong Xian,** China
139/X15 **Roniu** (peak), FrPol.
207/E2 **Ronkonkoma,** NY,US
62/F4 **Rønne,** Den.
72/C6 **Ronneburg,** Ger.
62/F3 **Ronneby,** Swe.
137/U **Ronne Entrance** (inlet), Ant.
137/W **Ronne Ice Shelf,** Ant.
67/G4 **Ronnenberg,** Ger.
123/B4 **Ron Phibun,** Thai.
132/B3 **Ronsard** (cape), Austl.
81/G2 **Ronsberg,** Ger.
68/C2 **Ronse,** Belg.
170/B2 **Ronuro** (riv.), Braz.
156/P13 **Roodeport-Maraisburg,** SAfr.
193/J4 **Roodhouse,** Il,US
156/B2 **Rooiberg** (peak), Namb.
118/C2 **Roorkee,** India
66/B5 **Roosendaal,** Neth.
137/N **Roosevelt** (isl.), Ant.
166/A4 **Roosevelt** (riv.), Braz.
178/D3 **Roosevelt** (mtn.), BC,Can
187/G4 **Roosevelt,** Az,US
206/D3 **Roosevelt,** NJ,US
207/L9 **Roosevelt,** NY,US
207/K8 **Roosevelt** (isl.), NY,US
190/E3 **Roosevelt,** Ok,US
185/J3 **Roosevelt,** Ut,US
182/G3 **Roosville,** BC,Can
177/L4 **Root** (mtn.), Ak,US
205/Q14 **Root** (riv.), Wi,US
208/F5 **Rootstown,** Oh,US
205/P14 **Root, West Branch** (riv.), Wi,US
130/D3 **Roper** (riv.), Austl.
201/J3 **Roper,** NC,US
130/D3 **Roper Valley,** Austl.
190/C4 **Ropesville,** Tx,US
82/D4 **Roquebillière,** Fr.
82/D5 **Roquebrune-Cap-Martin,** Fr.
82/C6 **Roquebrune-sur-Argens,** Fr.
82/A4 **Roquemaure,** Fr.
174/F2 **Roque Pérez,** Arg.
82/D5 **Roquestron,** Fr.
76/D4 **Roquetas de Mar,** Sp.
76/D4 **Roquetes,** Sp.
82/B6 **Roquevaire,** Fr.
165/F4 **Roraima** (state), Braz.
163/C2 **Roraima** (peak), Guy.
165/F3 **Roraima** (peak), Ven.
157/E3 **Rorke's Drift,** SAfr.
157/E3 **Rorke's Drift Battlesite,** SAfr.
194/E2 **Rorketon,** Mb,Can
61/D3 **Røros,** Nor.
81/F3 **Rorschach,** Swi.
141/W17 **Rosa** (cape), Alg.
162/C2 **Rosa** (lake), Bahm.
87/E1 **Rosà,** It.
202/B2 **Rosa,** La,US
80/D5 **Rosablanche** (peak), Swi.
76/A2 **Rosal,** Sp.
188/B3 **Rosales,** Mex.
191/F2 **Rosalia,** Ks,US
182/F4 **Rosalia,** Wa,US
202/N8 **Rosalie** (lake), Fl,US
173/F2 **Rosalina,** Par.
186/C3 **Rosamond,** Ca,US
86/A1 **Rosa, Monte** (mts.), It.
158/D4 **Rosamorada,** Mex.
81/G3 **Rosanna** (riv.), Aus.
82/B4 **Rosans,** Fr.
158/C3 **Rosa, Punta** (pt.), Mex.
174/E2 **Rosario,** Arg.
172/C2 **Rosario** (riv.), Arg.
169/E4 **Rosario,** Bol.
167/E3 **Rosário,** Braz.
158/C3 **Rosario,** Mex.
158/D4 **Rosario,** Mex.
173/E3 **Rosario,** Par.
125/C1 **Rosario,** Phil.
175/F2 **Rosario,** Uru.
158/A2 **Rosario de Arriba,** Mex.
172/C3 **Rosario de la Frontera,** Arg.
172/C3 **Rosario de Lerma,** Arg.
175/S11 **Rosario del Tala,** Arg.
173/F4 **Rosário do Sul,** Braz.
170/A2 **Rosário Oeste,** Braz.
158/B2 **Rosarito,** Mex.
186/D4 **Rosarito,** Mex.
83/B6 **Rosarno,** It.
164/B4 **Rosas,** Col.
77/G1 **Rosas** (gulf), Sp.
86/C2 **Rosate,** It.
164/B4 **Rosa Zárate,** Ecu.
87/G1 **Rosazzo, Corno di,** It.
67/H3 **Rosche,** Ger.
198/B3 **Roscoe,** Il,US
191/H2 **Roscoe,** Mo,US
188/D1 **Roscoe,** Tx,US
78/B3 **Roscoff,** Fr.
60/B2 **Roscommon,** Ire.
60/B2 **Roscommon** (co.), Ire.
198/D2 **Roscommon,** Mi,US
60/C4 **Roscrea,** Ire.
67/G6 **Rosdorf,** Ger.
139/J6 **Rose** (isl.), ASam.
177/M4 **Rose** (pt.), BC,Can
187/H4 **Rose** (peak), Az,US
162/F4 **Roseau** (cap.), Dom.
194/G3 **Roseau,** Mn,US
194/F3 **Roseau River,** Mb,Can
161/H2 **Roseaux,** Haiti
157/S15 **Rose Belle,** Mrts.
135/C4 **Rosebery,** Austl.
201/H3 **Roseboro,** NC,US
183/H2 **Rosebud** (riv.), Ab,Can
191/H3 **Rose Bud,** Ar,US
183/L4 **Rosebud,** Mt,US
189/F2 **Rosebud,** Tx,US
192/D2 **Rosebud Ind. Res.,** SD,US
184/B2 **Roseburg,** Or,US
198/D2 **Rose City,** Mi,US
186/C3 **Rosedale,** Ca,US
206/B5 **Rosedale,** Md,US
200/B4 **Rosedale,** Ms,US
201/G2 **Rosedale,** Va,US
191/J5 **Rosefield,** La,US
194/D4 **Roseglen,** ND,US
54/D1 **Rosehearty,** Sc,UK
191/F2 **Rose Hill,** Ks,US
200/C4 **Rose Hill,** Ms,US
201/F2 **Rose Hill,** Va,US
171/L7 **Roseira,** Braz.
149/G3 **Roseires** (dam), Sudan
194/E3 **Roseisle,** Mb,Can
202/C2 **Roseland,** La,US
207/H8 **Roseland,** NJ,US
82/C1 **Roselette, Aiguille de** (peak), Fr.
205/P16 **Roselle,** Il,US
207/D2 **Roselle,** NJ,US
207/H9 **Roselle Park,** NJ,US
184/B1 **Rose Lodge,** Or,US
200/C3 **Rosemark,** Tn,US
204/F7 **Rosemead,** Ca,US
197/N6 **Rosemère,** Qu,Can
195/P7 **Rosemount,** Mn,US
201/F1 **Rosemount,** Oh,US
70/D4 **Rosenberg,** Ger.
189/G3 **Rosenberg,** Tx,US
70/B6 **Rosenfeld,** Ger.
206/C5 **Rosenhayn,** NJ,US
64/G5 **Rosenheim,** Ger.
183/L2 **Rosenhof,** Sk,Can
194/F3 **Rosenort,** Mb,Can
202/B2 **Rosepine,** La,US
77/G1 **Roses,** Sp.
188/B3 **Rosetilla,** Mex.
206/C2 **Roseto,** Pa,US
85/E2 **Roseto degli Abruzzi,** It.
85/F5 **Roseto Valfortore,** It.
183/L2 **Rosetown,** Sk,Can
103/B4 **Rosetta** (Rashīd), Egypt
194/C1 **Rose Valley,** Sk,Can
205/M9 **Roseville,** Ca,US
193/J3 **Roseville,** Il,US
205/G6 **Roseville,** Mi,US
195/P6 **Roseville,** Mn,US
198/E5 **Roseville,** Oh,US
189/H2 **Rosevine,** Tx,US
130/C4 **Rosewood,** Austl.
189/M9 **Rosharon,** Tx,US
80/D1 **Rosheim,** Fr.
103/F7 **Rosh Ha'Ayin,** Isr.
103/D3 **Rosh HaNiqra** (pt.), Isr.
107/G2 **Roshkhvār,** Iran
194/F5 **Rosholt,** SD,US
198/B2 **Rosholt,** Wi,US
156/B2 **Rosh Pinah,** Namb.
200/C2 **Rosiclare,** Il,US
68/B4 **Rosières-en-Santerre,** Fr.
86/D6 **Rosignano Marittimo,** It.
86/D6 **Rosignano Solvay,** It.
166/B1 **Rosignol,** Guy.
73/C1 **Rosina,** Slvk.
93/G3 **Roşiori de Vede,** Rom.
93/H4 **Rositsa,** Bul.
72/C5 **Rositz,** Ger.
62/E4 **Roskilde,** Den.
64/F1 **Roskilde** (co.), Den.
63/T9 **Roskilde** (fjord), Den.
63/S7 **Roslags-Näsby,** Swe.
96/E1 **Roslavl',** Rus.
62/C3 **Roslev,** Den.
94/G1 **Roslyakova,** Rus.
95/K4 **Roslyatino,** Rus.
182/D4 **Roslyn,** Wa,US
66/C5 **Rosmalen,** Neth.
76/B3 **Rosmaninhal,** Port.
54/B4 **Rosneath,** Sc,UK
53/T10 **Rosny-sous-Bois,** Fr.
79/G2 **Rosny-sur-Seine,** Fr.
87/F2 **Rosolina,** It.
90/D4 **Rosolini,** It.
78/B5 **Rosporden,** Fr.
69/G2 **Rösrath,** Ger.
137/M **Ross** (isl.), Ant.
137/P **Ross** (sea), Ant.
135/C4 **Ross,** Austl.
197/T8 **Ross** (pt.), On,Can
136/B3 **Ross,** N.Z.
136/C3 **Ross** (peak), N.Z.
54/C1 **Ross** (dist.), Sc,UK
205/J11 **Ross,** Ca,US
189/F2 **Ross,** Tx,US
182/D3 **Ross** (lake), Wa,US
75/K3 **Rossa** (peak), It.
81/F5 **Rossa,** Swi.
57/E4 **Rossall** (pt.), Eng,UK
83/C3 **Rossano,** It.
83/C3 **Rossano Stazione,** It.
87/E1 **Rossano Veneto,** It.
71/F5 **Rossbach,** Ger.
200/C4 **Ross Barnett** (res.), Ms,US
80/D2 **Rossberg** (mtn.), Fr.
194/D2 **Rossburn,** Mb,Can
60/A6 **Ross Carbery,** Ire.
70/B3 **Rossdorf,** Ger.
138/E6 **Rossel** (isl.), PNG
69/F5 **Rosselange,** Fr.
194/F3 **Rosser,** Mb,Can
188/L7 **Rosser,** Tx,US
81/G2 **Rosshaupten,** Ger.
137/N **Ross Ice Shelf,** Ant.
199/J2 **Rossie,** NY,US
86/B3 **Rossiglione,** It.
196/E3 **Rossignol** (lake), NS,Can
154/B4 **Rössing,** Namb.
55/G9 **Rosskeeragh** (pt.), Ire.
72/B5 **Rossla,** Ger.
182/D3 **Ross Lake Nat'l Rec. Area,** Wa,US
182/F3 **Rossland,** BC,Can
60/D5 **Rosslare,** Ire.
60/D5 **Rosslare** (bay), Ire.
60/D5 **Rosslare** (pt.), Ire.
72/C4 **Rosslau,** Ger.
56/A3 **Rosslea,** NI,UK
72/B5 **Rossleben,** Ger.
195/K3 **Rosslyn Village,** On,Can
144/B2 **Rosso,** Mrta.
58/D3 **Ross on Wye,** Eng,UK
99/K2 **Rossosh',** Rus.
195/L3 **Rossport,** On,Can
177/M3 **Ross River,** Yk,Can
81/E4 **Rossstock** (peak), Swi.
70/D4 **Rosstal,** Ger.
191/H4 **Rosston,** Ar,US
198/C4 **Rossville,** Il,US
191/G1 **Rossville,** Ks,US
72/D5 **Rosswein,** Ger.
61/E2 **Røst,** Nor.
114/A4 **Rostāq,** Afg.
105/H5 **Rostāq,** Iran
60/B6 **Rostellan,** Ire.
183/L1 **Rosthern,** Sk,Can
64/G1 **Rostock,** Ger.
53/G4 **Rostov,** Rus.
99/K4 **Rostov** (int'l arpt.), Rus.
99/L3 **Rostov Obl.,** Rus.
78/B4 **Rostrenen,** Fr.
56/B3 **Rostrevor,** NI,UK
200/E3 **Roswell,** Ga,US
190/B4 **Roswell,** NM,US
208/F7 **Roswell,** Oh,US
81/F1 **Rot** (riv.), Ger.
138/D3 **Rota** (isl.), NMar.
76/B4 **Rota,** Sp.
188/D1 **Rotan,** Tx,US
67/G2 **Rotenburg,** Ger.
67/G7 **Rotenburg an der Fulda,** Ger.
71/E2 **Roter Main** (riv.), Ger.
81/F3 **Rote Wand** (peak), Aus.
72/D6 **Rote Weisseritz** (riv.), Ger.
69/F2 **Rötgen,** Ger.
81/G1 **Roth** (riv.), Ger.
72/C5 **Rötha,** Ger.
64/E3 **Rothaargebirge** (mts.), Ger.
80/D1 **Rothau,** Fr.
70/E4 **Roth bei Nürnberg,** Ger.
57/G1 **Rothbury,** Eng,UK
70/E4 **Röthenbach an der Pegnitz,** Ger.
70/B4 **Rothenberg,** Ger.
70/D4 **Rothenburg ob der Tauber,** Ger.
57/G5 **Rother** (riv.), Eng,UK
59/F5 **Rother** (riv.), Eng,UK
57/G5 **Rotherham,** Eng,UK
81/E3 **Rothernburg,** Swi.
54/C1 **Rothes,** Sc,UK
196/E3 **Rothesay,** NB,Can
54/A5 **Rothesay,** Sc,UK
69/E2 **Rotheux-Rimière,** Belg.
194/F4 **Rothsay,** Mn,US
193/K1 **Rothschild,** Wi,US
59/F2 **Rothwell,** Eng,UK
130/A2 **Roti** (isl.), Indo.
144/B4 **Rotifunk,** SLeo.
135/C2 **Roto,** Austl.
83/C3 **Rotonda,** It.
203/G4 **Rotonda,** Fl,US
83/C2 **Rotondella,** It.
84/D2 **Rotondo** (peak), It.
136/D2 **Rotorua,** N.Z.
69/D2 **Rotselaar,** Belg.
71/F6 **Rott** (riv.), Ger.
64/F5 **Rottach-Egern,** Ger.
71/F7 **Rott am Inn,** Ger.
69/F6 **Rotte** (riv.), Fr.
80/E5 **Rotten** (riv.), Swi.
70/C6 **Rottenacker,** Ger.
70/E4 **Röttenbach,** Ger.
70/C2 **Rottenberg,** Ger.
70/B6 **Rottenburg am Neckar,** Ger.
71/F5 **Rottenburg an der Laaber,** Ger.
66/B5 **Rotterdam,** Neth.
66/B5 **Rotterdam** (int'l arpt.), Neth.
199/K3 **Rotterdam** (South Schenectady), NY,US
70/D2 **Rottershausen,** Ger.
71/G6 **Rotthalmünster,** Ger.
59/F5 **Rottingdean,** UK
70/C3 **Röttingen,** Ger.
62/F3 **Rottne,** Swe.
132/B4 **Rottnest** (isl.), Austl.
86/C2 **Rottofreno,** It.
81/F1 **Rottum** (riv.), Ger.
66/D2 **Rottumeroog** (isl.), Neth.
66/D2 **Rottumerplaat** (isl.), Neth.
70/B6 **Rottweil,** Ger.
138/G6 **Rotuma** (isl.), Fiji
71/F4 **Rötz,** Ger.
68/C2 **Roubaix,** Fr.
74/F4 **Roubion** (riv.), Fr.
71/H2 **Roudnice nad Labem,** Czh.
79/G2 **Rouen,** Fr.
80/D2 **Rouffach,** Fr.
197/S8 **Rouge** (riv.), On,Can
199/J1 **Rouge** (riv.), Qu,Can
78/D5 **Rougé,** Fr.
205/F6 **Rouge** (riv.), Mi,US
80/C3 **Rougemont,** Fr.
80/C2 **Rougemont-le-Château,** Fr.
200/D2 **Rough** (riv.), Ky,US
200/D2 **Rough River** (lake), Ky,US
194/B2 **Rouleau,** Sk,Can
199/G4 **Roulette,** Pa,US
74/D4 **Roullet-Saint-Estèphe,** Fr.
200/E1 **Round** (hill), In,US
200/E2 **Round** (hill), Ky,US
196/C2 **Round** (mtn.), Me,US
208/G6 **Round** (hill), Oh,US
206/B3 **Round** (hill), Pa,US
184/C1 **Round Butte** (dam), Or,US
134/C4 **Round Hill** (pt.), Austl.
56/B1 **Round Knowe** (mtn.), NI,UK
205/P15 **Round Lake,** Il,US
205/P15 **Round Lake Beach,** Il,US
205/P15 **Round Lake Park,** Il,US
184/E4 **Round Mountain,** Nv,US
189/E2 **Round Mountain,** Tx,US
189/F2 **Round Rock,** Tx,US
191/J2 **Round Spring,** Mo,US
189/F2 **Round Top,** Tx,US
183/K4 **Roundup,** Mt,US
206/D2 **Round Valley** (res.), NJ,US
184/B4 **Round Valley Ind. Res.,** Ca,US
58/E4 **Roundway** (hill), Eng,UK
194/E3 **Rounthwaite,** Mb,Can
166/C1 **Roura,** FrG.
55/N13 **Rousay** (isl.), Sc,UK
134/G8 **Rouse Hill,** Austl.
199/K2 **Rouses Point,** NY,US
208/H5 **Rouseville,** Pa,US
68/D3 **Rousies,** Fr.
73/A1 **Rousínov,** Czh.
82/B6 **Rousset,** Fr.
82/A2 **Roussillon,** Fr.
82/B5 **Roussillon,** Fr.
196/D1 **Routhierville,** Qu,Can
79/E3 **Rouvre** (riv.), Fr.
69/E5 **Rouvres-en-Woëvre,** Fr.
69/E4 **Rouvroy,** Belg.
79/G1 **Rouxmesnil-Bouteilles,** Fr.
156/D3 **Rouxville,** SAfr.
176/K5 **Rouyn-Noranda,** Can.
179/J4 **Rouyn-Noranda,** Qu,Can
61/H2 **Rovaniemi,** Fin.
61/H2 **Rovaniemi** (int'l arpt.), Fin.
86/B1 **Rovasenda,** It.
86/D1 **Rovato,** It.
86/C1 **Rovello Porro,** It.
99/K3 **Roven'ki,** Rus.
99/K3 **Roven'ki,** Ukr.
191/H3 **Rover,** Ar,US
191/J2 **Rover,** Mo,US
87/D2 **Roverbella,** It.
87/D3 **Rovereto,** It.
87/E1 **Rovereto,** It.
84/D3 **Roviano,** It.
123/D3 **Rovieng Tbong,** Camb.
87/E2 **Rovigo,** It.
87/E2 **Rovigo** (prov.), It.
87/G2 **Rovinj,** Cro.
164/C3 **Rovira,** Col.
98/D2 **Rovno,** Ukr.
98/D2 **Rovno Obl.,** Ukr.
97/H2 **Rovnoye,** Rus.
155/H1 **Rovuma** (riv.), Moz.
190/B3 **Rowe,** NM,US
191/H4 **Rowell,** Ar,US
135/D1 **Rowena,** Austl.
159/E2 **Rowena,** Tx,US
201/H3 **Rowland,** NC,US
188/L7 **Rowlett,** Tx,US
188/L6 **Rowlett** (cr.), Tx,US
128/B3 **Rowley** (shoals), Austl.
179/J2 **Rowley** (isl.), NW,Can
121/J2 **Rowta,** India
144/B4 **Roxa** (isl.), GBis.
125/B3 **Roxas,** Phil.
125/C1 **Roxas,** Phil.
127/F1 **Roxas City,** Indo.
201/H2 **Roxboro,** NC,US
162/F5 **Roxborough,** Trin.
136/B4 **Roxburgh,** N.Z.
208/A2 **Roxbury,** Ct,US
191/F1 **Roxbury,** Ks,US
199/J3 **Roxbury,** NY,US
62/F2 **Roxen** (lake), Swe.
200/B5 **Roxie,** Ms,US
144/A3 **Roxo** (cape), Sen.
191/G4 **Roxton,** Tx,US
183/K4 **Roy,** Mt,US
190/B3 **Roy,** NM,US
185/G3 **Roy,** Ut,US
205/B3 **Roy,** Wa,US
82/D5 **Roya** (riv.), Fr.
60/D3 **Royal** (can.), Ire.
190/B1 **Royal** (gorge), Co,US
197/R9 **Royal Botanical Garden,** On,Can
198/C4 **Royal Center,** In,US
120/E2 **Royal Chitwan Nat'l Park,** Nepal
182/E4 **Royal City,** Wa,US
195/K3 **Royale, Isle** (isl.), Mi,US
59/E2 **Royal Leamington Spa,** Eng,UK
59/G4 **Royal Military** (can.), Eng,UK
156/E3 **Royal Natal Nat'l Park,** SAfr.
135/D2 **Royal Nat'l Park,** Austl.
205/F6 **Royal Oak,** Mi,US
113/D4 **Royal Paekje Tombs,** SKor.
202/P6 **Royal Palm Beach,** Fl,US
201/F3 **Royal Pines,** NC,US
123/D2 **Royal Tombs,** Viet.
200/C2 **Royalton,** Il,US
195/G5 **Royalton,** Mn,US
206/B3 **Royalton,** Pa,US
199/K3 **Royalton,** Vt,US
59/G4 **Royal Tunbridge Wells,** Eng,UK
158/E2 **Royalty,** Tx,US
74/C4 **Royan,** Fr.
68/B4 **Roye,** Fr.
80/C2 **Roye,** Fr.
206/C3 **Royersford,** Pa,US
132/C2 **Roy Hill,** Austl.
62/D2 **Røyken,** Nor.
188/L7 **Royse City,** Tx,US
182/B3 **Royston,** BC,Can
59/F2 **Royston,** Eng,UK
201/F3 **Royston,** Ga,US
57/F4 **Royton,** Eng,UK
92/E4 **Rožaje,** Yugo.
68/B6 **Rozay-en-Brie,** Fr.
78/C2 **Rozel,** Chl,UK
195/J5 **Rozellville,** Wi,US
155/H3 **Rozendo,** Moz.
98/C2 **Rozhishche,** Ukr.
71/H4 **Rožmberk** (lake), Czh.
71/G3 **Rožmital pod Třemšínem,** Czh.
65/L4 **Rožňava,** Slvk.
99/J4 **Rozovka,** Ukr.
68/D4 **Rozoy-sur-Serre,** Fr.
65/M3 **Roztoczański Nat'l Park,** Pol.
71/H2 **Roztoky,** Czh.
86/C2 **Rozzano,** It.
91/F2 **Rrëshen,** Alb.
91/F2 **Rrogozhinë,** Alb.
97/G1 **Rtishchevo,** Rus.
124/C2 **Ru** (cape), Malay.
57/E6 **Ruabon,** Wal,UK
154/B3 **Ruacana** (falls), Ang.
154/B3 **Ruacana,** Namb.
151/A3 **Ruaha Nat'l Park,** Tanz.
136/J9 **Ruamahanga** (riv.), N.Z.
136/B4 **Ruapuke** (isl.), N.Z.
136/B3 **Ruatapu,** N.Z.
79/F5 **Ruaudin,** Fr.
136/C2 **Ruawai,** N.Z.
106/E5 **Rub' al Khali** (des.), SAr.
151/B3 **Rubeho** (mts.), Tanz.
72/A4 **Rübeland,** Ger.
53/U11 **Rubelles,** Fr.
112/C2 **Rubeshibe,** Japan
99/K3 **Rubezhnoye,** Ukr.
77/G2 **Rubí,** Sp.
153/F2 **Rubi,** Zaire
153/F2 **Rubi** (riv.), Zaire
170/C2 **Rubiataba,** Braz.
204/C3 **Rubidoux,** Ca,US
87/D3 **Rubiera,** It.

80/D4 Rubigen, Swi.
171/E3 Rubim, Braz.
153/G3 Rubondo Nat'l Park, Tanz.
191/F4 Rubottom, Ok,US
71/G4 Rubřina (riv.), Czh.
114/D1 Rubtsovsk, Rus.
151/A3 Rubuga, Tanz.
177/G3 Ruby, Ak,US
189/H2 Ruby, La,US
185/G1 Ruby (riv.), Mt,US
184/F3 Ruby (lake), Nv,US
184/F3 Ruby (mts.), Nv,US
184/F3 Ruby Lake Nat'l Wild. Ref., Nv,US
134/B3 Rubyvale, Austl.
184/F3 Ruby Valley, Nv,US
63/J3 Rucava, Lat.
94/J2 Ruch'i, Rus.
65/L2 Ruciane-Nida, Pol.
66/B5 Rucphen, Neth.
132/D2 Rudall River Nat'l Park, Austl.
120/D2 Rūdarpur, India
120/C2 Rudauli, India
73/B2 Rudava (riv.), Slvk.
65/K2 Ruda Woda (lake), Pol.
183/L1 Ruddell, Sk,Can
57/G6 Ruddington, Eng,UK
63/M5 Rudensk, Bela.
73/A5 Rudersdorf, Aus.
72/D3 Rüdersdorf, Ger.
70/A3 Rüdesheim, Ger.
151/A4 Rudewa, Tanz.
151/B3 Rudi, Tanz.
86/C2 Rudiano, It.
63/L4 Rūdiškės, Lith.
98/B3 Rudki, Ukr.
62/D4 Rudkøbing, Den.
109/M3 Rudnaya Pristan', Rus.
65/M3 Rudnik, Pol.
98/E3 Rudnitsa, Ukr.
63/P4 Rudnya, Rus.
97/M1 Rudnyy, Kaz.
100/F1 Rudolf (isl.), Rus.
195/K5 Rudolph, Wi,US
72/B6 Rudolstadt, Ger.
115/E4 Rudong, China
93/G5 Rudozem, Bul.
105/G2 Rūdsar, Iran
57/H3 Rudston, Eng,UK
198/D1 Rudyard, Mi,US
183/J3 Rudyard, Mt,US
68/A3 Rue, Fr.
80/C4 Rue, Swi.
56/B1 Rue (pt.), NI,UK
76/C2 Rueda, Sp.
53/S10 Rueil-Malmaison, Fr.
54/A4 Ruell (riv.), Sc,UK
74/D4 Ruelle-sur-Touvre, Fr.
92/F4 Ruen (Rujen) (peak), Bul.
155/G3 Ruenya (riv.), Zim.
81/H3 Ruetzbach (riv.), Aus.
149/G2 Rufā'ah, Sudan
191/G3 Rufe, Ok,US
84/B2 Rufeno (peak), It.
91/F3 Ruffano, It.
74/D3 Ruffec, Fr.
201/G4 Ruffin, SC,US
151/B3 Rufiji (riv.), Tanz.
87/E5 Rufina, It.
174/E2 Rufino, Arg.
144/A3 Rufisque, Sen.
155/F2 Rufunsa, Zam.
182/E3 Rufus Woods (lake), Wa,US
63/M3 Rugāji, Lat.
115/E4 Rugao, China
59/E2 Rugby, Eng,UK
194/E3 Rugby, ND,US
58/E1 Rugeley, Eng,UK
65/G1 Rügen (isl.), Ger.
81/F3 Ruggell, Lcht.
79/F3 Rugles, Fr.
72/A3 Rühen, Ger.
72/D5 Ruhland, Ger.
71/F5 Ruhmannsfelden, Ger.
63/K3 Ruhnu saar (isl.), Est.
66/D6 Ruhr (riv.), Ger.
67/D6 Ruhrgebiet (reg.), Ger.
115/B4 Ruicheng, China
188/B3 Ruidosa, Tx,US
190/B4 Ruidoso, NM,US
190/B4 Ruidoso Downs, NM,US
117/H2 Ruihong, China
66/D3 Ruinen, Neth.
151/B4 Ruipa, Tanz.
151/B2 Ruiru, Kenya
68/C1 Ruiselede, Belg.
53/M7 Ruislip, Eng,UK
158/D4 Ruiz, Mex.
164/C3 Ruiz, Nevado del (peak), Col.
92/F4 Rujen (peak), Yugo.
92/F4 Rujen (Ruen) (peak), Bul., Macd.
63/L3 Rūjiena, Lat.
152/D3 Ruki (riv.), Zaire
130/B1 Rukua, Indo.
120/D1 Rukumkot, Nepal
151/A4 Rukwa (lake), Tanz.
153/G4 Rukwa (reg.), Tanz.
188/E1 Rule, Tx,US
200/B4 Ruleville, Ms,US
130/B3 Rulhieres (cape), Austl.
70/B4 Rülzheim, Ger.
81/H3 Rum, Aus.
162/C2 Rum (cay), Bahm.
73/A5 Rum, Hun.
195/H5 Rum (riv.), Mn,US
90/D3 Ruma, Yugo.
116/B4 Ruma Bāzār, Bang.
106/E3 Rumāḩ, SAr.
165/F3 Ruman, Ven.
151/A2 Ruma Nat'l Park, Kenya
149/G2 Rumaylah, Sudan
133/G3 Rumbalara, Austl.
149/F4 Rumbek, Sudan
105/N6 Rumeli Hisar, Turk.
68/C2 Rumes, Belg.
196/B3 Rumford, Me,US
65/K1 Rumia, Pol.
80/B6 Rumilly, Fr.
130/C3 Rum Jungle, Austl.
81/E3 Rumlang, Swi.
189/E2 Rumley, Tx,US
58/C4 Rumney, Wal,UK
199/L3 Rumney, NH,US
112/B2 Rumoi, Japan
155/G1 Rumphi, Malw.
207/E3 Rumson, NJ,US
68/D1 Rumst, Belg.
151/B1 Rumuruti, Kenya
56/B1 Runabay Head (pt.), NI,UK
115/C4 Runan, China
136/B3 Runanga, N.Z.
136/D2 Runaway (cape), N.Z.
57/F5 Runcorn, Eng,UK
63/M3 Rundēni, Lat.
71/F4 Runding, Ger.
151/A2 Runere, Tanz.
189/F3 Runge, Tx,US
63/T9 Rungsted, Den.
153/F2 Rungu, Zaire
151/A3 Rungwa, Tanz.
153/G4 Rungwa, Tanz.
151/A3 Rungwa (riv.), Tanz.
151/A3 Rungwa Game Rsv., Tanz.
151/A4 Rungwe (peak), Tanz.
78/C5 Runio (riv.), Fr.
70/B2 Runkel, Ger.
62/F1 Runn (lake), Swe.
202/D2 Runnelstown, Ms,US
206/C4 Runnemede, NJ,US
190/B1 Running (cr.), Co,US
204/C2 Running Springs, Ca,US
190/C3 Running Water Draw (stream), NM, Tx,US
154/C3 Runtu, Namb.
108/D3 Ruo (riv.), China
63/N1 Ruokolahti, Fin.
114/E4 Ruoqiang, China
122/D2 Rūpar, India
124/C2 Rupat (isl.), Indo.
93/G2 Rupea, Rom.
68/D1 Rupel (riv.), Belg.
179/J3 Rupert (riv.), Qu,Can
200/E4 Rupert, Ga,US
185/G2 Rupert, Id,US
201/G2 Rupert, WV,US
179/J3 Rupert House (Waskaganish), Qu,Can
69/G2 Ruppichteroth, Ger.
72/D2 Ruppiner (can.), Ger.
72/C2 Ruppiner (lake), Ger.
80/C2 Rupt-sur-Moselle, Fr.
166/B2 Rupununi (riv.), Guy.
69/F1 Rur (riv.), Ger.
201/G2 Rural Hall, NC,US
201/G2 Rural Retreat, Va,US
169/E4 Rurrenabaque, Bol.
139/K7 Rurutu (isl.), FrPol.
196/D3 Rusagonis, NB,Can
155/G3 Rusape, Zim.
149/G3 Ruşayriş, Khazzān Ar (res.), Sudan
80/D4 Rüschegg, Swi.
81/E3 Rüschlikon, Swi.
205/G7 Ruscom (riv.), On,Can
93/G4 Ruse, Bul.
121/F3 Rusera, India
60/D2 Rush, Ire.
190/B1 Rush, Co,US
192/C4 Rush (cr.), Co,US
195/N6 Rush (cr.), Mn,US
59/E4 Rushall, Eng,UK
115/E3 Rushan, China
195/H5 Rush City, Mn,US
59/F2 Rushden, Eng,UK
193/J2 Rushford, Mn,US
197/K2 Rushoon, Nf,Can
191/F3 Rush Springs, Ok,US
193/J3 Rushville, Il,US
198/D5 Rushville, In,US
189/G2 Rusk, Tx,US
202/L8 Ruskin, Fl,US
57/H5 Ruskington, Eng,UK
73/B3 Ruskovce, Slvk.
63/J4 Rusnė, Lith.
80/D1 Russ, Fr.
167/G4 Russas, Braz.
73/A3 Russbach (riv.), Aus.
178/F1 Russell (isl.), NW,Can
134/F7 Russell (isl.), Austl.
178/F3 Russell, Mb,Can
199/J2 Russell, On,Can
201/F3 Russell (lake), Ga, SC,US
190/E1 Russell, Ks,US
201/F1 Russell, Ky,US
208/B1 Russell, Ma,US
199/J2 Russell, NY,US
200/E3 Russell Cave Nat'l Mon., Al,US
198/E4 Russells Point, Oh,US
200/E2 Russell Springs, Ky,US
200/D3 Russellville, Al,US
191/H3 Russellville, Ar,US
200/D2 Russellville, Ky,US
191/H1 Russellville, Mo,US
201/F2 Russellville, Tn,US
70/B3 Rüsselsheim, Ger.
87/F4 Russi, It.
100/H3 Russia
186/A1 Russian (riv.), Ca,US
177/F3 Russian Mission, Ak,US
96/F1 Russkiy Brod, Rus.
189/J2 Russum, Ms,US
200/B5 Russum, Ms,US
73/A4 Rust, Aus.
53/H4 Rustavi, Geo.
201/H2 Rustburg, Va,US
156/D2 Rustenburg, SAfr.
189/H1 Ruston, La,US
205/B3 Ruston, Wa,US
153/G3 Rutana, Buru.
76/C4 Rute, Sp.
127/F5 Ruteng, Indo.
155/F4 Rutenga, Zim.
202/C2 Ruth, Ms,US
67/F6 Rüthen, Ger.
200/D4 Rutherford, Al,US
207/D2 Rutherford, NJ,US
200/C2 Rutherford, Tn,US
201/G3 Rutherfordton, NC,US
199/G1 Rutherglen, On,Can
54/B5 Rutherglen, Sc,UK
190/A2 Rutheron, NM,US
81/F3 Rüthi, Swi.
57/E5 Ruthin, Wal,UK
205/G7 Ruthven, On,Can
81/E3 Rüti, Swi.
81/F4 Rüti, Swi.
83/B2 Rutino, It.
208/C1 Rutland, Ma,US
194/E4 Rutland, ND,US
201/F1 Rutland, Oh,US
199/K3 Rutland, Vt,US
134/A1 Rutland Plains, Austl.
59/F1 Rutland Water (res.), Eng,UK
200/D5 Rutledge, Al,US
195/H4 Rutledge, Mn,US
201/F2 Rutledge, Tn,US
81/E4 Rütli, Swi.
114/C5 Rutog, China
153/G3 Rutshuru, Zaire
153/G3 Rutshuru (riv.), Zaire
66/C3 Rutten, Neth.
94/E2 Ruukki, Fin.
66/D4 Ruurlo, Neth.
90/E2 Ruvo di Puglia, It.
151/B3 Ruvu, Tanz.
151/B3 Ruvu (riv.), Tanz.
153/G3 Ruvubu (riv.), Buru., Tanz.
140/F6 Ruvuma (riv.), Afr.
151/B4 Ruvuma (reg.), Tanz.
155/H1 Ruvuma (riv.), Tanz.
155/F3 Ruwa, Zim.
105/F2 Ruwāndūz, Iraq
104/D3 Ruwaq, Jabal ar (mts.), Syria
153/G2 Ruwenzori (range), Ugan.
107/G4 Ruwī, Oman
192/C5 Ruxton, Co,US
82/B1 Ruy, Fr.
155/F3 Ruya (riv.), Zim.
115/C4 Ruyang, China
153/G3 Ruyigi, Buru.
117/G3 Ruyuan Yaozu Zizhixian, China
97/H1 Ruzayevka, Rus.
65/N2 Ruzhany, Bela.
98/E3 Ruzhin, Ukr.
153/G3 Ruzizi (riv.), Buru., Zaire
73/D1 Ružomberok, Slvk.
71/H2 Ruzyně (Prague) (int'l arpt.), Czh.
153/G3 Rwanda
153/G2 Rwenjaza, Ugan.
153/G3 Rwenzori Nat'l Park, Ugan.
99/L2 Ryabobskiy, Rus.
131/F3 Ryan (peak), Austl.
135/D2 Ryan (peak), Austl.
191/F3 Ryan, Ok,US
56/C2 Ryan, Loch (inlet), Sc,UK
192/A3 Ryan Park, Wy,US
53/G3 Ryazan', Rus.
94/J5 Ryazan' Obl., Rus.
96/G1 Ryazhsk, Rus.
61/K1 Rybachiy (pen.), Rus.
114/C3 Rybach'ye, Kyr.
94/H4 Rybinsk, Rus.
94/H4 Rybinsk (res.), Rus.
65/K3 Rybnik, Pol.
93/J2 Rybnitsa, Mol.
94/H5 Rybnoye, Rus.
62/F3 Ryd, Swe.
62/F3 Rydaholm, Swe.
134/H8 Ryde, Austl.
59/E5 Ryde, Eng,UK
63/T9 Rydebäck, Swe.
62/D3 Rydet, Swe.
59/G5 Rye, Eng,UK
59/G5 Rye (bay), Eng,UK
57/H3 Rye (riv.), Eng,UK
191/J4 Rye, Ar,US
190/B2 Rye, Co,US
207/L8 Rye, NY,US
189/G2 Rye, Tx,US
207/L7 Rye Brook, NY,US
183/K4 Ryegate, Mt,US
184/D3 Rye Patch (dam), Nv,US
184/D3 Rye Patch (res.), Nv,US
62/D2 Rygge, Nor.
65/L3 Ryki, Pol.
183/H1 Ryley, Ab,Can
99/H2 Ryl'sk, Rus.
135/D2 Rylstone, Austl.
63/J1 Rymättylä (isl.), Fin.
97/J2 Ryn-Peski (des.), Kaz.
111/F1 Ryōtsu, Japan
111/M9 Ryōzen-yama (peak), Japan
65/K2 Rypin, Pol.
93/H2 Ryshkany, Mol.
96/B2 Rysy (peak), Slvk.
57/G2 Ryton, Eng,UK
59/E2 Ryton on Dunsmore, Eng,UK
62/F4 Rytterknægten (peak), Den.
111/J7 Ryūgasaki, Japan
111/G3 Ryūgasaki, Japan
112/H8 Ryukyu (Nansei Shoto) (isls.), Japan
111/M9 Ryūō, Japan
65/M3 Rzeszów, Pol.
65/L3 Rzeszów (prov.), Pol.
94/G4 Rzhev, Rus.
98/F3 Rzhishchëv, Ukr.

## S

123/C2 Sa, Thai.
62/F2 Saab (int'l arpt.), Swe.
63/K1 Sääksjärvi (lake), Fin.
71/E5 Saal an der Donau, Ger.
70/B4 Saalbach (riv.), Ger.
71/E2 Saaldorf, Ger.
67/G4 Saale (riv.), Ger.
72/B4 Saale (riv.), Ger.
80/D1 Saales, Col de (pass), Fr.
72/B6 Saalfeld, Ger.
75/K3 Saalfelden am Steinernen Meer, Aus.
79/F1 Saâne (riv.), Fr.
80/D4 Saane (riv.), Swi.
80/D5 Saanen, Swi.
182/C3 Saanich, BC,Can
151/B1 Saanta (peak), Kenya
69/F5 Saar (riv.), Ger.
69/F5 Saarbrücken, Ger.
69/F4 Saarburg, Ger.
63/K3 Sääre, Est.
72/B3 Saare (riv.), Ger.
63/K2 Saaremaa (isl.), Est.
69/F5 Saarland (state), Ger.
69/F5 Saarlouis, Ger.
81/F4 Saas, Swi.
80/D5 Saas Fee, Swi.
80/D5 Saastal (vall.), Swi.
149/F2 Sa'ata, Sudan
97/J5 Saatly, Azer.
149/H1 Saatta, Eth.
123/D3 Sab (riv.), Camb.
162/F3 Saba (isl.), NAnt.
92/D3 Šabac, Yugo.
77/G2 Sabadell, Sp.
112/C3 Sabae, Japan
127/E2 Sabah (state), Malay.
120/A2 Sabalgarh, India
161/H1 Sabana, Cuba
161/F1 Sabana (arch.), Cuba
165/E2 Sabana de Uchire, Ven.
165/F3 Sabana, La Gran (plain), Ven.
164/C2 Sabanalarga, Col.
164/C3 Sabanalarga, Col.
159/H5 Sabancuy, Mex.
162/D3 Sabaneta, DRep.
164/D2 Sabaneta, Ven.
124/A1 Sabang, Indo.
161/G4 Sabanita, Pan.
170/E3 Sabará, Braz.
103/G7 Sabasţīyah, WBnk.
149/G3 Sabat (riv.), Eth., Sudan
85/E5 Sabato (riv.), It.
84/D5 Sabaudia, It.
84/D5 Sabaudia (lake), It.
172/B1 Sabaya, Bol.
86/D1 Sabbio Chiese, It.
86/D3 Sabbioneta, It.
116/D2 Sabdê, China
107/H2 Sāberī, Hāmūn-e (lake), Afg.
191/G1 Sabetha, Ks,US
146/B3 Sabhā, Libya
147/F3 Sabie, Egypt
157/F2 Sabie (riv.), Moz.
147/F3 Sabie, SAfr.
155/F5 Sabierivier (riv.), SAfr.
158/D3 Sabinas, Mex.
63/K3 Sabile, Lat.
194/F4 Sabin, Mn,US
161/G1 Sabinal (cay), Cuba
188/E3 Sabinal, Tx,US
188/E3 Sabinal (riv.), Tx,US
188/D4 Sabinas, Mex.
188/D4 Sabinas (riv.), Mex.
188/D4 Sabinas Hidalgo, Mex.
189/H3 Sabine (lake), La, Tx,US
189/H2 Sabine (riv.), La, Tx,US
202/B3 Sabine Nat'l Wild. Ref., La,US
189/H3 Sabine Pass, Tx,US
84/C3 Sabini (mts.), It.
190/B3 Sabinoso, NM,US
97/J5 Sabirabad, Azer.
106/F4 Sabkhat Maţţī (salt marsh), UAE
125/C2 Sablayan, Phil.
196/E4 Sable (cape), NS,Can
197/H3 Sable (isl.), NS,Can
203/H5 Sable (cape), Fl,US
196/B1 Sables (riv.), Qu,Can
79/E5 Sablé-sur-Sarthe, Fr.
77/H1 Sablon, Pointe du (pt.), Fr.
167/G4 Saboeiro, Braz.
145/H5 Sabon Gida, Nga.
145/G5 Sabongidda, Nga.
76/B2 Sabor (riv.), Port.
145/E3 Sabou, Burk.
167/M6 Saboyá, Col.
127/H4 Sabra (cape), Indo.
146/B1 Şabrātah, Libya
146/B1 Şabratha (ruins), Libya
137/J Sabrina (coast), Ant.
72/E3 Sabrodt, Ger.
121/H4 Sabrūm, India
116/B4 Sabual, India
76/B2 Sabugal, Port.
193/J2 Sabula, Ia,US
124/B3 Sabulubek, Indo.
97/J4 Sabunchi, Azer.
150/B1 Şabyā, SAr.
105/J2 Sabzevār, Iran
172/C1 Sacaca, Bol.
184/E1 Sacajawea (peak), Or,US
182/E4 Sacajawea (lake), Wa,US
163/D5 Sácama, Col.
152/C4 Sacandica, Ang.
174/E1 Sacanta, Arg.
76/A3 Sacavém, Port.
82/D4 Saccarello (peak), It.
86/A4 Saccarello, Monte (Mont Saccarel), Fr.
86/A4 Saccarel, Mont (Monte Saccarello) (mtn.), Fr.
85/F4 Saccione (riv.), It.
193/G2 Sac City, Ia,US
85/D4 Sacco (riv.), It.
76/D2 Sacedón, Sp.
93/G3 Săcele, Rom.
154/C2 Sachanga, Ang.
178/G3 Sachigo (riv.), On,Can
105/E1 Sachkhere, Geo.
169/E4 Sachojere, Bol.
187/H4 Sachse, Tx,US
81/E4 Sachseln, Swi.
70/D2 Sachsenbrunn, Ger.
67/G4 Sachsenhagen, Ger.
178/D1 Sachs Harbour, NW,Can
208/C3 Sachuest Point Nat'l Wild. Ref., RI,US
87/F1 Sacile, It.
80/D2 Säckingen, Ger.
53/S10 Saclay, Fr.
200/E5 Saco, Al,US
196/B4 Saco, Me,US
196/B4 Saco (bay), Me,US
199/L3 Saco (riv.), Me, NH,US
183/L3 Saco, Mt,US
154/B2 Saco do Giraul, Ang.
82/D2 Sacra di San Michele, It.
188/D4 Sacramento, Mex.
168/C2 Sacramento (plain), Peru
186/B1 Sacramento (cap.), Ca,US
205/M10 Sacramento (co.), Ca,US
205/L10 Sacramento (riv.), Ca,US
200/D2 Sacramento, Ky,US
188/B1 Sacramento, NM,US
190/B4 Sacramento (mts.), NM,US
205/L9 Sacramento Metro (arpt.), Ca,US
184/B4 Sacramento Nat'l Wild. Ref., Ca,US
205/L10 Sacramento River Deep Water Ship (can.), Ca,US
76/D4 Sacratif (cape), Sp.
57/G2 Sacriston, Eng,UK
83/B2 Sacro (peak), It.
85/G4 Sacro (peak), It.
86/B1 Sacro Monte, It.
159/L7 Sacromonte Nat'l Park, Mex.
157/H6 Sada, May.
156/D4 Sada, SAfr.
76/A1 Sada, Sp.
76/E1 Sádaba, Sp.
120/B2 Sadābād, India
150/B1 Şa'dah, Yem.
151/B3 Sadani, Tanz.
118/B2 Sadasar, India
105/G2 Sādāt Maḩalleh, Iran
105/F3 Saddam (int'l arpt.), Iraq
187/G2 Saddle (mtn.), Az,US
185/G1 Saddle (mtn.), Id,US
207/J8 Saddle (riv.), NJ,US
184/B1 Saddle (mtn.), Or,US
196/B3 Saddleback (mtn.), Me,US
196/C3 Saddleback (mtn.), Me,US
190/C3 Saddleback (mesa), NM,US
207/J8 Saddle Brook, NJ,US
182/E4 Saddle Mtn. Nat'l Wild. Res., Wa,US
207/J7 Saddle River, NJ,US
207/K8 Saddle Rock, NY,US
185/K1 Saddlestring, Wy,US
54/A2 Saddle, The (mtn.), Sc,UK
133/H5 Saddleworth, Austl.
57/G4 Saddleworth, Eng,UK
123/D4 Sa Dec, Viet.
116/B2 Sadêng, China
122/D2 Sādhaura, India
149/G3 Sadi, Eth.
107/G3 Sadīch, Iran
141/R16 Sāda, Alg.
144/C3 Sadiola, Mali
107/K3 Sādiqābād, Pak.
116/B3 Sadiya, India
157/J6 Sadjoavato, Madg.
191/F4 Sadler, Tx,US
111/F2 Sado (isl.), Japan
76/A3 Sado (riv.), Port.
91/J1 Sadovo, Bul.
97/H3 Sadovoye, Rus.
110/B4 Sadowara, Japan
118/B2 Sādri, India
125/D3 Sadripante (mtn.), Phil.
121/G3 Sādullāpur, Bang.
67/E4 Saerbeck, Ger.
69/E4 Saeul, Lux.
147/G3 Safājah, Bi'r (well), Egypt
144/E3 Safané, Burk.
114/B5 Safāpur, India
114/H3 Safāqis, Tun.
141/X18 Safāqis (gov.), Tun.
122/A1 Safed Koh (range), Pak.
202/K8 Safety Harbor, Fl,US
106/E3 Saffānīyah, Ra's as (pt.), SAr.
69/G3 Saffig, Ger.
62/E2 Säffle, Swe.
187/H4 Safford, Az,US
59/G2 Saffron Walden, Eng,UK
142/C2 Safi, Mor.
142/C2 Safi (cape), Mor.
142/D5 Safia, Hamada (plat.), Mali
107/H2 Safid (mts.), Afg.
107/J1 Safid (riv.), Afg.
107/K1 Safid Khers (mts.), Afg., Taj.
120/A1 Safidon, India
81/F4 Safien Platz, Swi.
120/C2 Safīpur, India
103/E2 Şāfītā, Syria
94/G5 Safonovo, Rus.
104/C1 Safranbolu, Turk.
121/E1 Saga, China
110/B4 Saga, Japan
110/A4 Saga (pref.), Japan
153/E5 Saga, Ang.
111/G1 Sagae, Japan
116/B4 Sagaing, Burma
116/B3 Sagaing (div.), Burma
111/H7 Sagami (bay), Japan
111/H7 Sagami (riv.), Japan
111/F3 Sagami (sea), Japan
111/F3 Sagamihara, Japan
111/H7 Sagamiko, Japan
207/E2 Sagamore Hill Nat'l Hist. Site, NY,US
208/F5 Sagamore Hills, Oh,US
127/H4 Sagan, Indo.
151/B2 Sagana, Kenya
195/J3 Saganaga (lake), On,Can, Mn,US
118/C3 Sāgar, India
65/G1 Sagard, Ger.
97/H4 Sagaredzho, Geo.
121/F2 Sagarmatha (zone), Nepal
121/F1 Sagarmatha (Everest) (mtn.), China, Nepal
121/F2 Sagarmatha Nat'l Park, Nepal
144/A3 Sagata, Sen.
121/E2 Sagauli, India
177/J2 Sagavanirktok (riv.), Ak,US
125/C3 Sagay, Phil.
125/D3 Sagay, Phil.
191/J2 Sage, Ar,US
183/J3 Sage (cr.), Mt,US
195/D1 Sagemace (bay), Mb,Can
60/D3 Saggart, Ire.
207/F2 Sag Harbor, NY,US
198/E3 Saginaw, Mi,US
198/E3 Saginaw (bay), Mi,US
184/B2 Saginaw, Or,US
188/K7 Saginaw, Tx,US
84/D3 Sagittario (riv.), It.
97/K2 Sagiz, Kaz.
182/F3 Sagle, Id,US
179/K3 Saglek (bay), Nf,Can
198/B1 Sagola, Mi,US
90/A1 Sagone (gulf), Fr.
76/A4 Sagres, Port.
114/E2 Sagsay (riv.), Mong.
67/E2 Sagter Ems (riv.), Ger.
130/A2 Sagu, Indo.
192/A4 Saguache, Co,US
192/A4 Saguache (cr.), Co,US
161/H1 Sagua de Tánamo, Cuba
161/F1 Sagua la Grande, Cuba
187/G4 Saguaro Nat'l Mon., Az,US
196/B1 Saguenay (riv.), Qu,Can
77/E3 Sagunto, Sp.
73/C6 Ságvár, Hun.
53/R9 Sagy, Fr.
121/G1 Sa'gya, China
97/K2 Sagyz (riv.), Kaz.
103/E4 Saḩāb, Jor.
147/F5 Sahaba, Sudan
164/C2 Sahagún, Col.
76/C1 Sahagún, Sp.
103/D3 Saḩam, Jor.
105/F2 Sahand (mtn.), Iran
140/B2 Sahara (des.), Afr.
107/L3 Sahāranpur, India
121/F3 Saharsa, India
120/B1 Sahaspur, India
120/B1 Sahaswān, India
157/J8 Sahavato, Madg.
118/B2 Sahāwar, India
141/T15 Sahel (riv.), Alg.
122/B2 Sāhibganj, India
93/H5 Şāhin, Turk.
93/H5 Şahinli, Turk.
122/B2 Sāhīwāl, Pak.
146/B3 Sahl, Bi'r as (well), Libya
105/F3 Şahneh, Iran
152/B2 Sahoué, Gabon
143/H4 Şaḩrā Awbārī (des.), Libya
143/H4 Şaḩrā Marzūq (des.), Libya
142/D3 Sahro, Jebel (mts.), Mor.
127/G3 Sahu, Indo.
158/C2 Sahuaripa, Mex.
187/G5 Sahuarita, Az,US
158/E4 Sahuayo de Díaz, Mex.
73/C3 Šahy, Slvk.
120/C2 Sai (riv.), India
111/E2 Sai (riv.), Japan
131/F2 Saibai (isl.), Austl.
123/C5 Sai Buri, Thai.
141/R16 Saïda, Alg.
141/R16 Saïda (wilaya), Alg.
149/E3 Sa'id Bundas, Sudan
141/N13 Saïdia, Mor.
131/G1 Saidor, PNG
121/G3 Saidpur, Bang.
120/D3 Saidpur, India
107/K2 Saidu, Pak.
80/D3 Saignelégier, Swi.
82/B5 Saignon, Fr.
110/C2 Saigō, Japan
123/D4 Saigon (Ho Chi Minh City), Viet.
110/C4 Saijō, Japan
110/A4 Saikai Nat'l Park, Japan
110/B4 Saiki, Japan
82/B3 Saillans, Fr.
68/B2 Sailly-sur-la-Lys, Fr.
127/H4 Sailolof, Indo.
118/C4 Sailu, India
113/C2 Saima, China
63/M1 Saimaa (lake), Fin.
158/E4 Saín Alto, Mex.
105/F2 Sā'īn Dezh, Iran
68/B2 Sainghin-en-Weppes, Fr.
68/D3 Sains-du-Nord, Fr.
68/C4 Sains-Richaumont, Fr.
54/D5 Saint Abbs, Sc,UK
54/D5 Saint Abb's Head (pt.), Sc,UK
194/F3 Saint Adolphe, Mb,Can
74/E5 Saint-Affrique, Fr.
196/C2 Saint Agatha, Me,US
58/A6 Saint Agnes, Eng,UK
58/A6 Saint Agnes (pt.), Eng,UK
79/G6 Saint-Aignan, Fr.
197/K2 Saint Alban's, Nf,Can
53/N6 Saint Albans, Eng,UK
53/M6 Saint Albans (val.), Eng,UK
199/K2 Saint Albans, Vt,US
201/G1 Saint Albans, WV,US
183/H1 Saint Albert, Ab,Can
58/D5 Saint Aldhelm's Head (pt.), Eng,UK
196/D2 Saint-Alexis-de-Matapédia, Qu,Can
199/K1 Saint-Alexis-des-Monts, Qu,Can
197/P6 Saint-Amable, Qu,Can
79/E2 Saint-Amand, Fr.
68/C3 Saint-Amand-les-Eaux, Fr.
79/G5 Saint-Amand-Longpré, Fr.
74/E3 Saint-Amand-Montrond, Fr.
80/D2 Saint-Amarin, Fr.
194/E2 Saint Ambroise, Mb,Can
196/B1 Saint-Ambroise, Qu,Can
80/C1 Saint-Amé, Fr.
80/B5 Saint-Amour, Fr.
196/D2 Saint-André, NB,Can
68/C2 Saint-André, Fr.
157/R15 Saint-André, Reun.
74/C4 Saint-André-de-Cubzac, Fr.
68/A6 Saint-André-de-l'Eure, Fr.
82/B1 Saint-André-le-Gaz, Fr.
82/C5 Saint-André-les-Alpes, Fr.
74/F2 Saint-André-les-Vergers, Fr.
82/A1 Saint-Andre, Signal de (mtn.), Fr.
196/D3 Saint Andrews, NB,Can
197/H2 Saint Andrew's, Nf,Can
54/D4 Saint Andrews, Sc,UK
54/D4 Saint Andrew's (bay), Sc,UK
199/J2 Saint-Anicet, Qu,Can
144/B5 Saint Ann (cape), SLeo.
78/C1 Saint Anne, Chl,UK
197/R9 Saint Anns, On,Can
58/A3 Saint Ann's (pt.), Wal,UK
161/G2 Saint Ann's Bay, Jam.
193/H2 Saint Ansgar, Ia,US
179/L3 Saint Anthony, Nf,Can
185/H2 Saint Anthony, Id,US
194/D4 Saint Anthony, ND,US
196/E2 Saint-Antoine, NB,Can
197/N6 Saint-Antoine, Qu,Can
196/C2 Saint-Antonin, Qu,Can
68/D6 Saint-Armand-sur-Fion, Fr.
135/B3 Saint Arnaud, Austl.
53/R11 Saint-Arnoult-en-Yvelines, Fr.
196/D2 Saint Arthur, NB,Can
56/E5 Saint Asaph, Wal,UK
58/C4 Saint Athan, Wal,UK
196/C2 Saint-Athanase, Qu,Can
82/C5 Saint-Auban, Fr.
196/B2 Saint-Aubert, Qu,Can
80/B3 Saint-Aubin, Fr.
80/C4 Saint-Aubin, Swi.
78/C1 Saint Aubin, Chl,UK
78/D4 Saint-Aubin-d'Aubigné, Fr.
78/D4 Saint-Aubin-du-Cormier, Fr.
79/G2 Saint-Aubin-lès-Elbeuf, Fr.
78/C2 Saint Aubin's (bay), Chl,UK
79/G2 Saint-Aubin-sur-Gaillon, Fr.
79/E2 Saint-Aubin-sur-Mer, Fr.
197/N6 Saint-Augustin, Qu,Can
157/G8 Saint-Augustin, Madg.
203/H3 Saint Augustine, Fl,US
203/H3 Saint Augustine Beach, Fl,US
58/B6 Saint Austell, Eng,UK
58/B6 Saint Austell (bay), Eng,UK
78/C5 Saint-Avé, Fr.
79/F6 Saint-Avertin, Fr.
69/F5 Saint-Avold, Fr.
196/A2 Saint-Barthélemy, Qu,Can
162/F3 Saint Barthélemy (isl.), Fr.
79/E6 Saint-Barthélémy-d'Anjou, Fr.
74/D5 Saint-Barthélemy, Pic de (peak), Fr.
196/C2 Saint-Basile, NB,Can
136/B4 Saint Bathans (peak), N.Z.
56/E3 Saint Bees, Eng,UK
56/E2 Saint Bees Head (pt.), Eng,UK
183/M1 Saint Benedict, Sk,Can
197/M6 Saint-Benoît, Qu,Can
74/D3 Saint-Benoît, Fr.
157/R15 Saint-Benoît, Reun.
202/D3 Saint Bernard, La,US
79/E4 Saint-Berthevin-sur-Vicoin, Fr.
197/P7 Saint Blaise, Qu,Can
80/C3 Saint-Blaise, Swi.
156/C4 Saint Blaize (cape), SAfr.
82/C3 Saint-Bonnet, Fr.
82/B1 Saint-Bonnet-de-Mure, Fr.
54/D5 Saint Boswells, Sc,UK
78/C6 Saint-Brevin-les-Pins, Fr.
78/C3 Saint-Briac-sur-Mer, Fr.
58/D3 Saint Briavels, Eng,UK
68/C5 Saint-Brice-et-Courcelles, Fr.
53/T10 Saint-Brice-sous-Forêt, Fr.
197/K2 Saint Bride's, Nf,Can
58/A3 Saint Brides (bay), Wal,UK
78/C3 Saint-Brieuc, Fr.
78/C3 Saint-Brieuc (bay), Fr.
183/M1 Saint Brieux, Sk,Can
197/P6 Saint-Bruno (co.), Qu,Can
197/P6 Saint-Bruno-de-Montarville, Qu,Can
79/F5 Saint-Calais, Fr.
82/B5 Saint-Cannat, Fr.
197/M6 Saint-Canut, Qu,Can
192/F3 Saint-Cassier (lake), Fr.
78/C3 Saint-Cast-le-Guildo, Fr.
199/G3 Saint Catharines, On,Can
162/F4 Saint Catherine (mtn.), Gren.
203/G3 Saint Catherine, Fl,US
59/E5 Saint Catherine's (hill), Eng,UK
59/E5 Saint Catherine's (pt.), Eng,UK
203/H2 Saint Catherines (isl.), Ga,US
74/D4 Saint-Céré, Fr.
80/C5 Saint-Cergue, Swi.
80/C5 Saint-Cergues, Fr.
79/F4 Saint-Chamas, Fr.
74/F4 Saint-Chamond, Fr.
196/E2 Saint-Charles, NB,Can
205/P16 Saint Charles, Il,US
201/J1 Saint Charles, Md,US
198/D3 Saint Charles, Mi,US
193/H2 Saint Charles, Mn,US
191/J1 Saint Charles, Mo,US
74/E4 Saint-Chély-d'Apcher, Fr.
53/S11 Saint-Chéron, Fr.
162/D4 Saint Christoffel (peak), NAnt.
198/E3 Saint Clair (lake), Can., US
198/E3 Saint Clair (riv.), Can., US
205/G7 Saint Clair (lake), On,Can, Mi,US
205/H6 Saint Clair (riv.), On,Can, Mi,US
205/H6 Saint Clair, Mi,US
205/G6 Saint Clair (co.), Mi,US
193/H1 Saint Clair, Mn,US
206/B2 Saint Clair, Pa,US
205/G7 Saint Clair Beach, On,Can
82/A2 Saint-Clair-du-Rhône, Fr.
205/G6 Saint Clair Shores, Mi,US
198/F4 Saint Clairsville, Oh,US
80/B5 Saint-Claude, Fr.
58/B3 Saint Clears, Wal,UK
53/S10 Saint-Cloud, Fr.
203/H3 Saint Cloud, Fl,US
195/G5 Saint Cloud, Mn,US
58/B6 Saint Columb Major, Eng,UK
54/E1 Saint Combs, Sc,UK
197/N7 Saint-Constant, Qu,Can
79/F4 Saint-Cosme-de-Vair, Fr.
78/D3 Saint-Coulomb, Fr.
132/B3 Saint Cricq (cape), Austl.
196/D3 Saint Croix, NB,Can
82/C5 Saint-Croix (lake), Fr.
195/H5 Saint Croix (riv.), Mn, Wi,US
195/G6 Saint Croix (co.), Wi,US
162/E3 Saint Croix (isl.), USVI
195/H5 Saint Croix Ind. Res., Mn,US
193/H1 Saint Croix Ind. Res., Wi,US
196/C2 Saint-Cyprien, Qu,Can
177/M3 Saint Cyr (mtn.), Yk,Can
79/G5 Saint-Cyr-en-Val, Fr.
196/A3 Saint-Cyrille, Qu,Can
53/S10 Saint-Cyr-l'École, Fr.
53/S11 Saint-Cyr-sous-Dourdan, Fr.
79/F6 Saint-Cyr-sur-Loire, Fr.
82/B6 Saint-Cyr-sur-Mer, Fr.
54/D3 Saint Cyrus, Sc,UK
196/D1 Saint-Damase, Qu,Can
196/B2 Saint-Damien-de-Buckland, Qu,Can
187/G5 Saint David, Az,US
196/B1 Saint-David-de-Falardeau, Qu,Can
58/A3 Saint David's, Wal,UK
58/A3 Saint David's Head (pt.), Wal,UK
53/T10 Saint-Denis, Fr.
157/R15 Saint-Denis, Reun.
80/B6 Saint-Denis-en-Bugey, Fr.
79/G4 Saint-Denis-les-Ponts, Fr.
82/B4 Saint-Didier, Fr.
80/A5 Saint-Didier-sur-Saône, Fr.
80/C1 Saint-Dié, Fr.
74/F2 Saint-Dizier, Fr.
78/C5 Saint-Dolay, Fr.
199/J1 Saint-Donat-de-Montcalm, Qu,Can
82/B2 Saint-Donat-sur-l'Herbasse, Fr.
74/E3 Saint-Doulchard, Fr.
199/J2 Sainte-Adèle, Qu,Can
79/F1 Sainte-Adresse, Fr.
194/F3 Sainte Agathe, Mb,Can
199/J1 Sainte-Agathe-des-Monts, Qu,Can
194/E2 Sainte Amélie, Mb,Can
194/F3 Sainte Anne, Mb,Can
78/C5 Sainte-Anne-d'Auray, Fr.
196/B2 Sainte-Anne-de-Beaupré, Qu,Can
196/C2 Sainte-Anne-de-Madawaska, NB,Can
196/D1 Sainte-Anne-des-Monts, Qu,Can
197/N6 Sainte-Anne-des-Plaines, Qu,Can
199/J1 Sainte-Anne-du-Lac, Qu,Can
196/B1 Sainte-Bernadette, Qu,Can
196/C1 Sainte-Blandine, Qu,Can
82/A4 Sainte-Cécile-les-Vignes, Fr.
196/B2 Sainte-Croix, Qu,Can
80/C4 Sainte-Croix, Swi.
80/D1 Sainte-Croix-aux-Mines, Fr.
82/C5 Sainte-Croix, Barrage de la (dam), Fr.
197/N7 Sainte-Édouard-de-Napierville, Qu,Can
196/E2 Saint Edward, PE,Can
192/F3 Saint Edward, Ne,US
196/D1 Sainte-Florence, Qu,Can
196/B2 Sainte-Foy, Qu,Can
82/A1 Sainte-Foy-lès-Lyon, Fr.
196/C1 Sainte-Françoise, Qu,Can
79/E6 Sainte-Gemmes-sur-Loire, Fr.
191/J2 Sainte Genevieve, Mo,US
196/A2 Sainte-Geneviève-de-Batiscan, Qu,Can
53/T11 Sainte-Geneviève-des-Bois, Fr.
82/B2 Sainte-Égrève, Fr.
196/B2 Sainte-Hénédine, Qu,Can
79/F4 Sainte-Jamme-sur-Sarthe, Fr.
197/P6 Sainte-Julie-de-Verchères, Qu,Can
199/K2 Sainte-Julienne, Qu,Can
196/F2 Saint Eleanors, PE,Can
178/B2 Saint Elias (mts.), Yk,Can, Ak,US
177/K4 Saint Elias (cape), Ak,US
177/K3 Saint Elias (mtn.), Ak,US
177/K3 Saint Elias (mts.), Yk,Can, Ak,US
177/K3 Saint Elias-Wrangell Nat'l Park and Prsv., Ak,US
199/K1 Sainte-Élie, Qu,Can
166/C1 Saint-Élie, FrG.
74/E3 Sainte-Éloy-les-Mines, Fr.
78/D6 Sainte-Luce-sur-Loire, Fr.
199/L1 Sainte-Marie, On,Can
196/B2 Sainte-Marie, Qu,Can
162/F4 Sainte-Marie, Mart.
69/F5 Sainte-Marie-aux-Chênes, Fr.
80/D1 Sainte-Marie-aux-Mines, Fr.
157/J7 Sainte Marie, Nosy (isl.), Madg.
199/K2 Sainte-Martine, Qu,Can
82/C6 Sainte-Maxime, Fr.
69/D5 Sainte-Menehould, Fr.
78/D2 Sainte-Mère-Église, Fr.
78/C6 Sainte-Reine-de-Bretagne, Fr.
68/C5 Sainte-Erme-Outre-et-Ramecourt, Fr.
196/B1 Sainte-Rose-du-Nord, Qu,Can
74/C4 Saintes, Fr.
197/M6 Sainte-Scholastique, Qu,Can
74/F4 Sainte-Sigolène, Fr.
197/N6 Saint-Esprit, Qu,Can
74/E5 Saint-Estève, Fr.
79/E4 Sainte-Suzanne, Fr.
196/A2 Sainte-Thècle, Qu,Can
197/N6 Sainte-Thérèse, Qu,Can
197/N6 Sainte-Thérèse-Ouest, Qu,Can
74/F4 Saint-Étienne, Fr.
68/A2 Saint-Étienne-au-Mont, Fr.
74/C5 Saint-Étienne-de-Baïgorry, Fr.
82/C2 Saint-Étienne-de-Cuines, Fr.
78/D6 Saint-Étienne-de-Montluc, Fr.
82/C4 Saint-Étienne-de-Tinée, Fr.
82/A5 Saint-Étienne-du-Grès, Fr.
79/G2 Saint-Étienne-du-Rouvray, Fr.
82/B3 Saint-Étienne-en-Dévoluy, Fr.
80/C1 Saint-Étienne-lès-Remiremont, Fr.
82/B5 Sainte-Tulle, Fr.
196/C2 Saint-Eusèbe, Qu,Ca
199/K2 Saint-Eustache, Qu,Can
162/F3 Saint Eustatius (isl.), NAnt.
199/J1 Sainte-Véronique, Qu,Can
196/C1 Saint-Fabien, Qu,Ca
53/T11 Saint-Fargeau-Ponthierry, Fr.
196/A1 Saint-Félicien, Qu,C
82/A2 Saint-Félicien, Fr.
80/B6 Saint-Félix, Fr.
54/E1 Saint Fergus, Sc,UK
196/B2 Saint-Ferréol-les-Neiges, Qu,Can
196/C2 Saint-Fidèle, Qu,Can
56/C3 Saintfield, NI,UK
82/C3 Saint-Firmin-en-Valgodemard, Fr.
74/E2 Saint-Florentin, Fr.
79/E6 Saint-Florent-le-Vie
74/E3 Saint-Florent-sur-Cher, Fr.
148/D3 Saint-Floris Nat'l Park, CAfr.
74/E4 Saint-Flour, Fr.
82/A1 Saint-Fons, Fr.
197/L2 Saint Francis (cape), Nf,Can
156/D4 Saint Francis (cape), SAfr.
191/J3 Saint Francis (riv.), Ar,US
200/B2 Saint Francis (riv.), A Mo,US
190/D1 Saint Francis, Ks,US
196/C2 Saint Francis, Me,U
192/D2 Saint Francis, SD,US
205/Q14 Saint Francis, Wi,US
200/D1 Saint Francisville, Il,US
202/C2 Saint Francisville, La,US
196/A3 Saint-François (riv.), Qu,Can
199/L2 Saint François (riv.), Qu,Can
191/J2 Saint Francois (mts.), Mo.
196/A2 Saint-François-du-Lac, Qu,Can
194/B1 Saint-Front, Sk,Can
196/B1 Saint-Fulgence, Qu,Can
199/K1 Saint-Gabriel, Qu,Ca
202/C2 Saint Gabriel, La,US
74/D5 Saint-Gaudens, Fr.
199/K3 Saint-Gaudens Nat'l Hist. Site, NH,US
79/E5 Saint-Gault, Fr.
199/L2 Saint-Gédéon, Qu,Ca
82/A1 Saint-Genis-Laval, F
80/C5 Saint-Genis-Pouilly, Fr.
82/B1 Saint-Genix-sur-Guiers, Fr.
82/B2 Saint Geoirs (Grenoble) (arpt.), Fr.
134/C5 Saint George, Austl.
196/D3 Saint George, NB,Ca
179/L4 Saint George (cape) Nf,Can
197/Q9 Saint George, On,Ca
177/E4 Saint George, Ak,US
177/E4 Saint George (isl.), Ak,US
203/F3 Saint George (cape) Fl,US
203/G2 Saint George, Ga,US
191/H2 Saint George, Mo,US
207/J9 Saint George, NY,US
201/G4 Saint George, SC,US
187/F2 Saint George, Ut,US
56/C6 Saint George's (char
199/L1 Saint-Georges, Qu,Can
197/H1 Saint George's, Nf,C
197/H1 Saint George's (bay) Nf,Can
197/G3 Saint George's (bay) NS,Can
196/A2 Saint-Georges, Qu,C
196/B2 Saint-Georges, Qu,C
166/D2 Saint-Georges, FrG.
162/F4 Saint George's (cap.), Gren.
55/H11 Saint George's (char Ire., UK
206/C4 Saint Georges, De,U
79/E4 Saint-Georges-Buttavent, Fr.
196/C2 Saint-Georges-de-Cacouna, Qu,Can
79/E3 Sainte-Georges-des-Groseillers, Fr.
79/F2 Saint-Georges-du-Vievre, Fr.
79/G6 Saint-Georges-sur-Cher, Fr.
79/G4 Saint-Georges-sur-Eure, Fr.
79/E6 Saint-Georges-sur-Loire, Fr.
78/D6 Saint-Géréon, Fr.
80/C2 Saint-Germain, Fr.
80/B4 Saint-Germain-du-Bois, Fr.
79/F4 Saint-Germain-du-Corbéis, Fr.
80/A4 Saint-Germain-du-Plain, Fr.
53/S10 Saint-Germain-en-Laye, Fr.
53/T11 Saint-Germain-lès-Corbeil, Fr.
53/U10 Saint-Germain-sur-Morin, Fr.
68/A5 Saint-Germer-de-Fly, Fr.
79/G5 Saint-Gervais-la-Forêt, Fr.
80/C6 Saint-Gervais-les-Bains, Fr.
68/C3 Saint-Ghislain, Belg.
78/C6 Saint-Gildas-des-Bois, Fr.
74/F5 Saint-Gilles, Fr.
74/C3 Saint-Gilles-Croix-de Vie, Fr.
80/C5 Saint-Gingolph, Swi.
74/D5 Saint-Girons, Fr.
68/C4 Saint-Gobain, Fr.
196/E1 Saint-Godefroi, Qu,Can

81/E4 Saint Gotthard (pass), Swi.
58/B3 Saint Govan's Head (pt.), Eng,UK
55/J11 Saint Govan's Head (pt.), Wal,UK
53/S10 Saint-Gratien, Fr.
78/D4 Saint-Grégoire, Fr.
197/H1 Saint Gregory (cape), Nf,Can
78/A5 Saint-Guénolé, Fr.
199/J1 Saint-Guillaume-Nord, Qu,Can
198/D2 Saint Helen, Mi,US
134/F6 Saint Helena (isl.), Austl.
156/B4 Saint Helena (bay), SAfr.
140/B6 Saint Helena (isl.), UK
205/K9 Saint Helena, Ca,US
205/J9 Saint Helena (mtn.), Ca,US
201/G4 Saint Helena (sound), SC,US
135/D4 Saint Helens, Austl.
135/D4 Saint Helens (pt.), Austl.
57/F5 Saint Helens, Eng,UK
182/C5 Saint Helens, Or,US
182/C4 Saint Helens (vol.), Wa,US
78/C2 Saint Helier, Chl,UK
198/D4 Saint Henry, Oh,US
78/D6 Saint-Herblain, Fr.
197/M6 Saint-Hermas, Qu,Can
196/B3 Saint-Herménégilde, Qu,Can
121/F4 Sainthia, India
194/F3 Saint Hilaire, Mn,US
79/D3 Saint-Hilaire-du-Harcouët, Fr.
80/C3 Saint-Hippolyte, Fr.
196/B1 Saint-Honoré, Qu,Can
196/B3 Saint-Honoré, Qu,Can
69/E3 Saint-Hubert, Belg.
197/P7 Saint-Hubert, Qu,Can
196/C2 Saint-Hubert-de-Témiscouata, Qu,Can
199/K2 Saint-Hugues, Qu,Can
196/A3 Saint-Hyacinthe, Qu,Can
195/L3 Saint Ignace (isl.), On,Can
198/D2 Saint Ignace, Mi,US
183/G4 Saint Ignatius, Mt,US
80/D3 Saint-Imier, Swi.
196/B2 Saint-Irénée, Qu,Can
196/E2 Saint-Isidore, NB,Can
197/N7 Saint-Isidore-de-Laprairie, Qu,Can
134/H8 Saint Ives, Austl.
58/A6 Saint Ives, Eng,UK
59/F2 Saint Ives, Eng,UK
58/A6 Saint Ives (bay), Eng,UK
196/C2 Saint-Jacques, NB,Can
78/D4 Saint-Jacques-de-la-Lande, Fr.
197/P7 Saint-Jacques-le-Mineur, Qu,Can
78/D4 Saint Jacques (Rennes) (int'l arpt.), Fr.
178/C3 Saint James (cape), BC,Can
78/D3 Saint-James, Fr.
191/J3 Saint James, Ar,US
198/D2 Saint James, Mi,US
193/G2 Saint James, Mn,US
191/J2 Saint James, Mo,US
207/E2 Saint James, NY,US
203/G4 Saint James City, Fl,US
197/P7 Saint-Jean (co.), Qu,Can
196/A1 Saint-Jean (lake), Qu,Can
196/E1 Saint-Jean (riv.), Qu,Can
166/C1 Saint-Jean, FrG.
82/D5 Saint-Jean-Cap-Ferrat, Fr.
74/C4 Saint-Jean-d'Angély, Fr.
78/D6 Saint-Jean-de-Boiseau, Fr.
82/B2 Saint-Jean-de-Bournay, Fr.
79/G5 Saint-Jean-de-Braye, Fr.
196/C2 Saint-Jean-de-Dieu, Qu,Can
79/G5 Saint-Jean-de-la-Ruelle, Fr.
80/B3 Saint-Jean-de-Losne, Fr.
74/C5 Saint-Jean-de-Luz, Fr.
199/K1 Saint-Jean-de-Matha, Qu,Can
82/C2 Saint-Jean-de-Maurienne, Fr.
82/A2 Saint-Jean-de-Muzols, Fr.
82/B2 Saint-Jean-en-Royans, Fr.
82/D5 Saint-Jeannet, Fr.
196/B2 Saint-Jean-Port-Joli, Qu,Can
199/K2 Saint-Jean-sur-Richelieu, Qu,Can
80/C5 Saint-Jeoire, Fr.
199/K2 Saint-Jérôme, Qu,Can
191/F4 Saint Jo, Tx,US
78/C6 Saint-Joachim, Fr.
191/H2 Saint Joe, Ar,US
182/F4 Saint Joe (riv.), Id,US
180/C2 Saint Joe (riv.), Id, Wa,US
196/D3 Saint John, NB,Can
196/D3 Saint John (riv.), NB,Can, Me,US
78/C2 Saint John, Chl,UK
191/E1 Saint John, Ks,US
202/C2 Saint John (lake), La,US
194/E3 Saint John, ND,US
182/F4 Saint John, Wa,US
162/E3 Saint John (isl.), USVI
162/F3 Saint John's (cap.), Anti.
197/L2 Saint John's (cap.), Nf,Can
197/L2 Saint John's (int'l arpt.), Nf,Can
56/C3 Saint John's (pt.), IM,UK
187/H3 Saint Johns, Az,US
203/H3 Saint Johns (marsh), Fl,US
203/H2 Saint Johns (riv.), Fl,US
198/D3 Saint Johns, Mi,US
199/K2 Saint Johnsbury, Vt,US
206/C5 Saint Jones (riv.), De,US
196/E3 Saint-Joseph, NB,Can
198/E1 Saint Joseph (isl.), On,Can
195/J2 Saint Joseph (lake), On,Can
157/R15 Saint-Joseph, Reun.
198/D4 Saint Joseph (riv.), US
203/F3 Saint Joseph (pen.), Fl,US
203/F3 Saint Joseph (pt.), Fl,US
202/C2 Saint Joseph, La,US
202/C1 Saint Joseph (lake), La,US
198/C3 Saint Joseph, Mi,US
191/G1 Saint Joseph, Mo,US
200/D3 Saint Joseph, Tn,US
196/B2 Saint-Joseph-de-Beauce, Qu,Can
196/C2 Saint-Joseph-de-Madawaska, NB,Can
196/A2 Saint-Joseph-de-Mékinac, Qu,Can
199/J1 Saint-Jovite, Qu,Can
74/E5 Saint-Juéry, Fr.
80/B3 Saint-Julien, Fr.
78/D5 Saint-Julien-de-Vouvantes, Fr.
80/C5 Saint-Julien-en-Genevois, Fr.
74/F2 Saint-Julien-les-Villas, Fr.
82/C2 Saint-Julien-Mont-Denis, Fr.
74/D4 Saint-Junien, Fr.
58/A6 Saint Just, Eng,UK
196/B2 Saint-Juste-de-Bretenières, Qu,Can
68/B5 Saint-Just-en-Chaussée, Fr.
58/A6 Saint Just in Roseland, Eng,UK
135/F5 Saint Kilda, Austl.
55/G8 Saint Kilda (isl.), Sc,UK
162/F3 Saint Kitts (isl.), StK.
162/F3 Saint Kitts and Nevis
197/P6 Saint-Lambert, Qu,Can
202/B2 Saint Landry, La,US
194/F2 Saint Laurent, Mb,Can
196/B2 Saint-Laurent, Qu,Can
68/B3 Saint-Laurent-Blangy, Fr.
74/E5 Saint-Laurent-de-Cerdans, Fr.
82/B1 Saint-Laurent-de-Mure, Fr.
82/A4 Saint-Laurent-des-Arbres, Fr.
166/C1 Saint-Laurent du Maroni, FrG.
166/C1 Saint-Laurent du Maroni (dist.), FrG.
82/B2 Saint-Laurent-du-Pont, Fr.
82/D5 Saint-Laurent-du-Var, Fr.
80/B4 Saint-Laurent-en-Grandvaux, Fr.
74/C4 Saint-Laurent-et-Benon, Fr.
79/G5 Saint-Laurent-Nowan, Fr.
196/C1 Saint-Laurent (Saint Lawrence) (riv.), Qu,Can
80/A5 Saint-Laurent-sur-Saône, Fr.
134/C3 Saint Lawrence, Austl.
179/K4 Saint Lawrence (gulf), Can.
197/G1 Saint Lawrence (gulf), Can
50/F3 Saint Lawrence (gulf), Can.
197/K2 Saint Lawrence, Nf,Can
197/P6 Saint Lawrence (riv.), Can.
176/K5 Saint Lawrence (riv.), Can., US
181/N2 Saint Lawrence (riv.), Can., US
199/L1 Saint Lawrence (riv.), Can., US
59/E5 Saint Lawrence, UK
177/D3 Saint Lawrence (isl.), Ak,US
206/C3 Saint Lawrence, Pa,US
188/D2 Saint Lawrence, Tx,US
199/H2 Saint Lawrence Is. Nat'l Park, On,Can
196/C1 Saint Lawrence (Saint-Laurent) (riv.), Qu,Can
197/M7 Saint-Lazare, Qu,Can
69/E4 Saint-Léger, Belg.
68/A5 Saint-Léger-du-Bourg-Denis, Fr.
68/B3 Saint-Léger-lès-Domart, Fr.
203/G3 Saint Leo, Fl,US
194/E3 Saint Leon, Mb,Can
135/G5 Saint Leonard (mtn.), Austl.
197/N6 Saint-Léonard, Qu,Can
59/H5 Saint Léonard, Fr.
68/A2 Saint-Léonard, Fr.
157/R15 Saint-Leu, Reun.
68/B5 Saint-Leu-d'Esserent, Fr.
53/S9 Saint-Leu-la-Forêt, Fr.
196/A3 Saint-Liboire, Qu,Can
79/D2 Saint-Lô, Fr.
197/N7 Saint Louis (lake), Qu,Can
80/D2 Saint-Louis, Fr.
157/R15 Saint-Louis, Reun.
144/A2 Saint-Louis, Sen.
144/B3 Saint-Louis (reg.), Sen.
198/D3 Saint Louis, Mi,US
195/H4 Saint Louis (riv.), Mn,US
191/J1 Saint Louis, Mo,US
197/N7 Saint-Louis-de-Gonzague, Qu,Can
196/E2 Saint-Louis-de-Kent, NB,Can
197/N6 Saint-Louis-de-Terrebonne, Qu,Can
161/H2 Saint Louis du Nord, Haiti
191/J1 Saint Louis-Lambert (int'l arpt.), Mo,US
195/P7 Saint Louis Park, Mn,US
80/C2 Saint-Loup-sur-Semouse, Fr.
68/A6 Saint-Lubin-des-Joncherets, Fr.
197/P7 Saint-Luc, Qu,Can
162/F4 Saint Lucia
157/F3 Saint Lucia (cape), SAfr.
157/F3 Saint Lucia Estuary, SAfr.
157/F3 Saint Lucia, Lake (lag.), SAfr.
162/F4 Saint Lucia Passage (chan.), Mart.,StL.
203/H4 Saint Lucie, Fl,US
203/H4 Saint Lucie (can.), Fl,US
203/H4 Saint Lucie (inlet), Fl,US
78/C3 Saint-Lunaire, Fr.
196/B2 Saint-Magloire, Qu,Can
55/P12 Saint Magnus (bay), Sc,UK
74/C3 Saint-Maixent-l'École, Fr.
196/B2 Saint-Malachie, Qu,Can
194/F3 Saint Malo, Mb,Can
78/C3 Saint-Malo, Fr.
78/C3 Saint-Malo (gulf), Fr.
78/C6 Saint-Malo-de-Guersac, Fr.
53/T10 Saint-Mandé, Fr.
82/B6 Saint-Mandrier-sur-Mer, Fr.
197/P6 Saint-Marc, Qu,Can
161/H2 Saint-Marc, Haiti
199/K1 Saint-Marc-des-Carrières, Qu,Can
68/A5 Saint-Marcel, Fr.
80/A4 Saint-Marcel, Fr.
166/C2 Saint-Marcel (peak), FrG.
82/A3 Saint-Marcel-lès-Valence, Fr.
82/B2 Saint-Marcellin, Fr.
79/D1 Saint-Marcouf, Iles (isls.), Fr.
161/H2 Saint-Marc, Pointe de (pt.), Haiti
53/U9 Saint-Mard, Fr.
78/A3 Saint Margaret's at Cliffe, Eng,UK
55/N13 Saint Margaret's Hope, Sc,UK
182/F4 Saint Maries, Id,US
156/D4 Saint Mark's, SAfr.
203/F2 Saint Marks, Fl,US
79/F4 Saint-Mars-la-Brière, Fr.
78/D5 Saint-Mars-la-Jaille, Fr.
194/E2 Saint Martin (lake), Mb,Can
162/F3 Saint Martin (isl.), Fr.
80/D5 Saint-Martin, Swi.
198/C2 Saint Martin (isl.), Mi,US
80/A5 Saint-Martin-Belle-Roche, Fr.
68/A2 Saint-Martin-Boulogne, Fr.
68/C6 Saint-Martin-d'Ablois, Fr.
82/A5 Saint-Martin-de-Crau, Fr.
78/B3 Saint-Martin-des-Champs, Fr.
82/B2 Saint-Martin-d'Hères, Fr.
53/T9 Saint-Martin-du-Tertre, Fr.
82/D5 Saint-Martin-du-Var, Fr.
116/A4 Saint Martins (isl.), Bang.
196/E3 Saint Martins, NB,Can
162/F3 Saint Martin (Sint Maarten) (isl.), Fr.
82/D4 Saint-Martin-Vésubie, Fr.
202/C2 Saint Martinville, La,US
183/H3 Saint Mary (riv.), Ab,Can, Mt,US
133/H4 Saint Mary (peak), Austl.
182/F3 Saint Mary (riv.), BC,Can
196/D3 Saint Mary (cape), NS,Can
144/A3 Saint Mary (cape), Gam.
135/D4 Saint Marys, Austl.
197/L2 Saint Mary's, Nf,Can
197/L2 Saint Mary's (bay), Nf,Can
197/K2 Saint Mary's (cape), Nf,Can
196/D3 Saint Mary's (bay), NS,Can
197/F3 Saint Mary's (riv.), NS,Can
55/N13 Saint Mary's, Sc,UK
177/F3 Saint Marys, Ak,US
203/H2 Saint Marys (riv.), Fl,US
203/H2 Saint Marys, Ga,US
198/D4 Saint Marys (riv.), In,US
191/F1 Saint Marys, Ks,US
193/K5 Saint Marys, Mo,US
198/D4 Saint Marys, Oh,US
198/D4 Saint Marys (riv.), Oh,US
199/G4 Saint Marys, Pa,US
201/G1 Saint Marys, WV,US
155/E2 Saint Mary's, Zam.
203/H2 Saint Marys Entrance (inlet), Ga,US
197/N7 Saint-Mathieu, Qu,Can
78/A4 Saint-Mathieu, Pointe de (pt.), Fr.
177/D3 Saint Matthew (isl.), Ak,US
201/G4 Saint Matthews, SC,US
138/E5 Saint Matthias (isls.), PNG
53/T10 Saint-Maur-des-Fossés, Fr.
196/A2 Saint-Maurice (riv.), Qu,Can
80/C5 Saint-Maurice, Swi.
202/B2 Saint Maurice, La,US
80/B6 Saint-Maurice-de-Gourdans, Fr.
82/A2 Saint-Maurice-l'Exil, Fr.
58/A6 Saint Mawes, Eng,UK
69/F6 Saint-Max, Fr.
82/B6 Saint-Maximin-la-Sainte-Baume, Fr.
78/C4 Saint-Méen-le-Grand, Fr.
200/D1 Saint Meinrad, In,US
58/C3 Saint Mellons, Wal,UK
68/D6 Saint-Memmie, Fr.
177/F3 Saint Michael, Ak,US
195/N6 Saint Michael, Mn,US
187/H3 Saint Michaels, Az,US
206/B6 Saint Michaels, Md,US
68/D4 Saint-Michel, Fr.
78/B4 Saint-Michel (mtn.), Fr.
78/C6 Saint-Michel-Chef-Chef, Fr.
82/C2 Saint-Michel-de-Maurienne, Fr.
199/K1 Saint-Michel-des-Saints, Qu,Can
80/C1 Saint-Michel-sur-Meurthe, Fr.
53/S11 Saint-Michel-sur-Orge, Fr.
69/E6 Saint-Mihiel, Fr.
82/B6 Saint-Mitre-les-Remparts, Fr.
54/D4 Saint Monance, Sc,UK
88/F1 Saint-Moritz, (Sankt Moritz), Swi.
80/C1 Saint-Nabord, Fr.
78/C6 Saint-Nazaire, Fr.
166/C1 Saint-Nazaire, FrG.
59/F2 Saint Neots, Eng,UK
69/E2 Saint-Nicolas, Belg.
68/A4 Saint-Nicolas-d'Aliermont, Fr.
78/B4 Saint-Nicolas-du-Pélem, Fr.
53/S10 Saint-Nom-la-Bretèche, Fr.
68/B2 Saint-Omer, Fr.
68/A4 Saint-Omer-en-Chaussée, Fr.
192/C1 Saint Onge (peak), SD,US
68/B3 Saint-Ouen, Fr.
53/S9 Saint-Ouen-l'Aumône, Fr.
78/C2 Saint Ouen's (bay), Chl,UK
78/A3 Saint-Pabu, Fr.
196/C2 Saint-Pacôme, Qu,Can
78/D3 Saint-Pair-du-Mer, Fr.
196/C2 Saint-Pamphile, Qu,Can
198/E4 Saint Paris, Oh,US
196/C2 Saint-Pascal, Qu,Can
79/F4 Saint-Paterne, Fr.
79/F5 Saint-Paterne-Racan, Fr.
53/U9 Saint-Pathus, Fr.
60/B4 Saint Patrickswell, Ire.
50/H5 Saint Paul (isls.), Braz.
178/E3 Saint Paul, Ab,Can
82/C3 Saint-Paul, Fr.
51/N7 Saint Paul (isl.), FrAnt.
145/F5 Saint Paul (cape), Gha.
144/C5 Saint Paul (riv.), Libr.
157/R15 Saint-Paul, Reun.
177/D4 Saint Paul, Ak,US
177/E4 Saint Paul (isl.), Ak,US
191/H3 Saint Paul, Ar,US
198/D5 Saint Paul, In,US
191/G2 Saint Paul, Ks,US
195/H5 Saint Paul, Mn,US
192/E3 Saint Paul, Ne,US
201/G4 Saint Paul, SC,US
199/K2 Saint-Paul-d'Abbotsford, Qu,Can
196/C1 Saint-Paul-du-Nord, Qu,Can
82/A2 Saint-Paul-en-Jarez, Fr.
74/C5 Saint-Paul-lès-Dax, Fr.
134/B1 Saint Pauls (peak), Austl.
201/H3 Saint Pauls, NC,US
207/E2 Saint Paul's Church Nat'l Hist. Site, NY,US
82/A4 Saint-Paul-Trois-Châteaux, Fr.
74/C5 Saint-Pé-de-Bigorre, Fr.
82/A3 Saint-Péray, Fr.
78/C6 Saint-Père-en-Retz, Fr.
133/G5 Saint Peter (isl.), Austl.
198/B5 Saint Peter, Il,US
190/D1 Saint Peter, Ks,US
193/H1 Saint Peter, Mn,US
78/C2 Saint Peter Port, Chl,UK
197/G3 Saint Peters, NS,Can
197/F2 Saint Peters, PE,Can
59/H4 Saint Peter's, Eng,UK
200/B1 Saint Peters, Mo,US
181/K6 Saint Petersburg, Fl,US
203/G4 Saint Petersburg, Fl,US
208/H5 Saint Petersburg, Pa,US
203/G4 Saint Petersburg Beach, Fl,US
202/K8 Saint Petersburg-Clearwater (arpt.), Fl,US
94/F4 Saint Petersburg (Leningrad), Rus.
63/N1 Saint Petersburg Obl., Rus.
196/B2 Saint Philémon, Qu,Can
197/P7 Saint-Philippe-de-La Prairie, Qu,Can
194/D2 Saint Philips, Sk,Can
199/K1 Saint-Pierre (lake), Qu,Can
196/E1 Saint-Pierre (pt.), Qu,Can
197/J2 Saint-Pierre, StP,Fr.
197/J2 Saint Pierre (isl.), StP,Fr.
82/D1 Saint-Pierre, It.
162/F4 Saint-Pierre, Mart.
157/R15 Saint-Pierre, Reun.
197/J2 Saint Pierre and Miquelon (terr. coll.), Fr.
82/C1 Saint-Pierre-d'Albigny, Fr.
82/C2 Saint-Pierre-d'Allevard, Fr.
82/A2 Saint-Pierre-de-Boeuf, Fr.
79/F6 Saint-Pierre-des-Corps, Fr.
79/F2 Saint-Pierre-des-Fleurs, Fr.
74/C4 Saint-Pierre-d'Oleron, Fr.
74/C5 Saint-Pierre-du-Mont, Fr.
53/T11 Saint-Pierre-du-Perray, Fr.
79/E3 Saint-Pierre-du-Regard, Fr.
78/D1 Saint-Pierre-Église, Fr.
80/C5 Saint-Pierre-en-Faucigny, Fr.
79/F1 Saint-Pierre-en-Port, Fr.
79/D4 Saint-Pierre-la-Cour, Fr.
79/G2 Saint-Pierre-lès-Elbeuf, Fr.
79/D6 Saint-Pierre-Montlimart, Fr.
78/B5 Saint-Pierre-Quiberon, Fr.
79/E2 Saint-Pierre-sur-Dives, Fr.
197/M6 Saint-Placide, Qu,Can
80/C4 Saint-Point (lake), Fr.
78/B3 Saint-Pol-de-Léon, Fr.
68/B1 Saint-Pol-sur-Mer, Fr.
68/B3 Saint-Pol-sur-Ternoise, Fr.
74/E5 Saint-Pons (mtn.), Fr.
74/E3 Saint-Pourçain-sur-Sioule, Fr.
80/C5 Saint-Prex, Swi.
82/A1 Saint-Priest, Fr.
196/A1 Saint-Prime, Qu,Can
53/S9 Saint-Prix, Fr.
196/B2 Saint-Prosper-de-Dorchester, Qu,Can
78/C3 Saint-Quay-Portrieux, Fr.
68/C4 Saint-Quentin, Fr.
68/C4 Saint Quentin, Canal de (can.), Fr.
68/A3 Saint-Quentin-Lamotte-Croix-au-Bailly, Fr.
82/A2 Saint-Rambert-d'Albon, Fr.
80/B6 Saint-Rambert-en-Bugey, Fr.
196/B2 Saint-Raphaël, Qu,Can
82/C6 Saint-Raphaël, Fr.
196/B2 Saint-Raymond, Qu,Can
199/J2 Saint Regis Ind. Res., NY,US
197/N7 Saint-Rémi, Qu,Can
82/A5 Saint-Rémy-de-Provence, Fr.
53/S10 Saint-Rémy-lès-Chevreuse, Fr.
68/A6 Saint-Rémy-sur-Avre, Fr.
78/A4 Saint-Renan, Fr.
196/D1 Saint-René-de-Matane, Qu,Can
68/A3 Saint-Riquier, Fr.
197/N6 Saint-Roch-de-l'Achigan, Qu,Can
79/F1 Saint-Romain-de-Colbosc, Fr.
82/B2 Saint-Romans, Fr.
196/B2 Saint-Romuald-d'Etchemin, Qu,Can
68/A4 Saint-Saëns, Fr.
78/C2 Saint Sampson's, Chl,UK
82/B5 Saint-Saturnin-d'Apt, Fr.
82/A5 Saint-Saturnin-lès-Avignon, Fr.
68/C3 Saint-Saulve, Fr.
80/C2 Saint-Sauveur, Fr.
82/C3 Saint-Sauveur-de-Montagut, Fr.
199/J2 Saint-Sauveur-des-Monts, Qu,Can
78/D2 Saint-Sauveur-Lendelin, Fr.
78/D2 Saint-Sauveur-le-Vicomte, Fr.
82/D4 Saint-Sauveur-sur-Tinée, Fr.
78/C2 Saint Saviour, Chl,UK
78/D6 Saint-Sébastien-sur-Loire, Fr.
196/B3 Saint-Sébastien, Qu,Can
199/L2 Saint-Sébastien, Qu,Can.
74/C5 Saint-Sever, Fr.
79/D3 Saint-Sever-Calvados, Fr.
197/L2 Saint Shotts, Nf,Can
82/B2 Saint-Siméon-de-Bressieux, Fr.
203/H2 Saint Simons (isl.), Ga,US
203/H2 Saint Simons Island, Ga,US
53/U9 Saint-Soupplets, Fr.
196/D3 Saint Stephen, NB,Can
58/B6 Saint Stephen in Brannel, Eng,UK
202/D2 Saint Stephens, Al,US
201/G3 Saint Stephens, NC,US
201/J2 Saint Stephens Church, Va,US
74/D5 Saint-Sulpice, Fr.
79/E5 Saint-Sylvain-d'Anjou, Fr.
79/F6 Saint-Symphorien (arpt.), Fr.
82/A1 Saint-Symphorien-d'Ozon, Fr.
199/K2 Saint-Théodore-d'Acton, Qu,Can
196/B3 Saint-Théophile, Qu,Can
198/F3 Saint Thomas, On,Can
191/H1 Saint Thomas, Mo,US
194/F3 Saint Thomas, ND,US
162/E3 Saint Thomas (isl.), USVI
197/M7 Saint-Timothée, Qu,Can
196/A2 Saint-Tite, Qu,Can
80/B5 Saint-Trivier-de-Courtes, Fr.
82/C6 Saint-Tropez, Fr.
82/C6 Saint-Tropez (gulf), Fr.
82/C6 Saint-Tropez, Cap de (cape), Fr.
196/A2 Saint-Ubalde, Qu,Can
80/B1 Saint-Urbain, Fr.
196/B2 Saint-Urbain-de-Charlevoix, Qu,Can
197/N7 Saint-Urbain-Premier, Qu,Can
80/D3 Saint-Ursanne, Swi.
82/A2 Saint-Uze, Fr.
78/D1 Saint-Vaast-la-Hougue, Fr.
79/F1 Saint-Valéry-en-Caux, Fr.
68/A3 Saint-Valéry-sur-Somme, Fr.
82/A2 Saint-Vallier, Fr.
82/C5 Saint-Vallier-de-Thiey, Fr.
74/D3 Saint-Vaury, Fr.
68/B2 Saint-Venant, Fr.
79/G5 Saint-Viâtre, Fr.
194/B3 Saint Victor, Sk,Can
82/B6 Saint-Victoret, Fr.
79/E2 Saint-Vigor-le-Grand, Fr.
133/H5 Saint Vincent (gulf), Austl.
135/C4 Saint Vincent (pt.), Austl.
86/A1 Saint Vincent, It.
162/F4 Saint Vincent (isl.), StV.
162/F4 Saint Vincent and the Grenadines
78/D5 Saint-Vincent-des-Landes, Fr.
74/C5 Saint-Vincent-de-Tyrosse, Fr.
203/F3 Saint Vincent Nat'l Wild. Ref., Fl,US
162/F4 Saint Vincent Passage (chan.), StL.,StV.
80/B3 Saint-Vit, Fr.
69/F3 Saint Vith, Belg.
53/T11 Saint-Vrain, Fr.
183/K1 Saint Walburg, Sk,Can
79/F1 Saint-Wandrille-Rançon, Fr.
53/T9 Saint-Witz, Fr.
183/L5 Saint Xavier, Mt,US
74/D4 Saint-Yrieix-la-Perche, Fr.
78/B5 Saint-Yvy, Fr.
82/B6 Saint-Zacharie, Fr.
120/C1 Saipal (mtn.), Nepal
138/D3 Saipan (isl.), NMar.
172/C1 Saipina, Bol.
141/M14 Saïss (Fez) (int'l arpt.), Mor.
111/F2 Saitama (pref.), Japan
110/B4 Saito, Japan
151/A1 Saiwa Swamp Nat'l Park, Kenya
123/B3 Sai Yok, Thai.
123/B3 Sai Yok Nat'l Park, Thai.
168/D5 Sajama, Bol.
172/B1 Sajama (peak), Bol.
172/B1 Sajama Nat'l Park, Bol.
141/W17 Sajānan, Tun.
92/E1 Sajószentpéter, Hun.
156/C3 Sak (riv.), SAfr.
111/H7 Sakado, Japan
111/J7 Sakae, Japan
123/C3 Sa Kaeo, Thai.
111/M9 Sakahogi, Japan
111/F2 Sakai, Japan
111/F2 Sakai, Japan
110/C3 Sakaide, Japan
110/C3 Sakaiminato, Japan
104/E4 Sakākah, SAr.
194/C4 Sakakawea (res.), ND,US
179/J3 Sakami (lake), Qu,Can
155/F2 Sakania, Zaire
131/G1 Sakar (isl.), PNG
157/H8 Sakaraha, Madg.
93/K5 Sakarya (prov.), Turk.
96/D4 Sakarya (riv.), Turk.
104/B2 Sakarya (str.), Turk.
112/A4 Sakata, Japan
110/C4 Sakawa, Japan
157/H7 Sakay (riv.), Madg.
104/D2 Sakçagöze, Turk.
113/C2 Sakchu, NKor.
121/H2 Sakden, Bhu.
155/E3 Sake, Zaire
157/H7 Sakeny (riv.), Madg.
127/G4 Sakesar, Pak.
145/F5 Sakété, Ben.
101/Q4 Sakhalin (gulf), Rus.
101/Q4 Sakhalin (isl.), Rus.
112/C1 Sakhalin Obl., Rus.
109/N2 Sakhalin-Zapando (mts.), Rus.
99/H3 Sakhnovshchina, Ukr.
106/F1 Sakht Sar (Ramsar), Iran
99/G5 Saki, Ukr.
63/K4 Šakiai, Lith.
112/G8 Sakishima (isls.), Japan
97/L1 Sakmara (riv.), Rus.
123/D2 Sakon Nakhon, Thai.
208/C3 Sakonnet (pt.), RI,US
107/J3 Sakrand, Pak.
156/C3 Sakrivier, SAfr.
97/M3 Saksaul'skiy, Kaz.
120/D4 Sakti, India
111/F2 Saku, Japan
111/J7 Sakura, Japan
111/L10 Sakurai, Japan
121/G1 Sakya Monastery, China
63/K1 Säkylä, Fin.
140/K10 Sal (isl.), CpV.
160/E3 Sal (pt.), Hon.
99/L4 Sal (riv.), Rus.
85/E6 Sala, It.
73/B3 Šal'a, Slvk.
62/G2 Sala, Swe.
86/D3 Sala Baganza, It.
126/D4 Salabangka, Indo.
199/J2 Salaberry-de-Valleyfield, Qu,Can
63/L3 Salacgrīva, Lat.
83/B2 Sala Consilina, It.
158/A1 Salada (dry lake), Mex.
172/E4 Saladas, Arg.
174/F2 Saladillo, Arg.
172/D3 Saladillo (riv.), Arg.
175/S12 Saladillo (riv.), Arg.
172/C3 Salado (riv.), Arg.
172/D3 Salado (riv.), Arg.
174/D3 Salado (riv.), Arg.
174/F2 Salado (riv.), Arg.
161/G1 Salado (riv.), Cuba
188/E4 Salado (riv.), Mex.
187/J3 Salado (riv.), NM,US
189/F2 Salado, Tx,US
172/C5 Salado del Norte (riv.), Arg.
145/E4 Salaga, Gha.
151/C1 Salagle, Som.
105/E3 Şalāḩ ad Dīn (gov.), Iraq
127/G4 Salahatu (mtn.), Indo.
139/H6 Sala'ilua, WSam.
65/M5 Sălaj (co.), Rom.
92/F2 Sălaj (co.), Rom.
98/B4 Sălaj (co.), Rom.
148/C2 Salal, Chad
144/C5 Salala, Libr.
106/F5 Şalālah, Oman
147/H4 Şalālah, Sudan
160/D3 Salamá, Guat.
174/D5 Salamanca (plain), Arg.
174/C1 Salamanca, Chile
159/E4 Salamanca, Mex.
76/C2 Salamanca, Sp.
199/G3 Salamanca, NY,US
148/D3 Salamat (pref.), Chad
148/C3 Salamat, Bahr (riv.), Chad
177/H3 Salamatof, Ak,US
140/K10 Sal (Amilcar Cabral) (int'l arpt.), CpV.
164/C2 Salamina, Col.
164/C3 Salamina, Col.
91/H3 Salamís, Gre.
91/L7 Salamís (isl.), Gre.
103/E2 Salamīyah, Syria
123/C1 Sala Mok, Laos
198/D4 Salamonie (riv.), In,US
85/G6 Salandra, It.
83/C2 Salandrella (riv.), It.
63/J3 Salantai, Lith.
123/C2 Sala Pac Thu, Laos
168/B2 Salas, Peru
76/B1 Salas, Sp.
76/D1 Salas de los Infantes, Sp.
77/G1 Salat (riv.), Fr.
124/E4 Salatiga, Indo.
53/J3 Salavat, Rus.
168/B3 Salaverry, Peru
138/B5 Salawati (isl.), Indo.
50/D7 Sala y Gomez (isls.), Chile
79/H6 Salbris, Fr.
168/C4 Salcantay (peak), Peru
162/D3 Salcedo, DRep.
125/D3 Salcedo, Phil.
74/E5 Salces, Fr.
63/L4 Šalčininkai, Lith.
58/C6 Salcombe, Eng,UK
76/C1 Saldaña, Sp.
156/B4 Saldanha, SAfr.
156/K10 Saldanhabaai (bay), SAfr.
63/K3 Saldus, Lat.
135/C3 Sale, Austl.
86/B3 Sale, It.
141/L13 Salé, Mor.
57/F5 Sale, Eng,UK
127/G3 Salebabu (isl.), Indo.
203/F2 Sale City, Ga,US
100/G3 Salekhard, Rus.
81/F2 Salem, Ger.
122/G3 Salem, India
154/B4 Salem, Namb.
63/R7 Salem, Swe.
191/J2 Salem, Ar,US
208/B3 Salem, Ct,US
193/K4 Salem, Il,US
200/D1 Salem, In,US
199/L3 Salem, Ma,US
205/E7 Salem, Mi,US
191/J2 Salem, Mo,US
199/L3 Salem, NH,US
206/C4 Salem, NJ,US
206/C4 Salem (co.), NJ,US
206/C4 Salem (cr.), NJ,US
187/J4 Salem, NM,US
208/G6 Salem, Oh,US
184/B1 Salem, Or,US
192/F2 Salem, SD,US
201/G2 Salem, Va,US
201/G1 Salem, WV,US
86/D1 Sale Marasino, It.
90/C4 Salemi, It.
90/F2 Salentina (pen.), It.
141/L13 Sale (Rabat) (int'l arpt.), Mor.
82/C5 Salernes, Fr.
85/E6 Salerno, It.
85/E6 Salerno (gulf), It.
85/E6 Salerno (prov.), It.
59/G3 Sales (pt.), UK
68/B4 Saleux, Fr.
103/D3 Salfit, WBnk.
57/F5 Salford, Eng,UK
173/G4 Salgado Filho (int'l arpt.), Braz.
95/K5 Salgan, Rus.
164/C3 Salgar, Col.
80/D5 Salgesch, Swi.
92/D1 Salgótarján, Hun.
167/G5 Salgueiro, Braz.
62/A1 Salhus, Nor.
92/B4 Sali, Cro.
186/B2 Salida, Ca,US
192/B4 Salida, Co,US
74/C5 Salies-de-Béarn, Fr.
77/F1 Salies-du-Salat, Fr.
150/B2 Şalīf, Yem.
104/B2 Salihli, Turk.
155/G2 Salima, Malw.
147/F4 Salīmah (oasis), Sudan
76/B1 Salime (res.), Sp.
151/B4 Salimes, Tanz.
116/B4 Salin, Burma
162/C2 Salina (pt.), Bahm.
83/A5 Salina (isl.), It.
191/F1 Salina, Ks,US
185/H4 Salina, Ut,US
160/C2 Salina Cruz, Mex.
164/A5 Salinas, Ecu.
159/E4 Salinas, Mex.
186/B2 Salinas, Ca,US
186/B2 Salinas (riv.), Ca,US
77/G3 Salinas, Cabo de (cape), Sp.
172/C1 Salinas de Garci Mendoza, Bol.
172/D1 Salinas de Santiago, Bol.
172/C3 Salinas Grande (salt pan), Arg.
172/C1 Salinas Grandes (salt pan), Arg.
190/A3 Salinas Nat'l Mon., NM,US
154/B2 Salinas, Ponta das (pt.), Ang.
188/D5 Salinas Victoria, Mex.
168/D4 Salinas y Aguada Blanca Nat'l Rsv., Peru
82/A6 Salin-de-Giraud, Fr.
87/D6 Saline, It.
90/D2 Saline (marsh), It.
54/C4 Saline, Sc,UK
191/G3 Saline (riv.), Ar,US
191/H4 Saline (riv.), Ar,US
190/E1 Saline (riv.), Ks,US
189/H1 Saline, La,US
189/H1 Saline (bayou), La,US
202/B2 Saline (lake), La,US
198/E3 Saline, Mi,US
205/E7 Saline (riv.), Mi,US
191/H3 Saline, Alum Fork (riv.), Ar,US
85/D2 Salinello (riv.), It.
188/E4 Salineno, Tx,US
208/G6 Salineville, Oh,US
167/E3 Salinópolis, Braz.
80/B4 Salins-les-Bains, Fr.
82/C2 Salins-les-Thermes, Fr.
133/M8 Salisbury, Austl.
196/E2 Salisbury, NB,Can
179/J2 Salisbury (isl.), NW,Can
59/E4 Salisbury, Eng,UK
58/D4 Salisbury (plain), Eng,UK
208/A2 Salisbury, Ct,US
201/K1 Salisbury, Md,US
191/H1 Salisbury, Mo,US
201/G3 Salisbury, NC,US
199/J3 Salisbury, NY,US
133/J4 Salisbury Downs, Austl.
182/G3 Salish (mts.), Mt,US
124/F4 Salitiga, Indo.
202/D2 Salitpa, Al,US
171/E1 Salitre (riv.), Braz.
164/B5 Salitre, Ecu.
73/C4 Salka, Slvk.
201/G4 Salkehatchie (riv.), SC,US
61/J2 Salla, Fin.
206/A1 Salladasburg, Pa,US
80/C6 Sallanches, Fr.
66/D4 Salland (reg.), Neth.
144/B4 Sallatouk (pt.), Gui.
68/B3 Sallaumines, Fr.
77/F2 Sallent, Sp.
68/D3 Salles, Belg.
60/D3 Sallins, Ire.
174/E3 Salliqueló, Arg.
191/G3 Sallisaw, Ok,US
147/H5 Sallūm, Sudan
120/D1 Sallyāna, Nepal
60/D3 Sally Gap (pass), Ire.
69/F3 Salm (riv.), Ger.
105/F3 Salmān Pāk, Iraq
105/F2 Salmās, Iran
63/K2 Salme, Est.
182/F3 Salmo (riv.), BC,Can
182/B2 Salmon (riv.), BC,Can
184/B3 Salmon (mts.), Ca,US
185/G1 Salmon, Id,US
185/F2 Salmon (dam), Id,US
184/F1 Salmon (riv.), Id,US
187/H2 Salmon (ruin), NM,US
188/D3 Salmon (peak), Tx,US
182/E2 Salmon Arm, BC,Can
197/L2 Salmon Cove, Nf,Can
185/F2 Salmon Creek (res.), Id,US
182/C5 Salmon Creek, Wa,US
185/F2 Salmon Falls (cr.), Id, Nv,US
132/D5 Salmon Gums, Austl.
185/F1 Salmon, Middle Fork (riv.), Id,US
196/D3 Salmon River, NS,Can
185/F1 Salmon River (mts.), Id,US
184/F1 Salmon, South Fork (riv.), Id,US
69/F4 Salmtal, Ger.
148/C5 Salo, CAfr.
63/K1 Salo, Fin.
86/D1 Salò, It.
150/A4 Salole, Eth.
187/F4 Salome, Az,US
80/B2 Salon (riv.), Fr.
120/C2 Salon, India
82/B5 Salon-de-Provence, Fr.
153/E3 Salonga (riv.), Zaire
153/E3 Salonga Nat'l Park, Zaire
91/H3 Salonika (Thermaic) (gulf), Gre.
92/E2 Salonta, Rom.
76/B3 Salor (riv.), Sp.
81/H5 Salorno (Salurn), It.
68/B4 Salouël, Fr.
144/B3 Saloum, Vallée du (wadi), Sen.
63/M1 Salpausselkä (mts.), Fin.
168/B3 Salpo, Peru
140/K10 Sal Rei, CpV.
53/H4 Sal'sk, Rus.
90/C4 Salso (riv.), It.
85/F4 Salsola (riv.), It.
86/C3 Salsomaggiore Terme, It.
122/B1 Salt (range), Pak.
156/C3 Salt (riv.), SAfr.
77/G2 Salt, Sp.
161/J1 Salt (cay), Trks.
187/G4 Salt (riv.), Az,US
205/Q16 Salt (cr.), Il,US
200/E2 Salt (riv.), Ky,US
191/J1 Salt (riv.), Mo,US
190/B4 Salt (cr.), NM,US
158/D2 Salt (cr.), Tx,US
188/B2 Salt (lakes), Tx,US
185/H2 Salt (riv.), Wy,US
172/C3 Salta, Arg.
172/C3 Salta (int'l arpt.), Arg.
172/C2 Salta (prov.), Arg.
182/B3 Saltair, BC,Can
207/E2 Saltaire, NY,US
58/B6 Saltash, Eng,UK
190/B5 Salt Basin (lake), Tx,US
57/H2 Saltburn, Eng,UK
194/C2 Saltcoats, Sk,Can
54/B5 Saltcoats, Sc,UK
188/B2 Salt Draw (cr.), Tx,US
60/D5 Saltee (isls.), Ire.
61/E2 Saltfjorden (fjord), Nor.
58/D4 Saltford, Eng,UK
63/T9 Saltholm (isl.), Den.
159/E3 Saltillo, Mex.
200/C3 Saltillo, Ms,US
200/C3 Saltillo, Tn,US
185/H3 Salt Lake City (cap.), Ut,US
185/H3 Salt Lake City (int'l arpt.), Ut,US
208/B3 Salt Meadow Nat'l Wild. Ref., Ct,US
193/H4 Salt, Middle Fork (riv.), Mo,US
193/H4 Salt, North Fork (riv.), Mo,US
174/E2 Salto, Arg.
170/D4 Salto, Braz.
84/D3 Salto (lake), It.
84/D3 Salto (riv.), It.
172/E4 Salto, Uru.
173/E3 Salto (dept.), Uru.
171/F3 Salto da Divisa, Braz.
159/G5 Salto de Agua, Mex.
173/F3 Salto del Guairá, Par.
173/E3 Salto Grande (res.), Arg.
186/E4 Salton Sea (lake), Ca,US
186/E4 Salton Sea Nat'l Wild. Ref., Ca,US
173/F2 Salto Santiago (res.), Braz.
173/F3 Saltos de Iguaçu (falls), Braz.
191/E2 Salt Plains Nat'l Wild. Ref., Ok,US
145/E5 Saltpond, Gha.
63/S7 Saltsjöbaden, Swe.
63/J1 Saltvik, Fin.
201/G2 Saltville, Va,US
97/H1 Saltykovka, Rus.
201/G3 Saluda, SC,US
201/G3 Saluda (riv.), SC,US
201/J2 Saluda, Va,US
125/C3 Salug, Phil.
86/B2 Saluggia, It.
206/B3 Salunga-Landisville, Pa,US
118/D4 Sālūr, India
81/H5 Salurn (Salorno), It.
191/H3 Salus, Ar,US
166/C1 Salut (isls.), FrG.
127/G3 Saluta, Indo.
86/A3 Saluzzo, It.
175/J7 Salvación (bay), Chile
171/F2 Salvador, Braz.
183/K1 Salvador, Sk,Can
202/C3 Salvador (lake), La,US
203/G4 Salvador Dali Museum, Fl,US
166/D3 Salvaterra, Braz.
76/A3 Salvaterra de Magos, Port.
76/A1 Salvatierra de Miño, Sp.
200/E2 Salvisa, Ky,US
116/C5 Salween (riv.), Asia
102/J8 Salween (riv.), Burma, China
119/G4 Salween (riv.), Burma,China
123/B2 Salween (riv.), Burma, Thai.
108/D5 Salween (riv.), China
97/J5 Sal'yany, Azer.
201/F2 Salyersville, Ky,US
65/H5 Salza (riv.), Aus.
64/G4 Salzach (riv.), Aus., Ger.
71/F6 Salzach (riv.), Ger.
87/F1 Salzano, It.
67/E4 Salzbergen, Ger.
75/K3 Salzburg, Aus.
75/K3 Salzburg (int'l arpt.), Aus.
75/K3 Salzburg (prov.), Aus.
67/H4 Salzgitter, Ger.
67/H2 Salzhausen, Ger.
67/G4 Salzhemmendorf, Ger.
67/F5 Salzkotten, Ger.
72/B4 Salzmünde, Ger.
72/B2 Salzwedel, Ger.
152/B2 Sam, Gabon
76/C1 Sama, Sp.
114/G1 Samagaltay, Rus.
172/D1 Samaipata, Bol.
124/D3 Samak (cape), Indo.
187/J5 Samalayuca, Mex.
188/A2 Samalayuca, Mex.
125/C4 Samales (isls.), Phil.
120/A1 Samālkha, India
118/D4 Sāmalkot, India
147/F2 Samālūt, Egypt
106/F3 Samān, Iran
162/C2 Samana (cay), Bahm.
167/K6 Samaná, Col.
162/D3 Samaná, DRep.
162/D3 Samaná (cape), DRep.
122/D2 Samāna, India
161/H1 Samana (Atwood) (cay), Bahm.
168/B3 Samanco, Peru
103/D1 Samandağı, Turk.
105/N7 Samandıra, Turk.
112/C2 Samani, Japan
164/B4 Samaniego, Col.
103/B4 Samannūd, Egypt
103/D3 Samar, Jor.
125/D2 Samar (isl.), Phil.
125/D2 Samar (sea), Phil.
53/J3 Samara, Rus.
97/K1 Samara (riv.), Rus.
138/E6 Samarai, PNG
97/J1 Samara Obl., Rus.
81/B1 Samarate, It.
109/M2 Samarga (riv.), Rus.
103/G7 Samaria (reg.), WBnk.
103/G7 Samaria Nat'l Park, WBnk.
164/E3 Samariapo, Ven.
91/H5 Samaria Gorge Nat'l Park, Gre.
127/E4 Samarinda, Indo.
100/G6 Samarkand, Uzb.
105/E3 Sāmarrā', Iraq
97/L1 Samarskoye, Rus.
107/K3 Samasata, Pak.
121/E3 Samastipur, India
127/H4 Samate, Indo.
144/D4 Samatiguila, IvC.
122/C1 Sāmba, India
153/E2 Samba, Zaire
153/F4 Samba, Zaire
167/E4 Sambaíba, Braz.
144/B3 Sambailo, Gui.
118/D3 Sambalpur, India
152/C5 Samba Lucala, Ang.
157/H7 Sambao (riv.), Madg.
126/D4 Sambar (cape), Indo.
126/C3 Sambas, Indo.
157/J6 Sambava, Madg.
127/J4 Samberbaba, Indo.
120/B1 Sambhal, India
148/D4 Sambili, Zaire
154/C2 Sambo, Ang.
127/E4 Sambo, Indo.
113/E2 Sambong-ni, NKor.
65/M4 Sambor, Ukr.
98/B3 Sambor, Ukr.
175/F2 Samborombón (bay), Arg.
175/T12 Samborombón (riv.), Arg.
123/D3 Sambor Prei Kuk (ruins), Camb.
64/C3 Sambre (riv.), Belg.

68/C3 Sambre (riv.), Belg.,Fr.
74/E1 Sambre (riv.), Belg., Fr.
68/C4 Sambre à l'Oise, Canal de (can.), Fr.
196/F3 Sambro, NS,Can
85/E3 Sambuceto, It.
85/F4 Sambuco (peak), It.
151/B2 Samburu, Kenya
151/B1 Samburu Nat'l Rsv., Kenya
82/C1 Sambury, Pointe de la (peak), Fr.
154/C3 Sambusu, Namb.
121/G2 Samchi, Bhu.
113/E4 Samch'ŏk, SKor.
113/E5 Samch'ŏnp'o, SKor.
121/H2 Samdrup Jongkhar, Bhu.
130/B2 Same, Indo.
151/B3 Same, Tanz.
81/F4 Samedan, Swi.
68/A2 Samer, Fr.
155/F1 Samfya Mission, Zam.
189/G2 Sam Houston Mem. Museum, Tx,US
116/B4 Sami, Burma
91/G3 Sámi, Gre.
94/H3 Saminskiy Pogost, Rus.
168/C2 Samiria (riv.), Peru
123/C4 Samit (cape), Camb.
113/E2 Samjiyŏn, NKor.
123/B1 Samka, Burma
123/C3 Sam Khok, Thai.
123/C3 Samkos (peak), Camb.
205/C2 Sammamish (lake), Wa,US
113/E5 Samnangjin, SKor.
81/G4 Samnaun, Swi.
123/B2 Sam Ngao, Thai.
190/D3 Samnorwood, Tx,US
146/B3 Samnū, Libya
172/B4 Samo Alto, Chile
92/B3 Samobor, Cro.
80/C5 Samoëns, Fr.
86/D4 Samoggia (riv.), It.
93/F4 Samokov, Bul.
77/Q10 Samora (riv.), Port.
77/Q10 Samora Correia, Port.
73/B3 Samorín, Slvk.
104/A2 Sámos, Gre.
89/K3 Sámos (isl.), Gre.
91/J2 Samothráki, Gre.
91/J2 Samothráki (isl.), Gre.
123/D2 Samouay, Laos
99/M2 Samoylovka, Rus.
174/D2 Sampacho, Arg.
124/F4 Sampang, Indo.
77/E2 Samper de Calanda, Sp.
82/D3 Sampeyre, It.
126/D4 Sampit, Indo.
126/D4 Sampit (riv.), Indo.
153/F5 Sampwe, Zaire
122/D2 Samrāla, India
189/G2 Sam Rayburn (dam), Tx,US
189/G2 Sam Rayburn (res.), Tx,US
150/A2 Samrē, Eth.
123/C3 Samrong Thap, Thai.
185/K4 Sams, Co,US
114/D5 Samsang, China
123/C1 Sam Sao (mts.), Laos, Viet.
62/D4 Samsø (isl.), Den.
62/D4 Samsø Bælt (chan.), Den.
134/E6 Samson (mtn.), Austl.
203/E2 Samson, Al,US
123/D2 Sam Son, Viet.
183/H1 Samson Ind. Res., Ab,Can
134/E6 Samsonvale (lake), Austl.
113/E2 Samsu, NKor.
104/D1 Samsun, Turk.
104/C1 Samsun (prov.), Turk.
120/B3 Samthar, India
130/D4 Samuel, Mount (peak), Austl.
182/F3 Samuels, Id,US
90/A3 Samugheo, It.
123/B4 Samui (isl.), Thai.
111/H7 Samukawa, Japan
122/B2 Samundri, Pak.
97/J4 Samur (riv.), Azer., Rus.
100/E5 Samur (riv.), Rus., Azer.
123/C3 Samut Prakan, Thai.
123/C3 Samut Sakhon, Thai.
123/C3 Samut Songkhram, Thai.
121/H1 Samye Monastery, China
123/D3 San (riv.), Camb.
109/H5 San (riv.), China
144/D3 San, Mali
65/M3 San (riv.), Pol.
92/C3 Sana (riv.), Bosn.
168/B2 Saña, Peru
150/C2 Sanaa (int'l arpt.), Yem.
150/C2 Sanaa (Şan'ā') (cap.), Yem.
187/J3 San Acacia, NM,US
76/A1 San Adrián, Cabo de (cape), Sp.
140/D4 Sanaga (riv.), Afr.
148/A4 Sanaga (riv.), Camr.
172/C2 San Agustín, Bol.
164/B4 San Agustín, Col.
125/D4 San Agustin (cape), Phil.
187/H4 San Agustin (plains), NM,US
164/B4 San Agustín Arch. Park, Col.
77/N8 San Agustín de Guadalix, Sp.
177/F5 Sanak (isl.), Ak,US
188/D4 San Alberto, Mex.
106/D4 Sanām, SAr.
127/G4 Sanama (isl.), Indo.
163/B5 San Ambrosio (isl.), Chile
105/F3 Sanandaj, Iran
172/D2 Sanandita, Bol.
186/B1 San Andreas, Ca,US
205/K11 San Andreas (lake), Ca,US
169/E4 San Andrés, Bol.
164/C3 San Andrés, Col.
161/F3 San Andrés (isl.), Col.
160/B1 San Andrés (lag.), Mex.
125/D2 San Andres, Phil.
187/J4 San Andres (mts.), NM,US
175/S12 San Andrés de Giles, Arg.
76/C1 San Andrés del Rabanedo, Sp.
161/F3 San Andrés Island (int'l arpt.), Col.
187/J4 San Andres Nat'l Wild. Ref., NM,US
159/G5 San Andrés Tuxtla, Mex.
173/G3 Sananduva, Braz.
188/D2 San Angelo, Tx,US
144/D3 Sanankoroba, Mali
205/J11 San Anselmo, Ca,US
161/H4 San Antero, Col.
174/D2 San Antonio, Arg.
175/F3 San Antonio (cape), Arg.
169/E4 San Antonio, Bol.
174/C2 San Antonio, Chile
164/B4 San Antonio, Ecu.
158/C4 San Antonio, Mex.
168/B4 San Antonio, Peru
125/C2 San Antonio, Phil.
175/T12 San Antonio, Uru.
204/C2 San Antonio (mtn.), Ca,US
186/B3 San Antonio (res.), Ca,US
190/A4 San Antonio, NM,US
190/A2 San Antonio (mtn.), NM,US
189/E3 San Antonio, Tx,US
189/F3 San Antonio (bay), Tx,US
189/E3 San Antonio (int'l arpt.), Tx,US
188/B2 San Antonio (mtn.), Tx,US
189/F3 San Antonio (riv.), Tx,US
165/E2 San Antonio, Ven.
165/F2 San Antonio, Ven.
77/F3 San Antonio Abad, Sp.
88/D3 San Antonio Abadi, Sp.
161/E1 San Antonio, Cabo de (cape), Cuba
159/M8 San Antonio Cañada, Mex.
174/F2 San Antonio de Areco, Arg.
164/D3 San Antonio de Caparo, Ven.
165/F2 San Antonio del Golfo, Ven.
172/C2 San Antonio de Lípez, Bol.
172/C3 San Antonio de los Cobres, Arg.
164/C3 San Antonio del Táchira, Ven.
165/F2 San Antonio de Tabasca, Ven.
167/O8 San Antonio de Tamanaco, Ven.
189/E3 San Antonio Missions Nat'l Hist. Park, Tx,US
174/D4 San Antonio Oeste, Arg.
158/B2 San Antonio, Punta (pt.), Mex.
82/C2 Sana, Pointe de la (peak), Fr.
186/B4 San Ardo, Ca,US
82/B6 Sanary-sur-Mer, Fr.
150/C2 Şan'ā (Sanaa) (cap.), Yem.
200/C5 Sanatorium, Ms,US
190/A4 San Augustin (pass), NM,US
189/G2 San Augustine, Tx,US
122/D2 Sanaur, India
106/F5 Sanāw, Yem.
118/C3 Sānāwad, India
168/B4 San Bartolo, Peru
142/B4 San Bartolomé de Tirajana, Canl.
87/E3 San Bartolomeo in Bosco, It.
85/F5 San Bartolomeo in Galdo, It.
175/U12 San Bautista, Uru.
87/E5 San Benedetto (mts.), It.
85/D4 San Benedetto dei Marsi, It.
85/D2 San Benedetto del Tronto, It.
87/E5 San Benedetto in Alpe, It.
87/D2 San Benedetto Po, It.
158/C5 San Benedicto (isl.), Mex.
186/B2 San Benito (mtn.), Ca,US
186/B2 San Benito (riv.), Ca,US
189/F4 San Benito, Tx,US
189/F3 San Bernard (riv.), Tx,US
159/R10 San Bernardino (riv.), Mex.
125/D2 San Bernardino (str.), Phil.
81/F5 San Bernardino, Swi.
204/C2 San Bernardino, Ca,US
204/C2 San Bernardino (co.), Ca,US
204/C2 San Bernardino (mts.), Ca,US
159/L7 San Bernardino Contla, Mex.
204/C2 San Bernardino Nat'l For., Ca,US
187/H5 San Bernardino Nat'l Wild. Ref., Az,US
189/G3 San Bernard Nat'l Wild. Ref., Tx,US
172/D3 San Bernardo, Arg.
174/C2 San Bernardo, Chile
174/Q9 San Bernardo, Chile
164/C3 San Bernardo, Col.
164/C2 San Bernardo (pt.), Col.
158/C3 San Blas, Mex.
158/D4 San Blas, Mex.
188/B4 San Blas, Mex.
203/F3 San Blas (cape), Fl,US
191/G3 San Bois (mts.), Ok,US
87/E2 San Bonifacio, It.
169/E4 San Borja, Bol.
193/G1 Sanborn, Mn,US
194/E4 Sanborn, ND,US
197/T9 Sanborn, NY,US
158/B3 San Bruno, Mex.
205/K11 San Bruno, Ca,US
108/E4 Sanbu, China
188/D4 San Buenaventura, Mex.
204/A2 San Buenaventura (Ventura), Ca,US
83/C5 San Calogero, It.
75/K3 San Candido (Innichen), It.
172/C3 San Carlos, Arg.
172/D1 San Carlos, Bol.
174/C3 San Carlos, Chile
167/L6 San Carlos, Col.
158/B3 San Carlos, Mex.
159/F3 San Carlos, Mex.
188/D3 San Carlos, Mex.
161/E4 San Carlos, Nic.
164/B2 San Carlos, Pan.
173/E2 San Carlos, Par.
125/C2 San Carlos, Phil.
175/G2 San Carlos, Uru.
187/G4 San Carlos, Az,US
187/G4 San Carlos (lake), Az,US
205/K11 San Carlos, Ca,US
164/D2 San Carlos, Ven.
174/C4 San Carlos de Bariloche, Arg.
164/D2 San Carlos del Zulia, Ven.
165/E4 San Carlos de Río Negro, Ven.
187/G4 San Carlos Ind. Res., Az,US
87/E5 San Casciano in Val di Pesa, It.
167/N8 San Casimiro, Ven.
91/F2 San Cataldo, It.
174/F3 San Cayetano, Arg.
167/L6 San Cayetano, Col.
87/E3 San Cesario sul Panaro, It.
108/E5 Sancha, China
117/F3 Sancha, China
116/E3 Sancha (riv.), China
113/B2 Sanchahe, China
175/T11 Sánchez Grande, Uru.
158/E4 Sánchez Román, Mex.
186/D5 Sanchez Toboada, Mex.
85/G6 San Chirico Nuovo, It.
83/C2 San Chirico Raparo, It.
113/D5 Sanch'ŏng, SKor.
174/C2 San Clemente, Chile
76/D3 San Clemente, Sp.
204/C4 San Clemente, Ca,US
186/C4 San Clemente (isl.), Ca,US
175/F3 San Clemente del Tuyú, Arg.
85/D3 San Clemente in Casauria, It.
188/D1 Sanco, Tx,US
86/C2 San Colombano al Lambro, It.
172/D4 San Cristóbal, Arg.
172/C2 San Cristóbal, Bol.
161/F1 San Cristóbal, Cuba
162/D3 San Cristóbal, DRep.
168/K7 San Cristóbal (isl.), Ecu.
160/E3 San Cristóbal (vol.), Nic.
138/F6 San Cristobal (isl.), Sol.
158/B1 San Cristobal (cr.), Az,US
187/F4 San Cristobal (wash), Az,US
190/B2 San Cristobal, NM,US
164/C3 San Cristóbal, Ven.
76/B1 San Cristóbal de Cea, Sp.
160/C2 San Cristóbal de las Casas, Mex.
174/E2 Sancti Spíritu, Arg.
161/G1 Sancti Spíritus, Cuba
62/B2 Sand, Nor.
156/D3 Sand (riv.), SAfr.
58/D4 Sand (pt.), Eng,UK
186/E4 Sand (hills), Ca,US
203/G4 Sand (key), Fl,US
192/C3 Sand (hills), Ne,US
192/E1 Sand (cr.), SD,US
110/D3 Sanda, Japan
56/C1 Sanda (isl.), Sc,UK
125/B4 Sandakan, Malay.
202/P8 Sandalfoot Cove, Fl,US
86/B3 San Damiano d'Asti, It.
82/D4 San Damiano Macra, It.
70/D3 Sand am Main, Ger.
123/D3 Sandan, Camb.
93/F5 Sandanski, Bul.
144/C3 Sandaré, Mali
62/G1 Sandarne, Swe.
190/D2 Sand Arroyo (cr.), Co, Ks,US
72/C2 Sandau, Ger.
55/N13 Sanday (isl.), Sc,UK
57/F5 Sandbach, Eng,UK
70/D2 Sandbergen, Ger.
200/D1 Sandborn, In,US
183/J4 Sand Coulee, Mt,US
192/D3 Sand Draw (cr.), Co, Ne,US
67/F2 Sande, Ger.
62/D2 Sandefjord, Nor.
83/C3 San Demetrio Corone, It.
85/D3 San Demetrio ne'Vestini, It.
137/Q Sanders (coast), Ant.
187/H3 Sanders, Az,US
188/C2 Sanderson, Tx,US
201/F4 Sandersville, Ga,US
200/C5 Sandersville, Ms,US
134/F6 Sandgate, Austl.
56/D2 Sandhead, Sc,UK
197/R8 Sandhill, On,Can
59/F4 Sandhurst, Eng,UK
168/D4 Sandia, Peru
187/J3 Sandia Mil. Res., NM,US
190/A3 Sandia Park, NM,US
187/J3 Sandia Peak Tramway, NM,US
175/L8 San Diego (cape), Arg.
172/C2 San Diego, Bol.
204/C5 San Diego, Ca,US
204/C5 San Diego (co.), Ca,US
204/C4 San Diego (aqueduct), Ca,US
204/C5 San Diego (bay), Ca,US
204/C4 San Diego (co.), Ca,US
204/C5 San Diego (riv.), Ca,US
189/E4 San Diego, Tx,US
204/C5 San Diego-Lindbergh Field (int'l arpt.), Ca,US
186/D4 San Diego Nav. Sta., Ca,US
204/C4 San Diego Wild Animal Park, Ca,US
204/C5 San Diego Zoo, Ca,US
204/C5 San Dieguito (riv.), Ca,US
104/B2 Sandıklı, Turk.
120/C2 Sandīla, India
79/H5 Sandillon, Fr.
204/C2 San Dimas, Ca,US
89/G3 San Dimitri (pt.), Malta
90/D4 San Dimitri, Ras (pt.), Malta
124/C3 Sanding (isl.), Indo.
208/A1 Sandisfield, Ma,US
127/E3 Sandkan, Malay.
188/L7 Sand Lake, Tx,US
192/E1 Sand Lake Nat'l Wild. Ref., SD,US
62/A2 Sandnes, Nor.
61/E2 Sandnessjøen, Nor.
153/E5 Sandoa, Zaire
65/L3 Sandomierz, Pol.
164/B4 Sandoná, Col.
87/F1 San Donà di Piave, It.
85/D4 San Donato Val di Comino, It.
87/E5 San Donnino, It.
92/E2 Sándorfalva, Hun.
87/G1 San Dorligo della Valle, It.
144/B3 Sandougou (riv.), Gam., Sen.
193/K4 Sandoval, Il,US
133/G2 Sandover (riv.), Austl.
116/B5 Sandoway, Burma
59/E5 Sandown, Eng,UK
177/F4 Sand Point, Ak,US
182/F3 Sandpoint, Id,US
157/J7 Sandrakatsy, Madg.
87/E1 Sandrigo, It.
135/F5 Sandringham, Austl.
59/G1 Sandringham, Eng,UK
155/F4 Sandrivier (riv.), SAfr.
157/H8 Sandrohy, Madg.
198/C1 Sands, Mi,US
207/L8 Sands (pt.), NY,US
177/M5 Sandspit, BC,Can
207/L8 Sands Point, NY,US
183/L4 Sand Springs, Mt,US
67/F2 Sandstedt, Ger.
132/C3 Sandstone, Austl.
195/H4 Sandstone Nat'l Wild. Ref., Mn,US
117/G2 Sandu, China
117/E3 Sandu Shuizu Zizhixian, China
198/E3 Sandusky, Mi,US
198/E4 Sandusky, Oh,US
198/E4 Sandusky (riv.), Oh,US
62/D2 Sandvika, Nor.
62/G1 Sandviken, Swe.
69/F4 Sandweiler, Lux.
134/B2 Sandwich (cape), Austl.
59/H4 Sandwich, Eng,UK
198/B4 Sandwich, Il,US
199/L4 Sandwich, Ma,US
199/L3 Sandwich, NH,US
121/H4 Sandwīp (isl.), Bang.
134/D4 Sandy (cape), Austl.
197/J1 Sandy (lake), Nf,Can
178/G3 Sandy (lake), On,Can
59/F2 Sandy, Eng,UK
208/F6 Sandy (cr.), Oh,US
208/H5 Sandy (cr.), Pa,US
208/C3 Sandy (pt.), RI,US
201/G4 Sandy (pt.), SC,US
185/H3 Sandy, Ut,US
199/H3 Sandy Creek, NY,US
201/F1 Sandy Hook, Ky,US
207/J10 Sandy Hook (bay), NJ,US
207/J10 Sandy Hook (pen.), NJ,US
207/D3 Sandy Hook (bay), NJ, NY,US
207/D3 Sandy Hook Lighthouse, NJ,US
107/H1 Sandykachi, Trkm.
208/G5 Sandy Lake, Pa,US
196/E4 Sandy Point, NS,Can
200/D4 Sandy Ridge, Al,US
200/E4 Sandy Springs, Ga,US
201/M7 Sandy Springs, Ga,US
208/F6 Sandyville, Oh,US
201/G1 Sandyville, WV,US
188/A2 San Elizario, Tx,US
69/E4 Sanem, Lux.
187/F5 San Emeterio, Mex.
173/E3 San Estanislao, Par.
76/D2 San Esteban de Gormaz, Sp.
174/C3 San Fabián de Alico, Chile
85/F6 San Fele, It.
84/D5 San Felice Circeo, It.
86/D1 San Felice del Benaco, It.
87/E3 San Felice sul Panaro, It.
174/C2 San Felipe, Chile
158/B2 San Felipe, Mex.
159/E4 San Felipe, Mex.
186/D4 San Felipe (cr.), Ca,US
164/C2 San Felipe, Ven.
164/D2 San Felipe, Ven.
188/A4 San Felipe de Jesús, Mex.
159/E5 San Felipe del Progresso, Mex.
168/A2 San Felipe de Vichayal, Peru
187/J3 San Felipe Ind. Res., NM,US
190/A3 San Felipe Pueblo, NM,US
163/A5 San Félix (isl.), Chile
83/B6 San Ferdinando, It.
85/G5 San Ferdinando di Puglia, It.
175/S12 San Fernando, Arg.
174/C2 San Fernando, Chile
159/F3 San Fernando, Mex.
125/C1 San Fernando, Phil.
125/C2 San Fernando, Phil.
76/B4 San Fernando, Sp.
165/F2 San Fernando, Trin.
204/B2 San Fernando, Ca,US
204/E7 San Fernando (val.), Ca,US
165/E3 San Fernando de Apure, Ven.
164/E3 San Fernando de Atabapo, Ven.
77/N9 San Fernando-de-Henares, Sp.
187/J3 San Fidel, NM,US
83/B6 San Filippo del Mela, It.
87/F1 San Fior di Sopra, It.
61/E3 Sånfjällets Nat'l Park, Swe.
194/F3 Sanford, Can
177/K3 Sanford (mtn.), Ak,US
187/K2 Sanford, Co,US
181/K6 Sanford, Fl,US
202/N6 Sanford, Fl,US
203/H3 Sanford, Fl,US
196/B4 Sanford, Me,US
202/D2 Sanford, Ms,US
201/H3 Sanford, NC,US
86/A2 San Francesco al Campo, It.
172/D4 San Francisco, Arg.
172/C1 San Francisco (riv.), Arg.
172/E1 San Francisco, Bol.
164/B4 San Francisco, Col.
160/D3 San Francisco, ESal.
158/B2 San Francisco, Mex.
125/D3 San Francisco, Phil.
187/G3 San Francisco (mts.), Az,US
187/H4 San Francisco (riv.), Az, NM,US
205/K11 San Francisco, Ca,US
205/K11 San Francisco (bay), Ca,US
205/K11 San Francisco (co.), Ca,US
205/K11 San Francisco (int'l arpt.), Ca,US
188/C3 San Francisco (cr.), Tx,US
164/D2 San Francisco, Ven.
205/K11 San Francisco Bay Nat'l Wild. Ref., Ca,US
164/A4 San Francisco, Cabo de (cape), Ecu.
160/E3 San Francisco de la Paz, Hon.
172/D4 San Francisco del Chañar, Arg.
188/B4 San Francisco del Oro, Mex.
162/D3 San Francisco de Macorís, DRep.
174/C2 San Francisco de Mostazal, Chile
165/E2 San Francisco de Tiznados, Ven.
172/B3 San Francisco, Paso de (pass), Chile
83/A6 San Fratello, It.
82/D3 Sanfront, It.
152/C5 Sanga, Ang.
153/G4 Sanga, Zaire
174/Q9 San Gabriel, Chile
164/B4 San Gabriel, Ecu.
204/B2 San Gabriel, Ca,US
204/B2 San Gabriel (mts.), Ca,US
204/C2 San Gabriel (res.), Ca,US
204/C2 San Gabriel (riv.), Ca,US
159/M8 San Gabriel Chilac, Mex.
158/B2 San Gabriel, Punta (pt.), Mex.
204/C2 San Gabriel, West Fork (riv.), Ca,US
204/C2 San Gabriel Wilderness, Ca,US
97/J4 Sangachaly, Azer.
84/B1 San Galgano, It.
118/B4 Sangamner, India
193/J3 Sangamon (riv.), Il,US
193/K4 Sangamon, South Fork (riv.), Il,US
107/H2 Sangān (mtn.), Afg.
82/D2 Sangano, It.
101/N3 Sangar, Rus.
144/C4 Sangardo, Gui.
144/B4 Sangaréya, Gui.
68/A2 Sangatte, Fr.
88/F3 San Gavino Monreale, It.
164/B5 Sangay (vol.), Ecu.
164/B5 Sangay Nat'l Park, Ecu.
148/B4 Sangbé, Camr.
153/G3 Sange, Zaire
108/F3 Sangejing, China
84/C2 San Gemini, It.
174/E2 San Genaro, Arg.
76/A1 Sangenjo, Sp.
186/C2 Sanger, Ca,US
189/F1 Sanger, Tx,US
72/B5 Sangerhausen, Ger.
161/G1 San Germán, Cuba
86/B2 San Germano Vercellese, It.
115/C2 Sanggan (riv.), China
116/D1 Sanggarmai, China
126/D3 Sanggau, Indo.
113/B4 Sanggou (bay), China
152/D2 Sangha (riv.), Afr.
148/E5 Sangha (pref.), CAfr.
148/C5 Sangha (riv.), CAfr.
152/C2 Sangha (pol. reg.), Congo
107/J3 Sanghar, Pak.
81/H4 San Giacomo (Sankt Jakob), It.
125/D5 Sangihe (isl.), Indo.
138/B4 Sangihe (isls.), Indo.
164/C3 San Gil, Col.
87/E6 San Gimignano, It.
85/D1 San Ginesio, It.
85/E6 San Giorgio a Cremano, It.
87/E1 San Giorgio delle Pertiche, It.
85/E5 San Giorgio del Sannio, It.
87/G1 San Giorgio di Nogaro, It.
87/E3 San Giorgio di Piano, It.
90/E2 San Giorgio Ionico, It.
83/C2 San Giorgio Lucano, It.
86/C3 San Giorgio Piacentino, It.
87/G1 San Giovanni al Natisone, It.
83/B2 San Giovanni a Piro, It.
86/C1 San Giovanni Bianco, It.
90/C4 San Giovanni Gemini, It.
86/D2 San Giovanni in Croce, It.
83/C4 San Giovanni in Fiore, It.
87/F5 San Giovanni in Marignano, It.
87/E3 San Giovanni in Persiceto, It.
85/E3 San Giovanni in Venere, It.
87/E2 San Giovanni Lupatoto, It.
85/F4 San Giovanni Rotondo, It.
87/E5 San Giovanni Valdarno, It.
86/B3 San Giuliano, It.
86/D5 San Giuliano Terme, It.
85/E6 San Giuseppe Vesuviano, It.
87/F5 San Giustino, It.
86/A2 San Giusto Canavese, It.
108/D2 Sangiyn Dalay (lake), Mong.
113/E4 Sangju, SKor.
123/C3 Sangkha, Thai.
123/B3 Sangkhla, Thai.
127/E3 Sangkulirang, Indo.
122/B2 Sāngla, Pak.
125/E6 Sangley Point Nav. Air Sta., Phil.
118/B4 Sāngli, India
148/B5 Sangmélima, Camr.
111/L10 Sangō, Japan
186/D3 San Gorgonio (mtn.), Ca,US
116/B3 Sangpang (mts.), Burma
190/B1 Sangre de Cristo (mts.), Co,US
190/B3 Sangre de Cristo (mts.), NM,US
174/E2 San Gregorio, Arg.
175/G2 San Gregorio, Uru.
205/K12 San Gregorio, Ca,US
85/F6 San Gregorio Magno, It.
162/F5 Sangre Grande, Trin.
121/J1 Sangri, China
85/E3 Sangro (lake), It.
85/E3 Sangro (riv.), It.
122/C2 Sangrūr, India
121/F1 Sangsang, China
161/G2 Sangster (int'l arpt.), Jam.
170/A1 Sangue (riv.), Braz.
76/E1 Sangüesa, Sp.
145/E4 Sanguie (prov.), Burk.
86/C2 San Guiliano Milanese, It.
172/D4 San Guillermo, Arg.
87/E2 Sanguinetto, It.
113/D3 Sangwŏn, NKor.
115/D3 Sanhe, China
158/B3 San Hipólito, Punta (pt.), Mex.
117/F3 Sanhuang, China
156/E3 Sani (pass), SAfr.
203/G4 Sanibel (isl.), Fl,US
120/D1 Sāni Bheri (riv.), Nepal
160/D2 San Ignacio, Belz.
172/D1 San Ignacio, Bol.
174/B3 San Ignacio, Chile
158/B3 San Ignacio, Mex.
158/D4 San Ignacio, Mex.
158/B2 San Ignacio (riv.), Mex.
173/E3 San Ignacio, Par.
168/B2 San Ignacio, Peru
125/C1 San Ildefonso (cape), Phil.
76/D2 San Ildefonso, Sp.
110/D3 San'in Kaigin Nat'l Park, Japan
144/C5 Saniquellie, Libr.
161/F4 San Isidro, CR
160/D2 San Isidro, Mex.
160/E3 San Isidro, Nic.
125/C4 Sanito, Phil.
164/C2 San Jacinto, Col.
125/C2 San Jacinto, Phil.
175/G2 San Jacinto, Uru.
186/D4 San Jacinto, Ca,US
204/C3 San Jacinto (riv.), Ca,US
185/F3 San Jacinto, Nv,US
189/G3 San Jacinto (dam), Tx,US
188/C3 San Jacinto (mtn.), Tx,US
189/M9 San Jacinto (riv.), Tx,US
189/M9 San Jacinto Mon., Tx,US
172/E4 San Jaime, Arg.
174/E4 San Javier, Arg.
169/E4 San Javier, Bol.
169/F5 San Javier, Bol.
174/C2 San Javier, Chile
77/E4 San Javier, Sp.
155/E2 Sanje, Zam.
167/K6 San Jerónimo, Col.
188/D3 San Jerónimo, Mex.
117/F4 Sanjia, China
116/E2 Sanjiang, China
111/F2 Sanjō, Japan
169/E4 San Joaquín, Bol.
169/F4 San Joaquín (riv.), Bol.
164/C3 San Joaquín, Col.
168/K7 San Joaquín (peak), Ecu.
160/C2 San Joaquín, Mex.
173/E3 San Joaquín, Par.
186/B2 San Joaquin, Ca,US
205/M11 San Joaquin (co.), Ca,US
204/G8 San Joaquin (hills), Ca,US
205/L10 San Joaquin (riv.), Ca,US
186/B2 San Joaquin (val.), Ca,US
167/N7 San Joaquín, Ven.
186/C2 San Joaquin, South Fork (riv.), Ca,US
190/C3 San Jon, NM,US
173/F2 San Jonquin (mts.), Par.
174/E1 San Jorge, Arg.
174/D5 San Jorge (cape), Arg.
174/D5 San Jorge (gulf), Arg.
164/C3 San Jorge (riv.), Col.
158/B2 San Jorge (bay), Mex.
160/E4 San Jorge, Nic.
77/F2 San Jorge (gulf), Sp.
172/C4 San José, Arg.
174/D4 San José (gulf), Arg.
159/H5 San Jose, Belz.
161/E4 San José (cape), CR
160/D3 San José, Guat.
158/B3 San José, Mex.
158/C3 San José (isl.), Mex.
168/B2 San Jose, Peru
168/D4 San José, Peru
125/C2 San Jose, Phil.
77/F3 San José, Sp.
175/F2 San José (dept.), Uru.
175/T12 San José (dept.), Uru.
175/T11 San José (riv.), Uru.
205/L12 San Jose, Ca,US
204/G7 San Jose (hills), Ca,US
205/L12 San Jose (int'l arpt.), Ca,US
193/K3 San Jose, Il,US
190/B3 San Jose, NM,US
187/J3 San Jose (riv.), NM,US
189/F4 San Jose (isl.), Tx,US
164/E3 San José, Ven.
165/F2 San José de Amacuro, Ven.
188/D4 San José de Aura, Mex.
125/C3 San Jose de Buenavista, Phil.
172/D1 San José de Chiquitos, Bol.
172/E4 San José de Feliciano, Arg.
158/C2 San José de Gracia, Mex.
165/E2 San José de Guanipa, Ven.
165/E2 San José de Guaribe, Ven.
172/B4 San José de Jáchal, Arg.
172/C1 San Jose de la Banda (int'l arpt.), Bol.
174/E2 San José de la Esquina, Arg.
158/C4 San José del Cabo, Mex.
164/C4 San José del Guaviare, Col.
125/F6 San Jose del Monte, Phil.
164/D3 San José del Ocune, Col.
168/C4 San Jose de Los Molinos, Peru
160/E3 San José de los Remates, Nic.
174/Q9 San José de Maipo, Chile
175/F2 San José de Mayo, Uru.
158/C2 San José de Pimas, Mex.
159/E3 San José de Raíces, Mex.
167/P7 San José de Río Chico, Ven.
164/D2 San José de Seque, Ven.
188/B4 San José de Sextín, Mex.
167/N8 San José de Tiznados, Ven.
159/E4 San José Iturbide, Mex.
159/F5 San José Tenango, Mex.
174/C1 San Juan, Arg.
175/M8 San Juan (cape), Arg.
172/C3 San Juan (prov.), Arg.
172/B3 San Juan (riv.), Arg.
172/E1 San Juan, Bol.
164/B3 San Juan (riv.), Col.
161/E4 San Juan (riv.), CR, Nic.
162/D3 San Juan, DRep.
152/B2 San Juan (cape), EqG.
160/D3 San Juan (pt.), ESal.
168/C4 San Juan, Peru
125/C2 San Juan, Phil.
125/D3 San Juan, Phil.
125/F6 San Juan (riv.), Phil.
162/E3 San Juan, PR
204/C3 San Juan (cr.), Ca,US
190/A2 San Juan (mts.), Co,US
190/A2 San Juan (riv.), Co, NM,US
187/J4 San Juan, NM,US
187/H2 San Juan (basin), NM,US
182/C3 San Juan (isl.), Wa,US
173/E3 San Juan Bautista, Par.
186/B2 San Juan Bautista, Ca,US
172/E3 San Juan Bautista de Ñeembucú, Par.
204/C3 San Juan Capistrano, Ca,US
77/E3 San Juan de Alicante, Sp.
76/B4 San Juan de Aznalfarache, Sp.
158/D5 San Juan de Lima, Punta (pt.), Mex.
125/F6 San Juan del Monte, Phil.
161/F4 San Juan del Norte, Nic.
164/D2 San Juan de los Cayos, Ven.
165/E2 San Juan de los Morros, Ven.
158/C4 San Juan de los Planes, Mex.
172/C2 San Juan del Piray, Bol.
172/C1 San Juan del Potrero, Bol.
158/D3 San Juan del Río, Mex.
165/E3 San Juan de Manapiare, Ven.
167/L7 San Juan de Ríoseco, Col.
204/C3 San Juan Hot Springs, Ca,US
158/B3 San Juanico, Punta (pt.), Mex.
159/M8 San Juan Ixcaquixtla, Mex.
159/M7 San Juan Ixtenco, Mex.
182/C3 San Juan Nat'l Wild. Ref., Wa,US
164/C2 San Juan Nepomuceno, Col.
173/F3 San Juan Nepomuceno, Par.
190/A2 San Juan Pueblo, NM,US
159/F5 San Juan Quiotepec, Mex.
159/R9 San Juan Teotihuacan, Mex.
175/L7 San Julián, Arg.
175/K7 San Julián, Gran Bajo de (val.), Arg.
172/D4 San Justo, Arg.
144/C4 Sankanbiriwa (peak), SLeo.
122/F4 Sankaranāyinarkovil, India
113/C2 Sankeyushu, China
120/E4 Sankh (riv.), India
144/C4 Sankoroni (riv.), Gui., Mali
121/G2 Sankosh (riv.), Bhu., India
107/K3 Sānkra, India
92/B2 Sankt Aegyd am Neuwalde, Aus.
71/G6 Sankt Agatha, Aus.
75/L3 Sankt Andrä, Aus.
73/A3 Sankt Andrä-Wördern, Aus.
67/H5 Sankt Andreasberg, Ger.
81/G3 Sankt Anton am Arlberg, Aus.
69/G2 Sankt Augustin, Ger.
80/E2 Sankt Blasien, Ger.
71/G6 Sankt Florian am Inn, Aus.
81/F3 Sankt Gallen, Swi.
81/F3 Sankt Gallen (canton), Swi.
81/F3 Sankt Gallenkirch, Aus.
71/F7 Sankt Georgen bei Salzburg, Aus.
71/G7 Sankt Georgen im Attergau, Aus.
70/B6 Sankt Georgen im Schwarzwald, Ger.
81/G5 Sankt Gertraud (Santa Gertrude), It.
69/G3 Sankt Goar, Ger.
70/A2 Sankt Goarshausen, Ger.
69/G5 Sankt Ingbert, Ger.
81/H4 Sankt Jakob (San Giacomo), It.
71/G6 Sankt Johann am Walde, Aus.
75/K3 Sankt Johann im Pongau, Aus.
75/K3 Sankt Johann in Tirol, Aus.
81/G3 Sankt Leonhard im Pitztal, Aus.
81/H4 Sankt Leonhard in Passeier (San Leonardo in Passiria), It.
73/A4 Sankt Margarethen im Burgenland, Aus.
71/H6 Sankt Marien, Aus.
73/A6 Sankt Martin an der Raab, Aus.
71/H6 Sankt Martin im Mühlkreis, Aus.
81/H4 Sankt Martin in Passeier (San Martino in Passiria), It.
75/L3 Sankt Michael in Obersteiermark, Aus.
81/H5 Sankt Michael (San Michele), It.
88/F1 Sankt Moritz (Saint-Moritz), Swi.
80/D5 Sankt Niklaus, Swi.
71/H6 Sankt Oswald bei Freistadt, Aus.
71/F6 Sankt Pantaleon, Aus.
67/G1 Sankt Pauli, Ger.
71/G6 Sankt Peter am Hart, Aus.
71/H6 Sankt Peter in der Au, Aus.
64/E1 Sankt Peter-Ording, Ger.
75/L2 Sankt Pölten, Aus.
80/D4 Sankt Stephan, Swi.
71/H6 Sankt Valentin, Aus.
75/L3 Sankt Veit an der Glan, Aus.
92/B1 Sankt Veit an der Gölsen, Aus.
69/G5 Sankt Wendel, Ger.
71/F6 Sankt Wolfgang, Ger.
172/E2 San Lázaro, Par.
158/B3 San Lázaro, Cabo (cape), Mex.
87/E4 San Lazzaro, It.
205/K11 San Leandro, Ca,US
205/K11 San Leandro (res.), Ca,US
189/N9 San Leon, Tx,US
81/H4 San Leonardo in Passiria (Sankt Leonhard in Passeier), It.
109/J5 Sanlong, China
169/E3 San Lorenzo, Bol.
169/E4 San Lorenzo, Bol.
175/J6 San Lorenzo (peak), Chile
164/B4 San Lorenzo, Ecu.
160/E3 San Lorenzo, Hon.
90/A3 San Lorenzo (cape), It.
158/D2 San Lorenzo, Mex.
158/D3 San Lorenzo (riv.), Mex.
160/E3 San Lorenzo, Nic.
170/A5 San Lorenzo, Par.
168/D3 San Lorenzo, Peru
205/K11 San Lorenzo, Ca,US
187/J3 San Lorenzo, NM,US
86/A5 San Lorenzo al Mare, It.
76/C2 San Lorenzo de El Escorial, Sp.
83/C3 San Lorenzo del Vallo, It.
87/F5 San Lorenzo in Campo, It.
83/C6 San Luca, It.
76/B4 Sanlúcar de Barrameda, Sp.
172/C2 San Lucas, Bol.
158/C4 San Lucas, Mex.
159/E5 San Lucas, Mex.
160/E3 San Lucas, Nic.
186/B2 San Lucas, Ca,US
158/C4 San Lucas, Cabo (cape), Mex.
83/C4 San Lucido, It.
174/D2 San Luis, Arg.
174/D2 San Luis (mts.), Arg.
174/D2 San Luis (prov.), Arg.
172/E1 San Luis, Bol.
169/E4 San Luis (lake), Bol.
167/K7 San Luis, Col.
167/L6 San Luis, Col.
161/H1 San Luis, Cuba
160/D2 San Luis, Guat.
168/B4 San Luis, Peru
186/E4 San Luis, Az,US
186/B2 San Luis (res.), Ca,US
190/B2 San Luis, Co,US
192/B5 San Luis (cr.), Co,US
190/B2 San Luis (val.), Co,US
192/A5 San Luis (val.), Co,US
164/D2 San Luis, Ven.
175/G2 San Luis al Medio, Uru.
203/F2 San Luis Arch. Site, Fl,US
159/E4 San Luis de la Paz, Mex.
187/F5 San Luisito, Mex.
186/B2 San Luis Nat'l Wild Ref., Ca,US
186/B3 San Luis Obispo, Ca,US
186/B3 San Luis Obispo de Tolosa (mission), Ca,US
159/E4 San Luis Potosí, Mex.
159/E4 San Luis Potosí (state), Mex.
180/F7 San Luis Potosi (state), Mex.
204/C4 San Luis Rey, Ca,US
204/C4 San Luis Rey (riv.), Ca,US
186/E4 San Luis Río Colorad[o], Mex.
172/B3 San Manuel, Chile
187/G4 San Manuel, Az,US
87/D4 San Marcello Pistoiese, It.
190/A4 San Marcial, NM,US
85/E5 San Marco (peak), It.
83/C3 San Marco Argentan[o], It.
83/A6 San Marco D'Alunzio, It.
85/E5 San Marco dei Cavot[i], It.
85/F4 San Marco in Lamis, It.
85/F4 San Marco la Catola, It.
164/C2 San Marcos, Col.
161/E4 San Marcos, CR
160/D3 San Marcos, Guat.
160/B2 San Marcos, Mex.
168/B2 San Marcos, Peru
168/B3 San Marcos, Peru
204/C4 San Marcos, Ca,US
189/F3 San Marcos, Tx,US
189/F3 San Marcos (riv.), Tx,US
87/G5 San Maria di Porto Novo, It.
125/C1 San Mariano, Phil.
87/F5 San Marino
87/F5 San Marino (cap.), SMar.
204/F7 San Marino, Ca,US
174/C2 San Martín, Arg.
175/J7 San Martín (lake), Ar[g].
169/F4 San Martín (riv.), Bol.
164/C4 San Martín, Col.
164/C5 San Martín, Peru
186/B2 San Martin, Ca,US
186/B3 San Martin (cape), Ca,US
159/L7 San Martín de las Pirámides, Mex.
174/C4 San Martín de los Andes, Arg.
76/C2 San Martín de Valdeiglesias, Sp.
168/B2 San Martín-La Libertad (dept.), Peru
172/E3 San Martín Número Dos, Arg.
84/C3 San Martino al Cimino, It.
87/E2 San Martino Buon Albergo, It.
90/A1 San Martino-di-Lota, Fr.
87/E1 San Martino di Lupari, It.
87/E2 San Martino di Venezze, It.
81/H4 San Martino in Passiria (Sankt Martin in Passeier), It.
85/F4 San Martino in Pensilis, It.
87/D3 San Martino in Rio, It.
86/C2 San Martino in Strada, It.
86/C2 San Martino Siccomario, It.
159/L7 San Martín Texmelucan, Mex.
145/E3 Sanmatenga (prov.), Burk.
168/B3 San Mateo, Peru
125/F6 San Mateo, Phil.
77/F2 San Mateo, Sp.
205/K11 San Mateo, Ca,US
205/K12 San Mateo (co.), Ca,US
204/C4 San Mateo (cr.), Ca,US
203/H3 San Mateo, Fl,US
187/J3 San Mateo, NM,US
187/J3 San Mateo (mts.), NM,US
187/J4 San Mateo (mts.), NM,US
165/E2 San Mateo, Ven.
159/K7 San Mateo Atenco, Mex.
174/D4 San Matías (gulf), Arg
169/G5 San Matías, Bol.
159/L7 San Matías Tlalancaleca, Mex.
165/E2 San Mauricio, Ven.
86/B1 San Maurizio d'Opaglio, It.
85/G7 San Mauro Forte, It.
83/C4 San Mauro Marchesato, It.
87/F4 San Mauro Pascoli, It.
86/A2 San Mauro Torinese, It.
115/B4 Sanmenxia, China
87/F1 San Michele al Tagliamento, It.
81/H5 San Michele (Sankt Michael), It.
172/E4 San Miguel, Arg.
169/E4 San Miguel, Bol.
169/F5 San Miguel, Bol.
172/D1 San Miguel (riv.), Bol.
164/B4 San Miguel (riv.), Col., Ecu.
160/D3 San Miguel, ESal.
188/C3 San Miguel, Mex.
161/G4 San Miguel, Pan.
161/G4 San Miguel (gulf), Pan.
168/B2 San Miguel, Peru
168/C4 San Miguel, Peru
125/C2 San Miguel (bay), Phil.
186/B3 San Miguel, Ca,US
186/B3 San Miguel (isl.), Ca,US
187/H1 San Miguel (riv.), Co,US
187/J4 San Miguel, NM,US
189/E3 San Miguel (cr.), Tx,US
186/B3 San Miguel Arcangel (mission), Ca,US
159/E4 San Miguel de Allende, Mex.

169/E4 San Miguel de Huachi, Bol.
174/F2 San Miguel del Monte, Arg.
164/B4 San Miguel de los Bancos, Ecu.
172/C3 San Miguel de Tucumán, Arg.
168/D3 San Miguelito, Bol.
169/F5 San Miguelito, Bol.
159/L6 San Miguel Regla, Mex.
159/K8 San Miguel Totomaloya, Mex.
159/K7 San Miguel Zinacantepec, Mex.
117/H3 Sanming, China
87/D5 San Miniato, It.
111/L9 Sannan, Japan
149/G2 Sannār, Sudan
86/B2 Sannazzaro de'Burgondi, It.
85/F4 Sannicandro Garganico, It.
83/C5 San Nicola da Crissa, It.
85/E5 San Nicola la Strada, It.
186/C4 San Nicolas (isl.), Ca,US
174/E2 San Nicolás de los Arroyos, Arg.
175/E2 San Nicolas de los Arroyos, Arg.
188/D5 San Nicolás Hidalgo, Mex.
159/M7 San Nicolás Terrenate, Mex.
159/E4 San Nicolás Tolentino, Mex.
86/C2 San Nicolò, It.
85/D2 San Nicolò a Tordino, It.
101/P2 Sannikova (str.), Rus.
85/E4 Sannio (mts.), It.
112/B3 Sannohe, Japan
53/S10 Sannois, Fr.
111/F2 Sano, Japan
172/C4 Sañogasta, Arg.
65/M4 Sanok, Pol.
164/C2 San Onofre, Col.
204/C4 San Onofre, Ca,US
204/C4 San Onofre (mtn.), Ca,US
187/H2 Sanostee, NM,US
172/C2 San Pablo, Bol.
174/B4 San Pablo, Chile
164/B4 San Pablo, Col.
168/B2 San Pablo, Peru
76/C4 San Pablo (int'l arpt.), Sp.
205/K11 San Pablo, Ca,US
205/K10 San Pablo (bay), Ca,US
205/K11 San Pablo (res.), Ca,US
190/B2 San Pablo, Co,US
165/E2 San Pablo, Ven.
158/D3 San Pablo Balleza, Mex.
205/K10 San Pablo Bay Nat'l Wild. Ref., Ca,US
125/C2 San Pablo City, Phil.
167/L6 San Pablo de Borbur, Col.
86/D2 San Paolo, It.
85/F4 San Paolo di Civitate, It.
125/C2 San Pascual, Phil.
188/D4 San Patricio, Mex.
190/B4 San Patricio, NM,US
84/H8 San Pawl il-Bahar, Malta
174/F2 San Pedro, Arg.
160/E2 San Pedro, Belz.
169/E3 San Pedro, Bol.
169/E4 San Pedro, Bol.
169/F5 San Pedro, Bol.
172/C1 San Pedro, Bol.
174/C2 San Pedro, Chile
174/Q9 San Pedro, Chile
172/B3 San Pedro (pt.), Chile
172/B2 San Pedro (vol.), Chile
167/K6 San Pedro, Col.
161/G1 San Pedro (riv.), Cuba
160/D2 San Pedro (riv.), Guat., Mex.
144/D5 San Pédro, IvC.
158/C4 San Pedro, Mex.
158/D3 San Pedro (riv.), Mex.
187/G4 San Pedro (riv.), Mex., US
173/E3 San Pedro, Par.
173/E2 San Pedro (dept.), Par.
76/B3 San Pedro (range), Sp.
158/C1 San Pedro (riv.), Az,US
204/F8 San Pedro, Ca,US
204/F8 San Pedro (bay), Ca,US
204/B3 San Pedro (chan.), Ca,US
160/D3 San Pedro Carchá, Guat.
164/D3 San Pedro de Arimena, Col.
168/C3 San Pedro de Cajas, Peru
165/F3 San Pedro de las Bocas, Ven.
158/E3 San Pedro de las Colinas, Mex.
168/B2 San Pedro de Lloc, Peru
161/E3 San Pedro de Lóvago, Nic.
173/E3 San Pedro del Paraná, Par.
77/E4 San Pedro del Pinatar, Sp.
162/D3 San Pedro de Macorís, DRep.
172/B2 San Pedro de Quemes, Bol.
158/B2 San Pedro Martir (mts.), Mex.
160/D3 San Pedro Sula, Hon.
86/C1 San Pellegrino Terme, It.
189/F4 San Perlita, Tx,US
83/B6 San Pier Niceto, It.
87/E5 San Piero a Sieve, It.
87/E5 San Piero in Bagno, It.
83/A6 San Piero Patti, It.
198/C4 San Pierre, In,US
90/A3 San Pietro (isl.), It.
83/C5 San Pietro a Maida, It.
87/E3 San Pietro in Casale, It.
87/E1 San Pietro in Gù, It.
83/C4 San Pietro in Guarano, It.
87/F4 San Pietro in Vincoli, It.
87/F2 San Pietro in Volta, It.
185/H4 San Pitch (riv.), Ut,US
86/D3 San Polo d'Enza, It.
87/F1 San Polo di Piave, It.
87/D3 San Possidonio, It.
115/K9 Sanqiao, China
205/K11 San Quentin, Ca,US
54/C6 Sanquhar, Sc,UK
164/B4 Sanquianga Nat'l Park, Col.
158/B2 San Quintín, Mex.
158/B2 San Quintín, Cabo (cape), Mex.
84/B1 San Quirico d'Orcia, It.
174/C2 San Rafael, Arg.
168/D4 San Rafael, Bol.
169/F5 San Rafael, Bol.
174/C2 San Rafael, Chile
167/K6 San Rafael, Col.
159/H4 San Rafael, Mex.
168/B2 San Rafael, Peru
168/B3 San Rafael, Peru
184/B5 San Rafael, Ca,US
204/F7 San Rafael (hills), Ca,US
186/C3 San Rafael (mts.), Ca,US
187/J3 San Rafael, NM,US
185/H4 San Rafael (des.), Ut,US
185/H4 San Rafael (riv.), Ut,US
185/H4 San Rafael (swell), Ut,US
161/J4 San Rafael, Ven.
164/D2 San Rafael del Moján, Ven.
167/O8 San Rafael de Orituco, Ven.
169/E4 San Ramón, Bol.
161/E4 San Ramón, CR
159/H4 San Ramón, Mex.
168/C3 San Ramón, Peru
175/G2 San Ramón, Uru.
205/L11 San Ramon, Ca,US
172/C2 San Ramón de la Nueva Orán, Arg.
86/A5 San Remo, It.
83/B6 San Roberto, It.
86/C2 San Rocco al Porto, It.
87/E6 San Rocco a Pilli, It.
162/D4 San Román (cape), Ven.
87/D5 San Romano, It.
167/K6 San Roque, Col.
76/C4 San Roque, Sp.
174/B3 San Rosendo, Chile
189/E2 San Saba, Tx,US
188/D2 San Saba (riv.), Tx,US
144/B4 Sansalé, Gui.
174/F1 San Salvador, Arg.
162/C1 San Salvador (isl.), Bahm.
168/J7 San Salvador (isl.), Ecu.
160/D3 San Salvador (cap.), ESal.
186/D5 San Salvador, Mex.
175/S11 San Salvador (riv.), Uru.
172/C3 San Salvador de Jujuy, Arg.
159/M7 San Salvador el Seco, Mex.
159/M8 San Salvador Huixcolotla, Mex.
86/B3 San Salvatore Monferrato, It.
85/E3 San Salvo, It.
191/G3 Sans Bois (mts.), Ok,US
175/K8 San Sebastián, Arg.
76/E1 San Sebastián, Sp.
167/N8 San Sebastián, Ven.
76/D2 San Sebastián de los Reyes, Sp.
77/N8 San Sebastian de los Reyes, Sp.
160/E3 San Sebastian de Yalí, Nic.
86/D1 San Sebastiano, It.
86/D3 San Secondo Parmense, It.
87/F5 Sansepolcro, It.
84/D1 San Severino Marche, It.
85/F4 San Severo, It.
117/J3 Sansha, China
108/F4 Sanshilipu, China
186/B3 San Simeon, Ca,US
169/F4 San Simón, Bol.
158/C3 San Simón, Mex.
187/H4 San Simon (riv.), Az,US
187/F4 San Simon (wash), Az,US
83/C3 San Sosti, It.
117/F3 Sansui, China
108/F2 Sant, Mong.
168/B3 Santa, Peru
168/B3 Santa (riv.), Peru
182/F4 Santa, Id,US
169/E4 Santa Ana, Bol.
169/F5 Santa Ana, Bol.
164/D4 Santa Ana, Col.
164/A5 Santa Ana, Ecu.
160/D3 Santa Ana, ESal.
160/D3 Santa Ana (vol.), ESal.
160/E3 Santa Ana, Hon.
158/C2 Santa Ana, Mex.
204/C3 Santa Ana, Ca,US
204/C3 Santa Ana (mts.), Ca,US
204/C3 Santa Ana (riv.), Ca,US
164/C3 Santa Ana, Ven.
159/L7 Santa Ana Chiautempan, Mex.
164/D2 Santa Ana, Falcón, Ven.
187/J3 Santa Ana Ind. Res., NM,US
189/E4 Santa Ana Nat'l Wild. Ref., Tx,US
164/D2 Santa Ana, Trujillo, Ven.
188/E2 Santa Anna, Tx,US
171/E3 Santa Bárbara, Braz.
174/B3 Santa Bárbara, Chile
164/C3 Santa Bárbara, Col.
160/D3 Santa Bárbara, Hon.
188/B4 Santa Bárbara, Mex.
125/C2 Santa Barbara, Phil.
204/A2 Santa Barbara, Ca,US
204/A2 Santa Barbara (chan.), Ca,US
204/A1 Santa Barbara (co.), Ca,US
186/C4 Santa Barbara (isl.), Ca,US
164/D2 Santa Bárbara, Ven.
164/D3 Santa Bárbara, Ven.
165/E4 Santa Bárbara, Ven.
170/D4 Santa Bárbara d'Oeste, Braz.
161/F4 Santa Catalina, Pan.
125/C3 Santa Catalina, Phil.
186/D4 Santa Catalina (gulf), Ca,US
204/B4 Santa Catalina (isl.), Ca,US
164/D3 Santa Catalina, Ven.
173/G2 Santa Catarina (isl.), Braz.
173/G2 Santa Catarina (state), Braz.
186/E5 Santa Catarina, Mex.
160/B2 Santa Catarina Juquila, Mex.
158/D3 Santa Catarina Tepehuanes, Mex.
159/Q9 Santa Cecilia Pyramid, Mex.
161/G1 Santa Clara, Cuba
158/B2 Santa Clara, Mex.
158/E3 Santa Clara, Mex.
76/A4 Santa Clara (res.), Port.
205/L12 Santa Clara, Ca,US
205/L12 Santa Clara (co.), Ca,US
204/B2 Santa Clara (riv.), Ca,US
187/F2 Santa Clara, Ut,US
165/E2 Santa Clara, Ven.
175/G2 Santa Clara de Olimar, Uru.
186/C3 Santa Clarita, Ca,US
200/D1 Santa Claus, In,US
168/C1 Santa Clotilde, Peru
77/G2 Santa Coloma de Farners, Sp.
77/L7 Santa Coloma de Gramanet, Sp.
76/A1 Santa Comba, Sp.
85/D5 Santa Croce (peak), It.
85/E4 Santa Croce di Magliano, It.
87/D5 Santa Croce sull'Arno, It.
152/D4 Santa Cruz, Ang.
175/K7 Santa Cruz, Arg.
175/K7 Santa Cruz (prov.), Arg.
175/K7 Santa Cruz (riv.), Arg.
172/D1 Santa Cruz, Bol.
167/G4 Santa Cruz, Braz.
174/C2 Santa Cruz, Chile
160/E4 Santa Cruz, CR
168/J7 Santa Cruz (isl.), Ecu.
187/G5 Santa Cruz, Mex.
187/G5 Santa Cruz (riv.), Mex., US
168/B2 Santa Cruz, Peru
168/C2 Santa Cruz, Peru
125/B2 Santa Cruz, Phil.
125/C1 Santa Cruz, Phil.
125/C2 Santa Cruz, Phil.
125/D4 Santa Cruz, Phil.
152/A2 Santa Cruz, SaoT.
138/F6 Santa Cruz (isls.), Sol.
186/A2 Santa Cruz, Ca,US
204/A2 Santa Cruz (isl.), Ca,US
77/S12 Santa Cruz da Graciosa, Azor.,Port.
77/R12 Santa Cruz das Flores, Azor.,Port.
164/D2 Santa Cruz de Bucaral, Ven.
142/A3 Santa Cruz de la Palma, Canl.
76/D3 Santa Cruz de la Zarza, Sp.
160/D3 Santa Cruz del Quiché, Guat.
161/G1 Santa Cruz del Sur, Cuba
76/D3 Santa Cruz de Mudela, Sp.
165/E2 Santa Cruz de Orinoco, Ven.
142/A3 Santa Cruz de Tenerife, Canl.
140/A2 Santa Cruz de Tenerife, Sp.
167/G4 Santa Cruz do Capibaribe, Braz.
154/D3 Santa Cruz do Cuando, Ang.
167/F4 Santa Cruz do Piauí, Braz.
170/C4 Santa Cruz do Rio Pardo, Braz.
173/F4 Santa Cruz do Sul, Braz.
160/D3 Santa Cruz, Sierra de (range), Guat.
160/B2 Santa Cruz Zenzontepec, Mex.
83/B3 Santa Domenica Talao, It.
77/L7 Sant Adrià de Besòs, Sp.
172/D4 Santa Elena, Arg.
172/E4 Santa Elena, Arg.
174/D5 Santa Elena (peak), Arg.
172/C2 Santa Elena, Bol.
160/E4 Santa Elena (bay), CR
160/E4 Santa Elena (cape), CR
164/A5 Santa Elena, Ecu.
160/E2 Santa Elena, Hon.
158/E3 Santa Elena, Mex.
159/E3 Santa Elena, Mex.
168/C2 Santa Elena, Peru
172/C1 Santa Elena de Turuchipa, Bol.
165/F3 Santa Elena de Uairén, Ven.
76/C4 Santaella, Sp.
83/C5 Santa Eufemia (arpt.), It.
83/C5 Santa Eufemia Lamezia, It.
76/A1 Santa Eugenia, Sp.
76/A1 Santa Eugenia de Ribeira, Sp.
77/F3 Santa Eulalia del Río, Sp.
174/E1 Santa Fé, Arg.
172/D3 Santa Fe (prov.), Arg.
169/E3 Santa Fe, Bol.
161/F1 Santa Fe, Cuba
76/D4 Santa Fé, Sp.
203/G3 Santa Fe (lake), Fl,US
203/H3 Santa Fe (riv.), Fl,US
180/E4 Santa Fe, NM,US
190/B3 Santa Fe (cap.), NM,US
190/B3 Santa Fe (mts.), NM,US
189/G3 Santa Fe, Tx,US
170/C4 Santa Fé do Sul, Braz.
204/B2 Santa Felicia (dam), Ca,US
204/F8 Santa Fe Springs, Ca,US
167/E5 Santa Filomena, Braz.
84/B2 Santa Fiora, It.
83/B6 Sant'Agata (riv.), It.
87/E3 Sant'Agata Bolognese, It.
83/A6 Sant'Agata di Militello, It.
85/F5 Sant'Agata di Puglia, It.
87/F5 Sant'Agata Feltria, It.
81/G5 Santa Gertrude (Sankt Gertraud), It.
188/B4 Santa Gertrudis, Mex.
81/H5 Santa Giustina (lake), It.
85/E6 Sant'Agnello, It.
87/E3 Sant'Agostino, It.
167/K6 Santaguida (arpt.), Col.
121/G3 Sāntāhār, Bang.
167/E3 Santa Helena, Braz.
170/C3 Santa Helena de Goiás, Braz.
171/F2 Santa Inês, Braz.
175/J8 Santa Inés (isl.), Chile
159/L7 Santa Inés Zacatelco, Mex.
174/D3 Santa Isabel, Arg.
174/E2 Santa Isabel, Arg.
172/C2 Santa Isabel, Bol.
171/K8 Santa Isabel, Braz.
161/F3 Santa Isabel, Col.
168/B1 Santa Isabel, Ecu.
160/D2 Santa Isabel (riv.), Guat.
158/C3 Santa Isabel, Mex.
138/E5 Santa Isabel (isl.), Sol.
165/E4 Santa Isabel, Ven.
168/C5 Santa Isabel de Sihuas, Peru
173/F2 Santa Isabel do Ivaí, Braz.
166/D3 Santa Isabel do Pará, Braz.
152/B2 Santa Isabel, Oico de (peak), EqG.
159/F3 Santa Juana, Mex.
170/D3 Santa Juliana, Braz.
87/F3 Sant'Alberto, It.
172/E4 Santa Lucía, Arg.
172/E3 Santa Lucía (riv.), Arg.
142/B4 Santa Lucia, Canl.
164/B5 Santa Lucia, Ecu.
168/D4 Santa Lucía, Peru
175/F2 Santa Lucía, Uru.
175/G2 Santa Lucia (riv.), Uru.
186/B2 Santa Lucia (range), Ca,US
164/D2 Santa Lucía, Ven.
83/B6 Santa Lucia del Mela, It.
87/F1 Santa Lucia di Piave, It.
171/F1 Santa Luz, Braz.
167/E3 Santa Luzia, Braz.
167/G4 Santa Luzia, Braz.
140/J10 Santa Luzia (isl.), CpV.
158/B3 Santa Magdalena (isl.), Mex.
174/E2 Santa Magdelena, Arg.
158/B3 Santa Margarita (isl.), Mex.
186/B3 Santa Margarita, Ca,US
204/C4 Santa Margarita (riv.), Ca,US
86/C4 Santa Margherita Ligure, It.
172/C3 Santa María, Arg.
169/F4 Santa María, Bol.
169/F5 Santa María, Bol.
172/D1 Santa María, Bol.
173/F4 Santa Maria, Braz.
173/F3 Santa Maria (riv.), Braz.
174/C2 Santa María, Chile
174/B3 Santa María (isl.), Chile
140/K10 Santa Maria, CpV.
168/J7 Santa María, Ecu.
168/J7 Santa María (isl.), Ecu.
159/L7 Santa María, Mex.
158/C3 Santa María (bay), Mex.
158/D2 Santa María (riv.), Mex.
160/A1 Santa María (riv.), Mex.
125/C1 Santa Maria, Phil.
125/D4 Santa Maria, Phil.
77/T13 Santa Maria (isl.), Azor.,Port.
186/B3 Santa Maria, Ca,US
87/D5 Santa Maria a Monte, It.
155/G5 Santa Maria, Cabo de (cape), Moz.
76/B4 Santa Maria, Cabo de (cape), Port.
85/E5 Santa Maria Capua Vetere, It.
171/F1 Santa Maria da Boa Vista, Braz.
170/D2 Santa Maria da Vitória, Braz.
76/D1 Santa María de Cayón, Sp.
165/E3 Santa María de Erebató, Ven.
84/C1 Santa Maria degli Angeli, It.
165/E2 Santa María de Ipire, Ven.
86/C3 Santa Maria della Versa, It.
165/E3 Santa María del Orinoco, Ven.
188/B5 Santa María del Oro, Mex.
159/E4 Santa María del Río, Mex.
168/C1 Santa María de Nanay, Peru
91/F3 Santa Maria di Leuca (cape), It.
166/E3 Santa Maria do Pará, Braz.
171/E3 Santa Maria do Suaçi, Braz.
160/B3 Santa María Huatulco, Mex.
81/G4 Santa Maria im Münstertal, Swi.
85/E5 Santa Maria la Fossa, It.
87/E3 Santa Maria Maddalena, It.
81/E5 Santa Maria Maggiore, It.
87/G6 Santa Maria Nuova, It.
84/B3 Santa Marinella, It.
164/C2 Santa Marta, Col.
173/G4 Santa Marta Grande, Cabo de (cape), Braz.
164/C2 Santa Marta, Nevada de (mts.), Col.
204/B2 Santa Monica, Ca,US
204/E8 Santa Monica (bay), Ca,US
204/B2 Santa Monica (mts.), Ca,US
204/B2 Santa Monica Mts. Nat'l Rec. Area, Ca,US
170/D2 Santana, Braz.
173/F3 Santana (hills), Braz.
167/F3 Santana (isl.), Braz.
142/A2 Santana, Madr.
77/P11 Santana, Port.
77/V15 Santana, Madr.,Port.
173/F4 Santana da Boa Vista, Braz.
167/F3 Santana do Acaraú, Braz.
167/G4 Santana do Cariri, Braz.
171/F1 Santana do Ipanema, Braz.
173/F4 Santana do Livramento, Braz.
85/E6 Sant'Anastasia, It.
164/B4 Santander, Col.
164/C3 Santander (dept.), Col.
125/C3 Santander, Phil.
76/D1 Santander, Sp.
159/F3 Santander Jiménez, Mex.
83/C5 Sant'Andrea Apostolo dello Ionio, It.
85/E5 Sant'Andrea del Pizzone, It.
85/F6 Sant'Andrea di Conza, It.
85/F6 Sant'Angelo dei Lombardi, It.
83/A6 Sant'Angelo di Brolo, It.
87/F5 Sant'Angelo in Vado, It.
86/C2 Sant'Angelo Lodigiano, It.
90/A3 Sant'Antioco, It.
88/E3 Sant' Antioco (isl.), It.
90/A3 Sant'Antioco (isl.), It.
82/D2 Sant'Antonino di Susa, It.
87/D2 Sant'Antonio, It.
85/E6 Sant'Antonio Abate, It.
77/G3 Santañy, Sp.
76/B4 Santa Olalla del Cala, Sp.
204/A2 Santa Paula, Ca,US
204/A2 Santa Paula (peak), Ca,US
77/E3 Santa Pola, Sp.
77/E3 Santa Pola, Cabo de (cape), Sp.
87/F4 Sant'Apollinare in Classe, It.
185/H4 Santaquin, Ut,US
167/F4 Santa Quitéria, Braz.
167/F3 Santa Quitéria do Maranhão, Braz.
83/C2 Sant'Arcangelo, It.
87/F4 Santarcángelo, It.
83/C2 Sant'Arcangelo (peak), It.
167/E3 Santarém, Braz.
76/A3 Santarém, Port.
76/A3 Santarém (dist.), Port.
167/E3 Santarém Novo, Braz.
167/E4 Santa Rita, Braz.
167/H4 Santa Rita, Braz.
159/E3 Santa Rita, Mex.
158/C1 Santa Rita, NM,US
164/D2 Santa Rita, Ven.
165/E2 Santa Rita, Ven.
170/D1 Santa Rita de Cássia, Braz.
171/L7 Santa Rita do Sapucaí, Braz.
174/D2 Santa Rosa, Arg.
174/D3 Santa Rosa, Arg.
174/D4 Santa Rosa (val.), Arg.
169/E3 Santa Rosa, Bol.
169/E4 Santa Rosa, Bol.
169/E5 Santa Rosa, Bol.
169/F5 Santa Rosa, Bol.
172/C1 Santa Rosa, Bol.
172/D1 Santa Rosa, Bol.
166/C4 Santa Rosa, Braz.
168/B1 Santa Rosa, Ecu.
159/F4 Santa Rosa, Mex.
159/H5 Santa Rosa, Mex.
188/D3 Santa Rosa, Mex.
173/E3 Santa Rosa, Par.
168/D4 Santa Rosa, Peru
175/T12 Santa Rosa, Uru.
187/F4 Santa Rosa (wash), Az,US
184/B4 Santa Rosa, Ca,US
186/A1 Santa Rosa, Ca,US
186/B4 Santa Rosa (isl.), Ca,US
186/D4 Santa Rosa (mts.), Ca,US
203/E2 Santa Rosa (isl.), Fl,US
190/B3 Santa Rosa, NM,US
184/E3 Santa Rosa (range), Nv,US
164/D2 Santa Rosa, Ven.
164/D3 Santa Rosa, Ven.
164/E3 Santa Rosa, Ven.
160/E3 Santa Rosa de Aguán, Hon.
165/E4 Santa Rosa de Amanadona, Ven.
167/K7 Santa Rosa de Cabal, Col.
174/D2 Santa Rosa de Calamuchita, Arg.
160/D3 Santa Rosa de Copán, Hon.
169/F5 Santa Rosa de la Roca, Bol.
169/F4 Santa Rosa del Palmar, Bol.
164/C3 Santa Rosa de Osos, Col.
173/H2 Santa Rosa de Viterbo, Braz.
158/B3 Santa Rosalía, Mex.
164/D2 Santa Rosalía, Ven.
165/E3 Santa Rosalía, Ven.
158/B2 Santa Rosalía, Punta (pt.), Mex.
160/E4 Santa Rosa Nat'l Park, CR
83/B2 Sant'Arsenio, It.
83/C4 Santa Severina, It.
87/E5 Santa Sofia, It.
204/B2 Santa Susana (mts.), Ca,US
133/G3 Santa Teresa, Austl.
170/C2 Santa Teresa, Braz.
171/E3 Santa Teresa, Braz.
170/C2 Santa Teresa (riv.), Braz.
159/H5 Santa Teresa, Mex.
167/O7 Santa Teresa, Ven.
133/G2 Santa Teresa Abor. Land, Austl.
83/B7 Santa Teresa di Riva, It.
175/G2 Santa Teresa Nat'l Park, Uru.
170/C1 Santa Teresinha, Braz.
175/F3 Santa Teresita, Arg.
172/D2 Santa Victoria, Arg.
170/C3 Santa Vitória, Braz.
175/G2 Santa Vitória do Palmar, Braz.
186/B3 Santa Ynez, Ca,US
204/A2 Santa Ynez (mts.), Ca,US
204/A1 Santa Ynez (riv.), Ca,US
186/B3 Santa Ynez Ind. Res., Ca,US
186/D4 Santa Ysabel Ind. Res., Ca,US
77/L7 Sant Boi de Llobregat, Sp.
77/F2 Sant Carles de la Ràpita, Sp.
77/G2 Sant Celoni, Sp.
77/G2 Sant Cugat del Vallès, Sp.
204/D5 Santee, Ca,US
201/G4 Santee (dam), SC,US
201/H4 Santee (pt.), SC,US
201/H4 Santee (riv.), SC,US
192/F2 Santee Ind. Res., Ne,US
201/G4 Santee Nat'l Wild. Ref., SC,US
85/D2 Sant'Egidio alla Vibrata, It.
85/E4 Sant'Elia a Pianisi, It.
85/D4 Sant'Elia Fiumerapido, It.
158/E5 San Telmo, Punta (pt.), Mex.
85/D1 Sant'Elpidio a Mare, It.
86/A3 Santena, It.
87/E4 Santerno (riv.), It.
83/B5 Sant'Eufemia (gulf), It.
83/B6 Sant'Eufemia d'Aspromonte, It.
77/L7 Sant Feliu, Sp.
77/G2 Sant Feliu de Guíxols, Sp.
77/G2 Sant Feliu de Llobregat, Sp.
77/F1 Sant Gervàs (peak), Sp.
86/B2 Santhia, It.
173/F4 Santiago, Braz.
174/C2 Santiago (cap.), Chile
174/Q9 Santiago (cape), Chile
168/B1 Santiago (riv.), Ecu., Peru
152/B2 Santiago (pt.), EqG.
158/C4 Santiago, Mex.
159/E3 Santiago, Mex.
176/G7 Santiago (riv.), Mex.
161/F4 Santiago, Pan.
161/F4 Santiago (mtn.), Pan.
173/E3 Santiago, Par.
168/C4 Santiago, Peru
125/C1 Santiago, Phil.
76/A1 Santiago de Compostela, Sp.
76/A1 Santiago (int'l arpt.), Sp.
204/C3 Santiago (peak), Ca,US
204/C3 Santiago (res.), Ca,US
188/C2 Santiago (mts.), Tx,US
188/C3 Santiago (peak), Tx,US
174/Q9 Santiago (Arturo Merino Benítez) (int'l arpt.), Chile
168/B2 Santiago de Cao, Peru
168/C4 Santiago de Chocorvos, Peru
168/B3 Santiago de Chuco, Peru
161/H1 Santiago de Cuba, Cuba
172/C3 Santiago del Estero, Arg.
172/D2 Santiago del Estero (prov.), Arg.
162/D3 Santiagode los Caballeros, DRep.
168/D5 Santiago de Machaca, Bol.
169/D4 Santiago de Pacaguaras, Bol.
76/A3 Santiago do Cacém, Port.
158/D4 Santiago Ixcuintla, Mex.
160/B2 Santiago Jocotepec, Mex.
160/B2 Santiago Juxtlahuaca, Mex.
159/M8 Santiago Miahuatlán, Mex.
158/D3 Santiago Papasquiaro, Mex.
174/C2 Santiago, Region Metropolitana de (reg.), Chile
159/G5 Santiago Tuxtla, Mex.
175/T12 Santiago Vázquez, Uru.
127/F3 Santigi, Indo.
86/D3 Sant'Ilario d'Enza, It.
164/D2 San Timoteo, Ven.
121/G4 Sāntipur, India
81/F3 Säntis (peak), Swi.
76/D3 Santisteban del Puerto, Sp.
77/K6 Sant Jeroni (mtn.), Sp.
77/F1 Sant Julià, And.
77/K6 Sant Llorenç del Munt Nat'l Park, Sp.
111/K9 Santō, Japan
189/E1 Santo, Tx,US
171/F2 Santo Amaro, Braz.
171/K8 Santo Amaro (isl.), Braz.
171/F1 Santo Amaro das Brotas, Braz.
173/G2 Santo Anastácio, Braz.
170/D4 Santo André, Braz.
173/F4 Santo Ângelo, Braz.
140/J9 Santo Antão (isl.), CpV.
152/A2 Santo António, SaoT.
164/E5 Santo Antônio do Içá, Braz.
170/A2 Santo Antônio do Leverger, Braz.
167/E4 Santo Antônio dos Lopes, Braz.
173/F3 Santo Antônio do Sudoeste, Braz.
173/F3 Santo Augusto, Braz.
172/E1 Santo Corazón, Bol.
169/E3 Santo Domingo, Bol.
174/Q9 Santo Domingo, Chile
161/F1 Santo Domingo, Cuba
162/D3 Santo Domingo (cap.), DRep.
158/B2 Santo Domingo, Mex.
159/E4 Santo Domingo, Mex.
76/D1 Santo Domingo de la Calzada, Sp.
164/B5 Santo Domingo de los Colorados, Ecu.
160/C2 Santo Domingo Petapa, Mex.
190/A3 Santo Domingo Pueblo, NM,US
158/B3 Santo Domingo, Punta (pt.), Mex.
165/E2 San Tomé, Ven.
77/E3 Santomera, Sp.
76/D1 Santoña, Sp.
84/C3 Sant'Oreste, It.
91/J4 Santorini (Thíra), Gre.
87/E1 Santorso, It.
170/D4 Santos, Braz.
171/E4 Santos Dumont, Braz.
171/E4 Santos Dumont (int'l arpt.), Braz.
169/E3 Santos Mercado, Bol.
160/B2 Santos Reyes Nopala, Mex.
85/D6 Santo Stefano (isl.), It.
86/B3 Santo Stefano Belbo, It.
86/C3 Santo Stefano d'Aveto, It.
86/C4 Santo Stefano di Magra, It.
83/B6 Santo Stefano in Aspromonte, It.
87/F1 Santo Stino di Livenza, It.
168/J7 Santo Tomás (vol.), Ecu.
158/A2 Santo Tomás, Mex.
186/D5 Santo Tomás, Mex.
168/B2 Santo Tomás, Peru
168/C4 Santo Tomás, Peru
125/C1 Santo Tomas (mtn.), Phil.
158/A2 Santo Tomás, Punta (pt.), Mex.
174/E1 Santo Tomé, Arg.
77/K7 Sant Pere de Ribes, Sp.
77/K7 Sant Sadurní d'Anoia, Sp.
167/K6 Santuario, Col.
86/B2 Santuario di Crea, It.
85/E6 Santuario di Monte Vergine, It.
86/A1 Santuario di Oropa, It.
115/J6 Santunying, China
76/D1 Santurce-Antiguo, Sp.
77/K6 Sant Vicenç de Castellet, Sp.
77/L7 Sant Vicenç dels Hort, Sp.
103/G7 Sānūr, WBnk.
174/B5 San Valentín (peak), Chile
87/G1 San Valentino, It.
174/E1 San Vicente, Arg.
174/C2 San Vicente, Chile
160/D3 San Vicente, ESal.
186/D5 San Vicente, Mex.
204/D5 San Vicente (res.), Ca,US
164/E3 San Vicente, Ven.
76/B3 San Vicente de Alcántara, Sp.
168/B4 San Vicente de Cañete, Peru
164/C4 San Vicente del Caguán, Col.
77/E3 San Vicente del Raspeig, Sp.
84/D1 San Vicino (peak), It.
87/G6 San Vicino, Monte (peak), It.
84/A1 San Vincenzo, It.
161/F4 San Vito, CR
83/D2 San Vito (cape), It.
87/F1 San Vito al Tagliamento, It.
85/E3 San Vito Chietino, It.
84/C4 San Vito Romano, It.
83/C5 San Vito sullo Ionio, It.
187/G4 San Xavier Ind. Res., Az,US
115/L8 Sanxing, China
117/F5 Sanya, China
117/H2 Sanyang, China
155/F3 Sanyati (riv.), Zim.
188/E4 San Ygnacio, Tx,US
204/C5 San Ysidro, Ca,US
190/A3 San Ysidro, NM,US
117/E1 Sanyuanba, China
113/C1 Sanyuanpu, China
83/B2 Sanza, It.
152/C4 Sanza Pombo, Ang.
170/D3 São Bartolomeu (riv.), Braz.
167/F3 São Benedito do Rio Prêto, Braz.
167/E3 São Bento, Braz.
167/G4 São Bento, Braz.
171/L7 São Bento do Sapucaí, Braz.
173/G3 São Bento do Sul, Braz.
171/F1 São Bento do Una, Braz.
170/D4 São Bernardo do Campo, Braz.
173/F4 São Borja, Braz.
152/C5 São Braz, Cabo de (cape), Ang.
170/D4 São Carlos, Braz.
171/F1 São Cristóvão, Braz.
170/D2 São Desidério, Braz.
170/D2 São Domingos, Braz.
170/D2 São Domingos (riv.), Braz.
144/A3 São Domingos, GBis.
166/E3 São Domingos do Capim, Braz.
167/E4 São Domingos do Maranhão, Braz.
167/F4 São Félix do Piauí, Braz.
166/D4 São Félix do Xingu, Braz.
171/E4 São Fidélis, Braz.
140/J11 São Filipe, CpV.
170/D2 São Francisco, Braz.
173/G2 São Francisco (isl.), Braz.
171/F1 São Francisco (riv.), Braz.
173/F4 São Francisco de Assis, Braz.
173/G4 São Fransisco de Paula, Braz.
173/F4 São Gabriel, Braz.
171/E3 São Gabriel da Palha, Braz.
171/N7 São Gonçalo, Braz.
171/L6 São Gonçalo do Sapucaí, Braz.
173/H1 São Gotardo, Braz.
151/A4 Sao Hill, Tanz.
170/D4 São Joachim da Barra, Braz.
169/F3 São João (mts.), Braz.
167/E3 São João Batista, Braz.
170/D2 São João da Aliança, Braz.
170/D4 São João da Boa Vista, Braz.
76/A2 São João da Madeira, Port.
76/B2 São João da Pesqueira, Port.
170/D2 São João da Ponte, Braz.
77/P10 São João das Lampas, Port.
170/D4 São João del Rei, Braz.
171/N7 São João de Meriti, Braz.
166/D4 São João do Araguaia, Braz.
167/G4 São João do Jaguaribe, Braz.
171/E2 São João do Paraíso, Braz.
167/F5 São João do Piauí, Braz.
167/F4 São João dos Patos, Braz.
171/E3 São João Evangelista, Braz.
171/N6 São João Nepomuceno, Braz.
173/G4 São Joaquim, Braz.
173/G4 São Joaquim Nat'l Park, Braz.
77/S12 São Jorge (isl.), Azor.,Port.
173/G3 São José, Braz.
171/F1 São José da Laje, Braz.
167/H4 São José de Mipibu, Braz.
167/G4 São José de Piranhas, Braz.
167/E3 São José de Ribamar, Braz.
167/G4 São José do Belmonte, Braz.
167/H4 São José do Campestre, Braz.
167/G4 São José do Egito, Braz.
167/E3 São José do Gurupi, Braz.
167/F4 São José do Peixe, Braz.
170/D4 São José do Rio Pardo, Braz.
173/G2 São José do Rio Preto, Braz.
170/D4 São José dos Campos, Braz.
171/L8 São José dos Campos (arpt.), Braz.
173/G3 São José dos Pinhais, Braz.
154/B2 São José, Ponta de (pt.), Ang.
167/F4 São Julião, Braz.
170/D4 São Lourenço, Braz.
170/A3 São Lourenço (riv.), Braz.
77/Q10 São Lourenço, Port.
173/F3 São Lourenço d'Oeste, Braz.
173/G4 São Lourenço do Sul, Braz.
152/D5 São Lucas, Ang.
167/E3 São Luís, Braz.
170/C3 São Luís de Montes Belos, Braz.
167/G3 São Luís do Curu, Braz.
167/H5 São Luís do Quitunde, Braz.
173/F4 São Luís Gonzaga, Braz.
167/G4 São Mamede, Braz.
167/E3 São Marcos (bay), Braz.
170/D3 São Marcos (riv.), Braz.
76/A3 São Martinho do Porto, Port.
171/F3 São Mateus, Braz.
171/E3 São Mateus (riv.), Braz.
167/E4 São Mateus do Maranhão, Braz.
173/G3 São Mateus do Sul, Braz.
167/G4 São Miguel, Braz.
77/T13 São Miguel (isl.), Azor.,Port.
170/C2 São Miguel do Araguaia, Braz.
173/F3 São Miguel d'Oeste, Braz.
167/E3 São Miguel do Guamá, Braz.
171/F1 São Miguel dos Campos, Braz.
167/F4 São Miguel do Tapuio, Braz.
162/D3 Saona (isl.), DRep.
80/C3 Saône, Fr.
80/B4 Saône (riv.), Fr.
80/B4 Saône-et-Loire (dept.), Fr.
140/J10 São Nicolau (isl.), CpV.
170/D4 São Paulo, Braz.
173/G1 São Paulo (state), Braz.
168/D1 São Paulo de Olivença, Braz.
167/H4 São Paulo do Potengi, Braz.
167/F4 São Pedro do Piauí, Braz.
173/F4 São Pedro do Sul, Braz.
76/A2 São Pedro do Sul, Port.
167/G4 São Rafael, Braz.
167/E4 São Raimundo das Mangabeiras, Braz.
171/E1 São Raimundo Nonato, Braz.
111/M9 Saori, Japan
170/D3 São Romão, Braz.
163/F3 São Roque, Cabo de (cape), Braz.
77/S12 São Roque do Pico, Azor.,Port.
171/L8 São Sebastião, Braz.
171/L8 São Sebastião (isl.), Braz.
155/G4 São Sebastião (pt.), Moz.
166/D3 São Sebastião da Boa Vista, Braz.
173/H2 São Sebastião do Paraíso, Braz.
166/D4 São Sebastião do Tocantins, Braz.
167/G5 São Sebastião do Umbuzeiro, Braz.
170/C3 São Simão, Braz.
170/C3 São Simão (res.), Braz.
169/F4 São Simão (riv.), Braz.
76/A4 São Teotónio, Port.
140/K10 São Tiago (isl.), CpV.
152/A2 São Tomé (cap.), SaoT.
152/A2 São Tomé (int'l arpt.), SaoT.
152/A2 São Tomé (isl.), SaoT.
152/A2 São Tomé and Príncipe
171/E4 São Tomé, Cabo de (cape), Braz.
143/E3 Saoura, Oued (dry riv.), Alg.
170/D4 São Vicente, Braz.
171/K8 São Vicente, Braz.
140/J10 São Vicente (isl.), CpV.
76/A4 São Vicente, Cabo de (cape), Port.
167/E3 São Vicente Ferrer, Braz.
123/C1 Sa Pa, Viet.
121/G3 Sapāhār, Bang.
91/J2 Sápai, Gre.
172/C2 Sapaleri (peak), Chile
168/C4 Sapallanga, Peru
93/K5 Sapanca, Turk.
91/H1 Sapareva Banya, Bul.
127/G4 Saparua, Indo.
121/H2 Sapatgrām, India
195/J3 Sapawe, On,Can
167/H4 Sapé, Braz.
145/G5 Sapele, Nga.
190/B3 Sapello, NM,US
203/H2 Sapelo (isl.), Ga,US
104/B4 Saphane, Turk.
91/G4 Sapiéndza (isl.), Gre.
80/D1 Sapin Sec, Roche du (mtn.), Fr.
113/D4 Sapkyo, SKor.
145/E3 Saponé, Burk.
153/E4 Sapo-Sapo, Zaire
161/G5 Sapo, Serranía de (range), Pan.
168/B2 Saposoa, Peru
97/G1 Sapozhok, Rus.
66/D2 Sappemeer, Neth.
134/B3 Sapphire, Austl.
112/B2 Sapporo, Japan
83/B2 Sapri, It.
121/F2 Sapt Kosi (riv.), Nepal
173/H1 Sapucaí (riv.), Braz.
124/F4 Sapudi (isl.), Indo.
191/F3 Sapulpa, Ok,US
125/B4 Sapulut, Malay.
141/W17 Sāqiyat Sī'di Yūsuf, Tun.
105/F2 Saqqez, Iran
168/C2 Saquena, Peru
164/B5 Saquisilí, Ecu.
92/E4 Šar (mts.), Yugo.
125/C3 Sara, Phil.
105/F2 Sarāb, Iran
123/C3 Sara Buri, Thai.
83/C3 Saracena, It.
83/A6 Saraceni, Monte de (peak), It.
85/E5 Saraceno (peak), It.
83/C3 Saraceno (riv.), It.
148/C2 Saraf Doungous, Chad
105/G3 Sarafjagān, Iran
188/C2 Saragosa, Tx,US
77/E2 Saragossa, Sp.
88/C2 Saragossa (Zaragoza), Sp.
168/B1 Saraguro, Ecu.
122/B1 Sarāi Alamgir, Pak.
121/E4 Saraikela, India
121/H3 Sarāil, Bang.
92/D4 Sarajevo (cap.), Bosn.
97/L2 Saraktash, Rus.
202/D2 Saraland, Al,US
153/F4 Saramabila, Zaire
166/C1 Saramacca (dist.), Sur.
116/B3 Saramati (mtn.), India
169/D4 Sarampiuni, Bol.
79/G5 Saran, Fr.
126/D4 Saran (peak), Indo.
114/B2 Saran', Kaz.
199/J2 Saranac Lake, NY,US
151/A3 Saranda, Tanz.
91/L6 Sarandapótamos (riv.), Gre.
91/G3 Sarandë, Alb.
173/F3 Sarandi, Braz.
175/G2 Sarandí Del Yí, Uru.
175/F2 Sarandí de Navarro, Uru.
175/F2 Sarandí Grande, Uru.
125/D4 Sarangani (isls.), Phil.
118/C3 Sarangpur, India
150/B5 Saranley, Som.
53/H3 Saransk, Rus.
53/J3 Sarapul, Rus.
164/D3 Sarare (riv.), Ven.
120/A3 Sāraskheri, India
203/G4 Sarasota, Fl,US
98/E4 Sarata, Ukr.
205/K12 Saratoga, Ca,US
185/K3 Saratoga, Wy,US
199/K3 Saratoga Nat'l Hist. Park, NY,US
199/K3 Saratoga Springs, NY,US
126/D3 Saratok, Malay.
53/H3 Saratov, Rus.
97/J1 Saratov (res.), Rus.
99/M2 Saratov Obl., Rus.
107/H3 Sarāvān, Iran

123/D3 Saravan, Laos
131/G1 Sarawaget (range), PNG
126/D3 Sarawak (state), Malay.
104/A1 Saray, Turk.
144/C3 Saraya, Sen.
164/B5 Sarayacu, Ecu.
120/C2 Sarāyan (riv.), India
104/B2 Saraykőy, Turk.
104/C2 Sarayönü, Turk.
107/H3 Sarbāz, Iran
121/H2 Sarbhāng, Bhu.
73/C6 Sárbogárd, Hun.
81/G5 Sarca (riv.), It.
172/C2 Sarcari, Bol.
53/T10 Sarcelles, Fr.
172/B4 Sarco, Chile
191/G2 Sarcoxie, Mo,US
120/C1 Sārda (can.), India
118/D2 Sarda (riv.), India
120/C1 Sārda (riv.), India
120/C2 Sārda, Hardoi Branch (can.), India
90/A3 Sardara, It.
118/B2 Sardārshahar, India
105/F2 Sar Dasht, Iran
90/A2 Sardegna (reg.), It.
120/A1 Sardhana, India
164/C2 Sardinata, Col.
82/C6 Sardinaux, Cap de (cape), Fr.
90/A2 Sardinia (isl.), It.
200/F1 Sardinia, Oh,US
201/G4 Sardis, Ga,US
200/C3 Sardis, Ms,US
200/C3 Sardis (dam), Ms,US
200/C3 Sardis (lake), Ms,US
191/G3 Sardis (lake), Ok,US
188/L7 Sardis, Tx,US
61/F2 Sareks Nat'l Park, Swe.
61/F2 Sarektjåkko (peak), Swe.
127/E4 Sarempaka (peak), Indo.
121/F4 Sārenga, India
81/H4 Sarentino, It.
189/H1 Sarepta, La,US
86/D1 Sarezzo, It.
81/F3 Sargans, Swi.
185/K4 Sargents, Co,US
122/B1 Sargodha, Pak.
140/D4 Sarh, Chad
105/H2 Sārī, Iran
124/C2 Sari (cape), Malay.
122/C1 Saria, India
127/J4 Saribi (cape), Indo.
104/B1 Sarıcakaya, Turk.
90/A2 Sari-di-Porto-Vecchio, Fr.
138/D3 Sarigan (isl.), NMar.
105/N7 Sarigazi (arpt.), Turk.
104/B2 Sarıgöl, Turk.
104/E1 Sarıkamış, Turk.
104/C2 Sarıkaya, Turk.
104/C2 Sarikaya (prov.), Turk.
126/D3 Sarikei, Malay.
134/C3 Sarina, Austl.
80/D4 Sarine (riv.), Swi.
77/E2 Sariñena, Sp.
104/C2 Sarıoğlan, Turk.
189/F4 Sarita, Tx,US
113/C3 Sariwŏn, NKor.
120/C2 Sarju (riv.), India
78/C2 Sark (isl.), UK
74/B2 Sark (isl.), Chl,UK
92/E2 Sarkad, Hun.
97/L4 Sarkamyshskoye (lake), Trkm., Uzb.
100/H5 Sarkand, Kaz.
73/C5 Sárkeresztúr, Hun.
104/B2 Şarkîkaraağaç, Turk.
104/D2 Şarkışla, Turk.
93/H5 Şarköy, Turk.
74/D4 Sarlat-La-Canéda, Fr.
71/G5 Sarleinsbach, Aus.
86/C2 Sarmato, It.
73/B6 Sármellék, Hun.
83/C2 Sarmento (riv.), It.
87/E2 Sarmeola, It.
127/J4 Sarmi, Indo.
174/C5 Sarmiento, Arg.
175/K8 Sarmiento (peak), Chile
62/E1 Särna, Swe.
85/D1 Sarnano, It.
120/D3 Sārnāth, India
80/E4 Sarnen, Swi.
205/H6 Sarnia, On,Can
86/C1 Sarnico, It.
85/E6 Sarno, It.
98/D2 Sarny, Ukr.
127/F4 Saroako, Indo.
112/B1 Sarobetsu-Rishiri-Rebun Nat'l Park, Japan
124/C3 Sarolangun, Indo.
112/C1 Saroma (lake), Japan
91/H4 Saronic (gulf), Gre.
91/L7 Saronikós (gulf), Gre.
86/C1 Saronno, It.
93/H5 Saros (gulf), Turk.
92/E1 Sárospatak, Hun.
62/D2 Sarpsborg, Nor.
69/G6 Sarralbe, Fr.
146/D4 Sarra, Ma'ṭan as (well), Libya
82/A2 Sarras, Fr.
69/F6 Sarre (riv.), Fr.
78/B5 Sarre (riv.), Fr.
69/G6 Sarrebourg, Fr.
69/G5 Sarreguemines, Fr.
69/G6 Sarre-Union, Fr.
76/B1 Sarria, Sp.
82/A4 Sarrians, Fr.
90/A3 Sarroch, It.
68/D6 Sarry, Fr.
87/F5 Sarsina, It.
67/G4 Sarstedt, Ger.
160/D3 Sarstún (riv.), Belz., Guat.
101/P3 Sartang (riv.), Rus.
84/B2 Sarteano, It.
195/G5 Sartell, Mn,US
90/A2 Sartène, Fr.
79/F4 Sarthe (dept.), Fr.
79/E5 Sarthe (riv.), Fr.
79/E4 Sarthon (riv.), Fr.
78/D3 Sartilly, Fr.
108/B2 Sartokay, China
53/S10 Sartrouville, Fr.
112/C1 Sarufutsu, Japan
104/A2 Saruhanlı, Turk.
73/A5 Sárvár, Hun.
208/H6 Sarver, Pa,US
105/H4 Sarvestān, Iran
73/C6 Sárvíz (riv.), Hun.
92/D2 Sárvíz (riv.), Hun.
114/A3 Saryagach, Kaz.
97/M3 Sarybasat, Kaz.
99/G5 Sarych (cape), Ukr.
114/G1 Saryg-Sep, Rus.
114/C2 Sary Ishikotrau (des.), Kaz.
114/B2 Saryshagan, Kaz.
114/A2 Sarysu (riv.), Kaz.
86/C4 Sarzana, It.
78/C5 Sarzeau, Fr.
187/G5 Sasabe, Az,US
195/G2 Sasaginnigack (lake), Mb,Can
124/B2 Sasak, Indo.
120/E3 Sasarām, India
111/L9 Sasayama, Japan
111/L9 Sasayama (riv.), Japan
92/D2 Sásd, Hun.
110/A4 Sasebo, Japan
178/F3 Saskatchewan (prov.), Can.
178/F3 Saskatchewan (riv.), Sk,Can
183/L1 Saskatoon, Sk,Can
161/E3 Saslaya (mtn.), Nic.
161/E3 Saslaya Nat'l Park, Nic.
120/B2 Sāsni, India
156/D2 Sasolburg, SAfr.
114/C5 Sasoma, India
53/H3 Sasovo, Rus.
206/C5 Sassafras, Md,US
206/B5 Sassafras (riv.), Md,US
201/F3 Sassafras (mtn.), SC,US
200/E3 Sassafras (mtn.), Tn,US
144/D5 Sassandra, IvC.
144/D5 Sassandra (riv.), IvC.
83/B2 Sassano, It.
90/A2 Sassari, It.
82/C4 Sasse (riv.), Fr.
86/B4 Sassello, It.
67/F5 Sassenberg, Ger.
66/B4 Sassenheim, Neth.
203/F2 Sasser, Ga,US
65/G1 Sassnitz, Ger.
87/F5 Sassocorvaro, It.
87/F6 Sassoferrato, It.
87/E4 Sasso Marconi, It.
145/H3 Sassoumbouroum, Niger
144/C5 Sasstown, Libr.
87/D3 Sassuolo, It.
77/E2 Sástago, Sp.
73/B2 Šaštín-Stráže, Slvk.
174/E1 Sastre, Arg.
66/A6 Sas Van Gent, Neth.
98/E5 Sasyk (lake), Ukr.
114/D2 Sasykkol (lake), Kaz.
144/C3 Satadougou Tintiba, Mali
110/B5 Sata-misaki (cape), Japan
118/B4 Sātāra, India
157/E2 Satararuskamp, SAfr.
138/E4 Satawan (isl.), Micr.
203/H3 Satellite Beach, Fl,US
148/D4 Satema, CAfr.
62/F1 Säter, Swe.
188/A4 Satevó, Mex.
204/A2 Saticoy, Ca,US
203/H2 Satilla (riv.), Ga,US
82/A2 Satillieu, Fr.
168/C3 Satipo, Peru
95/J5 Satis, Rus.
121/J4 Sātkānia, Bang.
121/G4 Sātkhira, Bang.
57/G2 Satley, Eng,UK
120/C3 Satna, India
82/B1 Satolas (Lyon) (int'l arpt.), Fr.
92/E1 Sátoraljaújhely, Hun.
114/A2 Satpayev, Kaz.
120/A5 Satpura (range), India
83/C5 Satriano, It.
202/D2 Satsuma, Al,US
189/G3 Satsuma, Tx,US
123/C3 Sattahip, Thai.
122/F4 Sāttānkulam, India
81/F3 Satteins, Aus.
70/D4 Satteldorf, Ger.
131/G1 Sattelberg, PNG
122/F4 Sāttūr, India
123/C3 Satuk, Thai.
92/F2 Satu Mare, Rom.
92/F2 Satu Mare (co.), Rom.
98/B4 Satu Mare (co.), Rom.
123/C5 Satun, Thai.
139/R9 Satupaitea, WSam.
182/C3 Saturna, BC,Can
84/B2 Saturnia, It.
122/F3 Satyamangalam, India
172/E4 Sauce, Arg.
168/B2 Sauce, Peru
172/E4 Sauce de Luna, Arg.
172/E3 Saucedo, Uru.
174/E3 Sauce Grande (riv.), Arg.
202/D2 Saucier, Ms,US
188/B3 Saucillo, Mex.
62/B2 Sauda, Nor.
61/N6 Saudhárkrókur, Ice.
106/D4 Saudi Arabia
64/D4 Sauer (riv.), Fr.
70/A5 Sauer (riv.), France
67/F5 Sauer (riv.), Ger.
69/F4 Sauer (riv.), Ger.
69/F4 Sauer (riv.), Lux.
81/H2 Sauerlach, Ger.
69/G1 Sauerland (reg.), Ger.
169/G4 Sauêruiná (riv.), Braz.
207/E1 Saugatuck (riv.), Ct,US
198/C3 Saugatuck, Mi,US
198/F2 Saugeen (riv.), On,Can
198/F2 Saugeen Ind. Res., On,Can
199/K3 Saugerties, NY,US
166/B3 Sauiá, Braz.
74/C4 Saujon, Fr.
193/G1 Sauk (riv.), Mn,US
195/G5 Sauk Centre, Mn,US
193/K2 Sauk City, Wi,US
193/G1 Sauk Rapids, Mn,US
166/C2 Saül, FrG.
62/C2 Sauland, Nor.
82/A3 Saulce-sur-Rhône, Fr.
79/G6 Sauldre (riv.), Fr.
70/C6 Saulgau, Ger.
70/B3 Saulheim, Ger.
74/F3 Saulieu, Fr.
63/L3 Saulkrasti, Lat.
196/D3 Saulnierville, NS,Can
196/C1 Sault aux Cochons (riv.), Qu,Can
82/B4 Sault-du-Vaucluse, Fr.
68/D5 Sault-lès-Rethel, Fr.
198/D1 Sault Sainte Marie, On,Can
198/D1 Sault Sainte Marie, Mi,US
69/E6 Saulx (riv.), Fr.
80/C2 Saulx-de-Vesoul, Fr.
80/C2 Saulxures-sur-Moselotte, Fr.
134/D3 Saumarez (reefs), Austl.
82/C3 Saume, Pointe de (peak), Fr.
130/C1 Saumlaki, Indo.
79/E6 Saumur, Fr.
132/E3 Saunders (peak), Austl.
136/B4 Saunders (cape), N.Z.
58/B3 Saundersfoot, Wal,UK
208/C2 Saunderstown, RI,US
208/C1 Saundersville, Ma,US
121/F3 Saura (riv.), India
153/E5 Saurimo, Ang.
83/C2 Sauro (riv.), It.
205/K11 Sausalito, Ca,US
53/S9 Sausseron (riv.), Fr.
82/B6 Sausset-les-Pins, Fr.
127/F4 Sausu, Indo.
152/D5 Sautar, Ang.
164/B3 Sautatá, Col.
82/B3 Sautet (lake), Fr.
162/F4 Sauteurs, Gren.
78/D6 Sautron, Fr.
166/C1 Saut-Tigre, FrG.
78/B6 Sauzon, Fr.
92/C3 Sava (riv.), Eur.
164/E4 Savá, Hon.
90/E2 Sava, It.
204/D5 Savage (dam), Ca,US
199/G5 Savage (mtn.), Md,US
195/P7 Savage, Mn,US
183/M4 Savage, Mt,US
135/C4 Savage River, Austl.
139/H6 Savai'i (isl.), WSam.
145/F5 Savalou, Ben.
193/J2 Savanna, Il,US
191/G3 Savanna, Ok,US
193/J2 Savanna Army Dep., Il,US
132/L6 Savannah (brook), Austl.
201/G4 Savannah, Ga,US
201/G4 Savannah (int'l arpt.), Ga,US
203/H1 Savannah (int'l arpt.), Ga,US
201/G4 Savannah (riv.), Ga, SC,US
193/G4 Savannah, Mo,US
208/E6 Savannah, Oh,US
200/C3 Savannah, Tn,US
201/G4 Savannah River Plant-Atomic Energy Commission, SC,US
119/H4 Savannakhet, Laos
123/D2 Savannakhet, Laos
161/G2 Savanna la Mar, Jam.
195/J2 Savant (lake), On,Can
195/J2 Savant Lake, On,Can
118/B4 Savantvādi, India
61/G3 Sävar, Swe.
104/A2 Savaştepe, Turk.
154/C3 Savate, Ang.
145/F4 Savé, Ben.
155/G4 Save (riv.), Moz., Zim.
105/G3 Sāveh, Iran
83/C4 Savelli, It.
87/E4 Savena (riv.), It.
78/D6 Savenay, Fr.
93/H2 Săveni, Rom.
74/D5 Saverdun, Fr.
69/G6 Saverne, Fr.
75/G3 Savièse, Swi.
86/A3 Savigliano, It.
87/F4 Savignano sul Rubicone, It.
79/F4 Savigné-l'Évêque, Fr.
53/T11 Savigny-le-Temple, Fr.
79/F5 Savigny-sur-Braye, Fr.
53/T10 Savigny-sur-Orge, Fr.
208/B2 Saville (dam), Ct,US
82/C3 Savines-le-Lac, Fr.
87/F5 Savio (riv.), It.
62/G2 Sävja, Swe.
81/F4 Savognin, Swi.
82/C1 Savoie (dept.), Fr.
182/D2 Savona, BC,Can
86/B4 Savona, It.
86/B4 Savona (prov.), It.
191/G2 Savonburg, Ks,US
61/J3 Savonlinna, Fin.
177/D3 Savoonga, Ak,US
88/E1 Savoy (hist. reg.), Fr.
82/C1 Savoy (reg.), Fr.
193/K3 Savoy, Il,US
183/K3 Savoy, Mt,US
194/C5 Savoy, SD,US
191/F4 Savoy, Tx,US
80/C6 Savoy Alps (mts.), Fr.
104/E1 Şavşat, Turk.
62/F3 Sävsjö, Swe.
130/A2 Savu (sea), Indo.
87/G2 Savudrija, Cro.
138/G6 Savusavu, Fiji
87/C4 Savuto (riv.), It.
124/C3 Sawahlunto, Indo.
147/H5 Sawākin, Sudan
123/C2 Sawang Daeh Din, Thai.
123/B2 Sawankhalok, Thai.
111/G3 Sawara, Japan
111/F2 Sawasaki-bana (pt.), Japan
190/A1 Sawatch (range), Co,US
59/G3 Sawbridgeworth, Eng,UK
106/D5 Sawdā', Jabal (mtn.), SAr.
146/B2 Sawdā', Jabal as (hills), Libya
149/F2 Sawdirī, Sudan
127/H4 Saweba (cape), Indo.
56/A2 Sawel (mtn.), NI,UK
150/B4 Sawena, Eth.
147/F3 Sawhāj, Egypt
147/F3 Sawhāj (gov.), Egypt
119/E6 Sāwi, India
146/B2 Sawkanah, Libya
155/F3 Sawmills, Zim.
185/J5 Sawpit, Co,US
106/G5 Sawqirah, Ghubbat (bay), Oman
107/G5 Şawqirah, Ra's (pt.), Oman
59/G2 Sawston, Eng,UK
135/E1 Sawtell, Austl.
185/F1 Sawtooth (range), Id,US
183/K3 Sawtooth (mtn.), Mt,US
185/F1 Sawtooth Nat'l Rec. Area, Id,US
130/A2 Sawu, Indo.
130/A2 Sawu (isl.), Indo.
130/A2 Sawu (isls.), Indo.
191/E2 Sawyer, Ks,US
194/D3 Sawyer, ND,US
184/B3 Sawyers Bar, Ca,US
77/E3 Sax, Sp.
63/T9 Saxån (riv.), Swe.
63/S7 Saxarfjärden (sound), Swe.
57/H5 Saxilby, Eng,UK
201/K2 Saxis, Va,US
177/M4 Saxman, Ak,US
59/H2 Saxmundham, Eng,UK
64/A2 Saxmundham, Eng,UK
80/D5 Saxon, Swi.
208/H6 Saxonburg, Pa,US
65/G3 Saxony (state), Ger.
72/B2 Saxony-Anhalt (state), Ger.
145/F3 Say, Niger
172/C1 Saya, Bol.
196/D1 Sayabec, Qu,Can
100/H5 Sayak, Kaz.
111/F3 Sayama, Japan
168/B3 Sayán, Peru
108/E1 Sayansk, Rus.
72/D6 Sayda, Ger.
104/C3 Şaydā, Leb.
103/D3 Şaydā (Sidon), Leb.
150/D2 Sayḥūt, Yem.
159/H4 Sayil (ruins), Mex.
116/D3 Sayingpan, China
97/H2 Saykhin, Kaz.
92/C3 Saynbach (riv.), Ger.
195/K5 Sayner, Wi,US
108/G3 Saynshand, Mong.
114/D3 Sayram (lake), China
190/E3 Sayre, Ok,US
199/H4 Sayre, Pa,US
207/D3 Sayreville, NJ,US
114/F3 Saysu, China
97/K3 Say-Utes, Kaz.
207/E2 Sayville, NY,US
150/D2 Saywūn, Yem.
91/F2 Sazan (isl.), Alb.
71/H3 Sázava (riv.), Czh.
97/J3 Sazdy, Kaz.
105/M6 Sazli Dere (riv.), Turk.
143/E3 Sbaa, Alg.
78/B4 Scaër, Fr.
85/E6 Scafati, It.
57/E3 Scafell Pikes (mtn.), Eng,UK
55/H8 Scalasaig, Sc,UK
57/H3 Scalby, Eng,UK
54/C5 Scald Law (mtn.), Sc,UK
83/B3 Scalea, It.
87/D4 Scale, Corno alle (peak), It.
81/F5 Scalino, Pizzo (peak), It.
55/P12 Scalloway, Sc,UK
177/E3 Scammon Bay, Ak,US
83/C4 Scandale, It.
183/H2 Scandia, Ab,Can
191/F1 Scandia, Ks,US
195/Q6 Scandia, Mn,US
205/B2 Scandia, Wa,US
87/D3 Scandiano, It.
87/E5 Scandicci, It.
195/H4 Scanlon, Mn,US
85/D4 Scanno, It.
84/B2 Scansano, It.
208/B2 Scantic, Ct,US
83/C2 Scanzano Jonico, It.
55/N13 Scapa Flow (chan.), Sc,UK
132/K6 Scarborough, Austl.
197/S8 Scarborough, On,Can
162/F5 Scarborough, Trin.
57/H3 Scarborough, Eng,UK
196/B4 Scarborough, Me,US
87/F3 Scardovari, It.
68/B3 Scarpe (riv.), Fr.
87/E5 Scarperia, It.
60/B4 Scarriff, Ire.
207/E1 Scarsdale, NY,US
56/E1 Scar Water (riv.), Sc,UK
197/H3 Scatarie (isl.), NS,Can
60/A4 Scattery (isl.), Ire.
85/D5 Scauri, It.
53/S10 Sceaux, Fr.
85/E3 Scerni, It.
80/B2 Scey-Saint-Albin, Fr.
206/B3 Schaefferstown, Pa,US
68/D2 Schaerbeek, Belg.
195/L5 Schaffer, Mi,US
81/E2 Schaffhausen, Swi.
81/E2 Schaffhausen (canton), Swi.
81/H2 Schäftlarn, Ger.
66/B3 Schagen, Neth.
66/C5 Schaijk, Neth.
71/G6 Schalchen, Aus.
70/E2 Schalkau, Ger.
67/E6 Schalksmühle, Ger.
193/K2 Schaller, Ia,US
135/C3 Schanck (cape), Austl.
80/D4 Schangnau, Swi.
81/F4 Scharans, Swi.
71/G5 Schardenberg, Aus.
71/F6 Schärding, Aus.
81/H2 Scharfreiter (peak), Aus.
67/F1 Scharhorn (isl.), Ger.
72/E3 Scharmützelsee (lake), Ger.
67/H2 Scharnebeck, Ger.
131/G1 Scharnhorst (pt.), PNG
81/H3 Scharnitz (pass), Ger.
71/G7 Scharnstein, Aus.
64/F1 Schashagen, Ger.
99/K3 Schast'ye, Ukr.
81/E4 Schattdorf, Swi.
73/A4 Schattendorf, Aus.
71/E2 Schauenstein, Ger.
205/P15 Schaumburg, Il,US
66/D2 Scheemda, Neth.
70/C6 Scheer, Ger.
67/G2 Scheessel, Ger.
179/K3 Schefferville, Qu,Can
65/H4 Scheibbs, Aus.
81/F2 Scheidegg, Ger.
70/D3 Scheinfeld, Ger.
68/C2 Schelde (Scheldt) (riv.), Belg.
68/C2 Scheldt (Schelde) (riv.), Belg.
70/C6 Schelklingen, Ger.
191/G1 Schell City, Mo,US
185/F4 Schell Creek (range), Nv,US
67/H4 Schellerten, Ger.
205/K10 Schellville, Ca,US
199/K3 Schenectady, NY,US
67/G3 Schenefeld, Ger.
205/R16 Schererville, In,US
70/D5 Schermbeck, Ger.
66/C3 Scherpenzeel, Neth.
189/E3 Schertz, Tx,US
81/F2 Scherzingen, Swi.
81/F3 Schesaplana (peak), Aus.
70/E3 Schesslitz, Ger.
66/B4 Scheveningen, Neth.
81/H1 Scheyern, Ger.
66/B5 Schiedam, Neth.
67/G5 Schieder-Schwalenberg, Ger.
54/B3 Schiehallion (mtn.), Sc,UK
71/F5 Schierling, Ger.
66/D2 Schiermonnikoog, Neth.
66/D2 Schiermonnikoog (isl.), Neth.
81/F4 Schiers, Swi.
70/B4 Schifferstadt, Ger.
69/G5 Schiffweiler, Ger.
66/C5 Schijndel, Neth.
72/C5 Schildau, Ger.
68/D1 Schilde, Belg.
66/D2 Schildmeer (lake), Neth.
67/F1 Schillighörn (cape), Ger.
70/D4 Schillingfürst, Ger.
70/B6 Schiltach, Ger.
69/G6 Schiltigheim, Fr.
69/E2 Schinnen, Neth.
80/E3 Schinznach-Dorf, Swi.
87/E1 Schio, It.
69/G6 Schipbeek (riv.), Neth.
66/B4 Schiphol (Amsterdam) (int'l arpt.), Neth.
80/D1 Schirmeck, Fr.
72/C5 Schkeuditz, Ger.
72/B5 Schkölen, Ger.
72/B5 Schkopau, Ger.
91/G2 Schkumbin (riv.), Alb.
67/H4 Schladen, Ger.
92/A2 Schladming, Aus.
81/G4 Schlanders (Silandro), It.
67/F5 Schlangen, Ger.
70/B2 Schlangenbad, Ger.
200/B4 Schlater, Ms,US
69/F2 Schleiden, Ger.
81/E2 Schleitheim, Swi.
71/E1 Schleiz, Ger.
71/F1 Schlema, Ger.
64/E1 Schleswig, Ger.
193/G2 Schleswig, Ia,US
67/H1 Schleswig-Holstein (state), Ger.
64/E1 Schleswig-Holsteinisches Wattenmeer Nat'l Park, Ger.
70/D2 Schleuse (riv.), Ger.
70/D1 Schleusingen, Ger.
72/D4 Schlieben, Ger.
80/D2 Schliengen, Ger.
71/H7 Schlierbach, Aus.
81/E3 Schlieren, Swi.
71/F7 Schloss Herrenchiemsee, Ger.
67/F5 Schloss Holte-Stukenbrock, Ger.
72/D3 Schloss Sansoucci, Ger.
67/G4 Schloss Wilhelmstein, Ger.
67/H6 Schlotheim, Ger.
80/E2 Schluchsee, Ger.
80/D1 Schlucht, Col de la (pass), Fr.
70/C2 Schlüchtern, Ger.
81/G4 Schluderns (Sluderno), It.
67/G6 Schlüsselfeld, Ger.
71/G6 Schlüsslberg, Aus.
64/F3 Schmalkalden, Ger.
67/F6 Schmallenberg, Ger.
70/C6 Schmeich (riv.), Ger.
81/F1 Schmeie (riv.), Ger.
69/F5 Schmelz, Ger.
72/D6 Schmiedeberg, Ger.
70/B2 Schmitten, Ger.
80/D4 Schmitten, Swi.
72/C6 Schmölln, Ger.
70/D6 Schmutter (riv.), Ger.
71/F6 Schnaitsee, Ger.
71/E3 Schnaittach, Ger.
71/F3 Schnaittenbach, Ger.
72/C5 Schnauder (riv.), Ger.
206/C2 Schnecksville, Pa,US
70/C3 Schneeberg, Ger.
71/F1 Schneeberg, Ger.
71/E2 Schneeberg (peak), Ger.
69/F3 Schneifel (plat.), Ger.
64/D4 Schneifel (upland), Ger.
67/G2 Schneverdingen, Ger.
190/E1 Schoenchen, Ks,US
193/K1 Schofield, Wi,US
199/J3 Schoharie, NY,US
175/L7 Scholl, Cerro (mtn.), Arg.
190/A3 Scholle, NM,US
72/C2 Schollene, Ger.
70/C2 Schöllkrippen, Ger.
70/B5 Schömberg, Ger.
70/B6 Schömberg, Ger.
70/C5 Schönaich, Ger.
80/D2 Schönau, Ger.
71/G5 Schönberg, Ger.
70/D1 Schönbrunn, Ger.
70/E6 Schondorf am Ammersee, Ger.
70/C2 Schondra (riv.), Ger.
72/B3 Schönebeck, Ger.
71/F2 Schöneck, Ger.
67/F3 Schönecken, Ger.
65/G2 Schönefeld (Berlin) (int'l arpt.), Ger.
72/D3 Schöneiche, Ger.
81/G2 Schongau, Ger.
72/C2 Schönhausen, Ger.
71/F2 Schönheide, Ger.
72/A3 Schöningen, Ger.
72/D2 Schönow, Ger.
71/F3 Schönsee, Ger.
71/F2 Schönwald, Ger.
198/D3 Schoolcraft, Mi,US
66/D3 Schoonebeek, Neth.
66/B5 Schoonhoven, Neth.
66/D3 Schoorl, Neth.
70/A3 Schopfheim, Ger.
70/D4 Schopfloch, Ger.
67/H4 Schöppenstedt, Ger.
72/D1 Schörfheide (reg.), Ger.
71/G7 Schörfling am Attersee, Aus.
70/C5 Schorndorf, Ger.
67/E1 Schortens, Ger.
68/D1 Schoten, Belg.
70/C2 Schotten, Ger.
135/D4 Schouten (isl.), Austl.
138/C5 Schouten (isls.), Indo.
66/A5 Schouwen (isl.), Neth.
74/D5 Schrader (peak), Fr.
70/B6 Schramberg, Ger.
81/H3 Schrankogel (peak), Aus.
72/B5 Schraplau, Ger.
80/E4 Schreckhorn (peak), Swi.
195/L3 Schreiber, On,Can
70/B4 Schriesheim, Ger.
202/C3 Schriever, La,US
70/E5 Schrobenhausen, Ger.
195/J4 Schroeder, Mn,US
156/B2 Schroffenstein (peak), Namb.
199/K3 Schroon Lake, NY,US
70/C4 Schrozberg, Ger.
81/F3 Schruns, Aus.
81/E3 Schübelbach, Swi.
64/E1 Schuby, Ger.
189/F3 Schulenburg, Tx,US
183/J2 Schuler, Ab,Can
191/G3 Schulter, Ok,US
67/H4 Schunter (riv.), Ger.
80/E4 Schüpfheim, Swi.
184/D4 Schurz, Nv,US
81/F2 Schussen (riv.), Ger.
81/F1 Schussenried, Ger.
70/A6 Schutter (riv.), Ger.
70/E5 Schutter (riv.), Ger.
70/A6 Schutterwald, Ger.
67/E4 Schüttorf, Ger.
193/F3 Schuyler, Ne,US
206/B2 Schuylkill (co.), Pa,US
206/C3 Schuylkill (riv.), Pa,US
206/B2 Schuylkill Haven, Pa,US
70/E4 Schwabach, Ger.
81/H1 Schwabhausen bei Dachau, Ger.
70/D5 Schwäbische Alb (range), Ger.
70/C5 Schwäbisch Gmünd, Ger.
70/C4 Schwäbisch Hall, Ger.
70/D6 Schwabmünchen, Ger.
70/C4 Schwaigern, Ger.
69/F5 Schwalbach, Ger.
70/B2 Schwalbach am Taunus, Ger.
67/G6 Schwalm (riv.), Ger.
66/D6 Schwalmtal, Ger.
81/F4 Schwanden, Swi.
71/F4 Schwandorf im Bayern, Ger.
72/B4 Schwanebeck, Ger.
71/G6 Schwanenstadt, Aus.
126/D4 Schwaner (mts.), Indo.
67/F2 Schwanewede, Ger.
70/D3 Schwanfeld, Ger.
81/G2 Schwangau, Ger.
67/G3 Schwarmstedt, Ger.
65/G3 Schwartz Elster (riv.), Ger.
154/C5 Schwartzerberg (peak), Namb.
72/B6 Schwarza, Ger.
72/B6 Schwarza (riv.), Ger.
71/F5 Schwarzach, Ger.
70/E4 Schwarzach (riv.), Ger.
71/F4 Schwarzach (riv.), Ger.
92/A2 Schwarzach im Pongau, Aus.
72/C4 Schwarzbach (riv.), Ger.
72/D4 Schwarze Elster (riv.), Ger.
71/E4 Schwarze Laber (riv.), Ger.
71/E2 Schwarzenbach am Wald, Ger.
67/H2 Schwarzenbek, Ger.
71/F1 Schwarzenberg, Ger.
70/E4 Schwarzenbruck, Ger.
80/D4 Schwarzenburg, Swi.
71/F4 Schwarzenfeld, Ger.
69/F3 Schwarzer Mann (peak), Ger.
71/F4 Schwarzer Regen (riv.), Ger.
72/D5 Schwarzheide, Ger.
81/H3 Schwarzhorn (peak), Aus.
154/C5 Schwarzrand (mts.), Namb.
70/B6 Schwarzwald (Black Forest) (for.), Ger.
75/J3 Schwaz, Aus.
73/A3 Schwechat, Aus.
73/A3 Schwechat (int'l arpt.), Aus.
65/H2 Schwedt, Ger.
69/F4 Schweich, Ger.
69/G6 Schweighouse-sur-Moder, Fr.
70/D2 Schweinfurt, Ger.
72/D4 Schweinitzer Fliess (riv.), Ger.
156/D2 Schweizer-Reneke, SAfr.
67/E6 Schwelm, Ger.
72/C4 Schwemsal, Ger.
70/C6 Schwendi, Ger.
206/C3 Schwenksville, Pa,US
64/F2 Schwerin, Ger.
64/F2 Schweriner (lake), Ger.
71/H6 Schwertberg, Aus.
67/E6 Schwerte, Ger.
70/B4 Schwetzingen, Ger.
72/E3 Schwielochsee (lake), Ger.
67/G1 Schwinge (riv.), Ger.
80/D2 Schwörstadt, Ger.
67/G5 Schwülme (riv.), Ger.
67/H4 Schwülper, Ger.
81/E3 Schwyz, Swi.
81/E3 Schwyz (canton), Swi.
90/C4 Sciacca, It.
90/D4 Scicli, It.
200/E2 Science Hill, Ky,US
195/P7 Science Museum of Minnesota, Mn,US
83/B6 Scilla, It.
55/H11 Scilly (isls.), Eng,UK
65/J3 Ścinawa, Pol.
208/F7 Scio, Oh,US
184/B1 Scio, Or,US
80/C5 Scionzier, Fr.
206/C2 Sciota, Pa,US
198/E5 Scioto (riv.), Oh,US
208/D1 Scituate, Ma,US
208/C2 Scituate (res.), RI,US
194/A2 Sclater, Mb,Can
183/M3 Scobey, Mt,US
185/H4 Scofield (res.), Ut,US
59/G1 Scolt (pt.), UK
135/D2 Scone, Austl.
200/C4 Scooba, Ms,US
86/B1 Scopello, It.
90/D4 Scordia, It.
78/B5 Scorff (riv.), Fr.
57/G3 Scotch Corner, Eng,UK
182/E2 Scotch Creek, BC,Can
182/F3 Scotchman (peak), Id,US
206/D2 Scotch Plains, NJ,US
137/W Scotia (sea), Ant.
184/A3 Scotia, Ca,US
55/J8 Scotland, UK
208/B2 Scotland, Ct,US
191/E4 Scotland, Tx,US
201/J2 Scotland Neck, NC,US
196/E3 Scots Bay, NS,Can
60/C1 Scotstown, Ire.
137/M Scott, Ant.
137/L Scott (coast), Ant.
130/C3 Scott (cape), Austl.
133/M9 Scott (cr.), Austl.
130/A3 Scott (reef), Austl.
178/D3 Scott (cape), BC,Can
179/R7 Scott (cape), NW,Can
178/F2 Scott (lake), NW,Can
183/K1 Scott, Sk,Can
184/B3 Scott (riv.), Ca,US
189/H2 Scott, La,US
195/P7 Scott (co.), Mn,US
191/E3 Scott (mtn.), Ok,US
184/C2 Scott (mtn.), Or,US
193/K4 Scott A.F.B., Il,US
157/E3 Scottburgh, SAfr.
190/D1 Scott City, Ks,US
200/C2 Scott City, Mo,US
201/M7 Scottdale, Ga,US
199/G4 Scottdale, Pa,US
132/B5 Scott Nat'l Park, Austl.
133/M9 Scotts (cr.), Austl.
192/C3 Scottsbluff, Ne,US
192/C3 Scotts Bluff Nat'l Mon., Ne,US
200/D3 Scottsboro, Al,US
200/E1 Scottsburg, In,US
135/C4 Scottsdale, Austl.
187/G4 Scottsdale, Az,US
200/C3 Scotts Hill, Tn,US
203/H3 Scottsmoor, Fl,US
135/C4 Scotts Peak (dam), Austl.
186/A2 Scotts Valley, Ca,US
200/D2 Scottsville, Ky,US
186/D2 Scotty's Castle, Ca,US
196/E2 Scoudouc, NB,Can
55/K7 Scrabster, Sc,UK
194/C4 Scranton, ND,US
206/C1 Scranton, Pa,US
201/H4 Scranton, SC,US
191/G2 Scraper, Ok,US
203/G2 Screven, Ga,US
193/F3 Scribner, Ne,US
204/C5 Scripps Aquarium/Museum, Ca,US
86/B3 Scrivia (riv.), It.
57/H4 Scunthorpe, Eng,UK
81/G4 Scuol, Swi.
205/N14 Scuppernong (riv.), Wi,US
55/K8 Scurdie Ness (pt.), Sc,UK
188/L7 Scurry, Tx,US
92/D4 Scutari (lake), Alb., Yugo.
78/D2 Scye (riv.), Fr.
103/F7 Sde Dov (arpt.), Isr.
201/G5 Sea (isls.), Ga, SC,US
205/B2 Seabeck, Wa,US
201/J2 Seaboard, NC,US
205/B2 Seabold, Wa,US
171/E2 Seabra, Braz.
199/L3 Seabrook, NH,US
206/C4 Seabrook, NJ,US
201/G4 Seabrook, SC,US
189/M9 Seabrook, Tx,US
206/B6 Seabrook-Lanham, Md,US
204/A2 Sea Cliff, Ca,US
207/E2 Sea Cliff, NY,US
189/F3 Seadrift, Tx,US
53/P6 Seaford, UK
201/K1 Seaford, De,US
207/M9 Seaford, NY,US
56/C3 Seaforde, NI,UK
134/C3 Seaforth, Austl.
198/F3 Seaforth, On,Can
207/D3 Sea Girt, NJ,US
188/L7 Seagoville, Tx,US
188/C1 Seagraves, Tx,US
57/G2 Seaham, Eng,UK
179/H2 Seahorse (pt.), NW,Can
205/C3 Seahurst, Wa,US
206/D5 Sea Isle City, NJ,US
178/G3 Seal (riv.), Mb,Can
174/B5 Seal (pt.), Chile
156/C4 Seal (cape), SAfr.
53/P8 Seal, Eng,UK
196/C4 Seal (isl.), Me,US
135/B2 Sea Lake, Austl.
204/B3 Seal Beach, Ca,US
204/F8 Seal Beach Nat'l Wild. Ref., Ca,US
196/D3 Seal Cove, NB,Can
197/J2 Seal Cove, Nf,Can
200/E4 Seale, Al,US
196/C4 Seal Island Nat'l Wild. Ref., Me,US
189/F3 Sealy, Tx,US
201/F1 Seaman, Oh,US
57/H3 Seamer, Eng,UK
87/E5 Seano, It.
203/H1 Sea Pines, SC,US
202/P7 Sea Ranch Lakes, Fl,US
186/E3 Searchlight, Nv,US
198/D1 Searchmont, On,Can
191/J3 Searcy, Ar,US
196/C3 Searsport, Me,US
56/E3 Seascale, Eng,UK
182/C5 Seaside, Or,US
207/D4 Seaside Heights, NJ,US
207/D4 Seaside Park, NJ,US
58/C5 Seaton, Eng,UK
58/B6 Seaton (riv.), Eng,UK
57/G2 Seaton Carew, Eng,UK
57/G1 Seaton Valley, Eng,UK
182/C4 Seattle, Wa,US
205/C2 Seattle Art Museum, Wa,US
205/C2 Seattle Center, Wa,US
205/C3 Seattle-Tacoma (int'l arpt.), Wa,US
207/E2 Seatuck Nat'l Wild. Ref., NY,US
208/F5 Sea World, Oh,US
203/H3 Sea World of Florida, Fl,US
130/A2 Seba, Indo.
160/E3 Sébaco, Nic.
196/B4 Sebago (lake), Me,US
141/T15 Sebaou (riv.), Alg.
203/H4 Sebastian, Fl,US
189/F4 Sebastian, Tx,US
158/B2 Sebastián Vizcaino (bay), Mex.
135/B3 Sebastopol, Austl.
184/B4 Sebastopol, Ca,US
200/C4 Sebastopol, Ms,US
189/G2 Sebastopol, Tx,US
125/B4 Sebatik (isl.), Malay., Indo.
126/D4 Sebayan (peak), Indo.
174/A2 Sebderat, Eth.
141/Q16 Sebdou, Alg.
152/C3 Sébé (riv.), Gabon
196/C3 Sebec (lake), Me,US
196/G4 Sebeka, Mn,US
144/C3 Sébékoro, Mali
93/K5 Seben, Turk.
93/F3 Sebeş, Rom.
149/H3 Sebeta, Eth.
198/E3 Sebewaing, Mi,US
63/N3 Sebezh, Rus.
155/E4 Sebina, Bots.
104/D1 Şebinkarahisar, Turk.
92/F2 Sebiş, Rom.
124/C3 Seblat, Indo.
65/H3 Sebnitz, Ger.
199/M2 Seboomook, Me,US
164/C2 Seboruco, Ven.
125/C4 Seboto (pt.), Phil.
142/D2 Sebou (riv.), Mor.
187/J3 Seboyeta, NM,US
200/D2 Sebree, Ky,US
203/H4 Sebring, Fl,US
208/F6 Sebring, Oh,US
125/B5 Sebuku (bay), Indo.
127/E4 Sebuku (isl.), Indo.
174/D3 Seca (plain), Arg.
72/B2 Secantsgraben (riv.), Ger.
207/J8 Secaucus, NJ,US
87/D3 Secchia (riv.), It.
182/C3 Sechelt, BC,Can
168/A2 Sechura, Peru
168/A2 Sechura (bay), Peru
168/A2 Sechura (des.), Peru
68/C2 Seclin, Fr.
175/L7 Seco (riv.), Arg.
187/G5 Seco (riv.), Mex.
188/E3 Seco (cr.), Tx,US
147/F4 Second Cataract (falls), Sudan
187/G3 Second Mesa, Az,US
206/B3 Second Mtn. (ridge), Pa,US
204/C2 Second San Diego (aqueduct), Ca,US
207/H8 Second Watchung (mts.), NJ,US
200/E3 Section, Al,US
156/E2 Secunda, SAfr.
118/C4 Secunderābād, India
169/E4 Secure (riv.), Bol.
192/B4 Security-Widefield, Co,US
73/C5 Séd (riv.), Hun.
63/K3 Seda, Lith.
183/J2 Sedalia, Ab,Can
192/B4 Sedalia, Co,US
191/H1 Sedalia, Mo,US
69/D4 Sedan, Fr.
191/F2 Sedan, Ks,US
190/C2 Sedan, NM,US
124/F4 Sedano (cape), Indo.
76/D1 Sedano, Sp.
123/B3 Sedaung (mtn.), Burma
124/F4 Sedayu, Indo.
57/F3 Sedbergh, Eng,UK
147/F4 Seddenga Temple (ruins), Sudan
136/C3 Seddon, N.Z.
136/B3 Seddonville, N.Z.
91/K2 Seddülbahir, Turk.
107/G2 Sedeh, Iran
82/B4 Séderon, Fr.
103/D4 Sederot, Isr.
57/G2 Sedgefield, Eng,UK
183/J1 Sedgewick, Ab,Can
177/L2 Sedgwick (mtn.), Yk,Can
191/F2 Sedgwick, Ks,US
144/B3 Sedhiou, Sen.
71/H3 Sedlčany, Czh.
72/E4 Sedlitz, Ger.
71/H1 Sedlo (peak), Czh.
187/G3 Sedona, Az,US
103/F7 Sedot Yam, Isr.
141/V17 Sedrata, Alg.
182/C3 Sedro-Woolley, Wa,US
63/K4 Šeduva, Lith.
65/L3 Sędziszów, Pol.
98/A2 Sędziszów Małopolski, Pol.
78/D3 Sée (riv.), Fr.
182/G2 Seebe, Ab,Can
92/A2 Seeboden, Aus.
185/J3 Seedskadee Nat'l Wild. Ref., Wy,US
81/H3 Seefeld in Tirol, Aus.
60/A6 Seefin (mtn.), Ire.
60/C5 Seefin (mtn.), Ire.
81/G2 Seeg, Ger.
72/B2 Seehausen, Ger.
156/B2 Seeheim, Namb.
70/B3 Seeheim-Jugenheim, Ger.
154/C4 Seeis, Namb.
71/G7 Seekirchen am Wallersee, Aus.
208/C2 Seekonk, Ma,US
156/D3 Seekooi (riv.), SAfr.
186/E4 Seeley, Ca,US
183/H4 Seeley Lake, Mt,US
65/H2 Seelow, Ger.
71/F7 Seeon-Seebruck, Ger.
79/F3 Sées, Fr.
67/H5 Seesen, Ger.
81/H2 Seeshaupt, Ger.
67/G2 Seeve (riv.), Ger.
71/G7 Seewalchen am Attersee, Aus.
73/A4 Seewinkel (reg.), Aus.
81/F4 Seewis im Prättigau, Swi.
82/C1 Séez, Fr.
104/C2 Şefaatli, Turk.
155/E4 Sefare, Bots.
202/L8 Seffner, Fl,US
105/G2 Sefīd Rūd (riv.), Iran
141/M14 Sefrou, Mor.
136/B3 Sefton (peak), N.Z.
150/B4 Segag, Eth.
125/B5 Segama (riv.), Malay.
124/C2 Segamat, Malay.
93/F3 Segarcea, Rom.
145/F4 Ségbana, Ben.
144/D4 Ségélo-Koro, IvC.
62/D1 Segelstad bru, Nor.
149/H4 Segen Wenz (riv.), Eth.
90/C4 Segesta (ruins), It.
127/H4 Seget, Indo.
94/G3 Segezha, Rus.
84/D4 Segni, It.
77/E3 Segorbe, Sp.
144/D3 Ségou, Mali
144/D3 Ségou (reg.), Mali
164/C3 Segovia, Col.
76/C2 Segovia, Sp.
188/E2 Segovia, Tx,US
94/G3 Segozero (lake), Rus.
86/C2 Segrate, It.
79/E5 Segré, Fr.
77/F2 Segre (riv.), Sp.
177/D5 Seguam (isl.), Ak,US
177/D5 Seguam (passg.), Ak,US
146/B4 Séguédine, Niger
144/D5 Séguéla, IvC.
145/E3 Séguénéga, Burk.
189/F3 Seguin, Tx,US
172/D3 Segundo (riv.), Arg.
76/D3 Segura (riv.), Sp.
87/E1 Segusino, It.
154/D4 Sehithwa, Bots.
67/G4 Sehnde, Ger.
156/E3 Sehonghong, Les.
120/A4 Sehore, India
107/J3 Sehwān, Pak.
69/G4 Seibersbach, Ger.
78/D5 Seiche (riv.), Fr.
79/E5 Seiches-sur-le-Loir, Fr.
92/B2 Seiersberg, Aus.
111/L10 Seika, Japan
112/B3 Seikan (tunnel), Japan
80/B4 Seille (riv.), Fr.
190/E2 Seiling, Ok,US
69/F6 Seille (riv.), Fr.
61/G3 Seinäjoki, Fin.
195/J3 Seine (riv.), On,Can
79/E1 Seine (bay), Fr.
53/S10 Seine (riv.), Fr.
53/U10 Seine-et-Marne (dept.), Fr.
79/F1 Seine-Maritime (dept.), Fr.
53/T10 Seine-Saint-Denis (dept.), Fr.
71/H6 Seitenstetten, Aus.
61/G3 Seitsemisen Nat'l Park, Fin.
111/M10 Seiwa, Japan
74/D5 Seix, Fr.
77/P10 Seixal, Port.
167/H4 Seixas (pt.), Braz.
127/E4 Sejaka, Indo.
62/D4 Sejerø (isl.), Den.
65/M1 Sejny, Pol.
124/D4 Sekampung (riv.), Indo.
124/C3 Sekayu, Indo.
151/A2 Seke, Tanz.
152/C4 Seke-Banza, Zaire
151/A3 Sekenke, Tanz.
111/E3 Seki, Japan
103/A1 Seki (riv.), Turk.
111/M9 Sekigahara, Japan
111/H6 Sekiyado, Japan
154/D5 Sekoma, Bots.
145/E5 Sekondi, Gha.
150/A2 Sek'ot'a, Eth.
182/D4 Selah, Wa,US
124/C1 Selama, Malay.
124/C2 Selangor (state), Malay.
123/C2 Selaphum, Thai.
90/A3 Selargius, It.
130/C2 Selaru (isl.), Indo.
126/D4 Selatan (cape), Indo.
177/F2 Selawik, Ak,US
177/F2 Selawik (lake), Ak,US
177/G2 Selawik Nat'l Wild. Ref., Ak,US
127/F5 Selayar (isl.), Indo.
71/F2 Selb, Ger.
71/E2 Selbitz, Ger.
71/E2 Selbitz (riv.), Ger.
61/D3 Selbu, Nor.
57/G4 Selby, Eng,UK
192/D1 Selby, SD,US
206/B6 Selby-on-the-Bay, Md,US
201/K1 Selbyville, De,US
87/F6 Selci, It.
104/A2 Selçuk, Turk.
190/D1 Selden, Ks,US
207/E2 Selden, NY,US
177/H4 Seldovia, Ak,US
85/F6 Sele (riv.), It.
155/E4 Selebi-Phikwe, Bots.
155/J2 Selela (pt.), Moz.
153/H5 Seleli (hill), Tanz.
109/L1 Selemdzha (riv.), Rus.
92/D3 Selenča, Yugo.
104/B2 Selendi, Turk.
108/F1 Selenduma, Rus.
108/F1 Selenga (riv.), Rus.
108/E2 Selenge, Mong.
108/E2 Selenge (riv.), Mong.
108/F1 Selenginsk, Rus.
91/F2 Selenicë, Alb.
80/D1 Sélestat, Fr.
114/B1 Selety (riv.), Kaz.
114/B1 Seletyteniz (lake), Kaz.
63/N1 Selezněvo, Rus.
61/N7 Selfoss, Ice.
194/D4 Selfridge, ND,US
144/B3 Sélibabi, Mrta.
99/J3 Selidovo, Ukr.
70/B2 Seligenstadt, Ger.
94/G4 Seliger (lake), Rus.
187/F3 Seligman, Az,US
191/H2 Seligman, Mo,US
155/F4 Selika, Bots.
126/D3 Selimbau, Indo.
104/A2 Selimiye, Turk.
124/C2 Selim River, Malay.
206/B2 Selinsgrove, Pa,US
90/C4 Selinunte (ruins), It.
62/C2 Seljord, Nor.
72/B4 Selke (riv.), Ger.
182/F2 Selkirk (mts.), BC,Can
194/F2 Selkirk, Mb,Can
54/D5 Selkirk, Sc,UK
71/F5 Selle (riv.), Fr.
205/D3 Selleck, Wa,US
203/E1 Sellers, Al,US
206/C3 Sellersville, Pa,US
79/G6 Selles-sur-Cher, Fr.
83/C5 Sellia Marina, It.
84/B4 Sellières, Fr.
187/G5 Sells, Az,US
92/C3 Sellye, Hun.
58/E2 Selly Oak, Eng,UK
67/E5 Selm, Ger.
200/D4 Selma, Al,US
191/J4 Selma, Ar,US
186/C2 Selma, Ca,US
201/H3 Selma, NC,US
190/E2 Selman, Ok,US
200/C3 Selmer, Tn,US
79/G5 Selommes, Fr.
80/B2 Selongey, Fr.
82/C4 Selonnet, Fr.
144/C4 Selouma, Gui.
177/M3 Selous (mtn.), Yk,Can
155/F3 Selous, Zim.

151/B4 Selous Game Rsv., Tanz.
59/F5 Selsey, Eng,UK
59/F5 Selsey Bill (pt.), Eng,UK
67/G2 Selsingen, Ger.
96/E1 Sel'tso, Rus.
69/H6 Seltz, Fr.
130/C1 Selu (isl.), Indo.
79/E3 Sélune (riv.), Fr.
142/A3 Selvagens (isls.), Port.
163/C3 Selvas (for.), Braz.
182/G4 Selway (falls), Id,US
185/F1 Selway (riv.), Id,US
133/J2 Selwyn, Austl.
131/E4 Selwyn (range), Austl.
70/B3 Selz (riv.), Ger.
142/C4 Semara, WSah.
124/E4 Semarang, Indo.
120/D4 Semarsot, India
130/A2 Semau (isl.), Indo.
125/B4 Sembakung (riv.), Indo.
152/C2 Sembé, Congo
144/B5 Sembehun, SLeo.
71/H2 Sembera (riv.), Czh.
124/C2 Semberong (riv.), Malay.
105/F2 Şemdinli, Turk.
74/D5 Séméac, Fr.
79/F4 Semelle (riv.), Fr.
152/D3 Semendua, Zaire
99/G3 Semënoka, Ukr.
95/K4 Semenov, Rus.
98/G1 Semenovka, Ukr.
124/F5 Semeru (peak), Indo.
124/F5 Semeru-Bromo-Tengger Nat'l Prsv., Indo.
177/G4 Semidi (isls.), Ak,US
99/L4 Semikarakorsk, Rus.
94/J5 Semilovo, Rus.
99/K2 Semiluki, Rus.
83/B6 Seminara, It.
185/K2 Seminoe (dam), Wy,US
185/K2 Seminoe (res.), Wy,US
202/K8 Seminole, Fl,US
203/F2 Seminole (lake), Ga,US
191/F3 Seminole, Ok,US
190/C4 Seminole, Tx,US
188/C1 Seminole Draw (cr.), Tx,US
203/H4 Seminole Ind. Res., Fl,US
114/D1 Semipalatinsk, Kaz.
125/C2 Semirara (isl.), Phil.
105/G4 Semīrom, Iran
177/B5 Semisopochnoi (isl.), Ak,US
126/D4 Semitau, Indo.
153/G2 Semliki (riv.), Ugan., Zaire
105/H3 Semnān, Iran
105/H3 Semnān (gov.), Iran
78/D5 Semnon (riv.), Fr.
69/E4 Semois (riv.), Belg.
80/C2 Semouse (riv.), Fr.
80/B1 Semoutiers, Fr.
79/G5 Sémoy, Fr.
69/D4 Semoy (riv.), Fr.
80/E3 Sempach, Swi.
80/E3 Sempacher See (lake), Swi.
125/B4 Semporna, Malay.
84/D4 Semprevisa (peak), It.
80/C4 Semsales, Swi.
94/B2 Semskefjellet (peak), Nor.
123/D3 Sen (riv.), Camb.
169/E3 Sena, Bol.
123/C3 Sena, Thai.
190/B3 Sena, NM,US
193/K3 Senachwine (lake), Il,US
167/G4 Senador Pompeu, Braz.
167/F3 Senador Sá, Braz.
150/A2 Sen'afē, Eth.
124/C2 Senai, Malay.
125/B4 Senaja, Malay.
170/D1 Sena Madureira, Braz.
154/D3 Senanga, Zam.
183/K3 Senate, Sk,Can
200/B2 Senath, Mo,US
200/C3 Senatobia, Ms,US
59/E2 Sence (riv.), Eng,UK
150/A3 Sendafa, Eth.
110/B5 Sendai, Japan
111/G1 Sendai (bay), Japan
111/G1 Sendai (int'l arpt.), Japan
110/B5 Sendai (riv.), Japan
110/D3 Sendai (riv.), Japan
67/E5 Senden, Ger.
70/D6 Senden, Ger.
67/E5 Sendenhorst, Ger.
78/C5 Séné, Fr.
124/C2 Senebui, Indo.
124/C2 Senebui (cape), Indo.
73/B3 Senec, Slvk.
191/F1 Seneca, Ks,US
191/G2 Seneca, Mo,US
190/C2 Seneca, NM,US
199/H3 Seneca (lake), NY,US
184/D1 Seneca, Or,US
201/F3 Seneca, SC,US
199/H3 Seneca Falls, NY,US
201/H1 Seneca Rocks Nat'l Rec. Area, WV,US
198/F5 Senecaville (lake), Oh,US
68/D2 Seneffe, Belg.
144/B3 Senegal
144/B2 Sénégal (riv.), Afr.
156/D3 Senekal, SAfr.
195/M4 Seney, Mi,US
198/C1 Seney Nat'l Wild. Ref., Mi,US
145/E5 Senfi, Gha.
72/E4 Senftenberg, Ger.
72/E5 Senftenberger Stockteich (lake), Ger.
153/G5 Senga Hill Mission, Zam.
71/E4 Sengenthal, Ger.
114/D5 Sênggê (riv.), China
97/J1 Sengiley, Rus.
124/G5 Sengkol, Indo.
121/H2 Sengor, Bhu.
174/C5 Senguerr (riv.), Arg.
155/F3 Sengwe (riv.), Zim.
171/E1 Senhor do Bonfim, Braz.
73/J2 Senica, Slvk.
87/G5 Senigallia, It.
87/E4 Senio (riv.), It.
104/B2 Senirkent, Turk.
83/C2 Senise, It.
92/B3 Senj, Cro.
61/F1 Senja (isl.), Nor.
104/E1 Şenkaya, Turk.
98/C2 Šenkevichevka, Ukr.
103/E1 Şenköy, Turk.
183/K1 Senlac, Sk,Can
74/E2 Senlis
68/B5 Senlis, Fr.
123/D3 Senmonorom, Camb.
111/L10 Sennan, Japan
149/G2 Sennar (dam), Sudan
68/D2 Senne (riv.), Belg.
80/A4 Sennecy-le-Grand, Fr.
70/D2 Sennfeld, Ger.
63/N4 Senno, Bela.
97/H1 Sennoy, Rus.
99/M2 Sennoy, Rus.
81/F3 Sennwald, Swi.
58/C3 Sennybridge, Wal,UK
145/F3 Séno (prov.), Burk.
73/B3 Senohrad, Slvk.
79/G3 Senonches, Fr.
80/C1 Senones, Fr.
90/A3 Senorbì, It.
144/D3 Senou (Bamako) (int'l arpt.), Mali
93/H4 Senovo, Bul.
74/E2 Sens, Fr.
78/D4 Sens-de-Bretagne, Fr.
160/D3 Sensuntepeque, ESal.
92/E3 Senta, Yugo.
127/K4 Sentani, Indo.
153/F4 Sentery, Zaire
187/F4 Sentinel, Az,US
190/E3 Sentinel, Ok,US
167/F5 Sento Sé, Braz.
145/E5 Senya Beraku, Gha.
138/E4 Senyavin (isls.), Micr.
72/D3 Senzig, Ger.
120/B1 Seohāra, India
80/E3 Seon, Swi.
120/B2 Seondha, India
120/B4 Seoni, India
120/A4 Seoni Mālwā, India
101/N6 Seoul (cap.), SKor.
113/G7 Seoul Grand Park, SKor.
113/D4 Seoul-Jikhalsi, SKor.
113/D4 Seoul (Sŏul) (cap.), SKor.
124/D2 Sepang (cape), Malay.
124/F4 Sepanjang (isl.), Indo.
187/H4 Separ, NM,US
136/C3 Separation (pt.), N.Z.
169/E3 Sepatini (riv.), Braz.
171/N8 Sepetiba (bay), Braz.
138/D5 Sepik (riv.), PNG
92/E5 Sepino, It.
127/G3 Sepo, Indo.
113/D3 Sep'o, NKor.
65/J2 Sepólno Krajeńskie, Pol.
154/D3 Sepopa, Bots.
82/B6 Septèmes-les-Vallons, Fr.
93/G4 Septemvri, Bul.
68/A6 Septeuil, Fr.
179/K3 Sept-Iles, Qu,Can
204/F7 Sepulveda (dam), Ca,US
76/B2 Sequeros, Sp.
182/C3 Sequim, Wa,US
205/A1 Sequim (bay), Wa,US
186/C2 Sequoia Nat'l Park, Ca,US
191/G3 Sequoyah Nat'l Wild. Ref., Ok,US
130/C1 Sera (isl.), Indo.
86/C1 Serada, Monte (peak), It.
99/M3 Serafimovich, Rus.
190/B3 Serafina, NM,US
69/E3 Seraing, Belg.
149/E2 Serambe, Sudan
80/B6 Séran (riv.), Fr.
124/D4 Serang, Indo.
124/C2 Serangoon, Sing.
126/C3 Serasan, Indo.
126/C3 Serasan (str.), Indo., Malay.
86/D5 Seravezza, It.
124/B2 Serbeulangit (mts.), Indo.
92/E4 Serbia (rep.), Yugo.
189/F2 Serbin, Tx,US
116/B4 Serchhīp, India
86/D5 Serchio (riv.), It.
124/D4 Serdang (cape), Indo.
150/B3 Serdo, Eth.
97/H1 Serdobsk, Rus.
177/D2 Serdtse-Kamen, Mys (pt.), Rus.
100/J5 Serebryansk, Kaz.
73/B3 Sered', Slvk.
94/H5 Serednikovo, Rus.
63/K4 Seredžius, Lith.
104/C2 Şereflikoçhisar, Turk.
73/C5 Seregélyes, Hun.
86/C1 Seregno, It.
74/F3 Serein (riv.), Fr.
69/F5 Serémange-Erzange, Fr.
124/C2 Seremban, Malay.
151/A2 Serengeti (plain), Tanz.
151/A2 Serengeti Nat'l Park, Tanz.
155/F2 Serenje, Zam.
78/C5 Sérent, Fr.
150/A2 Serere, Ugan.
95/K5 Sergach, Rus.
206/D3 Sergeantsville, NJ,US
93/H5 Sergen, Turk.
100/J2 Sergeya Kirova (isls.), Rus.
95/Q5 Sergeyevka, Kaz.
171/F1 Sergipe (state), Braz.
94/H4 Sergiyev Posad, Rus.
86/C2 Sergnano, It.
125/A4 Seria, Bru.
86/C1 Seriate, It.
85/G6 Serico (peak), It.
68/A5 Sérifontaine, Fr.
91/J4 Sérifos, Gre.
91/J4 Sérifos (isl.), Gre.
74/E5 Sérignan, Fr.
103/B1 Serik, Turk.
114/C4 Serikbuya, China
166/D4 Seringa (mts.), Braz.
103/E1 Serinyol, Turk.
86/C2 Serio (riv.), It.
75/H4 Serio, Orio al (int'l arpt.), It.
86/C1 Serio, Orio al (int'l arpt.), It.
143/G5 Serkout, Djebel (mtn.), Alg.
79/H4 Sermaises, Fr.
69/D6 Sermaize-les-Bains, Fr.
130/C2 Sermata (isl.), Indo.
130/C2 Sermata (isls.), Indo.
87/E3 Sermide, It.
84/C4 Sermoneta, It.
87/F1 Sernaglia della Battaglia, It.
97/J1 Sernovodsk, Rus.
95/L4 Sernur, Rus.
76/D4 Serón, Sp.
77/F2 Serós, Sp.
81/G5 Serottini, Monte (peak), It.
100/G4 Serov, Rus.
155/E4 Serowe, Bots.
76/B4 Serpa, Port.
90/A3 Serpeddi (peak), It.
135/C4 Serpentine (dam), Austl.
133/F4 Serpentine (lakes), Austl.
198/E5 Serpent Mound, Oh,US
165/F2 Serpent's Mouth (str.), Trin., Ven.
144/C3 Serpent, Vallée du (wadi), Mali
94/H5 Serpukhov, Rus.
79/F2 Serquigny, Fr.
171/E4 Serra, Braz.
167/G4 Serra Branca, Braz.
171/E1 Serra Capivara Nat'l Park, Braz.
85/F4 Serracapriola, It.
170/D4 Serra da Bocaína Nat'l Park, Braz.
170/D4 Serra da Canastra Nat'l Park, Braz.
167/F5 Serra da Capivara Nat'l Park, Braz.
173/H1 Serra de Canastra Nat'l Park, Braz.
85/G6 Serra del Corvo (lake), It.
171/E3 Serra do Cipo Nat'l Park, Braz.
166/D2 Serra do Navio, Braz.
171/N7 Serra dos Órgãos Nat'l Park, Braz.
85/G6 Serraficaia (peak), It.
91/H2 Sérrai, Gre.
83/C5 Serralta di San Vito (peak), It.
90/A3 Serramanna, It.
87/D4 Serramazzoni, It.
86/D5 Serra, Monte (peak), It.
167/G4 Serra Negra do Norte, Braz.
165/E4 Serrania de la Neblina Nat'l Park, Ven.
161/G3 Serranilla Bank (reef), Col.
174/E2 Serrano, Arg.
170/C3 Serranópolis, Braz.
83/C5 Serra San Bruno, It.
87/G6 Serra San Quirico, It.
83/C4 Serrastretta, It.
141/W17 Serrat (cape), Tun.
167/G4 Serra Talhada, Braz.
87/F3 Serravalle, It.
84/C1 Serravalle di Chienti, It.
86/B3 Serravalle Scrivia, It.
86/B1 Serravalle Sesia, It.
68/C4 Serre (riv.), Fr.
85/F6 Serre, It.
82/C3 Serre Chevalier (mtn.), Fr.
90/A3 Serrenti, It.
82/C4 Serre-Ponçon (lake), Fr.
82/C4 Serre-Ponçon, Barrage de (dam), Fr.
82/B4 Serres, Fr.
82/A2 Serrières, Fr.
80/A3 Serrigny, Fr.
171/F1 Serrinha, Braz.
167/G4 Serrita, Braz.
173/J1 Sêrro, Braz.
83/C4 Sersale, It.
76/A3 Sertã, Port.
167/G5 Sertânia, Braz.
170/D4 Sertãozinho, Braz.
103/C1 Sertavul (pass), Turk.
108/C4 Serteng (mts.), China
150/B4 Sēru, Eth.
127/J4 Serui, Indo.
155/E4 Serule, Bots.
154/E4 Serurumi (dry riv.), Bots.
124/B1 Seruwai, Indo.
126/D4 Seruyan (riv.), Indo.
80/C2 Servance, Fr.
78/B3 Servel (Lannion) (arpt.), Fr.
104/E2 Servi, Turk.
91/H2 Sérvia, Gre.
135/B3 Serviceton, Austl.
85/D1 Servigliano, It.
130/B2 Serwaru, Indo.
125/B5 Sesayap (riv.), Indo.
153/H3 Sese (isls.), Ugan.
147/F4 Sesebi (ruins), Sudan
127/G4 Sesepe, Indo.
154/B3 Sesfontein, Namb.
154/E3 Sesheke, Zam.
86/B2 Sesia (riv.), It.
76/A3 Sesimbra, Port.
63/N1 Seskar (isl.), Rus.
204/B2 Sespe, Ca,US
204/A1 Sespe (cr.), Ca,US
204/B1 Sespe Condor Sanct., Ca,US
85/D5 Sessa Aurunca, It.
193/K4 Sesser, Il,US
70/D2 Sesslach, Ger.
76/D1 Sestao, Sp.
86/B1 Sesto Calende, It.
85/E5 Sesto Campano, It.
87/E5 Sesto Fiorentino, It.
87/D4 Sestola, It.
86/C1 Sesto San Giovanni, It.
86/C2 Sesto Ulteriano, It.
86/C4 Sestri Levante, It.
63/N1 Sestroretsk, Rus.
90/A3 Sestu, It.
81/G4 Sesvenna, Piz (peak), It.
92/C3 Sesvete, Cro.
63/L4 Šeta, Lith.
112/A2 Setana, Japan
74/E5 Sète, Fr.
167/F4 Sete Cidades Nat'l Park, Braz.
170/D3 Sete Lagoas, Braz.
201/G1 Seth, WV,US
107/J3 Sethārja, Pak.
120/C1 Seti (riv.), Nepal
120/C1 Seti (zone), Nepal
141/U17 Sétif, Alg.
141/U17 Sétif (gov.), Alg.
141/T15 Sétif (wilaya), Alg.
111/E3 Seto, Japan
110/C3 Seto-Naikai Nat'l Park, Japan
111/K10 Seto-Naikai Nat'l Park, Japan
112/K6 Setouchi, Japan
142/D2 Settat, Mor.
152/B3 Setté-Cama, Gabon
84/C4 Settecamini, It.
86/B4 Settepani, Monte (peak), It.
86/A2 Settimo Torinese, It.
86/A1 Settimo Vittone, It.
57/F3 Settle, Eng,UK
162/B1 Settlement (pt.), Bahm.
111/L10 Settsu, Japan
76/A3 Setúbal, Port.
77/Q11 Setúbal (bay), Port.
76/A3 Setúbal (dist.), Port.
71/E4 Seubersdorf, Ger.
74/C4 Seudre (riv.), Fr.
74/C4 Seugne (riv.), Fr.
195/H2 Seul (lake), On,Can
124/A1 Seulimeum, Indo.
79/E2 Seulles (riv.), Fr.
80/B4 Seurre, Fr.
81/E2 Seuzach, Swi.
97/H4 Sevan, Arm.
97/H4 Sevan (lake), Arm.
105/F1 Sevan Nat'l Park, Arm.
53/G4 Sevastopol', Ukr.
81/F3 Sevelen, Swi.
183/J3 Seven (cr.), Ab,Can
57/H3 Seven (riv.), Eng,UK
60/B6 Seven Heads (pt.), Ire.
208/F5 Seven Hills, Oh,US
55/F10 Seven Hogs, The (isls.), Ire.
177/M2 Seven Islands Crossing, NW,Can
192/D2 Sevenmile (hill), Ne,US
53/P8 Sevenoaks, Eng,UK
189/G2 Seven Oaks, Tx,US
190/B4 Seven Rivers, NM,US
194/F2 Seven Sisters Falls, Mb,Can
182/D2 Seventy Mile House, BC,Can
206/B4 Seven Valleys, Pa,US
82/C3 Sévéraise (riv.), Fr.
178/G3 Severn (riv.), On,Can
55/K11 Severn (riv.), UK
58/D3 Severn (riv.), Eng,UK
206/B5 Severn, Md,US
206/B5 Severn (riv.), Md,US
206/B5 Severna Park, Md,US
95/K3 Severnaya Dvina (riv.), Rus.
95/P3 Severnaya Sos'va (riv.), Rus.
102/K2 Severnaya Zemlya (arch.), Rus.
58/C4 Severn, Mouth of the (est.), U. K.
95/Q2 Severnyy, Rus.
101/L4 Severobaykal'sk, Rus.
71/G2 Severočeský (reg.), Czh.
72/E6 Severočeský (reg.), Czh.
75/L1 Severočeský (reg.), Czh.
53/G4 Severodonetsk, Ukr.
94/H2 Severodvinsk, Rus.
101/R4 Severo-Kuril'sk, Rus.
65/J4 Severomoravský (reg.), Czh.
73/C1 Severo-Moravský (reg.), Czh.
75/M1 Severomoravský (reg.), Czh.
94/G1 Severomorsk, Rus.
101/M4 Severomuysk, Rus.
95/N3 Severoural'sk, Rus.
100/K3 Severo-Yeniseyskiy, Rus.
99/K3 Seversk, Ukr.
99/K5 Severskaya, Rus.
95/P4 Severukha, Rus.
191/F2 Severy, Ks,US
86/C1 Seveso, It.
185/G4 Sevier, Ut,US
185/G4 Sevier (des.), Ut,US
185/G4 Sevier (lake), Ut,US
187/F1 Sevier (plat.), Ut,US
185/G4 Sevier (riv.), Ut,US
187/F2 Sevier, E. Fork (riv.), Ut,US
201/F3 Sevierville, Tn,US
164/C3 Sevilla, Col.
135/G5 Seville, Austl.
76/C4 Seville, Sp.
208/F5 Seville, Oh,US
190/A3 Sevilleta Nat'l Wild. Ref., NM,US
93/G4 Sevlievo, Bul.
92/B2 Sevnica, Slov.
92/D4 Sevojno, Yugo.
53/T10 Sevran, Fr.
53/S10 Sèvres, Fr.
99/H1 Sevsk, Rus.
144/C5 Sewa (riv.), SLeo.
200/E3 Sewanee, Tn,US
177/J3 Seward, Ak,US
177/E2 Seward (pen.), Ak,US
191/E1 Seward, Ks,US
193/F3 Seward, Ne,US
207/H9 Sewaren, NJ,US
174/Q10 Sewell, Chile
177/M5 Sewell Inlet, BC,Can
208/G6 Sewickley, Pa,US
200/F2 Sextons Creek, Ky,US
105/F2 Seyah Cheshmeh, Iran
159/H5 Seybaplaya, Mex.
141/V17 Seybouse (riv.), Alg.
141/H5 Seychelles
72/C4 Seyda, Ger.
61/Q6 Seydhisfjördhur, Ice.
104/B2 Seydişehir, Turk.
103/D1 Seyhan (dam), Turk.
103/D1 Seyhan (riv.), Turk.
104/B2 Seyitgazi, Turk.
150/B3 Seylac, Som.
99/H2 Seym (riv.), Rus., Ukr.
135/C3 Seymour, Austl.
193/H3 Seymour, Ia,US
198/D5 Seymour, In,US
191/H2 Seymour, Mo,US
190/E4 Seymour, Tx,US
193/K1 Seymour, Wi,US
182/E2 Seymour Arm, BC,Can
201/J3 Seymour Johnson A.F.B., NC,US
82/C4 Seyne, Fr.
80/C6 Seynod, Fr.
80/B6 Seyssel, Fr.
82/B2 Seyssinet-Pariset, Fr.
105/N6 Şeytan (riv.), Turk.
87/G1 Sežana, Slov.
68/C6 Sézanne, Fr.
76/A3 Sezimbra, Port.
71/H4 Sezimovo Ústí, Czh.
84/D4 Sezze, It.
143/H2 Sfax El Maou (int'l arpt.), Tun.
93/G3 Sfîntu Gheorghe, Rom.
93/J3 Sfîntu Gheorghe, Rom.
141/Q16 Sfizef, Alg.
66/C4 's-Graveland, Neth.
66/B5 's-Gravendeel, Neth.
66/B4 's-Gravenhage (The Hague) (cap.), Neth.
54/A2 Sgurr a' Chaorachain (mtn.), Sc,UK
54/B2 Sgurr a' choire Ghlais (mtn.), Sc,UK
54/B1 Sgurr a' Mhuilinn (mtn.), Sc,UK
54/A1 Sgurr Mór (mtn.), Sc,UK
54/A2 Sgurr na Ciche (mtn.), Sc,UK
54/A2 Sgurr na Lapaich (mtn.), Sc,UK
115/C4 Sha (riv.), China
117/H3 Sha (riv.), China
117/F1 Shaanxi (prov.), China
153/F5 Shaba (Katanga) (pol. reg.), Zaire
151/B1 Shaba Nat'l Rsv., Kenya
149/G2 Shabasha, Sudan
121/H4 Shābāzpur (riv.), Bang.
150/C4 Shabeele, Webi (riv.), Som.
151/C1 Shabeelle, Webi (riv.), Som.
93/J4 Shabla, Bul.
98/F4 Shabo, Ukr.
153/F3 Shabunda, Zaire
150/C2 Shabwah, Yem.
114/C4 Shache, China
182/D2 Shackan Ind. Res., BC,Can
137/M Shackleton (coast), Ant.
137/G Shackleton Ice Shelf, Ant.
117/F2 Shadaogou, China
105/G4 Shādegān, Iran
194/C5 Shadehill, SD,US
192/C1 Shadehill (dam), SD,US
198/C4 Shadeland, In,US
206/A2 Shade Mtn. (ridge), Pa,US
95/P4 Shadrinsk, Rus.
116/C2 Shaduzup, Burma
184/B2 Shady Cove, Or,US
203/G2 Shady Grove, Fl,US
198/F5 Shadyside, Oh,US
201/G2 Shady Spring, WV,US
201/G2 Shady Valley, Tn,US
198/C4 Shafer (lake), In,US
95/M5 Shafranovo, Rus.
186/C3 Shafter, Ca,US
185/F3 Shafter, Nv,US
188/B3 Shafter, Tx,US
58/D4 Shaftesbury, Eng,UK
199/K3 Shaftsbury, Vt,US
145/F5 Shagamu, Nga.
114/C2 Shagan (riv.), Kaz.
113/B2 Shagang, China
98/F5 Shagany (lake), Ukr.
177/D3 Shageluk, Ak,US
196/E4 Shag Harbour, NS,Can
108/C1 Shagonar, Rus.
120/B1 Shāhābād, India
118/C2 Shāhābād, India
120/A2 Shāhābād, India
120/B2 Shāhābād, India
122/D2 Shāhābād, India
124/C2 Shah Alam, Malay.
107/J4 Shāhbandar, Pak.
105/J4 Shahdād, Iran
107/J3 Shāhdādkot, Pak.
107/J3 Shāhdādpur, Pak.
105/F4 Shāhdasht, Iran
120/C4 Shahdol, India
105/F5 Shahekan, China
120/D2 Shāhganj, India
148/D1 Shaḩḩāt, Libya
120/B2 Shāhjahānpur, India
120/B2 Shāh Kot, Pak.
120/A4 Shāhpur, India
122/B1 Shāhpur, Pak.
107/K3 Shāhpura, India
120/C4 Shāhpura, India
118/A2 Shāhpur Chākar, Pak.
105/G3 Shahrak, Iran
105/H4 Shahr-e Bābak, Iran
105/G3 Shahr-e Kord, Iran
105/G3 Shāhrūd, Iran
105/G3 Shahryār, Iran
121/G4 Shāhzādpur, Bang.
122/D2 Shāhzādpur, India
147/G3 Shā'ib al Banāt, Jabal (mtn.), Egypt
121/E3 Shaikhpura, India
121/H3 Shāistāganj, Bang.
118/C3 Shājāpur, India
116/D3 Shaji, China
117/H3 Shajian, China
113/C2 Shajianzi, China
122/C1 Shakargarh, Pak.
157/E3 Shakaskraal, SAfr.
154/D3 Shakawe, Bots.
208/F5 Shaker Heights, Oh,US
195/K3 Shakespeare (isl.), On,Can
97/H5 Shakhbuz, Azer.
109/N2 Shakhtërsk, Rus.
99/K3 Shakhtersk, Ukr.
100/H5 Shakhtinsk, Kaz.
53/H4 Shakhty, Rus.
53/H3 Shakhun'ya, Rus.
145/F4 Shaki, Nga.
150/A4 Shakīso, Eth.
193/H1 Shakopee, Mn,US
112/B2 Shakotan (pen.), Japan
95/N5 Shaksha, Rus.
177/F3 Shaktoolik, Ak,US
105/G3 Shāl, Iran
150/A4 Shala (lake), Eth.
151/D1 Shalaanbood, Som.
97/H4 Shalbuzdag, Gora (peak), Rus.
58/C5 Shaldon, Eng,UK
97/H4 Shali, Rus.
113/B2 Shaling, China
201/H4 Shallotte, NC,US
190/D4 Shallowater, Tx,US
133/M8 Shallow Reach (inlet), Austl.
94/H3 Shal'skiy, Rus.
116/C2 Shaluli (mts.), China
99/H2 Shalygino, Ukr.
151/A3 Shama (riv.), Tanz.
103/C4 Shamal Sīnā' (gov.), Egypt
95/N4 Shamary, Rus.
179/H3 Shamattawa (riv.), On,Can
149/F4 Shambe, Sudan
149/H3 Shambu, Eth.
152/D4 Shambungu, Zaire
118/C3 Shāmgarh, India
105/J5 Shamīl, Iran
97/H4 Shamkhor, Azer.
120/A1 Shāmli, India
104/E5 Shammar, Jabal (mts.), SAr.
206/B2 Shamokin, Pa,US
206/B2 Shamokin (cr.), Pa,US
206/B2 Shamokin Dam, Pa,US
120/A2 Shāmpur, India
177/L3 Shamrock (mtn.), Yk,Can
190/D3 Shamrock, Tx,US
201/F2 Shamrock-Mount Gay, WV,US
120/A4 Shamsābād, India
120/B2 Shamsābād, India
155/F3 Shamva, Zim.
116/C4 Shan (plat.), Burma
116/C4 Shan (state), Burma
117/H3 Shan (pass), China
143/H2 Sha'nabī, Jabal ash (mtn.), Tun.
60/A4 Shanagolden, Ire.
113/C1 Shanchengzhen, China
149/G1 Shandī, Sudan
186/B3 Shandon, Ca,US
115/D3 Shandong (pen.), China
113/A4 Shandong (prov.), China
155/F3 Shangani, Zim.
155/F3 Shangani (riv.), Zim.
115/C4 Shangcai, China
115/C5 Shangcheng, China
117/G4 Shangchuan (isl.), China
117/G3 Shangdu, China
117/H2 Shangfang, China
115/E5 Shanghai, China
115/E5 Shanghai (mun.), China
115/L9 Shanghai (prov.), China
115/D3 Shanghe, China
113/C2 Shanghekou, China
113/C2 Shangjiahe, China
117/H2 Shangjiaodao, China
117/H3 Shangjing, China
108/F5 Shangliang, China
119/J3 Shanglin, China
153/F5 Shangolume, Zaire
154/D3 Shangombo, Zam.
117/G3 Shangping, China
115/C4 Shangqiu, China
117/H2 Shangrao, China
115/C4 Shangshui, China
123/E1 Shangsi, China
115/C2 Shangyi, China
117/G3 Shangyou (riv.), China
117/J4 Shanhua, Tai.
148/B3 Shani, Nga.
59/E5 Shanklin, Eng,UK
117/F2 Shankou, China
201/H1 Shanks, WV,US
153/E3 Shankuru (riv.), Zaire
117/F3 Shanmatang (mtn.), China
117/F3 Shanmen, China
60/A3 Shannawona (mtn.), Ire.
116/C3 Shan-ngaw (range), Burma
208/C3 Shannock, RI,US
196/B2 Shannon, Qu,Can
60/B4 Shannon (int'l arpt.), Ire.
60/B4 Shannon (riv.), Ire.
136/C3 Shannon, N.Z.
200/C3 Shannon, Ms,US
182/D3 Shannon (lake), Wa,US
60/B3 Shannonbridge, Ire.
191/H3 Shannon Hills, Ar,US
108/C3 Shanshan, China
117/F3 Shantangyi, China
101/P4 Shantar (isls.), Rus.
117/H4 Shantou, China
199/G2 Shanty Bay, On,Can
151/A2 Shanwa, Tanz.
115/B3 Shanxi (prov.), China
117/H3 Shanyang, China
117/H3 Shanyao, China
115/C3 Shanyin, China
117/F3 Shaodong, China
117/G3 Shaoguan, China
117/J2 Shaoxing, China
117/F3 Shaoyang, China
57/F2 Shap, Eng,UK
117/F4 Shapa, China
137/L Shapeless (peak), Ant.
63/P2 Shapki, Rus.
95/M2 Shapkina (riv.), Rus.
108/B2 Shaqiuhe, China
105/F2 Shaqlāwah, Iraq
106/E3 Shaqrā', SAr.
150/C2 Shaqrā', Yem.
105/F2 Sharafkhāneh, Iran
95/M5 Sharan, Rus.
95/K4 Sharanga, Rus.
107/G5 Sharbatāt, Ra's ash (pt.), Oman
199/H2 Sharbot Lake, On,Can
108/D2 Sharga, Mong.
98/E3 Shargorod, Ukr.
112/D2 Shari, Japan
108/F2 Sharingol, Mong.
132/B3 Shark (bay), Austl.
162/A1 Shark (pt.), Fl,US
132/B3 Shark Bay, Austl.
63/M4 Sharkovshchina, Bela.
207/E3 Shark River (inlet), NJ,US
97/K1 Sharlyk, Rus.
104/C5 Sharm ash Shaykh, Egypt
147/G3 Sharm el Sheikh, Egypt
59/F2 Sharnbrook, Eng,UK
208/A2 Sharon, Ct,US
208/C1 Sharon, Ma,US
208/G5 Sharon, Pa,US
200/C2 Sharon, Tn,US
196/A4 Sharon, Vt,US
208/F5 Sharon Center, Oh,US
190/D1 Sharon Springs, Ks,US
198/D5 Sharonville, Oh,US
99/H2 Sharovka, Ukr.
192/E1 Sharpe (lake), SD,US
203/H3 Sharpes, Fl,US
200/F1 Sharpsburg, Ky,US
208/H7 Sharpsburg, Pa,US
208/G5 Sharpsville, Pa,US
122/C2 Sharqpur, Pak.
89/F4 Sharqī, Jazīrat ash (isl.), Tun.
53/H3 Shar'ya, Rus.
149/G4 Shasha, Eth.
155/E4 Shashe, Bots.
155/F4 Shashe (riv.), Bots., Zim.
150/A4 Shashemenē, Eth.
115/C5 Shashi, China
184/B3 Shasta (dam), Ca,US
184/B3 Shasta (lake), Ca,US
184/B3 Shasta (mtn.), Ca,US
184/B3 Shasta-Trinity-Whiskeytown Nat'l Rec. Area, Ca,US
94/G5 Shatalovo, Rus.
146/B3 Shāţi, Wādī ash (dry riv.), Libya
63/M5 Shatsk, Bela.
97/G1 Shatsk, Rus.
98/B2 Shatskiy Nat'l Park, Ukr.
105/F4 Shatt al Arab (riv.), Iran, Iraq
140/C1 Shatt al Jarīd (depr.), Tun.
148/D2 Shattāy, Sudan
190/E2 Shattuck, Ok,US
183/H3 Shaughnessy, Ab,Can
183/K3 Shaunavon, Sk,Can
189/E3 Shavano Park, Tx,US
186/C2 Shaver Lake, Ca,US
59/E4 Shaw, Eng,UK
189/J2 Shaw, La,US
200/B4 Shaw, Ms,US
196/B4 Shaw (mtn.), NH,US
201/G4 Shaw A.F.B., SC,US
117/H3 Shawan, China
193/K1 Shawano, Wi,US
197/M6 Shawbridge, Qu,Can
58/D1 Shawbury, Eng,UK
196/A2 Shawinigan, Qu,Can
196/A2 Shawinigan-Sud, Qu,Can
192/B4 Shawnee, Co,US
198/E5 Shawnee, Oh,US
191/F3 Shawnee, Ok,US
200/F2 Shawnee-Harrogate, Tn,US
200/C2 Shawneetown, Il,US
199/H2 Shawville, Qu,Can
117/F3 Shaxi, China
132/D2 Shay Gap, Austl.
105/E2 Shaykhān, Iraq
104/C3 Shaykh, Jabal ash (mtn.), Leb.
105/F3 Shaykh Sa'd, Iraq
150/C2 Shaykh 'Uthmān, Yem.
114/B4 Shaymak, Taj.
108/C4 Shazaoyuan, China
117/F2 Shazipo, China
96/C1 Shchara (riv.), Bela.
99/L5 Shchekino, Rus.
95/N2 Shchel'yabozh, Rus.
95/M2 Shchel'yayur, Rus.
100/H4 Shcherbakty, Kaz.
99/J2 Shchigry, Rus.
98/F2 Shchors, Ukr.
63/L5 Shchuchin, Bela.
114/B1 Shchuchinsk, Kaz.
95/P5 Shchuch'ye, Rus.
207/K8 Shea Stadium, NY,US
184/E2 Sheaville, Or,US
149/H4 Shebē, Eth.
99/J2 Shebekino, Rus.
140/G4 Shebelē Wenz, Wabē (riv.), Eth., Som.
107/J1 Sheberghān, Afg.
193/L2 Sheboygan, Wi,US
198/C3 Sheboygan Falls, Wi,US
109/N2 Shebunino, Rus.
184/B1 Shedd, Or,US
196/E2 Shediac, NB,Can
54/C3 Shee (riv.), Sc,UK
60/C2 Sheelin, Lough (lake), Ire.
183/G2 Sheep (riv.), Ab,Can
177/F2 Sheep (mtn.), Ak,US
184/F2 Sheep (cr.), Id, Ut,US
186/E2 Sheep (mts.), Nv,US
192/C2 Sheep Mtn. (peak), SD,US
207/K9 Sheepshead Bay, NY,US
66/D5 's-Heerenberg, Neth.
183/J2 Sheerness, Ab,Can
59/G4 Sheerness, UK
197/F3 Sheet Harbour, NS,Can
103/F7 Shefayim, Isr.
135/C4 Sheffield, Austl.
57/G5 Sheffield, Eng,UK
200/D3 Sheffield, Al,US
207/M7 Sheffield (isl.), Ct,US
193/H2 Sheffield, Ia,US
208/E1 Sheffield, Ma,US
208/E5 Sheffield, Oh,US
199/G4 Sheffield, Pa,US
188/D2 Sheffield, Tx,US
208/E5 Sheffield Lake, Oh,US
59/F2 Shefford, Eng,UK
117/G2 Shegangshi, China
94/J3 Shegovary, Rus.
150/A2 Shehēt, Eth.
150/B4 Shēh Husēn, Eth.
175/K7 Shehuen (riv.), Arg.
60/A6 Shehy (mts.), Ire.
150/C3 Sheikh, Som.
115/B3 Shejaping, China
116/B2 Shejiaping, China
118/B2 Shekhūpura, Pak.
97/H4 Sheki, Azer.
101/T2 Shelagskiy (cape), Rus.
191/H1 Shelbina, Mo,US
198/C5 Shelburn, In,US
131/F2 Shelburne (bay), Austl.
196/E4 Shelburne, NS,Can
198/F2 Shelburne, On,Can
199/K2 Shelburne, Vt,US
193/G3 Shelby, Ia,US
198/C3 Shelby, Mi,US
200/B4 Shelby, Ms,US
183/J3 Shelby, Mt,US
201/G3 Shelby, NC,US
198/E4 Shelby, Oh,US
193/K4 Shelbyville, Il,US
193/K4 Shelbyville (lake), Il,US
198/D5 Shelbyville, In,US
200/E1 Shelbyville, Ky,US
193/H4 Shelbyville, Mo,US
200/D3 Shelbyville, Tn,US
189/G2 Shelbyville, Tx,US
193/G2 Sheldon, Ia,US
198/C4 Sheldon, Il,US
191/G2 Sheldon, Mo,US
194/E4 Sheldon, ND,US
189/M9 Sheldon, Tx,US
199/K2 Sheldon, Vt,US
195/J5 Sheldon, Wi,US
184/D3 Sheldon Antelope Ra., Nv,US
177/F3 Sheldon Point, Ak,US
208/C1 Sheldonville, Ma,US
108/E1 Shelekhov, Rus.
101/R3 Shelekhov (gulf), Rus.
177/H4 Shelikof (str.), Ak,US
192/F3 Shell (cr.), Ne,US
183/L1 Shellbrook, Sk,Can
185/G2 Shelley, Id,US
206/B3 Shelley (isl.), Pa,US
189/J3 Shell Keys Nat'l Wild. Ref., La,US
183/L1 Shell Lake, Sk,Can
193/J1 Shell Lake, Wi,US
194/C3 Shell Lake Nat'l Wild. Ref., ND,US
200/E5 Shellman, Ga,US
59/G4 Shell Ness (pt.), UK
193/H2 Shell Rock, Ia,US
193/H2 Shell Rock (riv.), Ia,US
194/F4 Shelly, Mn,US
207/F1 Shelter (isl.), NY,US
207/F1 Shelter Island (sound), NY,US
208/A3 Shelton, Ct,US
192/E3 Shelton, Ne,US
205/A3 Shelton, Wa,US
97/J4 Shemakha, Azer.
121/H2 Shemgang, Bhu.
177/A5 Shemya (isl.), Ak,US
193/G3 Shenandoah, Ia,US
206/B2 Shenandoah, Pa,US
201/H1 Shenandoah, Va,US
201/J1 Shenandoah (riv.), Va, WV,US
201/H1 Shenandoah Nat'l Park, Va,US
201/H1 Shenandoah, North Fork (riv.), Va,US
201/H1 Shenandoah, South Fork (riv.), Va,US
208/G5 Shenango (riv.), Pa,US
208/G5 Shenango River (res.), Oh,Pa,US
115/C3 Shenchi, China
122/F4 Shencottah, India
145/H4 Shendam, Nga.
144/B5 Shenge (pt.), SLeo.
151/B3 Shengena (peak), Tanz.
115/H7 Shengfang, China
91/F2 Shëngjin, Alb.
116/E3 Shengjing (pass), China
114/E3 Shengli Daban (pass), China
115/L9 Shengze, China
117/H3 Shenhu, China
94/J3 Shenkursk, Rus.
115/B5 Shennongjia, China
150/A3 Sheno, Eth.
115/C4 Shenqiu, China
59/E1 Shenstone, Eng,UK
115/C3 Shen Xian, China
113/B2 Shenyang, China
115/E2 Shenyang (arpt.), China
109/J5 Shenzao, China
117/G4 Shenzhen, China
118/B2 Sheoganj, India
120/A3 Sheopur, India
183/H2 Shepard, Ab,Can
208/C2 Shepaug (dam), Ct,US
98/D2 Shepetovka, Ukr.
189/G2 Shepherd, Tx,US
138/F6 Shepherd (isls.), Van.
200/E2 Shepherdsville, Ky,US
191/E4 Sheppard A.F.B., Tx,US
135/C3 Shepparton, Austl.
59/G4 Sheppey (isl.), Eng,UK
59/E1 Shepshed, Eng,UK
58/D4 Shepton Mallet, Eng,UK
115/C4 Sheqi, China
179/H1 Sherard (cape), NW,Can
208/C1 Sherborn, Ma,US
58/D5 Sherborne, Eng,UK
144/B5 Sherbro (isl.), SLeo.
196/B3 Sherbrooke, Qu,Can
57/G2 Sherburn, Eng,UK
199/J3 Sherburne, NY,US
193/H1 Sherburne Nat'l Wild. Ref., Mn,US
60/D2 Shercock, Ire.
145/H4 Shere (hill), Nga.
94/H5 Sheremetyevo (int'l arpt.), Rus.
121/J2 Shergaon, India
121/E3 Sherghāti, India
191/H3 Sheridan, Ar,US
184/C4 Sheridan, Ca,US
198/B4 Sheridan, Il,US
198/C4 Sheridan, In,US
185/G1 Sheridan, Mt,US
184/B1 Sheridan, Or,US
180/E3 Sheridan, Wy,US
59/H1 Sheringham, Eng,UK
60/A6 Sherkin (isl.), Ire.
120/B1 Sherkot, India
108/H1 Sherlovaya Gora, Rus.
208/A2 Sherman, Ct,US
193/K4 Sherman, Il,US
196/C3 Sherman, Me,US
200/C3 Sherman, Ms,US
192/E3 Sherman (dam), Ne,US
192/E3 Sherman (res.), Ne,US
187/J4 Sherman, NM,US
206/A3 Sherman (cr.), Pa,US
191/F4 Sherman, Tx,US
196/C3 Sherman Mills, Me,US
204/F7 Sherman Oaks, Ca,US
196/C3 Sherman Station, Me,US
121/G3 Sherpur, Bang.
121/H3 Sherpur, Bang.
208/F7 Sherrodsville, Oh,US
122/F4 Shertallai, India
66/C5 's-Hertogenbosch, Neth.
196/F2 Sherwood, PE,Can
207/E1 Sherwood (pt.), Ct,US
194/D3 Sherwood, ND,US
198/D4 Sherwood, Oh,US
191/G3 Sherwood, Ok,US
200/D3 Sherwood, Tn,US
159/E2 Sherwood, Tx,US
183/H1 Sherwood Forest, Ab,Can
178/E3 Sherwood Park, Ab,Can
193/G1 Shetek (lake), Mn,US
117/F3 Shetianqiao, China
55/N12 Shetland (isls.), Sc,UK
97/K3 Shetpe, Kaz.
122/G3 Shevaroy (hills), India
97/J4 Shevchenko, Kaz.
97/J4 Shevchenko (int'l arpt.), Kaz.
99/J3 Shevchenkovo, Ukr.
149/H3 Shewa (reg.), Eth.
115/D5 She Xian, China
115/E4 Sheyang, China
115/D4 Sheyang (riv.), China
194/E4 Sheyenne, ND,US
194/E4 Sheyenne (riv.), ND,US
194/F4 Sheyenne Nat'l Grsld., ND,US
115/C4 Shi (riv.), China
205/E6 Shiawassee (riv.), Mi,US
150/D2 Shibām, Yem.
117/F2 Shibantan, China
111/F2 Shibata, Japan
112/D2 Shibecha, Japan
112/C1 Shibetsu, Japan
112/D2 Shibetsu, Japan
121/G3 Shibganj, Bang.
103/B4 Shibīn al Kaum, Egypt
103/B4 Shibīn al Qanāţir, Egypt
112/E2 Shibotsu (isl.), Rus.
110/B5 Shibushi (bay), Japan
113/C2 Shicheng, China
113/B2 Shicheng (isl.), China
206/B1 Shickshinny, Pa,US
113/B4 Shidao, China
114/B1 Shiderty (riv.), Kaz.
117/F2 Shidixi, China
191/F2 Shidler, Ok,US
110/D3 Shido, Japan
131/E3 Shield (cape), Austl.
198/D3 Shields, Mi,US
194/D4 Shields, ND,US
113/D2 Shi'erdaogou, China
58/D1 Shifnal, Eng,UK
111/L9 Shiga, Japan
111/E3 Shiga (pref.), Japan
111/M10 Shigaraki, Japan
97/J1 Shigony, Rus.
115/C3 Shigu Shan (mtn.), China
113/A3 Shihe, China
114/E3 Shihezi, China
91/F2 Shijak, Alb.
115/L9 Shijiaqiao, China
115/C3 Shijiazhuang, China
117/H3 Shijing, China
115/H7 Shijingshan, China
117/H2 Shijiu (lake), China
145/G4 Shika, Nga.
112/B2 Shikabe, Japan
120/B1 Shikārpur, India
107/J3 Shikārpur, Pak.
111/M9 Shikatsu, Japan
111/H7 Shiki, Japan
120/B2 Shikohābād, India
110/C4 Shikoku (isl.), Japan
110/C4 Shikoku (mts.), Japan
112/C2 Shikotan (isl.), Rus.
112/B2 Shikotsu (lake), Japan
112/B2 Shikotsu-Tōya Nat'l Park, Japan
117/G3 Shikou, China
150/C4 Shilabo, Eth.
57/G2 Shildon, Eng,UK
117/G2 Shilipu, China
108/H1 Shilka, Rus.
109/H1 Shilka (riv.), Rus.
107/L2 Shilla (mtn.), India
60/D4 Shillelagh, Ire.
206/C3 Shillington, Pa,US
103/G7 Shillo, Naḥal (dry riv.), WBnk.
121/H3 Shillong, India
152/C4 Shiloango (riv.), Afr.
206/C5 Shiloh, NJ,US
200/C3 Shiloh Nat'l Mil. Park, Tn,US
115/B3 Shilou, China
97/G1 Shilovo, Rus.
108/D2 Shilüüstey, Mong.
111/H7 Shima (pen.), Japan
110/B4 Shimabara, Japan
110/B4 Shimabara (bay), Japan
111/M10 Shimagahara, Japan
111/E3 Shima-Ise Nat'l Park, Japan
110/D3 Shimamoto, Japan
110/C3 Shimane (pref.), Japan
109/K1 Shimanovsk, Rus.
117/F4 Shimao (mtn.), China
111/M9 Shimasahi, Japan
151/B3 Shimba Hills Nat'l Rsvs., Kenya
150/C3 Shimber Berris (peak), Som.
115/H6 Shimen, China
117/F2 Shimenqiao, China
119/H2 Shimian, China
111/F3 Shimizu, Japan
110/C3 Shimizu, Japan
112/F3 Shimoda, Japan
111/F2 Shimodate, Japan
118/C5 Shimoga, India
111/L10 Shimoichi, Japan
112/B3 Shimokita (pen.), Japan
110/A5 Shimo-koshiki (isl.), Japan
110/B4 Shimonoseki, Japan
111/N9 Shimoyama, Japan
63/P2 Shimsk, Rus.
112/C2 Shimukappu, Japan
117/J2 Shinaibeidong (mtn.), China
123/E1 Shinan, China
111/F2 Shinano (riv.), Japan
107/G4 Shināş, Oman
113/D3 Shinch'ŏrwon, SKor.
107/H2 Shindand, Afg.
113/D4 Shindo, SKor.
189/F3 Shiner, Tx,US
119/G2 Shingbwiyang, Burma
198/C1 Shingleton, Mi,US
110/D4 Shingū, Japan
155/F4 Shingwidzi Ruskamp, SAfr.
110/A3 Shinhyŏn, SKor.
110/C3 Shinji (lake), Japan
112/B4 Shinjō, Japan
111/M9 Shinkawa, Japan
55/J7 Shin, Loch (lake), Sc,UK
111/E2 Shinminato, Japan
207/F1 Shinnecock (bay), NY,US
207/F2 Shinnecock Ind. Res., NY,US
201/G1 Shinnston, WV,US
60/C4 Shinrone, Ire.
111/M9 Shinsei, Japan
112/C2 Shintoku, Japan
151/A2 Shinyanga, Tanz.
151/A2 Shinyanga (reg.), Tanz.
111/G1 Shiogama, Japan
110/D4 Shio-no-misaki (cape), Japan
111/G2 Shioya-saki (pt.), Japan
186/B1 Ship (chan.), Ca,US
203/D2 Ship (isl.), Ms,US

117/H3 **Shipai,** China
207/D4 **Ship Bottom,** NJ,US
53/P8 **Shipbourne,** Eng,UK
117/F3 **Shiping,** China
93/G4 **Shipka,** Bul.
57/G4 **Shipley,** Eng,UK
201/H2 **Shipman,** Va,US
207/E1 **Shippan** (pt.), Ct,US
196/E2 **Shippegan,** NB,Can
196/E2 **Shippegan** (isl.), NB,Can
199/H4 **Shippensburg,** Pa,US
111/M9 **Shippo,** Japan
187/H2 **Shiprock,** NM,US
59/E2 **Shipston on Stour,** Eng,UK
114/C5 **Shipuqi Shankou** (pass), China
117/E2 **Shiqiao,** China
117/H3 **Shiqiao,** China
109/K3 **Shiqijie,** China
105/H4 **Shīr** (mtn.), Iran
111/H8 **Shirahama,** Japan
112/B3 **Shirakami-misaki** (cape), Japan
111/G2 **Shirakawa,** Japan
110/E3 **Shirakawa-tōge** (pass), Japan
111/F2 **Shirane-san** (mtn.), Japan
111/F3 **Shirane-san** (mtn.), Japan
112/D2 **Shiranuka,** Japan
112/B2 **Shiraoi,** Japan
111/H6 **Shiraoka,** Japan
151/A2 **Shirati,** Tanz.
105/H4 **Shīrāz,** Iran
105/H4 **Shiraz** (int'l arpt.), Iran
103/B4 **Shirbīn,** Egypt
155/G3 **Shire** (riv.), Malw.
57/G1 **Shiremoor,** Eng,UK
113/D2 **Shiren,** China
112/D1 **Shiretoko-misaki** (cape), Japan
112/D1 **Shiretoko Nat'l Park,** Japan
112/B3 **Shiriya-zaki** (pt.), Japan
115/C5 **Shirjiu** (lake), China
191/H3 **Shirley,** Ar,US
199/K4 **Shirley,** NY,US
185/K2 **Shirley Basin,** Wy,US
189/G2 **Shiro,** Tx,US
111/J7 **Shiroi,** Japan
111/G2 **Shiroishi,** Japan
99/G4 **Shirokoye,** Ukr.
111/F2 **Shirone,** Japan
111/H7 **Shiroyama,** Japan
105/J2 **Shīrvān,** Iran
115/D2 **Shi San Ling,** China
99/H3 **Shishaki,** Ukr.
177/F5 **Shishaldin** (vol.), Ak,US
117/H3 **Shishan,** China
117/H3 **Shishang,** China
120/B1 **Shīshgarh,** India
108/D1 **Shishhid** (riv.), Mong.
177/E2 **Shishmaref,** Ak,US
115/C5 **Shishou,** China
111/J7 **Shisui,** Japan
117/G3 **Shitang,** China
117/J2 **Shitang,** China
105/E3 **Shithātha,** Iraq
116/D2 **Shiting** (riv.), China
112/D2 **Shitsugen-Kishiro Nat'l Park,** Japan
116/E2 **Shituan,** China
93/H4 **Shivachevo,** Bul.
121/G4 **Shivalaya,** Bang.
60/B3 **Shiven** (riv.), Ire.
200/C5 **Shivers,** Ms,US
120/A3 **Shivpurī,** India
120/A3 **Shivpuri Nat'l Park,** India
187/F2 **Shivwits** (plat.), Az, Nv,US
119/K3 **Shixing,** China
115/B4 **Shiyan,** China
117/F4 **Shiyong,** China
108/F5 **Shizigoukou,** China
117/H2 **Shizipu,** China
116/D3 **Shizong,** China
112/B4 **Shizugawa,** Japan
108/F4 **Shizuishan,** China
112/B4 **Shizukuishi,** Japan
112/C2 **Shizunai,** Japan
111/F3 **Shizuoka,** Japan
111/F3 **Shizuoka** (pref.), Japan
63/P4 **Shklov,** Bela.
91/F1 **Shkodër,** Alb.
91/G2 **Shkumbin** (riv.), Alb.
92/E5 **Shkumbin** (riv.), Alb.
177/C2 **Shmidta, Mys** (pt.), Rus.
132/B4 **Shoal** (pt.), Austl.
193/K4 **Shoal** (cr.), Il,US
191/G2 **Shoal** (cr.), Ks, Mo,US
197/L1 **Shoal Harbour,** Nf,Can
135/D2 **Shoalhaven** (riv.), Austl.
200/D1 **Shoals,** In,US
134/C3 **Shoalwater** (bay), Austl.
134/C3 **Shoalwater Bay Mil. Trg. Area,** Austl.
182/B4 **Shoalwater Ind. Res.,** Wa,US
110/C3 **Shōbara,** Japan
110/D3 **Shōdō** (isl.), Japan
191/G3 **Shoe** (mtn.), Ok,US
59/G3 **Shoeburyness,** Eng,UK
206/C2 **Shoemakersville,** Pa,US
112/B2 **Shokanbetsu-dake** (mtn.), Japan
118/C4 **Sholāpur,** India
103/G7 **Shomron** (ruins), WBnk.
202/N7 **Shon** (can.), Fl,US
111/M9 **Shonai** (riv.), Japan
111/J7 **Shōnan,** Japan
187/G2 **Shonto,** Az,US
122/F3 **Shoranūr,** India
118/C4 **Shorāpur,** India
182/F3 **Shoreacres,** BC,Can
198/C3 **Shoreham,** Mi,US
194/G4 **Shoreham,** Mn,US
199/K3 **Shoreham,** Vt,US
59/F5 **Shoreham by Sea,** Eng,UK
195/P6 **Shoreview,** Mn,US
205/P16 **Shorewood,** Il,US
205/Q13 **Shorewood,** Wi,US
122/B2 **Shorkot,** Pak.
122/B2 **Shorkot Road,** Pak.
134/F6 **Shorncliffe,** Austl.
200/E3 **Short** (mtn.), Tn,US
200/E4 **Shorter,** Al,US
203/F2 **Shorterville,** Al,US
138/E5 **Shortland** (isl.), Sol.
59/E5 **Shorwell,** Eng,UK
186/D3 **Shoshone,** Ca,US
185/F2 **Shoshone,** Id,US
185/F2 **Shoshone** (falls), Id,US
184/E4 **Shoshone** (mts.), Nv,US
185/H1 **Shoshone** (lake), Wy,US
185/J1 **Shoshone** (riv.), Wy,US
155/E4 **Shoshong,** Bots.
185/J2 **Shoshoni,** Wy,US
99/G2 **Shostka,** Ukr.
59/H3 **Shotley,** Eng,UK
57/G2 **Shotton,** Eng,UK
54/C5 **Shotts,** Sc,UK
115/D3 **Shouguang,** China
115/D4 **Shou Xian,** China
115/C3 **Shouyang,** China
111/H7 **Shōwa,** Japan
187/G3 **Show Low,** Az,US
95/K2 **Shoyna,** Rus.
94/J3 **Shozhma,** Rus.
99/M5 **Shpakovskoye,** Rus.
112/E2 **Shpanberga** (chan.), Rus.
98/F3 **Shpola,** Ukr.
122/G4 **Shree Meenakshi Temple,** India
208/E6 **Shreve,** Oh,US
189/H1 **Shreveport,** La,US
189/H1 **Shreveport Reg.** (int'l arpt.), La,US
58/D1 **Shrewsbury,** Eng,UK
208/C1 **Shrewsbury,** Ma,US
206/B4 **Shrewsbury,** Pa,US
206/A2 **Shriner Mtn.** (ridge), Pa,US
58/D1 **Shropshire** (co.), Eng,UK
57/F6 **Shropshire Union** (can.), Eng,UK
60/A2 **Shrule,** Ire.
115/D4 **Shu** (riv.), China
115/D5 **Shu** (riv.), China
116/D3 **Shuangbai,** China
101/N5 **Shuangcheng,** China
115/L8 **Shuangfeng,** China
117/G2 **Shuanghe,** China
117/E2 **Shuanghechang,** China
115/E2 **Shuangliao,** China
119/K2 **Shuangpai,** China
117/G3 **Shuangpaishan,** China
117/H3 **Shuangxi,** China
109/K3 **Shuangyang,** China
109/L2 **Shuangyashan,** China
146/D2 **Shu'bah, Wādī ash** (dry riv.), Libya
97/L2 **Shubarkuduk,** Kaz.
97/K2 **Shubarshi,** Kaz.
196/F3 **Shubenacadie,** NS,Can
193/G3 **Shubert,** Ne,US
103/B4 **Shubrā al Khaymah,** Egypt
103/B4 **Shubrā Khīt,** Egypt
200/C5 **Shubuta,** Ms,US
115/D5 **Shucheng,** China
103/D4 **Shu'fāţ,** WBnk.
116/B3 **Shuganu,** India
95/M5 **Shugurovo,** Rus.
117/E2 **Shuibatang,** China
117/H3 **Shuibei,** China
117/H3 **Shuiche,** China
117/H3 **Shuiji,** China
117/E2 **Shuijiang,** China
117/G3 **Shuikou,** China
117/G4 **Shuikou,** China
117/H3 **Shuikou,** China
123/D1 **Shuikouguan,** China
116/D2 **Shuiluo** (riv.), China
113/B3 **Shuimenzi,** China
117/H3 **Shuinan,** China
108/F5 **Shuiping,** China
115/D5 **Shuiyang** (riv.), China
108/C4 **Shuizhan,** China
107/K3 **Shujāābād,** Pak.
182/D3 **Shuksan** (mtn.), Wa,US
109/K3 **Shulan,** China
108/D4 **Shule** (riv.), China
108/D3 **Shulehe,** China
201/H4 **Shulerville,** SC,US
177/F5 **Shumagin** (isls.), Ak,US
97/L4 **Shumanay,** Uzb.
93/H4 **Shumen,** Bul.
95/K5 **Shumerlya,** Rus.
95/P5 **Shumikha,** Rus.
99/L3 **Shumilinskaya,** Rus.
98/D2 **Shumskoye,** Ukr.
54/A3 **Shuna** (isl.), Sc,UK
114/B2 **Shunak, Gora** (peak), Kaz.
146/D2 **Shunayn, Sabkhat** (salt marsh), Libya
117/H3 **Shunchang,** China
94/G3 **Shun'ga,** Rus.
177/G2 **Shungnak,** Ak,US
115/D2 **Shunyi,** China
117/E4 **Shuoliang,** China
123/D1 **Shuolong,** China
115/C3 **Shuo Xian,** China
122/C1 **Shupīyan,** India
200/C4 **Shuqualak,** Ms,US
105/J4 **Shūr** (riv.), Iran
105/G3 **Shūr Āb,** Iran
149/G2 **Shurayk,** Sudan
155/F3 **Shurugwi,** Zim.
105/G3 **Shūsh,** Iran
114/F1 **Shushenskoye,** Rus.
105/G3 **Shūshtar,** Iran
182/E2 **Shuswap** (lake), BC,Can
182/E2 **Shuswap** (riv.), BC,Can
208/B1 **Shutesbury,** Ma,US
149/G2 **Shuwak,** Sudan
103/G7 **Shuwaykah,** WBnk.
146/C2 **Shuwayrib, Sabkhat ash** (salt marsh), Libya
94/J4 **Shuya,** Rus.
115/D4 **Shuyang,** China
94/G2 **Shuyeretskoye,** Rus.
116/B5 **Shwebandaw,** Burma
116/B4 **Shwebo,** Burma
116/B5 **Shwedaung,** Burma
116/C5 **Shwegun,** Burma
116/C5 **Shwegyin,** Burma
116/C4 **Shweli** (riv.), Burma
116/C5 **Shwemawdaw Pagoda,** Burma
123/B2 **Shwemawdaw Pagoda** (ruins), Burma
116/C5 **Shwethalyaung,** Burma
123/B2 **Shwethalyaung** (Reclining Buddha), Burma
107/L2 **Shyok,** India
114/C5 **Shyok** (riv.), India
82/C5 **Siagne** (riv.), Fr.
107/H2 **Siāh** (mts.), Afg.
124/C2 **Siak** (riv.), Indo.
124/C2 **Siaksriinderapura,** Indo.
122/C1 **Siālkot,** Pak.
131/G1 **Sialum,** PNG
120/B1 **Siana,** India
85/E6 **Siano,** It.
62/G4 **Sianów,** Pol.
124/D2 **Sianton** (isl.), Indo.
165/E4 **Siapa** (riv.), Ven.
125/D3 **Siargao** (isl.), Phil.
196/C5 **Siasconset,** Ma,US
125/C4 **Siasi,** Phil.
155/E3 **Siasikabole,** Zam.
131/G1 **Siassi,** PNG
125/C3 **Siaton,** Phil.
125/C3 **Siaton** (pt.), Phil.
127/G3 **Siau** (isl.), Indo.
63/K4 **Šiauliai,** Lith.
155/F3 **Siavonga,** Zam.
97/J4 **Siazan',** Azer.
125/C3 **Sibalom,** Phil.
155/E3 **Sibanyati,** Zam.
155/F4 **Sibasa,** SAfr.
97/L1 **Sibay,** Rus.
63/L1 **Sibbo** (Sipoo), Fin.
92/B4 **Šibenik,** Cro.
100/K3 **Siberia** (reg.), Rus.
124/B3 **Siberut** (isl.), Indo.
107/J3 **Sibi,** Pak.
131/F2 **Sibidiri,** PNG
124/A2 **Sibigo,** Indo.
84/D2 **Sibillini** (mts.), It.
151/B1 **Sibiloi Nat'l Park,** Kenya
109/L3 **Sibirtsevo,** Rus.
152/C3 **Sibiti,** Congo
93/G3 **Sibiu,** Rom.
93/G2 **Sibiu** (co.), Rom.
59/G3 **Sible Hedingham,** Eng,UK
193/G2 **Sibley,** Ia,US
202/C2 **Sibley,** Ms,US
124/B2 **Sibolga,** Indo.
127/F3 **Siboluton,** Indo.
116/B3 **Sibong,** India
124/B2 **Siborongborong,** Indo.
116/B3 **Sibsāgar,** India
121/G2 **Sibsoo,** Bhu.
126/D3 **Sibu,** Malay.
124/B2 **Sibuatan** (mtn.), Indo.
125/C4 **Sibuco,** Phil.
125/C4 **Sibuguey** (bay), Phil.
124/B2 **Sibuhuan,** Indo.
127/F2 **Sibuko,** Phil.
148/C4 **Sibut,** CAfr.
125/B4 **Sibutu** (chan.), Malay., Phil.
125/C2 **Sibuyan** (isl.), Phil.
127/F1 **Sibuyan** (sea), Phil.
125/C2 **Sibuyan** (str.), Phil.
144/E4 **Siby,** Burk.
182/E2 **Sicamous,** BC,Can
125/C1 **Sicapoo** (mtn.), Phil.
172/C1 **Sicasica,** Bol.
123/C2 **Si Chiang Mai,** Thai.
154/E3 **Sichifulo** (riv.), Zam.
123/B4 **Si Chon,** Thai.
115/B5 **Sichuan** (prov.), China
82/B6 **Sicié** (cape), Fr.
83/B6 **Sicilia** (reg.), It.
90/C3 **Sicily** (isl.), It.
90/B4 **Sicily** (str.), It., Tun.
202/C2 **Sicily Island,** La,US
202/C2 **Sicily Island** (mtn.), La,US
161/E3 **Sico** (riv.), Hon.
168/D4 **Sicuani,** Peru
92/D3 **Šid,** Yugo.
150/A4 **Sīdamo** (reg.), Eth.
113/D2 **Sidaogou,** China
53/P7 **Sidcup,** Eng,UK
118/C4 **Siddipet,** India
144/D4 **Sidéradougou,** Burk.
83/C6 **Siderno Marina,** It.
173/G4 **Sideropólis,** Braz.
204/C1 **Sidewinder** (mtn.), Ca,US
91/F3 **Sidhári,** Gre.
120/C2 **Sidhaulī,** India
120/C3 **Sidhi,** India
91/H2 **Sidhirókastron,** Gre.
118/B3 **Sidhpur,** India
141/S16 **Sidi Aïssa,** Alg.
141/L13 **Sidi Allal Tazi,** Mor.
147/E2 **Sīdī Barrānī,** Egypt
141/Q16 **Sidi Bel-Abbes,** Alg.
141/Q16 **Sidi Bel-Abbes** (wilaya), Alg.
142/C2 **Sidi Bennour,** Mor.
142/D3 **Sidi Bou Othmane,** Mor.
141/W18 **Sīdī Bū Zayd,** Tun.
141/W18 **Sidi Bū Zayd** (gov.), Tun.
90/A5 **Sīdī Bū Zayd** (gov.), Tun.
142/C3 **Sidi Ifni,** Mor.
141/M13 **Sidi Kacem,** Mor.
124/B2 **Sidikalang,** Indo.
141/X17 **Sīdī Nājī,** Tun.
146/C2 **Sīdī Şāliḩ, Thamad** (well), Libya
103/B4 **Sīdī Sālim,** Egypt
141/M13 **Sidi Slimane,** Mor.
142/C2 **Sidi Smaïl,** Mor.
141/X18 **Sīdī 'Umar Bū Ḩajalah,** Tun.
141/L13 **Sidi Yahya du Rharb,** Mor.
54/C4 **Sidlaw** (hills), Sc,UK
137/R **Sidley** (mtn.), Ant.
134/A1 **Sidmouth** (cape), Austl.
58/C5 **Sidmouth,** Eng,UK
195/K4 **Sidnaw,** Mi,US
182/C3 **Sidney,** BC,Can
191/J2 **Sidney,** Ar,US
193/G3 **Sidney,** Ia,US
196/C3 **Sidney,** Me,US
183/M4 **Sidney,** Mt,US
192/C3 **Sidney,** Ne,US
199/J3 **Sidney,** NY,US
198/D4 **Sidney,** Oh,US
192/C3 **Sidney Draw** (cr.), Co, Ne,US
200/E3 **Sidney Lanier** (lake), Ga,US
148/C3 **Sido,** CAfr.
124/F4 **Sidoharjo,** Indo.
104/C3 **Sidon,** Leb.
103/D3 **Sidon** (Şaydā), Leb.
146/C2 **Sidra** (gulf), Libya
170/B4 **Sidrolândia,** Braz.
157/E2 **Sidvokodvo,** Swaz.
72/D5 **Siebenlehn,** Ger.
87/E5 **Sieci,** It.
67/F3 **Siede** (riv.), Ger.
65/M2 **Siedlce,** Pol.
65/L2 **Siedlce** (prov.), Pol.
69/G2 **Sieg** (riv.), Ger.
69/G2 **Siegburg,** Ger.
182/G4 **Siegel** (mtn.), Mt,US
69/H2 **Siegen,** Ger.
71/E5 **Siegenburg,** Ger.
73/A4 **Siegendorf im Burgenland,** Aus.
144/C4 **Sielo,** Libr.
65/M2 **Siemianówka** (lake), Pol.
65/M2 **Siemiatycze,** Pol.
123/D3 **Siempang,** Camb.
123/C3 **Siemreab,** Camb.
87/E6 **Siena,** It.
84/B1 **Siena** (prov.), It.
78/D3 **Sienne** (riv.), Fr.
65/K3 **Sieradz,** Pol.
65/K3 **Sieradz** (prov.), Pol.
65/J2 **Sieraków,** Pol.
80/D2 **Sierentz,** Fr.
69/F5 **Sierk-les-Bains,** Fr.
73/A3 **Sierndorf,** Aus.
71/H6 **Sierning,** Aus.
65/K2 **Sierpc,** Pol.
204/C3 **Sierra** (peak), Ca,US
184/C3 **Sierra Army Dep.,** Ca,US
188/B2 **Sierra Blanca,** Tx,US
184/C4 **Sierra City,** Ca,US
174/D4 **Sierra Colorada,** Arg.
164/C4 **Sierra de la Macarena Nat'l Park,** Col.
188/C3 **Sierra del Carmen Nat'l Park,** Mex.
158/B2 **Sierra de San Pedro Martir Nat'l Park,** Mex.
172/B2 **Sierra Gorda,** Chile
174/D4 **Sierra Grande,** Arg.
144/B4 **Sierra Leone**
144/B4 **Sierra Leone** (cape), SLeo.
125/C1 **Sierra Madre** (mts.), Phil.
204/B2 **Sierra Madre,** Ca,US
186/B3 **Sierra Madre** (mts.), Ca,US
158/E3 **Sierra Mojada,** Mex.
186/B1 **Sierra Nevada** (range), Ca, Nv,US
164/C2 **Sierra Nevada de Santa Marta Nat'l Park,** Col.
164/D2 **Sierra Nevada Nat'l Park,** Ven.
174/E3 **Sierras Bayas,** Arg.
187/G5 **Sierra Vista,** Az,US
80/D5 **Sierre,** Swi.
203/G4 **Siesta** (key), Fl,US
77/M8 **Siete** (peak), Sp.
174/C2 **Siete Tazas Nat'l Park,** Chile
87/E5 **Sieve** (riv.), It.
150/B2 **Sīfenī,** Eth.
143/H3 **Sif Fatima,** Alg.
144/C4 **Siffray,** Gui.
144/D5 **Sifié,** IvC.
91/J4 **Sífnos** (isl.), Gre.
141/Q16 **Sig,** Alg.
151/A2 **Siga** (hills), Tanz.
74/E5 **Sigean,** Fr.
124/B3 **Sigep,** Indo.
124/B3 **Sigep** (cape), Indo.
84/H8 **Siggiewi,** Malta
93/F2 **Sighetu Marmaţiei,** Rom.
93/G2 **Sighişoara,** Rom.
57/F1 **Sighty Crag** (hill), Eng,UK
87/F6 **Sigillo,** It.
122/H5 **Sigiriya,** SrL.
141/T15 **Sigli** (cape), Alg.
124/A1 **Sigli,** Indo.
61/N6 **Siglufjördhur,** Ice.
70/C6 **Sigmaringen,** Ger.
81/F2 **Sigmarszell,** Ger.
87/E5 **Signa,** It.
97/H4 **Signakhi,** Geo.
192/C2 **Signal** (hill), SD,US
204/F8 **Signal Hill,** Ca,US
80/D4 **Signau,** Swi.
82/B6 **Signes,** Fr.
68/D4 **Signy-l'Abbaye,** Fr.
68/D4 **Signy-le-Petit,** Fr.
193/H3 **Sigourney,** Ia,US
80/D4 **Sigriswil,** Swi.
62/G2 **Sigtuna,** Swe.
63/R6 **Sigtunafjärden** (lake), Swe.
160/E3 **Siguatepeque,** Hon.
164/B4 **Sigüe,** Ecu.
76/D2 **Sigüenza,** Sp.
144/C4 **Siguiri,** Gui.
63/L3 **Sigulda,** Lat.
124/B2 **Sigura Gura** (falls), Indo.
185/H4 **Sigurd,** Ut,US
81/E3 **Sihl** (riv.), Swi.
81/E3 **Sihlsee** (lake), Swi.
159/H5 **Sihochac,** Mex.
115/D4 **Sihong,** China
120/C4 **Sihorā,** India
168/B3 **Sihuas,** Peru
61/H3 **Siilinjärvi,** Fin.
103/G8 **Si'īr,** WBnk.
104/E2 **Siirt,** Turk.
104/E2 **Siirt** (prov.), Turk.
113/D2 **Sijung,** NKor.
120/A1 **Sikandarābād,** India
120/E2 **Sikandarpur,** India
120/B2 **Sikandra Rao,** India
178/D3 **Sikanni Chief** (riv.), BC,Can
118/C2 **Sīkar,** India
144/D4 **Sikasso,** Mali
144/D4 **Sikasso** (reg.), Mali
116/C4 **Sikaw,** Burma
73/C3 **Sikenica** (riv.), Slvk.
191/H4 **Sikes,** La,US
200/C2 **Sikeston,** Mo,US
123/C3 **Si Khiu,** Thai.
109/M2 **Sikhote-Alin'** (mts.), Rus.
91/J4 **Síkinos,** Gre.
91/J4 **Síkinos** (isl.), Gre.
144/D5 **Sikinssa,** IvC.
121/G2 **Sikkim** (state), India
92/D3 **Siklós,** Hun.
91/H3 **Sikoúrion,** Gre.
101/N3 **Siktyakh,** Rus.
125/B4 **Sikuati,** Malay.
154/E5 **Sikwane,** Bots.
76/B1 **Sil** (riv.), Sp.
160/B2 **Silacayoapán,** Mex.
83/C4 **Sila Grande** (mts.), It.
83/C3 **Sila Greca** (mts.), It.
121/F4 **Silai** (riv.), India
63/K4 **Šilalė,** Lith.
81/G4 **Silandro** (Schlanders), It.
121/E3 **Silao,** India
159/E4 **Silao,** Mex.
83/C4 **Sila Piccola** (mts.), It.
125/C3 **Silay,** Phil.
116/B3 **Silchar,** India
121/F4 **Sildā,** India
93/J5 **Şile,** Turk.
87/F1 **Šilea,** It.
59/E1 **Sileby,** Eng,UK
150/B3 **Silel** (dry riv.), Som.
81/E4 **Silenen,** Swi.
201/H3 **Siler City,** NC,US
65/H3 **Silesia** (reg.), Pol.
143/G5 **Silet,** Alg.
184/B1 **Siletz,** Or,US
184/B1 **Siletz** (riv.), Or,US
120/C1 **Silgarhi,** Nepal
103/C1 **Silifke,** Turk.
121/G2 **Silīguri,** India
114/E5 **Siling** (lake), China
139/H6 **Silisili** (peak), WSam.
93/H3 **Silistra,** Bul.
93/J5 **Silivri,** Turk.
62/F1 **Siljan** (lake), Swe.
62/F1 **Siljansnäs,** Swe.
62/C3 **Silkeborg,** Den.
57/G2 **Silksworth,** Eng,UK
81/H3 **Sill** (riv.), Aus.
77/E3 **Silla,** Sp.
172/B1 **Sillajguay** (peak), Chile
172/B1 **Sillajhuay** (peak), Bol.
63/M2 **Sillamäe,** Est.
122/B2 **Sillānwāli,** Pak.
87/E4 **Sillaro** (riv.), It.
110/A3 **Silla Tombs,** SKor.
76/A1 **Silleda,** Sp.
79/E4 **Sillé-le-Guillame,** Fr.
75/K3 **Sillian,** Aus.
150/B3 **Sillil,** Som.
57/E2 **Silloth,** Eng,UK
168/D4 **Sillustani,** Peru
191/F3 **Silo,** Ok,US
191/G2 **Siloam Springs,** Ar,US
104/E2 **Silopi,** Turk.
189/G2 **Silsbee,** Tx,US
57/G4 **Silsden,** Eng,UK
81/F5 **Silsersee** (lake), Swi.
184/A2 **Siltcoos** (lake), Or,US
160/C3 **Siltepec,** Mex.
194/B2 **Silton,** Sk,Can
148/B1 **Siltou** (well), Chad
126/C3 **Siluas,** Indo.
145/G5 **Şiluko,** Nga.
63/J4 **Šilutė,** Lith.
191/J2 **Silva,** Mo,US
104/E2 **Silvan,** Turk.
104/E2 **Silvan** (dam), Turk.
120/B4 **Silvāni,** India
170/C3 **Silvânia,** Braz.
167/L7 **Silvania,** Col.
81/F5 **Silvaplana,** Swi.
118/B3 **Silvassa,** India
204/C1 **Silver** (mtn.), Ca,US
193/G3 **Silver** (cr.), Ia,US
193/K4 **Silver** (cr.), Il,US
205/F7 **Silver** (cr.), Mi,US
184/D2 **Silver** (cr.), Or,US
184/C2 **Silver** (lake), Or,US
188/D1 **Silver,** Tx,US
204/C3 **Silverado,** Ca,US
195/J4 **Silver Bay,** Mn,US
187/G4 **Silver Bell,** Az,US
187/H4 **Silver City,** NM,US
192/C1 **Silver City,** SD,US
190/B1 **Silver Cliff,** Co,US
177/L3 **Silver Creek,** Yk,Can
199/G3 **Silver Creek,** NY,US
57/F3 **Silverdale,** Eng,UK
205/B2 **Silverdale,** Wa,US
206/D2 **Silver Hill-Suitland,** Md,US
195/G5 **Silver Lake,** Mn,US
208/F5 **Silver Lake,** Oh,US
184/C2 **Silver Lake,** Or,US
205/P14 **Silver Lake,** Wi,US
206/C5 **Silver Lake Meadow** (lake), NJ,US
194/E3 **Silver Lake Nat'l Wild. Ref.,** ND,US
206/A4 **Silver Run,** Md,US
206/A6 **Silver Spring,** Md,US
203/G3 **Silver Springs,** Fl,US
184/D4 **Silver Springs,** Nv,US
183/H5 **Silver Star,** Mt,US
59/E2 **Silverstone,** Eng,UK
192/A4 **Silverthorne,** Co,US
133/J4 **Silverton,** Austl.
58/C5 **Silverton,** Eng,UK
185/K5 **Silverton,** Co,US
207/D3 **Silverton,** NJ,US
184/B1 **Silverton,** Or,US
190/D3 **Silverton,** Tx,US
182/D3 **Silverton,** Wa,US
198/E2 **Silver Water,** On,Can
204/C2 **Silverwood** (lake), Ca,US
166/B3 **Silves,** Braz.
76/A4 **Silves,** Port.
85/E2 **Silvi,** It.
164/B4 **Silvia,** Col.
184/D2 **Silvies** (riv.), Or,US
173/E3 **Silvio Pettirossi** (Asunción) (int'l arpt.), Par.
81/G4 **Silvretta** (mts.), Aus., Swi.
141/W17 **Silyānah,** Tun.
90/A4 **Silyānah** (gov.), Tun.
81/G3 **Silz,** Aus.
142/C3 **Sim** (cape), Mor.
157/H6 **Sima,** Com.
152/C3 **Sima,** Congo
126/D3 **Simanggang,** Malay.
116/D4 **Simao,** China
171/F1 **Simão Dias,** Braz.
105/F3 **Şimareh** (riv.), Iran
104/B2 **Simav,** Turk.
153/E2 **Simba,** Zaire
71/G6 **Simbach am Inn,** Ger.
131/G1 **Simbai,** PNG
53/H3 **Simbirsk,** Rus.
97/H1 **Simbirsk Obl.,** Rus.
153/G4 **Simbo,** Tanz.
84/C3 **Simbruini** (mts.), It.
198/F3 **Simcoe,** On,Can
199/G2 **Simcoe** (lake), On,Can
121/E4 **Simdega,** India
99/H5 **Simeiz,** Ukr.
149/H2 **Simēn** (mts.), Eth.
149/H2 **Simen Mts. Nat'l Park,** Eth.
83/C4 **Simeri** (riv.), It.
92/F3 **Simeria,** Rom.
89/G3 **Simeto** (riv.), It.
124/A2 **Simeulue** (isl.), Indo.
53/G4 **Simferopol',** Ukr.
99/G5 **Simferopol** (int'l arpt.), Ukr.
104/A2 **Sími,** Gre.
204/B2 **Simi** (hills), Ca,US
167/M6 **Simijaca,** Col.
118/D2 **Simikot,** Nepal
81/G4 **Similaun** (peak), Aus.
182/D3 **Similkameen** (riv.), BC,Can
115/E5 **Siming** (mtn.), China
164/C3 **Simití,** Col.
93/F5 **Simitli,** Bul.
204/B2 **Simi Valley,** Ca,US
151/A2 **Simiyu** (riv.), Tanz.
122/D2 **Simla,** India
92/F2 **Şimleu Silvaniei,** Rom.
80/D4 **Simme** (riv.), Swi.
71/E3 **Simmelsdorf,** Ger.
69/F2 **Simmerath,** Ger.
69/G4 **Simmerbach** (riv.), Ger.
69/G4 **Simmern,** Ger.
69/G4 **Simmertal,** Ger.
202/C2 **Simmesport,** La,US
191/H2 **Simmons,** Mo,US
113/C3 **Simni** (isl.), NKor.
61/H2 **Simo,** Fin.
167/F4 **Simões,** Braz.
171/F2 **Simões Filho,** Braz.
160/C2 **Simojovel,** Mex.
164/B5 **Simón Bolívar** (int'l arpt.), Ecu.
165/E2 **Simón Bolívar** (int'l arpt.), Ven.
87/F5 **Simoncello** (peak), It.
196/D2 **Simonds,** NB,Can
156/B4 **Simonstown,** SAfr.
66/D1 **Simonszand** (isl.), Neth.
189/G3 **Simonton,** Tx,US
73/C6 **Simontornya,** Hun.
124/D3 **Simpang,** Indo.
124/B2 **Simpang-kiri** (riv.), Indo.
124/C2 **Simpang Tiga** (int'l arpt.), Indo.
124/B1 **Simpangulim,** Indo.
69/E2 **Simpelveld,** Neth.
167/F4 **Simplício Mendes,** Braz.
80/E5 **Simplon,** Swi.
80/E5 **Simplon** (tunnel), Swi.
80/E5 **Simplonpass** (pass), Swi.
133/H3 **Simpson** (des.), Austl.
178/H2 **Simpson** (pen.), NW,Can
178/G2 **Simpson** (riv.), NW,Can
195/L3 **Simpson** (isl.), On,Can
194/B2 **Simpson,** Sk,Can
202/B2 **Simpson,** La,US
183/J3 **Simpson,** Mt,US
133/H3 **Simpson Des. Consv. Park,** Austl.
133/H3 **Simpson Des. Nat'l Park,** Austl.
133/G2 **Simpsons Gap Nat'l Park,** Austl.
62/F4 **Simrishamn,** Swe.
191/H3 **Sims,** Ar,US
189/M9 **Sims** (bayou), Tx,US
208/B2 **Simsbury,** Ct,US
125/B4 **Simunul,** Phil.
124/B2 **Sinabang,** Indo.
150/C4 **Sinadhago,** Som.
106/B3 **Sinafir** (isl.), SAr.
103/C4 **Sinai** (pen.), Egypt
125/C1 **Sinait,** Phil.
158/D3 **Sinaloa** (state), Mex.
158/C3 **Sinaloa de Leyva,** Mex.
84/B1 **Sinalunga,** It.
85/E4 **Sinarca** (riv.), It.
146/A2 **Sīnāwin,** Libya
155/E3 **Sinazongwe,** Zam.
104/C2 **Sincan,** Turk.
164/C2 **Sincé,** Col.
164/C2 **Sincelejo,** Col.
68/C4 **Sinceny,** Fr.
113/E2 **Sinch'ang,** NKor.
113/C3 **Sinch'ŏn,** NKor.
133/G5 **Sinclair** (pt.), Austl.
201/F4 **Sinclair** (lake), Ga,US
185/K3 **Sinclair,** Wy,US
120/B2 **Sind** (riv.), India
118/A2 **Sind** (prov.), Pak.
62/D3 **Sindal,** Den.
125/C3 **Sindañgan,** Phil.
124/D4 **Sindangbarang,** Indo.
70/C5 **Sindelfingen,** Ger.
121/E2 **Sindhūli Garhi,** Nepal
63/L2 **Sindi,** Est.
104/B2 **Sındırgı,** Turk.
149/E2 **Sindī, Wādī** (dry riv.), Sudan
144/D4 **Sindou,** Burk.
99/L4 **Sinegorskiy,** Rus.
93/H5 **Sinekçi,** Turk.
93/J5 **Sinekli,** Turk.
85/E3 **Sinello** (riv.), It.
99/H3 **Sinel'nikovo,** Ukr.
145/F4 **Sinendé,** Ben.
76/A4 **Sines,** Port.
76/A4 **Sines, Cabo de** (cape), Port.
144/D5 **Sinfra,** IvC.
124/C2 **Singapore**
124/C2 **Singapore** (cap.), Sing.
118/B2 **Singar,** India
124/F5 **Singaraja,** Indo.
123/C3 **Sing Buri,** Thai.
81/E2 **Singen,** Ger.
93/G2 **Sîngeorz-Băi,** Rom.
151/A3 **Singida,** Tanz.
151/A3 **Singida** (reg.), Tanz.
108/B3 **Singim,** China
91/H2 **Singitic** (gulf), Gre.
116/B3 **Singkaling Hkamti,** Burma
127/F4 **Singkang,** Indo.
126/C3 **Singkawang,** Indo.
124/D3 **Singkep** (isl.), Indo.
124/B2 **Singkil,** Indo.
124/B2 **Singkuang,** Indo.
135/D2 **Singleton,** Austl.
132/C4 **Singleton** (peak), Austl.
133/F2 **Singleton** (peak), Austl.
145/F4 **Singou Rsv.,** Ben.
121/G3 **Singra,** Bang.
116/C4 **Singu,** Burma
155/F4 **Singuédeze** (riv.), Moz.
113/D3 **Sin'gye,** NKor.
113/D2 **Sinhŭng,** NKor.
148/C3 **Siniaka-Minia Fauna Rsv.,** Chad
146/B2 **Sinidah, Bi'r as** (well), Libya
164/B5 **Sinincay,** Ecu.
90/A2 **Siniscola,** It.
99/K2 **Siniye Lipyagi,** Rus.
149/G2 **Sinjah,** Sudan
104/E2 **Sinjār,** Iraq
103/D3 **Sinjil,** WBnk.
147/H5 **Sinkāt,** Sudan
114/E3 **Sinkiang** (reg.), China
68/C3 **Sin-le-Noble,** Fr.
119/G3 **Sinlumkaba,** Burma
113/D3 **Sinmak,** NKor.
70/C2 **Sinn** (riv.), Ger.
166/C1 **Sinnamary,** FrG.
166/C1 **Sinnamary** (riv.), FrG.
113/D2 **Sinnam-dok-san** (mtn.), NKor.
118/B4 **Sinnar,** India
83/C2 **Sinni** (riv.), It.
92/E2 **Sînnicolau Mare,** Rom.
103/B5 **Sinnūris,** Egypt
113/E4 **Sinnyŏng,** SKor.
144/C5 **Sino** (co.), Libr.
93/J3 **Sinoe** (lake), Rom.
89/L1 **Sinoe, Lacul** (lag.), Rom.
170/B1 **Sinop,** Braz.
104/C1 **Sinop,** Turk.
104/C1 **Sinop** (prov.), Turk.
104/C1 **Sinop** (pt.), Turk.
173/G3 **Sinos** (riv.), Braz.
113/D2 **Sinp'a-ŭp,** NKor.
113/E2 **Sinp'o,** NKor.
113/D3 **Sinp'yŏng,** NKor.
70/B4 **Sinsheim,** Ger.
113/D5 **Sint'aein,** SKor.
113/E2 **Sint'ae-ri,** NKor.
126/D3 **Sintang,** Indo.
66/B5 **Sint Annaland,** Neth.
68/D2 **Sint-Genesius-Rode,** Belg.
68/D1 **Sint-Gillis-Waas,** Belg.
66/C5 **Sint Hubert,** Neth.
66/C2 **Sint Jacobiparochie,** Neth.
68/D1 **Sint-Katelijne-Waver,** Belg.
68/C1 **Sint-Laureins,** Belg.
162/F3 **Sint Maarten** (Saint Martin) (isl.), NAnt.
66/B5 **Sint Maartensdijk,** Neth.
69/E2 **Sint-Martens-Voeren,** Belg.
66/C5 **Sint-Michielsgestel,** Neth.
162/D4 **Sint Nicolaas,** Aru.
68/D1 **Sint-Niklaas,** Belg.
66/C5 **Sint-Oedenrode,** Neth.
189/F3 **Sinton,** Tx,US
68/D2 **Sint-Pieters-Leeuw,** Belg.
76/A3 **Sintra,** Port.
77/P10 **Sintra** (mts.), Port.
69/E2 **Sint-Truiden,** Belg.
161/H4 **Sinú** (riv.), Col.
164/B2 **Sinu** (riv.), Col.
113/C2 **Sinŭiju,** NKor.
150/D3 **Sinujif,** Som.
113/C3 **Sinwŏn,** NKor.
113/D3 **Sinyang,** NKor.
63/P2 **Sinyavino,** Rus.
70/B5 **Sinzheim,** Ger.
69/G2 **Sinzig,** Ger.
73/C6 **Sió** (riv.), Hun.
125/C4 **Siocon,** Phil.
73/C6 **Siófok,** Hun.
154/D3 **Sioma Ngwezi Nat'l Park,** Zam.
80/D5 **Sion,** Swi.
78/D5 **Sion-les-Mines,** Fr.
55/H9 **Sion Mills,** NI,UK
74/E4 **Sioule** (riv.), Fr.
193/F2 **Sioux Center,** Ia,US
193/F2 **Sioux City,** Ia,US
193/F2 **Sioux Falls,** SD,US
195/J2 **Sioux Lookout,** On,Can
195/G3 **Sioux Narrows,** On,Can
193/G2 **Sioux Rapids,** Ia,US
125/C3 **Sipalay,** Phil.
166/C2 **Sipaliwini** (dist.), Sur.
166/B2 **Sipaliwini** (riv.), Sur.
90/E1 **Šipan** (isl.), Cro.
162/F5 **Siparia,** Trin.
164/B3 **Sipí,** Col.
115/F2 **Siping,** China
124/B2 **Si Piso-Piso** (falls), Indo.
125/A4 **Sipitang,** Malay.
178/G3 **Sipiwesk** (lake), Mb,Can
137/Q **Siple** (coast), Ant.
137/R **Siple** (isl.), Ant.
125/C2 **Sipocot,** Phil.
85/F4 **Siponto** (ruins), It.
63/L1 **Sipoo** (Sibbo), Fin.
200/D4 **Sipsey** (riv.), Al,US
124/B3 **Sipura** (isl.), Indo.
124/B3 **Sipura** (str.), Indo.
170/C4 **Siqueira Campos,** Braz.
158/D4 **Siqueros,** Mex.
161/E3 **Siquia** (riv.), Nic.
125/C3 **Siquijar** (isl.), Phil.
164/D2 **Siquisique,** Ven.
62/B2 **Sira** (riv.), Nor.
82/C3 **Sirac** (mtn.), Fr.
123/C3 **Si Racha,** Thai.
90/D4 **Siracusa** (Syracuse), It.
121/G3 **Sirājganj,** Bang.
104/D1 **Şiran,** Turk.
150/A3 **Sīrē,** Eth.
131/E3 **Sir Edward Pellew Group** (isls.), Austl.
193/H1 **Siren,** Wi,US
85/D3 **Sirente** (peak), It.
93/H2 **Siret,** Rom.
93/H3 **Siret** (riv.), Rom.
121/F2 **Sirha,** Nepal
122/D2 **Sirhind,** India
105/J5 **Sīrīk,** Iran
126/D3 **Sirik** (cape), Malay.
116/D5 **Sirikit** (res.), Thai.
171/G1 **Sirinhaém,** Braz.
103/G7 **Sīrīs,** WBnk.
119/H4 **Sirit** (res.), Thai.
177/B5 **Sirius** (pt.), Ak,US
178/D2 **Sir James MacBrien** (peak), NW,Can
132/C5 **Sir James Mitchell Nat'l Park,** Austl.
105/H4 **Sīrjan,** Iran
135/D4 **Sir John** (cape), Austl.
122/G3 **Sirkali,** India
104/C1 **Sirkeli,** Turk.
86/D2 **Sirmione,** It.
120/A2 **Sir Muttra,** India
81/F3 **Sirnach,** Swi.
104/E2 **Şırnak,** Turk.
118/B3 **Sirohi,** India
87/G5 **Sirolo,** It.
124/B2 **Sirombu,** Indo.
120/A3 **Sironj,** India
91/J4 **Síros** (isl.), Gre.
99/M3 **Sirotinskaya,** Rus.
142/D3 **Siroua, Jebel** (mtn.), Mor.
91/K2 **Sırpsındığı,** Turk.
118/C2 **Sirsa,** India
120/B2 **Sirsāganj,** India
182/F2 **Sir Sandford** (mtn.), BC,Can
157/S15 **Sir Seewoosagur Ramgoolam** (int'l arpt.), Mrts.
154/E5 **Sir Seretse Khama** (Gaborone) (int'l arpt.), Bots.
120/B1 **Sirsi,** India
133/F3 **Sir Thomas** (peak), Austl.
146/C2 **Sirtica** (reg.), Libya
125/C2 **Siruma,** Phil.
105/F3 **Sīrvān** (riv.), Iran
63/L4 **Širvintos,** Lith.
92/C3 **Sisak,** Cro.
119/H4 **Si Sa Ket,** Thai.
123/D3 **Sisaket,** Thai.
160/D1 **Sisal,** Mex.
123/B2 **Si Satchanalai,** Thai.
123/B2 **Si Satchanalai** (ruins), Thai.
156/C2 **Sishen,** SAfr.
115/D4 **Sishui,** China
97/H5 **Sisian,** Arm.
194/E1 **Sisib** (lake), Mb,Can
81/E4 **Sisikon,** Swi.
50/G2 **Sisimiut,** Grld.
184/B2 **Siskiyou** (mts.), Ca, Or,US
123/C3 **Sisophon,** Camb.
80/D3 **Sissach,** Swi.
144/C4 **Sisséla,** Gui.
193/F1 **Sisseton,** SD,US
193/F1 **Sisseton-Wahpeton Ind. Res.,** SD,US
145/E4 **Sissili** (prov.), Burk.
68/C4 **Sissone,** Fr.
201/G1 **Sissonville,** WV,US
198/C2 **Sister Bay,** Wi,US
188/L6 **Sister Grove** (cr.), Tx,US
82/B4 **Sisteron,** Fr.
201/G1 **Sistersville,** WV,US
87/G1 **Sistina,** It.
84/D5 **Sisto** (riv.), It.
120/D2 **Siswā Bāzār,** India
168/B2 **Sitacocha,** Peru
121/H4 **Sītākund,** Bang.
121/H4 **Sitākunda,** Bang.
153/G4 **Sitalike,** Tanz.
121/E2 **Sītāmarhi,** India
120/C2 **Sītāpur,** India
120/B1 **Sitārganj,** India
157/E2 **Siteki,** Swaz.
77/F2 **Sitges,** Sp.
91/H2 **Sithoniá** (pen.), Gre.
91/K5 **Sitía,** Gre.
108/C3 **Sitian,** China
177/M2 **Sitidgi** (lake), NW,Can
117/E3 **Siting,** China
170/D2 **Sítio d'Abadia,** Braz.
167/E4 **Sítio Novo do Grajaú,** Braz.
177/L4 **Sitka,** Ak,US
98/E3 **Sitkovtsy,** Ukr.
73/C3 **Sitno** (peak), Slvk.
154/D3 **Sitoti,** Zam.
116/C5 **Sittang** (riv.), Burma
66/C7 **Sittard,** Neth.
67/G2 **Sittensen,** Ger.
81/F3 **Sitter** (riv.), Swi.
59/G4 **Sittingbourne,** Eng,UK
204/C3 **Sitton** (peak), Ca,US
116/B4 **Sittwe** (Akyab), Burma
124/F4 **Situbondo,** Indo.
130/A1 **Siumpu** (isl.), Indo.
184/B2 **Siuslaw** (riv.), Or,US
92/D3 **Sivac,** Yugo.
122/G4 **Sivaganga,** India
122/F4 **Sivakāsi,** India
109/K1 **Sivaki,** Rus.
105/H4 **Sīvand,** Iran
104/D2 **Sivas,** Turk.
104/D2 **Sivas** (prov.), Turk.
99/G4 **Sivash** (sound), Ukr.
144/B3 **Sivé,** Mrta.
104/D2 **Siverek,** Turk.
63/P2 **Siverskiy,** Rus.
80/C4 **Siviriez,** Swi.
95/P2 **Sivomaskinskiy,** Rus.
104/B2 **Sivrihisar,** Turk.
68/D3 **Sivry-Rance,** Belg.
147/E2 **Siwa** (oasis), Egypt
127/F4 **Siwa,** Indo.
147/E2 **Sīwah,** Egypt
122/D2 **Siwālik** (range), India
118/D2 **Siwalik** (range), Nepal
120/C1 **Siwālik** (range), Nepal
120/E2 **Siwān,** India
184/A2 **Sixes,** Or,US
206/D3 **Six Flags Great Adventure,** NJ,US
205/Q15 **Six Flags Great America,** Il,US
204/B2 **Six Flags Magic Mountain,** Ca,US
201/L7 **Six Flags Over Georgia,** Ga,US
188/K7 **Six Flags Over Texas,** Tx,US
82/B6 **Six-Fours-les-Plages,** Fr.
115/D4 **Si Xian,** China
202/C3 **Sixmile** (lake), La,US
60/B4 **Sixmilebridge,** Ire.
56/A2 **Sixmilecross,** NI,UK
149/G1 **Sixth Cataract** (falls), Sudan
177/K3 **Sixtymile,** Yk,Can
156/E2 **Siyabuswa,** SAfr.
120/B1 **Siyāna,** India
115/D4 **Siyang,** China
116/E2 **Siyichang,** China
108/F3 **Siyitang,** China
117/J2 **Sizhoutou,** China
108/G3 **Siziwang,** China
78/A4 **Sizun,** Fr.
95/M2 **Sizyahsk,** Rus.
61/D5 **Sjælland** (isl.), Den.
63/T9 **Sjælsø** (lake), Den.
92/E4 **Sjenica,** Yugo.
63/R7 **Sjöberg,** Swe.
62/E4 **Sjöbo,** Swe.
61/M6 **Sjónfridh** (peak), Ice.
61/F1 **Sjøvegan,** Nor.
62/E2 **Sjuntorp,** Swe.
99/G4 **Skadovsk,** Ukr.
61/P7 **Skaftafell Nat'l Park,** Ice.
62/D3 **Skagen,** Den.
62/D3 **Skagens** (cape), Den.
62/F2 **Skagern** (lake), Swe.
62/C3 **Skagerrak** (str.), Eur.
62/C1 **Skaget** (peak), Nor.
182/D3 **Skagit** (riv.), Wa,US
177/L4 **Skagway,** Ak,US
61/H1 **Skaidi,** Nor.
63/L3 **Skaistkalne,** Lat.
91/H4 **Skála,** Gre.
62/E3 **Skälderviken** (bay), Swe.
61/P6 **Skálfandafljót** (riv.), Ice.
73/B2 **Skalica,** Slvk.
71/H4 **Skalice** (riv.), Czh.
71/F2 **Skalka, Údolní nádrž** (res.), Czh.
62/D4 **Skælskør,** Den.
62/E4 **Skåne** (reg.), Swe.
199/H3 **Skaneateles,** NY,US
141/X18 **Skanes** (int'l arpt.), Tun.
62/F2 **Skänninge,** Swe.
62/E4 **Skanör,** Swe.
91/J3 **Skantzoura** (isl.), Gre.
62/E2 **Skara,** Swe.
62/E2 **Skaraborg** (co.), Swe.
62/F2 **Skärblacka,** Swe.
107/L1 **Skārdu,** Pak.
62/E2 **Skåre,** Swe.
62/H4 **Skarszewy,** Pol.
63/R6 **Skarven** (lake), Swe.
65/L3 **Skarżysko-Kamienna,** Pol.
54/D5 **Skateraw,** Sc,UK
62/E2 **Skattkärr,** Swe.
63/K4 **Skaudvilė,** Lith.
63/T9 **Skævinge,** Den.
65/K4 **Skawina,** Pol.
178/D3 **Skeena** (range), BC,Can
178/D3 **Skeena** (riv.), BC,Can
198/D2 **Skegemog** (lake), Mi,US
57/J5 **Skegness,** Eng,UK
154/B3 **Skeleton Coast Park,** Namb.
61/G2 **Skellefteå,** Swe.
61/F2 **Skellefteälv** (riv.), Swe.
61/G2 **Skelleftehamn,** Swe.
190/D3 **Skellytown,** Tx,US
57/G4 **Skelmanthorpe,** Eng,UK
57/F4 **Skelmersdale,** Eng,UK
54/B5 **Skelmorlie,** Sc,UK
57/H2 **Skelton,** Eng,UK
57/G2 **Skerne** (riv.), Eng,UK
60/D2 **Skerries,** Ire.
91/H3 **Skhimatárion,** Gre.
91/G4 **Skhiza** (isl.), Gre.
62/D2 **Ski,** Nor.
91/H3 **Skíathos,** Gre.
191/F2 **Skiatook,** Ok,US
60/A6 **Skibbereen,** Ire.
201/G5 **Skidaway Island,** Ga,US
57/E2 **Skiddaw** (mtn.), Eng,UK
177/M5 **Skidegate,** BC,Can
63/L5 **Skidel',** Bela.
91/H2 **Skídhra,** Gre.
193/G3 **Skidmore,** Mo,US
189/F3 **Skidmore,** Tx,US
198/D2 **Skidway Lake,** Mi,US
62/C2 **Skien,** Nor.
65/L3 **Skierniewice,** Pol.
65/K3 **Skierniewice** (prov.), Pol.
183/J3 **Skiff,** Ab,Can
141/V17 **Skikda,** Alg.
141/V17 **Skikda** (wilaya), Alg.
193/K4 **Skillet Fork** (riv.), Il,US
91/G4 **Skinári, Ákra** (cape), Gre.
62/F2 **Skinnskatteberg,** Swe.
54/A5 **Skipness,** Sc,UK
57/H4 **Skipsea,** Eng,UK
57/F4 **Skipton,** Eng,UK
57/F3 **Skirfare** (riv.), Eng,UK
91/J3 **Skíros,** Gre.
91/J3 **Skíros** (isl.), Gre.
62/C3 **Skive,** Den.
62/D2 **Skjærhollen,** Nor.
62/D2 **Skjeberg,** Nor.
94/B2 **Skjelåtinden** (peak), Nor.
62/C4 **Skjern,** Den.
62/C4 **Skjern** (riv.), Den.
92/B2 **Škofja Loka,** Slov.
62/E2 **Skoghall,** Swe.
62/G2 **Skogstorp,** Swe.
58/A3 **Skokholm** (isl.), Wal,UK
205/Q15 **Skokie,** Il,US
205/Q15 **Skokie** (riv.), Il,US
62/G2 **Skokloster,** Swe.
182/C4 **Skokomish Ind. Res.,** Wa,US
98/B3 **Skole,** Ukr.
62/F2 **Sköflersta,** Swe.
58/A3 **Skomer** (isl.), Wal,UK
123/D3 **Skon,** Camb.
182/G3 **Skookumchuck,** BC,Can
91/H3 **Skópelos,** Gre.
91/H3 **Skópelos** (isl.), Gre.
96/F1 **Skopin,** Rus.
92/E5 **Skopje** (cap.), Macd.
98/E2 **Skorodnoye,** Bela.
99/J2 **Skorodnoye,** Rus.
62/E2 **Skotterud,** Nor.
93/F5 **Skoútari,** Gre.
62/E2 **Skövde,** Swe.
109/J1 **Skovorodino,** Rus.
196/C3 **Skowhegan,** Me,US
194/E2 **Skownan,** Mb,Can
63/L3 **Skrīveri,** Lat.
63/M4 **Skrudaliena,** Lat.
63/K3 **Skrunda,** Lat.
177/L3 **Skukum** (mtn.), Yk,Can
157/E2 **Skukuza,** SAfr.
60/A6 **Skull,** Ire.
185/G3 **Skull** (val.), Ut,US
187/F3 **Skull Valley,** Az,US
185/G3 **Skull Valley Ind. Res.,** Ut,US
62/E2 **Skultorp,** Swe.
62/G2 **Skultuna,** Swe.
193/J3 **Skunk** (riv.), Ia,US
63/J3 **Skuodas,** Lith.
62/E4 **Skurup,** Swe.
62/G1 **Skutskär,** Swe.
98/E3 **Skvira,** Ukr.
177/H3 **Skwentna,** Ak,US
65/H2 **Skwierzyna,** Pol.
55/H8 **Skye** (isl.), Sc,UK
182/D4 **Skykomish,** Wa,US
205/D2 **Skykomish** (riv.), Wa,US
206/C1 **Skytop,** Pa,US
175/J8 **Skyway** (sound), Chile
131/F2 **Slade** (pt.), Austl.
73/B3 **Sládečkovce,** Slvk.
194/E4 **Slade Nat'l Wild. Ref.,** ND,US
73/B3 **Sládkovičovo,** Slvk.
95/Q4 **Sladkovskoye,** Rus.
62/D4 **Slagelse,** Den.
202/B2 **Slagle,** La,US
57/F4 **Slaidburn,** Eng,UK

71/F2 Slakovský Les (for.), Czh.
54/C5 Slamannan, Sc,UK
124/E4 Slamet (peak), Indo.
65/L4 Slaná (riv.), Slvk.
177/K3 Slana, Ak,US
60/D2 Slane, Ire.
60/D4 Slaney (riv.), Ire.
63/T9 Slangerup, Den.
93/G3 Slănic, Rom.
93/H2 Slănic-Moldova, Rom.
63/N2 Slantsy, Rus.
71/H2 Slaný, Czh.
73/A1 Slapanice, Czh.
71/H3 Slapy, Údolní nádrž (res.), Czh.
195/L3 Slate (isls.), On,Can
206/C2 Slatedale, Pa,US
193/H3 Slater, Ia,US
191/H1 Slater, Mo,US
93/G3 Slatina, Rom.
73/D2 Slatina (riv.), Slvk.
206/C2 Slatington, Pa,US
190/D4 Slaton, Tx,US
62/D1 Slattum, Nor.
202/C2 Slaughter, La,US
206/C6 Slaughter Beach, De,US
191/F3 Slaughterville, Ok,US
176/F5 Slave (riv.), Can.
145/F5 Slave Coast (reg.), Afr.
178/E3 Slave Lake, Ab,Can
114/C1 Slavgorod, Rus.
73/B1 Slavičín, Czh.
73/B2 Slavkov, Czh.
73/A1 Slavkov u Brna (Austerlitz), Czh.
92/C3 Slavonia (reg.), Cro.
92/C3 Slavonska Požega, Cro.
92/D3 Slavonski Brod, Cro.
98/D2 Slavuta, Ukr.
109/L3 Slavyanka, Rus.
93/G4 Slavyanovo, Bul.
99/J3 Slavyansk, Ukr.
99/K5 Slavyansk-na-Kubani, Rus.
65/J1 Sławno, Pol.
193/G2 Slayton, Mn,US
57/H6 Sleaford, Eng,UK
66/D3 Sleen, Neth.
179/H3 Sleeper (isls.), NW,Can
198/C2 Sleeping Bear Dunes Nat'l Lakesh., Mi,US
193/G1 Sleepy Eye, Mn,US
205/P15 Sleepy Hollow, Il,US
177/G3 Sleetmute, Ak,US
201/F2 Slemp, Ky,US
60/C2 Sliabh na Caillighe (mtn.), Ire.
73/D2 Sliač, Slvk.
73/D2 Sliač (Zvolen) (arpt.), Slvk.
199/J4 Slide (mtn.), NY,US
202/D2 Slidell, La,US
62/C1 Slidre, Nor.
66/B5 Sliedrecht, Neth.
84/J8 Sliema, Malta
60/C1 Slieve Anierin (mtn.), Ire.
60/B3 Slieve Aughty (mts.), Ire.
56/A3 Slieve Beagh (mtn.), NI,UK
60/B4 Slieve Bernagh (mtn.), Ire.
56/C3 Slieve Binnian (mtn.), NI,UK
60/C3 Slieve Bloom (mts.), Ire.
60/A4 Slievecallan (mtn.), Ire.
56/C3 Slieve Croob (mtn.), NI,UK
56/C3 Slieve Donard (mtn.), NI,UK
60/A3 Slieve Elva (mtn.), Ire.
60/B4 Slievefelim (mts.), Ire.
60/B1 Slieve Gamph (Ox) (mts.), Ire.
56/B3 Slieve Gullion (mtn.), NI,UK
60/B4 Slievekimalta (mtn.), Ire.
60/D1 Slieve Martin (mtn.), NI,UK
60/C5 Slievenamon (hill), Ire.
60/C5 Slieverve, Ire.
56/A1 Slieve Snaght (mtn.), Ire.
60/B1 Sligo, Ire.
60/B1 Sligo (arpt.), Ire.
60/B1 Sligo (bay), Ire.
60/B1 Sligo (co.), Ire.
54/A1 Slioch (mtn.), Sc,UK
208/G5 Slippery Rock, Pa,US
208/G6 Slippery Rock (cr.), Pa,US
63/H3 Slite, Swe.
93/H4 Sliven, Bul.
92/F4 Slivnitsa, Bul.
193/F2 Sloan, Ia,US
186/E3 Sloan, Nv,US
197/T10 Sloan, NY,US
207/D1 Sloatsburg, NY,US
98/E4 Slobodka, Ukr.
95/L4 Slobodskoy, Rus.
98/E4 Slobodzeya, Mol.
93/H3 Slobozia, Rom.
182/F3 Slocan, BC,Can
182/F3 Slocan (lake), BC,Can
182/F3 Slocan Park, BC,Can
66/D2 Slochteren, Neth.
203/F2 Slocomb, Al,US
208/C2 Slocum, RI,US
189/G2 Slocum, Tx,US
96/C1 Slonim, Bela.
66/C3 Sloten, Neth.
66/C3 Slotermeer (lake), Neth.
53/M7 Slough, Eng,UK
65/K4 Slovakia
98/E2 Slovechno, Ukr.
92/B3 Slovenia
92/B2 Slovenj Gradec, Slov.
92/B2 Slovenska Bistrica, Slov.
73/D2 Slovenska Ľupča, Slvk.
92/B2 Slovenske Konjice, Slov.
65/L4 Slovenské Rudohorie (mts.), Slvk.
65/J1 Słowiński Nat'l Park, Pol.
65/H2 Słubice, Pol.
98/D2 Sluch' (riv.), Ukr.
81/G4 Sluderno (Schluderns), It.
66/A6 Sluis, Neth.
65/J2 Słupca, Pol.
65/J1 Słupia (riv.), Pol.
65/J1 Słupsk, Pol.
65/J1 Słupsk (prov.), Pol.
96/C1 Slutsk, Bela.
55/F10 Slyne (pt.), Ire.
108/E1 Slyudyanka, Rus.
191/H4 Smackover, Ar,US
62/E3 Smålandsstenar, Swe.
185/G1 Small, Id,US
53/N8 Smallfield, Eng,UK
176/L4 Smallwood (res.), Can.
179/K3 Smallwood (res.), Nf,Can
200/E3 Smartt (mtn.), Tn,US
97/M1 Smaylovskiy, Kaz.
92/E3 Smederevo, Yugo.
92/E3 Smederevska Palanka, Yugo.
62/F1 Smedjebacken, Swe.
98/F3 Smela, Ukr.
141/V17 Smendou (riv.), Alg.
199/G4 Smethport, Pa,US
109/L2 Smidovich, Rus.
65/J2 Śmigiel, Pol.
201/F2 Smilax, Ky,US
66/D3 Smilde, Neth.
183/K2 Smiley, Sk,Can
189/F3 Smiley, Tx,US
63/L3 Smiltene, Lat.
109/N2 Smirnykh, Rus.
137/V Smith (pen.), Ant.
179/J2 Smith (isl.), NW,Can
201/K1 Smith (isl.), Md,US
183/J4 Smith (riv.), Mt,US
184/D4 Smith, Nv,US
189/N9 Smith (pt.), Tx,US
201/J2 Smith (pt.), Va,US
201/G2 Smith (riv.), Va,US
207/D3 Smithburg, NJ,US
191/E1 Smith Center, Ks,US
202/C2 Smithdale, Ms,US
178/D3 Smithers, BC,Can
189/M9 Smithers (lake), Tx,US
201/G3 Smithfield, NC,US
185/H3 Smithfield, Ut,US
201/J2 Smithfield, Va,US
200/C2 Smithland, Ky,US
201/H2 Smith Mountain (dam), Va,US
201/H2 Smith Mountain (lake), Va,US
184/A3 Smith River, Ca,US
200/E4 Smiths, Al,US
205/G6 Smiths Creek, Mi,US
199/H2 Smiths Falls, On,Can
200/D2 Smiths Grove, Ky,US
136/A4 Smiths Lookout (hill), N.Z.
135/C4 Smithton, Austl.
191/H1 Smithton, Mo,US
207/E2 Smithtown, NY,US
207/E2 Smithtown (bay), NY,US
197/R9 Smithville, On,Can
200/E5 Smithville, Ga,US
198/C5 Smithville, In,US
193/G4 Smithville, Mo,US
191/G1 Smithville (lake), Mo,US
208/F6 Smithville, Oh,US
191/G3 Smithville, Ok,US
200/E3 Smithville, Tn,US
189/F2 Smithville, Tx,US
206/D5 Smithville, Hist. Homes of, NJ,US
184/D3 Smoke Creek (des.), Nv,US
135/E1 Smoky (cape), Austl.
182/E1 Smoky (riv.), Ab,Can
197/G2 Smoky (cape), NS,Can
190/E1 Smoky (hills), Ks,US
133/G5 Smoky Bay, Austl.
191/E1 Smoky Hill (riv.), Co, Ks,US
190/C1 Smoky Hill, North Fork (riv.), Co, Ks,US
61/C3 Smøla (isl.), Nor.
191/F1 Smolan, Ks,US
94/G5 Smolensk, Rus.
94/F5 Smolensk Obl., Rus.
63/N4 Smolevichi, Bela.
91/G2 Smólikas (peak), Gre.
93/G5 Smolyan, Bul.
185/H2 Smoot, Wy,US
63/M4 Smorgon', Bela.
71/G5 Smrčina (peak), Czh.
71/H4 Smutná (riv.), Czh.
183/L1 Smuts, Sk,Can
93/H4 Smyadovo, Bul.
137/U Smyley (isl.), Ant.
206/C5 Smyrna, De,US
206/C5 Smyrna (riv.), De,US
200/E4 Smyrna, Ga,US
200/D3 Smyrna, Tn,US
97/J1 Smyshlyayevka, Rus.
56/D3 Snaefell (mtn.), IM,UK
177/M2 Snake (riv.), Yk,Can
182/E4 Snake (riv.), Id, Wa,US
195/H4 Snake (riv.), Mn,US
192/D2 Snake (riv.), Ne,US
192/E1 Snake (cr.), SD,US
185/H2 Snake, Henrys Fork (riv.), Id,US
182/E1 Snake Indian (riv.), Ab,Can
185/G2 Snake River (plain), Id,US
184/E2 Snake River Birds of Prey Nat. Area, Id,US
136/A5 Snares (isl.), N.Z.
61/E2 Snåsa, Nor.
203/F2 Snead, Al,US
201/J3 Sneads Ferry, NC,US
62/C3 Snedsted, Den.
66/C2 Sneek, Neth.
66/C2 Sneekermeer (lake), Neth.
156/D3 Sneeuberg (mts.), SAfr.
156/B4 Sneeuberg (peak), SAfr.
156/L11 Sneeuwkop (peak), SAfr.
185/K4 Sneffels (mtn.), Co,US
62/C3 Snejbjerg, Den.
197/R8 Snelgrove, On,Can
201/M7 Snellville, Ga,US
59/G1 Snettisham, Eng,UK
100/J3 Snezhnaya, Rus.
99/K3 Snezhnoye, Ukr.
65/H3 Sněžka (peak), Czh.
92/B3 Snežnik (peak), Yugo.
65/L2 Śniardwy (lake), Pol.
99/G4 Snigirëvka, Ukr.
98/B3 Snilow (int'l arpt.), Ukr.
98/B3 Snina, Slvk.
59/G4 Snodland, Eng,UK
61/D3 Snøhetta (peak), Nor.
205/C2 Snohomish, Wa,US
205/D2 Snohomish (co.), Wa,US
205/C2 Snohomish (riv.), Wa,US
189/F2 Snook, Tx,US
205/D2 Snoqualmie, Wa,US
205/D2 Snoqualmie (falls), Wa,US
205/D2 Snoqualmie (riv.), Wa,US
205/D3 Snoqualmie, Middle Fork (riv.), Wa,US
205/D3 Snoqualmie-Mount Baker Nat'l For., Wa,US
205/D2 Snoqualmie, North Fork (riv.), Wa,US
205/D3 Snoqualmie, South Fork (riv.), Wa,US
61/E2 Snøtind (peak), Nor.
196/B3 Snow (mtn.), Me,US
191/G3 Snow, Ok,US
182/E3 Snow (peak), Wa,US
182/F3 Snowcrest (mtn.), BC,Can
56/D5 Snowdon (mtn.), Wal,UK
56/D5 Snowdonia Nat'l Park, Wal,UK
203/E1 Snowdoun, Al,US
178/E2 Snowdrift, NW,Can
194/E3 Snowflake, Mb,Can
187/G3 Snowflake, Az,US
201/K1 Snow Hill, Md,US
201/J3 Snow Hill, NC,US
190/A1 Snowmass, Co,US
185/K4 Snowmass Village, Co,US
133/H5 Snowtown, Austl.
185/G3 Snowville, Ut,US
135/D3 Snowy (riv.), Austl.
177/K2 Snowy (peak), Ak,US
199/J3 Snowy (mtn.), NY,US
192/A3 Snowy Range (pass), Wy,US
135/D3 Snowy River Nat'l Park, Austl.
98/C3 Snyatyn, Ukr.
191/J4 Snyder, Ar,US
190/E3 Snyder, Ok,US
206/A2 Snyder (co.), Pa,US
188/D1 Snyder, Tx,US
206/B2 Snydertown, Pa,US
164/C3 Soacha, Col.
157/H7 Soalala, Madg.
157/G8 Soalara, Madg.
157/H8 Soamanonga, Madg.
86/A2 Soana (riv.), It.
157/J7 Soanierana-Ivongo, Madg.
157/H7 Soanindrariny, Madg.
57/G6 Soar (riv.), Eng,UK
87/E2 Soave, It.
157/H8 Soavina, Madg.
157/J8 Soavina, Madg.
157/H7 Soavinandriana, Madg.
145/H4 Soba, Nga.
113/D5 Sobaek (mts.), SKor.
169/E4 Soberania, Bol.
161/G4 Soberania Nat'l Park, Pan.
69/G4 Sobernheim, Ger.
71/H4 Soběslav, Czh.
127/K4 Sobger (riv.), Indo.
107/J3 Sobhādero, Pak.
75/L1 Sobotka, Czh.
170/D2 Sobradinho, Braz.
171/E1 Sobradinho (res.), Braz.
167/F3 Sobral, Braz.
98/B3 Sobrance, Slvk.
82/B5 Sobretta, Monte (peak), It.
111/M9 Sobue, Japan
87/G1 Soča (riv.), Slov.
168/D5 Socabaya, Peru
201/H4 Socastee, SC,US
65/L2 Sochaczew, Pol.
53/G4 Sochi, Rus.
96/F4 Sochi/Adler (int'l arpt.), Rus.
113/D4 Sŏch'ŏn, SKor.
71/F7 Söchtenau, Ger.
87/E5 Soci, It.
200/F4 Social Circle, Ga,US
139/K6 Society (isls.), FrPol.
201/H3 Society Hill, SC,US
172/B3 Socompa (vol.), Arg.
170/D4 Socorro, Braz.
164/C3 Socorro, Col.
158/C5 Socorro (isl.), Mex.
190/A3 Socorro, NM,US
187/J5 Socorro, Tx,US
164/C3 Socotá, Col.
168/B2 Socota, Peru
102/E8 Socotra (isl.), Yem.
123/D4 Soc Trang, Viet.
76/D3 Socuéllamos, Sp.
186/D3 Soda (dry lake), Ca,US
182/C1 Soda Creek, BC,Can
61/H2 Sodankylä, Fin.
185/H2 Soda Springs, Id,US
200/E3 Soddy-Daisy, Tn,US
111/H7 Sodegaura, Japan
62/F1 Söderbärke, Swe.
62/G1 Söderfors, Swe.
62/G1 Söderhamn, Swe.
62/G2 Söderköping, Swe.
62/G2 Södermanland (co.), Swe.
62/G2 Södertälje, Swe.
63/R7 Södertörn (pen.), Swe.
149/H4 Sodo, Eth.
63/R7 Södra Björkfjärden (bay), Swe.
63/S7 Södra Ljusterö (isl.), Swe.
199/H3 Sodus, NY,US
199/H3 Sodus Point, NY,US
130/B2 Soe, Indo.
156/Q12 Soekmekaar, SAfr.
67/F5 Soest, Ger.
66/C4 Soest, Neth.
67/E3 Soeste (riv.), Ger.
91/H3 Sofádhes, Gre.
155/G3 Sofala (prov.), Moz.
93/F4 Sofia (int'l arpt.), Bul.
157/J6 Sofia (riv.), Madg.
93/F4 Sofia (Sofiya) (cap.), Bul.
92/F4 Sofiya (reg.), Bul.
93/F4 Sofiya (Sofia) (cap.), Bul.
99/G3 Sofiyevka, Ukr.
109/L1 Sofiysk, Rus.
94/F2 Sofporog, Rus.
151/B3 Soga, Tanz.
145/F5 Sogakofe, Gha.
164/C3 Sogamoso (riv.), Col.
164/C3 Sogamoso, Col.
67/E3 Sögel, Ger.
131/F1 Sogeri, PNG
105/H4 Soghād, Iran
62/A1 Sognafjorden (fjord), Nor.
62/B1 Sogndal, Nor.
62/B2 Søgne, Nor.
62/A1 Sogn og Fjordane (co.), Nor.
125/D3 Sogod, Phil.
104/C1 Soğuksu Nat'l Park, Turk.
104/B2 Söğüt, Turk.
93/K5 Söğütlü, Turk.
151/A1 Sogwass (peak), Ugan.
109/K5 Sŏgwip'o, SKor.
105/G3 Soh, Iran
120/C3 Sohāgī, India
120/B4 Sohāgpur, India
59/G2 Soham, Eng,UK
69/G4 Sohren, Ger.
113/D3 Sŏhŭng, NKor.
68/D2 Soignies, Belg.
53/U11 Soignolles-en-Brie, Fr.
116/C2 Soila, China
79/G6 Soings-en-Sologne, Fr.
68/C5 Soissons, Fr.
53/T11 Soisy-sur-Seine, Fr.
110/C3 Sōja, Japan
118/B2 Sojat, India
113/C3 Sŏjosŏn (bay), NKor.
97/J1 Sok (riv.), Rus.
123/C3 Sok (pt.), Thai.
111/H7 Sōka, Japan
98/C2 Sokal', Ukr.
113/E3 Sokch'o, SKor.
104/A2 Söke, Turk.
114/B4 Sokh, Uzb.
108/F1 Sokhor (peak), Rus.
91/H2 Sokhós, Gre.
98/D3 Sokiryany, Ukr.
62/C1 Sokna, Nor.
92/E4 Sokobanja, Yugo.
145/F4 Sokodé, Togo
71/G4 Sokol (peak), Czh.
94/J4 Sokol, Rus.
65/M2 Sokółka, Pol.
144/D3 Sokolo, Mali
71/F2 Sokolov, Czh.
99/K4 Sokolovo-Kundryuchenskoye, Rus.
65/M2 Sokołów Podlaski, Pol.
145/G3 Sokoto, Nga.
145/G4 Sokoto (plains), Nga.
145/G4 Sokoto (riv.), Nga.
145/G3 Sokoto (state), Nga.
62/A2 Sola, Nor.
62/A2 Sola (int'l arpt.), Nor.
125/C1 Solana, Phil.
204/C5 Solana Beach, Ca,US
167/H4 Solânea, Braz.
164/B3 Solano (pt.), Col.
125/C1 Solano, Phil.
205/L10 Solano (co.), Ca,US
165/E4 Solano, Ven.
87/E4 Solarolo, It.
81/H3 Solbad Hall in Tirol, Aus.
98/C4 Solca, Rom.
76/C4 Sol, Costa del (coast), Sp.
77/P10 Sol, Costa do (reg.), Port.
81/H4 Sölden, Aus.
193/G3 Soldier (riv.), Ia,US
193/J2 Soldiers Grove, Wi,US
177/H3 Soldotna, Ak,US
65/K2 Solec Kujawski, Pol.
164/C2 Soledad, Col.
186/B2 Soledad, Ca,US
204/B2 Soledad (canyon), Ca,US
165/F2 Soledad, Ven.
167/G4 Soledade, Braz.
159/N7 Soledad de Doblado, Mex.
173/F4 Soledade, Braz.
194/D4 Solen, ND,US
59/E5 Solent (chan.), Eng,UK
144/D3 Solenzo, Burk.
87/E2 Solesino, It.
68/C3 Solesmes, Fr.
69/E4 Soleuvre (mtn.), Lux.
86/D2 Solferino, It.
104/E2 Solhan, Turk.
87/D3 Soliera, It.
94/J4 Soligalich, Rus.
87/F1 Soligo, It.
96/C1 Soligorsk, Bela.
59/E2 Solihull, Eng,UK
53/J3 Solikamsk, Rus.
97/K2 Sol'-Iletsk, Rus.
169/E1 Solimões (Amazon) (riv.), Braz.
67/E6 Solingen, Ger.
154/C4 Solitaire, Namb.
61/F3 Sollefteå, Swe.
62/G2 Sollentuna, Swe.
77/G3 Sóller, Sp.
63/T9 Sollerød, Den.
62/F1 Sollerön, Swe.
82/C6 Solliès-Pont, Fr.
67/G5 Solling (mts.), Ger.
147/E2 Sollum (gulf), Egypt, Libya
70/B2 Solmsbach (riv.), Ger.
61/D3 Søln (peak), Nor.
63/S7 Solna, Swe.
80/B5 Solnan (riv.), Fr.
99/J2 Solntsevo, Rus.
124/E4 Solo (riv.), Indo.
85/E6 Solofra, It.
124/C3 Solok, Indo.
96/F4 Solokh-Aul, Rus.
160/D3 Sololá, Guat.
138/E5 Solomon (sea), PNG, Sol.
177/F3 Solomon, Ak,US
187/H4 Solomon, Az,US
191/F1 Solomon, Ks,US
191/F1 Solomon (riv.), Ks,US
138/E6 Solomon Islands
190/D1 Solomon, North Fork (riv.), Ks,US
190/E1 Solomon, South Fork (riv.), Ks,US
109/J2 Solon, China
208/F5 Solon, Oh,US
97/L4 Solonchak Goklenkui (salt marsh), Trkm.
167/G4 Solonópole, Braz.
85/E5 Solopaca, It.
130/A2 Solor (isl.), Indo.
130/A2 Solor (isls.), Indo.
80/D3 Solothurn, Swi.
80/D3 Solothurn (canton), Swi.
98/B4 Solotvina, Ukr.
94/G2 Solovetskiy (isls.), Rus.
109/J1 Solov'yevsk, Rus.
68/D3 Solre-le-Château, Fr.
77/F2 Solsona, Sp.
73/D6 Solt, Hun.
92/B4 Šolta (isl.), Cro.
105/J2 Solṭānābād, Iran
67/G3 Soltau, Ger.
63/P2 Sol'tsy, Rus.
92/D2 Soltvadkert, Hun.
92/E5 Solunska (peak), Macd.
58/A3 Solva (riv.), Wal,UK
186/B3 Solvang, Ca,US
62/F3 Sölvesborg, Swe.
56/E2 Solway Firth (inlet), Eng, Sc,UK
155/E2 Solwezi, Zam.
73/C4 Solymár, Hun.
111/G2 Sōma, Japan
104/A2 Soma, Turk.
155/F3 Somabhula, Zim.
68/C3 Somain, Fr.
92/D3 Sombor, Cro.
205/H6 Sombra, On,Can
68/D2 Sombreffe, Belg.
158/E4 Sombrerete, Mex.
173/G4 Sombrio, Braz.
123/C2 Som Det, Thai.
57/G5 Somercotes, Eng,UK
66/C6 Someren, Neth.
63/K1 Somero, Fin.
208/B2 Somers, Ct,US
183/G3 Somers, Mt,US
205/Q14 Somers, Wi,US
194/E3 Somerset, Mb,Can
178/G1 Somerset (isl.), NW,Can
58/D4 Somerset (co.), Eng,UK
200/E2 Somerset, Ky,US
202/C1 Somerset, La,US
208/C2 Somerset, Ma,US
206/D3 Somerset, NJ,US
206/D2 Somerset (co.), NJ,US
197/T9 Somerset, NY,US
198/E5 Somerset, Oh,US
199/G4 Somerset, Pa,US
195/Q6 Somerset, Wi,US
135/C4 Somerset-Burnie, Austl.
156/D4 Somerset East, SAfr.
156/B4 Somerset West, SAfr.
59/F2 Somersham, Eng,UK
206/D3 Somers Point, NJ,US
208/B2 Somersville, Ct,US
199/L3 Somersworth, NH,US
58/D4 Somerton, Eng,UK
186/E4 Somerton, Az,US
208/C1 Somerville, Ma,US
206/D2 Somerville, NJ,US
200/C3 Somerville, Tn,US
189/F2 Somerville, Tx,US
189/F2 Somerville (lake), Tx,US
93/F2 Someș (riv.), Rom.
93/G2 Someșul Mare (riv.), Rom.
120/E2 Someswar (range), India, Nepal
204/B2 Somis, Ca,US
113/D5 Sŏmjin (riv.), SKor.
87/D2 Sommacampagna, It.
86/B1 Somma Lombardo, It.
141/T15 Sommam (riv.), Alg.
86/A3 Sommariva del Bosco, It.
74/D1 Somme (bay), Fr.
68/B4 Somme (dept.), Fr.
68/A3 Somme (riv.), Fr.
68/D6 Somme (riv.), Fr.
68/B4 Somme, Canal de La (can.), Fr.
69/E5 Sommedieue, Fr.
82/C2 Sommeiller (peak), Fr.
69/E3 Somme-Leuze, Belg.
66/B5 Sommelsdijk, Neth.
62/F3 Sommen (lake), Swe.
72/B5 Sömmerda, Ger.
72/B3 Sommersdorf, Ger.
68/D5 Somme-Soude (riv.), Fr.
80/A1 Sommevoire, Fr.
73/B6 Somogy (co.), Hun.
198/B4 Somonauk, Il,US
160/E3 Somoto, Nic.
99/K2 Somovo, Rus.
59/F5 Somptin, Eng,UK
81/E4 Somvix, Swi.
121/E3 Son (riv.), India
66/C5 Son, Neth.
87/D2 Sona, It.
152/C4 Sona-Bata, Zaire
121/G4 Sonāmukhi, Bang.
121/F4 Sonāmukhi, India
121/F4 Sonāmura, India
120/B4 Sonār (riv.), India
121/G3 Sonātala, Bang.
121/E2 Sonbarsa, India
113/C3 Sŏnch'ŏn, NKor.
86/C2 Soncino, It.
87/E5 Sondalo, It.
62/C4 Sønderborg, Den.
62/C4 Sønderborg (int'l arpt.), Den.
156/L11 Sonderend (riv.), SAfr.
62/C4 Sønderjylland (co.), Den.
62/C3 Sønder Nissum, Den.
72/A5 Sondershausen, Ger.
189/M1 Sondheimer, La,US
76/D1 Sondica (int'l arpt.), Sp.
81/F5 Sondrio, It.
81/F5 Sondrio (prov.), It.
120/A2 Sone Ka Gurja, India
120/A1 Sonepat, India
118/D3 Sonepur, India
123/E3 Song Cau, Viet.
113/D3 Sŏngch'ŏn, NKor.
117/H2 Songcun, China
123/D4 Song Dinh, Viet.
151/A4 Songea, Tanz.
79/G2 Songeons, Fr.
115/F1 Songhua (riv.), China
113/C3 Songhwa, NKor.
113/D4 Sŏnghwan, SKor.
108/D2 Songino, Mong.
115/E5 Songjiang, China
115/L8 Songjiang, China
113/D1 Songjianghe, China
113/D5 Songjŏng, SKor.
113/E5 Sŏngju, SKor.
114/B3 Song-Kel' (lake), Kyr.
123/C5 Songkhla, Thai.
123/C2 Songkhram (riv.), Thai.
109/J2 Songling, China
123/C1 Song Ma, Viet.
117/J2 Songmen, China
116/D3 Songming, China
113/D4 Songnam, SKor.
113/C3 Songnim, NKor.
152/C4 Songo, Ang.
155/G2 Songo, Moz.
152/C4 Songololo, Zaire
123/C3 Song Phi Nong, Thai.
121/H3 Songsak, India
117/F4 Songshan, China
115/C4 Song Shan (peak), China
113/B3 Songshu, China
113/D2 Songshuzhen, China
113/D4 Songt'an, SKor.
117/F5 Songtao, China
117/F2 Songtao Miaozu Zizhixian, China
113/C2 Songwŏn, NKor.
117/H3 Songxi, China
117/H3 Songxia, China
115/C4 Song Xian, China
117/E3 Songyan, China
115/B5 Songzi, China
117/G2 Songzi (pass), China
115/C5 Songzi Guan (pass), China
117/G2 Songzi Hudu (riv.), China
123/E3 Son Ha, Viet.
120/D4 Sonhāt, India
111/M10 Soni, Japan
108/G3 Sonid Youqi, China
108/G3 Sonid Zuoqi, China
123/C1 Son La, Viet.
107/J3 Sonmiāni, Pak.
107/J3 Sonmiāni (bay), Pak.
70/E2 Sonneberg, Ger.
70/E2 Sonnefeld, Ger.
183/M5 Sonnette, Mt,US
72/D4 Sonnewalde, Ger.
59/F4 Sonning, Eng,UK
84/D5 Sonnino, It.
81/H3 Sonnjoch (peak), Aus.
64/G5 Sonntagshorn (peak), Ger.
170/D1 Sono (riv.), Braz.
110/D3 Sonobe, Japan
187/G5 Sonoita, Az,US
205/K10 Sonoma, Ca,US
205/J10 Sonoma (co.), Ca,US
205/J10 Sonoma (cr.), Ca,US
184/B4 Sonoma (lake), Ca,US
205/J10 Sonoma (mts.), Ca,US
158/C2 Sonora (riv.), Mex.
187/F5 Sonora (state), Mex.
184/C5 Sonora, Ca,US
186/C1 Sonora (pass), Ca,US
188/D2 Sonora, Tx,US
188/D2 Sonora, Caverns of (cave), Tx,US
187/F5 Sonoyta, Mex.
187/F5 Sonoyta (riv.), Mex.
121/E3 Sonpur, India
105/F3 Sonqor, Iran
113/E4 Sŏnsan, SKor.
66/D5 Sonsbeck, Ger.
76/D3 Sonseca, Sp.
72/B5 Son Servera, Sp.
164/C3 Sonsón, Col.
160/D3 Sonsonate, ESal.
138/C4 Sonsorol (isls.), Palau
92/D3 Sonta, Yugo.
202/C2 Sontag, Ms,US
123/D1 Son Tay, Viet.
70/D7 Sontheim, Ger.
70/D5 Sontheim an der Brenz, Ger.
81/G2 Sonthofen, Ger.
67/G6 Sontra, Ger.
81/E5 Sonvico, Swi.
125/B4 Sook, Malay.
191/F2 Sooner (lake), Ok,US
151/C1 Sooyaac, Som.
172/C1 Sopachuy, Bol.
191/G3 Soper, Ok,US
201/F4 Soperton, Ga,US
164/C3 Sopetrán, Col.
123/D1 Sop Hao, Laos
166/C2 Sophie, FrG.
127/G3 Sopi (cape), Indo.
123/C1 Sopka, Laos
123/C1 Sop Kai, Laos
123/C1 Sop Nhom, Laos
167/M7 Sopó, Col.
149/E3 Sopo (dry riv.), Sudan
107/K2 Sopore, India
93/G4 Sopot, Bul.
65/K1 Sopot, Pol.
123/B2 Sop Prap, Thai.
73/A4 Sopron, Hun.
73/A4 Sopronkőhida, Hun.
186/B2 Soquel, Ca,US
58/D3 Sôr (riv.), Wal,UK
85/D4 Sora, It.
86/D3 Soragna, It.
113/E3 Sŏrak-san (mtn.), SKor.
113/E3 Sŏraksan Nat'l Park, SKor.
84/B2 Sorano, It.
168/D4 Sorata, Bol.
76/D4 Sorbas, Sp.
86/D3 Sorbolo, It.
69/E6 Sorcy-Saint-Martin, Fr.
196/A2 Sorel, Qu,Can
72/C2 Sorel (pt.), Chl,UK
135/C4 Sorell-Midway Point, Austl.
103/F8 Soreq, Nabel (dry riv.), Isr.
86/C2 Soresina, It.
62/G1 Sörforsa, Swe.
150/A4 Sorfta, Eth.
82/A5 Sorgues, Fr.
104/C2 Sorgun, Turk.
86/C4 Sori, It.
76/D2 Soria, Sp.
175/S11 Soriano, Uru.
175/S11 Soriano (dept.), Uru.
83/C5 Soriano Calabro, It.
84/C3 Soriano nel Cimino, It.
79/F6 Sorigny, Fr.
124/B2 Sorikmerapi (peak), Indo.
168/B2 Soritor, Peru
97/K3 Sor Karatuley (salt pan), Kaz.
97/K3 Sor Kaydak (salt marsh), Kaz.
97/K3 Sor Mertvyy Kultuk (salt marsh), Kaz.
68/D4 Sormonne (riv.), Fr.
170/D1 Soro (riv.), Braz.
62/D4 Sorø, Den.
83/A7 Soro (peak), It.
170/D4 Sorocaba, Braz.
97/K1 Sorochinsk, Rus.
73/A5 Sorok (riv.), Hun.
93/J1 Soroki, Mol.
73/C5 Soroksári-Duna (riv.), Hun.
138/D4 Sorol (isl.), Micr.
120/B2 Soron, India
127/H4 Sorong, Indo.
165/G3 Sororieng (mtn.), Guy.
153/H2 Soroti, Ugan.
61/G1 Sørøya (isl.), Nor.
61/G1 Sørøysundet (chan.), Nor.
67/E6 Sorpestausee (res.), Ger.
76/A3 Sorraia (riv.), Port.
182/E2 Sorrento, BC,Can
85/E6 Sorrento, It.
202/M6 Sorrento, Fl,US
202/C2 Sorrento, La,US
154/B4 Sorris-Sorris, Namb.
61/F2 Sorsele, Swe.
90/A2 Sorso, It.
125/D2 Sorsogon, Phil.
77/F1 Sort, Sp.
94/F3 Sortavala, Rus.
63/K3 Sõrve (pt.), Est.
113/D4 Sosa, SKor.
113/D4 Sŏsan, SKor.
113/C4 Sŏsan Haean Nat'l Park, SKor.
62/E3 Sösdala, Swe.
76/E1 Sos del Rey Católico, Sp.
67/H5 Söse (riv.), Ger.
96/E1 Sosenskiy, Rus.
96/E1 Soskovo, Rus.
96/F1 Sosna (riv.), Rus.
174/C2 Sosneado (peak), Arg.
98/G2 Sosnitsa, Ukr.
95/M3 Sosnogorsk, Rus.
94/G2 Sosnovets, Rus.
94/J2 Sosnovka, Rus.
95/L4 Sosnovka, Rus.
97/G1 Sosnovka, Rus.
63/P1 Sosnovo, Rus.
108/G1 Sosnovo-Ozerskoye, Rus.
94/J5 Sosnovskoye, Rus.
63/N2 Sosnovyy Bor, Rus.
65/K3 Sosnowiec, Pol.
200/C5 Soso, Ms,US
82/D5 Sospel, Fr.
86/D2 Sospiro, It.
148/B5 Sosso, CAfr.
162/D3 Sosúa, DRep.
120/B1 Sot (riv.), India
151/A2 Sotik, Kenya
159/F4 Soto la Marina, Mex.
145/F4 Sotouboua, Togo
79/G2 Sotteville-lès-Rouen, Fr.
87/F2 Sottomarina, It.
67/G2 Sottrum, Ger.
142/B5 Sotuf, Adrar (mts.), WSah.
159/H4 Sotuta, Mex.
152/C2 Souanké, Congo
144/D5 Soubre, IvC.
133/H2 Soudan, Austl.
78/D5 Soudan, Fr.
191/J3 Soudan, Ar,US
195/H4 Soudan, Mn,US
68/D6 Soude (riv.), Fr.
206/C3 Souderton, Pa,US
91/J5 Soúdha, Gre.
152/B2 Souellaba (pt.), Camr.
79/H6 Souesmes, Fr.
69/G6 Souffelweyersheim, Fr.
69/G6 Soufflenheim, Fr.
82/C3 Souffles, Pic de (peak), Fr.
91/K2 Souflion, Gre.
162/F3 Soufrière (peak), Guad.
162/F4 Soufrière (peak), StV.
144/B4 Sougéta, Gui.
74/D4 Souillac, Fr.
157/S15 Souillac, Mrts.
141/V17 Souk Ahras, Alg.
141/V17 Souk Ahras (gov.), Alg.
141/L13 Souk el Arba du Rharb, Mor.
74/C4 Soulac-sur-Mer, Fr.
197/M7 Soulanges (co.), Qu,Can
78/D2 Soulles (riv.), Fr.
186/B2 Soulsbyville, Ca,US
113/D4 Sŏul (Seoul) (cap.), SKor.
80/D2 Soultz-Haut-Rhin, Fr.
69/G1 Soultz-sous-Forets, Fr.
145/E3 Soum (prov.), Burk.
69/E2 Soumagne, Belg.
183/J2 Sounding (cr.), Ab,Can
74/E2 Souppes-sur-Loing, Fr.
148/D2 Sourbaral (peak), Chad
156/E3 Sources, Mont aux (peak), Les.
79/E3 Sourdeval, Fr.
182/G5 Sourdough (peak), Id,US
166/D3 Soure, Braz.
76/A2 Soure, Port.
41/S15 Sour El Ghozlane, Alg.
194/D3 Souris, Mb,Can
197/F2 Souris, PE,Can
180/F1 Souris (riv.), Can., US
194/D3 Souris, ND,US
194/C3 Souris (riv.), US, Can
189/G2 Sour Lake, Tx,US
144/E3 Sourou (prov.), Burk.
78/C6 Sœurs, Passage-de (chan.), Fr.
167/G4 Sousa, Braz.
76/B3 Sousel, Port.
142/C3 Sous, Oued (riv.), Mor.
74/C5 Soustons, Fr.
156/C3 Sout (dry riv.), SAfr.
134/G8 South (cr.), Austl.
196/E3 South (mts.), NS,Can
179/H2 South (bay), NW,Can
60/A3 South (sound), Ire.
151/B1 South (isl.), Kenya
136/A4 South (cape), N.Z.
136/C4 South (isl.), N.Z.
201/M7 South (riv.), Ga,US
202/C3 South (pt.), La,US
201/H3 South (riv.), NC,US
140/E7 South Africa
53/M7 Southall, Eng,UK
130/D3 South Alligator (riv.), Austl.
59/E2 Southam, Eng,UK
207/H10 South Amboy, NJ,US
163/* South America (cont.)
208/B1 South Amherst, Ma,US
208/E5 South Amherst, Oh,US
176/J3 Southampton (isl.), Can.
179/H2 Southampton (cape), NW,Can
179/H2 Southampton (isl.), NW,Can
198/F2 Southampton, On,Can
59/E5 Southampton, Eng,UK
208/B1 Southampton, Ma,US
207/F2 Southampton, NY,US
59/E5 Southampton (Eastleigh) (int'l arpt.), Eng,UK
59/E5 Southampton Water (inlet), Eng,UK
119/F5 South Andaman (isl.), India
201/J2 South Anna (riv.), Va,US
50/J6 South Atlantic (ocean)
201/F4 South Augusta, Ga,US
179/K3 South Aulatsivik (isl.), Nf,Can
128/E5 South Australia (state), Austl.
200/B3 Southaven, Ms,US
208/B1 South Barre, Ma,US
56/D3 South Barrule (mtn.), IM,UK
203/H4 South Bay, Fl,US
198/E2 South Baymouth, On,Can
193/K2 South Beloit, Il,US
198/C4 South Bend, In,US
189/E1 South Bend, Tx,US
182/C4 South Bend, Wa,US
208/C1 South Berlin, Ma,US
196/B4 South Berwick, Me,US
53/P8 Southborough, Eng,UK
208/C1 Southborough, Ma,US
201/H2 South Boston, Va,US
59/F5 Southbourne, Eng,UK
197/H2 South Branch, Nf,Can
58/C6 South Brent, Eng,UK
136/C3 Southbridge, N.Z.
208/B1 Southbridge, Ma,US
197/J1 South Brook, Nf,Can
153/G3 South Buganda (prov.), Ugan.
199/K2 South Burlington, Vt,US
208/A3 Southbury, Ct,US
161/J1 South Caicos (isl.), Trks.
201/G3 South Carolina (state), US
208/D2 South Carver, Ma,US
201/G1 South Charleston, WV,US
102/L8 South China (sea), Asia
182/D4 South Cle Elum, Wa,US
191/G2 South Coffeyville, Ok,US
205/B2 South Colby, Wa,US
199/J2 South Colton, NY,US
192/D1 South Dakota (state), US
58/D5 South Dorset Downs (uplands), Eng,UK
186/B2 South Dos Palos, Ca,US
59/F5 South Downs (hills), Eng,UK
121/G4 South Dum Dum, India
208/D1 South Duxbury, Ma,US
51/S8 South East (cape), Austl.
135/C3 South East (pt.), Austl.
162/C2 Southeast (pt.), Bahm.
156/D2 South-East (dist.), Bots.
161/G2 Southeast (pt.), Jam.
177/E3 Southeast (cape), Ak,US
208/A1 South Egremont, Ma,US
205/P16 South Elgin, Il,US
57/G4 South Elmsall, Eng,UK
59/G3 Southend (int'l arpt.), Eng,UK
56/C1 Southend, Sc,UK
59/G3 Southend-on-Sea, Eng,UK
131/F2 South Entrance (inlet), PNG
132/K7 Southern (riv.), Austl.
156/D2 Southern (dist.), Bots.
103/D4 Southern (dist.), Isr.
155/G2 Southern (reg.), Malw.
144/B5 Southern (prov.), SLeo.
149/F4 Southern (reg.), Sudan
153/G3 Southern (prov.), Ugan.
155/E3 Southern (prov.), Zam.
136/B4 Southern Alps (mts.), N.Z.
139/J6 Southern Cook (isls.), Cookls.
132/C4 Southern Cross, Austl.
197/L2 Southern Harbour, Nf,Can
131/F1 Southern Highlands (prov.), PNG
178/G3 Southern Indian (lake), Mb,Can
188/L7 Southern Methodist Univ. (SMU), Tx,US
201/H3 Southern Pines, NC,US
201/K2 Southern Shores, NC,US
54/C5 Southern Uplands (mts.), Sc,UK
56/D1 Southern Uplands (range), Sc,UK
95/N5 Southern Ural (mts.), Rus.
187/H2 Southern Ute Ind. Res., Co,US
59/G1 Southery, Eng,UK
135/C4 South Esk (riv.), Austl.
130/B4 Southesk (tablelands), Austl.
54/C5 South Esk (riv.), Sc,UK
54/D3 South Esk (riv.), Sc,UK
128/D3 South Esk Tablelands (plat.), Austl.
132/E2 Southesk Tablelands (plat.), Austl.
208/F4 South Euclid, Oh,US
194/B2 Southey, Sk,Can
199/J4 South Fallsburg, NY,US
207/M9 South Farmingdale, NY,US
208/A1 Southfield, Ma,US
205/F7 Southfield, Mi,US
59/H4 South Foreland (pt.), Eng,UK
185/K5 South Fork, Co,US
184/F3 South Fork Ind. Res., Nv,US
208/C2 South Foster, RI,US
198/D2 South Fox (isl.), Mi,US
200/C2 South Fulton, Tn,US
182/B2 Southgate (riv.), BC,Can
53/N7 Southgate, Eng,UK
203/H4 South Gate, Ca,US
201/J1 South Gate, Md,US
205/F7 Southgate, Mi,US
137/X South Georgia (isl.), UK
50/H8 South Georgia (isl.), UK
58/C4 South Glamorgan (co.), Wal,UK
130/D2 South Goulburn (isl.), Austl.
191/G1 South Grand (riv.), Mo,US
208/B1 South Hadley, Ma,US
58/C6 South Hams (plain), Eng,UK
121/H4 South Hātia (isl.), Bang.
191/F2 South Haven, Ks,US
198/C3 South Haven, Mi,US
59/F5 South Hayling, Eng,UK
194/C4 South Heart, ND,US
208/G6 South Heights, Pa,US
201/H2 South Hill, Va,US
66/B5 South Holland (prov.), Neth.
205/Q16 South Holland, Il,US
53/N8 South Holmwood, Eng,UK
151/B1 South Horr, Kenya
189/M9 South Houston, Tx,US
191/F1 South Hutchinson, Ks,US
208/B2 Southington, Ct,US
151/B1 South Island Nat'l Park, Kenya
208/A2 South Kent, Ct,US
208/C2 South Killingly, Ct,US
151/B2 South Kinangop, Kenya
57/G4 South Kirkby, Eng,UK
151/B2 South Kitui Nat'l Rsv., Kenya
121/E4 South Koel (riv.), India
113/D4 South Korea
188/K7 Southlake, Tx,US
184/D4 South Lake Tahoe, Ca,US
208/C1 South Lancaster, Ma,US
136/A4 Southland (reg.), N.Z.
188/D1 Southland, Tx,US
208/A1 South Lee, Ma,US
188/D2 South Llano (riv.), Tx,US
192/E3 South Loup (riv.), Ne,US
155/F2 South Luangwa Nat'l Park, Zam.
205/E7 South Lyon, Mi,US
137/K South Magnetic Pole, Ant.
198/C2 South Manitou (isl.), Mi,US
202/P8 South Miami, Fl,US
208/D2 South Middleboro, Ma,US
201/J2 South Mills, NC,US
205/Q14 South Milwaukee, Wi,US
59/G3 Southminster, Eng,UK
58/C4 South Molton, Eng,UK
198/E4 South Monroe, Mi,US
177/M5 South Moresby Nat'l Park Rsv., BC,Can
206/A3 South Mtn. (ridge), Pa,US
177/G4 South Naknek, Ak,US
199/J2 South Nation (riv.), On,Can
202/P7 South New River (can.), Fl,US
57/G5 South Normanton, Eng,UK
207/K7 South Nyack, NY,US
53/P7 South Ockenden, Eng,UK
185/H3 South Ogden, Ut,US
196/D4 South Ohio, NS,Can
207/F1 Southold, NY,US
207/H9 South Orange, NJ,US
137/W South Orkney (isls.), UK
50/G9 South Orkney (isls.), UK
97/G4 South Ossetian Aut. Obl., Geo.
53/M7 South Oxhey, Eng,UK
207/M9 South Oyster (bay), NY,US
138/G7 South Pacific (ocean)
189/F4 South Padre Island, Tx,US
133/M8 South Para (res.), Austl.
133/M8 South Para (riv.), Austl.
196/B3 South Paris, Me,US
204/F7 South Pasadena, Ca,US
202/K8 South Pasadena, Fl,US
193/K3 South Pekin, Il,US
132/K6 South Perth, Austl.
58/D5 South Petherton, Eng,UK
134/E6 South Pine (riv.), Austl.
206/D2 South Plainfield, NJ,US
190/D3 South Plains, Tx,US
190/C1 South Platte (riv.), Co, Ne,US
190/A1 South Platte, Middle Fork (riv.), Co,US
137/W South Polar (plat.), Ant.
137/A South Pole, Ant.
57/E4 Southport, Eng,UK
203/F2 Southport, Fl,US
201/H4 Southport, NC,US
199/H3 Southport, NY,US
196/B4 South Portland, Me,US
205/C3 South Prairie (cr.), Wa,US
205/C3 South Prairie, Wa,US
196/F3 South Pugwash, NS,Can
54/C5 South Queensferry, Sc,UK
185/G4 South Range (mil. res.), Ut,US
199/G2 South River, On,Can
206/D3 South River, NJ,US
205/F7 South Rockwood, Mi,US
55/N13 South Ronaldsay (isl.), Sc,UK
155/G1 South Rukuru (riv.), Malw.
208/F5 South Russell, Oh,US
195/P7 South Saint Paul, Mn,US
50/H8 South Sandwich (isls.), SGeo.

137/Y **South Sandwich** (isls.), UK
205/K11 **South San Francisco**, Ca,US
184/B1 **South Santiam** (riv.), Or,US
183/J2 **South Saskatchewan** (riv.), Ab,Can
183/L1 **South Saskatchewan** (riv.), Sk,Can
199/K3 **South Schenectady** (Rotterdam), NY,US
206/D5 **South Seaville**, NJ,US
137/W **South Shetland** (isls.), Ant.
57/G2 **South Shields**, Eng,UK
201/F1 **South Shore**, Ky,US
194/F5 **South Shore**, SD,US
200/D4 **Southside**, Al,US
200/D2 **Southside**, Tn,US
189/M9 **Southside Place**, Tx,US
184/C1 **South Sister** (peak), Or,US
193/H2 **South Skunk** (riv.), Ia,US
118/E3 **South Suburban**, India
191/G4 **South Sulphur** (riv.), Tx,US
136/C2 **South Taranaki** (bight), N.Z.
187/G4 **South Tucson**, Az,US
151/A1 **South Turkana Nat'l Rsv.**, Kenya
57/F2 **South Tyne** (riv.), Eng,UK
125/C4 **South Ubian**, Phil.
55/H8 **South Uist** (isl.), Sc,UK
184/B2 **South Umpqua** (riv.), Or,US
207/L9 **South Valley Stream**, NY,US
53/N7 **Southwark** (bor.), Eng,UK
57/H5 **Southwell**, Eng,UK
135/C4 **South West** (cape), Austl.
162/B1 **Southwest** (pt.), Bahm.
162/C2 **Southwest** (pt.), Bahm.
136/A4 **South West** (cape), N.Z.
191/G2 **South West City**, Mo,US
196/C3 **Southwest Harbor**, Me,US
196/D2 **Southwest Miramichi** (riv.), NB,Can
135/C4 **South West Nat'l Park**, Austl.
196/E4 **South West Port Mouton**, NS,Can
135/E1 **South West Rocks**, Austl.
196/B4 **South Weymouth Nav. Air Sta.**, Ma,US
204/F8 **South Whittier**, Ca,US
190/D4 **South Wichita** (riv.), Tx,US
208/B1 **Southwick**, Ma,US
206/B1 **South Williamsport**, Pa,US
208/B2 **South Willington**, Ct,US
59/H2 **Southwold**, Eng,UK
64/A2 **Southwold**, Eng,UK
59/G3 **South Woodham Ferrers**, Eng,UK
134/C4 **Southwood Nat'l Park**, Austl.
208/C2 **South Woodstock**, Ct,US
205/B2 **Southworth**, Wa,US
57/G5 **South Yorkshire** (co.), Eng,UK
198/E5 **South Zanesville**, Oh,US
155/F4 **Soutpansberg** (mts.), SAfr.
76/B3 **Souzel**, Port.
93/G2 **Sovata**, Rom.
83/C5 **Soverato** (riv.), It.
83/C5 **Soverato Marina**, It.
86/D1 **Sovere**, It.
83/C4 **Soveria Mannelli**, It.
63/J4 **Sovetsk**, Rus.
95/L4 **Sovetsk**, Rus.
99/L5 **Sovetskaya**, Rus.
109/N2 **Sovetskaya Gavan'**, Rus.
95/L4 **Sovetskiy**, Rus.
99/H5 **Sovetskiy**, Ukr.
97/H3 **Sovetskoye**, Rus.
154/E4 **Sowa Pan** (salt pan), Bots.
57/G4 **Sowerby Bridge**, Eng,UK
156/D2 **Soweto**, SAfr.
112/B1 **Sōya-misaki** (cape), Japan
94/J2 **Soyana** (riv.), Rus.
113/D4 **Soyang** (lake), SKor.
74/D4 **Soyaux**, Fr.
71/F6 **Soyen**, Ger.
80/D3 **Soyhières**, Swi.
152/C4 **Soyo**, Ang.
137/E **Soyuz**, Ant.
98/F1 **Sozh** (riv.), Bela.
96/D1 **Sozh** (riv.), Eur.
93/H4 **Sozopol**, Bul.
69/E3 **Spa**, Belg.
137/U **Spaatz** (isl.), Ant.
190/B4 **Space Ctr.**, NM,US
203/H3 **Spaceport USA**, Fl,US
205/D2 **Spada** (lake), Wa,US
83/B6 **Spadafora**, It.
70/B6 **Spaichingen**, Ger.
76/C2 **Spain**
66/C4 **Spakenburg**, Neth.
133/H5 **Spalding**, Austl.
183/J1 **Spalding**, Sk,Can
57/H6 **Spalding**, Eng,UK
195/L5 **Spalding**, Mi,US
182/E2 **Spallumcheen**, BC,Can
70/D4 **Spalt**, Ger.
205/C3 **Spanaway**, Wa,US
72/D2 **Spandau**, Ger.
67/G6 **Spangenberg**, Ger.
182/F4 **Spangle**, Wa,US
199/G4 **Spangler**, Pa,US
60/A4 **Spanish** (pt.), Ire.
185/H3 **Spanish Fork**, Ut,US
202/E2 **Spanish Fort**, Al,US
55/J9 **Spanish Head** (pt.), IM,UK
198/E1 **Spanish River Ind. Res.**, On,Can
161/G2 **Spanish Town**, Jam.
162/B1 **Spanish Wells**, Bahm.
81/E4 **Spannort** (peak), Swi.
85/E5 **Sparanise**, It.
190/A2 **Spar City**, Co,US
191/H4 **Sparkman**, Ar,US
203/G2 **Sparks**, Ga,US
184/D4 **Sparks**, Nv,US
189/F2 **Sparks**, Tx,US
205/G6 **Sparlingville**, Mi,US
62/G2 **Sparreholm**, Swe.
89/J3 **Sparta**, Gre.
201/F4 **Sparta**, Ga,US
193/K4 **Sparta**, Il,US
198/D3 **Sparta**, Mi,US
191/H2 **Sparta**, Mo,US
201/G2 **Sparta**, NC,US
206/D1 **Sparta**, NJ,US
200/E3 **Sparta**, Tn,US
193/J2 **Sparta**, Wi,US
201/G3 **Spartanburg**, SC,US
91/H4 **Sparti** (Spárti), Gre.
141/M13 **Spartel** (cape), Mor.
91/H4 **Spárti** (Sparta), Gre.
83/C7 **Spartivento** (cape), It.
90/A3 **Spartivento** (cape), It.
83/C3 **Sparviere** (peak), It.
182/G3 **Sparwood**, BC,Can
94/G5 **Spas-Demensk**, Rus.
94/G3 **Spasskaya Guba**, Rus.
109/L3 **Spassk-Dal'niy**, Rus.
91/H5 **Spátha, Ákra** (cape), Gre.
191/G2 **Spavinaw**, Ok,US
69/G3 **Spay**, Ger.
54/B3 **Spean** (riv.), Sc,UK
54/B3 **Spean Bridge**, Sc,UK
192/C1 **Spearfish**, SD,US
190/D2 **Spearman**, Tx,US
190/E2 **Spearville**, Ks,US
199/J3 **Speculator**, NY,US
198/C5 **Speedway**, In,US
81/F3 **Speer** (peak), Swi.
183/L1 **Speers**, Sk,Can
69/F4 **Speicher**, Ger.
81/F3 **Speicher**, Swi.
71/E3 **Speichersdorf**, Ger.
151/A2 **Speke** (gulf), Tanz.
57/F5 **Speke**, Eng,UK
57/F5 **Speke** (Liverpool) (int'l arpt.), Eng,UK
67/E4 **Spelle**, Ger.
84/C2 **Spello**, It.
178/G2 **Spence Bay**, NW,Can
133/H5 **Spencer** (cape), Austl.
133/H5 **Spencer** (gulf), Austl.
196/E3 **Spencer** (cape), NB,Can
177/E2 **Spencer** (pt.), Ak,US
193/G2 **Spencer**, Ia,US
198/C5 **Spencer**, In,US
208/C1 **Spencer**, Ma,US
201/G3 **Spencer**, NC,US
208/E5 **Spencer**, Oh,US
200/E3 **Spencer**, Tn,US
193/J1 **Spencer**, Wi,US
201/G1 **Spencer**, WV,US
198/D4 **Spencerville**, Oh,US
191/G3 **Spencerville**, Ok,US
182/D2 **Spences Bridge**, BC,Can
67/F4 **Spenge**, Ger.
57/G2 **Spennymoor**, Eng,UK
62/D3 **Spentrup**, Den.
72/D3 **Sperenberg**, Ger.
91/H3 **Sperkhiás**, Gre.
91/H3 **Sperkhios** (riv.), Gre.
85/D5 **Sperlonga**, It.
56/A2 **Sperrin** (mts.), NI,UK
70/C3 **Spessart** (range), Ger.
91/H4 **Spétsai**, Gre.
72/B3 **Spetze** (riv.), Ger.
54/C1 **Spey** (bay), Sc,UK
54/C1 **Spey** (riv.), Sc,UK
70/B4 **Speyer**, Ger.
70/B4 **Speyerbach** (riv.), Ger.
197/R8 **Speyside**, On,Can
86/C4 **Spezia, La** (prov.), It.
83/C3 **Spezzano Albanese**, It.
83/C4 **Spezzano della Sila**, It.
71/F2 **Spičák** (peak), Czh.
179/H2 **Spicer** (isl.), NW,Can
195/G5 **Spicer**, Mn,US
189/E2 **Spicewood**, Tx,US
193/H3 **Spickard**, Mo,US
60/A3 **Spiddle**, Ire.
67/E1 **Spiekeroog** (isl.), Ger.
80/D4 **Spiez**, Swi.
85/F4 **Spigno** (peak), It.
86/B3 **Spigno Monferrato**, It.
66/B5 **Spijkenisse**, Neth.
177/K2 **Spike** (mtn.), Ak,US
92/A2 **Spilimbergo**, It.
91/J5 **Spílion**, Gre.
182/F2 **Spillimacheen**, BC,Can
182/F2 **Spillimacheen** (riv.), BC,Can
57/J5 **Spilsby**, Eng,UK
63/L3 **Spilve** (int'l arpt.), Lat.
90/A2 **Spina, Bruncu** (peak), It.
85/G6 **Spinazzola**, It.
107/J2 **Spin Būldak**, Afg.
69/E5 **Spincourt**, Fr.
87/F1 **Spinea**, It.
86/B3 **Spinetta Marengo**, It.
208/C3 **Spinnerstown**, Pa,US
86/C2 **Spino d'Adda**, It.
86/C1 **Spirano**, It.
193/G2 **Spirit** (lake), Ia,US
193/J1 **Spirit**, Wi,US
193/G2 **Spirit Lake**, Ia,US
182/F4 **Spirit Lake**, Id,US
183/L1 **Spiritwood**, Sk,Can
191/G3 **Spiro**, Ok,US
65/L4 **Spišská Nová Ves**, Slvk.
97/H4 **Spitak**, Arm.
59/E5 **Spithead** (chan.), Eng,UK
122/D1 **Spiti** (riv.), India
100/B2 **Spitsbergen** (isl.), Sval.
75/K3 **Spittal an der Drau**, Aus.
201/M7 **Spivey** (lake), Ga,US
191/E2 **Spivey**, Ks,US
189/G2 **Splendora**, Tx,US
178/G3 **Split** (lake), Mb,Can
92/C4 **Split**, Cro.
186/C2 **Split** (mtn.), Ca,US
92/C4 **Split** (int'l arpt.), Yugo.
207/H8 **Splitrock** (res.), NJ,US
81/F4 **Splügen**, Swi.
81/F4 **Splügenpass** (pass), It.
63/M3 **Špoģi**, Lat.
191/H2 **Spokane**, Mo,US
182/F4 **Spokane**, Wa,US
182/F4 **Spokane Ind. Res.**, Wa,US
99/L5 **Spokoynaya**, Rus.
81/G5 **Spöl** (riv.), It.
84/C2 **Spoleto**, It.
85/E3 **Spoltore**, It.
193/J2 **Spook Cave**, Ia,US
193/K3 **Spoon** (riv.), Il,US
193/J1 **Spooner**, Wi,US
182/G5 **Spot** (mtn.), Id,US
86/B4 **Spotorno**, It.
206/D3 **Spotswood**, NJ,US
201/J1 **Spotsylvania C. H.**, Va,US
123/C3 **Spreng** (riv.), Camb.
195/G3 **Sprague**, Mb,Can
184/C2 **Sprague** (riv.), Or,US
182/F4 **Sprague**, Wa,US
66/C5 **Sprang-Capelle**, Neth.
182/D1 **Spranger** (mtn.), BC,Can
126/D2 **Spratly** (isls.)
184/D1 **Spray**, Or,US
72/E3 **Spree** (riv.), Ger.
72/E4 **Spreewald** (reg.), Ger.
70/A3 **Sprendlingen**, Ger.
87/F1 **Spresiano**, It.
69/E3 **Sprimont**, Belg.
200/B2 **Spring** (riv.), Ar,US
186/D3 **Spring** (dry lake), Ca,US
186/E2 **Spring** (mts.), Ca, Nv,US
192/D3 **Spring** (cr.), Co, Ne,US
203/F2 **Spring** (riv.), Ga,US
190/E2 **Spring** (riv.), Ks, Mo,US
200/B2 **Spring** (riv.), Mo,US
194/C4 **Spring** (cr.), ND,US
184/E3 **Spring** (cr.), Nv,US
192/E1 **Spring** (cr.), SD,US
189/G2 **Spring**, Tx,US
189/G2 **Spring** (cr.), Tx,US
156/B3 **Springbok**, SAfr.
155/F5 **Springbokvlakte** (val.), SAfr.
200/E1 **Springboro**, Oh,US
206/C3 **Spring City**, Pa,US
200/E3 **Spring City**, Tn,US
185/H4 **Spring City**, Ut,US
191/G2 **Springdale**, Ar,US
208/H6 **Springdale**, Pa,US
201/G3 **Springdale**, SC,US
187/F2 **Springdale**, Ut,US
182/F3 **Springdale**, Wa,US
67/G4 **Springe**, Ger.
190/B2 **Springer**, NM,US
191/F3 **Springer**, Ok,US
187/H3 **Springerville**, Az,US
190/C2 **Springfield**, Co,US
203/F2 **Springfield**, Fl,US
201/G4 **Springfield**, Ga,US
193/K4 **Springfield**, Il,US
200/E2 **Springfield**, Ky,US
208/B1 **Springfield**, Ma,US
196/C3 **Springfield**, Me,US
198/D3 **Springfield**, Mi,US
193/G1 **Springfield**, Mn,US
191/H2 **Springfield**, Mo,US
201/H9 **Springfield**, NJ,US
198/E5 **Springfield**, Oh,US
184/B1 **Springfield**, Or,US
192/F2 **Springfield**, SD,US
200/D2 **Springfield**, Tn,US
206/A6 **Springfield**, Va,US
199/K3 **Springfield**, Vt,US
156/D3 **Springfontein**, SAfr.
205/P15 **Spring Grove**, Il,US
193/J2 **Spring Grove**, Mn,US
206/B4 **Spring Grove**, Pa,US
196/E3 **Springhill**, NS,Can
191/H4 **Spring Hill**, Ar,US
202/K7 **Spring Hill**, Fl,US
203/G3 **Spring Hill**, Fl,US
191/G1 **Spring Hill**, Ks,US
189/H1 **Springhill**, La,US
203/H3 **Spring Hill**, Tn,US
201/H3 **Spring Lake**, NC,US
207/D3 **Spring Lake**, NJ,US
156/E2 **Springs**, SAfr.
199/K4 **Springs**, NY,US
194/C2 **Springside**, Sk,Can
134/C4 **Springsure**, Austl.
189/F1 **Springtown**, Tx,US
135/G5 **Springvale**, Austl.
196/C3 **Springvale**, Me,US
204/D5 **Spring Valley**, Ca,US
193/K3 **Spring Valley**, Il,US
193/H2 **Spring Valley**, Mn,US
207/D1 **Spring Valley**, NY,US
189/M9 **Spring Valley**, Tx,US
192/E2 **Springview**, Ne,US
200/D4 **Springville**, Al,US
186/C2 **Springville**, Ca,US
193/J2 **Springville**, Ia,US
199/G3 **Springville**, NY,US
185/H3 **Springville**, Ut,US
183/K2 **Springwater**, Sk,Can
199/H3 **Springwater**, NY,US
194/D4 **Springwater Nat'l Wild. Ref.**, ND,US
67/E6 **Sprockhövel**, Ger.
59/H1 **Sprowston**, Eng,UK
185/F3 **Spruce** (mtn.), Nv,US
201/H1 **Spruce** (mtn.), WV,US
204/F8 **Spruce Goose/Queen Mary**, Ca,US
201/H1 **Spruce Knob Nat'l Rec. Area**, WV,US
183/H1 **Spruce Lake**, Sk,Can
201/F3 **Spruce Pine**, NC,US
206/C2 **Spruce Run** (res.), NJ,US
194/E3 **Sprucewoods**, Mb,Can
66/B5 **Spui** (riv.), Neth.
83/C3 **Spulico** (cape), It.
190/D4 **Spur**, Tx,US
57/J4 **Spurn Head** (pt.), Eng,UK
182/D3 **Spuzzum**, BC,Can
182/C3 **Squamish**, BC,Can
182/C3 **Squamish** (riv.), BC,Can
196/C2 **Squa Pan** (lake), Me,US
183/J4 **Square Butte**, Mt,US
193/G3 **Squaw Creek Nat'l Wild. Ref.**, Mo, Ne,US
177/F4 **Squaw Harbor**, Ak,US
195/G4 **Squaw Lake**, Mn,US
186/C2 **Squaw Valley**, Ca,US
205/B3 **Squaxin I. Ind. Res.**, Wa,US
208/D3 **Squibnocket** (pt.), Ma,US
83/C5 **Squillace**, It.
83/C5 **Squillace** (gulf), It.
91/F2 **Squinzano**, It.
201/G2 **Squire**, WV,US
133/E3 **Squires** (peak), Austl.
191/H2 **Squires**, Mo,US
92/D3 **Srbobran**, Yugo.
123/C4 **Sre Ambel**, Camb.
92/D3 **Srebrenica**, Bosn.
93/G4 **Sredna** (mts.), Bul.
109/K1 **Srednebelaya**, Rus.
101/R3 **Srednekolymsk**, Rus.
99/K2 **Sredniy Ikorets**, Rus.
93/G4 **Srednogorie**, Bul.
97/H2 **Srednyaya Akhtuba**, Rus.
123/D3 **Sre Khtum**, Camb.
65/J2 **Śrem**, Pol.
92/E3 **Sremčica**, Yugo.
92/D3 **Sremska Mitrovica**, Yugo.
123/C3 **Sreng** (riv.), Camb.
123/D3 **Sre Noy**, Camb.
123/D3 **Srepok** (riv.), Camb.
109/H1 **Sretensk**, Rus.
107/K3 **Sri Dungargarh**, India
107/K3 **Sri Gangānagar**, India
118/D4 **Srīkākulam**, India
184/E2 **Srike, C.J.** (res.), Id,US
116/B5 **Sri Kshetra** (ruins), Burma
118/D6 **Sri Lanka**
121/H3 **Srimangal**, Bang.
107/K2 **Srīnagar**, India
122/G3 **Srīrangam**, India
122/F4 **Srīvaikuntam**, India
118/B4 **Srīvardhan**, India
122/F4 **Srīvilliputtūr**, India
65/J3 **Środa Śląska**, Pol.
65/J2 **Środa Wielkopolska**, Pol.
134/A2 **Staaten** (riv.), Austl.
134/A2 **Staaten River Nat'l Park**, Austl.
73/A2 **Staatz**, Aus.
61/H1 **Stabbursdalen Nat'l Park**, Nor.
62/D4 **Staberhuk** (pt.), Ger.
66/B6 **Stabroek**, Belg.
193/H2 **Stacyville**, Ia,US
67/G1 **Stade**, Ger.
68/C2 **Staden**, Belg.
66/D3 **Stadskanaal**, Neth.
70/D6 **Stadtbergen**, Ger.
67/G4 **Stadthagen**, Ger.
72/B6 **Stadtilm**, Ger.
70/D2 **Stadtlauringen**, Ger.
66/D5 **Stadtlohn**, Ger.
67/G5 **Stadtoldendorf**, Ger.
72/B6 **Stadtroda**, Ger.
73/A5 **Stadtschlaining**, Aus.
71/E2 **Stadtsteinach**, Ger.
81/E3 **Stäfa**, Swi.
62/E4 **Staffanstorp**, Swe.
70/E2 **Staffelberg** (peak), Ger.
80/E3 **Staffelegg** (pass), Swi.
80/D2 **Staffelfelden**, Fr.
81/H2 **Staffelsee** (lake), Ger.
70/D2 **Staffelstein**, Ger.
67/F3 **Staffhorst**, Ger.
86/C3 **Staffora** (riv.), It.
57/F6 **Stafford**, Eng,UK
208/B2 **Stafford**, Ct,US
191/E2 **Stafford**, Ks,US
189/M9 **Stafford**, Tx,US
201/J1 **Stafford**, Va,US
58/D2 **Stafford & Worcester** (can.), Eng,UK
57/F5 **Staffordshire** (co.), Eng,UK
208/B2 **Stafford Springs**, Ct,US
208/B2 **Staffordville**, Ct,US
86/D5 **Stagno**, It.
90/B4 **Stagnone** (isls.), It.
72/D3 **Stahnsdorf**, Ger.
63/L3 **Staicele**, Lat.
57/G2 **Staindrop**, Eng,UK
53/M7 **Staines**, Eng,UK
53/T10 **Stains**, Fr.
54/B5 **Stake, Hill of** (hill), Sc,UK
205/M12 **Stakes** (mtn.), Ca,US
53/G4 **Stakhanov**, Ukr.
58/D5 **Stalbridge**, Eng,UK
80/D5 **Stalden**, Swi.
83/C5 **Staletti**, It.
59/H1 **Stalham**, Eng,UK
64/A2 **Stalham**, Eng,UK
200/C4 **Stallo**, Ms,US
179/S6 **Stallworthy** (cape), NW,Can
65/M3 **Stalowa Wola**, Pol.
194/B2 **Stalwart**, Sk,Can
57/F5 **Stalybridge**, Eng,UK
198/B1 **Stambaugh**, Mi,US
93/G4 **Stamboliyski**, Bul.
134/A3 **Stamford**, Austl.
59/F1 **Stamford**, Eng,UK
207/E1 **Stamford**, Ct,US
199/J3 **Stamford**, NY,US
188/E1 **Stamford**, Tx,US
188/E1 **Stamford** (lake), Tx,US
57/H4 **Stamford Bridge**, Eng,UK
81/F5 **Stampa**, Swi.
184/C4 **Stampede** (res.), Ca,US
154/C5 **Stampriet**, Namb.
191/H4 **Stamps**, Ar,US
61/E1 **Stamsund**, Nor.
60/D2 **Stamullin**, Ire.
201/H1 **Stanardsville**, Va,US
193/G3 **Stanberry**, Mo,US
195/H5 **Stanchfield**, Mn,US
156/E2 **Standerton**, SAfr.
200/E1 **Standiford Field** (int'l arpt.), Ky,US
201/F3 **Standing Indian** (peak), NC,US
200/E4 **Standing Rock**, Al,US
192/D1 **Standing Rock Ind. Res.**, SD,US
196/B4 **Standish**, Me,US
198/E3 **Standish**, Mi,US
57/F4 **Standish-with-Langtree**, Eng,UK
187/G4 **Stanfield**, Az,US
184/D1 **Stanfield**, Or,US
200/E2 **Stanford**, Ky,US
183/J4 **Stanford**, Mt,US
59/G4 **Stanford le Hope**, Eng,UK
53/P6 **Stanford Rivers**, Eng,UK
62/D1 **Stange**, Nor.
195/L5 **Stangelville**, Wi,US
157/E3 **Stanger**, SAfr.
87/E2 **Stanghella**, It.
57/F2 **Stanhope**, Eng,UK
206/D2 **Stanhope**, NJ,US
99/K3 **Stanichno-Luganskoye**, Ukr.
92/D3 **Stanišić**, Yugo.
205/M12 **Stanislaus** (co.), Ca,US
186/B1 **Stanislaus** (riv.), Ca,US
93/F4 **Stanke Dimitrov**, Bul.
135/C4 **Stanley**, Austl.
133/F2 **Stanley** (peak), Austl.
196/D2 **Stanley**, NB,Can
175/N7 **Stanley**, Falk.
122/F3 **Stanley** (res.), India
57/G2 **Stanley**, Eng,UK
54/C4 **Stanley**, Sc,UK
194/C3 **Stanley**, ND,US
187/K3 **Stanley**, NM,US
201/H1 **Stanley**, Va,US
193/J1 **Stanley**, Wi,US
140/E4 **Stanley** (falls), Zaire
152/C4 **Stanley** (Malebo) (pool), Congo, Zaire
201/H2 **Stanleytown**, Va,US
201/G2 **Stanleyville**, NC,US
92/E4 **Stanovo**, Yugo.
101/N4 **Stanovoy** (range), Rus.
81/E4 **Stans**, Swi.
196/A3 **Stanstead Plain**, Qu,Can
53/P8 **Stansted**, Eng,UK
59/G3 **Stansted** (London) (int'l arpt.), Eng
59/G3 **Stansted Mountfitchet**, Eng,UK
135/D1 **Stanthorpe**, Austl.
59/G2 **Stanton**, Eng,UK
200/D4 **Stanton**, Al,US
204/C3 **Stanton**, Ca,US
206/C4 **Stanton**, De,US
193/G3 **Stanton**, Ia,US
200/F2 **Stanton**, Ky,US
198/D3 **Stanton**, Mi,US
193/F3 **Stanton**, Ne,US
206/D2 **Stanton**, NJ,US
200/C3 **Stanton**, Tn,US
188/D1 **Stanton**, Tx,US
53/M7 **Stanwell**, Eng,UK
182/C3 **Stanwood**, Wa,US
66/D3 **Staphorst**, Neth.
59/E4 **Stapleford**, Eng,UK
53/P7 **Stapleford Abbotts**, Eng,UK
59/G4 **Staplehurst**, Eng,UK
193/F3 **Staplehurst**, Ne,US
205/G7 **Staples**, On,Can
195/G4 **Staples**, Mn,US
202/E2 **Stapleton**, Al,US
201/F4 **Stapleton**, Ga,US
192/D3 **Stapleton**, Ne,US
65/L3 **Stąporków**, Pol.
96/E1 **Star'**, Rus.
200/B4 **Star**, Ms,US
189/E2 **Star**, Tx,US
188/C2 **Star** (mtn.), Tx,US
65/L3 **Starachowice**, Pol.
92/E3 **Stara Pazova**, Yugo.
92/F3 **Stara Planina** (mts.), Yugo.
73/B2 **Stará Turá**, Slvk.
97/J1 **Staraya Racheyka**, Rus.
63/P3 **Staraya Russa**, Rus.
98/C2 **Staraya Vyzhevka**, Ukr.
93/G4 **Stara Zagora**, Bul.
194/F3 **Starbuck**, Mb,Can
139/K5 **Starbuck** (isl.), Kiri.
195/G5 **Starbuck**, Mn,US
183/M1 **Star City**, Sk,Can
191/J4 **Star City**, Ar,US
134/B1 **Starcke Nat'l Park**, Austl.
73/B1 **Staré Město**, Czh.
65/H2 **Stargard Szczeciński**, Pol.
90/E1 **Stari Grad**, Cro.
191/G2 **Stark**, Ks,US
196/B3 **Stark**, NH,US
208/F6 **Stark** (co.), Oh,US
203/G3 **Starke**, Fl,US
184/D1 **Starkey**, Or,US
200/C4 **Starkville**, Ms,US
194/E3 **Starkweather**, ND,US
199/J2 **Star Lake**, NY,US
71/E7 **Starnberg**, Ger.
81/H2 **Starnbergersee** (lake), Ger.
99/K3 **Starobel'sk**, Ukr.
99/K4 **Staroderevyan-kovskaya**, Rus.
96/E1 **Starodub**, Rus.
65/K2 **Starogard Gdański**, Pol.
98/D3 **Starokonstantinov**, Ukr.
99/K4 **Starominskaya**, Rus.
99/K5 **Staronizhesteb-liyevskaya**, Rus.
99/K4 **Staroshcher-binovskaya**, Rus.
99/J5 **Starotitarovskaya**, Rus.
99/K5 **Starovelichkovskaya**, Rus.
58/C6 **Start** (bay), Eng,UK
58/C6 **Start** (pt.), Eng,UK
55/N13 **Start** (pt.), Sc,UK
189/J1 **Start**, La,US
205/D2 **Startup**, Wa,US
96/D1 **Staryye Dorogi**, Bela.
94/J5 **Staryy Kistruss**, Rus.
99/H5 **Staryy Krym**, Ukr.
99/J2 **Staryy Oskol'**, Rus.
53/G3 **Staryy Oskol'**, Rus.
95/L5 **Staryy Studenets**, Rus.
72/B4 **Stassfurt**, Ger.
65/L3 **Staszów**, Pol.
205/B3 **State Capitol**, Wa,US
199/G4 **State College**, Pa,US
206/C6 **State Fairgnds.**, De,US
188/L7 **State Fair Park** (Cotton Bowl), Tx,US
208/A1 **State Line**, Ma,US
202/D2 **State Line**, Ms,US
207/J9 **Staten** (isl.), NY,US
207/J9 **Staten Island** (Richmond) (co.), NY,US
203/G2 **Statenville**, Ga,US
201/G4 **Statesboro**, Ga,US
78/C2 **States** (Jersey) (int'l arpt.), ChI,UK
201/G3 **Statesville**, NC,US
200/F4 **Statham**, Ga,US
201/G1 **Statts Mills**, WV,US
207/J9 **Statue of Liberty Nat'l Mon.**, NY,US
64/E3 **Staufenberg**, Ger.
80/D2 **Staufen im Breisgau**, Ger.
58/D3 **Staunton**, Eng,UK
193/K4 **Staunton**, Il,US
201/H1 **Staunton**, Va,US
58/D2 **Staunton on Wye**, Eng,UK
81/G4 **Stausee Gepatsch** (lake), Aus.
71/E1 **Stausee-Hohenwarte** (res.), Ger.
62/A2 **Stavanger**, Nor.
57/F3 **Staveley**, Eng,UK
57/G5 **Staveley**, Eng,UK
69/E3 **Stavelot**, Belg.
183/H2 **Stavely**, Ab,Can
66/C3 **Staveren**, Neth.
62/D2 **Stavern**, Nor.
98/F3 **Stavishche**, Ukr.
53/H4 **Stavropol'**, Rus.
99/L5 **Stavropol' Kray**, Rus.
91/H2 **Stavrós**, Gre.
135/B3 **Stawell**, Austl.
198/F2 **Stayner**, On,Can
184/B1 **Stayton**, Or,US
190/C2 **Stead**, NM,US
205/L10 **Steamboat** (slough), Ca,US
185/K3 **Steamboat Springs**, Co,US
200/E2 **Stearns**, Ky,US
177/F3 **Stebbins**, Ak,US
98/B3 **Stebnik**, Ukr.
81/E2 **Steckborn**, Swi.
67/H3 **Stederau** (riv.), Ger.
81/G3 **Steeg**, Aus.
185/F2 **Steel** (mtn.), Id,US
135/F5 **Steele** (cr.), Austl.
200/C2 **Steele**, Mo,US
194/E4 **Steele**, ND,US
54/C4 **Steele's Knowe** (hill), Sc,UK
193/K4 **Steeleville**, Il,US
157/E2 **Steelpoortrivier** (riv.), SAfr.
206/B3 **Steelton**, Pa,US
191/J2 **Steelville**, Mo,US
66/B5 **Steenbergen**, Neth.
127/H4 **Steenkool**, Indo.
179/J1 **Steensby** (inlet), NW,Can
184/D2 **Steens Mtn. Rec. Lands**, Or,US
68/B2 **Steenvoorde**, Fr.
66/D3 **Steenwijk**, Neth.
132/B3 **Steep** (pt.), Austl.
58/C4 **Steep Holm** (isl.), Eng,UK
57/J5 **Steeping** (riv.), Eng,UK
194/E2 **Steep Rock**, Mb,Can
177/J2 **Steese Nat'l Rec. Area**, Ak,US
93/H2 **Ştefăneşti**, Rom.
73/B2 **Štefanov**, Slvk.
178/F1 **Stefansson** (isl.), NW,Can
174/C5 **Steffen** (peak), Chile
80/D4 **Steffisburg**, Swi.
80/D5 **Steg**, Swi.
62/E4 **Stege**, Den.
73/A5 **Stegersbach**, Aus.
92/A2 **Steiermark** (prov.), Aus.
70/D3 **Steigerwald** (for.), Ger.
75/J2 **Steigerwald** (reg.), Ger.
205/B3 **Steilacoom**, Wa,US
155/F4 **Steilloopbrug**, SAfr.
67/G3 **Steimbke**, Ger.
182/D2 **Stein** (riv.), BC,Can
64/F4 **Stein**, Ger.
69/E2 **Stein**, Neth.
72/E5 **Steina**, Ger.
81/E2 **Steina** (riv.), Ger.
70/E2 **Steinach**, Ger.
71/F5 **Steinach**, Ger.
70/E2 **Steinach** (riv.), Ger.
81/H3 **Steinach am Brenner**, Aus.
81/E2 **Stein am Rhein**, Swi.
70/C2 **Steinau an der Strasse**, Ger.
194/F3 **Steinbach**, Mb,Can
71/H7 **Steinbach an der Steyr**, Aus.
70/E4 **Stein bei Nürnberg**, Ger.
69/G6 **Steinbourg**, Fr.
170/B2 **Steinen** (riv.), Braz.
80/D2 **Steinen**, Ger.
71/G6 **Steinerkirchen an der Traun**, Aus.
73/A4 **Steinfeld** (reg.), Aus.
67/F3 **Steinfeld**, Ger.
69/H5 **Steinfeld**, Ger.
70/B4 **Steinfeld**, Ger.
70/C3 **Steinfeld**, Ger.
69/E4 **Steinfort**, Lux.
81/G2 **Steingaden**, Ger.
67/F5 **Steinhagen**, Ger.
203/G3 **Steinhatchee**, Fl,US
154/C4 **Steinhausen**, Namb.
81/E3 **Steinhausen**, Swi.
70/C6 **Steinhausen an der Rottum**, Ger.
70/E2 **Steinheid**, Ger.
67/G5 **Steinheim**, Ger.
70/D5 **Steinheim am Albuch**, Ger.
70/C5 **Steinheim an der Murr**, Ger.
67/H3 **Steinhorst**, Ger.
67/G4 **Steinhuder Meer** (lake), Ger.
61/D2 **Steinkjer**, Nor.
62/A1 **Steinsland**, Nor.
70/B4 **Steinweiler**, Ger.
68/D1 **Stekene**, Belg.
94/J4 **Steklyanka**, Rus.
156/D2 **Stella**, SAfr.
193/G3 **Stella**, Ne,US
83/B2 **Stella, Monte della** (peak), It.
81/F5 **Stella, Pizzo** (peak), It.
197/F3 **Stellarton**, NS,Can
67/H2 **Stelle**, Ger.
156/B4 **Stellenbosch**, SAfr.
75/H5 **Stello** (mtn.), Fr.
81/G5 **Stelvio Nat'l Park**, It.
81/G4 **Stelvio, Passo di** (pass), It.
69/E5 **Stenay**, Fr.
72/B2 **Stendal**, Ger.
63/K3 **Stende**, Lat.
93/G4 **Steneto Nat'l Park**, Bul.
63/R7 **Stenhamra**, Swe.
54/C4 **Stenhousemuir**, Sc,UK
63/T9 **Stenløse**, Den.
62/D2 **Stenungsund**, Swe.
53/H5 **Stepanakert**, Azer.
97/H4 **Stepanavan**, Arm.
60/D3 **Stepaside**, Ire.
192/E1 **Stephan**, SD,US
71/F5 **Stephansposching**, Ger.
136/C3 **Stephens** (cape), N.Z.
191/H4 **Stephens**, Ar,US
200/D2 **Stephensburg**, Ky,US
201/H1 **Stephens City**, Va,US
133/J4 **Stephens Creek**, Austl.
198/C2 **Stephenson**, Mi,US
197/H1 **Stephenville**, Nf,Can
189/E1 **Stephenville**, Tx,US
197/H1 **Stephenville Crossing**, Nf,Can
72/B1 **Stepnitz** (riv.), Ger.
95/P5 **Stepnoy**, Rus.
97/H2 **Stepnoye**, Rus.
97/H3 **Stepnoye**, Rus.
191/J3 **Steprock**, Ar,US
185/F4 **Steptoe** (val.), Nv,US
182/F4 **Steptoe**, Wa,US
156/D3 **Sterkspruit**, SAfr.
156/D3 **Sterkstroom**, SAfr.
177/H3 **Sterling**, Ak,US
192/C3 **Sterling**, Co,US
208/C2 **Sterling**, Ct,US
203/H2 **Sterling**, Ga,US
193/K3 **Sterling**, Il,US
191/E1 **Sterling**, Ks,US
208/C1 **Sterling**, Ma,US
198/D2 **Sterling**, Mi,US
208/F6 **Sterling**, Oh,US
188/D2 **Sterling City**, Tx,US
205/F6 **Sterling Heights**, Mi,US
189/H1 **Sterlington**, La,US
53/J3 **Sterlitamak**, Rus.
71/H5 **Sternstein** (peak), Aus.
81/H4 **Sterzing** (Vipiteno), It.
65/J2 **Stęszew**, Pol.
71/H2 **Štětí**, Czh.
195/J5 **Stetsonville**, Wi,US
183/H1 **Stettler**, Ab,Can
208/G7 **Steubenville**, Oh,US
59/F3 **Stevenage**, Eng,UK
133/G3 **Stevenson** (cr.), Austl.
177/H4 **Stevenson** (str.), Ak,US
208/A3 **Stevenson**, Ct,US
208/A3 **Stevenson** (dam), Ct,US
182/D5 **Stevenson**, Wa,US
193/K1 **Stevens Point**, Wi,US
54/B5 **Stevenston**, Sc,UK
177/J2 **Stevens Village**, Ak,US
206/B6 **Stevensville**, Md,US
198/C3 **Stevensville**, Mi,US
183/G4 **Stevensville**, Mt,US
66/C3 **Stevinsluizen** (dam), Neth.
193/K4 **Stewardson**, Il,US
128/E2 **Stewart** (cape), Austl.
182/F1 **Stewart** (mtn.), Ab,Can
177/N4 **Stewart**, BC,Can
177/L3 **Stewart** (riv.), Yk,Can
136/B4 **Stewart** (isl.), N.Z.
200/D4 **Stewart**, Al,US
200/C4 **Stewart**, Ms,US
177/L3 **Stewart Crossing**, Yk,Can
194/C4 **Stewart Lake Nat'l Wild. Ref.**, ND,US
54/B5 **Stewarton**, Sc,UK
177/L3 **Stewart River**, Yk,Can
56/B2 **Stewartstown**, NI,UK
206/B4 **Stewartstown**, Pa,US
183/L2 **Stewart Valley**, Sk,Can
193/H2 **Stewartville**, Mn,US
196/F3 **Stewiacke**, NS,Can
59/F5 **Steyning**, Eng,UK
156/D2 **Steynrus**, SAfr.
156/D3 **Steynsburg**, SAfr.
71/H6 **Steyr**, Aus.
71/H6 **Steyr** (riv.), Aus.
71/H6 **Steyregg**, Aus.
156/D4 **Steytlerville**, SAfr.
87/E5 **Stia**, It.
86/D5 **Stiava**, It.
73/C3 **Štiavnické vrchy** (mts.), Slvk.
205/D2 **Stickney** (mtn.), Wa,US
66/C2 **Stiens**, Neth.
191/G3 **Stigler**, Ok,US
83/C2 **Stigliano**, It.
62/G2 **Stigtomta**, Swe.
177/M4 **Stikine**, BC,Can
177/M4 **Stikine** (riv.), BC,Can
156/C4 **Stilbaai**, SAfr.
188/D2 **Stiles**, Tx,US
195/K5 **Stiles**, Wi,US
156/D2 **Stilfontein**, SAfr.
91/H3 **Stilís**, Gre.
206/C2 **Still Creek** (res.), Pa,US
62/D3 **Stilling**, Den.
201/F4 **Stillmore**, Ga,US
206/B5 **Still Pond**, Md,US
195/H5 **Stillwater**, Mn,US
195/Q6 **Stillwater**, Mn,US
185/J1 **Stillwater** (riv.), Mt,US
184/D4 **Stillwater** (range), Nv,US
199/J3 **Stillwater** (res.), NY,US
191/F2 **Stillwater**, Ok,US
206/B1 **Stillwater**, Pa,US
206/C1 **Stillwater** (lake), Pa,US
184/D4 **Stillwater Nat'l Wild. Ref.**, Nv,US
83/C6 **Stilo**, It.
83/C6 **Stilo** (pt.), It.
191/G3 **Stilwell**, Ok,US
92/E4 **Štimlje**, Yugo.
70/D4 **Stimpfach**, Ger.
183/H3 **Stimson** (mtn.), Mt,US
56/D1 **Stinchar** (riv.), Sc,UK
192/D3 **Stinking Water** (cr.), Ne,US
190/D3 **Stinnett**, Tx,US
92/F5 **Štip**, Macd.
69/F5 **Stiring-Wendel**, Fr.
71/G4 **Stírka** (peak), Czh.
132/K6 **Stirling**, Austl.
132/C4 **Stirling** (peak), Austl.
183/H3 **Stirling**, Ab,Can
199/H2 **Stirling**, On,Can
54/C4 **Stirling**, Sc,UK
132/C5 **Stirling Range Nat'l Park**, Austl.
86/C3 **Stirone** (riv.), It.
182/G4 **Stites**, Id,US
61/D3 **Stjørdal**, Nor.
54/B4 **Stob a' Choin** (mtn.), Sc,UK
54/B3 **Stob Choire Claurigh** (mtn.), Sc,UK
71/G2 **Stochov**, Czh.
81/F2 **Stockach**, Ger.
59/E4 **Stockbridge**, Eng,UK
201/M7 **Stockbridge**, Ga,US
208/A1 **Stockbridge**, Ma,US
198/D3 **Stockbridge**, Mi,US
193/K1 **Stockbridge Ind. Res.**, Wi,US
189/F3 **Stockdale**, Tx,US
73/A3 **Stockerau**, Aus.
206/C2 **Stockertown**, Pa,US
183/J4 **Stockett**, Mt,US
71/E2 **Stockheim**, Ger.
194/C2 **Stockholm**, Sk,Can
62/H2 **Stockholm** (cap.), Swe.
196/C2 **Stockholm**, Me,US
194/F5 **Stockholm**, SD,US
80/D4 **Stockhorn** (peak), Swi.
158/E2 **Stockton** (plat.), Tx,US
155/E4 **Stockpoort**, SAfr.
57/F5 **Stockport**, Eng,UK
57/F4 **Stocks** (res.), Eng,UK
57/G5 **Stocksbridge**, Eng,UK
70/C3 **Stockstadt am Main**, Ger.
70/B3 **Stockstadt am Rhein**, Ger.
202/E2 **Stockton**, Al,US
205/M11 **Stockton**, Ca,US
203/G2 **Stockton**, Ga,US
193/J2 **Stockton**, Il,US
190/E1 **Stockton**, Ks,US
191/H2 **Stockton**, Mo,US
191/H2 **Stockton** (dam), Mo,US
191/H2 **Stockton** (lake), Mo,US
206/D3 **Stockton**, NJ,US
188/C2 **Stockton** (plat.), Tx,US
57/G2 **Stockton-on-Tees**, Eng,UK
71/G3 **Stod**, Czh.
94/G5 **Stodolishche**, Rus.
123/D3 **Stoeng Treng**, Camb.
156/Q12 **Stoffberg**, SAfr.
58/B6 **Stoke** (pt.), Eng,UK
57/F5 **Stoke-on-Trent**, Eng,UK
135/B4 **Stokes** (pt.), Austl.
130/C4 **Stokes** (range), Austl.
136/C3 **Stokes** (peak), N.Z.
132/D5 **Stokes Nat'l Park**, Austl.
92/C4 **Stolac**, Bosn.
69/F2 **Stolberg**, Ger.
72/A4 **Stolberg**, Ger.
101/P2 **Stolbovoy** (isl.), Rus.
63/M5 **Stolbtsy**, Bela.
98/D2 **Stolin**, Bela.
72/C6 **Stollberg**, Ger.
62/E1 **Stöllet**, Swe.
72/E5 **Stolpen**, Ger.
67/G3 **Stolzenau**, Ger.
156/K10 **Stompneuspunt** (pt.), SAfr.
92/C4 **Ston**, Cro.
57/F6 **Stone**, Eng,UK
201/F2 **Stone**, Ky,US
208/G5 **Stoneboro**, Pa,US
199/H1 **Stonecliffe**, On,Can
208/F7 **Stone Creek**, Oh,US
116/D3 **Stone Forest**, China
200/C2 **Stonefort**, Il,US
189/G2 **Stoneham**, Tx,US
206/D5 **Stone Harbor**, NJ,US
54/D3 **Stonehaven**, Sc,UK
134/A4 **Stonehenge**, Austl.
59/E4 **Stonehenge** (ruins), Eng,UK
58/D3 **Stonehouse**, Eng,UK
54/C5 **Stonehouse**, Sc,UK
182/C2 **Stone Ind. Res.**, BC,Can
195/J5 **Stone Lake**, Wi,US
201/M7 **Stone Mountain**, Ga,US
201/M7 **Stone Mtn. Mem. Park**, Ga,US
200/D3 **Stones River Nat'l Bfld,**, Tn,US
201/H2 **Stoneville**, NC,US
192/C1 **Stoneville**, SD,US
194/F2 **Stonewall**, Mb,Can
201/L7 **Stonewall**, Ga,US
202/B1 **Stonewall**, La,US
200/C4 **Stonewall**, Ms,US
191/F3 **Stonewall**, Ok,US
54/C5 **Stoneyburn**, Sc,UK
197/R9 **Stoney Creek**, On,Can
205/G7 **Stoney Point**, On,Can
190/C2 **Stonington**, Co,US
208/C3 **Stonington**, Ct,US
196/C3 **Stonington**, Me,US
198/C2 **Stonington**, Mi,US
194/F1 **Stony** (pt.), Mb,Can
184/B4 **Stony** (cr.), Ca,US
205/F6 **Stony** (cr.), Mi,US
199/H3 **Stony** (pt.), NY,US
206/B3 **Stony** (cr.), Pa,US
194/B2 **Stony Beach**, Sk,Can
207/E2 **Stony Brook**, NY,US
206/B4 **Stonybrook-Wilshire**, Pa,US
205/F6 **Stony Creek** (lake), Mi,US
184/B4 **Stonyford**, Ca,US
182/G2 **Stony Ind. Res.**, Ab,Can
201/H1 **Stony Man** (mtn.), Va,US
201/G3 **Stony Point**, NC,US
207/E1 **Stony Point**, NY,US
177/G3 **Stony River**, Ak,US
100/K3 **Stony Tunguska** (riv.), Rus.
179/S7 **Stor** (isl.), NW,Can
67/G1 **Stör** (riv.), Ger.
62/F2 **Storå**, Swe.
62/D2 **Stora Le** (lake), Swe.
61/F2 **Stora Sjöfallets Nat'l Park**, Swe.
61/F2 **Storavan** (lake), Swe.
63/H1 **Storby**, Fin.
62/A2 **Stord** (isl.), Nor.
62/D4 **Store Bælt** (chan.), Den.
62/A1 **Storebø**, Nor.
62/D1 **Stor-Elvdal**, Nor.
61/D3 **Støren**, Nor.
135/C4 **Storeys Creek**, Austl.
62/F2 **Storfors**, Swe.
87/G1 **Štorje**, Slov.
72/D3 **Storkow**, Ger.
61/E3 **Storlien**, Swe.
135/C4 **Storm** (bay), Austl.
193/G2 **Storm Lake**, Ia,US
194/F4 **Storm Lake Nat'l Wild. Ref.**, ND,US
56/C2 **Stormont**, NI,UK
182/D4 **Stormy** (mtn.), Wa,US
85/F5 **Stornara**, It.
85/F5 **Stornarella**, It.
55/H7 **Stornoway**, Sc,UK
86/D1 **Storo**, It.
95/M3 **Storozhevsk**, Rus.
98/C3 **Storozhinets**, Ukr.
59/F5 **Storrington**, Eng,UK
208/B2 **Storrs**, Ct,US
55/H8 **Storr, The**, Sc,UK
62/G1 **Storsjön** (lake), Swe.
61/G1 **Storslett**, Nor.
61/F1 **Storsteinsfjellet** (peak), Nor.
62/D4 **Storstrøm** (co.), Den.
59/G3 **Stort** (riv.), Eng,UK
194/D3 **Storthoaks**, Sk,Can
61/F2 **Storuman**, Swe.
62/G1 **Storvik**, Swe.
62/G2 **Storvreta**, Swe.
185/K1 **Story**, Wy,US
193/H2 **Story City**, Ia,US
175/J7 **Stosch** (isl.), Chile
72/B5 **Stössen**, Ger.
59/F2 **Stotfold**, Eng,UK
81/G2 **Stötten**, Ger.
72/B5 **Stotternheim**, Ger.
199/G3 **Stouffville-Whitchurch**, On,Can
194/C3 **Stoughton**, Sk,Can
208/C1 **Stoughton**, Ma,US
198/B3 **Stoughton**, Wi,US
69/E3 **Stoumont**, Belg.
58/D5 **Stour** (riv.), Eng,UK
59/E2 **Stour** (riv.), Eng,UK
59/H3 **Stour** (riv.), Eng,UK
59/H4 **Stour** (riv.), Eng,UK
58/D2 **Stourbridge**, Eng,UK
55/M11 **Stour, Great** (riv.), Eng,UK
58/D2 **Stourport on Severn**, Eng,UK
189/G1 **Stout**, Tx,US
193/H5 **Stoutland**, Mo,US
191/H1 **Stover**, Mo,US
54/D5 **Stow**, Sc,UK
208/C1 **Stow**, Ma,US
206/C5 **Stow** (cr.), NJ,US
208/F5 **Stow**, Oh,US
208/C3 **Stowe**, Pa,US
199/K2 **Stowe**, Vt,US
189/G3 **Stowell**, Tx,US
59/G2 **Stowmarket**, Eng,UK
59/E3 **Stow on the Wold**, Eng,UK
98/B3 **Stoy** (peak), Ukr.
109/L1 **Stoyba**, Rus.
87/F2 **Stra**, It.
55/H9 **Strabane**, NI,UK
56/A2 **Strabane** (dist.), NI,UK
54/D2 **Strachan**, Sc,UK
54/A4 **Strachur**, Sc,UK
60/C3 **Stradbally**, Ire.
60/C5 **Stradbally**, Ire.
86/C2 **Stradella**, It.
66/D6 **Straelen**, Ger.
60/D3 **Straffan**, Ire.
191/H2 **Strafford**, Mo,US
135/C4 **Strahan**, Austl.
71/G4 **Strakonice**, Czh.
93/H4 **Straldzha**, Bul.
64/G1 **Stralsund**, Ger.
86/A2 **Strambino**, It.
156/B4 **Strand**, SAfr.
56/C3 **Strangford**, NI,UK
56/C3 **Strangford Lough** (inlet), NI,UK
94/C4 **Strängnäs**, Swe.
133/G2 **Strangways** (peak), Austl.
56/B1 **Stranocum**, NI,UK
56/C2 **Stranraer**, Sc,UK
183/M2 **Strasbourg**, Sk,Can
69/G6 **Strasbourg**, Fr.
80/D1 **Strasbourg** (Entzheim) (int'l arpt.), Fr.
194/D4 **Strasburg**, ND,US
208/F6 **Strasburg**, Oh,US
206/B4 **Strasburg**, Pa,US
201/H1 **Strasburg**, Va,US
93/J2 **Strasheny**, Mol.
69/F4 **Strassen**, Lux.
73/A3 **Strasshof an der Nordbahn**, Aus.
71/G7 **Strasswalchen**, Aus.
198/F3 **Stratford**, On,Can
136/C2 **Stratford**, N.Z.
186/C2 **Stratford**, Ca,US
208/A3 **Stratford**, Ct,US
207/L7 **Stratford** (har.), Ct,US
207/E1 **Stratford** (pt.), Ct,US
199/L2 **Stratford**, NH,US
206/C4 **Stratford**, NJ,US
199/J3 **Stratford**, NY,US
191/F3 **Stratford**, Ok,US
190/C2 **Stratford**, Tx,US
193/J1 **Stratford**, Wi,US
59/E2 **Stratford upon Avon**, Eng,UK
133/H5 **Strathalbyn**, Austl.
54/B5 **Strathaven**, Sc,UK
54/E1 **Strathbeg** (bay), Sc,UK
54/B5 **Strathblane**, Sc,UK
194/D2 **Strathclair**, Mb,Can
54/B5 **Strathclyde** (reg.), Sc,UK
54/C4 **Strathearn** (val.), Sc,UK
135/C4 **Strathgordon**, Austl.
183/H2 **Strathmore**, Ab,Can
54/D3 **Strathmore** (val.), Sc,UK
186/C2 **Strathmore**, Ca,US
54/B1 **Strathpeffer**, Sc,UK
198/F3 **Strathroy**, On,Can
54/C2 **Strathspey** (val.), Sc,UK
54/B4 **Strathyre**, Sc,UK
195/G3 **Stratton**, On,Can
58/B5 **Stratton**, Eng,UK
192/C4 **Stratton**, Co,US
196/B3 **Stratton**, Me,US
208/G6 **Stratton**, Oh,US
199/K3 **Stratton** (mtn.), Vt,US
71/F5 **Straubing**, Ger.
61/M6 **Straumnes** (pt.), Ice.
61/E1 **Straumsjøen**, Nor.
72/D2 **Strausberg**, Ger.
72/A5 **Straussfurt**, Ger.
206/B3 **Strausstown**, Pa,US
191/J3 **Strawberry**, Ar,US
191/J2 **Strawberry** (riv.), Ar,US
186/B1 **Strawberry**, Ca,US
204/B2 **Strawberry** (peak), Ca,US
184/D1 **Strawberry** (peak), Or,US
185/H3 **Strawberry** (res.), Ut,US
185/H3 **Strawberry** (riv.), Ut,US
193/J2 **Strawberry Point**, Ia,US
189/E1 **Strawn**, Tx,US
193/G4 **Strawn** (New Strawn), Ks,US
200/B3 **Strayhorn**, Ms,US
93/G4 **Strazhitsa**, Bul.
73/B2 **Strážnice**, Czh.
73/C2 **Strážovská hornatina** (mts.), Slvk.
128/E6 **Streaky** (bay), Austl.
133/G5 **Streaky Bay**, Austl.
205/P15 **Streamwood**, Il,US
53/N7 **Streatham**, Eng,UK
59/E3 **Streatley**, Eng,UK
193/K3 **Streator**, Il,US
71/H3 **Středočeská Žulová Vrchovina** (mts.), Czh.
71/G2 **Středočeský** (reg.), Czh.
73/C2 **Středoslovenský** (reg.), Slvk.
58/D4 **Street**, Eng,UK

206/B4 Street, Md,US
194/E4 Streeter, ND,US
188/E2 Streeter, Tx,US
189/F2 Streetman, Tx,US
208/F5 Streetsboro, Oh,US
197/R8 Streetsville, On,Can
93/F3 Strehaia, Rom.
72/D5 Strehla, Ger.
132/D4 Streich (peak), Austl.
73/C4 Strekov, Slvk.
65/G3 Strěla (riv.), Czh.
71/G3 Střela (riv.), Czh.
93/G4 Strelcha, Bul.
132/C2 Strelley Abor. Land, Austl.
63/P2 Strel'na, Rus.
94/H2 Strel'na (riv.), Rus.
72/C3 Stremme (riv.), Ger.
63/L3 Strenči, Lat.
71/H6 Strengberg, Aus.
80/D3 Strengelbach, Swi.
81/G3 Strengen, Aus.
86/B1 Stresa, It.
96/D1 Streshin, Bela.
57/F5 Stretford, Eng,UK
59/G2 Stretham, Eng,UK
86/D5 Strettoia, It.
70/D2 Streu (riv.), Ger.
100/H3 Strezhevoy, Rus.
62/C4 Strib, Den.
71/G3 Stříbro, Czh.
54/D1 Strichen, Sc,UK
131/F1 Strickland (riv.), PNG
191/G3 Strickler, Ar,US
81/H5 Strigno, It.
66/B5 Strijen, Neth.
184/F2 Strike, C.J. (dam), Id,US
91/H2 Strimón (gulf), Gre.
91/H2 Strimónas (riv.), Gre.
200/C5 Stringer, Ms,US
191/F3 Stringtown, Ok,US
54/A5 Striven (inlet), Sc,UK
99/M5 Strizhament (peak), Rus.
175/K7 Strobel (lake), Arg.
174/E4 Stroeder, Arg.
91/G4 Strofadhes (isl.), Gre.
89/J3 Strofádhes (isls.), Gre.
99/J2 Stroitel', Rus.
60/B2 Strokestown, Ire.
69/G4 Stromberg, Ger.
83/B5 Stromboli (isl.), It.
183/H1 Strome, Ab,Can
55/J8 Stromeferry, Sc,UK
62/D2 Strømmen, Nor.
55/N13 Stromness, Sc,UK
192/F3 Stromsburg, Ne,US
62/D2 Strömstad, Swe.
61/E3 Strömsund, Swe.
81/E6 Strona (riv.), It.
84/C2 Stroncone, It.
191/H4 Strong, Ar,US
196/B3 Strong, Me,US
200/C4 Strong (riv.), Ms,US
191/F1 Strong City, Ks,US
193/J3 Stronghurst, Il,US
83/D4 Strongoli, It.
208/F5 Strongsville, Oh,US
65/J3 Stronie Śląskie, Pol.
55/N13 Stronsay, Sc,UK
55/N13 Stronsay Firth (inlet), Sc,UK
71/H5 Stropnice (riv.), Czh.
86/B2 Stroppiana, It.
58/D3 Stroud, Eng,UK
191/F3 Stroud, Ok,US
206/C2 Stroudsburg, Pa,US
55/H8 Struan, Sc,UK
62/C3 Struer, Den.
92/E5 Struga, Macd.
63/N2 Strugi-Krasnyye, Rus.
156/C4 Struisbaai (bay), SAfr.
56/A2 Strule (riv.), NI,UK
193/J1 Strum, Wi,US
91/H2 Struma (riv.), Bul., Gre.
58/A2 Strumble Head (pt.), UK
92/F5 Strumica, Macd.
208/G5 Struthers, Oh,US
156/C3 Strydenburg, SAfr.
182/G3 Stryker, Mt,US
61/C3 Stryn, Nor.
98/B3 Stryy, Ukr.
65/J3 Strzegom, Pol.
65/H2 Strzelce Krajeńskie, Pol.
133/J4 Strzelecki (cr.), Austl.
133/G2 Strzelecki (peak), Austl.
130/D5 Strzelecki, Mount (peak), Austl.
65/J3 Strzelin, Pol.
65/K2 Strzelno, Pol.
65/L4 Strzyżów, Pol.
203/H4 Stuart, Fl,US
193/G3 Stuart, Ia,US
191/F3 Stuart, Ok,US
201/G2 Stuart, Va,US
182/D4 Stuart (mtn.), Wa,US
194/F3 Stuartburn, Mb,Can
182/B2 Stuart Island, BC,Can
201/H1 Stuarts Draft, Va,US
135/D2 Stuart Town, Austl.
62/E4 Stubbekøbing, Den.
65/G1 Stubbenkammer (pt.), Ger.
63/L3 Stučka, Lat.
201/H4 Stuckey, SC,US
59/E5 Studland, Eng,UK
59/E2 Studley, Eng,UK
81/E2 Stühlingen, Ger.
194/E4 Stump (lake), ND,US
194/E4 Stump Lake Nat'l Wild. Ref., ND,US
201/K3 Stumpy Point, NC,US
73/B2 Stupava (riv.), Czh.
73/B3 Stupava, Slvk.
94/H5 Stupino, Rus.
82/D2 Stura di Ala (riv.), It.
86/A4 Stura di Demonte (riv.), It.
86/A2 Stura di Lanzo (riv.), It.
82/D2 Stura di Val Grande (riv.), It.
82/D2 Stura di Viù (riv.), It.
208/B1 Sturbridge, Ma,US
195/F1 Sturgeon (bay), Mb,Can
195/J2 Sturgeon (lake), On,Can
198/F1 Sturgeon (riv.), On,Can
197/F2 Sturgeon, PE,Can
191/H1 Sturgeon, Mo,US
193/L1 Sturgeon Bay, Wi,US
198/G1 Sturgeon Falls, On,Can
195/H4 Sturgeon Lake, Mn,US
208/G7 Sturgeon-Noblestown, Pa,US
194/C2 Sturgis, Sk,Can
200/D2 Sturgis, Ky,US
198/D4 Sturgis, Mi,US
192/C1 Sturgis, SD,US
58/D5 Sturminster Newton, Eng,UK
73/C4 Štúrovo, Slvk.
59/H4 Sturry, Eng,UK
130/B4 Sturt (cr.), Austl.
134/A5 Sturt (des.), Austl.
133/J4 Sturt (peak), Austl.
133/M8 Sturt (riv.), Austl.
205/Q14 Sturtevant, Wi,US
133/J4 Sturt Nat'l Park, Austl.
62/E4 Sturup (int'l arpt.), Swe.
156/D4 Stutterheim, SAfr.
70/C5 Stuttgart, Ger.
191/J3 Stuttgart, Ar,US
70/C5 Stuttgart (Echterdingen) (int'l arpt.), Ger.
70/D1 Stützerbach, Ger.
73/B3 Štvrtok, Slvk.
73/B3 Štvrtok Na Ostrove, Slvk.
61/M6 Stykkishólmur, Ice.
98/C2 Styr (riv.), Ukr.
75/L3 Styria (prov.), Aus.
171/E3 Suaçui Grande (riv.), Braz.
130/B2 Suai, Indo.
147/H5 Suakin (arch.), Sudan
151/A1 Suam (riv.), Kenya
198/B2 Suamico, Wi,US
113/D3 Suan, NKor.
152/E4 Suana, Zaire
117/H3 Su'ao, China
117/J3 Suao, Tai.
169/E4 Suapi, Bol.
158/C2 Suaqui Grande, Mex.
120/B1 Suār, India
164/C3 Suárez (riv.), Col.
175/T12 Suárez, Uru.
63/L4 Subačius, Lith.
124/D4 Subang, Indo.
117/F3 Subao (mtn.), China
121/F4 Subarnarekhā (riv.), India
84/C1 Subasio (peak), It.
63/L3 Subata, Lat.
141/W18 Subayţilah, Tun.
108/C4 Subei, China
126/C3 Subi (isl.), Indo.
84/D4 Subiaco, It.
125/C2 Subic Bay Nav. Base, Phil.
190/D2 Sublette, Ks,US
92/D2 Subotica, Yugo.
124/B2 Subulusalam, Indo.
73/D1 Sučany, Slvk.
200/C4 Sucarnoochee (riv.), Al, Ms,US
206/D2 Succasunna-Kenvil, NJ,US
191/H2 Success, Mo,US
86/D4 Succiso, Alpe di (peak), It.
93/H2 Suceava, Rom.
93/G2 Suceava (co.), Rom.
78/D6 Sucé-sur-Erdre, Fr.
65/L3 Suchedniów, Pol.
168/D4 Suches, Bol.
160/C2 Suchilapan, Mex.
60/B3 Suck (riv.), Ire.
131/G2 Suckling (cape), PNG
131/H2 Suckling, Mount (peak), PNG
172/C1 Sucre (cap.), Bol.
164/C2 Sucre (dept.), Col.
164/A5 Sucre, Ecu.
165/F2 Sucre (state), Ven.
164/B5 Sucúa, Ecu.
166/B4 Sucunduri (riv.), Braz.
167/E4 Sucupira do Norte, Braz.
166/D2 Sucuriju, Braz.
170/B3 Sucuriú (riv.), Braz.
53/T10 Sucy-en-Brie, Fr.
148/A5 Sud (prov.), Camr.
142/C3 Sud (reg.), Mor.
94/H4 Suda (riv.), Rus.
99/H5 Sudak, Ukr.
140/E3 Sudan
140/C3 Sudan (reg.), Afr.
190/C3 Sudan, Tx,US
176/J5 Sudbury, Can.
198/F1 Sudbury, On,Can
59/G2 Sudbury, Eng,UK
208/C1 Sudbury, Ma,US
140/F4 Sudd (swamp), Sudan
165/G3 Suddie, Guy.
67/H2 Sude (riv.), Ger.
64/E1 Süderbrarup, Ger.
65/H3 Sudeten (mts.), Czh., Pol.
151/B4 Sudi, Tanz.
206/C5 Sudlersville, Md,US
66/D5 Südlohn, Ger.
94/J5 Sudogda, Rus.
145/H5 Sud-Ouest (prov.), Camr.
99/H2 Sudzha, Rus.
149/F4 Sue (riv.), Sudan
77/E3 Sueca, Sp.
93/G4 Sŭedinenie, Bul.
106/B3 Suez, Egypt
103/C4 Suez (can.), Egypt
103/C5 Suez (gulf), Egypt
103/C5 Suez (As Suways), Egypt
103/D3 Sūf, Jor.
106/D4 Şufaynah, SAr.
81/F4 Sufers, Swi.
207/D1 Suffern, NY,US
208/B2 Suffield, Ct,US
208/F5 Suffield, Oh,US
59/G2 Suffolk (co.), Eng,UK
208/C1 Suffolk (co.), Ma,US
207/F2 Suffolk (co.), NY,US
201/J2 Suffolk, Va,US
105/F2 Şūfīān, Iran
193/K2 Sugar (riv.), Il,US
198/C4 Sugar (cr.), In,US
208/F6 Sugar (cr.), Oh,US
208/H5 Sugar (cr.), Pa,US
205/P14 Sugar (cr.), Wi,US
193/K2 Sugar (riv.), Wi,US
193/K1 Sugarbush (hill), Wi,US
192/C4 Sugar City, Co,US
185/H2 Sugar City, Id,US
208/F7 Sugarcreek, Oh,US
208/H5 Sugarcreek, Pa,US
205/P16 Sugar Grove, Il,US
200/E3 Sugar Hill, Ga,US
189/G3 Sugar Land, Tx,US
129/J6 Sugarloaf (pt.), Austl.
58/C3 Sugar Loaf (mtn.), Wal,UK
203/H5 Sugarloaf (key), Fl,US
201/F1 Sugarloaf (mtn.), Ky,US
196/B3 Sugarloaf (mtn.), Me,US
201/H2 Sugarloaf (mtn.), Va,US
206/C1 Sugar Notch, Pa,US
189/G3 Sugar Valley, Tx,US
121/E2 Sugauli, India
125/C4 Sugbai (chan.), Phil.
70/D3 Sugenheim, Ger.
114/E3 Süget, China
104/C2 Suğla (lake), Turk.
95/P5 Sugoyak, Rus.
125/B4 Sugut (riv.), Malay.
125/B4 Sugut, Tanjong (cape), Malay.
107/G4 Şuhār, Oman
108/F1 Sühbaatar, Mong.
70/D1 Suhl, Ger.
67/H3 Suhlendorf, Ger.
104/B2 Şuhut, Turk.
123/B4 Sui (pt.), Thai.
170/B1 Suia-Missu (riv.), Braz.
109/L2 Suibin, China
119/K2 Suichuan, China
109/L3 Suifenhe, China
109/K2 Suihua, China
116/D2 Suijiang, China
109/K2 Suileng, China
115/D4 Suining, China
116/E2 Suining, China
174/F2 Suipacha, Arg.
172/C2 Suipacha, Bol.
115/C4 Suiping, China
68/D5 Suippe (riv.), Fr.
68/D5 Suippes, Fr.
60/C5 Suir (riv.), Ire.
146/A3 Suis, Hasy (well), Libya
112/D2 Suishō (isl.), Rus.
205/K10 Suisun (bay), Ca,US
205/K10 Suisun (cr.), Ca,US
205/K10 Suisun City, Ca,US
111/L10 Suita, Japan
206/B6 Suitland-Silver Hill, Md,US
115/D4 Suixi, China
117/F4 Suixi, China
115/C4 Sui Xian, China
117/E3 Suiyang, China
80/B2 Suize (riv.), Fr.
115/E2 Suizhong, China
117/G2 Suizhou, China
108/F3 Suj, China
118/B2 Sūjāngarh, India
113/B2 Sujiatun, China
124/D4 Sukabumi, Indo.
124/D4 Sukadana, Indo.
126/C4 Sukadana (bay), Indo.
111/G2 Sukagawa, Japan
126/D4 Sukamara, Indo.
126/D4 Sukaraja, Indo.
124/D4 Sukarno-Hatta (int'l arpt.), Indo.
125/B4 Sukau, Malay.
113/C3 Sukch'ŏn, NKor.
121/H4 Sukhcharer Hāt, Bang.
122/B2 Sukheke, Pak.
93/G4 Sukhindol, Bul.
96/E1 Sukhinichi, Rus.
97/J1 Sukhodol, Rus.
63/N1 Sukhodol'skoye (lake), Rus.
94/J4 Sukhona (riv.), Rus.
123/B2 Sukhothai, Thai.
123/B2 Sukhothai (ruins), Thai.
53/H4 Sukhumi, Geo.
107/J3 Sukkur, Pak.
93/J2 Sukleya, Mol.
92/D2 Sükösd, Hun.
110/C4 Sukumo, Japan
166/D3 Sul (chan.), Braz.
117/G3 Sul (riv.), China
127/G4 Sula (isls.), Indo.
95/L2 Sula (riv.), Rus.
99/G2 Sula (riv.), Ukr.
183/H5 Sula, Mt,US
107/J3 Sulaimān (range), Pak.
97/H4 Sulak, Rus.
104/C1 Sulakyurt, Turk.
108/F3 Sulanheer, Mong.
127/E4 Sulawesi (Celebes) (isl.), Indo.
130/A1 Sulawesi Tenggara (prov.), Indo.
141/X17 Sulaymān, Tun.
147/F4 Sulb Temple (ruins), Sudan
56/D3 Sulby (riv.), IM,UK
105/H2 Sūldeh, Iran
65/H2 Sulechów, Pol.
65/H2 Sulęcin, Pol.
145/G4 Suleja, Nga.
65/K3 Sulejów, Pol.
65/L2 Sulejówek, Pol.
73/B3 Šulekovo, Slvk.
95/N5 Suleya, Rus.
81/F2 Sulgen, Swi.
124/C3 Suliki, Indo.
93/J3 Sulina, Rom.
67/F3 Sulingen, Ger.
108/D4 Sulin Gol (riv.), China
61/F2 Sulitjelma (peak), Nor.
168/A2 Sullana, Peru
60/A6 Sullane (riv.), Ire.
200/C4 Sulligent, Al,US
183/J2 Sullivan (lake), Ab,Can
193/K4 Sullivan, Il,US
198/C5 Sullivan, In,US
191/J1 Sullivan, Mo,US
208/E5 Sullivan, Oh,US
205/N13 Sullivan, Wi,US
58/C4 Sully, Wal,UK
193/H3 Sully, Ia,US
74/E3 Sully-sur-Loire, Fr.
85/D3 Sulmona, It.
191/G4 Sulphur (riv.), Ar, Tx,US
202/B2 Sulphur, La,US
184/D3 Sulphur, Nv,US
191/F3 Sulphur, Ok,US
194/C5 Sulphur (cr.), SD,US
190/C4 Sulphur Draw (stream), Tx,US
187/H4 Sulphur Springs (val.), Az,US
204/A2 Sulphur Springs, Ca,US
189/G1 Sulphur Springs, Tx,US
190/C4 Sulphur Springs Draw (cr.), Tx,US
205/D2 Sultan, Wa,US
205/D2 Sultan (cr.), Wa,US
104/B2 Sultandağı, Turk.
151/B2 Sultan Hamud, Kenya
125/D4 Sultan Kudarat, Phil.
120/D2 Sultānpur, India
122/C2 Sultānpur, India
125/C4 Sulu (sea), Malay., Phil.
125/C4 Sulu (arch.), Phil.
104/C2 Sülüklü, Turk.
104/C1 Suluova, Turk.
146/D2 Sulūq, Libya
69/G2 Sülz (riv.), Ger.
71/E4 Sulz (riv.), Ger.
80/E2 Sulz, Swi.
70/D4 Sulzach (riv.), Ger.
70/B6 Sulz am Neckar, Ger.
69/G5 Sulzbach, Ger.
71/F6 Sulzbach (riv.), Ger.
70/C3 Sulzbach am Main, Ger.
70/C4 Sulzbach an der Murr, Ger.
71/E4 Sulzbach-Rosenberg, Ger.
81/G2 Sulzberg, Ger.
137/P Sulzberger (bay), Ant.
137/Q Sulzberger Ice Shelf, Ant.
80/D2 Sulzburg, Ger.
81/F3 Sulzfluh (peak), Aus.
70/D3 Sulzheim, Ger.
92/E3 Šumadija (reg.), Yugo.
172/D4 Sumampa, Arg.
125/B4 Sumangat, Tanjong (cape), Malay.
164/C4 Sumapaz Nat'l Park, Col.
92/C4 Sumartin, Cro.
182/C3 Sumas, Wa,US
124/C3 Sumatera Barat (prov.), Indo.
124/D3 Sumatera Selatan (prov.), Indo.
124/B2 Sumatera Utara (prov.), Indo.
124/D3 Sumatra (isl.), Indo.
203/F2 Sumatra, Fl,US
166/A4 Sumaúma, Braz.
71/G4 Sumava (uplands), Czh.
126/E5 Sumba (isl.), Indo.
127/E5 Sumba (str.), Indo.
152/D2 Sumba (isl.), Zaire
97/L5 Sumbar (riv.), Trkm.
126/E5 Sumbawa (isl.), Indo.
127/E5 Sumbawa Besar, Indo.
153/G4 Sumbawanga, Tanz.
168/D4 Sumbay, Peru
152/C5 Sumbe, Ang.
108/F2 Sümber, Mong.
152/C4 Sumbi, Zaire
124/E4 Sumbing (mtn.), Indo.
55/P13 Sumburgh Head (pt.), Sc,UK
144/C5 Sumbuya, SLeo.
177/M4 Sumdum (mtn.), Ak,US
167/G4 Sumé, Braz.
73/B6 Sümeg, Hun.
124/F4 Sumenep, Indo.
53/H4 Sumgait, Azer.
80/D3 Sumiswald, Swi.
200/D4 Sumiton, Al,US
198/C2 Summer (isl.), Mi,US
184/C2 Summer (lake), Or,US
182/E4 Summer (falls), Wa,US
57/G3 Summer Bridge, Eng,UK
154/C4 Summerdown, Namb.
189/H1 Summerfield, La,US
191/G3 Summerfield, Ok,US
184/C2 Summer Lake, Or,US
204/A2 Summerland, Ca,US
203/H5 Summerland Key, Fl,US
196/F2 Summerside, PE,Can
200/E2 Summersville, Ky,US
191/J2 Summersville, Mo,US
201/G1 Summersville, WV,US
201/G4 Summerton, SC,US
201/F4 Summertown, Ga,US
200/D3 Summertown, Tn,US
197/L1 Summerville, Nf,Can
200/E3 Summerville, Ga,US
201/G4 Summerville, SC,US
190/A2 Summit (peak), Co,US
202/C2 Summit, Ms,US
206/D2 Summit, NJ,US
208/F5 Summit (co.), Oh,US
191/G3 Summit, Ok,US
187/F2 Summit, Ut,US
206/C4 Summit Bridge, De,US
206/C2 Summit Hill, Pa,US
198/B2 Summit Lake, Wi,US
184/D3 Summit Lake Ind. Res., Nv,US
208/G6 Summitville, Oh,US
200/E3 Summitville, Tn,US
193/H2 Sumner, Ia,US
191/H1 Sumner, Mo,US
200/B4 Sumner, Ms,US
190/B3 Sumner (lake), NM,US
205/C3 Sumner, Wa,US
110/D3 Sumoto, Japan
127/E4 Sumpangbinangae, Indo.
65/J4 Šumperk, Czh.
119/G2 Sumprabum, Burma
191/H4 Sumpter, Ar,US
202/D2 Sumrall, Ms,US
94/G2 Sumskiy Posad, Rus.
202/L6 Sumter (co.), Fl,US
201/G4 Sumter, SC,US
124/C3 Sumurup, Indo.
99/H2 Sumy, Ukr.
99/G2 Sumy Obl., Ukr.
116/B4 Sun (peak), Burma
183/H4 Sun (riv.), Mt,US
112/B2 Sunagawa, Japan
122/C2 Sunām, India
121/H3 Sunāmganj, Bang.
111/M9 Sunami, Japan
113/C3 Sunan, NKor.
199/K3 Sunapee, NH,US
185/J3 Sunbeam, Co,US
185/F1 Sunbeam, Id,US
200/E2 Sunbright, Tn,US
183/J3 Sunburst, Mt,US
194/D4 Sunburst Lake Nat'l Wild. Ref., ND,US
135/C3 Sunbury, Austl.
53/M7 Sunbury, Eng,UK
201/J2 Sunbury, NC,US
206/B2 Sunbury, Pa,US
59/F4 Sunbury on Thames, Eng,UK
172/D4 Sunchales, Arg.
113/D5 Sunch'ang, SKor.
182/G1 Sunchild Ind. Res., Ab,Can
172/D3 Suncho Corral, Arg.
113/C3 Sunch'ŏn, NKor.
113/D5 Sunch'ŏn, SKor.
156/D2 Sun City, SAfr.
187/F4 Sun City, Az,US
204/C3 Sun City, Ca,US
202/L8 Sun City, Fl,US
202/L8 Sun City Center, Fl,US
187/F4 Sun City West, Az,US
199/L3 Suncook, NH,US
102/J10 Sunda (isls.), Indo.
124/D4 Sunda (str.), Indo.
192/B1 Sundance, Wy,US
121/G5 Sundarbans (reg.), Bang., India
120/E4 Sundargarh, India
122/D2 Sundarnagar, India
156/D4 Sundays (riv.), SAfr.
199/G2 Sunderland, On,Can
57/G2 Sunderland, Eng,UK
67/F6 Sundern, Ger.
80/D1 Sundhouse, Fr.
152/C4 Sundi-Mamba, Zaire
194/F3 Sundown, Mb,Can
190/C4 Sundown, Tx,US
135/D1 Sundown Nat'l Park, Austl.
183/G2 Sundre, Ab,Can
62/C3 Sunds, Den.
61/F3 Sundsvall, Swe.
63/R7 Sundyberg, Swe.
190/C1 Sunflower (mtn.), Ks,US
200/B4 Sunflower, Ms,US
124/C2 Sungaiapit, Indo.
124/D3 Sungaigerong, Indo.
124/C2 Sungaiguntung, Indo.
123/C5 Sungai Kolok, Thai.
124/C2 Sungai Lembing, Malay.
124/D3 Sungailiat, Indo.
124/C2 Sungaipakning, Indo.
124/C3 Sungaipenuh, Indo.
124/C1 Sungai Petani, Malay.
126/D4 Sungaipinang, Indo.
124/C3 Sungaisalak, Indo.
124/D3 Sungaiselan, Indo.
124/C1 Sungai Siput, Malay.
113/C3 Sŭngho, NKor.
113/D5 Sŭngju, SKor.
124/D3 Sungsang, Indo.
113/D3 Sŭngt'ong-ni, NKor.
93/H4 Sungurlare, Bul.
104/C1 Sungurlu, Turk.
115/C3 Suning, China
113/D1 Sunjiapuzi, China
203/G4 Sunken Gardens, Fl,US
121/F2 Sun Kosi (riv.), Nepal
204/F7 Sunland, Ca,US
187/J5 Sunland Park, NM,US
61/D3 Sunndalsøra, Nor.
62/E2 Sunne, Swe.
59/F4 Sunninghill, Eng,UK
183/J2 Sunnynook, Ab,Can
201/H3 Sunny Point Ordinance Dep., NC,US
197/L2 Sunnyside, Nf,Can
204/C5 Sunnyside, Ca,US
203/F2 Sunnyside, Fl,US
203/G2 Sunnyside, Ga,US
205/P15 Sunnyside, Il,US
182/E4 Sunnyside, Wa,US
200/D5 Sunny South, Al,US
205/K12 Sunnyvale, Ca,US
188/L7 Sunnyvale, Tx,US
205/L11 Sunol, Ca,US
111/H8 Su-no-saki (cape), Japan
193/K2 Sun Prairie, Wi,US
190/D2 Sunray, Tx,US
203/H4 Sunrise, Fl,US
206/D1 Sunrise (mtn.), NJ,US
202/B2 Sunset, La,US
189/F1 Sunset, Tx,US
204/B3 Sunset Beach, Ca,US
135/B2 Sunset Country (reg.), Austl.
187/G3 Sunset Crater Nat'l Mon., Az,US
135/F5 Sunshine, Austl.
202/C2 Sunshine, La,US
190/B4 Sunspot, NM,US
101/M3 Suntar, Rus.
101/P3 Suntar-Khayata (mts.), Rus.
67/G4 Süntel (mts.), Ger.
149/H3 Suntu, Eth.
204/F7 Sun Valley, Ca,US
109/K2 Sunwu, China
145/E5 Sunyani, Gha.
153/G5 Sunzu (peak), Zam.
110/B4 Suo (sea), Japan
123/D1 Suoi Rut, Viet.
63/L1 Suomenlinna, Fin.
61/H3 Suomenselkä (reg.), Fin.
123/D4 Suong, Camb.
94/G3 Suoyarvi, Rus.
187/F2 Supai, Az,US
167/L6 Supatá, Col.
121/F2 Supaul, India
199/J5 Supawna Meadows Nat'l Wild. Ref., NJ,US
168/B3 Supe, Peru
181/J2 Superior (lake), Can., US
187/G4 Superior, Az,US
182/G4 Superior, Mt,US
192/E3 Superior, Ne,US
195/H4 Superior, Wi,US
195/J4 Superior (upland), Wi,US
185/J3 Superior, Wy,US
187/G4 Superstition (mts.), Az,US
90/E1 Supetar, Cro.
123/C3 Suphan Buri, Thai.
167/K6 Supía, Col.
84/D4 Supino, It.
127/J4 Supiori (isl.), Indo.
113/C2 Sup'ung (res.), China, NKor.
113/C2 Sup'ung (dam), NKor.
150/B2 Sūq 'Abs, Yem.
105/F4 Sūq ash Shuyūkh, Iraq
103/E2 Şuqaylabīyah, Syria
115/D4 Suqian, China
205/B2 Suquamish, Wa,US
175/F3 Sur (pt.), Arg.
69/E4 Sûr (riv.), Belg.
71/F7 Sur (riv.), Ger.
107/G4 Şūr, Oman
186/B2 Sur (pt.), Ca,US
97/H1 Sura (riv.), Rus.
150/C3 Sura (cape), Som.
124/F4 Surabaya, Indo.
118/D4 Surada, India
62/G2 Surahammar, Swe.
124/E4 Surakarta, Indo.
105/G1 Surakhany, Azer.
125/D4 Surallah, Phil.
122/G3 Sūramangalam, India
80/B5 Suran (riv.), Fr.
73/C3 Šurany, Slvk.
134/C4 Surat, Austl.
118/B3 Surat, India
118/B2 Suratgarh, India
123/B4 Surat Thani, Thai.
63/P4 Surazh, Bela.
96/E1 Surazh, Rus.
69/G6 Surbourg, Fr.
175/J7 Sur, Campo de Hielo (glacier), Chile
92/E3 Surčin, Yugo.
92/F4 Surdulica, Yugo.
69/E4 Sûre (riv.), Belg., Lux.
82/B3 Sure (riv.), Fr.
151/C1 Sure, Lach (dry riv.), Kenya
118/B3 Surendranagar, India
201/J3 Surf City, NC,US
207/D4 Surf City, NJ,US
202/P8 Surfside, Fl,US
201/H4 Surfside Beach, SC,US
74/C3 Surgères, Fr.
201/F2 Surgoinsville, Tn,US
100/H3 Surgut, Rus.
121/F4 Sūri, India
77/F2 Súria, Sp.
125/D3 Surigao, Phil.
123/C3 Surin, Thai.
166/B1 Suriname
166/C2 Suriname (riv.), Sur.
193/K1 Suring, Wi,US
164/D3 Suripa, Ven.
120/C1 Surkhet, Nepal
114/A4 Surkhob (riv.), Taj.
121/H3 Surma (riv.), Bang.
146/B1 Şurmān, Libya
99/M3 Surovikino, Rus.
187/F4 Surprise, Az,US
206/B6 Surrattsville (Clinton), Md,US
142/A3 Sur Reina Sofia (int'l arpt.), Canl.
182/C3 Surrey, BC,Can
53/M8 Surrey (co.), Eng,UK
194/D3 Surrey, ND,US
201/J2 Surry, Va,US
80/E3 Sursee, Swi.
97/H1 Sursk, Rus.
95/K5 Surskoye, Rus.
146/C2 Surt, Libya
62/E3 Surte, Swe.
61/D3 Sur-Trøndelag (co.), Nor.
103/D3 Şūr (Tyre), Leb.
104/D2 Sürüç, Turk.
111/F3 Suruga (bay), Japan
124/C3 Surulangun, Indo.
165/F4 Surumu (riv.), Braz.
125/D4 Surup, Phil.
133/F3 Surveyor General's Corner, Austl.
53/T9 Survilliers, Fr.
165/F3 Surwakwima (falls), Guy.
67/E3 Surwold, Ger.
167/M6 Susa, Col.
82/D2 Susa, It.
141/X18 Sūsah, Tun.
90/B5 Sūsah (gov.), Tun.
110/C4 Susaki, Japan
184/C3 Susan (riv.), Ca,US
144/A3 Susana, GBis.
105/G4 Sūsangerd, Iran
63/P2 Susanino, Rus.
184/C3 Susanville, Ca,US
87/F1 Susegana, It.
104/D1 Suşehri, Turk.
115/B4 Sushui (riv.), China
71/G4 Sušice, Czh.
177/J3 Susitna (riv.), Ak,US
115/D5 Susong, China
111/F3 Susono, Japan
206/B4 Susquehanna (riv.), US
206/B5 Susquehanna Nat'l Wild. Ref., Md,US
206/A1 Susquehanna, West Branch (riv.), Pa,US
172/C2 Susques, Arg.
72/B4 Süsser (lake), Ger.
196/E3 Sussex, NB,Can
206/C6 Sussex (co.), De,US
206/D1 Sussex, NJ,US
206/D1 Sussex (co.), NJ,US
201/J2 Sussex, Va,US
185/K2 Sussex, Wy,US
196/E3 Sussex Corner, NB,Can
135/D2 Sussex Inlet, Austl.
59/F4 Sussex, Vale of (vall.), Eng,UK
81/E4 Sustenhorn (peak), Swi.
81/E4 Sustenpass (pass), Swi.
66/C6 Susteren, Neth.
127/F4 Susua, Indo.
101/Q3 Susuman, Rus.
104/B2 Susurluk, Turk.
65/K2 Susz, Pol.
164/C3 Sutamarchán, Col.
104/B2 Sütçüler, Turk.
134/H9 Sutherland, Austl.
136/A4 Sutherland (falls), N.Z.
156/C4 Sutherland, SAfr.
193/G2 Sutherland, Ia,US
192/D3 Sutherland, Ne,US
184/B2 Sutherlin, Or,US
92/D4 Sutjeska Nat'l Park, Bosn.
122/B2 Sutlej (riv.), India
122/B2 Sutlej (riv.), Pak.
93/H5 Sütlücc, Turk.
84/C3 Sutri, It.
205/L9 Sutter (co.), Ca,US
186/B1 Sutter Creek, Ca,US
57/H6 Sutterton, Eng,UK
199/K2 Sutton, Can.
196/A3 Sutton, Qu,Can
53/N7 Sutton, Eng,UK
53/N7 Sutton (bor.), Eng,UK
177/J3 Sutton, Ak,US
208/C1 Sutton, Ma,US
192/F3 Sutton, Ne,US
201/G1 Sutton, WV,US
57/J6 Sutton Bridge, Eng,UK
59/E1 Sutton Coldfield, Eng,UK
57/G5 Sutton in Ashfield, Eng,UK
57/J5 Sutton on Sea, Eng,UK
57/H5 Sutton on Trent, Eng,UK
112/B2 Suttsu, Japan
63/K2 Suur (str.), Est.
156/D4 Suurberge (mts.), SAfr.
156/C4 Suurbraak, SAfr.
63/L2 Suure-Jaani, Est.
138/G6 Suva (cap.), Fiji
63/L3 Suvainiškis, Lith.
139/Y18 Suva (Nausori) (int'l arpt.), Fiji
93/H4 Suvorovo, Bul.
150/B2 Suwa, Eth.
111/F2 Suwa, Japan
65/M1 Suwałki, Pol.
65/M2 Suwałki (prov.), Pol.
201/M6 Suwanee, Ga,US
119/H4 Suwannaphum, Thai.
203/G3 Suwannee, Fl,US
203/G3 Suwannee (riv.), Fl,US
112/K6 Suwanose (isl.), Japan
139/J6 Suwarrow (isl.), CookIs.
103/D3 Şuwaylih, Jor.
113/D4 Suwŏn, SKor.
113/G7 Suwŏn (arpt.), SKor.
168/B2 Suyo, Peru
80/D3 Suze (riv.), Swi.
82/A4 Suze-la-Rousse, Fr.
99/H1 Suzemka, Rus.
115/D4 Suzhou, China
115/E5 Suzhou, China
113/C2 Suzi (riv.), China
82/B2 Suzon (riv.), Fr.
111/E2 Suzu, Japan
110/E3 Suzuka, Japan
111/M10 Suzuka (range), Japan
111/M10 Suzuka (riv.), Japan
111/E2 Suzu-misaki (cape), Japan
87/D3 Suzzara, It.
100/C2 Svalbard (arch.), Nor.
63/U9 Svalöv, Swe.
98/B3 Svalyava, Ukr.
62/F4 Svaneke, Den.
62/F3 Svängsta, Swe.
61/G2 Svanstein, Swe.
63/R7 Svartsjölandet (isl.), Swe.
71/F2 Svatava (riv.), Czh.
99/K3 Svatovo, Ukr.
123/D4 Svay Rieng, Camb.
62/F2 Svealand (reg.), Swe.
62/E4 Svedala, Swe.
63/L4 Svėdasai, Lith.
61/E3 Sveg, Swe.
62/A2 Sveio, Nor.
62/C3 Svejbæk, Den.
63/J4 Švėkšna, Lith.
62/D2 Svelvik, Nor.
96/E1 Sven', Rus.
63/M4 Švenčionėliai, Lith.
63/M4 Švenčionys, Lith.
62/D4 Svendborg, Den.
179/S7 Svendsen (pen.), NW,Can
62/C2 Svenes, Nor.
62/E3 Svenljunga, Swe.
182/C4 Svensen, Or,US
62/C3 Svenstrup, Den.
97/H2 Sverdlovo, Rus.
99/K3 Sverdlovsk, Ukr.
95/P4 Sverdlovsk (Yekaterinburg), Rus.
179/S7 Sverdrup (chan.), NW,Can
179/R7 Sverdrup (isls.), NW,Can
100/H2 Sverdrup (isl.), Rus.
85/F1 Svetae (isl.), Cro.
109/M2 Svetlaya, Rus.
96/D1 Svetlogorsk, Bela.
63/J4 Svetlogorsk, Rus.
65/L1 Svetlogorsk, Rus.
99/M5 Svetlograd, Rus.
99/G3 Svetlovodsk, Ukr.
63/J4 Svetlyy, Rus.
97/H2 Svetlyy Yar, Rus.
63/N1 Svetogorsk, Rus.
92/E4 Svetozarevo, Yugo.
61/P7 Svíahnúkar (peak), Ice.
92/E3 Svilajnac, Yugo.
93/H5 Svilengrad, Bul.
63/Q1 Sviritsa, Rus.
108/E1 Svirsk, Rus.
93/G4 Svishtov, Bul.
63/N5 Svisloch', Bela.
65/J4 Svitavy, Czh.
109/K1 Svobodnyy, Rus.
93/F4 Svoge, Bul.
61/E1 Svolvær, Nor.
73/A2 Svratka (riv.), Czh.
92/F4 Svrljig, Yugo.
99/M2 Svyatoslavka, Rus.
101/Q2 Svyatyy Nos (cape), Rus.
59/E1 Swadlincote, Eng,UK
59/G1 Swaffham, Eng,UK
134/D3 Swain (reefs), Austl.
139/H5 Swains (isl.), ASam.
201/F4 Swainsboro, Ga,US
152/D4 Swa-Kibula, Zaire
154/B4 Swakop (dry riv.), Namb.
154/B4 Swakopmund, Namb.
57/G3 Swale (riv.), Eng,UK
59/H4 Swalecliffe, Eng,UK
59/G4 Swale, The (chan.), Eng,UK
201/H1 Swallow (falls), Md,US
66/D6 Swalmen, Neth.
133/G2 Swan (peak), Austl.
132/K7 Swan (riv.), Austl.
178/E3 Swan (range), Ab,Can
194/D1 Swan (lake), Mb,Can
194/C1 Swan (riv.), Mb, Sk,Can
161/F2 Swan (isls.), Hon.
184/E2 Swan (falls), Id,US
205/F7 Swan (cr.), Mi,US
193/G1 Swan (lake), Mn,US
183/H3 Swan (range), Mt,US
59/E5 Swanage, Eng,UK
135/B2 Swan Hill, Austl.
183/H4 Swan Lake, Mt,US
191/H1 Swan Lake Nat'l Wild. Ref., Mo,US
53/P7 Swanley, Eng,UK
59/G4 Swanley Hextable, Eng,UK
60/C1 Swanlinbar, Ire.
201/F3 Swannanoa, NC,US
205/F7 Swan, North Branch (cr.), Mi,US
194/C1 Swan Plain, Sk,Can
201/J3 Swanquarter, NC,US
201/J3 Swanquarter Nat'l Wild. Ref., NC,US
133/H5 Swan Reach, Austl.
194/D1 Swan River, Mb,Can
183/H4 Swan River Nat'l Wild. Ref., Mt,US
196/C3 Swans (isl.), Me,US
53/P7 Swanscombe, Eng,UK
135/D4 Swansea, Austl.
58/C3 Swansea, Wal,UK
58/C3 Swansea (bay), Wal,UK
193/K4 Swansea, Il,US
208/C2 Swansea, Ma,US
196/C3 Swans Island, Me,US
192/D3 Swanson (res.), Ne,US
198/E4 Swanton, Oh,US
199/K2 Swanton, Vt,US
195/G5 Swanville, Mn,US
206/C4 Swarthmore, Pa,US
156/D3 Swart Kei (riv.), SAfr.
156/D2 Swartruggens, SAfr.
206/D1 Swartswood (lake), NJ,US
205/E6 Swartz (cr.), Mi,US
198/E3 Swartz Creek, Mi,US
65/J2 Swarzędz, Pol.
71/E2 Swarzenbach an der Sächsischen Saale, Ger.
156/B2 Swarzrand (mts.), Namb.
195/H4 Swatara, Mn,US
206/B3 Swatara (cr.), Pa,US
56/B2 Swatragh, NI,UK
182/D4 Swauk (pass), Wa,US
59/E5 Sway, Eng,UK
121/E2 Swayambhunath, Nepal
157/E2 Swaziland
61/E3 Sweden
206/C4 Swedesboro, NJ,US
145/E5 Swedru, Gha.
189/G3 Sweeny, Tx,US
131/E4 Sweers (isl.), Austl.
183/K1 Sweet Grass Ind. Res., Sk,Can
184/B1 Sweet Home, Or,US
189/F3 Sweet Home, Tx,US
191/H1 Sweet Springs, Mo,US
200/D4 Sweet Water, Al,US
204/D5 Sweetwater (res.), Ca,US
204/C5 Sweetwater (riv.), Ca,US
202/P8 Sweetwater, Fl,US
194/E3 Sweetwater (lake), ND,US
190/E3 Sweetwater, Ok,US
200/E3 Sweetwater, Tn,US
188/D1 Sweetwater, Tx,US
185/J2 Sweetwater (riv.), Wy,US
156/C4 Swellendam, SAfr.
65/J3 Świdnica, Pol.
65/M3 Świdnik, Pol.
65/H2 Świdwin, Pol.
65/J3 Świebodzice, Pol.
65/H2 Świebozin, Pol.
65/K2 Świecie, Pol.
182/C1 Swift (riv.), BC,Can
183/L2 Swift Current, Sk,Can
66/C3 Swifterbant, Neth.
191/J3 Swifton, Ar,US
200/B4 Swiftown, Ms,US
135/C3 Swifts Creek, Austl.
55/H9 Swilly, Lough (inlet), Ire.
207/D3 Swimming River (res.), NJ,US
59/E3 Swindon, Eng,UK
57/H6 Swineshead, Eng,UK
60/B2 Swinford, Ire.
182/C3 Swinomish Ind. Res., Wa,US
65/H2 Świnoujście, Pol.
57/G5 Swinton, Eng,UK
80/D4 Swiss (plat.), Swi.
193/K2 Swiss Hist. Vill., Wi,US
184/B1 Swisshome, Or,US
69/F2 Swist Bach (riv.), Ger.
80/D4 Switzerland
81/G4 Switzerland Nat'l Park, Swi.
79/E2 Sword Beach, Fr.
60/D3 Swords, Ire.
206/C1 Swoyersville, Pa,US
121/E1 Syābru, Nepal
94/G3 Syamozero (lake), Rus.
63/Q1 Syas'stroy, Rus.
95/K4 Syava, Rus.
83/C3 Sybaris-Copia (ruins), It.
200/D4 Sycamore, Al,US
203/G2 Sycamore, Ga,US
193/K3 Sycamore, Il,US
184/C2 Sycan (riv.), Or,US
65/J3 Syców, Pol.
135/D2 Sydney, Austl.
135/D2 Sydney (int'l arpt.), Austl.
197/G2 Sydney, NS,Can
194/E4 Sydney, ND,US
134/H8 Sydney-Kingsford Smith (int'l arpt.), Austl.
139/H5 Sydney (Manra) (isl.), Kiri.
197/G2 Sydney Mines, NS,Can
67/F3 Syke, Ger.
194/E4 Sykeston, ND,US
206/B5 Sykesville, Md,US
53/J2 Syktyvkar, Rus.
200/D4 Sylacauga, Al,US
61/E3 Sylarna (peak), Swe.
121/H3 Sylhet, Bang.
121/H3 Sylhet (dist.), Bang.
64/E1 Sylt (isl.), Ger.
95/N4 Sylva (riv.), Rus.
201/F3 Sylva, NC,US
191/E1 Sylvan Grove, Ks,US
183/N1 Sylvania, Sk,Can
200/E3 Sylvania, Al,US
201/G4 Sylvania, Ga,US
198/E4 Sylvania, Oh,US
183/G1 Sylvan Lake, Ab,Can
205/F6 Sylvan Lake, Mi,US
81/H2 Sylvenstein-Stausee (lake), Ger.
131/E4 Sylvester (lake), Austl.
203/G2 Sylvester, Ga,US
188/D1 Sylvester, Tx,US
191/E2 Sylvia, Ks,US
130/B4 Synnott (range), Austl.
91/L6 Syntagma Square, Gre.
95/N2 Synya, Rus.
207/E2 Syosset, NY,US
137/C Syowa, Ant.
198/D4 Syracuse, In,US
190/D2 Syracuse, Ks,US
193/F3 Syracuse, Ne,US
199/H3 Syracuse, NY,US
201/G1 Syracuse, Oh,US
199/H3 Syracuse Hancock (int'l arpt.), NY,US
90/D4 Syracuse (Siracusa), It.
100/G5 Syrdar'ya (riv.), Asia
104/D3 Syria
119/G4 Syriam, Burma
104/D3 Syrian (des.), Asia
96/F1 Syrskiy, Rus.
63/L1 Sysmä, Fin.
95/L3 Sysola (riv.), Rus.
59/E1 Syston, Eng,UK
53/H3 Syzran', Rus.
73/D6 Szabadszállás, Hun.
92/E1 Szabolcs-Szatmár-Bereg (co.), Hun.
65/J2 Szamotuły, Pol.
92/E2 Szarvas, Hun.
73/C5 Százhalombatta, Hun.
65/M3 Szczebrzeszyn, Pol.
65/H2 Szczecin, Pol.
65/H2 Szczecin (prov.), Pol.
65/J2 Szczecinek, Pol.
75/M1 Szczytna, Pol.
65/L2 Szczytno, Pol.
92/E2 Szeged, Hun.
92/E2 Szeghalom, Hun.
92/E2 Szegvár, Hun.
73/C5 Székesfehérvár, Hun.
92/D2 Szekszárd, Hun.
73/D6 Szelidi tó (lake), Hun.
92/E1 Szendro, Hun.
73/D4 Szentendre, Hun.
73/D4 Szentendrei-Duna (riv.), Hun.
73/D4 Szentendrei-sziget (isl.), Hun.
92/E2 Szentes, Hun.
73/A6 Szentgotthárd, Hun.
73/C5 Szent László-vize (riv.), Hun.
92/C2 Szentlorinc, Hun.
92/E1 Szerencs, Hun.
65/M1 Szeskie (peak), Pol.
94/D5 Szeskie Wzgorza (peak), Pol.
73/A6 Szevíz (riv.), Hun.
73/B4 Szigetköz (isl.), Hun.
73/D5 Sziget-Szentmiklós, Hun.
92/C2 Szigetvár, Hun.
73/B5 Szil, Hun.
92/D2 Szirák, Hun.
73/C4 Szob, Hun.
92/E2 Szolnok, Hun.
73/A5 Szombathely, Hun.
65/H3 Szprotawa, Pol.
65/K2 Sztum, Pol.
65/J2 Szubin, Pol.
65/L3 Szydłowiec, Pol.

T

73/C6 Tab, Hun.
125/C2 Tabaco, Phil.
124/F5 Tabanan, Indo.
125/D3 Tabango, Phil.
162/F5 Tabaquite, Trin.
141/W17 Ţabarqah, Tun.
105/J3 Ţabas, Iran
161/F4 Tabasara, Serranía de (range), Pan.
158/E4 Tabasco, Mex.
159/G5 Tabasco (state), Mex.
170/D1 Tabatinga (hills), Braz.
189/N9 Tabbs (bay), Tx,US
151/C1 Tabda, Som.
142/E3 Tabelbala, Alg.
183/H3 Taber, Ab,Can
77/E3 Tabernes de Valldigna, Sp.
138/F5 Tabiang, Kiri.
131/G1 Tabibuga, PNG
124/C3 Tabing (int'l arpt.), Indo.
167/L7 Tabio, Col.
167/G4 Tabira, Braz.
138/G5 Tabiteuea (atoll), Kiri.
135/C2 Tabitta, Austl.
125/C2 Tablas (isl.), Phil.
125/C3 Tablas (str.), Phil.
88/C3 Tablas de Daimiel Nat'l Park, Sp.
60/D3 Table (mtn.), Ire.
136/D2 Table (cape), N.Z.
136/A4 Table (hill), N.Z.
156/B4 Table (bay), SAfr.
156/L10 Table (peak), SAfr.
182/D4 Table (mtn.), Wa,US
130/B4 Tableland, Austl.
191/H2 Table Rock (lake), Ar, Mo,US
191/H2 Table Rock (dam), Mo,US
131/G1 Tabletop, Mount (peak), PNG
145/F5 Tabligbo, Togo
76/B1 Taboada, Sp.
71/H4 Tábor, Czh.
151/A3 Tabora, Tanz.
151/B4 Tabora, Tanz.
151/A3 Tabora (reg.), Tanz.
201/H3 Tabor City, NC,US
144/D5 Tabou, IvC.
100/E6 Tabrīz, Iran
102/D6 Tabriz, Iran
105/F2 Tabrīz, Iran
139/K4 Tabuaeran (Fanning) (isl.), Kiri.
127/K5 Tabubil, PNG
125/C1 Tabuk, Phil.
104/D4 Tabūk, SAr.
167/G4 Tabuleiro do Norte, Braz.
90/A4 Ţaburbah, Tun.
85/E5 Taburno (peak), It.
90/A4 Tabursuq, Tun.
124/B2 Tabuyung, Indo.
138/F6 Tabwemasana (mt.), Van.
63/S6 Täby, Swe.
168/B2 Tacabamba, Peru
160/C3 Tacaná (vol.), Mex.
167/G5 Tacaratu, Braz.
161/G4 Tacarcuna (mtn.), Pan.
114/D2 Tacheng, China
117/J3 Tachia (riv.), Tai.
110/A4 Tachibana (bay), Japan
111/F3 Tachikawa, Japan
71/F7 Tachinger See (lake), Ger.
164/C2 Táchira (state), Ven.
117/J3 Tachoshui, Tai.
71/F3 Tachov, Czh.
83/C4 Tacina (riv.), It.
127/F4 Tacipi, Indo.
125/D3 Tacloban, Phil.
168/D5 Tacna, Peru
187/F4 Tacna, Az,US
172/C1 Tacobamba, Bol.
205/C3 Tacoma, Wa,US
208/A1 Taconic, Ct,US
172/C1 Tacopaya, Bol.
172/B1 Tacora (vol.), Chile
77/X16 Tacoronte, Canl.,Sp.
159/G5 Tacotalpa, Mex.
175/G1 Tacuarembó, Uru.
175/G2 Tacuarembó (dept.), Uru.
158/C2 Tacupeto, Mex.
125/D4 Tacurong, Phil.
165/F4 Tacutu (riv.), Braz., Guy.
111/F2 Tadami (riv.), Japan
111/L10 Tadaoka, Japan
57/G4 Tadcaster, Eng,UK
143/F3 Tademaït (plat.), Alg.
118/D4 Tādepallegūdem, India
139/V12 Tadine, NCal.
150/B3 Tadjoura, Djib.
150/C3 Tadjoura (gulf), Som.

# Tadley – Tefé

59/E4 **Tadley,** Eng,UK
104/D3 **Tadmur,** Syria
164/B3 **Tadó,** Col.
111/M9 **Tado,** Japan
113/C5 **Tadohae Hasang Nat'l Park,** SKor.
110/C3 **Tadotsu,** Japan
196/C1 **Tadoussac,** Qu,Can
118/C5 **Tādpatri,** India
146/A3 **Tadrart** (mts.), Alg., Libya
127/F4 **Taduno,** Indo.
53/N8 **Tadworth,** Eng,UK
145/F5 **Tadzewu,** Gha.
113/D4 **T'aean,** SKor.
113/D2 **T'aebaek** (mts.), NKor., SKor.
113/E4 **T'aebaek,** SKor.
113/F7 **Taebudo** (isl.), SKor.
113/C3 **T'aech'ŏn,** NKor.
113/D4 **Taech'ŏn,** SKor.
113/C4 **Taech'ŏng** (isl.), SKor.
113/D5 **Taedŏk,** SKor.
113/C3 **Taedong,** NKor.
113/D3 **Taedong** (riv.), NKor.
113/D3 **Taegang-got** (pt.), NKor.
113/E5 **Taegu,** SKor.
110/A3 **Taegu** (arpt.), SKor.
113/E5 **Taegu-Jikhalsi,** SKor.
110/A2 **Taegu-jikhalsi** (prov.), SKor.
113/C2 **Taegwan,** NKor.
113/C5 **Taehŭksan** (isl.), SKor.
113/D2 **Taehŭng,** NKor.
113/D5 **T'aein,** SKor.
113/D4 **Taejŏn,** SKor.
113/C2 **Taeryŏng** (riv.), NKor.
113/C3 **T'aet'an,** NKor.
58/B3 **Taf** (riv.), Wal,UK
76/E1 **Tafalla,** Sp.
143/H4 **Tafassasset** (dry riv.), Alg.
143/H5 **Tafassasset, Ténéré du** (reg.), Niger
58/C3 **Taff** (riv.), Wal,UK
144/D4 **Tafiré,** IvC.
172/C3 **Tafí Viejo,** Arg.
123/C1 **Ta Fou San,** Laos
142/C3 **Tafraout,** Mor.
105/G3 **Tafresh,** Iran
105/H4 **Taft,** Iran
125/D3 **Taft,** Phil.
186/C3 **Taft,** Ca,US
202/N7 **Taft,** Fl,US
191/G3 **Taft,** Ok,US
189/F4 **Taft,** Tx,US
107/H3 **Taftān** (mtn.), Iran
111/M9 **Taga,** Japan
121/G2 **Taga Dzong,** Bhu.
53/G4 **Taganrog,** Rus.
99/K4 **Taganrog** (gulf), Rus., Ukr.
144/C2 **Tagant** (reg.), Mrta.
105/J2 **Tagarav** (peak), Trkm.
110/B4 **Tagawa,** Japan
125/C3 **Tagbilaran,** Phil.
86/A5 **Taggia,** It.
143/E3 **Taghit,** Alg.
60/D5 **Taghmon,** Ire.
125/F6 **Tagig,** Phil.
177/M3 **Tagish,** Yk,Can
84/D3 **Tagliacozzo,** It.
87/G1 **Tagliamento** (riv.), It.
87/F2 **Taglio di Po,** It.
68/D5 **Tagnon,** Fr.
125/C3 **Tagolo** (pt.), Phil.
125/D3 **Tagoloan,** Phil.
142/D3 **Tagounit,** Mor.
161/G1 **Taguasco,** Cuba
170/C2 **Taguatinga,** Braz.
170/D2 **Taguatinga,** Braz.
125/C1 **Tagudin,** Phil.
138/E6 **Tagula** (isl.), PNG
125/D4 **Tagum,** Phil.
95/P4 **Tagun** (riv.), Rus.
76/C3 **Tagus** (Tajo) (riv.), Sp.
76/B3 **Tagus** (Tejo) (riv.), Port.
136/B4 **Tahakopa,** N.Z.
124/C1 **Tahan** (peak), Malay.
111/N10 **Tahara,** Japan
143/G5 **Tahat** (peak), Alg.
141/R16 **Tahat, Oued et** (riv.), Alg.
109/J1 **Tahe,** China
139/L6 **Tahenea** (atoll), FrPol.
104/E2 **Tahir** (pass), Turk.
139/L6 **Tahiti** (isl.), FrPol.
63/K2 **Tahkuna** (pt.), Est.
191/G3 **Tahlequah,** Ok,US
135/D2 **Tahmoor,** Austl.
142/D3 **Tahnaout,** Mor.
177/J3 **Tahneta** (pass), Ak,US
184/C4 **Tahoe** (lake), Ca, Nv,US
188/D1 **Tahoka,** Tx,US
182/B4 **Taholah,** Wa,US
145/G3 **Tahoua,** Niger
145/G3 **Tahoua** (dept.), Niger
198/D1 **Tahquamenon** (falls), Mi,US
147/F3 **Taḩtā,** Egypt
169/E4 **Tahua,** Bol.
168/D3 **Tahuamanu,** Peru
168/D3 **Tahuamanu** (riv.), Peru
139/L6 **Tahuata** (isl.), FrPol.
127/G3 **Tahulandang** (isl.), Indo.
125/D5 **Tahuna,** Indo.
205/A3 **Tahuya,** Wa,US
205/B3 **Tahuyo** (riv.), Wa,US
115/L8 **Tai** (lake), China
144/D5 **Taï,** IvC.
144/B4 **Taiama,** SLeo.
113/B2 **Tai'an,** China
115/D3 **Tai'an,** China
115/L8 **Tai'angang,** China
139/X15 **Taiarapu** (pen.), FrPol.
108/F5 **Taibai** (peak), China
115/C3 **Taibai Shan** (mtn.), China
190/B3 **Taiban,** NM,US
108/H3 **Taibus Qi,** China
115/E5 **Taicang,** China
117/J3 **Taichung,** Tai.
136/B4 **Taieri** (riv.), N.Z.
115/C3 **Taigu,** China
115/C3 **Taihang** (mts.), China
136/C2 **Taihape,** N.Z.
115/C4 **Taihe,** China
117/J4 **Taihsi,** Tai.
115/D5 **Taihu,** China
115/C4 **Taikang,** China
112/C2 **Taiki,** Japan
109/J2 **Tailai,** China
124/B3 **Taileleo,** Indo.
133/H5 **Tailem Bend,** Austl.
70/B5 **Tailfingen,** Ger.
111/L10 **Taima,** Japan
54/B1 **Tain,** Sc,UK
117/J4 **Tainan,** Tai.
89/J3 **Taínaron** (cape), Gre.
91/H4 **Taínaron, Ákra** (cape), Gre.
144/D5 **Taï Nat'l Park,** IvC.
86/B1 **Taino,** It.
173/G3 **Taió,** Braz.
171/E2 **Taiobeiras,** Braz.
139/L5 **Taiohae,** FrPol.
102/M7 **Taipei,** Tai.
117/J3 **Taipei** (cap.), Tai.
115/D5 **Taiping,** China
117/F4 **Taiping,** China
117/G1 **Taiping,** China
123/D1 **Taiping,** China
109/J2 **Taiping** (peak), China
124/C1 **Taiping,** Malay.
109/L2 **Taipinggou,** China
113/C2 **Taipingshao,** China
167/H4 **Taipu,** Braz.
124/C4 **Tais,** Indo.
110/C3 **Taisha,** Japan
117/G4 **Taishan,** China
111/L10 **Taishi,** Japan
117/H3 **Taishun,** China
71/G6 **Taiskirchen im Innkreis,** Aus.
68/D5 **Taissy,** Fr.
174/B5 **Taitao** (pen.), Chile
151/A1 **Taiti** (peak), Kenya
117/J4 **Taitung,** Tai.
117/J3 **Taiwan**
117/H4 **Taiwan** (str.), China, Tai.
115/E4 **Tai Xian,** China
115/E4 **Taixing,** China
91/H4 **Taíyetos** (mts.), Gre.
115/C3 **Taiyuan,** China
116/B2 **Taizhao,** China
115/D4 **Taizhou,** China
115/E2 **Taizi** (riv.), China
150/C2 **Ta'izz,** Yem.
126/C4 **Tajam** (peak), Indo.
146/B3 **Tajarhī,** Libya
100/H6 **Tajikistan**
111/F2 **Tajima,** Japan
111/E3 **Tajimi,** Japan
187/J3 **Tajique,** NM,US
111/L10 **Tajiri,** Japan
141/W18 **Tājirwīn,** Tun.
120/A2 **Tāj Mahal,** India
160/D3 **Tajmulco** (vol.), Guat.
76/C3 **Tajo** (Tagus) (riv.), Sp.
120/B1 **Tājpur,** India
105/G3 **Tajrīsh,** Iran
76/D2 **Tajuña** (riv.), Sp.
146/B1 **Tājūrā,** Libya
123/B2 **Tak,** Thai.
105/F2 **Takāb,** Iran
111/G2 **Takahagi,** Japan
110/D3 **Takahama,** Japan
110/C3 **Takahashi,** Japan
110/C3 **Takahashi** (riv.), Japan
111/G2 **Takahata,** Japan
111/L10 **Takaishi,** Japan
136/C3 **Takaka,** N.Z.
166/B1 **Takama,** Guy.
110/D3 **Takamatsu,** Japan
110/D3 **Takamatsu** (arpt.), Japan
111/M10 **Takami-yama** (peak), Japan
110/B4 **Takanabe,** Japan
112/B3 **Takanosu,** Japan
111/E2 **Takaoka,** Japan
136/C2 **Takapau,** N.Z.
136/C2 **Takapuna,** N.Z.
111/L10 **Takarazuka,** Japan
139/L6 **Takaroa** (isl.), FrPol.
111/F2 **Takasaki,** Japan
111/M9 **Takashima,** Japan
111/L10 **Takatori,** Japan
110/D3 **Takatsuki,** Japan
151/B2 **Takaungu,** Kenya
111/E2 **Takayama,** Japan
110/E3 **Takefu,** Japan
110/C3 **Takehara,** Japan
105/G2 **Tākestān,** Iran
110/B4 **Taketa,** Japan
111/M10 **Taketoyo,** Japan
123/D4 **Takev,** Camb.
122/D1 **Takh,** India
118/B2 **Takhatgarh,** India
120/C4 **Takhatpur,** India
119/H4 **Ta Khli,** Thai.
123/C3 **Takhli,** Thai.
123/D4 **Ta Khmau,** Camb.
99/M5 **Takhta,** Rus.
107/H1 **Takhta-Bazar,** Trkm.
109/J1 **Takhtamygda,** Rus.
105/H4 **Takht-e Jamshīd** (ruins), Iran
121/G4 **Tāki,** India
111/M10 **Taki,** Japan
145/H3 **Takiéta,** Niger
178/E2 **Takijuq** (lake), NW,Can
112/B2 **Takikawa,** Japan
124/B1 **Takingeun,** Indo.
111/K10 **Takino,** Japan
114/D4 **Takla Makan** (des.), China
146/D1 **Tāknis,** Libya
145/E5 **Takoradi,** Gha.
141/V17 **Takouch** (cape), Alg.
101/M4 **Taksimo,** Rus.
73/D5 **Taksony,** Hun.
145/H5 **Takum,** Nga.
152/D4 **Takundi,** Zaire
103/B4 **Talā,** Egypt
151/B2 **Tala,** Kenya
175/G2 **Tala,** Uru.
172/B4 **Talacasto,** Arg.
57/E5 **Talacre,** Wal,UK
122/B1 **Talagang,** Pak.
174/Q9 **Talagante,** Chile
141/W18 **Tālah,** Tun.
122/G4 **Talaimannar,** SrL.
118/B3 **Talāja,** India
145/G2 **Talak** (reg.), Niger
191/G2 **Talala,** Ok,US
99/G2 **Talalayevka,** Ukr.
161/F4 **Talamanca, Cordillera de** (range), CR
81/F5 **Talamona,** It.
152/D5 **Tala Mugongo,** Ang.
124/C3 **Talang** (peak), Indo.
160/E3 **Talanga,** Hon.
124/D4 **Talangbatu,** Indo.
124/D3 **Talangbetutu,** Indo.
69/F5 **Talange,** Fr.
80/A3 **Talant,** Fr.
168/A2 **Talara,** Peru
114/B3 **Talas** (riv.), Kaz.
114/B3 **Talas,** Kyr.
104/C2 **Talas,** Turk.
157/H8 **Talata Ampano,** Madg.
145/G3 **Talata Mafara,** Nga.
125/D4 **Talaud** (isls.), Indo.
76/C3 **Talavera de la Reina,** Sp.
76/B3 **Talavera la Real,** Sp.
118/D6 **Talawakele,** SrL.
149/F3 **Talawdī,** Sudan
116/C3 **Talawgyi,** Burma
158/C2 **Talayotes,** Mex.
76/C3 **Talayuela,** Sp.
135/D2 **Talbingo,** Austl.
128/D2 **Talbot** (cape), Austl.
132/E3 **Talbot** (peak), Austl.
183/J1 **Talbot,** Ab,Can
206/B6 **Talbot** (co.), Md,US
200/E4 **Talbotton,** Ga,US
174/C2 **Talca,** Chile
174/B3 **Talcahuano,** Chile
118/E3 **Tālcher,** India
145/F3 **Talcho,** Niger
189/G1 **Talco,** Tx,US
201/G2 **Talcott,** WV,US
208/B2 **Talcottville,** Ct,US
109/J1 **Taldan,** Rus.
97/J2 **Taldykuduk,** Kaz.
114/C3 **Taldy-Kurgan,** Kaz.
150/D3 **Taleex,** Som.
74/C4 **Talence,** Fr.
80/C4 **Talent** (riv.), Swi.
184/B2 **Talent,** Or,US
105/G2 **Tālesh,** Iran
81/H4 **Talfer** (Talvera) (riv.), It.
100/H5 **Talgar,** Kaz.
58/C3 **Talgarth,** Wal,UK
127/F4 **Taliabu** (isl.), Indo.
122/B2 **Tālibwāla,** Pak.
191/G3 **Talihina,** Ok,US
97/G4 **Talin,** Arm.
172/B3 **Talinay Nat'l Park,** Chile
142/D3 **Taliouine,** Mor.
125/C4 **Talipaw,** Phil.
149/F4 **Tali Post,** Sudan
127/E3 **Talisayan,** Indo.
125/D3 **Talisayan,** Phil.
95/P4 **Talitsa,** Rus.
127/E5 **Taliwang,** Indo.
63/N5 **Tal'ka,** Bela.
177/H3 **Talkeetna,** Ak,US
103/B4 **Ţalkhā,** Egypt
105/G3 **Ţālkhūncheh,** Iran
104/D2 **Tall Abyaḑ,** Syria
200/D4 **Talladega,** Al,US
104/E2 **Tall 'Afar,** Iraq
60/D3 **Tallaght,** Ire.
202/D2 **Tallahala** (cr.), Ms,US
203/F2 **Tallahassee** (cap.), Fl,US
200/B3 **Tallahatchie** (riv.), Ms,US
135/C3 **Tallangatta,** Austl.
60/D2 **Tallanstown,** Ire.
200/E4 **Tallapoosa** (riv.), Al, Ga,US
200/E4 **Tallapoosa,** Ga,US
82/C4 **Tallard,** Fr.
200/E4 **Tallassee,** Al,US
103/G8 **Tall 'Āsūr** (Ba'al Hazor) (mtn.), WBnk.
132/B4 **Tallering** (peak), Austl.
206/C4 **Talleyville,** De,US
63/L2 **Tallinn** (cap.), Est.
103/E2 **Tall Kalakh,** Syria
105/E2 **Tall Kayf,** Iraq
104/E2 **Tall Kūjik,** Syria
208/F5 **Tallmadge,** Oh,US
80/C6 **Talloires,** Fr.
60/C5 **Tallow,** Ire.
202/C1 **Tallulah,** La,US
185/H3 **Talmage,** Ut,US
87/G1 **Talmassons,** It.
195/H4 **Talmoon,** Mn,US
98/F3 **Tal'noye,** Ukr.
149/H3 **Talo** (peak), Eth.
118/B3 **Taloda,** India
190/E2 **Taloga,** Ok,US
107/J1 **Tāloqān,** Afg.
99/L2 **Talovaya,** Rus.
158/D4 **Talpa,** Mex.
188/E2 **Talpa,** Tx,US
63/K3 **Talsi,** Lat.
71/F1 **Talsperre Pöhl** (res.), Ger.
172/B3 **Taltal,** Chile
178/E2 **Taltson** (riv.), NW,Can
188/L7 **Talty,** Tx,US
124/C3 **Taluk,** Indo.
127/E3 **Talukbayur,** Indo.
123/C4 **Talumphuk** (pt.), Thai.
78/B5 **Talut, Pointe du** (pt.), Fr.
81/H4 **Talvera** (Talfer) (riv.), It.
122/C2 **Talwandi Bhāi,** India
122/C2 **Talwāra,** India
99/L3 **Taly,** Rus.
111/H7 **Tama,** Japan
111/H7 **Tama** (riv.), Japan
125/A5 **Tama Abu** (ra.), Malay.
111/H7 **Tama-Chichibu Nat'l Park,** Japan
111/H6 **Tamagawa,** Japan
191/G3 **Tamaha,** Ok,US
111/M10 **Tamaki,** Japan
136/G6 **Tamaki** (str.), N.Z.
164/C2 **Tamalameque,** Col.
145/E4 **Tamale,** Gha.
99/J5 **Taman',** Rus.
99/J5 **Taman** (bay), Rus.
164/B3 **Tamana** (peak), Col.
138/G5 **Tamana** (isl.), Kiri.
167/G8 **Tamanaco** (riv.), Ven.
142/C3 **Tamanar,** Mor.
143/G5 **Tamanghasset,** Alg.
143/F5 **Tamanghasset** (dry riv.), Alg.
143/F4 **Tamanghasset** (wilaya), Alg.
146/B3 **Tamanhint,** Libya
124/C1 **Taman Negara Nat'l Park,** Malay.
116/B3 **Tamanthi,** Burma
206/C2 **Tamaqua,** Pa,US
58/B5 **Tamar** (riv.), Eng,UK
112/H8 **Tamara** (isl.), Japan
202/P7 **Tamarac,** Fl,US
195/H4 **Tamarack,** Mn,US
195/G4 **Tamarack Nat'l Wild. Res.,** Mn,US
164/C3 **Tamar, Alto de** (peak), Col.
131/F2 **Tamarike,** Indo.
160/E4 **Tamarindo Nat'l Wild. Ref.,** CR
77/F2 **Tamarite de Litera,** Sp.
81/E5 **Tamaro, Monte** (peak), Swi.
172/B1 **Tamarugal** (plain), Chile
73/C6 **Tamási,** Hun.
144/B2 **Tamassoumît,** Mrta.
165/E4 **Tamatama,** Ven.
188/B4 **Tamaulipas** (state), Mex.
158/D3 **Tamazula,** Mex.
158/E5 **Tamazula,** Mex.
159/F4 **Tamazunchale,** Mex.
111/L9 **Tamba,** Japan
111/L9 **Tamba** (hills), Japan
151/A1 **Tambach,** Kenya
144/B3 **Tambacounda,** Sen.
144/B3 **Tambacounda** (reg.), Sen.
144/C3 **Tambakara,** Mali
155/G3 **Tambara,** Moz.
135/D1 **Tambar Springs,** Austl.
145/G3 **Tambawel,** Nga.
127/F4 **Tambea,** Indo.
126/C3 **Tambelan,** Indo.
126/C3 **Tambelan** (isls.), Indo.
132/C5 **Tambellup,** Austl.
100/H2 **Tambey,** Rus.
125/B4 **Tambisan,** Malay.
134/B4 **Tambo,** Austl.
168/C3 **Tambo** (riv.), Peru
168/C4 **Tambobamba,** Peru
168/C4 **Tambo Colorado,** Peru
168/B4 **Tambo de Mora,** Peru
168/A2 **Tambo Grande,** Peru
157/G7 **Tambohorano,** Madg.
168/D4 **Tambopata** (riv.), Bol., Peru
81/F5 **Tambo, Pizzo** (peak), Swi.
127/E5 **Tambora** (peak), Indo.
173/E4 **Tambores,** Uru.
167/F4 **Tamboril,** Braz.
135/C3 **Tamboritha** (peak), Austl.
53/H3 **Tambov,** Rus.
99/L2 **Tambov Obl.,** Rus.
76/A1 **Tambre** (riv.), Sp.
127/E4 **Tambu,** Indo.
131/F1 **Tambul,** PNG
125/B4 **Tambunan,** Malay.
149/E4 **Tambura,** Sudan
144/C2 **Tamchaket,** Mrta.
164/D3 **Tame,** Col.
59/E1 **Tame** (riv.), Eng,UK
76/B2 **Tâmega** (riv.), Port.
175/K7 **Tamel Aike,** Arg.
143/E4 **Tamentit,** Alg.
167/K6 **Támesis,** Col.
145/H2 **Tamgak** (peak), Niger
120/D2 **Tamghas,** Nepal
144/B3 **Tamgue, Massif du** (reg.), Gui., Sen.
159/F4 **Tamiahua,** Mex.
160/B1 **Tamiahua** (lag.), Mex.
202/P8 **Tamiami,** Fl,US
203/H4 **Tamiami** (can.), Fl,US
124/B1 **Tamiang** (pt.), Indo.
122/F3 **Tamil Nadu** (state), India
164/B4 **Taminango,** Col.
68/D3 **Tamines,** Belg.
103/B5 **Ţāmiyah,** Egypt
120/E2 **Tamkuhi,** India
123/E3 **Tam Ky,** Viet.
123/D2 **Tam Le,** Viet.
121/F4 **Tamlūk,** India
116/B3 **Tāmma,** India
206/C2 **Tammany** (mt.), NJ,US
85/E5 **Tammaro** (riv.), It.
63/K1 **Tammela,** Fin.
63/K2 **Tammisaari** (Ekenäs), Fin.
103/D3 **Ţammūn,** WBnk.
191/J3 **Tamo,** Ar,US
181/K6 **Tampa,** Fl,US
203/G4 **Tampa,** Fl,US
202/K8 **Tampa** (bay), Fl,US
203/G4 **Tampa** (int'l arpt.), Fl,US
191/F1 **Tampa,** Ks,US
122/H4 **Tampalakamam,** SrL.
159/F4 **Tampamolón Corona,** Mex.
124/D4 **Tampang,** Indo.
63/K1 **Tampere,** Fin.
63/K1 **Tampere-Pirkkala** (int'l arpt.), Fin.
159/F4 **Tampico,** Mex.
159/F4 **Tampico Alto,** Mex.
124/C2 **Tampin,** Malay.
166/C2 **Tampoc** (riv.), FrG.
157/J6 **Tampon Ambohitra** (peak), Madg.
124/B2 **Tampulonanjing** (peak), Indo.
123/E3 **Tam Quan,** Viet.
106/E4 **Tamrah,** SAr.
142/C3 **Tamri,** Mor.
63/M2 **Tamsalu,** Est.
168/C2 **Tamshiyacu,** Peru
75/K3 **Tamsweg,** Aus.
159/F4 **Tamuín,** Mex.
160/B1 **Tamuín** (riv.), Mex.
121/H2 **Tāmulpur,** India
121/F2 **Tamur** (riv.), Nepal
135/D1 **Tamworth,** Austl.
59/E1 **Tamworth,** Eng,UK
113/D5 **Tamyang,** SKor.
119/K3 **Tan** (riv.), China
149/H3 **Tana** (lake), Eth.
151/B2 **Tana** (riv.), Kenya
61/J1 **Tana,** Nor.
61/H1 **Tana** (riv.), Nor.
110/D4 **Tanabe,** Japan
173/G2 **Tanabi,** Braz.
177/K3 **Tanacross,** Ak,US
61/J1 **Tanafjorden** (fjord), Nor.
177/C6 **Tanaga** (isl.), Ak,US
177/C6 **Tanaga** (vol.), Ak,US
85/F6 **Tanagro** (riv.), It.
111/G2 **Tanagura,** Japan
124/D3 **Tanahbala** (isl.), Indo.
124/B3 **Tanahmasa** (isl.), Indo.
131/F1 **Tanahmerah,** Indo.
123/C5 **Tanah Merah,** Malay.
124/C2 **Tanahputih,** Indo.
120/C1 **Tanakpur,** India
157/J7 **Tanambe,** Madg.
133/F1 **Tanami,** Austl.
130/C4 **Tanami** (des.), Austl.
133/F2 **Tanami Des. Wild. Sanct.,** Austl.
123/D4 **Tan An,** Viet.
177/H2 **Tanana,** Ak,US
177/J3 **Tanana** (riv.), Ak,US
157/G8 **Tanandava,** Madg.
151/A3 **Tanangozi,** Tanz.
151/C2 **Tana River Primate Nat'l Rsv.,** Kenya
86/B3 **Tanaro** (riv.), It.
146/A2 **Tanārūt, Wādī** (dry riv.), Libya
174/E2 **Tancacha,** Arg.
79/F2 **Tancarville,** Fr.
115/D4 **Tancheng,** China
113/E2 **Tanch'ŏn,** NKor.
158/E5 **Tancítaro, Pico de** (peak), Mex.
118/C2 **Tānda,** India
118/D2 **Tāndā,** India
120/B1 **Tānda,** India
120/D2 **Tāndā,** India
144/E5 **Tanda,** IvC.
144/D3 **Tanda** (lake), Mali
125/D3 **Tandag,** Phil.
149/F2 **Tandaltī,** Sudan
93/H3 **Ţăndărei,** Rom.
122/D1 **Tāndi,** India
113/C2 **Tandian,** China
174/F3 **Tandil,** Arg.
148/C3 **Tandjilé** (pref.), Chad
145/F4 **Tandjoaré,** Togo
122/B2 **Tāndliānwāla,** Pak.
107/J3 **Tando Ādam,** Pak.
107/J3 **Tando Allāhyār,** Pak.
107/J3 **Tando Muhammad Khān,** Pak.
133/J5 **Tandou** (lake), Austl.
56/B3 **Tandragee,** NI,UK
157/H8 **Tandrano,** Madg.
136/D2 **Taneatua,** N.Z.
110/B5 **Tanega** (isl.), Japan
116/C5 **Tanem** (range), Burma, Thai.
119/G4 **Tanem** (range), Thai.
206/A4 **Taneytown,** Md,US
191/H2 **Taneyville,** Mo,US
143/E5 **Tanezrouft** (des.), Alg., Mali
115/C3 **Tang** (riv.), China
115/C4 **Tang** (riv.), China
151/B3 **Tanga,** Tanz.
151/B3 **Tanga** (prov.), Tanz.
121/G3 **Tangail,** Bang.
121/G3 **Tangail** (dist.), Bang.
157/H8 **Tangainony,** Madg.
144/C4 **Tangali,** Gui.
105/H2 **Tangalī,** Iran
117/G2 **Tangang,** China
153/G4 **Tanganyika** (lake), Afr.
170/A2 **Tangará da Serra,** Braz.
116/D3 **Tangdan,** China
177/G1 **Tangent** (pt.), Ak,US
72/B3 **Tanger** (riv.), Ger.
124/D4 **Tangerang,** Indo.
72/B3 **Tangerhütte,** Ger.
72/B2 **Tangermünde,** Ger.
141/M13 **Tanger** (Tangier), Mor.
115/J7 **Tangfang,** China
114/E5 **Tanggula** (mts.), China
114/F5 **Tanggula Shankou** (pass), China
115/C4 **Tanghe,** China
140/B1 **Tangier,** Mor.
201/J1 **Tangier** (sound), Md,US
201/K2 **Tangier,** Va,US
141/M13 **Tangier** (Boukhalf) (int'l arpt.), Mor.
141/M13 **Tangier** (Tanger), Mor.
202/C2 **Tangipahoa,** La,US
202/C2 **Tangipahoa** (riv.), Ms,US
113/D4 **Tangjin,** SKor.
124/C2 **Tangkak,** Malay.
205/B3 **Tanglewilde-Thompson Place,** Wa,US
208/A1 **Tanglewood,** Ma,US
116/B2 **Tangmai,** China
152/C5 **Tango,** Ang.
115/L9 **Tangqi,** China
114/E5 **Tangra** (lake), China
115/D3 **Tangshan,** China
117/F3 **Tangtou,** China
125/C3 **Tangub,** Phil.
145/F4 **Tanguiéta,** Ben.
117/F3 **Tangwan,** China
117/H2 **Tangxi,** China
117/F2 **Tangyan** (riv.), China
115/C4 **Tangyin,** China
109/K2 **Tangyuan,** China
171/E2 **Tanhaçu,** Braz.
116/C2 **Taniantaweng** (mts.), China
130/C2 **Tanimbar** (isls.), Indo.
80/C5 **Taninges,** Fr.
127/G4 **Taniwel,** Indo.
125/C3 **Tanjay,** Phil.
117/F2 **Tanjiachang,** China
124/C2 **Tanjong Malim,** Malay.
126/E4 **Tanjung,** Indo.
124/B2 **Tanjungbalai,** Indo.
124/C2 **Tanjungbatu,** Indo.
124/C3 **Tanjungenim,** Indo.
124/D4 **Tanjungkarang-Telukbetung,** Indo.
126/C4 **Tanjungpandan,** Indo.
124/D2 **Tanjungpinang,** Indo.
124/B2 **Tanjungpura,** Indo.
124/D2 **Tanjunguban,** Indo.
122/A1 **Tānk,** Pak.
188/D2 **Tankersley,** Tx,US
71/F6 **Tann,** Ger.
71/E2 **Tanna,** Ger.
138/F6 **Tanna** (isl.), Van.
111/L9 **Tannan,** Japan
206/C1 **Tannersville,** Pa,US
81/G3 **Tannheim,** Aus.
114/F1 **Tannu-Ola** (mts.), Mong., Rus.
145/E5 **Tano** (riv.), Gui., IvC.
145/H3 **Tânout,** Niger
117/G3 **Tanqiu,** China
187/G4 **Tanque Verde,** Az,US
159/F4 **Tanquián,** Mex.
120/D2 **Tānsing,** Nepal
103/B4 **Ţanţā,** Egypt
147/F2 **Ţanţā,** Egypt
116/C5 **Tantabin,** Burma
194/D2 **Tantallon,** Sk,Can
206/A6 **Tantallon,** Md,US
142/C3 **Tan-Tan,** Mor.
117/H2 **Tantou,** China
159/F4 **Tantoyuca,** Mex.
109/J2 **Tantu,** China
118/D4 **Tanuku,** India
62/D2 **Tanumshede,** Swe.
135/A2 **Tanunda,** Austl.
122/E3 **Tānūr,** India
113/E4 **Tanyang,** SKor.
125/E7 **Tanza,** Phil.
140/F5 **Tanzania**
111/H7 **Tanzawa-yama** (peak), Japan
117/G3 **Tanzishan,** China
117/G3 **Tao** (riv.), China
123/B4 **Tao** (isl.), Thai.
109/J2 **Tao'er** (riv.), China
117/F3 **Taochuan,** China
108/F4 **Taole,** China
117/G3 **Taolin,** China
109/J2 **Taonan,** China
90/D4 **Taormina,** It.
120/A1 **Tāoru,** India
191/H1 **Taos,** Mo,US
190/B2 **Taos,** NM,US
190/B2 **Taos Pueblo,** NM,US
142/E5 **Taoudenni,** Mali
141/M13 **Taounate,** Mor.
143/F4 **Taourirt,** Alg.
141/N13 **Taourirt,** Mor.
117/H2 **Taoxi,** China
119/K2 **Taoyuan,** China
117/J3 **Taoyuan,** Tai.
63/L2 **Tapa,** Est.
172/C1 **Tapacarí,** Bol.
160/C3 **Tapachula,** Mex.
124/C1 **Tapah,** Malay.
166/C3 **Tapajós** (riv.), Braz.
166/B4 **Tapajós** (Amazônia) Nat'l Park, Braz.
124/B2 **Tapaktuan,** Indo.
158/E5 **Tapalpa,** Mex.
124/C3 **Tapan,** Indo.
166/C2 **Tapanahoni** (riv.), Sur.
160/C2 **Tapantatepec,** Mex.
136/B4 **Tapanui,** N.Z.
166/C3 **Tapará** (mts.), Braz.
169/E2 **Tapauá,** Braz.
169/E2 **Tapauá** (riv.), Braz.
125/C3 **Tapaz,** Phil.
172/E2 **Tapenagá** (riv.), Arg.
166/C2 **Tapera do Jeronimo,** Braz.
167/G4 **Taperoá,** Braz.
144/C5 **Tapeta,** Libr.
123/C2 **Taphan Hin,** Thai.
123/C3 **Ta Phraya,** Thai.
76/B1 **Tapia de Casariego,** Sp.
175/K7 **Tapi Aike,** Arg.
168/C2 **Tapiche** (riv.), Peru
153/F2 **Tapili,** Zaire
116/C3 **Taping** (riv.), Burma
131/G2 **Tapini,** PNG
124/C1 **Tapis** (peak), Malay.
121/F2 **Taplejung,** Nepal
168/C3 **Tapo,** Peru
145/F3 **Tapoa** (prov.), Burk.
73/B6 **Tapolca,** Hun.
54/D2 **Tap O'Noth** (hill), Sc,UK
201/J2 **Tappahannock,** Va,US
207/K7 **Tappan** (lake), NJ, NY,US
207/E1 **Tappan,** NY,US
208/F7 **Tappan** (dam), Oh,US
198/F4 **Tappan** (lake), Oh,US
208/F7 **Tappan** (res.), Oh,US
207/E1 **Tappan Zee** (reach), NY,US
194/E4 **Tappen,** ND,US
85/E4 **Tappino** (riv.), It.
112/B3 **Tappi-zaki** (pt.), Japan
205/C3 **Tapps** (lake), Wa,US
120/A5 **Tāpti** (riv.), India
125/C4 **Tapul** (isls.), Phil.
116/C3 **Tapun,** India
147/F5 **Taqab,** Sudan
147/H5 **Taqātu' Hayyā,** Sudan
117/H2 **Taqian,** China
173/G4 **Taquari,** Braz.
170/A3 **Taquari** (riv.), Braz.
170/C4 **Taquaritinga,** Braz.
170/C4 **Taquarituba,** Braz.
173/F1 **Taquaruçu** (res.), Braz.
168/B1 **Taquil,** Ecu.
87/G2 **Tar,** Cro.
60/B5 **Tar** (riv.), Ire.
114/B3 **Tar** (riv.), Kyr.
201/J3 **Tar** (riv.), NC,US
134/C4 **Tara,** Austl.
92/D4 **Tara** (riv.), Bosn., Yugo.
100/H4 **Tara,** Rus.
155/E3 **Tara,** Zam.
145/H4 **Taraba** (riv.), Nga.
172/C1 **Tarabuco,** Bol.
103/D2 **Ţarābulus** (Tripoli), Leb.
146/B1 **Tarābulus** (Tripoli) (cap.), Libya
136/D2 **Taradale,** N.Z.
60/D2 **Tara, Hill of,** Ire.
56/B4 **Tara, Hill of** (hill), Ire.
172/D2 **Tarairí,** Bol.
127/E3 **Tarakan,** Indo.
151/A1 **Tarakit** (peak), Kenya
93/K5 **Taraklı,** Turk.
93/J3 **Tarakliya,** Mol.
120/D1 **Tārākot,** Nepal
112/E2 **Taraku** (isl.), Rus.
135/D2 **Taralga,** Austl.
130/B2 **Taramana,** Indo.
136/C2 **Taranaki** (reg.), N.Z.
76/D2 **Tarancón,** Sp.
151/A2 **Tarangire Nat'l Park,** Tanz.
135/C4 **Taranna,** Austl.
83/D2 **Taranto,** It.
83/C2 **Taranto** (gulf), It.
83/C2 **Taranto** (prov.), It.
172/B1 **Tarapacá** (reg.), Chile
164/D5 **Tarapacá,** Col.
164/B5 **Tarapoa,** Ecu.
168/B2 **Tarapoto,** Peru
74/F4 **Tarare,** Fr.
136/J8 **Tararua** (range), N.Z.
82/A5 **Tarascon,** Fr.
74/D5 **Tarascon-sur-Ariège,** Fr.
98/F3 **Tarashcha,** Ukr.
172/C1 **Tarata,** Bol.
168/D5 **Tarata,** Peru
168/D3 **Tarauacá,** Braz.
168/D2 **Tarauacá** (riv.), Braz.
139/M7 **Taravai** (isl.), FrPol.
138/G4 **Tarawa** (isl.), Kiri.
136/D2 **Tarawera** (vol.), N.Z.
76/E2 **Tarazona,** Sp.
76/E3 **Tarazona de la Mancha,** Sp.
114/D2 **Tarbagatay** (mts.), Kaz.
151/C1 **Tarbaj,** Kenya
54/C1 **Tarbat Head** (pt.), Sc,UK
55/K8 **Tarbat Ness** (pt.), Sc,UK
107/K2 **Tarbela** (res.), Pak.
60/A4 **Tarbert,** Ire.
54/A5 **Tarbert,** Sc,UK
55/H8 **Tarbert,** Sc,UK
74/D5 **Tarbes,** Fr.
74/D5 **Tarbes/Lourdes** (int'l arpt.), Fr.
54/B6 **Tarbolton,** Sc,UK
203/H2 **Tarboro,** Ga,US
201/J3 **Tarboro,** NC,US
92/A2 **Tarcento,** It.
133/G4 **Tarcoola,** Austl.
135/C2 **Tarcutta,** Austl.
74/E3 **Tardes** (riv.), Fr.
77/E2 **Tardienta,** Sp.
74/D4 **Tardoire** (riv.), Fr.
109/M2 **Tardoki-Jani** (peak), Rus.
135/E1 **Taree,** Austl.
208/H6 **Tarentum,** Pa,US
141/V18 **Tarf** (lake), Alg.
147/G2 **Ţarfā', Wādī al** (dry riv.), Egypt
147/F4 **Tarfâwi, Bîr** (well), Egypt
146/E2 **Ţarfāwī, Bi'r at** (well), Libya
77/Y17 **Tarfaya,** Mor.
56/D2 **Tarf Water** (riv.), Sc,UK
207/E2 **Target Rock Nat'l Wild. Ref.,** NY,US
141/M13 **Targuist,** Mor.
146/B1 **Tarhūnah,** Libya
131/F1 **Tari,** PNG
164/D4 **Tariana,** Col.
106/F4 **Tarīf,** UAE
168/B1 **Tarifa,** Ecu.
76/C4 **Tarifa,** Sp.
208/B2 **Tariffville,** Ct,US
172/C2 **Tarija,** Bol.
172/C1 **Tarija** (dept.), Bol.
172/C1 **Tarija** (int'l arpt.), Bol.
127/J4 **Tariku** (riv.), Indo.
127/J4 **Tariku-taritatu** (plain), Indo.
108/B4 **Tarim** (basin), China
114/D3 **Tarim** (riv.), China
150/D1 **Tarīm,** Yem.
151/A2 **Tarime,** Tanz.
114/E3 **Tarim Liuchang,** China
107/J2 **Tarin** (riv.), Afg.
124/B2 **Taring,** Indo.
127/J4 **Taritatu** (riv.), Indo.
156/D4 **Tarkastad,** SAfr.
98/G5 **Tarkhankut** (cape), Ukr.
96/E3 **Tarkhankut, Mys** (cape), Ukr.
193/G3 **Tarkio** (cr.), Ia, Mo,US
193/G3 **Tarkio,** Mo,US
100/H3 **Tarko-Sale,** Rus.
145/E5 **Tarkwa,** Gha.
125/C2 **Tarlac,** Phil.
54/D2 **Tarland,** Sc,UK
133/H2 **Tarlton Downs,** Austl.
168/C3 **Tarma,** Peru
67/G2 **Tarmstedt,** Ger.
74/D5 **Tarn** (riv.), Fr.
108/E2 **Tarna** (riv.), Mong.
107/J2 **Tarnak** (riv.), Afg.
63/T9 **Tårnby,** Den.
98/B3 **Tarnica** (peak), Pol.
65/L3 **Tarnobrzeg,** Pol.
65/L3 **Tarnobrzeg** (prov.), Pol.
95/J3 **Tarnogskiy Gorodok,** Rus.
65/L3 **Tarnów,** Pol.
65/L3 **Tarnów** (prov.), Pol.
62/G1 **Tärnsjö,** Swe.
122/C2 **Tarn Tāran,** India
114/D5 **Taro** (lake), China
86/D3 **Taro** (riv.), It.
112/B4 **Tarō,** Japan
117/J3 **Taroko Nat'l Park,** Tai.
105/H4 **Ţārom,** Iran
99/H3 **Taromskoye,** Ukr.
134/C4 **Taroom,** Austl.
76/B2 **Tarouca,** Port.
142/C3 **Taroudannt,** Mor.
64/E1 **Tarp,** Ger.
92/F1 **Tarpa,** Hun.
202/K7 **Tarpon** (lake), Fl,US
203/G3 **Tarpon** (lake), Fl,US
181/K6 **Tarpon Springs,** Fl,US
203/G3 **Tarpon Springs,** Fl,US
57/F5 **Tarporley,** Eng,UK
164/C5 **Tarqui,** Peru
84/B3 **Tarquinia,** It.
103/D4 **Tarqūmiyah,** WBnk.
140/K10 **Tarrafal,** CpV.
77/F2 **Tarragona,** Sp.
135/C4 **Tarraleah,** Austl.
200/D4 **Tarrant,** Al,US
188/K7 **Tarrant** (co.), Tx,US
77/F2 **Tàrrega,** Sp.
81/G3 **Tarrenz,** Aus.
190/B1 **Tarryall** (mts.), Co,US
207/E1 **Tarrytown,** NY,US
103/D1 **Tarsus,** Turk.
103/D1 **Tarsus** (riv.), Turk.
172/D2 **Tartagal,** Arg.
172/E4 **Tartagal,** Arg.
87/E2 **Tartaro** (riv.), It.
74/C5 **Tartas,** Fr.
63/M2 **Tartu,** Est.
103/D2 **Ţarţūs,** Syria
103/D2 **Ţarţūs** (dist.), Syria
111/M9 **Tarui,** Japan
110/B5 **Tarumizu,** Japan
96/F1 **Tarusa,** Rus.
123/B5 **Tarutao Nat'l Park,** Thai.
98/E4 **Tarutino,** Ukr.
124/B2 **Tarutung,** Indo.
108/D2 **Tarvagatay** (mts.), Mong.
57/F5 **Tarvin,** Eng,UK
188/D1 **Tarzan,** Tx,US
204/E7 **Tarzana,** Ca,US
103/B1 **Taşağıl,** Turk.
146/B3 **Tasawāh,** Libya
80/D5 **Täsch,** Swi.
104/C2 **Taşçı,** Turk.
182/C2 **Taseko** (mtn.), BC,Can
182/C2 **Taseko** (riv.), BC,Can
123/D3 **Ta Seng,** Camb.
114/E2 **Tashanta,** Rus.
97/L4 **Tashauz Obl.,** Trkm.
121/H2 **Tashigang,** Bhu.
105/H4 **Tashk** (riv.), Iran
114/A3 **Tashkent** (cap.), Uzb.
107/H1 **Tashkepri,** Trkm.
114/B3 **Tash-Kumyr,** Kyr.
176/P3 **Tasiilaq,** Grld.
124/E4 **Tasikmalaya,** Indo.
103/C1 **Taşkent,** Turk.
145/H3 **Tasker,** Niger
104/C1 **Taşköprü,** Turk.
105/E2 **Taşlıçay,** Turk.
138/E8 **Tasman** (sea)
135/C4 **Tasman** (cape), Austl.
135/C4 **Tasman** (pen.), Austl.
131/E3 **Tasman** (pt.), Austl.
136/C3 **Tasman** (bay), N.Z.
135/C4 **Tasmania** (isl.), Austl.
135/C4 **Tasmania** (state), Austl.
136/C3 **Tasman Nat'l Park,** N.Z.
92/F2 **Tăşnad,** Rom.
104/D1 **Taşova,** Turk.
159/K6 **Tasquillo,** Mex.
145/G2 **Tassara,** Niger
143/G4 **Tassili-n-Ajjer** (mts.), Alg.
63/T9 **Tåstrup,** Den.
95/N5 **Tastuba,** Rus.
177/M5 **Tasu,** BC,Can
103/C1 **Taşucu,** Turk.
123/B2 **Tasudi,** Burma
105/F2 **Tasūj,** Iran
73/C4 **Tata,** Hun.
142/D3 **Tata,** Mor.
149/F5 **Tata,** Zaire
127/F4 **Tataba,** Indo.
73/C4 **Tatabánya,** Hun.
139/M6 **Tatakoto** (isl.), FrPol.
108/D4 **Talalin** (riv.), China
130/B2 **Tata Mailau** (peak), Indo.
206/C2 **Tatamy,** Pa,US
109/N2 **Tatar** (str.), Rus.
95/L5 **Tatar Aut. Rep.,** Rus.
98/E5 **Tatarbunary,** Ukr.
93/H5 **Tatarlar,** Turk.
100/H4 **Tatarsk,** Rus.
126/D3 **Tatau,** Malay.
95/L4 **Tataurovo,** Rus.
143/H2 **Tatāwīn,** Tun.
143/H3 **Tatāwīn** (gov.), Tun.
200/E3 **Tate,** Ga,US
144/B4 **Tatéma,** Gui.
200/E2 **Tateville,** Ky,US
111/F3 **Tateyama,** Japan
111/E2 **Tate-yama** (mtn.), Japan
178/E2 **Tathlina** (lake), NW,Can
106/D5 **Tathlīth,** SAr.
135/D3 **Tathra,** Austl.
144/B2 **Tatilt** (well), Mrta.
177/J3 **Tatitlek,** Ak,US
123/B1 **Tatkon,** Burma
182/B2 **Tatlayoko Lake,** BC,Can
114/E4 **Tatlikbulak,** China
178/G3 **Tatnam** (cape), Mb,Can
145/H3 **Tatokou,** Niger
65/K4 **Tatranský Nat'l Park,** Slvk.
65/K4 **Tatrzański Nat'l Park,** Pol.
53/P8 **Tatsfield,** Eng,UK
99/L3 **Tatsinskiy,** Rus.
111/E3 **Tatsuno,** Japan
57/H5 **Tattershall,** Eng,UK
170/D4 **Tatuí,** Braz.
190/C4 **Tatum,** NM,US
189/G1 **Tatum,** Tx,US
135/C3 **Tatura,** Austl.
104/E2 **Tatvan,** Turk.
167/F4 **Tauá,** Braz.
170/D4 **Taubaté,** Braz.
70/C3 **Tauber** (riv.), Ger.
70/C3 **Tauberbischofsheim,** Ger.
168/B3 **Tauca,** Peru
72/C5 **Taucha,** Ger.
97/J3 **Tauchik,** Kaz.
75/K3 **Tauern, Hohe** (mts.), Aus.
71/F6 **Taufkirchen,** Ger.
71/G6 **Taufkirchen an der Pram,** Aus.
70/C1 **Taufstein** (peak), Ger.
136/J9 **Tauherenkau** (riv.), N.Z.
120/D2 **Taulihawa,** Nepal
136/C2 **Taumarunui,** N.Z.
191/J2 **Taum Sauk** (mtn.), Mo,US
156/D2 **Taung,** SAfr.
116/B4 **Taungdwingyi,** Burma
116/C4 **Taunggyi,** Burma
116/B3 **Taungthonlon** (peak), Burma
116/B5 **Taungup,** Burma
116/B5 **Taungup** (pass), Burma
123/B3 **Taungzun,** Burma
122/A2 **Taunsa,** Pak.
197/T8 **Taunton,** On,Can
58/C4 **Taunton,** Eng,UK
208/C2 **Taunton,** Ma,US
208/C2 **Taunton** (riv.), Ma,US
70/B2 **Taunus** (range), Ger.
70/B2 **Taunusstein,** Ger.
136/C2 **Taupo,** N.Z.
136/C2 **Taupo** (lake), N.Z.
63/K4 **Tauragė,** Lith.
136/D2 **Tauranga,** N.Z.
83/C6 **Taurianova,** It.
74/D3 **Taurion** (riv.), Fr.
136/C1 **Tauroa** (pt.), N.Z.
103/B1 **Taurus** (mts.), Turk.
76/E2 **Tauste,** Sp.
131/G1 **Tauta,** PNG
78/D2 **Taute** (riv.), Fr.
139/X15 **Tautira,** FrPol.
138/E5 **Tauu** (isls.), PNG
97/H4 **Tauz,** Azer.
80/D3 **Tavannes,** Swi.
203/H3 **Tavares,** Fl,US
87/E5 **Tavarnelle,** It.
87/E5 **Tavarnuzze,** It.
104/B2 **Tavas,** Turk.
80/B3 **Tavaux,** Fr.
86/C2 **Tavazzano,** It.
95/Q4 **Tavda,** Rus.
95/Q4 **Tavda** (riv.), Rus.
82/A4 **Tavel,** Fr.
59/H1 **Taverham,** Eng,UK
83/C4 **Taverna,** It.
86/C1 **Tavernerio,** It.
82/C5 **Tavernes,** Fr.
53/S9 **Taverny,** Fr.
151/B2 **Taveta,** Kenya
139/Z17 **Taveuni** (isl.), Fiji
76/B4 **Tavira,** Port.
58/B5 **Tavistock,** Eng,UK
85/E3 **Tavo** (riv.), It.
123/B3 **Tavoy,** Burma
123/B3 **Tavoy** (pt.), Burma
109/L3 **Tavrichanka,** Rus.
104/B2 **Tavşanlı,** Turk.
58/B5 **Tavy** (riv.), Eng,UK
58/B4 **Taw** (riv.), Eng,UK
136/H9 **Tawa,** N.Z.
127/E4 **Tawaeli,** Indo.
136/A4 **Ta Waewae** (bay), N.Z.
189/F1 **Tawakoni** (lake), Tx,US
111/L10 **Tawaramoto,** Japan
198/E2 **Tawas City,** Mi,US
125/B4 **Tawau,** Malay.
125/B4 **Tawau** (int'l arpt.), Malay.
58/C3 **Tawe** (riv.), Wal,UK
69/F4 **Tawern,** Ger.
122/C1 **Tāwi** (riv.), India
151/B4 **Tawi,** Tanz.
125/B4 **Tawi-tawi** (isl.), Phil.
147/H5 **Ţawkar,** Sudan
117/F2 **Tawo,** China
105/F3 **Ţawūq,** Iraq
146/B1 **Tāwurghā',** Libya
89/G4 **Tāwurghā', Sabkhat** (salt marsh), Libya
143/H2 **Tawzar,** Tun.
143/G2 **Tawzar** (gov.), Tun.
159/F5 **Taxco,** Mex.
159/K8 **Taxco de Alarcón,** Mex.
122/B1 **Taxila,** Pak.
122/B1 **Taxila** (ruins), Pak.
114/C4 **Taxkorgan Tajik Zizhixian** (Taxkorgan), China
114/C4 **Taxkorgan** (Taxkorgan Tajik Zizhixian), China
54/C4 **Tay** (firth), Sc,UK
54/C4 **Tay** (riv.), Sc,UK
168/B3 **Tayabamba,** Peru
130/C1 **Tayandu** (isls.), Indo.
160/D2 **Tayasal,** Guat.
94/G1 **Taybola,** Rus.
150/C4 **Tayeegle,** Som.
54/B3 **Tay, Loch** (lake), Sc,UK
203/F2 **Taylor,** Al,US
189/H1 **Taylor,** Ar,US
187/G3 **Taylor,** Az,US
190/A1 **Taylor** (riv.), Co,US
189/H1 **Taylor,** La,US
205/F7 **Taylor,** Mi,US
187/J3 **Taylor** (mt.), NM,US
199/J4 **Taylor,** Pa,US
189/F2 **Taylor,** Tx,US
201/F3 **Taylors,** SC,US
184/C3 **Taylorsville,** Ca,US
200/E1 **Taylorsville,** In,US
200/E1 **Taylorsville,** Ky,US
200/C5 **Taylorsville,** Ms,US
201/G3 **Taylorsville,** NC,US
185/H3 **Taylorsville-Bennion,** Ut,US
189/H1 **Taylortown,** La,US
191/G4 **Taylor Town,** Tx,US
193/K4 **Taylorville,** Il,US
104/D5 **Taymā',** SAr.
196/D2 **Taymouth,** NB,Can
101/L2 **Taymyr** (isl.), Rus.
100/K2 **Taymyr** (pen.), Rus.
100/K2 **Taymyr** (riv.), Rus.
100/J2 **Taymyr Aut. Okr.,** Rus.
123/D4 **Tay Ninh,** Viet.
158/D3 **Tayoltita,** Mex.
54/D4 **Tayport,** Sc,UK
164/C2 **Tayrona Nat'l Park,** Col.
100/K4 **Tayshet,** Rus.
54/C3 **Tayside** (reg.), Sc,UK
125/B3 **Taytay,** Phil.
124/E4 **Tayu,** Indo.
100/J3 **Taz** (riv.), Rus.
141/M13 **Taza,** Mor.
112/B4 **Tazawako,** Japan
141/M13 **Tazekka** (peak), Mor.
142/D3 **Tazenakht,** Mor.
201/F2 **Tazewell,** Tn,US
201/G2 **Tazewell,** Va,US
109/J2 **Tazicheng,** China
146/D3 **Tāzirbū** (oasis), Libya
100/H3 **Tazovskiy,** Rus.
143/G5 **Tazrouk,** Alg.
90/B4 **Tāzughrān,** Tun.
160/D3 **Tazumal** (ruins), ESal.
53/H4 **Tbilisi** (cap.), Geo.
99/L5 **Tbilisskaya,** Rus.
148/B3 **Tchamba,** Camr.
145/F4 **Tchamba,** Togo
145/F4 **Tchaourou,** Ben.
145/F5 **Tchetti,** Ben.
152/B3 **Tchibanga,** Gabon
154/C2 **Tchikala-Tcholohanga,** Ang.
154/B2 **Tchindjenje,** Ang.
145/G3 **Tchin Tabaradene,** Niger
148/B3 **Tcholliré,** Camr.
200/B4 **Tchula,** Ms,US
65/K1 **Tczew,** Pol.
165/E5 **Tea** (riv.), Braz.
158/D4 **Teacapán,** Mex.
189/F2 **Teague,** Tx,US
57/H5 **Tealby,** Eng,UK
136/A4 **Te Anau,** N.Z.
207/D2 **Teaneck,** NJ,US
85/E5 **Teano,** It.
136/A4 **Te Anu** (lake), N.Z.
159/G5 **Teapa,** Mex.
185/K2 **Teapot Dome Nav. Res.,** Wy,US
136/D2 **Te Araroa,** N.Z.
92/E4 **Tearce,** Macd.
136/C2 **Te Aroha,** N.Z.
185/H4 **Teasdale,** Ut,US
136/C2 **Te Awamutu,** N.Z.
124/D4 **Tebak** (peak), Indo.
97/G4 **Teberda,** Rus.
141/W18 **Tébessa,** Alg.
143/G2 **Tébessa** (wilaya), Alg.
141/W18 **Tebessa** (mts.), Alg., Tun.
145/F2 **Tebesselamane** (well), Mali
172/E2 **Tebicuary** (riv.), Par.
124/B2 **Tebingtinggi,** Indo.
124/C3 **Tebingtinggi,** Indo.
124/C2 **Tebingtinggi** (isl.), Indo.
97/H4 **Tebulos-mta** (peak), Rus.
158/E5 **Tecalitlán,** Mex.
159/M8 **Tecamachalco,** Mex.
186/D4 **Tecate,** Mex.
77/G1 **Tech** (riv.), Fr.
189/H2 **Teche** (bayou), La,US
93/J3 **Techirghiol,** Rom.
104/D2 **Tecirli,** Turk.
174/C4 **Tecka,** Arg.
174/C4 **Tecka** (riv.), Arg.
192/B2 **Teckla,** Wy,US
88/E4 **Tecklenberg,** Ger.
63/U9 **Teckomatorp,** Swe.
159/H4 **Tecoh,** Mex.
159/F4 **Tecolutla,** Mex.
160/B1 **Tecolutla** (riv.), Mex.
158/E5 **Tecomán,** Mex.
186/D3 **Tecopa,** Ca,US
158/C2 **Tecoripa,** Mex.
159/K6 **Tecozautla,** Mex.
160/C2 **Tecpatán,** Mex.
158/D4 **Tecuala,** Mex.
93/H3 **Tecuci,** Rom.
205/G7 **Tecumseh,** On,Can
198/E3 **Tecumseh,** Mi,US
193/F3 **Tecumseh,** Ne,US
191/F3 **Tecumseh,** Ok,US
150/B4 **Ted Ceidaar Dabole,** Som.
143/G5 **Tedjert** (well), Alg.
116/C5 **Tedodita Sakan,** Burma
107/H1 **Tedzhen,** Trkm.
100/G6 **Tedzhen** (riv.), Trkm.
57/G2 **Tees** (bay), Eng,UK
57/G2 **Tees** (riv.), Eng,UK
57/G2 **Teesside** (int'l arpt.), Eng,UK
141/Q16 **Tefaraoui** (arpt.), Alg.
169/E1 **Tefé,** Braz.
169/E1 **Tefé** (int'l arpt.), Braz.
169/E1 **Tefé** (lake), Braz.

169/E2 Tefé (riv.), Braz.
104/B2 Tefenni, Turk.
92/E4 Teferič, Yugo.
148/B2 Tefidinga, Éché (dry riv.), Niger
201/G3 Tega Cay, SC,US
124/E4 Tegal, Indo.
65/G2 Tegel (Berlin) (int'l arpt.), Ger.
66/D6 Tegelen, Neth.
72/D2 Tegeler (lake), Ger.
64/F5 Tegernsee, Ger.
83/B2 Teggiano, It.
146/A3 Tegheri, Bi'r (well), Libya
121/E3 Teghra, India
56/E6 Tegid, Llyn (lake), Wal,UK
145/G4 Tegina, Nga.
124/D4 Tegineneng, Indo.
81/G5 Teglio, It.
148/A2 Tegouma (dry riv.), Niger
145/H3 Tégouma (wadi), Niger
174/B4 Tegualda, Chile
160/E3 Tegucigalpa (cap.), Hon.
186/C3 Tehachapi, Ca,US
186/C3 Tehachapi (mts.), Ca,US
106/C5 Tehamiyam, Sudan
178/G2 Tehek (lake), NW,Can
146/B4 Tehiga'i (plat.), Niger
127/G4 Tehoru, Indo.
105/G3 Tehrān (cap.), Iran
105/G2 Tehrān (gov.), Iran
114/C5 Tehri, India
159/F5 Tehuacán, Mex.
189/F2 Tehuacana, Tx,US
160/C3 Tehuantepec (gulf), Mex.
159/G5 Tehuantepec (isth.), Mex.
160/C2 Tehuantepec (riv.), Mex.
159/M8 Tehuipango, Mex.
77/X16 Teide (peak), Canl.,Sp.
142/A3 Teide Nat'l Park, Canl.
142/A3 Teide, Pico de (mtn.), Canl.
58/B2 Teifi (riv.), Wal,UK
58/B2 Teifiside (vall.), Wal,UK
149/E2 Teiga (plat.), Sudan
58/C5 Teignmouth, Eng,UK
78/B6 Teignouse (str.), Fr.
71/F7 Teisendorf, Ger.
54/B4 Teith (riv.), Sc,UK
144/A3 Teixeira Pinto, GBis.
124/F5 Tejakula, Indo.
62/F4 Tejn, Den.
76/B3 Tejo (Tagus) (riv.), Port.
116/C3 Teju, India
193/F3 Tekamah, Ne,US
144/B2 Tékane, Mrta.
136/C1 Te Kao, N.Z.
136/B3 Tekapo (lake), N.Z.
136/D2 Te Karaka, N.Z.
121/E3 Tekāri, India
136/C2 Te Kauwhata, N.Z.
159/H4 Tekax, Mex.
93/J5 Teke, Turk.
114/C3 Tekeli, Kaz.
114/D3 Tekes (riv.), China
106/C6 Tekezē Wenz (reg.), Eth.
149/H2 Tekezē Wenz (riv.), Eth.
114/D4 Tekiliktag (peak), China
93/H5 Tekirdağ, Turk.
104/A1 Tekirdağ (prov.), Turk.
159/H4 Tekit, Mex.
118/D4 Tekkali, India
104/D1 Tekke, Turk.
104/D1 Tekkeköy, Turk.
104/E2 Tekman, Turk.
182/F4 Tekoa, Wa,US
136/C2 Te Kopuru, N.Z.
127/F4 Teku, Indo.
136/C2 Te Kuiti, N.Z.
118/D3 Tel (riv.), India
160/E3 Tela, Hon.
141/Q16 Télagh, Alg.
145/F2 Télataï, Mali
97/H4 Telavi, Geo.
103/D3 Tel Aviv (dist.), Isr.
103/F7 Tel Aviv (dist.), Isr.
103/D3 Tel Aviv-Yafo, Isr.
142/B4 Telde, Canl.
144/E2 Télé (lake), Mali
127/K5 Telefomin, PNG
188/E2 Telegraph, Tx,US
177/M4 Telegraph Creek, BC,Can
96/C1 Telekhany, Bela.
114/G2 Telem (lake), Mong.
170/C5 Telemaco Borba, Braz.
62/C2 Telemark (co.), Nor.
127/E3 Telen (riv.), Indo.
93/G4 Teleorman (co.), Rom.
191/F4 Telephone, Tx,US
143/G4 Telertheba, Djebel (mtn.), Alg.
186/D2 Telescope (peak), Ca,US
85/E5 Telese, It.
83/B6 Telesi (riv.), It.
166/B4 Teles Pires (riv.), Braz.
58/D1 Telford, Eng,UK
206/C3 Telford, Pa,US
81/H3 Telfs, Aus.
86/C1 Telgate, It.
78/A4 Telgruc-sur-Mer, Fr.
67/E5 Telgte, Ger.
160/E3 Telica, Nic.
142/E5 Télig (well), Mali
144/B4 Télimélé, Gui.
125/B4 Telipok, Malay.
160/B2 Telixtlahuaca, Mex.
103/G8 Tel Jericho Nat'l Park, WBnk.
149/E2 Teljo (peak), Sudan
190/D3 Tell, Tx,US
143/E2 Tell Atlas (mts.), Alg., Mor.
200/D2 Tell City, In,US
177/E2 Teller, Ak,US
122/E3 Tellicherry, India
200/E3 Tellico (lake), Tn,US
200/E3 Tellico Plains, Tn,US
174/D5 Tellier, Arg.
69/E3 Tellin, Belg.
185/K5 Telluride, Co,US
103/G6 Tel Megiddo Nat'l Park, Isr.
108/D2 Telmen (lake), Mong.
79/F5 Teloché, Fr.
124/C1 Telok Anson, Malay.
159/F5 Teloloapan, Mex.
114/E1 Telotskoye (lake), Rus.
174/D4 Telsen, Arg.
63/K4 Telšiai, Lith.
72/D3 Teltow, Ger.
72/D3 Teltow (reg.), Ger.
124/C3 Telukbayur, Indo.
124/B2 Telukdalem, Indo.
126/C4 Telukmelano, Indo.
124/C2 Telukmerbau, Indo.
124/C3 Teluk Punggur (pt.), Indo.
145/E5 Tema, Gha.
143/G2 Temacine, Alg.
198/F1 Temagami (lake), On,Can
124/E4 Temanggung, Indo.
124/C1 Teman Negara Nat'l Park, Malay.
127/J4 Tembagapura, Indo.
124/C3 Tembesi (riv.), Indo.
156/E2 Tembisa, SAfr.
165/F2 Temblador, Ven.
152/D4 Tembo, Zaire
152/D4 Tembo Aluma, Ang.
155/G2 Tembue, Moz.
55/K10 Teme (riv.), UK
58/D2 Teme (riv.), Eng,UK
204/C4 Temecula, Ca,US
91/H1 Temelkovo, Bul.
92/D3 Temerin, Yugo.
126/B3 Temerloh, Malay.
127/H4 Teminabuan, Indo.
97/L2 Temir, Kaz.
114/B1 Temirtau, Kaz.
199/G1 Témiscaming, Qu,Can
135/C4 Temma, Austl.
108/E1 Temnik (riv.), Rus.
139/M7 Temoe (isl.), FrPol.
135/C2 Temora, Austl.
158/C3 Temores, Mex.
187/G4 Tempe, Az,US
133/G3 Tempe Downs, Austl.
72/D3 Tempelhof, Ger.
72/D3 Tempelhof (Berlin) (arpt.), Ger.
189/E4 Temperance, Mi,US
201/K2 Temperanceville, Va,US
83/D4 Tempio di Hera Lacinia (ruins), It.
90/A2 Tempio Pausania, It.
131/F3 Temple (bay), Austl.
182/F2 Temple (mtn.), Ab,Can
189/H2 Temple, La,US
191/E3 Temple, Ok,US
206/C3 Temple, Pa,US
189/F2 Temple, Tx,US
60/C4 Templemore, Ire.
56/B2 Templepatrick, NI,UK
135/G5 Templestowe, Austl.
202/L7 Temple Terrace, Fl,US
186/B3 Templeton, Ca,US
60/C4 Templetouhy, Ire.
68/C2 Templeuve, Fr.
206/C5 Templeville, Md,US
72/D1 Templin, Ger.
72/D3 Templiner (lake), Ger.
159/F4 Tempoal, Mex.
160/B1 Tempoal (riv.), Mex.
160/B1 Tempoal de Sanchez, Mex.
154/C2 Tempué, Ang.
108/D4 Tēmpung, China
99/J5 Temryuk, Rus.
99/J5 Temryuk (gulf), Rus.
68/D1 Temse, Belg.
174/B3 Temuco, Chile
136/B4 Temuka, N.Z.
97/L1 Temyasovo, Rus.
164/B5 Tena, Ecu.
159/H4 Tenabó, Mex.
145/E3 Ténado, Burk.
207/K8 Tenafly, NJ,US
189/G2 Tenaha, Tx,US
177/L4 Tenakee Springs, Ak,US
118/D4 Tenāli, India
159/F5 Tenamaxtle, Mex.
159/F5 Tenancingo, Mex.
159/K7 Tenango, Mex.
160/B2 Tenango, Mex.
159/F5 Tenango de Río Blanco, Mex.
123/B3 Tenasserim, Burma
123/B3 Tenasserim (range), Burma
123/B4 Tenasserim (Thanintharyi) (div.), Burma
80/B6 Tenay, Fr.
66/D2 Ten Boer, Neth.
58/D2 Tenbury, Eng,UK
58/B3 Tenby, Wal,UK
87/E2 Tencarola, It.
86/A4 Tenda, Colle di (pass), It.
150/B3 Tendaho, Eth.
82/D4 Tende, Fr.
82/D4 Tende, Col de (pass), Fr.
82/D4 Tende, Colle di (pass), It.
98/F4 Tenderovsk (bay), Ukr.
98/F4 Tenderovsk (spit), Ukr.
111/G1 Tendō, Japan
185/G1 Tendoy, Id,US
143/E2 Tendrara, Mor.
80/C4 Tendre (peak), Swi.
144/D3 Ténenkou, Mali
173/F3 Tenente Portela, Braz.
145/H2 Ténéré (des.), Niger
146/A4 Ténéré du Tafassasset (des.), Niger
145/H2 Ténéré, 'Erg du (des.), Niger
146/A5 Ténéré, 'Erg du (des.), Niger
142/A3 Tenerife (isl.), Canl.
164/C2 Tenerife, Col.
143/F1 Ténès, Alg.
71/F6 Tenes (riv.), Sp.
116/C4 Teng (riv.), Burma
113/B2 Teng'aopu, China
116/C3 Tengchong, China
127/E4 Tenggarong, Indo.
108/E4 Tengger (des.), China
124/F5 Tengger-Bromo-Semeru Nat'l Psrv., Indo.
114/A1 Tengiz (lake), Kaz.
123/E2 Tengqiao, China
164/B5 Tenguel, Ecu.
115/D4 Teng Xian, China
82/C4 Tenibre (mtn.), Fr.
75/G4 Tenibres (peak), It.
172/D1 Teniente Enciso Nat'l Park, Par.
81/E4 Tenigerbad, Swi.
80/D1 Teningen, Ger.
182/C4 Tenino, Wa,US
92/D3 Tenja, Cro.
167/L7 Tenjo, Col.
122/F4 Tenkāsi, India
153/F5 Tenke, Zaire
191/G3 Tenkiller (lake), Ok,US
145/E4 Tenkodogo, Burk.
187/F4 Tenmile (wash), Az,US
200/E3 Ten Mile, Tn,US
188/L7 Tenmile (cr.), Tx,US
85/D1 Tenna (riv.), It.
130/D4 Tennant Creek, Austl.
200/D2 Tennessee (riv.), US
200/D3 Tennessee (state), US
200/D2 Tennessee Ridge, Tn,US
200/C3 Tennessee-Tombigbee Wtrwy., Al, Ms,US
69/E3 Tenneville, Belg.
203/F2 Tennille, Al,US
201/F4 Tennille, Ga,US
174/C2 Teno, Chile
61/H1 Tenojoki (riv.), Fin.
125/A4 Tenom, Malay.
159/H5 Tenosique, Mex.
111/L10 Tenri, Japan
111/E3 Tenryū, Japan
111/E3 Tenryū (riv.), Japan
189/J2 Tensas (basin), La,US
202/C2 Tensas (riv.), La,US
202/C1 Tensas River Nat'l Wild. Ref., La,US
142/C3 Tensift (reg.), Mor.
142/C3 Tensift, Oued (riv.), Mor.
185/K1 Ten Sleep, Wy,US
193/G4 Tenstrike, Mn,US
149/H3 Tenta, Eth.
127/F4 Tentena, Indo.
59/G4 Tenterden, Eng,UK
135/E1 Tenterfield, Austl.
203/H5 Ten Thousand (isls.), Fl,US
123/B2 Ten Thousand Buddhas, Cave of, Burma
127/F3 Tentolomatinan (peak), Indo.
142/A5 Tenuaiur, Uad (dry riv.), WSah.
151/A1 Tenus (peak), Kenya
76/A1 Teo, Sp.
158/E4 Teocaltiche, Mex.
159/N7 Teocelo, Mex.
158/E4 Teocuitatlán de Corona, Mex.
174/E2 Teodelina, Arg.
170/B4 Teodoro Sampaio, Braz.
171/E3 Teófilo Otoni, Braz.
153/G2 Te'Okutu, Ugan.
161/H4 Teorama, Col.
159/L7 Teotihuacán (ruins), Mex.
159/R9 Teotihuacan Pyramids, Mex.
130/C1 Tepa, Indo.
158/C2 Tepache, Mex.
158/E5 Tepalcatepec, Mex.
159/L8 Tepalcingo, Mex.
159/E4 Tepatitlán, Mex.
159/M7 Tepatlaxco de Hidalgo, Mex.
159/F5 Tepeaca, Mex.
159/F5 Tepeapulco, Mex.
103/C1 Tepebaşı, Turk.
158/E4 Tepechitlán, Mex.
190/E3 Tepee (mtn.), Ok,US
159/K7 Tepeji del Río, Mex.
91/G2 Tepelenë, Alb.
71/F2 Tepelská Plošina (mts.), Czh.
159/M8 Tepexi de Rodríguez, Mex.
158/E4 Tepezalá, Mex.
149/G4 Tēpī, Eth.
158/D4 Tepic, Mex.
71/F2 Teplá (riv.), Czh.
71/G5 Teplá Vltava (riv.), Czh.
72/D6 Teplice, Czh.
158/B2 Tepoca, Cabo (cape), Mex.
139/L6 Tepoto (isl.), FrPol.
159/Q9 Tepotzotlán, Mex.
159/K8 Tepoztlán, Mex.
158/E4 Tequila, Mex.
77/G1 Ter (riv.), Sp.
145/F3 Téra, Niger
76/B1 Tera (riv.), Sp.
66/B4 Ter Aar, Neth.
139/K4 Teraina (Washington) (isl.), Kiri.
149/F4 Terakeka, Sudan
85/D2 Teramo, It.
85/D2 Teramo (prov.), It.
135/B3 Terang, Austl.
67/E3 Ter Apel, Neth.
66/D5 Terborg, Neth.
99/K1 Terbuny, Rus.
104/E2 Tercan, Turk.
77/S12 Terceira (isl.), Azor.,Port.
174/E2 Tercero (riv.), Arg.
73/D1 Terchová, Slvk.
93/K2 Terderovsk (bay), Ukr.
93/K2 Terderovsk (spit), Ukr.
98/C3 Terebovlya, Ukr.
97/H4 Terek, Rus.
97/H4 Terek (riv.), Rus.
98/F1 Terekhovka, Bela.
97/J3 Terekli-Mekteb, Rus.
124/D2 Terempa, Indo.
124/C1 Terengganu (riv.), Malay.
124/C1 Terengganu (state), Malay.
87/G1 Terenzano, It.
164/D2 Terepaima Nat'l Park, Ven.
167/F4 Teresina, Braz.
171/E4 Teresópolis, Braz.
65/M2 Terespol, Pol.
172/D1 Terevinto, Bol.
68/C4 Tergnier, Fr.
108/D4 Tergun Daba (mts.), China
127/F2 Terhathum, Nepal
66/B5 Terheijden, Neth.
94/G1 Teriberka, Rus.
94/G1 Teriberskiy, Mys (pt.), Rus.
66/C2 Terkaplesterpoelen (lake), Neth.
93/H5 Terkirdağ (prov.), Turk.
81/H4 Terlano (Terlan), It.
81/H4 Terlan (Terlango), It.
188/C3 Terlingua, Tx,US
81/H5 Termeno (Tramin), It.
107/J1 Termez, Uzb.
79/G4 Terminiers, Fr.
90/C4 Termini Imerese, It.
84/C3 Terminillo (peak), It.
85/E6 Terminio (peak), It.
159/H5 Términos (lag.), Mex.
145/H3 Termit-Kaoboul, Niger
148/A1 Termit, Massif de (plat.), Niger
85/E3 Termoli, It.
60/D2 Termonfeckin, Ire.
66/E2 Termunten, Neth.
58/D1 Tern (riv.), Eng,UK
127/G3 Ternate, Indo.
82/A1 Ternay, Fr.
66/A6 Terneuzen, Neth.
109/M2 Terney, Rus.
84/C2 Terni, It.
84/C2 Terni (prov.), It.
74/F3 Ternin (riv.), Fr.
68/B3 Ternoise (riv.), Fr.
98/C3 Ternopol', Ukr.
98/C3 Ternopol' Obl., Ukr.
99/L2 Ternovka, Rus.
99/J3 Ternovka, Ukr.
135/C2 Terowie, Austl.
109/N2 Terpeniya (bay), Rus.
109/N2 Terpeniya (cape), Rus.
91/H2 Terpni, Gre.
186/C3 Terra Bella, Ca,US
202/C3 Terrabonne (bay), La,US
178/D3 Terrace, BC,Can
195/L3 Terrace Bay, On,Can
182/D4 Terrace Heights, Wa,US
202/K8 Terra Ceia, Fl,US
84/D5 Terracina, It.
197/R8 Terra Cotta, On,Can
87/E4 Terra del Sole, It.
61/E2 Terråk, Nor.
191/F4 Terral, Ok,US
90/A3 Terralba, It.
167/G5 Terra Nova, Braz.
83/C3 Terranova da Sibari, It.
83/C3 Terranova di Pollino, It.
197/K1 Terra Nova Nat'l Park, Nf,Can
87/E5 Terranuova Bracciolini, It.
173/F2 Terra Rica, Braz.
77/G2 Terrassa, Sp.
74/D4 Terrasson-la-Villedieu, Fr.
188/A3 Terrazas, Mex.
199/K2 Terrebonne, Qu,Can
197/N6 Terrebonne (co.), Qu,Can
198/C5 Terre Haute, In,US
206/B3 Terre Hill, Pa,US
189/F1 Terrell, Tx,US
197/K2 Terrenceville, Nf,Can
185/G2 Terreton, Id,US
134/H8 Terrey Hills, Austl.
59/G1 Terrington Saint Clement, Eng,UK
81/F4 Terri, Piz (peak), Swi.
191/J4 Terry, La,US
200/B4 Terry, Ms,US
183/M4 Terry, Mt,US
208/A2 Terryville, Ct,US
97/K5 Tersakan, Trkm.
114/A1 Tersakkan (riv.), Kaz.
66/C2 Terschelling (isl.), Neth.
90/A3 Tertenia, It.
77/E2 Teruel, Sp.
123/B5 Terutao (isl.), Thai.
93/H4 Tervel, Bul.
75/K3 Terza Grande (peak), It.
75/K4 Terzo d'Aquileia, It.
87/G1 Terzo d'Aquileia, It.
108/C1 Tes, Mong.
108/D2 Tes, Mong.
92/D3 Tešanj, Bosn.
191/F1 Tescott, Ks,US
74/D5 Tescou (riv.), Fr.
149/H2 Teseney, Eth.
81/H5 Tesero, It.
177/G1 Teshekpuk (lake), Ak,US
145/E5 Teshi, Gha.
112/D2 Teshikaga, Japan
112/B1 Teshio, Japan
112/C1 Teshio (riv.), Japan
112/C2 Teshio-dake (mtn.), Japan
108/D2 Tesiyn (riv.), Mong.
108/C1 Tes-Khem (riv.), Rus.
92/C3 Teslić, Bosn.
178/C3 Teslin (lake), BC,Can
177/M3 Teslin, Yk,Can
178/C2 Teslin (riv.), Yk,Can
63/P2 Tësovo-Netyl'skiy, Rus.
145/F1 Tessalit, Mali
145/G3 Tessaoua, Niger
79/E3 Tessé-la-Madeleine, Fr.
69/E1 Tessenderlo, Belg.
79/D3 Tessy-sur-Vire, Fr.
59/E4 Test (riv.), Eng,UK
85/G4 Testa del Gargano (pt.), It.
82/D1 Testa del Rutor (peak), It.
77/G1 Têt (riv.), Fr.
73/B4 Tét, Hun.
172/B2 Tetas (pt.), Chile
58/D3 Tetbury, Eng,UK
155/G3 Tete, Moz.
155/G2 Tete (prov.), Moz.
82/D5 Tête d'Alpe (peak), Fr.
80/D1 Tête de Faux (peak), Fr.
82/C4 Tête de l'Enchastraye (peak), Fr.
82/C4 Tête de l'Estrop (peak), Fr.
82/C4 Tête de Moïse (peak), Fr.
82/C4 Tête de Siguret (peak), Fr.
82/C3 Tête de Soulaure (peak), Fr.
80/C6 Tête du Torraz (peak), Fr.
182/E1 Tête Jaune Cache, BC,Can
136/D2 Te Teko, N.Z.
159/L8 Tetela del Volcán, Mex.
159/M7 Tetela de Ocampo, Mex.
82/C1 Tête Nord des Fours (peak), Fr.
80/D5 Tête Ronde (peak), Swi.
62/E5 Teterow, Ger.
93/G4 Teteven, Bul.
57/H5 Tetford, Eng,UK
139/L6 Tetiaroa (isl.), FrPol.
69/F5 Teting-sur-Nied, Fr.
98/E3 Tetiyev, Ukr.
99/H2 Tëtkino, Rus.
177/K3 Tetlin, Ak,US
177/K3 Tetlin Nat'l Wild. Ref., Ak,US
185/H2 Teton, Id,US
185/H2 Teton (riv.), Id, Wy,US
183/J4 Teton (riv.), Mt,US
185/H2 Teton (range), Wy,US
185/H2 Tetonia, Id,US
141/M13 Tétouan, Mor.
92/E4 Tetovo, Macd.
105/F1 Tetri-Tskaro, Geo.
81/F2 Tettnang, Ger.
77/N9 Tetuan, Sp.
121/G2 Tetulia, Bang.
121/H4 Tetulia (riv.), Bang.
73/B6 Tetves (riv.), Hun.
71/F4 Teublitz, Ger.
72/C5 Teuchern, Ger.
185/K5 Teuchezhsk, Rus.
172/D2 Teuco (riv.), Arg.
81/F3 Teufen, Swi.
90/A3 Teulada (cape), It.
158/E4 Teul de González Ortega, Mex.
194/F2 Teulon, Mb,Can
160/E3 Teupasenti, Hon.
72/D3 Teupitzer (lake), Ger.
112/B1 Teuri (isl.), Japan
71/E2 Teuschnitz, Ger.
67/F4 Teutoburger Wald (for.), Ger.
193/K4 Teutopolis, Il,US
72/B5 Teutschenthal, Ger.
84/C3 Tevere (Nera) (riv.), It.
87/F5 Tevere (Tiber) (riv.), It.
103/D3 Teverya (Tiberias), Isr.
54/D6 Teviot (riv.), Sc,UK
54/D6 Teviotdale (vall.), Sc,UK
134/D4 Tewantin-Noosa, Austl.
194/F4 Tewaukon Nat'l Wild. Ref., ND,US
58/D3 Tewkesbury, Eng,UK
182/B3 Texada (isl.), BC,Can
189/F3 Texana (lake), Tx,US
191/G4 Texarkana, Ar,US
191/G4 Texarkana, Tx,US
135/D1 Texas, Austl.
180/G5 Texas (state), US
188/L7 Texas, Tx,US
188/K7 Texas Christian Univ., Tx,US
189/G3 Texas City, Tx,US
189/H3 Texas Point Nat'l Wild. Ref., Tx,US
189/F2 Texas Safari Wild. Park, Tx,US
159/L7 Texcoco de Mora, Mex.
159/R9 Texcoco, Lago del (lake), Mex.
66/B2 Texel (isl.), Neth.
66/B3 Texelstroom (chan.), Neth.
190/D2 Texhoma, Ok,US
190/C3 Texico, NM,US
191/F3 Texoma (lake), Ok, Tx,US
156/D3 Teyateyaneng, Les.
94/J4 Teykovo, Rus.
84/C1 Tezio (peak), It.
159/F5 Teziutlán, Mex.
159/F5 Tezoatlán, Mex.
159/F5 Tezonapa, Mex.
159/L7 Tezontepec, Mex.
116/B3 Tezpur, India
87/E1 Tezze, It.
123/C1 Tha (riv.), Laos
178/G2 Tha-anne (riv.), NW,Can
156/E3 Thabana-Ntlenyana (peak), Les.
156/D3 Thaba Nchu, SAfr.
157/E2 Thabankulu (peak), SAfr.
156/D2 Thabazimbi, SAfr.
82/C2 Thabor (mtn.), Fr.
123/B3 Tha Chin (riv.), Thai.
106/E3 Thādiq, SAr.
123/B4 Thaen (pt.), Thai.
123/B2 Thagaya, Burma
123/D1 Thai Binh, Viet.
123/C3 Thailand
123/C4 Thailand (gulf), Thai.
123/D1 Thai Nguyen, Viet.
120/B1 Thākurdwāra, India
121/G2 Thākurgaon, Bang.
118/E3 Thākurmunda, India
122/A1 Thal, Pak.
122/A2 Thal (des.), Pak.
148/E2 Tha'l (mtn.), Sudan
123/B4 Thalang, Thai.
72/B4 Thale, Ger.
123/C5 Thale Ban Nat'l Park, Thai.
69/G5 Thaleischweiler-Fröschen, Ger.
75/L3 Thalerhof (int'l arpt.), Aus.
71/G7 Thalgau, Aus.
72/C6 Thalheim, Ger.
71/G6 Thalheim bei Wels, Aus.
203/H2 Thalmann, Ga,US
70/E4 Thalmässing, Ger.
81/E3 Thalwil, Swi.
123/C3 Tha Mai, Thai.
106/E6 Thamar, Jabal (mtn.), Yem.
59/F3 Thame, Eng,UK
59/F3 Thame (riv.), Eng,UK
198/F3 Thames (riv.), On,Can
136/C2 Thames, N.Z.
53/P7 Thames (riv.), Eng,UK
53/P7 Thames Barrier, Eng,UK
136/C2 Thames, Firth of (inlet), N.Z.
136/C2 Thames Valley (reg.), N.Z.
118/B4 Thāna, India
120/A1 Thāna Bhawan, India
120/A3 Thāna Kasbā, India
120/C3 Thanatpin, Burma
123/B3 Thanbyuzayat, Burma
121/H3 Thāneswar, Bang.
59/H4 Thanet, Isle of (isl.), Eng,UK
119/J5 Thang Duc, Viet.
121/G2 Thanggu, India
134/C4 Thangool, Austl.
123/D2 Thanh Hoa, Viet.
119/J4 Thanh Lang Xa, Viet.
123/D4 Thanh Phu, Viet.
123/D4 Thanh Tri, Viet.
123/B4 Thanintharyi (Tenasserim) (div.), Burma
122/G3 Thanjavur, India
121/E2 Thānkot, Nepal
80/D2 Thann, Fr.
70/D6 Thannhausen, Ger.
123/C3 Thanya Buri, Thai.
154/D3 Thaoge (riv.), Bots.
80/C1 Thaon-les-Vosges, Fr.
123/B4 Thap Put, Thai.
123/B4 Thap Sakae, Thai.
78/D3 Thar (riv.), Fr.
107/J3 Thar (des.), India, Pak.
118/B3 Tharād, India
72/D6 Tharandt, Ger.
134/A5 Thargomindah, Austl.
116/B5 Tharrawaddy, Burma
123/C3 Tha Rua, Thai.
123/B4 Tha Sala, Thai.
91/J2 Thásos, Gre.
91/J2 Thásos (isl.), Gre.
59/E4 Thatcham, Eng,UK
187/H4 Thatcher, Az,US
185/H2 Thatcher, Id,US
123/D1 That Khe, Viet.
116/C5 Thaton, Burma
123/D2 That Phanom, Thai.
123/C3 Tha Tum, Thai.
116/B3 Thaungdut, Burma
81/H3 Thaur, Aus.
119/H4 Tha Uthen, Thai.
123/C2 Tha Wang Pha, Thai.
57/G3 Thaxted, Eng,UK
200/C3 Thaxton, Ms,US
65/H4 Thaya (riv.), Aus.
193/K4 Thayer, Il,US
191/G2 Thayer, Ks,US
191/J2 Thayer, Mo,US
116/B5 Thayetmyo, Burma
119/G4 Thayetmyo, Burma
81/E2 Thayngen, Swi.
116/C4 Thazi, Burma
59/E4 Theale, Eng,UK
147/G3 Thebes (ruins), Egypt
180/B2 The Dalles, Or,US
123/B1 Thedaw, Burma
192/D3 Thedford, Ne,US
133/F2 The Granites (peak), Austl.
66/B4 The Hague ('s-Gravenhage) (cap.), Neth.
136/B3 The Hermitage, N.Z.
70/D3 Theilheim, Ger.
78/C5 Theix, Fr.
141/W18 Thelepte, Tun.
176/G3 Thelon (riv.), Can.
178/F2 Thelon (riv.), NW,Can
70/D2 Themar, Ger.
122/F4 Theni-Allinagaram, India
133/F2 Theo (peak), Austl.
134/C4 Theodore, Austl.
194/C2 Theodore, Sk,Can
202/D2 Theodore, Al,US
208/C2 Theodore Francis Green (st. arpt.), RI,US
187/G4 Theodore Roosevelt (lake), Az,US
194/C4 Theodore Roosevelt Nat'l Park, ND,US
191/H2 Theodosia, Mo,US
130/C5 Theo, Mount (peak), Austl.
201/F1 The Plains, Oh,US
68/B5 Thérain (riv.), Fr.
91/H3 Thermaic (Salonika) (gulf), Gre.
186/D4 Thermal, Ca,US
184/C4 Thermalito, Ca,US
91/H2 Thérmi, Gre.
91/H3 Thermopílai (Thermopylae) (pass), Gre.
185/J2 Thermopolis, Wy,US
91/H3 Thermopylae (Thermopílai) (pass), Gre.
53/U9 Thérouanne (riv.), Fr.
79/G6 Thésée, Fr.
91/G3 Thesprotikón, Gre.
198/E1 Thessalon, On,Can
91/H2 Thessaloníki, Gre.
92/F5 Thessaloníki (int'l arpt.), Gre.
91/H3 Thessaly (reg.), Gre.
59/G2 Thet (riv.), Eng,UK
59/G2 Thetford, Eng,UK
196/A4 Thetford, Vt,US
199/K3 Thetford Center, Vt,US
196/B2 Thetford Mines, Qu,Can
116/C5 Thetkala, Burma
156/D3 Theunissen, SAfr.
69/E2 Theux, Belg.
53/T9 Thève (riv.), Fr.
53/P7 Theydon Bois, Eng,UK
53/T10 Thiais, Fr.
91/G3 Thíamis (riv.), Gre.
62/B3 Thiant, Fr.
69/E6 Thiaucourt, Fr.
79/F2 Thiberville, Fr.
202/C3 Thibodaux, La,US
199/H4 Thick (mtn.), Pa,US
183/L1 Thickwood (hills), Sk,Can
194/F3 Thief River Falls, Mn,US
80/C4 Thielle (riv.), Swi.
184/B2 Thielsen (mtn.), Or,US
87/E1 Thiene, It.
120/D4 Thien Ngon, Viet.
70/D5 Thierhaupten, Ger.
74/E4 Thiers, Fr.
53/T9 Thieux-Saint-Thève, Fr.
69/E5 Thierville-sur-Meuse, Fr.
144/A3 Thiès, Sen.
144/A3 Thiès (reg.), Sen.
116/E4 Thiet Tra, Viet.
151/B2 Thika, Kenya
121/G2 Thimphu (cap.), Bhu.
61/N7 Thingvellir Nat'l Park, Ice.
138/F7 Thio, NCal.
69/F5 Thionville, Fr.
145/E3 Thiou, Burk.
91/J4 Thíra (isl.), Gre.
89/K3 Thíra (Sántorini), Gre.
147/F5 Third Cataract (falls), Sudan
205/P15 Third Lake, Il,US
57/E2 Thirlmere (lake), Eng,UK
79/G4 Thiron, Fr.
79/G4 Thironne (riv.), Fr.
57/G3 Thirsk, Eng,UK
132/D5 Thirsty (peak), Austl.
197/U9 Thirtymile (pt.), NY,US
80/C3 Thise, Fr.
62/C3 Thisted, Den.
61/P6 Thistilfjördhur (bay), Ice.
133/G5 Thistle (isl.), Austl.
177/M3 Thistle (mtn.), Yk,Can
139/Z18 Thithia (isl.), Fiji
91/H3 Thívai, Gre.
61/N7 Thjórsa (riv.), Ice.
116/B3 Thlanship, India
178/G2 Thlewiaza (riv.), NW,Can
123/B2 Thoen, Thai.
123/C2 Thoeng, Thai.
155/F4 Thohoyandou, SAfr.
123/D4 Thoi Binh, Viet.
80/A5 Thoissey, Fr.
66/B5 Tholen, Neth.
66/B5 Tholen (isl.), Neth.
69/G5 Tholey, Ger.
206/B6 Thomas (pt.), Md,US
191/E3 Thomas, Ok,US
201/H1 Thomas, WV,US
198/B4 Thomasboro, Il,US
188/D1 Thomas, J. B. (lake), Tx,US
200/D4 Thomaston, Al,US
208/A2 Thomaston, Ct,US
200/E4 Thomaston, Ga,US
60/C4 Thomastown, Ire.
191/J4 Thomastown, La,US
200/C4 Thomastown, Ms,US
200/D5 Thomasville, Al,US
203/G2 Thomasville, Ga,US
191/J2 Thomasville, Mo,US
201/G3 Thomasville, NC,US
206/B4 Thomasville, Pa,US
184/B4 Thomes (cr.), Ca,US
134/A4 Thompson (riv.), Austl.
182/D2 Thompson (riv.), BC,Can
178/G3 Thompson, Mb,Can
184/B3 Thompson (peak), Ca,US
208/C2 Thompson, Ct,US
193/H3 Thompson (riv.), Ia, Mo,US
198/C2 Thompson, Mi,US
182/G4 Thompson (riv.), Mt,US
194/F4 Thompson, ND,US
190/B3 Thompson (peak), NM,US
185/J4 Thompson, Ut,US
182/G4 Thompson Falls, Mt,US
205/B3 Thompson Place-Tanglewilde, Wa,US
200/C2 Thompsonville, Il,US
198/D2 Thompsonville, Mi,US
178/E1 Thomsen (riv.), NW,Can
138/D7 Thomson (riv.), Austl.
201/F4 Thomson, Ga,US
193/J3 Thomson, Il,US
123/C3 Thon Buri, Thai.
119/J4 Thon Cam Lo, Viet.
123/B2 Thongwa, Burma
123/E4 Thon Lac Nghiep, Viet.
80/B1 Thonnance-lès-Joinville, Fr.
80/C5 Thonon-les-Bains, Fr.
202/L7 Thonotosassa, Fl,US
202/L7 Thonotosassa (lake), Fl,US
123/E4 Thon Song Pha, Viet.
187/H3 Thoreau, NM,US
80/C6 Thorens-Glières, Fr.
53/U10 Thorigny-sur-Marne, Fr.
61/N7 Thorlákshöfn, Ice.
205/Q16 Thorn (cr.), Il,US
57/G2 Thornaby-on-Tees, Eng,UK
198/F2 Thornbury, On,Can
58/D3 Thornbury, Eng,UK
206/C4 Thorndale, Pa,US
189/F2 Thorndale, Tx,US
208/B1 Thorndike, Ma,US
199/G1 Thorne, On,Can
57/H4 Thorne, Eng,UK
177/M4 Thorne Bay, Ak,US
191/H2 Thornfield, Mo,US
197/S8 Thornhill, On,Can
54/B4 Thornhill, Sc,UK
56/E1 Thornhill, Sc,UK
206/C1 Thornhurst, Pa,US
57/G2 Thornley, Eng,UK
57/G3 Thornthwaite, Eng,UK
191/H4 Thornton, Ar,US
205/M10 Thornton, Ca,US
190/B1 Thornton, Co,US
189/F2 Thornton, Tx,US
57/E4 Thornton Cleveleys, Eng,UK
57/H3 Thornton Dale, Eng,UK
188/C2 Thorntonville, Tx,US
198/C4 Thorntown, In,US
197/S9 Thorold, On,Can
197/S9 Thorold South, On,Can
182/D4 Thorp, Wa,US
193/J1 Thorp, Wi,US
53/M7 Thorpe, Eng,UK
59/H3 Thorpe le Soken, Eng,UK
57/G2 Thorpe Thewles, Eng,UK
183/G1 Thorsby, Ab,Can
200/D4 Thorsby, Al,US
61/P6 Thórshöfn, Ice.
79/E6 Thouarcé, Fr.
78/D6 Thouaré-sur-Loire, Fr.
74/C3 Thouars, Fr.
116/B3 Thoubāl, India
74/C3 Thouet (riv.), Fr.
68/B5 Thourotte, Fr.
199/H2 Thousand (isls.), Can., US
204/B2 Thousand Oaks, Ca,US
185/F3 Thousand Springs (cr.), Nv.,Ut, US
151/B2 Thowa (dry riv.), Kenya
89/K2 Thrace (reg.), Eur.
96/C4 Thracian (sea), Gre., Turk.
205/E6 Thread (cr.), Mi,US
135/D3 Thredbo Village, Austl.
206/D2 Three Bridges, NJ,US
185/F2 Three Creek, Id,US
183/J5 Three Forks, Mt,US
177/L4 Three Guardsmen (mtn.), BC,Can
183/H2 Three Hills, Ab,Can
183/H2 Threehills (cr.), Ab,Can
135/C4 Three Hummock (isl.), Austl.
136/B1 Three Kings (isls.), N.Z.
198/B2 Three Lakes, Wi,US
206/B3 Three Mile (isl.), Pa,US
196/E3 Three Mile Plains, NS,Can
200/E4 Three Notch, Al,US
198/C4 Three Oaks, Mi,US
123/B3 Three Pagodas (pass), Burma
145/E5 Three Points (cape), Gha.
132/C3 Three Rivers, Austl.
208/B1 Three Rivers, Ma,US
198/D4 Three Rivers, Mi,US
187/J4 Three Rivers, NM,US
132/B4 Three Springs, Austl.
182/E2 Three Valley, BC,Can
188/E2 Thrifty, Tx,US
190/E4 Throckmorton, Tx,US
132/E3 Throssell (lake), Austl.
182/F3 Thrums, BC,Can
58/B5 Thrushel (riv.), Eng,UK
58/D2 Thruxton, Eng,UK
131/F3 Thud (pt.), Austl.
123/D4 Thu Dau Mot, Viet.
123/D4 Thu Duc, Viet.
68/D3 Thuin, Belg.
74/E5 Thuir, Fr.
70/C2 Thulba (riv.), Ger.
179/T7 Thule Air Base, Grld.
125/B3 Thumb (peak), Phil.
80/D4 Thun, Swi.
195/K3 Thunder (bay), On,Can
195/K3 Thunder (cape), On,Can
193/K1 Thunder (mtn.), Wi,US
185/L2 Thunder Basin Nat'l Grsld., Wy,US
195/K3 Thunder Bay, On,Can
194/B5 Thunder Bay Nat'l Grsld., Wy,US
192/C1 Thunder Butte (cr.), SD,US
80/D4 Thunersee (lake), Swi.
123/C2 Thung Chang, Thai.
70/C3 Thüngersheim, Ger.
123/C2 Thung Salaeng Luang Nat'l Park, Thai.
123/B4 Thung Song, Thai.
121/H2 Thunkar, Bhu.
81/E2 Thur (riv.), Swi.
81/F2 Thurgau (canton), Swi.
81/F3 Thüringen, Aus.
71/E1 Thüringer Schiefergebirge (mts.), Ger.
70/D1 Thüringer Wald (for.), Ger.
72/B6 Thuringia (state), Ger.
59/E2 Thurlaston, Eng,UK
60/C4 Thurles, Ire.
135/B1 Thurloo Downs, Austl.
183/L4 Thurlow, Mt,US
199/H5 Thurmont, Md,US
71/E2 Thurnau, Ger.
62/D4 Thurø By, Den.
131/F2 Thursday Island, Austl.
199/J2 Thurso, Qu,Can
55/K7 Thurso, Sc,UK
137/T Thurston (isl.), Ant.
205/A3 Thurston (co.), Wa,US
79/E3 Thury-Harcourt, Fr.
81/F4 Thusis, Swi.
137/S Thwaites Iceberg Tongue, Ant.
80/C5 Thyez, Fr.
155/G3 Thyolo, Malw.
72/A4 Thyra (riv.), Ger.
135/D1 Tia, Austl.
172/B1 Tiahuanacu, Bol.
172/B1 Tiahuanaco, Bol.
177/M5 Tian (pt.), BC,Can
117/H3 Tianbao, China
108/D3 Tiancang, China
115/D4 Tianchang, China
117/E4 Tiandeng, China
119/J3 Tian'e, China
167/F3 Tianguá, Braz.
117/G3 Tianhua, China
115/D3 Tianjin, China
115/D3 Tianjin (prov.), China
119/J3 Tianlin, China
115/C5 Tianmen, China
115/K9 Tianmu (mts.), China
117/F3 Tianping, China
117/F2 Tianqiao, China
100/H5 Tian Shan (range), Asia
113/C2 Tianshifu, China
108/F5 Tianshui, China
114/C4 Tianshuihai, China
115/C5 Tiantangzhai (mtn.), China
119/J3 Tianyang, China
115/C2 Tianzhen, China
117/F3 Tianzhu, China
113/B2 Tianzhuangtai, China
141/R16 Tiaret, Alg.
141/R16 Tiaret (wilaya), Alg.
144/D5 Tiassalé, IvC.
175/T11 Tiatucurá, Uru.
139/S9 Tiavea, WSam.
170/C5 Tibagi, Braz.
170/C4 Tibagi (riv.), Braz.
173/G1 Tibají (riv.), Braz.
164/C3 Tibaná, Col.
146/C4 Tibasti, Sarīr (des.), Libya
148/B4 Tibati, Camr.
200/C4 Tibbee (cr.), Ms,US
57/F6 Tibberton, Eng,UK
202/D2 Tibbie, Al,US
63/R7 Tibble, Swe.
144/C4 Tibé, Pic de (peak), Gui.
84/C4 Tiber (riv.), It.
183/J3 Tiber (dam), Mt,US
103/D3 Tiberias (Sea of Galilee) (lake), Isr., Syria
103/D3 Tiberias (Teverya), Isr.
82/D4 Tibert (peak), It.
87/F5 Tiber (Tevere) (riv.), It.
146/C4 Tibesti (mts.), Chad,Libya
114/D5 Tibet (reg.), China
77/L7 Tibidabo (peak), Sp.
145/G3 Tibiri, Niger
103/D3 Tibnīn, Leb.
133/J4 Tibooburra, Austl.
143/H1 Tīb, Ra's aṭ (cape), Tun.
90/B4 Tīb, Ra's aṭ (cape), Tun.
62/F2 Tibro, Swe.
57/G5 Tibshelf, Eng,UK
164/B3 Tibugá, Ensenada de (gulf), Col.
161/H2 Tiburon (cape), Haiti
158/B2 Tiburón (isl.), Mex.
161/G4 Tiburón (cape), Pan.
205/K11 Tiburon, Ca,US
168/D5 Ticaco, Peru
59/G4 Ticehurst, Eng,UK
205/P14 Tichigan (lake), Wi,US
144/C2 Tichît, Mrta.
144/C2 Tichît, Dhar (hills), Mrta.
142/C3 Tichka, Jebel (mtn.), Mor.
142/B5 Tichla, WSah.
191/J3 Tichnor, Ar,US
150/A4 Tīcho, Eth.
86/C2 Ticino (riv.), It.
81/E5 Ticino (canton), Swi.
81/E5 Ticino (riv.), Swi.
57/G5 Tickhill, Eng,UK
92/E4 Ticleni, Rom.
168/B3 Ticllos, Peru
199/K3 Ticonderoga, NY,US
159/H4 Ticul, Mex.
116/B4 Tiddim, Burma
62/E2 Tidaholm, Swe.
57/G5 Tideswell, Eng,UK
143/F4 Tidikelt (plain), Alg.
199/G4 Tidioute, Pa,US
144/C2 Tidjikdja, Mrta.
86/C3 Tidone (riv.), It.
127/G3 Tidore (isl.), Indo.
144/A2 Tidra (isl.), Mrta.
142/B5 Tidsit, Sebjet (dry lake), WSah.
145/E4 Tiébélé Corabie, Burk.
144/D5 Tiébissou, IvC.
146/C4 Tiéboro, Chad
113/D2 Tiechang, China
77/X16 Tiede Nat'l Park
81/F4 Tiefencastel, Swi.
72/D2 Tiefensee, Ger.
144/D4 Tiéfinzo, IvC.
69/E2 Tiège, Belg.
66/C5 Tiel, Neth.
109/K2 Tieli, China
113/B1 Tieling, China
77/N9 Tielmes, Sp.
68/C1 Tielt, Belg.
69/D2 Tielt-Winge, Belg.
144/D4 Tiemba (riv.), IvC.
114/E3 Tiemen Guan (pass), China
69/D2 Tienen, Belg.
144/D4 Tiénigbe, IvC.
117/H3 Tieniu (pass), China
102/H5 Tien Shan (range), China
123/D1 Tien Yen, Viet.
123/D2 Tien Yen, Viet.
200/C4 Tie Plant, Ms,US
79/E5 Tiercé, Fr.
134/C3 Tieri, Austl.
146/C4 Tieroko, Tarso (peak), Chad
62/G1 Tierp, Swe.
172/B3 Tierra Amarilla, Chile
190/A2 Tierra Amarilla, NM,US
159/F5 Tierra Blanca, Mex.
190/C3 Tierra Blanca (cr.), NM, Tx,US
175/L8 Tierra del Fuego (isl.), Arg., Chile
175/L8 Tierra del Fuego, Antártida e Islas del Atlántico Sur (prov.), Arg.
175/K8 Tierra del Fuego Nat'l Park, Arg.
164/B4 Tierradentro, Col.
159/E4 Tierranueva, Mex.
76/C2 Tiétar (riv.), Sp.
170/C4 Tietê (riv.), Braz.
182/D4 Tieton, Wa,US
182/D4 Tieton (peak), Wa,US
133/G3 Tieyon, Austl.
142/C4 Tifariti, WSah.
187/J2 Tiffany, Co,US
182/E3 Tiffany (mtn.), Wa,US
198/E4 Tiffin, Oh,US
198/D4 Tiffin (riv.), Oh,US
141/L14 Tiflet, Mor.
203/G2 Tifton, Ga,US
139/V12 Tiga (isl.), NCal.
124/C3 Tigapuluh (mts.), Indo.
194/E3 Tiger (hills), Mb,Can
165/G4 Tiger (fall), Guy., Sur.
202/N8 Tiger (lake), Fl,US
193/K1 Tigerton, Wi,US
54/A6 Tighvein (hill), Sc,UK
101/R4 Tigil', Rus.
201/F4 Tignall, Ga,US
148/B4 Tignère, Camr.
82/C1 Tignes, Barrage de (dam), Fr.
82/B1 Tignieu-Jameyzieu, Fr.
196/E2 Tignish, PE,Can
150/A2 Tigray (prov.), Eth.
175/S12 Tigre, Arg.
168/C1 Tigre (riv.), Peru
165/F2 Tigre (riv.), Ven.
154/A3 Tigres (bay), Ang.
102/D6 Tigris (riv.), Asia
100/E6 Tigris (riv.), Iraq, Turk.
144/B2 Tiguent, Mrta.
146/C5 Tigui (well), Chad
79/H5 Tigy, Fr.
150/B1 Tihāmat al Yaman (val.), Yem.
73/B6 Tihany, Hun.
62/C3 Tihøje (peak), Den.
159/F4 Tihuatlán, Mex.
61/J3 Tiilikkajärven Nat'l Park, Fin.
120/A2 Tijāra, India
146/A1 Tījī, Libya
144/B1 Tijirit (reg.), Mrta.
186/D4 Tijuana, Mex.
171/N8 Tijuca Nat'l Park, Braz.
173/G3 Tijucas, Braz.
173/G1 Tijuco (riv.), Braz.
159/H5 Tikal, Guat.
160/D2 Tikal (ruins), Guat.
160/D2 Tikal Nat'l Park, Guat.
120/B3 Tīkamgarh, India
114/E3 Tikanlik, China
118/D3 Tikarapāra, India
145/E3 Tikaré, Burk.
177/G3 Tikchik (lakes), Ak,US
139/L6 Tikehau (atoll), FrPol.
99/L5 Tikhoretsk, Rus.
94/G4 Tikhvin, Rus.
152/B1 Tiko, Camr.
105/E3 Tikrīt, Iraq
101/N2 Tiksi, Rus.
53/U6 Tikveš (lake), Macd.
159/G5 Tila, Mex.
66/C5 Tilburg, Neth.
205/H7 Tilbury, On,Can
53/O7 Tilbury, Eng,UK
133/J4 Tilcha, Austl.
200/C1 Tilden, Il,US
189/E3 Tilden, Tx,US
192/F1 Tilford, SD,US
206/B6 Tilghman, Md,US
206/B6 Tilghman (isl.), Md,US
120/B2 Tilhar, India
116/B4 Tilin, Burma
174/D2 Tilisarao, Arg.
54/D5 Till (riv.), Eng,UK
57/F5 Till (riv.), Eng,UK
145/F3 Tillabéry, Niger
184/B1 Tillamook, Or,US

184/A1 Tillamook (bay), Or,US
191/J4 Tillar, Ar,US
80/B3 Tille (riv.), Fr.
201/G3 Tillery (lake), NC,US
183/J2 Tilley, Ab,Can
54/C4 Tillicoultry, Sc,UK
205/B3 Tillicum, Wa,US
79/G3 Tillières-sur-Avre, Fr.
191/J5 Tillman, Ms,US
202/D2 Tillmans Corner, Al,US
198/F3 Tillsonburg, On,Can
130/B2 Tilomar, Indo.
172/B2 Tilopozo, Chile
135/C1 Tilpa, Austl.
62/D3 Tilst, Den.
194/D3 Tilston, Mb,Can
54/C3 Tilt (riv.), Sc,UK
135/C1 Tiltagara, Austl.
174/Q9 Tiltil, Chile
198/C4 Tilton, Il,US
199/L3 Tilton, NH,US
62/C3 Tim, Den.
99/J2 Tim, Rus.
104/B5 Ţimā, Egypt
95/L2 Timan (ridge), Rus.
164/C4 Timaná, Col.
172/E1 Timane (riv.), Par.
142/B3 Timanfaya Nat'l Park, Canl.
136/B4 Timaru, N.Z.
97/J1 Timashevo, Rus.
99/K5 Timashevsk, Rus.
91/J5 Timbákion, Gre.
202/C3 Timbalier (bay), La,US
167/H4 Timbaúba, Braz.
144/C2 Timbédra, Mrta.
188/C2 Timber (mtn.), Tx,US
192/D1 Timber Lake, SD,US
201/H2 Timberlake, Va,US
201/H1 Timberville, Va,US
164/B4 Timbiquí, Col.
167/F4 Timbiras, Braz.
173/G3 Timbó, Braz.
144/C4 Timbo, Gui.
135/B3 Timboon, Austl.
155/H3 Timbué (pt.), Moz.
144/E2 Timbuktu, Mali
127/H4 Timbuni (riv.), Indo.
165/G3 Timehri (int'l arpt.), Guy.
71/G7 Timelkam, Aus.
146/A3 Timenocalin, Hasy (well), Libya
145/E2 Timetrine, Mali
88/B4 Timetrout, Jebel (peak), Mor.
91/G3 Timfristós (peak), Gre.
141/V18 Timgad (ruins), Alg.
145/H2 Tîmia, Niger
143/F3 Timimoun, Alg.
144/A2 Timiris (cape), Mrta.
92/E3 Timiş (co.), Rom.
92/E3 Timiş (riv.), Rom.
92/E3 Timişoara, Rom.
92/E3 Timişoara (int'l arpt.), Rom.
145/G2 Ti-m-Mershoï (wadi), Niger
179/H4 Timmins, On,Can
201/H3 Timmonsville, SC,US
193/J1 Timms (hill), Wi,US
60/B6 Timoleague, Ire.
167/F4 Timon, Braz.
206/B5 Timonium, Md,US
138/B6 Timor (sea)
128/D2 Timor (sea), Austl.
130/B2 Timor (isl.), Indo.
130/B2 Timor (sea), Indo.
130/B2 Timor Timur (prov.), Indo.
171/E3 Timóteo, Braz.
192/C5 Timpas, Co,US
189/G2 Timpson, Tx,US
101/N4 Timpton (riv.), Rus.
61/F3 Timrå, Swe.
200/D3 Tims Ford (dam), Tn,US
200/D3 Tims Ford (lake), Tn,US
95/M3 Timsher, Rus.
203/H2 Timucuan Nat'l Prsv., Fl,US
120/A4 Timurnī, India
156/E3 Tina (riv.), SAfr.
125/D4 Tinaca (pt.), Phil.
164/D2 Tinaco, Ven.
60/D4 Tinahely, Ire.
143/H4 Tin Alkoum (well), Alg.
127/E4 Tinambung, Indo.
92/E2 Tinca, Rom.
134/D4 Tin Can Bay, Austl.
79/E3 Tinchebray, Fr.
185/K4 Tincup, Co,US
118/C5 Tindivanam, India
142/C4 Tindouf, Alg.
142/D3 Tindouf (wilaya), Alg.
82/C4 Tinée (riv.), Fr.
76/B1 Tineo, Sp.
148/D2 Tiné, Ouadi (dry riv.), Chad
145/F2 Ti-n-Essako, Mali
117/H3 Ting (riv.), China
148/D3 Tinga (peak), CAfr.
134/F7 Tingalpa (cr.), Austl.
134/F7 Tingalpa (res.), Austl.
135/D3 Tingaringy Nat'l Park, Austl.
135/D1 Tingha, Austl.
146/A2 Tinghert, Ḩamādat (upland), Libya
144/C4 Tingi (mts.), Gui., SLeo.
120/D1 Tingjegaon, Nepal
115/L9 Tinglin, China
177/F2 Tingmerkpuk (mtn.), Ak,US
168/C3 Tingo María, Peru
117/F3 Tingping, China
144/D4 Tingréla, IvC.
121/F1 Tingri, China
62/F3 Tingsryd, Swe.
174/C2 Tinguirrica (vol.), Chile
171/F2 Tinharé (isl.), Braz.
123/D2 Tinh Gia, Viet.
138/D3 Tinian (isl.), NMar.
206/C4 Tinicum Nat'l Env. Ctr., Pa,US
143/G4 Ti-n-Jedane, Oued (dry riv.), Alg.
191/F3 Tinker A.F.B., Ok,US
144/C4 Tinkisso (riv.), Gui.
205/Q16 Tinley Park, Il,US
136/C3 Tinline (peak), N.Z.
172/C4 Tinogasta, Arg.
91/J4 Tínos, Gre.
91/J4 Tínos (isl.), Gre.
68/C5 Tinqueux, Fr.
146/D1 Tín, Ra's at (pt.), Libya
143/G3 Tinrhert, Hamada de (plat.), Alg.
142/D3 Tinrhir, Mor.
191/H4 Tinsman, Ar,US
116/B3 Tinsukia, India
168/D4 Tinta, Peru
58/B5 Tintagel, Eng,UK
58/B5 Tintagel Head (pt.), Eng,UK
144/C2 Tîntâne, Mrta.
78/D4 Tinténiac, Fr.
58/D3 Tintern Abbey, Wal,UK
69/E4 Tintigny, Belg.
135/B2 Tintinara, Austl.
136/F6 Tintira Matangi (isl.), N.Z.
76/B4 Tinto (riv.), Sp.
54/C5 Tinto (mtn.), Sc,UK
207/D3 Tinton Falls (New Shrewsbury), NJ,US
148/A1 Ti-n-Toumma (reg.), Niger
57/G5 Tintwistle, Eng,UK
136/D3 Tinui, N.Z.
168/B3 Tinyahuarco, Peru
145/F2 Ti-n-Zaouâtene, Mali
186/C2 Tioga (pass), Ca,US
202/B2 Tioga, La,US
194/C3 Tioga, ND,US
199/H4 Tioga, Pa,US
191/F4 Tioga, Tx,US
201/G1 Tioga, WV,US
127/J4 Tiom, Indo.
124/D2 Tioman (isl.), Malay.
81/G5 Tione di Trento, It.
199/G4 Tionesta, Pa,US
166/D2 Tipac (hill), Braz.
141/S15 Tipaza, Alg.
198/D5 Tipp City, Oh,US
60/B5 Tipperary, Ire.
60/C4 Tipperary (co.), Ire.
186/C2 Tipton, Ca,US
193/J3 Tipton, Ia,US
198/C4 Tipton, In,US
191/E1 Tipton, Ks,US
191/H1 Tipton, Mo,US
190/E3 Tipton, Ok,US
199/G4 Tipton, Pa,US
200/C2 Tiptonville, Tn,US
195/L3 Tip Top (mtn.), On,Can
59/G3 Tiptree, Eng,UK
118/C5 Tiptūr, India
169/D4 Tipuani, Bol.
139/L6 Tiputa, FrPol.
168/D5 Tiquina, Bol.
189/G1 Tira, Tx,US
167/E4 Tiracambu (mts.), Braz.
147/G2 Tiran (strait), Egypt
104/C5 Tīrān (isl.), SAr.
91/F2 Tiranë (cap.), Alb.
147/G3 Tiran, Jazīrat (isl.), Egypt
81/G5 Tirano, It.
172/C1 Tiraque, Bol.
150/A2 T'irarē Shet' (riv.), Eth.
133/H4 Tirari (des.), Austl.
93/J2 Tiraspol', Mol.
122/D2 Tīra Sujānpur, India
104/A2 Tire, Turk.
96/F4 Tirebolu, Turk.
55/H8 Tiree (isl.), Sc,UK
145/F1 Tirest (well), Mali
149/G4 Tirgol, Eth.
93/G3 Tîrgovişte, Rom.
93/H3 Tîrgu Bujor, Rom.
93/F3 Tîrgu Cărbuneşti, Rom.
93/H2 Tîrgu Frumos, Rom.
93/F3 Tîrgu Jiu, Rom.
93/F2 Tîrgu Lăpuş, Rom.
93/G2 Tîrgu Mureş, Rom.
93/H2 Tîrgu Neamţ, Rom.
93/H2 Tîrgu Ocna, Rom.
93/H3 Tîrgu Secuiesc, Rom.
107/K1 Tirich Mīr (mtn.), Pak.
83/C5 Tiriolo, It.
142/B5 Tiris (reg.), WSah.
142/C4 Tiris Zemmour (reg.), Mrta.
95/N5 Tirlyanskiy, Rus.
93/G2 Tîrnava Mare (riv.), Rom.
93/G2 Tîrnava Mică (riv.), Rom.
93/G2 Tîrnăveni, Rom.
91/H3 Tírnavos, Gre.
144/C4 Tiro, Gui.
81/G3 Tirol (prov.), Aus.
86/D5 Tirrenia, It.
58/C1 Tir Rhiwiog (mtn.), Wa,UK
71/F3 Tirschenreuth, Ger.
90/A2 Tirso (riv.), It.
62/D3 Tirstup (int'l arpt.), Den.
174/B3 Tirúa, Chile
122/F3 Tiruchchendūr, India
122/G3 Tiruchchirāppalli, India
122/G4 Tiruchendūr, India
122/F4 Tirumangalam, India
122/F4 Tirunelveli, India
168/C2 Tiruntán, Peru
118/C5 Tirupati, India
122/G3 Tiruppattūr, India
122/F3 Tiruppūr, India
122/E3 Tirūr, India
120/B4 Tiruttani, India
122/G3 Tirutturaippūndi, India
122/F4 Tiruvalla, India
118/C5 Tiruvannāmalai, India
122/G3 Tiruvārūr, India
98/C3 Tisa (riv.), Eur.
93/G1 Tisa (riv.), Ukr.
89/J1 Tisa (riv.), Yugo.
58/D4 Tisbury, Eng,UK
183/M1 Tisdale, Sk,Can
98/F3 Tishkovka, Ukr.
97/J3 Tishkovo, Rus.
200/C3 Tishomingo, Ms,US
191/F3 Tishomingo, Ok,US
191/F3 Tishomingo Nat'l Wild. Ref., Ok,US
141/M13 Tissa, Mor.
141/R16 Tissemsilt, Alg.
141/R16 Tissemsilt (wilaya), Alg.
121/G2 Tista (riv.), Bang., India
63/T8 Tisvilde, Den.
92/E2 Tisza (riv.), Hun.
98/B3 Tisza (riv.), Hun.
92/E2 Tiszaföldvár, Hun.
92/E2 Tiszafüred, Hun.
92/E2 Tiszakécske, Hun.
92/E1 Tiszalök, Hun.
92/E2 Tiszavasvári, Hun.
143/F4 Tit, Alg.
87/F5 Titano, Monte (peak), SMar.
145/E3 Titao, Burk.
125/C4 Titay, Phil.
92/E3 Titel, Yugo.
85/E5 Titerno (riv.), It.
152/C3 Titi, Congo
168/D4 Titicaca (lake), Bol., Peru
208/A3 Titicus (mtn.), Ct,US
80/E2 Titisee Neustadt, Ger.
118/D3 Titlagarh, India
81/E4 Titlis (peak), Swi.
85/F6 Tito, It.
92/D4 Titograd, Yugo.
83/B6 Tito Menniti (arpt.), It.
92/D4 Titovo Užice, Yugo.
92/E5 Titov Veles, Macd.
92/E5 Titov vrh (peak), Macd.
133/G2 Ti-Tree Abor. Land, Austl.
53/P8 Titsey, Eng,UK
70/E5 Titting, Ger.
71/F6 Tittmoning, Ger.
93/G3 Titu, Rom.
153/F2 Titule, Zaire
203/H3 Titusville, Fl,US
206/D3 Titusville, NJ,US
199/G4 Titusville, Pa,US
122/D2 Tiuni, India
151/B2 Tiva (dry riv.), Kenya
144/A3 Tivaouane, Sen.
92/D4 Tivat, Yugo.
198/F2 Tiverton, On,Can
58/C5 Tiverton, Eng,UK
208/C2 Tiverton, RI,US
84/C4 Tivoli, It.
189/F3 Tivoli, Tx,US
63/T9 Tivoli Gardens, Den.
107/G4 Ţīwī, Oman
168/B1 Tixán, Ecu.
160/D1 Tixkokob, Mex.
159/L7 Tizayuca, Mex.
159/H4 Tizimín, Mex.
167/N8 Tiznados (riv.), Ven.
107/L1 Tiznap (riv.), China
142/C3 Tiznit, Mor.
62/C4 Tjæreborg, Den.
133/F4 Tjarutja-Maralinga Abor. Land, Austl.
62/A1 Tjeldstø, Nor.
66/C3 Tjeukemeer (lake), Neth.
62/D2 Tjøme, Nor.
62/D3 Tjorn (isl.), Swe.
99/K5 Tkhab (peak), Rus.
97/G4 Tkibuli, Geo.
97/G4 Tkvarcheli, Geo.
159/M7 Tlachichuca, Mex.
160/B2 Tlacolula, Mex.
159/P8 Tlacotalpan, Mex.
159/R10 Tláhuac, Mex.
158/E3 Tlahualilo de Zaragoza, Mex.
159/K6 Tlahuelilpa de Ocampo, Mex.
158/E4 Tlajomulco, Mex.
159/N8 Tlalixcoyan, Mex.
159/R10 Tlalmanalcó de Valásquez, Mex.
159/Q9 Tlalnepantla, Mex.
159/K7 Tlalnepantla de Galeana, Mex.
159/Q10 Tlaloc (mt.), Mex.
159/Q10 Tlalpan, Mex.
159/K8 Tlaltizapan, Mex.
159/F5 Tlapa, Mex.
159/F5 Tlapacoyan, Mex.
159/R10 Tlapacoya Pyramid, Mex.
159/E5 Tlapehuala, Mex.
158/E4 Tlaquepaque, Mex.
159/K8 Tlaquiltenango, Mex.
159/M7 Tlatlauquitepec, Mex.
159/E5 Tlatlaya, Mex.
159/F5 Tlaxcala, Mex.
159/F5 Tlaxcala (state), Mex.
159/L7 Tlaxcala de Xicohténcatl, Mex.
159/K6 Tlaxcoapan, Mex.
159/L7 Tlaxco de Morelos, Mex.
159/L8 Tlayacapan, Mex.
177/M5 Tlell, BC,Can
141/Q16 Tlemçen, Alg.
141/Q16 Tlemcen (wilaya), Alg.
154/E5 Tlokweng, Bots.
73/C2 Tlsta (peak), Slvk.
146/B3 Tmassah, Libya
161/F4 Toabré, Pan.
93/G2 Toaca (peak), Rom.
164/B4 Toachi (riv.), Ecu.
187/H2 Toadlena, NM,US
141/G6 Toamasina, Madg.
157/J7 Toamasina (prov.), Madg.
205/B2 Toandos (pen.), Wa,US
201/J2 Toano, Va,US
145/E5 Toasi, Gha.
201/G2 Toast, NC,US
139/L6 Toau (atoll), FrPol.
174/D3 Toay, Arg.
182/B2 Toba (inlet), BC,Can
182/B2 Toba (riv.), BC,Can
108/D5 Toba, China
124/B2 Toba (lake), Indo.
111/E3 Toba, Japan
162/F5 Tobago (isl.), Trin.
107/J2 Toba Kākar (range), Pak.
76/E3 Tobarra, Sp.
122/B2 Toba Tek Singh, Pak.
173/E3 Tobatí, Par.
86/B3 Tobbio, Monte (peak), It.
196/E3 Tobeatic Game Sanct., NS,Can
60/B1 Tobercurry, Ire.
56/B2 Tobermore, NI,UK
133/H2 Tobermorey, Austl.
198/F2 Tobermory, On,Can
55/H8 Tobermory, Sc,UK
112/B2 Tōbetsu, Japan
152/C5 Tobias, Ang.
171/F1 Tobias Barreto, Braz.
125/C3 Tobias Fornier, Phil.
132/E2 Tobin (lake), Austl.
196/D2 Tobique (riv.), NB,Can
111/M9 Tobishima, Japan
124/D3 Toboali, Indo.
97/M1 Tobol, Kaz.
95/Q4 Tobol (riv.), Kaz., Rus.
100/G4 Tobol'sk, Rus.
140/E1 Tobruk, Libya
146/D1 Tobruk (Ţubruq), Libya
95/M1 Tobseda, Rus.
95/K5 Toburdanovo, Rus.
206/C1 Tobyhanna, Pa,US
206/C1 Tobyhanna (cr.), Pa,US
206/C1 Tobyhanna (lake), Pa,US
206/C1 Tobyhanna St. Park, Pa,US
95/L2 Tobysh (riv.), Rus.
168/B3 Tocache, Peru
167/L7 Tocaima, Col.
170/C1 Tocantínia, Braz.
167/E4 Tocantinópolis, Braz.
166/D3 Tocantins (riv.), Braz.
166/D5 Tocantins (state), Braz.
201/F3 Toccoa, Ga,US
200/E3 Toccoa (riv.), Ga, Tn,US
85/D3 Tocco da Casauria, It.
81/E5 Toce (riv.), It.
111/F2 Tochigi, Japan
111/F2 Tochigi (pref.), Japan
159/L8 Tochimilco, Mex.
111/F2 Tochio, Japan
76/C4 Tocina, Sp.
62/D2 Töcksfors, Swe.
165/F2 Toco, Trin.
191/G4 Toco, Tx,US
172/D1 Tocomechi, Bol.
172/B2 Tocopilla, Chile
161/G4 Tocumen, Pan.
135/C2 Tocumwal, Austl.
164/D2 Tocuyito, Ven.
164/D2 Tocuyo (riv.), Ven.
111/H7 Toda, Japan
120/A2 Toda Bhīm, India
59/F3 Toddington, Eng,UK
149/G4 Todenyang, Kenya.
84/C2 Todi, It.
81/E4 Tödi (peak), Swi.
57/F4 Todmorden, Eng,UK
113/C5 Todohae Hasang Nat'l Park, SKor.
171/F2 Todos os Santos (bay), Braz.
169/E4 Todos Santos, Bol.
172/B1 Todos Santos, Bol.
158/C4 Todos Santos, Mex.
207/J9 Todt Hill, NY,US
80/E2 Todtmoos, Ger.
80/D2 Todtnau, Ger.
60/A7 Toe Head (pt.), Ire.
113/D3 T'oejo, NKor.
166/B1 Toekomstig (res.), Sur.
142/C5 Toffal (hill), Mrta.
145/F5 Toffo, Ben.
183/H1 Tofield, Ab,Can
61/E3 Töfsingdalens Nat'l Park, Swe.
139/H6 Tofua (isl.), Tonga
114/D4 Togatax, China
144/C2 Togba (well), Mrta.
81/F3 Toggenburg (vall.), Swi.
60/D3 Togher, Ire.
177/F4 Togiak, Ak,US
177/G4 Togiak Nat'l Wild. Ref., Ak,US
71/F6 Töging am Inn, Ger.
113/D2 Togno (riv.), NKor.
145/F4 Togo
194/D2 Togo, Sk,Can
111/N9 Tōgō, Japan
115/B2 Togtoh, China
113/D5 Tŏgyu-san Nat'l Park, SKor.
97/M3 Togyz, Kaz.
187/H3 Tohatchi, NM,US
206/C3 Tohickon (cr.), Pa,US
139/X15 Tohivea (peak), FrPol.
112/B3 Tōhoku (dist.), Japan
111/F2 Tōhoku (prov.), Japan
108/F3 Tohom, China
203/H3 Tohopekaliga (lake), Fl,US
124/C2 Tohor (cape), Malay.
145/F5 Tohoun, Togo
111/F3 Toi, Japan
119/F5 Toibalawe, India
111/M9 Tōin, Japan
184/E4 Toiyabe (range), Nv,US
110/C3 Tojō, Japan
111/L10 Tōjō, Japan
177/K3 Tok, Ak,US
112/C2 Tokachi (riv.), Japan
111/E3 Tōkai, Japan
92/E1 Tokaj, Hun.
111/F2 Tōkamachi, Japan
136/B4 Tokanui, N.Z.
147/H5 Tokar, Sudan
112/K6 Tokara (isls.), Japan
99/L2 Tokarevka, Rus.
147/H5 Tokar Game Rsv., Sudan
104/D1 Tokat, Turk.
104/D1 Tokat (prov.), Turk.
113/C4 Tŏkchŏk (arch.), SKor.
113/D3 Tŏkch'ŏn, NKor.
177/M4 Tokeen, Ak,US
182/C4 Tokeland, Wa,US
50/A6 Tokelau (isls.), N.Z.
139/H5 Tokelau (terr.), N.Z.
111/N9 Toki, Japan
111/N9 Toki (riv.), Japan
111/H6 Tokigawa, Japan
194/E4 Tokio, ND,US
123/B3 Tokkya Chaung, Burma
100/H5 Tokmak, Kyr.
99/H4 Tokmak, Ukr.
136/D2 Tokomaru Bay, N.Z.
111/M10 Tokoname, Japan
144/C4 Tokonou, Gui.
112/D1 Tokoro, Japan
112/C2 Tokoro (riv.), Japan
136/C2 Tokoroa, N.Z.
111/F3 Tokorozawa, Japan
113/E2 Tŏksŏng, NKor.
177/E3 Toksook Bay, Ak,US
63/P1 Toksovo, Rus.
108/B2 Toksun, China
114/B3 Toktogul, Kyr.
114/B3 Toktogul (res.), Kyr.
112/K7 Tokuno (isl.), Japan
112/K7 Tokunoshima, Japan
109/L1 Tokur, Rus.
110/D3 Tokushima, Japan
110/D3 Tokushima (arpt.), Japan
110/C4 Tokushima (pref.), Japan
110/B3 Tokuyama, Japan
155/F3 Tokwe (riv.), Zim.
111/H7 Tokyo (bay), Japan
111/F3 Tōkyō (cap.), Japan
111/F3 Tōkyō (pref.), Japan
111/H7 Tōkyō Disneyland, Japan
160/E4 Tola, Nic.
136/D2 Tolaga Bay, N.Z.
141/G7 Tôlanäro, Madg.
189/F1 Tolar, Tx,US
172/C3 Tolar Grande, Arg.
95/M5 Tolbazy, Rus.
108/C2 Tolbo, Mong.
93/H4 Tolbukhin, Bul.
172/C1 Toledo, Bol.
170/B5 Toledo, Braz.
164/C3 Toledo, Col.
125/C3 Toledo, Phil.
76/C3 Toledo, Sp.
76/C3 Toledo (mts.), Sp.
175/T12 Toledo, Uru.
193/H3 Toledo, Ia,US
198/B5 Toledo, Il,US
198/E4 Toledo, Oh,US
184/B1 Toledo, Or,US
182/C4 Toledo, Wa,US
202/B2 Toledo Bend (dam), La,US
202/B2 Toledo Bend (res.), La, Tx,US
189/H2 Toledo Bend (dam), Tx,US
85/D1 Tolentino, It.
84/B3 Tolfa, It.
84/B3 Tolfaccia (peak), It.
174/C3 Tolhuaca Nat'l Park, Chile
114/D2 Toli, China
157/G8 Toliara, Madg.
157/H8 Toliara (prov.), Madg.
164/C5 Tolima, Col.
164/C4 Tolima (dept.), Col.
159/F4 Tolimán, Mex.
164/C3 Tolima, Nevado del (peak), Col.
127/F3 Tolitoli, Indo.
60/D3 Tolka (riv.), Ire.
183/J1 Tolland, Ab,Can
208/B2 Tolland, Ct,US
208/B2 Tolland (co.), Ct,US
191/H4 Tollette, Ar,US
194/D3 Tolley, ND,US
85/E3 Tollo, It.
92/A2 Tolmezzo, It.
92/D2 Tolna, Hun.
73/C6 Tolna (co.), Hun.
194/E4 Tolna, ND,US
127/F4 Tolo (gulf), Indo.
152/D3 Tolo, Zaire
55/P13 Tolob, Sc,UK
63/N4 Tolochin, Bela.
131/G1 Tolokiwa (isl.), PNG
157/H8 Tolongoina, Madg.
193/K4 Tolono, Il,US
76/D1 Tolosa, Sp.
113/D5 Tolsan (isl.), SKor.
194/E5 Tolstoy, SD,US
98/C3 Tolstoye, Ukr.
205/D2 Tolt (res.), Wa,US
205/D2 Tolt (riv.), Wa,US
174/B3 Toltén, Chile
174/B3 Toltén (riv.), Chile
205/D2 Tolt, North Fork (riv.), Wa,US
205/D2 Tolt, South Fork (riv.), Wa,US
164/C2 Tolú, Col.
160/B2 Toluca, Mex.
159/Q10 Toluca (arpt.), Mex.
193/K3 Toluca, Il,US
159/Q10 Toluca de Laredo, Mex.
159/K7 Toluca de Lerdo, Mex.
160/B2 Toluca, Nevado de (peak), Mex.
164/C2 Tolúviejo, Col.
85/G6 Tolve, It.
53/H3 Tol'yatti, Rus.
97/M2 Tolybay, Kaz.
100/J4 Tom' (riv.), Rus.
191/G4 Tom, Ok,US
144/E3 Toma, Burk.
131/G2 Toma, PNG
193/J2 Tomah, Wi,US
182/G1 Tomahawk, Ab,Can
193/K1 Tomahawk, Wi,US
112/B2 Tomakomai, Japan
99/H4 Tomakovka, Ukr.
112/B1 Tomamae, Japan
125/D4 Tomanao, Phil.
138/G6 Tomanivi (peak), Fiji
76/A3 Tomar, Port.
109/N2 Tomari, Rus.
91/G3 Tómaros (peak), Gre.
104/C2 Tomarza, Turk.
168/C4 Tomás, Peru
172/C1 Tomás Barrón, Bol.
168/J7 Tomás de Berlanga, Ecu.
98/B2 Tomashëvka, Bela.
65/M3 Tomaszów Lubelski, Pol.
65/L3 Tomaszów Mazowiecki, Pol.
149/E3 Tomat, Sudan
54/C2 Tomatin, Sc,UK
158/D5 Tomatlán, Mex.
172/C2 Tomave, Bol.
169/G3 Tombador (mts.), Braz.
189/G2 Tomball, Tx,US
149/F4 Tombe, Sudan
200/C5 Tombigbee (riv.), Al, Ms,US
152/C4 Tomboco, Ang.
115/B4 Tomb of Qinshihuang, China
87/E1 Tombolo, It.
187/G5 Tombstone, Az,US
154/A2 Tombua, Ang.
174/B3 Tomé, Chile
78/B3 Tomé (isl.), Fr.
187/J3 Tome, NM,US
130/A1 Tomea (isl.), Indo.
166/D3 Tomé-Açu, Braz.
62/E4 Tomelilla, Swe.
76/D3 Tomelloso, Sp.
172/C1 Tomina, Bol.
135/D2 Tomingley, Austl.
127/F4 Tomini (gulf), Indo.
144/D3 Tominian, Mali
76/A2 Tomiño, Sp.
54/C2 Tomintoul, Sc,UK
111/H7 Tomiura, Japan
111/F3 Tomiyama, Japan
101/N4 Tommot, Rus.
164/D3 Tomo (riv.), Col.
108/C4 Tomorlog, China
92/D2 Tompa, Hun.
127/E4 Tompe, Indo.
183/K2 Tompkins, Sk,Can
200/E2 Tompkinsville, Ky,US
127/F3 Tompo, Indo.
132/C2 Tom Price, Austl.
207/D3 Toms (riv.), NJ,US
100/J4 Tomsk, Rus.
207/D4 Toms River, NJ,US
103/D1 Tömük, Turk.
177/K3 Tom White (mt.), Ak,US
160/C2 Tonalá, Mex.
187/G2 Tonalea, Az,US
81/G5 Tonale, Passo del (pass), It.
182/E3 Tonasket, Wa,US
166/C1 Tonate, FrG.
199/G3 Tonawanda, NY,US
197/T9 Tonawanda (cr.), NY,US
197/T9 Tonawanda Ind. Res., NY,US
53/P8 Tonbridge, Eng,UK
166/B1 Tonckens (falls), Sur.
160/E3 Toncontín (int'l arpt.), Hon.
111/L10 Tondabayashi, Japan
127/F3 Tondano, Indo.
62/C4 Tönder, Den.
122/G4 Tondi, India
145/F3 Tondi Kiwindi, Niger
152/D3 Tondo, Zaire
144/B4 Tondon, Gui.
154/C3 Tondoro, Namb.
82/C1 Tondu (mtn.), Fr.
111/J7 Tone, Japan
111/G3 Tone (riv.), Japan
58/C4 Tone (riv.), Eng,UK
105/G2 Tonekābon, Iran
60/D3 Tonelagee (mtn.), Ire.
108/F5 Tong (riv.), China
139/H7 Tonga
149/F3 Tonga, Sudan
157/E3 Tongaat, SAfr.
117/H3 Tong'an, China
139/K5 Tongareva (Penrhyn) (isl.), CookIs.
136/C2 Tongariro (reg.), N.Z.
136/C2 Tongariro (vol.), N.Z.
136/C2 Tongariro Nat'l Park, N.Z.
139/H7 Tongatupu (isl.), Tonga
115/C4 Tongbai, China
109/K2 Tongbei, China
113/C2 Tongch'ang, NKor.
117/G2 Tongcheng, China
117/H2 Tongcheng, China
113/D3 T'ongch'ŏn, NKor.
108/F4 Tongchuan, China
113/G6 Tongdaemun, SKor.
117/F3 Tongdao Dongzu Zizhixian, China
113/D4 Tongduch'on, SKor.
69/E2 Tongeren, Belg.
113/C2 Tonggou, China
119/K2 Tonggu, China
117/H3 Tonggu Zhang (peak), China
113/E4 Tonghae, SKor.
113/C2 Tonghua, China
121/H4 Tongi, Bang.
109/J3 Tongjiadian, China
113/D3 Tongjosŏn (East Korea) (bay), NKor.
115/E2 Tongliao, China
115/D5 Tongling, China
117/G3 Tongmu, China
113/E5 Tongnae, SKor.
116/E2 Tongnan, China
113/C3 Tongnim, NKor.
135/B1 Tongo, Austl.
127/E5 Tongo (peak), Indo.
157/H8 Tongobory, Madg.
117/F3 Tongren, China
121/H2 Tongsa (riv.), Bhu.
121/H2 Tongsa Dzong, Bhu.
115/C5 Tongshan, China
113/D2 Tongsin, NKor.
108/D5 Tongtian (riv.), China
55/J7 Tongue, Sc,UK
192/A1 Tongue (riv.), Mt,US
185/K1 Tongue (riv.), Mt, Wy,US
190/D4 Tongue (riv.), Tx,US
162/B1 Tongue of the Ocean (chan.), Bahm.
115/H7 Tong Xian, China
115/C4 Tongxu, China
115/E1 Tongyu, China
117/H2 Tongyuan, China
113/B2 Tongyuanpu, China
112/C1 Tonino-Anivskiy (pen.), Rus.
66/D6 Tönisvorst, Ger.
149/F4 Tonj, Sudan
149/F4 Tonj (riv.), Sudan
118/C2 Tonk, India
191/F2 Tonkawa, Ok,US
123/D1 Tonkin (gulf), China, Viet.
144/D5 Tonkoui (peak), IvC.
123/C3 Tonle Sap (lake), Camb.
74/D4 Tonneins, Fr.
74/E3 Tonnerre, Fr.
64/E1 Tönning, Ger.
112/B4 Tōno, Japan
187/F4 Tonopah, Az,US
184/E4 Tonopah, Nv,US
110/D3 Tonoshō, Japan
161/F5 Tonosí, Pan.
155/E4 Tonota, Bots.
120/C3 Tons (riv.), India
62/D2 Tønsberg, Nor.
62/B2 Tonstad, Nor.
187/G4 Tonto Nat'l Mon., Az,US
139/V13 Tontouta (Noumea) (int'l arpt.), NCal.
104/D1 Tonya, Turk.
132/C4 Toodyay, Austl.
185/G3 Tooele, Ut,US
202/K6 Tooke (lake), Fl,US
189/F1 Tool, Tx,US
185/G3 Toole Army Dep., Ut,US
133/J5 Tooleybuc, Austl.
201/F4 Toomsboro, Ga,US
200/C4 Toomsuba, Ms,US
135/G6 Toomuc (cr.), Austl.
60/B4 Toomyvara, Ire.
135/C3 Tooradin, Austl.
135/D1 Tooraweenah, Austl.
182/C2 Toosey Ind. Res., BC,Can
63/L2 Tootsi, Est.
134/C4 Toowoomba, Austl.
133/G2 Top (peak), Austl.
167/L6 Topaipí, Col.
204/B2 Topanga, Ca,US
204/B2 Topanga Beach, Ca,US
204/B2 Topanga St. Park, Ca,US
187/G5 Topawa, Az,US
198/D4 Topeka, In,US
193/G4 Topeka, Ks,US
191/G1 Topeka (cap.), Ks,US
158/D3 Topia, Mex.
84/C1 Topino (riv.), It.
105/M6 Topkapi Palace, Turk.
93/G2 Toplița, Rom.
186/E3 Topock, Az,US
192/B2 Top of the World (peak), Wy,US
168/D5 Topohoco, Bol.
73/C2 Topol'čany, Slvk.
73/B4 Topol'níky, Slvk.
158/C3 Topolobampo, Mex.
93/G3 Topoloveni, Rom.
93/H4 Topolovgrad, Bul.
94/F2 Topozero (lake), Rus.
182/D4 Toppenish, Wa,US
103/E1 Toprakkale, Turk.
196/D3 Topsfield, Me,US
58/C5 Topsham, Eng,UK
196/C4 Topsham, Me,US
130/C4 Top Springs, Austl.
206/C2 Topton, Pa,US
168/D5 Toquepala, Peru
187/F2 Toquerville, Ut,US
184/E4 Toquima (range), Nv,US
149/G4 Tor, Eth.
58/C6 Tor (bay), Eng,UK
153/G2 Tora, Zaire
111/M9 Torahime, Japan
114/F3 Toranggekuduk, China
83/C3 Torano Castello, It.
168/D5 Torata, Peru
127/G3 Torawitan (cape), Indo.
104/A2 Torbalı, Turk.
105/J3 Torbat-e Ḩeydarīyeh, Iran
197/L2 Torbay, Nf,Can
74/B1 Torbay, Eng,UK
161/H2 Torbeck, Haiti
177/H3 Torbert (mt.), Ak,US
97/G1 Torbeyevo, Rus.
83/C6 Torbido (riv.), It.
198/D2 Torch (lake), Mi,US
82/C2 Torches, Cime des (peak), Fr.
53/T10 Torcy, Fr.
64/E1 Törder, Den.
77/L6 Tordera (riv.), Sp.
76/C2 Tordesillas, Sp.
85/D2 Tordino (riv.), It.
62/F2 Töreboda, Swe.
77/G1 Torelló, Sp.
76/B1 Toreno, Sp.
99/K3 Torez, Ukr.
72/D4 Torgau, Ger.
65/G2 Torgelow, Ger.
62/F3 Torhamnsudde (pt.), Swe.
68/C1 Torhout, Belg.
121/E4 Tori, India
111/J7 Toride, Japan
79/E2 Torigni-sur-Vire, Fr.
111/E3 Torii-tōge (pass), Japan
76/A1 Toriñana (cape), Sp.
86/A3 Torino (prov.), It.
75/G4 Torino, Citta di (int'l arpt.), It.
86/A2 Torino, Citta di (int'l arpt.), It.
85/E3 Torino di Sangro, It.
86/A2 Torino (Turin), It.
138/D1 Tori-Shima (isl.), Japan
149/G4 Torit, Sudan
107/H1 Torkestān (mts.), Afg.
84/C3 Tor Lupara, It.
76/C2 Tormes (riv.), Sp.
73/B5 Torna (riv.), Hun.
132/C5 Torndirrup Nat'l Park, Austl.
57/H4 Torne (riv.), Eng,UK
61/G2 Torneälven (Torniojoki) (riv.), Swe.
67/G1 Tornesch, Ger.
92/D4 Tornik (peak), Yugo.
188/A2 Tornillo, Tx,US
61/G2 Torniojoki (Torneälven) (riv.), Fin.
76/C2 Toro, Sp.
186/D4 Toro (peak), Ca,US
172/B4 Toro, Cerro del (peak), Arg.
145/F3 Torodi, Niger
153/G2 Toro Game Rsv., Ugan.
148/B3 Torok, Chad
73/C5 Törökbálint, Hun.
92/E2 Törökszentmiklós, Hun.
144/B4 Toromélun, Gui.
91/H2 Toronaic (gulf), Gre.
172/C2 Toronao (peak), Arg.
164/D2 Torondoy, Ven.
199/G3 Toronto (cap.), On,Can
197/S8 Toronto (isl.), On,Can
191/G2 Toronto, Ks,US
191/G2 Toronto (lake), Ks,US
208/G7 Toronto, Oh,US
63/P3 Toropets, Rus.
153/H2 Tororo, Ugan.
63/N3 Toroshino, Rus.
77/N8 Torote (riv.), Sp.
172/C1 Torotoro, Bol.
62/D2 Torp (int'l arpt.), Nor.
62/E3 Torpa, Swe.
54/D2 Torphins, Sc,UK
58/B6 Torpoint, Eng,UK
107/G1 Ţorqebeh, Iran
135/C3 Torquay, Austl.
194/C3 Torquay, Sk,Can
58/C6 Torquay, Eng,UK
76/C1 Torquemada, Sp.
204/B3 Torrance, Ca,US
86/A2 Torrazza Piemonte, It.
85/E6 Torre Annunziata, It.
87/E1 Torrebelvicino, It.
77/F2 Torreblanca, Sp.
84/B3 Torre Ciana, Punta di (pt.), It.
76/D4 Torre del Campo, Sp.
85/E6 Torre del Greco, It.
86/D5 Torre del Lago Puccini, It.
76/B2 Torre de Moncorvo, Port.
85/D3 Torre dè Passeri, It.
76/D4 Torredonjimeno, Sp.
84/C4 Torre Gaia, It.
85/E6 Torregaveta, It.
87/E2 Torreglia, It.
83/B6 Torregrotta, It.
76/B3 Torrejoncillo, Sp.
76/D2 Torrejón de Ardoz, Sp.
76/D2 Torrelaguna, Sp.
76/C1 Torrelavega, Sp.
77/N8 Torrelodones, Sp.
85/F4 Torremaggiore, It.
84/C2 Torre Maggiore (peak), It.
83/A6 Torrenova, It.
134/B3 Torrens (cr.), Austl.
133/M8 Torrens (isl.), Austl.
133/H4 Torrens (lake), Austl.
133/M8 Torrens (riv.), Austl.
77/E3 Torrente, Sp.
158/E3 Torreón, Mex.
187/J3 Torreon, NM,US
83/B2 Torre Orsaia, It.
77/E4 Torre-Pacheco, Sp.
82/D3 Torre Péllice, It.
76/D3 Torreperogil, Sp.
131/F2 Torres (str.), Austl., PNG
173/G4 Tôrres, Braz.
138/F6 Torres (isls.), Van.
175/J7 Torres del Paine Nat'l Park, Chile
186/D4 Torres Martinez Ind. Res., Ca,US
76/A3 Torres Novas, Port.
131/F2 Torres Strait Is. Abor. Land, Austl.
76/A3 Torres Vedras, Port.
77/E4 Torrevieja, Sp.
185/H4 Torrey, Ut,US
56/B1 Torr Head (pt.), NI,UK
85/E3 Torricella Peligha, It.
58/B5 Torridge (riv.), Eng,UK
87/E1 Torri di Quartesolo, It.
76/C3 Torrijos, Sp.
183/H2 Torrington, Ab,Can
208/A2 Torrington, Ct,US
192/B2 Torrington, Wy,US
84/B1 Torrita di Siena, It.
77/G1 Torroella de Montgrí, Sp.
81/F5 Torrone Alto (peak), Swi.
135/B1 Torrowangee, Austl.
76/D4 Torrox, Sp.
121/G2 Torsa (riv.), Bhu.
62/F3 Torsås, Swe.
62/E1 Torsby, Swe.
197/L2 Tors Cove, Nf,Can
52/C2 Tórshavn, Den.
175/J6 Tortel, Chile
74/B2 Torteral, ChI,UK
78/C2 Torteval, ChI,UK
187/G4 Tortilla Flat, Az,US
84/C4 Torto (riv.), It.
162/E3 Tortola (isl.), BVI
90/A3 Tortolì, It.
86/B3 Tortona, It.
85/D2 Tortoreto Lido, It.
83/A6 Tortorici, It.
77/F2 Tortosa, Sp.
77/F2 Tortosa (cape), Sp.
161/H1 Tortue (Tortuga) (isl.), Haiti
161/H1 Tortuga (Tortue) (isl.), Haiti
161/F4 Tortuguero Nat'l Park, CR
104/E1 Tortum, Turk.
105/H3 Ţorūd, Iran
114/C3 Torugart, Pereval (pass), Kyr.
104/D1 Torul, Turk.
65/K2 Toruń, Pol.
65/K2 Toruń (prov.), Pol.
62/E3 Torup, Swe.
63/L3 Tõrva, Est.
84/C4 Torvaianica, It.
87/G1 Torviscosa, It.
55/G9 Tory (isl.), Ire.
65/L4 Torysa (riv.), Slvk.
94/G4 Torzhok, Rus.
110/C4 Tosa, Japan
110/C4 Tosa (bay), Japan
164/A5 Tosagua, Ecu.
113/D3 T'ŏsan, NKor.
110/C4 Tosashimizu, Japan
87/E4 Toscanella, It.
154/B4 Toscanini, Namb.
84/A2 Toscano (arch.), It.
75/J4 Tosco-Emiliano (range), It.
86/D1 Toscolano-Maderno, It.
112/A2 Toshibet (riv.), Japan
112/C2 Toshībetsu (riv.), Japan
95/M2 Toshviska, Rus.
63/P2 Tosno, Rus.
108/D4 Toson (lake), China
108/D2 Tosontsengel, Mong.
81/E3 Töss (riv.), Swi.
54/E6 Tosson (hill), Eng,UK
172/D4 Tostado, Arg.
63/L2 Tõstamaa, Est.
67/G2 Tostedt, Ger.
110/B4 Tosu, Japan
104/C1 Tosya, Turk.
76/E4 Totana, Sp.
154/D4 Toteng, Bots.
79/G1 Tôtes, Fr.
59/E5 Totland, Eng,UK
94/J4 Tot'ma, Rus.
58/C6 Totnes, Eng,UK
166/B1 Totness, Sur.
152/C4 Toto, Ang.
159/E5 Totolapan, Mex.
172/B3 Totora (mts.), Arg.
172/B3 Totoral, Chile
175/T11 Totoral, Uru.
174/E2 Totoras, Arg.
144/C5 Totota, Libr.
207/J8 Totowa, NJ,US
97/K1 Totskoye, Rus.
137/H Totten (glac.), Ant.
205/B3 Totten (inlet), Wa,US
135/C2 Tottenham, Austl.
53/N7 Tottenham, Eng,UK
207/H9 Tottenville, NY,US
57/F4 Tottington, Eng,UK
59/E5 Totton, Eng,UK
110/D3 Tottori, Japan
110/D3 Tottori (arpt.), Japan
110/C3 Tottori (pref.), Japan
159/N7 Totutla, Mex.
142/B5 Touâjîl, Mrta.
143/E4 Touat (reg.), Alg.
144/B4 Touba, Gui.
144/D4 Touba, IvC.
144/B3 Touba, Sen.
140/B1 Toubkal (peak), Mor.
142/D3 Toubkal, Jebel (mtn.), Mor.
142/D3 Toubkal Nat'l Park, Mor.
148/B4 Touboro, Camr.
117/J3 Toucheng, Tai.
182/E4 Touchet, Wa,US
194/B2 Touchwood (hills), Sk,Can
74/E3 Toucy, Fr.
113/D1 Toudao (riv.), China
117/J3 Toufen, Tai.
142/D4 Toufourine (well), Mali
144/E3 Tougan, Burk.
143/G2 Touggourt, Alg.
206/C4 Toughkenamon, Pa,US
144/C4 Tougué, Gui.
141/S16 Touiel (riv.), Alg.
144/C3 Touil, Mrta.
144/C3 Toukoto, Mali
69/E6 Toul, Fr.
144/C5 Toulépleu, IvC.
82/B6 Toulon, Fr.
193/K3 Toulon, Il,US
82/C6 Toulon/Hyères (Le Palyvestre) (arpt.), Fr.
82/B4 Toulourenc (riv.), Fr.
74/D5 Toulouse, Fr.
74/D5 Toulouse (Blagnac) (int'l arpt.), Fr.
146/B4 Toumo (well), Niger
144/D5 Toumodi, IvC.
117/J4 Tounan, Tai.
148/B3 Toungo, Nga.
116/C5 Toungoo, Burma
144/B4 Tounyifili, Gui.
115/L9 Toupeng, China
79/F2 Touques (riv.), Fr.
144/D5 Toura (mts.), IvC.
123/C2 Tourakom, Laos
68/C2 Tourcoing, Fr.
196/D1 Tourelle, Qu,Can
74/C5 Tourettes, Pic de (peak), Fr.
76/A1 Touriñan (cape), Sp.
78/D1 Tourlaville, Fr.
68/C2 Tournai, Belg.
82/D4 Tournairet (mtn.), Fr.
53/U10 Tournan-en-Brie, Fr.
168/C3 Tournavista, Peru
143/H5 Tourndo, Oued (dry riv.), Alg.
82/A2 Tournon, Fr.
80/A4 Tournus, Fr.
76/A1 Touro, Sp.
167/H4 Touros, Braz.
79/F3 Tourouvre, Fr.
79/F6 Tours, Fr.
82/B6 Tourves, Fr.
79/G2 Tourville-la-Rivière, Fr.
79/G4 Toury, Fr.
77/E3 Tous (res.), Sp.
78/B4 Toussaines, Signal de (peak), Fr.
144/D4 Toussiana, Burk.
146/C4 Toussidé (peak), Chad
82/B3 Toussière (mtn.), Fr.
148/D3 Toussoro (peak), CAfr.
156/C4 Touws (riv.), SAfr.
156/C4 Touwsrivier, SAfr.
71/G2 Toužim, Czh.
164/D2 Tovar, Ven.
96/F1 Tovarkovskiy, Rus.
59/E2 Tove (riv.), Eng,UK
108/E2 Tövshrüüleh, Mong.
207/H8 Towaco, NJ,US
111/G2 Towada, Japan
112/B3 Towada (lake), Japan
112/B3 Towada-Hachimantai Nat'l Park, Japan
199/H4 Towanda, Pa,US
121/H2 Towang, India
187/H2 Towaoc, Co,US
59/F2 Towcester, Eng,UK
185/H1 Tower (falls), Wy,US
194/F4 Tower City, ND,US
206/B2 Tower City, Pa,US
53/N7 Tower Hamlets (bor.), Eng,UK
198/B5 Tower Hill, Il,US
53/N7 Tower of London, Eng,UK
57/G2 Tow Law, Eng,UK
202/K7 Town and Country, Fl,US
189/G2 Town Bluff (dam), Tx,US
194/D3 Towner, ND,US
58/D2 Townhope, Eng,UK
206/C5 Townsend, De,US
199/L3 Townsend, Ma,US
183/J4 Townsend, Mt,US
200/F3 Townsend, Tn,US
201/K2 Townsend, Va,US
205/A2 Townsend (mt.), Wa,US
193/K1 Townsend, Wi,US
206/D5 Townsends (inlet), NJ,US
134/C3 Townshend (cape), Austl.
134/B2 Townsville, Austl.
149/G4 Towot, Sudan
107/H1 Towraghondi, Afg.
206/B5 Towson, Md,US
127/F4 Towuti (lake), Indo.
202/D2 Toxey, Al,US
114/C3 Toxkan (riv.), China, Kyr.
112/B2 Toya (lake), Japan
188/C2 Toyah, Tx,US
111/E2 Toyama, Japan
111/E2 Toyama (arpt.), Japan
111/E2 Toyama (bay), Japan
111/E2 Toyama (pref.), Japan
113/D5 Toyang, SKor.
112/B2 Tōya-Shikotsu Nat'l Park, Japan
111/N9 Toyoake, Japan
111/E3 Toyohashi, Japan
111/E3 Toyokawa, Japan
111/L10 Toyonaka, Japan
111/L10 Toyono, Japan
110/D3 Toyo'oka, Japan
111/M9 Toyosato, Japan
111/E2 Toyoshina, Japan
111/E3 Toyota, Japan
111/M9 Toyoyama, Japan
131/F3 Tozer, Mount (peak), Austl.
149/F3 Tozi, Sudan
177/H2 Tozi (mt.), Ak,US
97/H4 Tpig, Rus.
69/G4 Traben-Trarbach, Ger.
123/E3 Tra Bong, Viet.
204/C3 Trabuco, Arroyo (cr.), Ca,US
204/C3 Trabuco Canyon, Ca,US
104/D1 Trabzon, Turk.
104/D1 Trabzon (prov.), Turk.
196/E2 Tracadie, NB,Can
80/D3 Trachselwald, Swi.
123/D4 Tra Cu, Viet.
196/D3 Tracy, NB,Can
196/A2 Tracy, Qu,Can
205/M11 Tracy, Ca,US
193/G1 Tracy, Mn,US
200/E3 Tracy City, Tn,US
205/B2 Tracyton, Wa,US
86/B1 Tradate, It.
201/G3 Tradesville, SC,US
200/D2 Tradewater (riv.), Ky,US
193/H2 Traer, Ia,US
76/B4 Trafalgar (cape), Sp.
77/P10 Trafaria, Port.
208/H7 Trafford, Pa,US
81/G4 Trafoi, It.
146/B3 Trāghin, Libya
71/H6 Tragwein, Aus.
174/B3 Traiguén, Chile
182/F3 Trail, BC,Can
184/B2 Trail, Or,US
79/H5 Traînou, Fr.
171/F1 Traipu, Braz.
167/G3 Trairi, Braz.
75/L3 Traisen (riv.), Aus.
73/A3 Traiskirchen, Aus.
65/H4 Traismauer, Aus.
63/L4 Trakai, Lith.
123/D3 Trakan Phut Phon, Thai.
60/A5 Tralee, Ire.
63/S7 Trälhavet (bay), Swe.
123/D1 Tra Linh, Viet.

80/D3 **Tramelan,** Swi.
123/E3 **Tra Mi,** Viet.
81/H5 **Tramin** (Termeno), It.
201/F2 **Trammel,** Va,US
60/C5 **Tramore,** Ire.
60/C5 **Tramore** (bay), Ire.
190/C2 **Tramperos** (cr.), NM, Tx,US
183/K1 **Tramping Lake,** Sk,Can
83/B2 **Tramutola,** It.
62/F2 **Tranås,** Swe.
62/D3 **Tranbjerg,** Den.
76/B2 **Trancoso,** Port.
62/D4 **Tranebjerg,** Den.
62/E3 **Tranemo,** Swe.
54/D5 **Tranent,** Sc,UK
69/D4 **Tranet** (mtn.), Fr.
123/B5 **Trang,** Thai.
130/D1 **Trangan** (isl.), Indo.
135/C2 **Trangie,** Austl.
62/E1 **Trängsletsjön** (lake), Swe.
85/G5 **Trani,** It.
157/H9 **Tranoroa,** Madg.
122/G3 **Tranquebar,** India
173/F4 **Tranqueras,** Uru.
186/B2 **Tranquillity,** Ca,US
137/W **Transantarctic** (mts.), Ant.
98/B3 **Transcarpathian Obl.,** Ukr.
82/C6 **Trans-en-Provence,** Fr.
156/E3 **Transkei** (aut. rep.), SAfr.
156/E2 **Transvaal** (prov.), SAfr.
92/F2 **Transylvania** (reg.), Rom.
189/J1 **Transylvania,** La,US
92/F3 **Transylvanian Alps** (range), Rom.
123/D4 **Tra On,** Viet.
90/C3 **Trapani,** It.
123/D3 **Trapeang Veng,** Camb.
183/G5 **Trapper** (peak), Mt,US
53/S10 **Trappes,** Fr.
135/C3 **Traralgon,** Austl.
144/B2 **Trarza** (reg.), Mrta.
85/D4 **Trasacco,** It.
84/C1 **Trasimeno** (lake), It.
184/B1 **Trask** (mtn.), Or,US
191/H3 **Traskwood,** Ar,US
62/E3 **Träslövsläge,** Swe.
76/B2 **Trás-os-Montes e Alto Douro** (dist.), Port.
123/C3 **Trat,** Thai.
71/H6 **Traun,** Aus.
71/G6 **Traun** (riv.), Aus.
71/F7 **Traun** (riv.), Ger.
71/F7 **Traunreut,** Ger.
71/G7 **Traunsee** (lake), Aus.
71/F7 **Traunstein,** Ger.
86/D1 **Travagliato,** It.
64/F2 **Trave** (riv.), Ger.
86/B1 **Travedona Monate,** It.
196/C2 **Traveler** (mtn.), Me,US
201/F3 **Travelers Rest,** SC,US
133/J5 **Travellers** (lake), Austl.
195/F2 **Traverse** (bay), Mb,Can
177/G2 **Traverse** (peak), Ak,US
193/F1 **Traverse** (lake), Mn, SD,US
198/D2 **Traverse City,** Mi,US
86/D3 **Traversetolo,** It.
123/D4 **Tra Vinh,** Viet.
189/E2 **Travis** (lake), Tx,US
205/L10 **Travis A.F.B.,** Ca,US
92/C3 **Travnik,** Bosn.
58/C2 **Trawsalt** (mtn.), Wal,UK
56/E6 **Trawsfynydd,** Wal,UK
56/E6 **Trawsfynydd, Llyn** (lake), Wal,UK
76/A1 **Trazo,** Sp.
92/B2 **Trbovlje,** Slov.
133/G2 **Treachery** (peak), Austl.
202/K8 **Treasure Island,** Fl,US
87/F1 **Trebaseleghe,** It.
86/C3 **Trebbia** (riv.), It.
72/D3 **Trebbin,** Ger.
64/G1 **Trebel** (riv.), Ger.
72/C3 **Trebelsee** (lake), Ger.
71/G2 **Třebenice,** Czh.
78/B3 **Trébeurden,** Fr.
65/H4 **Třebíč,** Czh.
92/D4 **Trebinje,** Bosn.
83/C3 **Trebisacce,** It.
72/C4 **Trebitz,** Ger.
72/C5 **Trebnitz,** Ger.
71/H4 **Třeboň,** Czh.
134/B2 **Trebonne,** Austl.
76/B4 **Trebujena,** Sp.
70/B3 **Trebur,** Ger.
85/E5 **Trecase,** It.
86/B2 **Trecate,** It.
58/C3 **Tredegar,** Wal,UK
183/K3 **Treelon,** Sk,Can
194/E3 **Treesbank,** Mb,Can
58/C2 **Trefeglwys,** Wal,UK
67/H6 **Treffurt,** Ger.
56/E5 **Trefnant,** Wal,UK
58/C2 **Tregaron,** Wal,UK
78/B3 **Trégastel,** Fr.
87/E1 **Tregnago,** It.
195/J5 **Trego,** Wi,US
78/C4 **Trégueux,** Fr.
78/B3 **Tréguier,** Fr.
78/B5 **Trégunc,** Fr.
194/E3 **Treherne,** Mb,Can
64/E1 **Treia,** Ger.
87/G6 **Treia,** It.
54/B3 **Treig, Loch** (lake), Sc,UK
174/E3 **Treinta de Agosto,** Arg.
175/G2 **Treinta y Tres,** Uru.
175/G2 **Treinta y Tres** (dept.), Uru.
80/C6 **Tré-la-Tête** (mtn.), Fr.
155/F3 **Trelawney,** Zim.
79/E6 **Trélazé,** Fr.
58/B3 **Trelech,** Wal,UK
78/B3 **Trélévern,** Fr.
174/D4 **Trelew,** Arg.
74/D4 **Trélissac,** Fr.
62/E4 **Trelleborg,** Swe.
56/D6 **Tremadoc** (bay), Wal,UK
199/J1 **Tremblant** (mtn.), Qu,Can
53/T10 **Tremblay-lès-Gonesse,** Fr.
79/G3 **Tremblay-le-Vicomte,** Fr.
60/C2 **Tremblestown** (riv.), Ire.
69/D2 **Tremelo,** Belg.
190/B3 **Trementina,** NM,US
85/F3 **Tremiti** (isls.), It.
196/C3 **Tremont,** Me,US
206/B2 **Tremont,** Pa,US
185/G3 **Tremonton,** Ut,US
71/G3 **Třemošná** (riv.), Czh.
77/F1 **Tremp,** Sp.
193/J1 **Trempealeau** (riv.), Wi,US
71/G3 **Třemšín** (peak), Czh.
198/C1 **Trenary,** Mi,US
196/A1 **Trenche** (riv.), Qu,Can
73/C2 **Trenčín,** Slvk.
67/G5 **Trendelburg,** Ger.
174/D2 **Trenel,** Arg.
174/E2 **Trenque Lauquen,** Arg.
199/H2 **Trent** (riv.), On,Can
57/H5 **Trent** (riv.), Eng,UK
57/F6 **Trent and Mersey** (can.), Eng,UK
81/G5 **Trentino-Alto Adige** (reg.), It.
81/H5 **Trento,** It.
81/H5 **Trento** (prov.), It.
125/D3 **Trento,** Phil.
85/E6 **Trentola-Ducenta,** It.
197/F3 **Trenton,** NS,Can
199/H2 **Trenton,** On,Can
203/G3 **Trenton,** Fl,US
200/E3 **Trenton,** Ga,US
200/C1 **Trenton,** Il,US
200/D2 **Trenton,** Ky,US
205/F7 **Trenton,** Mi,US
193/H3 **Trenton,** Mo,US
201/J3 **Trenton,** NC,US
194/C3 **Trenton,** ND,US
192/D3 **Trenton,** Ne,US
192/D3 **Trenton** (dam), Ne,US
206/D3 **Trenton** (cap.), NJ,US
200/C3 **Trenton,** Tn,US
201/J3 **Trent Woods,** NC,US
86/D2 **Trenzano,** It.
58/C3 **Treorchy,** Wal,UK
197/L2 **Trepassey,** Nf,Can
91/F2 **Trepuzzi,** It.
82/B2 **Tréry** (riv.), Fr.
81/E6 **Tresa** (riv.), It.
174/E2 **Tres Algarrobos,** Arg.
175/T11 **Tres Arboles,** Uru.
174/E3 **Tres Arroyos,** Arg.
159/E5 **Tres Arroyos,** Mex.
206/C2 **Tresckow,** Pa,US
170/D4 **Três Corações,** Braz.
86/C1 **Trescore Balneario,** It.
86/C2 **Trescore Cremasco,** It.
172/B3 **Tres Cruces** (peak), Arg., Chile
173/F3 **Três de Maio,** Braz.
164/C4 **Tres Esquinas,** Col.
87/E3 **Tresigallo,** It.
86/D3 **Tresinaro** (riv.), It.
83/A2 **Tresino** (pt.), It.
173/G1 **Três Irmãos** (res.), Braz.
172/D3 **Tres Isletas,** Arg.
170/C4 **Três Lagoas,** Braz.
175/K7 **Tres Lagos,** Arg.
169/E3 **Tres Mapajos,** Bol.
170/D3 **Três Marias,** Braz.
170/D3 **Três Marias** (res.), Braz.
158/D4 **Tres Marías** (isls.), Mex.
174/B5 **Tres Montes** (cape), Chile
164/B3 **Tres Morros, Alto de** (peak), Col.
173/F3 **Três Passos,** Braz.
174/C4 **Tres Picos** (peak), Arg.
174/E3 **Tres Picos** (peak), Arg.
190/B2 **Tres Piedras,** NM,US
170/D4 **Três Pontas,** Braz.
152/C5 **Três Pontas, Cabo das** (cape), Ang.
174/D5 **Tres Puntas** (cape), Arg.
171/E4 **Três Rios,** Braz.
77/F1 **Tres Seigneurs, Pic de** (peak), Fr.
82/B1 **Tresserve,** Fr.
85/E4 **Treste** (riv.), It.
87/F6 **Trestina,** It.
82/B6 **Trets,** Fr.
70/D5 **Treuchtlingen,** Ger.
71/F1 **Treuen,** Ger.
72/C3 **Treuenbrietzen,** Ger.
62/C2 **Treungen,** Nor.
174/C4 **Trevelín,** Arg.
84/C2 **Trevi,** It.
86/C1 **Treviglio,** It.
87/F1 **Trevignano,** It.
84/C3 **Trevignano Romano,** It.
76/D1 **Treviño,** Sp.
87/F1 **Treviso,** It.
87/F1 **Treviso** (int'l arpt.), It.
87/F1 **Treviso** (prov.), It.
78/C5 **Trevolo** (riv.), Fr.
206/B2 **Trevorton,** Pa,US
206/D3 **Trevose-Feasterville,** Pa,US
58/A5 **Trevose Head** (pt.), Eng,UK
86/C1 **Trezzo sull'Adda,** It.
71/H5 **Trhové Sviny,** Czh.
135/C4 **Triabunna,** Austl.
206/A5 **Triadelphia** (res.), Md,US
201/J1 **Triangle,** Va,US
155/F4 **Triangle,** Zim.
83/C3 **Trianto** (riv.), It.
69/E6 **Triaucourt-en-Argonne,** Fr.
73/C3 **Tribeč** (mts.), Slvk.
70/B6 **Triberg,** Ger.
121/E2 **Tribhuvan** (int'l arpt.), Nepal
134/B2 **Tribulation** (cape), Austl.
81/H3 **Tribulaun** (peak), Aus.
190/D1 **Tribune,** Ks,US
174/D3 **Tricaco,** Arg.
85/G6 **Tricarico,** It.
91/F3 **Tricase,** It.
122/F3 **Trichūr,** India
184/B2 **Tri-City,** Or,US
127/J4 **Tricora** (peak), Indo.
68/B4 **Tricot,** Fr.
135/C2 **Trida,** Austl.
184/D3 **Trident** (peak), Nv,US
92/B2 **Trieben,** Aus.
72/C6 **Triebes,** Ger.
68/A5 **Trie Château,** Fr.
79/G2 **Trie-Château,** Fr.
53/S10 **Triel-sur-Seine,** Fr.
69/F4 **Trier,** Ger.
69/F4 **Trierweiler,** Ger.
81/F3 **Triesen,** Lcht.
87/G1 **Trieste,** It.
87/G1 **Trieste** (gulf), It.
87/G1 **Trieste** (prov.), It.
73/A4 **Triesting** (riv.), Aus.
69/E5 **Trieux,** Fr.
78/B3 **Trieux** (riv.), Fr.
71/G6 **Triftern,** Ger.
90/E2 **Triggiano,** It.
93/G4 **Triglav** (peak), Bul.
92/A2 **Triglav** (peak), Slov.
92/A2 **Triglav Nat'l Park,** Slov.
72/C1 **Triglitz,** Ger.
78/C6 **Trignac,** Fr.
85/E4 **Trigno** (riv.), It.
86/C2 **Trigolo,** It.
76/B4 **Trigueros,** Sp.
91/G3 **Tríkala,** Gre.
91/G3 **Trikhonís** (lake), Gre.
121/F3 **Trikut Parvat,** India
198/D4 **Tri-Lakes,** In,US
202/L7 **Trilby,** Fl,US
203/G3 **Trilby,** Fl,US
122/D1 **Triloknāth,** India
68/B6 **Trilport,** Fr.
60/D2 **Trim,** Ire.
80/D3 **Trimbach,** Swi.
57/G2 **Trimdon,** Eng,UK
81/F4 **Trimmis,** Swi.
81/F4 **Trin,** Swi.
122/H4 **Trincomalee,** SrL.
122/H4 **Trincomalee** (dist.), SrL.
170/C3 **Trindade,** Braz.
65/K4 **Třinec,** Czh.
59/F3 **Tring,** Eng,UK
196/B2 **Tring-Jonction,** Qu,Can
174/E3 **Trinidad** (isl.), Arg.
169/E4 **Trinidad,** Bol.
175/J7 **Trinidad** (chan.), Chile
175/J7 **Trinidad** (gulf), Chile
164/D3 **Trinidad,** Col.
162/F5 **Trinidad** (isl.), Trin.
175/F2 **Trinidad,** Uru.
184/A3 **Trinidad** (pt.), Ca,US
190/B2 **Trinidad,** Co,US
189/F1 **Trinidad,** Tx,US
162/F5 **Trinidad and Tobago**
85/G5 **Trinitapoli,** It.
197/L1 **Trinity,** Nf,Can
197/L2 **Trinity** (bay), Nf,Can
177/H4 **Trinity** (isls.), Ak,US
200/D3 **Trinity,** Al,US
184/B3 **Trinity** (dam), Ca,US
184/B3 **Trinity** (riv.), Ca,US
201/H3 **Trinity,** NC,US
184/D3 **Trinity** (range), Nv,US
189/G2 **Trinity,** Tx,US
189/N9 **Trinity** (bay), Tx,US
189/G2 **Trinity** (riv.), Tx,US
184/B3 **Trinity Center,** Ca,US
188/K7 **Trinity, Clear Fork** (riv.), Tx,US
188/L6 **Trinity, East Fork** (riv.), Tx,US
188/L6 **Trinity, Elm Fork** (riv.), Tx,US
190/A4 **Trinity Site,** NM,US
184/B3 **Trinity, South Fork** (riv.), Ca,US
188/K7 **Trinity, West Fork** (riv.), Tx,US
184/B3 **Trinity-Whiskeytown-Shasta Nat'l Rec. Area,** Ca,US
147/H5 **Trinkitat,** Sudan
86/B2 **Trino,** It.
152/C4 **Trinta-e-um de Janeiro,** Ang.
157/S15 **Triolet,** Mrts.
85/F4 **Triolo** (riv.), It.
200/E3 **Trion,** Ga,US
83/C3 **Trionto** (cape), It.
201/J2 **Triplet,** Va,US
106/C2 **Tripoli,** Leb.
140/D1 **Tripoli** (cap.), Libya
146/B1 **Tripoli** (int'l arpt.), Libya
91/H4 **Trípolis,** Gre.
146/A2 **Tripolitania** (reg.), Libya
103/D2 **Tripoli** (Tarābulus), Leb.
104/C3 **Tripoli** (Tarābulus), Leb.
146/B1 **Tripoli** (Tarābulus) (cap.), Libya
69/G5 **Trippstadt,** Ger.
72/B6 **Triptis,** Ger.
122/F4 **Tripunittura,** India
121/H4 **Tripura** (state), India
81/G3 **Trisanna** (riv.), Aus.
87/E1 **Trissino,** It.
50/J7 **Tristan da Cunha** (isls.), StH.
144/B4 **Tristao** (isls.), Guin.
174/D4 **Triste** (peak), Arg.
71/G5 **Třístoličník** (peak), Czh.
121/E2 **Trisuli** (riv.), Nepal
121/E2 **Trisūli Bāzār,** Nepal
123/D4 **Tri Ton,** Viet.
67/H1 **Trittau,** Ger.
202/D3 **Triumph-Buras,** La,US
169/E3 **Triunfo,** Bol.
167/G4 **Triunfo,** Braz.
122/F4 **Trivandrum,** India
122/F4 **Trivandrum** (int'l arpt.), India
85/E4 **Trivento,** It.
86/B1 **Trivero,** It.
73/A2 **Trkmanka** (riv.), Czh.
73/B3 **Trnava,** Slvk.
73/B3 **Trnávka** (riv.), Slvk.
79/E2 **Troarn,** Fr.
138/E5 **Trobriand** (isls.), PNG
70/C6 **Trochtelfingen,** Ger.
183/H2 **Trochu,** Ab,Can
85/D1 **Trodica,** It.
68/A5 **Troesne** (riv.), Fr.
75/L3 **Trofaiach,** Aus.
72/C5 **Tröglitz,** Ger.
62/D2 **Trøgstad,** Nor.
85/F5 **Troia,** It.
77/Q11 **Tróia,** Port.
69/G2 **Troisdorf,** Ger.
69/G6 **Troisfontaines,** Fr.
141/N13 **Trois Fourches, Cap des** (cape), Mor.
196/C1 **Trois-Pistoles,** Qu,Can
69/E3 **Trois-Ponts,** Belg.
196/A2 **Trois-Rivières,** Qu,Can
80/C5 **Troistorrents,** Swi.
69/E3 **Troisvierges,** Lux.
96/G1 **Troitsa,** Rus.
95/P5 **Troitsk,** Rus.
99/M2 **Troitskiy,** Rus.
95/N3 **Troitsko-Pechorsk,** Rus.
109/M2 **Troitskoye,** Rus.
97/K1 **Troitskoye,** Rus.
99/K3 **Troitskoye,** Ukr.
148/B2 **Trolla** (well), Chad
62/E2 **Trollhättan,** Swe.
166/B3 **Trombetas** (riv.), Braz.
51/M6 **Tromelin** (isl.), Fr.
141/H6 **Tromelin** (isl.), Reu.
86/B2 **Tromello,** It.
54/B3 **Tromie** (riv.), Sc,UK
61/F1 **Troms** (co.), Nor.
61/F1 **Tromsø,** Nor.
186/D3 **Trona,** Ca,US
174/C4 **Tronador** (peak), Arg.
174/C4 **Tronador** (peak), Chile
61/D3 **Trondheim,** Nor.
61/D3 **Trondheimsfjorden** (fjord), Nor.
85/D2 **Tronto** (riv.), It.
69/E6 **Tronville-en-Barrios,** Fr.
86/B2 **Tronzano Vercellese,** It.
103/C2 **Troodos** (mts.), Cyp.
56/D1 **Trool, Loch** (lake), Sc,UK
54/B5 **Troon,** Sc,UK
206/C3 **Trooper,** Pa,US
83/B5 **Tropea,** It.
182/E2 **Trophy** (mtn.), BC,Can
187/F2 **Tropic,** Ut,US
91/G1 **Tropojë,** Alb.
62/G2 **Trosa,** Swe.
63/L4 **Troškūnai,** Lith.
68/B5 **Trosly-Breuil,** Fr.
99/H1 **Trosna,** Rus.
194/B3 **Trossachs,** Sk,Can
70/B6 **Trossingen,** Ger.
56/B1 **Trostan** (mtn.), NI,UK
71/F6 **Trostberg an der Alz,** Ger.
98/E3 **Trostyanets,** Ukr.
99/H2 **Trostyanets,** Ukr.
53/Q8 **Trottiscliffe,** Eng,UK
161/H2 **Trou du Nord,** Haiti
189/G1 **Troup,** Tx,US
54/D1 **Troup Head** (pt.), Sc,UK
190/E2 **Trousdale,** Ks,US
178/D2 **Trout** (lake), NW,Can
195/H2 **Trout** (lake), On,Can
187/F3 **Trout** (cr.), Az,US
57/F3 **Troutbeck,** Eng,UK
198/B1 **Trout Creek,** Mi,US
182/G4 **Trout Creek,** Mt,US
185/G4 **Trout Creek,** Ut,US
182/F2 **Trout Lake,** BC,Can
198/D1 **Trout Lake,** Mi,US
182/D5 **Trout Lake,** Wa,US
200/E5 **Troutman,** Ga,US
201/G3 **Troutman,** NC,US
79/F2 **Trouville,** Fr.
58/D4 **Trowbridge,** Eng,UK
135/C4 **Trowutta,** Austl.
206/A2 **Troxelville,** Pa,US
200/E5 **Troy,** Al,US
186/D3 **Troy** (lake), Ca,US
200/D2 **Troy,** In,US
191/G1 **Troy,** Ks,US
205/F6 **Troy,** Mi,US
191/J1 **Troy,** Mo,US
182/G3 **Troy,** Mt,US
201/H3 **Troy,** NC,US
184/F4 **Troy** (peak), Nv,US
199/K3 **Troy,** NY,US
198/D4 **Troy,** Oh,US
184/E1 **Troy,** Or,US
199/H4 **Troy,** Pa,US
189/F2 **Troy,** Tx,US
199/K2 **Troy,** Vt,US
93/G4 **Troyan,** Bul.
93/G4 **Troyanski Prokhod** (pass), Bul.
205/P14 **Troy Center,** Wi,US
95/Q5 **Troyebratskiy,** Kaz.
74/F2 **Troyes,** Fr.
91/K3 **Troy** (Ilium) (ruins), Turk.
92/E4 **Trstenik,** Yugo.
80/D4 **Trub,** Swi.
81/F3 **Trübbach,** Swi.
96/E1 **Trubchëvsk,** Rus.
184/C4 **Truckee,** Ca,US
184/D4 **Truckee** (riv.), Ca, Nv,US
95/K2 **Trufanovo,** Rus.
177/M3 **Truitt** (peak), Yk,Can
160/E3 **Trujillo,** Hon.
168/B3 **Trujillo,** Peru
76/C3 **Trujillo,** Sp.
190/B3 **Trujillo,** NM,US
164/D2 **Trujillo,** Ven.
164/D2 **Trujillo** (state), Ven.
138/E4 **Truk** (isls.), Micr.
69/G5 **Trulben,** Ger.
193/G2 **Truman,** Mn,US
191/J3 **Trumann,** Ar,US
206/C3 **Trumbauersville,** Pa,US
187/F2 **Trumbull** (mt.), Az,US
208/A3 **Trumbull,** Ct,US
208/G5 **Trumbull** (co.), Oh,US
188/L7 **Trumbull,** Tx,US
80/D4 **Trümmelbachfälle** (falls), Swi.
124/B2 **Trumon,** Indo.
58/D2 **Trumpet,** Eng,UK
92/F4 **Trŭn,** Bul.
79/F3 **Trun,** Fr.
135/C2 **Trundle,** Austl.
123/D1 **Trung Khanh,** Viet.
99/M5 **Trunovskoye,** Rus.
196/F3 **Truro,** NS,Can
58/A6 **Truro,** Eng,UK
193/H3 **Truro,** Ia,US
190/E4 **Truscott,** Tx,US
98/B3 **Truskavets,** Ukr.
93/G4 **Trŭstenik,** Bul.
208/C3 **Trustom Pond Nat'l Wild. Ref.,** RI,US
187/J4 **Truth Or Consequences,** NM,US
65/H3 **Trutnov,** Czh.
74/E4 **Truyère** (riv.), Fr.
56/D6 **Trwyn Cilan** (pt.), Wal,UK
93/G4 **Tryavna,** Bul.
192/D3 **Tryon,** Ne,US
191/F3 **Tryon,** Ok,US
62/E1 **Trysil,** Nor.
62/D1 **Trysilelva** (riv.), Nor.
65/J2 **Trzcianka,** Pol.
65/H1 **Trzebiatów,** Pol.
65/J3 **Trzebnica,** Pol.
65/J2 **Trzemeszno,** Pol.
92/B2 **Tržič,** Slov.
108/D3 **Tsagaan Bogd** (peak), Mong.
114/E2 **Tsagaannuur,** Mong.
108/G2 **Tsagaan-Ovoo,** Mong.
108/E1 **Tsagaan-Üür,** Mong.
97/H3 **Tsagan Aman,** Rus.
187/H2 **Tsaile,** Az,US
203/G3 **Tsala Apopka** (lake), Fl,US
97/G4 **Tsalendzhikha,** Geo.
105/F1 **Tsalka,** Geo.
82/D2 **Tsanteleina** (mtn.), Fr.
157/J6 **Tsarahonenana,** Madg.
157/H7 **Tsaramandroso,** Madg.
157/H7 **Tsaratanana,** Madg.
157/J6 **Tsaratanana** (massif), Madg.
154/B5 **Tsarisberge** (mts.), Namb.
108/C2 **Tsast** (peak), Mong.
114/F2 **Tsast Uul** (peak), Mong.
156/E3 **Tsatsana** (peak), Les.
154/D4 **Tsau,** Bots.
151/B2 **Tsavo,** Kenya
151/B2 **Tsavo East Nat'l Park,** Kenya
151/B2 **Tsavo West Nat'l Park,** Kenya
81/F3 **Tschagguns,** Aus.
194/D4 **Tschida** (lake), ND,US
81/G4 **Tschierv,** Swi.
81/G4 **Tschlin,** Swi.
98/F4 **Tsebrikovo,** Ukr.
99/L4 **Tselina,** Rus.
95/P5 **Tselinnoye,** Rus.
97/H3 **Tselinnyy,** Rus.
114/B1 **Tselinograd,** Kaz.
108/F2 **Tsenhermandal,** Mong.
154/C5 **Tses,** Namb.
154/D4 **Tsetseng,** Bots.
108/D2 **Tsetsen-Uul,** Mong.
108/E2 **Tsetserleg,** Mong.
145/F5 **Tsévié,** Togo
154/D5 **Tshabong,** Bots.
153/G2 **Tshagbo,** Zaire
154/D5 **Tshane,** Bots.
157/E2 **Tshaneni,** Swaz.
153/F5 **Tshangalele** (res.), Zaire
152/C4 **Tshela,** Zaire
153/F4 **Tshele,** Zaire
155/E4 **Tshesebe,** Bots.
153/E4 **Tshianza,** Zaire
153/E5 **Tshibwika,** Zaire
156/D2 **Tshidilamolomo,** SAfr.
153/E4 **Tshikapa,** Zaire
153/E4 **Tshikapa** (riv.), Zaire
153/E4 **Tshilenge,** Zaire
153/E4 **Tshimbulu,** Zaire
155/E2 **Tshinsenda,** Zaire
155/F4 **Tshipise,** SAfr.
153/E4 **Tshisenga,** Zaire
153/E4 **Tshisenge,** Zaire
155/E3 **Tsholotsho,** Zim.
153/F2 **Tshopo** (riv.), Zaire
153/E3 **Tshuapa** (riv.), Zaire
154/D4 **Tshwaane,** Bots.
141/G6 **Tsiafajavona** (peak), Madg.
95/L2 **Tsil'ma** (riv.), Rus.
99/M4 **Tsimlyansk,** Rus.
53/H4 **Tsimlyansk** (res.), Rus.
156/C2 **Tsineng,** SAfr.
157/H6 **Tsinjomitondraka,** Madg.
157/H9 **Tsiombe,** Madg.
157/H7 **Tsiribihina** (riv.), Madg.
157/H7 **Tsiroanomandidy,** Madg.
97/H4 **Tsiteli-Tskaro,** Geo.
157/H8 **Tsitondroina,** Madg.
156/C4 **Tsitsikamma For. & Coast. Nat'l Park,** SAfr.
95/K5 **Tsivil'sk,** Rus.
157/H9 **Tsivory,** Madg.
104/E1 **Tskhaltubo,** Geo.
97/G4 **Tskhinvali,** Geo.
97/G4 **Tskhiri,** Geo.
94/G4 **Tsna** (riv.), Rus.
105/F1 **Tsnori,** Geo.
154/D3 **Tsodilo** (hills), Bots.
108/D2 **Tsogt,** Mong.
108/F3 **Tsogt-Ovoo,** Mong.
108/F3 **Tsogttsetsiy,** Mong.
108/F2 **Tsöh** (riv.), Mong.
156/D3 **Tsomo** (riv.), SAfr.
110/E3 **Tsu,** Japan
113/E5 **Tsu** (isl.), Japan
110/A3 **Tsu** (isls.), Japan
111/F2 **Tsubame,** Japan
110/E2 **Tsubata,** Japan
111/G2 **Tsuchiura,** Japan
111/M10 **Tsuchiyama,** Japan
112/B3 **Tsugaru** (pen.), Japan
112/B3 **Tsugaru** (str.), Japan
111/L10 **Tsuge,** Japan
112/B4 **Tsukidate,** Japan
111/M10 **Tsukigase,** Japan
111/H7 **Tsukui,** Japan
110/B4 **Tsukumi,** Japan
97/G4 **Tsulukidze,** Geo.
154/C3 **Tsumeb,** Namb.
154/D3 **Tsumkwe,** Namb.
111/K10 **Tsuna,** Japan
97/H4 **Tsurib,** Rus.
111/F3 **Tsuru,** Japan
110/E3 **Tsuruga,** Japan
111/H7 **Tsurugashima,** Japan
111/E2 **Tsurugi,** Japan
110/D4 **Tsurugi-san** (mtn.), Japan
112/A4 **Tsuruoka,** Japan
111/M9 **Tsushima,** Japan
110/A3 **Tsushima** (arpt.), Japan
110/D3 **Tsuyama,** Japan
155/E4 **Tswapong** (hills), Bots.
98/G4 **Tsyurupinsk,** Ukr.
150/B2 **T'T'o,** Eth.
126/C5 **Tua** (cape), Indo.
131/G1 **Tua** (riv.), PNG
76/B2 **Tua** (riv.), Port.
130/D1 **Tual,** Indo.
60/B2 **Tuam,** Ire.
131/G1 **Tuam** (isl.), PNG
174/B4 **Tuamapu** (chan.), Chile
139/L6 **Tuamotu** (arch.), FrPol.
115/B4 **Tuan** (riv.), China
124/B2 **Tuan** (pt.), Indo.
124/C2 **Tuan** (cape), Malay.
123/C1 **Tuan Giao,** Viet.
124/B2 **Tuangku** (isl.), Indo.
123/D2 **Tuan Thuong,** Viet.
125/C1 **Tuao,** Phil.
96/F3 **Tuapse,** Rus.
136/A4 **Tuatapere,** N.Z.
117/J5 **Tuba,** Phil.
187/G5 **Tubac,** Az,US
187/G2 **Tuba City,** Az,US
124/F4 **Tuban,** Indo.
106/D6 **Tuban** (riv.), Yem.
163/E5 **Tubarao,** Braz.
103/G7 **Ṭūbās,** WBnk.
125/C3 **Tubbataha** (reef), Phil.
66/D4 **Tubbergen,** Neth.
125/C3 **Tubigon,** Phil.
70/C5 **Tübingen,** Ger.
68/D2 **Tubize,** Belg.
144/C5 **Tubmanburg,** Libr.
138/H6 **Tubou,** Fiji
146/D1 **Ṭubruq** (Tobruk), Libya
139/K7 **Tubuaä** (isls.), FrPol.
139/K7 **Tubuaï** (isl.), FrPol.
161/G4 **Tubualá,** Pan.
125/C3 **Tuburan,** Phil.
125/C4 **Tuburan,** Phil.
158/C2 **Tubutama,** Mex.
162/D5 **Tucacas,** Ven.
182/F4 **Tucannon** (riv.), Wa,US
171/F1 **Tucano,** Braz.
172/E1 **Tucavaca,** Bol.
72/C3 **Tucheim,** Ger.
113/B2 **Tuchengzi,** China
65/J2 **Tuchola,** Pol.
65/L4 **Tuchów,** Pol.
206/C5 **Tuckahoe** (cr.), Md,US
206/D5 **Tuckahoe,** NJ,US
206/D5 **Tuckahoe** (riv.), NJ,US
207/K8 **Tuckahoe,** NY,US
201/F3 **Tuckasegee** (riv.), NC,US
191/J3 **Tucker,** Ar,US
201/M7 **Tucker,** Ga,US
191/J3 **Tuckerman,** Ar,US
207/D4 **Tuckerton,** NJ,US
69/E5 **Tucquegnieux,** Fr.
187/G4 **Tucson,** Az,US
187/G4 **Tucson** (int'l arpt.), Az,US
172/C2 **Tucumán** (prov.), Arg.
190/C3 **Tucumcari,** NM,US
172/B4 **Tucunuco,** Arg.
165/E2 **Tucupido,** Ven.
165/F2 **Tucupita,** Ven.
166/D3 **Tucuruí,** Braz.
166/D4 **Tucuruí** (res.), Braz.
175/K7 **Tucu Tucu,** Arg.
76/E1 **Tudela,** Sp.
76/C2 **Tudela de Duero,** Sp.
53/P8 **Tudeley,** Eng,UK
74/E5 **Tude, Rochers de la** (mtn.), Fr.
63/M2 **Tudu,** Est.
145/H4 **Tudun Wada,** Nga.
82/C4 **Tuébi** (riv.), Fr.
135/D2 **Tuena,** Austl.
81/H5 **Tuenno,** It.
104/D2 **Tufanbeyli,** Turk.
79/F4 **Tuffé,** Fr.
131/H2 **Tufi,** PNG
201/F3 **Tugaloo** (riv.), Ga, SC,US
108/F4 **Tugao,** China
157/E3 **Tugela,** SAfr.
156/E3 **Tugela** (falls), SAfr.
157/E3 **Tugela** (riv.), SAfr.
157/E3 **Tugela Ferry,** SAfr.
201/F1 **Tug Fork** (riv.), WV,US
120/A1 **Tughlakabad** (ruins), India
125/D3 **Tugnug** (pt.), Phil.
116/D3 **Tuguancun,** China
125/C1 **Tuguegarao,** Phil.
95/Q4 **Tugulym,** Rus.
124/B2 **Tuhemberua,** Indo.
109/K3 **Tuibo,** China
204/F7 **Tujunga,** Ca,US
124/B2 **Tuka,** Indo.
130/A1 **Tukangbesi** (isls.), Indo.
150/C3 **Tukayel,** Eth.
103/B4 **Ṭūkh,** Egypt
116/B4 **Tukkalh,** India
145/E5 **Tukobo,** Gha.
146/D1 **Tūkrah,** Libya
177/M2 **Tuktoyaktuk,** NW,Can
63/K3 **Tukums,** Lat.
126/D4 **Tukung** (peak), Indo.
151/A4 **Tukuyu,** Tanz.
205/C3 **Tukwila,** Wa,US
151/B2 **Tula** (dry riv.), Kenya
159/F4 **Tula,** Mex.
159/K6 **Tula** (riv.), Mex.
53/G3 **Tula,** Rus.
159/K6 **Tula de Allende,** Mex.
114/F4 **Tulagt Ar** (riv.), China
205/C1 **Tulalip Bay,** Wa,US
205/C1 **Tulalip Ind. Res.,** Wa,US
182/D3 **Tulameen** (riv.), BC,Can
159/F4 **Tula Nat'l Park,** Mex.
159/F4 **Tulancingo,** Mex.
124/D4 **Tulangbawang** (riv.), Indo.
96/F1 **Tula Obl.,** Rus.
186/C2 **Tulare,** Ca,US
186/C3 **Tulare** (dry lake), Ca,US
192/E1 **Tulare,** SD,US
190/A4 **Tularosa,** NM,US
188/A1 **Tularosa** (val.), NM,US
156/L10 **Tulbagh,** SAfr.
164/B4 **Tulcán,** Ecu.
93/J3 **Tulcea,** Rom.
93/J3 **Tulcea** (co.), Rom.
98/E3 **Tul'chin,** Ukr.
205/L9 **Tule** (can.), Ca,US
186/C2 **Tule** (riv.), Ca,US
184/C3 **Tulelake,** Ca,US
184/C3 **Tule Lake Nat'l Wild. Ref.,** Ca,Or,US
186/C2 **Tule River Ind. Res.,** Ca,US
82/A4 **Tulette,** Fr.
155/F4 **Tuli,** Zim.
155/F4 **Tuli** (riv.), Zim.
190/D3 **Tulia,** Tx,US
155/F4 **Tuli Block** (reg.), Bots.
177/E5 **Tulik** (vol.), Ak,US
138/E5 **Tulin** (isls.), PNG
191/H3 **Tulip,** Ar,US
103/D3 **Ṭūlkarm,** WBnk.
60/B4 **Tulla,** Ire.
200/D3 **Tullahoma,** Tn,US
54/B3 **Tulla, Loch** (lake), Sc,UK
135/C3 **Tullamarine** (int'l arpt.), Austl.
135/C2 **Tullamore,** Austl.
60/C3 **Tullamore,** Ire.
60/C4 **Tullaroan,** Ire.
74/D4 **Tulle,** Fr.
135/C2 **Tullibigeal,** Austl.
54/C4 **Tullibody,** Sc,UK
63/R7 **Tullinge,** Swe.
82/B2 **Tullins,** Fr.
65/J4 **Tulln,** Aus.
186/B2 **Tulloch** (res.), Ca,US
202/B2 **Tullos,** La,US
60/D4 **Tullow,** Ire.
149/E3 **Tullus,** Sudan
134/B2 **Tully,** Austl.
199/H3 **Tully,** NY,US
206/D3 **Tullytown,** Pa,US
94/G1 **Tuloma** (riv.), Rus.
206/B3 **Tulpehocken** (cr.), Pa,US
191/G2 **Tulsa,** Ok,US
177/M4 **Tulsequah,** BC,Can
120/D2 **Tulsīpur,** India
120/D1 **Tulsipur,** Nepal
63/T9 **Tulstrup,** Den.
159/K7 **Tultepec,** Mex.
164/B3 **Tuluá,** Col.
149/H3 **Tulu Bolo,** Eth.
177/F3 **Tuluksak,** Ak,US
160/E1 **Tulum,** Mex.
159/J4 **Tulum Nat'l Park,** Mex.
101/L4 **Tulun,** Rus.
124/E5 **Tulungagung,** Indo.
124/D3 **Tulungselapan,** Indo.
161/E3 **Tuma** (riv.), Nic.
187/G5 **Tumacacori,** Az,US
159/C2 **Tumacacori Nat'l Mon.,** Az,US
164/B4 **Tumaco,** Col.
96/E1 **Tumanovo,** Rus.
165/G3 **Tumatumari,** Guy.
62/G2 **Tumba,** Swe.
152/D3 **Tumba** (lake), Zaire
159/G5 **Tumbalá,** Mex.
126/D4 **Tumbangkaman,** Indo.
126/D4 **Tumbangsenamang,** Indo.
135/D2 **Tumbarumba,** Austl.
168/A1 **Tumbes,** Peru
135/D2 **Tumblong,** Austl.
123/C3 **Tumbot** (peak), Camb.
153/F5 **Tumbwe,** Zaire
133/H5 **Tumby Bay,** Austl.
115/B2 **Tumd Youqi,** China
115/B2 **Tumd Zuoqi,** China
109/K3 **Tumen,** China
113/E1 **Tumen** (riv.), China, NKor.
108/E4 **Tumenzi,** China
165/F3 **Tumeremo,** Ven.
165/F3 **Tumereng,** Guy.
118/C5 **Tumkūr,** India
54/C3 **Tummel** (riv.), Sc,UK
109/M1 **Tumnin** (riv.), Rus.
107/H3 **Tump,** Pak.
127/F3 **Tumpaan,** Indo.
124/C1 **Tumpat,** Malay.
127/F4 **Tumpu** (peak), Indo.
182/F4 **Tumtum,** Wa,US
145/E4 **Tumu,** Gha.
166/C2 **Tumuc-Humac** (mts.), SAm.
169/E4 **Tumupasa,** Bol.
172/C2 **Tumusla,** Bol.
135/D2 **Tumut,** Austl.
182/C4 **Tumwater,** Wa,US
145/E4 **Tuna,** Gha.
61/F3 **Tunadal,** Swe.
199/K3 **Tunbridge,** Vt,US
104/D2 **Tunceli,** Turk.
104/D2 **Tunceli** (prov.), Turk.
117/F5 **Tunchang,** China
154/C1 **Tunda Chissococua,** Ang.
155/F3 **Tundazi** (hill), Zim.
120/B2 **Tundla,** India
151/A4 **Tunduma,** Tanz.
151/B4 **Tunduru,** Tanz.
114/C1 **Tundyk** (riv.), Kaz.
92/H4 **Tundzha** (riv.), Bul.
89/K2 **Tundzha,** Bul., Turk.
63/T9 **Tune,** Den.
118/C4 **Tungabhadra** (res.), India
118/C4 **Tungabhadra** (riv.), India
135/C3 **Tungamah,** Austl.
149/F3 **Tungaru,** Sudan
125/C4 **Tuñgawan,** Phil.
125/B4 **Tungku,** Malay.
113/C4 **Tŭngsan-got** (pt.), NKor.
117/J3 **Tungshih,** Tai.
178/D2 **Tungsten,** NW,Can
164/B5 **Tungurahua** (prov.), Ecu.
100/K3 **Tunguska, Lower** (riv.), Rus.
100/K3 **Tunguska, Stony** (riv.), Rus.
108/F2 **Tünhel,** Mong.
202/C2 **Tunica,** La,US
200/B3 **Tunica,** Ms,US
90/B4 **Tūnis** (cap.), Tun.
90/B4 **Tunis** (gov.), Tun.
141/X17 **Tunis** (gulf), Tun.
143/H2 **Tunisia**
164/C3 **Tunjá,** Col.
196/C3 **Tunk** (mtn.), Me,US
199/J4 **Tunkhannock,** Pa,US
125/B4 **Tunku Abdul Rahman Nat'l Park,** Malay.
115/C3 **Tunliu,** China
130/B4 **Tunnel Creek Nat'l Park,** Austl.
200/E3 **Tunnel Hill,** Ga,US
167/E4 **Tuntum,** Braz.
177/F3 **Tuntutuliak,** Ak,US
179/K3 **Tunungayualuk** (isl.), Nf,Can
174/C2 **Tunuyán,** Arg.
174/C2 **Tunuyán** (riv.), Chile
116/E2 **Tuo** (riv.), China
117/F3 **Tuokou,** China
117/E4 **Tuolu,** China
186/B2 **Tuolumne** (riv.), Ca,US
186/B2 **Tuolumne City,** Ca,US
186/C2 **Tuolumne Grove,** Ca,US
123/D2 **Tuong Duong,** Viet.
116/E3 **Tuoniang** (riv.), China
84/C1 **Tuoro sul Trasimeno,** It.
114/F5 **Tuotuo** (riv.), China
108/C5 **Tuotuoheyan,** China
170/C4 **Tupã,** Braz.
173/G1 **Tupaciguara,** Braz.
105/F2 **Tūp Āghāj,** Iran
139/K6 **Tupai** (isl.), FrPol.
175/G2 **Tupambaé,** Uru.
167/G5 **Tupanatinga,** Braz.
164/D3 **Tuparro** (riv.), Col.
200/C3 **Tupelo,** Ms,US
191/F3 **Tupelo,** Ok,US
200/C3 **Tupelo Nat'l Bfld.,** Ms,US
94/G5 **Tupik,** Rus.
159/G5 **Tupilco,** Mex.
166/B3 **Tupinambarana** (isl.), Braz.
170/C4 **Tupi Paulista,** Braz.
172/C2 **Tupiza,** Bol.
186/C3 **Tupman,** Ca,US
199/J2 **Tupper Lake,** NY,US
202/N7 **Tupperware Exhibit,** Fl,US
174/C2 **Tupungato,** Arg.
174/C2 **Tupungato** (peak), Arg., Chile
109/J2 **Tuquan,** China
114/E4 **Tura,** China
121/H3 **Tura,** India
101/L3 **Tura,** Rus.
95/Q4 **Tura** (riv.), Rus.
106/D4 **Turabah,** SAr.
122/G3 **Turaiyūr,** India
136/C3 **Turakina,** N.Z.
114/F1 **Turan,** Rus.
109/L1 **Turana** (mts.), Rus.
136/J9 **Turanganui** (riv.), N.Z.
136/C2 **Turangi,** N.Z.
100/G5 **Turan Lowland** (plain), Uzb.
84/C3 **Turano** (lake), It.
84/C3 **Turano** (riv.), It.
73/D1 **Turany,** Slvk.
104/D4 **Ţurayf,** SAr.
164/C2 **Turbaco,** Col.
107/H3 **Turbat,** Pak.
81/E3 **Turbenthal,** Swi.
201/G4 **Turbeville,** SC,US
164/C2 **Turbo,** Col.
206/B1 **Turbotville,** Pa,US
73/C2 **Turčianske Teplice,** Slvk.
80/D1 **Turckheim,** Fr.
93/F2 **Turda,** Rom.
139/M7 **Tureia** (isl.), FrPol.
65/K2 **Turek,** Pol.
100/G5 **Turgay,** Kaz.
100/G4 **Turgay Obl.,** Kaz.
93/H4 **Tŭrgovishte,** Bul.
104/A2 **Turgutlu,** Turk.
104/D1 **Turhal,** Turk.
63/L2 **Türi,** Est.
77/E3 **Turia** (riv.), Sp.
167/E3 **Turiaçu,** Braz.
167/E3 **Turiaçu** (bay), Braz.
167/N7 **Turiamo,** Ven.
159/E5 **Turicato,** Mex.
73/C2 **Turiec** (riv.), Slvk.
52/D4 **Turin,** It.
86/A2 **Turin** (Torino), It.
98/C2 **Turiysk,** Ukr.
108/F1 **Turka,** Rus.
98/B3 **Turka,** Ukr.
149/G5 **Turkana** (lake), Eth., Kenya
104/C1 **Türkeli,** Turk.
114/A3 **Turkestan,** Kaz.
92/E2 **Túrkeve,** Hun.
104/C2 **Turkey**
198/F3 **Turkey** (pt.), On,Can
193/J2 **Turkey** (riv.), Ia,US
188/D3 **Turkey** (cr.), Tx,US
130/C4 **Turkey Creek,** Austl.
202/C2 **Turkey Creek** (lake), La,US
200/E4 **Turkey Heaven** (mtn.), Al,US
70/D6 **Türkheim,** Ger.
99/M2 **Turki,** Rus.
100/F6 **Turkmenistan**
107/H1 **Turkmen-Kala,** Trkm.
104/D2 **Türkoğlu,** Turk.
162/D2 **Turks** (isls.), Trks.
162/C2 **Turks and Caicos** (isls.), UK
162/D2 **Turks Island Passage** (chan.), Trks.
161/J1 **Turks Islands** (passg.), Trks.
61/G3 **Turku,** Fin.
63/K1 **Turku** (int'l arpt.), Fin.
63/K1 **Turku** (Åbo), Fin.
63/K1 **Turku Ja Pori** (prov.), Fin.
151/A1 **Turkwel** (riv.), Kenya
191/G2 **Turley,** Ok,US
188/C3 **Turlingua** (cr.), Tx,US
186/B2 **Turlock,** Ca,US
171/E3 **Turmalina,** Braz.
63/M4 **Turmantas,** Lith.
165/E2 **Turmero,** Ven.
136/D3 **Turnagain** (cape), N.Z.
54/B6 **Turnberry,** Sc,UK
187/G4 **Turnbull** (mt.), Az,US
184/E2 **Turnbull** (dry lake), Or,US
182/E4 **Turnbull Nat'l Wild. Ref.,** Wa,US
160/E2 **Turneffe** (isls.), Belz.
132/C2 **Turner** (peak), Austl.
196/B3 **Turner,** Me,US
183/K3 **Turner,** Mt,US
206/C4 **Turnersville,** NJ,US
189/F2 **Turnersville,** Tx,US
183/G2 **Turner Valley,** Ab,Can
66/B6 **Turnhout,** Belg.
65/H3 **Turnov,** Czh.
93/G4 **Turnu Măgurele,** Rom.
191/E2 **Turon,** Ks,US
135/D3 **Tuross Head,** Austl.
98/D1 **Turov,** Bela.
108/B3 **Turpan,** China
114/E3 **Turpan** (depr.), China
161/G2 **Turquino** (peak), Cuba
200/B3 **Turrell,** Ar,US
79/F1 **Turretot,** Fr.
87/G1 **Turriaco,** It.
82/C4 **Turriers,** Fr.
54/D1 **Turriff,** Sc,UK
83/C2 **Tursi,** It.
100/G6 **Tursunzade,** Taj.
130/C3 **Turtle** (pt.), Austl.
144/B5 **Turtle** (isls.), SLeo.
194/F3 **Turtle** (riv.), ND,US
192/E1 **Turtle** (cr.), SD,US
208/H7 **Turtle Creek,** Pa,US
183/K1 **Turtleford,** Sk,Can
194/D4 **Turtle Lake,** ND,US
194/E3 **Turtle Mountain Ind. Res.,** ND,US
195/G4 **Turtle River,** Mn,US
57/F4 **Turton,** Eng,UK
194/E5 **Turton,** SD,US
114/C3 **Turugart Shankou** (pass), China
100/J3 **Turukhansk,** Rus.
171/M6 **Turvo** (riv.), Braz.
173/G1 **Turvo** (riv.), Braz.
200/D4 **Tuscaloosa,** Al,US
200/D4 **Tuscaloosa** (lake), Al,US
84/B3 **Tuscania,** It.
90/B1 **Tuscano** (arch.), It.
86/D4 **Tuscany** (reg.), It.
208/F7 **Tuscarawas,** Oh,US
208/F7 **Tuscarawas** (co.), Oh,US
208/F6 **Tuscarawas** (riv.), Oh,US
184/E3 **Tuscarora,** Nv,US
197/T9 **Tuscarora Ind. Res.,** NY,US
206/A3 **Tuscarora Mtn.** (ridge), Pa,US
85/F6 **Tusciano** (riv.), It.
193/K4 **Tuscola,** Il,US
188/E1 **Tuscola,** Tx,US
200/D3 **Tuscumbia,** Al,US
191/H1 **Tuscumbia,** Mo,US
187/F1 **Tushar** (mts.), Ut,US
191/F3 **Tushka,** Ok,US
191/G3 **Tuskahoma,** Ok,US
200/E4 **Tuskegee,** Al,US
200/E4 **Tuskegee Institute Nat'l Hist. Site,** Al,US
196/E4 **Tusket,** NS,Can
191/F3 **Tussy,** Ok,US
204/C3 **Tustin,** Ca,US
65/K3 **Tuszyn,** Pol.
105/E2 **Tutak,** Turk.
94/H4 **Tutayev,** Rus.
57/G6 **Tutbury,** Eng,UK
122/G4 **Tuticorin,** India
92/E4 **Tutin,** Yugo.
167/F3 **Tutóia,** Braz.
125/A4 **Tutong,** Bru.
93/H3 **Tutrakan,** Bul.
194/E4 **Tuttle,** ND,US
191/F3 **Tuttle,** Ok,US
191/F1 **Tuttle Creek** (res.), Ks,US
70/B7 **Tuttlingen,** Ger.
130/B2 **Tutuala,** Indo.
151/A3 **Tutubu,** Tanz.
139/H6 **Tutuila** (isl.), ASam.
168/D5 **Tutupaca** (vol.), Peru
177/F2 **Tututalak** (mtn.), Ak,US
200/B3 **Tutwiler,** Ms,US
81/H2 **Tutzing,** Ger.
108/F2 **Tuul** (riv.), Mong.
63/L1 **Tuusula,** Fin.
100/K4 **Tuva Aut. Rep.,** Rus.
138/G5 **Tuvalu**
106/E4 **Ţuwayq, Jabal** (mts.), SAr.
194/B2 **Tuxford,** Sk,Can
57/H5 **Tuxford,** Eng,UK
158/D4 **Tuxpan,** Mex.
159/F4 **Tuxpan,** Mex.
159/F4 **Tuxpan** (riv.), Mex.
159/F5 **Tuxtepec,** Mex.
160/C2 **Tuxtla Gutiérrez,** Mex.
76/A1 **Túy,** Sp.
167/O7 **Tuy** (riv.), Ven.
123/E3 **Tuy An,** Viet.
123/D2 **Tuyen Hoa,** Viet.
123/D1 **Tuyen Quang,** Viet.
123/E3 **Tuy Hoa,** Viet.
95/M5 **Tuymazy,** Rus.
105/G3 **Tūysarkān,** Iran
114/C3 **Tuyuk,** Kaz.
104/C2 **Tuz** (lake), Turk.
95/K4 **Tuzha,** Rus.
187/F3 **Tuzigoot Nat'l Mon.,** Az,US
105/F3 **Ţūz Khurmātū,** Iraq
92/D3 **Tuzla,** Bosn.
105/N7 **Tuzla,** Turk.
105/E1 **Tuzluca,** Turk.
104/B2 **Tuzlukçu,** Turk.
98/F5 **Tuzly,** Ukr.
153/E4 **Tuzule,** Zaire
62/E3 **Tvååker,** Swe.
62/C2 **Tvedestrand,** Nor.
94/G4 **T'ver,** Rus.
63/P3 **Tver' Obl.,** Rus.
94/G4 **T'ver Obl.,** Rus.
94/G4 **Tvertsa** (riv.), Rus.
73/C3 **Tvrdošovce,** Slvk.
93/G4 **Tvŭrditsa,** Bul.
186/B1 **Twain Harte,** Ca,US
155/F2 **Twapia,** Zam.
65/J3 **Twardogóra,** Pol.
183/M1 **Tway,** Sk,Can
199/H2 **Tweed,** On,Can
55/K9 **Tweed** (riv.), UK
54/D5 **Tweed** (riv.), Sc,UK
135/E1 **Tweed Heads,** Austl.
54/D5 **Tweedmouth,** Eng,UK
208/B3 **Tweed-New Haven** (arpt.), Ct,US
54/C5 **Tweedsmuir,** Sc,UK
66/D4 **Twente** (can.), Neth.
66/D4 **Twente** (reg.), Neth.
197/R9 **Twenty Mile** (riv.), On,Can
186/D3 **Twentynine Palms,** Ca,US
186/D3 **Twentynine Palms Marine Corps Base,** Ca,US
195/H4 **Twig,** Mn,US
185/F2 **Twin** (falls), Id,US
185/G1 **Twin Bridges,** Mt,US
188/D2 **Twin Buttes** (res.), Tx,US
201/F4 **Twin City,** Ga,US
185/F2 **Twin Falls,** Id,US
155/F1 **Twingi,** Zam.
177/F4 **Twin Hills,** Ak,US
198/C3 **Twin Lake,** Mi,US
205/P14 **Twin Lakes,** Wi,US
206/D3 **Twin Rivers,** NJ,US
184/B1 **Twin Rocks,** Or,US
208/F5 **Twinsburg,** Oh,US
182/F1 **Twins, The** (mtn.), Ab,Can
194/F4 **Twin Valley,** Mn,US
67/E3 **Twist,** Ger.
67/G6 **Twiste** (riv.), Ger.
67/F3 **Twistringen,** Ger.
186/B3 **Twitchell** (res.), Ca,US
190/C2 **Two Butte** (cr.), Co,US
183/J4 **Twodot,** Mt,US
135/D3 **Twofold** (bay), Austl.
195/J4 **Two Harbors,** Mn,US
183/J1 **Two Hills,** Ab,Can
190/B4 **Two Rivers** (res.), NM,US
193/L1 **Two Rivers,** Wi,US
59/E1 **Twycross,** Eng,UK
154/B4 **Twyfelfontein Rock Engravings,** Namb.
59/F4 **Twyford,** Eng,UK
58/C1 **Twymyn** (riv.), Wal,UK
56/D2 **Twynholm,** Sc,UK
98/B3 **Tyachev,** Ukr.
116/B4 **Tyao** (riv.), Burma, India
112/E1 **Tyatya Gora** (mt.), Rus.
201/G4 **Tybee Nat'l Wild. Ref.,** Ga,US
65/K3 **Tychy,** Pol.
59/G1 **Tydd Saint Giles,** Eng,UK
188/E1 **Tye,** Tx,US
144/D4 **Tyémé,** IvC.
199/H2 **Tyendinaga,** On,Can
201/H1 **Tygart** (lake), WV,US
109/K1 **Tygda,** Rus.
201/G3 **Tyger** (riv.), SC,US
184/C1 **Tygh Valley,** Or,US
146/B4 **Tyi Grounto** (plat.), Niger
57/F4 **Tyldesley,** Eng,UK
193/F1 **Tyler,** Mn,US
189/G1 **Tyler,** Tx,US
206/A2 **Tylersville,** Pa,US

202/C2 Tylertown, Ms,US
109/N1 Tymovskoye, Rus.
75/L2 Týn, Czh.
60/B3 Tynagh, Ire.
189/F3 Tynan, Tx,US
101/N4 Tynda, Rus.
194/F2 Tyndall, Mb,Can
192/F2 Tyndall, SD,US
203/F2 Tyndall A.F.B., Fl,US
83/B6 Tyndaris (ruins), It.
54/B4 Tyndrum, Sc,UK
57/F2 Tyne (riv.), Eng,UK
54/D5 Tyne (riv.), Sc,UK
57/G2 Tyne & Wear (co.), Eng,UK
57/G1 Tynemouth, Eng,UK
200/F2 Tyner, Ky,US
196/F2 Tyne Valley, PE,Can
61/D3 Tynset, Nor.
177/H3 Tyonek, Ak,US
104/C3 Tyre, Leb.
62/H2 Tyresö, Swe.
63/S7 Tyresta (reg. park), Swe.
103/D3 Tyre (Şūr), Leb.
62/D1 Tyrifjorden (lake), Nor.
62/E3 Tyringe, Swe.
208/A1 Tyringham, Ma,US
109/L2 Tyrma (riv.), Rus.
97/G4 Tyrnyauz, Rus.
191/G2 Tyro, Ks,US
201/L8 Tyrone, Ga,US
187/H4 Tyrone, NM,US
190/D2 Tyrone, Ok,US
199/G4 Tyrone, Pa,US
191/J3 Tyronza, Ar,US
135/B2 Tyrrell (cr.), Austl.
133/J5 Tyrrell (lake), Austl.
60/C3 Tyrrellspass, Ire.
52/E4 Tyrrhenian (sea), It.
62/A1 Tysnes, Nor.
62/A2 Tysnesøy (isl.), Nor.
206/A6 Tysons Corner, Va,US
62/A1 Tysse, Nor.
62/G2 Tystberga, Swe.
63/K4 Tytuvėnai, Lith.
203/G2 Ty Ty, Ga,US
97/J3 Tyub-Karagan (pt.), Kaz.
97/J3 Tyulen'i (isls.), Kaz.
97/H3 Tyuleniy (isl.), Rus.
95/Q4 Tyumen', Rus.
95/Q4 Tyumen (int'l arpt.), Rus.
95/Q4 Tyumen' Obl., Rus.
114/C3 Tyup, Kyr.
58/B3 Tywi (riv.), Wal,UK
58/B1 Tywyn, Wal,UK
155/F4 Tzaneen, SAfr.
159/H4 Tzucacab, Mex.

U

125/C2 Uac (mt.), Phil.
150/D3 Uadi Uadaimo (dry riv.), Som.
139/M5 Ua Huka (isl.), FrPol.
152/D4 Uamba (riv.), Ang., Zaire
54/B4 Uamh Bheag (mtn.), Sc,UK
134/B3 Uanda, Austl.
139/L5 Ua Pou (isl.), FrPol.
130/B2 Uato-Lari, Indo.
166/B3 Uatumã (riv.), Braz.
171/F1 Uauá, Braz.
165/E5 Uaupés, Braz.
164/D4 Uaupés (riv.), Braz.
159/H5 Uaxactún, Guat.
160/D2 Uaxactún (ruins), Guat.
92/E3 Ub, Yugo.
171/E4 Ubá, Braz.
148/B3 Uba, Nga.
69/F2 Ubach over Worms, Neth.
69/F2 Übach-Palenberg, Ger.
95/Q5 Ubagan (riv.), Kaz.
171/F2 Ubaitaba, Braz.
167/F3 Ubajara, Braz.
167/F3 Ubajara Nat'l Park, Braz.
140/D4 Ubangi (riv.), Afr.
171/F2 Ubatã, Braz.
164/C3 Ubaté, Col.
170/D4 Ubatuba, Braz.
125/D3 Ubay, Phil.
82/C4 Ubaye (riv.), Fr.
82/C4 Ubayette (riv.), Fr.
66/C5 Ubbergen, Neth.
118/D4 Ube, Japan
110/B4 Ūbe (arpt.), Japan
76/D3 Úbeda, Sp.
169/G5 Uberaba (lake), Bol., Braz.
170/D3 Uberaba, Braz.
69/F5 Überherrn, Ger.
170/C3 Uberlândia, Braz.
81/F2 Überlingen, Ger.
81/F2 Überlingersee (lake), Ger.
127/J4 Ubia (peak), Indo.
145/G5 Ubiaja, Nga.
172/C2 Ubina, Bol.
168/D5 Ubinas, Peru
198/E3 Ubly, Mi,US
157/F2 Ubombo, SAfr.
123/D3 Ubon Ratchathani, Thai.
76/C4 Ubrique, Sp.
153/F3 Ubundu, Zaire
153/F3 Ubute, Zaire
174/E2 Ucacha, Arg.
168/C3 Ucayali (dept.), Peru
168/C2 Ucayali (riv.), Peru
64/C3 Uccle, Belg.
154/C3 Uchab, Namb.
107/H1 Uch-Adzhi, Trkm.
53/J3 Uchaly, Rus.
100/J5 Uch-Aral, Kaz.
130/D4 Ucharonidge, Austl.
112/B2 Uchiura (bay), Japan
168/B3 Uchiza, Peru
99/M6 Uchkeken, Rus.
100/G5 Uchkuduk, Uzb.
67/F4 Uchte, Ger.
72/B2 Uchte (riv.), Ger.
168/B2 Uchumarca, Peru
168/D5 Uchumayo, Peru
101/P4 Uchur (riv.), Rus.
204/G8 U.C.-Irvine, Ca,US
69/F5 Ückange, Fr.
72/D1 Ücker (riv.), Ger.
72/D1 Uckermark (reg.), Ger.
59/G5 Uckfield, Eng,UK
204/F7 U.C.L.A., Ca,US
185/H2 Ucon, Id,US
192/A1 Ucross, Wy,US
152/C5 Ucua, Ang.
172/C1 Ucumasi, Bol.
108/F1 Uda (riv.), Rus.
118/B3 Udaipur, India
120/B4 Udaipura, India
121/F2 Udaipur Garhi, Nepal
122/F3 Udamalpet, India
122/G4 Udankudi, India
145/G4 Udara, Nga.
62/D2 Uddevalla, Swe.
54/B5 Uddingston, Sc,UK
61/F2 Uddjaure (lake), Swe.
66/C5 Uden, Neth.
66/C5 Udenhout, Neth.
67/H6 Uder, Ger.
118/C4 Udgīr, India
122/C1 Udhampur, India
145/G5 Udi, Nga.
95/K3 Udimskiy, Rus.
87/G1 Udine, It.
87/G1 Udine (prov.), It.
118/B5 Udipi, India
95/L4 Udmurt Aut. Rep., Rus.
94/G4 Udomlya, Rus.
79/E3 Udon (riv.), Fr.
123/C2 Udon Thani, Thai.
105/F1 Udzhary, Azer.
72/D4 Uebigau, Ger.
65/H2 Ueckermünde, Ger.
111/F2 Ueda, Japan
153/E2 Uele (riv.), Zaire
177/E2 Uelen, Rus.
66/D4 Uelsen, Ger.
67/H3 Uelzen, Ger.
110/E3 Ueno, Japan
111/F3 Uenohara, Japan
153/F1 Uere (riv.), Zaire
80/D4 Uetendorf, Swi.
67/G1 Uetersen, Ger.
67/H4 Uetze, Ger.
53/J3 Ufa, Rus.
95/N5 Ufa (riv.), Rus.
70/D3 Uffenheim, Ger.
81/H2 Uffing, Ger.
59/E3 Uffington, Eng,UK
85/F5 Ufita (riv.), It.
105/H2 Ufra, Trkm.
154/B4 Ugab (dry riv.), Namb.
63/K3 Ugāle, Lat.
153/G4 Ugalla, Tanz.
153/G4 Ugalla (riv.), Tanz.
153/G4 Ugalla River Game Rsv., Tanz.
140/F4 Uganda
145/G5 Ugbobo Ani, Nga.
91/F3 Ugento, It.
145/H5 Ugep, Nga.
145/G5 Ughelli, Nga.
54/E1 Ugie (riv.), Sc,UK
76/D4 Ugíjar, Sp.
82/C1 Ugine, Fr.
109/N2 Uglegorsk, Rus.
99/K3 Uglegorsk, Ukr.
95/N4 Ugleural'skiy, Rus.
94/H4 Uglich, Rus.
75/L4 Ugljan (isl.), Cro.
109/L3 Uglovoye, Rus.
73/B5 Ugod, Hun.
101/T3 Ugol'nyye Kopi, Rus.
96/E1 Ugra (riv.), Rus.
108/F2 Ugtaaltsaydam, Mong.
93/G4 Ugŭrchin, Bul.
151/B2 Ugweno, Tanz.
73/B1 Uherské Hradiště, Czh.
73/B1 Uherský Brod, Czh.
70/C5 Uhingen, Ger.
189/F3 Uhland, Tx,US
71/G4 Úhlava (riv.), Czh.
71/F3 Úhlavka (riv.), Czh.
208/F7 Uhrichsville, Oh,US
82/D2 Uia di Ciamarella (peak), It.
72/B5 Uicheritz, Ger.
55/H7 Uig, Sc,UK
55/H8 Uig, Sc,UK
152/C4 Uige, Ang.
152/C4 Uige (prov.), Ang.
113/E4 Ŭihŭng, SKor.
113/D4 Ŭijŏngbu, SKor.
113/C2 Ŭiju, NKor.
97/K2 Uil, Kaz.
97/K2 Uil (riv.), Kaz.
156/L11 Uilkraal (riv.), SAfr.
97/G4 Uilpata, Gora (peak), Rus.
185/H3 Uinta (basin), Ut,US
185/J3 Uinta (riv.), Ut,US
185/H3 Uinta (mts.), Ut, Wy,US
185/H3 Uinta and Ouray Ind. Res., Ut,US
167/G4 Uiraúna, Braz.
113/E5 Ŭiryŏng, SKor.
113/E4 Ŭisŏng, SKor.
156/D4 Uitenhage, SAfr.
66/B3 Uitgeest, Neth.
66/B4 Uithoorn, Neth.
66/D2 Uithuizen, Neth.
138/F4 Ujae (atoll), Mrsh.
138/F4 Ujelang (atoll), Mrsh.
51/S5 Ujelang (isl.), Mrsh.
92/E2 Újfehértó, Hun.
120/B1 Ujhāni, India
111/L10 Uji, Japan
111/L10 Uji (riv.), Japan
153/G4 Ujiji, Tanz.
111/L10 Ujitawara, Japan
118/C3 Ujjain, India
126/E3 Ujohbilang, Indo.
124/D2 Ujunggading, Indo.
124/D4 Ujung Kulon Nat'l Park, Indo.
127/E5 Ujung Pandang, Indo.
151/A2 Ukara (isl.), Tanz.
153/G4 Ukata, Nga.
114/C5 Ukdungle, India
151/A2 Ukerewe (isl.), Tanz.
116/B4 Ukhiya, Bang.
53/J2 Ukhta, Rus.
184/B4 Ukiah, Ca,US
184/D1 Ukiah, Or,US
63/L4 Ukmergė, Lith.
98/F4 Ukraine
103/C2 U.K. Sovereign Base Area (poss.), Cyp.
151/A4 Ukwama, Tanz.
153/F3 Ukwatutu, Zaire
104/B2 Ula, Turk.
108/F2 Ulaanbaatar (cap.), Mong.
108/C2 Ulaangom, Mong.
108/B2 Ulaanhus, Mong.
108/F1 Ulan-Burgasy (mts.), Rus.
97/H3 Ulan Erge, Rus.
153/F3 Ulangati, Zaire
109/J2 Ulanhot, China
97/H3 Ulan-Kholl, Rus.
115/B2 Ulansuhai (salt lake), China
108/F1 Ulan-Ude, Rus.
114/F5 Ulan Ul (lake), China
104/D2 Ulaş, Turk.
205/L10 Ulatis (cr.), Ca,US
151/B3 Ulaya, Tanz.
183/L4 Ul Bend Nat'l Wild. Ref., Mt,US
113/E4 Ulchin, SKor.
92/D5 Ulcinj, Yugo.
168/C3 Ulcumayo, Peru
108/G2 Uldz (riv.), Mong.
62/C2 Ulefoss, Nor.
63/L2 Ülemiste (int'l arpt.), Est.
194/F4 Ulen, Mn,US
109/H2 Ulgain (riv.), China
118/B4 Ulhāsnagar, India
108/D2 Uliastay, Mong.
153/F3 Ulindi (riv.), Zaire
138/D3 Ulithi (isl.), Micr.
92/E3 Uljma, Yugo.
63/N4 Ulla, Bela.
76/A1 Ulla (riv.), Sp.
135/D2 Ulladulla, Austl.
121/G3 Ullāpāra, Bang.
55/J8 Ullapool, Sc,UK
63/G3 Ullared, Swe.
168/D4 Ulla Ulla, Bol.
168/D4 Ulla Ulla Nat'l Rsv., Bol.
77/F2 Ulldecona, Sp.
62/B1 Ullensvang, Nor.
172/B1 Ulloma, Bol.
61/F1 Ullsfjorden (fjord), Nor.
57/F2 Ullswater (lake), Eng,UK
110/B2 Ullŭng (isl.), SKor.
113/D3 Ŭllyul, NKor.
70/C6 Ulm, Ger.
191/J3 Ulm, Ar,US
191/H1 Ulman, Mo,US
135/E1 Ulmarra, Austl.
69/F3 Ulmen, Ger.
63/S7 Ulnasjön (lake), Swe.
155/G2 Ulongué, Moz.
62/E3 Ulricehamn, Swe.
81/E4 Ulrichen, Swi.
71/G5 Ulrichsberg, Aus.
70/C1 Ulrichstein, Ger.
66/D2 Ulrum, Neth.
113/E5 Ulsan, SKor.
70/C1 Ulster (riv.), Ger.
56/A3 Ulster (reg.), Ire.
199/H4 Ulster, Pa,US
56/A2 Ulster American Folk Park, NI,UK
127/G3 Ulu, Indo.
149/G3 Ulu, Sudan
160/E3 Ulua (riv.), Hon.
104/B2 Uluborlu, Turk.
103/D1 Uluçınar, Turk.
104/B1 Uludağ, Tepe (peak), Turk.
105/F2 Uludoruk (peak), Turk.
151/B3 Uluguru (mts.), Tanz.
104/C2 Ulukışla, Turk.
160/D2 Ulumal, Mex.
157/E3 Ulundi, SAfr.
108/B2 Ulungur (lake), China
108/B2 Ulungur (riv.), China
133/F3 Uluru (Ayers Rock) (peak), Austl.
133/F3 Uluru Nat'l Park, Austl.
114/A2 Ulutau, Gora (peak), Kaz.
57/E3 Ulverston, Eng,UK
135/C4 Ulverstone, Austl.
62/B1 Ulvik, Nor.
63/J1 Ulvila, Fin.
63/P2 Ul'yanovka, Rus.
98/F3 Ul'yanovka, Ukr.
96/E1 Ul'yanovo, Rus.
190/D2 Ulysses, Ks,US
193/F3 Ulysses, Ne,US
199/H4 Ulysses, Pa,US
87/G2 Umag, Cro.
172/C1 Umala, Bol.
159/H4 Umán, Mex.
98/F3 Uman', Ukr.
125/D3 Umanum (pt.), Phil.
97/G4 Umari, Braz.
167/G4 Umarizal, Braz.
118/D4 Umarkot, India
107/L2 Umāsi La (pass), India
203/H3 Umatilla, Fl,US
184/D1 Umatilla, Or,US
184/D1 Umatilla (riv.), Or,US
184/D1 Umatilla Army Dep., Or,US
184/D1 Umatilla Ind. Res., Or,US
182/E5 Umatilla Nat'l Wild. Ref., Wa,US
94/G2 Umba, Rus.
131/E3 Umbakumba, Austl.
133/G3 Umbeara, Austl.
84/C1 Umbertide, It.
172/D4 Umberto I, Arg.
157/E3 Umbogintwini, SAfr.
131/G1 Umboi (isl.), PNG
81/G4 Umbrailpass (pass), Swi.
81/G4 Umbrail, Piz (peak), Swi.
84/C2 Umbria (reg.), It.
84/C1 Umbro-Marchigiano, Appennino (mts.), It.
87/F5 Umbro-Marchigiano, Appennino (mts.), It.
155/F5 Umbuluze (riv.), Moz., Swaz.
148/D3 Um Dafuq, Sudan
100/B3 Ume (riv.), Swe.
155/F3 Ume (riv.), Zim.
61/G3 Umeå, Swe.
61/F2 Umeälv (riv.), Swe.
121/G4 Umedpur, Bang.
97/G1 Umët, Rus.
157/E3 Umfolozi (riv.), SAfr.
195/G2 Umfreville (lake), On,Can
155/F3 Umfuli (riv.), Zim.
157/E3 Umgeni (riv.), SAfr.
81/G3 Umhausen, Aus.
177/H2 Umiat, Ak,US
80/D1 Umkirch, Ger.
157/E3 Umkomaas, SAfr.
146/B3 Umm al Abī'd, Libya
146/B3 Umm al Arānib, Libya
106/C4 Umm al Birak, SAr.
146/B2 Umm al Ghirbāl, Bi'r (well), Libya
106/D5 Umm al Khashab, SAr.
107/G3 Umm al Qaywayn, UAE
107/F4 Umm as Samīm (salt dep.), Oman
148/D2 Umm Buru, Sudan
149/F2 Umm Dam, Sudan
149/F2 Umm Dhibbān, Sudan
149/G2 Umm Dhibbān, Sudan
149/G2 Umm Durmān (Omdurman), Sudan
103/D3 Umm el Fahm, Isr.
70/C6 Ummendorf, Ger.
147/G4 Umm Hibal, Bi'r (well), Egypt
149/F2 Umm Inderaba, Sudan
149/E2 Umm Kaddādah, Sudan
147/H3 Umm Lajj, SAr.
105/F4 Umm Qaşr, Iraq
149/E2 Umm Qawzayn, Sudan
149/F2 Umm Ruwābah, Sudan
149/F2 Umm Sayyālah, Sudan
177/E5 Umnak (isl.), Ak,US
177/E5 Umnak (passg.), Ak,US
155/F3 Umniati, Zim.
155/F3 Umniati (riv.), Zim.
123/B2 Umphang, Thai.
184/B2 Umpqua, Or,US
184/B2 Umpqua (riv.), Or,US
154/C2 Umpulo, Ang.
104/B2 Umraniye, Turk.
113/D4 Ŭmsŏng, SKor.
156/E3 Umtata, SAfr.
145/G5 Umuahia, Nga.
170/B4 Umuarama, Braz.
131/F2 Umuda (isl.), PNG
145/G5 Umu Duru, Nga.
145/G5 Umunede, Nga.
91/K2 Umurbey, Turk.
156/E3 Umzimvubu (riv.), SAfr.
155/F4 Umzingwani (riv.), Zim.
157/E3 Umzinto, SAfr.
92/B3 Una (riv.), Bosn., Cro.
171/F2 Una, Braz.
122/D2 Una, India
136/C3 Una (peak), N.Z.
200/F4 Unadilla, Ga,US
199/J3 Unadilla (riv.), NY,US
170/D3 Unaí, Braz.
200/F2 Unaka (mts.), NC, Tn,US
177/F3 Unalakleet, Ak,US
177/E5 Unalaska, Ak,US
177/E5 Unalaska (isl.), Ak,US
106/D3 'Unayzah, SAr.
104/D3 'Unāzah, Jabal (mtn.), SAr.
77/E1 Uncastillo, Sp.
189/G1 Uncertain, Tx,US
120/C3 Unchahra, India
185/K4 Uncompahgre (peak), Co,US
185/K4 Uncompahgre (pk.), Co,US
185/J4 Uncompahgre (plat.), Co,US
185/K4 Uncompahgre (riv.), Co,US
155/F2 Undaunda, Zam.
62/F2 Unden (lake), Swe.
70/B3 Undenheim, Ger.
156/E3 Underberg, SAfr.
133/J5 Underbool, Austl.
194/D4 Underwood, ND,US
200/D3 Underwood-Petersville, Al,US
139/Z17 Undu (pt.), Fiji
169/E5 Unduavi, Bol.
167/L7 Une, Col.
96/E1 Unecha, Rus.
177/F4 Unga (isl.), Ak,US
151/C2 Ungama (bay), Kenya
135/C2 Ungarie, Austl.
179/K3 Ungava (bay), Qu,Can
179/J2 Ungava (pen.), Qu,Can
108/D4 Ungeny, Mol.
109/L3 Unggi, NKor.
131/E3 Ungwariba (pt.), Austl.
71/H2 Unhošť, Czh.
113/E2 Unhŭng, NKor.
167/F4 União, Braz.
173/G3 União da Vitória, Braz.
171/F1 União dos Palmares, Braz.
177/E4 Unimak (isl.), Ak,US
177/E5 Unimak (passg.), Ak,US
165/F5 Unini (riv.), Braz.
168/C3 Unini, Peru
174/D2 Unión, Arg.
173/E3 Unión, Par.
54/C5 Union (can.), Sc,UK
200/D4 Union, Al,US
187/F3 Union (mt.), Az,US
208/B2 Union, Ct,US
191/J1 Union, Mo,US
200/C4 Union, Ms,US
207/D2 Union, NJ,US
206/C5 Union (lake), NJ,US
198/D5 Union, Oh,US
184/D1 Union, Or,US
206/A2 Union (co.), Pa,US
201/G3 Union, SC,US
201/G2 Union, WV,US
207/D3 Union Beach, NJ,US
206/B4 Union Bridge, Md,US
192/C1 Union Center, SD,US
205/K11 Union City, Ca,US
200/E4 Union City, Ga,US
198/D4 Union City, In,US
198/D3 Union City, Mi,US
207/D2 Union City, NJ,US
191/F3 Union City, Ok,US
199/G4 Union City, Pa,US
200/C2 Union City, Tn,US
184/B2 Union Creek, Or,US
156/C4 Uniondale, SAfr.
207/L9 Uniondale, NY,US
161/F1 Unión de Reyes, Cuba
158/D5 Unión de Tula, Mex.
205/P14 Union Grove, Wi,US
60/A6 Unionhall, Ire.
160/C2 Unión Hidalgo, Mex.
206/A4 Union Mills, Md,US
202/N6 Union Park, Fl,US
198/C4 Union Pier, Mi,US
201/H4 Union Point, Ga,US
193/G2 Union Slough Nat'l Wild. Ref., Ia,US
200/E4 Union Springs, Al,US
199/H3 Union Springs, NY,US
200/D4 Uniontown, Al,US
191/G3 Uniontown, Ks,US
200/C1 Uniontown, Ky,US
206/A4 Uniontown, Md,US
199/G5 Uniontown, Pa,US
197/S8 Unionville, On,Can
203/G2 Unionville, Ga,US
200/D1 Unionville, In,US
198/E3 Unionville, Mi,US
193/H3 Unionville, Mo,US
184/D3 Unionville, Nv,US
201/J1 Unionville, Va,US
106/F4 United Arab Emirates
55/* United Kingdom
207/K8 United Nations, NY,US
113/E5 United Nations Mem. Cemetery, SKor.
179/T6 United States (range), NW,Can
180/* United States of America
94/G3 Unitsa, Rus.
183/K1 Unity, Sk,Can
196/C3 Unity (pond), Me,US
184/D1 Unity, Or,US
193/J1 Unity, Wi,US
189/E3 Universal City, Tx,US
202/M7 Universal Studios Florida, Fl,US
203/H3 Universal Studios Florida, Fl,US
159/Q10 University City, Mex.
208/F5 University Heights, Oh,US
190/A4 University Park, NM,US
188/L7 University Park, Tx,US
195/N7 Univ. of Minnesota Landscape Arboretum, Mn,US
118/B3 Unjha, India
113/C3 Unjŏn, NKor.
69/G2 Unkel, Ger.
95/N5 Unkurda, Rus.
133/M8 Unley, Austl.
67/E5 Unna, Ger.
120/C2 Unnão, India
113/C3 Ŭnp'a, NKor.
113/C2 Unsan, NKor.
113/D3 Ŭnsan-ŭp, NKor.
60/B1 Unshin (riv.), Ire.
55/P12 Unst (isl.), Sc,UK
67/F3 Unstrut (riv.), Ger.
72/A5 Unstrut (riv.), Ger.
113/D2 Unsu-nodongjagu, NKor.
81/E3 Unterägeri, Swi.
81/F2 Unterargen (riv.), Ger.
71/G5 Untergriesbach, Ger.
81/E3 Unteriberg, Swi.
80/E3 Unterkulm, Swi.
67/H3 Unterlüss, Ger.
70/D3 Unterpleichfeld, Ger.
71/E6 Unterschleissheim, Ger.
81/E2 Untersee (lake), Ger., Swi.
75/G3 Unterseen, Swi.
81/E2 Untersiggenthal, Swi.
81/G2 Unterthingau, Ger.
81/F4 Untervaz, Swi.
80/E4 Unterwalden (canton), Swi.
71/H6 Unterweissenbach, Aus.
72/B6 Unterwellenborn, Ger.
114/F4 Unuli Horog, China
79/G4 Unverre, Fr.
104/D1 Ünye, Turk.
110/A4 Unzen-Amakusa Nat'l Park, Japan
110/B4 Unzen-dake (mtn.), Japan
95/K4 Unzha (riv.), Rus.
157/E3 Unzimkulu, SAfr.
165/F3 Uon-quen, Ven.
111/E2 Uozu, Japan
161/E4 Upala, CR
185/H3 Upalco, Ut,US
167/G4 Upanema, Braz.
165/F2 Upata, Ven.
153/F5 Upemba (lake), Zaire
153/F5 Upemba Nat'l Park, Zaire
151/A1 Upe-Pian Game Rsv., Ugan.
179/L1 Upernavik, Grld.
54/C5 Uphall, Sc,UK
125/D4 Upi, Phil.
156/C3 Upington, SAfr.
155/F3 Upiriwombe, Zam.
198/D4 Upland, In,US
206/C4 Upland, Pa,US
118/B3 Upleta, India
53/P7 Upminster, Eng,UK
180/U10 Upolu (pt.), Hi,US
139/H6 Upolu (isl.), WSam.
184/C3 Upper (lake), Ca,US
181/J2 Upper (pen.), Mi,US
185/H1 Upper (falls), Wy,US
198/E4 Upper Arlington, Oh,US
182/F2 Upper Arrow (lake), BC,Can
71/H6 Upper Austria (prov.), Aus.
196/E2 Upper Blackville, NB,Can
206/C4 Upper Darby, Pa,US
166/B1 Upper Demerara-Berbice (reg.), Guy.
59/G5 Upper Dicker, Eng,UK
145/E4 Upper East (reg.), Gha.
81/F5 Upper Engadine (vall.), Swi.
201/K1 Upper Fairmount, Md,US
206/B5 Upper Falls, Md,US
120/A1 Upper Ganges (can.), India
120/B2 Upper Ganges, Etāwah Branch (can.), India
201/G1 Upperglade, WV,US
136/C3 Upper Hutt, N.Z.
193/J2 Upper Iowa (riv.), Ia,US
184/B2 Upper Klamath (lake), Or,US
184/C2 Upper Klamath Nat'l Wild. Ref., Or,US
184/B4 Upper Lake, Ca,US
56/B2 Upperlands, NI,UK
60/C1 Upper Lough Erne (lake), NI,UK
185/H1 Upper Mesa (falls), Id,US
193/H1 Upper Mississippi Nat'l Wild. Ref., Mn, Wi,US
191/H4 Upper Ouachita Nat'l Wild. Ref., La,US
193/K3 Upper Peoria (lake), Il,US
195/G3 Upper Red (lake), Mn,US
205/F7 Upper Rouge (riv.), Mi,US
207/J7 Upper Saddle River, NJ,US
198/E4 Upper Sandusky, Oh,US
195/G5 Upper Sioux Ind. Res., Mn,US
194/D3 Upper Souris Nat'l Wild. Ref., ND,US
166/B2 Upper Takutu-Upper Essequibo (reg.), Guy.
59/E3 Upper Thames (vall.), Eng,UK
93/J2 Upper Trajan's (wall), (ruins),Mol.
98/E4 Upper Trajan's Wall (ruins), Mol.
196/E3 Upper Vaughan, NS,Can
145/E4 Upper West (reg.), Gha.
59/F1 Uppingham, Eng,UK
62/G2 Upplands-Väsby, Swe.
62/G2 Uppsala, Swe.
62/G1 Uppsala (co.), Swe.
177/D3 Upright (cape), Ak,US
195/J3 Upsala, On,Can
193/G1 Upsala, Mn,US
107/L2 Upshi, India
195/J4 Upson, Wi,US
134/B2 Upstart (bay), Austl.
134/B2 Upstart (cape), Austl.
200/E2 Upton, Ky,US
208/C1 Upton, Ma,US
192/B1 Upton, Wy,US
58/D2 Upton upon Severn, Eng,UK
105/F4 Ur (ruins), Iraq
164/B2 Urabá (gulf), Col.
165/F2 Uracoa, Ven.
112/D3 Urad Qianqi, China
111/H7 Uraga (chan.), Japan
112/C2 Urahoro, Japan
112/C2 Urakawa, Japan
100/F3 Ural (mts.), Rus.
100/F5 Ural (riv.), Rus., Kaz.
135/D1 Uralla, Austl.
97/J2 Ural'sk, Kaz.
97/J2 Ural'skiy, Rus.
97/J2 Ural'sk Obl., Kaz.
97/L1 Ural'skoye, Rus.
153/H4 Urambo, Tanz.
135/C2 Urana, Austl.
202/B2 Urania, La,US
178/F3 Uranium City, Sk,Can
130/D3 Urapunga, Austl.
154/B4 Uraras, Namb.
166/A2 Uraricoera, Braz.
165/F4 Uraricoera (riv.), Braz.
112/J7 Urasoe, Japan
185/J4 Uravan, Co,US
111/F3 Urawa, Japan
100/G3 Uray, Rus.
111/H7 Urayasu, Japan
95/K5 Urazovka, Rus.
99/K2 Urazovo, Rus.
72/C5 Urbach, Ger.
191/H4 Urbana, Ar,US
198/B4 Urbana, Il,US
206/A5 Urbana, Md,US
191/H2 Urbana, Mo,US
198/E4 Urbana, Oh,US
193/H3 Urbandale, Ia,US
87/F5 Urbania, It.
161/G1 Urbano Noris, Cuba
167/F3 Urbano Santos, Braz.
134/D5 Urbenville, Austl.
87/F5 Urbino, It.
84/C1 Urbino (peak), It.
168/D4 Urcos, Peru
97/H2 Urda, Kaz.
76/D3 Urda, Sp.
174/F2 Urdinarrain, Arg.
81/E3 Urdorf, Swi.
114/D2 Urdzhar, Kaz.
57/G3 Ure (riv.), Eng,UK
97/G4 Ureki, Geo.
100/H3 Urengoy, Rus.
158/C2 Ures, Mex.
111/M10 Ureshino, Japan
66/D2 Ureterp, Neth.
136/D2 Urewera Nat'l Park, N.Z.
104/D2 Urfa, Turk.
104/D2 Urfa (prov.), Turk.
67/G6 Urft (riv.), Ger.
109/L1 Urgal, Rus.
100/G5 Urgench, Uzb.
86/C1 Urgnano, It.
61/H1 Urho Kekkosen Nat'l Park, Fin.
81/E4 Uri (canton), Swi.
136/B3 Uriah (peak), N.Z.
202/E2 Uriah, Al,US
164/D3 Uribante (riv.), Ven.
164/C2 Uribia, Col.
98/B5 Uricani, Rom.
191/G1 Urich, Mo,US
54/D2 Urie (riv.), Sc,UK
165/F3 Urimán, Ven.
80/C1 Uriménil, Fr.
172/C2 Uriondo, Bol.
158/D3 Urique (riv.), Mex.
165/F3 Uriranteriña, Ven.
81/E4 Uri-Rotstock (peak), Swi.
100/G4 Uritskiy, Kaz.
63/K1 Urjala, Fin.
66/C3 Urk, Neth.
104/A2 Urla, Turk.
93/H3 Urlaţi, Rom.
60/C4 Urlingford, Ire.
95/N5 Urman, Rus.
122/C2 Urmar, India
109/L2 Urmi (riv.), Rus.
105/F2 Urmia (lake), Iran
69/G3 Urmitz, Ger.
57/F5 Urmston, Eng,UK
81/F3 Urnäsch, Swi.
81/E4 Urnersee (lake), Swi.
92/E4 Uroševac, Yugo.
56/E1 Urr Water (riv.), Sc,UK
71/E4 Ursensollen, Ger.
185/F5 Ursine, Nv,US
159/N7 Úrsulo Galván, Mex.
97/L1 Urtazym, Rus.
158/C3 Uruáchic, Mex.
170/C2 Uruaçu, Braz.
186/D5 Uruapan, Mex.
168/C4 Urubamba, Peru
168/C3 Urubamba (riv.), Peru
169/F4 Urubichá, Bol.
166/B3 Urubu (riv.), Braz.
166/C3 Urubuquara (hill), Braz.
167/G3 Uruburetama, Braz.
166/B3 Urucará, Braz.
169/E2 Urucu (riv.), Braz.
167/E4 Uruçuí, Braz.
170/D1 Uruçuí (hills), Braz.
167/E5 Uruçuí (mts.), Braz.
170/D3 Urucuia (riv.), Braz.
167/E5 Uruçuí Preto (riv.), Braz.
166/B3 Urucurituba, Braz.
163/D5 Uruguai (riv.), Braz.
163/D5 Uruguaiana, Braz.
171/F3 Uruguaiana, Braz.
173/F2 Uruguai (Chapecó) (riv.), Braz.
163/D6 Uruguay
163/D5 Uruguay (riv.), SAm.
164/D2 Urumaco, Ven.
108/B3 Ürümqi, China
135/E1 Urunga, Austl.
167/F3 Uruoca, Braz.
101/R5 Urup (isl.), Rus.
85/F4 Ururi, It.
97/H4 Urus-Martan, Rus.
173/G4 Urussanga, Braz.
97/K1 Urussu, Rus.
172/C1 Uru Uru (lake), Bol.
153/G4 Uruwira, Tanz.
165/F3 Uruyáen, Ven.
109/H1 Uruymkan (riv.), Rus.
99/M2 Uryupinsk, Rus.
95/L4 Urzhum, Rus.
93/H3 Urziceni, Rom.
53/R9 Us, Fr.
108/C1 Us (riv.), Rus.
110/B4 Usa, Japan
53/J2 Usa (riv.), Rus.
192/B4 U.S.A.F. Academy, Co,US
151/A2 Usagara, Tanz.
104/B2 Uşak, Turk.
104/B2 Uşak (prov.), Turk.
154/B4 Usakos, Namb.
191/F3 U.S. Army Amm. Plant, Ok,US
175/N7 Usborne (peak), Falk.
204/F7 U.S.C., Ca,US
206/D6 U. S. C. G. Receiving Ctr., NJ,US
86/C4 Uscio, It.
206/A5 U.S. Dept. of Energy, Md,US
65/G2 Usedom, Ger.
69/E4 Useldange, Lux.
132/B3 Useless Loop, Austl.
153/G4 Usevia, Tanz.
147/H4 'Usfān, SAr.
63/N4 Ushachi, Bela.
63/P2 Ushaki, Rus.
151/A2 Ushashi, Tanz.
106/D4 'Ushayrah, SAr.
153/H4 Ushetu, Tanz.
110/B4 Ushibuka, Japan
111/J7 Ushiku, Japan
153/G3 Ushirombo, Tanz.
63/N1 Ushkovo, Rus.
114/C2 Ushtobe, Kaz.
175/K8 Ushuaia, Arg.
109/K1 Ushumun, Rus.
113/C2 Usi, NKor.
177/J3 Usibelli, Ak,US
168/D4 Usicayos, Peru
122/F4 Usilampatti, India
153/G4 Usinge, Tanz.
70/B2 Usingen, Ger.
131/G1 Usino, PNG
53/H3 Usinsk, Rus.
58/D3 Usk, Wal,UK
58/D3 Usk (riv.), Wal,UK
93/J5 Üsküdar, Turk.
93/H5 Üsküp, Turk.
67/G5 Uslar, Ger.
71/G4 Uslava (riv.), Czh.
99/K1 Usman', Rus.
206/B6 U.S. Naval Academy, Md,US
162/E3 U.S. Naval Res., PR
204/F8 U.S. Nav. Weap. Sta., Ca,US
153/H4 Usoke, Tanz.
108/E1 Usol'ye-Sibirskoye, Rus.
125/C2 Uson, Phil.
174/C2 Uspallata, Arg.
174/C2 Uspallata (pass), Arg., Chile
99/K3 Uspenka, Ukr.
208/C2 Usquepaug, RI,US
168/B2 Usquil, Peru
202/E2 U.S.S. Alabama Battleship Park, Al,US
74/E4 Ussel, Fr.
70/D5 Ussel (riv.), Ger.
80/C5 Usses (riv.), Fr.
154/B2 Ussoque, Ang.
151/D3 Ussure, Tanz.
101/P5 Ussuri (riv.), Rus., China
109/L3 Ussuriysk, Rus.
108/F1 Ust'-Barguzin, Rus.
71/H1 Úštěk, Czh.
81/E3 Uster, Swi.
90/C3 Ustica, It.
90/C3 Ustica (isl.), It.
101/L4 Ust'-Ilimsk, Rus.
72/E6 Ústí nad Labem, Czh.
100/H4 Ust'-Ishim, Rus.
65/J1 Ustka, Pol.
101/S4 Ust'-Kamchatsk, Rus.
114/D2 Ust'-Kamenogorsk, Kaz.
109/H1 Ust'-Karsk, Rus.
95/M3 Ust'-Kulom, Rus.
101/L4 Ust'-Kut, Rus.
101/P2 Ust'-Kuyga, Rus.
99/K5 Ust'-Labinsk, Rus.
63/N2 Ust'-Luga, Rus.
95/P3 Ust'-Man'ya, Rus.
101/P3 Ust'-Maya, Rus.
101/Q3 Ust'-Nera, Rus.
95/L3 Ust'-Ocheya, Rus.
101/M2 Ust'-Olenëk, Rus.
101/Q3 Ust'-Omchug, Rus.
108/E1 Ust'-Ordynskiy, Rus.
94/J2 Ust'-Pinega, Rus.
100/J3 Ust'-Port, Rus.
95/N4 Ust'-Pozhva, Rus.
65/M4 Ustrzyki Dolne, Pol.
95/M2 Ust'-Tsil'ma, Rus.
108/E1 Ust'-Uda, Rus.
95/K3 Ust'ya (riv.), Rus.
97/K4 Ustyurt (Ust'-Urt) (plat.), Kaz., Uzb.
94/H4 Ustyuzhna, Rus.
114/D3 Usu, China
110/B4 Usuki, Japan
160/D3 Usulután, ESal.
149/E4 Usuma, Zaire
160/C2 Usumacinta (riv.), Guat., Mex.
127/J4 Uta, Indo.
79/D2 Utah (beach), Fr.
180/D4 Utah (state), US
185/H3 Utah (lake), Ut,US
185/G3 Utah Test & Trng. Ra., Ut,US
155/G2 Utale, Malw.
127/E5 Utan, Indo.
120/A2 Utangan (riv.), India
111/L10 Utano, Japan
112/C2 Utashinai, Japan
190/C2 Ute (cr.), NM,US
154/D3 Utembo (riv.), Ang.
187/H2 Ute Mtn. Ind. Res., Co,US
63/L4 Utena, Lith.
151/A4 Utengule, Tanz.
84/D2 Utero (peak), It.
71/G3 Uterský (riv.), Czh.
151/B3 Utete, Tanz.
123/C3 Uthai Thani, Thai.
167/L6 Utica, Col.
205/F6 Utica, Mi,US
193/H4 Utica, Mo,US
200/B4 Utica, Ms,US
193/F3 Utica, Ne,US
199/J3 Utica, NY,US
208/H5 Utica, Pa,US
76/E3 Utiel, Sp.
160/E2 Utila (isl.), Hon.
171/E2 Utinga, Braz.
138/G3 Utirik (atoll), Mrsh.
138/G5 Utiroa, Kiri.
99/H4 Utlyukskiy (estuary), Ukr.
118/C4 Utnūr, India
133/G2 Utopia, Austl.
188/E3 Utopia, Tx,US
133/G2 Utopia Abor. Land, Austl.
63/P2 Utorgosh, Rus.
120/D2 Utraulā, India
66/C4 Utrecht, Neth.
66/C4 Utrecht (prov.), Neth.
157/E2 Utrecht, SAfr.
76/C4 Utrera, Sp.
111/F2 Utsunomiya, Japan
97/H3 Utta, Rus.
122/F4 Uttamapālaiyam, India
123/C2 Uttaradit, Thai.
114/C5 Uttarkashi, India
121/G4 Uttarpara-Kotrung, India
121/G3 Uttar Patiata, Bang.
120/B2 Uttar Pradesh (state), India
70/C6 Uttenweiler, Ger.
57/G6 Uttoxeter, Eng,UK
63/R7 Uttran (lake), Swe.
162/E3 Utuado, PR
138/F6 Utupua (isl.), Sol.
139/K6 Uturoa, FrPol.
50/B6 Uturoa (isl.), FrPol.
80/D3 Utzenstorf, Swi.
108/G2 Uulbayan, Mong.
63/L2 Uulu, Est.
108/E1 Üür (riv.), Mong.
108/C1 Üüreg (lake), Mong.
108/C1 Uus (lake), Mong.
63/J1 Uusikaupunki, Fin.
63/L1 Uusimaa (prov.), Fin.
164/D4 Uva (riv.), Col.
201/D4 Uvalda, Ga,US
188/E3 Uvalde, Tx,US
100/E4 Uvals, Northern (upland), Rus.
71/H2 Uvaly, Czh.
99/M2 Uvarovo, Rus.
95/P5 Uvel'skiy, Rus.
165/E2 Uverito, Ven.
153/G4 Uvinza, Tanz.
153/G3 Uvira, Zaire
161/F4 Uvita (pt.), CR
157/E3 Uvongo Beach, SAfr.
114/F1 Uvs Nuur (lake), Mong.
110/C4 Uwajima, Japan
149/E3 Uwayl, Sudan
143/J3 'Uwaynat Wannin (well), Libya
127/F4 Uwekuli, Indo.
131/F1 Uwimmerah (riv.), Indo.
199/G2 Uxbridge, On,Can
53/M7 Uxbridge, Eng,UK
208/C1 Uxbridge, Ma,US
115/B3 Uxin Qi, China
159/H4 Uxmal (ruins), Mex.
95/P5 Uy (riv.), Kaz., Rus.
108/E2 Uyanga, Mong.
108/C2 Üyench, Mong.
145/G5 Uyo, Nga.
116/B3 Uyu (riv.), Burma
172/C2 Uyuni, Bol.
172/B1 Uyuni (salt pan), Bol.
103/F8 'Uza, Isr.
100/G5 Uzbekistan
154/D2 Uzcudún, Arg.
74/C5 Uzein (Pau) (int'l arpt.), Fr.
78/C4 Uzel, Fr.
97/K4 Uzen', Kaz.
74/D4 Uzerche, Fr.
74/F4 Uzès, Fr.
98/B3 Uzhgorod, Ukr.
98/B3 Uzhok (pass), Ukr.
98/F3 Uzin, Ukr.
96/F1 Uzlovaya, Rus.
81/E3 Uznach, Swi.
104/D2 Üzümlü, Turk.
104/C1 Uzunköprü, Turk.
63/K4 Užventis, Lith.
81/F3 Uzwil, Swi.

V

156/C3 Vaal (riv.), SAfr.
61/H2 Vaala, Fin.
156/E2 Vaaldam (res.), SAfr.
69/E2 Vaals, Neth.
69/E2 Vaalsberg (hill), Neth.
155/F5 Vaalwater, SAfr.
79/F5 Vaas, Fr.
61/G3 Vaasa (int'l arpt.), Fin.
61/G3 Vaasa (prov.), Fin.
61/G3 Vaasa (Vasa), Fin.
66/C4 Vaassen, Neth.
63/L4 Vabalninkas, Lith.
73/D4 Vác, Hun.
205/K10 Vaca (mtn.), Ca,US
205/K10 Vaca (mts.), Ca,US
173/F3 Vacacai (riv.), Braz.
173/G4 Vacaria, Braz.
173/F1 Vacaria (riv.), Braz.
205/L10 Vacaville, Ca,US
82/A6 Vaccares (lag.), Fr.
161/H2 Vache (isl.), Haiti
82/B3 Vachères (mtn.), Fr.
97/H4 Vachi, Rus.
179/J2 Vachon (riv.), Qu,Can
71/G4 Vacov, Czh.
95/K5 Vad, Rus.
86/D6 Vada, It.
122/F3 Vadakkāncheri, India
191/H4 Vaden, Ar,US
62/A1 Vadheim, Nor.
190/B2 Vadito, NM,US
195/P6 Vadnais Heights, Mn,US
86/B4 Vado Ligure, It.
81/F4 Vadret, Piz (peak), Swi.
61/J1 Vadsø, Nor.
62/F2 Vadstena, Swe.
93/J2 Vadul-Luy-Vode, Mol.
81/F3 Vaduz (cap.), Lcht.
61/D3 Vaernes (int'l arpt.), Nor.
94/J3 Vaga (riv.), Rus.
92/B3 Vaganski vrh (peak), Cro.
95/R4 Vagay (riv.), Rus.
62/F3 Vaggeryd, Swe.
85/F6 Vaglio Basilicata, It.
80/C1 Vagney, Fr.
76/A2 Vagos, Port.
73/C4 Váh (riv.), Slvk.
139/M6 Vahitahi (isl.), FrPol.
87/E5 Vaiano, It.
86/C2 Vaiano Cremasco, It.
54/B1 Vaich, Loch (lake), Sc,UK
200/C4 Vaiden, Ms,US
79/E5 Vaige (riv.), Fr.
79/E4 Vaiges, Fr.
70/B5 Vaihingen an der Enz, Ger.
107/K5 Vaijāpur, India
122/F4 Vaikam, India
63/M2 Väike-Maarja, Est.
187/G4 Vail, Az,US
192/A4 Vail, Co,US
68/C5 Vailly-sur-Aisnes, Fr.
207/J9 Vailsburg, NJ,US
82/B6 Vaine (lag.), Fr.
63/J3 Vaiņode, Lat.
80/B1 Vair (riv.), Fr.
85/E5 Vairano Patenora, It.
82/C4 Vaire (riv.), Fr.
53/T10 Vaires-sur-Marne, Fr.
120/B2 Vaisali (riv.), India
82/B4 Vaison-la-Romaine, Fr.
138/G5 Vaitupu (isl.), Tuv.
80/C2 Vaivre-et-Montoille, Fr.
148/D3 Vakaga (pref.), CAfr.
148/D3 Vakaga-Ouandjia Fauna Rsv., CAfr.
96/F4 Vakfıkebir, Turk.
100/J3 Vakh (riv.), Rus.
107/K1 Vākhān (mts.), Afg.
109/N2 Vakhrushev, Rus.
95/L4 Vakhrushi, Rus.
107/J1 Vakhsh (riv.), Trkm.
95/K4 Vakhtan, Rus.
73/C5 Vál, Hun.
80/D5 Valais (canton), Swi.
87/G2 Valalta, Cro.
73/C2 Valaská Belá, Slvk.
62/G1 Valbo, Swe.
196/D1 Val-Brillant, Qu,Can
66/C5 Valburg, Neth.
174/D4 Valcheta, Arg.
199/K2 Valcourt, Qu,Can
87/E1 Valdagno, It.
80/C3 Valdahon, Fr.
94/G4 Valdai (hills), Rus.
87/E5 Valdarno (val.), It.
199/J1 Val-David, Qu,Can
94/G4 Valday, Rus.
69/F6 Val-de-Bide, Fr.
76/C3 Valdecañas (res.), Sp.
166/D3 Val de Cans (int'l arpt.), Braz.
53/T10 Val-de-Marne (dept.), Fr.
63/K3 Valdemarpils, Lat.
62/G2 Valdemarsvik, Swe.
77/M8 Valdemorillo, Sp.
76/D3 Valdepeñas, Sp.
76/C2 Valderaduey (riv.), Sp.
76/C1 Valderas, Sp.
77/F2 Valderrobres, Sp.
174/E4 Valdés (pen.), Arg.
199/J2 Val-des-Monts, Qu,Can
76/C3 Valdeverdeja, Sp.
164/B4 Valdez, Ecu.
177/J3 Valdez, Ak,US
84/B1 Val di Chiana (val.), It.
82/C2 Val d'Isère, Fr.
174/B3 Valdivia, Chile
164/C3 Valdivia, Col.
87/F1 Valdobbiadene, It.
80/C2 Valdoie, Fr.
53/S9 Val-d'Oise (dept.), Fr.
68/A5 Val-d'Oise (dept.), Fr.
79/G2 Val d'Oise (dept.), Fr.
179/J4 Val d'Or, Qu,Can
203/G2 Valdosta, Ga,US
76/A1 Valdoviño, Sp.
97/G4 Vale, Geo.
78/C2 Vale, Chl,UK
184/E2 Vale, Or,US
92/F2 Valea lui Mihai, Rom.
87/D2 Valeggio sul Mincio, It.
182/E1 Valemount, BC,Can
171/F2 Valença, Braz.
76/A1 Valença, Port.
167/F4 Valença do Piauí, Braz.
82/A3 Valence, Fr.
74/D5 Valence-sur-Baïse, Fr.
164/B5 Valencia, Ecu.
55/F11 Valencia (isl.), Ire.
125/D3 Valencia, Phil.
125/D4 Valencia, Phil.
77/E3 Valencia, Sp.
77/E3 Valencia (aut. comm.), Sp.
77/F3 Valencia (gulf), Sp.
77/E3 Valencia (int'l arpt.), Sp.
190/A3 Valencia, NM,US
208/H6 Valencia, Pa,US
164/E2 Valencia, Ven.
167/N7 Valencia (int'l arpt.), Ven.
167/N7 Valencia (lake), Ven.
76/B3 Valencia de Alcántara, Sp.
76/C1 Valencia de Don Juan, Sp.
68/C3 Valenciennes, Fr.
81/F4 Valendas, Swi.
93/H3 Vălenii de Munte, Rom.
82/B5 Valensole, Fr.
82/B5 Valensole (plat.), Fr.
84/B2 Valentano, It.
80/C3 Valentigney, Fr.
109/L3 Valentin, Rus.
187/F3 Valentine, Az,US
192/D2 Valentine, Ne,US
188/B2 Valentine, Tx,US
192/D2 Valentine Nat'l Wild. Ref., Ne,US
175/G2 Valentines, Uru.
201/J2 Valentines, Va,US
53/T10 Valenton, Fr.
86/B2 Valenza, It.
125/E6 Valenzuela, Phil.
62/D1 Våler, Nor.
62/D2 Våler, Nor.
164/D2 Valera, Ven.
84/C1 Valfabbrica, It.
82/C5 Valferrière, Col de (pass), Fr.
80/D1 Valff, Fr.
63/M3 Valga, Est.
82/D2 Val Grande (riv.), It.
207/E1 Valhalla, NY,US

171/K7 Valhinos, Braz.
74/D5 Valier (mtn.), Fr.
200/C1 Valier, Il,US
183/H3 Valier, Mt,US
90/A2 Valinco (gulf), Fr.
73/C5 Váli víz (riv.), Hun.
92/D3 Valjevo, Yugo.
94/E4 Valka, Lat.
63/K1 Valkeakoski, Fin.
63/M1 Valkeala, Fin.
69/E2 Valkenburg, Neth.
66/C6 Valkenswaard, Neth.
99/H3 Valki, Ukr.
63/L4 Valkininkai, Lith.
159/H4 Valladolid, Mex.
76/C2 Valladolid, Sp.
85/F5 Vallata, It.
82/D5 Vallauris, Fr.
77/E3 Vall de Uxó, Sp.
172/C3 Valle (riv.), Arg.
164/B5 Valle, Ecu.
62/B2 Valle, Nor.
205/L11 Valle (arroyo), Ca,US
77/N9 Vallecas, Sp.
188/E4 Vallecillo, Mex.
190/A2 Vallecitos, NM,US
85/D5 Vallecorsa, It.
86/A5 Vallecrosia, It.
86/A1 Valle d'Aosta (prov.), It.
86/A1 Valle d'Aosta (reg.), It.
158/D3 Valle de Allende, Mex.
159/E5 Valle de Bravo, Mex.
164/B3 Valle de Cauca (dept.), Col.
172/B3 Valle de Encantado Nat'l Park, Chile
186/D4 Valle de Guadalupe, Mex.
165/E2 Valle de Guanape, Ven.
165/E2 Valle de la Pascua, Ven.
77/M8 Valle de los Caídos, Sp.
159/E4 Valle de Santiago, Mex.
158/D3 Valle de Zaragoza, Mex.
164/C2 Valledupar, Col.
199/L1 Vallée-Jonction, Qu,Can
83/C5 Vallefiorita, It.
172/C1 Vallegrande, Bol.
142/A3 Vallehermoso, Canl.
159/F3 Valle Hermoso, Mex.
77/X16 Vallehermoso, Canl.,Sp.
66/C4 Valleikanaal (can.), Neth.
205/K10 Vallejo, Ca,US
86/B2 Valle Lomellina, It.
86/B1 Valle Mosso, It.
172/B4 Vallenar, Chile
69/G3 Vallendar, Ger.
63/S6 Vallentuna, Swe.
63/S6 Vallentunasjön (lake), Swe.
69/E5 Valleroy, Fr.
193/J4 Valles Mines, Mo,US
84/J8 Valletta (cap.), Malta
200/E4 Valley, Al,US
182/F3 Valley, Wa,US
204/C4 Valley Center, Ca,US
183/L2 Valley Centre, Sk,Can
194/E4 Valley City, ND,US
207/E1 Valley Cottage, NY,US
198/F1 Valley East, On,Can
195/N7 Valleyfair, Mn,US
193/G4 Valley Falls, Ks,US
184/C2 Valley Falls, Or,US
208/C2 Valley Falls, RI,US
187/G4 Valley Farms, Az,US
197/M7 Valleyfield, Qu,Can
182/F4 Valleyford, Wa,US
206/C3 Valley Forge Nat'l Hist. Park, Pa,US
200/E3 Valley Head, Al,US
201/G1 Valley Head, WV,US
189/F2 Valley Mills, Tx,US
200/B4 Valley Park, Ms,US
194/D2 Valley River, Mb,Can
189/E2 Valley Spring, Tx,US
191/H2 Valley Springs, Ar,US
207/E2 Valley Stream, NY,US
162/F3 Valley, The, Angu.
178/F3 Valleyview, Ab,Can
208/F5 Valley View, Oh,US
191/F4 Valley View, Tx,US
87/F3 Valli Bertuzzi (lag.), It.
87/F3 Valli di Comacchio (lag.), It.
80/B4 Vallière (riv.), Fr.
174/E3 Vallimanca (riv.), Arg.
63/R7 Vällingen (lake), Swe.
83/B2 Vallo della Lucania, It.
82/C2 Valloire, Fr.
80/C4 Vallorbe, Swi.
77/F2 Valls, Sp.
81/G3 Valluga (peak), Aus.
183/L3 Val Marie, Sk,Can
77/M8 Valmayor (res.), Sp.
67/F6 Valme (riv.), Ger.
63/L3 Valmiera, Lat.
53/S9 Valmondois, Fr.
188/B1 Valmont, NM,US
84/C4 Valmontone, It.
184/E3 Valmy, Nv,US
78/D1 Valognes, Fr.
91/F2 Valona (bay), Alb.
203/H2 Valona, Ga,US
76/B2 Valpaços, Port.
122/F3 Välpārai, India
174/C2 Valparaíso, Chile
167/K6 Valparaíso, Col.
158/E4 Valparaíso, Mex.
198/C4 Valparaiso, In,US
193/F3 Valparaiso, Ne,US
174/C2 Valparíso (reg.), Chile
203/E2 Valparaiso, Fl,US
80/D6 Valpelline (riv.), It.
86/A2 Valperga, It.
92/D3 Valpovo, Cro.
82/A4 Valréas, Fr.
131/E2 Vals (cape), Indo.
156/D2 Vals (riv.), SAfr.
118/B3 Valsād, India
159/L8 Valsaquillo (res.), Mex.
156/B4 Valsbaai (bay), SAfr.
80/B5 Valserine (riv.), Fr.
81/F4 Valserrhein (riv.), Swi.
83/C2 Valsinni, It.
74/F4 Vals-les-Bains, Fr.
81/F4 Vals Platz, Swi.
81/G4 Valsura (riv.), It.
81/F5 Valtellina (vall.), It.
73/A2 Valtice, Czh.
99/K2 Valuyki, Rus.
122/H4 Valveddituraí, SrL.
142/A4 Valverde, Canl.
204/B2 Val Verde, Ca,US
76/B4 Valverde del Camino, Sp.
204/C2 Valyermo, Ca,US
62/F1 Vämhus, Swe.
155/J1 Vamizi (isl.), Moz.
63/K1 Vammala, Fin.
187/F5 Vamori (wash), US.,Mex.
91/J5 Vámos, Gre.
73/C4 Vámosmikola, Hun.
92/E2 Vámospércs, Hun.
105/E2 Van, Turk.
105/E2 Van (lake), Turk.
105/E2 Van (prov.), Turk.
184/D2 Van, Or,US
189/G1 Van, Tx,US
201/G2 Van, WV,US
63/K1 Vanajavesi (lake), Fin.
189/F1 Van Alstyne, Tx,US
183/L4 Vananda, Mt,US
101/L3 Vanavara, Rus.
139/L7 Vanavaro (isl.), FrPol.
166/C1 van Blommestein, W.J. (lake), Sur.
196/A2 Van Bruyssel, Qu,Can
191/G3 Van Buren, Ar,US
196/D2 Van Buren, Me,US
191/J2 Van Buren, Mo,US
191/F2 Vance A.F.B., Ok,US
190/D3 Vanceboro, Me,US
201/J3 Vanceboro, NC,US
201/F1 Vanceburg, Ky,US
82/C4 Vancom (riv.), Fr.
207/K8 Van Cortlandt Park, NY,US
159/E2 Vancourt, Tx,US
132/C5 Vancouver (cape), Austl.
182/C3 Vancouver, BC,Can
182/C3 Vancouver (int'l arpt.), BC,Can
176/D4 Vancouver (isl.), BC,Can.
182/C5 Vancouver, Wa,US
177/L3 Vancouver (mtn.), Yk,Can, Ak,US
137/L Vanda, Ant.
193/K4 Vandalia, Il,US
191/J1 Vandalia, Mo,US
183/L3 Vandalia, Mt,US
198/D5 Vandalia, Oh,US
81/F3 Vandans, Aus.
186/B3 Vandenberg A.F.B., Ca,US
186/B3 Vandenberg Village, Ca,US
156/D2 Vanderbijl Park, SAfr.
189/F3 Vanderbilt, Tx,US
207/E2 Vanderbilt Museum, NY,US
178/D3 Vanderhoof, BC,Can
131/E3 Vanderlin (isl.), Austl.
191/G3 Vandervoort, Ar,US
128/F2 Van Dieman (gulf), Austl.
130/C2 Van Diemen (cape), Austl.
131/E4 Van Diemen (cape), Austl.
130/C2 Van Diemen (gulf), Austl.
69/F6 Vandoeuvre-lès-Nancy, Fr.
63/L2 Vändra, Est.
85/E4 Vandro (riv.), It.
94/J3 Vandysh, Rus.
63/K4 Vandžiogala, Lith.
159/E4 Vanegas, Mex.
62/E2 Vänern (lake), Swe.
62/E2 Vänersborg, Swe.
151/B3 Vanga, Kenya
157/H8 Vangaindrano, Madg.
183/L3 Vanguard, Sk,Can
66/C2 Van Harinxmakanaal (can.), Neth.
123/D1 Van Hoa, Viet.
188/B2 Van Horn, Tx,US
179/R7 Vanier (isl.), NW,Can
199/J2 Vanier, On,Can
138/F6 Vanikoro (isl.), Sol.
80/D4 Vanil Noir (peak), Swi.
127/K4 Vanimo, PNG
109/N2 Vanino, Rus.
201/F2 Van Lear, Ky,US
61/F3 Vännäs, Swe.
191/J3 Vanndale, Ar,US
74/E2 Vanne (riv.), Fr.
78/C5 Vannes, Fr.
123/E3 Van Ninh, Viet.
204/E7 Van Norman (lakes), Ca,US
204/F7 Van Nuys, Ca,US
75/G4 Vanoise Nat'l Park, Fr.
78/A4 Van, Pointe du (pt.), Fr.
208/G6 Vanport, Pa,US
156/E3 Vanreenenpas (pass), SAfr.
127/J4 Van Rees (mts.), Indo.
156/B3 Vanrhynsdorp, SAfr.
131/F4 Vanrook, Austl.
201/F2 Vansant, Va,US
62/F1 Vansbro, Swe.
194/A2 Vanscoy, Sk,Can
62/B2 Vanse, Nor.
130/B3 Vansittart (bay), Austl.
179/H2 Vansittart (isl.), NW,Can
63/L1 Vantaa, Fin.
63/L1 Vantaa-Helsinki (int'l arpt.), Fin.
194/A3 Vantage, Sk,Can
182/E4 Vantage, Wa,US
138/G6 Vanua Levu (isl.), Fiji
138/F6 Vanuatu
53/S10 Vanves, Fr.
189/G3 Van Vleck, Tx,US
193/H3 Van Wert, Ia,US
198/D4 Van Wert, Oh,US
156/C3 Vanwyksvlei, SAfr.
123/D1 Van Yen, Viet.
191/H2 Vanzant, Mo,US
156/C2 Vanzylsrus, SAfr.
98/E3 Vapnyarka, Ukr.
82/C6 Var (dept.), Fr.
82/D5 Var (riv.), Fr.
86/C4 Vara (riv.), It.
62/E2 Vara, Swe.
161/F1 Varadero, Cuba
82/D3 Varaita (riv.), It.
63/M3 Varakļāni, Lat.
144/E4 Varalé, IvC.
105/G3 Varāmīn, Iran
118/D2 Vārānasi, India
120/D3 Vārānasi (Benares), India
95/N1 Varandey, Rus.
61/J1 Varangerfjorden (fjord), Nor.
61/J1 Varangerhalvøya (pen.), Nor.
69/F6 Varangéville, Fr.
85/F4 Varano (lake), It.
86/B1 Varano Borghi, It.
83/B6 Varapodio, It.
92/C2 Varaždin, Cro.
86/B4 Varazze, It.
62/E3 Varberg, Swe.
82/B2 Varces-Allières-et-Risset, Fr.
200/C4 Vardaman, Ms,US
89/J2 Vardar (riv.), Bul., Gre., Macd.
91/G2 Vardar (riv.), Gre.
92/E5 Vardar (riv.), Macd.
62/C4 Varde, Den.
97/H4 Vardenis, Arm.
91/G3 Várdha, Gre.
61/J1 Vardø, Nor.
67/F2 Varel, Ger.
63/L4 Varėna, Lith.
79/F1 Varengeville-sur-Mer, Fr.
99/J5 Varenikovskaya, Rus.
79/E3 Varenne (riv.), Fr.
79/G1 Varenne (riv.), Fr.
197/P6 Varennes, Qu,Can
68/A4 Varennes (riv.), Fr.
53/T10 Varennes-Jarcy, Fr.
74/E3 Varennes-Vauzelles, Fr.
92/D3 Vareš, Bosn.
86/B1 Varese, It.
86/B1 Varese (prov.), It.
86/C4 Varese Ligure, It.
82/A2 Varèze (riv.), Fr.
62/E2 Vårgårda, Swe.
171/K6 Vargem do Sul, Braz.
167/F3 Vargem Grande, Braz.
170/D4 Varginha, Braz.
62/A2 Varhaug, Nor.
91/H4 Vári, Gre.
91/L7 Vari, Gre.
190/B3 Variadero, NM,US
66/C5 Varik, Neth.
74/D5 Varilhes, Fr.
172/B3 Varillas, Chile
61/H3 Varkaus, Fin.
122/F4 Varkkallai, India
63/T9 Værløse, Den.
63/S7 Värmdo, Swe.
63/S7 Värmdolandet (isl.), Swe.
62/E2 Värmeln (lake), Swe.
62/E2 Värmland (co.), Swe.
93/H4 Varna, Bul.
93/H4 Varna (int'l arpt.), Bul.
93/H4 Varna (reg.), Bul.
95/P5 Varna, Rus.
62/F3 Värnamo, Swe.
95/P1 Varnek, Rus.
63/K4 Varniai, Lith.
201/G4 Varnville, SC,US
80/B3 Varois-et-Chaignot, Fr.
92/C3 Varoška Rijeka, Bosn.
73/C5 Várpalota, Hun.
82/C3 Vars, Fr.
82/C3 Vars, Col de (pass), Fr.
86/C3 Varsi, It.
63/M3 Värska, Est.
62/G2 Vårsta, Swe.
97/H4 Vartashen, Azer.
91/G4 Vartholomión, Gre.
104/E2 Varto, Turk.
60/D3 Vartry (res.), Ire.
60/D3 Vartry (riv.), Ire.
98/G2 Varva, Ukr.
105/H3 Varzaneh, Iran
167/G4 Várzea Alegre, Braz.
170/D3 Várzea da Palma, Braz.
170/A2 Várzea Grande, Braz.
86/C3 Varzi, It.
81/E5 Varzo, It.
94/H2 Varzuga (riv.), Rus.
73/A5 Vas (co.), Hun.
171/F1 Vasa Barris (riv.), Braz.
84/C3 Vasanello, It.
65/M4 Vásárosnamény, Hun.
61/G3 Vasa (Vaasa), Fin.
92/F2 Vaşcău, Rom.
95/K2 Vashka (riv.), Rus.
205/C3 Vashon, Wa,US
205/C3 Vashon (isl.), Wa,US
93/J3 Vasile Roaită, Rom.
98/E1 Vasilevichi, Bela.
91/H2 Vasiliká, Gre.
98/F2 Vasil'kov, Ukr.
99/H3 Vasil'kovka, Ukr.
99/H4 Vasil'yevka, Ukr.
93/H2 Vaslui, Rom.
93/H2 Vaslui (co.), Rom.
148/C3 Vassako-Bolo Nat. Rsv., CAfr.
196/C3 Vassalboro, Me,US
194/G3 Vassar, Mb,Can
198/E3 Vassar, Mi,US
62/B2 Vassdalsegga (peak), Nor.
91/G4 Vassés (Bassae) (ruins), Gre.
171/N7 Vassouras, Braz.
79/E3 Vassy, Fr.
52/E3 Västerås, Swe.
62/G2 Västerås, Swe.
61/F2 Västerbotten (co.), Swe.
62/E1 Västerdalälven (riv.), Swe.
62/H2 Västerhaninge, Swe.
61/F3 Västernorrland (co.), Swe.
62/G3 Västervik, Swe.
62/G1 Västmanland (co.), Swe.
94/C3 Västmanland (co.), Swe.
85/E3 Vasto, It.
62/E2 Västra Silen (lake), Swe.
73/A5 Vasvár, Hun.
99/K5 Vasyurinskaya, Rus.
73/A5 Vát, Hun.
71/E6 Vaterstetten, Ger.
84/C4 Vatican City (Città del Vaticano)
83/B5 Vaticano (cape), It.
84/C4 Vaticano, Città del (Vatican City)
61/P7 Vatnajökull (glac.), Ice.
61/M6 Vatneyri, Ice.
157/J7 Vatomandry, Madg.
93/G2 Vatra Dornei, Rom.
62/F2 Vättern (lake), Swe.
139/Y18 Vatukoula, Fiji
98/F3 Vatutino, Ukr.
82/B4 Vaucluse (dept.), Fr.
82/B5 Vaucluse (mts.), Fr.
201/G4 Vaucluse, SC,US
80/C4 Vaud (canton), Swi.
79/E4 Vaudelle (riv.), Fr.
199/J2 Vaudreuil, Qu,Can
197/M7 Vaudreuil-sur-le-Lac, Qu,Can
197/R8 Vaughan, On,Can
200/B4 Vaughan, Ms,US
183/J4 Vaughn, Mt,US
190/B3 Vaughn, NM,US
205/B3 Vaughn, Wa,US
80/C4 Vaulruz, Swi.
80/A6 Vaulx-en-Velin, Fr.
197/M7 Vaundreuil (co.), Qu,Can
78/D4 Vaunoise (riv.), Fr.
164/D4 Vaupés (comm.), Col.
164/D4 Vaupés (riv.), Col.
74/F5 Vauvert, Fr.
80/C2 Vauvillers, Fr.
68/D4 Vaux (riv.), Fr.
183/H2 Vauxhall, Ab,Can
53/R9 Vaux-sur-Seine, Fr.
69/E4 Vaux-sur-Sûre, Belg.
68/B3 Vaux-Vraucourt, Fr.
157/J7 Vavatenina, Madg.
50/A6 Vava'u (isls.), Tonga
139/H6 Vava'u Group (isls.), Tonga
182/E2 Vavenby, BC,Can
144/D5 Vavoua, IvC.
122/H4 Vavuniya (dist.), SrL.
122/H4 Vavuniya, SrL.
183/K1 Vawn, Sk,Can
63/S7 Vaxholm, Swe.
62/F3 Växjö, Swe.
62/F3 Växjö (int'l arpt.), Swe.
78/D5 Vay, Fr.
53/J2 Vaygach (isl.), Rus.
171/K8 Vázea Paulista, Braz.
95/K2 Vazhgort, Rus.
94/G5 Vazuza (res.), Rus.
87/F1 Vazzola, It.
194/F5 Veblen, SD,US
86/D5 Vecchiano, It.
67/H4 Vechelde, Ger.
80/D4 Vechigen, Swi.
66/D4 Vecht (riv.), Neth.
67/F3 Vechta, Ger.
67/E4 Vechte (riv.), Ger.
63/L3 Vecpiebalga, Lat.
73/D5 Vecsés, Hun.
63/L3 Vecumnieki, Lat.
86/B1 Vedano Olona, It.
122/G3 Vedāranniyam, India
62/E3 Veddige, Swe.
93/G3 Vedea (riv.), Rom.
87/F1 Vedelago, It.
105/F2 Vedi, Arm.
174/E2 Vedia, Arg.
76/A1 Vedra, Sp.
198/C4 Veedersburg, In,US
66/D2 Veendam, Neth.
66/C4 Veenendaal, Neth.
66/D2 Veenhuizen, Neth.
66/A5 Veere, Neth.
66/A5 Veersedam (dam), Neth.
66/A5 Veerse Meer (res.), Neth.
82/A1 Véga (riv.), Fr.
61/D2 Vega (isl.), Nor.
177/B6 Vega (pt.), Ak,US
190/C3 Vega, Tx,US
61/D2 Vegafjorden (fjord), Nor.
63/U8 Vegeån (riv.), Swe.
67/F2 Vegesack, Ger.
66/C5 Veghel, Neth.
91/G2 Vegorítis (lake), Gre.
79/E4 Vègre (riv.), Fr.
183/H1 Vègreville, Ab,Can
168/B3 Végueta, Peru
190/A3 Veguita, NM,US
63/M1 Vehkalahti, Fin.
79/F6 Veigné, Fr.
70/D2 Veilsdorf, Ger.
174/E2 Veinticinco de Mayo, Arg.
175/T12 Veinticinco de Mayo, Uru.
168/B1 Veintiocho de Mayo, Ecu.
175/J7 Veintiocho de Noviembre, Arg.
84/C3 Veio (ruins), It.
166/D3 Veira Grande (bay), Braz.
63/K4 Veisiejai, Lith.
65/H5 Veitsch, Aus.
70/C3 Veitshöchheim, Ger.
62/C4 Vejen, Den.
76/C4 Vejer de la Frontera, Sp.
62/C4 Vejle, Den.
62/C4 Vejle (co.), Den.
71/G3 Vejprnice, Czh.
71/G2 Vejprty, Czh.
69/E6 Velaines, Fr.
92/C4 Vela Luka, Cro.
80/D6 Vélan, Monte (peak), Swi., It.
190/B2 Velarde, NM,US
77/S12 Velas, Azor,Port.
164/B5 Velasco Ibarra, Ecu.
82/B5 Velaux, Fr.
175/G2 Velázquez, Uru.
66/E6 Velbert, Ger.
71/E4 Velburg, Ger.
156/B4 Velddrif, SAfr.
71/G6 Velden, Ger.
66/D6 Velden, Neth.
75/L3 Velden am Wörthersee, Aus.
66/C6 Veldhoven, Neth.
66/D5 Velen, Ger.
73/C5 Velence, Hun.
73/C5 Velencei hegy (hill), Hun.
73/C5 Velencei-tó (lake), Hun.
92/B2 Velenje, Slov.
92/E5 Veleśta, Macd.
91/H3 Velestínon, Gre.
164/C3 Vélez, Col.
76/D4 Vélez-Blanco, Sp.
141/M13 Vélez de la Gomera (isl.), Sp.
76/C4 Vélez-Málaga, Sp.
76/D4 Vélez-Rubio, Sp.
170/D3 Velhas (riv.), Braz.
83/B2 Velia (ruins), It.
92/C3 Velika Gorica, Cro.
92/B3 Velika Kladuša, Bosn.
92/E3 Velika Plana, Yugo.
63/N3 Velikaya (riv.), Rus.
98/F2 Velikaya Dymerka, Ukr.
99/G4 Velikaya Lepetikha, Ukr.
99/J4 Velikaya Novosëlka, Ukr.
98/B3 Velikiy Berëznyy, Ukr.
99/J2 Velikiy Burluk, Ukr.
98/C3 Velikiye Borki, Ukr.
63/P3 Velikiye Luki, Rus.
98/B3 Velikiy Lyuben', Ukr.
53/H2 Velikiy Ustyug, Rus.
98/F4 Velikodolinskoye, Ukr.
94/J5 Velikodvorskiy, Rus.
93/G4 Veliko Tŭrnovo, Bul.
95/M2 Velikovisochnoye, Rus.
168/D4 Velille, Peru
144/B3 Vélingara, Sen.
93/G4 Velingrad, Bul.
85/D3 Velino (peak), It.
84/D2 Velino (riv.), It.
63/P4 Velizh, Rus.
53/S10 Vélizy-Villacoublay, Fr.
65/J4 Vel'ke Leváre, Slvk.
65/J4 Velké Meziříčí, Czh.
92/C1 Vel'ké Zálužie, Slvk.
71/H1 Velké Žernoseky, Czh.
92/D1 Vel'ký Ďur, Slvk.
65/K4 Vel'ký Krtíš, Slvk.
71/F3 Velký Zvon (peak), Czh.
122/G3 Vellār (riv.), India
70/C4 Vellberg, Ger.
84/C4 Velletri, It.
62/E4 Vellinge, Swe.
67/G6 Vellmar, Ger.
77/N8 Vellón (res.), Sp.
118/C5 Vellore, India
191/F3 Velma, Ok,US
91/H4 Vélon, Gre.
66/C5 Velp, Neth.
66/B4 Velsen-Noord, Neth.
66/B4 Velsen-Zuid, Neth.
94/J3 Vel'sk, Rus.
72/D2 Velten, Ger.
66/C4 Veluwe (reg.), Neth.
66/C4 Veluwemeer (lake), Neth.
66/C4 Veluwezoom Nat'l Park, Neth.
194/D3 Velva, ND,US
71/H2 Velvary, Czh.
91/H2 Velvendós, Gre.
62/C3 Vemb, Den.
122/F3 Vembādi Shola (peak), India
122/F4 Vembanād (lake), India
92/D2 Vémend, Hun.
63/T9 Ven (isl.), Swe.
54/B4 Venachar, Loch (lake), Sc,UK
167/L7 Venadillo, Col.
159/E4 Venado, Mex.
159/L6 Venados, Mex.
174/E2 Venado Tuerto, Arg.
85/E5 Venafro, It.
165/F3 Venamo (peak), Ven.
173/F4 Venâncio Aires, Braz.
192/C3 Venango, Ne,US
208/H5 Venango (co.), Pa,US
134/A2 Vena Park, Austl.
86/A2 Venaria, It.
85/D2 Venarotta, It.
82/D5 Vence, Fr.
170/C4 Venceslau Brás, Braz.
155/F4 Venda (aut. rep.), SAfr.
76/A3 Vendas Novas, Port.
79/G5 Vendôme, Fr.
77/F2 Vendrell, Sp.
167/K6 Venecia, Col.
82/B5 Venelles, Fr.
82/C3 Vénéon (riv.), Fr.
87/F2 Veneta (lag.), It.
184/B1 Veneta, Or,US
83/B6 Venetico, It.
83/B6 Venetico Marina, It.
177/J2 Venetie, Ak,US
87/E1 Veneto (reg.), It.
96/F1 Venëv, Rus.
87/F2 Venezia (gulf), It.
87/F1 Venezia (prov.), It.
87/F2 Venezia, Po di (riv.), It.
87/F2 Venezia (Venice), It.
165/E3 Venezuela
164/D2 Venezuela (gulf), Ven.
118/B4 Vengurla, India
177/G4 Veniaminof (vol.), Ak,US
204/F8 Venice, Ca,US
203/G4 Venice, Fl,US
185/G4 Venice, Ut,US
87/F2 Venice (Venezia), It.
82/A1 Vénissieux, Fr.
62/E1 Venjan, Swe.
62/E1 Venjansjön (lake), Swe.
118/C5 Venkatagiri, India
66/D6 Venlo, Neth.
194/B2 Venn, Sk,Can
62/B2 Vennesla, Nor.
62/C3 Veno (bay), Den.
80/C4 Venoge (riv.), Swi.
85/F6 Venosa, It.
85/F5 Venosa (riv.), It.
81/G4 Venosta (vall.), It.
66/C5 Venray, Neth.
63/J3 Venta (riv.), Lat., Lith.
76/C2 Venta de Baños, Sp.
156/D3 Ventersburg, SAfr.
156/D2 Ventersdorp, SAfr.
156/P13 Venterspos, SAfr.
156/D3 Venterstad, SAfr.
139/L6 Vent, Iles du (isls.), FrPol.
139/K6 Vent, Iles sous le (isls.), FrPol.
86/A5 Ventimiglia, It.
90/A2 Ventiseri, Fr.
59/E5 Ventnor, Eng,UK
206/D5 Ventnor City, NJ,US
85/D6 Ventotene (isl.), It.
82/B4 Ventoux (range), Fr.
63/J3 Ventspils, Lat.
165/E3 Ventuari (riv.), Ven.
180/C5 Ventura, Ca,US
204/A2 Ventura (co.), Ca,US
204/A2 Ventura (riv.), Ca,US
204/A2 Ventura (San Buenaventura), Ca,US
84/A1 Venturina, It.
167/G5 Venturosa, Braz.
139/X15 Vénus (pt.), FrPol.
188/K7 Venus, Tx,US
160/C2 Venustiano Carranza, Mex.
188/D4 Venustiano Carranza (res.), Mex.
82/B3 Véore (riv.), Fr.
73/A5 Vép, Hun.
172/D4 Vera, Arg.
76/E4 Vera, Sp.
190/E4 Vera, Tx,US
159/F5 Veracruz, Mex.
159/F5 Veracruz (state), Mex.
164/B2 Vera Cruz, Pan.
159/N7 Veracruz Llave, Mex.
79/E6 Verades, Fr.
173/G4 Veranópolis, Braz.
118/B3 Verāval, India
86/B1 Verbania, It.
200/D4 Verbena, Al,US
68/B5 Verberie, Fr.
83/B3 Verbicaro, It.
94/J5 Verbovskiy, Rus.
86/B2 Vercelli, It.
86/B2 Vercelli (prov.), It.
80/C3 Vercel-Villedieu-le-Camp, Fr.
199/K2 Verchéres, Qu,Can
197/P6 Verchères (co.), Qu,Can
82/B3 Vercors (upland), Fr.
201/F2 Verda, Ky,US
189/H2 Verda, La,US
61/D3 Verdal, Nor.
174/E3 Verde (bay), Arg.
169/F4 Verde (riv.), Bol., Braz.
170/A2 Verde (riv.), Braz.
170/B3 Verde (riv.), Braz.
158/D3 Verde (riv.), Mex.
159/E4 Verde (riv.), Mex.
172/D1 Verde (riv.), Par.
140/A3 Verde (cape), Sen.
187/G3 Verde (riv.), Az,US
86/A5 Verde, Capo (cape), It.
76/B1 Verde, Costa (coast), Sp.
171/E2 Verde Grande (riv.), Braz.
125/C2 Verde Island (chan.), Phil.
67/G3 Verden, Ger.
91/G3 Verdhikoússa, Gre.
191/G2 Verdigris (riv.), Ks, Ok,US
82/B5 Verdon (riv.), Fr.
204/F7 Verdugo (mts.), Ca,US
197/N7 Verdun, Qu,Can
69/E5 Verdun-sur-Meuse, Fr.
201/F2 Verdunville, WV,US
156/D2 Vereeniging, SAfr.
194/C2 Veregin, Sk,Can
87/E1 Verena, Monte (peak), It.
95/M4 Vereshchagino, Rus.
98/B3 Veretskiy (pass), Ukr.
65/M4 Veretskiy Pereval (pass), Ukr.
144/B4 Verga (cape), Gui.
175/T12 Vergara, Arg.
76/D1 Vergara, Sp.
175/G2 Vergara, Uru.
194/G4 Vergas, Mn,US
87/E4 Vergato, It.
81/E5 Vergeletto, Swi.
199/K2 Vergennes, Vt,US
86/B1 Vergiate, It.
91/H2 Vergína (ruins), Gre.
95/K3 Verhknyáya Toyma, Rus.
188/D2 Veribest, Tx,US
81/F1 Verigenstadt, Ger.
76/B2 Verín, Sp.
70/C6 Veringenstadt, Ger.
63/M3 Veriora, Est.
97/J2 Verkhazovka, Rus.
99/J5 Verkhnebakanskiy, Rus.
99/H3 Verkhnedneprovsk, Ukr.
94/G5 Verkhnedneprovskiy, Rus.
63/M4 Verkhnedvinsk, Bela.
94/F1 Verkhnetulomskiy (res.), Rus.
95/N5 Verkhneural'sk, Rus.
101/R3 Verkhniy At Uryakh, Rus.
97/H2 Verkhniy Baskunchak, Rus.
95/N5 Verkhniye Kigi, Rus.
63/P1 Verkhniye Osel'ki, Rus.
99/L2 Verkhniy Mamon, Rus.
99/H4 Verkhniy Rogachik, Ukr.
95/N4 Verkhniy Tagil, Rus.
95/P4 Verkhniy Ufaley, Rus.
97/J1 Verkhnyaya Orlyanka, Rus.
95/P4 Verkhnyaya Pyshma, Rus.
95/P4 Verkhnyaya Salda, Rus.
95/P4 Verkhnyaya Sinyachikha, Rus.
95/N4 Verkhnyaya Tura, Rus.
94/J2 Verkhnyaya Zolotitsa, Rus.
99/H3 Verkhovtsevo, Ukr.
101/P3 Verkhoyansk, Rus.
101/N3 Verkhoyansk (range), Rus.
67/F5 Verl, Ger.
183/K2 Verlo, Sk,Can
68/C4 Vermand, Fr.
86/A4 Vermenagna (riv.), It.
183/J1 Vermilion, Ab,Can
183/J1 Vermilion (riv.), Ab,Can
183/L2 Vermilion (hills), Sk,Can
189/H3 Vermilion (bay), La,US
195/H4 Vermilion (dam), Mn,US
195/H4 Vermilion (lake), Mn,US
195/H4 Vermilion (range), Mn,US
208/E5 Vermilion, Oh,US
208/E5 Vermilion (riv.), Oh,US
195/H3 Vermilion Bay, On,Can
195/H4 Vermilion Ind. Res., Mn,US
195/H4 Vermilion Lake Ind. Res., Mn,US
185/J3 Vermillion (cr.), Wy.,Co, US
193/K3 Vermillion (riv.), Il,US
202/B3 Vermillion (bay), La,US
193/F2 Vermillion, SD,US
193/F2 Vermillion (riv.), SD,US
193/F2 Vermillion, East Fork (riv.), SD,US
193/F2 Vermillion, West Fork (riv.), SD,US
199/K3 Vermont (state), US
193/J3 Vermont, Il,US
198/D3 Vermontville, Mi,US
83/B6 Vernà (peak), It.
122/C1 Vernāg, India
82/B3 Vernaison (riv.), Fr.
185/J3 Vernal, Ut,US
86/A4 Vernante, It.
79/F6 Vernantes, Fr.
83/B6 Vernà, Pizzo di (peak), It.
80/D5 Vernayaz, Swi.
86/C4 Vernazza, It.
195/G4 Verndale, Mn,US
79/F3 Verneuil-sur-Avre, Fr.
53/R10 Verneuil-sur-Seine, Fr.
156/C3 Verneukpan (salt pan), SAfr.
80/C5 Vernier, Swi.
79/F6 Vernoil, Fr.
182/E2 Vernon, BC,Can
68/A5 Vernon, Fr.
200/C4 Vernon, Al,US
187/H3 Vernon, Az,US
208/B2 Vernon, Ct,US
203/F2 Vernon, Fl,US
198/D5 Vernon, In,US
202/B2 Vernon (lake), La,US
190/E3 Vernon, Tx,US
200/E1 Vernon Fork (riv.), In,US
205/Q15 Vernon Hills, Il,US
182/C5 Vernonia, Or,US
206/D1 Vernon Valley, NJ,US
206/D1 Vernon Valley/Great Gorge & Action Park, NJ,US
53/R10 Vernouillet, Fr.
82/A3 Vernoux-en-Vivarais, Fr.
78/D4 Vern-sur-Seiche, Fr.
69/F5 Verny, Fr.
203/H4 Vero Beach, Fl,US
73/D4 Verőcemaros, Hun.
91/H2 Véroia, Gre.
86/D2 Verolanuova, It.
86/D2 Verolavecchia, It.
86/A2 Verolengo, It.
85/D4 Veroli, It.
199/H2 Verona, On,Can
87/D2 Verona, It.
87/D2 Verona (int'l arpt.), It.
87/D1 Verona (prov.), It.
200/C3 Verona, Ms,US
194/E4 Verona, ND,US
207/J8 Verona, NJ,US
208/H6 Verona, Pa,US
201/H1 Verona, Va,US
175/F2 Verónica, Arg.
86/A1 Verrès, It.
80/C6 Verres, Pointe des (peak), Fr.
202/C3 Verret (lake), La,US
53/S10 Verrières-le-Buisson, Fr.
85/E4 Verrino (riv.), It.
85/G6 Verrutoli (peak), It.
86/B3 Versa (riv.), It.
53/S10 Versailles, Fr.
208/B2 Versailles, Ct,US
193/J4 Versailles, Il,US
198/D5 Versailles, In,US
200/E1 Versailles, Ky,US
191/H1 Versailles, Mo,US
198/D4 Versailles, Oh,US
208/H7 Versailles, Pa,US
53/S10 Versailles, Chateau de, Fr.
169/F4 Versalles, Bol.
108/H1 Vershino-Darasunskiy, Rus.
109/H1 Vershino-Shakhtaminskiy, Rus.
96/E2 Verskla (riv.), Rus., Ukr.
67/F4 Versmold, Ger.
80/C5 Versoix, Swi.
76/E1 Vert (riv.), Fr.
75/J3 Vertana (peak), It.
81/G4 Vertana, Cima (peak), It.
80/C6 Verte, Aiguille (peak), Fr.
86/C1 Vertemate, It.
73/C5 Vértes (hills), Hun.
98/F2 Verteyevka, Ukr.
53/T11 Vert-le-Grand, Fr.
53/T11 Vert-le-Petit, Fr.
74/C3 Vertou, Fr.
86/C1 Vertova, It.
53/T11 Vert-Saint-Denis, Fr.
68/D6 Vertus, Fr.
69/E2 Verviers, Belg.
68/C4 Vervins, Fr.
156/Q12 Verwoerdburg, SAfr.
59/E5 Verwood, Eng,UK
58/B6 Veryan (bay), Eng,UK
81/E5 Verzasca (riv.), Swi.
81/E5 Verzasca (Gerra), It.
79/D5 Verzée (riv.), Fr.
82/D2 Verzel (peak), It.
86/A2 Verzel, Punta (peak), It.
68/D5 Verzenay, Fr.
83/C4 Verzino, It.
86/A3 Verzuolo, It.
68/D5 Verzy, Fr.
90/A1 Vescovato, Fr.
86/D2 Vescovato, It.
74/F1 Vesdre (riv.), Belg.
69/F2 Vesdre (riv.), Ger.
71/H4 Veselí nad Lužnicí, Czh.
73/B2 Veselí nad Moravou, Czh.
98/F4 Veselinovo, Ukr.
99/H4 Vesëloye, Ukr.
99/L4 Veselyy (res.), Rus.
79/G3 Vesgre (riv.), Fr.
99/L3 Veshenskaya, Rus.
97/H1 Veshkayma, Rus.
63/L1 Vesijärvi (lake), Fin.
68/D5 Vesle (riv.), Fr.
80/C2 Vesoul, Fr.
86/B2 Vespolate, It.
62/B2 Vest-Agder (co.), Nor.
62/C3 Vestbjerg, Den.
62/D2 Vestby, Nor.
62/B2 Vestbygd, Nor.
61/E1 Vesterålen (isls.), Nor.
62/D3 Vesterø Havn, Den.
52/E2 Vestfjorden (bay), Nor.
61/E2 Vestfjorden (fjord), Nor.
62/C2 Vestfold (co.), Nor.
61/N7 Vestmannaeyjar, Ice.
86/D1 Vestone, It.
62/D4 Vest-Sjæland (co.), Den.
61/E1 Vestvågøya (isl.), Nor.
82/D5 Vésubie (riv.), Fr.
85/E6 Vesuvio (Vesuvius) (vol.), It.
201/H2 Vesuvius, Va,US
85/E6 Vesuvius (Vesuvio) (vol.), It.
94/H4 Ves'yegonsk, Rus.
73/B5 Veszprém, Hun.
73/B5 Veszprém (co.), Hun.
92/E2 Vészto, Hun.
156/D3 Vet (riv.), SAfr.
183/J2 Veteran, Ab,Can
96/D1 Vetka, Bela.
62/F3 Vetlanda, Swe.
95/K4 Vetluga (riv.), Rus.
95/K4 Vetluzhskiy, Rus.
93/H4 Vetovo, Bul.
84/C3 Vetralla, It.
80/C5 Vétraz, Fr.
63/N4 Vetrino, Bela.
71/H5 Větřni, Czh.
72/E4 Vetschau, Ger.
85/D2 Vettore (peak), It.
74/D3 Veude (riv.), Fr.
79/F1 Veulettes-sur-Mer, Fr.
68/B1 Veurne, Belg.
79/F5 Veuve (riv.), Fr.
200/E1 Vevay, In,US
148/G4 Veveno, Khawr (dry riv.), Sudan
80/C5 Vevey, Swi.
80/D5 Vex, Swi.
69/F2 Veybach (riv.), Ger.
80/B5 Veyle (riv.), Fr.
82/B3 Veynes, Fr.
187/F2 Veyo, Ut,US
80/C5 Veyrier, Swi.
80/C6 Veyrier-du-Lac, Fr.
80/C1 Vézelise, Fr.
74/D4 Vézère (riv.), Fr.
78/D4 Vezin-le-Coquet, Fr.
104/C1 Vezirköprü, Turk.
84/C3 Vezza (riv.), It.
81/G5 Vezza d'Oglio, It.
86/C4 Vezzano Ligure, It.
172/B1 Viacha, Bol.
86/D3 Viadana, It.
174/E1 Viale, Arg.
191/G3 Vian, Ok,US
152/C5 Viana, Ang.
167/E3 Viana, Braz.
76/B1 Viana del Bollo, Sp.
76/B3 Viana do Alentejo, Port.
76/A2 Viana do Castelo, Port.
76/A2 Viana do Castelo (dist.), Port.
69/F4 Vianden, Lux.
66/C5 Vianen, Neth.
123/C2 Viangchan (Vientiane) (cap.), Laos
123/C1 Viangphoukha, Laos
162/E3 Viaquez (Vieques) (isl.), PR
76/C4 Viar (riv.), Sp.
86/D5 Viareggio, It.
53/T9 Viarmes, Fr.
74/E4 Viaur (riv.), Fr.
194/C2 Vibank, Sk,Can
83/C5 Vibo Marina, It.
62/C3 Viborg, Den.
62/C3 Viborg (co.), Den.
193/F2 Viborg, SD,US
83/C5 Vibo Valentia, It.
79/F4 Vibraye, Fr.
191/J2 Viburnum, Mo,US
77/G2 Vic, Sp.
158/C3 Vicam, Mex.
76/D4 Vícar, Sp.
86/D5 Vicarello, It.
87/E5 Vicchio, It.
168/A2 Vice, Peru
77/F1 Vic-en-Bigorre, Fr.
204/F8 Vicente (pt.), Ca,US
158/B2 Vicente Guerrero, Mex.
158/E4 Vicente Guerrero, Mex.
175/S12 Vicente López, Arg.
87/E1 Vicenza, It.
87/E1 Vicenza (prov.), It.
81/H6 Vicenza (state), It.
194/B3 Viceroy, Sk,Can
74/D5 Vic-Fezensac, Fr.
164/D3 Vichada (comm.), Col.
164/D3 Vichada (riv.), Col.
175/G1 Vichadero, Uru.
172/B1 Vichaya, Bol.
94/J4 Vichuga, Rus.
74/E3 Vichy, Fr.
191/J1 Vichy, Mo,US
190/E2 Vici, Ok,US
202/B2 Vick, La,US
187/F4 Vicksburg, Az,US
198/D3 Vicksburg, Mi,US
200/B4 Vicksburg, Ms,US
200/B4 Vicksburg Nat'l Mil. Park, Ms,US
90/A1 Vico, Fr.
84/C3 Vico (lake), It.
85/F4 Vico del Gargano, It.
85/E6 Vico Equense, It.
86/D5 Vicopisano, It.
171/E4 Viçosa, Braz.
167/F3 Viçosa do Ceará, Braz.
81/F5 Vicosoprano, Swi.
91/G3 Vicou Gorge Nat'l Park, Gre.
84/C3 Vicovaro, It.
68/C5 Vic-sur-Aisne, Fr.
69/F6 Vic-sur-Seille, Fr.
183/L1 Victoire, Sk,Can
186/B1 Victor, Ca,US
190/B1 Victor, Co,US
193/H3 Victor, Ia,US
133/H5 Victor Harbor, Austl.
153/H3 Victoria (lake), Afr.
174/E2 Victoria, Arg.
130/C3 Victoria (riv.), Austl.
135/C3 Victoria (state), Austl.
160/D2 Victoria (peak), Belz.
116/B4 Victoria (peak), Burma
182/C3 Victoria (cap.), BC,Can
178/E1 Victoria (isl.), NW,Can
178/F2 Victoria (str.), NW,Can
197/R8 Victoria, On,Can
174/B3 Victoria, Chile
167/L6 Victoria, Col.
165/F1 Victoria, Gren.
144/B4 Victoria, Gui.
117/G4 Victoria (cap.), HK
160/E3 Victoria, Hon.
125/A4 Victoria, Malay.
125/C2 Victoria, Phil.
125/B3 Victoria (peak), Phil.
93/G3 Victoria, Rom.
190/E1 Victoria, Ks,US
195/N7 Victoria, Mn,US
200/B1 Victoria, Mo,US
200/C3 Victoria, Ms,US
189/F3 Victoria, Tx,US
201/H2 Victoria, Va,US
140/E6 Victoria (falls), Zam.
194/F2 Victoria Beach, Can
154/E3 Victoria Falls, Zim.
154/E3 Victoria Falls (int'l arpt.), Zim.
137/L Victoria Land (reg.), Ant.
154/E3 Victoria (Mosi-oa-Tunya) (falls), Zam.
153/G2 Victoria Nile (riv.), Ugan.
84/H7 Victoria (Rabat), Malta
130/C4 Victoria River Downs, Austl.
125/C3 Victorias, Phil.
196/B2 Victoriaville, Qu,Can
156/C3 Victoria West, SAfr.
174/D3 Victorica, Arg.
164/E4 Victorino, Ven.
158/E4 Víctor Rosales, Mex.
204/C1 Victorville, Ca,US
172/B4 Vicuña, Chile
174/D2 Vicuña Mackenna, Arg.
183/M4 Vida, Mt,US
157/F3 Vidal (cape), SAfr.
186/E3 Vidal, Ca,US
201/F4 Vidalia, Ga,US
202/C2 Vidalia, La,US
82/C6 Vidauban, Fr.
173/G3 Videira, Braz.
172/D4 Videla, Arg.
93/G3 Videle, Rom.
71/G4 Vidhošt (peak), Czh.
76/B3 Vidigueira, Port.
86/C2 Vidigulfo, It.
92/F4 Vidin, Bul.
120/A4 Vidisha, India
63/Q1 Vidlitsa, Rus.
87/F1 Vidor, It.
189/G2 Vidor, Tx,US
62/F3 Vidöstern (lake), Swe.
74/E5 Vidourle (riv.), Fr.
79/F3 Vie (riv.), Fr.
71/F4 Viechtach, Ger.
174/E4 Viedma, Arg.
175/J7 Viedma (lake), Arg.
71/H5 Viehberg (peak), Aus.
166/D3 Vieira Grande (bay), Braz.
76/C1 Vieja (mtn.), Sp.
188/B2 Vieja (peak), Tx,US
188/B2 Vieja, Sierra (mts.), Tx,US
168/B2 Viejo (peak), Peru
63/K3 Viekšniai, Lith.
72/B1 Vielank, Ger.
77/F1 Viella, Sp.
69/E3 Vielsalm, Belg.
67/H5 Vienenburg, Ger.
200/F4 Vienna, Ga,US
200/C2 Vienna, Il,US
191/J1 Vienna, Mo,US
208/G5 Vienna, Oh,US
206/A6 Vienna, Va,US
201/G1 Vienna, WV,US
73/A3 Vienna (Wien) (cap.), Aus.
82/A1 Vienne, Fr.
74/D3 Vienne (riv.), Fr.
123/C2 Vientiane (int'l arpt.), Laos
123/C2 Vientiane (Viangchan) (cap.), Laos
162/E3 Vieques (Viaquez) (isl.), PR
69/D6 Viere (riv.), Fr.
66/D5 Vierlingsbeek, Neth.
70/B3 Viernheim, Ger.
69/E4 Vierre (riv.), Fr.
66/D6 Viersen, Ger.
81/E3 Vierwaldstättersee (Lucerne) (lake), Swi.
79/H6 Vierzon, Fr.
158/E3 Viesca, Mex.
72/B6 Vieselbach, Ger.
63/L3 Viesīte, Lat.
85/G4 Vieste, It.
123/D2 Vietnam
85/F6 Vietri di Potenza, It.
85/E6 Vietri sul Mare, It.
123/D1 Viet Tri, Viet.
74/C5 Vieux-Boucau-les-Bains, Fr.
82/C3 Vieux Chaillol (mtn.), Fr.
80/C2 Vieux-Charmont, Fr.
68/C3 Vieux-Condé, Fr.
198/B1 Vieux Desert (lake), Mi, Wi,US
162/F4 Vieux Fort, StL.
80/D2 Vieux-Thann, Fr.
63/L4 Vievis, Lith.
54/B5 Viewpark, Sc,UK
175/T12 Vieytes, Arg.
80/C5 Vieze (riv.), Swi.
82/B2 Vif, Fr.
125/D2 Viga, Phil.
125/C1 Vigan, Phil.
87/E3 Vigarano Mainarda, It.
87/D2 Vigasio, It.
86/B2 Vigevano, It.
83/B2 Viggiano, It.
86/B1 Viggiù, It.
166/D3 Vigia, Braz.
86/B1 Vigliano Biellese, It.
85/D4 Viglio (peak), It.
68/B3 Vignacourt, Fr.
84/C3 Vignanello, It.
74/C5 Vignemale (mtn.), Fr.
69/E6 Vigneulles-lès-Hattonchâtel, Fr.
53/T10 Vigneux-sur-Seine, Fr.
87/E4 Vignola, It.
69/E6 Vignot, Fr.
79/G2 Vigny, Fr.
76/A1 Vigo, Sp.
87/E2 Vigodarzere, It.
86/A3 Vigone, It.
87/F2 Vigonovo, It.
87/E2 Vigonza, It.
62/A2 Vigrestad, Nor.
86/B3 Viguzzolo, It.
69/F5 Vigy, Fr.
61/H2 Vihanti, Fin.
107/K2 Vihāri, Pak.
63/L1 Vihti, Fin.
61/H3 Viitasaari, Fin.
63/M2 Viivikonna, Est.
116/C3 Vijayanagar, India
118/D4 Vijayawada, India
91/F2 Vijosë (riv.), Alb.
61/N7 Vík, Ice.
62/B1 Vik, Nor.
61/H2 Vikajärvi, Fin.
62/A2 Vikedal, Nor.
130/B2 Vikeke, Indo.
62/C2 Vikersund, Nor.
62/B2 Vikeså, Nor.
62/A2 Vikevåg, Nor.
93/F5 Vikhren (peak), Bul.
183/J1 Viking, Ab,Can
62/F1 Vikmanshyttan, Swe.
122/F4 Vikramasingapuram, India
138/F6 Vila (cap.), Van.
164/D5 Vila Bittencourt, Braz.
172/C1 Vilacaya, Bol.
155/H3 Vila da Maganja, Moz.
77/G2 Viladecans, Sp.
77/V14 Vila de Porto Santo, Madr.,Port.
155/G3 Vila de Sena, Moz.

76/A4 Vila do Bispo, Port.
76/A2 Vila do Conde, Port.
77/T13 Vila do Porto, Azor,Port.
77/K7 Vilafranca del Penedès, Sp.
76/A3 Vila Franca de Xira, Port.
77/T13 Vila Franca do Campo, Azor.,Port.
78/C5 Vilaine (riv.), Fr.
63/M3 Viļaka, Lat.
172/C1 Vilama (lake), Arg.
157/H7 Vilanandro (cape), Madg.
155/G4 Vilanculos, Moz.
63/M3 Viļāni, Lat.
76/B2 Vila Nova de Fozcoa, Port.
76/A2 Vila Nova de Gaia, Port.
76/A4 Vila Nova de Milfontes, Port.
152/C5 Vila Nova do Seles, Ang.
77/F2 Vilanova i la Geltrù, Sp.
77/K7 Vilanova i la Geltru, Sp.
76/B2 Vila Pouca de Aguiar, Port.
76/B2 Vila Real, Port.
76/B2 Vila Real (dist.), Port.
76/B4 Vila Real de Santo António, Port.
76/B2 Vilar Formoso, Port.
166/D2 Vila Velha, Braz.
171/E4 Vila Velha Argolas, Braz.
76/B3 Vila Velha de Ródão, Port.
76/A2 Vila Verde, Port.
76/B3 Vila Viçosa, Port.
172/B1 Vila-Vila, Chile
168/B3 Vilcabamba, Peru
93/F3 Vîlcea (co.), Rom.
98/E2 Vil'cha, Ukr.
76/D3 Vilches, Sp.
174/B4 Vilcún, Chile
63/M4 Vileyka, Bela.
61/F2 Vilhelmina, Swe.
169/F4 Vilhena, Braz.
63/M4 Viliya (riv.), Bela.
63/L2 Viljandi, Est.
156/D2 Viljoenskroon, SAfr.
63/K4 Vilkaviškis, Lith.
63/K4 Vilkija, Lith.
101/K2 Vil'kitsogo (str.), Rus.
93/J3 Vilkovo, Ukr.
81/F4 Villa, Swi.
172/C2 Villa Abecia, Bol.
174/C1 Villa Aberastain, Arg.
84/C4 Villa Adriana (ruins), It.
174/Q9 Villa Alemana, Chile
174/Q10 Villa Alhué, Chile
162/D3 Villa Altagracia, DRep.
172/E4 Villa Ana, Arg.
172/D3 Villa Ángela, Arg.
172/D4 Villa Atamisqui, Arg.
174/D2 Villa Atuel, Arg.
125/D3 Villaba, Phil.
76/E1 Villaba, Sp.
87/E2 Villa Bartolomea, It.
169/E3 Villa Bella, Bol.
172/D3 Villa Berthet, Arg.
76/B1 Villablino, Sp.
164/D2 Villa Bruzual, Ven.
174/E2 Villa Cañas, Arg.
76/D3 Villacañas, Sp.
86/D1 Villa Carcina, It.
172/C4 Villa Carlos Paz, Arg.
76/D3 Villacarrillo, Sp.
75/K3 Villach, Aus.
174/E2 Villa Chañar Ladeado, Arg.
172/B4 Villa Colón, Arg.
174/E2 Villa Constitución, Arg.
158/C3 Villa Constitución, Mex.
76/C1 Villada, Sp.
86/C1 Villa d'Almè, It.
158/E4 Villa de Cos, Mex.
76/A1 Villa de Cruces, Sp.
165/E2 Villa de Cura, Ven.
76/C4 Villa del Río, Sp.
172/D4 Villa del Rosario, Arg.
172/C4 Villa de Soto, Arg.
76/C1 Villadiego, Sp.
86/C1 Villa di Serio, It.
87/E2 Villadose, It.
81/E5 Villadossola, It.
172/C1 Villa E. Viscarra, Bol.
77/E2 Villafamés, Sp.
172/E4 Villa Federal, Arg.
160/C2 Villa Flores, Mex.
173/E3 Villa Florida, Par.
76/E1 Villafranca, Sp.
86/B3 Villafranca d'Asti, It.
76/B1 Villafranca del Bierzo, Sp.
77/E2 Villafranca del Cid, Sp.
76/D3 Villafranca del los Caballeros, Sp.
76/B3 Villafranca de los Barros, Sp.
87/D2 Villafranca di Verona, It.
86/C4 Villafranca in Lunigiana, It.
86/A3 Villafranca Piemonte, It.
83/B6 Villafranca Tirrena, It.
188/D4 Villa Frontera, Mex.
189/D4 Villa Frontera, Mex.
76/A1 Villagarcía, Sp.
191/H4 Village, Ar,US
191/J2 Village (cr.), Ar,US
188/K7 Village (cr.), Tx,US
189/G2 Village Mills, Tx,US
175/F3 Villa Gesell, Arg.
159/F3 Villagran, Mex.
192/B4 Villa Grove, Co,US
198/B5 Villa Grove, Il,US
86/C1 Villa Guardia, It.
174/F1 Villaguay, Arg.
172/E4 Villa Guillermina, Arg.
172/E3 Villa Hayes, Par.
167/K6 Villahermosa, Col.
159/G5 Villahermosa, Mex.
76/D3 Villahermosa, Sp.
172/E4 Villa Hernandarias, Arg.
158/C2 Villa Hidalgo, Mex.
158/D3 Villa Hidalgo, Mex.
174/D2 Villa Huidobro, Arg.
168/D5 Villa Industrial, Chile
79/E4 Villaines-la-Juhel, Fr.
174/E3 Villa Iris, Arg.
162/D3 Villa Isabela, DRep.
161/J2 Villa Jaragua, DRep.
77/E3 Villajoyosa, Sp.
174/C4 Villa La Angostura, Arg.
76/B1 Villalba, Sp.
76/B2 Villalcampo (res.), Sp.
188/D4 Villaldama, Mex.
85/E6 Villa Literno, It.
76/C1 Villalón de Campos, Sp.
174/E3 Villalonga, Arg.
158/D3 Villa López, Mex.
76/C2 Villalpando, Sp.
175/S11 Villa Mantero, Arg.
174/E2 Villa María, Arg.
167/K6 Villamaría, Col.
172/E4 Villa María Grande, Arg.
172/C2 Villa Martín, Bol.
76/C4 Villamartín, Sp.
172/C4 Villa Mazán, Arg.
172/D4 Villa Minetti, Arg.
86/D4 Villa Minozzo, It.
172/D2 Villa Montes, Bol.
84/A2 Villa Napoleone, It.
81/H4 Villandro, Monte (peak), It.
87/E4 Villanova, It.
87/F4 Villanova, It.
86/A3 Villanova d'Asti, It.
86/A4 Villanova Mondovì, It.
86/C2 Villanterio, It.
174/C2 Villa Nueva, Arg.
164/C2 Villanueva, Col.
160/D3 Villa Nueva, Guat.
160/E3 Villanueva, Hon.
158/E4 Villanueva, Mex.
160/E3 Villanueva, Nic.
190/B3 Villanueva, NM,US
76/A1 Villanueva de Arosa, Sp.
76/C3 Villanueva de Córdoba, Sp.
76/D3 Villanueva del Arzobispo, Sp.
76/C3 Villanueva de la Serena, Sp.
76/D3 Villanueva de los Infantes, Sp.
76/B1 Villanueva de Oscos, Sp.
86/D1 Villanuova sul Clisi, It.
92/D3 Villány, Hun.
159/Q10 Villa Obregon, Mex.
172/E4 Villa Ocampo, Arg.
158/D3 Villa Ocampo, Mex.
172/D4 Villa Ojo de Agua, Arg.
87/G1 Villa Opicina, It.
204/C3 Villa Park, Ca,US
205/Q16 Villa Park, Il,US
83/C3 Villapiana, It.
172/C1 Villar, Bol.
174/E2 Villa Ramírez, Arg.
76/D1 Villarcayo, Sp.
195/G5 Villard, Mn,US
82/B2 Villard-Bonnot, Fr.
82/B2 Villard-de-Lans, Fr.
77/E3 Villar del Arzobispo, Sp.
76/B2 Villardevós, Sp.
174/D3 Villa Regina, Arg.
130/A4 Villaret (cape), Austl.
168/C3 Villa Rica, Peru
200/E4 Villa Rica, Ga,US
85/E6 Villaricca, It.
164/C3 Villa Rosario, Col.
82/D3 Villar Perosa, It.
77/E3 Villarreal de los Infantes, Sp.
174/B3 Villarrica, Chile
174/B3 Villarrica (lake), Chile
174/C3 Villarrica (vol.), Chile
173/E3 Villarrica, Par.
174/C3 Villarrica Nat'l Park, Chile
76/D3 Villarrobledo, Sp.
76/D3 Villarrubia de los Ojos, Sp.
82/C3 Villar-Saint-Pancrace, Fr.
80/B5 Villars-les-Dombes, Fr.
80/D4 Villars-sur-Glâne, Swi.
82/D5 Villars-sur-Var, Fr.
206/D5 Villas, NJ,US
76/D1 Villasana de Mena, Sp.
161/E3 Villa Sandino, Nic.
83/B6 Villa San Giovanni, It.
174/F2 Villa San José, Arg.
172/C4 Villa San Martín, Arg.
86/C1 Villasanta, It.
85/E4 Villa Santa Maria, It.
174/D2 Villa Sarmiento, Arg.
172/C1 Villa Serrano, Bol.
86/A3 Villastellone, It.
172/C1 Villa Tunari, Bol.
172/B4 Villa Unión, Arg.
158/D4 Villa Unión, Mex.
188/D3 Villa Unión, Mex.
174/D2 Villa Valeria, Arg.
76/C4 Villaverde del Río, Sp.
87/E1 Villaverla, It.
87/F5 Villa Verucchio, It.
164/C3 Villavicencio, Col.
76/C1 Villaviciosa, Sp.
77/N9 Villaviciosa de Odon, Sp.
172/C2 Villazón, Bol.
79/G5 Villebarou, Fr.
53/T10 Villecresnes, Fr.
53/S10 Ville-d'Avray, Fr.
78/D3 Villedieu-les-Poêles, Fr.
82/B1 Villefontaine, Fr.
82/D5 Villefranche, Fr.
74/E4 Villefranche-de-Rouergue, Fr.
79/G6 Villefranche-sur-Cher, Fr.
74/F4 Villefranche-sur-Saône, Fr.
53/T10 Villejuif, Fr.
82/B5 Villelaure, Fr.
53/T10 Villemomble, Fr.
74/D5 Villemur-sur-Tarn, Fr.
77/E3 Villena, Sp.
80/C5 Villeneuve, Swi.
68/C2 Villeneuve-d'Ascq, Fr.
53/S10 Villeneuve-la-Garenne, Fr.
53/U10 Villeneuve-le-Comte, Fr.
53/T10 Villeneuve-le-Roi, Fr.
82/A5 Villeneuve-lès-Avignon, Fr.
82/D5 Villeneuve-Loubet, Fr.
68/B6 Villeneuve-Saint-Georges, Fr.
68/C5 Villeneuve-Saint-Germain, Fr.
74/D4 Villeneuve-sur-Lot, Fr.
74/E2 Villeneuve-sur-Yonne, Fr.
74/D5 Villeneuve-Tolosane, Fr.
53/R10 Villennes-sur-Seine, Fr.
53/T10 Villeparisis, Fr.
53/T10 Villepinte, Fr.
202/B2 Ville Platte, La,US
53/S10 Villepreux, Fr.
68/B4 Villers-Bocage, Fr.
68/B4 Villers-Bretonneux, Fr.
68/C5 Villers-Cotterêts, Fr.
80/C2 Villersexel, Fr.
69/E2 Villers-Le-Bouillet, Belg.
80/C3 Villers-le-Lac, Fr.
69/F6 Villers-lès-Nancy, Fr.
68/C3 Villers-Outreaux, Fr.
68/B5 Villers-Saint-Paul, Fr.
69/D4 Villers-Semeuse, Fr.
79/E2 Villers-sur-Mer, Fr.
69/E5 Villerupt, Fr.
167/L6 Villeta, Col.
80/A6 Villeurbanne, Fr.
53/T10 Villevaudé, Fr.
156/E2 Villiers, SAfr.
156/L10 Villiersdorp, SAfr.
69/D6 Villiers-en-Lieu, Fr.
53/T9 Villiers-le-Bel, Fr.
68/C6 Villiers-Saint-Georges, Fr.
53/T10 Villiers-sur-Marne, Fr.
80/B6 Villieu-Loyes-Mollon, Fr.
70/B6 Villingen-Schwenningen, Ger.
193/G3 Villisca, Ia,US
70/B2 Villmar, Ger.
86/C1 Villongo, It.
122/G3 Villupuram, India
63/L4 Vilnius (cap.), Lith.
63/L4 Vilno (int'l arpt.), Lith.
191/H3 Vilonia, Ar,US
61/H3 Vilppula, Fin.
81/G2 Vils, Aus.
71/E4 Vils (riv.), Ger.
71/F6 Vilsbiburg, Ger.
71/E3 Vilseck, Ger.
71/G5 Vilshofen, Ger.
81/F3 Vilters, Swi.
68/D2 Vilvoorde, Belg.
101/M3 Vilyuy (range), Rus.
101/N3 Vilyuy (riv.), Rus.
101/N3 Vilyuysk, Rus.
86/C1 Vimercate, It.
76/B1 Vimianzo, Sp.
76/B2 Vimioso, Port.
62/F3 Vimmerby, Swe.
86/C2 Vimodrone, It.
79/F3 Vimoutiers, Fr.
71/G4 Vimperk, Czh.
68/B3 Vimy, Fr.
148/B4 Vina (riv.), Camr.
174/C2 Viña del Mar, Chile
82/D4 Vinadio, It.
82/C6 Vinaigre (mtn.), Fr.
196/C3 Vinalhaven, Me,US
157/J6 Vinanivao, Madg.
77/F2 Vinaroz, Sp.
82/B2 Vinay, Fr.
137/H Vincennes (bay), Ant.
53/T10 Vincennes, Fr.
53/U10 Vincennes (res.), Fr.
198/C5 Vincennes, In,US
200/D4 Vincent, Al,US
204/B1 Vincent, Ca,US
188/D1 Vincent, Tx,US
206/D4 Vincentown, NJ,US
164/B5 Vinces, Ecu.
80/C1 Vincey, Fr.
85/E5 Vinchiaturo, It.
172/B3 Vinchina, Arg.
172/B3 Vinchina (riv.), Arg.
168/C4 Vinchos, Peru
87/D5 Vinci, It.
62/D4 Vindeby, Den.
61/F2 Vindeln, Swe.
120/A4 Vindhya (range), India
200/E2 Vine Grove, Ky,US
197/S9 Vineland, On,Can
195/H4 Vineland, Mn,US
206/C5 Vineland, NJ,US
197/S9 Vineland Station, On,Can
154/B4 Vineta, Namb.
79/G5 Vineuil, Fr.
208/D3 Vineyard (sound), Ma,US
62/F2 Vingåker, Swe.
154/B4 Vingerklip, Namb.
123/D2 Vinh, Viet.
76/B2 Vinhais, Port.
171/K8 Vinhedo, Braz.
123/D4 Vinh Long, Viet.
123/D2 Vinh Moc, Tunnels of, Viet.
123/D4 Vinh Quoi, Viet.
123/E3 Vinh Thanh, Viet.
123/D1 Vinh Yen, Viet.
92/F5 Vinica, Macd.
201/M7 Vinings, Ga,US
191/G2 Vinita, Ok,US
92/F3 Vînju Mare, Rom.
66/B4 Vinkeveen, Neth.
92/D3 Vinkovci, Cro.
98/C3 Vinniki, Ukr.
69/G5 Vinningen, Ger.
98/E3 Vinnitsa, Ukr.
98/D3 Vinnitsa Obl., Ukr.
98/B3 Vinogradov, Ukr.
82/B5 Vinon-sur-Verdon, Fr.
86/A3 Vinovo, It.
50/E9 Vinson (peak), Ant.
182/D2 Vinsulla, BC,Can
125/C1 Vintar, Phil.
193/H2 Vinton, Ia,US
63/Q2 Viny, Rus.
191/J2 Viola, Ar,US
206/C5 Viola, De,US
193/J3 Viola, Il,US
207/D1 Viola, NY,US
202/D3 Violet, La,US
182/G1 Violet Grove, Ab,Can
135/C3 Violet Town, Austl.
130/B4 Violet Valley Abor. Land, Austl.
78/D5 Vioreau, Grande-Res-de (res.), Fr.
53/R9 Viosne (riv.), Fr.
167/L7 Viotá, Col.
87/G1 Vipava, Slov.
81/H4 Vipiteno (Sterzing), It.
72/B5 Vippach (riv.), Ger.
125/D2 Virac, Phil.
170/D4 Viracopos (int'l arpt.), Braz.
104/D2 Viranşehir, Turk.
118/B4 Virār, India
63/K4 Virbalis, Lith.
194/D3 Virden, Mb,Can
193/K4 Virden, Il,US
187/H4 Virden, NM,US
79/E3 Vire, Fr.
79/D2 Vire (riv.), Fr.
154/B2 Virei, Ang.
62/F2 Viren (lake), Swe.
69/D3 Vireux-Wallerand, Fr.
183/J3 Virgelle, Mt,US
197/S9 Virgil, On,Can
162/E3 Virgin (isls.), UK, US
162/E3 Virgin Gorda (isl.), BVI
60/C2 Virginia, Ire.
156/D3 Virginia, SAfr.
201/H2 Virginia (state), US
193/J4 Virginia, Il,US
195/H4 Virginia, Mn,US
201/K2 Virginia Beach, Va,US
185/H1 Virginia City, Mt,US
184/D4 Virginia City, Nv,US
192/B3 Virginia Dale, Co,US
53/M7 Virginia Water, Eng,UK
162/E3 Virgin Islands, UK
162/E3 Virgin Islands, US
162/E3 Virgin Islands Nat'l Park, USVI
171/E3 Virgolândia, Braz.
80/B5 Viriat, Fr.
80/B6 Virieu-le-Grand, Fr.
123/D3 Virochey, Camb.
53/S10 Viroflay, Fr.
68/D3 Viroin (riv.), Belg.
193/J2 Viroqua, Wi,US
92/C3 Virovitica, Cro.
62/F3 Virserum, Swe.
69/E4 Virton, Belg.
63/K2 Virtsu, Est.
168/B3 Virú, Peru
122/F4 Virudunagar, India
63/M2 Viru-Jaagupi, Est.
153/G3 Virunga, Zaire
153/G3 Virunga Nat'l Park, Zaire
63/M2 Viru-Nigula, Est.
172/D1 Viru Viru (int'l arpt.), Bol.
53/T10 Viry-Châtillon, Fr.
85/G1 Vis, Cro.
85/G1 Vis (isl.), Cro.
118/D4 Visākhapatnam, India
186/C2 Visalia, Ca,US
82/A4 Visan, Fr.
125/C3 Visayan (sea), Phil.
67/F3 Visbek, Ger.
62/H3 Visby, Swe.
85/E6 Visciano, It.
171/E4 Visconde do Rio Branco, Braz.
179/R7 Viscount Melville (sound), NW,Can
69/E2 Visé, Belg.
92/D4 Višegrad, Bosn.
73/C4 Visegrád, Hun.
167/E3 Viseu, Braz.
76/B2 Viseu, Port.
76/B2 Viseu (dist.), Port.
93/G2 Vişeu de Sus, Rom.
95/L3 Vishera (riv.), Rus.
95/N3 Vishera (riv.), Rus.
98/C3 Vishnevets, Ukr.
93/J2 Vishnëvka, Mol.
96/D2 Vishnëvoye, Ukr.
156/B4 Vishoek, SAfr.
62/E3 Viskafors, Swe.
62/F3 Vislanda, Swe.
118/B3 Visnagar, India
92/D3 Višnjevac, Cro.
82/D3 Viso (peak), It.
92/D4 Visoko, Bosn.
80/D5 Visp, Swi.
80/D5 Visperterminen, Swi.
67/G3 Visselhövede, Ger.
62/D4 Vissenbjerg, Den.
80/D5 Vissoie, Swi.
204/C4 Vista, Ca,US
91/J2 Vistonís (lake), Gre.
65/K2 Vistula (Wisła) (riv.), Pol.
168/D5 Visviri, Chile
93/G4 Vit (riv.), Bul.
194/F3 Vita, Mb,Can
75/J5 Vitalba (peak), It.
86/D6 Vitalba, Monte (peak), It.
63/P4 Vitebsk, Bela.
63/N4 Vitebsk Obl., Bela.
84/C3 Viterbo, It.
84/B3 Viterbo (prov.), It.
92/C3 Vitez, Bosn.
123/D4 Vi Thanh, Viet.
131/G1 Vitiaz (str.), PNG
172/C2 Vitichi, Bol.
76/B2 Vitigudino, Sp.
138/G6 Viti Levu (isl.), Fiji
101/M4 Vitim, Rus.
108/G1 Vitim (plat.), Rus.
108/G1 Vitim (riv.), Rus.
101/M4 Vitimskiy, Rus.
84/C4 Vitinia, It.
71/H5 Vítkuv Kamen (peak), Czh.
92/E4 Vitomirica, Yugo.
168/D5 Vitor, Peru
163/E5 Vitória, Braz.
166/D4 Vitoría, Braz.
171/E4 Vitória, Braz.
76/D1 Vitoria, Sp.
171/E2 Vitória da Conquista, Braz.
167/H5 Vitória de Santo Antão, Braz.
167/E3 Vitória do Mearim, Braz.
167/E4 Vitorino Freire, Braz.
93/F4 Vitosha Nat'l Park, Bul.
83/D4 Vitravo (riv.), It.
78/D4 Vitré, Fr.
80/B2 Vitrey-sur-Mance, Fr.
82/B6 Vitrolles, Fr.
68/B3 Vitry-en-Artois, Fr.
68/D6 Vitry-le-François, Fr.
53/T10 Vitry-sur-Seine, Fr.
153/G3 Vitshumbi, Zaire
61/G2 Vittangi, Swe.
80/B1 Vittel, Fr.
90/D4 Vittoria, It.
75/K4 Vittorio Veneto, It.
85/E5 Vitulano, It.
85/E5 Vitulazio, It.
82/D2 Viú, It.
74/F4 Vivarais (mts.), Fr.
76/B1 Vivero, Sp.
86/B2 Viverone, It.
86/A2 Viverone (lake), It.
189/H1 Vivian, La,US
82/A4 Viviers, Fr.
74/D3 Vivonne, Fr.
172/C2 Vizcachilla, Bol.
158/B3 Vizcaíno, Sierra de (mts.), Mex.
202/P8 Vizcaya Museum, Fl,US
93/H5 Vize, Turk.
95/K2 Vizhas, Rus.
95/K2 Vizhas (riv.), Rus.
98/C3 Vizhnitsa, Ukr.
118/D4 Vizianagaram, India
82/B2 Vizille, Fr.
87/G2 Vižinada, Cro.
95/L3 Vizinga, Rus.
93/H3 Viziru, Rom.
73/B1 Vizovice, Czh.
66/B5 Vlaardingen, Neth.
92/F2 Vlădeasa (peak), Rom.
53/H4 Vladikavkaz, Rus.
53/H3 Vladimir, Rus.
94/J5 Vladimir Obl., Rus.
98/C2 Vladimir-Volynskiy, Ukr.
109/L3 Vladivostok, Rus.
67/E2 Vlagtwedde, Neth.
93/G2 Vlăhiţa, Rom.
92/E4 Vlajna (peak), Yugo.
92/D3 Vlasenica, Bosn.
65/H4 Vlašim, Czh.
92/F4 Vlasotince, Yugo.
71/G3 Vlastec (hill), Czh.
66/C4 Vleuten, Neth.
66/B2 Vlieland (isl.), Neth.
66/C2 Vliestroom (chan.), Neth.
66/C5 Vlijmen, Neth.
66/A6 Vlissingen, Neth.
91/F2 Vlorë, Alb.
67/F4 Vlotho, Ger.
71/H2 Vltava (riv.), Czh.
94/H5 Vnukovo (int'l arpt.), Rus.
86/D1 Vobarno, It.
159/F2 Voca, Tx,US
71/G6 Vöcklabruck, Aus.
71/G7 Vöcklamarkt, Aus.
92/B3 Vodice, Cro.
94/H3 Vodlozero (lake), Rus.
71/H4 Vodňany, Czh.
87/G3 Vodnjan, Cro.
62/D3 Vodskov, Den.
66/D5 Voerde, Ger.
145/F5 Vogan, Togo
194/E2 Vogar, Mb,Can
70/C1 Vogelsberg (mts.), Ger.
86/C3 Voghera, It.
81/E5 Vogogna, It.
81/E5 Vogorno (lake), Swi.
81/E5 Vogorno, Pizzo di (peak), Swi.
92/D4 Vogošća, Bosn.
71/F7 Vogtareuth, Ger.
71/E2 Vogtland (reg.), Ger.
139/U12 Voh, NCal.
71/E5 Vohburg an der Donau, Ger.
71/F3 Vohenstrauss, Ger.
157/H8 Vohilava, Madg.
157/J8 Vohilava, Madg.
157/J7 Vohimena, Madg.
157/H9 Vohimena (cape), Madg.
141/G7 Vohipeno, Madg.
157/H8 Vohiposa, Madg.
157/H8 Vohitrambo, Madg.
63/L2 Võhma, Est.
81/G1 Vöhringen, Ger.
151/B2 Voi, Kenya
69/E6 Void-Vacon, Fr.
205/C3 Voight (cr.), Wa,US
54/B4 Voil, Loch (lake), Sc,UK
144/C4 Voinjama, Libr.
82/B2 Voiron, Fr.
79/G3 Voise (riv.), Fr.
179/K3 Voisey (bay), Nf,Can
68/B5 Voisne (riv.), Fr.
80/B4 Voiteur, Fr.
73/C4 Vojnice, Slvk.
92/D5 Vojosë (riv.), Alb.
92/D3 Vojvodina (aut. prov.), Yugo.
152/C4 Voka, Congo
95/K4 Vokhma, Rus.
69/F5 Vöklingen, Ger.
87/E1 Volano, It.
87/E3 Volano, Po di (riv.), It.
208/G5 Volant, Pa,US
71/G5 Volary, Czh.
183/M5 Volborg, Mt,US
161/F4 Volcán Barú Nat'l Park, Pan.
138/C2 Volcano (isls.), Japan
180/U11 Volcano, Hi,US
161/E4 Volcán Poás Nat'l Park, CR
153/G3 Volcans Nat'l Park, Rwa.
99/J2 Volchansk, Ukr.
63/Q1 Volchiy Nos (cape), Rus.
61/C3 Volda, Nor.
66/C4 Volendam, Neth.
53/H4 Volga (riv.), Rus.
193/F1 Volga, SD,US
94/H3 Volga-Baltic Wtwy., Rus.
80/D1 Volgelsheim, Fr.
53/H4 Volgodonsk, Rus.
53/H4 Volgograd, Rus.
97/H2 Volgograd (int'l arpt.), Rus.
97/H2 Volgograd (res.), Rus.
99/M2 Volgograd Obl., Rus.
70/D3 Volkach, Ger.
70/D3 Volkach (riv.), Ger.
66/B5 Volkerakdam (dam), Neth.
75/L3 Völkermarkt, Aus.
81/E3 Volketswil, Swi.
63/Q2 Volkhov, Rus.
94/F4 Volkhov (riv.), Rus.
64/D4 Völklingen, Ger.
67/G6 Volkmarsen, Ger.
65/N2 Volkovysk, Bela.
157/E2 Volksrust, SAfr.
66/C3 Vollenhove, Neth.
69/G5 Volmunster, Fr.
99/J4 Volnovakha, Ukr.
100/K2 Volochanka, Rus.
109/L2 Volochayevka, Rus.
98/D3 Volochisk, Ukr.
99/J4 Volodarskoye, Ukr.
94/H4 Vologda, Rus.
94/J3 Vologda Obl., Rus.
80/C1 Vologne (riv.), Fr.
94/G4 Volokolamsk, Rus.
99/J2 Volokonovka, Rus.
82/C4 Volonne, Fr.
91/H3 Vólos, Gre.
91/H3 Volos (gulf), Gre.
63/N2 Volosovo, Rus.
63/P3 Volot, Rus.
98/B3 Volovets, Ukr.
96/F1 Volovo, Rus.
63/M4 Volozhin, Bela.
87/F1 Volpago del Montello, It.
86/A2 Volpiano, It.
72/B3 Völpke, Ger.
81/H3 Völs, Aus.
84/B2 Volsini (mts.), It.
53/H3 Vol'sk, Rus.
145/E4 Volta (lake), Gha.
145/F5 Volta (reg.), Gha.
140/C4 Volta (riv.), Gha.
145/F5 Volta (riv.), Gui.
130/B3 Voltaire (cape), Austl.
87/E3 Voltana, It.
170/D4 Volta Redonda, Braz.
87/D6 Volterra, It.
67/E4 Voltlage, Ger.
86/B4 Voltri, It.
85/E6 Volturara Irpina, It.
85/F5 Volturino, It.
83/B2 Volturino (peak), It.
85/E5 Volturno (riv.), It.
141/M13 Volubilis (ruins), Mor.
208/C2 Voluntown, Ct,US
86/A3 Volvera, It.
91/H2 Vólvi (lake), Gre.
82/B5 Volx, Fr.
71/G4 Volyně, Czh.
71/G4 Volyňka (riv.), Czh.
98/C2 Volyn Obl., Ukr.
98/D3 Volyno-Podol'sk (upland), Ukr.
95/L5 Volzhsk, Rus.
53/H4 Volzhskiy, Rus.
145/H4 Vom, Nga.
85/D2 Vomano (riv.), It.
194/A1 Vonda, Sk,Can
157/H8 Vondrozo, Madg.
69/D3 Vonêche, Belg.
177/H3 Von Frank (mtn.), Ak,US
91/G3 Vónitsa, Gre.
74/D3 Vonne (riv.), Fr.
63/M2 Võnnu, Est.
66/B4 Voorburg, Neth.
66/B5 Voorne (isl.), Neth.
66/B4 Voorschoten, Neth.
66/D4 Voorst, Neth.
61/P6 Vopnafjördhur, Ice.
81/F4 Vorab (peak), Swi.
81/F3 Vorarlberg (prov.), Aus.
70/C4 Vorbach (riv.), Ger.
71/G7 Vorchdorf, Aus.
66/D4 Vorden, Neth.
81/E4 Vorderrhein (riv.), Swi.
71/H5 Vorderweissenbach, Aus.
91/F2 Vorë, Alb.
82/B2 Voreppe, Fr.
53/K2 Vorkuta, Rus.
95/P2 Vorkuta (int'l arpt.), Rus.
63/K2 Vormsi (isl.), Est.
91/J5 Vóroi, Gre.
98/C3 Vorokhta, Ukr.
99/M2 Vorona (riv.), Rus.
53/G3 Voronezh, Rus.
99/K2 Voronezh (int'l arpt.), Rus.
96/F1 Voronezh (riv.), Rus.
99/K2 Voronezh Obl., Rus.
63/Q1 Voronov (cape), Rus.
98/E3 Voronovitsa, Ukr.
63/L4 Voronovo, Bela.
99/L2 Vorontsovka, Rus.
94/G1 Voron'ya (riv.), Rus.
63/M4 Voropayevo, Bela.
99/H2 Vorozhba, Ukr.
99/H3 Vorskla (riv.), Rus., Ukr.
69/E1 Vorst, Belg.
156/C2 Vorstershoop, SAfr.
63/L2 Vörts (lake), Est.
63/M3 Võru, Est.
98/F2 Vorzel', Ukr.
156/C3 Vosburg, SAfr.
73/A3 Vösendorf, Aus.
80/C1 Vosges (dept.), Fr.
80/C2 Vosges (mts.), Fr.
97/H2 Voskresenka, Rus.
94/H5 Voskresensk, Rus.
94/H4 Voskresenskoye, Rus.
95/K4 Voskresenskoye, Rus.
62/B1 Voss, Nor.
200/C5 Vossburg, Ms,US
109/L3 Vostochnyy, Rus.
137/V Vostock (cape), Ant.
137/H Vostok, Ant.
139/K6 Vostok (isl.), Kiri.
71/H3 Votice, Czh.
53/J3 Votkinsk, Rus.
95/M4 Votkinsk (res.), Rus.
170/D4 Votorantim, Braz.
170/C4 Votuporanga, Braz.
76/B2 Vouga (riv.), Port.
148/D4 Vougba, CAfr.
80/B5 Vouglans (lake), Fr.
80/B5 Vouglans, Barrage de (dam), Fr.
80/C3 Voujeaucourt, Fr.
79/F6 Vouvray, Fr.
80/C5 Vouvry, Swi.
91/H5 Voúxa, Ákra (cape), Gre.
69/D5 Vouziers, Fr.
79/H5 Vouzon, Fr.
79/G4 Voves, Fr.
149/E4 Vovodo (riv.), CAfr.
195/H3 Voyageurs Nat'l Park, Mn,US
137/J Voyeykov Ice Shelf, Ant.
95/M3 Voy-Vozh, Rus.
94/H3 Vozhe (lake), Rus.
94/J3 Vozhega, Rus.
95/K4 Vozherovo, Rus.
98/F4 Voznesensk, Ukr.
73/C3 Vráble, Slvk.
73/B2 Vracov, Czh.
98/F4 Vradiyevka, Ukr.
80/B1 Vraine (riv.), Fr.
93/H3 Vrancea (co.), Rom.
107/K1 Vrang, Taj.
102/S2 Vrangelya (isl.), Rus.
92/E4 Vranje, Yugo.
92/F4 Vranjska Banja, Yugo.
65/L4 Vranov nad Teplou, Slvk.
92/E5 Vrapčište, Macd.
93/F4 Vratsa, Bul.
92/C3 Vrbas (riv.), Bosn.
92/D3 Vrbas, Yugo.
73/B2 Vrbové, Slvk.
71/H4 Vrchy (peak), Czh.
156/E2 Vrede, SAfr.
156/D2 Vredefort, SAfr.
66/D4 Vreden, Ger.
156/B4 Vredenburg, SAfr.
200/D5 Vredenburgh, Al,US
156/B3 Vredendal, SAfr.
69/D4 Vresse-sur-Semois, Belg.
75/L4 Vrhnika, Slov.
122/G3 Vriddhāchalam, India
66/D2 Vries, Neth.
66/D4 Vriezenveen, Neth.
62/F3 Vrigstad, Swe.
64/B5 Vrin (riv.), Fr.
118/C2 Vrindāban, India
92/E4 Vrnjačka Banja, Yugo.
91/K3 Vrondádhos, Gre.
66/D4 Vroomshoop, Neth.
92/E3 Vršac, Yugo.
87/G2 Vrsar, Cro.
73/C1 Vrútky, Slvk.
156/D2 Vryburg, SAfr.
157/E2 Vryheid, SAfr.
65/K4 Vsetín, Czh.
177/E5 Vsevidof (mtn.), Ak,US
63/P1 Vsevolozhsk, Rus.
73/C2 Vtáčnik (mts.), Slvk.
73/C2 Vtáčnik (peak), Slvk.
149/G4 Vuca, Eth.
92/E4 Vučitrn, Yugo.
66/C5 Vught, Neth.
92/D3 Vukovar, Cro.
183/H2 Vulcan, Ab,Can
93/F3 Vulcan, Rom.
191/J2 Vulcan, Mo,US
83/B6 Vulcano (isl.), It.
93/F4 Vŭlchedrŭm, Bul.
93/H4 Vŭlchi Dol, Bul.
84/B3 Vulci (ruins), It.
85/F5 Vulgano (riv.), It.
123/D2 Vu Liet, Viet.
93/J3 Vulkaneshty, Mol.
85/F6 Vulture (peak), It.
123/D4 Vung Tau, Viet.
138/G7 Vunisea, Fiji
61/F2 Vuoggatjålme, Swe.
63/M1 Vuohijärvi (lake), Fin.
61/G2 Vuollerim, Swe.
63/N1 Vuoska (lake), Rus.
94/E1 Vuotso, Fin.
93/H4 Vŭrbitsa, Bul.
151/B2 Vuria (peak), Kenya
95/K5 Vurnary, Rus.
93/F4 Vŭrshets, Bul.
95/P5 Vvedenka, Kaz.
151/A4 Vwawa, Tanz.
118/B3 Vyāra, India
53/H3 Vyatka, Rus.
95/L4 Vyatka (riv.), Rus.
95/L4 Vyatka Obl., Rus.
95/L4 Vyatskiye Polyany, Rus.
94/J4 Vyatskoye, Rus.
109/L2 Vyazemskiy, Rus.
94/G5 Vyaz'ma, Rus.
95/N5 Vyazovaya, Rus.
63/N1 Vyborg, Rus.
63/N1 Vyborg (bay), Rus.
95/K3 Vychegda (riv.), Rus.
65/H3 Východočeský (reg.), Czh.
65/L4 Východoslovenský (reg.), Slvk.
94/G3 Vygozero (lake), Rus.
65/M4 Vyhorlat (peak), Slvk.
94/J5 Vyksa, Rus.
95/L3 Vym' (riv.), Rus.
94/G4 Vypolzovo, Rus.
63/P2 Vyritsa, Rus.
58/C1 Vyrnwy (riv.), Wal,UK
99/K5 Vyselki, Rus.
98/F2 Vyshgorod, Ukr.
63/N3 Vyshgorodok, Rus.
94/G4 Vyshniy Volochek, Rus.
65/J4 Vyškov, Czh.
73/C3 Vyškovce nad Ipl'om, Slvk.
109/M1 Vysokogornyy, Rus.
99/G4 Vysokopol'ye, Ukr.
94/H4 Vysokovsk, Rus.
65/M2 Vysokoye, Bela.
63/N1 Vysotsk, Rus.
71/H5 Vyšší Brod, Czh.
94/H3 Vytegra, Rus.
95/J5 Vyyezdnoye, Rus.
109/N2 Vzmor'ye, Rus.

W

145/E4 Wa, Gha.
150/B5 Waajid, Som.
70/D7 Waal, Ger.
66/C5 Waal (riv.), Neth.
66/C6 Waalre, Neth.
66/C5 Waalwijk, Neth.
131/E4 Waanyi-Garawa Abor. Land, Austl.
68/C1 Waarschoot, Belg.
196/D3 Waasis, NB,Can
131/F1 Wabag, PNG
183/G1 Wabamun, Ab,Can
183/G1 Wabamun (lake), Ab,Can
197/L2 Wabana, Nf,Can
178/E3 Wabasca (riv.), Ab,Can
198/C4 Wabash (riv.), Il, In,US
198/D4 Wabash, In,US
193/H1 Wabasha, Mn,US
193/G1 Wabasso, Mn,US
150/B4 Wabē Gestro Wenz (riv.), Eth.
193/K1 Wabeno, Wi,US
67/G6 Wabern, Ger.
150/B4 Wabē Shebelē Wenz (Webi Shabeele) (riv.), Eth.
195/H3 Wabigoon, On,Can
195/H3 Wabigoon (lake), On,Can
65/K2 Wąbrzeźno, Pol.
115/D4 Wabu (lake), China
113/G6 Wabu, SKor.
131/F2 Wabuda (isl.), PNG
201/H4 Waccamaw (riv.), NC, SC,US
203/G3 Waccasassa (bay), Fl,US
111/L9 Wachi, Japan
150/A4 Wach'īlē, Eth.
68/C1 Wachtebeke, Belg.
66/D6 Wachtendonk, Ger.
70/C2 Wächtersbach, Ger.
196/B4 Wachusett (mtn.), Ma,US
208/C1 Wachusett (res.), Ma,US
69/H4 Wackernheim, Ger.
71/F4 Wackersdorf, Ger.
189/F2 Waco, Tx,US
191/E1 Waconda (lake), Ks,US
195/N7 Waconia, Mn,US
195/N7 Waconia (lake), Mn,US
111/J7 Wada, Japan
149/G2 Wad al Ḩaddād, Sudan
149/G2 Wad an Nail, Sudan
149/E2 Wad Bandah, Sudan
135/D3 Wadbilliga Nat'l Park, Austl.
146/C2 Waddān, Libya
146/C2 Waddān, Jabal (hills), Libya
187/F4 Waddell (dam), Az,US
66/C2 Waddenzee (sound), Neth.
182/B2 Waddington (mtn.), BC,Can
57/F4 Waddington, Eng,UK
57/H5 Waddington, Eng,UK
66/B4 Waddinxveen, Neth.
134/D4 Waddy (pt.), Austl.
191/F4 Wade, Ok,US
58/B5 Wadebridge, Eng,UK
194/C2 Wadena, Sk,Can
195/G4 Wadena, Mn,US
81/E3 Wädenswil, Swi.
69/F4 Wadern, Ger.
67/F5 Wadersloh, Ger.
201/G3 Wadesboro, NC,US
69/F5 Wadgassen, Ger.
149/G1 Wad Ḩāmid, Sudan
59/G4 Wadhurst, Eng,UK
103/D4 Wādī As Sīr, Jor.
141/W17 Wādī Az Zarqā', Tun.
147/F4 Wādī Ḩalfā', Sudan
103/D4 Wādī Mūsá, Jor.
206/D4 Wading (riv.), NJ,US
207/F2 Wading River, NY,US
201/F4 Wadley, Ga,US
149/G2 Wad Medanī, Sudan
65/K4 Wadowice, Pol.
205/Q15 Wadsworth, Il,US
208/F5 Wadsworth, Oh,US
189/G3 Wadsworth, Tx,US
113/E5 Waegwan, SKor.
189/F3 Waelder, Tx,US
113/B3 Wafangdian, China
117/F1 Wafangdian, China
152/E3 Wafania, Zaire
70/D2 Waffenrod, Ger.
151/A1 Wagagai (peak), Ugan.
122/C2 Wāgah, Pak.
130/C3 Wagait Abor. Land, Austl.
123/B3 Wagaru, Burma
148/D2 Wagat, Ouadi (dry riv.), Chad
201/G4 Wagener, SC,US
64/E2 Wagenfeld, Ger.
67/F3 Wagenfeld-Hasslingen, Ger.
66/C5 Wageningen, Neth.
166/B1 Wageningen, Sur.
178/G2 Wager (bay), NW,Can
135/C2 Wagga Wagga, Austl.
132/B4 Waggrakine, Austl.
70/B4 Waghäusel, Ger.
132/C5 Wagin, Austl.
71/F7 Waging am See, Ger.
71/F7 Waginger See (lake), Ger.
81/E3 Wägitalersee (lake), Swi.
75/L3 Wagna, Aus.
192/E2 Wagner, SD,US
191/G3 Wagoner, Ok,US
184/D2 Wagontire, Or,US
65/J2 Wągrowiec, Pol.
107/K2 Wāh, Pak.
127/G4 Wahai, Indo.
147/F4 Wāḩat Salīmah (well), Sudan
195/H4 Wahkon, Mn,US
80/D4 Wahlern, Swi.
62/D4 Wahlstedt, Ger.
193/F3 Wahoo, Ne,US
194/F4 Wahpeton, ND,US
193/F1 Wahpeton-Sisseton Ind. Res., SD,US
67/H3 Wahrenholz, Ger.
185/G4 Wah Wah (mts.), Ut,US
118/B4 Wai, India
180/S10 Waialee, Hi,US
180/S10 Waialua, Hi,US
136/D2 Waiapu (riv.), N.Z.
136/C3 Waiau, N.Z.
136/C3 Waiau (riv.), N.Z.
136/D2 Waiau (riv.), N.Z.
127/E5 Waibakul, Indo.
115/D2 Waibamiao, China
70/B4 Waibstadt, Ger.
71/F3 Waidhaus, Ger.
75/L2 Waidhofen an der Thaya, Aus.
75/L3 Waidhofen an der Ybbs, Aus.
127/H3 Waigeo (isl.), Indo.
70/D3 Waigolshausen, Ger.
108/H3 Waigoumen, China
136/G6 Waiheke (isl.), N.Z.
136/C2 Waihou (riv.), N.Z.
153/F3 Waika, Zaire
127/E5 Waikabubak, Indo.
136/C3 Waikanae, N.Z.
136/C3 Waikari, N.Z.
136/C2 Waikato (reg.), N.Z.
136/C2 Waikato (riv.), N.Z.
133/H5 Waikerie, Austl.
180/T10 Waikiki, Hi,US
180/U11 Waikoloa Village, Hi,US
136/B4 Waikouaiti, N.Z.
180/T10 Wailuku, Hi,US
117/F4 Wailuo, China
136/C3 Waimangaroa, N.Z.
180/S10 Waimea, Hi,US
69/F3 Waimes, Belg.
197/S10 Wainfleet, On,Can
57/J5 Wainfleet All Saints, Eng,UK
120/B4 Waingangā (riv.), India
127/F5 Waingapu, Indo.
165/G2 Waini (riv.), Guy.
136/J9 Wainuiomata, N.Z.
136/H9 Wainuiomata (riv.), N.Z.
183/J1 Wainwright, Ab,Can
177/F1 Wainwright, Ak,US
191/G3 Wainwright, Ok,US
136/J8 Waiohine (riv.), N.Z.
180/S10 Waipahu, Hi,US
136/B4 Waipapa (pt.), N.Z.
136/C3 Waipara, N.Z.
136/D2 Waipawa, N.Z.
180/U10 Waipio, Hi,US
136/D2 Waipiro, N.Z.
136/C3 Waipukurau, N.Z.
136/J9 Wairarapa (lake), N.Z.
136/C3 Wairarapa (reg.), N.Z.
136/C3 Wairau (riv.), N.Z.
136/D2 Wairoa, N.Z.
136/C1 Wairoa (riv.), N.Z.
71/E3 Waischenfeld, Ger.
136/F6 Waitakere (range), N.Z.
136/B4 Waitaki (riv.), N.Z.
136/E3 Waitangi, N.Z.
136/C2 Waitara, N.Z.
196/D3 Waite, Me,US
136/F6 Waitemata, N.Z.
136/F6 Waitemata (har.), N.Z.
136/C2 Waitotara, N.Z.
182/E4 Waitsburg, Wa,US
136/C2 Waiuku, N.Z.
139/Z17 Waiyevu, Fiji
71/G6 Waizenkirchen, Aus.
111/E2 Wajima, Japan
151/C1 Wajir, Kenya
149/H4 Waka, Eth.
127/G4 Waka (cape), Indo.
152/E2 Waka, Zaire
152/E3 Waka, Zaire
136/B4 Wakapitu (lake), N.Z.
198/C4 Wakarusa, In,US
110/D3 Wakasa, Japan
110/D3 Wakasa (bay), Japan
183/M1 Wakaw, Sk,Can
110/D3 Wakayama, Japan
110/D4 Wakayama (pref.), Japan
138/F3 Wake (isl.), PacUS
190/E1 WaKeeney, Ks,US
57/G4 Wakefield, Eng,UK
191/F1 Wakefield, Ks,US
198/B1 Wakefield, Mi,US
193/F2 Wakefield, Ne,US
198/E5 Wakefield, Oh,US
208/C3 Wakefield-Peacedale, RI,US
116/B5 Wakema, Burma
208/E5 Wakeman, Oh,US
110/D3 Waki, Japan
191/F2 Wakita, Ok,US
112/B1 Wakkanai, Japan
111/H7 Wakō, Japan
135/C2 Wakool, Austl.
194/D5 Wakpala, SD,US
152/C5 Waku Kungo, Ang.
203/F2 Wakulla, Fl,US
112/B4 Wakuya, Japan
148/B4 Wal (peak), Camr.
151/A3 Wala (riv.), Tanz.
93/G3 Walachia (range), Rom.
93/G3 Walachia (reg.), Rom.
109/J1 Walagan, China
132/D2 Walagunya Abor. Land, Austl.
155/F2 Walamba, Zam.
149/F4 Wal Athiang, Sudan
65/J3 Wałbrzych, Pol.
65/J3 Wałbrzych (prov.), Pol.
59/E4 Walbury (hill), Eng,UK
135/D1 Walcha, Austl.
81/H2 Walchensee (lake), Ger.
66/A5 Walcheren (isl.), Neth.
185/G2 Walcott (lake), Id,US
194/F4 Walcott, ND,US
185/K3 Walcott, Wy,US
68/D3 Walcourt, Belg.
65/J2 Wałcz, Pol.
71/F4 Wald, Ger.
81/E3 Wald, Swi.
71/H6 Waldaist (riv.), Aus.
69/F4 Waldbillig, Lux.
69/G2 Waldbreitbach, Ger.
69/G2 Waldbröl, Ger.
70/B5 Waldbronn, Ger.
70/C3 Waldbrunn, Ger.
81/F2 Waldburg, Ger.
183/L2 Waldeck, Sk,Can
67/G6 Waldeck, Ger.
198/F1 Walden, On,Can
192/A3 Walden, Co,US
70/C5 Waldenbuch, Ger.
70/C4 Waldenburg, Ger.
72/C6 Waldenburg, Ger.
80/D3 Waldenburg, Swi.
71/F3 Waldershof, Ger.
69/G3 Waldesch, Ger.
69/G5 Waldfischbach-Burgalben, Ger.
72/D5 Waldheim, Ger.
80/D2 Waldighofen, Fr.
67/G6 Waldkappel, Ger.
70/A6 Waldkirch, Ger.
71/F6 Waldkraiburg, Ger.
69/G5 Waldmohr, Ger.
71/F4 Waldmünchen, Ger.
71/F3 Waldnaab (riv.), Ger.
191/H4 Waldo, Ar,US
203/G3 Waldo, Fl,US
184/B2 Waldo (lake), Or,US
201/J1 Waldorf, Md,US
184/A1 Waldport, Or,US
69/F4 Waldrach, Ger.
191/G3 Waldron, Ar,US
198/D5 Waldron, In,US
71/F3 Waldsassen, Ger.
81/E2 Waldshut-Tiengen, Ger.
70/C5 Waldstetten, Ger.
75/L2 Waldviertel (reg.), Aus.
207/J7 Waldwick, NJ,US
127/F4 Walea (str.), Indo.
127/F4 Waleabahi (isl.), Indo.
81/F3 Walensee (lake), Swi.
81/F3 Walenstadt, Swi.
179/H2 Wales (isl.), NW,Can
55/J10 Wales, UK
177/E2 Wales, Ak,US
208/B1 Wales, Ma,US
185/H4 Wales, Ut,US
205/P13 Wales, Wi,US
145/E4 Walewale, Gha.
69/F4 Walferdange, Lux.
208/G6 Walford (Bessemer), Pa,US
135/D1 Walgett, Austl.
137/T Walgreen (coast), Ant.
71/F4 Walhalla, Ger.
198/C3 Walhalla, Mi,US
194/F3 Walhalla, ND,US
201/F3 Walhalla, SC,US
194/F3 Walhalla Hist. Site, ND,US
208/E7 Walhonding (riv.), Oh,US
153/G3 Walikale, Zaire
156/L11 Walker (bay), SAfr.
198/D3 Walker, Mi,US
195/G4 Walker, Mn,US
191/G2 Walker, Mo,US
184/D4 Walker (lake), Nv,US
184/D4 Walker (riv.), Nv,US
195/P7 Walker Art Ctr., Mn,US
54/C5 Walkerburn, Sc,UK
184/D4 Walker River Ind. Res., Nv,US
155/G2 Walkers Ferry, Malw.
134/C3 Walkerston, Austl.
206/A5 Walkersville, Md,US
198/F2 Walkerton, On,Can
198/C4 Walkerton, In,US
201/G2 Walkertown, NC,US

206/D1 Walkill (riv.), NJ.,NY,US
192/C2 Wall, SD,US
188/D2 Wall, Tx,US
196/F3 Wallace, NS,Can
184/C4 Wallace, Ca,US
182/G4 Wallace, Id,US
192/D4 Wallace, Ks,US
201/J3 Wallace, NC,US
192/D3 Wallace, Ne,US
205/H6 Wallaceburg, On,Can
195/G2 Wallace Lake, Mb,Can
135/D2 Wallacia, Austl.
196/C2 Wallagrass, Me,US
132/D1 Wallal Downs, Austl.
132/D1 Wallal Station, Austl.
133/H5 Wallaroo, Austl.
57/E5 Wallasey, Eng,UK
135/C2 Walla Walla, Austl.
182/E4 Walla Walla, Wa,US
70/B4 Walldorf, Ger.
70/D1 Walldorf, Ger.
70/C3 Walldürn, Ger.
205/F6 Walled (lake), Mi,US
113/G7 Walled City, SKor.
205/F6 Walled Lake, Mi,US
135/D2 Wallendbeen, Austl.
72/C5 Wallendorf, Ger.
67/F4 Wallenhorst, Ger.
199/J4 Wallenpaupack (lake), Pa,US
189/G2 Waller, Tx,US
73/A4 Wallern im Burgenland, Aus.
68/C3 Wallers, Fr.
71/F5 Wallersdorf, Ger.
71/G7 Wallersee (lake), Aus.
70/D5 Wallerstein, Ger.
72/B5 Wallhausen, Ger.
59/E3 Wallingford, Eng,UK
208/B3 Wallingford, Ct,US
207/J8 Wallington, NJ,US
139/H6 Wallis (isls.), Wall.
138/G6 Wallis & Futuna (terr.), Fr.
81/E3 Wallisellen, Swi.
189/G3 Wallisville, Tx,US
184/E1 Wallowa (mts.), Or,US
184/E1 Wallowa (riv.), Or,US
55/P12 Walls, Sc,UK
185/H3 Wallsburg, Ut,US
57/G2 Wallsend, Eng,UK
182/E4 Wallula, Wa,US
134/C4 Wallumbilla, Austl.
57/E3 Walney, Isle of (isl.), Eng,UK
204/C2 Walnut, Ca,US
201/M8 Walnut (cr.), Ga,US
193/K3 Walnut, Il,US
190/E1 Walnut (cr.), Ks,US
191/F2 Walnut (riv.), Ks,US
200/C3 Walnut, Ms,US
188/K7 Walnut (cr.), Tx,US
187/G3 Walnut Canyon Nat'l Mon., Az,US
205/K11 Walnut Creek, Ca,US
208/F6 Walnut Creek, Oh,US
200/D3 Walnut Grove, Al,US
205/L10 Walnut Grove, Ca,US
200/F4 Walnut Grove, Ga,US
191/H2 Walnut Grove, Mo,US
200/C4 Walnut Grove, Ms,US
204/F8 Walnut Park, Ca,US
206/C2 Walnutport, Pa,US
191/J2 Walnut Ridge, Ar,US
189/F1 Walnut Springs, Tx,US
132/C5 Walpole, Austl.
208/C1 Walpole, Ma,US
199/K3 Walpole, NH,US
205/G6 Walpole I. Ind. Res., On,Can
132/C5 Walpole-Nornalup Nat'l Park, Austl.
177/F4 Walrus (isls.), Ak,US
58/E1 Walsall, Eng,UK
72/A5 Walschleben, Ger.
190/B2 Walsenburg, Co,US
134/A2 Walsh, Austl.
190/C2 Walsh, Co,US
179/K2 Walsingham (cape), NW,Can
59/G1 Walsingham, Eng,UK
67/G3 Walsrode, Ger.
202/M7 Walt Disney World, Fl,US
203/H3 Walt Disney World, Fl,US
81/G2 Waltenhofen, Ger.
201/G4 Walterboro, SC,US
206/C1 Walter, F.E. (res.), Pa,US
200/E4 Walter F. George (res.), Al, Ga,US
202/C2 Walters, La,US
191/E3 Walters, Ok,US
184/B1 Walterville, Or,US
200/C4 Walthall, Ms,US
208/C1 Waltham, Ma,US
53/P6 Waltham Abbey, Eng,UK
53/N7 Waltham Forest (bor.), Eng,UK
59/G3 Waltham Holy Cross, Eng,UK
193/F2 Walthill, Ne,US
201/G5 Walthourville, Ga,US
185/K2 Waltman, Wy,US
198/C4 Walton, In,US
200/E1 Walton, Ky,US
199/J3 Walton, NY,US
201/G1 Walton, WV,US
208/F5 Walton Hills, Oh,US
57/F4 Walton-le-Dale, Eng,UK
59/F4 Walton on Thames, Eng,UK
59/H3 Walton on the Naze, Eng,UK
67/E5 Waltrop, Ger.
121/F2 Walungchung Gola, Nepal
154/B4 Walvisbaai (Walvis Bay), SAfr.
154/B4 Walvis Bay (Walvisbaai), SAfr.
205/N14 Walworth, Wi,US
205/P14 Walworth (co.), Wi,US
132/C4 Walyahmoning (peak), Austl.
132/L6 Walyunga Nat'l Park, Austl.
81/F3 Walzenhausen, Swi.
154/B2 Wama, Ang.
193/K4 Wamac, Il,US
153/F4 Wamaza, Zaire
151/B1 Wamba, Kenya
145/H4 Wamba, Nga.
153/F2 Wamba, Zaire
191/F1 Wamego, Ks,US
66/C5 Wamel, Neth.
127/J4 Wamena, Indo.
151/B3 Wami (riv.), Tanz.
184/C1 Wamic, Or,US
57/E2 Wampool (riv.), Eng,UK
199/J3 Wampsville, NY,US
208/G6 Wampum, Pa,US
185/K3 Wamsutter, Wy,US
115/D5 Wan (riv.), China
135/C1 Wanaaring, Austl.
136/B4 Wanaka, N.Z.
136/B4 Wanaka (lake), N.Z.
207/D3 Wanamassa, NJ,US
193/H1 Wanamingo, Mn,US
182/E4 Wanapum (dam), Wa,US
207/D1 Wanaque, NJ,US
207/H7 Wanaque (res.), NJ,US
192/D2 Wanblee, SD,US
130/A1 Wanci, Indo.
109/L2 Wanda (mts.), China
132/C5 Wandering, Austl.
153/G2 Wandi, Ugan.
116/C3 Wanding, China
72/D2 Wandlitz, Ger.
113/D5 Wando, SKor.
134/C4 Wandoan, Austl.
67/H1 Wandsbek, Ger.
53/N7 Wandsworth (bor.), Eng,UK
191/F3 Wanette, Ok,US
67/H6 Wanfried, Ger.
113/B2 Wanfu, China
123/B2 Wang (riv.), Thai.
135/C2 Wanganella, Austl.
136/C2 Wanganui, N.Z.
136/C2 Wanganui (reg.), N.Z.
135/C3 Wangaratta, Austl.
145/E4 Wangasi Turu, Gha.
117/F2 Wangcun, China
115/C3 Wangdu, China
121/G2 Wangdü Phodrang, Bhu.
81/F2 Wangen, Ger.
80/D3 Wangen an der Aare, Swi.
80/D3 Wangen bei Olten, Swi.
67/E1 Wangerooge (arpt.), Ger.
67/E1 Wangerooge (isl.), Ger.
127/F6 Wanggamet (peak), Indo.
117/F3 Wanggao, China
113/A2 Wanghai (peak), China
113/A2 Wanghai Shan (peak), China
123/B4 Wang Hip (peak), Thai.
81/E3 Wängi, Swi.
130/A1 Wangiwangi (isl.), Indo.
115/D5 Wangjiang, China
113/B2 Wangjiapu, China
109/K2 Wangkui, China
117/G3 Wangling, China
117/F4 Wangmao, China
116/E3 Wangmo, China
123/C3 Wang Noi, Thai.
144/D4 Wangolodougou, IvC.
113/D1 Wangou, China
115/L9 Wangpan (bay), China
117/J2 Wangpang (sea), China
109/K3 Wangqing, China
113/C2 Wangqingmen, China
123/C2 Wang Saphung, Thai.
117/J2 Wangtan, China
116/D5 Wang Thong, Thai.
115/L8 Wangting, China
123/B1 Wān Hsa-la, Burma
116/C5 Wān Hwè-ün, Burma
127/F4 Wani (peak), Indo.
166/C1 Wanica (dist.), Sur.
153/F2 Wanie-Rukula, Zaire
133/G5 Wanilla, Austl.
198/F1 Wanipitie (lake), On,Can
198/F1 Wanipitie (riv.), On,Can
117/G2 Wanjiahu, China
113/B3 Wanjialing, China
81/H2 Wank (peak), Ger.
155/E3 Wankie (Hwange) Nat'l Park, Zim.
150/C5 Wanle Weyne, Som.
191/G2 Wann, Ok,US
195/G3 Wannaska, Mn,US
72/B3 Wanne (riv.), Ger.
119/K4 Wanning, China
146/B2 Wannīn, 'Uwaynat (well), Libya
111/M9 Wanouchi, Japan
115/C2 Wanquan, China
114/D5 Wanquan (lake), China
117/F5 Wanquan (riv.), China
115/B4 Wanrong, China
57/G1 Wansbeck (riv.), Eng,UK
117/E2 Wanshengchang, China
127/H4 Wansra, Indo.
53/P7 Wanstead, Eng,UK
59/E3 Wantage, Eng,UK
207/L9 Wantagh, NY,US
117/F2 Wantan, China
153/G5 Wantipa-Mweru Nat'l Park, Zam.
123/E1 Wanwei, China
117/F2 Wanxian, China
69/E2 Wanze, Belg.
72/B3 Wanzleben, Ger.
125/D4 Wao, Phil.
198/D4 Wapakoneta, Oh,US
200/B3 Wapanocca Nat'l Wild. Ref., Ar,US
191/F3 Wapanucka, Ok,US
182/D4 Wapato, Wa,US
194/D2 Wapella, Sk,Can
193/J3 Wapello, Ia,US
131/F1 Wapenamanda, PNG
153/E2 Wapinda, Zaire
185/J1 Wapiti, Wy,US
188/K7 Waples, Tx,US
127/J4 Wapoga (riv.), Indo.
200/B2 Wappapello (lake), Mo,US
199/K4 Wappingers Falls, NY,US
193/J3 Wapsipinicon (riv.), Ia,US
196/D2 Wapske, NB,Can
206/B1 Wapwallopen, Pa,US
206/B1 Wapwallopen (cr.), Pa,US
201/G2 War, WV,US
111/H7 Warabi, Japan
118/C4 Warangal, India
120/C3 Wārāseoni, India
135/C4 Waratah, Austl.
195/H4 Warba, Mn,US
59/F2 Warboys, Eng,UK
183/G1 Warburg, Ab,Can
67/G6 Warburg, Ger.
133/E3 Warburton, Austl.
133/H3 Warburton (cr.), Austl.
122/B2 Warburton, Pak.
133/E3 Warburton (Central Australia) Abor. Rsv., Austl.
133/E3 Warburton Range Abor. Rsv., Austl.
69/F3 Warche (riv.), Belg.
136/C3 Ward, N.Z.
200/B3 Ward, Ar,US
177/M4 Ward Cove, Ak,US
156/E2 Warden, SAfr.
59/G4 Warden (pt.), Eng,UK
182/E4 Warden, Wa,US
67/F2 Wardenburg, Ger.
118/C3 Wardha, India
131/H2 Ward Hunt (cape), PNG
183/J2 Wardlow, Ab,Can
127/J4 Wardo, Indo.
57/F3 Ward's Stone (mtn.), Eng,UK
193/H4 Wardsville, Mo,US
59/F3 Ware, Eng,UK
208/B1 Ware, Ma,US
208/B1 Ware (riv.), Ma,US
68/C2 Waregem, Belg.
58/D5 Wareham, Eng,UK
208/D2 Wareham, Ma,US
69/E2 Waremme, Belg.
64/G2 Waren, Ger.
127/J4 Waren, Indo.
67/E5 Warendorf, Ger.
201/F3 Ware Shoals, SC,US
207/D4 Waretown, NJ,US
66/D2 Warffum, Neth.
182/F3 Warfield, BC,Can
59/F3 Wargrave, Eng,UK
183/K4 War Horse Nat'l Wild. Ref., Mt,US
135/D1 Warialda, Austl.
123/D3 Warin Chamrap, Thai.
189/E3 Waring, Tx,US
56/B3 Waringstown, NI,UK
57/F1 Wark, Eng,UK
65/L3 Warka, Pol.
199/H2 Warkworth, On,Can
136/C2 Warkworth, N.Z.
58/D2 Warley, Eng,UK
53/N8 Warlingham, Eng,UK
130/D4 Warlmanpa Abor. Land, Austl.
194/A1 Warman, Sk,Can
156/B3 Warmbad, Namb.
156/E2 Warmbad, SAfr.
67/G6 Warmebach (riv.), Ger.
67/H5 Warme Bode (riv.), Ger.
66/B3 Warmenhuizen, Neth.
68/D5 Warmeriville, Fr.
65/K1 Warmia (reg.), Pol.
58/D4 Warminster, Eng,UK
206/C3 Warminster, Pa,US
184/F1 Warm Lake, Id,US
184/C1 Warm Springs, Or,US
184/D2 Warm Springs (res.), Or,US
201/H1 Warm Springs, Va,US
184/C1 Warm Springs Ind. Res., Or,US
64/G1 Warnemünde, Ger.
184/C3 Warner (mts.), Ca,US
191/G3 Warner, Ok,US
194/E5 Warner, SD,US
200/F4 Warner Robins, Ga,US
172/D1 Warnes, Bol.
64/G2 Warnow (riv.), Ger.
66/D4 Warnsveld, Neth.
132/B5 Waroona, Austl.
131/F1 Waropko, Indo.
133/G2 Warrabri, Austl.
133/G2 Warrabri Abor. Land, Austl.
135/C3 Warragamba, Austl.
131/D3 Warrakunta (pt.), Austl.
133/G2 Warramunga Abor. Land, Austl.
133/H3 Warrandirinna (lake), Austl.
135/G5 Warrandyte, Austl.
134/B4 Warrego (range), Austl.
135/C1 Warrego (riv.), Austl.
135/C1 Warren, Austl.
132/C5 Warren (riv.), Austl.
177/M2 Warren (pt.), NW,Can
191/H4 Warren, Ar,US
186/C2 Warren (mtn.), Ca,US
208/A2 Warren, Ct,US
184/F1 Warren, Id,US
198/D4 Warren, In,US
208/B1 Warren, Ma,US
205/F6 Warren, Mi,US
194/F3 Warren, Mn,US
183/H5 Warren (peak), Mt,US
206/D2 Warren, NJ,US
206/C1 Warren (co.), NJ,US
208/G5 Warren, Oh,US
182/C5 Warren, Or,US
199/G4 Warren, Pa,US
208/C2 Warren, RI,US
192/B3 Warren (F.E.) A.F.B., Wy,US
56/B3 Warrenpoint, NI,UK
193/J1 Warrens, Wi,US
191/H1 Warrensburg, Mo,US
199/K3 Warrensburg, NY,US
208/F5 Warrensville Heights, Oh,US
156/D3 Warrenton, SAfr.
201/F4 Warrenton, Ga,US
191/J1 Warrenton, Mo,US
201/H2 Warrenton, NC,US
182/C4 Warrenton, Or,US
201/J1 Warrenton, Va,US
208/B2 Warrenville, Ct,US
205/P16 Warrenville, Il,US
145/G5 Warri, Nga.
133/G4 Warrina, Austl.
57/F5 Warrington, Eng,UK
131/F2 Warrior (reefs), Austl.
200/D4 Warrior, Al,US
135/B3 Warrnambool, Austl.
195/G3 Warroad, Mn,US
135/D1 Warrumbungle Nat'l Park, Austl.
198/D4 Warsaw, In,US
200/E1 Warsaw, Ky,US
191/H1 Warsaw, Mo,US
201/H3 Warsaw, NC,US
199/G3 Warsaw, NY,US
208/E7 Warsaw, Oh,US
201/J2 Warsaw, Va,US
65/L3 Warsawa (prov.), Pol.
65/L2 Warsawa (Warsaw) (cap.), Pol.
65/H5 Warscheneck (peak), Aus.
150/C5 Warshiikh, Som.
57/G5 Warslow, Eng,UK
57/G5 Warsop, Eng,UK
72/B4 Warstein, Ger.
65/L2 Warszawa (Warsaw) (cap.), Pol.
65/H2 Warta (riv.), Pol.
71/H7 Wartberg an der Krems, Aus.
200/E2 Wartburg, Tn,US
201/F4 Warthen, Ga,US
200/D3 Wartrace, Tn,US
127/H4 Waru, Indo.
135/E1 Warwick, Austl.
59/E2 Warwick, Eng,UK
200/F5 Warwick, Ga,US
206/C5 Warwick, Md,US
207/D1 Warwick, NY,US
208/C2 Warwick, RI,US
59/E2 Warwickshire (co.), Eng,UK
182/G3 Wasa, BC,Can
145/G4 Wasagu, Nga.
185/H4 Wasatch (range), Id, Ut,US
122/B2 Wasāwewāla, Pak.
157/E3 Wasbank, SAfr.
183/M2 Wascana (riv.), Sk,Can
186/C3 Wasco, Ca,US
195/J4 Wascott, Wi,US
193/H1 Waseca, Mn,US
195/F2 Washaw (bay), Mb,Can
178/F1 Washburn (lake), NW,Can
57/G4 Washburn (riv.), Eng,UK
196/C2 Washburn, Me,US
194/D4 Washburn, ND,US
193/H2 Washburn, Wi,US
136/C4 Washdyke, N.Z.
57/H5 Washingborough, Eng,UK
57/G2 Washington, Eng,UK
182/D4 Washington (state), US
208/A2 Washington, Ct,US
206/A6 Washington (cap.), DC,US
201/F4 Washington, Ga,US
193/J3 Washington, Ia,US
193/K3 Washington, Il,US
198/C5 Washington, In,US
191/F1 Washington, Ks,US
200/F1 Washington, Ky,US
202/B2 Washington, La,US
208/A1 Washington, Ma,US
195/G6 Washington (co.), Mn,US
191/J1 Washington, Mo,US
202/C2 Washington, Ms,US
201/J3 Washington, NC,US
196/B3 Washington (mtn.), NH,US
206/D2 Washington, NJ,US
198/F4 Washington, Pa,US
208/G7 Washington (co.), Pa,US
208/C2 Washington (co.), RI,US
189/F2 Washington, Tx,US
187/F2 Washington, Ut,US
201/H1 Washington, Va,US
205/C2 Washington (lake), Wa,US
182/C4 Washington (mtn.), Wa,US
198/C2 Washington (isl.), Wi,US
198/F5 Washington, WV,US
206/B5 Washington-Baltimore (int'l arpt.), Md,US
198/E5 Washington C. H. (Washington), Oh,US
208/A2 Washington Depot, Ct,US
199/H5 Washington Dulles (int'l arpt.), Va,US
206/A6 Washington Nat'l (int'l arpt.), DC,US
139/K4 Washington (Teraina) (isl.), Kiri.
208/G6 Washingtonville, Oh,US
206/B1 Washingtonville, Pa,US
198/E5 Washington (Washington Court House), Oh,US
191/F3 Washita (riv.), Ok, Tx,US
191/E3 Washita Nat'l Wild. Ref., Ok,US
146/B2 Washkah, Bi'r al (well), Libya
205/E7 Washtenaw (co.), Mi,US
59/G1 Wash, The (bay), Eng,UK
182/E4 Washtucna, Wa,US
65/M2 Wasilków, Pol.
177/J3 Wasilla, Ak,US
127/H4 Wasior, Indo.
130/B1 Wasiri, Indo.
105/F3 Wāsit (gov.), Iraq
194/D3 Waskada, Mb,Can
179/J3 Waskaganish (Rupert House), Qu,Can
177/G4 Waskey (mtn.), Ak,US
130/C1 Wasletan, Indo.
161/F3 Waspam, Nic.
203/H2 Wassaw Nat'l Wild. Ref., Ga,US
69/G6 Wasselonne, Fr.
81/E4 Wassen, Swi.
66/B4 Wassenaar, Neth.
66/D6 Wassenberg, Ger.
154/C5 Wasser, Namb.
69/F4 Wasserbillig, Lux.
70/D6 Wasserburg, Ger.
71/F6 Wasserburg am Inn, Ger.
70/C2 Wasserkuppe (peak), Ger.
69/F4 Wasserliesch, Ger.
70/D4 Wassertrüdingen, Ger.
144/B4 Wassou, Gui.
186/C1 Wassuk (range), Nv,US
80/A1 Wassy, Fr.
57/E3 Wast Water (lake), Eng,UK
131/G1 Wasu, PNG
193/J3 Wataga, Il,US
127/F4 Watampone, Indo.
111/M10 Watarai, Japan
111/F2 Watarase (riv.), Japan
111/G1 Watari, Japan
201/G2 Watauga (lake), Tn,US
188/K7 Watauga, Tx,US
123/C2 Wat Bot, Thai.
58/C4 Watchet, Eng,UK
59/E3 Watchfield, Eng,UK
208/C3 Watch Hill (pt.), RI,US
207/H9 Watchung, NJ,US
207/H9 Watchung (mts.), NJ,US
59/G2 Waterbeach, Eng,UK
154/C4 Waterberg, Namb.
155/E5 Waterberge (mts.), SAfr.
154/C4 Waterberg Plat. Park, Namb.
208/A2 Waterbury, Ct,US
199/K2 Waterbury, Vt,US
197/R9 Waterdown, On,Can
201/G3 Wateree (lake), SC,US
187/H2 Waterflow, NM,US
60/C5 Waterford, Ire.
60/C5 Waterford (arpt.), Ire.
60/C5 Waterford (co.), Ire.
60/D5 Waterford (harb.), Ire.
186/B2 Waterford, Ca,US
208/B3 Waterford, Ct,US
205/F6 Waterford, Mi,US
205/P14 Waterford, Wi,US
206/D4 Waterford Works, NJ,US
48/B6 Watergate (bay), Eng,UK
60/B5 Watergrasshill, Ire.
194/E1 Waterhen (lake), Mb,Can
130/D3 Waterhouse (riv.), Austl.
130/C4 Waterloo, Austl.
68/D2 Waterloo, Belg.
198/F3 Waterloo, On,Can
196/A3 Waterloo, Qu,Can
165/G3 Waterloo, Sur.
193/H2 Waterloo, Ia,US
193/J4 Waterloo, Il,US
199/H3 Waterloo, NY,US
68/D2 Waterloo Battlesite (1815), Belg.
206/D2 Waterloo Vill., NJ,US
59/E5 Waterlooville, Eng,UK
68/D2 Watermael-Boitsfort, Belg.
202/C1 Waterproof, La,US
198/B1 Watersmeet, Mi,US
183/H3 Waterton-Glacier Int'l Peace Park, Can, US
183/H3 Waterton Lakes Nat'l Park, Ab,Can
183/H3 Waterton Park, Ab,Can
208/A2 Watertown, Ct,US
203/G2 Watertown, Fl,US
208/C1 Watertown, Ma,US
195/H7 Watertown, Mn,US
199/J3 Watertown, NY,US
194/F4 Watertown, SD,US
193/K2 Watertown, Wi,US
157/E2 Waterval-Bo, SAfr.
183/G3 Water Valley, Ab,Can
200/C2 Water Valley, Ky,US
200/C3 Water Valley, Ms,US
54/F11 Waterville, Ire.
196/C3 Waterville, Me,US
199/J3 Waterville, NY,US
198/E4 Waterville, Oh,US
182/D4 Waterville, Wa,US
68/C1 Watervliet, Belg.
199/K3 Watervliet, NY,US
198/F3 Watford, On,Can
53/M7 Watford, Eng,UK
194/C4 Watford City, ND,US
149/G3 Wa'th, Sudan
132/C4 Watheroo, Austl.
132/B4 Watheroo Nat'l Park, Austl.
57/G5 Wath-upon-Dearne, Eng,UK
193/G1 Watkins, Mn,US
199/H3 Watkins Glen, NY,US
201/F4 Watkinsville, Ga,US
162/C1 Watling (San Salvador) (isl.), Bahm.
59/F3 Watlington, Eng,UK
123/B2 Wat Mahathat, Thai.
130/C1 Watmuri, Indo.
191/E3 Watonga, Ok,US
193/G1 Watonwan (riv.), Mn,US
127/G3 Watowato (peak), Indo.
116/D5 Wat Phra Si Ratana Mahathat, Thai.
123/D3 Wat Phu, Laos
194/B2 Watrous, Sk,Can
190/B3 Watrous, NM,US
153/G2 Watsa, Zaire
198/C4 Watseka, Il,US
194/B1 Watson, Sk,Can
191/J4 Watson, Ar,US
198/B5 Watson, Il,US
178/D2 Watson Lake, Yk,Can
206/B1 Watsontown, Pa,US
186/B2 Watsonville, Ca,US
68/B2 Watten, Fr.
70/B3 Wattenscheid, Ger.
75/J3 Wattens, Aus.
68/E2 Wattignies, Fr.
59/G1 Watton, Eng,UK
68/C2 Wattrelos, Fr.
204/F8 Watts, Ca,US
200/E3 Watts Bar (dam), Tn,US
200/E3 Watts Bar (lake), Tn,US
81/F3 Wattwil, Swi.
208/C2 Watuppa (pond), Ma,US
123/C2 Wat Xieng Thong, Laos
131/G1 Wau, PNG
194/F5 Waubay, SD,US
192/F1 Waubay (lake), SD,US
192/F1 Waubay Nat'l Wild. Ref., SD,US
194/G4 Waubun, Mn,US
135/E1 Wauchope, Austl.
203/H4 Wauchula, Fl,US
205/P15 Wauconda, Il,US
185/F1 Waugh (mtn.), Id,US
132/D2 Waukarlycarly (lake), Austl.
203/G2 Waukeenah, Fl,US
205/Q15 Waukegan, Il,US
205/P13 Waukesha, Wi,US
205/P14 Waukesha (co.), Wi,US
191/F2 Waukomis, Ok,US
193/J2 Waukon, Ia,US
205/B3 Wauna, Wa,US
193/K2 Waunakee, Wi,US
192/D3 Wauneta, Ne,US
58/C3 Waun Fâch (mtn.), Wal,UK
58/C1 Waun Oer (mtn.), UK
193/K1 Waupaca, Wi,US
194/F5 Waupeton-Sisseton Ind. Res., SD,US
193/K2 Waupun, Wi,US
208/C2 Wauregan, Ct,US
191/F3 Waurika, Ok,US
191/E3 Waurika (lake), Ok,US
193/K1 Wausau, Wi,US
193/L1 Wausaukee, Wi,US
198/D4 Wauseon, Oh,US
193/K1 Wautoma, Wi,US
205/P13 Wauwatosa, Wi,US
130/C4 Wave Hill, Austl.
191/H3 Waveland, Ar,US
202/D2 Waveland, Ms,US
59/H2 Waveney (riv.), Eng,UK
57/E2 Waver (riv.), Eng,UK
196/F3 Waverley, NS,Can
136/C2 Waverley, N.Z.
135/B1 Waverley Downs, Austl.
135/G5 Waverly, Austl.
202/M8 Waverly, Fl,US
203/H2 Waverly, Ga,US
193/H2 Waverly, Ia,US
191/G1 Waverly, Ks,US
202/C1 Waverly, La,US
193/F3 Waverly, Ne,US
199/H3 Waverly, NY,US
198/E5 Waverly, Oh,US
200/D2 Waverly, Tn,US
200/E4 Waverly Hall, Ga,US
68/D2 Wavre, Belg.
68/B2 Wavrin, Fr.
149/E4 Wāw, Sudan
179/H4 Wawa, On,Can
145/G4 Wawa, Nga.
161/E3 Wawa (riv.), Nic.
146/C3 Wāw al Kabīr, Libya
194/E3 Wawanesa, Mb,Can
161/E3 Wawasang (mtn.), Nic.
207/H7 Wawayanda St. Park, NJ,US
127/F4 Wawo, Indo.
131/F1 Wawoi (riv.), PNG
194/C3 Wawota, Sk,Can
189/F1 Waxahachie, Tx,US
188/L7 Waxahachie (cr.), Tx,US
69/F3 Waxweiler, Ger.
114/E4 Waxxari, China
201/F3 Wayah (peak), NC,US
127/G4 Wayakuba, Indo.
127/G3 Wayamli, Indo.
135/C4 Wayatinah, Austl.
203/G2 Waycross, Ga,US
127/G4 Waygay, Indo.
127/F4 Wayhaya, Indo.
208/C1 Wayland, Ma,US
198/D3 Wayland, Mi,US
199/H3 Wayland, NY,US
199/J4 Waymart, Pa,US
205/P16 Wayne, Il,US
205/F7 Wayne, Mi,US
205/E7 Wayne (co.), Mi,US
193/F2 Wayne, Ne,US
207/D2 Wayne, NJ,US
199/H3 Wayne, NY,US
208/F6 Wayne (co.), Oh,US
191/F3 Wayne, Ok,US
206/C3 Wayne, Pa,US
206/C1 Wayne (co.), Pa,US
201/F1 Wayne, WV,US
193/K4 Wayne City, Il,US
205/F7 Wayne Co. (Detroit Metro.) (int'l arpt.), Mi,US
201/F4 Waynesboro, Ga,US
200/C5 Waynesboro, Ms,US
199/H5 Waynesboro, Pa,US
200/D3 Waynesboro, Tn,US
201/H1 Waynesboro, Va,US
208/F6 Waynesburg, Oh,US
198/F5 Waynesburg, Pa,US
191/H2 Waynesville, Mo,US
201/F3 Waynesville, NC,US
190/E2 Waynoka, Ok,US
200/B4 Wayside, Ms,US
117/G3 Wayuan, China
148/B3 Waza, Camr.
148/B3 Waza Nat'l Park, Camr.
68/C3 Waziers, Fr.
122/C1 Wazīrābād, Pak.
111/L10 Wazuka, Japan
64/K2 Wda (riv.), Pol.
145/F3 W du Niger Nat'l Park, Afr.
124/A1 We (isl.), Indo.
138/F7 Wé, NCal.
59/G4 Weald, The (grsld.), Eng,UK
57/F2 Wear (riv.), Eng,UK
199/L3 Weare, NH,US
57/F2 Wear Head, Eng,UK
191/E3 Weatherford, Ok,US
189/F1 Weatherford, Tx,US
188/K7 Weatherford (lake), Tx,US
206/C2 Weatherly, Pa,US
208/B2 Weatogue, Ct,US
193/H5 Weaubleau, Mo,US
194/F1 Weaver (lake), Mb,Can
57/F5 Weaver (riv.), Eng,UK
184/B3 Weaverville, Ca,US
201/F3 Weaverville, NC,US
183/K2 Webb, Sk,Can
203/F2 Webb, Al,US
200/B4 Webb, Ms,US
188/D1 Webb A.F.B., Tx,US
191/G2 Webb City, Mo,US
191/E1 Webber, Ks,US
191/G3 Webbers Falls, Ok,US
198/D3 Webberville, Mi,US
195/J4 Weber (mtn.), Mn,US
185/H3 Weber (riv.), Ut,US
150/B4 Webi Shabeele (Shabeelē Wenz) (riv.), Eth.
202/L6 Webster, Fl,US
203/G3 Webster, Fl,US
208/C1 Webster, Ma,US
208/C1 Webster (lake), Ma,US
194/B4 Webster, Mt,US
192/F1 Webster, SD,US
189/M9 Webster, Tx,US
193/H2 Webster City, Ia,US
191/J1 Webster Groves, Mo,US
201/G1 Webster Springs (Addison), WV,US
151/A1 Webuye, Kenya
137/W Weddell (sea), Ant.
175/M7 Weddell (isl.), Falk.
135/B3 Wedderburn, Austl.
67/F1 Wedde-Warden, Ger.
201/G3 Weddington, NC,US
135/C2 Weddin Mountains Nat'l Park, Austl.
67/G1 Wedel, Ger.
67/G3 Wedemark, Ger.
182/C2 Wedge (mtn.), BC,Can
196/E4 Wedgeport, NS,Can
58/D4 Wedmore, Eng,UK
58/D1 Wednesbury, Eng,UK
58/D1 Wednesfield, Eng,UK
200/E4 Wedowee, Al,US
130/D1 Weduar (cape), Indo.
149/E3 Wedweil, Sudan
155/F3 Wedza, Zim.
184/B3 Weed, Ca,US
59/E2 Weedon Bec, Eng,UK
196/B3 Weedon-Centre, Qu,Can
186/C3 Weedpatch, Ca,US
198/C5 Weedpatch (hill), In,US
199/G4 Weedville, Pa,US
207/J8 Weehawken, NJ,US
208/C3 Weekapaug, RI,US
194/C1 Weekes, Sk,Can
202/K6 Weeki Wachee, Fl,US
202/K6 Weeki Wachee Springs, Fl,US
203/G3 Weeki Wachee Springs, Fl,US
189/J3 Weeks, La,US
58/B5 Week Saint Mary, Eng,UK
201/F2 Weeksbury, Ky,US
201/J2 Weeksville, NC,US
157/E3 Weenen, SAfr.
189/F3 Weeping Water, Ne,US
66/D4 Weerselo, Neth.
66/C6 Weert, Neth.
189/F3 Weesatche, Tx,US
81/F3 Weesen, Swi.
66/C4 Weesp, Neth.
135/D1 Wee Waa, Austl.
66/D5 Weeze, Ger.
72/B3 Wefensleben, Ger.
72/B3 Weferlingen, Ger.
66/D6 Wegberg, Ger.
81/E3 Weggis, Swi.
65/L1 Węgorzewo, Pol.
65/M2 Węgrów, Pol.
71/G5 Wegscheid, Ger.
70/B6 Wehingen, Ger.
149/H2 Wehnī, Eth.
80/D2 Wehr, Ger.
80/D2 Wehra (riv.), Ger.
67/G6 Wehre (riv.), Ger.
70/B2 Wehrheim, Ger.
119/H4 Wei (riv.), China
70/C3 Weibersbrunn, Ger.
109/H3 Weichang, China
72/C6 Weida, Ger.
72/B5 Weida (riv.), Ger.
72/C6 Weida (riv.), Ger.
71/F3 Weiden, Ger.
70/B4 Weidenthal, Ger.
198/D3 Weidman, Mi,US
115/D3 Weifang, China
206/B4 Weigelstown, Pa,US
113/B4 Weihai, China
70/D4 Weihenzell, Ger.
70/C4 Weikersheim, Ger.
70/B2 Weil (riv.), Ger.
70/B2 Weilburg, Ger.
70/B5 Weil der Stadt, Ger.
81/F2 Weiler-Simmerberg, Ger.
67/F2 Weilerswist, Ger.
81/H2 Weilheim, Ger.
70/C5 Weilheim an der Teck, Ger.
70/B2 Weilmünster, Ger.
72/B6 Weimar, Ger.
189/F3 Weimar, Tx,US
72/D5 Weinböhla, Ger.
191/J3 Weiner, Ar,US
81/F2 Weinfelden, Swi.
70/B4 Weingarten, Ger.
81/F2 Weingarten, Ger.
70/B3 Weinheim, Ger.
70/C4 Weinsberg, Ger.
70/C5 Weinstadt, Ger.
73/A2 Weinviertel (reg.), Aus.
131/F3 Weipa, Austl.
131/F3 Weipa Abor. Rsv., Austl.
131/F3 Weipa South, Austl.
191/G2 Weir, Ks,US
200/C4 Weir, Ms,US
189/F2 Weir, Tx,US
203/H3 Weirsdale, Fl,US
208/G7 Weirton, WV,US
71/F2 Weischlitz, Ger.
70/D3 Weisendorf, Ger.
184/E1 Weiser, Id,US
184/E1 Weiser (riv.), Id,US
115/D4 Weishan, China
115/D4 Weishan (lake), China
115/C4 Weishi, China
69/F4 Weiskirchen, Ger.
72/D5 Weismain, Ger.
200/E3 Weiss (dam), Al,US
200/E3 Weiss (lake), Al,US
200/E3 Weiss (lake), Ga,US
70/B5 Weissach, Ger.
71/F2 Weisse Elster (riv.), Ger.
71/F4 Weisse Laber (riv.), Ger.
81/G3 Weissenbach am Lech, Aus.
70/D4 Weissenburg im Bayern, Ger.
72/B5 Weissenfels, Ger.
70/D6 Weissenhorn, Ger.
72/B5 Weissensee, Ger.
72/D2 Weissensee, Ger.
71/E2 Weissenstadt, Ger.
80/D3 Weissenstein (mtn.), Swi.
69/G3 Weissenthurm, Ger.
72/D5 Weisseritz (riv.), Ger.
71/E2 Weisser Main (riv.), Ger.
71/F4 Weisser Regen (riv.), Ger.
69/F3 Weisser Stein (peak), Ger.
80/D5 Weisshorn (peak), Swi.
72/D5 Weissig, Ger.
81/G4 Weisskugel (Palla Bianca) (peak), Aus., It.
80/D5 Weissmies (peak), Swi.
65/H3 Weisswasser, Ger.
71/H6 Weistrach, Aus.
69/G2 Weitefeld, Ger.
70/B3 Weiterstadt, Ger.
117/H3 Weitian, China
75/L2 Weitra, Aus.
72/D5 Weixdorf, Ger.
119/G2 Weixi, China
119/J2 Weixin, China
108/E4 Weiyuan, China
116/D4 Weiyuan (riv.), China
75/L3 Weiz, Aus.
117/F4 Weizhou (isl.), China
113/C2 Weiziyu, China
65/K1 Wejherowo, Pol.
123/B3 Wekame, Burma
202/N6 Wekiva (riv.), Fl,US
119/G2 Welatam, Burma
156/E2 Welbekend, SAfr.
192/B4 Welby, Co,US
191/G2 Welch, Ok,US
206/A3 Welch (hill), Pa,US
201/G2 Welch, WV,US
201/G3 Welcome, NC,US
191/G1 Welda, Ks,US
81/G1 Welden, Ger.
150/A3 Weldiya, Eth.
59/F2 Weldon, Eng,UK
186/C3 Weldon, Ca,US
193/H3 Weldon (riv.), Ia, Mo,US
189/G2 Weldon, Tx,US
191/F3 Weleetka, Ok,US
149/G3 Welega (reg.), Eth.
149/G3 Welel (peak), Eth.
134/A4 Welford, Austl.
59/E4 Welford, Eng,UK
53/N6 Welham Green, Eng,UK
118/D6 Weligama, SrL.
69/E2 Welkenraedt, Belg.
149/H3 Welk'īt'ē, Eth.
156/D3 Welkom, SAfr.
199/G3 Welland, On,Can
197/S10 Welland (can.), On,Can
59/F1 Welland (riv.), Eng,UK
197/S10 Wellandport, On,Can
203/G2 Wellborn, Fl,US
131/E4 Wellesley (isls.), Austl.
208/C1 Wellesley, Ma,US
196/B5 Wellfleet, Ma,US
201/F3 Wellford, SC,US
69/E3 Wellin, Belg.
59/F2 Wellingborough, Eng,UK
135/D2 Wellington, Austl.
135/C3 Wellington (inlet), Austl.
179/S7 Wellington (chan.), NW,Can
199/H3 Wellington, On,Can
197/Q8 Wellington (co.), On,Can
175/J7 Wellington (isl.), Chile
136/H9 Wellington (cap.), N.Z.
136/H9 Wellington (int'l arpt.), N.Z.
156/B4 Wellington, SAfr.
58/C5 Wellington, Eng,UK
58/D2 Wellington, Eng,UK
192/B3 Wellington, Co,US
191/F2 Wellington, Ks,US
184/D4 Wellington, Nv,US
208/E5 Wellington, Oh,US
190/D3 Wellington, Tx,US
193/J3 Wellman, Ia,US
188/C1 Wellman, Tx,US
132/D3 Wells (lake), Austl.
182/D1 Wells, BC,Can
58/D4 Wells, Eng,UK
196/B4 Wells, Me,US
193/H2 Wells, Mn,US
185/F3 Wells, Nv,US
199/J3 Wells, NY,US
189/G2 Wells, Tx,US
182/E4 Wells (dam), Wa,US
199/H4 Wellsboro, Pa,US
198/F4 Wellsburg, WV,US
136/C2 Wellsford, N.Z.
59/G1 Wells-next-the-Sea, Eng,UK
195/M5 Wellston, Mi,US
198/E5 Wellston, Oh,US
191/F3 Wellston, Ok,US
191/G1 Wellsville, Ks,US
191/J1 Wellsville, Mo,US
199/H3 Wellsville, NY,US
208/G6 Wellsville, Oh,US
206/B3 Wellsville, Pa,US
185/H3 Wellsville, Ut,US
187/E4 Wellton, Az,US
194/E2 Wellwood, Mb,Can
150/A3 Welo (prov.), Eth.
149/H2 Welo (reg.), Eth.
71/H6 Wels, Aus.
69/F4 Welschbillig, Ger.
72/E1 Welse (riv.), Ger.
202/B2 Welsh, La,US
81/H5 Welshofen (Nova Levante), It.
58/C1 Welshpool, Wal,UK
191/F3 Welty, Ok,US
67/E5 Welver, Ger.
150/C4 Welwel, Eth.
194/D2 Welwyn, Sk,Can
59/F3 Welwyn, Eng,UK
59/F3 Welwyn Garden City, Eng,UK
70/C5 Welzheim, Ger.
72/E4 Welzow, Ger.
57/F6 Wem, Eng,UK
151/A3 Wembere (riv.), Tanz.
53/N7 Wembley Stadium, Eng,UK
58/B6 Wembury, Eng,UK
70/D5 Wemding, Ger.
179/J3 Wemindji, Qu,Can
68/D2 Wemmel, Belg.
54/B5 Wemyss Bay, Sc,UK
149/H4 Wenago, Eth.
115/H7 Wen'an, China
182/D4 Wenatchee, Wa,US
182/D4 Wenatchee (mts.), Wa,US
117/F5 Wenchang, China
117/J3 Wencheng, China
145/E5 Wenchi, Gha.
67/H4 Wendeburg, Ger.
194/F4 Wendell, Mn,US
69/G2 Wenden, Ger.
187/F4 Wenden, Az,US
113/B4 Wendeng, China
117/F4 Wendi, China
152/D3 Wendji, Zaire
149/H4 Wendo, Eth.
144/B4 Wendou Borou, Gui.
59/F3 Wendover, Eng,UK
185/F3 Wendover, Nv,US
58/A6 Wendron, Eng,UK
192/D1 Wendte, SD,US
117/F3 Wengdong, China
117/G2 Wengjiang, China
119/G2 Wengshui, China
117/J2 Wengyang, China
119/G3 Wengyuan, China
58/D2 Wenlock Edge (ridge), Eng,UK
67/F6 Wenne (riv.), Ger.
67/G4 Wennigsen, Ger.
57/F3 Wennington, Eng,UK
198/B4 Wenona, Il,US
206/C4 Wenonah, NJ,US
114/F5 Wenquan, China
116/D2 Wenquan, China
117/E2 Wenquan, China
117/G3 Wenquanzhen, China
119/H3 Wenshan, China
115/D4 Wenshang, China
117/F3 Wenshi, China
115/C3 Wenshui, China
57/F3 Wensleydale (vall.), Eng,UK
59/H1 Wensum (riv.), Eng,UK
57/G4 Went (riv.), Eng,UK
117/G2 Wentang, China
133/J5 Wentworth, Austl.
201/H2 Wentworth, NC,US
115/B4 Wenxi, China
115/C4 Wen Xian, China
117/J3 Wenzhou, China
202/M8 Weohyakapka (lake), Fl,US
184/B3 Weott, Ca,US
156/D3 Wepener, SAfr.
69/D3 Wépion, Belg.
120/A2 Wer, India
72/D2 Werbellinsee (lake), Ger.
72/E4 Werben, Ger.
154/D5 Werda, Bots.
72/C6 Werdau, Ger.
150/C4 Werder, Eth.
72/C3 Werder, Ger.
67/E6 Werdohl, Ger.
150/A3 Were Īlu, Eth.
127/G4 Werinama, Indo.
66/B5 Werkendam, Neth.
67/E5 Werl, Ger.
67/E3 Werlte, Ger.
67/E6 Wermelskirchen, Ger.
72/C5 Wermsdorf, Ger.
70/C3 Wern (riv.), Ger.
71/F3 Wernberg-Köblitz, Ger.
67/E5 Werne an der Lippe, Ger.
70/D3 Werneck, Ger.
195/G2 Werner Lake, On,Can
72/D2 Werneuchen, Ger.
67/H5 Wernigerode, Ger.
135/D2 Werong (peak), Austl.
149/H3 Werota, Eth.
67/G6 Werra (riv.), Ger.
67/F4 Werre (riv.), Ger.
135/E1 Werrikimbe Nat'l Park, Austl.
133/J5 Werrimull, Austl.
57/F5 Werrington, Eng,UK
135/D1 Werris Creek, Austl.
67/E5 Werse (riv.), Ger.
70/D6 Wertach (riv.), Ger.
70/C3 Wertheim, Ger.
207/F2 Wertheim Nat'l Wild. Ref., NY,US
67/F4 Werther, Ger.
67/H6 Werther, Ger.
70/D5 Wertingen, Ger.
66/C3 Wervershoof, Neth.
68/C2 Wervik, Belg.
70/B3 Weschnitz (riv.), Ger.
66/D5 Wesel, Ger.
67/E5 Wesel-Datteln-Kanal (can.), Ger.
64/G2 Wesenberg, Ger.
72/E5 Wesenitz (riv.), Ger.
64/E2 Weser (riv.), Ger.
67/G4 Wesergebirge (ridge), Ger.
189/F4 Weslaco, Tx,US
193/H2 Wesley, Ia,US
196/D3 Wesley, Me,US
189/F3 Wesley E. Seale (dam), Tx,US
207/J7 Wesley Hills, NY,US
156/D2 Wes-Rand, SAfr.
131/E2 Wessel (cape), Austl.
131/E2 Wessel (isls.), Austl.
64/E1 Wesselburen, Ger.
69/F2 Wesseling, Ger.
156/D2 Wesselsbron, SAfr.
58/D4 Wessex (reg.), Eng,UK
192/E1 Wessington, SD,US
192/E1 Wessington Springs, SD,US
191/H4 Wesson, Ar,US
200/B5 Wesson, Ms,US
131/E3 West (isl.), Austl.
135/C4 West (pt.), Austl.
136/A4 West (cape), N.Z.
192/B4 West (mts.), Co,US
202/D3 West (bay), La,US
189/F2 West, Tx,US
189/G3 West (bay), Tx,US
205/C2 West (pt.), Wa,US
133/G3 Westall (pt.), Austl.
205/P13 West Allis, Wi,US
197/G3 West Arichat, NS,Can
201/F4 West Augusta, Ga,US
201/H1 West Augusta, Va,US
207/E2 West Babylon, NY,US
130/C4 West Baines (riv.), Austl.
124/F5 West Bali Nat'l Park, Indo.
103/D3 West Bank (occ. zone)
193/K2 West Baraboo, Wi,US
54/D5 West Barns, Sc,UK
208/C1 West Barrington, RI,US
197/G3 West Bay, NS,Can
194/C2 West Bend, Sk,Can
193/G2 West Bend, Ia,US
193/K2 West Bend, Wi,US
121/F5 West Bengal (state), India
59/G3 West Bergholt, Eng,UK
208/C1 West Berlin, Ma,US
192/B4 West Bijou (cr.), Co,US
200/D4 West Blocton, Al,US
193/J1 Westboro, Wi,US
208/C1 Westborough, Ma,US
194/E2 Westbourne, Mb,Can
208/C1 West Boylston, Ma,US
198/D2 West Branch, Mi,US
199/K3 West Brattleboro, Vt,US
208/C1 West Bridgewater, Ma,US
57/G6 West Bridgford, Eng,UK
59/E1 West Bromwich, Eng,UK
208/B3 Westbrook, Ct,US
193/G1 Westbrook, Mn,US
208/B1 West Brookfield, Ma,US
58/D4 Westbury, Eng,UK
207/E2 Westbury, NY,US
193/J2 Westby, Wi,US

161/H1 West Caicos (isl.), Trks.
54/C5 West Calder, Sc,UK
207/H8 West Caldwell, NJ,US
132/C5 West Cape Howe Nat'l Park, Austl.
199/J3 West Carthage, NY,US
202/P8 Westchester, Fl,US
207/E1 Westchester (co.), NY,US
207/E1 Westchester (co. arpt.), NY,US
207/L7 Westchester (co. arpt.), NY,US
206/C4 West Chester, Pa,US
205/P16 West Chicago, Il,US
151/B2 West Chyulu Game Consv. Area, Kenya
53/M8 West Clandon, Eng,UK
58/B3 West Cleddau (riv.), Wal,UK
192/B4 Westcliffe, Co,US
136/B3 West Coast (reg.), N.Z.
189/G3 West Columbia, Tx,US
208/C1 West Concord, Ma,US
57/G2 West Cornforth, Eng,UK
208/A2 West Cornwall, Ct,US
204/C2 West Covina, Ca,US
207/D4 West Creek, NJ,US
189/J1 West Crossett, Ar,US
58/C5 West Dart (riv.), Eng,UK
193/H3 West Des Moines, Ia,US
66/A6 Westdorpe, Neth.
196/F3 West Dover, NS,Can
52/F3 West Dvina (riv.), Eur.
190/A1 West Elk (mts.), Co,US
199/H3 West Elmira, NY,US
162/B1 West End, Bahm.
186/D3 Westend, Ca,US
66/D3 Westerbork, Neth.
70/A1 Westerburg, Ger.
53/P8 Westerham, Eng,UK
70/D6 Westerheim, Ger.
67/E1 Westerholt, Ger.
67/E4 Westerkappeln, Ger.
64/E1 Westerland, Ger.
69/D1 Westerlo, Belg.
208/C3 Westerly, RI,US
208/C3 Westerly (st. arpt.), RI,US
196/E4 Western (pt.), NS,Can
103/A5 Western (des.), Egypt
145/E5 Western (reg.), Gha.
151/A1 Western (prov.), Kenya
131/F1 Western (prov.), PNG
144/B4 Western (area), SLeo.
153/G2 Western (prov.), Ugan.
154/D2 Western (prov.), Zam.
128/B4 Western Australia (state), Austl.
154/D3 Western Caprivi Game Park, Namb.
110/A3 Western Channel (str.), Japan, SKor.
100/C4 Western Dvina (riv.), Lat., Rus.
118/B4 Western Ghats (mts.), India
131/G1 Western Highlands (prov.), PNG
199/G5 Westernport, Md,US
142/B4 Western Sahara (occ. zone)
108/C1 Western Sayan (mts.), Rus.
136/F6 Western Springs, N.Z.
66/A6 Westerschelde (chan.), Neth.
67/E2 Westerstede, Ger.
198/E4 Westerville, Oh,US
66/C5 Westervoort, Neth.
69/G2 Westerwald (for.), Ger.
67/F4 Westfalica, Porta (pass), Ger.
175/M8 West Falkland (isl.), Falk.
194/F4 West Fargo, ND,US
208/G5 West Farmington, Oh,US
138/D4 West Fayu (isl.), Micr.
196/D3 Westfield, NB,Can
208/B1 Westfield, Ma,US
208/B1 Westfield (riv.), Ma,US
196/D2 Westfield, Me,US
207/D2 Westfield, NJ,US
199/G3 Westfield, NY,US
199/H4 Westfield, Pa,US
198/B3 Westfield, Wi,US
208/F5 Westfield Center, Oh,US
197/Q9 West Flamborough, On,Can
68/B2 West Flanders (prov.), Belg.
208/B2 Westford, Ct,US
196/B4 Westford, Ma,US
208/G4 Westford, Pa,US
191/G3 West Fork, Ar,US
193/K5 West Frankfort, Il,US
66/C2 West Frisian (isls.), Neth.
58/C3 West Glamorgan (co.), Wal,UK
59/F1 West Glen (riv.), Eng,UK
208/B2 West Granby, Ct,US
208/B1 West Granville, Ma,US
203/G2 West Green, Ga,US
206/C4 West Grove, Pa,US
53/P7 West Ham, Eng,UK
201/F1 West Hamlin, WV,US
208/B1 Westhampton, Ma,US
207/F2 Westhampton, NY,US
207/F2 Westhampton Beach, NY,US
208/B2 West Hartford, Ct,US
70/D5 Westhausen, Ger.
208/B3 West Haven, Ct,US
207/E1 West Haverstraw, NY,US
195/G3 West Hawk Lake, Mb,Can
207/C2 West Hazleton, Pa,US
70/B4 Westheim, Ger.
191/J3 West Helena, Ar,US
207/L9 West Hempstead, NY,US
54/D2 Westhill, Sc,UK
207/M8 West Hills, NY,US
70/B3 Westhofen, Ger.
189/F3 Westhoff, Tx,US
204/F7 West Hollywood, Ca,US
194/D3 Westhope, ND,US
53/Q7 West Horndon, Eng,UK
53/M8 West Horsley, Eng,UK
57/F4 Westhoughton, Eng,UK
197/R8 West Humber (riv.), On,Can
199/J4 West Hurley, NY,US
137/F West Ice Shelf, Ant.
176/L7 West Indies (isls.), NAm.
129/J4 West Islet (isl.), Austl.
207/E2 West Islip, NY,US
201/G2 West Jefferson, NC,US
185/H3 West Jordan, Ut,US
66/A5 Westkapelle, Neth.
196/B3 West Kennebago (mtn.), Me,US
54/B5 West Kilbride, Sc,UK
53/P8 West Kingsdown, Eng,UK
208/C3 West Kingston, RI,US
57/E5 West Kirby, Eng,UK
54/D3 West Knock (mtn.), Sc,UK
198/C4 West Lafayette, In,US
198/F4 West Lafayette, Oh,US
189/H2 Westlake, La,US
208/F5 Westlake, Oh,US
189/F2 West Lake Hills, Tx,US
204/B2 Westlake Village, Ca,US
205/F7 Westland, Mi,US
136/B3 Westland Nat'l Park, N.Z.
198/C4 West Lebanon, In,US
193/J3 West Liberty, Ia,US
201/F2 West Liberty, Ky,US
198/E4 West Liberty, Oh,US
184/B1 West Linn, Or,US
54/C5 West Linton, Sc,UK
178/E3 Westlock, Ab,Can
198/F3 West Lorne, On,Can
154/E2 West Lunga (riv.), Zam.
154/E2 West Lunga Nat'l Park, Zam.
208/C2 West Mansfield, Ma,US
60/C3 Westmeath (co.), Ire.
203/H3 West Melbourne, Fl,US
200/B3 West Memphis, Ar,US
59/G3 West Mersea, Eng,UK
202/P8 West Miami, Fl,US
208/G5 West Middlesex, Pa,US
59/E2 West Midlands (co.), Eng,UK
208/H7 West Mifflin, Pa,US
207/D1 West Milford, NJ,US
201/G1 West Milford, WV,US
208/C1 West Millbury, Ma,US
206/B1 West Milton, Pa,US
204/B3 Westminster, Ca,US
192/B4 Westminster, Co,US
206/B4 Westminster, Md,US
201/F3 Westminster, SC,US
199/K3 Westminster, Vt,US
53/N7 Westminster Abbey, Eng,UK
53/N7 Westminster, City of (bor.), Eng,UK
189/H1 West Monroe, La,US
198/E4 West Monroe, Mi,US
205/Q16 Westmont, Il,US
199/G4 Westmont, Pa,US
206/C4 Westmont (Haddon), NJ,US
131/E4 Westmoreland, Austl.
57/F3 Westmoreland (reg.), Eng,UK
191/F1 Westmoreland, Ks,US
186/E4 Westmorland, Ca,US
197/G2 Westmount, NS,Can
197/N7 Westmount, Qu,Can
54/G3 Westmuir, Sc,UK
131/H1 West New Britain (prov.), PNG
207/J8 West New York, NJ,US
155/F4 West Nicholson, Zim.
66/A5 West-Nieuwland, Neth.
193/G3 West Nishnabotna (riv.), Ia,US
193/G3 West Nodaway (riv.), Ia,US
188/D3 West Nueces (riv.), Tx,US
207/E1 West Nyack, NY,US
198/C3 West Olive, Mi,US
125/A4 Weston, Malay.
190/B2 Weston, Co,US
208/A3 Weston, Ct,US
200/E5 Weston, Ga,US
185/H2 Weston, Id,US
208/C1 Weston, Ma,US
191/G1 Weston, Mo,US
198/E4 Weston, Oh,US
195/H5 Weston, Wi,US
201/G1 Weston, WV,US
194/B5 Weston, Wy,US
156/P13 Westonaria, SAfr.
58/D4 Weston-super-Mare, Eng,UK
58/D4 Weston Zoyland, Eng,UK
207/D2 West Orange, NJ,US
189/H2 West Orange, Tx,US
192/D2 Westover, SD,US
198/G5 Westover, WV,US
208/B1 Westover A.F.B., Ma,US
162/A1 West Palm Beach, Fl,US
202/P6 West Palm Beach, Fl,US
203/H4 West Palm Beach, Fl,US
202/P6 West Palm Beach (can.), Fl,US
196/B3 West Paris, Me,US
207/J8 West Paterson, NJ,US
53/Q8 West Peckham, Eng,UK
202/E2 West Pensacola, Fl,US
191/G1 Westphalia, Ks,US
208/G6 West Pittsburg, Pa,US
191/J2 West Plains, Mo,US
200/E4 West Point (lake), Al,US
186/B1 West Point, Ca,US
200/E4 West Point, Ga,US
200/E4 West Point (dam), Ga,US
200/E4 West Point (lake), Ga,US
193/J3 West Point, Ia,US
193/J3 West Point, Il,US
200/C4 West Point, Ms,US
193/F3 West Point, Ne,US
199/J4 West Point (Mil. Acad.), NY,US
194/A3 West Poplar, Sk,Can
196/D3 Westport, NS,Can
199/H2 Westport, On,Can
60/A2 Westport, Ire.
136/B3 Westport, N.Z.
207/E2 Westport, Ct,US
198/D5 Westport, In,US
182/B4 Westport, Wa,US
201/F1 West Portsmouth, Oh,US
55/N13 Westray (isl.), Sc,UK
206/C3 West Reading, Pa,US
208/A3 West Redding, Ct,US
182/E4 West Richland, Wa,US
182/B1 West Road (riv.), BC,Can
205/L9 West Sacramento, Ca,US
195/P7 West Saint Paul, Mn,US
200/C1 West Salem, Il,US
208/E6 West Salem, Oh,US
207/E2 West Sayville, NY,US
199/G3 West Seneca, NY,US
100/H3 West Siberian (plain), Rus.
200/F3 Westside, Ga,US
208/B2 West Simsbury, Ct,US
198/E4 West Sister I. Nat'l Wild. Ref., Oh,US
208/B1 West Springfield, Ma,US
208/A1 West Stockbridge, Ma,US
59/F4 West Sussex (co.), Eng,UK
189/F1 West Tawakoni, Tx,US
66/C2 West-Terschelling, Neth.
53/P7 West Thurrock, Eng,UK
208/D3 West Tisbury, Ma,US
193/J2 West Union, Ia,US
198/C5 West Union, Il,US
201/F1 West Union, Oh,US
201/G1 West Union, WV,US
198/D4 West Unity, Oh,US
189/M9 West University Place, Tx,US
185/H3 West Valley City, Ut,US
182/C3 West Vancouver, BC,Can
194/C2 Westview, Sk,Can
208/G6 West View, Pa,US
197/F3 Westville, NS,Can
203/F1 Westville, Ga,US
198/C4 Westville, Il,US
198/C4 Westville, In,US
191/G3 Westville, Ok,US
201/G3 Westville, SC,US
181/K4 West Virginia (state), US
184/D4 West Walker (riv.), Ca, Nv,US
58/B4 Westward Ho!, Eng,UK
208/D2 West Wareham, Ma,US
208/B1 West Warren, Ma,US
208/C2 West Warwick, RI,US
54/D3 West Water (riv.), Sc,UK
199/J3 West Winfield, NY,US
182/E2 Westwold, BC,Can
184/C3 Westwood, Ca,US
201/F1 Westwood, Ky,US
208/C1 Westwood, Ma,US
207/D2 Westwood, NJ,US
155/F2 Westwood, Zam.
188/K7 Westworth Village, Tx,US
135/C2 West Wyalong, Austl.
185/H1 West Yellowstone, Mt,US
206/B4 West York, Pa,US
57/G4 West Yorkshire (co.), Eng,UK
192/B4 Wet (mts.), Co,US
130/C1 Wetan (isl.), Indo.
130/B1 Wetar (isl.), Indo.
130/B2 Wetar (str.), Indo.
183/H1 Wetaskiwin, Ab,Can
151/B3 Wete, Tanz.
153/F4 Wete, Zaire
57/F2 Wetheral, Eng,UK
57/G4 Wetherby, Eng,UK
133/J5 Wetherell (lake), Austl.
208/B2 Wethersfield, Ct,US
123/A1 Wetlet, Burma
193/G4 Wetmore, Ks,US
67/E6 Wetter, Ger.
70/B2 Wetter (riv.), Ger.
70/C2 Wetterau (reg.), Ger.
68/C1 Wetteren, Belg.
80/E4 Wetterhorn (peak), Swi.
72/B4 Wettin, Ger.
81/E3 Wettingen, Swi.
67/E4 Wettringen, Ger.
191/F3 Wetumka, Ok,US
200/D4 Wetumpka, Al,US
135/B2 Wetuppa, Austl.
81/E3 Wetzikon, Swi.
70/B1 Wetzlar, Ger.
71/E2 Wetzstein (peak), Ger.
68/C2 Wevelgem, Belg.
203/F2 Wewahitchka, Fl,US
138/D5 Wewak, PNG
191/F3 Wewoka, Ok,US
60/D5 Wexford, Ire.
60/D5 Wexford (co.), Ire.
60/D5 Wexford (harb.), Ire.
53/M8 Wey (riv.), Eng,UK
202/C2 Weyanoke, La,US
198/B2 Weyauwega, Wi,US
59/H1 Weybourne, Eng,UK
53/M7 Weybridge, Eng,UK
194/C3 Weyburn, Sk,Can
193/J1 Weyerhaeuser, Wi,US
143/F4 Weygand (ruins), Alg.
67/H4 Weyhausen, Ger.
133/G5 Weyland (pt.), Austl.
131/F3 Weymouth (cape), Austl.
196/E3 Weymouth, NS,Can
58/D5 Weymouth, Eng,UK
58/D5 Weymouth (bay), Eng,UK
208/D1 Weymouth, Ma,US
196/E3 Weymouth North, NS,Can
136/D2 Whakatane, N.Z.
178/G2 Whale Cove, NW,Can
182/B2 Whaletown, BC,Can
57/G5 Whaley Bridge, Eng,UK
208/D2 Whaling Museum, Ma,US
57/F4 Whalley, Eng,UK
55/P12 Whalsey (isl.), Sc,UK
136/C2 Whangamata, N.Z.
136/F6 Whangaparaoa Head (pt.), N.Z.
136/C1 Whangarei, N.Z.
57/G3 Wharfe (riv.), Eng,UK
201/G2 Wharncliffe, WV,US
189/F3 Wharton, Tx,US
136/B3 Whataroa, N.Z.
136/D2 Whatatutu, N.Z.
208/B1 Whately, Ma,US
202/E2 Whatley, Al,US
191/H2 Wheatland, Mo,US
190/C3 Wheatland, NM,US
208/G5 Wheatland, Pa,US
192/B2 Wheatland, Wy,US
192/B3 Wheatland No. 2 (res.), Wy,US
205/H7 Wheatley, On,Can
59/E3 Wheatley, Eng,UK
191/J3 Wheatley, Ar,US
205/P16 Wheaton, Il,US
194/F5 Wheaton, Mn,US
191/G2 Wheaton, Mo,US
58/D1 Wheaton Aston, Eng,UK
206/A5 Wheaton-Glenmont, Md,US
206/C5 Wheaton Village, NJ,US
200/D3 Wheeler (lake), Al,US
200/C3 Wheeler, Ms,US
180/E4 Wheeler (peak), NM,US
190/B2 Wheeler (pk.), NM,US
185/F4 Wheeler (peak), Nv,US
184/B1 Wheeler, Or,US
190/D3 Wheeler, Tx,US
200/D3 Wheeler Nat'l Wild. Ref., Al,US
201/F1 Wheelersburg, Oh,US
204/A1 Wheeler Springs, Ca,US
190/C2 Wheeless, Ok,US
205/Q15 Wheeling, Il,US
193/H4 Wheeling, Mo,US
198/F4 Wheeling, WV,US
189/F2 Wheelock, Tx,US
174/E2 Wheelwright, Arg.
208/B1 Wheelwright, Ma,US
191/H4 Whelen Springs, Ar,US
136/F6 Whenuapai, N.Z.
57/F3 Whernside (mtn.), Eng,UK
57/G2 Whickham, Eng,UK
133/G5 Whidbey (pt.), Austl.
205/B1 Whidbey (isl.), Wa,US
60/A6 Whiddy (isl.), Ire.
203/F2 Whigham, Ga,US
133/F3 Whinham (peak), Austl.
184/B3 Whiskeytown-Shasta-Trinity Nat'l Rec. Area, Ca,US
182/C5 Whistler, BC,Can
201/J2 Whitakers, NC,US
197/L2 Whitbourne, Nf,Can
57/G2 Whitburn, Eng,UK
54/C5 Whitburn, Sc,UK
199/G3 Whitby, On,Can
57/H3 Whitby, Eng,UK
57/F6 Whitchurch, Eng,UK
59/E4 Whitchurch, Eng,UK
59/F3 Whitchurch, Eng,UK
58/C4 Whitchurch, Wal,UK
199/G3 Whitchurch-Stouffville, On,Can
136/B3 Whitcombe (peak), N.Z.
137/D White (isl.), Ant.
133/F2 White (lake), Austl.
182/G2 White (riv.), BC,Can
179/L3 White (bay), Nf,Can
195/M3 White (lake), On,Can
94/H2 White (sea), Rus.
177/L4 White (pass), Ak,US
191/J4 White, Ar,US
200/B3 White (riv.), Ar,US
191/J3 White (riv.), Ar, Mo,US
185/J3 White (riv.), Co, Ut,US
200/E3 White, Ga,US
198/D4 White (riv.), In,US
189/H3 White (lake), La,US
205/E6 White (lake), Mi,US
192/D2 White (riv.), Ne, SD,US
199/L2 White (mts.), NH,US
185/F4 White (riv.), Nv,US
192/E1 White, SD,US
190/D4 White (riv.), Tx,US
201/G2 White (peak), Va,US
182/D4 White (pass), Wa,US
205/D3 White (riv.), Wa,US
205/P14 White (riv.), Wi,US
54/D5 Whiteadder Water (riv.), Sc,UK
197/J1 White Bear (riv.), Nf,Can
183/K2 White Bear, Sk,Can
195/P6 White Bear (lake), Mn,US
195/P6 White Bear Lake, Mn,US
184/E1 White Bird, Id,US
200/D2 White Bluff, Tn,US
194/C4 White Butte (mtn.), ND,US
194/C5 White Butte, SD,US
196/C3 White Cap (mtn.), Me,US
202/C2 White Castle, La,US
203/F3 White City, Fl,US
203/H4 White City, Fl,US
191/F1 White City, Ks,US
133/J4 White Cliffs, Austl.
198/D3 White Cloud, Mi,US
54/C6 White Coomb (mtn.), Sc,UK
178/E5 Whitecourt, Ab,Can
206/A1 White Deer (cr.), Pa,US
194/G4 White Earth, Mn,US
194/C3 White Earth, ND,US
194/C3 White Earth (riv.), ND,US
195/G4 White Earth Ind. Res., Mn,US
54/C6 White Esk (riv.), Sc,UK
195/H4 Whiteface (res.), Mn,US
195/H4 Whiteface (riv.), Mn,US
199/K2 Whiteface (mtn.), NY,US
190/C4 Whiteface, Tx,US
57/F4 Whitefield, Eng,UK
196/B3 Whitefield, NH,US
198/D1 Whitefish (bay), Can., US
195/G4 Whitefish (lake), Mn,US
183/G3 Whitefish, Mt,US
195/L5 Whitefish (pt.), Wi,US
198/D1 Whitefish Point, Mi,US
177/L2 Whitefish Station, Yk,Can
58/B3 Whiteford (pt.), Wal,UK
206/B4 Whiteford, Md,US
60/B4 Whitegate, Ire.
60/B6 Whitegate, Ire.
55/N13 Whitehall, Sc,UK
200/D4 White Hall, Al,US
191/H3 White Hall, Ar,US
206/B4 White Hall, Md,US
198/C3 Whitehall, Mi,US
183/H5 Whitehall, Mt,US
199/K3 Whitehall, NY,US
198/E5 Whitehall, Oh,US
193/J1 Whitehall, Wi,US
206/C2 Whitehall (Fullerton), Pa,US
56/E2 Whitehaven, Eng,UK
206/C1 White Haven, Pa,US
56/C2 Whitehead, NI,UK
54/D1 Whitehills, Sc,UK
177/L3 Whitehorse, Yk,Can
59/E3 Whitehorse (hill), Eng,UK
192/D1 Whitehorse, SD,US
188/B2 White Horse Draw (cr.), Tx,US
198/E4 Whitehouse, Oh,US
200/D2 White House, Tn,US
189/G1 Whitehouse, Tx,US
199/H2 White Lake, On,Can
193/K1 White Lake, Wi,US
194/C4 White Lake Nat'l Wild. Ref., ND,US
198/C5 Whiteland, In,US
191/H1 Whiteman A.F.B., Mo,US
135/D4 Whitemark, Austl.
206/B5 White Marsh, Md,US
206/D2 White Meadow Lake, NJ,US
200/D2 White Mills, Ky,US
177/F3 White Mountain, Ak,US
186/C2 White Mountain (peak), Ca,US
177/J2 White Mountains Nat'l Rec. Area, Ak,US
194/G3 Whitemouth, Mb,Can
195/G3 Whitemouth (lake), Mb,Can
194/G3 Whitemouth (riv.), Mb,Can
149/G3 White Nile (riv.), Sudan
149/G2 White Nile (Khazzān Jabal Al Awliyā) (dam), Sudan
203/H2 White Oak, Ga,US
206/B5 White Oak, Md,US
198/D5 White Oak, Oh,US
189/G1 White Oak, Tx,US
189/M9 White Oak (bayou), Tx,US
189/G1 White Oak (cr.), Tx,US
190/B4 White Oaks, NM,US
195/J3 White Otter (lake), On,Can
198/D4 White Pigeon, Mi,US
185/K4 Whitepine, Co,US
201/F2 White Pine, Tn,US
201/G2 White Plains, NC,US
207/E1 White Plains, NY,US
195/L5 White Rapids (dam), Mi,US
195/M3 White River, On,Can
187/H4 Whiteriver, Az,US
192/D2 White River, SD,US
200/D1 White River, East Fork (riv.), In,US
191/J3 White River Nat'l Wild. Ref., Ar,US
200/D1 White River, West Fork (riv.), In,US
192/E4 White Rock (cr.), Ks,US
190/A3 White Rock, NM,US
201/G3 White Rock, SC,US
189/F1 White Rock, Tx,US
188/L6 White Rock (cr.), Tx,US
188/L7 White Rock (lake), Tx,US
182/D5 White Salmon, Wa,US
187/J4 White Sands, NM,US
187/J4 White Sands (des.), NM,US
190/A4 White Sands Miss. Ra., NM,US
190/A4 White Sands Nat'l Mon., NM,US
190/A4 White Sands Space Harbor, NM,US
191/G3 Whitesboro, Ok,US
191/F4 Whitesboro, Tx,US
201/F2 Whitesburg, Ky,US
190/B4 Whites City, NM,US
189/F1 White Settlement, Tx,US
190/D4 White Shield, ND,US
175/K8 Whiteside (chan.), Chile
196/F3 Whites Lake, NS,Can
203/G2 White Springs, Fl,US
194/E4 Whitestone Hill Bfld., ND,US
183/J4 White Sulphur Springs, Mt,US
201/G2 White Sulphur Springs, WV,US
200/D2 Whitesville, Ky,US
207/D3 Whitesville, NJ,US
199/H3 Whitesville, NY,US
182/D4 White Swan, Wa,US
194/B3 Whitetail, Mt,US
158/D1 Whitetail, NM,US
201/G2 Whitetop, Va,US
201/H3 Whiteville, NC,US
200/C3 Whiteville, Tn,US
145/E4 White Volta (riv.), Burk., Gha.
185/J4 Whitewater, Co,US
203/H5 Whitewater (bay), Fl,US
191/F2 Whitewater, Ks,US
181/L3 Whitewater, Mt,US
193/K2 Whitewater, Wi,US
187/H4 Whitewater Baldy (peak), NM,US
206/C2 Whitewater Kingdom/Dorney Park, Pa,US
205/D3 White, West Fork (riv.), Wa,US
192/D4 White Woman (cr.), Co, Ks,US
194/C2 Whitewood, Sk,Can
191/F4 Whitewright, Tx,US
56/D2 Whithorn, Sc,UK
136/C2 Whitianga, N.Z.
193/F2 Whiting, Ia,US
205/R16 Whiting, In,US
191/G1 Whiting, Ks,US
193/K1 Whiting, Wi,US
54/A6 Whiting Bay, Sc,UK
202/E2 Whiting Field Nav. Air Sta., Fl,US
208/C1 Whitinsville, Ma,US
58/B3 Whitland, Wal,UK
183/J3 Whitlash, Mt,US
57/G1 Whitley Bay, Eng,UK
200/E2 Whitley City, Ky,US
208/D1 Whitman, Ma,US
205/E7 Whitmore Lake, Mi,US
199/G2 Whitney, On,Can
186/C2 Whitney (mtn.), Ca,US
189/F2 Whitney, Tx,US
189/F2 Whitney (lake), Tx,US
199/J3 Whitney Point, NY,US
58/B6 Whitsand (bay), Eng,UK
189/E3 Whitsett, Tx,US
59/H4 Whitstable, Eng,UK
129/H4 Whitsunday (isl.), Austl.
134/C3 Whitsunday Is. Nat'l Park, Austl.
191/E4 Whitt, Tx,US
205/E7 Whittaker, Mi,US
177/J3 Whittier, Ak,US
204/B3 Whittier, Ca,US
135/G5 Whittlesea, Austl.
59/F1 Whittlesey, Eng,UK
195/J4 Whittlesey (mtn.), Wi,US
135/C2 Whitton, Austl.
57/G5 Whitwell, Eng,UK
200/E3 Whitwell, Tn,US
57/F4 Whitworth, Eng,UK
178/F2 Wholdaia (lake), NW,Can
187/F4 Why, Az,US
133/H5 Whyalla, Austl.
197/G3 Whycocomagh, NS,Can
133/J4 Whyjonta, Austl.
123/B2 Wiang Ko Sai Nat'l Park, Thai.
198/F2 Wiarton, On,Can
153/H2 Wiawer, Ugan.
145/E5 Wiawso, Gha.
194/B4 Wibaux, Mt,US
165/G4 Wichabai, Guy.
150/A3 Wich'alē, Eth.
68/C2 Wichelen, Belg.
123/C3 Wichian Buri, Thai.
191/F2 Wichita, Ks,US
190/E3 Wichita (mts.), Ok,US
190/E4 Wichita (riv.), Tx,US
191/E4 Wichita Falls, Tx,US
55/K7 Wick, Sc,UK
67/E6 Wickede, Ger.
67/E6 Wickede (Dortmund) (int'l arpt.), Ger.
187/F4 Wickenburg, Az,US
132/C5 Wickepin, Austl.
191/G3 Wickes, Ar,US
59/G3 Wickford, Eng,UK
132/C2 Wickham, Austl.
135/C3 Wickham (cape), Austl.
59/H2 Wickham Market, Eng,UK
184/C2 Wickiup (res.), Or,US
200/C2 Wickliffe, Ky,US
208/F4 Wickliffe, Oh,US
60/D4 Wicklow, Ire.
60/D4 Wicklow (co.), Ire.
60/D4 Wicklow (mts.), Ire.
60/D3 Wicklow Gap (pass), Ire.
56/C6 Wicklow Head (pt.), Ire.
67/F4 Wickriede (riv.), Ger.
192/B4 Widefield-Security, Co,US
132/D4 Widgiemooltha, Austl.
81/F3 Widnau, Swi.
57/F5 Widnes, Eng,UK
65/J2 Więcbork, Pol.
69/G2 Wied (riv.), Ger.
67/G2 Wiedau (riv.), Ger.
72/C5 Wiederitzsch, Ger.
67/F2 Wiefelstede, Ger.
67/F4 Wiehengebirge (ridge), Ger.
69/G2 Wiehl, Ger.
81/H2 Wielenbach, Ger.
65/J4 Wieliczka, Pol.
68/C2 Wielsbeke, Belg.
65/K3 Wieluń, Pol.
73/A3 Wien (prov.), Aus.
73/A3 Wien (riv.), Aus.
73/A3 Wiener Becken (basin), Aus.
73/A3 Wiener Neudorf, Aus.
73/A4 Wiener Neustadt, Aus.
73/A3 Wienerwald (reg.), Aus.
73/A3 Wien (Vienna) (cap.), Aus.
75/L2 Wienwald (reg.), Aus.
65/M3 Wieprz (riv.), Pol.
66/D4 Wierden, Neth.
67/H3 Wieren, Ger.
66/B3 Wieringermeerpolder (polder), Neth.
66/C3 Wieringerwerf, Neth.
66/D2 Wierum, Neth.
65/K3 Wieruszów, Pol.
70/B2 Wiesbaden, Ger.
80/D2 Wiese (riv.), Ger.
100/H2 Wiese (isl.), Rus.
70/B1 Wieseck (riv.), Ger.
73/A4 Wiesen, Aus.
72/C3 Wiesenburg, Ger.
81/E2 Wiesendangen, Swi.
70/C5 Wiesensteig, Ger.
70/D5 Wiesent (riv.), Ger.
70/D3 Wiesentheid, Ger.
70/B4 Wiesloch, Ger.
67/E2 Wiesmoor, Ger.
67/E3 Wietmarschen, Ger.
67/G3 Wietze, Ger.
67/G3 Wietze (riv.), Ger.
67/G3 Wietzendorf, Ger.
65/K1 Wieżyca (peak), Pol.
57/F4 Wigan, Eng,UK
202/D2 Wiggins, Ms,US
59/E5 Wight, Isle of (isl.), Eng,UK
68/D3 Wignehies, Fr.
63/K5 Wigry (lake), Pol.
59/E1 Wigston, Eng,UK
57/E2 Wigton, Eng,UK
56/D2 Wigtown, Sc,UK
56/D2 Wigtown (bay), Sc,UK
66/C5 Wijchen, Neth.
66/D4 Wijhe, Neth.
66/C5 Wijk bij Duurstede, Neth.
66/C5 Wijk en Aalburg, Neth.
187/F3 Wikieup, Az,US
150/A2 Wik'ro, Eth.
198/F2 Wikwemikong, On,Can
198/F2 Wikwemikong Ind. Res., On,Can
81/F3 Wil, Swi.
193/F3 Wilber, Ne,US
134/G8 Wilberforce, Austl.
131/E2 Wilberforce (cape), Austl.
57/H4 Wilberfoss, Eng,UK
208/B1 Wilbraham, Ma,US
208/D2 Wilbur (pt.), Ma,US
182/E4 Wilbur, Wa,US
70/D4 Wilburgstetten, Ger.
191/G3 Wilburton, Ok,US
135/B1 Wilcannia, Austl.
81/E2 Wilchingen, Swi.
194/B2 Wilcox, Sk,Can
199/G4 Wilcox, Pa,US
100/G1 Wilczek (isl.), Rus.
72/D3 Wildau, Ger.
70/B5 Wildbad im Schwarzwald, Ger.
70/B5 Wildberg, Ger.
201/F3 Wildcat (peak), NC,US
156/E4 Wild Coast (reg.), SAfr.
206/C2 Wild Creek (res.), Pa,US
73/A2 Wildendürnbach, Aus.
184/E2 Wilder, Id,US
200/C3 Wildersville, Tn,US
80/D4 Wilderswil, Swi.
66/D2 Wildervank, Neth.
67/F3 Wildeshausen, Ger.
72/D6 Wilde Weisseritz (riv.), Ger.
197/R8 Wildfield, On,Can
70/C2 Wildflecken, Ger.
81/G3 Wildgrat (peak), Aus.
81/F3 Wildhaus, Swi.
182/E1 Wildhay (riv.), Ab,Can
80/D5 Wildhorn (peak), Swi.
192/D3 Wild Horse (hill), Ne,US
204/C3 Wildomar, Ca,US
194/F4 Wild Rice (riv.), Mn, ND,US
194/C3 Wildrose, ND,US
198/B2 Wild Rose, Wi,US
81/G4 Wildspitze (peak), Aus.
80/D5 Wildstrubel (peak), Swi.
202/C2 Wildsville, La,US
182/G1 Wildwood, Ab,Can
203/G3 Wildwood, Fl,US
195/H4 Wildwood, Mn,US
206/D6 Wildwood, NJ,US
206/D6 Wildwood Crest, NJ,US
206/B6 Wild World, Md,US
192/C4 Wiley, Co,US
73/A2 Wilfersdorf, Aus.
156/E2 Wilge (riv.), SAfr.
131/G1 Wilhelm (mtn.), PNG
208/G5 Wilhelm (res.), Pa,US
137/F Wilhelm II (coast), Ant.
166/B2 Wilhelmina (mts.), Sur.
66/C5 Wilhelminakanaal (can.), Neth.
67/G2 Wilhelmsburg, Ger.
67/F1 Wilhelmshaven, Ger.
72/D3 Wilhelmshorst, Ger.
154/C4 Wilhelmstal, Namb.
71/H6 Wilhering, Aus.
72/C6 Wilkau-Hasslau, Ger.
206/C1 Wilkes-Barre, Pa,US
201/G2 Wilkesboro, NC,US
137/J Wilkes Land (reg.), Ant.
205/C3 Wilkeson, Wa,US
183/K1 Wilkie, Sk,Can
137/V Wilkins (sound), Ant.
208/H7 Wilkinsburg, Pa,US
201/G4 Wilkinson Heights, SC,US
208/C1 Wilkinsonville, Ma,US
177/N4 Will (mtn.), BC,Can
205/P16 Will (co.), Il,US
192/E3 Willa Cather Mem., Ne,US
203/G2 Willacoochee, Ga,US
184/B1 Willamette (riv.), Or,US
184/B2 Willamette, Middle Fork (riv.), Or,US
135/C2 Willandra Nat'l Park, Austl.
182/C4 Willapa (bay), Wa,US
182/C4 Willapa Nat'l Wild. Ref., Wa,US
191/H2 Willard, Mo,US
194/B4 Willard, Mt,US
190/A3 Willard, NM,US
198/E4 Willard, Oh,US
190/E2 Willard, Ok,US
185/G3 Willard, Ut,US
57/F5 Willaston, Eng,UK
135/B3 Willaura, Austl.
187/H4 Willcox, Az,US
187/H4 Willcox Playa (dry lake), Az,US
67/G5 Willebadessen, Ger.
68/D1 Willebroek, Belg.
162/D4 Willemstad (cap.), NAnt.
66/B5 Willemstad, Neth.
195/Q6 Willernie, Mn,US
130/C3 Willeroo, Austl.
69/D4 Willerzie, Belg.
53/N7 Willesden, Eng,UK
135/B3 William (peak), Austl.
132/C5 William Bay Nat'l Park, Austl.
201/M7 William B. Hartsfield Atlanta (int'l arpt.), Ga,US
202/E1 William Bill Dannely (res.), Al,US
133/H4 William Creek, Austl.
200/E1 William H. Taft Nat'l Hist. Site, Oh,US
189/M9 William P. Hobby (arpt.), Tx,US
132/C5 Williams, Austl.
187/F3 Williams, Az,US
195/G3 Williams, Mn,US
201/G4 Williams, SC,US
205/N14 Williams Bay, Wi,US
193/H3 Williamsburg, Ia,US
200/E2 Williamsburg, Ky,US
208/B1 Williamsburg, Ma,US
187/J4 Williamsburg, NM,US
207/K9 Williamsburg, NY,US
201/J2 Williamsburg, Va,US
208/G4 Williamsfield, Oh,US
176/E4 Williams Lake, Can.
182/C1 Williams Lake, BC,Can
182/D1 Williams Lake Ind. Res., BC,Can
184/C2 Williamson (riv.), Or,US
201/F2 Williamson, WV,US
198/C4 Williamsport, In,US
206/A1 Williamsport, Pa,US
206/B1 Williamsport-Lycoming (co. arpt.), Pa,US
201/J3 Williamston, NC,US
201/F3 Williamston, SC,US
135/F5 Williamstown, Austl.
200/E1 Williamstown, Ky,US
193/J3 Williamstown, Mo,US
206/D4 Williamstown, NJ,US
199/J3 Williamstown, NY,US
206/B2 Williamstown, Pa,US
199/K2 Williamstown, Vt,US
198/F5 Williamstown, WV,US
191/J2 Williamsville, Mo,US
197/T10 Williamsville, NY,US
66/D6 Willich, Ger.
208/B2 Willimantic, Ct,US
206/D3 Willingboro, NJ,US
67/F6 Willingen, Ger.
57/G2 Willington, Eng,UK
57/G6 Willington, Eng,UK
208/B2 Willington, Ct,US
191/F4 Willis, Ok,US
189/G2 Willis, Tx,US
80/D3 Willisau, Swi.
129/J3 Willis Islets (isls.), Austl.
178/D3 Williston (lake), BC,Can
156/C3 Williston, SAfr.
203/G3 Williston, Fl,US
194/C3 Williston, ND,US
201/G4 Williston, SC,US
200/C3 Williston, Tn,US
207/L8 Williston Park, NY,US
191/H4 Willisville, Ar,US
58/C4 Williton, Eng,UK
184/B4 Willits, Ca,US
195/G5 Willmar, Mn,US
208/F4 Willoughby Hills, Oh,US
183/H2 Willow (cr.), Ab,Can
182/D1 Willow (riv.), BC,Can
177/H3 Willow, Ak,US
190/E3 Willow, Ok,US
184/D1 Willow (cr.), Or,US
184/E1 Willow (cr.), Or,US
185/J4 Willow (cr.), Ut,US
195/K5 Willow (res.), Wi,US
204/F8 Willowbrook, Ca,US
205/Q16 Willowbrook, Il,US
194/B3 Willow Bunch, Sk,Can
194/D3 Willow City, ND,US
189/E2 Willow City, Tx,US
183/K3 Willow Creek, Sk,Can
184/B3 Willow Creek, Ca,US
183/J5 Willow Creek, Mt,US
206/C5 Willow Grove, De,US
206/C3 Willow Grove, Pa,US
206/C3 Willow Grove Nav. Air Sta., Pa,US
192/F1 Willow Lake, SD,US
194/D3 Willow Lake Nat'l Wild. Ref., ND,US
156/C4 Willowmore, SAfr.
188/K7 Willow Park, Tx,US
133/G2 Willowra, Austl.
133/G2 Willowra Abor. Land, Austl.
184/C3 Willow Ranch, Ca,US
184/B4 Willows, Ca,US
191/J2 Willow Springs, Mo,US
206/B4 Willow Street, Pa,US
135/D1 Willow Tree, Austl.
191/F3 Will Rogers World (int'l arpt.), Ok,US
130/C5 Wills (lake), Austl.
198/D4 Willshire, Oh,US
189/F1 Wills Point, Tx,US
80/D1 Willstätt, Ger.
133/H5 Willunga, Austl.
191/J4 Wilmar, Ar,US
182/F2 Wilmer, BC,Can
188/L7 Wilmer, Tx,US
72/D3 Wilmersdorf, Ger.
205/Q15 Wilmette, Il,US
133/H5 Wilmington, Austl.
53/P7 Wilmington, Eng,UK
204/F8 Wilmington, Ca,US
206/C4 Wilmington, De,US
193/K3 Wilmington, Il,US
201/J3 Wilmington, NC,US
198/E5 Wilmington, Oh,US
201/G5 Wilmington Island, Ga,US
193/G2 Wilmont, Mn,US
200/E2 Wilmore, Ky,US
196/F2 Wilmot, PE,Can
191/J4 Wilmot, Ar,US
208/F6 Wilmot, Oh,US
194/F5 Wilmot, SD,US
57/F5 Wilmslow, Eng,UK
69/H2 Wilnsdorf, Ger.
122/G4 Wilpattu Nat'l Park, SrL.
66/B6 Wilrijk, Belg.
183/J5 Wilsall, Mt,US
72/D5 Wilsdruff, Ger.
67/G2 Wilseder Berg (peak), Ger.
191/F1 Wilsey, Ks,US
206/B4 Wilshire-Stonybrook, Pa,US
179/H2 Wilson (cape), NW,Can
200/B3 Wilson, Ar,US
204/B2 Wilson (mtn.), Ca,US
185/K5 Wilson (mtn.), Co,US
191/E1 Wilson, Ks,US
191/E1 Wilson (lake), Ks,US
189/J2 Wilson, La,US
201/J3 Wilson, NC,US
199/G3 Wilson, NY,US
191/F3 Wilson, Ok,US
206/C2 Wilson, Pa,US
188/D1 Wilson, Tx,US
188/L6 Wilson (cr.), Tx,US
185/H2 Wilson, Wy,US
182/E4 Wilson Creek, Wa,US
196/D3 Wilsons Beach, NB,Can
129/H7 Wilsons Promontory (pen.), Austl.
135/C3 Wilsons Promontory Nat'l Park, Austl.
200/D4 Wilsonville, Al,US
192/D3 Wilsonville, Ne,US
67/G2 Wilstedt, Ger.
67/G1 Wilster, Ger.
66/D3 Wilsum, Ger.
130/D3 Wilton (riv.), Austl.
59/E4 Wilton, Eng,UK
200/D4 Wilton, Al,US
200/B3 Wilton, Ar,US
205/M10 Wilton, Ca,US
208/A3 Wilton, Ct,US
193/J3 Wilton, Ia,US
196/B3 Wilton, Me,US
194/D4 Wilton, ND,US
59/E4 Wiltshire (co.), Eng,UK
69/E4 Wiltz, Lux.
132/D3 Wiluna, Austl.
202/L8 Wimauma, Fl,US
189/E3 Wimberley, Tx,US
53/N7 Wimbledon, Eng,UK
194/E4 Wimbledon, ND,US
58/E5 Wimborne Minster, Eng,UK
68/A2 Wimereux, Fr.
203/F3 Wimico (lake), Fl,US
80/D4 Wimmis, Swi.
151/A2 Winam (gulf), Kenya
198/C4 Winamac, In,US
156/D3 Winburg, SAfr.
58/D4 Wincanton, Eng,UK
59/E3 Winchcombe, Eng,UK
59/G5 Winchelsea, Eng,UK
196/A4 Winchendon, Ma,US
199/J2 Winchester, On,Can
136/B4 Winchester, N.Z.
59/E4 Winchester, Eng,UK
191/J4 Winchester, Ar,US
204/C3 Winchester, Ca,US
208/A2 Winchester, Ct,US
193/J4 Winchester, Il,US
198/D4 Winchester, In,US
200/E2 Winchester, Ky,US
193/J3 Winchester, Mo,US
186/E2 Winchester, Nv,US
191/F3 Winchester, Ok,US
184/B2 Winchester, Or,US
200/D3 Winchester, Tn,US
201/H1 Winchester, Va,US
199/K4 Winchester Center, Ct,US
205/L12 Winchester Mystery House, Ca,US
190/A3 Wind (mesa), NM,US
190/A3 Wind (mtn.), NM,US
205/P14 Wind (lake), Wi,US
185/J2 Wind (riv.), Wy,US
81/H1 Windach, Ger.
81/G2 Windach (riv.), Ger.
199/G4 Windber, Pa,US
192/C2 Wind Cave Nat'l Park, SD,US
201/J3 Windemere, NC,US
200/F4 Winder, Ga,US
57/F3 Windermere, Eng,UK
57/F3 Windermere (lake), Eng,UK
202/M7 Windermere, Fl,US
69/G4 Windesheim, Ger.
206/C2 Wind Gap, Pa,US
208/B2 Windham, Ct,US
208/B2 Windham (co.), Ct,US
208/F5 Windham, Oh,US
154/C4 Windhoek (cap.), Namb.
154/C4 Windhoek (int'l arpt.), Namb.
71/F3 Windischeschenbach, Ger.
130/B4 Windjana Gorge Nat'l Park, Austl.
187/J2 Windom (peak), Co,US
193/G2 Windom, Mn,US
133/J3 Windorah, Austl.
187/H3 Window Rock, Az,US
205/Q14 Wind Point, Wi,US
185/J2 Wind River (range), Wy,US
185/J2 Wind River Ind. Res., Wy,US
59/E3 Windrush (riv.), Eng,UK
70/D4 Windsbach, Ger.
134/G8 Windsor, Austl.
197/K1 Windsor, Nf,Can
196/E3 Windsor, NS,Can
205/F7 Windsor, On,Can
205/G7 Windsor (arpt.), On,Can
196/B3 Windsor, Qu,Can
59/F4 Windsor, Eng,UK
184/B4 Windsor, Ca,US
192/B3 Windsor, Co,US
208/B2 Windsor, Ct,US
198/B5 Windsor, Il,US
208/B1 Windsor (dam), Ma,US
191/H1 Windsor, Mo,US
206/B4 Windsor, Pa,US
199/K3 Windsor, Vt,US
208/B2 Windsor Locks, Ct,US
194/C2 Windthorst, Sk,Can
191/E4 Windthorst, Tx,US
161/H2 Windward (passg.), Cuba, Haiti
162/F4 Windward (isls.), West Indies
201/H3 Windy Hill, SC,US
208/F6 Winesburg, Oh,US
183/G1 Winfield, Ab,Can
200/D4 Winfield, Al,US
193/J3 Winfield, Ia,US
191/F2 Winfield, Ks,US
206/A5 Winfield, Md,US
191/J1 Winfield, Mo,US
206/B2 Winfield, Pa,US
201/G1 Winfield, WV,US
59/F3 Wing, Eng,UK
194/D4 Wing, ND,US
130/C3 Wingate (mts.), Austl.
57/G2 Wingate, Eng,UK
201/G3 Wingate, NC,US
188/D1 Wingate, Tx,US
68/C1 Wingene, Belg.
197/S10 Winger, On,Can
135/E1 Wingham, Austl.
198/F3 Wingham, On,Can
59/H4 Wingham, Eng,UK
200/C2 Wingo, Ky,US
130/B2 Wini, Indo.
132/D2 Winifred (lake), Austl.
183/K4 Winifred, Mt,US
174/D3 Winifreda, Arg.
193/H3 Winigan, Mo,US
179/H3 Winisk, On,Can
179/H3 Winisk (riv.), On,Can
188/C2 Wink, Tx,US
66/B3 Winkel, Neth.
187/G4 Winkelman, Az,US
194/F3 Winkler, Mb,Can
189/F2 Winkler, Tx,US
182/F3 Winlaw, BC,Can
182/C4 Winlock, Wa,US
196/C3 Winn, Me,US
145/E5 Winneba, Gha.

193/G2 Winnebago, Mn,US
193/K2 Winnebago (lake), Wi,US
193/F2 Winnebago Ind. Res., Ne,US
193/J1 Winnebago Ind. Res., Wi,US
193/K1 Winneconne, Wi,US
184/E3 Winnemucca, Nv,US
184/D3 Winnemucca (lake), Nv,US
70/C5 Winnenden, Ger.
194/D1 Winnepegosis (lake), Mb,Can
196/B4 Winnepesaukee (lake), NH,US
192/E2 Winner, SD,US
205/Q15 Winnetka, Il,US
183/K4 Winnett, Mt,US
202/B2 Winnfield, La,US
195/G3 Winnibigoshish (lake), Mn,US
189/G3 Winnie, Tx,US
132/B2 Winning, Austl.
69/G3 Winningen, Ger.
194/F3 Winnipeg (cap.), Mb,Can
194/F3 Winnipeg (int'l arpt.), Mb,Can
178/G3 Winnipeg (lake), Mb,Can
195/G2 Winnipeg (riv.), Mb, On,Can
194/F2 Winnipeg Beach, Mb,Can
194/E2 Winnipegosis, Mb,Can
178/F3 Winnipegosis (lake), Mb,Can
199/L3 Winnipesaukee (lake), NH,US
202/C1 Winnsboro, La,US
201/G3 Winnsboro, SC,US
189/G1 Winnsboro, Tx,US
70/A3 Winnweiler, Ger.
197/R9 Winona, On,Can
187/G3 Winona, Az,US
193/J1 Winona, Mn,US
191/J2 Winona, Mo,US
200/C4 Winona, Ms,US
208/G6 Winona, Oh,US
189/G1 Winona, Tx,US
198/D4 Winona Lake, In,US
66/E2 Winschoten, Neth.
58/D4 Winscombe, Eng,UK
67/G3 Winsen, Ger.
67/F2 Winsen, Ger.
57/F5 Winsford, Eng,UK
58/D4 Winsley, Eng,UK
59/F3 Winslow, Eng,UK
191/G3 Winslow, Ar,US
187/G3 Winslow, Az,US
196/C3 Winslow, Me,US
206/D4 Winslow, NJ,US
205/B2 Winslow, Wa,US
208/A2 Winsted, Ct,US
193/G1 Winsted, Mn,US
202/L7 Winston, Fl,US
183/J4 Winston, Mt,US
187/J4 Winston, NM,US
184/B2 Winston, Or,US
201/G2 Winston-Salem, NC,US
66/D2 Winsum, Neth.
183/K1 Winter, Sk,Can
195/J5 Winter, Wi,US
67/F6 Winterberg, Ger.
156/D4 Winterberge (mts.), SAfr.
58/D3 Winterbourne, Eng,UK
72/B2 Winterfeld, Ger.
202/M6 Winter Garden, Fl,US
186/E4 Winterhaven, Ca,US
202/M7 Winter Haven, Fl,US
203/H3 Winter Haven, Fl,US
70/C6 Winterlingen, Ger.
202/N6 Winter Park, Fl,US
203/H3 Winter Park, Fl,US
196/C3 Winterport, Me,US
205/L9 Winters, Ca,US
206/B4 Winters (run), Md,US
188/E2 Winters, Tx,US
187/F4 Wintersburg, Az,US
193/G3 Winterset, Ia,US
202/N6 Winter Springs, Fl,US
81/F3 Winterstaude (peak), Aus.
208/G7 Wintersville, Oh,US
66/D5 Winterswijk, Neth.
81/E2 Winterthur, Swi.
206/C4 Winterthur Museum & Gdns., De,US
197/L2 Winterton, Nf,Can
156/E3 Winterton, SAfr.
201/J3 Winterville, NC,US
208/B3 Winthrop, Ct,US
208/D1 Winthrop, Ma,US
196/C3 Winthrop, Me,US
193/G1 Winthrop, Mn,US
182/D3 Winthrop, Wa,US
199/J2 Winthrop-Brasher Falls, NY,US
205/Q15 Winthrop Harbor, Il,US
134/A3 Winton, Austl.
136/B4 Winton, N.Z.
186/B2 Winton, Ca,US
201/J2 Winton, NC,US
116/C3 Wintong, India
80/D1 Wintzenheim, Fr.
72/A5 Wipper (riv.), Ger.
72/B4 Wipper (riv.), Ger.
67/H2 Wipperau (riv.), Ger.
67/H6 Wipperdorf, Ger.
67/E6 Wipperfürth, Ger.
72/B4 Wippra, Ger.
124/D3 Wiralaga, Indo.
70/A2 Wirges, Ger.
57/G5 Wirksworth, Eng,UK
133/H5 Wirrabara, Austl.
57/E5 Wirral (pen.), Eng,UK
133/G5 Wirrulla, Austl.
59/G1 Wisbech, Eng,UK
196/C3 Wiscasset, Me,US
80/D1 Wisches, Fr.
67/G1 Wischhafen, Ger.
181/H3 Wisconsin (state), US
193/K2 Wisconsin (lake), Wi,US
193/J2 Wisconsin (riv.), Wi,US
193/K2 Wisconsin Dells, Wi,US
193/K1 Wisconsin Rapids, Wi,US
201/H2 Wise, NC,US
188/K6 Wise (co.), Tx,US
201/F2 Wise, Va,US
177/H2 Wiseman, Ak,US
70/E1 Wisenta (riv.), Ger.
183/L2 Wiseton, Sk,Can
194/C2 Wishart, Sk,Can
54/C5 Wishaw, Sc,UK
194/E4 Wishek, ND,US
182/D5 Wishram, Wa,US
65/K4 Wisła, Pol.
63/H4 Wiślany (lag.), Pol.
65/K2 Wisła (Vistula) (riv.), Pol.
65/L4 Wisłok (riv.), Pol.
65/L4 Wisłoka (riv.), Pol.
64/F2 Wismar, Ger.
202/C2 Wisner, La,US
193/F3 Wisner, Ne,US
68/A2 Wissant, Fr.
69/G5 Wissembourg, Fr.
69/G2 Wissen, Ger.
59/G1 Wissey (riv.), Eng,UK
191/G3 Wister, Ok,US
156/E2 Witbank, SAfr.
154/B5 Witberg (peak), Namb.
154/C5 Witbooisvlei, Namb.
183/L1 Witchekan (lake), Sk,Can
59/G3 Witham, Eng,UK
57/H5 Witham (riv.), Eng,UK
199/K2 Witherbee-Mineville, NY,US
58/C5 Witheridge, Eng,UK
57/J4 Withernsea, Eng,UK
177/J3 Witherspoon (mtn.), Ak,US
187/J4 Withington (mtn.), NM,US
202/L6 Withlacoochee (riv.), Fl,US
202/L6 Withlacoochee St. For., Fl,US
57/F4 Withnell, Eng,UK
133/G3 Witjira Nat'l Park, Austl.
156/D3 Wit Kei (riv.), SAfr.
65/J2 Witkowo, Pol.
197/L2 Witless Bay, Nf,Can
59/E3 Witney, Eng,UK
65/H2 Witnica, Pol.
156/B2 Witputz, Namb.
68/D5 Witry-lès-Reims, Fr.
193/K4 Witt, Il,US
80/D2 Wittelsheim, Fr.
69/E2 Witten, Ger.
67/E6 Witten, Ger.
81/F3 Wittenbach, Swi.
72/C4 Wittenberg, Ger.
193/K1 Wittenberg, Wi,US
72/B2 Wittenberge, Ger.
64/F2 Wittenburg, Ger.
80/D2 Wittenheim, Fr.
132/C2 Wittenoom, Austl.
59/F1 Wittering, Eng,UK
72/C6 Wittgensdorf, Ger.
67/H3 Wittingen, Ger.
69/F4 Wittlich, Ger.
206/B6 Wittman, Md,US
187/F4 Wittmann, Az,US
67/E1 Wittmund, Ger.
65/G1 Witton (pen.), Ger.
72/C1 Wittstock, Ger.
151/C2 Witu, Kenya
154/C4 Witvlei, Namb.
154/B4 Witwatersberge (peak), Namb.
156/P12 Witwatersrand (reg.), SAfr.
67/G6 Witzenhausen, Ger.
58/C4 Wiveliscombe, Eng,UK
129/J5 Wivenhoe (lake), Austl.
59/G3 Wivenhoe, Eng,UK
113/D2 Wiwŏn, NKor.
65/L2 Wkra (riv.), Pol.
65/K1 Władysławowo, Pol.
65/K2 Włocławek, Pol.
65/K2 Włocławek (prov.), Pol.
65/K2 Włocławskie (lake), Pol.
65/M3 Włodawa, Pol.
65/K3 Włoszczowa, Pol.
154/B4 Wlotzkasbaken, Namb.
58/C1 Wnion (riv.), Wal,UK
153/H2 Wobulenzi, Ugan.
59/F3 Woburn Abbey, Eng,UK
59/F2 Woburn Sands, Eng,UK
135/C3 Wodonga, Austl.
65/K4 Wodzisław Śląski, Pol.
66/B4 Woerden, Neth.
69/G6 Woerth, Fr.
186/C3 Wofford Heights, Ca,US
66/C3 Wognum, Neth.
81/E3 Wohlen, Swi.
80/D4 Wohlen bei Bern, Swi.
204/D4 Wohlford (lake), Ca,US
69/F5 Woippy, Fr.
131/G2 Woitape, PNG
130/D1 Wokam (isl.), Indo.
109/K2 Woken (riv.), China
53/M8 Woking, Eng,UK
59/F4 Wokingham, Eng,UK
113/D5 Wŏlch'ul-san Nat'l Park, SKor.
208/B2 Wolcott, Ct,US
197/T9 Wolcottsville, NY,US
65/K3 Wołczyn, Pol.
195/P7 Wold Chamberlain (Minneapolis-Saint Paul) (int'l arpt.), Mn,US
53/N8 Woldingham, Eng,UK
138/D4 Woleai (isl.), Micr.
152/B2 Woleu (riv.), Gabon
152/B2 Woleu-Ntem (prov.), Gabon
182/F1 Wolf (cr.), Ab,Can
168/J6 Wolf (isl.), Ecu.
168/J7 Wolf (vol.), Ecu.
177/H2 Wolf (mtn.), Ak,US
205/R16 Wolf (lake), In,US
202/D2 Wolf (riv.), Ms,US
200/C3 Wolf (riv.), Ms, Tn,US
208/F5 Wolf (cr.), Oh,US
191/F3 Wolf, Ok,US
191/G3 Wolf (mtn.), Ok,US
190/D2 Wolf (cr.), Ok, Tx,US
208/G5 Wolf (cr.), Pa,US
193/K1 Wolf (riv.), Wi,US
70/B6 Wolfach, Ger.
70/B6 Wolfach (riv.), Ger.
134/B3 Wolfang (peak), Austl.
191/J3 Wolf Bayou, Ar,US
177/J3 Wolf Creek (mtn.), Ak,US
191/G1 Wolf Creek (res.), Ks,US
200/E2 Wolf Creek (dam), Ky,US
183/H4 Wolf Creek, Mt,US
184/B2 Wolf Creek, Or,US
198/F4 Wolfdale, Pa,US
189/F1 Wolfe City, Tx,US
130/B4 Wolfe Creek Crater Nat'l Park, Austl.
81/F2 Wolfegg, Ger.
199/H2 Wolfe Island, On,Can
72/C4 Wolfen, Ger.
67/H4 Wolfenbüttel, Ger.
71/H6 Wolfern, Aus.
70/B2 Wölfersheim, Ger.
190/C4 Wolfforth, Tx,US
67/G6 Wolfhagen, Ger.
198/C3 Wolf Lake, Mi,US
183/M3 Wolf Point, Mt,US
70/D4 Wolframs-Eschenbach, Ger.
81/H2 Wolfratshausen, Ger.
67/H4 Wolfsburg, Ger.
71/G6 Wolfsegg am Hausruck, Aus.
69/G4 Wolfstein, Ger.
81/F3 Wolfurt, Aus.
196/E3 Wolfville, NS,Can
65/G1 Wolgast, Ger.
80/E3 Wolhusen, Swi.
65/H2 Wolin, Pol.
65/H2 Woliński Nat'l Park, Pol.
73/A3 Wolkersdorf, Aus.
178/E2 Wollaston (pen.), NW,Can
178/F3 Wollaston (lake), Sk,Can
175/L8 Wollaston (isl.), Chile
59/F2 Wollaston, Eng,UK
135/D2 Wollemi Nat'l Park, Austl.
81/E3 Wollerau, Swi.
131/E4 Wollogorang, Austl.
135/E1 Wollomombi, Austl.
135/D2 Wollongong, Austl.
70/B2 Wöllstadt, Ger.
69/G4 Wöllstein, Ger.
156/D2 Wolmaransstad, SAfr.
72/B3 Wolmirstedt, Ger.
75/J3 Wolnzach, Ger.
65/L2 Wołomin, Pol.
65/J3 Wołów, Pol.
130/A2 Wolowaru, Indo.
66/A5 Wolphaartsdijk, Neth.
194/C2 Wolseley, Sk,Can
156/L10 Wolseley, SAfr.
192/E1 Wolsey, SD,US
57/G2 Wolsingham, Eng,UK
65/J2 Wolsztyn, Pol.
72/D3 Woltersdorf, Ger.
68/D2 Woluwé-St-Lambert, Belg.
66/D3 Wolvega, Neth.
58/D1 Wolverhampton, Eng,UK
205/F6 Wolverine Lake, Mi,US
59/F2 Wolverton, Eng,UK
194/F4 Wolverton, Mn,US
72/D3 Wolziger (lake), Ger.
60/B6 Womanagh (riv.), Ire.
135/C2 Womboota, Austl.
58/D1 Wombourne, Eng,UK
57/G4 Wombwell, Eng,UK
206/B3 Womelsdorf, Pa,US
199/H3 Women's Rights Nat'l Hist. Park, NY,US
144/B3 Wompou, Mrta.
134/C4 Wondai, Austl.
205/P15 Wonder (lake), Il,US
155/F2 Wonder Gorge, Zam.
113/E2 Wŏndong-ni, NKor.
71/F3 Wondreb (riv.), Ger.
70/D2 Wonfurt, Ger.
135/C1 Wongalarroo (lake), Austl.
132/C4 Wongan Hills, Austl.
152/B3 Wonga-Wongué Nat'l Park, Gabon
121/G2 Wong Chu (riv.), Bhu.
113/D4 Wŏnju, SKor.
135/C3 Wonnangatta-Moroka Nat'l Park, Austl.
124/E4 Wonogiri, Indo.
124/E4 Wonosari, Indo.
124/E4 Wonosobo, Indo.
130/B2 Wonreli, Indo.
113/D3 Wŏnsan, NKor.
135/C3 Wonthaggi, Austl.
132/C3 Wonyulgunna (peak), Austl.
183/L3 Wood (mtn.), Sk,Can
183/L3 Wood (riv.), Sk,Can
177/K3 Wood (mtn.), Yk,Can
192/E3 Wood (riv.), Ne,US
203/H2 Woodbine, Ga,US
193/G3 Woodbine, Ia,US
193/F4 Woodbine, Ks,US
200/E2 Woodbine, Ky,US
206/A5 Woodbine, Md,US
206/D5 Woodbine, NJ,US
197/R8 Woodbridge, On,Can
59/H2 Woodbridge, Eng,UK
205/M10 Woodbridge, Ca,US
208/A3 Woodbridge, Ct,US
207/D2 Woodbridge, NJ,US
201/J1 Woodbridge, Va,US
178/E2 Wood Buffalo Nat'l Park, Ab, Yk,Can
135/E1 Woodburn, Austl.
197/R9 Woodburn, On,Can
56/C2 Woodburn, NI,UK
184/B1 Woodburn, Or,US
208/A2 Woodbury, Ct,US
200/E4 Woodbury, Ga,US
195/Q7 Woodbury, Mn,US
206/C4 Woodbury, NJ,US
200/D3 Woodbury, Tn,US
207/J7 Woodcliff Lake, NJ,US
60/B4 Woodcock (hill), Ire.
130/D4 Woodcock, Mount (peak), Austl.
205/Q16 Wood Dale, Il,US
131/E3 Wooded (isl.), Austl.
60/D4 Woodenbridge, Ire.
135/C3 Woodend, Austl.
201/G3 Woodfield, SC,US
201/F3 Woodfin, NC,US
60/B3 Woodford, Ire.
134/D4 Woodgate, Austl.
134/D4 Woodgate Nat'l Park, Austl.
57/H5 Woodhall Spa, Eng,UK
205/F7 Woodhaven, Mi,US
193/J3 Woodhull, Il,US
197/F3 Wood Islands, PE,Can
186/C2 Woodlake, Ca,US
195/G5 Wood Lake, Mn,US
192/D3 Wood Lake, Ne,US
205/L9 Woodland, Ca,US
196/D3 Woodland, Me,US
195/H4 Woodland, Mn,US
200/C4 Woodland, Ms,US
182/C5 Woodland, Wa,US
198/G2 Woodland Beach, On,Can
204/E7 Woodland Hills, Ca,US
192/B4 Woodland Park, Co,US
194/F2 Woodlands, Mb,Can
189/G2 Woodlands, The, Tx,US
138/E5 Woodlark (isl.), PNG
193/K4 Woodlawn, Il,US
206/B5 Woodlawn, Md,US
200/D2 Woodlawn, Tn,US
201/G2 Woodlawn, Va,US
59/F4 Woodley, Eng,UK
207/E2 Woodmere, NY,US
208/B3 Woodmont, Ct,US
194/F3 Woodridge, Mb,Can
205/P16 Woodridge, Il,US
207/J8 Wood-Ridge, NJ,US
192/E3 Wood River, Ne,US
133/F3 Woodroffe (peak), Austl.
192/C4 Woodrow, Co,US
187/G3 Woodruff, Az,US
192/E4 Woodruff, Ks,US
201/F3 Woodruff, SC,US
185/H3 Woodruff, Ut,US
130/D4 Woods (lake), Austl.
200/E3 Woods (res.), Tn,US
205/D2 Woods (cr.), Wa,US
206/A4 Woodsboro, Md,US
189/F3 Woodsboro, Tx,US
57/F6 Woodseaves, Eng,UK
198/F5 Woodsfield, Oh,US
208/D2 Woods Hole, Ma,US
133/M8 Woodside, Austl.
194/E2 Woodside, Mb,Can
205/K12 Woodside, Ca,US
206/C5 Woodside, De,US
199/G5 Woodside, Pa,US
185/H4 Woodside, Ut,US
206/C2 Woodside-Drifton, Pa,US
195/G3 Woods, Lake of the (lake), Can., US
191/H3 Woodson, Ar,US
188/E1 Woodson, Tx,US
135/D2 Woodstock, Austl.
196/D2 Woodstock, NB,Can
198/F3 Woodstock, On,Can
59/E3 Woodstock, Eng,UK
208/C2 Woodstock, Ct,US
205/P15 Woodstock, Il,US
206/B5 Woodstock, Md,US
199/L3 Woodstock, NH,US
201/H1 Woodstock, Va,US
196/A4 Woodstock, Vt,US
190/E1 Woodston, Ks,US
206/C4 Woodstown, NJ,US
199/K2 Woodsville, NH,US
199/G2 Woodview, On,Can
136/C3 Woodville, N.Z.
203/F2 Woodville, Fl,US
208/C1 Woodville, Ma,US
189/J2 Woodville, Ms,US
202/C2 Woodville, Ms,US
189/G2 Woodville, Tx,US
195/H5 Woodville, Wi,US
193/H3 Woodward, Ia,US
190/E2 Woodward, Ok,US
189/F2 Woodway, Tx,US
201/F2 Woodway, Va,US
205/C2 Woodway, Wa,US
202/B2 Woodworth, La,US
194/E4 Woodworth, ND,US
186/C3 Woody, Ca,US
58/D5 Wool, Eng,UK
58/D4 Woolavington, Eng,UK
54/E5 Wooler, Eng,UK
134/A2 Woolgar, Austl.
135/E1 Woolgoolga, Austl.
135/E1 Wooli, Austl.
182/C3 Woolley-Sedro, Wa,US
206/A1 Woolrich, Pa,US
57/G1 Woolsington, Eng,UK
133/H4 Wooltana, Austl.
53/P7 Woolwich, Eng,UK
133/G4 Woomera, Austl.
133/G4 Woomera Prohibited Area, Austl.
132/L6 Woonoloo (brook), Austl.
208/C1 Woonsocket, RI,US
192/E1 Woonsocket, SD,US
134/C4 Woorabinda Abor. Community, Austl.
132/B3 Wooramel, Austl.
132/B3 Wooramel (riv.), Austl.
57/F6 Woore, Eng,UK
208/F6 Wooster, Oh,US
59/E3 Wootton Basset, Eng,UK
80/D4 Worb, Swi.
67/H6 Worbis, Ger.
156/B4 Worcester, SAfr.
58/D2 Worcester, Eng,UK
208/C1 Worcester, Ma,US
208/C1 Worcester (co.), Ma,US
208/C1 Worcester (mun. arpt.), Ma,US
199/J3 Worcester, NY,US
58/D2 Worcester & Birmingham (can.), Eng,UK
183/K5 Worden, Mt,US
208/C3 Worden (pond), RI,US
75/K3 Wörgl, Aus.
130/D1 Workai (isl.), Indo.
130/D1 Workai (riv.), Indo.
56/E2 Workington, Eng,UK
57/G5 Worksop, Eng,UK
66/C3 Workum, Neth.
185/K1 Worland, Wy,US
50/* World (Earth)
207/J9 World Trade Ctr., NY,US
72/C4 Wörlitz, Ger.
66/B4 Wormer, Neth.
68/B2 Wormhoudt, Fr.
53/N6 Wormley, Eng,UK
70/B3 Worms, Ger.
70/D5 Wörnitz (riv.), Ger.
208/B1 Woronoco, Ma,US
67/F2 Worpswede, Ger.
70/B3 Wörrstadt, Ger.
70/B2 Worsbach (riv.), Ger.
57/G4 Worsbrough, Eng,UK
205/Q16 Worth, Il,US
189/F2 Wortham, Tx,US
70/C3 Wörth am Main, Ger.
70/B4 Wörth am Rhein, Ger.
71/F4 Wörth an der Donau, Ger.
71/F5 Wörth an der Isar, Ger.
59/F5 Worthing, Eng,UK
198/C5 Worthington, In,US
208/B1 Worthington, Ma,US
195/G5 Worthington, Mn,US
198/E4 Worthington, Oh,US
70/E6 Wörthsee, Ger.
70/E6 Wörthsee (lake), Ger.
206/B5 Worton, Md,US
138/F3 Wotho (atoll), Mrsh.
130/B3 Wotjalum Abor. Land, Austl.
138/G4 Wotje (atoll), Mrsh.
58/D3 Wotton under Edge, Eng,UK
196/B3 Wottonville, Qu,Can
127/F4 Wotu, Indo.
66/C4 Woudenberg, Neth.
66/C5 Woudrichem, Neth.
161/F3 Wounta (lag.), Nic.
146/B4 Wour, Chad
152/B1 Wouri (riv.), Camr.
66/B5 Wouw, Neth.
127/F4 Wowoni (isl.), Indo.
57/H5 Wragby, Eng,UK
101/T2 Wrangel (isl.), Rus.
177/M4 Wrangell, Ak,US
177/A5 Wrangell (cape), Ak,US
177/J3 Wrangell (mts.), Ak,US
177/K3 Wrangell-Saint Elias Nat'l Park & Prsv., Ak,US
57/J5 Wrangle, Eng,UK
55/J7 Wrath (cape), Sc,UK
192/C3 Wray, Co,US
53/M7 Wraysbury, Eng,UK
53/M7 Wraysbury (res.), Eng,UK
57/H6 Wreake (riv.), Eng,UK
129/K4 Wreck (reef), Austl.
156/B3 Wreck (pt.), SAfr.
201/K2 Wreck (isl.), Va,US
58/D1 Wrekin, The (hill), Eng,UK
67/F1 Wremen, Ger.
57/F5 Wrenbury, Eng,UK
201/F4 Wrens, Ga,US
195/H4 Wrenshall, Mn,US
208/C1 Wrentham, Ma,US
57/F5 Wrexham, Wal,UK
72/E2 Wriezen, Ger.
195/N6 Wright (co.), Mn,US
192/B2 Wright, Wy,US
201/K2 Wright Brothers Nat'l Mem., NC,US
191/G3 Wright City, Ok,US
119/F5 Wrightmyo, India
189/G1 Wright Patman (lake), Tx,US
198/D5 Wright-Patterson A.F.B., Oh,US
201/J3 Wrightsboro, NC,US
206/D3 Wrightstown, NJ,US
191/H3 Wrightsville, Ar,US
201/F4 Wrightsville, Ga,US
201/J3 Wrightsville Beach, NC,US
204/C2 Wrightwood, Ca,US
178/D2 Wrigley, NW,Can
183/N3 Writing Rock, ND,US
194/C3 Writing Rock Hist. Site, ND,US
59/G3 Writtle, Eng,UK
65/J3 Wrocław, Pol.
65/J3 Wrocław (prov.), Pol.
194/F1 Wrong (lake), Mb,Can
53/P8 Wrotham, Eng,UK
178/D1 Wrottesley (cape), NW,Can
58/D1 Wroxeter, Eng,UK
59/H1 Wroxham, Eng,UK
194/D2 Wroxton, Sk,Can
65/J2 Września, Pol.
65/J3 Wschowa, Pol.
117/F3 Wu (riv.), China
117/G3 Wu (riv.), China
115/C3 Wu'an, China
132/C4 Wubin, Austl.
109/K3 Wuchang, China
115/C5 Wuchang, China
115/C5 Wuchang (lake), China
115/D3 Wucheng, China
117/H3 Wuchiu (isl.), Tai.
115/B2 Wuchuan, China
109/K2 Wudalianchi, China
117/F1 Wudang (mtn.), China
117/F1 Wudang (mts.), China
115/B4 Wudang Shan (mtn.), China
113/A3 Wudao, China
113/C1 Wudaogou, China
115/D3 Wudi, China
145/H4 Wudil, Nga.
115/B3 Wuding (riv.), China
133/G5 Wudinna, Austl.
115/B5 Wufeng, China
117/G3 Wufuting, China
117/G3 Wugong (mtn.), China
108/F4 Wuguzhang, China
108/F4 Wuhai, China
115/C5 Wuhan, China
115/C5 Wuhan (arpt.), China
115/D4 Wuhe, China
72/D2 Wuhle (riv.), Ger.
115/D5 Wuhu, China
109/J3 Wuhuanchi, China
144/C5 Wuilo, Libr.
108/F3 Wujia (riv.), China
115/E5 Wujiang, China
145/H5 Wukari, Nga.
108/D6 Wulang, China
72/B4 Wulfen, Ger.
66/E6 Wülfrath, Ger.
67/H5 Wulften, Ger.
108/F5 Wulian, China
109/H4 Wulian, China
115/D4 Wulian, China
116/D3 Wulian (mts.), China
116/D4 Wuliang (mts.), China
130/C1 Wuliara (isl.), Indo.
117/F2 Wuling (mts.), China
73/A4 Wulka (riv.), Aus.
73/A2 Wullersdorf, Aus.
119/J2 Wulong, China
113/C2 Wulongbei, China
130/C1 Wulur, Indo.
145/H5 Wum, Camr.
116/D3 Wumeng (mts.), China
67/F2 Wümme (riv.), Ger.
118/C3 Wūn, India
151/B2 Wundanyi, Kenya
132/L7 Wungong (brook), Austl.
132/L7 Wungong (res.), Austl.
67/F5 Wünnenberg, Ger.
80/D4 Wünnewil, Swi.
149/F3 Wun Rog, Sudan
72/D3 Wünsdorf, Ger.
149/F3 Wun Shwai, Sudan
71/F2 Wunsiedel, Ger.
67/G4 Wunstorf, Ger.
119/G3 Wuntho, Burma
187/G3 Wupatki Nat'l Mon., Az,US
67/E6 Wüpper (riv.), Ger.
67/E6 Wuppertal, Ger.
115/B3 Wuqi, China
114/C4 Wuqia, China
115/C3 Wuqiang, China
115/D3 Wuqiao, China
115/H7 Wuqing, China
72/D5 Wurgwitz, Ger.
81/H1 Würm (can.), Ger.
69/F2 Würm (riv.), Ger.
71/E6 Würm (riv.), Ger.
145/G3 Wurno, Nga.
72/C6 Wurschnitz (riv.), Ger.
69/F2 Würselen, Ger.
199/J4 Wurtsboro, NY,US
198/E2 Wurtsmith A.F.B., Paul B., Mi,US
71/E2 Wurzbach, Ger.
70/C3 Würzburg, Ger.
72/C5 Wurzen, Ger.
109/H5 Wushan (lake), China
117/H2 Wusheng, China
117/G2 Wusheng (pass), China
115/C5 Wusheng Guan (pass), China
114/C3 Wushi, China
115/L8 Wusong, China
67/G6 Wüstegarten (peak), Ger.
70/C4 Wüstenrot, Ger.
72/C2 Wusterhausen, Ger.
72/C3 Wusterwitz, Ger.
72/B2 Wustrow, Ger.
109/L2 Wusuli (riv.), China, Rus.
81/E2 Wutach (riv.), Ger.
115/C3 Wutai, China
115/C3 Wutai Shan (peak), China
144/C4 Wuteve (peak), Libr.
70/D1 Wutha-Farnroda, Ger.
114/E3 Wutonggou, China
81/E2 Wutöschingen, Ger.
66/B6 Wuustwezel, Belg.
108/F4 Wuwei, China
115/D5 Wuwei, China
115/L8 Wuxi, China
117/H2 Wuxi (riv.), China
115/C3 Wuxiang, China
115/C5 Wuxue, China
115/C4 Wuyang, China
115/C3 Wuyi, China
117/H3 Wuyi (mts.), China
109/K2 Wuying, China
108/F3 Wuyuan, China
109/K2 Wuyur (riv.), China
115/B3 Wuzhai, China
115/L9 Wuzhen, China
115/C4 Wuzhi, China
117/F5 Wuzhi (mts.), China
117/F5 Wuzhi (peak), China
115/D2 Wuzhi Shan (peak), China
117/F4 Wuzhou, China
132/C4 Wyalkatchem, Austl.
207/M8 Wyandanch, NY,US
205/F7 Wyandotte, Mi,US
191/G2 Wyandotte, Ok,US
205/F7 Wyandotte Nat'l Wild. Ref., Mi,US
134/B4 Wyandra, Austl.
135/D2 Wyangale (dam), Austl.
192/A1 Wyarno, Wy,US
135/B3 Wycheproof, Austl.
207/D1 Wyckoff, NJ,US
58/D3 Wye (riv.), UK
135/D2 Wyee, Austl.
206/B6 Wye Mills, Md,US
64/E1 Wyk, Ger.
201/G3 Wylie (lake), NC, SC,US
188/L6 Wylie, Tx,US
155/F4 Wyllie's (pass), SAfr.
201/H2 Wylliesburg, Va,US
58/D4 Wylye (riv.), Eng,UK
183/L2 Wymark, Sk,Can
57/G6 Wymeswold, Eng,UK
59/H1 Wymondham, Eng,UK
193/F3 Wymore, Ne,US
133/G4 Wynbring, Austl.
130/C3 Wyndham, Austl.
194/F4 Wyndmere, ND,US
80/D3 Wynigen, Swi.
182/F3 Wynndel, BC,Can
191/J3 Wynne, Ar,US
191/F3 Wynnewood, Ok,US
134/F6 Wynnum, Austl.
191/F2 Wynona, Ok,US
135/C4 Wynyard, Austl.
194/B2 Wynyard, Sk,Can
185/K1 Wyola, Mt,US
198/E3 Wyoming, On,Can
180/E3 Wyoming (state), US
206/C5 Wyoming, De,US
193/K3 Wyoming, Il,US
198/D3 Wyoming, Mi,US
195/H5 Wyoming, Mn,US
206/C1 Wyoming, Pa,US
208/C2 Wyoming, RI,US
206/C3 Wyomissing, Pa,US
135/D2 Wyong, Austl.
135/B2 Wyperfeld Nat'l Park, Austl.
132/D5 Wyralinu (peak), Austl.
57/F4 Wyre (riv.), Eng,UK
65/J2 Wyrzysk, Pol.
65/M2 Wysokie Mazowieckie, Pol.
199/H4 Wysox, Pa,US
65/J2 Wyszków, Pol.
201/G2 Wytheville, Va,US

X

150/D3 Xaafuun, Som.
123/D4 Xa Binh Long, Viet.
116/C2 Xabyaisamba, China
160/B3 Xadani, Mex.
84/H7 Xagħra, Malta
116/B2 Xagquka, China
114/E5 Xainza, China
121/G1 Xaitongmoin, China
155/G4 Xaiva, Moz.
155/G5 Xai-Xai, Moz.
150/D3 Xalin, Som.
160/E2 Xalpatlahuac, Mex.
116/E4 Xam (riv.), Laos
166/D4 Xambioá, Braz.
123/D1 Xam Nua, Laos
152/D5 Xá-Muteba, Ang.
123/D3 Xan (riv.), Viet.
152/D5 Xandel, Ang.
114/D5 Xangdoring, China
152/C5 Xangongo, Ang.
66/D5 Xanten, Ger.
91/J2 Xánthi, Gre.
173/F3 Xanxerê, Braz.
168/D3 Xapuri, Braz.
108/D4 Xarag, China
150/C4 Xarardheere, Som.
120/E1 Xarba (pass), China
108/E5 Xar'oi, China
123/E4 Xa Song Luy, Viet.
152/D5 Xassengue, Ang.
123/D3 Xa Tho Thanh, Viet.
154/D3 Xaudum (dry riv.), Bots.
170/C1 Xavantes (mts.), Braz.
170/C4 Xavantes (res.), Braz.
173/F2 Xavantina, Braz.
123/D4 Xa Vo Dat, Viet.
173/F3 Xaxim, Braz.
114/D3 Xayar, China
160/E2 Xcalak, Mex.
159/J4 X Can, Mex.
159/J4 Xel-há (ruins), Mex.
200/C1 Xenia, Il,US
198/E5 Xenia, Oh,US
123/D2 Xeno, Laos
77/F2 Xerta, Sp.
80/C1 Xertigny, Fr.
154/E4 Xhumo, Bots.
115/E2 Xi (lake), China
113/A2 Xi (riv.), China
117/E3 Xi'ao, China
115/H7 Xiadian, China
108/D3 Xiadong, China
116/D3 Xiaguan, China
117/F3 Xiahuaqiao, China
116/G6 Xiahuayuan, China
116/E3 Xiajia, China
117/F3 Xiajiang, China
113/C1 Xiajiapu, China
115/C3 Xiajin, China
113/C2 Xialuhe, China
117/H3 Xiamen, China
117/H3 Xiamen (int'l arpt.), China
108/F5 Xi'an, China
115/B5 Xianfeng, China
117/G3 Xiang (riv.), China
108/G5 Xiangcheng, China
117/G3 Xiangdong, China
115/C4 Xiangfan, China
115/B4 Xiangfen, China
115/D3 Xianghe, China
117/G3 Xianghua (mts.), China
123/C2 Xiangkhoang, Laos
123/C2 Xiang Khoang (plat.), Laos
117/H2 Xiangkou, China
117/F3 Xianglinpu, China
123/C2 Xiang Ngeun, Laos
115/B4 Xiangning, China
109/H5 Xiangshui, China
117/F3 Xiangshuiba, China
117/G2 Xiangtan, China
117/G3 Xiangtan, China
117/G3 Xiangyangqiao, China
115/C3 Xiangyuan, China
116/D3 Xiangyun, China
117/J2 Xianju, China
115/C5 Xianning, China
115/C5 Xiantao, China
117/H2 Xianxia, China
117/H2 Xianxia (mtn.), China
117/F3 Xianxizhen, China
108/F5 Xianyang, China
117/H2 Xianyuan, China
117/F3 Xianzijiao, China
115/C3 Xiao (riv.), China
116/D3 Xiao (riv.), China
117/F3 Xiao (riv.), China
109/J1 Xiaobole (peak), China
108/D4 Xiaodongliang, China
113/A2 Xiaofangshen, China
115/C5 Xiaogan, China
119/H2 Xiaoguanxi, China
113/B3 Xiaogushan, China
117/F3 Xiaohenglong, China
109/K2 Xiao Hinggang (mts.), China
117/G2 Xiaojiagang, China
119/K3 Xiaojiang, China
116/D2 Xiaojin (riv.), China
113/B1 Xiaoliangshan, China
117/G1 Xiaolindian, China
117/H3 Xiaomei, China
117/G3 Xiaomei (pass), China
116/E2 Xiaomianzhen, China
108/C4 Xiaonanchuan, China
108/D4 Xiao Qaidam, China
117/H2 Xiaoqiao, China
115/D3 Xiaoqing (riv.), China
115/L9 Xiaoshan, China
117/H3 Xiaosong, China
113/B1 Xiaotazi, China
115/C3 Xiaowutai Shan (peak), China
115/D4 Xiao Xian, China
116/E2 Xiaoxiba, China
119/H3 Xiaoyangjie, China
115/B3 Xiaoyi, China
117/G3 Xiaoyuan, China
117/F3 Xiapilin, China
117/E3 Xiasi, China
113/E1 Xiatianping, China
160/D2 Xiatil, Mex.
115/D4 Xiayi, China
117/E3 Xiazichang, China
121/J1 Xibaxa (riv.), China
108/F5 Xichahe, China
117/F4 Xichang, China
119/H2 Xichang, China
115/C4 Xicheng Shan (mtn.), China
119/H3 Xichou, China
115/B4 Xichuan, China
159/F4 Xicohténcatl, Mex.
159/F4 Xicotepec, Mex.
159/M6 Xicotepec de Juárez, Mex.
164/D4 Xicute, Col.
116/D2 Xide, China
117/J2 Xidian, China
117/J2 Xidongting (mtn.), China
115/C4 Xifei (riv.), China
108/F4 Xifeng, China
109/J3 Xifeng, China
115/J6 Xifengkou, China
121/G1 Xigazê, China
115/B4 Xiguan (arpt.), China
108/E5 Xihan (riv.), China
117/F2 Xihaoping, China
113/B3 Xihekou, China
115/C4 Xihua, China
150/C3 Xiis, Som.
117/H3 Xijin, China
108/C5 Xijir, China
114/F4 Xijir Ulan (lake), China
108/E4 Xijishui, China
117/H3 Xikouxu, China
115/E2 Xiliao (riv.), China
109/J3 Xilin, China
109/J1 Xilinji, China
91/H3 Xilókastron, Gre.
116/C4 Ximeng Vazu Zizhixian, China
108/E3 Ximiao, China
113/B2 Ximucheng, China
117/H2 Xin (riv.), China
115/C4 Xin'an, China
115/D5 Xin'an (riv.), China
117/H2 Xin'anjiang (res.), China
117/H2 Xin'anjiang, China
115/D5 Xin'anjiang (res.), China
155/G5 Xinavane, Moz.
115/G6 Xinbao'an, China
109/H2 Xin Barag Zuoqi, China
113/C2 Xinbin, China
115/F2 Xinbin, China
109/H2 Xin Bulag Dong, China
115/C4 Xincai, China
117/H2 Xinchang, China
117/J2 Xinchang, China
115/C3 Xincheng, China
113/B1 Xinchengzi, China
117/F4 Xindi, China
117/F4 Xindu, China
119/K3 Xinfeng, China
117/G4 Xinfengjiang (res.), China
117/F3 Xing'an, China
115/E2 Xingcheng, China
152/D5 Xinge, Ang.
115/D4 Xinghua, China
114/D3 Xingjiang Uygur (aut. reg.), China
109/L3 Xingkai (lake), China
115/D2 Xinglong, China
117/F2 Xinglongchang, China
117/F3 Xingping, China
116/D2 Xingqêngoin, China
115/B5 Xingshan, China
113/B3 Xingshutun, China
115/C3 Xingtai, China
166/D3 Xingu (riv.), Braz.
108/D3 Xingxingxia, China
115/C4 Xingyang, China
116/E3 Xingyi, China
114/D3 Xinhe, China
115/C3 Xinhe, China
115/L8 Xinhezhen, China
117/F3 Xinhuang Dongzu Zizhixian, China
108/E4 Xining, China
102/K6 Xining Shi, China
108/H4 Xinji, China
115/C3 Xinji, China
117/H2 Xinjian, China
115/B4 Xinjiang, China
102/J5 Xinjiang (reg.), China
123/E2 Xinjie, China
109/J4 Xinjin, China
113/A3 Xinjin, China
115/E3 Xinjin, China
113/B2 Xinkaihe, China
115/C3 Xinle, China
113/B2 Xinlitun, China
117/H3 Xinlong, China
109/J2 Xinmiao, China
113/B2 Xinmin, China
116/D3 Xinping Yizu, China
117/G2 Xinqiang, China
117/F4 Xinqiao, China
117/F3 Xinshao, China
115/L9 Xinshi, China
108/E5 Xinsi, China
115/D4 Xintai, China
115/C4 Xinxiang, China
109/J3 Xinxing, China
119/J3 Xinxu, China
115/C4 Xinyang, China
115/C4 Xinye, China
109/H5 Xinyi, China
115/D4 Xinyi, China
119/K3 Xinyi, China
117/G3 Xinyu, China
114/D3 Xinyuan, China
115/C4 Xinzheng, China
115/C5 Xinzhou, China
115/D3 Xiong Xian, China
113/B2 Xiongyuecheng, China
115/C4 Xiping, China
117/H3 Xiqin, China
108/E5 Xiqing (mts.), China
171/E1 Xique-Xique, Braz.
117/G2 Xishan, China
119/J2 Xishui, China
115/E5 Xitang, China
117/H2 Xitianmu (peak), China
115/D5 Xitiao (riv.), China
144/B4 Xitole, GBis.
117/G2 Xiu (riv.), China
115/D5 Xiuning, China
119/J2 Xiuwen, China
115/C4 Xiuwu, China
113/B2 Xiuyan, China
121/E1 Xixabangma (peak), China
117/H3 Xixi, China
116/D2 Xixi (riv.), China
115/B4 Xixia, China
116/E4 Xiyang (riv.), China
114/D5 Xizang (aut. reg.), China
121/F1 Xizang Aut. Reg., China
116/B2 Xizang (Tibet) (aut. reg.), China
117/J2 Xize, China
117/F2 Xizhai, China
115/E3 Xizhong (isl.), China
159/H5 Xmaben, Mex.
159/F4 Xochiatipan, Mex.
159/K8 Xochicalco (ruins), Mex.
159/Q10 Xochimilco, Mex.
159/M8 Xochitlán, Mex.
116/B2 Xoka, China
108/C4 Xorkol, China
160/D2 Xpujil, Mex.
117/H3 Xu (riv.), China
115/B5 Xuan'en, China
115/C2 Xuanhua, China
116/E3 Xuanwei, China
115/C4 Xuchang, China
150/B4 Xuddur (Oddur), Som.
116/C3 Xue (mts.), China
115/E5 Xuedou (peak), China
108/D4 Xugin Gol (riv.), China
115/L8 Xugou, China
115/L8 Xuguanzhen, China
113/B2 Xujiatun, China
115/B4 Xun (riv.), China
117/F4 Xun (riv.), China
121/E1 Xungru, China
117/F2 Xunjiansi, China
109/K2 Xunke, China
115/C4 Xun Xian, China
115/B4 Xunyang, China
117/J2 Xupu, China
108/D4 Xur, China
121/E1 Xuru (lake), China
115/G7 Xushui, China
117/F4 Xuwen, China
115/D4 Xuyi, China
116/E2 Xuyong, China
115/D4 Xuzhou, China

Y

116/D2 Ya'an, China
135/B2 Yaapeet, Austl.
151/C1 Yaaq-Baraawe, Som.
103/G7 Ya'bad, WBnk.
152/B1 Yabassi, Camr.
149/H4 Yabēlo, Eth.
153/E2 Yabia, Zaire
93/G4 Yablanitsa, Bul.
161/F3 Yablis, Nic.
98/C3 Yablonov, Ukr.
108/G1 Yablonovo, Rus.
99/K5 Yablonovskiy, Rus.
108/F1 Yablonovyy (ridge), Rus.
106/E4 Yabrīn, SAr.
103/G8 Yabrūd, WBnk.
162/E3 Yabucoa, PR
111/G2 Yabuki, Japan
172/E1 Yacaré Norte (riv.), Par.
125/D3 Yacgam (mt.), Phil.
184/A1 Yachats, Or,US
123/E2 Yacheng, China
116/E3 Yachi (riv.), China
111/J7 Yachiyo, Japan
111/K9 Yachiyo, Japan
175/J7 Yacimiento Rio Turbio, Arg.
172/C1 Yaco, Bol.
182/C5 Yacolt, Wa,US
167/L6 Yacopí, Col.
172/D2 Yacuiba, Bol.
169/E4 Yacuma (riv.), Bol.
164/D2 Yacumbu Nat'l Park, Ven.
148/B4 Yadé, Massif du (plat.), Camr., CAfr.
118/C4 Yādgīr, India
201/G2 Yadkin (riv.), NC,US
201/G2 Yadkinville, NC,US
121/G2 Yadong, China
95/K5 Yadrin, Rus.
112/G8 Yaeyama (isl.), Japan
146/B1 Yafren, Libya
104/B2 Yağcılar, Turk.
111/L9 Yagi, Japan
158/D4 Yago, Mex.
101/Q3 Yagodnoye, Rus.
98/F4 Yagorlytsk (gulf), Ukr.
98/F2 Yagotin, Ukr.
148/B3 Yagoua, Camr.
108/D4 Yagradagzê (peak), China
160/E3 Yaguale (riv.), Hon.
175/G2 Yaguarón (riv.), Uru.
169/F4 Yaguarú, Bol.
168/D1 Yaguas (riv.), Col., Peru
161/J2 Yague del Sur (riv.), DRep.
111/N10 Yahagi (riv.), Japan
182/F3 Yahk, BC,Can
115/H7 Yahongqiao, China
159/F4 Yahualica, Mex.
158/E4 Yahualica de Gonzalez Gallo, Mex.
104/C2 Yahyalı, Turk.
79/F2 Yainville, Fr.
91/G3 Yáios (Paxoí), Gre.
111/F2 Yaita, Japan
111/F3 Yaizu, Japan
160/C2 Yajalón, Mex.
103/E1 Yakacık, Turk.
103/D1 Yakapınar, Turk.
109/J2 Yakeshi, China
182/D4 Yakima, Wa,US
182/D4 Yakima (riv.), Wa,US
183/D4 Yakima Firing Ra., Wa,US
182/D4 Yakima Ind. Res., Wa,US
112/B1 Yakishiri (isl.), Japan
145/E3 Yako, Burk.
153/E1 Yakoma, Zaire
148/C4 Yakoma, CAfr.
93/F4 Yakoruda, Bul.
99/J2 Yakovlevo, Rus.
113/D2 Yaksu-nodongjagu, NKor.
110/B5 Yaku (isl.), Japan
110/B5 Yaku-Kirishima Nat'l Park, Japan
112/B2 Yakumo, Japan
111/K9 Yakuno, Japan
177/L4 Yakutat, Ak,US
177/K4 Yakutat (bay), Ak,US
101/N3 Yakut Aut. Rep., Rus.
101/N3 Yakutsk, Rus.
123/C5 Yala, Thai.
202/M6 Yalaha, Fl,US
160/E1 Yalahua (lag.), Mex.
182/C2 Yalakom (riv.), BC,Can
97/J4 Yalama, Azer.
103/E1 Yalangoz, Turk.
133/F4 Yalata Abor. Land, Austl.
160/D2 Yalbac (hills), Belz.
182/D3 Yale, BC,Can
198/E3 Yale, Mi,US
191/F2 Yale, Ok,US
132/C4 Yalgoo, Austl.
132/B5 Yalgorup Nat'l Park, Austl.
148/D4 Yalinga, CAfr.
135/C2 Yallock, Austl.
104/E1 Yalnızçam, Turk.
200/B4 Yalobusha (riv.), Ms,US
148/C4 Yaloké, CAfr.
116/D2 Yalong (riv.), China
93/H5 Yalova, Turk.
93/J5 Yalova, Turk.
98/E5 Yalpuh (lake), Ukr.
135/B1 Yalpunga, Austl.
53/G4 Yalta, Ukr.
109/J3 Yalu (riv.), China, NKor.
153/F3 Yaluwe, Zaire
104/B2 Yalvaç, Turk.
196/A2 Yamachiche, Qu,Can
112/B4 Yamada, Japan
110/B4 Yamaga, Japan
111/G1 Yamagata, Japan
111/G1 Yamagata (arpt.), Japan
111/F1 Yamagata (pref.), Japan
110/B3 Yamaguchi, Japan
110/B3 Yamaguchi (pref.), Japan
100/G2 Yamal (pen.), Rus.
100/G3 Yamal-Nenets Aut. Okr., Rus.
111/F3 Yamanashi (pref.), Japan
134/B2 Yamanie (falls), Austl.
134/B2 Yamanie Falls Nat'l Park, Austl.
100/F4 Yamantau (peak), Rus.
95/N5 Yamantau, Gora (peak), Rus.

# Yamao – Závora

111/N9 **Yamaoka,** Japan
132/D3 **Yamarna Abor. Rsv.,** Austl.
132/D4 **Yamarna Abor. Rsv.,** Austl.
111/L10 **Yamashiro,** Japan
196/A3 **Yamaska** (riv.), Qu,Can
111/F2 **Yamato,** Japan
111/L10 **Yamato** (riv.), Japan
111/L10 **Yamato-Kōriyama,** Japan
110/D3 **Yamatotakada,** Japan
111/M10 **Yamazoe,** Japan
135/E1 **Yamba,** Austl.
133/G2 **Yambah,** Austl.
153/E2 **Yambata,** Zaire
144/B4 **Yambéring,** Gui.
149/F4 **Yambio,** Sudan
93/H4 **Yambol,** Bul.
168/B2 **Yambrasbamba,** Peru
130/C1 **Yamdena** (isl.), Indo.
116/C4 **Yamethin,** Burma
184/B1 **Yamhill,** Or,US
127/K4 **Yamin** (peak), Indo.
63/N2 **Yamm,** Rus.
133/J3 **Yamma Yamma** (lake), Austl.
111/G1 **Yamoto,** Japan
144/D5 **Yamoussoukro** (cap.), IvC.
185/J3 **Yampa** (riv.), Co,US
98/D3 **Yampol',** Ukr.
98/E3 **Yampol',** Ukr.
120/C3 **Yamuna** (riv.), India
122/D2 **Yamunānagar,** India
121/H1 **Yamzho** (lake), China
119/E2 **Yamzho Yumco** (lake), China
115/B3 **Yan** (riv.), China
122/H4 **Yan** (riv.), SrL.
101/P3 **Yana** (riv.), Rus.
135/B3 **Yanac,** Austl.
110/B4 **Yanagawa,** Japan
110/C4 **Yanai,** Japan
168/D4 **Yanaoca,** Peru
95/M4 **Yanaul,** Rus.
119/H2 **Yanbian,** China
147/H3 **Yanbu' al Baḩr,** SAr.
133/J4 **Yancannia,** Austl.
188/E3 **Yancey,** Tx,US
201/H2 **Yanceyville,** NC,US
115/C4 **Yancheng,** China
115/E4 **Yancheng,** China
132/B4 **Yanchep Nat'l Park,** Austl.
135/C2 **Yanco,** Austl.
139/T12 **Yandé** (isl.), NCal.
132/C2 **Yandeearra Abor. Rsv.,** Austl.
145/H5 **Yandev,** Nga.
117/E3 **Yandong,** China
153/E2 **Yandongi,** Zaire
116/B5 **Yandoon,** Burma
144/C4 **Yanfolila,** Mali
148/D4 **Yangalia,** CAfr.
153/F2 **Yangambi,** Zaire
116/B2 **Ya'ngamdo,** China
148/B4 **Yangamo,** Camr.
116/C3 **Yangbi** (riv.), China
116/E3 **Yangchangba,** China
115/C4 **Yangcheng,** China
115/L8 **Yangcheng** (lake), China
117/G4 **Yangcun,** China
117/H3 **Yangdang** (mts.), Laos
113/D3 **Yangdŏk,** NKor.
113/D2 **Yanggang-do** (prov.), NKor.
115/C2 **Yanggao,** China
115/C3 **Yanggu,** China
113/D3 **Yanggu,** SKor.
117/F4 **Yangjiang,** China
116/E3 **Yangjiawan,** China
115/H7 **Yangliuqing,** China
117/G2 **Yangloudong,** China
113/A4 **Yangma** (isl.), China
117/J3 **Yangmei,** Tai.
117/F3 **Yangming** (peak), China
116/C5 **Yangon** (Rangoon) (cap.), Burma
113/D4 **Yangp'yŏng,** SKor.
108/F4 **Yangqiaopan,** China
115/C3 **Yangqu,** China
115/C3 **Yangquan,** China
113/E5 **Yangsan,** SKor.
119/K3 **Yangshan,** China
119/K3 **Yangshuo,** China
123/C2 **Yang Talat,** Thai.
116/C3 **Yangtouyan,** China
115/L8 **Yangtze** (riv.), China
117/H2 **Yangtze** (Chang) (riv.), China
115/D5 **Yangtze** (Jinsha) (riv.), China
150/B3 **Yangudi Rassa Nat'l Park,** Eth.
117/G3 **Yangxi,** China
115/D3 **Yangxin,** China
117/G2 **Yangxin,** China
116/E4 **Yangxu,** China
113/E3 **Yangyang,** SKor.
115/C2 **Yangyuan,** China
115/D4 **Yangzhong,** China
115/D4 **Yangzhou,** China
152/D3 **Yanja,** Zaire
109/K3 **Yanji,** China
113/A2 **Yanjia,** China
115/C4 **Yanjin,** China
116/E2 **Yanjin,** China
119/H2 **Yanjin,** China
116/C2 **Yanjing,** China
145/G4 **Yankara,** Nga.
145/H4 **Yankari Game Rsv.,** Nga.
208/G5 **Yankee Lake,** Oh,US
207/K8 **Yankee Stadium,** NY,US
192/F2 **Yankton,** SD,US
192/E2 **Yankton Ind. Res.,** SD,US
115/C4 **Yanling,** China
115/C3 **Yanmen Guan** (pass), China
153/F2 **Yanonge,** Zaire
115/G6 **Yanqing,** China
132/B2 **Yanrey,** Austl.
115/D3 **Yanshan,** China
119/H3 **Yanshan,** China
115/C4 **Yanshi,** China
117/H3 **Yanshi,** China
108/C5 **Yanshiping,** China
109/K2 **Yanshou,** China
135/C1 **Yantabulla,** Austl.
115/E3 **Yantai,** China
133/J4 **Yantara,** Austl.
63/H4 **Yantarnyy,** Rus.
116/E2 **Yanting,** China
191/G4 **Yantis,** Tx,US
200/C4 **Yantley,** Al,US
115/C2 **Yantong Shan** (mtn.), China
89/K2 **Yantra** (riv.), Bul.
191/G3 **Yanush,** Ok,US
116/C3 **Yanwa,** China
117/H3 **Yanxi,** China
135/G5 **Yan Yean** (res.), Austl.
116/D3 **Yanyuan,** China
115/D4 **Yanzhou,** China
148/C2 **Yao,** Chad
110/D3 **Yao,** Japan
119/H2 **Yao'an,** China
115/B3 **Yaodian,** China
117/G4 **Yaogu,** China
148/A5 **Yaoundé** (cap.), Camr.
138/C4 **Yap** (isls.), Micr.
165/E4 **Yapacana Nat'l Park,** Ven.
169/E5 **Yapacani** (riv.), Bol.
145/E4 **Yapei,** Gha.
127/J4 **Yapen** (isl.), Indo.
127/J4 **Yapen** (str.), Indo.
207/F2 **Yaphank,** NY,US
172/D1 **Yapirga,** Bol.
104/C1 **Yapraklı,** Turk.
117/F2 **Yaqueling,** China
158/C3 **Yaqui,** Mex.
158/C2 **Yaqui** (riv.), Mex.
184/A1 **Yaquina** (bay), Or,US
59/E5 **Yar** (riv.), Eng,UK
161/G1 **Yara,** Cuba
164/D2 **Yaracuy** (state), Ven.
134/B4 **Yaraka,** Austl.
104/C1 **Yaralıgöz** (peak), Turk.
127/J4 **Yaramaniapuka** (mtn.), Indo.
95/K4 **Yaransk,** Rus.
103/B1 **Yardımcı** (pt.), Turk.
206/D3 **Yardley,** Pa,US
206/D3 **Yardville-Groveville,** NJ,US
97/J5 **Yardymly,** Azer.
59/H1 **Yare** (riv.), Eng,UK
95/M3 **Yarega,** Rus.
98/C3 **Yaremcha,** Ukr.
95/L3 **Yarensk,** Rus.
93/J2 **Yargora,** Mol.
164/C4 **Yarí** (riv.), Col.
111/E2 **Yari-ga-take** (mtn.), Japan
150/C2 **Yarīm,** Yem.
93/J5 **Yarımca,** Turk.
164/D2 **Yaritagua,** Ven.
114/C4 **Yarkant** (riv.), China
95/Q4 **Yarkovo,** Rus.
132/B5 **Yarloop,** Austl.
114/F6 **Yarlung Zangbo** (riv.), China
121/G1 **Yarlung Zangbo** (Brahmaputra) (riv.), China
98/D3 **Yarmolintsy,** Ukr.
196/D4 **Yarmouth,** NS,Can
196/B5 **Yarmouth,** Ma,US
196/B4 **Yarmouth,** Me,US
187/F3 **Yarnell,** Az,US
53/G3 **Yaroslavl',** Rus.
94/H4 **Yaroslavl' Obl.,** Rus.
109/L3 **Yaroslavskiy,** Rus.
103/E1 **Yarpuz,** Turk.
135/G5 **Yarra** (riv.), Austl.
135/G5 **Yarra Glen,** Austl.
135/C3 **Yarram,** Austl.
134/D4 **Yarraman,** Austl.
135/C3 **Yarrawonga,** Austl.
205/C2 **Yarrow Point,** Wa,US
100/K3 **Yartsevo,** Rus.
94/G5 **Yartsevo,** Rus.
164/C3 **Yarumal,** Col.
116/C2 **Yarzhong,** China
153/E3 **Yasa,** Zaire
139/Y17 **Yasawa** (isls.), Fiji
138/G6 **Yasawa Group** (isls.), Fiji
96/C1 **Yasel'da** (riv.), Bela.
99/K4 **Yasenskaya,** Rus.
99/M4 **Yashalta,** Rus.
150/C2 **Yashbum,** Yem.
145/G3 **Yashi,** Nga.
145/F4 **Yashikera,** Nga.
112/B4 **Yashima,** Japan
111/H7 **Yashio,** Japan
111/K10 **Yashiro,** Japan
97/K1 **Yashkino,** Rus.
97/H3 **Yashkul',** Rus.
107/K1 **Yāsīn,** Pak.
99/J3 **Yasinovataya,** Ukr.
98/C3 **Yasinya,** Ukr.
99/J3 **Yasnogorka,** Ukr.
97/L2 **Yasnyy,** Rus.
123/D3 **Yasothon,** Thai.
135/D2 **Yass,** Austl.
106/F4 **Yas, Sir Bani** (isl.), UAE
111/M9 **Yasu,** Japan
111/M10 **Yasu** (riv.), Japan
110/C3 **Yasugi,** Japan
105/G4 **Yāsūj,** Iran
104/D1 **Yasun** (pt.), Turk.
164/B5 **Yasuni Nat'l Park,** Ecu.
146/B4 **Yat** (well), Niger
169/E4 **Yata,** Bol.
169/E4 **Yata** (riv.), Bol.
148/D3 **Yata** (riv.), CAfr.
111/G2 **Yatabe,** Japan
104/B2 **Yatağan,** Turk.
173/E3 **Yataity,** Par.
148/D3 **Yata-Ngaya Fauna Rsv.,** CAfr.
58/D3 **Yate,** Eng,UK
59/F4 **Yateley,** Eng,UK
145/E3 **Yatenga** (prov.), Burk.
191/G2 **Yates Center,** Ks,US
178/G2 **Yathkyed** (lake), NW,Can
172/C2 **Yatina,** Bol.
153/F2 **Yatolema,** Zaire
111/M9 **Yatomi,** Japan
111/E2 **Yatsuo,** Japan
110/B4 **Yatsushiro,** Japan
151/B2 **Yatta** (plat.), Kenya
103/D4 **Yattah,** WBnk.
58/D4 **Yatton,** Eng,UK
168/C4 **Yauca,** Peru
168/C4 **Yauca** (riv.), Peru
162/E3 **Yauco,** PR
168/B3 **Yauli,** Peru
164/D5 **Yaúna Moloca,** Col.
164/B5 **Yaupi,** Ecu.
201/H4 **Yaupon Beach,** NC,US
168/B3 **Yaután,** Peru
159/K7 **Yautepec,** Mex.
168/C4 **Yauyos,** Peru
187/F3 **Yavapai Ind. Res.,** Az,US
164/D4 **Yavaraté,** Col.
168/C2 **Yavarí** (riv.), Peru
158/C3 **Yavaros,** Mex.
118/C3 **Yavatmāl,** India
100/H2 **Yavay** (pen.), Rus.
160/C2 **Yaveo,** Mex.
165/E4 **Yávita,** Ven.
161/G4 **Yaviza,** Pan.
103/F8 **Yavne,** Isr.
98/B3 **Yavorov,** Ukr.
104/D2 **Yavuzeli,** Turk.
111/J7 **Yawahara,** Japan
111/L10 **Yawata,** Japan
110/C4 **Yawatahama,** Japan
159/H4 **Yaxcabá,** Mex.
160/D2 **Yaxchilán** (ruins), Mex.
123/E2 **Ya Xian,** China
123/E2 **Yaxing,** China
59/F2 **Yaxley,** Eng,UK
104/E2 **Yaygın,** Turk.
103/E2 **Yayladaği,** Turk.
104/E2 **Yayladere,** Turk.
97/L2 **Yaysan,** Kaz.
113/D2 **Yayuan,** China
105/H4 **Yazd,** Iran
105/H3 **Yazd** (gov.), Iran
95/K2 **Yazhma,** Rus.
117/E3 **Yazhou,** China
200/B4 **Yazoo** (riv.), Ms,US
200/B4 **Yazoo City,** Ms,US
200/B4 **Yazoo Nat'l Wild. Ref.,** Ms,US
97/H1 **Yazykovo,** Rus.
75/L2 **Ybbs,** Aus.
71/H7 **Ybbs** (riv.), Aus.
92/B1 **Ybbs an der Donau,** Aus.
65/H5 **Ybbsitz,** Aus.
202/L8 **Ybor City,** Fl,US
203/G4 **Ybor City,** Fl,US
173/E3 **Ybycuí,** Par.
74/C4 **Ychoux,** Fr.
62/C3 **Yding Skovhøj** (peak), Den.
123/B3 **Ye,** Burma
201/F2 **Yeaddiss,** Ky,US
57/G4 **Yeadon,** Eng,UK
58/B6 **Yealmpton,** Eng,UK
113/E4 **Yean,** SKor.
123/C4 **Yeay Sen** (cape), Camb.
146/C4 **YebbiBou,** Chad
146/C4 **Yébiqué, Enneri** (dry riv.), Chad
114/C4 **Yecheng,** China
113/E4 **Yech'ŏn,** SKor.
77/E3 **Yecla,** Sp.
158/C2 **Yécora,** Mex.
159/N7 **Yecuatla,** Mex.
123/B2 **Yedashe,** Burma
104/B1 **Yedigöller Nat'l Park,** Turk.
105/M6 **Yedikule,** Turk.
93/H1 **Yedintsy,** Mol.
103/E2 **Yeditepe,** Turk.
150/B4 **Yeed,** Som.
130/A4 **Yeeda River,** Austl.
132/D3 **Yeelirrie,** Austl.
94/G4 **Yefimovskiy,** Rus.
92/F5 **Yéfira,** Gre.
53/G3 **Yefremov,** Rus.
99/L5 **Yegorlak** (riv.), Rus.
99/L4 **Yegorlykskaya,** Rus.
159/M8 **Yehualtepec,** Mex.
103/F7 **Yehud,** Isr.
149/F4 **Yei,** Sudan
149/F4 **Yei** (riv.), Sudan
95/P4 **Yekaterinburg Obl.,** Rus.
95/P4 **Yekaterinburg** (Sverdlovsk), Rus.
109/K1 **Yekaterinoslavka,** Rus.
97/H1 **Yekaterinovka,** Rus.
112/E1 **Yekateriny** (chan.), Rus.
144/C5 **Yekepa,** Libr.
148/C1 **Yekia Sahal** (well), Chad
95/M5 **Yelabuga,** Rus.
152/C4 **Yelala, Chutes** (falls), Zaire
99/M2 **Yelan',** Rus.
135/D1 **Yelarbon,** Austl.
53/G3 **Yelets,** Rus.
149/G3 **Yelgu,** Sudan
144/C3 **Yélimané,** Mali
97/L2 **Yelizavetinka,** Rus.
63/N2 **Yelizavetino,** Rus.
97/M1 **Yelizavetopol'skoye,** Rus.
101/Q4 **Yelizavety** (cape), Rus.
101/R4 **Yelizovo,** Rus.
97/J1 **Yelkhovka,** Rus.
55/P12 **Yell** (isl.), Sc,UK
141/R16 **Yellel,** Alg.
109/J4 **Yellow** (sea), Asia
203/E2 **Yellow** (riv.), Al,US
201/M7 **Yellow** (riv.), Ga,US
208/G6 **Yellow** (cr.), Oh,US
193/J1 **Yellow** (riv.), Wi,US
206/A3 **Yellow Breeches** (cr.), Pa,US
183/M1 **Yellow Creek,** Sk,Can
195/L4 **Yellow Dog** (pt.), Mi,US
194/B3 **Yellow Grass,** Sk,Can
190/C4 **Yellow Horse Draw** (stream), Tx,US
115/D3 **Yellow** (Huang) (riv.), China
187/H2 **Yellow Jacket,** Co,US
178/E2 **Yellowknife,** NW,Can
178/E2 **Yellowknife** (riv.), NW,Can
208/G6 **Yellow, North Fork** (cr.), Oh,US
202/D2 **Yellow Pine,** Al,US
184/F1 **Yellow Pine,** Id,US
185/H1 **Yellowstone** (lake), Wy,US
185/J1 **Yellowstone, Clarks Fork** (riv.), Mt, Wy,US
185/H1 **Yellowstone Nat'l Park,** Mt, Wy,US
185/K1 **Yellowtail** (dam), Mt,US
191/H2 **Yellville,** Ar,US
182/C4 **Yelm,** Wa,US
94/G5 **Yel'nya,** Rus.
97/H2 **Yelshanka,** Rus.
98/E2 **Yel'sk,** Bela.
58/B6 **Yelverton,** Eng,UK
145/G4 **Yelwa,** Nga.
145/H4 **Yelwa,** Nga.
108/D4 **Yema** (riv.), China
152/C4 **Yema,** Zaire
113/B1 **Yemaotai,** China
201/G4 **Yemassee,** SC,US
106/E5 **Yemen**
94/J3 **Yemetsk,** Rus.
98/D2 **Yemil'chino,** Ukr.
145/G5 **Yenagoa,** Nga.
99/K3 **Yenakiyevo,** Ukr.
116/B4 **Yenangyaung,** Burma
116/B5 **Yenanma,** Burma
123/D1 **Yen Bai,** Viet.
135/C2 **Yenda,** Austl.
152/D2 **Yende,** Congo
144/C4 **Yende Millimou,** Gui.
145/E4 **Yendi,** Gha.
116/C4 **Ye-ngan,** Burma
153/E3 **Yenge** (riv.), Zaire
114/C4 **Yengisar,** China
152/C2 **Yengo,** Congo
152/B3 **Yengué,** Gabon
93/L5 **Yeniçağa,** Turk.
103/D1 **Yenice,** Turk.
93/H6 **Yenice,** Turk.
93/L5 **Yenice,** Turk.
96/E4 **Yenice** (riv.), Turk.
104/C2 **Yeniceoba,** Turk.
93/H5 **Yeniköy,** Turk.
93/J5 **Yenişehir,** Turk.
114/F1 **Yenisey** (riv.), Rus.
100/K4 **Yeniseysk,** Rus.
123/D1 **Yen Minh,** Viet.
152/B3 **Yeno,** Gabon
117/J4 **Yenshui,** Tai.
132/E3 **Yeo** (lake), Austl.
58/D5 **Yeo** (riv.), Eng,UK
107/K4 **Yeola,** India
132/E3 **Yeo Lake Nature Rsv.,** Austl.
135/D2 **Yeoval,** Austl.
58/D5 **Yeovil,** Eng,UK
117/H3 **Yeping,** China
134/C3 **Yeppoon,** Austl.
97/G1 **Yerakhtur,** Rus.
91/H3 **Yerakovoúni** (peak), Gre.
97/J4 **Yeraliyev,** Kaz.
158/E3 **Yerbanís,** Mex.
174/C2 **Yerbas Buenas,** Chile
105/J2 **Yerbent,** Trkm.
68/A4 **Yères** (riv.), Fr.
53/H4 **Yerevan** (cap.), Arm.
165/E3 **Yerichaña,** Ven.
184/D4 **Yerington,** Nv,US
104/C2 **Yerköy,** Turk.
93/H5 **Yerlisu,** Turk.
114/C1 **Yermak,** Kaz.
95/M5 **Yermekeyevo,** Rus.
100/H4 **Yermentau,** Kaz.
94/J5 **Yermish',** Rus.
95/M2 **Yermitsa,** Rus.
158/D3 **Yermo,** Mex.
186/D3 **Yermo,** Ca,US
97/K1 **Yermolayevo,** Rus.
109/J1 **Yerofey Pavlovich,** Rus.
103/D4 **Yeroḩam,** Isr.
91/H4 **Yerolimín,** Gre.
79/G4 **Yerre** (riv.), Fr.
53/T10 **Yerres,** Fr.
53/U11 **Yerres** (riv.), Fr.
66/B6 **Yerseke,** Neth.
97/J2 **Yershov,** Rus.
95/Q5 **Yershovka,** Kaz.
95/K3 **Yertoma,** Rus.
168/B3 **Yerupaja** (peak), Peru
103/D4 **Yerushalayim** (Jerusalem) (cap.), Isr.
79/F1 **Yerville,** Fr.
172/D1 **Yesa,** Bol.
116/B4 **Yesagyo,** Burma
113/D4 **Yesan,** SKor.
158/D4 **Yesca,** Mex.
114/A1 **Yesil',** Kaz.
103/C1 **Yeşildere,** Turk.
104/C2 **Yeşilhisar,** Turk.
96/F4 **Yeşilırmak** (riv.), Turk.
103/E1 **Yeşilkent,** Turk.
104/B2 **Yeşilova,** Turk.
104/C2 **Yeşilova,** Turk.
190/B3 **Yeso,** NM,US
103/F8 **Yesodot,** Isr.
113/D3 **Yesŏng** (riv.), NKor.
97/G3 **Yessentuki,** Rus.
101/L3 **Yessey,** Rus.
76/D3 **Yeste,** Sp.
152/E3 **Yete I,** Zaire
54/D5 **Yetholm,** Sc,UK
58/D5 **Yetminster,** Eng,UK
142/D4 **Yetti** (reg.), Alg., Mrta.
119/G3 **Ye-u,** Burma
74/B3 **Yeu** (isl.), Fr.
118/B3 **Yevla,** India
97/H4 **Yevlakh,** Azer.
53/G4 **Yevpatoriya,** Ukr.
79/G4 **Yèvres,** Fr.
99/K3 **Yevsug,** Ukr.
108/G5 **Ye Xian,** China
115/D3 **Ye Xian,** China
99/K4 **Yeya** (riv.), Rus.
53/G4 **Yeysk,** Rus.
99/K4 **Yeysk** (bay), Rus.
78/C4 **Yffinac,** Fr.
74/C5 **Ygos-Saint-Saturnin,** Fr.
115/C4 **Yi** (riv.), China
175/G2 **Yi** (riv.), Uru.
103/D2 **Yialousa,** Cyp.
113/B2 **Yiangkou,** China
91/H2 **Yiannitsá,** Gre.
91/H3 **Yiánnouli,** Gre.
91/J4 **Yiaros** (isl.), Gre.
116/E2 **Yibin,** China
115/B5 **Yichang,** China
115/B4 **Yicheng,** China
115/C5 **Yicheng,** China
115/C4 **Yichuan,** China
109/K2 **Yichun,** China
117/G3 **Yichun,** China
119/K2 **Yichun,** China
116/C2 **Yidun,** China
119/K2 **Yifeng,** China
93/K5 **Yıgılca,** Turk.
117/H3 **Yihuang,** China
109/K2 **Yilan,** China
104/D1 **Yıldız** (peak), Turk.
104/D2 **Yıldızeli,** Turk.
105/N6 **Yildiz Park,** Turk.
109/J1 **Yilehuli** (mts.), China
116/E3 **Yiliang,** China
108/C4 **Yiliping,** China
115/B4 **Yima,** China
116/D3 **Yimen,** China
109/J2 **Yimin** (riv.), China
108/F3 **Yin** (mts.), China
115/D4 **Yinan,** China
108/F4 **Yinchuan,** China
132/D4 **Yindarlgooda** (lake), Austl.
115/C4 **Ying** (riv.), China
117/G2 **Yingcheng,** China
119/K3 **Yingde,** China
113/C1 **Ying'emen,** China
123/E2 **Yinggehai,** China
113/B2 **Yingkou,** China
117/F4 **Yingpan,** China
117/G3 **Yingpanxu,** China
117/G3 **Yingqian,** China
115/C5 **Yingshan,** China
115/D4 **Yingshang,** China
115/H6 **Yingshouyingzi,** China
117/H2 **Yingtan,** China
152/B1 **Yingui,** Camr.
114/D3 **Yining,** China
115/L8 **Yinyang,** China
116/B2 **Yi'ong** (riv.), China
150/A4 **Yirga 'Alem,** Eth.
150/A4 **Yirga Ch'efē,** Eth.
149/F4 **Yirol,** Sudan
131/E3 **Yirrkala,** Austl.
109/H2 **Yirshi,** China
117/F3 **Yishan,** China
115/D4 **Yishui,** China
91/H4 **Yíthion,** Gre.
115/F2 **Yitong** (riv.), China
108/C3 **Yiwanquan,** China
108/C3 **Yiwu,** China
113/A2 **Yi Xian,** China
115/D5 **Yixing,** China
108/G5 **Yiyang,** China
115/C4 **Yiyang,** China
117/G2 **Yiyang,** China
119/F2 **Yiyu,** India
115/D3 **Yiyuan,** China
119/K2 **Yizhang,** China
115/D4 **Yizheng,** China
63/J3 **Ylakiai,** Lith.
56/E6 **Y Llethr** (mtn.), Wal,UK
63/K1 **Ylöjärvi,** Fin.
182/F3 **Ymir,** BC,Can
182/F3 **Ymir** (mtn.), BC,Can
62/G2 **Yngaren** (lake), Swe.
189/F3 **Yoakum,** Tx,US
150/B3 **Yoboki,** Djib.
172/C1 **Yocalla,** Bol.
113/D5 **Yŏch'ŏn,** SKor.
200/C4 **Yockanookany** (riv.), Ms,US
200/C3 **Yocona** (riv.), Ms,US
191/F2 **Yoder,** Ks,US
192/B3 **Yoder,** Wy,US
110/D3 **Yodo** (riv.), Japan
113/D3 **Yodŏk,** NKor.
101/P4 **Yoduma** (riv.), Rus.
125/D2 **Yog** (pt.), Phil.
93/H5 **Yoğuntaş,** Turk.
124/E4 **Yogyakarta,** Indo.
124/E5 **Yogyakarta** (prov.), Indo.
150/A2 **Yohannes IV** (int'l arpt.), Eth.
182/F2 **Yoho Nat'l Park,** BC,Can
112/B2 **Yoichi,** Japan
160/D3 **Yojoa** (lake), Hon.
113/D4 **Yŏju,** SKor.
148/B5 **Yokadouma,** Camr.
110/E3 **Yōkaichi,** Japan
153/E2 **Yokana,** Zaire
110/D3 **Yokawa,** Japan
200/B4 **Yokena,** Ms,US
110/E3 **Yokkaichi,** Japan
148/B4 **Yoko,** Camr.
111/F3 **Yokohama,** Japan
153/E3 **Yokolo,** Zaire
111/F3 **Yokosuka,** Japan
112/B4 **Yokote,** Japan
148/B3 **Yola,** Nga.
161/E4 **Yolaina, Serranías de** (range), Nic.
104/E2 **Yolboyu,** Turk.
205/L9 **Yolo,** Ca,US
205/L9 **Yolo** (co.), Ca,US
153/E3 **Yolombo,** Zaire
123/C2 **Yom** (riv.), Thai.
152/B3 **Yombi,** Gabon
113/C3 **Yŏmju,** NKor.
144/C5 **Yomou,** Gui.
117/F4 **Yon** (riv.), China
74/C3 **Yon** (riv.), Fr.
110/C3 **Yonago,** Japan
110/C3 **Yonago** (arpt.), Japan
112/G8 **Yonaguni** (isl.), Japan
112/K7 **Yonaha-dake** (peak), Japan
113/D4 **Yŏnan,** NKor.
184/B2 **Yoncalla,** Or,US
112/B3 **Yoneshiro** (riv.), Japan
111/G2 **Yonezawa,** Japan
113/D5 **Yŏngam,** SKor.
113/C3 **Yongamp'o,** NKor.
117/E2 **Yong'an,** China
117/H3 **Yong'an,** China
117/F3 **Yong'an** (pass), China
113/C3 **Yŏngbyŏn,** NKor.
108/E4 **Yongchang,** China
115/D4 **Yongcheng,** China
113/E5 **Yŏngch'ŏn,** SKor.
119/G3 **Yongde,** China
115/H7 **Yongding** (riv.), China
113/E4 **Yŏngdŏk,** SKor.
113/D4 **Yŏngdong,** SKor.
113/F6 **Yongdungpo,** SKor.
108/F5 **Yongfeng,** China
119/J3 **Yongfu,** China
113/C3 **Yonggang,** NKor.
113/D5 **Yŏnggwang,** SKor.
113/E4 **Yŏnghae,** SKor.
113/D3 **Yonghăng** (riv.), NKor.
115/B3 **Yonghe,** China
113/D3 **Yŏnghŭng,** NKor.
115/B4 **Yongji,** China
113/F6 **Yŏngjong** (isl.), SKor.
113/E4 **Yŏngju,** SKor.
116/E4 **Yongle,** China
113/C2 **Yongling,** China
113/D4 **Yongmun-san** (mtn.), SKor.
115/C3 **Yongnian,** China
123/E1 **Yongning,** China
113/A3 **Yongningjian,** China
153/E3 **Yongo,** Zaire
124/C2 **Yong Peng,** Malay.
108/F4 **Yongping,** China
117/H3 **Yongping,** China
117/J3 **Yongqiang,** China
115/D3 **Yongqing,** China
115/H7 **Yongqing,** China
119/H2 **Yongren,** China
113/D5 **Yŏngsan** (riv.), SKor.
116/D2 **Yongshan,** China
117/D3 **Yongsheng,** China
119/J2 **Yongshun,** China
113/E4 **Yŏngwŏl,** SKor.
113/D3 **Yŏngwŏn,** NKor.
119/K2 **Yongxin,** China
113/E4 **Yŏng-yang,** SKor.
117/F3 **Yongzhou,** China
144/B4 **Yonibana,** SLeo.
207/E2 **Yonkers,** NY,US
74/E2 **Yonne** (riv.), Fr.
111/H7 **Yono,** Japan
113/E2 **Yonsa,** NKor.
113/D3 **Yŏnsan,** NKor.
114/C4 **Yopurga,** China
204/C3 **Yorba Linda,** Ca,US
132/C4 **York,** Austl.
131/F2 **York** (cape), Austl.
130/B3 **York** (sound), Austl.
197/S8 **York,** On,Can
197/R8 **York** (co.), On,Can
196/E1 **York** (riv.), Qu,Can
57/G4 **York,** Eng,UK
200/C4 **York,** Al,US
192/F3 **York,** Ne,US
206/B4 **York,** Pa,US
206/B3 **York** (co.), Pa,US
201/G3 **York,** SC,US
201/J2 **York** (riv.), Va,US
133/H5 **Yorke** (pen.), Austl.
133/H5 **Yorketown,** Austl.
178/G3 **York Factory,** Mb,Can
206/B3 **York Haven,** Pa,US
176/H4 **York Landing,** Can.
57/G4 **York Minster,** Eng,UK
199/G3 **Yorkshire,** NY,US
57/F3 **Yorkshire Dales Nat'l Park,** Eng,UK
57/H3 **Yorkshire Wolds** (grassl.), Eng,UK
206/A3 **York Springs,** Pa,US
194/C2 **Yorkton,** Sk,Can
191/J3 **Yorktown,** Ar,US
198/D4 **Yorktown,** In,US
189/F3 **Yorktown,** Tx,US
201/J2 **Yorktown,** Va,US
207/E1 **Yorktown Heights,** NY,US
57/G3 **York, Vale of** (vall.), Eng,UK
205/P16 **Yorkville,** Il,US
160/E3 **Yoro,** Hon.
111/M9 **Yorō,** Japan
111/J7 **Yōrō** (riv.), Japan
111/M10 **Yoroi-zaki** (pt.), Japan
112/K7 **Yoron** (isl.), Japan
108/F2 **Yöröö,** Mong.
144/D3 **Yorosso,** Mali
57/F6 **Yorton,** Eng,UK
145/F4 **Yorubaland** (plat.), Nga.
186/C2 **Yosemite** (falls), Ca,US
186/C2 **Yosemite Nat'l Park,** Ca,US
110/C4 **Yoshida,** Japan
110/D3 **Yoshii** (riv.), Japan
111/H7 **Yoshikawa,** Japan
110/D3 **Yoshimo** (riv.), Japan
111/L10 **Yoshino,** Japan
111/L10 **Yoshino** (riv.), Japan
110/E3 **Yoshino-Kumano Nat'l Park,** Japan
53/H3 **Yoshkar-Ola,** Rus.
131/E1 **Yos Sudarso** (isl.), Indo.
113/D5 **Yŏsu,** SKor.
172/C1 **Yotala,** Bol.
169/F5 **Yotaú,** Bol.
112/B2 **Yōtei-san** (mtn.), Japan
111/J7 **Yotsukaidō,** Japan
117/G3 **You** (peak), China
117/E4 **You** (riv.), China
117/F2 **You** (riv.), China
182/B3 **Youbou,** BC,Can
108/C4 **Youdunzi,** China
60/C6 **Youghal,** Ire.
60/C6 **Youghal** (bay), Ire.
199/G5 **Youghiogheny** (riv.), Md, Pa,US
148/D4 **Youhamba** (riv.), CAfr.
135/D2 **Young,** Austl.
194/B2 **Young,** Sk,Can
175/F2 **Young,** Uru.
187/G3 **Young,** Az,US
195/N7 **Young America,** Mn,US
136/D2 **Young Nick's** (pt.), N.Z.
205/C3 **Youngs** (lake), Wa,US
183/J2 **Youngstown,** Ab,Can
203/F2 **Youngstown,** Fl,US
198/C5 **Youngstown,** In,US
197/S9 **Youngstown,** NY,US
208/G5 **Youngstown,** Oh,US
208/G5 **Youngstown** (mun. arpt.), Oh,US
208/G5 **Youngstown Steel Museum,** Oh,US
202/C2 **Youngsville,** La,US
187/J2 **Youngsville,** NM,US
199/G4 **Youngsville,** Pa,US
205/K10 **Yountville,** Ca,US
117/G3 **Youshui,** China
142/C2 **Youssoufia,** Mor.
117/F3 **Youxi,** China
117/H3 **Youxikou,** China
119/J2 **Youyang,** China
109/L2 **Youyi,** China
165/E3 **Yoví** (peak), Ven.
104/C2 **Yozgat,** Turk.
173/E1 **Ypané** (riv.), Par.
173/F2 **Ypé Jhú,** Par.
79/F1 **Yport,** Fr.
68/B2 **Ypres** (Ieper), Belg.
205/E7 **Ypsilanti,** Mi,US
194/E4 **Ypsilanti,** ND,US
56/D6 **Yr Eifl** (mtn.), Wal,UK
184/B3 **Yreka,** Ca,US
68/B2 **Yser** (riv.), Fr.
62/E4 **Ystad,** Swe.
58/C3 **Ystalyfera,** Wal,UK
58/C3 **Ystradgynlais,** Wal,UK
58/C3 **Ystrad Mynach,** Wal,UK
58/C2 **Ystwyth** (riv.), Wal,UK
54/D2 **Ythan** (riv.), Sc,UK
74/E4 **Ytrac,** Fr.
62/A1 **Ytre Sula** (isl.), Nor.
62/D3 **Ytterby,** Swe.
61/G2 **Ytterbyn,** Swe.
119/J3 **Yu** (riv.), China
117/J4 **Yü** (peak), Tai.
115/C5 **Yuan** (lake), China
117/F2 **Yuan** (riv.), China
117/G3 **Yuan** (riv.), China
115/B5 **Yuan'an,** China
108/F5 **Yuanba,** China
117/F3 **Yuanbao** (mtn.), China
115/C3 **Yuanping,** China
115/B4 **Yuanqu,** China
116/D4 **Yuan** (Red) (riv.), China
116/E2 **Yuanshan,** China
115/C3 **Yuanshi,** China
117/G4 **Yuantan,** China
117/H2 **Yuantan,** China
115/C4 **Yuanyang,** China
184/C4 **Yuba** (riv.), Ca,US
191/F4 **Yuba,** Ok,US
184/C4 **Yuba City,** Ca,US
112/B2 **Yūbari,** Japan
112/C1 **Yūbetsu,** Japan
112/C2 **Yūbetsu** (riv.), Japan
204/C2 **Yucaipa,** Ca,US
181/J7 **Yucatan** (chan.), Cuba, Mex.
160/E1 **Yucatan** (chan.), Mex.
159/H5 **Yucatán** (pen.), Mex.
160/D2 **Yucatan** (pen.), Mex.
159/H4 **Yucatan** (state), Mex.
160/D1 **Yucatán** (state), Mex.
181/J7 **Yucatan** (state), Mex.
176/J7 **Yucatan** (chan.), Mex., Cuba
187/E3 **Yucca,** Az,US
187/H2 **Yucca House Nat'l Mon.,** Co,US
186/D3 **Yucca Valley,** Ca,US
115/C4 **Yucheng,** China
115/D3 **Yucheng,** China
115/C3 **Yuci,** China
117/G3 **Yudu,** China
116/E2 **Yuechi,** China
117/G1 **Yuehedian,** China
116/E2 **Yuelaichang,** China
117/G2 **Yuelu** (mtn.), China
133/F2 **Yuendumu,** Austl.
133/F2 **Yuendumu Abor. Land,** Austl.
117/J2 **Yueqing,** China
108/H5 **Yuexi,** China
117/H2 **Yuexi,** China
119/H2 **Yuexi,** China
116/D2 **Yuexi** (riv.), China
117/G2 **Yueyang,** China
95/K3 **Yug** (riv.), Rus.
95/P1 **Yugorskiy** (pen.), Rus.
92/D3 **Yugoslavia**
115/L9 **Yuhang,** China
117/G3 **Yuhua** (mtn.), China
117/J2 **Yuhuan,** China
117/F2 **Yujiaxi,** China
111/F2 **Yūki,** Japan
152/D3 **Yuki Kengundu,** Zaire
177/F3 **Yukon** (riv.), Ak,US, Yk,Can
50/B2 **Yukon** (riv.), Us,Can.
178/B2 **Yukon** (riv.), Yk,Can, Ak,US
176/B3 **Yukon** (riv.), Can. ,US
191/J2 **Yukon,** Mo,US
177/K2 **Yukon-Charley Rivers Nat'l Prsv.,** Ak,US
177/L3 **Yukon Crossing,** Yk,Can
177/F3 **Yukon Delta Nat'l Wild. Ref.,** Ak,US
177/J2 **Yukon Flats Nat'l Wild. Ref.,** Ak,US
177/L2 **Yukon Territory** (terr.), Can.
105/F2 **Yüksekova,** Turk.
110/B4 **Yukuhashi,** Japan
113/A1 **Yulamasi,** China
133/F3 **Yulara,** Austl.
97/L1 **Yuldybayevo,** Rus.
134/C4 **Yuleba,** Austl.
203/H2 **Yulee,** Fl,US
114/E3 **Yuli,** China
145/H4 **Yuli,** Nga.
117/F4 **Yulin,** China
117/F5 **Yulin,** China
115/B3 **Yulin** (riv.), China
117/H2 **Yuling** (pass), China
115/D5 **Yuling Guan** (pass), China
116/D3 **Yulongxue** (peak), China
186/E4 **Yuma,** Az,US
186/E4 **Yuma** (des.), Az,US
192/C3 **Yuma,** Co,US
186/E4 **Yuma Marine Corps Air Sta.,** Az,US
186/E4 **Yuma Prov. Grnd.,** Az,US
133/G4 **Yumbarra Consv. Park,** Austl.
153/G2 **Yumbe,** Ugan.
174/B3 **Yumbel,** Chile
152/D2 **Yumbi,** Zaire
152/D3 **Yumbi,** Zaire
153/F3 **Yumbi,** Zaire
164/B4 **Yumbo,** Col.
121/H1 **Yumbu Lhakang,** China
108/D4 **Yumen,** China
108/D3 **Yumenzhen,** China
114/D2 **Yumin,** China
103/D1 **Yumurtalık,** Turk.
115/C5 **Yun** (riv.), China
132/B4 **Yuna,** Austl.
104/B2 **Yunak,** Turk.
115/B4 **Yuncheng,** China
115/C4 **Yuncheng,** China
144/A3 **Yundum,** Gam.
115/C2 **Yungang Caves,** China
172/C1 **Yungas** (reg.), Bol.
174/B3 **Yungay,** Chile
168/D5 **Yunguyo,** Peru
117/H2 **Yunhe,** China
117/F3 **Yunjiang,** China
117/F4 **Yunkai** (mts.), China
133/F2 **Yunkanjini Abor. Land,** Austl.
119/G2 **Yunlong,** China
116/D3 **Yunnan** (prov.), China
133/H5 **Yunta,** Austl.
115/D4 **Yuntai Shan** (peak), China
115/D2 **Yunwu Shan** (peak), China
115/B4 **Yunxi,** China
108/G5 **Yun Xian,** China
115/B4 **Yun Xian,** China
116/D3 **Yun Xian,** China
115/D4 **Yunyan** (riv.), China
115/B3 **Yunyanzhen,** China
115/C3 **Yunzhong Shan** (mtn.), China
119/J2 **Yuping,** China
165/G4 **Yupukari,** Guy.
166/B2 **Yupukarri,** Guy.
115/H7 **Yuqiao** (res.), China
172/C2 **Yura,** Bol.
110/D3 **Yura** (riv.), Japan
168/B2 **Yuracyacu,** Peru
63/L4 **Yuratishki,** Bela.
100/J4 **Yurga,** Rus.
95/Q5 **Yurgamysh,** Rus.
112/E2 **Yuri** (isl.), Rus.
168/B2 **Yurimaguas,** Peru
95/K2 **Yuroma,** Rus.
114/C4 **Yurongkax** (riv.), China
165/F3 **Yuruari** (riv.), Ven.
93/H5 **Yürük,** Turk.
95/L4 **Yur'ya,** Rus.
94/J4 **Yur'yevets,** Rus.
99/J3 **Yur'yevka,** Ukr.
94/H4 **Yur'yev-Pol'skiy,** Rus.
95/N5 **Yuryuzan',** Rus.
95/N5 **Yuryuzan'** (riv.), Rus.
160/E3 **Yuscarán,** Hon.
117/J4 **Yushan Nat'l Park,** Tai.
115/C3 **Yushe,** China
109/K3 **Yushu,** China
113/C2 **Yushu,** China
113/D4 **Yusŏng,** SKor.
104/E1 **Yusufeli,** Turk.
115/D4 **Yutai,** China
114/D4 **Yutian,** China
115/D3 **Yutian,** China
172/C2 **Yuto,** Arg.
173/E3 **Yuty,** Par.
69/F5 **Yutz,** Fr.
115/C3 **Yu Xian,** China
115/C4 **Yu Xian,** China
117/H2 **Yuxikou,** China
117/J2 **Yuyao,** China
112/A4 **Yuza,** Japan
112/B4 **Yuzawa,** Japan
112/D1 **Yuzhno-Kuril'sk,** Rus.
109/N2 **Yuzhno-Sakhalinsk,** Rus.
97/H3 **Yuzhno-Sukhokumsk,** Rus.
95/P5 **Yuzhnoural'sk,** Rus.
114/D1 **Yuzhnyy,** Rus.
99/L4 **Yuzhnyy,** Rus.
98/F4 **Yuzhnyy Bug** (riv.), Ukr.
78/C5 **Yvel** (riv.), Fr.
53/R10 **Yvelines** (dept.), Fr.
80/C4 **Yverdon,** Swi.
79/F1 **Yvetot,** Fr.
53/S10 **Yvette** (riv.), Fr.
69/D3 **Yvoir,** Belg.
80/C4 **Yvonand,** Swi.
79/F4 **Yvré-l'Évêque,** Fr.
123/B2 **Ywathit,** Burma
82/A1 **Yzeron** (riv.), Fr.
74/E3 **Yzeure,** Fr.

## Z

116/C1 **Za** (riv.), China
141/N13 **Za** (riv.), Mor.
66/B4 **Zaandam,** Neth.
66/B4 **Zaandijk,** Neth.
64/C2 **Zaanstad,** Neth.
109/H2 **Zabaykal'sk,** Rus.
84/J8 **Żabbar,** Malta
70/C4 **Zaber** (riv.), Ger.
150/B2 **Zabīd,** Yem.
150/B2 **Zabīd, Wādī** (dry riv.), Yem.
65/L2 **Ząbki,** Pol.
65/J3 **Ząbkowice Śląskie,** Pol.
92/D4 **Žabljak,** Yugo.
107/H2 **Zābol,** Iran
107/H3 **Zābolī,** Iran
145/E4 **Zabré,** Burk.
65/J4 **Zábřeh,** Czh.
65/K3 **Zabrze,** Pol.
97/J3 **Zaburun'ye,** Kaz.
145/F4 **Zabzuga,** Gha.
160/D3 **Zacapa,** Guat.
159/M7 **Zacapoaxtla,** Mex.
159/E5 **Zacapú,** Mex.
158/E4 **Zacatecas,** Mex.
158/E3 **Zacatecas** (state), Mex.
160/D3 **Zacatecoluca,** ESal.
159/K8 **Zacatepec,** Mex.
159/M7 **Zacatlán,** Mex.
202/C2 **Zachary,** La,US
159/F4 **Zacualtipán,** Mex.
160/D3 **Zaculeu,** Guat.
92/B3 **Zadar,** Cro.
123/B4 **Zadetkyi** (isl.), Burma
152/C4 **Zadi** (riv.), Ang.
123/B3 **Zadi,** Burma
108/D5 **Zadoi,** China
96/F1 **Zadonsk,** Rus.
76/B3 **Zafra,** Sp.
65/H3 **Żagań,** Pol.
63/K3 **Žagarė,** Lith.
84/C4 **Zagarolo,** It.
105/G3 **Zāgheh-ye Pā'īn,** Iran
141/X17 **Zaghwān,** Tun.
141/W17 **Zaghwān'** (gov.), Tun.
91/H3 **Zagorá,** Gre.
142/D3 **Zagora,** Mor.
92/B2 **Zagorjeob Savi,** Slov.
92/C3 **Zagreb** (cap.), Cro.
105/F2 **Zagros** (mts.), Iran
114/E5 **Za'gya** (riv.), China
107/H3 **Zāhedān,** Iran
118/C4 **Zahirābād,** India
103/D3 **Zaḩlah,** Leb.
72/C4 **Zahna,** Ger.
72/C4 **Zahna** (riv.), Ger.
92/F1 **Záhony,** Hun.
106/D5 **Ẕahrān,** SAr.
77/F2 **Zaidín,** Sp.
120/C2 **Zaidpur,** India
117/F3 **Zaima,** China
141/N13 **Zaïo,** Mor.
152/C4 **Zaire** (prov.), Ang.
140/E5 **Zaire** (Congo)
140/E4 **Zaïre** (Congo) (Lualaba) (riv.), Afr.
92/F4 **Zaječar,** Yugo.
155/F4 **Zaka,** Zim.
108/E1 **Zakamensk,** Rus.
97/H4 **Zakataly,** Azer.
91/G4 **Zakháro,** Gre.
105/E2 **Zākhū,** Iraq
145/H5 **Zaki Biam,** Nga.
91/G4 **Zákinthos,** Gre.
91/G4 **Zákinthos** (isl.), Gre.
65/K4 **Zakopane,** Pol.
148/C3 **Zakouma,** Chad
148/C3 **Zakouma Nat'l Park,** Chad
91/J5 **Zakro** (ruins), Gre.
152/C4 **Zala,** Ang.
149/H4 **Zala,** Eth.
73/A6 **Zala** (co.), Hun.
73/B6 **Zala** (riv.), Hun.
73/B6 **Zalaapáti,** Hun.
73/A6 **Zalaegerszeg,** Hun.
73/A6 **Zalalövő,** Hun.
76/C3 **Zalamea de la Serena,** Sp.
76/B4 **Zalamea la Real,** Sp.
145/H4 **Zalanga,** Nga.
109/J2 **Zalantun,** China
108/E1 **Zalari,** Rus.
73/B6 **Zalaszentgrót,** Hun.
92/F2 **Zalău,** Rom.
92/B2 **Žalec,** Slov.
98/C3 **Zaleshchiki,** Ukr.
106/D4 **Ẓalim,** SAr.
148/D2 **Zalingei,** Sudan
146/A1 **Zalţan,** Libya
146/C2 **Zalţan,** Libya
146/C2 **Zaltan, Bi'r** (well), Libya
146/D2 **Zaltan, Jabal** (mts.), Libya
66/C5 **Zaltbommel,** Neth.
116/B5 **Zalun,** Burma
123/B3 **Zalut,** Burma
73/B3 **Zálužie, Vel'ké,** Slvk.
111/H7 **Zama,** Japan
141/X18 **Zamālat As Sawāsī,** Tun.
120/D3 **Zamānia,** India
73/B6 **Zamárdi,** Hun.
155/G3 **Zambezi** (riv.), Afr.
154/D2 **Zambezi,** Zam.
155/H3 **Zambézia** (prov.), Moz.
155/E3 **Zambezi Escarpment** (cliff), Zam., Zim.
140/E6 **Zambia**
125/C4 **Zamboanga City,** Phil.
65/M2 **Zambrów,** Pol.
77/P11 **Zambujal de Cima,** Port.
145/G3 **Zamfora** (riv.), Nga.
123/B3 **Zami** (riv.), Burma
117/E4 **Zamiao,** China
149/E4 **Zamoi,** Zaire
153/F2 **Zamoi,** Zaire
168/B2 **Zamora,** Ecu.
168/B1 **Zamora** (riv.), Ecu.
76/C2 **Zamora,** Sp.
168/B2 **Zamora-Chinchipe** (prov.), Ecu.
158/E5 **Zamora de Hidalgo,** Mex.
65/M3 **Zamość,** Pol.
65/M3 **Zamość** (prov.), Pol.
81/G3 **Zams,** Aus.
146/B3 **Zāmūs, Bi'r** (well), Libya
97/H3 **Zam'yany,** Rus.
146/B2 **Zamzam, Wādī** (dry riv.), Libya
152/C3 **Zanaga,** Congo
76/D3 **Záncara** (riv.), Sp.
114/C5 **Zanda,** China
166/C1 **Zanderij,** Sur.
166/C1 **Zanderij** (int'l arpt.), Sur.
66/A5 **Zandkreekdam** (dam), Neth.
152/D4 **Zandu-Kansabala,** Zaire
66/B6 **Zandvliet,** Belg.
66/B4 **Zandvoort,** Neth.
87/E1 **Zanè,** It.
198/E5 **Zanesville,** Oh,US
145/H3 **Zango,** Nga.
115/C3 **Zanhuang,** China
105/G2 **Zanjān,** Iran
105/G2 **Zanjān** (gov.), Iran
73/B6 **Zánka,** Hun.
84/C6 **Zannone** (isl.), It.
132/D4 **Zanthus,** Austl.
95/L3 **Zanul'ye,** Rus.
151/B3 **Zanzibar,** Tanz.
151/B3 **Zanzibar** (isl.), Tanz.
151/B3 **Zanzibar** (Kisauni) (int'l arpt.), Tanz.
151/B3 **Zanzibar North** (prov.), Tanz.
151/B3 **Zanzibar South** (prov.), Tanz.
151/B3 **Zanzibar West** (prov.), Tanz.
151/A2 **Zanzuzi** (hill), Tanz.
117/G3 **Zaoheshi,** China
115/C3 **Zaoqiang,** China
111/G1 **Zaō-san** (mtn.), Japan
143/E2 **Za, Oued** (riv.), Mor.
143/E4 **Zaouiet Kounta,** Alg.
115/C4 **Zaoyang,** China
115/D4 **Zaozhuang,** China
94/F5 **Zapadnaya Dvina** (riv.), Bela., Rus.
71/G3 **Západočeský** (reg.), Czh.
73/B3 **Západoslovenský** (reg.), Slvk.
149/E4 **Zapai,** Zaire
174/C3 **Zapala,** Arg.
172/C2 **Zapaleri** (peak), Arg.
174/C2 **Zapallar,** Chile
109/N2 **Zapando-Sakhalin** (mts.), Rus.
161/F1 **Zapata** (pen.), Cuba
188/E4 **Zapata,** Tx,US
164/C3 **Zapatoca,** Col.
164/C2 **Zapatosa** (lake), Col.
161/H4 **Zapatosa, Ciénaga de** (lake), Col.
71/H4 **Záplatský Rybnik** (lake), Czh.
75/K2 **Západočeský** (reg.), Czh.
94/F1 **Zapolyarnyy,** Rus.
99/H4 **Zaporozh'ye,** Ukr.
99/H4 **Zaporozh'ye** (int'l arpt.), Ukr.
99/H4 **Zaporozh'ye Obl.,** Ukr.
164/B5 **Zapotal,** Ecu.
168/A2 **Zapotillo,** Ecu.
85/F5 **Zapponeta,** It.
92/B3 **Zaprešić,** Cro.
108/C5 **Zaqên,** China
146/C2 **Zaqqūţ, 'Ayn** (well), Libya
104/D2 **Zara,** Turk.
149/F3 **Zarāf, Baḩr Az** (riv.), Sudan
100/G5 **Zarafshan,** Uzb.
164/C3 **Zaragoza,** Col.
159/E2 **Zaragoza,** Mex.
159/E4 **Zaragoza,** Mex.
188/A2 **Zaragoza,** Mex.
188/D3 **Zaragoza,** Mex.
88/C2 **Zaragoza** (Saragossa), Sp.
105/J4 **Zarand,** Iran
145/H4 **Zaranda** (hill), Nga.
63/M4 **Zarasai,** Lith.
174/F2 **Zárate,** Arg.
76/D1 **Zarauz,** Sp.
165/E2 **Zaraza,** Ven.
105/H4 **Zārch,** Iran
105/G3 **Zard** (mtn.), Iran
105/F1 **Zardob,** Azer.
94/F2 **Zarechensk,** Rus.
98/D2 **Zarechnoye,** Ukr.
107/J2 **Zareh Sharan,** Afg.
105/H4 **Zargān,** Iran
145/G4 **Zaria,** Nga.
114/D1 **Zarinsk,** Rus.
107/H2 **Zarmast** (pass), Afg.
93/G3 **Zărnești,** Rom.
73/C3 **Žarnovica,** Slvk.
91/J5 **Zarós,** Gre.
67/H1 **Zarrentin,** Ger.
105/F2 **Zarrīneh** (riv.), Iran
105/G3 **Zarrin Shahr,** Iran
73/B3 **Záruby** (peak), Slvk.
168/B1 **Zaruma,** Ecu.
168/A1 **Ẓarumilla,** Peru
65/H3 **Żary,** Pol.
143/H3 **Zarzaïtine,** Alg.
164/B3 **Zarzal,** Col.
76/B3 **Zarza la Mayor,** Sp.
76/A1 **Zas,** Sp.
63/L3 **Zasa,** Lat.
107/L2 **Zāskar** (range), India
63/M5 **Zaslavl',** Bela.
156/D3 **Zastron,** SAfr.
95/K2 **Zasul'ye,** Rus.
71/G2 **Žatec,** Czh.
95/P5 **Zatobol'sk,** Kaz.
98/F4 **Zatoka,** Ukr.
72/C3 **Zauche** (reg.), Ger.
174/E2 **Zavalla,** Arg.
189/G2 **Zavalla,** Tx,US
105/H3 **Zavāreh,** Iran
103/F8 **Zavdi'el,** Isr.
68/D2 **Zaventem,** Belg.
93/H4 **Zavet,** Bul.
92/D3 **Zavidovići,** Bosn.
109/K1 **Zavitinsk,** Rus.
95/Q4 **Zavodoukovsk,** Rus.
155/G5 **Závora** (pt.), Moz.

65/K3 **Zawadzkie,** Pol.
155/F3 **Zawi,** Zim.
65/K3 **Zawiercie,** Pol.
146/B3 **Zawīlah,** Libya
146/D1 **Zāwiyat al Mukhaylá,** Libya
146/D2 **Zāwiyat Masūs,** Libya
73/A2 **Zaya** (riv.), Aus.
108/D6 **Zaya** (riv.), China
114/D2 **Zaysan,** Kaz.
114/D2 **Zaysan** (lake), Kaz.
116/C2 **Zayü,** China
116/C2 **Zayü** (riv.), China
161/G1 **Zaza** (riv.), Cuba
157/H8 **Zazafotsy,** Madg.
146/B2 **Zāzamt, Wādī** (dry riv.), Libya
164/D2 **Zazárida,** Ven.
98/C3 **Zbarazh,** Ukr.
65/H2 **Zbąszyń,** Pol.
71/G3 **Zbiroh,** Czh.
98/C3 **Zborov,** Ukr.
71/G3 **Zbůch,** Czh.
65/H4 **Žďár nad Sázavou,** Czh.
73/A2 **Zdánický les** (for.), Czh.
71/G3 **Zdice,** Czh.
98/D2 **Zdolbunov,** Ukr.
65/K3 **Zduńska Wola,** Pol.
196/D2 **Zealand,** NB,Can
183/L2 **Zealandia,** Sk,Can
174/C5 **Zeballos** (peak), Arg.
84/H8 **Żebbuġ,** Malta
156/E2 **Zebediela,** SAfr.
200/E4 **Zebulon,** Ga,US
141/R16 **Zeddine** (riv.), Alg.
68/C1 **Zedelgem,** Belg.
68/C1 **Zeebrugge,** Belg.
135/C4 **Zeehan,** Austl.
66/C5 **Zeeland,** Neth.
66/A5 **Zeeland** (prov.), Neth.
156/D2 **Zeerust,** SAfr.
72/D3 **Zeesen,** Ger.
66/C4 **Zeewolde,** Neth.
103/D3 **Zefat,** Isr.
65/L2 **Zegrzyńskie** (lake), Pol.
117/J2 **Zeguo,** China
72/D2 **Zehdenick,** Ger.
194/B2 **Zehner,** Sk,Can
72/D5 **Zehren,** Ger.
200/C2 **Zeigler,** Il,US
133/G2 **Zeil** (peak), Austl.
70/D2 **Zeil,** Ger.
66/C4 **Zeist,** Neth.
72/D5 **Zeithain,** Ger.
84/J8 **Żeitun,** Malta
72/C5 **Zeitz,** Ger.
103/F8 **Zekharya,** Isr.
68/D1 **Zele,** Belg.
97/G4 **Zelenchukskaya,** Rus.
94/G2 **Zelenoborskiy,** Rus.
53/H3 **Zelenodol'sk,** Rus.
99/G4 **Zeleñodol'sk,** Ukr.
63/N1 **Zelenogorsk,** Rus.
63/J4 **Zelenogradsk,** Rus.
97/G3 **Zelenokumsk,** Rus.
66/D4 **Zelhem,** Neth.
208/G6 **Zelienople,** Pa,US
73/C3 **Želiezovce,** Slvk.
144/C5 **Zelimai,** Libr.
69/G3 **Zell,** Ger.
80/D3 **Zell,** Swi.
192/E1 **Zell,** SD,US
70/D1 **Zella-Mehlis,** Ger.
80/E1 **Zell am Harmersbach,** Ger.
70/C3 **Zell am Main,** Ger.
71/G7 **Zell am Moos,** Aus.
75/K3 **Zell am See,** Aus.
71/G6 **Zell an der Pram,** Aus.
71/G7 **Zellersee** (lake), Aus.
81/E2 **Zellersee** (lake), Ger.
70/C3 **Zellingen,** Ger.
80/D2 **Zell in Wiesental,** Ger.
141/N13 **Zelouane,** Mor.
65/K3 **Zelów,** Pol.
69/G4 **Zeltingen-Rachtig,** Ger.
92/B2 **Zeltweg,** Aus.
65/N2 **Zel'va,** Bela.
63/L4 **Želva,** Lith.
68/C1 **Zelzate,** Belg.
63/J4 **Žemaičiu Naumiestis,** Lith.
90/B4 **Zembra** (isls.), Tun.
108/E5 **Zêmdasam,** China
92/F4 **Zemen,** Bul.
97/G1 **Zemetchino,** Rus.
149/E4 **Zemio,** CAfr.
69/F4 **Zemmer,** Ger.
141/R16 **Zemmora,** Alg.
149/E4 **Zémongo Fauna Rsv.,** CAfr.
159/N7 **Zempoala,** Mex.
159/Q10 **Zempoala** (mt.), Mex.
160/C2 **Zempoaltepec, Cerro** (mtn.), Mex.
68/D2 **Zemst,** Belg.
141/R16 **Zenata** (arpt.), Alg.
108/D5 **Zênda,** China
191/E2 **Zenda,** Ks,US
107/H2 **Zendeh Jān,** Afg.
92/C3 **Zenica,** Bosn.
205/C3 **Zenith,** Wa,US
99/H2 **Zen'kov,** Ukr.
70/D3 **Zenn** (riv.), Ger.
110/C3 **Zentsūji,** Japan
152/C5 **Zenza do Itombe,** Ang.
192/C1 **Zeona,** SD,US
92/D3 **Žepče,** Bosn.
72/D2 **Zepernick,** Ger.
189/E2 **Zephyr,** Tx,US
184/D4 **Zephyr Cove,** Nv,US
202/L7 **Zephyrhills,** Fl,US
203/G3 **Zephyrhills,** Fl,US
141/S15 **Zeralda,** Alg.
72/C4 **Zerbst,** Ger.
141/L13 **Zerga** (lake), Mor.
146/B4 **Zergamouchi, Enneri** (dry riv.), Niger
80/D5 **Zermatt,** Swi.
81/G4 **Zernez,** Swi.
67/H2 **Zernien,** Ger.
99/L4 **Zernograd,** Rus.
87/F1 **Zero Branco,** It.
91/G2 **Zerqan,** Alb.
97/G4 **Zestafoni,** Geo.
178/F1 **Zeta** (lake), NW,Can
121/H1 **Zêtang,** China
67/E2 **Zetel,** Ger.
72/B6 **Zeulenroda,** Ger.
72/D3 **Zeuthen,** Ger.
67/G2 **Zeven,** Ger.
66/D5 **Zevenaar,** Neth.
66/B5 **Zevenbergen,** Neth.
91/H4 **Zevgolatíon,** Gre.
87/E2 **Zevio,** It.
109/K1 **Zeya,** Rus.
109/K1 **Zeya** (res.), Rus.
109/K1 **Zeya** (riv.), Rus.
109/K1 **Zeya-Bureya** (plain), Rus.
104/A2 **Zeytindağ,** Turk.
76/A3 **Zêzere** (riv.), Port.
103/D2 **Zghartā,** Leb.
65/K3 **Zgierz,** Pol.
65/H3 **Zgorzelec,** Pol.
97/M2 **Zhabasak,** Kaz.
65/N2 **Zhabinka,** Bela.
97/M2 **Zhailma,** Kaz.
117/F4 **Zhaixu,** China
117/G3 **Zhajiang,** China
117/F4 **Zhakou,** China
109/K2 **Zhan** (riv.), China
121/H1 **Zhanang,** China
100/G5 **Zhanatas,** Kaz.
115/B5 **Zhang** (riv.), China
117/G3 **Zhang** (riv.), China
115/C5 **Zhangdu** (lake), China
109/K3 **Zhangguangcai** (mts.), China
115/C2 **Zhanghei,** China
117/F4 **Zhanghuang,** China
113/B4 **Zhangjiabu,** China
115/C2 **Zhangjiakou,** China
116/D1 **Zhangla,** China
117/F3 **Zhangmu,** China
115/D3 **Zhangqiu,** China
115/D3 **Zhangwei** (riv.), China
108/E4 **Zhangye,** China
117/H3 **Zhangzhou,** China
115/C3 **Zhangzi,** China
113/B3 **Zhangzi** (isl.), China
115/D3 **Zhanhua,** China
117/F4 **Zhanjiang,** China
97/K3 **Zhanterek,** Kaz.
109/J3 **Zhanyu,** China
115/H7 **Zhaobeikou,** China
109/K2 **Zhaodong,** China
117/E2 **Zhaojiachang,** China
119/H2 **Zhaojue,** China
119/K3 **Zhaoping,** China
117/G4 **Zhaoqing,** China
116/D3 **Zhaotong,** China
115/C3 **Zhao Xian,** China
109/J4 **Zhaoyuan,** China
109/K2 **Zhaoyuan,** China
115/E3 **Zhaoyuan,** China
109/K2 **Zhaozhou,** China
119/K3 **Zhapo,** China
115/L9 **Zhapu,** China
114/D5 **Zhari Namco** (lake), China
97/L2 **Zharkamys,** Kaz.
94/G5 **Zharkovskiy,** Rus.
114/D2 **Zharma,** Kaz.
97/K3 **Zharmysh,** Kaz.
98/F3 **Zhashkov,** Ukr.
101/N3 **Zhatay,** Rus.
121/G1 **Zhaxilhünbo,** China
108/D5 **Zhaxizê,** China
99/K3 **Zhdanovka,** Ukr.
97/H5 **Zhdanovsk,** Azer.
115/C4 **Zhecheng,** China
116/D2 **Zhedou** (pass), China
115/L9 **Zhejiang** (prov.), China
117/G4 **Zhelang,** China
100/G2 **Zhelaniya** (cape), Rus.
63/J4 **Zheleznodorozhnyy,** Rus.
99/H1 **Zheleznogorsk,** Rus.
101/L4 **Zheleznogorsk-Ilimskiy,** Rus.
97/G3 **Zheleznovodsk,** Rus.
115/L9 **Zhelin,** China
97/L2 **Zhëltoye,** Rus.
99/G3 **Zheltyye Vody,** Ukr.
117/F3 **Zhenbao** (mtn.), China
115/G7 **Zhenchang,** China
116/E3 **Zhenfeng,** China
113/A2 **Zheng'anpu,** China
115/C3 **Zhengding,** China
117/G4 **Zhengguo,** China
108/H3 **Zhenglan,** China
115/B4 **Zhengning,** China
115/C4 **Zhengyang,** China
115/L8 **Zhengyi,** China
115/C4 **Zhengzhou,** China
115/C4 **Zhengzhou** (arpt.), China
115/D4 **Zhenjiang,** China
119/G3 **Zhenkang,** China
109/J2 **Zhenlai,** China
117/F4 **Zhenlong,** China
119/J2 **Zhenning Bouyeizu Miaozu Zizhixian,** China
108/F5 **Zhenping,** China
108/G5 **Zhenping,** China
115/C4 **Zhenping,** China
117/H3 **Zhenqian,** China
115/C4 **Zhentou** (riv.), China
115/B3 **Zhenwu Shan** (mtn.), China
119/H2 **Zhenxiong,** China
119/H3 **Zhenyuan,** China
115/L9 **Zhenze,** China
99/L2 **Zherdevka,** Rus.
97/J2 **Zhestyanka,** Rus.
97/K4 **Zhetybay,** Kaz.
109/H4 **Zhewang,** China
116/E3 **Zhexiang,** China
115/B5 **Zhicheng,** China
98/C3 **Zhidachov,** Ukr.
101/L4 **Zhigalovo,** Rus.
101/N3 **Zhigansk,** Rus.
97/J1 **Zhigulevsk,** Rus.
121/H1 **Zhigung,** China
117/F3 **Zhijiag,** China
117/F2 **Zhijiang,** China
119/J2 **Zhijin,** China
101/M2 **Zhilinda,** Rus.
63/J4 **Zhilino,** Rus.
97/J4 **Zhiloy** (isl.), Azer.
97/K2 **Zhiren'kupa,** Kaz.
97/H2 **Zhirnovsk,** Rus.
96/C1 **Zhitkovichi,** Bela.
63/N1 **Zhitkovo,** Rus.
98/E2 **Zhitomir,** Ukr.
98/E2 **Zhitomir Obl.,** Ukr.
117/G3 **Zhixia,** China
117/H2 **Zhixia,** China
96/E1 **Zhizdra,** Rus.
96/D1 **Zhlobin,** Bela.
98/E3 **Zhmerinka,** Ukr.
107/J2 **Zhob,** Pak.
107/J2 **Zhob** (riv.), Pak.
63/N4 **Zhodino,** Bela.
101/R2 **Zhokhov** (isl.), Rus.
114/B1 **Zholymbet,** Kaz.
120/E1 **Zhongba,** China
117/F3 **Zhongdu,** China
117/F3 **Zhonghuang,** China
116/E2 **Zhongjiang,** China
115/B4 **Zhongnan Shan** (mtn.), China
117/G4 **Zhongshan,** China
117/F2 **Zhong Xian,** China
115/C5 **Zhongxiang,** China
117/E2 **Zhongxin,** China
117/G3 **Zhongxin,** China
115/B3 **Zhongyang,** China
117/G3 **Zhouhu,** China
115/C4 **Zhoukou,** China
116/E2 **Zhoulichang,** China
115/L8 **Zhoupu,** China
117/J2 **Zhoushan** (isl.), China
115/E5 **Zhoushan** (isls.), China
98/G4 **Zhovtnevoye,** Ukr.
99/H2 **Zhovtnevoye,** Ukr.
113/B3 **Zhuanghe,** China
116/E3 **Zhucang,** China
115/D4 **Zhucheng,** China
117/G4 **Zhuhai,** China
117/J2 **Zhujia** (isl.), China
115/L8 **Zhujiajiao,** China
96/E1 **Zhukovka,** Rus.
94/H5 **Zhukovskiy,** Rus.
115/C4 **Zhumadian,** China
108/E5 **Zhuokeji,** China
115/C2 **Zhuolu,** China
115/G6 **Zhuolu,** China
115/G7 **Zhuo Xian,** China
115/C2 **Zhuozi,** China
115/B4 **Zhushan,** China
117/G2 **Zhutan,** China
115/B4 **Zhuxi,** China
117/F1 **Zhuxi,** China
117/H2 **Zhuxi,** China
117/G2 **Zhuyu,** China
116/E1 **Zhuyuanba,** China
117/G3 **Zhuzhou,** China
117/F3 **Zi** (riv.), China
121/H4 **Zia** (int'l arpt.), Bang.
187/J3 **Zia Ind. Res.,** NM,US
73/C2 **Žiar nad Hronom,** Slvk.
144/D5 **Zia Town,** Libr.
107/K1 **Zībāk,** Afg.
115/D3 **Zibo,** China
116/B4 **Zibyu** (hills), Burma
88/D5 **Zid, Hassi bou** (well), Alg.
73/A1 **Židlochovice,** Czh.
65/J3 **Ziębice,** Pol.
71/E1 **Ziegenrück,** Ger.
65/H3 **Zielona Góra,** Pol.
65/H2 **Zielona Góra** (prov.), Pol.
70/D6 **Ziemetshausen,** Ger.
144/C5 **Zienzu,** Libr.
67/G6 **Zierenberg,** Ger.
66/A5 **Zierikzee,** Neth.
72/C3 **Ziesar,** Ger.
103/B4 **Ziftá,** Egypt
104/D1 **Zigana** (pass), Turk.
148/B2 **Zigey,** Chad
116/B5 **Zigon,** Burma
116/E2 **Zigong,** China
115/B5 **Zigui,** China
144/A3 **Ziguinchor,** Sen.
144/A3 **Ziguinchor** (int'l arpt.), Sen.
144/A3 **Ziguinchor** (reg.), Sen.
159/E5 **Zihuatanejo,** Mex.
117/F3 **Zijingguan,** China
115/B3 **Zijing Shan** (mtn.), China
103/F6 **Zikhron Ya'aqov,** Isr.
97/L1 **Zilair,** Rus.
104/C1 **Zile,** Turk.
73/C1 **Žilina,** Slvk.
146/C2 **Zillah,** Libya
182/D4 **Zillah,** Wa,US
75/J3 **Ziller** (riv.), Aus.
81/F4 **Zillis,** Swi.
80/D2 **Zillisheim,** Fr.
63/N3 **Zilupe,** Lat.
195/H4 **Zim,** Mn,US
108/E1 **Zima,** Rus.
160/B2 **Zimatlán,** Mex.
153/G4 **Zimba,** Tanz.
154/E3 **Zimba,** Zam.
155/F3 **Zimbabwe**
195/H5 **Zimmerman,** Mn,US
93/G4 **Zimnicea,** Rom.
93/H4 **Zimnitsa,** Bul.
99/M3 **Zimnyatskiy,** Rus.
99/M4 **Zimovniki,** Rus.
80/D5 **Zinal,** Swi.
159/E5 **Zinapécuaro de Figueroa,** Mex.
155/G4 **Zinave Nat'l Park,** Moz.
145/H3 **Zinder,** Niger
145/H3 **Zinder** (dept.), Niger
148/C5 **Zinga,** CAfr.
123/B2 **Zingyaik,** Burma
145/E3 **Ziniaré,** Burk.
150/C2 **Zinjibār,** Yem.
65/G1 **Zinnowitz,** Ger.
205/Q15 **Zion,** Il,US
206/C4 **Zion,** Md,US
187/F2 **Zion Nat'l Park,** Ut,US
201/G2 **Zionville,** NC,US
164/C3 **Zipaquirá,** Col.
105/H2 **Zīrāb,** Iran
159/E5 **Zirándaro,** Mex.
73/B5 **Zirc,** Hun.
92/B4 **Žirje** (isl.), Cro.
192/A3 **Zirkel** (mt.), Co,US
81/H3 **Zirl,** Aus.
70/D4 **Zirndorf,** Ger.
116/B3 **Ziro,** India
73/A2 **Zistersdorf,** Aus.
92/D1 **Žitava** (riv.), Czech.
73/C3 **Žitava** (riv.), Slvk.
65/H3 **Zittau,** Ger.
92/D3 **Živinice,** Bosn.
153/G3 **Ziwa Magharibi** (pol. reg.), Tanz.
150/A4 **Ziway,** Eth.
150/A3 **Ziway** (lake), Eth.
115/B4 **Ziwu** (mtn.), China
117/G3 **Zixing,** China
115/D3 **Ziya** (riv.), China
117/F1 **Ziyang,** China
117/H3 **Ziyundong** (mtn.), China
116/E3 **Ziyun Miaozu Bouyeizu Zizhixian,** China
142/D2 **Ziz, Oued** (dry riv.), Mor.
73/C3 **Zlaté Moravce,** Slvk.
93/F2 **Zlatna,** Rom.
93/G5 **Zlatograd,** Bul.
92/E4 **Zlatorsko** (lake), Yugo.
95/N5 **Zlatoust,** Rus.
109/L1 **Zlatoustovsk,** Rus.
73/B1 **Zlin,** Czh.
146/B1 **Zlīṭan,** Libya
71/H4 **Zliv,** Czh.
65/J2 **Złocieniec,** Pol.
92/E3 **Zlot,** Yugo.
65/H3 **Złotoryja,** Pol.
65/J2 **Złotów,** Pol.
71/G2 **Žlutice,** Czh.
92/D3 **Zmajevo,** Yugo.
65/J3 **Żmigród,** Pol.
87/G2 **Žminj,** Cro.
96/E1 **Znamenka,** Rus.
98/G3 **Znamenka,** Ukr.
98/G3 **Znamenka Vtoraya,** Ukr.
63/J4 **Znamensk,** Rus.
65/J2 **Żnin,** Pol.
73/A2 **Znojmo,** Czh.
208/F6 **Zoar,** Oh,US
73/A4 **Zöbernbach** (riv.), Aus.
153/F2 **Zobia,** Zaire
159/Q10 **Zocálo,** Mex.
87/D4 **Zocca,** It.
69/D1 **Zoersel,** Belg.
148/A5 **Zoétélé,** Camr.
66/B4 **Zoetermeer,** Neth.
80/D3 **Zofingen,** Swi.
153/F4 **Zofu,** Zaire
119/G2 **Zogang,** China
86/C1 **Zogno,** It.
116/C1 **Zogqên,** China
91/L7 **Zográfos,** Gre.
105/G4 **Zohreh** (riv.), Iran
151/B3 **Zoissa,** Tanz.
82/B5 **Zola** (lake), Fr.
87/E4 **Zola,** It.
203/H4 **Zolfo Springs,** Fl,US
81/E3 **Zollikon,** Swi.
98/C3 **Zolochev,** Ukr.
99/H2 **Zolochëv,** Ukr.
98/G3 **Zolotonosha,** Ukr.
99/K3 **Zolotoye,** Ukr.
99/J1 **Zolotukhino,** Rus.
155/G2 **Zomba,** Malw.
58/B6 **Zone** (pt.), UK
153/F2 **Zongia,** Zaire
108/D4 **Zongjiafangzi,** China
169/D5 **Zongo,** Bol.
148/C4 **Zongo,** Zaire
159/N8 **Zongolica,** Mex.
93/K5 **Zonguldak,** Turk.
93/K5 **Zonguldak** (prov.), Turk.
114/F6 **Zongxoi,** China
115/D5 **Zongyang,** China
69/E2 **Zonhoven,** Belg.
68/B2 **Zonnebeke,** Belg.
90/A2 **Zonza,** Fr.
146/B5 **Zoo Baba** (well), Niger
159/L7 **Zoquiapan y Anexas Nat'l Park,** Mex.
160/B2 **Zoquitlán,** Mex.
121/H4 **Zorārganj,** Bang.
72/C4 **Zörbig,** Ger.
67/H5 **Zorge** (riv.), Ger.
145/E3 **Zorgo,** Burk.
99/K3 **Zorinsk,** Ukr.
76/C3 **Zorita,** Sp.
75/G2 **Zorn** (riv.), Fr.
69/G6 **Zorn** (riv.), Ger.
70/B3 **Zornheim,** Ger.
168/A1 **Zorritos,** Peru
183/K4 **Zortman,** Mt,US
144/C5 **Zorzor,** Libr.
72/D3 **Zossen,** Ger.
68/C2 **Zottegem,** Belg.
145/F5 **Zou** (prov.), Ben.
146/C4 **Zouar,** Chad
142/B5 **Zouîrât,** Mrta.
145/E4 **Zoundwéogo** (prov.), Burk.
115/D3 **Zouping,** China
143/E3 **Zousfana, Oued** (dry riv.), Alg.
156/L10 **Zout** (riv.), SAfr.
66/D2 **Zoutkamp,** Neth.
115/D4 **Zou Xian,** China
92/E3 **Zrenjanin,** Yugo.
72/C4 **Zscherndorf,** Ger.
72/D6 **Zschopau,** Ger.
71/G1 **Zschopau** (riv.), Ger.
71/F1 **Zschorlau,** Ger.
72/C4 **Zschornewitz,** Ger.
72/C5 **Zschortau,** Ger.
165/E2 **Zuata,** Ven.
76/D4 **Zubia,** Sp.
97/G1 **Zubova Polyana,** Rus.
103/G6 **Zubūbā,** WBnk.
81/E5 **Zucchero, Monte** (peak), Swi.
81/H4 **Zuckerhütl** (peak), Aus.
144/D5 **Zuénola,** IvC.
81/E3 **Zug,** Swi.
81/E3 **Zug** (canton), Swi.
142/B5 **Zug,** WSah.
97/G4 **Zugdidi,** Geo.
81/E3 **Zugersee** (lake), Swi.
146/A2 **Zughrāṙ, Bi'r** (well), Libya
99/K3 **Zugres,** Ukr.
81/G3 **Zugspitze** (peak), Ger.
66/A6 **Zuidbeveland** (isl.), Neth.
66/C4 **Zuidelijk Flevoland** (polder), Neth.
66/D2 **Zuidhorn,** Neth.
66/D2 **Zuidlaardermeer** (lake), Neth.
66/D2 **Zuidlaren,** Neth.
66/C6 **Zuid-Willemsvaart** (can.), Belg.
66/D3 **Zuidwolde,** Neth.
68/C1 **Zuienkerke,** Belg.
76/D4 **Zújar,** Sp.
76/C3 **Zújar** (res.), Sp.
76/C3 **Zujar** (riv.), Sp.
150/A2 **Zula,** Eth.
164/C2 **Zulia** (riv.), Col., Ven.
164/C2 **Zulia** (state), Ven.
69/F2 **Zülpich,** Ger.
68/C2 **Zulte,** Belg.
157/E2 **Zululand** (reg.), SAfr.
76/D1 **Zumárraga,** Sp.
168/B2 **Zumba,** Ecu.
155/F2 **Zumbo,** Moz.
193/H1 **Zumbrota,** Mn,US
159/F5 **Zumpango de Ocampo,** Mex.
104/B2 **Zümrütkaya,** Turk.
66/B6 **Zundert,** Neth.
145/G4 **Zungeru,** Nga.
83/B5 **Zungri,** It.
115/D2 **Zunhua,** China
187/H3 **Zuni** (riv.), Az, NM,US
187/H3 **Zuni,** NM,US
187/H3 **Zuni** (mts.), NM,US
187/H3 **Zuni Ind. Res.,** NM,US
117/E3 **Zunyi,** China
117/E4 **Zuo** (riv.), China
123/D1 **Zuo Jiang** (riv.), China
117/F1 **Zuolonggou,** China
115/C3 **Zuoquan,** China
115/C3 **Zuoyun,** China
81/F4 **Zuoz,** Swi.
92/D3 **Županja,** Cro.
106/D6 **Zuqar, Jabal** (isl.), Yemen
92/E4 **Žur,** Yugo.
106/D3 **Zurayghiṭ,** SAr.
105/F3 **Zurbāṭīyah,** Iraq
81/E3 **Zürich,** Swi.
81/E2 **Zürich** (canton), Swi.
81/E3 **Zürich** (int'l arpt.), Swi.
81/E3 **Zürichsee** (lake), Swi.
73/B4 **Zurndorf,** Aus.
65/K2 **Żuromin,** Pol.
84/H8 **Żurrieq,** Malta
81/G3 **Zürs,** Aus.
145/G4 **Zuru,** Nga.
81/E2 **Zurzach,** Swi.
70/D5 **Zusam** (riv.), Ger.
111/H7 **Zushi,** Japan
70/D6 **Zusmarshausen,** Ger.
66/D4 **Zutphen,** Neth.
146/B1 **Zuwārah,** Libya
95/L4 **Zuyevka,** Rus.
98/F3 **Zvenigorodka,** Ukr.
95/L5 **Zvenigovo,** Rus.
99/L3 **Zverevo,** Rus.
95/Q5 **Zverinogolovskoye,** Rus.
92/D4 **Zvijesda Nat'l Park,** Yugo.
155/F4 **Zvishavane,** Zim.
73/D2 **Zvolen,** Slvk.
92/D3 **Zvorničko** (lake), Yugo.
92/D3 **Zvornik,** Bosn.
66/D2 **Zwaagwesteinde,** Neth.
66/B4 **Zwanenburg,** Neth.
66/C3 **Zwarte Meer** (lake), Neth.
66/D3 **Zwartsluis,** Neth.
144/C5 **Zwedru,** Libr.
69/G5 **Zweibrücken,** Ger.
80/D4 **Zweisimmen,** Swi.
72/C5 **Zwenkau,** Ger.
67/G6 **Zwesten,** Ger.
68/C2 **Zwevegem,** Belg.
72/C6 **Zwickau,** Ger.
71/F2 **Zwickauer Mulde** (riv.), Ger.
71/G4 **Zwiesel,** Ger.
66/B6 **Zwijndrecht,** Belg.
66/B5 **Zwijndrecht,** Neth.
67/F2 **Zwischenahn,** Ger.
67/F2 **Zwischenahner Meer** (lake), Ger.
81/F3 **Zwischenwasser,** Aus.
65/L3 **Zwoleń,** Pol.
66/D4 **Zwolle,** Neth.
202/B2 **Zwolle,** La,US
72/C6 **Zwönitz,** Ger.
72/C6 **Zwönitz** (riv.), Ger.
71/F2 **Zwota,** Ger.
65/K2 **Żychlin,** Pol.
65/L2 **Żyrardów,** Pol.
101/R3 **Zyryanka,** Rus.
108/A2 **Zyryanovsk,** Kaz.
97/J3 **Zyudev** (isl.), Rus.
65/K4 **Żywiec,** Pol.

165° W
150° W
135° W
120° W
105° W
90° W
75° W
60° W
45° W
30° W
15° W
0°
1 A.M.
2 A.M.
3 A.M.
4 A.M.
5 A.M.
6 A.M.
7 A.M.
8 A.M.
9 A.M.
10 A.M.
11 A.M.
NOON
ARCTIC OCEAN
GREENLAND
9 A.M.
11 A.M.
Nuuk
ICELAND
Reykjavik
3 A.M.
ALASKA
Anchorage
Whitehorse
CANADA
Edmonton
Winnipeg
NEWFOUNDLAND
8:30 A.M.
Montreal
Halifax
Seattle
Boise
Denver
UNITED STATES
Chicago
Detroit
New York
Washington
San Francisco
Los Angeles
Phoenix
Atlanta
Houston
BERMUDA
ATLANTIC OCEAN
AZORES
IRELAND
UNITED KINGDOM
London
Paris
FRANCE
MONACO
ANDORRA
PORTUGAL
Madrid
SPAIN
Algiers
MOROCCO
ALGERIA
CANARY Is.
W. SAHARA
MAURITANIA
MALI
CAPE VERDE
Dakar
SENEGAL
GAMBIA
GUINEA-BISSAU
GUINEA
BURKINA FASO
SIERRA LEONE
LIBERIA
IVORY COAST
GHANA
TOGO
BENIN
EQUAT. GUI
SÃO TOMÉ
PRÍNCIPE
Miami
BAHAMAS
MEXICO
Mexico City
CUBA
HAITI
DOM. REP.
PUERTO RICO
ANT. & BARB.
JAMAICA
ST. KITTS & NEVIS
DOMINICA
ST. LUCIA
BARBADOS
ST. VINC. & GRENS.
GRENADA
TRINIDAD AND TOBAGO
BELIZE
HONDURAS
GUATEMALA
EL SALVADOR
NICARAGUA
COSTA RICA
PANAMA
HAWAII
Honolulu
PACIFIC OCEAN
VENEZUELA
GUYANA
SUR.
FR. GUIANA
Bogota
COLOMBIA
ECUADOR
Manaus
BRAZIL
Recife
PERU
Lima
La Paz
BOLIVIA
PARAGUAY
Rio de Janeiro
CHILE
Santiago
URUGUAY
Buenos Aires
ARGENTINA
ASCENSION
TRISTAN DA CUNHA
FALKLAND Is.
SOUTH GEORGIA
KIRIBATI
2:30 A.M.
MARQUESAS Is.
TAHITI
FRENCH POLYNESIA
3:30 A.M.
PITCAIRN I.
EASTER I.
TIME ZONES OF THE WORLD
STANDARD TIME ZONES
3 A.M.
4 A.M.
5 A.M.
6 A.M.
AREAS USING HALF HOUR DEVIATIONS
5:30 P.M.